W9-ANZ-830

For Reference

Not to be taken from this room

Who Was Who in America®

Published by Marquis Who's Who®

Titles in Print

Who's Who in America®

Who's Who in America Junior & Senior High School Version

Who Was Who in America®

  Historical Volume (1607–1896)

  Volume I (1897–1942)

  Volume II (1943–1950)

  Volume III (1951–1960)

  Volume IV (1961–1968)

  Volume V (1969–1973)

  Volume VI (1974–1976)

  Volume VII (1977–1981)

  Volume VIII (1982–1985)

  Volume IX (1985–1989)

  Volume X (1989–1993)

  Volume XI (1993–1996)

  Index Volume (1607–1996)

Who's Who in the World®

Who's Who in the East®

Who's Who in the Midwest®

Who's Who in the South and Southwest®

Who's Who in the West®

Who's Who in American Education®

Who's Who in American Law®

Who's Who in American Nursing®

Who's Who of American Women®

Who's Who in Finance and Industry®

Who's Who in Medicine and Healthcare™

Who's Who in Science and Engineering®

Index to Marquis Who's Who® Publications

The *Official* ABMS Directory of Board Certified Medical Specialists®

Available on CD-ROM

The Complete Marquis Who's Who® on CD-ROM

ABMS Medical Specialists *PLUS*™

Who Was Who in America®
with world notables

1993-1996
Volume XI

MARQUIS
Who'sWho® 121 Chanlon Road
New Providence, NJ 07974 U.S.A.

Who Was Who in America®

Marquis Who's Who®

Vice President & Co-publisher   Sandra S. Barnes

Vice President, Database Production & Co-publisher   Dean Hollister

Vice President, Production—Directories   Leigh Yuster-Freeman

Editorial & Marketing Director   Paul Canning

Research Director   Judy Redel

Senior Managing Editor   Fred Marks

Senior Editor   Harriet Tiger

Associate Editor   Rose Marvin

Published by Marquis Who's Who, a division of Reed Elsevier, Inc.

Library of Congress Catalog Card Number 43-3789
International Standard Book Number   0-8379-0224-X (13-volume set)
                                     0-8379-0225-8 (volume XI)
                                     0-8379-0226-6 (Index volume)
                                     0-8379-0227-4 (volume XI and Index)
International Standard Serial Number 0146-8081

Manufactured in the United States of America

Table of Contents

Preface

The publication of Volume XI of *Who Was Who in America* answers an ongoing demand among biographical researchers for the books in the *Who's Who in America* series. *Who's Who in America*, the major component of the series, has continued to advance the highest standards of biographical compilation throughout nearly a century of continuous publication.

The *Was* books (to use the shortened form by which they are perhaps better known) have sought to reflect the history and genealogical heritage of America. These books have inherited the unique characteristics that have made *Who's Who in America* both an internationally respected reference work and a household word here in the country of its origin.

For example, sketches in each *Was* volume have not only been prepared from information supplied by the Biographees themselves, but have been approved personally—and frequently revised—before being printed in a Marquis publication during the subject's lifetime. As with all *Was* volumes, many of these sketches have been scrutinized and revised by relatives or legal representatives of the deceased Biographee.

The preface to the first volume of *Who's Who in America* stated: "The book is autobiographical, the data having been obtained from first hands." It follows that *Who Was Who in America* is also autobiographical to a distinctive degree. In that respect, it is unique among American biographical directories. And although condensed to the style that Marquis Who's Who has made famous, the sketches contain all essential facts.

Most of the sketches in Volume XI are of deceased Biographees from *Who's Who in America*. This volume also contains the sketches of deceased Marquis Biographees whose careers were of regional or international significance and whose listings were in Marquis publications other than *Who's Who in America*. Additionally, this volume includes sketches of some Marquis Biographees who were born in 1896 or earlier, and are believed to be deceased.

Continuously updated, and now published in thirteen volumes containing some 126,000 biographies, *Who Was Who in America* is a vital portion of American history from the early days of the colonies to the present. It is the autobiography of America.

The Editors
New Providence, N.J.
1996

Key to Information

[1] GIBSON, OSCAR JULIUS, [2] physician, medical educator; **[3]** b. Syracuse, N.Y., Aug. 31, 1918; **[4]** s. Paul Oliver and Elizabeth H. (Thrun) G.; **[5]** m. Judith S. Gonzalez, Apr. 28, 1939; **[6]** children: Richard Gary, Matthew Cary, Samuel Perry. **[7]** BA magna cum laude, U. Pa., 1940; MD, Harvard U., 1944. **[8]** Diplomate Am. Bd. Internal Medicine, Am. Bd. Preventive Medicine. **[9]** Intern Barnes Hosp., St. Louis, 1944-49, resident, 1950-66; clin. assoc. Nat. Heart Inst., NIH, Bethesda, Md., 1966-68; chief resident medicine U. Okla. Hosps., 1968-69; asst. prof. community health Okla. Med. Ctr., 1969-70, assoc. prof., 1970-74, prof., chmn. dept., 1974-80; dean U. Okla. Coll. Medicine, 1978-82; v.p. med. staff affairs Bapt. Med. Ctr., Oklahoma City, 1982-86, exec. v.p., 1986-88, chmn., 1988-96; **[10]** mem. governing bd. Ambulatory Health Care Consortium, Inc., 1979-80; mem. Okla. Bd. Medicolegal Examiners, 1985-90. **[11]** Contrb. articles to profl. jours. **[12]** Bd. dirs., v.p. Okla. Arthritis Found., 1982-86; trustee North Central Mental Health Ctr., 1985-90. **[13]** Served with U.S. Army, 1955-56. **[14]** Recipient R.T. Chadwick award NIH, 1968; Am. Heart Assn. grantee, 1985-86, 88. **[15]** Fellow Assn. Tchrs. Preventive Medicine; mem. Am. Fedn. Clin. Research, Assn. Med. Colls., AAAS, AMA, Masons, Shriners, Sigma Xi. **[16]** Republican. **[17]** Roman Catholic. **[18]** Avocations: swimming, weight lifting, travel. **[19]** Home: Oklahoma City **[20]** Died May 1, 1996; buried Tulsa, Okla.

KEY

[1]	Name
[2]	Occupation
[3]	Vital statistics
[4]	Parents
[5]	Marriage
[6]	Children
[7]	Education
[8]	Professional certifications
[9]	Career
[10]	Career-related
[11]	Writings and creative works
[12]	Civic and political activities
[13]	Military
[14]	Awards and fellowships
[15]	Professional and association memberships, clubs and lodges
[16]	Political affiliation
[17]	Religion
[18]	Avocations
[19]	Home address
[20]	Death information

Table of Abbreviations

The following abbreviations and symbols are frequently used in this book.

A Associate (used with academic degrees only)

AA, A.A. Associate in Arts, Associate of Arts

AAAL American Academy of Arts and Letters

AAAS American Association for the Advancement of Science

AACD American Association for Counseling and Development

AACN American Association of Critical Care Nurses

AAHA American Academy of Health Administrators

AAHP American Association of Hospital Planners

AAHPERD American Alliance for Health, Physical Education, Recreation, and Dance

AAS Associate of Applied Science

AASL American Association of School Librarians

AASPA American Association of School Personnel Administrators

AAU Amateur Athletic Union

AAUP American Association of University Professors

AAUW American Association of University Women

AB, A.B. Arts, Bachelor of

AB Alberta

ABA American Bar Association

ABC American Broadcasting Company

AC Air Corps

acad. academy, academic

acct. accountant

acctg. accounting

ACDA Arms Control and Disarmament Agency

ACHA American College of Hospital Administrators

ACLS Advanced Cardiac Life Support

ACLU American Civil Liberties Union

ACOG American College of Ob-Gyn

ACP American College of Physicians

ACS American College of Surgeons

ADA American Dental Association

a.d.c. aide-de-camp

adj. adjunct, adjutant

adj. gen. adjutant general

adm. admiral

adminstr. administrator

adminstrn. administration

adminstrv. administrative

ADN Associate's Degree in Nursing

ADP Automatic Data Processing

adv. advocate, advisory

advt. advertising

AE, A.E. Agricultural Engineer

A.E. and P. Ambassador Extraordinary and Plenipotentiary

AEC Atomic Energy Commission

aero. aeronautical, aeronautic

aerodyn. aerodynamic

AFB Air Force Base

AFL-CIO American Federation of Labor and Congress of Industrial Organizations

AFTRA American Federation of TV and Radio Artists

AFSCME American Federation of State, County and Municipal Employees

agr. agriculture

agrl. agricultural

agt. agent

AGVA American Guild of Variety Artists

agy. agency

A&I Agricultural and Industrial

AIA American Institute of Architects

AIAA American Institute of Aeronautics and Astronautics

AIChE American Institute of Chemical Engineers

AICPA American Institute of Certified Public Accountants

AID Agency for International Development

AIDS Acquired Immune Deficiency Syndrome

AIEE American Institute of Electrical Engineers

AIM American Institute of Management

AIME American Institute of Mining, Metallurgy, and Petroleum Engineers

AK Alaska

AL Alabama

ALA American Library Association

Ala. Alabama

alt. alternate

Alta. Alberta

A&M Agricultural and Mechanical

AM, A.M. Arts, Master of

Am. American, America

AMA American Medical Association

amb. ambassador

A.M.E. African Methodist Episcopal

Amtrak National Railroad Passenger Corporation

AMVETS American Veterans of World War II, Korea, Vietnam

ANA American Nurses Association

anat. anatomical

ANCC American Nurses Credentialing Center

ann. annual

ANTA American National Theatre and Academy

anthrop. anthropological

AP Associated Press

APA American Psychological Association

APGA American Personnel Guidance Association

APHA American Public Health Association

APO Army Post Office

apptd. appointed

Apr. April

apt. apartment

AR Arkansas

ARC American Red Cross

arch. architect

archeol. archeological

archtl. architectural

Ariz. Arizona

Ark. Arkansas

ArtsD, ArtsD. Arts, Doctor of

arty. artillery

AS American Samoa

AS Associate in Science

ASCAP American Society of Composers, Authors and Publishers

ASCD Association for Supervision and Curriculum Development

ASCE American Society of Civil Engineers

ASHRAE American Society of Heating, Refrigeration, and Air Conditioning Engineers

ASME American Society of Mechanical Engineers

ASNSA American Society for Nursing Service Administrators

ASPA American Society for Public Administration

ASPCA American Society for the Prevention of Cruelty to Animals

assn. association

assoc. associate

asst. assistant

ASTD American Society for Training and Development

ASTM American Society for Testing and Materials

astron. astronomical

astrophys. astrophysical

ATLA Association of Trial Lawyers of America

ATSC Air Technical Service Command

AT&T American Telephone & Telegraph Company

atty. attorney

Aug. August

AUS Army of the United States

aux. auxiliary

Ave. Avenue

AVMA American Veterinary Medical Association

AZ Arizona

AWHONN Association of Women's Health Obstetric and Neonatal Nurses

B. Bachelor

b. born

BA, B.A. Bachelor of Arts

BAgr, B.Agr. Bachelor of Agriculture

Balt. Baltimore

Bapt. Baptist

BArch, B.Arch. Bachelor of Architecture

BAS, B.A.S. Bachelor of Agricultural Science

BBA, B.B.A. Bachelor of Business Administration

BBB Better Business Bureau

BBC British Broadcasting Corporation

BC, B.C. British Columbia

BCE, B.C.E. Bachelor of Civil Engineering

BChir, B.Chir. Bachelor of Surgery

BCL, B.C.L. Bachelor of Civil Law

BCLS Basic Cardiac Life Support

BCS, B.C.S. Bachelor of Commercial
Science
BD, B.D. Bachelor of Divinity
bd. board
BE, B.E. Bachelor of Education
BEE, B.E.E. Bachelor of Electrical
Engineering
BFA, B.F.A. Bachelor of Fine Arts
bibl. biblical
bibliog. bibliographical
biog. biographical
biol. biological
BJ, B.J. Bachelor of Journalism
Bklyn. Brooklyn
BL, B.L. Bachelor of Letters
bldg. building
BLS, B.L.S. Bachelor of Library Science
BLS Basic Life Support
Blvd. Boulevard
BMI Broadcast Music, Inc.
BMW Bavarian Motor Works (Bayerische
Motoren Werke)
bn. battalion
B.&O.R.R. Baltimore & Ohio Railroad
bot. botanical
BPE, B.P.E. Bachelor of Physical Education
BPhil, B.Phil. Bachelor of Philosophy
br. branch
BRE, B.R.E. Bachelor of Religious
Education
brig. gen. brigadier general
Brit. British, Brittanica
Bros. Brothers
BS, B.S. Bachelor of Science
BSA, B.S.A. Bachelor of Agricultural
Science
BSBA Bachelor of Science in Business
Administration
BSChemE Bachelor of Science in Chemical
Engineering
BSD, B.S.D. Bachelor of Didactic Science
BSEE Bachelor of Science in Electrical
Engineering
BSN Bachelor of Science in Nursing
BST, B.S.T. Bachelor of Sacred Theology
BTh, B.Th. Bachelor of Theology
bull. bulletin
bur. bureau
bus. business
B.W.I. British West Indies

CA California
CAA Civil Aeronautics Administration
CAB Civil Aeronautics Board
CAD-CAM Computer Aided Design–
Computer Aided Model
Calif. California
C.Am. Central America
Can. Canada, Canadian
CAP Civil Air Patrol
capt. captain
cardiol. cardiological
cardiovasc. cardiovascular
CARE Cooperative American Relief
Everywhere
Cath. Catholic
cav. cavalry
CBC Canadian Broadcasting Company
CBI China, Burma, India Theatre of
Operations
CBS Columbia Broadcasting Company
C.C. Community College
CCC Commodity Credit Corporation

CCNY City College of New York
CCRN Critical Care Registered Nurse
CCU Cardiac Care Unit
CD Civil Defense
CE, C.E. Corps of Engineers, Civil Engineer
CEN Certified Emergency Nurse
CENTO Central Treaty Organization
CEO chief executive officer
CERN European Organization of Nuclear
Research
cert. certificate, certification, certified
CETA Comprehensive Employment
Training Act
CFA Chartered Financial Analyst
CFL Canadian Football League
CFO chief financial officer
CFP Certified Financial Planner
ch. church
ChD, Ch.D. Doctor of Chemistry
chem. chemical
ChemE, Chem.E. Chemical Engineer
ChFC Chartered Financial Consultant
Chgo. Chicago
chirurg. chirurgical
chmn. chairman
chpt. chapter
CIA Central Intelligence Agency
Cin. Cincinnati
cir. circle, circuit
CLE Continuing Legal Education
Cleve. Cleveland
climatol. climatological
clin. clinical
clk. clerk
C.L.U. Chartered Life Underwriter
CM, C.M. Master in Surgery
CM Northern Mariana Islands
CMA Certified Medical Assistant
cmty. community
CNA Certified Nurse's Aide
CNOR Certified Nurse (Operating Room)
C.&N.W.Ry. Chicago & North Western
Railway
CO Colorado
Co. Company
COF Catholic Order of Foresters
C. of C. Chamber of Commerce
col. colonel
coll. college
Colo. Colorado
com. committee
comd. commanded
comdg. commanding
comdr. commander
comdt. commandant
comm. communications
commd. commissioned
comml. commercial
commn. commission
commr. commissioner
compt. comptroller
condr. conductor
Conf. Conference
Congl. Congregational, Congressional
Conglist. Congregationalist
Conn. Connecticut
cons. consultant, consulting
consol. consolidated
constl. constitutional
constn. constitution
constrn. construction
contbd. contributed
contbg. contributing
contbn. contribution

contbr. contributor
contr. controller
Conv. Convention
COO chief operating officer
coop. cooperative
coord. coordinator
CORDS Civil Operations and Revolutionary
Development Support
CORE Congress of Racial Equality
corp. corporation, corporate
corr. correspondent, corresponding,
correspondence
C.&O.Ry. Chesapeake & Ohio Railway
coun. council
CPA Certified Public Accountant
CPCU Chartered Property and Casualty
Underwriter
CPH, C.P.H. Certificate of Public Health
cpl. corporal
CPR Cardio-Pulmonary Resuscitation
C.P.Ry. Canadian Pacific Railway
CRT Cathode Ray Terminal
C.S. Christian Science
CSB, C.S.B. Bachelor of Christian Science
C.S.C. Civil Service Commission
CT Connecticut
ct. court
ctr. center
ctrl. central
CWS Chemical Warfare Service
C.Z. Canal Zone

D. Doctor
d. daughter
DAgr, D.Agr. Doctor of Agriculture
DAR Daughters of the American Revolution
dau. daughter
DAV Disabled American Veterans
DC, D.C. District of Columbia
DCL, D.C.L. Doctor of Civil Law
DCS, D.C.S. Doctor of Commercial Science
DD, D.D. Doctor of Divinity
DDS, D.D.S. Doctor of Dental Surgery
DE Delaware
Dec. December
dec. deceased
def. defense
Del. Delaware
del. delegate, delegation
Dem. Democrat, Democratic
DEng, D.Eng. Doctor of Engineering
denom. denomination, denominational
dep. deputy
dept. department
dermatol. dermatological
desc. descendant
devel. development, developmental
DFA, D.F.A. Doctor of Fine Arts
D.F.C. Distinguished Flying Cross
DHL, D.H.L. Doctor of Hebrew Literature
dir. director
dist. district
distbg. distributing
distbn. distribution
distbr. distributor
disting. distinguished
div. division, divinity, divorce
divsn. division
DLitt, D.Litt. Doctor of Literature
DMD, D.M.D. Doctor of Dental Medicine
DMS, D.M.S. Doctor of Medical Science
DO, D.O. Doctor of Osteopathy
docs. documents
DON Director of Nursing

DPH, D.P.H. Diploma in Public Health
DPhil, D.Phil. Doctor of Philosophy
D.R. Daughters of the Revolution
Dr. Drive, Doctor
DRE, D.R.E. Doctor of Religious Education
DrPH, Dr.P.H. Doctor of Public Health, Doctor of Public Hygiene
D.S.C. Distinguished Service Cross
DSc, D.Sc. Doctor of Science
DSChemE Doctor of Science in Chemical Engineering
D.S.M. Distinguished Service Medal
DST, D.S.T. Doctor of Sacred Theology
DTM, D.T.M. Doctor of Tropical Medicine
DVM, D.V.M. Doctor of Veterinary Medicine
DVS, D.V.S. Doctor of Veterinary Surgery

E, E. East
ea. eastern
E. and P. Extraordinary and Plenipotentiary
Eccles. Ecclesiastical
ecol. ecological
econ. economic
ECOSOC Economic and Social Council (of the UN)
ED, E.D. Doctor of Engineering
ed. educated
EdB, Ed.B. Bachelor of Education
EdD, Ed.D. Doctor of Education
edit. edition
editl. editorial
EdM, Ed.M. Master of Education
edn. education
ednl. educational
EDP Electronic Data Processing
EdS, Ed.S. Specialist in Education
EE, E.E. Electrical Engineer
E.E. and M.P. Envoy Extraordinary and Minister Plenipotentiary
EEC European Economic Community
EEG Electroencephalogram
EEO Equal Employment Opportunity
EEOC Equal Employment Opportunity Commission
E.Ger. German Democratic Republic
EKG Electrocardiogram
elec. electrical
electrochem. electrochemical
electrophys. electrophysical
elem. elementary
EM, E.M. Engineer of Mines
EMT Emergency Medical Technician
ency. encyclopedia
Eng. England
engr. engineer
engring. engineering
entomol. entomological
environ. environmental
EPA Environmental Protection Agency
epidemiol. epidemiological
Episc. Episcopalian
ERA Equal Rights Amendment
ERDA Energy Research and Development Administration
ESEA Elementary and Secondary Education Act
ESL English as Second Language
ESPN Entertainment and Sports Programming Network
ESSA Environmental Science Services Administration
ethnol. ethnological
ETO European Theatre of Operations

Evang. Evangelical
exam. examination, examining
Exch. Exchange
exec. executive
exhbn. exhibition
expdn. expedition
expn. exposition
expt. experiment
exptl. experimental
Expy. Expressway
Ext. Extension

F.A. Field Artillery
FAA Federal Aviation Administration
FAO Food and Agriculture Organization (of the UN)
FBA Federal Bar Association
FBI Federal Bureau of Investigation
FCA Farm Credit Administration
FCC Federal Communications Commission
FCDA Federal Civil Defense Administration
FDA Food and Drug Administration
FDIA Federal Deposit Insurance Administration
FDIC Federal Deposit Insurance Corporation
FE, F.E. Forest Engineer
FEA Federal Energy Administration
Feb. February
fed. federal
fedn. federation
FERC Federal Energy Regulatory Commission
fgn. foreign
FHA Federal Housing Administration
fin. financial, finance
FL Florida
Fl. Floor
Fla. Florida
FMC Federal Maritime Commission
FNP Family Nurse Practitioner
FOA Foreign Operations Administration
found. foundation
FPC Federal Power Commission
FPO Fleet Post Office
frat. fraternity
FRS Federal Reserve System
FSA Federal Security Agency
Ft. Fort
FTC Federal Trade Commission
Fwy. Freeway

G-1 (or other number) Division of General Staff
GA, Ga. Georgia
GAO General Accounting Office
gastroent. gastroenterological
GATE Gifted and Talented Educators
GATT General Agreement on Tariffs and Trade
GE General Electric Company
gen. general
geneal. genealogical
geod. geodetic
geog. geographic, geographical
geol. geological
geophys. geophysical
geriat. geriatrics
gerontol. gerontological
G.H.Q. General Headquarters
GM General Motors Corporation
GMAC General Motors Acceptance Corporation
G.N.Ry. Great Northern Railway

gov. governor
govt. government
govtl. governmental
GPO Government Printing Office
grad. graduate, graduated
GSA General Services Administration
Gt. Great
GTE General Telephone and ElectricCompany
GU Guam
gynecol. gynecological

HBO Home Box Office
hdqs. headquarters
HEW Department of Health, Education and Welfare
HHD, H.H.D. Doctor of Humanities
HHFA Housing and Home Finance Agency
HHS Department of Health and Human Services
HI Hawaii
hist. historical, historic
HM, H.M. Master of Humanities
HMO Health Maintenance Organization
homeo. homeopathic
hon. honorary, honorable
Ho. of Dels. House of Delegates
Ho. of Reps. House of Representatives
hort. horticultural
hosp. hospital
H.S. High School
HUD Department of Housing and Urban Development
Hwy. Highway
hydrog. hydrographic

IA Iowa
IAEA International Atomic Energy Agency
IATSE International Alliance of Theatrical and Stage Employees and Moving Picture Operators of the United States and Canada
IBM International Business Machines Corporation
IBRD International Bank for Reconstruction and Development
ICA International Cooperation Administration
ICC Interstate Commerce Commission
ICCE International Council for Computers in Education
ICU Intensive Care Unit
ID Idaho
IEEE Institute of Electrical and Electronics Engineers
IFC International Finance Corporation
IGY International Geophysical Year
IL Illinois
Ill. Illinois
illus. illustrated
ILO International Labor Organization
IMF International Monetary Fund
IN Indiana
Inc. Incorporated
Ind. Indiana
ind. independent
Indpls. Indianapolis
indsl. industrial
inf. infantry
info. information
ins. insurance
insp. inspector
insp. gen. inspector general

inst. institute
instl. institutional
instn. institution
instr. instructor
instrn. instruction
instrnl. instructional
internat. international
intro. introduction
IRE Institute of Radio Engineers
IRS Internal Revenue Service
ITT International Telephone & Telegraph Corporation

JAG Judge Advocate General
JAGC Judge Advocate General Corps
Jan. January
Jaycees Junior Chamber of Commerce
JB, J.B. Jurum Baccalaureus
JCB, J.C.B. Juris Canoni Baccalaureus
JCD, J.C.D. Juris Canonici Doctor, Juris Civilis Doctor
JCL, J.C.L. Juris Canonici Licentiatus
JD, J.D. Juris Doctor
jg. junior grade
jour. journal
jr. junior
JSD, J.S.D. Juris Scientiae Doctor
JUD, J.U.D. Juris Utriusque Doctor
jud. judicial

Kans. Kansas
K.C. Knights of Columbus
K.P. Knights of Pythias
KS Kansas
K.T. Knight Templar
KY, Ky. Kentucky

LA, La. Louisiana
L.A. Los Angeles
lab. laboratory
L.Am. Latin America
lang. language
laryngol. laryngological
LB Labrador
LDS Latter Day Saints
LDS Church Church of Jesus Christ of Latter Day Saints
lectr. lecturer
legis. legislation, legislative
LHD, L.H.D. Doctor of Humane Letters
L.I. Long Island
libr. librarian, library
lic. licensed, license
L.I.R.R. Long Island Railroad
lit. literature
litig. litigation
LittB, Litt.B. Bachelor of Letters
LittD, Litt.D. Doctor of Letters
LLB, LL.B. Bachelor of Laws
LLD, LL.D. Doctor of Laws
LLM, L.L.M. Master of Laws
Ln. Lane
L.&N.R.R. Louisville & Nashville Railroad
LPGA Ladies Professional Golf Association
LPN Licensed Practical Nurse
LS, L.S. Library Science (in degree)
lt. lieutenant
Ltd. Limited
Luth. Lutheran
LWV League of Women Voters

M. Master
m. married

MA, M.A. Master of Arts
MA Massachusetts
MADD Mothers Against Drunk Driving
mag. magazine
MAgr, M.Agr. Master of Agriculture
maj. major
Man. Manitoba
Mar. March
MArch, M.Arch. Master in Architecture
Mass. Massachusetts
math. mathematics, mathematical
MATS Military Air Transport Service
MB, M.B. Bachelor of Medicine
MB Manitoba
MBA, M.B.A. Master of Business Administration
MBS Mutual Broadcasting System
M.C. Medical Corps
MCE, M.C.E. Master of Civil Engineering
mcht. merchant
mcpl. municipal
MCS, M.C.S. Master of Commercial Science
MD, M.D. Doctor of Medicine
MD, Md. Maryland
MDiv Master of Divinity
MDip, M.Dip. Master in Diplomacy
mdse. merchandise
MDV, M.D.V. Doctor of Veterinary Medicine
ME, M.E. Mechanical Engineer
ME Maine
M.E.Ch. Methodist Episcopal Church
mech. mechanical
MEd., M.Ed. Master of Education
med. medical
MEE, M.E.E. Master of Electrical Engineering
mem. member
meml. memorial
merc. mercantile
met. metropolitan
metall. metallurgical
MetE, Met.E. Metallurgical Engineer
meteorol. meteorological
Meth. Methodist
Mex. Mexico
MF, M.F. Master of Forestry
MFA, M.F.A. Master of Fine Arts
mfg. manufacturing
mfr. manufacturer
mgmt. management
mgr. manager
MHA, M.H.A. Master of Hospital Administration
M.I. Military Intelligence
MI Michigan
Mich. Michigan
micros. microscopic, microscopical
mid. middle
mil. military
Milw. Milwaukee
Min. Minister
mineral. mineralogical
Minn. Minnesota
MIS Management Information Systems
Miss. Mississippi
MIT Massachusetts Institute of Technology
mktg. marketing
ML, M.L. Master of Laws
MLA Modern Language Association
M.L.D. Magister Legnum Diplomatic
MLitt, M.Litt. Master of Literature, Master of Letters

MLS, M.L.S. Master of Library Science
MME, M.M.E. Master of Mechanical Engineering
MN Minnesota
mng. managing
MO, Mo. Missouri
moblzn. mobilization
Mont. Montana
MP Northern Mariana Islands
M.P. Member of Parliament
MPA Master of Public Administration
MPE, M.P.E. Master of Physical Education
MPH, M.P.H. Master of Public Health
MPhil, M.Phil. Master of Philosophy
MPL, M.P.L. Master of Patent Law
Mpls. Minneapolis
MRE, M.R.E. Master of Religious Education
MRI Magnetic Resonance Imaging
MS, M.S. Master of Science
MS, Ms. Mississippi
MSc, M.Sc. Master of Science
MSChemE Master of Science in Chemical Engineering
MSEE Master of Science in Electrical Engineering
MSF, M.S.F. Master of Science of Forestry
MSN Master of Science in Nursing
MST, M.S.T. Master of Sacred Theology
MSW, M.S.W. Master of Social Work
MT Montana
Mt. Mount
MTO Mediterranean Theatre of Operation
MTV Music Television
mus. museum, musical
MusB, Mus.B. Bachelor of Music
MusD, Mus.D. Doctor of Music
MusM, Mus.M. Master of Music
mut. mutual
MVP Most Valuable Player
mycol. mycological

N. North
NAACOG Nurses Association of the American College of Obstetricians and Gynecologists
NAACP National Association for the Advancement of Colored People
NACA National Advisory Committee for Aeronautics
NACDL National Association of Criminal Defense Lawyers
NACU National Association of Colleges and Universities
NAD National Academy of Design
NAE National Academy of Engineering, National Association of Educators
NAESP National Association of Elementary School Principals
NAFE National Association of Female Executives
N.Am. North America
NAM National Association of Manufacturers
NAMH National Association for Mental Health
NAPA National Association of Performing Artists
NARAS National Academy of Recording Arts and Sciences
NAREB National Association of Real Estate Boards
NARS National Archives and Record Service

NAS National Academy of Sciences
NASA National Aeronautics and Space Administration
NASP National Association of School Psychologists
NASW National Association of Social Workers
nat. national
NATAS National Academy of Television Arts and Sciences
NATO North Atlantic Treaty Organization
NATOUSA North African Theatre of Operations, United States Army
nav. navigation
NB, N.B. New Brunswick
NBA National Basketball Association
NBC National Broadcasting Company
NC, N.C. North Carolina
NCAA National College Athletic Association
NCCJ National Conference of Christians and Jews
ND, N.D. North Dakota
NDEA National Defense Education Act
NE Nebraska
NE, N.E. Northeast
NEA National Education Association
Nebr. Nebraska
NEH National Endowment for Humanities
neurol. neurological
Nev. Nevada
NF Newfoundland
NFL National Football League
Nfld. Newfoundland
NG National Guard
NH, N.H. New Hampshire
NHL National Hockey League
NIH National Institutes of Health
NIMH National Institute of Mental Health
NJ, N.J. New Jersey
NLRB National Labor Relations Board
NM New Mexico
N.Mex. New Mexico
No. Northern
NOAA National Oceanographic and Atmospheric Administration
NORAD North America Air Defense
Nov. November
NOW National Organization for Women
N.P.Ry. Northern Pacific Railway
nr. near
NRA National Rifle Association
NRC National Research Council
NS, N.S. Nova Scotia
NSC National Security Council
NSF National Science Foundation
NSTA National Science Teachers Association
NSW New South Wales
N.T. New Testament
NT Northwest Territories
nuc. nuclear
numis. numismatic
NV Nevada
NW, N.W. Northwest
N.W.T. Northwest Territories
NY, N.Y. New York
N.Y.C. New York City
NYU New York University
N.Z. New Zealand

OAS Organization of American States
ob-gyn obstetrics-gynecology

obs. observatory
obstet. obstetrical
occupl. occupational
oceanog. oceanographic
Oct. October
OD, O.D. Doctor of Optometry
OECD Organization for Economic Cooperation and Development
OEEC Organization of European Economic Cooperation
OEO Office of Economic Opportunity
ofcl. official
OH Ohio
OK Oklahoma
Okla. Oklahoma
ON Ontario
Ont. Ontario
oper. operating
ophthal. ophthalmological
ops. operations
OR Oregon
orch. orchestra
Oreg. Oregon
orgn. organization
orgnl. organizational
ornithol. ornithological
orthop. orthopedic
OSHA Occupational Safety and Health Administration
OSRD Office of Scientific Research and Development
OSS Office of Strategic Services
osteo. osteopathic
otol. otological
otolaryn. otolaryngological

PA, Pa. Pennsylvania
P.A. Professional Association
paleontol. paleontological
path. pathological
PBS Public Broadcasting System
P.C. Professional Corporation
PE Prince Edward Island
pediat. pediatrics
P.E.I. Prince Edward Island
PEN Poets, Playwrights, Editors, Essayists and Novelists (international association)
penol. penological
P.E.O. women's organization (full name not disclosed)
pers. personnel
pfc. private first class
PGA Professional Golfers' Association of America
PHA Public Housing Administration
pharm. pharmaceutical
PharmD, Pharm.D. Doctor of Pharmacy
PharmM, Pharm.M. Master of Pharmacy
PhB, Ph.B. Bachelor of Philosophy
PhD, Ph.D. Doctor of Philosophy
PhDChemE Doctor of Science in Chemical Engineering
PhM, Ph.M. Master of Philosophy
Phila. Philadelphia
philharm. philharmonic
philol. philological
philos. philosophical
photog. photographic
phys. physical
physiol. physiological
Pitts. Pittsburgh
Pk. Park
Pky. Parkway
Pl. Place

P.&L.E.R.R. Pittsburgh & Lake Erie Railroad
Plz. Plaza
PNP Pediatric Nurse Practitioner
P.O. Post Office
PO Box Post Office Box
polit. political
poly. polytechnic, polytechnical
PQ Province of Quebec
PR, P.R. Puerto Rico
prep. preparatory
pres. president
Presbyn. Presbyterian
presdl. presidential
prin. principal
procs. proceedings
prod. produced (play production)
prodn. production
prodr. producer
prof. professor
profl. professional
prog. progressive
propr. proprietor
pros. atty. prosecuting attorney
pro tem. pro tempore
PSRO Professional Services Review Organization
psychiat. psychiatric
psychol. psychological
PTA Parent-Teachers Association
ptnr. partner
PTO Pacific Theatre of Operations, Parent Teacher Organization
pub. publisher, publishing, published
pub. public
publ. publication
pvt. private

quar. quarterly
qm. quartermaster
Q.M.C. Quartermaster Corps
Que. Quebec

radiol. radiological
RAF Royal Air Force
RCA Radio Corporation of America
RCAF Royal Canadian Air Force
RD Rural Delivery
Rd. Road
R&D Research & Development
REA Rural Electrification Administration
rec. recording
ref. reformed
regt. regiment
regtl. regimental
rehab. rehabilitation
rels. relations
Rep. Republican
rep. representative
Res. Reserve
ret. retired
Rev. Reverend
rev. review, revised
RFC Reconstruction Finance Corporation
RFD Rural Free Delivery
rhinol. rhinological
RI, R.I. Rhode Island
RISD Rhode Island School of Design
Rlwy. Railway
Rm. Room
RN, R.N. Registered Nurse
roentgenol. roentgenological
ROTC Reserve Officers Training Corps

RR Rural Route
R.R. Railroad
rsch. research
rschr. researcher
Rt. Route

S. South
s. son
SAC Strategic Air Command
SAG Screen Actors Guild
SALT Strategic Arms Limitation Talks
S.Am. South America
san. sanitary
SAR Sons of the American Revolution
Sask. Saskatchewan
savs. savings
SB, S.B. Bachelor of Science
SBA Small Business Administration
SC, S.C. South Carolina
SCAP Supreme Command Allies Pacific
ScB, Sc.B. Bachelor of Science
SCD, S.C.D. Doctor of Commercial Science
ScD, Sc.D. Doctor of Science
sch. school
sci. science, scientific
SCLC Southern Christian Leadership Conference
SCV Sons of Confederate Veterans
SD, S.D. South Dakota
SE, S.E. Southeast
SEATO Southeast Asia Treaty Organization
SEC Securities and Exchange Commission
sec. secretary
sect. section
seismol. seismological
sem. seminary
Sept. September
s.g. senior grade
sgt. sergeant
SHAEF Supreme Headquarters Allied Expeditionary Forces
SHAPE Supreme Headquarters Allied Powers in Europe
S.I. Staten Island
S.J. Society of Jesus (Jesuit)
SJD Scientiae Juridicae Doctor
SK Saskatchewan
SM, S.M. Master of Science
SNP Society of Nursing Professionals
So. Southern
soc. society
sociol. sociological
S.P.Co. Southern Pacific Company
spkr. speaker
spl. special
splty. specialty
Sq. Square
S.R. Sons of the Revolution
sr. senior
SS Steamship
SSS Selective Service System
St. Saint, Street
sta. station
stats. statistics
statis. statistical
STB, S.T.B. Bachelor of Sacred Theology
stblzn. stabilization
STD, S.T.D. Doctor of Sacred Theology
std. standard
Ste. Suite
subs. subsidiary
SUNY State University of New York
supr. supervisor
supt. superintendent

surg. surgical
svc. service
SW, S.W. Southwest
sys. system

TAPPI Technical Association of the Pulp and Paper Industry
tb. tuberculosis
tchg. teaching
tchr. teacher
tech. technical, technology
technol. technological
tel. telephone
Tel. & Tel. Telephone & Telegraph
telecom. telecommunications
temp. temporary
Tenn. Tennessee
Ter. Territory
Ter. Terrace
TESOL Teachers of English to Speakers of Other Languages
Tex. Texas
ThD, Th.D. Doctor of Theology
theol. theological
ThM, Th.M. Master of Theology
TN Tennessee
tng. training
topog. topographical
trans. transaction, transferred
transl. translation, translated
transp. transportation
treas. treasurer
TT Trust Territory
TV television
TVA Tennessee Valley Authority
TWA Trans World Airlines
twp. township
TX Texas
typog. typographical

U. University
UAW United Auto Workers
UCLA University of California at Los Angeles
UDC United Daughters of the Confederacy
U.K. United Kingdom
UN United Nations
UNESCO United Nations Educational, Scientific and Cultural Organization
UNICEF United Nations International Children's Emergency Fund
univ. university
UNRRA United Nations Relief and Rehabilitation Administration
UPI United Press International
U.P.R.R. United Pacific Railroad
urol. urological
U.S. United States
U.S.A. United States of America
USAAF United States Army Air Force
USAF United States Air Force
USAFR United States Air Force Reserve
USAR United States Army Reserve
USCG United States Coast Guard
USCGR United States Coast Guard Reserve
USES United States Employment Service
USIA United States Information Agency
USMC United States Marine Corps
USMCR United States Marine Corps Reserve
USN United States Navy
USNG United States National Guard
USNR United States Naval Reserve

USO United Service Organizations
USPHS United States Public Health Service
USS United States Ship
USSR Union of the Soviet Socialist Republics
USTA United States Tennis Association
USV United States Volunteers
UT Utah

VA Veterans Administration
VA, Va. Virginia
vet. veteran, veterinary
VFW Veterans of Foreign Wars
VI, V.I. Virgin Islands
vice pres. vice president
vis. visiting
VISTA Volunteers in Service to America
VITA Volunteers in Technical Assistance
vocat. vocational
vol. volunteer, volume
v.p. vice president
vs. versus
VT, Vt. Vermont

W, W. West
WA Washington (state)
WAC Women's Army Corps
Wash. Washington (state)
WATS Wide Area Telecommunications Service
WAVES Women's Reserve, US Naval Reserve
WCTU Women's Christian Temperance Union
we. western
W. Ger. Germany, Federal Republic of
WHO World Health Organization
WI Wisconsin
W.I. West Indies
Wis. Wisconsin
WSB Wage Stabilization Board
WV West Virginia
W.Va. West Virginia
WWI World War I
WWII World War II
WY Wyoming
Wyo. Wyoming

YK Yukon Territory
YMCA Young Men's Christian Association
YMHA Young Men's Hebrew Association
YM & YWHA Young Men's and Young Women's Hebrew Association
yr. year
YT, Y.T. Yukon Territory
YWCA Young Women's Christian Association

zool. zoological

Alphabetical Practices

Names are arranged alphabetically according to the surnames, and under identical surnames according to the first given name. If both surname and first given name are identical, names are arranged alphabetically according to the second given name.

Surnames beginning with De, Des, Du, however capitalized or spaced, are recorded with the prefix preceding the surname and arranged alphabetically under the letter D.

Surnames beginning with Mac and Mc are arranged alphabetically under M.

Surnames beginning with Saint or St. appear after names that begin Sains, and are arranged according to the second part of the name, e.g. St. Clair before Saint Dennis.

Surnames beginning with Van, Von, or von are arranged alphabetically under the letter V.

Compound surnames are arranged according to the first member of the compound.

Many hyphenated Arabic names begin Al-, El-, or al-. These names are alphabetized according to each Biographee's designation of last name. Thus Al-Bahar, Neta may be listed either under Al- or under Bahar, depending on the preference of the listee.

Also, Arabic names have a variety of possible spellings when transposed to English. Spelling of these names is always based on the practice of the Biographee. Some Biographees use a Western form of word order, while others prefer the Arabic word sequence.

Similarly, Asian names may have no comma between family and given names, but some Biographees have chosen to add the comma. In each case, punctuation follows the preference of the Biographee.

Parentheses used in connection with a name indicate which part of the full name is usually deleted in common usage. Hence Chambers, E(lizabeth) Anne indicates that the usual form of the given name is E. Anne. In such a case, the parentheses are ignored in alphabetizing and the name would be arranged as Chambers, Elizabeth Anne. However, if the name is recorded Chambers, (Elizabeth) Anne, signifying that the entire name Elizabeth is not commonly used, the alphabetizing would be arranged as though the name were Chambers, Anne. If an entire middle or last name is enclosed in parentheses, that portion of the name is used in the alphabetical arrangement. Hence Chambers, Elizabeth (Anne) would be arranged as Chambers, Elizabeth Anne.

Where more than one spelling, word order, or name of an individual is frequently encountered, the sketch has been entered under the form preferred by the Biographee, with cross-references under alternate forms.

Who Was Who in America®

AARONSON, MARC A., astronomer, educator; b. Los Angeles, Aug. 24, 1950; s. Simon and Rena (Silverstein) A.; m. Marianne Gabrielle Kun, Aug. 20, 1972; children: Laura, Jamie. BS, Calif. Inst. Tech., 1972; MA, Harvard U., 1974, PhD, 1977. Research asst. Harvard Coll. Obs., Cambridge, 1974-76; research assoc. U. Ariz. Steward Obs., Tucson, 1977-80, asst. astronomer, 1980-82, assoc. astronomer, 1982-83, assoc. prof. astronomy, 1983-87. Contbr. articles to profl. jours. Recipient Bart J. Bok prize Harvard U., 1983, George Van Bresbroeck prize U. Ariz., 1981, Newton Lacy Pierce prize Am. Astron. Soc., 1984; grantee Smithsonian Astrophys. Obs., 1976. Home: Santa Monica Calif. Died 1987.

ABBOTT, ROBERT TUCKER, zoologist, author; b. Watertown, Mass., Sept. 28, 1919; s. Charles M. and Frances (Tucker) A.; m. Mary Sisler, Feb. 18, 1946 (dec. 1964); children: Robert T., Carolyn T., Cynthia Douglas; m. Cecelia White, May 13, 1977. B.S., Harvard, 1942; M.S., George Washington U., 1953, Ph.D., 1955. Asso. curator Smithsonian Instn., Washington, 1946-54; curator Acad. Natural Scis. of Phila., 1955-69, also chmn. dept. mollusks, 1955-69; asst. dir. Del. Mus. of Natural History, 1970-77; pres. Am. Malacologists, Inc., Melbourne, Fla., 1977-95; adj. prof. U. Del., 1973-79; founding dir. Bailey-Matthews Shell Mus., Sanibel Island, Fla., 1994-95. Author: American Seashells, 1954, 2d edit., 1974, Introducing Seashells, 1955, Seashells of the World, 1962,, 2d edit., 1985, How to Know the American Marine Shells, 1961, Seashells of North America, 1968, Kingdom of the Seashell, 1972, The Shell, (with H. Stix), 1968, Shells in Color, 1973, The Best of the Nautilus, 1976, Standard Catalog of Shells, (with R. Wagner) Compendium of Seashells, 1982, Collectible Florida Shells, 1984, Compensium of Landshells, 1989, Shells, 1989, Seashells of Southeast Asia, 1991, Seashells of the Northern Hemisphere, 1991, Field Guide to the Atlantic Coast Shells, 1995. Mem. Friends of the Gardens, Monmouth County, Bklyn. Botanic Gardens; bd. dirs. Tom's River (N.J.) C. of C., 1978-84; bd. dirs. N.J. Shade Tree Fedn., New Brunswick, 1982-95, pres., 1991-93; v.p. No. Hanover Twp. Bd. Edn., 1982-83, pres., 1985-86; chmn. No. Hanover Shade Tree Commn., 1985-95, Zoning Bd. of Adjustment, No. Hanover, 1985-95; mem. Sayreville Indsl. Commn.; past chmn. Ocean County Traffic Safety Commn., Raritan Valley C. of C.; life mem. Rep. Nat. Com., 1989-95; mem. Rep. Presdl. Task Force, 1989-95, Rep. Senatorial Com., 1988-95, at-large del. party platform planning com. Staff sgt. Signal Corps U.S. Army, 1950-53. Recipient Presdl. Legion of Merit, 1993. Mem. IEEE (sr. mem., life), NSPE, NRA (life), Internat. Soc. Arborists, Internat. Soc. Arbiculture, Am. Forestry Assn., N.J. Soc. Profl. Engrs., N.J. Fedn. Shade Tree Commsn., Air Force Assn. (life), Am. Legion (life), Pa. Horticulture Soc., N.J. Pesticide Assn., Raritan Valley Regional C. of C., Ocean County Employees Legis. Com., Burlington County Employees Legis. Com., Monmouth County Employees Legis. Com. Home: Melbourne Fla. Died Nov. 3, 1995.

ABBOTT, WOODROW ACTON, air force general officer; b. Eubank, Ky., Dec. 16, 1919; s. William Thomas and Susie Ellen (Gastineau) A.; m. Lois Marie Scobee, May 17, 1944; children: Woodrow Acton II, Celesta Ann, Teletha Gay. Student, Butler U., 1939-43; B.S., U. Md., 1955, postgrad., 1956; M.B.A., Golden State U., 1982, Ph.D, 1984. Commd. 2d lt. USAAF, 1943; advanced through grades to brig. gen. USAF, 1969; B-17 pilot ETO, 1944-45; assigned Far East Air Force, 1950-52; with SAC, 1956-71; comdr. 92d Wing, 1966-67, 93d Wing, 1968-69, 307th Strategic Wing and 4258th Strategic Wing, Thailand, 1969-70, 42d Air Div., 1970-71; insp. gen. SAC, 1971-73; dir. intelligence J-2, also insp. gen. U.S., Readiness Command, MacDill AFB, Fla., 1973-87; pres. Associated Internat. Group, San Diego, 1988, chief exec. officer, chmn. bd. Decorated D.S.M. with oak leaf cluster, Legion of Merit with 2 oak leaf clusters, D.F.C., Meritorious Service medal, Air medal with 6 oak leaf clusters, Air Force Commendation medal with 2 oak leaf clusters, Army Commendation medal, Purple Heart; Supreme Command Forward badge 1st class Thailand. Mem. Tampa Club (Fla.), Yacht and Country Club, Merced Racquet Club, Merced Golf and Country Club, Delta Sigma Pi. Home: Merced Calif. Died Dec. 29, 1994.

ABDALLAH, AHMED, president of Federal Islamic Republic of the Comoros; b. 1919. Former businessman; rep. Comoros Islands in French Senate, 1959-72; pres. Govt. Council, 1972-73, of Govt., 1973-75; leader Union democratique des Comoros, 1974, Parti pour l'Independence et l'Unité des Comoros, 1974-75; head of state, 1975, pres. Comoros, 1975; overthrown in coup, 1975; pres. Fed. Islamic Republic of Comoros, 1978-89, pres. politicomilitary directory, minister of justice and civil service, 1978-89. Died Nov. 27, 1989. Home: Moroni Comoros

ABE, KOBO, author; b. Tokyo, Japan, Mar. 7, 1924; grad. Tokyo U.; L.H.D., Columbia U., 1975. Recipient 25th Akutagawa prize, 1951, Post-war Lit. prize, 1950, Kishida prize for drama, 1958, Yomiuri Lit. prize, 1962, 75, Tanizaki prize for drama, 1967. Mem. Am. Acad. Arts and Scis. (fgn. hon.). Author: The Road Sign at the End of the Road, 1948; The Red Cocoon, 1950; The Crimes of S. Karma, 1951; Hunger Union, 1954; The Uniform, 1955; Hunt for a Slave, 1955; Animals are Forwarding to their Natives, 1957; The Fourth Unglacial Period, 1959; Here is a Ghost, 1959; Eyes of Stone, 1960; The Woman in the Dunes, 1962; The Face of Another, 1964; You are Guilty Too, 1965; Buyo Enomoto, 1965; Friends, 1967; The Ruined Map, 1967; The Man Who Turned Into a Stick, 1969; Inter Ice Age Four, 1970; Premeditated Act of Uncertain Consequences, 1971; Guidebook, 1971; The Box Man, 1973; Love's Spectacles are Colored Glass, 1973; Green Stocking, 1974; Wee, 1975; Secret Rendez-vous, 1977; Kozo wa Shinda, 1979; Ark Sakuramaru, 1984; Kangaroo Note, 1991; Beyond the Curve, 1991. Home: Tokyo Japan

ABEL, RAY, graphic artist; b. Chgo., Sept. 19, 1911; s. Harry and Etta A.; m. Ruth Herzman, June 20, 1941; children: Helen, Peter. A.B., U. Chgo., 1937; M.A., NYU, 1950. Artist in residence Kala Inst. Illustrator numerous childrens books including The New Sitter, 1950, The Extra Hand, 1953, Refugee Hero, 1957, Mystery of the Red Carnations, 1968, Coal-Energy and Crisis, 1974, The Turnabout Year, 1976, Escape King, 1978, (with others) The Complete Shakespeare, 1979, The Seven Ages of Man, Woodcuts, 1987. With USAAF, 1943-46. Mem. Soc. Illustrators, Art Students League N.Y. (life), Calif. Soc. Printmakers. Avocations: printmaking, piano. Died Aug. 9, 1995. Home: Berkeley Calif.

ABELL, THOMAS HENRY, judge; b. Wharton, Tex., May 7, 1909; s. Thomas James and Lyda (Horton) A.; m. Frances Norris Wright, June 24, 1934; children—Madeleine (Mrs. Robert C. Wither), Alex G., Tom J. Student, Tex. A. and M. Coll., 1926-27; LL.B., Tex. U., 1933. Bar: Tex. bar 1933, U.S. Supreme Ct 1937. Practice in Wharton, 1993-94; county atty. Wharton County, 1937-40, county judge, 1943-46; bd. dirs. Houston Lighting & Power Co.; bd. dirs. Tex. Mid-Coastal Water Devel. Assn., Palacios, 1961-79. Trustee Wharton Sch. Dist., 1949-58; trustee Runnells Fund, Bay City, Tex.; bd. dirs. Gulf Coast Med. Found., Wharton; pres. bd. trustees Wharton County Mus. Assn. Recipient 1989 Golden Book award World Simmental Fedn. Mem. Am. Simmental Assn. (trustee), Sigma Nu. Episcopalian. Home: Wharton Tex. Died June 9, 1996.

ABRAGAM, ANATOLE, physicist; b. Griva-Semagallen, USSR, Dec. 15, 1914; s. Simon and Anna (Maimin) A.; m. Suzanne Lequesme, 1944. Student, Lycee Jeanson, Sorbonne, Oxford U. Research assoc. Centre Nat. de la Recherche Scientifique, 1946; joined French Atomic Energy Commn., 1947, physicist, later sr. physicist, 1947-55, head magnetic resonance lab.,, 1955-58, head solid state physics and nuclear physics dept.,, 1959-65, dir. physics, 1965-70, dir. research, 1971-80; prof. nuclear magnetism Coll. de France, 1960—. Author: Discovery of Anomalous Hyperfine Structure in Solids, 1950; Dynamic Polarization in Solids, 1957, The Principles of Nuclear Magnetism, 1961, Nuclear Anti-ferromagnetism, 1969, Time Reversal: an Autobiography, 1989; (with B. Bleaney) Electron Paramagnetic Resonance of Transition Elements, 1970, Nuclear Pseudomagnetism, 1971, Nuclear Ferromagnetism, 1973, (with M. Goldman) Nuclear Magnetism: Order and Disorder, 1982, Time Reversal (autobiography), 1989. Decorated Grand Officier Ordre Nat. du Merite, Commandeur Legion d'Honneur; recipient Holweck prize London Phys. Soc., 1958, Grand Prix Cognac-Jay Acad. Scis., 1958, Lorentz medal, 1982. Fellow Am. Acad. Arts and Scis. (hon.), Royal Soc. (fgn.); mem. French Phys. Soc. (pres. 1967), U.S. Nat. Acad. Scis., French Acad. Sci.

ABRAHAM, GEORGE G., retired packing company executive; b. Scranton, Pa., June 15, 1906; s. Samuel H. and Anna (Arnof) A.; m. Celia G. Abraham, Dec. 1, 1928; children—Hubert A., Lee. Student, U. Chgo., 1924-25, U. Memphis Law Sch., 1925-28. Sec. Abraham Packing Co., Memphis, 1925-40, pres., 1940-50; plant mgr. Wilson & Co., Memphis, 1950-55; pres. Ill. Packing Co., Chgo., 1955-61; exec. Hygrade Packing Co., Detroit, 1961-66; chmn. bd. Abraham Cattle Co., Memphis, 1966-86; mem. Nat. War Meat Bd., 1942-46. Mem. Am. Meat Inst. (bd. dirs. 1942-50), Am. Cattlemen Assn. Republican. Jewish. Lodges: Rotary (bd. dirs. 1948-50), B'nai B'rith (pres. 1935-36). Home: Memphis Tenn. Died Dec. 9, 1994.

ABRAVANEL, MAURICE, musical director; b. Salonica, Greece, Jan. 6, 1903; came to U.S., 1936; s. Edouard and Rachel (Bitty) A.; m. Lucy Carasso, 1947 (dec. 1985); m. Carolyn Firmage, 1987. Student, Gymnasium, Lausanne, Switzerland, 1917-19, U. Lausanne, 1919-21, U. Zurich, 1921-22; PhD (hon.), Cleve. Music Inst.; LLD, U. Utah, State U., Westminster Coll. mem. music panel Nat. Endowment for Arts, 1968-70, 89-93; mem. Nat. Coun. for Arts, 1970-76. Began as orch. condr., 1924, has conducted leading symphony orchs. in U.S., Europe, Australia, condr. Met. Opera, N.Y.; Kurt Weill premieres Seven Deadly Sins, 1933; Knickerbocker Holiday, 1938, Lady in the Dark, 1940, One Touch of Venus, 1943, Street Scene, 1946, Marc Blitzstein's Regina, 1949, Utah Symphony Orch., 1947-79, music dir. Acad. of the West, Santa Barbara, Calif., acting music dir. Berkshire Music Ctr., Tanglewood, Mass., 1982, permanent artist-in-residence, Berkshire Music Ctr., Tanglewood, Mass.; condr. numerous rec. premieres: 1st studio recs. Mahler: Symphony #7 and #8; condr. complete orchestral works of Mahler, Brahms, Tchaikovsky and Grieg, complete symphonies of Sibelius. Recipient Antoinette Perry award, 1950, Kilenyi Mahler medal, 1965, Ditson Condr.'s award, 1971, Gold Baton award Am. Symphony Orch. League, 1981, Nat. medal of Arts Pres. and Mrs. Bush, 1991, Theodor Thomas award Condrs. Guild, 1992; 4 concert halls named in his honor. Mem. Internat. Gustav Mahler Soc. (hon.). Home: Salt Lake City Utah Died Sept. 22, 1993.

ABS, HERMANN J., banker; b. October 15, 1901. Honorary president Deutsche Bank AG, Frankfurt, W.Ger. Died Feb. 5, 1994. Home: Frankfurt Germany

ACKERMAN, JAMES NILS, lawyer; b. Pleasant Dale, Nebr., Mar. 16, 1912; s. Albert Ferdinand and Irma Marie (Berlet) A.; m. Jean Caroline Doty, Aug. 8, 1939; children: Thomas Richard, Mary Alice (Mrs. James Reents). A.B., Nebr. Wesleyan U., 1933, LL.D. (hon.), 1975; LL.B., Harvard U., 1938. Bar: Nebr. 1938. Practice of law Davis & Stubbs, 1938-41, Davis, Stubbs & Ackerman, 1941-42, Peterson & Devoe, 1947-48; ptnr. Peterson, Devoe & Ackerman, 1948-52, Peterson & Ackerman, Lincoln, Nebr., 1952-77, Pierson, Ackerman, Fichett, Akin & Hunzeker, 1977-87; of counsel Pierson Fitchett Hunzeker Blake & Loftis, 1988-94; with FBI, 1942-47; asst. gen. counsel Bankers Life Ins. Co. Nebr. (now Ameritas), 1947-55, gen. counsel, 1955-77, v.p., 1960-77, trustee, 1957-77; magistrate U.S. Dist. Ct. Nebr., Lincoln, 1979-81; dir. Farmers Mut. Ins. Co.; dir. Gateway Bank, 1971-83, chmn. bd., 1975-83; counsel Nebr. Ins. Fedn., 1978-85. Bd. dirs. Lincoln Community Chest, 1965-68, chmn. bd., 1967-68; bd. dirs. Lincoln Community Council, 1950-65, County-City Implementation Commn., 1974, Lancaster County Child Guidance Clinic, 1946-54, Lincoln Symphony. Orch. Assn., 1965-72; Chmn. Lancaster County Rep. Party, 1950; del. Rep. county and state convs.; mem. Pres.'s Adv. Com. for J.F. Kennedy Center for Performing Arts, 1970-77, Nebr. Coordinating Commn. for Post-Secondary Edn., 1977-82; bd. govs. Nebr. Wesleyan U., 1964-91, chmn., 1964-76. Mem. Nebr. Bar Assn. (v.p. 1942), Lincoln Bar Assn. (pres. 1957), Assn. Life Ins. Counsel (pres. 1969-70), Am. Life Conv. (chmn. legal sect. 1960), Nebr. Ins. Fedn. (pres. 1970-73), Lincoln C. of C. (dir. 1968-70). Presbyterian. Clubs: Lincoln Country, Nebraska (Lincoln). Lodge: Masons. Home: Lincoln Nebr. Died July 14, 1994.

ADAMS, JAMES LUTHER, theologian; b. Ritzville, Wash., Nov. 12, 1901; s. James Carey and Lella May (Barnett) A.; m. Margaret Ann Young, Sept. 21, 1927; children: M. Eloise, Elaine Adams Miller, Barbara Thomas Thompson. A.B., U.Minn., 1924; S.T.B., Harvard U., 1927, A.M., 1930; Ph.D., U. Chgo., 1945; D.D., Meadville Theol. Sch., Chgo., 1958; Theol. D., Marburg U., W. Ger., 1960; D.H.L., Middlebury Coll., 1979. Ordained to ministry Unitarian Ch., 1927. Minister Second Ch., Salem, Mass., 1927-34; instr. English dept. Boston U., 1929-32; minister 1st Unitarian Soc., Wellesley Hills, Mass., 1934-35; prof. religious ethics Meadville Theol. Sch., also Div. Sch., U. Chgo., 1936-56; prof. Christian ethics Div. Sch., Harvard U., Cambridge, Mass., 1956-68; prof. emeritus Div. Sch., Harvard U.; Disting. prof. social ethics Andover Newton Theol. Sch., Newton Centre, Mass., 1968-72; Disting. scholar in residence Meadville-Lombard Theol. Sch., 1972-73; prof. theology and religious ethics Div. Sch., 1972-76; minister adult edn. Arlington Street Ch., Boston, 1971-94; Noble lectr. Harvard U., 1953; lectr. Albert Schweitzer Coll., 1952, Internat. Assn. History of Religion, Tokyo, 1958, World Ctr. for Buddhistic Studies, Rangoon, 1958, Theol. Coll., Bangalore, 1958; Hibbert lectr. Oxford, Manchester, Liverpool univs., Eng., 1963. Author: Irving Babbitt: Man and Teacher, 1941; The Changing Reputation of Human Nature, 1943; Taking Time Seriously, 1956; Paul Tillich's Philosophy of Culture, Science and Religion, 1965; On Being Human Religiously, 1976; (with others) New Perspective on Peace, 1944, Together We Advance, 1946, Voices of Liberalism II, 1947, Orientation in Religious Education, 1950, Religion in the State University, 1950, The Theology of Paul Tillich, 1952, rev. edit., 1984, Authority and Freedom, 1952, The Meaning of Love, 1953, Man's Faith and Freedom: The Theological Influence of Jacobus Arminius, 1962, Interpreters of Luther, 1968, Political and Legal Obligation, 1970, Religion of the Republic, 1971, Festschrift for Erich Fromm, In the Name of Life, 1971, Festschrift for W. Alvin Pitcher, Ethics and Belief, 1978, Democracy and Mediating Structures: A Theological Inquiry, 1980, Readings on Professionalism, 1980; author: (with others) Pastoral Care in the Liberal Churches, 1970; editor: (with others) Christian Register, 1932, The Directive in History (H.N. Wieman), 1949, What Did Luther Understand by Religion ? (Karl Holl), 1977, Taking Times Seriously (John R. Wilcox), 1978, The Reconstruction of Morality, 1979, (with Roger L. Shinn) The Thought of Paul Tillich, 1985, The Prophethood of All Believers, 1986, Voluntary Associations, 1986, Festschrift for Harold Berman, The Weightier Matters of the Law, 1988, An Examined Faith, 1991; editor (with others) Phoenix series of vols. on sociology of politics and religion; editor, translator: (with others) What Is Religion? (Paul Tillich), 1969; Political Expectation, 1971; editor Jour. Liberal Religion, 1939-49; assoc. editor Faith and Freedom, 1950-94, Jour. Liberal Ministry, 1979; co-editor Jour. Religion, 1951-56; mem. editorial bd. Jour. Religious Ethics, 1973-94; translator: Dogma of Christ (Erich Fromm), 1963, Religion in History, Essays by Ernst Troelstch, 1991; transl. and introductory essay on Paul Tillich, The Protestant Era, 1948; contbr. to profl. publs. Chmn. adv. com. dept. social responsibility Unitarian-Universalist Assn., 1965-69; bd. dirs. Ctr. for Vol. Soc., F.I.R.S.T., Inc., Mass. chpt. ACLU, Ctr. Applied Ethics, Mass. chpt. Ams. for Dem. Action; chmn. bd. dirs. Fellowship Racial and Econ. Equality; mem. adv. bd. Americans United for Separation of Ch. and State. Fulbright research scholar U. Marburg, 1963; hon. fellow Manchester Coll., Oxford. Fellow Am. Acad. Arts and Sci.; mem. Soc. Sci. Study of Religion (pres. 1957-59), Am. Soc. Christian Ethics (pres. 1967-68), Am. Theol. Soc. (pres. 1972-73), Am. Sociol. Soc., Societe Europeenne de Culture (internat. council), Soc. Art Religion and Contemporary Culture (chmn. bd. 1971-73, pres. 1984-85, pres. emeritus 1986-94), Council Religion and Law (bd. dirs.), Assn. for Vol. Action Scholars (v.p. 1971-94), Soc. Polit. and Legal Philosophy. Home: Cambridge Mass. Died July 26, 1994; interred Cambridge Cemetary, Cambridge, M.A.

ADAMS, LEON DAVID, author; b. Boston, Feb. 1, 1905; s. Nathan and Augusta (Lager) A.; m. Corinne Leona Adams (div. 1953); children: Gerald David, Brian Arthur; m. Eleanor Rittman (div. 1975); children: Timothy Rittman, Susan Campbell. Student, U. Calif., Berkeley, 1923-25. From reporter to marine editor San Francisco News and San Francisco Bulletin, 1923-28; bur. chief McClatchy Newspapers, San Francisco, 1928-35; with Organized Grape Growers League of Calif., San Francisco, 1931-33, Organized Wine Inst., San Francisco, 1934-54, Organized Wine Adv. Bd., San Francisco, 1938-54; organizer, exec. sec., editor Soc. Med. Friends of Wine, San Francisco, 1939-89, editor, 1956-89. Author: Striped Bass Fishing in California and Oregon, 1952, 2nd rev. edit., 1954, Commonsense Book of Wine, 1958, 5th rev. edit., 1991, Commonsense Book of Drinking, 1960, The Wines of America, 1973, 4th rev. edit., 1990. Mem. Am. Wine Soc. (Merit award 1974), Am. Soc. of Viticulture and Enology (Merit award 1974), Wine and Food Soc. Republican. Home: San Francisco Calif. Died Sept. 14, 1995.

ADAMS, STANLEY, lyricist; b. N.Y.C., Aug. 14, 1907; s. Henry Charles and Nan (Josephs) A.; m. Janice Schwarts, Sept. 28, 1940 (div.); 1 child, Barbara Paula; m. Bernice Halperin. LL.B., N.Y. U., 1929. Mem. adv. bd. Am. Fedn. Musicians, Nat. Cultural Center, Washington, Kennedy Cultural Center; mem. adminstrv. council Confedn. Internat. Performing Rights Socs. Author of lyrics for There Are Such Things, What A Diff'rence A Day Made, Little Old Lady, La Cucaracha; many others; contributed songs to The Show is On, A Lady Says Yes, Everyday's a Holiday, Duel in the Sun, Strategic Air Command (motion pictures); others. Bd. dirs. Braille Inst.; trustee Great Neck Symphony Assn. Recipient Presdl. citation Nat. Fedn. Music Clubs, 1961; Gold medal Phila. Club Printing House Craftsmen; Vet. Hosp. Radio and TV Guild award, 1964; Medal of Honor Nat. Arts Club, 1965; named hon. citizen State of Tenn., 1966. Mem. Country Music Assn. (v.p.), Am. Guild Authors and Composers (v.p. 1943-44), ASCAP (dir. 1944—, pres. 1953-80), Nat. Music Council (v.p.), Songwriters Hall of Fame (Bd. Dirs. award for lifetime achirevement 1988), Confedn. Internat. Des Societes D'Auteurs et Compositeurs (mem. exec. bur. 1976-78, pres. 1978-80), Delta Beta Phi. Clubs: Friars (N.Y.C.), Alfalfa (Washington). Home: Great Neck N.Y. Deceased.

ADAMS, WILLIAM JACKSON, JR., lawyer; b. Carthage, N.C., Sept. 15, 1908; s. William Jackson and Florence (Wall) A.; m. Elizabeth Whitehead, May 1, 1937; children: Elizabeth Whitehead (Mrs. R. Edward Morrissett, Jr.), William Jackson III. Student, Woodberry Forest Sch., Orange, Va.; A.B., U. N.C., 1930, J.D., 1933. Bar: N.C. bar 1932. Practice in Rocky Mount, 1933- 39; chief div. legislative drafting and codification of statutes N.C. Dept. Justice, 1939-41; an asst. atty. gen. N.C., 1941-45; practice in Greensboro, 1945-93; Mem. steering com. to establish N.C. Constl. Study Commn., 1968-69; chmn. Spl. Liaison Tax Com. for S.E. Region, 1974. Student editor in chief: N.C. Law Rev, 1933; Contbr. profl. jours., yachting mags. Bd. dirs. Found. Greater Greensboro, 1984-93. Mem. Am. Bar Assn., N.C. Bar Assn. (pres. 1968-69), Greensboro Bar Assn. (pres. 1957-58), Am. Judicature Soc., Am. Coll. Probate Counsel, Nat. Conf. Bar Presidents, Phi Beta Kappa, Order of Coif, Phi Delta Phi. Democrat. Methodist. Clubs: Greensboro Country; Carolina Sailing (Henderson, N.C.) (charter, 1st commodore; Robinson cup 1959); Lake Norman Yacht (Mooresville, N.C.) (charter); Pamlico Sailing (Washington). Home: Greensboro N.C. Died Feb. 13, 1993.

ADISESHIAH, MALCOLM SATHIANATHAN, academic administrator; b. Madras, Tamilnadu, India, Apr. 18, 1910; s. Paul Veranaci and Nassamma A.; m. Dec. 26, 1952; 2 children. Ed. Voorhees Sch. and Coll., Vellore, India, Loyola Coll., Madras, London Sch. Econs., U. London, Kings Coll., Cambridge U. (Eng.); hon. degrees. From lectr. to prof. econs. U. Calcutta (India), U. Madras, 1931-46; dir. UNESCO, Paris, from 1946, asst. dir. gen., dep. dir. gen., to 1970; dir. Madras Inst. Devel. Studies, from 1971, chmn; vice chancellor Madras U., 1975-78. Author numerous books, the most recent being: Literacy Discussion, 1976; Towards a Functional Learning Society, 1976; Backdrop to Learning Society, 1980; Adult Education Faces Inequalities, 1981; Mid Year Review of the Economy 1974, 89; Mid Year Assessment of the VI Plan, 1983; Seventh Plan Perspectives, 1985; The Why, What and Whither of the Public Sector Enterprises, 1985; Shaping the National Events-The Economy as Seen in Parliamentary Statements, 1985; Comments on the Black Money, 1986, Tax Policy Proposals for Direct Tax Reform, 1987, Price Policy Analysis of Administered and Support Prices, 1988. Mem. Parliament Rajya Sabha, 1978-94; v.p. Tamil Nadu Bd. Continuing Edn. (India); pres. Tamil Nadu State Coun. for Sci. and Tech. Decorated Padma Bhushan (India). Mem. Indian Econ. Assn., Internat. Council for Adult Edn., Indian Adult Edn. Assn., Internat. Inst. for Ednl. Planning. Died Nov. 21, 1994. Home: Madras India

ADKINS, ARTHUR WILLIAM HOPE, humanities educator; b. Leicester, Eng., Oct. 17, 1929; s. Archibald Arthur and Nora (Hope) A.; m. Elizabeth Mary Cullingford, Sept. 16, 1961; children—Matthew, Deborah. BA, Oxford U., 1952, MA, 1955, DPhil, 1957. Asst. in humanities U. Glasgow, Scotland, 1954-56; lectr. Greek Bedford Coll., U. London, 1956-61; fellow in classical langs. and lit. Exeter Coll., Oxford U., 1961-65; prof. classics U. Reading, Eng., 1965-74; Edward Olson prof. depts. classical langs. and lit., philosophy and early Christian lit. U. Chgo., 1974-96; chmn. com. on ancient Mediterranean world, 1980-92; sr. vis. fellow Soc. Humanities, Cornell U., 1969-70. Author: Merit and Responsibility: A Study in Greek Values, 1960, From the Many to the One, 1970, Moral Values and Political Behavior in Ancient Greece, 1972, Poetic Craft in the Early Greek Elegists, 1985; co-editor: Univ. Chgo. Readings in Western Civilization, vol. I, The Greek Polis, 1986, Human Virtue and Human Excellence, 1991; contbr. articles to profl. jours. Mem. Am. Philological Assn., Classical Assn. Gt. Britain, Soc. Promotion of Hellenic Studies., Am. Philos. Assn. Home: Chicago Ill. Died Feb. 13, 1996.

ADKINS, HOWARD EUGENE, aluminum company executive; b. Depoy, Ky., Oct. 4, 1912; s. Elmer Eugene and Mattie Luvenia (Merrill) A.; m. Wilma Lucille Jenkins, Sept. 18, 1936; children: Howard Eugene Jr., Michael Ray, Wilma Carol, Martha Lee. B.A., Western Ky. State U., 1940; M.S., U. Wis., 1950. Tchr. pub. schs. Ky., 1934-42; asst. prof. to asso. prof. U. Wis., 1947-57; welding engr., then mgr. welding engring. tech. services Kaiser Aluminum and Chem. Sales, Inc., Rosemont, Ill., 1957-74; asst. dir. field tech. operations Kaiser Aluminum and Chem. Sales, Inc., 1974-77; pres. Howard E. Adkins and Assos. Inc., welding engring. firm, Park Ridge, Ill., 1978-93; cons., lectr. in field. Contbr. articles to profl. lit. Served with USAAF, AUS, 1943-45. Recipient Bronze medallion and certificate Lincoln Arc Welding Found., 1953, Tech. Services Engring. award of Merit Kaiser Aluminum, 1969. Mem. Am. Welding Soc. (hon., Howard E. Adkins' Instr. Mem. award 1964, Meritorious certificate 1967, Lincoln Gold medal 1963, certificate Madison sect. 1966, Nat. Meritorious certificate and award 1974, dir. 1970-73, 76-93, dir. aluminum assn. welding and joining com. 1970-71, 73), Am. Soc. Metals, Phi Delta Kappa. Republican. Methodist. Club: Mason. Home: Park Ridge Ill. Died Nov. 29, 1993.

ADVANI, SUNDER, engineering educator, university dean. BSME with first class honors, Bombay U., 1961; MSME, Stanford U., 1962, PhD, 1965. Design engr. Carco Electronics, Menlo Park, Calif., 1962; teaching and rsch. asst. mech. engring. Stanford U., 1962-64; sr. rsch. engr., mem. tech. staff Biodynamics Lab. Northrop Corp., Calif., 1965-67; assoc. prof., prof. mech. engring. and mechanics W.Va. U., 1967-78, assoc. chmn. grad. studies dept. mech. engring. and mechanics, 1975-78; prof., chmn. dept. engring. mechanics Ohio State U., 1978-91, assoc. dean acad. affairs Coll. Engring., 1984-91; dean Coll. Engring. and Applied Sci. Lehigh U., Bethlehem, Pa., 1991-93; mem. U.S. nat. rock mechanics com. NRC, 1983-89; assoc. editor ASME JOMAE, 1987-91, JERT, 1986-91; bd. dirs. Ohio State U. Rsch. Found., 1986-90; pres. Assn. Chmn. Dept. Mechanics, 1990-91. Author: (with others) Crashworthiness in Transportation Systems, 1978, Applied Physiological Mechanics, 1979, Electrical Properties of Bone and Cartilage, 1979, Human Body Dynamics, 1982, Finite Elements in Fluids, 1984; editor: (with C.H. Popelar and A.W. Leissa) Developments in Mechanics, 1985; contbr. numerous articles to profl. jours. Recipient Ralph P. Boyer Meritorious award, 1980, George Westinghouse award ASEE, 1985. Fellow ASME, Am. Acad. Mechanics. Home: Bethlehem Pa. Died Nov. 3, 1993.

AFANASYEV, VIKTOR GRIGORYEVICH, newspaper editor; b. Aktanysh, Tataria, USSR, Nov. 18, 1922; s. Grigory Yakovlevich and Ekaterina (Mikhailovna) A.; grad. Chita Pedagogical Inst., 1949; Ph.B., Chelyabinsk Pedagogicol Inst., 1953; Sc.D., Acad. Social Scis., 1964; m. Lyudmila Petrovna Yegorova, Jan. 7, 1946; children: Olga, Andrei. Instr. philosophy Chelyabinsk Pedagogical Inst., 1952-60; chmn. Acad. Social Scis., 1960-68; with Pravda, 1968-94, editor-in-chief, 1976-94. Dep. to Supreme Soviet USSR, 1977-94; chmn. USSR Journalists Union, 1976-94. Mem. central com. Communist Party of Soviet Union, 1976-94. Served with Russian Air Force, 1940-53. Decorated Order Lenin, Order Red Star, Order Oct. Revolution, Order Red Banner Labour. Mem. Acad. Scis. Author books, articles on politics, philosophy. Died April 10, 1994. Home: Moscow Russia

AGO, ROBERTO, judge, educator; b. Vigevano, Pavia, Italy, May 26, 1907; s. Pietro and Maria (Marini) A.; m. Luciana Cova, 1936; 5 children. LL.D., U. Naples, Italy; Dr. (hon.), univs. of Geneva, Nancy (France), Nice (France), Paris, Toulouse (France). Lectr. internat. law U. Cagliari, Italy, 1930-33, U. Messina, Italy, 1933-34; prof. internat. law U. Catania, Italy, 1934, U. Genoa, Italy, 1935, Milan U., Italy, 1938, Rome U., 1956—; pres. Italian Soc. Internat. Orgns.; Italian del. ILO Conf., from 1945, to UNESCO, 1949-50, Law of Sea Conf., 1958-60, Vienna Conf. on Diplomatic Relations, 1961; pres. Vienna Conf. Law of Treaties, 1968-69; mem. Com. for drafting European Constn., 1952; chmn. governing bd. ILO, 1954-55, 67-68; mem., former pres. Internat. Law Com. UN, 1957-79; mem. Permanent Ct. Arbitration, from 1957; hon. pres. World Fedn. UN Assns.; judge ad hoc Internat. Ct. Justice, 1959-60, judge, 1979—; pres. curatorium Hague Acad. Internat. Law, Arbitration Tribunal France-Germany, France-U.S.; mem. and pres. numerous other internat. tribunals and conciliation coms. Author: Teoria del diritto internazionale privato, 1934; Il requisito dell'effettivita dell'occupazione in diritto internazionale, 1934; Règles générales des conflits de lois, 1936; La responsabilità indiretta nel diritto internazionale, 1936; Lezioni di diritto internazionale privato, 1939; Le délit international, 1939; Lezioni di diritto internazionale, 1943; Scienza giuridica e diritto internazionale, 1950; Diritto positivo e diritto internazionale, 1955; International Organisations and their Functions in the Field of Internal Activities of States, 1957; Positive Law and International Law, 1957; Il Trattato istitutivo dell'Euratom, 1961; The State and International Organisation, 1963; La responsabilité internationale des Etats, 1963; La qualité de l'Etat pour agir en matière de protection diplomatique des sociétés, 1964; La Nazioni Unite per il diritto internazionale, 1965; La coopération internationale dans le domaine du droit international public, 1966; La codification du droit international et les problèmes de sa réalisation, 1968; Sur la protection diplomatique des personnes morales, 1969; La fase conclusiva dell'opera di codificazione del diritto internazionale, 1969; Premier, deuxieme, troisieme, quatrieme, cinquieme, sixieme, septieme et huiteme rapport à la C.D.I. sur la responsabilité des Etats, 1969-79; Nazioni Unite: venticinque anni dopo, 1970; Droit des traités à la lumière de la Convention de Vienne, 1971; Caratteri generali della communità internazionale e del suo diritto, 1974-75; Eccezioni non esclusivamente preliminari, 1975; Il pluralismo della communità internazionale alle sue origini, 1977; Pluralism and the Origins of International Community, 1978; The First International Communities in the Mediterranean World, 1982; Studi sulla responsabilità internazionale, 1979-1986; Le droit international dans la conception de Grotius, 1983; Positivism (International Law), 1984; I quaranta anni delle Nazioni Unite, 1986; individual and dissenting opinions in cases before the I.c.y., 1980, 82, 86, Nouvelles réflexions sur la codification du droit international, 1989; contbr. articles to profl. jours. Decorated grand croix Order of Merit (Italy); Order of Merit (W. Ger.); officier Legion d'honneur (France); comdr. Order Brit. Empire. Mem. Inst. de Droit International (v.p.), Accademia Nacionale dei Lincei, Am. Acad. Polit. and Social Scis., Inst. Hellenique Droit International, Societe Royale de Belgique, Indian Soc. Internat. Law (hon.), Am. Soc. Internat. Law (hon.). Home: Geneva Switzerland Died Feb. 24, 1995.

AGUILAR MAWDSLEY, ANDRÉS, judge; b. Caracas, July 10, 1924. Student, U. Ctrl. Venezuela, Caracas, McGill U., Montreal. Tchr. civil law U. Ctrl. Venezuela, 1948, prof. law, 1958-95; tchr. civil law U. Católica Andrés Bello, Caracas, 1954, prof., 1958, vice-rector, 1962-63; min. justice Venezuela, amb. to U.S., 1972-74; permanent rep. to European office UN, Geneva, 1963-65; permanent rep. UN, 1969-72; judge Internat. Ct. Justice, The Hague, 1991-95; legal adviser Venezuela Chamber Bldg., 1957-58; mem. governing bd. Banco Indsl. Venezuela, 1958-59; pres. Nat. Governing Bd. of Caritas, 1966-69; mem. governing bd. Inst. Higher Studies Adminstrn., 1966; head Venezuelan delegation Internat. Conf. Human Rights, Teheran, 1968; mem. panel legal experts INTELSAT, 1974; mem. com. inquiry UN, 1980. Author: Possession in the Civil Law of the Province of Quebec, La responsabilidad contractual del arquitecto y del empresario por vicios y defectos de la obra, Protección familiar, La delincuencia en Venezuela: su prevención, La obligación de alimentos en derecho venezolano; contbr. articles to profl. jours. Mem. ILO (mem. various coms., pres. conf. 1964), ICEM (pres. coun. 1964-65), Internat. Coun. Social Welfare (chair nat. coun. 1968), Venezuelan Assn. UN (pres. 1967-68), Inter-Am. Com. Human Rights (former chair), Internat. Com. Jurists (pres. 1986-95). Home: The Hague The Netherlands Died Oct. 24, 1995.

AGUSTA, BENJAMIN J., computer company executive; b. Bklyn., July 1, 1931; s. Michael and Stephanie (Gallo) A.; m. Josephine Galante, Aug. 30, 1953; children: Michael, Stephanie, Joseph. B.S.E.E., MIT, 1952, M.S. in Elec. Engring, 1954; D.Eng., Syracuse U., 1964. Functional mgr. advanced solid state monolithic device research IBM Corp., Burlington, Vt., 1967-77; exec. mgr. gen. tech. devel. IBM Corp., 1977-78, exec. mgr. div. tech. devel. staff, 1978-93; ret., 1993; instr. M.I.T., 1952-54. Mem. adv. bd.: IBM Jour. Research and Devel., 1974-94; contbr. articles to profl. jours. Coordinator Burlington Internat. Games, 1977-83; advisor NSF. Served to 1st lt. USAR, 1952-54. Fellow IEEE; mem. Sigma Xi, Tau Beta Pi, Eta Kappa Nu. Roman Catholic. Clubs: Burlington Country, Elks. Home: Durham N.C. Deceased.

AIELLO, SALVATORE, performing company executive. Artistic dir. N.C. Dance Theatre, Charlotte. Home: Charlotte N.C. Deceased.

AIRD, JOHN BLACK, lawyer, university official, former lieutenant governor; b. Toronto, Ont., Can., May 5, 1923; s. Hugh Reston and May (Black) A.; m. Lucile Jane Housser, July 27, 1944; children: Lucille Elizabeth Aird Menear, Jane Victoria Aird Blackmore, Hugh Housser, Katherine Aird Porter. BA, U. Toronto, 1946; LLB, Osgoode Hall Law Sch., 1949; LLD (hon.), Wilfrid Laurier U., 1975, Royal Mil. Coll. Can, 1980, U. Western Ont., 1983, Lakehead U., 1984, U. Toronto, 1984; DSL, Wycliffe Coll., 1985, U. St. Michaels Coll., 1992. Bar: Ont., 1949. Assoc. Wilton & Edison, 1949-53; ptnr. Edison, Aird & Berlis, 1953-74, Aird, Zimmerman & Berlis, 1974-78; ptnr. Aird & Berlis, Toronto, 1978-80, 85-93, hon. chmn., 1990, counsel, 1993; lt. gov. of Ont., 1980-85; chancellor emeritus Wilfrid Laurier U., 1985; chancellor U. Toronto, 1986-91, chancellor emeritus, 1991—, third visitor-Massey Coll., 1990; Gillette lectr. U. Western Ont., 1984; chmn. Can. sect. Can.-U.S. Permanent Joint Bd. Def., 1971-79; chmn. Inst. Rsch. Pub. Policy, 1974-80, Can. Inst. for Advanced Rsch., chmn. bd., chmn. emeritus, 1990; bd. dirs. Econ. Investment Trust Ltd.; hon. chmn. The Consumer's Gas Co., Ltd.; hon. chmn., bd. dirs. Algoma Ctrl. Corp.; hon. dir. The Molson Cos. Ltd.; spl. rep. Bermuda Comml. Bank Ltd. Hon. chmn. United Way Greater Toronto, 1987-91, Can. Liver Found., Gov. Royal Can. Geog. Soc.; mem. Senate of Can., 1964-74; mem. Duke of Edinburgh's Award World Fellowship. Lt. Royal Can. Navy, 1942-45, capt. Can. Forces Res., hon. col. 78th Fraser Highlanders, 1989. Decorated officer Order Can., promoted to companion; First recipient of the Order of Ont., recipient award of Merit-City of Toronto, Officer of the Order of Red Cross, 35th Humanitarian award Beth Shalom Brotherhood, Silver Acorn Boy Scouts of Can., Human Relations award Can. Council of Christians and Jews, Great Lakes Man of Yr., Knight of Justice of the Most Venerable Order of the Hosp. of St. John of Jerusalem, King Clancy award Can. Found. for Physically Disabled Persons, Paul Harris award Rotary Found.; Promise Hope award Can. Children's Found.; named Queen's Coun., 1960, Hon. Gov. Variety Village, Toronto. Mem. Naval Officers Assn. Can. (hon. pres., Gold award), Royal Can. Geog. Soc. (gov.), York Club (spl.), Toronto Club (hon.), Toronto Golf Club, Royal Can. Yacht Club, Royal and Ancient Golf Club St. Andrews, Royal Bermuda Yacht Club, Alpha Delta Phi (Samuel Eells award). Anglican. Home: Toronto Can. Died May 6, 1995.

AITKIN, W. ROY, mining company executive; b. Glasgow, Scotland, Apr. 5, 1932; m. Pamela Mary Evans, 1958; children: Neil, Richard. BS, Glasgow U., 1953; postgrad., U. Western Ontario, Can., 1973. With Inco Ltd., 1970-93, exec. v.p., 1984-92, asst. to the chmn. and ceo, 1992-93. Mem. Ontario Mining Assn. (bd. dirs.), Can. Mfrs. Assn. (bd. dirs., Can. com.). Home: Oakville Can. Deceased.

ALBERS, ANNI, artist, textile designer; b. Berlin, June 12, 1899; came to U.S., 1933, naturalized, 1937; d. Siegfried and Toni (Ullstein) (changed name to Farman) Fleischmann; m. Josef Albers, 1925. Art student under Martin Brandenburg,, Berlin, 1916-19; student, Kunstgewerbeschule, Hamburg, Germany, 1919-20, Bauhaus, Weimar and Dessau, Germany, 1922-29; Bauhaus diploma; DFA (hon.), Md. Inst. Coll. of Art, 1972, Phila. Coll. Art, 1976, U. Hartford, 1979, R.I. Sch. of Design, 1990; LLD, York U., Toronto, Ont., Can., 1973; D (hon.), Royal Coll. Art, London, 1990. Part-time instr., acting dir. Bauhaus weaving workshop, 1930-33; asst. prof. art Black Mountain Coll., N.C., 1933-49; free-lance work, Dessau and Berlin, 1930-33, New Haven, 1950-94; lectr. Minn. Sch. Art, R.I. Sch. Design, San Francisco Mus. Art, Carnegie Inst. Tech., Phila. Mus. Coll. Art, U. Hawaii, Contemporary Art Mus., Houston, Rice Inst., Yale. Exhbns. include Mus. Modern Art, N.Y.C., 1949, Wadsworth Atheneum, Hartford, Conn., 1953, Honolulu Acad. Arts, 1954, MIT, 1959, Carnegie Inst., Pitts., 1959, Balt. Mus. Art, 1959, Yale U. Art Gallery, New Haven, 1960, 1986, Colorado Springs Fine Arts Ctr., Colo., 1959, Contemporary Arts Mus., Houston, 1960, U. Bridgeport, Conn., 1971, Kunstmuseum, Dusseldorf, Fed. Republic Germany, 1975, Bauhaus-Archiv, Berlin, 1975, Bklyn. Mus., 1977, Queens Coll. Library, N.Y., 1979, Monmouth Mus., N.J., 1979, Hartford Art Sch., U. Hartford, 1979, Mattatuck Mus., Waterbury, Conn., 1979, Renwick Gallery, Smithsonian Instn., Washington, 1985, Villa Stück, Munich, 1989, Mus. Modern Art, 1990; represented in permanent collections, Mus. Modern Art, Met. Mus. Art, N.Y.C., Art Inst. Chgo., Busch-Reisinger Mus. at Harvard U., Balt. Mus. Art, Mus. Cranbrook Acad. Art, Currier Gallery Art, Bauhaus-Archiv, Jewish Mus., N.Y., Bklyn. Mus., Nat. Gallery, Washington, Seattle Art Mus., Israel Mus., Jerusalem, N.Y. Pub. Library, Grunwald Ctr. for Graphic Arts, UCLA, Kunstmuseum der Stadt Düsseldorf, Westfälisches Landesmuseum für Kunst und Kulturegeschichte, Münster, Fed. Republic Germany, Art Gallery Ont., Ft. Worth Art Mus., St. Louis Art Mus., Wadsworth Atheneum, Yale U. Art Gallery, also others, also pvt. collections; author: Anni Albers: on Designing, 1959 3d edit, 1971, Anni Albers: on Weaving, 1965, 2d edit., 1972, Pre-Columbian Mexican Miniatures; the Josef and Anni Albers Collection, 1970, also articles; subject of exhbn. catalogs and numerous articles. Recipient medal in craftsmanship AIA, 1961; citation Phila. Mus. Coll. Art, 1962; citation Decorative Arts Book Award, 1965; award for outstanding achievement as weaver, designer and printmaker Women's Caucus for Art, 1980; Gold medal Am. Craft Council, 1981; Tamarind Lithography Workshop fellow, 1964. Home: Orange Conn. Died May 9, 1994.

ALBERT, STEPHEN JOEL, composer; b. N.Y.C., Feb. 6, 1941. Pvt. lessons in composition with, Elie Siegmeister, 1956-58, Karl-Birger Blomdahl, Stockholm, 1960, Joseph Castaldo-Phila. Musical Acad., 1960-93, George Rochberg-U. Pa., 1963. Lectr. music Stanford U., Calif., 1970-71; mem. faculty dept. music Smith Coll., Northampton, Mass., 1974-76; composition faculty dept. music Julliard Sch., N.Y.C., 1988-93, Boston U., 1988-90; composer-in-residence Seattle Symphony and Opera, 1985-88. Works include: Illuminations for 2 Pianos, 2 Harps, Brass and Percussion, 1961, Supernatural Songs for Sorprano and Chamber Orchestra, 1963, Imitations for String Quartet, 1964, Winter Songs for Tenor and Orchestra, 1965, Wedding Songs for Soprano and Piano, 1965, Bacchae for Narrator, Chorus, and Orchestra, 1967-68, Prologue to the Bacchae for Orch., 1967, Wolf Time for Soprano and Chamber Orch. with amplifier, 1968, Cathedral Music for 2 Flutes, 2 Cellos, 2 Horns, 2 Trumpets, electric Guitar, Harpsichord, 2 Percussion, Electronic Piano, Electronic Organ and 2 Grand Pianos, 1972, Voices Within for Orchesta and Pit Band, 1975, To Wake the Dead for Soprano, Flute, Clarinet, Violin, Cello, and Piano (aux player for harmonium and assisting piano), 1978, (recorded Smithsonian Collection), Into Eclipse for Tenor and 12 instruments, 1981 (recorded), Into Eclipse for Tenor and Orch., 1981 (recorded), Treestone for Soprano, 10 and 12 instruments, 1984 (recorded), Riverrun for Orch., 1984 (recorded), Flower of the Mountain for Soprano and Chamber Orch., 1985 (recorded), In Concordiam for violin and orch., 1986, Anthem and Processionals for Orchestra, 1987, Songs From the Stone Harp, 1988, Sun's Heat (for tenor and 11 instruments), 1989, Cello Concerto, 1989 (recorded), Tapioca for Orch., 1990, Wind Canticle for clarinet and orch., 1991, Ecce Pier for soprano, ob,, 191, Symphony # 2 for orch., 1992; performed with Chgo. Symphony Orch. (commn.), N.Y. Philharm. Orch. (commn.), Nat. Symphony Orch. (commn.), Boston Symphony Orch., Pitts. Symphony Orch., Seattle Symphony Orch., Phila. Orch., St. Louis Orch., N.J. Symphony Orch., BBC Orch. of London, RAI of Rome Orch., Am. Composer's N.Y. Orch., Australian Broadcasting Co. Symphony of Sydney, Jerusalem Symphony, Balt. Symphony Orch., Rotterdam Orch., Berkshire Music Festival, N.Y. Chamber Orch. (commn.), L.A. Chamber Orch., L.A. Chamber Ensemble, Da Capo, Bklyn. Acad. Music, 20th Century Consort, San Francisco Contemporary Music Players, Lontano, Collage, Musica Viva & Alea III, Musical Elements, Music Today Series, various univs. and conservatories. Recipient Bearns prize, 1962, Pulitzer prize for music, 1985, also, honorable mention, 1987,1st Prize BMI Hemispheric Competition, 1961, Alfred I. duPont award, 1991, Lancaster award, 1991; works commd. N.Y. Philharm., Phila. Orch., Chgo. Symphony, Balt. Symphony, Pitts. Symphony Orch., Chamber Music Soc. Lincoln Ctr. , Seattle Symphony Orch./Nonesuch Records Joint Project, Paui; Fromm/Berkshire Mus. Festival Joint Commn., 1975, McKim Ford/Libr. Congress Commn., 1988; grantee Martha Baird Rockefeller Found. (4), Ford Found, CMP, Guggenheim Found., NEA (2); fellow MacDowell Found., 1964-65, 68, 71, Huntington Hartford Found. 1965, Am. Acad. in Rome (Prix de Rome), 1965-67. Home: Newtonville Mass. Died Dec. 27, 1993.

ALDERFER, OWEN HIRAM, educator, minister; b. Upland, Calif., June 7, 1923; s. Hiram R. and Mary Rebecca (Frymire) A.; m. Ardis Witter, June 15, 1945; children: Jill Annette, Eric Ray. AB, Upland (Calif.) Coll., 1945; BD, Asbury Theol. Sem., Wilmore, Ky., 1951; PhD, Claremont (Calif.) Grad. Sch., 1964. Ordained minister Brethren in Christ Ch., 1946. Pastor Brethren In Christ Ch., Springfield, Ohio, 1951-55; prof. religion Upland Coll., 1955-65; prof. ch. history Ashland (Ohio) Theol. Sem., 1965-80; prof. religion Messiah Coll., Grantham, Pa., 1980-84, C.N. Hostetter prof. theology, 1980-84; bishop Brethren in Christ Ch., West Milton, Ohio, 1984-90; ret., 1990. Author: Called to Obedience, 1974; editor Ashland Theol. Bull., 1969-79; contbr. articles to profl. jours. Recipient Disting. Alumnus award Messiah Coll., 1983; Danforth Found. grantee, 1961-63. Home: Mechanicsburg Pa. Died June 4, 1991.

ALDERSON, WILLIAM THOMAS, historian, consultant; b. Schenectady, May 8, 1926; s. William Thomas and Helen Martha (Knowlton) A.; m. Sylvia Caldwell Farrell, Sept. 14, 1953; children: William Thomas III, Virginia Ann, Rebecca Louise. AB, Colgate U., 1947; student, Howard Coll., 1944-45, Tulane U., 1945-46; MA, Vanderbilt U., 1949, PhD, 1952. Sr. archivist Tenn. State Libr. and Archives, 1952-57, asst. state libr. and archivist, 1959-61; exec. sec. Tenn. Hist. Commn., 1957-61, state librarian and archivist, chmn. commn., 1961-64; dir. Am. Assn. State and Local History; editor History News, Nashville, 1964-78; prof., dir. mus. studies, William Watson Harrington Disting. lectr. in history U. Del., Newark, 1978-82; dir. Margaret Woodbury Strong Mus., Rochester, N.Y., 1982-86; pres. Old Salem Inc., Winston-Salem, N.C., 1987-90; coord. seminar for hist. adminstrn. Colonial Williamburg Found., 1990-96; mem. adv. com. Library of Congress Nat. Union Catalog Manuscript Collections, 1965-70; adv. com. hist. socs. and humanistic mus. NEH, 1966; mus. adv. panel Nat. Endowment Arts, 1972-75, co-chmn., 1974-75; adv. com. Historic Am. Bldgs. Survey, 1967-71; mem. Nat. Museum Act adv. council Smithsonian Instn., 1971-76; instr. extension div. U. Tenn., 1954-61; vis. asst. prof. history Vanderbilt U., 1955-56, adj. prof., 1973-78; dir. Am. Heritage Pub. Co., 1965-78; mem. Hist. Commn. Met. Nashville and Davidson County, 1966-70; trustee Hist. Hudson Valley, 1981-91; adj. prof. history Wake Forest U., Winston-Salem, N.C., 1990-93. Author: Tennessee Historical Markers, 1958, (with R.H. White) A Guide to the Study and Reading of Tennessee History, 1959, (with R.M. McBride) Tennessee Historical Markers, 1962, (with H.G. Thomas) Historic Sites in Tennessee, 1963, Tennessee, A Student's Guide to Localized History, 1966, (with Shirley P. Low) Interpretation of Historic Sites, 1976, 2d edit., 1985; co-editor: Landmarks of Tennessee History, 1965; editor: American Issues, 1976, Mermaids, Mummies and Mastadons: The Emergence of the American Museum, 1992; asst. editor Tenn. Hist. Quar., 1953, assoc. editor, 1954-55, editor, 1956-65; contbr. to encys., profl. jours. Served with USNR, 1943-46. Fellow Soc. Am. Archivists (coun. 1963-67); mem. Am. Assn. for State and Local History (coun. 1959-64, award of distinction 1991), Am. Records Mgmt. Assn. (pres. S.E. chpt. 1963-64), Tenn. Assn. Mus. (pres. 1965-67), Assn. Preservation Tenn. Antiquities (trustee 1964-71), Colgate U. Alumni Assn. (pres. Tenn. chpt. 1962-66), Nashville Rose Soc. (pres. 1963), So. Hist. Assn., Tenn. Hist. Soc. (v.p. 1969-71), Am. Assn. Mus. (chmn. accreditation commn. 1970-73, councilor-at-large, 1987-89), Mid-Atlantic Assn. Mus. (v.p. 1978-80, pres. 1981-82, Katherine Coffey award 1988), Southeastern Mus. Conf. (James R. Short award 1987). Republican. Methodist. Home: Winston Salem NC Died April 4, 1996.

ALEKSANDROV, ANATOLIY PETROVICH, physicist; b. Tarashcha, Kiev Region, Ukraine, Feb. 13, 1903. Student Kiev U., 1925-30, Leningrad. Phys.-Tech.

Inst., 1930-46, Corr. mem. USSR Acad. Scis., 1943-53, mem., 1953-94, pres., 1976-86; dir. Inst. Physical Problems, USSR Acad. Scis., 1946-54; dir. Kurchatov Inst. Atomic Energy, 1960-94. Patentee anti-mine defense for ships during World War II, 1941-45. Mem. Communist Party Soviet Union, 1962-94, mem. central com., 1966-94, dep. to Supreme Soviet, 1960-66, from 1976. Recipient USSR State prize, 1942, 49, 51, 53, Lenin prize, 1959, Order of Lenin (9), Hero of Socialist Labour (3), Gold Star of Friendship Between Peoples, 1983, others. Died Feb. 3, 1994. Home: Moscow Russia

ALEXANDER, ROBERT EVANS, architect; b. Bayonne, N.J., Nov. 23, 1907; s. Edwin Hixson and Clara (Evans) A.; m. Eugenie Vigneron, June 13, 1931 (dec. 1952); children: Lynne Marie, Timothy Milne; m. Mary Starbuck, Aug. 29, 1953 (div. Mar. 1984); 1 child, Robert Evans II; m. Nancy Jaicks, July 28, 1984. BArch, Cornell U., 1930. Ptnr. Wilson, Merrill & Alexander, Los Angeles, 1935-41; asst. to works mgr. Lockheed Aircraft, Burbank, Calif., 1942-46; owner R.E. Alexander, Los Angeles, 1946-49; ptnr. R.J. Neutra & R.E. Alexander, Los Angeles, 1949-58; owner R.E. Alexander F.A.I.A. & Assocs., Los Angeles, 1959-81; cons. in field Berkeley, 1982-92; cons. Pub. Housing Adminstrn., 1950, Govt. India, 1951, Govt. Guam, 1951-52, FHA, 1958-59, U. Calif. San Diego, 1961-65, Calif. Inst. Tech, 1966-72, Claremont Colls., 1966-76, Ministry Culture & Edn. Brazil, 1977, Pacific Architects & Engrs., Tokyo, 1977-78, 1983. Author: The Rural City, 1952; co-author: Rebuilding the City, 1950, Environmental Quality and Amenity, 1966; contbr. numerous articles to profl. jours.; projects include Bunker Hill Towers, Caltech Ct. of Man, Orange Coast Coll., U. Calif. Elem. Demonstration Sch., Los Angeles, Baldwin Hills Village, U. Nev. Library, city plans for El Paso, San Fernando, Norwalk, Vista, Escondido, also dormitories, gen. services bldg., Sch. Medicine, Long-range devel. plans U. Calif. at San Diego, grad. student apartments U. So. Calif., Internat. Student Ctr., numerous others; architect (with Neutra), Am. Embassy, Karachi, Pakistan, also Gettysburg Cyclorama Bldg. and Petrified Forest Community for Nat. Park Service, art ctrs. for U. Nev. and San Fernando State Coll., Francis Scott Key Meml. and Mellon Sci. Labs. St. John's Coll., Annapolis, Md., Ctr. of Communicating and Performing Arts for Adelphi Coll., Library and residence halls Simpson Coll., redevel. of cen. bus. dist. Tulsa; (with others) County of Los Angeles Hall of Records; faculty Coll. Architecture U. So. Calif., 1952-61. V.p., then pres. Planning Comm. City of L.A., 1945-50; bd. govs. Town Hall City of L.A., 1965-67; pres. Willard Neighborhood Assn., 1985-87; support group leader Calif. Convicts in AIDS ward, Vacaville, 1985-92; bd. dirs. Calif. Planning and Conservation League, 1961-63. Recipient numerous awards for design. Fellow AIA (25 Yr. award); mem. So. Calif. Chpt. AIA (v.p., pres. 1969-70). Democrat. Home: Berkeley Calif. Died Nov. 17, 1992.

ALFORD, JOHN WILLIAM, bank executive; b. Balt., Oct. 21, 1912; s. James Perry and Lydia (Turner) A.; m. Mary Elizabeth Anderson, Jan. 3, 1951 (dec. Oct. 1987); children: Barbara Lynne Alford Cantlin, Ronald Bradford. AB, DePauw U., 1935, DHL (hon.), 1993; DHL (hon.), Denison U., 1988. With Park Nat. Bank, Newark, Ohio, 1935-96; v.p. Park Nat. Bank, 1946-56, pres., 1956-60, dir., 1952-96, chmn. exec. com.; bd. dirs. Contour Acquisition Co., W.E. Shrider Co.; chmn. bd. dirs. Park Nat. Corp. Mem. Licking County Hosp. Commn., 1962-96; gen. chmn. citizens com. for Licking County Meml. Hosp., 1962; mem. adv. bd. Salvation Army, 1946-96; chmn. Thomas J. Evans Found.; hon. trustee Dawes Arboretum; trustee Meth. Theol. Sch. in Ohio; life trustee Denison U. Served to lt. comdr. USNR, 1942-46. Mem. Ohio Bankers Assn. (pres. 1966-67), Am. Bankers Assn. (exec. council 1967-70, nat. bank div. exec. com. 1967-70), Newark C. of C. (pres. 1955-56), Ohio C. of C. (dir.), Am. Legion, VFW. Methodist. Clubs: Elks, Rotary, Columbus, Moundbuilders Country, Capital (Columbus). Home: Newark Ohio Died May 27, 1996.

ALFRINK, BERNARD JAN CARDINAL, former archbishop of Utrecht; b. July 5, 1900. Ordained priest Roman Catholic Ch., 1924; prof. sacred scripture Utrecht (Netherlands) maj. sem., 1933-45; cons. Pontificial Biblical Commn., Rome, 1944; prof. O.T. and Hebrew Cath. U. Nijmegen (Netherlands), 1945-51; titular archbishop of Tiana and coadjutor archbishop of Utrecht, 1951-55; consecrated archbishop of Utrecht, 1955-76; elevated to Sacred Coll. of Cardinals, 1960. Pub. numerous religious works. Died Dec. 17, 1987. Home: Utrecht The Netherlands

ALFVÉN, HANNES OLOF GOSTA, physicist; b. May 30, 1908. Ph.D., U. Uppsala, 1934. Prof. theory of electricity Royal Inst. Tech., Stockholm, 1940-45, prof. electronics, 1945-63, prof. plasma physics, 1963-73; prof. dept. applied physics, electrical engring. and info. sci. U. Calif., San Diego, 1967-88; mem. Swedish Sci. Adv. Coun., 1963-67; past mem. Swedish AEC; past gov. Swedish Def. Rsch. Inst., Swedish Atomic Energy Co.; past sci. adv. Swedish Govt.; pres. Pugwash Confs. on Sci. and World Affairs, 1970-75. Author: Cosmical Electrodynamics, 1950; On the Origin of the Solar System, 1954; Cosmical Electrodynamics: Fundamental Principles, 1963; Worlds-Antiworlds, 1966; The Tale of the Big Computer, 1968; Atom, Man and the Universe, 1969; Living on the Third Planet, 1972; Evolution of the Solar System, 1976; Cosmic Plasma, 1981. Recipient Nobel prize for physics, 1970, Lomonosov gold medal Russian Acad. Scis., 1971, Franklin medal, 1971, Bowie Golf medal Am. Geophys. Union, 1987, Dirac medal, 1994. Fellow Royal Soc. (Eng.); mem. Swedish Acad. Scis., Akademia NAUK (Russia), NAS (fgn. assoc.), and others. Died Apr. 2, 1995.

ALI, AHMED, poet, writer, critic, translator, diplomat; b. Delhi, India, July 1, 1908; s. syed Shuja-uddin and Ahmad Kaniz Begum; m. Bilqees Jehan Begum, Oct. 19, 1950; children: Eram, Orooj, Deed, Shahana. Student, Aligarh Muslim U., 1925-27; BA with honors, Lucknow U., 1930, MA magna cum laude, 1931; DLitt (hon.), U. Karachi, 1993. English lectr. Lucknow U., India, Allahabad U., India, Agra Coll., India, 1931-42; rep., listener rsch. dir. BBC, Delhi, India, 1942-45; prof. English, head dept. Presidency Coll. Bengal Sr. Ednl. Svc., Calcutta, India, 1945-47; dir. fgn. publicity Govt. of Pakistan, Karachi, 1948-49; various sr. posts Pakistan Fgn. Svc., China and Morocco, 1950-60; pub. rels. dir. to bus. and industry, 1960-70; chmn. Lomen Fabrics Ltd., 1970-94; advisor Akrash Publ., 1984-94; Brit. Coun. vis. prof. Nat. Ctrl. U. of China, Nanking, 1947-48; vis. prof. Mich. State U., 1975, Karachi (Pakistan) U., 1977-79, numerous other colls. and univs.; Fulbright vis. prof. Western Ky. U., 1978, So. Ill. U., 1979. Writings include: (play) Break the Chains, 1932, (with Sajjad Zahir and others) Angarey, 1932, Sholay, 1934, The Land of Twilight, 1937, Twilight in Delhi, 1940, 66, 73, 84, 91, with new introduction, 1994, translation, Urdu: Dilli ki Shaam, 1963, (French) Crepuscule a Delhi, 1989 (Spanish) Crepusculo en Delhi, 1991, (Portuguese), 1994, Mr. Eliot's Penny World of Dreams: An Essay in the Interpretation of Dreams: An Essay in the Interpretation of T.S. Eliot's Poetry, 1941, Hamari Gali, 1944, Qaid Khana, 1944, Maut se Pahle, 1945, Muslim China, 1949, The Flaming Earth: Poems from Indonesia, 1949, The Falcon and the Hunted Bird, 1950, The Bulbul and the Rose, 1960, Purple Gold Mountain: Poems from China, 1960, Ocen of Night, 1964, 72, Under the Green Canopy, 1966, Prima della Morte, 1966, The Failure of an Intellect, 1968, Problem of Style and Technique in Ghalib, 1969, Gahlib: Selected Poems, 1969, The Golden Tradition: An Anthology of Urdu Poetry, 1973, revised edit., 1991, The Shadow and the Substance: Principles of Reality, Art and Literature, 1977, Rats and Diplomats, 1985, The Prison-House, 1985, Slected Poems, 1988, Selected Short Stories from Pakistan, 1988, Al-Qur'an: A Contemporary Translation, 1984, 86, 87, revised definitive edit., 1988, 90, final revised edit., 1994, 95, (with others) First Voices, 1965; contbr. articles and poetry to profl. jours.; editor Indian Writing, 1939-42, Tomorrow, 1942-44, PEN Miscellany, 1950-51. Decorated Sitara-e-Imtiaz (Star of Distinction, Gov. of Pakistan); named Hon. Citizen, State of Nebr. Fellow Pakistan Acad. Letters (founding mem.); mem. Progressive Writers Assn. India (founding mem. 1936). Home: Karachi Pakistan Died Jan. 14, 1994.

ALICATA, JOSEPH EVERETT, microbiology researcher, parasitologist; b. Carlentini (Siracusa), Italy, Nov. 5, 1904; came to U.S., 1919, naturalized, 1926; s. Antonio and Concetta (Vaccaro) A.; m. Hannah L. Davis, Jan. 23, 1929 (div. 1954); children: Betty Mae, William D.; m. Earleen E. Moyer, June 30, 1958. AB, Grand Island Coll., 1927; MA, Northwestern U., 1929; PhD, George Washington U., 1934. Jr. zoologist Bur. Animal Industry USDA, Washington, 1928-35; parasitologist Hawaii Agrl. Exptl. Sta. U. Hawaii, Honolulu, 1935-37, head dept. animal scis. Parasitology Lab., 1937-70, prof. emeritus, 1970—; parasitologist Hawaii Dept. Health, Honolulu, 1936-37; parasitologist pub. health commn. Honolulu C. of C., 1940-42, Hawaii Sugar Planters' Assn., Honolulu, 1943; sr. scientist div. internat. health USPHS, Amman, Jordan, 1953-54. Author: (with others) Advances in Parasitology, 1965, (with K. Jindrak) Angiostrongylosis in the Pacific and Southeast Asia, 1970; contbr. chpt. to book, numerous articles to profl. jours. With USN, 1953-54. Fulbright scholar, 1950-51; NIH rsch. fellow, 1949-50, grantee. Fellow AAAS; mem. Am. Soc. Parasitologists, Am. Soc. Tropical Medicine and Hygiene, Hawaiian Acad. Scis., Washington Acad. Scis. (hon.), Sigma Xi (hon.), Phi Kappa Phi (hon.). Republican. Home: Honolulu Hawaii Died Oct. 20, 1994.

ALLEN, ARTHUR WILLIAM, pastor, educator; b. Eldora, Iowa, Apr. 6, 1914; s. William Alonzo and Ethel Pamelia (Doud) A.; m. Verna Marion Josephs, Jan. 24, 1942; children: Dorothy, Margaret, Robert, David. BTh, Northwestern Sem., 1941; DD, Bapt. Bible Coll., 1958; D in Lit., Pillsbury Bapt. Coll., 1983; ThM, Triune Bible Sem., 1986, ThD, 1987. Pastor Bapt. Chs., Baker, Dillon, Laurel, Mont., 1942-66; exec. sec. Minn. Bapt. Assn., Mpls., 1966-83; prof. Cen. Bapt. Sem., Mpls., 1966-75; editor North Star Bapt., Mpls., 1983-89; prof. Mtn. States Coll., Great Falls, Mont., 1983-89; tour leader Israel & Middle East, 1972-94. Pres. Castle Rock Baptist Camp, Bozeman, Mont., 1961-63; bd. dirs. Denver Bapt. Coll., 1960-66, San Francisco Bapt. Sem., 1960-66, Pillsbury Bapt. Coll., Owatonna, Minn., 1966-83. Republican. Home: Laurel Mont. Deceased.

ALLEN, MEL, broadcaster. Baseball broadcaster New York Yankees. Home: New York N.Y. Died June 16, 1996.

ALLEN, VERNON L(ESLIE), psychology educator; b. Lineville, Ala., June 6, 1933; s. Harvey N. and Hassie S.A.; m. Patricia S. Shumake, Dec. 31, 1956; children—Derek R., Craig R. B.A., U. Ala., 1955; M.S., Tufts U., 1958; Ph.D., U. Calif.-Berkeley, 1962. Asst. prof. U. Wis.-Madison, 1963-66, assoc. prof., 1966-69, prof. psychology, 1969—. Editor: Psychological Factors in Poverty, 1970; Children as Teachers, 1976; Cognitive Learning in Children, 1976; Role Transitions, 1983. Served to 1st lt. U.S. Army, 1956-58. Postdoctoral fellow NIMH, Stanford U., 1962-63; Fulbright fellow to Eng., 1969-70; fellow Netherlands Instn. for Advanced Study in Humanities and Social Sci., Wassenaar, 1979-80. Fellow Am. Psychol. Assn.; mem. Am. Sociol. Assn., Soc. for Psychol. Study of Social Issues, Soc. for Exptl. Social Psychology, Brit. Psychol. Soc. Home: Madison Wis. Deceased.

ALLEY, REWI, writer, poet, social activist; b. New Zealand, 1897. Author: (books) There Is a Way, 1952, The People Have Strength, 1954, Human China, 1957, Shandan: An Adventure in Creative Edn., 1959, Our Seven- Their Five, 1963, A Highway and an Old Chinese Doctor, 1973, Prisoners, 1973, The Rebels, 1973, Travels in China, 1973; (autobiography) At 90: Memoirs of My China Years, 1986; (poetry) Gung Ho, 1948, Leaves from a Shandan Notebook, 1950; (anthology) Light and Shadow Along a Great Road, 1984; translator ancient Chinese poets Li Bai, Du Fu and Bai Juyi; contbr. articles on travel in China. Mem. Chinese PEN. Home: Beijing People's Republic of China Deceased.

ALLISON, DAVID (DAVEY ALLISON), professional stock car driver; s. Robert Arthur and Judith A. Winner Coca Cola 600, 1991, NASCAR top money maker, 1992. Home: Hueytown Ala.

ALLPORT, PETER WARD, association executive; b. Vienna, Austria, July 28, 1920; s. Fayette Ward and Mildred Dorcas (Burt) A.; m. Margaret Hahr Nichols, Jan. 5, 1946; 1 son, George Nichols. B.A., Brown U., 1941. With Erwin, Wasey & Co. (advt.), N.Y.C., 1944-46; with Assn. Nat. Advertisers, N.Y.C., 1946-94; v.p., sec. Assn. Nat. Advertisers, 1958-60, exec. v.p., 1960, pres., 1960-86, pres. emeritus, 1986-94; Mem. adv. com. distbn. council Dept. Commerce, also U.S. council Internat. C. of C.; bd. dirs. Advt. Council, Advt. Research Found. Contbr. to: Handbook of Advertising Management, 1970. Mem. Alpha Delta Phi. Clubs: Union League (N.Y.C.); Am. Yacht (Rye, N.Y.). Home: Bronxville N.Y. Died Oct 3, 1994.

ALNES, ELLIS STEPHEN, journalist; b. Thief River Falls, Minn., Dec. 1, 1926; s. Lloyd T. and Shirley (Anderson) A.; m. Margaret Elizabeth Grinols, Dec. 17, 1948; children: Susan, Karen, Judith, Lee. BA, U. Minn., 1949. UPI reporter Bismarck, N.D., 1949-54; reporter, bus. editor, Sunday editor Pioneer Press & Dispatch, St. Paul, 1954-67; editorial writer Mpls. Star, 1967-71, assoc. editorial page editor, 1971-75, editorial page editor, 1975-79; exec. dir. Upper Midwest Council, 1979-82; editor Minn. Jour., 1983-91, ret., 1991. With USNR, 1944-46. Home: Saint Paul Minn. Died May 13, 1996.

ALPERN, MATHEW, physiological optics educator; b. Akron, Ohio, Sept. 22, 1920; s. Aaron Harry and Goldie (Ray) A.; m. Rebecca Ann Elsner, Aug. 17, 1951; children: Bowen Lewis, Goldie Ann, Barbara Rachel McGuinness, Aaron Harry. Student, U. Akron, 1937-38, 42; O.D., No. Ill. Coll. Optometry, 1941; B.M.E., U. Fla., 1946; Ph.D., Ohio State U., 1950; D.Sc. (hon.), SUNY, State Coll. Optometry, 1988. Asst. prof. optometry Pacific U., 1951-55; instr. ophthalmology U. Mich., 1955-56; asst. prof. physiol. optics Med. Sch.; also asst. prof. psychology Coll. Lit., Scis. and Arts, 1956-58, assoc. prof. physiol. optics, also assoc. prof. psychology, 1958-63, prof. physiol. optics dept. ophthalmology and physiology, also prof. psychology, 1963-91; prof. emeritus, 1991-96; NIH spl. fellow physiol. lab. U. Cambridge, Eng., 1961-62; mem. visual sci. study sect. NIH, Bethesda, Md., 1970-74; vis. prof. psychobiology Fla. State U., 1968-69; Anna Berliner lectr. Pacific U., 1978, Japanese Soc. Ophthalmic Optics, Kagoshima, Japan, 1980; vis. scientist physics divsn. NRC, Can., 1983-84; med. faculty Technion U., Haifa, Israel, 1990-91; mem. Am. Com. on Optics and Visual Physiology, 1969-88; mem. sci. adv. bd. Nat. Retinitis Pigmentosa Found., 1972-95. Author: (with others) Sensory Processes, 1966; Contbr. articles to profl. jours.; assoc. editor: Jour. of Optical Soc. Am., 1982-83. Recipient 19th Charles F. Prentice medal Am. Acad. Optometry, 1988, Rsch. to Prevent Blindness Sr. Sci. Investigator award, 1988. Fellow APA; mem. NAS, Optical Soc. Am. (Edgar O. Tillyer medal 1984), Am. Physiol. Soc., Soc. Exptl. Psychologists, Assn. Rsch. in Vision and Ophthalmology (Friedenwald award 1974, trustee 1979-83, v.p. 1983), Biophys. Soc. Jewish. Home: Ann Arbor Mich. Died May 16, 1996.

ALTER, DAVID EMMET, JR., author, artist, publisher, consultant; b. Mussoorie, U.P., India, July 14, 1921; s. David Emmet and Mary Martha (Payne) A. (parents U.S. citizens); m. Sarah G. McGinnis, July 25,

1981; children by previous marriage: Dismore J., David Emmet III; stepchildren: John A. Tinseth, Ruth K. Tinseth, Mary Tinseth. BA, Coll. Wooster, 1943; MA, Mills Coll., 1952; LHD (hon.), Am. Tolkien Soc., 1992. Fgn. service officer AID, 1954-75; alt. U.S. rep. to OAS, 1969-75; author, artist, pub. (ann.) The Wanderers Almanac, 1969-78, Fla.'s Christmas Legend, 1979; adj. prof. math. Flagler Coll., St. Augustine, Fla., spring 1983. Served with AUS, 1943-46, 50-54. Recipient meritorious honor award AID, 1959. Home: Saint Augustine Fla. Died Aug. 24, 1992.

AL-THANI, NASIR BIN KHALID (SHEIKH NASIR BIN KHALID AL THANI), Qatari minister economy and commerce, businessman; b. 1915; married. Businessman in Doha; agt. for Mercedes Benz; with Nat. Qatar Cinema Corp.; minister economy and commerce, from 1970. Pres., Qatar Israel Boycott Com. Deceased. Home: Doha Quatar

ALTSCHUL, AARON MAYER, nutrition educator emeritus; b. Chgo., Mar. 13, 1914; s. Philip and Sophie (Fox) A.; m. Ruth Braude, Oct. 24, 1937; children: Sandra Betty Altschul Norman, Judy Altschul Bonderman. B.S., U. Chgo., 1934, Ph.D., 1937; D.Sc. (hon.), Tulane U., 1968. Research assoc. dept. chemistry spectroscopic biol. investigations unit U. Chgo., 1937-41; scientist, adminstr. U.S. Dept. Agr. Lab., New Orleans, 1941-58; chief rsch. chemist Seed Protein Pioneering Rsch. Lab., New Orleans, 1958-67; spl. asst. to sec. of agr. for nutrition improvement and medicine Washington, 1967-71; prof. dept. community and family medicine Georgetown U., 1971-83, prof. emeritus depts. medicine and community and family medicine, 1983-94, dir. div. nutrition, 1975-83, dir. diet mgmt. eating disorders program, 1976-87, emeritus dir., 1987-94; Underwood-Prescott lectr., 1976; former cons. to Israeli govt.; former cons. UN agencies. Author: Proteins, Their Chemistry and Politics, 1965; editor: Processed Plant Protein Foodstuffs, 1958, New Protein Foods, Vol. 1, 1974, Vol. 2, 1976, (with H.L. Wilcke), Vol. 3, 1978, Vol. 4, 1981, Vol. 5, 1985, Weight Control: A Guide for Counselors and Therapists, 1987, Low-Calorie Foods Handbook, 1993; editor: (with N.S. Scrimshaw) Amino Acid Fortification of Protein Foods, 1971; contbr. articles to profl. jours. Pres. Temple Micah, Washington, 1977-78. Recipient Golden Peanut award, 1964; Distinguished Service award U.S. Dept. Agr., 1970; Rockefeller Public Service award, 1970. Fellow Am. Coll. Nutrition, Am. Inst. Nutrition; mem. Am. Chem. Soc. (Charles F. Spencer award 1966), Am. Soc. Biol. Chemists, Inst. Food Technologists (Internat. award 1971), Am. Soc. Clin. Nutrition, N.Am. Assn. Study Obesity, Phi Beta Kappa, Sigma Xi, Phi Tau Sigma. Club: Cosmos. Home: Arlington Va. Died July 4, 1994.

ALTSHUL, HAROLD MILTON, drug company executive; b. N.Y.C., June 19, 1909; s. Victor I. and Fannie (Kosven) A.; m. Anne Majette Grant, Feb. 13, 1959; children: Victor Anthony, Lindsey Grant. Student, Cornell U., 1928-29. With Ketchum & Co., Inc., Norwalk, Conn., 1930-93, sales mgr., 1933, ops. mgr., 1934, pres., from 1935, chmn. bd., chief exec. officer, 1978-93, dir., 1935-93. Fellow Aspen Inst. for Humanistic Studies; mem. Nat. Wholesale Druggists Assn. (v.p. 1938, mem. bd. control 1957-59), Am. Arbitration Assn. (mem. nat. panel 1946-59), Drug, Chem. and Allied Trades Assn. (exec. com. 1942-50, chmn. 1946, adv. council 1947-50), N.Y. Bd. Trade (dir. 1943-51, v.p. 1948-50), Young Pres. Orgn. (dir. 1951-55, chmn. exec. com. 1951-52, v.p. 1952-53), Chief Execs. Forum (dir., pres. 1962). Clubs: City Athletic (N.Y.C.); East Hampton (N.Y.); Yacht (gov. from 1965, commodore 1967-68), N.Y. Yacht, Wadawanuck Yacht. Home: Stonington Conn. Died Mar. 29, 1993.

ALWYN, WILLIAM, composer; b. Northampton, Eng., Nov. 7, 1905; m. Olive Pull (div.); 2 sons; m. Doreen Mary Carwithen. Ed., Royal Acad. Music, hon. doctorate in music, 1982. Prof. composition Royal Acad. Music, London, 1926-55, Composers Guild Gt. Brit. chair, 1949, 50, 54; composer: (opera) Juan, or the Libertine, 1975, Miss Julie, 1977; 5 Symphonies, 1950, 53, 56, 59, 73; Sinfonietta for Strings, 1970; 3 Concerti Grossi, 1942, 51, 64; Lyra Angelica Concerto for harp and strings, 1954; String Quartet No. 1 in D Minor, 1953, no. 2 Spring Waters, 1975, no. 3., 1984; Fantasy-Waltzes for Piano; Concerto for Flute and 8 Wind Instruments, 1980; (song cycle) Mirages, Invocations, A Leave-taking; (film score) Odd Man Out, Fallen Idol, The True Glory; Author: Ariel to Miranda—a Journal, 1968; An Anthology of 20th Century French Poetry, 1969; Winter in Copenhagen, Mirages, 1971; Daphne, or the Pursuit of Beauty, 1972; The World in My Mind, 1975; The Prayers and Elegies of Francis Jammes, 1978; Winged Chariot, 1983. Decorated comdr. Order Brit. Empire. Fellow Royal Acad. Music. Died Sept. 11, 1985; interred Blythburgh. Home: Suffolk Eng.

AMANO, HARUO, English language educator; b. Wako, Saitama, Japan, Sept. 30, 1920; s. Mitsuzo and Yoshi (Takahashi) A.; m. Emi Hanyu, Apr. 14, 1959; 1 child, Michiko Kodaira. Student, Tokyo Sch Fgn. Langs, 1940-43; B of Econs., Chuo U., Tokyo, 1946; B of Law, U. Tokyo, 1949; postgrad., U. Calif., Berkeley, 1952-53. Staff Shoko Trading Co. Ltd., Tokyo, 1949-54; sec, gen. Kyoto Br. Internat. Students Inst., 1970; staff translator Yuasa and Hara, Tokyo, 1970-87; prof. Fukuoka (Japan) Inst. Tech., 1987-89, Ibaraki Christian Coll., Hitachi, Japan, from 1989; Adviser Alpha Corp., Tokyo, from 1978; councilor Sino-Japanese Cultural and Scientific Exch. Assn., Tokyo, 1993; auditor Japan Assn. Current English, Tokyo, 1982. Co-editor: Dictionary of Current English, 1989. Deacon Setagaya Ch. of Christ, Tokyo, from 1960; mem. Internat. Gideon, Inc., Tokyo, from 1980. Mem. Soc. Teachng Japanese as a Fgn. Lang., Internat. House of Japan, Am.-Japan Soc., Smithsonian Inst. Home: Wako Japan Deceased.

AMAYA, NAOHIRO, government official; b. Fukui Prefecture, Japan, 1925. Grad., U. Tokyo, 1948. With Ministry of Commerce and Industry (now Ministry of Internat. Trade and Industry), 1948, dir.-gen. Internat. Econ. Affairs Dept. and Internat. Trade Bur., then councillor internat. trade and industry, then dir.-gen. Basic Industries Bur. and dir.-gen. Agy. of Natural Resources and Energy; vice-minister for internat. affairs, 1979-81, spl. adviser to minister and adv. Japan Indsl. Policy Research Inst., 1981-84; pres. Japan Econ. Found., 1984-87; exec. adviser Dentsu Inc., 1987-94; exec. dir. Dentsu Inst. for Human Studies, 1987-94, chmn., chief exec. officer, 1992-94. Home: Tokyo Japan Died Aug. 30, 1994; interred Fuji-Reien, Koyama-cho, Shizuoka Pref.

AMECHE, DON, actor; b. Kenosha, Wis., May 31, 1908; s. Felix and Barbara Etta (Hertel) A.; m. Honore Predergast; children: Don, Ronald, Thomas, Lawrence, Barbara, Cornelia. Student, Loras Coll., hon. doctorate, 1960; Student, Marquette U., Georgetown U., U. Wis. New York stage debut in Jerry for Short, 1930; appeared in theater prodn. Illegal Practice, 1930, Excess Baggage, 1930, Silk Stockings, 1956, Holiday for Lovers, 1958, Goldilocks, 1961, 13 Daughters, 1961, I Married an Angel, 1967, Henry Sweet Henry, 1968, The Odd Couple, 1972, No No Nanette, 1973, Never Get Smart with an Angel, 1976; toured in prodns. Silk Stockings, 1956, I Married an Angel, 1964, The Odd Couple, 1968, No, No, Nanette, 1973; appeared in films Ramona, 1936, Alexanders Ragtime Band, 1938, In Old Chicago, 1938, Swanee River, 1939, Story of Alexander Graham Bell, 1939, Lillian Russell, 1940, Heaven Can Wait, 1943, So Goes My Love, 1946, A Fever in the Blood, 1961, Rings Around the World, 1966, Suppose They Gave a War and Nobody Came, 1970, Cocoon (Acad. award for best supporting actor), 1986, Harry and the Hendersons, 1987, Cocoon: The Return, 1988, Things Change, 1988; appeared on TV Frances Langford Don Ameche Show, 1957; appeared in radio series The Chase and Sanborn Hour, 1937-39, The Charlie McCarthy Show, 1940, Don Ameche's Real-Life Stories, 1958. Republican. Roman Catholic. Home: Santa Monica Calif. Died Dec. 6, 1993.

AMEY, WILLIAM GREENVILLE, retired chief control systems engineer; b. Balt., Feb. 24, 1918; s. William Barton and Marie Sophia (Kittlein) A.; m. Hester Elizabeth Empie, 1941 (dec. June 1964); children: Kathryn Amey Graebner, Michael Barton; m. Julie Thelma Valkusky McCarthy, 1965; 1 stepchild, Margaret McCarthy Thatcher. BSEE, Johns Hopkins U., 1938, PhD in Elec. Engring., 1947. Instrument researcher Leeds & Northrup Co., North Wales, Pa., 1947-56, mgr., rsch. div., 1956-65, assoc. dir., corp. rsch., 1965-72; tech. and managerial cons. North Wales, 1972-74; chief control systems engr. Bechtel Power Corp., Ann Arbor, Mich., 1974-83, ret., 1983—. Contbr. articles to profl. jours. Sr. mentor Vol. program of Broward County Sch. Bd. Lt. comdr. USNR, 1941-46. Fellow IEEE, Instrument Soc. Am. Home: Palm City Fla. Died Mar. 13, 1994.

AMIRIKIAN, ARSHAM, engineering company executive; b. Armenia, May 17, 1899; came to U.S., 1919, naturalized, 1927; s. Paravon and Pearl (Delbarian) A.; m. Philomena Elizabeth Boardman, Aug. 8, 1925; children: Richard Armen, Joyce Eleanor (Mrs. Robert A. Harrison). B.S., Ecole superieure des Ponts et Chaussees, Constantinople, 1919; C.E., Cornell U., 1923; D.Tech.Sc., Technische Hochschule, Vienna, 1960. Steel fabricator draftsman and designer 1923-28; various engring. positions to chief engring. cons. Naval Facilities Engring. Command, U.S. Navy Dept., Washington, 1928-71; pres. Amirikian Engring. Co., from 1971; cons. engr. shore and floating structures, harbor and docking facilities; adj. prof. engring. George Washington U., 1965-66. Author: Analysis of Rigid Frames, 1942; contbr. articles tech. periodicals; inventor AMMI Lift Dock, a wingless floating dry dock and AMMI Stabilizer for floating and submersible structures. Recipient Fuertes Grad. gold medal Cornell U., 1943, Lincoln gold medal Am. Welding Soc., 1949, A.E. Lindau award Am. Concrete Inst., 1958, Distinguished Service award Dept. of Navy, 1966, Distinguished Service award Def. Dept., 1969, Civilian Career Achievement award Dept. Navy, 1971, Goethals medal Soc. Am. Mil. Engrs., 1971. Fellow Am. Concrete Inst., Soc. Am. Mil. Engrs.; mem. Nat. Acad. Engring., ASCE (hon., E.E. Howard award 1978), Am. Welding Soc. (hon.), Soc. Naval Architects and Marine Engrs., Internat. Inst. Welding (hon.), Sigma Xi. Home: Bethesda Md. Deceased.

AMIS, SIR KINGSLEY, novelist; b. Apr. 16, 1922; s. William Robert and Rosa A.; m. Hilary Ann Bardwell (div. 1965); 3 children; m. Elizabeth Jane Howard, 1965 (div. 1983). Ed., City of London Sch., St. John's, Oxford. Lectr. English U. Coll., Swansea, 1949-61; vis. fellow creative writing Princeton, 1958-59; fellow in English Peterhouse, Cambridge U., Eng., 1961-63. Author: verse A Frame of Mind, 1953, Lucky Jim, 1954 (filmed 1957), That Uncertain Felling, 1955; filmed as Only Two Can Play, 1961; verse A Case of Samples, 1956, I Like It here, 1958, Take A Girl Like You, 1960; non-fiction New Maps of Hell, 1960, My Enemy's Enemy, 1962, One Fat Englishman, 1963, The James Bond Dossier, 1965, (with Robert Conquest) The Egyptologists, 1965, The Anti-Death League, 1966, A Look Round the Estate (verse), 1967, I Want It Now, 1968, The Green Man, 1969, What Became of Jane Austen, 1970, Girl, 20, 1971, On Drink, 1972, The Riverside Villas Murder, 1973, Ending Up, 1974, Rudyard Kipling and His World, 1975, The Alteration, 1976, Jake's Thing, 1978, Collected Poems, 1979, Russian Hide-an-Seek, 1980, Stanley and the Women, 1984, The Old Devils, 1986 (Booker prize), Difficulties with Girls, 1988, The Folks That Live on the Hill, 1990, The Russian Girl, 1994, Mr. Barrett's Secret, 1993, You Can't Do Both, 1994, The Biographer's Moustache, 1994; collected Short Stories, 1980; editor: The New Oxford Book of Light Verse, 1978, The Faber Popular Reciter, 1978, The Golden Age of Science Fiction, 1981, Amis Anthology, 1988; contbr. to publs. Memoirs, 1991. With Brit. Army, 1942-45. Decorated comdr. Order Brit. Empire. Home: London Eng. Died Oct. 1995.

AMISSAH, JOHN KODWO, archbishop; b. Elmina, Ghana, Nov. 27, 1922; s. John Bentil and Mary Efua (Busumafi) A. JCD, Pontifical Urban U., Rome, 1954; DD honoris causa, LLD honoris causa, U. Cape Coast, Ghana, 1972. Asst. priest Sekondi (Ghana) Parish, 1950; tchr. St. Teresa's Minor Sem., Amisano, Elmina, Ghana, 1950-51, sr. Latin master, lectr. in canon law, 1954-57; aux. bishop Archdiocese of Cape Coast, Cen. Region, Ghana, 1957-59, archbishop, 1959—. Author: Fante Funeral Eulogy. Mem. Council of State, Accra, Ghana, 1969-72, Ghana Edn., Service Council, Accra, 1973-77. Recipient Grand medal Govt. of Ghana, 1975. Mem. Canon Law Soc. Am. Home: Cape Coast Central Ghana Died Sept. 22, 1991; interred St. Francis de Sales Cathedral, Cape Coast Central, Ghana.

AMUNDSON, JOHN MELVIN, JR., architect; b. Sunnyside, Wash., Mar. 4, 1926; s. John Malvin and Atta Faye (Swanay) A.; m. Janet Louise Barnard, June 19, 1947; children: Kathleen Faye, David William, Kristin Marie. BArch, U. Oreg., 1951; diploma in civic design, U. Liverpool, Eng., 1952. Registered architect, Oreg., Wash., Calif., Idaho, Alaska, Guam. Planner Bur. Govt. Svcs. U. Oreg., Eugene, 1955-57; prin. architect Lutes & Amundson, AIA, Springfield, Oreg., 1957-73, The Amundson Assocs., P.C., Springfield, 1973-95; pres. Nat. Archtl. Accrediting Bd., Washington, 1970-74; exam dir. Nat. Coun. Archtl. Registration Bds., Washington, 1967-73. Principle works include ch. design Our Saviour's Luth. Ch., 1959 (Merit award 1961), bank design Siuslaw Valley Bank, 1961 (Merit award 1963, bank design U.S. Nat. Bank, 1965 (Merit award 1967), sch. design Sheldon High Sch., 1961 (1st honor 1965), sch. design Churchill High Sch., 1966 (Merit award 1969), Coll. Union, Inst. Tech., 1978 (Honor award 1981). Citizen coord. Eugene (Oreg.) Bus. Assistance Team , 1983; mem. Com. for Econ. Devel., Eugene, 1984. With USN, 1944-46, PTO. Fulbright scholar, U.S. Govt., Liverpool, Eng., 1951-52, AIA fellow, Washington, 1975; named Future First Citizen, Eugene Jaycees, 1961, One of Outstanding Young Men of Oreg., Oreg. Jaycees, 1961; recipient Dean Gustafson award Nat. Coun. Archtl. Accrediting Bds., 1978. Fellow AIA; mem. Constrn. Specifications Inst., Quiet Birdmen, Lions Internat., Elks. Congregationalist. Home: Eugene Oreg. Died Feb. 17, 1995.

ANAGNOST, MARIA ATHENA, surgeon; b. Chgo., Oct. 21, 1943; d. Themis John and Catherine (Cook) A.; BA, Northwestern U., 1965; MD, U. Ill., 1973. Resident in surgery U. Chgo. Hosps. and Clinics, 1973-74; gen. surgery resident Michael Reese Med. Center, Chgo., 1975-79, chief resident, 1979-80; pvt. practice surgery; surg. staff Oak Park (Ill.) Hosp., Westlake Community Hosp., Melrose Park, Ill., Gottlieb Meml. Hosp., Melrose Park, Good Samaritan Hosp., Downers Grove, Ill., St. Elizabeth's, Chgo., Ravenswood Hosp., Chgo.; chmn. dept. surgery Loretto Hosp., Chgo. Diplomate Nat. Bd. Med. Examiners, 1974; cert. Am. Bd. Surgery. Recipient Physicians' Recognition award AMA. Fellow ACS, Internat. Coll. Surgeons (vice regent, sec. qualifications and interim coun.), Am. Soc. Abdominal Surgeons; mem. AMA, Ill. Med. Soc., Chgo. Med. Soc., InterAm. Coll. Physicians and Surgeons, Hellenic Med. Soc., U. Ill. alumni Assn., Northwestern U. Alumni Assn. Contbr. articles to profl. jours. Died Dec. 2, 1992. Home: Chicago Ill.

ANDERSEN, DANIEL JOHANNES, lawyer; b. Jamestown, N.Y., Nov. 3, 1909; s. Christian Johannes and Maria Bodil (Hansen) A.; m. Alice Klopstad, June 28, 1937; 1 child, Dianne Andersen Tecklenberg. AB, George Washington U., 1937, JD, 1940; grad. JAG Sch., 1942, Army War Coll., 1965. Bar: D.C. 1939, U.S. Ct. Claims 1953, U.S. Tax Ct. 1953, U.S. Supreme Ct. 1947. Assoc. Baker, Beedy & Magee, 1940-42; ptnr.

Magee, Bulow & Andersen, 1946-52; pvt. practice, Washington, 1952-94; pres., treas. Dr. O.E. Howe Found., Washington. Col. USAFR, 1965; bd. trustees Gettysburg Coll., 1963-80, trustee emeritus, 1980-94. Mem. D.C. Bar Assn., Fed. Bar Assn., Air Force Judge Advocates Assn. (past pres.), Washington Bd. Trade, Christian Businessmen's Assn., Religious Heritage of Am., Nat. Lawyers Club, Chevy Chase Club, Sigma Chi. Republican. Lutheran. Died June 22, 1994. Home: Kingsville Md.

ANDERSON, ALDON J., judge; b. Salt Lake City, Jan. 3, 1917; s. Aldon J. and Minnie (Egan) A.; m. Virginia Barbara Weilenmann, Nov. 5, 1943; children—Jeffrey Lance, Aldon Scott, Craig W., Paul Christian, Kevin E., Rebecca C., Douglas K. B.A., U. Utah, 1939, J.D., 1943. Bar: Utah 1943. Ptnr. King, Anderson & Durham, King, Anderson & Brown, 1943-57; dist. atty. 3d dist. Dist. Ct. of Utah, 1953-57; judge state dist. ct. State of Utah, 1957-71; judge U.S. Dist. Ct. Utah, 1971-96, chief judge, from 1978, sr. judge; vice chmn. State Bar Com. on Uniform Cts., Utah, 1970, chmn.; subcom. on Jud. Improvement, Jud. Adminstrv. Conf., 1979-96; vice chmn. State Bar Com. on Compiling State Rules of Evidence; past chmn. ad hoc com. of judicial conf. Am. Inns of Ct.; past chmn. Am. Inns of Ct. Found. Active Mormon Ch. Named Judge of Yr. Utah Bar Assn., 1980, 85. Mem. ABA, Am. Bar Found. (past pres.), Dist. Attys. Assn. Utah, U.S. Dist. Judges Assn. (past pres. 10th cir.), Order of Coif (hon.), Pi Kappa Alpha, Phi Delta Phi. Home: Salt Lake City Utah Died Mar., 1996.

ANDERSON, ARTHUR ROLAND, engineering company executive, civil engineer; b. Tacoma, Mar. 11, 1910; s. Eivind and Aslaug (Axness) A.; BS, U. Wash., 1934; MS, MIT, 1935, DSc, 1938; LLD (hon.), Gonzaga U., 1983; m. Barbara Hinman Beck, June 5, 1938; children: Martha Anderson Nelson, Karl, Richard, Elisabeth Anderson Zerzan, Deborah Anderson Ray. Mem. staff MIT, Cambridge, 1936-38, 39-41; design engr. Klonne Steel Co., Dortmund, Germany, 1938-39; head tech. dept. Cramp Shipyard, USN Bur. Ships, Phila., 1941-46; pvt. practice cons. civil engr., Stamford, Conn., 1946-51; co-founder Concrete Tech. Corp., Tacoma, 1951, sr. v.p., 1956-95; pres. Anderson Enterprises Corp., Tacoma, 1957-87; vis. lectr. U. Wash., 1954-55; chmn. bd. Anderson, Birkeland, Anderson & Mast, Engrs., Inc. (now ABAM Engrs. Inc.), Tacoma, 1951-77. Pres. Puget Sound (Wash.) Sci. Fair, 1954-58; mem. Tacoma Pub. Utility Bd., 1954-69, chmn., 1968-69; mem. ednl. council MIT, 1954-86, vis. com., 1960-70; mem. Pacific Luth. U. Collegium, 1976-95; mem. vis. com. U. Wash.; mem. Wash. State Coun. for Post-Secondary Edn., 1977-84. Registered profl. engr., Wash.; named Alumnus Summa Laude Dignatus, U. Wash., 1980. Mem. Am. Concrete Inst. (hon. mem., dir. 1962-69, pres. 1966-67, Constrn. Practice award 1962, Alfred E. Lindau medal 1970, Roger Corbetta award 1974, Charles S. Whitney award 1975, Turner medal 1977, Arthur J. Boase award 1979), ASCE (hon., life mem., mem. tech. com. 1963-66, T.Y. Lin award 1971), Soc. Exptl. Stress Analysis (charter), ASTM, Nat. Soc. Profl. Engrs., Soc. Naval Architects and Marine Engrs., Internat. Assn. Bridge and Structural Engrs. (hon.), Prestressed Concrete Inst. (pres. 1970-71), N.E. Coast Shipbuilders and Engrs., Japan Concrete Inst. (hon.), Fedn. Internat. de la Precontrainte (F.I.P. medal 1974), Comité European de Beton, Nat. Acad. Engring., Sigma Xi, Chi Epsilon, Beta Gamma Sigma, Tau Beta Pi. Contbr. numerous articles in tech. of concrete and research on welded steel ships to profl. jours.; patentee in field. Died June 23, 1995. Home: Tacoma Wash.

ANDERSON, CAROLYN JENNINGS, columnist; b. Franklin, Tenn., Apr. 8, 1913; d. Robert Harmon and Carrie (Estes) Jennings; m. Thomas Jefferson Anderson, Dec. 24, 1936; 1 child, Carol Anderson Porter. Student, Woman's Coll. Ala., 1931-33; B.A., Vanderbilt U., 1935. Asso. woman's editor Farm & Ranch, Nashville, 1962-72; syndicated columnist American Way Features, Pigeon Forge, Tenn., 1967-93; treas. So. Farm Publs. Author: Collector's Items, 1965. Mem. Davidson County (Tenn.) Republican Exec. Com., 1965; asst. to chmn. American Party, 1972-78; local chmn. Stop ERA, Pigeon Forge, 1978. Elected Miss Woman's Coll. Ala., 1932, Miss Vanderbilt, 1934. Mem. DAR (mem. nat. resolutions com, early 1960s), Colonial Dames Am., Delta Delta Delta. Home: Jupiter Fla. Died June 1, 1993.

ANDERSON, GEORGE CORLISS, retired aerospace executive; b. Los Angeles, Dec. 3, 1921; s. Gustave Emil and Nellie Elizabeth (Bengtson) A.; B.S. in Applied Physics, U. Calif., Los Angeles, 1949; m. Edna Dorothy Westergard, Aug. 2, 1952; 1 dau., Judith Annette Anderson Hindes. Research engr. sound and acoustics Don Lee Broadcasting System, Hollywood, Calif., 1948-51; engring. mgr. field dir., asst. to exec. v.p. N.Am. Aviation, Inc., Downey, Calif., 1951-64; engring. dir. Saturn II/Apollo program Space div. N.Am. Rockwell, Inc., Downey, 1964-72; engring. mgr. strategic missile systems Autonetics div. Rockwell Internat. Corp., Anaheim, Calif., 1972-88; ret., 1988; econs. acoustics and electronics; instr. math. and electronics Compton (Calif.) Coll., 1952-55; comml. airplane pilot; cons. in field. Served with USNR, 1944-46. Recipient Apollo program achievement award NASA, 1969. Mem. Am. Inst. Physics, Acoustical Soc. Am., Aircraft Owners and Pilots Assn., Am. Radio Relay League. Republican. Presbyterian. Clubs: East Whittier Radio, Autonetics Radio, Airventurers So. Calif. Patentee precision frequency regulator. Died June 5, 1995. Home: Whittier Calif.

ANDERSON, GLENN MALCOLM, congressman; b. Los Angeles; m. Lee Dutton; children: Melinda (Mrs. Michael Keenan), Evan, Glenn Michael. BA, UCLA. Mayor City of Hawthorne, Calif., 1940-43; mem. Calif. Assembly from South Bay Area, Los Angeles, 1943-51; lt. gov. State of Calif., 1958-68; mem. 91st-102d Congresses from 32d Calif. dist., 1969-94; chmn. State Lands Commn., 1959-67; chmn. pub. works and transp. com., 1988-90; past mem. Commn. Califs., Calif. Council Urban Growth; past chmn. Calif. Interstate Cooperation Commn. Hon. life mem. PTA.; Regent U. Calif., 1959-67. Served with AUS, World War II. Mem. Secondary Sch. Adminstrs. Assn., Am. Legion, DAV, Amvets, Native Sons Golden West, Redmen, Hawthorne C. of C. Democrat. Clubs: Elks, Kiwanis. Home: Hawthorne Calif. Died Dec. 13, 1994.

ANDERSON, GRANT THRALLS, lawyer; b. Portland, Oreg., Apr. 5, 1910; s. James Clifford and Nettie Avis (Thralls) A.; m. Mildred Lucille Shields, June 19, 1937 (dec. July 1961); children: Sharon Shields (Mrs. John R. Greiner), Franklin Vance (killed in action in Vietnam); m. Maryesther Agnew, July 1, 1967. B.A., U. Oreg., 1933, J.D., 1936. Bar: Oreg. 1936. Practiced in Portland; assoc. firm Miller, Nash, Wiener, Hager & Carlsen and predecessors, 1936-48; partner Miller, Nash, Wiener, Hager & Carlsen (and predecessors), 1948-80, of counsel, from 1980; instr. Northwestern Coll. Law, 1944-48. Mem. Am., Multnomah County bar assns., Am. Judicature Soc., Oreg. State Bar, Lang Syne Soc., Phi Delta Phi. Republican. Clubs: Mason (Portland) (32 deg.), Waverley Country (Portland), Multnomah Athletic (Portland); Thunderbird Country (Rancho Mirage, Calif.); Rotary. Home: Wilsonville Oreg. Deceased.

ANDERSON, LAWRENCE BERNHART, architect, educator; b. Geneva, Minn., May 7, 1906; s. Andrew S. and Lena (Christianson) A.; m. Rosina duPont, July 30, 1936; children: Judith, Karen, Lawrence. B.S., U. Minn., 1926, B.S. in Architecture, 1927; M.Arch., MIT, 1930; student, Ecole des Beaux-Arts, Paris, 1930-33. Architecture practice, 1936-73; ptnr. H.L. Beckwith, Cambridge, Mass., 1938-54, Anderson, Beckwith and Haible, Boston, 1954-73; mem. faculty MIT, 1933-76, chmn. dept. architecture, 1947-65; dean Sch. Architecture and Planning, 1965-71, prof. emeritus, sr. lectr., 1971-76; vis. prof. Universidad Católica, Santiago, Chile, 1975, T. Jefferson prof. U. Va., 1976; vis. prof. U. Utah, 1977, U. Ariz., 1980, U. Calif.-Berkeley, 1981. Academician NAD. Fellow AIA, Am. Acad. Arts and Sci.; mem. Assn. Collegiate Schs. Architecture (pres. 1953-55). Home: Lincoln Ctr Mass. Died Apr. 6, 1994.

ANDERSON, LEO E., lawyer; b. Gettysburg, S.D., Feb. 20, 1902; s. Laurits Martin and Leonora (Ellis) A.; m. Hollis Norris, Nov. 1, 1931 (dec. 1959); children: Denise, David H.; m. Pauline Murray, Feb. 12, 1961. Student, U. Redlands, 1921-22; B.S., B.A., U. So. Calif., 1924, LL.B., 1927. Bar: Calif. Assoc. Meserve, Mumper & Hughes, L.A., 1927-38, ptnr., 1938-89, ret., 1989; bd. dirs. Lennox Industries. Chmn. Los Angeles County Republican Central Com., 1936-40, Calif. Rep. Central Com., 1946-48; Pres., dir. Forest Lawn Meml. Parks; chmn. bd. govs. Shriners Hosps. for Crippled Children Los Angeles Unit, 1973-74; trustee U. Redlands (Calif.), 1968-72, Los Angeles Philanthropic Found., 1968-75; pres. Orange Grove Terr. Owners Assn., 1976-77. Clubs: Los Angeles Univ. (bd. dirs. 1956-59); San Gabriel Country (bd. dirs. 1943-54, pres., 1952-53. Lodges: Mason (grandmaster Calif. and Hawaii 1958), Shriner (potentate temple 1968). Home: Pasadena Calif. Deceased.

ANDERSON, LINDSAY GORDON, film and theater director; b. Bangalore, India, Apr. 17, 1923; s. Alexander Vass and Estelle Bell (Gasson) A.; ed. Cheltenham Coll., Wadham Coll., Oxford. Dir. films: (documentaries) Meet the Pioneers, 1948, O Dreamland, (with Guy Brenton) Thursday's Children, Everyday Except Christmas, Raz Dwa Trzy, If You Were There..., Is That All There Is?; (theatrical) This Sporting Life, The White Bus, If ..., O Lucky Man!, In Celebration, Britannia Hospital, The Whales of August; dir. theatrical prodns. include The Long and The Short and the Tall, Sergeant Musgraves Dance, The Fire Raisers, Billy Liar, In Celebration, The Contractor, Home, The Changing Room, The Farm, Early Days, The Cherry Orchard, The Sea Gull, The Bed Before Yesterday, What the Butler Saw, Hamlet, The Playboy of the Western World, Holiday, The March on Russia, The Fishing Trip, Stages; dir. for TV include The Old Crowd, 1979, Glory! Glory!, 1989. Recipient Acad. award for Thursday's Children, 1953, Venice Grand prix for Every Day Except Christmas, 1957, Grand prix Cannes Internat. Film Festival for If . . ., 1969, Spl. Jury prize Florence Festival, 1991, Grand prix Uppsala Documentary Festival for Is That All There Is?, 1992; performances in films and TV include The Parachute, 1967, Chariots of Fire, 1982, Prisoners of Honor, 1991. Author: Making a Film, 1952; About John Ford, 1981; co-founder, editor Sequence, 1947-51. Died Aug. 30, 1994. Home: London Eng.

ANDERSON, MARIAN, contralto; b. Phila., Feb. 27, 1902; d. John Berkeley and Anna Anderson; ed. Phila. pub. schs.; mus. edn. pvt. study in Phila., N.Y. and abroad; hon. degrees 23 Am. ednl. instns., 1 Korean; m. Orpheus H. Fisher, July 24, 1943 (dec.). As child sang in Union Bapt. Ch. choir, Phila.; a fund raised through a church concert enabled her to take singing lessons under an Italian instr.; won 1st prize in competition with 300 others at N.Y. Lewisohn Stadium, 1925; began singing career, 1924; debut in Un Ballo in Maschera, Met. Opera, 1955; has made many concert tours of the U.S. and Europe; one of the leading contraltos in world; appearances in all famous concert halls, stadia, now ret. U.S. del. to UN, 1955, also 13th Gen. Assembly. Recipient Bok Award, 1940, Congl. Medal of Honor, 1977, Nat. Medal of Arts, 1986; awarded Finnish decoration "probenignitate humana", 1940; decorations from Sweden, Philippines, Haiti, Liberia, France, numerous states and cities in U.S.; Yokus Lo medal (Japan). Mem. Alpha Kappa Alpha. Author: My Lord, What a Morning. Died Apr. 8, 1993. Home: Danbury Conn.

ANDERSON, ROBERT DENNIS, lawyer; b. Dallas, May 13, 1947; s. C.L. and Bobbie (Belote) A.; m. Molly Crouch, Sept. 23, 1972. BA, So. Meth. U., 1969, JD, 1972. Bar: Tex. 1972. Assoc. Fulbright & Jaworski L.L.P., Houston, 1972-80; ptnr. Fulbright & Jaworski, Houston, 1980-95. Contbg. author: Formalities of Corporate Operations, 1986. Fellow Am. Coll. Investment Counsel, Tex. Bus. Law Found. (chmn. bd.); mem. Am. Judicature Soc., Tex. State Bar Assn. (mem. corp. law com., mem. legal opinions com.), Tex. Assn. Bank Counsel, Tex. Bar Found., Houston Bar Assn., Houston Bar Found. Democrat. Home: Houston Tex.

ANDOLSEK, LUDWIG J., association executive; b. Denver, Nov. 6, 1910; s. Ludvig and Frances (Gouze) A.; m. Regina A. Burnett, Nov. 25, 1945; 1 child, Kathryn. B.E., St. Cloud State U., 1935. Area dir. Nat. Youth Adminstrn., Duluth, Minn., 1936-42; asst. to personnel officer VA Hosp., St. Cloud, Minn., 1947-50; civilian personnel officer Ellsworth AFB, Weaver, S.D., 1950-51; adminstrv. asst. to Congressman John Blatnik U.S. Ho. of Reps., D.C., 1951-62; chief clk. pub. works com. U.S. Ho. of Reps., 1963; commr. U.S. Civil Svc. Commn., D.C., 1963-77; nat. sec. Nat. Assn. Retired Fed. Employees, D.C., 1980-81; pres. Nat. Assn. Retired Fed. Employees, 1982-86. Recipient Gold medal of Merit, VFW, 1972, Disting. Alumni award St. Cloud U., 1973. Mem. Am. Legion, AMVETS (named Civil Servant of Yr. 1966), KC, Kiwanis. Democrat. Roman Catholic. Home: Durham N.C. Died Mar. 3, 1995.

ANDRÉ, OSCAR JULES, lawyer; b. Charleroi, Belgium, May 15, 1900; came to U.S., 1908, naturalized, 1914; s. Oscar Jean and Aline (Bastin) A.; m. Ruby E. Cox, June 14, 1932; children: Nancy André Hatton, Elise, David J. A.B. magna cum laude, Salem Coll., 1925, LL.D., 1977; LL.B., U. Va., 1929. Bar: W.Va. 1929, Va. 1978, U.S. Supreme Ct. 1973. Mem. firm Steptoe & Johnson, Clarksburg, 1929-93; partner Steptoe & Johnson, 1934-93, sr. partner, 1950-76; counsel firm André & Fowler, Winchester, Va., 1978-93; Vice pres., dir. Osborn Machinery Co., Inc. Pres. Clarksburg Community Concert Assn., 1950-78; past pres., bd. dirs. W.Va., Harrison County Tb and health assns.; bd. dirs. Salem Coll., 1930-51, Union Protestant Hosp., United Hosp. Center, Clarksburg; adv. bd. Clarksburg YWCA. Fellow Am. Coll. Trial Lawyers; mem. W. Va. State Bar (bd. govs. 1957-60, v.p. 1960-62, pres. 1962-63), Va. State Bar, Am. Bar Assn., W. Va. Bar Assn., Harrison County Bar Assn. (past pres.), Winchester-Frederick County Bar Assn., Fed. Jud. Conf. 4th Circuit, Order of Coif, Phi Beta Kappa. Republican. Presbyterian. Home: Winchester Va. Died 1993.

ANDREWS, FRANK MEREDITH, social scientist, educator; b. N.Y.C., Apr. 2, 1935; s. Frank Emerson and Edith Lilian (Severance) A.; m. Ann Katharine Skilling, July 6, 1962; children: Kenneth Skilling, Steven Severance. BA, Dartmouth Coll., 1957; postgrad., U. Sydney, Australia, 1958, New Sch. for Social Rsch., 1959; PhD, U. Mich., 1962. Asst. study dir. Inst. for Social Rsch. U. Mich., Ann Arbor, 1959-61, study dir., 1962-67, sr. study dir., 1968-70, program dir., 1971-92, rsch. sci., 1973-89, univ. disting. rsch. scientist, 1990-92, lectr. psychology, 1963-66, asst. prof., 1967-70, assoc. prof., 1971-75, prof., 1976-92, prof. population planning and internat. health, 1979-92; cons. Pan-Am. Health Orgn., UNESCO, AID, UN Rsch. Inst. Social Devel., Korea Devel. Inst., Can. Coun., Philippine Inst. Devel. Studies, Chinese Acad. Scis., Egyptian Cen. Agy. Stats., Norwegian Inst. Applied Social Rsch., various other corps. and univs. Author: (with D.C. Pelz) Scientists in Organizations, 1966, Japanese edit., 1971, Russian edit., 1973, rev. English edit., 1976; (with others) Justifying Violence, 1972; (with S.B. Withey) Social Indicators of Well-Being, 1976; A Study of Company Sponsored Foundations, 1959; (with others) Multiple Classification Analysis, 1967, 2d edit., 1973; (with R.C. Messenger) Multivariate Nominal Scale Analysis, 1973; (with others) A Guide for Selecting Statistical Techniques for Analyzing Social Science Data, 1974, 2d edit., 1981, Hebrew edit., 1976, French edit., 1977, Chinese edit., 1988; (with others) Tranquilizer Use and Well-being, 1984; editor: Scientific Productivity, 1979; editor: Research on the Quality of Life, 1986; co-editor: Quality of Life: Comparative Studies, 1980; contbr. chpts. to books, articles to profl. jours. Bd. dirs. Whitmore Lake Homeowners Assn., 1972-92, Whitmore Lake Health Clinic, 1981-92. Rotary Found. Internat. fellow U. Sydney, Australia, 1958, Rackham fellow U. Mich., 1962; grantee NSF, NIMH, NASA, UNESCO, Nat. Inst. Child Health and Human Devel. Mem. Am. Statis. Assn., Am. Psychol. Assn., Am. Sociol. Assn., Internat. Sociol. Assn., Am. Pub. Health Assn., Population Assn. Am., Am. Fertility Soc., Phi Beta Kappa, Sigma Xi. Home: Whitmore Lake Mich. Died Dec. 23, 1992.

ANDREWS, MARK EDWIN, lawyer, industrialist; b. Houston, Oct. 17, 1903; s. Jesse and Celeste (Bujac) A.; m. Marguerite McLellan (dec. 1946); m. Lavone Dickensheets, July 23, 1948; children: Marguerite McLellan, Mark Edwin. A.B., Princeton U., 1927; LL.B., So. Tex. Coll. Law, 1934; postgrad., U. Colo., 1931-34. Pres. Andrews, Loop & Co., 1928-34, Ryan & Andrews, 1936-42, Westmoreland Mfg. Co., 1936-42, M.E. Andrews, Ltd., 1951-92, Ancon Oil & Gas, Inc., 1951-92; adv. dir. Bank of Southwest; faculty So. Tex. Coll. Law, 1934-42. Author: Law vs. Equity in The Merchant of Venice, 1965, Buying a Navy, 1946, Wildcatters Handbook, 1952; contbr. articles to legal publs. Chmn. Bayou Bend Mus. Adv. Com.; trustee, ex-officio mem. exec. com. Mus. Fine Arts, Houston. Served USNR, 1942-46; advancing lt. to capt., serving in Office Procurement and Material, Exec. Office of Sec. Navy Dept.; chief of procurement USN, 1945-46; asst. sec. of navy 1947-49. Decorated Legion of Merit, 1946. Mem. Houston Com. on Fgn. Relations (Carnegie Found.), English Speaking Union (v.p. Houston chpt.), Japan-Am. Soc. Houston (pres.). Republican. Episcopalian. Clubs: River Oaks, Bayou, Allegro, Houston (Houston); Links (N.Y.C.), River (N.Y.C.); Tiger Inn (Princeton, N.J.), Right Wing (Princeton, N.J.); Fishers Island (N.Y.) Country); Shannon Golf (Ireland). Home: Houston Tex. Died Aug. 22, 1992.

ANFINSEN, CHRISTIAN BOEHMER, biochemist; b. Monessen, Pa., Mar. 26, 1916; s. Christian Boehmer and Sophie (Rasmussen) A.; m. Florence Bernice Kenenger, Nov. 29, 1941 (div. 1978); children: Carol Bernice, Margot Sophie, Christian Boehmer; m. Libby Shulman Ely, 1979. B.A., Swarthmore Coll., 1937, D.Sc., 1965; M.S., U. Pa., 1939; Ph.D., Harvard, 1943; D.Sc. (hon.), Georgetown U., 1967, N.Y. Med. Coll., 1969, Gustavus Adolphus Coll., 1975, Brandeis U., 1977, Providence Coll., 1978; M.D. (hon.), U. Naples Med. Sch., 1980, Adelphi U., 1987. Asst. prof. biol. chemistry Harvard Med. Sch., 1948-50, prof. biochemistry, 1962-63; chief lab. cellular physiology and metabolism Nat. Heart Inst., Bethesda, Md., 1950-62; chief lab. chem. biology Nat. Inst. Arthritis and Metabolic Diseases, Bethesda, 1963-82; prof. biology Johns Hopkins U., Balt., 1982—; vis. prof. Weizmann Inst. Sci., Rehovot, Israel, 1981-82, bd. govs. 1962. Author: The Molecular Basis of Evolution, 1959; contbr. articles to profl. jours. Am. Scandinavian fellow Carlsberg Lab., Copenhagen 1939; sr. cancer research fellow Nobel Inst., Stockholm, 1947; Markle scholar 1948; Guggenheim fellow Weizmann Inst., 1958; recipient Rockefeller Pub. Service award, 1954-55, Nobel prize in chemistry, 1972. Mem. Am. Soc. Biol. Chemists (pres. 1971-72), Am. Acad. Arts and Scis., Nat. Acad. Scis., Washington Acad. Scis., Am. Philos. Soc., Fedn. Am. Scientists (treas. 1958-59, vice chmn. 1959-60, 73-76), Pontifical Acad. Sci. Home: Baltimore Md. Died May 14, 1995.

ANGEVINE, GEORGE BRAUD, steel company executive; b. Newark, June 26, 1918; s. Lewis James and Eugenia Marie (Braud) A.; m. Margaret Muse Collin, Apr. 3, 1976; children by previous marriage—Paula Angevine Craig, Sheryl, Katherine Angevine Burneko, Barbara Angevine Klein. B.A., Rutgers U., 1940; LL.B., U. Pitts., 1948. Bar: Pa. 1948. Mgr. labor relations West Penn Power Co., Pitts., 1948-56; ptnr. Thorp, Reed & Armstrong, Pitts., 1956-63, of counsel, 1987—; v.p., gen. counsel, sec. Nat. Steel Corp., Pitts., 1963-87, ret., 1987; now vice chmn. Nat. Steel Corp. Bd. dirs. Allegheny Trails council Boy Scouts Am., Pitts; trustee Chatham Coll., Pitts. Served with USAAF, 1942-46. Decorated D.F.C., Air medal. Mem. Am. Iron and Steel Inst., Am., Pa., Mich., Allegheny County bar assns., Pa. Soc. Presbyterian (deacon). Clubs: Duquesne (Pitts.); Allegheny Country (Sewickley, Pa.); Rolling Rock (Ligonier, Pa.); Bath and Tennis, Everglades (Palm Beach, Fla.). Home: Sewickley Pa.

ANGLEMIRE, KENNETH NORTON, retired publishing company executive, writer, environmentalist, lawyer; b. Chgo.; s. Fred Rutherford and Isabel (Alguire) A.; m. Anne Hayes. (dec.); m. Geraldine Payne. Student, Northwestern U.; B.S., U. Ill., Urbana; LL.B., J.D., Chgo.-Kent Coll. Law, Ill. Inst. Tech. Bar: Ill. Pvt. practice of law, to 1936; atty. Chgo. Title and Trust Co., 1936-42; chief acct., office mgr. Graphic Arts Displays, Inc., Chgo., 1942-50; comptroller Marshall Industries, Chgo., 1950-59, Marquis-Who's Who, Inc., Chgo., 1953-59; v.p. Marquis-Who's Who, Inc., 1958-59, exec. v.p., chief ops. officer, 1959-69, chmn. bd., pub., 1969-70; pres., dir. A.N. Marquis Co., Inc., Chgo., 1964-69; Mem. Ill. State Scholarship Commn., 1966-69; charter mem. Bus. Adv. Council, Chgo. Urban League; hon. mem. staff N.Mex. Atty. Gen., 1971-74; mem. Adult Edn. Council Greater Chgo., bd. dirs., 1968-70. Writer articles on music, natural history and conservation, mountain adventure. Mem. ACLU, Ill. Audubon Soc. (v.p. fin., dir. 1961-65), Greater North Michigan Ave. Assn. (dir. 1966-70), Dickens Fellowship, Santa Fe Opera Guild, Internat. Alban Berg Soc., Sangre de Cristo Audubon Soc. N.Mex. (founder, pres. 1972-73, dir. 1972-75), Friends of Santa Fe (N.Mex.) Public Library, Historic Santa Fe Found., Wilderness Study Com. N.Mex., Santa Fe Concert Assn., Bus. Execs. Move for Peace in Viet Nam, Ridges Sanctuary, Bailey's Harbor, Wis., Armory for the Arts, Guadalupe Hist. Found., Santa Fe. Trail Assn. (End of the Trail chpt.), Pi Kappa Alpha, Delta Theta Phi, Sierra Club (founder, chmn. Great Lakes chpt. 1959-61, 64-66, exec. com. 1959-69, Rio Grande chpt., N.Mex.). Club: N.Mex. Mountain. Home: Santa Fe N.Mex. Died Jan. 5, 1994; cremated Santa Fe, N.M.

ANNIGONI, PIETRO, painter; b. Milan, Italy, June 7, 1910; attended Accademia di Belle Arti, Florence, Italy; m. Anna Maggini, 1937 (dec. 1968); m. 2d, Rosella Segreto, 1976; 2 children. Exhbns. include: Florence, 1932, Milan, 1936, Wildenstein's, London, 1950, Paris, London, 1954, N.Y.C., 1957, Bklyn. Museum, 1969, Calif. Palace of Legion of Honor, San Francisco, 1969, Galleria Levi, Milan, 1971; works include: Portraits of The Duchess of Devonshire, Miss Margaret Rawlings, Lord and Lady Howard de Walden, Dame Margot Fonteyn, Deposition of Christ with Dominican Saints 1936-40, Say You This is Man?, 1953, Way to the Sermon on the Mount, 1954, Portrait of H.M. Queen Elizabeth II, 1955, Portrait of H.R.H. Princess Margaret, 1958, Life, 1961, Portrait of President Kennedy, 1961, fresco Crucifix in S. Martino Castagno, Florence, Portrait of Pope John XXIII, altarpiece Ch. of Claretian Fathers, Hayes, Middlesex, The Immaculate Heart of Mary, 1962, Portrait of H.M. Queen Elizabeth, the Queen Mother, 1963, St. Joseph altarpiece Ch. of S. Lorenzo, Florence, 1964, Resurrection fresco in Ch. of S. Michele, Ponte Buggianese (Montecatini), 1967, Apocalypse fresco, 1973, The Last Supper, 1975, St. Benedict altarpiece Ch. of Montecassino, 1975, Portraits of Shah of Iran and Queen Farah Diba, 1968, second portrait of H.M. Queen Elizabeth II, 1970, Il Misericordioso for Venerabile Arciconfraternita della Misericordia, Florence, 1970, Portrait of H.R.H. the Duchess of Kent, 1971, The Gold Age frescos, Sala Pontormo, 1972-73, Portrait of H.R.H. Prince Henrik of Denmark, 1977, Portrait of H.M. Queen Margrethe II of Denmark, 1978, Abraham and Moses, Apotheosis of St. Benedict fresco Ch. of Montecassino, 1978, Facts of St. Benedict's Life fresco on dome, 1979, Facts of St. Anthony's Life fresco in Basilica del Santo, Padua, 1982-83, Last Supper Fresco in Basilica del Santo Padva, 1984, The Prodigal Son, 1987, St. Anthony Preaching Fresco in Basilica del Santo Padva, 1985. Mem. Accademia di S. Luca, Arti del Disegno. Author: An Artist's life. Home: Florence Italy

ANRIG, GREGORY RICHARD, educational testing company executive; b. Englewood, N.J., Nov. 18, 1931; m. Charlotte Schlott, June 29, 1957; children: Gregory Jr., Susan, Christopher. AB, Western Mich. U., 1953; MA in Teaching, Harvard U., 1956, EdD, 1963; DHL (hon.), Northeastern U., 1978; DL (hon.), Amherst Coll., 1978; D.Public Service (hon.), Simmons Coll., 1979; DL (hon.), Williams Coll., 1982; DHL (hon.), Syracuse U., 1982; LittD (hon.), Rider Coll., 1987; DL (hon.), U. Md. Ea. Shore, 1988. Tchr. history, asst. to prin. East View Jr. High Sch., White Plains, N.Y., 1956-60; prin. Battle Hill Elem.-Jr. High Sch., White Plains, 1960-64; supt. Mt. Greylock Regional Sch. Dist., Williamstown, Mass., 1964-67; dir. div. equal ednl. opportunities U.S. Office Edn., 1967-69, exec. asst. to commr. edn., 1969-70; dir. Inst. Learning and Teaching, U. Mass., Boston, 1970-73; commr. edn. Commonwealth of Mass., 1973-81; pres. Ednl. Testing Service, 1981-93. Author numerous papers, reports. Served to 1st lt. AUS, 1953-55, Korea. Recipient Disting. Svc. award White Plains C. of C., 1963; Superior Svc. award, HEW, 1970, Friend of Edn. award Mass. Tchrs. Assn., 1978, Outstanding Educator award Mass. Jr. High/Mid. Sch. Prins. Assn., 1980, Disting. Alumnus award Western Mich. U., 1981, Disting. Contbn. to Edn. award Harvard U. Grad. Sch. Edn. Alumni Coun., 1989, medal disting. svc. award Tchr's. Coll. Columbia U., 1993. Mem. Nat. Acad. Edn. Home: Princeton N.J. Died Nov. 14, 1993.

ANSTEY, EDGAR (HAROLD MACFARLANE), film director, producer, critic; b. Watford, Eng., Feb. 16, 1907; s. Percy Edgar and Kate (Clowes) A.; m. Daphne Lilly, Apr. 2, 1949; children: John Edgar, Caroline. Student, U. London. Founder Shell Film Unit, 1934; dir. prodns., then fgn. editor March of Time, 1936-38; film critic The Spectator, 1941-47; film producer Ministry of Info. and Armer Services, London, 1939-46; producer, supr. Brit. Transp. Commn. Film Unit, 1949-74; lectr. Temple U., Phila., 1978-85; chmn. prodn. com. Children's Film Found., 1981-83. Dir.: (films) Unchartered Waters, Eskimo Village, 1933, Housing Problems, Enough to Eat?, 1935, On the Way to Work, 1936; prodr.: (films) Journey into Spring, 1957 (Brit. Film Acad. award, Venice Film award 1957), Between the Tides, 1958 (Brit. Film Acad. award, Venice Film award 1958), Terminus, 1961 (Venice Film award 1961), Wild Wings, 1965 (Acad. award 1965, Hollywood Oscar, 1966); former film critic for the Spectator; regularly appeared on BBC radio program The Critics. Recipient Order of the Brit. Empire, 1969. Mem. Brit. Film Acad. (chmn. 1956), Internat. Sci. Film Assn. (pres. 1961-63), Brit. Assn. Film and TV Arts (chmn. 1967), Brit. Indsl. and Sci. Film Assn. (pres. 1974-81), Brit. Film Inst. (gov. 1965-75), Royal Coll. of Art (sr. fellow), Brit. Kinematograph Soc. (hon. fellow), Acad. Motion Picture Arts and Scis., Brit. Acad. Film and TV Arts. Club: Saville (London). Home: London Eng. Died Sept. 27, 1987; cremated Crematorium, London.

ANTALL, JOZSEF, government official. Prime min. Budapest, Hungary, 1990-93; pres. Hungarian Democratic Forum, 1991-93. Recipient Robert Schuman prize. Home: Budapest Hungary Died Dec. 12, 1993.

ANTONELLI, FERDINANDO GIUSEPPE, Italian ecclesiastic; b. Subbiano, Italy, July 14, 1896. Joined Order of Friars Minor, Roman Cath. Ch., 1914, ordained priest, 1922; tchr. ch. history Antonianum, 1928-32, instr. Christian archeology, 1932-65, rector magnificus, 1937-43, 53-59; definator gen. Friars Minor, 1939-45; various offices Roman Curia, sec. Congregation of Rites, 1965-69, Congregation for Causes of Saints, 1969-73; consecrated titular archbishop of Idicra, 1966; elevated to Sacred Coll. of Cardinals, 1973. Died July 12, 1993. Home: Vatican City Vatican City

ANTONIADES, HARRY NICHOLAS, educator, research biochemist; b. Thessaloniki, Greece, Mar. 12, 1923; came to U.S., 1953; s. Nicholas Harry Antoniades and Eustratia E. Antoniades Manos; m. Maria Tomaras, Dec. 27, 1953; children: Harry Nicholas Jr., Anna Maria. BS in Chemistry, Athens U., Greece, 1948, PhD in Biochemistry, 1952; MA (hon.), Harvard U., 1990. Research assoc. Ctr. Blood Research, Boston, 1954-57, assoc. investigator, 1957-61, sr. investigator, 1961-95; research assoc. Harvard Med. Sch., Boston, 1956-65; asst. prof. biochemistry Harvard Sch. Pub. Health, Boston, 1965-70, assoc. prof. biochemistry, 1971-81, prof. biochemistry, 1981-95; assoc. in biochemistry, Dudley House Harvard U., Cambridge, Mass., 1971-95; vis. prof. U. So. Calif. Med. Sch., L.A., 1961, U. Ala. Med. Ctr., Birmingham, 1963, Buenos Aires Med. Sch., 1966, Ain Shams Med. Sch., Cairo, Alexandria Med. Sch., Egypt, Zagazig Med. Sch., Egypt, 1971-81, U. Tex. Med. Sch., San Antonio, 1986. Editor: Hormones in Human Plasma, 1960, Hormones in Human Blood, 1976; contbr. over 200 sci. articles to profl. jours. Assoc. trustee New Eng. Conservatory of Music, Boston, 1980-85; bd. dirs. Commonwealth Charitable Fund, Boston, 1980-95; chmn., bd. dirs. Inst. Molecular Biology, Boston, 1984-95; v.p. Boston Cancer Rsch. Assn., pres., 1986-88. Recipient Fulbright Travel award MIT, 1953, Lilly award Am. Diabetes Assn., 1962. Fellow AAAS, N.Y. Acad. Scis.; mem. Soc. Biochemistry and Molecular Biology, Endocrine Soc., Athens Acad., Harvard Club (Boston), St. Botolph Club (Boston). Home: Newton Mass. Died Nov. 1, 1995.

ANTONINUS, BROTHER See EVERSON, WILLIAM OLIVER

APFALTER, HERIBERT FELIX, steel executive; b. Pregarten, Austria, Sept. 22, 1925; s. Felix and Leopoldine A.; Diplomkaufmann, Coll. Internat. Commerce; m. Hermine Burgstaller, 1949; children—Ingrid, Gunther. With Voest, Linz, Austria, 1949-85, (now Voest Alpine AG), v.p. fin., bus. adminstrn., EPD, to 1977, ret. as pres., chmn. bd. mgmt. hon. consul Republic of Senegal, Upper Austria. Decorated Gold medal of merit Republic of Austria, comdr. Nat. Order So. Cross (Brazil), gran maestre de la Orden del Merito Civil (Spain). Home: Linz Austria

ARAKI, YOSHIRO, banker; b. Aichi Prefecture, Japan, July 9, 1921; s. Danzo and Mitsuyo A.; m. Kimiko, Dec. 17, 1952; children: Akiko, Masao. Ed. Faculty of Law, Kyoto Imperial U. (Japan), 1944. Chief mgr. The Fuji Bank, Ltd., Hiroshima, Japan, 1968-70, dir. and chief mgr. bus. devel. div., Tokyo, 1970-73, mng. dir., 1973-75, dep. pres., 1975-81, pres., 1981-90; v.p. Japanese Com. for Econ. Devel., 1982-90. Mem. Fedn. Bankers Assn. Japan (dir. 1981-90, chmn. 1982-83, 86-90), Japan Fedn. Econ. Orgns. (exec. mem. bd. from 1982). Deceased. Home: Yokahama Japan

ARASTEH, ABDAL-REZA, psychologist, psychotherapist, educator, author; b. Shiraz, Iran, Sept. 27, 1927; came to U.S., 1951, naturalized, 1976; s. Mirza Khalil A. and Sarah Bigum Sadat; m. Josephine Durkatz, July 14, 1957; children: Dariush K., Roya Louise. B.A., U. Tehran, 1948, M.A. in Psychology and Philosophy, 1951; Ph.D., La. State U., 1953; postgrad., U. Chgo., 1953-54. Assoc. prof. U. Tehran and Inst. for Pub. Adminstrn., 1954-57; lectr. dept. near Eastern studies Princeton U., N.J., 1958-60; collaborator with Erich Fromm, 1960-62; mem. faculty dept. psychiatry and social behavior George Washington U., 1962-69; dir. interdisciplining research and tng. Psychiat. Inst. Washington, 1966-69; vis. prof. social and analytical psychology U. Tehran, 1969-71, advisor to mgmt. and social devel., 1969-71; vis. prof. Princeton U., 1971-72; internat. lectr. and advisor in devel. and tng. various univs. U.S., Can., Asia, Iran, India, Japan, 1972-88; mem. adj. faculty Grad Sch. Dept. Agr., 1962-75; advisor Indian Inst. Tech., 1972-78, UN Inst. for Research and Devel., 1971-72, NIH, 1968-69, Med. Women's Internat. Assn., 1975; dir. Inst. for Perspective Tng. and Devel., Bethesda and Berkeley, Calif., Md., 1973-92; vis. prof. Jung Inst., Zurich, Switzerland, 1982, Tokyo and Komazawa U., 1988. Author: Education and Social Awakening in Iran, 1960, Rebirth of Youth in the Age of Cultural Change, 1961, Final Integration in the Adult Personality, 1965, Creativity in the Life Cycle, vol. 66, vol. II, 1967, Teaching Through Research, 1968, Man and Society in Iran, 1969, Role of Science and Technology in Human Society, 1969, Faces of Persian Youth, 1970, Development of Western Psychology, 1970, Rumi the Persian, The Sufi, 1974 (English and (Spanish edits.), Toward Final Personality Integration, 1975, Creativity and Human Development, 1976, Growth to Selfhood, 1980, rev. edit., 1991, Anxious Search: The Way to Universal Self, 1984, (in Persian) The Process of Human Growth, 1986; poems Mankind, 1989; contbr. numerous articles on Persian culture and psycho-cultural analyses and human devel. to profl. jours. including Am. Jour. Psychoanalysis, Confenia Psychiatrica, Bern, Switzerland, Psychologia, Tokyo, World Union, India. Recipient Medal of Knowledge (Iran), 1950; UNESCO grantee, 1972; Fulbright scholar, 1951. Fellow Royal Soc. Medicine (affiliate), London Internat. Ctr. for Integrative Studies; mem. Am. Psychol. Assn., Congress for Asian Psychology (founding mem.), Inst. Advanced Islamic Studies (hon.), Internat. Congress Psychotherapy, Soc. for Interdevel., World Union and Consortium for Rural Tech. (adv. bd.), World Affairs Coun. (planetary citizen, adv. bd.). Home: Oakland Calif. Died Aug. 7, 1992; interred Colma, Calif.

ARCENEAUX, GEORGE, JR., federal judge; b. New Orleans, May 17, 1928; s. George and Louise (Austin) A. B.A., La. State U., 1949; J.D., Am. U., 1957. Bar: La. 1959. Partner Duval, Arceneaux, Lewis and Funderburk, Houma, La., 1960-79; spl. counsel La. Mineral Bd., Baton Rouge, 1960-62; city atty. City of Houma, 1970-71; judge U.S. Dist. Ct. (ea. dist.) La., New Orleans, 1979—. Mem. Houma-Terrebonne Regional Planning Commn., 1963-65, chmn., 1963-71; mem. La. Ho. of Dels., 1973-74. Mem. Fed. Terrebonne Parish Bar Assn. (pres. 1964-65). Home: Houma La.

ARDOLINO, EMILE, director, producer. dir. (films): He Makes Me Feel Like Dancin', 1984 (Oscar, Emmy awards), Dirty Dancing, 1987, Chances Are, 1989, (TV) The Most Happy Fella, 1978, When Hell Freezes Over I'll Skate, 1979, Leonard Berstein's Mass, 1980, Alice at the Palace, 1981, The Dance and The Railroad, 1982, Fairie Tale Theatre-Rumpelstiltskin, 1982, A Midsummer Night's Dream, 1982, Gala of Stars, 1984, Good Morning Mr. Orwell, 1984, Am. Playhouse-The Rise and Rise of Daniel Rocket, 1986; multi-media producer: Oh, Calcutta! (Obie award, 1969), Astarte, Makropoulus Affair, The Seagull; producer: Three by Balanchine, 1974-75, City Ctr. Joffrey Ballet, Sue's Leg/Remembering the 30s, Martha Graham Dance Co., Pa. Ballet, 1975-76, Am. Ballet Theater, Merce Cunningham Dance Co., Dance Theater of Harlem, Pilobolus Dance Theater, 1976-77, Choreography by Balanchine parts 1 & 2, Paul Taylor Dance Co., San Francisco Ballet: Romeo and Juliet, Am. Ballet Theater: Live from Lincoln Ctr., 1977-78, Martha Graham Dance Co.: Clytemnestra, Choreography by Balanchine part 3, 1978-79; producer, dir.: Baryshnikov at the White House, 1978-79, Two Duets with Choreography by Jerome Robbins and Peter Martins, 1979-80, The Tempest, Nureyev & The Joffrey Ballet in Tribute to Nijinsky, The Spellbound Child (DGA award), 1980-81, Paul Taylor Dance Co.: Three Modern Classics, Two Landmark Dances, 1981-82; dir.: Trailblazers of Modern Dance, 1976-77, The Joffrey Ballet: Live from Artpark, 1977-78, Paul Taylor Dance Co. Summerfest, The Feld Ballet, Choreography by Balanchine part 4 (Emmy award), Stravinsky & Balanchine: Genius Has a Birthday, Vaudeville Alive & Dancing, The Green Table with The Joffrey Ballet, Balanchine Celebrates Stravinsky, N.Y.C. Ballet Tribute to George Balanchine, 1982-83, Choreography by Jerome Robbins, The San Francisco Ballet: Cinderella, 1985-89; editor: On Loan from Russia, 1973, A Time to Live, 1973, A Desert's Dream (Golden Eagle award CINE), Threatened Paradise, 1972, Charlie Pride, Cherry Tree Carol, Luther, Seafall, 1969. Recipient Peabody award for 28 programs for Dance in America series. Home: Los Angeles Calif. Died Nov. 20, 1993.

AREEDA, PHILLIP, lawyer, educator; b. Detroit, Jan. 28, 1930; s. Elias Herbert and Selma (Cope) A. A.B., Harvard U., 1951, LL.B., 1954; Harvard travelling fellow, 1954-55. Bar: Mich. 1954. Mem. White House staff, asst. spl. counsel to Pres. U.S., 1956-61; mem. faculty Harvard Law Sch., 1961, prof. law, 1963-95, Langdell prof., 1981-95; counsel to Pres. U.S., 1974-75; exec. dir. U.S. Cabinet Task Force on Oil Import Control, 1969. Author: (with co-author on some volumes) Antitrust Analysis, 1967, 4th edit., 1988, Antitrust Law; 10 vols. and supplement, 1978-94. Served to 1st lt. USAF, 1955-57. Mem. Am. Law Inst., Am. Acad. Arts and Scis. Home: Cambridge Mass. Died Dec. 24, 1995.

ARGERSINGER, WILLIAM JOHN, JR., chemistry educator; b. Chittenango, N.Y., Apr. 14, 1918; s. William John and Elsie M. (Hosley) A.; m. Marjorie R. Hayes, Sept. 12,1 942; children: William John III, Peter Hayes, Ann Elizabeth. A.B., Cornell U., 1938, Ph.D., 1942. Instr. chemistry Cornell U., 1942-44; chemist, research chemist, group leader Monsanto Chem. Co., Manhattan Project, 1944-46; mem. faculty U. Kans., Lawrence, 1946-92, prof. chemistry, 1956-88, assoc. dean Grad. Sch., 1956-63, assoc. dean faculties, 1963-70, dean research adminstrn., 1970-72, vice chancellor for research and grad. studies, dean Grad. Sch., 1972-78, prof. emeritus, dean emeritus Grad. Sch., 1988-92. Author textbook on advanced inorganic chemistry; contbr. articles on thermodynamics of electrolytes and phys. chemistry to profl. publs. Fellow AAAS, Am. Inst. Chemists; mem. Soc. Engring. Sci., Am. Chem. Soc., AAUP, Kans. Acad. Sci., N.Y. Acad. Scis., Phi Beta Kappa, Sigma Xi, Phi Kappa Phi, Phi Lambda Upsilon, Alpha Chi Sigma. Home: Lawrence Kans. Died Dec. 14, 1992; buried Pioneer Cemetery, Lawrence, Kans.

ARGIRIS, SPIROS, conductor; b. Athens, Greece, Aug. 24, 1952; s. Iannis Argiris and Lydia Kaplani. Studied composition with Nadia Boylanger (Paris), Hans Swarowsky (Vienna). Music dir. Teatro G. Verdi, Trieste, Italy, 1987-90, Opera & Orch. Philharm., Nice, Italy, 1988-89; artistic dir. Teatro Bellini, Catania, Italy, 1990-96; music dir. Spoleto Festival Italy/U.S.A., 1987-96. Recipient Pegaso D'Oro Mobil Oil Italiana, 1988. Home: Monte Carlo Monaco Died May 19, 1996.

ARGUE, HAZEN R., Canadian government official; b. Moose Jaw, Sask., 1921; s. Howard B and Legia (Scharf) A.; m. Jean Ignatescu, 1945; 4 children. B.S. in Agr. with distinction, U. Sask., 1944. Mem. Can. Ho. of Commons. for Assiniboia, 1945-63; parliamentary leader, then nat. leader Coop. Commonwealth Fedn., 1958-62; mem. Can. Senate, from 1963, chmn. com. agr., 1972-80; mem. privy cabinet, minister of state for Can. Wheat Bd., from 1980; also minister for Two-Price Wheat Act and Western Grain Stblzn. Act; chmn. Grains Group. Mem. numerous internat. dels.; engaged in farming, Kayville, Sask. Home: Ormiston Can. Deceased.

ARISAWA, HIROMI, association executive; b. Feb. 16, 1896, Kochi, Japan; s. Mototaro and Hide Arisawa; m. Shizuko Kooriyama, 1930; 4 children. B.Econs., U. Tokyo, 1922, Dr.Econs., 1950; hon. doctorate Chinese Acad. Social Scis., Beijing, 1985. Prof., U. Tokyo, 1945-56; pres. Hosei U., Tokyo, 1959-62; mem. Japan Acad., Tokyo, from 1961, pres., from 1980; chmn. Japanese Atomic Indsl. Forum, Tokyo, from 1973. Author: Analytical Studies on the Control of Industries in Japan, 1937; Some Problems on Inflation and Socialization, 1948. Named Person of Cultural Merit, Japanese Govt., 1981; decorated officer Legion of Honor (France), 1985, comdr.'s Cross of Order of Merit (Fed. Republic of Germany). Avocation: go. Deceased. Home: Tokyo Japan

ARLINGHAUS, EDWARD JAMES, health administration educator; b. Cin., Jan. 6, 1925; s. Edward A. and Irene (Custer) A.; m. Ilse Denninger, Aug. 10, 1974; 1 child, Toni Gail. BBA, U. Cin., 1948, PhD, 1981; MBA, Xavier U., 1958, M.Ed., 1971, MS, 1973. Dir. personnel tng. Mabley & Carew Co., Cin., 1948-51; sales researcher John Shillito Co., Cin., 1951-53; personnel devel. specialist Gen. Elec. Co., Cin., 1953-57; dir. personnel, pub. relations and security Jewish Hosp. of Cin., 1957-66; dir. grad. program in hosp. and health adminstrn. Xavier U., Cin., 1966-92; mem. health care sect. Cath. Conf. Ohio; sec. bd. trustees Providence Hosp., 1968-77, St. Francis Hosp., 1968-75, St. Mary's Hosp., 1968-72 (all Cin.); trustee Epp Meml. Hosp., 1983-89, Otterbeni Homes, 1981-84; chmn. health manpower com. CORVA, Cin., 1970-75, Mercy St. Theresa Nursing Home System, 1991-92; mem. Ohio Bd. Examiners Nursing Home Adminstrs., 1974-76; trustee Lincoln Nat. Health Plan Ohio, 1983-89. Served with AUS, 1943-45; col. Res. (ret.). Fellow Royal Soc. Health; Am. Coll. Healthcare Execs., Am. Acad. Med. Adminstrs.; mem. Assn. Mental Health Adminstrs., Cath. Hosp. Assn., Am. Public Health Assn., Scarbard and Blade, Phi Delta Kappa. Died May 11, 1992. Home: Cincinnati Ohio

ARMSTRONG, HERBERT STOKER, retired university dean; b. Toronto, Ont., Can., Nov. 23, 1915; s. George Reidy and Ethel (Stoker) A.; m. Kathleen Halbert, Sept. 6, 1941; children: Catherine, Margaret. B.A., U. Toronto, 1938, M.A., 1939; Ph.D., U. Chgo., 1942; D.Sc., McMaster U., 1967; D.U.C., U. Calgary, 1972; hon. fellow, U. Guelph, 1985. Mem. faculty McMaster U., 1941-62, prof. geology, 1948-62, dean arts and scis., 1950-62; dean sci. U. Alta., 1962-63, v.p. acad., 1963-64; pres. U. Alta. at Calgary, 1964-66; pres., vice chancellor U. Calgary, 1966-68; prof. geology U. Guelph, Ont., 1968-82; dean grad. studies U. Guelph, 1968-80, presdl. spl. asst., 1980-88; from asst. to field geologist Ont. Dept. Mines, summers 1937-46, 52, 55, 56; chmn. com. on distance edn. Council Ont. Univs., 1983-85. Contbr. articles to profl. jours. Mem. bd. mgmt. Art Gallery Hamilton, 1949-62, pres., 1957-59; mem. council Hamilton Assn., 1946-53, pres., 1951-52; chmn. camp com. Hamilton YMCA, 1958-61, bd. dirs., 1961-62; bd. dirs. Hamilton Philharm. Orch., 1959-62, Edmonton Symphony Soc., 1963-64, Calgary Philharmonic, 1965-68. Fellow Royal Soc. Can., Royal Can. Geog. Soc., Geol. Assn. Can. (charter); mem. Can. Inst. Mining and Metallurgy (life, mem. Fifty-Yr. Club), Can. Soc. Petroleum Geologists (emeritus), Geol. Soc. Finland, Heraldry Soc. Can. (dir. 1974-78), Masons. Mem. United Ch. Can. Home: Guelph Can. Died Mar. 5, 1993.

ARMSTRONG, JOHN DALE, lawyer; b. Petersburg, Va., Dec. 7, 1918; s. William Davis and Ethel Kathryn (Walter) A.; m. Geneva Pratt, Aug. 3, 1951; children: Dale Armstrong James, William Taylor. B.S. in Bus. Adminstrn, U. Fla., 1941; LL.B., U. Va., 1948; LL.M. in Taxation, NYU, 1951. Bar: N.Y. 1949, Fla. 1950. Assoc. firm Cadwalader, Wickersham & Taft, N.Y.C., 1948-49, Shutts & Bowen, Miami, 1949-50; trial atty. Office Regional Counsel IRS, Phila., 1951-56; assoc. firm Mershon, Sawyer, Johnston, Dunwody & Cole, Miami, 1956-60, ptnr., 1960-87, of counsel, 1987-92; Pres. Estate Planning Council of Greater Miami, 1970-71; chmn. planning and program com. U. Miami Ann. Tax Conf., 1960-79; bd. dirs. Wilmington Trust Fla. N.A. Chmn. bd. mgrs. S.W. YMCA, 1970-71, now bd. dirs.; bd. dirs. Lighthouse for the Blind, 1983-88. Served to col., Transp. Corps AUS, 1941-46. Decorated Bronze Star. Fellow Am. Coll. Tax Counsel (bd. regents); mem. Am. Law Inst., ABA (past chmn. regional liaison com., sect. taxation, chmn. coordinator with orgns. coms.), N.Y. Bar, Fla. Bar (chmn. tax sect. 1962-63), Dade County Bar Assn. (bd. dirs. 1988-90), Mil. Order World Wars (comdr. Miami chpt.), Res. Officers Assn. (life), Phi Delta Phi, Sigma Nu. Democrat. Christian Scientist. Clubs: Miami, Riviera Country. Home: Oviedo Fla. Died May 11, 1992.

ARMSTRONG, RICHARD ALFORD, retired magazine editor; b. D'Lo, Miss., Aug. 29, 1929; s. Thomas Richard and Mildred (Alford) A.; m. Nancy Trimble Ray, Oct. 1, 1957; 1 dau., Lucy Isabelle. Student, U. Ala., 1946-47; B.J., U. Mo., 1950; M.A. in English, Columbia U., 1955. Reporter Gadsden (Ala.) Times, 1950-54; contbg. editor Time Mag., 1956-61, Saturday Evening Post, 1962-69; mng. editor USA-1 mag., 1961-62; with Fortune mag., N.Y.C., 1969-89, asso. editor, bd. editors, 1971-75, asst. mng. editor, 1975-77, exec. editor, 1977-89, ret. Served to 1st lt. U.S. Army, 1951-52, Korea. Decorated Bronze Star. Presbyterian. Home: New York N.Y. Died Aug. 16, 1992; interred Ewards, Miss.

ARMSTRONG, WALTER PRESTON, JR., lawyer; b. Memphis, Oct. 4, 1916; s. Walter Preston and Irma Lewis (Waddell) A.; m. Alice Kavanaugh McKee, Nov. 3, 1949; children: Alice Kavanaugh, Walter Preston III. Grad., Choate Sch., Wallingford, Conn., 1934; A.B., Harvard U., 1938, J.D., 1941; D.C.L. (hon.), Southwestern at Memphis, 1961. Bar: Tenn. 1940. Practiced in Memphis, 1941-96; assoc. firm Armstrong, Allen, Prewitt, Gentry, Johnston & Holmes (and predecessor firms), 1941-48, ptnr., 1948-86, of counsel, 1986-96; Commr. for Promotion of Uniformity of Legislation in U.S. for Tenn., 1947-67. Author law rev. articles. Pres. bd. edn. Memphis City Schs., 1956-61; mm. Tenn. Higher Edn. Commn., 1967-84, chmn., 1974-75; mem. Tenn. Hist. Commn., 1969-80, hon. French consul, 1978-88; mem. Tenn. Arts Commn., 1988-93, 95-96. With AUS, 1941-46. Fellow Am. Bar Found. (sec. 1960-62), Tenn. Bar Found. (chmn. 1983-84), Am. Coll. Trial Lawyers; mem. ABA (ho. of dels. 1952-75), Tenn. Bar Assn. (pres. 1972-73), Memphis and Shelby County Bar Assn., Assn. of Bar of City of N.Y., Am. Law Inst., Nat. Conf. Commrs. on Uniform State Laws (pres. 1961-63), Harvard U. Law Sch. Assn. (sec. 1957-58), Order of Coif, Scribes (pres. 1960-61), Phi Delta Phi, Omicron Delta Kappa. Home: Memphis Tenn. Died Mar. 5, 1996.

ARNALL, ELLIS GIBBS, lawyer, former governor; b. Newnan, Ga., Mar. 20, 1907; s. Joe Gibbs and Bessie Lena (Ellis) A.; m. Mildred DeLaney Slemons, Apr. 6, 1935 (dec. June 29, 1980); children: Alvan Slemons, Alice Slemons Arnall Harty (dec. May 20, 1984); m. Ruby Hamilton McCord, July 15, 1981. Student, Mercer U., 1924; A.B., U. of South, 1928, D.C.L., 1947; LL.B., U. Ga., 1931; LL.D., Atlanta Law Sch., 1942, Piedmont Coll., 1943, Bryant Coll., 1948. Bar: Ga. 1931. Mem. Ga. Ho. of Reps., speaker pro tem, 1933-37; atty. gen. Ga., 1939-43, gov., 1943-47; pres. Columbus Nat. Life Ins. Co. (formerly Dixie Life Ins. Co.), Newnan, 1946-60, Soc. Ind. Motion Picture Producers, Beverly Hills, Calif., 1948-60, Ind. Film Producers Export Corp., Beverly Hills, 1953-60; sr. partner law firm Arnall, Golden & Gregory, Atlanta; chmn. bd. Coastal States Life Ins. Co., Atlanta, 1956-87, Atlanta Americana Motor Hotel Corp., 1949-86; vice chmn., dir. Sun Life Group, Inc.; dir. First Nat. Bank in, Newnan, 1949-85, Alterman Foods Inc., 1950-81, Midland Capital Corp., 1951-85, The Rushton Co., 1950-80, Simmons Plating Works, 1950-82, U.S. Office Price Stblzn., Feb.-Sept. 1952; mem. Nat. Commn. for UNESCO, 1947-51, 63-67; mem. U.S. del. Fifth Conf. UNESCO, Paris, 1949; mem. U.S. del. Anglo-Am. Film Conf., London, 1950, 53-56; nat. dir. U.S. Office Price 1953 Stabilization, Washington. Author: The Shore Dimly Seen, 1946, What the People Want, 1947. Mem. Franklin D. Roosevelt Warm Springs Meml. Commn., 1970—; trustee U. South, 1946-50, Mercer U., 1960-70. Named to Transp. Hall of Fame, 1977. Fellow Internat. Inst. Arts and Scis.; mem. Am. Judicature Soc., Nat. Assn. Life Ins. Co. (chmn. bd. 1955-81), Am., Fed., Ga. bar assns., Soc. Motion Picture Arts and Scis., Phi Beta Kappa, Phi Delta Phi, Kappa Alpha. Democrat. Club: Atlanta Lawyers. Home: Atlanta Ga. Died Dec. 13, 1992.

ARNOLD, HARRY LOREN, JR., dermatologist, editor, author; b. Owosso, Mich., Aug. 7, 1912; s. Harry L. and Meda (Sheldon) A.; m. Blanche G. Wetherald, 1934 (div. 1941); hildren: Sara Arnold-Taylor, Charles R.; m. Jeanne M. Prevost, July 11, 1942 (dec. Jan. 1983); children: Harry Loren III, John P., Susan M. Von Geldern; m. Jeanne S. Herman, Dec. 16, 1983. A.B. cum laude, U. Mich., 1932, M.D. cum laude, 1935; M.S., 1939. Diplomate: Am. Bd. Dermatology (mem. bd. 1966-76, pres. 1972-73). Intern U. Mich. Hosp., 1935-36, resident, 1936-37, instr. dermatology, 1937-39; chief dermatology Straub Clinic, Honolulu, 1939-69; clin. prof. medicine U. Hawaii.; clin. prof. dermatology U. Calif., San Francisco; pres. Straub Med. Research Inst., 1961-63; Frederick G. Novy, Jr. vis. scholar in dermatology U. Calif. Med. Sch., Davis, 1975; cons. emeritus U.S. Army Health Services Command, 1980. Author: Modern Concepts of Leprosy, 1953, Raibyo Gentaiteki Kaisen, 1956, (with P. Fasal) Leprosy, 1973, (with R.B. Odom and W.D. James) Andrews' Diseases of the Skin, 8th edit, 1990; also numerous articles, editorials, columns, and chpts. in textbooks.; editor Hawaii Med. Jour, 1941-83, founding editor, 1983-91; editor Straub Clinic Procs., 1941-77, editor emeritus, 1978-91; editor The Schoch Letter, 1975-91, Internat. Jour. Dermatology, 1978-91; corr. editor: Internat. Jour. of Leprosy, 1950-84; editorial bd. Cutis, 1965-91, Group Practice, 1966-74, Jour. Internat. Med. Research, 1972-91, Archives Dermatology, 1973-83, Jour. AMA, 1973-74. Named Practitioner of Yr. Dermatol. Found., 1983, Janssen Master of Dermatology, 1987. Fellow ACP, AAAS, Royal Soc. Medicine; mem. Hawaii Med. Assn. (past pres.), Honolulu County Med. Assn. (past pres.), Hawaiian Acad. Sci. (past pres.), Am. Acad. Dermatology (hon.; pres. 1975-76), Internat. Soc. Dermatology (v.p. 1960-65), Internat. Leprosy Assn., Hawaii Dermatol. Soc. (hon. 1986), Pacific Dermatol. Assn. (hon. mem., pres. 1968), AMA (past del., sect. chmn., del. sect. dermatology), Am. Dermatol. Assn. (bd. dirs. 1969-70, pres. 1971), Sociedad Argentina de Leprología (corr.), Sociedad Cubana de Dermatología y Sifilografía (corr.), Asociacion Argentina de Dermatología (corr.), Sociedad Venezolana de Dermatología, Venereología y Leprología (corr.), Sociedad Mexicana de Dermatología (hon.), Sociedad Brasileira de Dermatologia (hon.), S. African Dermatol. Assn. (hon.), N.Y. Dermatol. Assn. (hon.), Swedish Dermatol. Soc. (corr.), Honolulu chpt. Internat. Wine and Food Soc. (pres. 1977), Social Sci. Assn. Honolulu (pres. 1984, hon. mem.), Sigma Xi, Kappa Beta Phi, Alpha Omega Alpha, Nu Sigma Nu, Phi Kappa Psi, Zeta Psi. Home: San Francisco Calif. Died Aug. 13, 1991.

ARNOLD, PHILIP MILLS, retired oil company executive; b. Springfield, Mo., Feb. 9, 1911; s. Anthony L. and Mary Genevieve (Hodnett) A. B.S., Washington U., 1932, Chem. E., 1941, Sc.D. hon., 1983. Chem. engr. research div. Philips Petroleum Co., 1937-45, asst. mgr. chem. engring. div., 1946-48, asst. mgr. chem. dept., 1948-50, mgr. research and devel. dept., 1950-64, v.p. research and devel., 1964-76; exec. com. div. chemistry and chem. tech. NRC, 1961-65; mem. U.S. nat. com. Internat. Union Pure and Applied Chemistry, 1961-75, chmn. fin. com. 1964-68, mem. bur., 1969-75; dir. Coordinating Rsch. Coun., 1964, pres., 1969-71; pres. Indsl. Rsch. Inst., 1964-65, bd. dirs. 1958-61; mem. Com. on Scholarly Communication with People's Rep. of China. Mem. World Petroleum Congresses (permanent council 1965-71), AAAS, Dirs. Indsl. Research, Nat. Acad. Engring., Sigma Chi, Tau Beta Pi, Alpha Chi Sigma. Republican. Home: Bartlesville Okla. Died Oct. 28, 1994.

ARNON, DANIEL I(SRAEL), biochemist, educator; b. Poland, Nov. 14, 1910; s. Leon and Rachel (Chodes) A.; m. Lucile Jane Soule, Feb. 24, 1940 (dec. Mar. 1986); children: Anne Arnon Hodge, Ruth Arnon Hanham, Stephen, Nancy Arnon Agnew, Dennis. BS, U. Calif., 1932; PhD, 1936; Docteur honoris causa, U. Bordeaux, France, 1975, U. Seville, Spain, 1992. Instr. U. Calif. at Berkeley, 1936-41, asst. prof., assoc. prof., 1941-50, prof. plant physiology, 1950-60, prof. cell physiology, 1960-78, prof. emeritus, research biochemist, 1978-94; founding chmn. dept. cell physiology, 1961-78; biochemist Calif. Agrl. Expt. Sta., 1958-78; Guggenheim fellow, Cambridge U., Eng., 1947-48; lectr. Belgian Am. Found., U. Liège, Belgium, 1948; Mary Snow lectr. Oxford U., England, 1982; Fulbright research scholar Max-Planck Inst., Berlin-Dahlem, Germany, 1955-56. Author over 300 sci. articles. Served from lt. to maj. AUS, 1943-46. Recipient Gold medal U. Pisa, 1958, Charles F. Kettering research award Kettering Found.-Nat. Acad. Scis.-NRC, Nat. medal of Sci., Finsen medal Assn. Internationale de Photobiologie, 1988; Guggenheim fellow, 1962-63. Fellow Am. Acad. Arts and Scis., AAAS (Newcomb Cleveland prize 1940); mem. NAS , Royal Swedish Acad. Scis., Acad. d'Agriculture de France, Deutsche Akademie der Naturforscher Leopoldina, Am. Chem. Soc., Am. Soc. for Biochemistry and Molecular Biology, Biochem. Soc. (London), Am. Soc. Photobiology, Am. Soc. Plant Physiologists (pres. 1952-53, Stephen Hales prize, Charles Reid Barnes life membership award, Kettering award in photosynthesis), Scandinavian Soc. Plant Physiologists, Spanish Biochem. Soc. (hon.). Home: Berkeley Calif. Died Dec. 20, 1994.

ARNOTT, PETER DOUGLAS, drama educator; b. Ipswich, England, Nov. 21, 1931; came to U.S., 1958; s. George William and Audrey (Smith) A.; m. Eva Schenkel; children: Catherine, Christopher, Jennifer. BA, U. Wales, 1952; MA, Oxford U., 1954; PhD, U. Wales, 1958; DHL (hon.), Suffolk U., 1978. Prof. drama U. Iowa, Iowa City, 1958-69, Tufts U., Medford, Mass., 1969—; adj. prof. of classics, Carleton U., Ottawa, 1988—. Active Marionette Theater: performing ancient Greek drama, 1950—; author: Public and Performance in the Greek Theater, 1989, Theater In Its Time, 1984. Mem. Oxford and Cambridge U. Club, Winchester Boat Club, Phi Beta Kappa (traveling prof. 1984). Roman Catholic. Home: Winchester Mass.

ARNOW, WINSTON EUGENE, federal judge; b. Micanopy, Fla., Mar. 13, 1911; s. J. Leslie and Mable (Thrasher) A.; m. Frances Day Cease, Jan. 11, 1941; 1 child, Ann Moulton. B.S. in Bus. Adminstrn, U. Fla., 1932. Bar: Fla. bar 1933. J.D., 1933; research clk. Supreme Ct. of Fla., 1934; gen. practice Gainesville, Fla., 1935-42; mem. firm Clayton, Arnow, Duncan, Johnston, Clayton & Quincey, Gainesville, 1946-67; judge U.S. Dist. Ct., No. Dist. Fla., Pensacola, 1968-94; chief judge U.S. Dist. Ct., No. Dist. Fla., 1969-81, sr. judge, 1981-94. Contbr. articles profl. jours. Chmn. steering com. Fla. Civil Practice before trial. Served to maj. AUS, 1942-46. Recipient Disting. Alumni award U. Fla., 1972, Disting. Svc. award Fla. Coun. on Crime and Delinquency, 1981. Fellow Am. Coll. Probate Counsel; mem. ABA, Fla. Bar (bd. govs. 1955-58), Escambia-Santa Rosa Bar Assn., Am. Law Inst., Am. Judicature Soc., Order of Coif (hon.), Scabbard and Blade, Fla. Blue Key, Sigma Phi Epsilon, Phi Delta Phi, Tau Kappa Alpha, Phi Delta Epsilon. Clubs: Pensacola Rotary, Exec. Home: Pensacola Fla. Died Nov. 28, 1994.

ARONIN, JEFFREY ELLIS, architect, author; b. London, Eng., Aug. 16, 1927; s. Joseph and Bertha (Danziger) A. (father Am. citizen). BArch, U. Manitoba, Winnipeg, Can., 1949; MArch magna cum laude, McGill U., Winnipeg, Can., 1951. Architect Frank Grad and Sons, Architects, Newark, 1951-52; architect Shreve Lamb and Harmon, Architects, N.Y.C., 1952-53, Voorhees, Walker, Foley and Smith, then Voorhees, Walker, Smith and Smith, Architects, N.Y.C., 1954-56, Kahn and Jacobs, N.Y.C., 1956-57; pvt. practice N.Y.C., 1957-77, 81—; chief architect Kingdom of Lesotho, 1977—; prof. Ecole d'Architecture U. Montreal, 1976-77; lectr. 95 archtl. schs. at univs. in N. Am., Europe, Australia, S. Pacific; moderator WNYC Architecture in the Space Age; mem. N.Y.C. Mayor's Panel of Architects, 1961-76; mem. Mayor's Com. for Better Housing. Treas. Scandinavian-Americans for Rockefeller, 1968. Author: Climate and Architecture, N.Y., 1953, Climate and Architecture, Moscow, 1959, Climate and Architecture, Boston, 1977, 79. With Canadian Army, 1944-47. Fellow Royal Inst. Brit. Architects; mem. AIA, (chmn., mem. many local state, nat. coms., sec., 1968, v.p., 1969,74), N.Y. State Assn. of Architects, Royal Archtl. Inst. Can., La Sociedad de Arquitectos Mexicanos, La Sociedad Venezolana de Arquitectos, Inst. South African Architects, Lesotho Architects, Engrs. and Surveyors Assn., Nat. Inst. for Archtl. Edn., Brit.-Am. C. of C., Danish-Am. Soc., Rebild Nat. Park Soc., Swedish C. of C. of U.S.A., Am. Arbitration Assn. (mem. nat. panel of arbitrators), St. George's Soc., Internat. Solar Energy Soc., French Engrs. in U.S.A., Masons, Scottish Rite. Canadian University Club, Hamilton Club. Home: New York N.Y.

ARONSON, SIDNEY HERBERT, sociology educator; b. Boston, Aug. 11, 1924; s. Max and Lena (Shuffer) A.; m. Selma Bornstein, Dec. 25, 1949; children: Nancy, Mark. A.B., Harvard U., 1949, A.M., 1958; A.M., Tufts U., 1949; Ph.D., Columbia U., 1961. Assoc. prof., chmn, dept. sociology NYU, N.Y.C., 1967-72; prof. sociology Bklyn. Coll. and Grad. Ctr.-CUNY, 1972-93; Fulbright prof. Israel and India, 1978-79; Fulbright prof. Bharathiar U., Coimbatore, India, 1984-85; cons. Children's TV Workshop; 1989. Author: Status and Kinship in the Higher Civil Service, 1964, Life in Society, 1965; assoc. editor: Social Problems, 1953-58; adv. editor: Sociol. Inquiry, 1982-86, History of Sociol., 1984-93. Bd. dirs. New Rochelle (N.Y.) Mental Health Assn., 1963-64; mem. exec. com. Westchester County Anti-Defamation League, 1972-93; trustee Tarnakath Das Found., 1986-93. Served with inf. U.S. Army, 1943-45. Decorated Bronze Star; postdoctoral fellow Harvard U., 1961-62; NIMH fellow Cornell U., 1956-57. Mem. Am. Sociol. Assn., Eastern Sociol Soc., Soc. Study Social Problems. Democrat. Jewish. Club: Harvard of Westchester. Home: Larchmont N.Y. Died Mar. 6, 1993; interred Sharon Gardens, Valhalla, N.Y.

ARRAJ, ALFRED ALBERT, federal judge; b. Kansas City, Mo., Sept. 1, 1906; s. Elias and Mary (Dervis) A.; m. Madge L. Connors, Nov. 12, 1929; 1 dau., Sally Marie. LLB, U. Colo., 1928, JD, 1965, LLD (hon.), 1977. Bar: Colo. 1928. Gen. practice law Denver, Springfield, Colo., 1928-36; county atty. Baca County, Colo., 1936-42, 46-48; dep. dist. atty. Baca County, 1946-48; dist. judge 15th Jud. Dist. Colo., 1949-57; U.S. judge Dist. of Colo., 1957-59, chief judge, from 1959, sr. judge. Bd. dirs. Fed. Jud. Center. Served from 1st lt. to maj. USAAF, 1942-46, CBI. Recipient Norlin recognition award for disting. achievement U. Colo., 1968, William Lee Knous award U. Colo. Sch. Law, 1979. Mem. ABA, Colo. Bar Assn., S.E. Colo. Bar Assn. (pres. 1940), Fed. Bar Assn., Denver Bar Assn., Am. Judicature Soc. (Herbert Harley award 1990), Order of Coif (hon.), Jud. Conf. U.S., Phi Delta Phi. Episcopalian. Club: University. Home: Denver Col. Died 1993.

ASHBY, HAL, film director; b. Ogden, Utah, Sept. 2, 1929. Ed., Utah State U. Film editor, asso. producer, dir., 1970-88. Films directed include The Landlord, 1970, Harold and Maude, 1971, The Last Detail, 1973, Shampoo, 1974, Bound for Glory, 1976, Coming Home, 1978, Being There, 1979, Lookin' To Get Out, 1982, Let's Spend the Night Together, 1983, The Slugger's Wife, 1985, 8 Million Ways to Die, 1987. Home: Fresno Calif. Died Dec. 27, 1988.

ASHE, ARTHUR ROBERT, JR., tennis player, sports consultant; b. Richmond, Va., July 10, 1943; s. Arthur Robert Sr. and Mattie C. (Cunningham) A.; m. Jeanne-Marie Moutoussamy, Feb. 20, 1977; 1 child, Camera Elizabeth. BS in Bus. Adminstrn., UCLA, 1966; LHD (hon.), Princeton U., Dartmouth U., Le Moyne U., Va. Union U., Bryant Coll., Trinity U., Hartford, Conn. Profl. tennis player, 1969-79; mem. U.S. Davis Cup Team, capt., 1981; dir. tennis Doral Country Club, Miami, Fla.; bd. dirs. Aetna Life and Casualty; chmn. adv. staff Head Sports USA; v.p. internat. mktg. LE COQ Sportif USA; sports cons., 1979-93. Author: (with Frank DeFord) Portrait in Motion, 1973, (with Neil Amdur) Off the Court, 1981, A Hard Road To Glory, (3 rols) 1988; creator video (with Stan Smith and Vic Braden) Tennis Our Way, 1986. Campaign chmn. Am. Heart Assn., Dallas, 1981-82. Served to 1st lt. U.S. Army, 1967-69. Named Player of Yr. Assn. Tennis Profls., 1975; winner two U.S. Intercollegiate championships during coll.; winner U.S. Men's Hard Court championship, 1963; U.S. Men's Clay Ct., 1967, U.S. Amateur title, 1968, U.S. Open championship, 1968, Australian Open, 1970, French Open Doubles, 1972, Wimbledon Singles, 1975, World Championship Tennis Singles, 1975, Australian Open Doubles, 1970, 77. Mem. U.S. Tennis Assn., Kappa Alpha Psi, Sigma Pi Phi. Home: New York N.Y. Died Feb. 6, 1993.

ASHFORD, DOUGLAS ELLIOTT, comparative politics educator; b. Lockport, N.Y., Aug. 28, 1928; s. Howard John and Doris (Saunders) A.; m. Margaret Anderson, May 25, 1955 (div. 1970); children: Elizabeth, Douglas, David, Michael; m. 2d Karen V. Knudson, June 8, 1974; 1 child, Matthew. B.A., Brown U., 1950; M.A., Oxford U., (Eng.), 1952; Ph.D., Princeton U., 1961. Asst. prof. comparative politics Ind. U., Bloomington, 1961-63; assoc. prof. Johns Hopkins U., Balt., 1963-64; assoc. prof. Cornell U., Ithaca, N.Y., 1964-68, prof., 1968-82; Andrew W. Mellon prof. comparative politics U. Pitts., 1982—; cons. NSF, Washington, 1968—, NEH, Washington, 1972—; mem. steering com. Council for European Studies, N.Y.C., 1974-78. Author: Financing Cities in the Welfare State, 1980, Policy and Politics in Britain: Limits of Consensus, 1981, British Dogmatism and French Pragmatism, 1982, Policy and Politics in France: Living with Uncertainty, 1982, The Emergence of the Welfare States, 1986, Discretionary Politics, 1990, History and Context in Comparative Public Policy, 1991; mem. editorial bd. Policy, 1988—, Govt. and Policy, 1978—, Jour. Policy History, 1992—. Served to 1st lt.

USAF, 1952-55. Rhodes scholar, 1950, Fulbright scholar, 1992; fellow The Netherlands Inst. Advanced Study, 1977, Simon fellow U. Manchester, Eng., 1980; fellow Guggenheim Found., 1982, Ctr. for Interdisciplinary Studies, U. Bielefeld, Federal Republic of Germany, 1989. Mem. mem. Am. Polit. Sci. Assn., Am. Oxonian Soc., Policy Studies Assn., Brit. Studies Group (mem. exec. com. 1979-82), Tocqueville Soc. Democrat. Presbyterian. Home: Pittsburgh Pa. Died June 20, 1993.

ASHTON, WENDELL JEREMY, publisher; b. Salt Lake City, Oct. 31, 1912; s. Marvin Owen and Rae (Jeremy) A.; m. Marian Reynolds, Apr. 24, 1940 (dec. Mar. 1963); children: Wendy Jane (Mrs. Neil Christiansen), Susan, Ellen (Mrs. J. Robert Van Orman), Marged, Owen, Kay; m. Belva Barlow, June 26, 1964; 1 dau., Allyson Louise. B.S. magna cum laude, U. Utah, 1933; LL.D., Westminster Coll., 1980. Reporter Salt Lake City Telegram, 1931-34; asso. editor Millennial Star, London, Eng., 1935-36; salesman for bldg. materials co., 1936-42; gen. sec. Sunday Schs., Ch. of Jesus Christ of Latter Day Saints, 1942-46; mng. editor Deseret News, Salt Lake City, 1947-48; v.p. Gillham Advt., Inc., Salt Lake City, 1951-72; mng. dir. pub. communications Ch. of Jesus Christ of Latter Day Saints, 1972-77; pub. Deseret News Pub. Co., Salt Lake City, 1978-95; partner Oneida Investment Co., 1952-95; chmn. bd. Salt Lake br. Fed. Res. Bank San Francisco, 1979-95. Author: (with Ab Jenkins) Salt of the Earth, 1939, Theirs is the Kingdom, 1945, Voice in the West, 1950, It's Your Life to Enjoy, 1955, In Your Own Image, 1959, Bigger Than Yourself, 1965, To Thine Own Self, 1972. Pres., chief exec. officer Utah Symphony, 1966-95; pres. Sons Utah Pioneers, 1946-47; chmn. Utah Cancer Crusade, 1964; v.p. Great Salt Lake council Boy Scouts Am., 1957-60; vice chmn. Utah Bicentennial Commn. for Am.'s Ind., 1972-95; state adv. com. Citizens for Better Utah, 1968-95; mem. Utah Travel Commn., 1975-95; bd. govs. DS Hosp., 1975-95, Stevens Henager Coll., 1957-72, Deseret Utah Art Found., 1974-95; adv. bd. dept. journalism U. Utah, 1967-95; mem. nat. adv. bd. Brigham Young U. Coll. Bus., 1972-95; exec. com. Utahns Against Pornography, 1976-95; bd. dirs. Newspaper Agy. Corp. Recipient Distinguished Alumni award U. Utah, 1968, Service to Journalism award, 1967; Silver medal Am. Advt. Fedn., 1967; Silver Beaver award Boy Scouts Am., 1957; Meritorious Service award Dept. Communications Brigham Young U., 1975; Disting. Service award U. Utah Coll. Bus., 1979; Disting. Service to Edn. award Phi Delta Kappa, 1983. Mem. Salt Lake Area C. of C. (bd. govs. 1976-79, 1st v.p., pres. 1978-79), Sigma Nu (Utah Hall of Fame 1976). Republican. Mem. Ch. of Jesus Christ of Latter Day Saints (stake pres. 1960-62; regional rep. of 12, 1967-73). Home: Salt Lake City Utah Died Aug. 31, 1995.

ASTON, JAMES WILLIAM, banker; b. Farmersville, Tex., Oct. 6, 1911; s. Joseph Alexander and Jimmie Gertrude (Jackson) A.; m. Sarah Camilla Orth, June 29, 1935 (dec. Mar. 1989); 1 child, James William Jr.; m. Pat I. Harris, Feb. 14, 1991. BSCE, Tex. A&M U., 1933. Apprentice city mgr. City of Dallas, 1933-34, asst. city mgr., 1934-39, city mgr., 1939-41; city mgr. City of Bryan, Tex., 1939; v.p. Republic Nat. Bank, Dallas, 1945-55, exec. v.p., 1955-57, pres., 1957-61, pres., chief exec. officer, 1961-65, chief exec. officer, 1965-77, chmn. bd. dirs exec. com., 1977-87, cons., 1987-95; bd. dirs. Indsl. Properties Corp., Dallas; ret. chmn. NationsBank, 1988-95. Bd. dirs. Hoblitzelle Found., Dallas, Trinity Improvement Assn., Dallas; chmn. bd. Southwestern Med. Found., Dallas, 1981-88, chmn. emeritus, 1988-95; ex-official dir. Cotton Bowl Athletic Assn., Dallas; mem. Gov.'s Energy Adv. Counc., 1973; mem. adv. com. Dallas Citizens Coun. Recipient Disting. Am. award Nat. Football Found. and Hall of Fame, 1984, J. Erik Jonsson award for Voluntarism United Way, 1985. Mem. Dallas Clearing House Assn., Tex. Bankers Assn. (past pres.), Assn. Former Students Tex. A&M U. (pres. 1961), Tau Beta Phi, Beta Gamma Sigma. Home: Dallas Tex. Died Oct. 2, 1995.

ATANASOFF, JOHN VINCENT, physicist; b. Hamilton, N.Y., Oct. 4, 1903; s. John and Iva Lucina (Purdy) A.; m. Lura Meeks, June, 1926 (div. 1949); children: Elsie Whistler, Joanne Gathers, John Vincent; m. Alice Crosby, June 17, 1949. BSEE, U. Fla., 1925, DSc (hon.), 1974; MS, Iowa State U., 1926; PhD, U. Wis., 1930, DSc (hon.), 1987; DSc (hon.), Moravian Coll., Bethlehem, Pa., 1981; LittD, Western Md. Coll., 1984; LHD (hon.), Mount St. Mary's Coll., 1990. Asst. prof. to assoc. prof. physics Iowa State U., Ames, 1930-42; chief acoustics div. Naval Ordnance Lab., White Oak, Md., 1942-49; dir. fuses Naval Ordnance Lab., White Oak, 1951-52; sci. advisor Chief Army Field Forces, Fort Monroe, Va., 1949-51; pres. Ordnance Engring. Corp., Frederick, Md., 1952-56; v.p. Aerojet Gen. Corp., Azusa, Calif., 1956-61; pres. Cybernetics Inc., Frederick, 1961-82; cons. scientist Stewart-Warner Corp., Chgo., 1961-63, Honeywell Inc., Mpls., 1968-71, Control Data Corp., Washington, 1968-71. Contbr. articles to acoustical, phys. and seismol. jours.; inventor 1st electronic digital computer, 1935, binary alphabet, 1943; patentee in field. Decorated Order of Cyril and Methodius 1st class (Bulgaria), 1970; recipient Disting. Civilian Service award U.S. Navy, 1945; citation Seismol. Soc., 1947, citation Bur. Ordnance, 1947; Disting. Achievement award Iowa State U. Alumni, 1983; Computing Appreciation award EDUCOM, 1985, IEEE elec. engring. milestone, 1990; named to Iowa Inventors Hall of Fame, 1978, Computer Pioneer medal IEEE, 1984, Iowa Gov.'s Sci. medal, 1985, medal of Bulgaria, 1985, Holley medal ASME, 1985, Nat. medal Technology U.S. Dept. Commerce Tech. Adminstrn., 1990. Mem. Bulgarian Acad. Sci. (fgn. mem.), Phi Beta Kappa, Pi Mu Epsilon, Tau Beta Pi. Democrat. Club: Cosmos (Washington). Home: Monrovia Md. Died June 15, 1995.

ATWATER, JAMES DAVID, journalist, educator; b. Westfield, Mass., Oct. 25, 1928; s. William Henry and Vesta Buffum (Gannett) A.; m. Patricia Anne Levington, Jan. 15, 1955; children: Mary Elizabeth, Stephen Gannett, Christopher Perry, Andrew, Katharine, Jennifer. B.A., Yale U., 1950. Corr., writer Time mag., 1953-62, 73-77, sr. editor, 1978-83; sr. journalist-in-residence Duke U., Durham, N.C., spring 1981; contbg. editor Saturday Evening Post, 1963-66, sr. editor, 1966-69; corr. The Reader's Digest, London, 1970-72; dean Sch. Journalism, U. Mo., Columbia, 1983-89, prof. of journalism, 1989-96; Atwood prof. journalism U. Alaska, Anchorage, 1991-93. Author: novel Time Bomb, 1977. Spl. asst. to Pres. U.S., 1969-70; mem. sch. bd. Union Free Sch. Dist. 2, Town Greenburgh, N.Y., 1965-69, 74-76, pres., 1968, 75. Served to 1st lt. USAF, 1950-53. Home: Columbia Mo. Died Mar. 1, 1996.

ATWOOD, ANN MARGARET, author; b. Heber, Calif., Feb. 12, 1913; d. Howard C. and Marie (Jones) A. B.A., U. Redlands, 1934; student, Art Center Sch., Los Angeles, summer 1935. Co-owner Ann Atwood Studio Children's Portraiture, Riverside, Calif., 1937-40, San Marino, Calif., 1940-60, South Laguna, Calif., 1960-67; founder, dir. adult edn. class in poetry writing, Riverside, 1938-40; tchr. poetry Hollywood (Calif.) High Sch., 1943-44. Author, illustrator (or author-photographer): (poetry) Being Made of Earth, 1940, The Little Circle, 1967; author, illustrator: (poetry) New Moon Cove, 1969 (awards 1969, 70), The Wild Young Desert, 1970, Haiku: The Mood of Earth, 1971 (award So. Calif. Council on Lit. for Children and Young People), The Kingdom of the Forest, 1972, My Own Rhythm, 1973; author-photographer: filmstrips Sea, Sand and Shore series, 1969, The Making of a Desert, 1970, Life Conquers the Desert, 1970, The Little Circle, 1970 (Silver medal Internat. Film and TV Festival), The Heart of Haiku, 1971, Haiku: A Photographic Interpretation, 1971 (Chris award Columbus Internat. Film Festival), The Gods Were Tall and Green, 1972 (Silver medal Internat. Film and TV Festival N.Y.), Haiku: The Hidden Glimmering, 1973 (Gold medal Atlanta Film Festival), (with Elizabeth B. Hazelton) Sammy, the Crow, 1970, Tahiti is My Island, 1969, Teeka, the Otter, 1971, My Forty Years with Beavers, 1975, For All That Lives, 1975, Day Into Night, 1981; photographer: (with Elizabeth B. Hazelton) filmstrips Sammy, The Crow Who Remembered, 1969; (with Erica Anderson) book For All That Lives, 1975; film strips Inscape: The Realm of Haiku, 1976 (Gold Cindy award Informational Film Producers Assn.), Haiku-Vision (named Best of Yr., Previews), book, 1977 (ALA Notable Book 1978), Fly With the Wind-Flow With the Water, 1979; (with Günther Klinge) book Im Kreis des Jahres, 1982; book Lebe den Tag, 1983. Mem. Sierra Club. Home: Laguna Calif. Died Sept. 13, 1992.

ATWOOD, DONALD JESSE, JR., former deputy secretary of defense, former automobile manufacturing company executive; b. Haverhill, Mass., May 25, 1924; s. Donald Jesse and Doris Albertine (French) A.; m. Curina Harian, Sept. 8, 1946; children: Susan Albertine, Donald Jesse. BSEE, MIT, 1948, MSEE, 1950. With AC Electronics div. GM, 1961-70, dir. Milw. ops., 1968-70, mgr. Indpls. ops. Detroit Diesel Allison div., 1970-73, 1st gen. mgr. Transp. Systems div., 1973-74; gen. mgr. Delco Electronics div. GM, Kokomo, Ind., 1974-78; gen. mgr. Diesel div. GM, 1978-80, v.p., group exec., 1981-83, exec. v.p., 1984-87, vice-chmn., 1987-89, pres. GM Hughes Electronic Corp. div., 1985-89; dep. sec. of def. Washington, 1989-93; pres. Atwood Assocs. Cons. Firm, Franklin; bd. dirs. Charles Stark Draper Lab. Corp., Stewart and Stevenson, LMI; mem. Corp. of MIT. Bd. dirs. Automotive Hall of Fame Inc. Served with AUS, 1943-46. Mem. AIAA, NAE (council), Soc. Automotive Engrs. Home: Franklin Mich. Died Apr. 24, 1994.

AUCLAIR, JACQUES LUCIEN, entomologist, educator; b. Montreal, Que., Can., Apr. 2, 1923; s. Alfred and Clothilde (Boucher) A.; m. Suzanne Strub, Apr. 28, 1951; children: Danielle, France; m. Monique Marsil, May 31, 1975. B.Sc., U. Montreal, 1942; M.Sc., McGill U., 1945; Ph.D., Cornell U., 1949. Asst. prof. dept. biology U. Montreal, 1949-53, prof., 1967-93, chmn. dept. biol. scis., 1967-73; Research entomologist Can. Agr. Dept., St. Jean, Que., 1949-64; research prof. N.Mex. State U., Las Cruces, 1964-67. Contbr. 100 sci. articles to profl. jours. Fellow Entomol. Soc. Can., Entomol. Soc Que.; mem. Entomol. Soc. Am., Am. Inst. Biol. Scis. Home: Saint Lambert Can. Deceased.

AUERBACH, ISAAC L., information systems and management consultant; b. Phila., Oct. 9, 1921; s. Philip and Rose (Levin) A.; m. Naomi Bernstein, Dec. 1951 (div. Nov. 1957); 1 child, Philip B.; m. Carol Fischer, Nov. 19, 1976; children: Alan Philip, Rachel. BSEE, Drexel U., 1943; MS in Applied Physics, Harvard U., 1947. Registered engr. N.Y., Pa. Rsch. engr. Eckert Mauchly Computer Corp., Phila., 1947-49; founder, dir. def., space and spl products div. Burroughs Corp., Paoli, Pa., 1949-57; pres., chief exec. officer Auerbach Corp. for Sci. and Tech., Phila., 1957-82, Auerbach Assocs., Inc., Phila., 1957-76, Auerbach Pubs., Pennsauken, N.J., 1960-81; pres. Auerbach Cons., Narberth, Pa., 1976-92; adj. prof. Wharton Sch., U. Pa., Phila., 1974-77, sr. fellow SEI Ctr. Advanced Studies Mgmt., 1989-92; bd. dirs. Baupost Group, Cambridge, Mass., 1982-92. Contbr. numerous articles to profl. jours. Mem. Jewish Fedn. Greater Phila., 1940-92, bd. dirs. 1963-92, exec. com. 1969-76, 88-92, v.p., 1990-92; v.p. Fedn. Endowment Corp., 1983-92; co-founder Am. Technion Soc., Phila, 1948, bd. dirs. 1948-80, chmn. nat. technol. com. 1949-57; founder Am. Friends of Boys Town Jerusalem, Phila. chpt. 1974, bd. govs. 1974-84, hon. chmn. 1974-84, creator of Isaac L. Auerbach Sch. for Computer Tech., 1973; nat. pres. Am. Assocs. Ben Gurion Univ. of the Negev, 1987-89, nat. v.p., chmn. mid-Atlantic region, 1985-87; bd. govs. Ben Gurion U. of Negev, 1985-92, vice chmn. 1988-92; alumni assn. bd. govs. Drexel U., 1964-78, assoc. trustee, 1975-87, trustee 1988-92, vice chmn. bd. trustees, 1990-92. Lt. USNR, 1943-46. Recipient A.J. Drexel Paul medal Drexel U., 1981, Drexel Centennial medal, 1992. Fellow IEEE (founder first pres. Phila. chpt. of Computing Soc. 1949), Brit Computer Soc. (disting. fellow); mem. Am. Fedn. Info. Processing Socs. (co-founder, rep. to UNESCO and Internat. Fedn. Info. Processing 1957-65), Internat. Fedn. Info. Processing (hon. mem. 1969, founder, first pres. 1960-65), Nat. Acad. Engring. (chmn. pub. awareness adv. com. 1985-91), The Charles Babbage Inst. (co-founder, dir. 1975-92), Sigma Xi, Tau Beta Pi, Eta Kappa Nu. Democrat. Jewish. Home: Narberth Pa. Died Dec. 24, 1992.

AUGER, ARLEEN, concert artist, soprano; b. L.A., Sept. 13, 1939. BA, Calif. State U. Long Beach, 1963. Singer of classical music, 1967-93; prof. singing Goethe U., Frankfurt, Germany, 1971-83. Coloratura soprano debut with Vienna State Opera, 1967, N.Y.c. Opera, 1969, Met. Opera, 1978, 13 world tours, over 200 recordings; gala soloist for internat. events including royal wedding Prince Andrew, 1986. Recipient Edison award for best vocal recording of yr., 1992; named Grammy Nominee, Ovation Award Winner, 1988; Grammy award, Best Classical Vocal for "The Art of Arleen Auger (Works of Larsen, Purcell, Schumann, Mozart)", 1994. Home: Hartsdale N.Y. Died June 10, 1993; buried Ferncliff Cemetery, Hartsdale, N.Y.

AULT, THOMAS JEFFERSON, III, manufacturing company executive, manufacturing consultant; b. Portland, Ind., June 23, 1911; s. Ross Earl and Olga (Sattler) A.; m. Mary Carr, June 30, 1938; 1 child, Brian Carr. AS, Cumnock Coll., 1932; BA in Econs., UCLA, 1934; student Los Angeles Stock Exchange Inst., 1930-33; cert. Am. Mgmt. Assn. With Borg-Warner Corp., Chgo., 1935-58, trainee Warner Gear div. Borg-Warner Corp., Muncie, Ind., 1935-37, buyer 1937-41; asst. purchasing agt., 1941-51, dir. purchasing, 1951-52, v.p. and asst. gen. mgr. Detroit Gear div., 1953-54, pres., 1954-57, pres., gen. mgr. Long mfg. div., Detroit, 1954-58; pres., chief exec. officer Saco-Lowell Shops, Boston, 1958-60, also dir.; pres., gen. mgr. The Budd Co., Detroit, 1960-64, dir. automotive div. Can., Mex., Argentina, 1960-64; v.p. McCord Corp., Detroit, 1965-68; pres., chief exec. officer Avis Indsl. Corp., Madison Heights, Mich., 1968-70, also dir.; pres., gen. mgr. Flyer Industries Ltd., Winnipeg, Man., Can., 1970-73; chmn. bd., chief exec. officer Saunders Aircraft Corp. Ltd., Gimi, Man., Can., 1972-73; chmn. bd., dir Austinite Corp., Southfield, Mich., 1970-74; chief exec. officer Superior Kendrick Bearings, Inc., Detroit, 1974-76, also dir.; chief exec. officer Washington (Ind.) Heat Transfer, Inc., 1976-79, also dir.; exec. v.p. Duffy Tool and Stamping Corp., Muncie, 1979-80, also sr. exec. in residence lectr. and exec. in residence Ball State U. Coll. Bus., Muncie, Ind., 1979-84; pres. The T.J. Ault Co., 1987-93; chmn., chief exec. officer Team R&D, Inc., Muncie, 1990-93; chmn. bd. Versatile Video Svcs., Inc., Yorktown, Ind., 1991—; cons. to mgmt. Arthur D. Little Consulting, Inc., 1959-93; bd. dirs. Halteman Villa Assn., 1984-86, 90-93. Bd. dirs. United Found. of Southeastern Mich., 1961-64, ARC, Detroit, 1961-64, Jr. Achievement of Southeastern Mich., 1960-63, Employers Assn. of Detroit, 1955-58, Boston Mus. Sci., 1958-60, Mass. Meml. Hosp., 1958-60; chmn., Muncie Ind. Transit System, 1983-87 . Served to capt. U.S. Army, 1934-47. Recipient Purchasing Progress award Purchasing News, 1953, Outstanding Service award Jr. Achievement of Detroit, 1963, S.A.M. award, 1982; named to Automotive Hall of Fame, 1988, Coll. Bus. Prof. of Yr. Ball State Univ., 1983, All Univ. We-ness award Student Leadership Devel. Bd. Ball State Univ., 1984. Mem. President's Profl. Assn., Engring. Soc. Detroit, NAM, Mich. Mfrs. Assn., Soc. for Advancement Mgmt., Nat. Safety Council, Acad. of Mgmt., Am. Inst. Mgmt., Nat. Assn. Purchasing Mgmt., Am. Textile Machinery Assn., Automotive Parts Mfg. Assn., Farm Equipment Assn., Am. Ordinance Assn., Am. Soc. for Metals, Soc. Mfg. Engrs. (robotics internat.), Am. Prodn. and Inventory Control Soc., Am. Soc. Quality Control, U.S. C. of C., Air Conditioning and Refrigeration Inst., Econ. Club of Detroit (dir. 1961-64), Ind.

Hist. Soc., Am. Security Council, La Coquille, Rotary, Elks, Masons, Shriners, Country Club of Detroit, Univ. Club, Delaware Country Club, Muncie Club, Columbia Club, Sigma Nu, Sigma Iota Epsilon, Delta Sigma Pi, Beta Gamma Sigma. Contbr. articles on material control, long range planning and mgmt. to indsl. publs. Died Jan. 10, 1993. Home: Muncie Ind.

AUSTIN, DARREL, artist; b. Raymond, Wash., June 25, 1907; s. Albert and Ella (Caruthers) A.; m. Margot Helser, Feb. 24, 1933; 1 son, Darrel. Ed. pub. schs.; studied art at, Oregon and Notre Dame univs., European Sch. Art, and with Emile Jacques. Began painting, 1925; painted murals for, Med. Coll. U. Oreg., 1934; one-man shows, Perls Gallery, N.Y.C., 12 times 1940-64, Mus. Modern Art, N.Y.C., A.C.A. Gallery, N.Y.C., 1970, Harmon Gallery, Naples, Fla., 1973, 79, Perls Gallery, N.Y.C., 1979, Harmon Gallery, Sarasota, Fla., 1983, Harmon-Meek Gallery, Naples, Fla., 1983, one-man retrospective show, McNay Inst., San Antonio, 1982, Perls Gallery, N.Y.C., 1982, group shows, Whitney Mus., N.Y.C., Carnegie Inst., Pitts., Art. Inst., Chgo., Inst. Modern Art, Boston, City Art Mus., St. Louis, Springfield, Mass., Mus. Fine Arts, Soc. Four Arts, Palm Beach, Fla.; spl. exhbn. Contemporary Painting in the U.S. at, Met. Mus., N.Y.C.; later on tour of Latin Am. countries spl. exhbn.; represented in permanent collections, Met. Mus., N.Y.C., Mus. Modern Art, Mus. Fine Arts, Boston, Detroit Inst. Art, Albright Art Gallery, Buffalo, Smith Coll. Mus. Art, Phillips Meml. Gallery, Washington, Nelson Gallery Art, Kansas City, Mo., Rochester Meml. Art Gallery, Clearwater (Fla.) Mus., Pa. Acad. Art, Phila., Permanent Collection (Walter Lippincott award), Montclair (N.J.) Mus. Art, IBM Collection, Portland (Oreg.) Mus. Art, U. Nebr., Sarah Lawrence Coll., Norton Gallery Art, Omaha Mus. Art, Ency. Brit., U. Del., Los Angeles County Mus. Art, Ga. Mus. Fine Arts, Morse Gallery Art. Home: New Fairfield Conn. Died Aug. 16, 1994.

AVDELSAYED, GABRIEL, priest. Home: Jersey City N.J. Died Dec. 2, 1993.

AWTRY, NELL CATHERINE, real estate executive; b. Dallas, Sept. 29, 1900; d. Henry Hibbler and Laura Jane (Harris) Jacoby; B.A., So. Meth U., 1935; postgrad. Columbia, 1941-42; m. John Hix Awtry, Apr. 24, 1922; 1 dau., Nell C. (Mrs. William W. Gilchrist) (dec.). Real estate saleswoman Prince & Ripley, Scarsdale, N.Y., 1948, Midgeley Parks, Scarsdale, 1949, Cleveland E. Van Wert, Inc., Scarsdale, 1954-60, Julia B. Fee, Inc., Scarsdale, 1960-73. Former mem. Scarsdale Realty Bd., Westchester Realty Bd. Mem. Am. Legion Aux. (vice comdr.), Leisure World Am. Aux., Zeta Tau Alpha. Republican. Baptist. Mem. Order Eastern Star (worthy matron 1961, 67). Clubs: Scarsdale Golf, Dallas Athletic, Leisure World Republican. Author poems and lyrics. Deceased. Home: Laguna Hills Calif.

AXELROD, DAVID, public health physician, state health official; b. Gt. Barrington, Mass., Jan. 7, 1935; m. Janet Claire Ross, Aug. 30, 1964; 1 son, Jonathan. A.B. magna cum laude, Harvard U., 1956, M.D., 1960. Intern Strong Meml. Hosp., Rochester, N.Y., 1960-61, resident in medicine, 1961-62; research asso. public health service Lab. Biology of Viruses, Nat. Inst. Allergies and Infectious Disease, NIH, Washington, 1962-65; virologist NIH, 1965-68; dir. infectious disease ctr. Div. Labs. and Research, N.Y. State Dept. Health, Albany, 1968-77, dir., 1977-79, commr. of health, 1979-91; pres. Health Research, Inc.; com. mem. NRC Assembly of Life Scis.; mem. Inst. Medicine, Nat. Acad. Scis. Chmn. N.Y. State Disaster Preparedness Commn. Served with USPHS, 1962-68. Mem. Assn. State and Territorial Health Ofcls. Home: Albany N.Y. Died July 4, 1994; interred Barrington, M.A.

AYERS, RICHARD WINSTON, architect; b. Jefferson, Ga., Nov. 23, 1910; s. Jere Sanford and Eva Pierce (McNeill) A.; m. Vaughan Benz, Nov. 14, 1941; children: Richard Allan, Allan Winston, Claire Vaughan. Student, Piedmont Coll., 1926-28; B.F.A., Yale U., 1932, M.F.A., 1934; fellow, Am. Acad. in Rome, 1936-38. Draftsman Frederick A. Godley, Architect, N.Y.C., 1934-36; mem. Buckler & Fenhagen, Architects, Balt., 1938-42; ptnr. Buckler, Fenhagen, Meyer & Ayers, Balt., 1946-55, Meyer & Ayers, Balt., 1955-64, Meyer, Ayers & Saint, Balt., 1964-70, Meyer Ayers Saint Stewart, Balt., 1970-75, Ayers/Saint, Balt., 1975-86, Ayers Saint Gross, Balt., 1986-95. Mem. Balt. Art Commn., 1955-68, 80-88; chmn. bldg. com. Balt. Mus. Art, 1955-60; chmn. Mt. Vernon Place Archtl. Adv. Commn., 1958-62; mem. Selection Com. for Fulbright Fellows, 1959-62; bd. archtl. rev. Md., 1947-55, 63-75, chmn. bd. archtl. rev., 1963-68; bd. archtl. rev. Baltimore County, 1952-57, 64-67, chmn. archtl. rev., 1952-57; trustee Balt. Bldg. Congress, 1956-58. Served to lt. USNR, 1942-46. Recipient Prix de Rome, 1936; Garland fellow, 1933-34. Fellow AIA (sec. Balt. chpt. 1948-50); mem. NAD (assoc.). Home: Baltimore Md. Died March 31, 1995.

AYLESWORTH, THOMAS GIBBONS, editor, author; b. Valparaiso, Ind., Nov. 5, 1927; s. Carrol Wells and Margaret Ruth (Gibbons) A.; m. Virginia Lillian Boelter, Aug. 13, 1949; children: Carol Jean, Thomas Paul. A.B., Ind. U., 1950, M.S., 1953; Ph.D., Ohio State U., 1959. Tchr. Harvard High Sch., Ill., 1951-52, New Albany Jr. High Sch., Ind., 1952-54; head sci. dept. Battle Creek High Sch., Mich., 1955-57; asst. prof. Mich. State U., East Lansing, 1957-61; spl. lectr. Wesleyan U., Middletown, Conn., 1961-64; sr. editor Doubleday & Co., Inc., N.Y.C., 1964-80; pres. Update Pub. Corp., 1976-95; editor-in-chief, dir. Bison Books Corp., Greenwich, Conn., 1981-86; vis. prof. Ohio State U., Columbus, 1962, Whitewater State U., Wis., 1964. Author: Planning for Effective Science Teaching, 1963, Our Polluted World, 1964, This Vital Air, This Vital Water, 1968, (rev. edit.), 1973, It Works Like This, 1968, Teaching for Thinking, 1969, Into the Mammal's World, 1970, Traveling Into Tomorrow, 1970, Servants of the Devil, 1970, Mysteries From the Past, 1971, Werewolves and Other Monsters, 1971; Vampires and Other Ghosts, 1972; Monsters from the Movies, 1972, The Alchemists, 1973, Astrology and Fortelling the Future, 1973, Who's Out There?, 1975, The World of Microbes, 1975, Cars, Boats, Trains and Planes of Today and Tomorrow, 1975, ESP, 1975, The Search for Life, 1975, Movie Monsters, 1975, Palmistry, 1976, Graphology, 1976, Science Update, 1977, 78, Science at the Ball Game, 1977, The Story of Vampires, 1977, The Story of Werewolves, 1978, Understanding Body Talk, 1978, The Story of Witches, 1979, The Story of Dragons and Other Monsters, 1980, Storm Alert, 1980, Animal Superstitions, 1981, Science Looks at Mythical Monsters, 1982, The Mount St. Helens Disaster, 1983, America: This Beautiful Land, 1984, History of Movie Musicals, 1984, America's National Parks, 1984, Chicago, 1985, Indiana, 1985, Broadway to Hollywood, 1985, Minnesota, 1986, Washington, D.C., 1986, The Best of Warner Bros., 1986, rev. edit., 1992, Monster and Horror Movies, 1986, America's Southwest, 1986, Television in America, 1986, Chicago: The Glamour Years, 1986, Great Moments of Television, 1987, The World Almanac Who's Who of Film, 1987, New York: The Glamour Years, 1987, Hollywood Kids, 1987, Let's Find Out About the States (17 vols.), 1987, World Series Baseball, 1988, The Encyclopedia of Baseball Managers, 1989, The Cubs, 1990, rev. edit., 1991, The Kids' World Almanac of Baseball, 1990, rev. edition 1993, The Kids' World Almanac of the United States, 1990, Moving Continents, 1990, Chicago, 1990, State Capitols, 1990, World Guide to Film Stars, 1991, The Kid's Almanac of Professional Football, 1992, Government and the Environment, 1993; New Eng. editor: Am. Biology Tchr., 1962-64; sr. editor: Current Sci., 1961-64. Served with AUS, 1946-47. Mem. N.Y. Acad. Scis., Nat. Sci. Tchrs. Assn., Nat. Assn. Biology Tchrs., Nat. Assn. Research Sci. Teaching, Nat. Assn. Sci. Writers, Authors Guild, Phi Delta Kappa. Club: Stamford Yacht (Conn.). Home: Stamford Conn. Died July, 1995.

BACH, GEORGE LELAND, economist, emeritus educator; b. Victor, Iowa, Apr. 28, 1915; s. James Everett and Ethel (Sies) B.; m. Ruth Bartoo, Sept. 7, 1939; children: Christopher Leland, Barbara Kathleen, Susan Louise, Timothy Lee. A.B., Grinnell Coll., 1936, LL.D., 1956; Ph.D., U. Chgo., 1940; LL.D., Carnegie Inst. Tech., 1967. Instr. Iowa State Coll., 1939-41; spl. asst. and sr. economist Bd. Govs. Fed. Res. System, 1941-44; prin. economist U.S. Dept. Commerce, 1946; prof., head dept. econs. Carnegie Inst. Tech., 1946-62; dean Grad. Sch. Indsl. Adminstrn., 1949-62, Maurice Falk prof. econs., 1962-66; Ford research prof. Stanford U., 1963-64, Frank Buck prof. econs., 1966-83, prof. econs. emeritus, 1983-94; chmn. bd. Pitts. br. Fed. Res. Bank Cleve., 1961-66; cons. Commn. on Orgn. of Exec. Br. Govt., U.S. Treasury and; bd. govs. Fed. Res. System., Ford Found. Author: Federal Reserve Policy Making, 1950, Economics, 1954, 11th edit., 1987, Inflation: A Study in Economics, Ethics, and Politics, 1958, Making Monetary and Fiscal Policy, 1971, The New Inflation, 1973; co-author: Economic Analysis and Public Policy, 1943, 49, Management and Corporations, 1960, Economic Analysis and Policy, 1963, 66, 74, Microeconomics, 1966, 80, Macroeconomics, 1966, 80, Improving the Monetary Aggregates, 1976; contbr. articles to various profl. jours.; bd. editors Am. Econ. Rev., Rev. Environ. Stats., Calif. Mgmt. Rev. Vice chmn. trustees Joint Council on Econ. Edn.; bd. dirs. Nat. Bur. Econ. Research. Served with USNR, 1944-46. First Recipient AACSB-Dow Jones award for disting. contbn. to mgmt. edn., Bower award for outstanding contributions to econ. edn.; recipient Walter Gores award for outstanding teaching; Faculty Research Fellow, 1958-59. Fellow Am. Acad. Arts and Scis.; mem. Am. Econ. Assn. (exec. com. 1959-62, chmn. com. on econ. edn. 1966-79), Nat. Task Force Econ. Edn. (chmn.), Phi Beta Kappa, Phi Kappa Phi. Home: Portola Valley Calif. Died Sept. 29, 1994.

BACHMEYER, ROBERT WESLEY, retired hospital administration consultant; b. Cin., Jan. 11, 1915; s. Arthur C. and Lulu K. (Troeger) B.; m. Margaret L. Knickerbocker, Jan. 25, 1942 (dec. Sept. 1988); children: Susan Lee, Janet Lynne, Margaret Ann. AB, U. Cin., 1939; MBA, U. Chgo., 1947. Asst. adminstr. St. Luke's Hosp., N.Y.C., 1940; asst. dir. Hosp. for Spl. Surgery, N.Y.C., 1941; hosp. specialist USPHS, Washington, 1942-43; asst. dir. Children's Hosp., Boston, 1946; dir. Aultman Hosp., Canton, Ohio, 1947-54, St. Barnabas Hosp. and St. Andrews Hosp., Mpls., 1954-63; exec. dir. Youngstown (Ohio) Hosp. Assn., 1963-68; prin. Herman Smith Assocs., hosp. cons., Hinsdale, Ill., 1968-71; v.p. adminstrn. Am. Coll. Hosp. Adminstrs., Chgo., 1971-78; field rep., cons. Joint Commn. on Accreditation Hosps., Chgo., 1978-85; instr. hosp. adminstrn. U. Minn, 1955-63; preceptor hosp. adminstrn. course, U. Chgo., 1949-69; lectr. in field George Washington U., Med. Coll. Va. Contbr. articles to profl. jours. Sec.-treas. St. Barnabas Hosp. Rsch. Found.; asst. treas. bd. trustee Youngstown Hosp.; trustee Blue Cross Youngstown, 1963-88, Mpls. War Meml. Blood Bank, 1955-63; mem. Village Med. and Health Com., 1985-89. Lt. AUS, 1943-46. Fellow ACHA (life, regional regent 1957-62, pres. 1963-64); mem. APHA, Am. Protestant Hosp. Assn. (trustee 1954-63), Am. Hosp. Assn. (life), Ohio Hosp. Assn. (life, pres. 1954, v.p. 1965), U. Chgo. Program Hosp. Adminstrn. Alumni Assn. (pres. 1964-65), Royal Soc. Health (Eng.), Hosp. Adminstrs. Study Soc., Hot Springs Village Camera Club (pres. 1985-87, 92-93), Village 9-Hole Golf Assn. (pres. 1989). Home: Canfield Ohio Died Aug. 27, 1995.

BACH-Y-RITA, PAUL, neurophysiologist, rehabilitation medicine specialist; b. N.Y.C., Apr. 24, 1934; s. Pedro and Anne (Hyman) Bach-y-R.; m. Esther Wicab Gutierrez, Apr. 2, 1977; children: Jacqueline Anne, Carol Jean, Laura, Andrea. MD, Universidad Nacional Autonoma de Mex., 1959. Diplomate: Am. Bd. Phys. Medicine and Rehab. Pub. health officer Tilzapotla, Mex., 1958-59; intern Presbyterian Hosp., San Francisco, 1960-61; resident in phys. medicine and rehab. Santa Clara Valley Med. Center, Stanford U., San Jose, Calif., 1977-79; prof. Sch. Med. Sci., U. Pacific, San Francisco, 1967-79; chief rehab. medicine service Martinez (Calif.) VA Hosp., 1979-83; prof., vice chmn. dept. phys. medicine and rehab., prof. dept. human physiology U. Calif., Davis, 1979-83; prof. U. Wis. Sch. Medicine-Madison, 1983—, dept. chmn., 1983-88; assoc. dir. Smith-Kettlewell Inst. Visual Scis., San Francisco, 1967-79, Centre Nat. de Recherche Scientifique, Paris, 1994—; dir. San Francisco Rehab. Engrng. Center, 1974-78; vis. prof. U. Pisa, Italy, 1970-71, Universidad Nacional Autonoma de Mex., 1974, 86, Universidad Autonoma Metropolitana, Mex., 1975-76, Karolinska Inst., Stockholm, 1989-90, Poste Rouge, Centre National de Recherche Scientifique, Paris, 1994-95. Author: Brain Mechanisms in Sensory Substitution, 1972, Nonsynaptic Neurotransmission, 1995; editor 5 books; assoc. editor: Perception, 1974-78; mem. editorial adv. bd.: Internat. Jour. Neurosci, 1977-85, Internat. Rehab. Medicine, 1978—, Annales Medicine Physique, 1981—, Jour. Neurol. Rehab., 1986—, Am. Jour. Phys. Med. and Rehab., 1987-90; editorial bd. Archivio Italiano di Riabilitazione e Scienze Neurologiche, Rome. Recipient Silver Hektoen medal AMA, 1972; Bronze Hektoen medal, 1977; Franceschetti-Liebrecht prize German Ophthal. Soc., 1974; Médaille d' Honneur de la ville de Bordeaux, France, 1991; Bank of Am.-Giannini fellow, 1961-62, USPHS postdoctoral fellow, 1962-63; NIH rsch. grantee, 1963-78, 92—. Mem. AAAS, Internat. Rehab. Medicine Assn., Am. Physiol. Soc., Soc. Neurosci. Democrat. Home: Madison Wis. Died July 13, 1995.

BADER, ALBERT XAVIER, JR., lawyer; b. Bklyn., Oct. 19, 1932; s. Albert Xavier and Elizabeth Dolores (Campion) B.; m. Patricia Anne Keeler, June 27, 1959; children: Albert X. III, Christopher F., Thomas J., Paul L. BS magna cum laude, Georgetown U., 1953; LLB, Columbia U., 1956. Bar: N.Y. 1956, U.S. Supreme Ct. 1965. Assoc. Simpson Thacher & Bartlett, N.Y.C., 1956-69, ptnr., 1969—. Bd. dirs. St. Christopher-Jennie Clarkson Child Care Svcs., Dobbs Ferry, N.Y., 1980—, Tolentine-Zeiser Community Life Ctr., Bronx, N.Y. Served with U.S. Army, 1956-58. Mem. ABA, N.Y. State Bar Assn., Assn. of Bar of City of N.Y., Fed. Bar Coun., Larchmont Shore Club, Down Town Assn.. Home: Bronxville N.Y.

BADER, FRANZ, artist, retired gallery administrator; b. Vienna, Austria, Sept. 19, 1903; s. David and Elsa (Steindler) B.; educated Vienna; D.F.A. (hon.), George Washington U., 1984; L.H.D. (hon.), Corcoran Sch. Art, 1984; m. Antonia Blaustein, Dec. 2, 1928; m. Virginia Forman, July 31, 1971. Owner, Wallishausser Book Shop, Vienna, until 1939; v.p., gen. mgr. Whyte Gallery, Washington, 1939-53; pres. Franz Bader Gallery, specializing in contemporary art, Washington, 1953-85; photographer, exhibited Corcoran Gallery Art, Washington, 1973, Nat. Acad. Scis., Washington, 1975; one-man shows Phillips Collection, Washington, 1977, Am. U., Washington, 1981, Cheekwood, Nashville, 1980, Brody Gallery, Washington, 1989, Susan Conway Gallery, 1991, Addison-Ripley Gallery, 1993, Austrian Embassy, Washington, 1993; represented in collections Air and Space Mus., Washington, U.S. Ct. Gen. Sessions, Washington, Phillips Collection, Washington, Corcoran Gallery, Washington, Mus. Am. History, Libr. Congress, Nat. Mus. Am. Art, George Washington U., also pvt. collections. Decorated Goldene Ehrenzeichen fuer Verdienste (Austria); Verdienstkreuz Erster Klasse (Germany); recipient (Washington) Mayor's Art award, 1981. Died Sept. 15, 1994. Home: Washington D.C.

BAGGIO, SEBASTIANO CARDINAL, archbishop; b. Rosà, Italy, May 16, 1913; s. Giovanni Battista and Pierina B. Ed., Seminario Vescovile di Vicenza, Pontificia Universita Gregoriana, Pontificia Accademia Ecclesiastica and Scuola di Paleografia e Biblioteconomia in Vaticano. Ordained priest Roman Catholic Ch.,

1935. Sec. Nunciatures in El Salvador, Bolivia, Venezuela, 1938-46, with sec. state, 1946-48; chargé d'Affaires Colombia, 1948-50, Sacra Congregazione Concistoriale, 1950-53; titular archbishop of Ephesus, 1953-93; apostolic nuncio, Chile, 1953-59; Apostolic del., Can., 1959-64; Apostolic Nuncio, Brazil, 1964-69; elevated to Cardinal, 1969; archbishop of Cagliari, 1969; head Sacred Congregation for Bishops of Roman Cath. Ch., 1973-84; pres. Pontifical Commn. for Latin Am., 1973, for Vatican City's State, 1984; Chamber of the Roman Ch., 1985; cardinal patron Sovereign Mil. Order of Malta, 1984. Decorated orders from Bolivia, Brazil, Chile, Colombia, Ecuador, Venezuela, Portugal; Bailli Great Cross Order of Malta. Home: Rome Italy Died Mar. 22, 1993.

BAHM, ARCHIE JOHN, philosophy educator; b. Imlay, Mich., Aug. 21, 1907; s. John Samuel and Lena (Kohn) B.; m. Luna Parks Bachelor, Feb. 13, 1930; children—Raymond John, Elaine Lucia (Mrs. C.R. Cundiff). A.B., Albion Coll., 1929; M.A., U. Mich., 1930, Ph.D., 1933. Instr. to asso. prof. Tex. Technol. Coll., 1934-46; asso. prof. philosophy U. Denver, 1946-48; prof. philosophy U. N.Mex., Albuquerque, 1948-73; prof. emeritus U. N.Mex., 1973-96; Fulbright rsch. scholar U. Rangoon, 1955-56, Banaras Hindu U., 1962-63; founder ctr. for Archie J. Bahm comparative philosophy studies Inst. Philosophy, Jiangsu Acad. Social Scis., Nanjing, 1994, Inst. for World Philosophy Albuquerque, 1995. Author: Philosophy, An Introduction, 1953, Philosophy of the Buddah, 1958, What Makes Acts Right?, 1958, Tao Teh King by Lao Tzu, 1958, Logic for Beginners, 1960, Types of Intuition, 1961, Yoga: Union with the Ultimate, 1961, The World's Living Religions, 1964, Yoga for Business Executives, 1965, The Heart of Confucius, 1969, Directory of American Philosophers vols. I-XVI, 1962-92, Bhagavad Gita, The Wisdom of Krishna, 1970, Metaphysics, An Introduction, 1974, Ethics as a Behavioral Science, 1974, Comparative Philosophy, 1977, The Specialist, 1977, The Philosopher's World Model, 1979, Why Be Moral, 1980, Axiology: The Science of Values, 1980, Ethics: The Science of Oughtness, 1980, Computocracy, 1985, editor: Interdependence, 1977, Epistemeology, 1995; contbr. articles to profl. jours. Mem. Am. Philos. Assn., AAAS, Planetary Citizens, Phi Beta Kappa, Phi Kappa Phi, Phi Sigma Tau. Home: Albuquerque N. Mex. Died Mar. 12, 1996.

BAHN, IRENE ELIZA SCHUYLER, writer; b. Borodino, N.Y., June 19, 1895; d. William Scott and Carrie Eugene (Kennedy) Schuyler; A.B., Syracuse U., 1918; m. Chester Bert Bahn, June 25, 1921 (dec. 1962); children: Gilbert Schuyler, Chester Bert, Jerrold Philip. News reporter Syracuse (N.Y.) Jour., 1918-21; free lance poet and news corr. various newspapers, N.Y., Pa., 1921-32; publicity agt. Loew's Theatre, Syracuse, 1932-34, RKO Theatres, Syracuse, 1934-36; vol. publicity agt. various charitable orgns., Malverne, N.Y., 1936-60, Thousand Oaks, Calif., 1960-82. Vol., S. Nassau Communities Hosp. Malverne Aux., 1944-62, pres., 1956-57; organizer Save the Name referendum upon incorporation Thousand Oaks, 1964; founding pres. Conejo Valley Hosp. Aux., 1963-68; vol. Los Robles Hosp. Aux., 1968-90; founding mem. Conejo Valley Debutantes Ball Com., 1968-81; bd. dirs. Conejo Valley Hist. Soc., 1968-80, named Dona Conejo, 1970. Recipient Community Service medal Thousand Oaks C. of C., 1963; life mem. Conejo Players, 1976. Mem. AAUW, Alpha Chi Omega. Republican. Presbyterian. Clubs: Conejo Valley Garden (hon. mem. 1975); Las Patronas. Died January 16, 1994. Home: Thousand Oaks Calif.

BAILAR, JOHN CHRISTIAN, JR., chemist, educator, consultant; b. Golden, Colo., May 27, 1904; s. John Christian and Rachel Ella (Work) B.; m. Florence L. Catherwood, Aug. 8, 1931 (dec. Mar. 13, 1975); children: John Christian III, Benjamin Franklin; m. Katharine R. Ross, June 12, 1976. B.A., U. Colo., 1924, M.A., 1925, D.Sc., 1959; Ph.D., U. Mich., 1928; D.Sc., U. Buffalo, 1959, Lehigh U., 1973; L.H.D., Monmouth Coll., 1983. Asst. in chemistry U. Mich., 1926-28; instr. chemistry U. Ill., Urbana, 1928-30; asso. U. Ill., 1930-35, asst. prof., 1935-39, assoc. prof., 1939-43, prof., 1943-72, prof. emeritus, 1972—, sec. chem. dept., 1937-51; vis. prof. chemistry U. Colo., summer 1962, U. Ariz., 1970, U. Wyo., 1970, U. São Paulo, 1972, Kyushu U., Japan, 1974, Wash. State U., 1975, U. Guanajuato, Mexico, 1976, 78-82, U. W.Fla., 1979; lectr. in field. Author: (with B S. Hopkins) General Chemistry for Colleges, 1951, 56, Essentials of College Chemistry, 1946, (with Therald Moeller and Jacob Kleinberg) University Chemistry, 1965, (with Therald Moeller, Jacob Kleinberg, Cyrus Guss, Mary Castellion, Clyde Metz) Chemistry, 1978, 3rd edit., 1989; editor: The Chemistry of the Coordination Compounds, 1956; editor-in-chief: Vol. IV Inorganic Syntheses; mem. editorial bds. several chem. jours; also contbr. articles and revs. to chem. jours. Bd. dirs. Monmouth Coll., 1958-76. Recipient Sci. Apparatus Makers award in chem. edn., 1961, John R. Kuebler award Alpha Chi Sigma, 1962, Priestley medal Am. Chem. Soc., 1964; Frank Dwyer medal Chem. Soc. New South Wales, 1965; Alfred Werner gold medal Swiss Chem. Soc., 1966; Teaching award Mfg. Chemists Assn., 1968; Am. Chem. Soc. award in inorganic chemistry, sponsored by Mallinckrodt Chem. Works, 1972; Midwest award St. Louis sect. Am. Chem. Soc., 1971; J. Heyrovski medal Czechoslovak Acad. Scis., 1978; Monie Ferst medal Sigma Xi, 1983; 1st recipient John C. Bailar Jr. medal U. Ill.; Jubilee medal Order of Lenin Gen. and Inorganic Chemistry, 1989; named Distinguished Alumnus U. Mich., 1967. Fellow Indian Chem. Soc. (hon.); mem. Am. Chem. Soc. (chmn. div. chem. edn. 1946-47, chmn. div. phys. and inorganic chemistry 1949-50, chmn. div. inorganic chem. 1956-57, pres. 1959, dir. 1958-60), Internat. Union Pure and Applied Chemistry (treas. 1963-71), Chem. Soc. Japan (hon.), Phi Beta Kappa, Sigma Xi, Phi Lambda Upsilon, Alpha Chi Sigma. Presbyterian. Home: Urbana Ill.

BAILEY, JOEL FURNESS, mechanical engineering educator; b. Pittsfield, Mass., Mar. 7, 1913; s. John Bowen and Clara (Cogswell) B.; m. Arlene Sara Lynn, Mar. 29, 1940 (dec. Sept. 1981); children: Richard John, Betty Jo.; m. Sharon P. White, June 12, 1982; children: Joy Annette and Carol Nanette (twins). BS, Purdue U., 1935; MS, Lehigh U., 1939, PhD, 1949. Instr. mech. engring. Lehigh U., 1939-42; asst. prof. mech. engring. Oreg. State Coll., 1942-43, Northwestern U., 1943-49; prof. mech. engring. U. Tenn., Knoxville, 1949-83, prof. emeritus, 1983-95; head dept. U. Tenn., 1952-73; dir. grad. study program at Arnold Engring. Devel. Center, 1956-57, Alumni Disting. Service prof., 1967-83; cons. Union Carbide Nuclear Co., 1951-70. Fellow ASME; mem. Am. Soc. Engring. Edn., Tau Beta Pi, Pi Tau Sigma, Phi Kappa Phi. Presbyterian. Home: Louisville Tenn. Died Feb. 13, 1995.

BAILEY, STURGES WILLIAMS, geologist, educator; b. Waupaca, Wis., Feb. 11, 1919; s. Ralph Williams and Katharine (Simmons) B.; m. Marilyn Lorraine Jones, Feb. 19, 1949; children: David S., Linda M. B.A., U. Wis., 1941, M.A., 1948; Ph.D., Cambridge (Eng.) U., 1955. Faculty U. Wis., Madison, 1951-89, prof. geology, 1961-89, Roland D. Irving prof. geology, 1976-89, emeritus, 1989, chmn. dept. geology and geophysics, 1968-71. Editor: Clays and Clay Minerals, 1964-69, Procs. Internat. Clay Congress, 1972-75; Contbr. articles to profl. jours. Served with USNR, 1942-46. Fulbright scholar, 1949-51. Fellow Mineral Soc. Am. (coun. 1970-72, v.p. 1972-73, pres. 1973-74, Roebling medal 1990-94; mem. Clay Minerals Soc. (exec. com. 1964-69, v.p. 1970-71, pres. 1971-72, Disting. mem. 1974), Assn. Internationale pour l'Etude des Argiles (editor 1972-75, pres. 1975-78, medal 1993), Nat. Assn. Geology Tchrs. (Neil Miner award 1990), Mineral. Soc. Gt. Britain (hon.), Phi Beta Kappa. Home: Madison Wis. Died Nov. 30, 1994.

BAILY, NORMAN ARTHUR, radiology educator; b. N.Y.C., July 2, 1915; s. Louis D. and Ida (Bolet) B.; m. Rose Levine, Nov. 21, 1940; children: Philip, Barbara Baily Black. BS in Sci., St. Johns Univ., 1941; MA in Edn., NYU, 1943; PhD in Physics, Columbia U., 1952. Diplomate Am. Bd. Radiology, Am. Bd. Health Physics (comprehensive panel, diagnostic imaging panel). Chief physicist, prin. cancer research scientist Roswell Park Meml. Inst., Buffalo, 1954-59; mgr. space sci. dept. Hughes Research Labs., Malibu, Calif., 1959-67; prof. radiology UCLA, 1959-68, Emory U., Atlanta, 1967-68; prof. U. Calif., San Diego, 1968-92; cons. USN Regional Med. Ctr., San Diego, from 1968, VA Med. Ctr., San Diego, from1971; vis. scientist CERN European Orgn. Nuclear Research, Switzerland, 1970; vis. prof. Hebrew U. Hadassah Med. Ctr., Israel, 1972; vis. prof. Korea Advanced Inst. of Sci. and Tech., 1982. Contbr. numerous articles to profl. jours. Named Henry Goldberg Prof., The Technion, 1980. Fellow Am. Coll. Radiology, Am. Assn. Physicists in Medicine; mem. AAAS, Am. Phys. Soc., Am. Endocurietherapy Soc., Radiation Rsch. Soc., Radiol. Soc. N.Am., Soc. Photo-Optical Instrumentation Engrs., Am. Coll. Med. Physics. Home: La Jolla Calif. Died Oct. 7, 1992.

BAIR, FRIEDA AUGUSTA, poet; b. Bowbells, N.D., Oct. 22, 1904; d. Rinehold Frederick and Bertha Marie (Ruhnke) Migge; m. F. Burke Bair, June 4, 1930 (dec. Sept. 1971); 1 child, Byron Burke. Student, Drake U., Des Moines, 1924-25; BS, U. N.D., 1928. Tchr. nursing Luth. Hosp., Hampton, Iowa, 1923-24; tchr. English and Latin Donnybrook (N.D.) High Sch., 1928-30; elem. tchr. North Versailles Twp., East McKeesport, Pa., 1944-48; elder First Presbyn. Ch., East Aurora, N.Y., 1952-55, clk., 1964-67, assoc. pres., pres. Women's Assn., 1960-64; pres. Western N.Y. Presbyterial Orgn., Buffalo, 1960-63; v.p., trustee Western N.Y. Presbyterial Nursing Homes, Buffalo, 1956-71, ch. historian, 1963-86; sec. Golden Agers Salvation Army, Tonawanda, N.Y., 1986-91; mem. League of Mercy, Salvation Army, Tonawanda, 1983-92; rep. Coun. of Aging, Erie County, 1987-90; mem., sec., chmn. Salvation Army Youth and Camp Commn., Buffalo, 1974-91. Author: Church Directory, 1956, Cracker Barrel Verse, 1973, Feather in the Wind, 1975, Twilight Tapestry, 1977, Weathere Years, 1984, Musings, 1991; contbr. articles to profl jours. Vol. U.S. War Bonds and Ration Bd., Eas McKeesport, Pa., 1945-47; inspector elections, Eas Aurora, N.Y., 1949-59; pres. PTA, East McKeesport 1942-43, East Aurora, 1949-50. Recipient awar Presbyn. Nat. Hdqrs., East Aurora, 1957, Woman c Yr. award Presbyn. Ch., East Aurora, 1963, Blue Bon nett award Buffalo Salvaiton Army, 1963, Plaque c Appreciation award U. N.D. Found., 1990. Mem. NEA (life, award 1947), AAUW (charter East Aurora, chmn tour of homes), Am. Bell Assn., Order Eastern Star. Democrat. Home: North Tonawanda N.Y. Died Sep 14, 1993.

BAIRD, JOSEPH ARMSTRONG, JR., retired ar history educator, appraiser, art consultant; b. Pitts. Nov. 22, 1922; s. Joseph Armstrong and Lulu Charlott (Fuller) B. B.A., Oberlin Coll., 1944; M.A., Harvar U., 1947, Ph.D., 1951. Lectr., instr. U. Toronto, Ont. Can., 1949-53; mem. faculty U. Calif.-Davis, 1953-85 prof. art, 1968-85; ret.; curator, art cons. Calif. Hist Soc., San Francisco, 1962-63, 68-71; catalogue Honeyman Collection Bancroft Library U. Calif. Berkeley, 1964-65; owner North Point Gallery, Sa Francisco, 1972-85; vis. prof. U. So. Calif., 1952, 70, U Mex., Mexico City, 1957, U. Oreg., 1963; art cons. mus. civic and hist. orgns.; lectr. cultural instns., includin Toronto Art Gallery, Royal Ont. Mus. Art, Nat. Gal lery, Washington, Crocker Art Mus., Sacramento. Author: Time's Wondrous Changes: San Francisc Architecture, 1776-1915, 1962, The Churches of Mexico 1962, California's Pictorial Lettersheets, 1849-1869 1967, Historic Lithographs of San Francisco, 1972, Th West Remembered, 1973, Wine and the Artist, 1979 archtl. commentary: Sacred Places, 1985, Los Retable del Siglo XVIII, 1987, A History of Rincon Hill, 1988 If Pictures Could Talk, 1989; catalogues Samuel Mar sden Brookes: 1816-1892, 1962, Catalogue of Origina Paintings, Drawing and Watercolors in the Robert E Honeyman, Jr. Collection, 1968, Pre-Impressionism 1860-1869: A Formative Decade in French Art an Culture, 1969, California Art: An Interpretive Bib liography, 1977; editor monographs, exhbn. catalogues contbr. articles to profl. jours. Recipient award of Meri Calif. Hist. Soc., 1961. Mem. Soc. Archtl. Historians Phi Beta Kappa. Home: Belvedere Tiburon Calif. Die Dec. 1992.

BAKER, BENJAMIN JOSEPH, lawyer; b. N.Y.C. Jan. 5, 1954; s. Harry and Stella Baker; m. Carmelyn D Civiletto, Aug. 7, 1975; children: Matthew, Lauren. BS Pa. State U., 1973; MS, Ohio State U., 1974; MBA, JD U. Ill., 1979. Bar: Ill. 1979. Ptnr. Vedder, Price Kaufman & Kammholz, Chgo., 1991-95. Home: North brook Ill. Died March 3, 1995.

BAKER, ELBERT HALL, II, newspaper publisher; b Quincy, Mass., July 18, 1910; s. Frank Smith and Ge trude (Vilas) B.; m. Betye Martin, May 27, 1936; chi dren: Suzanne Baker Bethke, Martine Baker. Grad Culver (Ind.) Mil. Acad., 1930; student, Rensselae Poly. Inst., 1932. With classified sales dept. Tacom News-Tribune Pub. Co., 1932-40, with advt. sales dep 1940-42, 45-50, circulation mgr., 1950-60, pub., 1960-8 pub. emeritus, 1986-95; pres. Tribune Pub. Co., 1969-7 chmn., 1977-86, also dir. Bd. dirs. United Go Neighbor Fund, Pierce County, Wash., Tacoma Com munity Fund. Served to capt. inf. U.S. Army, 1942-45 Mem. Sigma Delta Chi, Delta Kappa Epsilon. Epi copalian. Clubs: Tacoma Country and Golf, Tacom Bohemian (San Francisco). Home: Tacoma Wash. Di Feb., 1995.

BAKER, FRANK HAMON, education and researc administrator; b. Stroud, Okla., May 2, 1923; s. DeW and Maude Emma (Hamon) B.; m. Melonee Gayne Gray, May 25, 1946; children: Rilda, Necia, Twi Dayna. BS, Okla. State U., 1947, MS, 1951, Ph 1954. County agt. Del. County, Okla., 1947-48; gra asst. Okla. State U., Stillwater, 1951-53, extension live tock specialist, 1958-62, dean agr., prof., 1974-79, pro officer internat. program, 1979-81; asst. prof. animal s Kans. State U., 1953-55; assoc. prof. animal nutrition Ky., 1955-58; nat. coordinator extension animal s USDA, Washington, 1962-66; prof., chmn. animal s dept. U. Nebr., 1966-74; dir. Internat. Stockmen's Sc Winrock Internat., Morrilton, Ark., 1981—, dir. U program, 1985—. Contbr. articles to profl. jours. Wi AUS, 1943-45. Decorated Purple Heart. Fello AAAS, Am. Soc. Animal Sci. (pres. 1974); me Council Agr. Sci. and Tech. (pres. 1979), Nat. Beef Im provement Fedn. (sec. 1968-74), Am. Meat Sci. Ass Am. Inst. Biol. Sci., Sigma Xi, Gamma Sigma Del Epsilon Sigma Phi, Alpha Zeta. Democrat. Methodis Home: Conway Ariz.

BAKER, JOHN ALEXANDER, retired foreign servi officer, federal official; b. Bridgeport, Conn., Oct. 1927; s. John A. and Adelaide (Nichols) B.; m. Sarah Bragg, July 2, 1955 (dec. Sept. 1962); m. Katharine Gratwick, June 30, 1965; children: John, Kendall, A drew, Malcolm, Mitchell (dec.). B.A., Yale U., 19 Licence Scis. Politiques, Geneva (Switzerland) U., h.D. in Internat. Relations, Am. U., 1985. Joined U.S. gn. Service, 1950; assigned Belgrade, 1951-52, Voice of m., 1954-56; assigned Munich, 1956-57, Moscow, 957-58, Washington, 1958-60, Rome, 1960-63; assigned J.S. mission to UN, 1963-67; fellow Harvard Center nternat. Affairs, 1967-68; counselor of embassy, dep. hief mission Prague, 1968-70; dir. East European Af-airs, Dept. State, Washington, 1970-74, UN polit. af-airs, 1974-75; dep. asst. sec. internat. orgn. affairs, 975-77; minister to UN Agys. for Food-Agr., Rome, 977-79; dir. refugee bureau Dept. State, 1979-80, dep. sst. sec. for current intelligence, 1980; faculty Nat. War Coll., 1981-84; sr. research fellow Nat. Def. U., 1984-85; et. U.S. Fgn. Service, 1986; dir. civil-mil. and edn. rograms Atlantic Council of U.S., 1990, v.p., 1993. Contbr. articles to profl. publs. Served to 2d lt. AUS, 946-48. Recipient Meritorious Service award Dept. tate, 1960, George C. Marshall award 1994. Home: Vashington D.C. Died Aug. 16, 1994.

AKER, LENOX DIAL, orthopaedist, genealogist; b. DeKalb, Tex., Nov. 10, 1902; s. James D. and Dorothy Iamilton (Lenox) B.; m. Virginia Flowers, Aug. 22, 933 (dec.); children: Robert Flowers, Lenox Dial; m. Margaret Copeland, Apr. 22, 1967 (dec.). Student, St. Edwards Coll., Austin., Tex., 1912-13, Pierce Sch. Bus. Adminstrn., Phila., 1920-21, Carver Chiropractic Coll., 922-24, U. Tenn., 1925-29, Sch. Medicine, U. N.C., 929-30; M.D., Duke U., 1934. Diplomate: Am. Bd. Orthopaedic Surgery. Athletic trainer U. Tenn., 1925-9, asst. in zoology, 1927-29; athletic trainer Duke U., 929-33; ofcl. So. Football Conf., 1933-40; orthopaedic ntern Johns Hopkins Hosp., 1933-34, surg. intern, 934-35, asst. resident orthopaedics, 1935-36, resident rthopaedics, 1936-37; asst., instr. orthopaedic surgery, ch. med. Johns Hopkins U., 1935-37; asst. orthopaedics Duke U., Durham, N.C., 1937-38, assoc., 1938-39, asst. rof., 1940-42, assoc. prof., 1942-46, prof., 1947-72, meritus, 1972-95, Pres.'s assoc., 1974-95; orthopaedist Duke Hosp., 1937-72, founder and dir. div. phys. herapy, 1943-62; co-op. orthopaedic surgeon crippled hildren's div. N.C. Bd. Health; also vocational rehab. iv. N.C. Dept. Pub. Instrn., 1937-74; orthopaedist incoln Hosp., 1937-74, trustee, 1939-74, exec. com., 941-74, chmn. exec. com., 1951-74; vis. orthopaedist Vatts Hosp., 1937-95; faculty div. pub. health and soc. ork U. NC., 1938-41; founder, med. dir. Lenox Baker Children's Hosp. N.C., Durham, 1949-72, N.C. Cerebral alsy Hosp., 1948-95; established Virginia Flowers Baker chair of Orthopaedic Surgery Duke U., 1968; nem. gov.'s cabinet, sec. human resources, State of J.C., 1972; orthopaedic cons. to several hosps., founds., anitaria, govtl. agys.; active in cerebral palsy work, res. League for Crippled Children, 1941-43; mem. N.C. d. Health, 1956-72, pres., 1963-68, v.p., 1968-72. Author: Treatment of Minor Injuries of Baseball, Bone umors, 1952, (with others) History of Medicine in North Carolina, 1972; Mem. editorial com.: (with thers) Jour. Bone and Joints Surgery, 1960-61; trustee with others), 1967-95; Contbr. (with others) articles to rofl. publs. Recipient U.S. President's Physician's ward, 1958, Citizenship award Triangle chpt. Nat. Football Hall of Fame, 1969, Am. Legion 50th An-iversary Physician of Half-Century award, 1969, Ser-ice to Athletics award Atlantic Coast Sportswriters, 970, N.C. Gov.'s Baseball award, 1979, N.C. Order of he Long Leaf Pine, 1979, 88, Derby Day Dedication ward Sigma Chi, 1983, Cannon Cup award N.C. His-ory and Preservation Soc., Disting. Alumnus award Duke U. Sch. Medicine, 1989, Mr. Sports Medicine ward Am. Orthopaedic Soc. Sports Medicine, 1989, Disting. Svc. award So. Med. Assn., 1990, Svc. award m. Assn. for State and Local History, 1991, Hope ward Nat. Multiple Sclerosis Soc., 1991, Disting. Alumnus award Duke U., 1992, Disting. Alumnus ward Texarkana Tex. Ind. Sch. Dist., 1993; named Durham Father of Yr., Exchange Club Book of Golden Deeds; named N.C. Tar Heel of Wk.; named to Duke U. ports Hall of Fame, 1979, N.C. Sports Hall of Fame, 983, East Tenn. chpt. Nat. Football Found. Hall of ame, 1992, Hon. Order Ky. Cols.; Ortho Clinic Duke Med. Ctr. named in his honor, 1966, Lenox Baker Lec-ureship established at Duke Med. Ctr., 1966. Mem. AMA (chmn. orthopaedic sect. 1958-59), and other nat., egional, state, local profl. and sci. orgns., including m. Acad. Cerebral Palsy (pres. 1954-55), Am. Orthopaedic Assn. (pres. 1963-64), So. Med. Assn. editorial com. 1960-95, past. chmn. orthopaedic sect., Disting. Svc. award 1990), So. Surg. Assn., Med. Soc. N.C. (pres. 1959), N.C. Orthopaedic Assn. (pres. 1947, Outstanding Svc. award 1990), Tex. Orthopaedic Assn. non.), Internat. Cerebral Palsy Soc. (spl. mem.), Guatemala Orthopaedic Assn. (hon.), Internat. Soc. Orthopaedic Surgery and Traumatology, N.C. Geneal. oc. (dir. 1974-76, v.p. 1978, pres. 1982-83), Friends of Archives of N.C. (pres. 1980-95), Ky. Col., Soc. of the Cincinnati, Wake Forest Monogram Club (hon.), Kappa igma, Nu Sigma Nu, Alpha Omega Alpha. Presbyter-an. Clubs: Hope Valley Country (Durham, N.C.); ertoma (hon.); Wake Forest U. Monogram (hon.). Home: Durham N.C. Died June 2, 1995.

AKER, MELVIN C., advertising executive; b. Sioux City, Iowa, Nov. 9, 1920; s. Robert Cleve and Louise Cecilia (Moran) B.; m. Ann Mead Payne, July 10, 1943 div. 1984); children: Michael, Deborah, Alison, Mark, ohn, Geoffrey, Courtney. Student, U. S.D., 1939; B.S., Northwestern U., 1946; grad., Advanced Mgmt. Program, Harvard, 1959. Advt. exec. Procter & Gamble Co., 1946-54; with Gen. Foods Corp., 1954-68; v.p., gen. mgr. Gen. Foods Corp. (Post div.), 1964-67, v.p. mktg., 1968; v.p., dir. Thomas J. Lipton, Inc., 1968-69; v.p., pres. gen. edn. div. (N.Am.) FAS Internat., Inc., N.Y.C., 1969-71; sr. asst. postmaster gen. U.S. Postal Service, Washington, 1971-73; pres. Mktg. Services Inc., Washington, 1973-79; v.p. Am. Advt. Fedn., 1979-81, sr. v.p., 1981-87; pres. The Baker Group, Washington, 1987-95; adj. prof. George Washington U., Washington, 1987-95. Served to lt. USNR, 1941-45. Home: Senoia Ga. Died Aug. 3, 1995.

BAKER, ROBERT L(AWRANCE), Russian educator, consultant; b. Denver, Aug. 17, 1928; s. Robert Marion and Genevieve (Mummery) B.; m. Alexandra Tkachenko, May 27, 1962; children: Lawrence, Elizabeth Anne. BA in Modern Langs., U. Colo., 1950; MA in Russian Lang., U. Mich., 1960, PhD in Slavic Langs., 1962. Instr. Russian Ind. U., Bloomington, 1960-62, asst. prof. Russian, 1962-67; assoc. prof. Russian Middlebury (Vt.) Coll., 1967-70, prof. Russian, 1970-90, dir. Russian Sch., 1968-80, assoc. dir. Lang. Schs., 1980-82, C.V. Starr disting. prof. Russian, 1987-90, ret., 1990. Author: (with others) Russian for Everybody, 1984; contbr. numerous articles to profl. jours. With U.S. Army, 1953-56. Mem. Am. Assn. Tchrs. Slavic and East European Langs. (v.p.), MLA, Am. Assn. for Advancement Slavic Studies, Am. Coun. on Teaching Fgn. Langs., Northeast Conf. on Teaching Fgn. Langs (bd. dirs. 1987-90). Home: Middlebury Vt. Deceased.

BALKIND, ALVIN LOUIS, writer, former curator; b. Balt., Mar. 28, 1921; s. Benjamin and Nessie (Bers) B. Student, Sorbonne U., Paris, 1954-55; BA, Johns Hopkins U., 1953; diploma in fine arts (hon.), Emily Carr Coll. of Art and Design, 1991. Curator Fine Arts Gallery U. B.C., Vancouver, Can., 1962-73; curator contemporary art Art Gallery of Ont., Toronto, Can., 1973-75; chief curator Vancouver Art Gallery, 1975-78; head visual art studio Banff (Alta.) Sch. Fine Arts, Can., 1985-87; freelance writer, 1987-92; mem. arts adv. com. Can. Coun., Ottawa, Ont., 1971-73; mem. vis. com. Nat. Gallery Can., Ottawa, 1969-71. Served with USN, 1943-46. Named winner of $50,000 Viva award, 1992. Home: Vancouver Can. Died Dec. 21, 1992.

BALL, GEORGE WILDMAN, lawyer, investment banker, author, diplomat; b. Des Moines, Dec. 21, 1909; s. Amos and Edna (Wildman) B.; m. Ruth Murdoch, Sept. 16, 1932; children: John Colin, Douglas Bleakley. B.A., Northwestern U., 1930, J.D., 1933. Bar: Ill. 1934, D.C. 1946. With Gen. Counsel's Office, Dept. Treasury, Washington, 1933-35; pvt. practice Chgo., 1935-42, Washington, 1946-61; founder, ptnr. Cleary, Gottlieb, Steen & Hamilton; assoc. gen. counsel Lend-Lease Adminstrn., then Fgn. Econ. Adminstrn., 1942-44; dir. U.S. Strategic Bombing Survey, London, 1944-45; gen. counsel French Supply Council, Washington, 1945-46; Undersec. of State for econ. affairs, 1961, dep. sec., 1961-66; of counsel firm Cleary, Gottlieb, Steen & Hamilton (attys.), 1966-68, 69-94; chmn. Lehman Bros. Internat., Ltd., 1966-68; U.S. permanent rep. to UN, 1968; sr. ptnr. Lehman Bros., Jan-May 1968, 69-82. Author: The Discipline of Power, 1968, Diplomacy for a Crowded World, 1976, The Past Has Another Pattern, 1982, Error and Betrayal in Lebanon, 1984, The Passionate Attachment: America's Involvement with Israel 1947 to Present, 1992. Decorated officer Legion of Honor France; grand cross Order of Crown, Belgium; Medal of Freedom U.S.; grand ufficiale Order of Merit, Italy). Home: Princeton N.J. Died May 26, 1994.

BALLANTINE, THOMAS AUSTIN, JR., federal judge; b. Louisville, Ky., Sept. 22, 1926; s. Thomas Austin and Anna Marie (Pfeiffer) B.; m. Nancy A. Armstrong, June 10, 1953; children: Thomas A., Nancy Adair, Brigid A., Joseph A. Student, Northwestern U., 1944-46; B.A., U. Ky., 1948; J.D., U. Louisville, 1954. Bar: Ky. 1954. Asso. firm McElwain, Dinning, Clarke & Winstead, Louisville, 1954-64; dep. commr. Jefferson Circuit Ct., 1958-62; commr. Jefferson Fiscal Ct., 1962-64; judge Jefferson Circuit Ct., 1964-77, U.S. Dist. Ct. (we. dist.) Ky., 1977—; instr. U. Louisville Law Sch., 1969-75. Bd. dirs. Louisville Urban League, 1958-64, chmn., 1963-64; bd. dirs. NCCJ, 1960-65, Health and Welfare Council, 1969, Louisville Theatrical Assn., 1970, Father Maloney's Boys Haven, 1983—. Mem. Louisville Bar Assn., Ky. State Bar. Democrat. Roman Catholic. Club: Pendennis. Home: Louisville Ky. Died Feb. 18, 1992; interred Louisville, K.Y.

BALLEW, LEIGHTON MILTON, education educator, consultant, theatre director; b. Des Arc, Ark., Feb. 17, 1916; s. Lawrence Durant and Allie (Schnebly) B.; m. Despy Karlas, Mar. 30, 1949 (div.); 1 child, Christopher Durant. AB, Memphis State U., 1937; MA, Case Western Res. U., 1941; PhD, U. Ill., 1955. Actor The Cleve. Playhouse, 1940-41; exec. dir. Jacksonville (Fla.) Little Theatre, 1941-42; chair drama dept. U. Ga., Athens, 1942-82, prof. emeritus, 1983-93; theatre cons. Vestlandske Teaterlag, Bergen, Norway, 1977-78, theatre cons. Riksteatret, Oslo, Norway, 1988-93; producer, dir. films on aging U. Ga., 1979-81; vis. dir. Sogn og Fjordane Teater, Forde, Norway, 1979-80, guest dir., 1982-83; donor SETC Fund in Play Direction, U. N.C., Greensboro, 1988, Memphis State U., 1989. Dir.: The Lark, 1984, Inherit the Wind, 1984. Docent State Mus. of Ga., Athens, 1982-93; vol. Emmanuel Episcopal Ch., Athens, 1985-93. With USAAF, 1942-46, ETO. Mem. Nat. Theatre Conf. (life), Ga. Theatre Conf. (life, past pres.), Southeastern Theatre Conf. (life, past pres. 1968, Suzanne Davis Career award 1975, pres., dir. over 260 prodns.). Democrat. Home: Athens Ga. Died Jan. 12, 1993.

BALLOU, JAMES HOWLAND, architect; b. Salem, Mass., Oct. 27, 1920; s. Franklin Burgess and Sarah Edwards (Spofford) B.; m. Phyllis Winifred Clarke, July 12, 1947; children: Charlotte, Elise, Susan, Elizabeth, Heidi. Student, U.S. Merchant Marine Acad., New London, Conn., Boston Archtl. Ctr., MIT, 1951. Registered architect Mass., N.H., Fla. With Emery-Smith Assocs., Boston, James J. O'Shaughnessy, Boston, Campbell & Aldrich, Boston; pvt. practice Manchester by the Sea, Mass.; dir., pres. Ho. of Seven Gables. Prin. works include restoration Faneuil Hall Markets, Boston, , The Govs. Shirley Eustis Ho., Roxbury, Mass., U.S.S. Constitution Mus. at the Charlestown Navy Yard, Boston, Dormitory at LaSallette Sem., Ipswich, chptel St. Lukes at Danvers State Hosp., Masonic Temple, Wakefield, Am. Legion Bldg., Manchester, restoration of Pickman Ho. and Gedney Ho., Salem; architect for more that a hundred residences in New England area, L.I., New Brunswick, Can. and West Indies. Mem. Nat. Trust for Historic Preservation, Mass.; Capt. U.S. Army, 1942-46. Recipient Charles Bullfinch award Doric Dames of Mass. Mem. AIA (emeritus, Honor award New England chpt.), Mass. State Assn. of Architects, Boston Soc. of Architects, Mason, Shriner, Eastern Yacht Club (former mem. race com.). Home: Salem Mass. Died Aug. 3, 1995.

BALSAM, ARTUR, pianist; b. Warsaw, Poland, 1906; m. Ruth R. Balsam. Ed., Berlin. tchr. piano and chamber music Manhattan Sch. Music, N.Y.C., Eastman Sch. Music, Rochester, N.Y.; mem. jury piano competitions in Leeds, Eng. (3), Montreal, Can. (2), N.Y.C., Corpus Christi, Tex., Balt., South Bend., Ind., and Rubinstein Competition Tel Aviv. Editor: Mozart Concertos, Oxford U. Press and Schirmer; Debut, 1918, appearances in concerts and recitals throughout, U.S. and Europe, has accompanied, Menuhin, Milstein Francescatti, Morini, many others; former mem., Balsam-Kroll-Heifetz Trio, sonata recitals and recs. with, Szigeti, Oistrach, Rostropowitch, also others; soloist with, NBC, BBC, London Symphony, Royal Philharmonic, London Philharmonia orchs., radio orchs. of, Milan, Warsaw, Berlin, Hamburg, Cardiff, Munich, also others; recorded complete piano works of, Mozart and Haydn, all Beethoven violin sonatas with, Fuchs, all cello sonatas with, Nelsova, all Mozart violin sonatas with, Shumsky. Home: New York N.Y. Died Sept. 1, 1994.

BALSAM, MARTIN HENRY, actor; b. N.Y.C., Nov. 4, 1919; s. Albert and Lillian (Weinstein) B.; m. Pearl L. Somner, Oct. 1952 (div. 1954); m. Joyce Van Patten, Aug. 1959 (div. 1962); 1 dau.; m. Irene Miller, Nov. 1963. Ed., New Sch. Social Research, 1946-48. Profl. acting debut in The Play's the Thing, Locust Valley, N.Y., 1941; N.Y.C. debut in Ghost for Sale, 1941; stage appearances include Lamp at Midnight, N.Y.C., 1947, The Wanhope Building, N.Y.C., High Tor, A Sound of Hunting, Macbeth, N.Y.C., 1948, Sundown Beach, 1948, The Closing Door, 1949, You Know I Can't Hear You When the Water's Running, 1967 (Tony award), Cold Storage (Obie award); appeared in summer stock, 1949-96; appearances include The Iceman Cometh; motion pictures include On the Waterfront, 1954, 12 Angry Men, 1957, Marjorie Morningstar, 1957, Al Capone, 1959, Middle of the Night, 1959, Psycho, 1960, All at Home, 1960, Breakfast at Tiffany's, 1961, Ada, 1961, Cape Fear, 1962, The Captive City, 1962, Who's Sleeping in My Bed, 1963, Seven Days in May, 1963, The Carpetbaggers, 1963, 1000 Clowns, 1964 (Acad. award), Bedford Incident, Harlow, After the Fox, 1965, Hombre, 1966, Among the Paths to Eden, 1967, Me, Natalie, 1969, Good Guys and Bad Guys, 1969, 2001: A Space Odyssey, 1968, Catch 22, 1970, Tora Tora Tora, 1970, Little Big Man, 1969, The Anderson Tapes, The Commissioner, 1970, Murder on the Orient Express, 1974, Death Wish, 1974, All the President's Men, 1976, The Sentinel, 1977, Silver Bears, 1978, Cuba, 1979, There Goes the Bride, 1980, St. Elmo's Fire, 1985, The Goodbye People, 1986, The Delta Force, 1986, Whatever It Takes, 1986, Private Investigations, 1987, Two Evil Eyes (The Black Cat), 1991, Cape Fear (Martin Scorsese remake), 1991; regular on TV series Archie Bunker's Place, 1979; most recent TV movies include: Little Gloria....Happy at last, 1982, I Want to Live, 1983, Kids Like These, 1987; TV miniseries include: Queenie, 1987. Served with AUS, 1941-45. Mem. Actors Equity Assn., AFTRA, Screen Actors Guild, Actor's Studio. Home: New York N.Y. Died Feb. 13, 1996.

BAMFORD, DAVID ELLERY, lawyer; b. New Salem, Pa., Sept. 5, 1921; s. George Kyle and Hazel (Reid) B.; m. Theodora Mary Kenny, Jan. 7, 1949; children: Mary Ann, David Reid, James Douglas. LLB with honors, George Washington U., 1949. Bar: D.C. 1949, Ill. 1960. Assoc. Law Offices C.S. Rhyne, Washington, 1949-51; counsel Gen. Electric Co., N.Y.C., 1951-66; v.p., gen. counsel Gen. Electric Credit Corp., Stamford, Conn.,

1966-76; corp. counsel Gen. Electric Co., Fairfield, Conn., from 1976. Served to sgt. U.S. Army, 1942-46, CBI. Mem. Ill. State Bar Assn., D.C. Bar Assn., Order of Coif. Presbyterian. Home: Westport Conn. Deceased.

BAND, DAVID, investment banker; b. Edinburgh, Scotland, Dec. 14, 1942; s. David and Elisabeth (Aitken) B.; m. Olivia Rose Brind, June 1, 1973; children—David Robert Benjamin, Isabelle Olivia Eve. MA, Oxford U. Mng. dir. Morgan Guaranty, Ltd., London, 1986-87; exec. v.p. Morgan Guaranty Trust Co.; chmn. J.P. Morgan Securities, Ltd., London, 1987-88; dir. Barclays PLC and Barclays Bank PLC; chief exec. officer Barclays de Zoete Wedd, London, 1988-96; securities and futures authority The Securities Assn., London; dep. chmn. The Securities Assn., 1986-88; bd. dirs. The Inst. of Internat. Fin.; mem. govt. deregulation task force; chmn. adv. bd. St. Edmund Hall Oxford. Fellow Royal Soc. Arts; mem. Internat. Inst. for Strategic Studies, Pilgrims Soc. Gt. Britain, The Hon. Co. Edinburgh Golfers. Home: London Eng. Died Mar. 28, 1996.

BANK, STEVEN BARRY, mathematics educator; b. N.Y.C., Mar. 14, 1939; s. Abraham and Yetta (Slovis) B.; m. Connie Jane Thomas, June 16, 1972; 1 son, Seth Robert. AB, Columbia Coll., 1959; PhD, Columbia U., 1964. Instr. U. Ill., Urbana-Champaign, 1964-66; asst. prof. U. Ill., 1966-68, asso. prof., 1968-71, prof. math., 1971-94; prin. investigator NSF grants, 1976-94. Contbr. articles to math. jours. Mem. Am. Math. Soc. Home: Urbana Ill. Died Apr. 10, 1994.

BANKS, LOUIS LAYTON, editor, educator; b. Pitts., June 17, 1916; s. Louis Layton and Laura S. (Shrom) B.; m. Mary Margaret Campbell, Apr. 21, 1945; children: Robert, William, Theodore, Margaret Czekaj. A.B., U. Calif. at Los Angeles, 1937, postgrad., 1938-40; D.H.L., Rollins Coll., 1968, Wilkes Coll., 1980; D.H.L. Nieman fellow, Harvard U., 1969-70. Corr., editor Time mag., 1945-61; asst. mng. editor Fortune mag., 1961-65, mng. editor, 1965-70; editorial dir. Time Inc., 1970-73, dir.; dir. Harvard Mag., Foote, Cone & Belding Communications Inc.; Carroll Ford Found.; vis. prof. Bus. Sch., Harvard, 1973-76; adj. prof. mgmt. Sloan Sch. Mgmt. Mass. Inst. Tech., 1976-93. Served as naval aviator USNR, 1941-45. Mem. N.Y.C. Council on Fgn. Relations. Clubs: Naples (Fla.) Yacht; Indian Creek Country (Kilmarnock, Va.); St. Botolph's (Boston). Home: Cambridge Mass. Deceased.

BANNER, STEPHEN EDWARD, company executive, lawyer; b. N.Y.C., July 22, 1938; s. Harry and Stella (Altman) B.; m. Ellen Kleinman, July 15, 1962; children: Stuart, Wendy, Deborah, Emily. BA, Yale U., 1960; LLB, Harvard U., 1963. Bar: N.Y. 1964, U.S. Ct. Appeals (2nd cir.) 1965. Law clk. to judge U.S. Ct. Appeals (2d cir.), N.Y.C., 1963-64; assoc. Kaye, Scholer, Fierman, Hays & Handler, N.Y.C., 1964-68, Simpson, Thacher & Barlett, N.Y.C., 1968-70; ptnr. Simpson, Thacher & Bartlett, N.Y.C., 1971-91; sr. exec. v.p., bd. dirs. The Seagram Co. Ltd., N.Y.C., 1991—; lectr. Practicing Law Inst., N.Y.C., 1980—. Mem. Assn. Bar City N.Y. Home: New York N.Y. Died May 15, 1995.

BANSE, ROBERT LEE, lawyer; b. Phila., Mar. 11, 1927; s. Robert John and Esther Elizabeth (Warren) B.; m. Anne Windels, Dec. 17, 1955; children—Robert L., Amy L., John W. B.S., U. Pa., 1949; LL.B. cum laude, Washington and Lee U., 1953. Bar: N.Y. 1954, Pa. 1971. Mem. firm Townsend & Lewis, 1953-55; with Merck & Co., Inc., Rahway, N.J., 1955-92; counsel Merck Sharp & Dohme div. Merck & Co., Inc., Rahway, N.J., 1960-73, sr. counsel, 1973-75; gen. counsel Merck & Co., Inc., 1975-91; v.p. Merck & Co., Inc., Rahway, N.J., 1977-86, sr. vp., 1986-92; of counsel Drinker, Biddle and Reath, Phila. and Princeton, N.J., 1992—. Trustee Food and Drug Law Inst., Washington and Lee U. Mem. ABA, Am. Law Inst., Assn. of Bar of City of N.Y., Pharm. Mfrs. Assn. (chmn. Law sect. 1977-78), Assn. Gen. Counsel. Clubs: Phila. Cricket, Eagles Mere Country. Home: Lawrenceville N.J. Died June 16, 1995.

BANYARD, ALFRED LOTHIAN, bishop; b. Merchantville, N.J., July 31, 1908; s. Lothian Rupert and Emma May (Irwin) B.; m. Sarah Alice Hammer, Sept. 1, 1938; 1 son, Richard David. A.B., U. Pa., 1929; student, Gen. Theol. Sem., 1929-31, S.T.B., 1933, S.T.D., 1946; postgrad., Phila. Div. Sch., 1932, D.D., 1947. Ordained to ministry Episcopal Ch., N.J., 1931; pastor St. Lukes Ch., Westville, N.J., 1932-36; rector Christ Ch., Bordentown, N.J., 1936-43; archdeacon Episcopal Diocese N.J., 1943-55; suffragan bishop, 1945-55, bishop of N.J., 1955-73, ret., 1973; Mem. Bd. Examining Chaplains, 1938-55, chmn., 1941-55; dep. to provincial synod, 1940-46; sec. Ho. of Bishops, 2d Province, 1945-48; trustee Diocesan Found., 1941-43, ex-officio, 1945-92, pres., 1955-92; pres. Procter Found., 1955-92; master of Young Men's Conf., 1936-37, dean, 1941; mem. Bd. Religious Edn., 1939-41, 43-46, Bd. Social Service, 1940-42, 44-46; field, publicity dept., 1943-45; trustee Burlington Coll., 1945-53, v.p., 1946-53; Bd. mgrs. St. Martins Ho. of Retreats, Bernardsville, N.J., 1948-92; trustee, Evergreens, Moorestown, pres., 1955; v.p. Corp. for Relief Widows and Orphans of Clergymen, 1945-92; pres. Mission Advancement, 1955-92; trustee Phila. Div. Sch. Mem. Newcomen Soc., Philomathean Soc. of U. Pa. (scriba 1929), Phi Beta Kappa, Eta Sigma Phi. Republican. Home: Moorestown N.J. Died Dec. 6, 1992; interred St. Mary's, Burlington, N.J.

BARAN, CAROLYN JONES, military officer, nurse practitioner; b. Valdosta, Ga., Apr. 26, 1942; d. Charles Brooks and Melba Onee (Dameron) Jones; m. Stephen T. Baran, Apr. 7, 1973. RN, Grady Hosp., Atlanta, 1963; BSN, William Carey Coll., 1982; MA in Human Relations, Webster U., 1984, M in Health Svc. Mgmt., 1986. Cert. nurse practitioner. Commd. 2d lt. USAF, 1969, advanced through grades to col.; clin. nurse various USAF hosps., 1969-86; chief nursing svc. adminstrn. Hdqrs. 14th AF, Dobbins AFB, Ga., 1886-89; nurse practitioner 347th Med. Group, Moody AFB, Ga., 1989-94. Decorated Meritorious Svc. medal with 2 oak leaf clusters, Commendation medal with oak leaf cluster; recipient Humanitarian Svc. medal USAF, 1979, numerous others. Mem. Air Force Assn., AAUW, NAACOG, Uniformed Svcs. Nurse Practitioner Assn., ANA. Home: Valdosta Ga. Died Jan. 11, 1994.

BARATI, GEORGE, musician, conductor, composer; b. Györ, Hungary, Apr. 3, 1913; s. Miksa B. and Regina (Schreiber) B.; 1 child by previous marriage, Stephen G.; m. Ruth Carroll, Oct. 31, 1948; children: Lorna, Donna. Grad., Royal Hungarian Franz Liszt Conservatory of Music, Budapest, 1935; diploma, State Tchrs. Coll., 1937; diploma state artist diploma in cello, 1938; studies with, Georges Couvreur and Henry Switten, 1938-40, Roger Sessions, 1940-43; postgrad., Princeton U., 1939-43; MusD (hon.), U. Hawaii, 1954, Music and Arts Inst., 1969. mem. jury Mitropoulos Competition for Condrs., N.Y., Met. Opera, San Francisco Opera, 1957-70. Mem., Budapest Concert Orch., 1933-36, first cellist, Budapest Symphony and Municipal Opera House Orch., 1936-38, cellist, founder, Pro Ideale String Quartet, 1935-40; instr. Westminster Choir Coll., Princeton, N.J., 1938-40, Lawrenceville Sch., Princeton, also, N.J. State Tchrs. Coll., 1939-43; condr., founder, Princeton Ensemble, 1940-43, condr., Princeton Choral Union, 1942-43, mem., guest condr., San Francisco Symphony, mem., Calif. String Quartet, 1946-50, musical dir., Barati Chamber Orch. of San Francisco, (formation of Barati Chamber Orch. Soc. 1950), 1948-52, Honolulu Symphony Orch., lectr., U. Hawaii, 1950-68, world tours annually; exec. dir., Montalvo Center for the Arts, 1968-78; music dir. Santa Cruz County Symphony, Aptos, Calif., 1971-80; guest condr. orchs. worldwide, New York debut conducting, Madame Butterfly, Bklyn. Opera Co., 1961; compositions for orch. include Symphony, Chamber Concerto, Confluence, Polarization, film The Ugly Duckling, concertos for Piano, Violin, Cello, Guitar, chamber music Indiana Triptych (4 players), 3 string quartets, 4 trios, music for solo instruments B.U.D. Piano Sonata, harp, piano, cello, flute, violin, opera Noelani, chamber orch. Serenata.; recorded by the London Philharmonic, Noelani; chamber music Octet with Harpsichord; music solo instruments for harp, piano, cello, 3 trios, Serenata for chamber orch. Est. George Barati Archive, U. Calif., Santa Cruz; Rec. artist, Lyrichord, Decca, Columbia, CRI. Bd. govs. Pacific and Asian Affairs Council. Served with AUS, 1943-46. Guggenheim fellow, 1965-66; recipient Naumburg award, 1959, Ditson award, 1966,. Mem. Am. Musicol. Soc., Composers Forum, MacDowell Colony, Am. Composers Alliance, Berlioz Soc. Am. (founding mem.), Bruckner Soc. (hon.). Club: San Francisco Croquet. Home: Soquel Calif. Died June 22, 1996.

BARBASH, JOSEPH, lawyer, arbitrator; b. Jersey City, Dec. 31, 1921; s. Nathan and Lena (Brody) B.; m. Heather Livingston, Nov. 30, 1957 (dec. 1981); children: Ilisa L., Thomas L.; m. Carol Lamberg, July 3, 1985; stepchildren: Andrew A. Bernstein, Donna Lamberg Bernstein. AB, Rutgers U., 1941; LLB, Harvard U., 1948. Bar: N.Y. 1949;. Law clk. to Judge Learned Hand U.S. Ct. Appeals (2d cir.), N.Y.C., 1948-49; law clk. to Justice Stanley F. Reed U.S. Supreme Ct., 1949-50; assoc. Debevoise & Plimpton, 1950-59, ptnr., 1960-87, of counsel, 1987-90; mem. task force NLRB, 1976-77; chmn. Employment Disputes Task Force of Ctr. for Pub. Resources, 1983-91; lectr. Practising Law Inst.; speaker NYU and other law confs. Contbr. articles to profl. jours. V.p., bd. dirs. Goodwill Industries of Greater N.Y., Inc.; vice chair sr. employment adv. coun. N.Y.C. Dept. for Aging. Lt. USNR, 1942-46, ETO. Mem. ABA (chmn. adminstrv. law sect. 1979-80), Assn. of Bar of City of N.Y. (chmn. com. on minorities in profession 1985-88, chmn. com. on legal edn. and admission to bar 1983-85, chmn. com. on labor and social security 1969-72, mem. exec. com. 1991-95), N.Y. State Bar Assn. (chmn. com. on legal edn. and admission to bar 1972-77). Clubs: Harvard of N.Y.C. Home: New York N.Y. Died May 10, 1996.

BARCLAY, STANTON DEWITT, engineering executive, consultant; b. Pa., Apr. 27, 1899; s. James Arthur Barclay and Elsie Arvilla Gore; married; children: Stanton D. Jr., Gail Dee (dec.). BS, Pa. State U., 1922, M in Engring., 1926; LHD (hon.), Lycoming Coll., 1986. Lic. profl. engr. Instr. engring. Rensselaer Poly. Inst., 1922-25; asst. head dept. mech. engring. Pratt Inst., Bklyn., 1922-31; founder, pres. Barclay Chem. Co., Watertown, Mass., from 1931. Pres. local PTA. With SATC, 1918. Mem. ASME, Charlton R.R. Assn. (gen. mgr. 1991), Pioneer Valley R.R. Assn., Rotary, Masons. Republican. Home: Olmsted Falls Ohio Deceased.

BARGER, A(BRAHAM) CLIFFORD, physiology educator; b. Greenfield, Mass., Feb. 1, 1917; s. Paul and Rose (Solomon) B.; m. Claire S. Basch, June 6, 1943; children: Craig, Shael, Curtis. AB, Harvard U., 1939, MD, 1943; DSc (hon.), U. Cin., 1977, U. Mass., 1993. Research asst. Harvard Fatigue Lab., Boston, 1938-41; research fellow Harvard Med. Sch., Boston, 1946-47, instr. physiology, 1948-50, assoc. prof., 1955-61, prof physiology, 1961-87, prof. emeritus, 1987-96, Robert Henry Pfeiffer prof. physiology, 1963-87; pres. Elbanobscot Found., Mass., Harvard Apparatus Found. Boston, William Townsend Porter Found.; chmn Harvard Med. Alumni Fund; cons. Brigham & Women's Hosp., Boston, 1959-87. Author: Cardiovascular and Renal Physiology, Dictionary of Scientific Biography 1978, Walter B. Cannon: The Life and Times of a Young Scientist, 1987; assoc. editor Circulation Research, 1963-66; author films on cardiovascular and renal physiology, 1975. Mem. fellowship com. NRC 1955-57; mem. med. fellowship bd. NRC, 1957-62 mem. physiology study sect. NIH, 1960-64. 1st lt. U.S Army, 1944-45. Recipient Paul Dudley White award Mass. affiliate chpt. Am. Heart Assn., 1987, Assn. o Chmn. of Depts. Physiology Service award, 1985. Fellow AAAS; mem. NAS Inst. Medicine, Am. Physiol Soc. (chmn. Porter devel. com. 1966-89, pres. 1970-71 Carl J. Wiggers award 1982, Ray G. Daggs award 1985), Am. Soc. Nephrology, Am. Acad. Arts and Sci. Internat. Soc. Hypertension, Mass. Soc. for Med Research (pres. 1957-85, chmn. 1985-86, hon. chmn 1986-96), Harvard Club. Democrat. Jewish. Home Brookline Mass. Died Mar 13, 1996.

BARHAM, ROBERT YOUNG, JR., communication company executive; b. Houston, Feb. 5, 1930; s. Robert Young Sr. and Helen Lucy (McDonald) B.; m. Juli Radebaugh, June 9, 1951 (div. Sept. 1959); children David, William; m. Rose Mary Carro; 1 child Lisa. AB, Princeton U., 1952; MBA, Harvard U., 1954 Various positions to v.p. IBM Europe, S.A. IBM Corp 1957-85; pres., CEO, bd. dirs. IVANS Inc., Greenwich Conn., from 1985; bd. dirs. ISC, Greenwich. Contbr articles to profl. jours. Bd. dirs. Byran Civic Assn Greenwich, 1973-76, 84, 94, pres., 1973-75, 85-86. Republican. Home: Greenwich Conn. Deceased.

BARKATE, JOHN ALBERT, microbiologist, food scientist; b. Sulphur, La., Dec. 4, 1936. MS, Northwestern State U., 1963; PhD in food microbiology, La. Stat U., 1967. Dir. microbiology dept., asst. dir. ctr. rsch Ralston Purina Co., 1979-94. Mem. Am. Soc Microbiology, Inst. Food Technologists, Internat. Assn Milk, Food & Environ. Sanitarians, Inc., Am. Soc Cereal Chemists, Sigma Xi. Home: New Orleans La Deceased.

BARKER, C(LARENCE) AUSTIN, finance executive economist; b. Centralia, Wash., Dec. 2, 1911; s. Clarenc G. and Susan (McElroy) B.; m. Mary Ellen Brown Mar. 29, 1941; children: Beverly Jean, Stephen Warne AB, Stanford U., 1934; postgrad. Columbia U. Grad Sch. Bus., 1935-36; MBA, NYU, 1939. Acct., regulator analyst Pub. Svc. Electric & Gas Co. of N.J., Newark 1936-44; sr. economist charge fin. and econ. rsch. Cleve Electric Illuminating Co., 1944-59, sec. to fin. com. bd dirs., 1954-59; dir. rsch. Hornblower, Weeks Noyes & Trask Inc. (name changed to Loeb, Rhoades, Hornblower & Co.), N.Y.C., 1959-65, gen. ptnr., 1962-71 pub. utility cons., 1965-78, v.p., cons. economist 1972-78, fin. cons., 1978-79; pres. Barker Cons., Inc., 1979-93 fin. cons. Noyes Ptnrs., Inc., 1980-93; bd. dir. Western Mining & Exploration Co., Inc., 1977-93, v.p., 1983-93 lectr. corp. fin. and investment analysis Case-Western Res. U. Grad. div., 1955-59; lectr. pub. utility seminar Irving Trust Co., 1959-76; prepared testimony on stock splits SEC. Bd. dirs. Rye Conservation Soc.. 1965-80 pres., 1965-68; mem. nat. adv. council Stanford Alumni 1952-57; trustee Mt. Gulian Soc., 1972-91; founder sponsor Nat. Tax Limitation Com., 1976-85, mem. fed amendment drafting com., 1978-82. Chartered fin analyst. Mem. Acad. Polit. Sci. (life), Com. for Monetary Rsch. and Edn. (life), Nat. Assn. Bus. Economists (charter mem.), N.Y. Soc. Security Analysts, SAR (pres Westchester chpt. 1988-89, chaplain 1990-93), Desc Colonial Govs., Founders and Patriots (treas. 1965-6 councillor 1970-81, dep. gov. 1981-88, chaplain 1988-9 historian gen. 1983-84, dep. genealogist gen. 1988-93 Stanford Club (N.Y.C.), Rowfant Clu (Cleve.). Republican. Episcopalian. Assoc. edito Financial Analysts Jour., 1969-70; contbr. articles profl. jours. Died Dec. 27, 1993; buried Centrali Wash. Home: Rye N.Y.

BARKLEY, PAUL C., airline holding company executive; b. 1929; married. BS, San Diego State Coll., 1958 With Arthur Young & Co., 1958-67, with Pacif Southwest Airlines, San Diego, 1967-93, v.p. fin., 196 73, sr. v.p. fin., chief operating officer, 1973-79, pres chief operating officer, 1979-84, pres., chief exec. office 1984-89, now chmn. exec. com., also bd. dirs.; bd. di Pancrete Inc. Served with USAF, 1951. Mem. An Inst. CPA's, Nat. Assn. Accts. Died Mar. 15, 199 Home: San Diego Calif.

BARLOW, WILLIAM EDWARD, publishing company executive; b. Indpls., Dec. 6, 1917; s. Edward Stevens and Eva (Eustis) B.; m. Marguerite Emily Holcombe, Oct. 4, 1943 (div. 1975); children: Gloria Barlow Bernhardt, Christopher, James; m. Mildred Deveraux Sage, July 16, 1987. Grad., Phillips Acad., Andover, Mass., 1936; B.S., Hamilton Coll., 1940; postgrad., William Coll., 1940. With Pan Am. Airways, 1941-45, Time Inc., 1945-48; founder, pres. Vision Inc. (pub. Spanish and Portugese news mags. for Latin Am., other internat. publs.), N.Y.C., 1948-75, Middle East Enterprises, N.Y.C., 1975-79; owner, pres. MIN Pub., N.Y.C., 1978-91. First pres. Council of the Americas, 1963-71, hon. pres.; bd. dirs. Internat. Univ. Found., 1965-91; v.p. Interam. Council Commerce and Prodn., 1968-70; bd. dirs. Fund for Multinat. Mgmt. Edn., 1968-94; chmn. Land Coun., 1991-94. Recipient Maria Moors Cabot Gold Medal award Columbia U. Grad. Sch. Journalism, 1963; Cordier fellow Columbia U. Sch. Internat. Affairs, 1977-88. Mem. Coun. on Fgn. Rels., Pan Am. Soc. (bd. dirs. 1963-75), Ctr. Inter-Am. Rels. (bd. dirs. 1966-74), Univ. of N.Y. Club, L.I.-Wyandanch Club. Home: New York N.Y. Died May 10, 1994.

BARNES, GEORGE ELTON, stockbroker; b. Garner, Iowa, Mar. 17, 1900; s. Charles M. and Cora (Staver) B.; m. Florence Herrcke, Oct. 5, 1922 (dec. Aug., 1989); 1 child, Ruth Adele. Grad., Hamilton U., Mason City, Iowa, 1918. With LaSalle Nat. Bank, Ill., 1918-30; ptnr. A.C. Baur & Co., 1930-31; co-founder, ltd. ptnr. Wayne Hummer & Co., from 1931; mem. N.Y. Stock Exchange; bd. govs., chmn. exec. com. Chgo. Stock Exchange, 1946; chmn. bd. Midwest Stock Exchange, 1956-58. Author: Pay-as-you-go and Other Fed. Tax Plans. Chmn. budget fin. com. Oak Park and River Forest Community Chest, 1941-49, pres., 1950-51; mem. nat. budget com. Community Chests Councils Am., 1956-60; bd. dirs. LaSalle Extension U., 1952-60, Infant Welfare Soc. Chgo., 1956-60; chmn. corporate large gifts div. Chgo. Community Fund, 1946; v.p., bd. govs. Nat. Assn. Stock Exchange Firms, 1942-46; pres. Chgo. Tennis Assn., 1947-48; pres. U.S. Tennis Assn., 1960-61, mem. exec. com., 1958-79; mem. com. on mgmt. 1955 Davis Cup championships; nat. chmn. sponsors com. 1955 Davis Cup; pres. Nat. Tennis Ednl. Found., Inc., 1958-66; bd. dirs. Nat. Tennis Found. Hall of Fame, from 1958; founder, past pres. Chgo. Tennis Patrons, Inc. Named Sportsman of Yr., Chgo. Press Club, 1961, Sportsman of Yr., U.S. Jr. C. of C., 1961; recipient Hardy award for contbn. to tennis edn. U.S. Lawn Tennis Assn., 1962, 68; named to Western Tennis Hall of Fame, 1987. Mem. Ill. C. of C. (dir. 1964-68). Home: Stuart Fla. Deceased.

BARNES, L(OUIE) BURTON, III, lawyer; b. Jackson, Miss., Sept. 5, 1948; s. Louie Burton Jr. and Julia (Hering) B.; m. Melanie Barrentine, Aug. 18, 1973; children: Carlyle, Sidney, Christopher. BA, Miss. State U., 1970, MA, 1974; JD, Cornell U., 1976. Staff atty. Compt. Currency, Washington, 1976-77; regional coun. Compt. Currency, Cleve., 1977-78; assoc. Lange, Simpson, Robinson & Somerville, Birmingham, Ala., 1979-82, ptnr., 1982-85; gen. counsel, corp. sec. First Ala. Bancshares Inc. and First Ala. Bank, Birmingham, 1985—; bd. dirs. Secor Bank, First Ala. Investments Inc., Birmingham, First Ala. Ins./Co., Inc., FAB Agy. Inc. Counsel Jefferson County Rep. Party, Birmingham, 1984-87, mem. exec. com., 1984-89; mem. adv. com. Birmingham Mus. Art; bd. dirs. Birmingham Chamber Music Soc., 1991—, YMBC Civic Forum, 1992—, Leadership Birmingham,. Mem. ABA, Ala. Bar Assn., Ala. Law Inst. (chmn. securities law com. 1986-89), Birmingham Coun. Fgn. Rels., Ala. Bankers Assn. (govt. rels. com.), Miss. State U. Coll. Arts and Scis. Alumni Assn. (pres. 1989-92, Alumni fellow 1990, deans adv. bd. 1990—), Miss. State U. Alumni Assn. (bd. dirs. 1992—), Mountain Brook Club, Order of Red Ribbon. Mem. ABA, Ala. Bar Assn., Ala. Law Inst., Securities Law Com. (chmn. 1986-89), Birmingham Com. Fgn. Rels., Ala. Bankers Assn. (govt. rels. com.). Episcopalian. Home: Birmingham Ala.

BARNES, STANLEY NELSON, federal judge; b. Baraboo, Wis., May 1, 1900; s. Charles Luling and Janet (Rankin) B.; m. Anne Fisk, Oct. 18, 1929 (dec.); children: Janet Anne Hansen (dec.), Judith Fisk Melkesian, Joyce Rankin Robinson; m. Elizabeth MacDonald, Nov. 6, 1987. AB, U. Calif., 1922, JD, 1925, LLD, 1961; postgrad. in law, Harvard U., 1923-24. Bar: Calif. 1925. Sole practice San Francisco, 1925-28, Los Angeles, 1928-46; lectr. law U. So. Calif., 1947-52, lectr. forensic medicine, 1949-51; judge Superior Ct. of Los Angeles, 1947-53, presiding judge, 1952-53; asst. U.S. atty. gen.; with anti-trust div. Dept. Justice, 1953-56; judge U.S. Ct. Appeals (9th cir.), 1956-70, sr. judge, 1970—; Mem. Pres.'s Conf. Adminstrv. Proc., 1953; co-chmn. Atty. Gen.'s Nat. Com. Study Antitrust Laws, 1953-55; adv. council appellate rules jud. Conf. U.S., 1963-68; adv. council Practising Law Inst. Bd. dirs. S.W. Mus., Los Angeles, Calif. Inst. for Cancer Research, UCLA Med. Sch., 1949-75; regent U. Calif., 1946-48; trustee Sigma Chi Found., 1955—. Named Alumnus of Year U. Calif., 1966; recipient award Boalt Hall Sch. Law, U. Calif., Berkeley, 1967, St. Thomas More award Loyola Law Sch., Los Angeles, 1973; named to Nat. Collegiate Football Hall Fame, 1954, Helms Athletic Found. Hall of Fame, San Diego Hall of Champions; Berkeley fellow, 1969. Fellow Am. Bar Found., Am. Coll. Trial Lawyers, Am. Acad. Forensic Sci.; mem. Fed. Bar Assn. (nat. pres. 1954-55), ABA (chmn. sect. jud. adminstrn. 1966-67, mem. judges adv. commn. to ABA com. on profl. ethics 1957-63), Calif. Bar Assn., San Francisco Bar Assn., Los Angeles Bar Assn. (Shattuck-Price distinguished service award 1971), N.Y.C. Bar Assn., Am. Judicature Soc., Inst. Jud. Adminstrn., Calif. Alumni Assn. (pres. 1946-48), Phi Delta Phi., Sigma Chi (nat. pres. 1952-55, nat. trustee 1950-52, trustee Found. 1955—). Episcopalian. Clubs: Rotary (hon.), Nat. Lawyers (hon.); Univ., Calif. (Los Angeles); Bohemian (San Francisco). Home: Palm Springs Calif.

BARNETT, DAVID LEON, editorial consultant; b. Savannah, Ga., Jan. 21, 1922; m. Jeanne Kahn, Dec. 29, 1946; children: Randel, Megan, Jane. B.S. with honors in Govt, Harvard U., 1943; M.S., Columbia U., 1947. Mem. staff Richmond (Va.) News Leader, 1947-54, chief statehouse bur. and polit. corr., 1950-51, asst. city editor, 1951-54; regional corr. Business Week mag., 1951-54; Washington corr. N.Am. Newspaper Alliance, 1954-55, chief Washington bur., columnist, 1955-65; Washington news editor Hearst Newspapers, 1966-76; asst. mng. editor U.S. News & World Report, Washington, 1976-87, editorial cons., 1987-95. Contbr. articles to mags. Served with USAAF, 1943-46. Mem. White House Corr. Assn. Clubs: Gridiron (Washington), Harvard (Washington), Nat. Press (Washington), Federal City (Washington). Home: Alexandria Va. Died Jan. 18, 1995.

BARNETT, EUGENE VICTOR, physician, educator; b. N.Y.C., Mar. 28, 1932; s. Morris M. and Helen (Milrod) B.; m. Carole Lynn Kern, Sept. 7, 1958; children: David Marshall, Jonathan Bruce, Robin Leslie, Sharon Elizabeth. BA magna cum laude, Buffalo State Coll., 1955, MD, 1956. Diplomate Am. Bd. Internal Medicine. Intern Mt. Sinai Hosp., N.Y.C., 1956-57; resident U. Rochester (N.Y.) Med. Ctr., 1959-60; investigator, sr. asst. surgeon USPHS, 1957-59, trainee, 1960-61, sr. instr., fellow medicine and microbiology, 1962-63, asst. prof. medicine, sr. instr. microbiology, 1963-65; fellow rheumatic diseases Med. Rsch. Coun. Rheumatism Ctr., Taplow, Eng., 1961-62; pvt. practice specializing in internal medicine and rheumatology L.A., 1965—; assoc. dir. Clin. Path. Lab. UCLA, 1967—, dir. Inst. Rehab. and Chronic Diseases, 1970-78; mem. staff UCLA Hosp., 1970—; prof. rheumatology UCLA Med. Sch., 1970—. Fellow ACP, Am. Acad. Allergy; mem. L.A. Soc. Internal Medicine, Western Soc.Clin. Rsch., Am. Fedn. Clin. Rsch., Am. Assn. Immunologists, Am. Rheumatism Assn., Gibson Anat. Soc., Am. Soc. Clin. Investigation, Western Assn. Physicians, Phi Beta Kappa, Alpha Omega Alpha, Phi Lambda Kappa. Home: Los Angeles Calif. Deceased.

BARNETT, RICHARD BLAIR, lawyer; b. Topeka, July 12, 1927; s. Laurin Clark and Frances (Blair) B. BA, Yale U., 1950; JD, U. Mich., 1953. Bar: Kansas, 1953, N.Y., 1954. Assoc. Haight, Gardner, Poor & Havens, N.Y.C., 1953-66, ptnr., 1966-95; chmn. Internat. Ship Fin., London, 1989. Author: (with others) Asset Based Financing, 1986. Pres. Greenwich Village Soc. for Historic Preservation, N.Y.C., 1987-91. Mem. Maritime Law Assn. (chmn. ship fin. com.), Washington Sq. Assn. (honoree 1992, v.p. 1994-95). Republican. Episcopalian. Home: New York N.Y. Died Dec. 5, 1995.

BARNETT, WALTER MICHAEL, lawyer; b. New Orleans, Apr. 12, 1903; s. Walter Michael and Fannie Edith (Lion) b.; m. Virginia Mae Fuerst, Sept. 24, 1930; children: Linda Barnett Mintz, Walda Barnett Besthoff. AB, Tulane U., 1923, MA, JD, 1925. Bar: La. 1925. Practiced in New Orleans, from 1925; ptnr. Montgomery, Barnett, Brown, Read, Hammond & Mintz, 1950-96; asst. city atty., New Orleans, 1930-35; atty. Dept. Pub. Welfare, 1935-46. Bd. dirs. Cmty. Chest, Officers Town House, Eye, Ear, Nose and Throat Hosp.; pres. United Fund Greater New Orleans Area, 1958; chmn. Mayor's Adv. Com. on Cmty. Improvement, Urban Renewal Commn., New Orleans, New Orleans War Recreation Com.; pres. Family Svc. Soc., Coun. Social Agys., Citizens Housing Coun. Greater New Orleans Area, Touro Infirmary, 1960-64; treas. Mental Health Soc. Lt. (j.g.) USCGTR. Recipient Disting. Alumnus award Tulane U. Law Sch., 1992, Judah Touro award Touro Infirmary, 1993. Mem. ABA, La. Bar Assn., New Orleans Bar Assn. (pres. 1965-66, Pres.'s award 1992), Am. Law Inst., Tulane U. Alumni Assn. (nat. pres. 1939-40), Phi Beta Kappa. Home: New Orleans La. Died March 10, 1996.

BARNHARD, SHERWOOD ARTHUR, printing company executive; b. Newark, Mar. 14, 1921; s. Charles L. and Blanche (Tarnow) B.; m. Esther Lasky, Feb. 21, 1946; children: Ronald Harris, Paul Ira. BS, Franklin & Marshall Coll., 1942. With Lasky Co., Millburn, N.J., 1946-94, exec. v.p., 1956-61, pres., 1961—, chmn., 1986—; with N.J. Web and Sheetfed Color Lithographers; v.p. Daus. of Israel Geriatric Ctr., West Orange; N.J.; past trustee Temple Sharey Tefilo-Israel, South Orange, N.J.; bd. overseers NYU Ctr. Graphic Arts Mgmt. and Tech. Mem. Printing Industries N.J. (past pres.), Assn. Graphic Arts (past pres., past bd. dirs.), Met. Lithographers Assn. (past pres., mem. labor com.), Mktg. Communications Execs., Advt. Club N.Y., Crestmont Golf and Country Club (West Orange), Delaire Country Club (Delray, Fla.), Zeta Beta Tau. Home: Short Hills N.J. Died June 22, 1994.

BARNS, WILLIAM DERRICK, historian, emeritus educator; b. Fayette County, Pa., Apr. 3, 1917; s. William Post and Lida (Williams) B.; m. Doretha Mae Clayton, Sept. 3, 1947. A.B., Pa. State U., 1939, M.A., 1940; Ph.D., W.Va. U., 1947. Instr. history Pa. State U., 1939-40, vis. prof., 1949; mem. faculty W.Va. U., Morgantown, 1940-91; prof. history W.Va. U., 1977-85, prof. emeritus, 1985-91; vis. prof. Marshall U., Huntington, W.Va., 1951, McMaster U., Hamilton, Ont., Can., 1957, 59, 61. Author: The Granger and Populist Movements in West Virginia, 1873-1914, 1947, Highlights in West Virginia's Agricultural History, 1863-1963, 1963, The West Virginia State Grange: The First Century, 1873-1973, 1973; also articles. Field agt. Am. Friends Service Com., 1944-46; co-founder, dir. W.Va. Civil Liberties Union, 1970-79, v.p., 1979-81. Mem. Am. Hist. Assn., Orgn. Am. Historians, Agrl. History Soc., AAUP (co-founder W.Va. conf. 1961, dir. 1961-71), W.Va. Hist. Assn. Coll. and Univ. Tchrs. (co-founder 1959, pres. 1962-63, archivist, adv. 1973-91), English Speaking Union, Phi Kappa Phi, Phi Alpha Theta, Pi Gamma Mu, Alpha Tau Omega. Libertarian. Mem. Soc. of Friends. Home: Morgantown W.Va. Died Jan. 8, 1991; buried Oak Grove Cemetery, Morgantown, W. Va.

BARONE, EUGENE J., medical products executive; b. 1937; married. Grad., U. Pitts. Sales rep. Veritus, Inc., Pitts., 1958-61, staff asst. mktg. dept., 1961-65, dir. special accounts, 1965-68, dir. enrollment, 1968-69, asst. v.p. mktg. divsn., 1969-72, v.p. mktg., 1972-80, sr. v.p. mktg., 1980-83, pres., bd. dirs., from 1983. Home: Pittsburgh Pa. Deceased.

BAROODY, WILLIAM JOSEPH, JR., research institute executive; b. Manchester, N.H., Nov. 5, 1937; s. William Joseph and Nabeeha (Ashooh) B.; m. Mary Margaret Cullen, Apr. 23, 1960; children—William Joseph, III, Mary Nabeeha, David, Jo Ellen, Christopher, Andrew, Thomas, Philip, Paul. A.B. in English, Holy Cross Coll., 1959; postgrad. in polit. sci., Georgetown U., 1961-64; LL.D. (hon.), Seattle U., Marist Coll., Assumption Coll.; Litt.D. (hon.), St. Mary of Woods Coll. Legis. asst. and press sec. to Congressman Melvin R. Laird, 1961-68; research dir. House Republican Conf., 1968-69; asst. to Sec. and Dep. Sec. of Def., 1969-73; spl. asst. to Pres. U.S., 1973-74; asst. to Pres., 1974-76; exec. v.p. Am. Enterprise Inst. for Public Policy Research, Washington, 1977-78; pres. Am. Enterprise Inst. for Public Policy Research, 1978-96; chmn. bd. Woodrow Wilson Internat. Center for Scholars; bd. dirs. Center for Study of Presidency, St. Anselm Coll., Sem. of St. Gregory the Theologian, Dole Found. Pub.: Public Opinion mag, 1977-96, Regulation mag, 1977-96, AEI Foreign Policy and Def. Rev, 1977-96, The AEI Economist, 1978-96. Served with USN, 1959-61. Recipient Disting. Civilian Public Service award Dept. Def., 1973. Republican. Melkite Catholic. Home: Alexandria Va. Died June 8, 1996.

BARR, JOSEPH WALKER, retired corporate director; b. Vincennes, Ind., Jan. 17, 1918; s. Oscar Lynn and Stella Florence (Walker) B.; m. Beth Williston, Sept. 3, 1939; children—Bonnie (Mrs. Michael Gilliom), Cherry, Joseph Williston, Elizabeth Eugenia (Mrs. Andrew LoSasso), Lynn Hamilton (Mrs. Keith Fineberg). AB, DePauw U., 1939; MA, Harvard, 1941; LLD, Vincennes U., 1966, DePauw U., 1967. Partner J&J Co., 1976-94; retired 86th Congress, 11th Ind. Dist., 1994; asst. to sec. of treasury, 1961-64; chmn. FDIC, 1964-65; under sec. of treasury, 1965-68, sec. of treasury, 1968-69; pres. Am. Security & Trust Co., Washington, 1969-72; chmn. bd. Am. Security & Trust Co., 1972-74; bd. dirs. Manor Care. Bd. dirs. Student Loan Marketing Assn.; bd. regents Georgetown U. Served to lt. comdr. USN, 1942-45. Decorated Bronze Star. Mem. Phi Beta Kappa. Democrat. Home: Hume Va. Died Feb. 23, 1996.

BARRETT, CHARLES MARION, insurance company executive, physician; b. Cin., Mar. 10, 1913; s. Charles Francis and May (Ryan) B.; m. May Belle Finn, Apr. 27, 1942; children: Angela Barrett Eynon, Charles, John, Michael, Marian Barrett Leibold, William. AB, Xavier U., 1934, LLD (hon.), 1974; MD, U. Cin., 1938. Assoc. med. dir. Western & So. Life Ins. Co., Cin., 1942, med. dir., 1951-73, exec. v.p., 1965-73, pres., 1973-84, chmn. bd., chief exec. officer, 1984-88, chmn., 1988—; prof. depts. surgery and radiology U. Cin. Coll. Medicine, 1957-74, prof. emeritus, 1974—; chmn. Columbus Mut. Life Ins. Co., 1982—; bd. dirs. Procter & Gamble Co., Cin. Bell Inc. Bd. dirs. Our Lady of Mercy Hosp., Bethesda Hosp. and Deaconess Assn.; chmn. bd. trustees U. Cin., 1977, chmn. emeritus, 1987—; chmn. Cin. Bus. Com., 1986-87. Recipient Taft medal U. Cin., 1973, spl. award Ohio Radiol. Soc., 1974, Daniel Drake award, 1985; named Great Living Cincinnatian, 1987. Fellow Am. Coll. Radiology; mem. AMA, Life Ins. Assn. Am., Greater Cin. C. of C. (chmn. 1985-86), Knights of Malta, Alpha Omega Alpha. Home: Cincinnati OH Died May, 13, 1989.

BARRETT, RAYMOND JAMES, retired foreign service officer, educator; b. North Wildwood, N.J., July 22, 1924; s. James A. and Helen Knight (Ozmon) B.; m. Eleanore M. Spring, Sept. 5, 1948; children—Grainger,

Cherilyn Barrett Ensby, Clark, Melanie Barrett Smith, Holly Barrett Gross. A.B., Columbia U., 1946; M.A., U. Wis., 1959; Ph.D., Trinity Coll., Dublin, Ireland, 1958. Joined U.S. Fgn. Service, 1948; 3d sec. Am. embassy, Mexico City, 1949-51; 2d sec. Am. embassy, Managua, Nicaragua, 1951-53, Dublin, 1954-58, Cairo, UAR, 1959-61; with Office Eastern and So. African Affairs State Dept., 1961-63, Canadian desk officer, 1963-65; 1st sec. Am. embassy, Madrid, 1965-67; dep. chief program staff Office Internat. Confs. Dept. State, 1967-69; dep. chief global plans div. Hdqrs. U.S. Air Force, 1969-71; State Dept. adviser U.S. Army John F. Kennedy Center for Mil. Assistance, Ft. Bragg, N.C., 1971-73; instr. history N.C. State U., Ft. Bragg, 1971-73; assoc. prof. mgmt. Glassboro (N.J.) State Coll., 1973-85, prof. emeritus, 1985-91; prof. Franklin Coll., Lugano, Switzerland, 1985-86; sec. U.S. sect. U.S.-Can. Permanent Joint Bd. Def., 1963-65; U.S. sec. U.S.-Can. Joint Civil Emergency Planning Com., 1963-65. Author: Introduction to Management, 1975, 81; contbr. articles to profl. jours. Mem. U.S. Naval Inst. (1st prize essay 1972), Am. Mgmt. Assn., Soc. for Preservation and Encouragement of Barbershop Quartet Singing in Am., Rotary. Episcopalian. Home: Durham N.C. Died Dec. 31, 1991.

BARRETT, ROBERT JOHN, JR., management consultant; b. Bayonne, N.J., Dec. 20, 1917; s. Robert John and Neta (Clark) B.; m. Jane Sponseller, Jan. 24, 1942; children—Betsy Adams, Robin Selmier. B.S., Ohio U., 1940; postgrad., U. Calif. at Los Angeles, 1961-62. Mem. staff Price Waterhouse & Co., Cleve., 1940-42; exec. v.p., dir. Leach Relay Co., Los Angeles, 1947-54; dir. adminstrn. Ramo-Wooldridge Corp., Los Angeles, 1954-62; dir. adminstrn. and fin. Northrop Corp., Anaheim, Calif., 1962-65; treas., chief fin. officer Aeronca, Inc., Torrance, Calif., 1965-75, v.p., treas., 1969-75; v.p. adminstrn. and fin., treas. Pacific Am. Industries Inc., Gardenia, Calif., 1975-76; v.p., chief fin. officer Intermark Inc., La Jolla, Calif., 1976-81, v.p., chief adminstrv. officer, 1981-83; v.p., chief fin. officer, asst. sec. Mgmt. Analysis Co., San Diego, 1983-87; mgmt. cons., 1987-88; v.p., chief fin. officer, asst. sec. Mgmt. Analysis Co., San Diego, 1988-89, mgmt. cons., 1989-94, also bd. dirs. Served from 2d lt. to maj. AUS, 1942-46. Mem. Fin. Execs. Inst. (past Western area v.p., chpt. pres., nat. dir.), Corp. Fin. Council San Diego (chmn.). Clubs: La Jolla Beach and Tennis; Breakfast (Palos Verdes) (past pres.). Home: La Jolla Calif. Died Dec. 21, 1994.

BARROW, BERNARD ELLIOTT, actor, educator; b. N.Y.C., Dec. 30, 1927; s. Samuel and Sophie (Halpern) B.; m. Joan Kaye, Sept. 15, 1963; children: Susan M., Thomas E. B.A., Syracuse U., 1947; M.A., Columbia U., 1948; Ph.D., Yale U., 1957. Mem. faculty dept. theatre Lincoln U., Pa., 1948-51; mem. faculty Bklyn. Coll., 1955-83, prof., until 1983, prof. emeritus, 1983-93. Appeared in leading roles in TV daytime drama Where The Heart Is, 1969, Secret Storm, 1970-73, Edge of Night, 1974, Ryan's Hope, 1975-88, Loving, 1989-93; TV movies including Women at West Point, 1979, Senior Trip, 1981, also films; various off-Broadway theatre appearances; dir. (off-Broadway) Modern Romance, 1985. Mem. AAUP, Screen Actors Guild, AFTRA, Actors Equity Assn. Club: Yale. Home: New York N.Y. Died Aug. 3, 1993.

BARROW, ERROL WALTON, lawyer; b. Barbados, W.I., Jan. 21, 1920; s. Reginald Grant and Ruth Alberta (O'Neal) B.; student Harrison Coll. (Barbados), 1934-39; B.Sc. in Econ., U. London, 1950; LL.D. (hon.), McGill U., 1967, Sussex U., 1970; m. Carolyn Plaskett, Nov. 18, 1945; children: Lesley, David O'Neal. Prime minister Barbados, 1966-76, leader of opposition, 1978-86, prime minister, from 1986; practice law, Barbados and Eastern Caribbean, 1951-61, 77-86; Queen's counsel; disting. vis. prof. Fla. Internat. U., Miami, 1973. Fellow London Sch. Econs., 1974; liveryman Guild of Air Pilots and Air Navigators. Democratic Labour Party (gen. sec. 1978-80). Deceased. Home: Paradise Beach Barbados

BARROW, DAME RUTH NITA, government official; b. St. Lucy, Barbados, Nov. 15, 1916; d. Reginald Grant and Ruth Alberta (O'Neal) B. RN, Barbados Gen. Hosp., 1940, Port-of-Spain Hosp.; diploma in nursing edn., U. Toronto, 1943, diploma in pub. health, 1945; diploma, Edinburgh U., 1951; BS, Columbia U.; LLD (hon.), U. West Indies, U. Toronto, U. Mantobia, Spellman Coll., York U., Smith Coll., Queen's U. of Can., Adelphi U., 1994; DSc (hon.), Macmaster U.; DHun (hon.), Morris Brown U.; HHD, Mt. St. Vincent; LittD, Wilfrid Laurier U., 1994. Mem. various staff, teaching and adminstrv. posts in nursing and pub. health Barbados and Jamaica, 1940-56; prin. nursing officer Jamaica, 1956-62; nursing advisor Pan Am. Health Orgn., 1967-71; assoc. dir. Christian Med. Commn. World Coun. Chs., Geneva, 1971-75, dir., 1975-80; health cons. WHO, 1981-86; amb. to UN, 1986-90; gov.-gen. Barbados, 1990—; convenor Eminent Persons Group 1st UN Global Conf. on Sustainabe Devel. of Small Island Developing States, 1994. Mem. exec. com. World of YWCA, 1955-67, v.p., 1963-67, pres., 1975-83; pres. Quadrennial Coun., 1975-79, 83, Internat. Coun. for Adult Edn., 1982-90, WCC, 1983-91; participant numerous internat. confs. on population, health and women; chmn. health sect. Forum '80, Copenhagen; convenor UN Forum, Nairobi, Kenya, 1985, Eminent Persons Group, 1st UN Global Conf. Sustainable Devel. Small Island Developing States, 1994; mem. Commonwealth Group Eminent Persons on S.A., 1986; dir. Global Fund for Women, USA, 1986—, L.A. chpt.; bd. dirs. Found. for Internat. Tng. Can., 1986-90; mem. Internat. Adv. Synergos Inst., U.S.A., 1987-88, 89-90; mem. Jury Liberty Medal, 1988-90, steering com. on leadership and devel. Rockefeller Found. Internat., 1992. Recipient Caribbean prize Caribbean Coun. Chs., 1986, Caricom award Commonwealth Caribbean, 1987, Christine Reisman award Internat. Coun. Nurses, 1989, Louise McManua award Columiba U., 1989, award Afro Am. Inst., 1991, Women First award YWCA, 1993, Order of the Caribbean Cmty., 1994; named Dame Grand Cross of the Most Disting. Order of St. Michael and St. George, Dame of St. Andrew in the Order of Barbados. Fellow Royal Coll. Nursing (London); mem. Jamaica Nurses Assn. (founder, pres.), Internat. Peace Acad. (bd. dir. 1986-90). Home: Bridgetown Barbados Died Dec. 19, 1995.

BARROWS, STANLEY, interior designer, educator; b. Palacios, Tex., Dec. 5, 1914; s. William Stanley and Margaret Stuart (Sartwelle) B. B.A., Washington and Lee U., 1937; diploma in design, Parsons Sch. Design, N.Y. and Paris, 1940. Designer Joseph Platt Assocs., N.Y.C., 1941-42; prof. interior design, dir. European study program Parsons Sch. Design, N.Y.C., 1946-68; prof. interior design specializing in design histor Fashion Inst. Tech., N.Y.C., 1968—, chmn. dept. interior design, 1980—. Contbr. articles, Archtol. Digest, N.Y. Times, Inside Design. Mem. Mayor's com. for promotion of N.Y.C. as center for home furnishings resources, 1980. Served with AUS, 1942-45. Mem. Am. Soc. Interior Designers (edn. affiliate DeWolfe award), Irish Georgian Soc., Victorian Soc., Nat. Trust for Hist. Preservation, Kappa Phi Kappa. Republican. Presbyterian. Club: Princeton of N.Y. Home: New York N.Y. Died Jan. 31, 1995.

BARRY, JOHN KEVIN, lawyer; b. Akron, Ohio, Mar. 23, 1925; s. John Henry and Mary Ellen (O'Hara) B.; m. Ann L. Trainer, June 14, 1952 (div. 1958); children: Mona A., Barry de Sayve; m. Barbara Ann Lacek, Dec. 15, 1973; children: J. Kevin, Nicholas A., Liza M. A.B., Princeton U., 1947; J.D., Northwestern U., 1951. Bar: Ohio 1951, Pa. 1963. Assoc. Brouse, McDowell Inc., Akron, 1951-54; trial atty. IRS, Washington, 1954-57; atty., mem. legal adv. staff U.S. Treasury Dept., Washington, 1957-60, mem. office of tax legis. counsel, 1960-62; assoc. Reed Smith Shaw & McClay, Pitts., 1962-66, ptnr., 1966-86; tax counselnr. Jones Day Reavis & Pogue, Pitts., 1989-90. Bd. dirs. Pitts. Symphony Soc., 1981-89; trustee Sewickley (Pa.) Acad., 1982-88; co-chmn. bd. visitors Western Res. Acad., 1990-92. Served with USN, 1943-46. Mem. ABA, Fed. Bar Assn., Pa. Bar Assn., Northwestern U. Sch. Law Alumni Assn. (regional v.p. 1979-87). Republican. Roman Catholic. Clubs: Allegheny Country (Sewickley Heights, Pa.); Duquesne, Harvard-Yale-Princeton (Pitts.); Columbia Country (Chevy Chase, Md.); Princeton (N.Y.C.). Home: Sewickley Pa. Died Jan., 1995.

BARRY, THOMAS HUBERT, publishing company executive; b. Phillips, Wis., Mar. 18, 1918; s. John Sumner and Helen (Maloney) B.; m. Rosemary Klein, July 8, 1944 (dec. May 1983); children: Kathleen Barry Ingram, Patricia Barry Turriff (dec.), Mary Beth Barry O'Donnell, Julie Barry Carden; m. Marylyn P. Dorsett, Nov. 2, 1991. Student, U. Notre Dame, 1936-38; BA, Marquette U., 1941. Western mgr., welding engr. McGraw Hill Pub. Co., Chgo., 1947-53; Western mgr. Iron Age, Chilton Co., Chgo., 1953-66, Control Engring., Tech. Pub. (a Dun and Bradstreet Co.), Chgo., 1966-69; sales mgr. Control Engring., Tech. Pub. (a Dun and Bradstreet Co.), N.Y.C., 1969-72; assoc. pub. Control Engring., Tech. Pub. (a Dun and Bradstreet Co.), Chgo., 1972-76; pub. Control Engring., Tech. Pub. (a Dun and Bradstreet Co.), Barrington, Ill., 1977-86; v.p., pub. Control Engring., Cahners Pub. Co. div. Reed Pub. Co. USA, Des Plaines, Ill., 1986-93. Bd. dirs. Boys' Hope. Served with USMC, 1941-47. Decorated Bronze Star, Purple Heart. Mem. Nat. Indsl. Advertisers Assn., Assn. Indsl. Advertisers (dir. Chgo. chpt. 1963-65), Bus.-Profl. Advt. Assn., Indsl. Mktg. Club St. Louis, Rockford Advt. Club, Marine Corps Res. Officers Assn., 1st Marine Div. Assn. (officer, dir. 1954-93, pres. 1979-84), Holy Name Soc., Army and Navy Club (Washington), KC, Notre Dame Club of Chgo., Marquette U. Club Chgo. Roman Catholic. Home: Arlington Heights Ill. Died Oct. 20, 1993.

BARTELL, LEE, entrepreneur, lawyer; b. Milw., 1910; s. Benjamin and Lena (Beznor) B.; m. Ina Berginn, Jan. 13, 1934; children: Michael, Rusti, Richard. Student, Milw. State Tchrs. Coll., 1932, Marquette U., 1933; LLB, U. Wis., 1936. Bar: Wis. 1936, Calif. 1960. With Wis. Atty. Gen. Office; counsel Wis. Devel. Authority; trial atty. U.S. Govt.; founder Bartell Broadcasting Corp.; former pres. Bartell Media Corp., Sta. KCBQ, Inc.; sec., bd. dirs. Bartell Broadcasters, Inc., Bartell Broadcasters N.Y., Inc.; pres. McDodd Corp., Interstate 8 Hotel, Inc.; gen. ptnr. Bartell Hotels; sec. Sta. KMJC, San Diego. Editor Wis. Law Rev. Lt. (j.g.) USNR, 1943-44. Mem. Am. Legion (past post comdr.), Order of Coif. Home: San Diego Calif. Died Nov. 6, 1991.

BARTHE, RICHMOND, artist, sculptor; b. Bay St Louis, Miss., Jan. 28, 1901; s. Richmond and Mari Clementine (Raboteau) B. B.A., Xavier U., 193 D.F.A., St. Francis Coll., 1946. Exhibited one-ma shows, William Grant Still Community Art Cente 1978, Inst. Jamaica, 1959, Montclair (N.J.) Art Mus 1949, Margaret Brown Galleries, Boston, 1947, Gran Central Art Galleries, N.Y.C., 1947, Sayville (L.I. Playhouse, 1945, Internat. Print Soc., 1945, DePorre Interracial Ctr., 1945, South Side Art Ctr., Chgo., 194 Arden Galleries, N.Y.C., 1939, Delphic Studios, 193 U. Wis.-Madison, 1931, 32, 33,, Ranking Art Gallerie Washington, 1931, Women's City Club, Chgo., 193 Grand Rapids (Mich.) Art Gallery, 1930, numerou others, group shows, Met. Mus., Guggenheim Mus Whitney Mus., Nat. Urban League, Sculptor's Guil Audubon Artists, all N.Y.C., Phila. Mus. Art, Afr Am. Hist. and Cultural Mus., both Phila., Los Angel County Art Mus., Dallas Mus. Fine Arts, Century Progress, Chgo., High Mus. Art, Atlanta, Bklyn. Mus Beverly Hilton Hotel, others; represented: in permane collections maj. Museums, including Met. Mus.; permanent collections maj. museums, including Whitne Mus. Am. Art, Schomber Collection, Countee Colle Library, IBM, Arthur Brisbane Meml., all N.Y.C., A Inst. Chgo., Smithsonian Instn., Jamaican Pub. Librar Theosoph. Soc., Va. Mus. Fine Arts, Los Angel County Art Mus., Gibbs Mus., Oberlin Coll. Mus., Ya U. Mus., Howard U. Gallery of Art, Tuskegee U. Ga lery Art, Fisk U. Gallery of Art, Atlanta U. St. Augu tines Sem., Coll. St. Mary of the Springs, U. So. Mis Ch. St. Jude, Montgomery, Ala., South Bend, Ind numerous others; commd. bust: Booker T. Washingto Dr. George Washington Carver, Hall of Fame Gre Americans, 1976, Social Security Bldg., Washingto Dessalaines Monument, Haitian Govt., others. Hom Pasadena Calif. Died March 6, 1989.

BARTHOLOMEW, HENRY HOMER, surgeon; Fayette, Utah, Mar. 13, 1921; s. Henry L. and Ire (Rallison) B.; m. Betty Ann Deakin, Mar. 6, 1953 (de 1973); children: Brent H., Susan, Diane, David S.; Ellen Nielsen, Apr. 18, 1977. BA, Brigham Young U 1946; MD, U. Pa., 1949. Diplomate, Am. B Ophthalmology, Am. Bd. Med. Examiners. Inter Latter-Saints Hosp., Salt Lake City, 1949-50; resident ophthalmology Stanford U., San Francisco, 1953-5 instr. dept. ophthalmology, 1955-56; pvt. practice Sa Lake City, 1956-88, ret., 1988; chief dep ophthalmology Salt Lake Clinic, 1961-88; cons. Worl Wide Missionary Dept., Latter-Day Saints Ch., 1988— mem. staff, Latter-day Saints Hosp., Primary Children Med. Ctr.; clin. prof. ophthalmology, U. Utah, Sa Lake City, 1957—. Lt. USN, 1951-53, Korea. Fello ACS, Am. Acad. Ophthalmology; mem. AMA, Pacif Coast Ophthalmology Soc. Mormon. Home: Salt La City UT

BARTLETT, (HERBERT) HALL, motion pictu producer, director; b. Kansas City, Mo., Nov. 27, 192 s. Paul Dana and Alice (Hiestand) B.; m. Lupita Ferre Apr. 30, 1977 (div.); children: Cathy Bartlett Lync Laurie Bartlett Schrader. BA, Yale U., 1948. Owne operator Hall Bartlett Prodn., L.A., 1960-93; pre Jonathan Livingston Seagull Mcht. Co.; bd. dirs. Jame Doolittle Theatre, Hollywood, Calif., founder Mus Ctr., Los Angeles. Producer, dir. (films) Navajo, 195 Crazylegs, 1958, Unchained, 1957, All the Young Me 1961, Durango, 1959, Zero Hour, 1961, The Caretaker 1963, A Global Affair, 1968, Changes, 1968, Sandp Generals, 1971, Jonathan Livingston Seagull, 1973, Th Children of Sanchez, 1979, Catch Me If You Can, 198 The Search of Zubin Mehta, 1975, The Cleo Lai Story, 1978, Comeback, 1983; author: The Rest of O Lives, 1987. mem. Friends of Library, L.A., Cinem Circulus; assoc. founder Pub. TV Music Ctr. Lt. USN 1949-51. Recipient 11 Acad. award nominations, Fil Festival awards from Cannes, 1961, 63, Venice, 19 65, Edinburgh, 1963, San Sebastian, 1969, Mosco 1971, NCCJ, 1955, Jimmy Stewart award for Care Achievement in Motion Pictures, 1992, Fgn. Pre awards. Mem. Motion Picture Acad. Arts and Sci Acad. TV Arts and Scis., Phi Beta Kappa. Republica Presbyterian. Clubs: Bel-Air Country, Kansas Ci Country. Home: Los Angeles Calif. Died Sept. 8, 199

BARTLETT, THOMAS EDWARD, industrial e gineer; b. Tulsa, Sept. 3, 1920; s. Michael Leo a Elizabeth (Stadden) B.; BA, U. Okla., 1942; M Columbia U., 1947; postgrad. Purdue U., 1957-59, Fla., 1965, Ariz. State U., 1966. Engr., Montgome Ward & Co., 1947-48; chief indsl. engr. Bank of A 1948-50; mem. tech. staff Hughes Rsch. and Deve 1950-54, Ramo-Wooldridge, 1954; prof. Purdue 1955-63; mem. teaching staff Calif. State Poly. Co 1964-65; ops. rsch. cons., 1965-67; dir. ops. rsch. Lest Gorstene Assocs., 1967-68; pres., chmn. bd. di Wyvern Rsch. Assos., Inc., Mill Valley, Calif., 1968— dir., chmn. bd. JEBOR, Inc. Served with CIC, U. Army, 1942-46. Registered profl. engr., Calif. Me Am. Inst. Indsl. Engrs., Inst. Mgmt. Scis., Ops. Rs Soc. Am., Fedn. Am. Scientists, Soc. Indsl. and Appli Math., Scis., AAAS, Am. Soc. Personnel Adminstr Am. Math. Assn., San Francisco Press Club, Sigma Phi Kappa Phi, Phi Kappa Psi. Home: Stockton Calif

BARTLEY, WILLIAM WARREN, III, philosoph biographer; b. Pitts., Oct. 2, 1934; s. William Warr and Elvina (Henry) B. A.B., Harvard U., 1956, A.M., 1958; Ph.D., London (Eng.) Sch. Econs. and Polit. Sci., 1962. Lectr. logic London Sch. Econs., 1960-63; lectr. history of philosophy of sci. Warburg Inst. U. London, 1961-64; vis. assoc. prof. philosophy U. Calif.-Berkeley, 1963-64; assoc. prof. U. Calif.-San Diego, 1964-67, co.-dir. humanities program, 1965-66; S.A. Cook Bye fellow Gonville and Caius Coll., Cambridge U., 1966-67; assoc. prof. philosophy U. Pitts., 1967-69; assoc. prof. U. Pitts. (Population Div.), 1967-69; prof. philosophy and history and philosophy of sci., sr. research assoc., assoc. dir. Philosophy of Sci. Center U. Pitts., 1969-73; prof. philosophy Calif. State U. at Hayward, 1970-89, Outstanding prof., 1979—; vis. scholar Hoover Instn. War, Revolution and Peace, Stanford U., 1984, sr. research fellow, 1985—; fellow, adj. scholar Inst. Humane Studies, George Mason U., 1984—; cons., mem. Centro Superiore di Logica e Scienza Comparate, Bologna, Italy, 1972—; treas. Struction, Inc., 1978—; dir. N.Y. Tribune, 1981—; fellow Ludwig Boltzmann Research Inst., Vienna, 1986-87; staff philosopher, est, ednl. corp., 1975-78; Neil Arnott lectr. Robert Gordon's Inst. Tech., Aberdeen, Scotland, 1982; seminar leader Austrian Coll., Alpbach, 1961, 65, 75, 80, 82, 85; spl. lectr. Royal Inst. Philosophy, London, 1961, 68, Institut für Wissenschaftstheorie U. Salzburg, Austria, 1962; vis. asso. prof. U. Ill., 1964; spl. lectr. U. Karlsruhe, 1965; adj. prof. philosophy L.I. U., 1966; bd. dirs. Salzburg Seminar in Am. Studies, 1956-58, History and Theory, 1960-65, Centro Superiore di Logica e Scienze Comparate, Bologna, Italy, 1972—, Werner Erhard Charitable Settlement, Jersey, Channel Islands, 1976-81, est, an ednl. co., Ltd., London, 1977-81, Internat. Conf. on Unity of Scis., 1979-84, Inst. on Comparative Polit. and Econ. Systems, Georgetown U., 1980—, Inst. Methodology and Philosophy Sci., Turin, Italy, 1982—, Carl Menger Inst., Vienna, 1984—; mem. adv. bd. Washington Inst. Values in Pub. Policy, 1988—. Author: The Retreat to Commitment, 1962, 64, 84, Flucht ins Engagement, 1964, 86, Morality and Religion, 1971, Wittgenstein, 1973, 74, 75, 77, 83, 85, 86, Die Notwendigkeit des Engagements, 1974, 77, Wittgenstein e Popper, 1976, Lewis Carroll's Symbolic Logic, 1977, 78, 86, Werner Erhard, 1978, The Philosophy of Karl Popper, 1982, Evolutionary Epistemology, Rationality, and the Sociology of Knowledge, 1987, Ecologia della Razionalita, 1989, Unfathomed Knowledge, Unmeasured Wealth, 1990; assoc. editor: History and Theory, 1958-65; editor: Sir. Karl Popper's Postscript, 1982, 83, The Collected Works of F.A. Hayek, 1984—, The Fatal Conceit (F.A. Hayek), 1988; bd. editors: Soundings, 1967-69, Philos. Forum, 1967—, Critical Rev., 1986—, The Collected Works Karl Popper, 1986—. Contbr. articles profl. jours. Danforth Found. fellow, 1956-61, 66-67; U. Calif. Inst. for Humanities fellow, 1966-67; Am. Council Learned Socs. fellow, 1972-73, 79-80; Am. Philos. Soc. fellow, 1979-80; est Found. fellow, 1982-83; DAAD fellow, 1983; Thyssen Found. fellow, 1984; Earhart Found. fellow, 1984; Morris Found. fellow, 1984; Inst. Humane Studies fellow, 1984—; Wincott Found. fellow, 1984; Adam Smith Inst. fellow, 1984; Parshad award, 1952,; Fulbright award, 1958-60, 83; Dana Reed award, 1956; Bowen prize Harvard, 1958. Mem. Oxford and Cambridge Soc., Signet Soc., Brit. Soc. Philosophy of Sci. (mem. exec. com. 1964), Am. Philos. Assn., AAUP, Phi Beta Kappa. Clubs: Harvard, Commonwealth (San Francisco); Mont Pèlerin Soc. Home: Stanford Calif.

BARTON, LEON SAMUEL CLAY, JR., architect; b. Orangeburg, S.C., Jan. 9, 1906; s. Leon Samuel Clay and Georgia (Hadley) B.; m. Alice Barbara Mosher, Dec. 2, 1941 (dec. Sept. 3, 1971); 1 child, Mary Jane (Mrs. Thomas C. Murray). B.S. in Architecture, Clemson U., 1928; postgrad., NYU, 1932-34, Atelier Morgan, N.Y.C., 1932-35, Inst. Effective Speaking & Human Relations, N.Y.C., 1952, N.Y. Med. Coll., 1966, Columbia U., 1970, Eastern Sch. Real Estate, N.Y.C., 1971; cert., U.S. Civil Def. Preparedness Agy., 1974, Summer Seismic Inst., U. Ill., 1978. Registered architect, Colo., Fla., Md., N.J., N.Y., S.C. certified Nat. Council Archtl. Registration Bds. Designer, draftsman engring. div. E.R. Squibb & Sons, 1928-35, dir. master planning, asst. to chief exec. engr., 1944-47; partner Barton & Pilafian, Architects & Engrs., Teheran, Iran; also cons. to Iranian Govt. Barton & Pilafian, Architects & Engrs., 1935-38; prin. Leon S. Barton, 1939-41; chief architect head archtl. dept. Robert & Co., Inc., Atlanta, 1941-44; naval architect shipbldg. div. Bethlehem Steel Co., 1944; with Vitro Corp. Am.(formerly The Kellex Corp. of Am.), N.Y.C.; chief architect nuclear energy projects U.S. AEC, 1948-54; sr. partner Barton and Pruitt and Assocs. (Architects, Engrs. and Planners), N.Y.C., 1954—; chmn. bd. pres. Walton Resiliant Floors, Inc., N.Y.C., 1968—. Project architect in charge: design Peter Cooper br. Chase Manhattan Bank, Shreve Lamb & Harmon Assocs., N.Y.C., 1947-48; Prin. works include Engring. and Maintenance Facilities Bldg, E.R. Squibb & Sons, New Brunswick, N.J., Vitro Research Lab. Facilities, Silver Spring, Md., Gen. Nuclear Research Lab. Facilities and Radiation Effects Research Lab. Facilities, Lockheed Aircraft Corp., Dawsonville, Ga., U.S. Food and Drug Adminstrn. Research Lab. and Office Facilities, Bklyn.; assoc. architect: (with Gen. Charles B. Ferris, Engrs.) Barnert Meml. Hosp. Center, Paterson, N.J. Recipient First Hon. mention Nat. WGN Broadcasting Theater Competition, 1934; Grand prize Internat. Teheran Stock Exchange (Bourse) Competition, 1935; First Hon. mention Prix de Rome archtl. Competition, 1935; Certificate of Merit for loyal and efficient services during World War II def. projects Robert & Co., Inc., 1944. Mem. AIA (corp. mem., mem. nat. task force for devel. health facilities research 1969-77, mem. publ. com. 1957-58, mem. pub. affairs com. 1967-68, mem. speakers bur. 1967-71, mem. hosp. and health com. 1967—, mem. sch. and coll. archtl. com. 1971-78, mem. urban planning com. 1972-78, mem. LeBrun Scholarship com. 1972-78, mem. criminal justice facilities com. 1974-75, mem. W. Side Hwy. subcom. 1973-75), N.Y. State Assn. Architects (corp. mem., mem. housing and urban devel. planning com. 1971-78, mem. sch. and coll. com. 1971-78, mem. honors and awards com. 1974-75, mem. environmental and community planning com. 1974-78), Am. Arbitration Assn. (nat. panel arbitrators 1970—), Greater N.Y. Hosp. Assn. (engring. adv. com. 1978—). Episcopalian. Home: Cape Canaveral Fla.

BARUT, ASIM ORHAN, physicist, educator; b. Malatya, Turkey, June 24, 1926; came to U.S., 1953, naturalized, 1962; m. Pierrette Helene Gervaz, July 2, 1954. Diploma, Swiss Fed. Inst. Tech., 1949, DSc, 1952, D (hon.), 1982, 87. Mem. faculty U. Chgo., 1953-54, Reed Coll., Portland, Oreg., 1954-55, U. Montreal, Que., Can., 1955-56, Syracuse (N.Y.) U., 1956-61, U. Calif., Berkeley, 1961-62; prof. physics U. Colo., Boulder, 1962-94, rsch. lectr., 1982; lectr. ednl. instns., various countries. Editor, mem. editorial bd. Found. of Physics, Reports in Math. Physics, Hadronic Jour., Annales Fondat L. de Broglie, Com. Theoretical Physics. Mem. staff Internat. Ctr. for Theoretical Physics, Trieste, Italy, 1964-65, 68-69, 72-73, 86-87; bd. dirs. NATO Advanced Study Insts., 1966, 67, 70, 72, 77, 83, 84, 89, 94. Recipient Alexander von Humboldt award, 1974-75, 76, 85, Medal of Sci., Turkey, 1982, Rsch. Lectureship award, 1983; faculty rsch. fellow, 1968, 72, 78, 85; Erskine fellow U. Canterbury, New Zealand, 1970. Fellow Am. Phys. Soc. Home: Boulder Colo. Died Dec. 5, 1994.

BARZINI, LUIGI, author, journalist; b. Milan, Italy, Dec. 21, 1908; s. Luigi and Mantica (Pesavento) B.; m. Giannalisa Gianzana, 1940; m. 2d, Paola Gadola, 1949; 5 children. Student Sch. Journalism Columbia U., N.Y.C. Spl. corr. Corriere della Sera, 1931-40, columnist, 1978—; editor, pub. Il Globo, Rome, 1944-47; contbr. to Italian and other mags. Author: Americans are Alone in the World, 1953, I Disarmati, 1957, Mosca Mosca, 1961, The Italians, 1964, L'Europa Domani Mattina, 1964, From Caesar to the Mafia, 1971, L'Antropometro Italiano, 1973, O America: When You and I Were Young, 1977, The Europeans, 1984, O America: When You & I Were Young, 1985. Mem. Italian Chamber of deps., 1958-72. Liberal. Home: Rome Italy

BASCOM, EARL WESLEY, artist, sculptor, writer; b. Vernal, Utah, June 19, 1906; s. John W. and Rachel C. (Lybbert) B.; m. Nadine Diffey, Dec. 20, 1939; children: Denise, Glen, Doris, John, Dona. BS, Brigham Young U., 1940, postgrad., 1965, 66; postgrad., U. Calif., Riverside, 1969. Profl. rodeo cowboy, 1918-40; producer 1st rodeo State of Miss., 1935, 36, 37; pres. Bascom and Wilkerson, 1947-51; owner Two Bar Qtr. Circle Ranch, 1951-95; pres. High Desert Artists, Inc., 1964-65, Bascom Fine Arts, 1967-95; owner Diamond B Ranch, 1975-95; pres. Buckaroo Artists Am., 1978; tchr. art Barstow (Calif.) High Sch., 1966, 67, John F. Kennedy High Sch., 1966, 67; inventor rodeo equipment. Exhibited in group shows at Utah Artists, 1971, Cowboy Artists, 1972, Desert S.W. Artists, 1974, Mormon Festival of Arts, 1975, Cochise Mus., 1976, Wells Fargo Exhibit, 1976, Frank Tenney Johnson Invitational, 1979, Sun Valley, 1980, New Hibernia Exhibit, 1981, Santa Anita Nat. Horse Show, 1982, Cheyenne Frontier Days, 1983, Weighorst-Bascom Exhibit, 1984, Old Time Athletes, 1985, Golden Boot Exhibit, 1986, Nat. Salon, 1986, 87, 88, Internat. Art Exhibit, 1990, Equestrian Art Festival, 1991, Hollywood Park Exhibit, 1992, World Cup Exhibit (Las Vegas), 1993, A Bar A Ranch, Wyo., 1993; represented in pvt. collections including Ronald Reagan, Roy Rogers, Gene Autrey, J.W. Marriott, Ezra Taft Benson, Louis L'Amour, Barry Goldwater, Charlton Heston, Thomas Sarnoff; represented in permanent collections including Remington Mus. Art, Ogdensburg, N.Y., Nat. Cowboy Hall Fame Mus., Oklahoma City, N.Am. Cowboy Mus., Ft. Worth, Old West Mus., Cheyenne, Wyoming, Can. Rodeo Hall of Fame Mus., Calgary, Alberta, Can., U. Iowa Art Mus., Brigham Young U. Art Mus., Provo, Utah, Utah Mus. Fine Art, Salt Lake City, Whitney Mus. Art, Tucson Mus. Art, Will Rogers Meml. Ctr., Ft. Worth, Am. Vet. Med. Assn., Schaumberg, Ill.; actor movie The Lawless Rider, 1954; appeared in commls. and documentarys; designed and made rodeo's first Hornless Bronc Saddle, 1922, also first One-Hand Bareback Rigging, 1924, Rodeo Chaps, 1926; invented Rodeo Exercizer, 1928; author, illustrator The History of Bareback Bronc Riding Western Horseman, 1990. Grand marshall Apple Valley Frontier Days Rodeo, 1993. Reserve champion, holder world record steer decorating N.Am. Championship, 1933; bareback, all-around champion, Lethbridge, Alb., Can., 1934; saddle bronc, steer decorating, all-around champion, Raymond, Alb., 1935, saddle bronc, bareback, all-around champion, 1940; all-around champion, Nephi, Utah, 1936; saddle bronc, bareback, bull riding, all-around champion, Pocatello, Idaho, 1937; bareback, bull riding, all-around champion, Portland, Oreg., 1938; inducted Can. Rodeo Hall Fame, 1984, Utah Sports Hall Fame, 1985, Raymond Sports Hall Fame, 1987; named honorary parade marshall, Cardston, Alb., 1982, Raymond, Alberta, 1984, Columbia, Miss., 1985, Vernal, Utah, 1989; honored as Legendary Cowboy various rodeo coms.; honored as Am. Hero U.S. Congl. Record, 1985; honored in resolutions various state and city govts.; named Outstanding Sr. Citizen Dept. Gerontology, 1987. Fellow Royal Soc. Arts (London); mem. Western Writers Am., Old Time Athletic Assn. (life), Profl. Rodeo Cowboys Assn. (hon. life), Nat. Outlaw and Lawman Assn. (life), Can. Rodeo Cowboys Assn. (hon. life), Can. Rodeo Hist. Assn. (founder), Pro Rodeo Hist. Soc. (life), Nat. Soc. Sons Utah Pioneers (life), U.S. Mormon Battalion Soc. (life), Assn. Latter-Day Media Artists, Old Timers Rodeo Assn., Cowboys Turtle Assn., Outlaw Trail History Assn., Brigham Young Univ. Emeritus Club (Spl. Recognition award 1992), Nat. Huguenot Soc., Basque Soc. Republican. Mormon. Home: Victorville Calif. Died Aug. 28, 1995.

BASS, ARTHUR CHARLES, business executive; b. N.Y.C., Mar. 11, 1932; s. Irving and Doris (Cole) B.; m. Paula Campbell, Nov. 13, 1977; children: Cole C., Kaolin McC. BA in English, Middlebury Coll., 1954; postgrad., N.Y. Law Sch., 1960-61. Pres. Aerospace Advance Planning Group, N.Y.C., 1965-71; pres., vice chmn. bd. Fed. Express Corp., Memphis, 1972-82; chmn., chief exec. officer Midway Airlines, Inc., Chgo., 1982-85, Starmark Energy Systems, Inc., Memphis, 1985-88, The Cooper Cos., Inc., Palo Alto, Calif., 1989-90, 92-93, Emery Worldwide, 1990; bd. dirs. Interand Corp., Chgo. Author articles, contbg. editor various aviation mags., 1961-68. Capt. USMC, 1954-58. Home: Memphis Tenn. Died Aug. 22, 1993.

BASS, MARY ANNA, dietitian; b. Clanton, Ala., June 1, 1930; d. Crawford Dixon and Gatie Mae (Williams) Owen; m. William Marvin Bass, III, Aug. 8, 1953; children: Charles Edward, William, James Owen. BS, U. Montevallo, 1951; MS, U. Ky., 1956; PhD, Kans. State U., 1972. Registered dietitian. Cons. various nursing homes Lawrence, Kans., 1960-70; instr. U. Nebr., Lincoln, 1960; cons. Standing Rock Reservation, Ft. Yates, S.D., 1970-74; instr. U. Kans., Lawrence, 1960-68; dir. Community Food and Nutrition Svcs., Knoxville, 1970—; nutrition cons. Cherokee Tribe, 1974—; asst. prof. home econs. U. Tenn., Knoxville, 1971-77, asst. prof. dept. anthropology, 1977—; cons. Sertoma Learning Ctr., 1988—. Mem. bd. editors Jour. Nutrition Edn., 1975-79; sr. author: Community Nutrition and Individual Food Behavior, 1979; contbr. articles to profl. jours. 1st lt. U.S. Army, 1951-53. Mem. Am. Dietetic Assn., Soc. Nutrition Edn., AAAS, Am. Anthropol. Assn., Omicron Nu, Sigma Xi, Gamma Sigma Delta. Presbyterian. Home: Knoxville Tenn. Died Mar. 24, 1993.

BASS, SAUL, graphic designer, filmmaker; b. N.Y.C., May 8, 1920; s. Aaron and Pauline (Feldman) B.; m. Elaine Makatura, Sept. 30, 1961; children: Jennifer, Jeffrey. Student, Art Students League, 1936-39, Bklyn. Coll., 1944-45; hon. doctorates, Phila. Mus. Coll. Art, L.A. Art Ctr. Coll. Design, Otis/Parsons Art Inst. Freelance graphic designer N.Y.C., 1936-46; propr. Saul Bass & Assocs., Inc., Los Angeles, 1946-96; Regents lectr. UCLA, 1986; Guardian lectr. Brit. Film Inst.; mem. exec. bd. Internat. Design Conf., Aspen, Colo.; hon. mem. faculty Royal Designers for Industry, Royal Soc. Arts, Eng., 1965; leader seminars, lectr. univs., colls., various instns. Dir. short films, TV commls., motion picture titles, prologues, epilogues; spl. sequences for feature films including shower sequence in Psycho, 1960, maj. battle in Spartacus, 1962, all races in Grand Prix, 1968, live action epilogue West Side Story, 1961, animated equilogue Around the World in Eighty Days, 1956; graphic designs Man With the Golden Arm, 1955, Anatomy of a Murder, 1960, Exodus, 1961, Bonjour Triestesse, 1957, Such Good Friends, 1974, The Shining, 1980, Broadcast News, 1987, Big, 1988, War of the Roses, 1990, Goodfellas, 1991, Cape Fear, 1992, Mr. Saturday Night, 1992, The Age of Innocence, 1993; dir. opening titles for Vertigo, 1958, North by Northwest, 1959, Walk on the Wild Side, 1962, It's a Mad, Mad, Mad, Mad World, 1963; dir. feature film Phase IV, 1974; film retrospectives include Cinemateque Francais, Paris, Rotterdam Film Festival, Zagreb Film Festival, L.A. Film Festival, Jerusalem Cinemateque, Braunschweig, Germany, Toyama, Japan; represented permanent collections, Plakatu Mus., Warsaw, Poland, Lahti Art Mus., Finland, Mus. Modern Art, N.Y.C., Library of Congress, Smithsonian Instn., Prague Mus., Stedelijk Mus., Amsterdam, The Cooper Hewitt Mus., N.Y.C., Israel Mus., Jerusalem, Kunstsammlungen Mus., Munich; exhibited one-man and group shows, U.S., Europe, S.Am., Far East; designer, developer: numerous corp. identification systems for indsl. enterprises including Bell System, AT&T, Getty Trust, Celanese Corp., United Airlines, Alcoa, Quaker Oats, Rockwell Internat., Warner Communications, Minolta, Girl Scouts U.S.A., United Way; architect, designer world-wide network, BP, Exxon-Esso Gasoline stas., 1983; designer packages for comml. products, Wesson Oil, 1983, Dixie Paper Products, Lawry's Foods, Hunt's

Foods, symbol, Pres.'s White House Council for Energy Efficiency, 1981, U.S. Post Office Commorative Stamp for Art and Industry, 1983; contbr. numerous articles to profl. publs. Bd. dirs. Internat. Design Conf., Aspen; bd. govs. Acad. Motion Picture Arts and Scis., L.A.; founding trustee Sundance Film Inst.; bd. dirs. Internat. Documentary Assn., Internat. Design Edn. Found.; design arts policy panel Nat. Endowment for the Arts; adv. bd. Getty Trust Arch. Program, Met.Mus. Art/ Getty Trust Program for Art on Film; others. Hon. fellow Bezalel Acad.; recipient award for high artistic value in all work Mus. de Arte Moderna, Rio de Janiero, 1959, citation for distinction brough to profession Phila. Mus. Art, 1960; inducted N.Y. Art Dirs. Hall of Fame, 1977; recipient numerous gold medals various nat. and internat. design competitions, Grand award for The Searching Eye Venice Film Festival, Gold Hugo for From Here to There Chgo. Film Festival, Oscar for documentary Why Man Creates, 1969, Gold medal Moscow Film Festival, U.S. Govt. Fed. Design Achievement award Fifth Ave. Soc., Silver medal Tokyo Met. Govt. Mem. Soc. Typog. Arts, Am. Inst. Graphic Arts (Gold medal), Assn. Graphic Designers Sweden, Package Designers Coun., Alliance Graphique Internat. Home: Los Angeles Calif. Died Apr. 25, 1996.

BASSETT, C(HARLES) ANDREW L(OOCKERMAN), orthopaedic surgeon, educator; b. Crisfield, Md., Aug. 4, 1924; s. Harold Reuben and Vesta (Loockerman) B.; m. Nancy Taylor Clark, June 15, 1946; children: Susan, David Clark, Lee Sterling. Student, Princeton U., 1941-43; MD, Columbia U., 1948, ScD, 1955; LHD (hon.), SUNY, 1988. Diplomate: Am. Bd. Orthopedic Surgery. Intern, resident St. Lukes Hosp., N.Y.C., 1948-50; asst. resident orthopedic surgery N.Y. Orthopaedic Hosp., 1950, Annie C. Kane fellow, 1953-55; asst. attending orthopedic surgeon Presbyn. Hosp., 1955-60, assoc. attending orthopedic surgeon, 1960-63, attending orthopedic surgeon, 1963-83, cons., 1983-88; instr. orthopedic surgery Columbia U., 1955-59, dir. orthopedic rsch. labs., 1957-86, asst. prof., 1959-61, assoc. prof., 1961-67, prof., 1967-83, prof. emeritus, spl. lectr., 1983-86; dir. Bioelectric Rsch. Ctr., 1986-94; cons. Naval Med. Rsch. Inst., Bethesda, Md., 1952-54; spl. cons. NIH, Nat. Inst. Neurol. Diseases and Blindness, Bethesda, 1959-62; career scientist N.Y.C. Health Research Council, 1961-71; vis. scientist Strangeway Research Lab., Cambridge, Eng., 1965-66; cons. div. med. scis., cons., exec. sec. com. on skeletal system NRC-Nat. Acad. Scis., 1963-71; sci. advisors Schwerizerischen Abeitsgemeinschaft fur Osteosynthesefragen, 1959-75; bd. sci. advisors Inst. Calot, Berck-Plage, France, 1969-89; cons. N.Y. State Rehab. Hosp., West Haverstraw, 1968-86; cons. on med. devices FDA, HEW, 1970-77; founder, cons., bd. dirs. Electro-Biology, Inc., 1975-87; chmn. bd. dirs., founder Osteodyne, Inc., 1988-94. Contbr. chpts. to books, articles to profl. jours.; patentee in field. Served to lt. (j.g.) USNR, 1950-54. Recipient Nat. award Paralyzed Vets. Am., 1959, Max Weinstein award United Cerebral Palsy, 1960, James Mather Smith prize Columbia Coll. Phys. and Surg., 1971, Galvani award U. Bologna, 1989. Fellow ACS, N.Y. Acad. Scis.; mem. AMA, Am. Acad. Orthopaedic Surgeons, Am. Orthopaedic Assn., Am. Soc. Cell Biology, Bioelectromagnetics Soc. (bd. dirs. 1991—, d'Arsonval medal 1991), Bioelectric Repair and Growth Soc. (Kappa Delta award 1988, pres.-elect 1993, pres. 1994), Internat. Soc. Orthopedic Surgery and Traumatology (sci. adv. bd. internat. orthopedics), N.Y. State, N.Y. County med. socs., Orthopaedic Research Soc. (pres.), Can. Orthopaedic Assn. (hon.), Royal Coll. Medicine (Eng.), Royal Micros. Soc., Tissue Culture Assn., Can. Orthopaedic Research Soc. (hon.), Soc. Exptl. Biology and Medicine, Harvey Soc., S.C. Orthopaedic Assn. (hon.), Société Belge de Chirurgie Orthopédique et de Traumatologie (hon.), Sigma Xi (Ann. award), Alpha Omega Alpha. Home: Bronxville N.Y. Died Nov. 14, 1994.

BATES, SIR DAVID ROBERT, physicist; b. Omagh, No. Ireland, Nov. 18, 1916; s. Walter V. and Mary O. (Shera) B.; m. Barbara B. Morris, 1956; two children. Student, Royal Belfast Acad. Inst.; MSc, Queen's U., 1938; student U. Coll., London, 1938-39; DSc (hon.), Ulster U., 1972, Nat. U. Ireland, 1975, U. Dublin, 1979; LLD (hon.), U. Glasgow, 1979, U. York, 1983, others. With Admiralty Rsch. Lab., Teddington, 1939-42; with Mine Design Dept. H.M.S. Vernon, 1941-45; lectr. in math. Univ. Coll., London, 1945-50, reader in physics, 1951; cons. U.S. Naval Ordnance Test Sta., Inyokern, Calif., 1950; prof. applied math. Queen's U., Belfast, 1951-68, prof. theoretical physics, 1968-74, spl. rsch. chmn., 1968-82; Smithsonian Regent's fellow Ctr. for Astrophysics, Cambridge, Mass., 1982-83, rsch. assoc. Harvard U., 1982-83. Recipient Hughes medal Royal Soc., 1970, Gold medal Royal Astronomical Soc., 1977, Chree medal Inst. Physics, 1973, Fleming medal Am. Geophysics Union, 1987. Fellow Royal Soc.; mem. Royal Irish Acad., AAAS (fgn.), Nat. Acad. Scis. U.S. (fgn. assoc.), Royal Acad. Belgium; mem. Brit. Assn. Advancement Sci. (pres. physics section 1977), European Geophys. Soc. (hon., est. Sir David Bates medal 1992). Died Jan. 5, 1994; interred Omagh City Cemetary. Home: Belfast No. Ireland

BATHEN, KARL HANS, oceanography educator; b. New Haven, Nov. 28, 1934; s. John H. and Jane H. (Koscinski) B.; m. Nancy J., Dec. 29, 1963 (div. 1980); children: Heidi, J., Erik K., Kristin E. BSME cum laude, U. Conn., 1956; postgrad., Orange Coast Coll., 1964, U. Calif., Davis, 1964-65; MS in Oceanography, U. Hawaii, 1968, PhD in Oceanography, 1970. Enlisted USAF, 1956; advanced through grades to capt. USAF, San Francisco, 1963; resigned USAF, 1966; project engr. Colorvision Inc., Glendale, Calif., 1961-57; project research and devel. engr., Philco, Aeronutronic div. Ford Motor Co., Newport Beach, Calif., 1963-64; research asst. in oceanography U. Hawaii, Honolulu, 1966-70, assoc. prof., assoc. researcher, 1971-76, prof., researcher, 1976-95; mgr. Dillingham Environ. Co., Honolulu, 1970-71; pres. Sci. Environ. Analyses, Ltd.; cons., lectr. in field. Contbr. numerous articles to profl. jours. Fellow Hawaiian Electric Oceanographic, 1967-68; recipient Internat. Underwater Photographic awards, 1964-66. Mem. Underwater Photographic Soc. Am., Conservation Council for Hawaii, Marine Tech. Soc., Am. Water Resources Assn., Internat. Assn. Water Pollution Research, Am. Geophys. Union, Sigma Xi. Home: Honolulu Hawaii Died Nov. 23, 1995.

BATTAN, LOUIS JOSEPH, meteorology educator, scientist, author; b. N.Y.C., Feb. 9, 1923; s. Anibale and Louise (Webber) B.; m. Jeannette A. Waitches, June 8, 1952; children: Suzette, Paul. Student, CCNY, 1941-43, Harvard U., MIT, 1944; B.S., NYU, 1946; M.S., U. Chgo., 1949, Ph.D., 1953. Research meteorologist U.S. Weather Bur., 1947-51; research meteorologist, lectr. U. Chgo., 1951-58; prof. atmospheric scis. Inst. Atmospheric Physics, U. Ariz., from 1958; cons. NSF, 1964-71, U.S. Weather Bur., 1957-59, U.S. Air Force, 1963-65, U.S. Army, 1954, NIH, 1965; chmn. com. atmosphere sci. Nat. Acad. Scis., 1973-76; mem. bd. on atmospheric sci. and climate, 1983-86; mem. U.S. nat. com. Internat. Union Geodesy and Geophysics, 1974-76, 78-84, chmn., 1980-84; mem. Nat. Adv. Com. on Oceans and Atmosphere, 1978-81; trustee Univ. Corp. Atmospheric Research, 1983-86. Author: Radar Meteorology, 1959, The Nature of Violent Storms, 1961, Radar Observes the Weather, 1962, Cloud Physics and Cloud Seeding, 1962, The Unclean Sky, 1966, The Thunderstorm, 1964, (with others) Earth and Space Sciences, 1966, 71, Laboratory Manual for Earth and Space Science, 1966, 71, Harvesting the Clouds, 1969, Radar Observation of the Atmosphere, 1973, Weather, 1974, 85, Fundamentals of Meteorology, 1979, 84, Weather in Your Life, 1983; also numerous articles.; Assoc. editor: Jour. Meteorology, 1961, Jour. Atmospheric Sciences, 1962-66; mem. editorial adv. bd. Britannica Yearbook of Science and the Future, from 1969; cons. editor Weatherwise, from 1978; mem. editorial com. Il Nuovo Cimento C, from 1978. Served to capt. USAAF, 1943-46. Fellow Am. Meteorol. Soc. (pres. 1966-68, councilor 1959-61, Meisinger award 1962, Brooks award 1971, Second Half Century award 1975), Am. Geophys. Union (pres. meteorol. sect. 1974-75), AAAS (sec. sect. on atmospheric and hydrospheric scis. 1968-74); mem. Sigma Xi. Roman Catholic. Home: Tucson Ariz. Deceased.

BATTENHOUSE, ROY WESLEY, English educator; b. Nevinville, Iowa, Apr. 9, 1912; s. Henry Martin and Sarah Louise (Krill) B.; m. Marian Gaber, Feb. 2, 1952; 1 dau., Anna. A.B., Albion Coll., 1933; B. Div., Yale U., 1936, Ph.D., 1938; D. Litt. (hon.), Ripon Coll., 1964; L.H.D., St. Michael's Coll., 1974. Instr. English Ohio State U., 1938-40; asst. prof. ch. history Vanderbilt U., 1940-43, assoc. prof., 1943-46; assoc. prof. ch. history Episcopal Theol. Sch., Cambridge, Mass., 1946-49; assoc. prof. English Ind. U., Bloomington, 1950-56; prof. English Ind. U., 1956-82, prof. emeritus, 1982-95; priest-in-charge St. Paul's Episcopal Ch., Franklin, Tenn., 1942-46; pres. Conf. on Christianity and Lit., 1977-82; vis. prof. English U. Western Ont., 1963-64, NYU, U. Notre Dame, U. Wash. Baylor U. Author: Marlowe's Tamburlaine: A Study in Renaissance Moral Philosophy, 1941, Shakespearean Tragedy: Its Art and Its Christian Premises, 1969; editor: Shakespeare's Christian Dimension: An Anthology of Commentary, 1994; editor, contbg. author: A companion to the Study of St. Augustine, 1955. Guggenheim fellow, 1958; recipient disting. alumni award Albion Coll., 1983; Kent fellow, 1937; Ford faculty fellow, 1954. Mem. Phi Beta Kappa, MLA (chmn. Shakespeare sect. 1951, chmn. drama sect. 1973, chmn. religious approaches to lit. div. 1981). Home: Bloomington Ind. Died Feb. 17, 1995; interred Edgerton, Ohio.

BATTISTA, ORLANDO ALOYSIUS, scientist, author, executive, inventor; b. Cornwall, Ont., Can., June 20, 1917; s. James L. and Carmel (Infante) B.; m. Helen Frances Keffer, Aug. 25, 1945; children: William Keffer, Elizabeth Ann. B.Sc., McGill U., Montreal, 1940; Sc.D. (hon.), St. Vincent Coll., Latrobe, Pa., 1955, Clarkson U., 1985. With Am. Viscose Corp., Phila., 1940-63, asst. dir. corporate research, 1961-63; asst. dir. central research dept. FMC Corp., Princeton, N.J., 1963-71; v.p. sci. and tech. Avicon, Inc., Ft. Worth, 1971-74; chmn., pres. Research Services Corp., 1974-95, O.A. Battista Research Inst.; editorial cons. McGraw-Hill Book Co., 1975-77; adj. prof. chemistry U. Tex., Arlington, 1976-79; editor, pub. Knowledge Mag., 1976-95; founder Olympiads of Knowledge Found., 1977-95. Author: How to Enjoy Work and Get More Fun Out of Life, 1957, God's World and You, 1957, Fundamentals of High Polymers, 1958, The Challenge of Chemistry, 1959, Commonscience in Everyday Life, 1960, Mental Drugs: Chemistry's Challenge to Psychotherapy, 1960, The Power to Influence People, 1960, Toward the Conquest of Cancer, 1961, Synthetic Fibers in Papermaking, 1964, Dictionary of Quotoons, 1966, Childish Questions?, 1973, Research for Profit, 1974, 2d edit., 1988, rev. hardcover, 1990, Microcrystal Polymer Science, 1975, Work For Profit, 1975, People Power, 1977, Speakers' Dictionary of Quotoons, 1977, Olympiads of Knowledge-1984, How to Enjoy Life 365 Days of the Year, 1984, 1989, Research for Profit, 1989, Microcrystal Polymer Sci., 1975, 2d edit., 1993, EPIGRAMERICA: 10,000 Quotations at Their Best, 1991, Grow Richer Through People Power, 1993, Uphill All the Way, 1993; contbr. articles to profl. jours. Recipient Napoleon Hill Gold Medal for Creative Achievement, 1986. Fellow Am. Inst. Chemists (Chem. Pioneer award 1969, pres., chief exec. officer 1977-79), N.Y. Acad. Scis., Nat. Assn. Sci. Writers; mem. Am. Acad. Achievement (Golden Plate award 1971), Am. Chem. Soc. (James T. Grady Gold Medal award 1973, 87, Creative Invention award 1983, Anselme Payen award 1985, Applied Poymer Sci. Gold medal 1987). Home: Fort Worth Tex. Died Oct. 3, 1995.

BATTISTI, FRANK JOSEPH, federal judge; b. Youngstown, Ohio, Oct. 4, 1922; s. Eugene and Jennie (Dalesandro) B. B.A., Ohio U., 1947; LL.B., Harvard U., 1950. Bar: Ohio 1950. Asst. atty. gen. Ohio, 1950; atty. adviser C.E. U.S. Army, 1951-52; 1st asst. dir. law Youngstown, 1954-59; judge Common Pleas Ct., Mahoning County, Ohio, 1959-61; judge U.S. Dist. Ct. (no. dist.) Ohio, Cleve., 1961-69, chief judge, 1969-94. Served with C.E., U.S. Army, 1943-45; ETO. Mem. ABA, Mahoning County Bar Assn., Cleve. Bar Assn., Am. Judicature Soc. Roman Catholic. Home: Cleveland Ohio Died Oct. 19, 1994.

BATTLE, WILLIAM RAINEY, insurance company executive; b. Santa Ana, Tex., July 10, 1924; s. Fred and Margaret (Rainey) B.; m. Jane Nichol Brown, Jan. 6, 1951; children: Rebecca Brown, William Lee. Student, U. Tex. at El Paso, 1941-43; B.A., U. Iowa, 1947, M.S., 1948. Mgr. actuarial dept. Nat. Life & Accident Ins. Co., Nashville, 1948-51; asso. actuary Southwestern Life Ins. Co., Dallas, 1951-58; actuary Shenandoah Life Ins. Co., Roanoke, Va., 1959-62, v.p., actuary, 1962-70, v.p. fin. ops., 1970-71, also bd.dirs., exec. v.p., 1971-72, pres., CEO, 1972-89, 93—, chmn. bd., 1989-93, chmn. exec. com., 1993—; bd. dirs. Chesapeake and Potomac Telephone Co. Va., Crestar Fin. Corp.; mem. advisory council Coll. Bus., Va. Poly. Inst. and State U., 1973-89. Mem. advisory bd. Salvation Army; bd. dirs. Community Hosp. of the Roanoke Valley, 1974—; area chmn. U.S. Savs. Bonds, 1986, 87; mem. Va. Coun. Econ. Edn., Richmond, 1979—, chmn.-elect, 1988, chmn., 1989; trustee Joint Coun. Econ. Edn., N.Y.C., 1987-90; mem. Va. Tech. Adv. Coun. Roanoke Valley, Blacksburg, 1987-90; bd. dirs. Blue Ridge Regional Health Care Coalition, 1984-89, Carilion Health System, 1990—. 1st lt. USAAF, 1943-46. Fellow Soc. Actuaries; mem. Middle Atlantic Actuarial Club (pres. 1967), Am. Acad. Actuaries, Roanoke Valley C. of C. (pres. 1973). Home: Roanoke Va. Deceased.

BAUDOUIN I (BAUDOUIN ALBERT CHARLES LEOPOLD AXEL MARIE GUSTAVE), King of Belgium; b. Brussels, Sept. 7, 1930; s. King Leopold III and Queen Astrid, Princess of Sweden; m. Dona Fabiola Mora y Aragon, Dec. 15, 1960. During invasion of Belgium by Germany, 1940, went to France, later to Spain, returning to Belgium, 1940; was removed to Germany, 1944, liberated after Allied invasion of Normandy, May 1945; lived in Switzerland until Leopold returned to Belgium as king, 1950; Prince Royal, Aug. 1950; held office as Chief of State until accession to throne; became king upon abdication of King Leopold, July 1951. Home: Brussels Belgium Died July 31, 1993.

BAYLES, SAMUEL HEAGAN, advertising agency executive; b. Port Jefferson, L.I., N.Y., Nov. 10, 1910; s. Edward Post and Mary Jane (Lerch) B.; m. Gladys Grinnell, Sept. 25, 1933 (dec. Dec. 1980); children: Elizabeth Jane Wheeler, Samuel Heagan, Christina Mary Callahan; m. Jane Curry, Feb. 11, 1984; step-children: John Romeo, Mary Elizabeth Schoeneman, Susan Martin, Katherine Dedejong, Steve Romeo, Peter Romeo. Student, Stony Brook Prep. Sch., 1928; B.A., Dartmouth, 1933. With Ruthrauff & Ryan, Inc., 1933-46, v.p., dir., co-dir. radio and television, 1940-46; a prin., chief exec. officer, founder chmn. Lintas Worldwide Inc. and predecessors, N.Y.C., 1946-96; mem. policy, ops. coms. SSC & B Lintas Internat., Ltd. Author and pub.: Modern Man's Quest for Identity, The Golden Book on Writing, The Power of Intersensory Selling; writer foreword to Slogans. Bd. overseers Hanover Inn, Dartmouth Coll.; chmn. bd. dirs. Advt. Research Found. Mem. Lauderdale Yacht Club, Phi Beta Kappa, Psi Upsilon. Home: Fort Lauderdale Fla. Died Jan. 30, 1996.

BAZARGAN, MEHDI, Iranian political organization administrator; b. Teheran, Iran, 1907; s. Abbasagholi and Sedigheh B.; m. Malak Tabatabai, 1939; 5 children. From asst. prof. to dean Teheran U.; former mng. dir. Nat. Oil Co. of Iran; mem. Nat. Resistance Movement of Iran, 1953; arrested, 1955, 57, 62, 78; mng. dir. YAD Consulting Engrs., Safyad Air Conditioning

Equipment Mfg. Co.; leader Freedom of Iran Movement; mem. Islamic Revolutionary Coun., 1979-81; former prime min. Govt. of Iran, M.P., 1981-84; gen. sec. Liberation Movement of Iran. Author over 60 books and pamphlets on engring., industry, sci. and thermodynamics theory. Mem. Assn. Def. of Freedom and Soveriegnty of Iranian People. Home: Teheran Iran Died Jan. 21, 1995.

BAZELON, DAVID LIONEL, judge; b. Superior, Wis., Sept. 3, 1909; m. Miriam M. Kellner, June 7, 1936; children: James A., Richard Lee. B.S. in Law, Northwestern U., 1931, LL.D., 1974; LL.D. (hon.), Colby Coll., 1966; LL.D., Boston U., 1969, Albert Einstein Coll. Medicine of Yeshiva U., 1972, U. So. Calif., 1977, Syracuse U., 1980, Georgetown U. Law Center, 1980, U. Santa Clara, 1982, Northeastern U. Sch. Law, 1982, John Jay Coll. Criminal Justice, 1982. Bar: practice in Ill 1932. Asst. atty. gen. U.S. Lands Div., 1946-49; judge U.S. Ct. of Appeals for D.C. Circuit, 1949-93, chief judge, 1962-78, sr. circuit judge, 1979-93; lectr. psychiatry Johns Hopkins U. Sch. Medicine, 1964-93; mem. nat. adv. mental health council USPHS, 1967-71; mem. U.S. mission on mental health, USSR, 1967; mem. adv. com. child devel. NRC, 1971-78; adv. bd. div. legal, ethical and ednl. aspects of medicine Inst. Medicine, Nat. Acad. Scis., 1977-78; mem. sci. adv. bd. Salk Inst. Alcohol Research Center, 1979-93; bd. dirs. Washington Sch. Psychiatry, Nat. Council Crime and Delinquency. Cons.: Children Today, 1973-93. Trustee Salk Inst. for Biol. Studies. Recipient Isaac Ray award Am. Psychiat. Assn., 1960. Hon. fellow Am. Psychiat. Assn. (Distinguished Service award 1975), Am. Coll. Legal Medicine; fellow Am. Acad. Arts and Scis.; mem. Am., Fed., D.C. bar assns., Am. Orthopsychiat. Assn. (pres. 1969-70, dir.), UN Assn. (panel on human rights and U.S. fgn. policy 1978-79), Am. Correctional Assn. (commn. on accreditation for corrections 1980-82), Inst. of Medicine of Nat. Acad. Scis. Democrat. Jewish. Club: Cosmos. Home: Washington D.C. Died Jan. 19, 1993.

BEAM, THOMAS ROGER, JR., physician, researcher; b. Elizabeth, N.J., July 12, 1946; s. Thomas Roger Sr. and Lillian (Norloff) B.; Janice Victoria Niesz, Aug. 15, 1970; children: Nancy Victoria, Thomas Roger III. AB in Biology, U. Pa., 1968, MD, 1972. Diplomate Am. Bd. Internal Medicine; bd. eligible infectious diseases; lic., N.Y. Intern in medicine SUNY, Buffalo, 1972-73, resident in medicine, 1973-74, chief teaching fellow, instr. in medicine, 1974-75, postdoctoral fellow, rsch. assoc., clin. instr. in medicine, 1975-77, asst. prof. medicine, 1977-84, clin. asst. prof. pharmacy, adj. clin. asst. prof. nursing, 1979-94, assoc. prof. medicine, 1984-92, prof., 1992-94, assoc. prof. microbiology, 1988-94; chief infectious diseases sec. VA Med. Ctr., Buffalo, 1977-88, assoc. chief of staff for edn., 1987-94; chmn. FDA Adv. Com. on Anti Infective Drug Products, 1989-94; chmn. antibiotic use and monical trials Com. IDSA, 1993-94; cons. J. N. Adam Devel. Ctr., N.Y. State Dept. Mental Retardation and Devel. Disabilities, 1981-94, West Seneca Devel. Ctr., 1982-94, Craig Devel. Ctr., 1986-94, Buffalo Gen. Hosp., 1984-92, Roswell Park Meml. Inst., 1985-91, N.Y. State Dept. Edn. AIDS program for Secondary Schs. in Western N.Y., Kaiser Permanente Health Care Program, San Francisco Control of Infections in Open Heart Surgery; lectr. nat. and internat. confs. Author: (with Allen, J.C.) Infectious Diseases for the House Officer, 1982, (with others) Clinical Guidelines for Antimicrobial Use, 1986; contbr. numerous chpts. to books including Antimicrobial Therapy, 1980, Primary Care, 1981, Conn's Current Therapy, 1984, Antibiotics and Chemotherapy Surgical Prophylaxis, 1985, Immunity and Illness in the Elderly, 1987, Principles and Practice of Nursing Home Care, 1989, Current Therapy in Infectious Diseases, 1990; editor-in-chief: Infections in Medicine, 1987-94, editorial rev. bd. 1984-87; editorial reviewer: JAMA, Archives of Internal Medicine, Jour. of Infectious Diseases, Respiratory Infections, Revs. of Infectious Diseases, Rsch. Communications in Chem. Pathology and Pharmagology, Am. Jour. Kidney Diseases; contbr. numerous articles to profl. publs. including European Jour. Clin. Microbiol. Infectious Diseases, Antimicrobic Newsletter, Am. Jour. Pub. Health, Archives Internal Medicine, Drug Info. Jour., Archives Dermatology, Archives Surgery, Am. Jour. Kidney Disease, Am. Jour. Med. Sci. Mem. of session N. Presbyn. Ch., 1985, bd. dirs. Amherst (N.Y.) Hockey Assn., 1986-88; chmn. Nat. Anti-Infective Adv. Com., 1990-94. Fellow ACP, Infectious Diseases Soc. of Am.; mem. AAAS, APHA, Am. Soc. Microbiology (v.p. Western N.Y. br. 1987-89, pres. 1989-91), Am. Fedn. Clin. Rsch., Assn. for Practitioners of Infection Control, Alliance for Prudent Use of Antibiotics, Am. Geriatrics Soc., Am. Coll. Clin. Pharmacology, Am. Acad. Med. Dirs.-Am. Coll. Physician Execs., Am. Soc. Clin. Pharmacology and Therapeutics, Am. Soc. Hosp. Pharmacists, Drug Info. Assn., N.Y. Acad. Sci., Buffalo Acad. Medicine. Home: Buffalo N.Y. Died Aug. 17, 1994.

BEAN, ELIZABETH HARRIMAN, county legislator, civic worker; b. Buffalo, Sept. 23, 1923; d. Lewis Gildersleeve and Grace (Bastine) Harriman; m. Charles Palmer Bean, Sept. 13, 1947; children: Katherine Bean Yancey, Bruce P., Margaret Bean Busby, Sarah Bean Amour, Gordon T. B.A. in History, Smith Coll., 1945; M.A. in Polit. Sci., SUNY-Albany, 1985; cert. in social welfare adminstrn. U. Ill., 1948. Claims adjustor Liberty Mutual Ins. Co., Washington, 1945; instr. U.S. Armed Forces Inst., Manila and Okinawa, 1946; social caseworker Family Service Agy., Urbana, Ill., 1948-50; legislator Schenectady County Legis., N.Y., 1976-90, chmn. ways and means com. 1980-85, majority leader, 1986-87, vice chmn., 1988-90; commr. Capital Dist. Regional Planning Commn., 1976-80; vice chmn. Schenectady County Indsl. Devel. Agy., 1986-90. Chmn., N.Y. State Citizens Info. Service, 1968-72; bd. govs. Albany Med. Ctr. Hosp., N.Y., 1977-90; bd. dirs. Sunnyview Hosp., Schenectady, 1979-90, N.E. Parent and Child Soc., Schenectady, 1981-90, Schenectady Symphony Orch., 1983-86, Schenectady Mus., 1986-87, Hospice of Schenectady, 1988-90; chmn. N.Y. State Legis. Forum, Albany, 1967-69, commn. budget com., 1983-90; chmn. blood svcs. com. ARC, Schenectady chpt., 1989-90. Recipient Pub. Service Recognition award YWCA, 1979; Susan B. Anthony award LWV, 1980. Mem. N.Y. State Suprs. and County Legislators Assn. (legis. chmn. 1982-87), N.Y. State Assn. of Counties, Bus. and Profl. Women's Club of Schenectady, AAUW (issues chmn. 1985-86), NAACP, Planned Parenthood. Republican. Episcopalian, LWV, Jr. League Schenectady. Clubs: Niskayuna Rep. (pres. 1984-86), Torch. Lodge: Zonta. Avocations: dancing, tennis, hiking. Died July 9, 1990. Home: Niskayuna N.Y.

BEATY, JAMES RALPH, minister; b. Evansville, Ind., May 16, 1929; s. James Clifford and Amanda Ann (Apgar) B.; m. Emma Jean Galloway, June 13, 1950; children: Ralph Norman, James Robert, Ann Lynn, Jerri Elizabeth, William Clifford. B.A., Franklin Coll. Ind., 1951, D.D., 1979. M.Div., So. Bapt. Theol. Sem., 1954; D.D., Judson Coll., 1970. Ordained to ministry Am. Baptist Chs. U.S.A., 1952. Asst. to pastor 1st Bapt. Ch., Evansville, 1948; pastor Exeter Ave. Bapt. Ch., Indpls., 1949-52, Veale Creek Bapt. Ch., Washington, Ind., 1952-54, 1st Bapt. Ch., Salem, Ind., 1954-57; field counselor Div. World Mission Support, Am. Bapt. Conv., 1958-66; exec. minister Indpls. Bapt. Assn., 1966-67; regional minister Am. Bapt. Chs. of the Great Rivers Region, 1977-94; assoc. gen. sec. Am. Bapt. Chs. in U.S.A., 1989-94. Mem. alumni coun. Franklin Coll., 1960-70; mem. Ch. Fedn. Greater Indpls., 1966-67; mem. Ill. Conf. Chs., 1977-94, Mo. Coun. of Chs., 1977-94; bd. dirs. Shurtleff Fund, 1977-94; trustee No. Bapt. Theol. Sem., 1977-94, Franklin Coll., 1982-94, Judson Coll., 1971; mem. Midwest commn. on ministry Am. Bapt. Conv., 1966-94, mem. Regional Exec. Ministers Coun., 1966-94, mem. Gen. Staff Coun., 1972-94. Recipient citations Christian Higher Edn. Challenge, Am. Bapt. Conv., 1960, Franklin Coll. Alumni Council, 1971, Ch. Fedn. Greater Indpls., 1975, Ind. Bapt. Conv., 1976, Indpls. Bapt. Assn., 1977; Alumni of Yr. citation So. Bapt. Theol. Sem., 1981; Certificate of Appreciation, World Mission Campaign of Am. Bapt. Conv., 1968. Mem. Lambda Chi Alpha. Died July 7, 1994. Home: Indianapolis Ind.

BEAUFORT, JOHN DAVID, journalist; b. Edmonton, Alta., Can., Sept. 23, 1912; came to U.S., 1922, naturalized, 1943; s. Ernest and Margaret Mary (Crawley) B.; m. Francesca Bruning, June 28, 1940. Student, Boston U., 1930-33, 35-39, Rollins Coll., 1933-35. With The Christian Science Monitor, Boston, 1930-33, 35-39; asst. reviewer The Christian Science Monitor, 1937-39, N.Y.C. drama and film critic, 1939-43, war corr. for Pacific, 1943-46, chief N.Y.C. news bur., 1946-50, arts and mag. editor, 1950-51, N.Y.C. drama and film critic, 1951-58, 59-61, arts-entertainment editor, 1959-61, chief London bur., 1962-65; feature editor The Christian Science Monitor, Boston, 1965-70; N.Y.C. drama critic The Christian Science Monitor, 1971-74, contbg. drama critic, feature writer, 1975—. Author: 505 Theatre Questions Your Friends Can't Answer; BBC European Service panelist, 1962-65. Recipient Critics award Dirs. Guild Am., 1961. Mem. N.Y. Drama Critics Circle, Am. Theatre Critics Assn., Drama Desk, Critics Circle of London (hon.), Nat. Theatre Conf. (hon.). Christian Scientist. Home: New York N.Y.

BEAVER, PAUL CHESTER, parasitologist, educator; b. Glenwood, Ind., Mar. 10, 1905; s. John Chester and Blanche Emma (Murphy) B.; m. Lela E. West, Oct. 16, 1931; 1 dau., Paula Jean Beaver Chipman. A.B., Wabash Coll., 1928, D.Sc. (hon.), 1963; M.S., U. Ill., 1929, Ph.D., 1935. Diplomate Am. Bd. Microbiology. Asst. zoology U. Ill., 1928-29, 31-34; instr. zoology U. Wyo., 1929-31; instr. biology Oak Park Jr. Coll., 1934-37; asst. prof. biology Lawrence Coll., 1937-42; investigator U. Mich. Biol. Sta., summer 1938, 39, 42; biologist Wis. Dept. Health, summer 1940, Ga. Dept. Pub. Health, 1942-45; asst. prof. parasitology Tulane U. Med. Sch., 1945-47, assoc. prof., 1947-52, prof., 1952-93, head dept. parasitology, 1956-71, William Vincent prof. tropical diseases and hygiene, 1958-76, prof. emeritus, 1976-93; dir. Internat. Center Med. Research and Tng. in Colombia, 1967-76; vis. prof. Eastern Mont. Normal Sch., summers 1935-37, Colo. State Coll., 1941, U. Mich., 1954-56, 58, U. Natal Med. Sch., Durban, South Africa, 1957; hon. vis. prof. Universidad del Valle, Cali, Colombia, 1970-76; cons. Ga. Dept. Pub. Health, 1946-53, USPHS Hosp., New Orleans, 1949-72, WHO, 1960-77; mem. com. standards and exams. Am. Bd. Microbiology, 1960-67; mem. commn. parasitic diseases Armed Forces Epidemiol. Bd., 1953-73, dir. commn. parasitic diseases, 1967-73; mem. Am. Found. Tropical Medicine, 1960-66; microbiology fellowships rev. panel NIH, 1960-63; mem. WHO expert com. on intestinal helminths, 1963, temp. adv., 1960, 61, 65, 66, 80, 81, 86, WHO expert panel on parasitic diseases, 1963-77; bd. sci. counselors Nat. Inst. Allergy and Infectious Diseases, NIH, 1966-68; mem. NIH parasitic diseases panel U.S.-Japan Coop. Med. Sci. Program, 1965-69; mem. adv. sci. bd. Gorgas Meml. Inst. Tropical and Preventive Medicine, 1970-91. Co-author: Animal Agents and Vectors of Human Disease, 5th edit., Craig & Faust's Clinical Parasitology, 9th edit.; contbg. author: Am. Pub. Health Assn.'s Control of Communicable Diseases in Man, 14th edit.; editorial bd. Am. Jour. Tropical Medicine and Hygiene, 1958-60, 67-70, editor, 1960-66, 72-84; asso. editor: Am. Jour. Hygiene, 1961-64, Jour. Parasitology, 1965-76, Am. Jour. Epidemiology, 1966-88; editorial bd.: Transactions of Am. Micros. Soc, 1966-73, Ceskoslovenska Parasitologie, 1966-72; contbr. articles to profl. jours. Fellow Am. Acad. Microbiology (bd. govs. 1966-75), AAAS; mem. Internat. Filariasis Assn. (hon.), Am. Soc. Tropical Medicine and Hygiene (councilor 1956-57, v.p. 1958, pres. 1969), Royal Soc. Tropical Medicine and Hygiene, Am. Soc. Parasitologists (councilor 1952-54, 56-59, pres. 1968), Am. Micros. Soc. (v.p. 1953, exec. com. 1955-59, 61-62), Soc. Exptl. Biology and Medicine, Am. Pub. Health Assn., Société Belge de Medicine Tropicale de Parasitologie et de Mycologie, Société de Pathologie Exotique (France; hon.), Sociedad Mexicana de Parasitologia (hon.), New Orleans Acad. Sci., Brazilian Soc. Tropical Medicine (hon.), Sigma Xi, Delta Omega, Alpha Omega Alpha (hon.). Club: Round Table (New Orleans). Home: Indianapolis Ind. Died Dec. 23, 1993; buried East Hill Cemetary, Rushville, I.N.

BEAVERS, ALVIN HERMAN, soil science educator; b. Addington, Okla., Jan. 1, 1913; s. Orlando Franklin and Willie (Morris) B.; m. Edith Sarah Moody, Dec. 24, 1940; children—James Franklin, John Alvin, Nancy Ann. B.S., N.Mex. State U., 1940; M.S. in Soil Sci; grad. asst., U. Mo., 1948, Ph.D., 1950. Soil scientist U.S. Dept. Agr., 1941-43; asst. prof. soil mineralogy and chemistry U. Ill., 1950-58, asso. prof., 1958-63, prof., 1963-83; prof. emeritus, 1983-95; cons. Served with U.S. Army, 1943-46. NSF grantee, lectr., 1967. Mem. Am. Soc. Agronomy, Sigma Xi, Alpha Zeta, Gamma Sigma Delta. Methodist. Home: Champaign Ill. Died May 22, 1995.

BECHANAN, WILLIAM BRYAN, electric utility company executive; b. Hodgenville, Ky., Oct. 18, 1925; s. Lucien Bryan and Ruby Jane B.; m. Ann L. Goins, May 10, 1947; children: Gary, Karen. BSEE, U. Ky., 1949. Asst. v.p. Ky. Utilities Co., Lexington; former v.p., pres. Old Diminion Power Co., Lexington, chmn., chief exec. officer, also bd. dirs.; bd. dirs. 1st Security Nat. Bank, Electric Energy, Inc., Edison Electric Inst., Ohio Valley Electric Corp. Mem. IEEE. Home: Lexington Ky. Died Nov. 3, 1995.

BECKER, RALPH ELIHU, lawyer, diplomat; b. N.Y.C., Jan. 29, 1907; s. Max Joseph and Rose (Becker) B.; m. Ann Marie Watters; children: William Watters, Donald Lee, Pamela Rose, Ralph Elihu Jr. LL.B., St. John's U., 1928; L.L.D., St. Johns U., 1983; LL.D. (hon.), South Eastern U., Washington. Bar: N.Y. 1929, U.S. Supreme Ct. 1940, D.C. 1949. Practice in Washington, 1948-86; of counsel Landfield and Becker, Washington, 1986-94; asst. counsel to U.S. Senate Subcom. Elections and Privileges, 1951; founding trustee, gen. counsel John F. Kennedy Ctr. for Performing Arts, 1958-76, hon trustee, 1980-94; U.S. ambassador to Honduras, 1976-77; Disting. lectr. Strom Thurmond Inst. Clemson U., S.C.; assoc. mem. coun. NASA Task Force for Comml. Use Space. Author: Miracle on the Potomac: Kennedy Center from the Beginning, 1990; co-author: Hail to the Candidate: Presidential Campaigns from Banners to Broadcast, 1992; also numerous booklets, articles on constl. law, ins., space law, atomic energy. Chmn. cultural devel. com. Met. Washington Bd. of Trade, 1958, former bd. dirs., gen. counsel, 1964-71; dir. emeritus, bd. dirs., gen. counsel, sec. Albert Schweitzer Found., 1955; pres. bd. dirs. Voice Found., 1976-94, Friends of LBJ Library; adv. com. L.B. Johnson Meml. Grove on the Park; founding dir., former gen. counsel Wolf Trap Found., 1964-76; mem. adv. com. Sec. Interior Wolf Trap Farm Park for Performing Arts; rep. of Pres. L.B. Johnson with rank spl. ambassador Independence Ceremonies, Swaziland, 1968; mem. Arctic Expdn. for polar bears Washington Zoo, 1962, Antarctic-South Pole Operation Deepfreeze, 1963; nat. chmn. Young Republicans, 1946-49; mem. Rep. Nat. Exec. Com., 1948-51, Pres.'s Inaugural Com., 1953, 57, 69, 73, 80, 83, Vice Pres. Rockefeller Inaugural Medal Com., Rep. Senatorial Inner Circle, fin. com. Rep. Eagle, Presdl. Task Force; charter mem. Nat. Rep. Congl. Com.; donor collection polit. Americana to Smithsonian Instn., Dartmouth Coll., St. Albans Sch., L.B.J. Library, U. Tex., Austin., Strom Thurmond Inst., Clemson U. (S.C.); founder, dir. Inter-Am. Music Festival; founding mem. Friends of the Nat. Zoo, 1958; mem. St. Albans Parish. Served to capt. JAGS, AUS, 1942-45 (ass't and acting judge advocate 30th Infantry Div.), ETO. Decorated Bronze Star medal U.S.; chevalier Legion of Honor; Croix de Guerre with palm France; Belgian Fourragere; Order Morazon 1st class Honduras; chevalier and officer So. Cross of Brazil;

Knighthood of Order of Dannebrog, Denmark; Gt. Cross for Meritorious Services to Austrian Republic; Royal Order de Vasa Sweden; Netherlands Resistance Meml. Cross; Order Rising Sun Japan; Vets. of Battle of Bulge; recipient Smithsonian Instn. Benefactor medal, 1975; Antarctic Service medal; Mt. Becker Antarctic; honored with award by OAS, 1968, Man of Yrs. award Metropolitan (Wash.) Bd. Trade, 1989; N.Y. State Good Conduct medal. Fellow Corcoran Gallery Art, Aspen Inst. Humanistic Studies; mem. ABA (mem. major coms., del. Internat. Bar Assn. com. meeting Monte Carlo 1954, Oslo, 1956, chmn. Vienna post conv. ABA meeting London 1957), D.C. Bar Assn., N.Y. State Bar Assn., Westchester County Bar Assn., Internat. Bar Assn., Fed. Bar Assn. (nat. council), Am. Law Inst. (life mem.), 30th Inf. Div. Assn. (pres. 1958), U.S. Capitol Hist. Soc. (founding dir.), N.Y. State Soc. (pres. 1963-64), Hist. Soc. Washington, Arctic Polar Inst. (hon.), Smithsonian Assn. (nat. mem.), Supreme Ct. Hist. Soc. (founding dir., mem. exec. com., chmn. ann. meetings 1978, 79, 80), Am. Fedn. Musicians (hon.), James Smithson Soc. of Smithsonian Assocs. (life), Friends of the Folger Library, Friends of Nat. Zoo (founding), Ctr. For Study of Presidency, Dwight D. Eisenhower Soc. (hon. trustee), Nat. Wildflower Research Ctr., Dacor-Bacon House Found., Choral Arts Soc. (hon.), Coun. Am. Ambs., Am. Fgn. Service Officers Assn., Diplomatic and Consular Officers Ret., Capitol Hill Club, Masons (32 degree). Home: Washington D.C. Died Aug. 24, 1994.

BECKER, WILLIAM HENRY, federal judge; b. Brookhaven, Miss., Aug. 26, 1909; s. William Henry and Verna (Lilly) B.; m. Geneva Moreton, June 9, 1932; children: Frances Becker Mills, Patricia Becker Hawkins, Nancy Becker Hewes, Geneva Becker Jacks, William Henry III. Student, Whitworth Coll., 1926-27, La. State U., 1927-28; LLB, U. Mo., 1932. Bar: Miss. 1930, Mo. 1932, U.S. Supreme Ct. 1937. Assoc. Clark, Boggs, Cave & Peterson, Columbia, Mo., 1932-36, Clark & Becker, Columbia, 1936-44, 46-61; judge U.S. Dist. Ct. (we. dist.) Mo., 1961—, chief judge, 1965-77, sr. judge, 1977—; judge U.S. Temp. Emergency Ct. Appeals, 1977—; spl. master Supreme Ct. of U.S., 1979-83; counsel to Gov. Lloyd Stark in Kansas City Criminal Investigation, 1938-39, Judge Allen C. Southern, 1939, Gov. Forrest C. Donnell, 1941-42; spl. asst. to dir. econ. stblzn. Office of War Mobilization and Reconversion, Washington, 1945-46; spl. commr. Mo. Supreme Ct., 1954-58; spl. counsel Mo. Ins. Dept., 1936-44; chmn. Mo. Supreme Ct. Com. to Draft Rules of Civil Procedure for Mo., 1952-59, mem. coordinating com. for multiple litigation, 1962-68, vice chmn., 1967-68; com. on operation of jury system, chmn. subcom. drafting Jury Selection and Svc. Act, 1968; mem. jud. panel on multidist. litigation Jud. Conf. U.S., 1968-77, mem. com. on operation of jury system, 1966-68; faculty Fed. Jud. Ctr. seminars and workshops for U.S. Dist. judges, 1968081. Bd. editors: Original Manual for Complex Litigation, 1968-85 ; chmn., 1977-81. Lt. with USN, 1944-45, PTO; with Res. 1944-52. Decorated Phillipines Liberation Ribbon with Bronze Star, Naval Commendation Ribbon and Medal for Mil. Merit. Fellow Am. Bar Found., Am. Coll. Trial Lawyers, Am. Coll. Probate Counsel; mem. ABA, Am. Judicature Soc., Fed. Bar Assn. (award 1977), Mo. Bar Assn., Kansas City Bar Assn. (spl. award 1977), Lawyers Assn. Kansas City (Charles Evans Whittaker award 1977). Home: Columbia Mo.

BECKMAN, MILLARD WARREN, investment securities company executive; b. Lodi, Calif., Jan. 8, 1926; s. Sherwood W. and Christine (Koenig) B.; m. Lucille Stark, May 23, 1948; children—Bruce, Don, Joan. Student, Am. Inst. Banking, also Stockton Jr. Coll., Sacramento Jr. Coll., 1949-60. Founder Beckman & Co., 1954, pres., chmn. bd., 1961-72, pres., dir., 1972-95; chmn. bd., v.p. Beckman Capital Corp., 1972-95. Home: Lodi Calif. Died Sept. 28, 1995.

BECKWITH, WILLIAM HUNTER, clergyman; b. Noank, Conn., Oct. 8, 1896; s. Walter Howard and Annie Elizabeth (Keddy) B. Mus.B. magna cum laude, N.Y. U., 1929, A.M., 1931, Ph.D., 1936; postgrad., U. Poitiers, France. Organist and choir master Ch. of the Transfiguration, N.Y.C., 1917-18, Trinity Ch., Lenox, Mass., 1918-19, Trinity Chapel (Trinity Parish), N.Y.C., 1919-43; instr. French Washington Sq. Coll., N.Y. U., 1931-36; instr. French Hofstra Coll., 1936-38, asst. prof., 1938-39, assoc. prof., 1939-40; prof. French and dean of Coll., 1941-48; prof., past dir. div. gen. studies Coll. Agr. and Mechanic Arts, Universidad de Puerto Rico, Mayaguez, P.R.; ordained priest Protestant Episcopal Ch. of U.S., 1954; asst. San Andrés Episcopal Mission, Mayaguez; ordained priest Antiochian Orthodox Christian Ch., 1981. Author: The Formation of the Esthetic of Romain Rolland, 1935. Served in U.S. Navy, 1918. Fellow Am. Guild Organists; mem. MLA, AAUP, Eastern Assn. Deans, Phi Beta Kappa. Republican. Home: Clearwater Fla. Died Feb. 3, 1996.

BEDELL, RALPH CLARION, psychologist, educator; b. Hale, Mo., June 4, 1904; s. Charles E. and Jennie (Eaton) B.; m. Stella Virginia Bales, Aug. 19, 1929 (dec. 1968); m. Ann Barclay Sorency, Dec. 21, 1968 (dec. 1975); m. Myra Jervey Hoyle, Feb. 14, 1976. BS in Edn., Cen. Mo. State U., 1926; AM, U. Mo., 1929, PhD, 1932. Tchr. Hale Pub. Schs., 1922-24; tchr. sci. and math. S.W. High Sch., Kansas City, Mo., 1926-30, 32-33; asst. prof. ednl. psychology N.E. Mo. State U., 1933-34, prof. ednl. psychology, 1934-37, dir. Bur. Guidance, 1934-37; dean, faculty and student pers. Cen. Mo. State U., 1937-38; freshman counselor, dir. reading labs., assoc. prof. ednl. psychology and measurements U. Nebr., 1938-46, prof., counselor educator, 1946-50; chmn. dept. psychology and edn. Sch. Social Scis. and Pub. Affairs, Am. U., Washington, 1950-52; dir. program planning and rev. br. internat. div. U.S. Office Edn., HEW, 1952-55; sec.-gen. South Pacific Commn. Noumea, New Caledonia, 1955-58; dir. counseling and guidance insts. br. U.S. Office of Edn., Washington, 1959-67; prof. edn., dir. nat. edn. studies U. Mo., Columbia, 1967, prof. emeritus, 1974—; rsch. assoc. Ctr. for Ednl. Improvement, 1974-75; cons. faculty devl. Lincoln U. of Mo., 1976-77; mem. study group to Surinam, 1954; adviser U.S. del. UN, 1953, 62; U.S. del. Caribbean Commn. and West Indian Conf., 1952, 53; cons. Stephens Coll., Columbia, 1974; chmn. tech. com. access and retention for master planning Mo. Coordinating Bd. Higher Edn., 1976-78; edn. cons. Prince of Songkla U., Pattani, Thailand, 1980-88. Author or co-author sch. textbooks and achievement tests in sci. and aviation, 1930-40; dir. tng. manuals preparation Chief of Naval Air Tng., 1941-45; contbr. articles to profl. jours. V.p., trustee Sigma Tau Gamma Found., 1972-74; co-founder (with Myra Hoyle Bedell) Bedell Fund to Support Sch. Counseling; dean Sigma Tau Gamma Leadership Inst., 1973. Comdr. USNR, 1942-46. Named Honored Alumnus, Cen. Mo. State U., 1971, Disting. Alumnus Cen. Mo. State U., 1984, Outstanding Contbn. award Assn. Counselor Edn. and Supervision, 1967, Disting. Contbn. award, 1984, Award of Merit, Mo. Assn. Sch. Librarians, 1971, Outstanding Achievement and Meritorious Service in Edn. citation U. Mo., Columbia Alumni Assn., 1979, Profl. award Mo. Coll. Personnel Assn., 1982, Appreciation award Prince of Songkla U., 1986. Fellow Am. Psychol. Assn. (Disting. Sr. Contbr. Div. 17 1985); mem. NEA (life), AACD (life), Nat. Soc. for Study Edn. (life), Mil. Order World Wars (perpetual), Am. Assn. Higher Edn., Mo. Tchrs. Assn., Mo. Guidance Assn. (Merit award 1971), Mo. Assn. Counseling and Devel., Kappa Delta Pi, Sigma Tau Gamma (Top Tau 1970, Wilson C. Morris fellow 1982, pres. Wilson C. Morris fellowship 1985-86, Soc. Seventeen Disting. Achievement award 1985), Explorers Club, Army and Navy Club, Country Club Mo. Home: Columbia Mo.

BEERY, NOAH, actor; b. N.Y.C., Aug. 10, 1916; s. Noah and Marguerite Beery; m. Lisa Beery; children: Maxine, Melissa, Bucklind; 3 stepchildren. Student, North Hollywood (Calif.) High Sch. Actor: (films) Father and Son, Road Back, 1937, Only Angels Have Wings, 1939, Doolins of Oklahoma, 1949, Davy Crockett, Indian Scout, 1950, Savage Horde, Rocketship XM, 1950, Two Flags West, 1950, Last Outpost, 1951, Cimarron Kid, 1951, Wagons West, Story of Will Rogers, 1952, Wings of the Hawk, 1953, War Arrow, 1953, Tropic Zone, 1953, The Yellow Tomahawk, 1954, Black Dakotas, 1954, White Feather, 1955, Jubal, 1956, Fastest Gun Alive, 1956, Journey to Shiloh, 1968, Heaven with a Gun, 1969, Walking Tall, 1973, The Spikes Gang, 1974, The Best Little Whorehouse in Texas, 1982, Waltz Across Texas, others, (TV series) Circus Boy, 1956-57, 58, Riverboat, 1960-61, Hondo, 1967, Doc Elliot, 1973-74, The Rockford Files, 1974-80, (TV miniseries) The Bastards, 1978, (TV movies) Sidekick, 1974, Savages, 1974, Francis Gary Powers, 1976, Gridlock, 1980, The Capture of Grizzly Adams, 1982, The Yellow Rose. Home: Tehachapi Calif. Died Nov. 1, 1994.

BEGUN, SEMI JOSEPH, management consultant; b. Free City of Danzig, Dec. 2, 1905; came to U.S., 1935; s. Wolf Begun and Elizabeth Wishniak; m. Ruth Natalie Weltmann. MSEE, Inst. Tech., Charlottenburg, Germany, 1929, D in Elec. Engring., 1933. Registered profl. engr., Ohio. Sr. devel. engr. Guided Radio Inc., N.Y.C., 1935-37; v.p. Acoustic Cons. Inc., N.Y.C., 1937-38; v.p. engring. Brush Devel. Co., Cleve., 1938-51; v.p., mem. bd. dirs. Clevite Corp., Cleve., 1951-69, Gould Inc., Cleve., 1969-70; pres., chief exec. officer Auctor Assocs. Inc., Cleve., 1970-95; bd. dirs. Pyromatics Inc., Bally Gaming Internat., Las Vegas; cons. various corps. in Cleve., Pitts., Chgo.; lectr. in field. Author: Magnetic Recording; over 50 patents in field; contbr. articles to tech. jours. Founder, pres. Soc. for Prevention of Violence, Cleve., 1983-95, Begun Inst. for Studies of Violence and Aggression, John Carroll U., University Heights, Ohio, 1974-84. Recipient Presdl. Cert. Merit Nat. Def. Rsch. Com., 1948; Emil Berliner award Audio Engring. Soc., 1960, John Potts Meml. award, 1960; inducted into Ohio Sci., Tech. and Industry Hall of Fame, 1993. Fellow IEEE (life), Acoustical Soc.; mem. Astron. Soc. Home: Cleveland Heights Ohio Died Jan. 5, 1995.

BEHL, WOLFGANG, sculptor, retired educator; b. Berlin, Germany, Apr. 13, 1918; came to U.S., 1939, naturalized, 1947; s. C.F.W. and Ellida (Schmidt) B.; m. Lula Marie Brock, June 20, 1948; 1 dau., Elizabeth. Student, Acad. Fine Arts, Berlin, 1936-39, R.I. Sch. Design, 1939-40. Mem. faculty Richmond Profl. Inst., Coll. William and Mary, 1945-53; prof. Hartford Art Sch., U. Hartford, Conn., 1955-83, prof. emeritus, 1987-94; Bd. dirs. Sculptors Guild, N.Y.C.; mem. adv. bd. Internat. Sculptors Conf., Washington. Exhibited in one-man shows at Bertha Schaefer Gallery, 1950, 55, 63, 68, 73, New Britain Mus. Am. Art, 1969, Rosenfield Gallery, Phila., 1979, others; exhibited in group shows at Plastics U.S.A.-USSR, 1960, Carnegie Inst., 1964, Pa. Acad., 1964, Fogg Mus., 1966, Greater Hartford Jewish Ctr., 1994, Chase Freeman Gallery; represented in museum and pvt. collections; represented in book Masters of Wood Sculpture, 1980. Nat. Inst. Arts and Letters grantee, 1963. Mem. Nat. Sculpture Soc. Home: Hartford Conn. Died Oct. 17, 1994.

BEIGEL, ALLAN, psychiatry educator; b. Hamilton, Ohio, Apr. 4, 1940; s. Alfred and Mary (Schachter) B.; children: Jennifer, Jill; m. Nancy Sher. A.B., Harvard U., Cambridge, Mass., 1961; M.D., Albert Einstein Coll., Bronx, 1965. Diplomate Am. Bd. Psychiatry and Neurology. Intern Mount Sinai Hosp., N.Y.C., 1965-66, resident in psychiatry, 1966-68; clin. assoc. Nat. Inst. Mental Health, Rockville, Md., 1968-70; dir. So. Ariz. Mental Health Ctr., Tucson, 1970-83; prof. psychiatry U. Ariz., Tucson, 1970-96, v.p., 1983-93; vis. prof. psychiatry Harvard Med. Sch., 1994-95; cons. in field; mem. Pres.'s Commn. on Mental Health, 1977. Author: Community Mental Health, 1972, Understanding Human Behavior for Effective Police Work, 1975, 81, 90, Beneath the Badge, 1978; contbr. articles to profl. jours., chpts. to books. Served as surgeon USPHS, 1968-70. Recipient Copper Letters, City of Tucson, 1973, 77, 89. Fellow Am. Psychiat. Assn. (v.p. 1987-89), Am. Coll. Psychiatrists (v.p. 1987-89, pres.-elect 1989-90, pres. 1990-91); mem. NAS, AMA (chmn., sec. coun. on psychiatry 1985-88), Group for Advancement Psychiatry (sec. 1981-89, pres.-elect 1989-91, pres. 1991-93), Nat. Coun. Community Mental Health (pres. 1976-77), Inst. Medicine, World Psychiat. Assn. (sec. 1989-96). Home: Tucson Ariz. Died June 22, 1996.

BELDEN, H. REGINALD, lawyer; b. Arnold, Pa., Dec. 23, 1907; s. Arthur Ernest and Otilla Christiana (Sode) B.; m. Irene, Jan 15, 1938; children: H. Reginald Jr., Marcia I. Belden Lappas. BS in Econs., Thiel Coll., 1929, LLD, 1989; postgrad., U. Pa., 1932. Bar: Pa. 1933, U.S. Dist. Ct. (we. dist.) Pa. 1943, U.S. Ct. Appeals (3d cir.) 1954, U.S. Supreme Ct. 1960. Ptnr. Belden, Belden, Persin, Johnston & Zuzik, Greensburg, Pa. Author: (with others) Lawyers Professional Liability, 1981. Recipient Disting. Alumnus award Thiel Coll., 1973. Fellow Am. Bar Found. (life), Pa. Bar Found. (life), Am. Coll. Trial Lawyers (state chmn. 1975-76); mem. ABA (mem. Ho. Dels. 1971-72), Pa. Bar Assn. (pres. 1971-72, mem. Ho. Dels.), Westmoreland Bar Assn. (pres. 1961), Westmoreland Acad. Trial Lawyers (co-founder, pres. 1969-70), Internat. Assn. Def. Counsel (state chmn. 1972-86), Nat. Conf. Bar Pres., Jud. Conf. for 3rd cir. U.S. (life), Def. Rsch. Inst., Pa. Def. Inst., Greensburg (Pa.) Country Club, Pinehurst (N.C.) Country Club, Belleair Country Club (Fla.), James Wilson Law Club, Delta Sigma Phi. Republican. Lutheran. Home: Greensburg Pa. Died March 27, 1993.

BELL, GEORGE DE BENNEVILLE, investment banker; b. Phila., Feb. 6, 1924; s. John Cromwell and Sarah (Baker) B.; m. Roberta Howard McVey, May 2, 1953; children: Sophie Bell Ayres, George de Benneville Jr., James T. BA, Yale U., 1948; postgrad., U. Pa. Law Sch., 1948-49. With Drexel & Co., Phila., 1949-66, ptnr., 1956-66; sr. v.p., dir. Drexel Harriman Ripley, Phila., 1967-70; v.p. Dillon Read & Co., N.Y.C., 1971-73; sr. v.p., dir. Janney Montgomery Scott Inc., Phila., 1974-78, exec. v.p., dir., 1978-82, co-chmn., dir., 1982-90, chmn., 1991—; vice-chmn. JMS Resources, Phila.; v.p. K.B. Equities, Inc.; mem. regional firms adv. com. N.Y. Stock Exch., 1983-86; bd. govs. Am. Stock Exch., Inc.; bd. dirs. Airgas, Inc., AccuLase, Inc. Trustee The Lankenau Hosp., Phila., The Lankenau Med. Rch. Ctr., Fox Chase Cancer Ctr., Inst. for Cancer Rsch., Main Line Health, Inc., Soc. Home for Children, 1956-66. Served as 2d lt. USAF, 1943-45. Mem. Investment Bankers Assn. (past v.p., bd. dirs.), Assn. Stock Exch. Firms (past gov.), Phila. Stock Exch. (past vice chmn., bd. dirs.), Bond Club Phila. (past. gov.), Bond Club N.Y. (past gov.), Racquet Club (pres. 1976-79), Pine Valley Golf Club, Links Club, Augusta Nat. Golf Club, Merion Cricket Club, The Courts Club, Gulph Mills Golf Club. Republican. Episcopalian. Home: Gladwyne Pa.

BELL, J. A. GORDON, retired banker; b. Rivers, Man., Can., Aug. 16, 1929; s. John Edwin and Mary MacDonald (McIlraith) B. LLD (hon.), Brock U., St. Mary's U. With Bank of N.S., from 1948, dep. chief gen. mgr., 1969-72, exec. v.p., chief gen. mgr., 1972-79, pres., COO, 1989-96, dep. chmn., 1982-96; bd. dirs. Bank of N.S., Toronto; ret.; bd. dirs. Bosch Inc., Cameco Corp., Devtek Corp., Hudson's Bay Co., D.A. Stuart Ltd. Gov. St. Mary's U.; trustee Spencer Hall Fedn. Mem. Nat. Club, Toronto Club. Home: Toronto Can. Died Mar. 1996.

BELL, JAMES FREDERICK, physicist, educator; b. Melrose, Mass., Apr. 21, 1914; s. John Joseph and Hester (Walsh) B.; m. Perra Somers, Aug. 30, 1940; children: Jane Elizabeth, Christopher James. BA in Math., NYU, 1940. Design engr. Arma Corp., 1940-45; prof. solid mechanics Johns Hopkins U., Balt., 1945-85; prof. emeritus Johns Hopkins U., 1979-95, vis. prof.

1985-95; faculty physics of music Peabody Conservatory Music, 1985-95; vis. prof. U. Va., summers 1951, 52; sr. visitor dept. applied math., theoretical physics U. Cambridge (Eng.), 1962-63; ricercatore associato Istituto Matematico U. Bologna, Italy, 1970-71; sr. visitor Inst. Math., Rumanian Acad. Sci., 1970; invited lectr. in over 70 univs. in U.S., Europe, Africa and Asia; cons. U.S. Govt. Author: The Physics of Large Deformation of Crystalline Solids, Springer Tracts in Natural Philosophy, vol. 14, 1968, Experimental Foundations of Solid Mechanics, Handbuch der Physik, vol. VIa/1, 1973, republished as Mechanics of Solids, I, 1984, Russian translation, 1984; sr. editor Internat. Jour. Plasticity, 1985-95; also numerous sci. papers on physics of solids; contbr.; sect. to Grove's Dictionary of Music and Musicians, 1981. Recipient Pres.'s medal Johns Hopkins U. Fellow Am. Acad. Mechanics, Soc. Exptl. Mechanics (B.J. Lazan award 1974, William J. Murray medal 1989); mem. AAUP, Soc. Natural Philosophy, Chamber Music Soc. (bd. govs. 1957-95). Home: Baltimore Md. Died Jan. 15, 1995.

BELL, TERREL HOWARD, education educator; b. Lava Hot Springs, Idaho, Nov. 11, 1921; s. Willard Dewain and Alta (Martin) B.; m. Betty Ruth Fitzgerald, Aug. 1, 1957; children—Mark Fitzgerald, Warren Terrel, Glenn Martin, Peter Fitzgerald. B.A., So. Idaho Coll. Edn., 1946; M.S., U. Idaho, 1953; Ed.D. (Ford fellow), U. Utah, 1961. Tchr. high sch. chemistry and physics Eden, Idaho, 1946-47; supt. schs. Rockland (Idaho) Valley Schs., 1947-54, Star Valley Sch. Dist., Afton, Wyo., 1955-57, Weber County (Utah) Sch. Dist., 1957-62; prof. sch. adminstrn. Utah State U., 1962-63; supt. pub. instruction State of Utah, 1963-70; assoc. commr. for regional office coordination U.S. Office Edn., HEW, 1970, acting commr. edn., 1970, dep. commr. sch. systems, 1971, commr. edn., 1974-76; supt. Granite Sch. System, Utah, 1971-74; commr. higher edn. State of Utah, Salt Lake City, 1976-81; sec. Dept. Edn., Washington, 1981-85; prof. U. Utah, 1985-96; chmn. Utah Textbook Commn., Utah Course Study Commn.; mem. Utah Land Bd.; exec. officer Utah Bd. Edn. Author: novel The Prodigal Pedagogue, 1956, Effective Teaching: How to Recognize and Reward Competence, 1962, A Philosophy of Education for the Space Age, 1963, Your Child's Intellect: A Guide to Home-Based Preschool Education, 1972, A Performance Accountability System for School Administrators, 1974, Active Parent Concern, 1976, The 13th Man: A Reagan Cabinet Memoir, 1988, How To Shape Up Our Nation's Schools, 1991, Keys to Your Child's Intellect, 1992. Served with USMCR, 1942-46, PTO. recipient Harold W. McGraw, Jr. Prize in Education, McGraw-Hill, 1994. Mem. Am. Assn. Sch. Adminstrs., Council Chief State Sch. Officers, Phi Delta Kappa. Mem. Ch. Jesus Christ of Latter-day Saints. Home: Salt Lake City Utah Died June 22, 1996.

BELLAMY, ROBERT K., lawyer; b. San Francisco, July 6, 1950; s. John Benton and Marion (Kendrick) B.; m. Suzanne Sahagan, June 2, 1974; children: Erica Michelle, Blair Alyssa. BA cum laude in Econs., U. Rochester, 1972; JD, U. Va., 1975. Bar: U.S. Dist. Ct. (so. dist.) Ind. 1975, U.S. Ct. Appeals (7th cir.) 1978, U.S. Ct. Appeals (6th cir.) 1980, U.S. Dist. Ct. (no. dist.) Ind. 1992. Assoc. Barnes & Thornburg, Indpls., 1975-81, ptnr., 1982-94, chmn. dept. labor and employment, mem. coms. mgmt., long range planning; bd. dirs. Hillenbrand Industries, Inc., Batesville, Ind., mem. coms. audit, compensation and performance compensation; presenter numerous seminars. Contbr. articles to profl. jours. Trustee Indpls. Mus. Art, 1989-94, instl. advancement com., chmn. human resources com.; bd. dirs. Hooverwood/Indpls. Jewish Home, 1993; regional mgr. ann. giving program U. Va. Sch. Law. Named Sagamore of Wabash Gov. Ind., 1993. Mem. ABA (labor and employment law sect., litigation sect., com. practice and procedure under Nat. Labor Rels. Act), Ind. State Bar Assn. (labor and employment law sect., chmn. 1983-84), Ind. State C. of C. (legis. com.), Seventh Cir. Bar Assn., Indpls. C. of C. (substance abuse task force). Home: Indianapolis Ind. Died June 5, 1994; buried Crown Hill Cemetary, Indpls., Ind.

BELLOWS, CHARLES SANGER, lawyer; b. Mpls., Oct. 20, 1915; s. Henry Adams and Mary (Sanger) B. A.B., Harvard U., 1937; LL.B., Yale U., 1940. Bar: N.Y. 1941, Minn. 1946. Ptnr. Best & Flanagan, Mpls., 1946-86, of counsel, 1987-93. Pres., Mpls. Citizens League, 1952, Minn. Orch. Assn., 1959-62; chmn. bd. dirs. Abbott Northwest Hosp., 1971-74; bd. dirs. Lifespan, Inc., 1982-87; life mem. bd. dirs. Minn. Orch. Assn., 1959-93; hon. trustee Macalester Coll. Served with AUS, 1941-46. Mem. Am., N.Y. State, Minn., Hennepin County bar assns. Home: Minneapolis Minn. Died June 12, 1993.

BELLOWS, JOHN G., ophthalmologist; b. N.Y.C., Aug. 22, 1906; s. Louis G. and Rose (Goldfreed) B.; m. Mary Trueblood, Apr. 4, 1945; children: Randall, Diane, Deborah, Sandra, David. B.S., U. Ill., 1927, M.D., 1930; M.S., Northwestern U., 1935, Ph.D., 1938. Diplomate: Am. Bd. Ophthalmology. Intern Cook County Hosp., Chgo., 1929-30; resident Cook County Hosp., 1930-33; practice medicine, specializing in ophthalmology Chgo., 1933-93; clin. prof. ophthalmology Chgo. Med. Sch.; asso. prof. ophthalmology Northwestern U.; prof. ophthalmology Cook County Grad. Sch. Medicine, 1946; attending ophthalmologist Cook County Hosp., 1946-93, Columbus, Henrotin hosps., 1960-93; dir. Mediphone (med. consultation by telephone); vis. prof. U. Central de Venezuela; founder, exec. sec. Soc. for Cryo-surgery; hon. pres. El Consejo Directivo del Instituto de Oftalmologicas, Caracas. Author: Cataract and Anomalies Crystalline Lens, 1944, Cryotherapy of Ocular Diseases, 1966, Contemporary Ophthalmology (honoring Sir Stewart Duke-Elder), 1972, Cataract and Abnormalities of the Lens, 1975, Glaucoma: Contemporary International Concepts, 1980; chief editor: Jour. Ocular Surgery, Annals of Ophthalmology, Glaucoma, Comprehensive Therapy; editorial bd.: Excerpta Medica, Klinische Monatsblatter fur Augenheilkunds. Served to lt. col. AUS, World War II; chief eye sect. Wakeman Gen. Hosp. Ind. Recipient Lucien Howe medal U. Buffalo, 1938. Fellow A.C.S., Internat. Coll. Surgeons; mem. Am. Assn. Research Ophthalmology, N.Y. Soc. Clin. Ophthalmology, Pan Am. Med. Assn., Pan-Pacific Surg. Assn., Internat., Am. acads. ophthalmology, Soc. Cryobiology, Soc. Française D'Ophtalomologie, Am. Assn. Ophthalmology, Academia Ophtalmologica Internationalis, Am. Soc. Contemporary Ophthalmology (dir., founder), Internat. Glaucoma Congress (founder, dir.), Am. Soc. Contemporary Medicine and Surgery (dir., founder), Internat. Assn. Ocular Surgeons (founder, dir. 1981), Royal Soc. Medicine. Home: Chicago Ill. Died Feb. 1, 1993.

BELLUSCHI, PIETRO, architect; b. Ancona, Italy, Aug. 18, 1899; naturalized, 1929; s. Guido and and Camilla (Dogliani) B.; m. Helen Hemmila, Dec. 1, 1934 (dec. Mar. 1962); children: Peter, Anthony; m. Marjorie Bruckner, June 25, 1965. Student, U. Rome Sch. Engring., 1919-22; doctor's degree in civil engring.; C.E., Cornell U.; C.E. (Italian scholarship), 1924; LLD (hon.), Reed Coll., Portland, Oreg., 1950; ScD (hon.), Christian Bros. Coll., Memphis, 1957; D.F.A. (hon.), U. R.I., 1963, U. Mass., 1967, U. Portland, 1977, Pacific N.W. Coll. Art, 1983, Notre Dame U., 1985, Whitman Coll., 1986; D.Arch. (hon.), U. Mich., 1967; L.H.D. (hon.), Oklahoma City U., 1968; DFA (hon.), George Fox Coll., 1992. Insp. housing devel. Rome, 1923; elec. engr. work Bunker Hill and Sullivan Mining Co., Kellogg, Idaho, 1924-25; draftsman A.E. Doyle (architect), Portland, 1925-27; chief designer A.E. Doyle & Assoc. (architects), 1927-42, mem. firm, 1932-42; dean, architecture and planning Mass. Inst. Tech. Sch., 1951-65; practice architecture under own name Portland, 1943-90; mem. Nat. Fine Arts Commn., 1950; adviser State Dept. on design fgn. bldgs.; Am. del. conv. Inst. Intellectual Coop. of League of Nations, Madrid, 1934. Past pres. bd. trustees Portland Art Mus. N.A.; past trustee Boston Mus. Fine Arts. Recipient Nat. medal of the Arts, 1991. Fellow AIA (Gold medal 1972), Danish Royal Acad. Fine Arts, Am. Acad. Arts and Scis., Nat. Inst. Arts and Letters (v.p.); mem. NAD. Home: Portland Oreg. Died Feb. 14, 1994.

BELLWOOD, SHERMAN JEAN, arbitrator, consultant, retired judge; b. Sugar City, Idaho, June 13, 1917; s. Ollie J. and Myrtle J. (Polson) B.; m. Eleanor Jane Lee, May 14, 1938 (dec.); 1 child, Sherman Lee (dec.). AB, U. Idaho, 1938; JD, U. Mich., 1941; grad., Nat. Coll. State Judiciary, 1969. Bar: Idaho 1942. Pvt. practice Hailey, Idaho, 1942-47, Rupert, Idaho, 1947-57, 60-66; pros. atty. Minidoka County, 1951-57; judge 11th Jud. Dist., Idaho, 1957-60, 5th Jud. Dist., 1966-81; cons., 1981-95, arbitrator, 1990-95; grad. faculty adviser Nat. Coll. State Judiciary, 1975. Author: The Judge, 1979. Capt. CAC, AUS, World War II. Recipient Disting. Citizen award Idaho Statesman, 1970, 1st Annual Chase A. Clark Meml. award, 1971. Mem. 5th Jud. Dist. Bar Assn. (past pres.), Idaho Bar Assn. (commr. 1957-60, pres. 1960), Am. Judicature Soc., Masons (32 deg., knight comdr. Ct. Honor), Shriners, Elks, Beta Theta Pi. Home: Rupert Ind. Died Aug. 14, 1995.

BELZER, FOLKERT OENE, surgeon; b. Soerabaja, Indonesia, Oct. 5, 1930; came to U.S., 1951, naturalized, 1956; s. Peter and Jacoba H. (Gorter) B.; Aug. 4, 1956; children—Ingrid J., John B., G. Eric, Paul O. A.B., Colby Coll., Waterville, Maine, 1953; M.A., Boston U., 1954, M.D., 1958. Diplomate: Am. Bd. Surgery. Intern Grace-New Haven Hosp., 1958-59; asst. resident 1960-62; chief resident U. Oreg. Med. Sch., 1962-63, instr. surgery, 1963-64; asst. research surgeon U. Calif. Med. Center, San Francisco, 1964; asst. prof. surgery U. Calif. Med. Center, 1966-69, asst. prof. ambulatory and community medicine, 1966-69; asst. chief Transplant Service, 1967-69, co-chief, 1969-72, chief, 1972-74, asso. prof. surgery, 1969-72, asso. prof. ambulatory and community medicine, 1969-72, prof. surgery, 1972-74; dir. Exptl. Surgery Labs., 1973-74; sr. lectr. Guys Hosp., London, Eng., 1964-66; prof., chmn. dept. surgery U. Wis., Madison, 1974-95. Contbr. articles to med. jours. Recipient Samuel Harvey award as outstanding resident, 1960. Mem. A.C.S., Am., Calif. med. assns., Am. Soc. Transplant Surgeons (pres. 1975), Calif. Soc. Transplant Surgeons (pres. 1970-72), Am., Central surg. assns. (pres. 1993), Calif. Acad. Medicine, Halsted Soc., C. Naffziger Surg. Soc., Madison Surg. Soc., Pacific Coast Surg. Soc., San Francisco Surg. Soc. (chmn. program com. 1973-74), Wis. surg. socs), Nat. Kidney Found. (vice chmn. com. on dialysis and transplantation 1974-76), Société Internationale de Chirurgie, Soc. Vascular Surgery, Soc. Surg. Chairmen, Soc. U. Surgeons, Surg. Biology Club III, Transplantation Soc., Whipple Soc. Republican. Home: Madison Wis. Died Aug. 6, 1996.

BENADE, LEO EDWARD, lawyer, retired army officer; b. Dubuque, Iowa, July 29, 1916; s. Nicholas A. and Jennie (Bruno) B.; m. Marietta Taylor, Mar. 20, 1943; children: Leonard E., Lawrence M. Student, U. Mich. Sch. Law, 1946; J.D., Am. U., 1952. Bar: Va. bar 1951. Enlisted as pvt. U.S. Army, 1941, advanced through grades to lt. gen., 1972; adj. gen. U.S. Army Europe, 1966-67; dep. asst. sec. def. for personnel policy Washington, 1968-74; sr. v.p., gen. counsel United Way Am., Alexandria, Va., 1975-87. Decorated D.D.S.M., D.S.M. with 2 oak leaf clusters, Legion of Merit with 2 oak leaf clusters, Commendation medal with 2 oak leaf clusters. Mem. ABA, Va. State Bar, Am. Judicature Soc., Va. Trial Lawyers Assn., Army-Navy Country Club (chmn. bd. govs. 1970-73, 76-80), Sigma Nu Phi. Home: Whispering Pines N.C. Died Dec. 10, 1994.

BENDITT, EARL PHILIP, educator, medical scientist; b. Phila., Apr. 15, 1916; s. Milton and Sarah (Schoenfeld) B.; m. Marcella Wexler, Feb. 18, 1945; children: John, Alan, Joshua, Charles. B.A., Swarthmore Coll., 1937; M.D., Harvard U., 1941. Intern Phila. Gen. Hosp., 1941-43; resident pathology U. Chgo. Clinics, 1944; mem. faculty U. Chgo. Med. Sch., 1945-57, asso. prof. pathology, 1952-57; asst. dir. research LaRabida Children's Sanitarium, Chgo., 1950-56; prof. pathology U. Wash. Sch. Medicine, 1957-86, prof. emeritus, 1986-96, chmn. dept., 1957-81; mem. sci. adv. bd. St. Jude Children's Research Hosp.; cons. USPHS-NIH, 1957-80; Commonwealth Fund fellow, vis. prof. Sir William Dunn Sch. Pathology, U. Oxford, Eng., 1965, Macy faculty scholar, 1979-80, Litchfield lectr., 1980; chmn. bd. sci. counselors adv. com. Nat. Inst. Environ. Health Scis., 1976-79, 83-87, council mem., 1971-74. Mem. editorial bds. scis. publs. Recipient Med. Alumni award univ. Chgo., 1968; Rous-Whipple award Am. Assn. Pathologists, 1980; Gold Headed Cane Am. Assn. Pathologists, 1984. Fellow AAAS; mem. Am. Soc. Exptl. Pathology (council 1971-77, sec. treas. 1972-73, pres. 1975-76), Nat. Acad. Scis., Am. Soc. Pathologists and Bacteriologists (council 1972-77), Soc. Exptl. Biology and Medicine, Am. Soc. Cell Biology, Am. Soc. Biol. Chemists, Histochem. Soc. (pres. 1963-64), Phi Beta Kappa, Sigma Xi. Home: Seattle Wash. Died May 27, 1996.

BENEDICT, FREDRIC ALLEN, architect, planner; b. Medford, Wis., Mar. 15, 1914; s. Fredric Seth and Mary (Billack) B.; m. Fabienne Cravan Lloyd, Mar. 1, 1949; children: Charlotte St. Clair, Emilie, Marie-Fabienne, Nicholas. BS, U. Wis., 1936, MS, 1938, postgrad., 1938-41. Registered architect, Colo. Ptnr. Benedict Assocs. Architects, Aspen, Colo., 1945-95. Chmn. Aspen Music Festival, 1985-95; pres. Pks. Assn., Aspen, 1982-88; founder, pres. 10th Mountain Trail Assn., Aspen, 1980; chmn. City Planning and Zoning Commn., Aspen, 1952-62; bd. dirs. Colo. Hist. Soc., Denver. 1st lt. U.S. Army, 1941-45, ETO. Recipient Stewardship award Pitkin County, 1971, Greg Mace award City of Aspen, 1988, Outstanding Alumnus award U. Wis., 1989; named to Aspen Hall of Fame City of Aspen, 1988. Fellow AIA; mem. Am. Soc. Landscape Architects, The Nature Conservancy (hon. life). Democrat. Lutheran. Home: Aspen Colo. Died July 8, 1995.

BENNETT, ALLAN ROBERT, chemical company executive; b. N.Y.C., June 3, 1930; s. Ben and Gay (Leslie) B.; m. June Finn; children: Gay, Richard, Lizbeth. BS in Acctg., L.I. U., 1951, MS in Bus., 1957. Pres., chief exec. officer Helena Chem. Co. (acquired by Marubeni Am. Corp., 1987), Memphis, 1976-95, also bd. dirs. Mem. Univ. Golden Circle Christian Bros. U., Memphis, 1985-95. Served to 1st lt. USAF, 1952-56. Mem. Nat. Agrl. Chems. Assn. (bd. dirs. 1982-95). Republican. Club: Econs. (Memphis) (bd. dirs. 1984-95). Home: Memphis Tenn. Died June 15, 1995.

BENNETT, RICHARD JOSEPH, corporate executive; b. Bklyn., Jan. 20, 1917; s. Richard and Gertrude (McGuire) B.; m. Eileen P. O'Neill, May 4, 1946; children: Susan, Richard. AB, Fordham Coll., 1938, JD, 1942. Bar: N.Y. 1942. Ptnr. Whedon & Bennett, N.Y.C., 1945-46; staff atty. Schering Corp., 1947-55, asst. sec., asst. gen. counsel, 1955-59, sec., gen. atty., 1959-70, v.p., sec., gen. counsel, 1970-72; v.p., sec., gen. counsel Schering-Plough Corp., Madison, N.J., 1971-73, sr. v.p. adminstrn., 1973-76, pres., 1976-80, chief operating officer, 1976-78, chief exec. officer, 1978-82, chmn., 1980-83. Trustee emeritus Fordham U.; vice chmn. bd. trustees Cathedral Healthcare System Inc. Served with USAAF, 1942-45. Mem. ABA, N.Y. State Bar Assn. Home: Portland Oreg.

BENSON, CHARLES SCOTT, education educator; b. Atlanta, May 20, 1922; s. Marion Trotti and Sallie May (Bagley) B.; m. Dorothy Ruth Merrick, June 8, 1946; children: Michele, Charles Scott, Sally Merrick. A.B., Princeton U., 1943; M.A., Columbia U., 1948, Ph.D., 1950. Mem. faculty Bowdoin Coll., Brunswick, Maine, 1950-55, Harvard U., Cambridge, Mass., 1955-64; assoc. prof. U. Calif., Berkeley, 1964-68, prof. econs. of edn., 1968-94, assoc. dean, 1986-89; vis. prof. dept. edn.

Stanford U., 1980-81; cons. NAACP, San Francisco, R.I. Spl. Commn. on Edn., Calif. Bd. Edn., Com. Econ. Devel., Conn. Gov.'s Commn. on Tax Reform, Govt. Pakistan Planning Commn., World Bank, AID; staff dir. N.Y. State Edn. Commn.; mem. Pres.'s Adv. Panel on Financing Elem. and Secondary Edn., 1979-81; mem. com. on vocat. edn. Nat. Acad. Scis.; dir. Nat. Ctr. for Research in Vocat. Edn., 1988-94. Author: The Economics of Public Education, 1961, 3d edit., 1978, The Cheerful Prospect, 1965, The School and the Economic System, 1966, (with others) Planning for Educational Reform: Financial and Social Alternatives, 1974; editor: (with others) Perspectives on the Economics of Education, 1963. Served with USN, 1943-46. Recipient Berkeley citation, 1994. Mem. Am. Econ. Assn., Am. Ednl. Fin. Assn. (pres. 1977-78, disting. service award 1987), Phi Delta Kappa. Home: Kensington Calif. Died July 2, 1994.

BENSON, EZRA TAFT, church executive, former secretary of agriculture; b. Whitney, Idaho, Aug. 4, 1899; s. George Taft and Sarah (Dunkley) B.; m. Flora Smith Amussen, Sept. 10, 1926; children: Reed, Mark, Barbara, Beverly, Bonnie, Flora Beth. Student, Utah State Agrl. Coll., Logan, 1918-21; BS, Brigham Young U., 1926, Dr. Pub. Service (hon.), 1955; MS in Agrl. Econs., Iowa State Coll., 1927, D Agrl. (hon.), 1953; postgrad., U. Calif., 1937-38; HHD, Coll. Osteo. Physicians and Surgeons, 1951; LLD, U. Utah, 1953, Bowdoin Coll., 1955, U. Maine, 1956; D Agr. (hon.), Mich. State Coll., 1955; DSc (hon.), Rutgers U., 1955. Mission Ch. Jesus Christ Latter-day Saints, Brit. Isles and Europe; pres. Newcastle dist. Ch. Jesus Christ Latter-day Saints, 1921-23; farm operator, 1923-30; county agrl. agt. U. Idaho Extension Service, Preston, 1929-30; extension economist and mktg. specialist in charge econ. and mktg. work State of Idaho, 1930-38; organizer, sec. Idaho Coop. Council, 1933-38; exec. sec. Nat. Council Farmer Coops., 1939-44; mem. exec. com., bd. trustees Am. Inst. Co-op, 1942-52, vice chmn. bd. trustees, 1942-49, chmn., 1952; sec. agr. U.S. Dept. Agr., Washington, 1953-61; dir. Olson Bros., Inc.; bd. dirs. Farm Found., 1946-50; mem. Nat. Agrl. Adv. Com., World War II; mem. Nat. Farm Credit Com., 1940-43; U.S. del. 1st Internat. Conf. of Farm Orgns., London, 1946. Contbr. to agrl., coop. and church jours. Mem. nat. exec. bd. Boy Scouts Am., 1948-66, awarded Silver Antelope, 1951, Silver Buffalo award, 1954; mem. Boise Stake Presidency, Ch. of Jesus Christ of Latter-day Saints, Idaho, 1935-39, pres. Boise Stake, 1938-39; pres. Wash. Dist. Council, Eastern States Mission, 1939-40, Washington Stake, 1940-44; ordained apostle of Ch., mem. Council of Twelve, 1943, pres. European Mission, 1946, 63-65, mem. Gen. Ch. Bd. Edn.; pres. Ch. Jesus Christ Latter-day Saints, Salt Lake City, 1985-94; br. trustees Brigham Young U. Recipient testimonial for disting. service to agr. U. Wis., 1952; scholarship Gamma Sigma Delta, hon. soc. agr. Iowa State Coll.; fellow U. Calif., Berkeley. Mem. Am. Mktg. Assn., Farm Econs. Assn., Delta Nu, Alpha Zeta. Home: Salt Lake City Utah Died May 30, 1994.

BENTINCK-SMITH, WILLIAM, former university administrator; b. Boston, Jan. 22, 1914; s. William Frederick and Marion (Jordan) Bentinck-S.; m. Phebe Keyes, June 26, 1937; children: Michael, Judy, Nancy, Peter. A.B., Harvard U., 1937; M.S., Columbia U., 1938. Reporter Boston Globe, 1938-40; mng. editor Harvard Alumni Bull., 1940-46, editor, 1946-54, editorial adv. com., 1954-76; asst. to pres. Harvard, 1954-71, sr. assoc., 1971-84; editor Harvard Today, 1957-69, editorial chmn., 1969-72, adv. com., 1971-75; hon. curator type specimens and letter design Harvard Coll. Library. Author: The Harvard Book, 1953, rev., 1982, Building A Great Library, The Coolidge Years At Harvard, 1976, Lives of Harvard Scholars, 1986, History of Harvard Named Chairs, 1991. Dir. Cambridge Trust Co.; Sec. Harvard Class of 1937. Served to lt. comdr. USNR, 1942-45. Decorated Bronze Star; recipient Harvard medal, 1987. Mem. Am. Antiquarian Soc., Mass. Hist. Soc., Colonial Soc. Mass., Phi Beta Kappa (hon.). Home: Groton Mass. Died Jan. 19, 1993; interred Groton, Mass.

BENTLEY, GERALD EADES, author, retired, English literature educator; b. Brazil, Ind., Sept. 15, 1901; s. Layton Coval and Josephine Cynthia (Eades) B.; m. Esther Greenwood Felt, Sept. 12, 1927 (dec. 1961); 1 child, Gerald Eades; m. Ellen Voigt Stern, Aug. 25, 1965 (dec. 1990). AB, DePauw U., 1923, LittD (hon.), 1949; AM, U. Ill., 1926; PhD, U. London, 1929; MA (hon.), Cambridge (Eng.) U., 1952; LittD (hon.), U. Birmingham, Eng., 1959, L.I. U., 1975; LHD (hon.), U. Ind., 1970. Instr. English U. Ill., 1923-26; instr. English N.Mex. Mil. Inst., 1926-27; from instr. to prof. English U. Chgo., 1929-45; prof. English Princeton U., N.J., 1945-70, Murray prof., 1952-70, librarian rare books and spl. collections, 1971-72, bibliographer, cons., 1972-74; lectr. Lent term Cambridge U., Eng., 1953, Postgrad. Sch. Elizabethan Studies, U. Birmingham, summers 1947, 53, 57, 62, Harvard U., summer 1955. Author: (with Millett) The Art of the Drama, 1935, The Jacobean and Caroline Stage, 7 vols., 1941-68, Shakespeare and Jonson, 2 vols., 1945, 65, The Swan of Avon and the Bricklayer of Westminster, 1948, The Development of English Drama, 1950, Shakespeare, A Biographical Handbook, 1961, 85, Shakespeare and His Theater, 1964, The Profession of Dramatist in Shakespeare's Time, 1972, 85, (with others) The Revels History of Drama in English, vol. IV, 1981, The Profession of Player in Shakespeare's Time, 1984, 86; also articles; editor: (with Fred B. Millett) The Play's the Thing, 1936, The Alchemist (Jonson), 1947, The Arte of Angling, 1956, Shakespeare's Othello, 1957, The Seventeenth Century Theater, 1968, William Shakespeare: His World, His Work, His Influence, 1985. (with others) The Legacy of R.P. Blackmur, 1987. Rector scholar DePauw U., 1919-23; research fellow Huntington Library, 1938-39; Guggenheim Found. fellow, 1944-45; Fulbright sr. research fellow Cambridge U., 1952-53; sr. research fellow Clark Library, UCLA, 1976-77. Mem. Jesus Coll. (Cambridge) Soc., Modern Humanities Research Assn., Shakespeare Soc. Am. (pres. 1972-74), Malone Soc. (pres. 1970-89), Bibliog. Soc., Am. Philos. Soc., Am. Acad. Arts and Sci., Am. Soc. Theatre Research, Phi Kappa Psi. Clubs: Century (N.Y.C.); Nassau (Princeton). Home: Hightstown N.J. Died July 25, 1994.

BENUA, RICHARD SQUIER, nuclear physician, educator; b. Bexley, Ohio, Aug. 11, 1921; s. Albert Ray and Ruth (Squier) B.; m Mary Consilia Ralston, June 15, 1945 (div. 1954); m. Joan MacLellan, Oct. 16, 1954; children: David Peter, Daniel Ray, Margaret Anne, Laura Helen. B.S. magna cum laude, Western Res. U., 1942; M.D., Johns Hopkins U., 1946; M.S., U. Minn., 1952. Am. Bd. Nuclear Medicine. Intern N.Y. Polyclinic Hosp., N.Y.C., 1946-47; resident fellow in medicine Mayo Clinic, Rochester, Minn., 1950-53; asst. Sloan-Kettering Inst., N.Y.C., 1955-60, assoc. mem., 1960-66; assoc. prof. medicine and radiology U. Tex. Med. Ctr., Galveston, 1966-70; asst. prof. medicine Cornell Med. Coll., N.Y.C., 1970-81, assoc. prof. radiology, 1972-87, prof. clin. medicine, 1981-87, emeritus prof. clin. medicine, from 1987; attending physician, chief nuclear medicine svc. Meml. Hosp., N.Y.C., 1970-87; attending radiologist N.Y. Hosp., from 1989; chmn. adv. bd. Bur. of Labs., N.Y.C., 1976-79. Mem. editorial bd. Yr. Book of Cancer, 1976-88, Jour. Nuclear Medicine, 1988-90. Chmn. Citizen Adv. Com. on Permanent Disposal Facilities Siting and Disposal Method Selection, Dept. Environ. Conservation, N.Y. State, from 1992. Served to capt. AUS, 1947-49. Recipient Research award Mayo Found., 1962. Fellow N.Y. Acad. Med.; mem. Endocrine Soc., Am. Thyroid Assn., Soc. Nuclear Medicine (pres. edn. and research found. 1974-76, pres. Greater N.Y. chpt. 1976-77), Am. Coll. Nuclear Physicians, Phi Beta Kappa, Sigma Xi. Unitarian. Club: Horseshoe Harbor Yacht (Larchmont, N.Y.). Home: Larchmont N.Y. Deceased.

BERAS ROJAS, OCTAVIO ANTONIO CARDINAL, former archbishop of Santo Domingo; b. El Seybo, Dominican Republic, Nov. 16, 1906; s. Octavio and Teresa (Rojas) B. Ordained priest Roman Catholic Ch.; pastor Cathedral of Santo Domingo; dir. Verdad Catolica Sem.; archbishop co-adjutor of Santo Domingo, 1945-61, archbishop of Santo Domingo, 1961-81; elevated to Sacred Coll. of Cardinals, 1976; founder Cath. Action, Santiago; pres. Tribunal; chancellor, then provicar gen., Santo Domingo; sec.-gen. 1st Conf. Latin Am. Episcopate; mem. central commn. II Vatican Conf.; pres. Dominican Episcopal Conf., 1963-75. Died Nov. 30, 1990. Home: Santo Domingo Dominican Republic

BÉRÉGOVOY, PIERRE EUGENE, French prime minister; b. Dévilleles-Rouen, France, Dec. 23, 1925; s. Adrien and Irène (Baudelin) B.; m. Gilberte Bonnet, 1948; 3 children. Educated, U. Strasbourg, France. Head subdiv. then asst. to dir. Soc. pour le devel. de l'industrie du gaz; chargé de mission Gaz de France, 1978-81; mem. Econ. and Social Coun., 1979-81; sec.-gen. to presidency, 1981-82; min. Ministry of Social Affairs and Nat. Solidarity, 1982-84; min. Ministry of Economy, Fin. and Budget, 1984-86, min. of state, 1988-92; prime min. French Govt., 1992—; founder-mem. Parti Socialist Autonome, 1958; Socialist dep., 1986-88, Maire de la Nièvre, 1983—; mem. Sec. Parti Socialiste Unifié, 1963-67; mem. manpower com. and exec. bd. Parti Socialiste, 1969, Nat. Soc. for Social Affairs, 1973-75, in charge of fgn. affairs, 1975-81; responsible for party to Liaison Com. of the Left. Home: Paris France

BERG, DON LEROY, editorial director; b. Wildrose, N.D., Feb. 8, 1934; s. Clifford Berg and Florence (Mobley) Rundhaug; m. Dona Rae Cooper, June 24, 1956; children: Marilyn Berg Bolognese, Kevin, Nadine. BA, Pacific U., 1956. Reporter Longview (Wash.) Daily News, 1956-60; editor night news sect. Salt Lake Tribune, Salt Lake City, 1960-69; editor Med. Econs. Mag., Montvale, N.J., 1969-91; editorial dir. Med. Econs. Co., Montvale, 1991; chairperson Neal Com., Am. Bus. Press, N.Y.C., 1977-78 (Neal cert. in editorial writing 1982). Contbr. numerous articles to profl. jours. Former mem. sch. facilities evaluation com. River Edge Sch. Dists., N.J. Mem. Am. Soc. Mag. Editors, Am. Bus. Press (past chmn. Jesse H. Neal awards com., Jesse H. Neal cert. for editorial writing). Republican. Home: Montvale N.J. Died Dec. 4, 1991.

BERGEN, DANIEL PATRICK, librarian, retired educator; b. Albert Lea, Minn., May 25, 1935; s. Francis Joseph and Grace Frances (Donovan) B.; m. Carol Lee Janson, Apr. 11, 1958; children: Mary Clare, Paula Maureen, Brent Daniel, Gregory Joseph. A.B. in History-Philosophy, U. Notre Dame, 1957, M.A. in Polit. Sci., 1962; M.A. in Librarianship, U. Chgo., 1961, cert. advanced study librarianship, 1968, postgrad., 1963; M.A. in Am. Studies, U. Minn., 1968, Ph.D. in Am. Studies, 1970, postgrad. in. Philosophy, 1973-75; postgrad., U. Conn. Law Sch., 1977. Grad. asst. dept. polit. sci. U. Notre Dame, 1957-58, 61-62; asst. librarian, instr. polit. sci. St. Benedict's Coll., 1962-63; asst. dean, lectr. Sch. Library Sci.-Syracuse U., 1964-65; asst. prof. library sci. U. Md., 1965-66; assoc. prof. library sci. U. Miss., 1966-70, chmn. dept. library sci., 1966-68; assoc. prof. U. R.I., Kingston, 1970-75, prof., 1975-87, teaching fellow, 1981-82, chmn. faculty senate, 1976-77, prof. emeritus library and info. studies, 1988-96; vis. fellow Sch. Library and Info. Studies, U. Wis.-Madison, 1984. Contbr. articles to profl. jours. Past pres., bd. dirs. R.I. Libr. Assn.; trustee Upper Iowa U., Fayette, 1983-85, South Kingstown (R.I.) Pub. Library, Peace Dale, R.I., 1983-86, Village of Hamilton, 1990-96; dept. mayor Village of Hamilton, 1991-96; bd. dirs. Hamilton Sr. Citizens Ctr., 1990-96. With USAF, 1958-60. Fellow R.I. Bd. Regents for Edn., 1981; U. Chgo. fellow, 1963; U. Minn. fellow, 1967-70; U. R.I. teaching effectiveness grantee, 1975. Mem. So. Madison County C. of C. (bd. dirs. 1991-93), Hamilton Club (sec. 1990-91, pres. 1991-92), Hamilton Club (pres. 1991-92, bd. govs. 1990-93). Home: Hamilton N.Y. Died Jan. 6, 1996.

BERGER, SYDNEY L., lawyer; b. N.Y.C., May 29, 1917; s. Abraham I. and Ruth (Levine) B.; m. Jean Danenberg, May 16, 1985; children: Charles Lee, Jeri Beth. B.S., Coll. City N.Y., 1936; J.D., Columbia U., 1940. Bar: N.Y. 1941, Ind. 1947, U.S. Supreme Ct. 1952. Atty. REA, 1941-43; individual practice law Evansville, Ind., 1946-72; ptnr. firm Berger & Berger, 1972-88; adj. instr. law and polit. sci. Ind. State U., Evansville, 1971-88; adj. lectr. legal medicine Ind. U. Med. Sch., Evansville, 1973-88; adj. prof. law Ind. Law Sch., Indpls., 1974-88. Mem. Mayor's Commn. on Human Relations; mem. Gov.'s advisory com. for Evansville State Psychiat. Treatment Center for Children, 1961-68; pres. Legal Aid Soc., Evansville, 1965. Served with AUS, 1943-45. Recipient James Bethel Gresham freedom award, 1971; Human Rights award City of Evansville, 1978. Mem. Am. Judicature Soc., ABA, Ind. Bar Assn. (Presdl. citation 1975, chmn. Ho. of Dels. 1980-81), Evansville Bar Assn. (pres. 1966), Am. Trial Lawyers Assn. (editor law jour. 1959-69, bd. govs. 1968-70), Ind. Trial Lawyers Assn. (pres. 1971-72), Am. Polit. Sci. Assn., Am. Arbitrators Assn. (nat. panel), Wilderness Soc., U. Evansville Acad. Arts and Scis. Home: Evansville Ill. Died July 31, 1988.

BERGER, WILHELM GEORG, composer, musicologist; b. Rupea, Brasov, Dec. 4, 1929. Studied violin Bucharest Conservatoire. Mem. Bucharest Philharmonic Orch., 1948-58; mem. Composers' Union Quartet, 1953-57; sec. Romanian Composers' Union, 1968-90; prof. Acad. Music Bucharest, 1991-93 Composer: 24 symphonies, concerts for several instruments and orchestras, chamber music including 21 string quartets, sonatas; author: Studies: Moduri si proportii; Structuri sonore si aspectele lor armonice (Modes and proportions; Sonorous structures and their harmonic aspects), Model Dimensions, 1979; Ghid pentru muzica instrumentala de camera (Guidebook for instrumental chamber music), 1965; Muzica simfonica (Baroque-Classical 1967, Romantic 1972, Modern 1974, Contemporary 1976); Quartetul de coarde de la Haydn la Debussy (The string quartet from Haydn to Debussy), 1970, The Aesthetic of Classical Sonata, 1981, The Aesthetic of Romantic Sonata, 1982, The Aesthetic of the Modern Sonata, 1983 The Aesthetic of Baroque Sonata, The Aesthetic of the Contemporary Sonata, 1985, The Classicism from Bach to Beethoven, 1990, Mozart: Culture and Style, 1991, A General Aesthetic of the Sonata, 1987. Recipient Prince Rainier III of Monaco prize, Monte Carlo, 1964; Concours internat. de composition d'oeuvres pour quatuor a cordes prize, Liege, 1965; Reine Elisabeth de Belgique, Internat. Musical Contest prize, 1966; George Enescu prize of Romanian Acad., 1966; Composers' Union prize, 1969. Mem. Romanian Acad. (corr.), Internat. Music Coun. Romania (pres. 1991-93). Died Mar. 8, 1993; buried Evangelical Cemetary, Bucharest, Romania. Home: Bucharest Romania

BERGOLD, HARRY EARL, JR., diplomat; b. Olean, N.Y., Nov. 11, 1931; s. Harry Earl and Juniata V. (Glosser) B.; m. Karlene Knieps Bergold. BA, Yale U., 1953, MA, 1957. Commd. fgn. service officer Dept. State, 1957, Econ. officer, 1958-60; 3d. sec. embassy Tegucigalpa, Honduras, 1960-62; 2d sec. embassy Mexico City, 1962-64; polit. officer Dept. State, 1964-67; polit. mil. counsellor U.S. Embassy, Madrid, Spain, 1967-72; dep. asst. sec. def. for NATO/European affairs Dept. Def., Washington, 1973-75; prin. dep. asst. sec. def. for legis. affairs NATO/European affairs Dept. Def., 1976-77; asst. sec of energy for internat. affairs Dept. Energy, Washington, 1977-79; amb. to Hungary, Budapest, 1980-84, Nicaragua, Managua, 1984-87; vis. prof. Inst. for European Studies, Vienna. Served with U.S. Army, 1954-56. Home: Paris France Died May 16, 1995; interred Dearborn Meml. Park, Poway, Calif.

BERGSMA, WILLIAM LAURENCE, composer; b. Oakland, Calif., Apr. 1, 1921; s. William Joseph and Helen Margaret (Doepfner) B.; m. Nancy Nickerson 1946. Student, Stanford U., 1938-40; teaching fellow

Eastman Sch. Music, 1942-44; A.B., U. Rochester, 1942, Mus.M., 1943. Faculty Juilliard Sch. Music, N.Y.C., 1946-63, chmn. composition dept., also chmn. dept. lit. and materials of music, assoc. dean, 1961-63, prof., 1963-86; dir. Sch. Music, U. Wash., Seattle, 1963-71; vis. prof. Bklyn. Coll., CUNY, 1972-73. Composer: ballet Gold and the Señor Commandante, 1942, First Quartet, 1942, Symphony for Chamber Orchestra, 1942, Music on a Quiet Theme, 1943, Three Fantasies (piano solo), 1943, rev., 1983, Second Quartet, 1944, Six Songs, 1945, Suite from Children's Film, 1945, Symphony, 1949, string orch. The Fortunate Islands, 1947, rev. 1956, piano solo Tangents, 1951, Third Quartet, 1953, orch. A Carol on Twelfth Night, 1953, 3 act opera The Wife of Martin Guerre, 1955, rev. 1958, 3 choruses Riddle Me This, 1956, band March with Trumpets, 1957, Concerto for Woodwind Quintet, 1958, orch. Chameleon Variations, 1960, viola and piano Fantastic Variations, 1961, orch. In Celebration: Toccata for the Sixth Day, 1962, Confrontation from the Book of Job, orch. Documentary One, 1963, Serenade to Await the Moon, 1965, Concerto for Violin and Orchestra, 1966, for chorus, brass, percussion The Sun, The Soaring Eagle, The Turquoise Prince, The God, 1967; Orch. Documentary Two, 1967; clarinet, percussion Illegible Canons, 1969, 1969; Fourth Quartet, 1970, rev., 1974; solo woodwind quintet, harp, percussion, strings Changes, 1971; Changes for Seven, 1971; cello, percussion Clandestine Dialogues, 1972; two-act opera The Murder of Comrade Sharik, 1973; chorus, instruments Wishes, Wonders, Portents, Charms, 1974; soprano, instruments In Space, 1975; chorus and orch. Second Symphony: Voyages for Soloists, 1976; solo viola and orch. Sweet Was the Song the Virgin Sung/Tristan Revisited, 1977; trombone and percussion Blatent Hypotheses, 1977; 3 instruments, percussion Four All, 1979; Quintet for Flute and String Quartet, 1979, The Voice of the Coelacanth, 1980; oboe concertante, 2 bassoons and strings In Campo Aperto, 1981; medium voice, clarinet, bassoon and piano Four Songs, 1981; Fifth Quartet, 1982; Piano Variations, 1984, woodwind quintet Masquerade, 1986; four songs for voice and marimba I Toad You So, 1986, A Lick and a Promise for saxophone and chimes, 1988, Sixth Quartet, 1991. Recipient Town Hall commn. for Symphony for Chamber Orch., 1942; Bearns prize for String Quartet No. 1, 1943; Koussevitzky Found. commn., 1943-44; grant AAAL and Nat. Inst. Arts and Letters, 1945; award Soc. for Publ. Am. Music, 1945; Guggenheim fellow, 1946, 51; Collegiate Chorale commn., 1946; commn. from Carl Fischer, Inc., for 25th anniversary of League of Composers, 1947; Juilliard Found. commn., 1953, 62; Louisville commn., 1953; Elizabeth Sprague Coolidge commn., 1956; Collegiate Chorale of Ill. Wesleyan U. commn., 1956; 1st ann. Edwin Franco Goldman Meml. commn., 1957; Harvard Mus. Soc. commn., 1961; Portland Jr. Symphony commn., 1960; Mid-Am. Chorale commn., 1963; Mus. Arts Soc. La Jolla commn., 1965; Phi Beta commn., 1966; Am. Choral Dirs. Assn. commn., 1967; Kansas City Youth Symphony commn., 1967; U. Ala. for Cadek Quarter, 1970; Poncho and Brechemin Family Found. commn., 1971; New Dimensions in Music, 1972; Nat. Chorale and N.Y. State Council on Arts commn., 1974; Gt. Falls Symphony and Symphonic Choir, Mont. Bicentennial Adminstrn., 1975; Seattle Symphony Orch. commn., 1977; Chamber Music Soc. of Lincoln Center commn., 1980; Nat. Endowment Arts commn., 1979, Nat. Endowment Arts grantee, 1985; Wash. State Music Educators grantee, 1988. Mem. AAAL, Phi Beta Kappa, Phi Mu Alpha. Home: Seattle Wash. Died Mar. 18, 1994.

BERING, EDGAR ANDREW, JR., neurosurgeon; b. Salt Lake City, Feb. 18, 1917; s. Edgar Andrew and Ilse (Billing) B.; B.A., U. Utah, 1937; M.D., Harvard U., 1941; postgrad. Columbia U., 1947; m. Harriet Crocker Aldrich, Nov. 3, 1944; children: Edgar Andrew, Charles C., Harriet A. Surg. house officer Boston City Hosp., 1941-42; spl. research assoc. Dept. Phys. Chemistry, Harvard Med. Sch., Boston, 1942-44; asst. in neurosurgery, spl. research assoc., demonstrator in anatomy N.Y. Med. Coll. and Flower Fifth Ave. Hosp., N.Y.C., 1946-48; Moseley travelling fellow of Harvard Med. Sch., Nat. Hosp., Queens Sq., London, and clin. clk., 1948-49; resident in neurosurgery Childrens Hosp. and Peter Bent Brigham Hosp., Boston 1949-50; practice medicine, Easton, Md., 1974-85; teaching fellow in surgery Harvard Med. Sch., Boston, 1949-50, asst. in surgery, 1952, clin. asso. in surgery, 1956-59, asst. clin. prof. surgery, 1959-65; research fellow in neurosurgery Children's Hosp., Boston, 1950-51, asst. neurosurgeon, 1950-55, dir. neurosurg. research lab., 1952-63, asso. neurosurgeon, 1955-64; Harvey Cushing fellow Peter Bent Brigham Hosp., Boston, 1950-51, jr. asso. in neurol. surgery, 1950-63; sr. fellow in polimoyelitis, NRC, 1951-52; cons. in surgery of nervous system Lemuel Shattuck Hosp., Jamaica Plain, Mass., 1953-55; attending neurosurgeon West Roxbury VA Hosp., 1954-63; vis. lectr. neurosurgery UCLA Med. Sch., 1958; vis. scientist Nat. Inst. Neurol. Diseases and Blindness, NIH, Bethesda, Md., 1963-65; spl. asst. to dir. for program analysis Nat. Inst. Neurol. Diseases and and Stroke, NIH, 1965-71; cons. to adv. com. on coagulation components Commn. on Plasma Fractionation and Related Products, 1954-94; chief spl. programs br. Collaborative and Field Research, Nat. Inst. Neurol. Diseases and Stroke, NIH, Bethesda, 1971-74; assoc. clin. prof. neurol. surgery Georgetown U., Washington, 1968-84; cons. neurol. and electroencephalographic dept. Eastern Shore Hosp., Cambridge, Md., 1975-94; cons. Neurosurg. Dept., Johns Hopkins Hosp., Balt., 1975-84 active staff neurosurg. and electroencephalographic dept. Meml. Hosp. of Easton, 1974-94, vice chief of staff, 1981-83, chief staff, 1983-85. Served with M.C., USN, 1942-46. Rockefeller fellow, 1940; diplomate Am. Bd. Neurol. Surgery. Mem. Am. Acad. Neurology, AAAS, Am. Assn. Neurol. Surgeons, Soc. for Neurosci. (founding mem.), Internat. Soc. for Pediatric Neurosurgery (founding mem.), Soc. Neurology, Psychiatry and Neurosurgery (Argentina), Chilean Soc. Neurosurgery and Neurology, Neurosurg. Soc. Am., Scandinavian, New Eng. neurosurg. socs., N.Y. Acad. Sci., Am. Assn. Neurol. Surgeons, Research Soc. Neurosurg. (founding mem.), Sigma Xi. Patentee fibrin foam used in surgery; contbr. numerous articles in field to profl. jours. Died Aug. 11, 1994. Home: Oxford Md.

BERK, ALLEN JOEL, lawyer; b. N.Y.C., Nov. 5, 1940; s. William and Sarah Berk; m. Barbara S. Levine, May 30, 1964; children: Dara Brett, Carrie Robyn. B.A., CUNY, 1962; LLB, George Washington U., 1965, LLM, 1967. Bar: D.C. 1966, U.S. Ct. Appeals (4th, 5th and D.C. cirs.) 1967, U.S. Supreme Ct. 1969. U.S. Ct. Appeals (2d, 6th, 7th, 8th and 9th cirs.) 1968, Calif. 1974. Grad. fellow Inst. Law, Psychiat. and Criminology, Washington, 1965-67; litigation atty. NLRB, Washington, 1967-69; asst. dir. legal dept. Airline Pilots Assn., Los Angeles and Washington, 1969-71, spl. asst. to pres., Washington, 1971-74; ptnr. Corbett, Kane & Berk, San Francisco, 1971-84; ptnr., head San Francisco labor dept. Pettit & Martin, 1984-93; lectr. various area law schs., 1974-93; mem. faculty Practising Law Inst., 1975-93, Employment Law Inst., 1991-93. Contbr. chpts. to atty. edn. books, 1978, 81. Mem. adv. bd. Kiahuna Home Owners Assn., Kauai, Hawaii, 1976-82; judge U. Calif.-Berkeley and San Francisco U. competitions, 1976-93; guest speaker various interest groups; mem. faculty Employment Law Inst. Mem. ABA (liaison mem. to NLRB of practice and procedures com. 1976-93), San Francisco Bar Assn., , Bankers Club. Jewish. Died July 1, 1993. Home: Berkeley Calif.

BERKE, ANITA DIAMANT, literary agent; b. N.Y.C., Jan. 15; d. Sidney J. and Lea (Lyons) Diamant; m. Harold Berke, Dec. 22, 1945 (dec. 1972); 1 child, Allyson. B.S., NYU. Mem. editorial bd. Forum Mag., N.Y.C., McCalls Mag.; reporter Macy Newspapers; literary agt., pres. Anita Diamant Lit. Agy., N.Y.C.; adj. prof. L.I.U. Contbr. articles to profl. jours. Mem. Women in Communications, Inc. (past pres. N.Y. chpt.), Nat. Assn. Newspaper Women, Soc. Author's Reps. Club: Overseas Press (pres. 1981-86). Home: Weston Conn.

BERKMAN, MARSHALL L., manufacturing company executive; b. Steubenville, Ohio, 1936; (married). A.B., Harvard U., 1958, M.B.A., 1960, J.D., 1963. Pres. Rust Craft Greeting Cards, Inc., 1967-79; with Ampco-Pitts. Corp., 1979-94, chmn., chief exec. officer, 1979-94, also dir.; bd. dirs. Louis Berkman Co. Home: Pittsburgh Pa. Died Sept. 8, 1994.

BERMAN, BUD, textile manufacturing company executive; b. 1917. Student, Wayne State U. Mdse. mgr. IT & T, 1946-47; founder Bud Berman Sportswear, Inc., 1947-63; with Dynasty-Hong Kong Ltd., 1973-84; with Kellwood Co., Chesterfield, Mo., 1977-91, v.p., 1984; now v.p. corp. devel. Kellwood Co., Chesterfield; also pres. Kellwood Interat., St. Louis. With U.S. Army, 1942-45. Home: Saint Louis Mo. Died March 7, 1991.

BERMAN, RICHARD LEE, publishing consultant; b. N.Y.C., Apr. 1, 1929; s. Louis K. and Marie Jeanette (Kellner) B.; m. Constance Kaufmann, Oct. 2, 1952; children: Patricia, Anthony, Anne, Donald. BS in Applied Econs., Yale U., 1950. Prodn. mgr. TV NBC, N.Y.C., 1954-55, bus. mgr. weekday radio, 1955-56, bus. mgr. opera, 1956-57, mgr. internat. facilities, 1957-63; internat. adminstr. Screen Gems, Inc., N.Y.C., 1963-64; mgr. prodn. Solocast Co., Stamford, Conn., 1964-67; mgr. program prodn. Graflex, Inc., Rochester, N.Y., 1967-69; pub. media Harper & Row, Pubs., Inc., N.Y.C., 1969-79, v.p. planning and devel., 1979-87; assoc. Moseley Assocs., Inc., N.Y.C., 1987-93. Chmn. Jewish Child Care Assn. N.Y., 1983-85, pres. 1986-93; mem. bd. edn. Mt. Pleasant Cottage Sch., Pleasantville, N.Y., 1980-93. Mem. Assn. Am. Pubs. (chmn. media com. 1974-76). Died Sept. 5, 1993.

BERNAYS, EDWARD L., public relations counsel; b. Vienna, Austria, Nov. 22, 1891; came to U.S., 1892; s. Ely and Anna (Freud) B.; m. Doris E. Fleischman, Sept. 16, 1922 (dec. July 1986); children: Doris Fleischman Bernays Held, Anne Fleischman Bernays Kaplan. BS, Cornell U., 1912; HHD (hon.), Boston U., 1966; LL.D. (hon.), Babson Coll., 1977, Ball State U., 1987, Northeastern U., 1989. Pub. relations counsel to govt., industry, corps., profl. and trade orgns., individuals, 1919-95; pub. relations counsel N.Y. World's Fair, 1939; instr. 1st course and 1st book pub. rels. NYU, 1923, adj. prof. pub. rels., 1949-50; prof. U. Hawaii, 1950; adj. prof. Sch. Pub. Relations Boston U., 1968-69; cons. HEW, 1976, U.S. Dept. Commerce, 1977; fgn. affairs officer, cons. Bur. Ednl. and Cultural Affairs U.S. State Dept., 1970-75; former mem. Am. advisory council Ditchley Found., 1962-69; Tallents lectr. Brit. Inst. for Pub. Rels., 1966; founder Edward L. Bernays Found., N.Y.C., 1940-95; staff mem. U.S. com. on pub. info. U.S. and Paris Peace Conf., 1918-19; carried out wide range of svc. for nat. and state govt. including cons. to U.S. War Dept., 1919, U.S. Army, USN, U.S. Air Force, U.S. Treasury Depts. WWII, 1941-45; assoc. commr. U.S. Dept. Commerce; mem. Pres. Hoover's Emergency Com. for Employment, 1931-32; mem. Citizens Morale Com. of N.Y. State Def. Coun., N.Y. State Com. on Discrimination in Employment, 1942; mem., pub. rels. advisor on Pub. Info. Com. of ARC War Fund, 1942-49; chmn. Nat. Adv. Com. of the Third U.S. War Loan, 1943-45; mem. Sixth War Fin. Com., 1944, Joint Civilian Orientation Conf. of U.S. Dept. Def., 1951, Exec. Res. U.S. Info. Agy., 1956-64; cons. Mental Health Dept. Mass., 1970-75. Author numerous books including Crystallizing Public Opinion, 1923, An Outline of Careers, 1927, Propaganda, 1928, Careers for Men, 1939, Speak up for Democracy, 1940, Take Your Place at the Peace Table, 1945, Public Relations 1952, The Engineering of Consent, 1955, Your Future in Public Relations, 1961, Biography of an Idea, Memoirs of Public Relations Counsel Edward L. Bernays, 1965; editor: numerous books, latest being The Later Years, 1986; contbr. articles to profl. jours.; subject of book Public Relations, The Edward L. Bernayses and the American Scene, Edward L. Bernays Later Years, 1986. Chmn. Sr. Citizens Month Com., N.Y.C., 1956; mem. pub. rels. com. Whitney Mus. Am. Art, N.Y.C., 1958; trustee Hosp. for Joint Diseases, N.Y.C., 1957-63, N.Y. Shakespeare Festival, 1959, Carnegie Hall Corp., 1960-62; co-chmn. Emergency Com. to Save Meml. Drive, 1964-65; bd. dirs. Nat. Multiple Sclerosis, Edward R. Murrow Ctr. Pub. Diplomacy, 1966-95, Fletcher Sch. Law and Diplomacy, Tufts U., Com. on Performing Arts, N.Y.C., 1955; hon. chmn. USO, 1985-95, United Svc. Orgn., 1987-90, Careers for Later Yrs., 1990; hon. trustee Interfaith Counseling Svc.; hon. chmn. United Svc. Orgn., Boston, 1988-90. Decorated Officer of Pub. Instrn. France, 1946; recipient King Christian medal (Denmark) 1946, bronze medallion of honor City of N.Y., 1961, Southwest Press award So. Meth. U., 1954, Honor award Ohio U., 1970, Disting. Svc. award Nat. Pub. Rels. Coun. Health and Welfare Svcs., 1975, Leadership award Chgo. chpt., 1976, Outstanding Alumnus award Cornell U., 1980, Pub. Rels. Tchr. award Assn. for Edn. in Journalism, 1980, Golden Trumpet award Chgo. Publicity Club, 1981, Presdl. citation N.Y.U., 1985. Hosp. Pub. Rels. Assn., 1983, Pres. citation N.Y.U., 1985, United Service Orgn. award, 1985, Nat. Pub. Rels. Achievement award Ball State U., 1986, award Mich. Sci. Trail Blazer Light's Golden Jubilee, 1929, Mich. Sci. Trail Blazer award, 1987, award Detroit Sci. Ctr., 1988, official citation Commonwealth of Mass. State Senate, 1986, Cert. of Appreciation U.S. Navy Office of Info., Life Achievement in Pub. Rels. award Mortgage Bankers Assn. Am., 1989, Dist. Prof. award We. Ky. U. Presa chpt., 1989, Cert. of Recognition Cambridge, 1989, Plaque Nat. Assn. Vocat. Tech. Edn. Communications, 1989, Crystall Bell award Pub. Club New Eng., 1990, Joseph E. Connor Meml. award, Emerson Coll, 1990, Lifetime Achievement award Tampa Bay chpt. Pub. Rels. Soc. Am., 1991; named to New Eng. Advt. Hall of Fame, 1986, Acad. Disting. Bostonians, Boston U., 1987; Benjamin Franklin fellow Royal Soc. Arts. 1969; Assn. Edn. Journalism and Mass Comms. award for significant contbns. to devel. pub. rels., 1992. Mem. ACLU (publicity chmn. 1941), Overseas Press Club, Coun . for Democracy (bd. dirs. 1942), Soc. Psychol. Study of Social Issues (Charter Mem. award 1988), Internat. Pub. Rels. Assn. (Pres.'s award 1979), Pub. Soc. Assn. Am. (Golden Anvil award 1976, Lincoln award New Eng. chpt. 1976, Spl. Troth award Nat. Capital chpt. 1984, advancing pub. rels. award So. New Eng. chpt. 1988, Appreciation award 1988, Lifetime Achievement award Tampa chpt., bd. dirs.), Nat. Assn. Ednl. Broadcasters (chmn. pub. interest com. 1950-58), DeWitt Clinton Alumni Assn. (award 1940, v.p. 1982-95), Boston UN Assn. (bd. dirs. 1987), Acad. Disting. Bostonians, Inter-Faith Cons. Service, Inc. (hon. trustee 1988), Cornell U. Club (N.Y.C., Boston), Harvard Faculty Club, Tau Mu Epsilon (hon.), Phi Alpha Tau. Home: Cambridge Mass. Died Mar. 9, 1995.

BERNDT, RONALD MURRAY, anthropologist, ethnologist; b. Adelaide, Australia, July 14, 1916; s. Alfred Henry Berndt; m. Catherine Berndt, Apr. 1941. Diploma in anthropology, Sydney U., 1943, BA, 1950, MA with 1st class honors, 1951; PhD, London Sch. Econs. and Polit. Sci., 1955. Anthropologist No. Territory Pastoral Firm, Australia, 1944-46; temp. lectr. U. Sydney, Australia, 1951-53; lectr. anthropology U. Sydney, 1954; sr. lectr. U. Western Australia, Nedlands, 1956-58, reader, 1958-63, found. prof. anthropology, 1963-81, emeritus prof., from 1981, hon. rsch. fellow, from 1982; condr. fieldwork in aboriginal Australia, from 1939, New Guinea, 1951-53; hon. assoc., min. aboriginal affairs com. Western Australian Mus., 1962-85; adviser aboriginal affairs Law Reform Commn., from 1979. Author: (with C.H. Berndt and A.P. Elkin) Art in Arnhem Land, 1950, (with C.H. Berndt) From Black to White in South Australia, 1951, Sexual Behavior in Western Arnhem Land, 1951, The First Australians, 1952, Arnhem Land: Its History and Its People, 1954, The World of the First Australians, 1964, Man, Land, and Myth in North Australia: The Gunwinggu People, 1970, The Barbarians: An Anthropological View, 1971, Pioneers and Settlers: The Aboriginal Australians, 1978, Aborigines in Australian Society, 1985, The Speaking Land: Myth and Story in Aboriginal Australia, 1989, (with Stanton) Australian Aboriginal Art, 1981 (with C.H. Berndt and J.E. Stanton) Aboriginal Australian Art: A Visual Perspective, 1982; author: Kunapipi: A Study of an Australian Aboriginal Religious Cult, 1951, Djanggawul: An Aboriginal Cult of North-Eastern Arnhem Land, 1952, Excess and Restraint: Social Control Among a New Guinea Mountain People, 1962, An Adjustment Movement in Arnhem Land, 1962, A Question of Choice: An Australian Aboriginal Dilemma, 1971, Australian Aboriginal Religion, 1974, Love Songs of Arnham Land, 1976, Three Faces of Love, 1976, End of an Era: Aboriginal Labour in the Northern Territory, 1987; contbr. Australian Aboriginal Studies, 1963; editor, contbr.: Australian Aboriginal Art, 1964, Australian Aboriginal Anthropology, 1970, Aborigines and Change: Australia in the Seventies, 1977, others; editor: Aboriginal Sites, Rights and Resource Development, 1982; contbr. American People's Encyclopedia, Encyclopaedia Britannica, Encyclopaedia of Papua and New Guinea; gen. editor Anthrop. Forum; contbr. over 200 articles to profl. jours. Recipient Wellcome medal, 1958; Univ. Grants Commn. grantee Govt. of India, 1965, grantee Australian U., from 1985; Nuffield fellow, 1953-54, Carnegie Traveling fellow, 1955-56. Fellow Am. Anthrop. Assn. (fgn.), Royal Anthrop. Soc. Great Britain and Ireland (hon.), Australian and New Zealand Assn. Advancement Sci. (v.p. anthropology sect. 1959, 61, pres. 1962), Acad. Social Scis. Australia; mem. Assn. Social Anthropologists (mem. Brit. br., pres. Australian br. 1962-64), Royal Soc. Western Australia (medal 1979), Anthrop. Soc. NSW, Anthrop. Soc. Western Australia (hon. life., chmn., pres. 1959, 60, v.p. 1961, medal 1983), Australian Inst. Aboriginal Studies (mem. adv. pnael social anthropology 1961—, mem. interim com. 1962-64, mem. coun. from 1964). Home: Peppermint Grove Australia Deceased.

BERNOUDY, WILLIAM ADAIR, architect; b. St. Louis, Dec. 4, 1910; s. Jerome Baudy and Elizabeth (Maddox) B.; m. Gertrude Charlotte Tornofsky, June 14, 1956. Student, Taliesin Fellowship, 1930-36. Registered architect, Mo. Pres. Bernoudy Assocs., Inc., St. Louis, from 1947; v is. artist in residence Am. Acad., Rome, 1982. Trustee St. Louis Art Mus., 1981-83; bd. dirs. Laumier Sculpture Park, from 1980; mem. exec. bd. Mo. Bot. Gardens, 1983. Fellow AIA. Clubs: University (St. Louis); Metropolitan (N.Y.C.). Home: Saint Louis Mo. Deceased.

BERNSTEIN, EUGENE FELIX, vascular surgeon, medical educator; b. N.Y.C., Oct. 9, 1930; s. Mayer H. and Sarah (Marmerstein) B.; m. Joan Jordan, Oct. 10, 1954; children: Diane, Steven, Susan. Student, Coll. Arts and Pure Scis., NYU, 1947-50; M.D., Downstate Med. Center, SUNY, 1954; M.S., U. Minn., 1961, Ph.D., 1964. Diplomate Am. Bd. Surgery, Am. Bd. Thoracic Surgery, Am. Bd. Vascular Surgery. Intern King's County Hosp., Bklyn., 1954-55; resident U. Minn., 1957-64; instr. dept. surgery U. Minn. Med. Sch., 1963-64, asst. prof., 1964-67, asso. prof., 1967-69; prof. surgery U. Calif. at San Diego Sch. Medicine, 1969-82, head vascular surgery; surgeon Scripps Clinic and Research Found., La Jolla, Calif., 1982-95, sr. con. in vascular surgery, 1993; mem. study sect. NIH, 1976-79. Editor: Vascular Diagnosis, 1985, 4th edit. 1993, Amaurosis Fugax Vascular Diagnosis, 1988, Cerebral Revascularization, 1993; mem. editl. bd. Jour. Vascular Surgery, VASA, Recent Advances in Non-invasive Diagnostic Techniques in Vascular Disease, 1990. Served to capt. M.C. AUS, 1955-57. Postdoctoral research fellow Nat. Heart Inst., 1959-62; Advanced research fellow Am. Heart Assn., 1962-64; John and Mary R. Markle scholar acad. medicine, 1963-68. Mem. ACS, Am. Heart Assn., Am. Soc. Artificial Internal Organs (past pres.), Assn. Acad. Surgery, Am. Surg. Assn., Ctrl. Surg. Assn., Pacific Coast Surg. Assn., San Diego Soc. Gen. Surgeons, Internat. Cardiovasculaar Soc., Soc. Univ. Surgeons, Soc. Clin. Vascular Surgery, Soc. Thoracic Surgery, Soc. Vascular Surgery, So. Calif. Vascular Soc. (past pres.), Western Vascular Soc. (past pres.), Mpls. Surg. Soc., James E. Moore Surg. Soc., Alpha Omega Alpha, Beta Lambda Sigma. Home: La Jolla Calif. Died June 21, 1995.

BERNSTEIN, SIDNEY RALPH, editor, columnist; b. Chgo., Jan. 29, 1907; s. Charles and Jennie R. (Greenblatt) B.; m. Adele Bass, Oct. 5, 1930; children: Janet Bernstein Wingis, Henry. Student, U. Ill., 1924-25; MBA, U. Chgo., 1956. Assoc. editor and mng. editor Hosp. Mgmt., Chgo., 1925-31; mng. editor Advt. Age, Chgo., 1932-38; editor Advt. Age, 1939-57, editorial dir., 1958-64, pub., 1964-70; dir. rsch. and promotion Crain Communications Inc.; v.p. formerly Advt. Pubs., Inc., 1938-60, exec. v.p., gen. mgr., 1961-64, pres., 1964-73, chmn. exec. com., 1973—; pres. Red Tag News Publs., Chgo., 1971-77; chmn. bd. Crain Automotive Group, Detroit, 1973-86, Am. Trade Mags., Chgo., 1973—, Crain Associated Enterprises, 1987—; lectr. U. Coll., U. Chgo., Mich. State U., 1950-58; mem. nat. mktg. adv. com. U.S. Dept. Commerce, 1969-71; bd. dirs. Am. Bus. Press, 1970-73, Mag. Pubs. Assn., 1970-76. Author: This Makes Sense to Me, 1976. Named Advt. Man of Year Chgo. Post 170 Am. Legion, 1957; Chgo. Federated Advt. Club, 1961; Communications Man of Year Chgo. Jr. Assn. Commerce and Industry; Communications Man of Year U. Chgo., 1962; elected to Distbn. Hall of Fame Boston Conf. on Distbn., 1962; named Man of Year Nat. Advt. Agy. Network, 1964, Communications Man of Year Chgo. Soc. Communicating Arts, 1976; named Communicator of Year U. Chgo. Alumni Assn., 1975; recipient Humanitarian award Am. Jewish Com., 1976; Torch of Truth award Advt. Club of Indpls., 1979, Mktg. Man of Yr. Mktg. Communications Execs. Internat., 1980, Paid Circulation Achievement award Assn. Paid Circulation Pubs., 1984; elected to Advt. Hall of Fame, 1989. Mem. Am. Mktg. Assn. (dir. 1946-47, v.p. mktg. mgmt. 1963-64, Distinguished Svc. award 1979), Arts Club, Tavern Club, Nat. Press Club, Chgo. Press Club, Phi Epsilon Pi, Alpha Delta Sigma, Sigma Delta Chi, Beta Gamma Sigma. Home: Chicago Ill. Died May 29, 1993; interred Westlawn Cemetary, Chicago, Ill.

BERRY, KEITH ORAN, chemistry educator; b. Ft. Collins, Colo., Aug. 6, 1938; s. John Allen and Ruby (Good) B.; m. Marian Louise Warner, Aug. 20, 1960; children: Krista, Jana. BA, U. No. Colo., Greeley, 1960; PhD, IA State U., Ames, 1966. Professor U. Puget Sound, Tacoma, from 1965; cons. pvt. practice, Tacoma, from 1974, Kendall/Hunt Pub. Co., Dubuque, IA, from 1985. Editor: Puget Sound Chemist newsletter, 1972; contbr. articles to profl. jours. Mem. Am. Acad. of Forensic Sci., Am. Chem.Soc., The Forensic Sci. Soc. Mem. United Methodist. Home: Tacoma Wash. Deceased.

BERS, LIPMAN, mathematician, educator; b. Riga, Latvia, May 22, 1914; came to U.S., 1940, naturalized, 1949; s. Isaac and Bertha (Weinberg) B.; m. Mary Kagan, May 15, 1938; children: Ruth, Victor. Dr. Rerum Naturalium, U. Prague, 1938; D.Sci (hon.), SUNY-Stony Brook, 1984. Rsch. instr. Brown U., 1942-45; asst. prof., then assoc. prof. Syracuse U., 1945-49; mem. Inst. Advanced Study, 1948-50; prof. NYU, 1950-64, chmn. grad. dept. math., 1959-64; prof. Columbia U., 1964—, chmn. dept. math., 1972-75, Davies prof. math., 1973-82, Davies prof. math. emeritus, 1982—, spl. prof., 1982-84; vis. prof. Stanford U., summer 1955; CUNY Grad. Ctr., 1984-88; vis. Miller rsch. prof. U. Calif., Berkeley, 1968; chmn. Com. Support on Rsch. on Math. Scis., NAS-NRC, 1966-68; chmn. div. math. scis. NRC, 1969-71; chmn. U.S. Nat. Com. for Math., 1977-81. Author math. books.; contbr. articles to math. jours. Recipient N.Y. Mayor's award in sci. and tech., 1985. Fulbright fellow, 1959-60; Guggenheim fellow, 1959-60, 79. Fellow AAAS (chmn. math. sect. 1973, 83), Am. Acad. Arts and Scis., Am. Philos. Soc.; mem. NAS (chmn. math. sect. 1967-70, chmn. com. on human rights 1979-84), Am. Math. Soc. (v.p. 1963-65, Steele prize 1975, pres. 1975-77), Fedn. Am. Scientists (coun. 1977-79, sponsor 1980—), Finnish Acad. Sci. and Letters (fgn.), N.Y. Acad. Scis. (hon. life, Recognition of Svcs. award 1986), London Math. Soc. (hon.). Home: New Rochelle N.Y.

BESSINGER, JESS BALSOR, JR., retired English language educator; b. Detroit, Sept. 25, 1921; s. Jess Balsor and Elaine (Brown) B.; m. Elizabeth Lieber Duvally, July 12, 1956 (div. 1979); children: Anthony DuVally, Jess Balsor III. B.A., Rice U., 1943; M.A. Harvard U., 1947, Ph.D., 1952. Teaching asst. MIT, Cambridge, 1947-48; teaching fellow, tutor Harvard U., Cambridge, 1948-50; hon. teaching asst. Univ. Coll., London, 1950-52; asst. prof. English Brown U., Providence, 1952-56; assoc. prof. English Univ. Coll., Toronto, 1956-60; prof. Univ. Coll., 1960-63; prof. English NYU, 1964-92. Author: A Short Dictionary of Anglo-Saxon Poetry, 1960; editor: Procs. of a Literary Data Processing Conference, 1964, (with Robert P. Creed) Franciplegius: Medieval and Linguistic Studies in Honor of F. P. Magoun, Jr, 1965, (with Stanley J. Kahrl) Essential Articles for the Study of Old English Poetry, 1968, A Concordance to Beowulf, 1969, (with Robert R. Raymo) Medieval Studies in Honor of L. H. Hornstein, 1976, A Concordance to the Anglo-Saxon Poetic Records, 1978, (with Robert F. Yeager) Approaches to the Teaching of Beowulf, 1983; gen. editor: Harvard Old English Series, 1965—; co-founder, editor Old English Newsletter, 1966-69; long-playing records and cassettes (Caedmon) include Wellsprings of Drama, 1958, Chaucer: The Canterbury Tales General Prologue, Prologue to the Parson's Tale, Retraction, 1964, Caedmon's Hymn and Other Poems in Old English including Beowulf, 1964, Chaucer: The Miller's Tale, The Reeve's Tale, 1965, The Poetry of Geoffrey Chaucer, 1966, A History of the English Language, 1973; (with Marie Boroff) Sir Gawain and the Green Knight and Pearl, 1967. Served with U.S. Army, 1943-46. Fulbright scholar, 1950-52; Can. Council fellow, 1960; Guggenheim Found. fellow, 1963, 74. Mem. Mediaeval Acad. Am., MLA, Internat. Assn. Univ. Profs. English, Medieval Soc. So. Africa. Home: Middletown R.I. Died June 23, 1994.

BETCHKAL, JAMES JOSEPH, editor; b. Racine, Wis., Mar. 11, 1935; s. Herbert M. and Frances (Cetrano) B.; m. Ann Vernon, June 23, 1956; children: Janet Ann, Mark James. B.S., U. Miami, 1956; postgrad., U. Wis., 1957, Northwestern U., 1959. Asst. editor Actual Specifying Engr., Chgo., 1956-58; mng. editor Nation's Schs. Mag., Chgo., 1959-63; editor The Record, Oak Park, Ill., 1963; exec. editor Pioneer Newspapers, Inc., Oak Park, 1964-68; editor, pub. Am. Sch. Bd. Jour., Evanston, Ill., then Am. Sch. Bd. Jour., Washington, 1968-78; editor-in-chief, pub. The Exec. Educator and asso. exec. dir. Nat. Sch. Bds. Assn., Washington, 1978-89; instr. folio Nat. Mag. Conf., 1977-78; instr. Sci. Research Assocs., Chgo., 1964, No. Ill. U., DeKalb, summer 1966; judge nat. mag. awards Columbia U. Gen. chmn. Schaumburg Twp. (Ill.) United Fund, 1966, Stars and Stripes charity cotillion, 1966; mem. Hoffman Estates (Ill.) Police Commn., 1966-67; bd. dirs. Pathfinder council Boy Scouts Am., 1965; judge Nat. Mag. award competition, 1986-87. Recipient Editorial award Ill. Press Assn., 1966, award of Merit, Boy Scouts Am., 1966, award of Merit, Assn. Sch. Bus. Ofcls. U.S. and Can., 1960; All-Am. award Ednl. Press Assn. Am., 1970, 71, 72, 75, 76, 80, 82, 85, Editorial award, 1983, 84. Mem. Nat. Newspaper Assn., Edn. Writers Assn. Am., Am. Soc. Assn. Execs., Soc. Nat. Assn. Publs. (dir. 1972-89, pres. 1977-78, Life Time Achievement award 1989), Am. Soc. Mag. Editors, Mag. Pubs. Assn., Am. Soc. Assn. Execs. Home: Washington D.C. Died Apr. 21, 1989.

BETTS, WILBUR WARD, mechanical engineer, author, historian; b. Rockford, Ill., Aug. 28, 1904; s. Fred Grant and Edith Belle (Beach) B.; BS with honors in Mech. Engring., U. Ill., 1935; m. Sarah Elizabeth Farrey, June 2, 1928 (div.); children: Mary Edith, Sharon Ann; m. Mary Roberta Van DeWalker, Oct. 19, 1970. Design engr. Ingersoll Milling Machine Co., Rockford, 1922-32; asst. sales mgr. Barnes Drill Co., Rockford, 1935-37; sales engr. English & Miller Machinery Co., Detroit, 1937-38; design engr. Farrel Birmingham Gear Corp., Buffalo, 1938-40; group leader Bell Aircraft Corp., Buffalo, 1940-42, W. Coast Engring. rep. B-29 Com., 1942-44; product analyst Webster-Brinkley Co., Seattle, 1944-46; chief engr. Kirsten Pipe Co., Seattle, 1946-48; adminstrn. engr. B47 and Bomarc Functional tests Boeing Co., Seattle, 1948-61; test devel. engr. DynaSoar Gliders, Seattle, 1962, charge test verification saturn booster, New Orleans, 1963-65, adminstrn. engr. 747 airplane, 1965-69; test procedures cons., Seattle, 1969—. Chmn. adv. com. Office of Price Adminstrn., State of Wash., 1944-46. Recipient Bronze Tablet award U. Ill., 1935. Mem. Soc. Automotive Engrs. (25-Yr. Membership award 1969), Am. Indian Profl. Assocs., Mayflower Soc., Sons of Union Vets. of Civil War, SAR, Gen. James A. Longstreet Meml. Assn., James Willard Schultz Soc., Jet Pioneers Assn. U.S.A., Phi Eta Sigma, Pi Tau Sigma, Theta Tau, Tau Beta Pi, Horseless Carriage Club (pres. 1958), N.W. Intertribal Club. Methodist. Author: (with Schultz) Bear Chief's War Shirt, 1983. Contbr. articles to profl. jours., also short story. Home: Seattle Wash.

BIANCHI, DONALD ERNEST, academic administrator, biology educator; b. Santa Cruz, Calif., Nov. 22, 1933; s. Ernest A. and Florence A. Bianchi; m. Georgia Louise McCush, June 3, 1933; children: Diana, David, William. AB, Stanford U., 1955, AM, 1956; PhD, U. Mich., 1959. Asst. prof. biology Calif. State U., Northridge, 1959-63, assoc. prof., 1963-66, prof., 1966—, acting dean, 1973-74, dean, 1974-91, 93-96, acting v.p. for acad. affairs, 1991-93; vis. asst. prof. Western Wash. State Coll., summer 1962; adj. prof. biology U. Calif., Santa Barbara, 1990-92; mem. bd. govs. So. Calif. Ocean Studies Consortium, 1977—, vice chmn. bd., 1979-80, 85-91, chmn. bd., 1991-92, bd. govs. Desert Studies Consortium, 1976-96, chmn., 1983-84; mem. edn. and rsch. coun. Assoc. Western Univs. Inc., chmn.-elect, 1986-87, bd. trustees. Author: (with P. Sheeler) Cell Biology, 1980, 3d edit., 1987 ; profl. papers pub. in numerous sci. jours. Bd. dirs. Soc. of Exptl. Test Pilots Scholarship Found., 1985-96. NIH predoctoral fellow 1957-59, NIH research grantee, 1950-65; Bache Found research grantee, 1962; NSF Sci. Faculty fellow, U. Geneva, 1965-66; recipient outstanding tchr. award Calif. State U., Northridge, 1972. Mem. Am. Arachnological Soc., So. Calif. Soc. Microbiology, Mycological Soc. Am., Sigma Xi (chpt. pres. 1971-72). Home: Northridge Calif.

BICH, MARCEL L. (BARON BICH), industrialist; b. Turin, Italy, July 29, 1914; s. Aime-Mario and Marie (Muffat de Saint-Amour de Chanaz) B.; m. Louise Chamussy (dec.); children: Claude, Marie-Caroline Bich Martin, Bruno, Francois; m. Laurence Courier de Mere children: Antoine, Marie Aimee, Marie-Charlotte Marie-Henriette, Marie-Pauline, Xavier. Ed., Coll. St Elmeà Arcachon, Faculté de Droit de Paris. Founder former pres., chmn. bd., now hon. chmn. bd. Bic Co. chmn. bd., dir. Bic Corp., Milford, Conn. Decorated chevalier Legion of Honor. Home: Milford Conn. Died May 30, 1994.

BIERMAN, EDWIN LAWRENCE, physician, educator; b. N.Y.C., Sept. 17, 1930; s. J.M. and Bella (Smolens) B.; m. Marilyn Joan Soforan, July 1, 1956 children: Ellen M., David J. B.A., Bklyn. Coll., 1951; M.D. (Schepp, Shapiro, Grand St. Boys founds. scholar, Thorne Shaw scholar), Cornell U., 1955. Diplomate Nat. Bd. Med. Examiners, Am. Bd. Internal Medicine. Intern N.Y. Hosp., N.Y.C., 1955-56; resident N.Y. Hosp., 1959-60; asst. Rockefeller Inst., N.Y.C., 1956-57; asst. prof. Rockefeller Inst., 1960-62; assoc. prof. medicine U. Wash. Med. Sch., Seattle, 1963-68; prof medicine U. Wash. Med. Sch., 1968—; chief div metabolism and gerontology VA Hosp., Seattle, 1967-75, head div. metabolism, endocrinology and nutrition, 1975—. Editor Arteriosclerosis, 1980-90; assoc. editor Diabetes, 1984-86; contbr. numerous articles to profl. jours. Served to capt. M.C. AUS, 1957-59. Mead Johnson postgrad. scholar A.C.P., 1959; Guggenheim fellow, 1972. Fellow ACP, AAAS; mem. AMA (Goldberger award 1988), Inst. Medicine (food and nutrition bd. 1989-95), Am. Fedn. Clin. Rsch., Am. Diabetes Assn., Western Soc. for Clin. Investigation (Mayo Soley award 1993), Am. Soc. for Clin. Investigation, Assn. Am. Physicians, Endocrine Soc., Am. Physiology Soc., Am. Soc. Clin. Nutrition (Robert S. Herman award 1985, v.p. 1990-91, pres. 1991-92), Western Assn. Physicians (pres. 1980), Am. Heart Assn. (vice chmn. coun. on arteriosclerosis 1981-83, chmn. 1983-85, chmn. sci. adv. com. 1990-93, Award of Merit 1984, Gold Heart award 1990, Spl. Recognition award 1993, Disting. Achievement award). Home: Seattle Wash. Died July 5, 1995.

BIEZUP, JOHN THOMAS, lawyer; b. Wilkes-Barre, Pa., June 25, 1929; s. Frank W. and Nellie (Moroski) B.; m. Georgia M. Medley, Aug. 20, 1959; children: Jennifer L., Laura M., Mark A. Grad. cum laude, Wyo. Sem., 1947; BS with honors., U.S. Mcht. Marine Acad., Kings Point, N.Y., 1951; LLB, Yale U., 1955. Bar: Pa. 1959, U.S. Dist. Ct. (ea. dist.) Pa. 1959, U.S. Ct. Appeals (3d cir.) 1959, U.S. Supreme Ct. 1977, U.S. Dist. Ct. (we. dist.) Pa. 1987, U.S. Dist. Ct. (mid. dist.) Pa. 1993, Md. 1994, U.S. Dist. Ct. Md. 1992, N.Y., N.J. 1994, U.S. Dist. Ct. (ea. and so. dist.) N.Y. 1994, U.S. Dist. Ct. N.J. Assoc. Rawle & Henderson, Phila., 1958-63, ptnr., 1964-79; ptnr. Palmer Biezup & Henderson, Phila., 1979-94; permanent mem. Jud. Conf. 3d Cir. Ct. Appeals, Phila., 1971-94; emeritus trustee Balch Inst. for Ethnic Studies, Greater Phila. Philosophy Consortium, Operation Smile, Phila. chpt. Mem. bd. adv. editors The Maritime Law Jour., Tulane U., 1983-94; assoc. editor Am. Maritime Cases, 1987-94; mem. bd. advisors, maritime advisor Ct. Case Digest, 1991-94; contbr. articles to profl. Jours. Lt. USNR, 1955-57. Mem. ABA, Pa. Bar Assn., Phila. Bar Assn. Maritime Law Assn. (exec. com., bd. dirs. 1990-93, Maritime Advisor of U.S.), Port Phila. Maritime Soc., Assn. Marine Average Adjusters U.S., Assn. Average Adjusters Gt. Britain, Union League, Merion Cricket Club, Trucking Industry Def. Assn. (founder, bd. dirs. 1993-94), Yale Club of N.Y., Westmoreland Club (Wilkes-Barre, Pa.), Downdown Club (Phila.). Republican. Episcopalian. Home: Gladwyne Pa. Died July 23, 1994.

BILL, MAX, architect, sculptor, painter; b. Winterthur, Switzerland, Dec. 22, 1908; s. Erwin and Marie (Geiger) B.; m. Binia Spoerri, 1931 (dec. 1988); m. Angela Thomas, 1991. Student, Zurich Sch. Art and Craft, 1924-27, Dessau Bauhaus, 1927-29; Dr. honoris causa, U. Stuttgart, 1979. Pvt. practice architecture and graphic artist Zurich, 1929-94, publicist, 1936; dir. Inst. for Design, Ulm, Fed. Republic Germany, 1951-56; chief architect educating and creating sect. Swiss Nat. Exhbn., Lausanne, 1961-64; prof. environ. design Inst. Fine Arts, Hamburg, 1967-75; mem. Swiss Parliament, Berne, 1967-71. Over 200 one-man shows include Albright-Knox Art Gallery, Buffalo, N.Y., 1974; represented in permanent collections Kunstmuseum, Basle, Kunstmuseum, Berne, Art Inst. Chgo., Hirshhorn Mus., Washington, Musee d'Art Moderne, Paris, Gallery Naz d'Arte Moderna, Rome, Kunsthaus, Zurich. Mem. Zurich City Coun., 1961-67. Recipient Grand Prix Triennale Milan, 1936, 51, Biennale Sao Paulo, 1951, 1st prize City of Goslar, 1982, Kandinsky prize, 1949, Gold medal Italian Chamber of Deps., Verucchio, 1966, 1st prize Internat. Biennale Small Sculpture, Budapest, 1971, Internat. Leonardo prize, 1987, Marconi prize, 1988, Diploma of Honmor graphic biennale Lubliana, 1991; named comdr. Ordre of Arts and Letters, France, 1985; ordre 1st class (Germany). Fellow AIA (hon.); mem. Acad. Arts (Berlin), Acad. Architecture (France, corr.), Acad. Arts and Letters (Belgium). Home: Zumikon Switzerland Died Dec. 9, 1994.

BILLINGS, BRUCE HADLEY, physicist, aerospace company executive; b. Chgo., July 6, 1915; s. Thomas H. and Grace (Hadley) B.; m. Sarah Winslow (div.); children: Sally Frances, Bruce Randolph, Jane Winslow, Peter Fayssoux; m. Fannie Hu. A.B., Harvard U., 1936, A.M., 1937; Ph.D., Johns Hopkins U., 1943; hon. Ph.D., China Acad. Tchr. math. sci. Am. Community Sch., Beirut, 1937-40; jr. instr. physics Johns Hopkins U., Balt., 1940-41; physicist Polaroid Corp., Cambridge, Mass., 1941-47; mem. radiol. safety sect. atomic bomb test Bikini, 1946; dir. research Baird-Atomic, Inc., Cambridge, 1947-63; exec. v.p. Baird-Atomic, Inc., 1955-59, v.p. and tech. dir., 1960-63; v.p., gen. mgr. labs. operation Aerospace Corp., Los Angeles, 1963-68; v.p. corp. planning Aerospace Corp., 1973-74; v.p. Aerospace Corp., Washington, 1974-76; pres. Thagard Research Corp., 1976-80; chmn. bd. Internat. Tech. Assocs., Inc., 1977-92, dir. research, 1980-92; commr. Joint Commn. on Rural Reconstrn.; spl. asst. to Am. ambassador for sci. and tech., Taipei, Taiwan, 1968-73; mem. sci. adv. com. Bell & Howell; dir. Ealing Corp., Diffraction, Ltd., Inc., Altovac Tech., Inc.; mem. Air Force Sci. Adv. Bd., 1962-72; asst. dir. def. research and engring. Dept. Def., 1959-60; U.S. del. Marseille Conf. on Thin Films, 1949; U.S. rep. on UN Adv. Com. on Application of Sci. and Tech. to Devel., 1973-78; mem. U.S. nat. com. Internat. Commn. Optics; research asso. Harvard Coll. Obs.; cons. Dept. State, 1973-82; adj. prof. physics Harvey Mudd Coll., 1986-92; adj. prof. East Asian studies Calif. State U., Long Beach, 1991-92; fellow East Asian Studies Ctr., U. So. Calif.; bd. dirs. Laser Sci., Inc., Phys. Optics Corp. Assoc. editor: Am. Inst. Physics Handbook; subject editor: Applied Optics; Contbr. tech. articles to profl. jours. Decorated Order of Brilliant Star Republic of China. Fellow Am. Acad. Arts and Scis. (sec.), Am. Phys. Soc., Optical Soc. Am. (asso. editor jour. 1956-60, pres. 1971, v.p. internat. commn. of optics 1973); mem. Acoustical Soc. Am., AAAS, Sigma Xi. Club: St. Botolph. Home: Long Beach Calif. Died Nov. 21, 1992.

BINFORD, CHAPMAN HUNTER, physician; b. Darlington Heights, Va., Oct. 3, 1900; s. Charles F. and W. Ava (Chilton) B.; m. Thelma Lynette Beauchamp, June 8, 1929; children—Charles C., M. Lynette. A.B., Hampden-Sydney Coll., 1923, D.Sc. (hon.), 1962; M.D., Med. Coll. Va., 1929; D.Sc. (hon.), Va. Commonwealth U., 1979. Diplomate: Am. Bd. Pathology.; Registrar for leprosy Am. Registry Pathology, 1951-75. Commd. officer USPHS, 1930, advanced through grades to med. dir., 1948; cancer investigator Harvard Med. Sch., 1931-32; with Leprosy Research Inst., Honolulu, 1933-36; pathology investigations NIH, 1936-37; pathologist USPHS hosps., 1937-51; rep. USPHS at Armed Forces Inst. Pathology, Washington, 1951-60; ret., 1960; chief geog. pathology div. Armed Forces Inst. Pathology, 1960-62; med. dir. Leonard Wood Meml. (Am. Leprosy Found.), 1963-72; chief spl. mycobacterial diseases br. Armed Forces Inst. Pathology, 1963-74; expert com. leprosy WHO, 1964-77; chmn. U.S. coordinating com. Internat. Com. Socs. Pathology, 1966-69; Maude Abbott lectr. Internat. Acad. Pathology, 1973; cons. to leprosy registry Armed Forces Inst. Pathology. Author: (with Emmons Utz and Kwon-Chung) Medical Mycology, 1977; also numerous articles; editor: (with Connor) The Pathology of Tropical and Extraordinary Diseases, 1976. Recipient F.K. Mostofi award Internat. Acad. Pathology, 1978; Damien Dutton award in Leprosy, 1970. Mem. Wash. Soc. Pathologists (pres. 1954-55), Coll. Am. Pathologists, AMA, Am. Assn. Pathologists, Am. Soc. Clin. Pathologists (Ward Burdick award 1968), Internat. Acad. Pathology (pres. 1958-59, rep. to internat. intersoc. com. pathology 1962-70, editor bull. 1960- 65), Internat. Leprosy Assn. (hon. v.p. from 1973), Am. Soc. Tropical Medicine and Hygiene, Société Belge de Medicine Tropicale (asso.), Phi Beta Kappa, Sigma Xi, Alpha Omega Alpha. Club: Cosmos. Home: Arlington Va. Deceased.

BINKLEY, THOMAS EDEN, music educator, conductor; b. Cleve.; s. Robert Cedric and Frances (Williams) B.; m. Raglind Herrel; children: Leonor, Isabel, Beatriz. MusB, U. Ill., 1956, postgrad., 1958-59; postgrad., U. Munich, 1957-58. Founding mem., dir. Studio der fruhen Musik (Early Music Quartet), Munich, 1960-80; tchr., performer medieval program Schola Cantorum Basiliensis, Basel, Switzerland, 1973-77; vis. prof. Stanford U., 1977, 79; prof. music, dir. Early Music Inst. Ind. U., Bloomington, 1979—; producer Focus Records, Early Music Inst. Editor: (book series) Music: Scholarship and Performance; contbr. articles to profl. jours.; performer (middle ages and renaissance music recordings) Orlando di Lasso, Guillaume de Machaut, Chansons der Troubadour, Roman de Fauvel, Heiteres Mittelalter, 1300-1600, Guillaume Dufay, Minnesang und Spruchdichtung, Weltliche Musik um 1300, Das Grosse Passionspiel, Florid Song, Musica Iberica, Vox Humana, Carmina Burana I, II, Geistliche Lieder, Cantigas De Santa Maria, Fruhe Musik in Italien, numerous others. Recipient Edison award Amsterdam, 1964, 74, Preis der deutschen Schallplattenkritik Berlin 1965, 68, 73, 79, Grand Prix du Disques Paris, 1968, 69, 72, 74, Deutscher Schallplattenpreis Baden Baden, 1981, 82, Dickenson Coll. Arts award, 1983. Mem. Am. Musicol. Soc., Early Music Am. (v.p.), Greenburg Awards Com. Home: Bloomington Ind. Died Apr. 28, 1995.

BIRD, FRANCIS MARION, lawyer; b. Comer, Ga., Sept. 4, 1902; s. Henry Madison and Minnie Lee (McConnell) B.; m. Mary Adair Howell, Jan. 30, 1935; children: Francis Marion, Mary Adair Bird Kennedy, Elizabeth Howell Bird Hewitt, George Arthur. AB, U. Ga., 1922, LLB, 1924; LLM, George Washington U., 1925; LLD, Emory U., 1980, U. St. Andrews, 1982. Bar: Ga. bar 1924, D.C. bar 1925. Since practiced in Atlanta; with U.S. Senator Hoke Smith, 1925; pvt. practice, 1930-45; assoc. Bird & Howell, 1945-59, Jones Bird & Howell, 1959-82, Alston & Bird, 1982—; served as part-time U.S. referee in bankruptcy, 1945-54; spl. asst. to U.S. atty. gen. as hearings officer Nat. Selective Svc. Act.; Mem. commn. for preparation plan of govt. City of Atlanta and county area; mem. permanent rules com. Ga. Supreme Ct.; mem. Met. Atlanta Commn. Crime and Juvenile Delinquency, chmn., 1969-70; formerly Ga. co-chmn. Tech.-Ga. Devel. Fund.; Trustee Young Harris Coll., U. Ga. Found., Atlanta Lawyers Found., Interdenominational Theol. Ctr.; trustee, past mem. exec. com. Emory U., Atlanta.; Chmn. Ga. Bd. Bar Examiners, 1954-61. Mem. permanent editorial bd.: Uniform Comml. Code, 1962-77, Fed. Jud. Conf., 5th Circuit, Fed. Jud. Conf., 11th Circuit, 1960-81, 1981—. Recipient Disting. Svc. citation U. Ga. Law Sch.; Disting. Svc. award Atlanta Bar Assn., 1977; Pres.'s award Assn. Pvt. Colls. and Univs., 1979, GA award Harvard Law Sch. Assn., 1984. Fellow Am. Bar Found; mem. Am. Judicature Soc. (past dir.), Am. Law Inst. (council 1949-82, emeritus, past chmn. com. membership), ABA, Ga. (past pres.), Atlanta Bar Assns., N.Y.C. Bar Assn., Atlanta C. of C. (past pres., Atlanta Civic Svc. award 1957), U. Ga. Alumni Assn. (past pres., certificate of merit 1952), George Washington U. Alumni Assn. (achievement award 1965), Peachtree Golf Club, Atlanta Athletic Club (past pres.), Kiwanis, Piedmont Driving Club, Capital City Club, Lawyers Club (past pres.), Augusta Nat. Golf Club (gov.), Phi Kappa Phi, Sigma Chi, Phi Delta Phi. Methodist. Home: Atlanta Ga.

BIRDWHISTELL, RAY L., retired folklore and communication educator; b. Cin., Sept. 29, 1918; s. Robert N. and Hattie Queen (Hughes) B.; m. Anne Davison; children: Jill Read Birdwhistell Pierce, Nancy Mead Birdwhistell Rothberg. A.B., Miami U., Oxford, Ohio, 1940; M.A., Ohio State U., 1941; Ph.D., U. Chgo., 1951. Lectr. in anthropology U. Toronto, 1944-46; instr. sociology U. Louisville, 1946-48, asst. prof. anthropology, dept. sociology, 1948-52, assoc. prof. anthropology, dept. psychology and sociology, 1952-56; assoc. prof. anthropology, dept. anthropology and linguistics U. Buffalo, 1956-59; coordinator Inst. for Research in Human Communication, 1956-59; sr. research scientist Eastern Pa. Psychiat. Inst., 1959-77; prof. research in anthropology, dept. psychiatry Health Scis. Center, Temple U., Phila., 1959-66; clin. prof. psychiatry, dept. psychiatry, adj. prof. anthropology, dept. behavioral sci. Health Scis. Center, Temple U., 1966-68; vis. prof. communication Annenberg Sch. Communications, U. Pa., 1969-70, prof. communication, 1970-83, prof. folklore and communication, 1983-88, prof. emeritus, 1988-94; vis. lectr. U. Chgo., summer 1951; rsch. assoc. Fgn. Service Inst., Dept. State, 1952; rsch. cons. Center for Advanced Study in Behavioral Scis., Palo Alto, Calif., 1956, fellow, 1968-69; vis. prof. dept. anthropology U. B.C., Vancouver, 1968; Cons., dept. psychiatry Western Psychiat. Inst., Pitts., 1957-64, Emory U. Med. Sch., Atlanta, 1963-64, U. Louisville, Syracuse U., SUNY, Worcester (Mass.) State Hosp., VA Hosp., Palo Alto, Langley Porter Clinic, U. Kans., Ind. U., NIMH, U. Ill., U. Mich.; ptnr. Heron Point Folklore Arts: Native Am. Textile Repair. Author: Kinesics and Context; co-author: Natural History of an Interview; Adv. editor: Family Processes; Mem. editorial adv. bd.: Miss. Quar; mem. editorial bd. Communication; contbr. numerous articles, reviews to profl. jours. Fellow Am. Anthrop. Assn., AAAS, Soc. for Applied Anthropology; mem. Phila. Anthrop. Soc., Am. Acad. Polit. and Social Sci., Phi Beta Kappa, Alpha Kappa Delta, Kappa Pi Epsilon. Home: Brigantine N.J. Died Oct. 19, 1994.

BIRKETT, JOHN HOOPER, accounting and consulting company executive; b. Montreal, Que., Can., Oct. 16, 1925; s. Leonard Harris and Gertrude (Caughill) B.; m. Joan Louise Macklaier, Dec. 27, 1952; children: Peter, Jennifer, Timothy, Elisa. B.Commerce, McGill U., Montreal, 1949. Dist. supr. Canadian Liquid Air Co., 1949-54; sales service mgr. Canadian Chm. & Cellulose Co., Ltd., Montreal, 1955-57; asst. sec. Canadian Chm. & Cellulose Co., Ltd., 1959-61, Columbia Cellulose Co. Ltd., 1958-59, Canadian Chem. Co. Ltd., Montreal, 1962-63, Celanese Can. Inc., Montreal, 1963-64; sec. Celanese Can. Inc., 1964-71, v.p., sec., 1971-72, v.p. adminstrn., 1972-79, dir., 1973-79; v.p. adminstrn., sec. Wabasso Inc., Montreal, 1980-83, v.p. fin. and adminstrn., 1983-87; pres. Woods Inc., 1982-83; sr. assoc. Peat Marwick Stevenson & Kellogg, Montreal, 1986-92. Co-chmn. fin. campaign Montreal YMCA, 1969-71, bd. mgmt., 1969-73, exec. com., 1970-73. Served with Royal Canadian Navy, 1944-45. Mem. Swiss Canadian C. of C. (dir. 1975-80), Can. Textile Inst. (dir.), Can. Chem. Producers Assn.(dir.). Mem. Anglican Ch. Clubs: St. James's (Montreal), Royal Montreal Golf (Montreal), Red Birds Ski (Montreal). Home: Senneville Can. Died Dec. 19, 1992.

BISHOP, BARRY CHAPMAN, professional society executive, scientist; b. Cin., Jan. 13, 1932; m. Lila Mueller; children: Tara Anderson, Brent Russell. BS in Geology, U. Cin., 1954; MS in Geography, Northwestern U., 1957; PhD in Geography, U. Chgo., 1980. Nat. lectr., 1958-59; picture editor illustrations divsn. Nat. Geog. Soc., Washington, 1959-60, mem. photog. staff, 1960-63, fgn. editorial staff, 1963-64, mem. com. rsch. and exploration, 1964, sec. com. rsch. and exploration, 1964-66, mem. editorial staff, 1972-77, chief geog. liaison, office of pres., 1980-89, vice chmn. com. rsch. and exploration, 1984-89, chmn. com., 1989-91, v.p., chmn. com., 1992-94; vis. lectr. dept. geography and Ctr. Asian Studies, U. Mich., 1971-72; adj. assoc. prof. dept. geography Ariz. State U., 1979; vis. geog. scientist Gamma Theta Upsilon/AAG program, 1981-94; bd. dirs. Woodlands Mountain Inst., Yosemite Nat. Insts., Population Reference Bur.; founder, hon. dir. Mountain Travel, 1989-94; del. to numerous convs.; speaker in field. Mem. editorial bd. The Professional Geographer, 1985-87; contbr. articles to profl. jours. With USAF, 1955-58. Recipient Franklin L. Burr award Nat. Geog. Soc., 1961, Hubbard medal Nat. Geog. Soc., 1963, Spl. award Nat. Press Photographers Assn./U. Mo., 1963, Disting. Svc. award Chgo. Geog. Soc., 1963, Merit award Northwestern U., 1963, William Howard Taft medal U. Cin., 1963, McMicken Coll. Arts and Scis. Disting. Alumni award U. Cin., 1990. Fellow Royal Geog. Soc.; mem. Am. Alpine Club (coun. 1965-67),

Am. Soc. Photogrammetry and Remote Sensing, Assn. Am. Geographers (Honors award 1993), Alpine Club (Eng.), Himalayan Club (life), Internat. Mountain Soc. (mem. coun.), Explorers Club N.Y. (bd. dirs. 1983-87, v.p. 1984-85, Club medal 1987), Univ. Club (Washington), Sigma Xi. Home: Bethesda Md. Died Sept. 24, 1994.

BISSELL, RICHARD MERVIN, JR., economist; b. Hartford, Conn., Sept. 18, 1909; s. Richard Mervin and Marie (Truesdale) B.; m. Ann Cornelia Bushnell, July 6, 1940; children: Richard Mervin, Ann Harriet, Winthrop Bushnell, William George, Thomas Ericsson. Student, Kingswood Sch., 1916-22, Groton Sch., 1922-28, London Sch. Econs., 1932-33; AB, YaleU., 1932, PhD, 1939, MA (hon.), 1949. Research asst. Yale U., New Haven, 1934, instr. econs., 1935-39, asst. prof., 1939-42; mem. staff Bur. Fgn. and Domestic Commerce, Dept. Commerce, Washington, 1941-42; economist Combined Shipping Adjustment Bd.; asst. to dep. adminstr. War Shipping Adminstrn., Washington, 1942-43; U.S. exec. officer Combined Shipping Adjustment Bd., 1942-45, dir. ship requirements, 1943-45; econ. adviser to dir. War Moblzn. and Reconversion, Washington, 1945-46, dep. dir., 1946; asso. prof. econs. MIT, Boston, 1942-48, prof., 1948-52; exec. sec. Pres.'s Com. Fgn. Aid (Harriman Com.), Washington, 1947-48; asst. adminstr. program Econ. Cooperation Adminstrn. Washington, 1948-51; acting adminstr., 1951; mem. staff Ford Found., 1952-54; spl. asst. to dir. CIA, Washington, 1954-59, dep. dir. plans, 1959-62; pres. Inst. for Def. Analyses, Washington, 1962-64; dir. marketing and econ. planning United Aircraft Corp., East Hartford, Conn., 1964-74; bus. cons. Farmington, Conn., 1974-94; cons. to dir. Mut. Security, 1952; cons. various intervals Conn. Pub. Utilities Commn., Fortune Mag., Social Sci. Research Council, Cosmopolitan Shipping Co., U.S. Steel Corp., Scudder, Stevens & Clark, Brightwater Paper Co., Asiatic Petroleum Co. Author articles econ. jours.; Prin. editor, contbr. (report of President's Com. Fgn. Aid) European Recovery and American Aid. Recipient Nat. Security medal, 1962. Mem. Am. Acad. Arts and Scis., Am. Econ. Assn., Econometric Assn., Council on Fgn. Relations, Washington Inst. Fgn. Affairs, Conn. Acad. Arts and Scis. Clubs: Hartford; Graduate Club Assn. (New Haven); Yale (N.Y.C.). Home: Farmington Conn. Died Feb. 7, 1994.

BIXBY, BILL, actor, director; b. San Francisco, Jan. 22, 1934; m. Brenda Benet (dec.); 1 child (dec.); m. Laura Michaels, 1990. Student, U. Calif., Berkeley. Appeared in films including Irma La Douce, 1963, Under the Yum Yum Tree, 1963, Ride Beyond Vengeance, 1966, Doctor You've Got to be Kidding, 1967, Speedway, 1968, The Apple Dumpling Gang, 1975, Kentucky Fried Movie, 1977; star of TV series including My Favorite Martian, 1963-65, The Courtship of Eddie's Father, 1969-72, The Magician, 1973-74, (host) Once Upon a Classic, 1976-79, The Incredible Hulk, 1978-81, Goodnight, Beantown, 1983-84, others; dir. TV films: The Barbary Coast, 1975, Three on a Date, 1978, (also actor) The Incredible Hulk Returns, 1988, Another Pair of Aces: Three of a Kind, 1991, Baby of the Bride, 1991; dir. TV series Blossom, 1991-93. Home: Beverly Hills Calif. Died Nov. 22, 1993.

BIZINSKY, (HYMAN) ROBERT, artist; b. Atlanta, June 17, 1915; s. Robert and Jennie Bizinsky; m. Eleanor Anita Guggenheim, 1952. Grad. high sch., Atlanta; student, High Mus. Art, Atlanta, 1936-42; studied with Hans Hofmann, 1942-46, studied with Louis Bouche, 1942-46, studied with Eves Brayer, 1946-50, studied with Emile-Othon Friesz. Mem. art staff Atlanta Constn., 1936-42; columnist The Pacer newspaper, L.A., 1952-55; mem. staff art dept. Beverly Hills (Calif.) Adult Edn., 1955-75. Exhibited in group shows at High Mus. Art, Atlanta, 1944, 45, Nat. Gallery Art, Washington, 1945, Riverside Mus., 1945, Provincetown (Mass.) Mus., 1946, Prix dela Critique, 1948, Pershing Hall, Paris, 1948, Foyer Montparnasse, Paris, 1948, European Ctr., Paris, 1948, Gallery Sainte-Placide, Paris, 1949, Gallery Casteluche, Paris, 1949, traveling exhbn., France, North Africa, Germany, Finland, 1950-51, Gallery Else Clausen, Paris, 1950-51, Societé Nat. des Beaux-Arts, 1950-51, Gallery Zak, Paris, 1950-51, L.A. County Mus. Art, 1952, Francis Lynch Gallery, L.A., 1953, All-City Art Festival, L.A., 1954, Brentwood Art Festival, 1957, pvt. exhbns., 1960-75, others; permanent collection in Nat. Mus. of U.S. Army, Washington, Army Med. Mus., Washington; commd. by U.S. Army to paint historical murals documenting 1st Armored Div., 1942, Feingarten Galleries, L.A., 1990, Armory show, N.Y.C., 1992, Pepperdine U. Art Gallery, One-Man Retrospective, Malibu, Calif., 1992. Appointed mem. Mayor's Art Community Adv. Com. of L.A., 1966. With U.S. Army, 1942-46. Recipient commendation medal from US Army and Red Cross, 1946, Bronze medal All-City Art Festival, 1954; Huntington Hartford Found. scholar, 1951-52. Home: Los Angeles Calif. Died Feb. 20, 1982.

BLACK, ROBERT EMENS, construction company executive; b. Honolulu, July 26, 1920; s. Everett Earl and Ruth Alene (Emens) B.; divorced; children—Elizabeth J., William R.; m. Lucile Mortimer, Dec. 24, 1977. M.E., U. Cin., 1942. Engr., supt. E.E. Black Ltd., Honolulu, 1946-49, gen. supt., 1949-54, v.p., 1954-62, pres., 1962-72, chmn., chief exec. officer, 1972—. Chmn. Hawaii Pacific Coll., Honolulu, 1976—; dir. Hawaiian Trust Co., Ltd., Honolulu, 1972—, Hawaii Employers Council, Honolulu, 1973—, Bishop Mus., Honolulu, 1984—, Hawaiian Found., Honolulu, 1978—, Oahu Devel. Conf., Honolulu, 1978—; active in Hawaii Bus. Roundtable, 1983—; nat. committeeman Republican Party Hawaii, Honolulu, 1982-83. Hon. fellow of Pacific Hawaii Pacific Coll., 1982. Episcopalian. Club: Pacific Honolulu), Oahu Country (Honolulu). Home: Honolulu Hawaii

BLACK, RUSSELL, food store company executive. Chmn. Assoc. Food Stores, Inc., Pocatello, Idaho. Home: Pocatello Idaho

BLACKBURN, MARTHA GRACE, corporate executive, publisher; b. London, Ont., Can., Oct. 9, 1944; d. Walter Juxon and Marjorie Ludwell (Dampier) Blackburn; children: Richard Antony Frederick, Sarah Dampier, Annabelle Grace. B.A. in French, U. Western Ont., London, 1969. Chmn. bd., pres. The Blackburn Group Inc., London, Ont., 1984; also bd. dir. Blackburn Group Inc, London, Ont.; chmn. Blackburn Mktg. Svcs. Inc., Blackburn Holdings Ltd.; pub., dir. London Free Press Printing Co. Ltd., 1984; bd. dirs. CFPL Broadcasting Ltd., London, Netmar Inc. (formerly Pennysaver Publs.), CKNX Broadcasting Ltd., Compusearch Market and Social Rsch. Ltd.; pres. Kilbyrne Investments Inc. Founding mem. Walter J. Blackburn Found.; dir.-at-large Jr. Achievement of Can., Can. Equestrian Team; hon. patron Kidney Found. Can.; mem., hon. bd. dirs. Alan Thicke Centre for Juvenile Diabetes Rsch.; adv. bd. Vanier Cup; past chmn. adv. bd. Performing Arts Ctr.; mem. adv. coun. Orch. London; bd. dirs. World Wildlife, 1985—, The Michener Awards, Ont. Press Coun.; mem. hon. com. Can. Meml. Found.; mem. nat. adv. coun. IMAGINE, Can. Ctr. for Philanthropy; mem. adv. coun. Elgin and Winter Garden Project; mem. adv. com. to Prime Minister on Bus./Govt. Exec. Exchange Program. Mem. Can. Press, Internat. Assn. for Students in Econs. and Bus. Mgmt. (Western adv. com.), Can. Assn. Family Enterprises, U. Western Ont. Women in Mgmt. (adv. com. rsch. project), London Hunt and Country Club, Univ. Club of Toronto. Anglican. Home: London Can. Died Aug. 15, 1992.

BLACKWELL, EARL, publishing executive, writer; b. Atlanta, May 3, 1913; s. Samuel Earl and Carrie (Lagomarsino) B. Student, Culver Mil. Acad., 1928; A.B., Oglethorpe U., 1933; student, Columbia U.; D (hon.), 1980. Co-founder Celebrity Svc. Inc. (offices N.Y.C., London, Paris, Rome, Hollywood), pres., 1939-85, chmn., 1985-95; editor-in-chief Celebrity Register; contbg. editor Town & Country mag., N.Y.C., 1964-95; editorial cons. Town & Country mag.; pres. Embassy Found., Inc., 1958-67, French-Am. Found. Med. Research, 1987; radio commentator Celebrity Table, 1955-56; founder, v.p. Doubles Club, N.Y.C.; lectr. on celebrities, 1963-95. Author: play Aries is Rising, 1939; novels Crystal Clear, 1978, Skyrocket, 1980; contbr. articles on celebrities to mags. Producer Pres. Kennedy's Birthday Celebration, Madison Sq. Garden, 1962; Founder, pres. Nine O'Clocks of N.Y.; dir. Mayor N.Y.C. Com. for Scholastic Achievement, 1957-65; bd. dirs. Soldiers, Sailors, Airmen's Club, N.Y.C.; organizer, pres. Theater Hall of Fame; organizer Salute to Israel's 25th Anniversary. Decorated Knight of Malta. Mem. Pi Kappa Phi, The Boar's Head. Republican. Roman Catholic. Clubs: N.Y. Athletic (N.Y.C.); Tamboo (Bahamas). Home: New York N.Y. Died Mar. 1, 1995.

BLAKE, JOHN FRANCIS, former government agency official, consultant; b. San Francisco, July 10, 1922; s. Richard Daniel and Catherine Genevieve B.; m. Frances Olive Foley, June 25, 1949; children: Kathleen, Barbara, Mary, Joan, Margaret. B.S., U. San Francisco, 1943; M.A., George Washington U., 1965; D (hon.), Def. Intelligence Coll., 1990. With CIA, 1947-79, dep. dir. adminstrn., 1974-79; staff dir. U.S. Senate Select Com. on Intelligence, Washington, 1981-82; v.p. Electronic Warfare Assocs. Inc., McLean, Va., 1982-86; adj. prof. Def. Intelligence Coll., Washington, 1986-93. Served in U.S. Army, 1943-46. Recipient Career Service award U.S. Civil Service League, 1978. Mem. Assn. Former Intelligence Officers (dir.), CIA Retirees Assn. Home: Alexandria Va. Died Mar. 27, 1995.

BLAKELY, ROBERT JOHN, retired journalist, educator; b. nr. Ainsworth, Nebr., Feb. 24, 1915; s. Percy Lee and Mary Frances (Watson) B.; m. Alta M. Farr, 1964; 3 children. B.A. with highest distinction, State U. Iowa, 1937; scholar, Harvard Grad. Sch., 1937-38. Editorial writer Chgo. Daily News, 1964-67, editor sch. page, 1967-68; with Register and Tribune, Des Moines, 1938-42, 46-48; asst. to dir. domestic br. O.W.I., 1942-43; charge bur. spl. operations, editorial page editor St. Louis Star Times, 1948-51; mgr. cen. regional office Fund for Adult Edn., 1951-56, v.p., 1956-61; dean extension State U. Iowa, 1961-62; adj. assoc. prof. adult edn. Syracuse U., 1969-77, prof., 1977-84; Exec. com. Adult Edn. Council, Des Moines, 1939-41, St. Louis, 1948-51. Appeared numerous radio, TV broadcasts; author scripts for films.; Author: Adult Education in a Free Society, 1958, Toward a Homeodynamic Society, 1965, Knowledge Is the Power to Control Power, 1969, The People's Instrument: A Philosophy for Public Television, 1971, Fostering the Growing Need to Learn, 1974, To Serve the Public Interest, 1979; contbr. chpts. to profl. publs., articles to mags. Served from pvt. to 1st lt. USMCR, 1943-46. Home: Chicago Ill. Died Nov. 14, 1994.

BLANCH, STUART YARWORTH, archbishop; b. Blakeney, Gloucestershire, Eng., Feb. 2, 1918; s. William Edwin and Elizabeth Blanch; m. Brenda Gertrude Coyte, 1943; children—Susan, Hilary, Angela, Timothy, Alison. BA, Oxford U., 1948, MA, 1952; LLD, Liverpool U., 1975; DD (hon.), Hull U., 1977, Wycliffe Coll., Toronto, 1979, U. Manchester, 1984; D (hon.), U. York, 1979. Ordained priest Ch. of Eng. With Law Fire Ins. Soc. Ltd., 1936-40; curate, then vicar chs. in Oxford, 1949-57; vice prin. Wycliffe Hall, 1957-60; Oriel canon Rochester Cathedral, warden Rochester Theol. Coll., 1960-66; bishop of Liverpool, 1966-75; archbishop of York, 1975-83; prochancellor Hull U., 1975-83, York U., 1977-83; mem. House of Lords, 1972—, privy counsellor, 1975—, subprelate Order St. John, 1975—. Served as navigator RAF, 1940-46. Hon. fellow St. Catherine's Coll., Oxford, 1975, St. Peter's Coll., Oxford, 1983; decorated Baron, 1983. Mem. Royal Commonwealth Soc. Author: The World Our Orphanage, 1972; For All Mankind, 1976; The Christian Militant, 1978; The Burning Bush, 1978; The Trumpet in Morning, 1979; The Ten Commandments, 1981; Living by Faith, 1983; Way of Blessedness, 1985, Encounters with Jesus, 1988.

BLANCHETTE, JAMES EDWARD, psychiatrist; b. Syracuse, N.Y., Aug. 28, 1924; s. Joseph M. and Margaret (Vincent) B.; m. Shirley Ruth Brisco, Sept. 1, 1948 (dec. May 1981). BA, Syracuse U., 1950; MD, SUNY-Syracuse Sch. Med., 1953. Diplomate Am. Bd. Med. Examiners, Am. Bd. Psychiatry and Neurology. Intern St. Vincent's Hosp., N.Y.C., 1953-54; resident Patton (Calif.) State Hosp., 1954-55, Met. State Hosp., Norwalk, Calif., 1957-59; pvt. practice psychiatry Redlands, Calif., 1959—; chief profl. edn. Patton State Hosp., 1960-64, teaching. cons., 1964-69; mem. staff San Bernardino Community Hosp., St. Bernadine Hosp. (both San Bernardino). With USAAF, 1945-47. Fellow Am. Psychiat. Assn. (life), AAAS, Pan.-Am. Med. Assn., Royal Soc. Health; mem. AMA, Calif. Med. Assn., San Bernardino Med. Soc., Internat. Platform Assn., So Calif. Psychiat. Soc. (pres. Inland chpt. 1963-64, pres. 1983-84), Am. Med. Soc. Vienna, Phi Mu Alpha Symphonia, Nu Sigma Nu. Home: San Bernardino Calif.

BLAND, EDWARD FRANKLIN, physician; b. West Point, Va., Jan. 24, 1901; s. James Edward and Mary L. (Bowden) B.; m. Frances Poinier, Sept. 7, 1935 (dec.); children: Frances B. Youngblood, James Edward (dec.), Robert Poinier; m. Caroline B. Thayer, Dec. 31, 1984. B.S., U. Va., 1923, M.D., 1927; research fellow, Univ. Coll. Hosp., London, 1930-31. Intern Mass. Gen. Hosp., 1927-29, resident, 1929-30, chief cardiac unit, 1949-64; cons. vis. physician, 1960-86, pvt. practice specializing in cardiology, Boston, 1932-86; sr. vis. physician House of Good Samaritan, Children's Med. Center, 1962-86; mem. cons. staff W. Roxbury, VA, Winchester, Malden, Brockton, Framingham, Gloucester hosps.; assoc. clin. prof. medicine Harvard Med. Sch., 1954-64, clin. prof. medicine, 1964-67, clin. prof. medicine emeritus, from 1967; ret. 1986; civilian cons. to surgeon gen. U.S. Army, 1946-50. Mem. editorial bd. Cardiology Digest, 1965-92. Mem. tng. rev. com. Nat. Heart Inst., 1965-92. Served to lt. col., M.C. AUS, 1942-45, MTO. Decorated Bronze Star. Mem. Am. Soc. Clin. Investigation, Am. Clin. and Climatol. Assn., Assn. Am. Physicians, New Eng. Cardiovascular Soc. (past pres.), Am. Heart Assn. (past dir., Paul D. White award 1975), Mass. Heart Assn. (past pres.). Clubs: Aesculapian (Boston); Brookline Country (Mass.). Home: Chestnut Hill Mass. Died Sept., 1992.

BLANTON, JOE, supermarket company executive. Pres. Publix Super Markets, Inc., Lakeland, Fla. Home: Lakeland Fla.

BLAUSTEIN, ALBERT PAUL, lawyer, law educator, author; b. N.Y.C., Oct. 12, 1921; s. Karl Allen and Rose (Brickam) B.; m. Phyllis Migden, Dec. 21, 1948; children: Mark Allen, Eric Barry, Dana Blaustein Litke. AB, U. Mich., 1941; JD, Columbia U., 1948; hon. doctorate, Academia Nacional de Derecho y Cincias Sociales de Cordoba. Bar: N.Y. 1948, N.J. 1962. Reporter, rewriteman Chgo. Tribune and City News Bur., 1941-42; ptnr. Blaustein and Blaustein, N.Y.C., 1948-50, 52-55; asst. prof. law N.Y. Law Sch., N.Y.C., 1953-55; assoc. prof. law Rutgers U., Camden, N.J., 1955-59, prof. law, 1959-91, prof. emeritus, 1991-94; counsel Dilworth, Paxson, Kalish & Kauffman, Phila., 1990-93; sr. assoc. van Kloberg & Assocs., Washington, 1993-94; mem. Civil Rights Reviewing Authority, U.S. Dept. Edn., 1984-94; chief exec. officer, sec. gen., Phila. Constn. Found., 1988-90, pres., 1990-94; pres. Constns. Rsch. Ctr., Fribourg, Switzerland; v.p., chmn. adv. bd. Internat. Ctr. Constitutions Studies, Athens, Greece, 1984-94; pres., chmn. Constns., Assocs., N.Y.C., 1979-94; counsel-advisor, draftsman Constns. of Bangladesh, Bolivia, Brazil, Canada, Namibia, Cambodia, Liberia, Niger, Peru, Uganda, Zimbabwe, Fiji, Romania, Poland, Nepal, Nicaragua, Russia, Republic South Africa, Trinidad and Tobago,

Georgia, Macedonia, Mi'Kmag Indian Nation, Can., Cuban-Am. Nat. Found., 1966-94; cons. law sch. devel. Internat. Legal Ctr. and Asia Found., Nigeria, Liberia, Ethiopia, Kenya, Vietnam, Taiwan, Tanzania, Uganda, Zaire, 1963-73; cons. U.S. CRC, Washington, 1962-63, N.J. Div. Civil Rights, Trenton, 1971-72; pres., chmn. Human Rights Advocates Internat., N.Y.C., 1979-94; academico honoris causa La Academia Mexicana de Derecho Internacional; Miembro correspondiente (hon.), Revista Uruguaya de Derecho Constitucional; sr. assoc. Jerusalem Ctr. for Pub. Affairs; prof. Miembro (hon.) Inst. Derecho Politico y Constn., Argentina; founder Law Day, U.S. Author or co-author: Public Relations for Bar Associations, 1953, The American Lawyer, 1972, Fiction Goes to Court, 1954, 1977, Desegregation and the Law, 1957, 2d edit., 1962, 85, Doctors' Choice, 1957, Deals with the Devil, 1958, Invisible Men, 1960, Civil Affairs Legislation, Selected Cases and Materials, 1960, Fundamental legal Documents of Communist China, 1962, Manual on Foreign Legal Periodicals and their Index, 1962, Civil Rights U.S.A.: Public Schools in Cities in the North and West, Philadelphia, 1962, Human and Other Beings, 1963, Civil Rights U.S.A., 1963, Public Schools in Camden and Environs, 1964, Civil Rights and the American Negro, 1968, Civil Rights and the Black American, 1970, Law and the Military Establishment, 1970, Cataloging Manual for Use in Vietnamese Law Libraries, 1971, Constitutions of the Countries of the World, 22 vols., 1971-94, Housing Discrimination in New Jersey, 1972, Human Rights and the Bangladesh Trials, 1973, A Bibliography on The Common Law in French, 1973, Intellectual Property: Cases and Materials (1960-70), 1973, Constitutions of Dependencies and Special Sovereignties, 8 vols., 1975-94, Independence Documents of the World, 2 vols., 1977, The Arab Oil Weapon, 1977, The First 100 Justices: Statistical Studies on the Supreme Court of the U.S., 1978, The Military and American Society, 1978, 2d edit., 1984, Disinvestment, 1985, Influence of the U.S. Constitution Abroad, 1986, Resolving Language Conflicts: A Story of the World's Constitutions, 1986, Human Rights Sourcebook, 1987, Constitutions That Made History, 1988, Civil Rights and African Americans, 1991, The Bicentennial Concordance, 1992, Constitutions of the World, 1993. Served to maj. U.S. Army, 1942-46, 1950-52. Fellow Ford Found., 1962, Centre Internat. Studies, London Sch. Econs., 1984-85. Mem. Assn. Bar City N.Y., World Jurist Assn. (chmn. com. constns. 1982-94), Scribes (co-founder), Internat. Bar Assn., Internat. Law Assn., Soc. Mil. Law and Law of War, Internat. Assn. Jewish Lawyers and Jurists (UN rep. 1975-92), Woodcrest Country Club (Cherry Hill, N.J.). Republican. Jewish. Home: Cherry Hill N.J. Died Aug. 21, 1994; interred Crescent Meml. Cemetery, Pensauken N.J.

BLAXTER, SIR KENNETH LYON, agriculturist, educator; b. June 19, 1919; s. Gaspard Culling and Charlotte Ellen B. Student. Reading (Eng.), U. Ill.; B.Sc. in Agr., Ph.D., D.Sc., NDA (hons.); D.Sc. (hon.), QUB, 1974, Leeds, 1977; D.Agr. (hon.), Agrl. U. Norway; LL.D. (hon.), U. Aberdeen, 1981; D.Sc. (hon.), U. Newcastle, 1984; m. Mildred Lillington Hall, 1957; 3 children. Sci. officer Nat. Inst. for Rsch. in Dairying, 1939-40, 41-44; rsch. officer Ministry Agr. Vet. Lab., 1944-46; Commonwealth fellow U. Ill., 1946-47; head dept. nutrition Hannah Inst., Ayr, Scotland, 1948-65; chmn. Individual Merit Promotion Panel, Cabinet Office, 1983-89; dir. Rowett Rsch. Inst., Bucksburn, Aberdeen, Scotland and cons. dir. Commonwealth Bur. Nutrition (formerly Animal Nutrition), 1965-82; vis. prof. dept. agrl. biochemistry U. Newcastle-upon-Tyne, 1982—; pres. Inst. Biology, 1986-88. With RA, 1940-41. Decorated knight; recipient Thomas Baxter prize, Gold medal, 1960, Gold medal RASE, 1964, Wooldridge Gold medal Brit. Vet. Assn., 1973, De Laval medal Royal Swedish Acad. Engring. Scis., 1976, Messel medal Soc. Chem. Industry, 1976, Massey Ferguson award, 1977, Wolf Found. Internat. prize, 1979. Fellow Royal Soc., Royal Svc. Edinburgh (Keith medal and prize 1977, pres. 1979-91), Royal Agrl. Soc., Royal Soc. Arts; mem. Brit. Soc. Animal Prodn. (pres. 1970-71), Nutrition Soc. (pres. 1974), Lenin Acad. Agrl. Scis. (fgn.), French Acad. Agrl. Sci. (fgn.), Am. Inst. Nutrition (hon.), Dutch Soc. Scis. (fgn.), Royal Coll. Vet. Sci. (hon.). Author: Energy Metabolism of Ruminants, 1962; Energy Metabolism, 1965; People, Food and Resources, 1986, Energy Metabolism of Animals and Man, 1989; contbr. articles to profl. jours.; rsch. in vet. sci. and other profl. fields. Died Oct. 4, 1991. Home: Suffolk Eng.

BLEDSOE, WOODROW WILSON, mathematics and computer sciences educator; b. Maysville, Okla., Nov. 12, 1921; s. Thomas Franklin and Eva (Matthews) B.; m. Virginia Norgaard, Jan. 29, 1944; children: Gregory Kent, Pamela Nelson, Lance Woodrow. B.S. in Math., U. Utah, 1948; Ph.D. in Math., U. Calif., 1953. Lectr. in math. U. Calif.-Berkeley, 1951-53; mathematician, staff mem. Sandia Corp., Albuquerque, 1953-60, head math. dept., 1957-60; mathematician, researcher Panoramic Research Inc., Palo Alto, Calif., 1960-65, pres., 1963-65; prof. math. computer sci. U. Tex., Austin, 1966-95, acting chmn. dept. math., 1967-69, chmn. dept. math., 1973-75, Ashbel Smith prof. math. and computer sci., 1981-84; on leave U. Tex., 1984-87; Peter O'Donnell Jr. Centennial chair in computing systems U. Tex., Austin, 1987-94; v.p., dir. artificial intelligence Microelectronics and Computer Tech. Corp., Austin, 1984-87; gen. chmn. Internat. Joint Conf. Artificial Intelligence, MIT, Cambridge, Mass., 1975-77; trustee Internat. Joint Conf. on Artificial Intelligence, 1978-83; mem. subcom. for computer sci. Adv. Com. Math. and Computer Sci., NSF, 1979-82, 88-90; vis. prof. MIT, 1970-71, Carnegie-Mellon U., Pitts., 1978. Editor: (with Donald Loveland) Automated Theorem Proving, 1984; bd. editors Internat. Jour. of Artificial Intelligence, 1972-95, also rev. editor, 1973-77; author numerous tech. papers in refereed jours., confs. Vice-pres. Capitol Area council Boy Scouts Am., Austin, 1979-83. Served to capt. U.S. Army, 1940-45, ETO. NSF research grantee, 1972-95; NIH research grantee, 1967-72. Mem. Am. Math. Soc., Assn. Computing Machinery, Am. Assn. Artificial Intelligence (pres. 1984-85). Mem. LDS Ch. Home: Austin Tex. Died Oct. 4, 1995.

BLISS, ROBERT LANDERS, public relations consultant; b. Binghamton, N.Y., Nov. 19, 1907; s. George Calvin Sherwood and Katherine Barbara (Scheider) B.; m. Friede Smidt, May 16, 1942; children: John Smidt, Friede Sherwood (Mrs. Thomas Mark Brayton). A.B., Cornell U., 1930. With Gen. Tire & Rubber Co., N.Y.C., 1933-36, Arthur B. Treman & Co.; mem. N.Y. Stock Exchange, N.Y.C., 1936-38; asst. chief press Bur. J. Walter Thompson, N.Y.C., 1938-40; asst. to pub. and promotion mgr. PM Newspaper, 1940, Compton Advt., Inc., 1941-46; dir. pub. relations Nat. Assn. Ins. Agts., N.Y.C., 1946-49; exec. v.p. Pub. Relations Soc. Am., N.Y.C., 1949-56; mng. editor pub. Pub. Relations Jour., 1950-56; editor Pub. Relations Register, 1949-56; pres. Robert L. Bliss Inc. (now Robert L. Bliss Assos., Inc.), public relations cons., 1956-95; pres. New Canaan Neighborhoods, Inc.; chmn. bd. Helicopter Assocs. Inc.; Chmn. Ardn-House on Bus. and Politics, 1959, Am. Bus. Conf. on Practical Local Politics, N.Y., 1960; mem. Republican town com. New Canaan, 1951-80, chmn., 1951-62; life mem. Rep. Nat. Com.; mem. Rep. State Central Com., 1954-56; treas., chmn. Fairfield County Rep. Com., 1960-64; mem. Conn. Senate, 1963-67, Conn. Transp. Authority, 1974-75, Commn. on Conn.'s Future; founder, mem. Presdl. Task Force; founder, chmn. New Canaan ann. Gridiron Dinner, 1961-80; life mem., mem. public relations adv. com. Cornell U. Council. Co-author: Handbook of Public Relations, 2d edit, 1971. Served from 2d lt. to maj. USAAF, 1942-46. Mem. Pub. Relations Soc. Am. (charter), Internat. Pub. Relations Assn. (founding council mem. 1955, chmn. research com., mem. council, v.p., pres. 1965-68, gen. rapporteur 2d World Congress on Pub. Relations, Venice 1961, exec. com., program chmn. 3d World Congress, Montreal, Que. 1964, presiding officer 4th World Congress, Rio de Janeiro, Brazil 1967, emeritus mem. 1980-95), Nat. Soc. State Legislators (founder, charter mem., 1st v.p.), Pub. Relations Soc. N.Y., Pub. Relations Soc. Am. (pres. N.Y.C. chpt. 1962-63), SAR, Psi Upsilon. Baptist. Clubs: Woodway Country (Darien, Conn.); Cornell (N.Y.C.). Home: New Canaan Conn. Died Apr. 12, 1995.

BLOCH, ROBERT ALBERT, author; b. Chgo., Apr. 5, 1917; s. Raphael A. and Stella A. (Loeb) B.; m. Eleanor Alexander, Oct. 16, 1964; 1 dau. by previous marriage, Sally Ann. Student public schs., Maywood, Ill. and Milw. Free lance writer, 1934-42, 53-94; copywriter Gustav Marx Advt. Agy., Milw., Wis., 1942-53; lectr. various schs. and community orgns., 1946-94. Author numerous books of fantasy and suspense fiction, 1945-94, including Sea-Kissed, 1945, The Opener of the Way, 1945, The Scarf, 1947, The Kidnapper, 1954, Spiderweb, 1954, The Will to Kill, 1954, Shooting Star, 1958, Terror in the Night, 1958, Pleasant Dreams, Nightmares, 1959, Psycho, 1959, The Dead Beat, 1960, Firebug, 1961, Nightmares, 1961, More Nightmares, 1961, Blood Runs cold, 1961, Yours Truly, Jack the Ripper, 1962, Atoms and Evil, 1962, The Couch, 1962, Terror, 1962, Horror, 7, 1963, Bogey Men, 1963, The Skull of the Marquis de Sade, 1965, Tales in a Jugular Vein, 1965, Chamber of Horrors, 1966, The Living Demons, 1967, This Crowded Earth, 1967, The Star Stalker, 1968, The Todd Dossier, 1969, Dragons and Nightmares, 1969, (with Ray Bradbury) Bloch and Bradbury, 1969, Fear Today, Gone Tomorrow, 1971, It's All in Your Mind, 1971, Sneak Preview, 1971, Night-World, 1972, American Gothic, 1974, Cold Chills, 1977, The King of Terrors, 1977, The Best of Robert Bloch, 1977, Out of the Mouths of Graves, 1978, Strange Eons, 1979, Such Stuff as Screams Are Made Of, 1979, There is a Serpent in Eden, 1979, La Boîteà Malefices de Robert Bloch, 1981, Mysteries of the Worm, 1981, Psycho II, 1982, La Scène Finale, 1982, Parlez-moi d'horreur, 1982, Le Démon Noir, 1983, Dr. Holmes Murder Castle, 1983, Twilight Zone-The Movie, 1983, Les Yeux de la Momie, 1984, The Night of the Ripper, 1984, Récitade Terreur, 1985, L'Homme qui Criah au Loup, 1985, Out of My Head, 1986, Unholy Trinity, 1986, Lost in Time and Space with Lefty Feep, 1987, Midnight Pleasures, 1987, Selected Short Stories of Robert Bloch, 1987, Fear and Trembling, 1989, Lori, 1989, Screams, 1990, Psycho House, 1990, (with Andre Norton) The Jekyll Legacy, 1990, Once Around the Bloch, 1993, Tales From Arkham, 1993; author screenplays The Couch, 1961, The Cabinet of Caligari, 1962, Straitjacket, 1963, The Night Walker, 1964, The Skull, 1964, The Psychopath, 1965, (with Anthony Marriott) The Deadly Bees, 1966, Torture Garden, 1967, The House That Dripped Blood, 1970, Asylum, 1972 (Cannes Fantasy Film Festival First Prize); also numerous radio scripts and teleplays; contbr. numerous short stories to various mags. and lit. jours.; editor: The Best of Fredric Brown, 1977, Psycho-Paths, 1991, Monsters In Our Midst, 1993. Recipient E.E. Evans Meml. award, 1959; Hugo Award, World Science Fiction Convention, 1959; Screen Writer's Guild award, 1960; Mystery Writers of Am. Edgar Allen Poe Scroll, 1960; Ann Radcliffe Award for Lit., 1960; Trieste Film Festival award, 1965; Ann Radcliffe Award for television, 1966; Convention du Cinema Fantastique de Paris Prize, 1973; Award for Service to Field of Sci. Fantasy, Los Angeles Sci. Fantasy Soc., 1974; Comicon Inkpot Award, 1975; World Fantasy convention Life Achievement Award, 1975; Fritz Leiber Fantasy award, 1978; Lifetime Achievement award, 1984; Lifetime Career award Atlanta Fantasy Fair, 1984; Twilight Zone Dimension award, 1985; Bram Stoker award for Lifetime Career, Horror Writers of Am., 1990; Grand Master award World Horror Conv., 1991. Mem. Writers Guild Am., Sci. Fiction Writers Am., Mystery Writers Am. (pres. 1970-71), Acad. of Motion Pictures Arts and Scis. Home: Los Angeles Calif. Died Sept. 23, 1994.

BLOCK, GEORGE EDWARD, surgeon, educator; b. Joliet, Ill., Sept. 16, 1926; s. Edward J. and Florence (Hyland) B.; m. Mary Cobb, Nov. 26, 1966; children: George, John, Edward. B.S., Northwestern U., 1947; M.D., U. Mich., 1951, M.S. in Surgery, 1958. Diplomate: Am. Bd. Surgery. Intern U. Mich. Hosp., 1951, resident, 1951-58; mem. faculty U. Chgo. Med. Sch., 1961-94, prof. surgery, pres. med. staff, 1979-83, Thomas D. Jones prof. surgery, 1984-94, chmn. dept., 1991-93, head. surg. oncology, 1970-85, chief sect. gen. surgery, 1993-94. Author articles in field. Served to col. M.C. USAR, 1952-54, Korea. Decorated Bronze Star, Combat Medic badge; recipient McClintock award, 1965, Pybus medal, 1977, Edwin S. Hamilton Teaching award, 1978. Fellow ACS (gov. 1985-94, adv. coun. for gen. surgery, chmn. adv. coun. for surgery 1990-94, Disting. Svc. award 1985); mem. AMA, Am. Surg. Assn. (v.p. 1988-89), Coller Surg. Soc. (pres. 1971-72), Soc. Surg. Oncology, Soc. Surgery Alimentary Tract (v.p. 1976-77, Founders medal 1994), Western Surg. Assn. (pres. 1992-93), Soc. Head and Neck Surgeons, Colegium Internat. Chirurgiae, Cen. Surg. Assn. (pres. 1984), Ill. Surg. Soc. (pres. 1979-80), Chgo. Surg. Soc. (pres. 1978-79), Ill. Med. Soc., Chgo. Med. Soc., Sigma Xi, Alpha Omega Alpha. Republican. Roman Catholic. Clubs: Chgo. Athletic Assn; Plimsoll (New Orleans). Home: Yorkville Ill. Died July 17, 1994.

BLOCK, ROBERT JACKSON, investment banker; b. Seattle, Oct. 20, 1922; s. Max Harry and Esther Ida (Parker) B.; m. Dorothy Wolens, Aug. 11, 1946 (dec.); children: Jonathan, Adam, Daniel, Kenan, Susanna, Mary Judith; m. Mary Lou Moats, Dec. 26, 1972; children: Melinda Mulvaney, Newton Moats, Christina Moats, Tamara Moats. Student Stanford U., 1940-42, U. Wash., 1942-43. Asst. to pres. Block Shoe Stores, Inc., Seattle, 1946-56, pres., 1956-58; pres. Columbia-Cascade Securities Corp., Seattle, 1958-77; pres. Nat. Securities Corp., Seattle, 1977-80, chmn., chief exec. officer, 1980-85, founding dir., chmn. bd., from 1985; founding dir. North West Bank (merged with Old Nat. Bank); cons. Area Redevel. Adminstrn., 1961-62; exec. reservist policy secretariat Nat. Def. Exec. Res.; GSA, from 1968. Named to Seattle Ctr. Legion of Honor Seattle Ctr. Adv. Commn. & Seattle Ctr. Found., 1987. Pres. Block Found., Inc., Allied Arts Found.; former chmn. Puget Sound chpt. Nat. Found. March of Dimes; mem. nat. exec. council Am. Jewish Com.; former mem. Seattle Bd. Park Commrs.; chmn., dir. Cornish Inst., 1980-82; former trustee Pilchuck Sch., Stanwood, Wash.; bd. dirs. Seattle Pub. Library Found.; chmn. King County (Wash.) USO Com., 1950-52; chmn. Civic Ctr. Com., Seattle, 1954; co-chmn. Metro Campaign Com., Seattle, 1958; alt. del. Democratic Nat. Conv., 1956; King County co-chmn. Vols. for Stevenson, 1956; elected King County Freeholder, 1967. Mem. Wash. State Bar Assn. (fee arbitration panel, vis. cons.), College Club (Seattle), Rainier Club. Deceased. Home: Seattle Wash.

BLOCK, S. LESTER, department store executive; b. Trenton, N.J., Jan. 10, 1917; s. Maurice R. and Jeanne (Finkle) B.; m. Ruth Harris, Mar. 21, 1942; children: John D., Richard H. AB, Princeton, 1938; LLB, U. Pa., 1941. Bar: N.Y. 1945, N.J. 1947. Assoc. Proskauer, Rose, Goetz & Mendelsohn, N.Y.C., 1945-54; labor atty. R.H. Macy & Co., Inc., N.Y.C., 1954-67, v.p., labor atty., 1967-70, sr. v.p. govt. relations, labor counsel, 1970-84, now cons., 1984-92; arbitrator N.Y. Stock Exch., 1992-93; lectr. N.Y. State Sch. Indsl. and Labor Relations; chmn. labor-mgmt. law com. Am. Arbitration Assn., 1967, mem. arbitration com., 1959; mem. N.Y. State Bus. Adv. Com. Mgmt. Improvement, 1970-93; mem. planning com. NYU 24th Ann. Conf. Labor, 1970; mem. regional adv. conf. adminstrn. NLRB, 1960-63; mem. Fed. Adv. Council Employment Security, 1960-62; chmn. adv. council Office Personnel Services, Princeton U., N.J.; mem. exec. bd., adv. council Pace U.-Labor Mgmt. Relations Inst. Mem. Bergen County Jewish Welfare Coun., 1958-66, Teaneck (N.J.) Jewish Community Coun., 1954-60, Princeton Civil Rights Commn.; sec., trustee Princeton Med. Ctr.; bd. dirs. Stonybrook Millstone Watershed Assn., also pres.; bd. dirs. Friends Princeton Libr. Capt., Signal Corps AUS, 1941-45. Mem. Assn. of Bar of City of N.Y., Am. Retail Fedn. (exec. com., dir.), Am. Mgmt. Assn., U.S. C. of C. (labor relations com.), N.Y. State C. of C. and Industry (chmn. nat. affairs com.), Indsl. Relations Soc., Nat. Retail Mchts. Assn., Nat. Acad. Arbitrators, Bus. Roundtable, Phi Beta Kappa, Order of Coif. Home: Princeton N.J. Died Sept. 1, 1993.

BLOKHIN, NIKOLAI NIKOLAEVITCH, medical research scientist; b. May 4, 1912. Grad. Gorky Med. Inst., 1934. Surgeon, oncologist, prof. Med. Inst. Gorky, 1947-52; dir. Inst. Exptl. and Clin. Oncology (now All Union Cancer Research Ctr.), Acad. Med. Scis. USSR, Moscow; mem. council Internat. Union Against Cancer, governing council Internat. Agy. for Research on Cancer. Chmn. com. Internat. Lenin prize for Strengthening of Peace among Nations; pres. Inst. Soviet-Am. Relations, from 1960. Decorated Order of Lenin (4), Order of Red Star, Order of October Revolution, Order of Labour Red Banner; named Hero Socialist Labour. Mem. Acad. Sci. USSR, (pres. 1960-68, 77-87), Polish Acad. Scis., Am. Assn. Cancer Research, N.Y. Acad. Sci., Cancer Soc. Italy. Researcher on malignant neoplasms treatment; organizer of med. scientists for internat. coop. in field. Mem. Communist Party, 1948. Died May 12, 1993. Home: Moscow Russia

BLOSSER, PATRICIA ELLEN, science educator; b. Wayne County, Ohio, Apr. 17, 1931; d. Russell Ford and Mabel Ellen (Kastor) B. BA, Wooster Coll., 1953; MA, U. No. Colo., 1956; MA in Liberal Studies, Wesleyan U., 1962; PhD, Ohio State U., 1970. Cert. secondary sch. sci. tchr., Ohio, Colo., Ill. Tchr. secondary sch. sci., 1953-67; teaching and research assoc. Ohio State U., Columbus, 1967-70, prof. sci. edn., 1970-94; rsch. assoc. Edn. Resources Info. Ctr. Clearing House for Sci., Math. and Environ. Edn., 1970; dir. user svcs. Edn. Resources Info. Ctr., 1979-91, acting dir. Clearinghouse for Sci., Math. and Environ. Edn., 1990-91; sci. assoc. Eisenhower Clearinghouse for Math. and Sci. Edn., 1994; presenter in-service tchr. workshops. Editor: Investigations in Science Education, 1978-89; mem. editorial bd. Sci. Edn., 1978-92; contbr. articles to profl. jours. Named Master Tchr. Jennings Found., 1964; U.S. Office Edn. grantee, 1970, 72. Mem. ASCD, NSTA (bd. dirs. 1966-68, 76-77, 78-80, 88-89), Am. Ednl. Rsch. Assn., Assn. Edn. Tchrs. in Sci. (pres. 1976-77), Assn. Tchr. Educators, Nat. Assn. Rsch. in Sci. Teaching (bd. dirs. 1984-87, pres. 1988-89), Nat. Sci. Suprs. Assn., Sch. Sci. and Math. Assn. (bd. dirs. 1988-91, pres.-elect 1993-94), Phi Delta Kappa (pres. Ohio State U. chpt. 1976-77), Delta Kappa Gamma (Margaret I. White fellow 1967, 69). Home: Columbus Ohio Died Mar. 17, 1994.

BLUM, MICHAEL STEPHEN, financial services executive; b. N.Y.C., Aug. 30, 1939; s. Louis and Jeanne (Dubow) B.; m. Sandra Ruth Saul, Aug. 21, 1960; children: Jan Allen, Emily June, Jennifer Ann. BCE, CCNY, 1960; MBA, Rutgers U., 1965. Mgr. NE region So. Gulf Utilities, Bound Brook, N.J., 1966-67; sr. auditor Gen. Electric Corp., Schenectady, 1967-72; dept. gen. mgr., Gen. Electric Credit Corp., Stamford, Conn., 1979-83, v.p., 1980-86, sr. v.p., div. gen. mgr., 1984-86; pres., CEO Abacus Real Estate Fin. Group, Chgo., 1986-95; vice chmn. Heller Fin. Inc., Chgo., 1987-95; group subs. Fuji Bank, Ltd., Chgo., 1986-95; chmn., CEO Heller Internat. Corp., Heller Fin. Inc., Heller Internat. Group Inc., 1990-95; bd. dirs. Fuji Bank & Trust Co., Fuji Securities, Inc., bd. govs., Am. Jewish Com., 1995, City Schs., Providence St. Mel Sch., Chgo., Chgo. Alliance Latinos and Jews; mem. adv. bd. Kellog Sch. Northwestern U. Mem. Urban Land Inst. Died Oct. 29, 1995. Home: Chicago Ill.

BLUM, WALTER J., lawyer, educator; b. Chgo., Aug. 17, 1918; m. Natalie Richter (dec.); children: Wendy (Mrs. David R. Coggins, Jr.), Catherine (Mrs. James Dennis Scott). AB, U. Chgo., 1939, JD, 1941. Bar: Ill. 1941, D.C. 1941. Atty. OPA, 1941-43; faculty U. Chgo. Law Sch., 1946-91, prof., 1953-91, prof. emeritus, 1991-94, mem. planning com. tax conf., 1947-91; legal counsel Bull. Atomic Scientists, 1949-94; prof. emeritus, 1991-94; mem. steering com. IRS project Adminstrv. Conf. of U.S., 1974-76. Author: (with Harry Kalven, Jr.) The Uneasy Case for Progressive Taxation, 1953, Public Law Perspectives on a Private Law Problem, Auto Compensation Plans, 1964, (with Stanley A. Kaplan) Corporate Readjustments and Reorganizations, 1976; also articles. Trustee Coll. Retirement Equity Fund, 1970-82. Mem. ABA (coun. tax sect. 1972-75), Chgo. Bar Assn. (past bd. mgrs.), Am. Law Inst. (cons. fed. income tax project 1974-94), Am. Acad. Arts and Scis., Chgo. Fed. Tax Forum, Order of Coif, Phi Beta Kappa. Club: Law (Chgo.). Home: Chicago Ill. Died Dec. 18, 1996.

BLUM, WILLIAM LEE, lawyer; b. Cin., Dec. 25, 1920; s. Charles J. and Julia J. (Knock) B.; m. Mary B. Janszen, Feb. 15, 1947; children: Mary Lee Blum Olinger, W. Charles, Christine L., John A., Margaret A. Grubbs. AB, Georgetown U., 1942; Indsl. Adminstrn., Harvard U., 1943, MBA, 1949, JD, 1949. Bar: Ohio 1949. Since practiced in Cin.; ptnr. firm Dinsmore & Shohl, 1953-95, adminstrv. ptnr., 1978-90, chmn. litigation dept., 1974-82, chmn. mgmt. com., 1978-90; bd. dirs. Allen Co., Downing Displays Inc. Pres., chmn. trustees Greater Cin. Community Chest and Council, 1966-69; pres. Cin. Bd. Health, 1970-72; trustee United Appeal, 1965-77, Nat. Cath. Laymen's Retreat Conf., 1958-72, Queen City Found., 1975-79, McDonald Found., 1962-79, Cin. Community Action Commn., 1969-72, Catholic Social Services S.W. Ohio, 1970-83, Athenaeum of Ohio, 1970-83; trustee Cin. Zoo, 1977-90, pres., 1980-84 ; trustee St. Xavier High Sch., Cin., 1977-87 ; mem. president's council Georgetown U., 1979; trustee St. Margaret Hall, 1975-90. Served to maj. AUS, 1943-46. Decorated Knight of Malta, 1970, Knight of Holy Sepulchre, 1983, Knight Grand Cross, 1993; recipient Xavier Insignis award, 1976, St. Margaret Hall Disting. Svc. award, 1987, Disting. Svc. award NCCJ, 1988. Mem. U.S. Cath. Conf. Diocesan Attys. Assn., Ohio Bar Assn., Cin. Bar Assn., Mil. Order Knights Malta., Mil. Order Knights of Holy Sepulchre. Roman Catholic. Clubs: Cin. Country, Bankers, K.C. Home: Cincinnati Ohio Died Mar. 28, 1995.

BLUMENTHAL, NORMAN BRAD, appellate judge; b. Phila., Sept. 22, 1942; s. Samuel and Beatrice (Brodsky) B.; m. Sara Kister, Sept. 24, 1968; children: Amanda, Gery. B.S., NYU, 1965; J.D., Dickinson Law Sch., 1968. Bar: D.C. 1968. Atty. FCC, Washington, 1968-72, legal asst., 1972-77, asst. gen. counsel, 1977-79, assoc. gen. counsel, 1979-80, mem. rev. bd., 1980-94. Exec. dir. Montgomery Citizens for Edn., Montgomery County, Md., 1982. Mem. St. Thomas More Soc. Died May 11, 1994. Home: Bethesda Md.

BOBULA, EDWARD MICHAEL, container company executive; b. Lakewood, Ohio, Sept. 28, 1915; s. George Albert and Anna Agnes (Szlaga) B.; m. Helen Joyce (Matson) B.; Mar. 2, 1940; children: Lynne Michele, Katherine Ann. Student Spencerian Bus. Coll., Cleve., 1933-34. Various positions, Cleve., 1935-36; mem. sales office Iron Fireman Mfg. Co., Cleve., 1936-40; salesman Remington Rand, Cleve., 1940-41; estimator Johns Manville, Cleve., 1941-43; machinist Aircraft Fitting Co., Cleve., 1943-45; v.p. Greif Bros. Corp., Delaware, Ohio, 1945-95. Republican. Lodges: Elks, Masons. Died Oct. 19, 1995. Home: Elliottsburg Pa.

BODDEN, WILLIAM MICHAEL, retired publishing company executive; b. Lafayette, Ind., Oct. 15, 1929; s. William Albert and Dorothy Catherine (Schlacks) B.; m. Louise-Marie Therese Longpre, June 12, 1951; children—Susan Louise, Michael Peter, Sarah Longpre, Jacob Andrew. B.A., Yale, 1951; M.B.A., U. Pa., 1953. With Houghton Mifflin Co., Boston, 1956-95; prodn. mgr. Houghton Mifflin Co., 1963-70, mgr. art and prodn. depts., 1970-74, v.p., 1974-93; Lectr. on pub. Harvard Grad. Sch. Bus. Adminstrn., 1968, Radcliffe Coll., 1968, 69; visitor Boston Mus. Fine Arts, 1966; mem. Adv. Commn. on Textbook Specifications, 1972-95. Contbr. articles to bus. and mil. jours. Mem. Town Meeting, Wellesley, Mass., 1972-80; pres. Wellesley Sr. High Sch. P.T.A., 1974-75; trustee Wellesley Free Library, 1969-75, chmn., 1972-74; pub. and prodn. exec. Hall of Fame, 1991; mem. Friends of Wellesley Free Library, pres., 1967-69, Yale class agt., 1975-84, alumni schs. com., 1978-86; lay mass reader, eucharistic minister St. Paul's Ch.; citizen rev. com. United Way of Mass. Bay, 1984-87, sect. chmn., 1989. Served to lt. (j.g.) Supply Corps USNR, 1953-56; comdr. Res. ret. Named New England Tennis Family of Yr., 1984. Mem. Soc. Printers Boston (pres. 1972-74), New Eng. Printing and Pub. Council (gen. chmn. 1969-70, Benjamin Franklin award 1984), Bookbuilders of Boston (pres. 1964-66, William A. Dwiggins award 1974), Am. Inst. Graphic Arts (dir. 1971-74), Assn. Am. Pubs. (chmn. textbook specifications com. 1978-80, 90-95), Assoc. Grantmakers of Mass. (dir. 1983-85), Wellesley Tennis Assn. (treas. 1974-77), Boston Recorder Soc. (pres. 1991-95). Republican. Roman Catholic. Home: Wellesley Mass. Died Jan. 24, 1995.

BODE, CARL, writer, educator; b. Milw., Mar. 14, 1911; s. Paul and Celeste Helene (Schmidt) B.; m. Margaret Lutze, Aug. 3, 1938 (dec.); children: Barbara, Janet, Carolyn; m. Charlotte W. Smith, 1972. Ph.B., U. Chgo., 1933; M.A., Northwestern U., 1938, fellow, 1940-41, Ph.D., 1941; hon. doctorate, U. Balt., 1987, Salisbury State U., 1987, Western Md. Coll., 1988. Tchr. Milw. Vocat. Sch., 1933-37; asst. prof. English UCLA, 1946-47; prof. English U. Md., College Park, 1947-82, emeritus, 1982-93; exec. sec. Am. Civilization program U. Md., 1950-57; cultural attache Am. embassy, London, 1957-59 (on leave from U. Md); chmn. U.S. Ednl. Commn. in U.K., 1957-59; vis. prof. Calif. Inst. Tech., Claremont Colls., Northwestern U., U. Wis., Stanford. Author: (poems) The Sacred Seasons, 1953, The Man Behind You, 1959, Practical Magic, 1981; (books) The American Lyceum, 1956, The Anatomy of American Popular Culture, 1840-1861, 1959 (repub. as Antebellum Culture, 1970), The Half-World of American Culture, 1965; Mencken, 1969, 73, re-issue 86, Highly Irregular (newspaper columns), 1974, Maryland: A Bicentennial History, 1978; Maryland (photographs by Steve Uzzell), 1983; editor: Collected Poems of Henry Thoreau, 1943, enlarged edit., 1964, The Portable Thoreau, 1947, rev. edit., 1964, 82, 87; American Life in the 1840s, 1967, The Selected Journals of Henry David Thoreau, 1967, The Best of Thoreau's Journals, 1971, Ralph Waldo Emerson, A Profile, 1969, Midcentury America: Life in the 1850's, 1972, The Young Mencken, 1973, The New Mencken Letters, 1977, Barnum, Struggles and Triumphs, 1982; Alger, Ragged Dick & Struggling Upward, 1985; The Editor, the Bluenose, and the Prostitute: H.L. Menchen's History of the "Hatrack" Censorship Case, 1988; co-editor: American Heritage, 2 vols., 1955, The Correspondence of Henry David Thoreau, 1958, American Literature, 3 vols, 1966, The Portable Emerson, 1981; co-editor, contbr. The Young Rebel in Am. Lit., 1959, The Great Experiment in Am. Lit., 1961; editor: American Perspectives: The United States in the Modern Age, 1990; contbr. articles to encys., poetry and revs. to Brit. and Am. jours.; Columnist: Balt. Evening Sun. Mem. Md. State Arts Council, 1971-79, chmn., 1972-76; mem. Md. Humanities Council, 1981-90, chmn., 1984-86; mem. Marshall Scholarship Adv. Council, 1960-69. Served with AUS, 1944-45. Ford Found. fellow, 1952-53; Newberry Library fellow, 1954; Guggenheim Found. fellow, 1954-55. Fellow Royal Soc. Lit. U.K. (hon.); mem. AAUP (council 1965-68), Am. Studies Assn. (founder, 1st pres. 1952), Modern Lang. Assn., Thoreau Soc. Am. (dir. 1955-57, pres. 1960-61), Popular Culture Assn. Am. (v.p. 1972-75, pres. 1978-79), Mencken Soc. (founder, 1st pres. 1976-79), Phi Beta Kappa (hon.), Alpha Tau Omega. Democrat. Episcopalian. Clubs: Cosmos (Washington); Hamilton St. (Balt.). Home: Chestertown Md. Died Jan. 5, 1993; interred St. Paul's Church, Rockhall, M.D.

BOE, NILS ANDREAS, federal judge; b. Baltic, S.D., Sept. 10, 1913; s. Nils and Sissel C. (Finseth) B. AB, U. Wis., 1935, LLB, 1937; LLD (hon.), Huron Coll., Augustana Coll., S.D., 1986. Bar: Wis. 1937, S.D. 1938, U.S. Supreme Ct. 1944, D.C. 1970. Practice in Sioux Falls, S.D., 1938-65; lt. gov. S.D., 1963-65; gov., 1965-67, 67-69; dir. Office of Intergovtl. Relations, Exec. Office of Pres., Washington, 1969-71; judge U.S. Ct. Internat. Trade, 1971-94, chief judge, 1971-77, sr. judge, 1984-94; Mem. S.D. Ho. of Reps., 1951-59, speaker, 1955, 57. Served with USN, 1942-46. Mem. Phi Alpha Delta. Republican. Lutheran. Club: Elks. Home: Sioux Falls S.D. Died July 30, 1992.

BOGERT, HENRY LAWRENCE, banker; b. N.Y.C., Oct. 7, 1911; s. Henry Lawrence and Elizabeth Blodget (Sanford) B.; m. Margaret Milbank, Apr. 25, 1936; children: Henry Lawrence III, Jeremiah M. Grad., St. Paul's Sch., Concord, N.H., 1930; B.A., Yale U., 1934. With Bankers Trust Co., N.Y.C., 1934-42; with Blyth, Eastman, Paine, Webber Inc. (and predecessors), 1946-92, gen. partner, 1948-56; gen. partner Eastman Dillon, Union Securities & Co., Inc., 1956-71, sr. v.p., dir., 1971-73, sr. subordinated debenture holder, 1973-92. Trustee Provident Loan Soc. N.Y.; Hon. trustee Buckley Sch. of N.Y., Boys Club N.Y. Mem. Investment Bankers Assn. Am. (pres. 1966-67, gov.), Soc. of Cincinnati. Clubs: Links (N.Y.C.), River. (N.Y.C.); Fishers Island (N.Y.) (gov., pres. 1957-59); Hobe Sound Country (Fla.) (dir., pres. 1974-81). Home: New York N.Y. Died June 15, 1992.

BOGORAD, SAMUEL NATHANIEL, English educator; b. New Bedford, Mass., Apr. 7, 1917; s. Sidney and Rebecca (Eisenstadt) B.; m. Ruth Pollack, Sept. 10, 1944. AB summa cum laude, Brown U., 1939, AM, 1941; PhD, Northwestern U., 1946; LittD (hon.), U. Vt., 1989. Instr. English Northwestern U., Evanston, Ill., 1942-45; instr. U. Vt., Burlington, 1946-47; asst. prof. U. Vt., 1947-52, asso. prof., 1952-57, prof., 1957-93, Frederick Corse prof. English lang. and lit., 1968-93, chmn. English dept., 1961-1969; Vis. asst. prof. Brown U., 1948-49; vis. prof. William and Mary Coll., summer 1951, U. Colo., summer 1958; mem. Jud. Nominating Bd., State of Vt., 1985-91. Author: (with J. Trevithick) The College Miscellany, 1952, (with C. Graham) Atlantic Essays, 1958, (with R.G. Noyes) Samuel Foote's Primitive Puppet Shew, 1973. Chmn. planning commn., South Burlington, Vt., 1952-55, town moderator, 1955-61, justice of peace, 1973-93; mem. commn. on insts. of higher edn. New Eng. Assn. Colls. and Secondary Schs., 1963-71; commr. New Eng. Bd. Higher Edn., 1973-79; mem. bd. govs. Vt. Health Found., 1985-93; Vt. Holocaust Human Rights Edn. Com., 1985-93. Fellow Vt. Acad. Arts and Scis.; mem. MLA, Nat. Council Tchrs. English, Coll. English Assn. (pres. New Eng. 1966-67, nat. dir. 1968-71, v.p. 1971-73, pres. 1973), AAUP (pres. U. Vt. chpt. 1954-55), Phi Beta Kappa (pres. New Eng. dist. United chpts. 1961-76, com. on Qualifications United chpts., mem. Senate 1970-76). Home: Shelburne Vt. Died Dec. 31, 1993; interred New Bedford, M.A.

BOGUSLAW, ROBERT, sociologist, educator, researcher; b. N.Y.C., June 19, 1919; s. Max and Eva (Zaslavsky) B.; m. Wanda Steinberg, Apr. 23, 1956; children: Chelle, Janet, Lisa. A.B., Bklyn. Coll., 1940, M.A., 1947; Ph.D., NYU, 1954. Sr. staff scientist Rand Corp. and Systems Devel. Corp., Santa Monica, Calif., 1953-65; research prof., sr. social scientist Am. U., Washington, 1965-66; prof. sociology Washington U., St. Louis, 1966-85; prof. emeritus Washington U., 1985-93; research prof. Ctr. Tech. and Policy Boston U., 1985-86; vis. scholar London Sch. Econs., 1973; cons. Nat. Acad. Sci., 1963, Office Advanced Systems, U.S. Social Security Adminstrn., Washington, 1978-79; mem. adv. panel Office Tech. Assessment, U.S. Congress, 1976-77. Author: Systems Analysis and Social Planning, 1982, The New Utopians, 1965, 2d edit., 1981 (C. Wright Mills award), (with George Vickers) Prologue to

Sociology, 1977, (with William Berg) Communication and Community, 1985, (with Warren Pelton and Sonja Sackmann) Tough Choices: The Decision-Making Styles of America's Top 50 CEOs, 1990; contbr. Ency. Sociology, 1991; contbr. articles to profl. jours. Mem. adv. bd. City Community Mental Health Service, Santa Monica, Calif., 1958-63; chmn. Santa Monica Welfare Council, Calif., 1958-59. Served to 1st lt. U.S. Army, 1941-45. Decorated Bronze Star medal; Fulbright fellow Paris, 1972-73; NEH sr. fellow, 1973-74; Camargo Found. research fellow, 1980-81. Mem. Am. Sociol. Assn., Soc. for Study Social Problems (chmn. com. on internat. tensions 1964-66). Democrat. Jewish. Home: Fort Lauderdale Fla. Died Nov. 21, 1993.

BOISFONTAINE, CURTIS RICH, lawyer; b. New Orleans, June 30, 1929; s. Albert Sidney and Margaret (Toomer) B.; m. Cheryl Reynaud; children: Suzanne Baker, Curtis Rich Jr., Eugenie Wright, Stephanie Brett, Arthur Maxwell. B.A., Tulane U., 1951, LL.B., 1952. Bar: La. 1952. Practice in New Orleans, 1952-53; assoc. Porteous & Johnson, New Orleans, 1955-61; ptnr. Sessions & Fishman, New Orleans, 1961-93. Served with Judge Adv. Gen.'s Corps USAF, 1953-55. Fellow Am. Bar Found. (state chmn.), Am. Coll. Trial Lawyers; mem. ABA (ho. of dels. 1976-92), La. Bar Assn. (pres. 1976-77), New Orleans Bar Assn., Am. Judicature Soc., Internat. Assn. Ins. Counsel, Fed. Ins. Counsel, La. Assn. Def. Counsel (pres. 1972-73), New Orleans Assn. Def. Counsel. Home: Metairie La. Deceased.

BOJANIC, MILENKO, Yugoslavian minister of foreign trade; b. Aradac, Vojvodina, Yugoslavia, 1924. Grad. Faculty of Law, Belgrade U., 1951; doctorate in Polit. Scis., 1976. Active Nat. Liberation Struggle, from 1943; mem. League of Communists of Yugoslavia, 1944—, del. to various Congresses; formerly: sec. to county com. League of Communists in Zrenjanin and Becej; mem. bur. of dist. com. League of Communists in Zrenjanin; elected several times dep. and/or del. to Serbian Assembly; v.p., then pres. Republican Chamber of Agr. and Forestry; pres. bd. mgmt. Republican Fund for Devel. Underdeveloped Regions; mem. central bd. Socialist Alliance of Working People of Serbia; mem. council Nat. Def. Yugoslavia; del. to several Congresses, League of Communists of Serbia; mem. exec. council and commr. for fin. Autonomous Province of Vojvodina; mem. and pres. exec. council Serbian Assembly; gen. mgr. Yugoslav Investment Bank; now assoc. prof. econs. U. Kragujevac; gen. mgr. Crvena Zastava car works, Kragujevac, 1974—; Yugoslavian minister of fgn. trade, Belgrade; del. to fed. chamber Yugoslavian Assembly; mem. exec. bd. Yugoslav Bank for Econ. Cooperation with Fgn. Countries. Various decorations. Died 1987. Home: Belgrade Yugoslavia

BOLENDER, CARROLL HERDUS, retired air force officer, consultant; b. Cin., Nov. 2, 1919; s. Oscar H. and Kathryn L. (Baughman) B.; m. Virginia I. McWilliams, Nov. 7, 1942; children—Carol S. (Mrs. James B. Walden), Robert A. B.S., Wilmington Coll., 1941; M.B.A., Ohio State U., 1949. Commd. 2d lt. USAAF, 1941; advanced through grades to brig. gen. USAF, 1965; dep. chief of staff plans and operations Eglin Air Force Base, Fla., 1963-64; study coordinator Office of Vice Chief of Staff, Hdqrs. USAF, Washington, 1964-65; Apollo Mission dir. NASA, Washington, 1965-67; program mgr. for lunar module NASA, Houston, 1967-69; dep. dir. devel. and acquisition Dep. Chief of Staff Research and Devel., Hdqrs. USAF, Washington, 1969-72; asst. mgr. Hampton (Va.) ops. Systems Devel. Corp., 1972-73; mgr. Hampton (Va.) ops. Systems Devel. Corp. (Hampton ops.), 1973-78; cons. Engring. Inc., Hampton, 1979-80; mgr. System Devel. Corp., Newport News, Va., 1984-86; cons. Unisys, 1987-88. Decorated Air Force D.S.M. with oak leaf cluster, Legion of Merit, D.F.C. with oak leaf cluster, Air medal with 8 oak leaf clusters, Air Force Commendation Medal; Croix de Guerre with palm and gold star France; recipient Apollo Achievement award, exceptional service medal, distinguished service medal, Apollo Program Mgmt. Team award, Group Achievement award all NASA. Home: Williamsburg Va. Died Aug. 3, 1995.

BOLT, ROBERT OXTON, playwright; b. Manchester, Eng., Aug. 15, 1924; s. Ralph and Leah (Binnion) B.; m. Celia Anne Roberts, Nov. 1948 (div. 1967); children: Sally, Benedict, Joanna; m. Sarah Elizabeth Miles, 1967 (div. 1975 remarried 1988); 1 son, Thomas; m. Ann Zane, 1980 (div. 1985). BA with honors in History, Manchester U., 1950; LLD, Exeter U., 1977. Office-boy Sun Life Assurance Office, Manchester, 1941-42; tchr. village sch., Bishopsteignton, Devonshire, 1950-51; tchr., head English dept. Millfield Sch., Sommerset, Devonshire, 1952-58. Author: (plays) A Man for All Seasons, 1954 (New York Drama Critics Circle award best foreign play 1962, Tony award 1962), The Last of the Wine, 1956, The Critic and the Heart, 1957, Flowering Cherry, 1957 (Evening Standard Drama award 1957), The Tiger and the Horse, 1960, Gentle Jack, 1960, Three Plays, 1963, The Thwarting of Baron Bolligrew, 1966, Brothers and Sister, 1967, Vivat! Vivat Regina!, 1970 (Tony award nomination 1972), State of Revolution, 1977; (radio plays) The Master, 1953, Fifty Pigs, 1953, Ladies and Gentlemen, 1954, The Last of the Wine, 1955, Mr. Sampson's Sundays, 1955, The Window, 1958, The Drunken Sailor, 1958, The Banana Tree, 1961; (screenplays) Lawrence of Arabia, 1962 (Academy award nomination best adapted screenplay 1962, British Film Academy award 1962), Dr. Zhivago, 1965 (Academy award best adapted screenplay 1965, Golden Globe award 1966), A Man for All Seasons, 1966 (Academy award best adapted screenplay 1966, British Academy of Film and Television Arts award 1967, Golden Globe award 1967), Ryan's Daughter, 1970, Lady Caroline Lamb, 1972, The Bounty, 1984, The Mission, 1986 (Cannes Film Festival Palme d'Or 1986, Christopher award 1987, Golden Globe award 1987); (teleplays) The James Brady Story, HBO, 1991. Served with RAF and Brit. Army, 1943-46. Decorated comdr. Order Brit. Empire. Home: London Eng.

BOLTÉ, BROWN, advertising executive, inventor, designer, writer; b. Winnetka, Ill., Dec. 23, 1908; s. John Willard and Jessie (Brown) B.; m. Bernice Nicholson, Jan. 4, 1930 (dec.); 1 child, Celia (Mrs. John William Griesé, Jr.); m. Baronessa Erminia Amaru-Landau, 1987. Student, Butler U., 1930, U.S. Army Sch. for Spl. Services, Washington and Lee U., 1943. Western and So. sales mgr. Rytex Co., Indpls., 1930-35; asst. to pres. mktg. Beecham Products, Inc., Bloomfield, N.J., 1935-39; account exec., exec. v.p., chmn. plans bd. Benton & Bowles, Inc., N.Y.C., 1939-57; pres. SSC&B, Inc., 1958-60, vice chmn. bd., 1965; owner Bolté Advt. Cos., N.Y., Conn., Tex., 1961-73; chmn. Bolté-Lukin & Assocs., Inc., Palm Beach, 1970-94; v.p., dir. World of Plastics, Inc., Ft. Pierce, Fla., 1973-94. Composer: Allies Victory March, Army Fighting Song, Bring Peace O Lord, others; author (poetry) Men of Transportation, Two Letters, Thanksgiving Prayer, Prayer for Peace; contbr. articles to N.Y. Times; holder numerous patents in clothing, cookware, medical fields. Trustee Norwalk Hosp. Assn., 1958-65, YMCA, New Canaan, 1967-94; bd. dirs. New Canaan ARC, 1953-54, New Canaan YMCA, 1967-94, Eleanor Roosevelt Cancer Found., 1961, Child Welfare League Am., 1962-63, Community Mental Health Center, West Palm Beach, 1961, hon. dir., 1963-94; bd. govs. Gulfstream Goodwill Industries, 1973-94; trustee Palm Beach-Martin County Med. Center, Inc., Jupiter, Fla., 1974-94, life mem., 1977-94; bd. dirs. Boys Club of Palm Beach County, 1973-94, pres., 1985-88, life chmn., 1988. Served from 2d lt. to maj. AUS, 1942-46. Mem. ASCAP, SAR, Am. Assn. Advt. Agys. (gov. 1956, chmn. Eastern Region 1957), Am. Guild Authors and Composers, Nat. Def. Transp. Assn. (bd. dirs., exec. com. 1956-58), Inst. Outdoor Advt. (dir., chmn. bd. 1967-68), Advt. Coun. (dir. 1966-94), Sailfish Club, Beach Club (Palm Beach), Club Ltd., Sigma Chi (Significant Sig). Home: Palm Beach Fla. Died Jan. 17, 1994.

BOLTON, EARL CLINTON, lawyer, consultant; b. L.A., Aug. 22, 1919; s. John R. and Hazel A. (Van Order) B.; m. Jean Studley, June 27, 1942; children: Barbara Bolton Poley, Elizabeth Ann Bolton Newell, William Earl. A.B. magna cum laude, U. So. Calif., 1941, J.D., 1948; LL.D. (hon.), U. San Diego, 1963. Bar: Calif. 1949, U.S. Supreme Ct. 1958. Staff, Coordinator Inter-Am. Affairs, N.Y.C., also Washington, 1941; v.p., treas. Nat. Public Discussions, Inc., N.Y.C., 1942; lectr. polit. sci. dept. U. So. Calif., 1946-48; asst. prof. U. So. Calif. (Coll. Liberal Arts and Sch. Commerce), 1948-50, asso. prof. law and v.p. planning, 1952-60; spl. asst. to pres. U. Calif., Berkeley, 1960-61; v.p. univ. relations U. Calif., 1962-64, v.p. adminstrn., 1964-66, v.p. govtl. relations, 1966-68, v.p. adminstrn., 1968-70; v.p. Booz, Allen & Hamilton, Inc., Chgo., 1970-79; of counsel firm Willis Butler & Scheifly, Los Angeles, 1979-81, Pepper, Hamilton & Scheetz, 1981-84, Earl C. Bolton & Assocs., 1984-93. Mem. editorial bd. Law Rev., U. So. Calif., 1947-48. Mem. Calif. Gov.'s Mental Health Adv. Com., Citizens' Legis. Adv. Com.; past chmn., founding mem. Calif. Scholarship Com. Served to capt. USNR, 1942-46, 50-52. Mem. State Bar Calif., Order of Coif, Phi Beta Kappa, Phi Kappa Phi. Home: Alameda Calif. Died Aug. 10, 1993.

BOLZ, RAY EMIL, retired engineering educator; b. Cleve., Oct. 24, 1918; s. William and Amelia Anne (Waechter) B.; m. Jean Kathryn Hoeft, Oct. 4, 1944; children: Elaine Kathryn, Nancy Jane, Patricia Lynn, Janet Gail. B.S. in Engring., Case Inst. Tech., 1940; M.S., Yale U., 1942, D. Engring., 1949; D. Engring. (hon.), Worcester Poly. Inst., 1984. Research scientist NACA, 1942-46, head jet engine combustion sect., 1944-46; asst. prof. aero. engring. Rensselaer Poly. Inst., 1947-50; faculty Case Western Res. U., 1950-73, prof. aero. engring., coordinator research, 1952-55, head dept. mech. engring., 1956-60, head engring. div., 1960-67; dean Case Western Res. U. (Sch. Engring.), 1967-73; v.p., dean faculty Worcester (Mass.) Poly. Inst., 1973-84; Cons. to industry, 1950-91; mem. adv. panel to engring. div. NSF, 1958-61, adv. panel to course content and improvement sect., 1961-66; applied mechanics reviewer. Adv. com. Air Force Inst. Tech., 1971-74. Trustee Worcester Craft Ctr., 1978-91, pres., 1983-91. Recipient award for advancement basic and applied sci. Yale U., 1957; Outstanding Alumni award Case Western Res. U., 1968. Fellow ASME (v.p., chmn. policy bd. edn. 1968-70); mem. Am. Soc. Engring. Edn. (mem. bd. engring. coll. council 1975-80), Am. Inst. Aero. and Astronautics, Cleve. Engring. Soc. (bd. govs. 1972-73), Engring. Council Profl. Devel. (chmn. region II 1963-68), Sigma Xi. Unitarian (trustee 1964-68, pres. bd. trustees 1967-68). Home: Indian River Mich. Died Sept. 11, 1991.

BOMBECK, ERMA LOUISE (MRS. WILLIAM BOMBECK), author, columnist; b. Dayton, Ohio, Feb. 21, 1927; d. Cassius Edwin Fiste and Erma (Fiste) Harris; m. William Lawrence Bombeck, Aug. 13, 1949; children: Betsy, Andrew, Matthew. BA, U. Dayton, 1949; holder 16 hon. degrees. Columnist Newsday Syndicate, 1965-70, Pubs.-Hall Syndicate (now N.Am. Syndicate), 1970-85, Los Angeles Times Syndicate, 1985-88, Universal Press Syndicate, Kansas City, Mo., 1988-96; contbg. editor: Good Housekeeping mag., 1969-74. Author: At Wit's End, 1967, Just Wait Till You Have Children Of Your Own, 1971, I Lost Everything In The Post-Natal Depression, 1974, The Grass Is Always Greener Over The Septic Tank, 1976, If Life is a Bowl of Cherries, What Am I Doing in the Pits?, 1978, Aunt Erma's Cope Book, 1979, Motherhood: The Second Oldest Profession, 1983, Family: The Times That Bind...and Gag!, 1987, I Want to Grow Hair, I Want To Grow Up, I Want To Go To Boise, 1989, When You Look Like Your Passport Photo, It's Time To Go Home, 1991, A Marriage Made in Heaven...or Too Tired for an Affair, 1993, All I Know About Animal Behavior I Learned in Loehmann's Dressing Room, 1995. Mem. Am. Acad. Humor Columnists, Theta Sigma Phi (Headliner award 1969). Died Apr. 22, 1996.

BOMBERG, THOMAS JAMES, dental educator; b. Curtis, Nebr., May 31, 1928; s. Robert Joseph and Alpha Marie (Fairburn) B.; m. Arthurene Edens, Apr. 29, 1954; children—Bryan Craig, Scott Edens. B.S., U. Denver, 1951; D.D.S., U. Mo., Kansas City, 1961. Pvt. practice dentistry Colorado Springs, 1961-72; asst. prof. U. Ky. Coll. Dentistry, 1972-73; assoc. prof. U. Okla. Coll. Dentistry, 1973-74; prof. U. Colo. Sch. Dentistry, Denver, 1974-95; dean U. Colo. Sch. Dentistry, 1977-80, assoc. dean, 1988-95. Contbr. articles to dental related jours. Bd. dirs. El Paso County (Colo.) Mental Health Assn., 1967-70. Served with USN, 1946-48; to 1st lt. USAF, 1951-56. Fellow Internat. Coll. Dentists, Am. Coll. Dentists; mem. Am. Dental Assn., Pierre Fauchard Acad., Am. Assn. Dental Schs., Am. Assn. for Dental Rsch. Republican. Episcopalian. Home: Denver Colo. Died May 15, 1995.

BOND, THOMAS See BURNAM, TOM

BONDARCHUK, SERGEY FEDOROVICH, actor, director; b. Byelozerka, Odessa Region, Russia; Sept. 25, 1920. Student All Union State Inst. Cinematography. Appeared as Othello, Shevchenko in Taras Shevchenko, Valko in the Young Guard, Dymov in The Grasshopper, Yershov in An Unfinished Tale, Ivan Franko in Ivan Franko, Matvei Krylov in The Soldiers Go On, Sokolov in Destiny of a Man, Korostylov in Seryozha, Pierre Bezukhov in War and Peace, Astrov in Uncle Vanya, Sergey Tutarinov in Gold Star Winner, Fyodor in It Was Night in Rome, Martin Evens in The Silence of Doctor Evens, Ivan Nikolayevich in This High Mountain, Kurchatov in Choosing the Goal, Zvyagintsev in They fought for the Motherland, Emelyan in Steppe; dir. (films) including Destiny of a Man, War and Peace, 1968 (Best fgn. lang. film Acad. award), Waterloo, 1970, Uncle Vanya, 1974, They Fought for the Motherland, 1975, Steppe, 1979, Father Sergius, 1979, Mexico in Flames, 1982, Boris Godunov, 1987, (miniseries) And Quiet Flows the Don, 1992, (opera) Mazepa, 1987. Recipient numerous awards including: Order of Lenin (2), People's Artist of USSR, Order of Red Banner, Hero of Soviet Labour, 1980, USSR State prize, 1984. Author: Intimate Thoughts, 1979. Died Oct. 20, 1994. Home: Moscow Russia

BONDS, ALFRED BRYAN, JR., college president; b. Monroe County, Ark., Nov. 3, 1913; s. Alfred Bryan Sr. and Nellie Belle (Hasley) B.; m. Georgianna Arnett, Feb. 23, 1939; children: Anna Belle, Alfred Bryan, III, Alexandra Burke, Stephen Arnett. AB, Henderson State Tchrs. Coll., Arkadelphia, Ark., 1935; MA, La. State U., 1936, postgrad., 1936-38; Julius Rosenwald fellow, U. N.C., 1940-41; LLD, Ohio Wesleyan U., Cleve.-Marshall Law Sch., 1956. Asst. to dean Grad. Sch., La. State U, 1936-41; coordinating officer So. Grad. Sch. Survey and Work Conf., Tulane U., 1941-42; chief ednl. surveys br. Nat. Roster Sci. and Specialized Personnel, War Manpower Commn., Washington, 1942-43; chief edn. div. retng. and re-employment adminstrn. U.S. Dept. Labor, 1946; asst. exec. sec. Pres.'s Commn. on Higher Edn., 1946-48; dir. tng. AEC, Washington, 1948-49; Ark. commr. edn. Little Rock, 1949-53; chief U.S. Ednl. Commn., Egypt; co-dir. Egyptian-Am. Joint Commn. for Edn., 1953-55; pres. Baldwin-Wallace Coll., 1956-81, pres. emeritus, 1981—; Cons. FSA; council advisers U.S. Commn. Edn.; gov.'s adviser Council on Land Utilization; mem. exec. com. Bd. Control for So. Regional Edn.; dir. Ark. Tchrs. Retirement System; mem. Cleve. Com. Higher Edn. Prepared basic plan and survey for, UNESCO publs., Study Abroad, 1948; Editor: Essays on Southern Life and Culture, 1941; Contbr. articles to profl. jours. Bd. dirs. Cuyahoga Co. Library; bd. dirs. Lake Erie Jr. Mus., St. Luke's Hosp., Cleve., YMCA; chmn. S.W. Gen. Hosp. Found.; mem. World Council on Methodism; v.p. Ohio Council Chs.; mem. coordinating council Gen. Conf. Meth. Ch., mem. program council; del. World Meth. Council, London, Eng., 1966, World Family Life Conf., London, 1966; del. to Consultation on Evangelism, World Meth. Council, Frankfurt, 1970; Trustee Lake Erie Opera

Assn. Served from ensign to lt. (s.g.) USNR, 1943-46. Decorated officer's cross Order of Merit West Germany; recipient medal of honor Nat. Assn., League of New Eng. Women, Grindstone award City of Berea, 1972, Disting. Alumnus award Henderson State U., 1977, Rufus Putnam award Masons, Disting. Alumnus award La. State U. Mem. Ohio Coll. Assn. (pres. 1970), Am. Soc. Internat. Law, Am. Polit. Sci. Assn., NEA, Am. Assn. Sch. Adminstrs., Ark. Edn. Assn., Phi Gamma Mu, Omicron Delta Kappa. Methodist. Clubs: Rotarian, Mason (33 degree), Union, University, Midday. Home: Cleveland Ohio Died Sept. 4, 1989; interred Woodvale Berea, O.H.

BONICA, JOHN JOSEPH, anesthesiologist, educator; b. Filicudi Messina, Italy, Feb. 16, 1917; came to U.S., 1927, permanent resident, 1947, naturalized, 1928; s. Antonino and Angela (Zagame) B.; m. Emma Louise Baldetti, June 7, 1942; children: Angela C., Charlotte E., Linda L., John A. Student, L.I. U., 1934-37; B.S., NYU, 1938; M.D., Marquette U., 1942; D.Med.Scis. (hon.), U. Siena, 1972; D.Sc. (hon.), Med. Coll. Wis., 1977, NW U. Chgo., 1989. Diplomate Am. Bd. Anesthesiology; lic. surgeon, N.Y., Wash. Intern St. Vincent's Hosp., N.Y.C., 1942; resident St. Vincent's Hosp., 1942-44; practice medicine specializing in anesthesiology U. Wash. Med. Center, Seattle, 1960-77; dir. dept. anesthesiology Tacoma Gen. Hosp., 1947-63, Pierce County Hosp., 1947-60; clin. prof. dept. anatomy U. Wash., Seattle, 1948-60; attending anesthesiologist Mary Bridge Children's Hosp., Tacoma, 1955-60; prof. U. Wash., 1960-94, chmn. dept. anesthesiology, 1960-77, chmn. emeritus and prof., 1978-87, prof., chmn. emeritus, 1987-94; founder and dir. Pain Clinic, Med. Center and affiliated hosps., 1961-79; dir. Anesthesia Research Center, 1968-77, Pain Center, U. Wash., Seattle, 1980-83; vis. prof. and lectr. various Am., Canadian, Middle East, Zimbabwe, European, Latin Am., Australian, N.Z., Asiatic, Near Eastern, South African univs.; chief sect. anesthesiology and operating theatre Madigan Army Hosp., Ft. Lewis, Wash., 1944-46, sr. cons., 1947-77, U.S. Penitentiary, McNeil Island, Wash., 1948-60, No. Pacific Beneficial Assn. Hosp., Tacoma, 1948-60, VA Hosp., Seattle, 1960-77, Children's Hosp. and Med. Ctr., Seattle, 1961-77; mem. anesthesia tng. com. NIH, 1965-69, chmn. gen. med. research program-project com., 1970-72, chmn. ad hoc com. on acupuncture, 1972-75; cons. ministries of health, Argentina, 1955, Brazil, 1959, Italy, 1954, 60, Sweden, 1969; cons. ministries of health Ministry Edn. Japan, 1969, Ministry Edn. and Health Venezuela, 1966, 69; mem. adv. com. Com. on Scholarly Communication with People's Republic of China, Nat. Acad. Scis., 1973-74; mem. Am. Med. Mission to People's Republic of China, 1973. Author: Management of Pain, 1953, 2d edit., 1990, Il Dolore, 1959, Tratamiento del Dolor, 1959, Clinical Applications of Diagnostic and Therapeutic Blocks, 1955, Manual of Anesthesiology for Medical Students, Interns and Residents, 1947, Anesthesia for Obstetrical Complications, 1965, Principles and Practice of Obstetric Analgesia and Anesthesia, Vol. 1, 1967, 2nd edit., 1994, Vol. 2, 1969, Vol. 3, 1994, Regional Anesthesia, 1969, Obstetric Analgesia and Anesthesia, 1972, 2d edit., 1980, Blocks of the Sympathetic Nervous System, 1981; also articles profl. jours.; Editor: (with P. Procacci, C. Pagni) Recent Advances on Pain, Pathophysiology and Clinical Aspects, 1974, Proc. Internat. Symposium on Pain, 1974, Obstetric Analgesia-Anesthesia, Recent Advances and Current Status, 1975, (with D. Albe-Fessard) Proc. First World Congress on Pain, 1976, Advances in Pain Research and Therapy, 1976, (with D. Albe-Fessard, J. Liebeskind) Proc. 2d World Congress on Pain, Vol. 3, 1979, (with V. Ventafridda) Proc. Internat. Symposium on Pain of Advanced Cancer, 1979, Proc. ARNMD-Ann. Meeting, 1979; (with L. Ng) Proc. NIH Conf. of 1979 Pain, Discomfort and Humanitarian Care, 1980; assoc. editor: Survey of Anesthesiology, 1957-72, Current Contents, 1972-78, Am. Jour. Chinese Medicine, 1973-76, Survey of Anesthesiology, 1957-72; editor: Pain, 1975-85; fgn. editor: Revista Mexicana de Anestesiologia, 1958-66. Bd. dirs. Tacoma Symphony, 1951-59, Seattle Opera, 1977-86 . Served from lt. to maj. U.S. Army, 1944-46. Decorated comdr. Order of Merit Italy, hereditary chevalier at rank of baronet Noble Order of Cingolo Militare; recipient Silver medal Swedish Med. Soc., 1969; Gold medal for neuroscis. German Neurophysiologic Soc., 1972; Gold medal U. Palermo, 1954; Disting. Service award Am. Soc. Anesthesiologists, 1973; Disting. Achievement award Modern Medicine, 1975, medal Intra-Sci. Rsch. Found., 1983, Karl Koller Gold medal European Soc. Regional Anesthesia, 1985, Achievement medal Alpha Omega, 1988, Alumni Merit award Marquette U., 1989, Humanitarian award, 1989; Disting John J. Bonica medal and lecture named in his honor, Am. Soc. Regional Anesthesiologists, 1988, John J. Bonica Fellowship named in his honor, Internat. Pain Found, City of Paris gold medal 7th World Congress on Pain, 1993; 1st recipient John J. and Emma Bonica Pub. Svc. award Am. Pain Soc., 1994. Fellow Am. Coll. Anesthesiologists, Internat. Coll. Anesthetists, Am. Acad. Anesthesiology, Faculty of Anaesthetists of Royal Coll. Surgeons (hon.); mem. AMA, King County, Wash. State med. socs., Am. Soc. Anesthesiologists (2d v.p. 1961, 1st v.p. 1964, pres. 1966), Assn. Univ. Anesthetists (pres. 1969), Internat. Assn. for Study of Pain (founder, mem. various coms. and couns., chmn. orgn. com. 1973-75, pres. 1978-81, hon. life pres. 1990-94), AAAS, World Med. Assn., Wash. State Soc. Anesthesiologists (pres. 1952), Internat. Anesthesia Research Soc., N.Y. Internat. Pain Found. (chmn. adv. bd. 1987, bd. dirs. 1992), Acad. Scis., Seattle, Tacoma surg. socs., Assn. des Anesthesiologistes Européens (hon.), Soc. Academic Anesthesia Chairmen, Assn. Am. Med. Colls., Am. Soc. Pharm. and Exptl. Therapy, Am. Pain Soc. (founder 1978, bd. dirs. 1978-86), Royal Coll. Medicine, World Fedn. Socs. Anaesthesiologists (chmn. sci. adv. com. 1968-72, sec.-gen. 1972-80, pres. 1980-84), Alpha Omega Alpha; hon. mem. Cuban Anesthesiology Soc., Mexican Anesthesiology Soc., Italian Anesthesiology Soc. (hon. pres. 1954), Argentinian Anesthesiology Soc. (hon. pres. 1955), Venezuelan Anesthesiology Soc., Colombian Anesthesiology Soc., Brazilian Anesthesiology Soc., Chilean Anesthesiology Soc., Swedish Anesthesiology Soc., Assn. Anaesthetists of Gt. Brit. and Ireland, Assn. Research on Nervous and Mental Diseases (pres. 1978). Home: Mercer Island Wash. Died Aug. 15, 1994.

BONNER, WALTER D(ANIEL), JR., physical biochemist; b. Salt Lake City, Oct. 22, 1919; s. Walter Daniel and Grace Amber (Gaylord) B.; m. Josephine Annette Silberberg, May 13, 1944; children: Andrew Daniel, Brian Timothy. BSc in Chemistry, U. Utah, 1940; PhD in Biology, Calif. Inst. Tech., 1946; MA (hon.), U. Pa., 1971. Research assoc. in biology Harvard U., 1946-49; Am. Cancer Soc. and USPHS fellow Moltneo Inst. U. Cambridge, Eng., 1949-52; biochemist Smithsonian Instn., Washington, 1952-53; asst. prof. botany Cornell U., 1953-57, assoc. prof., 1957-59; prof. phys. biochemistry Johnson Rsch. Found. U. Pa., 1959-75, prof. biochemistry and biophysics Sch. Medicine, 1975-90, prof. emeritus, 1990-95; mem. molecular biology panel NSF, 1960-63, biochem. program dir., 1974-76. Contbr. numerous articles to profl. jours. Guggenheim fellow and Churchill Coll. overseas fellow, 1967-68. Mem. Am. Chem. Soc., Am. Soc. Biol. Chemistry, Am. Soc. Plant Physiology, Biochem. Soc. (London), Biophys. Soc., N.Y. Acad. Sci., Sigma Xi. Home: Boyertown Pa. Died Aug. 6, 1995.

BONO, PHILIP, aerospace consultant; b. Bklyn., Jan. 14, 1921; s. Julius and Marianna (Culcasi) B.; m. Gertrude Camille King, Dec. 15, 1950; children: Richard Philip, Patricia Marianna, Kathryn Camille. B.E., U. So. Calif., 1947; postgrad., 1948-49. Research and systems analyst N.Am. Aviation, Inglewood, Calif., 1947; engrng. design specialist Douglas Aircraft Co., Long Beach, Calif., 1948-49; preliminary design engr. Boeing Airplane Co., Seattle, 1950-59; dep. program mgr. Douglas Aircraft Co., Santa Monica, Calif., 1960-62; tech. asst. to dir. advanced launch vehicles and space stas. Douglas Aircraft Co., Huntington Beach, Calif., 1963-65; br. mgr. advanced studies, sr. staff engr. advanced tech. McDonnell Douglas Astronautics Co., Huntington Beach, 1966-73; sr. engr.-scientist Douglas Aircraft Co., Long Beach, 1973-83; engrng. specialist Northrop Advanced Systems Div., Pico Rivera, Calif., 1984-86; mgr. Cal-Pro Engrng. Cons., Costa Mesa, 1986-93; lectr. seminars, univs. and insts. including Soviet Acad. Scis., 1965. Author: Destination Mars, 1961, (with K. Gatland) Frontiers of Space, 1969; contbr. articles to profl. jours., chpts. in books. Served with USNR, 1943-46. Recipient Golden Eagle award Council Internat. Events, 1964, A.T. Colwell merit award Soc. Automotive Engrs., 1968, M.N. Golovine award Brit. Interplanetary Soc., 1969, cert. of recognition NASA, 1983, Heritage medallion Project Italia, 1988; named engr. of distinction Engrs. Joint Council, 1971, Knight of Mark Twain, 1979. Fellow AAAS, Royal Aero. Soc. (sr.), Brit. Interplanetary Soc. (editorial adv. bd.), AIAA (assoc.); mem. Am. Astron. Soc. (sr.), N.Y. Acad. Scis., Internat. Acad. Astronautics (academician), ASME, Soc. Automotive Engrs. (chmn. space vehicle com.). Home: Costa Mesa Calif. Died May 1993.

BONSAL, DUDLEY BALDWIN, federal judge; b. Bedford, N.Y., Oct. 6, 1906; s. Stephen and Henrietta Fairfax (Morris) B.; m. Lois Abbott Worrall, May 16, 1931 (dec. Aug. 1981); children: Lois (Mrs. Frederic B. Osler, Jr.), Stephen.; m. Lucia Turner Faithfull, Mar. 5, 1983. A.B., Dartmouth Coll., 1927; LL.B., Harvard, 1930. Bar: N.Y. bar 1932. Asso. firm Curtis, Mallet-Prevost, Colt & Mosle, N.Y.C., 1930-38; mem. firm Curtis, Mallet-Prevost, Colt & Mosle, 1938-42, 45-61; U.S. dist. judge So. dist. N.Y., 1961-95; judge Temporary Emergency Ct. Appeals of U.S., 1977-87; chief counsel Office Inter-Am. Affairs, Washington, 1942-45; mem. U.S. del. Inter-Am. Conf. on Problems of War and Peace, Mexico City, 1945; legal adviser Fgn. Bondholders Protective Council, Conf. on German Debts, London, 1951, 52; mem. Internat. Commn. of Jurists, Geneva, Switzerland, 1953-73; chmn. spl. com. on fed. loyalty-security program Assn. Bar City N.Y., 1955-57; mem. com. on criminal justice act Jud. Conf. of U.S., 1964-79, chmn., 1974-79. Trustee Inst. Internat. Edn., 1948-64, Sterling and Francine Clark Art Inst., Williamstown, Mass., 1960-73, William Nelson Cromwell Found., Practising Law Inst., 1969-85. Fellow Am. Bar Found. (dir. 1967-75); mem. Am., N.Y. bar assns., Assn. Bar City N.Y. (pres. 1958-60), N.Y.C. Council on Fgn. Relations. Club: Century Assn. (N.Y.C.). Home: Bedford N.Y. Died July 22, 1995.

BOOLOS, GEORGE STEPHEN, philosophy educator; b. N.Y.C., Sept. 4, 1940; s. Stephen George and Blanche (Salomon) B.; 1 child, Peter. BA, Princeton U., 1961; BPhil, Oxford U., Eng., 1963; PhD, MIT, 1966. Asst. prof. philosophy Columbia U., 1966-69; asst. prof. philosophy MIT, 1969-73, assoc. prof., 1973-80, prof., 1980-96. Author: The Logic of Probability, 1993, The Unprovability of Consistency, 1979, (with R.C. Jeffrey) Computability and Logic, 1974; editor: Jour. Symbolic Logic, 1987, Meaning and Method, 1990. NEH fellow, 1984; Fulbright scholar, 1961-63; Guggenheim Found. fellow, 1996; NSF grantee, 1986, 88-89. Fellow Am. Acad. Arts and Scis.; mem. Assn. Symbolic Logic (pres. 1995-96), Am. Philos. Assn., Math. Assn. Am. Home: Cambridge Mass. Died May 27, 1996.

BOORDA, JEREMY MICHAEL (MIKE BOORDA), naval officer; b. South Bend, Ind., Nov. 26, 1939; s. Herman J. and Gertrude Frank (Wallis) B.; m. Bettie May Moran, Apr. 13, 1957; children: David Arthur, Edward Morris, Anna Elizabeth, Robert Nathan. BA in Polit. Sci., U. R.I., 1971; postgrad., Naval War Coll., Newport, R.I., 1971, 83; Ph.D. of Laws (hon.), U. of R.I., 1994. Commd. ensign USN, 1962, advanced through grades to adm., 1984; exec. officer USS Brooke, 1973-75; comdg. officer USS Farragut, 1975-81; comdr. Destroyer Squadron 22, 1983; exec. asst. Chief Naval Pers., Washington, 1983-84, Chief Naval Ops., Washington, 1984-86; comdr. Cruiser Destroyer Group 8, Norfolk, Va., 1986-88; chief naval pers. Navy Dept., Washington, 1988-91; comdr. allied forces So. Europe NATO, 1991-94; chief naval ops. Washington, 1994-96; mem. Joint Chiefs of Staff, 1994-96; pres. (ex officio) U.S. Naval Inst.; mem. of the bd. (ex officio) Navy/Marine Corps Relief Society, 94-96. Decorated D.S.M., Legion of Merit. mem. Coun. on Foreign Affairs (Rels.); Fleet Reserve Assoc.; Bluejacket Assoc. Home: Washington D.C. Died May 16, 1996.

BOREI, HANS GEORG, zoology educator, academic administrator; b. Stockholm, Feb. 7, 1914; m. 1938; 3 children. PhD in Zoology, U. Stockholm, 1941, DSc in Biochemistry, 1945. Rsch. asst. biophysics and exptl. biology U. Stockholm, 1937-45, assoc. prof., 1945-52, head dept. devel. physiology and genetics Wenner-Gren Inst., 1947-50, acting head Wenner-Gren Inst., 1948, 50, head dept. biophysics, 1948-52; prof. zoology U. Pa., Phila., 1953-84, prof. gen. physiology, 1955-60, chmn. major biol. programs, undergrad. chmn., 1964-84, prof. emeritus, 1984-93; vis. prof. zoology Calif. Inst. Tech., 1951; researcher Carlsberg Lab., Copenhagen, 1946, Kristinebergs Zool. Sta., Sweden, 1946-52, 61, Millport (Scotland) Marine Sta., 1948, Molteno Inst., Cambridge, Eng., 1948-49, Woods Hole, Mass., 1951, 53, Mt. Desert Island (Maine) Biol. Lab., 1955-64; researcher Swans Island (Maine) Marine Sta., 1965-84, pres., 1966-84. Recipient Aquist award, Stockholm, 1945, 46. Fellow AAAS, Am. Soc. Zoologists, Am. Soc. Limnololgy and Oceanography, Internat. Soc. Cell Biology, Sigma Xi. Home: Minturn Maine Died Mar. 10, 1993.

BORGSTEDT, HAROLD HEINRICH, pharmacologist, toxicologist; b. Hamburg, Germany, Apr. 21, 1929; came to U.S., 1956, naturalized, 1962; s. Gustav Johannes and Anni (Wulf) B.; m. Agneta D. von Rehren, Apr. 3, 1957; children: Eric von R., Astrid Anne. MD, U. Hamburg, 1956. Intern, Rochester (N.Y.) Gen. Hosp., 1956-57; fellow in pharmacology and anatomy U. Rochester, 1957-59, instr. pharmacology, 1959-63, sr. instr., 1963-65, research sr. instr. anesthesiology, 1963-65, asst. prof. pharmacology, rsch. asst. prof. anesthesiology, 1965-83; v.p. medicine and toxicology Health Designs, Inc., Rochester, N.Y., 1983-91; v.p. toxicology Compudrug USA, Inc., Rochester, N.Y., 1991-92, Compudrug Chemistry Budapest, 1991-94; pres. Compudrug N.A., Inc., Rochester, N.Y., 1992-94; tech. cons. Mitsubishi Chems. Am., San Jose, Calif., 1994-96; vis. staff U. Surrey, Guildford, Eng.; assoc. James W. Bunger Assocs., Salt Lake City, 1994-96. Mem. AAAS, N.Y. Acad. Scis., Am. Soc. Pharmacology and Exptl. Therapeutics, Soc. Toxicology, Leica Hist. Soc., Photog. Hist. Soc. (pres. 1986-88), Leica Historica (Germany), Internat. Soc. Study of Xenobiotics, Am. Chem. Soc., European Soc. of Toxicology (Eurotox), Sigma Xi. Unitarian. Contbr. to sci. jours., books. Died Feb. 16, 1996. Home: Henrietta N.Y.

BORISH, BERNARD M., lawyer; b. Phila., Sept. 20, 1916; s. Barney and Helen (Mandel) B.; m. Annette Peck, Jan. 24, 1943; children: Steven M., Arnold P., Rachel R. A.B., U. Pa., 1937, LL.B., 1943. Assoc. Wolf, Block, Schorr and Solis-Cohen, Phila., 1946-53, ptnr., 1954-87, of counsel, from 1987; permanent del. jud. conf. U.S. Ct. Appeals (3d cir.), from 1962; mem. adv. com. on appellate ct. rules Supreme Ct. Pa., 1973-80, chmn., 1980-86; founding chmn. Pub. Interest Law Ctr. Phila., 1974-77, also dir. Dep. city solicitor City of Phila., 1951-52; pres. Phila. Housing Assn., 1967-70; chmn. Phila. Gas Commn., 1980-83; adv. com. Women's Way, Phila., 1981-87; trustee William Goldman Found. 1st lt. USAAF, 1943-46. Fellow Am. Coll. Trial Lawyers, Am. Bar Found., Phila. Bar Found.; mem. Phila. Bar Assn. (chancellor 1977), Pa. Bar Assn. (ho. of dels. 1967-87), Am. Law Inst., Am. Judicature Soc. (bd. dirs. 1980-83), Law Alumni Soc. U. Pa. Law Sch. (pres. 1981-83). Democrat. Jewish. Clubs: Philmont Country (Huntingdon Valley, Pa.); Locust (Phila.); The Polo (Boca Raton, Fla.). Home: Boca Raton Fla. Deceased.

BORTOLUZZI, PAOLO, ballet dancer, choreographer; b. Genoe, Italy, May 17, 1938; m. Jaleh Kerendi, 1970; 2 children. Student of Ugo Dell'Ara, Genoe, 1954. With Del Balletio Italiano, Milan, 1957, Leone Massine's Festival de Nervi, 1960, Maurice Béjart's Ballet of the 20th Century, 1960-72; permanent guest artist Am. Ballet Theater, 1972, La Scala, Milan, Dusseldorf Opera; artistic adviser, choreographer La Scala, Milan. Repertoire includes Romeo and Juliet, Les Sylphides, Giselle, The Sleeping Beauty, Orpheo, The Nutcracker, Cinderella, Swan Lake, Firebird, Nomos Alpha, Apollo. Musagéte, Albinoni Adagio, L'Aprés-midi d'un faune, Sheherazade, Spectre-de-al-Rose, Mess Baudelaire, IXe Symphonie.

BOTTS, GUY WARREN, banker, lawyer; b. Milton, Fla., July 12, 1914; s. Alonzo O'Hara and Margaret (L) B.; m. Edith M. Huddleston, Nov. 4, 1939 (dec. Apr. 1978); children: Edith, William; m. Suzanne L. Crist, Sept. 12, 1987. J.D., U. Fla., 1937; LL.B. (hon.), Jacksonville U., 1967. Bar: Fla. 1937. Mem. firm Fleming, Hamilton, Diver & Jones, Jacksonville, 1937-39, 40-42; with law dept. Fla. br. Prudential Ins. Co. Am., Lakeland, Fla., 1939-40; mem. firm Fleming, Scott & Botts, and predecessor, 1942-55, sr. ptnr., 1955-57; sr. ptnr. Botts, Mahoney, Chambers & Adams (and predecessor), Jacksonville, 1957-63; gen. counsel, dir. Barnett Nat. Bank of Jacksonville, 1955-63, pres., chief exec. officer, dir., 1963-70, vice chmn., 1970-73, chmn., 1973-82; pres., CEO The Charter Co., 1960-63; chmn., bd. dirs. Charter Mortgage & Investment Co., 1960-63; pres. Barnett Banks, Inc. (formerly Barnett Nat. Securities Corp.), 1963-72, chmn. bd., 1973-84; chmn. bd. Nat. Bankamericard, Inc. (now VISA), 1973-75; ptnr. Culverhouse & Botts, and predecessors, 1983-93. Compiled: Brit. Statutes in Force in Florida, 1943; editor: Banks and banking statutes sect. Fla. Law Practice. Past mem. Fla. Devel. Commn.; commr. Uniform State Laws Fla., 1955-59; Chmn. bd. trustees Jacksonville U.; dir., past pres. Duval County Legal Aid Assn.; chmn. bd. dirs. Bok Tower Gardens Found., Inc. Recipient Gold Key award U.S. Jr. C. of C., 1946; Ted Arnold award Jacksonville Jr. C. of C., 1963, 78. Mem. Am. Coll. Probate Counsel (past regent), Jr. C. of C. (past pres.), U.S. C. of C., Jacksonville Area C. of C. (past pres.), ABA, Jacksonville Bar Assn. (past pres.), Fla. Bar (gov.), Am. Bankers Assn. (governing council), Fla. Bankers Assn., Assn. Bank Holding Cos. (past pres.), Phi Eta Sigma, Phi Alpha Delta, Alpha Kappa Psi, Delta Tau Delta. Clubs: River, Fla. Yacht, Ponte Vedra, Timuquana Country (Jacksonville); Quail Hollow Country (Charlotte, N.C.); Linville Golf, Grandfather Country (Linville, N.C.). Lodge: Rotary. Home: Jacksonville Fla. Died Jan. 1, 1993.

BOUCHER, MAYO TERRY, lawyer, judge; b. Stephenville, Tex., July 15, 1918; s. Terry S. and Henryetta (Turley) B.; m. Mary Catherine Lake, July 31, 1942; children: Phillip Larry, Terri Sue. Student, Tex. Tech, 1937-41; LLB, U. N.Mex., 1952, JD, 1969. Bar: N.Mex.; ordained deacon Bapt. Ch. With Atchison, Topeka & Santa Fe Ry., Belen, N.Mex., 1946-52; sole practice Belen, 1952-80; dist. judge 13th Jud. Dist., 1980-92; mem. ho. of reps. State of N.Mex., 1957-64; v.p. Belen Broadcasting Co., 1963-64; city atty. City of Belen, 1956-57; sec.-treas. First Belen Escrow Co., 1986-88; bd. dirs. First Nat. Bank Belen, 1956-81. Served with USNR, 1942-45. Mem. C. of C. (dir. 1954-57, pres. 1955), Pi Sigma Alpha. Lodges: Masons (past master), Order Eastern Star (past patron Jessamine chpt., 1954, 78, 89—, past grand patron, grand jurisdiction N.Mex., 1984-85), Rotary (pres. 1961-62, Paul Harris award, 1991). Home: Belen N. Mex. Died Oct. 24, 1992.

BOULDING, KENNETH EWART, economist, educator; b. Liverpool, Eng., Jan. 18, 1910; came to U.S., 1937, naturalized, 1948; s. William Couchman and Elizabeth Ann (Rowe) B.; m. Elise Bjorn-Hansen, Aug. 31, 1941; children: Russell, Mark, Christine, Philip, William. Student, Oxford U., 1928-32, BA with 1st class honors, 1931, MA, 1939; postgrad., U. Chgo., 1932-34; over 30 hon. degrees. Asst. U. Edinburgh, Scotland, 1934-37; instr. Colgate U., 1937-41; economist League of Nations Econ. and Fin. Sect., 1941-42; prof. Fisk U., 1942-43; assoc. prof. Iowa State Coll., 1943-46, prof., 1947-49; Angus prof. polit. economy McGill U., 1946-47; prof. econs. U. Mich., 1949-68, rsch. dir. Ctr. for Rsch. in Conflict Resolution, 1964-66; vis. prof. U. Colo., Boulder, 1967-68, prof., 1968-77, disting. prof., 1977-80, disting. prof. emeritus, 1980-93, dir. program on gen. social and econ. dynamics Inst. Behavioral Sci., 1967-81, rsch. assoc., project dir. program on polit. and econ. change, 1981-93; vis. prof. Univ. Coll. West Indies, Kingston, Jamaica, 1959-60, U. Natal, 1970, U. Edinburgh, fall 1972, Joseph H. Lauder Inst., U. Pa., June 1984, Butler U., fall 1984, U. Colo., fall 1986, Adlai E. Stevenson Coll., U. Calif., Santa Cruz, spring 1987, Fort Lewis Coll., Durango, Colo., spring 1987; Danforth vis. prof. Internat. Christian U., Tokyo, 1963-64, Aoyama Gakuin U., Tokyo, May, June 1991, July 1992; vis. lectr. Japanese Broadcasting Co., Tokyo, 1970, Patten lectr. Ind. U., Bloomington, fall 1973; Andrew D. White prof.-at-large Cornell U., 1974-79; Barnette Miller vis. prof. Wellesley Coll., fall 1975; Disting. Vis. Tom Slick prof. world peace L.B. Johnson Sch., U. Tex., Austin, 1976-77; Montgomery vis. prof. Dartmouth Coll., fall 1978; disting. vis. prof. Sch. Pub. Adminstrn., Ohio State U., spring 1981; Winegard vis. prof. U. Guelph, Ont., Can., fall 1981; Downing fellow Melbourne (Australia) U., spring 1982; Eugene M. Lang vis. prof. social change Swarthmore Coll., 1982-83; A. Lindsay O'Connor vis. prof. Am. instns. Colgate U., fall 1983; 1st vis. scholar UN Univ., Tokyo, spring 1984; Aspinall vis. prof. Mesa Coll., Apr. 1984; Mitchell disting. vis. prof. Trinity U., spring 1985; disting. vis. prof., George Mason U., fall 1985; vis. scholar Russell Sage Found., N.Y., spring 1986; friend in residence Pendle Hill, Wallingford, Pa., fall 1988; Hitchcock vis. prof. U. Calif., 1989; Robinson vis. prof. George Mason U., Fall 1989. Author: Economic Analysis, 1941, 4th rev. edit., 1966, Economics of Peace, 1945, reissued, 1972, There is a Spirit (The Naylor Sonnets), 1945, rev. edit., 1992, A Reconstruction of Economics, 1950, The Organizational Revolution, 1953, reissued, 1984, The Image, 1956, Principles of Economic Policy, 1958, The Skills of the Economist, 1958, Conflict and Defense, 1962, reissued, 1988, The Meaning of the Twentieth Century, 1964, reissued, 1988, The Impact of the Social Sciences, 1966, Beyond Economics, 1968, Economics as a Science, 1970, reissued, 1988, A Primer on Social Dynamics, 1970, The Prospering of Truth (Swarthmore Lecture), 1970, Collected Papers, Vols. 1-5, 1971-75, Vol. 6, 1985, The Appraisal of Change (in Japanese), 1972, The Economy of Love and Fear, 1973, Sonnets from the Interior Life and Other Autobiographical Verse, 1975, Stable Peace, 1978, Ecodynamics, 1978, Beasts, Ballads and Bouldingisms, 1980, Evolutionary Economics, 1981, A Preface to Grants Economics, 1981, Human Betterment, 1985, The World as a Total System, 1985, Sonnets on Courtship, Marriage, and Family, 1987, 2d edit. 1990, Three Faces of Power, 1989, Towards a New Economics, 1991, The Structure of Modern Economy: The United States 1929-89, 1993; author: (with Elise Boulding and Guy M. Burgess) The Social System of Planet Earth, 1977, 80; editor: (with George J. Stigler) Readings in Price Theory, 1952; (with W.A. Spivey) Linear Programming and the Theory of the Firm, 1960; (with Emile Benoit) Disarmament and the Economy, 1963; (with Tapan Mukerjee) Economic Imperialism, 1972; (with Martin Pfaff) Redistribution to the Rich and the Poor, 1972; (with Martin and Anita Pfaff) Transfers in an Urbanized Economy, 1973; (with Thomas F. Wilson) Redistribution through the Financial System, 1978; (with H.R. Porter) General Systems Yearbook, vol. 23, 1979; (with Lawrence Senesh) The Optimum Utilization of Knowledge: Making Knowledge Serve Human Betterment, 1983; edited Peace and the War Industry, 1970, 73, The Economics of Human Betterment, 1984; Bibliography of Published Works by Kenneth E. Boulding (1932-84) compiled by Vivian L. Wilson, 1985. Recipient prize for disting. scholarship in humanities Am. Coun. Learned Socs., 1962, Frank E. Seidman disting. award in polit. economy, 1976, Rufus Jones award World Acad. Art and Sci., 1979, John R. Commons award Omicron Delta Epsilon, 1985, (with Elise Boulding) 18th Boise Peace Quilt, 1988, award Assn. for Integrative Studies, 1990; co-recipient Lentz Internat. Peace Rsch. award, 1976; Commonwealth fellow U. Chgo., 1932-34; fellow Ctr. Advanced Study in Behavior Scis., Palo Alto, 1954-55. Fellow Am. Acad. Arts and Scis., Am. Philos. Soc., Brit Acad. (corr.); mem. Am. Econ. Assn. (John B. Clark medal 1949, pres. 1968), NAS (sr. mem. Inst. Medicine), Soc. Gen. Systems Rsch. (pres. 1957-59, Leadership award 1984), Internat. Studies Assn. (v.p. 1969-70, pres. 1974-75), AAAS (v.p., chmn. sect. K 1966-67, pres. 1979, chmn. bd. dirs. 1980), Peace Rsch. Soc. Internat. (pres. 1969-70), Assn. Study Grants Economy (pres. 1969-89), Brit. Assn. Advancement of Sci. (pres. sect. on econs. 1982-83). Democrat. Mem. Soc. of Friends. Home: Boulder Colo. Died Mar. 19, 1993; cremated.

BOURGEOIS, ANDRE MARIE GEORGES, French educator; b. Orleans, France, Dec. 1, 1902; came to U.S., 1927, naturalized, 1936; s. Maurice M. and Yvonne (Assire) B.; m. Dorothea de la Barre 1930; 1 child, Maxime William; m. May Hander, 1940; 1 child, June Katherine Marie. B.A., U. Paris, 1921, LL.B., 1923; certicats etudes superieures, 1930, doctorat, 1945; M.A., U. Tex., 1934. Mem. faculty Rice U., 1928-94, prof. French, 1954-72, prof. emeritus, 1972-94, acting chmn. dept., 1957-61, Favrot prof. French lit., 1969-94, chmn. dept., 1970-72; vis. prof. U. Houston, 1947, 60, U. Tex., 1940, Tulane U., 1939. Author: Ballades Louisianaises, 1938, Practical French Grammar, 1940, Pastels and Sanguines, 1947, Rene Boylesve, le peintre de la Touraine, 1945, Rene Boylesve, et le probleme de l'amour, 1950, La vie de Rene Boylesve, 1958, Rene Boylesve, le Poete, 1967. Asst. dir. Le Petit Theatre Français de Houston, 1933-38; assoc. pub. Le Bayou, 1936-61. Served to maj. M.I., AUS, 1942-45, ETO. Decorated Bronze Star; Croix de Guerre (France); officer Ouissam Alaouite Cherifien, Corona d'Italia; comdr. Palmes Academiques; recipient Medaille d'Honneur U. Nancy (France). Mem. South Central Modern Lang. Assn. (hon.), Société des Gens de Lettres de France, Houston Philos. Soc., Alliance Française, Chevaliers du Tastevin. Roman Catholic. Home: Houston Tex. Died Jan. 28, 1994.

BOURNE, MARY BONNIE MURRAY (MRS. SAUL HAMILTON BOURNE), music publishing company executive; b. Salix, Iowa, Sept. 13, 1903; d. Thomas William and Kathryn (McDermott) Murray; student Morningside Normal Coll., 1922-23; student Am. Banking Inst., N.Y.C.; m. Saul Hamilton Bourne, Apr. 12, 1928; 1 dau., Mary Elizabeth. Appeared with George White Scandals, Ramblers, Cocoanuts, Ziegfield Follies, 1925-28; owner, mgr. Bourne Co., N.Y.C., 1960-93. Mem. social work recruiting com. United Hosp. Fund. Trustee S.H. Bourne Found., Coll. New Rochelle; trustee N.Y. Infirmary, 1945-93, chmn. social service youth bd., 1947-93, bd. visitors Sch. Music, Catholic U. Am., Washington. Recipient Abe Olman Pub. award. Mem. A.S.C.A.P. (dir., pubs. adv. com.). Died March 20, 1993. Home: New York N.Y.

BOUYGUES, FRANCIS GEORGES, industrialist; b. Paris, Dec. 5, 1922; Dipolma in E.C.P. Sch. of Engring, diploma in C.P.A. Bus. Tng. Ctr., diploma of C. of C., Paris; s. Georges B. and Edmée née Regnault (Marr) B.; m. Monique Teze, Oct. 26, 1946; children: Corinne, Nicolas, Martin, Olivier. Founder Bouygues Group, France, 1951; v.p. found. pour entreprendre. chmn. chief exec. officer Bouygues Co., first French TV Sta. Decorated Officer of the Legion of Honour, Comdr. of Nat. Order of Merit. Ach. yachting, hunting, fishing. Died July 25, 1993. Home: Paris France

BOVE, JANUAR D., JR., lawyer; b. Wilmington, Del., Aug. 17, 1920; s. Januar D. and Teresa (A.) B.; m. Lillian Briggs, 1949; children: Jeffrey, Nancy, Kathryn. Grad. with honors, U. Del.; J.D., Harvard U., 1948. Bar: Del. 1949, U.S. Supreme Ct. 1959. Pvt. practice Wilmington, 1949-91; ptnr. Connolly, Bove, Lodge & Hutz, Wilmington, 1953-91, sr. ptnr., 1990; asst. city solicitor Wilmington, 1949-50, city solicitor, 1953-57; Dep. Atty. Gen. Del., 1950-53, Atty. Gen., 1958-62; bd. dirs. Del. Citizen's Crime Commn., 1962-71, Del. Council on Crime and Justice, 1977-81. Trustee Tatnall Sch., 1962-73; past sec. Republican Com. of Del.; chmn. Crusade for Freedom, Del., 1958. Served from 2d lt. to maj. AUS, World War II. Recipient Good Govt. award Com. of 39, 1962, Wyman award Nat. Assn. Attys. Gen., 1962; inducted posthumously into U. Del. Alumni Hall of Fame, 1992. Mem. Am., Del. bar assns., Harvard Law Sch. Assn. (pres. Del. 1962-63), Del. C. of C. (dir. 1967-70), U. Del. Alumni Assn. (treas. 1979-81), Phi Kappa Phi. Club: Harvard (Wilmington). Home: Wilmington Del. Died Oct. 16, 1991.

BOWEN, ALBERT REEDER, lawyer; b. Logan, Utah, Apr. 13, 1905; s. Albert Ernest and Aletha (Reeder) B.; m. Lucile Ross, Nov. 17, 1934 (dec. 1952); children: Barbara (Mrs. Ted O. Brunker), David Ross, Beverly (Mrs. Michael W. Walker), Albert Ross, Robert K. Bowen; m. Margret Jenson, Mar. 29, 1954; children: Mark J., Julie (Mrs. Curtis D. Elton), Stephen J. A.B., U. Utah, 1930; J.D., Leland Stanford Jr. U., 1932. Bar: Utah bar 1932. Since practiced in Salt Lake City; partner firm Ray, Quinney & Nebeker (and predecessors), 1945-85, of counsel, 1985-93; Sec., mem. Utah Sch. Study Com., 1963-64; del. Republican Nat. Conv., 1964; Bd. regents U. Utah, 1951-55. Fellow emeritus Am. Coll. Trial Lawyers; mem. ABA, Utah Bar Assn. Mem. Ch. of Jesus Christ of Latter Day Saints. Clubs: Timpangogas (pres. 1975-76), Bonneville Knife and Fork (dir. 1962-65). Home: Salt Lake City Utah Died 1993.

BOWERSOCK, JUSTIN DEWITT, III, banker; b. Kansas City, Mo., Dec. 27, 1907; s. Justin Dewitt and Frances (Matteson) B.; m. Betty Bruce Van Antwerp, Oct. 25, 1930; children: Justin Dewitt IV (dec.), Chiles V. (dec.), Frances and Caroline (twins). A.B., Harvard, 1929. Asst. cashier Fidelity Nat. Bank, Kansas City, Mo., 1929-33; v.p. Union Nat. Bank, Kansas City, 1933-49; exec. v.p. 1st Am. Bank (NA), Washington, 1949-67; pres. 1st Am. Bank (NA), 1967-70, chmn. bd., 1970-75, chmn. exec. com., from 1975; dir., mem. audit com. First Am. Bankshares, Inc., Washington, from 1974; dir. Fed. Services Fin. Corp., Washington, 1957-67, Group Hospitalization, Inc., 1960-70. Served to lt. (j.g.) USNR, 1944-46, PTO. Mem. Am. Bankers Assn. (v.p. D.C. 1957, 62-63, exec. council 1965-68), D.C. Bankers Assn. (pres. 1958-59). Republican. Episcopalian. Clubs: Chevy Chase (Md.); Metropolitan (Washington), Alfalfa (Washington). Home: Middleburg Va. Deceased.

BOWLES, JOHN, retired sales executive; b. Monroe, N.C., Nov. 16, 1916; s. Hargrove and Kelly Bess (Moneyhun) B.; m. Norma Louise Landwehr, Oct. 6, 1950; children: Carol Louise, Kelly Louise, John Hargrove, Norma. BS, U. N.C., 1938; DBA, Woodbury Coll., 1963; DBA (hon.), Wingate Jr. Coll., 1960. With Rexall Drug Co., Los Angeles, 1949-66; v.p. Rexall Drug Co., 1953-55, pres., 1955-65, chmn. bd., 1965-66; v.p., dir. Rexall Drug & Chem. Co., 1955-66; chmn. Sunstates, Inc., Raleigh, N.C.; dir. A.S. Haight Co. Inc.; mem. Pres.'s Com. for Community Relations; mem. nat. sponsoring com. Duke; mem. pharmacy adv. com. Coll. Pacific; founder Free Enterprise Day; chmn. Los Amigos del Pueblo de Los Angeles, Los Amigos de Los Charros; founding pres. Calif. Wine Patrons. Trustee U. Calif. at Los Angeles Found., Southwest Mus.; adv. bd. Pepperdine U.; bd. govs. Am. Found. Religion and Psychiatry; bd. regents St. John's Hosp. Served as lt. comdr. USNR, 1941-46. Recipient Horatio Alger award, 1962; named El Padrino del Pueblo de Los Angeles Bd. Suprs. of Los Angeles, 1981. Mem. Sales and Marketing Execs. (trustee), Confrerie des Chevaliers du Tastevin (grand officer), Calif. Wine Patrons (pres.),

Master of Foxhounds Assn., Beta Theta Pi. Methodist (steward). Clubs: Los Angeles Country; Kildare Hunt (Ireland); Santa Ynez Hunt; Valley Hunt; Rancheros Vistadores (Santa Barbara); Bohemian (San Francisco). Lodge: Masons. Home: Los Angeles Calif. Died Oct. 20, 1993; cremated; ashes interred Gifford Co. Cemetery, Greensboro & Selu Conservancy, Montgomery Co., Va.

BOWMAN, VICTOR, manufacturing executive; b. Morrow, Ohio, Mar. 31, 1894; s. Alva C. and Nannie (Hicks) B.; m. Maddah Craven, Jan. 7, 1922. A.B., Twin Valley Coll., 1912; postgrad., in Europe. Spl. fgn. rep. Dennison Mfg. Co., 1914-21; traveling in Dennison Mfg. Co., Cuba, P.R., other W.I. Islands, Mex., Central Am. countries, Argentina, Brazil, other South Am. countries; operated in Hawaii, South Sea Islands, Australia, New Zealand, Africa, Dutch East Indies, Malay States, China, Japan, Philippines, France, Spain, other European countries; domestic dist. sales mgr. N.Y.C., 1921; gen. sales mgr. domestic and fgn. sales Framingham, Mass., 1922-27; organizer 1st internat. sales orgn., gen. sales mgr. Pacific Mills, N.Y.C., 1927-33; gen. field supr. Schenley Distillers Corp., N.Y.C., 1933; gen. sales mgr. Mohawk Carpet Mills, N.Y., 1933, N.Y.C., 1933; dir., v.p. Mohawk Import and Export Co., 1940-42; v.p., dir. Am. Steel Export Co., 1942, 1st v.p., exec. v.p., 1943-53, v.p., dir. domestic and fgn. subsidiaries, from 1942; Mem. Spl. Econ. Mission, Dept. State to, French North Africa, Middle East and Italy, 1944-45. Treas. Fountain House Found., N.Y.C. Served with Mil. Intelligence to observe pro-German activities in Latin America, 1917-18. Mem. Commerce and Industries Assn. N.Y. (fgn. trade com.), N.Y. State C. of C. (com. on fgn. commerce 1949-52, now chmn.), Ohio Soc. N.Y., Am. Legion, Soc. for Advancement Mgmt. (mgr. N.Y. chpt.), Mktg. Execs. Soc. (charter), English-Speaking Union, Taylor Soc., Vet. Corps of Arty., Mil. Soc. War 1812, Order Ky. Cols., Civic Assn. Palm Beach (Fla.), Alpha Chi Sigma. Clubs: Yale (N.Y.C.), N.Y. Export Managers (N.Y.C.), Metropolitan (N.Y.C.); Sleepy Hollow Country (Scarborough); Mexico City Country, Circumnavigators; Everglades (Palm Beach, Fla.); Circle Interallie (Paris). Home: Allenhurst N.J. Deceased.

BOWMAN, WARD SIMON, JR., economist, educator; b. Everett, Wash., Oct. 29, 1911; s. Ward Simon and Charity E. (Rice) B.; m. Maxine Beal, Feb. 14, 1937; children: Gary W., George T. A.B., U. Wash., 1933; M.A. (hon.), Yale, 1959. Economist Dept. Justice, 1938-46; research asso. U. Chgo. Law Sch., 1946-56; mem. faculty Yale Law Sch., New Haven, 1956-91; prof. law and econs. Yale Law Sch., 1959-73, Ford Found. prof. law and econs., 1973-79, prof. emeritus, 1979-91. Author: Patent and Antitrust Law: A Legal and Economic Appraisal, 1973; Contbr. articles to profl. jours. Mem. Am. Econ. Assn. Home: Guilford Conn. Died Sept. 10, 1991.

BOWN, OLIVER HUTCHINS, psychology educator; b. Denver, Aug. 6, 1921; s. Albert George and Henrietta Hutchins (Punshon) B.; m. Evelyn Elizabeth Struble, Dec. 11, 1943; children: J. Michael, Jennifer L. Bown Keogh, Kathleen Bown Duck, Kimberly A. Pugh. AB in Psychology, U. Denver, 1943; MA in Clin. Psychology, U. Chgo., 1948, PhD in Clin. Psychology, 1954. Cert. and lic. psychologist, Tex. Staff counselor U. Chgo. Counseling Ctr., 1947-49, coord. profl. svcs., 1949-51; lectr. psychology dept. ednl. psychology U. Tex., Austin, 1951-59, assoc. prof., 1959-66, prof. dept. ednl. psychology, from 1966, asst. dir. Testing and Counseling Ctr., 1951-58, assoc. dir. Personality Rsch. Ctr. Coll. Edn., 1962-77, assoc. dir. then dir. R&D Ctr. Tchr. Edn., 1965-84, sr. scholar in residence R&D Ctr. Tchr. Edn., 1984-86; mem. coun. ednl. personal devel. Tex. Edn. Agy., 1967-73; mem. med.-profl. adv. and evaluation bd. United Cerebral Palsey Tex., Inc., 1962-68; nat. adv. and policy coun. Ednl. Resources Info. Ctr. Clearinghouse Tchr. Edn., Washington, 1968-84, chmn., 1978-79. Author: (with others) Client-Centered Therapy, 1951, Counselor Education and Supervision: Readings in Theory, Practice and Research, 1982; contbr. articles to profl. jours. Lt. USN, 1943-46, PTO. Mem. APA, Nat. Soc. Study Edn., Tex. Pers. and Mgmt. Assn. (program chmn. edn. sect. 1955), Sigma Xi, Phi Beta Kappa, Omicron Delta Kappa. Home: Austin Tex. Deceased.

BOYD, HOWARD TANEY, lawyer, former gas company executive; b. Woodside, Md., June 5, 1909; s. Howard and Mary Violet (Stewart) B.; m. Lucille Belhumeur, June 15, 1935; children: Dennis Brooke, Sharon Ann Boyd Rodriguez, Deborah Boyd Fitch (dec.). Grad., Georgetown Prep. Sch., Garrett Park, Md.; A.B. magna cum laude, Georgetown U., 1932, J.D., 1935, LL.D., 1977. Bar: D.C. 1934, Tex. 1953. Sec. to U.S. atty. gen., 1934; spl. atty. U.S. Dept. Justice, 1935; asst. U.S. atty. for D.C., 1935-39; prof. Nat. Law Ctr. (formerly Nat. Law Sch.), Am. U. (formerly Washington Coll. Law), Washington; ptnr. firm Hogan & Hartson, Washington, 1939-52; officer, dir. El Paso Co. (formerly El Paso Natural Gas Co.), 1952-79, chmn. bd., chief exec. officer, 1964-79; ptnr. Liddell, Sapp, Zivley, Hill & LaBoon, Houston, 1979-89, ret., 1989. Regent emeritus Georgetown U.; past bd. dirs. Houston Symphony Soc.; former trustee U. So. Calif.,U.S.-USSR Trade and Econ. Council, U.S. Nat. Com. World Energy Conf., Exec. Service Corps of Houston, Nat. Petroleum Council; mem. nat. corp. cabinet Am. Heart Assn., also Tex. affiliate, Nat. Council Salk Inst.; mem. bd. advisors Inst. Bioscis. and Tech. Tex. A&M U.; mem. devel. council Tex. A&M U. Coll. Bus. Adminstrn. Decorated chevalier Legion of Honor France, Order of Malta; recipient Golden Plate award Am. Acad. Achievement, 1977. Mem. ABA, State Bar Tex., Bar Assn. D.C. (dir. 1950), Houston Bar Assn., Independent Natural Gas Assn. (pres. 1967-68), Groupe Internat. des Importateurs de Gaz Naturel Liquefié (pres. emeritus), Tex. Philos. Soc. Clubs: Barristers, Burning Tree, Chevy Chase, Columbia Country, Metropolitan (Washington); River Oaks Country, Houston Country, Petroleum, Ramada (Houston); Kissing Camels Golf (Colo. Springs). Home: Houston Tex. Died Feb. 10, 1992; interred Houston, Tex.

BOYD, JAMES BROWN, molecular genetics educator; b. Denver, June 25, 1937; s. James and Ruth Ragland (Brown) B.; m. Susie Fay Staats, Apr. 23, 1960; children: Randall Ragland, Pamela Ann. BA, Cornell U., 1959; PhD, Calif. Inst. Tech., 1965. Postdoctoral fellow Max-Planck Institut for Biologie, Tubingen, W.Ger, 1965-68; asst. prof. dept. genetics U. Calif., Davis, 1969-71, asso. prof., 1971-77, prof., 1977-93; vis. scholar Stanford (Calif.) U., 1988-89; mem. genetics study sect. NIH, 1976-80. Served with M.S.C. U.S. Army, 1959-60. Helen Hay Whitney fellow, 1965-68; NATO sr. scientist fellow, 1974; Guggenheim fellow, 1975-76; Sr. Am. von Humboldt prize, 1981-82. Mem. Genetics Soc. Am., Sierra Club, Sigma Xi. Home: Davis Calif. Died Oct. 7, 1993.

BOYD, WILLIAM RICHARD, airline company executive; b. Newark, May 13, 1916; s. Samuel and Marion (Suchoy) B.; m. Katherine Louise Myer, Apr. 24, 1942. Student, U. N.C., 1933-35. Vice pres., gen. mgr. Nationwide Air Transport Service, Miami, Fla., 1947-49; pres., dir., gen. mgr. Frontier Airmotive, Inc., 1950-51; v.p., asst. pres. Resort Airlines, 1951-52; dir., pres., gen. mgr. All Am. Airways, 1952-53, Riddle Airlines, 1953-55; exec. v.p., gen. mgr., dir. Aerovias Sud Americana, 1955-56; exec. v.p., dir. World Airways, 1956-63; v.p. Continental Air Lines, 1964-68; pres., gen. mgr., dir. Airlift Internat., Inc., Miami, Fla., 1968-70; chief exec. officer, dir. Holiday Airlines, Inc., Los Angeles, 1970-71; v.p. Tracinda Investment Co., 1971—; dir. Metro-Goldwyn-Mayer, Inc., Western Airlines Inc. Served to flying officer RAF, 1940-42; to maj. USAAF, 1942-45. Decorated Air medal, D.F.C. U.S. and Eng.). Home: Beverly Hills Calif.

BOYER, ERNEST LEROY, foundation executive; b. Dayton, Ohio, Sept. 13, 1928; s. Clarence and Ethel (French) B.; m. Kathryn Tyson, Aug. 26, 1950; children: Ernest LeRoy, Beverly, Craig, Stephen. AB, Greenville Coll., 1950; MA, U. So. Calif., 1955, PhD, 1957; postdoctoral, U. Iowa Hosp., 1959; over 130 hon. degrees including, Fordham U., U Rochester, Hamilton Coll., Coll. William and Mary,; Yeshiva U., U. Mo., Mich. State U., Earlham Coll., Miami U.,, CUNY, Haverford Coll., De Paul U., Mt. Union Coll., U. Portland,, U. Utah, Williams Coll. Former mem. faculty Upland (Calif.) Coll., acad. dean, prof. speech pathology, 1956-60; teaching asst. U. So. Calif., 1950-55; asst. prof., dir. forensics Loyola U., Los Angeles, 1955-56; dir. commn. to improve edn. tchrs. Western Coll. Assn., 1960-62; dir. Ctr. Coordinated Edn., U. Calif., Santa Barbara, 1962-65; exec. dean univ.-wide activities SUNY, 1965-68, vice chancellor, 1968-70, chancellor, 1970-77; U.S. commr. of edn., 1977-79; pres. Carnegie Found. for Advancement of Teaching, Princeton, N.J., 1979—; sr. fellow Woodrow Wilson Sch., Princeton U., 1983-90; columnist higher edn. supplement London Times, 1983-92; scholar-in-residence Aspen Inst. Humanistic Studies, 1974-76; vis. fellow Wolfson Coll. Cambridge (Eng.) U., 1976; mem. exec. com. Nat. Adv. Bd. of The Ctr. for the Book, Library of Congress, 1980—; mem. Nat. Commn. Financing of Postsecondary Edn., 1972-73, Commn. on Critical Choices for Ams., 1973-74, Carnegie Council on Policy Studies in Higher Edn., 1974-77, Presdl. Com. on Edn. Women, 1975, Pres.'s Adv. Council on Women's Ednl. Programs, 1975-77, Cities in Schs., Inc., Council Fin. Aid to Edn.; chmn. bd. Am. Coll. Testing; bd. dirs. Am. Council for the Arts, Council for Aid to Edn., EDUCATION 1st!, Nat. Alliance Bus.; bd. dirs. Com. Econ. Devel., Aspen Inst., Princeton Child Devel. Inst.; chair adv. group Nat. Edn. Goals Panel; mem. nat. adv. com. Children's Initiative of Pew Found. mem. editorial bd. Jour. Am. Assn. Univ. Adminstrs. Bd. mgrs. Haverford Coll., 1980—; mem. Nat. Adv. Com. on the Arts, Council on Fgn. Relations; trustee Messiah Coll., Guilford Coll., U. Pa. Med. Ctr., Very Spl. Arts with the Kennedy Ctr., 1980—; chair Dept. State Overseas Schs-Adv. Coun., 1989—, Mus. Am. Indian, Nat. Arts Edn., Nat. Faculty of Humanities, Arts and Scis., N.J. Literacy in Arts Task Force; bd. dirs. Lincoln Ctr. Inst. for Arts in Edn., Lincoln Ctr. Performing Arts, Am. Council Arts, N.J. Performing Arts Ctr. Recipient Pres.'s medal Tel Aviv U., 1971, Gov.'s award State of Ohio, 1978, Achievement in Life award Ency. Britannia, 1978, N.Y. Acad. Pub. Edn. Ann. award, 1979, spl. citation PUSH-EXCEL, 1979, William Moss Inst. award, 1982, Pi Lambda Theta award, 1983, James Conant award Edn. Commn. of the States, 1994; named one of Am.'s Two Outstanding Leaders in Edn., U.S. News and World Report mag., 1978; Presdl. fellow Aspen Inst. Humanistic Studies, 1978, Disting. Fulbright prof., India, 1985, Disting. Fulbright lectr. Chile, 1989,1990 Educator of the Year US News & World Report, 1990 Horatio Alger award, Regents lectr. U. Calif., Santa Barbara, 1992, Disting. Svc. medal Teachers Coll. Columbia U., 1988, Disting. Svc. award N.Y. State United Teachers, 1993, Charles Frankel prize NEA, 1994, Edn. Leadership award Coun. Am. Pvt. Edn., 1995. Fellow AAAS, Nat. Acad. Edn. (chair adv. group, nat. edn. goals panel), Internat. Coun. Ednl. Devel. (bd. dirs., mem. exec. com. 1980—), Nat. Assn. State Univs. and Land-Grant Colls. (pres. 1974-75), Internat. Higher Edn. Acad. Scis., Soc. Friends, Pi Kappa Delta, Alpha Kappa Sigma, Kappa Delta Pi, N.Y. Univ. Club. Home: Princeton N.J.

BOYLAN, WILLIAM ALVIN, lawyer; b. Marshalltown, Iowa, Sept. 18, 1924; s. Glen D. and Dorothy I. (Gibson) B.; m. Nancy Dickson, Aug. 5, 1950; children: Ross, Laura. Student, U. Iowa, 1943-44; BA, Drake U., 1947; LLB, Harvard U., 1950. Bar: Ill. 1950, N.Y. 1952. Practiced in N.Y.C., 1952-93; mem. Gould & Wilkie, N.Y.C., 1987-93. Contbr. articles to profl. jours. Served with USAAF, 1943-46. Mem. ABA, N.Y. State Bar Assn., Assn. of Bar of City of N.Y., Phi Beta Kappa, Sigma Alpha Epsilon. Episcopalian. Clubs: Harvard, The Down Town Assn. Home: New York N.Y. Died Mar. 26, 1993.

BOYLE, KAY, writer; b. St. Paul, Feb. 19, 1902; d. Howard Peterson and Katherine (Evans) B.; m. Richard Brault, June 24, 1923 (div.); m. Laurence Vail Apr. 2, 1931 (div.); children: Sharon Walsh, Apple-Joan, Kathe, Clover, Faith Carson, Ian Savin; m. Baron Joseph von Franckenstein, Feb. 24, 1943 (dec. 1963); 1 child, Joseph. Student, Ohio Mechanics Inst., 1917-19; LittD (hon.), Columbia U., 1971; LHD (hon.), Skidmore Coll., 1977, So. Ill. U., 1978; student, Ea. Wash. U., 1982; LHD (hon.), Bowling Green State U., 1986. Prof. English and creative writing San Francisco State U., 1963-79; LHD (hon.). Author: poems A Glad Day, 1930, Wedding Day; short stories, 1930, Plagued by the Nightingale; novel, 1931, Year Before Last; novel, 1932, Gentlemen, I Address You Privately; novel, 1933, My Next Bride; novel, 1934, Death of a Man; novel, 1936, The White Horses of Vienna; short stories, 1937, Monday Night; novel, 1938, His Human Majesty: novel, 1939, The Crazy Hunter; 3 short novels, 1940, Primer for Combat; novel, 1942, Avalanche, 1943, A French Man Must Die; novel, 1945, American Citizen; poem, 1944, Thirty Stories, 1946; 1939, novel, 1947, His Human Majesty, 1949, The Smoking Mountain; essays, 1951, The Seagull on the Step; novel, 1955, Three Short Novels, 1958, children's book The Youngest Camel, 1959, novel, Generation Without Farewell, 1960, Collected Poems, 1962, essay, Breaking the Silence, 1962, Nothing Ever Breaks Except the Heart; short stories, 1966, (children's book) Pinky, the Cat Who Likes to Sleep, 1966, editor: The Autobiography of Emanuel Carnevali, 1967, Being Geniuses Together; memoir, 1968, (children's book) Pinky in Persia, 1968, Testament For My Students; poems, 1970, The Long Walk at San Francisco State; essays, 1970, The Underground Woman; novel, 1975, Fifty Stories, 1980, Words That Must Somehow Be Said: The Selected Essays of Kay Boyle 1927-1984, 85, This is Not a Letter, Life Being the Best, Short Stories, 1988, Poems, 1985, Collected Poems, 1992. Recipient O. Henry Meml. prize, 1936, 1941; San Francisco Art Commn. award, 1978, Columbus Found. Am. Book award, 1983, The Los Angeles Times Robert Kirsch award, 1986, Lannan Found. award, 1989, Fred Cody award, 1992; Guggenheim fellow, 1934, 61; sr. citizen grantee Nat. Endowment for Arts, 1980. Mem. Am. Acad. Arts and Letters. Home: Mill Valley Calif. Died Dec. 27, 1992.

BOZEMAN, ADDA BRUEMMER, international relations scholar, educator, consultant, author; b. Geistershof, Latvia, Dec. 17, 1908; came to U.S., 1936, naturalized, 1941; d. Leon and Anna (von Kahlen) von Bruemmer; m. Virgil Bozeman, Mar. 26, 1937 (div. 1947); 1 dau., Anya Bozeman Taylor; m. Arne Barkhuus, Feb. 8, 1951. Diplomée, Sect. Diplomatique Ecole Libre des Scis. Politiques, Paris, 1934; barrister at law, Middle Temple Inn of Ct., London, 1936; J.D., So. Meth. U., 1937; postgrad., Stanford U., Hoover Inst. With law offices Charles H. Huberich, Berlin, Paris, The Hague and London, 1933-36; assoc. prof. history Augustana Coll., 1943-47; prof. internat. history Sarah Lawrence Coll., Bronxville, N.Y., 1947-77, prof. emeritus, 1977—; vis. prof. Northwestern U., 1945, NYU, 1948, 49; Benedict disting. vis. prof. Carleton Coll., Minn., 1978; Leon lectr. U. Pa., 1978; mem. grad. faculty New Sch. Social Research, 1954, 55, 63; dir. postdoctoral seminars on diplomacy internat. history NEH, 1975, 76, 78, dir. postdoctoral seminars on internat. relations in multicultural world, 1981, 82; curricular cons. in intercultural relations Marlboro Coll., Vt., 1982—; lectr. cons. for postdoctoral seminars in intelligence Consortium for Study of Intelligence, 1981, 82, 84, 86, 88, 89, 90; cons. studies on war and clash of ideas Ctr. for Aerospace Doctrine, Rsch. and Edn., Air U., Maxwell Air Base, Ala., 1989-90; mem. bd. founding dirs. Consortium for Study of Intelligence; cons. NEH, 1970—; mem. faculty seminar study peace Columbia U., 1953—; mem. U.S. Global Strategy Council for Congl. Study of Am.'s Role in Internat. Soc.; mem. nat. adv.

council on fgn. policy East-West com. Nat. Republican Com., mem. human rights and Africa coms.; pub. mem. USIA Generalist Selection Bd. for Fgn. Ser. Author: Regional Conflicts around Geneva, 1948, Politics and Culture in International History: From the Ancient Near East to the Opening of the Modern Age, 1960, 2nd edit., 1994, The Future of Law in a Multicultural World, 1971, Conflict in Africa: Concepts and Realities, 1976, How To Think about Human Rights, 1978, Strategic Intelligence and Statecraft, 1991; monograph The Roots of American Commitment to the Rights of Man, 1980, The Relevance of Hugo Grotius and De Jure Belli ac Pacis for Our Times, 1980, Foreign Policy and Covert Action, 1981, Human Rights and National Security, 1983, The Future of International Law in the Multicultural World, 1983, The Study of Foreign Intelligence in Non-Western Societies, 1987; sr. editor: Society; mem. editorial bd.: Conflict: An Internat. Jour. Studies in Conflict & Terrorism: Comparative Strategy, Comparative Civilizations Rev., Orbis, Def. Intelligence Jour.; contbr. articles, revs., essays, book revs. to profl. jours. and encys., chpts. to books; featured in Autobiographical Reflections of Distinguished Scholars, 1989. Bd. dirs. Chinese Culture Ctr., Security and Intelligence Found.; bd. dirs., mem. exec. coun. Com. on Present Danger; mem. Main St. adv. com. The Rockford Inst., Consortium for Study of Intelligence (bd. founding mems.); bd. trustees Internat. Ctr. for Protection of Minority Rights and Cultural Diversity in Africa. Recipient Recognition award Internat. Soc. Ednl., Cultural, and Scientific Interchanges, 1984, 85; rsch. grantee Carnegie Endowment Internat. Peace, 1952, Rockefeller Found., 1960. Fellow Inter-Univ. Seminar on Armed Forces and Soc.; mem. Am. Soc. Internat. Law, Am. Polit. Sci. Assn., Am. Hist. Assn., Internat. Sociol. Assn., Internat. Studies Assn., Internat. Law Assn., Internat. Soc. Comparative Study of Civilizations (dir., exec. council). Home: Bronxville N.Y. Died Dec. 3, 1994.

BRADLEY, LEE CARRINGTON, JR., lawyer; b. Charlottesville, Va., Sept. 27, 1897; s. Lee C. and Eleanor (Lyons) B.; m. Mary Allen Northington, Jan. 9, 1924; children—Lee Carrington, Merrill Northington, Mary Earle (Mrs. Murray). Litt.B., Princeton, 1918; LL.B., Harvard, 1921. Bar: Ala. bar 1921. Practiced in Birmingham; partner firm Bradley, Arant, Rose & White (and predecessors), from 1922. Mem. Phi Beta Kappa. Episcopalian. Club: Rotarian. Home: Birmingham Ala. Deceased.

BRADLEY, STUART B., lawyer; b. Chgo., Jan. 29, 1907; s. Alexander S. and Laura (Bevans) B.; m. Patricia Goodhue, Mar. 15, 1935; children: Stuart, Barbara, Carolyn, Laura. Student, Wash. State Coll., 1923-25, U. Chgo., 1927-30; Ph.B., J.D., U. Chgo. Bar: Ill. 1931. Partner firm Bradley, McMurray, Black & Snyder, and predecessors, Chgo., 1934-84; partner firm Bradley, McMurray, Black & Snyder, and predecessors, Deerfield, Ill., 1984-90, ret., 1990; promoter St. Lawrence Seaway, Calumet-Sag projects; dir. Deerfield Savs. & Loan Assn.; mem. adv. com. on admiralty rules U.S. Supreme Ct., 1960-72. Author articles mags., law revs. Scoutmaster Boy Scouts Am., 1949-52; chmn. planning bd. North Shore Area Council, 1953; trustee Glencoe Pub. Library, 1964-73. Served from capt. to lt. col. U.S. Army, 1943-46. Decorated Bronze Star; recipient citation for pub. service U. Chgo., 1955. Mem. Chgo. Assn. Commerce (chmn. harbors and waterways com. 1948-52), Maritime Law Assn. (exec. com. 1963-66), ABA, Ill. Bar Assn., Chgo. Bar Assn. (chmn. admiralty com. 1958-59), Am. Coll. Trial Lawyers, Phi Delta Phi, Kappa Sigma. Methodist. Clubs: Propeller (Chgo.) (pres. Port of Chgo. 1948), Jackson Park Yacht (Chgo.), Law (Chgo.), Legal (Chgo.), Lit. (Chgo.); Skokie Country (Glencoe). Home: Glencoe Ill. Died Apr. 9, 1990; interred Fryeburg, Maine.

BRADSHAW, RICHARD BURNETT, marketing consultant; b. Berkhamstead, Eng., Mar. 4, 1927; s. Sidney Basil and Marjorie (Hewett) B.; m. Jayne McGraw, June 11, 1955; children: David, Brian, Bruce, Dean, Tracey. B.S. in Journalism, U. Ill., 1951. With Foote, Cone & Belding, Chgo., 1951-79, research analyst, 1951-53, account exec., 1953-60; pres. Canadian Co., Toronto, Ont., 1960-68, sr. v.p., dir. parent co., 1968-78, pres. internat. co., Brussels, 1969-72, chmn. bd., Toronto, 1972-79; chmn. and pres. Palmetto Mktg. & Mgmt., 1980-89; dir. Churchill Steel; pres. Dolphin Plantation Homes; pres. Palmar Homes; dir. Carolina Sales Corp. Served with Brit. Royal Navy, 1943-46. Home: Hilton Head Island S.C. Died Mar. 7, 1989.

BRANDBORG, LLOYD LEON, retired medical educator; b. Wheatland, Wyo., Oct. 16, 1924; s. Sten Sture and Alma Elizabeth (Lovberg) B.; m. Donna Marie Fagerstrom, Jan. 28, 1950; children: Terry A., Scott L. Student, U. Ala., 1943-44; AB in Physiology, U. Calif., Berkeley, 1950; MD, U. Chgo., 1955. Diplomate Nat. Bd. Med. Examiners. Rsch. asst. Calif. Rsch. Corp., Richmond, 1946-51; intern King County Hosp., Seattle, 1955-56; asst. resident in medicine VA Hosp., Seattle, 1956-57, chief resident medicine, 1960-61; trainee gastroenterology Nat. Cancer Inst., U. Wash. Sch. Medicine, 1957-60; fellow and asst. medicine King County Hosp., Seattle, 1957-60; spl. med. staff appt. Children's Orthopedic Hosp., Seattle, 1959-61; chief gastroenterology sect. VA Hosp., San Francisco, 1961-85, acting chief med. svc., 1966-68; clin. instr. dept. medicine U. Calif., San Francisco, 1961-64, asst. clin. prof. medicine dept. medicine, 1964-68, asst. prof. medicine in residence, 1968-69, asst. dir. grad. rsch. tng. program in gastroenterology, 1968, clin. prof. medicine, 1969-95, lectr. in pathology dept. pathology, 1969-95; asst. physiology U. Chgo. Sch. Medicine, 1953; asst. in medicine dept. medicine U. Wash., 1956-61; mem. tumor bd. VA Hosp., San Francisco, 1961-95, mem. rsch. and edn. com., 1961-65, 66-68, dep. chmn. rsch. adn edn. com., 1962-63, chmn. rsch. and edn. com., 1963-64; responsible investigator Pacific VA Cancer Chemotherapy Group, 1961-64; prin. investigator VA Coop. Study of Esophagogastric Varices, Cirrhosis and Related Liver Disease, 1962-95, VA Gastroenterology Study Group, 1962-95; cons. gastroenterology USPHS, San Francisco, 1962-95, Surgeon Gen.'s Office, Letterman Army Med. Ctr., Presidio, San Francisco, 1965-95, David Grant USAF Med. Ctr., Travis AFB, Calif., 1966-82, William Beaumont Gen. Hosp., El Paso, Tex., 1970-95, U.S. Naval Hosp., Oakland, Calif., 1972; vis. prof. Cmty. Hosp., Sonoma County, Santa Rosa, Calif., 1970, Monroe County Cancer Soc., Genesee Hosp., U. Rochester, N.Y., 1970, William Beaumont Gen. Hosp., 1970, Brooke Gen. Hosp., San Antonio, 1970, Madigan Gen. Hosp., Ft. Lewis, Wash., 1972; mem. utilization rev. com. VA Hosp., San Francisco, 1972, chmn. com. on therapeutic agts. and pharmacy rev., 1972-77, com. on cancer, 1973, med. svc. audit com. mem., 1973, med. svc. audit com., 1975, nutrition com. mem., 1977-95, hosp. cancer com. mem., 1977-81; spkr. in field. Editl. bd. mem. Gastroenterology, 1968-73; contbr. articles to profl. jours. 2d lt. USAAF, 1943-45. Home: San Francisco Calif. Died Aug. 6, 1995.

BRANDON, DOUG, state senator; b. Aug. 23, 1932; m. Elizabeth Riggs, 1958; 4 children. BA, U. Ark; grad. Command and Gen. Staff Sch. Former mem. Ark. Ho. of Reps., chmn. legis. council, joint budget com., revenue and taxation com.; mem. Ark. Senate, 1980-92; owner, CEO Brandon Furniture Co. Dem. nominee U.S. Congress, 1978; v.p. bd. dirs. Ark. Children's Hosp.; mem. adv. bd. U. Ark. Coll. Bus.; Mem. Am. Legion, Nat. Home Furnishing Bd. (exec. com.), Inst. Politics and Govt., Dallas Home Furnishing Mart (adv. bd.). Died July 12, 1992. Home: Little Rock Ark.

BRANDON, HENRY OSCAR, writer, consultant; b. Mar. 9, 1916; s. Oscar and Ida (Farta) B.; m. Mable Hobart, Apr. 4, 1970; 1 child, Fiona. Litt.D. (hon.), Williams Coll., 1979. Chief Am. corr. Sunday Times of London, 1949-83; internat. cons., Washington, 1982-93; columnist N.Y. Times World Syndicate; guest scholar Brookings Instn., Washington. Author: As We Are, 1961; In the Red, 1968; The Anatomy of Error, 1969; The Retreat of American Power, 1973. Recipient Hannen Swaffer award, London, 1964. Clubs: Nat. Press (Washington); Overseas Writers. Died Apr. 20, 1993. Home: Washington D.C.

BRANDT, BILL, photographer; b. London, 1904. Photography student Switzerland; studied with Man Ray, Paris, 1929; D. (hon.), Royal Coll. of Art, London, 1977. Freelance photographer, Paris; mem. faculty Royal Designers for Industry. Retrospective exhbns. include travelling exhbn. Mus. Modern Art, N.Y.C., London, other cities, 1969; Marlboro Gallery travelling exhbn., N.Y.C. and London, 1976, N.Y.C., 1981, Royal Photog. Soc., 1981; works featured in numerous mags. and newspapers; represented in permanent collections: Victoria and Albert Mus., London, Mus. Modern Art, N.Y.C., Bibliothèque Nationale, Paris, Internat. Mus. Photography, Rochester, N.Y., Art Inst. Chgo. Named Royal Designer for Industry, Royal Soc. Arts, 1978; recipient Silver Progress medal Royal Photog. Soc., 1979. Publs. include: The English at Home, 1936; A Night in London, 1938; Camera in London, 1948; Literary Britain, 1951; The Land: Twentieth Century Landscape Photography, 1975; Perspective of Nudes, 1961; Shadow of Light, 1977; Nudes 1945-80, 1980. Fellow Royal Photog. Soc. Gt. Britain (hon.). Deceased. Home: London Eng.

BRANNON, H(EZZIE) RAYMOND, JR., petroleum engineer, oil company scientist; b. Midland, Ala., Jan. 23, 1926; s. Hezzie Raymond and Cora Mae B.; m. Rita Alice Newville, Oct. 19, 1957; 1 dau., Sarah Elaine. B. Engring. Physics, Auburn (Ala.) U., 1950, M.S., 1951. Research asso. Auburn Research Found., 1951-52; engr. Exxon Prodn. Research Co., Houston, 1952-94; sr. research scientist Exxon Prodn. Research Co., 1982-86, cons., 1986-92; ret., 1992. Contbr. articles to profl. jours. Served with USNR, 1943-46. Mem. Am. Phys. Soc., Soc. Petroleum Engrs. of AIME (Disting. Lectr. 1976-77), Soc. Exploration Geophysicists, NRC (marine bd.), Nat. Acad. Engring., Sigma Xi, Phi Kappa Phi, Tau Beta Pi, Sigma Pi Sigma. Republican. Home: Houston Tex. Died Aug. 9, 1994.

BRANSON, HERMAN RUSSELL, retired physicist, former university president; b. Pocahontas, Va., Aug. 14, 1914; s. Harry C. and Gertrude (Brown) B.; m. Corolynne M. Gray, Sept. 4, 1939; children: Corolynne G., Herman E. Student, U. Pitts., 1932-34; B.S., Va. State Coll., 1936, Sc.D., 1967; Ph.D., U. Cin., 1939, Sc.D., 1967; Sc.D., Lincoln U., Pa., 1969, Northeastern U., 1985; L.H.D., Brandeis U., 1972, Shaw Coll., Detroit, 1978; LL.D., Western Mich. U., 1973; Litt.D., Drexel U., 1982. Instr. Dillard U., New Orleans, 1939-41; faculty Howard U., 1941-68, prof. physics, 1942-68, head dept., 1955-68; pres. Central State U., 1968-70, Lincoln U., Lincoln University, Pa., 1970-85; dir. precoll. sci. and math. rsch. program Howard U., Washington, 1986-89; mem. Inst. Medicine Nat. Acad. Scis., 1975, Nat. Sea Grant Coll. Program, 1980-95; mem. energy research adv. bd. U.S. Dept. Energy, 1981-95. Mem. Bicentennial Commn. Pa., 1975; trustee Carver Found., Woodrow Wilson Nat. Fellowship Found., 1975-95; bd. dirs. Nat. Med. Fellowships, Inst. for Services to Edn., 1973-95, Am. Found. for Negro Affairs, 1973-95; mem. corp. M.I.T., 1979-95; mem. Middle Atlantic Consortium for Energy Research, 1980-95; mem. council Nat. U. of Lesotho, Africa, 1985-95; mem. task force to study higher edn. Council of Pres. U. Del. Sr. fellow NRC, 1948-49; fellow NSF, 1962-63. Mem. Am. Assn. State Colls. and Univs., Commn. Coll. Physics, Biophysics Soc. (council), Am. Phys. Soc., AAAS (council 1971-95), Am. Assn. Physics Tchrs., Pa. Assn. Colls. and Univs. (govt. relations com. 1979-95), Middle States Assn. Colls. and Secondary Schs. (com. on higher edn. 1970-76), Nat. Assn. for Equal Opportunity in Edn. (pres. 1970-73, dir.), Sigma Xi. Home: Silver Spring Md. Died June, 1995.

BRAUER, GERHARD MAX, chemist; b. Berlin, Feb. 5, 1919; came to U.S., 1939, naturalized 1942; s. Ernst Moritz and Alice Therese (Brauer) B.; m. Inge Wolf, June 1, 1969. B.Chem., U. Minn., 1941; M.A., U. N.C., 1948, Ph.D., 1950. Research fellow U. N.C., Chapel Hill, 1948-50; chemist Nat. Bur. Standards, Gaithersburg, Md., 1950—; guest prof. Freie U. Berlin, 1974-75; mem. biomaterials adv. com. Nat. Inst. Dental Research, Bethesda, Md., 1967-71. Contbr. articles to profl. jours., chpts. to books. Patentee in field. Served with U.S. Army, 1942-46. Recipient gold medal U.S. Dept. Commerce, 1975; U.S. Sr. Scientist award Humboldt Found., 1974. Fellow Washington Acad. Sci., Am. Coll. Dentists (hon.), Acad. Dental Materials; mem. Am. Chem. Soc. (sect. pres. 1967, Charles Gordon award), Internat. Assn. Dental Research (Souder award 1969), AAAS, Adhesion Soc., ASTM (exec. com. 1977—, com. F-4, 1982—), Soc. Biomaterials (corr.), Sigma Xi, Alpha Chi Sigma (sect. pres. 1966). Avocations: sports; stamps. Home: Bethesda Md.

BRAUN, DANIEL CARL, physician; b. San Diego, July 2, 1905; s. Daniel Jacob and Frida (Lorch) B.; m. Hazel Winfield Beckley, Aug. 10, 1929. Student, Carnegie Inst. Tech., 1923-31; B.S., U. Pitts., 1933, M.D., 1937; postgrad., L.I. Coll. Medicine, 1942, Columbia U., 1945. Diplomate Am. Bd. Preventive Medicine. Intern Mercy Hosp., Pitts., 1937-38; practice medicine specializing in occupational medicine Pitts., 1938-94; med. dir. Pitts. Coal Co., 1944-50, cons. occupational medicine, 1950-52; med. dir. Indsl. Hygiene Found., Pitts., 1952-58, Homestead dist. works U.S. Steel Corp., Munhall, Pa., 1958-61; asst. med. dir. U.S. Steel Corp., 1961-70; mgr. occupational med. svcs. Indsl. Health Found., 1970-72, pres., 1972-89; lectr. in indsl. hygiene U. Pitts. Sch. Medicine, 1948-94; lectr. in occupational medicine Grad. Sch. Pub. Health, U. Pitts., 1950-94. Contbr. articles to profl. jours. Mem. Mayor Pitts. Com. Reorgn. Pitts. Dept. Health, 1948-50, President's Com. Employment Handicapped, 1958-80; mem. SSS appeal bd. Western Fed. Jud. Dist. Pa., 1962-68; active, Allegheny council Boy Scouts Am.; Bd. dirs. St. Clair Meml. Hosp.; trustee Indsl. Health Found. Am. Fellow Am. Coll. Chest Physicians, Am. Acad. Occupational Medicine (chmn. standards com. 1967-70), Am. Occupational Med. Assn. (dir. 1950-52), Am. Coll. Preventive Medicine, Am. Inst. Chemists; mem. AMA (recognition award 1976), Pa., Allegheny County med. socs., Alpha Omega Alpha. Club: University (Pitts.). Lodge: Masons. Home: Pittsburgh Pa. Died June 11, 1994.

BRAUN, SHELDON RICHARD, medical educator; b. Cleve., Apr. 11, 1943; s. Jerome Milton and Rosalind Florence (Stern) B.; m. Katy L. Tessler, Aug. 19, 1967; children: Sheara Joy, Joshua Solomon. BA, Western Res. U., 1965; MD, U. Pitts., 1968. Diplomate Am. Bd. Internal Medicine (pulmonary diseases, critical care sects.). Intern Mt. Sinai Hosp., Cleve., 1968-69; resident U. Wis. Sch. Medicine, Madison, 1969-71; pulmonary fellow U. Wis., Madison, 1971-73; asst. clin. prof. medicine U. Wis. Sch. Medicine, Madison, 1975-77, asst. prof. medicine, 1977-83, assoc. prof. medicine, 1983-84; dir. div. pulmonary, environ. and critical care U. Mo., Columbia, 1984-93, assoc. prof. medicine, 1984-90, prof., 1990-93. Editor: Concise Textbook of Pulmonary Disease, 1989. Chmn. Coalition of Smoking and Health, Mo., 1985-91; pres. Congregation of Beth Shalom, Columbia, 1988-90; bd. dirs. Ea. Mo. region Am. Lung Ass., Columbia Entertainment Com., 1989-93, Maplewood Barn Community Theater, 1989-93. Recipient Preventive Pulmonary Acad. award NIH, 1991-96, Lifestyle award Am. Lung Assn. Eastern Mo. Fellow Am. Coll. Chest Physicians (regent 1987-88, chmn. clin. problems assembly Chgo., 1986-88, gov. Mo. chpt. 1989-93, Young Physicians of Future award 1971); mem. Am. Thoracic Soc., Phi Delta Epsilon. Democrat. Jewish. Home: Columbia Mo. Died, Jan. 13, 1993; interred Columbia, Mo.

BRECHNER, JOSEPH LOUIS, broadcast executive; b. Fall River, Mass., May 18, 1915; s. Barney and Dora

(Woltman) B.; m. Marion Brody, July 10, 1941; 1 child, Berl M. Student, Wayne State U., 1934-35, George Washington U., 1940-41, Rollins Coll., Orlando, Fla., 1979-80; LLD (hon.), Salisbury State Coll., 1986, U. Fla., 1990. Script writer radio br., Bur. Pub. Rels. Dept. War, Washington, 1941-43; dir., radio and TV VA, Washington, 1945-46; gen. mgr., part owner Sta. WGAY, Silver Spring, Md., 1946-58; founder, pres. Mid-Fla. TV Corp., Orlando, 1958-84, Brechner Mgmt. Co., Orlando, 1984-90; gen. mgr., pres. Sta. WFTV, Orlando, 1958-70; owner Sta. WMDT-TV, Salisbury, Md., Sta. KTKA-TV, Topeka, Sta. WKFI-AM/WSWO-FM, Wilmington, Ohio. Columnist Orlando Sentinel, 1968-78; contbr. articles to profl. jours. Mem. Orlando Human Rels. Commn., 1962-79; bd. dirs. Ellis Island Restoration Commn., 1978-90; donor Brechner Ctr. for Freedom Info., Coll. Journalism, U. Fla., Gainesville, 1984-85. Recipient Youth Fellow award B'nai Brith, 1965, Leonard L. Abess Human Rels. award Anti-Defamation League, 1966, Best Newspaper Interpretive Report Greater Orlando Press Club, 1970, Fla. Patriot award Fla. Gov.'s Bicentennial Com., 1976, Silver Beaver award Boy Scouts Am., 1989. 1st lt. USAAF, 1943-45. Mem. Nat. Assn. Broadcasters, Md.-Del.-D.C. Broadcasters Assn., Soc. Profl. Journalists (pres. cen. Fla. chpt. 1973-75), Broadcast Pioneers, Elks. Democrat. Jewish. Died Feb. 26, 1990.

BREEN, WALTER HENRY, numismatic writer; b. San Antonio, Sept. 5, 1928; m. Marion Zimmer Bradley, Feb. 14, 1964; children: Patrick Russell Donald, Moira Evelyn Dorothy. AB, Johns Hopkins, 1952; MA, U. Calif., Berkeley, 1966. Researcher Wayte Raymond, Inc., N.Y.C, 1951-52; cataloguer New Netherlands Coin Co., Inc., N.Y.C, 1952-60, Lester Merkin, Inc., N.Y.C, 1968-72; mng. editor Twin Worlds Publs., N.Y.C, 1970-71; sr. v.p. research First Coinvestors, Inc., Albertson, N.Y., 1973-87; contbg. editor Guidebook of U.S. Coins, 1953—; cons. Smithsonian Inst., U.S. Secret Service, U.S. Treasury, 1961—; trustee New Eng. Jour. Numis. Author: A Coiner's Caviar: Walter Breen's Encyclopedia of U.S. and Colonial Proof Coins, 1722-1977, 1977, The Darkover Concordance: A Reader's Guide, 1979; (with Anthony Swiatek) Encyclopedia of U.S. Gold and Silver Commemorative Coins, 1981 (Book of Yr. award Numis. Lit. Guild 1982); (with Ron Gillio) California Pioneer Fractional Gold, 1983, Walter Breen's Encyclopedia of United States Half Cents, 1793-1857, 1984 (Book of Yr. award Numis. Lit. Guild, 1985), Walter Breen's Comprehensive Encyclopedia of United States Coins, 1988 (Book of Yr. award Numis. Lit. Guild, 1988, Friedberg Meml. award Profl. Numis. Guild, 1988); also articles, essays, monographs and revs. Recipient Silver Medal of Honor Roosevelt U., 1966, Order of the Laurel Soc. for Creative Anachronism, 1969, Silver Medal of Merit Soc. for Internat. Numis, 1991. Mem. AAAS, Am. Numis. Assn. (life, mem., Heath award 1952, 91), Am. Numis. Soc.,Numis. Lit. Guild (Clemy award 1985). Democrat. Home: Berkeley Calif. Died April 28, 1993.

BRENNAN, JAMES JOSEPH, lawyer; b. San Francisco, Apr. 13, 1936; s. Joseph Bernard and Dorothy Ann (Smith) B.; m. Sarah Anne Cahill, Aug. 29, 1959; children: Mary, Joseph, Michael, Catherine. BS, Marquette U., 1957; LLB magna cum laude, Harvard U., 1963. Bar: Ill. 1963. Assoc. Sidley & Austin, Chgo., 1963-69, ptnr., 1970-93. Served to lt. (j.g.) USN, 1957-60. Mem. Chgo. Bar Assn., Legal Club Chgo. Republican. Clubs: Chicago, Tavern, Saddle and Cycle (Chgo.). Home: Chicago Ill. Died July 4, 1993.

BRENNAN, WILLIAM ROBERT, JR., banker; b. N.Y.C., Mar. 8, 1921; s. William R. and Margeret (Healy) B.; children: William, John Paul, Ellen, Christopher, Vincent, Timothy, Andrew. B.B.A., Manhattan Coll., 1943; J.D., Fordham U., 1948. Bar: N.Y. 1948, U.S. Dist. Ct. (so. and eastern dist. N.Y.) 1949-52, U.S. Ct. Appeals (2d circuit N.Y.) 1952. Ptnr. Hanrahan & Brennan, N.Y.C., 1948-55; dep. supt., counsel N.Y. State Banking Dept., 1955-59, acting supt. banks, 1959; justice N.Y. State Supreme Ct., N.Y.C., 1960-68; ptnr. Reavis & McGrath, N.Y.C., 1968-70; chmn. bd., chief exec. officer Apple Bank for Savings, N.Y.C., 1970-93. Served with U.S. Army, 1942-45, ETO. Mem. N.Y. Bar Assn., Nassau County Bar Assn. Clubs: Garden City Country, Sky. Home: Manhasset N.Y. Died Mar. 30, 1993.

BRENT, ADALIE M. (JOLEENE), artist; b. Dallas, Nov. 27, 1920; d. Joseph Herman and Bertha B. (Raphiel) Margules; m. Allan Rudolph Brent, Dec. 19, 1941; 1 child, Joanna Raphiel Brent Leake. Student, U. Tex., 1937-38; BEd, UCLA, 1941; postgrad., La. State U., 1948-49. Art tchr., supr. Calif. Pub. Sch. System, 1941-43; art tchr. St. Joseph Acad., 1952-64; instr. art edn. La. State U., 1950-52, instr. sch. landscape architecture, 1980-83; dir. La. Arts and Sci. Center, 1962-80; interior designer Karl Harvey Assocs., 1980-93; cons. gifted and talented program La. Dept. Edn., 1978-85; adv. coun. Artist-in-Residence Program, 1977-83; mem. vis. com. Loyola U., New Orleans, 1989-93. Prin. works include: (leaded and faceted stained glass-windows) Convent Chapel, Sisters of St. Joseph, St. Joseph Cathedral Sacristy, Cath. Life Ctr., Bishop's Chapel, La. State U. Law Ctr., Woman's Club House, St. Paul Luth. Ch., Blackwater United Meth. Ch., Baton Rouge Gen. Med. Ctr. Chapel, St. Jules Ch., Belle Rose, La., (murals) St. Aloysius Convent, Cath. Life Ctr., St. Joseph Prep. Sch. (now Bishop Tracy Ctr.), St. Alphonsus Ch., Am. Bank, Eglise Assumption, Baton Rouge Gen. Md. Ctr., Stas. of Cross, Our Lady of Lake Med. Ctr. Chapel, Baton Rouge, (mural panels) Sta. WBRZ-TV, Baton Rouge, Madonna and Child, Bishop's Chapel Cath. Life Ctr., 1992; exhibited in La. Arts and Sci. Ctr., 1993. Co-chmn. Plz. Com., 1970-84; pres. Bicentennial Commn., 1976. Decorated Orden del Merito Civil Govt. of Spain, 1979; recipient Mayor-Pres.'s award for excellence in the arts, 1989. Mem. Baton Rouge City Club, Delta Kappa Gamma, Delta Epsilon. Home: Baton Rouge La. Died Apr. 8, 1993; interred Baton Rouge, L.A.

BRESEE, PAUL KIRK, diversified businesses company executive; b. Etna, Ill., July 1, 1901; s. Byrd Elma and Bertha (Kirchgraber) B.; m. Dorothy F. Weber, July 20, 1969; children: Joanne, Jeanne, Paula, Marvin. B.S., Coll. Agriculture, U. Ill., 1923. Cert. tax cons., Calif. Ptnr. Bresee Bros. Cleaners, Champaign, Ill., 1925-40; v.p. System Fin. Co., Champaign, 1934-67; pres. Continental Loan Co., Champaign, 1938-67; ptnr. Byrd Realty Co., Champaign, from 1938; pres. Bresee-Warner, Inc., Champaign, from 1926; chmn. bd. Arrowhead Lanes, Inc., Champaign, from 1926, Kickapoo Broadcasting Co., Champaign, from 1969; pres. Univ. Fed. Savs. and Loan Assn., Champaign, 1927-79; aux. bd., from 1979, Bloomington Fed. Savs. and Loan Assn., from 1977. Mem. tribal council grants-in-aid U. Ill., from 1982. Mem. Nat. Soc. SAR, C. of C., Alpha Gamma Rho (grand treas. 1948-68), Phi Kappa Psi, Alpha Kappa Psi, Alpha Gamma Rho (grand pres. 1968). Republican. Presbyterian. Club: Quarterback. Home: Boiling Springs N.C. Deceased.

BREST, ALEXANDER, television executive, consulting engineer; b. Boston, Nov. 4, 1894; s. Simon and Sarah (Rosenthal) B.; children: Paul Andrew, Peter Ronald. B.S., MIT, 1916; D.Civil Law (hon.), Jacksonville U., 1974. Registered profl. engr., land surveyor, Fla. San. engr. Fla. Bd. Health, 1919-21; asst. prof. civil engring. U. Fla., Gainesville, 1921-23; sec.-treas. Duval Engring. & Contracting Co., Jacksonville, Fla., 1923-72; founder, pres., treas. WTLV Channel 12, Jacksonville, from 1954; cons. engr. Harbor Engring., from 1975; dir. Flagship Banks, WesJax Corp. Bd. dirs. Mus. Arts and Scis., from 1973, St. Vincent's Hosp., from 1979; mem. No. Fla. council Boy Scouts Am.; trustee Jacksonville U., from 1954; founder, trustee Alexander Brest Planetarium, 1973. Served to lt. col. C.E., U.S. Army, 1942-45. Decorated Legion of Merit; recipient Disting. Service award Fla. Assn. Colls., 1982; Disting. Citizen award Boy Scouts Am., 1983. Mem. ASCE (life; World War II award 1945), Fla. Road Builders Assn. (life), Asphalt Contractors Assn. Fla. (hon. life). Jewish. Club: River of Jacksonville (dir.). Lodge: Shriners, Jesters.

BRETT, THOMAS MARSHALL, judge; b. Norman, Okla., Feb. 7, 1916; s. Rutherford and Gertrude (Whitaker) B.; m. Evelyn Kane, Mar. 9, 1941 (div. 1946); 1 child, Bonnie Kay; m. Ida Maude Emery, June 1, 1946; children: Marsha, William Thomas. BSBA, U. Okla., 1940, LLB, 1948; PhD in Psychology, Nat. Christian U., 1969. Bar: Okla. 1948, U.S. Dist. Ct. (we. dist.) Okla. 1948. Pvt. practice Norman, 1948-50; of counsel, dir. Okla. Civil Def. Agy., Oklahoma City, 1952-62; counsel, exec. sec. Okla. Sheet Metal Industry Fund, Oklahoma City, 1962-65; judge Okla. Ct. Criminal Appeals, Oklahoma City, 1965—. Bd. dirs. Redlands council Girl Scouts U.S., Oklahoma City, 1962-69; post supr. Explorer Post Boy Scouts Am., Oklahoma City, 1971-73. Maj. U.S. Army, 1940-46, 50-52, Korea; with USAFR. Decorated Silver medal, Purple Heart medal. Mem. Conf. Chief Judges, Masons, N.W. Optimist Club, Phi Delta Phi. Democrat. Methodist. Home: Oklahoma City Okla. Deceased.

BRIDGES, JAMES, film writer-director; b. Little Rock, Feb. 2, 1936; s. Doy and Celestine (McKeen) B. Student, Ark. Tchrs. Coll., U. S.C. Actor 7 feature films including Johnny Trouble, 1957; writer (tv shows) 18 Alfred Hitchcock Shows (Mystery Writers award for Unlocked Window), (TV pilot) The Paper Chase, 1978, (feature films) Appaloosa, 1966, Colossus: The Forbin Project, 1969, Limbo, 1972, White Hunter, Black Heart, 1990, others, (plays) Days of the Dancing, 1964; writer, dir. (feature films) The Baby Maker, 1970, The Paper Chase (Best Screenplay, Best Picture, Best Dir., Atlanta Film Festival, Best Screenplay, Acad. and nomination 1973), September 30, 1955, 1977, The China Syndrome (Best Writer, Am. Movie award, Best Writer, Best Dir., Christopher award, Best Screenplay, Japanese Acad. award, Best Screenplay, Acad. award nomination, Best Writer, Best Dir., Best Picture, Golden Globe nomination, Best Drama, Writers Guild award 1979), Urban Cowboy, 1980, Mike's Murder, 1984, Perfect, 1985; dir. The Candied House, 1966, Cherry, Larry, Sandy, Doris, Jean, Paul, 1969, A Meeting by the River, 1972, The Bum's Show, 1970, A Streetcar Nmaed Desire, 1973, The Soldier's Tale, 1977, Bright Lights, Big City, 1988. Mem. Writers Guild, Dirs. Guild, Screen Actors Guild, AFTRA. Home: Los Angeles Calif.

BRIGGS, RODNEY ARTHUR, agronomist, consultant; b. Madison, Wis., Mar. 18, 1923; s. George McSpadden and Mary Etta (McNelly) B.; m. Helen Kathleen Ryall, June 1, 1944; children: Carolyn, Kathleen, David, Andrew, Amy. Student, Oshkosh (Wis.) State Coll., 1941-42; B.S. in Agronomy, U. Wis., 1948; Ph.D. in Field Crops, Rutgers U., 1953. Extension asso. farm crops Rutgers U., New Brunswick, N.J., 1949-50, 52-53; mem. faculty U. Minn., 1953-73; supt. West Central Sch. and Expt. Sta., Morris, Minn., 1959-60; prof. agronomy, dean U. Minn.; administrv. head, provost U. Minn. (Morris Campus), 1960-69, sec. bd. regents, 1971-72, exec. asst. to pres., 1971-73; on leave of absence Ford Found. as asso. dir., dir. research Internat. Inst. Tropical Agr., Ibadan, Nigeria, 1969-71; pres. Eastern Oreg. State Coll., La Grande, 1973-83; exec. v.p. Am. Soc. Agronomy/Crop Sci. Soc. Am./Soil Sci. Soc. Am., Madison, Wis., 1982-85; ind. cons., 1985-95; chmn. Nat. Silage Evaluation Com., 1957; sec. Minn. Corp Improvement Assn., 1954-57; columnist crops and soils Minn. Farmer mag., 1954-59; judge grain and forage Minn. State Fair, 1954-61; mem. ednl. mission to Taiwan, Am. Assn. State Colls. and Univs., 1978, chmn. ednl. mission to Colombia, 1982, state rep., 1974-76, mem. spl. task force of pres.'s on intercollegiate athletics, 1976-77, mem. nat. com. on agr., renewable resources and rural devel., 1978-82, nat. sec.-treas., 1980-82; mem. com. on govt. relations Am. Council Edn. Com., 1981; mem. Gov.'s Commn. on Fgn. Lang. and Internat. Studies, State Oreg., 1980-83; Mem. Gov.'s Commn. Law Enforcement, 1967-69; adv. com. State Planning Agy., 1968-69, Minn. Interinstnl. TV, 1967-69; invited participant The Role of Sci. & Emergency Societies in Devel., African Regional Seminar AAAS, 1984. Com. mem. African sci. jour. AAAS, 1986-88. Bd. dirs. Rural Banking Sch., 1967-69; bd. dirs. Channel 10 ETV, Appleton, Minn., Grande Ronde Hosp., 1980-83; chmn. policy adv. com. Oreg. Dept. Environ. Quality, 1979-81. Served with inf. AUS, 1942-46, 50-52. Recipient Staff award U. Minn., 1959, spl. award U. Minn. at Morris, 1961; commendation Soil Conservation Soc. Am., 1965; Rodney A. Briggs Library named in his honor U. Minn., Morris, 1974. Fellow AAAS, Am. Assn. State Colls. and Univs., Soil Conservation Soc. Am. (pres. emeritus Ea. Oreg. State Coll. chpt. 1988); mem. ACLU, Am. Soc. Agronomy, Am. Inst. Biol. Scis. (bd. dirs. 1982-83), Pres.' Club U. Minn., Sigma Xi, Alpha Gamma Rho. Congregationalist. Home: Shoreview Minn. Died May 10, 1995.

BRIGHT, SIMEON MILLER, retired government official; b. Keyser, W.Va., Sept. 11, 1925; s. Simeon Miller and Agnes Virginia (Bane) B.; m. Lorna Mae Stewart, June 10, 1950; children: Sheryl McCarty Bright McWhorter, Simeon Miller, Scott Randolph. A.A., Potomac State Coll., 1946; B.A., W.Va. U., 1949, M.A., 1950. With Dept. of Army, 1951-62, with ordnance tng. command, 1958-62; with Post Office Dept., Washington, 1962-69; spl. asst. to postmaster gen. Post Office Dept., 1965-69; pres. Bright Assocs., Keyser, 1970-93, Sim Bright Real Estate, Keyser, 1971-77; mem. Postal Rate Commn., Washington, 1977-84; cons. Nat. Assn. Postmasters U.S., 1985-93; instr. history U. Md., 1952-62, 69-70, Potomac State Coll., 1973-76; bd. dirs. Nat. Bank Keyser, WM Bancorp. Spl. asst. to conv. mgr. Democratic Nat. Conv., Miami Beach, 1972; mem. Mineral County Extension Svc. Com. Served with USAAF, 1944-45, 51. Mem. Nat. Assn. Regulatory Utility Commrs. (exec. com.), Nat. Assn. Postmasters U.S. (hon.), Am. Legion., C. of C. Methodist. Club: Touchdown (Washington). Lodges: Moose, Lions (past pres. Keyser club), Shriners. Home: Keyser W.Va. Died Jan. 29, 1993.

BRINGS, LAWRENCE MARTIN, publisher; b. St. Paul, Sept. 29, 1897; s. Lee Brings and Bertha (Haugen) B.; m. Ethel Mattson, Aug. 26, 1921 (dec.); 1 son, Keith; m. Nettie A. Johnson, Jan. 9, 1961. A.B., Gustavus Adolphus Coll., 1920, A.M., 1925. High sch. tchr., 1920- 21; head dept. speech No. State Tchrs. Coll., Aberdeen, S.D., 1921- 23; instr. speech U. Minn., 1923-26; pres., dir. dept. oratory Mpls. Sch. Music, Oratory and Dramatic Art, 1923-25; prof. speech Luther Theol. Sem., St. Paul, 1923-46, Northwestern Theol. Sem., Mpls., 1925-49; founder, pres. Northwestern Coll. Speech Arts, Mpls., 1926-51, Northwestern Press, 1926-95, T.S. Denison & Co., 1944-95, Brings Press, 1951-77, Denison Yearbook Co., 1952-76; dir. Graphic Arts Cons. Svc., 1977-95; lectr., dramatic reader. Compiler, editor: numerous books, most recent being Minnesota Heritage, 1960, One-Act Dramas and Contest Plays, 1962, Rehearsal-less Skits and Plays, 1963, Gay Nineties Melodramas, 1963, Golden Book of Christmas Plays, 1963, What God Hath Wrought, 1969. Pres. Minn. Ch. Found., Central Luth. Ch. Found.; pres. Golden Valley Coll. Found.; regent emeritus Golden Valley Luth. Coll., Count Folke Bernadotte Meml. Found. Served in U.S. Army, World War I. Mem. USCG League, Internat. Platform Assn., Nat. Assn. Tchrs. Speech, Nat. Thespian Dramatic Soc. (hon.), Am. Legion, Phi Kappa Delta, Phi Beta (hon.). Republican. Lutheran. Clubs: Mpls. Auto; Minnetonka Country. Lodges: Mason (32 deg., Shriner), Rotary. Home: Bloomington Minn. Died Feb. 15, 1995.

BRINKLEY, WILLIAM CLARK, writer; b. Custer, Okla., Sept. 10, 1917; s. Daniel Squire and Ruth (Clark) B. Student, William Jewell Coll., 1936-37; B.A., U. Okla., 1940; spl. student, Yale Drama Sch., 1961-62. Reporter Daily Oklahoman, Oklahoma City, 1940-41, Washington Post, 1941-42, 49-51; successively corr., asst. editor, staff writer Life mag., 1951-58. Author: Quicksand, 1948, The Deliverance of Sister Cecilia, 1954, Don't Go Near the Water, 1956, The Fun House, 1961, The Two Susans, 1962, The Ninety and Nine, 1966, Breakpoint, 1978, Peeper, 1981, The Last Ship, 1988. Served to lt. USNR, 1942-46. Recipient Citation for Achievement award William Jewell Coll., 1986. Mem. Phi Beta Kappa. Club: Nat. Press (Washington). Home: McAllen Tex. Died Nov. 22, 1993; cremated.

BRITT, HENRY MIDDLETON, retired judge; b. Olmsted, Ill., June 9, 1919; s. Henry Middleton and Sarah Theodosia (Roach) B.; m. Barbara Jean Holmes, Oct. 29, 1942 (Feb. 1987); children: Nancy Marsh, Sarah Barbara, Melissa Middleton. AB, U. Ill., 1941, JD, 1947. Bar: Ill. 1947, Ark. 1948, U.S. Dist. Ct. (we. dist.) Ark. 1948, U.S. Dist. Ct. (ea. dist.) Ark. 1958, U.S. Ct. Appeals (8th cir.) 1951, U.S. Supreme Ct. 1954. Pvt. practice law Hot Springs, Ark., 1948-67; asst. U.S. Atty. Western Dist. Ark., 1953-58; cir. judge 18th Jud. Cir. Ark., Hot Springs, 1967-83, ret., 1983; pres. Ark. Jud. Coun., 1982-83; mem. Ark.-Fed. Jud. Coun., 1973-74; fellow Nat. Coll. Advocacy, Harvard U., 1974; faculty adviser Nat. Coll. State Judiciary, 1973, Nat. Coll. Dist. Attys., U. Houston, 1976, Am. Acad. Jud. Edn., U. Va., 1976; mem. Midwestern Tng. Conf. Organized Crime and Law Enforcement at U. Notre Dame, 1972, Ark. Coll. Juvenile Justice, 1972; mem. exec. com. Ark. Commn. Crime and Law Enforcement, 1968-71; mem. cen. planning coun. Ark. Crime Commn. Republican candidate for Gov. of Ark., 1960; gen. counsel Rep. Party of Ark., 1962-64; permanent mem. Ark. State Rep. Com.; alt. del. Rep. Nat. Conv., 1968; mem. Garland County Bd. Election, 1962-64; chmn. Garland County Rep. Com., 1962-64; bd. dirs. United Fund, 1951-52; bd. trustees The Univ. of Ozarks, 1982-95, Evergreen Found.; exec. bd. Boy Scouts Am., Ouachita Area Coun.; pres. Garland County Community Coll. Found., 1988-90, Garland County Coun. on Aging Coun., Inc., Lakewood Convalescent Home, Inc., Lakewood Residential Care Facility Inc. Capt. JAGC AUS, 1941-46. Recipient Svc. to Mankind award Sertoma Club, 1973; Paul Harris fellow Rotary Internat. Fellow Nat. Coll. State Trial Judges, Ark. Bar Found.; mem. ABA (ex-officio mem., exec. coun. 1982-83), Ill. Bar Assn., Ark. Bar Assn. (Award of Merit 1983), Garland County Bar Assn. (pres. 1961-62), Am. Legion, VFW, U.S. Navy League (life, pres. Hot Springs coun. 1966-68, state pres. 1968-70), Hot Springs Jr. C. of C. (life, pres. 1951-52), Delta Phi, Phi Alpha Delta, Am. Judicature Soc., Am. Judges Assn., Kiwanis (pres. Hot Springs Club 1969-70), Masons, Shriners, Elks. Presbyterian (elder, deacon, trustee). Home: Hot Springs National Park Ariz. Died Feb. 17, 1995.

BRITT, JAMES THOMAS, lawyer; b. Kansas City, Mo., Feb. 27, 1904; s. Aylett T. and Katherine B. (Henderson) B.; JD, Washington U., St. Louis, 1926; m. Ruth E. Burgin. Sept. 18, 1930; children: Thomas Burgin, Robert McCammon. Bar: Mo. 1926. Practiced in Kansas City, 1926-95; sr. ptnr. firm Spencer, Fane, Britt & Browne, 1951-95; instr. Real Estate Bd. Inst., 1945-66; mem. bar com. 16th Jud. Circuit Mo., 1942-49; legal adviser local SSS, 1939-75; sec., dir. Commonwealth Theatres, Inc., 1965-77. Mem. bd. visitors Jackson County, 1948-53; chmn. Recreation Adv. Com. Kansas City, 1955-62; chmn. citizens adv. bd. City-County Office of Aging, 1969-72; co-founder, dir. Nat. Council on Alcoholism, Kansas City, area pres., 1966-67, exec. v.p., 1967-68; bd. dirs. Kansas City Social Health Agy., 1969-72; mem. Mo. Adv. Council Alcoholism and Drug Abuse, 1965-77; bd. dirs., mem. exec. com., pres. Starlight Theatre Assn., 1977-79. Mem. Am., Mo., Kansas City bar assns., Lawyers Assn. Kansas City, Kappa Alpha, Phi Delta Phi. Clubs: Rotary, Kansas City, River. Contbr. articles to legal jours. Died Jan. 18, 1995. Home: Kansas City Mo.

BROADUS, JAMES MATTHEW, research center administrator; b. Mobile, Ala., Feb. 24, 1947; m. Victoria Anne Gordon; children: Matthew Lee, Victoria Rose, Joseph Gordon. BA, Oberlin Coll., 1969; MA, Yale U., 1972, M.Phil., 1974, PhD, 1976. Economist U.S. Dept. Justice, Washington, 1975-79; vis. asst. prof. econs. U. Ky., Lexington, 1979-81; rsch. fellow Marine Policy Ctr., Woods Hole (Mass.) Oceanographic Instn., 1981-82; policy assoc. Marine Policy Ctr., 1982-84, social scientist, 1984—, dir., 1986—; mem. marine bd. NRC, Washington, 1989—, Panel on the Law Ocean Uses, N.Y.C., 1988—; bd. govs. Bigelow Lab., W. Boothbay Harbor, Maine, 1983-89; vis. assoc. prof. sci. and soc. Wesleyan U., 1986; adj. prof. marine policy U. Del., 1990—; adv. com. U.S.-Japan Nat. Resources Agreement, 1991—; mem. UN Group of Experts on Sci. Aspects of Marine Pollution (GESAMP), 1986-89; mem. UN Regional Working Groups on Implications of Climatic Change, 1989-91. Editorial bd. Jour. Aquatic Conservation; editorial advisor Oceanus; assoc. editor Jour. Coastal Rsch. Grad. fellow Yale U., 1971-75. Mem. Am. Econ. Assn., Assn. Environ. Resource Economists, Marine Tech. Soc., AAAS, Nat. Man and the Biosphere Program, Marine & Coastal Ecosystems Directorate (chmn.). Home: Falmouth Mass. Died Sept. 1994.

BROCCOLI, ALBERT ROMOLO, motion picture producer; b. N.Y.C., Apr. 5, 1909; s. Giovanni and Cristina (Vence) B.; m. Dana Natol Wilson, June 21, 1959; children: Michael Wilson, Anthony, Christina, Barbara. Student pub. schs., N.Y.C. Asst. dir. 20th Century Fox, 1941-42; RKO under Howard Hughes, 1947-48; theatrical agt. Charles Feldman, 1948-51; producer Warwick Films, 1951-60, Eon Prodns., Inc., 1960-96. Prodr.: Red Beret, 1952, Hell Below Zero, 1953, Black Knight, 1954, Prize of Gold, 1955, Cockleshell Heroes, 1956, Safari, 1956, April in Portugal, 1956, Fire Down Below, 1956, Odongo, 1956, Pickup Alley, 1957, Arrivederci Roma, 1957, Interpol, 1957, How to Murder a Rich Uncle, 1957, High Flight, 1958, No Time to Die, 1958, The Man Inside, 1958, Killers of Kilimanjaro, 1958, Bandit of Zhobe, 1958, In The Nick, 1959, Jazz Boat, 1960, Let's Get Married, 1960, The Trials of Oscar Wilde, 1960, Idol in Parade, 1960, Johnny Nobody, 1961, Call Me Bwana, 1963, Chitty Chitty Bang Bang, 1967 (Family Film award So. Calif. Motion Picture Coun. 1968); James Bond films Dr. No, 1962, From Russia With Love, 1963 (Screen Prodrs. Guild cert. of nomination as best picture 1964), Goldfinger, 1963 (Screen Prodrs. Guild cert. of nomination as best picture 1964), Thunderball, 1964 (Mkkin Kogyo Tsushin cert. of award 1966), You Only Live Twice, 1966 (Mkkin Kogyo Tsushin cert. of award 1967), On Her Majesty's Secret Service, 1969, Diamonds Are Forever, 1971, Live and Let Die, 1972, The Man with the Golden Gun, 1974, The Spy Who Loved Me, 1977, Moonraker, 1979, For Your Eyes Only, 1981, Octopussy, 1983, A View to a Kill, 1985, The Living Daylights, 1987, License to Kill, 1988, Goldeneye, 1995. Bd. Dirs. Boys Club of Queens, Inc., 1968, recipient Man of the Yr. award. Served to lt. (j.g.) USN, 1942-47, PTO. Decorated grand officer Order of Crown (Italy), Order St. Constantine (Italy), Caballero De Merito 1970 Order of Constantinana de St. Jorge of Spain, 1970, Commandatore Order of the Crown Grand Officer of Italy, Order of Brit. Empire HRH Queen Elizabeth II, 1987, Commandeur des Arts et Des Lettres Le Ministre de la Culture et de France la Communication, 1987; recipient Irving G. Thalberg Meml. award 54th ann. Acad. Awards, 1982, Dwight D. Eisenhower Admirable Am. Achievement and Wisdom award of honor, 1990, Winston Churchill Medal of Wisdom Soc., 1990; honored in Hollywood Walk of Fame, 1990. Mem. Producers Guild, Am. Film Inst. Roman Catholic. Club: Metropolitan (N.Y.C.). Died June 27, 1996.

BRODE, MARVIN JAY, lawyer, former state legislator; b. Memphis, Aug. 26, 1931; s. Howard M. and Erniece J. (Jacob) B.; m. Freda Cohn, June 24, 1965; children—William Howard, Robert Mark, Laura Mary. B.A., Vanderbilt U., 1953, LL.B., 1954; postgrad. law, U. Chgo., 1954, Harvard U., 1962. Bar: Tenn. 1955. Since practiced in Memphis; assoc. Brode and Fisher, 1958-65, Brode & Dunlap, 1965-70, Brode & Smith, 1970-72; spl. judge City Ct. Memphis, 1957-63; asst. city atty. City of Memphis, 1965-68; spl. officer, 1991; mem. Pres.'s Nat. Traffic Adv. Com., 1963-64; drafted legis. creating Tenn. Arts Commn., 1965, and authored Tenn. seat belt law, 1963. Co-editor: Memphis Municipal Code. Mem. Tenn. Art Commn., 1965-72, Mayor's Community Action Com., 1965; past guarantor Met. Opera Memphis; hon. col. on staff Tenn. Gov., 1967-95; del. So. Regional Edn. Conf., 1964, 65, 66; mem. Tenn. Ho. of Reps., 1962-65, Shelby County Democratic Exec. Com., 1966-95; hon. dep. sheriff, Shelby County, 1978-95; bd. dirs. West Tenn. chpt. Arthritis and Rheumatism Found., Memphis and Shelby County Multiple Sclerosis Soc., 1978-95. Named Amb. of the Arts, Tenn. Arts Commn., 1985. Mem. ABA, Tenn. Bar Assn., Shelby County Bar Assn., Memphis Bar Assn., Assn. Trial Lawyers Am., Tenn. Trial Lawyers Assn., Am. Trial Lawyers Assn., Am. Judicature Soc., Memphis Art Coun., Masons (32 deg.), Scottish Rite, Shriners, Phi Alpha Delta. Jewish (dir. temple brotherhood). Home: Memphis Tenn. Died July 20, 1995.

BRODERICK, DANIEL THOMAS, III, lawyer; b. Duluth, Minn., Nov. 22, 1944; s. Daniel Thomas Jr. and Yolande (Gordon) B. BS, U. Notre Dame, 1966; MD, Cornell U., 1970; JD, Harvard U., 1973. Bar: Calif. 1973. Assoc. Gray, Cary, Ames & Frye, San Diego, 1973-78; sole practice San Diego, 1978—; lectr. Continuing Edn. of the Bar, San Diego, 1981—, Rutter Group, San Diego, 1981—. Mem. Am. Coll. Legal Medicine, Calif. Trial Lawyers Assn., San Diego County Bar Assn. (bd. dirs. 1983-87, pres. 1987), San Diego County Trial Lawyers Assn. (bd. dirs. 1979-83). Republican. Roman Catholic. Club: Friendly Sons of St. Patrick (San Diego) (pres. 1986). Lodge: Rotary. Home: San Diego Calif.

BRODERICK, VINCENT LYONS, federal judge; b. N.Y.C., Apr. 26, 1920; s. Joseph A. and Mary Rose (Lyons) B.; m. Sally Brine, Apr. 15, 1950; children: Kathleen, Vincent, Mary, Ellen, Joan, Justin. A.B., Princeton U., 1941; LL.B., Harvard U., 1948. Bar: N.Y. 1948. Assoc. Hatch, Root and Barrett, N.Y.C., 1948-54; dep. commr. charge legal matters N.Y.C. Police Dept., 1954-56; gen. counsel Nat. Assn. Investment Cos., N.Y.C., 1956-61; chief asst. U.S. atty. U.S. Dist. Ct. (so. dist.), N.Y., 1961-62, 62-65, U.S. atty., 1962; judge U.S. Dist. Ct. (so. dist.) N.Y., 1976-95; police commr. N.Y.C., 1965-66; mem. firm Phillips, Nizer, Benjamin, Krim & Ballon, 1966-71, Forsyth, Decker, Murray & Broderick, 1971-76; chmn. com. on criminal law Jud. Conf. U.S., 1990-93. Home: Pelham N.Y. Died Mar. 3, 1995.

BRODEUR, ALPHONSE TONER, industrialist; b. Montreal, Que., Can., Feb. 20, 1902; s. Alphonse and Nellie (Toner) B.; m. Nora Hope, June 14, 1928 (dec. 1979); children: Michael T.H., Alphonse William, James, Christopher John; m. 2d Marguerite Rathbun, June 12, 1981. Chmn. Continental Mfrs. Can. Ltd., Cassidy's Ltd., Montreal, Terminal Sheet Metal Works Ltd., Vancouver, B.C., Can., 1973-93. Gov. Montreal Children's Hosp., 1953-93; past pres., dir. Que. Assn. Retarded Children; bd. hon. govs. Can. Assn. Mentally Retarded, 1950-93; dir. Canadian Council Internat. C. of C. Served with Royal Militia, 1925-47. Mem. Canadian Importers Assn. (past pres.), Hotel and Restaurant Suppliers Assn. (past pres.). Clubs: Royal Montreal Golf, Royal Montreal Curling, Royal St. Lawrence Yacht, Mt. Royal, Montreal Badminton and Squash. Home: Westmount Can. Died Dec. 1, 1993.

BRODKEY, HAROLD ROY, writer; b. Staunton, Ill., Oct. 25, 1930; s. Max and Ceil (Glazer) Weintrub; adopted s. Joseph and Doris (Rubenstein) B.; m. Joanna Brown, June, 1952 (div. 1962); 1 child, Ann Emily; m. Ellen Rosenberg Schwamm, Oct. 21, 1980. BA, Harvard U., 1952. Adj. assoc. prof. dept. English Cornell U., Ithaca, N.Y., 1977-78, spring 79, 81; staff writer The New Yorker mag., 1987-96; writer-in-residence English dept., CCNY, spring, 1987. Author: (short story collections) First Love and Other Sorrows, 1958, 2d edit., 1986, Women and Angels, 1985, Stories in an Almost Classical Mode, 1988 (Present Tense mag. award 1989), (novel) The Runaway Soul, 1991, Profane Friendship, 1994; contbr. poetry, essays and fiction to New Yorker mag., Esquire, Vanity Fair, Partisan Rev., Paris Rev., numerous other mags.; work anthologized in over 20 books. Recipient Prix de Rome Am. Acad., 1959-60, Nat. Mag award for fiction, 1974, Brandeis U. award, 1975, Pushcart prize Pushcart Press, 1975, O'Henry First prize, 1975, 76, O'Henry prize best Am. short story, 1978; Guggenheim fellow, 1987; Creative Artists Pub. Svc. Program grantee, 1972-73, Nat. Endowment Arts grantee, 1984-85. Mem. PEN Am. (freedom to write com. 1988-89). Democrat. Jewish. Home: New York N.Y. Died Jan. 26, 1996.

BRODSKY, JOSEPH (ALEXANDROVICH), poet, educator; b. Leningrad, USSR, May 24, 1940; sentenced to 5 years in exile in Arkhangelsk, 1964; sentence commuted, 1966; involuntary exile, 1972; came to U.S.; naturalized, 1977.; s. Alexander I. and Maria (Volpert) B. Student, Russian secondary schs., until 1956; D.Litt. (hon.), Yale U., 1978, Dartmouth Coll., U. Keele, Amherst Coll., Uppsala U., U. Rochester, Williams Coll., Colchester U., Oxford (Eng.) U. Poet-in-residence U. Mich., Ann Arbor, 1972-73, 74-80; Andrew W. Mellon prof. Mount Holyoke Coll., South Hadley, Mass., 1990-96; U.S. poet laureate, 1991. Author: Velka Elegie, 1968, A Halt in the Desert, 1970, Selected Poems, 1973, End of a Beautiful Era, 1977, A Part of Speech, 1977, 1980 (Nat. Book Critics Circle award nomination 1980), Novye stansky k Avguste: stikhi k M.B., 1962-1982, 1983, To Uraniia: Selected Poems, 1965-85, A Part of Speech: Collected Poems, 1990, The Works of Joseph Brodsky, 1992-95, In the Neighborhood of Atlantis, 1995; (plays) Mramor, 1984, Marbles (translated by Alan Myers and author), 1980, Watermark, 1992, Democracy, 1993; Less than One: Selected Essays, 1986, 1995; contbr. numerous articles to profl. jours. Decorated Legion d'Honneur (France); knight Order of St. John of Malta; recipient Premio Mondello, Italy, 1979, Nobel Prize for Lit., 1987; John D. and Catherine T. MacArthur Found. fellow, 1981; Guggenheim fellow, N.Y. Inst. Humanities fellow NYU. Jewish. Home: New York N.Y. Died Jan. 28, 1996; buried N.Y.C.

BROGLIE, LOUIS-VICTOR DUC DE, scientist; b. Dieppe, France, Aug. 15, 1892; s. Victor duc de Broglie and Pauline de la Forest d'Armaille. Ed. U. Paris, D.Sc. Prof. theoretical physics Inst. Henri Poincaré, U. Paris, 1932-62; mem. Acad. Française, from 1943; mem. sci. com. AEC, from 1946; mem. Comité d'action sci. de defense nationale, 1950-67. Recipient Nobel prize for physics, 1929; decorated Grand Croix, Légion d'honneur, comdr. des Palmes académiques. Author: La theorie de Quanta, 1924; Ondes et Mouvements, 1930; Introduction a l'etude de la mécanique ondulatoire, 1926; Consequences de la relativité dans le developpement de la mecanique ondulatoire, 1933; Matière et Lumière, la Physique moderne et les quanta, 1937; Une nouvelle de la lumière, 1940; Continue et Discontinue, 1941; Mé canique ondulatoire à la théorie du Noyau, 1943; Physique et Microphysique, 1957; Sur les Sentiers de la Science, 1960; Certitudes et Incertitudes de la Science, 1977; La Ré interpretation de la Mécanique Ondulatoire, 1972; Recherches d'un demi-siècle, 1976; Jalons pour une nouvelle microphysique, 1978. Mem. Inst. de France, Acad. des Scis., from 1933, life sec. Acad. des Scis., 1942-75. Mem. Nat. Acad. Scis. (U.S.), Roya. Soc., Romanian Acad. (hon.). Deceased. Home: Neuilly-sur-Seine France

BROME, ROBERT HARRISON, lawyer; b. Basin, Wyo., June 28, 1911; s. Charles L. and Margaret (Kennedy) B.; m. Mary E. Reed, Aug. 28, 1937; children: Thomas R., Robert H. AB, Whitman Coll., 1933,

LLD, 1970; LLB, Columbia U., 1936. Bar: N.Y. 1936, Wyo. 1946. Asst. counsel, asst. sec. Fed. Res. Bank of N.Y., 1936-46, 48-50; resident counsel Bankers Trust Co., N.Y.C., 1950-62; sec. Bankers Trust Co., 1955-66, gen. counsel, 1962-66, sr. v.p., gen. counsel, 1966-68, sr. v.p., 1968-74; v.p., sec. Bankers Internat. Corp., 1962-70, also dir.; sec., gen. counsel BT N.Y. Corp., 1966-68, sr. v.p., 1968-75, exec. v.p., 1975-77; chmn., chief exec. officer, dir. Bankers Trust Co. of Hudson Valley, 1975-77, dir., 1975-78; counsel Eaton & Van Winkle, N.Y.C., 1978-88. Bd. overseers Whitman Coll.; adv. council Columbia U. Grad. Sch. Bus., 1976-78. Mem. Tuxedo Club (N.Y.), Quail Ridge Country Club (Boynton Beach, Fla.), The Little Club (Gulfstream, Fla.), Phi Beta Kappa, Delta Sigma Rho. Home: Delray Beach Fla. Died Nov. 24, 1995.

BROOKHUIS, JOHN G. K., chemical company executive; b. Enschede, The Netherlands, 1921; married. Grad., Enschede Textile Inst., 1941. Pres. Hoechst-Holland N.V., 1960-70, Am. Hoechst Corp., Somerville, N.J., 1970-82; vice chmn. Am. Hoechst Corp., Somerville, 1982—, also bd. dirs.; bd. dirs. Bank N.Y. Home: Somerville N.J.

BROOKINS, DOUGLAS GRIDLEY, geochemist, educator; b. Healdsburg, Calif., Sept. 27, 1936; s. Rex McKain and Ellyn Caroline (Hitt) B.; m. Barbara Flashman, Sept. 16, 1961 (div. 1990); children: Laura Beth, Rachel Sarah. AA, Santa Rosa Jr. Coll., 1956; AB, U. Calif.-Berkeley, 1958; PhD, MIT, 1963. Geologist Bear Creek Co., San Francisco, 1957-59; research asst. MIT, Cambridge, 1958-63; physicist Avco Corp., Wilmington, Mass., 1961; asst. prof. geology Kans. State U., Manhattan, 1963-65; assoc. prof. Kans. State U., 1965-70; prof. geology U. N.Mex., Albuquerque, 1971—; acting chmn. U. N.Mex., 1972, chmn. dept., 1976-79. Author: Earth Resources, Energy and the Environment, 1980, Geochemical Aspects of Radioactive Waste Disposal, 1984, Physical Geology, 1982, Eh-ph Diagrams for Geochemists, 1987, The Geological Disposal of High Level Radioactive Wastes, 1988, Earth, Energy Resources and Their Environmental Impact, 1989, The Indoor Radon Problem, 1990; contbr. 600 articles to profl. jours. Bd. dirs. Jewish Community Council Albuquerque, 1974; trustee Congregation Albert, 1975-81 , v.p., 1983-84, pres., 1985-87. Named Researcher-Tchr. of Year, 1971. Fellow Geol. Soc. Am., Am. Inst. Chemists, Mineral Soc. Am.; mem. LWV, Geochem. Soc., Meteoritical Soc., Am. Geophys. Union, N.Y. Acad. Sci., Albuquerque Geol. Soc.(pres. 1973), N.Mex. Geol. Soc., N.Mex. Inst. Chemists (councillor 1974-75), Am. Assn. Petroleum Geologists, Internat. Assn. Geochemistry and Cosmochemistry, Soc. Econ. Geologists, Soc. Exploration Geochemists, Materials Rsch. Soc., Am. Chem. Soc., B'nai B'rith (sec. 1974-75), Phi Beta Kappa (pres. Alpha Assn. Kans. 1967-68), Sigma Xi. Home: Albuquerque N. Mex.

BROOKS, CLEANTH, English educator, writer; b. Murray, Ky., Oct. 16, 1906; s. Cleanth and Bessie Lee (Witherspoon) B.; m. Edith Amy Blanchard, Sept. 12, 1934 (dec. Oct. 1986). A.B., Vanderbilt U., 1928; A.M., Tulane U., 1929; Rhodes scholar, Oxford U., La. and Exeter, Eng., 1929-32; B.A. (hon.), Oxford U., 1931, B.Litt., 1932; D.Litt. (hon.), Upsala Coll., 1963, U. Ky., 1963, U. Exeter, 1966, Washington and Lee U., 1968, Tulane U., 1969, U. of South, 1975, Newberry Coll., 1979, Ind. State U., 1992; L.H.D. (hon.), St. Louis U., 1968, Centenary Coll., 1972, Oglethorpe U., 1976, St. Peter's Coll., 1978, Lehigh U., 1980, Millsaps Coll., 1983, U. New Haven, 1984, U. S.C., 1984, Adelphi U., 1992. Prof. English La. State U., 1932-47; mng. editor (with R. P. Warren) So. Rev., Baton Rouge, 1935-41; editor (with R. P. Warren) So. Rev., 1941-42; vis. prof. U. Tex., summer 1941, U. Mich., summer 1942, U. Chgo., 1945-46, U. So. Calif., Los Angeles, 1953, Bread Loaf Sch. English, 1963; fellow Library of Congress, 1951-62; cultural attache Am. Embassy, London, 1964-66; Gray prof. rhetoric emeritus Yale U., New Haven; Lamar lectr., 1984; Jefferson lectr., 1985; mem. council of scholars for Library of Congress, 1984-87; chancellor Fellowship of So. Writers, 1986-91. Author: Modern Poetry and the Tradition, 1939, The Well Wrought Urn, 1947; (with R.P. Warren) Understanding Poetry, 1938, Modern Rhetoric, 1950; (with W. K. Wimsatt, Jr.) Literary Criticism: A Short History, 1957, The Hidden God, 1963, William Faulkner: The Yoknapatawpha Country, 1963, A Shaping Joy: Studies in the Writer's Craft, 1972; (with R. W. B. Lewis and R. P. Warren) American Literature: the Makers and the Making, 1973, William Faulkner: Toward Yoknapatawpha and Beyond, 1978, William Faulkner, First Encounters, 1983, The Language of the American South, 1985, On the Prejudices, Predilections, and Firm Beliefs of William Faulkner, 1987, Historical Evidence and the Reading of Seventeenth Century Poetry, 1991, also other books; editor: The Correspondence of Thomas Percy and Richard Farmer, 1946, Thomas Percy and William Shenstone, 1977; gen. editor (with David N. Smith and Alex Falconer) The Percy Letters, 10 vols. projected from 1942; mem. adv. com. for Boswell Papers, 1950; contbr. articles, revs. to lit. mags., jours. Named research prof. Bostick Found., 1975; Guggenheim fellow, 1953, 60, sr. fellow NEH, 1975. Mem. MLA, Royal Soc. Lit., Am. Acad. Arts and Scis., Nat. Acad. Arts and Letters, Am. Philos. Soc., Phi Beta Kapa. Democrat. Anglican Catholic. Club: Athenaeum (London). Home: New Haven Conn. Died May 10, 1994.

BROOKS, EVANS BARTLETT, retired graphic arts company executive; b. New Albany, Ind., Jan. 28, 1900; s. William Wilson and Bertha (Evans) B.; m. Margaret Marby, Mar. 6, 1926; children: Marcia Jayne Brooks Browne, Sandra Lee Brooks Jordan. Student bus. adminstrn., Louisville YMCA Extension and Ind. U. Extension. Vice pres. Del. Engraving Co., Muncie, Ind., 1926-30, Ditzel-Brooks Co., Dayton, Ohio, 1931-32; v.p.-sec. Wayne Colorplate Co. Ohio, Dayton, 1932-37; pres., treas. Wayne Colorplate Co. Ohio, 1937-84; v.p., treas. Brooks Investment Co., Dayton, 1953-84; emeritus chmn. bd. Third Nat. Bank & Trust Co., Dayton. Charter mem. Dayton Area Progress Council, 1961; chmn. Montgomery County Bldg. Commn.; founder, mem. 1st pres. All- Dayton Com., 1945-47; past chmn. Montgomery County chpt. ARC; past pres. Dayton Philharmonic Assn.; mem., past chmn. Bd. Mental Retardation; trustee, exec. com. Air Force Mus.; trustee Dayton and Montgomery County Pub. Library (past pres.); pres. Dayton Art Inst., 1951-53; emeritus trustee U. Dayton. Mem. Am. Photoengravers Assn. (past pres.), Photo-Engravers Research Inst. (dir., past pres.), Dayton Printing Industry Assn. (past pres.), Dayton C. of C. (past pres.), Research and Engring. Council Graphic Arts (dir.), Newcomen Soc. Presbyterian (past pres. Ohio Bd. Home Missions; ch. elder). Clubs: Moraine Country, Engineers. Lodges: Masons, Rotary (past pres.). Home: Columbus Ohio Deceased.

BROOKS, JOHN, writer; b. N.Y.C., Dec. 5, 1920; s. John Nixon and Bessie (Lyon) B.; m. Anne Curtis Brown, Mar. 6, 1948 (div. 1952); m. Rae Alexander Everitt, Aug. 15, 1953 (div. 1975); children: Carolyn, John Alexander.; m. Barbara Smith Mahoney, Jan. 29, 1982. A.B., Princeton U., 1942. Contbg. editor Time mag., 1945-47; staff contbr. New Yorker mag., 1949-93. Author: The Big Wheel, 1949, A Pride of Lions, 1954, The Man Who Broke Things, 1958, The Seven Fat Years, 1958, The Fate of the Edsel, 1963, The Great Leap, 1966, Business Adventures, 1969, Once in Golconda, 1969, The Go-Go Years, 1973, Telephone, 1976, The Games Players, 1980, Showing Off in America, 1981, The Takeover Game, 1987; also articles and revs.; editor: The One and the Many, 1962, The Autobiography of American Business, 1974. Trustee N.Y. Pub. Library, 1978-84. Served with AUS, 1942-45, ETO. Poynter fellow Yale, 1974-75. Mem. Authors Guild Am. (treas. 1964-71, v.p. 1971-75, pres. 1975-79), P.E.N. (v.p. 1962-66), Soc. Am. Historians (v.p. 1984-87, pres. 1987-93). Clubs: Coffee House, Century Assn. (N.Y.C.). Home: East Hampton N.Y. Died July 27, 1993.

BROOME, GEORGE CALVIN, III, physicist; b. Hattiesburg, Miss., July 31, 1938; s. George Calvin, Jr. and Ruth (Hudson) B.; m. Margaret Virginia Weeks, May 30, 1962; 1 son, Matthew Calvin. B.S. in Physics, Miss. State U., 1960, M.S., 1962. Mem. staff Langley Research Center, NASA, Hampton, Va., 1962-93; mgr. sci. payload studies, advanced space projects Langley Research Center, NASA, 1967-69, lander sci. instruments mgr. Viking project, 1969-76, Viking project mgr., 1976-78, mgr. earth radiation budget expts. project, 1978-83, mem. sr. staff, 1983-87, mgr. projects devel. br., 1987-91, chief engineer projects div., 1991-93. Recipient Outstanding Leadership medal NASA, 1977. Methodist. Home: Hampton Va. Died Apr. 15, 1993.

BRORBY, MELVIN, advertising agency executive; b. Decorah, Iowa, Sept. 20, 1894; s. Martin J. and Louise (Wimmer) B.; m. Rowena Williams, Jan. 1, 1927; children: Harry, Virginia (Mrs. Wesley Horner). Student, Oxford U., 1919; A.B., U. Wis., 1920; student, U. Strasbourg, 1920, The Sorbonne, 1920-21, Free Sch. Polit. Scis., Paris, 1921-22. Sr. vice pres. Needham Harper Worldwide, Inc. (formerly known as Needham, Louis & Brorby, Inc., Chgo., from 1925; sr. vice pres. then Needham, Harper & Steers, Inc., Chgo., %. Gov., life mem. Art Inst. Chgo.; mem. citizens coms. U. Chgo., U. Ill.; mem. Orchestral Assn.; bd. dirs. Nat. Outdoor Advt. Bur.; Sponsor Nat. Soc. Crippled Children and Adults; mem. Stevenson Com.; trustee, v.p. Johnson Found. Mem. Soc. of Contemporary Am. Art (past pres.), Inst. Internat. Edn. (trustee; mem. midwest adv. com.), Am. Assn. Advt. Agys. (past chmn.), Art Club Chgo., Oxford Soc. (past br. sec.), Chgo. Council Fgn. Relations (dir. past pres.), N.Y. Council Fgn. Relations, Phi Beta Kappa, Phi Gamma Delta, Artus. Clubs: Tavern (Chgo.), Arts (Chgo.), Lake Shore (Chgo.) (past pres.), Mid-America (Chgo.); Century (N.Y.C.). Home: Tucson Ariz. Deceased.

BROWN, ALBERT CLARENCE, former mayor; b. Los Angeles, Oct. 25, 1918; s. Albert C. and Wanda (Albright) B.; m. Virginia Little, 1941; children—Cheryl Kinsman, Susan Baltagi, Becky Westerdahl. A.A., Riverside City Coll., 1939. Owner, mgr. Brown's Engine, Riverside, Calif., 1948-84; mayor City of Riverside, 1978-90. Trustee Riverside City Coll., 1964-78. Served with USN, 1940-45, PTO. Recipient Alumnus of Yr. award Riverside City Coll., 1977, Outstanding Service award Catholic Athletic League, Riverside. Republican. Lodges: Elks, Masons, Shriners, Lions (past pres.). Home: Riverside Calif. Died Aug. 26, 1995.

BROWN, ALBERT JACOB, lawyer; b. San Francisc May 6, 1914; s. Charles and Rose (Lape) B.; m. Sylvi Esther Kotok, June 16, 1940; children: Katherine Rut David Julian. AB, U. Calif., Berkeley, 1937, JD, 1940. Bar: Calif. 1940, U.S. Dist. Ct. (no. dist.) Calif. 194 U.S. Ct. Appeals (9th cir.) 1940. Sole practice Jackso Calif., 1941-42; assoc. Pillsbury, Madison & Sutro, Sa Francisco, 1942-51, ptnr., 1951-95. Bar: ABA, Cali Bar Assn., San. Francisco Bar Assn. Clubs: Sa Francisco Yacht, San Franciso Exchange. Hom Lafayette Calif. Died Nov. 3, 1995.

BROWN, ARTHUR THOMAS, architect; b. Tarki Mo., May 6, 1900; s. John Vallance and Ada (Moor B.; m. Margaret Caroline Munn, Dec. 23, 1927; chil dren: Gordon Vallance, Arthur Thomas. B.S., Tarki Coll., 1923; B.Arch., Ohio State U., 1927; scholar, Lak Forest Found. Architecture and Landscape Archite ture, 1927; D.F.A. (hon.), U. Ariz., 1985. Draftsma Office David Adler, Chgo., 1928-32; with Century Progress Expn., Chgo., 1932-34, Richard A. Mors Tucson, 1936-39; partner Richard A. Morse, 1939-4 pvt. practice architecture Tucson, 1942-70; ptnr. Gordo V. Brown, 1970-91; ret., 1991; Dir. Tucson Fine Ar Assn., 1948-52. Author: Arthur T. Brown, Architec Artist, Inventor, 1985; contbr. to archtl. books an mags. Recipient mention for Rosenberg Hous Progressive Architecture awards, 1946, award of mer A.I.A., 1949, Western Mountain Dist. awards fo Winsor House, Ariz. Biltmore Motor Hotel, 1st Chris tian Ch. A.I.A., 1953, 54; Smith Meml. Chapel exhibite Pan Am. Congress of Architects, Lima, Peru, 194 Alumni citation Tarkio Coll., 1958; Disting. Alumnu award Ohio State U., 1960; Disting. Citizen award U Ariz. Alumni Assn., 1977. Fellow AIA (mem. nat. com on sch. bldgs. 1948-50, pres. Ariz.chpt. 1946, Silve Medal award Western Mountain Region 1986), Palet and Brush Club, So. Ariz. Watercolor Guild, Tucso Gem and Mineral Soc.; mem. Rotary. Presbyterian. Home: Tucson Ariz. Died Oct. 24, 1993.

BROWN, ARTHUR WILLIAM, JR., lawyer; b. Chgo July 11, 1939; s. Arthur W. and Henriette (Degen) B m. Anita Shulman, June 16, 1963; children: Michael A Joel F. BBA, U. Mich., 1961; JD magna cum laud Northwestern U., 1964. Bar: Ill. 1964, U.S. Dist. C (no. dist.) Ill. 1964. Assoc. Altheimer and Gray, Chgo 1964-71, ptnr., 1971-93; lectr. in field. Active Jewis Fedn. of Met. Chgo., 1967, pres., 1991-93. Mem. Am Coll. Trust and Estate Counsel; mem. ABA, Ill. Ba Assn., Chgo. Bar Assn., Chgo. Estate Planning Cour (pres. 1990-91), Standard Club. Home: Highland Par Ill. Deceased.

BROWN, DAVID SPRINGER, retired public ad ministration educator; b. Bangor, Maine, Dec. 27, 191 s. Lyle Lincoln and Myra Jane (Springer) B.; m. Evely Lovett, May 1, 1943 (dec. 1967); children: Davi Springer, Christopher, Robert, Adele; m. Anne Elizo 1968. A.B., U. Maine, 1936; Ph.D., Syracuse U., 1955 Newspaper reporter Bangor Daily News, 1931-3 teaching asst. Syracuse U., 1937-40; with Dept. Agr 1940, 42, N.Y. State Dept. Edn., 1941, CAA, 1946-4 Air Coordinating Com., 1948-50, ECA, 1950-52; exe sec. pub. adv. bd. Mut. Security Agy., 1952-53; ass exec. dir. Com. Nat. Trade Policy, 1953-54; asso. pro pub. adminstrn. George Washington U., Washingto 1954-57; prof. George Washington U., 1957-69, pro mgmt., 1969-86, prof. emeritus, 1986-96, chmn. dep pub. adminstrn., 1972-76; pres. Leadership Resource 1970-75; dir. USAF adv. mgmt. program, 1954-61; vi prof. Royal Coll. Sci. and Tech., Glasgow, Scotlan 1958. Author: Federal Contributions To Managemen 1971, Managing the Large Organization, 198 Management's Hidden Enemy-and What Can be Don About It, 1987, Management Concepts and Practice 1989; also articles, monographs. Sec. U.S. delegatio Internat. Civil Aviation Orgn., Montreal, Que., Can 1950; mem. U.S. delegation Internat. Inst. Adminstr Scis., Brussels, Belgium, 1958; adv. com. tng. Intern Revenue Service, 1959-60; dep. chief U. So. Cal. Party Pub. Adminstrn., Lahore, Pakistan, 1961-62. Mem Am. Soc. for Pub. Adminstrn., Am. Soc. Mil. Comp trollers, Am. Soc. Tng. and Devel., Acad. Mgmt. Democrat. Home: Washington D.C. Died Mar. 1 1996.

BROWN, EDMUND GERALD (PAT BROWN lawyer, former governor of California; b. San Francisc Apr. 21, 1905; s. Edmund Joseph and Ida (Schuckma B.; m. Bernice Layne, Oct. 30, 1930; children: Barba Brown Casey, Cynthia Brown Kelly, Edmund Geral Kathleen Brown Sauter. LLB, San Francisco Law Sch 1927; LLD, U. San Francisco, 1959, U. San Diego, 196 U. Santa Clara, 1961; D.C.L., Calif. Coll. Medicine, Lo Angeles, 1964. Bar: Calif. bar 1927. Practiced in Sa Francisco, 1927-43; dist. atty. City and County Sa Francisco, 1943-47, 47-50; atty. gen. Calif., 1951-5 gov. of Calif., 1959-66; head Nat. Commn. Reform Fe Criminal Laws; sr. ptnr. firm Ball, Hunt, Hart, Brown Baerwitz., 1970-90; of counsel Ball, Hunt, Hart, Brow and Baerwitz, 1990-91. Author: Public Justice, Priva Mercy, 1989. Mem. Franklin Delano Roosevelt Mem Commn.; del Dem. Nat. Conv., 1940, 44, 48, 52, 56, 6 64, 88; mem. Golden Gate Bridge and Hwy. Dis chmn. San Francisco Coordinating Council, 1947; ho chair Edmund G. "Pat" Brown Inst. of Pub. Affair Calif. State U., L.A.; emeritus trustee U. Calif. Berkel 'ound. Fellow Am. Coll. Trial Lawyers; mem. Dist. ıttys. Assn. Calif. (pres. 1950-51), Western Assn. Attys. ;en. (past pres.), Nat. Assn. Attys. Gen. (exec. bd.), ım., Beverly Hills bar assns., State Bar Calif.)emocrat. Roman Catholic. Clubs: Native Sons Golden Vest, Bel-Air Country, Olympic, La Quinta Country. Iome: Los Angeles Calif. Died Feb. 16, 1996.

ıROWN, ELLIS L., chemical company executive; b.)uncan, Okla., 1915. Grad., Okla. U., 1939. Ind. oil roducer, 1946-66; with Petrolite Corp., St. Louis, 1966-2; chmn. Petrolite Corp., 1981-92. Home: Saint Louis Io. Died Feb. 15, 1992.

ıROWN, EMERSON LEE, textbook publisher; b. Iemple, Mo., Dec. 28, 1901; s. Aubrey S. and Della Holmes) B.; m. Marguerite Bangs, June 6, 1926; chilren: Emerson Lee, Robert Tindall. A.B., Baker U., 924; M.A., U. Kans., 1929; postgrad., Sch. Bus. 'olumbia, 1956. Instr. history Marion (Kans.) High ch., 1924-26, prin., 1926-30; field rep. Harcourt, Brace : Co., 1930-38, social studies editor, 1938-52; gen. mgr. ch. dept. McGraw-Hill Book Co., N.Y.C., 1952-63; litorial dir. McGraw-Hill Book Co. (Webster div.), 963-67, v.p., dir., 1954-67; sr. v.p. BCMA Assos., 967-81; v.p. Moseley Assocs., from 1981; Del. NESCO internat. seminar on improvement textbooks, russels, Belgium, 1950; mem. Govt. Adv. Com. on Iat. Book Programs, 1964-66; Pres. Am. Textbook ubs. Inst., 1964-65; Bd. dirs. CEMREL, Inc., St. ouis, 1972-81. Mem. Nat. Council Social Studies, Phi)elta Kappa. Democrat. Congregationalist. Home: ireenwich Conn. Deceased.

ıROWN, GEORGE MACKAY, poet; b. Stromness, ırkney Islands, Scotland, Oct. 17, 1921; s. John and Iary Jane (Mackay) B. BA, U. Edinburgh, Scotland, 960, postgrad., 1962-64. Author: (poetry) The Storm nd Other Poems, 1954, Loaves and Fishes, 1959, The ear of the Whale, 1965, The Five Voyages of Arnor, 966, Twelve Poems, 1968, Fishermen with Ploughs: A oem Cycle, 1971, Lifeboat and Other Poems, 1971, oems New and Selected, 1971, (with Iain Crichton mith and Norman MacCaig) Penguin Modern Poets 1, 1972, Winterfold, 1976, Voyages, 1983, Christmas oems, 1984, Stone, 1987, Tryst on Egilsay, 1988, The Vreck of the Archangel, 1989, Selected Poems 1954-83, 992, The Lost Village, 1992, Foresterhill, 1992, Orfeo, 995, Following a Lark, 1996; (novels) Greenvoe, 1972, Iagnus, 1973, Time in a Red Coat, 1984, Vinland, 992, Beside the Ocean of Time, 1994; (short fiction) A alendar of Love, 1967, A Time To Keep and Other tories, 1969, Hawkfall and Other Stories, 1974, The un's Net, 1976, Witch and Other Stories, 1977, An-ina and Other Stories, 1982, Christmas Stories, 1985, he Hooded Fishman: A Story, 1985, Selected Stories, 986, The Golden Bird: Two Orkney Stories, 1987, Vinter Tales, 1995; (children's books) The Two Fid-ıers: Tales from Orkney, 1974, Pictures in the Cave, 977, Six Lives of Fankle the Cat, 1980, Keepers of the Iouse, 1986, The Sea King's Daughter, 1991, Beside the cean and Time, 1994; (plays) Witch, 1969, A Time to eep, 1969, A Spell for Green Corn, Orkney, 1971, The oom of Light, 1972, The Storm Watchers, 1976, ibretto) The Martyrdom of St. Magnus, 1977, Miss arraclough, 1977, Four Plays for Schools, 1978, The wo Fiddlers, 1978, The Well, 1981, The Voyage of aint Brandon, 1984, Andrina, 1984, Three Plays, 1984, he Road to Colonus, 1989; (other writings) Let's See ıe Orkney Islands, 1948, Stromness Official Guide, 956, An Orkney Tapestry, 1969, Letters from Iamnavoe, 1975, Edwin Muir: A Brief Memoir, 1975, rom Stone to Thorn, 1975, Claddagh, 1977, Under rinkie's Brae, 1979, Portrait of Orkney, 1981, 89, The cottish Bestiary, 1986, Letters to Gypsy, 1990, In the Iargins of a Shakespeare, 1991; editor: Selected Prose f Edwin Muir, 1987. Fellow Royal Soc. Lit. Home: ırkney Scotland Died Apr. 13, 1996.

ıROWN, HOWARD MAYER, music educator; b. .A., Apr. 13, 1930; s. Alfred Ralph and Florence ophie (Mayer) B. BA magna cum laude, Harvard U., 951, MA, 1954, PhD, 1959; MusD (hon.), Bates Coll., ewiston, Maine, 1989. Asst. prof. Wellesley (Mass.) 'oll., 1958-60; from asst. prof. to prof. U. Chgo., 1960-2, Ferdinand Schevill disting. svc. prof., 1974-93; King dward prof. of music King's Coll., London, 1972-74; 'r. Collegium Musicum U. Chgo., 1960-82; cons., as-oc. curator mus. instruments Smithsonian Inst., Wash-gton, 1964-65. Author of numerous books, including Florentine Chansonnier from the Time of Lorenzo the Iagnificent, Florence, Biblioteca Nazionale Centrale, IS Banco Rari 229. Pres. Renaiance Soc. Am., 1990-I. Guggenheim fellow, 1963-64, Harvard U. Ctr. for alian Renaissance Studies fellow, 1969-70; recipient olikes Galilei prize, U. Pisa, 1988. Fellow Am. Acad. ırts and Scis.; mem. Am. Mus. Soc. (hon., v.p. 1966-68, ıem. at large exec. bd. 1970-72, pres. 1978-80, mem. dit. bd. jour. 1969-71), Am. Recorder Soc. (pres. 1965-6), Am. Music Soc. (hon.), Internat. Musicological Soc. :.p. 1982-87), Royal Music Assn. (hon. fgn.), Renais-ance Soc. Am. (music rep. in coun. 1970-72, pres. 1990-1), Reform Club (London). Home: Chicago Ill. Died 'eb. 21, 1993.

ıROWN, JACK ERNEST, information scientist; b. dmonton, Alta., Can., Mar. 1, 1914; s. Ernest William nd Maud Alice (Jarman) B.; m. Estelle A. Coles, Dec. 26, 1944; children: Keith, Frances. B.A., U. Alta., 1938; B.L.S., McGill U., 1939; M.A.; ALA fellow, U. Chgo., 1940; LL.D. (hon.), U. Waterloo, 1965, McMaster U., 1978. Reference librarian Edmonton (Alta., Can.) Pub. Library, 1940-42; library asst. N.Y. Pub. Library, N.Y.C., 1942-45; first asst. sci. and tech. div. N.Y. Pub. Library, 1947-52; asst. librarian Brown U., Providence, 1946-47; dir. Nat. Sci. Library, Ottawa, Ont., Can., 1957-74, Can. Inst. Sci. and Tech. Info., Ottawa, 1974-77; prof. McGill U. Grad. Sch. Library Sci., 1978-82; sci. info. cons., 1982-88; v.p. Internat. Fedn. Documentation, 1964-68; mem. adv. coun. Pahlavi Nat. Library, Iran, 1974-96. Contbr. articles to library jours. Mem. ALA, Can. Library Assn. (Outstanding Service award 1979), Spl. Libraries Assn., Can. Assn. Info. Sci., Assn. Library and Info. Services (award for Spl. Librarianship in Can. 1979). Anglican. Home: Ottawa Can. Died Jan. 17, 1996.

BROWN, JOHN ROBERT, federal judge; b. Funk, Nebr., Dec. 10, 1909; s. E.E. and Elvira (Carney) B.; m. Mary Lou Murray, May 30, 1936 (dec. 1977); 1 child, John R.; m. Vera Smith Riley, Sept. 14, 1979. AB, U. Nebr., 1930, LLD, 1965; JD, U. Mich., 1932, LLD, 1959; LLD, Tulane U., 1979. Bar: Tex. 1932. Mem. Royston & Rayzor, Houston and Galveston, 1932-55; judge 5th Circuit U.S. Ct. Appeals, 1955-92, chief judge, 1967-79. Chmn. Harris County Republican Com., 1953-55. Served from lt. to maj. Transp. Corps USAAF, 1942-46. Mem. ABA, Tex. Bar Assn., Houston Bar Assn., Am. Judicature Soc., Am. Law Inst., Am. Soc. Average Adjusters (hon.), Maritime Law Assn. U.S., Assn. ICC Practitioners, Order of Coif, Phi Delta Phi, Sigma Chi. Presbyn. (elder). Clubs: Houston, Houston Country. Home: Houston Tex. Died Jan. 22, 1993.

BROWN, JOSEPH SIMON, JR., food company executive; b. Jeanerette, La., June 1, 1907; s. Joseph Simon and Septima Alexandrine (Fortier) B.; m. Mary Sylvia Sandoz, June 18, 1930; children: Gordon Sandoz, Norman Sandoz, Joseph Simon III, Sylvia Sandoz Brown Putnam. Grad., St. Peter's Coll., New Iberia, La., 1924. Ptnr., founder J.S. Brown & Son, New Iberia, La., 1926-56; founding ptnr., chmn. bd. Bruce Foods Corp., New Iberia, La., 1956—; founder, dir., v.p. City Bank Trust Co., New Iberia, La., 1958—. Recipient award of Appreciation, City Bank and Trust Co. of New Iberia, 1983. Mem. New Iberia C. of C., Nat. Food Processors Assn., La. Yam Council, Internat. Trade Mart. (New Orleans, Plimsoll div.), World Trad Ctrs. Assn. (New Orleans), Internat. House of New Orleans. Democrat. Roman Catholic. Home: New Iberia La.

BROWN, LEON, retired architect, educator; b. Blackville, S.C., Sept. 25, 1907; s. Isador and Sadie (Cohen) B.; m. Marguerite Kahn, Aug. 30, 1944; 1 child, Warren Lee. Student, Cornell U., 1924-25; BS in Architecture, Ga. Inst. Tech., 1929; MArch, U. Pa., 1933. Registered architect various states. Designer-draftsman R. Brognard Okie, Phila., 1929-31, 33-34; designer Thalheimer and Weitz, Phila., 1934-42; pvt. practice architecture Washington, 1946-80; prof. architecture Howard U., Washington, 1947-72; ptnr. Brown & Wright, Washington, 1950-80, Brown, Wright & Mano, Washington, 1968-71; mem. nat. panel arbitrators Am. Arbitration Assn., Washington, 1962-92; pres. Registration Bd. Architects, Washington, 1967-69; guide Hillwood Mus., Washington, 1980-92; cons. and lectr. in field. Co-author: R. Brognard Okie, Architect of Philadelphia, 1955; also articles. Chmn. bd. appeals and rev. D.C. Govt., 1956-60; co-chmn. Nat. Conf. Christians and Jews, Washington, 1966-69; bd. dirs. N.W. Settlement House, Washington, 1956-72. Served to capt. C.E., U.S. Army, 1943-46. Recipient Meritorious Pub. Service award Mil. Dist. Washington, 1946. Fellow AIA (pres. Washington chpt. 1956-58, elected Coll. Fellows 1969, Archtl. Washington Post award, Merit award, Centennial award 1991), Cosmos Club (Washington). Democrat. Jewish. Home: Washington D.C. Died Mar. 20, 1992.

BROWN, PETER CAMPBELL, retired lawyer; b. Aug. 12, 1913; s. Peter P. and Ellen (Campbell) B.; m. Joan Gallagher, June 8, 1943; children: Peter Campbell, Patricia, Thomas, Michael, Robert. A.B., Fordham Coll., 1935, LL.B., 1938; LL.D., St. Bonaventure U., New York, 1951. Bar: N.Y. 1938. Practiced in Bklyn., 1938-41; asst. U.S. atty. for Eastern Dist. of N.Y., Bklyn., 1946; 1st. asst. criminal div. Dept. of Justice, 1947-48; exec. asst. to atty. gen. U.S., 1948, spl. asst. to atty. gen., 1949-50, mem. subversive activities control bd. (under the Internal Security Act of 1950), 1950-53, chmn., 1952-53; commr. investigation N.Y.C., 1954-55; corp. counsel City of N.Y., 1955-58; mem. Manning, Hollinger & Shea, 1958-65; ptnr. Brown, Carlino & Emmanuel, 1965-72; counsel Winer, Neuburger & Sive, 1972-78; sole practice N.Y.C., 1978-88; dir. Thomas Pub. Co., Fedn. Bank & Trust Co. Bd. dirs. St. Mary's Coll., South Bend, Ind. Served to maj. AUS, 1942-45, ETO. Decorated 6 Battle Stars on European African Middle Eastern ribbon, Fourragere of Belgium for Battle of Ardennes (The Bulge); named Knight Holy Sepulchre Knight Malta. Fellow Am. Coll. Trial Lawyers, Bar Supreme Ct. U.S., Fed. Dist. Cts., U.S. Ct. Appeals, Am., N.Y. State bar assns., V.F.W., Legion, Catholic Lawyers Guild, Assn. Bar City of N.Y., St. Patrick Soc. Bklyn. (past pres., dir.), Friendly Sons St. Patrick City N.Y., Fordham Coll. Alumni Assn. (past pres.). Democrat. Roman Catholic. Clubs: Lawyers (Bklyn.), Montauk (Bklyn.); Manhattan (N.Y.C.), New York Athletic (N.Y.C.), Pinnacle (N.Y.C.); Army-Navy (Washington); Pelham Country; Westchester Country (Rye, N.Y.). Home: Port Chester N.Y. Died July 23, 1994.

BROWN, ROBERT CURTIS, retired city official; b. Peabody, Kans., Oct. 27, 1920; s. Orville Curtis and Rena Margaret (Runyon) B.; m. Helen Robinson Hale, Aug. 24, 1944; children: Dennis, Carol, Steven. Student public schs., Topeka. Laborer Internat. Harvester, Topeka, Kans., 1939-41; truck salesman, br. mgr. Internat. Harvester, Topeka and Lubbock, Tex., 1945-54; ter. mgr. White Motor Co., Dallas, 1954-56; v.p. to chmn. bd. Wichita (Kans.) White Truck Sales, 1956-78; v.p. Wichita Truck Lease & Fin., 1956-78; pres. Jaybo Leasing, Wichita, 1956-78; city commr. Wichita, 1979-81, 82-83, 1983-85, 86-87; mayor, 1981-82, 85-86. Served with USN, 1941-45, PTO. Mem. VFW, Am. Legion. Republican. Methodist. Clubs: Masons, Shriners, Lions. Home: Wichita Kans. Died Mar. 8, 1993; interred Old Mission Mausoleum, Wichita, Kans.

BROWN, ROBERT HAROLD, retired geography educator; b. Rochester, N.Y., Sept. 16, 1921; s. Harold Cecil and Marion (Johnson) B.; m. Helene Adeline Zukey, Sept. 1, 1945; children: Suzanne Odette, Kurtis Johnson. BS, U. Minn., 1948, MA, 1949; PhD, U. Chgo., 1957. Mem. faculty St. Cloud (Minn.) State Coll., 1949-64; prof. geography dept. U. Wyo., 1964-85. Author: Political Areal Functional Organization, 1957, (with Phillip Tideman) Atlas of Minnesota Occupancy, 3d edit., 1969, Wyoming Occupance Atlas, 1970, Wyoming: A Geography, 1980, The Global-Economy Urban Heirarchy, 1991, The Pervasive Spirit: Concepts for a Personal Religious Philosophy, 1992, Sedona: Arizona's Red Rock Community, 1993, Hopscotch for Two -- A Novel, 1994. Served to 1st lt. AUS, 1939-45; with USAF, 1951-52. Mem. Assn. Am. Geographers. Home: Sun City Ariz. Died Dec. 23, 1994.

BROWN, ROBERT MICHAEL, lawyer; b. Pitts., Oct. 18, 1929; s. Richard Thomas and Wilhelmina (Baehr) B.; m. Rita Claire Tepe, Aug. 11, 1951; children: Karen Claire, Paul M., Maureen A. Werwie. BA, Duquesne U., 1951, LLB, 1958, postgrad. in theology. Bar: Pa. 1959, U.S. Ct. Appeals (3d cir.) 1962, U.S. Supreme Ct. 1982. Law clk. Ct. of Common Pleas, Allegheny County, Pa., 1960-63; assoc. atty. Burgwin, Ruffin, Perry & Pohl, Pitts., 1963-65, atty. ptnr., 1965-83; atty. ptnr. Eckert Seamans Cherin & Mellott, Pitts., 1983-93; chmn. task force Am. Pub. Transit Assn. to rev. bid protest procedures of UMTA, chmn. legal affairs com., 1990-93; mem. adv. com. to Pa. task force of joint State Govt. Commn. on state Model Procurement Code; bd. dirs. Interform Corp., Consolidated Bus. Forms Co. Gen. counsel Port Authority of Allegheny County, Pub. Auditorium Authority Pitts. and Allegheny County; spl. counsel Urban Redevel. Authority Pitts.; ex-officio mem., bd. dirs. Duquesne U., 1979-82; trustee Andrew Carnegie Free Libr. of Carnegie, Pa., 1984-89; mem. adv. bd. Three Rivers Shakespeare Festival, 1985-90; mem. steering com. leadership Pitts. Project of Greater Pitts. C. of C., 1986-93. Mem. ABA, Pa. Bar Assn., Allegheny County Bar Assn., Duquesne U. Alumni Assn. (pres. 1979-82, chmn. Century Club of Disting. Duquesne Alumni, 1983-84, recognition award Duquesne U. Old Main Alumni, 1984), Pitts. Club (bd. govs.), Chartiers Country Club, Rotary (Paul Harris fellow, 1984, past pres. Three Rivers Club, Pitts. 1986-87). Democrat. Roman Catholic. Home: Carnegie Pa. Died May 7, 1993; buried Queen of Heaven Cemetery, Pitts., Pa.

BROWN, RONALD HARMON, government official, political organization administrator, lawyer; b. Washington, D.C., Aug. 1, 1941; s. William Harmon and Gloria (Osborne) B.; m. Alma Arrington, Aug. 11, 1962; children: Michael, Tracey. BA, Middlebury Coll., 1962; JD, St. John's U., 1970, LLD (hon.), 1989; LLD (hon.), Hunter Coll., 1989; Dr. Pub. Svc. (hon.), R.I. Coll., 1989. Bar: N.Y. 1971, D.C. 1973, U.S. Supreme Ct. 1975. Gen. counsel Nat. Urban League, Washington, 1971-73, chief Washington spokesperson, 1973-79, dep. exec. officer, 1974-76, v.p. Washington ops., 1976-79; chief counsel Com. on Judiciary U.S. Senate, Washington, 1980; gen. counsel, staff dir. Office Sen. Edward Kennedy, Washington, 1981; ptnr. Patton, Boggs & Blow, Washington, 1981-92; chmn. Dem. Nat. Com., Washington, 1989-93; sec. Dept. of Commerce, Washington, 1993-96; dist. leader Dem. Party Mt. Vernon, N.Y., 1971-73; legis. chmn. Leadership Conf. on Civil Rights, 1976-79; mem. U.S. Nat. Commn. UNESCO, 1977-79; mem. adv. coun. Fed. Home Loan Bank, 1978-79; Middle East rep. Nat. Urban Leage, 1979; dep. nat. campaign mgr. Kennedy for Pres., 1979-80, dir. Calif. campaign, 1980; chief counsel task force on voting rights and voter participation Dem. Nat. Com., 1981, dep. chmn., 1982-85, chmn., 1986-88; mem. exec. com. Dem. Nat. Com., 1988; sr. polit. advisor Dukakis-Bentsen Campaign, 1988; mgr. Dem. Convention Jesse Jackson Campaign; chmn. sr. adv. com. John F. Kennedy Sch. Gov. Inst. Politics Harvard U., 1986-96. Trustee Middlebury Coll., 1988-96, chmn. bd. trustees, 1976-80, 82-85. Capt. U.S. Army, 1963-67. Fellow Harvard U. Inst. Politics, 1980. Mem. ABA (standing com. on law and electoral process). Home: Washington D.C. Died April 3, 1996.

BROWN, SAM C., psychology educator; b. N.Y.C., Apr. 16, 1935; s. Michael and Rose (Roth) B.; m. Judith Marfleet, June 14, 1958. B.B.A., CCNY, 1957; M.A., U. Va., 1961, Ph.D., 1963. From asst. prof. to prof. psychology Kans. State U., 1963-73; prof. psychology U. Mo., Columbia, 1973—; chmn. dept. U. Mo., 1973-85. Contbr. articles to profl. jours. Served with U.S. Army, 1958-59. NIMH grantee, 1964-70, NIMH fellow, 1962-63; NDEA fellow, 1959-62. Mem. Am. Psychol. Assn., Eastern Psychol. Assn., Midwest Psychol. Assn., Rocky Mountain Psychol. Assn., AAAS, Psychonomic Soc., Sigma Xi. Home: Columbia Mo. Deceased.

BROWN, TERENCE MICHAEL, university president; b. Charleston, W.Va., Nov. 16, 1941; s. Charles Wilkerson and Pauline Marie (Pell) B.; m. Janet Elizabeth Hart, May 21, 1966; children: Elizabeth Michelle, Terence Michael II, Cara Susan. B.S., Lamar U., 1963; M.A. in English, Stephen F. Austin State U., 1965; Ph.D. in English, So. Ill. U., 1975. Instr. English So. Ill. U., Carbondale, 1966-72, asst. dean, asst. prof., 1972-77; Am. Council on Edn. fellow U. Ark., Fayetteville, 1977-78; v.p. acad. affairs Ark. State U., Jonesboro, 1978-82; pres. No. State U., Aberdeen, S.D., 1982-92. Editor: New Directions in Post-Secondary Education, 1974; author poetry; contbr. articles on English and Am. lit to profl. jours. Mem. Am. Council on Edn., Am. Assn. State Colls. and Univs., Aberdeen C. of C. (bd. dirs.), Pi Gamma Mu, Phi Kappa Phi, Beta Gamma Sigma, Sigma Phi Epsilon. Lodges: Rotary (Aberdeen); Masons, York Rite, Scottish Rite (32 degs.), Shrine. Home: Aberdeen S.D. Died Oct. 4, 1992; interred Aberdeen, S.D.

BROWN, WILLIAM CLIFFORD, publishing company executive; b. Ottumwa, Iowa, Nov. 12, 1911; s. Walter Mahlin and Zella Audrey (Mathews) B.; m. Eunice Mary Farley, May 20, 1936; children: Lawrence W., Cheryl (Mrs. Mark Falb). Grad. high sch.; LL.D., Bowling Green State U., 1970. Dist. sales mgr. John S. Swift Co., Inc., St. Louis, 1934-44; founder, chmn. William Brown Co., Pubs., Dubuque, Iowa, 1944-92; Chmn. Dubuque Bank & Trust Co., 1968-82; chmn. exec. com. Life Investors, Inc., Cedar Rapids, Iowa, 1967-82; chmn. Heartland Bancorp., 1982-88; bd. dirs. Retirement Investment Corp. Bd. dirs. U. Dubuque, 1969-95. Mem. Dubuque Shooting Soc. Clubs: Masons, Shriners, Elks, Dubuque Golf and Country; Vero Beach (Fla.) Golf and Country. Home: Vero Beach Fla. DIed Jan., 1995.

BROWN, WILSON GORDON, physician, educator; b. Bosworth, Mo., Jan. 18, 1914; s. Arthur Grannison and Clemma (Frock) B.; m. Anne Buckalew; 1 child, Gordon Alan. A.B., William Jewell Coll., 1935; M.D., Washington U., St. Louis, 1939. Diplomate: Am. Bd. Clin. Pathology, Am. Bd. Anatomic Pathology. Intern pathology Barnes Hosp., St. Louis, 1939-40; resident in pathology St. Louis City Hosp., 1940-41; instr. pathology Washington U., 1945-51; clin. assoc. prof. Baylor U. Coll. Medicine, Houston, 1951-90; clin. prof. U. Tex. Med. Sch. at Houston, 1972-90, mem. com. on lab. medicine; Pathologist, dir. labs. Hermann Hosp., Houston, 1951-71, apptd. disting. physician, 1986; dir. labs. Twelve Oaks Hosp., Houston, 1965-6, Polly Ryon Hosp., Richmond, Tex., 1954-90, Park Plaza Hosp., Houston, 1975-86; cons. Bellville Hosp., Ft. Bend Hosp., Katy Community Hosp., Navasota Regional Hosp., Parkway Hosp., Sharpstown Hosp.; ptnr. Brown & Assocs. Med. Labs., Houston, 1954-88; ptnr. Brown and Kott Med. Labs., 1988-90; mem. Anderson Assocs., U. Tex., 1988-90; mem. adv. bd. Living Bank, Houston, 1968-90; mem. adv. bd. InterFirst Fannin-Bank, mem. devel. bd., 1987; founding mem., trustee Mus. Med. Sci., Houston, 1969-90, pres. bd. trustees, 1974-75; bd. dirs. Ewing Ctr. Inc., Am. Cancer Soc. Harris County (Tex.) Br., 1952, pres, 1967-68. Contbr. articles to med. publs. Mem. William Greenleaf Elliott Soc. Washington U. Sch. Medicine. Served to maj. M.C. AUS, 1942-46, ETO, MTO. Decorated Bronze Star medal. Mem. Am., Tex. med. assns., Harris County Med. Soc., Coll. Am. Pathologists, Am. Soc. Clin. Pathology, Houston, Tex. socs. pathologists, Sigma Xi, Beta Beta Beta, Theta Chi Delta, Aeons, Phi Gamma Delta. Clubs: Warwick (Houston), Forum (Houston). Home: Spring Tex. Died Dec. 23, 1990.

BROWNE, ALLAN ROLAND, lawyer; b. El Paso, Tex., Nov. 18, 1900; s. Cecil W. and Anne (Welsh) B.; m. Blanche Longan, June 27, 1925; children: Virginia Browne Mount, Carol Harrington; m. Phoebe Mosman Harrington, July 5, 1958 (dec. 1984). A.B., Harvard U., 1922; J.D., U. Mo., Kansas City, 1925; grad., Command and Gen. Staff Coll., Ft. Leavenworth, Kans. Bar: Mo. 1923, Hawaii 1956, Kans. 1962, U.S. Supreme Ct., Ct. Appeals, Dist. Ct. 1962. Practice law Kansas City, Mo., 1923-42, from 56; served from capt. to col. U.S. Army, 1942-56; acting judge adv. gen. for Pacific Ocean area, 1945-46; judge adv. 8th Army Japan, 1946-49; presiding officer Bd. Review, Washington, 1949-53; judge adv. U.S. Army Pacific, 1953-56; ret., 1956; of counsel Ennis, Browne & Jensen. Mem. ABA, Kansas City Met. Bar Assn. (pres. 1962-63, chmn. grievance com., fee disputes com., Service award, Litigator Emeritus award), Mo. Assn. Trial Attys. (v.p. 1970, pres. 1973), Mo. Bar, Alumni Assn. Sch. Law U. Mo. at Kansas City (pres. 1967, v.p. alumni bd. 1973), Delta Theta Phi, Alpha Sigma Phi. Home: Shawnee Mission Kans. Deceased.

BROWNE, JOHN PATRICK, legal educator; b. East Cleveland, Ohio, Dec. 17, 1935; s. Patrick Joseph and Margaret Anne (O'Grady) B. BS in Social Sci., John Carroll U., 1957; JD, U. Detroit, 1960; MLS, Case Western Res. U., 1965. Bar: Ohio 1960, Mich. 1960, U.S. Dist. Ct. (no. dist.) Ohio 1966, U.S. Dist. Ct. (ea. dist.) Mich. 1966. Assoc. Gallagher, Sharp, Fulton & Norman, Cleve., 1965-69; prof. law Cleve.-Marshall Coll. Law, from 1969. Author: Browne on Ohio Civil Procedure, 1987, Basic Ohio Motion Practice, 1988; co-author: Baldwin's Ohio Civil Practice, 1988, Ohio Civil Rule II and Other Sanctions, 1989; editor Ohio Sanctions Reporter, 1990, Ohio Civil Practice jour., 1990; contbr. articles to profl. jours. Capt. JAGC, U.S. Army, 1960-64. Mem. ABA, Ohio Bar Assn., Mich. Bar Assn., Cleve. Bar Assn., Def. Research Assn., Delta Theta Phi. Democrat. Roman Catholic. Home: Cleveland Ohio Deceased.

BROWNELL, HERBERT, lawyer, former federal official; b. Peru, Nebr., Feb. 20, 1904; s. Herbert and May A. (Miller) B.; m. Doris A. McCarter, June 16, 1934 (dec.); children: Joan, Ann, Thomas McCarter, James Barker; m. Marion R. Taylor, Dec. 23, 1987. AB, U. Nebr., 1924; LLD; LB, Sch. Law, Yale, 1927; LLD, U. Nebr., Am. U., U. Notre Dame, LaFayette Coll., Hamilton Coll., Fordham U., Union Coll., Dickerson Coll., Peru State Coll., Nat. U. of Ireland. Bar: N.Y. 1927. With Root, Clark, Buckner & Ballantine, 1927-29; with Lord, Day & Lord, 1929-53, 57-77, of counsel, 1977-89; atty. gen. of U.S., 1953-57. Vice-chmn. Commn. on Bicentennial of U.S. Constn.; bd. dirs. Ludwig Found. for Cancer Rsch., DIA Art Found., Burkett White Miller Ctr. Mem. Am. Judicature Soc., Assn. Bar City New York, Pilgrims Soc., Order of Coif, Phi Beta Kappa, Sigma Delta Chi, Delta Upsilon. Republican. Methodist. Clubs: Century Assn., Links (N.Y.C.), Metropolitan (Washington). Home: New York N.Y. Died May 1, 1996.

BRUBAKER, CARL H., JR., chemistry educator; b. Passaic, N.J., July 13, 1925; s. Carl H. and Lillian (Rochow) B.; m. Mary Ellen Fiske, June 24, 1949; children: Peter, Carl Fiske. B.S., Franklin and Marshall Coll., 1949; Ph.D., Mass. Inst. Tech., 1952. Asst. prof. Mich. State U., 1952-58, assoc. prof., 1958-61, prof., 1961-92, prof. emeritus, 1992; research assoc. Mass. Inst. Tech., 1952, summer 1955, Argonne Nat. Lab., summer 1957; Smith-Mundt-Fulbright lectr. radiochemistry U. Chile, 1958. Asst. editor: Jour. American Chem. Soc, 1964-69; asso. editor, 1969-70, 73-88, bd. editors, 1970-73; editorial adv. bd. Inorganica Chimica Acta. Served with AUS, 1943-46. Mem. Am. Chem. Soc. (council 1971-74), Royal Soc. Chemistry, AAAS, Sigma Xi, Phi Beta Kappa. Home: Okemos Mich. Died Sept. 24, 1992.

BRUCE, LAWRENCE EVERETT, JR., government representative; b. Huntington, W.Va., Nov. 26, 1945; s. Lawrence Everett and Jo Ann (Tyler) B. BA, Marshall U., 1967; JD, W.Va. U., 1971. Bar: W.Va. 1971. Legis. asst. rep. Ken Hechler, Washington, 1971-73; dir., legal counsel Mortgage Bankers Assn. Am., Washington, 1973-77; gen. counsel, dir. Congl. rels. Inter-Am. Found., Washington, 1978-83; exec. v.p., chief oper. officer AFS Internat., N.Y.C., 1983-85; pres., chief exec. officer U.S. Com. for UNICEF, N.Y.C., 1985-92; former global chair standing group exec. com. UNICEF Nat. Coms., Geneva, Coun. Fgn. Rels., N.Y.C.; bd. dirs. U.S. Com. for UNIFEM, InterAction, Washington. Trustee Internat. Devel. Conf., Washington, 1985-92. Mem. ABA, W.Va. Bar Assn., Internat. Law Assn., The Ams. Soc. Democrat. Mem. Church of Christ, Scientist. Home: New York N.Y. Died Dec. 25, 1992.

BRUENN, HOWARD GERALD, physician; b. Youngtown, Ohio, June 6, 1905; s. Alexander H. and Fanny (Bergstein) B.; m. Dorothy Conner, June 10, 1937; children: Stephen, Nancy Bruenn Clement, James. A.B., Columbia U., 1925, M.S., 1934, D.M.S., 1934; M.D., Johns Hopkins U., 1929. Diplomate: Am. Bd. Internal Medicine, Am. Bd. Cardiovascular Disease. Intern. Boston City Hosp., 1929-31; asst. resident Presbyn. Hosp., N.Y.C., 1932-34; chief med. resident Presbyn. Hosp., 1934-35, attending physician, 1961—; chief cardiology Bethesda Naval Med. Center and 3d Naval Dist., 1961-75; chief Vanderbilt Cardiac Clinic, N.Y.C., 1946-70; asso. attending physician Vanderbilt Cardiac Clinic, 1946-61; clin. prof. medicine Columbia U., N.Y.C., 1962-70; cons. in medicine Columbia Med. Center, 1970—; physician to Pres. F. Roosevelt, 1944-45. Contbr. articles on cardiology to profl. jours. Served to comdr. USNR, 1942-46. Markle fellow medicine, 1935-37. Fellow Am. Heart Assn., Am. Med. Assn., Coun. of Clin. Cardiology; mem. AMA, Soc. Med. Cons. to Armed Svcs., N.Y. County Med. Soc., N.Y. Acad. Medicine, N.Y. Acad. Sci., Harvey Soc. Home: Bronx N.Y. Died July 29, 1995.

BRUNNER, JOHN (K.H.), writer; b. Oxfordshire, England, Sept. 24, 1934; s. Anthony and Felicity (Whittaker) B.; m. Marjorie Rosamond Sauer, July 12, 1958 (dec. 1986); m. Li Yi Tan, Sept. 27, 1991. Attended, Cheltenham Coll., 1948-51. Science fiction novelist songwriter, poet, free-lance writer, 1958-95; abstracto Indsl. Diamond Info. Bur., 1956; editor Spring Book Ltd., 1956-58; Hampstead chmn. Campaign for Nuclea Disarmament, 1961; mem. London Reg. Coun., 1962-63 Nat. Coun., 1964-65; guest novelist in res. U. Kans. Lawrence, 1972; lectr. on sci. fiction to univs. and profl groups in the U.S., Eng. and Italy. Author: (as Keit Woodcott) I Speak for Earth, 1961, The Ladder in Th Sky, 1962, The Psionic Menace, 1963, The Martia Sphinx, 1965, Horses at Home, 1958, The Brink, 1959 Echo in the Skull, 1959, The Hundreth Millennium 1959, Threshold of Eternity, 1959, The World Swappers 1959, Slavers of Space, 1960, The Skynappers, 1960 Sanctuary in the Sky, 1960, The Atlantic Abomination 1960, Meeting at Infinity, 1961, Secret Agent of Terra 1962, The Super Barbarians, 1962, Times Withou Number, 1962, No Future in It, and Other Science Fic tion Stories, 1962, The Dreaming Earth, 1963, The As tronauts Nust Not Land (and) The Rites of One, 1963 Listen! The Stars!, 1963, The Rites of One, 1963, En dless Shadow, 1964, The Crutch of Memory, 1964, T Conquer Chaos, 1964, The Whole Man, 1964, Th Squares of the City, 1965, The Long Result, 1965, Now Then: Three Stories, 1965, Wear The Butcher's Meda 1965, The Altar on Asconel, 1965, Enigma Fro Tantalus, 1965, The Repairmen of Cyclops, 1965, Th Day of the Star Cities, 1965, A Planet of Your Own 1965, No Other God's But Me, 1966, Out of My Mind 1967, The Productions of Time, 1967, Quicksand, 1967 Born Under Mars, 1967, Bedlam Planet, 1968, Catch Falling Star, 1968, Into the Slave Nebula, 1968, No Before Time, 1968, Stand on Zanzibar, 1968 (Hug award 1968), Father of Lies, 1968, A Plague on Bot Your Causes, 1969, Black is the Color, 1969, Double Double, 1969, The Evil That Men Do, 1969, Timescoop 1969, The Jagged Orbit, 1969, Good Men Do Nothing 1970, The Gaudy Shadows, 1970, The Devil's Work 1970, Honky in the Woodpile: A Max Curfew Thriller 1971, The Wrong End of Time, 1971, Traveler in Black 1971, The Sheep Look Up, 1972, Entry to Elsewhen 1971, From This Day Forward, 1972, The Dramaturge of Yan, 1972, Age of Miracles, 1973, The Stone Tha Never Came Down, 1973, Web of Everywhere, 1974 The Shockwave Rider, 1975, Total Eclipse, 1975, Th Book of John Brunner, 1976, Intersteller Empire, 1978 Tomorrow May Even Be Worse, 1978, Foreign Conste lations: The Fantastic Worlds of John Brunner, 1979 The Infinitive of Go, 1980, Players at the Game of Pe ople, 1980, A New Settlement of Old Scores, 1983, Th Great Steamboat Race, 1983, The Tides of Time, 1984 The Compleat Traveller in Black, 1986, The Shift Key 1987, The Best of John Brunner, 1988, Children of th Thunder, 1989, A Maze of Stars, 1992, Muddle Earth 1993. Pilot Officer Royal Air Force, 1953-55. Recipien British Fantasy award, 1966, British Sci. fiction awards Prix Apollo, Bronze Porgie award West Coast Review c Books, Grand Prix du Festival de l'Insolite (France) Cometa d'Argento (twice), Premio Italia, Best Wester SF Writer award European SF Convention, Gilgames award for Sci. Fiction (Spain), Clark Ashton Smit award for Fantasy Poetry, elected Knight of Mar Twain (twice). Mem. European Sci. Fiction Soc. (pas joint pres.), Sci. Fiction Writers of Am., Soc. Author Sci. Fiction Found. (past v.p.), British Sci. Fiction Ass (past chmn.), Herb Soc. Home: Somerset Eng. Die Aug. 25, 1995.

BRUNO, JOSEPH S., meat products company execu tive; b. 1914. With Bruno Bros., Birmingham, Ala 1933-35; ptnr. Bruno's, Birmingham, 1935-46; owne Bruno's Inc., Birmingham, 1946-96, chmn. bd., CEC dir. Died Jan. 21, 1996. Home: Birmingham Ala.

BRUSCA, JACK, artist; b. N.Y.C., Nov. 18, 1939; s John Joseph and Rosemary (Miraglia) B. BFA, Sch. c Visual Arts, 1967. One-man shows include Bonin Gallery, N.Y., 1969-70, 73, 75-77, 83-84, 87, Galeri Bonino, Rio de Janerio, 71, 81, 83, Galeria Arte-Pura Rio de Janerio, 1985, Mulsanne Gallery, Palm Beach Fla., 1986, Paraty Gallery, N.Y. 1989, Carlson Gallery San Francisco; exhibited in group shows at Galeri Bonino, Rio de Janeiro, 1987, Bonino Gallery, N.Y. 1988; represented in permanent collections The Whitne Mus., N.Y., The Queens Mus., N.Y., Chrysler Mus. a Norfolk, Va., Chase Manhattan Bank, N.Y., AT&T N.Y.; and numerous others. Sgt. USAF, 1956-61. Democrat. Roman Catholic. Home: New York N.Y Died July 31, 1993.

BRUTON, JAMES DEWITT, JR., retired judge; b Magazine, Ark., Feb. 2, 1908; s. James David and Patti Lee (Bruton) B.; m. Quintilla Geer, June 11, 1932. J.D U. Fla., 1931. Bar: Fla. 1931. Practiced law Plant City 1931-61; asst. criminal court solicitor Tampa, 1934-37 elected to Fla. Ho. of Reps., 1935-36; municipal judg Plant City, 1937-57; corp. and civil lawyer, 1931-61 probate judge Tampa, 1961-64; circuit judge 13th Jud Circuit Fla., 1964-75; founder, owner Bruton's Audubo Acres Bird Sanctuary (donated to U. Fla. Law Coll. Plant City, 1952-95; dir. Tampa Abstract and Title In Co., Hillsboro Bank, Plant City, Fla. Bd. dirs. Chi dren's Home, Tampa, 1947-67, Tampa Mental Healt Assn., 1962-68, Inter-Profl. Family Council, Inc Tampa chpt. ARC, 1967-68; bd. dirs., life mem. Tamp Humane Soc.; mem. Fla. State Bd. Law Examiner 1950-54; chmn. bd. editors Fla. Bar Jour., 1950-52. Recipient Trustee's award U. Fla. Law Coll., Disting lumnus award U. Fla., 1988. Fellow Am. Coll. Probate Counsel (jud. fellow 1961), Am. Bar Found. (life ellow 1961); mem. Fla. Mcpl. Judges Assn. (pres. 1956-7), C. of C. (dir.), Plant City Civic Music Assn. (pres. 939), Tampa Symphony Soc. (dir. 1952), Jr. C. of C. res. 1940), Fla. County Judges Assn. (v.p. 1962), U. la. Alumni Assn. (v.p. 1948), ABA (ho. of dels. 1951-5), Fla. Bar Assn. (state chmn. com. on integration, ov. 1949-50, chmn. com. on citizenship 1952-53, hmn. com. on co-operation with Am. Bar Assn. 1956-9, chmn. com. on world peace through law 1959-63), ampa Bar Assn., Fla. Bar (del. to Am. Bar Assn. Conf. n World Peace 1959, chmn. com. on memls. 1962-72), eldon Soc. London, Am. Judicature Soc. (dir. 1953-58), .udubon Soc. (life), Am. Ornithologists Union (life), la. Cattle Assn., Fla. Hist. Soc. (life, dir. 1967-68), ast Hillsborough County Hist. Soc. (life patron), SAR, ons Confederate Vets., Blue Key, Chi Phi. Methodist. lubs: Elk; Kiwanian (past lt. gov. Plant City club), ampa Executives (Tampa) (pres. 1951-52, dir. 1948-5), Tampa Audubon (Tampa), University (Tampa). ome: Plant City Fla. Died Jan. 10, 1995.

RYANT, DOUGLAS WALLACE, librarian; b. isalia, Calif., June 20, 1913; s. Albert George and thel (Wallace) B.; m. Rene Leilani Kuhn, Apr. 6, 1953; dau., Heather Corbally Bryant Jordan. Student, U. lunich, Germany, 1932-33; A.B., Stanford, 1935; A.M. L.S., U. Mich., 1938. Asst. curator printed books Villiam L. Clements Library, U. Mich., 1936-38; sr. eference asst., tech. dept. Detroit Pub. Library, 1938-1; asst. chief Burton Hist. Collection, 1941-42; asst. brarian U. Calif. at Berkeley, 1946-49; attache Am. mbassy, London, 1949-52; adminstrv. asst. librarian arvard Coll. Library, 1952-55; asso. dir. Harvard U. ibrary, 1955-64; univ. librarian Harvard, 1964-72, dir. niv. library, prof. bibliography, 1972-79, prof. bibography, librarian emeritus, 1979-94; trustee, exec. dir. m. Trust for Brit. Library, 1979-90, pres., 1990-94; em. U.S. nat. commn. for UNESCO, 1953-55; v.p. nternat. Fedn. Library Assns., 1952-58, Internat. Fedn. or Documentation, 1956-58; cons. Ford Found., nkara, Turkey, 1954, Rockefeller Found., London, 956; lectr., cons. Japanese univ. libraries, 1963; cons. st. Am. Studies, Free U., Berlin, 1964-66, London ch. Econs., 1965-66; chmn. bd. dirs. Center Research ibraries, 1969-70. Served to lt. comdr. USNR, World Var II; head tech. data br. Bur. Aeros. Navy Dept., Vashington. Fellow Am. Acad. Arts and Scis., Royal oc. Arts; mem. ALA (chmn. internat. relations com. 952-55, chmn. coordinating com. on Slavic and East uropean library resources 1959-61), Assn. Research ibraries chmn. Com. on preservation research library aterials 1960-68, pres. 1969-70, Mass. Hist. Soc., olonial Soc. Mass., Am. Antiquarian Soc. Clubs: rolier (N.Y.), Harvard (N.Y.); Odd Volumes (Boston). Home: Lexington Mass. Died June 12, 1994; interred oncord, Mass.

RYANT, ROBERT EDWARD, architect; b. Palmetto, a., Sept. 14, 1931; s. James Madison and Oda Bell .ong) B.; m. Shirley Mae Smothers, July 17, 1954. .Arch., Howard U., 1954. Registered architect, D.C. rchitect in tng. B.L. Frishman & Assocs., Washington, 956-58; project architect, assoc. E.W. Dreyfuss & As-ocs., Washington, 1958-69; ptnr. Bryant & Bryant, Vashington, 1969-95; guest critic U.S. Army War Coll., 974; internat. exchange del. to China, People to People, 982. Mem. Community Adv. Group Pa. Ave. Devel. orp., Washington, 1974; bd. dirs. Boys' & Girls' Club f Greater Washington, 1981-83, v.p., 1984; mem. amond-Riggs Civic Assn., Washington, 1961; active at. fin. com. Ted Kennedy for Pres., Washington, 1980. ecipient Achievement award NAACP, 1968. Fellow IA; mem. Nat. Ctr. for Barrier Free Soc., Am. Arbiation Assn., D.C. Council Black Architects, Nat. ech. Assn. Democrat. Methodist. Died Feb. 2, 1995. ome: Washington D.C.

RYND, SCOTT RICHARD, screen writer, artist anagement executive; b. Chgo., Oct. 29, 1954; s. ichard J. and Betty L. (Schluraff) B. B.F.A. in Com-unications, Pacific Lutheran U.; M.F.A. in Theatre 1gmt., UCLA. Formerly pres. Am Theatrical Prodns., os Angeles, fin. v.p. Hollywood's New View (Calif.), roducing mgr. UCLA's Resident Theatre Co.; former gr. Los Angeles Ballet; former exec. dir. Circuit letwork; Recipient Amoco Oil award of Excellence, ohn F. Kennedy Ctr., Hollywood Wall of Fame ward. Lutheran. Died Sept. 17, 1993. Home: San afael Calif.

UCHANAN, JOHN CHALKLEY, physician, state xecutive; b. Darwin, Va., Jan. 20, 1911; s. Noah Jackson nd Minnie (Willis) B.; B.S., U. Va., 1933, M.D., 1951; . Carol King Phipps, July 17, 1945. Intern, Jefferson-Iillman Hosp., Birmingham, Ala., 1951-52; resident in ternal medicine U. Va. Hosp., Charlottesville, 1952-55; ractice medicine specializing in internal medicine, Wise, a., 1956-86; mem. Va. Senate, 1972-91. Mem. adv. bd. linch Valley Coll., 1971-75; mem. Wise County lousing and Devel. Authority, 1971-91. Served in USN, 942-46. Diplomate Am. Bd. Internal Medicine. Mem. lat. Conf. State Legislatures. Democrat. Died Apr. 15, 991. Home: Wise Va.

UCHANAN, WILLIAM EUGENE, former wire orks corporation executive; b. Appleton, Wis., Jan. 11,

1903; s. Gustavus E. and Josephine (Pond) B.; m. Josephine Breneman, Jan. 3, 1931; children: Charles, William Eugene, Jean, Robert. B.S., Dartmouth, 1924, M.A.; hon., 1962, LL.D., 1977; M.B.A., Harvard U., 1926; M.A. (hon.), Lawrence U., 1959, LL.D. (hon.), 1978. With Appleton Wire Works, Inc. (merged with Albany Felt Co. (N.Y.), 1969, name now Albany Internat. Corp.), 1926-75, v.p., 1935-38, pres., chief exec. officer, 1938-69, chmn. bd., dir., 1969-75; chmn., dir. Outagamie Corp., Appleton, 1958-83; chmn., dir. Fox Valley Corp., 1974-92, dir. emeritus, 1992-93. Trustee Lawrence U., Appleton, 1938-77; trustee Dartmouth Coll., 1961-73. Mem. Sigma Nu. Republican. Conglist. Clubs: Mason, Rotarian, Riverview Country, North Shore Golf; Gulf Stream Golf (Delray Beach), Country Club of Fla. (Delray Beach). Home: Village of Golf Fla. Deceased.

BUCHBINDER, GEORGEDA, physician, educator; b. N.Y.C., Feb. 2, 1939; d. Jacob H. and Gertrude (Rose) B. BA, Sarah Lawrence Coll., 1960; MA, Columbia U., 1966, PhD, 1973; MD, U. Chgo., 1981; MPH, Johns Hopkins U., 1984. Diplomate Am. Bd. Med. Examiners, Am. Bd. Preventive Medicine. Teaching asst. anthropology Columbia U., N.Y.C., 1962; lectr. White Plains (N.Y.) Adult Edn. Ctr., 1962, CUNY, 1963-65, Bklyn. Coll., 1965-70; asst. prof. Queens (N.Y.) Coll., 1970-77; cons. nutritional anthropology So. Highlands Devel. Project World Bank, Papua, New Guinea, 1977-79; vis. lectr. dept. psychiatry Chgo. Med. Sch., 1979-80; resident in ob-gyn. Columbia Presbyn. Med. Ctr., N.Y.C., 1981-83; resident in gen. preventative medicine Johns Hopkins, Balt., 1983-85, adj. instr. internat. health, 1984; assoc. prof. internat. health Sch. Pub. Health U. Hawaii, Honolulu, 1985—, assoc. prof. epidmiology, 1986; cons. many health care project in Hawaii, Asia and the Pacific, 1985—. Contbr. articles to profl. jours. Recipient numerous rsch. scholarships, fellowships and grants, 1956—. Mem. AMA, Hawaii Med. Assn., Nat. Council for Internat. Health, Am. Pub. Health Assn., AAAS, Am. Anthrop. Assn., Am. Assn. Phys. Anthropologists, Med. Anthropology Assn., Assn., Social Anthropologists in Oceania, Sigma Xi. Home: Honolulu Hawaii

BUCHSBAUM, SOLOMON JAN, physicist; b. Stryj, Poland, Dec. 4, 1929; came to U.S., 1953, naturalized, 1957; s. Jacob and Berta (Rutherfoer) B.; m. Phyllis N. Isenman, July 3, 1955; children: Rachel Joy, David Joel, Adam Louis. B.S., McGill U., 1952, M.S., 1953; Ph.D., Mass. Inst. Tech., 1957. Mem. tech. staff Bell Labs., Murray Hill, N.J., 1958-61; dept. head Bell Labs., 1961-65, dir., 1965-68; v.p. Sandia Labs., Albuquerque, 1968-71; exec. dir. Bell Labs., 1971-76, v.p., 1976-79, sr. v.p., 1979-93; research in gaseous and solid state plasmas, communications; sr. cons. Def. Sci. Bd., chmn., 1972-77, 81-93; mem. AEC Controlled Thermonuclear Fusion Com., 1965-72, Pres.'s Sci. Adv. Com., 1970-73, Pres.'s Com. on Sci. and Tech., 1975-76; mem. fusion power coordinating com. ERDA, 1972-76, adv. group sci. and tech. NSF, 1976-77; chmn. Energy Research Adv. Bd., 1978-81; mem. Naval Research Adv. Com., 1978-81; mem. vis. com. MIT, 1977-93, mem. corp. devel. com., 1980-93; cons. Office Sci. and Tech., 1976-82; chmn. White House Sci. Council, 1982-89; trustee Rand Corp., 1982-92; mem. Draper Lab. Corp., 1983-93, bd. dirs.; bd. Govs. Argonne Nat. Lab., 1985-92; mem. Pres.'s Coun. Advisors on Sci. and Tech., 1990-93; mem. DOE Inertial Confinement Fusion Adv. Com./Defense Programs (ICFAC/DP), 1992-93. Assoc. editor: Revs. Modern Physics, 1968-72, Jour. Applied Physics, 1968-70, Physics of Fluids, 1963-64; co-author: Waves in Plasmas, 1963; contbr. numerous articles to profl. jours. Trustee Argonne Univs. Assn., 1979-82. Moyse traveling fellow, 1953-54; IBM fellow, 1954-56; recipient Anne Molson Gold medal, Soc. of Def. medal for Outstanding Pub. Service, 1977; Sec. of Energy award for exceptional pub. svc., 1981; Nat. Medal of Sci., 1986; Arthur M. Bueche award, 1990. Fellow Am. Phys. Soc. (chmn. div. plasma physics 1968, mem. council 1973-76), IEEE (Frederk Philips award 1987), Am. Acad. Arts and Scis., AAAS; mem. NAS, NAE (exec. com. 1975-76). Home: Westfield N.J. Died Mar. 8, 1993; interred B'Nai Abraham, Union, N.J.

BUCKINGHAM, LISLE MARION, lawyer; b. Monroeville, Ohio, July 20, 1895; s. Jesse and Bretna (Latham) B.; m. Mildred Heter, Dec. 9, 1920 (dec. Sept. 1951); m. Ruth Heter, Feb. 25, 1959. A.B., Western Res. U., 1917, LL.B., 1919. Bar: Ohio bar 1919. And since practiced trial law and served as corp. counsel Akron; sr. partner firm Buckingham, Doolittle & Burroughs, from 1942; asst. county prosecutor, 1922; gen. counsel Ohio Motor Trucking Assn. Assn. of Motor Carries of Ohio, 1951; dir. 1st Nat. Bank, Roadway Express (many other corps.); Trial counsel for entire rubber industry in hearings at Washington and before War Labor Bd., 1943- 45; chief counsel in Big 4 Negotiations for Firestone, B. F. Goodrich, Goodyear and U.S. Rubber Cos., 1946-47. Trustee Community Chest; chmn. drive, 1933, Y.M.C.A.; Peoples Hosp., Summit County Tb Assn.; pres. Akron Community Trusts; trustee U. Akron, pres. devel. found.; trustee The GAR Found.; gov. Western Res. U., 1947-69; mem. Ohio State Bar Examiners, 1938-43, chmn., 1943. Mem. ABA, Ohio Bar Assn., Akron Bar Assn. (pres. 1931), Akron C. of C. (pres. 1935), Phi Beta Kappa, Delta Upsilon, Order of Coif, Phi Delta Phi, Delta Sigma Rho.

Presbyn. (trustee). Clubs: Mason, Rotary (trustee). Home: Akron Ohio Deceased.

BUCKLEY, JOSEPH PAUL, pharmacologist, educator; b. Bridgeport, Conn., Jan. 12, 1924; m. Shirley Elizabeth Jane Shipman, Aug. 16, 1947. B.S., U. Conn., 1949; M.S., Purdue U., 1951, Ph.D., 1952. Registered pharmacist, Conn., Tex. Asst. prof. pharmacology U. Pitts., 1952-55, assoc. prof., 1955-58, prof., head dept. pharmacology, 1958-73; prof. Sch. of Dentistry, 1963-73; assoc. dean Sch. Pharmacy U. Pitts., 1969-73, dean Coll. Pharmacy, 1973-87; prof. pharmacology Inst. for Cardiovascular Studies U. Houston, 1973-91, dir., 1977-91; staff pharmacologist St. John's Gen. Hosp., Pitts., Western Pa. Hosp.; cons. pharmacologist Carter-Wallace Labs., Cranberry, N.J., E.R. Squibb & Sons, Princeton, N.J., VA Hosp., Houston; hon. prof. San Carlos U., Guatemala City, Guatemala, 1967-93; trustee U.S. Phamacopeial Conv., 1985-90; vis. prof. U. Calif., San Diego, 1987; adj. prof. dept. medicine Baylor U. Coll. of Medicine, Houston, 1987-93;. Author: (with Ferrario) Central Actions of Angiotension and Related Hormones, 1977; Central Nervous System Mechanisms in Hypertension, 1981, Brain Peptides and Catecholamines in Cardiovascular Regulation, 1987; cons. editor: Jour. Behavioral Pharmacology; editor in chief Jour. Clin. and Exptl. Hypertension; mem. editorial bd. Jour. of Ethnopharmacology, Rsch. Communications in Chem. Pathology and Pharmacology; contbr. articles to profl. jours. Served as 2d lt. USAAF, 1943-45. Decorated Air medal with clusters; recipient award Angiology Research Found., 1965, award Am. Pharmacodynamics Assn., 1966; Disting. Alumnus award Purdue U. Sch. Pharmacy, 1984; Am. Found. Pharm. Edn. fellow, 1950-52. Mem. Acad. Pharm. Scis. (chmn. sect. pharmacology and bio-chemistry 1965-67, v.p. 1969-70), Am. Soc. Pharm. and Exptl. Therapeutics, Tex. Pharmacologists Assn. (pres. 1982-91), Am. Pharmacodynamics Assn. (Pharmacodynamics award 1966), AAAS (sec. sect pharm. scis. 1961-67, chmn. sect., v.p. 1969, 76), N.Y. Acad. Sci., Interam. Soc. Hypertension (dir.), Council High Blood Pressure Research(med. adv. bd.), Phi Kappa Phi, Sigma Xi, Rho Chi, Phi Sigma, Phi Lambda Upsilon, Kappa Psi. Presbyterian. Home: Durham N.C. Died May, 17, 1993; interred East Cemetery, Manchester, Conn.

BUCKLEY, PAGE SCOTT, manufacturing consultant; b. Hampton, Va., June 23, 1918; s. Walter Arthur and Cora Byrd (Edwards) B.; m. Betty Hill, Jan. 29, 1948; children: Ann, Kebba, Judith, Elizabeth. BA, Columbia U., 1939, BS, 1940; DEng (hon.), Lehigh U., 1975. Registered profl. engr., Del., Calif. Prin. cons. engring. dept. DuPont, Newark, Del., 1962-87. Author 3 books. Fellow Am. Inst. Chem. Engrs., Instrument Soc. Am. Home: Wheat Ridge Colo. Died July 25, 1995.

BUCKNAM, JAMES ROMEO, consultant labor-management relations; b. Livermore Falls, Maine, Apr. 26, 1911; s. Howard Leland and Rose Alma (Deschenes) B.; m. Adrienne Meteyer, Aug. 6, 1934 (div. Dec. 1965); children: Beverly Anne Buckman Marcou, Howard V., James L., Nancy R. Bucknam Weidinger; m. Cecile LeBlanc, Jan. 14, 1967 (dec. Dec. 1975); m. Myrna Nicholas, May 23, 1981. Student, U. N.H., 1930-33. Reporter-editor Berlin (N.H.) Reporter, 1933-43; deskman Manchester (N.H.) Union Leader, 1943-49, night editor, 1949-62, mng. editor, 1962-69, exec. editor, 1969-79, personnel mgr., labor relations dir., 1971-79; cons. labor-mgmt. relations, 1979—; editor, pub. The Bow (N.H.) Times, 1987—; mem. Appeals Tribunal N.H. Dept. Employment Security; mem. ad hoc panel N.H. Pub. Employees Labor Relations Bd. Mem. Gov.'s Traffic Safety Commn., 1963-65; chmn. N.H. Traffic Safety Commn., 1965-85; mem. CJIS adv. bd. to N.H. Commn. on Crime and Delinquency, 1972-73; mem. bd. rev. Boy Scouts Am., 1968-70; mem. Joint Hosp. Commn., Manchester, 1969-71,Bow (N.H.) Bus. Assn.; pres., bd. govs., mem. adv. bd. Notre Dame Hosp., 1969-71; former bd. dirs. N.H. Heart Assn., Nat. Kidney Found. N.H.; trustee Castle Jr. Coll., Windham, N.H., 1971—, chmn. 1987-88; moderator Town of Bow, N.H., 1980-83. Served with USMCR, World War II, PTO. Mem. Am. Assn. Automotive Medicine, Internat. Assn. Accident and Traffic Medicine, Am. Legion, VFW, Marine Corps Combat Corrs. Assn., Marine Corps Res. Officers Assn., Res. Officers Assn. U.S. (pres. Concord chpt.), Bow Club (Citizen of Yr. award 1991), Community Men's Club, KC (4th degree), Rotary (Paul Harris fellow 1991). Home: Bow N.H. Died Aug. 25, 1993.

BUDA, ALEKS, science administrator, history researcher, educator; b. Elbasan, Albania, Sept. 7, 1910; s. Dhimiter and Elena (Kasapi) B.; m. Vasilika Stratoberdha, Nov. 24, 1941; children: Tatjana, Liro. Student, U. Vienna, Austria, 1938; prof., U. Tirana, Albania, 1958; academician, Acad. Sci. Tirana, Albania, 1972; fgn. mem., Bulgarian Acad. Sci., Sofia, 1979. History educator Gymnasium, Tirana, Albania, 1938-40, Lycium, Korca, Albania, 1940-41; dir. Nat. Libr., Tirana, Albania, 1945-46; history rsch. Inst. of Scis., Tirana, Albania, 1947-55, Inst. Linguistics, History, Tirana, Albania, 1955-57; prof. history U. Tirana, 1957-72; pres. Acad. Sci. Tirana, 1972-93. Author: Historical Notes, vol. 1, 2, 1986; co-author: (chief ed.) History of Albania , vol. 1, 1959, vol. 2, 1965; contbr. articles to profl. jours. Mem. Gen. Coun. Dem. Front,

Tirana, 1985; deputy People's Coun., 1950-91. Recipient Tchr. of People's award Presidium of People's Coun., 1977, Great Golden medal Pres. Austria, 1991. Mem. Internat. Soc. for South-East Europe Studies (vice-chmn. 1966, medal 1973), German Soc. for South-East Europe (hon., diploma 1981). Home: Tiranë Albania Died July 7, 1993; interred Sharre, Tirane, Albania.

BUELL, TEMPLE HOYNE, architect; b. Chgo., Sept. 9, 1895; s. Charles Clinton and Modrea (Hoyne) B.; children: Callae Mackey Buell Gilman, Temple Hoyne, Beverly Milne Buell More, Marjorie Daphne Buell Groos. Grad., Lake Forest Acad., 1912; BS, U. Ill., 1916; MS, Columbia U., 1917, DHL (hon.), 1986; DHL (hon.), U. Colo., 1987. Registered architect, Colo., N.Mex., Tex., Wyo., Nebr., Utah. Founder, pres. Buell & Co., architects & engrs., Denver, from 1923, Buell Devel. Corp., from 1949; doing bus. as Buell & Co. (real estate devel.), from 1985; pres. Sandex Equities, Ltd., from 1985. Spl. works include univ. bldgs. secondary and elementary schs., municipal, state and fed. bldgs., shopping ctrs., housing devels., others. Chmn. Cherry Hills Planning Commn., from 1937, Arapahoe County Planning Commn., from 1939, Tri-County Planning Commn. and Upper Plate Valley Planning Commn., 1940-42; founder Temple Hoyne Buell Found., 1963. Served to 1st lt. U.S. Army, 1917-19. Recipient Alumni medal Columbia U., 1932, Deans medal Sch. Architecture, 1938; Alumni Achievement award U. Ill., 1977, Disting. Service award U. Colo., 1985. Fellow AIA; Mem. Colo. Soc. Engrs., Soc. Mil. Engrs., Nat. Council Archtl. Registration Bds., Chi Psi (pres. from 1967). Clubs: Denver, Denver Athletic, Country, City (Denver); Cherry Hills Country (pres. 1943); Metropolitan (N.Y.C.); Camp Fire of Am. (Chappaqua, N.Y.); Regency (N.Y.C.); California (Los Angeles). Lodges: Masons (32 deg.); Shriners; K.T; Jesters; Rotary. Home: Englewood Colo. Deceased.

BUENO Y MONREAL, JOSÉ MARIA CARDINAL, archbishop emeritus of Seville (Spain); b. Zaragoza, Spain, Sept. 11, 1904. Ordained priest Roman Catholic Ch., 1927; ordained bishop of Jaca, Mar. 19, 1946; bishop of Vitoria, 1950; titular archbishop of Antioch in Pisidia and coadjutor archbishop of Seville, 1957-81, archbishop emeritus, 1981—, archbishop of Seville, 1957—, elevated to Sacred Coll. of Cardinals, 1958; titular ch. Sts. Vitus, Modestus and Crescentia. Died Aug. 20, 1987. Home: Seville Spain

BUERGER, DAVID BERNARD, lawyer; b. Phila., Dec. 1, 1909; s. Charles B. and Ada (Fischel) B.; m. Anne M. Fortun, June 30, 1946; children: David C., Charles A. AB, U. Pitts., 1928, AM, 1929; LLB, Columbia U., 1932, JD, 1969; LLD, Davis & Elkins Coll., 1995. Bar: Pa. 1932, U.S. Supreme Ct. Practiced in Pitts.; mem., sr. ptnr. Buchanan, Ingersoll, Rodewald, Kyle & Buerger (and predecessors), 1932-83; sole practice, 1983-96, litigation in 48 states; lectr. taxation and corp. law Com. Continuing Legal Edn., Am. Law Inst., 1951-96; pres., dir. Fourteen Bell Corp., Jersey City Investment Co.; bd. dirs. Geston Milway; sec., Elmhurst Co.; sec., bd. dirs. Vantage Broadcasting Co., Heritage Hills Realty, Munroe Enterprises, Inc., Power Assocs., Inc.; gen. counsel, trustee Davis and Elkins Coll.; gen. counsel Magee Women's Hosp., Hunt Found., Roy A. Hunt Found., Allegheny Acad.; trustee Helen Clay Frick Found. Editor Columbia Law Rev, 1930-32. Pres. Hampton Civic Assn., 1956-57. Fellow Am. Bar Found.; mem. ABA, Am. Law Inst. (life), Am. Arbitration Assn., Am. Judicature Soc., Wildwood Golf Club (hon.), Sigma Alpha Mu, Omicron Delta Kappa, Delta Sigma Rho. Home: Sewickley Pa. Died Jan. 5, 1996.

BUGG, JUNE MOORE, state legislator; b. Altoona, Ala., Oct. 7, 1919; d. Sims Smith and Bertie Edith (Powell) Moore; m. Bill Knight Bugg (dec. 1987); children: Barbara Bugg, Bill Jr. BA in Edn., U. Ala., 1940, postgrad., 1970; MS in Edn., Jacksonville (Ala.) State U., 1970, postgrad., 1970. Librarian Gadsden (Ala.) High Sch., 1941-46, tchr. English, 1952-65; librarian Ala. Tech. Coll., Gadsden, 1949-51; mem. Ala. Ho. of Reps., Montgomery, 1983-93; mem. com. on devel. of cultural resources Ala. Ho. of Reps., vice chair edn. com., mem. budget com.; libratian Gadsden Ctr., U. Ala.; student-tchr. supr., U. Ala., Birmingham, 1975-80. Chair Project Our Town, Gadsden; mem. Ala. Dem. Exec. Com., 1982-90; mem. adv. coun. Ret. Sr. Vol. Program, Etowah County, Ala.; mem. adv. bd. Commun. Intensive Treatment for Youth of Etowah County, RSVP Etowah County. Recipient Pres.'s award Downtown Action Council, 1976-77, award AAUW, 1981; inducted into Ala. Sr. Citizens' Hall of Fame, 1990. Mem. Alpha Xi Delta (Order of Rose 1987). Methodist. Home: Gadsden Ala. Died May 18, 1993.

BUHSE, HOWARD EDWARD, financial consultant; b. Prairie du Chien, Wis., June 4, 1906; s. Maximilian E. and Caroline (Grelle) B.; m. Virginia Dixon, Sept. 30, 1933; children: Howard, Joan, Deborah. J.D., U. Minn., 1929. Chmn. bd. Nat. Aviation & Tech. Corp.; chmn. Chgo. Assn. Stock Exchange Firms, 1948; chmn. bd. govs. Nat. Assn. Securities Dealers, 1951; bd. govs. N.Y. Stock Exchange, 1961-67; mng. ptnr. Hornblower & Weeks-Hemphill, Noyes, 1959-71; sr. mng. dir. Loeb Rhoades, Hornblower & Co., 1978-79; chmn. bd. Nat. Telecommunications and Tech., Nat. Aviation and Tech. Pres., Fairfield Found. Diocese of Bridgeport; mem. Winnetka Bd. Edn., Ill., 1952-58, pres., 1957-58. Decorated Knight of St. Gregory. Mem. Sigma Phi Epsilon, Phi Alpha Delta. Clubs: Metropolitan, Bond (N.Y.C.) (pres. 1969); Silver Springs Country (Ridgefield, Conn.). Lodge: Knights of Malta. Home: Danbury Conn. Died June 9, 1994.

BUIE, BENNETT FRANK, geologist, educator; b. Patrick, S.C., Jan. 9, 1910; s. Daniel Franklin and Mary Julia (Smith) B.; m. Susanna Townsend Peirce, Aug. 9, 1938; children: Susanna (Mrs. Susanna Matthews), Julia (Mrs. Julia B. Steinitz), Carolyn (Mrs. Carolyn B. Erdener), Margaret (Mrs. J. Duncan Keppie). BS, U. S.C., 1930; MS (research fellow 1930-32), Lehigh U., 1932; MA, Harvard U., 1934, PhD, 1939; grad., Command and Gen. Staff Coll., 1939. Asst. in geology Harvard U., 1932-37, resident adv., proctor, 1935-37; mem. Shaler Meml. Expdn., summers 1933-35; geologist subs. Seaboard Oil Co., Iran and Afghanistan, 1937-38; mem. subs. Standard Oil Co., Calif., Brit. India and Tex., 1939-42; prof. geology U. S.C., Calif., Brit. India and Tex., 1946-56; geologist S.C. Devel. Bd., Calif., Brit. India and Tex., 1946-56; prof. geology Fla. State U., 1956-81, emeritus prof., 1981—, chmn. dept., 1956-64; cons. geologist J.M. Huber Corp., 1958-88. Research on world resources of kaolin and phosphate. Condr. del. geologists to USSR and Middle East, People-to-People Internat. Citizen Ambassador Program, 1979. Served to maj. C.E., AUS, 1942-46; col. Res. ret. Decorated Bronze Star and Order Red Star for work in Persian Gulf Command (USSR); recipient Algernon Sydney Sullivan award U. S.C., Pres. Bush Task Force medal, 1990. Fellow Geol. Soc. Am., Explorers Club, Mineral. Soc. Am.; mem. Soc. Econ. Geologists, AIME, Soc. Mining Engrs., Am. Assn. Petroleum Geologists, Carolina Geol. Soc. (pres. 1958), Sigma Xi, Omicron Delta Kappa. Episcopalian. Home: Tallahassee Fla. Died Apr. 9, 1992; buried Oak Grove Meth. Ch., Cheraw, S.C.

BUKOWSKI, CHARLES, author; b. Andernach, Ger., Aug. 16, 1920; came to U.S., 1923; m. Linda Beighle; 1 child, Marina Louise. Student, Los Angeles City Coll., 1939-41. Editor: Laugh Literary and Man the Humping Guns, 1970; author (novels): Post Office, 1971, Factotum, 1975, Women, 1978, Ham on Rye, 1982, Hollywood, 1989, Pulp, 1994; (short stories) Confessions of a Man Insane Enough to Live with Beasts, 1965, All the Assholes in the World and Mine, 1966, Notes of a Dirty Old Man, 1969, Erections, Ejaculations and General Tales of Ordinary Madness, 1972, South of No North, 1973, You Kissed Lilly, 1978, Hot Water Music, 1983, There's No Business, 1984; (poetry) Flower, Fist and Bestial Wail, 1960, Poems and Drawings, 1962, Longshot Pomes for Broke Players, 1962, Run with the Hunted, 1962, It Catches My Heart in Its Hands, 1963, Crucifix in a Deathhand, 1965, Cold Dogs in the Courtyard, 1965, The Genius of the Crowd, 1966, At Terror Street and Agony Way, 1968, Poems Written Before Jumping Out of an 8 Story Window, 1968, The Days Run Away Like Wild Horses Over the Hills, 1969, Fire Station, 1970, Mockingbird Wish Me Luck, 1972, Me and Your Sometimes Love Poems, 1972, While the Music Played, 1973, Burning in Water, Drowning in Flame, 1974, Africa, Paris, Greece, 1975, Scarlet, 1976, Maybe Tomorrow, 1977, We'll Take Them, 1978, Love is a Dog from Hell, 1978, Play the Piano, 1979, Dangling in the Tournefortia, 1981, Horsemeat, 1982, War All The Time, 1984, You Get So Alone At Times That It Just Makes Sense, 1986, (poems) The Roominghouse Madrigals, 1988, (stories and poems) Septagenarian Stew, 1990, (poems) In the Shadow of the Rose, 1991, The Last Night of the Earth Poems, 1992, Screams From the Balcony (Letters from the Sixties), 1993; (screenplay) Barfly, 1979, film produced from, 1987; (travel book) Shakespeare Never Did This, 1979; narrator: (documentary film) Poetry in Motion (Ron Mann), 1983; film produced from short stories: Tales of Ordinary Madness (Marco Ferreri), 1982. Nat. Endowment for Arts grantee, 1974. Home: San Pedro Calif. Died Mar. 9, 1994.

BULKELEY, JOHN DUNCAN, retired naval officer; b. N.Y.C., Aug. 19, 1911; s. Frederick Fiske and Elizabeth (MacCuaig) B.; m. Hilda Alice Wood, Nov. 10, 1938; children—Joan Bulkeley Stade, John, Peter, Regina Bulkeley Day, Diana Bulkeley Lindsay. B.S., U.S. Naval Acad., 1933. Commd. ensign U.S. Navy, 1934, advanced through grades to vice adm., 1988; comdr. PT boats Philippines and Normandy Invasion; comdr. USS Endicott, Stribling, 1941-44; mem. staff Naval Acad., Annapolis, Md., 1946-48; exec. officer USS Mt. Olympus, 1948-49; chief weapons div. mil. liaison com. to AEC Washington, 1950-52; comdr. destroyer div. 132 Korea, 1952-54; chief of staff to comdr. cruiser div. 5, 1954-55, mem. joint staff, Joint Chiefs of Staff, 1956-58, comdr. Tolovana, 1958, comdr. destroyer squadron 12, 1958-59, comdr. Clarksville (Tenn.) Base, 1960-62; comdr. Naval Base Guantanamo Bay, Cuba, 1963-65, comdr. cruiser-destroyer flotilla 8, 1966-67; pres. Bd. Insp. and Survey, Washington, 1967-88, ret., 1988. Decorated Congl. Medal of Honor, Navy Cross, D.S.C. (23, D.S.M. (3), Silver Star (2), Legion of Merit (2), Purple Heart; Croix de Guerre with Crimson Star (France); recipient Chairman's award Am. Assn. Engring. Socs., 1980, Harold E. Saunders award for outstanding contbns. to naval engring. Am. Soc. Naval Engrs., 1981, Outstanding Leadership award in Engring., ASME, 1982. Home: Silver Spring Md. Died Apr. 6, 1996.

BULLARD, EDWARD PAYSON, IV, non-profit executive; b. Bridgeport, Conn., Feb. 23, 1935; s. Edward Payson III and Jane (Alling) B.; m. Gail Elizabeth Grew, June 22, 1957 (div. 1973); children: Jennifer Jane, Amy Brewster; m. Carol Mary Harrison, Mar. 2, 1974; 1 child, Payson Harrison. Diploma, Deerfield acad., Mass., 1953; BS, Yale U., 1957; LHD (hon.), Sacred Heart U., 1982; DEng (hon), Bridgeport Engring. Inst., 1983. Design engr. The Bullard Co., Bridgeport, 1958-61, chief devel. engr., 1961-63; mission assoc. United Ch. Bd. World Ministries, Ghana, W. Africa, 1963-64; D of Engring The Bullard Co., Bridgeport, 1964-65, mgr. prodn. engr., 1965-67; prin., founder Technoserve Inc., Norwalk, Conn., 1968-96; dir. Am. Coun. Voluntary Internat. Action, N.Y., 1988-96. co-inventor machine tool patents, 1962-68. Pres. United Neighbors Self Devel., Conn., 1965-67, Shelter for the World Inc., Conn., 1967-68; trustee Sacred Heart U., Conn., 1983-89. Recipient Heritage award Deerfield Acad., Mass., 1984, John W. Gardner Leadership award Ind. Sector, Washington, 1990; honoree Newcomen Soc., 1993. Mem. Coun. Fgn. Rels. Inc., Bretton Woods Com., Overseas Devel. Coun., Yale Club N.Y.C., Wilton Riding Club. Mem. United Ch. of Christ. Died May 30, 1996.

BULLOCK, H. RIDGELY, management and investment executive, lawyer; b. N.Y.C., June 16, 1934; s. H. Ridgely and Marian (Batterman) B.; m. Leslie Kitchell deBraux, Sept. 26, 1973 (div. June 1990); children: James William, Sylvia Marian, David Duncan Ridgely, Ariane deBraux, Sabrina Carpenter, Karena Ridgely. BA, Colby Coll., 1955, LLD (hon.), 1991; JD, U. Va., 1967. Bar: Va. 1967, N.Y. 1970. Ptnr. Mudge Rose Guthrie, Alexander & Ferdon, N.Y.C., 1970-75, of counsel, 1976-94; chmn., pres., chief exec. officer UniDynamics Corp., Stamford, Conn., 1969-85; pres., chief exec. officer Montchanin Mgmt. Corp., N.Y., 1985-94; chmn., chief exec. officer Bank of New Eng., 1990; pres., CEO Michel Vineyards, Inc., N.Y.C., 1978-94. Theatrical producer 1955-94. Bd. dirs., mem. exec. com., co-chair spl. litigation com. Dart Group Corp.; bd. dirs. Crown Books Corp., Trac Auto Corp, Nat. Boys' Clubs Am.; corporator Jordan Oil & Gas., Jordan Vineyards and Winery; trustee Colby Coll., Waterville, Maine, 1978-94, chmn. bd., 1982-91. Capt. USAF, 1957-59. Mem. ABA, N.Y. State Bar Assn., Va. State Bar Assn., Assn. Bar City N.Y., League Am. Theaters & Producers, Piping Rock Country Club, N.Y. Yacht Club, Down Town Assn., Greenwich Country Club, Indian Harbor Yacht Club, Lyford Cay Club. Republican. Episcopalian. Home: New York N.Y. Died Dec. 19, 1994.

BUNCE, DONALD FAIRBAIRN MACDOUGAL, II physician, anatomist; b. Harrisburg, Pa., July 15, 1920 s. Wesley Hibbard and Jean (Fairbairn) B.; m. Lorraine Pelch, May 1, 1954 (dec. Nov. 1975); children: Chip Gregory Alan, Dale Graham Alison; m. Suzanne Brockman, July 13, 1978. B.S., U. Miami, 1951; M.Sc. U. Ill., 1959, Ph.D., 1960; grad. with honors, Indsl Coll. of Armed Forces, 1965; D.O., Coll. Osteo Medicine and Surgery, 1973. Pres., Bunce Sch. Lab Technique, Coral Gables, Fla., 1945-48; clin. physiologist Armour Labs., Chgo., 1953-56; dir. research Chgo Pharmacal Co., 1956-57; instr. anatomy Tulane Sch Medicine, 1960-62; research prof. physiology Coll. Osteo. Medicine and Surgery, Des Moines, 1962-67; dir grad. sch. Coll. Osteo. Medicine and Surgery, 1962-73 prof. pathology, acting chmn. dept., 1966-68, prof physiology, chmn. dept., 1967-73; intern, house physician Des Moines Gen. Hosp., 1973-74; gen. practice medicine Forest City, Iowa, 1974-78, Dubuque Iowa, 1978-80; clin. assoc. prof. dept. medicine U. Ala Sch. Medicine, Tuscaloosa, 1982-90; chief of staff Forest City Hosp., 1977-78; chief physician Acute Med. Car Unit, Bryce Hosp., Tuscaloosa, Ala., 1980-90; vice-chie of staff Bryce Hosp., 1984-85, chief staff, 1985-90; pres med. staff Hale Meml. Hosp., 1986-90; former mem staff Mercy, Finley and Xavier hosps., Dubuque; nov mem. staff depts. internal medicine Hale and Druid Cit hosps., Tuscaloosa; vis. fellow Inst. Exptl. Surgery Copenhagen, 1962; vis. prof. Karolinska Inst Stockholm, 1965, Edinburgh, Scotland, 1966, Kenned Inst. Rheumatology, London, 1969-70; travelling fellov NSF-Internat. Union Physiology; program dir. grac tng. program in med. scis. NIH; ofcl. del. 4th Interna Congress Angiology. Mem. editorial bd. Angéiologie Paris, 1960-90, Jour. Psychiat. Medicine, 1984—author: Laboratory Guide to Microscopic Anatomy 1964, The Nervous System in Canine Medicine, 3d edit 1968, Atlas of Arterial Histology, 1973; also articles. Bd. dirs. Mus. Sci. and Industry, Des Moines, 1971-75 Recipient Billups Meml. Research award La. Hea Assn., 1960. Fellow Am. Coll. Angiology, AAAS N.Y., Iowa acads sci., Royal Soc. Medicine; mem AMA, Iowa Med. Soc., Dubuque County Med. Soc Ala. Med. Assn., Tuscaloosa County Med. Soc., Am Osteo. Assn., So. Med. Assn., Am. Assn. Anatomist Anat. Soc. Gt. Britain, So. Soc. Anatomists (exec. se 1960-62), Path. Soc. Gt. Britain, Soc. Exptl. Biology an Medicine, Am. Assn. U. Profs., Instn. Nuclear Engrs L'Union Internationale d'Angéiologie, Société Franç d'Angéiologie et d'Histopathologie, Mensa, U.S. Nav ıst., Sigma Xi, Sigma Alpha Epsilon. Club: Mason. Iome: Melbourne Fla.

URCIAGA, JUAN GUERRERO, federal judge; b. oswell, N.Mex., Aug. 17, 1929; s. Melesio Antonio ıd Juana (Guerrero) B.; m. Carolyn Jacoby, Oct. 28, 958 (dec.); children: Lisa Anne, Lora Anne, Amy irginia, Carlos Antonio, Pamela. BS, U.S. Mil. Acad., 952; JD, U. N.Mex., 1963. Bar: N.Mex. 1964. Assoc., ıen ptnr. firms in Albuquerque, 1964-79; judge U.S. ›ist. Ct. N.Mex., 1979-95; lectr. U. N.Mex. Sch. Law, 970-71. Bd. dirs. Albuquerque YMCA, 1964-74, CCJ, Albuquerque, 1969-73; urban renewal commnr. ity of Albuquerque, 1972-76. Served as officer USAF, 952-60. Mem. Am. Bar Assn., Am. Judicature Soc. lir.), Def. Research Inst., Am. Bd. Arbitration, Am. rial Lawyers Assn., Am. Bd. Trial Advocates, Albu- uerque Bar Assn. Democrat. Roman Catholic. Home: lbuquerque N.Mex. Died Mar. 5, 1995.

URG, GEORGE ROSCOE, journalist; b. New Lex- ıgton, Ohio, Apr. 1, 1916; s. Roscoe E. and Erie Kreider) B.; m. Mary Vesta Ford, Oct. 31, 1941; chil- ren: George F., Mary Jane Burg Coffyn. BS in ournalism, Ohio State U., 1938, BS in Edn., 1939. chr. Pike Twp. High Sch., Madison County, Ohio, 939-40; engaged in newspaper work, 1948-96; mng. litor Kansas City (Mo.) Star, 1967-75, assoc. editor, sst. to pub., 1975-95. Mem. Mayor's Corps of rogress; past trustee U. Mo., Kansas City; bd. dirs. ansas City Econ. Devel. Corp., Sci. Pioneers, Greater ansas City Area Safety Coun., Downtown Coun. /ith AUS, 1940-48. Mem. Mid-Am. Press Inst., ansas City C. of C., AP Mng. Editors Assn., N.W. lo. Press Assn., Kans. Press Assn., Mil. Order World /ars, Res. Officers Assn., Tau Kappa Epsilon. lethodist. Clubs: Kansas City Press, Kansas City, omestead. Lodge: Elks. Home: Shawnee Mission ans. Died Feb. 26, 1995.

URGAN, JOHN SYDNEY, library director; b. Balt., ept. 25, 1930; s Harry Clark and Ethel Huntington Fox) B.; m. Anne Shaw; stepchildren: Sarah Siskin, lartha Shaw. BA, John Hopkins U., 1957; MLS, utgers U., 1959. Prin. librarian Linden (N.J.) Pub. ibrary, 1959-62; adult specialist Baltimore County Pub. ibrary, Towson, Md., 1962; administrv. asst., br. noch Pratt Free Library, Balt., 1963, asst. to asst. dir., 963-65, head county svcs., 1965-67, chief extension v., 1967-73, chief cen. library, 1973-83; chief librarian artford (Conn.) Pub. Library, 1984-89; pres. Md. Libr. ssn., Balt., 1970-71; mem. ALA/Reference and Adult vcs. Div. com. on Wilson Indexes, Bronx, 1985-89, onn. State Adv. Counc. on Libr. Planning and Devel., artford, 1988-89. Trustee Stowe Day Found., artford, 1989; corporator Hartford Hosp., 1985-89. lem. Am. Library Assn., Conn. Library Assn., New ngland Library Assn., John Hopkins Club, Beta Phi lu. Democrat. Episcopalian. Home: Hartford Conn. ›ied July 1991.

URGER, WARREN EARL, former chief justice of nited States supreme court, academic administrator; b. . Paul, Sept. 17, 1907; s. Charles Joseph and atharine (Schnittger) B.; m. Elvera Stromberg, Nov. 8, 933; children: Wade Allan, Margaret Mary lizabeth. Student, U. Minn., 1925-27; LL.B. magna ım laude, St. Paul Coll. Law (now Mitchell Coll. Law), 931; LL.D. (hon.), William Mitchell Coll. Law, U. linn., NYU, Columbia U., U. Pa., N.Y. Coll. Law, eorgetown U., Am. U., Coll. William and Mary, lercer U., Yeshiva U., Howard U., Ripon Coll., Wash- gton Coll., Brigham Young U., George Washington ., W.Va. U., Pace U.; H.H.D. (hon.), other colls. and nivs. Bar: Minn. 1931. Mem. firm Boyeson, Otis, Brill Faricy (and successor firm Faricy, Burger, Moore & ostello), St. Paul, 1931, ptnr., 1933-53; asst. atty. gen., vil litigation div. U.S. Dept. Justice, 1953-56; judge .S. Ct. Appeals D.C., 1956-69; Chief Justice U.S. upreme Ct., 1969-86; chancellor Coll. William and lary, Williamsburg, Va., 1985-94; adj. prof. Mitchell oll. Law, 1931-46; chmn. Jud. Conf. of U.S., 1969-95; ımn. Fed. Judicial Ctr. by tradition; hon. chmn. Inst. ıd. Adminstrn.; chmn. Commn. on Bicentennial of .S. Constitution, 1985-92. Chancellor emeritus Smith- ›nian Instn.; trustee emeritus Mitchell Coll. Law, Ma- alester Coll., St. Paul, Mayo Found., Rochester, Minn.; ustee Nat. Geog. Soc.; hon. chmn. Nat. Jud. Coll. U. lev., Nat. Ctr. for State Cts., Williamsburg; hon. chmn. upreme Ct. Hist. Soc.; trustee and chmn. Nat. Gallery f Art, 1969-86; pres. emeritus Bentham Club, London, 971-72. Hon. Bencher Middle Temple, London and ings Inn, Dublin; recipient Thomas Jefferson award U. a., John Marshall award Coll. William and Mary, ımes Madison award Princeton U., Presl. medal of reedom, 1987. Home: Washington D.C. Died June 25, 995.

URGESS, ALFRED FRANKLIN, lawyer; b. Greer, C., June 1, 1906; s. Franklin and Minnie (Cun- ıngham) B.; m. Mary Wyche, June 25, 1938; children: lary Wyche Burgess Lesesne, Caroline Burgess An- ›acher, Alfred Franklin, Granville Wyche, Victoria urgess Pitman. A.B. cum laude, Davidson (N.C.) oll., 1928; LL.B. cum laude, U. Va., 1931. Bar: S.C. 931. Practiced in Greenville; partner firm Wyche, urgess, Freeman & Parham, P.A., 1931-92; spl. circuit ıdge, 1948, 50, 55, 61; spl. hearing officer Dept. Justice, Greenville, 1956-92; mem. com. rules of practice U.S. Dist. Cts., 1965. Numerous appearances in little theatre prodns. Chmn. Greenville County Democratic Com., 1940-42; del. Dem. Nat. Conv., 1944; bd. dirs. Green- ville Community Youth Commn., 1955, Greenville Children's Center, 1954-55, Friends of Bach Choir, 1940-45, Greenville Community Concert Assn., 1960-63, St. Francis Community Hosp., Greenville, 1966, Shriners Hosp., 1973-78, Greenville United Fund, 1961- 66, The Savoyards, 1979-92, Greenville Community Re- lations Bi-Racial Com., 1964-66, Greenville County Found., 1965-66, Greenville Little Theatre, 1973-92, Greenville Met. Arts Council, 1975-76, Roc Found.; pres. Greenville Symphony Assn., 1958-59. Mem. Am. Bar Assn., Am. Judicature Soc., Am. Fedn. Ins. Counsel (Law Sci. Acad.), S.C. Bar Assn., Greenville Bar Assn. (pres. 1947). Episcopalian (former vestryman). Clubs: Green Valley Country, Greenville Country, Poinsett, Thirty-Nine. Lodges: Shriners; Rotary (past pres., dist. gov.). Home: Greenville S.C. Died Jan. 1, 1992.

BURGESS, ANTHONY, author; b. Manchester, Eng., Feb. 25, 1917; s. Joseph and Elizabeth (Wilson) B.; m. Llewela Isherwood Jones, Jan. 23, 1942 (dec. 1968); m. Liliana Macellari, 1968. B.A. with honours, Manchester U., 1940, LLD; D. Litt., Birmingham U. Lectr., schoolmaster, 1946-54; edn. officer in Malaya and Borneo, 1954-59; composer, 1933-93, play producer, 1947-93, jazz pianist, 1941-93; vis. fellow Princeton U., 1970-71; Disting. prof. CCNY, 1972-73. Author: Time for a Tiger, 1956, English Literature: A Survey for Students, 1958, The Enemy in the Blanket, 1958, Beds in the East, 1959, The Right to an Answer, 1960, The Doctor is Sick, 1960, The Worm and the Ring, 1961, Devil of a State, 1961, One Hand Clapping, 1961, The Wanting Seed, 1962, A Clockwork Orange, 1962, Honey for the Bears, 1963, Inside Mr. Enderby, 1963, The Novel Today, 1963, Nothing Like the Sun, 1964, The Eve of Saint Venus, 1964, Language Made Plain, 1964, The Long Day Wanes, 1965, Re Joyce, 1965, A Vision of Battlements, 1965, The Doctor is Sick, 1965, Tremor of Intent, 1966, The Novel Now, 1967, Enderby, 1968, Urgent Copy, 1968, Shakespeare, 1970, MF, 1971, Joysprick: An Introduction to the Language of James Joyce, 1973, Napoleon Symphony, 1974, The Clockwork Testament, 1974, Moses, 1975, A Long Trip to Teatime, 1976, Beard's Roman Women, 1976, ABBA ABBA, 1976, Nineteen Eighty-Five, 1978, Ernest Hemingway and His World, 1978, Man of Nazareth, 1979, The Land Where Ice Cream Grows, 1979, Earthly Powers, 1980, On Going to Bed, 1981, This Man and Music, 1982, The End of the World News, 1982, Enderby's Dark Lady, 1983, The Clockwork Testament, 1984, The Kingdom of the Wicked, 1984, Homage to Qwert Yuiop, 1985, The Pianoplayers, 1986, (autobiography) Little Wilson and Big God: The First Part of the Confession, 1987, Any Old Iron, 1989, The Devil's Mode, 1990, You've Had Your Time: The Second Part of the Confessions, 1991, On Mozart: A Paean for Wolfgang, 1991, A Mouthful of Air: Language, Languages...Especially English, 1993; editor: Coaching Days of England, 1966, A Journal of the Plague Year, 1966, A Shorter Finnegan's Wake, 1966, (with F. Haskell) The Age of the Grand Tour, 1967; translator: Oedipus the King, 1972, Cyrano de Bergerac, 1984, Carmen, 1986, Oberon, 1986. Served with British Army, 1940-46. Home: Monte Carlo Monaco Died Nov. 25, 1993.

BURKE, E. AINSLIE, artist, educator; b. Omaha, Jan. 26, 1922; s. Charles Alvin and Flora (Glanville) B.; m. Barbara Chase, Sept. 26, 1947. Student, Md. Inst. Fine Arts, 1938-41, Johns Hopkins U., 1939-41, Art Students League, N.Y.C., 1945-47. Vis. artist-in-residence Syracuse (N.Y.) U., 1962-63, assoc. prof., 1963-65, prof. art, 1965-86, chmn. dept. studio art, 1970-80; ret., 1986; vis. artist Exeter (N.H.) Acad., 1970; chmn. Woodstock Artists Assn., 1960-62. One-man shows AAA Galleries, N.Y.C., L.I. U., Polari Gallery, Woodstock, N.Y., Storm King Art Ctr., Mountainville, N.Y., Philips Ex- eter Acad., N.Y., Albany (N.Y.) Inst. History and Art, Lehigh (Pa.) U., Gorham State Coll., U. Maine, Deer Isle Artist Assn., Stonington, Maine, 1975-77, 78, 80, 88, 89, Kraushaar Galleries, N.Y.C., 1960, 63, 67, 71, 74, 77, 80, 85, LeMoyne Coll., Syracuse, 1973, Lowe Art Center, Syracuse U., 1974, 86, Manlius (N.Y.) Library, 1975, Oxford Gallery, Rochester, N.Y., 1977, 81, 87, Munson Williams Proctor Mus., Utica, N.Y., 1979, Everson Mus., Syracuse, 1979, 80, U. Maine, Orono, 1980, Cazenovia (N.Y.) Coll., 1981, Leighton Gallery, Blue Hill, Maine, 1986, Petrucci Gallery Saugerties, N.Y., 1987, Hawthorn Gallery, Woodstock, N.Y., 1989; group shows include New Acquisitions Gallery, Syracuse, 1985; Toledo Mus., Bklyn. Mus., Riverside Mus., N.Y.C., Pa. Acad., Phila., Schneider Gallery, Rome, U. Nebr., Mary Washington Coll., Am. Acad. Arts and Letters, Albany Inst. History and Art, Proctor Mus., Springfield (Mass.) Mus., Columbia (S.C.) Art Mus., Columbus (Ohio) Gallery Art, Corcoran Gallery, Washington, Stamford (Conn.) Mus., Phila. Mus., Marietta (Ohio) Coll., Nat. Acad., N.Y.C., Audubon Artists, N.Y.C., Ill. Wesleyn U., Smithsonian Instn. Traveling Exhn., Va. Mus. Fine Art, Everson Mus., Nat. Arts Club; represented in permanent collec- tions Columbia U., N.Y.C., Syracuse U., Springfield Mus., Lehigh U., Munson-Williams Proctor Inst., Utica, St. Lawrence U., others. Served in USN, 1942-45. Fulbright fellow Italy, 1957-58; Creative Artists Public Service grantee, 1976-77; recipient numerous awards NAD, N.Y. Worlds Fair, 1st prize Kirkland Art Ctr., 1978, numerous other awards. Mem. AAUP, Art Students League, Maine Coast Artists, Audubon Artist (Emily Lowe prize 1984, Alice Melrose award 1985, Fabri Medal of Merit 1988, Gold medal and prize 1989), Assoc. Artists Syracuse, Woodstock Artists Assn., also others. Home: Woodstock N.Y.

BURKE, KENNETH (DUVA), English language edu- cator, author; b. Pitts., May 5, 1897; s. James Leslie and Lillyan May (Duva) B.; m. Lily Mary Batterham, May 19, 1919 (div.); children: Jeanne Elspeth, Eleanor Duva, Frances Batterham; m. Elizabeth Batterham, Dec. 18, 1933; children: James Anthony, Kenneth Michael. Student, Ohio State U., Columbia U.; D.Litt. (hon.), Bennington Coll., 1966, Rutgers U., 1968, Dartmouth Coll., 1970; L.H.D. (hon.), Fairfield U., 1970, Rochester U., 1972, Northwestern U., 1972, Ind. State U., 1976, Kenyon Coll., 1979, Emory U., 1982, Queens Coll., 1985. Researcher Laura Spelman Rock- efeller Meml., 1926-27; music critic The Dial, 1927-29; editorial worker Bur. Soc. Hygiene, 1928-29; vis. prof. English U. Chgo., 1949-50, lect. psychology of lit. form and on Samuel Taylor Coleridge, 1938; music critic The Nation, 1934-36; lectr. on practice and theory of lit. criticism New Sch. for Soc. Research, 1937; educator course in theory and practice, lit. criticism Bennington Coll., 1943-61;; lit. critic Drew U., 1962, 64; modern lit. critic Pa. State U., 1963; Regents prof. U. Calif.-Santa Barbara, 1964-65; prof. Central Wash. State Coll., 1966; educator lit. theory Harvard U., Cambridge, Mass., 1967; lit. critic, Fannie Hurst vis. prof. Wash. U., 1970- 71; critic Ctr. for Humanities, Wesleyan U., 1972; An- drew W. Mellon vis. prof. English U. Pitts., 1974; tchr. seminar in lit. criticism Princeton U., N.J., 1975, U. Nev., Reno, 1976; Walker-Ames vis. prof. English U. Wash., 1976; fellow Ctr. for Advanced Study Behavioral Scis., 1957-58; vis. prof. Grad. Inst. Liberal Arts, Emory U., winters 1981-85. Author: The White Oxen and Other Stories, 1924, Counter-Statement, 1931, rev. edit., 1953, 68, (novel) Towards a Better Life; a Series of Declamations, or Epistles, 1932, rev. edit., 1966, Permanence and Change Anatomy of Purpose, 1935, rev. edit., 1954, Attitudes Toward History (Vol. I, Ac- ceptance and Rejection: The Curve of History, Vol. II, Analysis of Symbolic Structure), 1937, rev. 1 vol. edit., 1959, Philosophy of Literary Form, Studies in Symbolic Action, 1941, abridged edit., 1957, rev. unabridged edit., 1967, A Grammar of Motives, 1945, new edit., 1969, A Rhetoric of Motives, 1950, new edit., 1969, Book of Moments, Poems 1915-54, 1955, The Rhetoric of Reli- gion, 1961, new edit., 1970, Perspectives by Incongruity, Terms for Order, 1964, Language as Symbolic Action, 1966, Collected Poems, 1915-67, 68; (short stories) The Complete White Oxen, 1968, Dramatism and Develop- ment, 1972; translator several books; contbr. to numerous mags. Recipient Dial award for disting. ser- vice to Am. Letters, 1928, Creative Arts award Brandeis U., 1967, Poet of Year award N.J. Assn. Tchrs. English, 1968, award NEA, 1969, Horace Gregory award New Sch. Soc. Research, 1970, award Ingram Merrill Found., 1970, gold medal for eminence in belles lettres and criticism Nat. Inst. Arts and Letters, 1975; Guggenheim Meml. fellow, 1935; grantee Am. Acad. Arts and Letters and Nat. Inst. Arts and Letters, 1946, Rockefeller Found., 1966. Fellow MLA (hon.); mem. Am. Acad. and Inst. Arts and Letters, Am. Acad. Arts and Scis. (emeritus, award for contbn. to humanities 1977, Nat. Medal for Lit. 1981), Kenneth Burke Soc. (eponymous founder). Home: Andover N.J. Died Nov. 1993.

BURKHARDT, HANS GUSTAV, artist; b. Basel, Switzerland, Dec. 20, 1904; came to U.S., 1924, naturalized, 1930; s. Gustav and Anna (Schmidt) B.; m. Louise Thile, Mar. 25, 1929 (div. 1938); 1 dau., Elsa Burkhardt Brown; m. Thordis Olga Westhassel, June 18, 1955. Student, Cooper Union, 1924-25, Grand Central Sch. Art, N.Y.C., 1928-29; pvt. student, with Gorky, 1930-37. Assoc. prof. art Long Beach State U., 1959; prof. art U. So. Calif., 1959-60; parttime instr. UCLA, 1960-63; asso. prof. U. Calif., Northridge, 1963-73, Chouinard Art Inst., 1962-94; prof. emeritus Calif. State U., Northridge. Collaborator: (with Ray Bradbury) Man Dead? Then God is Slain, prints, 1977; (with Wil- liam Everson) prints Rattlesnake August, 1978, (with Ray Bradbury) The Kiss, 1983; One-man exhbns. in- clude, Los Angeles County Mus., Oreg. State U., Museo de Bellas Artex, Guadalajara, Mexico, Occidental Coll., Inst. de Allende, San Miguel de Allende, Mexico, Mt. St. Mary Coll., Palos Verdes Community Art Assn., Pasadena Art Mus., U. So. Calif., Santa Barbara Mus. Art, Palace Legion of Honor, Los Angeles Municipal Art Gallery, La Jolla Art Center, Pierce Coll., Los Angeles, Freie Schule, Basel, Switzerland, San Fernando Valley State Coll., Bay City Jewish Community Center, Laguna Beach Mus. Art, San Diego Art Inst. (forty year retrospective), ACA-American Masters Gallery, Los Angeles, San Diego Fine Arts Gallery, Michael Smith Gallery, Los Angeles, Long Beach Mus. Art (retrospec- tive 1950-72), Calif. State U., Northridge, 1973, 75, Santa Barbara Mus. Art, Pasquale Ianetti, San Francisco, 1977, Palm Springs Desert Mus., 1979, Robert Schoelkopf Gallery, N.Y.C., 1979, Alana Gal- lery, Oslo, Norway, 1978, 80, C.H. Wenger Gallery, Basel, 1981, Jack Rutberg Fine Arts, Los Angeles, 1982, 83, 84, 87, 88, 90, 91, , Muhlenberg Coll., Pa., 1990, Galway Arts Festival, Ireland, 1990, 91, Laguna Art Mus., 1990, 92, Portland Art Mus., Oreg., 1991, Sid

Deutsch Gallery, N.Y.C., 1987, Graduate Theological Union, Berkeley, 1993; group shows Los Angeles Inst. Contemporary Art, San Francisco Mus. Art, Blue Point Gallery, Berlin, 1993 numerous others; represented in permanent collections, Mus. Modern Art Stockholm, Oakland Mus., Palm Springs Desert Mus., Corcoran Gallery, Washington, Guggenheim Mus., N.Y.C., St. Louis Mus. Art, Tamarin Inst., U. N.Mex., Los County Art Mus., Pasadena Art Mus., Santa Barbara Mus. Art, Long Beach Art Mus., La Jolla Art Mus., San Diego Fine Art Center, Jocelyn Art Center, Lincoln, Nebr., Kunstmuseum, Basel, Switzerland, Ahmanson collection, Hirshhorn Mus.; subject documentary film Hans Burkhardt: The Artist's World, 1987. Recipient purchase prize in oil Los Angeles County Mus., 1946, cash awards, 1954, 57; award Terry Art Inst., Miami, Fla., 1951; purchase prize Santa Barbara Mus. Art, 1957; award Calif. Watercolor Soc., 1961; purchase oil Los Angeles All-City Show, 1958,61; purchase watercolor, 1961; purchase watercolor Long Beach Mus.; purchase watercolor Pasadena Art Mus.; purchase watercolor Los Angeles County Mus.; purchase watercolor Santa Barbara Mus. Art; purchase watercolor La Jolla Art Center; purchase watercolor Emily and Joe Lowe Meml.; Outstanding Tchrs. award Calif. State U., Northridge, 1973, Lifetime Achievement Art award Am. Acad. and Inst. Arts and Letters, N.Y.C., 1992; Hans Burkhardt Week proclaimed by Mayor Tom Bradley, L.A., 1991; Hans Burkhart Art and Humanities Ctr. at Calif. State U., Northridge named in his honor, 1992; recipient Lifetime Achievement award L.A. Artcore, Calif., 1992. Mem. Santa Barbara Mus. Art, Los Angeles Art Assn., Long Beach Art Mus., Kappa Pi, Phi Kappa Phi (hon.). Home: Los Angeles Calif. Died 1994.

BURKHART, CHARLES BARCLAY, outdoor advertising executive; b. Atchison, Kans., May 18, 1914; s. Charles Bert and Claudene (Barclay) B.; m. Elinor Karr, Apr. 19, 1936 (dec. mar. 1991); children: Sherry (Mrs. Peter C. John), Janette (Mrs. W. Scott Miller). Grad., Ft. Scott Jr. Coll., 1932. Pres. Stalcup, Inc., Kansas City, Mo., 1945-54, Cream City Outdoor Advt. Co., Milw., 1954-58, Naegele Outdoor Advt. Co., Milw., 1958-62, Outdoor Advt. Assn. Am., Chgo., 1962-64; chmn. bd. Burkhart Advt., Inc., South Bend, Ind., 1964-95; pres. Barclay Corp., 1970-95; former mem. advt. com. U.S. Dept. Commerce; past dir. Am. Fedn. Advt., Advt. Council Am., Traffic Audit Bur. N.Y., Nat. Sign Assn.; past chmn. Notre Dame Outdoor Advt. Assn. Am. Found. Mem. at large nat. coun. Boy Scouts Am.; Chmn. founding bd. govs. Inst. Outdoor Advt.; bd. dirs., exec. com. Cen. Outdoor Markets; vice chmn. Outdoor Advt. Assn. Edn. Fund. Mem. Outdoor Advt. Assn. Am. (recipient Myles Standish award; inducted into Hall of Fame 1991), Outdoor Advt. Assn. Ind. (bd. dirs.), Transit Advt. Assn. (past dir.), Young Pres. Orgn., South Bend-Mishawaka C. of C. (past bd. dirs.), South Bend Country Club, Summit Club (South Bend), Univ. (South Bend), Chgo. Athletic Assn. Home: South Bend Ind. Died Jan. 7, 1995.

BURKITT, DENIS PARSONS, surgeon; b. Enniskillen, Ireland, Feb. 28, 1911; s. James Parsons and Gwendoline (Hill) B.; m. Olive Mary Rogers, July 28, 1943; children: Judith, Carolyn, Rachel. MB, Dublin U., Ireland, 1935, MD, 1938; DSc (hon.), U. East Africa, 1970, U. Ulster, 1981, U. Leeds, 1982, U. London, 1984, U. W.Va., 1985; MD (hon.), U. Bristol, 1979; DSc (hon.), Bristol U., Leeds U., U. Ulster, U. East Africa; MD (hon.), U. S.C. Gov. surgeon, surgery lectr. Makerere U. Coll. Med. Sch., Uganda, 1946-64; sr. cons. surgeon Ministry Health, Uganda, 1961-64; with external scientific staff Med. Rsch. Coun., Uganda, 1964-66, London, 1966-76; hon. sr. rsch. fellow St. Thomas' Hosp. Med. Sch., London, 1976-93; hon. fellow Trinity Coll., Dublin, Ireland. Co-editor: (books) Treatment of Burkitt's Lymphoma, 1967, Burkitt's Lymphoma, 1970, Refined Carbohydrate Foods and Disease, 1975, Don't Forget the Fibre in Your Diet, 1979, Western: Diseases: Their Emergence and Prevention, 1981, Dietary Fibre: Fibre-Depleted Foods and Disease, 1985; contbr. articles to profl. jours. Maj. Royal Army Med. Corps, 1941-46. Decorated companion Order of St. Michael and St. George. Recipient Harrison prize Royal Soc. Medicine, 1964, Stuart prize Brit. Med. Assn., 1966, Walker prize Royal Coll. Surgeons, 1971, Gold Medal The Soc. Apothecaries, 1972, Gold Medal The Brit. Med. Assn., 1978, Arnott Gold Medal Irish Hosps. and Med. Schs. Assn., 1968, Katherine Berkan Judd award The Sloan Kettering Inst., 1969, Robert de Villiers award Am. Leukaemia Soc., 1970, 72, The Bristol-Myers award, 1982, The Charles Mott G.M. award, 1982, Gairdner Found. award, 1973, Paul Ehrlich-Ludwig Darmstaedter Gold medal, 1972, Gold Medal Acad. Medicine, 1982, Bower award Achievement Sci. Franklin Inst., 1992. Fellow Royal Soc., Royal Can. Coll. Physicians and Surgeons (hon.); mem. East African Assn. Surgeons (hon.), Brazilian Soc. Surgery (hon.), Sudan Assn. Surgeons (hon.), Internat. Christian Med. and Dental Assn. (v.p., French Acad. Scis., Internat. Med. Club (hon.). Evangelical Anglican. Home: Bisley Eng. Died Mar. 23, 1993.

BURKSTRAND, C. CLAYTON, retail discount company executive; b. Kimball, Minn., Mar. 11, 1934; s. Clarence and Evelyn Ida B.; m. Linda Kay Hardas, Nov. 15, 1973; children: David, Jeff, Steve, Beth. Student, U. Minn., 1952-54, U. Alaska. Trainee, ops. mgr. Target, Mpls., 1962-64, mdse. mgr., 1964-65, store mgr., 1965-68, dist. mgr., sr. dist. mgr. then regional mgr., 1968-74; v.p. ops. Globe div. Walgreen Drug Co., Inc., Houston, 1975, pres. Globe div. and v.p. parent co., 1975-78; pres., chief operating officer Pamida, Inc., Omaha, 1978-81, chmn., pres., chief exec. officer, 1981-85, also bd. dirs., chmn., chief exec. officer, 1985—. Past mem. bd. advisors Discount Store News. Mem. fin. com. Hal Daub Senatorial campaign, 1987; active Nebr. Rep. Party; participant local membership drive Ak-Sar-Ben. Served with AUS, 1954-56. Named Man of Yr. Boys and Young Men's Apparel Lodge B'nai B'rith, 1982. Mem. Nat. Mass Retailing Inst. (bd. dirs. 1982-86). Lutheran. Home: Omaha Nebr.

BURLEW, JOHN SWALM, research scientist; b. Washington, Sept. 10, 1910; s. Ebert Keiser and Marion Kate (Swalm) B.; m. Grace Anne Schaum, June 16, 1934; children: David Schaum, Thomas Ebert. A.B., Bucknell U., 1930, Sc.D., 1955; Ph.D. in Chemistry, Johns Hopkins, 1934; Sc.D., Drexel Inst. Tech., 1956. Sterling Fellow in chemistry Yale, 1934-36; phys. chemist Geophys. Lab., Carnegie Instn. of Washington, 1936-43, 47-52; tech. aide NDRC, 1943-47; tech. dir. Cambridge Corp., 1952-54; asst. dir. Franklin Inst., 1954-55, dir., 1955-56, exec. v.p., 1956-59; dir. research Carrier Corp., 1960-66; dir. Conn. Research Commn., 1966-71; pres. New Directions Inc., Glastonbury, Conn., 1971-91. Editor: Algal Culture from Laboratory to Pilot Plant, 1953, Connecticut Walk Book, 16th edit., 1990, 17th edit., 1993. Decorated Presdl. Medal for Merit, 1948. Fellow AAAS; mem. Am. Chem. Soc. (chmn. Connecticut Valley sect. 1982, gen. chmn. Northeast regional meeting 1983, exec. officer Northeast regional meetings 1984-90), Ops. Research Soc. Am., Conn. Acad. Sci. and Engring. (incorporator 1976), Am. Geophys. Union, Phi Beta Kappa, Sigma Xi. (pres. Hartford chpt. 1984-85). Home: Forest Grove Oreg. Died Jan. 6, 1996.

BURNAM, TOM (THOMAS BOND), English language educator, author; b. Swan Lake, Mont., Oct. 2, 1913; s. Clarence Miles and Ora Harmer (Bond) B.; m. Phyllis Anderson, Mar. 29, 1940. B.A., U. Idaho, 1936, M.A., 1937; Ph.D., U. Wash., 1949. Instr. Lewis-Clark State Coll., 1938-42; ground sch. supr. FAA, 1942-44; instr. B-29 sch. Boeing Airplane Co., 1944-45; assoc. dept. English U. Wash., Seattle, 1946-49; asst. prof. to prof. English U. No. Colo., 1950-63; prof. Portland (Oreg.) State U., 1963-94; vis. Fulbright prof. U. Helsinki, 1961; spl. lectr. U. Caen, France, Leangkollen, Norway, 1961; guest prof. San Jose State U., 1964. Author: The Dictionary of Misinformation, 1975, rev. edit., 1986, (with Claude Vallette) Encyclopédie des idées recues, 1978, More Misinformation, 1980; mem. editorial bd. Harvest mag., 1974-76; contbr. articles, stories and poems to Am. Quar., Modern Fiction Studies, Tex. Quar., Harper's, Esquire, others. Portland State U. research grantee, 1970. Mem. MLA, AAUP, AFTRA, Philol. Assn. Pacific Coast, Rocky Mountain Am. Studies Assn. (pres. 1952), Rocky Mountain MLA (pres. 1953), Authors Guild, Phi Beta Kappa (alumnus mem. U. Idaho). Home: Lake Oswego Oreg. Died Sept. 6, 1994.

BURNETT, WILLIAM EARL, JR., insurance company executive; b. Louisville, Feb. 15, 1927; s. William Earl and Bessie (Davis) B.; m. Margaret Alberta Erny Crenshaw, Mar. 21, 1975; children: Bruce E., Cindy C., Suzanne L., John A. B.S., U. Louisville, 1949. Treas. Louisville Fire & Marine Ins. Co., 1949-54; asst. sec.-treas. Ky. Ins. Agy., Lexington, 1955-59; sec.-treas. Ky. Central Life Ins. Co., Lexington, 1959-74, exec. v.p., 1975-76, pres., 1976—, mem. exec. and fin. coms., 1961—, dir., 1961—; pres. Ky. Central Life Ins. Co. and Property and Casualty Co. subs., Lexington, pres., chmn., 1984—; dir. Central Bank, Lexington, Peoples Comml. Bank, Winchester, Ky., First Nat. Bank, Georgetown, Ky., Ky. Fin. Co., Lexington; sec., dir. Triangle Found.; bd. dirs. Cen. Bank, Lexington, Ky. Fin. Co., Lexington. Sec., bd. dirs. Triangle Found.; bd. dirs. United Way Bluegrass, Lexington Trolley, Lexington United; trustee, vice chmn. bd. trustees U. Ky., also mem. adv. coun. Coll. Bus. and Econs. With U.S. Army, 1945-47. Fellow U. Ky. Mem. Ins. Accts. and Statisticians Assn., Life Officers Mgmt. Assn., Nat. Assn. Life Underwriters, Ky. C. of C., Lexington C. of C., Georgetown Coll. Assocs., Lafayette Club, Masons, Shriners. Presbyterian. Home: Lexington Ky. Died Dec., 1993.

BURNS, GEORGE (NATHAN BIRNBAUM), actor, comedian; b. N.Y.C., Jan. 20, 1896; m. Gracie Allen, Jan. 7, 1926 (dec. Aug. 1964); adopted children: Sandra Jean, Ronald John. Student pub. schs., N.Y.C.; HHD (hon.), U. Hartford, 1988. Began as dancer, vaudeville performer; formed team with Gracie Allen, 1923, touring U.S. and Europe, making radio debut with B.B.C. and co-star radio show, 1932-50; screen debut, 1932; films include The Big Broadcast, 1932, 36, 37, International House, 1933, Love in Bloom, 1933, College Humor, 1933, Six of a Kind, 1934, We're Not Dressing, 1934, Here Comes Cookie, 1935, Love in Bloom, 1935, College Holiday, 1936, A Damsel in Distress, 1937, College Swing, 1938, Many Happy Returns, 1939, Honolulu, 1939, Two Girls and a Sailor, 1944,
The Sunshine Boys, 1975 (Oscar, Best Supporting A
tor), Oh God!, 1977, Sgt. Pepper's Lonely Hearts Cl
Band, 1978, Going in Style, 1979, Just You and M
Kid, 1979, Two of a Kind, 1979, Oh God! Book Tw
1980, Oh God, You Devil!, 1984, Eighteen Again, 19
co-star TV show George Burns and Gracie Allen Sho
1950-58; star TV show George Burns Show, 1958-
appeared on TV show Wendy and Me, 1964-65 (al
prodr.); numerous TV and personal appearances i
cluding host TV series George Burns Comedy Wee
CBS-TV, 1985; featured TV spl. for 90th birthday, CB
TV, 1986; producer Meet Mona McCluskey, NB
1965; record albums include I Wish I Was You
Again, 1981, George Burns in Nashville, 1981; author
Love Her, That's Why!, 1955, Living It Up, or, Th
Still Love Me in Altoona, 1976, The Third Ti
Around: Confessions of a Happy Hoofer, 1980, How
Live to be One Hundred or More, 1983, Dear Geor
Advice and Answers from America's Leading Expert
Everything from A to B, 1985, Gracie: A Love Sto
1988, (with David Fisher) All My Best Friends, 19
(with Hal Goodman) Wisdom of the 90s, 1991
Recipient Kennedy Ctr. Honor, 1988. Home: Beve
Hills Calif Died March 9, 1996.

BURNS, JOHN TOLMAN, consultant, form
manufacturing company executive; b. Montgome
Ala., May 16, 1922; s. Loren J. and Harriett (McFerra
B.; m. Patricia Jacques, Sept. 25, 1954; children: Sco
Kent. B.S., U. Louisville, 1943. Asst. hydraulic gro
engr. Douglas Aircraft Co., 1946-56; dist. sales m
aerospace div. Vickers, Inc., Torrance, Calif., 1956-
gen. sales mgr. Vickers, Inc., 1958-61, marketing mg
1961-62; gen. mgr. Vickers, Inc. (European div. intern
div.), 1962-64, v.p., gen. mgr., 1964-68; pres. Vick
div. Sperry Rand Corp., Troy, Mich., 1968-81; con
1980-93. Served to lt. (j.g.) USNR, 1944-46. Home:
Canada Flintridge Calif. Died Aug. 1993.

BURNS, ROGER GEORGE, mineralogist, educator;
Wellington, N.Z., Dec. 28, 1937; s. Alexander Par
and Jean Gertrude (Rodgers) B.; m. Virginia Anne M
Sept. 7, 1963; children: Kirk George, Jonath
Roger. BSc (Sir George Grey scholar 1958, Em
Lilias Johnson scholar 1959), Victoria U. of Wellingt
1959, MSc, 1961; PhD (Sci. fellow), U. Calif., Berkel
1965; MA in Geology (Brit. Council scholar 1965-
Natural Environ. Research Council, Eng. fellow 196
Oxford U., 1968, DSc, 1984. Demonstrator chemis
dept. Victoria U. of Wellington, 1959-60, sr. lectr.
ochemistry, 1967; sci. officer Dept. Sci. and Indsl. Rsc
Wellington, 1961; rsch. assoc. dept. engring. scis.
Calif., Berkeley, 1965; sr. rsch. visitor dept. mineral
and petrology Cambridge U., Eng., 1966; lectr.
ochemistry Oxford U., 1968-70; assoc. prof.
ochemistry MIT, Cambridge, 1970-72; prof. mineralo
and geochemistry MIT, 1972-94; vis. prof. Scripps Ins
Oceanography, La Jolla, Calif., 1976; UNESCO pr
Jadavpur U., Calcutta, India, 1981; Hallimond lec
Mineral. Soc. Eng., 1987; Guggenheim prof. Manches
U., England, 1991; prin. investigator lunar sam
analysis team Apollo program NASA, 1970-94, me
lunar and planetary proposal rev. panel, 1978-81; me
exec. com. Manganese Nodule Project Seabed Asse
ment Program Internat. Decade Ocean Explorati
NSF, 1974-80; mem. adv. panel Marine Minerals Offi
1976; mem. rev. panel Nat. Scis. and Engring. Rs
Can., 1985; mem. steering com. NASA MSATT proje
1990-94. Author: Mineralogical Applications of Crys
Field Thepry, 2d edit., 1993; editor: Chem. Geolo
1968-85, Canadian Mineralogist, 1988-90; assoc. edit
Geochimica et Cosmochimica Acta, 1978-94; cont
articles to profl. publs. Fulbright travel grantee U
Govt., 1961; Sci. Research fellow Com. for Exhbn.
1851, London, 1961-63; Pacific scholar English Speak
Union, San Francisco, 1961-63; fellow Wolfson C
Oxford U., 1970, Guggenheim fellow, 1990-91. Fell
Mineral. Soc. Am. (life; award 1976, councillor 1978-
rep. for Geol. Soc. Am. abstracts rev. com. 1984-8
mem. Mineral. Soc. Gt. Britain; Mem. Am. Geoph
Union (mineral physics com. 1984-86), Geochem. So
N.Z. Geochem. Group. Presbyterian. Home: Ca
bridge Mass. Died Jan. 7, 1994.

BURNS, WILLIAM HAYWOOD, lawyer, dean, ec
cator; b. Peekskill, N.Y., June 15, 1940; s. Junic
Haywood and Josephine (Clark) B.; m. Jennifer El
Dohrn, May 1, 1988; children: Seth, Amilcar, Jeremi
Haydee, Atariba. BA with honors, Harvard Co
1962; postgrad. fellowship, Cambridge U., 1962-63; J
Yale U., 1966. Bar: N.Y. 1967, U.S. Supreme Ct. 197
Assoc. Paul, Weiss, Rifkind, Whaston & Garris
N.Y.C., 1966; law clk. U.S. Dist. Ct. Judge C.
Motley, N.Y.C., 1966-67; asst. counsel NAACP Le
Def. and Edn. Fund, N.Y.C., 1967-69; nat. dir. N
Conf. of Black Lawyers, N.Y.C., 1970-73; vis. pr
SUNY at Buffalo (N.Y.) Law Sch., 1974-75; assoc. p
NYU Law Sch., N.Y.C., 1975-77; vice provost and de
Ctr. for Legal Edn. CCNY, N.Y.C., 1977-87; de
CUNY Law Sch. at Queens Coll., N.Y.C., from 19
v.p. Ctr. for Constnl. Rights, N.Y.C., from 1981; p
Nat. Inst., N.Y.C., from 1984. Author: Voices of Ne
Protest in America, 1963; contbr. articles, chpts. a
poetry. Vice chair Prisoner Legal Svcs. N.Y.; dir. V
Inst. for Justice, 21st Century Found., Boehm Foun
chmn. Neighborhood Defender Svc. Harlem, all N.Y.
Recipient Pres.'s award Malcolm-King Coll., N.Y.
1983, Florina Lasker award N.Y. Civil Liberties Uni

.Y.C., 1986, Human Rights award Bronx Community oll., N.Y.C., 1988, Lawyer for Justice award Bklyn. N.Y.) Legal Svcs., 1988. Mem. ABA (pro bono profl. sponsibilities award litigation sect. 1989), Nat. Bar ssn., Assn. of the Bar of the City of N.Y., Nat. Conf. ack Lawyers (chmn. 1982-85, Founders award 1973), at. Lawyers Guild (nat. pres. 1986-88), Queens County ar Assn., Coun. on Fgn. Rels. Home: New Rochelle .Y. Deceased.

URR, RAYMOND, actor; b. New Westminster, Can., ay 21, 1917. Student, Stanford U., U. Calif., olumbia, U. Chungking. Formerly radio actor. Ap-eared on stage, numerous countries, in Night Must all, Mandarin, Crazy with the Heat, Duke in Darkness; r. Pasadena Community Playhouse, 1943; star TV ries Perry Mason Show, 1961, 62 (recipient Emmy ward as best actor), Ironside, 1967-75, Kingston: Con-dential, 1977; appeared in numerous motion pictures cluding They Were So Young, 1955, You're Never oo Young, 1955, A Man Alone, 1955, Count Three d Pray, 1955, Please Murder Me, 1956, Godzilla King the Monsters, 1956, Great Day in the Morning, 1956, cret of Treasure Mountain, 1956, Cry in the Night, 56, Criss Cross, 1949, P.J, 1968, Rear Window, odzilla, 1985, Airplane II: The Sequel, 1982, others; peared in TV movies Kingston: The Power Play, 76, Mallory: Circumstantial Evidence, 1976, 79 Park venue, 1977, Centennial, 1978, Disaster on the oastliner, 1979, The Curse of King Tut's Tomb, 1980, ne Night the City Screamed, 1980, Peter and Paul, 81, Return of Perry Mason, 1985, Perry Mason: The ase of the Avenging Ace, 1988, The Case of the Lady the Lake, The Case of the Scandalous Scoundrel, ial by Jury, The Case of the Lethal Lesson. Home: erman Oaks Calif. Died Sept. 12, 1993.

URROUGHS, THOMAS, state education of-cial. Chmn. Bd. Edn. State of Ill. Home: Springfield . Deceased.

URROWS, GATES WILSON, retired architect; b. nta Paula, Calif., Apr. 17, 1899; s. Hubert Gates and llie Josephine (Wilson) B.; m. Lucinda Margaret Grif-h; 1 child, Gates Wilson Jr. Student, Stanford U., 18-21; BS, MIT, 1925; student, Fontainbleau Sch. ne Arts, France, 1926. Prin. Gates W. Burrows, rchitect, Laguna Beach, Calif., 1937-42, Santa Ana, alif., 1945-62; prin. Burrows and Allen Architects, nta Ana, 1962-73. Pres. Laguna Beach Art Mus., 45-46; mem. Episcopal Bishops Archtl. Commn., A., 1953-90. Fellow AIA (pres. Orange County chpt. 55-56); mem. Laguna Beach Art Assn. (life), Marine eml. (life), University Club (L.A.). Republican. iscopalian. Home: Laguna Hills Calif. Died May, 95.

URTON, CLAYTON B., SR., lawyer; b. Rock Island, ., Dec. 8, 1932; s. Benjamin Clayton and Beatrice arpole) B.; m. Joan Hubbel, Sept. 6, 1956; children: ayton B., Joan Lowell. B.A., U. Md., 1957, J.D., 60. Bar: Md. 1960, U.S. Ct. Mil. Appeals 1962, Fla. 67, U.S. Supreme Ct. 1975. Vice pres. Am. Internat. and Corp., Miami, Fla., 1962-63; corp. counsel Jack ckerd Corp., Clearwater, Fla., 1963-64, Li'l Gen. ores, Tampa, Fla., 1964-67; pres. Burton Profl. Assn., d predecessor firms, Clearwater, 1968-94. Author: tate Planning Understood, 1985, Before You Invest, 85, Before (and After) You Invest, 1986, new edit., 87, You Can Take It With You, 1988; author vide-apes. Served with JAGC, USAF, 1960-62, col. Res. . Recipient USAF Res. Lawyer of Yr. award, 1981, eservist of Yr. award, 1981, Lawyer of Yr. award actical Air Command, USAF, 1980, 81, Civilian Medal r Outstanding Pub. Service U.S. Sec. Def., 1988; hon. em. staff and faculty JAG's Sch. U.S. Army, 1985-94 . Mem. ABA (standing com. on legal assistance for mil. rsonnel 1981-87, chmn. 1984-87, vice chmn. mil. law m. gen. practice sect. 1981-94 , mem. consortium on gal services and the pub. 1984-87, vice chmn. estate anning com. gen. practice sect. 1985-87, chmn. 1987-), Res. Officers Assn. (life), Air Force Assn. (life), abbard and Blade (past nat. v.p.), Fla. Bar Assn. hmn. mil. law com. 1979-81), Sigma Nu, Phi Alpha elta. Republican. Episcopalian. Home: Clearwater a. Died 1994.

URTON, COURTNEY, mining and shipping com-any executive; b. Cleve., Oct. 29, 1912; s. Courtney and rita (Oglebay) B.; m. Marguerite Rankin, Sept. 7, 33 (dec. Apr. 1976); children: Sarita Ann Burton ith, Marguerite Rankin Burton Humphrey; m. Mar-ret Butler Leitch, Dec. 20, 1978. Student, Mich. Coll. ining and Tech., 1933-34, B.S., 1956. Dir. E.W. glebay Co., Cleve., 1934-57; pres. E.W. Oglebay Co., 47-57; v.p. Ferro Engrng. Co., Cleve., 1950-57; pres. ortuna Lake Mining Co., Cleve., 1950-57; treas., dir. olumbia Transp. Co., Cleve., 1950-57; v.p. Montreal ining Co., Cleve., 1950-57; pres. North Shore Land ., Cleve., 1950-57; v.p., dir. Brule Smokeless Coal ., Cleve., 1950-57; chmn. bd., chmn. exec. com. glebay Norton Co., 1957—; 1dir. Nat. Bank W.Va., 51-59, Central Nat. Bank Cleve., 1941-42, Cleve. ust Co., 1950-76. Dir. Ohio Civilian Def. and Ra-oning, 1941-42; exec. asst. Office Coordinator Inter-m. Affairs, 1942-44; mayor Village of Gates Mills, hio, 1948-61; mem. Cleve. Met. Park Bd., 1969-74; mn. Ohio Republican Finance Com., 1954-61, Rep. Nat. Finance Dir., 1961-64; former trustee, founder, mem. adminstrv. bd. Nat. Recreation and Park Assn.; bd. dirs. Nat. Park Found.; trustee Bethany Coll.; hon. trustee Univ. Hosp., Cleve., Oglebay Inst., Wheeling, W.Va.; pres. America's Future Trees Found. Served to lt. USNR, 1944-46. Mem. Am. Iron and Steel Inst., Nat. Coal Assn., Cleve. Zool. Soc. (pres. 1968-76). Episcopalian. Clubs: Chagrin Valley Hunt (Gates Mills) (master of hounds 1946-54); Tavern, Union (Cleve.); Fort Henry; Wheeling (W.Va.) Country; Kirtland Country (Willoughby, Ohio); Outrigger Canoe (Honolulu). Home: Cleveland Ohio

BUSCH, BENJAMIN, lawyer, educator; b. N.Y.C., June 12, 1912; s. S. Henry and Dorothy (Busch) B.; m. Phyllis Toby Schnell, Nov. 8, 1935; children: Frederick Matthew, Eric Edwin. Student, CCNY, 1928-30; LL.B., St. Lawrence U., 1933. Bar: N.Y. 1934. Ptnr. Katz & Sommerich, 1946-76; counsel Hamburger, Weinschenk, Molnar & Busch, from 1976; Adj. prof. comparative and internat. law N.Y. Law Sch., from 1973; appointed to Arbitration Panel for the U.S. Dist. Ct. (ea. dist.) N.Y., 1986. Author: (with Otto C. Sommerich) Foreign Law-A Guide to Pleading and Proof, 1959; also articles. Explorer, adviser Boy Scouts Am. Served with AUS, 1944-45. Decorated Bronze Star, Purple Heart. Mem. ABA (chmn. sect. internat. law 1972-73, observer to UN 1974-79), N.Y.C. Bar Assn. (mem. internat. law com. 1973-76, fgn. law com. 1978-79), N.Y. State Bar Assn., Am. Judicature Soc., Am. Fgn. Law Assn. (pres. 1969-70, Ann. award 1981), Consular Law Soc., Am. Soc. Internat. Law, 10th Mountain Div. Assn. Club: Appalachian Mountain (life). Home: Lakeville Conn. Died Sept. 15, 1989.

BUSENBERG, STAVROS NICHOLAS, mathematics educator; b. Jerusalem, Israel, Oct. 16, 1941; came to U.S. 1957; s. George Eurybiades and Panayota (Kotopoulea) B.; m. Bernadette Eleanor Egan, June 21, 1969; children: George, John. BME, Cooper Union, N.Y.C., 1962; MS, Ill. Inst. Tech., Chgo., 1964; PhD, Ill. Inst. Tech., 1967. Instr. math. Loyola U., Chgo., 1966-67; rsch. fellow Sci. Ctr. of Rockwell Internat., Thousand Oaks, Calif., 1967-68; asst. prof. Harvey Mudd Coll., Claremont, Calif., 1968-73; assoc. prof. Harvey Mudd Coll., 1973-79, prof. math., 1979—; mem. grad. faculty Claremont Grad. Sch., 1971—; dir. Math. Clinic, Harvey Mudd Coll., 1981-82, 1990—; cons. Oak Ridge Nat. Lab., 1979-82. Author: Models and Analysis of Vertically Transmitted Diseases, 1992; editor: Differential Equations and Applications, 1981, Delay Differential Equations and Dynamical Systems, 1991; contbr. articles to profl. jours.; assoc. editor Jour. Math. Analysis and Applications; editorial bd. Jour. Math. Biology. NSF grantee, 1971—; Fulbright Rsch. prof., 1988. Mem. Am. Math. Soc., Math. Assn. Am. (sci. policy com. 1987—), Soc. for Indsl. and Applied Math. Home: Claremont Calif.

BUSH, DOROTHY VREDENBURGH, political party executive; b. Baldwyn, Miss., Dec. 8, 1916; d. Will Lee and Lany (Holl) McElroy; m. Peter Vredenburgh, 3d, Dec. 27, 1940 (dec.); m. John W. Bush, Jan. 13, 1962; stepchildren: Peter (dec.), Jan Jennings, Emily Zuckett. Student, George Washington U., summer 1935; B.S., Miss. State Coll. for Women (now Miss. U. for Women), 1937. Sec. to dir. ins. bur. Tenn. Coal, Iron & R.R. Co. (subsidiary U.S. Steel), Birmingham, Ala., 1937-40; Nat. committeewoman Ala. Young Democrats, 1941-50; asst. sec. conv. Young Dems. Am., 1941, v.p., 1943-48; co-chmn. Jackson Day dinners of Ala., 1944; sec. Dem. Nat. Com., 1944-89, sec. emeritus, 1989-91; (1st woman to hold this position); acting pres. Young Dems. Am., 1944; sec. Dem. Nat. Convs., 1944, 48, 52, 56, 60, 64, 68, 72, 76, 80, 84, 88. Trustee North Collier County Hosp., 1991. Recipient Career Achievement award U.S. Govt., 1991. Mem. Ark. Traveler (life), Beta Sigma Phi. Baptist. Home: Naples Fla. Died Dec. 21, 1991.

BUSH-BROWN, ALBERT, architectural, educational and financial consultant; b. West Hartford, Conn., Jan. 2, 1926; s. James and Louise (Carter) Bush-B.; m. Frances Wesselhoeft, Aug. 28, 1948; children: David, Frances, Lesley, Martha. AB, Princeton U., 1947, MFA, 1949, PhD, 1958; LLD, Emerson Coll., 1965; HHD, Providence Coll., 1966; DFA, Mercy Coll., 1976. Instr. art and archaeology Princeton U., 1949-50; jr. fellow Soc. of Fellows, Harvard U., 1950-53; prof. art and architecture Western Res. U., Cleve., 1953-54; prof. architecture and humanities MIT, 1954-62; pres. R.I. Sch. Design, 1962-68; prof., v.p. SUNY, Buffalo, 1968-71; chancellor L.I. U., 1971-85; chmn. Barclays Bank of N.Y., 1981-88, chmn. regional adv. bd., 1989-91; sr. counselor Hill & Knowlton Internat., N.Y.C., 1988-91; sr. cons. Paul R. Ray Co., N.Y.C., 1987-90; chmn. bd. dirs. The Barrel Hill Group, 1983-94; pres. Albert Bush-Brown Assocs., 1980-94; advisor Toshiba Found., 1989-94; vis. scholar MIT, 1993-94. Author: Louis Sullivan, 1960; (with J.E. Burchard) The Architecture of America: A Social Interpretation, 1961, Books, Bass, Barnstable, 1967, King Khalid Military City, 1978, Skidmore, Owings and Merrill 1973-83, 1983, (with Dianne Davis) Hospitable Design for Healthcare and Senior Communities, 1991; editor architecture sect. Ency. Brit., 1955-94; contbr. articles to profl. jours. Active Providence City Planning Commn., 1962-67; spl. advisor to sec. Dept. of Housing and Urban Devel., 1968-69, U. Mass, 1970-71; mem. White House Nat. Council on Arts, 1965-70, Trilateral Commn., Bretton Woods Conf.; bd. govs. Sch. of Arts, U. Pa., 1975-85; bd. dirs. Recording for the Blind, 1976-81; bd. mng. dirs. Met. Opera, 1976-85. Woodrow Wilson fellow Princeton U., 1947-48; Howard Found. fellow Brown U., 1959-60; fellow Inst. Politics, J.F. Kennedy Sch. Govt., Harvard, 1968-69. Mem. AIA (hon.), Council on Fgn. Relations, N.Y. Acad. Scis. Clubs: Century Assn. Home: Barnstable Mass. Died July 22, 1994.

BUTENANDT, ADOLF FRIEDRICH JOHANN, physiological chemist; b. Bremerhaven, Germany, Mar. 24, 1903; s. Otto and Wilhelmine (Thomfohrde) B.; m. Erika von Ziegner, 1931; 2 sons, 5 daus. PhD; student, Oberrealschule Bremerhaven, U. Marburg, U. Göttingen. Sci. asst. Chem. Inst. Göttingen U., 1927-30, docent in organic and biol. chemistry, 1931; prof. chemistry, dir. Organic Chemistry Inst. Danzig (Germany) Inst. Tech., 1933-36; dir. Kaiser Wilhelm Inst. Biochemistry, Berlin; dir. Max Planck Inst. Biochemistry, Tubingen and Munich, Munich, 1936-72; prof. physiol. chemistry Munich U., 1956-71, prof. emeritus, 1971—. Author: Biochemie der Wirkstoffe; also articles. Recipient Nobel prize for chemistry, 1939; Adolf von Harnack medal Max Planck Soc., 1973; decorated Orden pour le Mérite, 1962, comdr. Légion d'Honneur, Ordr Palmes Académiques; Österreichisches Ehrenzeichen für Wissenschaft und Kunst. Mem. Max Planck Soc. (pres. 1960-72, hon. pres. 1972), Acad. Scis. Paris (fgn.). Home: Munich Germany Died Jan. 18, 1995.

BUTLER, BROADUS NATHANIEL, university administrator; b. Mobile, Ala., May 28, 1920; s. John Nathaniel and Mary Lillian B.; m. Lillian P. Rutherford, Dec. 27, 1947; children: Bruce N., Janet Cecile (Mrs. Reid). BA, Talladega (Ala.) Coll., 1941; MA, U. Mich., 1947, PhD, 1952. Instr. philosophy St. Augustine's Coll., Raleigh, N.C., 1953; dean guidance, asst. prof. humanities Talladega Coll., 1953-56; grad. officer Coll. Liberal Arts Wayne State U., Detroit, 1957-68, asst. to dean, 1956-68, asst. to U.S. commr. edn., 1964-65, spl. asst. to assoc. commr. for higher edn., 1965-66; dean Coll. Arts and Scis. Tex. So. U., 1969; pres. Dillard U., New Orleans, 1969-73; dir. Office Leadership Devel. in Higher Edn., Am. Council on Edn., Washington, 1974-77; pres. Robert Russa Moton Meml. Inst., 1977-80; dir. Office Internat. Affairs and Research, NAACP Spl. Contbn. Fund, Washington, 1981-96; acad. v.p. U. D.C.; disting. scholar-in-residence Ky. State U., 1984; disting. scholar-at-large MacArthur Found., United Negro Coll. Fund, 1987-88; dir. archives DeMartin Luther King, Jr. Meml. Ctr., Atlanta, 1988-89; bd. dirs. New Orleans br. Fed. Res. Bank Atlanta. Author, editor, lectr., research scholar. Mem. New Orleans Mayor's Com. on Internat. Trade Relations, La. Commn. for Performing Arts; commr. La. Ednl. TV Authority, La. Museum Commn.; adv. com. NSF; bd. dirs. Assn. Study Negro Life and History, NAACP, Nat. Merit Scholarship Corp., Internat. Trade Mart, New Orleans Philharmonic Soc., New Orleans Children's Bur., CEMREL St. Louis; trustee Lane Coll., Center for Study of the Presidency, N.Y.C., Internat. Inst. Public Mgmt.; pub. mem. Assn. Fgn. Svc. Selection Bds. U.S. Dept. of State and U.S. Info. Agy. Served with USAAF, 1942-45. Named Citizen of Yr. Mich. Chronicle, 1962, Hon. Citizen New Orleans and Mobile, Ala.; recipient Social Action award Phi Beta Sigma, 1961, Pan-Africa Student Union Service award, 1963, William H. Hastie Disting. Svc. award Nat. Bar Assn.; decorated grand comdr. Order Star of Africa, Liberia; named to Hon. Order of Ky. Cols.; others. Mem. NAACP (life), Assn. U.S. State Dept. (dir.), Nat. Urban League, New Orleans C. of C. (dir.), Hist. Soc. Mich., Am. Acad. Polit. and Social Sci., Assn. Fgn. Service (pub. mem. dir.), Am. Pub. Health Assn., Tuskegee Airmen World War II (pres. East Coast chpt. 1994-96), Omega Psi Phi (Founders award), Sigma Pi Phi, Phi Delta Kappa. Mem. Protestant Episcopal Ch. Clubs: Internat. House (New Orleans); Cosmos (Washington). Home: Silver Spring Maryland Died Jan. 9, 1996.

BYAM, SEWARD GROVES, JR., financial executive; b. Bridgeport, Conn., Jan. 9, 1928; s. Seward Groves and Marjorie W. (Cotton) B.; student Princeton U., 1949, U. Del., 1951; m. Constance Patricia Randell, Feb. 28, 1981; children: Pamela E. Byam Tinsley, John T. Mktg. exec. duPont Co., 1951-67; bus. mgr. Dow Badische Co., 1967-76; mktg. dir. Borg Textile Corp., 1976-79; v.p. Tower Securities Inc., 1979-81; pres., prin. Seward, Groves, Richard & Wells, Inc., 1985—; pres. Randell-Byam Assocs., Inc., Rye, N.Y., 1987—; mng. dir. Fiduciary Counsel Inc., 1981—, Econ. Analysts, Inc., 1983—. Chmn. Williamsburg (Va.) Sch. Bd., 1973-76. With USMC, 1946-47, USMCR, 1947-51. Mem. SAR, Mensa, Union League, Princeton Club, Nassau Club, Apawamis Club. Episcopalian. Home: New York N.Y.

BYERS, BUCKLEY MORRIS, business executive; b. Pitts., Jan. 7, 1917; s. John Frederic and Caroline Mitchell (Morris) B.; m. Rosamond Farrell Murray, Nov. 19, 1940 (dec. Oct. 21, 1984); children: Buckley Morris, Joseph Murray, Christopher Farrell; m. Mary Helen Herndon Powell, Nov. 21, 1987. A.B., Yale U., 1940. Salesman A.M. Byers Co., Pitts., 1940-42; asst.

mgr. A.M. Byers Co., Washington, 1942; asst. mgr. A.M. Byers Co., N.Y.C., 1945-51, mgr. export dept., 1946-51, asst. mgr. steel sales, 1951-53, gen. mgr. wrought iron sales, 1953-54, v.p. charge sales, 1954-57, pres., 1957-62, dir., 1948-70; v.p., spl. asst. to pres. Blaw-Knox Co., Pitts., 1962-64; pres., dir. Byers McManus Assocs. Inc., Washington, 1965-89. Dep. fin. chmn. Rep. Nat. Com., 1976-81, cons. to the chmn., 1981-89; cons. to the pres. of Boys Clubs of Am., 1981-89. Served from ensign to lt. USN Intelligence, 1942-45, overseas 4 major invasions in ETO, PTO. Recipient Presl. citation and Individual commendation. Mem. Nat. Steeplechase and Hunt Assn. Clubs: F St. (Washington), Capitol Hill (Washington), Carlton (Washington), Internat. (Washington), Met. (Washington); Rolling Rock (Pitts.), Duquesne (Pitts.), Allegheny Country (Pitts.); Fence, Book and Snake (Yale); Racquet and Tennis (N.Y.C.). Home: Washington D.C. Died Jan. 20, 1989.

BYRNES, DONALD J., consumer products company executive; b. Glendive, Mont., May 5, 1926; s. Charles Joseph and Amanda Marie (Halvorson) B.; m. Carol Jean Dana, Aug. 14, 1949; children—Donald, Karen, David, Ronald. BBA, U. Mont., Missoula, 1949. With phys. damange ins. dept. Gen. Motors Corp., Gt. Falls, Mont., 1949-57; mgr. mktg. Gen. Electric. Co., Louisville, 1957-71; mgr. mktg. Evenflo Juvenile Products Co., Ravenna, Ohio, 1971-72, v.p. mktg., 1972-73; v.p. ops. Evenflo Juvenile Furniture Co., L.A., 1973-77; pres. Questor Juvenile Furniture Co., L.A., 1977-80, L.A. and Ravenna, 1980-81; sr. v.p., chief oper. officer Questor Corp., Tampa, Fla., 1982-84; pres., chief oper. officer Spalding and Evenflo Cos., Inc., Tampa, 1984-95, also bd. dirs.; pres. E & S Holdings Corp., Tampa. Served with USN, 1944-46; PTO. Home: Tampa Fla. Died Sept. 5, 1995.

BYRNES, GEORGE BARTHOLOMEW, pension-insurance consultant; b. Kansas City, Mo., Oct. 19, 1911; s. James C. and Hannah (Haffey) B.; m. Grace E. Mehren, Apr. 11, 1942; children: Marygrace, Patrick, Robert, Brian, Kathleen. Student, Rockhurst Coll., Kansas City, 1929-31; grad., U. N.Mex., 1935. Rep. Equitable Life Assurance Soc., Albuquerque, 1935-42; dist. mgr. Equitable Life Assurance Soc., Phoenix, 1942-45, Pasadena, Calif., 1945-54; gen. agt. New Eng. Mut. Life Ins. Co., N.Y.C., 1954-60; cons. pension and profit-sharing planning, bus. and personal estate plans Los Angeles, 1960-91. Pres. Pasadena Tb Assn., 1954, Nat. Epilepsy League, 1960; Bd. dirs. Million Dollar Round Table Found., Des Plaines, Ill.; Mem. bd. fellows U. Santa Clara, Calif.; trustee Little Co. of Mary Hosp. Found.; v.p., bd. dirs. Knights of Malta Free Clinic. Decorated knight magistral grace Sovereign Mil. Order of Malta; named Honor agt. Equitable Life Assurance Soc., 1949. Mem. C.L.U.'s Assn. Los Angeles (v.p. 1952-53, nat. bd. 1958-60), Life Ins. and Trust Council Los Angeles (sec.-treas. 1951-52, v.p. 1952-53, pres. 1953-54), Million Dollar Round Table (exec. com. 1952-54, pres. 1955), Pasadena C. of C. (mem. bd. 1950, 53, sec.-treas. 1952, 2d v.p. 1953, 1st v.p. 1954), Tournament of Roses Assn., Phi Kappa Phi, Sigma Chi. Roman Catholic. Club: California (Los Angeles). Home: Palos Verdes Peninsula Calif. Died Dec. 6, 1991.

BYRNES, VICTOR ALLEN, ophthalmologist; b. Tipton, Iowa, June 4, 1906; s. Victor Warren and Wilhelmina (Brauch) B.; m. Ethel M. Ahlberg-Seebach, June 6, 1929 (div. Aug. 1949); children: Donn A., Diane E.; m. Jean Beryl Crowly, Aug. 13, 1949. BS, U. Iowa, 1927, MD, 1929. Diplomate Am. Bd. Ophthalmology, Am. Bd. Preventive Medicine. Commd. 1st lt. U.S. Air Force, 1929, advanced through grades to brig. gen., 1956; asst. commandant USAF Sch. Aviation Medicine, 1943-44; comdr. Air Base and Convalescent Hosp., Nashville, Plattsburg Barracks, N.Y., 1944-45; staff surgeon Fifth Air Force, Okinawa, Japan, 1945-46; dir. edn. and clin. medicine div. USAF Sch. Aviation Medicine, 1946-53; dep. surgeon U.S. Air Forces in Europe, 1953-55; dir. profl. svcs. Office Air Surgeon Gen., USAF, Washington, 1955-59; dir. med. edn. Mound Park Hosp., St. Petersburg, Fla., 1959-61; practice medicine specializing in ophthalmology, St. Petersburg, 1961-74; med. adjudicator VA, St. Petersburg, 1979-86; ret. Mem. editorial adv. bd. Jour. Aerospace Medicine, 1955-68; sect. editor Survey of Ophthalmology, 1959-68; mem. editorial adv. bd. Armed Forces Med. Jour., 1954-60; bd. editors Sight Saving Rev., 1961-70. Contbr. articles on ophthalmology to profl. jours. Decorated Legion of Merit with oak leaf cluster; recipient Gorgas medal Assn. Mil. Surgeons, 1955, Liljencrantz award Aerospace Med. Assn., 1958. Fellow Aerospace Med. Assn. (exec. council 1956-59), ACS (bd. govs. 1957-59), AMA (com. on aviation medicine 1957-59); mem. Am. Acad. Ophthalmology and Otolaryngology (exec. council 1957-61, honor award 1959), Am. Ophthal. Soc., Soc. Mil. Ophthalmologists, Assn. for Rsch. in Ophthalmology and Vision, Assn. Mil. Surgeons, Pan Am. Ophthal. Soc. (com. on space ophthalmology 1957), Mexican Ophthal. Soc. (hon.), Cuban Ophthal. Soc. (hon.), Alpha Omega Alpha. Republican. Lodge: Rotary. Died Aug. 10, 1994. Home: San Antonio Tex.

CABOT, PAUL CODMAN, investment company executive; b. Brookline, Mass., Oct. 21, 1898; s. Henry B. and Anne M. (Codman) C.; m. Virginia Converse, Sept. 20, 1924; children: Virginia Wood, Elizabeth Minot, Paul C., Frederick C., Edmund C. A.B., Harvard U., 1921, M.B.A. with distinction, 1923, LL.D., 1966; LL.D., Yale U., 1965. Treas. Harvard U., Cambridge, Mass., 1948-65; former chmn. bd. State St. Investment Corp., 1924-94; sr. ptnr. State St. Research & Mgmt. Co., Boston, 1924-94, ret. Served to 2d lt. arty. U.S. Army, World War-I; served with War Production Bd., World War II. Mem. Bus. Council. Republican. Clubs: Harvard (Boston); Porcellian (Cambridge); Dedham Country and Polo (Mass.). Home: Needham Mass. Died Sept. 1, 1994.

CABOT, THOMAS DUDLEY, chemical company executive; b. Cambridge, Mass., May 1, 1897; s. Godfrey Lowell and Maria Buckminster (Moors) C.; m. Virginia Wellington, May 15, 1920; children: Louis Wellington, Thomas Dudley, Robert Moors, Linda, Edmund Billings. AB, Harvard, 1919; LHD, Tufts U., 1951, Boston U., 1961; LLD, Northeastern U., 1952, Morris Harvey Coll., 1953, Harvard, 1970; DSc, Loughborough U., 1980. Former pres. United Fruit Co., Boston; pres. Godfrey L. Cabot, Inc. (name changed to Cabot Corp., 1960), chmn. bd., 1960-68, hon. chmn. bd., 1968-95; dir. Controlled Risk Ins. Co., Ltd.; former dir. John Hancock Mut. Life Ins. Co., First Nat. Bank of Boston, Am. Mut. Liability Ins. Co.; Chmn. Mass. Aero Commn., 1944-45; dir. office Internat. Security Affairs, Dept. of State, 1951; cons. Spl. Mission to Egypt, 1953. Author: Beggar on Horseback. Bd. overseers Harvard, 1953-59, 62-68; mem. governing bd. Harvard-Mass. Inst. Tech. Div. in Health Scis. and Tech., 1977-95; trustee Radcliffe Coll., Escuela Agricola Panamericana; mem. corp. emeritus Mass. Inst. Tech.; hon. trustee Com. Econ. Devel.; trustee Children's Med. Center; hon. bd. dirs. Brigham and Women's Hosp. Served as 2d lt., A.S. U.S. Army; flying instr. 1917-18. Decorated chevalier Legion of Honor France; commendatore Al Merito della Republica Italiana. Fellow AAAS; mem. Council Fgn. Relations, Internat. C. of C. (trustee U.S. council). Republican. Unitarian. Home: Weston Mass. Died June 8, 1995.

CADDEN, VIVIAN LIEBMAN, magazine editor; b. N.Y.C., Mar. 29, 1917; d. Harry and Jennie (Gus) Liebman; m. Joseph E. Cadden, June 16, 1940 (dec. 1980); children: Joan, Wendy, Frank. BA, Vassar Coll., 1938; PhM, Columbia U., 1940. Sr. editor Redbook mag., N.Y.C., 1960-68; sr. editor, writer McCall's mag., N.Y.C., 1968-78, editor-at-large, 1986-95; editor Working Mother mag., N.Y.C., 1978-86; editor-at-large Working Mother mag., 1986-95; v.p. McCall Pub. Co., N.Y.C., 1978-86, editor-at-large, 1986-95. Co-author: The Intelligent Man's Guide to Women, 1951; contbr. articles to mags. Bd. dirs. Child Care Action Campaign. Univ. fellow Columbia U., 1940. Home: New York N.Y. DIed May, 1995.

CADY, GEORGE HAMILTON, chemistry educator; b. Lawrence, Kans., Jan. 10, 1906; s. Hamilton P. and Stella (Gallup) C.; m. Alpha Marsh, June 2, 1929 (dec. June 1982); children: Howard H., Carl M.; m. Agnes Irene Hoving, Feb. 15, 1986. AB, U. Kans., 1927, AM, 1928; PhD, U. Calif., Berkeley, 1930. Asst. prof. U. S.D., Vermilion, 1930-31; instr. MIT, Cambridge, 1931-34; rsch. chemist U.S. Rubber Co., Passaic, N.J., 1934-35, Pitts. Plate Glass Co., Barberton, Ohio, 1935-38; asst. prof. U. Wash., Seattle, 1938-41, assoc. prof., 1941-47, prof., 1947-72, prof. emeritus, 1972-93, chmn. chemistry dept., 1961-65; with Manhattan Project Columbia U., N.Y.C., 1942-43; Centenary lectr. The Chem. Soc., London, 1959, G.N. Lewis Meml. lectr., U. Calif., 1967. Recipent citation USN, 1970, Disting. Svc. award U. Kans., 1972, Prix Henri Moissan, 1988. Mem. AAAS, Am. Chem. Soc. (Disting. Svc. award 1966, rsch. in fluorine chemistry award 1972), Deutsche Akademie der Naturforsher Leopoldina, Phi Beta Kappa, Sigma Xi, Alpha Chi Sigma, Phi Lambda Upsilon. Home: Seattle Wash. Died Mar. 18, 1993.

CAFFREY, ANDREW AUGUSTINE, federal judge; b. Lawrence, Mass., Oct. 2, 1920; s. Augustine J. and Monica A. (Regan) C.; m. Evelyn F. White, June 26, 1946; children: Augustine J., Andrew A., James E., Mary L., Francis J., Joseph H. AB cum laude, Holy Cross Coll., 1941; LLB cum laude, Boston Coll., 1948; LLM, Harvard U., 1948. Bar: Mass. 1948, U.S. Supreme Ct. 1958. Assoc. prof. law Boston Coll. Law Sch., 1948-55; asst. U.S. atty., chief civil div. Dist. Mass., 1955-59, 1st asst. U.S. atty., 1959-60, U.S. dist. judge, 1960-93, chief judge, 1972-86, sr. dist. ct. judge, 1986-93; Mem. Jud. Panel on Multidist. Litigation, 1975-90, chmn., 1980-90. Served with AUS, World War II, ETO. Named Alumnus of Yr. Boston Coll. Law Sch., 1986. Mem. ABA, Jud. Conf. U.S. (exec. com. 1973-79), Fed. Bar Assn., Mass. Bar Assn., Boston Bar Assn., Am. Law Inst., Harvard Law Sch. Assn. Mass., Order of Coif (hon.), Alpha Sigma Nu, Delta Epsilon Sigma. Clubs: Merrimack Valley, Holy Cross Alumni (past pres., dir.). Home: Boston Mass. Died Oct. 6, 1993.

CAHILL, JOHN CONWAY, air transportation company executive; b. Ruislip, Jan. 8, 1930; arrived in U.S., 1976; s. Francis Conway and Dorothy Winifred (Mills) Cahill; m. Giovanna Caterina Leonardon, May 7, 1956; children: Karen, Ann, Mary. Salesman London, 1952-54; with BTR Industries, 1955-91; salesman BTR Ltd., London, 1954-58; mgr. BTR Can. Ltd., Toronto, 1958-
62; mgr. BTR Ltd., London, 1962-66, divsn. pres., 196
76; CEO BTR Inc., Providence, 1976-86; mng. dir. BT
PLC, London, 1986-91; chmn. British Aerospace PL
London, 1992-94, TWA Inc., St. Louis, from 1994; b
dirs. BTR plc. With Brit. Army, 1947-50. Hom
Longboat Key Fla. Deceased.

CAHN, JULIUS NORMAN, publishing company e
ecutive; b. N.Y.C., Oct. 26, 1922; s. Richard David ar
Frieda (Cohen) C.; m. Ann Foote, Oct. 20, 1946; chi
dren: Gary Alan, Glenn Evan, Linda Jan, Carol D
ane. B.S.S., CCNY, 1942; M.A., Am. U., 1948. A
minstrv. analyst U.S. Office for Emergency Mgm
1942-44; asst. to U.S. Senator Alexander Wiley, 1945-5
54-58; cons. U.S. Senate Fgn. Relations Com., 1952-5
staff dir. Govt. Ops. Subcom., 1958-64; asst. to Vi
Pres. Hubert Humphrey, 1965-69; pub. assoc. Fami
Health mag., 1969-74; pres. Family Media Enterprise
Inc., N.Y.C., 1975-86, Goals Inc., N.Y.C., 1971-93; b
dirs. Washingtonian mag., 1974-79, Family Media, Inc
1978-86; chmn. editorial adv. bd. Futurist mag., 197
93, Fin. Planner mag., 1974-75; lectr. Am. U., 1952-53
Contbr. articles to profl. publs. Dep. nat. chmn. C
tizens for Humphrey-Muskie presdl. campaign, 1968
Mem. Soc. Fin. Counseling (past chmn. bd.), Sales Exe
Club N.Y. (dir.), Nat. Press Club. Democrat. Jewis
Club: Atrium (N.Y.C.). Home: Rockville Md. Di
May 5, 1993.

CAHN, SAMMY, lyric songwriter; b. N.Y.C., June
1913; s. Abraham and Alice (Reiss) Cohen; m. Glor
Delson, Sept. 5, 1945 (div. May 1964); children—Steve
Laurie; m. Tita Curtis, Aug. 2, 1970. Student pu
schs., N.Y.C. Pres., Songwriters Hall of Fame, 1975—
Violinist since boyhood; organizer of (with Sa
Chaplin) a band; songwriter for motion picture
1940—; writer for: stage shows Walking Happy, Hig
Button Shoes, Skyscraper; songs written include Lo
and Marriage (TV Emmy award, Christopher award
Rhythm in My Nursery Rhymes, Bei Mir Bist Schoe
Until the Real Thing Comes Along, Be My Love, Plea
Be Kind, I've Heard That Song Before, I'll Walk Alon
Shoe Shine Boy, Victory Polka, Because You're Min
Let It Snow, Let It Snow, Let It Snow, It's Magi
Teach Me Tonight, Three Coins in the Fountain (Aca
award 1954), The Tender Trap, All the Way, (Aca
award 1957), High Hopes, (Acad. award 1959), Secor
Time Around, Call Me Irresponsible, (Acad. awa
1963). Named to Songwriters Hall of Fame. Hom
Beverly Hills Calif. Died Jan. 16, 1993.

CAIN, WALKER O., architect; b. Cleve., Apr. 1
1915; s. Oscar Clyde and Meta Mathilde (Gusse) C.;
Abby Jane Huston, June 1941 (div.); children: Sus
Berry Cain Gould, Tamma Huston Cain; m. Elizabe
McCall Houhgton, July 27, 1973. Diploma
Architecture, Ecole de Beaux Arts Americain
Fontainebleu, France, 1937; B.Arch., Western Res. U
1938; M.F.A., Princeton, 1940; fellow, Am. Aca
Rome, 1947-48. With firm McKim, Mead & Whi
architects, N.Y.C., 1940-51, assoc., 1951-61; ptr
Steinmann, Cain & White (architects), N.Y.C., 1961-6
Steinmann & Cain (architects), N.Y.C., 1965-67, Walk
O. Cain & Assocs., 1967-78, Cain, Farrell and Be
1978-86. Prin. works include Campus Plan, Dormit
ries, Bethel, Maine, Maine State Cultural Bld
Schenectady Mus., Jafet Library, Engring. Sch, Hos
addition, faculty apts., Am. U., Beirut, Lebanon, Ball
Hall, Tufts Coll., campus plan dormitories, Liberal Ar
Ctr., Sci. Ctr., Union Coll., Schenectady, Museum Hi
tory and Tech. at Smithsonian Instn., library, fie
house, Computer Ctr., Princeton, library, Bowdo
Coll., St. Vartan Cathedral and cultural ctr. Armeni
Ch. Am, N.Y.C., Casco Bank & Trust Co. office bld
Portland, Maine, additions to New Eng. Ctr. Hos
Boston, Fine Arts Bldg., Lehman Coll., Athletics co
plex, York Coll.; illustrator archtl. mags. and books
Mem. Manhattan Boro Pres. Community Planning B
1965-67; dir. Park Assn. N.Y.C., 1962-65; chmn. Ci
Parks Week, 1962-63; mem. Taconic State Pa
Commn., 1966-72, Nat. Capitol Com., 1969-70, Ea
Hudson Pkwy. Authority, 1966-72; chmn. Am. Aca
Rome, 1973-83; hon. chmn. bd. trustees Garrison
Landing Assn. Museum Transp.; mem. vis. com. vis
arts Western Res. U., 1963-66. Served to lt. USN
1943-46. Recipient Prix de Rome, 1940. Fellow AI
(chmn. urban design com. N.Y. chpt. 1963-65); me
NAD, Am. Arbitration Assn., Soc. Archtl. Historian
Nat. Inst. Archtl. Edn. Clubs: Century Assn. (N.Y.C
Meadow (Southampton, N.Y.). Home: New York N.
Died June 1, 1993.

CAIRNS, THEODORE LESUEUR, chemist;
Edmonton, Alta., Can., July 20, 1914; came to U.S
1936, naturalized, 1945; s. Albert William and Theodo
(MacNaughton) C.; m. Margaret Jean McDonald, Au
17, 1940; children: John Albert, Margaret Eleanor (M
William L. Etter), Elizabeth Theodora (Mrs. Ernest
Reveal III), James Richard. BS, U. Alta., 1936, LL
1970; PhD, U. Ill., 1939. Instr. organic chemistry
Rochester, 1939-41; rsch. chemist cen. rsch. dept. E
duPont de Nemours & Co., Wilmington, Del., 1941-4
rsch. supr., 1945-51, lab. dir., 1951-63, dir. basic sci
1963-66, dir. rsch., 1966-67, asst. dir. cen. R & D dep
1967-71, dir., 1971-79; Regents prof. UCLA, 1965-6
mem. adv. bd. Organic Syntheses, from 1958; me
Pres.'s Sci. Adv. Com., 1970-73, Pres.'s Com. N
Medal Sci., 1974-75; chmn. Office of Chemistry a

Chem. Tech., NRC, 1979-81. Editorial bd.: Organic Reactions, from 1959, Jour. Organic Chemistry, 1965-69. Recipient award for creative work in synthetic organic chemistry Am. Chem. Soc., 1968; Perkin medal, 1973; Cresson medal Franklin Inst., 1974. Mem. NAS, AAAS, Am. Chem. Soc. (chmn. organic divsn. 1964-65), Sigma Xi, Phi Lambda Upsilon, Alpha Chi Sigma, Phi Lambda Upsilon (hon.). Home: Greenville Del. Died Sept. 26, 1995.

CALAMARI, JOHN DANIEL, retired law educator; b. June 22, 1921; s. Agostino and Margaret Elizabeth (Cassella) C.; m. Louise Rose Marzano, June 18, 1955; children: Paul Gerard, Cynthia Louise. A.B., Fordham U., 1942, J.D., 1947; LL.M., N.Y. U., 1950. Bar: N.Y. 1947, U.S. Dist. Ct. (so. dist.) N.Y. 1950, U.S. Dist. Ct. (ea. dist.) N.Y. 1956, U.S. Supreme Ct. 1951. Asst. to gen. counsel U.S. Trucking Corp., N.Y.C., 1947-52; asst. prof. law Fordham U., 1952-57, assoc. prof., 1957-59, prof., 1959-71, Wilkinson prof. law, 1971-91, ret. 1991; cons. to state commns. Served with U.S. Army, 1942-46; with JAGC, U.S. Army, 1951-52. Mem. ABA, Fordham Law Rev. Assn. Club: N.Y. Athletic (N.Y.C.). Author: (with Perillo) Contracts, 1970, 3d edit., 1987, Contracts Cases and Problems, 1978, 2d edit., 1989. Died Nov. 4, 1994. Home: Pelham N.Y.

CALAPAI, LETTERIO, artist; b. Boston, May 29, 1902; s. Biagio and Emanuela (Planeta) C.; m. Jean Hilliard, Jan. 5, 1962. Grad., Mass. Coll. Art, Boston Sch. Fine Arts and Crafts, Art Students League N.Y.C. Head graphics Albright Art Sch., Buffalo, 1949-54; became asso. Contemporaries Graphic Art Center, 1956; faculty mem. New Sch. Social Research, N.Y.C., 1957-61; founder, dir. Intaglio Workshop, N.Y.C., 1960-65; lectr. dept. art edn. N.Y.U., 1962-65; asso. prof. Brandeis U., 1964-65; vis. asso. prof. Kendall Coll., Evanston, Ill., 1965-69; lectr. dept. art and architecture U. Ill., Chgo. Circle, 1966; Mem. art adv. com. Field Mus. Natural History, Chgo., 1973-74; mem. adv. panel Ill. Arts Council, 1971-73. Publs.: 25 Wood Engravings by Letterio Calapai, 1948, A Portfolio of Wood Engravings inspired by Thomas Wolfe's Look Homeward, Angel, 30 Aesop's Fables Printed by Letterio Calapai from the Original Blocks of Thomas Bewick, 1973, A Negro Bible; wood engravings, 1946; Mural Historical Development of Military Signal Communication; commd. by Mural, Works Progress Adminstrn., 1939, acquired by, U.S. Army Signal Corps Mus., Ft. Gordon, Ga., 1980; one-man shows in N.Y.C., Nat. Gallery of Art, Smithsonian Instn., Washington, Paris and London; 50-yr. retrospective Boston Pub. Libr., 1991, Wiggin Gallery, 1991; represented in permanent collections Met. Mus. Art, Boston Mus. Fine Arts, Chgo. Art Inst., Fogg Mus., Bklyn. Mus., Albright Art Gallery, Library of Congress, N.Y. Pub. Library, Boston Pub. Library, Free Library Phila., Rose Mus., Brandeis U., the Biblioteque Nationale, Paris, Princeton U. Library, the Houghton Library (Harvard), Va. Mus. Fine Arts, Columbia U., Wichita (Kans.) State U., Washington U. Gallery Art, St. Louis, Ill. State Mus., Nat. Mus. of Bezalel, Nat. Mus. Jerusalem, Israel, Tokyo Mus., Japan, Civic Gallery Modern Art, Palermo, Italy, Gorakhpur U. Mus. Art, India, Kunsthaus, Zurich, Switzerland, Rosenwald Collection, British Mus., series intaglios " The Seven Last Words of Christ" in Collection of Modern Art Pontifical Monuments, Mus. and Galleries, Vatican Mus., 1987; illustrator: with wood engravings One Hundred Years Ago; restrospective "50 Years of Printmaking" at Palazzo Venezia, Rome, Italian Ministry Fgn. Affairs, 1986; 50-yr. retrospective The Prints of Letterio Calapai, Boston Pub. Libr., 1991. Recipient prize award America In the War Exhibition, 1943; work chosen for Fifty Best Prints of the Year, 1944; Albert H. Wiggins purchase prize First Boston Printmakers Exhbn., 1948; John Taylor Arms prize Soc. Am. Graphic Artists, 1954; Library of Congress purchase prize, 1950, 51, 54; William J. Keller prize Western N.Y. Exhbn., 1954; Tiffany Found. grant in graphic arts, 1959; Audubon Artists medal for creative graphics, 1967; purchase prize 27th Ill. Invitational Exhbn. Ill. State Mus., 1974; purchase awards Art Inst. Chgo., 1972-73; Gold medal for graphics Italian-Am. Artists in U.S.A., 1977, 79; hon. mention Ill. Regional Print Show, 1977; purchase award Northwestern U., 1978; purchase award U. Ill., 1978; Excellence award N. Shore Art League, Chgo., 1982; selected among Chgo.'s North Shore Celebrities in the Arts for a video tape documentary about the artist's work under auspicies of Archival Collection of Highland Pk. (Ill.) Pub. Libr. video-prodn. dept., 1988; selected one of "Seven Venerable Masters" Exhbn., David Adler Cultural Ctr., 1989; invited by Smithsonian Instn. Archives Am. Art. to submit papers and materials relative to life work, 1990. Mem. Soc. Am. Graphic Artists, Boston Printmakers, Deer Isle Artists Assn. (pres. 1979-81). Home: Wilmette Ill. Died Mar. 29, 1993.

CALCAGNO, LAWRENCE, artist; b. San Francisco, Mar. 23, 1913; s. Vincent and Anna (de Rosa) C. Student, Calif. Sch. Fine Arts, San Francisco, 1947-50, Academie de la Grande Chaumiere, Paris, Academia degli Belle Arte, Florence, Italy. Asst. prof. art U. Ala., 1955-56, Albright Art Sch. of U. Buffalo, 1956-58; vis. artist in residence U. Ill., 1958-59; part-time tchr. N.Y.U., 1960; Andrew Mellon prof. painting Carnegie Inst. Tech., 1965-68; vis. artist in residence Honolulu Acad. Arts, 1968-69. One-man shows include LaBaudt Gallery, San Francisco, 1948, 54, Galleria Numero, Florence, Italy, 1951, 52, Galeria Clan, Madrid, 1955, Studio Paul Fachetti, Paris, 1955, Martha Jackson Gallery, N.Y.C., 1955, 58, 60, 62, U. Ala., 1956, Albright Art Gallery, 1956, Inst. de Arte Contemporaneo, Lima, Peru, 1957, U. Ill., 1959, Fairweather-Hardin Gallery, Chgo., 1959, Phila. Art Alliance, 1960, New Arts Gallery, Houston, 1960, Ciudad Universitaria, Mexico City, 1961, McRoberts & Tunnard, London, 1961, Carnegie Inst. Tech., 1965, Houston Mus. Fine Arts, 1965, Yares Gallery, Scottsdale, Ariz., 1973, 75, 77, Talley Richard Gallery, Taos, N.Mex., 1976, Stables Gallery, Taos, 1978, Ulrich Mus., Wichita, 1979, Lincoln Ctr., Ft. Collins, Colo., 1979, Downtown Gallery, Honolulu, 1979, More-Rubin Gallery, Buffalo, 1980, retrospective exhibit, Westmoreland County Mus., Greensburg, Pa., 1967, Honolulu Acad. Arts, 1968-69, Franklin Siden Gallery, Detroit, 1965, 67, 69, Smithsonian Instn. traveling exhbn., 1973-75, Contemporary Art Ctr., Honolulu, 1976, Roko Gallery, N.Y.C., 1974-77, Stables Gallery, 1978, The New Gallery, Taos, 1981-83, Anita Shapolsky Gallery, N.Y.C., 1987-88, David Anderson Gallery, Buffalo, 1992; U.S. Mus. tour, 1973-75, 83-85; traveling retrospective exhibit, 1982-83; represented in permanent collections include Honolulu Acad. Arts, Santa Barbara Mus., Rochester Meml. Gallery, Houston Mus. Fine Arts, Carnegie Inst., Albright-Knox Gallery, Whitney Mus., U. Nebr., Inst. Contempory Art, Lima, San Francisco Mus. Modern Art, Walker Art Center, Krannert Mus., U. Ill., Mus. Modern Art, N.Y.U., Phoenix Art. Mus., Denver Mus. Art, U. Ala., Chase Manhattan Bank, Nat. Mus. Am. Art, Smithsonian Instn., Nat. Gallery Art, Washington, Balt. Mus., Mus. of N.Mex., Santa Fe, also numerous pvt. collections. Recipient 2d Drawing prize Nat. Army Arts Contest Nat. Gallery Art, 1945; resident fellow Yaddo Corp., 1965, Ford Found. Humanities Program, 1965, Macdowell Colony, 1967-68, 74-76, Wurlitzer Found., 1972-73; USIA fellow Soviet Union, 1988, Nat. Endowment of Arts Painting fellow, 1989. Home: New York N.Y. Died Apr. 22, 1993.

CALDER, DANIEL GILLMORE, English language educator; b. Lubec, Maine, Feb. 10, 1939; s. Gillmore Daniel and Margaret Hasty (Burr) C. BA, Bowdoin Coll., 1960; MA, U. Iowa, 1962, Ind. U., 1967; PhD, Ind. U., 1969. Instr. English Bowdoin Coll., Brunswick, Maine, 1962-64; asst. prof. U. Wash., Seattle, 1969-71; asst. prof. English UCLA, 1971-75, assoc. prof., 1975-80, prof., 1980-94, chmn. English dept., 1983-90, assoc. dean Sch. Theater, Film and TV, 1990-92, dean honors Coll. Letters and Sci., 1975-78, acting dean humanities Coll. Letters and Sci., 1992. Author: Cynewulf, 1981; co-author: Sources and Analogues of Old English Poetry, Vol. I, 1976, Vol. II, 1983, New Critical History of Old English Literature, 1986; editor: Old English Poetry: Essays on Style, 1979. Mem. MLA, Medieval Assn. Pacific Coast, New Chaucer Soc., Internat. Soc. Anglo-Saxonists (co-founder, exec. dir. 1981-87). Democrat. Home: Sherman Oaks Calif. Died Aug. 2, 1994.

CALDWELL, JAMES WILEY, lawyer; b. Arkadelphia, Ark., Dec. 14, 1923; s. Joseph Allison and Beulah (Wright) C.; m. Marie Cole, July 11, 1947; children: Susan, Carolyn, James Wiley. B.A., Ouachita Bapt. Coll., 1947; J.D. with honors, U. Tex., 1950. Bar: Tex. Assoc. McGregor & Sewell, Houston, 1950-51; atty. City of Houston, 1951-52; sr. ptnr. Fulbright & Jaworski, Houston. Trustee, gen. counsel Baylor Coll. Medicine; chmn. Houston Tax Research Assn.; originator program for state med. edn. funds Baylor Med., 1969; financing for control of pollution on Houston Ship Channel, 1971. Served to 1st lt. inf. AUS, 1943-46, ETO. Named Ouachita Bapt. U. Disting. Alumnus, 1975. Mem. Houston Bar Assn., ABA, Nat. Assn. Bond Lawyers, State Bar of Tex. Baptist. Clubs: River Oaks Country (pres. 1983); Coronado (Houston) (pres. 1975). Home: Houston Tex. Died July 23, 1995.

CALFEE, WILLIAM HOWARD, sculptor, painter; b. Washington, Feb. 7, 1909; s. Lee Price and Carrie L. (Whitehead) C.; children: Adriana, Richard, Judy, Helme, William, Alan Edward. Studied sculpture, Beaux Arts, Paris, also Cranbrook Acad., Mich.; H.L.D. (hon.), Am. U., 1979. Instr. spl. skills div. Resettlement Adminstrn., Cumberland Homesteads, Tenn., 1935; executed murals, sculptures, fine arts sect. procurement div. U.S. Treasury Dept., 1936-41; psychotherapy worker St. Elizabeth's Hosp., Washington, 1942-43; Tchr. mural technique Centre d'Art, Port au Prince, Haiti, 1949; guest asso. prof. painting U. Calif. at Berkeley, 1951; chmn. dept. painting and sculpture Am. U., Washington, until 1954, adj. prof. dept. art. Works exhibited most museums, one-man show painting, Wehye Gallery, N.Y.C., sculpture, Graham Gallery, Balt. Mus., Corcoran Gallery, Philbrook Art Mus., Tulsa; rep. in Root Collection, Phillips Gallery, Honolulu Acad., Corcoran Gallery, Nat. Collection Fine Arts, retrospective exhbn., Nat. Acad. Scis., 1978; initiated: Watkins Meml. Collection, Watkins Gallery; executed altar, font, candle sticks, St. Augustine's Chapel, Washington, D.C., 1968, Rockville (Md.) Civic Ctr. sculpture, 1980. Home: Chevy Chase Md. Died Dec. 2, 1995.

CALLAHAN, CARROLL BERNARD, lawyer; b. Montello, Wis., June 14, 1908; s. John and Rose (Reardon) C.; m. Phyllis Luchsinger, Sept. 27, 1939. LLB, U. Wis., 1931. Bar: Wis. 1931. Sole practice Columbus, Wis., 1931-41; ptnr. E. Clarke Arnold, 1941-95. Served to 1st lt. AUS, 1943-46. Fellow Am. Coll. Trial Lawyers; mem. ABA, State Bar Wis. (pres. 1960-61), Am. Legion, Phi Alpha Delta. Lodge: KC (4th deg.). Home: Columbus Wis. Died Nov. 26, 1995.

CALLAND, DIANA BAKER, broadcasting executive; b. Columbus, Ohio, Oct. 24, 1935; d. Paul Allen and Helena (Schwartz) Baker; m. Frederick Fremont, Sept. 23, 1966. B.A., Ohio State U., 1957, M.A., 1962, postgrad., 1966. Writer, producer Sta. WOSU-FM, Columbus, 1957-62; pub. relations dir. Ohio State Nurses Assn., Columbus, 1962-63; rsch. assoc., adminstrv. rsch. Ohio State U., Columbus, 1963-66; mgr. cultural affairs programming Sta. WFCR-FM, Amherst, Mass., 1966-71; with radio activities dept. Corp. for Pub. Broadcasting, Washington, 1971-81, also; dir. radio activities Corp. for Pub. Broadcasting; radio mktg. mgr. Adler Enterprises, Ltd., McLean, Va., 1981-82; NPR PLUS mktg. dir. Nat. Pub. Radio, Washington, 1982-84; dir. network mktg. Action Line Group, Washington, 1985-87; mgr. sales Wold Communications, Inc., Washington, 1987-89; pres. Calland Assocs., Washington, 1989-94. Co-author: Writing to People, 1963. Recipient 1st pl. award for children's radio Inst. for Edn. by Radio and TV, 1959; Cris award Film Council of Greater Columbus, 1965; award Council on Internat. Non-Theatrical Events, 1965. Mem. Alpha Epsilon Rho. Died Jan. 28, 1994.

CALLENDER, JOHN HANCOCK, architect; b. Kansas City, Mo., Jan. 18, 1908; s. Alonzo Lee and Lola (Hancock) C.; m. Mary Carnwath, Aug. 5, 1933; 1 dau., Janet. B.A., Yale, 1928; student, Sch. Architecture, 1928-30; BArch, NYU, 1939. Research methods and materials low-cost housing John B. Pierce Found., N.Y.C., 1931-43; individual practice architecture, specializing in residences, 1945-95; mem. faculty Columbia U., 1953-54, Princeton U., 1954-57; member faculty Pratt Inst., 1954-73, assoc. prof., 1958-63, prof., 1963-73; cons. architect for Nat. Housing Agency, Staff Army Engrs., Manhattan project, Columbia, 1943-45; Vis. prof. Cheng Kung U., Taiwan, China, 1967-68. Author: Before You Buy a House, 1953, (with others) Curtain Walls of Stainless Steel, 1955; Editor-in-chief: Time-Saver Standards for Architectural Design Data, 1982; Contbr. to popular mags., profl. publs. Home: Lansdale Pa. Died Mar. 30, 1995.

CALVO, HORACE L(AWRENCE), judge; b. Chgo., Jan. 4, 1927; s. Horace Laurence and Mary Cecilia (Drew) C.; m. Josephine Erika Beth, June 28, 1947; children: Larry Alan, Mary Elizabeth, Linda Beth. LL.B., St. Louis U., 1954. Bar: Ill. 1956, U.S. Dist. Ct. (ea. dist.) Ill. 1958, U.S. Supreme Ct. 1968. Tax auditor and clk. U.S. Treasury, Springfield and East St. Louis, Ill., 1947-54; solo practice law, 1956-75; mem. Chapman & Calvo, Granite City, Ill., 1956-75; cir. judge State of Ill., Edwardsville, 1975-91. Mem. Ill. Gen. Assembly, 1969-75. Served agt. CIC USAAF, 1944-47, W.Ger. Fellow ABA, Ill. State Bar Assn., Ill. Trial Lawyers, TriCity Bar Assn. (pres. 1960-62), Madison County Bar Assn.; mem. Ill. Judges Assn. (dir. Chgo. 1980-91, treas. 1983-91, 2d v.p. 1986). Democrat. Roman Catholic. Home: Edwardsville Ill. Died June 3, 1991.

CAMINOS, HORACIO, architect, educator; b. Buenos Aires, Argentina, Apr. 5, 1914; came to U.S., 1952, naturalized, 1965; s. Carlos N. and Maria E. (Crottogini) C.; m. Elena Ines Chapman, Sept. 13, 1943; children: Carlos H., José, Miguel, Maria I.. Maria P., Ana M. Arquitecto, U. Buenos Aires, 1939. Prof. architecture and town planning U. Tucuman, Argentina, 1946-50; chief architect Univ. City, Tucuman, 1948-50; prof. architecture Archtl. Assn., London, Eng., 1951-52, U. N.C., 1952-61, Harvard, fall 1962; prof. architecture Mass. Inst. Tech., 1962-84, prof. emeritus, 1984—. Prin. works include univ. campus plans and bldgs., U. Buenos Aires, 1961-67, U. Los Andes-Merida, Venezuela, 1963-67, campus plan, U. Carabobo, Valencia, Venezuela.; Author: (with John Turner and John Steffran) Urban Dwelling Environments, (with Carlos Caminos) Gente, Vivienda, Tierra, (with Reinhard Goethert) Urbanization Primer. Home: Newton Mass. Died 1990.

CAMINOS, RICARDO AUGUSTO, Egyptologist, educator; b. Buenos Aires, Argentina, July 11, 1915; s. Carlos Norberto and Maria (Crottogini) C. M.A., U. Buenos Aires, 1938; Ph.D., U. Chgo., 1947; D.Phil., U. Oxford, 1952. Research asst. Oriental Inst., U. Chgo., 1943-44; Rockefeller Found. fellow U. Chgo. and Oxford (Eng.) U., 1944-46; Oriental Inst. research fellow U. Chgo., 1946-47; epigraphist, expdn. at Luxor U. Chgo., Upper Egypt, 1947-50; asst. prof. Egyptology, Brown U., 1952-57, assoc. prof., 1957-64, prof., 1964-72, Charles E. Wilbour prof. Egyptology, 1972-80, chmn. dept., 1971-80, C.E. Wilbour prof. emeritus Egyptology, 1980-92; field dir. Egypt Exploration Soc. and Brown U. expdn. to Gebel es-Silsilah, Upper Egypt, 1955-82, Egypt Exploration Soc. and Brown U. expdn. to, Semna, Sudanese Nubia, 1962-63, Kumma, Sudanese Nubia, 1963-65; field dir. Egypt Exploration Soc. expdn. to Wadi el-Shatt el-Rigal, Upper Egypt, 1982-83; Guggenheim Meml. Found. fellow, Europe and Egypt, 1958-

59; vis. prof. Egyptology, U. Buenos Aires, 1960; vis. prof. Egyptology U. Leningrad, 1973; vis. lectr. USSR Acad. Scis., Moscow, 1973, Collège de France, Paris, 1981-92. Author: Late-Egyptian Miscellanies, 1954, Literary Fragments in the Hieratic Script, 1956, The Chronicle of Prince Osorkon, 1958, Gebel es-Silsilah, Vol. I, 1963, Shrines and Rock-Inscriptions of Ibrim, 1968, The New-Kingdom Temples of Buhen, Vols. I and II, 1974, A Tale of Woe, 1977, (with H.G. Fischer) Ancient Egyptian Epigraphy and Palaeography, 1976, The New Kingdom Temples of Semna-Kumma, Vols. I and II, 1987; bd. dirs., co-editor Aula Orientalis: Jour. for Study Ancient Near East, 1982-92; articles in field. Mem. Oxford Soc., Egypt Exploration Soc. (corr. mem.). Home: London Eng. Died May 26, 1992.

CAMMANN, SCHUYLER VAN RENSSELAER, author, emeritus educator; b. N.Y.C., Feb. 2, 1912; s. Herbert Schuyler and Katharine Van Rensselaer (Fairfax) C.; m. Marcia de F. Post, Feb. 6, 1943 (div. 1972); children: Frances Cammann Hrynio, Stephen Van Rensselaer, Hamilton F., Elizabeth Cammann Holcombe, William B.; m. Mary Lyman Cox; Dec. 29, 1980. AB, Yale U., 1935; MA, Harvard U., 1941; PhD, Johns Hopkins U., 1949. Tchr. Yale-in-China, Changsha, Hunan, 1935-37; asst. prof. U. Pa., Phila., 1949-50, assoc. prof., 1950-66, prof. East Asian studies, 1966-82, prof. emeritus, 1982-91; asst. curator Univ. Mus., Phila., 1948-50, assoc. curator, 1950-55, hon. curator, 1979-82, curator emeritus, 1982-91; NATO prof. to Denmark, U. Copenhagen, 1969; prof. Internat. Sch. Am. around the world, 1962-63; mem. panel CBS-TV show What In The World, Phila., 1950-55. Author: The Land of the Camel, 1951, Trade Through the Himalayas, 1951, Substance and Symbol in Chinese Toggles, 1962, Miniature Art From Old China, 1982; contbr. over 200 articles to profl. jours. Served to lt. USNR, 1941-46, CBI. Mem. Am. Oriental Soc. (v.p. 1956-57, assoc. editor jour. 1948-50). Democrat. Episcopalian. Club: Phila. Oriental (twice pres.). Home: Lisbon N.H. Died Sept. 10, 1991; interred Sugar Hill, N.H.

CAMPBELL, DONALD THOMAS, psychologist, educator; b. Grass Lake, Mich., Nov. 20, 1916; s. Arthur Lawrence and Hazel (Crafts) C.; m. Lola Sheaff, June 6, 1942 (div. Mar. 1983); children: Thomas Sheaff, Martin Crafts.; m. Barbara Frankel, Mar. 19, 1983. A.B., U. Calif. at Berkeley, 1939, Ph.D., 1947; M.A. (hon.), Oxford, 1969; LL.D., U. Mich., 1974; Sc.D., U. Fla., 1975, U. So. Calif., 1979, Northwestern U., 1983; D.Social Sci., Claremont Grad. Sch., 1978; D.H.L., U. Chgo., 1978; D. Philosophy (hon.), U. Oslo, 1986. Asst. prof. psychology Ohio State U., 1947-50, U. Chgo., 1950-53; mem. faculty Northwestern U., Evanston, Ill., 1953-79; prof. psychology Northwestern U., 1958-73, Morrison prof., 1973-79; N.Y. State Bd. Regents Albert Schweitzer prof. Maxwell Sch., Syracuse (N.Y.) U., 1979-82; univ. prof. social rels. and psychology Lehigh U., 1982-94; Fellow Center Advanced Study Behavioral Scis. Stanford, Calif., 1965-66; Fulbright lectr., vis. prof. social psychology Oxford U., 1968-69; William James lectr. Harvard U., 1977; Hovland Meml. lectr. Yale U., 1977. Author: Methodology and Epistemology for Social Science, 1988; co-author: Experimental and Quasi-Experimental Designs for Research, 1966, Unobtrusive Measures: Nonreactive Research in the Social Sciences, 1966, The Influence of Culture on Visual Perception, 1966, Ethnocentrism: Theories of Intergroup Conflict, Ethnic Attitudes and Group Behavior, 1972, Social Experimentation: A Method for Planning and Evaluating Social Intervention, 1974, Ethnocentrism and Intergroup Attitudes: East African Evidence, 1976, Quasi-Experimentation, 1979, Nonreactive Measures in the Social Sciences, 1981; also numerous articles. Served to lt. USNR, 1943-46. Recipient Kurt Lewin Meml. award Soc. Psychol. Study Social Issues, 1974, Myrdal Sci. Contbn. award Evaluation Rsch. Soc., 1977, award for disting. contbn. Am. Ednl. Rsch. Assn., 1981, Disting. Scientist award Soc. Exptl. Social Psychology, 1988, award for disting. svc. to measurement Ednl. Testing Svc., 1988. Fellow Am. Acad. Arts and Scis.; mem. NAS, APA (pres. 1975, pres. divsn. personality and social psychology 1968-69, Disting. Sci. Contbn. award 1970), Midwestern Psychol. Assn. (pres. 1966-67), Am. Philos. Soc. Home: Bethlehem Pa. Died May 7, 1996.

CAMPBELL, EDMUND DOUGLAS, lawyer; b. Lexington, Va., Mar. 12, 1899; s. Henry Donald and Martha (Miller) C.; m. Esther Butterworth, June 9, 1925 (dec. July 1934); children: Edmund D., Virginia (Mrs. Everett W. Holt); m. Elizabeth Pfohl, June 16, 1936; children: H. Donald, Benjamin P. AB, Washington and Lee U., 1918, LLB, 1922, LLD (hon.), 1989; MA, Harvard U., 1920. Bar: D.C. 1922, Va. 1922. Practice in Washington, 1924—, Arlington, Va., 1924—; mem. firm Jackson & Campbell, Washington. Pres. Arlington Council Chs., 1949, Arlington Community Chest, 1951; Mem. D.C. Police Complaint Rev. Bd., 1966-69; mem. Arlington County Bd. Suprs., 1941-47; chmn. Arlington Pub. Utilities Commn., 1935, Arlington Civil Service Commn., 1964-67; Democratic candidate for Congress, 1952; Trustee Mary Baldwin Coll., chmn., 1945-62; bd. dirs. Washington Council Chs., 1967. Served as pvt. U.S. Army, 1918. Recipient Algernon Sydney Sullivan award Mary Baldwin Coll., 1949. Fellow Am. Coll.

Trial Lawyers; mem. ABA (ho. dels. 1964-75, gov. 1972-75), Va. Bar Assn., D.C. Bar Assn. (Distinguished Lawyers Award 1965, pres. 1961-62, mem. disciplinary bd. 1979-84), Met. Club, Barristers Club, Lawyers Club (Washington), Order of Coif, Phi Beta Kappa, Omicron Delta Kappa, Phi Delta Phi, Alpha Tau Omega. Episcopalian. Home: Arlington Va. Died Dec. 7, 1995.

CAMPBELL, JAMES ARTHUR, professional baseball team executive; b. Huron, Ohio, Feb. 5, 1924; s. Arthur A. and Vanessa (Hart) C.; m. Helene G. Mulligan, Jan. 16, 1954 (div. July 1969). B.S., Ohio State U., 1949. Bus. mgr. Thomasville (Ga.) Baseball Club, 1950, Toledo Baseball Club, 1951, Buffalo Baseball Club, 1952; bus. mgr. Detroit Minor League System, 1953; asst. farm dir. Detroit Baseball Club, 1954-56, v.p., farm dir., 1957-61, v.p., gen. mgr., 1962-65; exec. v.p., gen. mgr. Detroit Tigers, 1965-78, pres., gen. mgr., 1978-84, pres., chief exec. officer, 1984-92, chmn., chief exec. officer, 1990-92; ret., 1992-95. Served with AC USNR, 1943-46. Named Maj. League Exec. of Yr., 1988; named to Mich. Sports Hall of Fame, 1987, Ohio Baseball Hall of Fame, 1989, Huron (Ohio) High Sch. Hall of Fame, 1994. Mem. Ohio State U. Varsity "O" Assn., Nat. Baseball Hall of Fame (bd. dirs.), Detroit Athletic Club, Detroit Press Club, Detroit Golf Club, Lone Palm Golf Club, Delta Upsilon. Presbyterian. Home: Lakeland Fla. Died Oct. 31, 1995.

CAMPBELL, LEONARD GENE, university administrator; b. Krebs, Okla., Oct. 15, 1933; s. Thomas Allen and Tempie (Woodall) C.; m. Linda Lou Bailey, May 22, 1958; 1 dau., Kristi Lynn. BS, Southeastern Okla. State Coll., 1958; MA, U. Okla., 1964, EdD, 1970. Tchr., coach Amarillo (Tex.) pub. schs., 1960-61, Moore (Okla.) High Sch., 1961-63; prin. Moore (Okla.) Jr. High Sch. and Moore High Sch., 1963-65; asst. supt. Moore (Okla.) pub. schs., 1965-70; supt. Western Heights Pub. Schs., Oklahoma City, 1970-75; pres. Southwestern Okla. State U., Weatherford, 1975-90. Served with USN, 1952-54. Mem. NEA, Okla. Edn. Assn., Am. Assn. Sch. Adminstrs., Okla. Assn. Sch. Adminstrs., Cen. Dist. Okla. Edn. Assn. (pres. 1973-74), Okla. Textbook Commn. (chmn. 1972-74). Democrat. Baptist. Lodges: Lions; Kiwanis; Rotary. Home: Weatherford Okla. Died Feb. 16, 1996.

CAMPION, CLIFFORD, screenwriter, producer; b. Santa Monica, Calif., Dec. 25, 1949; s. Royal A. and Jean (Hendricks) C. BA, U. So. Calif., 1972. Screenwriter: (TV series) Westbrook Hospital: This is the Life, Rituals (also co-creator), (TV movies) Image in a Glass, Hallmark Hall of Fame, 1981 (also co-producer), Love, Mary, 1985, Samaritan, 1985 (also producer), Growing Up, 1985 (also producer), Race Against Time, 1986, Celebration Family, Kingsley, (TV documentaries) Having a Baby, Portrait of a First Lady, (animated spls.) The Little Troll Prince, Blue Whale, Captain Caveman, Dinky Dog, The Witch Who Stole Marineland, Clyde's Ride, (TV spl.) Upbeat Aesop, (screenplay) The Bottom Line. Recipient Christopher award, FAB award, Luminas award. Mem. Writers Guild Am. (Best Original Anthology award), Acad. TV Arts and Scis., Delta Kappa Alpha. Home: San Diego Calif. Died Dec. 24, 1991.

CANDY, JOHN FRANKLIN, actor; b. Toronto, Ont., Can., Oct. 31, 1950; s. Sidney James and Evangeline (Aker) C.; m. Rosemary Margaret Hobor, Apr. 27, 1979; children: Jennifer Anne, Christopher Michael. Student, Centennial Coll., Toronto, 1969-71. Co-owner Toronto Argonauts. TV writer, performer SCTV, 1975-87 (2 Emmy awards for writing); appeared in numerous films including Class of 44, 1973, Face Off, It Seemed Like A Good Idea at the Time, Clown Murders, Find the Lady, Silent Partner, Lost and Found, Tunnel Vision, Double Negative, 1941, 1979, Blues Brothers, 1980, Stripes, 1982, (voice) Heavy Metal, It Came from Hollywood, 1982, National Lampoon's Vacation, 1983, Going Beserk, 1983, Splash, 1984, Brewster's Millions, 1985, Volunteers, 1985, Summer Rental, 1985, Follow That Bird, Little Shop of Horrors, 1986, Armed and Dangerous, 1986, Spaceballs, 1987, Planes, Trains and Automobiles, 1987, The Great Outdoors, 1988, (voice) Hot to Trot, 1988, Speed Zone, 1989, Uncle Buck, 1989, (also exec. prodr.) Who's Harry Crumb, 1989, Home Alone, 1990, (voice) The Rescuers Down Under, 1990, Nothing But Trouble, 1991, Career Opportunities, 1991, Only the Lonely, 1991, Delirious, 1991, JFK, 1991, Once Upon A Crime, 1992, Cool Runnings, 1993, Wagons East, 1994; appeared on numerous television shows; live theatre Second City Chgo., Toronto, Los Angeles. Recipient Emmy award Acad. TV Arts and Scis., 1981, 1982. Mem. Alliance Canadian Cinema, TV and Radio Artists (award 1978, 84), Screen Actors Guild, Writers Guild Am., AFTRA.

CANETTI, ELIAS, author; b. Russe, Bulgaria, July 25, 1905; Jacques and Mathilda Arditi C.; m. Venetia Toubner-Calderon, 1934 (dec. 1963); now remarried. PhD, U. Vienna. Author: Hochzeit, 1932, Die Blendung, 1935, Fritz Wotruba, 1955, Masse und Macht, 1960, Welt im Kopf, 1962, Komoedie der Eitelkeit, 1964, Die Befristeten, 1964, Aufzeichnungen 1942-48, 1965, Die Stimmen von Marrakesck, 1967, Der Andere Prozess, 1969, Die gespaltene Zukunft, 1972, Macht und Überleben, 1972, Die Provinz des Menschen, 1973, Der Ohrenzeuge, 1974, Das Gewissen der Worte,

1975, The Human Province, 1978, Earwitness, 1979, The Conscience of Words, 1979, The Tongue Set Free, 1981, The Torch in My Ear, 1982, Crowds & Power, 1982, Kafka's Other Trial, 1983, Comedy of Vanity and Life-Terms, 1983, Auto-da-Fe, 1984, The Voices of Marrakesh, 1984, The Play of the Eyes, 1985. Recipient Nobel prize for lit., 1981; numerous French and German lit. awards. Home: London Eng. Died Aug. 13, 1994.

CANFIELD, MURIEL JEAN NIXON, Spanish linguistics educator; b. Batavia, N.Y., Apr. 12, 1928; d. Robert and Amy Beatrice (Coultas) Nixon; m. Delos Lincoln Canfield, Aug. 2, 1971; children: Gerald Richard, Susan Nixon. BA, U. Rochester, 1949, MA 1965; PhD, So. Ill. U., 1984. Prof. English Colegio Metodista Cen., Havana, Cuba, 1949-50; tchr. Spanish and Latin N.Y. State Pub. Schs., 1950-59; dir., owner Tutoring Sch., Rochester, N.Y., 1960-64; instr. English linguistics U. Rochester, 1964-65, dir. internat. student and scholar affairs, 1967-69; instr. Spanish and English chmn. fgn. langs. Rochester Inst. Tech., 1964-67, assoc. registrar, dir. fgn. students, 1965-67; asst. dir. pub. relns. City of Rochester, 1969-71; researcher, writer, translator, evaluator Am. Assn. Tchrs. Spanish and Portuguese, Chgo. Press.; researcher, writer, translator, evaluator So. Ill. U., Carbondale, 1972-87. prof. Spanish linguistics, 1981-89; prof. Spanish linguistics Grupo Canfield, from 1986; dir., owner Grupo Canfield, from 1993; prodr., writer various cultural shows dept. adult vocat. and tech. edn. Ill. Bd. Edn., 1981. Author: Adjustment Experiences of Non-Immigrant Foreign Students, 1968, Criminal Justice Standards for Nonmetropolitan Area, 1977, Vocational English as Second Language Guidelines, 1981, Latin American Institute at Southern Illinois University at Carbondale 1958-73, 1985; translator (monographs) Criminology in Spain, Criminology in Mexico, both in Internationa Handbook of Contemporary Developments in Criminology, 1983; also monograph. Pres., editor yearbook Carbondale Garden Club, from 1971; pres., treas. Carbondale Found. for Better Environ., 1973-81; vestrywoman St. Andrew's Episcopal Ch., 1974-81; mem. Commn. on Ministry, Episcopal Diocese of Springfield, 1974-80; coord. George Bush for Pres. Campaign Jackson County, Ill., 1980; Rep. candidate for count clk. and recorder, Jackson County, 1978; fund raiser Jackson County Boosters Club, from 1979; pres. Carbondale Coun. Garden Clubs, 1980-81. Recipient Bicentennial award State of Ill., 1976, Disting. Svc award City of Carbondale, 1977; Genesee scholar, 1945, Vassar Coll. scholar, 1945, U. Rochester scholar, 1963. Mem. Am. Assn. Tchrs. Spanish and Portuguese (program evaluator 1973-75, researcher, writer, translator, evaluator), Nat. Assn. Fgn. Student Affairs (bd. dirs. 1969-70), AAUW, LWV (chmn. criminal justice Carbondale 1975-84), Phi Kappa Phi, Phi Sigma Iota (life). Episcopalian. Home: El Paso Tex. Deceased.

CANTOR, MURIEL GOLDSMAN, sociologist, educator; b. Mpls., Mar. 2, 1923; d. Leo and Bess Goldsman; m. Joel M. Cantor, Aug. 6, 1944 (Nov 1988); children: Murray Robert, Jane Cantor Shefler, James Leo. B.A., UCLA, 1964, M.A., 1966, Ph.D. 1969. Lectr. dept. econs. and sociology Immaculata Heart Coll., L.A., 1966-68; faculty Am. U., Washington 1968-93, instr., 1968-69, asst. prof. sociology, 1969-7 assoc. prof., 1972-76, prof., 1976-95, prof. emerita, from 1993, chmn. dept., 1973-75, 77-79, dir. women's studie 1989-93; vis. prof. communication studies UCLA, 198 cons. agys. including NIMH; cons. Corp. for Public Broadcasting, 1974-75, 80-81, Women, Men and Media U. S.C., 1990-91. Author: The Hollywood T Producer: His Work and His Audience, 1971, 2d editi with new intro., 1987, (with Phyllis L. Stewart) Varieties of Work Experience, 1974, 82), Prime Time Television Content and Control, 1980, (with Joel M. Cantor) 2 rev. and enlarged edit., 1992, (with Suzanne Pingree The Soap Opera, 1983, (with Sandra Ball-Rokeach Media, Audiences and Social Structure, 1986, (wit Cheryl Zollars) Creators of Culture: Descriptions an Professions in Culture Industries, 1993; editor Nat. SW newsletter. Bd. dirs. Population Inst., 1978-80; trustee WETA, 1972-76. NIMH grantee, 1979-81; recipien Premio Diego Fabbri for Soap Opera in Rome, 1988 Mem. Am. Sociol. Assn. (chair soc. culture sect. 1990 91, co-editor newsletter 1991-93), D.c. Sociol. Soc. (pres 1977-78, Stewart A. Rice Merit award 1987), Sociolo gists for Women in Soc. (pres.-elect 1994, pres. 1995 Ea. Sociol. Soc. (exec. coun. 1981-83, 89-92), So. Socio Soc. (exec. coun. 1991-93), Internat. Sociol. Assn., In ternat. Inst. Sociology. Home: Bethesda Md. Died Jul 19, 1995.

CAPPS, RICHARD HUNTLEY, physicist, educator; Wichita, Kans., July 1, 1928; s. Charles M. and Ann (Palmer) C.; m. Joan P. Salatino, June 18, 1955; ch Thelma L. Blair, June 3, 1975; stepchildren: Hollis Bla Westler, Patricia Blair Bollinger, Elizabeth I Kreuzmann. B.A., U. Kans., 1950, M.A., U. Wis 1952, Ph.D., 1955. Rsch. assoc. U. Calif. at Berkele 1955-57; faculty U. Wash., 1957-58; rsch. assoc. Corne U., 1958-60; faculty Northwestern U., Evanston, Ill 1960-67; prof. Northwestern U., 1965-67; prof. physic Purdue U., Lafayette, Ind., 1967-94. Contbr. articles profl. jours. Mem. Am. Phys. Soc. Home: We Lafayette Ind. Died Feb. 24, 1994.

ARAPETYAN, ARMEN, editor, musicologist; b. Oct. 1, 1908; came to U.S., 1928, naturalized, 1942; s. ackertoum and Mariam (Khazarian) C.; m. Harriette sther Norris, Nov. 4, 1937; children: Francelle, Peter nthony. Diploma, Am. Coll., Teheran, 1927; student , Paris, France, then N.Y.C.; M.A., Harvard U., 1940, h.D., 1945. Founder Am. Inst. Musicology (specializing Medieval and Renaissance music), Cambridge, ass., 1945, dir.; spl. work in fostering research and ubls. in field, directing project. Dir. Corpus criptorum de Musica, Corpus of Early Keyboard usic, Corpus Mensurabilis Musicae, Musicological udies and Documents, Musica Disciplina (yearbook), enaissance Manuscript Studies, Miscellanea. Mem. m. Musicol. Soc., Internat. Musicol. Soc. (hon.). ome: Granada Spain Died Sept. 5, 1992.

ARBONE, ALFONSO ROBERT, construction executive; b. Cleve., Jan. 17, 1921; s. Rosario P. and armela (Mandalfino) C.; student Sch. Architecture, ase Western Res. U. and Case Inst. Tech., 1940-42; Arch, 1946; m. Anna Mae Simmons, June 16, 1945; hildren—Carmela, Florence Roberta, Rosario P. II, nne Marie. Ptnr., v.p. estimator R.P. Carbone Conrn. Co., Cleve., 1940-77, owner, pres., 1977-82, chmn. d., 1983—. Alt. builder rep. mem. City of Cleve., Bd. dg. Standards and Bldg. Appeals, 1953-64, builder p. mem., 1964-74, chmn., 1965-74; past chmn. Cleve. ir Pollution Appeals Bd. Mem. Bus. Men's Club, entral YMCA, Cleve.; mem. Nat. UN Day Com., 971-80; trustee, past chmn. resources and personnel om. Alta House, pres. bd. trustees, 1981-83, chmn. evel. and govt. relations com., 1983—; bd. dirs. eighborhood Ctrs. Assn., 1981-84; trustee Parmadale-. Anthony Svc. Village, 1982—; del. Assembly of nited Way Services of Cleve., 1981-84; commd. extraordinary minister for adminstrn. of Holy Communion y Cath. Ch., 1974, also councilman, pres. parish ouncil, 1985-87 . Served with U.S. Coast and Geodetic urvey, Washington, 1942-45. Recipient Alpha Rho Chi edal, 1946; decorated cavalier Order Star Solidarity taly); papal cavaliere Order St. Gregory. Mem. Cleve. ngring. Soc., Assoc. Gen. Contractors Am., Builders xchange Cleve., Holy Name Soc., Ohio Bldg. Insps. ssn., Citizen League Cleve., Greater Cleve. Growth ssn., Internat. Platform Assn., Order Sons Italy Am. ast grand orator, past pres. lodge, grand trustee ofcer, state parliamentarian), Epsilon Delta Rho. Home: leveland Ohio

ARDWELL, HORACE MILTON, communications ompany executive; b. Oklahoma City, Feb. 3, 1919; s. orace M. and Lona (Bridges) C.; m. Fran Sicola, Nov. 3, 1993; children by previous marriage: Barbara Ann, everly Kay, Horace Milton III. B.S. in Econs, Tex. A. nd M. Coll., 1941. Asst. adminstr. Herman Hosp., ouston, 1946-48; adminstr. Meml. Hosp., Lufkin, Tex., 948-85; chmn. Hosp.-Ins.-Physicians Joint Adv. Com. ex., 1954-94; pres. Hosp.-Med. Communications, Inc., 985-95; mem. Tex. Commn. Patient Care, 1957-61; res. Tex. Bd. Vocational Nurse Examiners, 1962-68; r. Med. Info., 1968-78; mem. Joint Commn. on Accreditation, 1975-85; mem. adv. com. on allied health MA, 1975-82. Chmn. Lufkin United Fund, 1961-76; em. med. adv. com. Tex. Dept. Pub. Welfare, 1968-70; d. dirs. Blue Cross Tex., 1962-95. Served with AUS, 941-46, ETO, PTO. Fellow Am. Coll. Healthcare Ex-s. (Gold Medal award 1992); mem. Am. Health Conress (chmn. bd. govs. 1974), Am. Hosp. Assn. (del. 955-72, chmn. trustees 1974, speaker ho. of dels. 1975, istin. Svc. award 1979), Tex. Hosp. Assn. (pres. 1956-7, chmn. bldg. com. 1965-75, Earl M. Collier award 970), Tex. Assn. Hosp. Accts. (pres. 1953-54), Lufkin . of C., Rotary (local pres. 1969-70). Home: Lufkin ex. Died Sept. 15, 1996.

AREY, MACDONALD, actor; b. Sioux City, Iowa, ar. 15, 1913; s. Charles S. and Elizabeth (Macdonald) .; m. Elizabeth Heckscher, May 4, 1941 (div. 1967); hildren: Lynn, Lisa, Steve, Teresa, Edward Macdonald, aul. Student, U. Wis., 1931-32; B.A., U. Iowa, 1935, ostgrad., 1935-36. Mem., Old Globe Shakespeare Co., 936-37, NBC Radio Stock Co., Chgo., 1937-38, free nce radio actor, N.Y.C.; stage appearances include ady in the Dark, 1939, Anniversary Waltz, 1954; films clude Dr. Broadway, 1942, Take a Letter Darling, 942, Wake Island, 1942, Suddenly It's Spring, 1947, ream Girl, 1948, Streets of Laredo, 1949, Copper anyon, 1950, Great Missouri Raid, 1951, Excuse My ust, 1951, Let's Make It Legal, 1951, My Wife's Best riend, 1952, Count the Hours, 1953, Fire Over Africa, 954, Stranger at My Door, 1956, Tammy and the octor, 1963, Broken Sabre, 1965, End of the World, 977, American Gigolo, 1980; star: TV series Lock Up, 956, Dr. Christian, 1956, Days of Our Lives, 1965-94; her TV appearances on Roots, 1977, The Girl, The old Watch and Everything, 1980, Condominium, 1980; ost-narrator: radio program Heartbeat Theater; Recipient Emmy award (2) for Best Actor in Daytime rama Series Acad. TV Arts and Scis. 1974, 75); uthor: A Day in The Life, 1982, That Further Hill, 987. Bd. dirs. Cath. Big Bros., 1962-64; lector, inister of Eucharist, 1983. Served to 1st lt. USMCR, 942-45. Recipient Knight of Holy Sepulchre Papal rder, 1986. Mem. Screen Actors Guild (v.p. 1960), cad. Motion Picture Arts and Scis. (asst. treas. 1970), FTRA, Actors Equity Assn., Alpha Delta Phi. Democrat. Roman Catholic. Home: Beverly Hills Calif. Died Mar. 21, 1994.

CAREY, WILLIAM JOSEPH, retired controller; b. N.Y.C., May 15, 1922; s. Cornelius Montague and Ellen Katherine (Gannon) C.; m. Barbara L. Garrison, Aug. 24, 1946; children: Kathleen, Eileen, Christine, Robert. B.S., Rider Coll., 1949; postgrad., NYU, 1952-53. C.P.A., N.Y. Mgr. Ernst and Ernst, N.Y.C., 1949-59; controller Reynolds and Co., N.Y.C., 1959-61; exec. v.p. Bache and Co., N.Y.C., 1961-69; exec. ptnr. Goodbody and Co., N.Y.C., 1970-71; v.p. Paine Webber, N.Y.C., 1971-73; controller, treas., and chief fin. officer J. Henry Schroder Bank and Trust Co., Franklin Lakes, N.J., 1973-84; arbitration panel mem. Nat. Assn. Securities Dealers, N.Y.C. Trustee emeritus Rider Coll. Served with USN, 1942-45, PTO. Decorated Purple Heart. Mem. N.Y. State Soc. C.P.A.s, Am. Inst. C.P.A.s, Fin. Execs. Inst. (ops. com., internat. com). Clubs: Franklin Lakes, Indian Trail. Home: Mahwah N.J. Died Sept. 16, 1994.

CARLOUGH, EDWARD J., labor union official. Pres. Sheet Metal Workers' Internat. Assn. Home: Washington D.C. Died June 29, 1994.

CARLSON, HARRY, business and marketing communications consultant; b. Des Moines, Mar. 23, 1919; s. Anton and Minnie (Berquist) C.; m. Helen Brutsch, Aug. 7, 1946; children: Christopher, Marc, Eric. Student, Augustana Coll., Rock Island, Ill., 1937-40. Bur. mgr. UPI, Seattle, 1945-50; acct. exec. Carl Byoir & Assocs., San Francisco, 1950-52; pres. Gen. Pub. Rels. (subs. Benton & Bowles, Inc.), N.Y.C., 1957-64, Wolcott, Carlson & Co., N.Y.C., 1964-73, Carlson, Rockey & Assocs., N.Y.C., 1973-87. Mem. Pub. Rels. Soc. Am., San Diego Press Club, Vista Valley Country Club. Home: San Clemente Calif. Died June 4, 1993.

CARLSON, REYNOLD ERLAND, former foundation executive, former ambassador; b. Chgo., Sept. 7, 1912; s. Amel Reynold and Lillian (Evald) C.; m. Patricia Proctor, July 27, 1964; 1 dau., Marie Louise Roehm. B.S., Northwestern U., 1936, M.A., 1937; Ph.D., Harvard U., 1946. Asst. prof. econs. Johns Hopkins U., 1940-48; econ. cons. UN, 1946-47, Econ. Commn. Latin Am., Santiago, Chile, 1948; assoc. prof. econs., dir. Inst. Brazilian Studies, Vanderbilt U., 1949-53; economist Joint Brazilian-U.S. Devel. Commn., Inst. Inter-Am. Affairs, Rio de Janeiro, 1951-52; sr. economist Western Hemisphere operations World Bank, 1953-58; prof. econs., dir. grad. program econ. devel. Vanderbilt U., 1958-63, adj. prof., 1978-79; vis. prof. Grinnell Coll., 1979-80, Franklin Pierce Coll., 1980-81; cons. Ford Found., 1959-61, rep. in, Rio de Janeiro, 1961-65; assoc. dir. Ford Found. (Latin Am. program), 1965-66; U.S. ambassador to, Colombia, 1966-69; rep. Ford Found. in, Buenos Aires, 1969-72, regional program adviser, Lima, Peru, 1972-75. Served to 2d lt. USAAF, 1942-45. Decorated Cruzeiro de Sul (Brazil). Mem. Am. Econ. Assn., Phi Beta Kappa, Delta Sigma Pi. Clubs: Cosmos (Washington); University (Nashville). Home: Medomak Maine Died Oct. 27, 1993.

CARLTON, WINSLOW, health association administrator; b. London, Dec. 27, 1907; came to U.S., 1910; s. Newcomb Carlton and Josephine Woodruff (Winslow) Smith; m. Margaret Mary Gillies, Jan. 18, 1935; children: Mary Gillies Carlton Swope, Ann Winslow, Rhona Newcomb Carlton-Foss. AB cum laude, Harvard Coll., 1929; postgrad., Columbia U. Sch. of Bus., 1930-32. With Emergency Exchange Assn., N.Y., 1932-33; field rep. Bureau Self-Help Coops. Fed. Emergency Relief Adminstrn., Washington, 1933-34; dir. divsn. self-help coop. svcs. Calif. State Emergency Relief Adminstrn., San Francisco, 1934-36; with Group Health, Inc. (formerly Group Health Ins.), N.Y., 1937-38, co-organizer, exec. dir., 1938-44, chmn. exec. com., 1945-48, chmn. bd., 1948-67, hon. chmn., 1967-94, dir., 1945-78; co-founder, sec., dir. Group Health Dental Ins., Inc., N.Y., 1948-53, chmn. bd., 1953-60, chmn. exec. com., 1961-67, dir., 1948-67; co-founder, gen. ptnr. A.W. Jones Co., A.W. Jones and Assocs., A.W. Jones Mgmt., 1949-94; sec. Mayor's Health Plan Com., N.Y.C., 1944-45; exec. sec. Health Ins. Plan Greater N.Y., 1944-45; cons. health svcs., 1945-78; sec., dir. Pub. Health Rsch. Inst. N.Y., 1950-72. Mem. settlement com. Henry Street Settlement, 1937-44, bd. dirs., 1931-33, 44-78, pres., 1953-65, chmn., 1966-72, hon. dir., 1979-94; mem. devel. com. Consumer Coop. Svc., N.Y., 1951-53; chmn., bd. trustees Found. for Coop. Housing, Inc., N.Y., 1952-94; chmn. bd., dir. FCH Svcs., Inc., 1952-94; hon. chmn. Coop. Housing Found., 1985-94; vice chmn. sub-com. health and hosps. Mayor's Adv. Coun., N.Y.C., 1954-55, chmn., 1955-58; dir. United Neighborhood Houses, 1954-72, v.p., 1966-72; sec., dir. Com. to Protect our Children's Teeth, 1956-63; bd. dirs. Nat. Fedn. Settlements, 1958-72, pres., 1964-66; chmn., bd. dirs. Mobilization for Youth, 1958-70; pres. Nat. Social Welfare Assembly, Inc., 1960-63, chmn., bd. dirs., 1963-67; v.p., mem. exec. com. Nat. Assembly for Social Policy and Devel., 1968-72, bd. dirs., 1968-73; mem. adv. coun. Pres.' Com. Juvenile Delinquency and Youth Crime, 1962-65; sec., treas. Nat. Com. Health Care of Aged, 1962-63; mem. distribution com. Greater N.Y. Fund, 1962-63; dir. Gouveneur Gardens Housing Corp., Inc., 1964-68, pres., 1964-67, hon. pres., 1968; mem. program com. Nat. Conf. Social Welfare, 1964-66; mem. N.Y.C. Coun. Against Poverty, 1965-67; bd. dirs. United Community Funds and Couns. Am., 1969-71; trustee The Coop. Found., 1969-74; dir., pres. Settlement Housing Fund, N.Y., 1970-72; mem. sub-com. on liaison with pub. and pvt. agys., departmental coms. for ct. adminstrn., appellate divsn., 1st and 2d jud. depts. State of N.Y., 1971-73; founder, chmn., pres. Selcore Labs., Inc., 1985-88. Recipient Jane Addams award Nat. Fedn. Settlements, 1966, Disting. Svc. award Nat. Conf. Social Welfare, 1973, Disting. Svc. award Rochdale Inst., 1973, Disting. Svc. award Nat. Housing Conf., 1980, Hall of Fame award N.Y. Settlements, 1986. Home: Woods Hole Mass. Died Dec. 6, 1994.

CARMICHAEL, HUGH, physicist; b. Farr, Sutherland, Scotland, Nov. 10, 1906; s. Dugald and Agnes Macmillan (Macaulay) C.; m. Margaret Elizabeth May Maclennan (dec.), Oct. 23, 1937; children: Dugald Macaulay, Margaret Lind Carmichael Stuart, Elizabeth Agnes Carmichael Cooper, Hugh Alexander Lorne. B.Sc. with 1st class honors in Physics, U. Edinburgh, Scotland, 1929; Ph.D., U. Cambridge, Eng., 1936; M.A., U. Cambridge, 1939. Demonstrator in physics U. Cambridge, 1937-44; sr. prin. sci. officer Ministry of Supply Atomic Energy Mission to Can., 1944-50; prin. rsch. officer, head gen. physics br. Atomic Energy Can. Ltd., 1950-71; cons., 1971-95; mem. Wordie expedition to N.W. Greenland and the Can. Arctic, 1937; physicist Brit. Meteorol. Office, 1939-40, Hankey Scheme, 1941-44. Made 1st cosmic ray measurements at balloon altitudes near north magnetic pole, 1937; designed for the 1964-65 Internat. Quiet Sun Yrs. cosmic ray monitor NM-64, 1964 and promoted its installation worldwide; contbr. numerous articles and research papers to profl. publs. Carnegie research fellow U. Edinburgh, 1929-33; Clark Maxwell research scholar U. Cambridge, 1933-37, fellow St. John's Coll., 1936-40. Fellow Royal Soc. Can.; mem. Can. Assn. Physicists, Am. Geophys. Union. Home: Deep River Can. Died Jan. 16, 1995.

CARMICHAEL, MARY MULLOY, foreign service officer, educator; b. Miles City, Mont., Aug. 6, 1916; d. John William and Laura (Maher) Mulloy; m. John Buford Carmichael (dec. June 1949); m. Roger Goiran, Mar. 13, 1981. Ph.B., Marquette U., 1939, M.A., 1940; postgrad., Am. U., Washington, 1943-49. Asst. to dean Women Marquette U., 1935-40; dean women Thompson Falls (Mont.) pub. schs., 1940-42; personnel officer War Dept., Washington, 1942-44; chief overseas classification and wage adminstrn. OWI, Washington and, London, 1944-45; successively chief salary adminstrn. sect., asst. planning adviser, asst. chief pay leave and retirement br. State Dept., 1945-56; fgn. service officer, 1956-69; 1st sec., consul Brussels, Belgium, 1959-64; 1st. sec., econ. officer Am. embassy, Leopoldville, Congo, 1964-65; econ. officer U.S. delegation OECD, Paris, 1964-65; asst. econ. adviser U.S. del. NATO, 1965-66, spl. asst. to ambassador, also U.S. rep. to coordinating com. of govt. experts, 1966-69; also U.S. relocation coordinator NATO, Paris, Brussels, 1967-69; chmn. internat. bus. adminstrn. and econs. dept., vis. prof. Am. Coll. Switzerland, Leysin, 1969—; also cons. Recipient Superior Service award Dept. State, 1968; Merit award Marquette U., 1978. Mem. Fgn. Svc. Assn., Countryside Tennis and Social Club (Clearwater, Fla.), Dunedin Boat Club, Alpha Kappa Delta. Home: Spokane Wash. Died Jan. 1, 1995.

CAROSSO, VINCENT PHILLIP, historian, educator; b. San Francisco, Mar. 19, 1922; s. Vincent G. and Lucia M. (Barale) C.; m. Rose Celeste Berti, Aug. 23, 1952; 1 child, Steven Berti. A.B., U. Calif.-, Berkeley, 1943, M.A., 1944, Ph.D. (Panama-Pacific fellow in History), 1945-46, LeConte Meml. fellow, 1946-47, 1948. Instr. history San Jose (Calif.) State Coll., 1949-50; asst. prof. Carnegie Inst. Tech., Pitts., 1950-53, N.Y. U., N.Y.C., 1953-56; assoc. prof. N.Y. U., 1956-62, prof. history, 1962-76; William R. Kenan prof. history NYU, 1976-88, William R. Kenan prof. history emeritus, 1989-93; vis. assoc. research prof. Harvard U., 1961-62; vis. lectr., 1963-64; Fulbright-Hays sr. lectr., Italy, 1973, 76.

Author: California Wine Industry, 1830-95, 1951, reprinted, 1976, (with George Soule) American Economic History, 1957, (with Henry Parkes) Recent America, 2 vols, 1963, Investment Banking in America, 1970; reprinted 1979, More Than a Century of Investment Banking: The Kidder, Peabody & Co. Story, 1979, The Morgans: Private International Bankers, 1854-1913, 1987; editor: Wall Street and Security Markets, 1975, The United States in the Twentieth Century, 1979; coeditor: Companies & Men: Business Enterprise in America, 1976, Small Business Enterprise in America, 1979, Rise of Commercial Banking, 1980; asso. editor Jour. Econ. History, 1955-61; mem. editorial bds. Business Hist. Rev., 1957-61, Jour. Am. History, 1968-71; contbr. articles to profl. jours. Harvard postdoctoral fellow, 1948-49; NEH fellow, 1976-77; Am. Council Learned Socs. research grantee, 1978; John Simon Guggenheim fellow, 1980-81; Alfred P. Sloan Found. grantee, 1983; recipient Kenan Enterprise award, 1988. Mem. Am. Hist. Assn., Orgn. Am. Historians, Econ. History Assn., Bus. and Econ. History Conf. (trustee 1973-76, 85-87). Home: New York N.Y. Died June 24, 1993.

CARPENTER, FRANK MORTON, zoologist; b. Boston, Sept. 6, 1902; s. Edwin Arthur and Maude Frances (Wall) C.; m. Ruth Frances Scace, June 1, 1932; children: Alden Bliss, Ellen Ruth, Cynthia. A.B. magna cum laude, Harvard, 1926, M.S., 1927, D.Sc., 1929. NRC fellow biol. scis., 1928-31; asso. entomology Harvard, 1931-32; research asso. Carnegie Inst., 1931-32; asst. curator invertebrate paleontology Harvard, 1932-36; curator fossil insects Mus. of Comparative Zoology, Harvard, 1936-94; asst. prof. paleontology Mus. of Comparative Zoology, 1936-39, assoc. prof. entomology, 1939-45, prof. entomology, Agassiz prof. zoology, 1945-69, Fisher prof. natural history, 1969-73. Author tech. articles on insect evolution. Fellow Am. Acad. Arts and Scis. (v.p. 1961-63); mem. Palentol. Soc. (medal 1975), Phi Beta Kappa, Sigma Xi (nat. pres.). Home: Lexington Mass. Died Jan. 18, 1994.

CARPINO, FRANCESCO CARDINAL, former archbishop of Palermo; b. Palazzolo Acreide, Italy, May 18, 1905; Ordained priest Roman Catholic Ch., 1927; ordained titular archbishop of Nicomedia and coadjutor archbishop of Monreale, 1951, archbishop of Monreale, 1951-61; titular archbishop of Sardica, 1961; assessor Sacred Consistorial Congregation, 1961; pro-prefect of Sacred Congregation of the Council, 1967; elevated to Sacred Coll. of Cardinals, 1967; archbishop of Palermo, 1967-70; entered order of cardinal bishops as titular bishop of Albano, 1978. Referendary of the Congregation of Bishops, 1970. Mem. Council for Public Affairs of the Ch., Congregation, Tribunal, Causes of Saints, Apostolic Signatura. Home: Rome Italy

CARR, GEORGE C., federal judge; b. 1929. BS, BA, U. Fla., 1951, LLB, 1954. Bar: Fla. 1954. Pvt. practice law, 1954-51; mem. firm Carr, Chiles & Ellsworth, 1957-63, Bently, Miller, Sinder, Carr, Chiles & Ellsworth, 1963-67, Carr & Chiles, 1967-69, Peterson, Carr & Harris, 1969-77; atty. Polk County, 1973-78; judge U.S. Dist. Ct. (mid. dist.) Fla., Tampa, 1977-90, chief judge, 1989-90. Mem. ABA. Home: Tampa Fla. Died Jan. 26, 1990; buried Oak Hill Cemetery, Lakeland, Fla.

CARR, MARTIN DOUGLAS, television producer, director, writer; b. Flushing, N.Y., Jan. 20, 1932; s. Irving Conovitz and Isabel (Hochdorf) C. B.A. summa cum laude, Williams Coll., 1953; postgrad., Neighborhood Playhouse Sch. Theatre, 1956. Producer, CBS News, N.Y.C., 1957-69, NBC News, N.Y.C., 1969-71, ABC News, N.Y.C., 1973-75; exec. producer PBS Smithsonian World, 1981-85; producer: (stage) The Saturday Night Kid, N.Y.C., 1959; major TV prodns. Smithsonian World, CBS Reports, Hunger in America, NBC White Paper: Migrant, This Child Is Rated X, The Search for Ulysses, Gauguin in Tahiti, Leaving Home Blues, Five Faces of Tokyo, Dublin Through Different Eyes, ABC Closeup: The Culture Thieves, ABC News-20/20. Served to lt (j.g.) USN, 1953-55. Recipient Emmy awards Nat. Acad. TV Arts and Scis. 1966, 67, 68, 71, 85, Peabody award U. Ga. Sch. Journalism 1968, 70, 71, Robert F. Kennedy Journalism award Robert F. Kennedy Found. 1970, Sidney Hillman Found. award 1971, DuPont/Columbia Journalism awards 1971, Gavel award Am. Bar Assn. 1972, Cine Golden Eagle 1980, 85, Blue Ribbon, Am. Film Festival, 1984, 86. Club: Williams (N.Y.C.). Home: New York N.Y.

CARR, MICHAEL, secondary education educator; b. Stockton, Calif., Sept. 20, 1951; s. Frank Edward and Eleanor (Adair) C. AA, San Joaquin Delta Community, 1971; BA, Calif. State U., Long Beach, 1975; MA, Pacific Oaks Coll., 1977; postgrad., U. Calif., Irvine, 1981. Cert. tchr./trainer, Calif. Tchr. Carlsbad (Calif.) Unified Schs.; presenter workshops on writing process, accelerated learning and learning styles. Contb. author: Thinking/Writing, Practical Ideas for Teaching Writing as a Process, CBEST Preparation Guide, Guiding Young Children's Learning: An Activities Handbook, (audio tape series) Success Through Writing; cons. film series. Mem. NEA, Calif. Tchrs. Assn., Internat. Reading Assn., SCTE. Home: Oceanside Calif. Died July 27, 1993.

CARR, RONALD GENE, lawyer; b. Chgo., Jan. 19, 1946; s. Harry Bertram and Marion Esther (Adlam) C.; m. Mary Laurie Azcuenaga, Aug. 24, 1968. A.B., Stanford U., 1968; M.A., U. Calif.-Berkeley, 1970; J.D., U. Chgo., 1973. Law clk. to chief judge U.S. Ct. Appeals (D.C. cir.), Washington, 1973-74; law clk. to Justice Lewis F. Powell U.S. Supreme Ct., Washington, 1974-75; spl. asst. to Atty. Gen. Edward H. Levi U.S. Dept. Justice, Washington, 1975-76; assoc. ptnr. Morrison & Foerster, San Francisco, 1977-81; ptnr. Morrison & Foerster, San Francisco, Washington, 1983-95; dep. asst. atty. gen. antitrust div. U.S. Dept. Justice, Washington, 1981-83; lectr. fed. jurisdiction Law Sch., U. Calif.-Berkeley, 1978; vis. prof. law Boston U., 1985. Editor-in-chief: U. Chgo. Law Rev., 1972-73. Mem. ABA, Am. Law Inst., Order of Coif, Phi Beta Kappa. Home: Washington D.C. Died June 1995.

CARRARA, ARTHUR ALFONSO, architect, designer, painter, graphic designer; b. Chgo., Apr. 8, 1914; s. Cesare and Georgia (Marcucci) C.; m. Charlotte A. Bartels, Sept. 23, 1944. B.A. in Arch, U. Ill., 1937; apprenticeship, John S. VanBergen, Prairie Sch. Architect, Highland Park, Ill., 1938. Pvt. practice architecture Chgo., 1946-95; tchr., lectr. various archtl. schs. and museums; mem. editorial staff Inland Architect, 1964-67; Mem. Nat. Council Architects Registration Bd. Collector, curator, Prairie Sch. Architects work.; one-man archtl. shows include, Milw. Art Center, 1960, Walker Art Center, Mpls., 1962, Albright-Knox Art Mus., 1965, Munson-Williams-Proctor Mus. Art, Utica, N.Y., 1965; exhibited in group show, Milw. Art Center, 1977-78, introduction hydraulic/moving parts to architecture, Cafe Borranical, Melbourne, Australia, 1944; architect master plan, Manila, P.I., 1944, Cebu, P.I., 1945, 1st magnetic sculpture exhbn., Renaissance Soc., U. Chgo., 1947, design 1st magnetic lamp, 1946; designer, inventor magnet master playtool, 1947, inflata lamp, 1954, transfer print, 1957, one man show prints, Gilman Gallery, 1963; exhibited in: group show An Am. Architecture: Its Roots, Growth and Horizons, Milw. Art Center, 1977; introduction paper flexagon, Chgo. Art Inst., 1957, prin. magnetic and electro-magnetic into modern architecture, 1960; designer sky-spider duct column, Graphic Controls Bldg., 1962, 1st large scale one piece fibre-glass skylite into modern architecture, 1963; introduced air supported forms into architecture, 1964; designed 1st continuous light-rift Architects Workshop, Kettle Moraine, Wis., 1969; introduced large-scale indsl. fiberglass light-rift controles Graficas, S.A., Mexico City, 1970; pioneer large-scale fibreglass archtl. mech. forms; designer first stapled plywood furniture, first paper-core houses with paper-core furniture; work appears in book The Prairie Sch. Tradition, 1979, The Small House, 1986; introduced art glass done with water jet and bonding material; contbr. articles to profl. jours.; One man show Can. Ctr. for Architecture, Montreal, Can., 1994. Served to maj. AUS, 1942-45. Mem. A.I.A., Alpha Rho Chi. Home: Whitewater Wis. Died Oct. 2, 1996.

CARRIER, ESTELLE STACY, drilling company executive; b. near Anderson, Tex., Sept. 3, 1913; d. David D. and Rosa (Miller) Mabry; m. Jack Leonard Stacy, Dec. 24, 1933 (dec. May 1963); 1 child, Richard Allen; m. John B. Carrier, Mar. 2, 1974. Grad. high sch. V.p. Stacy Drilling Co., Douglas, Wyo., 1948-63, pres., from 1963; pres. Teno United, 1963-80; Treas. Converse County (Wyo.) Found., 1952-77; Vice chmn. Wyo. Republican Com., 1960-66; mem. Wyo. Fedn. Rep. Women (past pres.); Rep. nat. committeewoman for Wyo., 1965-76; sec. Rep. Nat. Com., 1972-76, Rep. Western States Conf., 1974-76; Mem. Def. Adv. Com. for Women in Services, from 1970, chmn., from 1972; mem. U.S. State Dept. Adv. Com., Western area, 1971-73, Nat. Adv. Council Safety in Agr., 1974-76; sec. Def. Adv. Com. on Women in Services, 1970-72, chmn., 1972; pres. bd. trustees Converse County Library, 1965-72; mem. Rep. Nat. Com. Adv. Com. on Energy and Environ. Trustee, mem. legis. coun. Wyo. Safety Found.; trustee Del. for Friendship among Women, 1975-87; del. Rep. Nat. Conv., Houston, 1992. Mem. C. of C., Am. Women for Internat. Understanding, Epsilon Sigma Alpha. Clubs: Women of the Moose, Douglas Sorority, Douglas Civic (past pres.), Federated Women's. Lodge: Order Eastern Star (past matron). Home: Douglas Wyo. Deceased.

CARRINGTON, PAUL, lawyer; b. Mexico, Mo., Sept. 24, 1894; s. William Thomas and Mary (Holloway) C.; m. E. Frances DeWitt, Nov. 5, 1921; children: Frances (Lee), Paul DeWitt. A.B., U. Mo., 1914; LL.B., Harvard U., 1917; LL.D. (hon.), So. Meth. U., 1980. Bar: Mo. 1917, Tex. 1919. Since practiced civil law Dallas; mem. firm Carrington, Coleman, Sloman & Blumenthal, until 1974; adj. prof. law So. Meth. U., 1974-80; reporter, Judicial Conf. Adv. Com. on Fed. Rules of Civil Procedure, from 1985. Author: (with William A. Sutherland) Articles of Partnership for Law Firms, 1962; contbr. numerous articles on corp. law, arbitrations and legal subjects to profl. jours. Chmn. N. Tex. Com. on Econ. Devel., 1943-46, Allen Enemy Hearing Bd. for North Tex., 1942-45; pres. Greater Dallas Planning Council, 1948-53; chmn. bd. Dallas Council on World Affairs, 1953-54; v.p., nat. councilor Dallas Boy Scouts Am., 1945-63; pres. Dallas YMCA, 1946-49; trustee S.W. Legal Found., 1948-74, life trustee, 1974—; trustee Dallas Boy Scout Found., 1946-78; bd. dirs. Am. Bar Endowment, 1963-70, dir. emeritus, 1970-79. Served as 2d lt., instr. primary flying U.S. Army, 1918-19. Recipient Hatton W. Sumners award S.W. Legal Found., 1963, Distinguished Alumnus award U. Mo., 1967, 50-yr. award for distinguished service to law profession Am. Bar. Found., 1973. Fellow Am. Bar Found. (chmn. 1965-66); mem. E. Tex. C. of C. (pres. 1950-51), Dallas C. of C. (pres. 1940-42, chmn. legislative com. 1943-70), Tex. Assn. Commerce (pres. 1946-49), ABA (house of dels. 1957-70, assembly del. 1958, 61, 64, 67, chmn. com. postwar planning 1943-45, chmn. sect. corp. banking and bus. law 1955-56, chmn. com. on lawyer referral 1959-63), Dallas Bar Assn. (pres. 1939-40), State Bar Tex. (pres. 1960-61, 50-yr. award for distinguished service to legal profession 1977, 1st chmn. sect. corp. banking and bus. law 1954-55, chmn. com. rev. Tex. corp. law 1948-57), Am. Soc. Internat. Law (exec. council 1961-67), Am. Arbitration Assn. (dir. 1935-75), World Peace Through Law Center (chmn. corporate law commn. 1963-72), Am. Law Inst., Am. Judicature Soc., Harvard Law Sch. Assn. (pres. 1959-61, nat. council from 1953), SAR, Order of Coif (hon.). Independent. Mem. Christian Ch. (elder emeritus). Clubs: Mason (32 deg.), Dallas Country, Petroleum (Dallas); Harvard (N.Y.C.); Metropolitan (Washington Home: Dallas Tex. Deceased.

CARROLL, DAVID SHIELDS, physician; b. Morri town, Tenn., Jan. 3, 1917; s. Charles Thomas and Z Marvin (Wells) C.; m. Mary Kathryn McGuire, Nov. 1941 (dec. May 1960); children: Kathryn (Mrs. Hal V Canary), Elizabeth Jane (Mrs. Stephen P. Busch), Davi Shields; m. Peggy Land Leppert, Nov. 10, 1961. B.S U. Tenn., 1938, M.D., 1940. Diplomate: Am. B Radiology. Intern John Gaston Hosp., Memphis, 194 41; resident radiology U. Tenn. Hosp., 1946-47; chm dept. radiology City of Memphis Hosps., 1947-64; pro chmn. dept. radiology U. Tenn. Coll. Medicine, 1957-6 clin. prof., 1964-90, ret.; staff radiologist Meth. Hosp cons. Oak Ridge Inst. Nuclear Studies, 1952-62, I Bonheur Children's Hosp., 1965-92, Kennedy V. Hosp., 1959-92, Meth. Hosp., 1962-92, St. Jude Chi dren's Hosp., 1963-92. Conbtr. articles to med. jours Pres. bd. dirs. Les Passees Treatment Center, 1960-6 pres. Memphis and Shelby County unit Am. Canc Soc., 1963, bd. dirs. Tenn. div., 1960-92; bd. dirs. We Tenn. Cancer Clinic, 1954-92. Served to maj. M. AUS, 1941-46, ETO. Fellow Am. Coll. Radiolog (chmn. bd. chancellors 1963, pres. 1964); mem. Radic Soc. N.Am. (v.p. 1956, chmn. bd. 1971, pres. 1973, go medal 1978), Am., So. med. assns., Tenn. Radiol. So (pres. 1958), Memphis and Shelby County Med. So Am. Radium Soc. Episcopalian. Club: Memphis Cou try. Home: Memphis Tenn. Died Oct. 25, 1992.

CARTER, DAVID MARTIN, dermatologist; Doniphan, Mo., June 10, 1936; s. Joseph and Elizabe (Estes) C.; m. Anne Babson; children: Anna, Chri topher, Elizabeth. AB, Dartmouth Coll., 1955-58; M Harvard U. Med. Sch., 1961; PhD, Yale U., 1971 Diplomate Am. Bd. Dermatology. Intern U. Rocheste 1961-62, asst. resident, 1962-63; teaching fellow USPH Ctr. for Disease Control, Atlanta, 1963-65; dermatolo resident U. Pa., Phila., 1965-67; postdoctoral fellow Ya U. Sch. Medicine, New Haven, Conn., 1967-70; a tending physician Yale-New Haven Hosp., New Have 1970-81; prof. dermatology Yale U. Sch. Medicine, Ne Haven, 1977-81; co-head div. dermatology N.Y. Hos Cornell Med. Ctr., N.Y.C., 1981-93; prof., sr. physici The Rockefeller U., N.Y.C., 1981-93; bd. dirs. Soc. I vestigative Dermatology, N.Y.C., pres. 1985-86; me adv. council Nat. Inst. for Arthritis, Musculoskele and Skin Diseases, 1988-91; mem. Nat. Commn. Orph Diseases, 1987-89; lectureships and vis. professorsh include Am. Physicians Fellowship, Inc. for Medicin Israel, Coll. Physicians and Surgeons of Columbia U N.Y.C., Ind. U., Indpls., U. Ala., Birmingham, Barn Usher vis. prof. McGill U., Montreal, Washington U St. Louis , Kyushu U., Japan, 1984, Kobe U., Japa 1984, Kitasato U., Japan, 1984, U. Pitts. Sch. Medicin 1984, U. Ariz., Tucson, 1985, U. Calif., San Francisc 1985, British Soc. Investigative Dermatology Oxford U 1985, M.H. Samitz lectr. U. Pa., 1986, U. Conn., 198 All India Inst. Medicine, 1986, Columbia U., 198 Robert N. Buchanan vis. prof. Vanderbilt U., 198 Taiwan, New Delhi. Author numerous books and a ticles in field; assoc. editor Yale Jour. Biology ar Medicine, 1977-81, Jour. Investigative Dermatolog 1977-82, Jour. of Am. Acad. Dermatology, 1979-84 Daniel Webster Nat. scholar Dartmouth Coll., 1954-5 Howard Hughes med. investigator Yale U., 1971-78 Fellow AAAS, Coll. Physicians of Phila.; mem. A Acad. Dermatology, Am. Dermatol. Assn. (edn. com Soc. Investigative Dermatology (pres. 1985-86, bd. di 1975-80, 84-87), Nat. Program Dermatology (task for on genetics), New England Dermatol. So Dermatology Found. (med. and sci. com. for grants a fellowships), Am. Fedn. Clin. Research, Internat. P ment Cell Soc., N.Y. Acad. Sci., N.Y. Acad. Medici (pres. sect. on dermatology and syphilology, 1986-8 sec. 1985-86), Assn. Profs. Dermatology (genetics co bd. dirs.), NIH (adv. com. on formation of nat. in arthritis, musculoskeletal, and skin diseases), Japan Soc. for Investigative Dermatology (hon.), French Sc Dermatology and Syphilology (hon.). Home: New Yo N.Y. Died Nov. 7, 1993.

CARTER, EDWARD WILLIAM, retail executive; Cumberland, Md., June 29, 1911; s. S. and Rose P. m. Christine Dailey; children: William Dailey, A Carter Huneke; m. Hannah Locke Caldwell, 1963. A UCLA, 1932; MBA cum laude, Harvard, 1937; LL (hon.), Occidental Coll., 1962. Account mgr. Scudd Stevens & Clark, L.A.; mdse. mgr. May Co., L.A chmn. emeritus bd. dirs. Carter Hawley Hale Stor Inc., L.A.; emeritus bd. dirs. Stanford Rsch. Inst., Pa Alto, Calif., Businessmen's Coun., N.Y.C.; emerit chmn. bd. regents U. Calif., Berkeley. Emeritus trust Occidental Coll., Brookings Instn., Los Angeles Cou Mus. Art, Nat. Humanities Ctr. Com. Econ. Deve emeritus bd. dirs. Assocs. Harvard Grad. Bus. Sc Santa Anita Found., L.A. Philharm Assn.; mem. v com. UCLA Grad. Sch. Mgmt.; mem. Woodrow Wils Internat. Ctr. Coun., Coun. on Fgn. Rels. Mem. B Coun., Harvard U. Bus. Sch. Alumni Assn. Clu Calif. (Los Angeles), Los Angeles Country; Paci Union, Bohemian, Burlingame Country (San Francisc Cypress Point (Pebble Beach). Home: Bel Air Ca Died Apr. 25, 1996.

CARTER, JAMES EDWARD, JR., dentist, associati official; b. Augusta, Ga., July 1, 1906; s. James Edwa d Emma (Barnett) C.; D.D.S., Howard U., 1930; stgrad. Haines Normal and Indsl. Inst., 1920-24; m. arjorie Butler, Jan. 7, 1928; 1 son, James Edward III. t. practice dentistry, Augusta, 1930-81. Mem. Nat. uncil YMCA, 1958-64, 67-69; chmn. 9th St. YMCA, igusta, 1950-57; active United Coll. Fund, Cancer ., United Chest Fund, Boy Scouts Am. Del. Repub- an Nat., Conv., 1960. Bd. dirs. Augusta-Richmond unty Library. Recipient Achievement award in pub. vice Upsilon Sigma chpt. Omega Psi Phi, 1949, hitney M. Young Jr. Service award Boy Scouts Am., Year award Omega Psi Phi, 1986, Eastern Dist. ental Soc. Service award, 1986, 50 Year and Hon. llowship award Ga. Dental Assn., 1980, Dentist of . award Ga. Dental Soc., 1980, Achievement award oney Med. Dental & Pharm. Soc., 1980; award of erit Georgia Dental Soc., 1961; 55 Year award ankful Bapt. Ch., 1973; Howard U. Alumni Dental hievement award, 1982; Spl. award Stoney Med., ental and Pharm. Soc., 1983. Fellow Internat. Coll. entists, Am. Coll. Dentists, Royal Soc. Health, Acad. en. Dentistry, World Wide Acad. Scholars, Acad. entistry Internat.; mem. Nat. (life; past pres.; mem. ec. bd. 1940-52), Am. (life), Ga. (life, pres. 1940-41, -year service plaque) dental assns., Stoney-Med. and ental Soc. (pres. 1961-63), Ga. Dental Soc. (life mem. 87-93), Acad. Gen. Dentistry, John A. Andrew Clin, c. (pres. dental sect. 1947), Fedn. Dentaire Interna- nale, Pierre Fauchard Acad., Omega Psi Phi (past silius Psi Omega chpt. 1936-37, treas. 7th dist. 1943- ; recipient achievement award human relations Psi nega chpt. 1963, 50 Year Pin), Sigma Pi Phi, Omicron appa Upsilon. Republican. Baptist (chmn. bd. trustees 37-77, chmn. emeritus, deacon 1961-93). Clubs: ontiers (Augusta, Ga.); Optimist Internat. Died May , 1993. Home: Augusta Ga.

ARTER, JOHN COLES, lawyer; b. Eolia, Mo., Jan. , 1920; s. Charles William and Ollie (Brown) C.; m. orothy Mary Strong, Jan. 29, 1944; children: Carolyn , Charles W. AB, Lake Forest (Ill.) Coll., 1943, MA, 79; LLB, Chgo.-Kent Coll. Law, 1950. Pub. acct. ice Waterhouse & Co., Chgo., 1946-47, Paul Pettingill ., Waukegan, Ill., 1950-51; instr. Lake Forest Coll., 47-50; with Inland Steel Co., Chgo., 1951-79; sec. land Steel Co., 1962-79; prof. law Memphis State U., 79-90, prof. law emeritus, 1990-93; ptnr. Glankler, own, Gilliland, Chase, Robinson & Raines, Memphis, 90-92; mem. Benham, Schatz & Tucker, P.C., emphis, 1992-93; instr. John Marshall Sch. Law, 1964. ommr., past pres. Lake Bluff (Ill.) Park Dist.; past es. Lake Bluff Village Library.; past bd. dirs. Am. ng Assn., Chgo. Lung Assn., Lake Forest Hosp., ncerts Internat.; bd. dirs. Tenn. Lung Assn.; pres. emphis Lung Assn.; former trustee Village of Lake uff, Lake Forest Coll. Served to lt. (j.g.) USNR, 1943- , PTO. Decorated Presdl. Commendation Medal. em. ABA, Tenn. Bar Assn., Memphis Bar Assn., Am. w Inst., Am. Soc. Corp. Secs. (pres. 1964-65, nat. dir. 66-77, nat. v.p. 1967, nat. pres. 1975-76), Lake Forest umni Assn. (past pres. exec. bd.), Scholarship and iidance Assn. (pres. 1972-73, dir.), Legal Club, Law ub, Farmington Club (Charlottesville, Va.), Chick- aw Club (Memphis). Home: Memphis Tenn. Died t. 5, 1993.

ARTER, MARSHALL SYLVESTER, foundation ecutive, former army officer; b. Ft. Monroe, Va., Sept. , 1909; s. Clifton Carroll and Mai (Coleman) C.; m. éot Nichols; children: Josephine Stoney, Marshall chols, Mary Coleman. BS, U.S. Mil. Acad., 1931; S, MIT, 1936; grad., Nat. War Coll., 1950. Commd. lt. U.S. Army, 1931, advanced through grades to lt. n., 1962; with plans and operations div. War Dept. en. Staff, 1942-45; dep. and asst. chief of staff G-5 dqrs., China Theater, 1945-46; spl. rep. for Gen. Mar- all Office Sec. State, Washington, 1946-47, spl. asst. to . state, 1947-49; minister Am. Embassy, London, 49; comdg. officer 138th AAA Group and AA Of- er, Cen. Japan, 1950; dir. exec. office Sec. Def., Wash- gton, 1950-52; dep. comdg. gen., asst. div. comdr. 71st f. Div., Alaska, 1952-55; comdg. gen. 5th AA Re- onal Command, Ft. Sheridan, Ill., 1955-56; chief of aff N.Am. Air Def. Command, Colorado Springs, 56-59, U.S. 8th Army, Republic of Korea, 1959-60; mdg. gen. Army Air Def. Ctr., Ft. Bliss, Tex., 1961- ; dep. dir. CIA, Washington, 1962-65; dir. Nat. curity Agy., Washington, 1965-69, cons., 1969—; es. George C. Marshall Research Found., Lexington, ., 1969-85, pres. emeritus, 1985-93. Trustee Cheyenne ountain Zool. Soc., 1970-90. Decorated Disting. In- ligence medal, D.S.M. with two oak leaf clusters, Le- on of Merit with oak leaf cluster, Bronze Star; cipient Spl. Breast Order of Yun Hui with Rosette hina), 1945, with oak-leaf cluster, 1947; named omdr., Order of Orange Nassau with swords (Nether- nds), to Order of Service Merit (Korea). Mem. Va. st. Soc. (hon. life), Sigma Xi. Roman Catholic. ubs: Boone and Crockett (N.Y.C.); Cheyenne ountain Country,, Cooking, Country of Colo. olorado Springs); Army-Navy Country (Arlington, .); Army-Navy (Washington). Home: Colorado rings Colo. Died Feb. 18, 1993.

ARTIER, GEORGES, library director; b. L'Assomp- n, Quebec, Can., Apr. 4, 1929; s. Rosaire D. and arguerite (Mathieu) C.; m. Céline Robitaille, Nov. 29, 52; children: Nathalie, Guillaume. BA, U. Montreal, Quebec, 1948, L.L., 1951, B of Libr. Sci., 1952; LittD (hon.), U. Moncton (New Brunswick), 1988. Asst. dir. libris. Cath. Schs. Commn., Montreal, 1952-57; dir. libr. Coll. Sainte-Marie, Montreal, 1958-61; dir. svc. distbn. press div. UNESCO, Paris, 1961-64; conservator St.-Sulpice Libr., Montreal, 1964-67; chief conservator Nat. Libr. Que., Montreal, 1967-73; dir., prof. Sch. Libr. Sci. U. Montreal, 1973-77; gen. dir. dept. arts and letters Minister of Cultural Affairs, Govt. of Que., 1977-83; dir. Ctr. Pub. and Adminstrv. Studies, 1983-86; gen. dir. Nat. Libr. Que., Montreal, 1986-89. Author: (fiction) Le Poisson Pêché, 1964 (Prix du Cercle du Livre de France 1964), Notre-Dame du Colportage, 1987, Jacques Cartier: l'odyssée intime, 1991, Dans les fougères de l'enfance, 1993, (poetry) Hymnes/Isabelle, 1954, La Mort à Vivre, 1954 (Prix InterFrance 1955), Laves et Neiges, 1954, Obscure Navigation du Temps, 1956, Chanteaux, 1976. Home: Ville de Saint-Laurent Can.

CARVAJAL PRADO, PATRICIO, Chilean minister of defense, naval officer, politician; b. Sept. 13, 1916; m. Teresa Carvallo; 4 children. Ed. Liceo Aleman de Santiago and naval coll. Commdr. Lautaro (patrol-boat) 1953; staff course 1955-56, anti-submarine tactics course 1958. Capt. Esmeralda (training ship), 1961; dir. gunnery sch. and naval attache, U.K., 1964; chief of Naval Gen. Staff, 1970; dir.-gen. of services, 1972; min.of def., 1973-74, 83-94, min. of fgn. affairs, 1974-78. Died July 15, 1994. Home: Santiago Chile

CASANOVA, MARC, oil co. exec.; b. Jan. 14, 1926; Lycee-Mangin, Morocco; m. Daisy Pistorelli, Apr. 7, 1954; 3 children. With Mobil Oil Co., various locations, from 1946, exec. v.p., Tokyo, 1968-71, v.p., regional exec., N.Y.C., 1972-73, pres., gen. mgr., Istanbul, Turkey, 1973-78, pres., mng. dir. Mobil Oil Italiana, Rome, 1979-84, Mobil Oil Franç aise, Paris, from 1984. Served with 2d French Armored Div., 1943-45. Deceased. Home: La Défense France

CASARTELLI, FABIO, Olympic athlete. Recipient Gold medal individual road race men's cycling XXV Summer Olympic Games, Barcelona, Spain, 1992. Home: New Tripoli Pa. Died July 18, 1995.

CASE, JAMES HUGHSON, mathematics educator; b. Franklinville, N.Y., May 25, 1928; s. Hughson Lester and Ella Jane (Maxwell) C.; m. Joanna Elsie Hogue, Sept. 15, 1951; children: Judith, Thomas, Eliot. BS, Auburn U., 1950; PhD, Tulane U., 1954. Asst. prof. U. Rochester, N.Y., 1959-61; asst. prof. U. Utah, Salt Lake City, 1954-59, assoc. prof., 1961-69, prof., from 1969; cons. Gen. Dynamics Corp., Rochester, 1960-61, CIS Corp., Manhattan, Kans., from 1983. Patentee in field. Served with U.S. Army, 1955-56. Mem. Am. Math. Soc., AAAS. Home: Salt Lake City Utah Deceased.

CASEY, ETHEL LAUGHLIN, concert and opera singer; b. Tarboro, N.C., Jan. 14, 1926; d. Maurice Lee and Mary Irene (Williams) Laughlin; m. Willis Robert Casey, May 23, 1946; children: Willis Robert, Walker Laughlin. Student, Va. Intermont Coll., 1944-45; BA, Greensboro Coll, 1946-47; postgrad., U. N.C., 1948, 62, Meredith Coll., 1949, Northwestern U., 1961. Founder, owner Carolina Records Co.; founder concert series N.C. State Art Mus. Performed at numerous convs. and festivals; oratorio soloist, conv. and mus. comedy performer; author: Claude de France, 1963, Psalms (160 psalm poems), 1987; composer Christmas Night, 1971, America Will Endure, 1972, U.S.A., 1972; N.Y. debut Town Hall, 1961; concert singer performing at Carnegie Hall, all-Debussy concert, 1961, Tribute to Galli-Curci, 1965, Composer's Showcase, N.Y., 1965, Electronic Concert, Ann Arbor, Mich., 1966, Webern World Premieres Internat. Webern Festivals, Seattle, Buffalo, 1962-66, World Premieres of Graphic Music, 1965, command performance Greek Royal Princess, 1966, New Vistas, World Premieres of Am. Music, 1968; performance of Babbitt's electronic opera Philomel, 1968; Gov.'s Concerts, Judson Hall, N.Y., 1969, 70, Nat. Congress, Constn. Hall, Washington, 1970; World Premieres Webern and Earls Music Carnegie Hall, 1971, world premieres own music and Webern Lincoln Ctr., N.Y.C., 1971, Internat. Platform Assn., Washington, 1972, performed in Leningrad, USSR, 1975; TV and radio performer, 1936-95. Founder, God's Ministry, Christian Broadcast Network, 1981-82. Named Alumna of Year, Va. Intermont Coll., 1967, Singer of Year, Nat. Assn. Tchrs. Singing, 1963; honored as singer All-Am. City Celebrations, Tarboro, N.C., 1978; recipient award Greensboro Coll. Concert, 1980. Mem. N.C. State Music Soc. (founder). Home: Raleigh N.C. Died Nov. 22, 1995.

CASEY, JOHN JOSEPH, airline executive; b. Boston, Oct. 3, 1918; s. John Joseph and Norine (Doyle) C.; m. Mary June Reipe, Apr. 21, 1945; children: John Joseph, David Vaughan, Janet Marjorie, Mary June; m. Dawn Anderson Bryan, May 27, 1984. S.B., M.I.T., 1940; postgrad., Cornell U., 1942. Stress engr. Curtiss-Wright Corp., Buffalo, 1940-42; mgr. air cargo engring. Am. Airlines, St. Joseph, Mo., 1946-47; service engr. Am. Airlines, N.Y.C., 1947-49; asst. v.p. maintenance Am. Airlines, Tulsa, 1950-56; v.p. R. Dixon Speas Assos., Manhasset, N.Y.; aviation cons., 1956-62; sr. v.p. operations, dir. Seaboard World Airlines, N.Y.C., 1962-68; group v.p., vice chmn. bd., dir. Braniff Internat., Dallas, 1968-81; pres., chmn. bd. Braniff Internat., 1981-82; exec. v.p. ops. Pan Am. World Airways, 1982-84; pres., chief exec. officer Pan Am. World Services, 1984-85; pres., chmn., chief exec. officer Pan Am Comml. Services, 1986-88; prin. John J. Casey & Assocs., Port Washington, N.Y., 1988—. V.p. then pres. Circle 10 coun. Boy Scouts Am., also mem. exec. bd. N.E. Region, mem. nat. coun., internat. com. With USAAF, 1942-46; comdg. officer 320th Squadron, 509th Composite Bomb Group 1945-46. Mem. AIAA, Soc. Automotive Engrs., Mass. Inst. Tech. Alumni Assn., Air Force Assn. Clubs: Wings (N.Y.C.); Manhasset Bay (N.Y.) Yacht. Home: Huntington Station N.Y. Died Feb. 15, 1994.

CASEY, SAMUEL ALEXANDER, lawyer, paper manufacturer; b. Peoria, Ill., Sept. 10, 1914; s. Richard C. and Chloris (Thomason) C.; m. Ardean Alexander, Nov. 7, 1942; children: John A., Suzanne E., Page E. AB, Bradley U., 1936; JD, U. Ill., 1939; DSc (hon.), Clarkson U., 1972. Bar: Ill. bar 1939, Wis. bar 1946. Pvt. practice, 1939-92; with Chapman & Cutler, Chgo., 1940-42; exec. v.p., treas. Nekoosa-Edwards Paper Co., Port Edwards, Wis., 1946-61; pres., dir. Nekoosa-Edwards Paper Co., 1962-70, Gt. No. Nekoosa Corp., Stamford, Conn., 1971-78; chief exec. officer Gt. No. Nekoosa Corp., 1972-79, chmn., 1974-80, chmn. exec. com., 1980-84, ret., 1984; past dir. U.S. Trust Co. N.Y., Greyhound Corp., Gen. Signal, Pitney Bowes, Moore McCormack Resources, Armstrong Rubber, Marshall & Ilsley Bank, Employers Ins. of Wausau, Trane Co. Former trustee Bradley U.; former trustee Lawrence U. With Army Intelligence, 1942-43, Judge Adv. Gen.'s Dept., U.S. Army, 1944-46. Mem. Links Club, Phi Delta Phi. Home: Wickenburg Ariz. Died Oct. 15, 1992; interred Port Edwards, Wis.

CASSIDY, SCOTT MICHAEL, lawyer; b. Winona, Minn., Apr. 10, 1933; s. Joseph Michael and Marion (Scott) C.; m. Mary Kenney, Jan. 26, 1962; children: Maureen, Bridget, Joseph, Nora. BS in Polit. Sci., St. Thomas Coll., St. Paul, Minn., 1955; LLB, Marquette U., 1958. Assoc. Tilg & Koch, Milw., 1959-65; ptnr. Margolis & Cassidy, Milw., 1965—; lectr. family law Marquette U., Milw., 1975—, Continuing Legal Edn. State Bar Wis., 1985—; ct. commr. Milwaukee County Cir. Ct., 1971—. Solicitor donation com. United Fund, Milw. Mem. ABA, Am. Acad. Matrimonial Lawyers (pres. Wis. chpt. 1987-88), Wis. Bar Assn., Milwaukee County Bar Assn. (pres. 1986-87), Marquette U. Alumni Assn. (bd. dirs. 1988-91, pres. 1983), Western Racquet Club, Milw. Athletic Club. Roman Catholic. Home: Waukesha Wis.

CASTELLAN, GILBERT WILLIAM, chemistry educator; b. Denver, Nov. 21, 1924; s. John and Eleanor (Pavella) C.; m. Joan Margaret McDonald, Sept. 8, 1956; children: Stephen Joseph, William Andrew, David Matthew, Susan Marie. B.S. summa cum laude, Regis Coll., 1945, Sc.D., 1967; Ph.D., Cath. U. Am., 1949. Instr. chemistry Cath. U. Am., Washington, 1950-54, asst. prof., 1954-58, asso. prof., 1958-64, asst. head dept., 1963-65, prof. chemistry, 1964-69; assoc. dean phys. scis. and engring. U. Md. Grad. Sch., College Park, 1969-74; prof. chemistry U. Md., College Park, 1969-91, prof. emeritus, 1991-96, assoc. chmn. dept. chemistry, 1974-79, 86-87, 89-90; cons. electrochemistry br. U.S. Naval Rsch. Lab., 1956-63, Melpar, Inc., Falls Church, Va., 1963-67. Author: Physical Chemistry, 1964, 3d edit., 1983, Solutions Manual to Accompany Physical Chemistry, 3d edit., 1983; co-author: Study Guide to Accompany The World of Chemistry, Faculty Manual; mem. acad. team for TV course The World of Chemistry, 1986-89, co-dir., 1989-96; contbr. articles to profl. jours. Bd. dirs. The Campus Sch., Washington, 1969-70, treas., 1969-70. AEC fellow phys. scis. U. Ill., 1949-50; NSF fellow Max Planck Institut für Physikalische Chemie, Göttingen, Fed. Republic Germany, 1962-63. Mem. Am. Chem. Soc., Am. Phys. Soc., Electrochem. Soc. (pres. sect. 1964-65), Sigma Xi. Home: Silver Spring Md.

CASTELLAN, N(ORMAN) JOHN, JR., psychologist, educator; b. Denver, Jan. 21, 1939; s. Norman John and Mary Victoria (Biebl) C.; m. Diane Cecile Swift, July 18, 1964; children: Caryn Lynn, Norman John, Tanya Cecile. A.B., Stanford U., 1961; Ph.D., U. Colo., 1965. Prof. psychology Ind. U., Bloomington, 1965-93, psychology editor Conduit curriculum com., 1974-92, assoc. dean rsch. and grad. devel. Ind. U., 1977-93, mem. adv. bd. Conduit, 1986-88; program dir. decision, risk and mgmt. scis. NSF, 1991-93; vis. prof. computer sci. U. Colo., summers 1971-73; vis. rsch. assoc. Oreg. Rsch. Inst., 1972; mem. steering com. Soc. Computers in Psychology, 1973-76, 83-85, 89-93, conf. chmn., 1974, 88, pres., 1979-80. Author: (with Hammond and Householder) Introduction to the Statistical Method, 1970, (with S. Siegel) Nonparametric Statistics, 1988, Individual and Group Decision Making: Current Issues, 1993; Cognitive Theory, Vol. I, 1974, Vol. 2, 1977, Vol. 3, 1978; editor: Judgement/Decision Making Newsletter, 1981-91, Behavior Rsch. Methods, Instruments, and Computers, 1989-93; assoc. editor: Computers and The Social Scis., 1985-88; contbr. sci. articles to profl. jours. Active noise subcom. Bloomington Environ. Commn.; mem. Monroe County Dem. Ctrl. Com., 1968-73, 75-78, 80-83. Research grantee and fellow NSF, 1971-73, 81-83; Research grantee and fellow NIMH, 1966, 73-75.

Fellow AAAS, Am. Psychol. Assn., Am. Psychol. Soc.; mem. Am. Statis. Assn., Psychonomic Soc., Assn. Computing Machinery, Sigma Xi. Home: Bloomington Ind. Died Dec. 21, 1993.

CATER, DOUGLASS, former college president, former presidential assistant, writer, editor; b. Montgomery, Ala., Aug. 24, 1923; s. Silas D. and Nancy (Chesnutt) C.; m. Libby Anderson, Dec. 20, 1950; children: Silas Douglass III, R. Sage, L. Morrow, Benjamin W. Grad., Phillips Exeter Acad., 1942; A.B., Harvard U., 1947, M.A., 1948. Washington editor The Reporter Mag., 1950-63; nat. affairs editor Reporter mag., 1963-64; spl. asst. to Pres. Johnson, 1964-68; spl. asst. to sec. army, 1951; cons. to dir. Mut. Security Agy., 1952; Ferris chair pub. affairs Princeton, 1959; fellow, assoc. dir. Ctr. for Advanced Studies; vis. prof. pub. affairs Wesleyan U., Middletown, Conn., 1963; Regent prof. U. Calif. at San Francisco, 1971-72; cons. prof. Stanford, 1972-77; dir. program council Aspen Inst., sr. fellow, trustee, 1978-91, trustee emeritus, 1991-95; pres. Washington Coll., Chestertown, Md., 1982-90, pres. emeritus, 1990-95; vice chmn. The Observer, London, 1976-81; pres. Observer Internat., 1976-81. Author: (with Marquis Childs) Ethics in a Business Soc., 1953, (with Stephen Strickland) TV Violence and the Child, 1975; author: The Fourth Branch of Government, 1959, Power in Washington, 1964, Dana: The Irrelevant Man, 1970, A Sense of Stewardship, 1990; bd. editors Ency. Brit. Served with World War II, OSS. Guggenheim fellow, 1955; Eisenhower exchange fellow, 1957, sr. fellow Nat. Humanities Ctr.; recipient George Polk Meml. award, 1961; N.Y. Newspaper Guild Page One award, 1961. Mem. Sigma Delta Chi. Methodist. Clubs: Century Assn. (N.Y.C.), Univ. (N.Y.C.). Home: Montgomery Ala. Died Sept. 15, 1995.

CATES, JOHN MARTIN, JR., lawyer; b. Denver, Jan. 20, 1912; s. John Martin and Mary Arden (Randall) C.; m. Mary Perkins Raymond, July 4, 1942 (div. 1973); 1 son, John Martin III; m. Nelia Barletta, Nov. 19, 1976; 1 dau., Nelia M. Barletta Anselin. Grad., Phillips Andover Acad., 1932; B.A., Yale, 1936, J.D., 1939. Bar: Calif. bar 1940, D.C. bar 1946, N.Y. State bar 1976. With McCutchen, Olney, Mannon & Greene, San Francisco, 1939-41; labor relations San Francisco Warehousemen's Assn., 1941-42; with U.S. Maritime Commn. and War Shipping Adminstrn., Washington, 1942-47; fgn. affairs specialist on UN and specialized agencies U.S. Dept. State, 1947-53; with Nat. War Coll., 1952-53; legal adviser Am. embassy U.S. Dept. State, Bonn; also mem. War Criminal Parole Bd., 1953-55; legal advisor, 1st sec., negotiator compensation for agrl. land confiscated from U.S. citizens Am. Embassy, Mexico, 1955-57; chief polit. officer Am. embassy Venezuela, 1957-61; alternate U.S. rep. Council OAS, Washington, 1961-63; counsellor, adviser on Latin Am. Affairs and Liason U.S. Mission to UN, 1963-70; counsellor U.S. Mission to Geneva, 1970-71; pres., dir. Center for Inter-Am. Relations, 1971-75; cons., atty., 1976-94; London counsel firm Pettit & Martin, San Francisco; adj. prof. Fairleigh Dickinson U. Contbr. articles to profl. jours. Mem. Latin Am. adv. council State Dept.; Committeeman Boy Scouts Am., N.Y.C., also Mexico, Venezuela, 1963-94; mem. Am. Ch. Council, Bad Godesburg, Germany, 1953-55; mem. council Yale U., 1968-77; bd. dirs. Youth for Understanding, Incon Internat. Inc., Americas' Found., Programme for New World Anthropology, Ecuador; trustee Am. Aid Soc., London; asso.-cons. Phillips Acad. Bicentennial, 1978. Recipient medal of merit Venezuela Boy Scouts, 1960, superior honor award Dept. of State, 1967, gran cruz Vasco Nuñez de Balboa Panama, 1975; Order Francisco de Miranda Venezuela, 1976, Order St. John of Jerusalem (U.K.). Mem. Council Fgn. Relations, ABA, Inter-Am. Bar Assn., Calif. Bar Assn., D.C. Bar Assn., Bar City N.Y., London Law Soc., Bolivian Soc. (dir. 1971-94), Pan Am. Soc. (dir. 1974-94), Am. Arbitration Assn. (mem. comml. panel), Cercle le de la Presse et Amitie Etrangere (Geneva), Am. Polit. Sci. Assn., English Speaking Union (London), S.R., Soc. Colonial Wars (exec. com.), Pilgrims, St. Nicholas Soc. (exec. com 1969), Phelps Assn. Wolfs Head (exec. com.), Am. Arbitration Assn., Phi Delta Phi. Clubs: Mason (N.Y.C.), Union (N.Y.C.), Century (N.Y.C.); Bucks (London), Am. (London), The Pilgrims (London); Met. (Washington); Bohemian (San Francsico); Lyford Cay (Nassau); Travellers (Paris), Circle de l'Union Interalliée (Paris). Home: Nassau Bahamas Died July 14, 1994.

CAU, JEAN, writer, journalist; b. Bram, Aude, France, July 8, 1925; s. Etienne and Rose (Olivier) C. Licencie Philosophie, Sorbonne, U. Paris. Sec. to Jean-Paul Sartre, 1947-56; editor Les Tempes Modernes, 1949-54; journalist L'Express, Le Figaro litteraire, Candide, France-Observateur, Paris-Match, also others; writer Figaro-Dimanche, 1978-93. Author novels: Le coup de barre; Les paroissiens; La pitie de Dieu; Les enfants, 1975; stories: Mon village; chronicle: Les oreilles et la queue, L'incendie de Rome, 1964; plays: Les parachutistes; Le maitre du monde; Dans un nuage de poussiere, 1967; Les yeux creves, 1968; Pauvre France, 1972; transl.: Who's Afraid of Virginia Woolf; Lettre ouverte aux tetes de chiens de l'Occident, 1967; L'agonie de la vieille, 1969; Tropicanas, 1970; Le tempes des esclaves, Les entrailles du taureau, 1971; Traite de moraleI: les ecuries de l'occident, 1973, II: la grande prostituee, 1974; Toros, 1973; Pourquoi la France, 1975; Les otrages, 1976; Le chevalier; la mort et le diable; Une nuit a Saint-Germaine des pres; La conquete de Zanzibar et Nouvelles du Paradis, 1980; Le grand soleil, 1981; Une rose à la mer, 1983, Proust, le chat et moi, 1984, Croquis de memoire, 1985, Mon lieutenant, 1985, Sevillanes, 1987, les Culottes Courtes, 1988, la Grande maison, 1989; film scripts: La curee, 1966; Don Juan, 1973. Decorated chevalier Legion d'honneur; recipient prix Goncourt, 1961. Died June 18, 1993. Home: Paris France

CAWLEY, EDWARD PHILIP, physician, educator; b. Jackson, Mich., Sept. 1, 1912; s. Michael and Gertrude (Klein) C.; m. Virginia Anne Cohen, June 17, 1939; children: Janet Anne, Philip Edward. A.B., U. Mich., 1936, M.D., 1940. Diplomate: Am. Bd. Dermatology (pres., dir.). Intern Mercy Hosp., Jackson, 1940-42; teaching fellow, instr. dermatology and syphilology Med. Sch., U. Mich., 1945-48, asst. prof., 1948-51; prof., chmn. dept. dermatology and syphilology Sch. Medicine, U. Va., Charlottesville, 1951-95; Disting. prof. Sch. Medicine, U. Va., 1977; practice medicine, specializing in dermatology and syphilology Charlottesville, 1951-95. Contbr. articles to med. jours. Served from 1st lt. to maj. M.C. AUS, 1942-45. Decorated Bronze Star. Fellow A.C.P.; mem. Assn. Profs. Dermatology (pres.), Am. Dermatol. Assn. (pres., dir.), A.M.A., Va., Albemarle County med. socs., Am. Acad. Dermatology (pres.), Soc. for Investigative Dermatology, Chgo. Dermatology Soc., Balt.-Washington, Southeastern dermatol. socs., So. Med. Assn., Am. Soc. Dermatopathology (pres., dir.), Sigma Xi, Alpha Omega Alpha. Roman Catholic. Club: Farmington Country (Charlottesville). Home: Charlottesville Va. Died Jan. 20, 1995.

CEAUSESCU, ELENA, Romanian government official; b. Jan. 7, 1919; ed. Coll. Indsl. Chemistry Poly. Inst., Bucharest; Dr. (hon.), U. Buenos Aires, 1974, U. Malta, 1983, U. Islamabad, 1984, others; m. Nicolae Ceausescu. Active, Union Communist Youth; mem. Romanian Communist Party, 1937-89, mem. central com., 1972-89, mem. exec. com., 1973-89, mem. polit. exec. com., 1974-89, mem. standing bur., 1979-89; mem. Grand Nat. Assembly, 1975-89; 1st dept. prime minister Govt. of Romania, 1980-89; prof. extraordinary Nat. Autonomous U. Mex., 1978. Dir., Inst. of Chemistry, 1964-65; gen. dir. Central Inst. Chemistry, 1975-80; dep. chair Supreme Council of Socio-Econ. Devel., 1982-89; Decorated Hero Socialist Labour, Order Victory of Socialism, Star Socialist Republic of Romania, Hero of Socialist Republic of Romania. Fellow Royal Inst. Chemistry; mem. Nat. Council Front of Socialist Democracy and Unity, 1980-89, Central Inst. Chem. Research, Nat. Council Sci. and Tech. (mem. exec. bur. 1972-89, chmn., 1979-89), Romanian Acad., N.Y. Acad. Scis., Athens Acad., Internat. Inst. Indsl. Chemistry, Internat. Soc. Indsl. Chemistry France, Royal Inst. Chemistry (U.K.), Acad. of Sci. (Ill.), Chem. Soc. Méx., Acad. Scis. III. Author: Research on the Synthesis and Characterizationof Macromolecular Compounds, 1974, Stereospecific Polymerization of Isoprene, 1979, New Research Work on Macromolecular Compounds, 1981, Studies on Chemistry and Technology of Polymers, 1983, Encyclopedia of Chemistry, vol. 1, 1983, vols. 2 and 3, 1986, vol. 4, 1987, vol. 5, 1988, Advances in Polymer Chemistry and Technology, 1986, Hydrocarbon Resins, 1988; contbr. articles to profl. jours. Home: Bucharest Romania

CEAUSESCU, NICOLAE, president of Romania; b. Scornicesti-Olt, Romania, Jan. 26, 1918; m. Elena Ceausescu; children: Valentin, Elena, Nicolae. Zoe, Nicu. State Diploma, Acad. Econ. Studies, Bucharest; D. Polit. Sci., D. Econs, mem. Acad., Acad. Socialist Republic of Romania, 1978, PhD (hon.) univs., 1978; PhD (hon.), univs. Bucharest, Bogotá, Quito, 1973, univs. Lima, Beirut, Buenos Aires,Bahia Blanca, 1974, univs. Nice, Quezon City, Yucatán, Teheran, 1975, U. Liberia, 1988. Participant in working revolutionary movement, 1930—; mem. Union Communist Youth, 1930, sec. central com., 1939-40, sec.-gen., 1944-46; mem. Romanian Communist Party, 1933—, mem. central com., 1945—, sec. gen. Cen. Com., 1954-65, sec.-gen. party, 1969—, mem. polit. exec. com., 1974—; dep. minister of agr., 1948-50, dep. minister of armed forces, 1950-54; dep. Grand Nat. Assembly, 1946—; pres. Council of State of Socialist Republic of Romania, 1967—, pres. republic, 1974—; pres. Nat. Council Socialist Unity Front, 1968—, Def. Council, 1969—; supreme comdr. Armed Forces, 1969—; chmn. Supreme Council Social and Econ. Devel., Nat. Council Working People. Author: Romania on the Way to Building Up the Multilaterally Developed Society, 1931, vols., 1969-87; Selected Works, vols. 1-5, 1965-88, Interviews, Statements and Press Conferences, vols. 1-4, 1966-85. Hon. pres. Acad. Social and Polit. Scis. Socialist Republic of Rumania, 1970—; hon. pres. Acad. Socialist Republic of Romania, 1985—. Named Hero of Socialist Republic of Romania, 1971, 78, 81; decorated orders and distinction of 64 states, including Order Karl Marx (E.Ger.); Order Lenin (USSR); Gold Medal Frederic Joliot-Curie Peace award, 1977; named hon. mem. Anversane Acad., 1983—. Home: Bucharest Romania Died Dec. 25, 1989.

CECIL, JOHN LAMONT, retired bank executiv lawyer; b. Fredricktown, Ky., May 15, 1909; s. Robe Logan and Dorothea Bovard (Griffith) C.; m. Hel Madigan Breen, Sept. 21, 1954; children: Patricia M Cecil Bikai, Elaina M. Cecil Coyne, Anita J. Ce O'Donovan (dec.), Barbara L. Cecil Peterson, Jol Lamont Jr. Student, St. Charles Jr. Coll., 1930, Ca U. Am., 1930; LL.B., Georgetown U., 1935, LL.M 1937. Bar: D.C. 1935, Md. 1962. Contr. Hamilt Hotel, Washington, 1934-35; asst. counsel FDI Washington, 1936-42, counsel, 1946-53, asst. ge counsel, 1953-62; v.p., sec., gen. counsel Weste Bancorp., L.A., 1962-64; v.p., asst. sec. United Ca Bank Internat., 1962-70; exec. v.p., sec., gen. couns Western Bancorp., L.A., 1964-74; corp. sec. Pacific Ar Income Shares, Inc., Western Asset Mgmt. C Pasadena, Calif., 1974-93; mem. staff Alien Proper Custodian, Washington, 1941-42. Mem. bd. rege Georgetown U., 1965-67; mem. bd. regents, fin. co Mount St. Mary's Coll., Los Angeles, 1966-85; bd. dir mem. exec. com. Cath. Social Services, Archdiocese Los Angeles, 1975-86; bd. dirs., mem. exec. com. Ca Assn. Utility Shareholders, 1975-91. Served to comdr. USNR, 1942-46; to capt. Res. 1958. Recipie John Carroll Alumni award Georgetown U., 1969, S Citizen award Los Angeles Expo for Life, 1984. Me D.C., Am. bar assns., Gamma Eta Gamma. Clu Congl. Country (Washington); Newman (pres. 196 Jonathan (L.A.). Home: Los Angeles Calif. Died Ju 21, 1995.

CEDERSTROM, JOHN ANDREW, artist; b. Phil Apr. 26, 1929; s. Albert Gustav and Emilie (Laessig) C m. Eleanor Susanne Ross, June 17, 1960 (dec. 198 children: Andrew Eric, Jeffrey David. Pvt. art instr 1943-48; student, Phila. Coll. Art, 1948-50, Pa. Aca Fine Arts, 1950-51. Children's program dir., exec. di treas. Bryn Mawr Art Center, 1951-62; art dir. S Peters Sch., Phila., 1953-55, Episcopal Acad., Meric Pa., 1955-59; art therapist Inglis House, Home for t Disabled, Phila., 1955-63; chmn. art dir. Friends Cent Sch., Phila., 1963-81; chief conservator Hahn Galle Phila., 1975—, Erikson Gallery, Reisterstown, M 1981—, numerous others; vis. lectr. art and art histo Art Inst., Phila., Hammond Mus., Mass., Woodme Mus., Pa., Pa. Acad. Fine Arts, Phila. Represented permanent collections: Phila. Mus. Art, Allentown M Art, N.C. Mus. Art, Noyes Mus. Art., N.J.; painti commissioned by Price Waterhouse Inc., Phila., 199 Recipient 1st prize 1990 Earth Art Chester County A Assn. Mem. Artists Equity Assn. Phila. (chmn. eth com. 1972-80, bd. dirs., v.p.), Am. Color Print So Phila. Water Color Soc. (assoc.), Am. Artists Pro League, Fellowship of Pa. Acad. Fine Arts (bd. dirs Nat. Trust Hist. Preservation (assoc.), Phila. Watercol Club, Pa. Acad. Fine Arts Alumni Assn. (bd. dirs. Home: Gloucester Mass. Died, Aug. 25, 1992.

CELIO, NELLO, lawyer, political official; b. Feb. 1914. Ed., U. Basel, U. Berne. Sec. Cantonal De Interior, Switzerland, 1941-45; Public Procura Switzerland, 1945-46, mem. Council of States, 1946- mem. Swiss Nat. Council, 1963-95, mem. Swiss Fe Council, 1967-73, v.p. Swiss Fed. Council, 1971, pre 1972, head Fed. Def. Dept., 1967-68, Head Fin. a Customs Dept., 1968-73; chmn. Swiss Aluminum, Lt 1987-96, also bd. dirs.; former pres. Swiss Radical De Party; chmn. Interfood, Banco Rasini of Milan, 1984- Home: Lugano Switzerland Died Dec. 29, 1995.

CHAKOVSKY, ALEKSANDR BORISOVICH, writ b. St. Petersburg, Russia, Aug. 26, 1913; s. Bo Matveevich and Nina Michailovna (Chakovskaia) C.; Raisa Chakovskaya, Sept. 20, 1945; 1 child, Sergei. rad., Gorky Lit. Inst. Moscow, 1938. War corr., 194 45; chief editor jour. Inostrannaya literatura, 1954- Literaturnaya Gazeta, 1962-88. Sec., USSR Uni Writers, 1963-94; dep. to Supreme Soviet of the USS 1966-89; alt. mem. Central Com., Communist Pa Soviet Union, 1971-86, mem., 1986-89. Author: It W in Leningrad, 1944, Lyda, 1945, Peaceful Days, 19 It's Already Morning With Us, 1950, Khvan Cher Is Guard, 1952, A Year of One Life, 1956, Roads Take, 1960, Light of a Distant Star, 1962, Fiancée, 19 Blockade (5 vols.), 1968-75, Complete Works (6 vol 1974-76, Victory (3 vols.), 1980-81, Unfinished Portra 1984, The Nüremberg Phantoms, 1987; also essays a articles. Decorated Order Red Star; recipient US State prize, 1950, 83, Order of Lenin, 1967, 73, Or Oct. Revolution, 1973, Lenin prize, 1978; named H Socialist Labour, 1973. Home: Moscow Russia D Feb. 17, 1994.

CHALMERS, FLOYD SHERMAN, publishing a broadcasting executive; b. Chgo., Sept. 14, 1898; James K. and Anna (Dusing) C.; m. Jean Albe Boxall, Apr. 28, 1921; children: Wallace G. (dec.), Joan. LLD, U. Western Ont., London, Can., 19 Waterloo Luth. U. (now Wilfred Laurier U.), 19 LittD, Trent U., Peterborough, 1968; BFA (hon.), Yo U., 1973. Jr. Bank N.S., 1914; reporter Toronto Wo and Toronto News, Ont., 1916; joined Fin. Post, 19 Montreal editor, 1923-25, editor, 1925-42; exec. v Maclean-Hunter Ltd., Toronto, 1942-52, pres., 1952- chmn. bd., 1964-69, hon. chmn., 1978—. Author: Gentleman of the Press, 1969, Two Sides of the Stre 1983. Chmn. Toronto War Hosps. Com., 1939-46; pr Can. Opera Co., 1957-61, Stratford Shakespearean F al Can., 1965-67, Can. Opera Found., 1969-72, Floyd Chalmers Found., 1963-79; chancellor York U., oronto, 1968-73. Served with Can. Army, World War Decorated officer Order of Can., 1972, companion, 85, liveryman Worshipful Co. Stationers and Newapermakers, London, freeman City of London; cipient Centennial medal, 1967, Queen's Jubilee medal, 77, Diplome d'Honneur Can. Conf. Arts, 1974, spl. ard Can. Music Council, 1977, Civic medal, Order of nt., 1988. Fellow Internat. Inst. Arts and Letters. ubs: Arts and Letters, York, Canadian, Ticker oronto). Home: Toronto Can.

HALMERS, THOMAS CLARK, physician, educanal and research administrator; b. Forest Hills, N.Y., ec. 8, 1917; s. Thomas Clark and Elizabeth (Ducat) ; m. Frances Crawford Talcott, Aug. 31, 1942; chilen: Elizabeth Ducat Chalmers Wright, Frances lcott Chalmers Smith, Thomas Clark, Richard atthew. Student, Yale U., 1936-39; M.D., Columbia , 1943. Diplomate: Am. Bd. Internal Medicine. Inn Presbyn. Hosp., N.Y.C., 1943-44; research fellow YU Malaria Research Unit, Goldwater Meml. Hosp., .Y.C., 1944-45; resident Harvard Med. Services of ston City Hosp., 1945-47; pvt. practice internal edicine Cambridge, Mass., 1947-53; asst. physician horndike Meml. Lab., 1947-53; chief med. services muel Shattuck Hosp., Boston, 1955-68; asst. chief ed. dir. for research and edn. VA, Washington, 1968-; asso. dir. clin. care NIH, also dir. clin. center NIH, ethesda, Md., 1970-73; pres. Mt. Sinai Med. Ctr., 73-83; prof. medicine, dean Mt. Sinai Sch. Medicine, .Y.C., 1973-83, Disting. Service prof., dir. clin. trials nit, 1983-86, pres. emeritus, dean emeritus, 1983-95; . prof. Harvard Sch. Pub. Health, 1983-86, lectr. dept. ealth policy and mgmt., Tech. Assessment Group, 86-95; disting. physician Boston VA Hosp., 1987-92; under, chmn. Metaworks Inc., Boston; pres. Meta nalysis Consulting Inc., West Lebanon, N.H.; prof. edicine Tufts U., 1961-68, George Washington U., 70-73; mem. ethics adv. bd., spl. cons. NIH, HHS, 80; lectr. dept. medicine, Tufts U., 1987-93, dept. idemiology and biostatistics Boston U., 1987-95; vis. egents prof. stats., U. Calif., Berkeley, 1990; adj. prof. edicine Tufts U., 1992-95, Dartmouth Sch. Medicine, 92-95. Contbr. numerous articles profl. jours. Bd. rs. New Eng. Home for Little Wanderers, 1960-65; bd. gents Nat. Library Medicine, 1978-79; trustee artmouth Hitchcock Med. Ctr., 1987-95, chmn. bd., 83-87. Served as capt., M.C. AUS, 1953-55. Mem. m. Assn. Study Liver Diseases (pres. 1959), Am. Clin. d Climatol. Assn., ACP, Am. Fedn. Clin. Research, m. Gastroent. Assn. (pres. 1969), Am. Soc. Clin. Instigation, Assn. Am. Physicians, N.Y. Acad. edicine, Inst. Medicine of Nat. Acad. Scis., Internat. ysicians for the Prevention of Nuclear War, Soc. for in. Trials (pres. 1987), Eastern Gut Club, Physicians r Social Responsibility, Am. Acad. Arts and Scis. ome: West Lebanon N.H. Died Dec. 27, 1995.

HAMBERLAIN, JOHN RENSSELAER, columnist; New Haven, Oct. 28, 1903; s. Robert Rensselaer and mily (Davis) C.; m. Margaret Sterling, Apr. 22, 1926 ec.); children: Elizabeth, Margaret; m. Ernestine odelle, June 29, 1956; 1 son, John; stepchildren: anya, Chris, Ben. Ph.B., Yale, 1925. Advt. writer, 25; reporter N.Y. Times, 1926-28, daily book lumnist, 1933-36; editor Fortune Mag., 1936-41; asso. of. Columbia Sch. Journalism, 1941-44; asst. editor .Y. Times Book Rev., 1928-33; asso. editor Saturday ev. Lit., 1933; book editor Scribners Mag., 1936-38, arper's Mag., 1939-47; lectr. Columbia Sch. urnalism, 1934-35, New Sch. for Social Research, 35, Columbia U. Summer Sch., 1937; contbg. daily ok columnist Times, 1942-44; editor Life mag., 1945-, The Freeman rev. politics, econs., arts, 1950-52; so. editor Barron's Mag., 1953-55; staff writer Wall St. ur., 1955; dean Troy (Ala.) Sch. Journalism, 1972-77; lumnist These Days King Features Syndicate, N.Y.C., 62-85. Author: Farewell to Reform, 1932, The merican Stakes, 1940, MacArthur, 1941-1951, (with eneral Charles Willoughby), 1954, The Roots of apitalism, 1959, The Enterprising Americans: A Busiess History of the U.S, 1963, Freedom and Inependence: The Hillsdale Story, 1979, A Life with the inted Word, 1982, The Turnabout Years, 1992; ontbr. to: Critique of Humanism, 1930, Challenge to e New Deal, 1934, After the Genteel Tradition, 1937, ooks That Changed Our Minds, 1939, America Now; ading mags. Home: Cheshire Conn. Died Apr. 9, 95.

HAMBERS, FRED, electrical engineer; b. Carbon ill, Ala., Feb. 17, 1912; s. Bunnier Greater and Zora McCollum) C.; m. Margaret Armstrong, Nov. 29, 1933 ec. 1986); 1 son, Fred; m. Kathleen Martin, Oct. 10, 87. B.S. in Elec. Engring, Auburn U., 1930; postad., Mass. Inst. Tech., 1930-31. Registered profl. gr., La., Tenn. With Gen. Electric Co., 1930-32, sso. Gas and Electric Co., Elmira, N.Y., 1932, Tenn. lectric Power Co., 1933-39, Chattanooga Electric ower Bd., 1939; with TVA, 1939-71, asst. mgr. power, 70-71; with Bovay Engrs., Inc., 1971-73, Pub. Service ommn. State N.Y., Albany, 1973-74; elec. engr. ouston, 1974-93. Author tech. papers. Served with SNR, 1943-45. Fellow IEEE; mem. Internat. Conf. arge High Tension Electric Systems, Tenn. Soc. Profl. ngrs., Houston Engring. and Sci. Soc., Houston C. of C. Democrat. Episcopalian. Home: Houston Tex. Died Sept. 17, 1993.

CHANCELLOR, JOHN WILLIAM, news correspondent; b. Chicago, Ill., July 14, 1927; s. Estil Marion and Mollie (Barrett) C.; m. Constance Herbert; 1 child, Mary; m. Barbara Upshaw, Jan. 25, 1958; children: Laura, Barnaby. Student, DePaul Acad., Chgo., U. Ill. Reporter Chgo. Sun-Times; staff NBC News, 1950-93; Midwest correspondent NBC, 1953-57, Vienna correspondent, 1958, London correspondent, 1959-60, Moscow correspondent, 1960-61; host NBC's Today, 1961-62; Brussels correspondent NBC, 1962-63, chief White House correspondent, 1964-65; dir. Voice of Am., Washington, 1965-67; anchorman NBC Nightly News, 1970-82; sr. commentator NBC News, 1982-93. Author: Peril and Promise: A Commentary on America, 1990, (with Walter Mears) The News Business, 1983, The New News Business, 1994. Honored by the Overseas Press Club of America for 'distinguished and exemplary service,' 1993. Club mem., Century (N.Y.C), Metropolitan (Washington), Garrick (London). Died July 12, 1996.

CHANDRASEKHAR, SUBRAHMANYAN, astrophysicist, educator; b. Lahore, India, Oct. 19, 1910; came to U.S., 1936, naturalized, 1953; m. Lalitha Doraiswamy, Sept. 1936. M.A., Presidency Coll., Madras, 1930; Ph.D., Trinity Coll., Cambridge, 1933, Sc.D., 1942; Sc.D., U. Mysore, India, 1961, Northwestern U., 1962, U. Newcastle Upon Tyne, Eng., 1965, Ind. Inst. Tech., 1966, U. Mich., 1967, U. Liege, Belgium, 1967, Oxford (Eng.) U., 1972, U. Delhi, 1973, Carleton U., Can., 1978, Harvard U., 1979. Govt. India scholar in theoretical physics Cambridge, 1930-34; fellow Trinity Coll., Cambridge, 1933-37; rsch. assoc. Yerkes Obs., Williams Bay and U. Chgo., 1937, asst. prof., 1938-41, assoc. prof., 1942-43, prof., 1944-47, Disting. Service prof., 1947-52, Morton D. Hull Disting. Service prof., 1952-86, prof. emeritus, 1986-95; Nehru Meml. lectr., Padma Vibhushan, India, 1968; laureate Lincoln Acad. Ill., 1993. Author: An Introduction to the Study of Stellar Structure, 1939, Principles of Stellar Dynamics, 1942, Radiative Transfer, 1950, Hydrodynamic and Hydromagnetic Stability, 1961, Ellipsoidal Figures of Equilibrium, 1969, The Mathematical Theory of Black Holes, 1983, Eddington: The Most Distinguished Astrophysicist of His Time, 1983, Truth and Beauty: Aesthetics and Motivations in Science, 1987, Selected Papers, 6 vols., 1989-90, Newton's Principia: For the Common Reader, 1995; mng. editor: The Astrophysical Jour., 1952-71; contbr. various sci. periodicals and articles to profl. jours. Recipient Bruce medal Astron. Soc. Pacific, 1952, gold medal Royal Astron. Soc., London, 1953; Rumford medal Am. Acad. Arts and Scis., 1957; Nat. Medal of Sci., 1966; Nobel prize in physics, 1983; Dr. Tomalla prize Eidgenössiches Technische Hochschule, Zurich, 1984; R.D. Birla Mem. award Indian Physics Assn., 1984; S. Ramanujan medal 1962; Vainu Bappu Mem. award Indian Nat. Acad. Sci., 1986. Fellow Royal Soc. (London) (Royal medal 1962, Copley medal 1984); mem. Nat. Acad. Scis. (Henry Draper medal 1971), Am. Phys. Soc. (Dannie Heineman prize 1974), Am. Philos. Soc., Cambridge Philos. Soc., Am. Astron. Soc. (v.p. 56-58), Am. Acad. Arts and Sci., Royal Swedish Acad., Royal Astron. Soc. Club: Quadrangle (U. Chgo.). Home: Chicago Ill. Died Aug. 21, 1995.

CHAPMAN, GROSVENOR, architect; b. Paris, July 9, 1911; s. Frederick Burnham and Helen Grosvenor (Kenyon) C.; m. Rose-Marie de Foix Edmunds, Sept. 25, 1937; children: Alexander Kenyon, Eleanor Preston (Mrs. Edmund Randolph). B.A., Yale, 1934, M.Arch., 1937. Pvt. practice architecture N.Y.C., 1940-41, Washington, 1946-54; partner Brown, Chapman, Taher & Miller, Washington, 1954-63, Chapman & Miller, Washington, 1963-76; mem. NRC, 1965-68; participant Sec. Interior's Symposium on Nat. Capital, 1979. Mem. Washington Urban Renewal Council, 1957-58; pres. Georgetown Planning Council, 1968-69, Citizens' Assn. Georgetown, 1950-51, 73-76; chmn. Com. of 100 of Federal City, 1968-70; mem. Georgetown Adv. Neighborhood Commn., 1976-77; mem. D.C. steering com. Whitehurst Freeway Corridor Study, 1983-84. Served to lt. comdr. USNR, 1942-45. Recipient award in architecture Washington Bd. Trade, 1960, 63, 68, award in architecture Am. Assn. Sch. Adminstrs.-AIA, 1969, 74; Excellence in Architecture award Sec. Def., 1972. Fellow AIA (pres. Washington Met. chpt. 1957, local awards 1954, 55, 56, 74); mem. Constrn. Specifications Inst. (dir. 1953-57). Clubs: Cosmos (Washington), Chevy Chase (Washington). Home: Washington D.C. Died July 23, 1993.

CHAPMAN, JAMES EDWARD, lawyer; b. Wadsworth, Ohio, Apr. 27, 1927; s. Horace Vernon and Sarah Lucille (Thompson) C.; m. Anita Louise Esbenshade, July 3, 1954; children: Ann Frances, Thomas Marshall, David Abram. Student, Mexico City Coll., Mex., 1950; BBA cum laude, Ohio State U., 1953, JD cum laude, 1954. Bar: Ohio 1954, U.S. Dist. Ct. (no. dist.) Ohio 1954, U.S. Supreme Ct. 1970. Assoc. Baker & Hostetler (and predecessor firm Baker, Hostetler & Patterson), Cleve., 1954-64, ptnr., 1964-93, chmn. legal services, 1979-81, mng. ptnr., 1981-86; sec. Preformed Line Products Co., Cleve., 1958-93; bd. dirs. McGean-Rohco Inc., Cleve., Cleve. Inst. Electronics Inc., Euclid Industries Inc., Cleve.; serjeant Ct. Nisi Prius, Cleve., 1975-93. Chmn. regional steering com. Ohio State U., Cleve., 1985-93, mem. steering com. nat. campaign, Columbus, 1986-90; trustee Mystic (Conn.) Seaport Mus. Inc., 1981-93, Great Lakes Mus.; mem. steering com. Linnean Soc. Cleve. Mus. Natural History, 1987; mem. USS Constn. Mus., Boston, 1982-93; trustee, sec. Thomas F. Peterson Found., Cleve., 1960-93, Mellen Found., Cleve., 1983-93, Philip B. and Celia B. Arnold Found., Cleve., 1965-93, Elizabeth G. and John D. Drinko Charitable Found., 1984-93, Standard Products Found., Cleve., 1968-93; trustee, chmn. Cleve. Octet, 1986-93. Served with U.S. Army, 1945-47, PTO. Mem. ABA, Ohio Bar Assn., Cleve. Bar Assn., Nat. Assn. for Mental Health (bd. dirs. 1966-72, sec. 1967-68, v.p. 1969, pres. 1970-71), N.Am. Soc. for Oceanic History, Nat. Maritime Hist. Soc., U.S. Naval Inst., Great Lakes Hist. Soc., Suburban Symphony Orch., Shaker Symphony Orch., Order of Coif. Clubs: Ohio State U. Pres.'s (mem. exec. com. 1982-88), Ohio State Faculty (Columbus); Cleve. Athletic, Cleve. Playhouse, Ohio State U. Alumni Cleve. (pres. 1987), Union, Canterbury Golf. Lodge: Masons. Home: Cleveland Ohio Deceased.

CHARNES, ABRAHAM, mathematics, economics and business educator, researcher; b. Hopewell, Va., Sept. 4, 1917; s. Harry and Rebecca (Levatin) C.; m. Kathryn Francis, May 1950; children: Deborah, Daniel, William. A.B., U. Ill.-Urbana, 1938, M.Sc., 1939, Ph.D., 1947; cert. applied math., Brown U., 1941. Asst. prof. math. Carnegie Inst. Tech., Pitts., from 1948, assoc. prof., to 1955; prof. math., econs. and transp. Purdue U., 1955-57; prof. math., econs., engring. scis., Murphy prof., univ. prof. Northwestern U., 1957-68; univ. prof. U. Tex. System, Austin, from 1968; now Harbin chair U. Tex. System, dir. Ctr. Cybernetic Studies, from 1968; cons. in field. Author books and articles; assoc. editor Chinese Jour. Ops. Research, from 1982, Jour. Info. and Optimization Scis., from 1984. Mem. final expert rev. com. NSF for U.S. Congress, Laxenburg, Austria, 1978. Served to lt. USNR, 1942-46. Ford Found. fellow, 1960; recipient von Neumann Theory award ORSA-TIMS, 1982, Disting. lectr. Soviet Acad. Scis., 1976, Disting. lectr. Chinese Acad. Sci., 1981, 84, 86, Disting. lectr. Technion-Israel Inst. Tech., 1982, Highest Civilian award U.S. Navy, 1977. Fellow AAAS, Econometric Soc., Ops. Research Soc. Am.; mem. Inst. Mgmt. Scis. (pres.), Nat. Acad. Engring. Mex. (sec. internat. affairs from 1974), Am. Math. Soc. Home: Austin Tex. Deceased.

CHARTERIS, LESLIE, author; b. Singapore, May 12, 1907; naturalized, 1946; m. Pauline Schishkin, 1931 (div. 1937); 1 dau., Patricia Ann; m. Barbara Meyer, 1938 (div.); m. Elizabeth Bryant Borst, 1943 (div.); m. Audrey Long, 1952. Student, Cambridge U., 1926; studied art in, Paris. Author: numerous books including Meet the Tiger, 1928, Saint to the Rescue, 1959, Trust the Saint, 1962, The Saint in the Sun, 1963, Vendetta for the Saint, 1964, The Saint on TV, 1968, The Saint Returns, 1968, The Saint Abroad, 1969, The Saint in Pursuit, 1971, Catch the Saint, 1975, The Saint and The Hapsburg Necklace, 1976, Send for the Saint, 1977, The Saint in Trouble, 1978, The Saint and the Templar Treasure, 1978, Count on the Saint, 1980; collection The Fantastic Saint, 1981; Salvage for the Saint, 1983. Contbr. to numerous mags.; author motion pictures Midnight Club, 1933, River Gang, 1945, Two Smart People, 1945. Recipient Golden Dagger award Crime Writers' Assn., 1992. Fellow Royal Soc. Arts; mem. Mensa, Yacht de Cannes. Home: London Eng. Died Apr. 15, 1993.

CHATTOPADHYAYA, HARINDRANATH AGORNATH, poet, film actor; b. Hyderabad, India, Apr. 2, 1898; s. Agornath Mathuranath and Varada Sundari C.; m. Kamila Dhareshwar (div.) ; 1 child, Ram; m. Sundarvali Achari, Aug. 15, 1947; 1 child, Lakshman. LittD (hon.), Andhra U., Hyderabad, 1980; D B.C. (hon.) Royal Nat. award for lit., Delhi, India, 1982. Producer emritus Doordarshan India, TV and Radio of India, Bombay, 1975-78. Author: (poems) Feast of Youth, 1916, Perfume of Earth, 1920, Magic Tree, 1925, Feast of Thirsts, Iconoclast, A Bird Sang on a Bough, Reflections, 1988. Mem. Parliament, Vijaywada, Andhra Pradesh, India, 1950-55. Recipient Padmabhushan Govt. of India, 1972, Dr. B.C. Roy Nat. Lit. award, New Delhi, 1982. Home: Bombay India Deceased.

CHAUCHOIN, LILY See COLBERT, CLAUDETTE

CHAUNCEY, TOM, retired radio and television executive.; b. Houston, Jan. 20, 1913; s. Brinkley and Lucille Dunn (Weber) C.; 6 children; student pub. schs.; LHD (hon.) Ariz. State U., 1983. Owner, Tom Chauncey Jeweler, 1940-61; v.p., gen. mgr. Sta KPHO, 1941-48; pres. Sta. KOPO, Tucson, 1947-76; v.p., mng. dir. KOOL Radio-TV, Inc., 1948-55, exec. v.p., gen. mgr., 1955-57, pres., gen. mgr., 1957-61, pres., 1961-81, chmn. bd., pres., chief exec. officer, 1981-82, owner, chief exec. officer Sta. KOOL-AM-FM, 1982-86; owner, 26 Bar Ranch, Ceear Creek Cattle Co., Tom Chauncey Arabians, Tom Chauncey Properties; pres., mng. dir. Old Pueblo Broadcasting Co., (KOLD-TV), Tucson, 1957-69; daily columnist TV Views, Ariz. Republic, Phoenix Gazette, (weekly) Broadcasting mag., 1960-61;

former chmn. bd. CBS TV Network Affiliates 1961-62; dir. Valley Nat. Bank; mem. nat. com. Support Free Broadcasting; rep. of pres. U.S., ambassador, Nigeria, 1960. Grand marshal J.C. World Championship Rodeo and Parade, 1963; former nat. trustee City of Hope; former mem. Ariz. Nat. Livestock Show; past Ariz. chmn. Radio Free Europe; former mem. bd. Phoenix Symphony Assn., Phoenix Art Mus., Muscular Dystrophy Assn. Am.; gen. campaign. chmn. Greater Phoenix-Scottsdale United Fund Campaign; former mem. bd., v.p., pres. Phoenix Better Bus. Bur.; mem. Citizen's Action Com.; voting mem. Ariz. State U. Found.; former mem. Phoenix Baseball Stadium Com., U. Ariz. Found., chmn. Ariz. com. A.R.C.; past dir. at large for Ariz. Am. Cancer Soc.; past dir. and pres. Community Council; exec. v.p., mem. bd., Incorporator, co-founder Barrow Neurol. Inst.; mem. Com. for Phoenix Civic Plaza Dedication Ceremonies, 1972, Ariz. Commn. on Nat. and Internat. Commerce; past nat. chmn. Broadcaster's adv. com. U.S. Savs. Bonds; past dir. United Cerebral Palsey Assn. Central Ariz.; past mem. Phoenix All-Am. City Com.; chmn. Ariz. Motion Picture Adv. Bd.; past chmn. adv. bd. on radio and TV, Ariz. State U.; bd. dirs. Central Ariz. Water Conservation Dist.; Nat. Cowboy Hall of Fame bd. dir. 1979-96; pres., bd. dirs. Ariz. Children's Found. Named Man of Yr., City of Hope, 1962, NCCJ, 1967, B'nai B'rith Anti-Defamation League, 1975; Citizen of Yr., Phoenix Real Estate Bd., 1965; recipient Nat. Sch. Bell award, 1961; award U.S. Treasury Dept., 1961; Tom Chauncey award United Fund, 1962; Jesse Owens award; George Foster Peabody award, Disting. Achievement award Coll. Pub. Programs Ariz. State U., 1984. Mem. Ariz. (past pres., past dir., past mem. legis. com.), Met. Phoenix (past pres., dir.) broadcasters assns., Nat. Assn. Broadcasters, Nat. Acad. TV Arts and Scis. (Bd. Govs. award Phoenix chpt. 1962, past Ariz. bd. gov.), Mus. Broadcasting (hon.), Nat. Retail Jewelers Assn. (past dir.), Phoenix C. of C., Ariz. Quarterhorse Breeders Assn., Ariz. State Horseman's Assn., Ariz. Heart Inst. 1974-96, Arabian Horse Assn. Ariz. (dir. 1972), Ariz. Hereford Assn., Ariz. Retail Jewelers Assn., Am. Gem Soc., TV Pioneers, Phoenix Press Box Assn. (life), Phoenix Thunderbirds, Navy League, Newcomen Soc. N. Am., Sigma Delta Chi. Elk. Clubs: Phoenix Country, Phoenix Execs.; Paradise Valley Country; Rancheros Vistacores; Cowman's. Author: Educational Contributions of Commercial Television, 1960. Tom Chauncey Student Loan Fund established at Ariz. State U. Died June 29, 1996. Home: Scottsdale Ariz.

CHAVEZ, CESAR ESTRADA, union official; b. nr. Yuma, Ariz., Mar. 31, 1927; m. Helen Favila; 8 children. Mem. staff Community Svc. Orgn., Calif., 1952-58; gen. dir. Community Svc. Orgn., 1958-62; organized Nat. Farm Workers Assn., 1962; merged 1966 with Agrl. Workers Organizing Com. of AFL-CIO to form United Farm Workers Organizing Com., dir. 1966-73, Delano, Calif.; pres. United Farm Workers Am. AFL-CIO, Keene, Calif., 1973-93. Served with USNR, 1944-45. Roman Catholic. Home: Keene Calif. Died Apr. 22, 1993.

CHEN, HAN-SENG, historian, economist; b. Wuxi, Jiangsu, People's Republic of China, Feb. 5, 1897; m. Gu Shu-Xin, Apr. 20, 1922 (div. 1968). BA, Pomona Coll., 1920; MA, U. Chgo., 1922; PhD, U. Berlin, Germany, 1924. Prof. history Peking U., Beijing, 1924-66; dep. pres. Inst. Social Scis., Acad. Sinica, 1929-33; prof. Wash. State U., Pullman, 1946-51; v.p. Chinese People's Inst. of Fgn. Affairs, Beijing, 1951-66, Sino-Indian Friendship Assn., Beijing, 1952-66; dep. dir. Rsch. Inst. Internat. Rels., Beijing, 1956-66; chmn. Chinese Soc. for Central Asian Studies, Beijing, from 1979; mem. Chinese People's Polit. Consultative Conf., Beijing, 1951-62, 78-82; cons. Chinese Acad. Social Scis., from 1977; hon. chmn. Inst. World History, Beijing, from 1978; vis. prof. Peking U., from 1978; pres. Acad. Internat. Culture, from 1989. Author: The Agrarian Regions of India and Pakistan, 1959, My Life through Four Epochs, 1988; contbr. articles to profl. jours. Home: Beijing China Deceased.

CHENG, CHUNG-CHIEH, astrophysicist; b. Chungqing, China, Nov. 7, 1938; s. Ti-Chuan and Wen-Hsu (Shu) C.; m. Min-Hwa Ho, June 21, 1968; children: Guang-Shing, Guang-Ien, Guang-Yeu (dec.). BS, Nat. Taiwan U., Taipei, 1960; MA in Applied Physics, Harvard U., 1963, PhD, 1970. Postdoctoral rsch. assoc. dept. physics and astronomy U. Md., 1970; rsch. assoc. lab. for solar physics NRC-NASA Goddard Space Flight Ctr., Greenbelt, Md., 1970-72; solar physicist Ball Brother Rsch. Corp. and Naval Rsch. Lab., Washington, 1972-78, NASA Marshall Space Flight Ctr., Huntsville, Ala., 1979-81; rsch. astrophysicist E.O. Hulburt Ctr. for Space Rsch., Nat. Rsch. Lab., Washington, 1982-88, sr. astrophysicist, 1988-95; vis. scientist Academia Sinica, China, 1981, 83; vis. prof. Arcetri Astrophys. Obs., Florence, 1982, 85, U. Oslo, Norway, 1989, 94; sr. fellow Ctr. for Space Plasma and Aeronomic Rsch., 1987-95; founding mem. Inst. for Astronomy and Astrophysics, Academia Sinica, Sinica, Taiwan, 1994; prin. investigator NASA, 1978-88, 89-94, 89-90, 87-95; tchg. fellow in applied physics Harvard U., 1963-64, in astronomy, 1964-69; hon. vis. prof. Beijing U. Observatory, 1994. Grad. fellow Harvard U., 1962-64, tchg. fellow Harvard U., 1964-66, Harvard Obs. fellow, 1966-68; Smithsonian predoctoral fellow, 1968-69; honor scholar Nat. Waitan U., 1957-60. Home: Potomac Md. Died Mar. 10, 1995.

CHERNISS, NORMAN ARNOLD, newspaper editor; b. Council Bluffs, Iowa, July 16, 1926; s. David P. and Esther (Arenson) C.; B.A., State U. Iowa, 1950; post-grad. (Nieman fellow) Harvard, 1958-59, (Haynes fellow) U. Calif. at Los Angeles, 1960-61. Reporter, Council Bluffs Nonpareil, 1942-44; newswriter Sta. KOIL, Omaha, 1946; corr. Internat. News Service, Iowa City, 1948-49; editorial writer Des Moines Register and Tribune, 1949; Evansville (Ind.) Courier, 1951-53; editor editorial pages Riverside (Calif.) Press and Enterprise, 1953-67, asso. editor, 1967-71, exec. editor, 1971-—. Vis. lectr. U. Calif. at Los Angeles, 1965-66, U. So. Calif., 1968-69, 71, 79; vis. prof., editor in residence Columbia Grad. Sch. Journalism, 1969-70. Served with USNR, 1944-46. Mem. Am. Soc. Newspaper Editors, Nat. Conf. Editorial Writers, Soc. Nieman Fellows, Kappa Tau Alpha. Home: Riverside Calif.

CHERNOFF, DANIEL PAREGOL, patent lawyer; b. Washington, Jan. 24, 1935; s. Bernard M. and Goldie S. (Paregol) C.; m. Nancy M. Kuehner, June 17, 1965; children: Scott, Graham. B.E.E. with distinction, Cornell U., 1957, LL.B., 1959. Bar: N.Y. 1959, D.C. 1959, Oreg. 1968. Instr. Cornell U., 1957-59; practiced in N.Y.C., 1959-67; assoc. firm Fish, Richardson & Neave (now Fish & Neave), N.Y.C., 1961-67; practiced in Portland, 1967—; assoc. firm Davies, Biggs, Strayer, Stoel & Boley (now Stoel Rivers Boley Jones & Grey), Portland, 1967-70; patent atty., sr. mem. Chernoff, Vilhauer, McClung & Stenzel, Portland, 1970—, pres., 1988—; patent counsel Polarad Electronics Corp., L.I., N.Y., 1959-61. Author: (annual updates) Federal Circuit Patent Case Digests, 1990. Bd. dirs. Cardio-Pulmonary Rsch. Inst., 1974-80, Learning Resource Ctr., Inc., chmn., 1975-79, pres., 1988-89; mem. adv. coun. Cornell Law Sch., 1981-90; bd. dirs. Pacific Ballet Theatre, 1985-89, pres., 1988-89; bd. dirs. Oreg. Ballet Theatre, 1989-94; mem. N.W. Bus. Com. for Arts, 1991—. Mem. Oreg. Bar Assn., N.Y. Bar Assn., D.C. Bar Assn., Am. Intellectual Property Law Assn., N.Y. Patent Law Assn., Oreg. Patent Law Assn. (pres. 1973-74), Internat. Trademark Assn., Cornell Law Assn., Cornell U. Coun., Multnomah Athletic Club, Cornell Club N.Y.C., Order of Coif, Tau Beta Pi, Eta Kappa Nu. Home: Portland Oreg. Died July 22, 1995.

CHERNY, WALTER B., obstetrician, gynecologist, educator; b. Montreal, Que., Can., Apr. 13, 1926. BSc, McGill U., 1948, MD, CM, 1950. Diplomate Am. Bd. Ob-Gyn. Rotating intern Montreal Gen. Hosp., 1950-51, asst. resident in gen. surgery, 1951-52; resident in ob-gyn Duke U., Durham, N.C., 1952-55; prof. ob-gyn Duke U. Sch. Medicine, 1955-70, U. Ariz., Tucson, 1971-88; dir. ob-gyn edn. Good Samaritan Med. Ctr., Phoenix, 1970-89; mem. cons. staff, 1955-91. Fellow Am. Coll. Obstetricians and Gyncologists (coun. on residency edn. 1981-87), Cen. Assn. Ob-Gyn (v.p. 1986-87). Home: Paradise Vly Ariz. Died Nov. 11, 1991.

CHESTER, GIRAUD, television executive; b. N.Y.C., Apr. 4, 1922; s. Harry and Minnie (Lachman) C.; m. Marjorie J. Fatt, 1962; children: Christopher, Katherine. B.A., Bklyn. Coll., 1942; M.A., U. Wis., 1943, Ph.D., 1947; D.C.S. (hon.), St. John's U., 1980. Asst. prof. speech Cornell U., 1947-49, U. Mich., summers 1947-49, Queens Coll., 1949-53; gen. program exec. NBC-TV, 1954-57; asso. Sylvester L. Weaver, Jr., 1957; dir. new TV program devel. Ted Bates & Co., Inc., 1958; v.p. charge network daytime programming ABC-TV, 1958-62; v.p. charge network program adminstr. NBC-TV, 1962-64; exec. v.p. Goodson-Todman Prodns. (now Mark Goodson Prodns.), N.Y.C., 1964-93. Author: Embattled Maiden: The Life of Anna Dickinson, 1951, (with G.R. Garrison) Radio and Television, 1950, Television and Radio, 1956, (with G.R. Garrison and E.E. Willis), 1963, 1971, 78, The Ninth Juror, 1970; also articles.; Asso. editor: Quar. Jour. Speech, 1948-54. Trustee Guild Hall, East Hampton, 1980-86. Served to lt. (j.g.) USNR, 1943-46. Recipient Edgar Allan Poe award Mystery Writers Am., 1971; H. V. Kaltenborn radio news scholar, 1946-47; Ford Found. fellow, 1953-54. Mem. Internat. Radio and TV Soc. (pres. 1977-80), Acad. TV Arts and Scis., Nat. Assn. Ind. TV Prodrs. and Distbrs. (chmn. 1974-86), East Hampton Tennis Club, Univ. Club. Home: East Hampton N.Y. Died Dec. 23, 1995.

CHI, RICHARD SEE-YEE, educator; b. Peking, China, Aug. 3, 1918; came to U.S., 1965; s. Mi Kang and Pao (Ten) C. B.S., Nankai U., China, 1937; M.A., Oxford (Eng.) U., 1962, D.Phil., 1964; Ph.D., Cambridge (Eng.) U., 1964. Exec. industry China and Hong Kong, 1938-56; instr. Air Ministry, Eng., 1957-60; lectr. Cambridge (Eng.) U., 1960-62; univ. lectr. Oxford (Eng.) U., 1962-65; curator Oriental art City Art Gallery, Bristol, Eng., 1965; asso. prof. Ind. U., Bloomington, 1965-71; prof. Ind. U., from 1971, acting chmn., summer, 1972; asso. adviser Centro Superiore di Logica e Scienze Comparate, Italy, from 1972; vis. asso. prof. U. Mich., summer 1968; fellow participant Linguistic Inst., UCLA, 1966; contbg. specialist Summer Faculty Seminar on Buddhism, Carleton Coll., Minn., 1968; mem. Workshop in Problems on Meaning and Truth, Oakland U., 1968; adviser film Buddhism in China, N.Y.C., 1972; cons. Inst. Advanced Studies World Religions, 1972—; session chmn. East-West Philosophers Conf., 1973; panelist Internat. Conf. on Indian Philosophy, U. Toronto, 1974, 5th Internat. Symposium Multiple-valued Logic, Ind. U., 1974, Internat. Seminar on History of Buddhism, U.Wis., 1976, 30th Internat. Congress Human Scis. in, Asia, Mexico City, 1976; mem. sub-com. Buddhist philos. materials Nat. Endowment for Humanities, 1974; rep. State of Ind. Nat. Reconstrn. Conf., China, 1975. Author: The Bracket Complex in Chinese Architecture, 1946, Palatial Architecture of the Ching Dynasty, 1947, A General Theory of Operators, 1967, Buddhist Formal Logic, 1968, A Comparative Study of Propositions in the Western and Indian Logic, 1972, Topics on Being and Logical Reasoning, 1974, A Semantic Study of Propositions, East and West, 1976, The Art of Chinese Calligraphy, 1977, Dignaga and Post-Russell Logic, 1983, The Art of War of Sun Tzu, 1983; editor: Jour. Buddhist Philosophy, from 1978; editorial bd.: History and Philosophy of Logic, from 1978; dir.: Classical Chinese Architecture, from 1978; reviewer: Nat. Endowment Humanities, from 1979. Fellow China Acad., 1969. Mem. Cambridge U. Buddhist Soc. (v.p. 1961-62), Royal Asiatic Soc., Aristotelian Soc., Decorative Art Soc. Indpls., Mind Assn., Assn. Brit. Orientalists, Assn. for Symbolic Logic, Linguistic Soc. Am., Soc. Asian and Comparative Philosophy (bd. mem.-at-large 1975-86), Oriental Art Soc. (founding mem.), Kings Coll. Assn. (Eng.), Asian Studies Inst. (mem. adv. com. from 1975), Indpls. Mus. Art. Club: Lake Havasu Golf and Country. Lodge: Rotary. Home: Bloomington Ind. Died Feb. 17, 1986.

CHIANG, CHING-KUO, president Republic of China; b. Fenghua, Chekiang Province, China, Mar. 18, 1910; s. Chiang Kai-shek; ed. Sun Yat-sen U., 1927, USSR Mil. and Polit. Inst., 1929; m. Chiang Fang-liang, Mar. 1935; children: Chiang Hsiao-wen, Chiang Hsiao-chang, Chiang Hsiao-wu, Chiang Hsiao-yung. Various position in mines and factories in Russia, 1929-37; adminstrv. commr. for So. Kiangsi Province, 1939-45; fgn. affair commr. Mil. and Polit. Adminstrn. for N.E. China, 1945-47; dep. econ. control supr. for Shanghai, 1948; dir. gen. polit. warfare dept. Ministry of Nat. Def., 1950-54; dep. sec. gen. Nat. Security Council, 1954-67; chmn. Vocat. Assistance Comm. for Ret. Servicemen, 1957-64; minister of state, 1958-65; dep. minister of nat. def., 1964-65; minister nat. def., 1965-69; vice premier concurrently chmn. Council for Internat. Econ. Cooperation and Devel., 1969-72; premier, 1972-78; pres. Taiwan, Republic of China, 1978-88. Chmn. Kuomintang Taiwan Provincial Hdqrs., 1949-50; mem. Kuomintang Reform Com., 1950-52; mem. Central Standing Com., 1952-88; chmn. Central Com., 1975-88; dir. Chinese Youth Corps, 1952-73. Author: Wo ti sheng huo (My Life), 1947; Wo ti fu ch'in (My Father), 1956; Fu chung chih yuan (Bearing the Burden and Carrying It a Long Way), 1960; Feng yu chung te ning ching (Calm in the Eye of a Storm), 1967; Sheng li chih lu (Road to Victory), 1967; Shou fu ling i yueh ch (Thoughts About My Father at Tsuhu), 1975; Mei Ta szu ch'in (Thoughts of My Father at Plum Terrace), 1976; Chi chieh ju shih (As Firm as Rock), 1977; Sz ch'in, li chih, pao kuo (Thinking of My Father), 1978; Shih yueh yu kan (Sentiments in October), 1979; Na wang te i nien (A Year to Remember), 1980. Died Jan. 13, 1988. Home: Taipei Taiwan

CHILDRESS, ALICE, playwright; b. Charleston, S.C. Oct. 12, 1920. Student public schs. Playwright. Joined American Negro Theatre, Harlem, 1941; appeared in On Strivers Row, 1940, Natural Man, 1941, Three's A Family, 1943, Anna Lucasta, 1944, Rain, 1947, Almost Faithful, 1948, Florence, 1949, The Candy Story, 195 The Emperor's Clothes, 1953, The Cool World, 196 directed Florence, 1949, Trouble in Mind, 1955 (Obie award best original play 1956), Wedding Band, 1966 (film appearance) Uptight, 1968; plays and stories include Florence, 1949,Just a Little Simple, 1950, Gold Through the Trees, 1952, Trouble in Mind, 1955, Wedding Band, 1966, The World on a Hill, 1968, String 1969, Martin Luther King at Montgomery, Alabama 1969, A Man Bearing a Pitcher, 1969, String, 196 Young Martin Luther King, 1969-71, Mojo: A Black Love Story, 1970, The African Garden, 1971, When the Rattlesnake Sounds, 1975, Let's Hear It for the Queen 1976, Sea Island Song, 1977, (mus. play) Gullah, 198 Moms, 1986; playwright, scholarplays and stories for children Radcliffe Inst., 1966-68; author: (novels) Like One of the Family: Conservations from a Domestic Life, 1956, A Hero Ain't Nothin but a Sandwich, 197 (New York Times outstanding book of the year citation 1973, Woodward School Book award 1974, Jane Addams Children's Book Honor award 1974, Nat. Book award nomination 1974, Lewis Carroll Shelf Award U Wisc. 1975, Best Young Adult Book citation Amer. Li Assn. 1975), A Short Walk, 1979, Rainbow Jordan 1981 (School Library Journal best book 1981, New York Times outstanding book of the year citation 198 Coretta Scott King honorable mention award 198 Many Closets, 1987, Those Other People, 198 (screenplays) Wine in the Wilderness, 1969, Wedding Band, 1973, A Hero Ain't Nothin but a Sandwich, 19 (Best Screenplay award Virgin Islands Film Festiv 1977, First Paul Robeson award for Outstandin Contbns. to the performance Arts Black Filmmake Hall of Fame 1977), String, 1979; (radio plays) Wine the Wilderness, 1969. Recipient John Golden Fund F

Playwrights grant, 1957, Rockefeller Grant, 1967, Sojourner Truth Award, Nat. Assn. of Negro Business and Professional Women's Clubs, 1975, Paul Robeson award, 1980, Radcliffe Grad. Soc. Medal, 1984, Audelco Pioneer award 1986, Lifetime Achievement awd., Assn. for Theatre in Higher Education, 1993. Mem. PEN, Harlem Writers Guild, Dramatists Guild, Writers Guild Am. Home: New York N.Y. Died Aug. 14, 1994.

CHILES, (HARRELL) EDDIE, professional baseball team executive, corporate executive; b. Itasca, Tex., 1910; married. B.S. in Petroleum Engring., U. Okla., 1934. With Reed Roller Bit Co., 1934-39; founder Western Co. of N.Am., Ft. Worth, 1939-93, former chief exec. officer, pres., from 1985, chmn., 1985-93, also bd. dirs.; pres., chief exec. officer Tex. Rangers Baseball Team, Arlington, Tex., 1980-93, also chmn. bd. dirs. Mem. AIME, Am. Petroleum Inst., Mid-Continent Oil and Gas Assn. Home: Fort Worth Tex. Died Aug. 22, 1993.

CHIMY, JEROME ISIDORE, bishop; b. Radway, Alta., Can., Mar. 12, 1919; s. Stanley and Anna (Y-ahnij) C. J.C.D., Lateran U., Rome, 1966. Ordained priest Ukrainian Cath. Ch., 1944; consecrated bishop, 1974; consultor to Provincial Superior, 1958-61; sec. to Superior Gen. of Basilian Order, Rome, 1961-63; consultor Superior Gen. of Basilian Order, 1963-74; rector St. Josaphat Ukrainian Pontifical Coll., Rome, 1966-74; former consultor to Sacred Congregation for Eastern Chs.; former commissario for matrimonial cases at Sacred Congregation for Doctrine of Faith; bishop of New Westminster B.C., Can., 1974-92; consultor to Pontifical Comm. for Revision Oriental Canon Law. Author: De Figura Luridica Archiepiscopi Maioris in Iure Canonico Orientali Vigenti, 1968. Home: New Westminster Can. Died Sept. 19, 1992.

CHIN, GILBERT YUKYU, metallurgist; b. Kwangtung, China, Sept. 21, 1934; s. George Shee Ng and Liawah (Gee) C. (father Am. citizen); m. Ginie Wong, June 26, 1960; children: Patrick Ken, Michael Philip, Grace Fay, Karen Jean. S.B., MIT, 1959, Sc.D., 1963. Mem. tech. staff AT&T Bell Labs, Murray Hill, N.J., 1962-91; head phys. metallurgy and crystal growth research dept. AT&T Bell Labs, 1973-75, head phys. metallurgy and ceramics research and devel. dept., 1975-84, dir. Materials Research Lab., 1984-87, dir. Materials Physics Research Lab., 1987-90, dir. Passive Components Research Lab., 1990-91. Author. Recipient Achievement award Chinese Inst. Engrs. of U.S.A., 1980, Chinese Engrs. and Scientists Assn. of So. Calif., 83. Fellow Metall. Soc. of AIME (Mathewson Gold medal 1974), Am. Soc. Metals; mem. AAAS, NAE, Am. Ceramics Soc., Magnetics Soc. of IEEE, Am. Phys. Soc., Sigma Xi, Tau Beta Pi, Phi Lambda Upsilon. Episcopalian. Home: New Providence N.J. Died May 1991.

CHOATE, JOSEPH, lawyer; b. Santa Ana, Calif., Jan. 14, 1900; s. Walter Addison and Nellie E. (Jurd) C.; m. Dorothy Drew, 1939; 1 child, Joseph Jr. Student, Pomona Coll., 1919-21; A.B., LL.B., U. So. Calif., 1925; LL.M. in Internat. Law, Harvard U., 1935; postgrad. intramural session, Oxford U., Internat. Law Seminar, U. Mich., 1937; LL.D., Salem (W.Va.) Coll., 1937. Bar: Calif. 1927, U.S. Supreme Ct. 1935. Dep. dist. atty. Los Angeles County, Calif., 1927-34; in gen. practice of law Los Angeles; pvt. internat. law; mem. Choate & Choate & Assocs. Author: Qualifying for Destiny, 1937, Douglas MacArthur, As I Knew Him, 1985, Death Valley Scotty, of California, 1990, Miracles of My Life, 1992; also numerous legal articles. Mem. pub. panel War Labor Bd. Mem. ABA, Los Angeles County, Internat. bar assns., Japan-Am. Soc. So. Calif., Am. Soc. Internat. Law, U.S. Naval Inst., Internat. Platform Assn., Delta Theta Phi. Presbyterian. Clubs: Masons (Shriners, K.T.), Lincoln (Los Angeles); Harvard of Calif. Home: Los Angeles Calif. Deceased.

CHON, MYRON EDWARD, advertising executive; b. Chgo., Dec. 12, 1901; s. Benjamin W. and Anna (Bransky) C.; m. Bernice Larson, July 30, 1937 (dec. 1959). A.B., U. Mich., 1923. Copywriter J. Walter Thompson, Chgo., 1923-25; copy dir. William H. Rankin Co., Chgo., 1926-33; exec. creative dir. Arthur Meyerhoff Assos., Inc., Chgo., from 1934; exec. v.p. Arthur Meyerhoff Assos., Inc., from 1962; owner Jade House.; Music and advt. cons. Composer musicals, compositions and commls.; saxophone performer. Recipient numerous awards for mus. commls. Mem. ASCAP, Composers Hall of Fame. Home: Chicago Ill. Deceased.

CHRISTENSEN, ROBERT A., lawyer; b. Kansas City, Mo., Sept. 12, 1940; s. Marion Medsker and Dorothy Alice (Arnold) C.; m. Sandra Lynn Towne, Aug. 3, 1963; children: Eric R., Kirsten M. BA, U. Kans., 1961; JD, Stanford U., 1966. Bar: Wis. 1966, U.S. Ct. Appeals (7th cir.) 1969, U.S. Supreme Ct. 1977. Assoc. Foley & Lardner, Milw., 1966-73, ptnr., 1973-95; bd. dirs. FWD Corp., Clintonville, Wis., 1979-95. Pres. Legal Aid Soc., 1977-79. Lt. (j.g.) USNR, 1961-63. Mem. ABA. Home: Thiensville Wis. Died May 22, 1995.

CHRISTIE, ANDREW DOBBIE, state chief justice, deceased; b. Cin., Feb. 11, 1922; s. John W. and Ruth (Bigelow) C.; m. Carol Graves, July 20, 1946; children: Anne C. Plochman, Andrew Dobbie Jr., George D., Elizabeth M. AB, Princeton U., 1944; LLB, U. Pa., 1949; LLD, Widener Law Sch., 1988. Bar: Del. 1949. Pvt. practice law Wilmington, Del., 1949-57; chief atty. Del. Gen. Assembly, Dover, 1953-57; judge Del. Superior Ct., Wilmington, 1957-83; justice Del. Supreme Ct., Wilmington, 1983-85, chief justice, 1985-92; ret.; instr. Nat. Coll. State Trial Judges, 1967, Nat. Coll. State Judiciary, 1969, 72, 73, 74; pres. Legal Aid Soc., Wilmington, 1957-67. Former trustee Westminster Presbyn. Ch., Family Ct. Assn., Child Guidance Clinic, Florence Crittendon Home. Served with USAAF, 1943-46. Mem. ABA, Am. Judicature Soc., Del. Bar Assn., Wilmington Club, Greenville Country Club, Nassau Club. Republican. Home: Wilmington Del. Died May 28, 1993; interred Meml. Garden of Westminster Presbyterian Church, Wilmington, Del.

CHRISTOFF, BORIS, opera singer, basso; b. Plovdiv, Bulgaria, May 18, 1919; s. Kyril and Raina (Teodorova) C.; law degree U. Sofia; studied with Riccardo Straccìari, Rome; scholarship Mozarteum, Salzburg; m. Franca de Rensis. Soloist Bulgarian Gussia choir, Sofia Cathedral choir; profl. debut Italy, 1945; soloist opera La Boheme, 1946; appeared Salzburg and Edinburgh festivals; Am. debut with San Francisco Opera Co.; prin. roles include: Borix Godunoff, Dossiteus, Galitzky, Konchak, Philip II, Don Quixote, Ivan the Terrible. Decorated comdr. Order of Italian Republic; comdr. Order San Pietro e Paolo de Rio de Janeiro; recipient award Academie du Disque Francais, 1953, Academie Charles Cros, 1953, 59; prize Am. Acad. Arts and Scis. Hon. mem. Opera-Paris, Academie du Musique. Numerous recordings opera, Russian folk songs and religious selections. Died June 28, 1993. Home: Rome Italy

CHRISTOPHER, ROBERT COLLINS, journalist; b. Thomaston, Conn., Mar. 3, 1924; s. Gordon Newton and Ruth Mignon (Adams) C.; m. Rita Joan Goldstein, May 17, 1970; children: Alistair David, Gordon Francis Benjamin; children by previous marriage: Ulrica Boyd, Thomas Adams, Valerie, Nicholas. B.A. with exceptional distinction, Yale, 1948. Staff Investment Dealers Digest, 1949-50; with Time mag., 1950-63, asso. editor, 1956-61; sr. editor Time mag. (U.S. and world bus. sects.), 1961-63; dir. fundamental econ. research Corning Glass Works, N.Y.C., 1963; fgn. editor Newsweek mag., 1963-69, exec. editor, 1969-72, editor internat. edit., 1972-77, contbg. editor, 1977-79; mng. editor GEO mag., 1979-80, contbg. editor, 1980-81; adminstr. Pulitzer Prizes, 1981-92. Author: The Japanese Mind: The Goliath Explained, 1983, Second to None: American Companies in Japan., 1986, Crashing the Gates: The De-WASPing of America's Power Elite, 1989. Trustee Corrs. Fund. Served with AUS, 1943-46, 50-52, PTO. Mem. Council on Fgn. Relations, Phi Beta Kappa. Clubs: Century (N.Y.C.); Elizabethan (New Haven). Home: Old Lyme Conn. Died June 15, 1992.

CHRISTOPHERSON, WESTON ROBERT, retired bank executive; b. Walum, N.D., May 5, 1925; s. Carl and Ermie (Larsen) C.; m. Myrna Christensen, June 8, 1951; children: Mia Karen Kammerer, Mari Louisa Morsch, Kari Marie. B.S., U. N.D., 1949, J.D., 1951. Bar: N.D. 1951, Ill. 1952. With Jewel Cos., Inc., Chgo., 1951-84, pres., 1970-80, chief exec. officer, 1979-84, also dir.; chmn. bd., chief exec. officer No. Trust Corp., 1984-89, chmn. bd., 1989-90; also dir.; dir. Ameritech, GATX Corp., Quaker Oats Co. trustee U. Chgo. Presbyn. Clubs: Economic, Chicago, Onwentsia, Old Elm, Commercial. Died May 29, 1994.

CHURCH, ABIAH A., retired broadcasting company executive, lawyer; b. St John's Park, Fla., Aug. 3, 1922; s. Harrison C. and Emile R. (Goss) C.; A.B. in Govt., George Washington U., 1948, J.D. with honors, 1950; m. Bety Morrison, Sept. 13, 1947; children: Harry, Susan, Sharon. Admitted to Fla. bar, 1950, D.C. bar, 1950; law clk. U.S. Ct. of Claims, Washington, 1950-51; atty. Nat. Assn. Broadcasting, Washington, 1951-54; staff atty. Storer Communications Inc Miami Beach, Fla., 1954-57, asst. sec., 1957-79, v.p. corp. law, sec., 1979-80, v.p., gen. counsel, sec., 1980-88, ret., 1988. Pres. Dade Assn. Retarded Citizens, Dade County, Fla., 1959-61. Served with USCG, 1942-45. Mem. Fla. Bar, Fed. Communications Bar Assn., Com. of 100. Democrat. Presbyterian. Clubs: Surf (Miami Beach); Jockey (Miami, Fla.); Nat. Lawyers, (Washington), Coral Gables Exec.'s. Died Oct. 10, 1995. Home: Naples Fla.

CHUSMIR, JANET, newspaper editor. Exec. bd. Miami (Fla.) Herald. Home: Miami Fla. Died Dec. 22, 1990.

CHUTE, MARCHETTE, author; b. Wayzata, Minn., Aug. 16, 1909; d. William Young and Edith Mary (Pickburn) C. A.B., U. Minn., 1930; Litt.D., Western Coll. for Women, 1952, Carleton Coll., 1957, Dickinson Coll., 1964. Author: Rhymes About Ourselves, 1932, The Search for God, 1941, Rhymes About the Country, 1941, The Innocent Wayfaring, 1943, Geoffrey Chaucer of England, 1946, Rhymes About the City, 1946, The End of the Search, 1947, Shakespeare of London, 1950, An Introduction to Shakespeare, 1951, Ben Jonson of Westminster, 1953, The Wonderful Winter, 1954, Stories from Shakespeare, 1956, Around and About, 1957, Two Gentle Men: The Lives of George Herbert and Robert Herrick, 1959, Jesus of Israel, 1961, (with Ernestine Perrie) The Worlds of Shakespeare, 1963, The First Liberty: A History of the Right to Vote in America, 1619-1850, 1969, The Green Tree of Democracy, 1971, P.E.N. American Center: A History of the First Fifty Years, 1972, Rhymes About Us, 1974. Exec. com. Nat. Book Com.; judge non-fiction Nat. Book Awards, 1952, 59. Recipient Author Meets the Critics award for best non-fiction of, 1950; Chap-Book award Poetry Soc. Am., 1954; N.Y. Shakespeare Club award, 1954; Secondary Edn. Bd. book award, 1954; Outstanding Achievement award U. Minn., 1957. Fellow Royal Soc. Arts; mem. Am. P.E.N. (pres. 1955-57), Am. Acad. Arts and Letters, Phi Beta Kappa. Home: Morris Plains N.J. Died May 6, 1994.

CIARANELLO, ROLAND DAVID, biochemist; b. Schenectady, N.Y., Feb. 7, 1943; s. Roland Victor and Carmella (Vertucci) C.; m. Nancy Jane Rogers, June 29, 1968; 1 child, Andrea Lynne. BS, Union Coll., 1965; MD, Stanford U., 1970. Rsch. assoc. NIH, Bethesda, Md., 1971-74; resident in psychiatry Stanford (Calif.) U., 1974-78, asst. prof. psychiatry, 1978-81, assoc. prof. psychiatry, 1981-84, prof. psychiatry, from 1984; Nancy Friend Pritzker prof. Stanford U. Sch. Medicine, from 1990; sci. adv. bd. NIMH, Bethesda, from 1988; sci. cofounder Neurex Corp., Menlo Pk., Calif., from 1986, bd. dirs., from 1986. Contbr. 132 sci. articles to profl. jours. Lt. Comdr. USPHS, 1971-74. Recipient Rsch. Scientist award NIMH, from 1990, Rsch. Career Devel. award NIMH, 1978-88, Daniel Efron Rsch. award Am. Coll. Neurpsychopharmacology, 1988. Fellow Am. Coll. Neuropsychopharmacology; mem. Am. Soc. Biochemistry Molecular Biology. Home: Palo Alto CA Deceased.

CLAMPITT, AMY KATHLEEN, writer, editor; b. New Providence, Iowa, June 15, 1920; d. Roy Justin and Lutie Pauline (Felt) C. B.A. with honors in English, Grinnell Coll., 1941, DHL (hon.), 1984; DHL (hon.), Bowdoin Coll., 1992. Sec., writer Oxford Univ. Press, N.Y.C., 1943-51; reference libr. Nat. Audubon Soc., N.Y.C., 1952-59; free-lance writer, N.Y.C., 1960-77; editor E.P. Dutton, N.Y.C., 1977-82; writer-in-residence Coll. William & Mary, Williamsburg, Va., 1984-85; vis. writer Amherst Coll., 1986-87; Grace Hazard Conkling disting. writer Smith Coll., 1993. Author (poetry) The Kingfisher, 1983, What the Light Was Like, 1985, Archaic Figure, 1987, Westward, 1990, A Silence Opens, 1994, (essays) Predecessors, Et Cetera, 1991. Recipient Lit. award Am. Acad. Arts and Letters, 1984, Writer's award Lila Wallace-Reader's Digest, 1991; Guggenheim fellow, 1982-83, Acad. Am. Poets fellow, 1984, MacArthur fellow, 1992. Mem. AAAL, PEN, Authors Guild. Democrat. Home: New York N.Y. Died Sept. 10, 1994.

CLARENBURG, RUDOLF, anatomy and physiology educator; b. Utrecht, The Netherlands, May 3, 1931; came to U.S., 1959; s. Adolf and Hetty Josephine (Meijer) C.; m. Margalith H.J. Rothschild, Dec. 16, 1958; 1 child, Nathan Victor. Kandidaat in Chemistry, Rijks U., Utrecht, 1955, Kandidaat in Pharmacy, 1955, Dr in Chemistry, 1959, DSc, 1965. Asst. researcher dept. physiology U. Calif., Berkeley, 1959-65, assoc. researcher, 1965-66; assoc. prof. anatomy and physiology Kans. State U., Manhattan, 1966-73, prof., from 1973. Contbr. numerous articles to profl. jours. Bd. dirs., v.p. Unified Sch. Dist. 383 Bd. Edn., Manhattan, 1985-87; bd. dirs. Pawnee Mental Health, Manhattan, from 1987, Riley County chpt. Kans. Heart Assn., from 1989, Manhattan Assoc. Christian and Jewish Congregations, from 1988. Recipient citation Poultry Sci. Conv., Fayetteville, Ark., 1971, Norden Disting. Tchr. award 1983; numerous rsch. grants, including NIH, USDA, Kans. Agrl. Expt. Sta., Tevcon Industries, Gen. Mills. Mem. Am. Physiol. Soc., Soc. for Exptl. Biology and Medicine, Fedn. Am. Socs. for Exptl. Biology, AAAS, Sigma Xi, Phi Zeta, Gamma Sigma Delta. Democrat. Jewish. Home: Manhattan Kans. Deceased.

CLARK, EDWARD, lawyer, banker, former ambassador; b. San Augustine, Tex., July 15, 1906; s. John David and Leila (Downs) C.; m. Anne Metcalfe, Dec. 27, 1927; 1 child, Leila Downs Clark Wynn. LL.D., Southwestern U., 1966; D.Sc., Cleary Coll., 1972. Bar: Tex. 1928. County atty. San Augustine County, 1929-30; asst. atty. gen. Tex., 1931-34; pvt. practice law Austin, 1939-92; sr. partner Clark, Thomas, Winters & Newton, 1939-92; chmn. bd. Tex. Commerce Bank, Austin, 1960-92, First Nat. Bank, San Augustine, 1959-92; U.S. ambassador to Australia Canberra, 1965-68; fed. commr. for HemisFair, San Antonio, 1968; Am. exec. dir. Inter-Am. Devel. Bank, Washington, 1968-69; gen. adv. com. U.S. ACDA, 1974-77; dir. San Benito Bank & Trust Co., Tex, Employers Casualty Ins. Co., Dallas, Employers Nat. Life Ins. Co., Tex. Commerce Bank, Tex. Commerce Bancshares; sec. to gov. Tex., 1935-36, sec. of state Tex., 1937-39. Trustee U. Tex. Law Sch. Found.; bd. regents U. Tex. System for State Tex., 1973-79; chmn. devel. bd. Inst. Texan Cultures, San Antonio; mem. devel. bd. U. Tex. Med. Br., Galveston; mem. adv. council McDonald Obs., U. Tex. Served to capt. AUS, World War II. Mem. ABA, State Bar Tex., Tex. Philos. Soc., Tex. Hist. Assn. (pres.), SAR, Knights San Jacinto, Sons Republic Tex., Kappa

Sigma, Phi Delta Phi. Episcopalian. Clubs: Headliner, University; Ramada (Houston). Home: Austin Tex. Died Sept. 16, 1992.

CLARK, ELEANOR, author; b. Los Angeles, July 6, 1913; d. Frederick Huntington and Eleanor (Phelps) C.; m. Robert Penn Warren, Dec. 7, 1952 (dec. 1989); children: Rosanna, Gabriel. B.A., Vassar Coll., 1934. Mem. Corp. of Yaddo. Author: (novels) The Bitter Box, 1946, Baldur's Gate, 1970, Dr. Heart: A Novella, and Other Stories, 1974, Gloria Mundi, 1979, Camping Out, 1986; (children's books) The Song of Roland, 1960; (non-fiction) Rome and a Villa, 1952, expanded edit., 1975, The Oysters of Locmariaquer, 1964 (National Book award 1965), Eyes, Etc.: A Memoir, 1977, Tamrart: 13 Days in the Sahara, 1984; translator: Ramon Jose Sender's Dark Wedding, 1943; editor: (with Horace Gregory) New Letters in America, 1937; contbr. stories, essays and revs. to numerous publs. Served with OSS, 1943-45. Guggenheim fellow, 1946-47, 49-50; National Inst. of Arts and Letters grantee, 1947. Mem. Nat. Inst. Arts and Letters. Home: Boston Mass. Died Feb. 16, 1996.

CLARK, JACK LELAND, health and fitness center executive; b. San Bernardino, Calif., Oct. 11, 1930; s. Lealand Quency and Faye Lorretta (Vaughn) Kindstrom; m. Marcella Newton, 1951 (div.); children—Jack L., Larry, Colleen; m. 2d, Lee D. Clark, Nov. 4, 1973. Student San Bernardino Valley Coll., 1948-50, U. Redlands, 1951-54. With Santa Fe R.R., 1954-56; exec. v.p. Vic Tanny Internat., N.Y.C., and Calif., 1956-62; founder, pres. Chgo. Health Clubs, 1962—; exec. v.p. Health & Tennis Corp., Chgo. and Calif., 1970—; pres. Health Spa Fin.; v.p., dir. Finco Corp., Detroit; ptnr., investor Richard Simmons Anatomy Asylum. Mem. Phys. Fitness Assn. Am. Republican. Clubs: LaJolla Beach and Tennis, Kona Kai (San Diego). Inventor gov.'s working bench Santa Fe R.R., kicking toe for football conversions. Home: Lions View Calif.

CLARK, STEPHEN P., mayor; b. Florence, Kans., Nov. 19, 1923; children: Peter, Jimmy, Therese, John, Paul, Cecile. Student, Univ. Miami. Former mem. planning and zoning bd. Miami, Fla.; mem. Miami City Commn., 1963; chmn. Downtown Devel. Authority; mayor Miami, Fla., 1967-96; co-founder Clark Constrn. Co., Inc., 1957. With USAF. Decorated Order of Vasco Nunez de Balboa, Republic Panama, 1970, Order of Duarte Sanchez and Mella, Pres. Joaquin Balaguer Dominican Republic, 1977, La Orden de Isabel la Catolica, King Juan Carlos, 1982; recipient Spirit of Life award City of Hope. Mem. Dade County League of Cities (former dir.), Fla. Conf. Mayors (founder), Bldg. and Trades Union, AFL-CIO, Am. Pub. Works Assn., VFW. Roman Catholic. Home: Miami Fla. Died June 4, 1996.

CLARK, SUSAN LOUISE, educator; b. Canton, Ohio, Apr. 21, 1948; d. R.W. and Miriam L. (Windle) C.; m. Charles B. Lovekin, May 6, 1986. BA, Mont. U., 1969; MPhil, Rutgers U., 1972, PhD, 1973. Prof. Rice U., Houston, 1973-93; dir. Teutonic Prodns., Houston, 1981-93, Student Adv. Rice U., 1983-85. Author: Poetics of Conversion, 1976, Thomas Hardy and The Tristan Legend, 1979, Landscapes of Mind, 1989; contbr. numerous articles and book reviews. Mem. South Cen. Modern Lang. Assn., Southeast Medieval Assn. (sec./treas. 1987-90), Modern Lang. Assn., Renaissance Soc. Home: Houston Tex.

CLARK, THOMAS HENRY, geology educator; b. London, Dec. 3, 1893; s. Thomas and Elisabeth Lydia (Anstiss) C.; m. Olive Marguerite Melvenia Prichard, Apr. 1, 1927; 1 child, Joan. A.B., Harvard U., 1917, A.M., 1921, Ph.D., 1923. Asst. in geology Harvard U., Cambridge, Mass., 1915-18, instr. in geology, 1920-23; asst. prof. McGill U., Montreal, Que., Can., 1924-27, assoc. prof., 1927-29, Logan prof. geology, 1929-64, prof. emeritus, from 1964; geologist Que. Dept. Mines, 1938-60, Que. Dept. Natural Resources, 1960-63; advisor geology Redpath Mus. McGill U., from 1964; cons. in field. Author: (with others) Geological Evolution of North America, 1979; contbr. articles to profl. jours. Served to 2d lt. U.S. Army, 1917-19. Recipient Can. Centennial medal, 1967. Fellow Royal Soc. Can. (pres. sect. 4 1954-55), Geol. Assn. Can. (pres. 1958-59, Logan Gold medal 1970), Geol. Soc. Am.; mem. Paleontol. Soc. (v.p. 1951-52), Sigma Xi (pres. 1944). Home: Town Mount Royal Can. Deceased.

CLARKE, CLIFFORD MONTREVILLE, health foundation executive; b. Ludowici, Ga., July 20, 1925; s. Clifford Montreville and Lella Bertrue (Hightower) C. A.B. in Polit. Sci., Emory U., 1951. Radio engr., announcer Sta. WSAV, Savannah, 1941-43; pub. relations dir. Ga. dept. Am. Legion, 1945-47; instr. Armstrong Coll., Savannah, 1947-48; asst. supt. Savannah Park and Tree Commn., 1951; instr., supr. tng. dept. Lockheed Aircraft Corp., Marietta, Ga., 1951-52; mgr. employee services dept. Lockheed Aircraft Corp., 1952-53; exec. v.p. Asso. Industries, Ga., 1953-68; pres. Ga. Bus. and Industry Assn., Atlanta, 1968-73; exec. dir. Bicentennial Council Thirteen Original States, Atlanta, 1973-75; pres. Arthritis Found., 1975-90, pres. emeritus, 1991-94; mem. Am. Soc. Assn. Execs., 1955-94, bd. dirs., 1958-67, mem. exec. com., 1960-67, treas., 1962-64, sr. v.p., 1964-65, pres., 1965-66; pres. Ga. Soc. Assn. Execs., 1958-60; v.p., chmn. state assn. group Nat. Indsl. Council, 1970-72. Mem. Ga. Urban and Tech. Assistance Adv. Council, 1965-70, Ga. Intergovtl. Relations Commn., 1966; mem. Ga. Ednl. Improvement Council, 1964-69, chmn., 1967-69, vice chmn., 1970-71; mem. Forward Ga. Commn., 1969-72; vice chmn. Ga. Commn. for Nat. Bicentennial Celebration, 1969-72, chmn., 1973-75; chmn. Chartered Exec. Chartering Bd., 1969-71; mem. Cert. Assn. Exec. Bd., 1978-80; mem. policy com. U. Ga. Grad. Sch. Bus.; adv. bd. Ga. Vocat. Rehab.; mem. Nat. Arthritis Adv. Bd., 1977-80; bd. dirs. Arthritis Found. Ga., 1965-71, Atlanta Community Services to Blind, Coop. Services for Blind, 1964-71, Atlanta Sch. Art, Atlanta Conv. Bur., 1968-71, Nat. Health Council, 1978-81; trustee Am. Soc. Assn. Execs. Found. Served with inf. AUS, World War II. Decorated Purple Heart with 2 oak leaf clusters. Home: Shiloh Ga. Died Nov. 17, 1994.

CLARKE, JAMES PHILIP, medical educator, physician; b. Denver, Nov. 25, 1922; s. Philip and Grace (Lilly) C.; m. Doris Jean O'Brien, Jan. 5, 1946; children: Philip, Bernard, Nancy, Ted, Paul, Maureen, Mark, Mary, Patricia, Peggy, Libby. BS, U. Notre Dame, 1945; MD, U. Colo., 1946. Diplomate Am. Bd. Internal Medicine, 1955, 74. Co-founder Denver Clinic, 1956, ptnr., 1956-85; clin. prof. U. Colo. Sch. Medicine, Denver, 1977—, assoc. dean, 1985—; bd. dirs. Nat. Alumni Bd., U. Notre Dame; founder Conf. Med. Ethics U. Notre Dame, 1986—. Contbr. articles to profl. jours. Mem. Nat. Commn. on Future Regis Coll., Denver, 1980-82; bd. dirs. Denver Bd. Health and Hosp. (chmn.), 1973-75. Lt. U.S. Navy, 1947-49. Recipient Robins award Colo. Med. Soc., 1972, Outstanding Clin. Faculty award U. Colo. Health Sci. Ctr., Denver, 1983, Edward Sorin award U. Notre Dame, 1987. Fellow AMA, Am. Coll. Physician (gov. 1981-85, chmn. 1985-86, regent 1986—), Am. Soc. Internal Medicine, Denver Med. Soc., Colo. Med. Soc., Serra (pres. 1968), Denver Country Club. Democrat. Roman Catholic. Home: Englewood Colo.

CLAVELL, JAMES, author, screenwriter, producer, director, playwright; b. Sydney, Australia, Oct. 10, 1924; came to U.S., 1953; naturalized, 1963; s. Richard Charles and Eileen (Collis) C.; m. April Stride, Feb. 20, 1951. Student, Birmingham U., 1946-47. Screenwriter: films The Fly, 1958, Watussi, 1959, 633 Squadron, 1964, The Satan Bug, 1965; writer, producer, dir. films Five Gates to Hell, 1959, Walk Like A Dragon, 1960, The Great Escape, 1963 (Writers Guild award for screenplay 1963), To Sir, With Love, 1967, Where's Jack, 1968, The Last Valley, 1971, (with Eric Bercovicci) Shogun, 1980, The Children's Story, 1982; dir. various TV programs; author: (novellette) The Children's Story, 1981; (novels) King Rat, 1962, Tai-Pan, 1966, Shogun, 1975, Noble House, 1981, Thrump-O-Moto, 1985, Whirlwind, 1986, Gai-Jin, 1993; (play) Countdown at Armegeddon, 1966; also poetry. Served to capt. Royal Arty., 1941-46. Home: Vevey Switzerland Died Sept. 6, 1994.

CLAY, GEORGE HARRY, lawyer; b. Kansas City, Kans., Feb. 14, 1911; s. G. Harry and Linnie Winn (Phillips) C.; m. Harriett Hawley, Feb. 17, 1940; children: Constance Lucille (Loosli), Martha Linnie (McDermott), Charles Hawley, Catherine Louise (Winston), James Nicholas. AB, JD, U. Mo., 1934. Bar: Mo. 1934. Gen. practice law Borders, Borders & Warrick, 1935, Parker & Knipmeyer, 1935-40, Winger, Reeder & Barker, 1940-44; exec. asst. Trans World Airlines, Inc., Kansas City, Mo., 1944-47; sec. Trans World Airlines, Inc., 1947-54, v.p., sec., 1954-57, v.p. adminstrv. service, 1957-58, dir., 1956-58; v.p., gen. counsel Fed. Res. Bank Kansas City, 1958-61, pres., 1961-76; chmn. bd., dir. ISC Fin. Corp., 1980-88; of counsel Morris, Larson, King, & Stamper, P.C., 1984-87. Pres. Regional Health and Welfare Council, 1965-67; asso. mem. Civic Council Kansas City, 1960-76; bd. dirs. Kansas City (Mo.) YMCA, 1950-58, 71-74, pres., 1955-56; bd. dirs. Starlight Theatre Assn., pres., 1968-69; bd. dirs. U. Mo.-Columbia Devel. Fund, 1969-74, United Funds, Mid-Am. Regional Council, 1968-85, Helping Hand Inst., Urban Reinvestment Task Force; mem. adv. bd. Salvation Army; bd. govs. Am. Royal Live Stock and Horse Show; trustee Conservatory Music chmn., 1967-75. Mem. Mo., Kansas City bar assns., Chancery, Kansas City C. of C., Nat. Alliance Businessmen, Phi Gamma Delta. Presbyterian (elder). Clubs: Kansas City, Mission Hills Country, Rotary, Mercury, Palmbrook Country. Home: Shawnee Mission Kans. Died Oct. 11, 1995.

CLAYTON, JACK, film director; b. Brighton, Sussex, Eng., Mar. 1, 1921; m. Christine Norden (div.); m. 2d, Katherine Kath (div.). Prodn. mgr. (film) An Ideal Husband; assoc. producer Queen of Spades, Flesh and Blood, Moulin Rouge, Beat the Devil, The Good Die Young, I am a Camera; producer, dir. The Bespoke Overcoat, 1955; dir. Room at the Top, 1958; producer, dir. The Innocents, 1961, Our Mother's House, 1967; dir. The Pumpkin Eater, 1964, The Great Gatsby, 1974, Something Wicked This Way Comes, 1983, The Lonely Passion of Judith Hearne, 1989, TV films include: Memeuto Muri,1992. Served to flight lt. RAF, 1940-45. Deceased. Home: London Eng.

CLAYTOR, ROBERT BUCKNER, retired railroad executive; b. Roanoke, Va., Feb. 27, 1922; s. William Graham and Gertrude Harris (Boatwright) C.; m Frances Tice, Sept. 25, 1943 (dec. June 1989); childrer Jane Gordon (Mrs. Samuel J. Webster), Robert Harris John Preston. A.B. cum laude, Princeton U., 194 J.D., Harvard U., 1948; L.H.D. (hon.), Hollins Coll 1982. Bar: Mass. 1948, N.Y. 1949, Va. 1952. Atty AT&T, 1948-51; solicitor Norfolk & Western, Roanok 1951-54, asst. gen. solicitor, 1954-56, asst. gen. counse 1956-60, gen. solicitor, 1960- 64, v.p. law, 1964-68, s v.p., 1968-70, exec. v.p., 1970-80, also chmn., pres., chi exec. officer, 1980-82; chmn., chief exec. officer Norfol So. Corp., 1982-87, chmn. exec. com., bd. dirs., 1987-9 bd. dirs. Ashland Coal Inc. Chancellor Episcopal D ocese Southwestern Va., 1969-74; trustee Hollins Coll 1968-90, chmn. bd. 1972-82, Va. Theol. Sem. Bd.; Eas tern Va. Med. Found., 1983-90; bd. visitors Va. Pol Inst. and State U., 1982-90; chmn., bd. regents Merce sburg Acad., 1988-90; chmn. Va. Found. for Ind. Colls 1987-89. Served to 1st lt. AUS, 1943-46. Mem. ABA Va. Bar Assn., Roanoke Bar Assn., Norfolk Bar Assn Va. Opera Assn. (bd. dirs.), Phi Beta Kappa. Epis copalian. Clubs: Princeton (N.Y.C.); Metropolita (Washington); Harbor (Norfolk); Norfolk Yacht an Country; Shenandoah (Roanoke); Links (N.Y.C. Sarasota (Fla.) Yacht. Home: Norfolk Va. Died Apr. 1993.

CLAYTOR, WILLIAM GRAHAM, JR., railroad ex ecutive; b. Roanoke, Va., Mar. 14, 1912; s. Willian Graham and Gertrude Harris (Boatwright) C.; m Frances Murray Hammond, Aug. 14, 1948; childrer Frances Murray, William Graham III. BA, U. Va 1933; JD summa cum laude, Harvard U., 1936; LLD U. Miami, 1985. Bar: N.Y. 1937, D.C. 1938. Law cl U.S. Judge Learned Hand, 1936-37, Mr. Justic Brandeis, 1937-38; assoc. firm Covington & Burlin Washington, 1938-47; partner Covington & Burlin 1947-67, counsel, 1981-82; v.p. law So. Ry. Co., 196 67, chief exec. officer, 1967-77, pres., 1967-76, chm bd., 1976-77; chmn. bd., pres. Nat. R.R. Passeng Corp., Washington, 1982-94; former chief exec. office dir. various cos. comprising So. Ry. System; sec. Nav Washington, 1977-79, acting sec. Transp., 1979, de sec. Def., 1979-81; bd. dirs. Assn. Am. R.R.s, 1967-7 82-94. Pres. Harvard Law Rev, 1935-36. Trustee Epis copal Home Children, Washington, 1960-65, v.p., 196 63; trustee Ctr. for Strategic and Internat. Studies, 198 94; govs. Beauvoir Sch., Washington, 1958-61, St. A bans Sch., 1961-67; mem. adv. bd. Center for Advance Studies, U. Va., 1974-80; trustee Eisenhower Fellow ships, Inc., 1981-94; mem. adv. com. Mt. Vernon (Va Ladies Assn. of the Union, 1980-86. Served to lt. comd USNR, 1941-46. Mem. ABA, Am. Law Inst. A Judicature Soc., Harvard Law Sch. Assn., Am. So Corp. Execs. (assoc. mem.), Met. Club, City Tave Assn. (bd. govs. 1961-64), Chevy Chase Club, Sh nandoah Club. Democrat. Episcopalian. Home: Wash ington D.C. Died May 14, 1994; interred Roanoke, Va

CLEARY, FRITZ, editor, sculptor; b. N.Y.C., Sept. 2 1913; s. Francis Xavier and Minnie (Walsh) C.; m. Ho Harris Kielland, 1959; children: Catherine, Christophe Cyrus. BA, St. Johns's U., 1936; student, NAD N.Y.C., Beaux Arts. Editor Nat. Sculpture Rev., In terlaken, N.J.; reporter, photographer, editor Asbur Park (N.J.) Press, 1946-72. Commns. include Worl War II Meml., Point Pleasant, N.J., John F. Kenned Meml., Asbury Park, N.J., others; exhbns. include Na Acad. Design, N.Y., Pa. Acad. Fine Arts, Phila., Oa land (Calif.) Art Mus., Nat. Sculpture Soc., Allied A tists, Hudson Valley Art Assn. Ann., also in col. a mus. and city mus. in Ea. U.S., others; contbr. articl to profl. jours. With AUS, 1943-46. Recipient Ann Hyatt Huntington award for Sculpture Hudson Valle Art Assn., 1975, Herbert Adams Meml. award Na Sculpture Soc., 1991. Fellow Nat. Sculpture Soc. (Joh Spring award 1974); mem. Allied Am. Artist Salamagundi Club, Nat. Arts Club, Asbury Park So Fine Arts. Home: Interlaken N. J. Died Feb. 24, 1993.

CLEARY, JOHN VINCENT, JR., utility company ex ecutive; b. N.Y.C., June 14, 1928; s. John Vincent an Lillian V. (Dacy) C.; m. Ann E. Farley, Jan. 28, 195 children: John V., Eileen, Patricia, Karen, Mary E len. B.S. in Civil Engring., Manhattan Coll., 1954. Chief cost engr. Consol. Edison Co., N.Y.C., 1968-6 v.p. Bklyn. div., 1971-74, v.p. Staten Island div., 196 71, 74-77; exec. v.p. Green Mountain Power Corp Burlington, Vt., 1977-81, pres., chief operating office 1981-83, pres., chief exec. officer, 1983-90; dir. Gree Mountain Power Corp., Vt. Electric Power Co Rutland, Electric Council N.E., Bedford, Mass., Great Burlington Indsl. Corp., Assn. of Edison Illuminatin Cos., N.Y.C. Served with U.S. Army, 1950-52, Korea. Mem. Electric Power Research Inst., Edison Electri Inst. Clubs: Ethan Allen, Burlington Country. Hom Charlotte Vt. Died July 23, 1990.

CLEAVER, VERA ALLEN, author; b. Virgil, S.D Jan. 6, 1919; d. Fortis Alonzo and Beryl Naiome (Rei inger) Allen; m. William Joseph Cleaver, Oct. 4, 194 (dec. 1981). Student pub. schs. Freelance pub. a countant, 1945-54; with U.S. Air Force, Tachikaw Japan, 1954-56, Chaumont, France, 1956-58. Autho (with Bill Cleaver) Ellen Grae, 1967, Lady Ellen Gra 1968, Where the Lilies Bloom, 1969 (Nat. Book awar nominee), Grover, 1970 (Nat. Book award nominee) The Mimosa Tree, 1970, I Would Rather Be a Turni

1971, The Mock Revolt, 1971, Delpha Green & Company, 1972, Me Too, 1973, The Whys and Wherefores of Littabelle Lee, 1973 (Nat. Book award nominee), Dust of the Earth (Western Writers of Am. Spur award Best Western Juvenile Novel, Lewis Carroll Bookshelf award), Trial Valley, 1977, Queen of Hearts, 1978 (Nat. Book award nominee), A Little Destiny, 1979, The Kissimmee Kid, 1981, Hazel Rye, 1983, Sugar Blue, 1984, Sweetly Sings the Donkey (Children's Choice award), 1986, Moon Lake Angel, 1987, Belle Pruitt, 1988 (Junior Library Guild Selection 1988). Died Aug. 11, 1992.

CLELAND, ROBERT LINDBERGH, research chemist, educator; b. St. Francis, Kans., June 10, 1927; s. Robert Earl and Dorothy (Voss) C.; m. Monique Cecile Tremege, Aug. 20, 1956; children: Chantal C., Maryke A., Andrew N., Francis A. B.S., A. and M. Coll. Tex., 1948; M.Ch.E., Mass. Inst. Tech., 1951, Ph.D., 1956. Research assoc. Cornell U., 1956-58; Fulbright research scholar U. Leiden, The Netherlands, 1958-59; USPHS Spl. Research fellow Retina Found., Boston, 1959-60; asst. prof. chemistry Dartmouth Coll., 1960-65, assoc. prof., 1965-71, prof., 1971-90; guest rsch. prof. BMC U. Uppsala, Sweden, 1991-93; professeur associe U. Strasbourg, France, 1968-69; vis. prof. U. Uppsala, 1977-78, 90-93. Assoc. editor: Macromolecules, 1974-76. Home: Norwich Vt. Died Apr. 29, 1993.

CLÉMENT, RENÉ JEAN, film director; b. Bordeaux, France, Mar. 18, 1913; s. Jean Clément and Marguérite Bayle; m. Bella Gurwich, Aug. 10, 1940 (dec. Feb. 1986); m. Johanna Harwood, Apr. 14, 1987. Student, Sch. of Architecture, Paris. Founder mem. Inst. des hautes études cinématographiques. Films include Bataille du rail, 1946, Les Maudits, 1947, Walls of Malapaga, 1948, Chateau de verre, 1950, Au delà des grilles (Oscar award for Best Fgn. Film 1951), Jeux interdits (Oscar award for Best Fgn. Film 1952), Lion d'or, 1952, Monsieur Ripois, 1954, Gervaise, 1956, Sea Wall, 1958, Demain est un autre jour, 1962, Quelle joie de vivre, Purple Noon (Plein Soleil), 1960, The Love Cage (Les félins), 1964, Paris brule-t-il?, 1965, Le passager de la pluie, 1970, La maison sous les arbres, 1971, La course du lièvre à travers les champs, 1971, The Baby-Sitter, 1975; author: (with C. Audry) Bataille du rail, 1947. Decorated Officier Légion d'honneur, Grand Officer Ordre Nat. Mérite, Comdr. des Arts et des Lettres; recipient prize Cannes Festival, 1946, 47, 52, 54, Grand Internat. Venice Biennale, 1952, César d'honneur, 1984. Mem. Acad. Fine Arts, de l'Inst. de France. Home: Paris France Died Mar. 17, 1996.

CLEMENTS, THOMAS, consulting geologist; b. Chgo., June 7, 1898; s. George Henry and Caroline Barbara (Nathan) C.; m. Lydia Pryce Brooks, Oct. 14, 1922; 1 dau., Anne. E.M., Tex. Sch. Mines, 1922; M.S., Calif. Inst. Tech., 1929, Ph.D., 1932. Metallurgist Compañia Minera de Peñoles, S.A., Torreón, Mexico, 1922-25; engr. Security Title Ins. & Guarantee Co., Los Angeles, 1925-28; teaching fellow Calif. Inst. Tech., 1928-29; teaching staff U. So. Calif., Los Angeles, 1929-64; Hancock prof. geology U. So. Calif., 1945-64, head dept., 1933-63; chmn. com. research Hancock Found., 1952-60; curator of mineralogy and petrology Los Angeles County Mus., 1955-60; condr. research in Mexico on source of ancient Mexican jade, from 1957; geologist Los Angeles County Mus. Expdn. to Lake Chapala, Jalisco, Mexico, 1956, Nat. Geog. Soc. archeol. site, Calico, Calif., from 1964; cons. mining engr., geologist, from 1930; cons. geologist Dept. Petroleum, Ministerio de la Economia Nacional, Bogotá, Colombia, 1939; mem. geol. hazards com., City Los Angeles, 1957-63; mem. grading cons. bd. Bldg. and Safety Commn., 1963-73; pres. Qualifications Bd. Engring. Geologists, 1960-70; mem. Adv. Com. on Engring. Geology, 1979-82. Author: Geological Story of Death Valley, 1954, 11th edit., 1982; contbr. tech. articles to sci. jours. Served with USN, 1917-19. Fellow Geol. Soc. Am., So. Calif. Acad. Scis.; mem. Sociedad Geológica Mexicana, Death Valley Fortyniners (dir., past pres. 1955), Los Angeles Mineral. Soc. (founder, 1st pres. 1932), Soc. Econ. Geologists, Am. Inst. Mining and Metall. Engrs. (Legion of Honor 1987), Am. Assn. Petroleum Geologists, Branner Geol. Club (hon. life, past pres.), Acacia, Phi Kappa Phi. Home: Los Angeles Calif. Deceased.

CLEMONS, WALTER, writer; b. Houston, Nov. 14, 1929; s. Walter C. and Margaret (Ewing) C. A.B., Princeton U., 1951; M.A. (Rhodes scholar), Magdalen Coll., Oxford U., 1953. Free lance writer, 1955-65; editor McGraw-Hill Book Co., N.Y.C., 1966-68, New York Times Book Rev., 1968-71; editor, book critic Newsweek, N.Y.C., 1971-77; sr. writer Newsweek, 1978-82, 83-88; editor, writer Vanity Fair mag., N.Y.C., 1982-83; writer-in-residence Alley Theater, Houston, Ford Found. Program for Poets and Fiction Writers, 1963-64; dir. Nat. Book Critics Circle, 1978-86; Hodder fellow Princeton, 1959-60. Author: The Poison Tree and Other Stories, 1959. Recipient Prix de Rome Am. Acad. in Rome, 1960-62. Mem. Century Assn., The Players. Home: Long Island City N.Y. Died July 6, 1994.

CLEVELAND, CARL S(ERVICE), JR., academic administrator, educator, physician; b. Webster City, Iowa, Mar. 29, 1918; s. Carl S. Sr. and Ruth R. (Ashworth) C.; m. Mildred G. Allison, Mar. 28, 1939 (dec. 1979). D in Chiropractic, Cleveland Chiropractic Coll., Kansas City, 1945; BS in Physiology, U. Nebr., 1947. Cert. tchr., Kans., Calif. Instr. Cleveland Chiropractic Coll., Kansas City, Mo., 1939-95, dean, 1945-55, pres., 1976-82, prof. physiology, 1975-95; exec. v.p. Cleveland Chiropractic Coll., L.A., 1976-82, pres., 1982-92, chancellor, 1992-95; pres. bd. trustees Unity Temple, Kansas City, 1969-78; pres. bd. trustees Unity Sch. Practical Christianity, Kansas City, 1969-78; speaker nat., internat. lecture tours The Sci. Award Medallion, Rsch. Award World Chiro Congress, Montreaux, Switzerland, 1970. Mem. Internat. Chiropractors Assn. (bd. control), Mo. Chiropractic Assn. (pres. 1962-63), North Ctrl. Assn. Colls. and Schs., Delta Sigma Chi, Beta Chi Rho, Sigma Chi, Sigma Chi Psi. Republican. Home: Los Angeles Calif. Died July 23, 1995.

CLEVELAND, JAMES COLGATE, lawyer, former congressman; b. June 13, 1920; s. Mather and Susan (Colgate) C.; m. Hilary Paterson, Dec. 9, 1950; children: Cotton Mather, James Colby, David Paterson, Lincoln Mather, Susan Sclater. Student, Deerfield Acad., 1933-37; B.A. magna cum laude, Colgate U., 1941; LL.B., Yale, 1948. Bar: N.H. bar 1948. Practice law Concord, New London, 1949-95; sr. partner Cleveland, Waters & Bass; of counsel; mem. 88th-96th congresses from 2d N.H. dist.; Organizer, incorporator, officer, dir. New London Trust Co.; Rep. 7th Dist. to N.H. Senate, 1950-62. Co-author: We Propose A Modern Congress, 1966. Served with AUS, World War II, Korean War. Decorated Bronze Star for Valor. Mem. Am. Legion, Nat. Rifle Assn., Phi Beta Kappa. Home: New London N.H. Died Dec. 3, 1995.

CLINE, RAY STEINER, political scientist, historian; b. Anderson, Ill., June 4, 1918; s. Charles and Ina May (Steiner) C.; m. Marjorie Wilson, June 4, 1941; children: Judith, Sibyl. A.B., Harvard U., 1939, M.A., 1941, Ph.D., 1949; postgrad., Balliol Coll., Oxford (Eng.) U., 1939-40. Jr. fellow Harvard U., 1941-42; with OSS, 1943-46, Office Chief Mil. History, Dept. Army, 1946-49, CIA, 1949-51; attaché Am. Embassy, London, 1951-53; with CIA, 1954-58; dir. U.S. Naval Aux. Communications Ctr., Taipei, 1958-62; dep. dir. for intelligence CIA, 1962-66; spl. adviser Am. embassy, Bonn, Germany, 1966-69; dir. Bur. Intelligence and Rsch., Dept. State, 1969-73; dir. world power studies Georgetown U. Ctr. Strategic and Internat. Studies, Washington, 1973-86; chmn. U.S. Global Strategy Coun., Washington, 1986-94; pres. Nat. Intelligence Study Ctr., Washington; adj. prof. Georgetown U., 1974-94. Author: Washington Command Post, 1951, World Power Assessment, 1975, Secrets, Spies and Scholars, 1976, World Power Trends and U.S. Foreign Policy for the 1980's, 1980, The CIA: Reality vs. Myth, 1982, (with Yonah Alexander) Terrorism: the Soviet Connection, 1984, Terrorism as State-Sponsored Covert Warfare, 1986; editor: Europe in Soviet Global Strategy, 1987, Asia in Soviet Global Strategy, 1987, Metastrategy: National Security Memorandum for the President, 1988, Chiang Ching-Kuo Remembered, 1989, Foreign Policy Failures in China, Cuba and Nicaragua, 1992, The Power of Nations in the 1990s: A Strategic Assessment, 1994; contbr. articles to profl. jours. Mem. Oxford Soc., Coun. Fgn. Rels., Washington Inst. Fgn. Affairs, Harvard Club (Washington and N.Y.C.), Phi Beta Kappa. Home: Arlington Va. Died Mar. 15, 1996.

CLINTON, JOHN HART, editor, lawyer; b. Quincy, Mass., Apr. 3, 1905; s. John Francis and Catherine Veronica (Hart) C.; m. Helen Alice Amphlett, Feb. 18, 1933 (dec. 1965); children: Mary Jane (Mrs. Raymond Zirkel), Mary Ann (Mrs. Christopher Gardner, Jr.), John Hart; m. Mathilda A. Schoorel van Dillen, Feb. 22, 1969. A.B., Boston Coll., 1926; J.D., Harvard U., 1929. Bar: Calif. 1930, Mass. 1930. Since practiced in San Francisco; assoc. Morrison, Foerster, Holloway, Clinton & Clark, and predecessor, 1929-41, ptnr., 1941-72; of counsel Morrison & Foerster, 1972-93; vice pres., gen. counsel Indsl. Employers and Distbrs. Assn., Emeryville, 1944-72; pres. Leamington Hotel, Oakland, Calif., 1933-47, Amphlett Printing Co., San Mateo, Calif., 1943-93; pub. San Mateo Times, 1943-87, editor, 1960-93. Hon. mem. exec. com. San Mateo County council Boy Scouts Am.; bd. dirs., pres. Bay Meadows Found.; regent emeritus Notre Dame Coll., Belmont, Calif. Decorated Knight Equestrian Order of Holy Sepulchre of Jerusalem. Mem. FCC, Am., San Francisco, San Mateo County bar assns., State Bar Calif. (past chmn. fair trial/free press com., past co-chmn. Calif. bench/bar media com.), Am. Judicature Soc., Nat. Lawyers Club, Am. Law Inst., San Mateo County Devel. Assn (pres. 1963-65), San Mateo County Hist. Assn. (pres. 1960-64), Calif. Press Assn. (pres. 1970, chmn. membership com.), Am. Newspaper Pubs. Assn. (govt. affairs com., press/bar relations com.; Am. Bar Assn.-Am. Newspapers Pubs. Assn. task force), Calif. Newspaper Pubs. Assn. (pres. 1969), Wine and Food Soc. San Francisco, Am. Soc. Newspaper Editors, Assn. Cath. Newsmen, Nat. Press Photographers Assn., Internat. Platform Assn., Newcomen Soc. Clubs: Commonwealth of Calif. (San Francisco) (past pres.), San Francisco Comml. (San Francisco), Bohemian (San Francisco); Bombay Bicycle Riding (Burlingame, Calif.); Sequoia (Redwood City, Calif.). Lodges: Elks; Rotary (San Mateo past pres.). Home: San Mateo Calif. Died June 1992.

CLOAR, CARROLL, artist; b. Earle, Ark., Jan. 18, 1913; s. Charles W. and Eva (David) C. A.B., Southwestern Coll., Memphis, 1934; A.B. hon. doctorate, 1978; student, Memphis Acad. Art, 1935, Art Students League, N.Y.C., 1936-40. Author: Hostile Butterflies and Other Paintings, 1977; Contbr. to: Delta Rev; One man shows include, Alan Gallery, N.Y.C., 1956, 58, 60, 62, 64, 66, Brooks Meml. Gallery, Memphis, 1955, High Mus., Atlanta, 1959, M. H. De Young Gallery, San Francisco, 1967, Ark. Art Ctr., Little Rock, 1956, exhbns. include, Pitts. Internat., 1955, Whitney Ann., 1960, Phila. Ann., 1962, retrospective exhbn., N.Y. State U., 1968; represented in permanent collections, Met. Mus., Mus. Modern Art, Whitney Mus., Library of Congress, Wadsworth Atheneum, others, also pvt. collections. Former trustee Brooks Meml. Gallery Art, Memphis. Served with USAAF, 1942-45. Guggenheim fellow, 1946; named Ark. traveller, 1956. Hon. mem. Phi Beta Kappa. Home: Memphis Tenn. Died Apr. 10, 1993.

CLOGG, CLIFFORD COLLIER, statistician, educator; b. Oberlin, Ohio, Oct. 16, 1949; s. Richard Gould and Margaret Narise (Puder) C.; m. Vicki Lynne Bowman, Dec. 20, 1971 (div. 1974); m. Judy Marie Ellenberger, Sept. 24, 1977; children: Katye, Edna, Roberta, Edith. BA, Ohio U., 1971; MA, MS, U. Chgo., 1974, PhD, 1977. From asst. prof. to prof. Pa. State U., University Park, 1976-86, disting. prof., from 1990. Author: Measuring Underemployment, 1979; editor J. Am. Statis. Assn., 1989-91; contbr. over 50 articles to profl. jours. Recipient Spl. Creativity award NSF, 1982; Fellow Ctr. for Advanced Study, Stanford (Calif.) U., 1983-84. Fellow AAAS; Am. Statis. Assn.; mem. Population Assn. Am. (bd. dirs. from 1992), Am. Sociol. Assn. (chair methodology sect. 1990-91, Lazarsfeld award 1987), Biometric Soc. Republican. Home: Bellefonte Pa. Deceased.

CLURMAN, RICHARD MICHAEL, journalist; b. N.Y.C., Mar. 10, 1924; s. Will N. and Emma (Herzberg) C.; divorced; children: Susan Emma, Carol Mae; m. Shirley Potash, Apr. 13, 1957; 1 child, Richard Michael. PhB, U. Chgo., 1946. Asst. editor Commentary mag., 1946-49; press editor Time mag., 1949-55; editorial dir. Newsday, 1955-58; dep. chief corr. Time and Life mag., N.Y.C., 1958-60; chief Time and Life mag., 1960-69; v.p. Time Inc., 1969-72; chmn. bd. Time-Life Broadcast, 1971-72; adminstr. Parks, Recreation and Cultural Affairs Adminstrn. and Commn. Parks, City N.Y., 1972-73; cons. Am. Revolution Bicentennial Adminstrn., 1974; dir. E.M. Warburg, Pincus & Co., Inc., 1976-81; pres. Richard M. Clurman Assocs., Inc., 1975-88; pub. policy advisor Office of Chmn., Joseph E. Seagram & Sons, Inc., 1980-84. Author: Beyond Malice: The Media's Years of Reckoning, 1988, To the End of Time: The Seduction and Conquest of a Media Empire, 1992, Who's in Charge? CEOs and Boards Shuffle Power, 1993. Chmn. bd. N.Y.C. Ctr. Music and Drama, Inc., 1968-75; pres. N.Y. Found. for Arts, Inc., 1971-72; bd. dirs. Lincoln Ctr. for Performing Arts, 1968-75, Sch. Am. Ballet, 1970-76, Parks Coun., 1975-77; chmn. Gov.'s Task Force on Arts and Cultural Life, 1975; mem. adv. coun. NYU Sch. Arts, 1974-89; chmn. adv. com. WNCN, chmn., 1975-76; bd. dirs. Citizens Com. N.Y.C., 1976-96; chmn. bd. govs. Columbia U. Grad. Sch. Journalism media and soc. seminars, 1981-92. With U.S. Army, 1942-46. Sr. fellow Columbia U. Media Studies Ctr., N.Y.C., 1995. Mem. Coun. Fgn. Rels., Century Assn. N.Y.C., Fed. Club, City Club Washington. Home: New York N.Y. Died May 15, 1996.

CLYDE, EDWARD WILBUR, lawyer, b. Heber City, Utah, Nov. 23, 1917; s. Lionel Dean and Ardell (Buhler) C.; m. Betha Jensen, Aug. 14, 1941; children—Carolyn, Susan, Steven, Thomas. B.S., Brigham Young U., 1939; J.D., U. Utah, 1942, LL.D. (hon.), 1981. Bar: Utah. Law clk. Utah Supreme Ct., Salt Lake City, 1941-45; asst. atty. gen. State of Utah, Salt Lake City, 1945-48, Utah Land Bd., Salt Lake City, 1956-60; commr. Utah Oil and Gas Commn., 1956-60; ptnr. Clyde and Pratt, Salt Lake City, 1943—; chmn. Utah Constl. Revision Commn., 1970-74. Contbr. numerous articles to profl. jours. Mem. bd. regents U. Utah, 1964-69, chmn. bd. regents, 1966-68; chmn. Instl. Council, 1969-81. Mem. Am. Coll. Trial Attys., ABA (chmn. natural resources law sect. 1976-77), Soc. Bar and Gavel, Phi Kappa Phi. Home: Salt Lake City Utah

COBLE, ROBERT LOUIS, material sciences educator; b. Uniontown, Pa., Jan. 22, 1928; s. Gomer Lawrence and Dorothy Marguerite (Phillippi) C.; m. Joan Walker, Apr. 14, 1952; children: David, Eric, Catherine, Stefan, Jan. B.S., Bethany (W.Va.) Coll., 1950; Sc.D., M.I.T., 1955. Research assoc. Gen. Electric Co. Research and Devel. Center, Schenectady, 1955-61; faculty dept. materials sci. and engring. M.I.T., Cambridge, 1961-92; emeritus prof. ceramics M.I.T., 1992; cons. govt. adv. coms. Contbr. tech. articles to profl. jours. Recipient Pace award Nat. Inst. Ceramic Engrs., 1970, U.S. Sr. Scientist, von Humboldt award Fed. Republic of Germany, 1984. Fellow Am. Ceramic Soc. (Ross Coffin Purdy award); mem. Nat. Acad. Engring. Home: Cambridge Mass. Died Jan. 22, 1992.

COCKLIN, ROBERT FRANK, professioal society administrator; b. Lincoln, Nebr., Feb. 13, 1919; s. Frank

Dietrich and Helen Catherine (Sampson) C.; m. Ruth Elizabeth Castner, June 25, 1942; children: John Andrew, Mary Collison (dec.). Student, U. Nebr., 1938-41, U.S. Army Command and Staff Coll., 1964, Army War Coll., 1969. Commd. 2nd lt. U.S. Army, 1941, advanced through grades to maj. gen., 1977; assoc. editor Field Arty. Jour., Washington, 1946-48; bus. mgr. N.G. Assn., Washington, 1948-50; dir. public affairs Assn. U.S. Army, Arlington, Va., 1950-77; exec. v.p. Assn. U.S. Army, 1977-88, sr. fellow, 1988-96; dir. United Services Life Ins. Co., USLICO Corp. Author: Battery Duties, 1950, also pamphlets and articles. Trustee George C. Marshall Research Found. Decorated D.S.M., Bronze Star, Air medal, Purple Heart; recipient Disting. Civilian Svc. award, Disting. Svc. medal SSS, Disting. Svc. medal Nat. Guard Assoc. U.S. Fellow Inst. LAnd Warfare; mem. Army-Navy Club. Roman Catholic. Home: Arlington Va. Died Jan., 1996.

COFFRIN, ALBERT WHEELER, federal judge; b. Burlington, Vt., Dec. 21, 1919; s. Morris Daniel and Florence Belle (Browe) C.; m. Elizabeth Ann MacCornack, May 14, 1943; children: Peter S., Albert W., III, James W., Nancy (Mrs. Michael G. Furlong). AB, Middlebury Coll., 1941, LLD, 1990; LLB, Cornell U., 1947. Bar: Vt. bar 1948. Assoc. Black & Wilson, Burlington, 1947-51, 52-56, Black, Wilson, Coffrin & Hoff, 1956-60; ptnr. Coffrin & Pierson, 1962-68, Coffrin, Pierson & Affolter, 1968-72; judge U.S. Dist. Ct. Vt., 1972-93. Trustee Middlebury Coll., 1973-88, overseer, 1988-93. With USN, 1942-45, 51-52; comdr. Res. 1952-66. Fellow Am. Bar Found.; mem. ABA, Vt. Bar Assn., Chittenden County Bar Assn., Burlington Tennis Club, Phi Delta Phi, Kappa Delta Rho. Republican. Unitarian. Home: Burlington Vt. Died Jan. 14, 1993.

COFFY, ROBERT CARDINAL, archbishop; b. Le Biot, Haute Savoie, France, Oct. 24, 1920; s. Jean and Henriette (Morand) C. Student, Petit Séminaire de Thonon Les Bains, Haute Savoie, Grand Séminaire d'Annecy, Haute Savoie; grad., Faculté de Théologie de Lyon, Rhone; Licentiate in Theology. Ordained priest Roman Cath. Ch., 1944, bishop, 1967, created cardinal, 1991. Vicar à Bernex Roman Cath. Ch., 1946-48, prof. au Petit Séminaire de Thonon les Bains, 1948-49, prof. de dogme au Grand Séminaire d'Annecy, 1949-52, supérieur du Grand Séminaire d'Annecy, 1952-67, vicaire général du diocèse d'Annecy, 1956, eveque de Gap, 1967-74, archbishop d'Albi, 1974-85, archbishop de Marseille, 1985—, cardinal, 1991—; former mem. Conseil Permanent Episcopat Francais, Paris. Author: Dieu des Athées: Theilhard de Chardin et le Socialisme, Eglise, signe de salut, Une Eglise qui cèlébre et qui prie. Home: Marseilles France Died 7/15/95.

COFIELD, HOWARD JOHN, lawyer; b. Rising Sun, Ind., July 14, 1926; s. Howard Francis and Grace Augusta (Barricklow) C.; m. Helen Adams, Sept. 4, 1949; children: Anne Cofield Clark, John Adams. BS in Bus., Ind. U., 1950, LLB, 1952. Bar: Ind. 1952, U.S. Dist. Ct. (so. dist.) Ind. 1952, U.S. Ct. Appeals (7th cir.) 1954. Assoc. Barnes Hickam Pantzer & Boyd, now Barnes & Thornburg, Indpls., 1952-60, ptnr., 1960-92, of counsel, 1993-95; bd. dirs. Ind. Energy, Inc., Indpls., Ind. Gas Co., Inc., Indpls. Editor-in-chief Ind. Law Jour., Bloomington, 1951-52. 1st lt. U.S. Army, 1944-46, ETO. Mem. ABA, Ind. Bar Assn., Indpls. Bar Assn., 7th Cir. Bar Assn., Meridian Hills Country Club (Indpls.), Lawyers Club (Indpls.), Order of Coif, Beta Gamma Sigma. Methodist. Home: Indianapolis Ind. Died Oct. 16, 1995.

COGAN, DAVID GLENDENNING, physician, educator; b. Fall River, Mass., Feb. 14, 1908; s. James Joseph and Edith (Ives) C.; m. Frances Capps, July 14, 1934; children: Christy (dec.), Frances, Ann (dec.), Priscilla. AB, Dartmouth, 1929, med. student, 1930-31; MD, Harvard, 1932; MD Moseley travelling fellow, 1937-38; DSc (hon.), Duke U., 1990, U. Ind., 1991. Intern U. Chgo. Clinics, 1931-32; resident Mass. Eye and Ear Infirmary, Boston, 1932-34, assoc. surgeon, 1943-54, surgeon, 1954-60, chief ophthalmology, 1963-68; practiced medicine Boston, 1934-73; dir. Howe Lab. Ophthalmology, Harvard, 1940-74, asso. prof. ophthalmic research, 1943-55; prof. ophthalmology Harvard Med. Sch., 1955-74, chmn. dept., 1963-68, Henry Willard Williams prof., 1963-70, emeritus, 1974-93; chief neuro-ophthalmic sect. Nat. Eye Inst., 1974-85; sr. med. officer NIH, 1985-93; Mem. council Nat. Inst. Neurologic Diseases and Blindness, Council Nat. Eye Inst., NIH; trustee Mass. Eye and Ear Infirmary. Author: Neurology of the Ocular Muscles, 1946, rev. edit., 1958, Neurology of the Visual System, 1966, Ophthalmic Manifestations of Systematic Vascular Disease, 1974; editor-in-chief: Archives of Ophthalmology, 1960-66; cons. editor, 1966-70; mem. editorial bd.: Graefes Archiv für Ophthalmologie, 1972-81. Mem. sci. coun. Rsch. to Prevent Blindness. Recipient Warren Triennial prize Mass. Gen. Hosp., 1944; Proctor award, 1954; Knapp prize A.M.A., 1955; Howe medal Am. Ophthal. Soc., 1965; Research to Prevent Blindness award, 1969; Gonin Medal, 1974; Vail award, 1976, Alexander von Humboldt Sr. Scientist award, 1987; Pisart award, 1988; Ophthalmic Pathology Labs. named in his honor Mass. Eye and Ear Infirmary, 1983; library named in his honor Nat. Eye Inst., 1985. Mem. Am. Acad. Arts and Sci., Am. Ophthal. Soc., Am. Soc. Clin. Research, Nat. Soc. Prevention Blindness (dir.); hon. mem. Can. Ophthal. Soc., Irish Ophthal. Soc., Japanese Ophthal. Soc., German Ophthal. Soc. Club: Cosmos. Home: Bethesda Md. Died Sept. 9, 1993.

COHEN, AUDREY C., college president; b. May 14; d. Abe and Esther (Morgan) C.; children: Dawn Jennifer, Winifred Alisa. BA magna cum laude, U. Pitts., 1953; postgrad. in polit. sci. and edn. George Washington U., 1957-58; DHL (hon.), U. New Eng., 1988; D of Sci. (hon.), Coll. Human Svcs., 1988. Founder, pres. Part-Time Rsch. Assocs., 1958-64; exec. dir. Women's Talent Corps., 1964-68; founder, pres. Audrey Cohen Coll (formerly Coll. Human Svcs.), N.Y.C., 1964-96; creator of new above entry level career categories Audrey Cohen Coll., 1964; participant pres. owner mgmt. program Harvard Grad. Sch. Bus. Adminstrn., 1982; lectr. in field; cons. Commn. Occupational Status Women in Nat. Vocat. Guidance Assn.; founder Am. Coun. Human Svc., 1974; key speaker X Triennial Conf. Internat. Assn. U. Pres., Kobe, Japan, 1993. Developer ednl. paradigm Purpose-Centered System of Edn., 1970-74; speaker in field; contbr. articles to profl. jours.; adv. bd. Glamour Mag.'s Woman of Yr. Awards, 1990-91. Active subcom. higher edn. N.Y.C. Partnership; chmn. Com. on Yr. 2000, N.Y. World Future Soc.; nat. adv. com. Horizons-Bicentennial Commn.; mem. planning com. Hemispheric Congress Women, Miami, Fla., 1975-76; chairperson Nat. Task Force on Women, Edn. and Work, 1975; active Manhattan Borough Pres.'s Adv. Com. on Health Careers for Disadvantaged, Pub. Edn. Assn. Project for Restructured Edn. System N.Y.C.; mem. exec. com. Assn. Better N.Y. Recipient Stanley M. Isaacs award Am. Jewish Com., 1959, George Champion award Chase Manhattan Bank, 1970, Disting. Vis. prof. award U. Mass., 1975, Ednl. Devel. Cert. of Achievement award Atlantic Richfield Co., 1979; Otty award Our Town newspaper, 1981; Mina Shaughnessy scholarship award U.S. Office Edn., 1983; Empire State award, 1984-85; Outstanding Leadership in Higher Edn. award Commn. Ind. Colls. and Univs., 1984-85; Giraffe Club award, 1989; Pres.'s award Nat. Orgn. Human Svcs. Edn., 1993; Anti-bias award Nat. Westminister Bancorp and N.Y.C. Job and Career Ctr., 1993; named in a Commending Resolution N.Y. State Legis., 1994. Mem. Support Services Alliance, Inc. (bd. dirs.), Fin. Women's Assn., Am. Jewish Com. (exec. com., bd. dirs.), Council Higher Ednl. Instns. Clubs: Economic, Harvard, Lotos, Women's Forum. Died Mar. 10, 1996. Home: New York N.Y.

COHEN, IRA STANLEY, psychologist, educator, association administrator; b. N.Y.C., Sept. 1, 1922; s. Herbert H. and Minnie (Raden) C.; m. M. Carolta Baca, June 16, 1984; children: Rachel, Sarah. BA, Queens Coll., 1948; PhD, Ind. U., 1953. Asst. prof. psychology SUNY, Buffalo, 1952-58, assoc. prof., 1958-63, prof., 1963-85, prof. emeritus, 1985-92; acting provost Faculty Social Scis. and Adminstrn., 1968-69, provost, 1969-71, chmn. psychology dept., 1978-80; dir. ednl. affairs APA, Washington, 1987-90, ednl. cons. in psychology, 1990-92; vis. prof. psychiatry Harvard U., 1972-73. With AUS, 1942-46. Mem. AAUP, APA, Eastern Psychol. Assn. Home: Santa Fe N. Mex. Died Dec. 2, 1992; buried Nat. Cemetery, Santa Fe, N. Mex.

COHEN, ISRAEL, chain store executive; b. 1912; married. With Giant Food Inc., Landover, Md., 1935-95, exec. v.p., 1974-75, exec. v.p., chief operating officer, from 1975, pres., chief exec. officer, chmn. bd., dir. Home: Landover Md. Died Nov., 1995.

COHEN, PHILIP PACY, biochemist, educator; b. Derry, N.H., Sept. 26, 1908; s. David Harris and Ada (Cottler) C.; m. Rubye Herzfeld Tepper, June 15, 1935; children: Philip T., David B., Julie A., Milton T. B.S., Tufts Coll., 1930; Ph.D., U. Wis., 1937, M.D., 1938; D.Sc. (hon.), U. Mex., 1979. NRC fellow Sheffield, Eng., 1938-39; NRC fellow Yale, 1939-40, instr., 1940-41; intern Wis. Gen. Hosp., 1941-42; asst. prof. clin. biochemistry U. Wis., 1942-45, asso. prof. physiol. chemistry, 1945-47, prof., 1947-92, chmn. dept. physiol. chemistry, 1948-75, H.C. Bradley prof., 1968-92; acting dean U. Wis. (Med. Sch.), 1961-63; Chmn. com. on growth, mem. exec. com. div. med. scis. NRC, 1954-56; bd. sci. counselors Nat. Cancer Inst., 1957-59, chmn., 1959-61; mem. physiol. chemistry study sect. NIH, 1959-62, nat. adv. cancer council, 1963-67, mem. adv. com. to dir., 1966-70. Mem. Nat. Adv. Arthritis and Metabolic Disease Council, 1970-74; adv. com. biology and medicine AEC, 1963-71; mem. adv. com. on med. research Pan Am. Health Orgn., 1967-75; mem. Nat. Commn. on Research, 1978-80; hon. mem. Med. Sch. Faculty, U. Chile. Commonwealth Fund fellow Oxford U., Eng., 1958. Fellow A.A.A.S.; mem. Nat. Acad. Scis., Am. Soc. Biol. Chemists (treas. 1951-56), Am. Chem. Soc., Biochem. Soc. (Eng.)., Sigma Xi; hon. mem. Harvey Soc., Chiba Med. Soc. (Japan), Argentina Biochem. Soc., Nat. Acad. Med. (Mex.), Japanese Biochem. Soc. Home: Madison Wis. Died Oct. 25, 1992.

COHEN, STEPHEN HOWARD, lawyer; b. Phila., Nov. 22, 1938; s. Joseph Allen and Sylvia (Bellak) C.; m. Ann Rothman, Sept. 2, 1962; children: Lynn Marcia, Sandra Jean. AB cum laude, U. Wis., 1960; LLB cum laude, Harvard U., 1963. Bar: Ill. 1963, Minn. 1970. Assoc. Lord, Bissell and Brook, Chgo., 1963-70; ptnr. Robins, Kaplan, Miller & Ciresi and predecessor, Mpls., 1970-89, McElroy, Deutsch & Mulvaney, Morristowr N.J., 1989—. Author: Religion and the Schools, 197 contbr. articles to various legal publs.; lectr. and speake various ins. and environ. issues. Chmn. Religion an the Schools Com., St. Louis Pk., Minn., 1974. Mem ABA, Hennepin County, Ill. and Chgo. bar assns. Home: Morristown N.J. Deceased.

COHEN, WALLACE M., retired lawyer; b. Norto Va., July 11, 1908; s. Jacob Edward and Annie (Hyma C.; m. Sylvia J. Stone, Sept. 7, 1932; children: Anne F (Mrs. Steven A. Winkelman), Edward S., Davi W. Grad., Lake Forest Acad., 1925; SB, Harvard U 1929; postgrad., Law Sch., 1930-31; Cornell Law Sch 1931-32. Bar: Mass. 1933, Md. 1952, D.C. 1946, U.S Supreme Ct. 1946. Assoc. Fox, Orlov & Cowin, Bostor 1932-38; mem. staff NLRB, Dept. Labor, Shipbldg Stablzn. Commn., Adv. Commn. Council Nat. Def OPA, Lend Lease Adminstrn., Fgn. Econ. Adminstrn 1938-45; dep. administrv. asst. to Pres.; ptnr. Landis Cohen, Rauh & Zelenko, Washington, 1951-90; Forme mem. adv. bd. Clinch Valley Coll. of U. Va.; Fellow Brandeis U. Served with USCGR, 1943-45. Mem ABA, Fed. Bar Assn., D.C. Bar Assn., Mass. Bar Assn Md. Bar Assn., Fed. Communications Bar Assn Harvard Club, Nat. Press Club. Home: Washingto D.C. Deceased.

COHN, HASKELL, lawyer; b. Concord, N.H., Dec. 4 1901; s. Abraham I. and Miriam (Caro) C.; m. Harrie Segal, Mar. 27, 1928; children: Marjorie (Mrs. Willian H. Wolf), Susan (Mrs. David A. Bensinger). A.E magna cum laude, Dartmouth Coll., 1922; LL.B Harvard U., 1925. Bar: Mass. 1926, D.C. 1972. Prac ticed in Boston; sr. partner firm Mintz, Levin, Cohr Ferris, Glovsky & Popeo (and predecessors), 1933-93. Author articles on taxation. Bd. dirs. Greater Bosto YMCA, 1956-71. Recipient Alumni award Dartmout Coll., 1977. Fellow Am. Bar Found., Am. Coll. Trus and Estate Counsel, Am. Coll. Tax Counsel; mem. AB (vice chmn. estate and gift tax com. of tax sect. 1966-6 ho. of dels. 1968-79, com. on specialization 1975-8 task force on lawyer competence 1981-83, consortium o lawyer competency 1983), Nat Conf. Chief Justice (mem. coordinating council), Mass. Bar Assn. (bd. del 1969-71), Boston Bar Assn. (chmn. family law 1959-6 pres. 1969-71), Am. Law Inst. (com. on revision esta and gift taxes 1964-67, joint com. continuing profl. edr 1965-93, chmn. adv. com. peer rev. 1978-80, chmn. pe rev. inst., co-chmn. com. on law practice evaluatio project, Svc. award 1988), Harvard Law Sch. Assn. (re gional v.p., mem. council 1966-70), Boston Bar Found (pres. 1969-74, Pub. Svc. award 1988), Dartmout Alumni Assn. (pres. Boston 1954), Phi Beta Kappa. Clubs: Harvard (Boston and N.Y.C.); Union, Curtis The Law; The Country (Brookline, Mass.). Home Westwood Mass. Died July 4, 1993.

COHN, RONALD DENNIS, lawyer; b. Chgo., Oct. 2 1942; s. Victor and Bette (Green) C.; m. Bobbi Sherman June 7, 1964; children: David E., Jonathan B. BSEE U. Ill., 1965, postgrad. in law, 1965-66; JD, Georg Washington U., 1969. Bar: D.C. 1969. Patent examine U.S. Patent and Trademark Office, Washington, 1965 66; patent atty. Johns Hopkins U., Balt., 1966-6 Stevens, Davis, Miller & Mosher, 1968-69; patent atty Fleit Gipple & Jacobson (now Fleit Jacobson Coh Price Holman & Stern), Washington, 1969-71, ptnr. 1972-92; ptnr. Keck, Mahin & Cate, Washington, 1992 94. Mem. ABA, IEEE (patent editor Engring. i Medicine and Biology 1985-94), Patent and Tradema Inst. Can., Am. Intellectual Property Law Assn., D.C Bar Assn. Home: Potomac Md. Died Oct. 30, 1994.

COHN, ZANVIL ALEXANDER, scientist, educato physician; b. N.Y.C., Nov. 16, 1926; s. David an Esther (Schwartz) C.; m. Fern R. Dworkin, Dec. 1 1948; children: David, Ellen. BS, Bates Coll., 194 DSc (hon.), 1987; MD summa cum laude, Harvard U 1953; MA (hon.), Oxford U., Eng., 1988; Dr honori causa, Rijksuniversiteit, Leiden, The Netherlands, 1990. Intern, asst. resident Mass. Gen. Hosp., Boston; chie div. rickettsial biology Walter Reed Army Hosp Washington, 1955-57; assoc. prof. Rockefeller Inst N.Y.C., 1958-66; prof., sr. physician dept. cellula physiology and immunology, Rockefeller U., N.Y.C 1966-93; v.p. med. affairs Rockefeller U., 1992; co-di M.D./Ph.D. joint program Rockefeller U. and Corne U. Med. Coll., N.Y.C., 1973-78; adj. prof. medicin Cornell U. Med. Coll., N.Y.C., 1977-93; mem. comm on radiation and infection Armed Forces Epidemiolog Bd.; mem. study sect. on immunology NIH; cons. Na Cancer Inst.; Harvey Soc. lectr., 1982. Recipient Boyl ston medal Harvard U., 1961, Basic Sci. award Am Soc. for Cytology, 1970; 5th Ann. Squibb award Infec tious Diseases Soc. Am., 1972, Joseph E. Smadel award 1990; award NAS, 1975, 7th Ann. Rsch. award Samue Noble Found., 1982, Ciba-Geigy award, Barcelona Spain, 1990. Home: New York N.Y. Died June 28 1993.

COLBERT, CLAUDETTE (LILY CHAUCHOIN) actress; b. Paris, Sept. 13, 1903; came to U.S.; d. Ge orges and Jeanne (Loew) Chauchoin; m. Norma Foster, Mar. 13, 1928 (div. 1935); m. Joel Pressman 1935 (dec. 1968). Grad., Washington Irving High Sch. 1920. Debut as Sibyl Blake in Wild Westcotts, Fraze Theatre, 1923; later appeared in plays including Th

Marionette Man, Leah Kleschna, High Stakes, The Kiss in a Taxi, The Ghost Train, Pearl of Great Price, Tin Pan Alley, See Naples and Die, Eugene O'Neill's Dynamo, A Talent for Murder; 1st appearance in London in the Barker, 1928; appeared in motion pictures, 1929—, including: The Lady Lies, Manslaughter, The Smiling Lieutenant, Sign of the Cross, Cleopatra, Private Worlds, Maid of Salem, It Happened One Night, The Gilded Lily, I Met Him in Paris, Bluebeard's Eighth Wife, Zaza Midnight, Drums Along the Mohawk, Skylark, Remember the Day, Palm Beach Story, No Time for Love, So Proudly We Hail, Parrish, Since You Went Away, Three Came Home, Bride for Sale, Arise My Love, Sleep My Love; starred in Broadway plays: Marriage-Go-Round, 1958-60, The Irregular Verb To Love, 1963, The Kingfisher, 1978; tour A Community of Two, 1973-74, Chgo. performances Marriage-Go-Round, 1976; appeared in Aren't We All at Theatre Royal Haymarket, London, 1984, N.Y., 1985. Appeared in TV spls. Best of Broadway, Including Royal Family, The Guardsman, Blythe Spirit, Private Worlds, 1954-56, The Kingfisher, N.Y. and tour, 1981-82 (Sarah Siddons best actress award, Chgo.). Recipient Oscar award for best actress Nat. Acad. Motion Picture Arts and Scis., 1934; Rose award, N.Y.C., 1983, Lincoln Ctr. honor, 1985, Goldlen Globe award, 1987; officier Legion of Honor, 1988, recipient Life Achievement award Kennedy Ctr. for Performing Arts, 1989, Kennedy Ctr. Honors award, 1989. Home: Saint Peter Barbados

COLBERT, LESTER LUM, investor, lawyer, former automobile executive; b. Oakwood, Tex., June 13, 1905; s. Lum and Sallie (Driver) C.; m. Daisy Gorman, Nov. 23, 1928 (dec. Aug. 1970); children—Lester Lum, Sarah Colbert Noble, Nicholas; m. Robert Ellen Hoke, Oct. 5, 1972. B.B.A., Tex. U., 1925; J.D., Harvard U., 1929; LL.D., Bethany Coll., 1954. Buyer cotton Tex., 1921-29; atty. Larkin, Rathbone & Perry, N.Y.C., 1929-33; with Chrysler Corp., 1933-65, mem. operation com., 1933-61, resident atty., 1933-42, v.p. Dodge div., 1935-45, operating mgr. Dodge Chgo. plant, 1942, gen. mgr. Dodge Chgo. plant, 1943-46, pres. Dodge div., 1946-51, v.p., 1949-50, pres., 1950-61, chmn., 1960-61; chmn. bd., dir. Chrysler Corp. of Can., Ltd., 1961-65; trustee Hanover Bank, N.Y.C., 1955-61. Chmn. United Found., Detroit, 1959-60, dir., 1951-62; mem. Nat. Indsl. Conf. Bd., 1958-61; trustee Automotive Safety Found., 1955-61, Com. for Econ. Devel., 1956-61; dir. devel. bd. U. Tex., 1958-95; overseers com. to visit Harvard Law Sch., 1952-58. Decorated chevalier Legion of Honor France, 1959; Texan of Distinction award, 1953; recipient Brother-hood award NCCJ, 1957; award Am. Soc. Tool Engrs., 1958; Distinguished Alumnus award U. Tex., Austin, 1977. Mem. Am. Ordnance Assn. (life), Automobile Old Timers (life), Am., Automobile Mfrs. Assn. (pres. 1958-61), Beta Gamma Sigma. Methodist. Clubs: Royal Poinciana, Naples Yacht, Naples Athletic (pres. 1987), Harvard (Naples, Fla.). Home: Naples Fla. Died Sept. 15, 1995.

COLBY, KENNETH POOLE, insurance company executive; b. Keene, N.H., June 21, 1908; s. Everett Nahum and Grace (Poole) C.; m. Bernece Esther Wilson, July 17, 1933 (dec. Sept. 1990); 1 son, Kenneth P. Student, Clark U., 1927-30. With Nat. Grange Mut. Ins. Co., Keene, 1930-95; successively claims adjuster and underwriter, agy. dir., exec. in charge casualty underwriting Nat. Grange Mut. Ins. Co., 1930-55, v.p., 1955-63, dir., exec. com., 1957-95, exec. v.p., 1963-66, pres., 1966-72, chief exec., 1966-73, chmn. bd., 1972-82, hon. chmn. bd., dir., mem. exec., fin. and compensation cons., 1982-95; past pres., trustee Keene Savs. Bank.; Past dir. Am. Mut. Ins. Alliance, Nat. Assn. of Mut. Ins. Cos.; past chmn. bd. dirs. N.H. Ins. Guaranty Assn. Del. N.H. Constl. Conv., 1974-95; mem. assembly overseers Mary Hitchcock Hosp., 1974-95; former pres., dir. Cheshire Sr. Svcs. Inc. Mem. SAR, Nat. Grange, Odd Fellow. Home: Keene N.H. Died Feb. 25, 1995.

COLBY, WILLIAM EGAN, lawyer, international consultant; b. St. Paul, Jan. 4, 1920; s. Elbridge and Margaret (Egan) C.; m. Barbara Heinzen, Sept. 15, 1945 (div. Nov. 1984); children: Jonathan, Catherine (dec.), Carl, Paul, Christine; m. Sally Shelton, Nov. 20, 1984. BA, Princeton U., 1940; LLB, Columbia U., 1947; D in Pub. Svc. (hon.), Norwich U., 1992. Bar: N.Y. 1947, D.C. 1976. Atty. Donovan Leisure Newton & Irvine, N.Y.C., 1947-49; counsel Donovan Leisure Newton & Irvine, Washington, 1987-96; with NLRB, Washington, 1949-50; attaché Am. Embassy, Stockholm, 1951-53, Rome, 1953-58; 1st sec. Am. Embassy, Saigon, Vietnam, 1959-62; chief Far East div. CIA, Washington, 1963-68, exec. dir., 1972-73, dep. dir. ops., 1973, dir., 1973-76; pvt. practice legal and internat. cons. Washington, 1978-96; editor Colby Report for Internat. Bus., 1994-96; amb., dir. Civil Ops. and Rural Devel. Support, Saigon, 1968-71. Author: Honorable Men-My Life in the CIA, 1978, Lost Victory, 1989. Maj. AUS, 1941-45. Decorated Silver Star, Bronze Star; St. Olaf's medal Norway; Croix de Guerre France; Nat. Order Vietnam; mentioned in dispatches Britain; recipient Nat. Security medal; Disting. Honor award Dept. State; Disting. Intelligence medal; Intelligence medal of Merit; Career Intelligence medal CIA. Mem. Coun. Fgn. Rels., Washington Inst. Fgn. Affairs, Cosmos Club, Princeton Club N.Y.C., Spl. Forces Club (London), Linge Klubben (Oslo), Phi Beta Kappa. Home: Washington D.C. Died Apr. 27, 1996.

COLE, JOSEPH EDMUND, specialty retail company executive; b. Cleve., Jan. 4, 1915; s. Solomon and Sarah (Miller) C.; m. Marcia Newman, Oct. 31, 1937; children: Jeffrey, Stephan. Student, Ohio State U., 1932, Fenn Coll., Cleve., 1933. Salesman Waldorf Brewing Co., 1933-35; office mgr., then gen. mgr. Nat. Key Shops, Inc., 1935-44; partner, sales dir. Curtis Industries, 1944-50; pres., chmn., sr. chmn. Cole Nat. Corp., Cleve., 1950-95; past chmn. Shelter Resources Corp.; past dir. BancOhio Nat. Bank, Cleve. Past pub. The Cleveland Press. Active Jewish Welfare Fund, Cleve., 1963-64; Chmn. Ohio Citizens for Kennedy, 1960; chmn. Hubert Humphrey for Pres., 1972; mem. Cuyahoga County Democratic Exec. Com., 1960-95; chmn. finance com. Dem. Nat. Com., 1973-74; Bd. dirs. Jewish Community Fedn., Cleve., Notre Dame Coll., Playhouse Sq. Found., Cleve., Palm Beach Ctr. for the Performing Arts, Fla.; past trustee Cleve. State U.; past chmn. scholarship fund Ohio State Coll.; life mem. Brandeis U. Mem. Cleve. C. of C. Jewish (trustee temple). Clubs: Masons, (32 deg.), Shriners, Oakwood Country City (Cleve.); Standard (Chgo.); Palm Beach (Fla.) Country. Home: Cleveland Ohio Died Jan. 7, 1995.

COLE-BEUGLET, CATHERINE MARIE, radiology educator; b. Windsor, Ont., Can.; came to U.S., 1962; d. John McKay Cole and Mary Electa Downey; m. Charles Paul Beuglet, May 29, 1973; 1 child, Charles Cole. BS, U. Western Ont., London, 1958, MD, 1962. Diplomate Am. Bd. Radiology. Asst. prof. radiology McGill U., Montreal, Que., Can., 1970-75; asst. prof. U. Wash., Seattle, 1975-76; assoc. prof. Thomas Jefferson U., Phila., 1978-82, prof., 1982-85; prof. U. Calif. Irvine, Orange, from 1985. Mem. editorial bd. Jour. Health Care Tech.; jour. reviewer Jour. Am. Med. Assn., Jour. Clin. Ultrasound, Jour. Ultrasound in Medicine, Roentgen Ray Jour.; contbr. articles to profl. jours. Fellow Am. Coll. Radiology, Royal Coll. Physicians and Surgeons of Can., Am. Inst. Ultrasound Medicine; mem. AMA, Am. Roentgen Ray Soc., Can. Assn. Radiologists, Radiological Soc. North Am. (editorial bd. jour. from 1980), Assn. Univ. Radiologists, Breast Imaging Soc., Soc. Study of Breast Disease. Home: Newport Beach Calif. Deceased.

COLEMAN, CLARENCE WILLIAM, banker; b. Wichita, Kans., Mar. 24, 1909; s. William Coffin and Fanny Lucinda (Sheldon) C.; m. Emry Regester Ingham, Oct. 2, 1935; children: Rochelle, Pamela, Kathryn Sheldon. Student, U. Kans., 1928-32; DHL, Friends U.; D. Laws, Ottawa U. With Coleman Co., Inc., Wichita, 1932-89; v.p. charge mfg. Coleman Co., Inc., 1944; bd. dirs.; dir. Coleman Co., Inc., 1935-89, asst. gen. mgr., 1951-54; pres. Union Nat. Bank, Wichita, 1957-72; vice chmn. bd. Union Nat. Bank, 1972-90; chmn. bd. dirs. Cherry Creek Inn, Inc., Denver, 1961-69, Kans. Devel. Credit Corp. Bd. dirs. Inst. Logopedics, 1940-74, chmn. bd., 1947-48; bd. dirs. Wichita Symphony Soc.; trustee Wichita Symphony Soc. Found.; bd. dirs. Found. for Study of Cycles, Irvine, Calif., chmn., 1988; bd. dirs. Wichita Mental Health Assn., 1956-74, United Fund Wichita and Sedgewick County, 1957-74, Friends U., 1956-74; bd. dirs. Wichita Crime Commn., 1953-74, pres., 1958; mem. Nat. Budget Com., 1952; chmn. State Mental Health Fund Kans., 1953; trustee Peddie Sch., Hightstown, N.J., chmn. bd. trustees, 1972-76, chmn. emeritus, 1981-92. Mem. Mid-Ark. Valley Devel. Assn. (treas.), Wichita C. of C. (pres. 1956, dir. 1947-74), Rotary, Phi Kappa Psi. Home: Wichita Kans. Died Dec. 13, 1992.

COLEMAN, JAMES SAMUEL, sociologist, educator; b. Bedford, Ind., May 12, 1926; s. James Fox and Maurine (Lappin) C.; m. Lucille Richey, Feb. 5, 1949 (div. Aug. 1973); children: Thomas Sedgwick, John Samuel, James Stephen.; m. Zdzislawa Walaszek, 1973; 1 son, Daniel Wlodzimierz. Student, Emory and Henry Coll., 1944-46; BS, Purdue U., 1949; PhD, Columbia U., 1955; hon. degree, Purdue U., SUNY, Hebrew U. Jerusalem, U. So. Calif., Free U. Brussels, U. Erlangen-Nuremberg, Marquette U., Haifa U., U. Notre Dame. Research asso. Bur. Applied Social Research, Columbia U., 1953-55; fellow Center Advanced Study Behavorial Scis., Palo Alto, Calif., 1955-56; asst. prof. sociology U. Chgo., 1956-59, prof., 1973-95; from assoc. prof. to prof. social relations Johns Hopkins U., 1959-73; mem. Pres.'s sci. adv. com., 1970-72, sci. adv. com. Gen. Motors, 1972-83; hon. prof. U. Vienna. Author: (with Lipset, Trow) Union Democracy, 1956, Community Conflict, 1957, The Adolescent Society, 1961, Introduction to Mathematical Sociology, 1964, Models of Change and Response Uncertainty, 1964, Adolescents and the Schools, 1965, (with others) Equality of Education Opportunity, 1966, Medical Innovation, 1967, Resources for Social Change, 1972, Mathematics of Collective Action, 1973, Power and the Structure of Society, 1973, (with others) Youth: Transition to Adulthood, 1973, Longitudinal Data Analysis, 1981, (with others) High School Achievement, 1982, The Asymmetric Society, 1982; Individual Interests and Collective Action, 1986; (with Hoffer) Public and Private High Schools: The Impact of Communities, 1987, Foundations of Social Theory, 1990, Equality and Achievement in Education, 1990. Guggenheim fellow, 1966-67; fellow Wizzenschaftskolleg Berlin, 1981-82; fellow Russell Sage Found., 1982; Fulbright sr. scholar European Univ. Inst., 1993. Mem. NAS, Nat. Acad. Edn., Am. Acad. Arts and Scis., Royal Acad. Scis. Sweden, Polish Sociol. Assn., Am. Philos. Soc. Home: Chicago Ill. Died March, 1995.

COLEMAN, JAMES SMOOT, political science educator; b. Provo, Utah, Feb. 4, 1919; s. Jacob and Allie (Smoot) C.; m. Margaret Tate, Feb. 4, 1944; children: James S. Jr., Robert L.; m. 2d, Ursula Maria Finken, June 20, 1965. B.A., Brigham Young U., 1947; M.A., Harvard U., 1948, Ph.D., 1953. Teaching fellow Harvard U., 1949-50, 53; from instr. to prof. polit. sci. UCLA, 1953-65, dir. African Studies Ctr., 1960-65; rep. Rockfeller Found. in East Africa and Zaire, 1967-78; prof. polit. sci., chmn. council internat., comparative studies UCLA, from 1978; cons. Rockefeller Found. Served to lt. col. U.S. Army, 1941-46. Decorated M.B.E. (Brit. Commonwealth); recipient Woodrow Wilson Found. award Am. Polit. Sci. Assn., 1959; Ctr. Advanced Study Behavioral Scis. fellow, 1963-64; grantee Carnegie Corp., Ford Found., Rockefeller Found. Fellow Am. Acad. Arts and Scis.; mem. Am. Polit. Sci. Assn., Council Fgn. Relations N.Y.C., Internat. Studies Assn., Comparative and Internat. Edn. Soc. Democrat. Unitarian. Club: Harvard (N.Y.C.). Author: Nigeria: Background to Nationalism, 1958; co-editor/co-author: The Politics of the Developing Areas, 1960; Political Parties and National Integration in Tropical Africa, 1964; Government and Rural Development in East Africa, 1977; Social Science and Public Policy in the Developing World, 1981; editor and co-author Education and Political Development, 1971. Deceased. Home: Los Angeles Calif.

COLEN, DONALD JEROME, public affairs specialist, writer; b. N.Y.C., Apr. 9, 1917; s. Bernard Daniel and Beth (Shere) C.; m. Marcia Elizabeth Sufrin, Apr. 17, 1943; 1 son, Bernard Daniel. B.S. cum laude, Harvard U., 1938; M.S. in Engring, 1942. Public issues analyst Gen. Electric Co., 1955-60; v.p. Ruder & Finn, N.Y.C., 1960-65; v.p. public affairs Citibank (N.A.), N.Y.C., 1965-80; pub. affairs cons., writer, 1980-94. Author: The Money Movers, 1978, The ABC's of Armageddon, 1988. Served with USNR, 1943-46. Democrat. Club: Harvard of N.Y. Home: Chapel Hill N.C. Died Dec. 10, 1994.

COLES, (CHARLES) HONI, tap dancer; b. Phila., 1911. Studied with, Bill (Bojangles) Robinson, John W. Bubbles. guest lectr., tchr. various colls. and univs.; former prodn. mgr. Apollo Theatre, N.Y.C. Toured with Miller Bros., Lucky Seven Trio; performed with numerous big bands including Cab Calloway, Count Basie, Fats Waller; Broadway shows include Gentlemen Prefer Blondes, 1949, My One and Only, 1983 (Tony award Best Actor in Mus.); mem. nat. touring co. Bubbling Brown Sugar, My One and Only; film appearances include The Cotton Club, 1989; regional prodns. includ Kiss Me Kate, Girl Crazy, Melody Fair; performances include Carnegie Hall, Newport Jazz Festival, Joffrey Ballet; TV appearances includ The Tap Dance Kid. Home: Elmhurst N.Y. Died 1993.

COLLADO, EMILIO GABRIEL, energy company executive, consultant; b. Cranford, N.J., Dec. 20, 1910; s. Emilio Gabriel and Carrie (Hansee) C.; m. Janet Gilbert, June 30, 1932 (dec.); children: Emilio Gabriel, Lisa; m. Maria Elvira Tanco, Oct. 6, 1972. Student, Phillips Acad., Andover, Mass., 1925-27; S.B., Mass. Inst. Tech., 1931; A.M., Harvard, 1934, Ph.D., 1936. With printing and pub. firm, 1931; econ. analyst U.S. Treasury Dept., 1934-36; economist Fed. Res. Bank N.Y., 1936-38; with Dept. State, 1938-46; asst. chief div. Am. Republics, 1940, spl. asst. to under sec. state, 1941-44; exec. sec. Bd. Econ. Operations, 1941-43, asso. adviser internat. econ. affairs, 1943-44, chief div. financial and monetary affairs, 1944-45; dir. Office Fin. and Devel. Policy, also dep. to asst. sec. for econ. affairs, 1945-46; U.S. exec. dir. Internat. Bank for Reconstrn. and Devel., 1946-47; trustee Export-Import Bank, Washington, 1944-45; with Exxon Corp., 1947-75, asst. treas., 1949-54, treas., 1954-60, dir., 1960-75, v.p., 1962-66, exec. v.p., 1966-75; pres., chief exec. officer Adela Investment Co. S.A., 1976-79; also dir.; chmn., chief exec. officer, dir. Grace Geothermal Corp., 1981-84, dir., cons., 1984-95; chmn., dir. Internat. Planning Corp., 1981-84; mem. adv. coun. Morgan Guranty Trust Co., N.Y., U.S. alt. mem. Inter-Am. Fin. and Econ. Adv. Com., former chmn. OECD, mem. bus. and industry adv. com. U.S. Army; past vice chmn. Atlantic Coun. U.S.; bd. dirs. J.P. Morgan & Co. Former chmn. vis. com. Sch. Pub. Health, Harvard U.; bd. visitors Fletcher Sch. Internat. Diplomacy; trustee, chmn. Com. Econ. Devel., 1972-75; trustee Hispanic Soc.; past chmn. Ctr. for Inter-Am. Relations; bd. dirs. emeritus Ams. Soc., Work in Am. Inst.; bd. govs., exec. com. Atlantic Inst. Internat. Affairs. Mem. USA/BIAC (bus. and industry adv. com.), OECD (former chmn.), PGA, Am. Acad. arts and Scis., Am. Econ. Assn., Internat. C. of C. (mem. exec. com. U.S. coun. internat. bus.), Atlantic Coun. U.S. (past vice chmn.), Acad. Polit. Sci. (past chmn.), Met. Club (Washington), Piping Rock Club (Locust Valley), Nat. Golf and Sports Club (Palm Beach Gardens), Phi Mu Delta. Home: Palm Bch Gdns Fla. Died Feb. 9, 1995.

COLLEDGE, CHARLES HOPSON, broadcasting consultant; b. Paterson, N.J., June 3, 1911; s. William Arthur and Mary (Hopson) C.; m. Margaret Whittaker, Sept. 2, 1931; children: Charles Edmund, William Arthur. Student, Newark Coll. Engring., Mass. Inst. Tech., Columbia U. Registered profl. engr., D.C. Engr. NBC, 1933-43; supr. TV operations NBC, Washington, 1947-49; dir. color operations RCA Labs., 1949-50; chief engr. NBC, Washington, 1950-52; dir. spl. events, news operations NBC-TV network, 1952-53; dir. operations and engring. NBC-TV network (NBC owned stas.), 1953-56, v.p. operations, 1956-59; gen. mgr. broadcasting and TV equipment div. RCA, 1959-60, v.p., gen. mgr., broadcast and TV equipment div., 1960-61; v.p., gen. mgr. RCA (Broadcast & Communications Products div.), 1961-68; mgmt. and engring. cons., 1968-93. Served from lt. (j.g.) to comdr. USNR, 1943-47. Mem. Nat. Soc. Profl. Engrs., TV Pioneers, Quarter Century Wireless Assn., Elks. Clubs: Radio Amateur Old Old Timers; Talbot Country (Easton, Md.); Poplar Island Yacht; Seven Rivers Country (Crystal River, Fla.). Lodge: Masons, Elks. Home: Bozman Md. Died Feb. 13, 1993.

COLLEY, NATHANIEL SEXTUS, lawyer; b. Carlowsville, Ala., Nov. 21, 1918; s. Lou Daniel and Fannie F. (Jones) C.; m. Jerlean J. Jackson, May 16, 1942; children: Jerlean E. (Mrs. Jack L. Daniel), Ola Marie (Mrs. Alfred O. Brown), Natalie S. (Mrs. Gary P. Lindsey), Sondra A., Nathaniel Sextus. BS, Tuskegee Inst., 1941; JD, Yale U., 1948; LLD (hon.), Calif. State U., Sacramento, 1988, U. of Pacific, 1989, Tuskegee U., 1991. Bar: Calif. 1949. Practiced in Sacramento.; ptnr. Colley, Lindsey & Colley; lectr. Calif. Continuing Edn. of Bar; adj. prof. McGeorge Sch. Law, U. of Pacific. Assoc. editor: Calif. Trial Lawyers Jour, 1967-74; Contbr. articles to profl. jours. Mem. Calif. Bd. Edn., 1960-63; mem. Pres.'s Commn. on Discrimination in U.S. Armed Services, 1961-63; bd. dirs. Calif. Jour., Charles F. Kettering Found., Dayton, Ohio; trustee Tuskegee Inst., Tuskegee U.; chmn. Calif. Horse Racing Bd., 1976-83; bd. dirs. Sacramento Regional Found.; bd. dirs. Sacramento Regional Found., chmn. spl. contbn. bd. NAACP. Served to capt. AUS, World War II, PTO. Recipient Civil Rights award Nat. Med. Assn., 1985, Equal Justice award Nat. Bar Assn., 1987; named Sacramento Man of Yr., 1981; named to Nat. Bar Assn. Hall of Fame, 1991; Nathaniel S. Colley Sr. Day declared by Sacramento County Bd. Suprs., 1991. Mem. ABA, ATLA, Calif. Bar Assn., Sacramento County Bar Assn. (Humanitarian award 1992), Am. Bd. Trial Advocates, Calif. Trial Lawyers Assn., Yale Law Sch. Assn. (exec. com.), Calif. Jud. Coun. Club: Sporgents. Home: Sacramento Calif. Died May 20, 1992; buried Veterans Cemetery, Sacramento, Calif.

COLLIER, FELTON MORELAND, architect, planner, developer, detention, and recreation consultant, lecturer; b. Bessemer, Ala., Mar. 20, 1924; s. Felton and Grace (Moreland) C.; m. Elizabeth Pettus Buck, Oct. 22, 1955 (dec. June 1966); children: Felton Moreland, Marcus Ashby Moreland. Student, Birmingham-So. Coll., 1942-43, Howard Coll. (now Samford U.), 1943; B.A., U. N.C., 1945; postgrad., N.C. State U., 1948-50; B.Arch., Auburn U., 1954; cert., Nat. War Coll. (name now Nat. Def. Coll.), 1963; certificate, Naval War Coll., 1964, Armed Forces Staff Coll., 1966. Archtl. experience with firms in Birmingham, Ala. and Durham, N.C., 1949-51, 54-57; architect Felton Moreland Collier, Birmingham, 1958-94, Felton Moreland Collier and Carroll C. Harmon (Asso. Architects), Birmingham, 1965-94; chmn. bd. Harmon, Collier, Bondurant Assos., Inc., Architects/Planners/Designers, 1977-84, Harmon, Collier Assocs., Inc., 1984-94; chmn. bd. Regent Townhomes, Inc., 1979-84; ptnr. Collier-Traylor Properties, 1985-87; propr. Collier Properties, 1987-94; owner-developer Dorchester Place; chief lectr. Naval Res. Officers Sch., Birmingham, 1957-69; mem. U.S. cultural exch. del. architects to Russia, 1972. Prin. works include McAlpine Community Ctr., new campus Daniel Payne Coll., Spain Park, Birmingham Zoo 10 year master plan, entrance bldg. and children's zoo, Bro. Bryan Park, Episc. Cathedral Ch. of Advent Parish House, U. Ala. Diabetes Hosp., (assoc. with Carroll C. Harmon), all Birmingham, Jefferson County Youth Detention Ctr., other recreational, ednl., med. and comml. projects; lit. editor Ala. Architect, 1969-70; editor: AIA/DATA, 1976-79; contbr. articles to recreational and archtl. jours.; surveyor Caribbean recreational facilities, 1969, 72, 79, 92; photographer ancient Greek monuments, architecture, Greece, Agean Islands, Crete, Malta, 1974. Democratic primary candidate Ala. Ho. Reps., 1970; bd. dirs. Ala. Zool. Soc., 1975-78, Advent Episcopal Day Sch., 1977-86; pub. mem. U.ALA.-Birmingham Univ. Coll. Senate, 1977-78, 79-80; v.p. Redmont Neighborhood Assn., Birmingham, 1984-86; mem. Birmingham Zoning Bd. Adjustment, 1977-88, chmn. 1987-88. Served with USNR, 1945-46, PTO, ETO; to lt. 1951-53, Korea; lt. comdr. Res. Recipient Regional Merit award A.I.A., 1962, Honor award Birmingham chpt. A.I.A., 1965, 81. Mem. Explorers Club, Newcomen Soc., English Speaking Union, Alpha Tau Omega. Episcopalian (lay reader, vestryman 1969-71, 75-77, 81-83, parish architect 1977-85). Home: Birmingham Ala. Died Dec. 19, 1994.

COLLIER, GAYLAN JANE, drama educator; b. Fluvanna, Tex., July 23, 1924; d. Ben V. and Narcis (Smith) C. BA, Abilene Christian U., 1946; MA, U. Iowa, 1949; postgrad., Cornell U., 1953; PhD, U. Denver, 1957. Instr. speech and drama U. N.C., Greensboro, 1947-48; asst. prof., acting chairperson speech and drama Greensboro Coll., 1949-50; asst. prof. Abilene (Tex.) Christian U., 1950-57, assoc. prof., 1957-60, dir. theatre, 1950-60; assoc. prof., chairperson acting studies Idaho State U., Pocatello, 1960-63; assoc. prof. drama Sam Houston State U., Huntsville, Tex., 1963-65, prof., 1965-67; prof. theatre arts Tex. Christian U., Ft. Worth, 1967-91, prof. emeritus, 1991-94, dir. acting and directing program, 1967-91; guest prof. Tex. Wesleyan U., Ft. Worth, 1992-93; condr. directing workshop Community Theatre Flagstaff, Ariz., 1993. Dir. Scott Actors Repertory Co., 1968, 69, Ft. Worth Repertory Theatre, summer, 1970, 72; over 150 major theatrical prodns. in coll. and community theatres, 1948-94, latest being , She Stoops To Conquer, 1986, Deathtrap, 1987, The Foreigner, 1987, The Two Gentlemen of Verona, 1988, The Importance of Being Earnest, 1988, Desire Under the Elms, 1989, Our Town, 1989, Tartuff, 1990, Steel Magnolias, 1990; judge drama performance Ft. Worth Community Theatre, 1978-79 ; author: Assignments in Acting, 1966; mem. play reading com. Cir. Theatre, 1991; guest dir. Lake Charles (La.) Little Theatre, 1992, Morning's a Seven; guest dir. Dial "M" for Murder, Rococo Theatre, Abilene, Tex., 1993; condr. vocal and dialects workshop Tex. Non-profit Theatres Conv., 1991, 93, also Flagstaff (Ariz.) Cmty. Theatre; adjudicator Texas Interscholastic League One Act Play Contests, 1992; contbr. articles to profl. jours. guest dir. Rococco Theatre, 1993. Recipient Svc. in Theatre award named to honor at Tex. Christian U., 1991, scholarship in performing Arts named to honor Outstanding Contributions in Theatre at Abilene Christian U., 1992. Mem. AAUP, Assn. Theatre in Higher Edn., S.W. Theatre Assn., Tex. Ednl. Theatre Assn., Tex. Non-profit Theatre Inc. Democrat. Mem. Ch. of Christ. Home: Abilene Tex. Died Nov. 2, 1994.

COLLINS, HORACE CLAYTON, lawyer; b. Atlanta, June 3, 1950; s. Horace Clayton and Helen Chase (Johnson) C. MA, Stanford U., 1974; BA magna cum laude, Harvard U., 1972, JD, 1977. Bar: N.Y. 1978, U.S. Dist. Ct. (so. dist.) N.Y. Assoc. Cahill, Gordon & Reindel, N.Y.C., 1977-79; assoc. counsel Home Box Office, Inc., N.Y.C., 1979-82, sr. counsel film, 1982-84, v.p., chief counsel film, 1984-94. Home: New York N.Y. Died July 13, 1994.

COLLINS, LESTER ALBERTSON, landscape architect; b. Moorestown, N.J., Apr. 19, 1914; s. Lester and Anne (Albertson) C.; m. Petronella leRoux, July 8, 1947; children: Abigail Anne (dec.), Lester Adrian, (dec.) Oliver Michael. Grad., Choate Sch., 1933; student, Princeton, 1933-35; A.B., Harvard, 1938; postgrad. outdoor design, India, Japan, China, 1939-40; M.L.A., Harvard, 1942; postgrad. outdoor design, Scandanavia, Finland, The Netherlands, England, 1969. Chmn. dept. landscape architecture Harvard, 1950-53; prin. Collins, Simonds and Simonds, Washington, 1955-70, Lester Collins Assos., 1971-93. Important projects include new town Miami Lakes, Fla., master plan and execution, 1958-93, Innisfree Garden, Millbrook, N.Y., redisigning and adapting 200 acre garden for public use and enjoyment: campus planning: U.S. Naval Acad., Ft. Detrick, Md., NASA Goddard Space Flight Ctr., Am. U., Georgetown U., Va. Mil. Inst., U. Vas., U. Fla., Coral Gables; city planning of Alexandria, Va., Roanoke, Va., Ashville, Va., Savannah, Ga.; landscape design for pub. blds. Am. Embassy, Cairo, John F. Kennedy Ctr. for the Performing Arts, Holy Cross Hosp., Md., East Lyme Libr. and Community Ctr., Ct., Hood Art Gallery, Dartmouth, N.H., Nat. Maritime Ctr., Va.; landscape design for gardens and pks.: Nat. Pk. Svc., Pa. Ave. 29 pks., Gunston Hall Plantation, Va., Washington Zoo, Balt. Zoo., Hirshhorn Sculpture Garden, Enid A. Haupt Garden, Smithsonian Instn. Pres. Innisfree Found. Bd. dirs., Hubbard Endl. Trust. Served with Am. Field Service, 1942-45. Fulbright scholar Japan, 1953-54. Fellow Am. Soc. Landscape Architects. Mem. Soc. of Friends. Clubs: Cosmos (Washington); Century Assn. (N.Y.C.). Home: Key West Fla. Died July 7, 1993.

COLLINS, ROBERT JOSEPH, journalist; b. Indpls., Jan. 22, 1927; s. Patrick Joseph and Evelyn (Mattingly) C.; m. Kristin S. Mobley; children: Kathleen, Carolyn, Cynthia, Mary Louise, Evelyn, Michael, Kevin, Linda; stepchildren: Angela, Amy. Student, Butler U., 1946-49. With Indpsl. Star, 1948-95, columnist, 1960-95, sports editor, 1964-95. Author: Best of Bob Collins, 1963, Boilermakers: A History of Purdue Football, 1976, (with Mario Andretti) What's It Like Out There, 1970, Thought You'd Never Ask, 1984. Served with USNR, World War II. Named to Ind. Basketball Hall of Fame, 1988, Ind. Journalism Hall of Fame, 1990. Roman Catholic. Club: Indpls. Press (pres. 1963). Home: Indianapolis Ind. Died May 15, 1995.

COLLINSON, JOHN THEODORE, former railroad company executive; b. Pitts., July 29, 1926; s. John Gordon and Katherine (Bichy) C.; m. Patricia Ann Davison, Nov. 15, 1947; children: John G. II, Donald L., Nancy Ann. B.S. in Civil Engring., Cornell U., 1946. Project engr. Dravo Corp., Pitts., 1946; various engring. positions Balt. & Ohio R.R. Co., Pitts., 1946-65, Newark, 1946-65, Akron, Ohio, 1946-65; chief engr. Balt. & Ohio R.R. Co., 1965; with Chessie System, Inc., Cleve., 1965-88, v.p. ops., 1973-76, exec. v.p., 1976-78, pres., chief exec. officer C & O Ry., Balt. & Ohio R.R., Cleve., 1978-85; vice chmn. CSX Corp., Richmond, Va., 1985-88, also bd. dirs.; chmn. Chessie System & Seaboard R.R.s, 1985-92; bd. dirs. Nat. City Bank, RFBP Corp. Served to lt. (j.g.) USN, 1943-46. Republican. Presbyterian. Clubs: Country of Cleve.; Quail Creek (Naples, Fla.). Lodges: Masons, Shriners. Home: Naples Fla.

COLLISHAW, ROBERT JAMES, banker; b. Suffern, N.Y., Aug. 14, 1934; s. James Albert and Dorothy (Conover) C.; m. Jacquelyn Jarrett, June 18, 1955; children: Daniel, Thomas, Robert, Karen, Stacey. BA, Colgate U., 1955. With exec. tng. Chem. Bank, N.Y.C., 1955-57, asst. sec. to regional v.p. nat. div., 1957-71, sr. v.p. metro div., 1971-77, sr. v.p. govt. affairs, 1977-87, sr. v.p., asst. to chmn., 1987—. Trustee Valley Hosp., Ridgewood, N.J., 1987—. Mem. Bus. Council N.Y. State (dir. 1972-82). Republican. Presbyterian. Home: Pasadena Calif.

COLOMBO, GIOVANNI CARDINAL, former archbishop; b. Milan, Dec. 6, 1902. Ordained to priesthood, 1926. Consecrated Titular Bishop of Phillipopolis in Arabia, 1960, Archbishop of Milan, 1963-79, created Cardinal, 1965; mem. Com. of the Ecumenical Council on Cath. Sems. and Edn. Home: Milan Italy

COMPTON, WALTER A., manufacturing company executive; s. Herman A. and Grace (Cooper) C.; m. Phoebe Emerson, June 22, 1935; children: Cynthia, Joan, Phoebe, Walter Ames, Gordon. BS, Princeton U., 1933; MD, Harvard U., 1937. With Miles, Inc., Elkhart, Ind., 1938-81, v.p. research med. div., 1946-61, exec. v.p., 1961-64, chief exec. officer, 1964-81, pres., 1964-73, chmn. bd. dirs., 1973-81, hon. chmn. bd. dirs., from 1981. Served to lt. col. AUS, 1942-46. Home: Elkhart IN Died Oct. 11, 1990.

CONDON, RICHARD THOMAS, author; b. N.Y.C., Mar. 18, 1915; s. Richard Aloysius and Martha Irene (Pickering) C.; m. Evelyn Rose Hunt, Jan. 14, 1938; children: Deborah Evelyn, Wendy Ann. Grad. high sch., N.Y.C. Ind. novelist, non-fiction writer, screenwriter, 1958-96; cons. Internat. Confederation of Book Actors. Playwright: Men of Distinction, 1953; writer children's record albums The Horse Stories, 1947; novelist (pub. 25 langs.), The Oldest Confession, 1958, The Manchurian Candidate, 1959, Some Angry Angel, 1960, A Talent for Loving, 1961, An Infinity of Mirrors, 1964, Any God Will Do, 1966, The Ecstasy Business, 1967, Mile High, 1969, Vertical Smile, 1971, Arigato, 1972, And Then We Moved to Rossenarra, 1973, The Mexican Stove, 1973, Winter Kills, 1974, The Star Spangled Crunch, 1974, Money is Love, 1975, The Whisper of the Axe, 1976, The Abandoned Woman, 1977, The Bandicoot, 1978, Death of a Politician, 1978, The Entwining, 1980, Prizzi's Honor, 1982, A Trembling Upon Rome, 1983, Prizzi's Family, 1986, Prizzi's Glory, 1988, Emperor of America, 1990, The Final Addiction, 1991, The Venerable Bread, 1992, Prizzi's Money, 1994; screenplays: (with Janet Roach) Prizzi's Honor, 1984 (Acad. award nom. 1986, Best Screenplay award Brit. Motion Picture Acad. 1986, Best Screenplay award Writers Guild Am. 1986), Arigato, 1985; contbr. to nat. mags. Decorated chevalier La Confrérie du Tastevin, 1968, commanderie du Bontemps, 1969, chevalier Chaine des Rotisseurs, 1976. Home: Dallas Tex. Died April 9, 1996.

CONE, CARL BRUCE, history educator; b. Davenport, Iowa, Feb. 22, 1916; s. Carl S. and Lena (Peterson) C.; m. Mary Louise Regan, Dec. 20, 1942; 1 child, Timothy. B.A., U. Iowa, 1936, M.A., 1937, Ph.D., 1940; DLitt (hon.), U. Ky., 1984. Instr. history Allegheny Coll., Meadville, Pa., 1940-41; research asst. Iowa Hist. Soc., 1941-42; asst. prof. history La. State U., 1942-47; faculty U. Ky., Lexington, 1947-95; prof. history U. Ky., 1956-81, chmn. dept., 1965-70; Summer vis. prof. U. Mo., 1952, La. State U., 1960, Miami U., Oxford, Ohio, 1964; dir. U. Ky. summer seminar Nat. Endowment Humanities, 1975. Author: Torchbearer of Freedom, 1952, Burke and the Nature of Politics: The Age of the American Revolution, 1957, Burke and the Nature of Politics: The Age of the French Revolution, 1964, The English Jacobins, 1968, Hounds in the Morning, 1981, A Pictorial History of the University of Kentucky, 1989; also articles. Mem. Lexington Civil Service Commn., 1958-68; bd. dirs. Lexington Library, 1978-83. Recipient Nat. Book award Phi Alpha Theta, 1965; Sang award U. Ky., 1968; Disting. Citizen award City of Lexington, 1981; Hallam prof. U. Ky.; also Faculty fellow Fund Advancement Teaching, 1951-52; Guggenheim fellow, 1963-64; Am. Council Learned Socs. grantee, 1971. Mem. Am. Hist. Assn., So. Hist. Assn. (exec. coun. 1977-80, chmn. European History sect. 1972, Disting. Svc. award European History sect. 1989), Am. Cath. Hist. Assn. (pres. 1967), So. Conf. Brit. Studies (pres. 1972), Omicron Delta Kappa, Phi Beta Kappa, Phi Alpha Theta (internat. coun. 1975-81). Republican. Roman Catholic. Lodge: Kiwanis. Home: Lexington Ky. Died Feb. 2, 1995.

CONE, SPENCER BURTIS, architect, engineer; b. Garden City, Kans., Jan. 12, 1910; s. Roy Spencer and Gertrude Ella (Burtis) C.; m. Nancy Howard, July 29,

1946; children: Catherine Howard, John Spencer. B.S., Armour Inst. Tech., 1933. Pvt. practice architecture Vt., N.H., 1934-37; partner Cone/Vogelgesang Architects, Chgo., 1937-41; ptnr. Cone/Dornbusch (Architects/Engrs.), Chgo., 1947-82, Cone and Kalb (Architects), Chgo., 1983-92. Works include Bryan Jr. High Sch, Elmhurst, Hubbard Woods Fashion Center (archtl. awards), Madison Elementary Sch, Skokie, Ill. (honor awards Chgo. chpt. AIA, Chgo. Assn. Commerce and Industry), Barrington Middle Sch, Forest Elementary Sch, (distinguished bldg. awards Chgo. chpt. AIA), Chgo. Assn. Commerce and Industry.). Pres. Chgo. Fine Arts Music Found., 1966-68; mem. Mayor's Adv. Coms. on Bldg. Code Amendments and Standards and Tests, 1967-79. Served with USN, 1941-44, PTO. Fellow AIA (pres. Chgo. chpt. 1969, chmn. nat. com. ednl. facilities planning 1968-69). Clubs: Dunham Wood Riding (Wayne, Ill.); Arts (Chgo.) (dir.). Home: Batavia Ill. Died Sept. 23, 1993.

CONGER, FRANKLIN BARKER, oil company executive; b. San Francisco, Oct. 20, 1929; s. Franklin Barker and Katherine S. C.; m. Pat Russell, Sept. 1985; children: Anne M., Lisa W., Donald H., Stephen B. B.A., U. Calif., Berkeley, 1951. With Shell Oil Co., 1951-80; geologist, sr. geologist, dist. geologist, mgr. exploration econs., sr. staff geologist western U.S., Alaska and Gulf Coast areas, 1951-65; established Pecten Internat. Cos. as mgr. of new ventures and ops., chief geologist Pacific Coast, Mid Continent, Western and Internat. regions, div. exploration mgr. Calif., So. Rocky Mountains, Mid Continent and Internat. divs., 1965-80; sr. v.p. Ashland (Ky.) Oil Inc., 1980-86; pres. Ashland Exploration Inc., Houston, 1980-86; chief exec. officer CONGEREX, Houston, 1986-95. Fellow Geol. Soc. Am.; mem. Am. Assn. Petroleum Geologists, Am. Petroleum Inst. (exploration com.), Pine Forest Country Club. Republican. Home: Houston Tex. Died Apr. 30, 1995.

CONKLIN, HUGH RANDOLPH, management consultant; b. Battle Creek, Mich., Oct. 20, 1911; s. Hugh William and Ida Charlotte (Maier) C.; m. Mary Alice Kendel, Mar. 12, 1938 (dec. Mar. 1988); children: Hugh Randolph, Drue Kendel; m. Mary Phipps Shepherd, Sept. 2, 1989. BS in Engring., U. Mich., 1933; postgrad. Advanced Mgmt. Program, Harvard U.; PhD in Bus. Adminstrn. (hon.), Colo. State Christian Coll., 1973. With Gen. Foods Corp., 1933-57, Eastern regional Sales mgr., 1954-55; nat. sales mgr. Gen. Foods Corp. (Post Cereals div.), 1955-57; with Lever Bros. Co., 1957-71, v.p. sales, 1962-71; v.p. nat. sales Pepsicola Co., Purchase, N.Y., 1971-72; pres. Hugh Conklin Assocs., 1972-93; broker-assoc. Century 21 Spinning Wheel Realtors, Tierra Verde, Fla., 1983-93; past v.p., dir. Econ. and Market Research Co., Inc. Past trustee Osteo. Hosp. and Clinic of N.Y.; past trustee Post Grad. Inst. Osteo. Medicine and Surgery; past bd. dirs. Found. for Research, N.Y. Acad. Osteopathy; past mem. bd. govs. N.Y. Coll. Osteo. Medicine and Surgery; past gov. Clinton Youth Center, N.Y.C.; past vice chmn. trustees 101 Assn. Served to capt., inf. AUS, 1942-46, CBI. Decorated Bronze Star, Combat Inf. badge. Mem. St. Petersburg-Suncoast Assn. Realtors (legis. com.), Delta Kappa Epsilon. Clubs: U.S. Power Squadron, Pass-A-Grill Yacht. Home: Saint Petersburg Fla. Died Sept. 26, 1993.

CONMY, PETER THOMAS, public library executive; b. San Francisco, July 8, 1901; s. Thomas Cherry and Mary Henrietta (Richter) C.; m. Emiliette Constance Storti, July 11, 1928 (dec. Dec. 1983); children—Constance Louise, Thomas Peter. A.B., U. Calif., 1924, M.A., 1927, Ed.D., 1937, B.L.S., 1947; M.A., Stanford, 1941; LL.B., U. San Francisco, 1952. Tchr. jr. high schs. San Francisco, 1926, tchr., counselor, debate coach, evening sch. tchr. evening high sch. registrar and evening high sch. prin., 2 pub. schs., 1927-43; serving at Horace Mann Fr. High Sch., Mission High Sch., Evening High Sch. of Commerce and; Galileo Evening High Sch.; named city librarian of Oakland, Calif., 1943; charge Oakland Pub. Library dept. including; Oakland Pub. Mus., Snow Mus., Oakland Art Gallery. Author: History of the Entrance Requirements of the University of California, 1928, Aids to the Study of Government, 1928, History of Public School Finance in California, 1937, Self Determination and the Paris Peace Conference, 1941, Public School-Public Library Relationships, 1945, Studies in English Education during the 18th Century, 1946, The Date of the Founding of San Francisco, 1947, A Centennial Evaluation of the Treaty of Guadalupe Hidalgo, 1848-1948, The Queen of the Avenue, the History of St. Francis Church, 1949, The Public Library and The State, 1962, also numerous articles on Calif. History pub. by, Native Sons of Golden West. Mem. Selective Service Bd. 100., San Francisco, 1943, chmn., from 1944, city historian, Oakland, from 1969. Decorated Knight of Saint Gregory, 1963, Knight of Malta, 1976. Mem. A.L.A., Calif. Library Assn. (pres. 1961), N.E.A., Calif. Tchrs. Assn., Calif. Hist. Soc., Am. Polit. Sci. Assn., Native Sons of Golden West (grand pres. 1949-50, dir. hist. research from 1954), Young Men's Inst., Phi Delta Kappa, Phi Delta Kappa. Clubs: K.C. (4 deg.), Elk, Serra (pres. 1952). Lodge: Rotary. Home: Oakland Calif. Deceased.

CONN, ARTHUR LEONARD, energy consultant; b. N.Y.C., Apr. 5, 1913; s. Nathan Avram and Jennie (Harmel) C.; m. Bernice Robbins, Sept. 2, 1937 (dec. May 1970); children: Robert Harmel, Elizabeth (Mrs. J. Geoffrey Magnus), Alex Paul; m. Irene Sekely Farkas, June 10, 1972. S.B. in Chem. Engring., MIT, 1934, S.M., 1935; grad., Inst. Mgmt., Northwestern U., 1959. Asst. to dir. research Blaw-Knox Co., Pitts., 1936; exptl. chemist ALCO Products div. Am. Locomotive Co., 1936-39; with Standard Oil Co. Ind. and Amoco Oil Co. subs., 1939-78; group and sect. leader in charge Boron isotope separation Manhattan Project, 1943-46, div. dir., 1950-59, supt. tech. service, 1959; dir. process devel. Amoco Oil Co., 1960-62, research coordinator, 1962-64, sr. cons. engr., 1964-67, dir. govt. contracts, 1967-78; pres. Arthur L. Conn & Assocs., Ltd., internat. cons. in new energy techs., research and devel. mgmt. and info. resource mgmt., 1978-95; cons. AEC, 1951-53, Office Coal Research, ERDA, Dept. Energy, 1968-82, Synthetic Fuels Corp., 1983; mem. indsl. adv. com. U. Ill.-Chgo., 1971-78; indsl. com. advising CUNY on coal research, 1972-79; mem. com. on coal liquefaction, chmn. com. on processing coal and shale liquids Nat. Acad. Engring., 1975-80; trustee Engring. Info. Inc., 1982-85. Contbr. articles to profl. jours. Thorp fellow, 1935. Fellow AAAS (council 1970-73), Am. Inst. Chem. Engrs. (dir. 1966-71, v.p. 1969, pres. 1970, Founders award 1976); mem. Am. Chem. Soc. Home: Chicago Ill. Died Jan. 5, 1995.

CONN, JEROME W., physician, educator; b. Sept. 24, 1907; s. Joseph and Dora (Kobrin) C.; m. Elizabeth Stern, June 17, 1932; children: Phyllis, J. William. Student, Rutgers U., 1925-28, D.Sc., 1964; M.D., U. Mich., 1932. Diplomate Am. Bd. Internal Medicine. Intern U. Hosp., Ann Arbor, Mich., 1932-33; asst. resident U. Hosp., Ann Arbor, 1933-34, instr. medicine, 1935-38, asst. prof. medicine, 1938-44, assoc. prof., 1944-50, prof. internal medicine, 1950-68, disting. prof. internal medicine, 1968-73, prof., dir. dept. metabolism and endocrinology, also metabolism research unit, 1943-73, prof. emeritus, 1973-94; disting. physician VA, 1973-76; cons. to surgeon gen. U.S. Army, 1945-54, surgeon gen. USPHS, 1947-58; holder numerous named lectureships, including Banting Meml. lectr. Am. Diabetes Assn., 1958; Russell lectr. U. Mich., 1961, Gordon Wilson lectr. Am. Clin. and Climatological Assn., 1962, Lawson lectr. Royal Coll. Physicians and Surgeons of Can., 1964, Phillips lectr. A.C.P., 1965, Joslin Meml. lectr. New Eng. Diabetes Assn., 1965, Harvey lectr., N.Y.C., 1967, Ramon Guiteras lectr. Am. Urol. Assn., 1967, Ricketts lectr. U. Chgo., 1967, Loeb lectr. St. Louis U., 1970; mem. com. on metabolism in trauma U.S. Army Dept. Research and Devel., 1953-61; drug research bd. div. med. scis. Nat. Acad. Scis. NRC, 1963-64; mem. expert adv. panel on chronic degenerative disease WHO, 1964-94; mem. bd. sci. dirs. Ctr. Research Diseases of Heart. Contbr. to books, jours. in field of metabolism and endocrinology. Recipient Modern Medicine award, 1957, citation for contbrn. to medicine Mich. Med. Soc., 1962, Banting award Am. Diabetes Assn., 1963, Phillips award A.C.P., 1965, Joslin award New Eng. Diabetes Assn., 1965, Internat. prize Gairdner Found., 1965, Ricketts award U. Chgo., Taylor award Am. Therapeutics Soc., 1967, Stouffer prize, 1969, gold medal Internat. Soc. for Progress in Internal Medicine, 1969. Mem. ACP (master), A.C.S. (hon.), Am. Soc. Clin. Investigation (council 1949-52), Central Soc. Clin. Research (v.p. 1953, pres. 1954), Am. Inst. Nutrition, Am. Diabetes Assn. (pres. 1962, chmn. com. research 1964-71), Nat. Acad. Scis., Inst. Medicine (charter, Med. Ctr. Alumni award 1987), Assn. Am. Physicians, Endocrine Soc., Sigma Xi, Alpha Omega Alpha, Phi Kappa Phi; hon. mem. Nat. Acad. Medicine Argentina, Endocrine Soc. Columbia, Peruvian Soc. Cardiology, Peruvian Soc. Angiology, Med. Soc. Santiago. Home: Naples Fla. Died June 11, 1994.

CONNALLY, JOHN B., III, former governor, former federal official; b. Floresville, Tex., 1917; s. John Bowden and Lela. Bachelor's, U. Texas, JD. Sec. of the Navy, 1961-62, governor of Texas, 1963-69, sec. of the Treasury, 1971-73. Address: Houston Texas.

CONNARE, WILLIAM GRAHAM, retired bishop; b. Pitts., Dec. 11, 1911; s. James J. and Nellie T. (O'Connor) C. BA, Duquesne U., 1932, LittD, 1961; MA, St. Vincent Coll., Latrobe, Pa., 1934, LHD, 1962; LLD, Seton Hill Coll., 1960. Ordained priest Roman Cath. Ch., 1936. Named domestic prelate, 1955; asst. pastor St. Canice, Pitts., 1936-37, St. Paul's Cathedral, 1937-49; adminstr. St. Richard's Ch., Pitts., 1949-55; pastor St. Richard's Ch., 1955-60; chaplain Univ. Cath. Club, Pitts., 1947-60, Cath. Interracial Council Pitts., 1953-60; dir. Soc. Propagation of Faith, 1950-59; vicar for religious as rep. Bishop of Pitts., 1959-60; consecrated bishop of Greensburg Pa., 1960-87. Bd. dirs., chmn. community services com. Urban League Pitts., 1950-60; mem. Pitts. Commn. Human Relations, 1953-60; mem. Allegheny County Council Civil Rights, 1953-60, bd. dirs., 1958-60; bd. dirs. Pitts. br. NAACP, 1959-60; Episcopal chmn. Nat. Cath. Com. on Scouting, Boy Scouts Am., 1962-70; Episcopal moderator div. youth activities U.S. Cath. Conf., 1968-70; mem. Bishop's Commn. for Liturgical Apostolate, 1967-72; chmn. commn. on missions Nat. Conf. Cath. Bishops, 1967-71, mem. adminstrv. bd., 1967, chmn. com. for inter-rite affairs, 1975-95; mem. Bishop's Com. on Missions, 1971; mem. council Christian Assos. Southwest Pa., 1972; chmn. Am. Bd. Cath. Missions, 1972; mem. Episcopal adv. bd. Word of God Inst., 1974; Episcopal adviser Nat. Cath. Stewardship Council, 1974; exec. bd. Cath. Relief Services, 1979-84. Home: Greensberg Pa. Died June 12, 1995.

CONNELLY, DONALD WEBB, former military officer, business executive; b. Washington, Apr. 7, 1930; s. Gerald John and Anne L. (Webb) C.; m. Barbara Ann Graddy, Feb. 6, 1954; children: Marian, Donna, Sharon, Alys, Forrest, Dolores, James, John. BA, George Washington U., 1963, MA in Pers. Adminstrn., 1966; MS in Counseling, Shippenburg State Coll., 1972; grad. Advanced Mgmt. Program, Harvard U., 1973. Commd. officer U.S. Army, 1949, advanced through grades to brig. gen., 1976; dep. comdr. Army Adminstrn. Ctr., Ft. Benjamin Harrison, Ind., 1976-77; dep. adj. gen. Dept. Army, Washington, 1977-78; dep. commdr. Army Recruiting Command, Ft. Sheridan, Ill., 1978-81; dir. mil. pers. mgmt. Dept. Army, Washington, 1981-82; mem. faculty U.S. Army War Coll.; ret., 1982; exec. v.p. Star Network, Inc., Alexandria, Va., 1982-91, pres., 1991-96; mayor City of Georgetown (Ga.), 1996. Decorated Legion of Merit with oak leaf cluster, Bronze Star with oak leaf cluster, D.S.M., DFC, Air medal, others. Roman Catholic. Home: Georgetown Ga. Died Jan. 14, 1996.

CONNELLY, FRANCIS JOHN, university dean, business administration educator; b. N.Y.C., Jan. 13, 1942; s. Thomas M. and Madeline V. (Devlin) C. B.B.A., CUNY, 1964; M.B.A., Wash. State U., 1966; D.B.A., Ind. U., 1972. Dir. grad. studies Howard U., Washington, 1974-75; assoc. dean Washington U., St. Louis, 1970-79; asst. v.p. Baruch Coll.-CUNY, N.Y.C., 1979-81, dean Sch. Bus. and Pub. Adminstrn., 1981-96; pres. Potomac Cons. Group, Fairfax, Va., 1975-96; cons. Co-author contract research projects; contbr. writings to profl. publs.; editor: Am. Assembley Collegiate Schs. Bus. Jour., 1975-78. Advisor pub. adminstrn. U.S. Dept. Treasury, Washington, 1974-75. Fellow Ind. U., 1967-68. Fellow Acad. Mktg. Sci.; mem. Am. Mktg. Assn., Inst. Mgmt. Sci., Beta Gamma Sigma, Phi Kappa Phi. Home: Flushing N.Y. Died Jan. 19, 1996.

CONRAD, BARRY L., hotel and restaurant executive. Chmn. CEO Hotels and Restaurants Worldwide Barrington Internat. Holdings, Ltd., Miami. Home: Miami Fla. Deceased.

CONRAD, PAM, author; b. N.Y.C., June 18, 1947; d. Robert Fredrick and Doris Elizabeth (Dowling) Stampf; m. Robert Raymond Conrad, June 25, 1967 (div. 1982); children: Johanna, Sarah Loretta. BA, New Sch. Social Rsch., N.Y.C., 1984. Author: I Don't Live Here!, 1984, Prairie Songs, 1985 (Spur award Western Writers Am. 1985, Internat. Reading Assn. award 1986, Boston Globe-Horn Book award 1986, Judy Lopez Meml. award Women's Nat. Book Assn. 1986), Holding Me Here, 1986, What I Did for Roman, 1987, Seven Silly Circles, 1987, Taking the Ferry Home, 1988, Staying Nine, 1988, My Daniel, 1989 (Spur award Western Writers Am. 1989), The Tub People, 1989, Stonewords: A Ghost Story, 1990 (Edgar award Mystery Writer's Am. 1991, Boston Globe-Horn Book award 1990), Prairie Vision: The Life and Times of Solomon Butcher, 1991, Pedro's Journal, 1991, The Lost Sailor, 1992, The Tub Grandfather, 1993, Pumpkin Moon, 1994, Molly and the Strawberry Day, 1994, Doll Face Has a Party!, 1994, The Rooster's Gift, 1995, Call Me Ahnighito, 1995, Animal Lingo, 1995. Mem. Authors Guild, Soc. Childrens Book Writers. Home: Rockville Centre N.Y. Died Jan. 22, 1996.

CONRAD, WILLIAM, actor, producer, director; b. Louisville, Sept. 27, 1920. Attended Fullerton Jr. Coll. Radio announcer KMPC, Los Angeles, till 1943. Starred in radio series Gunsmoke, 1949-60; film debut in The Killers, 1946; other film appearances include Body and Soul, 1947, Sorry, Wrong Number, 1948, East Side, West Side, 1949, The Naked Jungle, 1954, The Conqueror, 1956, 30, 1959, Moonshine County Express, 1977; prod. films Two On a Guillotine (also dir.), 1965, Brainstorm (also dir.), 1965, An American Dream, 1966, A Covenant With Death, 1967, First to Fight, 1967, The Cool Ones, 1967, Countdown, 1968, Chubasco, 1968, Assignment to Kill, 1969; TV appearances The Brotherhood of the Bell, 1970, Conspiracy to Kill, 1970, Night Cries, 1978, The Rebels, 1979, Shocktrauma, 1982, In Like Flynn, 1985; producer, dir.: Klondike; dir. 77 Sunset Strip, 1963, 35 episodes True, 1962-63, film The Man form Galveston, 1964; star TV series The D.A, 1971-72, O'Hara, U.S. Treasury, 1971-72, Cannon, 1971-76, Nero Wolfe, from 1981, Jake and the Fat Man, 1987—; appeared in TV movies The Rebels, Return of Frank Cannon, 1980, Shocktrauma, 1982; narrator TV shows: Return of the King; producer TV movie: Turnover Smith. Served with USAAF, 1943-45. Home: Sherman Oaks Calif.

CONSTANTINE BERENG SEEISO See **MOSHOESHOE, II**

CONTE, RICHARD NICHOLAS, architect; b. Pitts., Sept. 14, 1918; s. Phillip and Margaret (Del Gauido) C.; m. Ida Weinstein, June 18, 1956. B.S., U. Ill., 1947; student, Royal Academia de Bella Arts, Italy, 1945, Roosevelt U., 1948-49. With planning dept. U. Ill.

Med. Campus, Chgo., 1941; draftsman Harza Engring Co., Chgo. and Wyo., 1942, Traveleti & Suter, Chgo., 1946; architect Leickenko & Esser, 1947-50; partner Barancik, Conte & Assos., Chgo., 1950-93; retired, 1993; archtl. instr. U. Ill., 1946-47. Served with AUS, 1942-45. Mem. A.I.A. Home: Chicago Ill. Dec. Sept. 17, 1995.

CONTERATO, BRUNO PAUL, architect; b. Chgo., June 12, 1920; (married); 3 children. B.S., Ill. Inst. Tech., 1948. Registered architect, Ill. Partner Office of Mies Van Der Rohe, Chgo., 1969-75; prin. firm Fujikawa, Conterato, Lohan & Assocs., Chgo., 1975-91; chmn. bd. Fujikawa, Conterato, Lohan & Assos., Chgo., 1986-91, FCL Assocs., Chgo., 1983-91; ret., 1991. Pres. alumni bd. Ill. Inst. Tech., 1984-95, life trustee; pres. Chgo. Archtl. Assistance Ctr., 1986-87. Capt. USAAF, 1941-45, 51-53. Fellow AIA (dir., v.p., pres. Chgo. chpt. 1970-75, v.p. Ill. council 1974, dir. Ill. council 1973). Home: Geneva Ill. Died Nov. 20, 1995.

CONWAY, JAMES F., JR., printing company executive; m. Grace Conway; children: James, Peter, Michael, Stephen, Ruth, John. Grad., Harvard U., 1947, postgrad. in bus. adminstrn., 1949. Now chmn., chief exec. officer Courier Corp., Lowell, Mass.; bd. dirs. Blue Cross and Blue Shield of Mass., EMC Corp., State St. Bank & Trust Co., State St. Boston Fin. Corp., State Street Boston Corp.; chmn. Lowell Plan. Bd. dirs. Assoc. Industries Mass., Lowell Plan; trustee Lowell Gen. Hosp. Named Bus. Leader of Yr., North Middlesex C. of C., 1980. Mem. Printing Industries Am. (chmn. internat. activities com., Lewis Meml. Man of Yr. in Graphic Arts 1978), Internat. Bus. Forms Industries (past chmn., past pres.), Printing Industries New Eng. (past v.p.). Clubs: Racquet and Tennis (N.Y.C.), Sky (N.Y.), Harvard, Commercial, Algonquin (Boston), Carleton (Chgo.), Vesper Country (Tyngsboro, Mass.). Home: Lowell Mass. Died Dec. 1992.

CONWAY, THOMAS JAMES, lawyer; b. Kansas City, July 20, 1913; s. Thomas James and Nell M. (O'Sullivan) C.; m. Eleanor M. Nolan, June 4, 1938; children—Terry N., Brian J., Diana S. LL.B., Washington U., St. Louis, 1935. Bar: Mo. bar 1935. Atty. Kansas City Park Dept., 1936-42; asst. city counselor Kansas City, 1942-50; chief trial atty. City Counselor's Office, 1950-59; pres. Popham Law Firm P.C., Kansas City, 1959—. Decorated knight Holy Sepulchre. Mem. ABA, Mo. Bar Assn., Kansas City Bar Assn. (1st ann. litigator emeritus award), Internat. Soc. Barristers, Pi Epsilon Delta, Kappa Alpha. Roman Catholic. Clubs: K.C, Carriage, Kansas City Racquet. Home: Kansas City Mo. Deceased.

COOK, DON, author, retired foreign correspondent; b. Bridgeport, Conn., Aug. 8, 1920; s. Paul J. and Nelle Brown (Reed) C.; m. Cherry Mitchell, Oct. 31, 1943 (dec. 1983); children: Christopher, Jennifer, Adrienne, Deborah, Caron, Danielle, Dominique. Student pub. schs., Abington, Pa. With St. Petersburg (Fla.) Times, 1938-40, Jenkintown (Pa.) Times-Chronicle, 1940-41; with Phila. bur. Trans-radio Press Service, 1941, Washington bur., 1941-43; with N.Y. Herald Tribune, Washington, 1943-45, London, 1945-49; corr. N.Y. Herald Tribune, West Germany, 1949-52; roving European corr. Paris, 1952-55; chief London bur., 1956-60; chief European corr. N.Y. Herald Tribune, Paris, 1960-65; Paris corr. Los Angeles Times, 1965-83, European diplomatic corr., 1983-88. Author: Floodtide in Europe, 1965, The War Lords: Eisenhower, 1975, Ten Men and History, 1981, Charles de Gaulle, A Biography, 1983, Forging the Alliance, NATO 1945-50, 1989, The Long Fuse, England and the American Revolution, 1995; contbr. to popular mags. Trustee Am. Sch. Paris, 1972-80. Recipient William the Silent award for journalism, 1956; English Speaking Union award for better understanding, 1957; citation Overseas Press, 1966. Mem. Authors Guild, Internat. Inst. Strategic Studies (London), Council on Fgn. Relations (N.Y.C.). Clubs: Garrick (London); Century (N.Y.C.); Franklin Inn (Phila.). Home: Philadelphia Pa. Died Mar. 7, 1995.

COOK, HAROLD J., lawyer; b. Poplar Grove, Ill., Oct. 4, 1905; s. James B. and Anna (Padden) C.; m. Irene J., Sept. 1, 1934. Ph.B., Marquette U., 1929, LL.B., 1930, J.D., 1968. Bar: Wis. 1930. Sole practice, Milw., 1930-34; atty. Fed. Home Owners Loan Corp., Madison, Wis., 1934-36; sole practice, Beloit, from 1936. Mem. Rock County (Wis.) Bd. Suprs., 1940-46; sec., trustee Our Lady of Assumption Ch., Beloit. Mem. Delta Theta Phi. Deceased. Home: Beloit Wis.

COOK, PETER EDWARD, actor, comedian, writer, film producer; b. Torquay, Devonshire, Eng., Nov. 17, 1937; s. Alexander E. and Margaret Cook; m. Wendy Snowden, Oct. 28, 1964 (div.); m. Judy Huxtable, Feb. 14, 1974. Student, Cambridge (Eng.) U. Owner The Establishment Theatre Co., 1962-95; dir. Private Eye mag. Appeared in (stage prodns.) Beyond the Fringe, 1959, 61, 62, 64, Behind the Fringe, 1972, Good Evening, 1973-75, (films) The Wrong Box, 1966, The Bed Sitting Room, 1969, Pleasure at Her Majesty's, 1976, The Hound of the Baskervilles, 1977, Yellowbeard, 1983, Supergirl, 1984, (TV) The New London Palladium Show, Alice in Wonderland; producer (stage) The Establishment, 1963, The Mad Show, 1966, (film) The Haunted, 1983; author (plays) Pieces of Eight, Beyond the Fringe, 1959, The Establishment (with Alan Bennett, Dudley Moore and Paxton Whitehead), 1963, Good Evening, 1973 (screenplays) The Secret Policeman's Other Ball, 1981, (teleplays) Not Only...But Also, 1964-66, (books) Dud and Pete, The Dagenham Dialogues (both with Dudley Moore), 1971; contbr. various humorous and satirical periodicals. Best Mus. or Revue award London Evening Standard, 1962, Comedian of Yr. award Guild TV Producers and Dirs., 1973, Antoinette Perry award , 1974. Mem. Actors' Equity Assn., AFTRA, AGVA, Screen Actors Guild. Club: Footlights. Home: London Eng. Died Jan. 9, 1995.

COOK, WILLIAM RICHARD JOSEPH, physicist; b. Trowbridge, Eng., Apr. 10, 1905; s. John and Eva Emily (Boobyer) C.; M.Sc., Bristol U., 1926; D.Sc. (hon.), U. Strathclyde, 1967, U. Bath, 1975; m. Gladys Rose Allen, June 10, 1939; children—Robert Anthony, Elizabeth Mary. Engaged in ballistics research War Office, Woolwich, 1928-35, in rocket devel. Projectile Devel. Establishment, Aberporth, 1935-47; chief Royal Naval Sci. Service, London, 1947-54; dep. dir. Atomic Weapons Research Establishment, Aldermarston, 1954-58; mem. Atomic Energy Authority, 1958-64; chief sci. adv. Ministry Def., 1964-70, cons., 1970-81; dir. Rolls-Royce Ltd., 1970-76, cons., 1976-80; dir. GEC Marconi Ltd., 1972-76, Buck & Hickman Ltd., 1970-83. Created knight bachelor, 1958, knight comdr. Order Bath, 1970. Fellow Royal Soc., Inst. Physics. Club: Athenaeum (London). Home: Newbury Eng.

COOLBAUGH, FRANK, mining executive, consultant; b. Rapid City, S.D., Dec. 21, 1908; s. Melville Fuller and Osie (Smith) C.; m. Dallos Inez Davies, Aug. 17, 1947; 1 son, Melville James. E.M., Colo. Sch. Mines, 1933; grad., Advanced Mgmt. Program, Harvard U., 1947. Coal miner U.S. Fuel Co., Mohrland, Utah, 1928-30; from mine helper to asst. mill supt. Climax Molybdenum Co., Climax, Colo., 1933-42; planning dir., asst. gen. supt., resident mgr., gen. mgr., v.p. Climax Molybdenum Co., 1946-59, pres., 1959-60, dir., 1955-58; pres., dir. Climax Uranium Co.; v.p. Am. Metal Climax, Inc., 1958-60, pres., 1960-65, chmn., chief exec. officer, 1966-67, cons., 1967-68, dir., 1958-68; pres., dir. Coolbaugh Mining Corp., 1969-91; pres. Peabody Holding Co. Inc., 1977-82; mine developer, cons. industry, 1968-91; dir. Newmont Mining Corp., Ranchers Exploration & Devel. Corp., Lakewood Colo. Nat. Bank.; chmn., dir. Peabody Coal Co. Trustee Colo. Sch. Mines Research Inst. Served to capt., C.E. AUS, 1942-46. Mem. Am. Inst. Mining and Metall. Engrs., Mining and Metall. Soc. Am., Am. Mining Congress. Presbyterian. Home: Lakewood Colo. Died Mar. 8, 1991.

COOPER, GEORGE BRINTON, historian, educator; b. Phila., Apr. 14, 1916; s. Lloyd W. and Esther L. (Cooper) C. B.A. in Social Scis. with highest honors, Swarthmore Coll., 1938; B.A. Lockwood fellow, Univ. Coll., London, Eng., 1938-39; M.A., Yale U., 1942, Ph.D., 1948; L.H.D. (hon.), Trinity Coll., 1983. Mem. faculty Trinity Coll., Hartford, Conn., 1941-95; prof. history Trinity Coll., 1958-83, Northam prof., 1964-83, prof. emeritus, 1983-95, chmn. dept., 1964-74, sec. of Coll., 1974-83; lectr. elderhostel program Trinity Coll., Rome, Perugia and Sorrento, Padua, Lake Garda, Verona, Venice, Italy, 1985-95; mng. editor Jour. Brit. Studies, 1961-79; Sir Arnold Lunn Meml. lectr. London, 1982; Am. vice consul, London, 1944-46; mem. internat. adv. com. Yale edit. Walpole Memoirs, 1975-95; Mem. Hartford Bd. Edn., 1959-65, pres., 1961-62. Chmn. Gov. Conn. Bi-Partisan Com. Redistricting Conn. Senate, 1960; nat. adv. cancer council USPHS, 1961-64; Bd. dirs. Hartford Pub. Library, 1964-71, corporator, 1962-95; corporator St. Francis Hosp., 1982-95; trustee Lewis-Walpole Library of Yale U., Farmington, Conn., 1979-95; trustees Cesare Barbieri Found., 1970-95, chmn., 1976-82; trustee Historic Deerfield, Inc., 1976-95; bd. overseers U. Hartford Library, 1987-95. Served with USNR, 1943-44. Mem. Conf. Brit. Studies, Am. Hist. Assn., Colonial Soc. Mass., Royal United Svcs. Inst., Phi Beta Kappa, Pi Gamma Mu, Delta Upsilon. Democrat. Clubs: Yale (N.Y.C.), Grolier (N.Y.C.); Ski of Gt. Brit. (London); Monday Evening (Hartford), Twilight (Hartford). Home: West Simsbury Conn. Died Oct. 18, 1995.

COOPER, THEODORE, pharmaceutical company executive, physician; b. Trenton, N.J., Dec. 28, 1928; s. Victor and Dora (Popkin) C.; m. Vivian Cecilia Evans, June 16, 1956; children: Michael Harris, Mary Katherine, Victoria Susan, Frank Victor. BS, Georgetown U., 1949; MD, St. Louis U., 1954, PhD, 1956. USPHS fellow St. Louis U. Dept. Physiology, 1955-56; clin. asso. surgery br. Nat. Heart Inst., Bethesda, Md., 1956-58; faculty St. Louis U., 1960-66, prof. surgery, 1964-66; prof., chmn. dept. pharmacology U. N.Mex., Albuquerque, 1966-68, on leave, 1967-69; assoc. dir. artificial heart, myocardial infarction programs Nat. Heart Inst., Bethesda, 1967-68; dir. Nat. Heart and Lung Inst., 1968-74; dep. asst. sec. for health HEW, 1974-75, asst. sec. health, 1975-77; dean Med. Coll., Cornell U., N.Y.C., 1977-80; provost for med. affairs Cornell U., 1977-80; exec. v.p. Upjohn Co., Kalamazoo, 1980-84, vice chmn. bd., 1984-87, chmn. bd., chief exec. officer, 1987-89, chmn. bd., pres., chief exec. officer, 1990-91, chmn. bd., chief exec. officer, 1991-93; mem. USPHS Pharmacology and Exptl. Therapeutics Study Sect., 1964-67; Bd. overseers Meml. Sloan-Kettering Cancer Center. Author: (with others) Nervous Control of the Heart, 1965, Heart Substitutes, 1966, The Baboon in Medical Research, Vol. II, 1967, Factors Influencing Myocardial Contractility, 1967, Acute Myocardial Infarction, 1968, Advance in Transplantation, Prosthetic Heart Valves, 1969, Depressed Metabolism, 1969; Editorial bd.: Jour. Pharmacology and Exptl. Therapeutics, 1965-68, 77-93, Circulation Research, 1966-71; editor: Supplements to Circulation, 1966-71; sect. co-editor for: Jour. Applied Physiology, 1967-73; contbr. numerous articles med. jours.; discoverer new techniques of denervating heart which have helped delineate role of nerves in heart, on its ability to function under a wide variety of circumstances, and on its ability to respond to drugs. Bd. govs. ARC, 1980. Recipient Borden award, 1954; Albert Lasker Spl. Public Service award, 1978; Ellen Browning Scripps medal, 1980; medal for Disting. Pub. Service, Dept. Def., 1985. Mem. AAAS, AAUP, Am. Soc. Pharmacology and Exptl. Therapeutics, Am. Physiol. Soc., Soc. Exptl. Biology and Medicine, Am. Soc. Clin. Investigation, Am. Fedn. Clin. Research, Am. Soc. Artificial Internal Organs, Internat. Cardiovascular Soc., Am. Coll. Chest Physicians, Am. Coll. Cardiology, Sigma Xi. Home: Kalamazoo Mich. Died Apr. 22, 1993; interred Ventnor, N.J.

COORAY, THOMAS CARDINAL, clergyman; b. Negombo, Sri Lanka, Dec. 28, 1901; s. Jayalath Aratchige Jacob and Marguerita (Silva) C.; B.A., U. London, 1924; Degree in Philosophy, St. Bernard's Sem., Colombo, 1925-26; Ph.D., Acad. St. Thomas, Rome, 1928; Ph.D. in Div., Angelicum U., Rome, 1931. Ordained priest Roman Catholic Ch., 1929, archbishop, 1946, cardinal, 1965. Prof. botany St. Joseph's Coll. Colombo, Sri Lanka, 1931-37; warden Roman Cath. Hostel for Undergrads., Colombo, 1932-37; supr. Oblate Sem., Colombo, 1937-46; co-adjutor Archbishop of Colombo, 1946-47; archbishop of Colombo, 1947-76 archbishop emeritus, 1976—; pres. Roman Cath. Bishops Conf. Sri Lanka, 1947-76; planned Nat. Basilica/Sanctuary Our Lady of Lanka, 1948-75; established Aquinas U. Coll. Higher Edn., 1954, Nat. Seminary Ecclesiastical Studies in Sri Lanka, 1955, Cath. Radio Ctr., 1970; mem. ante prep. council Vatican Council, 1959-62, participant, 1962-65; mem. Sacred Congregations of Propaganda Fide and Oriental Chs. 1965-70; mem. Pontifical Commn. for Revision of Canon Law, 1968-83; founder, mem. Fedn. Asian Bishops Confs., 1970-76. Writer pamphlets on sanctity and family planning. Named Asst. at the Pontifical Throne, Holy Father Pope Pius XII, Rome, 1954. Home: Tewatta Ragama Sri Lanka

COPE, OLIVER, surgeon, educator; b. Germantown Pa., Aug. 15, 1902; s. Walter and Eliza Middleton (Kane) C.; m. Alice DeNormandie, Dec. 28, 1932; children: Robert DeNormandie, Eliza Middleton. A.B. Harvard U., 1923, M.D., 1928; Dr. honoris causa, U. Toulouse, 1950; D.H.L. (hon.), Haverford Coll., Pa. 1984; D.Sc. (hon.), U. R.I., 1984. Diplomate Am. Bd. Surgery. Intern, resident in surgery Mass. Gen. Hosp. Boston, 1928-32, asst. to assoc. surgeon, 1934-46, vis. surgeon, 1946-69, acting chief surg. services, 1968-69 mem. bd. consultation, 1969-94; traveling fellow Harvard U., 1933, instr., later assoc. in surgery, asst. prof. surgery, 1934-38, assoc. prof., 1948-63, prof., 1963-69, prof. emeritus, 1969-94, acting head dept. surgery 1968-69; chief of staff Boston unit Shriners Burn Inst. 1964-69, chief staff emeritus, 1969-94; responsible investigator Office Sci. Research and Devel., 1942-45; mem. subcom. burns NRC, 1943-45, dir. research under contract with Office Naval Research, 1947-52. Fellow ACS; mem. Am. Surg. Assn. (pres. 1962-63), Harvard Med. Alumni Assn. (pres. 1968-69), New Eng. Surg. Soc., Internat. Soc. Surgery, AAAS, Soc. Clin. Surgery Soc. Clin. Investigation, Soc. U. Surgeons, AMA, Mass. Med. Soc., Boston Surg. Soc. (pres. 1965), Boylston Med. Soc. (pres. 1964), Inst. Medicine of Nat. Acad. Scis., Am. Acad. Arts and Scis. Home: Lincoln Mass. Died Apr. 30, 1994.

CORBETT, JAMES WILLIAM, physicist, educator; b. N.Y.C., Aug. 25, 1928; s. Amos Bryant and Julia (Holmes) C.; m. M.E. Grenander, May 5, 1972. BS, U. Mo., 1951, MA, 1952; PhD, Yale U., 1955; DSc (hon.) King Meml. Coll., 1979, U. Mo., 1989, Novosibirsk (USSR) State U., 1990; Moscow Inst Electronic Tech 1991. Research assoc. Yale U., New Haven, 1955 physicist Gen. Electric Research and Devel. Ctr. Schenectady, 1955-68; mem. faculty physics dept. SUNY, Albany, 1968-94, prof., 1968-81, Disting. Service prof., 1981-94, chmn. dept. physics, 1969-70, lectr. oe nology and turology Coll. Gen. Studies, 1972-78,80, dir. Inst. Study of Defects in Solids, 1973-94, co-dir. Joint Lab. for Advanced Materials, 1987-94; adj. prof. Rensselaer Poly. Inst., 1964-68; Disting. vis. prof. Am. U. Cairo, 1973; vis. prof. Ecole Normale Superieure, 1976 U. Paris VII, 1976, U. Linköping, 1984-85, Beijing U. 1986, Fudan U., 1986, Sichuan U., 1986; sr. Fulbright prof. Tbilisi State U., USSR, 1979; Disting. lectr. Rude Boskovic Inst., Zagreb, Yugoslavia, 1983; active in ternat. confs. Author: (with others) Chaos an Stabilization Defect Processes in Semi-Conductors, 199 Democratic Committeeman, 1960-63; internat. sec. Bo Tie Wearers' Anti-Defamation League. Served to 2d l Signal Corps U.S. Army, 1946-48. Recipient Ivanr Javakishvili medal Tbilisi State U., 1977, A.I. Shok medal Moscow Inst. for Electronic Tech., 1990; O.M. Stewart fellow, 1951-52, Charles Coffin fellow, 1954-55, Guggenheim fellow, 1979; Wissenschaftlichen Mitglieder, Kaiserlich-Konigliche Bohmisch Physikalische Gesellschaft, 1982; named Citizen Laureate Univ. Found.-Albany, 1982. Fellow N.Y. Acad. Scis., Am. Phys. Soc. (vice chmn. N.Y. State sect. 1975-77, sect. 1977-79); mem. AAAS, IEEE (sr.), Am. Assn. Physics Tchrs., Materials Research Soc. (co-chair symposium on defects in semiconductors, Boston 1982, symposium on hydrogen, oxygen, carbon and nitrogen in silicon, Boston 1985, mem. pub. com. 1983-85) Electrochem. Soc., Am. Cryptogram Assn., Am. Solar Energy Soc., Am. Physicists Assn., Soc. Wine Educators (charter), Fulbright Assn., Soc. for Preservation Nat. Bow Tie, Phi Beta Kappa (chpt. pres. 1978-79), Sigma Xi. Home: East Berne N.Y. Died Apr. 25, 1994.

CORBETT, WILLARD JASON, food company executive; b. Pearl City, Ill., Oct. 29, 1912; s. William and Margaret (Schasker) Corbett; m. Alice Carman, Aug. 12, 1936; children: Ann, John. B.S., U. Ill., 1934, Ph.D., 1942; M.S., U. Wis., 1935. Research asst. U. Ill., Urbana, 1935-41; dir. lab. Nat. Dairy Products, Cleve., 1941-42; tech. dir. Dean Foods, Rockford, Ill., 1943-70, dir., 1947-80, v.p., 1957-70, sr. v.p., 1980-95. Mem. Sigma Xi. Lodge: Kiwanis (pres.). Home: Rockford Ill. Died Feb. 8, 1995.

CORBETT, WILLIAM LYNNWOOD, clergyman; b. Springfield, S.C., Sept. 27, 1927; s. Albert S. and Margaret (Tarrant) C.; m. Hazel Clark Crosby, Feb. 12, 1949; children—Patricia Lynn, Robert Stokes. Cert. in Bible, Columbia Bible Coll., S.C., 1947. Ordained to ministry So. Methodist Ch., 1946. Pres. So. Meth. Ch., Orangeburg, S.C., 1955-66, minister, 1962-82, pres., 1982—. Recipient Christian Service award So. Meth. Coll., Orangeburg, 1966, 69, 70. Mem. Evangel. Tchrs. Tng. Assn., Am. Council Christian Chs. (officer 1956-66). Lodge: Lions (bd. dirs. Orangeburg 1985). Deceased. Home: Orangeburg S.C.

CORCORAN, MARY BARBARA, language educator; b. Pasadena, Calif., May 22, 1924; d. George Ernest Morrison and Ina Pearl (Thomas) Phippen; m. James Leonard Corcoran, Dec. 22, 1956; children: Ann Morrison, Elizabeth Phippen DeGroodt. BA, Wellesley Coll., 1946; MA, Radcliffe Coll., 1949; postgrad., U. Munich, 1949-50; PhD, Bryn Mawr Coll., 1958. Translator U.S. War Dept., Nuremberg, Fed. Republic of Germany, 1946-47; prof. German Vassar Coll., Poughkeepsie, N.Y., 1953-90; part-time instr. Wellesley (Mass.) Coll., 1947-48. Translator: The Romantic Fairy Tale, 1964. Mem. Am. Assn. Tchrs. German, AAUP, MLA. Mem. United Ch. of Christ. Home: Poughkeepsie N.Y. Died June 11, 1992.

CORDEIRO, JOSEPH CARDINAL, archbishop of Karachi; b. Bombay, India, Jan. 19, 1918. BA, U. Bombay, 1939; MA, Oxford (Eng.) U., 1950. Ordained priest Roman Catholic Ch., 1946. Archbishop of Karachi Pakistan, 1958—, created cardinal, 1973. Mem. congregation Religious and Secular Insts.; mem. Secretariate Non-Christian Religions. Home: Karachi Pakistan Died Feb. 11, 1994.

CORNELL, GEORGE W., journalist; b. Weatherford, Okla., July 24, 1920; s. Charles H. and Gladys (Cameron) C.; m. Jo Ann Reeves, Apr. 1, 1944; children: Marion Emma, Harrison Reeves. AB, U. Okla., 1943; LHD, Defiance Coll., 1962; LittD, Gonsaga U., 1992. Reporter Daily Oklahoman, Oklahoma City, 1943-44; newsman A.P., N.Y.C., 1947-51; religion columnist A.P., 1951-94. Author: They Knew Jesus, 1957, The Way and its Ways, 1963, Voyage of Faith, 1964, (with Douglas Johnson) Punctured Preconceptions, 1972, Behold the Man, 1974, The Untamed God, 1975. Served to 2d lt., inf. AUS, 1944-47. Recipient Nat. Religious Pub. Rels. Coun. award, 1953, Religion Heritage in Am. Faith and Freedom award, 1960, Religion Newswriters Assn. Supple Meml. award, 1961, Jim Merrell Religious Liberty Meml. award, 1977, William E. Leidt award, 1978, Templeton Reporter of Yr. award, 1987, Wilbur award, 1993. Mem. Am. Newspaper Guild, Religious Newswriters Assn. Episcopalian. Home: New York N.Y. Died Aug. 10, 1994.

CORNEVIN, ROBERT, language professional, educator; b. Malesherbes, Loiret, France, Aug. 26, 1919; s. Maurice and Geneviéve (Chameaux) C.; m. Rau Marianne; children: François, Geneviéve, Bernard, Hubert, Etienne, Heléne. Student, Ecole Nat. France D"Outre Mer, Paris; Docteur es Lettres, U. Paris Sorbonne. Adminstr. France D'Outre Mer, successively Togo, Dahomey, Senegal, cambodgia, 1941-56; civl adminstr. Minister Nat. Edn., Paris, 1958-60; adminstr. Documentation Francaise, Paris, 1960-85; pres. Assn. Ecrivains Langue Francaise, Paris, 1974—; permanent sec. Acad. Sci. D'outre Mer, Paris, 1971—. Author: 30 books on history of Togo, Africa, Zaire, African Lit., theatre, others. Served to lt. French Infantry, 1940-47. Home: Paris France

CORREZE, JACQUES H., cosmetics executive; b. 1912. Chmn. Cosmair Inc., Clark, N.J., until 1991. Home: New York N.Y. Died June 27, 1991.

CORRIGAN, DANIEL, clergyman; b. Pontiac, Mich., Oct. 25, 1900; s. Herbert James and Katherine (Burns) C.; m. Elizabeth Waters, Sept. 21, 1926. BD, Nashotah (Wis.) Theol. Sem., 1926, STM, 1943, DD, 1955. Ordained to ministry P.E. Ch., 1924; pastor in Portage, Wis., 1925-31, Oconomowoc, Wis., 1931-43, Balt., 1944-48, St. Paul, 1948-58; chaplain St.Francis House, U. Wis., 1944; suffragan bishop Colo., 1958-60; dir. home dept. Nat. Council P.E. Ch., 1960-68; minister to coll. Amherst (Mass.) Coll., 1968-69; dean Bexley Hall, Rochester (N.Y.) Centre for theol. studies, 1969-71; assisting bishop of Los Angeles, 1972-94, ret. Chmn. dept. Christian social relations Diocese of Minn., 1952-58; pres. Am. Ch. Inst. for Negroes, from 1960; mem. joint commn. P.E. Gen. Conv. Edn. Holy Orders, from 1958; Vice pres. Minn. Indian Commn., 1955-58; pres. St. Paul Council Human Relations, 1954-58; mem. Gov. of Minn. Commn. on Resettlement, 1955-58; Trustee Nashotah Theol. Sem. Recipient Bishop William Scarlett award, 1979; John Nevin Sayre award, 1979. Fellow Am. Soc. Religion and Culture. Home: Santa Barbara Calif. Died Sept. 21, 1994.

CORRIGAN, FREDRIC H., retired corporate executive; b. Grand Forks, N.D., Dec. 2, 1914; s. Thomas S. and Bertha (Wolff) C.; m. Mary Leslie, Dec. 30, 1939; children: Leslie (Mrs. John G. Turner), Fredric Wolff, Nancy (Mrs. Kenneth B. Woodrow). Student, U. Minn., 1933-36. Grain merchandiser Peavey Co., Mpls., 1936-43, Duluth, Minn., 1946-55, Mpls., 1955-77; exec. v.p. Peavey Co., 1959-65, pres., 1965-77, chief exec. officer, 1968-77, chmn. bd., 1975-77; pres. Duluth Bd. Trade, 1954-55, Mpls. Grain Exchange, 1967-68. Bd. dirs. United Fund Mpls., 1967-72, Mpls. YMCA, 1970-78, Mpls. Urban Coalition, 1971-74, U. Minn. Found., 1976-85 , Vikings Childrens Fund, 1979-95, Minn. Orch., 1974-80, Animal Humane Soc., 1987-95, also Western, Minn. golf assns.; bd. dirs. Northwestern Hosp., 1975-88, chmn., 1977-79; trustee Evans Scholars Found., 1968-72. Served with USNR, 1942-46. Mem. Greater Mpls. C. of C. (bd. dirs. 1972-75), Sigma Chi. Methodist (trustee). Clubs: Minneapolis, Minikahda; Desert Forest (Carefree, Ariz.); Desert Mountain (Scottsdale, Ariz.). Home: Carefree Ariz. Died Oct. 16, 1995.

CORRIGAN, ROBERT WILLOUGHBY, university dean; b. Portage, Wis., Sept. 23, 1927; s. Daniel and Elizabeth (Waters) C.; m. Mary Katherine Kolling, Dec. 18, 1953 (div. Sept. 1960); m. Elizabeth Trevor Seneff, June 15, 1963 (div. June 1969); m. Jane Langley, Aug. 1, 1969 (div. Feb. 1979); m. JoAnn Johnson, Aug. 11, 1979; children: Michael Edward, Timothy Patrick. BA, Cornell U., 1950; MA, Johns Hopkins U., 1952; PhD, U. Minn., 1955. Instr. drama Johns Hopkins U., Balt., 1950-52; instr. English, dir. Drama Dept. The Gilman Sch., Balt., 1950-52; instr. theatre and classics U. Minn., Mpls., 1952-54; asst. prof. drama Carleton Coll., Northfield, Minn., 1954-57; assoc. prof. Tulane U., New Orleans, 1957-61; Andrew Mellon Prof., head Dept. Drama Carnegie-Mellon U., Pitts., 1961-64; prof. dramatic lit. NYU, 1964-68, dean Sch. of Arts, 1965-68; pres. Calif. Inst. of the Arts, Valencia, 1968-72; prof. English and theater U. Mich., 1973-74; dean Sch. Fine Arts U. Wis., Milw., 1974-84; dean Sch. Arts and Humanities U. Tex. at Dallas, Richardson, 1984-93; vis. regents lectr. State U. of Va., 1968; mem. faculty U. for Presidents, Young Pres.'s Orgn., 1973; Avery Hopgood lectr. U. Mich., Ann Arbor, 1973, vis. prof., 1973-74; cons. Samuel F. Rubin Found., N.Y.C., 1973-76, Chandler Pub. Co., Dell Pub. Co., Houghton Mifflin; lectr. for U.S. Dept. State in Austria, the Netherlands, Belgium, Denmark, 1976, for USIA in Europe, Sweden, Greece, Germany, Denmark, 1982, Austria, Romania, Yugoslavia, USSR, Finland, 1983, The Netherlands, Belgium, 1986; panelist summer drama teaching program NEH, 1978-80; sr. Fulbright lectr. in Am. drama U. Innsbruck, Austria, 1980; chmn. theatre panel CIES-Fulbright Scholar Awards in Theatre Arts, 1985-88; vis. prof. theatre U. Skopje, Yugoslavia, 1987. Author: The Theatre in Search of a Fix, 1973, The World of the Theatre, 1979, 2d edit., 1992; translator: Chekhov: Six Plays, 1962, Appia: Music and the Art of the Theatre, 1962; editor: Tulane Drama Review, 1957-62, Euripides: Hippolytus, 1962, The New Theatre of Europe, Vol. 1, 1962, Vol. 2, 1964, Vol. 3, 1968, The Theatre in the Twentieth Century, 1962, The Modern Theatre, 1964, Laurel Classical Drama series, 1964-65, Laurel Brit. Drama series, 1965, Greek Comedy, 1965, Euripides, 1965, Sophocles, 1965, Aeschylus, 1965, New Am. Plays, Vol. 1, 1965, Comedy, Meaning and Form, 1965, 1980, Tragedy: Vision and Form, 1965, 2d edit., 1981, 20th Century, 1965, Strindberg: A Dream Play and the Ghost Sonata, 1966, Roman Drama, 1966, 19th Century, 1967, Masterpieces of the Modern Theatre, 9 vols., 1966, Arthur Miller: Twentieth Century Views, 1969, Comedy: A Critical Anthology, 1971, Tragedy: A Critical Anthology, 1971, The Forms of Drama, 1972, The Making of Theatre: From Drama to Performance, 1981, (with James C. Rosenberg) The Art of the Theatre, 1964, The Context and Craft of Drama, 1964, Classical Comedy, 1987, Classical Tragedy, 1990; contbr. more than 100 articles to profl. jours.; contbr. essays to books; dir. 40 student and profl. stage plays, 1951-62. Mem. Pres.'s Council Vassar Coll., Poughkeepsie, N.Y., 1964-68; assoc. trustee U. Pa., 1967-72; trustee Simon's Rock Early Coll., Gt. Barrington, Mass., 1976-79, Milw. Art Mus., 1976-84, Pabst Theatre, Milw., 1979-81; bd. dirs. SPACE for Innovative Devel., N.Y.C., chmn., 1973-76, Arts Devel. Council, Milw., 1977-81, pres., 1979-81, KoThi Dance Co., Milw., 1978-84, Peoples Theatre, Milw., 1979-81, Lincoln Ctr. for the Arts, Milw., 1979-84, Milw. Artists Found., pres., 1981-84. Recipient Hon. Citation of Merit, Niagara U., 1967, Citation for Disting. Service to Theatre, Ill. Theatre Assn., 1979, Citation for Merit, Ky. Theatre Assn., 1979. Fellow Am. Theatre Assn.; mem. NEH (dir. critics program 1966-68), Univ./Coll. Theatre Assn. of Am. Theatre Assn. (v.p. for publs. 1983-87), Nat. Council of the Arts in Edn., Nat. Theatre Conf., Internat. Council of Fine Arts Deans (rep. to Nat. Council of the Arts), Nat. Choral Council (bd. dirs. 1966-77), Sigma Delta Chi, Sigma Phi. Episcopalian. Home: Dallas Tex. Died Sept. 1, 1993.

CORRY, ANDREW FRANCIS, consulting engineering executive; b. Lynn, Mass., Oct. 28, 1922; s. Andrew Francis and Julia Agnes (Gaynor) C.; m. Mildred M. Dunn, Sept. 16, 1950 (dec. 1977); children—Andrea, Janice, James; m. Diane Kinch, June 27, 1986; 1 stepchild, Melissa. BSEE, MIT, 1947; postgrad. Advanced Mgmt. Program, Harvard U., 1966. Registered profl. engr., Mass. With Boston Edison Co., 1947-83, asst. to exec. v.p., 1969-72, dir. engring., planning, nuclear and systems ops., 1972-75, v.p. engring. and distbn., 1975-79, sr. v.p., 1979-83; cons. engr. Boston, 1983-94; v.p. Power Mgmt. Assocs., 1987-88; gen. mgr. U.S. Nat. Com., Internat. Conf. Large High Voltage Electric Systems, 1985-94. Served with S.C., U.S. Army, 1942-46. Recipient Attwood award U.S. nat. com. CIGRE, 1993. Fellow IEEE (Habirshaw award 1983, Centennial medal 1984), NAE, Harvard Club (Boston). Roman Catholic. Home: West Hyannisport Mass. Died Dec. 22, 1994.

CORYELL, ROGER CHARLES, retired newspaper executive; b. Alliance, Nebr., May 21, 1916; s. Rex Laverne and Evangeline (Richardson) C.; m. Julia Lewis Hornady, Sept. 21, 1956; children: Coreen Coryell Haydon, Roger Charles, Julia Coryell Lange, Elizabeth Eve. Student, St. Ambrose Coll., Davenport, Iowa, 1937-41; spl. studies, UCLA, NYU. Advt. exec. Lee Syndicate, Davenport, Iowa, 1938-46, Miami News (Fla.), 1947-56; gen. mgr. Met. Asso. Services, N.Y.C., 1957-58; asst. pub. Capitol Newspapers Albany, N.Y., 1959-69; v.p., gen. mgr. Hartford (Conn.) Times, 1970-71, pres., pub., 1971-73; gen. mgr. Fresno (Calif.) Bee, 1974-83; past mem. bd. dirs. journalism adv. bd. and bus. adv. council Sch. Bus., Calif. State U., Fresno. Past bd. dirs. Albany area ARC, Fresno C. of C.; past bd. dirs. Hartford area ARC, Conn. Opera Assn.; past pres. Fresno Philharm. Assn. Served with U.S. Army, 1944-45. Decorated Army Commendation medal; recipient Silver Medal award Printers Ink, 1966. Mem. Am. Newspaper Pubs. Assn.,. Republican. Congregationalist. Home: New Baltimore N.Y. Died Dec. 26, 1992.

COSFORD, WILLIAM CLARK, film critic, columnist; b. Phila., July 7, 1946; s. William Clark and Mary Louise (Kohler) C.; m. Judith Ann Robertson, Aug. 31, 1971 (div. 1980). Film critic Miami (Fla.) Herald, 1979—, columnist, 1981—; commentator Sta. WPBT-TV, Miami, 1985-90, Sta. WLVE-FM, Miami, 1990—; adj. prof. film studies U. Miami, Coral Gables, Fla., 1985—; correspondent various stas., N.Y.C., 1980—. Conbtg. editor Self Mag., N.Y.C., 1988-90; freelance writer various mags. including Rolling Stone, US, Entertainment Weekly, Weightwatchers, 1984—. Recipient First Prize Criticism Fla. Newspaper Editors, 1984, 87, 90; named hon. chmn. Key West (Fla.) Literary Seminar, 1991. Mem. Sigma Delta Chi. (first prize criticism, 1981). Home: Chatham N.J.

COSTELLO, RUSSELL HILL, newspaper executive; b. Lewiston, Maine, Oct. 22, 1904; s. Louis B. and Sadie (Brackett) C.; m. Jane H. Cassidy, May 5, 1928; children: Alice Ann (Mrs. Robert E. Dillingham), James Russell, Jane Mary (Mrs. Daniel J. Wellehan, Jr.). Student, Bates Coll., 1924-26, Mass. Inst. Tech., 1927-30. With Lewiston Daily Sun, from 1930, treas., from 1955, pres., 1959-93, also dir., 1959-93; incorporator Androscoggin Savs. Bank. Former mem. Gov.'s Council on Art and Culture; devel. council U. Maine. Served to maj. Maine State Guard, 1943-46. Mem. Maine Publishers Assn. (past pres.), New Eng. Publishers Assn., Am. Publishers Assn., New Eng. Council (dir.), Lewiston C. of C. (dir., past pres.), New Eng. Mech. Assn. (past pres.). Home: Lewiston Maine Died June 5, 1993.

COSWAY, RICHARD, legal educator; b. Newark, Ohio, Oct. 20, 1917; s. Paul Taunton and Edith Harriet (Crawford) C.; m. Serena Boland, June 8, 1957; children: Robert Gordon, Paul Richard. A.B., Denison U., 1939; J.D., U. Cin., 1942. Bar: Ohio 1942. Prof. law U. Cin., 1946-58; prof. law U. Wash., Seattle, 1958-84, prof. emeritus, 1984-95; atty. Dept. Justice, Washington, 1952-53; vis. prof. law So. Meth. U., Dallas, 1954, 67-68, U. Puget Sound, Tacoma, Wash., 1965, 66; vis. prof. Hasting's Coll. Law, 1981-82; commr. on uniform state laws State of Wash., 1967-85; mem. Nat. Conf. of Commr. on Unified State Laws. Author: (with Warren Shattuck) Washington Practice, vols. 7 and 8, 1967, (with Warren Shattuck and Herbert Ma) Trade and Investment in Taiwan, 1973. Served with U.S. Army, 1942-46. Recipient Disting. teaching award U. Wash.,

1980. Lodges: Elks, Masons. Home: Seattle Wash. Died Dec. 2, 1995.

COTTEN, JOSEPH, actor; b. Petersburg, Va.; s. Joseph and Sally (Willison) C.; m. Lenore Kip (dec.); m. Patricia Medina, 1960. Student, Robert Nugent Hickman Dramatic Sch., Washington. pres. Mercury Theatre, 1944. Actor in: David Belasco prodns. Dancing Partners, Tonight or Never, 1930-31; in stock, Copley Theater, Boston, 1931-32; actor in popular stage plays, 1932-40, including, The Philadelphia Story, 1939-40, Calculated Risk, 1962; writer and appeared as actor in: Mercury Theatre of Air, 1938-39; radio actor: Lockheed Aircraft weekly radio program America Ceiling Unlimited, 1943-44; actor in motion pictures, 1940—, the first being, Citizen Kane, Lydia; later films include The Third Man, 1948, September Affair, Half-Angel, 1951, Special Delivery, 1955; other films Caravans; stage plays Sabrina Fair, N.Y.C., 1953-54, Once More With Feeling, N.Y.C., 1958-59, Hush, Hush, Sweet Charlotte, 1964; nat. road tour Seven Ways of Love, 1964; host, narrator: nat. road tour 20th Century-Fox TV Hour, 1955-56; narrator: TV show Hollywood and the Stars, 1963-64; appeared in: TV series On Trial, 1957-58, Angel Wore Red, 1959, Gun in Hand, 1960. Home: Los Angeles Calif.

COTTER, WILLIAM JOSEPH, retired grain company executive; b. Bayonne, N.J., Jan. 24, 1921; s. Michael and Nora Agnes (Sullivan) C.; m. Virginia Alicia McMahon, 1949 (dec. 1962); children: William Joseph, Alicia Ann Cotter Wilson; m. Almedia Jo Ford, June 28, 1966; children: Kathleen Jo Walker, Christopher Michael. BBA, Coll. City N.Y., 1947; postgrad., Georgetown U., 1950-52; LLB, N.Y. U., 1955. Spl. agt. FBI, 1947-51; with CIA, 1951-69; chief postal insp. U.S. Postal Service, 1969-75; v.p., chief compliance officer Bunge Corp., N.Y.C., 1975-86; v.p. Lauhoff Grain Co., Danville, Ill., 1979-86; spl. magistrate Arlington County, Va., 1978. Served to capt. USAAF, 1942-46, CBI. Mem. Soc. Former Spl. Agts. FBI, Cen. Intelligence Retiree's Assn., Mil. Order Fgn. Wars U.S. Roman Catholic. Home: Fairfax Va. Died Mar., 1995.

COUGHLAN, (JOHN) ROBERT, author, journalist; b. Kokomo, Ind., July 7, 1914; s. William Henry and Lucile DeNevers (Ernsperger) C.; m. Patricia Ann Collins, June 30, 1939; children: John Robert, Brian Christopher, Kevin Brooks, Cynthia Davis. BS, Northwestern U., 1936; DHL (hon.), Ind. U., 1988. Mem. staff Fortune mag., 1937-43, assoc. editor, 1938-43; text editor Life mag., 1943-49, mem. editorial staff, writer-editor, 1943-70; editorial assoc. Kennedy Found., 1971-73; freelance writer, contbr. various jours. and publs. Author: The Wine of Genius, 1951, The Private World of William Faulkner, 1954, Tropical Africa, 1962, The World of Michaelangelo, 1966, Elizabeth and Catherine, 1974; collaborator: Times to Remember (Rose Kennedy memoirs), 1974; contbr. anthologies, other publs. Recipient Benjamin Franklin award, 1953, Benjamin Franklin citation, 1954, Lasker award for med. journalism, 1954, 59, citation for excellence Overseas Press Club, 1957, Disting. Service to Journalism award Sigma Delta Chi, 1959, merit citation Nat. Edn. Writers Assn., 1961, Recognition award Northwestern U., 1962, Heywood Broun citation Am. Newspaper Guild, 1963, Ann. Book award Nat. Assn. Ind. Schs., 1967, Putnam award, 1974; Austin scholar, Northwestern U., 1936. Mem. Century Assn. Home: Sag Harbor N.Y. Died May 9, 1992.

COUGHLIN, SISTER MAGDALEN, college chancellor; b. Wenatchee, Wash., Apr. 16, 1930; d. William Joseph and Cecilia Gertrude (Diffley) C. BA, Coll. St. Catherine, Mpls., 1952; MA, Mount St. Mary's Coll., L.A., 1962; PhD, U. So. Calif., 1970; LHD (hon.), Loyola Marymount U., 1983, Holy Family Coll., 1989, Dominican Coll., 1991. Joined Sisters of St. Joseph, Roman Catholic Ch., 1956. Tchr. history Alemany High Sch., San Fernando, Calif., 1960-61; tchr. history St. Mary's Acad., Los Angeles, 1961-63; asst. prof. history Mount St. Mary's Coll., L.A., 1963-70, dean acad. devel., 1970-74, pres., 1976-89, chancellor, from 1989; provincial councilor Sisters of St. Joseph, L.A., 1974-76; trustee Marianne Frostig Ctr., Los Angeles, 1976-90, also bd. dirs.; trustee St. Catherine's Coll., Mpls., 1982-91; bd. dirs., vice chmn. Calif. Council for Humanities, 1984-88. Contbr. articles and revs. to profl. jours. Pres. Commn. on Status of Women, L.A., 1984-90; bd. dirs. Doheny Found., from 1987; trustee J. Paul Getty Trust, from 1991. Fulbright scholar U. Nijmegen, 1952-53; Haynes dissertation fellow, 1969-70. Mem. Calif. Hist. Soc., Am. Hist. Soc., Fulbright Alumni Assn., Women in Bus., Women's Trusteeship, Assn. Ind. Calif. Colls. (bd. dirs. 1979), Ind. Colls. So. Calif. (bd. dirs. 1976), Am. Coun. Edn. (bd. dirs. from 1986), So. Calif. Assn. Philanthropy (bd. dirs. from 1991), Phi Alpha Theta, Pi Gamma Mu, Delta Epsilon Sigma. Deceased.

COUGHRAN, TOM BRISTOL, banker; b. Visalia, Calif., Mar. 18, 1906; s. William L. and Rose (Bristol) C.; m. Florence Montgomery, Mar. 29, 1930; 1 child, Jane N. AB, Stanford U., 1927. With Bank of Am. Nat. Trust & Savs., 1927-57, v.p. internat. banking, 1946-57; exec. v.p., CEO Bank of Am. (Internat.), N.Y.C., 1959-70, vice chmn., 1970-71; mem. export adv. com. Dept. Commerce, 1953-57; asst. sec. for internat. affairs U.S. Treasury, 1957-58; U.S. exec. dir. IBRD, 1957-58, Internat. Fin. Corp., 1957-58; dir. U.S. Devel. Loan Fund, 1958; bd. dirs. Capitol Industries, EMI, Tenneco Internat.; chmn. bd. dirs. Wobaco Holding Co., Luxembourg, and its 5 banking, trust and fin. cos. in Luxembourg, Bahamas, Jersey, London, Cayman, 1971-75. Mem. presdl. commns. to NATO, Latin Am. and Colombo Conf., 1957, 58; chmn. U.S.A. bus. and industry adv. com. OECD, 1966-68. Served as lt. col. AUS, 1942-46, ETO. Clubs: F Street, Metropolitan (Washington); Pacific Union, Bohemian (San Francisco); Links (N.Y.C.). Home: Falls Church Va. Died Oct. 2, 1993; interred Woodlake, Calif.

COUSINS, SOLON B., association executive; b. Richmond, Va.. B.A. in Sociology, U. Richmond, 1947; M.A. in Sociology, U. Chgo., 1951; Hon. Dr. Humanics, Springfield Coll., 1982; Dr. Social Services, U. Richmond, 1983. Personnel mgr. chain dept. stores Chgo., in past; exec. dir. United Way of Met. Chgo., in past; past exec. dir. The Urban Group, Greater Boston YMCA; personnel and planning dir. (past) YMCAs of Met. Chgo.; nat. exec. dir. YMCA of U.S., to present. trustee George Williams Coll.; past trustee Springfield Coll., YMCA Retirement Fund; bd. Am. Humanics, Lincoln Filene Inst. of Tufts U.; bd. dirs. Chgo. Theol. Sem. Home: Chicago Ill. Died Feb. 29, 1996.

COVER, ROBERT M., law educator; b. Boston, July 30, 1943; s. Jacob L. and Martha (White) C.; m. Diane Bornstein, Oct. 29, 1967; children: Avidan, Leah. B.A., Princeton U., 1965; LL.B., Columbia U., 1968. Asst. prof. law Columbia U., N.Y.C., 1968-71; vis. sr. lectr. law and Am. studies Hebrew U., Jerusalem, 1971-72, vis. prof. law, 1975; assoc. prof. law Yale U., New Haven, 1973—, Chancellor Kent prof. law and legal history, dir. Law and Humanities Inst., 1981—. Author: (with Owen Fiss) Structure of Procedure, 1979. Pres. Yale Friends of Hillel, New Haven, 1980—. Fellow Guggenheim Found., 1981-82. Democrat. Jewish. Home: New Haven Conn.

COVEY, F. DON, energy company executive; b. Lubbock, Tex., June 19, 1934; s. Foy Wallace and Letha Beatrice (Dumas) C.; m. Mary Helen Key, Nov. 5, 1955; children: Frank P., Don W. B.S. in Petroleum Engring., Tex. Tech. U., 1955. Various engring. positions Shell Oil Co., Tex., Okla. and La., 1955-64; div. petroleum engr. Shell Oil Co., Houston and Bakersfield, Calif., 1964-68; chief petroleum engr. Shell Oil Co., New Orleans, 1968-70; div. prodn. mgr. Shell Oil Co., 1970-76; sr. v.p. prodn. Mitchell Energy Corp., Houston, 1976-79; pres. exploration and prodn. div. Mitchell Energy & Devel. Corp., The Woodlands, Tex., 1979-93, now also sr. v.p.; exec. v.p. Mitchell Energy Corp., The Woodlands, Tex. Mem. Soc. Petroleum Engrs., Am. Petroleum Inst., Tex. Mid-Continent Oil and Gas Assn. Republican. Mem. Ch. of Christ. Club: Woodlands Country. Home: Magnolia Tex. Died 1993.

COWART, WILLIAM SLATER, JR., utility executive; b. Cowart, Va., Oct. 31, 1917; s. William Slater and Alice (Sherman) C.; m. Pauline Sara Cox, Aug. 3, 1944; children—William S. III, Paula Alyce, Zilla Virginia (Mrs. David Forsythe), Bryan Charles. B.S. in Engring, Va. Poly. Inst., 1940; postgrad., Harvard, 1941, Mass. Inst. Tech., 1942; M.S. in Nuclear Physics, Ohio State U., 1947; postgrad., George Washington U., 1949. Commd. 2d lt. USAAF, 1940; advanced through grades to col. USAF, 1949; dir. operations joint Task force armed forces and AEC, Eniwetok and Bikini atolls, 1951-54; comdr. Tactical Strike Force, Langley AFB, Va., 1955-56; chief air research and devel. Tactical Systems Div., 1957-58; dir. Nat. Aviation Facilities Exptl. Center, Atlantic City, 1958-60; ret., 1960; with Atlantic Electric Co., 1960-81, sr. v.p. prodn., operations, sales, 1966-68, sr. v.p. customer and employee relations, sales, 1968-81; pres. Atlantic Housing, Inc., Atlantic City, 1969-95; v.p. Overland Realty, Inc., Atlantic City, 1971-95; pres. Traffic Technologies Research & Devel. Corp., Stamford, Conn., 1981. Chmn. West Jersey Bicentennial Corp., 1970-95, Mayor's Airport Com., 1962-95; pres. Atlantic County chpt. Am. Cancer Soc., 1965-69; pres. Miss Am. Pageant, 1968-72, bd. dirs.; mem. air-land service com., bd. dirs. N.J. Citizens' Transp. Council, 1971-95; pres. Transfair, N.J. Transp. Expns.; Bd. dirs. Atlantic Area council Boy Scouts Am., 1960-68, Atlantic-Cape May council Girl Scouts U.S., 1962-68; bd. dirs. Del. Valley council, 1969-95, v.p., 1974-95; trustee So. N.J. Devel. Council; chmn. Atlantic County Pvt. Industry Council, 1979-95; met. chmn. Nat. Alliance of Bus., 1978-95; v.p., sec. Atlantic City TV Corp., 1978-95; regional adv. Nat. Community Bank. Mem. Atlantic City C. of C. (pres., dir.), S. Jersey C. of C. (dir.), Edison Electric Inst. (hon. mem. sale's exec. conf.). Lodge: Rotary. Home: Lottsburg Va. Died June 4, 1995.

COX, GILBERT EDWIN, lawyer, diversified industry executive; b. 1917; married;. B.B.A., U. Tex., 1938, LL.B., 1940. Bar: Hawaii bar, Tex. bar. Past mem. firm Cades, Cox, Schutte, Fleming & Wright, Honolulu; exec. v.p. Amfac Inc., 1969-74, pres., COO, 1974-78; pres., CEO Alexander & Baldwin, Inc., 1978-80; of counsel firm Cades, Schutte, Fleming & Wright, Honolulu, 1980-90. Served to maj. USAF, 1940-46. Clubs: Silverado Country (Napa, Calif.); Pacific (Honolulu). Home: Napa Calif. Died Jan. 10, 1994; interred Honolulu, Hawaii.

COXE, LOUIS OSBORNE, educator, poet; b. Manchester, N.H., Apr. 15, 1918; s. Charles Shearman and Helen Eyre (Osborne) C.; m. Edith Winsor, June 28, 1946; children: Robert Winsor, Louis Osborne, Charles Shearman, Helen Eyre. A.B., Princeton U., 1940. Instr. Princeton (N.J.) U., 1946; Briggs-Copeland fellow Harvard U., Cambridge, Mass., 1948-49; asst., then assoc. prof. U. Minn., 1949-55; prof. English Bowdoin Coll., Brunswick, Maine, 1955-83, Pierce prof. English, 1956-65. Author: The Sea Faring, 1947, The Second Man, 1955, The Wilderness, 1958, The Middle Passage, 1960, The Last Hero, 1965; (with Robert Chapman) (play) Billy Budd, 1952, Nikal Seyn and Decoration Day, 1966; Edwin Arlington Robinson: The Life of Poetry, 1969, Enabling Acts: Selected Essays in Criticism, 1976, Passage: Selected Poems, 1979. Past trustee N.Y. Sch. Interior Design. Served with USNR, 1942-46. Recipient Creative Arts award Brandeis U., 1961; Sewanee Rev. fellow, 1955; Fulbright fellow, 1959-60, 71-72. Mem. P.E.N., Dramatists Guild. Home: Brunswick Maine Died May 25, 1993.

COYNE, RICHARD DALE, computer engineer; b. L.A., Oct. 24, 1940; s. Michael Thomas and Alma Coleen (Eagles) C.; m. Sandra Kay Humphrey Riley, Nov. 23, 1961 (div. 1968); children: Tandy, Richard, Randal; m. Jeannette Marie Tischler, Sept. 21, 1980; 1 child, Andre Michael. AS, Phoenix Coll., 1967; BS, Ariz. State U., 1970. Res. engr. Motorola Res. Labs., Phoenix, 1964-69, 73-76; lithography mgr. Semiconductor Electronic Memories, Phoenix, 1969-72; prin. engr. Electronic Memories and Magnetics, Phoenix, 1976-78, Motorola Semiconductor Sector, Mesa, Ariz., 1978-80; engring. mgr. Siliconix, Inc., Santa Clara, Calif., 1980-81; sr. scientist GCA Corp., Sunnyvale, Calif., 1981-86; res. scientist Hughes Res. Labs., Malibu, Calif., 1985-88; sr. prin. engr. Shipley Co., Inc., Tempe, Ariz., 1988—; tech. mktg. cons. Dataquest, San Jose, Calif., 1984, Sonotek, Inc., Poughkeepsie, N.Y., 1985; res. cons. Data Gen., Sunnyvale, 1984, Karl Suss, Munich, 1985. Contbr. articles to profl. jours; inventor vapor sheathed baking apparatus, phosphorus vapor deposition. Recipient IR 100 award Res. and Devel. Mag., 1985. Mem. Electrochem. Soc., Soc. Photo-Optical Instrumentation Engrs., IEEE, Scientists Interested in Growth (sec. 1965-69), Hughes/Pepperdine Recreational Club, Phoenix Chess Club, Sierra Club. Republican. Roman Catholic. Home: Mesa Ariz.

CRAIB, RALPH GRANT, reporter; b. Oakland, Calif., Jan. 31, 1925; s. Alexander Leslie and Martha O.C. (Clerk) C.; m. Karola Maria Saekel, Dec. 4, 1962; children: Lisa Maria, Anne. B.A. with honors, San Francisco State Coll., 1950. From copy person, reporter and feature writer Oakland Tribune, 1942-59; mem. staff San Francisco Chronicle, 1959-91, editorial writer, 1968-70, mem. editorial bd., 1978-91; ret., contbr., 1990-95; information officer, mem. staff gov. Am. Samoa, Pago Pago, 1965-66. Bd. dirs. No. Calif. chpt. Americans for Democratic Action, 1967-68. Served with AUS, World War II, ETO. Decorated Combat Infantrymans Badge Bronze star; recipient Joseph R. Knowland newswriting award, 1952, 57, Edward McQuade journalism award, 1977, Lifetime Excellence in Journalism award No. Calif. chpt. Soc. Profl. Journalists, 1990; Reid Found. fellow, New Guinea, Australia, 1955. Mem. San Francisco-Oakland Newspaper Guild (exec. com. 1976-78), Explorers Club (N.Y.C.). Democrat. Home: Berkeley Calif. Died Sept. 28, 1995.

CRAIG, BEN J., banker. Pres. 1st Union Corp., Charlotte, N.C., also bd. dirs.; chmn., chief exec. officer 1st Union Bank N.C. subs. 1st Union Corp., Charlotte, also bd. dirs. Home: Charlotte N.C.

CRAIG, GEORGE BROWNLEE, JR., entomologist; b. Chgo., July 8, 1930; s. George Brownlee and Alice Madeline (McManus) C.; m. Elizabeth Ann Pflum, Aug. 7, 1954; children: James Francis, Mary Catherine (dec.), Patricia Ann, Sarah Lynn. BA, Ind. U., 1951; MS, U. Ill., 1952, PhD, 1956. Rsch. asst. entomology U. Ill., 1951-53; entomologist Mosquito Abatement Dist., summers 1951-53; rsch. entomologist Chem. Corps Med. Labs., Army Chem. Ctr., Md., 1955-57; asst. prof. biology dept. U. Notre Dame, Ind., 1957-61, assoc. prof., 1961-64, prof., 1964-74, George and Winifred Clark disting. prof. biology, 1974-95, dir. WHO Internat. Reference Ctr. for Aedes; vis. rsch. dir. Internat. Ctr. for Insect Physiology and Ecology, Nairobi, Kenya, 1968-76; mem. NIH study sect. on tropical medicine and parasitology, 1970-77; mem. med. rsch. adv. com. U.S. Army., 1980-88. Contbr. 550 articles on Aedes mosquitoes to profl. publs. Chmn. Ind. Vector Control Adv. Coun., 1975-95. Served as 1st lt., Med. Svc. Corps U.S. Army, 1954-55. Rsch. grantee NIH, Ctr. Disease Control, AEC, WHO, NSF, Dept. Def. Fellow NAS (rsch. grantee), Am. Acad. Arts and Scis., Ind. Acad Scis., Entomol. Soc. Am. (bd. govs. 1969-75, Disting Tchg. medal 1975, fellow 1986, Meml. lectr. 1988) mem. Am. Mosquito Control Assn. (Outstanding Rsch award 1976, Meml. lectr. 1984, pres. 1987), Am. Soc Tropical Medicine and Hygiene (councilor 1978-83 councilor Am. com. on med. entomology 1985—Walter Reed medal 1993), Ind. Pub. Health Found. fo Accomplishment Environ. Health (Hulman meda 1991), Soc. Vector Ecology (Career Achievement meda 1995), Sigma Xi. Home: South Bend Ind. Died Dec. 21 1995.

CRAIG, ROBERT CHARLES, educational psychology educator; b. Sault Sainte Marie, Mich., Mar. 9, 1921; s. Frank Lyle and Sylva (Crowell) C.; m. Rosalie Esther DeBoer, Sept. 2, 1950; children: Bruce R., Stephen F. (dec.), Jeffrey A., Barbara Anne. B.S., Mich. State U., 1943, M.A., 1948; Ph.D., Tchrs. Coll., Columbia U., 1952. Research assoc. Columbia U. Tchrs. Coll., 1950-52; asst. prof. State U. Wash., Pullman, 1952-55; research scientist Am. Insts. for Research, Pitts., 1955-58; cons. for ednl. research Am. Insts. for Research, 1958-70; assoc. prof. Marquette U., Milw., 1958-62; prof. Marquette U., 1962-66; prof. ednl. psychology Mich. State U., East Lansing, 1966-89, prof. emeritus, 1989-90, chmn. dept. counseling and ednl. psychology, 1966-81; dir. U.S. Office Edn. Grad. research tng. program, 1966-72; Lectr. psychology U. Pitts., 1956-57; dir. Project TALENT, 1957-58; rsch. on discovery versus reception learning. Author: Transfer Value of Guided Learning, 1953, (with A.M. Dupuis) American Education, Origins and Issues, 1963, Psychology of Learning in the Classroom, 1966, (with H. Clarizio, William Mehrens) Contemporary Issues in Educational Psychology, 1969, 74, 77, 81, 87, Contemporary Educational Psychology, 1975, (with V.H. Noll and D.P. Scannell) Introduction to Educational Measurement, 1979. Served to lt. (j.g.) USNR, 1943-46. Fellow Am. Psychol. Assn.; mem. Am. Ednl. Research Assn., Nat. Council Measurement in Edn., Sigma Xi, Phi Delta Kappa, Phi Kappa Phi. Home: East Lansing Mich. Died Mar. 20, 1990; interred St. Josephs, Lansing, Mich.

CRAIN, BLUFORD WALTER, JR., architect; b. Longview, Tex., Jan. 31, 1914; s. Bluford Walter and Ethel (Smith) C.; m. Ann Lacy, Dec. 28, 1946; children: Lacy Crain, Bluford Walter III, Rogers Lacy. B.Arch., U. Tex., 1937; M.Arch., Harvard U., 1939. Exec. v.p. Rogers Lacy, Inc., Longview, 1947-95; dir. Longview Nat. Bank. Served to lt. USNR, 1941-45. Fellow AIA (pres. NE Tex. chpt. 1957); mem. Tex. Soc. Architects (dir. 1966), Kappa Sigma. Presbyterian. Home: Longview Tex. Died Apr. 27, 1995.

CRAMER, WILLIAM F., capitol goods executive; b. Oak Park, Ill., Aug. 9, 1923; s. Alfred W. and Flora M. (Countier) C.; m. Nancy Elizabeth Ward, Nov. 18, 1944; children: William F. Jr., Kenneth A. B.S.M.E., U. Tex., 1950. V.p., gen. mgr. LTV Aerospace Corp. Range Systems div. Tech. Svcs., Dallas, 1966-72; pres., chief exec. officer Ozone Industries, Inc., N.Y.C., 1972-75; group v.p. Joy Mfg. Co., Pitts., 1975-76, sr. v.p., 1976-78, exec. v.p., 1978-85; pres., chief operating officer Joy Indsl. Equipment Co., Pitts., 1978-85; pres., chief oper. officer Wheeling Machine Products Co., Wheeing, W.Va., 1977-84, Joy Petroleum Equipment Co., Houston, Tex., 1985-86; pres. CRA-KIN Inc., 1987-95. Served to 1st lt. U.S. Army, 1940-46, PTO. Republican. Club: Optimist (pres. 1957-60). Home: Mc Kinney Tex. Died June 17, 1995.

CRANE, ROBERT SELLERS, JR., plastics company executive, civic worker; b. Dayton, Ohio, June 9, 1922; s. Robert Sellers and Helen (Jameson) C.; m. Lois Ann Woods, Aug. 14, 1948; children: Robert Sellers III, Thomas W., Ann B., Mary Jameson. BSBA, Ohio State U., 1948, LLD (hon.), Franklin U., 1992. Pres. Crane Plastics Co., Columbus, Ohio, 1963-67, chmn., 1967-92; chmn. Crane Plastics Co. (formerly Taytec Corp.), Columbus, 1976-92; bd. dirs. State Savs., Columbus. Trustee, immediate past chmn. Franklin U., Columbus, 1986-88; trustee Battelle Meml. Inst.; pres. United Way Franklin County, Columbus, 1977, campaign chmn., 1974, hon. chmn. of 1989 and 1990 campaign; chmn. governing bd. 1st Community Ch., Columbus, 1976, mem. governing com. Columbus Found., vice chmn., 1982-83, chmn., 1984-86. 2d lt. U.S. Army, 1945-46. Mem. Soc. Plastic Industry, Presidents Club Ohio State, Presidents Assn. Am. Mgmt. Assn., Columbus Area C. of C. (vice chmn. 1979-83, Columbus award 1977), Phi Gamma Delta. Republican. Died Dec. 6, 1992. Home: Columbus Ohio

CRANK, CHARLES EDWARD, JR., retired clergyman; b. Richmond, Va., July 20, 1923; s. Charles Edward and Mary Frances (Cochran) C.; m. Melba Louise Cornett, June 7, 1947; children: Charles Edward III, Stephen Lee, Brian Cornett, Melba Kathryn. Student Hampden-Sydney Coll., 1940-42; B.A., Lynchburg Coll., 1947; B.D., Lexington Theol. Sem., 1950; D.D. (hon.), Bethany Coll., 1970. Ordained to ministry Christian Ch., 1947. Pastor, Ky. and Va., 1945-58; dist. minister N.E. Mo., 1958-65; assoc. prof. religion Culver-Stockton Coll., Canton, Mo., 1958-65; regional minister Christian Ch., Parkersburg, W.Va., 1965-88; dir. Div. Homeland Ministries, 1971-80, W.Va. Council Chs., 1965-88; chaplain Lions Club, 1952-55, Am. Legion, 1944-45. Dir. Hazel Green Acad., 1972-83; chmn. Shenandoah County (Va.) ARC, 1954; mem. PTA, 1955-73; worker Community Little League, 1959-65, Tb, Assn., 1956-58. Served with U.S. Army, 1943-44. Recipient Outstanding Alumni award Lexington Theol. Sem., 1971; Assoc. award Bethany Coll., 1969; Ch. Exec. Devel. Bd. scholar, 1968. Mem. Disciples Peace Fellowship, Council Christian Unity, Disciples of Christ Hist. Soc., Am. Philatelic Soc., Congress Disciples Clergy, Blennerhasset Hist. Found., Blennerhasset Stamp Soc. Democrat. Lodge: Masons. Editor W.Va. Christian Ch. News, 1965-88. Died Apr. 6, 1995. Home: Lynchburg Va.

CRANSTON, JOHN MONTGOMERY, lawyer; b. Denver, Oct. 5, 1909; s. Earl Montgomery and Florence Terry (Pitkin) C.; m. Pearl M. Kreps, June 21, 1934; children: Theodore J., Jacqueline G., Harold D. A.B., Stanford U., 1929, J.D., 1932; LL.D., Calif. Western Law Sch., 1977; D.H.L., U.S. Internat. U., 1980. Bar: Calif. 1932, U.S. Supreme Ct. 1970. Asso. firm Gray, Cary, Ames and Driscoll, San Diego, 1932-45; partner Gray, Cary, Ames & Frye, 1945-91; lectr. Stanford U. Law Sch., 1946; Spl. Master U.S. Dist. Ct., 1958-61. Dir. San Diego County Water Authority, 1965-90, chmn., 1978-80; dir. Met. Water Dist. So. Calif., 1975-87, vice chmn., 1982-84; mem. Colo. River Bd. Calif., 1975-82; bd. trustees U.S. Internat. U., 1965-90. Mem. ABA (state del. 1968-74), Internat. Bar Assn., San Diego County Bar Assn. (past treas., dir.), State Bar Calif. (exec. com. Conf. State Bar Dels. 1961-64, bd. govs. 1964-67, mem. commn. on jud. qualifications 1968-73), World Assn. Lawyers, Am. Law Inst., Am. Coll. Probate Counsel, Am. Judicature Soc., Am. Bar Found., Order of Coif, Phi Alpha Delta. Republican. Methodist. Home: Solana Beach Calif. Died Aug. 5, 1995.

CRANSTON, MAURICE (WILLIAM), political science educator, author; b. London, May 8, 1920; s. William and Catherine (Harris) C.; m. Helga May, July 20, 1940 (div. Oct. 1949); m. Baroness Maximiliana von und zu Fraunberg, Nov. 11, 1958; children: Nicholas, Stephen. B.A., St. Catherine's Coll, Oxford U., 1948, M.A., 1951, B.Litt., 1951. Lectr. in polit. sci. London Sch. Econs., 1959-64, reader, 1964-68, prof., 1968-77, 82-86; head dept. polit. sci. European Univ. Inst., Florence, Italy, 1978-82; vis. prof. U. Calif., San Diego, 1986-93; lit. adviser Methuens, London, 1959-69. Author books, the most recent being: Philosophy and Language, 1969; La Quintessence de Sartre, 1970; The Mask of Politics, 1972; Jean-Jacques: the early life and work of J.J. Rousseau, 1983; Philosophers and Pamphleteers, 1986, The Noble Savage, 1991, The Romantic Movement, 1992; editor books, the most recent being: (with R.S. Peters) Hobbes and Rousseau, 1972; (with Peter Mair) Ideologie et Politique, 1980, Langage et Politique, 1982; translator: (J.J. Rousseau) The Social Contract, 1964, Discourse on Inequality, 1983; (J. Hartnack) Wittgenstein and Modern Philosophy, 1965. Hon. fellow St. Catherine's Coll., Oxford U., 1984, London Sch. Econs., 1991; named Commandeur Ordre des Palmes Académiques, Paris, 1987. Fellow Royal Soc. Lit; mem. Alliance Francaise (v.p. London chpt. 1964-93), Internat. Inst. Polit. Philosophy (pres. 1978-81), Am. Acad. Arts and Scis. (hon. fgn.). Mem. Ch. of England. Clubs: Garrick, Internat. PEN (London). Died Nov. 5, 1993; died Nov. 5, 1993; cremated. Home: London Eng.

CRAVEN, DONALD NEIL, former finance company executive; b. Springfield, Mass., Aug. 18, 1924; s. C.S. and Edna (Blanchard) C.; m. Betty L. Rodda, July 16, 1947; 1 dau., Patricia Craven Matheson. Student, Williams Coll., 1942-43, Grad. Sch. Bus., Columbia U., 1967. Advt. sales staff Springfield Newspapers, 1946-51; fin. br. mgr. Assocs. Investment Co., South Bend, Ind., 1951-62; br. mgr. Ford Motor Credit Co., Boston, 1962-64; br. mgr., then regional mgr. Chrysler Fin. Corp., 1964-69; v.p. Eastern U.S., 1969-80; dir. Indsl. Components Corp., Wilbraham, Mass. Bd. dirs., mem. fin. com. Springfield chpt., N.E. Regional Blood Svcs., dist. rep. for Mass. ARC, mem. Svc. Corps Ret. Execs. Served with USMC, 1943-46, 50-51. Clubs: Landmark (Stamford, Conn.); Dennis (Mass.) Yacht. Lodges: Masons, Shriners. Home: Springfield Mass. Died Sept. 13, 1992; interred Hillcrest Park, Springfield, M.A.

CRAWFORD, VICTOR LAWRENCE, lawyer; b. Richmond, Va., Apr. 19, 1932; s. Joseph and Elizabeth C. (Lawrence) C.; m. Clare W. Crawford, June 18, 1958 (div. 1973); children: Victor L. Jr., Charlene; m. Linda P. Crawford, Mar. 28, 1983. BA, U. Md., 1957; JD, Georgetown U., 1960. Bar: Md., D.C. State senator Md. Gen. Assembly, Annapolis, 1967-83; ptnr. Victor L. Crawford & Assocs., Rockville, Md., 1960—; Lobbyist for Tobacco Inst. until diagnosed with cancer, then activist for anti-smoking restrictions. Contbr. articles to profl. jours. Lobbyist Montgomery County Coun., Rockville, 1987—; mem. Md. Ho. of Dels., Annapolis, 1967-69; chmn. Montgomery County Senate Del., Annapolis, 1974-82, Budget and Taxation Subcom., Annapolis, 1979-82. Named Conservationist of Yr., Md. Conservation Coun., 1973; recipient achievement award Md. Fedn. for Retarded Children, achievement award Pub. Affairs Inst., Frostburg State Coll. Mem. ABA, Md. State Bar Assn. (bd. govs. 1985-86, exec. com. 1983-84), Montgomery County Bar Assn., D.C. Bar Assn., Montgomery County C. of C. (chmn. legis. com. 1989—). Democrat. Roman Catholic. Home: Bethesda Maryland Died March, 1996.

CREEL SISNIEGA, SALVADOR JOSÉ, banker; b. Mexico City, Oct. 10, 1927; s. Salvador and Carolina (Sisniega) C.; m. Marí a Luisa Ryan, May 28, 1955; children—Ines Maria, Salvador, Ricardo, Maria Cristina. LL.D., U. Mex., 1951; postgrad. in money and banking Columbia U., 1952-53. Bar: Mex. 1951. Founder, head nat. law dept. Banco Commercial Mexicano, S.A., 1954-63; founder, sr. ptnr. Creel, Garcia and Cruz, Mexico, 1955—; prof. econs. U. Chihuahua, Mex., 1955-65; pres. Financiera y Fiduciaria de Chihuahua, S.A., 1955-68; chmn. bd. Grupo Econó mico Mexicano, S.A., Banco Cré dito Mexicano S.A., Cré dito Financiero S.A., Harinas S.A. de C.V., Fomento Indsl. y Bursatil, S.A. de C.V., Inversiones y Valores Mexicanos, S.A. de C.V., Auto Camoines de Chihuahua, S.A., Ganado del Norte, S.A., Impulsora de Restaurantes S.A., Albergues y Hoteles Mexicanos, S.A., Tecnica Hotelera del Norte, S.A., Parques Industriales Mexicanos, S.A., Planeacion Inmobiliaria de Chihuahua, S.A., Chihuahua Futuro, S.A., Hogares, Comercio e Industria, S.A. de C.V., Seguros La Republica, S.A., Union de Seguros, S.A.; dir. Seguros La Comercial de Chihuahua, S.A., Aceros de Chihuahua, S.A., Banco Capitalizador de Chihuahua, S.A., Mueblerias Villareal, S.A. Author: Hacia Una Suma Jurí dica, 1951. Contbr. articles to profl. jours. Bd. dirs. Found. Educacion Chihuahuense, Found. Inmuebles Escolares de Chihuahua; pres. Hispanic Culture Inst., Chihuahua; founding mem., dir. Chihuahua Inst. Social Studies. Decorated knight Equestrian Order of Holy Sepulcher of Jerusalem, knight Hispanic-Am. chpt. Knights of Corpus Christi of Toledo; recipient award Inst. Hispano-Am. Culture; Disting. Exec. of Yr. award, Chihuahua, 1976. Mem. Numisatic Soc. Mex. Roman Catholic. Clubs: Casino de Chihuahua, Chihuahua Country. Home: Chihuahua Mexico

CREER, PHILIP DOUGLAS, architect, educator; b. Phila., Aug. 31, 1903; s. Robert C. and Ada L. (Skinner) C.; m. Esther B. Allen, Dec. 1, 1933; children: Philip Douglas, Robert Craine; m. Cleon Adair Kerr, Oct. 25, 1951. BArch, U. Pa., 1927. Instr. architecture U. Pa., 1928-31; head dept. architecture Wanamaker Inst., 1927-32; head. dept. architecture RISD, Providence, 1933-56; pvt. practice Providence, 1935-61; sr. ptnr. Creer, Kent, Cruise and Aldrich, Providence, 1946-61; ptnr. Creer and Roessner, Austin, 1958-63; prin. P.D. Creer, Austin, 1963-89; R.I. dist. officer Historic Am. Bldgs. Survey, 1935-41; dir. Sch. Architecture, U. Tex., Austin, 1956-67; mem. architects adv. com. Providence Bldg. Code, 1953-54, mem. Mayor's adv. com. to write minimum housing standards code, 1953-56, mem. exec. com., chmn. subcom. screening, 1953-56; sec.-treas. Tex. Archtl. Found., 1957-63; architect's adv. com. Tex. Bldg. Commn., 1958-60; mem. Austin Pks. and Recreations Bd., 1966-70, chmn., 1969; exec. dir. Tex. Bd. Architect Examiners, 1974-84, cons., 1984-89. Archtl. works include schs., hosps., pub. housing, overseas army bases, comml., indsl. and instl. bldgs. Past pres. R.I. Soc. Crippled Children and Adults; chmn. Austin Hist. Landmark Commn., 1974-81. Recipient award for Hartford Pk. Publ. Housing Project, Providence, 1951; named author of one of ten best projects in U.S. by architects adv. com. Pub. Housing Authority, 1951, Landmark award presented posthumously by City of Austin Hist. Landmark Commn., 1994; Philip Creer grad. fellowship for hist. preservation established in his name U. Tex., Austin, 1988. Fellow AIA (past pres. R.I. chpt., pres. N.E. regional coun., 1952-55, nat. dir. nat. judiciary com. 1952-55, chmn. com. 1954-55, 58-59, mem. centennial subcom. Commemorative stamp 1956, pres. Cen. Tex. chpt. 1960, chmn. honors awards com. 1966-67, Edward C. Kemper award 1960); mem. Tex. Soc. Architects (chmn. fellowship nominating com., mem. profl. devel. com., Pitts award 1975), R.I. Hist. Soc., Soc. Colonial Wars, Shakespeare's Head Assn., Austin Heritage Soc. (pres. 1964)Art Club (past gov.), Univ. Club (Providence), Headliners Club, Austin Club, Phi Sigma Kappa. Home: Austin Tex. Died Oct. 8, 1993.

CRIMI, ALFRED DIGIORGIO, artist; b. Italy, Dec. 1, 1900; s. Filadelfio and Maria (DiGiorgio) C.; m. Mary Timpano, Apr. 11, 1935. Student, NAD, Beaux Arts Inst. Design, both N.Y.C., Scuola Preparatoria a le Arti Ornamentali, Rome. Tchr. CCNY, 1947-53, Pratt Inst., 1948-51, Pa. State U., 1963, privately; lectr. Columbia U., Pratt Inst., CCNY, Fordham U., others. Featured in art mags.; one-man shows, Babcock Galleries, N.Y.C., 1928, Portland (Oreg.) Mus. Art, 1933, DeYoung Mus., San Francisco, 1933, Holyoke (Mass.) Mus., 1962, Fordham U., N.Y.C., 1966, Ringwood Manor Mus., N.J., 1971, Wichita (Kans.) State U., 1980, St. Lawrence U., Canton, N.Y., 1981, Bradley Air Mus., Windsor Locks, Conn.; group shows include, Whitney Mus. Am. Art, N.Y.C., Met. Mus. Art, N.Y.C., 1952-53, Mus. Modern Art, N.Y.C., 1936, Chgo. Art Inst., Bklyn. Mus., Smithsonian Instn., Washington, Internat. Littoriale, Bologna, Italy, First Internat. Liturgical Arts Exhbn., Trieste, Italy, 1961, Butler Inst. Am. Art, Youngstown, Ohio, DeYoung Meml. Mus., 1933, S.I. Mus, 1956, NAD, Am. Watercolor Soc., Audubon Artists, Mainstreams Internat., Marietta, Ohio, 1968, 69, 72, 74, Am. Artists in Paris Exhbn., 1975-76, numerous others, mosaic and fresco commns. include, Open Air Aquarium, Key West, Fla., Harlem Hosp., N.Y.C., Washington (D.C.) Post Office Dept. Bldg., Rutgers Presbyn. Ch., N.Y.C., Christian Herald Bldg., N.Y.C., various public schs. in N.Y.C.; represented in permanent collections Holyoke Mus., Columbia (S.C.) Mus., N.Y. Publ. Libr., Mus. Fine Arts, Springfield, Mass., U. Md., Springfield (Mo.) Art Mus., Library of Congress, Nat. Mus. Am. Art, Smithsonian Instn., Washington, S.I. Mus., Norfolk (Va.) Mus., Butler Inst. Am. Art, Wolfson Mus., Miami,

Fla., represented in, St. Lawrence U., Syracuse U., Wichita State U., Mus. City of N.Y., Bronx Bot. Garden Mus., Rose Art Mus., Brandeis U., Waltham., Mass., U. Rochester (N.Y.) Meml. Art Gallery, Ctr. for Migration Studies, S.I., N.Y., others; author: A Look Back-A Step Forward, 1987. Recipient awards and prizes; including Allied Artists Am., 1947, N.Y. State Fair, 1951, Art League L.I., 1954, 55, 56, 61, 62, Allied Artists Am., 1956, 60, 64, 74, 75, Grumbacher award Knickerbocker Ann., 1957, Grumbacher award Am. Watercolor Soc., 1968, Grumbacher award Butler Inst. Am. Art, 1969, Grumbacher award Nat. Arts Club, 1969; cert. of merit City of Northampton, Mass., 1980. Mem. Nat. Soc. Mural Painters (v.p. 1937-41), Louis Comfort Tiffany Found., Am. Watercolor Soc., Audubon Artists (pres. 1951-52), Coll. Art Assn., Artists Fellowship (officer), Allied Artists Am., Painters and Sculptors Assn. N.J., Internat. Platform Assn., Fedn. Modern Painters and Sculptors. Home: Bronx N.Y. Died Jan. 7, 1994; interred St. Raymond Cemetery, N.Y.C.

CRIQUI, WILLIAM EDMUND, lighting company financial executive; b. Irvington, N.J., June 25, 1922; s. William Valentine and Josephine Anna (Dotterweich) C.; m. Margaret Elizabeth Burke, Apr. 22, 1950 (dec. Feb. 1976); children: William John, Robert Joseph; m. Joyce Morse McLaughlin, Aug. 14, 1980. B.S. in Accounting, Rutgers U., 1955; certificate machine accounting, N.Y. U., 1958; M.B.A., Seton Hall U., 1966. Certified internal auditor. Sr. auditor Worthington Corp., Harrison, N.J., 1958-62; dir. internal auditing Worthington Corp., 1962-67, asst. treas., 1967-69; asst. treas. Studebaker-Worthington, Inc.; also treas. Worthington Corp., N.Y.C., 1969-72; v.p., treas. Worthington Pump Internat., 1971-74; asst. sec., gen. auditor Novo Corp., 1974-75; mgr. fin. services U.S. Radium Corp., Morristown, N.J., 1976-78; asst. treas. U.S. Radium Corp., 1978-81, USR Lighting, Inc., Parsippany, N.J., 1981-95, AeroPanel Corp., 1985-87. Treas. Nutley (N.J.) County Com., 1969-77; pres. Nutley Republican Club, 1972; committeeman Essex County, 1968-77; bd. dirs., v.p. Nutley Family Service Bur. Served with AUS, 1942-46. Decorated Purple Heart, Bronze Star medal, Combat Inf. badge. Mem. Inst. Internal Auditors (pres. 1962-63, bd. govs. 1964-66), Holy Name Soc. Elk (mem. crippled childrens com. 1969-71). Home: Largo Fla. Died Oct. 29, 1995.

CRONE, RICHARD IRVING, retired physician, retired army officer; b. Salt Lake City, June 6, 1909; s. Maurice B. and Mildred (Rheinstrom) C.; m. Alla M. Ernst, Mar. 26, 1946; children: Richard A., William E. Student, UCLA, 1927-30; AB, U. Calif., San Francisco, 1931, MD, 1935. Diplomate: Am. Bd. Internal Medicine. Rotating intern Alameda County Hosp., Oakland, Calif., 1934-35; med. resident U. Calif. Hosp., San Francisco, 1935-36; surg. resident U. Calif. Hosp., 1937-38; practice medicine specializing in internal medicine San Francisco, 1936-37; clin. instr. medicine U. Calif. Med. Sch., 1936-37; commd. 1st lt. M.C. U.S. Army, advanced through grades to brig. gen., 1965; contract surgeon Letterman Gen. Hosp., San Francisco, 1939; resident internal medicine Madigan Gen. Hosp., Tacoma, 1947-48, asst. chief med. svc., chief dept. medicine, 1948-49; chief med. service 130th Sta. Hosp., Heidelberg, Germany, 1949-51, 51-52; comdg. officer 130th Sta. Hosp., 1951; med. cons. Hdqrs. U.S. Army in Europe, Heidelberg, 1952-53; asst. chief dept. medicine, asst. dir. med. edn. Letterman Gen. Hosp., San Francisco, 1953-56, chief dept. medicine, asst. dir. med. edn., 1956-57; chief med. service, chief profl. services, dir. med. edn. 2d Gen. Hosp., Landstuhl, Germany, 1957-58; chief dept. medicine, cons. to surgeon gen. on internal medicine Walter Reed Gen. Hosp., Washington, 1963-65; comdg. gen. Madigan Gen. Hosp., 1965-69, ret., 1969; dir. edn. Group Health Coop., Puget Sound, 1969-71; med. cons. State of Calif. Dept. Health, 1972-76. Decorated D.S.M., Legion of Merit with oak leaf cluster, Bronze Star medal, Air medal; Order Yun Hui Nationalist China. Fellow A.C.P.; mem. Tacoma Acad. Internal Medicine (hon.), Phi Beta Pi. Home: Santa Rosa Calif. Died Feb. 13, 1994.

CROSS, CLYDE CLEVELAND, lawyer; b. Brownsville, Tenn., Aug. 17, 1918; s. Clyde C. and Jessie (Mann) C.; m. Helen Cross, June 21, 1941; children: Ann, Clyde, Richard, Jane, Frank, Katherine. B.A., U. Wis., 1940, J.D., 1942. Bar: Wis. 1942, U.S. Supreme Ct. 1960. Ptnr. Langer and Cross, Baraboo, Wis., 1945-80, Cross, Jenks, Mercer and Maffei, Baraboo, 1988—; instr. trial advocacy U. Wis., 1973-80; bd. dirs., mem. faculty Ct. Practice Inst., 1974-83. Contbr. articles to legal jours. Served to lt. USN, 1943-45. Fellow Am. Coll. Trial Lawyers, Am. Bar Found.; mem. State Bar Wis. (pres. 1971-72), Sauk County Bar Assn. (pres. 1960-61), U. Wis. Law Alumni Assn. (pres. 1965-66). Home: Baraboo Wis. Died Oct. 19, 1994.

CROSS, EARLE ALBRIGHT, entomologist, educator; b. Memphis, Nov. 23, 1925; s. Earle Albright and Florence Irene (Hale) C.; m. Dorthy Jean Showalter, Aug. 15, 1948; children: John Broughton, Stephen Earle, Robert Randall, Scott Lewis. BS in Forestry, Utah State U., 1951; MA in Entomology, U. Kans., 1955, PhD, 1962. Instr. Purdue U., West Lafayette, Ind., 1957-58; instr. U. Kans., Lawrence, 1958-59, rsch. assoc., 1959-60; asst. prof. Northwestern State U. La., Natchitoches, 1960-63, assoc. prof., 1964-66, prof., 1967-70; assoc. prof. U. Ala., Tuscaloosa, 1970-73, prof., from 1974. Editorial bd. Internat. Jour. Acarology; contbr. numerous articles to profl. jours. Served with USN, 1943-46. Mem. Entomol. Soc. Am., Cen. States Entomol. Soc. Home: Tuscaloosa Ala. Deceased.

CROTTI, JOSEPH ROBERT, aviation executive; b. Azzio, Italy, June 11, 1923; came to U.S., 1924; s. John Roberto and Teresa (Tabacchini) C.; m. Beverly J.DeGraff; children: Dennis, Laura Ann Rosio. Student, U. Calif., Berkeley, 1960-91; grad., Delahanty Inst. Fire Adminstrn., 1953. Accredited airport executive 1964. Dep. chief Merced (Calif.) Fire Dept., 1946-59; airport mgr./city mgr. pro tem Merced, 1959-67; dir. aeronautics State of Calif., Sacramento, 1967-74; dep. dir. Calif. Dept. Transp., Sacramento, 1974-75; exec. dir. Calif. Air Tankers Assn., Sacramento, 1975-79; cons. Pan Am. World Svc., Teterboro, N.Y., 1979-80; western region rep. Aircraft Owners & Pilots Assn., Frederick, Md., from 1981; v.p. Calif. Fire Chief's Assn., Merced, 1958-59, Calif. Assn. Airport Execs., Merced, 1967; vice chmn. Gov.'s Aerospace-Aviation Task Force, Sacramento, 1970; pres. No. Calif. Div. of CD, Merced, 1963; accident prevention counselor FAA, Sacramento, from 1980; mem. Calif. Divsn. Aeronautics Advisory Coun., Sacramento, from 1988. Contbr. numerous manuals and plans for airport regulations and safety. Scout master Boy Scouts Am. Air Explorers, Merced, 1954-65; gen. chmn. Mercy Hosp. Bldg., Merced, 1959; bd. dirs. United Givers, Merced, 1962; chmn. County Heart Fund Drive, Merced, 1967; v.p. Sacramento Youth Band, 1969. Recipient Nat. Flight Safety award, Nat. Fire Protection Assn., 1957-58, Harris Aviation Safety award, We. States Assn. Sheriff's Air Squadron, 1970, Bronze medal, Am. Meteorol. Soc., 1972, CD Commendation, Office of Emergency Svcs., 1986, Paul Harris Fellow, Rotary Internat., 1990, Gen. Aviation Sharples award, 1988, Disting. Svc. award FAA, 1994. Mem. Am. Assn. Airport Execs. (Outstanding Svc. award 1994), Nat. Assn. State Aviation Ofcls. (pres. 1972), Profl. Helicopter Pilots Assn., Aircraft Owners and Pilots Assn. (Joe Crotti Perpetual Trophy 1994), Calif. Assn. Airport Execs. (Outstanding Svc. award 1994), Calif. State Sheriffs Assn., Am. Legion, Cameron Park Rotary Club (pres. 1980), Delta Marina Yacht Club (commodore 1989). Home: Shingle Springs Calif. Deceased.

CROWLEY, JOHN JOSEPH, JR., ambassador; b. Albuquerque, Feb. 10, 1928; s. John Joseph and Myrtis (Duffield) C.; m. Ileana Rivera Cintron, June 12, 1953; children: Gail Marie, Ileana Marie. A.B., W.Va. U., 1949; M.A., Columbia U., 1950; grad., Nat. War Coll., 1970. Instr. U. P.R., 1950-52; joined U.S. Foreign Service, 1952; vice-consul Maracaibo, 1952-55; vice-consul, 3d sec. Lima, Peru, 1955-59; 1st sec. Am. embassy, Brussels, Belgium, 1960-64; officer charge Venezuelan affairs Dept. of State, 1964-66; counselor, dep. chief of mission Quito, Ecuador, 1966-69; charge d'affairs, 1967-68; counselor, dep. chief of mission Santo Domingo, Dominican Republic, 1970-74; dir. Office No. European Affairs Bur. European Affairs, Dept. State, 1974-77; dep. chief of mission U.S. Embassy, Caracas, Venezuela, 1977-80; U.S. ambassador to Suriname, 1980-82; sr. insp. Dept. State, 1982-84; dep. permanent rep. to OAS, 1984-86, U.S. rep. to Inter-Am. Coun. on Sci., Edn. and Culture, 1985, ret., 1986; cons., writer, lectr. in field. With U.S. Army, 1946-48. Decorated Order of Merit Ecuador Govt., 1969. Mem. Am. Fgn. Service Assn., Nat. War Coll. Alumni Assn. (pres. 1990-92). Roman Catholic. Home: Bethesda Md. Died Mar. 28, 1995.

CROWLEY, JOHN POWERS, lawyer, judge; b. Chgo., Oct. 5, 1936; s. William Beaudry and Mary (Powers) C.; m. Elizabeth Gwenellian Davies, Jan. 12, 1963; children: Helen Mary, Margaret Jane, Catherine Anne. Student, U. Notre Dame, 1954-57; LLB, DePaul U., Chgo., 1960; LLM, NYU, 1961. Bar: Ill. 1960. Asst. U.S. atty. No. Dist. Ill., 1961-65; pvt. practice Chgo., 1965-70; ptnr. firm Crowley, Burke, Nash & Shea, 1970-76; judge U.S. Dist. Ct., No. Dist. Ill., Chgo., 1976-81; ptnr. Cotsirilos & Crowley, 1981-89; instr. DePaul U. Coll. Law, 1962-63, adj. prof., 1976-89; mem. vis. com. Northwestern U. Sch. Law. Mem. vis. com. DePaul U. Coll Law. Fellow Am. Coll. Trial Lawyers, Internat. Acad. Trial Lawyers; mem. ABA, Ill. Bar Assn., Chgo. Bar Assn. (chmn. criminal law com. 1974-75, bd. mgrs. 1976-78), Chgo. Bar Found. (bd. dirs., v.p.), Blue Circle Soc., Blue Key. Roman Catholic. Home: Evanston Ill. Died Jan. 10, 1989.

CROWLEY, THOMAS B., marine transportation company executive; b. 1914; married. With Crowley Maritime Corp., San Francisco, 1935-94, chmn., formerly pres., dir. Recip. Vice-Admiral Jerry Land Medal, Soc. Naval Architects and Marine Engrs., 1985. Home: Piedmont Calif. Died July 7, 1994.

CSAVINSZKY, PETER JOHN, physicist, educator; b. Budapest, Hungary, July 10, 1931; came to U.S., 1959, naturalized, 1964; s. Lajos and Ida (Kiss) C.; m. Barbara J. Fraser, Oct. 1976. Diploma Ing. Chem., Tech. U. Budapest, 1954; Ph.D. in Physics, U. Ottawa, Ont., Can., 1959. Research physicist Hughes Aircraft Co., Newport Beach, Calif., 1959-60, Gen. Dynamics Corp., Rochester, N.Y., 1960-62, Tex. Instruments Inc., Dallas, 1962-65, TRW Systems, Redondo Beach, Calif., 1965-70; assoc. prof. physics U. Maine, Orono, 1970-74; prof. U. Maine, 1974-95; vis. lectr. U. Calif., Berkeley, summer 1971, UCLA, summers 1972, 73, 74, 75, 76, 77; vis. prof. U. So. Calif., 1977-78. Contbr. articles to profl. jours. Recipient Presdl. Research Achievement award U. Maine, Orono, 1978. Fellow Am. Phys. Soc. (v.p. New Eng. sect. 1986-87, pres. 1988, advisor sect. to the coun. 1990); mem. AAAS, Soaring Soc. Am., Sigma Xi. Home: Old Town Maine Died Dec. 31, 1995.

CULHANE, SHAMUS, producer, author; b. Ware, Mass., Nov. 12, 1908; s. James Henry and Alma (LaPierre) C.; m. Juana Hegarty, June 30, 1958; children: Brian, Kevin. Inker Bray Studio, N.Y.C., 1924-28, Krazy Kat Studio, N.Y.C., 1928-30; animator Fleischer Studio, N.Y.C., 1930-32; dir. Miami, Fla., 1939-41, Iwwerks Studio, Hollywood, Calif., 1932-34; animator Walt Disney Studios, Hollywood, 1934-39; dir. Walt Lantz Studio, Hollywood, 1942-46; owner, producer Shamus Culhane Prodns., Inc., Hollywood and N.Y.C., 1946-66, 69-89; producer Paramount Famous Studio, N.Y.C., 1966-67; exec. prod., dir. MG Films, N.Y.C., 1972-76; prod., dir. Westfall Prodns., N.Y.C., 1975-77; writer N.Y.C., 1980-96. Author: (autobiography) Talking Animals and Other People, 1986, (textbook) Animation from Script to Screen, 1988; animator: (films) Pinnochio and Snow White, (Oscar award 1939), Hemo the Magnificent (Christopher award 1959); dir. numerous animate shorts. Mem. Internat. Animated Film Assn. (bd. dirs., 50 Yrs. award 1985, Hollywood Disting. Svc. award 1986), Dirs. Guild Am. Home: New York N.Y. Died Feb. 2, 1996.

CULLINAN, VINCENT, lawyer; b. San Francisco, Jan 22, 1911; s. Eustace and Katherine (Lawler) C.; m Elizaberh Erlin, Oct. 16, 1937; children—Terrence Kathleen Cullinan Merchant, Sheila Cullinan Wheeler. A.B. magna cum laude, U. Santa Clara, 1933, LL.D., Stanford U., 1936. Bar: Calif. bar, U.S. Supreme Ct. bar, Fed. Ct. bars of Calif. Partner firm Cushing Cullinan, Duniway & Gorrill, San Francisco, 1936-41 Cullinan, Hancock, Rothert and Burns, 1946-71, Cullinan Brown and Helmer, San Francisco, 1971-77, Cullinan and Lyons, San Francisco, 1978—; dir. Schlage Lock Co. Served with M.I., USN, 1941-45. Mem ABA, San Francisco Bar Assn. (pres. 1968), Am. Law Inst., State Bar Calif. (v.p. 1969). Republican. Roman Catholic. Club:, Bohemian. Home: San Francisco Calif.

CULVERHOUSE, HUGH FRANKLIN, lawyer professional sports team executive; b. Birmingham, AL Feb. 20, 1919; s. Harry Georg and Grace Mae (Daniel) C.; m. Joy McCann, Nov. 14, 1942; children: Gay Hugh Franklin Jr. B.S., U. Ala., 1941, LL.B., 1947 LL.D. (hon.), Jacksonville U., Stetson U., 1984; DHL (hon.), U. So. Fla. Bar: Fla. 1955, Ala. 1947. Asst atty. gen. State of Alabama, Montgomery, AL, 1947-49 spl. atty., asst. regional counsel Office of Chief Counsel IRS, Atlanta and Jacksonville, FL, 1949-56; mem. firm Culverhouse & Botts, Tampa, Fla., 1956-94; mem. adv com. to commr. internal revenue, 1962-63; owner NFL franchise Tampa Bay Buccaneers, Tampa, FL, 1974-94 bd. dirs. Time Warner, Inc., PGA Tour, Chiquita Brands Internat., Penn Ctrl. Corp.; owner, developer various real estate projects, Fla., Ind., Ohio; endowed chair U. So. Fla. Contbr. articles to legal jours. Mem faculty U. Ala. Sch. Bus. Adminstrn.; Co-founder, 1st pres. Family Consultation Service, Jacksonville; vice chmn. bd. trustees Jacksonville U.; bd. visitors Coll Commerce and Bus. Adminstrn., U. Ala.; bd. overseers Stetson U. Coll. Law; del., U.S. Ambassador 1976 Winter Olympics, Innsbruck, Austria; mem. Fla Council of 100, Fla. Council Econ. Edn., Fla. Speaker's Adv. Com. on the Future. Served with USAAF, 1941-46; Served with USAF, 1951-53. Recipient Top Mgmt award Sales and Mktg. Execs. of Jacksonville, Chief award Ind. Colls. and Univs. in Fla., Fin. Achievement award U. Ala.; Fla. Enterprise award, Endowed Chair in bus. adminstrn. Jacksonville U., Stetson U. Coll Law, Eminent Scholar Chair U. Fla., Eminent Scholar Chair named for him U. Ala. Sch. Accountancy; inducted Ala. Sports Hall of Fame, 1990, Tampa Bus. Hall of Fame, 1991, Ala. Bus. Hall of Fame, 1991, Fla Sports Hall of Fame, 1993. Mem. ABA, Am. Judicature Soc., Ala. Bar Assn., Fla. Bar Assn., Dade County Bar Assn., Miami Bar Assn., Jacksonville Bar Assn (chmn. tax sect. 1957-59), Am. Acad. Achievement Knights of Malta, Avila Golf and Country Club, Center Club, Fla. Yacht Club, Indian Creek Country Club LaGorce Country Club, Surf Club, Univ. Club, Palma Ceia Golf and Country Club, Nat. Golf Links Club. Republican. Episcopalian. Home: Tampa Fla. Died Aug. 25, 1994.

CUMMINGS, CONSTANCE PENNY, public relations executive; b. Morristown, N.J., Feb. 12, 1948; d. Renwick Speer and Juliana Diane (Novotny) C.; B.A. U. Md., 1970. With Kaiser Aluminum, Washington 1970-71, Manning, Selvage & Lee, pub. relations Washington, 1971-77; dir. pub. relations Sheraton Washington Hotel, 1977-82, area dir. pub. relations Sheraton Corp., Washington, 1982-84, dir. pub. relations N.Am., 1984-87, Sheraton Corp. Hotels, Md., Va. Washington, 1987—. Recipient Sheraton Corp. Pres. award, 1978, Pub. Relations award, 1981, 82, 87. Bd. dirs. Big Sisters of Met. Washington, 1984. Mem. Am. News Women's Club (pres. 1982-83), Am. Women in Radio and TV (pres. chpt. 1976), Pub. Relations Soc.

Am. (dir. 1977). Contbr. articles in field. Home: Washington D.C.

CUNNINGHAM, MARILYN ALICE ENEIX, corporate executive; b. Warren, Minn., Mar. 8, 1917; d. Frederick C. and Mary (Boman) Eneix; m. Marcus E. Cunningham, Oct. 1, 1966. B.A., U. Mich., 1937. Account supr. Grant Advt., Inc., Detroit, Chgo. and N.Y.C., 1945-60; dir. advt. Cunningham-Limp Co., Detroit, 1960-69; v.p., dir. Cunningham-Limp Co., Birmingham, Mich., 1969-72; vice chmn. bd., dir., 1972-78; vice chmn. bd. dirs. Cunningham-Limp Holding Co., 1978—; v.p., dir. Brady Hill Co., Detroit, 1960—; vice chmn. bd., v.p., dir. Cunningham-Limp Internat., 1971—; vice-chmn. bd., dir. Cunningham-Limp de Las Americas, 1972—, Cunningham-Limp Ltd., 1972—. Author: The Right Plant on the Right Site for Maximum Profit, 1962, The Comprehensive Approach to Facility Expansion, 1967, Design and Engineering, 1970, The Facility Planning Services of Cunningham-Limp, 1973, Total Responsibility in Facility Expansion, 1975, Planning, Designing, Engineering and Building, 1976, Design-Engineering-Construction, 1977, Comprehensive Design, Engineering and Construction, 1978; Contbr. articles to profl. jours.; Author, pub.: SCOPE mag. Active civic, philanthropic activities. Mem. Fine Arts Soc. Detroit (Silver Anniversary mem.), Alpha Phi. Republican. Presbyn. Clubs: Kenilworth (Bal Harbour, Fla.); Jockey (Miami Beach, Fla.); Le Mirador Country (Switzerland). Home: Miami Fl.

CURRAN, FRANK EARL, former mayor; b. Cleve., Dec. 19, 1912; s. William E. and Anna (Hayer) C.; m. Florence McKenney, Apr. 15, 1936. Student, San Diego Jr. Coll., Balboa Law Sch., San Diego State Coll., U. Calif. extension. Dep. county assessor San Diego (Calif.) County, 1935-41; city storekeeper Oceanside, Calif., 1937-38; supr. procurement critical materials Dept. Navy, 1940-49; sec.-mgr. Fraternal Order Eagles, San Diego, 1949-60; with Shoreline Ins. Co., San Diego, 1960-63; councilman San Diego, 1955-63; vice mayor, 1957, 58, 61, 62, mayor, 1963-72; exec. v.p. Central City Assn. San Diego, Inc., 1989-92; Gen. chmn. Inter-Am. Municipal Orgn. Congress, San Diego, 1960; presiding officer Punta del Este, Uruguay, 1962-72, mem. nat. bd. dirs., 1962-72; bd. dirs. League Calif. Cities, 1964-72, dir.-at-large exec. com., 1964-72, mem. resolutions coms., 1964-72; city rep. to league com. on internat. municipal coop., 1961-72; mem. policy com. San Diego-Border Area Program, after 1963; bd. dirs. Palm City Sanitation Dist., after 1964; mem. Gov. Calif Adv. Com., after 1963; spl. rep. gov. Calif. to Commn. Californias, after 1964; mem. community relations com. U.S. Conf. Mayors, 1965-72; chmn. com. internat. mcpl. coop. Nat. League Cities, 1965-72, v.p., 1969, pres., 1970, bd. dirs., 1971; chmn. Coop. Area Manpower Planning System, 1970; mem. Govt. Task Force on Coastline Preservation, 1970. Contbr. articles to newspapers and mags. Bd. dirs. Nat. Center Voluntary Action, 1970, Epilepsy Soc., 1984—; treas. San Diego Coalition for Econ. and Environ. Balance, 1983-89; chmn. bd. dirs. Harbor View Med. Ctr., 1986—; founder Harbor View Urban Found., 1989—. Recipient Mayor La Guardia Civic award, 1964, Elsie Wittmore award, 1966; decorated Order Queen Isabella The Catholic (Spain); Prince Henry The Navigator (Portugal); Cavaliere Order Stella della Solidarieta Italiana (Italy). Democrat. Home: San Diego Calif. Died October 18, 1982; buried Eternal Hills Memorial Park, Oceanside, California.

CURRIE, CLIFFORD WILLIAM HERBERT, librarian, art historian; b. Ramsgate, Kent, Eng., Nov. 24, 1918; s. William Albert and Gladys Irene (Slingsby) C.; m. Inga-Britta Olsson, Oct. 14, 1972. B.A., Fitzwilliam Coll., Cambridge (Eng.) U., 1949; LL.M., Cambridge (Eng.) U., 1950, M.A., 1954; M.A., St. Edmund Hall, Oxford (Eng.) U., 1973, B.C.L., 1974. Asst. libr. Cambridge U., 1951-53; pub. libr. dir. London Borough of Bromley, Eng., 1953-59; libr. Imperial Coll. Sci. and Tech., London, 1959-68; exec. dir. Can. Libr. Assn., Ottawa, Ont., 1968-71; libr. Ashmolean Libr., Oxford, Eng., 1972-78; univ. libr. Coll. William and Mary, Williamsburg, Va., 1978-86. Author: Prospects in Librarianship, 58, 63; editor: Can. Library Jour, 1968-71; adv. editor: Eighteenth Century Life, 1980. Served with Brit. Army, 1939-45. Fellow Libr. Assn. Eng. (bd. advanced studies 1966-68); mem. Internat. Assn. Tech. Univ. Librs. (v.p. 1968, sec. 1962-67, dir.), Working Party Librs. and the Book Trade (founding mem.), Soc. Bookmen. Clubs: Athenaeum, Arts, Authors, London, Frewen, Oxford; Grolier (N.Y.C.). Home: Marlborough England Died February 9, 1994.

CURRIE, GLENNE, performing arts critic; b. Mar. 1, 1926; s. Donald and Winifred Amenia (Spaul) C.; m. Irene Ramsey, Jan. 10, 1953 (div. 1978). Student, U. Toronto, Can., 1943-46. Critic UPI, from 1975. Mem. N.Y. Drama Critics Circle, Am. Theatre Critics Assn. (treas. from 1979), Internat. Assn. Theater Critics, Dance Critics Assn. Home: New York N.Y. Deceased.

CURRY, JOHN ANTHONY, professional ice skater, choreographer; b. Birmingham, Eng., Sept. 9, 1949; s. Joseph Henry and Rita Agnes (Pritchard) C. Studied with, Alison Smith, Eng., Carlo Fassi, Denmark. Founder, dir. Theatre of Skating, 1976-77, Theatre of Skating 2, 1977, Ice Dancing, 1977-78, John Curry Sch. Skating, N.Y.C., 1978-94. Choreographer: Glides, Skater's Waltz, William Tell, Winter Storms, Nightmare, Russian Sailor's Dance, On the Waterfront, Gershwin Pieces, others; appeared in Broadway revival Brigadoon, A Symphony on Ice, 1984, in Cinderella, Liverpool Playhouse, 1986; appeared in PBS-TV prodns. Peter and the Wolf, The Snow Queen (co-choreographer); author: John Curry, 1978. Decorated comdr. Order Brit. Empire; winner Jr. Brit. Skating Championship, 1967, Jennings trophy for free skating, 1968, Brit. Nat. Championship, 1970, European Championship, 1976, World Championship, 1976, gold medal Winter Olympics, Innsbruck, Austria, 1976. Mem. Pro-Skate. Home: London Eng. Died Apr. 15, 1994.

CURRY, NORVAL HERBERT, agricultural engineer; b. St. Francis, Kans., Oct. 10, 1914; s. Charles Edward and Florence Eleanor (Ward) C.; m. Helen Maurine Smith, June 8, 1938; children: Sharon Gay Curry Morgret, Janice Kay Curry Dalal. Student, Ft. Hays State U., 1934-36; BS in Archtl. Engring., Iowa State U., 1940, MS in Agrl. Engring., 1946. Field engr. Structural Clay Products Inst., Ames, Iowa, 1940-44; rsch assoc. Iowa State U., Ames, 1944-46, instr., 1946-47, asst. prof., 1947-49, assoc. prof., 1949-54, prof. agrl. engring., 1954-59; pvt. practice Ames, 1959-79; founder, chief exec. officer Curry-Wille Consulting Engrs. P.C., Ames, 1979-80; sci. aide Rockefeller Found., Colombia, 1955-56, Chile, 1961. Named life mem. Iowa Engring. Soc., 1980. Fellow Am. Soc. Agrl. Engrs. (life; nat. pres. 1969-70, Cyrus Hall McCormick Gold medal 1980); mem. NAE, Iowa Engring. Soc. (life), Izaak Walton League (pres. 1953), Lions Club (dir. 1987-89). Republican. Home: Ames Iowa Died July 3, 1995; buried Ames Mcpl. Cemetery, Ames, Iowa.

CURTI, MERLE EUGENE, historian, educator; b. Papillion, Nebr., Sept. 15, 1897; s. John and Alice (Hunt) C.; m. Margaret Wooster, June 16, 1925 (dec. Sept. 1961); children: Nancy Alice Holub (dec.), Sister Felicitas Curti; m. Francis Bennett Becker, Mar. 9, 1968 (dec. Feb. 1978). A.B. summa cum laude, Harvard, 1920, Ph.D., 1927; student, Sorbonne, 1924-25; L.H.D., Northwestern U., 1950, U. Pa., 1962, Western Res. U. (now Case Western Res. U.), 1962, U. Mich., 1964, Adelphi U., 1965, U. Nebr., Drake U., 1967, U. Wis. at Milw., 1969; Litt.D., Rider Coll., 1970, Doane Coll., 1976; L.H.D., Beloit Coll., 1979. Vis. prof. Clark U., U. Chgo., UCLA, U. Vt.; instr. history Beloit Coll., 1921-22; asst. prof. Smith Coll., 1925-27, prof., 1929-35, Dwight Morrow prof., 1936-37; prof. history Tchrs. Coll., Columbia, 1937-42; prof. history U. Wis., 1942-68, Frederick Jackson Turner prof., 1947-68, emeritus; Guggenheim fellow, 1929-30; vis. prof. Watumull Found. to univs. India, 1946-47; vis. prof. history U. Tokyo, 1959-60, U. Melbourne, 1964; vis. scholar Huntington Library, 1936-37, 69; Fulbright Conf. Am. Studies Cambridge, 1952, Hyderabad, 1964; mem. adv. com. to U.S. mem. commn. history Pan Am. Inst. History and Geography, 1949-54; emeritus advisor Friends Hist. Library Swarthmore Coll., 1975. Author: Austria and the U.S. 1948-1852, 1927, American Peace Crusade, 1929, Bryan and World Peace, 1931, Social Ideas of American Educators, 1935, The Learned Blacksmith: Letters and Jours. of Elihu Burritt, 1937, Growth of American Thought, 1943, 64, 87 (Pulitzer award), Introduction to America, 1944, Roots of America Loyalty, 1946, (with Vernon Carstensen) University of Wisconsin, a history, 1949, (with L. P. Todd) America's History, 1950, (with W. Thorp and C. Baker) American Issues, 1950, (with R.H. Shryock, T.C. Cochran and F.H. Harrington) An American History, 1950, (with others) American Scholarship in the Twentieth Century, 1953, (with Kendall Birr) Prelude to Point Four, 1954, Probing Our Past, 1955, The American Paradox, 1956, The Making of an American Community, 1959, (with Paul Todd) Rise of the American Nation, 1960, 66, 74, 76, 84, American Philanthropy Abroad: A History, 1963, (with Roderick Nash) Philanthropy in the Shaping of American Higher Education, 1965, Human Nature in American Historial Thought, 1969, Human Nature in American Thought, A History, 1980; also articles. Bd. dirs. Harry S. Truman Library, 1958-61; Fellow Center Advanced Study in Behavioral Scis., 1956. Recipient award for distinguished scholarship Am. Council Learned Socs., 1960. Hon. fellow Wis. Acad. Sci., Arts and Letters, Wis. Hist. Soc.; mem. Swedish Order No. Star, Soc. Am. Historians (bd. editors 1936-40, pres. 1951-52), Soc. Sci. Rsch. Coun., Am. coun. Learned Socs. (vice chmn. bd. dirs. 1958-59), Am. Philos. Soc., Am. Acad. Arts and Scis., Am. Antiquarian Soc., Univ. Club, Phi Beta Kappa (senator 1947-52, pres. Wis. 1957-58). Home: Madison Wis. Died Mar. 9, 1996.

CURTIN, WILLIAM JOSEPH, lawyer; b. Auburn, N.Y., Mar. 9, 1931; s. William Joseph and Edith A. (Murray) C.; m. Helen Bragg White, Aug. 3, 1956; children: Helen Bragg, Caroline Goddard, William Joseph III, Christopher Newport. BS, Georgetown U., 1953, JD, 1956, LLM, 1957. Bar: D.C. 1956, U.S. Supreme Ct. 1962. Sr. ptnr. Morgan, Lewis & Bockius, Washington, 1960-95, chmn. labor and employment sect., 1973-95, chmn. firm exec. com., 1977, 82, 88, 89; public mem. Adminstrv. Conf. U.S., 1968-72; mem. adv. panel NLRB, 1994-95, Am. Law Inst., 1994, Phi Beta Kappa, 1995. Contbr. articles to legal jours. Bd. dirs. Georgetown U., Washington, 1990-95; chmn. bd. dirs. Georgetown U., Washington, 1992-95. Recipient Labor Mgmt. Peace and Outstanding Svc. award Am. Arbitration Assn., 1966, John Carroll award Georgetown U. alumni Assn., 1973, Charles A. Dukes award Duke U., 1992, John Carroll medal of merit Georgetown U., 1994. Fellow Am. Bar Found.; mem. ABA (chmn. spl. com. nat. strikes in transp. industries 1968-70, chmn. pub. utility comms. and transp. law sect. 1982-83), D.C. Bar Assn. (chmn. labor law com. 1969-70). Home: Potomac Md. Died Dec. 19, 1995.

CURTIS, MARK HUBERT, historian, former educational association executive; b. Medford, Minn., July 7, 1920; s. James Hubert and Lydia Ethel (Krueger) C.; m. Maria Isabel Bird y Zalduondo, Nov. 7, 1945 (dec. 1990); children: Mary Katherine, Thomas Mark; m. Katherine Kirn Lund, Apr. 1991. BA, Yale U., 1942, MA, 1947, PhD, 1953; LHD (hon.), Washington and Jefferson U., 1978, Ill. Coll., 1979, Beaver Coll., 1979, Centre Coll., 1980, Rhodes Coll., 1981, Gettysburg Coll., 1982, Towson State U., 1985. Instr. history Williams Coll., 1950-53; asst. prof. UCLA, 1953-59, assoc. prof. history, 1959-64, assoc. dean grad. div., 1962-64; pres. Scripps Coll., Claremont, Calif., 1964-76; cons. various colls. and orgns., 1976-78; pres. Assn. Am. Colls., Washington, 1978-85, pres. emeritus, 1985—; Danforth lectr. Pacific Sch. Religion, Berkeley, Calif., 1957; Folger Libr. rsch. prof., 1964; dir. postdoctoral seminar William Andrews Clark Libr., L.A., 1969; Kettering Found. fellow, 1985—; bd. dirs. Atlantic Coun. U.S., 1987—, chmn. com. on edn. and successor generation, 1985—; mem. Montgomery County Commn. on Humanities, 1988—, chmn., 1991—. Author: Oxford and Cambridge in Transition, 1558-1642, 1959 (Robert Livingston Schuyler prize 1961); contbr. articles to profl. jours. Served to lt. comdr. USNR, 1942-46. Social Sci. Research Council fellow, 1948-49; Guggenheim Found. fellow, 1959-60; Folger Shakespear Library fellow, 1962. Mem. Am. Hist. Assn., Yale Club of N.Y.C., Cosmos Club (Washington). Presbyterian. Home: Bethesda Md. Died Sept. 12, 1994.

CURTIS, THOMAS BRADFORD, lawyer; b. St. Louis, May 14, 1911; s. Edward Glion and Isabel (Wallace) C.; m. Susan R. Chivvis, June 28, 1941; children: Elizabeth, Leland, Allan, Charles, Jonathan. A.B., Dartmouth Coll, 1932, M.A. (hon.), 1951; J.D., Washington U., St. Louis, 1935, LL.D., 1969; LL.D., Westminster Coll., 1962. Bar: Mo. 1934. Ptnr. Curtis & Crossen, St. Louis, 1934-69, 74-87, Curtis, Bamburg, Oetting, Brackman & Crossen, 1987-90, Curtis, Oetting, Heinz, Garrett & Soule, 1990-93; v.p., gen. counsel Ency. Brit., 1969-74; mem. 82d Congress 12th Dist. Mo., 83d-90th Congresses 2d Dist Mo.; chmn. bd. Lafayette Fed. Savs. & Loan, 1974-82, Brooking Park Geriatrics, Inc., 1974-93. Am. Tech. Inst., 1979-93; Mem. Pres. Nixon's Task Force on Internat. Devel., Com. on All-Vol. Armed Forces, Nat. Commn. Founds. and Pvt. Philanthropy; chmn. Corp. for Pub. Broadcasting, 1973-74, Fed. Election Commn, 1975-76; chmn. Mo. del. Rep. Nat. Conv., 1964, 76, 80; trustee Dartmouth Coll., 1951-72, William Woods Coll., 1962-93; Westminster Coll., 1966-79, Nat. Coll. Edn., 1970-83, Lincoln Found., 1970-80, Lincoln Inst., 1976-80, Dartmouth Inst., 1972-82, Ctr. for Strategic and Internat. Studies, Georgetown U., 1972-82; bd. dirs. Webster U. 1979-90, Agri-Energy Roundtable, Inc., 1979-90; chmn. bd. Agri-Bus. Council, Inc., 1987-90; vice chmn., Internat. Great Lakes Coalition, 1988-90, chmn. U.S. sect., 1988-90 Served with U.S. Navy 1942-45. Recipient Congl. Disting. Service award Am. Polit. Sci. Assn., 1963-64, Perry award Nat. Fedn. for Blind, 1961, Silver Beaver award Boy Scouts Am., 1964, Disting. Eagle award Boy Scouts Am., 1973. Mem. Comf. Bd. (sr. adv. council 1973-75), ABA, Am. Polit. Sci. Assn., Assn., Order of Coif, Phi Delta Phi, Phi Sigma Kappa. Unitarian. Author: 87 Million Jobs: A Dynamic Solution for Unemployment, 1964; The Kennedy Round: The Future of U.S. Trade, 1970. Died Jan. 10, 1993. Home: Saint Louis Mo.

CUSACK, CYRIL JAMES, actor, writer; b. Durban, Nov. 26, 1910; s. James Walter and Alice Violet (Cole) C.; ed. Univ. Coll., Dublin, Nat. U.; m. Mary Margaret Kiely, 1945; 6 children. Joined Abbey Theatre, Dublin, 1932; actor Nat. Theatre, Dublin, 1932, 45, 46, asso., shareholder, 1966-93; producer Gaelic Players, 1935-36; mng. dir. Cyril Cusack Prodns., 1946-61; 1st London appearance in Ah Wilderness, 1936; leading roles in Ireland, U.K., Broadway, including Playboy of the Western World, The Moon for the Misbegotten, Julius Caesar, The Physicists, Andorra, The Cherry Orchard, Mr. O, Arms and the Man (Internat. Critics' award 1961), Krapp's Last Tape (Internat. Critics' award 1961), The Plow and the Stars, A life; films include: The Small Back Room, Odd Man Out, The Elusive Pimpernel, The Man Who Never Was, Ill Met by Moonlight, A Terrible Beauty, The Blue Veil, Johnny Nobody, The Waltz of the Toreadors, I Thank a Fool, 80,000 Suspects, One Spy Too Many, The Spy Who Came in from the Cold, The Taming of the Shrew, Oedipus Rex, Galileo Galilei, King Lear, David Copperfield, Country Dance, Day of the Jackal, Juggernaut, The Temptation of Mr. O, True Confession, 1981, Little Dorritt, 1987; also TV appearances. Author: Timepieces (Poems), 1970, Between the Acts and Other Poems, 1991. Died Oct. 8, 1993. Home: Dublin Ireland

CUSHING, PETER WILTON, actor; b. Kenley, Surrey, Eng., May 26, 1913; s. George Henry and Nellie Maria (King) C.; m. Violet Helene Beck, Apr. 10, 1943. ed. Purley County Schs. Actor in plays: War and Peace, 1943; Richard III, 1948; The School for Scandal, 1949; The Soldier and the Lady, 1954; The Silver Whistle, 1956; The Heiress, 1975; films include The Man in the Iron Mask, 1939; Alexander the Great, 1955; The Curse of Frankenstein, 1957; The Hound of the Baskervilles, 1959; Dr. Terror's House of Horrors, 1964; Star Wars, 1976; Touch of the Sun, 1978; A Tale of Two Cities, 1980; She, 1984; others; numerous TV appearances and radio broadcasts. Author: Peter Cushing: An Autobiography, 1986, Past Forgetting—Memoirs of the Hammer Years, 1988. Recipient Daily Mail TV award, 1954; TV Guild award, 1955; award 2d Conv. Française du Cinema Fantastique, 1973; named to Officer Brit. Empire, 1989. Died Aug. 11, 1994. Home: London Eng.

CUTKOSKY, RICHARD EDWIN, physicist, educator; b. Mpls., July 29, 1928; s. Oscar F. and Edna M. (Nelson) C.; m. Patricia A. Klepfer, Aug. 28, 1952; children: Mark, Carol, Martha. B.S., Carnegie Inst. Tech., 1950, M.S., 1950, Ph.D., 1953. Asst. prof. physics Carnegie-Mellon U., Pitts., 1954-61, prof. physics, 1961-93, Buhl prof., 1963-93. Fellow Am. Phys. Soc., AAAS. Home: Pittsburgh Pa. Died June 17, 1993.

CUTLER, HOWARD ARMSTRONG, economics educator, chancellor; b. Webster City, Iowa, Apr. 27, 1918; s. Harry O. and Myrtle (Armstrong) C.; m. Enid Ellison, Jan. 2, 1943; children: Cheryl Varian, Kristen Ellison, Sherwood Thor. A.B., U. Iowa, 1940, M.A., 1941; grad. certificate, Harvard U., 1943; Ph.D., Columbia U., 1952. Instr. econs. U. Iowa, 1946; asst. to economist Irving Trust Co., N.Y.C., 1946-47; instr. econs. U. Ill., Urbana, 1948-50; asst. prof. U. Ill., 1950; asst. to dean U. Ill. (Coll. Commerce), 1949-51; asst. prof. econs. Pa. State U., 1951-53, assoc. prof., 1953-56, prof., 1956-62, head dept., 1953-58, dir. gen. edn., 1957-62, asst. to v.p. academic affairs, 1958-61, asst. to pres., 1961-62; acad. v.p., prof. econs. U. Alaska, 1962-66, chancellor, 1976-81, chancellor emeritus, 1983-95, Regents' prof. econs., 1981-83, Regents' prof. emeritus, 1983-95; exec. v.p. Inst. Internat. Edn., N.Y.C., 1966-76; vis. prof. U. Chgo., 1955-56. Editor: Jour. Gen. Edn, 1960-62. Mem. Martin Luther King, Jr., Fellowship Selection Com., 1968-70; mem. pub.-at-large Ednl. Commn. for Fgn. Med. Grads., 1970-85; mem. chancellor's panel on univ. purposes State U. N.Y., 1970-72; mem. Nat. Liaison Com. Fgn. Student Admissions, 1968-75; mem. adv. com. Carl Duisberg Soc., 1968-75; bd. dirs. Nat. Council for Community Services to Internat. Visitors, 1971-75, Internat. Schs. Services, 1971-75, Axe-Houghton Found., 1970-85, bd. dirs. Alaska Council on Economic Edn., 1977-95. Served to lt. USNR, 1942-46. Recipient Disting. Alumnus Achievement award U. Iowa, 1989, Howard A. Cutler award for Oustanding Contbn. to Econ. Edn. in Alaska, 1987. Mem. Phi Beta Kappa, Beta Gamma Sigma, Pi Gamma Mu, Omicron Delta Epsilon. Home: Fairbanks Alaska Died Nov. 17, 1995.

CUTLER, ROBERT WARD, architect; b. Ridgway, Pa., June 27, 1905; s. Robert Ward and Olga (Holmberg) C.; m. Doris Saxton, June 29, 1929 (dec.); children: Denise Cutler Kimball, Robert Ward; m. Morene Parten, Apr. 27, 1954. B.Arch., Syracuse U., 1928. Employed in various archtl. offices N.Y.C., 1928-37; asso. Skidmore & Owings, N.Y.C., 1937-49; partner Skidmore, Owings & Merrill, N.Y.C., 1949-72; Mem. Art Commn. of City of N.Y., 1958-66; trustee Community Service Soc., N.Y.C., 1962-72, Syracuse U., 1964-72; cons. N.Y.C. Civic Center; mem. adv. council Architecture Found., U. Tex., Austin, 1979-86. Recipient George Arents pioneer medal Syracuse U., 1968. Fellow AIA (pres. N.Y. chpt. 1956-58); mem. Archtl. League N.Y. (pres. 1961-63), Bldg. Research Inst. (pres. 1963-65), N.Y. Bldg. Congress (life; pres. 1965-69), Fifth Ave Assn. (pres. 1969-71), Sigma Chi, Tau Sigma Delta, Phi Kappa Phi. Episcopalian. Clubs: Century Assn. (N.Y.C.), Met. (N.Y.C.), N.Y. Athletic (N.Y.C.). Home: Salado Tex. Died Dec. 17, 1993; interred Salado, Tex.

CZUBEK, JAN ANDRZEJ, nuclear geophysicist; b. Oct. 20, 1935; s. Stanisław and Maria (Birnbaum) C.; m. Danuta Degorska, June 3, 1961; children: Henryk, Irena. MSc, Acad. Mining & Metallurgy, Cracow, Poland, 1957; Doctor degree in physics, Inst. Nuclear Rsch., Warsaw, 1961; habilitation in exploration geophysics, Acad. Mining & Metallurgy, Cracow, 1967. Rsch. asst. Acad. Mining and Metallurgy, Cracow, 1954-62, lectr., 1960-62; rsch. staff mem. Inst. Nuclear Rsch., Cracow, 1962-66, head lab., 1966-70; prof. head divsn. Inst. Nuclear Physics, Cracow, 1970-93, prof., 1994-95; rschr. Commissariat à l'Energie Atomic, France, Commonwealth Sci., Indsl. and Rsch. Orgn., Australia, 1963-91; expert in nuclear geophysics Internat. Atomic Energy Agy., Vienna, 1967-95. Mem. editl. bd. Acta Geophys. Polonica, 1971-95, Uranium, Holland, 1982-88, Nuclear Geophysics, U.K., 1986-95; contbr. articles to profl. jours. Mem. Soc. Profl. Well Log Analysts, Polish Physics Soc. Home: Cracow Poland Died Dec. 19, 1995.

DABNEY, VIRGINIUS, author; b. University, Va., Feb. 8, 1901; s. Richard Heath and Lily Heth (Davis) D.; m. Douglas Harrison Chelf, Oct. 10, 1923; children: Douglas Gibson (Mrs. James S. Watkinson), Lucy Davis (Mrs. Alexander P. Leverty), Richard Heath II. A.B., U. Va., 1920, A.M., 1921; D.Litt. (hon.), U. Richmond, 1940; LL.D., Lynchburg Coll., Coll. William and Mary, 1944; L.H.D., Va. Commonwealth U., 1976. Tchr. French Episcopal High Sch., 1921-22; reporter Richmond News Leader, 1922-28; editorial staff Richmond Times-Dispatch, 1928-34, chief editorial writer, 1934-36, editor, 1936-69; contbr. to N.Y. Times, Dictionary Am. Biography, Ency. Brit., London Economist.; spent 6 months in Cen. Europe in 1934 under grant from Oberlaender Trust.; lectr. on New South Princeton U. session, 1939-40; lectr. Fulbright Conf. Am. Studies, Cambridge U., 1954. Author: Liberalism in the South, 1932, Below the Potomac, 1942, Dry Messiah: The Life of Bishop Cannon, 1949, Virginia: The New Dominion, 1971, Richmond: The Story of a City, 1976, Across the Years: Memories of a Virginian, 1978, The Jefferson Scandals, 1981, Mr. Jefferson's University, 1981, Bicentennial History and Roster of the Society of the Cincinnati in the State of Virginia, 1783-1983, 1983, The Last Review, 1984, Virginia Commonwealth University: A Sesqicentennial History, 1987, Pistols and Pointed Pens, 1987; editor: The Patriots, 1975, Architecture in Downtown Richmond, 1982, Virginius Dabney's Virginia, 1986; contbr. to nat. mags. Chmn. adv. bd. U.S. Hist. Soc.; bd. dirs. U. Press Va., 1966-70; chmn. Gov.'s Statewide Conf. on Edn., 1966; 1st rector Va. Commonwealth U., 1968-69, trustee, 1969-79. Recipient Lee Editorial award for disting. editorial writing Va. Press Assn., d Lee Sch. Journalism, Washington and Lee Univ., 1937; Pulitzer Prize for editorial writing, 1948; Nat. Editorial award Sigma Delta Chi, 1948, 52; Thomas Jefferson award for pub. service, 1972; Raven award for service U. Va., 1973; Distinguished Service award Va. Social Sci. Assn., 1975; Jackson Davis medal for service to higher edn., 1975; spl. award Va. C. of C., 1975; Liberty Bell award Richmond Bar Assn., 1976; Guggenheim fellow. Mem. Am. Soc. Newspaper Editors (dir. 1946-59, pres. 1957-58), So. Acad. Letters, Arts and Scis., Va. Hist. Soc. (pres. 1969-72), Raven, Omicron Delta Kappa, Delta Kappa Epsilon, Phi Beta Kappa, Sigma Delta Chi (fellow). Episcopalian. Club: Country of Virginia. Home: Richmond Va. Died Dec. 28, 1995.

DAESCHNER, RICHARD WILBUR, former food company executive; b. Preston, Nebr., July 5, 1917; s. Richard T. and Elma (Beckenhauer) D.; m. Prudence Armstrong, June 6, 1942; children: Richard, Rebecca, Martha. B.S. Edn., Kans. State Tchrs. Coll., 1937; J.D., Washburn U., 1941. Bar: Kans. 1941. Spl. agt. FBI, Washington, Boston, N.Y.C., Chgo., 1941-48; with employee relations dept. Beatrice Foods Co., Chgo., 1948-83; dir. employee relations Beatrice Foods Co., 1963-68, dir. personnel and indsl. relations, asst. sec., 1968-73, asst. v.p., 1973-78, v.p., 1978-83. Mem. Chgo. Crime Commn. Mem. Chgo. Bar Assn., Grocery Mfrs. Assn., Ill. C. of C., Chgo. Assn. Commerce and Industry, Am. Mgmt. Assn., Chgo. Better Bus. Bur. (bd. dirs.), Phi Delta Theta. Republican. Presbyterian. Clubs: Exec. (Chgo.); Inverness Golf. Lodge: Elks. Home: Palatine Ill. Died June 15, 1995.

DAHLBERG, ALBERT, dentist, dental and forensic bio-anthropologist; b. Chgo., Nov. 20, 1908; s. Albert Edward and Edith Ann (Carlson) D.; m. Thelma Elizabeth Ham, Jan. 2, 1934; children: Cordelia Thelma, Albert Edward, James Eric. BS, DDS, Loyola U., Chgo., 1932; D Odontologicae honoris causa, U. Turku, Finland, 1974. Intern, then resident, instr. U. Chgo. Clinic, 1932-36; rsch. assoc., prof. dept. anthropology U. Chgo., 1949-73, prof. evolution biology, 1950-73, acting dir. Zoller Dental Clinic, 1967-68, prof. emeritus, 1974-93; attending dental surgeon Chgo. Meml. Hosp., 1937-53; rsch. assoc. Mus. Natural History, Chgo., 1942-93; mem. Nat. Commn. on Study of Dentistry, Washington, 1957; mem. Oriental Inst. U. Chgo. archaeol. expdn., Iran, 1959-60, U. Wis. anthrop. expdn., Alaska and Greenland; adj. prof. Ariz. State U., Tempe, 1981-93; pvt. practice forensic bioanthropology, 1945-93. Author: International Symposium of Dental Morphology, 1967, Dental Morphology/Evolution, 1971; (with Graber) Orofacial Growth and Development, 1977; contbr. articles to profl. jour. Comdr. USPHS, 1943-46. Recipient Order of Rising Sun Minister of Edn. for Emperor of Japan, 1973; named Mem. of Honor GIRS Rsch. Soc. Europe, 1963. Fellow Chgo. Inst. Medicine, Internat. Coll. Dentists, Am. Coll. Dentists; mem. ADA (emeritus), Am. Assn. Phys. Anthropology, Internat. Symposium Dental Morphology, Internat. Assn. Dental Rsch. (craniofacial biology rsch. award Scotland 1992), Am. Acad. Forensic Scis., Forensic Odontology, Odontographic Soc. Chgo., Quadrangle Club, Delta Sigma Delta. Home: Franklin Grove Ill. Died July 30, 1993; cremated.

DAHLKE, WALTER EMIL, electrical engineering educator; b. Berlin, Aug. 24, 1910; came to U.S., 1964; s. Hermann Emil and Marie Emilie (Kunert) D.; m. Anneliese Mossler (dec. Jan. 1967); m. Ruth Ursula Brand. PhD, Berlin U., 1936; D Habililate, Jena U., Thuringia, Germany, 1939; hon. degree, Karlsruhe U., Fed. Republic Germany, 1961. Postdoctoral fellow in
physics U. Jena, 1936-40; lab. dir. aviation co. Berlin
1940-45; rsch. dir. AEG-Telefunken, Ulm, Fed
Republic Germany, 1949-65; prof. elec. engring. Lehig
U., Bethlehem, Pa., 1965-85, prof. emeritus, 1985-95.
Contbr. numerous publs. to profl. jours. and books.
Fellow IEEE; mem. German Phys. Soc., Info. Tech. Soc
Home: Allentown Pa. Died Oct. 8, 1995.

DALE, FRANCIS LYKINS, foundation executive
former performing arts officer, former sports executive
lawyer, former newspaper publisher, diplomat; b
Urbana, Ill., July 13, 1921; s. Charles Sherman an
Sarah (Lykins) D.; m. Kathleen Hamlin Watkins, Ma
20, 1947; children: Mitchell Watkins, Myron Lykins
Kathleen Hamlin, Holly Moore. AB, Duke U., 194
LLB, U. Va., 1948; cert., Acad. Internat. Law, Th
Hague, 1958; LLD (hon.), Eastern Ky. U., U. Cin
Ohio Wesleyan U., Salmon P. Chase Coll. of Law
Bloomfield Coll., Pepperdine Sch. of Bus., Whittier Col
Bar: Ohio 1948. Assoc. Frost & Jacobs, Cin., 1948-5
ptnr., 1953-65; asst. sec. Cin. Enquirer, Inc., 1952-6
pres., pub., 1965-73; pres. The Cin. Reds, Inc., 1967-7
vice-chmn., 1973-76; pub. L.A. Herald Examiner, 197
85; commr. Major Indoor Soccer League, 1985-86; pre
The Music Ctr. of L.A. County, 1986-88, Maureen an
Mike Mansfield Found., 1988-90; sr. assoc. Moxham
Carver & Assocs., Pasadena, Calif., 1990-93; bd. dirs
pres. Citizens for Water and Power for N.Am
Pasadena, Calif., 1991-93; chmn. Nat. Coun. Crime an
Delinquency, 1973-74, vice chmn., 1975-91; chm
Commn. White House fellows, 1973-74; U.S. ambas
sador and rep. to European Office of UN and othe
internat. orgns., Geneva, 1974-76; spl. asst. to asst. se
state, 1976; spl. adviser U.S. del. 31st Gen. Assembly
bd. dirs. ICN Biomeds., New Economy Fun
Coachman Inc., Smallcap World Fund; pres. Rep. As
socs. Active United Appeal, Cin., L.A. ; bd. dir
Goodwill Industries, Cin., v.p., 1968; bd. dirs., men
exec. com. Cin. area chpt. ARC; bd. dirs. Boys Club
Am., Bethesda Hosp., Boys' Club Cin., Taft Inst., Ci
Natural History Mus., also symphony, opera, ball
cos.; trustee Am. U., 1982-87, Occidental Coll., 1977-9
Claremont Sch. Theology, 1983-93; chmn. b
councilors U. So. Calif. Coll. Continuing Edn.; b
councilors Sch. Internat. Rels. and Sch. Bus.; asso
Calif. Poly. U., bd. dirs. Los Angeles chpt. ARC, Cen
tral City Assn., 1978-84, Meth. Hosp. So. Calif. Found
1980-93, Huntington Meml. Research Inst., 1985-9
Operating Co.-Music Center, 1982-86, Los Angele
World Affairs Coun., Los Angeles chpt. NCCJ, Tow
Hall Calif., Greater Los Angeles Visitors and Con
Bur.; bd. dirs., pres. Los Angeles Area council Bo
Scouts Am., 1983-84, mem. nat. adv. bd., 1984-93; b
dirs. Coun. Am. Ambssadors; mem., vice-chmn. S
Calif. Salvation Army; v.p. USAIM; assoc. chmn. Worl
Media Assn. With USNR, World War II. Name
Outstanding Young Man of Year Cin., 1951; recipien
Gov.'s award for adding prestige Ohio, 1968, Superio
Honor award State Dept., 1976, Freedoms Foun
award, 1976, Silver Beaver award Boy Scouts Am
1969, Disting. Citizen's award U.S. Olympic Com
1984; named to Wisdom Hall of Fame, 1987. Fello
ABA; mem. Ohio Bar Assn. (pres. 1961-62), L.A. C.
C. (v.p., bd. dirs. 1961-63), Coun. Chs. Greater Ci
(pres. 1959-61), Frat. of Friends (v.p. 1986-88), Order
Coif, Phi Kappa Psi, Sigma Nu Phi. Methodist (dis
lay leader 1958-64; mem. bd. publs. 1977-82). Club
Lincoln, Rotary; Comml. (Cin.); Annandale Golf (L
Angeles), Calif. (Los Angeles); Bohemian (San Franci
co); Valley Hunt (Pasadena). Home: Pasadena Cal
Died Nov. 28, 1993.

DALE, JOHN DENNY, economist, business executiv
b. N.Y.C., May 16, 1916; s. Francis Colegate ar
Imogen Hall (James) D.; m. Louise Boyd Lichtenstei
Oct. 22, 1938 (dec.); children: Anne Boyd (dec.), Joh
Denny Jr.; m. Madeline Houston McWhinney, June 2
1961; 1 child, Thomas Denny. AB, Hamilton Col
1936; MBA, NYU, 1954, PhD, 1962. Diplomate U.
Army Command and Gen. Staff Coll., 1967. Divs
mgr. Am. Steel Export Co., N.Y.C., 1936-40; asst.
pres. Charles Hardy Inc., N.Y.C., 1940, v.p., sec., treas
1941-45, pres., 1945-55; tech. dir. Charles Hardy Ltc
London, 1946-63; chmn. Mfrs. Mktg. Co., N.Y.C
1949-50; pres. Dale Elliott & Co. Inc., N.Y.C., 1955-6
71-76, chmn., 1976-93; fin. economist Litton Industri
Inc., Beverly Hills, Calif., 1965-68; fin. economist Ar
Export Industries, Inc., N.Y.C., 1968-70; v.p. Litt
Industries Leasing Corp., Beverly Hills, 1965-6
economist Dept. Labor and Industry, State of N.
Trenton, 1976-82; advisor to WPB, 1941, to Gov. N.Y
1948-51, to Chief Ordnance U.S. Army, 1952-55, Go
Monmouth Med. Ctr., 1954-71, to Port Authori
N.Y./N.J., N.Y.C., 1985-86. Author: Managerial A
counting in the Small Company, 1961. Trustee Mann
Coll. Music, 1957-69; mem. adv. bd. Root Art Ct
Whitney Mus. Am. Art; adviser mgmt. dept. Brookda
Coll., Holmdel, N.J., 1983-93; bd. dirs. Hudson Riv
Conservation Soc., 1936-83, Internat. Schs. Svcs
Princeton, N.J., 1985-90, Hamilton Coll. Alumni Cour
1948-52, 86-91; mem. Chamber Music Am. Maj. AU
1942-45, ETO, 1951-52, Korea, to col. USAR, ret
Decorated Legion of Merit; recipient Conspicious Se
vice medal Gov. State N.Y., 1948, Alumni Merit Servi
award NYU Alumni Fedn., 1962. Mem. Am. De
Preparedness Assn. (past pres., bd. dirs.), Order S
John, Knights Malta, Soc. Mayflower Descs., So
Colonial Wars, Soc. War of 1812, Huguenot Soc. (exe

coun. 1982-90), Mil. Order Fgn. Wars (past comdr.-gen. U.S.), Vet. Corps Arty., Soc. Am. Wars, S.R. St. Nicholas Soc., Res. Officers Assn., The English Speaking Union, NYU Grad. Sch. Bus. Adminstrn. Alumni Assn. (bd. dirs. 1953-65, pres. 1961-62), The Pilgrims, Psi Upsilon. Republican. Episcopalian. Clubs: University Glee, Racquet and Tennis, N.Y. Athletic (N.Y.C.), Rumson (N.J.) Country. Lodge: Masons. Home: Red Bank N.J. Died Apr. 20, 1993; buried Woodlawn Cemetery, Bronx, N.Y.

D'ALESSANDRO, ANGELO MICHAEL, financial services executive; b. Bklyn., Apr. 28, 1930; s. Dominic and Catherine (Siragusa) D'A.; m. Rosemarie Joan Rotondi, Apr. 30, 1955; children—Stephen, Paul, Gregory, Karen, Michael. B.B.A., St. John's U., 1954; M.B.A., NYU, 1956. Corp. sec. Lukens, Savage, Washburn & Rosenbaum, Phila., 1955-63; founder, exec. v.p. Rothman & D'Alessandro Inc., N.Y.C., 1963-70; sr. v.p. Martin E. Segal Co., N.Y.C., 1970-75; v.p., dir., mem., exec. com. A.S. Hansen, Inc., N.Y.C., 1975-78; founder, pres. A.M. D'Alessandro & Co., Inc., Fair Lawn, N.J., 1978-81; sr. v.p. Alexander & Alexander, Inc., N.Y.C., 1981-85, dir., 1982—, exec. v.p., mem. mgmt. com., ops. com., 1985—, chief exec. officer human resource mgmt. group, 1985—, chmn., chief exec. officer, 1986—; chmn. bd. dirs. Benefacts, N.Y.C., 1985—; dir., mem. exec. com., chmn. personnel com. Interchange State Bank, Saddle Brook, N.J., 1981—. Contbr. articles to profl. jours. Mem. adv. council St. John's U., Jamaica, N.Y., 1975—; trustee Bergen Community Coll., 1980—, chmn. bd. trustees, 1982-84. Served as spl. agt. USAF, 1951-55. Recipient cert. of merit Pres.' Commn. on Pension Reform; Meritorious Service award Bergen Community Coll., 1982. Mem. Am. Pension Conf., Employee Benefits Research Inst. (trustee), Internat. Found. Employee Benefit Plans, Am. Mgmt. Assn., Washington Forum. Democrat. Roman Catholic. Club: Union League (N.Y.C.). Home: Franklin Lakes N.J. Deceased.

DALY, JAMES JOSEPH, newspaper executive; b. Jersey City, June 11, 1916; s. Bernard B. and Anna (Leiner) D.; m. Catherine Mary Adams, June 26, 1937; children: Ann Daly Heller, Catherine Daly Kline. Student, St. Peters Coll. Classified advt. mgr. N.Y. Sun, 1946-49, World Telegram Sun, 1950-55; with Washington Post, 1955-94, v.p., gen. mgr., 1965-72; exec. v.p. Washington Star, 1975-77, chmn. exec. com., dir., 1977-78; mem. exec. com. Newspaper I. Mem. exec. com. Washington Conv. and Visitors Bur., 1969-72; chmn. v.p. Tenafly (N.J.) Community Chest, 1955; budget com. Washington Health and Welfare Council, 1961-64; Bd. dirs. United Givers Fund, Washington Bd. Trade, Better Bus. Bur., ARC; trustee Am. Cancer Soc., Fed. City Council, 1977-78. Served with AUS, 1943-45. Mem. Washington Advt. Club, John Carroll Soc., Silurians. Clubs: Rotary. (Washington), Columbia Country (Washington), Pisces (Washington); Boca Raton (Fla.); Delray Beach Yacht (Fla.); Boca Raton Hotel and Club. Home: Rockville Md. Died Apr. 17, 1994.

DAMSEL, RICHARD A., transportation company executive; b. 1942; married. BSBA, John Carroll U., 1964. Audit mgr. Deloitte Haskins and Sells, to 1974; with Leaseway Transp. Corp., Cleve., from 1974, mgr. fin. analysis, then treas., 1975-80, v.p. fin., 1980-82, CFO, sr. v.p. fin., 1982-87, sr. v.p. fin. and adminstrn., 1987-88, chmn., CEO, from 1988, also bd. dirs. Home: Cleveland Ohio Deceased.

DANIELS, WILBUR, lawyer; b. Detroit, Jan. 23, 1923; s. Max and Dora (Miller) D.; m. Patricia Heyman, Dec. 22, 1963; 1 child, Ann G. B.S., CCNY, 1942; J.D., NYU, 1950. Bar: N.Y. 1950, U.S. Supreme Ct. 1951. Rsch., asst. dir. rsch. Internat. Ladies' Garment Workers' Union, N.Y.C., 1943-50; assoc. gen. counsel Internat. Ladies' Garment Worker's Union, N.Y.C., 1950-59, asst. to pres., 1959-61, dir. master agreements dept., 1965-87, v.p., 1969-73, exec. v.p., 1973-87; ptnr. firm Vladeck & Elias, N.Y.C., 1961-63; exec. dir. Nat. Bd. Coat and Suit Industry, N.Y.C., 1963-65, S.H. and Helen R. Scheuer Family Found., 1987-93; assoc. adj. prof. grad. div. NYU Law Sch., 1979-84; vice chmn. N.Y. State Job Devel. Authority; mem. Nat. Commn. Unemployment Commn., 1977-80, U.S. Adv. Coun. on Employee Welfare and Pension Benefit Plans, 1961-69, Fed. Adv. Coun. Unemployment Inst., 1975-82. Bd. mng. dirs., chmn. exec. com. Met. Opera Assn.; mem. bd. visitors Grad. Ctr., CUNY; past bd. dirs. Lincoln Ctr. for Performing Arts; chmn. N.Y. State Adv. Coun. on Employment and Unemployment Ins.; bd. dirs. United Housing Found., 1977-87, N.Y. Urban Coalition, 1970-73, UN Assn.; alt. mem. N.Y.C. Office Collective Bargaining, 1986-87. With U.S. Army, 1945-46. Mem. ABA, Assn. of Bar of City of N.Y., Am Arbitration Assn. (bd. dirs.), Phi Beta Kappa. Home: New York N.Y. Died Mar. 20, 1993.

DANISH, ABRAHAM, retired gastroenterologist, medical educator; b. Phila., Dec. 25, 1916; m. Sophie Levinson, 1947 (dec.); children: Barbara, Judith, Katherine. AB, George Washington U., 1938, MD, 1941; postgrad., U. Pa., 1947-48. Diplomate Am. Bd. Internal Medicine. Intern. St. Francis Hosp., Pitts., 1941-42; pvt. practice medicine Phila., 1945-48; resident in internal medicine Gallinger Mcpl. Hosp., Washington, 1948-49; pvt. practice internal medicine, gastroenterology Silver Spring, Md., 1950-92; prof. emeritus George Washington U.; chief medicine Washington Adventist Hosp., Takoma Park, Md., 1961-66, hon. mem. staff with admitting privileges; pres. Community Psychiatric Clinic, Bethesda, Md., 1969-71; chief medicine Holy Cross Hosp., Silver Spring, 1974-76, chief gastroenterology, 1970-83, hon. mem. staff with admitting privileges. Pres. Montgomery County unit Am. Cancer Soc., 1964-67; bd. dirs. Md. Coll. Art and Design, Silver Spring, 1990-92, pres. 1992—. Capt. U.S. Army Med. Corps, 1942-45. Fellow George Washington U., Am. Cancer Soc., 1949-50. Fellow Am. Coll. Physicians; mem. Am. Soc. Internal Medicine, Am. Soc. Gastrointestinal, MEd. Chirurgical Faculty, Montgomery County Med. Soc. (Henry P. Laughlin award, 1970, Clinician of Yr., 1982). Home: Silver Spring Md.

DANISHEFSKY, ISIDORE, biochemist; b. Poland, Apr. 3, 1923; s. Jacob and Anna (Gorelik) D.; m. Madeleine Weinstein, Sept. 5, 1951; children: Kenneth, Avis. BA, Yeshiva U., 1944; PhD, NYU, 1951. Rsch. assoc. Poly. Inst., Bklyn., 1951-52, Columbia U., N.Y.C., 1952-55; asst. prof. N.Y. Med. Coll., Valhalla, 1955-60, assoc. prof., 1960-65, prof., 1965-77, prof., chmn. dept. biochemistry, 1977-88, prof., chmn. dept. biochemistry and molecular biology, 1988-94; cons. NIH, Bethesda, 1975, 77-80, 84-86, WHO, Geneva, Switzerland, 1989. Author: Biochemistry for Medical Sciences, 1980; editor Thrombosis Rsch., 1988-94; contbr. articles to sci. rsch. jours. Recipient Honors-Achievement award Am. Coll. Angiology, 1964, Bernard Revel award Yeshiva U., 1962, Outstanding Educator award, 1974; rsch. grantee NIH, 1960-94. Fellow AAAS; mem. Am. Soc. Biol. Chemists, N.Y. Acad. Scis., Internat. Soc. Thrombosis. Home: Bronx N.Y. Deceased.

DANZIG, SARAH PALFREY, retired advertising agency executive, writer; b. Sharon, Mass., Sept. 18, 1912; d. John Gorham and Methyl (Oakes) Palfrey; m. Jerome A. Danzig, Apr. 27, 1951; children—Diana, Jerome Palfrey. Grad., Winsor Sch., 1930; spl. studies, Radcliffe Coll. Advt. cons. World Tennis mag., 1967-91; sports editor NBC-TV Home program, 1956-57; sports commr. N.Y.C., 1966-96; exec. com. Nat. Tennis Found. and Hall of Fame Inc. Author: Winning Tennis and How to Play It, 1946, Tennis for Anyone, 1966, rev. paperback, 1972, 80, also articles. Chmn. spl. events Child Study Assn. Am., 1963-67; chmn. ann. benefit Vis. Nurse Service, N.Y.C., 1961-63; mem. spl. events com. People to People Sports Com., 1962-64, Eastern Tennis Patrons, 1962-67; Trustee Community Service Soc. N.Y., 1966-76. Won U.S. Women's Nat. Singles titles 1941, 45; recipient Svc. Bowl award USTA, 1981; elected Mass. Greatest Woman Athlete, Helms Hall of Fame, 1963, inducted into the Internat. Tennis Hall of Fame, 1963, Ea/ Tennis Assn. Hall of Fame, 1988, into New Eng. Law Tennis Assn. Hall of Fame, 1990; named Outstanding Mother, 1985. Mem. Lawn Tennis Writers Assn. Am., Internat. Lawn Tennis Club U.S.A. (hon., emeritus 1994), Internat. Tennis Hall of Fame (hon.). Clubs: 7th Regiment Tennis (hon.), Jr. League, Town Tennis (hon.); Longwood Cricket (Chestnut Hill, Mass.) (hon.); West Side Tennis (hon.). Home: New York N.Y. Died Feb. 27, 1996.

DARLING, BYRON THORWELL, physicist, educator; b. Napoleon, Ohio, Jan. 4, 1912; s. Frank Ellsworth and Evalyn Louise (Young) D.; m. Barbara Anne Borgogni, Aug. 24, 1946. B.Sc., U. Ill., 1933, M.Sc., 1936; postgrad., U. Mich., 1936-38, Ph.D., 1939; postgrad., U. Wis., 1938-39. Instr. math. Mich. State Coll., 1939-41; instr. physics Pa. State Coll., 1941; research physicist U.S. Rubber Co., Detroit, 1941-46; research assoc. U. Wis., 1946-47; research asso. with rank of instr. Yale U., 1947; asst. prof. physics Ohio State U., 1947-51, assoc. prof., 1951-53; prof. theoretical physics Laval U., Quebec, PQ, Can., 1955-79, disting. prof. emeritus, 1988-91; adj. vis. prof. U. Fla., Gainesville, 1980-91. Contbr. articles to sci. jours. Mem. Am. Phys. Soc., Can. Assn. Physicists, Assn. Canadienne Francaise pour l'Avancement des Sciences, N.Y. Acad. Scis., AAAS, Am. Assn. Physics Tchrs., Soc. Profl. Engrs. Que. Home: Gainsville Fla. Died Jan. 7, 1991.

DARLING, GEORGE BAPST, JR., retired medical educator; b. Boston, Dec. 30, 1905; s. George Bapst and Alice Emma (Smith) D.; m. Ann F. Shaw, June 25, 1931 (dec. 1989). Ed., Phillips Acad., Andover Mass.; SB, MIT, 1927; Dr. P.H., U. Mich., 1931, LLD (hon.), 1975; MA (hon.), Yale U., 1947. Research assoc., asst. epidemiologist Dept. Health, Detroit, 1927-32; with W. K. Kellogg Found., Battle Creek, Mich., 1932-43; beginning as asso. dir., mem. bd. trustees and asso. sec.-treas. W. K. Kellogg Found., 1934-37, comptroller, 1937, pres., 1940-43; dir. Atlas Properties, Inc., 1934-43, pres., 1940-43; dir. Kellogg Co., 1941-43; exec. sec. coms. on mil. medicine NRC, 1943-45, vice chmn. div. med. scis., 1944-45, 47-48; exec. sec. Nat. Acad. Sci. and NRC, 1946; dir. med. affairs Yale U., 1946-52, prof. human ecology, 1952-74, prof. emeritus, 1974-95, life fellow emeritus Timothy Dwight Coll., 1974-95; on leave as dir. Atomic Bomb Casualty Commn. NRC-Nat. Acad. Sci., Hiroshima and Nagasaki, Japan, 1957-72; on leave as Fogarty scholar Fogarty Internat. Center for Advanced Study in Health Scis., NIH, Bethesda, Md., 1973-74; vis. lectr. Hiroshima Sch. Medicine, Hiroshima Sch. Nursing.; chmn. health div. New Haven Council Social Agys., 1954-57; bd. dirs. Grace New Haven Community Hosp., 1946-59, exec. com., 1946-53; bd. dirs. Conn. Health League. Civilian observer Joint Task Force 1, Bikini Atom Bomb test, 1946. Contbr. articles on public health and edn. to jours. Asso. Yale Med. Library; asso. Art Gallery, Peabody Mus. Recipient Golden Orchid Supreme award Japan Med. Soc., 1967; Japan Red Cross medallion, 1967; Citation medal AEC, 1970; cert. of appreciation AEC, 1972; citations Japan Tb Assn.; citations Combined Rotary Clubs, Hiroshima; citations gov. Hiroshima; citations mayor Hiroshima; citations U. Hiroshima; citations Hiroshima Med. Assn.; citations Japan Ministry Health and Welfare, 1972; citations U.S. sec. state, 1972; medallion Atomic Bomb Casulty Commn.-Japan Nat. Inst. Health; award for distinguished contbns. to research adminstrn. Soc. Research Adminstrs., 1974; Paul Harris fellow (thrice), Japan, New Haven. Fellow Am. Pub. Health Assn. (mem. com. adminstrv. practice); mem. Washington Acad. Medicine, AAAS (life), Conn. Med. Soc. (Asso.), Radiation Research Soc. of Japan, Japan Pub. Health Assn., Hiroshima Med. Soc. (hon.), Am. C. of C. of Japan, Japan-Am. socs. Nagasaki, Hiroshima, Washington, Acad. Polit. Sci., N.Y. Acad. Scis., Delta Omega (past pres.), Pi Delta Epsilon, Theta Chi, Mortar and Ball, Ursa Major. Unitarian. Clubs: Mory's Assn. (New Haven), Rotary (Hiroshima and New Haven) (Paul Harris fellow); Beaumont Medical (New Haven), Yale Faculty (New Haven); Yale (N.Y.C.); Cosmos (Washington). Home: Hamden Conn. Died March 30, 1996.

DARLING, LOIS MACINTYRE, illustrator, author, artist; b. N.Y.C., Aug. 15, 1917; d. Malcolm and Grace (Hamilton) McIntyre; m. Louis Darling, June 3, 1946 (dec. Jan. 1970). Student, Grand Central Sch. Art, N.Y.C.; pvt. studies, 1935-40; student zoology, Columbia U.,, 1947-51. Staff artist dept. paleontology, Am. Mus. Natural History, N.Y.C., 1952-54, illustrator, 1945—; lectr. natural history, ecology. Author-illustrator: (with Louis Darling) Before and After Dinosaurs, 1959, Sixty Million Years of Horses, 1960, The Science of Life, 1961, Bird, 1962, Turtles, 1962, 1962, Coral Reefs, 1963, The Sea Serpents Around Us, 1965, A Place in the Sun, 1968, Worms, 1972; author-illustrator: The Beagle-A Search for a Lost Ship, 1960, H.M.S. Beagle-Further Research or Twenty Years a-Beagling, 1977, H.M.S. Beagle, 1820-1870, Voyages Summarized, Research and Reconstruction, 1984; illustrator: Yachting, Time-Life, Sou'West and by West of Cape Cod, 1948, 1987, Evolution of the Vertebrates, 1955, 69, 80, 88, The Middle Road, 1961, Where the Sea Breaks Its Back, 1966, others; illustrator: (with Louis Darling) Silent Spring, 1962, 87, The Birds, 1963, Animal Behavior, 1965, The Appalachians, 1965, others. Manuscripts and illustrations in permanent collections Beinecke Library, Yale U., Kerlan Collection, U. Minn. Served with WAVES, 1943-45. Recipient Govs. award for Outstanding Women of Conn., 1977; named among 350 celebrities in Conn., Hartford, 1986. Mem. Conn. Conservationists, Inc. (treas. 1955-56), Nat. Audubon Soc., Westport Audubon Soc. (conservation chmn. 1955-61), Nature Conservancy, Am. Inst. Biol. Scis., Thames Sci. Ctr., Soc. Illustrators, Essex Art Assn. (award 1981, 83), Catboat Assn. Conn. River Oar and Paddle Assn. Home: Old Lyme Conn.

DARMOJUWONO, JUSTIN CARDINAL, retired archbishop; b. Godean, Yogyakarta, Indonesia, Nov. 2, 1914; s. Yoseph Surodikoro and Mary Ngatinah. Diploma, Tchr. Sch., Muntilan, Indonesia, 1935, Minor Sem., Yogyakarta, 1942, Major Sem., Yogyakarta, 1947, Gregorian U., Rome, 1955. Ordained Roman Cath. priest, 1947. Tchr. Minor Sem., 1947-48; priest local parish Yogyakarta, 1948-50, Klaten, Indonesia, 1950-54, Surakarta, Indonesia, 1956-62; priest, vicar gen. Semarang, Indonesia, 1962-63; archbishop Semarang, 1963-81; ret., 1981; bishop Indonesian Army, 1964-81; cardinal 1967-94. Home: Semarang Indonesia Died Feb. 1994.

DARNALL, DENNIS WAYNE, biochemistry educator, corporate official; b. Glenwood Springs, Colo., Dec. 14, 1941; s. Harvey Glen and Lois Marie (Coleman) D.; m. Judy Marcell Thornton, May 31, 1963; children: Nichol Michelle, Beth Denise. BS in Chemistry, N.Mex. Inst. Mining and Tech., 1963; PhD in Biochemistry, Tex. Tech U., 1966. Asst. prof. biochemistry N.Mex. State U., Las Cruces, 1968-72, assoc. prof., 1972-74, prof., 1974—, head dept. chemistry, 1991—, assoc. dean, 1983-86, dir. rsch. ctr., 1983-86; pres. Bio-Recovery Systems, Inc., Las Cruces, 1985-89. Editor: Methods for Determining Metal Ion Environments in Proteins, 1979; contbr. articles to profl. jours.; inventor chem. method mineral recovery. NIH fellow Northwestern U., Evanston, Ill., 1966-68. Fellow AAAS; mem. Am. Chem. Soc., Am. Soc. Biol. Chemists, Soc. Research Adminstrs., Nat. Council of Univ. Research Adminstrs. Home: Mesilla N.Mex.

DASHEN, ROGER FREDERICK, physics educator, consultant; b. Grand Junction, Colo., May 5, 1938; m. Mary Kelleghan; children: Monica, Melissa. AB summa cum laude, Harvard U., 1960; PhD, Calif. Inst. Tech., 1964. Rsch. assoc. Calif. Inst. Tech., Pasadena, 1964-65, asst. prof., 1965-66, prof. theoretical physics, 1966-69; prof. Inst. for Advanced Study, Princeton,

N.J., 1969-86; prof. U. Calif. San Diego, La Jolla, 1986—, chmn. dept. physics, 1988-94; mem. steering com. Heart Island Global Program, 1991—; mem. Superpar Consortium, 1988—; mem. JASON, 1966—, Def. Sci. Bd. Panel on Anti-Submarine Warfare and SSBN Security, 1980-88; mem. planning and steering adv. com. of the advanced tech. panel Dept. of the Navy, 1984—; mem. adv. bd. Applied Physics Lab., U. Wash., Seattle, 1987-91; cons. Los Alamos Sci. Lab., 1975—; rsch. cons. Schlumberger, 1978-83; advisor Alfred P. Sloan Found., 1985-91; Amos de Shalit lectr. Weizmann Inst. Sci., Israel, 1981. Contbr. 115 articles to profl. jours. Fellow Alfred P. Sloan Found., 1966-73; Green Scholar Scripps Instn. Oceanography, 1977. Mem. NAS, Am. Acad. Arts and Scis. Home: La Jolla Calif. Died May 24, 1995.

DA SILVA, CARLOS E. VALLES, retired architect, historian, art critic; b. Cebu City, Philippines, May 12, 1908; m. Mary Betts, 1932 (div. 1955); children: Enrique, Ricardo, Miren; m. Martha Dizon, July 4, 1979. B.S. in Architecture, Mapua Inst. Tech.; postgrad. Adamson U., U. Philippines. Pvt. practice architect, Philippines, 1948-86; prof. architecture Nat. U. Coll. of Engring.; then with Adamson U. Sch. Arch., Manila. Researcher, numerous awards for archtl. projects. Fellow Philippine Inst. Arch.; mem. AIA, De la Salle Alumni Assn., Nat. Assn. Mapua Alumni (bd. dirs.), San Carlos Coll. Alumni Assn., Philippines Inst. Architects (pres. 1954-55), Art Assn. Philippines. Died Apr. 29, 1986. Home: Manila The Philippines

D'ATRI, JOSEPH EUGENE, researcher, mathematics educator; b. N.Y.C., Apr. 20, 1938; s. Americus Justin and Agnes Marie (Roesch) D'A.; m. Sheila Sherman, Jan. 19, 1963; children: Aileen Rebecca, Henry Evald. AB, Columbia U., 1959; PhD, Princeton U., 1964. Instr. summer sch. Columbia Coll., N.Y.C., 1959-61, Princeton (N.J.) U., 1962-63; lectr., asst. prof. Rutgers U., New Brunswick, N.J., 1963-69, assoc. prof., 1969-75, prof. math., 1975—, chmn. dept., 1985-90. Contbr. articles to profl. jours. Mem. Am. Math. Soc., Math. Assn. Am., Phi Beta Kappa. Home: Trenton N.J. Died Apr. 29, 1993.

DAUBENSPECK, ROBERT DONLEY, advertising agency executive; b. Butler, Pa., Nov. 5, 1926; s. Frank Thorne and Virginia (Donley) D.; m. Susan Mary Alcorn, Oct. 28, 1967; children: Nancy, Joan, Jean, Thorne. A.B. in Econs. and Social Instns, Princeton U., 1949. Supr. Benson & Benson (mktg. research), Princeton, N.J., 1949-51; sales analyst Lever Bros., N.Y.C., 1951-52; mgr. sales devel. NBC, Chgo., 1952-61; with Foote, Cone & Belding Advt., Inc., 1961-95; v.p., dir. media and programming Foote, Cone & Belding Advt., Inc., Chgo., 1974-79; broadcast media cons. Foote, Cone & Belding Advt., Inc., N.Y.C., 1979-90; pres. The Delphi Group (media cons.), 1990-95. Author: Recall Technique As Measurement of Broadcast Audiences, 1949. Served with USAAF, 1945. Mem. Internat. Radio and TV Soc., Broadcast Advt. Club, Menninger Found., Pres. Franklin Creek Assn. (pres. 1994-95), Boyer Club, Whitehall Club, Barclay Club, St. Charles Country Club, Aspetuck Valley Country Club, Princeton Club, The Landings. Home: Savannah Ga. Died Aug. 28, 1995.

D'AULAIRE, EDGAR PARIN, artist, lithographer, author; b. Munich, Germany, Sept. 30, 1898; came to U.S., 1929, naturalized, 1939; s. Gino and Ella (d'Aulaire) Parin; m. Ingri Sandsmark Mortenson, July 24, 1925 (dec. 1980); children: Per Ola, Nils Maarten. Student, Inst. Tech., Munich, 1917-19, Sch. Applied Arts, Munich, 1919-22, Hans Hofman Sch., Munich, 1922-24, Ecole André Lhote, Paris, 1925-26, Ecole Pola Gauguin, Paris, 1926—. lectr. with wife. Illustrator 17 books in, Germany, 1922-26; author-illustrator (with wife), 26 children's books, from 1931; painter, exhibited in, Norway and Paris; executed 2 frescoes, Norway, 1926-27; Author, illustrator: (with Ingri d'Aulaire) The Magic Rug, 1931, Ola, 1932, Ola and Blakken, 1933, Conquest of the Atlantic, 1933, The Lord's Prayer, 1934, Children of the Northlights, 1935, George Washington, 1936, East of the Sun and West of the Moon, 1938, Abraham Lincoln, 1939, Animals Everywhere, 1940, Leif the Lucky, 1941, The Star Spangled Banner, 1942, Don't Count Your Chicks, 1943, Wings for Per, 1944, Too Big, 1945, Pocahontas, 1946, Nils, 1948, Foxie, 1949, Benjamin Franklin, 1950, Buffalo Bill, 1952, The Two Cars, 1954, Columbus, 1955, The Magic Meadow, 1958, d'Aulaires' Book of Greek Myths, 1962, d'Aulaires' Norse Gods and Giants, 1967, d'Aulaires Trolls, 1972, The Terrible Troll Bird, 1976. Recipient Caldecott award A.L.A., 1940, Regina award Cath. Library Assn., 1970. Home: Georgetown Conn. Deceased.

DAVIE, DONALD ALFRED, humanities and English educator, author; b. Barnsley, Eng., July 17, 1922; s. George Clarke and Alice (Sugden) D.; m. Doreen John, Jan. 13, 1945; children:—Richard Mark, Diana Margaret, Patrick George. B.A., St. Catharine's Coll., Cambridge, Eng., 1947, M.A., 1948, Ph.D., 1951; D.Litt (hon.), U. So. Calif., 1978. Lectr. Dublin U., Ireland, 1950-57; fellow Trinity Coll., Dublin, Ireland, 1954-57; vis. prof. U. Calif.-Santa Barbara, 1957-58; lectr. English U. Cambridge, 1958-64; fellow Gonville and Caius Coll., 1959-64; prof. lit. U. Essex, Colchester, Eng., 1965-68,

dean comparative studies, 1964, pro-vice-chancellor, 1965; vis. prof. Grinnell Coll., 1965; Leo S. Bing prof. English and Am. lit. U. So. Calif., 1968-69; prof. English Stanford U., 1969-74, Olive H. Palmer prof. humanities, 1974-78; Andrew W. Mellon prof. humanities, prof. English Vanderbilt U., Nashville, 1978-88; hon. fellow Trinity Coll., Dublin, 1978. Author: Purity of Diction in English Verse, 1952, 2d edit.; 1976; The Heyday of Sir Walter Scott, 1961; Articulate Energy, 1957; Ezra Pound; Poet as Sculptor, 1964; Thomas Hardy and British Poetry, 1972; Ezra Pound, 1976; A Gathered Church, 1978, The Poet in the Imaginary Museum, 1978; Trying to Explain, 1980; Dissentient Voice, 1982, Czeslaw Milosz and the Insufficiency of Lyric, 1986; These the Companions: Reflections, 1982; (poetry) Brides of Reason, 1955; A Winter Talent, 1957; The Forests of Lithuania, 1960; New and Selected Poems, 1961; Events and Wisdoms, 1965; Essex Poems, 1969; Six Epistles to Eva Hesse, 1970; Collected Poems, 1950-70, 1972; The Shires, 1974; In the Stopping Train, 1977, Three for Water-Music, 1981; Collected Poems, 1971-83, 1983, To Scorch or Freeze, 1989; (verse-translations) The Poems of Doctor Zhivago, 1965; editor: The New Oxford Book of Christian Verse, 1982. Served with Royal Navy, 1941-46. Fellow (hon.) Trinity Coll., Dublin, 1978. Fellow Am. Acad. Arts and Scis., St. Catharine's Coll. (hon.), London Library. Home: Nashville Tenn. Died September 18, 1995.

DAVIES, ROBERT ERNEST, biochemist, educator; b. Barton-upon-Irwell, Eng., Aug. 17, 1919; s. William Owen and C. Stella (Spencer) D.; m. Helen Jean Rogoff, Sept. 8, 1961; children: Daniel J., Richard D. B.Sc., U. Manchester, 1941, M.Sc., 1942, D.Sc., 1952; Ph.D., U. Sheffield, 1949; M.A., Oxford U., 1956, U. Pa., 1971. Mem. faculty U. Manchester, Eng., 1941-42, U. Sheffield, Eng., 1942-54, U. Heidelberg, Germany, 1954, Oxford (Eng.) U., 1954-59; mem. faculty U. Pa., 1955-93, prof. biochemistry, 1955-70, Benjamin Franklin prof. molecular biology, 1970-93, chmn. Benjamin Franklin profs., 1978-93, Univ. prof. molecular biology, 1977-93, chmn. grad. group molecular biology, 1962-71, chmn. dept. animal biology, 1962-73, chmn. faculty senate, 1989-90. Mem. editorial bd.: Biochem. Jour, 1951-56; asso. editor: Jour. Mechanochemistry and Cell Motility, 1970-93. Mem. Brit. Home Guard, 1940-45, Brit. Nat. Fire Service, 1940-45. Fellow Royal Soc.; mem. Am. Chem. Soc., Am. Soc. Biol. Chemists, Am. Physiol. Soc., N.Y. Acad. Scis. (hon. life), Sigma Xi, Phi Zeta. Home: Philadelphia Pa. Died Mar. 7, 1993.

DAVIES, ROBERTSON, author; b. Thamesville, Ont., Can., Aug. 28, 1913; m. Brenda Mathews, 1940; three children. Student, Upper Can. Coll., Queen's U., Kingston, Ont.; LLD, Queen's U., Kingston, Ont., 1962; BLitt, Oxford U., (Eng.), 1938; LLD, U. Alta., Edmonton, 1957, U. Man., 1972, U. Calgary, 1975, U. Toronto, 1981, U. P.E.I., 1989; DLitt, McMaster U., Hamilton, Ont., 1959, U. Windsor, Ont., 1971, York U., 1973, Mt. Allison U., 1973, Meml. U., 1974, U. Western Ont., 1974, McGill U., 1974, Trent U., 1974, U. Lethbridge, 1981, U. Waterloo, 1981, U. B.C., 1983, U. Santa Clara, 1985, Trinity Coll., Dublin, 1990, U. Oxford, 1991; U. Wales, 1995; DCL, Bishop's U., Lennoxville, Que., 1967; LHD, U. Rochester, 1983, Dowling Coll., N.Y., 1992, Loyola U., Chgo., 1994; DSL, Thornloe Coll. U. Sudbury, 1988. Tchr., actor Old Vic Theatre Sch. and Repertory Co., London, Eng., 1938-40; lit. editor Saturday Night, Toronto, Ont., 1940-42; editor and pub. Examiner, Peterborough, Ont., 1942-68; prof. English U. Toronto, 1960-81; master Massey Coll., 1962-81; Past bd. govs. Stratford Ontario Shakespeare Festival. Author: Shakespeare's Boy Actors, 1939, Shakespeare for Young Players: A Junior Course, 1942, The Diary of Samuel Marchbanks, 1947, The Table Talk of Samuel Marchbanks, 1949; plays Hope Deferred, 1949, Fortune My Foe, 1949, Eros at Breakfast, 1949, Overlaid, 1949, At My Heart's Core, 1950, A Masque of Aesop, 1952, A Jig for the Gypsy, 1954, A Masque of Mr. Punch, 1963, Hunting Stuart and Other Plays, 1972, Question Time, 1975; novels Tempest-Tost, 1951, Leaven of Malice, 1954, A Mixture of Frailties, 1958, Fifth Business, 1970, The Manticore, 1972; World of Wonders, 1975, (with Tyrone Guthrie) Renown at Stratford: A Record of the Shakespearean Festival in Canada, 1953, Twice Have the Trumpets Sounded: A Record of the Stratford Shakespearean Festival in Canada, 1954, Thrice the Brinded Cat Hath Mew'd: A Record of the Stratford Shakespearean Festival in Canada, 1955, A Voice from the Attic, 1960, The Personal Art: Reading to Good Purpose, 1961, Samuel Marchbanks' Almanack, 1967, Stephen Leacock: Feast of Stephen, 1970, (with others) The Revels History of Drama in English, Vol. VI, 1975, One Half of Robertson Davies, 1977, The Rebel Angels, 1981, The Enthusiasms of Robertson Davies (Judith S. Grant editor), 1979, Robertson Davies: The Well-Tempered Critic (Grant editor), 1981, High Spirits, 1982, The Mirror of Nature, 1983, What's Bred in the Bone, 1985, The Papers of Samuel Marchbanks, 1985, The Lyre of Orpheus, 1988, Murther & Walking Spirits, 1991, Reading and Writing, 1993, The Cunning Man, 1994; transls. in 19 langs. Decorated Companion Order of Can., 1972; recipient Louis Jouvet prize for directing Dominion Drama Festival, 1949, Leacock medal, 1955, Lorne Pierce medal, 1961, Gov. Gen.;s award for fiction, 1973, Lifetime Achievement award Toronto Arts, 1986, City of Toronto Book award, 1986, Lit. award Can.

Authors Assn., 1986, Nat. award Banff Centre Sch. Fine Arts, 1986, Medal of Honor for lit. Nat. Arts Club, N.Y.C., 1987, Order of Ont., 1988, Diplôme d'honneur Can. Conf. of Arts, 1988, Molson prize in arts Can. Coun., 1988; hon. fellow Balliol Coll., Oxford, 1986, Neil Gunn internat. fellow Scottish Arts Coun., 1988, Hon. fellowship Royal Conservatory of Music, Toronto, 1994, Pierpong Morgan Libr., N.Y.C. Fellow Royal Soc. Can., Royal Soc. Lit.; mem. Am. Acad. and Inst. Arts and Letters (hon.). Home: New York N.Y. Died Dec. 2, 1995.

DAVIES, RONALD NORWOOD, federal judge; b. Crookston, Minn., Dec. 11, 1904; s. Norwood S. and Minnie M. (Quigley) D.; m. Mildred M. Doran, Oct. 10, 1933; children: Timothy Q., Mary Jo, Thomas A., Catharine A., Jean M. A.B., U. N.D., 1927, LL.D. (hon.), 1961; LL.B., Georgetown U., 1930, LL.D. (hon.), 1982. Practiced in Grand Forks, N.D., 1930-55; judge Municipal Ct., Grand Forks, 1932-40; lectr. U. N.D. Sch. Law, 1952-55; U.S. dist judge Dist. of N.D., Fargo, 1955-96; sr. judge; Mem. N.D. Bd. Pardons, 1933, N.D. Athletic Commn., 1935. Served from 1st lt. to lt. col. AUS, 1942-46. Recipient Outstanding Alumnus award Georgetown U. Law Center, 1958, U. N.D., 1979; named to U. N.D. Athletic Hall of Fame, 1980. Fellow Am. Bar Found.; mem. N.D. Bar Assn. (Disting. Service award 1980, exec. dir. 1947-55), Grand Forks C. of C. (pres. 1953), Am. Legion, Am. Bar Assn., 40 and 8, Order of Coif, Sigma Nu, Phi Alpha Delta. Roman Catholic. Clubs: Elk, K.C. Home: Fargo N.D. Died Apr. 18, 1996.

DAVIES, THEODORE PETER, artist; b. Bklyn., 1928. Student, Art Students League, N.Y.C. Exhbns. include Print Club Phila., Queens Mus., Mus. Modern Art, N.Y.C., Boston Printmakers, 1959, SUNY, Albany, Art Students League, Brigham Young U., U. South, Columbia Coll., Guild Hall Mus.; represented in permanent collections Mus. Modern Art, Phila. Mus. Art, Nat. Gallery Art, Washington, Brigham Young U., N.Y. Stock Exchange, U. South, Guild Hall Mus. Caps fellow in printmaking, 1973-74. Mem. Art Students League (past rec. sec.). Home: Sag Harbor N.Y. Died Jan. 5, 1993.

DAVIS, BERNARD DAVID, medical scientist; b. Franklin, Mass., Jan. 7, 1916; s. Harry and Tillie (Shain) D.; m. Elizabeth Menzel, June 19, 1955; children: Franklin A., Jonathan H., Katherine J. AB, Harvard U., 1936, MD, 1940. Intern, fellow Johns Hopkins Hosp., 1940-41; commd. officer USPHS, 1942-54; successively assigned NIH, Columbia U., Pub Health Research Inst. of N.Y., Rockefeller Inst., and charge; USPHS Tb Research Lab. at Cornell U. Med. Sch., 1947-54; prof. pharmacology, chmn. dept. NYU Med. Sch., 1954-57; prof. bacteriology, chmn. dept. Harvard Med. Sch., 1957-68, Adele Lehman prof. bacteriology and immunology, 1963-68, Adele Lehman prof. bacterial physiology, dir. bacterial physiol. unit, 1968-84, prof. emeritus, 1984-94; vis. investigator Pasteur Inst., Paris, 1954, Weizmann Inst., 1968, U. Tel Aviv, 1983; vis. prof. U. Calif., Berkeley, 1984-85, Nat. Taiwan U. Med. Sch., 1987; mem. div. com. for biology, medicine NSF, 1954-57; mem. med. adv. bd. Hebrew U., 1956-70. Author: Storm over Biology, 1986; co-author: Microbiology, 4th edit., 1989; editor: The Genetic Revolution, 1991; mem. editorial bd. Perspectives Biol. Medicine. Past trustee Worcester Found. for Exptl. Biology. Recipient Waksman medal Soc. Am. Bacteriologists, 1952; Ctr. for Advanced Study in Behavioral Scis. fellow, 1973-74; Fogarty scholar NIH, 1988-89. Mem NAS (Waksman award 1989), AAAS, Am. Soc. Biochemistry and Molecular Biology, Am. Acad. Arts and Scis. (v.p. 1977-79), Inst. of Medicine, Am. Soc. Microbiology (Hoechst-Roussel award 1989), Soc. Gen. Physiology (pres. 1964-65), Harvey Soc., Phi Beta Kappa, Sigma Xi, Alpha Omega Alpha. Home: Belmont Mass. Died Jan. 14, 1994.

DAVIS, BERTRAM GEORGE, lawyer, association executive; b. N.Y.C., Mar. 30, 1919; s. Maurice Bertram and Grace Elizabeth Davis; m. Violet Timothy, Mar. 7, 1941; children: Grace Elizabeth Hopper, Anne Whitfield Bland, Vivian Mary Starr, Christine Anderson, Gregory George. Student, St. Johns U., Am. U., 1949-51; LLB, George Washington U., 1955. Bar: D.C. 1957, U.S. Supreme Ct. 1963. Passenger agt. Cunard White Star Ltd., N.Y.C., 1936-41; with The Am. Legion, Indpls., 1945-95; nat. judge advocate The Am. Legion, 1960-95; pub. Am. Legion mag., 1978-95, asst. nat. treas., 1963-95; legal counsel Am. Legion Aux.; chmn. Am. Legion Retirement Com.; individual practice law Washington, 1957-59. Served with U.S. Army, 1942-45. Mem. ABA, D.C. Bar Assn., Army, Navy and Air Force Vets. Can., Am. Legion, Delta Theta Phi. Democrat. Roman Catholic. Home: Saint Augustine Fla. Died Aug. 11, 1995.

DAVIS, CHARLES FRANCIS, JR., retired architect; b. Montgomery, Ala., Dec. 13, 1908; s. Charles Francis and Catherine (West) D.; m. Helen Sellers, Nov. 1, 1935; children: Charles Francis, Helen West, Neil Edward. BArch, Auburn U., 1931, B in Archtl. Engring. 1932; LLD honoris causa, Samford U., 1982. Draftsman Miller, Martin & Lewis, 1935-38; designer E.B. Van Keuren, 1938-46, ptnr., 1946-49; ptnr. Van Keuren, Davis & Co., 1949-57, Davis, Speake and

Thrasher, Birmingham, Ala., 1957-63; ptnr. Davis, Speake and Assocs., Birmingham, 1964-71, pres., 1971-93. Works include all bldgs. Samford U., Bapt. Med. Ctr., Birmingham, library, Haley Ctr. and plant scis. bldgs. Auburn U., dormitory complex and library Birmingham-So. Coll. Chmn. bd. mgmt. Five Points YMCA, 1963; adv. bd. Salvation Army; bd. dirs. Birmingham Baoys Club, pres. 1978-79; trustee Montreat (N.C.)-Anderson Coll. Recipient William Booth award Salvation Army, 1977. Fellow AIA; mem. Country Club(Birmingham), Phi Kappa Phi, Omicron Delta Kappa, Lambda Chi Alpha. Home: Birmingham Ala. Died July 21, 1993.

DAVIS, GALE ELWOOD, insurance company executive; b. Omaha, July 18, 1909; s. Stanley A. and Frances Mary (Evans) D.; m. Margaret Nell Lavelle, Nov. 30, 1933; children: Stanley L., Sally K., Molly F. LL.B., U. Nebr., 1931. Bar: Nebr. 1931. With Mut. Omaha Ins. Co., 1932-65, v.p., 1950-59, exec. v.p., 1959-65; pres. United of Omaha Life Ins. Co., 1965-75, dir., 1959-92. Trustee, dir. Clarkson Hosp.; trustee, past pres. Omaha Home for Boys; trustee, mem. investment com. U. Nebr. Found.; bd. dirs. Dr. C.C. and Mabel L. Criss Found. Mem. Nebr. Bar Assn., Omaha Country Club, Garden of Gods Club, Plaza Club, Delta Upsilon, Phi Delta Phi. Home: Omaha Nebr. Died Oct. 23, 1992.

DAVIS, HAROLD TRUSCOTT, retired lawyer; b. Worcester, Mass., June 15, 1895; s. Charles Francis and Eva Leolen (Truscott) D.; m. Ruth M. Lent, Oct. 26, 1956; 1 dau. (by previous marriage), Eleanor Davis Claff. A.B. magna cum laude, Harvard U., 1918, J.D., 1921. Bar: Mass. 1921. Pvt. practice law Boston; ptnr. firm Nutter, McClennen & Fish, 1930-76, of counsel, 1977-91; ret., 1991; counsel, Town of Hingham, Mass., 1955-74; bd. dirs. Carter Family Corp., EPP Corp.; bd. dirs. emeritus Hollingsworth & Vose Co.; past bd. dirs. other corps. Former corporator New Eng. Bapt. Hosp.; trustee Hingham Pub. Library, 1939-87; hon. mem. Dean Found. Little Children. Mem. ABA, Mass. Bar Assn., Boston Bar Assn., Phi Beta Kappa, Alpha Sigma Phi. Republican. Congregationalist. Clubs: Union (Boston), Harvard (Boston); Hingham Yacht (Hingham), Harvard (Hingham). Home: Hingham Mass. Died Dec. 27, 1995.

DAVIS, HARTWELL, lawyer; b. Auburn, Ala., Dec. 18, 1906; s. Christopher Hartwell and Elizabeth Myrick (Dowdell) D.; m. Elizabeth Mardre, Feb. 24, 1933; children: Hartwell, Letitia Dowdell Davis Hamill. Student, U. Fla., 1923-24; B.S., Auburn U., 1928; postgrad. (Woodrow Wilson Meml. scholar), U. Va. Law Sch., 1929-30; J.D., Emory U., 1931. Bar: Ga., Ala., Fla. bars 1931. Clk. Bradenton Bank & Trust Co., Fla., 1924-25; practiced at Opelika and Montgomery, Ala., ret.; asst. U.S. atty. Middle Dist. Ala., 1932-51, U.S. atty., 1953-62; city atty. Montgomery, 1951-53; spl. asst. atty. gen. Ala., 1964-71. Del. S.E. jurisdictional confs. Meth. Ch., 1948, 52, 56; mem. Meth. Gen. Bd. Evangelism, 1952-56; sec.-treas. Meth. Ala. Conf. Bd. Lay Activities, 1945-60; Pres. Montgomery YMCA, 1939-40, dir., 1935-57; chmn. Ct. of Honor, Tuckabatchee area Boy Scouts Am., 1951-52, chmn. merit badge com., 1953; Trustee George Wheeler Meml. Scholarship Fund, 1941-71; bd. dirs. Ala. Meth. Children's Home, 1953-76, 1st v.p., 1973-74. Mem. ABA, Ala. Bar Assn., Montgomery Bar Assn., Ala. Hist. Assn., C. of C., Sigma Nu, Phi Alpha Delta, Theta Alpha Phi. Republican. Clubs: Kiwanian (pres. 1938), Tuesday Evening Social, Fresh Air Domino. Home: Montgomery Ala. Died Mar. 18, 1992.

DAVIS, LAURENCE LAIRD, coal company executive; b. Cin., June 6, 1915; s. Thomas Jefferson and Jane (Brown) D.; m. Charlotte Rowe Nichols, Oct. 12, 1940 (dec. Sept. 1973); children: Sally Laird (Mrs. Arthur D. Pratt), Laurence Laird, Thomas Jefferson II; m. Onlee Partin, Nov. 7, 1973; 1 child, Nancy Matilda Kathleen; stepchildren: Rickey Lee Foland, Stella Logan Turner, Samuel J. Logan, Gregory C. Logan. Grad., St. Mark's Sch., 1934; A.B., Harvard, 1938; postgrad., London (Eng.) Sch. Econs., 1939. With First Nat. Bank Cin., 1939-42, 46-70, v.p., 1964-70, vice chmn. bd., dir., 1951-89; dir., vice consul, econ. analyst State Dept., 1943-45; fin. cons., 1970-95; pres., dir. Roberta Coal Co.; pres., dir., chmn. Elkhorn Collieries Co.; gen. ptnr. The 474 Group, Cin., 1987-95; bd. dirs. 1st Nat. Bank Cin. Chmn. English Speaking Union, 1965-72; pres. Symphony Orch., 1965-68; bd. dirs. Christ Hosp. Mem. Greater Cin. C. of C. (pres. 1965-68). Clubs: Commonwealth (Cin.), Camargo (Cin.), Queen City (Cin.). Home: Homosassa Fla. Died Sept., 1996.

DAVIS, SHELBY CULLOM, investment banker, former ambassador; b. Peoria, Ill., Apr. 1, 1909; s. George Henry and Julia Mabel (Cullom) D.; m. Kathryn Edith Waterman, Jan. 4, 1932; children: Shelby Moore Cullom, Diana Cullom, Priscilla Alden (dec.). Student, Lawrenceville (N.J.) Sch., 1924-26; A.B., Princeton U., 1930; A.M., Columbia U., 1931; D. Polit. Sci., U. Geneva, 1934. Spl. corr., also asso. with Columbia Broacasting Co., Geneva, 1932-34; economist Investment Corp. Phila., 1934-37; treas. Delaware Fund, Inc., 1937-39; econ. adviser Thomas E. Dewey, 1940; presdl. campaigns; mem. N.Y. Stock Exchange, 1941-94; chief fgn. requirements sect. WPB, Washington, 1942; chief div. statistics and research WPB, N.Y., No. N.J., 1943; 1st dep. supt. ins. N.Y. State, 1944-47; mng. partner Shelby Cullom Davis & Co. (investment bankers), N.Y.C., 1947-69, 75-94; U.S. ambassador to Switzerland, Bern, 1969-75; dir. Plimouth Plantation; chmn. history adv. coun. Princeton U.; bd. dirs. Hoover Instn., Fletcher Sch. Diplomacy, Rockford Coll.; chmn. emeritus Heritage Found.; past chmn. Nat. Right to Work. Author: Your Career in Defense, 1942, others; former bus. editor: Current History and Forum mags; contbr. articles to several jours. Mem. Fin. Analysts Assn. (pres. 1955-56), Gen. Soc. SR, Soc. Colonial Wars (gov.), Mayflower Soc. Republican. Clubs: Knickerbocker, Univ., Sleepy Hollow Country, Princeton, Players (N.Y.C.); Hartford; Harbor (Maine); Down Town Assn., Charter (Princeton); Everglades (Palm Beach, Fla.). Home: Tarrytown N.Y. Buried May 26, 1994.

DAWES, GEOFFREY SHARMAN, medical researcher; b. Derbyshire, Eng., Jan. 21, 1918; s. William and Olive (White) D.; m. Margaret Joan Monk, Apr. 15, 1941; children—Caroline Harriet, Alison Jennifer, Nicholas William, Martin Geoffrey. B.A., Oxford (Eng.) U., 1939, M.Sc., 1940, B.M., B.Ch., 1943, D.M., M.A., 1947; D.Med. (hon.), Gothenburg U., 1978. Fellow Worcester Coll., Oxford U., 1947; dir. Nuffield Inst. Med. Research, 1948-85, Charing Cross Sunley Med. Rsch. Ctr., 1984-89; mem. Med. Rsch. Coun., 1978-82; vis. prof. U. Calif. at San Francisco, 1966. Author: Foetal and Neonatal Physiology, 1967. Gov. Sir John Port's Charity, Repton Sch., 1959-88, chmn., 1971-84; gov. Lister Inst. Preventive Medicine, chmn., 1988-94. Decorated comdr. Order Brit. Empire; recipient Max Weinstein award United Cerebral Palsy Assn., 1963, Gairdner Found. annual award, 1966, James Spence medal Brit. Pediatric Assn., 1969, Maternité award European Assn. Perinatal Medicine, 1976; Blair Bell medal, 1981, Osler Meml. medal Oxford U., 1990; Rockefeller fellow Harvard, 1946. Fellow Royal Soc. (v.p. 1975-77), Royal Coll. Physicians, Royal Coll. Obstetricians and Gynecologists, Am. Coll. Obstetricians and Gynecologists (hon.), Am. Acad. Pediatrics (hon., Virginia Apgar award 1980); mem. Neonatal Soc. (pres. 1965-69). Home: Oxford England Died May 6, 1996.

DAWSON, WILLIAM JAMES, JR., orthodontist; b. San Francisco, May 16, 1930; s. William James and Augusta (Rude) D.; m. Judith Elizabeth Riede, Aug. 11, 1962; children: William James, Wendy, Nancy Garms, Sarah Rankin, Evelyn Elizabeth. AB, U. Calif. at Berkeley, 1948-52; DDS, U. Calif. Med. Ctr., San Francisco, 1956. Pvt. practice orthodontics, San Rafael, Calif., 1958-92; clin. instr. oral histology, U. Calif. Med. Ctr., San Francisco, 1958-61; clin. instr. orofacial anomolies, 1964-75, asst. rsch. dentist, 1968-75; mem. Calif. Bd. Dental Examiners, 1985-92, sec. 1987-88, v.p., 1990, pres., 1990-92; bd. dirs. Bank of Marin. Mem. bd. adminstrn. Calif. Pub. Employees Retirement System, 1969-76. Mem. adv. com. Marin coun. Boy Scouts Am., 1965-92; chmn. citizen's adv. com. Dominican Coll. San Rafael, 1974-76; mem. city council, Ross, Calif., 1967-69; assoc. mem. Calif. Rep. Cen. Com., 1967-68, 85-87, regular mem., 1971-73; pres. Marin County Property Owners Assn., 1980-82; bd. dirs. Marin County Coalition, 1980-86, chmn., 1983-84; mem. adv. bd. Terwilliger Nature Ctr.; trustee Marin Gen. Hosp. Found., 1985-91, trustee emeritus, 1991-92; bd. dirs. Marin Health Care Systems, 1987-92. Served with USAF, 1951-54. Recipient Disting. Vol. award Marin County United Way, 1985, certs., 1986, 88 and resolutions of commendation for pub. svc., Calif. State Assembly, 1988, resolution of commendation for publ svc., Calif. State Senate, 1988. Diplomate Am. Bd. Orthodontics (charter mem. Coll. of Diplomates). Fellow Royal Soc. Health, Am. Coll. Dentists, Internat. Coll. Dentists, Acad. Dentistry Internat. (sec., treas. No. Calif. chpt. 1987-91, chmn. 1991-92), Pierre Fauchard Acad.; mem. ADA, Am. Assn. Orthodontists, Am. Assn. Dental Examiners (chmn. continued competency com. 1990-91, long range planning com. 1991-92, Citizen of Yr. award 1991), Fedn. Dentaire Internationale, Marin Forum, Marin County C. of C. (bd. dirs. 1976-90, pres. 1986-88), U. Calif. Alumni Assn. (life), Am. Rifle Assn. (life), Sierra Club (life), Trout Unltd. (life), Omicron Kappa Upsilon, Chi Phi, Xi Psi Phi. Republican. Episcopalian. Lodge: Rotary (dir. San Rafael 1971-73, pres. 1978-79, Paul Harris fellow). Clubs: Lagunitas Country (pres. 1973-75), Bohemian; Meadow. Contbr. articles to profl. jours. Died July 19, 1992; interred Johnsville, Calif.

DAWSON, WILLIAM LEVI, composer, conductor; b. Anniston, Ala., Sept. 26, 1899; s. George W. and Eliza M. (Starkey) D.; m. Cornella D. Lampton, May 25, 1927 (dec. Aug. 1928); m. Cecile D. Nicholson, Sept. 21, 1935. Student composition, orchestration, Washburn Coll.; Mus. B., Horner Inst. Fine Arts, Kansas City, Mo., 1925; M. Composition, Am. Conservatory Music, Chgo., 1927; Mus. D., Tuskegee Inst., 1955, Ithaca Coll., 1982; postgrad., Eastman Sch. Music; LL.D., Lincoln U., 1978. Dir. music, Topeka, Kansas City, 1921-25, then 1st trombonist, Chgo. Civic Symphony Orch., dir., Tuskegee Inst. Sch. Music, Tuskegee Choir; led: opening Tuskegee Choir at, Radio City Music Hall, 1932-33, on many tours, in concert series, NBC, CBS, ABC; guest condr. numerous state choral festivals, choral groups in, Spain, under auspices, Dept. State, 1956, Kansas City Philharmonic Orch., 1966, Nashville Symphony Orch., 1966, Talladega Choir and Mobile Symphony Orch., 1968, Wayne State U. Glee Club, 1970, 74, Balt. Symphony Orch., 1975; condr. symposium choral music, Huntingdon Coll., Montgomery, Ala., 1976 (Winner Rodman Wanamaker contest for composition 1930, 31, Chgo. Daily News contest for band condrs. 1929); Composer: numerous arrangements Negro folk songs for voices Break, Break; with orch. Trio in A; violin, cello, piano Sonata in A; violin and piano Negro Folk Symphony. Recipient award and citation U. Pa. Glee Club, 1967; recipient Alumni Achievement award U. Mo. at Kansas City, 1963, award and citation Am. Choral Dirs. Assn., 1975; named to Ala. Arts Hall of Fame, 1975; recipient Paul Heinecke citation of merit, 1983, Alumni Merit award Tuskegee Inst., 1983. Mem. Phi Mu Alpha Sinfonia (hon.). Home: Wilmington Del. Deceased.

DAWSON, WILLIAM WALLACE, JR., lawyer, state legislator; b. Vinita, Okla., Aug. 13, 1943; s. William Wallace and Imogene Marie (Cagle) D.; m. Marie Theresa Rim, Aug. 15, 1970; children—William Anthony, Thomas Gregory. B.A., Okla. State U., 1966, M.A., 1968; J.D., U. Tenn., 1973; postgrad. Ohio State U., 1970. Methodist minister, Earlsboro, Cushing and Glencoe, Okla., 1962-66; instr. Central State U., Edmond, Okla., 1967-69; asst. prof. Pa. State U., Erie, 1970-71; staff Okla. Ct. Criminal Appeals, 1973; ptnr. Dawson, Cadenhead & Kite, Seminole, Okla., 1973—; mem. Okla. State Senate, 1974-78, 82—; real estate broker, auctioneer, 1981—. Recipient U. Okla. Pres.'s Leadership award; U. Tenn. Coll. Law Cert. Outstanding Achievement, Legal Clinic Cert. of Merit; Nat. Found. March of Dimes Disting. Vol. Leadership award, 1975. Mem. Seminole County Bar Assn., Okla. Bar Assn., ABA, Okla. Assn. Auctioneers, Nat. Assn. Auctioneers. Democrat. Methodist. Died Jan. 17, 1987; interred Seminole, O.K. Home: Seminole Okla.

DAY, JOSEPH DENNIS, librarian; b. Dayton, Ohio, Sept. 23, 1942; s. John Albert and Ruth (Pearson) D.; m. Mary Louise Herbert, Oct. 10, 1964; children: Cindy, Jeff, Chris, Steve, Tom. B.A., U. Dayton, 1966; M.L.S., Western Mich. U., 1967; degree in Libr. Mgmt., U. Miami, 1975. Community libr. Dayton-Montgomery Pub. Libr., 1967-70; dir. Troy-Miami County Pub. Libr., Troy, Ohio, 1970-76, Salt Lake City Pub. Libr., 1976-95; chmn. Miami Valley Library Orgn., 1971-73; pres. Ohio Library Assn., 1975-76; project dir. planning and constrn. first solar powered library in world, 1973-76; exec. devel. program Miami, Ohio, libr., 1975. Pres. Troy Area Arts Coun., 1973-74; v.p. SLC Salvation Army Bd., 1986-91. Recipient Disting. Community Service award Troy C. of C., 1974; John Cotton Dana award, 1975, 77, 83, 85; AIA-ALA architecture award, 1977. Mem. ALA (chmn. intellectual freedom com. 1981-84, exec. bd. 1987-93, rep. to Internat. Fedn. Libr. Assn. 1989-95), ASPA, Utah Libr. Assn. (pres. 1979-80, Disting. Svc. award 1985), Mountain Plains Libr. Assn. (pres. 1990-91, Disting. Svc. award 1993), Kiwanis Club (pres. Troy 1975-76, Disting. Svc. award Troy 1973, pres. Salt Lake-Foothil 79-80), Snowbird Leadership Dustinte (exec. dir. 1991-95). Home: Salt Lake City Utah Died Aug. 3, 1995.

DAY, L. B., labor union ofcl., state senator; b. Omaha, Feb. 22, 1932; s. L. B. and Neva E. (Grimwod) D.; student U. Nebr., 1949-50; B.A. in Polit. Sci. and Econs., Willamette U., 1958, postgrad. (sr. scholar with honors) Law Sch., 1959, Ph.D. in Civil Law (hon.), 1975; m. Cynthia Rose Lang, Feb. 17, 1961; 1 son, Frank. With Master Service Tire Shop, Salem, Oreg., 1955-59; bus. rep. Cannery Local No. 670, Salem, 1956-70; regional dir. N.W. region U.S. Dept. Interior, Portland, 1970-71; dir. Oreg. Dept. Environ. Quality, 1971-72; public relations dir. Joint Council Teamsters No. 37, 1973; sec.-treas., head adminstrv. officer Teamster Local 670, Salem, 1974—. Mem. Manpower and Vocat. Tng. Devel. Adv. Com., 1962; mem., chmn. Marion County CSC, 1962; legis. council Oreg. Gov.'s Planning Council on Arts and Humanities, 1962; chmn. Portland Fed. Exec. Bd., 1971, Oreg. Land Conservation and Devel. Commn., 1973, Oreg. Task Force on Youth Unemployment, 1980; mem. Oreg. Gov.'s Com. on Fgn. Lang. and Internat. Studies, 1982. Active Family Counseling Service, Marion-Polk County United Good Neighbors, Marion County Health Council, Salem Boys Club, Marion County Juvenile Council, Vol. Services Bur., Marion County Juvenile Bd.; v.p. Oreg. State Fair Savers; mem. adv. com. Salem Vocat. Sch. Mem. Oreg. Ho. of Reps., 1964-70, Oreg. Senate, 1978—. Past mem. bd. dirs. Thomas Kay Hist. Park; bd. dirs. Salem Family YMCA, 1981; bd. cons. Goodwill Industries Oreg., 1981; former mem. Salem Econ. Devel. Commn., chmn., 1982. Served with USNR, 1951-55; Korea. Named Salem's Jr. 1st Citizen, 1966; One of 4 Outstanding Legislators, Oreg. Press, 1966; One of Top 10 Young Men in Oreg., 1967; Salem's 1st Citizen, 1968; recipient Disting. Alumni award Willamette U., 1972; Citizen of Yr. award Oreg. Assn. Chiropractic Physicians, 1972; Spl. Achievement award River Basins Commn., 1972; tribute of appreciation EPA, 1972; perpetual trophy Oreg. Wildlife Fedn., 1973; Clatsop Environ. Council award as public adminstr. of yr. Public Adminstrs. Oreg., 1973; Oreg. Cup award for conservation achievement, 1973; Leadership in Am. award Time mag., 1974; citation of appreciation Am. Legion, 1981;

named Outstanding Legislator of 1981 Session, Oreg. Homebuilders Assn., 1981. Mem. Salem Art Assn. (past pres.), Farmers Union, Grange, Salem C. of C. Clubs: Salem City, Masons, Elks. Home: Salem Oreg.

DAY, ROBERT ADAMS, English and comparative literature educator; b. Providence, Oct. 3, 1924; s. Irving Woodman and Mabel Evelyn (Adams) D. AB, Brown U., 1948; MA, Harvard U., 1949, PhD, 1952. Instr. Dartmouth Coll., Hanover, N.H., 1952-54; instr. Queens Coll., Flushing, N.Y., 1954-62, asst. prof., 1962-65, assoc. prof., 1965-70, prof., from 1970; prof. English City U. N.Y., from 1970; mem. staff grad. ctr. CUNY, from 1970, prof. comparative lit., from 1974. Author: Told in Letters, 1966, Pompey the Little, 1974, History of an Atom, 1989. With U.S. Army, 1943-45. Senior fellow NEH, 1993, NEH Huntington Libr., San Marino, Calif., 1984, 93. Home: New York N.Y. Deceased.

DEAKIN, EDWARD B., foundation administrator; b. Spokane, Wash., Sept. 10, 1943; s. Edward B. and Katherine S. Deakin. AB, Muhlenberg Coll., 1965; MBA, Drexel U., 1969; PhD, U. Ill., 1972. CPA, Ill., Tex. Staff acct. Coopers & Lybrand, Phila., 1965; systems analyst First Pa. Bank, Phila., 1967-68; grad. asst. U. Ill., Champaign, 1970-72; asst. prof. U. Tex., Austin, 1972-76, assoc. prof., 1976-81, prof., from 1981, Price Waterhouse prof., from 1984, Univ. Disting. Enterprise prof., 1986-89; dir. Petroleum Acctg. Rsch. Inst., U. North Tex., Denton, Tex., 1987-89; vis. assoc. prof. Stanford U., Palo Alto, Calif., 1978-79; vis. prof. Kuwait U., 1978; cons. U.S. Dept. Energy, Washington, 1979, Dept. Law, State of Alaska, Juneau and Anchorage, 1981-84, 89, State of N.J. Div. Law, Trenton, 1984, IRS, Houston, 1985-86, Exxon Corp., 1988-90, AT&T, 1992. Author: Cost Accounting, 1984, 3d edit., 1991; also 50 articles on acctg. topics. Benefactor AIDS charities; chmn. Edward B. Deakin LIFE Found., Inc. Recipient Elijah Watts Sells Found. award, 1972, Notable Contbns. to Research award U. Tex., 1985. Fellow Am. Acctg. Assn. (editorial bd. 1976-80). Home: Carlisle Pa. Deceased.

DEAN, CHARLES HENRY, JR., retired government official; b. Knoxville, Tenn., Oct. 22, 1925; s. Charles Henry and Helen (Ford) D.; m. Lottie Lavender, Dec. 30, 1947; children: Helen, James Miles, Camille. Student, U. Tenn., 1943-44; B.S., U.S. Naval Acad., 1947. Sales rep. Knoxville Fertilizer Co., Dean-Planters Warehouses, 1950-59; with Knoxville Utilities Bd., 1959-81, gen. mgr., 1971-81; chmn. bd. TVA, 1981-88, also bd. dirs.; ret.; bd. dirs. Magnetek, Inc., Environ. Systems Corp. Past pres. Knoxville Tourist Bus.; past chmn. Chancellors' Assocs., U. Tenn.; bd. dirs. Electric Power Rsch. Inst., 1982-90. Served with USMC, 1947-50. Recipient Profl. Mgrs. Citation Soc. Advancement Mgmt., 1972, Eminent Engr. award Tau Beta Pi, 1983. Mem. NSPE, Am. Pub. Power Assn. (past bd. dirs.), Tenn. Valley Pub. Power Assn. (past pres.), Civitan (past pres.), Racquet Club Knoxville (past pres.). Republican. Presbyterian. Home: Knoxville Tenn. Died Nov. 12, 1995.

DEAN, PETER, artist; b. Berlin, July 9, 1934; s. William F. and Roza (Nathan) D.; m. Lorraine Otterson; 1 son, Gregory. Student, Cornell U., 1957-58; B.A., U. Wis., 1959. One man shows include Darthea Speyer Gallery, Paris, 1981, Allan Stone Gallery, N.Y.C., 1970, 73, 78, 80, Bienville Gallery, 1975, 77, 79, 81, Semaphore Gallery, N.Y.C., 1981, 86, Bellman Gallery, N.Y.C., 1984, Osuna Gallery, Washington, 1984, Struve Gallery, Chgo., 1984, Koplin Gallery, L.A., 1985, 88, 90, Traver-Sutton Gallery, Seattle, 1985, 89, Kerr Gallery, N.Y.C., 1986, San Antonio Art Inst., 1988, Katzen-Brown Gallery, N.Y.C., 1989, Rena Branstein Gallery, San Francisco, Ca., 1987, 89, N.D. Mus. Art, 1989, 90, Alt. Mus. N.Y., 1990, 91, Mus. Art, U. Ariz., Tucson, 1991, U. Wis. Art. Mus., Milw., 1992; exhibited in group shows Nat. Inst. Arts and Letters, N.Y.C., 1973, Corpus Christi Mus., 1981, Chrysler Mus., Norfolk, Va., 1981, Chgo. Art Inst., 1982, Venice Bienniale, 1984, Tucson Mus., U. Ariz., 1991; represented in permanent collection Nat. Collection, Washington, Chgo. Art Inst., Madison (Wis.) Art Center, New Orleans Mus., Gray Gallery, N.Y. U.; vis. artist, Yale U., La. State U., N.D. U., U. Wis., Skidmore Coll., U. Tex., Yale U., Princeton U., Cranbrook Acad., Richard H. Love Gallery, Chgo., 1992. Founding mem. Rhino Horn Group, co-chmn., 1969-79. Fellow Nat. Endowment for the Arts, 1981, 87; N.Y. Council Arts grantee, 1975-76. Home: New York N.Y. Died Mar. 13, 1993; interred Gate of Heaven Cemetary, Valhalla, N.Y.

DEANE, FREDERICK, JR., retired banker; b. Boston, Aug. 5, 1926; s. Frederick and Julia (Coolidge) D.; m. Dorothy Legge, Dec. 21, 1948; children: Dorothy Porcher, Eleanor Dodds, Frederick III. MBA with distinction, Harvard U., 1951. With Signet Bank/Va., Richmond, 1953-90, chief exec. officer, 1973-89, ret., chmn. bd. dirs., 1973-90; mem. exec. com., bd. dirs. Signet Banking Corp., Richmond, ret.; bd. dirs. CSX Corp., Marriott Corp., Cir. City Stores, Inc.; mem. fed. adv. council Fed. Res. System; past chmn. MasterCard Internat. Bd. dirs. Va. Mus. Found., Va. Found. Ind. Colls., United Way Greater Richmond, Chesapeake Bay Found., Scott Found., Va. Diocesan Ctr., Battle Abbey Coun.; former vice rector Coll. William and Mary, mem. bd. Sch. Bus. Adminstrn. Sponsors; co-chmn. Richmond chpt. NCCJ. Mem. Assn. Res. City Bankers (past bd. dirs.), Assn. Bank Holding Cos. (past chmn. 1979-80, gov.'s adv. bd. on revenue estimates), Richmond Soc. Fin. Analysts (past pres.), Alexis de Toqueville Soc. (past founding chmn.), Scott Found. Republican. Episcopalian. Clubs: Harvard of Va. (former pres.), Harvard Bus. Sch. of Va.; Hasty Pudding-Inst. 1770, Delphic (Harvard); Commonwealth, Country of Va. (Richmond); Harvard, Brook (N.Y.C.); Mid Ocean (Bermuda); Burning Tree (Bethesda, Md.); Metropolitan (Washington); Country of Fla., Ocean Club Fla. Home: Richmond Va. Deceased.

DEARBORN, ROBERT D., lawyer; b. Lawrence, Kans., 1949. AB, U. N.C., 1971, JD with honors, 1975. Bar: N.C. 1975. Atty. Moore & Van Allen, Charlotte, N.C.; mem. comml. and constrn. panel of arbitrators Am. Arbitration Assn. Assoc. editor: N.C. Law Rev., 1974-75. Mem. ABA, Order of Coif. Home: Charlotte N.C. Deceased.

DEBARTOLO, EDWARD J., SR., real estate developer; b. Youngstown, Ohio, May 17, 1919; s. Michael and Rose (Villani) DeB.; m. Maria Patricia Montani, Dec. 18, 1943 (dec.); children: Edward J. Jr., Marie D. Grad., U. Notre Dame; DSc (hon.), Fla. Inst. Tech., 1981; D Bus. Adminstrn. (hon.), Youngstown State U., 1984. Registered profl. engr., registered surveyor. Ptnr. Michael DeBartolo Constrn. Co., Youngstown, 1936-41; pres. Michael DeBartolo Constrn. Co., 1946-48, Edward J. DeBartolo Corp., Youngstown, 1948-79; chmn. bd., chief exec. officer Edward J. DeBartolo Corp., 1979-94; owner Thistledown Racing Club, Cleve., Louisiana Downs race tracks, Remington Pk., Oklahoma City. Mem. adv. coun. U. Notre Dame; founder Italian Scholarship League. 2d lt. C.E., U.S. Army, 1941-46, PTO. Decorated Order of Merit (Italy); named Man of Yr., Youngstown West Side Mchts. and Civic Assn., 1953, Fraternal Order Police, Boardman, Ohio, 1975, Mahoning Valley Econ. Devel. Corp., 1983, City of Pitts., 1983, Pitts. chpt. Nat. Am. Sports Hall of Fame, 1986; named hon. citizen City of St. Petersburg, Fla., 1973; recipient Honor medal Ellis Island, 1986, Gov.'s award State of Ohio, 1984, Disting. Citizen award Youngstown State U., 1984, Achievement award Horsemen's Benevolent and Protection Assn., 1986, Achievement award Ohio Thoroughbred Breeder's and Owners, 1986. Mem. Urban Land Inst., Nat. Realty Com., Thoroughbred Racing Assn. (Eclipse award 1989), Internat. Coun. Shopping Ctrs., Italian-Am. War Vets. (life). Roman Catholic. Home: Youngstown Ohio Died Dec. 19, 1994.

DEBEVOISE, THOMAS MCELRATH, lawyer, educator; b. N.Y.C., Aug. 10, 1929; s. Eli Whitney and Barbara (Clay) D.; m. Ann Taylor, Nov. 1951; children: Eli Whitney II, Albert Clay, Thomas McElrath III, Anne Elizabeth. B.A., Yale U., 1950; LL.B., Columbia U., 1954; LL.D. (hon.), Vt. Law Sch., 1984. Bar: N.Y. 1954, Vt. 1957, D.C. 1963. Asst. U.S. Atty. So. Dist. N.Y., 1954-56; sole practice law Woodstock, Vt., 1957-59, 82-95; dep. atty. gen. State of Vt., 1959-60, atty. gen., 1960-62; asst. gen. counsel Fed. Power Commn., 1962-64; pvt. practice law D.C., 1964; partner Debevoise & Liberman, 1965-74, counsel, 1975-82, partner, 1982-84; dean Vt. Law Sch., South Royalton, 1974-82, dean emeritus, 1982, trustee emeritus, 1983-95. Pres. Woodstock Found., 1982-95. Fellow Am. Bar Found.; mem. ABA, Vt. Bar Assn., Phi Delta Phi. Republican. Episcopalian. Clubs: Lakota, National Lawyers, Century; University, Yale (N.Y.C.). Lodge: Masons. Home: Woodstock Vt. Died Feb. 1, 1995.

DE BRUYN KOPS, JULIAN, lawyer; b. Savannah, Ga., Nov. 8, 1908; s. Julian and May (Woodberry) de B.K.; m. Mary Virginia Thompson, July 1, 1939; children: Julianna, Virginia, Julian III. A.B., Harvard, 1929, LL.B., 1932. Bar: Md. bar 1932, Ohio bar 1946. Practice of law Balt., 1932-41; also service with U.S. Govt., 1934-35; counsel Dayton Power & Light Co., Ohio, 1946-69; gen. counsel Dayton Power & Light Co., 1969-73; pvt. practice Dayton, 1974-92. Served with AUS, 1941-46. Mem. Am., Fed., Fed. Energy, Ohio, Dayton bar assns. Clubs: Lawyers (Dayton), Engineers (Dayton), Dayton Bicycle. Home: Glendale Calif. Died May 30, 1993.

DECHAMPS, BRUNO JOSEF GERHARD, newspaper editor; b. Aachen, Germany, Apr. 4, 1925; s. Paul and Kitty (Herman) D.; m. Annemarie Rueben, Aug. 7, 1952; children: Claudius, Nicola, Daniel, Madeleine. MA, Fordham U., 1949; PhD, Heidelberg (Fed. Republic Germany) U., 1952. Copy editor Deutsche Zeitung-Wirtschafts Zeitung, Stuttgart, Fed. Republic Germany, 1952-56; copy editor Frankfurter Allgemeine Zeitung, 1956-66, editor, 1966-88. Author: Macht und Arbeit der Ausschuesse, 1954, Ueber Pferde, 1957. Recipient German Fed. Order of Merit, 1985, Order of St. Gregorius Pope John Paul II, 1985. Roman Catholic. Home: Dreieich Germany Died Apr. 15, 1992.

DECK, JOSEPH FRANCIS, chemist, educator; b. St. Louis, Mar. 19, 1907; s. Michael and and Anna (Westerheide) D.; m. Lillian M. Schwalbe, June 30, 1937; children: Jerry Bothe, Mary Victory, Peter Mitchel. AB, St. Louis U., 1928, MS, 1930; PhD, U. Kan., 1932; DS (hon.), Santa Clara U., 1986. With Stewart Inso Board Co., S. St. Joseph, Mo., 1932-36; quality supr. U.S. Gypsum Co., 1936; faculty U. Santa Clara Calif., 1936-93; dept. chemistry U. Santa Clara, 1945-93 chmn. dept., 1936-72; lectr. U. San Francisco, summers 1948, 49; research chemist Richmond Chase Co., 1940-49, Moyer Chem. Co., 1957-59, Food Machinery Corp. 1959-61. Named Chemist of Year St. Louis U Chemists Club, 1965. Mem. Am. Chem. Soc., Sigma Xi. Club: Rotarian (past pres. Santa Clara). Home San Jose Calif. Died Dec. 30, 1993.

DECKER, BERNARD MARTIN, retired federal judge b. Highland Park, Ill., Apr. 2, 1904; s. Martin C. and Florence (Bryant) D.; m. Louise Armstrong, Aug. 15 1928; children—Janine L. (Mrs. Jack G. Collins) Martin C. II. Student, Northwestern U., 1922-23; A.B. U. Ill., 1926; LL.B., Harvard, 1929. Bar: Ill. bar 1929. Law clk. Ralph J. Dady, 3d and 4th dists. Appellate Ct Ill., 1938-43; ptnr. Decker & Decker, Waukegan, Ill. 1929-51; judge Cir. Ct. (17th cir.) Ill., 1951-57; presiding judge Cir. Ct. (19th cir.) Ill., 1957-62; judge U.S. Dist Ct. (no. dist.) Ill., Chgo., 1962—; Chmn. organizing com. Ill. Jud. Conf., 1957, mem. exec. com., 1958-62 chmn. conf., 1959; exec. com. Nat. Conf. State Trial Judges, 1961-63, del., 1961, 62; mem. com. ct. adminis-trn. U.S. Cts., 1968-75, mem. rev. com., 1974-78, mem jud. ethics com., 1978-87. Pres. bd. edn. Waukegan Twp. High Sch., 1946-49. Mem. Harvard Law Soc Chgo. (pres. 1964-65), ABA, Ill. Bar Assn., Lake County Bar Assn. (pres. 1955), Phi Beta Kappa, Delta Tau Delta. Home: Chicago Ill. Died Nov. 1993.

DE CONINGH, EDWARD HURLBUT, electric company executive; b. Chgo., July 2, 1902; s. Frederic Benjamin Edward and Lucy (Peck) de C.; m. Virginia Scott Mueller, Nov. 7, 1927 (dec. 1964); children—Mary (Mrs. Oliver F. Emerson), Edward Hurlbut, Virginia (Mrs. Harold C. Fleming); m. Martha Hooker Washburn, 1965. A.B., Princeton, 1922; student, U Grenoble (France), 1922; B.S., Mass. Inst. Tech., 1925. Apprentice Am. Steel Foundries, 1925; sec. Laudryette Mfg. Co., Cleve., 1926-27; tech. editor Dust Recovering and Conveying Co., Cleve., 1928-33; ptnr., chief engr. Mueller Electric Co. (now Mueller Electric Co., Inc.) Cleve., 1933-66, chmn. bd., 1966-91; dir. emeritus Emerson Press, Inc., Midwest Screw Products, Inc. Pres. Cleve. Welfare Fedn., 1956-59; campaign chmn Cleve. United Appeal, 1961, 62; pres. Cleve. Community Chest, 1964-65; Vice chmn. trustees Smith Coll., 1962-72; trustee Greater Cleve. Asso. Found., 1967-70, Cleve. Inst. Music; vice chmn. bd. trustees Case Western Res. Univ., 1973-75; trustee Laurel Sch., 1970-76. Recipient Outstanding Service award Cleve. Welfare Fedn., 1959, Distinguished Service award Cleve. United Appeal, 1963; 1967 Cleve. medal for pub. service. Mem. Phi Beta Kappa, Tau Beta Pi, Chi Phi. Clubs: Cleveland Skating, Union, University (Cleve.). Home: Cleveland OH Died May 5, 1991; interred Cleveland, Ohio.

DE COSTA, EDWIN J., physician, surgeon; b. Chgo., Mar. 25, 1906; s. Lewis M. and Grace (Myers) DeC; m. Mari H. Bachrach, Jan. 5, 1935 (dec. 1970); children: Mari Jane De Costa Terman, Catherine De Costa Burstein, Louise De Costa Wides, John Lewis; m. Alyce H Heller, Feb. 1, 1971. B.S., U. Chgo., 1926; M.D., Rush Med. Coll., 1929. Diplomate: Am. Bd. Obstetricians and Gynecologists (examiner 1955—). Intern Cook County Hosp., Chgo., 1929-30; resident obstetrics and pathology Cook County Hosp., 1930-32; resident gynecology Michael Reese Hosp., Chgo., 1932-33; attending Northwestern Meml. Hosp., Prentice Women's Hosp., Cook County Hosp.; prof. ob-gyn Northwestern U. Med. Sch., 1946-95. Author: (with J.I. Brewer) Gynecology, 4th edit., 1967. Served as officer USNR, 1933-66; capt. ret. Mem. Chgo. Gynecol. Soc., Central Assn. Obstetricians and Gynecologists, Am. Coll. Obstetricians and Gynecologists, Am. Gynecol. and Obstetrical Soc., ACS, AMA, Ill., Chgo. Med. Socs., Central Travel Club, Chgo. Inst. Medicine, Pan-Pacific Surg. Assn., Pan-Am. Med. Assn., Phi Beta Kappa, Sigma Xi, Alpha Omega Alpha; hon. mem. Ark., Nebr. Obstetrical and Gynecol. Socs., Am.-Brit. Cowdray Med. Soc., Tex. Assn. Obstretricians and Gynecologists. Home: Chicago Ill. Died Jan. 26, 1996.

DECOURTRAY, ALBERT CARDINAL, archbishop; b. Wattignies, France, Apr. 9, 1923; s. Paul and Marie Louise (Pouille) D. D in Theology. Ordained priest Roman Cath. Ch. 1947. Consecrated bishop Titular Ch. of Ippona Zárito, 1971; with Titular Ch. of Dijon, 1974; archbishop of Lyons, 1981-94, created cardinal, 1985. Chmn. French Episcopal Conf., 1987-90; élu mem. Académie Française, 1993. Mem. French Acad. Home: Lyon France Died Sept. 16, 1994.

DE FURSTENBERG, MAXIMILIEN CARDINAL, ecclesiastic; b. Heerlen, Netherlands, Oct. 23, 1904. Ordained priest Roman Catholic Ch., 1931; titular archbishop of Palto and apostolic del. to Japan, 1949; internuncio, 1952, when Japan established diplomatic relations with Vatican; apostolic del. to Australia, N.Z. and Oceania, 1960; nuncio to Portugal, 1962-67; elevated to Sacred Coll. Cardinals, 1967; prefect of Congregation for Oriental Chs., 1969-74; chamberlain Sacred Coll. Cardinals, 1983—; mem. Council for Public Affairs of Ch. Grand master Equestrian Order Holy Sepulchre of Jerusalem. Home: Rome Italy

DEGNAN, HERBERT RAYMOND, financial executive, lawyer, accountant; b. N.Y.C., Mar. 16, 1921; s. John T. and Florence R. (Schoonmaker) D.; m. Gertrude J. Fretterd, Oct. 3, 1943; children—Donald J., Regina (Mrs. Paul Maurer), Raymond H., Robert V. Student, Columbia, 1938-40, postgrad., 1946-48; B.S., St. John's Coll., 1943; LL.B., Fordham U., 1955. Bar: N.Y. 1955. Accountant Scovell Wellington Co., N.Y.C., 1946-55; atty. Seghers & Reinhart, N.Y.C., 1955-57; sr. v.p., dir. Empire State Bldg. Corp., N.Y.C., 1957-62; v.p., dir. Nat. Car Rental System, N.Y.C., 1962-65; chief exec. officer, dir. 1st Fed. Savs. & Loan Assn., Tampa, Fla., 1965-67; pres., dir. Bermec Corp., N.Y.C., 1967-72; sr. v.p., chief fin. officer Tech. Tape, Inc., New Rochelle, N.Y., 1972-76; fin. cons., 1976-77; pres., dir. Cliffside Food Distbrs., Inc., Cliffside Park, N.J., 1977-84; pres. Degnan & Assocs., Ridgewood, N.J., 1984-91, River Bend, N.C., 1991-95. Served to lt. comdr. USNR, 1943-45. Decorated Bronze Star. Mem. ABA, N.Y. State Bar Assn., AICPA, N.Y. State Soc. CPAs, Skull and Circle, Delta Phi. Home: New Bern N.C. Died Aug. 7, 1995.

DEGNAN, RONAN E., law educator; b. 1942. BS in law, U. Minn., LLB. Asst. prof. Drake U., Des Moines, 1951-53, U. Minn., Mpls., 1953-54; from assoc. to full prof. U. Utah, Salt Lake City, 1955-62; prof. U. Calif., Berkeley, 1962—; vis. prof. Harvard U., Cambridge, Mass., 1973-74. Home: Berkeley Calif.

DE GREY, SIR ROGER, artist, arts academy executive; b. Apr. 18, 1918; s. Nigel and Florence Emily Frances (Gore) deG; m. Flavia Hatt Irwin, 1942; 3 children. Ed. Eton Coll., Chelsea Sch. Art. 1936-39; D in Civil Law (hon.) U. Kent, 1989; LLD (hon.) U. Reading, 1992. Lectr., dept. fine art King's Coll., Newcastle upon Tyne, Eng., 1947-51; master of painting, 1951-53; sr. tutor, later reader in painting Royal Coll. Art, 1953-73; prin. City and Guilds of London Art Sch., 1973-95. Represented in permanent collections Tate Gallery, Nat. Portrait Galler, Arts Council, Govt. Arts Collections Fund, Contemporary Arts Soc., Chantrey Bequest, Queensland Gallery, Brisbane, Manchester, Carlisle, Bradford and other provincial galleries, also pvt. collections. Served with Brit. Army, 1939-42, RAC, 1942-45. Decorated Bronze Star (US), Knight Comdr. Royal Victorian Order, 1991. Fellow Royal Inst. Brit. Archs. (hon.), City and Guilds of London Inst. (hon.); mem. Royal Acad. Arts London (pres. 1984-93). Died Feb. 14, 1995. Home: Meopham Eng.

DEHAY, JOHN CARLISLE, JR., lawyer; b. Jones Prairie, Tex., Mar. 30, 1922; s. John Carlisle and Valda (Drury) DeH.; m. Barbara Jean Smith, Nov. 30, 1956; 1 dau., Leslie. B.B.A., So. Meth. U., 1949, LL.B., 1949. Bar: Tex. 1948. Mem. legal dept. Employers Casualty Co., Dallas, 1949-51; pvt. practice law Gardere, Porter & DeHay, Dallas, 1951-79, DeHay & Blanchard, Dallas, 1979-91. Served with AUS, 1942-45. Decorated D.S.M. Mem. Dallas Bar Assn., Am. Coll. Trial Lawyers, Internat. Acad. Trial Lawyers, Internat. Assn. Def. Counsel, Tex. Assn. Def. Counsel (bd. dirs., pres.). Baptist. Clubs: Woodvale Fishing (Mineola, Tex.); Dallas Idlewild; Brookhollow Golf. Home: Dallas Tex. Died Nov. 15, 1991; interred Restland, Dallas, Tex.

DEJARNATT, ARLIE URBAN, senator; b. Glezen, Ind., Nov. 13, 1923; s. Clyde Oscar and Clara Etta (Weeks) DeJ.; m. Donna Lee Stoffel, Sept. 4, 1946; children: Judith Ann, John Douglas, Steven Herrick, Susan Lee, Lise Jeanne. AB, Cornell Coll., 1948; MA, U. No. Colo., 1951. Cert. tchr., Colo., Wash. Social sci. tchr. Sterling (Colo.) High Sch., 1948-53, Longview (Wash.) Schs., 1953-76; fed. program analyst, supt. pub. instrn. Olympia, Wash., 1976-78; dist. asst. Congressman Don Bonker, Longview, 1980-85; state Senator Olympia, 1985-90. Chmn. Logan County Dem. com., Colo., 1952-53; pres. Cowlitz County Young Dems., Wash., 1956-57; state committeeman Cowlitz Dem. Cen. Com., Wash., 1976. Served as cpl. U.S. Marine Corps, 1943-46. Mem. Phi Delta Kappa. Mem. Unitarian Ch. Lodge: Rotary. Home: Longview Wash. Died Aug. 19, 1990; interred Longview, Wash.

DE KOCK, GERHARDUS PETRUS CHRISTIAAN, banker; b. Cape Town, South Africa, Feb. 14, 1926; s. Michiel Hendrik and Christina Magdalena (De Jongh) De Kock; m. Jocé ne Hitchcock Visser, Feb. 5, 1949; children: Michael Hendrik, Charles Andries, Marié. B.A., U. Pretoria, 1945, M.A. in Econs., 1947; M.A., Harvard U., 1949, Ph.D. in Econs., 1950; Dr.Econs., U. Natal, 1982. Head econ. dept. South African Res. Bank, Pretoria, 1956-61; spl. econ. advisor South African Treasury, Pretoria, 1966-67; alt. exec. dir. Internat. Monetary Fund, Washington, 1968-71; dep. gov. South African Res. Bank, Pretoria, 1971-76; sr. dep. gov., spl. econ. advisor to minister of fin., Pretoria, 1976-80; gov. South African Res. Bank, Pretoria, 1981-89; chmn. Commn. of Inquiry into the Monetary System and Monetary Policy in South Africa, Pretoria, 1977-89; gov. for South Africa Internat. Bank for Reconstrn. and Devel., Washington, 1981-89; gov. Devel. Bank of South Africa, Johannesburg, 1983-89. Author: History of the South African Reserve Bank, 1920-52, 1950; (with C.G.W. Schuman and D.G. Franzsen) Ekonomie-'n Inleidende Studie. Named Bus. Statesman of Yr., Harvard Bus. Sch. Club of South Africa, 1979; Tinie Louw award, Afrikaanse Handelsinstituut, 1979; Top Five Businessmen of Yr., Sun Times, 1979; Wits Bus. Sch. Mgmt. award U. Witwatersrand Bus. Sch., 1983. Mem. Die Afrikaanse Akademie vir Wetenskap en Kuns (Stals prize for econs. 1983), Econ. Soc. South Africa (pres. 1980-81), Inst. of Bankers in South Africa (pres. 1984). Mem. Dutch Reformed Ch. Clubs: Pretoria Country, Pretoria. Died August 7, 1989. Home: Pretoria Republic of South Africa

DE KOSTER, HENRI JOHAN, industrialist, Netherlands politician; b. Leiden, Netherlands, Nov. 5, 1914; C.Econ., Amsterdam U., 1936. Asst. commr. gen. Netherlands Govt. Food Purchasing Bur., N.Y.C., 1945-46; mng. dir. Desleutels Flour Mill, Leiden, 1947-67; pres. Netherlands Flour Milling Assn., 1954-67, Netherlands Fedn. Industries, 1961-67, Union Indsl. Fedns. of EEC, 1962-67; mem. Dutch Parliament, 1967-77; sec. state for fgn. affairs, 1967-71; minister of def., 1971-73; v.p. Fedn. Liberal and Democratic Parties in EEC, 1975-79; mem. Senate of States Gen. of Netherlands, 1977-80; state councillor, 1980-85; pres. Europa Nostra, 1984—; pres. Parliamentary Assembly of Council of Europe, 1978-81. Served with the Resistance, World War II. Decorated Mil. Bronze Lion, grand officer Order Orange Nassau, knight Netherlands Lion; grand cordon Order Merit (Luxembourg); comdr. Order Couronne (Belgium); gt. cross 1st class Fed. Republic Ger.; comdr. 1st class Order Austria. Died Nov. 24, 1992; buried Little Green Church, Oestgeest, Netherlands. Home: The Hague The Netherlands

DELCHAMPS, ALFRED FREDERICK, JR., retail grocery chain executive; b. Mobile, Ala., June 30, 1931; s. Alfred Frederick and Sara Lucile (Crowell) D.; m. Carolyn Ann Weaver, Aug. 2, 1953; children: Alfred Frederick III, Thomas W., Carolyn M. Student, Duke U., 1948-50; B.S. in Commerce and Bus. Adminstrn, U. Ala., 1953. Supr. Delchamps, Inc., Mobile, Ala., 1953-58, asst. sec., 1958-63, v.p. service ops., 1963-65, exec. v.p., 1965-76, pres., 1976—; dir. 1st Nat. Bank, Mobile.; Mem. bus. adv. council U. South Ala.; vice chmn. bd. trustees Huntingdon Coll., Montgomery, Ala. Past pres. Jr. Achievement of Mobile, Inc.; past 1st v.p. Community Chest and Council of Mobile County, past pres., Mobile Symphony and Civic Music Assn.; past disaster chmn. Mobile chpt. ARC; past gen. chmn. Group Aid for Retarded Children, Inc.; treas. Mobile Hist. Devel. Found., Mobile Track and Field Assn. Mem. Am. Mgmt. Assn. Republican. Methodist. Clubs: Country of Mobile, Isle Dauphine, Mystic Socs. Home: Mobile Ala. Died Oct. 1989.

DELCHAMPS, OLIVER H., SR., manufacturing executive; b. Mobile, Ala., 1900; married;. Vice chmn., chief fin. officer Delchamps, Inc., Mobile, also bd. dirs.; bd. dirs. Mchts. Nat. Bank Mobile, Topco Assocs. Vice chmn., bd. dirs. U.S. C. of C. Home: Mobile Ala. Deceased.

DELFONT, BERNARD (LORD DELFONT OF STEPNEY), business executive, impresario, film executive; b. Tokmak, Russia, Sept. 5, 1909; s. Isaac and Olga (Winogradsky) D.; m. Carole Lynne, 1946; children: Susan, Jennifer, David. Entered theatrical mgmt. in Britain, 1941; 1st London prodn., 1942; since presented numerous shows in London; re-introduced variety to West End at London Casino, 1947-48, presenting Laurel and Hardy, Sophie Tucker, Lena Horne, Olsen and Johnson, Mistinguett; presented London Experience, Piccadilly, summer shows in seaside resorts; presenter ann. Royal Variety Performance, 1958-78; converted London Hippodrome into Talk of the Town theatre restaurant, 1958, also presented entertainment; chmn. First Leisure Corp. Plc., 1992, pres., 1992-94; dir. Bernard Delfont Orgn., Blackpool Tower Co.; chmn., chief exec. officer Trust House Forte Leisure Ltd., 1981-82 others; v.p. Asso. Film Distbn. Corp., Inc., 1978; recent prodns. include: (with David Merrick) The Roar of the Greasepaint-The Smell of the Crowd, 1965, Pickwick, 1965; (with Arthur Lewis) Barefoot in the Park, 1965, Funny Girl, 1966; (with Michael Codron) The Killing of Sister George, 1965; (with Geoffrey Russel) The Matchgirls, 1966; (with others) The Odd Couple, 1966, Martha Graham Dance Co., 1967, Sweet Charity, 1967, The Four Musketeers, 1967, Golden Boy, 1968, Hotel in Amsterdam, 1968, Time Present, 1968, Mame, 1969, Your Own Thing, 1969, What the Butler Saw, 1969, Cat Among the Pigeons, 1969, Carol Channing with Her 10 Stout-Hearted Men, 1970, The Great Waltz, 1970, Danny La Rue at the Palace, 1970, Kean, 1971, Rabelais, 1971, Children of the Wolf, 1971, Lulu, 1971, Applause, 1972, Threepenny Opera, 1972, The Good Old Bad Old Days, 1972, The Unknown Soldier and his Wife, 1973, The Danny La Rue Show, 1973, The Wolf, 1973, Brief Lives, 1974, The Good Companions, 1974, Sammy Cahn's Songbook, 1974, Cinderella (Twiggy), 1974, Harvey, 1975, 1975, Dad's Army, 1975; The Plumber's Progress, Queen Danniella, 1975; Mardi Gras, 1976; LeGrande Eugene, 1976; Tommy Steele Anniversary Show nat. tour, 1976; Val Doonican tour, 1977; Danny LaRue Show tour, 1977; An Evening with Tommy Steele, 1979; It's All Right If I Do It, 1977; Beyond the Rainbow, 1978; Charley's Aunt, 1979; Tommy Steele, 1980; It's Magic, Best Little Whorehouse in Texas, 1981; Underneath the Arches, 1982; Little Me, 1984. Pres., Entertainment Artistes Benevolent Fund. Named companion Grand Order Water Rats; knighted, 1974; created life peer, 1976. Mem. Saints and Sinners. Club: Variety of Gt. Britain (past pres.). Died July 28, 1994. Home: London Eng.

DELL, J. HOWARD, bishop; b. 1902. Founder, min. Christ Temple, Atlanta; bishop, Ch. of God in Christ, No. Ga., Atlanta. Died 1992. Home: Atlanta Ga.

DEL MESTRI, GUIDO CARDINAL, cardinal; b. Banja Luka, Yugoslavia, Jan. 13, 1911. Elevated to the Sacred Coll. Cardinals, 1991; cardinal Titular Ch. of Tusania, 1991-93. Home: Rome Italy Died Aug. 2, 1993.

DE LORENZO, ANTHONY GEORGE, public relations executive; b. Edgerton, Wis., Aug. 26, 1914; s. Joseph and Anna (Pipitoni) de L.; m. Josephine Paratore, Sept. 28, 1940; children: Annette M., Anthony J., Josephine M., Peter M. B.A., U. Wis., 1936; D.Sc. in Bus. Adminstrn. (hon.), Cleary Coll., 1958. Editorial staff Racine Jour.-Times, 1933-35; staff United Press Assn., Madison, Wis., Milw., Chgo., 1935-41; automotive editor, Mich. mgr. Detroit, 1941-44; pub. relations staff various accounts Kudner Agy., Inc., advt., 1944-49; staff dept. pub. relations Gen. Motors Corp., Detroit, 1949-56; v.p. charge public relations staff Gen. Motors Corp., 1957-79. Chmn. U. Wis. Found., 1979. Recipient Disting. Achievement in Journalism citation U. Wis., 1958. Mem. U. Wis. Alumni Assn. (nat. pres. 1965-66), Public Relations Soc. Am., Sigma Delta Chi. Roman Catholic. Clubs: 1925 F St. (Washington); Detroit, Detroit Athletic, Recess (Detroit); Flint City, Bloomfield Hills Country; University (N.Y.C.). Home: Birmingham Mich. Died May 15, 1993.

DEL REY, LESTER, author, editor; b. Saratoga, Minn., June 2, 1915; s. Franc and Jane (Sidway) del R.; m. Judy-Lynn Benjamin, Mar. 21, 1971. Student, George Washington U., 1931-33. Author, 1937—; sheet metal worker McDonnell Aircraft Corp., St. Louis, 1942-44; author's agt. Scott Meredith Lit. Agy., N.Y.C., 1947-50; tchr. fantasy fiction NYU, 1972-73; former editor sci. fiction mags.; editor Best Sci. Fiction Stories of Yr. E.P. Dutton & Co., 1971-75; fantasy editor Ballantine Books, 1975—, v.p., 1988—. Author: sci. fiction and children's books including Marooned on Mars, 1952, Attack from Atlantis, 1953, Mission to the Moon, 1956, Step to the Stars, 1954, Cave of Spears, 1957, Mysterious Earth, 1960, The Mysterious Sea, 1961, Moon of Mutiny, 1961, Mysterious Sky, 1964, Outpost of Jupiter, 1963, Runaway Robot, 1965, Infinite Worlds of Maybe, 1966, Rocket from Infinity, 1966, Tunnel Through Time, 1966, Prisoners of Space, 1968, The Eleventh Commandment, 1970, Nerves, 1970, Pstalmate, 1970, Gods and Golems, 1973, Early del Rey, 1975, Police Your Planet, 1975, The World of Science Fiction: 1926-76, 1980; others; Editor: Fantastic Science-Fiction Art, 1926-54, 1975, Garland Library of Science Fiction, 1975, The Best of John W. Campbell, 1976. Named guest of honor World Sci. Fiction Conv., N.Y.C., 1967; named Grand Master Sci. Fiction, Sci. Fiction Writers Am. Conv., 1991. Home: New York N.Y. Died May 10, 1993.

DELUCCIA, EMIL ROBERT, civil engineer; b. Brighton, Mass., Sept. 20, 1904; s. Emil James and Edna Laura (Hewes) de L.; m. Margaret McCutcheon, Jan. 16, 1932; children: Margaret Crichton, Jane Hewes. BS in Civil Engring, Mass. Inst. Tech., 1927. Registered profl. engr., D.C., Oreg. Surveyman and transitman Met. Water Supply Commn., Enfield, Mass., 1927-29; engr. designer Stone and Webster Engring. Corp., 1929-31; engr. insp. and designer U.S. Engr. Office, Charleston, W.Va., 1931-33; assoc. engr. and chief of design sect. U.S. Engr. Office, Huntington, W.Va., 1933-38, FPC, 1938-51; commd. capt. AUS, 1942, advanced through grades to lt. col., 1945; with SHEAF, Europe, 1944; ret., 1956; gen. engring. cons. and mgr. Yale hydroelectric project and others Pacific Power & Light Co., 1951, v.p., chief engr., 1952-66, sr. v.p., 1966-69; pres. Oreg. Grad. Ctr., 1969-72; life trustee Oreg. Grad. Ctr. (now Oreg. Grad. Inst.), 1989-92; cons. engr., 1969-92; v.p. Overseas Adv. Assos., Inc., 1973-92; sr. engr. cons. on dams and hydroelectric projects, 1938-40; chief, power supply br. Nat. Def. Power staff, 1940-41; asst. dir. Nat. Def. Power staff and asst. chief Bur. of Elec. Engring. (also cons. on power to OPM and WPB), chief Bur. of Power, 1944-92; head group econ. and energy studies South Vietnam, 1971-72, 74-75; U.S. del. Internat. Conf. on High Dams, Stockholm, 1948, Internat. Conf. on High Tension Elec. Systems, Paris, 1948; chief U.S. delegation Internat. Conf. High Tension Lines, Paris, 1950; U.S. del. World Power Conf., London, Eng., 1950; U.S. ofcl. Negotiation Treaty with Canada for division of water at Niagara Falls; cons. to UN, Japan, 1961, AEC, Nat. Security Resources Bd.; chmn. Internat. Passamaquoddy Bd. Engrs., U.S. Com. on Large Dams; mem. Tech. Indsl. Disarmament Com. for German and Japan Elec. Power Industry; vice-chmn. bd. dirs. Oreg. chpt. Am. Automobile Assn. Contbr. to Ency. Brit., Ency. Americana. Life trustee Oreg. Grad. Motivate, 1989. Decorated medal of merit Legion of Merit; medal of Merit 1st class South Vietnam; named Oreg. Engr. of Year, 1962; recipient Aubrey R. Watzek award Lewis and Clark Coll., 1986. Fellow IEEE, ASCE; mem. Soc. Am. Mil. Engrs. (dir., recipient Goethals medal award 1963), AIM, VFW, Am. Geophys. Union, Am. Legion, Internat. Assn. High Tension Lines, Internat. Assn. Hydraulic Research, Internat. Assn. Large Dams, Am. Automobile Assn., Army-Navy Country Club (Arlington, Va.), Cosmos (Washington), Arlington University, Wavery Country (Portland), Masons (Ware, Mass. chpt.), Shriners. Home: Lake Oswego Oreg. Died Dec. 17, 1992.

DEMARK, RICHARD REID, insurance company executive; b. Detroit, May 15, 1925; s. Charles and Hazel (Reid) DeM.; m. Dorothy Ann Goodin, Sept. 25, 1948; children: Deborah L., Richard R. B.A., U. Mich., 1947. Advt. mgr. Kemper Group, Chgo., 1960-65; resident v.p., New Eng. mgr. Kemper Group, Quincy, Mass., 1967-72, v.p., div. pres., 1972-83. Former pres. Advt. Execs. Club of Chgo.; bd. dirs. ARC of Massachusetts Bay, Boston, 1982; co-chmn. Rep. Town Com., Boxford, Mass., 1970; trustee Meml. Hosp., North Conway, N.H.; vestryman Christ Episcopal Ch., North Conway. Lt. USNR, 1943-52, PTO, Korea. Mem. South Shore C. of C. (bd. dirs. 1978). Home: North Conway N.H. Died June 27, 1995.

DE MILLE, AGNES, choreographer; d. William Churchill and Anna (George) de M.; m. Walter F. Prude, June 14, 1943; 1 child, Jonathan. A.B. cum laude, U. Calif.; Litt.D. (hon.), Mills Coll., 1952, Russell Sage Coll., 1953, Smith Coll., 1954, Western Coll., 1955, Hood Coll., 1957, Northwestern U., 1960, Goucher Coll., 1961, Clark U., 1962, UCLA, 1964, Franklin and Marshall, 1965, Western Mich. U., 1967, Nasson Coll., 1971; L.H.D., Dartmouth Coll., 1974, Duke U., 1975, U. N.C., 1980, NYU, 1981. Dance recitalist U.S., Eng., France, Denmark, 1928-42; choreographer and dancer The Black Crook, 1929; choreographer (film) Romeo and Juliet, 1936; (musicals) Nymph Errant, 1933, Hooray for What, 1937, Oklahoma, 1943, One Touch of Venus, 1943, Bloomer Girl, 1944, Carousel, 1945, Brigadoon, 1947, Gentlemen Prefer Blondes, 1949, Paint Your Wagon, 1951, The Girl in Pink Tights, 1954, Goldilocks, 1958, Juno, 1959, Kwamina, 1961; (ballets) OBeah Black Ritual, 1940, Three Virgins and a Devil, 1941, Drums Sound in Hackensack, 1941, Rodeo, 1942, Tally-Ho, 1944, Fall River Legend, 1948, The Harvest According, 1952, Oklahoma (film), 1955, The Wind in the Mountains, 1965, The Four Mary's, 1965, The Informer, 1988, The Other, 1992; choreographer, dir. Allegro, 1947; dir. Rape of Lucrecia, 1949, Out of this World, 1950, Come Summer, 1969; choreographer (musical) 110 In the Shade, 1963; head Agnes de Mille Dance Theatre, presented by S. Hurok, 6 mos. tour, 126 cities, 1953-54, Agnes de Mille Heritage Dance Theater, 1973, 74, Conversations About the Dance, 1974, 75, Omnibus lectrs. and ballets, 1956-57; choreographer for Ballet Russe de Monte Carlo, 1942, Royal Winnipeg Ballet, 1972; author: Dance to the Piper, 1952, And Promenade Home, 1958, To A Young Dancer, 1962, The Book of the Dance, 1963, Lizzie Borden Dance of Death, 1968, Dance in America, 1970, Russian Journals, 1970, Speak to Me, Dance with Me, 1974, Where the Wings Grow, 1978, America Dances, 1980, Reprieve, 1981, Portrait Gallery, 1990, Martha: The Life and Work of Martha Graham, 1991. Contbr. to McCalls, Atlantic Monthly, N.Y. Times mag., Vogue, Good Housekeeping, Esquire, Horizon mags. Recipient N.Y. Cirtics prize, 1942-46, Donaldson award, 1943-47, Madamoiselle Merit award, 1944, Antoinette Perry award, 1947, 62, Lord and Taylor award, 1947, Dancing Masters award of merit, 1950, Dance Mag. award, 1957, Capezio award, 1966, Handel award Mayor N.Y.C., 1975, Kennedy award Pres. U.S., 1980, Commonwealth award in dramatic arts, 1980, Nat. Medal of Arts, 1986; named Woman of Yr. Am. Newspaper Woman's Guild, 1946, named to Theatre Hall of Fame, 1973; Agnes de Mille Theatre, N.C. Sch. Arts, Winston-Salem named in her honor, 1975. Mem. Soc. Stage Dirs. and Choreographers (pres. 1965-66). Home: New York N.Y. Died Oct. 7, 1993.

DEMING, W(ILLIAM) EDWARDS, statistics educator, consultant. BS, U. Wyo., 1921, LLD (hon.), 1958; MS, U. Colo., 1924, LLD (hon.), 1987; PhD, Yale U., 1928, hon. degree, 1991; ScD (hon.), Rivier Coll., 1981, Ohio State U., 1982, Md. U., 1983, Clarkson Inst. Tech., 1983; D in Engring. (hon.), U. Miami, 1985; LLD (hon.), George Washington U., 1986, D in Engring. (hon.), 1987; DSc (hon.), U. Colo., 1987, U. Ala., 1988, Fordham U., 1988, U. Oreg., 1989, U. S.C., 1991, Am. U., 1991, Howard U., 1993, Boston U., 1993, Harvard U., 1993. Instr. engring. U. Wyo., 1921-22; asst. prof. physics Colo. Sch. Mines, 1922-24, U. Colo., 1924-25; instr. physics Yale U., 1925-27; math. physicist USDA, 1927-39; adviser in sampling Bur. of Census, 1939-45; prof. stats Stern Sch. Bus., NYU, N.Y.C., from 1946; Disting. prof. in mgmt. Columbia U., 1986-93; cons. research, industry, 1946-93; statistician Allied Mission to Observe Greek Elections, 1946; cons. sampling Govt. India, 1947, 51, 71; adviser in sampling techniques Supreme Command Allied Powers, Tokyo, 1947-50, High Commn. for Germany, 1952, 53; mem. UN Sub-Commn. on Statis. Sampling, 1947-52; lectr. various univs., Germany, Austria, 1953, London Sch. Econs., 1964, Institut de Statistique de U. Paris, 1964; cons. Census Mex., 1954, 55; cons. Statistisches Bundesamt, Wiesbaden, Fed. Republic Germany, 1953, Central Statis. Office Turkey, 1959-93, China Productivity Ctr., Taiwan, 1970, 71; Inter Am. Statis. Inst. lectr., Brazil, Argentina. Author: Statistical Adjustment of Data, 1943, Some Theory of Sampling, 1950, Statistical Design in Business Research, 1960, Quality, Productivity, and Competitive Position, 1982, Out of the Crisis, 1986, The New Economics, 1993; contbr. numerous articles to profl. publs. Decorated 2d Order medal of the Sacred Treasure (Japan), 1960; elected Most Disting. Grad., U. Wyo., 1972; recipient Taylor Key award Am. Mgmt. Assn., 1983, Nat. Medal Tech., Pres. of U.S., 1987, Edison award. 1989; enshrined in the Engring. and Sci. Hall of Fame, 1986. Fellow Am. Statis. Assn., Royal Statis. Soc. (hon.), Inst. Math. Stats.; mem. NAE, ASTM (hon.), Am. Soc. Quality Control (hon. life, Shewhart medal 1955), Internat. Statis. Inst. (hon. life), Philos. Soc. Washington, World Assn. Pub. Opinion Rsch., Market Rsch. Coun., Biometric Soc. (hon. life), Union Japanese Scientists and Engrs. (hon. life) (tchr. and cons. to Japanese industry 1950-52, 55, 60, 65-93, honored in establishment of Deming prizes in Japan), Japanese Statis. Assn. (hon. life), Deutsche Statistische Gesellschaft (hon. life), Ops. Rsch. Soc. Am., Dayton Hall of Fame. Home: Washington D.C. Died Dec. 20, 1993; interred D.C.

DEMMLER, RALPH HENRY, lawyer; b. Pitts., Aug. 22, 1904; s. Otto and Maud (Theobald) D.; m. Catherine Hollinger, Oct. 5, 1929; 1 child, John Henry. AB, Allegheny Coll., Meadville, Pa., 1925, LLD, 1965; LLB, U. Pitts., 1928. Bar: Pa. 1928, Pa. and U.S. cts. 1928. Faculty fellow Law Sch., U Pitts., 1928-30; practiced law in Pitts., 1928—; ptnr. Reed, Smith, Shaw & McClay, 1948-53, 55-74, counsel, 1974—; chmn. U.S. SEC, 1953-55, Fed. Home Loan Bank of Pitts., 1959-61; Mem. adv. com. on enforcement SEC, 1972; writer, lectr. securities regulation, 1953-80. Author: The First Century of an Institution, 1977; editor: Beaches & Battles, 1995. Mem. Sch. Bd. of, Ross Twp., 1933-45, Allegheny County, Pa., 1938-45; treas. Pitts. Presbytery, 1941-45; trustee Allegheny Coll., 1957—, chmn. bd., 1968-72; trustee Inst. Internat. Edn., 1958-60, Hist. Soc. Western Pa., 1977-87. Fellow Am. Bar Found.; mem. Am., Pa., Allegheny County bar assns., Am. Law Inst. (adv. com. on securities codification 1969-80—), Order of Coif, Phi Beta Kappa, Delta Theta Phi, Delta Sigma Rho, Phi Gamma Delta. Presbyterian. Clubs: Duquesne (Pitts.) (dir. 1957-60), Rolling Rock (Ligonier, Pa.), University (Pitts.). Lodge: Masons. Home: Pittsburgh Pa. Died Dec. 23, 1995.

DEMSKE, JAMES MICHAEL, college chancellor; b. Buffalo, Apr. 10, 1922; s. Albert J. and Augusta (Nagel) D. BA, Canisius Coll., Buffalo, 1947, DHL (hon.), 1981; PhL, Woodstock (Md.) Coll., 1951; STL, U. Innsbruck, Austria, 1958; PhD, U. Freiburg, West Germany, 1962; LittD (hon.), D'Youville Coll., 1986. Joined S.J., 1947, ordained priest Roman Cath. Ch., 1957. Fingerprint technician FBI, 1942-43; instr. philosophy St. Peter's Coll., Jersey City, 1951-54; prof. theology, dir. students Bellarmine Coll., Plattsburgh, N.Y., 1963-66; pres. Canisius Coll., 1966-93. Author: Introductory Metaphysics, 1955, Encounters with Silence, 1960, Sein, Mensch und Tod, 1963, Being, Man and Death, 1970, A Promise of Quality: the First 100 Years of Canisius College, 1970, The Irish and I, 1976, Alive and Well in Germany, 1977. Trustee Buffalo Studio Arena Theatre. Capt. AUS, 1943-46. Recipient Centennial Regents award Canisius Coll., 1970, 125th Anniversary Award for Distinguished Service State U. N.Y. at Buffalo, 1971, Educator or Yr., 1970, Distinguished Educator's award Urban Ctr., SUNY at Buffalo, 1971, Administrator of Yr. W.N.Y. chpt. Am. Assn. U. Adminstrn., 1975, Higher Education Leadership award Commn. Ind. Colls. and Univs., 1983, Distinguished Friend of College award Trocaire Coll., 1983, Nat. Conf. Christians and Jews citation, 1988, McAuley award Trocaire Coll., 1989, Theodore Roosevelt award, 1989, Chancellor Charles P. Norton medal, 1984, Brotherhood award Nat. Conf. Christians and Jews, 1973, Liberty Bell award Erie County Bar Assn., 1973, Silver Good Citizenship medal SAR, 1978; named Educator of Year, Univ. Club Buffalo, 1970, Goodfellow of Year, Buffalo Courier Express, 1971, Outstanding Citizen of Year, Buffalo Evening News, 1971, Man of Year, Bros. of Mercy, 1976, Gen. Agents & Mgrs. Assn. Western N.Y., 1970, Western New Yorker of Yr., Buffalo Area C. of C., 1986; recipient Edn. Service award Diocesan Union Holy Names Socs., 1984, Signum Fidei award St. Joseph's Collegiate Inst., 1985, Centennial medal John Carroll U., 1985, Bishop James A. McNulty Meml. award Diocese of Buffalo Youth Dept., 1985, Spl. Achievement award U.S. Dept. Justice, 1986, Citation, Buffalo Philharmonic Orch. Soc., 1986, Toast to Buffalo award YMCA of Greater Buffalo, 1986, Red Jacket award Buffalo and Erie County Hist. Soc., 1985, Communication award St. Mary's Sch. Deaf, 1991; Paul Harris fellow Buffalo Rotary, 1991, citation Buffalo Coun. on World Affairs, 1993, Disting. Citizen award Canisius Coll. Bd. Regents, 1994, Svc. for Mankind award Leukemia Soc., 1994; named to Canisius Coll. Sports Hall of Fame, 1993; honoree Dinner of Champions, Nat. Multiple Sclerosis Soc., 1993. Mem. Buffalo Fine Arts Acad. (hon. trustee), Buffalo Mus. Natural Sci., Buffalo and Erie County Hist. Soc., Buffalo Jazz Assn., Am. Fedn. Musicians, KC, Buffalo Club, Cherry Hill Club. Home: Buffalo N.Y. Died June 15, 1994.

DE NAGY, TIBOR JULIUS, art dealer; b. Debrecen, Hungary, Apr. 25, 1910; came to U.S., 1948, naturalized, 1953; s. Alexander and Anne (Kanitz de nagyecser) de N.; 1 dau., Marianne. Dr. Econs. and Philosophy, Basel U., 1931. Dir. Nat. Bank of Hungary, Budapest, 1931-47; pres. Tibor de Nagy Gallery Inc., N.Y.C., 1950-93; fgn. dep. Mfrs. Hanover Trust, N.Y.C., 1953-70. Author: Die Ungarische National Bank, 1932; contbr. articles to profl. jours. Recipient Arts award Syracuse U., 1980. Mem. Art Dealers Assn. Am., Mus. Modern Art, Whitney Mus. Home: New York N.Y. Died Dec. 25, 1993.

DENBY, PETER, lawyer; b. Phila., Dec. 15, 1929; s. Charles and Rosamond (Reed) D.; m. Peggy Ann O'Hearn, May 19, 1956; children: Charles, Peter, Le Curtis Marshall. A.B., Princeton U., 1951; J.D. Harvard U., 1954. Bar: N.Y. 1957, Pa. 1960. Assoc. Davis Polk & Wardwell, N.Y.C., 1954-59; assoc. Reed Smith Shaw & McClay, Pitts., 1959-62, ptnr., 1962-91; mayor Borough of Edgeworth, Pa., 1989-91. Trustee Pressley Ridge Sch., Pitts., 1962-77, pres., 1965-72; bd. dirs. Western Pa. Sch. for Blind Children, 1965-91, pres., 1970-82; term trustee Carnegie Inst. Fine Arts Com., Pitts., 1965-72; trustee Sarah Scaife Found., Pitts., 1969-91, Pitts. Plan for Art, 1970-73; mem. exec. com. Western Pa. Golf Assn., 1976-91, sec., 1978-86, pres. 1990-91; bd. dirs. Pitts. Regional Planning Commn. 1971-91; pres. Pitts Regional Planning Commn., 1974-91. Mem. ABA, Allegheny County Bar Assn. Home: Sewickley Pa. Died Apr. 17, 1991.

DENISOFF, R. SERGE, sociologist, writer; b. San Francisco, June 2, 1939; s. Serge Alexander and Irene (Golubev) D.; m. Ursula Weber, July 25, 1976; children: Allegra, Rachel. A.A. in Sociology, San Francisco City Coll., 1964; B.A. in Sociology, San Francisco State Coll., 1965, M.A., 1967; Ph.D. in Sociology, Simon Fraser U., 1969. Teaching asst. San Francisco State Coll., 1965-67; research asst. Sausalito Tchr. Edn. Project, Calif., 1966-67; research asst. Simon Fraser U. 1967-68, teaching asst., 1968-69; asst. prof. Calif. State U.-Los Angeles, 1969-70; assoc. prof. sociology Bowling Green State U., Ohio, 1970-78, prof., 1978-94. Author: Great Day Coming: Folk Music and the American Left, 1971, Sing a Song of Social Significance: A Sociological View of Protest, 1972, 2d edit., 1983, (with Ralph Wahrman) An Introduction to Sociology, 1975, 3d edit. 1983, Solid Gold: The Popular Record Industry, 1975, Waylon: A Biography, 1983, Tarnished Gold, 1986, Inside MTV, 1988, (with William Romanowski) Rock in Film, 1991, Risky Business, 1991, (with Donald McQuarie) Readings in Contemporary Sociological Theory, 1994; editor Popular Music and Society; adv. editor Jour. Popular Culture, Critical Issues in Mass Communications; author numerous articles and revs. contbr. material to anthologies. Recipient best article award Am. Studies Assn. Am. Quar., 1971; Joseph K. Balogh award, 1974; Pres.'s Spl. Achievement award 1975; Deems-Taylor award ASCAP, 1975. Mem. Popular Culture Assn., Am. Sociol. Assn. Home: Bowling Green Ohio Deceased.

DENTON, MELINDA FAY, botany educator; b. Horton, Kans., Mar. 27, 1944; d. John Edward and Helen Dorene (Shupe) D.; m. Donn Charnley, June 16, 1984; 1 child, Alan Denton Charnley. BS, Emporia State Tchrs. Coll., 1965; AM, U. Mich., 1967, PhD, 1971. Vis. asst. prof., acting curator dept botany/plant pathology Mich. State U., East Lansing, 1971-72; assoc. prof., curator dept. botany U. Wash., Seattle, 1972-78, assoc. chair dept. botany, 1979-82, acting chair dept. botany, 1983-84, prof., curator dept. botany, 1983-94, asst. prof., curator dept. botany, 1978, chair dept. botany, 1987-94. Contbr. sci. articles to profl. jours. Trustee The Nature Conservancy, Seattle, 1980-86, treas., 1981-85. Mem. Am. Soc. Plant Taxonomists (pres. 1990-91, editor jour. Systematic Botany 1983-85, editorial bd. Systematic Botany 1976-80, Cooley award 1978), Am. Soc. Plant Taxonomists (sec., program chair 1976-79), Bot. Soc. Am., Internat. Assn. for Plant Taxonomy, Calif. Bot. Soc., AAAS, Sigma Xi. Home: Seattle Wash. Died Mar. 5, 1994; interred Lopez Island, Wash.

DENTON, RICHARD TODD, electrical engineering educator; b. York, Pa., July 13, 1932; s. John Hugh Denton and Gertrude Eva (Todd) Farmer; m. Jeanette Marie Ibbotson, June 6, 1953; children: Michael Thomas, Theresa, Susan, John, Matthew, Stephen, Amelia, Christopher, Elizabeth, Eileen. BS, Pa. State U., State Coll., 1953, MS, 1954; PhD, U. Mich., 1961. Mem. tech. staff Bell Telephone Labs., Murray Hill and Whippany, N.J., 1954-63; tech. supr. Bell Telephone Labs., Murray Hill, 1963-69; dept. head Bell Telephone Labs., Whippany, 1969-85; prof. Lehigh U., Bethlehem, Pa., 1985-93; cons. Weston Controls, Wilkes Barre, Pa. 1986-87. Contbr. 21 tech. articles on optical modulators McGraw Hill Encyclopaedia of Science and Technology; patentee solid state devices. Treas. Morris County Homeless Shelter, Morristwon, N.J., 1983, 84. Fellow IEEE. Home: Bethlehem Pa. Died Apr. 9, 1993.

DE SOLA, RALPH, author, editor, educator; b. N.Y.C., July 26, 1908; s. Solomon and Grace (von Geist) DeS.; m. Dorothy Clair, Dec. 24, 1944. Student Columbia U., 1927, 29, 31, Swarthmore Coll., 1928. Collector N.Y. Zool. Soc., N.Y.C., 1928-29, 30-33, Am. Mus. Natural History, N.Y.C., 1930, Tropical Biology Soc., Miami, Fla., 1933-34; zool. editor Fed. Writers Project, N.Y.C., 1935-39; tech. dir. U.S. Microfilm Corp., N.Y.C., 1939-49; hist. dir. Travel U.S. 90 and Mex. Border Trails Assn., Del Rio, Tex., 1951-54; publs editor Convair div. Gen. Dynamics Corp., San Diego, 1955-68; instr. tech. English San Diego Unified Colls., 1962-88. Author: (with Fredrica De Sola) Strange Animals and Their Ways, 1933, Microstat Technicians Handbook, 1943, Microfilming, 1944, Worldwide What and Where, 1975; compiler Abbreviations Dictionary, 1991, Crime Dictionary, 1982, rev. edit., 1990, (booklet) Great Americans Discuss Religion, 1963, (booklet) Quotations from A to Z for freethinkers and other skeptics, 1985, (with Dorothy De Sola) A Dictionary of Cooking, 1969; Great Americans Examine Religion, 1983; editor: International Conversion Tables, 1961; compiler-editor Whitman books, specializing in zool. juveniles, 1937-41, Abbreviations Dictionary, 8th edit., augmented internat. 7th, edit., 1991; translator: Beethoven-by-Berlioz, 1975, World Wide What and Where Geographic Glossary and Traveller's guide, 1975; editor in chief The Truth Seeker, 1988-89; cons. on microfilming to USN, on abbreviations to Dept. Def.; contbr. articles to Copeia, 1928-32, revs. to classical records and concerts to Freeman, Del Rio News-Herald, San Diego Engr., Downtown. Home: San Diego Calif.

DESPATIE, ROGER, bishop; b. Sunbury, Ont., Can., Apr. 12, 1927. Ordained priest Roman Catholic Ch., 1952; Titular bishop Usinaza, 1968-73; aux. bishop Sault Ste. Marie, Can., 1968-73; bishop Hearst, Ont., 1973—. Home: Hearst Can. Deceased.

DESSAUER, JOHN HANS, chemist; b. Aschaffenburg, Germany, May 13, 1905; came to U.S., 1929, naturalized, 1936; s. Hans and Bertha (Thywissen) D.; m. Margaret B. Lee, June 29, 1935; children: John Philip, Margot, Thomas David. B.S., Inst. Tech., Munich, Germany, 1924-26; M.S., D.Eng., Inst. Tech., Aachen, Germany, 1929; L.H.D., Le Moyne Coll., 1963; D.Sc. (hon.), Clarkson Coll., 1975; LL.D. (hon.), Fordham U., 1979. Chemist Ansco, Binghamton, N.Y., 1929-35; chemist Haloid Co., Rochester, N.Y., 1935-38; research dir. Haloid Co., 1938-46, v.p. charge research and product devel., dir., 1946-59; (name changed to Haloid Xerox, Inc., 1958); exec. v.p. research and engring. div. Xerox Corp., 1959-68, vice chmn. bd., until 1970, dir., until 1973. Co-author: Xerography and Related Processes; author: My Years with Xerox, or the Billions Nobody Wanted. Trustee emeritus Fordham U. Fellow Photog. Soc. Am., Am. Inst. Chemists; mem. Am. Chem. Soc., Nat. Acad. Engring. Roman Catholic. Home: Pittsford N.Y. Died Aug. 12, 1993.

DETHIER, VINCENT GASTON, zoology educator, biologist; b. Boston, Feb. 20, 1915; s. Jean Vincent and Marguerite Frances (Lally) D.; m. Lois Evelyn Check, Jan. 23, 1960; children: Jehan Vincent, Paul Georges. A.B., cum laude, Harvard U., 1936, A.M., 1937, Ph.D., 1939; Sc.D. (hon.), Providence Coll., 1964, Ohio State U., 1970, U. Mass., 1984; Dhc, U. Pau, France, 1986. Instr., assoc. prof. John Carroll U., Cleve., 1939-42; prof. zoology and entomology Ohio State U., Columbus, 1946-47; prof. biology Johns Hopkins U., Balt., 1947-58; prof. zoology and psychology U. Pa., Phila., 1958-67; prof. biology Princeton U., N.J., 1967-75; prof. zoology U. Mass., Amherst, 1975-93; sci. adv. Whitehall Found., Palm Beach, Fla., 1973-93; mem. Nat. Adv. Coun. Monell Chem. Senses Ctr., Phila., 1982-93. Author: To Knov A. Fly, 1962, Fairweather Duck, 1970, The Ant Heap, 1979, The Tent Makers, 1980, Newberry, The Life and Times of Maine Clam, 1981, The Ecology of a Summer House, 1984, Ten Masses, 1988, Crickets and Katydids, Concerts and Solos, 1992; contbr. articles to profl. jours. Pres. bd. trustees Chapin Sch., Princeton, 1971-74; mem. adv. council Kneisel Hall Sch. Music, Blue Hill, Maine, 1976-93. Served to lt. col. U.S. Army, 1942-46, WWII. Fulbright scholar, 1954; Belgian-Am. Edn. Found. fellow, 1952, Guggenheim fellow, 1964, 72. Fellow Royal Soc. Arts London, Royal Entomol. Soc. of London (hon.); mem. Am. Philos. Soc., Nat. Acad. Scis., Am. Acad. Arts and Sci., Explorers Club. Home: Amherst Mass. Died Sept. 8, 1993; interred Blue Hill, Maine.

DETLEFSEN, GUY-ROBERT, management consultant; b. Chgo., May 3, 1919; s. Gustav C. and Elsa L. (Larrieu) D.; m. Merry Campbell, May 30, 1941; children: Guy-Robert, Keith Campbell, Joan Andre. B.A. cum laude, Harvard U., 1941. Cert. chem. dependency counselor. With shipbldg. div. Bethlehem Steel Co., Quincy, Mass., San Francisco, 1941-44; rsch. tech. Pillsbury Co., 1945-52, dir. comml. R & D, 1952-58, v.p. growth and tech., 1959-66, v.p. comml. devel. div., 1966-69; exec. v.p., gen. mgr., dir. Maple Island, Inc., Mpls., 1970-73; pres., chmn. Barberio Cheese Houses, Inc., Mpls., 1973-77; pres. Detlefsen and Assocs., Mpls., 1977-95; ptnr. Chem. Dependency Recovery Assocs.: Program Devel. Cons., Mpls., 1983-95; mem. research adv. council The Conf. Bd. Mem. Hennepin County Human Svcs. Planning Bd., Hennepin Youth and Drugs Task Force, Exec. Com. Suburban Alliance, Neighbors Acting Together, St. Paul. Mem. Am. Mktg. Assn. (past v.p. mktg. mgmt. div., nat. award for advancement of sci. of mktg.), Am. Econ. Assn. Home: Wayzata Minn. Died Sept. 25, 1995.

DETWILLER, LLOYD FRASER, hospital administrator; b. Maple Creek, Sask., Can., Aug. 8, 1917; s. Daniel Benjamin and Georgina Edith (Davis) D.; m. Margaret Jean, May 3, 1941; children: Gordon Bruce, Douglas Fraser. Student, U. Minn., 1955-57; B.A., U. B.C. with honors in Econs. and Govt., 1939, M.A. with 1st class honors in Econs. and Stats., 1940; M.H.A., U. Minn. with 1st class honors in Hosp. Adminstrn., 1957; diploma hosp. orgn. and mgmt. Can. Hosp. Assn., 1957. Lectr. in econs. and stats. U. B.C., Vancouver, 1939-40, 45-46, spl. lectr. med. econs., 1961-69, clin. prof. health care and epidemiology, prof. emeritus, 1983—; acting asst. adminstr. UCLA Hosp., 1956-56; asst. adminstr. B.C. Hosp., 1956-57; spl. lectr. med. econs. U. Minn., Mpls. 1958-69, 70-80; spl. lectr. med. and hosp. econs. U. Toronto, 1960, 61; spl. lectr. health econs. U. Man., Winnipeg, 1960, 80; spl. lectr. med. and hosp. econs. George Washington U., 1961; hon. lectr. U. Alta., 1969; research statistician Treasury Dept., Province of B.C., 1946-48, commr. sales tax, 1948-50; cons. in field; commr. B.C. Hosp. Ins. Service, 1950, asst. dept. minister hosp. ins., 1957-62; adminstr. U. B.C. Health Scis. Centre, Vancouver, 1962-82; staff cons. James Hamilton Assocs., Inc., Mpls., 1966-76. Contbr. articles to profl. jours. Mem. adv. com. Greater Vancouver Regional Hosp. Dist.; bd. dirs. Goodwill Enterprises for Handicapped, The Save the Children Fund; hon. gov. Cedar Lodge Soc.; bd. dirs. Alcoholism Found. B.C.; cons. Pan Am. Health Orgn. Fellow Royal Soc. Promotion of Health; mem. U. B.C. Alumni Assn., U. Minn. Alumni Assn., Am. Coll. Hosp. Adminstrs., Am. Pub. Health Assn., Internat. Hosps. Fedn., Burnaby Hosp. Soc., Can. Hosp. Assn., Assn. Am. Med. Colls., Internat. Fedn. Vol. Health Service Funds, Assn. Can. Teaching Hosps., Assn. Hosp. Adminstrs. B.C., Can. Pub. Health Assn., B.C. Hosp. Assn.

DEUTCH, BERNHARD IRWIN, physicist; b. N.Y.C., Sept. 29, 1929; s. Ernest and Amelia D.; m. Marguerite Goetke, June 15, 1951 (div. June 6, 1962); m. Bente Pedersen, Dec. 19, 1963; children: Ann Birgitte, Susanna. BA, Cornell U., 1951, MS, 1953; PhD, U. Pa., 1959. Physicist Bartol Rsch. Found., Swarthmore, Pa., 1958-62, Nobel Inst. Physics, Stockholm, 1965; prof. Inst. Physics Aarhus, Denmark, 1962-94; hon. prof. Fudan U., Shanghai, China, 1983. Editor Hyperfine Interaction, 1975-94; assoc. editor Nuclear Physics, 1973-94; patentee in field. Home: Risskov Denmark Died Sept. 7, 1994.

DEUTSCH, HAROLD CHARLES, history educator; b. Milw., June 7, 1904; s. Herman and Julia (Wettendorff) D.; m. Marie Margaret Frey, Aug. 25, 1923 (dec. Feb. 1989); children: Janet Leaf, Dorothy Thews, Harold Jr.; m. Elisabeth Gertrud Marquardt, Sept. 5, 1991. BA, U. Wis., 1924, MA, 1925; MA, Harvard U., 1927, PhD, 1929. Prof. history U. Minn., Mpls., 1929-72, 89-90; prof. Nat. War Coll., Washington, 1948, 50, 72-74, U.S. Army War Coll., Carlisle, Pa., 1974-85; vis. prof. Free U. Berlin, 1963; cons. Dept. of State, Washington, 1968-71; subdivsn. chief Office Strategic Svcs., Washington, 1943-45; sect. chief Bd. Econ. Warfare, Washington, 1942-43. Author: Letters and Diaries of Colonel Grosscurth, 1970, Conspiracy Against Hitler in the Twilight War, Hitler and His Generals, Genesis of Napoleonic Imperialism, 1988. Chmn. Minn. Com. Against the Bricker Amendment, Mpls., 1969-71, Com. on Atlantic Studies, Washington, 1968-73; com. mem. Fulbright Fellowship, Washington, 1954-58. Named Disting. fellow U.S. Army War Coll., 1989; recipient Bundes Verdienst Kreuz award German Fed. Govt., Bonn, 1971, Medal of Freedom award Office Strategic Svcs., 1946, Exceptional Civilian Svcs. award Dept. The Army, Washington, 1985. Mem. St. Paul-Mpls. Com. on Fgn. Rels., St. Paul World War II Round Table (advisor from 1988). Home: Saint Paul Minn. Deceased.

DEUTSCH, KARL W(OLFGANG), political scientist; b. Prague, Czechoslovakia, July 21, 1912; came to U.S., 1938, naturalized, 1948; s. Martin M. and Maria (Scharf) D.; m. Ruth Slonitz, Apr. 2, 1936; children: Mary Elizabeth Deutsch Edsall, Margaret Deutsch Carroll. Candidatus Juris, German U., Prague, 1934; D. Law and Polit. Sci., Charles U., Prague, 1938; Ph.D. in Govt., Harvard U., 1951; D. Econs. and Social Scis. (hon.), U. Geneva, 1973; LL.D. (hon.), U. Mich., 1975, U. Ill., 1976, Northwestern U., 1980; Ph.D. (hon.), U. Mannheim (Germany), 1977, Tech. U. Berlin, 1983; D.Litt. (hon.), U. Pitts., 1980. From instr. to prof. MIT, Cambridge, Mass., 1942-52, prof. history and polit. sci., 1952-58; prof. polit. sci. Yale U., New Haven, 1958-67; prof. govt. Harvard U., Cambridge, 1967-71, Stanfield prof. internat. peace, 1971-83, emeritus prof., 1983—; also dir. Internat. Inst. Comparative Social Research, West Berlin, 1976-85, dir. program devel., 1985-87; Sasakawa prof. internat. peace Carter Ctr. Emory U., 1985-90; vis. prof. Princeton (N.J.) U., 1953-54, U. Chgo., 1954, Heidelberg (Germany) U., 1960, Frankfurt (Germany) U., 1968, U. Geneva, 1971, 72, 74, 75, U. Paris, 1973, 74, U. Zurich, 1975; U. Mich., 1977, U. Hamburg, 1983, Emory U., 1984, Free U. Berlin, 1987; chmn. faculty Am. seminar, Salzburg, 1981; vis. fellow Nuffield Coll., Oxford U., Eng., 1962; specialist U.S. Dept. State, India, 1963, 73, Poland, 1967, Afghanistan and Nepal, 1973; mem. U.S. del. to Internat. Conf. on Czechoslovak Constl. Reform, Prague and Salzburg, 1990. Author: Nationalism and Social Communication, 1953, rev. edit., 1966, The Nerves of Government, 1963, rev. edit., 1966, Arms Control and the Atlantic Alliance, 1967, The Analysis of International Relations, 1968, rev. edit., 1978, Nationalism and Its Alternatives, 1969, Politics and Government: How People Decide Their Fate, 1970, rev. edits., 1974, 80, Tides Among Nations, 1979; co-author or contbg. author: Political Community and the North Atlantic Area, 1957, Germany Rejoins the Powers, 1959, World Handbook of Political and Social Indicators, 1964, France, Germany and the Western Alliance, 1967, Mathematical Approaches to Politics, 1973, Mathematical Political Analysis, 1976, Eco-Social Systems and Eco-Politics, 1977, Problems of World Modelling, 1977, Decentralization, 1980, Fear of Science-Trust in Science, 1980, Comparative Government, 1981, Advances in the Social Sciences, 1986; introduction to The Globus Model, 1987; mem. editorial bd.: Behavioral Sci., 1965—, Comparative Studies in Society and History, 1966-80, Polit. Theory, 1975—, Zeitschrift für Politik, 1976—, Jerusalem Jour. Internat. Relations, 1976—. Mem. adv. bd. UN U., Tokyo, 1986-88. Decorated Grand Cross of Merit (W. Ger.), 1977, with star, 1982; recipient Sumner prize Harvard U., 1951; Sudeten German prize of culture, 1977; in Medias Res research prize, 1979; Prix de Talloires, 1982; Guggenheim fellow, 1954, 71; fellow Carter Ctr., Emory U. Fellow Nat. Acad. Scis., Am. Acad. Arts and Scis.; mem. Am. Polit. Sci. Assn. (pres. 1969-70), Internat. Polit. Sci. Assn. (pres. 1976-79), Soc. for Gen. Systems Research (pres. 1983-84), Peace Sci. Soc. (pres. 1973-74), Internat. Inst. Polit. Philosophy (pres. 1983-84), Am. Unitarian Assn., Austrian Acad. Sci., Finnish Acad. Sci. Home: Cambridge Mass. Died Nov. 1, 1992.

DEVANEY, JOHN FRANCIS, retired aluminum company executive; b. Toronto, Ont., Can., Sept. 19, 1924; s. Leo Murray and Mary Margaret (Campbell) DeV.; m. Gertrude Iona Stuart, June 18, 1949; 1 child, Lynn Elizabeth. B.S.A.E.M.E., Cornell U., 1949. With U.S. Steel Corp., Reynolds Metals, Harvey Aluminum, Hunter Engring, Amax, Nat. Steel; pres. Nat. Aluminum Corp., Pitts. to 1984. Mem. Aluminum Assn. (dir., exec. com.). Clubs: Duquesne, Met, Field. Home: Solana Beach Calif. Died May 10, 1995.

DE VAUCOULEURS, GERARD HENRI, astronomer, educator; b. Paris, Apr. 25, 1918; came to U.S., 1957, naturalized, 1962; m. Antoinette Pietra, 1944 (dec. Aug. 1987); m. Elysabeth Bardavid, 1988. Ph.D., U. Paris, 1949; D.Sc., Australian Nat. U., Canberra, 1957. Research attache Nat. Center Sci. Research, Sorbonne and Astrophysics Inst., Paris, 1943-49; research fellow Australian Nat. U. Mt. Stromlo Obs., 1951-54; observer-in-charge Yale-Columbia So. Sta., 1954-57; astronomer Lowell Obs., Flagstaff, Ariz., 1957-58; research asso. Harvard U. Obs., 1958-60; asso. prof. astronomy U. Tex., Austin, 1960-63; prof. U. Tex., 1964-80, Ashbel Smith prof., 1981-82, Blumberg prof., 1983-88, emeritus, 1988-95; vis. prof. Cordoba Obs., Argentina, 1970, Coll. de France, Paris, 1976, Royal Obs., Edinburgh, Scotland, 1976; cons. in field. Author 20 books, 400 research papers in field. Grantee NSF; Grantee NASA; Grantee others. Mem. NAS, Nat. Acad. Sci. Argentina (fgn. assoc.), Internat. Astron. Union, Am. Astron. Soc. (Russell lectr. 1988), Astron. Soc. Pacific, Royal Astron. Soc. (Herschel medal 1980), French Phys. Soc., French Astron. Soc. (Janssen medal 1988). Home: Austin Tex. Died Oct. 7, 1995.

DEVOLL, RAY, tenor singer. Studies with Clytie Mundy, Norman Notley, Mark Pearson. Mem. New Eng. Conservatory. Performed thoughout U.S., South Am., Europe, The USSR; appeared st major Am. Bach festivals; tenor soloist rec. Berlioz Requiem. Home: Boston Mass. Died Aug. 24, 1993.

DE VRIES, PETER, writer, editor; b. Chgo., Feb. 27, 1910; s. Joost and Henrietta (Eldersveld) De V.; m. Katinka Loeser, Oct. 16, 1943; children: Jan, Peter Jon, Emily, Derek. A.B., Calvin Coll., 1931; student, Northwestern U., summer 1931. Editor community newspaper Chgo., 1931; freelance writer, 1931; assoc. editor Poetry Mag., 1938, co-editor, 1942; mem. editorial staff New Yorker Mag., 1944-87. Author: No But I Saw the Movie, 1952, The Tunnel of Love, 1954, Comfort Me with Apples, 1956, The Mackerel Plaza, 1958, The Tents of Wickedness, 1959, Through the Fields of Clover, 1961, The Blood of the Lamb, 1962, Reuben, Reuben, 1964, Let Me Count the Ways, 1965, The Vale of Laughter, 1967, The Cat's Pajamas and Witch's Milk, 1968, Mrs. Wallop, 1970, Into Your Tent I'll Creep, 1971, Without a Stitch in Time, 1972, Forever Panting, 1973, The Glory of the Hummingbird, 1974, I Hear America Swinging, 1976, Madder Music, 1977, Consenting Adults, or The Duchess Will Be Furious, 1980, Sauce for the Goose, 1981, Slouching Towards Kalamazoo, 1983, The Prick of Noon, 1984, Peckham's Marbles, 1986. Mem. Am. Acad. and Inst. Arts and Letters. Home: Westport Conn. Died Sept. 28, 1993.

DEWALD, ERNEST LEROY, landscape architect; b. Cleve., Oct. 15, 1907; s. Frank Ernest and Bessie Mary (Stutzman) D.; m. Edna E. Kummer, Oct. 9, 1935. B.F.A. in Landscape Architecture, Ohio State U., 1931; postgrad. (Found. scholar), Lake Forest Found. for Architects and Landscape Architects, 1931. Registered landscape architect, Calif., N.Y., Ohio, Pa. Landscape architect U.S. Forest Service and Nat. Park Service, McGregor, Iowa, Lynn and Hinckly, Minn., 1933-38; Works Progress adminstr. Cleve. City Parks and City of East Cleveland, 1938-41, Albert D. Taylor, Cleve., 1941-43, City of Cleve., 1945-56, Outcalt,

Guenther (Architects), Cleve., 1956-59; pvt. practice landscape architecture Shaker Heights, Ohio, 1959-86, ret., 1987. Co-author: Cleve. Region Airport Plan, 1946. Active Nat. Council Landscape Archtl. Registration Bds., 1967-74, pres., 1968-69, 72-73; mem. Nat. Interprofl. Council Registration, 1972-73; exec. sec. Ohio Roadside Council, 1959-67, vice chmn., 1968-95; mem. Forest Hill Park Adv. Commn., 1977-95, People to People Internat., 1981-95, del. to China, 1981. Fellow Am. Soc. Landscape Architects (nat. 2d v.p. 1969-71, sec.-treas. Council Fellows, Ky-Ohio chpt. medal 1974); mem. Cleve. Mus. Art (life), Internat. Fedn. Landscape Architects, Ohio State Alumni Assn. (life). Home: Cleveland Ohio Died May 17, 1995.

DIAMANT, ANITA, literary agent; b. N.Y.C., Jan. 15; d. Sidney J. and Lea (Lyons) D.; m. Harold Berke, Dec. 22, 1945 (dec. 1972); 1 child, Allyson. B.S., NYU. Former mem. editor bd. Forum mag., N.Y.C., McCall's mag., N.Y.C.; reporter Macy Newspapers, N.Y.; prin. Anita Diamant Lit. Agy., N.Y.C.; lectr. at writers' confs. throughout U.S.; adj. prof. Journalism, L.I. Univ., 1967. Contbr. articles to McCall's Mag., Writer, Women's News, others. Mem. Women in Comm. (past pres. N.Y. chpt.), Nat. Assn. Newspaper Women, Assn. Authors' Reps., Overseas Press Club Am. (pres. 1981-86, Meritorious Svc. award 1970), Williams Club. Home: Weston Conn. Died Jan. 13, 1996.

DIBBLE, GEORGE SMITH, JR., petroleum company executive, lawyer; b. Salt Lake City, July 29, 1933; s. George Smith and Cleone (Atwood) D.; m. Ilene Jensen, June 24, 1964; children: Andrea, George S. III. BS, U. Utah, 1954, JD, 1960; MBA, Brigham Young U., 1963. Bar: Utah 1960, Wyo. 1974, U.S. Ct. Appeals (10th cir.) 1960, U.S. Supreme Ct. 1971. Ins. atty. U.S. Fidelity & Guaranty Co., Salt Lake City, 1960-61; sole practice, Salt Lake City, 1961-64; ptnr., Tuft, Marshall & Dibble, Salt Lake City, 1964-66; corp. atty. Husky Oil Co./Husky Internat., Cody, Wyo. and Calgary, Alta., Can., 1966-73, asst. corp. sec., corp. officer, Cody and Englewood, Colo., 1973-84; vice chmn. Grambling Energy/RMT Properties, from 1984; pres., chief exec. office Sirius Energy, from 1984. Contbr. articles on pub. lands and resources to trade jours. Chmn. Gov. Com. on Employment of Handicapped, 1975-77; patrol leader, div. officer, nat. legis. chmn. Nat. Ski Patrol System, from 1976. Served to capt. USAF, 1954-56. Mem. Rocky Mountain Oil and Gas Assn. (pres. 1975-79), Am. Petroleum Inst. (bd. dirs. 1977-79), Ind. Petroleum Assn. Am. (chmn. com. western regional council from 1977; issues com.), Petroleum Assn. Wyo. (pres. 1973-75). Mormon. Deceased.

DI CENZO, COLIN DOMENIC, engineering educator, consultant; b. Hamilton, Ont., Can., July 26, 1923; s. Ferdinando and Kathleen (Quickenden) di C.; m. Patricia Evelyn Wright, Sept. 12, 1950; children: Colin, Eileen, Brian, Mark, Peter, Pamela. B.Sc. in Elec. Engring., U. N.B., 1952; D.I.C., Imperial Coll. Sci. and Tech., London, 1954; M.Sc. in Elec. Engring., U. N.B., 1957; DSc (hon), McMaster U., 1991. Comd. artificer apprentice Can. Navy, 1941, advanced through grades to comdr., 1965; trans. Naval Res., 1966; Control engr. Met. Vickers, Eng., 1953-54; lectr. Royal Mil. Coll. Can., 1954-57; dep. head sonar engring. Naval Hdqrs., Ottawa, Ont., 1957-60; head underwater fire control system design group Naval Hdqrs., 1960-62; squadron staff officer 2d Destroyer Squadron, Pacific, 1962-64; project engr. hydrofoil ship HMCS Bras d'Or, Naval Hdqrs., 1964-65; Comdg. officer HMCS Star, 1969-71; assoc. prof. McMaster U., Hamilton, 1965-72; prof. elec. engring. McMaster U., 1972-79, founding chmn. computer engring. program, 1978-79, prof. elec. and computer engring., 1979-80, dir. studies faculty engring., 1968-75, assoc. dean engring., 1975-79, prof. emeritus, 1980; dean engring. and applied sci. Meml. U. Nfld., St. John's, 1980-83; ptnr. James F. Hickling Mgmt. Cons., 1983-85; chmn. Colpat Enterprises, 1983-89; prin. Colin di Cenzo Assocs., Hamilton, 1989-92; dir. Can. continuing engring. edn. George Washington U., 1984-87; dir. Canadian Inst. for Advanced Engring. Studies, 1985-92; vis. fgn. expert People's Republic China, 1988-91, rsch. adviser Chengou U. Sci. and Tech., 1990-92. Bd. govs. Labrador Inst. No. Studies, 1980-83, Centre for Cold Oceans Resource Engring., 1980-83. Decorated Order Can.; recipient Can. Decoration, 1953, Centennial medal, 1967; Queen's Silver Jubilee medal, 1977; award Public Servants Invention Act; Gov.-Gen.'s Commemorative medal, 1978; Athlone fellow, 1952-54; Brydone-Jack scholar, 1952. Fellow IEEE (asso. editor transactions 1975-78), Engring. Inst. Can. (Julian C. Smith medal 1977, pres. 1979-80), Can. Acad. Engring.; mem. Can. Soc. Elec. Engring. (pres. 1976-78), Assn. Profl. Engrs. Ont. (Engring. medal 1977), Commonwealth Engrs. Council, Pan Am. Union Engring. Socs. (dir. 1981-84), Instn. Engrs. (Australia). Home: Hamilton Can. Died Dec. 15, 1992.

DICKEY, WILLIAM (HOBART DICKEY), humanities educator, poet; b. Bellingham, Wash., Dec. 15, 1928; s. Paul Condit and Anne Marie (Hobart) D. B.A., Reed Coll., 1951; M.A. (Woodrow Wilson fellow), Harvard, 1955; M.F.A., U. Iowa, 1956; postgrad., Jesus Coll. U. Oxford, Eng., 1959-60. Instr. Cornell U., Ithaca, N.Y., 1956-59; asst. prof. English Denison U., 1960-62; asst. prof. San Francisco State U., 1962-65, assoc. prof., 1966-69, prof. English and creative writing, 1970-91, prof. emeritus, 1991-94, chmn. creative writing, 1974-77; vis. prof. English U. Hawaii, 1972. Author: Of the Festivity, 1959, Interpreter's House, 1964, Rivers of the Pacific Northwest, 1969, More Under Saturn, 1971, The Rainbow Grocery, 1976 (Juniper prize), The Sacrifice Consenting, 1981, Six Philosophical Songs, 1983, Joy, 1983, Brief Lives, 1985, The King of the Golden River, 1986, Metamorphoses, 1991, Night Journey, 1992, In the Dreaming: Selected Poems, 1994. Recipient Union League prize Poetry mag., 1961, Commonwealth Club of Calif. medal, 1972, Juniper prize U. Mass. Press, 1978, Creative Writing award Am. Inst. Arts and Letters, 1980, Poetry award Bay Area Book Reviewers, 1986; fellow Fulbright Found., 1959-60, NEA, 1978-79. Mem. Calif. Assn. Tchrs. English (Classroom Excellence award 1985), Philol. Assn. Pacific Coast, MLA, (del. assembly 1974-76), PEN Am. Ctr., Phi Beta Kappa. Home: San Francisco Calif. Died May 3, 1994; interred Silverton, O.R.

DICKINSON, PATRIC (THOMAS), poet; b. Nasirabad, India, Dec. 26, 1914; s. Arthur Thomas and Eileen (Kirwan) D.; m. Shila Dunbar Shannon, Dec. 19, 1945; children: David Dunbar, Virginia Kirwan. BA (with hons.), St. Catharine's Coll., Cambridge, 1936. Schoolmaster, 1936-39; prodr. transcription svc. British Broadcasting Corp., London, 1942-45, poetry editor Home Svc. and Third Programme, 1945-48; freelance writer, broadcaster and critic, 1948-94; Gresham prof. rhetoric City U., London, 1964-67; lectr. and reader; dir. Poetry Festival Royal Court Theater, 1963. Author: (poetry) The Seven Days of Jericho, 1944, Theseus and the Minotaur, and Poems, 1946, Stone in the Midst, and Poems, 1948, The Sailing Race, and Other Poems, 1952, The Scale of Things, 1955, The World I See, 1960, This Cold Universe, 1964, The Good Minute: An Autobiographical Study, 1965, Selected Poems, 1968, More Than Time, 1971, A Wintering Tree, 1973, The Bearing Beast, 1976, Our Living John, 1979, Poems From Rye, 1980, To Go Hidden, 1980, Winter Hostages, 1981, A Rift in Time, 1983, To Go Hidden, 1984, A Sun Dog, 1988, Two Into One, 1989, Not Hereafter, 1991, Shadow of the Earth: Poems From Forty Years, 1992, (plays) Stone in the Midst, 1948, The Golden Touch, 1956, The First Family, 1960, A Durable Fire, 1962, Wilfred Own, 1970, The Pensive Prisoner, 1970, (librettos) (with Bernard Rose) Ode to St. Catharine, 1973, (with Alan Ridout) Creation, 1973, (with Stephen Dodgson) The Miller's Secret, 1973, The Return of Odysseus, 1977, Good King Wenceslaus, 1979; editor: Soldier's Verse, 1945, Poems of Byron, 1949, Poems to Remember: A Book For Children, 1958, Poet's Choice: An Anthology of English Poetry from Spenser to the Present Day, 1967, Selected Poems of Henry Newbolt, 1984; adaptor: (Jules Supervielle) Robinson, 1953, (Plautus) Pseudous, 1966; translator: (Aristophanes) Aristophanes against War: Three Plays, 1957, (Virgil) The Aeneid, 1962, (Aristophanes) The Complete Plays, 1970; adaptor, translator: (Plautus) Mercator, 1982. Recipient Atlantic award in Literature, 1948, Cholmondeley award for Poets, 1973. Mem. Savile Club. Home: Rye Eng. Died Jan. 28, 1994.

DIEBENKORN, RICHARD CLIFFORD, JR., painter; b. Portland, Oreg., Apr. 22, 1922; s. Richard Clifford and Dorothy (Stephens) D.; m. Phyllis Gilman, June 16, 1943; children: Gretchen Gilman, Christopher. B.A., Stanford, 1949; student, U. Calif. at Berkeley, 1943, Calif. Sch. Fine Arts, 1946; M.A., U. N.Mex., 1952. Tchr. San Francisco Art Inst., 1961-66; prof. art UCLA, 1966-73; artist-in-residence Stanford U., 1963-64. Author: Drawing, 1965, Richard Diebenkorn: Works on Paper, 1987; one-man shows: Calif. Palace of Legion of Honor, San Francisco, 1948, 60, San Francisco Mus. Art, 1954, 72, Oakland Arts Mus., 1956, Pasadena Mus. Art, 1960, Phillips Collection, Washington, 1961, Nat. Inst. Arts and Letters, N.Y.C., 1962, Washington Gallery Modern Art, 1964, Pa. Acad. Fine Arts, Phila., 1968 (Carol H. Beck Gold Medal award), Los Angeles County Mus. Art, 1969, UCLA, 1976, Albright-Knox Art Gallery, Buffalo, retrospective, 1976-77, M. Knoedler & Co., N.Y.C., 1977, 79-80, 82, 84-85, 87, 91, Mpls. Inst. Arts, 1981, San Francisco Mus. Modern Art, 1983, Sheldon Meml. Art Gallery, Lincoln, Nebr., 1985, Mus. Modern Art, retrospective, 1988, Hara Mus. Contemporary Art, Tokyo, 1989, Whitechapel Art Gallery, London, retrospective, 1992, Juan March Fondacion, Madrid, retrospective, 1992, others; exhibited: Venice Biennale, 1968, 78; works represented in permanent collections: Bklyn. Mus., Chgo. Art Inst., Met. Mus. Art, Mus. Modern Art, Whitney Mus., N.Y.C., Toronto Mus., Nelson Gallery, Kansas City, Phoenix Mus., Albright-Knox Art Gallery, Santa Barbara (Calif.) Mus., Cleve. Art Mus., Milw. Mus., Stanford U., Houston Mus., Oberlin Coll. Gallery, San Francisco Mus. Art, Pasadena Art Mus., Phillips Meml. Gallery, Hirschorn Mus., Washington, Carnegie Inst., U. Iowa, U. Mich., Los Angeles County Mus. Art. Recipient Gold medal PA. Acad. Fine Arts, 1968, Edwin MacDowell medal, 1978, Skowhegan medal for painting Skowhegan Sch. Art, 1979, Nat. Medal of Arts award Nat. Endowment for Arts, 1991; Gold Medal for Painting, AAAL, 1993. Mem. Nat. Found. on Arts and the Humanities, Nat. Inst. Arts and Letters, Am. Acad. Arts and Letters, Am. Acad. Design. Home: New York N.Y. Died Mar. 30, 1993.

DIEDERICHS, JOHN KUENSTING, investme company executive; b. Chgo., July 16, 1921; m. Jar Barbara Wood, Sept. 16, 1953. Student, MI Northwestern U., 1948-52; AB, U. Chgo., 1953. Sal and market planning adminstr. Pan Am. Wor Airways, N.Y.C. and Chgo., 1946-49; regional sal mgr. Pan Am.-Grace Airways, N.Y.C. and Chgo., 194 52; mem. profl. mgmt. cons. staff Booz Allen ar Hamilton, Chgo., 1952-55; chmn. techno-econs. dep Ill. Inst. Tech. Rsch., Chgo.; v.p. Johnson and Assoc Mgmt. Cons., 1962-63; v.p. rsch. and corp. devel. Chg Mill and Lumber Co., 1962-65; v.p. corp. planning ar devel. Sunbeam Corp., Chgo., 1965-82; owner, inves ment counselor Diederichs & Assocs., 1982-95; asso ated with John C. Stanley, London, 1982-95, Eric vo Stolzenberg, Zurich, Pacific Corp. Group Inc., La Jol Calif.; chmn., chief exec. officer WFMT, Inc., Chg Mag., 1985-86, bd. dirs. WFMT, Inc., 1975-92; bd. di Mich. Bldg. Corp., 1975-92; trustee WTTW-TV, Chgo Mem. Nat. Assn. Securities Dealers (profl. arbitrato Investment Co. Inst., Tech. Assn. of the Graphic Ar Photographic Scientists and Engrs., Internat. Sc Econometricians, Am. Arbitration Assn. (profl. ar trator), Chicago Club, Tavern Club, River Cl (N.Y.C.). Home: Chicago Ill. Died July 29, 199

DIEHL, GERALD GEORGE, architect; b. Highla Park, Mich., July 24, 1916; s. George Frederick a Alice Veronica (Nolan) D.; m. Marie Josephine Irvi (dec. Feb. 1987); children: Rosemary, Martha, Patric Elizabeth, Paul, James, Daniel, Frederick; m. Jo Martha Rogers Kuzinski, Jan. 28, 1989. Studer Lawrence Inst. Tech.; LHD (hon.), Siena Heights Co 1976. Registered architect, Mich., 20 other states Draftsman Giffels & Vallet, Detroit, 1941-44, Harl Ellington & Day, Detroit, 1944-45, Saarinen, Swans & Saarinen, Bloomfield Hills, Mich., 1954-47; v.p. Di & Diehl, Arch., Detroit, 1947-76, pres., 1976-95; chm planning com. Siena Heights Coll., Adrian, Mic 1974-95. Chmn. properties com. Boys' & Girls' Club Southeastern Mich., 1982-95, torch drive div. Unit Found., Detroit, 1955-86; chmn., mem. City Pl Commn., Detroit. Fellow AIA (pres. Detroit chp Gold Medal Detroit chpt. 1961); mem. Mich. Sc Architects (sec.), Engring. Soc. Detroit. Rom Catholic. Clubs: Detroit Athletic, Renaissance (D troit). Home: Dearborn Mich. Died Aug. 4, 199

DIETZ, ROBERT SINCLAIR, retired geology ed cator; b. Westfield, N.J., Sept. 14, 1914; s. Louis A drew Dietz and Bertha Staiger; m. Nanon Grinstea 1954 (div. 1974); children: Drew Loren, Robe Rex. BS, U. Ill., 1937, MS, 1939, PhD, 1941; D (honoris causa), Ariz. State U., 1988. With USN Ele tronic Lab., 1946-54. 59-63; asst. dir. Office Nav Rsch., London, 1954-59; with U.S. Coast and Geode Survey, 1963-70, Nat. Oceanic and Atmospheric A minstrn., 1970-77; prof. geology Ariz. State U., Temp 1977-85, prof. emeritus, 1985—; vis. prof. U. Ill., 197 Wash. State U., 1975, Washington U., 1976, Farlei Dickenson U., 1976, Tuebingen U., Fed. Republ Germany, 1978, U. Tokyo, 1980; adj. prof. Scripps Ins Oceanography, 1949-53, U. Miami, 1963-73. Auth about 250 sci. papers and articles and 4 books, includir ((with Jacques Piccard) Seven Miles Down: Story Bathyscaph Trieste, 1961, Creation/Evolution Satirico Creationism Bashed, 1987; co-author Present State Plate Tectonics, 1977. Patron Nat. Ctr. for Sci. Edi Berkeley, Calif., 1987—. Lt. col. USAF, 1941-45 Decorated World War II, 5 medals; recipient Superi Civilian Svc. award USN, 1960, Antarctic Svc. med Navy-Byrd Expedition, 1946-47, Outstanding Sci. Pap award U.S. Coast and Geodetic Survey, 1968, Go medal U.S. Dept. Commerce, Alexander von Humbol prize Fed. Republic Germany, 1978, Francis P. Shepa medal Soc. Econ. Paleontologists and Mineralogis 1979, Barringer medal and prize, 1985, Founders Plate Tectonics award Tex. A&M, 1988, Sigma Xi Sp award for integrity of sci., 1986, Disting. Achieveme award Ariz. State U., 1990. Fellow Geol. Soc. Ar (Penrose medal 1988), Geol. Soc. London (hon.), Ar Geophys. Union (Walter H. Bucher medal 197 Mineral. Soc. Am., Meteoritical Soc. (v.p. 1970-7 Geol. Soc. India; mem. Phi Beta Kappa. Home: Tem Ariz. Died May 19, 1995.

DIKOV, BISHOP JOSEPH (METROPOLITA BISHOP JOSEPH), bishop; b. Pelovo, Pleven, Bu garia, July 11, 1907; s. Diko Ivanov and Valka Bale (Marinova) D. Grad., Spiritual Sem., Sofia, Bulgari 1930. Ordained priest Bulgarian Orthodox Ch., 193 sec. Rila Monastery, 1935-36; protosingel of Metr politan of Vratza, 1936-41, Plovdiv, 1941-42; chief cu tural dept. Holy Synod, 1943-45, 51-57; rector Spiritu Sem., Plovdiv, Bulgaria, 1947-51; vicor bishop to Bu garian Patriarch Kiril, 1957-70; adminstr. Bulgaria Akron, Ohio diocese, 1970-72; metropolitan N.Y. D oceses N.Y.C., 1972-86; del. to Prague Peace Conf. Home: New York N.Y. Died Sept. 6, 1986; interr Sofia, Bulgaria.

DILLON, EILIS, writer; b. Galway, Ireland, Mar. 1920; d. Thomas and Geraldine (Plunkett) D.; r Cormac O'Cuilleanain, Mar. 28, 1940 (dec. 1970); ch dren: Eilean, Maire (dec.), Cormac; m. Vivian Mercie Apr. 5, 1974 (dec. 1989). DLitt (hon.), Nat. U. Irelan 1992. lectr. creative writing Trinity Coll. Dublin U 1971-72, Univ. Coll., Dublin, 1988; lectr. at Am. univ d colls. Author: (children's fiction) Midsummer agic, 1949, The Lost Island, 1952, The San Sebastian, 53, The House on the Shore, 1955, The Wild Little ouse, 1955, The Island of Horses, 1956, Plover Hill, 57, Aunt Bedelia's Cats, 1958, The Singing Cave, 59 (Honorable Mention citation N.Y. Herald Tribune ildren's Spring Book Festival 1960), The Fort of old, 1961, King Big-Ears, 1961, A Pony and a Trap, 62, The Cats' Opera, 1962, The Coriander, 1963 lonorable Mention citation N.Y. Herald Tribune ildren's Spring Book Festival 1964), A Family of oxes, 1964 (German Juvenile Book Prize Honor List ation 1968), The Sea Wall, 1965, The Lion Cub, 1966, ne Road to Dunmore, 1966, The Key, 1967, The uise of the Santa Maria, 1967, Two Stories: The Road Dunmore and The Key, 1967, The Seals, 1968, Under e Orange Grove, 1968, A Herd of Deer, 1969 onorable Mention citation N.Y. Herald Tribune ildren's Spring Book Festival 1970, Notable Book ation ALA 1970, Lewis Carroll Shelf award 1970), ne Wise Man on the Mountain, 1969, The Voyage of ael Duin, 1969, The King's Room, 1970, The Five undred, 1972, The Shadow of Vesuvius, 1978, Down the World, 1983, The Horse Fancier, 1985, The ekers, 1986, The Island of Ghosts, 1989 (Irish Book of award 1991), (adult fiction) Death at Crane's Court, 53, Sent to His Account, 1954, Death in the uadrangle, 1956, The Bitter Glass, 1958, The Head of e Family, 1960, Bold John Henebry, 1965, Across the ter Sea, 1973, Blood Relations, 1977, Wild Geese, 80, Citizen Burke, 1984, The Interloper, 1987, (plays) anna, 1962, A Page of History, 1966, The Cats' era, 1981, (others) An Choill bheo, 1948, Oscar agus Coiste se nEasog, 1952, Ceol na Coille, 1955, Living Imperial Rome, 1974, Inside Ireland, 1982; editor: e Hamish Hamilton Book of Wise Animals, 1973. llow Royal Soc. Lit.; mem. Irish Writers Ctr. (mem. ec. bd.), Irish Children's Book Trust (chair), Irish pyright Collection Agy. (sec.), Irish Writers Union air), Societa Dante Alighieri. Irish Nationalist. man Catholic. Home: Dublin Ireland Died July 19, 94.

LLON, JAMES LEE, media company executive, wspaper publisher; b. Martinsville, Va., Dec. 17, 1928; Alton Milton and Betty Ruth (Thomas) D.; m. zabeth Leeming, Mar. 23, 1957 (div. May 1978); ldren—Christopher S., Mark T.; m. Rhoda Fern omas, June 7, 1980. B.S., Va. Commonwealth Univ., 52; M.M.P., Harvard Univ., 1958. Mgr. planning and vice Norfolk (Va.) Newspaper, 1955-61; mgr. advt. chmond (Va.) Newspapers, 1961-72, bus. mgr., 1972- v.p., gen. mgr., 1973-77; v.p. Media Gen., Inc., chmond, 1977-95, Media Gen. Bus. Communications, ., 1985-95; pub. Va. Bus. Mag., 1985-95; v.p. Early d Satellite Service, Fairfax County, Va., 1982-95. Bd. s. Va. Home for Boys, Richmond, 1980-95; vice chair etro Richmond Coalition against Drugs, 1992-95; s. Robert E. Lee Coun. Boy Scouts Am., Richmond, 80-85, area pres., 1985, bd. dirs. So. region, 1992-95. aj. USMC, 1953-55. Recipient Silver Beaver award y Scouts Am., 1982, Silver Antelope award, 1982. em. Info. Industry Assn. (vice chmn. Future Tech. d Innovation Coun. 1982-89), Richmond C. of C. (dir. 80-84), Commonwealth Club, Country Club of Va., rmington Country Club (Charlottesville, Va.). publican. Presbyterian. Home: RIchmond Va. Died ne 24, 1995.

MON, JOHN E., lawyer; b. Roebling, N.J., May 14, 16; s. George and Mary (Vrabel) D.; m. Virginia Lee eece, Sept. 6, 1946; children: Patricia Frazier, Blake, vid, Mark, Matthew. B, Villanova U., 1937; LLB, mple U., 1940. Bar: N.J. 1946. Ptnr. Dimon, Haines d Bunting, 1952-73, Dimon & Eleuteri, 1973-79, mon Eleuteri & Gilanyi, Mt. Holly, N.J., 1979; sole actice Roebling, 1979-93; chmn. bd. dirs. Bank Mid ., Bordentown; bd. dirs. BMJ Fin., Bordentown, Mt. lly State Bank; corp. counsel Burlington County, ., 1980-82. Chmn. Burlington County Reps., Mt. lly, 1964-71, N.J. Rep. Orgn., Trenton, 1970-73, N.J. apportionment Commn.; del. N.J. Constl. Conv., New unswick, 1966-67, Nat. Rep. Conv., 1964, 68, 72, 76, staff mem., 1984, 88,; mem. N.J. Racing Commn., enton, 1986-93. Served to maj. U.S. Army, 1940-46. publican. Byzantine Catholic. Elks. Home: ebling N.J. Died Sept. 19, 1993.

NGMAN, MAURICE J., bishop; b. St. Paul, Iowa, . 20, 1914; s. Theodore and Angela (Witte) D. Ed., Ambrose Coll., Davenport, Iowa, 1936, N.Am. Coll. Gregorian U., Rome, Catholic U. Am. Ordained est Roman Cath. Ch., 1939; instr. St. Ambrose ad., 1940-43; vice chancellor Diocese of Davenport, va, 1942-45; prin. Hayes High Sch., Muscatine, Iowa, 50-53; domestic prelate, 1956; appointed bishop Di- se of Des Moines, 1968-87. Home: Saint Paul Iowa

SANTO, GRACE JOHANNE DEMARCO, poet; Derby, Conn., July 12, 1924; d. Richard and Fannie Marco; m. Frank Michael Di Santo, Aug. 30, 1946; ldren: Frank Richard, Bernadette Mary, Roxanne ith. Student in journalism, NYU, 1941-43; AB in glish, Belmont Abbey Coll., 1974. Newswriter Aus- ian Assn. Press, N.Y.C., 1942-43; staff reporter An- a Sentinel, Derby, 1943-45; feature writer, drama ic Bridgeport Herald, New Haven, 1945-46; editor nthly bull. Pa. State Coll. Optometry, Phila., 1947-48; free-lance writer, 1949-54; founder, pres. bd. dirs. Investors Ltd., Morganton, N.C., 1966-67; freelance writer. Author: (poetry) The Eye is Single, Portrait of the Poet as Teacher: James Dickey; contbr. The Dream Book: An Anthology of Writings by Italian-American Women. Pres., Burke County chpt. N.C. Symphony Soc., 1968-70; mem. exec. bd. Community Concerts Assn., 1962-71; trustee N.C. Symphony Soc., 1965-68, 69-70, North State Acad., Hickory, N.C., 1974-93; bd. advisors Belmont Abbey Coll., 1986-93. Recipient Oscar Arnold Young Meml. award, 1982. Republican. Roman Catholic. Clubs: Grandfather Golf and Country (Linville, N.C.); Mimosa Hills Golf. Died June 4, 1993.

DITOLLA, ALFRED W., international union executive; b. N.Y.C., Sept. 21, 1926; s. Alfred Joseph and Mary (O'Shaugnessy) DiT.; m. Kathleen Marie DiTolla, Sept. 24, 1949; children: M. Lourdes, Alfred J., Jane D. (dec.), Kathleen M., Daniel E., Andrea M. Student, Fordham U., N.Y. Law Sch. Bus. rep. Internat. Alliance of Theatrical Stage Employees, N.Y.C., 1951-94, internat. rep., 1974-78, asst. to pres., 1978-86, internat. pres., 1986-94; bd. dirs. Will Rogers Memorial Fund, White Plaines, N.Y., Motion Picture Pioneers, N.Y.; trustee Richard F. Walsh Found., N.Y., Internat. Alliance Theatrical Stage Employees Benefit Funds, N.Y. Served with US Naval AF, 1943-45. Recipient Honorary Citizen award City of Winnipeg (Can.), 1982, City of New Orleans (La.), 1986, Entertainment Industry Man of Yr. award Theatrical Mutual Assn., N.Y., 1985, Democratic Heritage award Am. Jewish Com., N.Y., 1987. Mem. Internat. Alliance Theatrical Stage Employees (Locals #1, 659, 706, 844, and 917), N.Y. Variety Clubs, Am. Theatre Wing, N.Y., Cath. Interracial Council, N.Y., Vets. Bedside Network N.Y., Motion Picture Pioneers N.Y. Democrat. Roman Catholic. Home: Glen Rock N.J. Died Dec. 20, 1994.

DIXON, GEORGE FRANCIS, JR., retired manufacturing company executive; b. Jersey City, Feb. 24, 1918; s. George F. and Frances (Martin) D.; m. Lottie Ivy Carter, Dec. 1, 1950; children: George Francis III, Richard Elliott, Marshall Lawrence, Charlotte Ivy. B.S., U.S. Mil. Acad., 1940; M.S., Cornell U., 1947; D.Eng., Grenoble U., France, 1949. Dist. engr. Vicksburg Dist. Corps Engrs., 1949-53; pres. Dart Truck Co., Kansas City, Mo., 1955-57; dir. Carlisle Corp., Pa., 1954-93; pres., CEO Carlisle Corp., 1957-70, chmn. bd., 1970-91, dir.; dir. Dauphin Deposit Trust Co., Harrisburg, Pa., CDI Corp., Phila.; Chmn. Pa. Div. Trauma. Trustee Dickinson Sch. Law; trustee Gettysburg Coll. Served as lt. col. AUS, World War II; div. engr., comdg. officer 65th Engrs., 25th Inf. Div. Mem. ASCE, Assn. Grads. U.S. Mil. Acad. (trustee, pres.), Soc. Automotive Engrs., Soc. Am. Mil. Engrs., Nat. Cathedral. Home: Fort Lauderdale Fla. Died Aug. 8, 1993; buried Zion Cemetery, Boiling Springs, Pa.

DIXON, LOUIS M., gaming consultant, lawyer. Chmn. Harrah's Hotels and Casinos, Reno, Nev., 1978-86; of counsel Vargas & Bartlett, Reno and Las Vegas, Nev.; bd. dirs. Showboat Hotels and Casinos, Las Vegas and Atlantic City. Home: Reno Nev. Deceased.

DOCKING, ROBERT BLACKWELL, former governor, banker; b. Kansas City, Mo., Oct. 9, 1925; s. George and Mary Virginia (Blackwell) D.; m. Meredith Martha Gear, 1950; children: William Russell, Thomas Robert. BS with honors, U. Kans., 1948; grad., U. Wis.; LLD, Washburn U. With Union State Bank, Arkansas City, Kans., 1956-59, pres., 1959—; mayor City of Arkansas, 1963-66; gov. State of Kans., 1967-75; prin. Docking Ins. Agy., Arkansas City, Docking Devel. Co., Oxford, Kans.; chmn. Kans. Venture Capital, Inc.; pres. City Nat. Bank & Trust Co., Guymon, Okla.; asst. treas., dir. Kans. Pub. Svc. Co.; pres., dir. Union State Bank, Arkansas City; dir. 4th Nat. Bank & Trust Co., Wichita, Kans., 1st Kans. Life Ins. Co., Newton, Cimmarron (Kans.) Investment Co., Inc., Cimmarron Ins. Co., Inc., Cimmarron Life Ins. Co., Plains Ins. Co., Cimmarron Fin. Co.; former chmn. Interstate Oil Compact Commn.; chmn. Midwest Gov.'s Conf., 1971-73; mem. Kans. Bank Mgmt. Commn. Mem. City Commn. Arkansas City, Winfield, 1963-66; past pres. Community Chest; pres. United Fund; chpt. chmn. ARC, 1961; chmn. Kans. Cancer Crusade, 1975, Douglas County Dem. Com., 1954-56; v.p. Kans. Dem. Vets., 1957; trustee Wesley Hosp. Found., U. Kans. Endowment Assn., Menninger Found., Midwest Rsch. Inst. 1st lt. USAAF, 1943-46. Recipient Disting. Svc. citation U. Kans., Ellsworth medallion, 1981, Disting. Kansan award, 1981. Mem. Arkansas City C. of C. (pres.), Am. Legion (comdr. Arkansas City chpt.), Cowley County Bankers Assn., Am. Bankers Assn., Ind. Oil and Gas Assn., Kans. Livestock Assn., Internat. Platform Assn., Am. G.I. Forum, Am. Assn. for UN, U. Kans. Alumni Assn. (pres.), Am. Assn. Criminology, Masons (32 degree, Shriner), Elks, Eagles, Rotary, Beta Theta Pi, Beta Gamma Sigma, Delta Sigma Pi.

DOE, SAMUEL K., former head of state of Liberia; b. Tuzon, Liberia, May 6, 1952; ed. Marcus Garvey Meml. High Sch.; m. Nancy Doe; 2 children. With Liberian Army, from 1973, acting 1st sgt., Monrovia, 1973-75, adj. 3d Bn., 1975-79; overthrew Pres. William Tobert in coup d'etat, 1980; head of state, chmn. People's Redemption Council, 1980-90. Died Sept. 10, 1990. Home: Monrovia Liberia

DOHENY, DONALD ALOYSIUS, SR., lawyer, business executive; b. Milw., Apr. 20, 1924; s. John Anthony and Adelaide (Koller) D.; m. Catherine Elizabeth Lee, Oct. 25, 1952; children: Donald Aloysius, Celeste Hazel Doheny Kennedy, John Vincent, Ellen Adelaide Doheny Cornwell, Edward Lawrence II, William Francis, Madonna Lee. Student U. Notre Dame, 1942-43; BME, Marquette U., 1947; JD, Harvard, 1949; M in Indsl. Engring. Washington U., St. Louis, 1956. Bar: Wis. 1949, Mo. 1949, U.S. Supreme Ct. 1970, U.S. Tax Ct., U.S. Ct. Mil. Appeals, U.S. Ct. Appeals (D.C. cir.), U.S. Dist. Ct. (ea. dist.) Wis., U.S. Ct. Appeals (fed. cir.); registered prof. engr., Mo. Asst. to civil engr. Shipbuilding div. Froemming Bros., Inc., Milw., 1942-43; draftsman, designer The Heil Co., Milw., 1944-46; assoc. Igoe, Carroll & Keefe, St. Louis, 1949-51; asst. to v.p. and gen. mgr., chief prodn. engr., gen. adminstr., dir. adminstrn. Granco Steel Products subsidiary Granite City Steel, Granite City, Ill., 1951-57; asst. to pres. Vestal Labs., Inc., St. Louis, 1957-63; exec. v.p., dir. Moehlenpah Engring., Inc., Hydro-Air Engring., Inc., 1963-67; pres. dir. Foamtex Industries, Inc., St. Louis, 1967-75; exec. v.p., dir. Seasonal Industries, Inc., N.Y.C., 1973-75; sole practice, St. Louis, 1967-81; ptnr., Doheny & Doheny, Attys., St. Louis, 1981—, Doheny & Assocs. Mgmt. Counsel, St. Louis, 1967—; pres., dir. Mktg. & Sales Counsel, Inc., St. Louis, 1975—; pres., dir. Mid-USA Sales Co., St. Louis, 1976—; pres., bd. dirs. Profl. Bus. Exchange, Inc., St Louis, 1988—, Prestige Offices and Properties, Inc., St. Louis, 1987—; dir. St. Louis Airport Area Devel. Corp., 1988—; sec., bd. dirs. St. Louis Airport Area Devel. Corp., St. Louis, 1988—; lectr. bus. orgn. and adminstrn. Washington U., 1950-74; lectr. Grad. Sch. Bus., St. Louis U., 1980—. Contbr. articles to profl. jours. Police and Fire Commn. mem. Frontenac Mo., 1989-92. Served with AUS, 1943-44; 1st lt. res., 1948-52. Mem. ABA, Am. Judicature Soc., Am. Marketing Assn. (nat. membership chmn. 1959), Mo. Bar Assn., Wis. Bar Assn., Fed. Bar Assn., Bar Assn. St. Louis (gen. chmn. pub. relations 1955-56, vice chmn., sec.-treas. jr. sect. 1950, 51), Marquette Engring. Assn. (pres. 1946-47), Engring. Knights, Am. Legion, Tau Beta Pi, Pi Tau Sigma. Clubs: Notre Dame (pres. 1955, 56), Marquette (pres. 1961), Harvard (St. Louis); Stadium, Engineers, Mo. Athletic. Died June 26, 1995. Home: Saint Louis Mo.

DOHERTY, JAMES MARTIN, advertising consultant; b. Sharon, N.D., June 23, 1916; s. David James and Anne (Westlund) D.; m. Virginia Mae Deitch, June 20, 1956 (div. 1961); m. Rosella Marie Rauh, Feb. 2, 1963; children: Shawn, Dennis, Randall. Student, Buena Vista Coll., Storm Lake, Iowa, 1938-40. Underwriter Nationwide Ins. Co., Columbus, Ohio, 1948-51, dir. advt. and promotion, 1952-72, v.p. advt. and promotion, 1973-81; advt. cons. Columbus, 1982-95. Served with U.S. Mcht. Marine, 1943-45. Recipient best of show awards Life Ins. Advertisers Am., 1976, 77, 78. Mem. Sales Promotion Execs., Advt. Fedn. Am., Columbus Advt. Fedn. Democrat. Roman Catholic. Club: Brookside Country (Columbus) (dir. 1960-63). Home: Columbus Ohio Died June 8, 1995.

DOI, HERMAN SATOSHI, ombudsman, lawyer; b. Kealia, Hawaii, Nov. 6, 1926; s. Daijiro and Takao (Tateishi) D.; m. Helen Teruko Hirose, June 9, 1951; children—Bryan Cary, Sheryl Lynne. B.A., U. Hawaii, 1950; J.D., U. Minn., 1954. Bar: Hawaii 1955. Ptnr. law firm, Honolulu, 1955-63; chief clk. judiciary com. Ho. of Reps., Honolulu, 1959; spl. dep. atty. gen. State of Hawaii, 1959-60; chief clk., legal counsel fin. com. Ho. of Reps., Honolulu, 1959-62; researcher Legis. Reference Bur. State of Hawaii, Honolulu, 1963-65, acting dir., 1965, dir., 1966-69; ombudsman State of Hawaii, Honolulu, 1969-84; mem. Commn. Govt. Orgn., Honolulu, 1975-77; mem. Citizens' Adv. Com. Basic Skills and Real-Life Skills, Honolulu, 1977-78. Contbr. articles to profl. jours. Mem. Internat. Bar Assn. (Ombudsman Adv. Bd.), Hawaii Bar Assn., Am. Soc. Pub. Adminstrn. (bd. dirs. Honolulu chpt. 1971-73, Hawaii Pub. Adminstrn. award, 1969). Home: Honolulu Hawaii

DOISNEAU, ROBERT SYLVAIN, photographer; b. Gentilly, France, Apr. 14, 1912; s. Gaston and Sylvie (Duval) D.; m. Pierrette Reine Chaumaison, 1932; children: Annette, Francine. Ed., Ecole Estienne, Paris, 1925-29. Free-lance photographer Agence Rapho, Paris, 1946-94. One-man shows include La Fontaine des Quatre Saisons, Paris, 1951, Limelight Gallery, N.Y., 1959, Art Inst. Chgo., 1960, Bibliothèque Nationale, Paris, 1968, Internat. Mus. Photography, Rochester, N.Y., 1972, Witkin Gallery, N.Y., 1974, 78, La Galerie et Fils, Brussels, 1975, Photo Art, Basle, 1976, Galerie Agathe Gaillard, Paris, 1978, Musee d'Art Moderne, Paris, 1979, Gallery for Fine Photography, New Orleans, 1981, Datar, 1985, Un Ceraui R.D., Rome, 1986, 88; represented in permanent collections Musée d'Art Moderne, Paris, Bibliothèque Nationale, Paris, Musée Nicéphore Niepce, Chalon-Sur-Saône, France, Victoria and Albert Mus., London, Mus. Modern Art, N.Y.C., Internat. Mus. Photography, Rochester, N.Y., New Orleans Mus. Art, Center for Creative Photography, U. Ariz., Tucson; author 27 books, including 3 Seconds from Eternity, 1981, Doisuar, 1983.

Decorated chevalier Légion d'Honneur, 1992. Home: Montrouge France Died Apr. 1, 1994.

DOLINAY, THOMAS V., bishop; b. Uniontown, Pa., July 24, 1923. Student, St. Procopius Coll., Ill. Ordained priest Roman Catholic Ch., 1948. Ordained titular bishop Tiatira and aux. bishop Byzantine rite Diocese of Passaic, 1976-81; aux. bishop Byzantine rite Diocese of Van Nuys Calif., 1981; installed, 1982—. Editor: Eastern Cath. Life, 1966-82. Home: Pittsburgh Pa. Deceased.

DONCHIAN, RICHARD DAVOUD, investment firm executive; b. Hartford, Conn., Sept. 21, 1905; s. Samuel B. and Armenouhi A. (Davoud) D.; m. Alma C. Gibbs, Feb. 9, 1957. A.B., Yale U., 1928. Chartered fin. analyst U. Va. and Inst. Chartered Fin. Analysts, 1964. Market technician Hemphill Noyes & Co., N.Y.C., 1933-35; v.p. Samuel Donchian Rug Co., Hartford, Conn., 1933-38; pres. Fin. Supervision, Inc., N.Y.C., 1938-42; econ. analyst, market letter writer Shearson Hammill & Co., N.Y.C., 1946-48; pvt. investment adviser N.Y.C., 1948-60; pres. Futures, Inc., N.Y.C., 1948-60; account exec., dir. commodity rsch., v.p. Shearson, Lehman, Hutton, Inc.; Am. Express Co., 1960-93; sr. v.p. fin. cons. Hayden Stone, Inc. (named changed to Shearson, Lehman, Hutton, Inc.), Greenwich, Conn., 1971-93. Author articles and monographs. Served as statis. control officer with USAAF, 1942-45. Mem. Commodity Exchange, Inc., N.Y. Cotton Exchange, N.Y. Futures Exchange, N.Y. Soc. Securities Analysts, Am. Statis. Assn., Nat. Assn. Futures Trading Advs., Managed and Futures Trade Assn., Wall Street Forum, Fin. Forum, Rug Soc., Yale Club (N.Y.C. and Ft. Lauderdale), Scarsdale Golf Club, Deerfield Country Club (Fla.), Appalachian Mountain Club. Republican. Presbyterian (elder, trustee). Home: Pompano Beach Fla. Died Apr. 24, 1993.

DONEGAN, THOMAS JAMES, retired federal administrative law judge; b. Bklyn., Feb. 27, 1907; s. Thomas James and Mary F. (Carey) D.; m. Dorothy N. Reynolds, May 2, 1936; 1 child, Thomas James Jr.; m. Darlene D. Looney, Aug. 23, 1986. AB, Columbia U., 1928; LLB, Fordham U., 1931. Bar: N.Y. 1932, U.S. Supreme Ct., U.S. Dist. Ct. (so. and ea. dists.) N.Y. Pvt. practice N.Y.C., 1932-33, 46-57; with FBI, 1933-46, spl. agent in charge, 1942-46; spl. asst. atty. gen. U.S., 1947-57; chmn. interdeptl. com. internal security Nat. Security Council, 1953-54; chmn. personnel security adv. com. Exec. Office Pres., 1954-57; mem. U.S. Subversive Activities Control Bd., 1957-67; exec. dir. Indian Claims Commn., Washington, 1968-70; fed. adminstrv. law judge, 1972-77, ret., 1977. Lt. USNR, 1937-40. Mem. ABA. Home: Bainsbridge Island Wash. Died Mar. 1993; interred Bainbridge Island, Wash.

DONNELLY, CHARLES LAWTHERS, JR., retired air force officer; b. Barberton, Ohio, Aug. 24, 1929; s. Charles Lucius and Flora (Riley) D.; m. Carolyn Marie Vandersall, Mar. 30, 1952; 1 dau., Linda Marie. B.A., Otterbein Coll., 1950; grad., Air Command and Staff Coll., 1964, Royal Coll. Def. Studies, London, 1971; M.P.A., George Washington U., 1964; LLD (hon.), Otterbein Coll., 1987. Served as aviation cadet USAF, 1951-52, commd. 2d lt., 1952, advanced through grades to gen., 1984; fighter interceptor pilot Selfridge AFB, Mich. and Wheelus Air Base, Libya, 1952-56; jet instr., asst. ops. officer for USAF Acad. Ops. Squadron, 1956-60; a.d.c. to comdr. (Air Tng. Command), 1960-63; instr. Squadron Officer Sch., Maxwell AFB, Ala., 1964-66; F-4 tng. George AFB, Calif., 1966; combat pilot S.E. Asia, 1966-67; served in various staff positions Hdqrs. USAF, Washington, 1967-70; vice comdr., comdr. 401st Tactical Fighter Wing, Torrejon Air Base, Spain, 1972-75; dep. dir. plans Hdqrs. USAF, Washington, 1975-77; comdr. Sheppard Tech. Tng. Ctr., Sheppard AFB, Tex., 1978-79; chief U.S. Mil. Tng. Mission, Saudi Arabia, 1979-81; comdr. U.S. Force in Japan and 5th Air Force, Yokota Air Base, 1981-84; comdr.-in-chief U.S. Air Force in Europe; comdr. Allied Air Forces, Cen. Europe, Ramstein Air Base, Fed. Republic Germany, 1984-87; ret. USAF, 1987. Decorated D.S.M., D.S.M. with oak leaf cluster, Legion of Merit with 2 oak leaf clusters, D.F.C., Air medal with 12 oak leaf clusters, Air Force Commendation medal with one oak leaf cluster; King Abdulaziz Badge 2d grade (Saudi Arabia); Order of Nat. Security Merit Gugseon medal (Republic of Korea); 1st Class Order of Sacred Treasure (Japan); knight Comdrs. Cross of Order of Merit (Fed. Republic Germany); officer Legion de Honour (France). Mem. Air Force Assn., Order Daedalians, Eta Phi Mu. Episcopalian. Home: Arlington Va. Died July 3, 1994.

DONOVAN, ALLEN FRANCIS, aerospace company executive; b. Onondaga, N.Y., Apr. 22, 1914; s. Paul Andrew and May (Hudson) D.; m. Beverly Fay, Aug. 14, 1940 (div.); 1 son, Allen Michael; m. Doris Mildred Efram, Apr. 17, 1953 (div.); children: Kathryn Ellen, Marshall Stephen; m. June Wallace Healy, Aug. 30, 1974. BS in Aero. Engring., U. Mich., 1936, MS, 1936, ScD (hon.), 1964. Structures engr. Curtiss Airplane Div. Curtiss-Wright Corp., Buffalo, 1936-38, asst. to chief design engr. Curtiss Airplane Div., 1941-42, asst. head structures dept. Curtiss-Wright Rsch. Lab., 1942-44; head structures dept. Curtiss-Wright Corp., Buffal0, 1944-46; sr. structures engr. Glenn L. Martin Co., Balt., 1939; asst. chief of structures Stinson Aircraft Co., Wayne, Mich., 1939-40; chief structures engr. Vultee Aircraft, Nashville, 1940-41; head aeromechanics dept. Cornell U. Aero. Lab. (former Curtiss-Wright Rsch. Lab.), Buffalo, 1946-55; dir. aero. rsch. and devel. staff/ Guided Missiles Rsch. Div. Ramo-Woolridge Corp., Inglewood, Calif., 1955-58; v.p. Space Tech. Labs, Inc. (formerly guided Missiles Rsch. Divsn. Ramo-Woolridge Corp.), Inglewood, Calif., 1958-60; founding sr. v.p. tech. The Aerospace Corp., El Segundo, Calif., 1960-78, trustee, 1961-63; exec. cons., 1978-95; cons. Pres.'s Sci. Adv. Com., 1957-72; mem. Air Force Sci. Adv. Bd., 1948-57, 59-68, chmn. propulsion panel, 1959-60, 63-68; U.S. del. Geneva Conf. on suspension of nuclear testing, 1959; mem. space systems com. NASA, 1972-77; cons. Sci. and Tech. Policy Office, NSF, 1973-76. Editor vols. on high speed aerodynamics, jet propulsion.; Author tech. papers on space vehicles, aeronautics. Recipient Medal for exceptional civilian services U.S. Air Force, 1968; recipient Sci. award Air Force Assn., 1961. Fellow AIAA (hon.); mem. NAE, AAAS, Calif. Yacht Club, Sigma Xi. Club: Calif. Yacht. Home: Corona Del Mar Calif. Died Mar. 11, 1995.

DONOVAN, JOHN ANTHONY, bishop; b. Chatham, Ont., Can., Aug. 5, 1911; s. John J. and Mary C. (O'Rourke) D. B.A., Sacred Heart Sem., 1932; post-grad., N.A. Coll., Rome, 1936; J.C.L., Pontifical Athenaeum of Lateran, Rome, 1947; LL.D., U. Detroit, 1952. Ordained priest Roman Cath. Ch., 1935, domestic prelate, 1949; pastor St. Aloysius' Ch., Detroit, also chancellor Archdiocese of Detroit, 1951-58, St. Veronica's Ch., East Detroit, 1958-67; Titular Bishop of Rhasus and Aux. Bishop of Detroit, 1954-67; vicar gen. Archdiocese of Detroit, 1959-67; bishop of Toledo, 1967-81. Home: Toledo Ohio Died Sept. 18, 1991.

DOOLIN, JOHN B., state supreme court justice; b. Alva, Okla., May 25, 1918; s. John B. and Leo M. (Museller) D.; m. Marilyn B. Bruck, Oct. 3, 1981; children from previous marriage: John William, Mary L. Doolin Trembley, Katherine, Carole and Colleen (twins), Martha. BS in Bus. Adminstrn, Okla. U., 1941, LLB, 1947. Bar: Okla. 1942. Pvt. practice law Alva, 1947-63, Lawton, 1963-73; justice Okla. Supreme Ct., 1973-93, vice chief justice; mem. Okla. Hwy. Commn., 1959-63. Trustee Comanche County (Okla.) Meml. Hosp., 1967-73, chmn., 1968-73. Served to capt. AUS, 1941-45. Mem. Phi Delta Phi. Home: Edmond Okla. Deceased.

DOOLITTLE, JAMES HAROLD (JIMMY DOOLITTLE), retired military officer, aviator, insurance company executive; b. Alameda, Calif., Dec. 14, 1896; s. Frank H. and Rosa C. (Shephard) D.; m. Josephine E. Daniels, Dec. 24, 1917; children: James H., John P. AB, U. Calif., 1918 (1922); MS, MIT, 1924, ScD, 1925. Aviator U.S. Army, 1917-30, resigned, 1930; maj. Res. Corps; teaching fellow aero. engring. MIT, 1925; mgr. aviation dept. Shell Petroleum Corp., 1930-40; apptd. mem. Army AC Investigating Com. (Baker Bd.), 1934; apptd. maj. USAAF, 1940, advanced through grades lt. col. to maj. gen., 1942, lt. gen., 1944; comdr. 12th Air Force USAAF, North Africa; comdr. Strategic Air Force, 15th and 8th Air Forces; comdr. 8th Air Force Okinawa, 1945; inactive duty, 1946-58, ret., 1959, gen. Res., 1985; v.p. Shell Oil Co., 1946-58, dir., 1946-67; chmn. bd. Space Tech. Labs., 1959-62; cons. TRW Systems, 1961-66, dir. parent co., 1961-69; dir. Mut. of Omaho Ins. Co. (and affiliates); trustee Aerospace Corp., 1963-69, vice chmn. bd. trustees, chmn. exec. com., 1965-69; Pres. Air Force Assn., 1946-47, chmn., 1948-49; apptd. chmn. Sec. War's Bd. on Enlisted Men-Officer Relationships; mem. NACA, 1948-56, chmn., 1956-58; adviser to Com. on Nat. Security Orgn. and Joint Congl. Aviation Policy Bd.; mem. adv. bd. Nat. Air Mus., Smithsonian Inst., 1956-65; chmn. Pres.'s Airport Commn., 1952, Pres.'s Task Group on Air Inspection, Stassen Disarmament Com., 1955, Pres.'s Bd. on Fgn. Intelligence, 1955-65, Air Force Sci. Adv. Bd., 1955-58; mem. Def. Sci. Bd., 1957-58, Pres.'s Sci. Adv. Com., 1957-58, Nat. Aeros. and Space Council, 1958. Contbr. sci., aero. articles to profl. jours. Decorated Congl. Medal of Honor, D.S.M. with oak leaf cluster, Silver Star, D.F.C. with two oak leaf clusters, Bronze Star, Air medal with three oak leaf clusters; Bolivian Order of Condor medal; Yon-Hwei Class III; grande officier French Legion d'Honneur, Croix de Guerre with palm; knight comdr. Order of the Bath; grande officer Order of Crown with Palm and Croix de Guerre with palm both Belgium, 1948; recipient Harmon Internat. Aviation award; winner Schneider Trophy Race, 1925; awarded Mackay trophy, 1926; Harmon trophy, 1930; winner Bendix Trophy Race, Burbank, Calif. to Cleve., 1931, Thompson Trophy Race, 258.68 miles per hr., 1932; Disting. Honoree NAE, 1992. Hon. fellow AIAA (pres. 1940, hon.), Royal Aero. Soc.; mem. Nat. Aero. Assn. Clubs: Explorers, Boone and Crockett, Bohemian, Wings, Lotos. Home: Carmel Calif. Died Sept. 27, 1993.

DOOLITTLE, JIMMY **See DOOLITTLE, JAMES HAROLD**

DORF, PHILIP, public relations executive; b. N.Y.C.; s. Max and Minnie (Siegelbaum) D.; m. Nathalie S. Bernstein, Mar. 30, 1947; children: Robert L., Lewis R., Margaret Sue. BA, NYU, 1942. Reporter, writer, editor United Press Assn., N.Y.C., 1946-56; accour exec. pub. rels. dept. N.W. Ayer & Son, Inc., N.Y.C 1956-58; account supr. Tex. McCrary, Inc., N.Y.C 1958-60; v.p. Rowland Co., Inc., 1960-63, sr. v.p., 196 70; v.p. Harshe-Rotman & Druck, Inc. (pub. rels. firm N.Y.C., 1970-71; sr. v.p. Harshe-Rotman & Druck, In (pub. rels. firm), 1971-73, exec. v.p., 1973-79, pres. ea tern region, 1979-80; exec. v.p. Robert Marston & A sos., Inc., N.Y.C., 1980-88; pres. Robert Marston Cor Communications, Inc., N.Y.C., 1989-91, vice chmr 1991-93. Capt. AUS, 1942-46. Decorated Silver Sta Bronze Star, Purple Heart. Mem. Pub. Rels. Soc. Am Nat. Investor Rels. Inst., Overseas Press Club Am Home: New York N.Y. Died May 30, 1993.

DOSLAND, WILLIAM BUEHLER, lawyer; b. Chgo Nov. 10, 1927; s. Goodwin Leroy and Beatrice Floren (Buehler) D.; m. Donna Mae Mathisen, Sept. 15, 195 children: David William, Susan Elizabeth. BA, Co cordia Coll., 1949; JD, U. Minn., 1954. Bar: Min 1954, U.S. Ct. Appeals (8th cir.) 1978. Ptnr. Dosland Dosland, 1954-68; sr. ptnr. Dosland, Dosland Nordhaugen, 1968-89; sr. ptnr. Dorland, Dorland Nordhougen, 1989-91, of counsel, 1990-91; of couns Dosland, Nordhougen, Lillihaug & Johnson P.A Moorhead, Minn., 1957-89; gen. counsel, corp. sec. A Crystal Sugar Co., 1973-89; gen. counsel, sec. No. Gra Co., 1975-84; gen. counsel Am. Bank & Trust, 1969-8 bd. dirs., 1969-83; regent U. Minn., 1979-85. Me Minn. State Senate, 1959-73. Capt. USNR, 1945-46, 5 53. Recipient Alumni Achievement award, Concorc Coll., 1979. Mem. Minn. State Bar Assn., Clay Coun Bar Assn., Lions, Masons. Republican. Lutheran Lodges: Masons, Lions. Home: Fargo N.D. Died A 6, 1993.

DOTY, GORDON LEROY, hematologist-oncologist; Belding, Mich., Apr. 3, 1931; s. George Henry a Frances Louie (Witt) D.; m. Joanne Ranell, June 1953 (div. 1982); m. Nancy Joyce Moorman, Nov. 1983. BS, Mich. State U., 1952; MD, Wayne State 1956. Diplomate Am. Bd. Internal Medicine. Rotati intern Detroit Receiving Hosp., 1956-57, asst. reside then chief resident internal medicine, 1961-64; USP trainee in hematology Tufts U., Boston, 1964-65; rsc fellow hematology Boston City Hosp., 1964-65; p practice Suburban Med. Clinnic, Portland, Oreg., 196 67, Hematology Clinic, Portland, 1967-92; clin. ins medicine U. Oreg. Health Scis. U., 1967-72, clin. as prof., 1972-93; attending physician hematolog oncology, Portland VA Hosp., 1967-93; cons. P vidence Med. Ctr., 1965-93, med. dir. cancer progra 1985-93, chmn. cancer com., 1985-92; clin. pr medicine Oreg. Health Scis. U., 1987-93; prin. inves gator Columbia River CCOP, 1987-93. Capt. MC, U Army, 1957-61. Mem. ACP, Am. Soc. Inter Medicine, Am. Soc. Hematology, Am. Soc. Cl Oncology, Oreg. Med. Assn., Oreg. Soc. Clin. Oncolo Multnomah County Med. Soc., Am. Alpine C (chmn. Oreg. sect. 1980), Mazamas (climbing lea 1971-80), Phi Kappa Phi, Alpha Omega Alpha. Hor Portland Oreg. Died Sept. 3, 1993.

DOUGLAS, LEE WAYLAND, association executive; Spokane, Wash., Dec. 9, 1931; s. Theodore Wayla and Lee Paynter (Bohan) D.; m. Patricia Murphy; child, Elizabeth Lee Douglas Bell; m. Simone C lier. AB, Harvard U., 1953. U.S. govt. messenger H & Mouth Disease Commn., Mexico City, 1948-49; g mgr. Cromo y Terminados, S.A., Mexico City, 1956- exec. v.p. Chem. Linings de Mexico, Mexico City, 19 59; gen. mgr. The Dorsey Co., Mathews, La., 1972- sys./program analyst U.S. Dept. Energy, Washingt 1973-82; recorder gen. Naval Order of the U.S., Wa ington, 1983-95. Author: The Log of Naval Rese Association, 1984, revised, 1995. Past nat. histor Naval Res. Assn., 1979-93. Lt. comdr. USN, 1953- 60-71, Korea, Vietnam. Recipient Nat. award of me Naval Res. Assn., 1976, 79. Mem. Harvard Club S Diego. Democrat. Episcopal. Home: San Diego Ca Died July 14, 1995.

DOW, HERBERT HENRY, II, foundation executi b. Midland, Mich., Aug. 6, 1927; s. Willard Henry a Martha (Pratt) D.; m. Barbara Clarke, Sept. 16, 19 children: Dana Dow Schuler, Willard Henry II, Pam G. B.S., MIT, 1952; LL.D., Central Mich. U., 19 H.H.D. (hon.), Saginaw Valley State Coll., 1975; D.P (hon.), Service Albion Coll., 1977. Mem. staff Midla div. Dow Chem. Co., 1952-54, mgr. fabric produ 1954-64, sec. exec. com., 1964-87, corp. sec., 1968- v.p., 1986-92; trustee The Herbert H. and Grace Dow Found., Midland, Mich., 1949-96, pres., 1970-9 Home: Midland Mich. Died Jan. 26, 1996.

DOZIER, THOMAS AUGUSTUS, editor, writer; Athens, Ga., Jan. 3, 1915; s. Olin Arnold and Mild (Carson) D.; m. Florence Elizabeth Peyton, Oct. 1936; children: Michele, David Thomas, Peter M quis. BA in Journalism, U. Ga., 1935. Asst. night editor Atlanta Constn., Atlanta, 1935-36; telegr editor Nashville Banner, 1936-37; corr. United Press ternat., Atlanta, 1937-38, Washington, 1938-41; c press div. Nelson Rockefeller Office, Washington, 19 44; corr. Time-Life, N.Y., London, Paris, Ro Madrid, 1947-89; intelligence analyst Office of D Chief of Staff, Washington, 1944. Author: Danger Sea Creatures, 1975, Whales and Other Sea Mamm

)75, Creatures of the Coral Reef, 1976; editor The Asia ſag., 1971-73; contbr. articles to mags. (Jose Marti ·ize, 1959). Sec. Lowndes County Dem. Exec. Com., aldosta, Ga., 1976-80. Served with M.I. Corps, 1944-5. Democrat. Roman Catholic. Clubs: Biftad (sec.)33-35), Savile (London), The Overseas Press (N.Y.C.). Iome: Valdosta Ga. Died 1989.

RAKE, (BRYANT) STILLMAN, history educator; b. ɛrkeley, Calif., Dec. 24, 1910; s. Bryant Stillman and ora Ornis (Frickstad) D.; m. Eda Doreen Salzmann, ov. 14, 1936; children: Mark Ernest, Daniel Lee; m. ucille Daneri Jarrell, Feb. 22, 1950; m. Florence Selvin asaroli, Apr. 1, 1967. AB, U. Calif., Berkeley, 1932; LD, U. Calif., 1968; LLD (hon.), U. Toronto, 1979; ɔn. degree, Universita di Padova. Vice pres. Calif. ſunicipal Statistics, San Francisco, 1934-41; finance ɒns. U.S. Def. Pub. Work, Los Angeles, 1941-42; re-onal statistician WPB, San Francisco, 1943-44; ac-ɒuntant Navy Price Adjustment Bd., San Francisco,)44-45; municipal statistician Heller Bruce & Co., San ·ancisco, 1946-56; asst. v.p. govt. devel. Bank of P.R., ın Juan, 1956-58; cons. municipal financing Blyth & ɔ., San Francisco, 1958-67; prof. history of sci. U. ɔronto, Ont., Can., 1967-78; prof. emeritus U. ɔronto, 1979-93. Author: Discoveries and Opinions of alileo, 1957, Galileo Studies, 1970, Galileo Against the ɪilosophers, 1976, Galileo At Work, 1978, Galileo,)80, Cause, Experiment, and Science, 1981, Telescopes, des, and Tactics, 1983, History of Free Fall, 1989, alileo: Pioneer Scientist, 1990; translator: Dialogue,)53, Mechanics, 1960, Assayer, 1960, Two New ɪiences, 1974, Geometric and Military Compass, 1978, I. edit., 1989. Recipient Premio Galileo Galilei, Italy,)84, George Sarton medal, 1988; John Simon Gug-ɒnheim Meml. Found. fellow, 1971-72, 76-77. Fellow ɒm. Acad. Arts and Scis., Royal Soc. Can.; mem. In-ɒrnat. Acad. History of Sci. Home: Toronto Can. Died ɔt. 6, 1993.

RAPER, EARLE SUMNER, planning and housing ɒnsultant; b. Falmouth, Mass., Oct. 19, 1893; s. ·ederic Ward and Bertha (Sumner) D.; m. Norma ɒrwell, May 26, 1917; children: Frederic Farwell, Earle ɒmner, Norman Clafin (dec.), Charles Alfred, Norma ɛc. 1934); m. Elizabeth Jordan (dec.). B.S., Mass. ate Coll., 1915; D.Landscape Architecture (hon.), U. ass., 1950. Landscape architect Cambridge, Mass.,)15; Charlotte, N.C., 1917; planning and housing ɒns.; vis. prof. Lowthorpe Sch. Landscape Architec-re, 1931-32, Harvard U. Sch. Landscape Architecture,)32; dir. land planning and housing TVA, 1933-37, dir. pt. regional planning studies, 1937-40; asst. adminstr. ɛd. Housing Adminstrn., 1940-41, dep. commr., 1942-; housing and planning cons., 1945-94; cons. Nat. ɛsources Com. and Md. Planning Bd., 1936-37, Ga. d Ala. planning bds., 1937; acting regional counselor r S.E., Nat. Resources Planning Bd., 1937-40; lectr. ɪn. works include estates and towns throughout so. S. Fellow Am. Soc. Landscape Architects (past v.p., I. dirs.); mem. Am. Inst. Planners (pres. 1940-42), Am. ɛc. Planning Ofcls. (past bd. dirs.), Phi Kappa Phi, lpha Sigma Phi. Clubs: Cosmos (Washington); Vero ɛach Country (Fla.). Lodge: Masons. Home: Vero ɛach Fla. Died July 1, 1994.

REIFUSS, ARTHUR, film director, writer; b. ·ankfurt, Germany, Mar. 25, 1908. Ed., U. Frankfurt ı Main, 1924, Conservatory of Music, 1920-26; ɪdent, Columbia U., 1928-29. Assoc. video editor ·eative Editing, Inc., 1979-80; dir. lit. dept. George ɪchaud Agy., 1981-86. Dir. numerous films including ɔuble Deal, 1939, Mystery in Swing, 1940, Murder on ɛnox Avenue, 1941, Baby Face Morgan, 1942, Sarong ɪrl, 1943, The Sultan's Daughter, 1944, Eddie Was a ɪdy, 1945, Prison Ship, 1945, Junior Prom, 1946, ɛddie Steps Out, 1946, Vacation Days, 1947, Glamour ɪrl, 1948, Manhattan Angel, 1948, Shamrock Hill,)49, There's a Girl in My Heart, 1949, Secret File,)55, Assignment Abroad, 1956, Life Begins at 17, 58, The Last Blitzkrieg, 1959, Juke Box Rhythm, 59, The Quare Fellow, 1962, Riot on Sunset Strip, 67, The Love-Ins, 1967, For Singles Only, 1968, A ɪme to Sing, 1968, The Young Runaways, 1968; assoc. ɒoducer, dir. TV series Wildlife in Crisis, 1978, Viacom. ſlem. Dirs. Guild Am., Writers Guild Am. West. ɔme: Burbank Calif.

REIZEN, SAMUEL, oncologist; b. N.Y.C., Sept. 12, 18; s. Charles and Rose (Schneider) D.; m. Ellie Jo ılley, Aug. 3, 1956; 1 child, Pamela L. BA, Bklyn. ɔll., 1941; DDS, Western Reserve U., 1945; MD, ɔrthwestern U., 1958. Lic. MD Tex., Ill.; lic. DDS a., N.Y. Rsch. assoc. U. Cin. Med. Sch., ɪmingham, Ala., 1945-47; instr. Northwestern Med. h., Chgo., 1947-49, asst. prof., 1949-58, assoc. prof., 58-65; prof. U. Tex. Health & Sci. Ctr., Houston, 65-89, prof. emeritus, 1989-94; asst. dir. Nutrition inic Hillman Hosp., Brimingham, 1950-65. Contbr. ɪicles to profl. jours. Capt. U.S. Army, 1953-60. llow Am. Assn. Advanced Sci.; mem. Am. Assn. ɪysical Anthropology, Internat. Assn. Dental Rsch., ɛ. Rsch. Child Devel. Home: Houston Tex. Died ɔr. 26, 1994.

RENNAN, CHARLES N., lawyer; b. Gideon, Mo., ɔv. 19, 1946. AB, U. Mo., 1969, JD, 1971; LLM, YU, 1974. Bar: Mo. 1971, Alaska 1974. Law clk. to Hon. Lawrence Holman Mo. Supreme Ct., 1971-72; mem. Faulkner, Banfield, Doogan & Holmes P.C., Juneau, Alaska. Note and comment editor Mo. Law Rev., 1970-71. Mem. ABA, Alaska Bar Assn., Mo. Bar, Juneau Bar Assn., Order of Coif, Phi Delta Phi. Home: Juneau Alaska Died Aug. 6, 1994.

DRENNAN, G(EORGE) ELDON, utility company executive, consultant; b. Walla Walla, Wash., Mar. 22, 1921; s. George I. and Ella B. (Myrick) D.; m. Jane Nilsson, June 16, 1943 (dec. June 1976); children: Michael E., Barbara A. Student, Whitman Coll., 1938-39; B.S., Wash. State U., 1943; grad., Advanced Mgmt. Program, Harvard U., 1970. With Pacific Power & Light Co., Portland, Oreg., 1946-91; v.p. Pacific Power & Light Co., 1971-74, sr. v.p., 1974-76, exec. v.p., 1976-79, pres., 1979-82, vice chmn. bd., 1982-84, cons., 1984-91. Served to lt. USNR, 1943-46. Clubs: Arlington, Univ., Portland Golf, Elks. Home: Lake Oswego Oreg. Died Oct. 22, 1991; buried Riverview Cemetery, Portland, Oreg.

DREWSEN, EDMOND TITUS, JR., banker; b. Bklyn., Oct. 29, 1932; s. Edmond Titus and Dorothy W. (MacDonald) D.; B.A., Cornell U., 1954; M.B.A., Columbia, 1958; m. Eunice L. Hull, Aug. 22, 1955; children: Karla H., Edmond Titus. With U.S. Trust Co. of N.Y., N.Y.C., 1958-92, sr. v.p., 1976-92. Trustee, Gould Acad., Bethel, Maine, 1968-80. Served to 1st lt., Adj. Gen. Corps. U.S. Army, 1955-57. Mem. N.Y. Soc. Security Analysts, Fin. Analyst Fedn., Union League of N.Y., Belle Haven Club (Greenwich, Conn.), St. Andrews Soc., Brays Island Plantation Club, Quaker Hill Country Club (Pawling, N.Y.). Died Nov. 6, 1992. Home: Greenwich Conn.

DREYFUS, MARC GEORGE, physicist, optical engineer, educator; b. Bklyn., Mar. 5, 1926; s. Louis and Frances (Weintraub) D.; m. Ruth Schechtman, July 25, 1954 (div. Sept. 1977); children: Katherine Ann, David Harry; m. Joan King, Dec. 16, 1978. AB magna cum laude, Harvard U., 1947, SM, 1949; postgrad., MIT, 1947-50. Rsch. physicist Am. Optical Co., Southbridge, Mass., 1950-54; head optics sect. Librascope Inc., Glendale, Calif., 1954-59; mgr. spectroscopy sect. Barnes Engring. Co., Stamford, Conn., 1959-63; chief scientist North Am. Philips Corp., Briarcliff Manor, N.Y., 1964-67, BAI Corp., Stamford, 1967-75; pres. Dreyfus-Pellman Corp., Stamford, 1975-80; sr. scientist Am. Cystoscope Makers, Inc., Stamford, 1980-86; cons. in optics various, Fairfield, Conn., from 1986; prof., head optics dept. Norwalk (Conn.) State Tech. Coll., from 1987. Patentee in field; author tech. papers. With U.S. Army, 1944-45. Fellow Optical Soc. Am.; mem. SPIE, Phi Beta Kappa. Home: Fairfield Conn. Deceased.

DRIGGS, DOUGLAS HARMON, savings and loan association executive; b. Driggs, Idaho, Apr. 8, 1901; s. Don C. and May (Robison) D.; m. Effie Killian, Aug. 31, 1926; children: John Douglas, Lois, Gary Harmon, Anne. Sec. Western Savs. & Loan Assn., Phoenix, 1929-33; pres. Western Savs. & Loan Assn., 1933-65, chmn. bd., 1966-72, chmn. fin. com., from 1975; chmn. exec. com. Western Fin. Corp., Phoenix. Past pres., mem. adv. bd. Theodore Roosevelt council Boy Scouts Am.; Bd. dirs. Phoenix Symphony Assn., pres., 1971-73, vice chmn., 1974-75; mem. nat. adv. council Coll. Bus., Brigham Young U. Recipient Jessie Knight Indsl. Citizenship award Brigham Young U., 1977. Mem. Ch. of Jesus Christ of Latter-day Saints. Club: Rotarian (dist. gov. 1969-70). Home: Paradise Valley Ariz. Deceased.

DRUCKMAN, JACOB RAPHAEL, composer; b. Phila., June 26, 1928; s. Samuel and Miriam (Golder) D.; m. Muriel Helen Topaz, June 5, 1954; children: Karen, Daniel. B.S., Juilliard Sch. Music, 1954, M.S., 1956; student, Ecole Normale de Musique, Paris, 1954-55; studied composition with, Aaron Copland, Louis Gessensway, Peter Mennin, Vincent Persichetti, Bernard Wagenaar. Mem. faculty Juilliard Sch. Music, N.Y.C., 1956-72, Bard Coll., 1961-67; dir. Electronic Music Studio, Yale U. Sch. Music, 1971-72, Bklyn. Coll., 1972-76; prof. composition dept. Yale U. Sch. Music, 1976-96; assoc. Columbia-Princeton Electronic Music Center, 1966-96; composer-in-residence N.Y. Philharm., 1983-86 , artistic dir. Horizons Festivals '83, 84, 86. Composer music for: Joffrey City Ctr. Ballet Co.'s Animus, 1969, Valentine, 1971, Jackpot, 1973; composer: Animus I, 1966, Animus II, 1968, Animus III, 1969, String Quarter no. 2, 1966, Incenters, 1968, Windows (orch.), 1972, Lamia, 1974, Mirage, 1976, Chiaroscuro, 1977, Viola Concerto, 1978, Aureole, 1979, Prism, 1980, String Quartet no. 3, 1981, Tromba Marina, 1981, Vox Humana, 1983, Athanor, 1986, In Memorium Vincent Persichetti, 1987, That Quickening Pulse, 1988, Brangle, 1989, Nor Spell Nor Charm, 1990, Shog, 1990, Summer Lightning, 1991, Seraphic Games, 1992, ComeRound., 1992, Demos, 1992, With Bells On, 1993, Counterpoise, 1994, Duo, 1995, Glint, 1996; guest condr. N.Y. Philharm., L.A. Philharm., Buffalo Symphony, New Orleans Symphony, Akron Symphony, The B.B.C. Philharm., The Netherland Radio Orch. and the Krakow Radio and TV Orch. Bd. dirs. Koussevitzky Found., 1972-96, pres., 1980-96; pres. Aaron Copland Fund for Music, 1991-96; chmn. composer-librettist panel Nat. Endowment for Arts, 1980-82; bd. dirs. ASCAP, 1979-90; artistic dir. New Music New Haven, 1988-96. Recipient Soc. for Publ. Am. Music award, 1967; Am. Acad./Nat. Inst. Arts and Letters award, 1969; Pulitzer prize for Windows, 1972; citation in music Brandeis U. Creative Arts Commn., 1975; Fulbright grantee, 1954; Guggenheim grantee, 1957, 68; Juilliard String Quartet Commn. through LADO, 1966; Library of Congress, Koussevitzky Found. commn., 1969; Bicentennial NEA commn. St. Louis and Cleve. orchs., 1976; N.Y. Philharm. commn. for Viola Concerto, 1978; Aureole, 1979. Mem. Am. Acad. Arts and Letters. Home: Milford Conn. Died May 24, 1996.

DRUMMOND, DONALD FRANCIS, retired university dean; b. Kalamazoo, Sept. 24, 1917; s. Merle Vaughn and Phyllis (DeWindt) D.; m. Elizabeth Ruth Biddle, Aug. 30, 1944; 1 son, Robert Ward. A.B., Western Mich. U., 1938; A.M., U. Mich., 1939, Ph.D., 1949. Instr., asst. prof. history U. Mich., Ann Arbor, 1948-57; prof. Geneseo, 1957-58; head dept. history and social scis. Ea. Mich. U., Ypsilanti, 1958-65, dean Coll. Arts and Scis., 1965-77, 79-86, interim v.p. for acad. affairs, 1977-79, ret., 1986. Author: Passing of American Neutrality, 1937-41, 1955; co-author: Five Centuries in America, 1964. Served with U.S. Army, 1941-45. Mem. Phi Beta Kappa, Phi Kappa Phi. Republican. Club: Forum (pres. 1971-72). Home: Ann Arbor Mich. Died April 12, 1991.

DRYSDALE, DONALD SCOTT, sports broadcaster; b. Van Nuys, Calif., July 23, 1936; s. Scott Sumner and Verna Ruth (Ley) D.; 1 dau., Kelly Eugenia; m. Ann Elizabeth Meyers, Nov. 1, 1986; children: Donald Scott Jr., Darren John. Student pub. schs., Van Nuys. Profl. baseball player Bklyn. and Los Angeles Dodgers, 1954-69; sports broadcaster Montreal Expos, 1970-71, Tex. Rangers, 1972, Calif. Angels, 1973-82, Chgo. White Sox and Sportsvision, from 1982, ABC Sports, N.Y.C., 1978-86, L.A. Dodgers, 1988-93; dir. tng. camp Vero Beach, Fla. Served with U.S. Army, 1957-58. Recipient Cy Young award, 1962; named to Baseball Hall of Fame, 1984; mem. Nat. League All-Star Team, 9 times. Home: Los Gatos Calif. Died June 3, 1993.

D'SOUZA, ANTHONY FRANK, mechanical engineering educator, consultant, researcher; b. Bombay, India, May 9, 1929; came to U.S., 1958; s. Manuel Joseph and Laurentina (Ataide) D'S.; m. Cecilia Verdejo, Dec. 28, 1965; children: Geraldine, Raissa. B.E., U. Poona, India, 1954; M.S., U. Notre Dame, 1960; Ph.D., Purdue U., 1963. Jr. engr. Mahindra & Mahindra, Ltd., India, 1954-55; indsl. engr. Internat. Bus. Cons., India, 1955-57; trainee Ransome & Rapier, Ltd., Eng., 1957-58; teaching asst. U. Notre Dame, Ind., 1958-60; research asst. Purdue U., West Lafayette, Ind., 1960-63; from asst. prof. to prof. mech. and aerospace engring. Ill. Inst. Tech., Chgo., 1963-94; cons. Argonne Nat. Labs., 1973-94, Par Enterprise, Inc., Fairfax, Va., 1980-94, Small and Medium Corp., Republic of Korea, 1982-94. Author: Advanced Dynamics, 1984, Design of Control Systems, 1987; contbr. articles to profl. jours. Research grantee NSF, 1963, 70; research Dept. of Energy, 1978-94, U.S. Air Force Office Sci. Research, 1977-94, Assn. Am. R.R.s, 1980-82. Mem. ASME, Sigma Xi, Pi Tau Sigma. Roman Catholic. Home: Chicago Ill. Died Oct. 14, 1994.

DUANE, MORRIS, lawyer; b. Phila., Mar. 20, 1901; s. Russell and Mary Burnside Morris; m. Maud S. Harrison, June 11, 1927; children: Margaretta Sergeant, Russell. Student, Episcopal Acad., Phila., 1913-15, St. George's Sch., Newport, R.I., 1915-19; A.B., Harvard U., 1923; postgrad., U. Pa. Law Sch., 1923-25; LL.B., Stetson U., 1927, LL.D., 1965; LL.D., Bucknell U., 1967, LaSalle Coll., 1970, Drexel U., 1976; L.H.D., Women's Med. Coll. Pa., 1967; Litt.D., Beaver Coll., 1969. Former ptnr., chmn. law firm of Duane, Morris & Hechscher, Phila.; former Pa. legal counsel Del. River Port Authority; former dir. Girard Trust Bank, Penn. Mut. Life Ins. Co., Phila. Saving Fund Soc., The Phila. Contributionship; and other corps., Ednl. Facilities Labs., Inc. Author: New Deal in Court, 1934; Contbr. articles to legal and other periodicals. Vice chmn. Cardinal's Com. to Study Phila. Catholic Schs., 1972; mem. Com. on Tri State Regional Devel., Pa., N.J., Del.; bd. dirs., past co-chmn. Greater Phila. Movement; chmn. Phila. Adv. Council, 1974-77; bd. dirs. Univ. City Sci. Center, United Fund, 1955-69, Phila. Orch. Corp., 1976 Bicentennial Corp., 1967-71, Phila. Urban Coalition; former pres., trustee Presser Found.; pres. bd. trustees Episcopal Acad., 1948-51; bd. dirs. Hosp. Survey Com., Phila., 1960-72, chmn., 1960-64, 72; chmn. Christian R. and Mary F. Lindback Found., from 1955; mem. Harvard Fund Council, 1949-55. Served from lt. to comdr. USNR, 1943-45; head materials and resources group, bur. aeros. U.S. Navy, 1944-45; rep. naval aviation on War Prodn. Bd. requirements com., Army and Navy munitions bd. exec. com. 1944-45; mem. Naval Air Res. Adv. Council (chmn.) 1947. Awarded Commendation Ribbon, 1945. Mem. Am. Philos. Soc., Am. Lawn Tennis Assn. (chmn. inter-collegiate com. 1928-33), Am., Pa., Phila. bar assns., Juristic Soc., Com. of Seventy (1938-46), Salvation Army (past mem. exec. bd., Phila.), Delta Psi. Republican. Episcopalian. Clubs: Gulph Mills Golf, Legal, Harvard (Phila.); Fly (Cambridge); Sharswood Law (U. Pa.). Home: Newton Square Pa. Deceased.

DUANE, THOMAS DAVID, ophthalmologist, educator; b. Peoria, Ill., Oct. 10, 1917; s. Joseph Francis and Alexa (Fischer) D.; m. Julia McElhinney, Mar. 22, 1944; children: Alexa Duane Bresnan, Joseph McElhinney, Rachel Duane Lee, Andrew Thomas. B.S., Harvard U., 1939; M.D., Northwestern U., 1943, M.S., 1943; Ph.D., State U. Iowa, 1948. Diplomate Am. Bd. Ophthalmology, Am. Bd. Preventive Medicine. Intern Evanston (Ill.) Hosp., 1943-44; resident ophthalmology U. Iowa, 1944-47, instr. physiology, 1947-48; practice medicine, specializing in ophthalmology Bethlehem, Pa. and Phila., 1949-81; instr. physiology U. Pa., 1952-58, instr. ophthalmology, 1958-62; prof. Jefferson Med. Coll., 1962-89, chmn. ophthalmology, 1962-81, emeritus prof., 1989-93; ophthalmologist-in-chief Wills Eye Hosp., 1973-81, cons. surgeon, 1981-93; mem. Nat. Adv. Eye Council; cons. USN, 1958-74, NASA, 1966-74. Author: Ophthalmic Research, USA, 1965; editor textbook: Clinical Ophthalmology, 5 vols., 1976, Biological Foundations of Ophthalmology, 3 vols., 1982; contbr. articles to profl. publs. Served to lt. USNR, 1950-53. Fellow ACS; mem. AMA (chmn. ophthalmol. sect., Howe medal 1982), Am. Bd. OPhthalmology, Am. Acad. Ophthalmology (councillor, residency rev. com.), Assn. Rsch. Ophthalmology, Am. Ophthal. Soc. (Howe medal 1988), Assn. Univ. Profs. Ophthalmology. Home: Bedminster Pa. Died June 20, 1993.

DUARTE FUENTES, JOSÉ NAPOLEÓN, president of El Salvador; b. Nov. 23, 1925; m. Inés Durán; children: Inés Guadalupe, José Napoleón, José Alejandro, María Eugenia, María Elena, Ana Lorena. M in Engring., U. Notre Dame. Founder Christian Dem. Party, 1960, sec.-gen., 1960-64, 68-70, pres., 1972—; practicing civil engr., before 1964; mayor San Salvador, 1964-70; elected pres. Republic of El Salvador, 1972; imprisoned, then exiled to Venezuela, 1972-79, returned to El Salvador, 1979, after mil. coup served as mem. Ruling Junta, 1980-82; pres. Republic of El Salvador, 1984-89. Home: San Salvador El Salvador

DU BOIS, WILLIAM PENE, author, illustrator; b. Nutley, N.J., May 9, 1916; s. Guy Pene and Florence (Sherman) duB.; m. Willa Kim; 1955. Student, Miss Barstow's Sch., N.Y.C., Lycée Hoche, Versailles, Lycée de Nice, France. Former corr. Yank Mag; former art editor; designer Paris Rev; author and illustrator books for children including Elizabeth the Cow Ghost, 1936, The Twenty-One Balloons, 1947, Lion, 1956, Pretty Pretty Peggit Moffitt, 1968, Bear Circus, 1971, The Forbidden Forest, 1978, Mother Goose for Christmas, 1979; (with Lee Po) The Hare and the Tortoise and the Tortoise and the Hare, 1972, Gentleman Bear, 1985. Served with AUS, 1941-45. Recipient Festival award N.Y. Herald Tribune, 1947, 56, Newberry medal, 1948, N.Y. Time award for illustration, 1971. Home: New York N.Y. Died Feb. 5, 1993.

DUBRIDGE, LEE ALVIN, physicist; b. Terre Haute, Ind., Sept. 21, 1901; s. Frederick Alvin and Elizebeth Rebecca (Browne) DuB.; m. Doris May Koht, Sept. 1, 1925 (dec. Nov. 1973); children: Barbara (Mrs. David MacLeod), Richard Alvin; m. Arrola Bush Cole, Nov. 30, 1974. A.B., Cornell Coll., Iowa, 1922, Sc.D., 1940; A.M., U. Wis., 1924, Ph.D., 1926; Sc.D., Wesleyan U., 1946, Poly. Inst. Bklyn., 1946, Washington U., 1948, U. B.C., 1947, Occidental Coll., 1952, U. Md., 1955, Columbia, 1957, Ind. U., 1957, U. Wis., 1957, Pa. Mil. Coll., De Pauw U., 1962, Pomona Coll., Rockefeller Inst., Carnegie Inst. Tech., 1965, Syracuse U., 1969, Rensselaer Poly. Inst., 1970; LL.D., U. Calif., 1948, U. Rochester, 1953, U. So. Calif., 1957, Northwestern U., 1958, Loyola U. of Los Angeles, 1963, U. Notre Dame, 1967, Ill. Inst. Tech., 1967; L.H.D., Redlands U., 1958, U. Judaism, 1958; D.C.L., Union Coll., 1961. Asst. in physics U. Wis., 1922-25, instr., 1925-26; NRC fellow Calif. Inst. Tech., 1926-28; asst. prof. physics Washington U., St. Louis, 1928-33; assoc. prof. Washington U., 1933-34; prof. physics, chmn. dept. physics U. Rochester, 1934-46, dean faculty arts scis., 1938-41; investigator Nat. Def. Research Com.; dir. radiation lab. MIT, 1940-45; pres. Calif. Inst. Tech., 1946-69; pres. emeritus, 1970-94; sci. adviser to Pres. U.S., 1969-70; Trustee Rand Corp., Santa Monica, Calif., 1948-61; mem. sci. adv. com. Gen. Motors, 1971-75; Mem. gen. adv. com. A.E.C., 1946-52; Naval Research Adv. Com., 1945-51, Air Force Sci. Adv. Bd., 1945-49; sci. advisor Weingart Found., 1979-94; mem. Pres.'s Communications Policy Bd., 1950-51, Nat. Sci. Bd., 1950- 54, 58-64; chmn. sci. adv. com. Office Defense Moblzn., 1952-56. Author: (with A.L. Hughes) Photoelectric Phenomena, 1932, New Theories of Photoelectric Effect, 1935, Introduction to Space, 1960; Contbr. numerous sci. and ednl. articles to mags. Mem. Nat. Manpower Council, 1951-64; mem. Nat. Adv. Health Council, 1960-61; mem. distinguished civilan service awards bd. U.S. Civil Service Commn., 1963-65; chmn. Greater Los Angeles Urban Coalition, 1968-69; mem. Pres.'s Air Quality Adv. Bd., 1968-69, Pres.'s Sci. Adv. Com., 1970-72; bd. dirs. Nat. Merit Scholarship Corp., 1963-69, Nat. Ednl. TV, N.Y., 1962-69; Trustee Mellon Inst., 1958-67, Rockefeller Found., 1956-67, Nutrition Found., 1952-63, Carnegie Endowment Internat. Peace, 1951-57, Community TV So. Calif., Los Angeles, 1962-69, Henry E. Huntington Library and Art Gallery, 1962-69, Thomas Alva Edison Found., 1960-69, Pasadena Hall Sci., 1977-78. Recipient Research Corp. award, 1947; Medal for Merit U.S., 1948; King's Medal for Service Gt. Britain, 1946; Recipient Vannevar Bush award NSF, 1982; Benjamin Franklin fellow Royal Soc. Arts. Fellow Am. Phys. Soc. (pres. 1947); mem. AAAS, NAS, Am. Philos. Soc., Phi Beta Kappa, Sigma Pi Sigma, Eta Kappa Nu, Sigma Xi, Tau Kappa Alpha, Tau Beta Pi. Presbyterian. Home: Duarte Calif. Died Jan. 23, 1994.

DUBUFFET, JEAN, painter; b. LeHavre, France, July 31, 1901; s. George S. and Jeanne (Paillettle) D.; degree, Le Havre Sch. Fine Arts; m. Paulette Bret, Feb. 25, 1927; 1 child; m. 2d, Lill Dubuffet. Wholesale wine mcht., Paris, 1924-42; painter, from 1942; exhibited Galerie Rene Drouin, Paris, 1944, Pierre Matisse, Cordier-Warren galleries, Mus. Modern Art, N.Y.C.; executed murals Vue de Paris, Grand Paysage, 1945-46; exhibited statuettes Galeries Rive Gauche 1954; retrospective exhbns. Cerde Volney, 1954, Musée des arts decoratifs, Paris, also Italy, Holland, Germany, Mus. Modern Art, N.Y.C., 1961, Tate Gallery, London, 1966, Guggenheim Mus., N.Y.C., 1966, Musée des Beaux-Arts de Montreal, 1969, Kunsthalle de Bâle, 1970, Art Inst. Chgo., 1971, Musée d'Art Moderne de la Ville de Paris, 1972, Mus. Modern Art, N.Y., 1972, Walker Art Center, Mpls., 1973, Guggenheim Mus., N.Y.C., 1973, Grand Palais, Paris, 1973, Kröler-Müller Mus., Amsterdam, 1974, Pace Gallery, N.Y.C., 1975, Waddington Galleries, London, 1975, Fundacion Juan March, Madrid, 1976, Musée des Beaux Arts André Malraux, Le Havre, 1977, Badischer Kunstverein, Karlsruhe, Germany, 1977, Galerie Rudolf Zwinner, Cologne, Germany, 1977, Albert White Gallery, Toronto, Ont., Can., 1977, Karl Ernst Osthaus Mus., Hagen, Germany, 1978, Galerie Berjeler, Turin, 1978, Galerie Zuriner, Cologne, 1977, 80, Palazzo Medici-Riccardi, Florence, 1981, Centre Georges Pompidou, Paris, 1981, Stedelijk Mus., Amsterdam, 1982; prin. paintings include: Mirobolus, Macadam et Cie, Sols et terrains, Hautes Pates, Corps de dames, Paysages du mental, Tables paysagées, Pierres philosophiques, Paris Circus; L'Hourloupe, sculptures, Monuments; Thé â tres de Mémoire, assemblages. Author: Prospectus et tous Ecrits Suivants, 1967; L'Homme du Commun a l'Ouvrage, 1973; La Botteànique, 1973. Catalogue integral des travaux I-XXXII. Deceased. Home: Paris France

DUCKENFIELD, THOMAS ADAMS, gas company executive, lawyer, consultant; b. Richmond, Va., July 30, 1935; s. John Samuel Sr. and Florence (Davis) D.; m. Evelyn Roberta Newman, May 11, 1963; children: Thomas A., David A., Pace A. BS in Math., Hampton U., 1957; JD, Georgetown U., 1970; MBA, So. Ill. U., 1977. Bar: D.C. 1972, U.S. Supreme Ct. 1984. Mathematician and divsn. head Taylor Ship Research & Devel., Carderock, Md., 1960-69; systems analyst Wolf Research and Devel. Co., Riverdale, Md., 1969-70; mgmt. intern Nat'l Savings and Trust Co., Washington, 1970-72; asst. v.p. United Nat. Bank Washington, 1972-73; chief dep. register of wills D.C. Superior Ct., 1973-80; clk. D.C. Superior Ct., Washington, 1980-85; v.p. and gen. mgr. D.C. Natural Gas Co., Washington, 1985-92. Bd. dirs., co-chmn. Neighborhood Legal Services Program, Washington, D.C. 1979; bd. dirs. Combined Health Appeal, Bethesda, Md., 1979, Council for Ct. Excellance, Washington, 1983. Served to 1st lt. U.S. Army, 1957-59. Mem. ABA, Nat. Bar Assn. (pres. 1989-90), Washington Bar Assn. (pres. 1980-82, Service awrd 1982, Ollie May Cooper award 1990), Bar Assn. D.C., Nat. Inst. for Consumer Edn. in Law (bd. dirs.), Am. Gas Assn., Md.-D.C. Pub. Utilities Conf., Lawyers Club. D.C., Alpha Phi Alpha, Beta Kappa Chi, Alpha Kappa Mu, Sigma Pi Phi. Democrat. Baptist. Home: Washington D.C. Died July 31, 1992; buried Fort Lincoln Cemetery, Brentwood, Md.

DUDLEY, HORACE CHESTER, scientist; b. St. Louis, June 28, 1909; s. Horace Chester and Rhoda Olivette (Mc Adoo) D.; A.B., SW Mo. State Coll., 1931; Ph.D. in Chemistry, Georgetown U., 1941; postgrad. U. Calif., 1948, N.Y. U., 1957; m. Thelma Avis Scott, June 13, 1935 (dec.); children: Jeanette, David; m. 2d, Joan Marie Kallenback, Nov. 6, 1954; children: Robert, Susan. Lab. asst. U.S. Bur. Standards, Washington, 1931-32; jr. chemist Bur. Chemistry, U.S. Dept. Agr., Washington, 1933-34; asst. chemist div. med. research Chem. Warfare Service, Edgewood Arsenal, Md., 1934-36; biochemist USPHS, Bethesda, Md., 1936-42; commd. lt., U.S. Navy, 1942, advanced through grades to capt., 1955; explosives specialist, comdg. officer units PTO, 1942-47; head div. biochemistry Naval Med. Research Inst., Bethesda, 1947-52; head sect. allied sci. Med. Service Corps, Washington, 1949-52; head radioisotope lab., dept. radiology Naval Hosp., St. Albans, N.Y., 1952-62; ret., 1962; prof. physics, chmn. dept. physics, U. So. Miss., Hattiesburg, 1962-69; prof. radiation physics, chief physicist U. Ill. Med. Center, Chgo., 1969-77, ret., 1977; with Rad. Safety Assocs., 1976-85; mem. com. coop. clin. studies, mem. med. library staff VA Med. Center, Hines, Ill., 1980-85. cons. in field. Decorated Bronze Star, Sec. Navy Medal; recipient Nat. prize Am. Chem. Soc., 1929; Outstanding Alumnus award Southwest Mo. State U., 1982; grantee AEC, 1963-64, NSF, 1963, 65, U. Ill., 1970, 72, U. So. Miss., 1965, 66, 67. Fellow AAAS; mem. Am. Phys. Soc., Health Physics Soc., Am. Assn. Physics Tchrs., Am. Assn. Physicists in Medicine, Am. Bd. Health Physics (cert.), Sigma Xi. Club: Masons. Author: New Principles in Quantum Mechanics, 1959; Morality Nuclear Planning, 1976; Theory of Neutrino Sea Generalized, Energy-Rich Medium, 1977. Contbr. a ticles to profl. publs. Patentee in field. Died May 2 1994; military burial Arlington Nat. Cemeter Arlington, Va. Home: Hinsdale Ill.

DUERK, WILLIAM ADAM, lawyer; b. Indpls., No 12, 1942; s. William Adam Duerk; m. Anne Mitche May 15, 1993; children from previous marriage: V Adam, Joshua M. AB, Ind. U., 1967; MBA, Pace U 1968; JD, DePaul U., 1972. Bar: D.C. 1973, U.S. C Claims 1976, U.S. Supreme Ct. 1976, U.S. Tax Ct. 197 Adminstr. Ill. Drug Abuse Council, Chgo., 1968-7 spl. counsel Exec. Office of Pres., Washington, 1971-7 ptnr. Perito, Duerk & Pinco, Washington, 1973-8 counsel Finley, Kumble, Wagner, Heine, Underber Manley & Casey, Washington, 1985-86; ptnr. Ross Duerk P.C., Washington, 1986-93; adj. prof. G orgetown U., Washington, 1976-78. Mem. Endowme Bd., DePaul U., Chgo., 1981-82; bd. dirs. Abrax Found., Pitts. Mem. ABA, Fed. Bar Assn, Nat. O Timers Game (Washington). Home: Alexandria V Died 1993.

DUFFY, JACQUES WAYNE, engineering educator; Nimes, France, July 1, 1922; s. Edward F. and Eveli (Lagier) D.; m. Angeline Coultas, June 17, 1950; ch dren: Jacqueline, Philip, Paul. A.B., Columbia U 1947, B.S., 1948, M.S., 1949, Ph.D., 1957; D.Sc. (hon U. Nantes, France, 1980. Mem. research de Grumman Aircraft Engring. Corp., 1950-52; resear asst. Columbia U., 1952-54; prof. engring. Brown U 1954-93, chmn. Center for Biomed. Engring., 1969-7 vis. prof. U. Nantes, France, 1985-86; editorial adv. b Inst. Sci. Info., 1970-93. Author 100 articles in fielc Served with AUS, 1943-46. Guggenheim fellow Ca bridge (Eng.) U., 1964-65; Engring. Found. fello 1978-79; recipient Ross Coffin Purdy award for b paper Am. Ceramic Soc., 1992. Fellow ASME; me ASTM, Soc. Exptl. Stress Analysis, Am. Soc. Meta European Assn. on Dynamic Material Behavior (hon. Home: Providence R.I. Deceased.

DUFOUR, R(ICHARD) W(ILLIAM), JR., lawyer; Mpls., Apr. 11, 1940; s. Richard William and Maxine (Kerr) DuF.; m. Mary E. Spooner, Apr. 3, 1971; ch dren: Nicole R., Richard W., III. BA, U. Minn., 19 JD cum laude, 1967. Bar: Minn. 1967, U.S. Dist. C Minn. 1968. Assoc. Dorsey, Marquart, Windhorst, W & Halladay, 1967-70; sole practice, Mpls., 1970-7 ptnr. Dorfman, Rudquist & DuFour, Mpls., 1972-7 sole practice, Mpls., 1976-81; ptnr. DuFour & Oli P.A. and predecessor, Mpls., 1982-94; instr. U. Min 1970-71, William Mitchell Coll. Law, 1970-71. Serv with U.S. Army, 1960-61. Mem. ABA, Minn. State B Assn., Hennepin County Bar Assn., Order Coif. Clu Masons. Died July 10, 1994. Home: Minneapolis Mir

DUGGAN, J(AMES) ROY, food company executive; Jacksonville, Fla., June 29, 1916; s. J. Roy and Oze (Booth) D.; m. Mabel Bryant Rogers, July 14, 19 children: John L. Williams, Margaret Manning, Jeni Brandon Duggan Flynn. BSBA in Acctg., U. F 1938. Office mgr. Burroughs Corp., Jacksonville, 19 40; corp. sec., contr. Gibbs Corp., Jacksonville, 1940- pres. Hubbard Printing Co., Atlanta, 1946-50; exec. v pres. Sea Pak Corp., St. Simons Island, Ga., 1950- pres., chmn., chief exec. officer King & Prince Seafo Corp., Brunswick, Ga., 1961-95; mem. adv. com. De State, Washington, 1957-63; mem. presdl. adv. co GATT, Washington, 1964. With USAAF, 1939. Me Nat. Fisheries Inst. (pres. 1970-71, chmn. 1971-72, M of Yr. award 1960), Timuquana Country Club (Ja sonville), Sapphire (N.C.) Lakes Country Club, Sea land Club. Home: Sea Island Ga. Died Sept. 30, 1995

DUGMORE, EDWARD, artist; b. Hartford, Con Feb. 20, 1915; s. Walter and Ellen (Spragg) D.; m. Ed Oslund, Aug. 20, 1938; 1 child, Linda Carol. One-m shows include Stable Gallery, N.Y.C., 1953, 54, 56, augural show Holland-Goldowsky Gallery, Chgo., 19 Howard Wise Gallery, N.Y.C., 1960, 61, 63, I Moines Art Center, 1972, Green Mountain Galle N.Y.C., 1971, 73, Carlson Gallery, San Francisco, 19 Manny Silverman Gallery, L.A., 1991, 92, 93, 94; 2-m shows (with Ernest Briggs) Anita Shapolsky Galle N.Y.C., 1991; group exhbns. include Pitts. Interr Exhbn. of Contemporary Painting, Carnegie Inst., 19 Am. Abstract Expressionists and Imagists, Guggenh Mus., 1961, 65th Ann, Art Inst. Chgo., 1962 (M Kohnstamm award), Painting and Sculpture in Ca The Modern Era, San Francisco Mus. Art, 1976- Nat. Fine Arts Collection, Washington, 1975, Kansas City Art Inst., Mo., 1982, Vintage N.Y. C Penn Plaza, 1983-84, The Ingber Gallery, 19 Vanderwoude Tananbaum Gallery, 1989, An Shapolsky Gallery, N.Y.C., 1989, Carlson Gallery, S Francisco, 1990, Manny Silverman Gallery, L.A., 19 93, 94, Snyder Fine Arts, N.Y.C., 1993, inaugural sh Santa Cruz Mus., Calif., 1993, Corcoran Gallery of A Washington, 1994, IBM Gallery, N.Y.C., 1995, Lagu Art Mus., 1996, San Francisco Mus. Modern Art, 19 represented in permanent collections Albright-Knox Gallery, Buffalo, Worcester (Mass.) Art Mus., Lagu Art Mus., Calif., Walker Art Center, Mpls., Des Moi Art Center, Weatherspoon Art Gallery, Greensbo N.C., Kresge Art Center, East Lansing, Mich., Ci eigy Corp., N.Y.C., Mobil Oil Corp., Arlington, Va., irshhorn Mus. and Sculpture Garden, Washington, enil Collection Houston, Tex., Zimmerle Art Mus. utgers U., New Brunswick, N.J. With USMC, 1943-. Recipient award Am. Acad. and Inst. Arts and etters, 1980, Ingram Merrill Found. award for life-ne's work as painter, 1992, Lee Krasner award Pol-ck-Krasner Found., 1995; grantee Nat. Endowment r Arts, 1976, fellow, 1985-86, Guggenheim fellow, 66-67. Home: Minneapolis Minn. Died June 13, 96.

UKE, ANGIER BIDDLE, retired diplomat; b. Y.C., Nov. 30, 1915; s. Angier Buchanan and ordelia (Biddle) D.; m. Robin Chandler Lynn, May 12, 62; 1 son, Angier Biddle Jr.; children by previous arriage: A. St. George B. Pony, Maria-Luisa B. Duke, ario B. Student, Yale U., 1934-37; LL.D., Iona Coll., 57, Duke U., 1969; L.H.D., L.I. U., 1967; LLD on.), Rocky Mountain Coll., 1991, Drexel U., 1992. es. Duke Internat. Corp., N.Y.C., 1945-48; apptd. 2d c. U.S. Fgn. Service, 1949; with Am. embassy, Buenos res, Argentina, 1949; spl. asst. to ambassador Am. nbassy, Madrid, 1951; U.S. ambassador to El lvador, 1952-53; v.p. CARE, 1958-60; chief of otocol White House and Dept. State, 1961-65; nbassador to Spain, 1965-68; chief of protocol Dept. ate, 1968; ambassador to Denmark, 1968-69; commr. ic affairs and pub. events N.Y.C., 1973-76; chmn. Y.C. Dem. Com., 1976-77; pres. The Spanish Inst., Y.C., 1977-79, chmn., 1983-87; chmn. N.Y. State ouncil on Ethnic Affairs, 1978-79; pres. Nat. Com. on n. Fgn. Policy, Inc., N.Y.C., 1978-79; ambassador to orocco, 1979-81; chmn. U.S.-Japan Found., N.Y.C., 81-86; pres. Internat. Rescue Com., 1954-60; chmn. em. State Com. Nationalities and Intergroup Rela-ns, 1960, Appeal of Conscience Found., 1974—. ommr. L.I. State Park, 1955-61; trustee L.I. U., 1981-, chancellor Southampton Coll. of L.I. U., 1986-90; mn. World Affairs Coun. L.I., 1981—. Served from t. to maj. AUS, 1940-45; officer in charge Paris sect. r Transport Command, 1945. Decorated by govts. . Britain, France, Spain, Haiti, Morocco, Sweden, reece and Denmark. Mem. SAR, Coun. Fgn. Rels., n. Acad. Diplomacy (dir. 1994), Assn. for Diplomatic udies and Tng. (dir. 1994—), Fgn. Policy Assn., eedom House, Coun. Am. Ambs. (pres. 1992—), UN ssn. of N.Y. (bd. dirs. 1995—), The Pilgrims, Soc. olonial Wars, Duke Family Assn. N.C. (chmn. 88—), Brook Club (N.Y.C.), River Club (N.Y.C.), acquet and Tennis Club 9N.Y.C.), Bucks Club ondon). Home: New York N.Y. Died April 29, 1995.

JKLER, ABRAHAM EMANUEL, chemical en-eer; b. Newark, Jan. 5, 1925; s. Louis and Netty harles) D.; children—Martin Alan, Ellen Leah, alcolm Stephen. B.S., Yale U., 1945; M.S., U. Del., 50, Ph.D., 1951. Devel. engr. Rohm & Haas Co., ila., 1945-48; research engr. Shell Oil Co., Houston, 50-52; mem. faculty dept. chem. engring. U. Houston, m 1952, prof., from 1963, chmn. dept., 1967-73, dean gring., 1976-83; dir. State of Tex. Energy Council, 73-75; cons. Schlumberger-Doll Research Co., ookhaven Nat. Lab., Shell Devel. Co., Exxon, others. ntbr. chpts. to books, articles to profl. jours. ecipient Research award Alpha Chi Sigma, 1974. llow Am. Inst. Chem. Engrs. (Alpha Chi Sigma rsch. ard 1974, D.Q. Kern rsch. award 1989), Nat. Acad. gring., Am. Soc. Engring. Edn. (research lectureship ard 1976); mem. Am. Inst. Chem. Engrs., ASME, AAS, Am. Chem. Soc., AAUP, Sigma Xi, Tau Beta Home: Houston Tex. Deceased.

JLY, LESLIE C., academic administrator. Pres. midsi State U. Home: Bemidji Minn.

JNBAR, MAXWELL JOHN, oceanographer, edu-or; b. Edinburgh, Scotland, Sept. 19, 1914; s. William d Elizabeth (Robertson) D.; m. Joan Jackson, Aug. 1, 45; children: Douglas, William; m. Nancy Wosstroff, c. 14, 1960; children: Elisabeth, Andrew, Christine, obyn. B.A., Oxford (Eng.) U., 1937, M.A., 1939; .D., McGill U., 1941; DSc (hon.), Meml. U., Nfld., 79, U. Copenhagen, 1991. Mem. faculty McGill U., ontreal, 1946-95, prof., 1959-95; also chmn. dept. rine sci., dir. Marine Sci. Ctr.; climate rsch. group pt. atmospheric and oceanic scis. McGill U, 1987-95; Eastern Arctic Investigations, Can., 1947-55. thor: Eastern Arctic Waters, 1951, Ecological velopment in Polar Regions, 1968, Environment and od Sense, 1971, Essays from a Life: Scotland, nada, Greenland, Denmark, 1995; contbr. articles ofl. jours. Decorated officer Order of Can.; Gug-nheim fellow Denmark, 1952-53; recipient Bruce dal Royal Soc. Edinburgh, 1950, Fry medal Can. Soc. ologists, 1979, Arctic Sci. prize North Slope Borough, 86, No. Sci. award (Can.), 1987, J.P. Tully medal n. Meteorol. and Oceanography Soc., 1988. Fellow yal Soc. Can., Linnaean Soc. London, Arctic Inst. Am. (gov., past chmn., recipient Fellows award 73). Home: Westmount Can. Died Feb. 14, 1995.

NCAN, KENT WHITNEY, retired banker; b. incy, Ill., Feb. 13, 1915; s. Laurance Morgan and argaret (Kent) D.; m. Deuel Rowan, Jan. 13, 1946; ildren: Cole Rowan, Sarah Whitney. B.A., Grinnell ll., 1936; postgrad., U. Wis., 1947-49, U. Ind., 1954- With Harris Trust & Savs. Bank, Chgo., 1936-80; v.p. Harris Trust & Savs. Bank, 1958-68, sr. v.p., 1968-73, exec. v.p., 1973-80; also dir.; exec. v.p., dir. Harris Bankcorp Inc., 1974-80; dir. Consolidated Papers, Inc., Wisconsin Rapids, Wis. Trustee Ravinia Festival Assn., chmn., 1979-81. Served to lt. col. C.E. U.S. Army, 1941-46. Clubs: University (Chgo.); Westmoreland Country (Wilmette, Ill.). Home: Winnetka Ill. Died Dec. 18, 1994.

DUNCAN-SANDYS, DUNCAN EDWIN (BARON DUNCAN-SANDYS), corporate executive; b. Jan. 24, 1908; s. George Sandys and Mildred; m. Diana, 1935 (dissolved 1960); 3 children; m. 2d Marie-Claire Schmitt, 1962; 1 child. Student Eton, Magdalen Coll., Oxford, Eng. Entered Diplomatic Service, 1930; served in Fgn. Office and Brit. Embassy, Berlin; M.P. for Norwood div. of Lambeth, 1935-45, Streatham, 1950-74; polit. columnist Sunday Chronicle, 1937-39; mem. Nat. Exec. of Conservative Party, 1938-39; fin. sec. to War Office, 1941-43; parliamentary sec. Ministry of Supply, responsible for armament prodn., 1943-44; chmn. War Cabinet Com. for def. against German flying bombs and rockets, 1943-45; minister of Works, 1944-45; minister of Supply, 1951-54; minister of Housing and Local Govt., 1954-57; minister of Def., 1957-59; minister of Aviation, 1959-60; sec. of State for Commonwealth Relations, 1960-64, also Sec. State for the Colonies, 1962-64; founder European Movement, 1947, chmn. internat. exec., 1947-50; chmn. Parliamentary Council of European Movement, 1950-51 (pres. of Honour 1980—); mem. Parliamentary Assembly of Council of Europe and of WEU, 1950-51, 65—, leader Brit. del. 1970-72; chmn. Brit. sect. Franco Brit. Council, 1972-78; chmn. Internat. Organising com. European Archtl. Heritage Yr., 1975; mem. gen. adv. council BBC, 1947-51; dir. Ashanti Goldfields Corp., 1947-51, 66-72; v.p. Assn. of Dist. Councils, 1979—; founder Civic Trust, pres., 1956—; pres. Europa Nostra, 1969—; chmn. Lonrho Ltd., 1972-84, pres., 1984—. Author: European Movement and the Council of Europe, 1949; The Modern Commonwealth, 1961. Hon. v.p. Nat. Chamber of Trade, 1951—. Decorated Grand Cross Order of Merit, Italy; Order of Sultanate of Brunei; Grand Cross of Order of Crown (Belgium); comdr. Legion d'Honneur (France), 1979; Grand Cross Order of Merit (Federal Republic Germany), 1981; recipient Medal of Honour, City of Paris; Gold Cup of European Movement, 1975; Goethe Gold Medal, Hamburg Found., 1975. Died Nov. 26th, 1987. Home: London Eng.

DUNGAN, MALCOLM THON, lawyer; b. Butler County, Kans., Mar. 17, 1922; s. Quintin Randolph and Henrietta Mathilde (Blumer) D.; m. Nancy Murray Traverso, Feb. 7, 1950; children: Nicholas William Fitz-Randolph, Sally Murray. A.A., Bartlesville Jr. Coll., 1941; B.A., Stanford U., 1947, LL.B., 1948. Bar: Calif. 1949, U.S Supreme Ct. 1956. Assoc. Brobeck, Phleger & Harrison, San Francisco, 1949-58, ptnr., 1958-92, of counsel, from 1992. Contbr. articles to legal jours. Served to 1st lt. USMCR, 1942-46, PTO. Decorated Air medal, D.F.C. Fellow Am. Bar Found.; mem. Am. Law Inst., ABA (fellow sect. of litigation), Bohemian, Presidio Golf Club. Republican. Episcopalian. Home: San Francisco Calif. Deceased.

DUNN, ANDREW FLETCHER, physicist; b. Sydney, N.S., Can., Jan. 17, 1922; s. Harold Stuart and Tomasina Marion (Fletcher) D.; m. Xenia Mills Reid, Feb. 9, 1943 (dec. June 15, 1982); children: Marion Elizabeth, John Andrew; m. Josephine Lucy Graham, Apr. 6, 1985. B.Sc., Dalhousie U., Halifax, N.S., Can., 1942; M.Sc., Dalhousie U., Can., 1947; Ph.D., U. Toronto, 1950. With electricity sect., div. physics Nat. Research Council Can., Ottawa, 1950-87; head electricity sect. Nat. Research Council Can., 1971-80, co-head elec. and time standards sect., 1981-87; pres. Measurements Internat. Ltd., Prescott, Ont., 1987-93; pres. Dunn Constrn. Co., Baddeck, N.S., 1964-70, dir., 1948-70. Contbr. articles to profl. jours. Nat. chmn. scout program subcom. Boy Scouts Can., 1969-70. Served to capt. Royal Can. Arty., 1942-45. Fellow IEEE (life); mem. Assn. Profl. Engrs. Ont., Canadian Assn. Physicists. Home: Manotick Can. Died Oct. 28, 1993; interred Capital Meml. Gardens, Nepean, Ont., Can.

DUNN, FRANCIS JOHN, bishop; b. Elkader, Iowa, Mar. 22, 1922; s. Peter A. and Josephine (Feeney) D. B.A., Loras Coll., Dubuque, Iowa, 1944; degree in philosophy, Kenrick Sem., St. Louis, 1948; J.C.L., Angelicum U., Rome, Italy, 1960. Ordained priest, Roman Cath. Ch., 1948. Asst. pastor in Iowa, 1948-56; asst. chancellor Archdiocese of Dubuque, 1956-60, chancellor, 1960-84, aux. bishop, 1969—, vicar gen., 1969—, bishop Cedar Rapids region, 1987—; pastor St. Joseph's Ch., 1969-76; dir. Family Life Program Archdiocese Dubuque, 1956-69, Cemetery Assn., 1960-69; chairperson Region IX, 1987-89. Trustee United Fund Dubuque; trustee Divine Word Coll., Epworth, Iowa, 1982—; com. mem. N.Am. Coll., Louvain, Belgium, 1984—; mem. governing bd. N.Am. Coll., Rome, 1987; bd. dirs. N.E. Iowa council Boy Scouts Am., Hawkeye area, 1988—; Episcopal moderator Worldwide Marriage Encounter, 1983—. Mem. Nat. Coun. Cath. Bishops (edn. com., pro life activities com. 1972—), Dubuque C. of C., Cath. Order Foresters. Club: K.C. (4 deg.). Home: Dubuque Iowa Died Nov. 17, 1989.

DUNNAM, SPURGEON M., III, minister, editor; b. Panama City, Fla., Jan. 20, 1943; s. Spurgeon M. Jr. and Thelma (Byers) D.; m. Dottie Cox, Aug. 5, 1966; children: Delilah Denise, Delayna Dawn, Daniel Spurgeon. BA, Tex. Wesleyan U., 1965, LHD, 1977; ThM, So. Meth. U., 1969. Editor, chief exec. officer The United Meth. Reporter, Dallas, 1969—; trustee Tex. Meth. Found., Austin, 1988—; chmn. bd. Religious News Svc., N.Y.C., 1984—; bd. dirs. Global Ministries, United Meth. Ch.; mem. North Tex. Conf. Bd. of Ordained Ministry, Dallas, 1984—. Home: Dallas Tex.

DUNNE, JAMES ARTHUR, space scientist; b. N.Y.C., Mar. 5, 1934; s. Arthur James and Anna Cecelia (McCarthy) D.; children: Michael Sean, Eric James. B.A. magna cum laude, Hofstra U., 1955; M.A., Columbia U., 1957, Ph.D., 1960. Geologist Texaco Inc., Houston, 1958-59; chief physicist Philips Electronic Instruments, Mt. Vernon, N.Y., 1960-64, prin. scientist, 1967-68; sr. scientist Jet Propulsion Lab., Pasadena, Calif., 1964-67; project scientist Mariner Venus-Mercury, 1970-74; ocean expts. mgr. Seasat-A Project, 1974-80, Office Tech. and Space Program Devel., 1980-83; sci. ops. chief Project Galileo, 1983—, chief scientist flight project support office, 1987-89; chmn. working group 3 Interagy. Consultive Group on Halley Comet Missions, 1982-84; mgr. Jet Propulsion Lab. USSR Phobos Project, 1987-88; mgr. Office of Sci. and Mission Design, Project Galileo, 1991—. Contbr. articles to profl. jours. Served with U.S. Army, 1957-58. Mem. AAAS, Sigma Xi. Home: Altadena Calif. Died Sept. 12, 1992.

DUNSTON, ALFRED GILBERT, JR., bishop; b. Coinjock, N.C., June 25, 1915; s. Alfred Gilbert and Cora Lee (Charity) D.; m. Permilla Rollins Flack, June 18, 1940 (div. 1947); children—Carol Dunston Goodrich, Aingred Dunston James, Armayne Dunston Pratt. A.B., Livinstone Coll., 1938; student, Drew U., 1938-39, 41-42. Ordained elder A.M.E. Zion Ch., 1938, then minister and consecrated bishop; minister Advance, N.C., 1936, Thomasville, N.C., 1937-38, Atlantic City, 1941-43, Summit, N.J., 1946-48, Knoxville, Tenn., 1948-52; minister Wesley A.M.E. Zion Ch., Phila., 1952-63, Mother A.M.E. Zion Ch., N.Y.C., 1963-64; prof. Black Ch. History Inst. for Black Ministries, 1971-95; bishop 2d Episcopal area A.M.E. Zion Ch., Phila. Author: Black Man in Old Testament and Its World. Mem. Alpha Phi Alpha. Home: Philadelphia Pa. Died June 24, 1995.

DUNWIDDIE, CHARLOTTE, sculptor; b. Strasbourg, France, June 19, 1907. Student, Acad. Fine Arts, Berlin, Mariano Benlliure, Madrid, Alberto Lagos, Buenos Aires, Argentina. Nat. Academician. Editorial bd.: Nat. Sculpture Rev; One-woman shows, Kennedy Galleries, N.Y.C., Salon de Bellas Artes, Buenos Aires, Nat. Horse Show, Madison Sq. Garden, N.Y.C., Aqueduct Racetrack, N.Y.C., Pimlico Racetrack, Balt., Nat. Arts Club, N.Y.C., group shows include, NAD, N.Y.C., Nat. Sculpture Soc. N.Y.C., Allied Artists Am., N.Y.C., Am. Artists Profl. League, N.Y.C., Hudson Valley Art Assn., Pen and Brush, N.Y.C.; represented in permanent collections including, Mus. Brookgreen Gardens, Myrtle Beach, S.C., Marine Corps Mus., Washington, Mus. Am. Art, New Britain, Conn., O'Bannon Hall, USMC, Quantico, Va., Sem. of Redemptorist Fathers, Suffield, Conn., Ch. of Good Shepherd, Lima, Peru, Nuncio Palace, Lima, also pvt. collections. Recipient numerous awards including 15 gold medals, Herbert Adams Meml. med. for svc. to Am. sculpture, 1990. Fellow Allied Artists, Nat. Sculpture Soc. (pres. 1982—), Royal Soc. Arts (London); mem. Am. Artists Profl. League, Pen and Brush (pres. 1964-68). Club: Cosmopolitan. Home: New York N.Y. Deceased.

DUPREE, FRANKLIN TAYLOR, JR., federal judge; b. Angier, N.C., Oct. 8, 1913; s. Franklin T. and Elizabeth Mason (Wells) D.; m. Rosalyn Adcock, Dec. 30, 1939; children: Elizabeth Rosalyn, Nancy Alice (Mrs. Philip R. Miller, Jr.). A.B., U. N.C. at Chapel Hill, 1933, LL.B., 1936. Bar: N.C. 1936. Practiced in Angier, 1936-39; asso. firm A.J. Fletcher, Raleigh, N.C., 1939-48; practiced in Raleigh, 1948-52; partner firm Dupree, Weaver, Horton, Cockman & Alvis (and predecessor firm), Raleigh, 1952-70; judge U.S. Dist. Ct. (ea. dist.) N.C., Raleigh, 1971-95; sr. judge. Mem. Wake County (N.C.) Bd. Elections, 1961-67; chmn. Wake County Republican Com., 1967-70; mem. N.C. Rep. Exec. Com., 1968-70. Served to lt. USNR, 1943-46. Mem. ABA, N.C. Bar Assn., Wake County Bar Assn., Am. Judicature Soc., Elks, Lions, Carolina Country Club, Stag Club, Capital City Club, Royster Stadium Tennis Club. Baptist. Home: Raleigh N.C. Died Dec., 1995.

DUPUY, TREVOR NEVITT, historian, research executive; b. S.I., N.Y., May 3, 1916; s. Richard Ernest and Laura (Nevitt) D.; m. Jonna Sløk Bjerggaard, Oct. 16, 1968 (dec. Apr. 1982); 1 child, Signe Sløk; children (by previous marriage): Trevor Nevitt, Richard Ernest II, George McVicar, Laura Nevitt, Charles Geissbuhler, Mirande Elisabeth, Arnold Christian, Fielding Davis. Student, St. Peter's Coll., 1933-34; B.S., U.S. Mil. Acad., 1938; grad., Joint Services Staff Coll., Latimer, Eng., 1948-49; student, Harvard Grad. Sch. Pub. Adminstrn., 1953-54. Commd. 2d lt. U.S. Army, 1938, advanced through grades to col., 1953; prof. mil. sci. and tactics Harvard, 1952-56, mem. original faculty Def. Studies program, 1954-56; dir. mil. history program Ohio State U., 1956, 57; ret., 1958; vis. prof. internat. relations program Rangoon (Burma) U., 1959-60; mem. internat. studies div. Inst. Def. Analyses, 1960-62; pres., exec. dir., bd. dirs. Hist. Evaluation and Research Orgn., 1962-90; pres. The Dupuy Inst., 1992-95; pres. bd. dirs. T.N. Dupuy Assocs., Inc., 1971-83, 90-91; pres., chmn.. bd. dirs. Data Memory Sys., Inc., 1983-90; pres., chmn. bd. dirs. HERO-TNDA, Pubs. and Rschrs., Inc., 1990-91. Author: (with R.E. Dupuy) To The Colors, 1942, Faithful and True, 1949, (with R.E. Dupuy) Military Heritage of America, 3d edit., 1992, Campaigns of the French Revolution and of Napoleon, 1956, (with R.E. Dupuy) Brave Men and Great Captains, 1960, 84, 93, Compact History of the Civil War, 1960 (Fletcher Pratt award, 1992), Civil War Land Battles, 1960, Civil War Naval Actions, 1961, Military History of World War II, 19 vols, 1962-65, (with R.E. Dupuy) Compact History of the Revolutionary War, 1963, Military History of World War I, 12 vols, 1967, The Battle of Austerlitz, 1968, Modern Libraries for Modern Colleges: Research Strategies for Design and Development, 1968, Ferment in College Libraries: The Impact of Information Technology, 1968, Military History of the Chinese Civil War, 1969, (with R.E. Dupuy) Encyclopedia of Military History, 4th edit, 1993, Military Lives, 12 vols, 1969, (with Grace P. Hayes) Revolutionary War Naval Battles, 1970, (with Gay M. Hammerman) Revolutionary War Land Battles, 1970; editor, contbr. to Holidays, 1965, (with John A. Andrews and Grace P. Hayes) Almanac of World Military Power, 1970, 72, 74, 80, (with Gay M. Hammerman) Documentary History of Arms Control and Disarmament, 1973, (with Gay M. Hammerman) People and Events of the American Revolution, 1974, (with R.E. Dupuy) An Outline History of the American Revolution, 1975, A Genius for War: The German Army and General Staff, 1807-1945, 1977, 4th edit., 1993, Numbers, Prediction and War, 1978, 85, Elusive Victory: The Arab-Israeli Wars, 1947-1974, 1978, 84, 89, 92, The Evolution of Weapons and Warfare, 1980, 84, (with Paul Martell) Great Battles of the Eastern Front, 1982, Options of Command, 1984, (with Paul Martell) Flawed Victory: The Arab-Israeli Conflict and the 1982 War in Lebanon, 1986, Understanding War: Military History and Theory of Conflict, 1986, (with Curt Johnson, Grace P. Hayes) Dictionary of Military Terms, 1986, Understanding Defeat, 1990, Attrition: Forecasting Battle Casualties and Equipment Losses in Modern War, 1990, If War Comes, How to Defeat Saddam Hussein, 1991, Future Wars, 1992, (with Curt Johnson, David L. Bongard) Encyclopedia of Military Biography, 1992; editor in chief Brassey's International Military and Defense Encyclopedia, 6 vols., 1992, (with David L. Bongard, Richard C. Anderson) Hitler's Last Gamble, 1994. Trustee Coll. Potomac. Decorated Legion of Merit, Bronze Star with combat V, Air medal; Brit. Distinguished Service Order; Chinese Nat. Govt. Cloud and Banner (2 grades); hon. col. 7th Field Arty. Regiment, 1988-95. Mem. Am. Mil. Inst. (pres. 1958-59), Assn. U.S. Army, Internat. Inst. Strategic Studies, U.S. Naval Inst. Home: Vienna Va. Died June 5, 1995.

DURAS, MARGUERITE, writer; b. Giadinh, Indochina, Apr. 4, 1914; d. Henri and Marie (Legrand) Donnadieu; m. Robert Antelme, 1939 (div. 1946). Ed., Saigon and Paris. Sec. Ministry of Colonies, Paris, 1935-41; writer, 1943-96. Writings include: (fiction) Les Impudents, 1943, La Vie tranquille, 1944, Un Barrage contre le Pacifique, 1950 (pub. as The Sea Wall, 1952), Le Marin de Gibraltar, 1952 (pub. as The Sailor from Gibraltar, 1966), Les Petits Chevaux da Tarquinia, 1953 (pub. as The Little Horses of Tarquinia, 1960), Des Journées entières dans les arbres, 1954 (pub. as Whole Days in the Trees, 1983), Le Square, 1955 (pub. as The Square, 1959), Moderato cantabile, 1958, Dix Heures et demi du soir en été, 1960 (pub. as Ten-Thirty on a Summer Night, 1962), L'Après-midi de Monsieur Andesmas, 1962 (pub. as The Afternoon of Monsieur Andesmas, 1964), Le Ravissement de Lol V. Stein, 1964 (pub. as The Ravishing of Lol V. Stein, 1967), Le Vice-Consul, 1966 (pub. as The Vice-Consul, 1968), L'Amante anglaise, 1967, Détruire, dit-elle, 1969 (pub. as Destroy, She Said, 1970), Abahn Sabana David, 1970, L'Amour, 1971, Ah! Ernesto, 1971, La Maladie de la mort, 1983 (pub. as The Malady of Death, 1986), L'Amant, 1984 (pub. as The Lover, 1985), Les Yeux bleus cheveux noirs, 1986 (pub. as Blue Eyes, Black Hair, 1987), Emily L., 1987, La Pluie d'été, 1990 (pub. as Summer Rain, 1992), L'Amant de la Chine du nord, 1991; (plays) Le Viaducs de la Seine-et-Oise, 1960, Théâtre I, 1965, Les Eaux et forets, 1965, La Musica, 1965, Des journées entières dans les arbres, 1965, Three Plays, 1967, Théâtre 2, 1968, Le Shaga, 1968, Susanna Andler, 1969, Yes, peut-être, 1968, La danse de mort, d'après August Stringberg, 1970, India Song, 1973, Home, 1973, L'Eden Cinéma, 1977, Le Navire Night, 1979, L'Homme assis dans le couloir, 1980, Agatha, 1981, L'Homme Atlantique, 1982, Savannah Bay, 1982, Théâtre III, 1984, La Musica deuxième, 1985; (adapations of novels into plays) Le Square, 1957, Les Papiers d'Aspern, 1961, Miracle en Alabama, 1961, La Bête dans la jungle, 1962, L'Amante Anglaise, 1969; (screenplays) Hiroshima mon amour, 1959 (Academy award nomination best original screenplay 1960), Moderato cantabile, 1960, Une Aussie Longue Absence, 1961, 10:30 P.M. Summer, 1966, La Musica, 1966, Les Rideaux blancs, 1966, Détruire, dit-elle, 1969, Jaune le soleil, 1971, Nathalie Granger, 1972, La ragazza di passaggio/La Femme du Gange, 1973, Ce que savait Morgan, 1974, India Song, 1975 (Cannes Film Festival spl. prize 1975), Des journées entières dans les arbres, 1976, Son nom de Venises dan Calcutta désert, 1976, Véra Baxter, 1977, Le Camion, 1977, La Navire Night, 1978, L'Homme assis dans le couloir, 1980, Agatha et les lectures illimitées, 1981, L'Homme Atlantique, 1981, Dialogue de Rome, 1982; (other) Les Parleuses, 1974 (pub. as Woman to Woman, 1987), Étude sur l'oeuvre littéraire, théâtrale, et cinématographique de Marguerite Duras, 1975, Territoires du féminin, 1977, Les Lieux de Marguerite Duras, 1978, L'Été 80, 1980, Outside: papiers d'un jour, 1981 (pub. as Outside: Selected Writings, 1986), Marguerite Duras à Montréal, 1981, La Douleur, 1985 (pub. as The War, 1986), La Pute de la côte normande, 1986, La Vie matérielle: Marguerite Duras parle à Jérôme Beaujour, 1987 (pub. as Practicalities: Marguerite Duras Speaks to Jérôme Beaujour, 1990, Les Yeux verts, 1987 (pub. as Green Eyes, 1990); dir.: (film) Les enfants, 1985; translator: Anton Chekhov's La Mouette, 1985. Recipient Prix Jean Cocteau, 1955, Ibsen prize, 1970, French Academy grand prize for theatre, 1983, Goncourt prize, 1984, Ritz Paris Hemingway prize, 1986. Home: Paris France Died March 3, 1996.

DURRELL, GERALD MALCOLM, zoologist, author; b. Jamshedpur, India, Jan. 7, 1925; s. Lawrence Samuel and Louisa Florence (Dixie) D.; m. Jacqueline Sonia Rasen, 1951 (div.); m. 2d, Lee Wilson McGeorge, 1979. Ed. pvt. tutors; LHD (hon.), Yale U., 1972; DSc (hon.) U. Durham, 1988, U. Kent, 1989. Student keeper Whipsnade Park, 1945-46; leader zool. collecting expdn., Brit. Cameroons, 1947, 48, Brit. Guiana, 1949, Argentina, Paraguay, 1953, Brit. Cameroons, 1956, Trans-Argentine, 1958, N.Z., Australia, Malaysia, 1961, Sierra Leone, 1964, Mexico, 1968, Mauritius, 1976, 77, India/Assam, 1978, Madagascar, 1981, 90; established own zoo, Jersey, Channel Islands, 1959; founder Jersey Wildlife Preservation Trust, 1964, dir., 1964-95; founder Wildlife Preservation Trust Internat., 1973, Wildlife Preservation Trust Can., 1986; lectr. in field; appeared on broadcasts, BBC; 4 maj. TV series on animals; author: The Overloaded Ark, 1952, Three Singles to Adventure, 1953, The Bafut Beagles, 1953, The Drunken Forest, 1955, My Family and Other Animals, 1956, Encounters with Animals, 1959, A Zoo in My Luggage, 1960, The Whispering Land, 1962, Menagerie Manor, 1964, Two in the Bush, 1966, Rosy is my Relative (novel), 1968, Birds, Beasts and Relatives, 1969, Fillets of Plaice, 1971, Catch Me a Colobus, 1972, Beasts in my Belfry, 1973, The Stationary Ark, 1976, Golden Bats and Pink Pigeons, 1977, The Garden of the Gods, 1978, The Picnic and Suchlike Pandemonium, 1979, The Mockery Bird, 1981, The Amateur Naturalist, 1982, How to Shoot an Amateur Naturalist, 1984, Durrell in Russia, 1986, The Ark's Anniversary, 1990, Marrying Off Mother, 1991, The Aye-aye and I, 1992; children's books: The New Noah, 1956, Island Zoo, 1961, Look at Zoos, 1961, My Favourite Animal Stories, 1963, The Donkey Rustlers, 1968, The Talking Parcel, 1974, The Fantastic Flying Journey, 1987, Fantastic Dinosaur Adventure, 1989, Keeper, 1990, Toby the Tortoise, 1991. Decorated Order Brit. Empire. Fellow Internat. Inst. Arts and Letters, Inst. Biology, Zool. Soc.; mem. Brit. Ornithologists Union. Died Jan. 30, 1995. Home: Jersey Channel Islands

DURSIN, HENRY LOUIS, opinion survey company executive, retired; b. Woonsocket, R.I., May 3, 1921; s. Henry and Mary Regina (Butler) D.; m. Margaret Alice Smith, Apr. 20, 1943 (dec.); children: Henry Peter, Philomene Louise, Margaret Elizabeth , Stefanie Marie; m. Marie Ann Novosedlik, May 22, 1982. AB with honors, Brown U., 1942; MBA, Harvard U., 1948. Supr. corp. research Gen. Electric Co., N.Y.C., 1948-63; supr. corp. research Harper-Atlantic Sales Co., N.Y.C., also dir. research and promotion, 1963-67; dir. research ORC Caravan Surveys Co., Princeton, N.J., 1968-70, pres., 1970-92; v.p. Opinion Research Corp., Princeton, 1970-74, sr. v.p., 1974-91. Chmn. agy. com. United Fund No. Westchester, 1960-68, pres. 1967-68; v.p. Westchester County United Fund, co-chmn. agy. com. 1966-67. Served with USAAF, 1942-46. Mem. Am. Assn. Pub. Opinion Research. Roman Catholic. Club: Harvard (N.Y.C). Home: Princeton N.J. Died 1992.

DURYEE, A. WILBUR, retired physician; b. North Hackensack, N.J., July 5, 1899; s. Abram and Margaret (Clarke) D.; m. Helen Deborah Moore; children: A. Wilbur, Deborah Jane, Mary Ellen. B.Sc., Rutgers Coll., 1921; M.D., Columbia, 1925. Intern N.Y. Post-grad. Hosp., 1925-28; formerly attending physician Univ. Hosp., Bellevue Hosp., N.Y.C.; formerly cons. Samaritan Bklyn., Prospect Heights, Englewood, St. Claire hosps.; formerly prof. clin. medicine N.Y. U. Served as pvt. U.S. Army, World War I. Mem. Am. Heart Assn. (exec. com.; dir.; v.p. 1959), N.Y. Heart Assn. (pres.), Am. Therapeutic Soc. (pres. 1947), Am. Acad. Compensation Medicine (pres. 1955), Phi Beta Kappa. Club: University (N.Y.C.). Home: Great Barrington Mass. Died June 1, 1994.

DUVAL, LÉON-ETIENNE CARDINAL, archbishop; b. Chenex, France, Nov. 9, 1903. Ordained priest Roman Catholic Ch., 1926, bishop of Constantine, A geria, 1947; archbishop of Algiers, Algeria, 1954-89; ret 1989; elevated to Sacred Coll. Cardinals, 1965; titula ch. St. Balbina. Died May 30, 1996. Home: Bologhin Algeria

DYER, WILLIAM ALLAN, JR., newspaper executiv b. Providence, Oct. 23, 1902; s. William Allan and Clar (Spink) D.; m. Marian Elizabeth Blumer, Aug. 9, 193 children: Allan H., William E. B.Ph., Brown U., 192 LL.D., 1984; LL.D. (hon.), Ind. U., 1977; H.L.D (hon.), Butler U., 1983, U. Indpls., 1986. Report Syracuse (N.Y.) Jour., 1923; various advt. positior Syracuse Post-Standard, 1925-41; v.p., gen. mgr. St Pub. Co., Indpls., 1944-49; v.p., gen. mgr. Indpls. New spapers, Inc., 1949-74, pres., 1975-93; pres. Munc Newspapers, Inc., 1975-93; dir. Cen. Newspapers, Inc Indpls., 1949-93, exec. v.p., 1964-73; N.Y.C. dir Me Sunday Newspapers, 1951-75, pres., 1969-75; pres. Ce Newspapers Found. Indpls., 1969-93, Ind. Journalis Hall of Fame, 1979. Mem. exec. com. United Fu Indpls., 1954-77, pres., 1970, chmn. bd., 1971; v. Community Service Council, Indpls., 1967-68; trust Brown U., 1952-59; pres. Indpls. Community Hos Found., 1976-83, hon. bd. dirs., 1983-93; pres. Goodw Industries Found., 1980-86; bd. dirs., v.p. In Symphony Soc., 1977-86. Lt. comdr. USNR, 1941-44 Recipient Brown Bear award Brown U., 1968; Torch Truth award Advt. Club, 1975; Silver medal Am. Adv Fedn., 1971. Mem. Better Bus. Bur. Indpls. (bd. dir 1950-93, pres. 1958, 65), Nat. Better Bus. Bur. (bd. dir 1950-70), Council Better Bus. Burs. (bd. dirs. 1970-7 80-86), Indpls. C. of C. (bd. dirs. 1967-93, v.p. 1970-7 Am. Newspaper Pubs. Assn. (labor relations com. 195 63, bd. dirs., bur. advt. 1963-69, Research Inst. 1955-6 pres. 1963-64), Indpls. Advt. Club (bd. dirs. 1952-5 pres. 1952-53), Indpls. Community Hosp. (bd. dir 1952-54, 66-69, v.p. 1954). Club: Brown U. Ind. (se 1946-52, pres. 1952-54). Home: Indianapolis Ind. Di Mar. 21, 1993.

DYKEMA, JOHN RUSSEL, retired lawyer; b. Was ington, June 1, 1918; s. Raymond Kryn and Marge (Russel) D.; m. Rosemary McDonald, June 21, 19 children—Mary McDonald, John Russel, Pe Kryn. A.B., Princeton, 1940; J.D., U. Mich., 1947 Bar: Mich. 1947. Assoc. firm Dykema, Gosse Spencer, Goodnow & Trigg (and predecessor), Detro 1947-48, 49-51, 53-58; mem. firm Dykema Gossett (a predecessor), 1958-95; law clk. to Justice Murphy, U. Supreme Ct., 1948-49; corp. and securities comm Mich., 1951-53. Trustee Western Mich. U., 1964-8 chmn., 1976-77. Served with USNR, 1941-45. Me State Bar Mich., Am., Detroit bar Assns. Hom Grosse Pointe Mich. Died June, 1995.

DYMENT, JOHN JOSEPH, financial executive; Ottawa, Ont., Can., Apr. 16, 1933; s. John Talbot a Josephine Beatrice (Bull) D.; m. Judith Gayle Jowse Feb. 25, 1961; children: John Dexter, Jeffrey Lor Jennifer Lynn. B Commerce, McGill U., 1953; MB with high distinction, Harvard U., 1962. Auditor Pri Waterhouse, Montreal, Que., Can., 1953-55; mgm cons. Urwick Currie Ltd., Montreal, Que., Can., 19 62, Arthur Young & Co., N.Y.C., 1962-63; con Hemphill Noyes & Co., N.Y.C., 1964; mgmt. co Arthur Young & Co., N.Y.C., 1965-68; ptnr. Arth Young & Co., N.Y., London, Paris, 1968-87; exec. v. MML Internat. Inc., N.Y.C., 1987-90; v.p. fin. tre Bruncor Inc., Saint John, N.B., Can., 1990-92; C Lease Adminstrn. Corp., Toronto, Ont., Can., 1994-9 bd. dirs. Maritime Life Assurance, Halifax. Auth Meet the Men Who Sailed The Seas, 1967; also article Mem. bd. govs. Downtown Bklyn. Rep. Orgn., 1963-6 Baker Scholar Harvard U., 1961. Mem. Can. In Chartered Accts., L'ordre des comptables agrees Que., N.B. Inst. Chartered Accts., Fin. Execs. In Planning Forum. Died Sept. 6, 1995.

EASLEY, JOHN ALLEN (JACK EASLEY), scie educator; b. Manning, S.C., Jan. 15, 1922; s. John All and Eleanor Martin (Robertson) E.; m. Elizabe Fumiko Fujioka, Aug. 15, 1948; children: Allen K Robert Fumio, David Fumitaka, John Makoto. B.S. Physics, Wake Forest Coll., 1943; M.Ed. in Sci. Edn, Hawaii, 1952; Ph.D., Harvard, 1955. Radio engr. de terrestrial magnetism Carnegie Inst., Washington, Baf Island, Hawaii, 1942-46; prin. Marshall Islands termediate Sch., 1949-50; instr. sci. edn. U. Haw 1950-52, asst. prof. sci., 1955-60, assoc. prof., 1960- acad. chmn., 1960-61; assoc. prof. edn. U. Ill., Urba 1962-67, prof. secondary edn., 1967-69, prof. tchr. e 1969-89, prof. emeritus tchr. edn., 1989-94, chmn. c on culture and cognition, 1975-76, 82-94, dir. S Tutoring Lab., 1977-82, mem. Bur. Ednl. Resear 1979-82, mem. Ctr. Instructional Research and C riculum Evaluation; cons. Peace Corps, 1961- UNESCO, 1970, D.C. Pub. Schs., 1987, Orland (Pub. Sch. Dist. 135, 1988, AAAS, 1989, Oakland Mich., 1989-90, Warrensburg-Latham (Ill.) Cmty. U Sch. Dist. # 11, 1990; chmn. rsch. adv. com. CEMR Aesthetics Edn. Program, 1978-81; mem. U.S.-Jap Seminar on Sci. Edn. Author: (with Maurice Tatsuo Scientific Thought: Cases from Classical Physics, 19 (with Robert E. Stake and others) Case Studies Science Education, 1978, (with J. Gallagher) Piaget a Education, 1978, (with E. Duckworth, D. Hawkins a A. Henriques) Science Education: A Minds-On oach for the Elementary Years, 1990, (with E. Easley) ıanging Mathematics Teaching in the Elementary hool, 1992. Danforth assoc., 1969-94. Fellow AAAS; em. AAUP, Jean Piaget Soc. (mem. internat. bd. adsers 1974-78), Nat. Assn. Rsch. in Sci. Teaching (exec. . 1979-82, Disting. Contbns. to Sci. Edn. Through sch. award 1993), Nat. Coun. Tchrs. Math., N.Y. ad. Scis., Internat. Group for Psychology of Math. In., Assn. Supervision and Curriculum Devel., Assn. Edn. of Tchrs. in Sci., Am. Ednl. Rsch. Assn., Sch. i. and Math. Assn., Phi Delta Kappa. Mem. United . of Christ. Home: Champaign Ill. Died Dec. 10,)4.

ATON, LEWIS SWIFT, savings and loan executive; San Francisco, Aug. 10, 1919; s. Edwin M. and Gerde (Swift) E.; m. Virginia Stammer, Apr. 21, 1950; ildren: William L., Joan E., John W. B.A., Stanford , 1942. With Guarantee Savs. & Loan Assn., Fresno, lif., 1946-87; v.p. Guarantee Savs. & Loan Assn., 50-56, pres., 1956-86, also chmn. bd.; chmn. No. lif. group Glendale Fed. Bank, Fresno, 1987—; dir. d. Home Loan Bank, San Francisco, 1964-70, MGIC vestment Corp., Milw., Pacific Gas & Electric Corp.; . dirs. Sta. KVPT Pub. TV Broadcasting, Fresno, enfed, Inc., Grundfos Pumps Corp. Pres. Fresno ol. Soc., 1967-68; mem. Fresno City Bd. Edn., 1958- , pres., 1959-62; chmn. bd. govs. Fresno Regional und., 1972-79; Yosemite Nat. Insts., 1986-90; trustee esno Community Hosp., 1965-81, vice chmn. Fresno ate Coll. Found., 1969—, Jr. Achievement, 1951-85, lif. Mus. Found., 1970-80; mem. adv. bd. Fresno ate Coll., 1965-75; chmn. bd. dirs. Fresno Met. Mus., 80-86; chmn. Nat. Parks Adv. Bd. Western Region, 72-79. Capt. AUS, 1942-46. Mem. Calif. Savs. and an League (pres. 1959-60), U.S. Savs. and Loan ague (pres. 1970-71), Calif. C. of C. (dir. 1977-89), C. C. Fresno City and County (pres. 1967), Natural story Assn. (dir. 1977-79), Calif. Nature Conservancy 1. dirs. 1991—), Stanford Alumni Assn. (pres. 1975-), Beta Gamma Sigma, Lambda Alpha. Home: esno Calif.

BERHART, JOHN CAROL, federal government ence official; b. Lima, Ohio, Dec. 26, 1907; s. Frank d Morna (Davis) E.; m. Sylvia Rothman, Feb. 8, 37; 1 son, Jonathan. B.A., U. Oreg., 1929; M.A., orthwestern U., 1931, Ph.D., 1934. Instr., asst. prof. ychology Northwestern U., 1936-43; tng. specialist, ief research grants and fellowships br. NIMH, thesda, Md., 1947-54, dir. intramural rsch., 1961-81; adviser, dep. dir. NIH, Bethesda, Md., 1981-90. ec. assoc. Commonwealth Fund, N.Y.C., 1954-61; bd. s. Found. for Advanced Edn. in Scis., 1962-89. Lt SNR, 1943-46. Decorated Bronze Star medal; Social . Research Council fellow, 1940-41, 46; recipient perior Service award HEW, 1965, Disting. Service ard, 1969, Career Civil Service award Nat. Civil Sere League, 1974, Presdl. Meritorious Exec. Rank ard, 1980. Mem. Am. Psychol. Assn. (Harold H. ldreth Meml. award 1968), Phi Beta Kappa, Sigma . Club: Cosmos (Washington). Home: Bethesda Md. ed Mar. 11, 1990.

BERT, ROBERT HIGGINS, physician, educator, undation consultant; b. Mpls., Sept. 10, 1914; s. ichael and Lilian (Gilbertson) E.; m. Emily Hirsch, ne 17, 1939 (dec. 1986); children: Elizabeth Schmidtowara, John, Thomas; m. Barbara Bacheller, Oct. 21, 89. BS, U. Chgo., 1936, MD, 1942; DPhil, Oxford , 1939; AM (hon.), Harvard U., 1964; DSc (hon.), ortheastern U., 1968, U. Md., 1970, Notre Dame U., 77, N.Y. Med. Coll., 1983; LLD (hon.), U. Toronto, 70; LHD (hon.), Rush Med. Coll., 1974. Intern, asst. sident medicine Boston City Hosp., 1942-44; asst., in- ., asst. prof., assoc. prof. dept. medicine U. Chgo., 46-55, prof., 1955-56; Hanna Payne prof. medicine estern Res. U., 1956-58, John H. Hord prof. medicine, 58-66; dir. medicine Univ. Hosps., 1956-64; Jackson of. clin. medicine Harvard U., 1964-65, prof. medicine, 65-73, Caroline Shields Walker prof. of medicine, 73-77, emeritus, 1977-96, dean Med. Sch. and faculty medicine, 1965-77; head Harvard dept. medicine ass. Gen. Hosp., 1964-65; pres. Harvard Med. Center, 65-77; pres. Harvard Cmty. Health Plan, 1968-74, em. bd. dirs., 1968-94, chmn. bd., 1974-84, chmn. und., 1983-96, chmn. bd. of overseers, 1985-96; exainer Am. Bd. Internal Medicine, 1961-64; vice chmn. es.' Biomed. Rsch. Panel, 1975-76; dir. Squibb Corp., 77-87; trustee Population Coun., 1966-96, chmn. bd., 78-88; pres. Milbank Meml. Fund, 1978-84, 88-89, . dirs., 1972-84, 88-96, mem. tech. bd., 1966-77; spl. ns. Robert Wood Johnson Found., 1984-88; mem. it. Adv. Commn. on Health Manpower, 1966-67, em. bd. dirs. Nat. Med. Fellowships, 1984-94; trustee ockefeller Found., 1966-76, Coun. for Divsn. Biol. s. Pritzker Sch. Medicine, 1990-95; mem. vis. com. on lls. U. Chgo., 1967-70; bd. regents Nat. Libr. edicine, 1967-71, chmn., 1970-71; mem. bd. visitors U. . Sch. Medicine, 1968-71; mem. adv. com. to dir. H, 1968-71; trustee Meharry Med. Coll., 1969-74, rnard Coll., 1977-87, Mt. Sinai Med. Sch., Hosp. and ed. Ctr., 1978-85; mem. bd. regents Uniformed Svcs. Health Scis., 1980-84; chmn. bd. overseers artmouth Med. Sch., 1983-86; spl. adv. The Comonwealth Fund, 1984-94; dir. Mind-Body Med. Inst., 92-96, chmn. bd. dirs., 1993-96; trustee Edn. Devel. r., 1992-96; chmn. vis. com. Health Sci. Ctr. SUNY, Bklyn., 1988-93. Lt. USNR, 1944-46. Recipient Alumni Achievement medal U. Chgo., 1968, also Disting. Svc. award, 1962, Flexner award Assn. Am. Med. Colls., 1982; Rhodes scholar, 1936-39, Markle scholar, 1948. Fellow AMA, AAAS, Am. Pub. Health Assn.; mem. ACP (master), Am. Soc. Clin. Investigation, Am. Thoracic Soc. (chmn. com. med. rsch. 1955, pres. 1961-62), Am. Clin. and Climatol. Assn., Assn. Am. Physicians (recorder 1962-66, councillor 1966, pres. 1972-73), Mass. Med. Soc., Phi Beta Kappa, Sigma Xi, Delta Kappa Epsilon, Alpha Omega Alpha, Omicron Kappa Upsilon (hon.), Kappa Pi Eta. Clubs: Century (N.Y.C.), Harvard (N.Y.C.). Home: Wayland Mass. Died Jan. 29, 1996.

ECHOLS, CHARLES ERNEST, civil engineer; b. Alderson, W.Va., Dec. 5, 1924; s. Frank and Dorothy (Guy) E.; m. Alexes Olgivie, Feb. 22, 1960 (div. 1975); children: Darcy, Carter, Heather, Charlester; m. Catherine May Adams, Dec. 1, 1978. BC, U. Va., 1949, JD, 1954, MCE, 1955. Registered profl. engr., surveyor, ins. agt., real estate broker; bar. V.p., sec. A.B. Torrence Co., Elkton, Va., 1945-83, cons., from 1983; instr. Mich. State U., East Lansing, 1955-57; prof. U. Va., Charlottesville, 1957—; examiner U.S. Patent Office, Washington, 1956; pres. Nereus Corp., Charlottesville, Va., 1987—; mem. Bituminous Rsch. Advisory com., Richmond, Va., from 1968. With USN, 1945-46. Mem. Am. Arbitration Assn. (arbitrator from 1972), Va. Soc. Civil Engrs. (pres. 1969-70), Blue Ridge Chpt. Soc. Profl. Engrs., Va. Assn. Surveyors (v.p. 1971), ABA, Tau Beta Pi. Republican. Presbyterian. Home: Charlottesville Va. Deceased.

ECHOLS, HARRISON, molecular biology educator; b. Charlottesville, Va., May 1, 1933; s. Gessner Harrison and Ann Shippen (Young) E.; m. Jean Harford Crutchfield, Dec. 18, 1954 (div. 1973); children: Catharine, Elizabeth, Jean, Robert; m. Carla Anne Babcock, Sept 11, 1977 (div. 1989). BA in Physics, U. Va., 1955; MA in Physics, U. Wis., Madison, 1957, PhD, 1959. Postdoctoral fellow MIT, Cambridge, Mass., 1959-60; asst. prof. U. Wis., Madison, 1960-63, assoc. prof., 1963-67, prof. biochemistry, 1967-69; prof. molecular biology U. Calif., Berkeley, 1969-93. Contbr. chpts. to books, articles to profl. jours. Guggenheim fellow, 1981-82. Mem. Nat. Acad. Scis., 1991, Am. Soc. Biol. Chemists, Genetics Soc. Am., Am. Soc. Microbiology. Democrat. Home: Berkeley Calif. Died Apr. 11, 1993.

ECKMAN, JOHN WHILEY, business executive; b. Forest Hills, N.Y., July 20, 1919; s. Samuel Whiley and Anna (Wolffram) E.; children: Alison Elizabeth, Stephen Keyler. Student, Yale U., 1937-38; B.S., U. Pa., 1943, LL.D. (hon.), 1984; L.H.D. (hon.), Pa. Coll. Podiatric Medicine, 1979; LL.D. (hon.), Phila. Coll. Pharmacy and Sci., 1981. With mktg. Smith Kline & French Labs., Inc., Phila., 1947-52; v.p. Thomas Leeming & Co., Inc., N.Y.C., 1952-62; exec. v.p. Rorer Group Inc. and predecessors, Ft. Washington, Pa., 1962-70, pres., 1970-80, chmn., chief exec. officer, 1976-85, chmn., 1985-86; bd. dirs. Rhône-Poulen Rorer Inc., Chattanooga Group, Inc., Nantucket Shellfish Aqua Farm, Inc., Hither Creek Boat Yard, Inc., U.S. Biosci., Inc.; chmn. audit com. Rittenhouse Trust Co., 1984-93. Trustee U. Pa., 1967-93, chmn. bd. overseers Univ. Librs., 1982-93; bd. mgrs. Winterthur Corp. Coun., 1984-93; bd. dirs. Independence Hall Assn., 1986-93, chmn., 1991-93; Nantucket Hist. Assn., 1987-93, Nantucket Land Coun., 1987-93, Coll. Physicians of Phila., 1986-93, Orthopedic Surgery Inst., 1989. Lt. USNR, 1943-46. Recipient Alumni award of merit U. Pa., 1972, Valley Forge Trail award Boy Scouts Am., 1985, Phila. Caring award Community Home Health Svcs. Phila., 1986, Louis Braille award Associated Svcs. for Phila. Blind, 1987; named Industrialist of Yr., Soc. Indsl. Realtors, 1975. Fellow N.Y. Acad. Sci., Coll. of Physicians of Phila.; mem. Pharm. Advt. Club N.Y. (pres. 1959-60), Pharm. Mfrs. Assn. (dir. 1975-85, chmn. 1981-82), Pharm. Advt. Coun. (hon. life), Greater Phila. C. of C. (dir. 1972-83), Hist. Soc. Pa. (dir., pres. 1980-86), Nantucket Hist. Assn., Nantucket Land Coun., German Soc. Pa. (hon. life), Internat. House (devel. com., human resource com., 1988-93), AAAS, Pa. Soc., Wharton Sch. Alumni Assn (dir. 1966-70, pres. 1968-70), Phila. Com. on Fgn. Rels., S.R., St. Andrews Soc., Confrerie de la Chaine des Rotisseurs, Faculty Club U. Pa. Nantucket Yacht Club, Rittenhouse Club (Phila., v.p. 1988-93), Union League (Phila.), Yale Club (N.Y.C.), Mask and Wig Club (hon.), Sigma Chi (Significant Sig award 1981), Beta Gamma Sigma. Republican. Presbyterian. Home: Collegeville Pa. Died Dec. 17, 1993.

ECKSTINE, BILLY (WILLIAM CLARENCE ECKSTINE), singer; b. Pitts., July 8, 1914. Student, Howard U. Night club singer, emcee, Buffalo, Detroit, then, Club de Lisa, Chgo., vocalist, Earl Hines Band, 1939-43, night club soloist, 1943, with, Budd Johnson, organized band featuring bop music, 1944; orch. leader, singer, trombone player, popular ballad singer, 1948-93, also jazz music; numerous appearances include, Mill Run Theatre, Niles, Ill.; appeared (motion picture) Let's Do It Again, 1975; now with Enterprise Records; recs. include Prime of My Life, 1963, For the Love of Ivy, My Way, 1967, Senior Soul, Stormy, Feel the Warm, If She Walked Into My Life, The Legendary Big Band of Billy Eckstine-Together, The Soul Sessions vol. 6 Newport in New York, 1972, Billy Eckstine Sings With Benny Carter; albums (with Quincy Jones) At Basin Street East, 1990, I Want To Talk About You, 1987. Home: New York N.Y. Died Mar. 8, 1993.

EDELSTEIN, JEROME MELVIN, bibliographer; b. Balt., July 31, 1924; s. Joseph and Irene (Schwartz) E.; m. Eleanor Rockwell, Nov. 5, 1950; children: Paul Rockwell, Nathaniel Benson. A.B. cum laude (teaching fellow 1946-49), Johns Hopkins U., 1947, postgrad., 1947-49; M.L.S., U. Mich., 1953. Italian Govt. fellow, Fulbright grantee U. Florence, Italy, 1949-50; reference librarian rare book div. Library of Congress, 1955-62; bibliographer Medieval and Renaissance studies UCLA, 1962-64, humanities bibliographer, lectr. bibliography, 1966-72; chief librarian Nat. Gallery Art, Washington, 1972-86; asst. dir., sr. bibliographer Getty Ctr. for History of Art and Humanities, Santa Monica, Calif., 1986-94; disting. bibliographer-in-residence John Carter Brown Libr. Brown U., Providence, 1994-96, adj. prof. dept. modern culture and media, 1994-96; lectr. rare book librarianship Cath. U. Am., Washington, 1975-83. Author: A Bibliographical Checklist of Thornton Wilder, 1959; editor, contbr. A Garland for Jake Zeitlin, 1967, The Library of Don Cameron Allen, 1968, Wallace Stevens: A Descriptive Bibliography, 1974; contbr. articles, revs. to profl. jours. Pres. bd. trustees Crossroads Sch., Santa Monica, Calif., 1970-72, hon. mem. bd. trustees ex officio, 1972-96. With AUS, 1943-46. Herzog August Bibliothek fellow, Wolfenbüttel, Fed. Republic Germany, 1985; Guggenheim Meml. fellow, 1986-87. Mem. Am. Antiquarian Soc., Ateneo Veneto, Bibliog. Soc. Am. (notes editor 1964-81), Assn. Internat. Bibliophile, Wallace Stevens Soc. (cons. editor jour. 1976-90), Am. Printing History Assn., Jargon Soc. (bd. dirs. 1976-85), Grolier Club (N.Y.C.), Century Assn. (N.Y.C.), Rounce and Coffin Club (L.A.), Club of Odd Volumes (Boston), Phi Beta Kappa. Home: Bristol R.I. Died June 12, 1996.

EDGERTON, NORMAN EDWARD, business executive; b. Raleigh, N.C., June 14, 1898; s. Noah Edward and Alma (Wynne) E.; m. Mishew Rogers, Feb. 9, 1929; 1 child, Mishew Ellen (Mrs. Mishew Edgerton Smith). Student, Duke U., 1917-19. Founder Raleigh Bonded Warehouse, Inc., 1923, pres., 1923-95. Hon. mem. N.C. Conf. Meth. Bd. Publ. Inc.; Former chmn. com. on improvement state care of mental patients 1st chmn., N.C. Hosps. Bd. Control.; Trustee emeritus Duke U.; former trustee Eastern Carolina Sch. Boys. Mem. Raleigh C. of C. (past pres.), Raleigh YMCA (past pres.), Duke U. General Alumni Assn. (past pres.), S.A.R., Am. Legion, Omicron Delta Kappa, Pi Kappa Alpha. Clubs: Mason (Shriner, past potentate), Kiwanian (past pres.), Carolina Country. Home: Raleigh N. C. Died Mar. 6, 1995.

EDLUND, MILTON CARL, physicist, educator; b. Jamestown, N.Y., Dec. 13, 1924. B.S., M.S., U. Mich., 1948, Ph.D., 1966. Physicist reactor physics, gaseous diffusion plant, 1948-49, Oak Ridge Nat. Lab., 1949-50; physicist, lectr. Sch. Reactor Tech., 1950-51, sr. physicist and sect. chief, 1953-55; mgr. devel. dept. Babcock & Wilcox Co., 1955-65, asst. mgr. atomic energy div., 1965-66; prof. U. Mich., 1966-67; planning cons. AEC, 1967-68; exec. v.p. Nuclear Assurance Corp., Atlanta, 1968-70; chmn. nuclear engring. Va. Poly. Inst. and State U., Blacksburg, 1970-74; dir. Center for Energy Research, 1974-78, prof. nuclear engring., 1978-89, prof. emeritus nuclear engring., 1989-93; vis. lectr. Swedish Atomic Energy Com., 1953. Author: (with S. Glasstone) Elements of Nuclear Reactor Theory, 1952, (with J. Fried) Desalting Technology, 1971. Recipient Ernest Orlando Lawrence award, 1965. Fellow Am. Nuclear Soc.; mem. Nat. Acad. Engring. Home: Blacksburg Va. Died Nov. 10, 1993.

EDMONDSON, JEANNETTE B., state official; b. Muskogee, Okla., June 6, 1925; d. A. Chapman and Georgia (Shutt) Bartleson; m. J. Howard Edmondson, May 15, 1946 (dec.); children—James H. (dec.), Jeanne E. Watkins, Patricia E. Zimmer. B.A., U. Okla., 1946. Sec. of state State of Okla., Oklahoma City, 1979-87. Chmn. bd. Okla. affiliate Am. Heart Assn., 1979. Democrat. Methodist. Home: Oklahoma City Okla. Deceased.

EDWARDS, GEORGE CLIFTON, JR., retired judge; b. Dallas, Aug. 6, 1914; s. George Clifton and Octavia (Nichols) E.; m. Margaret McConnell, Apr. 10, 1939; children: George Clifton III, James McConnell. BA, So. Meth. U., 1933; MA, Harvard U., 1934; JD, Detroit Coll. Law, 1949. Bar: Mich. 1944. Coll. sec. League Indsl. Democracy, 1934-35; prodn. worker Kelsey Hayes Wheel Co., 1936; rep. UAW-CIO, 1937, dir. welfare dept., 1938-39; dir., sec. Detroit Housing Commn., 1940-41; mem. Detroit Common Council, 1941-49, pres., 1945-49; with firm Edwards & Bohn, Detroit, 1946-50, Rothe, Marston, Edwards and Bohn, 1950-51; probate judge charge Wayne County Juvenile Ct., 1951-54; judge Jud. Circuit, Wayne County, 1954-56; justice Supreme Ct., Mich., 1956-62; commr. of police City Detroit, 1962-63; judge U.S. Ct. Appeals 6th Circuit, 1963-95, chief judge, 1979-83; chmn. com. adminstrn. criminal laws Jud. Conf. U.S., 1966-70; mem. Nat. Com. Reform of Fed. Criminal Laws, 1967-71. Author: The Police on the Urban Frontier, 1968, (with others) The Law of Criminal Correction, 1963, Pioneer-at-Law, 1974; also articles on crime and delinquency. Chmn. S.E. Mich. Cancer Crusade, 1950-51; active VFW, Am. Legion; chmn. 13th Congrl. Dist. Dem. Party, Wayne County, 1950-51. Lt. inf. AUS, 1943-46. Recipient award for community work for social progress Workmen's Circle, 1949; award for community work for civil rights St. Cyprian's Episcopal Ch., 1950; Americanism award Jewish War Vets., 1953; award for outstanding achievement juvenile rehab. VFW, 1953; St. Peter's medal for outstanding service to youth St. Peter's Episcopal Ch., Detroit, 1956; August Vollmer award Am. Soc. Criminology, 1966; Judiciary award Assn. Fed. Investigators, 1971. Mem. ABA, Mich. Bar Assn., Detroit Bar Assn., Nat. Coun. Judges, Nat. Coun. Crime and Delinquency, Am. Law Inst., Masons, Phi Beta Kappa, Kappa Sigma. Episcopalian. Home: Cincinnati Ohio Died Apr., 1995.

EDWARDS, JOSEPH CASTRO, physician; b. Springfield, Mo., Dec. 24, 1909; s. Lyman Paul and Lela (Bedell) E.; m. Virginia Anne Moser, Jan. 8, 1942; children: Virginia Lee, Joseph Byron, Jonathan Paul. A.B., U. Okla., 1930; M.D., Harvard U., 1934. Diplomate Am. Bd. Internal Medicine, Am. Bd. Cardiology. Tutorial fellow cardiology with Dr. Paul D. White Mass. Gen. Hosp., 1934; intern Springfield (Mass.) Hosp., 1935; house physician med. svc. Barnes Hosp., St. Louis, 1936-37; Stroud fellow, resident Pa. Hosp., Phila., 1937-38; Eli Lilly fellow in pneumonia rsch. Washington U. Med. Sch., St. Louis, 1939, Smith Kline and French fellow in hypertension, 1940, instr. clin. medicine, 1939-60, asst. prof. clin. medicine, 1960-88, assoc. prof., 1988-94, cons. clinics and div. gerontology, assoc. clin. prof. medicine emeritus, 1988-90; mem. staff Barnes Hosp.; vis. physician St. Louis City Hosp.; mem. staff Deaconess Hosp.; mem. cons. staff St. Joseph Hosp., St. Louis; cardiologist, dir. high blood pressure clinic St. Luke's Hosp.; area med. cons. hearings and appeals div. U.S. Social Security Adminstrn.; med. cons. R.R. Retirement Bd.; cardiovascular cons. div. gerontology Washington U. Sch. Medicine, St. Louis.; med. cons. Fifth Army U.S.A., Chgo.; cons. in field. Author: Hypertensive Disease and Clinical Management, 1959, Management of Hypertensive Disease, 1960; also chpt. in Drugs of Choice, 1959, chpt. in Folia Clinica Internacional, Barcelona, Spain., others; contbr. articles to profl. jours. Bd. dirs. Boys Town, Mo.; former bd. dirs. Speech and Hearing Soc. St. Louis; pres. Doctors Med. Found., St. Louis, 1964; mem. steering com. U.S. Senatorial Bus. Adv. Bd., 1981-88. Lt. col. M.C., AUS, 1942-46, 65. Decorated Legion of Merit. Joseph C. Edwards, M.D. Fund established in his honor Barnes Hosp. Fellow ACP, Am. Coll. Cardiology (gov. Mo. 1962-65), Royal Soc. Medicine (London); mem. Miss. Valley Med. Soc. (pres. 1958), St. Louis Med. Soc. (pres. 1970), Am. Heart Assn., Mo. Heart Assn. (dir.), St. Louis Heart Assn., St. Louis Cardiac Club (dir.), Cen. Soc. Clin. Rsch., A.M.A. (cons. council on drugs), So. Med. Assn., Am. Diabetes Assn., Endocrine Soc., Am. Therapeutic Soc. (v.p. 1961, treas. 1962), Constantinian Soc. (pres. 1978), Paul Dudley White Soc., Soc. for Acad. Achievement (mem. adv. and editorial bd.), S.A.R., Skeet and Trap Club, Internists Club, University Club, Marshland Duck Club, Phi Beta Kappa, Alpha Omega Alpha. Methodist (ofcl. bd.). Home: Saint Louis Mo. Died Jan. 9, 1994.

EDWARDS, WALTER MEAYERS, editor, photographer; b. Leigh-on-Sea, Essex, Eng., July 21, 1908; came to U.S., 1930, naturalized, 1936; s. Walter James and Lillian Emma (Meayers) E.; m. Mary Woodward Worrall, Feb. 11, 1937. Student, Lindisfarne Coll., Westcliff, Essex, Eng., 1917-26. Staff Paris bur. N.Y. Times-Wide World Photos, 1926-27; with Topical Press Agy., London, 1927-29, Harris & Ewing, photographers, Washington, 1930-31; sec.-treas. Pioneer Air Transport Operators Assn., N.Y.C., Washington, 1931-33. Mem. illustrations staff Nat. Geog. mag., 1933-54, illustrations editor, 1955-58, mem. fgn. editorial staff, 1958-62, chief pictorial rsch. div., 1963-73; contbr. articles to Nat. Geog. mag.; contbr. color photographs for Great American Deserts, 1972, America's Beginnings, 1974. Recipient Americanism medal DAR, 1968, Picture of Yr. award Nat. Press Photographers Assn., 1969, 72. Mem. Explorers Club (N.Y.C.), Masons. Christian Scientist. Home: Sedona Ariz. Died Apr. 2, 1994.

EGEKVIST, W. SOREN, corporate consultant, educator; b. Mpls., Dec. 9, 1918; s. Soren Andersen and Lillian (Anderson) E.; m. Margaret Stang, Oct. 21, 1948. A.B., Carleton Coll., 1941; M.B.A., Harvard, 1943; postgrad., Sch. Mil. Govt., U. Va., 1944, U. Chgo., 1945, 51; LL.D., Jamestown Coll., 1975. Chief economist U.S. Civil Service, also chief price control and rationing div. GHQ-SCAP, Tokyo, Japan, 1945-47; ptnr. Robert Heller & Assocs., Cleve., 1948-52; asst. to pres. J. Kayser Co., N.Y.C., 1952-55; v.p., gen. mgr. Munsingwear, Inc., Mpls., 1955-58; pres., dir. Sorenco, Inc. (also doing bus. as W.S. Egekvist & Assocs.), Mpls., 1958-94; sr. corp. advisor Ward & Co., Mpls., 1989-94; interim pres. Jamestown (N.D.) Coll., 1974-76, prof. history, 1976-94, hon. chancellor, 1978-94, also trustee; consul gen., Japan, Mpls., 1976-94; del. FAO-UN, India, 1947. Author: Economic Stabilization Plan for Japan, 1947, Legislation for Economic Stabilization Board, 1947, Economic Controls During Occupation of Japan, 1952. Bd. dirs. Twin City area Internat. Exec. Service Corps; recipient citation for distinguished service, 1970; trustee Jamestown Med. Found., 1975-94, Bishop Whipple Schs., 1976-79. Served to capt. AUS, 1943-46. Decorated Legion of Merit; recipient Meritorious Civilian Service medal War Dept., 1947; decorated Order of the Sacred Treasure with Gold Rays and Neck Ribbon by Emperor of Japan, 1987. Mem. Japan Soc. Minn. (pres. 1975, chmn. bd. 1977-94), Minn. Consular Assn. (v.p. 1994-94), Newcomen Soc., U.S. C. of C. (exec. res. 1958-68), Beta Gamma Sigma. Clubs: Mason (Mpls.) (32 deg., Shriner, Jester), Rotarian. (Mpls.), Harvard Bus. Sch. (Mpls.) (pres. 1962-63), Minneapolis Skylight (Mpls.), Six O'clock (Mpls.), Torske Klubben (Mpls.), Danish-Am. Fellowship (Mpls.), Interlachen Country (Mpls.) (gov. 1963-69), Minneapolis (Mpls.). Home: Minneapolis Minn. Died July 4, 1994.

EGGERS, DAVID FRANK, JR., chemistry educator; b. Oak Park, Ill., July 8, 1922; s. David Frank and Anne Elizabeth (Anderson) E.; m. Vera Ethel Dalton, Jan. 23, 1945; children: Daniel David, Richard Carl, Ann Mabel. BS, U. Ill., 1943; PhD, U. Minn., 1951. Chemist Tenn. Eastman Corp., Oak Ridge, 1944-47; mem. faculty U. Wash., Seattle, 1950-95; assoc. prof. chemistry U. Wash., 1956-63, prof., 1963-90, prof. emeritus, 1990-95; Cons. Jet Propulsion Lab., Pasadena, Calif., 1966. Author: (with Gregory, Halsey, Rabinovitch) Physical Chemistry, 1964; Contbr. profl. jours. Com. chmn. Chief Seattle coun. Boy Scouts Am., 1956-64. Recipient research grants USAF, NSF, Petroleum Research Fund. Mem. Am. Chem. Soc. Presbyn. Home: Seattle Wash. Died Aug. 21, 1995.

EGGERS, MELVIN ARNOLD, educational administrator, economist; b. Ft. Wayne, Ind., Feb. 21, 1916; s. Frederick Carl and Minnie (Kiel) E.; m. Mildred Grace Chenoweth, Apr. 5, 1941; children: Nancy Louise, William David, Richard Melvin. A.B., Ind. U., 1940, A.M., 1941; Ph.D., Yale U., 1950; LL.D. (hon.), Nazareth Coll., 1981; L.H.D. (hon.), SUNY, 1985, Georgetown U., 1986. Clk. Peoples Trust & Savs. Co., Ft. Wayne, 1934-38; instr. econs. Yale, 1947-50; mem. faculty Syracuse U., 1950-70, prof. econs., 1963-70, chmn. dept., 1960-70, vice chancellor for acad. affairs, also provost, 1970-71, chancellor, 1971-94, also pres.; mem. faculty Pacific Coast Banking Sch., 1955-70; cons. financial instns. Mem. Commn. on Ind. Colls. and Univs.; mem. exec. com. N.Y. State Edn. Commrs. Adv. Council on Post-Secondary Edn.; trustee SUNY Coll. Environ. Sci. and Forestry; bd. dirs. Syracuse Symphony, Nat. Kidney Found., Met. Devel. Assn. Served to lt. USNR, 1942-46. Mem. Assn. Am. Univs., Nat. Assn. Ind. Colls. and Univs., Am. Council on Edn.; Mem. Assn. Colls. and Univs. of N.Y. State, Phi Beta Kappa. Home: DeWitt N.Y. Died Nov. 20, 1994.

EHRENKRANZ, SHIRLEY MALAKOFF, university dean, social work educator; b. N.Y.C., Nov. 9, 1920; d. Isidore and Diana Frances (Lewis) Malakoff; m. Gilbert Ehrenkranz, Mar. 29, 1946 (dec.); children: Jean, Joel, Pamela; m. Fred Kasoff, July 11, 1982. A.B., Hunter Coll., 1939; M.A., Bryn Mawr Coll., 1943; M.S.W., U. Pa., 1945; D.S.W., Columbia U., 1967. Case worker Jewish Welfare Soc., Phila., 1943-44; case supr. S.I. Social Svc., N.Y., 1945-48, United Family and Children's Svc., Plainfield, N.J., 1949-53; field instr. Rutgers U., 1960-62; rsch. asst. Columbia U., N.Y.C., 1964-65; asst. prof. social work NYU, N.Y.C., 1966-68, assoc. prof. social work, 1968-73, prof. social work, 1973-94, assoc. dean Sch. Social Work, 1969-76, acting dean, 1976-77, 1977-94; pres. dean's coun. NYU, 1988-90. Co-editor: Clinical Social Work with Maltreated Children and Their Families, 1989; contbr. book revs., articles on social work to profl. jours., chpts. to textbooks. Mem. Commn. on Human Svcs. in Pub. Housing, N.Y.C. Housing Authority, 1991-94. Recipient Disting. Alumna award U. Pa., 1979, ann. award for svc. to community NYU Jewish Culture Found., 1988; NIMH grantee, 1963-64, 65. Mem. NASW (Cert. of Appreciation for Outstanding Contbn. to the Profession 1991), N.Y. State Assn. Deans (v.p. 1979-80, 87-88, pres. 1980-81, 88-89), Acad. Cert. Social Workers, NYU Deans' Coun. (pres. 1988-90). Home: South Orange N.J. Died Aug. 25, 1994.

EHRLICH, CLARENCE EUGENE, obstetrician/gynecologist, educator; b. Rosenberg, Tex., Oct. 19, 1938; s. Oscar Lee and Gertrude Gen (Walzel) E.; m. Sonna Anne Springer; children: Tracey J., Bradley S., Suzanne M. BA, U. Tex., 1961; MD, Baylor U., 1965. Diplomate Am. Bd. Ob-Gyn (mem. gynecology-oncology div. 1982-88, dir. 1985-88, elected organizational mem. 1989-95). Rotating intern Phila. Gen. Hosp., 1965-66; resident in ob-gyn. Tulane U.-Charity Hosp., New Orleans, 1966-69; fellow in gynecologic oncology M.D. Anderson Hosp. and Tumor Inst., Houston, 1971-73; chief sec. gynecologic oncology Ind. U. Med. Ctr., Indpls., 1973-84, from asst. to assoc. prof. ob-gyn., 1973-81, interum chmn. ob-gyn., from 1981, prof., from 1981, med. co-dir. nurse practitioner program, from 1982, William H. and Salie E. Coleman prof. ob-gyn., from 1982, chmn. dept., from 1982, adj. prof. nursing, from 1984. Co-author numerous books; contbr. numerous articles and profl. jours. Served to maj. M.C., USAF, 1969-71. Fellow Am. Coll. Obstetricians and Gynecologists; mem. AAAS, Am. Assn. Cancer Rsch., Am. Chem. Soc., AMA, Am. Radiur Soc., Am. Soc. Clin. Pharmacology and Therapeutic Am. Soc. Parental and Enteral Nutrition, Am. Soc Clin. Oncology, Am. Soc. Colposcopists an Colpomicroscipists, Assn. Profs. Ob-Gyn., Am. Ob Gyn. Soc., Sigma Xi. Home: Indianapolis Ind Deceased.

EHRLICH, RICHARD, bacteriologist, consultant; b Bedzin, Poland, Jan. 19, 1924; came to U.S., 194 naturalized, 1952; s. Jacob and Gela E.; m. Jun Beinhorn, June 2, 1950; children: Glenn J., Jeffre P. M.S., Tech. U. Munich, W. Ger., 1948, Ph.D., 194 Lab. dir. Am. Butter Inst., Chgo., 1949-52; bacteriolo gist Ill. Inst. Tech. Research Inst., Chgo., 1952-57, sup biol. research, then assoc. dir. life scis. research, 1957-6 dir. life sci. research, 1963-77, v.p. life scis. researcl 1977-89, sr. tech. advisor, 1989-90; cons. enviror health, rsch. mgmt. Skokie, Ill., 1990-93; mem. NO subcom. NRC-Nat. Acad. Scis., 1975; mem. rev. con air quality criteria EPA, 1970. Mem. editorial bd.: Ad vances in Modern Environ. Toxicology, Inhalation Tox icology; Author papers in field. Mem. AAAS, Air an Waste Mgmt. Assn., N.Y. Acad. Sci., Soc. Occupationa and Environ. Health (founding mem.), Pan Am. Mec Assn. (life), Soc. Française de la Tuberculose an Maladies Respiratoires (fgn. asso.), Sigma Xi. Hom Skokie Ill. Died Mar. 20, 1993.

EICHENBAUM, E. CHARLES, lawyer; b. Litt Rock, Ark., May 30, 1907; s. E.H. and Sadie C. (Cohr E.; m. Helen Lockwood; 1 child, Peggy Eichenbau Jalenak. LLB, Washington U., St. Louis, 1928; JI Washington U., 1928. Bar: Ark. 1928. Ptn Eichenbaum, Scott, Miller, Liles & Heister, Little Rock Fellow Am. Bar Found. (chmn. Ark. Fellows 1973-9 vice chmn. com. quality lawyer's life, sect. gen. practic 1979-80, mem. adv. com. 1982-84, 50 Yr. award 1988 Ark. Bar Found. (trust com. 1980-93, Lawyer Citizer award 1978-79); mem. ABA (chmn. standing con lawyer retirement benefits 1979-83, taxation, ins., ne ligence and compensation law sects., gen. practice, com corp. stockholder relationship 1975-84, implementir recommendations 1975-78, spl. com. retirement benefi 1976-78, chmn. sr. lawyers div. 1990-91), Ark. B Assn. (chmn. com. taxation 1946-50, chmn. com. tax tion, trusts and estate planning 1953-55, chmn. con fed. legis. and procedures 1969-93, chmn. sr. task for 1982-93, co-chmn. task force on constnl. revision of ju article, Golden Gavel award 1982, 91), Pulaski Coun Bar Assn., Am. Law Inst., Am. Judicature Soc., An Coll. Tax Counsel. Home: Little Rock Ark. Died Jur 28, 1993.

EKERN, GEORGE PATRICK, lawyer; b. Mexic Mo., June 12, 1931; s. Paul Chester and Sallie Ma (McCoy) E.; m. Anita Elizabeth Poynton, June 3, 196 children—Stephen G., Nigel P., Adrienne E. BA, Mo., 1953, JD, 1958. Bar: Mo. 1958, N.Y. 1962, Con 1995. Assoc. Dewey, Ballantine, Bushby, Palmer Wood, N.Y.C., 1960-68; asst. gen. atty. Cerro Corp N.Y.C., 1968-71; asst. sec. Freeport Minerals Co N.Y.C., 1971-75, assoc. gen. counsel, 1975-83; v.p. leg services Homequity, Inc., Wilton, Conn., 1984; sec., ge counsel Handy & Harman, N.Y.C., 1984-87, v.p., se and gen. counsel, 1987-92, of counsel, asst. sec., 199 95. Mem. Darien Bd. Edn., Conn., 1978-81. Fulbrig scholar The Netherlands, 1955-56; fellow Rotary I ternat., London, 1959-60. Mem. ABA, N.Y. State B Assn. (mem. exec. com. corp. counsel sect. 1981—, se 1994-95), Assn. Bar City N.Y. (mem. com. on corp. la depts. 1988-91, com. on lectures and continuing ed 1991-93, com. on corp. law 1993, sec. 1994, chmn. 199 com. on sr. lawyers 1993, sec. 1994—), Am. Soc. Cor Secs., Am. Corp. Counsel Assn., Phi Beta Kappa. Republican. Presbyterian. Home: Madison Conn. Di Aug. 8, 1995.

EKSTROM, CHARLES ALBERT, college president; Long Branch, N.J., June 30, 1936; s. Albert Isadore ar Katherine Anna (Bruning) E.; m. Sandra Louise Kaise June 16, 1962; children: Lisa Ann, Kristin Mar Charles Arthur, Dawn Allison. AAS, Broome Tec Community Coll., Binghamton, N.Y., 1956; BS, SUN Albany, 1960, MS, 1961; postgrad., U. Bridgeport Chem. technician ANSCO, Binghamton, 1956-57; gra teaching asst. SUNY, Albany, 1960-61; mem. facult chmn. dept. Rockland Community coll., Suffern, N.Y 1961-67; dean, exec. dean Housatonic Community Col Bridgeport, Conn., 1967-80; pres. Waterbury (Conn State Tech. Coll., 1980—; pres., sec., mem. exec. co New Eng. Community Jr. Tech. Coll. Coun., Warwic R.I., 1980—; sec. Conn. Learning Network, Ne Haven, 1987—. Mem. edn. com. Waterbury Area P Industry Coun., 1983—; mem. bd. assocs. Bridgeport, 1986—. Mem. New Eng. Assn. Schs. ar Colls. (commr. 1986—), Greater Waterbury C. of C Home: Stratford Conn.

ELFSTROM, DOROTHY LILLIAN BE TENCOURT (MRS. WALTER WILLIA ELFSTROM), author; b. Galveston, Tex.; d. Hen Joseph and Margaret (Rowan) Bettencourt; gra Draughon's Bus. Coll.; m. Walter William Elfstro (dec.); children: Dorothy Elfstrom Bailey, Bill, Hen Weekly columnist Texas City Sun, since 1972; po laureate Galveston County; former poet laureate State Tex.; contbr. poetry to Galveston mag., Travelho mag., IDEALS mag. Recipient 1st pl. awards Nat. Fedn. Press Women, 1963, Tex. Press Women, 1963. Author: Challenge of the Seasons, 1963, Fireside Fancies, 1960, Voyager on the Sea of Life, 1971, Seeker, 1974, In Touch, 1987. Writer various songs including But I Just Can't Say Goodbye, You're Way Behind the Beat, Lovely Galveston, What Are you Trying to Find, At Taps Time I Have a Date With You, Not for Keeps, You Have Shaken Up My World, I Know You've Got to Go, Now You Won't Let Me Be, No Plastic Heart for Me, I Have Captured an Old-Fashioned Christmas, I Fell in Love with You in Old San Antonio, That Good Old-Fashioned 14 Karat Band, You're Destroying a World You Can Never Replace, I Need A Hug From Santa; contbr. to numerous mags. including Sat. Evening Post, Goodhouskeeping, also newspapers. Died May 25, 1993. Home: Galveston Tex.

ELIA, CLAUDIO, manufacturing executive; b. 1943. With The Boston Consulting Group, Mass., 1968-73, Gen. Elec. Co., Fairfield, Conn., 1973-82, IFINT USA Inc., N.Y.C., 1982-88; with Anjou Internat. Co., N.Y.C, 1988-96, pres., ceo; chmn., CEO Air and Water Technologies, 1994-96. Home: New York N.Y. Deceased.

ELION, HERBERT A., optoelectronics and bioengineering executive, physicist; b. N.Y.C., Oct. 16, 1923; s. Robert and Bertha (Cohen) E.; m. Sheila Thall, June 16, 1945; children: Gary Douglas, Glenn Richard, Jonathon Lee, Maxine Yael Gold. BSME, CCNY, 1945; MS, Bklyn. Poly. Inst., 1949, grad. in physics, 1954; grad. cert. X-ray Microanalysis, MIT, 1960; PhD (hon), Hamilton State U., 1973; cert., Cambridge U., Eng., U. Bordeaux, France, Pa. State U., Rutgers U., M.I.T., Northeastern U.; MA, U. Calif., Santa Barbara, San Francisco and Davis; postgrad., Coll. of Marin, Calif., Revere Acad. Jewelry Arts, San Francisco; cert., MacDowell Labs., Aldie, Va. Registered profl. engr., Mass., Pa., N.Y.; MacDowell Labs. VA Cert. Group leader RCA, Camden, N.J., 1957-59; pres. Elion Instruments, Inc., Burlington, N.J., 1959-64; assoc. dir. space sci. GCA Corp., Bedford, Mass., 1965-67; mng. dir. electro-optics Arthur D. Little Inc., Cambridge, Mass., 1967-79; pres., chief exec. officer Internat. Communications and Energy, Inc., Framingham, Mass., 1979—; pres. Aetna Telecommunications Cons., Centerville, Mass., 1981-85; also ptnr. Aetna Telecommunications Cons., Hartford, Conn., 1981-85; pres., chief exec. officer Internat. Optical Telecommunications, Mill Valley, Calif., 1981-93; co-founder Kristallchemie M & Elion GmbH, Meudt, Fed. Fepublic Germany, 1961-64; lectr. on communications to Japanese, French, Can., Korean and Brazilian govts., 1970-93; lectr. on optical communication to govt. depts. in Japan, France, Can., Korea, Brazil, 1970-93; cons. on data communications Exec. Office of Pres., Washington, 1978-79; cons. Ministry Internat. Trade and Industry, Tokyo, 1975-88; chmn. internat. conf. European Electro-optics Conf., Heeze, The Netherlands, 1972-78; Mont. amb. Clean Coal Energy com., 1990-93; internat. lectr. in field. Author, editor 27 books including 11 on lightwave info. networks; co-editor: Progress in Nuclear Energy in Analytical Chemistry Series, 1964-75; mem. adv. bd. Photonics Mag.; several Japanese and internat. world records in geothermal energy devel. activities in clean energy by GeoGas (R) process and clean air by elimination of methane and carbon dioxide gases and econ. prodn. of methyl alcohol from geothermal gases and econ. prodn. of methyl alcohol from geothermal gases; devel. supervision in 100% high strength organically biodegradable or smokeless burning plastic; contbr. articles to profl. jours. Pres. Elion Found., Princeton, N.J., 1960-67; founder Rainbow's End Camp, Ashby, Mass., 1960; elder Unitarian Ch., Princeton, 1963-64, Wellesley Soc. of Friends, 1970. With USN, 1944-46. Decorated Chevalier du Tastevin (France); recipient Presdl. awards Arthur D. Little Inc. Fellow Am. Phys. Soc.; mem. AAAS, IEEE (life mem., sr.), Optical Soc. Am., Soc. Photo Instrumentation Engrs., Am. Vacuum Soc., Nat. Security Industrial Assn., Soc. for Nondestructive testing, Am. Chem. Soc., Geothermal Resources Coun., Sigma Xi, Epsilon Nu Gamma, United Fedn. of Doll Clubs. Home: San Fransisco Calif. Died Nov. 14, 1993.

ELKIN, STANLEY LAWRENCE, author, literature educator; b. N.Y.C., May 11, 1930; s. Philip and Zelda (Feldman) E.; m. Joan Marion Jacobson, Feb. 1, 1953; children: Philip Aaron, Bernard Edward, Molly Ann. AB, U. Ill., 1952, MA, 1953, PhD, 1961, LHD (hon.), 1986; LittD (hon.), Bowling Green State U., 1992. Faculty Washington U., St. Louis, 1960; prof. Am. lit., 1969-95, Merle Kling prof. modern letters, 1983-95; vis. lectr. Smith Coll., 1964-65; vis. prof. U. Calif. at Santa Barbara, 1967, U. Wis. at Milw., 1969, U. Iowa, 1974, Yale U., 1975, Boston U., 1976. Author: Boswell, 1964, Criers and Kibitzers, Kibitzers and Criers, 1966, A Bad Man, 1967, The Dick Gibson Show, 1971, The Making of Ashenden, 1972, Searches and Seizures, 1973, The Franchiser, 1976, The Living End, 1979, Stanley Elkin's Greatest Hits, 1980, George Mills, 1982, The Magic Kingdom, 1985, Early Elkin, 1985, The Rabbi of Lud, 1987, The Six-Year-Old Man, 1987, The Coffee Room, 1988, The MacGuffin, 1991, Pieces of Soap, 1992, Van Gogh's Room at Arles, 1993, Mrs. Ted Bliss, 1995; contbg. author: The Best American Short Stories, 1963, 65, 78; editor: Stories from the Sixties, 1971, Best American Short Stories of 1980, 1980; essays included in: The Best American Essays, 1989, 90, 92, 94. Served with AUS, 1955-57. Recipient humor prize Paris Rev., 1966, Longview Found. award, 1962, Am. Acad. and Inst. Arts and Letters award, 1974, Richard and Hinda Rosenthal award, 1980, So. Rev. award for short fiction, 1981, Nat. Book Critics Cir. award, 1982, Creative Arts award Brandeis U., 1986, Elmer Holmes Bobst award NYU, 1991; fellow Guggenheim Found., 1966-67, Rockefeller Inst., 1988; grantee Rockefeller Found., 1968-69, NEH, 1972. Mem. Am. Acad. Arts and Letters. Home: Saint Louis Mo. Died May 31, 1995.

ELLINGTON, MERCER KENNEDY, trumpeter, conductor, composer; b. Washington, Mar. 11, 1919; s. Edward Kennedy (Duke) and Edna (Thompson) E.; children: Mercedes, Edward, Gaye, Ralph, Paul. Student, Columbia U., Juilliard Sch. Music, NYU. Condr. Duke Ellington Band. Radio commentator Sta. WLIB, N.Y.C., 1962-65; leader own band, until 1949; road mgr., trumpeter Cootie Williams Orch., 1954; gen asst. to Duke Ellington, 1955-59; trumpeter, mgr. band, Duke Ellington Orch., 1965-74, leader orch., 1974-96; composer: (with Duke Ellington) The Three Black Kings; author: (with Stanley Dance) Duke Ellington in Person: An Intimate Memoir, 1978. With AUS, World War II. Home: Beverly Hills Calif. Died Feb. 8, 1996.

ELLIOTT, JOHN FRANK, engineering educator; b. St. Paul, July 31, 1920; s. Stowe E. and Helen (Grube) E.; m. Frances Pendleton, May 4, 1946; children: William S., Dorothy E. Sempolinski. B.S., U. Minn., 1942; Sc.D., MIT, 1949. Phys. chemist Fundamental Research Lab. U.S. Steel Corp., Kearny, N.J., 1949-51; research metallurgist Inland Steel Co., East Chicago, Ind., 1951-54; asst. supt. quality control Inland Steel Co., 1954-55; asso. prof. dept. metallurgy MIT, Cambridge, 1955-60; prof. metallurgy dept. materials sci. and engring. MIT, 1960—, AISI Disting. prof., 1981-87; dir. MIT (Mining and Mineral Resources Research Inst.), 1978—. Author: Thermochemistry for Steelmaking, vol. I, 1960, vol. II 1963, Steelmaking: The Chipman Conference, 1965; editor: The Physical Chemistry of Steelmaking, 1958; contbr. articles to profl. jours. Served to lt. comdr. USNR, 1942-46. Guggenheim fellow, 1965; Disting. mem. Iron and Steel Soc., 1976. Fellow Metall. Soc., Am. Acad. Arts and Scis., AIME (hon. mem. 1982, Douglas Gold medal 1976, Howe Meml. lectr. 1963, extractive metallurgy lectr. 1975, Educator award 1987), Am. Soc. Materials (White disting. teaching award 1971), Am. Inst. Chem. Engrs., AAAS; mem. Nat. Acad. Engring., Iron and Steel Inst. Japan (hon., Tawara Gold medal 1990), Can. Inst. Mining and Metallurgy, Japan Inst. Metals (hon.), Venezuelan Soc. Mining and Metall. Engrs. (hon.), Société Française de Métallurgie (hon.), Sigma Xi, Tau Beta Pi. Home: Winchester Mass. Died Apr. 15, 1991.

ELLIS, SPENCER PERCY, landscape architect; b. Joaquin, Tex., Dec. 17, 1923; s. Nathan Percy and Audrey (Cole) E.; m. Frances Pierce Schulter, Apr. 1, 1977. B.S. in Architecture, Tex. A&M U., 1943, M.Landscape Architecture, 1948. Supt. parks City of Corpus Christi, 1948-54; dir. parks and recreation City of Wichita Falls, Tex., 1954-63; dir. forests and parks State of Md., Annapolis, 1963-71; asst. sec. Md. Dept. Natural Resources, Annapolis, 1971-83; chmn. Ellis Design Group, Ltd., Annapolis, 1984-92; ret., 1992; Md. Gov.'s rep. Public Land Law Rev. Commn.; mem. Appalachian Nat. Trail Adv. Council; state liaison officer Dept. Interior; mem. Susquehanna River Study Group, Chespeake Bay Task Force (C.E.), Chesapeake and Delaware Canal Master Plan Team, Potomac Nat. River Group, Nat. Park Service, Islands Task Force, Bur. Outdoor Recreation, Adv. Commn. on Potomac River Basin, Adv. Com. on Susquehanna River; sec. Md. Bd. Landscape Architects; chmn. Md. Scenic Rivers Rev. Bd.; mem. Md. Bicentennial Commn., Md. Mine Land Reclamation Com., Md. Scenic Beauty Commn., Md. Soil Conservation Com., Md. Interagency Task Force on Outdoor Edn., Md. Rural Safety Commn., Md. Pesticide Commn. Designer various state and mcpl. parks, sub-divs., golf courses; contbr.: articles to Landscape Architecture, Parks and Recreation. Pres. Md. Fedn. of Art, Inc., 1965-69, YMCA of Anne Arundel County, Md., 1966-68, Woods Landing Community Service Assn., 1980-84; bd. dirs. Patuxent 4-H Found., 1965-94. Served with U.S. Army, 1943-47. Decorated D.S.M., Silver Star, Legion of Merit, Bronze Star with V device, Army Commendation medal, Purple Heart; recipient Disting. Service award Am. Inst. Park Execs., 1964. Fellow Am. Acad. Park Adminstrn., Am. Soc. Landscape Architects (pres. S.W. chpt. 1961-63, Md. chpt. 1978-79, trustee 1974-78, 79-80, nat. treas. 1976-77, nat. v.p. 1977-78, sec.-treas. council of fellows 1980-82, chmn. 1983-85), Am. Inst. Park Execs.; mem. Am. Recreation Soc., Nat. Assn. State Outdoor Recreation Liaison Officers (pres. 1971-72), Am. Inst. Park Mgmt. (fellow mem.), Nat. Recreation and Parks Assn. (Meritorious Service award 1966), Am. Park and Recreation Soc., Nat. Soc. Park Resources, Bay Hills Golf Club (charter), Watergate Village Yacht Club (founder), Ft. Collins Country Club, Annapolis Yacht Club, Rotar. Democrat. Home: Fort Collins Colo. Deceased.

ELLISON, RALPH (WALDO), writer; b. Oklahoma City, Mar. 1, 1914; s. Lewis Alfred and Ida (Millsap) E.; m. Fanny McConnell, July, 1946. Student, Tuskegee Inst., 1933-36; Ph.D. in Humane Letters (hon.), 1963; Litt.D. (hon.), Rutgers U., 1966, U. Mich., 1967, Williams Coll., 1970, L.I. U., Coll. William and Mary, 1972, Wake Forest U., 1974, Harvard U., 1974, Brown U., 1980; L.H.D. (hon.), Grinnell Coll., 1967, Adelphi U., 1971. Participant N.Y.C. Writer's Project; lectr. Am. Negro culture, folklore, creative writing NYU, Columbia U., Fisk U., Antioch Coll., Princeton U., Bennington Coll., others; tchr. Russian, Am. lit. Bard Coll., Annandale-on-Hudson, N.Y., 1958-61; Alexander White vis. prof. U. Chgo., 1961; vis. prof. writing Rutgers U., 1962-64; Albert Schweitzer prof. humanities NYU, 1970-79, prof. English emeritus, 1979-94; Hon. cons. in Am. letters Library of Congress, 1966-72; mem. Carnegie Commn. Ednl. TV, 1966-67; vis. fellow Am. studies Yale U., 1966; bd. vis. Wake Forest U., 1972-85; bd. advisors Ossabaw Island Project, 1972-75. Author: (novel) Invisible Man, 1952 (Nat. Book award 1953, Nat. newspaper pubs. Russwurm award 1953), (essays) Shadow & Act, 1964, (essays) Going to the Territory, 1986; editorial bd. Am. Scholar, 1966-69; contbr. short stories, articles, book revs. to pop., profl. mags., 1939-94. Trustee John F. Kennedy Ctr. Performing Arts, 1967-77, New Sch. Social Research, 1969-82, Bennington Coll., 1970-75, Colonial Williamsburg Found., 1971-84; bd. dirs. Ednl. Broadcasting Corp., 1968-79, Mus. City of N.Y., 1970-85; nat. adv. council Hampshire Coll.; mem. Carnegie Commn. on Ednl.TV, 1966-67, Nat. Portrait Gallery Commn., Nat. Council Arts. Served with U.S. Mcht. Marine, 1943-45. Decorated chevalier Ordre et Lettres France; recipient Medal of Freedom U.S., Nat. Medal of Arts, 1985; Ralph Ellison Br. Library, Oklahoma City, named in his honor, 1975; Rosenwald fellow, 1945; Nat. Am. Acad. Arts and Letters fellow Rome, 1955-57. Mem. AAAS, AAAL, PEN, Inst. Jazz Studies (bd. advisers), Nat. Inst. Arts and Letters (chmn. lit. grants com. 1964-67), The Century Assn. Home: New York N.Y. Died Apr. 16, 1994.

ELMS, JAMES CORNELIUS, IV, retired electronics and aerospace executive; b. East Orange, N.J., May 16, 1916; s. James Cornelius and Iva Marguerite (Corwin) E.; m. Patricia Marguerite Pafford, Jan. 4, 1942; children: Christopher Michael, Suzanne, Francesca, Deborah. B.S. in Physics, Calif. Inst. Tech., 1948; M.A. in Physics, UCLA, 1950. Registered profl. engr., Calif. Stress analyst Consol. Aircraft Corp., San Diego, 1940-42; chief devel. engr. G.M. Giannini & Co., Pasadena, Calif., 1948-49; research assoc. in geophysics UCLA, 1949-50; mgr. dept. armament systems, div. autonetics N.Am. Aviation Co., Downey, Calif., 1950-57; asst. chief engr. Martin Co., Denver, 1957-59; exec. v.p. Crosley div. AVCO Corp., Cin., 1959-60; gen. ops. mgr. aeronutronic div. Ford Motor Co., Newport Beach, Calif., 1960-63; dep. dir. Manned Spacecraft Center NASA, Houston, 1963-64; dep. assoc. adminstr. for manned space flight NASA Hdqrs., Washington, 1965-66; dir. Electronics Research Ctr. NASA, Cambridge, Mass., 1966-70; cons. to adminstr. NASA as dep. dir. Space Shuttle Assessment Team NASA, Washington, 1975; corp. v.p., gen. mgr. div. space and info. systems Raytheon, Sudbury, Mass., 1964-65; dir. Trans. Systems Center, Dept. Transp., Cambridge, 1970-74; cons. to adminstr. ERDA, 1975-77; cons. to mgmt. of aerospace and energy cos. Newport Beach, 1975-81; advisor to adminstr. NASA, 1981-85; mem. space systems com. space adv. council NASA, 1970-77; advisor to dir., mem. adv. com. Strategic Def. Initiative Orgn., 1984-88. Patentee in instrumentation, computers, radars and mechanisms. Served to capt. USAAF, 1942-46. Recipient Spl. award NASA, 1964, Exceptional Service medal, 1969, Outstanding Leadership medal, 1970; Sec.'s award for meritorious service Dept. Transp., 1974. Fellow IEEE, AIAA; mem. Nat. Acad. Engring., Am. Phys. Soc., Air Force Assn., Assocs. of Calif. Inst. Tech. (life), Res. Officers Assn., Soaring Soc. Am., Am. Legion. Episcopalian. Clubs: Balboa Yacht; Army and Navy; USMC Open Mess. Home: Newport Beach Calif. Died May 7, 1993; cremated.

EL SAFFAR, RUTH SNODGRASS, Spanish language educator; b. N.Y.C., June 12, 1941; d. John Tabb and Ruth (Wheelwright) Snodgrass; m. Zuhair M. El Saffar, Apr. 11, 1965; children: Ali, Dena, Amir. BA, Colo. Coll., 1962; PhD, Johns Hopkins U., 1966; DHL (hon.), Colo. Coll., 1987; PsyD, Chgo. Sch. Profl. Psychology, 1990. Instr. Spanish, Johns Hopkins U., Balt., 1963-65; instr. English Univ. Coll. Baghdad, 1966-67; asst. prof. Spanish U. Md.-Baltimore County, 1967-68; asst. prof. U. Ill.-Chgo., 1968-73, assoc. prof., 1973-78, prof., 1978-83, rsch. prof. Spanish, 1983-88; prof. Northwestern U., Evanston, Ill., 1988-89; rsch. prof. U. Ill., Chgo., from 1989; dir. summer seminar on Spanish Golden Age lit. NEH, 1979, 82. Author: Novel to Romance: A Study of Cervantes's Novelas Ejemplares, 1974, Distance and Control in Don Quixote, 1975, Cervantes's Casamiento engañoso and Coloquio de los perros, 1976, Beyond Fiction, 1984; editor Critical Essays on Cervantes, 1986, Studies in Honor of Elias Rivers; adv. bd. PMLA; editorial bd. Cervantes, The Comparatist, Hispanic Issues. Woodrow Wilson fellow, 1961, NEH fellow, 1970-71, Guggenheim fellow, 1975-76, Newberry Libr. fellow, 1982, U. Ill. Inst. Humanities fellow, 1985-86, NEH fellow, 1990-91, Danforth assoc., 1973-79, Am. Coun. Learned Socs. grantee, 1978, sr. univ. scholar U.

Ill., from 1986. Mem. MLA (exec. coun. 1974-78, commn. on future of the profession 1980-82, exec. com. div. on Spanish Golden Age poetry and prose 1977-82), Am. Assn. Tchrs. Spanish and Portuguese, Midwest MLA, Cervantes Soc. Am. (exec. com. 1979-82, 86—, v.p. 1989-92, pres. 1992-95). Home: Oak Park Ill. Deceased.

ELSON, EDWARD LEE ROY, minister; b. Monongahela, Pa., Dec. 23, 1906; s. Lee Roy and Pearl (Edie) E.; m. Frances B. Sandys, May 22, 1929 (dec. Dec. 1933); m. Helen Louise Chittick, Feb. 8, 1937; children: Eleanor F., Beverly L., Mary F., David Edward. BA, Asbury Coll., 1928; MTh, U. So. Calif., 1931, postgrad., 1932-33, LHD, 1954; DDiv, Wheaton Coll., 1934, Occidental Coll., 1947; postgrad. Am. sem. in Europe and Russia, 1936; LittD, Centre Coll., 1952, Lafayette Coll., 1958, Gettysburg Coll., 1960; LLD, Norwich U., 1953, Davis and Elkins Coll., 1955, Ashbury Coll., 1958, Hope Coll., 1961; STD, Coll. Emporia, 1955, Ripon Coll., 1956; DHum, Parsons Coll., 1955; LHD, Washington and Jefferson Coll., 1960, Wooster Coll., 1960; DMinistry, Salem Coll., 1974. Ordained to ministry Presbyn. Ch., 1930. Asst. minister ad interim 1st Ch., Santa Monica, Calif., 1930-31; minister 1st Presbyn., La Jolla, Calif., 1931-41; pastor Nat. Presbyn. Ch., Washington, 1946-73, pastor emeritus, 1973-93; chaplain U.S. Senate, Washington, 1969-81; moderator Presbytery of Los Angeles, 1938; commr. Gen. Assembly Presbyn. Ch. U.S.A., 1933, 38, 51, 56, 67; nat. chaplain D.A.V., 1950-51; pres. Washington Fedn. Chs., 1952-54; Western Region dir. Presbyn. post-war Restoration Fund., 1946; mem. bd. pensions, 1948-57; also com. chaplains and service personnel Presbyn. Ch. 1947-57; moderator Presbytery of Washington City, 1966; lectr. Nat. Indsl. War Coll.; Mem. com. John F. Kennedy Ctr. Performing Arts. Speaker at colls. and univs.; author: One Moment with God, 1951, America's Spiritual Recovery 1954 (Freedoms Found. award 1954); And Still He Speaks, 1960; The Inevitable Encounter, 1962; Wide Was His Parish, 1986; Prayers Offered by the Chaplain the Senate of the U.S., 91st Congress, 92d-97th Congresses. Bd. dirs. Freedoms Found. at Valley Forge, Damavand Coll. Ass., Am. Near East Relief; v.p. Am. Friends Middle East 1950-73; v.p. Religious Heritage Am.; pres. bd. dirs. Am. Colony Charities Assn.; trustee Wilson Coll., 1953-73; pres. 1961-72; adv. council Ctr. Study Presidency. Chaplain U.S. Army Res., 1930, advanced through grades to col., 1944, active duty, 1941-46; ret., 1961. Decorated Legion of Merit, Bronze Star, Army Commendations medal; Croix de Guerre avec Palme, Arms City of Colmar (France); gold medal Lebanese order of Merit; Silver Star (Jordan); comdr. Order Medal of Freedom (France); recipient Freedoms Found. award, sermon category, 1951, 54, 57, 58, 59, 60, 62, 64, 72, 73, prin. sermon award, 1965-72; Clergy-Churchman of Yr. citation Ch. Mgmt. and Wash. Pilgrimage of Am. Churchmen, 1954; Edward L.R. Elson monumental wall at Nat. Presbyn. Ch. dedicated in his honor, 1971; named Disting. Citizen of Yr., Los Angeles, 1975; recipient Key to City, Knoxville, Tenn., 1976. Mem. St. Andrews Soc., Am. Friends of Middle East (chaplain), DAV, Acad. Religion and Mental Health, Am. Soc. Ch. History, Ch. Service Soc., World Alliance Ref. Chs., VFW, Am. Legion, Mil. Order World Wars (chaplain), Mil. Chaplains' Assn. (nat. pres. 1957-59), English-Speaking Union, Assn. U.S. Army, Newcomen Soc. N.Am., Internat. Platform Assn., Scottish Am. Heritage, U.S. Capitol Hist. Soc., Res. Officers' Assn. (chaplain Calif. dept. 1937-38), Phi Chi Phi, Chi Alpha, Theta Sigma. Clubs: Cosmos (Washington); Kiwanis (past pres., hon. life mem.) (La Jolla). Home: Fort Belvoir Va. Died Aug. 25, 1993.

EMERSON, JOE C., lawyer; b. 1946. AB with highest distinction, Ind. U., 1969, JD summa cum laude, 1973. Bar: Ind. 1973, U.S. Dist. Ct. (so. dist.) Ind. 1973, U.S. Ct. Appeals (5th, 6th, 7th cirs.) 1973, U.S. Supreme Ct. Law clk. to Hon. Hastings Seventh Cir. Ct. Appeals, 1973-74; now ptnr. Baker & Daniels, Indpls., 1994; mem. local rules adv. com. So. Dist. Ind., 1990-92, chair civil justice adv. group, 1991-92. Fellow Ind. Bar Assn.; mem. ABA, Seventh Cir. Bar Assn., Ind. State Bar Assn., Indpls. Bar Assn., Ind. U. Law Sch. Alumni Assn. (bd. dirs. 1985-87, officer 1988-90, pres. 1990-91), Order Coif, Phi Beta Kappa. Home: Indianapolis Ind. Deceased.

EMERSON, WILLIAM, congressman; b. St. Louis, Jan. 1, 1938; s. Norvell Preston and Marie (Reinemer) E.; m. Jo Ann Hermann, June 21, 1975; children: Victoria Marie, Katharine; children by previous marriage: Elizabeth, Abigail. B.A., Westminster Coll., 1959; LL.B., U. Balt., 1964. Mem. congressional staffs, 1961-70; dir. govt. relations Fairchild Industries, Germantown, Md., 1970-74; dir. public affairs Interstate Natural Gas Assn., Washington, 1974-75; exec. asst. to chmn. Fed. Election Commn., 1975; dir. fed. relations TRW Inc., Washington, 1975-79; public affairs cons. William Emerson & Assn., 1979-80; mem. 97th-103rd Congresses from 8th Dist. Mo., 1981-96; chmn. agriculture subcom. on nutrition & fgn. ag., mem. transp. and infrastructure com., mem. joint com. orgn. of Cong. Served to capt. USAF. Republican. Presbyterian. Home: Kansas City Mo.

EMERY, EDWIN, journalist, educator; b. Chino, Calif., May 14, 1914; s. William E. and Laura A. (Miller) E.; m. Mary Margaret McNevin, Dec. 28, 1935; children: Michael Charles, Laurel Christine, Alison Clare. B.A., U. Calif., Berkeley, 1935, Ph.D., 1943. Mem. editorial staff Daily Californian, 1931-35, editor, 1935; Mem. editorial staff San Francisco Examiner, 1935-36; asst. editor Calif. Monthly mag., 1936-41, mng. editor, 1941-43; lectr. journalism U. Calif., Berkeley, 1938-41; staff writer, war desk editor and bur. chief UP, San Francisco, 1943-45; lectr. journalism and mass communication U. Minn., 1945-46, asst. prof., 1946-50, asso. prof., 1950-54, prof., 1954-93, dir. grad. study, 1973-79; vis. prof. journalism and mass communication U. Wash., Seattle, 1959, Nat. Chengchi U., Taiwan, 1972-73, U. de Navarra, Spain, 1973, Nanyang U., Singapore, 1979-80, Inst. Journalism, Beijing, China, 1984-85; vis. scholar Moscow State U., 1971; Fulbright vis. lectr., Afghanistan, 1973, USIS lectr., Asia, Europe, 1972-73, 79-80; cons. UNESCO, USIA, Am. Newspaper Pubs. Assn., Gannett Found., Freedom Forum, various publishers, 1954-93; editorial writer St. Paul Pioneer Press and Dispatch, summers, 1946-54. Author: The Press and America: An Interpretative History of the Mass Media, 1954, 7th edit. with Michael Emery, 1992, History of the American Newspaper Publishers Assn, 1950, (with P.H. Ault) Reporting the News, 1959, (with P.H. Ault and W.K. Agee) Introduction to Mass Communications, 1960, 10th edit., 1991, 11th edit., 1993, Perspectives on Mass Communications, 1982, Reporting and Writing the News, 1983, Maincurrents in Mass Communications, 1986, 2d edit., 1989, (with J.P. McKerns) AEJMC: 75 Years in the Making, 1988; editor: Journalism Quar. research jour, 1964-73; editorial bd.: Journalism Quar, 1973-93, Journalism History, 1973-93. Mem. Citizens League of Mpls., 1960-93; mem. exec. com. Democratic-Farmer-Labor party, 1948-50. Decorated Order of the Golden Bear; Guggenheim fellow, 1959-60. Mem. Assn. Edn. in Journalism (pres. 1974-75, Bleyer history award 1980, Blum research award 1986), Soc. Profl. Journalists (Nat. Disting. Teaching award 1980), Am. Journalism Hist. Assn. (Kobre rsch. award 1992), Newspaper Guild, Internat. Press Inst., Internat. Assn. for Mass Communication Research, Am. Soc. of Newspaper Editors (mem. edn. com. 1965-68, history com. 1989-93), A.P. Mng. Editors Assn. (mem. research com. 1970-72), Public Relations Soc. Am. (pres. Minn. chpt. 1956), AAUP, Minn. Hist. Soc., Minn. Press Club, Singapore Press Club, Minn. Soc. Fine Arts, UN Assn. of Minn., Minn. Public TV, Sigma Delta Chi (Research award 1950, 54), Phi Beta Kappa, Phi Alpha Theta, Kappa Tau Alpha, Phi Kappa Tau, Pi Delta Epsilon. Democrat. Club: U. Minn. Campus. Home: Minneapolis Minn. Died Sept. 15, 1993.

EMMANUEL, MICHEL GEORGE, lawyer; b. Clearwater, Fla., May 16, 1918; s. George M. and Alexandra (Damianakes) E.; m. Betty Boring, Dec. 19, 1942; children: George Michel II, Martha Alexandra. BS, U. Fla., 1940, LLB, 1948; LLM, NYU, 1949. Bar: Fla. 1948. Research fellow NYU, N.Y.C., 1948-49; ptnr. Mabry, Reaves, Carlton, Fields & Ward, Tampa, 1951-63; mem. firm Carlton, Fields, Ward, Emmanuel, Smith & Cutler, 1963-92; mem. adv. com., lectr. NYU Tax Inst.; lectr. Estate Planning Inst. U. Miami. Contbr. articles to profl. jours. and yachting mags. Bd. dirs., past pres. Hillsborough County Crime Commn.; chmn. Mayor's Com. on Juvenile Delinquency; pres. Crime Stoppers of Cen. Fla.; bd. dirs. Anclote Found., U. South Fla. Found., Univ. Community Found., U. Tampa, Saunders Found., Morrison Found., Fla. Hist. Soc., Univ. Community Hosp., Fla. Yacht Club Coun., United Fund, Tampa Improvement Found., Fales Com., U.S. Naval Acad. Comdr. USNR, World War II. Decorated D.F.C., Air medal with 2 stars, Purple Heart; recipient Gov.'s award for distinguished service to State of Fla. Fellow Am. Coll. Trust and Estate Counsel, Am. Coll. Tax Counsel; mem. ABA, Hillsborough County Bar Assn., Tampa Bar Assn., D.C. Bar Assn., Fla. Bar Assn. (past chmn. tax sect.), Am. Judicature Soc., Tampa C. of C. (past pres.), U.S. C. of C. (taxation com.), Ancient and Secret Order of Quiet Birdman, Ye Mystic Krewe of Gasparilla Club (past king), Univ. Club (past pres.), Tampa Execs. Club, Tampa Club., Tampa Yacht and Country Club, Tower Club, Gainesville Golf and Country Club, Cruising Club of Am., Rotary (past pres.), Sigma Chi, Phi Delta Phi. Episcopalian. Home: Tampa Fla. Died Dec. 11, 1992.

ENDERS, THOMAS OSTROM, U.S. ambassador to Spain; b. Hartford, Conn., Nov. 28, 1931; s. Ostrom and Alice Dudley (Talcott) E.; B.A., Yale U., 1953; Docteur de l'Université , U. Paris, 1955; M.A., Harvard U., 1957; m. Gaetana Elena Mathilde Constanza Marchegiano, July 6, 1955; children: Domitilla Elena, Alice Talcott, Claire Whitmore, Ostrom. Joined U.S. Fgn. Service, 1958; assigned Washington, 1958-60, 63-69, Stockholm, 1961-63; spl. asst. to under sec. state for polit. affairs, 1966-68; dep. asst. sec. state internat. monetary affairs, 1968-69; dep. chief mission, Belgrade, 1969-70; dep. chief mission, Phnom Penh, 1971-73, chargé d'affaires, 1973-74; asst. sec. state for econ. and bus. affairs, Washington, 1974-76; ambassador to Can., 1976-79; ambassador to European Communities, Brussels, 1979-81; asst. sec. state for inter-Am. affairs, Washington, 1981-83; ambassador to Spain, 1983-96. Recipient Arthur S. Flemming award, 1969. Died March 17, 1996. Home: New York N.Y.

ENELL, JOHN WARREN, association executive, educator; b. N.Y.C., June 24, 1919; s. William Howard and Cristabel (Baumann) E.; m. Anna Louise Lefferts, June 4, 1949; children: Margaret Ann, Janet Ellen, Kathryn Laurel, Mark William. B.S., U. Pa., 1940, M.E., 1948; M.Adminstrv. Engring., NYU, 1947, D.Eng. Sci., 1949. Test engr., asst. project engr., sr. exptl. engr. Wright Aero. Corp. div. Curtiss-Wright Corp., Paterson, N.J., 1940-45; from instr. to prof. mgmt. engring. NYU, 1946-58; dir. info. svc. and surveys Am. Mgmt. Assn., 1954-61, dir. rsch., 1961-66, v.p. rsch., 1967-83; v.p. rsch. Juran Inst., Inc., 1983-88; mem. U.S. Mut. Security Adminstrn. mission to Italy, 1952-53; dir. research Am. Found. Mgmt. Research, 1961-67, v.p., 1970-73; mem. AID mission to Vietnam, 1972, IESC missions to Greece, 1973, to Colombia, 1978. Author: (with others) Quality Control Handbook, 1951, rev. edit., 1988, Production Handbook, 1972, (with G.H. Haas) Setting Standards for Executive Performance, 1960; mem. editorial bd. Jour. Indsl. Engring. Trustee Wayne Pub. Library; mem. adv. bd. N.Y. U., N.J. Inst. Tech., Bradley U., Adelphi U. Accreditation Bd. Engring. Tech. fellow, 1992. Fellow Am. Inst. Indsl. Engrs. (nat. v.p. 1966-68, nat. pres. 1968-69); mem. Acad. Mgmt., Am. Mgmt. Assn., Am. Assn. Engring. Socs. (sec.-treas. 1980), ASME, Am. Soc. Quality Control, Am. Statis. Assn., Council on the Continuing Edn. Unit (v.p. 1977-80, pres. 1980-82), Engrs. Council Profl. Devel. (dir., nat. treas. 1973-77), Engrs. Joint Council (nat. treas. 1979), Inst. Cert. Profl. Mgrs. (bd. regents 1981-83), Sigma Xi, Alpha Pi Mu. Home: Cleveland Ohio Died Mar. 6, 1993.

ENGEL, ROBERT GEHRELS, banker; b. Teaneck, N.J., Feb. 7, 1932; s. Daniel Currie and Margaret Mary (Sweeney) E.; m. Jane Virginia Coe, June 20, 1953; children: Jennifer Margaret, Robert Andrew, Elizabeth Hunter. AB, Cornell U., 1953; postgrad., Columbia U. Grad. Sch. Bus., 1957-59. Sales engr. Corning (N.Y.) Glass Works, 1953-55; asst. treas. Morgan Guaranty Trust Co. N.Y. (formerly J.P. Morgan & Co.), N.Y.C., 1957-61, asst. v.p., 1961-64, v.p., 1964-71, sr. v.p., 1971-78, exec. v.p., treas., 1979-86, group. exec., corp. fin., 1986-89, group exec., 1990-91; also group exec. J.P. Morgan & Co. Inc.; sr. advisor Dillon Read & Co., N.Y.C., 1991-93; bd. dirs. Rockefeller Group, Inc., N.Y.C., Raychem Corp., Menlo Park, Calif., Ditchley Found., N.Y.C. Trustee Cornell U.; bd. dirs. N.Y. Hosp.-Cornell Med. Ctr., Teagle Found.; mem. Bergen County (N.J.) Rep. Com., HoHoKus (N.J.) Bd. Edn. Cpl. CIC AUS, 1955-57. Mem. Psi Upsilon. Republican. Episcopalian. Clubs: Union League, Laurel Valley Golf, Hackensack Golf, Meadow Brook, Mid Ocean. Home: Hohokus N.J. Died Aug. 17, 1993.

ENGLEHORN, DAVID WESLEY, architect; b. Cleve., Mar. 20, 1925; s. E. H. and Lucile (Roberts) E.; m. Peggy F. Williams Sept. 4, 1948 (div. May 1984); children: Chris Fortin, Dale, Caryl; m. Sharon Lynn Waggoner, Nov. 2, 1985. BA, Ohio State U., 1950. Registered architect, Ohio, Colo. Pres. C-E Assocs., Inc., Cleve., 1951-88, Englehorn and Assocs. Inc., 1988-90; v.p. HWH Inc., Cleve., 1990-95. Prin. works include Marathon Oil Co. Nat. Hdqrs. Bldg., Findlay, Ohio, Hobart Corp. World Hdqrs. Bldg., Troy, Ohio, Alltel Hdqrs. Bldg., Hudson, Ohio, United Telephone Co. Ohio Hdqrs. Bldg., Mansfield, Ohio, Blanchard Valley Hosp. complex, Findlay, Ohio. Served with U.S. Army, 1943-46. Mem. AIA, Architects Soc. Ohio, Nat. Coun. Archtl. Registration Bds., YMCA (bd. dirs. 1985-86). Republican. Protestant. Clubs: Atwood Yacht, University. Home: Cleveland Ohio Died Feb. 19, 1995.

ENGLISH, WOODRUFF JONES, lawyer; b. Elizabeth, N.J., Apr. 28, 1909; s. Conover and Sara Elizabeth (Jones) E.; m. Carolyn Barton, Dec. 19, 1942; children: Woodruff Jones II, Virginia English Sprenkle, Barton Conover, Elizabeth Cooper, Carolyn Whitaker. A.B., Princeton U., 1931; LL.B., Harvard U., 1934. Bar: N.J. 1935. Since practiced in Newark; ptnr. McCarter & English, 1947-82, of counsel, 1982-96; lectr. trusts and estates. Pres. Summit (N.J.) United Appeal, 1947-48; mem. Summit Environ. Commn., 1971-76; trustee Presbyn. Hosp., Newark, 1947-58; trustee United Hosps. Newark, 1959-70, chmn. bd., 1967-70; trustee Overlook Hosp., Summit, 1949-55, pres., 1953-55; trustee United Community Fund Newark, 1957-71, pres., 1961-65; trustee Frost Valley YMCA, 1959-96, pres., 1967-84, chmn. bd., 1984-96; trustee Overseas Ministries Study Ctr., 1958-89 , sec., 1958-70, pres., 1970-88; bd. dirs. Summit YMCA, 1935-39; bd. dirs. Newark YM-YWCA, 1951-84, pres., 1957-61; mem. internat. com. nat. bd. YMCA, 1953-72, exec. com., 1953-72, sec. exec. com., 1960-64, vice chmn. student work com., nat. bd., 1952-62, mem. nat. council, 1973-82, exec. com. internat. div. nat. bd., 1972-81; chmn. student work com. Central Atlantic Area, 1955-60; trustee N.J. region NCCJ, 1961-72; trustee Colonial Symphony Soc., 1951-61, v.p., 1959-61; trustee, mem. exec. com. Drew U., 1972-88; pres. Summit Council Chs., 1948-50. Served to lt. comdr. USNR, 1941-45. Hon. award NCCJ, 1973. Fellow Am. Coll. Probate Counsel; mem. Am. Law Inst., ABA, N.J. Bar Assn., Essex County Bar Assn., N.J. Soc. Hosp. Attys. (v.p. 1972). Republican. Presbyterian (ruling elder 1951-96). Clubs: Nassau (Princeton, N.J.), Baltusrol Golf. Home: Hightstown N.J. Died Mar. 3, 1996.

ENGMAN, LEWIS AUGUST, lawyer, trade association executive, former government official; b. Grand Rapids, Mich., Jan. 6, 1936; s. H. Sigurd and Florence C. (Lewis) E.; m. Patricia Lynne Hanahan, Dec. 2, 1978; children: Geoffrey Ponton, Jonathan Lewis, Richard Ransford. A.B., U. Mich., 1957; postgrad., Univ. Coll. and London Sch. Econs., 1957-58; LL.B., Harvard U., 1961. Assoc., then ptnr. law firm Warner Norcross & Judd, Grand Rapids, 1961-70, Washington, 1976-79; pres. Pharm. Mfrs. Assn., Washington, 1979-84; ptnr. Winston & Strawn, Washington, 1985-93; pres. Generic Pharm. Industry Assn., Washington, 1993-95, Nat. Drug Trade Conf., 1980; dir. legis. affairs Pres.'s Com. Consumer Interests, Washington, 1970; gen. counsel White House Office Consumer Affairs, Washington, 1970-71; asst. dir. Domestic Council, The White House, Washington, 1971-73; chmn. FTC, Washington, 1973-75; mem. Council Adminstrv. Conf. of U.S., 1974-75, pub. mem., 1986-95, sr. conf. fellow, 1995; chmn. Blue Ribbon Com. on Generic Medicines, 1990; mem. U.S. Congress Office Tech. Assessment Adv. Panel on Govt. Policies and Pharm. Rsch. and Devel., 1989-92; life mem. 6th Cir. Jud. Conf. U.S.; Bd. advisors Columbia U. Ctr. for Law and Econ. Studies, 1975-79, Mich. Franchise Adv. Com., 1977-79; mem. Western Mich. Areawide Comprehensive Health Planning Unit, 1969-70; chmn. Kent County (Mich.) Health Planning unit, 1969-70. Mem. Friends of Art adv. bd. Grand Valley State Coll., 1969-70; mem. Kent County Republican Fin. Com., 1965-70; bd. dirs. Opera Assn. Western Mich., 1967-69; bd. dirs. Grand Rapids Symphony Soc., 1964-70, pres., 1968-70; trustee Blodgett Meml. Hosp., 1968-70, sec., 1969-70; bd. dirs. Dyer-Ives Found., 1964-95, sec., 1961-70; bd. trustees Nat. Found. for Advancement in the Arts, 1992-95. Mem. ABA (mem. council sect. anti-trust law 1973-75), D.C. Bar Assn., State Bar Mich., Phi Beta Kappa, Delta Sigma Rho, Phi Kappa Phi, Phi Eta Sigma. Presbyterian. Clubs: Kent Country (Grand Rapids), University (Grand Rapids); George Town (Washington), Metropolitan (Washington). Home: Mc Lean Va. Died July 12, 1995.

ENLOE, CORTEZ FERDINAND, JR., magazine publisher, physician; b. Jefferson City, Mo., June 1, 1910; m. Mary Josephine Greenlee, May 4, 1963 (dec. Aug. 1990); children: Margaret Mary Greenlee, David Goodridge, Cynthia Holden. B.A., U. Mo., Columbia, 1932; postgrad., Ruperto Carola U. Heidelberg, Ger., Ludwig Maximillians U. Munich, Ger.; M.D. cum laude, U. Berlin, 1937; grad., Sch. Aviation Medicine, 1942, Command and Gen. Staff Coll., 1943. Diplomate: Am. Bd. Preventive Medicine. Research intern Charity Clinic, Berlin, 1936-37; intern St. Anthony Hosp., St. Louis, 1937-38; practice medicine, specializing in internal medicine; asst. med. dir. Winthrop Chem. Co., N.Y.C.; exec. v.p., gen. mgr. G.F. Harvey Co., Saratoga Springs, N.Y.; dir. profl. services and clin. research William R. Warner, Inc., N.Y.C.; v.p. Murray Breese Assos., N.Y.C.; chmn. bd., pres. Cortez F. Enloe, Inc., N.Y.C.; pres. Mediphone, Inc., Washington; sr. partner Enloe, Stalvey & Assocs., Washington; chmn. bd., pres. Nutrition Today, Inc., Annapolis, Md., 1964-86; editor, pub. Nutrition Today mag., 1964-86; mem. med. adv. bd. Nat. Assn. Human Devel., Washington, 1980-95; hon. Militare Samfunn lectr. Oslo, 1980; v.p. Chindits Old Comrades Assn., Wolverhampton, U.K.; dir. Antarctic Nutrition Survey, 1968-95; chmn. sci. adv. com. Am./Norwegian Trans Polar Expdn., 1968-69; ofcl. observer NATO High Arctic Exercises, 1980; Central European corr. Kansas City Star, 1933-37; cons. fed. adminstr. CD and dir. Office of Emergency Planning; adminstr. N.Y. State CD; cons. mem. Council Nat. Def., AMA; cons. Surgeon Gen. USAF; mem. N.Y. Gov's Adv. Com. Emergency Health Resources. Editor: The Flight Surgeon's Manual, 1954; contbr. articles to sci. jours. and yachting mags. Trustee Geriatrics Research Found. Served to maj. USAAF, 1946, CBI, PTO, ETO; med. advisor to Admiral Lord Louis Mountbatten, comdr. CBI. Decorated Legion of Merit, Air medal, Bronze Star, Antarctic medal, numerous others; recipient Faculty-Alumni Gold medal U. Mo., 1973, citation Jefferson City Public Schs., Nat. Air Power award Air Force Assn., 1955, Nat. Leica Photographers medal, 1939; Churchill scholar Westminster Coll., 1988; Churchill fellow Westminster Coll., Fulton, Mo. (life), fellow Churchill Meml. and Library, 1988. Fellow N.Y. Acad. Medicine, Royal Soc. Medicine (London), Royal Geog. Soc. (London), Aerospace Med. Assn., Am. Coll. Angiology, Am. Geriatrics Soc.; mem. AMA, N.Y. State Med. Soc. (chmn. space medicine sect.), County N.Y. Med. Soc., Am. Coll. Preventive Medicine, Am. Chem. Soc., AAAS, Endocrine Soc. (emeritus), Space Med. Soc., World Med. Assn., Hollywood (Calif.) Acad. Medicine (hon. life), Hakluyt Soc. (London), Air Force Assn. (life, past dir.), Soc. Med. Friends of Wine (hon. life), N.Y. Yacht Club (Atlantis trophy 1964, D.S.M. 1967), Annapolis Yacht Club, Explorers of N.Y., Spl. Forces Club (London). Home: Annapolis Md. Died Mar. 14, 1995.

ERDELYI, MIKLOS, conductor; b. Budapest, Hungary, Feb. 9, 1928; s. Ernö and Ida (Friedrich) E.; m. Katalin Miklōs, July 28, 1952. Student, Music Acad. Budapest, 1949. Condr. Hungarian State Opera, Budapest, 1951-93. Condr. concerts with Berlin Philharm. Orch., 1974-75, 78, Bamberg Symphony Orch., 1976, 78; toured throughout Europe, also concerts in San Antonio, 1972, Japan, 1966-88; guest condr. Finland Nat. Opera, 1986-88, Helsinki Nat. Opera, Tokyo Yomiuri Nippon Orch. Recipient Liszt prize, 1960, Merited Artist award, 1967, Kossuth prize, 1975, Outstanding Artist award, 1985, Eternal Mem. of the Hungarian State Opera, 1989. Roman Catholic. Home: Budapest Hungary Died Sept. 2, 1993; interred Cemetery Farkasret, Budapest, Hungary.

ERI, VINCENT, Papau New Guinean government official. Gov. gen. Govt. of Papua New Guinea, Port Moresby, 1990-93. Home: Port Moresby Papua New Guinea Died May 25, 1993.

ERIKSON, ERIK HOMBURGER, psychoanalyst; b. Frankfurt-am-Main, Germany, June 15, 1902; came to U.S., 1933, naturalized, 1939; (parents Danish citizens); m. Joan Mowat Serson, Apr. 1, 1930; children: Kai T., Jon M., Sue Erikson Bloland. Grad., Vienna Psychoanalytic Inst., 1933; MA (hon.), Harvard, 1960, LLD (hon.), 1978; LLD, U. Calif., 1968, Brown U., 1972; DSc (hon.), Loyola U. at Chgo., 1969; D in Social Sci. (hon.), Yale, 1971, U. Lund, 1980; DHL (hon.), U. San Francisco; D Social Sci. (hon.), Copenhagen U., 1987. Psychoanalyst, 1933-94, tng. psychoanalyst, 1942-94; teaching, research Harvard Med. Sch., 1934-35, Yale Sch. Medicine, 1936-39, U. Calif. at Berkeley and San Francisco, 1939-51; sr. staff mem. Austen Riggs Center, Stockbridge, Mass., 1951-60; vis. prof. U. Pitts. Sch. Medicine, 1951-60; prof. human devel., lectr. psychiatry Harvard, 1960-70, prof. emeritus, 1970-94, disting. vis. prof. Erikson Ctr., 1982-94; sr. cons. in psychiatry Mt. Zion Hosp., San Francisco, 1972-94. Author: Childhood and Society, 1950, 2d edit., 1963, 35th anniversary edit., 1985, Young Man Luther, 1958, Insight and Responsibility, 1964, Identity; Youth and Crisis, 1968, Gandhi's Truth, 1969 (Nat. Book award 1970, Pulitzer prize 1970, Melcher award 1970), Dimensions of a New Identity, 1973, Jefferson Lectures, 1974, Life History and the Historical Moment, 1975, Toys and Reasons: Stages in the Ritualization of Experience, 1977, Identity and the Life Cycle, 1980, The Life Cycle Completed, 1982, (with Joan Erikson and Helen Kivnick) Vital Involvement in Old Age, 1986; Editor: Youth: Change and Challenge, 1963, Adulthood, 1978; editor: (with Smelser) Themes of Work and Love in Adulthood, 1980. Recipient Foneme prize Milan, 1969, Aldrich award Am. Acad. Pediatrics, 1971, Montessori medal Am. Montessori Soc., 1973, McAlpin Research award Nat. Assn. for Mental Health, 1974. Fellow Am. Acad. Arts and Scis.; mem. Nat. Acad. Edn. (emeritus), Am. Psychoanalytic Assn. (life), Cambridge Sci. Club, Signet Soc., Phi Beta Kappa (hon.). Home: Cambridge Mass. Died May 12, 1994.

ERWIN, FREDERICK JOSEPH, broadcast executive; b. Waterbury, Conn., Feb. 23, 1925; s. Frederick J. and Gertrude (O'Connell) E.; m. Patricia Deeley, Nov. 27, 1955; children: David, Steven, Dana, Judith, Joseph. BS, Bryant Coll., 1949. With sales dept. IBM, Bridgeport, Conn., 1953-55; salesman Sta. WATR, Waterbury, 1955-68; gen. mgr. Stas. WATR, WWYZ-FM, Waterbury, 1968-94. Served to 1st sgt. U.S. Army, 1943-46, 50-52. Democrat. Roman Catholic. Home: Waterbury Conn. Died May 31, 1993.

ESAU, KATHERINE, retired botanist, educator; b. Ekaterinoslav, Russia, Apr. 3, 1898; naturalized. Ph.D., U. Caif., 1931, LL.D. (hon.), 1966; D.Sc. (hon.), Mills Coll., 1962. Instr. botany, jr. botanist U. Calif.-Davis, 1931-37, asst. prof., asst. botanist, 1937-43, assoc. prof., assoc. botanist, 1943-49, prof., botanist, 1949-63; prof. botany U. Calif.-Santa Barbara, 1963-65, emeritus prof. botany, from 1965; Prather lectr. Harvard U., 1960. Recipient U.S. Nat. Medal of Sci., 1989; Guggenheim fellow, 1940. Fellow Am. Acad. Arts and Scis.; mem. NAS, AAAS, Swedish Royal Acad. Sci., Am. Philos. Soc., Bot. Soc. Am. (pres. 1951). Deceased. Home: Santa Barbara Calif.

ESHBACH, WILLIAM WALLACE, architect; b. Allentown, Pa., Mar. 12, 1917; s. William W. and Annie (Krum) J.; m. Hilda Kern Campbell, Nov. 5, 1943; 1 son, William Wallace, Jr. B.Arch., U. Pa., 1941. Lic. architect, Pa., N.J., Del., Md. With DuPont Co., Wilmington, 1941-43, George Daub (architect), Phila., 1946-47; assoc. and project mgr. Vincent G. Kling, Phila., 1947-52; ptnr. William W. Eshbach (architect and assocs.), Phila., 1952-54, Eshbach, Pullinger, Stevens & Bruder (architects and engrs.), 1954-72, Eshbach Glass Kale and Assos. (architects, engrs. and planners), 1972-79; chmn. bd. TEI Cons. Engrs., Inc., 1970-72, pres., 1972-81; ptnr. Eshbach-Kale & Assos., 1979-87; cons. architect, 1988-94; chmn. bd., pub. interest dir. Fed. Home Loan Bank Pitts., 1973-75; mem. panel Am. Arbitration Assn., 1958-60; mem. pub. adv. panel on archtl. services GSA, 1969-73; mem. adv. panel on new sch. arch. Temple U., Phila., 1970-74. Prin. archtl. projects include State Office Bldg. and Plaza (Honor award Pa. Soc. Architects), Harrisburg, Arts and Humanities Bldg., Pa. State U., housing complex, U. Pa., Kent & Queen Anne's Hosp., Chestertown, Md. (selected as example of master planning & design of a rural hosp. in U.S., Dir. Mus. Modern Art, N.Y.C., also 2 awards of merit Pa. Soc. Architects and Phila. chpt. AIA), Class and Adminstrn. Bldg., Rutgers U., Camden, N.J. (1st Honor award Pa. Soc. Architects), Law School and Social Sci., Temple U., Mus. at Valley Forge Nat. Park, St. Paul's E. & R. Ch., Harrisburg, Pa. (award for master planning and design of first increment Nat. Ch. Conf.), dormitories Glasboro Coll., N.J. (design award of merit N.J. Soc. Architects, AIA, Dr. Samuel Rossman's residence, Pa.; prin. engring. projects include: regional mass transp. study for Buffalo area, extension to subway system Phila. N.E. Freeway, Phila. Mem. adv. com. Temple U., Phila. Lt. USNR, 1943-46, PTO. Fellow AIA (v.p. 1964-65, mem. vis. nat. archtl. accreditation teams, chmn. various coms. regional dir. nat. bd. 1961-63, Edward C. Kemper award 1966), Pa. Soc. Architects (dir. 1956-57, sec. 1957-58, pres. 1959-60, dir. 1956-60, chmn. com. Pa. interprofl.-govt. relations com. 1967-71). Club: Harbour League (Camden). Home: Springfield Pa. Died May 18, 1994; cremated.

ESKOFF, RICHARD JOSEPH, life insurance company executive. V.p., chief exec. officer Transamerica Life Ins. & Annuity Co., L.A., chmn. bd., pres., chief exec. officer. Home: Los Angeles Calif. Deceased.

ESPINOSA, AUGUSTO, Colombian government official, foreign service officer; b. Bucaramanga, Colombia, June 5, 1919; s. Abdon and Isabel (Valderrama) E.; m. Myriam Silva, Feb. 5, 1944; children: Augusto, Javier, Daniel Fernando. D. in Law and Polit. Sci., Universidad Nacional, Bogota, Colombia. Mgr., Banco de Bogota, Bucaramanga, 1943-46; mem. Colombia Ho. Reps., Bogota, 1947-51, 74-78; gen. mgr. Agr. Indsl. and Mining Credit Bank, Bogota, 1959-61; pres. Senate of Colombia, 1963-64, senator, 1958-74, 78-90, pres. 1st commn. of senate, 1982; minister agr. Colombian Govt., 1958-59; ambassador and permanent rep. to UN, N.Y.C., 1970-73, A.E. and P. to Eng., 1982-90. Author: The Economic and Political Thought in Colombia. Decorated Great Cross Order of Merit (France). Liberal. Roman Catholic. Clubs: Jockey, Country (Bogota). Deceased. Home: Bogota Columbia

ESPOSITO, ALBERT CHARLES, ophthalmologist, state legislator; b. Pitts., Nov. 9, 1912; s. Charles Micali and Elizabeth (Cuda) E.; m. V. Elizabeth Dodson, July 17, 1940; children: Bettina (Mrs. Peter F. Kelly), Mary Alice (Mrs. Andrew Tartler), Gregory C. B.S., U. Pitts., 1933; M.D. cum laude, Loyola U., 1938; D.Sc. (hon.), Marshall U., 1976. Diplomate: Am. Bd. Ophthalmology. Intern St. Francis Hosp., Pitts., 1938-39; resident Ohio State U. Med. Coll. Hosp., 1940-43, Wilmer Eye Inst., 1941-43; practice medicine specializing in ophthalmology Huntington, W.Va., 1946-95; instr. ophthalmology Ohio State U. Med. Coll., 1943-45, asso. prof., 1945-47; chmn. dept. ophthalmology St. Mary's Hosp., Huntington, 1950—; pres. staff St. Mary's Hosp., 1966-67; cons. VA Hosp., C. & O. Ry.; attending ophthalmologist Cabell Huntington, Huntington and Morris Meml. hosps.; clin. prof., chmn. dept. ophthalmology Sch. Medicine, Marshall U., 1976—; Pres. S. W.Va. Blue Shield; dir. First City Bank, Huntington; mem. W.Va. Ho. of Reps., 1974-95; minority whip, minority chmn. health, welfare, edn., banking and ins. coms.; alt. del. Rep. Nat. Conv., Detroit, 1980; exec. com. W.Va. State Rep. Com., 1982-95, 4th Congl. Dist., 1982-95, 5th State Senatorial Dist., 1982-95, 13th Del. Dist., 1982-95; elected del., mem. polit. orgn. com. to Rep. Nat. Conv., New Orleans, 1988. Originator of Veterans Administration Medical School Assistance Act, 1972; contbr. articles to profl. jours. Chmn. med. sch. com., bd. dirs., mem. faculty Marshall U. Found.; trustee Doctors Meml. Hosp., C. & O. R.R. Employees' Hosp. Assn.; sec.-treas. Norval Carter Trust Fund; bd. dirs. Shipyard Plantation, Hilton Head, S.C. Maj. M.C., AUS, World War II. Recipient Outstanding Ophthalmologist in South award, 1970, Marshall U. Disting. Svc. award, 1973, Appreciation award City of Huntington, 1974, Stritch medal, 1974, Disting. West Virginian award, 1976, Southern Med. Assn. Disting. Svc. award, 1988; inducted into Wall of Fame, City of Huntington, 1989. Fellow Internat. Coll. Surgeons (regent W.Va. chpt.), A.C.S., Oxford (Eng.) Congress Ophthalmology, Am. Acad. Ophthalmology (teaching staff 1967-95, Honor award 1977), Am. Assn. Ophthalmology (pres.), Southeastern Surgical Congress; mem. AMA, So. Med. Assn. (past pres., trustee, chmn. sect. ophthalmology, Disting. Svc. award 1988), W.Va. Med. Assn. (past pres.), Assn. Univ. Profs., Ophthalmology, Société Française d'Opthalmologie, Greater Huntington C. of C. (dir.), W.Va. Acad. Ophthalmology (pres.), Alpha Omega Alpha. Clubs: Elk, Guyan Golf and Country, Huntington Gun, Serena Yacht. Home: Huntington W. Va. Died Sept. 20, 1995.

ESTCOURT, VIVIAN FITZGEORGE, consulting electrical and mechanical engineer; b. London, May 31, 1897; came to U.S., 1912, naturalized, 1921; s. Rowland Metzner and Constance A. (Swain) E.; m. Helen Grant, June 21, 1929 (dec. Dec. 1977). A.B., Stanford U., 1922. Lic. profl. elec. and mech. engr., Calif. Mech. draftsman Consol. Copper Co., 1922-23; efficiency engr. Pacific Gas and Electric Co., San Francisco, 1923-36, asst. supt. steam dept., 1936-39; asst engr. ops. Pacific Gas and Electric Co., 1939-45; engr. steam and gas Pacific Gas and Electric Co., San Francisco, 1945-50, gen. supt. steam generation dept., 1950-60, mgr. steam generation dept., 1960-62, cons. engr., 1962-64; cons. engr. Bechtel Power Corp., San Francisco, from 1963; mem. accreditation of engring. colls. com. Engrs.' Council for Profl. Devel., N.Y.C., 1958-64; mem. com. on furnace safeguards Nat. Fire Protection Assn., Boston, from 1958; mem. tech. adv. com. on sea water conversion U. Calif.-Berkeley, 1960-64; chmn. joint steering com. on stack plume opacity Edison Electric Inst. and USPHS, Washington, 1960-64. Contbr. articles, sect. to profl. publs., from 1953. Recipient Newcomen Soc. Gold medal in steam Franklin Inst., Phila., 1966. Fellow ASME (chmn. San Francisco sect. 1940-41 Prime Movers Com. award, hon. mem. 1963 Centennial medal), Power Engring. Soc. of IEEE (hon. mem. generation com. 1983), IEEE (sr. mem.); mem. ASTM, Nat. Acad. Engring. Clubs: Commonwealth of No. Calif. (San Francisco), Engrs.' of San Francisco (San Francisco). Lodge: Masons. Home: San Francisco Calif. Deceased.

ETHEREDGE, ROBERT FOSTER, lawyer, state legislator; b. Birmingham, Ala., July 14, 1920; s. Joel H. and Nell (Cain) E.; m. Joanna Carson, Aug. 28, 1948; children: Robert Foster, Carson, Nancy. A.B., U. Ala., 1946, LL.B., 1949. Bar: Ala. 1949. Practiced in Birmingham; of counsel Spain, Gillon, Grooms, Blan & Nettles (and predecessors), 1949-92. Mem. Ala. Ho. of Reps. from Jefferson County, 1963-92; mem. adv. com. Family Ct.; Pres. Ala. Soc. for Crippled Children and Adults, 1972-73; bd. dirs. Jefferson County Soc. Crippled Children and Adults, No. Ala. Rehab. Facility. Served to 1st lt. AUS, 1943-46. Recipient citation for meritorious service Rotary Found. Mem. Am., Birmingham bar assns., Ala. State Bar, Internat. Assn. Ins. Counsel, Ala. Law Inst., Ala. Def. Lawyers Assn., Farrah Law Soc., Newcomen Soc. N.Am., Am. Legion, VFW, Omicron Delta Kappa, Pi Kappa Alpha. Democrat. Methodist. Clubs: Elks (Birmingham), Eagles (Birmingham), Rotary (Birmingham) (pres. 1981-82), Birmingham Country (Birmingham), Relay House (Birmingham). Died Apr. 11, 1992.

ETTINGER, GEORGE HAROLD, physiologist; b. Kingston, Ont., Can., May 9, 1896; s. John George and Elizabeth Jane (Watts) E.; m. Pearl Elizabeth Blyth, Dec. 21, 1920 (dec. 1958); 1 dau., Barbara Joan Ettinger Hinton; m. Margaret Elizabeth Mackay Sawyer, Apr. 19, 1969. B.A. Queen's U, Kingston, 1916, M.D., C.M., 1920, LL.D. (hon.), 1967; postgrad., U. Chgo., 1923, U. Edinburgh, Scotland, 1928-29; D.Sc. (hon.), U. Western Ont., London, 1958; M.D. (hon.), U. Ottawa, Ont., 1963. Lectr. in physiology Queen's U., 1920-29, asst. prof. physiology, 1929-33, asso. prof., 1933-35, prof., 1935-62, dean medicine, 1949-62; dir. med. planning Addiction Research Found., Toronto, Ont., 1962-70; ret. 1970; research asso. U. Toronto, 1931-35; hon. sec. Asso. Com. on Med. Research, Nat. Research Council Can., Ottawa, 1939-46, asst. dir. div. med. research, 1946-58. Author: History of the Associate Committee on Medical Research of NRC, 1946, History of the Canadian Physiological Society, 1970. Served with Royal Canadian Army M.C., 1918-19. Decorated mem. Order Brit. Empire; Queen's Jubilee medal Can. Govt. Fellow Royal Soc. Can.; mem. Am. Physiol. Soc., Physiol. Soc. Gt. Brit., Am. Assn. Anatomists, Can. Physiol. Soc., Can. Med. Assn. (sr.). Mem. United Ch. of Canada. Home: Kingston Can. Died Sept. 12, 1992; buried Cataraqui Cemetery, Kingston, Ont., Can.

EURE, THAD, retired state official; b. Gates County, N.C., Nov. 15, 1899; s. Tazewell A. and Armecia (Langstun) E.; m. Minta Banks, Nov. 15, 1924; children: Armecia (Mrs. J. Norman Black, Jr.), Thad. Student, U. N.C., 1917-19, Law Sch., 1921-22; LL.D., Elon Coll., 1958. Lawyer; mayor City of Winton, N.C., 1923-28; atty. Hertford County, N.C., 1923-31; prin. clk. N.C. Ho. of Reps., 1931, 33, 35, 36; sec. state State of N.C., Raleigh, 1936-89, ret., 1989; Mem. N.C. Ho. of Reps., 1929; keynote speaker N.C. Democratic Conv., 1950, permanent chmn., 1962. Chmn. bd. trustees Elon Coll. Mem. Nat. Assn. Secs. of State (pres. 1942, dean 1961), Am. Legion, 40 and 8, Theta Chi. Mem. United Ch. of Christ. Club: Elk. Home: Raleigh N.C. Deceased.

EVANS, ALFRED SPRING, physician, educator; b. Buffalo, Aug. 21, 1917; s. John H. and Ellen (Spring) E.; m. Brigitte Kluge, July 26, 1952 (dec. Oct. 1985); children: John Kluge, Barbara Spring Evans Paganelli, Christopher Paul. AB, U. Mich., 1939, MPH, 1960; MD, U. Buffalo, 1943; MA (hon.), Yale U., 1966. Diplomate Am. Bd. Internal Medicine. Intern U. Pitts. Hosps., 1943-44; resident Goldwater Hosp., N.Y.C., 1944; USPHS postdoctoral research fellow Yale Med. Sch., 1947-48, from instr. to asst. prof. medicine, 1949-50, prof. epidemiology, dir. WHO serum reference bank, dept. epidemiology and pub. health, 1966-89, John Rodman Paul prof. epidemiology, 1982-88, emeritus prof., lectr., 1988-94, dir. div. infectious disease, 1982-85; resident Buffalo Gen. Hosp., 1948-49; assoc. prof. preventive medicine and med. microbiology U. Wis. Sch. Medicine, 1952-59; prof., chmn. dept. preventive medicine, also dir. Wis. State Lab. Hygiene, 1959-66; mem. microbiology fellowship panel NIH, 1960-64; mem. microbiol. panel space flight NRC/NASA; cons. Philippine Health Dept., WHO, 1962, 1964, cons. tropical diseases, 1977-82; cons. epidemiology Surgeon Gen. U.S. Army, 1969-85, USN Bur. Medicine, 1973-76, viral epidemiology sect. Nat. Cancer Inst. NIH, 1988, 92. Author: (with M.J. Kelsey and D. Thompson) Observational Methods in Epidemiology, 1985, Causation and Disease A Chronological Journal, 1993; editor: Yale Jour. Biology and Medicine, 1971-73; editor-in-chief, 1973-76, Viral Infections of Humans, 1976, 82, 89; (with H.A. Feldman) Bacterial Infection of Humans, 1982; (with P.A. Brachman) 2d edit., 1991; contbr. articles on med. history, infectious diseases and epidemiology to profl. jours. Served to capt. M.C. AUS, 1944-46, 50-52. Recipient Best Book for Physicians award Am. Med. Writers Assn., 1977, Thomas Frances Jr. lectureship and award Sch. Pub. Health, U. Mich., 1986, Harrington lectureship and award U. Buffalo, 1988, Disting. Med. Alumnus award U. Buffalo, 1992, Tchr. of Yr. award Yale U. Sch. Pub. Health, 1993. Fellow AAAS, APHA (Abraham Lilienfeld award for teaching excellence 1990), Am. Coll. Epidemiology (bd. dirs., pres. 1989-90, Abraham Lilienfeld Disting. award 1986); mem. Soc. Epidemiol. Rsch., Am. Epidemiol. Soc. (sec.-treas. 1968-73, pres. 1973-74), Infectious Disease Soc. Am. (Kass Lecture and award 1995), Internat. Epidemiol. Assn., Am. Assn. History of Medicine, Soc. Med. Cons. to Armed Forces (chmn. preventive medicine 1973-76, coun. 1976-84, v.p. 1979-80, pres. 1980-81, John R. Seal award 1987). Home: North Branford Conn. Died Jan. 21, 1996.

EVANS, BLACKWELL BUGG, SR., pediatric urologist; b. Forksville, Va., Nov. 5, 1927; s. Clarence Meredith and Saluda Ann Rebecca (Bugg) E.; m. June Helen Banks, Oct. 8, 1949; 1 child, Blackwell Bugg, Jr. BA, U. Va., 1955; MD, Med. Coll. Va., 1959. Diplomate Am. Bd. Urology. Intern, resident in surgery Johnston-Willis Hosp., Richmond, Va., 1959-61; resident in urology, rsch. fellow in urology Tulane U. Med. Ctr., 1961-65; clin. asst. urology Med. Coll. S.C., 1965-67; mem. faculty Tulane U. Med. Ctr., 1967-94, prof. pediatrics, 1975-94, prof. urology, 1974-82, Sobin prof. pediatric urology, 1982-94, chief sect. pediatric urology, 1978-82, chmn. dept. urology, 1982-94, acting dean, 1988-89, acting vice dean, 1989, vice chancellor acad. affairs, 1989-93; dir. urologic edn. Children's Hosp., New Orleans, 1978-85; pres. med. staff Children's Hosp., 1981-83; med. adv. bd. La. Kidney Found., 1973-74; med. adv. com. La. Handicapped Children's Service Program, 1976-94; cons. in field. Active Bur. Govtl. Affairs, New Orleans, 1972-94, New Orleans Met. Area Commn., 1982-94, bd. dirs., 1993, exec. com., 1973, co-chair human rels. com., 1993-94. Officer USAF, 1951-53. Fellow ACS, Am. Acad. Pediatrics, Internat. Coll. Pediatrics; mem. AMA, Am. Urol. Assn. (dir., chmn. fin. com. Southeastern sect. 1979-83), Soc. Pediatric Urology, Soc. Univ. Urologists, Royal Soc. Medicine, Societe Internationale d'Urologie, Soc. GU Reconstructive Surgeons, Soc. Nephrology, Pan-Am. Med. Assn., So. Med. Assn., Am. Assn. Med. Colls., N.Y. Acad. Scis., So. Soc. Pediatric Research, La. Urol. Assn. (pres. 1977-78), United Ostomy Assn. (profl. adv. bd. 1974-79), Greater New Orleans Ostomy Assn. (med. adv. bd. 1980-94), Soc. Nuclear Medicine, Sigma Xi. Home: New Orleans La. Died Mar. 9, 1994.

EVANS, JOHN JAMES, management consultant; b. N.Y.C., Aug. 12, 1923; s. James J. and Mary (Galan) E. Student, U. Nebr., 1943; B.B.A. cum laude, CCNY, 1948, M.B.A., 1950; postgrad., NYU, 1951. Certified mgmt. cons. Mgr. Roman Silversmiths, 1946-49; systems Addressograph-Multigraph Corp., 1949-53; mgmt. cons., v.p. Fairbanks Assos., Greenwich, Conn., Fairbanks Assocs., N.Y.C. and Washington, 1953-59; pres., 1959-94. Contbr. articles to profl. jours. Served with AUS, 1943-46, ETO. Mem. Inst. Mgmt. Cons., Am. Soc. Assn. Execs., Beta Gamma Sigma. Home: Alamo Calif. Died 1994.

EVANS, ROBLEY DUNGLISON, physicist; b. University Place, Nebr., May 18, 1907; s. Manley Jefferson and Alice (Turner) E.; m. Gwendolyn Elizabeth Aldrich, Mar. 10, 1928; children: Richard Owen, Nadia Ann, Ronald Aldrich; m. Mary Margaret Shanahan, Feb. 24, 1990. B.S., Calif. Inst. Tech., 1924-28, M.S., 1929, Ph.D., 1932. Cert. health physicist, Am. Bd. Health Physics, 1961. With rsch. lab. C.F. Braun & Co., Alhambra, Calif., 1929-31; instr. Poly. Sch., Pasadena, Calif., 1931-32; nat. rsch. fellow U. Calif., Berkeley, 1932-34; asst. prof. MIT, Cambridge, 1934-38, assoc. prof., 1938-45, prof., 1945-72, prof. emeritus, 1972-95; dir. Radioactivity Ctr., MIT, 1935-72, cons., 1972-81; advisor U. N.Mex. Uranium Epidemiology Study, 1978-89; vis. prof. Ariz. State U., 1966-67; staff cons. Peter Bent Brigham Hosp., Boston, 1945-72; cons. surgeon gen. Dept. Army, 1962-69, USN Radiol. Def. Lab., 1952-69; cons. divsn. biology and medicine AEC, 1950-75; mem. Internat. Union of Pure and Applied Physics, 1947, AEC Adv. Com. on Isotope Distbn., 1948-53, chmn. 1952-53, Joint Commn. Stds., Units and Constants of Radioactivity, 1961; spl. project assoc. Mayo Clinic, 1973-81; cons. divsn. biol. and environ. rsch. ERDA, Dept. Energy, 1975-81; cons. physics Mass. Gen. Hosp., 1948-73, USPHS, 1969-71, Fed. Radiation Coun., 1965-69, Roger Williams Hosp., Providence, 1965-72; chmn. Internat. Conf. Applied Nuclear Physics, Cambridge, 1940; vice chmn. com. on nuclear sci. Nat. Rsch. Coun., 1946-72; mem. Nat. Acad. Scis.-Nat. Rsch. Coun. panel 231 adv. to Nat. Bur. Stds. on radiation physics, 1963-66, chmn., 1964; chmn. standing com. for radiation biology aspects of supersonic transport FAA, 1967; mem. com. on radioactive waste mgmt. Nat. Acad. Scis., 1968-70; adviser U. Chgo., 1964-68; sci. adv. bd. New Eng. Deaconess Hosp., 1963-69; sr. U.S. del. Internat. Assn. Radiation Rsch., Cortina, 1966; mem. organizing com. U.S. Nat. Com. Med. Physics, 1966-69; vis. com. med. dept. Brookhaven Nat. Lab., 1965-68; cons. Blood Rsch. Inst., 1967-74; vice chmn. adv. com. to U.S. Transuranium and Uranium Registries, 1968-86; mem. tech. adv. com. Ariz. Atomic Energy Commn., 1971-72. Author: The Atomic Nucleus, 1955; Editorial bd.: Internat. Jour. Applied Radiation and Isotopes, 1955-69, hon. mem. editorial bd., 1976-95; editorial bd.: Mt. Washington Obs. Bull, 1962-70, Health Physics, 1962-70, Physics in Medicine and Biology, 1963-66; editor physics: Radiation Research, 1959-62; Contbr. sci. research papers to various publs. Vice pres. Found. for Study and Aid of Emotionally Unstable, 1948-95. Recipient Theobald Smith medal in Med. Scis., AAAS, 1937; U.S. Presdl. Cert. of Merit, 1948; Hull award and Gold medal AMA, 1963; Silvanus Thompson medal Brit. Inst. Radiology, 1966; William D. Coolidge award Am. Assn. Physicists in Medicine, 1984, Enrico Fermi award U.S. Dept. Energy, 1990. Fellow AAAS, Am. Phys. Soc., Am. Acad. Arts and Scis., N.Y. Acad. Scis. Am. Assn. Physicists in Medicine; mem. Radiation Research Soc. (v.p., pres. 1965-67), Am. Roentgen Ray Soc. (asso.), Am. Indsl. Hygiene Assn., Am. Assn. Physics Tchrs., Am. Nuclear Soc., Health Physics Soc. (pres. 1972-73, Disting. Achievement award 1981, fellow 1984), Nat. Council Radiation Protection and Measurements (council 1965-71, hon. mem. 1975-95), Soc. Nuclear Medicine (hon. mem.), Royal Sci. and Lit. Soc. (hon.), Kungliga Vetenshapoch Vitterhets Samhallet (Goteborg, Sweden), Sigma Xi, Kappa Gamma, Tau Beta Pi, Pi Kappa Delta. Republican. Home: Paradise Vly Calif. Died Dec. 31, 1995.

EVARTS, CHARLES MCCOLLISTER, orthopaedic surgeon; b. Dunkirk, N.Y., Aug. 16, 1931; s. Charles Melville and Laura (McCollister) E.; m. Nancy Joan Lyons, July 2, 1955; children: Cynthia Ann, Charles Mark, Robert Alan. AB cum laude, Colgate U., 1953; MD, U. Rochester, 1957. Diplomate Am. Bd. Orthopaedic Surgery (pres. 1985-86). Intern Strong Meml. Hosp., 1957-58, resident in orthopaedic surgery, 1961-64; with Cleve. Clinic Found., 1964-74, chmn. dept. orthopaedic surgery, 1970-74; prof., chmn. dept. orthopaedics U. Rochester, 1974-86, Dorris H. Carlson prof., 1975-86, v.p. devel. Med. Ctr., 1985-86; dean Coll. of Medicine, sr. v.p. health affairs Pa. State U., Hershey, 1987—. Editor: Orthopaedic Clinics of North America, Vol. 12, 1971, Vol. 15, 1973, Clinical Orthopaedics and Related Research, Vol. 107, 1975, Proc. of the Hip Society, 1976, Reconstructive Surgery of the Knee, 1977, Instructional Course Lectures, 19839, Surgery of the Musculoskeletal System, 5 vols., 1989; contbr. articles to profl. jours. With USNR, 1959-61. Nat. Found. fellow, 1964. Fellow ACS (gov., chmn. adv. coun. for orthopedics); mem. AMA, Assn. Am. Med. Colls., Assn. Acad. Health Ctrs., Am. Acad. Orthopaedic Surgeons, Orthopaedic Rsch. Soc., Internat. Knee Soc., Hip Soc. (pres. 1982), Scoliosis Rsch. Soc., Am. Orthopaedic Assn. (pres. 1984-85), Assn. Orthopedic Chmn. (pres. 1982-83), Internat. Hip Soc., Am. Rheumatism Assn., Société Internationale de Chirurgie Orthopedique et de Traumatologie, Continental Orthopaedic Soc., Interurban Orthopaedic Soc., Am. Bd. Orthopaedic Surgery (pres. 1985), Am. Orthopaedic Assn. (pres. 1984), Soc. Med. Adminstrs., Alpha Omega Alpha, Fortnightly Club. Home: Hummelstown Pa.

EVERSON, WILLIAM OLIVER (BROTHER ANTONINUS), poet; b. Sacramento, Sept. 10, 1912; s. Louis Waldemar and Francelia Marie (Herber) E.; m. Edwa Poulson, 1938 (div. 1948); m. Mary Fabilli, 1948 (div. 1960); m. Susanna Rickson, Dec. 13, 1969; 1 stepson, Jude. Student, Fresno State Coll., 1931, 34-35. With Civilian Conservation Corps, 1933-34; with Civilian Public Service, 1943-46; dir. Fine Arts Group Waldport, Oreg., 1944-46; with U. Calif. Press, 1947-49; Catholic Worker Movement, 1950-51, Dominican Order Province of West, 1951-69; poet-in-residence Kresge Coll., U. Calif., Santa Cruz, 1971-81; master printer Lime Kiln Press, U. Calif., Santa Cruz, 1971-81. Author: (as Brother Antoninus) Novum Psalterium Pii XII, 1955, At the Edge, 1958, A Fragment for the Birth of God, 1958, The Age Insurgent, 1959, The Crooked Lines of God: Poems 1949-54, 1959 (Pulitzer Prize nominee 1959), The Hazards of Holiness: Poems 1957-60, 1962, The Poet is Dead: A Memorial for Robinson Jeffers, 1964, The Roses of Solitude, 1964 (Calif. Silver medal Commonwealth Club 1968), The Vision of Felicity, 1967, The Achievement of Brother Antoninus, 1967, A Canticle to the Waterbirds, 1968, The Springing of the Blade, 1968, The City Does Not Die, 1969, The Last Crusade, 1969, Who is She That Looketh Forth as the Morning?, 1972; (as William Everson) These are the Ravens, 1935, San Joaquin, 1939, The Masculine Dead: Poems 1938-40, 1942, X War Elegies, 1943, The Waldport Poems, 1944, The Residual Years: Poems 1940-41, 1944, Poems MCMXLII, 1945, A Privacy of Speech: Ten Poems in Sequence, 1949, Triptych for the Living, 1951, There Will Be Harvest, 1960, The Year's Declension, 1961, Single Source, 1966, The Blowing of the Seed, 1966, In the Fictive Wish, 1967, Poems of Nineteen Forty Seven, 1968, Tendril in the Mesh, 1973, Black Hills, 1973, Man-Fate: The Swan Song of Brother Antoninus, 1974, River-Root, A Syzygy for the Bicentennial of the States, 1976, Missa DeFunctorum, 1976, The Mate: Flight of Eagles, 1977, Blackbird Sundown, 1978, Rattlesnake August, 1978 (Shelley Meml. award 1978, Book of Yr. award Conf. on Christianity and Lit. 1978), The Veritable Years: Poems 1949-1966, 1978, Cutting the Firebreak, 1978, Blame it on the Je

Stream, 1978, The Masks of Drought, 1979, Eastward the armies: Selected War Poems, 1935-42, 1980, Sixty-Five, 1980, On Writing the Waterbirds, 1935-81, 1983, Renegade Christmas, 1984, In Medias Res: Canto One: Dust Shall Be the Serpent's Food, 1984, The High Embrace, 1986, The Engendering Flood, 1990, The Blood of the Poet: Selected Poems of William Everson, 1993; prose (with Brother Kurt) Friar Among Savages: Father Luis Cancer, 1958, (with J. Burns) If I Speak Truth, 1968, Archetype West, 1976, Earth Poetry: Selected Essays and Interviews, 1980, Birth of a Poet: The Santa Cruz Meditations, 1982, On Writing the Waterbirds, Collected Forewords and Afterwords, 1983, The Excesses of God: Robinson Jeffers as a Religious Figure, 1988, Naked Heart: Selected Interviews, 1992, (with Laurence C. Powell) Take Hold Upon the Future: Letters on Writers and Writing, 1994; editor: Roberson Jeffers: Fragments of an Older Fury (Jeffers), 1968, Cawdor and Medea (Jeffers), 1970, Californians (Jeffers), 1971, The Alpine Christ (Jeffers), 1973, Tragedy Has Obligations (Jeffers), 1973, Brides of the South Wind (Jeffers), 1974, Granite and Cypress (Jeffers), 1975; sound recordings: The Savagery of Love: Brother Antonious Reads His Poetry, 1968, Poetry of Earth, 1970, Roberson Jeffers, 1972. Recipient Oreg. Inst. Lit. Arts award, 1988, Lifetime Achievement award Nat. Poetry Assn., 1988, Body of Work award PEN Am. Ctr. West, 1989; Fred Coty Meml. award Bay Area Book Revs. Assn., 1991; Artist of Yr. award Santa Cruz Art Commn., 1991; Guggenheim fellow, 1949, Robinson Jeffers Tor House fellow, 1979; NEA grantee, 1981. Home: Davenport Calif. Died June 3, 1994.

EWART, GAVIN BUCHANAN, poet, writer; b. London, Feb. 4, 1916; s. George Arthur and Dorothy Hannah (Turner) E.; m. Margaret Adelaide Bennett, Mar. 24, 1956; children: Jane Susan, Julian Robert. BA, Christ's Coll., Cambridge U., 1937, MA, 1942. Salesman Contemporary Lithographs Ltd., London, 1938; editor Editions Poetry London, 1946; with book reviews dept. The Brit. Coun., London, 1946-52; copywriter various advt. agys., London, 1952-71; freelance writer, 1971—. Author: The Collected Ewart 1933-1980, 1980, Collected Poems 1980-1990, 1990, 85 Poems, 1993; editor: The Penguin Book of Light Verse, 1978. Capt. Royal Arty., 1940-46. Recipient Cholmondeley award, 1971, Michael Braude award for light verse Am. Acad., 1991. Fellow Royal Soc. Lit., Soc. Authors, The Poetry Soc. (chmn. 1974). Home: London Eng. Died Oct. 23, 1995.

EXLEY, SHECK, geologist. Recipient William J. Stephenson Outstanding Svc. award Nat. Speleological Soc., 1992. Home: Jacksonville Fla. Died Apr. 6, 1994; interred Jacksonville, Fla.

EYNARD, ITALO, agricultural engineering educator, researcher; b. Torre Pellice, Italy, Sept. 3, 1932; s. Carlo and Lidia Giulia (Pöet) E.; m. Giuliana Gay, Aug. 1, 1959; children: Carlo, Anna. Laurea, Turin U., Torino, Italy, 1957; libera docenza, Rome, 1965. Rsch. asst. Turin U., Torino, Italy, 1959-64, assoc. prof. viticulture, 1966-76, full prof. viticulture, 1976-93; field officer FAO, Viedma, Argentina, 1964-66; pres. Istituto Sperimentale Enologia, Asti, Italy, 1991-93; cons., expert in viticulture FAO, Egypt, Cyprus, Argentina, Iraq, CNR, China, 1983; former dean of agronomy faculty Turin U. Author: Viticulture, 1991. Home: Pinerolo Torino Italy Died Feb. 10, 1993.

FABER, GEORGES, corporate executive; b. Luxembourg, Luxembourg, Dec. 4, 1926; m. Carosati Josée, Oct. 13, 1949; children: Carlo, Christiane, Marie-Louise. Student law, U. Fribourg, Switzerland and Paris; doctorate, 1951; postgrad., Geneva and The Hague, Netherlands. With ARBED S.A., Luxembourg, 1952-93, head of dept., 1966-72, dep. mgr., 1972-73, mgr. legal dept., 1973-77, mem. bd. mng. dirs., 1977-86, chief exec., 1986-92, chmn., 1992-93; bd. dirs SIDMAR S.A., Belgium, Banque Internat. of Luxembourg S.A., Société Générale de Belgique, Belgium, Fedn. of Luxembourg Industrialists; mem. coun. State of Luxembourg, Inst. Grand-Ducal; mem. adv. com. ECSC Internat. Fiscal Assn. Contbr. articles in econ., legal and fiscal publs. Named Grand Officier de l'Ordre de la Couronne de Chene, Luxembourg, Commandeur d l'Ordre de Leopold II, Belgium. Home: Luxembourg Luxembourg Died Oct. 1, 1993.

FABIAN, LEONARD WILLIAM, anesthesiologist, educator; b. Little Rock, Nov. 12, 1923; s. Leonard Edward and Susan Ellen (Chitwood) F.; m. Elizabeth Mardelle Bishop, Jan. 8, 1947; children: Beverly, Susan, Leonard William, Edward, Ronald. BS, U. Ark., 1950, MD, 1951. Diplomate Am. Bd. Anesthesiology. Intern U. Ark. Hosp., 1951-52, resident in anesthesiology, 1952-54; instr. in anesthesiology U. Ark., 1954-55; fellow Phila. Children's Hosp., 1954; asst. prof. Duke U., 1955-58; prof., chmn. dept. U. Miss. Med. Ctr., 1958-71; prof. Washington U., St. Louis, 1971-94; mem. staff Barnes and Associated Hosps., St. Louis, St. Louis Children's Hosp.; nat. cons. emeritus in anesthesiology Surgeon Gen. USAF. Editor: Anesthesia and the Circulation, 1964; Clin. Anesthesia, 1965-94, Survey of Anesthesiology, 1965-94; contbr. articles to profl. jours. With USN, 1942-46, PTO. Fellow AMA, Am. Coll. Anesthesiologists, Internat. Anesthesia Rsch. Soc., Mo. Med. Soc., St. Louis Med. Soc., Mo. Soc. Anesthesiolo-

gists, St. Louis Soc. Anesthesiologists, Assn. Univ. Anesthetists, Am. Fedn. Clin. Rsch. Home: Saint Louis Mo. Died Mar. 25, 1994; buried St. John Cemetery, Marchester, Mo.

FAIN, PAUL KEMP, JR., financial planner; b. Augusta, Ga., Jan. 31, 1939; s. Paul Kemp and Carolyn (Wall) F.; student in architecture Clemson U., 1957-58, BME Ga. Inst. Tech., 1962; MS U. Tenn., 1970; PhD Calif. Coast U., 1984; m. Donna Jane Jay, Mar. 23, 1958; children: Paul Kemp III, Courtney Lee. Cert. fin. planner, chartered fin. cons., reg. investment advisor, lic. ins. agt., real estate broker, securities broker, fin. prin., CLU, fund specialist. Mktg. rep. Eastman Chem. Products, Inc., Kingsport, Tenn., 1962-67; stockbroker J.C. Bradford & Co., Kingsport, 1967-68; dist. dir. Fin. Service Corp., Knoxville, 1969-71, regional dir., 1972-75; chmn. Asset Planning Corp., Knoxville, 1975-94; instr. personal money mgmt. U. Tenn., 1972-94; adj. faculty mem. Coll. Fin. Planning, Knoxville, 1979-94. Bd. dirs. Knoxville Beautification Bd., 1978-80, Tenn. Valley Unitarian Ch., 1981-82. Co-author: Your Book of Financial Planning, 1983, The Expert's Guide to Managing and Marketing a Successful Financial Planning Practice, 1988. Grad. Realtors Inst. Recipient Spoke award Jaycees. Mem. Inst. Cert. Fin. Planners (dir., treas., v.p., pres., chmn., recipient Disting. Svc. award), Int. Assn. for Fin. Planning, Internat. Bd. Standards and Practices for Cert. Fin. Planners (chmn., past vice chmn.), Rotary (dir. Farragut chpt., pres.), Knoxville Track Club (dir.), Fairview Tech. Ctr. (chmn. bd. 1987-88), Farragut 2000 Planning Task Force (chmn. econ. devel. com.), Knoxville Bd. Realtors (edn. com.), AOK Assn. (pres. 1986-88), Am. Soc. CLUs, Knoxville Estate Planning Coun., Knoxville Assn. Life Underwriters, Toastmasters, MENSA, Concord-Farragut Optimist Club, Greater Knoxville C. of C. (econ. devel. com.), Beta Gamma Sigma. Died Aug. 29, 1994. Home: Knoxville Tenn.

FALCO, LOUIS, dancer, choreographer, dance company director; b. N.Y.C., Aug. 2, 1942. Studied with, Jose Limon, Charles Weidman, Martha Graham, Am. Ballet Theatre Sch. Participant Nat. Endowment Dance Touring Program; artist-in-residence numerous colls. and univs. throughout U.S. Prin. dancer Jose Limon Dance Co., 1960-70, toured Cen. and S.Am., N.Am., Europe and Far East, formed The Louis Falco Dance Co. Inc., 1967, since toured with co. throughout U.S., Can., Mexico and Europe, 10th tour, 1975; presents ann. seasons, N.Y.C.; works include Argot, 1967, Huescape, 1968, Timewright, 1969, Caviar, 1970, Ibid, 1970, Sleepers, 1971, Soap Opera, 1972, Avenue, 1973, Twopenny Portrait, 1973, Storeroom, 1974, Eclipse, 1974, Caterpillar, 1975, Pulp, 1975, Champagne, 1976, Hero, 1977, Tiger Rag, 1977, Escargot, 1978, Saltimbocca, 1979, Early Sunday Morning, 1979, Kate's Rag, 1980, Service Compris, 1980, Black & Blue, Little Boy; revived with Rudolph Nureyev Moor's Pavane, 1974, filmed for Dutch and German TV, choreographer: La Scala Opera Ballet, Alvin Ailey Dance Theatre, Boston Ballet, Washington Opera Soc., Caramoor Festival, Australian Ballet, Les Ballets Jazz de Montreal, Ballet Rambert and the, Netherlands Dance Theatre, Paris Opera Ballet Co.; choreographer: films Fame, 1979, Angel Heart, Leonard Part 6, (TV) Collisions, Photo Finish, Superfalco, Mixed Media Special, The Sleepers, Hero; choreographer, performer 6 episodes of TV series for RAI-TV of Italy, 1981; The Louis Falco Dance Co. Inc. is a non-profit corp. supported in part by Nat. Endowment for Arts, N.Y. State Coun. on Arts, many works are collaborations with prominent artists including Robert Indiana, Stanley Landsman, William Katz, Marisol; incorporates spoken dialogue in works. Recipient Harkness award, 1979. Home: New York N.Y. Died Mar. 26, 1993.

FALICOV, LEOPOLDO MAXIMO, physicist, educator; b. Buenos Aires, June 24, 1933; came to U.S., 1960, naturalized, 1967; s. Isaias Felix and Dora (Samoilovich) F.; m. Marta Alicia Puebla, Aug. 13, 1959; children: Alexis, Ian. Licenciado in chemistry, Buenos Aires U., 1957; PhD in Physics, Cuyo U. Instituto J. A. Balseiro, Argentina, 1958, Cambridge U., 1960; ScD, Cambridge U., 1977. Rsch. assoc. dept. physics Inst. Study Metals, U. Chgo., 1960-61, instr. physics, 1961-62, asst. prof. physics, 1962-65, assoc. prof., 1965- 68, prof., 1968-69; prof. physics U. Calif., Berkeley, 1969-95; Miller rsch. prof. U. Calif., 1979-80, chmn. dept. physics, 1981-83; cons. in field. Author: Group Theory and Its Physical Applications, 1966, La Estructura Electronica de los Solidos, 1967; contbr. articles to profl. jours. Alfred P. Sloan Found. fellow, 1964-68; vis. fellow Fitzwilliam Coll., Cambridge, Eng., 1966; Fulbright fellow, 1969; OAS vis. prof. Argentina, 1970; Nordita vis. prof. U. Copenhagen, 1971-72, 87; Fulbright lectr. Spain, 1972; Guggenheim fellow, 1976-77; vis. fellow Clare Hall, Cambridge, Eng., 1976-77; exchange prof. U. Paris, 1977, 84. Fellow Third World Acad. Scis.; mem. NAS, Royal Danish Acad. Scis. and Letters (fgn.), Academia Nacional de Ciencias Exactas, Fisicas y Naturales Argentina (corres. mem.). Home: Berkeley Calif. Died Jan. 24, 1995.

FANG, JOSEPH PE YONG, chemistry educator; b. Lie-yong, Jiangsu, China, June 30, 1911; came to U.S., 1941; s. Foo-tze Fang and Ling-tseng Huang; m. Yu Hou Liu, Mar. 9, 1940; children: Helen C., Elizabeth-

Linda, Josephine-Ann, Catherine, Mou-yi. PhD, Poly. of Milan, 1941. Registered profl. engr. Rsch. engr. Bell Tel. Labs., Summit, N.J., 1942-47; prof. Nantung (China) Coll., 1947-50; prof., dept. head China Textile U., Shanghai, 1951-87; prof., sr. advisor Super Material Rsch. Inst., Rockville, Md., 1987-95; founder faculty environ. sci. and tech. China Textile U., co-founder chem. fibers faculty; cons. editor Chinese Etymolog. Dictionary, Comprehensive Ency. Author: (Italian) Chemistry of Rayon, 1941, (Chinese) Organic Nomenclature Handbook, 1954, Man-made Fibers Technology, 1959, Isotactic Polypropylene Fibers, 1960; contbr. articles to profl. jours. Recipient Letter of Appreciation and Insignia for Disting. Svc. from Pres. Roosevelt, Bronze medal Gen. Alumni Assn. Poly. Milan, 1991, cert. of honor for disting. svc. China Textile U. Mem. AAAS, Am. Chem. Soc. (sr.), N.Y. Acad. Scis., Shanghai Environ. Sci. Soc. (co-founder, past editor, spl. adviser jour.), Am. Alumni Assn. China Textile U. (pres. 1992-95). Home: Rockville Md. Died Mar. 15, 1995.

FARBER, SEYMOUR MORGAN, physician, university administrator; b. Buffalo, June 3, 1912; s. Simon and Matilda (Goldstein) F.; children: Burt, Margaret, Roy. B.A., U. Buffalo, 1931; M.D. Harvard U., 1939; D.H.L. (hon.), St. Mary's Coll., Moraga, 1964; LL.D. (hon.), Pepperdine U., 1977. Individual practice medicine, specializing in chest diseases San Francisco, 1946-95; instr. dept. medicine U. Calif. at San Francisco, 1942-47, asst. prof., 1947-53, assoc. prof., 1953-61, prof. clin. medicine, 1961-95, asst. dean for continuing edn. medicine and health scis., 1956-63, dir. instrn. in extension, 1960-61, dir. continuing edn. medicine and health scis., 1963-70, dean ednl. services, 1963-70, dean continuing edn. in health scis., 1970-73, vice-chancellor pub. programs and continuing edn., 1973-95; lectr. U. Calif. Sch. Pub. Health, Berkeley, 1948—; chief U. Calif. Tb and chest service San Francisco Gen. Hosp., 1945-65, sr. cons., 1965-95; exec. dir. Howard Florey Inst. Am.; fellow Howard Florey Inst. Melbourne, Australia; spl. cons. Nat. Cancer Inst., 1958-60; nat. cons. continuing edn. and chest diseases to surg. gen. USAF, 1962. Author: Cytological Diagnosis of Lung Cancer, 1950, Lung Cancer, 1954; Editor: The Air We Breathe, 1961, Control of the Mind, 1961, Man and Civilization: Conflict and Creativity, 1963, The Potential of Woman, 1963, Man Under Stress, 1964, The Challenge to Women, 1966, Food and Civilization, 1966, Teen-Age Marriage and Divorce, 1967, Sex Education and the Teen-Ager, 1967; Editorial board: Diseases of Chest, 1948-61, General Practice, 1958- 61; bd. cons.: Pre-Med. Jour., 1965-95; Contbr. to profl. publs. Mem. Pres.'s Commn. on Status of Women, 1962-63; mem. Coun. Med. TV, Bay Area Coun. on Alcoholism; commr. Asian Art Commn. San Francisco, 1977-95; commr. Calif. Postsecondary Edn. Commn., vice chmn., 1978-81, chmn., 1983-95; mem. Air Quality Adv. Com. San Francisco Bay Area, 1979-95; mem. nat. planning com., nat. adv. bd. John Muir Med. Film Festival, 1980-95; chmn. com. on health maintenance White House Conf. on Aging, 1981-95; v.p. bd. trustees Nat. Hispanic U. Fellow Am. Coll. Chest Physicians (past pres.), Am. Coll Cardiology; mem. AMA (chmn. chest diseases sect. 1959-60), Calif. Med. Assn., San Francisco County Med. Soc., Calif. Soc. Internal Medicine, Am. Fedn. Clin. Research, N.Y. Acad. Scis., Am. Trudeau Soc., Internat. Acad. Pathology, AAAS, Pan Am. Med. Assn. (pres. sect. chest diseases), Assn. Am. Med. Colls., Am. Geriatrics Soc. Home: Los Altos Calif. Died Dec. 18, 1995.

FARNSWORTH, DAVID L., manufacturing company executive; b. McPherson, Kans., Aug. 31, 1937; s. Wayne E. and Dorothy (Mosing) F.; m. Patricia Ann Fanning, Sept. 14, 1963; children: Laura, Andrew, Katherine. BSBA, Emporia State Coll., 1959; MBA, Harvard U., 1970. Enlisted USN, 1959, advanced through grades to comdr., resigned, 1979; exec. v.p. adminstrn. Chief Industries, Grand Island, Nebr., 1979-81; pres. Sealrite Windows, Inc., Lincoln, Nebr., 1981-85; exec. v.p. mfg. ops. Indal Ltd., Weston, Ont., Can., 1986—; also bd. dirs. Indal Ltd. Mem. Can. Mfrs. Assn. (bd. dirs. Toronto chpt. 1988). Home: King City Can.

FARR, JAMES FRANCIS, lawyer; b. Ludlow, Mass., Mar. 17, 1911; s. Charles H. and Stella (Greene) F.; AB, Harvard U., 1933, LLB. 1936. Bar: Mass. 1937. Pvt. practice Boston, 1937-93; sr. ptnr. Haussermann, Davison & Shattuck, 1948-89, Peabody & Arnold, 1989-93; bd. dirs. clk. Durkee-Mower, Inc.; bd. dirs. H F G Co., Chgo., Babson Bros. Co., Robert McF. Brown & Sons, Inc., Currier Cons., Inc. Former bd. dirs., clk. Scottish Rite Mus. and Libr., Inc.; former pres. Cambridge YMCA; former chmn. bd. dirs. New Eng. Deaconess Hosp.; bd. dirs. New Eng. Edn. Soc. Served to lt. USCGR, World War II. Methodist (trustee), Mason (33 deg., Shriner, dir. grand lodge). Clubs: Cambridge Economy (past pres.), Cambridge, Harvard (Boston). Author: (with Mayo A. Shattuck) An Estate Planner's Handbook, 1953; Loring, A Trustee's Handbook Farr Revision, 1961; An Estate Planner's Handbook, 1966, co-author 1979 edit., supplement, 1982, 85, 87, 88-92. Deceased. Home: Cambridge Mass.

FARRELL, GEORGE T., banker; b. 1931; married. BS, U. Notre Dame, 1953. With Mellon Bank,

N.A., Pitts., 1955—, asst. cashier credit dept., 1959-64; asst. v.p. internat. dept. Mellon Bank, Pitts., 1964-66, v.p. internat. dept., 1966-74, sr. v.p. head internat. dept., 1974-78, exec. v.p., 1978-80, vice-chmn., 1978-80, pres., 1980-83, 85-89; also bd. dirs. Pitts., 1980-83, 85-89. Served with U.S. Army, 1953-55. Home: Pittsburgh Pa.

FARRINGTON, WILLIAM BENFORD, investment analyst; b. N.Y.C., Mar. 10, 1921; s. Harold Phillips and Edith C. (Aitken) F.; B.C.E., Cornell U., 1947, M.S., 1949; Ph.D., Mass. Inst. Tech., 1953; m. Frances A. Garratt, 1949 (div. 1955); children: William Benford, Phyllis Ashley, Timothy Colfax; m. Gertrude E. Eby, Jan. 3, 1979. Radio engr. Naval Research Labs., 1942-43; dir. Read Standard Corp., 1948-55; plant engr. Hope's Windows, Inc., 1950-51; instr. geology, geophysics U. Mass., 1953-54; research geophysicist Humble Oil & Refining Co., 1954-56; lectr. U. Houston, 1955-56; sr. investment analyst Continental Research Corp., N.Y.C., 1956-61; pres., dir. Farrington Engring. Corp., 1958-67; partner Farrington & Light Assos., Laguna Beach, Calif., 1967-82, Farrington Assocs., 1982-93; v.p. Empire Resources Corp., 1961-62; asst. v.p. Empire Trust Co., 1962-64; dir. Commonwealth Gas Corp., N.Y.C.; sci. dir. Select Com. on Govt. Research, U.S. Ho. of Reps., 1964-65; lectr. U. Calif. at Los Angeles, 1968-72; sr. cons. Trident Engring. Assos., Annapolis, Md., 1965-93; corporate asso. Technology Assos. So. Calif., 1971-93. Chmn. crusade Am. Cancer Soc., Jamestown, N.Y., 1951. Chartered fin. analyst; registered geologist, Calif. Fellow AAAS, Fin. Analysts Fedn.; mem. Am. Assn. Petroleum Geologists, Am. Inst. Aeros. and Aeronautics, Geol. Soc. Am., Los Angeles Soc. Fin. Analysts, Sigma Xi. Episcolalian. Author articles in field. Died July 17, 1993; interred Woodlawn Cemetery, Bronx, N.Y. Home: Laguna Beach Calif.

FASANO, CLARA, sculptor; b. Castellaneta, Italy, Dec. 14, 1900; emigrated to U.S., 1907, naturalized, 1939; d. Pasquale and Julia (de Feudis) F.; m. Jean de Marco, July 8, 1936. Student, Cooper Union Art Inst., Art Students League, N.Y.C., 1917-21, Julien Academie and Colarossi Academie, Paris, 1924-26; scholar, Rome, Italy, 1922-24. Tchr. sculpture adult edn. Bd. Edn., N.Y., 1948-58; tchr. Manhattanville Coll. Exhibited at, Salon d'Automne, Paris, 1925; worked in own studio, exhibited in, Rome, 1926-32; exhibited in numerous shows, including, Worlds Fair, N.Y.C., 1939, Whitney Museum, NAD, Pa. Acad., Art Inst. Chgo., Met. Mus. Art, Am.-Brit. Center N.Y.C., Ferragil, Buckholz galleries; works represented in permanent collections at, Met. Mus. Art, N.Y.C., Manhattanville Coll. Sacred Heart, Purchase, N.Y., Norfolk Mus. Arts and Scis., Smithsonian Instn., Washington, Syracuse U., also pvt. collections, U.S., abroad; important works include series of twelve portraits in bronze, the last being of His Excellency Giuseppe Cataldi, pres. Corte dei Conti of Italy. Grantee, recipient citation Nat. Inst. Arts and Letters, 1952; recipient medal of Honor with citation Am. Artists Mag., Audubon Annual Exhbn., 1956, hon. mention Archtl. League N.Y., Gold Medals Exhbn., 1956, Daniel Chester French medal NAD, 1965, Peter Caesar Alberti award Italian Execs. Am. Inc., 1967, Dessie Greer award for sculpture NAD, 1968, 2d pl. sculpture competitions for entrance Supreme Ct. of Bklyn., for fountain sculpture for lobby 100 Church St. bldg., N.Y.C., sculpture commn. for relief Middleport (Ohio) Post Office U.S. Treasury Dept. competition for Apex Bldg. in Washington. Academician NAD.; Fellow Nat. Sculpture Soc. (hon. mention 1956); mem. Audubon Artists (M. Grumbacher prize 1954), Sculptors Guild, Nat. Assn. Women Artists (Anonymous prize 1945, Marcia Brady Tucker prize 1950, medal of Honor for sculpture 63d ann. exhbn. 1955). Subject of articles, works reproduced in Am. Artist mag., Nat. Sculpture Rev., also books Sculpture in Modern America, Contemporary American Scultpure, The Materials and Methods of Sculpture. Deceased. Home: Cervaro Italy

FATE, MARTIN EUGENE, JR., utility company executive; b. Tulsa, Jan. 9, 1933; s. Martin Eugene and Frances Mae (Harp) F.; m. Ruth Ann Johnson, Aug. 28, 1954; children: Gary Martin, Steven Lewis, Mary Ann. B.E.E., Okla. State U., 1955; grad. Advanced Mgmt. Program, Harvard U., 1981. With Pub. Svc. Co. of Okla., Tulsa, 1955-93, v.p. power, 1973-76, exec. v.p., 1976-82, pres., CEO, 1982-92, vice chmn. bd., 1992-95, also bd. dirs., 1992-93; retired, cons. and pvt. investor, 1993-95; bd. dirs. 1st State Fin., Inc., Liberty Bancorp, citizens Bank of Lawton, Okla. Trustee, vice chair Tulsa Regional Med. Ctr., Phillips Grad. Sem., Tulsa Airport Authority; pres. Tulsa Libr. Trust; chair Tulsa Regional Med. Ctr. Found. Mem. Tulsa C. of C., Tulsa Summit Club, Phi Kappa Phi, Eta Kappa Nu, Tau Beta Pi. Mem. Christian Ch. Home: Tulsa Okla. Died May 10, 1995.

FAUBUS, ORVAL EUGENE, state official, former governor of Arkansas; b. Combs, Ark., Jan. 7, 1910; s. John Samuel and Addie (Joslen) F.; m. Alta Haskins, Nov. 21, 1931; 1 son, Farrell Eugene; m. Elizabeth Drake Thompson, Mar. 21, 1969 (died Mar. 1983); children: Kim Elizabeth, Frederick King; m. Jan Hines Wittenburg, Nov. 23, 1986; children: Donita Jan, Jeffrey Lyn Wittenburg. Student pub. schs. Rural sch. tchr., 1928-38; cir. clk., county recorder Huntsville, Ark., 1939-42; acting postmaster Huntsville, 1946-47, postmaster, 1953-54; editor, owner, pub. Madison County Record, Huntsville, 1947-69; owner Ark. Statesman, Little Rock, 1960-69; hwy. commr., adminstrv. asst. to gov., dir. hwys. for Ark., 1949-53; gov. State of Ark., 1955-67; pres. Recreational Enterprises, Inc., operating theme pk. Dogpatch U.S.A., in Ozarks, 1969-70; dir. Vets. Affairs Dept., State of Ark., 1981-83. Author: In This Faraway Land, Down From the Hills, 2 vols, Man's Best Friend-The Little Australian, The Faubus Years. Chmn. So. Gov.'s Conf., 1963; rural scout commr. N.W. Ark., 1924-38. Maj. inf. AUS, 1942-46. Decorated Bronze Star. Mem. Madison County C. of C. (pres. 1953-54), Am. Legion, VFW, DAV, SCV, 35th Div. Assn. (pres. 1954-55), Vets. of Battle of Bulge, 40 et 8 Club, Huntsville Lions Club (sec.-treas. 1939), Masons. Baptist. Home: Conway Ariz. Died Dec. 14, 1994.

FAULKNER, MAURICE ERVIN, educator, conductor; b. Fort Scott, Kans., Feb. 2, 1912; s. Ervin Phyletus and Minnie Mae (Munday) F.; m. Ellen Stradal, May 24, 1934 (div. 1951); children: Katherine Sydney, Barbara Ellen; m. Suzanne Somerville, Oct. 18, 1958. BS in Music, Fort Hays State U., 1932; postgrad. Interlochen U., 1933; MA in Music, Tchrs. Coll., N.Y.C., 1936; PhD, Stanford U., 1956. Instr. music pub. schs., Kans., 1932-37; assoc. prof. instrumental music Columbia U., summers 1934-40; asst. prof. San Jose (Calif.) State Coll., 1937-40; from asst. prof. to assoc. prof. to prof. emeritus U. Calif., Santa Barbara, 1940-94, also chmn. dept.; rsch. papers on Bronze Age musical instruments presented Biennial Archeol. Musicology Symposiums, Congress of Traditional Music of UNESCO, Stockholm, 1984, Hanover, Fed. Republic Germany, 1986, Internat. Trumpet Guild Conf., Rotterdam, The Netherlands, summer 1992; vis. prof. U. Tex., summer 1947; music critic Salzburg (Austria) Festival, 1951-94 (Reinhardt award 1969, Golden Svc. award 1981), Santa Barbara Star, 1951-56, Santa Barbara News-Press, 1956-82; rsch. musicologist Inst. for Environ. Stress, U. Calif., Santa Barbara, 1979-94; participant Vienna (Austria) Philharm. Orch. Symposium, 1990, Internat. Trumpet Guild Conf., Rotterdam, The Netherlands, 1992; condr. Santa Barbara Symphony Orch., 1941-44, All-Calif. High Sch. Symphony Orch., 1941-73, Kern County Honor Band of Calif.; guest condr. Seoul (Korea) Symphony Orch., 1945-46, officer in charge Seoul Nat. U., 1945-46; mus. dir. Santa Barbara Fiesta Bowl Mus. Show, 1951-53. Contbg. editor The Instrumentalist, 1964-86; contbr. articles and criticisms to Mus. Courier, Sat. Rev., Christian Sci. Monitor. Chmn. Santa Barbara Mayor's Adv. Com. on Arts, 1966-69. Lt. (j.g.) to lt. USNR, 1944-46. Fellow Internat. Inst. Arts and Letters (life); mem. Music Acad. West (pres. 1949-54, pres. emeritus 1954-94, sustaining dir. 1985-94), So. Calif. Sch. Band and Orch. Assn. (hon. life, v.p. 1955), Am. Fedn. Musicians (hon. life), Nat. Music Educators Conf., Internat. Trumpet Guild, U. Calif. Emeriti Assn., Masons, Phi Mu Alpha (life), Phi Delta Kappa. Republican. Presbyterian. Avocation: world traveling. Died Aug. 7, 1994. Home: Goleta Calif.

FAURE, EDGAR JEAN, lawyer, educator, French government official; b. Beziers (Herault), Aug. 18, 1908; s. Jean Baptiste and Claire (Lavit) F.; Agrege in law. Coll. de Verdun and Coll. de Narbonne, 1962; diplomate Ecole Nationale des Langues Orientales Vivantes; m. Lucie Meyer, Oct. 12, 1931 (dec.); children: Sylvie (Mrs. Pragier), Agnes (Mrs. Oppenheimer); m. 2d, Marie-Jeanne Vuez, 1980. Barrister, Ct. Paris, 1929-88; 2d sec. Conf. du Stage, 1928-29; dep. sec. gen. in charge legislative services Office of Pres. of French Liberation Com., then provisional govt. of Algiers, 1944; French dep. prosecutor gen. Nurnberg Internat. Mil. Tribunal, 1945; radical-socialist dep. for Jura. 1946-58; mayor of Port-Lesney, 1947, reelected, 1953-59, 65; past gen. councillor Canton of Villiers-Farlay; pres. Gen. Council of Iura, 1949-67; gen. councillor Canton of Pontarlier, 1967-88; v.p. Gen. Council of Doubs, 1967-88; sec. of state for finance, then budget minister, 1949-51; minister justice in Rene Pleven cabinet, 1951; pres. Council, minister finance, 1952; pres. Fgn. Affairs Commn. of Nat. Assembly, 1952-53; minister finance and econ. affairs in cabinet Joseph Laniel, 1953; minister finance, econ. affairs and planning cabinet of Pierre Mendes France, 1954; minister fgn. affairs in revised Mendes France cabinet, 1955; pres. Council of Ministers, 1955-56; minister finance cabinet of Pierre Pflimlin, 1958; senator from Jura, 1959-66. Pres., Com. for Econ. Expansion of Franche-Comte and Ter. of Belfort, 1951, later Econ. Devel. Commn. of Franche-Comte Region, 1964; prof. faculty law Dijon U., 1962; pres. Internat. Commn. on Devel. of Edn., UNESCO, 1971-88; Went on mission to Chinese People's Republic, 1963; minister agr. 3d, 4th cabinets Pompidou, 1966-68; dep. 5th Republic from 3d constituency of Doubs, 1967-88; minister nat. edn. Couve de Murville cabinet, 1968-69; minister social affairs P. Messmer cabinet, 1972-73; pres. Nat. Assembly, 1973-78; mayor of Pontarlier, 1971; mem. Assembly of European Community, 1979-88. Elected to French Acad., 1978; recipient Prix Historia, 1977. Clubs: Racing of France; Golf de la Boulie. Author: La Politique francaise du petrole, M.Langlois n'est pas toupours egal a lui-meme, le Serpent et la Tortue, 1957; la Disgrace de Turgot, 1961; Etude sur la capitation sous Diocletien d'apres le panegyrique, VIII. Prevoir le present. 1966; Education nationale et Participation, 1968; Philosophie d'une Reforme, 1969; L'ame du Combat, 1970; Ree que je Crois, 1971; Pour un Nouveau Contrat Social, 1973; La Banqueroute de Laws, 1977; author police novels under pseudonym Edgar Sanday. Died Mar. 30, 1988. Home: Paris France

FEARON, ROBERT HENRY, banker; b. Oneida, N.Y., Aug. 7, 1900; s. Henry D. and Mary A. (Fuller) F.; m. Ruby J. Kilts, Aug. 27, 1926 (dec. Mar. 1985); children—Robert Henry, Patricia A. (Mrs. Richard H. Howarth) (dec. Dec. 1984). B.S., Syracuse U., 1922. With Blair & Co., 1922-24; with Oneida Valley Nat. Bank, 1924-85, pres., 1942-71, chmn., 1971-85; pres. Sylvan Spring Water Co., Sylvan Beach, N.Y., 1942-86, also bd. dirs.; bd. dirs., treas. Marcellus Lumber Co., Oneida, 1942-70. Trustee N.Y. State Bankers Retirement System, 1939-67; Treas. Madison County council Boy Scouts Am., 1930-58; Treas., bd. dirs. bd. dirs. Oneida Library, Oneida Area Industries. Served with USNR, 1918. Recipient Silver Beaver award Boy Scouts Am., 1935, 80. Mem. N.Y. State (past chmn. group IV, past treas. assn.), Madison County (past pres.), bankers assns., Delta Kappa Epsilon. Republican. Methodist (past trustee, trustee Central N.Y. Conf. 1960-72). Clubs: Elk (Oneida), Rotarian (Oneida) (past pres.). Home: Oneida N.Y. Deceased.

FEENEY, CHARLES STONEHAM, retired professional baseball executive; b. Orange, N.J., Aug. 31, 1921; s. Thaddeus and Mary Alice (Stoneham) F.; m. Margaret Ann Hoppock, July 10, 1948; children: Katharine Willard, Charles Stoneham, John Hoppock, William McDonald, Mary Patrick. B.A., Dartmouth Coll., 1943; LL.B., Fordham U., 1949. Vice pres. San Francisco Giants, 1946-69; pres. Nat. League Profl. Baseball Clubs, San Francisco, 1970-77, N.Y.C., 1977-87, San Diego Padres, 1987-89; ret. Served to lt. USNR, 1943-46. Mem. Casque and Gauntlet, Phi Kappa Psi. Clubs: Pacific Union, Burlingame (Calif.) Country. Home: San Francisco Calif. Died Jan. 10, 1994.

FEHRLE, CARL CHRISTIAN, elementary education educator, consultant; b. Kent, Iowa, June 11, 1923; s. Fred and Margaretha (Eberle) F.; m. Norma Pauline Schaffer, Nov. 27, 1950; children: Kimberly Lynn, Margaret Joleen. BS, Drake U., 1955, MEd, 1959; PhD, U. Iowa, 1964. Tchr. Union County Schs., Kent, Iowa, 1942-43, Griswold (Iowa) Pub. Sch., 1943-44; elem. prin. Corning (Iowa) Pub. Schs.), 1944-49; tchr. Des Moines Pub. Schs., 1950-52, asst. to prin., 1952-59, elem. prin., 1959-63, 64-66; elem. prin. Chilren's Hosp. U. Iowa, Iowa City, 1963-64; asst. prof. elem., early childhood, and gifted edn. Drake U., Des Moines, 1966-68; prof. edn., ednl. specialist U. Mo., Columbia, 1968-86, prof. emeritus. Contbr. articles to profl. jours. Sgt. U.S. Army, 1949-51, Korea. Decorated Bronze Star, 1951; recipient State PTA award Lucas Elem. Sch., Des Moines, 1966, Citation Merit award Outstanding Achievement and Meritorious Svc. to Edn. Coll. Edn. Alumni Assn. U. Mo., 1990. Mem. NEA (life), Nat. Elem. Prins. (life.), Phi Delta Kappa. Methodist. Home: Columbia Mo.

FEITELSON, DINA, education educator; b. Vienna, May 28, 1926; arrived in Israel, 1934; d. Joseph and Hedwig Rachel (Koralek) Schur; m. Jehuda Leo Feitelson, July 24, 1950; children: Eran Isaac, Dror Gershon. Diploma, David Yellin Tchrs. Coll., Jerusalem, 1946; MA, Hebrew U., Jerusalem, 1951, PhD, 1956; postgrad., Cambridge U., 1954-55. Tchr. David Yellin Sch., 1946-51; rsch. officer Henrietta Szold Found., Jerusalem, 1951-54; teaching and rsch. fellow Hebrew U., Jerusalem, 1956-64, lectr., 1965-73; supr. spl. projects Ministry of Edn., Jerusalem, 1962-67, dir. infants sch. project, 1973-79, 82-90; sr. lectr. U. Haifa, Israel, 1973-76, assoc. prof., 1976-80, prof. edn., 1980-92; vis. scholar U. Chgo., 1964-65, NYU, 1980, 83, Ednl. Testing Service, Princeton, N.J., 1985, Johns Hopkins U., 1990, U. Mich., 1990; rsch. assoc., vis scholar Harvard U., Cambridge, Mass., 1970-71, 79-80; vis. prof. U. Minn, Mpls., 1975; speaker in field. Author several books including Facts and Fads in Beginning Reading: A Cross Language Perspective, 1988; edited several books; contbr. articles to profl. jours. Active Com. on Early Childhood, Israel, 1968-70, Com. on Children and Youth in Distress, 1971-73, Israel Nat. Com. Internat. Year of Child, 1978-79, exec. com. Assn. for Advancement of Play in Israel, 1980-92. Recipient Israel Prize for Ednl. Rsch., 1953. Mem. Internat. Reading Assn. (chmn. program com. 1976 world congress), Am. Ednl. Rsch. Assn., Internat. Soc for Study Behavioral Devel. (exec. com. 1979-85), Israel Reading Assn. (pres. 1968-70, 78-82), Israeli Psychol and Anthrop. Assn. Jewish. Home: Haifa Israel Died Apr. 1992.

FELD, FRITZ, actor, writer, director; b. Berlin Germany, Oct. 15, 1900; came to U.S., 1923, naturalized, 1930; s. Heinrich and Martha (Guttman) F.; m Virginia Christine, Nov. 10, 1940; children: Steven Danny. Ed., Gymnasium, Germany, 1907-17. chmn So. Calif. chpt. Am. Nat. Theatre ANTA, 1968-93. Performer in The Miracle, Prof. Max Reinhard Theaters, Berlin, 1917-23, Century Theatre, N.Y.C. 1923-27; actor, writer, dir., Hollywood motion picture studios, 1923-93; actor, dir. Grand Hotel, Nat. Theatre

1930-93, Berlin, George M. Cohan Theatre, N.Y.C., 1931-93; latest feature films include Homer and Eddy, Barfly, Get Smart, Again. Recipient award for 60 years in movies, 1977; award Nat. Film Soc.; award L.A. Bd. Dirs. "AFTRA" AFL-CIO, 1990; named KNX Radio Citizen of Week; hon. mayor of Brentwood Calif. Brentwood C. of C., 1979. Mem. Screen Actors Guild (dir. 1970-93, chmn. Hollywood Mus. project com. 1976-93), Acad. Motion Picture Arts and Scis. Home: Los Angeles Calif. Died Nov. 18, 1993.

FELKER, DONALD WILLIAM, consumer and family science educator. AB in History, Geneva Coll., 1954; AM in Journalism, Ind. U., 1963, PhD in Ednl. Philosophy and Psychology, 1965. Dean Sch. Consumer and Family Sci. Purdue U., West Lafayette, Ind., 1987-93; asst. prof. Inst. for Child Study U. Md., College Park, 1966-68; prof., head Ednl. Psychology sect., Dept. Edn. Purdue U., West Lafayette, Ind., 1973-74, prof., head Dept. Child Devel. and Family Studies, 1974-80, dean School Consumer and Family Scis., oprof. Child Devel. and Family Studies, 1987-93; pres. Geneva Coll., Beaver Falls, Pa., 1980-83; prof., chmn. Dept. Ednl. Psychology U. S.C., Columbia, 1983-87. Author: Building Positive Self-Concepts, 1974, (with E.H. Felker) Adoption Beginning to End, 1987; contbr. articles to jours. in field. Mem. Assn. Adminstrs. Home Econs. (strategic planning com.), Assn. Tchr. Educators (commn. on moral and ethical dimensions of teaching), Nat. Assn. State Univs. and Land-Grant Colls. (commn. on home econs.), Nat. Assn. Extension Home Economists (adv. coun.). Home: West Lafayette Ind. Died 1993.

FELLINI, FEDERICO, film director, writer; b. Rimini, Italy, Jan. 20, 1920; s. Urbano and Ida (Barbiani) F.; m. Giulietta Masina, Oct., 1943. Student, U. Rome. Journalist, 1937-39, writer radio dramas, 1939-42, screen writer, 1943-93, dir., 1952-93. Writer: films, including Open City (N.Y. Film Critics Circle award 1946), Paisan, (N.Y. Film Critics Circle award 1948), Ways of Love, 1950 (N.Y. Film Critics Circle award 1950), Senza Pieta, 1950; dir.: films, including The White Sheik, 1952, I Vitelloni, 1953, La Strada, 1954 (Acad. award 1957), Il Bidone, 1955, Notti di Cabiria, 1957 (Acad. award for best fgn. film 1958), La Dolce Vita, 1959 (Cannes Festival Gold Palm award 1960, N.Y. Film Critics Circle award 1961), 8 1/2, 1963 (Acad. award for best fgn. film 1964, N.Y. Film Critics Circle award 1963), Juliet of the Spirits, 1965, Never Bet the Devil Your Head, 1968, Histoires Extraordinairies, 1968, Satyricon, 1969, The Clowns, 1970, Fellini's Roma, 1972, Amarcord, 1974 (Acad. award for best fgn. film 1975), Casanova, 1977, Orchestra Rehearsal, 1979, City of Women, 1981, And the Ship Sails On, 1984, Ginger and Fred, 1986, Interview, 1987, Voce della Luna, 1989; author: films, including Amarcord, 1974, Quattro Film, 1975, Fellini on Fellini, 1977. Recipient Prix du 40th Anniversaire Cannes Film Festival, award Moscow Film Festival, Honorary Lifetime Achievement Academy award, 1993. Home: Rome Italy Died Oct. 31, 1993.

FELT, IRVING MITCHELL, foundation executive, corporation executive; b. N.Y.C., Jan. 25, 1910; s. Abraham and Dora (Mandel) F. B.S., U. Pa., 1929. Chmn. Felt Found., Inc., N.Y.C., 1941-94; hon. chmn. bd. dirs. Madison Sq. Garden Corp., N.Y.C.; bd. dirs., former chmn. , mem. exec. com. Republic Corp., L.A.; bd. dirs. DWG Corp. Hon. chmn., former pres. Fedn. Jewish Philanthropies; bd. dirs., mem. exec. com. Met. Opera Assn.; hon. chmn. nat. exec. bd. NCCJ; hon. chmn., past pres. Jewish Child Car Assn.; bd. dirs. Joffrey Ballet; founding patron Lincoln Ctr. for Performing Arts, N.Y.C.; founder L.A. Music Ctr.; former chmn. N.Y. Rangers Hockey Club, N.Y. Knickerbockers Basketball Club. Clubs: Morningside (Rancho Mirage, Calif.); Hillcrest Country (Los Angeles); Friars (N.Y.C.). Home: Los Angeles Calif. Died Sept. 22, 1994.

FENVESSY, STANLEY JOHN, management consultant; b. Rochester, N.Y., Oct. 30, 1918; s. John H.W. and Bessie Ruth (Weber) F.; m. Doris Goodman, July 10, 1943; children: Alice Fenvessy Healy, Barbara Fenvessy Kahlow. BS in Econs., U. Pa., 1940; LLB, Georgetown U., 1943. Bar: Ill. 1947. With Aldens, Inc. Chgo., 1945-50; prin. Cresap, McCormick and Paget, N.Y.C., 1950-55; exec. v.p. Am. Merchandising div. Rapid Am. Corp., N.Y.C., 1955-60; adminstrv. v.p. Ethan Allen, Inc., Danbury, Conn., 1960-65; pres. Fenvessy Assocs., Inc., Mgmt. Cons., N.Y.C., 1965-82; chmn. Fenvessy & Schwab, Inc., N.Y.C., 1982-86, Fenvessy & Silbert, Inc., N.Y.C., 1987-88, Fenvessy Consulting, N.Y.C., 1988—; bd. dirs. The Sharper Image, The Lighthouse, Inc. Author: Keep Your Customers and Keep Them Happy, 1976, Fenvessy On Fufillment, 1988; contbr. to Graphic Arts Manual, Mag. Public Mgmt., Direct Mail Advt., Selling for Retailers, Direct Mktg. Handbook, also bus. publs.; patentee addressing methods. Served to lt. (s.g.) Intelligence Corps, USNR, 1941-45. Named to Hall of Fame Fulfillment Mgmt. Assn. Mem. Chgo. Bar Assn., Inst. Mgmt. Cons., Direct Mktg. Assn. (bd. dirs.), Am. Arbitration Assn., Univ. Club, Penn Club, Govs. Club (Palm Beach, Fla.). Republican. Home: New York N.Y. Died May 25, 1994. Buried at sea.

FERDEN, BRUCE, conductor; b. Fosston, Minn., Aug. 19, 1949; s. Maurice Raymond and Irene Geneva (Torgerson) F. Student, Moorhead State U., 1967-70; B Music summa cum laude, U. Miami, Coral Gables, Fla., 1971; M Music summa cum laude, U. So. Calif., 1973; LittD (hon.), Gonzaga U., 1990. Asst. condr. N.Y. Philharmonic, N.Y.C., 1975-76; guest condr. Santa Fe Opera, 1977-81, San Francisco, Detroit, St. Louis Symphony Orchs., 1981-85, Scottish Chamber Orch., Edinburgh, 1983, Opera Theatre of St. Louis, 1978-86, Netherlands Opera Co., Amsterdam, 1980-86, Brabants (The Netherlands) Symphony Orch., 1987, 88, Pacific Symphony Orch., 1989-90, Seattle Opera, 1988-92; guest condr. Cin. Opera Debut, 1989, Kiel, Fed. Republic Germany, 1990; guest condr. Pitts. Symphony Orch., San Diego Symphony Orch., 1989-90; music dir. Nebr. Chamber Orch., Lincoln, 1983-90, Spokane (Wash.) Symphony Orch., 1985-90; generalmusik dir. AAchen (Fed. Republic Germany) Stadttheater, 1991-93. Debut appearance with San Francisco Opera, 1987, 89; condr. European debut of Philip Glass The Making of the Representation for the Planet 8, Amsterdam, 1989; condr., generalmusikdirektor Stadttheater Aachen Opera and Symphony, 1989. Mem. artistic adv. com. Olga Forrai Found., N.Y.C., 1987-93; adv. com. Cathedral and the Arts Assn., Spokane, 1985-91. Recipient Outstanding Young Alumnus award Moorhead State U., 1983, Outstanding Alumnus award U. So. Calif., 1985. Home: New York N.Y. Died Sept. 19, 1993; interred Fossten, M.A.

FERGUSON, FRANCES HAND, volunteer, civic worker; b. N.Y.C., Apr. 9, 1907; d. Learned and Frances (Fincke) Hand; m. Robert Munro Ferguson, Nov. 10, 1933; children: Patty M., Robert H.M., Phyllis M. AB, Bryn Mawr Coll., 1929; MA in Psychology, Columbia U., 1931, postgrad., 1933-35. Tchr. Brearley Sch., 1936-38; dir. courses N.Y. chpt. Am. Women's Vol. Svc., 1939-40; successively N.Y. chpt. pres., nat. chmn. field com., exec. com. Planned Parenthood Fedn. Am., 1940-51, pres., 1953-56, chmn., 1st pres., 1959-65; vol. rsch. technician Meml. Hosp., 1941-42; bd. dirs. Internat. Planned Parenthood Fedn., 1953-95, v.p., 1959-62, treas., 1970-73; bd. dirs. Euthanasia Soc., 1955-62, Am. Eugenics Soc., 1957-63; mem. nat. com. Maternal Health, 1957-63, Human Betterment Assn., 1956-64, Assn. for Vol. Sterilization, 1964-85, Assn. for Study Abortion, 1967-70, Assn. for Vol. Surg. Contraception, 1985-95. Recipient Disting. Svc. award Bryn Mawr Coll., 1960, Internat. Planned Parenthood, 1992, Dirs. award Planned Parenthood Fedn. Am., 1965. Mem. Assn. for Vol. Surg. Contraceptive. Home: New York N.Y. Died Aug. 11, 1995.

FERGUSON, FRANCIS EUGENE, retired insurance company executive; b. Batavia, N.Y., Feb. 4, 1921; s. Harold M. and Florence (Munger) F.; m. Patricia J. Reddy, Aug. 11, 1945; children: Susan Lee, Patricia Ann. Student, Cornell U., 1938-39; B.S., Mich. State U., 1947, LLD (hon.), 1972; DCL (hon.), Ripon Coll., 1978; LLD (hon.), Cardinal Stritch Coll., 1983. Asst. sec.-treas. Fed. Land Bank Assn., Lansing, Mich., 1947-48; appraiser Fed. Land Bank, St. Paul, 1948-50; specialist agrl. econs. Mich. State U. Extension, 1951; with Northwestern Mut. Life Ins. Co., Milw., 1951-85; specialist Northwestern Mut. Life Ins. Co., 1951-52, asst. mgr. farm loans, 1952-56, mgr. farm loans, 1956-62, gen. mgr. mortgage loans, 1962-63, v.p. mortgage loans, 1963-67, pres., 1967-80, chmn., chief exec. officer, 1980-83, chmn. bd., 1983-85; bd. dirs. Bradley Ctr. Corp., Green Bay Packing Inc., Ralston Purina Co. Gen. campaign chmn. United Fund, 1965; corp. mem. Milw. Children's Hosp.; hon. trustee Com. for Econ. Devel.; sr. mem. The Conf. Bd.; trustee Hastings (Nebr.) Coll.; adv. trustee Greater Milw. Com.; bd. dirs. Columbia Health Systems Inc. Decorated Purple Heart. Mem. Conf. Bd. (sr.). Republican. Methodist. Clubs: Milwaukee, Milwaukee Country. Home: Milwaukee Wis.

FERNANDEZ, JOSE BARTOLOME, JR., banking executive; b. Manila, Sept. 22, 1923; s. Jose Zorilla and Erundina (Bartolome) F.; m. Ma. Dulce Cacho, Nov. 25, 1952; children: Enrique, Jaime, jose Manuel, Roberto, Ma. Elena. BS in Bus. Adminstrn., Fordham U., 1947; MBA, Harvard U., 1949. Asst. v.p. Philippine Bank Commerce, 1949-59; pres., founder Far East Bank & Trust Co., Intramuros, Manila, 1960-72, chmn. bd. dirs., 1972-80, chmn., pres., 1981-84; mem. internat. adv. bd. Chemical Bank; gov. Central Bank of Philippines, Mabini, Manila, 1984-94; gov. Internat. Monetary Fund, Washington, 1984-94; alternate gov. Asian Devel. Bank, Manila., 1984-94; mem. coun. govs. S.E. Asian Cen. Banks, 1984; mem. Cen. Banks S.E. Asia, New Zealand, Australia, 1984; Chmn. bd. dirs. Philippine Chess Fedn., Makati, Metro Manila, 1989; mem. Manila Jaycee Senate, Paco, Metro Manila; trustee Metro Manila, 1989-94. Mem. Manila Golf and Country Club, Baguio Country Club. Avocation: golf. Died June 19, 1994; interred Sanctuario de San Antonio, Manila.

FERNANDEZ ORDONEZ, FRANCISCO, former Spanish government official; b. Madrid, June 22, 1930; m. Maria Paz Garcia Mayo. LL.B., U. Madrid, 1952; diploma internat. tax program, Harvard U., 1967. Bar: Spain 1975. Mem. corps state tax lawyers Spain, 1954-59, mem. corps state fin. and taxation inspectors, 1959-69; tech. sec.-gen. Ministry of Fin., Spain, 1969-73, under sec. fin. economy, 1973-74; pres. Nat. Inst. Industry, Spain, 1974; founder, pres. Fedn. Social Democrat Parties, 1974-77; minister of Finance, 1977-79, minister of justice, 1980-81; chmn. bd. dirs. Banco Exterior de Espana, 1982-83; founder Democratic Action Party, 1982, mem. Parliament for Madrid, minister fgn. affairs, 1985-92; sub-dir. Inst. Fiscal Studies; dir. studies Centre Tax Studies; pres. Spanish del. OCED, 1969-73; Spanish rep. GATT, IMF, EEC, numerous other internat. coms.; mem. Internat. Com. of Twenty for Monetary Reform; mem. Com. of Nine. Author: The Necessary Spain, 1980; Words in Freedom, 1982. Editor Economia Financiera Espanola. Contbr. articles to profl. jours. Home: Madrid Spain Died Aug. 8, 1992.

FERRARA, BERNARD EUGENE, retired surgeon, educator; b. Charleston, S.C., Nov. 19, 1924; s. Seth Joseph and Ermine (Frain) F.; m. Emily Calhoun McDuffie, June 3, 1949; children: Marie, Bernard Jr., Clifford, Martin, Ronald, Charles. BS, Coll. of Charleston, 1944; MD, Med. Coll. State of S.C., 1948. Intern Roper Hosp., Charleston, S.C., 1948-49, resident, 1950-53; resident Med. Ctr. Hosps., Charleston, 1954-56, teaching fellow in gen. surgery, 1955-56; pvt. practice Charleston, 1956-86; assoc. in surgery Med. U. S.C., 1956-63; pvt. practice New London, Conn., 1963-65; staff surgeon VA Med. Ctr., Lake City, Fla., 1986-93; clin. prof. surgery U. Fla. Coll. Medicine, Gainesville, 1987-93. Author: F.E. Kredel Master Surgeon for South Carolina, 1987; contbr. articles to profl. jours. Lt. USNR. Fellow ACS; mem. S.C. Surg. Soc. (pres. 1985-86). Republican. Roman Catholic. Home: Daufuskie Island SC Deceased.

FERRELL, WILLIAM WILSON, pipeline company executive; b. Danville, W.Va., Mar. 9, 1924; s. Robert F. and Isabel (Childress) F.; m. B. Annette Robinson, Dec. 27, 1947; children: Barbara Ann, William Wilson, Robert R. Student, Georgetown Coll., 1941-42; B.S. in Mining Engring, W.Va. U., 1949. Registered profl. engr., W.Va. Jr. engr. United Fuel Gas Co., 1949-56, asst. production supt., 1956-59, production and storage supt., 1959-62, v.p. ops., 1962-67; v.p. Charleston Group Cos.—Columbia Gas System, 1967-68, pres., 1968-72, pres., chief exec. officer, 1972-73; pres. Columbia Gas Transmission Corp., Charleston, W.Va., 1973-74; pres., chief exec. officer Columbia Gas Transmission Corp., 1974-76, chmn. bd., chief exec. officer, 1976-83, chmn. bd./pres., chief exec. officer, 1983-95, dir., 1962-95; pres., dir. Big Marsh Oil Co.; dir. Columbia Gas System Service Corp. Mem. vis. com. Coll. Mineral and Energy Resources, W.Va. U. Served with Q.M.C. USNR, 1943-46. Mem. W.Va. C. of C. (dir.). Clubs: Rotary (Charleston); Edgewood Country, Berry Hills Country. Home: Charleston W. Va. Died Jan. 17, 1995.

FERRER, ESTEBAN A., lawyer; b. Cuba, Sept. 20, 1925; s. Esteban A. and Carola (Ruiz) F.; m. Susan W. Stone, Apr. 15, 1970; children: Esteban, Cristina, Carlos, Geoffrey. LL.D., U. Havana, 1947; Cert. of Law, U. Fla., 1976. Ptnr. Salaya y Casteleiro, Havana, 1948-60; v.p., sr. advisor Council of the Americas, N.Y.C., 1961-95; ptnr. Shutts & Bowen, Miami, Fla., 1977-95. Pres., Internat. Ctr. of Fla., 1977, 84; bd. dirs. St. Thomas Sch. Law. Mem. ABA, Interam. Bar Assn., Cuban-Am. Bar Assn. Roman Catholic. Clubs: Key Biscayne Yacht, Bankers, American (Miami); Larchmont Yacht (N.Y.). Died Oct. 18, 1995. Home: Miami Fla.

FETTER, THEODORE HENRY, entertainment consultant; b. Ithaca, N.Y., June 10, 1906; s. Frank Albert and Martha (Whitson) F.; m. Suzanne Merandon Pleven, Apr. 26, 1946; children: Frank Albert II, (foster son) Patrick Alfred Pleven. Student, The George Sch.; A.B., Swarthmore Coll., 1928. v.p., nat. dir. programs ABC TV Network, 1956-68; curator theatre and music collection Mus. of City of N.Y., 1974-79, entertainment cons., 1979-96. Actor: Abraham Lincoln, 1929, Garrick Gaieties, 1930, Jubilee, 1935, Many Mansions, 1936; lyric writer: The Little Show, 1930, The Show Is On, 1936, Naughty Naught, 1937, The Fireman's Flame, 1937, The Girl from Wyoming, 1938, Billy Rose's Aquacade, 1939, Cabin in the Sky, 1939; TV prodns. Your Hit Parade, 1950-53, Jack Paar Show, 1954-56, One Man Show, 1969-70, Secret Challenge, 1970-71; Published songs include Taking a Chance on Love. Served to maj. U.S. Army, 1941-46. Mem. ASCAP, Nat. Acad. TV Arts and Scis., Am. Arbitration Assn., Soc. of Friends. Clubs: Seabright Lawn Tennis and Cricket, Seabright Beach, Coffee House. Home: New York N.Y. Died Mar. 13, 1996.

FICHTER, JOSEPH H., priest, sociology educator; b. Union City, N.J., June 10, 1908; s. Charles J. and Victoria (Weiss) F. AB, St. Louis U., 1935, MA, 1939; PhD, Harvard U., 1947; D (hon.), Marquette U., Rockhurst Coll., Spring Hill Coll. Entered Soc. Jesus, 1930; ordained priest Roman Cath. Ch., 1942; instr. Spring Hill Coll., 1935-36, Loyola U., New Orleans, 1944-45; prof., chmn. dept. sociology Loyola U., 1947-64, 72—; Chauncey Stillman prof. Harvard U., Boston, 1965-70; vis. prof. sociology Muenster U., Germany, 1953-54; vis. prof. sociology, dir. research Notre Dame U., 1956-57, U. Chile, Santiago, 1961-62; vis. prof. sociology U. Chgo., 1964-65; Stillman prof. Harvard U., 1965-70; vis. prof. State U. N.Y. at Albany, 1971-72;

Favrot prof. Tulane U., 1974-75. Author: Roots of Change, 1939, Man of Spain, 1940, Christianity, 1947, Social Relations in the Urban Parish, 1954, Sociology, 1957, Soziologie der Pfarrgruppen, 1958, Parochial School, 1958, Religion as an Occupation, 1961, Cambios Sociales en Chile, 1962, Priest and People, 1965, America's Forgotten Priests, 1968, One-Man Research, 1973, Organization Man in the Church, 1974, Catholic Cult of the Paraclete, 1975, The Rehabilitation of Clergy Alcoholics: Ardent Spirits Subdued, 1981, Religion and Pain, 1982, The Holy Family of Father Moon, 1985, The Health of American Catholic Priests, 1985, A Sociologist Looks at Religion, 1988, The Pastoral Provisions: Married Catholic Priests, 1989, The Wives of Catholic Clergy, 1992, others; contbr. numerous articles in field of Sociology to profl. jours. Founder Southeastern Region Coll. Students Inter-racial COmmn., 1948; mem. New Orleans Commn. Human Rights, 1948, New Orleans Com. Race Rels.; bd. trustees U. Bridgeport. Mem. AAUP, Am. Sociol. Soc. (mem. exec. coun.), So. Sociol. Soc. (past pres.), Assn. for Sociology Religion, Soc. Sci. Study of Religion (past pres.), Soc. Study Social Problems, Religious Rsch. Assn., Nat. Urban League. Home: New Orleans La.

FIELDS, BERNARD NATHAN, microbiologist, physician; b. Bklyn., Mar. 24, 1938; s. Julius and Martha F.; m. Ruth Peedin, Sept. 10, 1966; children: John, Edward, Michael, Daniel, Joshua. A.B., Brandeis U., 1958; M.D., N.Y. U., 1962; A.M. (hon.), Harvard U., 1976. Intern Beth Israel Hosp., Boston, 1962-63; resident in medicine Beth Israel Hosp., 1963-64; officer USPHS, Nat. Communicable Disease Center, Atlanta, 1965-67; fellow Albert Einstein Coll. Medicine, N.Y.C., 1967-68; asst. prof. medicine and cell biology Albert Einstein Coll. Medicine, 1968-71, asso. prof., 1971-75, chief infectious disease, 1971-75; prof. microbiology and molecular genetics Harvard Med. Sch., 1975-84, chmn. dept. microbiology and molecular genetics, 1982-87, Adele H. Lehman prof. microbiology and molecular genetics, 1984-95; chief infectious diseases Peter Bent Brigham Hosp., Boston, 1975-80; chief infectious disease div. Brigham and Women's Hosp., Boston, 1980-87; mem. and chmn. exptl. virology study sect. NIH, 1977-81; mem. Multiple Sclerosis Adv. Commn. on Fundamental Rsch., 1976; mem. coun. Nat. Inst. Allergy and Infectious Disease, 1987-91. Contbr. articles to profl. jours. Recipient Faculty Research Asso. award Am. Cancer Soc., 1969-74, Irma T. Hirschel scholar, 1974-76; Career Scientist award Health Research Council N.Y., 1974-75; 12th Ann. Redway medal N.Y. State Med. Soc., 1974; Dyer lecture award NIH, 1987; Bristol-Myers Suibb award Disting. Achievement Infectious Disease Rsch., 1993; grantee NIH, 1969-95. Fellow AAAS; mem. Am. Soc. Microbiology, Am. Soc. Virology (pres. 1990-91), Am. Soc. Clin. Investigation, Harvey Soc., Am. Assn. Immunologists, Infectious Disease Soc. Am., Assn. Am. Physicians, Nat. Acad. Scis., Inst. Medicine, Am. Acad. Arts & Scis. Home: Newton Mass. Died Jan. 31, 1995.

FIELDS, FREDRICA HASTINGS, artist; b. Phila., Jan. 10, 1912; d. Theodore Mitchell and Carolyn Corlies (Baily) Hastings; student Wellesley Coll., 1930-32, Art Students League, 1933; m. Kenneth E. Fields, July 10, 1934; children: David Edward (dec.), Luellen, Stephen Francis. Designer craftsman in stained glass, 1948-92; exhibited in one man show Artists Mart, Washington, 1955, First Presbyn. Ch., Stamford, Conn., 1976, Concordia Coll., Bronxville, N.Y., 1982, Greenwich (Conn.) YWCA, 1982; exhibited in group shows Nat. Soc. Arts and Letters, Washington, 1951, Smithsonian Instn., 1951, 53, 54, 57, 58, Corcoran Gallery Art, 1955, 56, Nat. Conf. on Religious Architecture, N.Y.C., 1967, Washington, 1970, Greenwich (Conn.) Art Soc. Ann. Exhbns., 1968-78, Stamford (Conn.) Art Soc., 1972, Danbury (Conn.) Public Library, 1974, Stained Glass Internat., N.Y.C., 1982, Stained Glass Assn. Am.-Corning Mus. Glass, 1987, The Gallery at Hastings-on-Hudson, N.Y., 1990; represented in permanent installations at Washington Cathedral, Marie Cole Auditorium, Greenwich Library, YWCA, Greenwich, Assn. for Research and Enlightenment Meditation/Prayer Center, Virginia Beach, Va., Conn. Hospice Inc., Branford, Concordia Coll., Bronxville, N.Y., Ch. of Holy Comforter, Kenilworth, Ill., many pvt. collections; tchr. classes in stained glass, Washington, 1950, YWCA, Greenwich, 1966, at studio, 1968-71. Recipient awards in stained glass Corcoran Gallery Art, 1955, 56, B.F. Drakenfeld award 6th Internat. Exhbn. of Ceramic Arts, Nat. Collections Fine Arts, Smithsonian Instn., 1957, 1st prize for autonomous panel in Beautiful Glass Show, Dallas, 1991, award of Excellence Stained Glass Assn. Am., 1991. Mem. Stained Glass Assn. Am. (contbr. to reference and tech. manuals vols. 1 and 2), Greenwich Art Soc. Died Mar. 4, 1992. Home: Greenwich Conn.

FIGG, ROBERT MCCORMICK, JR., lawyer; b. Radford, Va., Oct. 22, 1901; s. Robert McCormick and Helen Josephine (Cecil) F.; m. Sallie Alexander Tobias, May 10, 1927; children: Robert McCormick, Emily Figg Dalla Mura, Jefferson Tobias. A.B., Coll. of Charleston, 1920, Litt.D., 1970; law student, Columbia U., 1920-22; LL.D., U. S.C., 1959. Bar: S.C. 1922. Practiced in Charleston, 1922-59; gen. counsel S.C. State Ports Authority, 1942-72; circuit solicitor 9th Jud. Circuit of S.C., 1935-47; spl. circuit judge, 1957, 75, 76; dean Law Sch., U. S.C., 1959-70; sr. counsel Robinson, McFadden, Moore, Pope, Williams, Taylor & Brailsford, Columbia, from 1970; dir. Home Fed. Savs. & Loan Assn., Charleston. Co-author: Civil Trial Manual (joint com. Am. Coll. Trial Lawyers-Am. Law Inst.-Am. Bar Assn.), 1974. Mem. S.C. Reorgn. Commn., from 1948, chmn., 1951-55, 71-75; elector Hall Fame for Gt. Americans, 1976; mem. S.C. Ho. of Reps., 1933-35; first pres., now hon. life chmn. Coll. of Charleston Found.; trustee Saul Alexander Found., Columbia Mus. Art. Recipient DuRant award for disting. pub. service S.C. Bar Found., 1982; Founders medal Coll. of Charleston, 1986. Fellow Am. Coll. Trial Lawyers; mem. Am. Soc. Internat. Law, Am. Acad. Polit. Sci., Am. Law Inst. (life), Am. Judicature Soc., Inst. Jud. Adminstrn., World Assn. Lawyers, Inter-Am. Bar Assn., Charleston County Bar Assn. (pres. 1953), ABA (ho. of dels. 1971-72, com. fair trial-free press 1965-69, com. spl. study legal edn. from 1974), S.C. Bar Assn., S.C. State Bar (pres. 1971), Order Coif, Blue Key (hon.), Phi Beta Kappa (hon.), Phi Delta Phi (hon.). Clubs: Forum, Forest Lake, Palmetto U. S.C. Faculty. Lodge: Masons (33 degree, grand master S.C. 1972-74). Home: Columbia S.C. Deceased.

FILER, JOHN HORACE, lawyer; b. New Haven, Sept. 3, 1924; s. Harry Lambert and Ehrma (Green) F.; m. Marlene A. Klick, Feb. 2, 1977; children: Susan, Cynthia, Kathryn, Ann. B.A., Depauw U., 1947, LL.D., 1970; LL.B., Yale U., 1950. Bar: Conn. 1950. Practice in New Haven, 1950-58; law clk. to U.S. dist. judge, 1950-51; assoc., partner Gumbart, Corbin, Tyler & Cooper, 1951-58; gen. counsel Aetna Life & Casualty Co., Hartford, Conn., 1958-68; exec. v.p. Aetna Life & Casualty Co., 1968-72, chmn. bd., chief exec. officer, 1972-84; ptnr. law firm Tyler, Cooper & Alcorn, Hartford, 1984-85; bd. dirs. USX Corp. Chmn. Bd. Edn. Farmington, 1963-67; mem. Conn. Commn. to Study Met. Govt., 1966-67, Conn. Senate, 1957-58; trustee Mt. Holyoke Coll., 1971-77. Served to ensign USNR, 1943-46. Mem. ABA, Conn. Bar Assn., Assn. Life Ins. Counsel, Sigma Chi. Episcopalian. Home: West Hartford Conn. Died Sept 18, 1994.

FINCH, HAROLD BERTRAM, JR., wholesale grocery company executive; b. Grand Forks, N.D., Oct. 13, 1927; s. Harold Bertram and Ruth M. F.; m. Catherine E. Cole, Sept. 6, 1950; children: Mark, James, Sarah, Martha (dec.), David. BBA, U. Minn., 1952, BChemE, 1952. Div. mgr. Archer-Daniels-Midland Co., Mpls., 1960-66; dir. long-range planning, then v.p. sales and ops. Nash Finch Co., Mpls., 1966-78, pres., 1978-85, chief exec. officer, from 1982, chmn., from 1985; officer, bd. dirs. Nat. Assn. Wholesale Grocers Am., from 1989. Bd. dirs. Jr. Achievement Mpls., 1977-84, Mpls. YMCA, 1965-80, Wilderness Inquiry, from 1987; trustee Westminster Presbyn. Ch., 1985-92, Courage Ctr. Found., from 1991, Alfa Trading Co., Budapest, Hungary, from 1992. With U.S. Maritime Svc., 1945-47. Mem. Food Mktg. Inst. Presbyterian. Home: Wayzata Minn. Deceased.

FINDLAY, JOHN WILSON, retired physicist; b. Kineton, Eng., Oct. 22, 1915; came to U.S., 1956, naturalized, 1963; s. Alexander Wilson and Beatrice Margaret (Thornton) F.; m. Jean Melvin, Dec. 14, 1953; children: Stuart E.G., Richard A.J. B.A., Cambridge U., 1937, M.A., 1940, Ph.D., 1950. With British Air Ministry, 1939-40; fellow, lectr. in physics Queens' Coll., Cambridge, Eng., 1945-52; asst. dir. for electronics research Ministry of Supply, London, 1952-56; with Nat. Radio Astronomy Obs., Charlottesville, Va., 1956-85; dep. dir. Nat. Radio Astronomy Obs., 1961-65; dir. Arecibo Obs., 1965-66, sr. scientist, 1978-85; mem. space sci. bd. Nat. Acad. Scis., 1961-71; chmn. lunar and planetary missions bd. NASA, 1967-71; chmn. space sci. bd. study Scientific Uses of the Space Shuttle, 1973. Contbr. articles to profl. jours. Served with RAF, 1940-45. Decorated Order of Brit. Empire. Fellow IEEE, AAAS; mem. Internat. Sci. Radio Union, Internat. Astron. Union. Clubs: Cosmos, Farmington. Home: Greenwood Va. Died Mar. 22, 1994.

FINE, PHIL DAVID, lawyer; b. Brookline, Mass., Aug. 20, 1925; s. Joseph H. and Ann M. (Rosenblum) F.; m. Norma Loew, Dec. 28, 1952; children: Susan Ellen, Lauri Joan Friedman, Debra Jane. Student Northeastern U., Boston, 1942-43. 46-47, Norwich U., 1943-90; LL.B., Boston U., 1950; LL.D. (hon.), St. Michael's Coll., 1972. Bar: Mass. 1950, U.S. Dist. Ct. Mass. 1952, U.S. Ct. Appeals (1st cir.) 1952, U.S. Dist. Ct. (D.C. cir.) 1961, U.S. Tax Ct. 1962, U.S. Supreme Ct. 1961. Assoc. Parker Coulter, Daley & White, Boston, 1950-55, ptnr., 1955-57; ptnr. Peabody, Koufman & Brewer, Boston, 1957-59, Fine & Ambrogne, Boston, 1959-88, counsel, 1989-90; ptnr. White, Fine & Verville, Washington, 1967-88, counsel, 1989-90; dep. adminstr. SBA, Washington, 1961-63; cons. Dept. Commerce, Washington, 1964-67; chmn. bd. Commonwealth Nat. Corp., 1969-82, Stadium Realty Trust, 1970-80; Commonwealth Bank & Trust Co., Boston, 1964-82; bd. govs. Mass Gen. Hosp., 1983-90; hon. trustee Joslin Diabetes Center, 1983-90; trustee Boston U., 1973-78; hon. consul Republic of Costa Rica to Boston; past pub. mem. bd. govs. Boston Stock Exchange. Vice chmn. Housing Authority, Newton, Mass., 1961-63; trustee Pub. Library, Newton, 1964-70, Fund for the Arts, 1985-90; co-chmn. Democratic Congl. Campaign Com., Washington, 1975; bd. overseers Northeastern U., 1986-90; cons. dept. constrn. and housing Govt. of Israel. Mem. ABA, Boston Bar Assn. (chmn. banking law com. 1981-83). Democrat. Jewish. Lodge: Mason. Died July 31, 1990. Home: Waltham Mass.

FINGER, JOHN HOLDEN, lawyer; b. Oakland, Calif., June 29, 1913; s. Clyde P. and Jennie (Miller) F.; m. Dorothy C. Riley, Dec. 30, 1950; children: Catherine, John Jr., David, Carol. AB, U. Calif., 1933. Bar: Calif. 1937. Pvt. practice of law San Francisco, 1937-42; prof. U.S. Army Judge Advocate Gen.'s Sch., 1942-46; chief mil. commn. sect. Far East Hdqrs. War Dept., Tokyo, 1946-47; atty. Hoberg Finger Brown Cox & Molligan, San Francisco, 1989-91, of counsel, 1989-91; investigative hearing officer Office of Citizen Complaints, San Francisco, 1990-91; trustee Pacific Sch. Religion, bd. chmn., 1969-78; bd. dirs. Calif. Maritime Acad., San Francisco Legal Aid Soc., 1955-70; bd. visitors Judge Adv. Gen. Sch., Charlottesville, Va., 1964-76, Stanford U. Law Sch., 1969-71. Pres. Laymen's Fellowship, No. Calif. Conf. Congl. Chs., 1951-53, moderator, 1954-55. Served to maj. JAGC AUS, 1942-46; col. Res. ret.; comdg. officer 5th Judge Adv. Gen. Detachment, 1962-64; U.S. Army Judiciary, 1967-68. Decorated Legion of Merit. Mem. Am. Bar Found., Am. Coll. Trial Lawyers; mem. ABA (ho. of dels. 1970-78, coun. jud. adminstrn. divsn. 1972-77, standing com. assn. comms.), Am. Judicature Soc., Bar Assn. San Francisco (dir. 1960-62, recipient John A. Sutro award for legal excellence 1980), Judge Adv. Assn. (past bd. dirs., pres. 1964-65), Lawyers Club San Francisco (pres. 1953, past bd. dirs.), State Bar Calif. (bd. govs. 1965-67, pres. 1967-67), Sierra Club (exec. com. legal def. fund), Phi Alpha Delta, Sigma Phi Epsilon, Alpha Kappa Phi. Home: Monument Colo. Died Dec. 19, 1991.

FINGER, JUSTIN JOSEPH, lawyer, association executive; b. N.Y.C., Feb. 2, 1927; s. Joseph and Sophie (Purchin) F.; m. Sophia Blanche Geller, May 19, 1957; children: Janet, Laurel. B.A., NYU, 1949; J.D., Fordham U., 1952. Bar: N.Y. 1953, U.S. Supreme Ct. 1977, Ga. 1962. Law asst. N.Y. State Crime Commn., N.Y.C., 1952-53; asst. counsel Waterfront Commn. N.Y. Harbor, N.Y.C., 1953-57; atty., jud. inquiry Supreme Ct., Kings County, N.Y.C., 1957-58; asst. counsel N.Y. State Commn. Investigation, N.Y.C., 1958-59; dir. nat. civil rights div. Anti-Defamation League of B'nai B'rith, N.Y.C., 1960-96. Chmn. Manhattan Dist. 2 Sch. Bd., 1972-74; mem. Mayor's Commn. on Edn., N.Y.C., 1975; mem. bd. Stuyvesant Adult Ctr., N.Y.C., 1975-96; chmn. bd. Town and Village Synagogue, N.Y.C., 1978-96. Served with USN, 1944-47. Mem. ABA. Democrat. Jewish. Lodge: B'nai B'rith. Died May 6, 1996. Home: New York N.Y.

FINGER, KENNETH FRANKLIN, academic administrator; b. Antigo, Wis., Jan. 2, 1929; s. Otto Edward and Elsie (Kuehn) F.; m. Lois Eleanor Hoppe, Nov. 16, 1951; 1 child, William Lee. B.S., U. Wis., 1951, M.S., 1953, Ph.D., 1955. Sr. investigator Chas. Pfizer & Co. Bklyn., 1955-57, 1959-60, research supr., 1960-61, research mgr., 1961-63; assoc. prof. Sch. Pharmacy, U. Wis., Madison, 1963-67, prof., 1967-68; dean Coll. Pharmacy, U. Fla., Gainesville, 1968-78, assoc. v.p. health affairs, 1974-94; guest worker Nat. Heart Inst., 1957-59; mem. HEW Nat. Adv. Council on Alcoholism and Alcohol Abuse. Author publs. on adrenergic drugs. Recipient Teaching award Sch. Pharmacy, U. Wis., 1967, citation of Merit award, 1977, Human Svc. award of the decade United Ways Fla., 1990. Mem. Am. Soc. Pharmacology and Exptl. Therapeutics., Am. Pharm. Assn., Wis. Acad. Sci., Arts and Letters, Am. Assn. Colls. Pharmacy, Acad. Pharm. Scis., Sigma Xi, Rho Chi. Home: Gainesville Fla. Died July 11, 1994.

FINK, DONALD GLEN, engineering executive, editor; b. Englewood, N.J., Nov. 8, 1911; s. Harold Gardner and Margaret (Glen) F.; m. Alice Marjorie Berry, Apr. 10, 1948; children: Kathleen Marion, Stephen Donald, Susan Carol Fink Rudman. B.S., MIT, 1933; M.S., Columbia U., 1942. Research asst. MIT, 1933-34; staff radiation lab. Mass. Inst. Tech., 1941-43, head Loran div., 1943; bd. dirs. McGraw-Hill Book Co., Inc., 1947-52; vice chmn. Nat. TV System Com., 1950-52, panel chmn., 1950-53; chmn. prep. com. TV Dept. State, 1951-55; with Philco Corp., 1952-62, dir. research, 1952-58, dir., gen. mgr. research div., 1959-62, v.p.-research, 1961; exec. dir., gen. mgr. IEEE, N.Y.C., 1963-74; exec. cons. IEEE, 1975-76, dir. emeritus, 1974-96; ops. dir. Assn. Coop. Engring., 1975-76; cons., Belgium, 1952; mem. bd. for internat. orgns. and programs Nat. Acad. Scis.; chmn. com. on internat. sci. and tech. info. NRC, 1975-78; chmn. com. UNESCO sci. programs NRC, 1976-81; mem. exec. com. World Fedn. Engring. Orgns., 1973-77; mem. U.S. Commn. for UNESCO, 1976-81; trustee Met. Reference and Research Library Agy., 1974-83; chmn. Study Group High Definition TV Soc. Motion Picture and TV Engrs., 1977-83; expert cons. on radar and electronic nav. Office Sec. War, 1943-45; cons. to comdr. atom bomb tests, Bikini, 1946; mem. Army Sci. Adv. Panel, 1957-69; mem. com. nav. research and devel. bd. Dept. Def., 1948-51. Mem. editorial staff Electronics, 1934-52, editor in chief, 1946-52; author: Engineering Electronics, 1938, Principles of TV Engineering, 1940, Microwave Radar, 1942, Radar Engineering, 1947, TV Engineering, 1952, Color Television Standards, 1955, Television Engineering Handbook,

1957, Physics of Television, 1960, Computers and the Human Mind, 1966, Standard Handbook for Electrical Engineers, 1987, Electronics Engineers' Handbook, 1988, Engineers and Electrons, 1984, High Definition Television, 1990. Recipient Medal of Freedom, 1946; Presdl. Certificate Merit for wartime service, 1948; plaque for contbns. to TV IRE, 1951; Am. Technologists award N.Y. Inst. Tech., 1958; Outstanding Civilian Service medal U.S. Army, 1969; Citation for Outstanding Service to TV Internat. TV Symposium, Montreux, 1971. Fellow IEEE (editor Proc. IRE 1956-57, pres. IRE 1958, Founders medal 1978, Consumer Electronics award 1978), Soc. Motion Picture and TV Engrs. (jour. award 1956, Progress medal 1979); mem. Nat. Acad. Engring., Radio Club Am. (Sarnoff citation 1979, Batcher Meml. award 1985), Sigma Xi, Tau Beta Pi, Eta Kappa Nu (eminent mem.), Phi Mu Delta. Home: Somers N.Y. Died May 3, 1996.

FINK, JOHN, editor, newspaper; b. Farmington, Ill., Mar. 15, 1926; s. Walter Phillip and Alta Blanche (Payton) F.; m. Eloise Darlene Bradley, Aug. 8, 1949; children—Sara, Joel, Alison. B.A., Millikin U., 1949; M.A., U. Ill., 1950; postgrad., U. Wis., 1950-51. Reporter City News Bur. Chgo., 1952-53; mem. staff Chgo. Tribune, 1953—, asst. Sunday editor, 1961-67. Editor: Tribune mag, 1963—; Editor: WGN, a Pictorial History, 1961. Served USNR, 1944-46. Mem. Chgo. Press Club, Chgo. Headline Club, Sigma Delta Chi. Home: Winnetka Ill. Died Dec. 10, 1995.

FINKS, JAMES EDWARD, professional football club executive, consultant; b. St. Louis, MO, Aug. 31, 1927; s. William T. and Margaret (Hays) F.; m. Maxine Anne Stemmons, Sept. 24, 1951; children: James Edward Jr., Daniel K., David W., Thomas P. B.A., Tulsa U., 1949. Quarterback Pitts. Steelers Profl. Football Club, 1949-55; asst. coach U. Notre Dame, IN, 1956-57; gen. mgr. Calgary (Can.) Canadian Football League, 1957-64; gen. mgr. Minnesota Vikings, Minneapolis, MN, 1964-74, v.p., 1969-73, exec. v.p., 1973-74; v.p., gen. mgr., chief operations officer Chicago Bears, Chicago, IL, 1974-83; pres., chief exec. officer Chicago Cubs, Chicago, IL, 1983-84; pres., gen. mgr. New Orleans Saints, New Orleans, LA, 1986-93; consultant New Orleans Saints, 1993-94; cons. New Orleans Saints, New Orleans, LA, 1993-94. Named to Profl. Football Hall of Fame, 1995, Exec. of the Yr., 1973, 1987. Home: Metairie La. Died May 8, 1994; interred Metairie Lake Lawn Cemetary, Metairie, L.A.

FINLEY, CHARLES OSCAR, insurance company executive, former baseball executive; b. Birmingham, Ala., Feb. 22, 1918; s. Oscar A. and Burmah E. (Fields) F.; m. Shirley McCartney, May 9, 1941 (div. 1979); children: Sharon, Charles O., Kathryn, Paul, Martin, Luke, David. From laborer to foreman U.S. Steel Corp. mills, Gary, Ind., 1936-41; with Kingsbury Ordnance Plant, 1941-45, div. supt., 1945; pres., owner Charles O. Finley & Co., Inc. (gen. ins. brokers), Chgo., 1945-96; chmn. bd., pres., owner Oakland (Calif.) A's Baseball Club (American League), 1960-80; Assoc. mem. So. Med. Assn. for devel. group ins. for doctors and families, 1960. Nat. chmn. Christmas Seal campaign Nat. Tb Assn., 1961. Recipient trophy World Series, 1972, 73, 74; named sportsman of the yr., St. Louis Sporting News, 1973; named to Ala. Sports Hall of Fame, 1993, Chgo. Sports Hall of Fame, 1990. Presbyterian. Club: Chicago Athletic. Lodge: Mason (32 deg., Shriner). Home: La Porte Ind. Died Feb. 19, 1996.

FINLEY, LEON, lawyer; b. Bklyn., Nov. 22, 1907; s. Morris and Leah (Pikofski) Finklestein; m. Rosemary Watkins (divorced). LLB, St. John's U., 1929, LLD (hon), 1985; LLD (hon), Pace U., 1978, Fisk U., 1983. Bar: N.Y., U.S. Dist. Ct. (ea., so. dists.) N.Y., U.S. Ct. Appeals, U.S. Supreme Ct. 1942. Founding ptnr. Finley, Kumble, Heine, Underberg, N.Y.C., 1969-87; of counsel Baer Marks & Upham, N.Y.C., 1988-96. Trustee St. John's U.; vice-chmn. N.Y. State Dormitory Authority, 1978-83; founder Hebrew U., Israel, 1963, Albert Einstein Coll. Medicine, 1964. Recipient James Madison award St. John's U., 1987; Brandeis U. fellow, 1969. Mem. The Lotos Club (bd. dirs.), Univ. Club. Home: New York N.Y. Died Mar. 2, 1996.

FINN, THOMAS JAMES, food company executive; b. Chgo., June 8, 1940; s. Thomas James and Nora (O'Leary) F.; m. Evelyn Delores Grim; 1 child, Kristina. Account trainer Nabisco Co., Chgo., 1961-62; office mgr. Nabisco Co., St. Louis, 1963-64; internat. auditor Nabisco Co., Chgo., 1965-66; internat. auditor Nabisco Co., Toledo, 1966-67, grain buyer, 1967-68; corp. grain buyer Nabisco Co., N.Y.C., 1969-73; mgr. commodity purchasing Keebler Co., Elmhurst, Ill., 1973, dir. purchasing, 1974, v.p. purchasing, 1974-76, sr. v.p. purchasing, 1977—. Served with U.S. Army, 1959-61. Republican. Roman Catholic. Home: Long Grove Ill. Died Aug. 22, 1993.

FINN, WILLIAM FRANCIS, obstetrician, gynecologist; b. Union City, N.J., July 23, 1915; s. Neil and Catherine Marie (Hearn) F.; m. Doris Ida Henderson, Sept. 21, 1943; children: Neil C., Sharon R., David. AB summa cum laude, Holy Cross Coll., 1936; MD, Cornell U., 1940; MA in Philosophy, NYU, 1986; postgrad. CUNY, 1986-92. Diplomate Am. Bd. Obstetrics and Gynecology. Intern Albany Hosp., 1940-41; resident obstetrics and gynecology N.Y. Hosp., 1941-44, asst. attending obstetrician and gynecologist, 1946-48, assoc. attending obstetrician and gynecologist 1948-67; asst. prof. obstetrics and gynecology Cornell Med. Coll., 1948-67, assoc. clin. prof., 1967-92; attending obstetrics and gynecology North Shore Univ. Hosp., also founder com. medicine, soc. and ethics; cons. obstetrics and gynecology Mercy Hosp. Editor: Women and Loss; contbr. articles on dying, death, bereavement and biomed. Bd. mgrs. Episcopal Health Svcs., Episcopal Diocese of L.I.; chmn. ethics com. EMS, Diocesan Commn. Life and Health. J. Withridge Williams fellow, 1947. Recipient Bishop's Cross for disting. svc. Fellow ACS, AMA, Am. Coll. Obstetricians, Am. Soc. Colposcopy; mem. N.Y. Obstet. Soc., Queens Obstet. Soc. (pres.), Nassau Obstet. Soc. (pres.), Am. Acad. Obstetrics and Gynecology, N.Y. State Med. Soc., N.Y. County Med. Soc., Found. of Thanatology Inst. Soc., Ethics and Life Scis. Died Aug. 4, 1992. Home: Manhasset N.Y.

FINNEBURGH, MORRIS LEWIS, electronic manufacturing executive; b. Ft. Worth, Sept. 3, 1900; s. Lewis Henry and Lillie (Lewis) F.; m. Frieda Fox, Oct. 17, 1920; 1 child, Morris L. LLD, Ariz. Valley Tech. Coll., 1975. Ptnr., adminstrv. exec. Finney Co., Bedford, Ohio, 1952-94; chmn. exec. com., chmn. bd. Finney Mfg. Co., 1952-94, Bedford Realty Corp., 1952-94. Author: The Black Book. Contbr. articles to profl. jours. Trustee, mem. exec. com. Superior Ind. TV Service Fund; mem. Heritage Found., Washington; sustaining mem. G.O.P. Fund. Decorated knight Royal Order Rosarians; recipient Bernon Humanitarian award, 1969; Friends of Service awards (13); Community Improvement award City of Cleve., 1976; hon. Ky. col.; 25 Yr. Recognition award City of Toledo; Man of Yr. award in electronics industry, 1978; recipient (with wife) Second Wind Hall of Fame award for accomplishments in name of goodwill, humanity and charity; named to Electronic Hall of Fame, 1969; recipient Electronics Man of Yr. award, 1977, Silver Beaver award Boy Scouts Am., 50 Yr., 65 Yr., 70 Yr. Masonic awards, Hon. mem. Tex. Navy; named (with wife) Persons of Yr., Calif. Svc. Electronic Assn., 1992; apptd. by gov. Ind. as chieftain of Sagamore of the Wabash. Mem. All-Industry Electronics Conf. (nat. chmn. speakers bur. 1961-94), Electronics Industry Council (chmn.), Nat. Alliance Technicians and Electricians Assns., Nat. Electronics Distbrs. Assn., Technicians Service Assn., Electronic Technicians Guild; hon. life mem. Nat. Alliance TV and Electronic Service Assns. (chmn. nat. merger com. with Nat. Electronics Assn.), Ariz. Electronic Service Assn., Nat. Electronics Assn., Calif. Electonics Assn., Kans. Electronics Assn. (life), La. Electronics Assn., Va. Electronics Assn., Electronics Industry Assn., Maine Electronics Technicians Assn., Ky. Electronics Technicians Assn.; mem. TV Reception Industry Program (nat. chmn.), Tex. Electronics Assn., Nat. Heritage Assn. Found., Order of Turtle; hon. life mem. State Electronic Service assns. of Ill., Ind., Wis., Miss., Ark., Wash., N.Y., Ga., Va., Ohio, Calif., Mich., N.C. Service assns. Nat. Electronics Service Dealer Assn. (Excellence award 1986). Clubs: Lake Forest Country, Forest Hills. Lodges: Masons, Rotary of P.R. (hon.). Home: Cleveland Ohio Died Nov. 17, 1994.

FIRESTONE, RAYMOND CHRISTY, former rubber company executive; b. Akron, Ohio, Sept. 6, 1908; s. Harvey S. and Idabelle (Smith) F.; m. Laura An Lisk, Aug. 25, 1934 (dec. July, 1960); m. Jane Allen Messler, Apr. 28, 1962; children—Christy An Firestone Gordon-Creed, Judith An Firestone Thiel. A.B., Princeton U., 1933; LL.D., U. Akron, 1957; H.H.D., U. Liberia, 1960. Joined sales dept. Firestone Tire & Rubber Co., 1933; dist. store supr. Firestone Store, Los Angeles, 1934; asst. mgr. Southeastern sales zone Akron, 1934-35; dist. mgr. Richmond, Va., 1935-36; staff Firestone plant Memphis, 1936; pres. subs. Firestone Tire & Rubber Co., 1937-49, v.p. research and devel., 1949-54, exec. v.p., 1954-57, pres., 1957-63, pres., chief exec. officer, 1963-64, chief exec. officer, 1964-74, chmn. exec. com., 1964-76, chmn. bd., 1966-76, ret., 1976. Bd. dirs. 4-H Service Com., 1953-76, v.p., 1958-76; bd. dirs. Le Bonheur Children's Hosp., Inc., Memphis. Served as maj. USAF, 1942-44. Recipient Humanitarian Service award Eleanor Roosevelt Found., 1961, Ohio Gov.'s award, 1964; distinguished fellow Cleve. Clinic Found., 1971; decorated grand band Order Star of Africa, knight grand cross Order of Merit of Italy, 1971. Episcopalian. Clubs: Detroit Athletic (Detroit); Union (Cleve.), Chagrin Valley (Cleve.); Indpls. Athletic; Genesee Valley (Rochester, N.Y.), Rochester Country (Rochester, N.Y.); Country of N.C. (Pinehurst), Pinehurst Country (Pinehurst); Portage Country (Akron). Home: Bath Ohio Died Sept. 9, 1994.

FIRKUŠNY, RUDOLF, pianist, music educator; b. Napajedla, Czechoslovakia, Feb. 11, 1912; came to U.S., 1940; s. Rudolf and Karla (Šindelařová) F.; m. Tatiana Nevole, June 9, 1965; children: Véronique, Igor. Student coll., Conservatory of Music, Brno, Praha, 1922-1930; MA, Acad. Music, Prague, 1929; PhD (hon.), Charles U., Prague, 1990, Masaryk U., Brno, 1991, Bard Coll., 1993, Janáček Acad. Performing Arts, Brno, Czech Republic, 1993. Mem. piano faculty Juilliard Sch., N.Y.C., 1964-94. First appeared with Czech Philharm. Orch., 1922; appeared with symphony orchs. including N.Y., Boston, Phila., Chgo., Detroit, Mpls., Cleve., San Francisco, Los Angeles, Toronto, Montreal; played in recitals in all sects. U.S., also S.Am. tours, 1943-94, ann. tours in Europe, 30-39, 1950-94, tours of Australia and Far East, 1959, 67, Japan, 1978, 83, 85, 87, 89, 92; composer piano concerto in Prague, Czechoslovakia, piano pieces, songs. Recipient Honorary award Czechoslovak Soc. Arts and Scis. in Am., N.Y.C., Spl. award for Disting. Achievement in Music Third Street Music Sch. Settlement, N.Y.C., 1984, Ethnic New Yorker award Mayor Koch, 1989; T.G. Masaryk Order 1st Class Pres. Vaclav Havel, 1991; Hon. Citizen of Prague and Napajedla, 1990, Brno, 1991, Uherské Hradiště, 1993. Clubs: Century (N.Y.C.), Bohemians. Home: Staatsburg N.Y. Died July 19, 1994.

FIRST, JOSEPH MICHAEL, retired legal and management consultant; b. Phila., Apr. 1, 1906; s. Louis and Sarah (Selig) F.; m. Helen Gross, Dec. 27, 1931; children: Elsa, Abigail First Farber, Jonathan. BS in Econs. cum laude, Wharton Sch., U. Pa., 1927, JD cum laude, 1930, LLM (Gowen fellow 1930-32), 1932; LLD (hon.), Temple U., 1980. Bar: Pa. bar 1930. V.p., gen. counsel Triangle Publs., Inc., 1940-75, Phila. Inquirer, 1940-75; also dir. Triangle Publs., Inc.; v.p. Triangle Fin., Inc., 1970-75, also dir.; legal, mgmt. cons. Triangle Publs., 1975-84. Case editor U. Pa. Law Rev., 1929-30. First pres., hon. chmn. bd. dirs. Albert Einstein Med. Center, 1951-55; bd. dirs., life trustee emeritus dir. Albert Einstein Health Care Found., hon. chmn.; v.p., sec. Annenberg Sch. Communications, 1958-80, hon. trustee, 1980-95; v.p., sec. M.L. Annenberg Found., 1944-84; sec., treas. Annenberg Fund, Inc., 1951-84; bd. dirs. Merion Civic Assn., 1951-77, Fedn. Jewish Philanthropies Phila., 1950-80; hon. life trustee Fed. Jewish Philanthropies Phila. 1980-95; trustee Temple U., 1966-80, hon. life trustee, also mem. exec. com., mem. ednl. policies com., 1968-80; trustee Dropsie Coll., 1950-53; assoc. trustee U. Pa., 1968; hon. trustee Akiba Hebrew Acad. Recipient Outstanding Alumnus award McKean Law Club, U. Pa., 1959, alumni award of merit, 1958, life achievement award Albert Einstein Med. Ctr., 1993. Mem. Brandeis Lawyers Soc., ABA, Pa. Bar Assn. (editor quar. 1941-68, emeritus editor 1968-95, chmn. publs. com. 1960-67, Distinguished Service award 1961, spl. citation 1968), Phila. Bar Assn., Jewish Publ. Soc. (pres. 1966-69, hon. pres. 1970-95), Order of Coif. Jewish (life trustee Temple Har Zion). Home: Merion Station Pa. Died Sept. 6, 1995.

FISHER, CARL A., bishop; b. Pascagoula, Miss., Nov. 24, 1945. AA, Epiphany Apostolic Coll., Newburgh, N.Y., 1965; BA, St. Joseph's Sem., 1967; MA, Oblate Coll., 1970; MS, Am. U., 1974. Ordained priest Roman Cath. Ch., 1973. Titular bishop of Tlos, aux. bishop of L.A., 1987-93. First African-Am. Catholic Bishop in Western U.S. Home: Lakewood Calif. Died Sept. 3, 1993.

FISHER, HERBERT, retail executive; b. N.Y.C., Nov. 14, 1921; s. Arthur and May (Schnitzer) F.; m. Florence Temkin, Nov. 17, 1951; children: Meredith, Judith, Lesley. Student, CCNY, 1940-42. Co-owner A. Fisher & Sons, N.Y.C., 1945-50; owner Franklyn Shops, 1950-59, Royal Factory Outlet, Pittsfield, Mass., 1959-60; with Jamesway Corp., Secaucus, N.J., 1960-94, chmn. bd., 1962-94; nat. retail chmn. State of Israel Bonds, 1989-94; chmn. Bergen Health Svc., Inc., 1989-94; bd. dirs. Hillcrest Health Svcs. Inc. Exec. adv. Coll. Bus. Adminstrn., Fairleigh Dickinson U., Madison, N.J., 1982-94. With USAAF, 1942-45. Mem. Nat. Mass Retailing Inst. (chmn. 1973-75, chmn. polit. action com. 1980-88), Muscular Dystrophy Assn. (nat. v.p. 1985-94). Home: Oradell N.J. Died 1994.

FISHER, LEONARD ROBERT, shoe manufacturing company executive; b. N.Y.C., Nov. 16, 1922; s. Benjamin and Anna (Kleinstein) F.; m. Phyllis June Hyde, Dec. 9, 1946; children: John Hyde, Merrill Jane Fisher Gottesman. BS in Econs., U. Pa., 1943. With Hyde Athletic Industries, Inc., Cambridge, Mass., 1963—, asst. v.p., 1963-66, v.p., 1966-68, exec. v.p., 1968-77, pres., chmn. bd., 1977-85, chmn. bd. dirs., chief exec. officer, 1985—. Bd. dirs. Family Counseling and Guidance Ctrs., 1984-86. With USAAF, World War II; with M.I., Korean War. Mem. Sporting Goods Mfrs. Assn. (chmn. 1978-79), World Fedn. Sporting Goods Industry (pres. 1980-83), Univ. Club of Boston, Belmont Country Club. Home: Chestnut Hill Mass.

FISHER, SAUL HARRISON, psychiatrist, educator; b. Bklyn., Feb. 20, 1913; s. David and Anna (Klieger) F.; m. Isobel McBride, Nov. 28, 1945; 1 child, Rachel. BS, CCNY, 1932; MD, NYU, 1936. Diplomate Am. Bd. Psychiatry and Neurology, Am. Bd. Internal Medicine. Asst. physiology NYU Sch. Medicine, N.Y.C., 1936-37; intern medicine Bellevue Hosp., N.Y.C., 1937-40; rsch. resident Goldwater Meml. Hosp., N.Y.C., 1941; instr. medicine NYU Sch. Medicine, N.Y.C., 1944-46; resident psychiatry Bellevue Hosp., N.Y.C., 1946-49; clin. prof. psychiatry NYU Sch. Medicine, N.Y.C., 1972-93; cons. psychiatry Fountain House Found., N.Y.C., 1955-80. Contbr. articles to profl. jours.; author of profl. papers. Fellow Am. Psychiat. Assn. (life), Am. Orthopsychiat. Assn. (life), Am. Acad. Psychoanalysis, Soc. Med. Psychoanalysts (pres. 1955-56); mem. Harvey Soc. Jewish. Home: Ardsley N.Y. Died Feb. 13, 1993.

FISHKO, BELLA, art gallery executive; d. Abram and Anna (Kanterman) Gold; m. Sol Fishko, Aug., 1950; children: Robert S., Sara. Student, CUNY. Dir. Forum Gallery, N.Y.C., 1960-95. Mem. Art Dealers Assn. Am. Home: New York N.Y. Died Mar. 7, 1995.

FITCH, R. JAY, banker; b. Olmsted, Ohio, July 27, 1900; s. Rufus J. and Della K. (Kendal) F.; m. Alberta Spiegelberg, Sept. 15, 1925; 1 child, William J. Grad., Wooster Coll. Exec. v.p. Elyria Savs. & Trust Nat. Bank, Elyria, Ohio, 1945-83, chmn. bd., 1983-84, now chmn. bd. emeritus; v.p., dir. Elyria Telephone Co., Ohio, from 1947; treas., dir. Elyria Broadcasting Co. Treas. City of Elyria, 1937-41; trustee Lorain County Community Coll. Found., 1977-85. Republican. Lodge: Rotary (pres. 1950-51). Home: Elyria Ohio Deceased.

FITZGERALD, ALICE IRENE, educator emeritus; b. Miller County, Mo., June 9, 1911; d. J. W. and Ida Alice (Cotten) F. BS in Edn., Mo. U., 1938, MEd, 1954, EdD, 1960. Pub. sch. tchr. Rural Miller County, Eldon, Mo., 1932-36; elem. tchr. Eldon Pub. Schs., 1936-54; instr. Mo. U., Columbia, 1954-60; assoc. prof. N.E. Mo. State Tchrs. Coll., Kirksville, 1960-61; prof. Mo. U., Columbia, Mo., 1961-81, prof. emeritus, 1981-94. Author: Missouri's Literary Heritage, 1981; contbr. articles to profl. jours. Mem. Mo. United Meth. Ch., Columbia, 1962-94, various coms. Recipient Disting. Alumni award Mo. U. Coll. of Edn., 1982. Mem. AAUW (v.p. Mo. div. 1954-56, treas. 1952-54, mem. ednl. found. internat. fellowship com. 1969-73, past pres. Columbia and Eldon, Mo. brs.), State Hist. Soc. Mo. (Alice Irene Fitzgerald Collection of Mo.'s Lit. Heritage 1982), Delta Kappa Gamma, Pi Lambda Theta, Kappa Delta Pi (Tchr. of Yr. Mu chpt. 1981). Republican. Methodist. Home: Columbia Mo. Died Apr. 26, 1994; interred Dooley Cemetary, Eldon, M.O.

FITZGERALD, ELLA, singer; b. Newport News, Va., Apr. 25, 1918; m. Ray Brown (div. 1953); 1 child, Ray. Began singing with Chick Webb Orch., 1934-39; tours throughout U.S., Japan, Europe; with Jazz at the Philharmonic troupe, 1948-57; rec. artist for Decca, 1936-55, Verve, from 1956, now Pablo Records; appeared in motion picture Pete Kelly's Blues, 1955; nightclub appearances include Sahara Hotel, Caesar's Palace, both Las Vegas, Fairmont Hotel, San Francisco, Ronnie Scott's Club, London; appeared on TV in spls. with Frank Sinatra; also on All Star Swing Festival, 1972, concert with Boston Pops, 1972; later with more than 40 symphony orchs. throughout U.S.; records include At Duke's Place, 1966, Best, 1967, Clap Hands, 1961, Cote d' Azur, (with Ellington), 1967, Ella, Ella Fitzgerald; In Hamburg, 1965, Mack the Knife, Ella in Berlin, 1960, Sunshine of Your Love, Things Ain't What They Used to Be, Tribute to Porter, 1965, Whisper Not, 1966, Watch What Happens, 1972, Take Love Easy, 1975, Ella in London, 1975, Lady Time, 1978, A Perfect Match (with Count Basie), 1979, A Tisket a Tasket, 1985, Montreux Ella, The Intimate Ella, 1990, All That Jazz, 1990, Brighten The Corner, 1991, Misty Blue, 1991, Pure Ella, 1994, Verve Jazz Master 6: Ella Fitzgerald, 1994, The Best of the Songbooks: The Ballads, 1994, numerous others. Recipient 12 Grammy awards, numerous popularity awards from Down Beat mag., Metronome mag., Musicians Poll, JAY Award Poll; named number 1 female singer 16th Internat. Jazz Critics Poll, 1968, Commander of Arts and Letters, Paris, 1990; recipient Am. Music award, 1978, Kennedy Center honor, 1979, Grammy award as best female jazz vocalist, 1981, 84; recipient Nat. Medal of the Arts, 1987. Home: Beverly Hills Calif. Died June 15, 1996.

FITZSIMMONS, RICHARD M., lawyer; b. New Haven, Apr. 4, 1924; s. Irving F. and Nina G. (Moore) FitzS.; m. Estelle M. Naughton, Nov. 27, 1954; children: Estelle F. Thorson, Anne H. B.A., Hamilton Coll., 1947; J.D., Yale U., 1950. Bar: N.Y. 1950, U.S. Supreme Ct. 1954, Wis. 1958, Ill. 1964, Ky. 1966. Assoc. Winthrop, Stimson, Putnam & Roberts, N.Y.C., 1950-51, Satterlee, Warfield & Stephens, N.Y.C., 1951-54; counsel Gen. Electric Co., various locations, 1954-70; counsel Hotpoint div. Gen. Electric Co., various locations, Chgo., 1963-66; appliance and TV group Gen. Electric Co., various locations, Louisville, 1966-70; gen. counsel, sr. v.p., sec. Allis-Chalmers Corp., Milw., 1970-85; mem. firm Cook & Franke S.C., 1986-93; bd. dirs. Bank One Wis. Trust Co., N.A.; mem. adv. bd. Internat. and Comparative Law Center, Southwestern Legal Found., Dallas, 1970-93; mem. panel neutrals Asbestos Claims Facility; adj. prof. Marquette Law Sch., 1986-93. Editor Yale Law Jour., 1948-50; contbr. articles to profl. jours. Trustee Hamilton Coll., 1975-79. Served to capt. USAAF, 1943-46. Mem. Am., Wis., N.Y.C., Chgo., Ky. bar assns., Am. Arbitration Assn. (panel arbitrators), Corbey Ct., Yale Law Sch. Assn. (exec. com. 1978), Delta Kappa Epsilon, Phi Delta Phi. Clubs: Milwaukee Country, University of Milwaukee; Shenorock (Rye, N.Y.); Yale (N.Y.C.). Home: Milwaukee Wis. Died July 23, 1993; buried Holy Cross Cemetery, Milwaukee, Wis.

FLAGG, ROBERT FARRINGTON, advertising agency executive; b. Houston, Mar. 22, 1924; s. Joseph Walker and May Del (Farrington) F.; m. Nancy White, Sept., 1949; children: Robert Farrington, Betsy, Gael, Charles. Student, Tex. A&M U., 1941-42, Tex. A&I U., 1942-43; BA with honors, Rice U., 1949. Newspaper reporter, book pub., pub. relations dir. Elsvier Press, Houston and Amsterdam, 1951-54; account exec. Boone & Cummings, Houston, 1954-64; pres. Flagg Advt. Agy., Houston, 1964-95, Flagg Enterprises, Houston, 1967-95; editor, pub. Flagg's Gardening Almanac, also Flagg's Gardening Newsletter, Houston, 1972-95; gardening editor Houston Post, 1977-95; gardening radio host KSEV, Houston, 1977-95; precinct chmn., dist. and state del. Rep., 1960-74. Author: Gulf Coast Gardener, 1961; rev. edit., 1967; contbr. gardening articles to various publs. Decorated Bronze Star with cluster, Combat Infantryman's badge, Purple Heart with oak leaf clusters; various campaign ribbons; recipient award State of Israel, 1976; also various advt. awards. Mem. Garden Writers Am., Rice U. Alumni Assn. Episcopalian. Home: Houston Tex. Deceased.

FLAHERTY, GLORIA, writer, history educator; b. Kearny, N.J.; d. John Robert and Jean F. Student, Douglass Coll., 1955-57; BA, Rutgers U., 1959; MA, Johns Hopkins U., 1960, PhD, 1965. Jr. instr. Johns Hopkins U., Baltimore, 1960-63; asst. prof. Northwestern U., Evanston, Ill., 1964-71; assoc. prof. Bryn Mawr (Pa.) Coll., 1971-84; prof. 18th century studies U. Ill., Chgo., 1984-92. Fulbright scholar, 1981-82; Ford Found. grantee, 1984; fellow Inst. for the Humanities, U. Ill., Chgo. Mem. Am. Soc. for 18th Century Studies (v.p. 1986-87, pres. 1987-88). Home: Glen Ellyn Ill. Died Aug. 3, 1992.

FLANAGAN, JOHN CLEMANS, research psychologist; b. Armour, S.D., Jan. 7, 1906; s. Charles Gibbons and Gertrude (Clemans) F.; m. Katherine Ross, Jan. 18, 1930; children: John Ross, Scott Calhoun; m. Ruth Colonna; June 21, 1962. B.S., U. Wash., 1929; M.A., 1932; Ph.D., Harvard U., 1934. Diplomate: in personnel psychology Am. Bd. Examiners in Profl. Psychology. Tchr. sci. and math. Renton (Wash.) High Sch., 1929-30; tchr. math. Cleveland High Sch., Seattle, 1930-32; asst. in edn. Harvard U., 1934-35; lectr. Columbia Tchrs. Coll., 1936-41; assoc. dir. Coop. Test Service, N.Y.C., 1935-41; prof. psychology U. Pitts., 1946-66; founder, pres. Am. Inst. Rsch., Pitts., 1945-66, 1969-72, chmn. bd., 1972-89. Served to col. USAAF, 1941-46; dir. aviation psychology program. Decorated Legion of Merit, 1946; recipient Raymond F. Longacre award Aero. Med. Assn., 1954, Edward Lee Thorndike award Am. Psychol. Assn., 1972, Profl. Practice award Am. Psychol. Assn., 1982, Distinguished Contbn. award, 1976; Meritorious Contbn. award Phi Delta Kappa, 1977; Disting. Profl. Service award Ednl. Testing Service, 1978. Mem. AAAS (chmn. edn. sect.), Am. Ednl. Research Assn. (v.p. 1973), Am. Psychol. Assn. (pres. div. eval. and measurement 1956-57, pres. div. mil. psychology 1961-62, div. gen. psychology 1963-64, div. ednl. psychology 1969-70), Am. Statis. Assn., N.Y. Acad. Scis. (v.p. 1936), Psychometric Soc. (pres. 1952), Sigma Xi. Home: Menlo Park Calif. Died Apr. 15, 1996.

FLANDERS, DWIGHT PRESCOTT, economist; b. Rockford, Ill., Mar. 14, 1909; s. Daniel Bailey and Lulu Iona (Nichol) F.; m. Mildred Margaret Hutchison, Aug. 27, 1939 (dec. Dec. 1978); children: James Prescott, Thomas Addison. BA, U. Ill., 1931, MA, 1937; teaching cert., Beloit (Wis.) Coll., 1934; PhD in Econs., Yale U., 1939. With McLeish, Baxter & Flanders (realtors), Rockford, 1931-33; instr. U.S. history and sci. in secondary schs. Rockford, 1934-36; asst. prof. econs. Coll. Liberal Arts and Scis.; prof. statistics Maxwell Grad. Sch. Syracuse (N.Y.) U., 1939-42; acad. staff econs. dept. social sci. U.S. Mil. Acad., West Point, N.Y., 1942-46, lt. col. in charge of econs., 1945-46; mem. faculty U. Ill., Urbana, 1946-94; prof. econs. U. Ill., 1953-77; prof. emeritus dept. econs. Coll. Commerce and Bus. Adminstrn., 1977-94; prof. emeritus dept. family and consumer econs. Coll. Agr., 1980-94; chmn. masters research seminar, 1947-74, cons. in field; ptnr. McLeish and Flanders, 1978-94; mem. nominating com. Nobel award in econs.; cons. Dept of Pub. Works and Bldgs., Ill., 1959-65. Author: Science and Social Science, 2d edit, 1962, Status of Military Personnel as Voters, 1942, Collection Rural Real Property Taxes in Illinois, 1938; co-author: Contemporary Foreign Governments, 1946, The Conceptual Framework for a Science of Marketing, 1964; contbr. numerous articles to profl. jours. Pres. Three Lakes (Wis.) Waterfront Homeowners Assn., 1969-71, dir., 1971-75, ofcl. bd., 1975-84. Served to lt. col. AUS, 1942-46. Univ. fellow U. Ill., 1936-37; Univ. fellow Yale U., 1937-39; recipient Bronze tablet U. Ill., 1931, Excellence in Teaching award, 1977. Mem. Am. Econ. Assn., Midwest Econs. Assn., Royal Econ. Soc., Econometric Soc., Phi Beta Kappa, Beta Gamma Sigma (chpt. pres. 1959-61), Phi Kappa Phi, Alpha Kappa Psi. Methodist (ofcl. bd.). Club: Yale (Chgo.). Home: Champaign Ill. Deceased.

FLANDERS, EDWARD PAUL, actor; b. Mpls., Dec. 29, 1934; s. Francis Micheal Grey and Bernice (Brown) F.; children: Scott, Suzanne, Ian. Student pub. schs. Mem. Globe Theatre company, San Diego, 1952—. Appeared in numerous plays; film appearances include The Grasshopper, 1970, The Trial of the Catonsville Nine, 1972, MacArthur, 1977, The Ninth Configuration, 1980, Twinkle, Twinkle, Killer Kane, True Confessions, 1981; TV appearances include: Special Bulletin, Backstairs at the White House, Things in their Season, Mary White, The Amazing Howard Hughes, Harry S. Truman: Plain Speaking, also in TV series St. Elsewhere 1982—. Served with U.S. Army, 1956-58. Recipient Emmy awards, Tony award, Drama Desk award. Home: Eureka Calif.

FLATT, ERNEST ORVILLE, choreographer, director; b. Denver, Oct. 30, 1918; s. Ernest Scorrow and Della May (Allen) F. Grad. high sch. Dir. Ernatt Corp. Dancer in films including Singin' in the Rain; choreographer: film Anything Goes; TV shows Your Hit Parade, 1955-58, Garry Moore Show, 1958-63 (Emmy award), Carol Burnett Show, 1968-77 (Emmy award 1971); assoc. producer: TV spl. Julie and Carol at Carnegie Hall (Golden Rose award); dir.-choreographer Broadway shows include Fade In Fade Out, It's A Bird It's Plane It's Superman, Lorelei, Sugar Babies, 1979, Honky Tonk Nights, 1984, (Can. prodn.) Durante 1989-90. Served with AUS, 1941-45. Mem. AFTRA, Actors' Equity, Soc. Dirs. and Choreographers, Dirs. Guild Am. Home: Palm Springs Calif. Died June 10, 1995.

FLAVIN, GLENNON P., retired bishop; b. St. Louis, Mar. 2, 1916. Grad., St. Louis Prep. Sem., Kendrick Sem. Ordained priest Roman Catholic Ch., 1941; sec. to archbishop St. Louis, 1949-57; consecrated bishop 1957; ordained titular bishop of Joannina and aux. bishop St. Louis, 1957-67; bishop Diocese of Lincoln Nebr., 1967-92; retired, 1992-95. Died Aug. 27, 1995.

FLEMING, CHARLES ALEXANDER, naturalist; b. Auckland, N.Z., Sept. 9, 1916; s. George Herbert and Winifred (Hardy) F.; B.A., U. N.Z., 1940, M.Sc., 1941, D.Sc., 1952; D.Sc. (hon.), Victoria U., Wellington, 1967, U. Auckland, 1974; m. Margaret Alison Chambers, Apr. 12, 1941; children: Robin Margaret, Winifred Mary, Jean Sutherland. Mem. staff N.Z. Geol. Survey, Lower Hutt, 1940-77, chief paleontologist, 1952-77; hon. lectr. geology Victoria U., Wellington, 1975-85, hon. fellow Research Sch. Earth Scis., 1986-87. Mem. N.Z. Nat. Parks Authority, 1970-81; mem. council Nat. Mus. 1976-85. Decorated officer and knight comdr. Order Brit. Empire; recipient Sir George Fowlds Meml. medal 1941; Hamilton prize, 1943; Hutton Meml. medal, 1956, Hector Meml. medal, 1963; N.Z. Research medal, 1951, Service to Sci. medal, 1969, N.Z. Assn. Scientists; Walter Burfitt prize Royal Soc. New South Wales, 1965; McKay Hammer award Geol. Soc. N.Z., 1957; Herbert E. Gregory medal Pacific Sci. Assn., 1979. Fellow Royal Soc. London, Royal Soc. N.Z. (pres. 1962-66), Art Galleries and Mus. Assn. N.Z. Ornithologists Union, Brit. Ornithologists Union, Am. Ornithologists Union (corr.), Zool. Soc. London (hon.), Australian-N.Z. Assn. for Advancement Sci. (pres. 1969, medal 1972), Geol. Soc. London (hon.), Royal Australian Ornithologists Union; mem. Auckland Inst. and Mus., Bishops Mus. Assn., Geol. Soc.Australia, Soc. for Bibliography Natural History, Paleontol. Soc., Paleontol. Assn. (London), Am. Philos. Soc. (fgn. hon.), Geol. Soc. Australia (hon.), Entomol. Soc. N.Z. (hon.). Author: Geology of Wanganui Subidivision, 1953; The Genus Pecten in New Zealand, 1957; (with D. Kear) The Jurassic Sequence at Kawhia Harbour, 1960; (with others) Checklist of New Zealand Birds, 1953; The Geological History of New Zealand and its Life, 1979; George Edward Lodge: The Unpublished New Zealand Bird Paintings, 1982; also numerous articles; translator Geology of New Zealand (Hochstetter) 1959. Research on New Zealand birds, cicadas and molluscs, history of life in N.Z. Died Sept. 11, 1987; cremated. Home: Wellington New Zealand

FLEMING, JAMES DOUGLAS, manufacturing company executive; b. San Bernardino, Calif., Dec. 30, 1896; s. James and Elida (Wagner) F.; A.B. in Engring., Stanford U., 1918; m. Grace Willson, June 20, 1927. With Grinnell Co. of Pacific, 1919-40, br. mgr., San Francisco, Oakland, Calif., 1930-35, v.p., gen. mgr. Pacific Coast, 1935-40, gen. sales mgr. Grinnell Corp., Providence, 1940-42, exec. v.p., 1942-48, pres., 1948-68, chmn. bd., 1968-70, chmn. bd. ITT Grinnell Corp., Providence, from 1970. Trustee R.I. Hosp., Providence. Served with A.C. USN, 1918. Mem. Providence Engring. Soc. Republican. Episcopalian. Clubs: Agawam Hunt (E. Providence); Hope, Turks Head (Providence), Bohemian (San Francisco); Union League (N.Y.C.), Sakonnet Golf, Warren's Point Beach (Little Compton, R.I.); Mid Ocean (Tucker's Town, Bermuda). Deceased. Home: Cranston R.I.

FLEMKE, KARL, economic education association executive; b. New Britain, Conn., June 17, 1931; s. Karl and Catherine (Hilliard) F.; m. Dr. Mary Margaret Flynn, July 12, 1958; children—Ellen, Ann, Ned. BA, U. Pitts., Pa., 1972; LLHD (hon.), Green Mt. Coll., 1986. Indsl. engr. Pratt & Whitney, West Hartford, Conn., 1954-58; exec. dir. Junior Achievement of Greater New Bedford, Mass., 1958-62; exec. v.p. Jr. Achievement Southwestern Pa., Pitts., 1962-73; pres. Jr. Achievement Los Angeles, 1973-80; exec. v.p. Jr. Achievement, Inc., Stamford, Conn., 1980-82, pres., chief exec. officer, 1982-94; dir. Jr. Achievement of Canada, Toronto; bd. dirs. Am. Humanics, Kansas City, Mo., bd. dirs. Alfred U. Developer applied economics course for high sch. students, 1980. Mem. U.S. Olympic Organizing Com., Los Angeles, 1980. Named Outstanding Young Man Jaycees, New Bedford, 1971; Hon. mem. Delta Sigma Pi, 1983; recipient Charles R. Hook award Jr. Achievement Inc., 1970, 75. Mem. Am.

Mgmt. Assn., Independent Sector, U.S. C. of C. Republican. Lutheran. Home: Colorado Springs Colo. Died 1994.

FLETCHER, ALLEN, stage director; b. San Francisco, July 19, 1922; s. Allen and Jessica Laurestine (Dinmoor) F.; B.A., Stanford U., 1947, M.A., 1949; postgrad. Yale Univ., Bristol Old Vic Theatre Sch., London Acad. Music; m. Anne Lawder, Dec. 20, 1953; children—John Crandall, Julia Kathryn. Instr., then asst. prof. drama Carnegie-Mellon Inst., Pitts., 1951-59; stage dir. N.Y.C. Opera, 1959-65; dir. plays Oreg. Shakespeare Festival, 1948-49, 1950-52, 1953-54, 1956, San Diego Shakespeare Festival, 1955, 57-64, 72, Assn. Producing Artists, 1959-61; artistic dir. Am. Shakespeare Festival, 1961-65, Seattle Repertory Theatre, 1965-70; resident dir., conservatory dir. Am. Conservatory Theatre, San Francisco, 1965-84; conservatory dir. Nat. Theater Conservatory, resident dir. Denver Ctr. Theater Co., 1984—; guest dir. Pacific Conservatory Performing Arts. Served with U.S. Army, 1942-46. Fulbright scholar, 1957-58; Ford Found. grantee, 1959-60. Mem. Soc. Stage Dirs. and Choregraphers, Inc., Actors Equity Assn., Am. Guild Mus. Artists, Ibsen Soc. Am. Episcopalian. Club: Marines Memorial (San Francisco). Translator plays by Ibsen. Home: Denver Colo.

FLETCHER, DONALD JOSEPH, airport manager; b. Piqua, Ohio, Dec. 9, 1944; s. Joseph Nevin and Florence Helen (Darr) F.; m. Juanita Mary Jones, Oct. 7, 1977; children: David Jonathan, Kelly Lynn. BBA, U. Toledo, 1970, MA in Polit. Sci., 1972. Dir. adminstrn. Toledo-Lucas Co. Port Authority, 1971-73, airport mgr., 1973-75, dir. aviation, 1975-86; airport mgr. Dept. Aviation City of Houston, 1986-94. With USAF, 1963-67. Mem. Airport Ops. Coun. Internat. (bd. dirs. 1985-86), Ohio Airport Mgrs. Assn. (v.p. 1984-86), Am. Soc. Pub. Adminstrn. (pres. Toledo chpt. 1977, bd. dirs. Houston chpt. 1987, treas. 1990-94), Pearland/Hobby Area C. of C. (bd. dirs. 1988-93), Am. Assn. Airport Execs. (accredited airport exec.), Am. Legion, KC (grand knight 1975-76). Republican. Roman Catholic. Home: Humble Tex. Died Nov. 13, 1994.

FLEXNER, LOUIS BARKHOUSE, anatomist, educator; b. Louisville, Jan. 7, 1902; s. Washington and Ida (Barkhouse) F.; m. Josefa Barba Gosé, Aug. 23, 1937. B.S., U. Chgo., 1923; M.D., Johns Hopkins, 1927; LL.D., U. Pa. Fellow medicine Johns Hopkins Hosp., 1928-29; resident physician U. Chgo. Clinics, 1929-30; instr. and asso. anatomy Johns Hopkins Med. Sch., 1930-39; with dept. physiology Cambridge (Eng.) U., 1933-34; staff mem. dept. embryology Carnegie Instn., Washington, 1939-51; research assoc. Carnegie Instn., 1951-96; prof. anatomy Sch. Med. U. Pa., 1951-96, chmn. dept., 1951-67; dir. Inst. Neurol. Scis., 1953-66. Contbr. articles to profl. jours. Sci. adv. bds. USPHS, United Cerebral Palsy, Nat. Council to Combat Blindness, Nat. Paraplegic Soc., NRC, Nat. Found. Mem. Am. Assn. Anatomists, Nat. Acad. Scis., Am. Physiol. Soc., Am. Soc. Biol. Chemists, Am. Acad. Arts and Scis., Am. Philos. Soc. Home: Philadelphia Pa. Died Mar. 29, 1996.

FLICK, SOL E., retired watch company executive, lawyer; b. N.Y.C., May 4, 1915; s. Joseph and Anna (Mednick) F.; m. Stella Hurwitz, Jan. 14, 1940; children: Susan, Jonathan. B.A., Bklyn. Coll., 1937; LL.B., St. Lawrence U., 1939. Bar: N.Y. bar 1941. Practice in N.Y.C.; chmn. exec. com., chief exec. officer Bulova Watch Co., Inc., 1977-79; gen. counsel, dir. N.Am. Watch Corp., 1980-92; pres. N.Am. Watch Internat. Ltd., 1985-92; pres., dir. Movado Watch Co. S.A. Switzerland, 1980-92. Mem. Am. Bar Assn. Clubs: Twenty-Four Karat (N.Y.C.). Home: Roslyn Heights N.Y. Died Feb. 5, 1994.

FLOYD, OTIS L., academic administrator. Chancellor Tenn. Bd. Regents, Nashville, 1990-93. Home: Smyrna Tenn. Died May 19, 1993.

FLYNN, JUDITH ANNE, public relations executive; b. Hartford, Conn.; d. Jere J. and Helen P. (Kelly) F. B.A., U. Pa., 1959; M.A., Trinity Coll., Hartford, 1963. Pub. health edn. cons. Conn. Dept. Health, Hartford, 1962-64; assoc. editor Macmillan Co., N.Y.C., 1964-66; staff publicist Pub. Rels. Soc. Am., N.Y.C., 1966-68; asst. v.p. pub. rels. Bankers Trust Co., N.Y.C., 1968-75, asst. v.p., pub. rels. Marine Midland Bank, N.Y.C., 1978-80; nat. dir. pub. rels. Arthur Young & Co., N.Y.C., 1980-83; owner, dir. Flynn Communications Group, N.Y.C., 1983-94; bd. dirs. Brownstone Revival Commn., N.Y.C. Mem. New Eng. Soc. (N.Y.C.), Pub. Rels. Soc. Am., English Speaking Union, Princeton Club (N.Y.C.). Deceased. Home: New York N.Y.

FOISIE, PHILIP MANNING, journalist, media consultant; b. Seattle, Mar. 14, 1922; s. Francis Patrick and Wynifred (Shaw) F.; m. Margaruitte van Tschurin, Apr. 3, 1948; children: Gregory, Geoffrey, Christina, Timothy. BA, Harvard U., 1947. City editor China Press, Shanghai, 1948-49; reporter, telegraph editor Santa Rosa (Calif.) Press-Democrat, 1949-53; copy editor Louisville Courier-Jour., 1953-56; cable editor Washington Post, 1956-60, fgn. editor, 1960-68, asst. mng. editor, 1968-81; exec. editor Internat. Herald Tribune, Paris, 1981-87; pvt. practice internat. media cons., 1987-89; news ombudsman Dept. Def., 1989-92; ret., 1992. With AUS, 1942-46. Home: Alexandria Va. Died Apr. 18, 1995.

FOLEY, ROGER D., federal judge; b. 1917; s. Roger T. and Helen (Drummond) F. LL.B., U. San Francisco. Bar: Nev. bar 1946. Former atty. gen. Nev.; chief judge U.S. Dist Ct. Nev., Las Vegas, to 1980; judge U.S. Dist Ct. Nev., 1980-96. Home: Las Vegas Nev. Died Jan. 7, 1996.

FOLGATE, HOMER EMMETT, JR., lawyer; b. Rockford, Ill., Nov. 10, 1920; s. Homer Emmett and Hazel J. (Grissinger) F.; m. Letty Rae Huber, Apr. 28, 1944; children: Randall Lind, Jill, John Ernest. J.D., U. Ill., 1948. Bar: Ill. bar 1948. Asst. states atty. Winnebago County, Ill, 1948-55; partner firm Reno, Zahm, Folgate, Lindberg & Powell, Rockford, 1955-93. Chmn. Winnebago County Republican Central Com., 1955-64. Served with AUS, 1943-46. Decorated Purple Heart, Silver Star. Club: Mason (Shriner). Home: Rockford Ill. Died Sept. 24, 1993.

FOLLANSBEE, DOROTHY LELAND, publisher; b. St. Louis, Mar. 24, 1911; d. Robert Leathan and Minnie Cowden (Yowell) Lund; grad. Sarah Lawrence Coll., 1931; m. Austin Porter Leland, Apr. 24, 1935 (dec. 1975); children: Mary Talbot Leland MacCarthy, Austin Porter Jr. (dec.), Irene Austin Leland Barzantny; m. 2d, Robert Kerr Follansbee, Oct. 20, 1979. Pres., Station List Publ. Co., St. Louis, 1975-90; dir. Downtown St. Louis Inc. Hon. chmn. Old Post Office Landmark Com., 1975-89; bd. dirs. Services Bur. St. Louis, 1943, pres., 1951; bd. dirs. Robert E. Lee Meml. Assn.; mem. St. Louis County Parks and Recreation Dept., 1969-85; bd. dirs. Stratford Hall, Va., 1953-92 , pres., 1967-70, treas., 1970-89; bd. dirs. Historic Bldgs. Commn. St. Louis County, 1959-85, Mo. Hist. Soc., 1960-77, Mo. Mansion Preservation Com., 1975-80, Chatillon DeMenil House, 1977-79. Recipient Landmarks award Landmarks Assn. St. Louis, 1974; Pub. Service award GSA, 1978; Crownenshield award Nat. Trust for Hist Preservation, 1979. Mem. Colonial Dames Am., Daus. of Cin. Episcopalian. Clubs: St. Louis Country, Fox Chapel Golf, St. Louis Jr. League. Deceased. Home: Saint Louis Mo.

FOLLETT, ROY HUNTER, agronomy educator; b. Cowdrey, Colo., Feb. 27, 1935; s. Roy Lawrence and Frances (Hunter) F.; m. Barbara Ann Delehoy, June 28, 1959; children: Kevin, Karen. BS, Colo. State U., 1957, MS, 1963, PhD, 1969. Soil scientist Soil Conservation Svc., Ft. Collins, Colo., 1963-64; extension agronomist Colo. State U., Ft. Collins, 1964-70; asst. prof. Ohio State U., Columbus, 1970-74; prof. agronomy Kans. State U., Manhattan, 1974-81, Colo. State U., Ft. Collins, 1981-93. Author: Our Soils and Their Management, 1990, Fertilizers and Soil Amendments, 1981. Recipient Disting. Educators award, Plant Food Assn., 1989, Meritorious Svc. award, Epsilon Sigma Phi, 1989, Honor Alumni award Colo. State U., 1992. Fellow Am. Soc. Agronomy, Soil Sci. Soc. Am., Soil and Water Conservation Soc.; mem. Alpha Zeta, Sigma Xi, Gamma Sigma Delta (Faculty award 1992). Presbyterian. Home: Fort Collins Colo. Died Nov. 17, 1993.

FOLSOME, CLAIR EDWIN, microbiology educator; b. Ann Arbor, Mich., June 26, 1935; s. Clair Edwin and Leah (Carter) F.; m. Jo Grubawicz, Sept. 26, 1956 (div. Oct. 1980); children: Russell S., Wyn, Alexander, Theodore; m. Geraldine DeBenedetti, June 20, 1982; children: Cassandra, Grant. AB, Harvard U., 1956, MA, 1959, PhD, 1960. Research asst. prof. Boston U., 1960-62; sr. lectr. Melbourne (Australia) U., 1962-64; prof. microbiology U. Hawaii, Honolulu, from 1964; v.p. Biofoods Inc., Honolulu, from 1981; pres. Ecoculture Assn., Honolulu, from 1980; bd. dirs. Islenet Inc., Honolulu. Author: Origins of Life, 1979, rev. edit. 1982; editor: Genetics and the Origins of Life, 1956-86; contbr. articles to profl. jours. Research grantee NASA, Honolulu, from 1971; sr. research fellow Nat. Acad. Sci., Honolulu, 1971. Fellow Brit. Interplanetary Soc.; mem. AAAS, Am. Chem. Soc., Internat. Soc. Study Origin Life, Mensa, Sigma Xi. Clubs: Waikiki Yacht, Outrigger Canoe, Honolulu (Honolulu). Home: 916 Kana Pl Honolulu HI 96816-3644 Office: U Hawaii 2538 The Mall Honolulu HI 96822-2233 Deceased.

FONG, HAROLD MICHAEL, federal judge; b. Honolulu, Apr. 28, 1938; m. Judith Tom, 1966; children: Harold Michael, Terrence Matthew. A.B. cum laude, U. So. Calif., 1960; J.D., U. Mich., 1964. Bar: Hawaii 1965. Dep. pros. atty. City and County of Honolulu, 1965-68; assoc. Mizuha and Kim, Honolulu, 1968-69; asst. U.S. atty. Dist. Hawaii, 1969-73; U.S. atty., 1973-78; ptnr. Fong and Miho, Honolulu, 1978-82; judge U.S. Dist. Ct. Hawaii, 1982-95, chief judge, 1984-91. Home: Honolulu Hawaii Died Apr. 20, 1995.

FORD, JESSE HILL, author; b. Troy, Ala., Dec. 28, 1928; s. Jesse Hill and Lucille (Musgrove) F.; m. Lillian Pellettieri, Nov. 15, 1975; children: Jay, Charles Davis, Sarah Ann, Elizabeth. BA, Vanderbilt U., 1951; MA, U. Fla., 1955; postgrad. (Fulbright scholar), U. Oslo, Norway, 1961-62; LittD (hon.), Lambuth Coll., 1968. Reporter The Nashville Tennessean, 1950-51; news writer U. Fla., 1953-55; dir. pub. relations Tenn. Med. Assn., 1955-56; asst. dir. pub. relations AMA, Chgo., 1956-57; vis. fellow Center for Advanced Study, Wesleyan U., Middletown, Conn., 1965; guest editorialist USA Today, 1986-92. Author: Mountains of Gilead, 1961, The Conversion of Buster Drumwright, 1964, The Liberation of Lord Byron Jones, 1965, Fishes, Birds, and Sons of Men, 1968, The Feast of St. Barnabas, 1969, The Raider, 1975; playwright: (musical) Drumwright, 1982; screenwriter: (films) (with Stirling Silliphant) The Liberation of L. B. Jones, 1970, (TV movies) The Lynching of Michael Donald, CBS-TV, 1988, Murder in the Chapel, NBC, 1989. Served with USNR, 1951-53. Atlantic Monthly grantee, 1959; Guggenheim fellow, 1966; included in O. Henry Prize Collection Short Stories, 1961, 66, 67; Best Detective Stories, 1972-76; recipient Atlantic Monthly award for " The Surest Thing in Show Business", 1959, O. Henry award for "How the Mountains Are", 1961, Edgar award for "The Jail" Mystery Writers Am., 1975. Mem. Cum Laude Soc. Episcopalian. Club: Overseas Press. Home: Nashville Tenn. Died June 1, 1996.

FORD, LOUIS HENRY, bishop, pastor; b. Clarksdale, Miss., May 23, 1914; s. Cleveland and Chaney (Joiner) F.; m. Margaret Little, 1933; children: Charles, Janet Oliver. Student, Saints Coll., Lexington, Miss., 1928-33. Pastor St. Paul Ch. of God in Christ, Chgo., 1934-95, first asst., presiding bishop, 1976-90; presiding bishop Ch. of God in Christ, Memphis, 1990-95. Recipient Charles Harrison Mason award, 1957, Ch. Fedn. of Chgo. Leadership award, Alumnus award Saints Coll., 1954. Home: Chicago Ill. Died Mar. 31, 1995.

FORER, LOIS G., judge; b. Chgo., Mar. 22, 1914; d. Harry Goldstein and Lorraine (Beilman) Goldstein Forer; m. Morris L. Forer, June 30, 1940; children: Stuart, John, Hope Abigail Forer Ross. A.B. with honors, Northwestern U., 1935, J.D., 1938. Bar: Ill. 1938, Pa. 1945, U.S. Dist. Ct. (ea. dist.) Pa. 1945, U.S. Ct. Appeals (3d cir.) 1945, U.S. Supreme Ct. 1942. Legal staff US Senatte Com. Edn. and Labor, Washington, 1938-39, REA, Washington, 1939-42; law clk. to presiding judge U.S. Ct. Appeals (3d cir.) 1942-46; legal staff, Office of Price Stabilization, Phila., 1948; dep. atty. gen. Commonwealth of Pa., Harrisburg, 1955-63; atty.-in-charge Office for Juveniles, Community Legal Services, Phila., 1966-68; sole practice, Phila., 1946-71; judge Ct. of Common Pleas, Phila., 1971-87; cons. Kerner Commn. Author: No One Will Listen: How Our Legal System Brutalizes the Youthful Poor, 1970; The Death of the Law, 1975, Criminals and Victims: A Trial Judge Reflects on Crime and Punishment, 1980, paperback edit., 1984, Money and Justice: Who Owns the Courts, 1982, paperback edit., 1992, A Chilling Effect: The Mounting Threat of Libel and Invasion of Privacy Actions to the First Amendment, 1987, paperback edit., 1989, Unequal Protection: Women, Children, and the Elderly in Court, 1991, paperback edit., 1993, What Every Woman Needs to Konw Befor (adn After) She Gets Involved With Men and Money, 1994, Rage to Punish: The Unintended Consequences of Mandatory Sentencing, 1994; also articles. Editor-in-chief Jour. Nat. Assn. of Women Lawyers, 1966-67. Nat. bd. dirs. ACLU, 1960-80; mem. Lawyers Com. on Civil Rights under Law; mem. Lehman Com. on Immigration and Naturalization, Pa. Gov.'s Com. on Children and Youth; mem. drafting com. Interstate Compact on Del. River. Recipient Criminal Justice Thurgood Marshall award Phila. Bar Assn. Mem. Nat. Law Sci. Council, ABA (Ross Essay award 1950). Democrat. Jewish. Died May 9, 1994. Home: Philadelphia Pa.

FORMAN, SYLVIA HELEN, anthropologist, educator; b. Tacoma Park, Md., Dec. 31, 1943; d. Sidney and Mary Frances (O'Kelly) F. BA, U. Calif., Berkeley, 1968, PhD, 1972. Asst. prof. U. Mass., Amherst, 1972-78, assoc. prof., 1979-89, prof., from 1989; cons. Pan-Am. Health Orgn., Quito, Ecuador, 1979, Jet Propulsion Lab., Pasadena, Calif., 1979, Solar Energy Rsch. Inst., Golden, Colo., 1980. Contbr. articles to profl. jours. Danforth Found. fellow, 1968-72. Fellow Am. Anthrop Assn. (exec. com. 1986-88, program editor 1981), Soc. for Applied Anthropology, AAAS; mem. Assn. for Feminist Anthropology (organizing bd. 1987-88), Sci. Rsch. Soc., Sigma Xi. Home: Amherst Mass. Deceased.

FORMENTON, MARIO MACOLA, publishing and printing company executive; b. Teheran, Apr. 21, 1928; came to Italy, 1940; s. Luigi Macola and Cloe (Brasolin) F.; m. Cristina Mondadori, June 2, 1952; children: Luca, Silvia, Pietro, Mattia. Student, U. Milan. Gen. mgr. Mondadori Printing Plant, Verona, Italy, 1961-64; mng. dir. Mondadori Group, Milan, Italy, 1964-68, exec. v.p., mng. dir., 1968-82, chmn., CEO, from 1982; pres. Club degli Editori, Milan; bd. dirs. Cartiera di Ascoli, Ascoli Piceno, Editoriale La Repubblica, Rome, FIEG, Roma. Decorated Cavaliere del Lavoro, grand ofcl. Italian Republic; recipient Achille Marazza award, Domus Mercatorum award. Lodge: Rotary. Avocation: sailing. Died Mar. 29, 1987; interred Milan. Home: Segrate Italy

FORSTER, CORNELIUS PHILIP, priest, graduate school dean, history educator; b. N.Y.C., Oct. 27, 1919; s. Cornelius and Mary Catherine (Collins) F. A.B., Fordham U., 1941, Ph.D., 1963; M.A., Cath. U., 1951; S.T.L., S.T.Lr., Pontifical U., Washington, 1949; M.A. (hon.), Providence Coll., 1959. Joined Dominican Order Roman Cath. Ch., 1941, ordained priest, 1948. Instr.

Providence Coll., 1949-52, asst. prof., 1952-55, assoc. prof., 1955-58, prof., 1958-93, chmn. dept. history, 1962-92, dean Grad. Sch., 1964-93, exec. v.p., 1982-85, acting pres., 1982; archivist for Dominican Province of St. Joseph, 1988-93. Mem. Johannine Soc., History Club (founder, moderator), Nat. Cath. Edn. Assn., Am. Hist. Assn., Am. Cath. Hist. Assn., Am. Assn. Colls. for Tchr. Edn., Am. Assn. Univ. Adminstrs., New Eng. Assn. Grad. Schs., Delta Epsilon Sigma, Phi Alpha Theta. Home: Providence R.I. Died Nov. 18, 1993; buried The Dominican Faculty Cemetary, Providence, R.I.

FORTESS, KARL EUGENE, artist, lithographer; b. Antwerp, Belgium, Oct. 13, 1907; came to U.S., 1915, naturalized, 1923; s. David and Sara (Jukowska) F.; m. Lillian Fine (dec.). Student, Chgo. Art Inst., Art Students League N.Y., Woodstock Sch. of Painting; studied painting with, Y. Kuniyoshi. Faculty Art Students League, Bklyn Mus. Art Sch., La. State U., Am. Art Sch.; prof. emeritus Boston U. Sch. for the Arts. Contbg. author: The Funnies: An American Idiom, 1963; Contbr. articles to profl. jours.; works exhibited, Nat. Inst. Arts and Letters, Art Inst. Chgo., Carnegie Inst., Whitney Mus. Am. Art, Corcoran Gallery Art, Mus. Modern Art, N.A.D., Pa. Acad., one-man shows, Asso. Am. Artists Galleries, N.Y.C., Ganso Gallery, N.Y.C., Vose Galleries, Boston, Krasner Gallery, Mirski Gallery, also others; represented in permanent collections, Butler Inst. Am. Art, Nat. Mus. Am. Art, Smithsonian Instn., Munson-Williams-Proctor Inst., Newark Mus., Bklyn. Mus., Mus. Modern Art, print collection, Hudson Walker, Wichita Art Mus., Cedar Rapids Mus. Art, Herbert F. Johnson Mus. Art, Tamarind Inst., Anchorage Hist. and Fine Arts Mus., other pvt., pub. collections. Recipient E. Keith Meml. award Woodstock Artists Assn., 1935; hon. mention Carnegie Inst., 1941; Salmagundi prize NAD, 1973; Adolph and Clara Obrig prize, 1979;Audubon Medal of Honor, 1988; Guggenheim fellow, 1946. Mem. Artists Equity Assn., Coll. Art Assn., Art Students League N.Y. (life), Soc. Am. Graphic Artists, AAUP, Brit. Film Inst., Mus. Modern Art. Home: Woodstock N.Y. Deceased.

FOSTER, LUTHER HILTON, former university president, educational consultant; b. Lawrenceville, Va., Mar. 21, 1913; s. Luther Hilton and Daisy (Poole) F.; m. Vera Adrienne Chandler, Aug. 27, 1941; children: Adrienne Maria, Luther Hilton III. BS, Va. State Coll., 1932, LLD (hon.), 1959; BS, Hampton Inst., 1934, LHD (hon.), 1985; MBA, Harvard U., 1936; MA, U. Chgo., 1941, PhD, 1951; D of Pub. Svc. (hon.), Adams State Coll., 1957; LLD (hon.), U. Liberia, 1958, U. Mich., 1967, Colby Coll., 1971, U. Ala., 1978, Tuskegee Inst., 1981, Lincoln U., Pa., 1985; LHD (hon.), Loyola U., Chgo., 1970, Northeastern U., 1974, Howard U., 1983, Winston-Salem State U., 1983. Budget officer Howard U., 1936-40; bus. mgr. Tuskegee Inst. (name now Tuskegee U.), 1941-53, pres., 1953-81, pres. emeritus, 1981-94; chmn., CEO Robert R. Moton Meml. Inst., 1981-86, Foster Assocs., Inc., 1986-94; trustee Tchrs. Ins. and Annuity Assn., 1957-61; mem. U.S. Pres.' Adv. Commn. on Internat. Ednl. and Cultural Exch., 1962-68, Pres.' Gen. Adv. Com. on Fgn. Assistance Program, AID, 1965-68, Nat. Adv. Com. on Black Higher Edn., U.S. Dept. Edn., 1979-82; chmn. bd. Race Rels. Info. Ctr., Nashville, 1968-71; dir. Joint Ctr. for Polit. and Econ. Studies, 1983-94. Pres. United Negro Coll. Fund, 1961-63, chmn. fin. com., 1979-94, bd. dirs.; trustee Resources for the Future, 1961-79, Tchrs. Ins. and Annuity Assn., 1957-61; trustee Coll. Retirement Equities Fund, 1965-84, TIAA Stock; mem. CREF, 1984-87; dir. Acad. Ednl. Devel., 1976-94, Ctr. Creative Leadership, 1982-88, Norton Simon Inc., 1974-83, Sears Roebuck and Co., 1975-83; mem. Am. Revolution Bicentenniel Commn. 1966-73. Recipient Alumni award Hampton Inst., 1954, Star of Africa, Govt. of Liberia, 1958, Alumni medal U. Chgo., 1986, Alumni award Harvard Bus. Sch., 1988; named to Ala. Acad. of Honor, 1974. Mem. So. Regional Coun., Overseas Devel. Coun., Tuskegee Airmen, Alpha Phi Alpha, Sigma Pi Phi Boule. Episcopalian. Home: Alexandria Va. Died Nov. 29, 1994.

FOUNTAIN, KENNETH PAUL, lawyer, oil company executive; b. Timpson, Tex., Oct. 21, 1934; s. Joe Graham and Hazel VanDora (Magness) F.; m. Sylvia Elaine Worthington, Dec. 20, 1957; children: Paula, Kenneth, Douglas, David. Student So. Meth. U., 1953-54; B.S. in Mech. Engring., La. Poly. U., 1957; J.D., S. Tex. Coll. Law, 1966. Bar: Tex. Mech. engr. Interstate Oil Pipe Line Co., Shreveport, La., 1957-61, Humble Pipe Line Co., Houston, 1961-66; atty. Humble Oil & Refining Co., Southwest Enco region, Dallas, 1966-68; mgr. contracts and law Trans Alaska Pipeline System, Houston, 1968-70; coordinator legis. and polit. affairs Exxon Co. U.S.A., Houston, 1970-73; mgr. pub. affairs Western div., Los Angeles, 1973-74, trial counsel, law dept., Houston, 1974-81; gen. counsel, dir. Exxon Pipeline Co., Houston, 1981-86; sr. staff counsel Exxon Co. USA, Houston, 1986-87; trustee South Tex. Coll. Law; bd. dirs. Southwestern Legal Found. Served as capt. USAFR, 1958-61. Mem. ABA, Houston Bar Assn. Republican. Baptist. Clubs: Kingwood Country, Inns of Ct. Deceased. Home: Houston Tex.

FOWLER, DANIEL EISON, lawyer; b. Hopkinsville, Ky., Nov. 20, 1908; s. William Thomas and Ila (Earle) F.; m. Louisa Bickel, Apr. 14, 1932; 1 son, Robert Bickel. B.A., U. Ky., 1932, J.D., 1933. Bar: Ky. bar 1933. Practiced in Lexington; partner Fowler & Fowler, 1933-52, Fowler & Bell, 1952-54, Fowler, Bell, Cox & Hancock, 1958-59, Fowler, Rouse, Measle & Bell, 1959-77, Fowler, Measle & Bell, from 1977; Sec. F. & C. R.R. Co., 1933-60, Old Lewis Hunter Distillery Co., 1935-42; pres. Properties, Inc., 1959-80; sec. Spindletop Research, Inc., 1968-72; County judge Fayette County, 1954-58. Bd. dirs. Spindletop Hall, 1979-83. Served to lt. comdr. USNR, 1942-45. Mem. Ky. Soc. S.R., Am., Ky. bar assns., Thoroughbred Club Am., Delta Tau Delta, Phi Delta Phi. Presbyterian (deacon). Clubs: Spindletop Hall, Lafayette (Lexington). Home: Lexington Ky. Deceased.

FOWLER, WILLIAM ALFRED, retired physics educator; b. Pittsburgh, Penn., Aug. 9, 1911; s. John McLeod and Jennie Summers (Watson) F.; m. Ardiane Olmsted, Aug. 24, 1940 (dec. May 1988); children: Mary Emily Fowler Galowin, Martha Summers Fowler Schoenemann; m. Mary Dutcher, Dec. 14, 1989. B of Engring. Physics, Ohio State U., 1933, DSc (hon.), 1978; PhD, Calif. Inst. Tech., 1936; DSc (hon.), U. Chgo., 1976, Denison U., 1982, Ariz. State U., 1985, Georgetown U., 1986, U. Mass., 1987, Williams Coll., 1988; Doctorat honoris causa, U. Liège (Belgium), 1981, Observatoire de Paris, 1981. Asst. prof. physics Calif. Inst. Tech., 1939-42, asso. prof., 1942-46, prof. physics, 1946-70, Inst. prof. physics, 1970-82; prof. emeritus, 1982-95; conducted rsch. on nuclear forces and reaction rates, nuclear spectroscopy, structure of light nuclei, thermonuclear sources of stellar energy and element synthesis in stars and supernovae and the early universe, including recently proposed inflationary model; study of gen. relativistic effects in quasar and pulsar models, nuclear cosmochronology; Fulbright lectr. Pembroke Coll. and Cavendish lab. U. Cambridge, 1954-55; Guggenheim fellow, 1954-55; Guggenheim fellow St. John's Coll. and dept. applied math. and theoretical physics U. Cambridge, 1961-62; vis. fellow Inst. Theoretical Astronomy, summers 1967-72; vis. scholar program Phi Beta Kappa, 1980-81; asst. dir. rsch. sect. L Nat. Defense Rsch. Com., 1941-45; tech. observer, office of field service OSRD, South Pacific Theatre, 1944; sci. dir., project VISTA, Dept. Def., 1951-52; mem. nat. sci. bd. NSF, 1968-74; mem. space sci. bd. Nat. Acad. Scis., 1970-73, 77-80; chmn. Office of Phys. Scis., 1981-84; mem. space program adv. council NASA, 1971-73; mem. nuclear sci. adv. com. Dept. Energy/Nat. Sci. Found., 1977-80; E.A. Milne Lectr. Milne Soc., 1986; named lectr. univs., colls.; hon. fellow Pembroke Coll., Cambridge U., 1992. Contbr. numerous articles to profl. jours. Bd. dirs. Am. Friends of Cambridge U., 1970-78. Rsch. fellow Calif. Inst. Tech., Pasadena, 1936-39; recipient Naval Ordnance Devel. award USN, 1945, Medal of Merit, 1948; Lammé medal Ohio State U., 1952; Liège medal U. Liège, 1955; Calif. Co-Scientist of Yr. award, 1958; Barnard medal for contbn. to sci. Columbia, 1965; Apollo Achievement award NASA, 1969; Vetlesen prize, 1973; Nat. medal of sci., 1974; Bruce gold medal Astron. Soc. Pacific, 1979; Nobel prize for physics, 1983; Légion d'Honneur, 1989; Benjamin Franklin fellow Royal Soc. Arts; named to Lima Ohio City Schs. Disting. Alumni Hall of Fame, Ohio Sci. and Tech. Hall of Fame; named hon. fellow Pembroke Coll., Cambridge U., 1992. Fellow Am. Phys. Soc. (Tom W. Bonner prize 1970, pres. 1976, 1st recipient William A. Fowler award for excellence in physics So. Ohio sect. 1986), Am. Acad. Arts and Scis., Royal Astron. Soc. (assoc., Eddington medal 1978); mem. NAS (council 1974-77), AAAS, Am. Astron. Soc., Am. Inst. Physics (governing bd. 1974-80), AAUP, Am. Philos. Soc., Soc. Royal Sci. Liège (corr. mem.), Brit. Assn. Advancement Sci., Soc. Am. Baseball Research, Mark Twain Soc. (hon.), Naturvetenskapliga Foreiningen (hon.), Sigma Xi, Tau Beta Pi, Tau Kappa Epsilon. Democrat. Clubs: Athenaeum (Pasadena); Cosmos (Washington). Home: Pasadena Calif. Died Mar. 14, 1995.

FOX, CHARLES LEWIS, JR., physician, emeritus educator; b. N.Y.C., Jan. 16, 1908; s. Charles Lewis and Esther (Jacobs) F.; m. Emily A. Silk; children: Paul L., Susan M., Andrew C. AB, Harvard U., 1928; MD, SUNY, Bklyn., 1934. Intern Jewish Hosp., Bklyn., 1934-37; asst. Harvard U. Med. Sch., Boston, 1938-39; from asst. prof. to prof. microbiology assigned to surgery Columbia U. Coll. Physicians and Surgeons, N.Y.C., 1939-77, emeritus prof., from 1977; assoc. prof. N.Y. Med. Coll., 1956-60; adj. prof. burn unit surgery Valhalla, N.Y., from 1956; cons. Burn Ctr. Westchester County Med. Ctr., Valhalla, also bd. dirs.; dir. sci. adv. bd. Daltex Med. Scis. Inc., West Orange, N.J., from 1985. Patentee for SILVADENE in burns; contbr. articles to profl. jours. Recipient Cardinal Terrence Cooke award N.Y. Med. Coll., 1985. Mem. Am. Burn Assn. (emeritus, E.I. Evans award 1977), Am. Physiol. Soc. (emeritus), Am. Assn. Immunologists (emeritus), Surg. Infection Soc. (emeritus). Clubs: Harvard (N.Y.C.); Candlewood Yacht (New Fairfield, Conn.). Home: Fort Lauderdale Fla. Deceased.

FOX, MARVIN, philosophy educator, rabbi; b. Chgo., Oct. 17, 1922; s. Norman and Sophie (Gershengorn) F.; m. June Elaine Trachtenberg, Feb. 20, 1944; children: Avrom Baruch, Daniel Jonathan, Sheryl Deena. BA, Northwestern U., 1942, MA, 1946; PhD, U. Chgo., 1950. Ordained rabbi, 1942. Faculty Ohio State U., Columbus, 1948-74, instr., 1948-52, asst. prof., 1952-56, assoc. prof., 1956-61, prof. philosophy, 1961-73, Leo Yassenoff prof. philosophy and Jewish studies, 1973-74; Philip W. Lown prof. Jewish philosophy, dir. Lown Sch. Nr. Ea. and Judaic Studies Brandeis U., Waltham, Mass., 1974-93; prof. emeritus Jewish philosophy, from 1993; vis. prof. Hebrew Theol. Coll. Chgo., 1955, Hebrew U., Jerusalem, 1970-71, Bar-Ilan U., Ramat-Gan, Israel, 1970-71; Shoolman Disting. vis. prof. Hebrew Coll., Brookline, Mass., 1990-92; mem. exec. com. Conf. Jewish Philosophy, 1963-69, Inst. for Judaism and Contemporary Thought, Israel, from 1971; mem. acad. bd. Melton Rsch. Ctr., Jewish Theol. Sem. Am., 1972-90; mem. Internat. Coun. of Yad Yashem, Jerusalem, 1983-90. Author: Modern Jewish Ethics-Theory and Practice, 1975, Interpreting Maimonides. Studies in Methodology, Metaphysics and Moral Philosophy, 1990; editor: Kant's Fundamental Principles of the Metaphysic of Morals, 1949; cons. editor Jour. History of Philosophy, 1970-76; mem. editorial bd. Libr. of Living Philosophers, 1946-90, Judaism, from 1953, Tradition, 1956-89, AJS Rev., 1976-84, Daat, from 1978, Jewish Edn. Yearbook, from 1979; bd. editors Studies in Judaism, from 1986; contbr. articles to profl. jours. With USAAF, 1942-46. Elizabeth Clay Howald Found. fellow, 1956-57, Am. Coun. Learned Socs fellow, 1962-63, NEH fellow, 1980-81. Mem. AAUP, Am. Philos. Assn., World Union Jewish Studies (governing coun.), Assn. Jewish Studies (bd. dirs. from 1970, v.p. 1973-75, pres. 1975-78), Nat. Commn. B'nai Brith Hillel Founds. (exec. com.), Medieval Acad. Am., Metaphys. Soc. Am., Am. Acad. Jewish Rsch., Conf. Jewish Philosophy. Home: Newton Mass. Deceased.

FOX, ROBERT PHILLIP, manufacturing company executive; b. Duluth, Minn., June 20, 1917; s. Phillip and Christine (Peterson) F.; m. Alice Sten, Sept. 6, 1947; children—Phillip, James. B.M.E., U. Minn., 1939. Chief engr. Clyde Iron Works, Duluth, 1939-59; with Am. Hoist & Derrick Co., St. Paul, 1959-95; v.p. ops. Am. Hoist & Derrick Co., 1971-73, exec. v.p., 1973, pres., 1973, chief exec. officer, 1974-95, also dir.; dir. First Trust Co. St. Paul. Trustee Minn. Mut. Ins. Co.; Bd. dirs. Dunwoody Tech. Inst., Mpls. Served to lt. (j.g.) USNR, 1944-46. Clubs: Minnesota, North Oaks Golf. Home: Saint Paul Minn. Died Jan. 27, 1995.

FRAGALE, JOHN STEPHEN, information service executive; b. Bklyn., Apr. 16, 1931; s. Joseph Fragale and Mary Szema; m. Janet Audrey Caldwell; children: Marc, Laurie. Grad. in Bus., Pace U., 1959. Sales trainee Gen. Motors Acceptance Corp., N.Y.C., 1957; dir. circulation, then dir. mktg. Bill Communications Inc., N.Y.C., 1958-86; pres. Single Source, Inc., N.Y.C., 1987. With USAF, 1952-58; capt. USAFR, 1958-72. Mem. Assn. Bus. Pubs. (chmn. N.Y. chpt. 1975-76). Republican. Roman Catholic. Home: Norwalk Conn Deceased.

FRANCIS, SAM, artist; b. San Mateo, Calif., June 25, 1923; m. Margaret Smith, 1985; children: Osamu, Kayo, Shingo, Augustus. BA, U. Calif., Berkeley, 1949, MA, 1950, PhD (hon.), 1968; postgrad., Académie Fernand Leger, Paris, 1950. Works in permanent collection Mus Modern Art, N.Y.C., Whitney Mus., N.Y.C., Nat. Gallery, Washington, Albright-Knox Art Gallery, Buffalo, Tate Gallery, London, Mus. Nationale d'Art Moderne Paris, Stedelyk Mus., Amsterdam, Idemitsu Mus. of Art, Tokyo, others; one-person shows include San Francisco Mus. Art, 1958, Moderna Museet, Stockholm, 1960, Kunsthalle, Berne, 1960, Minami Gallery, Tokyo 1961-64, Kornfeld and Klipstein, Bern, Galerie Benador, 1961-64, 75-77, Pasadena Art Mus., 1964, Stedelyk Mus., Amsterdam, 1968, Albright-Knox Art Gallery, Buffalo, 1972, Ctr. Georges Pompidou, Paris, 1978, Hong Kong Arts Ctr., 1981, Galerie Niepel, Dusseldorf, Fed. Republic Germany, 1982, Flow Ace Gallery, Venice, 1982, Andre Emmerich Gallery, N.Y.C., 1983 86-90, Thomas Babcox Gallery, La Jolla, Calif., 1984 Galerie Kornfeld, Bern, 1985, Brussels Opera House ceiling mural, 1987, Nantenshi Gallery, Tokyo, 1988 Smith-Andersen Gallery, Palo Alto, 1988, 90, Greenberg Gallery, St. Louis, 1988, Galerie de Seoul, Korea, 1988, Mus. Modern Art, Seibu Takanawa, Japan, 1988, Galerie Jean Fournier, Paris, 1989, 91, Bernard Jacobson Gallery, London, 1989, Sun Valley Ctr. Gallery, Idaho, 1989, Linda Farris Gallery, Seattle, 1989, Cantor/Lemberg Gallery, Birmingham, Mich., 1989, Knoedler Gallery, London, 1989, Associated Am. Artists, N.Y.C., 1990, 91, Gallery Delaive, Amsterdam, 1990, Heland Wetterling Gallery, Stockholm, 1990, Ogawa Art Found., Tokyo, 1990, Ochi Gallery, Sun Valley, Calif., 1990, Talbot Rice Gallery, Edinburgh, Scotland, 1990, James Corcoran Gallery, L.A., 1991, Gagosian Gallery, N.Y.C., 1991, numerous others; retrospective exhbn.: Inst. Contemporary Art, Boston, 1979; 40-yr. retrospective exhbn.: Galerie Kornfeld, Bern, Switzerland, 1991, Kunst und Ausstellungshalle der Bundesrepublik Deutschald, Bonn, Germany, 1993 Galerie Pudelko, Bonn, Manny Silverman Gallery, L.A. Michael Cohen Gallery, N.Y.C., Denis Ochi Gallery Boise; commissioned New Bonn Parlament Bldg., 1993 represented in permanent collection: Mus. Modern Contemporary Art, L.A. Recipient 1st prize 3d Internat. Biennial Exhibit Prints, Tokyo, 1962; Dunn Internat. prize Tate Gallery, London, 1963; Tamarind fellow, 1963. Home: Santa Monica Calif. Died Nov. 4, 1994; interred Pt. Reyes Station, Calif.

FRANCK, MICHAEL, lawyer, association executive; b. Berlin, Oct. 6, 1932; came to U.S., 1941, naturalized, 1950; s. Wolf and Marga (Oppenheimer) F.; m. Carol E. Eichert, May 29, 1965; children: Michele, Lauren, Rebecca, Jennifer. BA, Columbia U., 1954, JD, 1958. Bar: N.Y. 1958, Mich. 1970. Trial counsel Liberty Mut. Ins. Co., Bklyn., 1958-60; chief litigator com. on grievances Assn. of Bar of City of N.Y., 1960-70; cons. spl. com. on disciplinary procedures, bd. governance Pa. Supreme Ct., 1969-72; spl. counsel Phila. Ct. Common Pleas, 1970-73; exec. dir. State Bar Mich., Lansing, 1970-94; mem. Commn. on Uniform State Laws, 1975-94, Mich. Malpractice Arbitration Adv. Com., 1975-94; mem. coordinating coun. on lawyer competence Conf. Chief Justices, 1981-87; mem. task force on gender issues in the cts. Mich. Supreme Ct., 1987-89. Contbr. articles to bar jours. With U.S. Army, 1954-56. Mem. ABA (reporter spl. com. on evaluation of disciplinary enforcement 1968-70, com. on nat. coordination disciplinary enforcement 1970-73, com. profl. discipline 1973-79, chmn. 1979-82, chmn. sect. bar activities 1975-76, del. 1976-78, 82-94, task force on lawyer advt. 1977, liaison to Commn. on Evaluation Profl. Standards 1977-83, ALI-ABA adv. com. on model peer rev. 1978-79, long-range planning coun. 1979-81, com. on ethics and profl. responsibility 1982-83, 88-91, com. on lawyer referral and info. svcs. 1991-94, coun. sect. on individual rights and responsiblities 1982-87, chmn. com. to implement model rules of profl. conduct 1983-88, house select com. 1989-92, ALI-ABA adv. com. to the practice evaluation project 1989-91), State Bar Mich., Women Lawyers Assn., Wolverine Bar Assn., Ingham County Bar Assn., Am. Judicature Soc. (bd. dirs. 1988-91), Am. Law Inst., Mich. Supreme Ct. Hist. Soc. (bd. dirs. 1988-94). Home: Mason Mich. Died June 28, 1994; buried Maple Ridge Cemetery, Holt, Mich.

FRANK, CLINTON EDWARD, advertising executive; b. St. Louis, Sept. 13, 1915; s. Arthur A. and Daisy Marian (Irwin) F.; m. Frances Calhoun Price, July 25, 1941 (div. 1967); children: Marcia Case, Clinton Edward, Laurie Anne, Cynthia Calhoun, Arthur A. III; m. Margaret Rathje Mullins, May 25, 1967. A.B., Yale, 1938. Account exec. Blackett-Sample-Hummert, 1938-41; Dancer-Fitzgerald-Sample, 1947-48; sales promotion mgr. E. J. Brach & Sons, Chgo., 1948-49; v.p., treas., partner Price-Robinson & Frank, Inc., 1949-53; pres. Clinton E. Frank, Inc., Chgo., 1954-67; chmn. exec. com., dir. Clinton E. Frank, Inc., 1967-77, chmn. bd., 1973-77, hon. chmn., 1977-92; chmn. Bridlewood Corp., Chgo., 1977-92. Trustee Eye Research Inst., Boston; vice-chmn., trustee Brain Research Found.; chmn. Am. Acad. Art, Chgo., 1978-92. Served with USAAF, 1941-45; aide to Lt. Gen. James H. Doolittle exec. officer 98th Bomb Group Africa, Italy; ret. as lt. col. Clubs: Chicago, Yale of Chgo. (dir.), University; Indian Hill, Old Elm. Home: Chicago Ill. Died July 7, 1992.

FRANK, MILTON, academic official, former U.S. ambassador; b. Reno, Dec. 18, 1919; 1 child. BA, U. Calif., Berkeley, 1941; MS, Boston U., 1958. Commd. U.S. Air Force, 1946, advanced through grades to col., ret., 1968; dir. pub. affairs Calif. State U. System, Long Beach, 1969-83; pub. relations and pub. affairs cons. Santa Monica, Calif., 1983-86; asst. to pres. Adelphi U., Garden City, N.Y., 1985-86; ambassador Nepal, 1987-89; personal asst. to pres. Adelphi U., Garden City, N.Y., 1990-93; mem. Presdl. del. to the coronation of His Majesty the King of Swaziland, 1986-87; vice-chmn. bd. dirs. African Devel. Found. Served with U.S. Army Air Corps, 1942-45. Home: Condon City N.Y. Died Jan. 13, 1993.

FRANK, ZOLLIE SYDNEY, automobile dealer; b. Dayton, Ohio, Jan. 1, 1907; s. Charles and Lena (Kessler) F.; m. Elaine Spiesberger, Jan. 1, 1938; children—Laurie Lieberman, James S., Nancy Lee Kaplan, Charles E. Student, Ohio State U., Columbus. Pres. Z Frank-Inc., Chgo., 1936—; pres. Four Wheels Inc., Chgo., 1939—, Laurie James Inc., Chgo., 1944—, Five Wheels Inc., Chgo., 1950—, Globe Auto Leasing, Chgo., 1953—, Wheels Inc, Chgo., 1953—; chmn C. James Inc., Chgo., 1952—; chmn. bd. dirs. Frank Consol. Enterprises Inc., Chgo., Wheels Car Rental Inc., Chgo., Wheels Leasing Co. Ltd., Chgo., Sunniday Chevrolet, Chgo., Sunniday Subaru, Chgo., Dealer's Acceptance Corp., Chgo., Wheels Funding Inc., Chgo., Z-J Investments, Chgo., Heather Terrace Inc., Chgo., C-N-L Holding Co., Chgo., C-N Life Ins. Co. Inc, Chgo., E-Z Ins. Co., Chgo., Z Frank Oldsmobile, Chgo.; bd. dirs. Nat. Car Rental, Chgo. Life mem. Brandeis U.; bd. dirs. North Shore Congregation Israel; trustee Steven David Epstein Found.; mem. pres.'s adv. com. Gen. Motors Corp.; bd. dirs. Michael Reese Hosp., charter mem., officer Michael Reese Research; bd. dirs. Lyric Opera; mem. citizens bd. Loyola U.; mem. North Town C. of C.; mem. Chgo. bd. Nat. Jewish Hosp., Denver; bd. dirs. High Ridge YMCA; active Combined Jewish Appeal, Jewish Fedn., Jewish Community Ctrs.; bd. dirs. Ben Gurion U., Israel. mem. U.S. Congl. Adv. Bd. Recipient Regional Quality Dealer award Time Mag., 1976; Disting. Service citation, Automotive Hall of Fame; Chgo. Police Dept. Sr. Adv. Council award; Chevrolet award as World's Largest Chevrolet Dealer. Mem. Am. Automobile Assn., Chevrolet Dealers Assn., Chgo. Automobile Trade Assn. Chgo. Assn. Commerce, Ill. C. of C. Jewish. Home: Des Plaines Ill.

FRANKE, CHARLES H(ENRY), mathematics educator, department chair; b. Jersey City, Dec. 28, 1933; s. Charles Henry Sr. and Lydia Agusta (Francis) F.; m. Evelyn Judith Walp, Aug. 8, 1959; children: Linda Jean, Bonnie Louise, Charles Henry III. AB, Rutgers U., 1955, PhD, 1961, MS, 1984; MA, Yale U., 1956. Instr. Rutgers U., Newark, 1958-62; mem. tech. staff Bell Telephone Labs., Whippany, N.J., 1962-66; prof., chair math. dept. Seton Hall U., South Orange, N.J., 1966-83, prof., coord. computer sci., 1983-85; prof., chair maths., stat. and computer sci. dept. Ea. Ky. U., Richmond, 1985-94. Contbr. articles to profl. jours. Mem. Am. Math. Soc., Math. Assn. Am., Assn. for Computing Machinery, Ky. Acad. Scis., Sigma Xi. Home: Richmond Ky. Deceased.

FRANKLIN, GEORGE S., private commission executive; b. N.Y.C., Mar. 23, 1913; s. George Small and Elizabeth (Jennings) F.; m. Helena Edgell, June 24, 1950; children: Helena, George III, Cynthia, Sheila. Student, U. Grenoble, 1931-32; A.B., Harvard, 1936; LL.B., Yale, 1939. Law clk. Davis, Polk, Wardwell, Gardiner & Reed, 1939; asst. Nelson A. Rockefeller, 1940; div. world trade intelligence Dept. State, 1941-44; assoc. Coun. on Fgn. Rels., 1945-71; asst. exec. dir. Council on Fgn. Relations, 1951-53, exec. dir., 1953-71; N.Am. sec. Trilateral Commn., 1972-76, coordinator, 1977-82; pres. Trilateral Commn. N. Am., 1982-85, vice-chmn., 1985-88, sr. advisor, 1988-96. Life trustee Internat. House, N.Y.C.; former trustee Brearley Sch., N.Y. Soc. Library, Boys Brotherhood Republic, N.Y.C., Robert Coll., Istanbul, Turkey, Cou. on Fgn. Rels.; trustee Atlantic Council U.S., Commn. United World Colls., Salzburg Seminar Am. Studies, French Am. Found.; hon. trustee American Ditchley Found.; hon. chmn. Mid-Atlantic Club; past sec., trustee Am. Com. on United Europe; chmn. bd. Erick Hawkins Dance Co. Presbyterian. Clubs: Century (N.Y.C.), River N.Y.C.), Seawanhaka (Oyster Bay). Home: New York N.Y. Died Mar. 5, 1996.

FRANKOVICH, GEORGE RICHARD, jewelers supply company executive; b. Pitts., Aug. 17, 1920; s. George and Anna (Subasic) F.; m. Madelaine E. Ruest, Jan. 29, 1944; children: Richard E., Diane A. Frankovich Lusk. B.A., U. Pitts., 1941. Cert. assn. exec. Indsl. engr. Mfg. Jewelers and Silversmiths of Am., Inc., Providence, 1946-48, exec. dir., 1948-86, v.p., 1958-86, ret. v.p., exec. dir. emeritus, 1986; pres. Asian Jewelers Supply Co.; owner Frankovich Inc.; bd. dirs 1st Bank and Trust, Providence, Antaya Inc.; past bd. dirs. Silver Users' Assn., New Eng. Trade Adjustment Ctr; past mem. industry adv. com. U.S. Dept. Commerce, former chief Am. del. to Internat. Confederation of Jewelry, Silverware, Diamonds, Pearls and Stones; assoc. mem. Worshipful Co. of Goldsmiths, London; cofounder, former chief exec. officer Jewelry Inst.; hon. dir. Jewelers' Shipping Assn., Providence, 1986-93; vol. cons. Internat. Exec. Svc. Corps., Thailand, 1988. Mem., past chmn. R.I. Apprentice Coun., Providence. Served to maj. U.S. Army, 1941-46; to col. USAR; ret. Decorated Bronze Star; Croix de Guerre. Mem. Res. Officers' Assn., Naval War Coll. Assn., Am. Legion, 24KT Club of N.Y., Providence Jewelers Club, World Brotherhood of Fashion Jewelry Mfrs., Squantum Assn. R.I., East Bay Anglers Club. Roman Catholic. Home: Rumford R.I. Died Apr. 17, 1993.

FRANTZ, ROBERT LEWIS, lawyer; b. Wilkinsburg, Pa., Aug. 24, 1925; s. Charton Christopher and Gladys Baird (Lewis) F.; m. Suzanne Holton Allen, Nov. 20, 1948; children: Charton Christopher II, Rodgers Allen, Ruth Patterson. BS, U.S. Mil. Acad., 1946; LLB, Harvard U., 1954. Bar: D.C. 1954, Pa. 1958. Commd. 2d lt. U.S. Army, 1946, advanced through grades to capt., 1950; with JAGC 24th Inf. Div., Korea, JAG Sch., Charlottesville, Va., 1954-58; resigned JAG Sch., 1958; assoc. Buchanan, Ingersoll, Rodewald, Kyle & Buerger, Pitts., 1958-66; ptnr. Buchanan, Ingersoll, Rodewald, Kyle & Buerger (and its successor Buchanan Ingersoll P.C.), Pitts., 1966-91, Raphael, Gruener, Horoho & Frantz, PC, Pitts., 1991-93, Raphael, Ramsden, Behers and Frantz, P.C., Pitts., 1993; bd. dirs. Weaver Assocs. Inc., Pitts., Eye and Ear Inst., Pitts. Trustee Valley Forge Mil. Acad. and Jr. Coll., Wayne, Pa., 1986-90; vestryman Calvary Episcopal Ch., Pitts., 1985-88. Mem. ABA, Pa. Bar Assn., Allegheny County Bar Assn., Harvard-Yale-Princeton Club, Pitts. Golf Club. Republican. Home: Pittsburgh Pa. Died Mar. 16, 1993; interred U.S.M.A., West Point, N.Y.

FRANZ, FREDERICK WILLIAM, religious organization official; b. Covington, Ky., Sept. 12, 1893; s. Frederick Edward and Ida Louise (Krueger) F. Student, U. Cin., 1911-14. Ordained to ministry Jehovah's Witnesses, 1914, mem. internat. hdqrs. staff, 1920-92; bd. dirs. Watchtower Bible and Tract Soc. N.Y., 1932-92, v.p., 1949-77, pres., 1977-92; bd. dirs. Watch Tower Bible and Tract Soc. Pa., 1943-92, v.p., 1945-77, pres., 1977-92. Home: Brooklyn N.Y. Died Dec. 22, 1992.

FRANZ JOSEF, II, Prince of Liechtenstein; b. Frauenthal, Aug. 16, 1906; s. Alois and Elisabeth, Archduchess of Austria; m. Georgine, countess Wilczek, Mar. 7, 1943 (dec. Oct. 1989); children: Hans-Adam, Philipp, Nikolaus, Nora, F.J. Wenzel. Student, Schottengymnasium Wien, forest engring. U. Wien. Succeeded grand-uncle Prince Francis I, as reigning prince of Liechtenstein, 1938—. Home: Vaduz Liechtenstein

FRASER, ALEXANDER V., Canadian provincial politician. Mem. Province of B.C. Legislative Assembly; minister of transp. and hwys. Died 1989. Home: Victoria Can.

FRASURE, ROBERT CONWAY, diplomat; b. Morgantown, W. Va., Apr. 20, 1942; m. Katharina Witting; children: Sarah, Virginia. BA, MA, W. Va. U., 1965; student, London Sch. Econs.; PhD, Duke U. With Fgn. Svc., 1974; chargé d'affairs U.S. Dept. State, Estonia, 1991; amb. to Estonia, 1992; mem. Sr. Fgn. Svc., 1989-95; Africa dir. Nat. Security Coun., 1990-91. Recipient Superior Honor award State Dept., 1982, 85, Presdl. medal Exceptional Svc., Washington, 1991. Mem. Phi Beta Kappa. Home: Washington D.C. Died Aug. 19, 1995.

FRAWLEY, DANIEL SEYMOUR, mayor; b. Fulton, N.Y., Nov. 9, 1943; s. John F. and Margaret (Seymour) F.; m. Bonita Buchele, Aug. 29, 1970; children: Marcus, Matthew, Marjorie. BS in Chemistry, LeMoyne Coll., Syracuse, N.Y., 1965; JD, U. Toledo, 1969; MBA, U. Pa., 1972. Bar: Ohio 1969, Pa. 1970. Atty. E.I. DuPont de Nemours & Co., Wilmington, Del., 1972-84; mayor City of Wilmington, 1985-93; ptnr. Curry, Frawley, Poole & Assocs., 1993-94. Active Big Bros./Big Sisters of Del., 1970-94, Wilmington Sch. Bd., 1975-78, Wilmington Design Commn., 1979-80, Wilmington City Coun., 1980-84, YMCA of Del., Boy Scouts Am.; founder Housing Renovation 1st Urban Homesteader Program, 1975. Recipient Disting. Alumnus award LeMoyne Coll., 1984; N.Y. State Regents scholar, 1961. Mem. Wilmington Rugby Club (co-founder 1974). Democrat. Home: Wilmington Del. Died Feb. 2, 1994.

FRAZIER, JOHN WARREN, civil engineer; b. Columbus, Ohio, May 20, 1913; s. Forrest Faye and Maybelle E. (Warren) F.; m. Edna E. Johnson, May 25, 1935; 1 dau., Mary Faye Frazier Bradley. B.S. in Civil Engring, Kans. State U., 1935. With Kans. Hwy. Commn., 1935-46; cons. engr. Finney & Turpinseed, Topeka, 1946-94; mng. partner Finney & Turpinseed, 1968-83. Mem. Kans. State Bd. Edn., 1966-79, chmn. 1971-77, vice-chmn., 1977-79; mem. Kans. Master Planning Commn. (edn.) 1972-79, Nat. Assn. State Bds. Edn., Bd. Examiners and Appeals, Topeka, 1967-77, Bd. Bldg. and Fire Appeals, 1977-93, chmn. 1987-93; trustee Kans. State U. Found., 1961; alumni rep. intercollegiate Athletic Coun. Kans. State U., 1961-85. Recipient Nat. Civil Govt. award, 1974, Edmund Friedman Profl. Engring. award ASCE, 1975, Citizenship award Kans. Engring. Soc., 1981, Disting. Svc. award Kans. State U. Coll. Engring., 1983, inducted into Coll. Engring. Hall of Fame, 1989. Fellow ASCE (dist. dir. 1968-70, v.p 1971-73); mem. Kans. State U. Alumni Assn. (pres. 1961-62), C. of C. U.S., Kans. Assn. Commerce and Industry, Chi Epsilon (hon.). Club: Pres.'s, Golden K (nat. pres. 1985-86) (Kans. State U.). Home: Topeka Kans. Died Nov. 12, 1994.

FREED, BERT, actor; b. N.Y.C., Nov. 3, 1919; s. Ely and Hannah (Fried) F.; m. Nancy Lee Wurzburger, Feb. 12, 1956; children: Carl Robert, Jennifer. B.S., Pa. State U., 1940. Trustee for SAG producers, pension & Health. Broadway Debut: Johnny 2X4, 1942; Featured in 75 motion pictures including Halls of Montezuma, Paths of Glory, Billy Jack, Norma Rae, Detective Story. Pres. Brentwood Dem. Club, 1968-69; treas. Theatre Authority West, 1983-94; chmn. AFTRA/SAG Fed. Credit Union, 1978-94. Mem. Acad. Motion Picture Arts and Scis. (mem. exec. com. fgn. films 1978-94), SAG (v.p. 1975-77, dir. 1968-89, chair srs. com. 1987-94). Jewish. Home: Los Angeles Calif. Died Aug. 2, 1994.

FREEDMAN, DANIEL X., psychiatrist, educator; b. Lafayette, Ind., Aug. 17, 1921; s. Harry and Sophia (Feinstein) F.; m. Mary C. Neidigh, Mar. 20, 1945. B.A., Harvard U., 1947; M.D., Yale U., 1951; grad., Western New Eng. Inst. Psychoanalysis, 1966; D.Sc. (hon.), Wabash Coll., 1974, Indiana U., 1982; DSC (hon.), Wabash Coll., 1974, Indiana U., 1982. Intern pediatrics Yale Hosp., 1951-52, resident psychiatry, 1952-55; from instr. to prof. psychiatry Yale U., 1955-66; chmn. dept. U. Chgo., 1966-83, Louis Block prof. biol. scis., 1969-83; Judson Braun prof. psychiatry and pharmacology UCLA, 1983-93, acting chair psychiatry and dir. NPI, 1989-91; career investigator USPHS, 1957-66; dir. psychiatry and biol. sci. tng. program Yale U., 1960-66; cons. NIMH, 1960-93, U.S. Army Chem. Center, Edgewood, Md., 1965-66; chmn. panel psychiat. drug efficacy study NAS-NRC, 1966; mem. adv. com. FDA, 1967-78; rep. to div. med. scis. NRC, 1971-82, mem. NAS com. on brain scis., 1971-74, mem. com. on problems of drug dependence, 1971-83; mem. com. problems drug dependence NRC-NAS, 1971-76, chmn. CPDD, Inc. 1977-78, NAS-IOM; com. substance abuse, and habitual behavior, 1976-84; advisor Pres.'s Biomed. Research Panel, 1975-76; mem. selection com., coordinator research task panel Pres.'s Commn. Mental

Health, 1977-78; mem. Joint Commn. Prescription Drug Use, Inc., 1977-80; bd. dirs. Sci. Counselors NIMH, 1982-93, chair from 1984; bd. dirs. Sci. Counselors NIDa Addiction Rsch. Ctr., chair 1989-93. Author: (with N.J. Giarman) Biochemical Pharmacology of Psychotomimetic Drugs, 1965, On the Use and Abuse of LSD, 1968, (with F.C. Redlich) The Theory and Practice of Psychiatry, 1966, (with D. Offer) Modern Psychiatry and Clinical Research, 1972; editor: (with J. Dyrud) American Handbook of Psychiatry, Vol. V, 1975, The Biology of the Major Psychoses: A Comparative Analysis, 1975, Hallucinogenic Drug Research: If so, so what?, 1986; chief editor: Archives Gen. Psychiatry, 1970-93. Bd. dirs. Founds. Fund for Research in Psychiatry, 1969-72, Drug Abuse Council, 1972-80; vice chmn. Drug Abuse Council Ill., 1972-82. Served with AUS, 1942-46. Recipient Disting. Achievement award Modern Medicine, 1973, William C. Menninger award ACP, 1975, McAlpin medal for rsch. achievement, 1979, Vestermark award for edn., 1981, Salmon medal N.Y. Acad. Medicine, 1990; Rhoda and Bernard G. Sarnat Mental Health award APA-IOM, 1992. Fellow Am. Coll. Neuropsychopharmacology (pres. 1970-71); mem. NIMH (bd. sci. counselors, chair 1984-86), Inst. Medicine NAS, Ill. Psychiat. Soc. (pres. 1971-72), Social Sci. Research Council (dir. 1968-74), Chgo. Psychoanalytic Soc., Western New Eng. Psychoanalytic Inst., Am. Soc. Pharmacology and Exptl. Therapeutics, AAAS, Am. Assn. Chairmen Depts. Psychiatry (pres. 1972-73), Coun. Acad. Socs., Assn. Am. Med. Colls. (adminstrv. bd. 1975-81, chmn. 1980-81, disting. svc. mem. 1980-93), Am. Psychiat. Assn. (chmn. com. drug abuse, 1971-78, v.p. 1975-77, pres.-elect 1980-81, pres. 1981-82), Group Advancement Psychiatry, Psychiat. Research Soc., Am. Psychosomatic Soc. (councillor 1970-73), Assn. Research in Nervous and Mental Disease (pres. 1974), Soc. Biol. Psychiatry (pres. 1985-86), NIDA Addiction Rsch. Ctr. (bd. sci. counsellors, chair 1989-93), Sigma Xi, Alpha Omega Alpha. Home: Los Angeles Calif. Died June 3, 1993.

FREEHLING, NORMAN, stockbroker; b. Chgo., Oct. 15, 1905; s. Isaac and Pearl (Eichberg) F.; m. Edna Wilhartz, Feb. 14, 1934; children: William W., Paul E. A.B., U. Mich., 1927; J.D., Chgo. Kent Coll. of Law, 1932. Mem. Chgo. Stock Exchange, 1927-49, Midwest Stock Exchange, 1949-94; partner Norman Freehling & Co., 1936-47, Freehling, Meyerhoff & Co., 1947-63, Freehling & Co., 1963-86; ltd. ptnr. Cowen & Co., 1986-94; Past chmn. bd. Midwest Stock Exchange. Clubs: Standard (Chgo.); Northmoor Country (Highland Park, Ill.) (past pres.). Home: Chicago Ill. Died Dec. 9, 1993.

FREEHLING, WILLARD MAXWELL, stockbroker; b. Chgo., Oct. 16, 1913; s. Isaac and Pearl (Eichberg) F.; m. Elaine Stadeker, June 27, 1947; children: Susan Freehling Axelrad-Lentz, Patricia Freehling O'Loughlin. Student, U. Mich., 1930-33. Ptnr. Norman Freehling & Co., Chgo., 1934-47, Freehling, Meyerhoff & Co., Chgo., 1947-69, Freehling & Co., Chgo., 1969-86; with Cowen and Co., Chgo., 1986-95. Served with AUS, 1941-45. Clubs: Standard (Chgo.) (pres. 1974-76, dir. 1968-78); Northmoor Country (Highland Park, Ill.). Home: Winnetka Ill. Died July 10, 1995.

FREEMAN, JAMES DARCY CARDINAL, former archbishop of Sydney; b. Sydney, Australia, Nov. 19, 1907; s. Robert and Margaret (Smith) F.; grad. St. Columba's Coll., Springwood, 1924, St. Patrick's Coll., Manly, 1927. Ordained priest Roman Catholic Ch., 1930; asst. priest in country and city parishes, 1930-37; mem. cathedral staff, Sydney, 1938-41; pvt. sec. to Archbishop of Sydney, 1941-46; dir. Cath. Info. Bur. Australia, 1946-49; pastor, Haymarket, 1949-54; parish priest, Stanmore, 1954-68; named domestic prelate, 1949, aux. bishop, 1957; bishop of Armidale, 1968-71; archbishop of Sydney, 1971-83; elevated to Sacred Coll. of Cardinals, 1973. Decorated knight Order Brit. Empire, 1977. Home: Randwick Australia

FREEMAN, MAURICE TRACY, retired investment executive; b. Somerville, Mass., Feb. 8, 1904; s. Maurice James and Catharine (Tracy) F.; m. Ruth Moulton, Sept. 12, 1931; children: Louise Freeman Ahearn, Elizabeth J. Freeman Spiller, Ruth M. Freeman O'Neill. Jean Tracy. B.S., Mass. Inst. Tech., 1925; M.B.A., Harvard, 1927. Staff research dept. Loomis, Sayles & Co., Inc., 1927-42, dir. investment research dept., 1942-63, exec. v.p., 1958-63, pres., 1963-68, chmn. bd., chief exec. officer, 1963-69; dir. Loomis, Sayles Mut. Fund, 1930-77, pres., 1951-70; pres., dir. Loomis, Sayles Can. Internat. Fund, 1959-70, Loomis, Sayles Capital Devel. Fund., 1960-70; dir. Standard Shares, Inc.; Centennial life fellow Mus. Fine Arts. Chmn. bd. trustees Winchester Hosp., 1947-74. Home: Winchester Mass. Died Oct. 7, 1992.

FREEMAN, WILLIAM ERNEST, JR., architect; b. Greenwood, S.C., Apr. 11, 1913; s. William Ernest and Julia (Griffin) F.; m. Othella Leonard, Dec. 11, 1937; children—William Ernest III, Allen Leonard, John Thomas. B.S. in Architecture, Clemson U., 1934. Draftsman, designer William R. Ward (Architect), Greenville, S.C., 1935-39; archtl. examiner FHA, Columbia, S.C., 1939-40; owner W.E. Freeman, Jr. & Assos., Greenville, 1940-65; ptnr. Freeman, Wells & Major (Architects), Greenville, 1965-78; dir. First Fed. Savs. & Loan Assn., Greenville, So. Service Corp.; v.p., dir. Freeman's, Inc., Greenville; mem. S.C. Bd. Archtl. Examiners, 1954-59, Greenville; Archtl. Commn., 1967-70. Archtl. works include Hillcrest High Sch, 1957, St. Mark Meth. Ch, Seneca, 1960, 1st Bapt. Ch, Valdese, N.C., 1965, 5 dormitory bldgs., Clemson U., 1966, St. Mathew Meth. Ch, Greenville, 1967, Visitor's Center, Keowee-Toxaway Nuclear Devel, 1969, First Fed. Savs. & Loan Assn. Main Office Bldg, Greenville, 1973, Henderson Advt. Inc. Bldg, Greenville, 1978. Gov. S.C. Beautification and Community Devel. Bd., 1969-72; chmn. Greenville Planning and Zoning Bd. Adjustments, 1953-60; trustee Greenville Bapt. Retirement Community, 1978-83; pres., trustee Archtl. Found., Clemson U., 1955-59, mem. engrng. adv. bd., 1954-55. Fellow AIA (nat. dir. 1962-65, pres. S.C. chpt. 1951-52, regional dir. 1962-65); mem. Greenville C. of C. (dir. 1959-61), Greenville Art Assn. (pres. 1956-57). Baptist (deacon). Clubs: Rotarian, Greenville Country; Lake Toxaway (N.C.) Country. Home: Greenville S.C. Died June 10, 1994.

FREIDEL, FRANK BURT, JR., historian; b. Bklyn., May 22, 1916; s. Frank Burt and Edith (Heacock) F.; m. Elisabeth Margo, 1938 (div. 1955); children: Linda Beth, Dorothy Edith, David Alan, Charles Robinson; m. Madeleine Bicskey, Feb. 23, 1956; children: Philip (dec.), Paul, Christine, Irene. B.A., U. So. Calif., 1937, M.A., 1939, D.Litt. (hon.), 1985; Ph.D., U. Wis., 1942; M.A., Oxford U., 1954, Harvard U., 1955; D.H.L., Roosevelt U., 1975. Faculty, assoc. prof. Shurtleff Coll., 1941-43; asst. prof. U. Md., 1943-45, Pa. State Coll., 1946-48, Vassar Coll., 1948-49; asst. prof. U. Ill., 1949-52, assoc. prof., 1952-53; assoc. prof. Stanford U., 1953-55; Harmsworth prof. Am. history Oxford U., 1955-56; prof. Harvard U., 1955-81, Charles Warren prof. Am. history, 1972-81, prof. emeritus, 1981-93; Bullitt prof. Am. history U. Wash., 1981-86, prof. emeritus, 1986-93; tchr. summers George Washington U., 1946, 49, Mich. State U., 1948, Columbia U., 1952, U. Calif., Berkeley, 1959; lectr. Salzburg (Austria) Seminar in Am. Studies, 1955-56; fellow Center for Advanced Study in Behavioral Scis., 1959-60; Cons. Office Naval Research, summer 1949; historian NSF, summer 1951; mem. Nat. Study Commn. Records and Documents Fed. Ofcls., 1976-77. Author: Francis Lieber, Nineteenth Century Liberal, 1947, Franklin D. Roosevelt: The Apprenticeship, 1952, Roosevelt: The Ordeal, 1954, Roosevelt: The Triumph, 1956, Roosevelt: Launching the New Deal, 1973, The Splendid Little War, 1958, America in the Twentieth Century, 196O, Over There, 1964, The Presidents of the United States, 1964, F.D.R. and the South, 1966, Our Country's Presidents, 1966, Franklin D. Roosevelt: A Rendezvous with Destiny, 1990; co-author: A History of the United States, 1959, America, A Modern History of the United States, 1970, Dissent in Three American Wars, 1970, America Is, 1978; editor: The Golden Age of American History, 1959, The New Deal and the American People, 1964, Union Pamphlets of the Civil War, 1967, American Epochs series, Franklin D. Roosevelt and the Era of the New Deal series, Modern American History series; Co-editor: Builders of American Institutions, 1963, American Issues in the Twentieth Century, 1966, Harvard Guide to American History, 1974. Served with USNR, 1945-46. Guggenheim fellow, 1964-65; Nat. Endowment for Humanities fellow, 1975-76. Fellow Am. Acad. Arts and Scis. (librarian, 1985-93); mem. Orgn. Am. Historians (pres. 1975-76). Home: Belmont Mass. Died Jan. 25, 1993.

FRELENG, FRIZ, writer, producer; b. Kansas City, Mo., Aug. 21, 1906. Animator Walt Disney Studio, 1928-29, Charles Mintz Studio, 1929-30; prod., dir. Warner Bros., 1930-63; ptnr. with David DePatie, 1963-95. Works include (cartoon films) Bugs Bunny series, Daffy Duck, Sylvester, Yosemite Sam, Porky Pig, Tweetie Pie, Speedy Gonzales, Halloween is Grinch Night, Pink Pather in Olympinks, Dr. Suess' Pontoffel Pock, other works The Looney Looney Bugs Bunny Movie, Bugs Bunny's 3d Movie: 1001 Rabbit Tales; numerous TV shows. Recipient 5 Academy awards, 3 Emmy awards. Home: Los Angeles Calif. Died May 26, 1995.

FRENCH, DAVID HEATH, anthropologist, educator; b. Bend, Oreg., May 21, 1918; s. Delbert Ransom and Ellen Evelyn (Fatland) F.; m. Kathrine McCulloch Story, May 15, 1943. Student, Reed Coll., 1935-38; B.A., Pomona Coll., 1939; M.A., Claremont Grad. Sch., 1940; Ph.D., Columbia U., 1949. Jr. profl. asst. United Pueblos Agy., Albuquerque, 1941-42; community analyst War Relocation Authority, Poston, Ariz., 1943-46; Amerindian research Reed Coll., Portland, Oreg., 1947-49, from asst. prof. to assoc. prof. anthropology, 1947-59, prof., 1959-88; prof. emeritus Reed Coll., Portland, 1988-94, cons. anthropologist, 1988-94; reviewer research proposals NSF, Washington, 1961-94, NIH, Washington, 1963-94; co-investigator pharmacognosy Oreg. State U., Corvallis, 1963-64. Author: Factionalism in Isleta Pueblo, 1948; contbr. chpts. to books, numerous articles to profl. publs. Grantee Wenner-Gren Found., 1951-52, Am. Philos. Soc., 1955, NIH, 1964-67; resident fellow Ctr. for Advanced Study in Behavioral Scis., Stanford, Calif., 1967-68; recipient Cert. Appreciation Confederated Tribes of Warm Springs, Oreg., 1989. Fellow Am. Anthrop. Assn. (exec. bd. 1965-68, Disting. Svc. award 1988), AAAS (coun. 1966-68), Royal Anthrop. Inst.; mem. Soc. Econ. Botany (chmn. membership com. 1964-68), Linguistic Soc. Am., Soc. for Anthropology of Europe, Soc. Ethnobiology, Soc. for Linguistic Anthropology, Sigma Xi. Democrat. Home: Portland Oreg. Died Feb. 12, 1994.

FRENCH, JOHN HENRY, JR., banker; b. Detroit, July 2, 1911; s. John Henry and Elsie (Mott) F.; m. Katharine Baker, Sept. 15, 1934; children: John Henry III, Dainforth Baker (dec. 1990), Henry Welling. AB, Brown U., 1933; MBA, Babson Coll., 1934. With City Nat. Bank of Detroit, 1949-77, pres., dir., 1953-77, chmn. bd., 1970-77; chmn. bd. No. States Bancorp., Inc., 1972-81; v.p., dir. Fed. Res. Bank, 1964-70. Pres. Detroit Clearing House, 1967, Leader Dogs for Blind, 1959-62; mem. adv. bd. and corp. gifts com. United Found., 1973-77; trustee Hutzel Hosp.; trustee, pres. United Health Orgn., 1967-77; mem. corp. Babson (Mass.) Coll., 1974. Mem. Am. Bankers Assn. (exec. coun. 1958), Country Club of Detroit, Yondotega Club, Grosse Pointe Club, Fontinalis Club (Vanderbilt, Mich.). Episcopalian. Home: Grosse Pointe Farms Mich. Died Aug. 3, 1994; interred Christ Church, Grosse Pointe Farms, Mich.

FRERICHS, WAYNE MARVIN, retired veterinarian; b. Bloomington, Nebr., Apr. 9, 1933; s. Weert Jacob and Esther Sophie Marie (Janssen) F.; m. Audrey Louise Henry, (div. Dec. 1972); children: Michael, Pamela; m. Jane Brunig Coffman, Dec. 15, 1972, (div. Mar. 1991); children: Eric Coffman, Steve Coffman. BS, Kans. State U., 1957, DVM; PhD, Washington State U., 1966. Diplomate Am. Coll. Vet. Preventive Medicine. Vet. livestock insp. USDA, Webster, S.D., 1957-58; pvt. practice Franklin, Nebr., 1958-62; USPHS fellow Washington State U., Pullman, 1962-65, jr. vet., 1965-66; rsch. vet. USDA, Beltsville, Md., 1966-79; section head Regional Agr. & Water Rsch. Ctr., Riyadh, Saudi Arabia, 1980-84; rsch. vet. USDA, Pullman, 1984-85; supervisory vet. USDA, Ames, Iowa, 1985-93, ret., 1993; lab. cons. Food and Agr. Orgn., Cairo, Egypt, 1988. Contbr. over 40 articles on equines to profl. jours. Mem. AAAS, AVMA, Am. Soc. Microbiology, N.Y. Acad. Sci. Lutheran. Home: Burke Va. Died Mar. 10, 1995.

FRESE, WALTER WENZEL, publisher; b. Mt. Vernon, N.Y., Sept. 28, 1909; s. Walter Adolf and Clara (Wenzel) F.; m. Margaret Penny, June 20, 1931; children: Alan David Rogers, Frederick Wenzel, Diana Elaine. Student, Columbia U., 1927-31. With Archtl. Book Pub. Co., Inc., 1927-95, v.p., 1930-53, pres., 1953-95; founder, pres. Hastings House, pubs., 1936-85, Archives Pub. Co. of Pa., Inc., 1945-56; partner Arnold & Frese (securities), 1936-39. Pres. Stamford (Conn.) Hills Assn., 1945-48; mem. adv. council Sch. Gen. Studies, Columbia U., chmn., 1963-71; mem. Conn. adv. com. on UN Orgn. Hdqrs. Site. Recipient Columbia Alumni Owl citation for distinguished pub. service, 1964. Mem. Am. Inst. Graphic Arts (pres. 1945-47), New Eng. Soc. City N.Y. (pres. 1976-77). Episcopalian. Clubs: Century, Coffee House, Princeton U. (N.Y.C.); Stamford Yacht (commodore 1971-73), Dutch Treat (sec.-treas. 1971-92, chmn. bd. 1992-95, gold medal 1991), Pilgrims. Home: Stamford Conn. Died Jan. 24, 1995.

FRICANO, JOHN CHARLES, lawyer; b. Rochester, N.Y., Oct. 10, 1930; s. Anthony J. and Lena (O'Geen) F.; m. Mary Elizabeth Kelly, Sept. 11, 1954; children: Lisa C., Christopher A. BS cum laude, Mt. St. Mary's Coll., Emmitsburg, Md., 1953; JD, Fordham U., 1956. Bar: D.C. 1977, N.Y. 1956, U.S. Supreme Ct. 1961, U.S. Ct. Appeals (D.C. and 2d cirs.) 1978, U.S. Ct. Appeals (3d cir.) 1985, U.S. Ct. Appeals (4th cir.) 1958, U.S. Ct. Appeals (8th and 9th cirs.) 1981, U.S. Dist. Ct. D.C. 1977, U.S. Dist. Ct. Md. 1957, U.S. Dist. Ct. (we. dist.) Pa. 1974, U.S. Dist. Ct. (so. dist.) N.Y. 1976, U.S. Dist. Ct. (ea. dist.) N.Y. 1986. Trial atty. antitrust div. Dept. Justice, Washington, 1956-73; chief trial sect. antitrust div. Dept. Justice, 1973-76; ptnr. Skadden, Arps, Slate, Meagher & Flom, Washington, 1976-93; mem. antitrust and trade adv. bd. Bur. Nat. Affairs, Washington, 1979-93, corp. practice series adv. bd., 1986-93, civil editor Racketeer Influenced and Corrupt Orgns. Act Law Reporter, 1984-93, chmn. civil adv. bd. Racketeer Influenced and Corrupt Orgn. Report, Bur. of Nat. Affairs, 1985-93; faculty trial practice programs for lawyers Columbia Law Sch., 1978-81. Editor: RICO Strategies, 1986; editor Fordham Law Rev., 1956; contbr. articles to profl. jours. Mem. ABA, City Club. Republican. Roman Catholic. Home: Arlington Va. Died Mar. 14, 1993.

FRIDAY, HERSCHEL HUGAR, lawyer; b. Lockesburg, Ark., Feb. 10, 1922; s. Herschel Hugar and Rosa Lee (Scarborough) F.; m. Nancy Elizabeth Hammett, Feb. 26, 1943; children: Gregory David, Steven Herschel, Pamela Friday Freeman (dec.). Student Little Rock Jr. Coll. (now U. Ark.-Little Rock), 1939-41, LLD (hon.), 1981; student air force program U. Minn., 1943; JD, U. Ark., 1947. Bar: Ark. Law clk. to judge U.S. Dist. Ct. we. dist. Ark., 1947-52; assoc. Friday, Eldredge & Clark, and predecessors, Little Rock, 1952, sr. ptnr., 1974-94; lectr. in law U. Ark.-Fayetteville, 1951-52; mem. Ark. Bd. Law Examiners, 1960-66; trustee Southwestern Legal Found., 1977-89; mem. Am. Bar Audit Com., 1987-92, chmn., 1991-92; sec. bd. dirs.

Oaklawn Jockey Club, Inc., 1973-94; bd. dirs. First Comml. Corp. in Little Rock, Gt. Lakes Chem. Corp., Dillard Dept. Stores, Inc. Trustee Ark. Children's Hosp., Little Rock, 1955-94, pres. 1962-64, chmn. steering com., 1979-80; bd. dirs. Pulaski County (Ark.) chpt. ARC, 1977-81. With USAF, 1943-46; maj. res. Named Man of Yr. in Ark., Ark. Democrat, 1971; named Disting. Alumnus and recipient Shield of Trojan award U. Ark.-Little Rock Alumni Assn., 1976; recipient Harrison Tweed award Assn. Continuing Legal Edn. Adminstrs., 1979, Disting. Citizen award Ark. Community Svc. Sta. KARK-TV, Office of Gov., divsn. volunteerism, 1992; named Citizen of Yr., Ark. chpt. March of Dimes, 1981; recipient Builders award U. Ark.-Little Rock, 1983; named Ark. Citizen of Yr. Easter Seals, 1989. Fellow Am. Bar Found.; mem. ABA (ho. of dels. 1954-94, gov. 1968-71, 85-86, chmn. cons. panel on advanced jud. and legal edn. 1978-81, chmn. task force on lawyer competence 1981-83, Am. Law Inst./ABA com. on continuing profl. edn. 1972-77, 83-86, ABA standing com. on edn. of bar 1973-79, chmn. 1976-79), Pulaski County Bar Assn., Ark. Bar Assn. (exec. com. 1954-68, chmn. exec. com. 1963-64, pres. 1976-77, chmn. law sch. com.; Outstanding Lawyer award 1971), Am. Judicature Soc., Am. Bar Endowment (pres. 1991-93), Am. Coll. Trial Lawyers, Greater Little Rock C. of C. (chmn. 1993), Pleasant Valley Country Club (pres. 1964-65), Little Rock Club, Country Club of Little Rock. Baptist. Died Mar. 1, 1994. Home: Little Rock Ark.

FRIEDERICI, HARTMANN H.R., physician, educator; b. Asuncion, Paraguay, Jan. 25, 1927; came to U.S., 1957, naturalized, 1960; s. H. Gerhard H. and Annaliese (Wacker) F.; m. Erica Y. Bachem, Mar. 23, 1958; children: Claudia Friederici Petersen, Peter G., Andrea Friederici Ross. B.S., Colegio de Goethe, Asuncion, 1946; M.D., U. La Plata, Argentina, 1953. Intern U. Ill. Research and Edn. Hosps., Chgo., 1960-61; resident U. Ill. Research and Edn. Hosps., 1957-59, U. Bonn (Germany) Hosp., 1955-56; practice medicine specializing in pathology; asso. pathologist U. Ill. Hosps., Chgo., 1961-69; pathologist, attending physician Evanston (Ill.) Hosp., 1969-71, sr. attending physician, chmn. dept. pathology and lab. medicine, 1971-95; asso. prof. pathology U. Ill., 1966-69; prof. pathology, assoc. chmn. dept. pathology Northwestern U., 1969-95, prof. biology, 1970-78; ret., 1994. Fellow Am. Heart Assn., Am. Soc. Clin. Pathologists; mem. AAAS, Internat. Acad. Pathology, Electron Microscopy Soc. Am., Assn. Am. Pathologists, Am. Soc. Cell Biology, Coll. Am. Pathologists, Assn. Pathology Chmn. (program dirs.' sect.). Home: Glencoe Ill. Died Jan. 28, 1995.

FRIEDLAENDER, ANN FETTER, economics educator; b. Phila., Sept. 24, 1938; d. Ferdinand Fetter and Elizabeth Head; m. Stephen Friedlaender, Dec. 28, 1960; children: Lucas Ferdinand, Nathaniel Marc. B.A., Radcliffe Coll., 1960; Ph.D. (Woodrow Wilson fellow, 1960-62), MIT, 1964. Asst. prof., assoc. prof., then prof. Boston Coll., 1965-74; prof. econs. MIT, Cambridge, 1974—, Class of 1941 prof., 1987—, chmn. dept. econs., 1983-84, dean Sch. Humanities and Social Sci., 1984-90; Fulbright lectr., Helsinki, Finland, 1964-65; bd. dirs. Consol. Rail Corp., Ins. Svcs. Office Inc.; bd. trustees Rand Corp. Author: The Dilemma of Freight Transportation, 1969, (with R.H. Spady) Freight Transport Regulation, 1981, (with John F. Due) Government Finance, 1981. NSF grantee, 1968, 76, 77, 79, 81, 83, 87. Mem. Am. Econ. Assn. (chmn. com. on status of women in the econs. profession 1978-80, exec. com. 1982-84, v.p. 1987). Home: Newton Mass. Died Oct. 19, 1992.

FRIEND, EDWARD MALCOLM, JR., lawyer; s. Edward Malcolm and May (Gusfield) F.; m. Hermione Frances Curjel, Sept. 22, 1938; children: Ellen Friend Elsas, Edward M. A.B., U. Ala., 1933, LL.B., 1935; LL.D. (hon.), Birmingham So. Coll., 1986, U. Ala., 1988. Bar: Ala. 1935. Practice in Birmingham; pres. Legal Aid Soc., Birmingham, 1954-55, Jefferson County (Ala.) Family Counseling Assn., 1958-59. Hon. editor: Ala. Law Rev. Gen. co-chmn. Jefferson County United Fund, 1959; gen. chmn. Jefferson-Shelby-Walker Counties United Way, 1982; trustee Ala. Law Sch. Found., pres., 1969-71; former trustee Children's Hosp.; bd. dirs. Jefferson County chpt. ARC; nat. bd. dirs. NCCJ, 1969-71; pres. Birmingham Area council Boy Scouts Am., 1980; mem. pres.'s cabinet U. Ala., 1975—, chmn., 1980-85; bd. dirs. Met. Arts Council, pres., 1991—; past mem. distbn. com. Greater Birmingham Found.; former bd. govs. The Club; bd. dirs. Leadership Birmingham, 1987—; pres. United Jewish Fund, 1971, Temple Emanu-El, 1971. Served with AUS, 1941-45; Normandy; brig. gen. Res. ret. Decorated Legion of Merit, Bronze Star with cluster; Croix de Guerre with palm France; recipient Daniel J. Meador Outstanding Alumnus award U. Ala. Law Sch., 1971; Outstanding Civilian Service award U.S. Army; Disting. Eagle award Boy Scouts Am.; Silver Beaver award, 1978; Brotherhood award NCCJ, 1981; Man of Yr. award Young Men's Bus. Club Birmingham, 1982; Outstanding Civic Leader award Nat. Assn. Fund Raising Execs., Ala. Chpt., 1983, Sam W. Pipes disting. alumnus award Farrah Law Soc., U. Ala., 1984, Ednl. Advocate award Birmingham Pub. Sch., 1993; inducted Ala. Acad. of Honor, 1987. Fellow Am. Bar Found.; mem. Ala. State Bar Assn. (chmn. joint coml lawyers and interested citizens to study Ala. correctional instns. and procedures 1975), Birmingham Bar Assn. (v.p. 1970, pres. 1971, Outstanding Lawyer award 1990), Order of Coif, Phi Beta Kappa, Omicron Delta Kappa, Zeta Beta Tau. Club: Rotary (pres. Birmingham 1974-75). Home: Birmingham Ala. Died June 5, 1995.

FRIIS, HENNING KRISTIAN, social scientist; b. Copenhagen, Oct. 11, 1911; s. Aage and Benedicte (Blichfeldt) F. Ed. U. Copenhagen. Social Sci. adviser Ministry Social Affairs, 1941-58; sec.-gen. Danish Govt. Youth Commn., 1945-52, Com. on Sci. and Tech. Personnel, 1956-59; exec. dir. Danish nat. Inst. Social Research, 1958-79; dir. EEC Study on Poverty in Denmark, 1979-80; WHO cons. on elderly, 1980-82; dir. Study on Social Changes in Next 20 Yrs., 1982-85; chmn. Future Study on Elderly in Denmark's Next Century, 1985—; chmn. European Social Research Com., Internat. Gerontol. Assn., 1954-60; chmn. OECD Com. for Sci. and Tech. Personnel, 1958-65; chmn. bd. trustees Danish Schs. Social Work, 1966-71; vice chmn. Danish Social Sci. Council, 1968-77, European Centre for. Coordination in Social Scis., 1968-82; trustee UN Inst. on Tng. and Research, 1965-76; mem. exec. com. Internat. Social Sci. Council, 1970-73, 79-83. Author: Social Policy and Social Trends, 1958; Longstanding Public Assistance Clients, 1960; Developments of Social Research in Ireland, 1965; Social Policy and Social Research in India, 1968; National and International Policies for Social Research, 1972; Pensions and Retirement up to the Year 2000, 1980; Poverty and Poverty Policies in Denmark, 1980, The Uncertain Future, 1985, Work and Retirement, 1990; co-author: Old People in Three Industrial Societies, 1968; editor Scandinavia between East and West, 1950, Family and Society, 1964. Deceased. Home: Frederiksberg Denmark

FROESCHLE, ROBERT EDWARD, professional association administrator; b. Davenport, Iowa, Apr. 9, 1918; s. Theodore Edward and Grace Marie (Hunn) F.; m. Marjorie A., Apr. 24, 1943; children: Judith Marjorie, James Robert, Jeffery Alan. Student, DePauw U., 1936, St. Ambrose Coll., 1937-38; BJ, U. Mo., 1940. Various def. work Rock Island (Ill.) Arsenal, 1940-42; advt. mgr. Herman Nelson Corp., Moline, Ill., 1943-50; sales mgr. Sta. KSTT-Radio, Davenport, Iowa, 1950-52; mng. dir. Bettendorf (Iowa) C. of C., 1952-55; aux. services dir. Iowa Meml. Union, U. Iowa, Iowa City, 1955-82; mng. dir. BCA, Iowa City, 1982-90; organizer, dir. billiard program Assn. Coll. Unions Internat., various campuses, 1957-77; internat. mng. dir. Billiard Congress of Am., various cities, 1966-83. Justice of the peace City of Bettendorf, 1950-55. With USN, 1943-45. Decorated Purple Heart, 1944; recipient Billard and Bowling Inst. Am. Industry Svc. award, 1989, Will J. Hayek award, Iowa City, 1994. Republican. Methodist. Lodge: Masons. Home: Iowa City Iowa Died Mar. 14, 1995.

FROST, FRANK L., utility executive, lawyer; b. Crescent, Iowa, July 12, 1898. LL.B., U. Omaha, 1923. Bar: Nebr. 1923. Ptnr. firm Frost & Meyers, Omaha; chmn. bd. Met. Utilities Dist., Omaha. Chmn. bd. dirs. 1st Christian Ch.; pres. Travelers Protective Assn. Named Dad Order of Rainbow; named Dad Order of DeMolay. Mem. Omaha C. of C. (big chiefs Tribe of Yessir). Clubs: Downtown Optimist (pres.), Business and Prof. Men's Breakfast Omaha (pres.). Home: Omaha Nebr. Deceased.

FROST, WILLIAM, English educator; b. N.Y.C., June 8, 1917; s. John William and Christina (Gurlitz) F.; m. Marjorie Hayes Pangburn, Aug. 5, 1942; children—Marjorie Augusta Frost McCracken, Christina Emily, Clifford William. A.B., Bowdoin Coll., 1938, D.Litt. (hon.), 1980; M.A., Columbia U., 1942; Ph.D., Yale U., 1946. Instr., Carnegie Inst. Tech., 1942-44; instr. Yale U., 1946-47, vis. assoc. prof., 1958-59; asst. prof. Wesleyan U., 1947-51; asst. prof. U. Calif., Santa Barbara, 1951-55, assoc. prof., 1955-58, 59-61, acting chmn. dept. English, 1965-66, chmn., 1974-79, prof. English, 1961—, co-editor Works of John Dryden, Vol. IV, 1974. Guggenheim fellow, 1959, 79-80, Am. Council Learned Socs. fellow, 1966-67, Nat. Endowment for Humanities fellow, 1972-73; Am. Philos. soc. grantee, 1982-83. Mem. MLA, Philol. Assn. of Pacific Coast, Medieval Acad. Am., Calif. State Employees Assn., Phi Beta Kappa. Club: Elizabethan (Yale U.). Author: Fulke Greville's Caelica: An Evaluation, 1942; Dryden and the Art of Translation, 1955, 69; Dryden and Future Shock, 1976; editor, co-editor, assoc. editor: English Masterpieces, 1950, 61; Selected Works of Dryden, 1953, 71; Pope's Homer, 1967; Dryden's Juvenal and Persius and Other Poems, 1974, Dryden's Virgil, 1987; contbr. articles on Chaucer, Shakespeare, Pope, Persius, others to publs. Home: Santa Barbara Calif.

FRYDENLUND, KNUT, Norwegian Minister of Foreign Affairs; b. Drammen, Norway, Mar. 31, 1927; s. Carl Herman and Kjellaug F.; m. Grethe Nilsen; children—Hans Jacob, Thomas, Jens Christian. Degree in Law, Oslo U., 1950. Joined Norwegian Fgn. Service, 1953, sec. Norwegian Embassy, Bonn, 1953-55, sec., then counsellor, Fgn. Ministry, 1956-62, press counselor Norwegian Embassy, Brussels, 1962-63, permanent rep. to Council of Europe, 1963-65, head of sect. Ministry of Fgn. Affairs, 1966-69; cons. Labour Party Research Office, 1967-69, mem. exec. com. Labour Party, Oslo, 1968-74, chmn. internat. com., 1971-73; mem. Parliament for Oslo, 1969-85; mem. del. to Consultative Assembly, Council of Europe, 1970-73; Minister of Fgn. Affairs, Norway, 1973-81, 86—, chmn. standing com. on def., 1981-85. Deceased. Home: Oslo Norway

FRYLING, GEORGE RICHARD, manufacturing company executive; b. St. Marys, Pa., Mar. 24, 1901; s. George Percy and Emma Elisabeth (Spratt) F.; m. Florence K. McCauley, Sept. 22, 1927; children: Florence Elisabeth, George Percy II, Richard McCauley, Mary Patricia. Student, Mercersburg Acad., 1917-18, Rensselaer Poly. Inst., 1918-23; LL.D., Gannon Coll., 1957. Salesman Speer Carbon Co., St. Marys, Pa., 1923-26; v.p., gen. mgr. Elk Graphite Milling Co., St. Marys, 1926- 32; pres. Erie Technol. Products, Inc. (formerly known as Erie Resistor Corp.), Pa., 1928-62; chmn. bd., treas. Erie Technol. Products, Inc. (formerly known as Erie Resistor Corp.), 1962-64, chmn. bd., pres., 1964-72; chmn., chief exec. officer Erie Technol. Products, Inc., 1966-72, chmn. bd., from 1972; chmn. Fryling Mfg., Inc., Electron Research, Inc., Tech. Materials Div., Erie Technol. Products Can., Ltd., Erie Technol. Products, Ltd., London, all until 1972; chmn. bd., pres. Fryling and Co., Inc., Erie, Pa., from 1972; chmn. bd. Preferred Fin. Services, Inc., Erie, from 1973; dir. Security Peoples Trust Co., Keithley Instruments, Inc., Cleve.; v.p. Pa. Mfrs. Assn. Casualty & Fire Ins. Co. Mem. Pa. Planning Bd., 1948-55; Bd. mgrs. Hamot Hosp., Erie; mem. bd. Gannon Coll., from 1960. Recipient Gold Medallion award Pa. State U. Behrend Coll., 1988. Mem. Pa. Mfrs. Assn. (dir.), NAM (dir.), Mfrs. Assn. Erie (dir., past pres.), Pa. C. of C. (dir., pres. 1957-59), Theta Chi. Republican. Episcopalian. Clubs: Erie (Erie) (dir., past pres.), Kahkwa Country (Erie). Home: Erie Pa. Deceased.

FUCHS, FRITZ, physician, educator, researcher; b. Denmark, Nov. 27, 1918; came to U.S., 1964; s. Josef and Sofie (Petersen) F.; m. Seere Anna-Rita Olsson, May 19, 1948; children: Anneli, Martin, Peter Erik, Lars Frederik. M.D., U. Copenhagen, 1944, D. Med. Scis., 1957; Postgrad. tng. ob-gyn and surgery, Danish and Swedish hosps., 1945-58. Gynecologist-in-chief Kommunehospital, Copenhagen, 1958-65; obstetrician, gynecologist-in-chief N.Y. Hosp., 1965-78, attending obstetrician, gynecologist, 1979-88, hon. attending obstetrician, gynecologist, 1989-95; prof. ob-gyn Cornell U. Med. Coll., 1965-89, prof. emeritus, 1989-95, Given Found. prof., chmn. dept., 1965-78, Uris prof. reproductive biology, 1977-80; cons. Rockefeller U., 1968-78, WHO, 1972-73, 1978-83; vis. prof. Chulalongkorn U., Bangkok, Thailand, 1972-73. Editor: Endocrinology of Pregnancy, Preterm Birth: Causes, Prevention, Management; contbr. over 200 articles to profl. jours., chpts. to books. Mem. bd. Found. for Child Devel., 1970-76. Served with Danish Brigade, 1945. Decorated knight of Dannebrog. Fellow Royal Coll of Obstetricians and Gynaecologists; mem. N.Y. Obstetrical Soc. (pres. 1981-82), Am. Gynecol. and Obstetrical Soc., Endocrine Soc.; hon. mem. Finnish Gynecol. Soc. Home: New York N.Y. Died Feb. 17, 1995.

FUKUNAGA, GEORGE JOJI, corporation executive; b. Waialua, Oahu, Hawaii, Apr. 13, 1924; s. Peter H. and Ruth (Hamamura) F.; BA, U. Hawaii, 1948; cert. Advanced Mgmt. Program Harvard U./U. Hawaii, 1955; HHD (hon.) U. Hawaii, 1985; m. Alice M. Tagawa, Aug. 5, 1950; 1 son, Mark H. Adminstrv. asst., dir. Svc. Motor Co., Ltd. (named changed to Servco Pacific Inc. 1969), Honolulu, 1948-52, v.p., 1952-60, pres., 1960-81; chmn., 1981-93, also chmn., bd. dirs. 15 subs. and affiliates, Svc. Fin., Ltd. (name now Servco Fin. Corp.), Servco Svcs. Corp., Am. Ins. Agy. Inc., Servco Ins. Agy. Inc., Servco Securities Corp., Servco Investment Corp., Servco Calif. Inc., Servco Japan, Inc. (Osaka), Servco Fgn. Sales Corp. (Guam), Hawaiiana Advt. Agy., Pacific Internat. Co. Inc. (Guam), Pacific Fin. Corp. (Guam), Pacific Motors Corp. (Guam), Pacific Internat. Marianas Inc., (Saipan), Pacific Marshalls Inc., (Majuro); CFO, bd. dirs. Cal-Pac Rice Milling Co., Inc., Sacramento; bd. dirs. Fender Music Corp., Phoenix. Mem. Japan-Hawaii Econ. Coun.; trustee Fukunaga Scholarship Found., Servco Found., Oceanic Inst. 2d lt. AUS, 1945-47, to 1st lt., 1950-52. Named Dealer of Yr. Time mag., 1978, Disting. Citizen of Yr. Boy Scouts Am., 1990. Mem. C. of C. Hawaii (v.p. 1970, 83-84, bd. dirs. 1970-75, 82-84), Honolulu Japanese (pres. 1969, bd. dir. 1963-93) C. of C., Bus. Roundtable Hawaii (bd. dirs.), Hawaii Econ. Study Club (pres. 1962), U.S.-Japan Soc. (dir. 1983-93), Plaza Club (bd. dirs.), Club 200, Deputies Club, Oahu Country Club, Pacific Club, Rotary. Methodist. Deceased. Home: Honolulu Hawaii

FUKUNAGA, KENJI, Japanese politician. Mem. Ho. Reps. for Saitama Prefecture, Japan; chief sec. to cabinet to Premiers Yoshida and Sato; Minister of Labor, 1961-62, Minister of Health and Welfare, 1974, Minister of Transport, 1977-78; speaker Ho. of Reps., 1983-84; chmn. Liberal-Democratic Party Presdl. Election Com., 19--; spl. envoy to UN, 1971, to Israel, 1972; chmn. Tokyo meeting of Internat.-Parliamentary Union. Home: Tokyo Japan

FULBRIGHT, JAMES WILLIAM, former senator; b. Sumner, Mo., Apr. 9, 1905; s. Jay and Roberta (Waugh) F.; m. Elizabeth William, June 15, 1932 (dec. 1985); children: Elizabeth (Mrs. John Winnacker), Roberta (Mrs. Edward Thaddeus Foote II); m. Harriet Mayor, Mar. 10, 1990. A.B., U. Ark., 1925; B.A., Oxford (Eng.) U., 1928, M.A., 1931; LL.B., George Washington U., 1934. Bar: D.C. 1934. Spl. atty. Anti-Trust Div. U.S. Dept. Justice, 1934-35; instr. in law George Washington U., 1935-36; lectr. in law U. Ark., 1936-39, pres., 1939-41; mem. 78th congress from 3d Dist. Ark.; U.S. senator from Ark., 1945-74; mem. com. on fin., mem. joint econ. com., chmn. com. on fgn. relations; of counsel firm Hogan & Hartson, Washington, 1975-93; ret., 1993; Del. 9th Gen. Assembly UN, 1954. Recipient Onassis Internat. prize, 1989, Presdl. medal of Freedom. Mem. Sigma Chi. Democrat. Mem. Disciples of Christ Ch. Club: Rotarian. Home: Washington D.C. Died Feb. 22, 1995.

FULLER, WANDA LOU, state legislator; b. Browning, Mo., Sept. 12, 1938; d. Harry L. and Alta Eulavea (Browning) Longwell; divorced; children: Carla E., John C. and Lori K. Student, Kansas City Jr. Coll., 2956, Wichita State U., 1974. Dept. sec. Hallmark Cards Inc., Kansas City, Mo., 1955-57, U. Mo., Rolla, 1957-59; assoc. tchr. Wichita Preschool for Blind, Kans., 1975; program coord. State Republican Party of Kansas, Wichita, 1978; office adminstr. Downtown Lions Club, Wichita, Kans., 1980-82; state representative Kansas, 1981-93; cons. State Republican Party, Wichita, Kans., 1982-93. Recipient Woman of Yr. award Wichita Zonta Club, 1985, Thanks badge, Wichita Area Girl Scout Coun., 1974, Citizenship award Princeton (Mo.) C. of C. Mem. Citizen Participation Orgn., Wichita, Normandy Republican Women, Nat. Fedn. Republican Women, Nat. Order Women Legislators, Nat. Conf. State Legislators, Wichita Childrens Home Bd., Booth Family Svcs. Adv. Coun., Sedgwick County Mental Health Adv. Bd., Kansas Ombudsman for Corrections, Wichita-Sedgwick County (Bus. Edn. Success Team Bd.), League of Women Voters (bd. dirs. 1974-78), Womans Soc. Christian Svc. (pres. 1964-66), Girl Scout Alumni and Friends Inc. (pres. 1987-93). Mem. Christian Ch. Home: Witchita Kans. Died Oct. 14, 1993.

FUMAGALLI, BARBARA MERRILL, artist, printmaker; b. Kirkwood, Mo., Mar. 15, 1926; d. Harold C. and Mary Louise (Fitch) Ellison; m. Orazio Fumagalli, Aug. 15, 1948; children: Luisa, Piera, Elio. B.F.A., State U. Iowa, 1948, M.F.A., 1950; student, Mauricio Lasansky, Iowa City, 1945-50, Garo Antreasian, John Sommers, Jim Kraft, Albuquerque, 1980-81. Solo shows, Tweed Gallery, U. Minn., Duluth, 1955, 82, U. Minn., St. Paul, 1964, Mpls., 1965, Concordia Coll., Moorhead, Minn., 1965, Suzanne Kohn Gallery, St. Paul, 1967, Hamline U., St. Paul, 1969, 84, Paine Art Center and Arboretum, Oshkosh, Wis., 1973, St. Johns U., Collegeville, Minn., 1984, U. Louisville, 1993; group shows, Baylor U., Waco, Tex., 1990, Abilene (Tex.) Christian U., 1991, Multnomah County Libr., Portland, Oreg., 1991, Hesston (Kans.) Coll., 1991, Henry Ford C.C., Dearborn, Mich., 1991, Grinnell (Iowa) Coll. Gallery, 1993, One West Contemporary Arts Ctr., Ft. Collins, Colo., 1994; represented in permanent collecions Mus. Modern Art, N.Y.C., Nelson A. Rockefeller Collection, N.Y.C.; included in: Drawing on Dance, Cork Gallery, Lincoln Ctr., N.Y.C., 1982; Illustrator: Swing Around the Sun (Barbara J. Esbensen), 1965. Home: Menomonie Wisc. Died Jan. 12, 1994.

FURNESS, BETTY, broadcast journalist, consumer adviser; b. N.Y.C., Jan. 3, 1916; d. George Choate and Florence (Sturtevant) F.; m. John Waldo Green, Nov. 27, 1937 (div. Aug. 1943); 1 child, Barbara Sturtevant; m. Hugh B. Ernst, Jr., Jan. 3, 1945 (dec. Apr. 1950); m. Leslie Midgley, Aug. 15, 1967. Student, Brearly Sch., N.Y.C., 1925-29, Bennett Sch., Millbrook, N.Y., 1929-32; LLD (hon.), Iowa Wesleyan Coll., 1968, Pratt Inst., 1978, Marymount Coll., 1983; DCL (hon.), Pace U., 1973, Marymount Coll. Manhattan, 1976. Movie actress, 1932-37; appeared in stage plays Doughgirls, My Sister Eileen, commls. for Westinghouse Corp., 1949-60; appeared on CBS radio in Dimension of a Woman's World, Ask Betty Furness, 1961-67; columnist McCall mag., 1969-70, 72; consumer reporter NBC News, 1974-92. Spl. asst. to Pres. of U.S. for consumer affairs, 1967-69; chmn. Pres.'s Com. Consumer Interests, 1967-69; chmn., exec. dir. N.Y. State Consumer Protection Bd., 1970-71; commr. N.Y. C. Dept. Consumer Affairs, 1973; bd. dirs. Consumers Union, 1969-93, Common Cause, 1971-75. Home: Hartsdale N.Y. Died Apr. 2, 1994.

FURST, NORMA FIELDS, academic administrator; b. N.Y.C., Feb. 26, 1931; d. Nathan B. Fields and Anne (Cooper) Platzer; m. M. Lawrence Furst, Sept. 9, 1951; children: Merrick Lee, Laura Furst Jacobs. BA cum laude, Bklyn. U., 1951; MEd, Temple U., 1963, EdD, 1967; LHD (hon.), Combs Coll. of Music, 1986. Registrar Pakistan Mission to the United Nations, N.Y.C., 1952-55; tchr., guidance counselor Harcum Jr. Coll., Bryn Mawr, Pa., 1962-63; instr., Coll. Edn. Temple Univ., Phila., 1963-65; project assoc., Joint Ednl. Psychology USOE Rsch., Temple Univ., Phila., 1965-67; asst. div. dir., Coll. of Edn. Temple Univ., Phila., 1966-68, coord., Coll. of Edn., 1967-70, assoc. prof., 1969-73, dir., Coll. Rels. and Student Devel., 1970-74, prof., Coll. Edn., 1973-83, dean student affairs, 1974-83; pres. Harcum Jr. Coll., Bryn Mawr, 1983-92; interim pres. Balt. Hebrew U., 1992-93, pres., 1993-95; cons. to over 25 sch. dists., univs., community colls. and ednl. consortia; lectr. in field; bd. dirs. Nat. Assn. State Univs. and Land Grant Colls. (past sec./senator, exec. com. of urban affairs div.), Nat. Assn. Ind. Jr. Colls. (v.p.), Am. Assn. of Jr., Tech. and Community Colls. (commn. on ind. colls.), Higher Edn. Referral Svc./Mid-Am. (founding dir.), Internat. B'nai B'rith/Hillel Commn. (past sec. and v.p.), Jewish Pub. Soc. (past. v.p. and sec.), Coun. Jewish Fed. & Welfare Funds. Editor: Review of Educational Research, Am. Educational Research; reviewer, editor for six pub. books; contbr. chpt. to book and articles to profl. jours. Mem. Mayor's Commn. on Literacy, Mayor's Task Force on Transit Safety, Ch. and World Instn., Jewish Campus Activities Bd. (past pres.), United Way, Nat. Coun. of Christians and Jews, Police Athletic League, Flag Day Assn., Chapel of Four Chaplains; exec. com. Cen. Agy. for Jewish Edn.; trustee Fedn. of Jewish Agys. (chmn. com. on Jewish edn., vice-chmn. com. on allocations and planning, exec. com., long range planning com.). Recipient Lindback award for Disting. Coll. Teaching, 1969, Netsky award B'nai B'rith Career and Counseling Svcs. for Dedication to Students' Ednl. and Career Needs, 1976, Humanitarian award B'nai B'rith Educators Chpt., Phila., 1983, Disting. Svc. to Counseling and Guidance, Guidance Assn. of Pa., 1987, Rosh Pina award for disting. svcs. to edn. Am. Jewish Congress, 1989, Pacesetter award Nat. Coun. for Mktg. and Pub. Rels. Dist. I, 1990, and others. Mem. Am. Edn. Rsch. Assn., Am. Psychol. Assn., Nat. Assn. for Student Pers. Adminstrs., Pa. Assn. for Student Pers. Adminstrs., Am. Assn. for Higher Edn., Nat. Assn. Ind. Colls. and Univs. Jewish. Home: Wynnewood Pa. Died Mar. 7, 1995.

GABRIELLI, DOMENICK L., judge; b. Rochester, N.Y., Dec. 13, 1912; s. Rocco and Veronica (Battisti) G.; m. Dorothy Louise Hedges, July 2, 1938; children: Veronica A. Gabrielli Dumas, Michael E. B.S., St. Lawrence U., 1936, LL.D. (hon.), 1973; LL.B., Albany Law Sch., 1936, J.D., 1968; LL.D. (hon.), Union Coll., 1973; H.L.D., Siena Coll., 1974; LL.D., Bklyn. Law Sch., 1975, Nazareth Coll., 1980. Bar: N.Y. 1937. Corp. counsel Village of Bath, N.Y., 1939-53; dist. atty. Steuben County, N.Y., 1953-57; judge Steuben County Ct. and Family Ct., Bath, 1957-61; justice Supreme Ct. N.Y., Albany, 1961-67; asso. justice appellate div. Supreme Ct. N.Y., 1967-73; asso. judge Ct. of Appeals N.Y. State, Bath, 1973-94; sr. counsel firm Nixon, Hargrave, Devans & Doyle, Rochester; presiding judge Extraordinary Spl. and Trial Term, Erie County, 1965-67; past dir. Bath Nat. Bank, Prattsburg (N.Y.) State Bank. Chmn. bd. trustees Albany Law Sch. Served to lt. USN, 1942-45, NATOUSA. Decorated comdr. Order of Merit Pres. of Italy, 1975; invested as knight Mil. Order Malta, 1974; Recipient 1st Hall of Fame award Steuben County, 1976, gold medal Albany Law Sch., 1983. Mem. ABA, N.Y. Bar Assn. (past pres., gold medal 1983), Steuben County Bar Assn. (past pres.), Bath Bar Assn. (past pres.), Am. Law Inst., Am. Judicature Soc., N.Y. State County Judges Assn. (pres. 1961), N.Y. State Children's Ct. Judges Assn., Juvenile Ct. Found., Am. Justinian Soc. Jurists (chmn. appellate cts. com.). Republican. Roman Catholic. Home: Bath N.Y. Died Mar. 25, 1994.

GAERTNER, JOHANNES ALEXANDER, retired art history educator, author; b. Berlin-Lichterfelde, Germany, Apr. 26, 1912; came to U.S., 1945, naturalized, 1952; s. Carl Eugen and Fanny (Horwitz) G.; m. Gerda Meyer, May 31, 1941; 1 dau., Susanna Barbara. Student, U. Berlin, 1930-33; Th.D., U. Heidelberg, 1936. Asst. mgr. Libreria Internacional del Peru, Lima, 1939-45; researcher, editor Frederick Ungar Pub. Co., N.Y.C., 1945-47; instr. Lafayette Coll., Easton, Pa., 1947-48; asst. prof. Lafayette Coll., 1948-58, assoc. prof., 1958-65, prof. art history, head dept. art and music, 1965-77. Author: Vox Humana, 1954, Prisma der Demokratie, 1961, Diapason, 1961, Cantus Firmus, 1966, Zur Deutung des Junius-Bassus-Sarkophages in Jahrbuch des Deutschen Archaeol. Instituts, 1968, Worldly Wisdom: A Catalog of Virtues, 1990, Worldly Virtues: A Catalogue of Reflections, 1994; Contbr. articles profl. jours. Home: Bethlehem Pa. Died Jan 28, 1996.

GAGGE, ADOLF PHARO, physics educator; b. Columbus, Ohio, Jan. 11, 1908; s. Axel Christian Pharo and Edith (Smith) G.; m. Edwina Winter Mead, Dec. 23, 1936; children: Peter Mead, Eleanor (Mrs. James St. John Martin), John Pharo, Ann (Mrs. Gerry H. Vogt). B.A., U. Va., 1929, M.A. in Physics, 1930; Ph.D. in Physics, Yale, 1933. Biophysicist Lab. Hygiene, John B. Pierce Found., New Haven, 1933-41; fellow Lab. Hygiene, John B. Pierce Found., 1963-78, dep. dir., 1970-78, cons., fellow emeritus, 1978-93; mem. faculty Yale U., 1933-41, 63-93, prof. environ. physiology, 1969-77, emeritus prof. epidemiology, 1977-93; chief biophysics, dir. research Aeromed. Lab., Wright Field, 1941-50; with Research and Devel. Hdqrs. USAF, Washington, 1950-55, Air Force Office Sci. Research, 1955-60, Office Sec. Def. Advanced Research Projects Agy., 1960-63; chmn. com. hearing, bioacoustics and biomechanics Nat. Acad. Scis.-NRC, 1967-68. Assoc. editor, sect. editor: Jour. Applied Physiology, 1970-83. Served to col. USAF, 1941-63. Decorated Legion of Merit with oak leaf cluster. Fellow Aerospace Med. Assn., AAAS, ASHRAE; mem. Am. Phys. Soc., Am. Physiol. Soc., Nat. Acad. Engring. (bioengring. sect.), Conn. Acad. Sci. and Engring. Club: Cosmos (Washington). Home: Branford Conn. Died Feb. 13, 1993.

GALEENER, FRANK LEE, physicist; b. Long Beach, Calif., July 31, 1936; s. Floras Frank and Daisy Elizabeth (Lee) G.; m. Janet Louise Trask, June 7, 1959. S.B., MIT, 1958, S.M., 1962; Ph.D. in Physics, Purdue U., 1970. Physicist Lincoln Lab. MIT, Cambridge, 1959-61, physicist Nat. Magnet Lab., 1961-64; scientist Xerox, Palo Alto (Calif.) Research Ctr., 1970-73, mgr. semicondr., research, 1973-77, prin. scientist, 1977-87; prof. dept. physics Colo. State U., Ft. Collins, 1987-93; mem. com. on recommendations U.S. Army Basic Sci. Research, 1976-79; co-chmn. adv. panel on amorphous materials div. materials sci. Dept. Energy, 1980; mem. adv. panel solid state physics Office Naval Research, 1980. Editor: (with G. Lucovsky) Structure and Excitations of Amorphous Solids, 1976, (with Lucovsky and S.T. Pantelides) The Physics of MOS Insulators, 1980, (with D.L. Griscom and M.J. Weber) Defects in Glasses, 1986. Recipient George W. Morey award Excellence in Glass Rsch., 1993. Fellow Am. Phys. Soc. (life), Am. Ceramic Soc. (life); mem. Optical Soc. Am., Sigma Xi, Sigma Pi Sigma. Home: Fort Collins Colo. Died June 6, 1993.

GALERSTEIN, CAROLYN LIPSHY, educational administrator, educator, researcher; b. Amarillo, Tex. Aug. 14, 1931; d. Harry and Tillie (Swartz) Lipshy; m. Sylvan Busch, Apr. 13, 1952 (dec. Aug. 1966); children—Susan Gail, Alan Lipshy, Saralynn, Lauren Kay; m. George Galerstein, Oct. 31, 1971. BA, U. Mo. 1951; MA, Columbia U., 1957; PhD, U. Md., 1965. Exec. dir. Zale Found., Dallas, 1963-67; asst. prof. U Tex., Arlington, 1968-74, assoc. prof., 1975; dean sch gen. studies U. Tex., Richardson, 1975-91. Author (with others) Profile of the Dallas Woman, 1976; editor Woman Writers of Spain, 1985, Un Noviazgo, 1973. Bd. dirs. Nat. Assembly Social Policy and Devel., N.Y 1964-66, Tex. Coun. Girl Scouts U.S., 1984-91; chairwoman Dallas Commn. Status Women, 1975-77. Mem. Assn. Gen. and Liberal Studies (exec. coun. 1981-83), MLA, AAUW. Democrat. Jewish. Home: Dallas Tex. Deceased.

GALEY, JOHN TAYLOR, geologist; b. Beaver, Pa. Aug. 30, 1907; s. George Banks and Vera MacDonald (Taylor) G.; Blanche Georgene Fishback, Nov. 19, 1938; children: Margaret Elizabeth, John Taylor Jr. BS Princeton U., 1932. Cert. profl. geologist. discoverer first oriskany sand natural gas prodn., Western Pa., Beaver County, 1935, Hancock County, W.Va., 1941 Knox Twp., Columbiana County, Ohio, 1944 Mahoning County, Ohio, 1945, Bedford County, Pa. 1953, W.Va., Ohio, Va.; cons. various gas cos., ind. gas producer; chmn. steering com. Nat. Conf. on Environ Geology, 1969, Nat. Interdisciplinary Conf. on Planning a New Town's Environment, 1971. Trustee Carnegie Mus. Nat. History, Pitts. Fellow Geol. Soc. Am.; mem. Am. Inst. Profl. Geologists (pres. 1968, Ben H. Parker medal 1978), Am. Assn. Petroleum Geologists (pres. Ea sect. 1968-72, hon. mem., Disting. Svc. award 1974, Founders award, 1987, Sidney Powers Meml. medal 1990), Pa. Natural Gas Men's Assn. (pres. 1961-62), Pitts. Geol. Soc. (pres. 1948), Pa. Gas Assn. (hon. life dir.). Home: Somerset Pa. Died May 5, 1992.

GALLAHER, STUART WILLIAM, architect; b. Appleton, Wis., Apr. 11, 1931; s. William U. and Winifred S. (Stuart) G.; m. Emmy Bunks, June 9, 1956; children Stacia Leigh, William Stuart. Student Lawrence U., 1949-50; Barch, U. Ill., 1955. Mem. staff, Shattuck & Siewert Assos. Neenah, Wis., 1957-60; architect John J Flad & Assos., Madison, 1960-64, Fritz & Rosenthal & Assos., Madison, 1964-65; pres. Stuart William Gallaher, Architect, Inc., Madison, 1965-96; U.S. rep Voglauer Mobelwerk, Abtenau, Austria. Mem. City of Madison Bldg. Bd. Examiners and Appeals, 1978-89 mem. City of Madison Bldg. and Fire Code Rev. and Appeals bd., 1989—. 1st lt. 11th Combat Group, C.E. U.S. Army, 1955-57, Europe. Allerton Travelling fellow 1954. Designer: Garner Park Pavilion, Madison, 1975; Hilton Inn, Lake Geneva, Wis., 1976; Olbrich Bot Center Complex, Madison, 1977; Office-Store-Factory Avanti Foods Co., Walnut, Ill., 1978; entrance bldg wiss Hist. Village, New Glarus, Wis., 1979; Chalet andhaus Hotel, New Glarus, 1980; Islamic Student enter Complex, Madison, 1981, Senner Chalet, eamboat Springs, Colo., 1984, Saile Chalet, Galena, ., 1985, Swiss Valley Pavillion, New Glarus, Wis., 86, Lenzlinger Chalet, New Glarus, 1987, Olbrich ot. Complex and Conservatory, Madison, 1989, Chalet andhaus, New Glarus, Wis., 1991. Mem. AIA. Con-egationalist. Died July 27, 1991. Home: Madison Wis.

ALLEGOS, ALPHONSE, bishop; b. Albuquerque, eb. 20, 1931; s. Jose Angel and Caseana (Apodaca) . B.S., St. Thomas Aquinas Coll., 1971; M.S., St. ohn's U., Jamaica, N.Y., 1972; M.E., Loyola U., Los ngeles, 1979. Ordained priest Roman Catholic Ch., 958. Pastor San Miguel Ch., Los Angeles, Our Lady Guadalupe Ch., Sacramento; vicar Hispanics in acramento area; first hispanic bishop Sacramento; Aux. shop of Sacramento, 1981—; pastor Guadalupe Ch., acramento; Vicar gen. Roman Catholic Ch., Sacra-ento, vicar for Hispanics; active campaign for human evel. U.S. Catholic Conf., Washington. Mem. Calif. ovs. Com.; bd. dirs. Sacramento Concilio, Boy Scouts m.; mem. Sacramento Mayor's Hispanic Adv. Com., ounty of Sacramento Multi-Cultural Park Com.; mem. dv. bd. Calif. Hispanic Cath. Inst.; mem. supt. of edn.'s dv. council on Hispanic affairs State of Calif. Recipient lver Beaver award. Home: Sacramento Calif.

ALLO, DEAN ANDERSON, congressman; b. Hack-asack, N.J., Nov. 23, 1935; s. Dean and Selma Anderson) G.; children: Susan, Robert. Ptnr. Gallo-eCroce Real Estate, Parsippany, N.J., 1956-94; v.p. arsippany-Troy Hills Twp. Council, 1968-69, pres., 970; dep. Morris County Bd. Chosen Freeholders, 971-72, dir., 1973-75; mem. N.J. Gen. Assembly 26th ist., 1976-84, minority leader, 1982-84; mem. 99th-03rd Congresses from 11th N.J. dist., Washington, .C., 1985-94; regional whip, mid-Atlantic, New En-and states U.S. House of Reps., Washington, 1985-94; em. appropriations com. U.S. Ho. of Reps., 1989-94, -chair N.E.-Midwest Congl. Coalition, 1991-94. hmn. heart fund N.J. chpt. Am. Heart Assn. of orthwest, Parsippany, 1985-94; vol. Cystic Fibrosis 'alk-a-Thon, March of Dimes. Named Legislator of r., Nat. Republican Legislators Assn., 1982, N.J. ssn. Counties, 1978. Mem. Morris County Bd. ealtors, Parsippany C. of C. Lodge: Elks (charter em.). Home: Morris Plains N.J. Died Nov. 6, 1994.

ALLO, JULIO, vintner; b. 1910; m. Aileen Gallo; 1 ild, Bob. Co-owner E & J Gallo Winery, Modesto, alif. Home: Modesto Calif. Died May 2, 1993.

ALVIN, THOMAS FRANCIS, architect; b. N.Y.C., ct. 18, 1926; s. Thomas J. and Ruth (Cronin) G.; m. Margaret Rowland, Sept. 6, 1948; children: Susan Hall, tephen; m. Gladys Lozano, Aug. 1974; children: homas Francis, Andrew. B.Arch., Pratt Inst., 1950. egistered architect, N.Y., Conn., N.J., Md., Maine, ex. certified Nat. Council Archtl. Registration Bd. 'ith Kokkins & Lyras (architects), 1950-60, assoc., 956-60; also sec. Kolyer Constrn. Corp., N.Y.C.; ptnr. yras, Galvin & Anaya (architects), N.Y.C., 1960-63; so exec. v.p. Lyras-Adams Ltd. Investment Builders, .Y.C.; pvt. practice Thomas F. Galvin, AIA, N.Y.C., 963-64; ptnr. Brown Guenther Battaglia Galvin rchitects), N.Y.C., 1965-70; chmn. N.Y.C. Bd. tandards and Appeals, 1970-72; exec. v.p. N.Y.C. onv. and Exhbn. Ctr. Corp., 1972-74; sr. v.p., chief perating officer Battery Park City Authority, N.Y.C., 974-80; sr. v.p. Olympia & York Equity Corp., N.Y.C., 980-81; pres. Bramalea Tex. Inc., Dallas, 1981-83; res., chief exec. officer N.Y. Conv. Ctr. Devel. Corp. nd N.Y. Conv. Ctr. Operating Corp., 1983-86, Xerox ealty Corp., Stamford, Conn., 1986-93; adj. prof. rchitecture CCNY, 1971-76; cons. on utilization air ghts over govt. owned real property N.Y. Legislature, 964; mem. archtl. adv. com. U. City N.Y., 1967-70, mn., 1970. Rep. candidate Ho. of Reps., 1962, N.Y. enate, 1965; Rep.-Conservative candidate for Pres. of ity Council N.Y.C., 1973; Rep.-Conservative candidate ueens Borough Pres., 1977; trustee Manhattan Coll., .Y.C., St. Vincent's Hosp. and Med. Ctr.; mem. adv. om. Pratt Inst. Sch. Engring., Wharton Sch. Econs. eal Estate Inst., dir. Stamford Partnership. Served ubmarine service with USNR, 1944-46. Fellow AIA ores. N.Y. chpt. 1972-73), N.Y. State Assn. Architects f AIA (pres. 1971-72); mem. Urban Land Inst. Roman atholic. Club: City (N.Y.C.). Home: Flushing N.Y. ied May 1993.

AMBEE, ELEANOR BROWN, deceased writer, ocial services volunteer; b. N.Y.C., Apr. 10, 1904; d. obert Rankins and Elizabeth (Turner) Brown; m. A. umner Gambee, June 1, 1928; children: Sumner Brown, raig, Eleanor Fay, Robert Rankin; dec. Dec. 2, 995. AB, Vassar Coll., 1925; postgrad., Columbia U., 926. Free-lance writer, lectr. on herbs, horticulture, lants in industry various orgns., 1961-95; cons. sect. erbs Nat. Geographic mag., 1983, Reader's Digest uide to Gardening, 1978; researcher, chmn. Chemurgic arden. Author: (collection of essays) A Garden dyssey, 1996; contbr. numerous articles to hort. publs.; ditl. bd. Vassar Alumnae Mag., 1954-56. Trustee wight Sch., Englewood, N.J., 1957-63, First Presbyn. h., Englewood, 1992-95; publicity chair Maternal ealth Ctr. Bergen County, Englewood, 1934-38; v.p., mem. bd. Planned Parenthood Assn. Bergen County, 1938-46; publicity chair No. valley chpt. ARC, 1939-43; 1st v.p. Social Svc. Fedn., Englwood, 1948-52; Englewood Hosp. Devel. Com., 1965-75. Recipient Garden Club Am. Hort. award, 1962, Merit award, 1979, Disting. Svc. award N.Y. Bot. Garden, 1980, Spl. honor The Friends of Horticulture Wave Hill, 1993. Mem. Herb Soc. Am. (past pres.), Corp. N.Y. Bot. Garden, Garden Club Englewood (past pres., hon. mem.). Home: Englewood N.J. Died Dec. 2, 1995.

GAMBLE, GEORGE CLINTON, architect; b. Newark, Mar. 15, 1910; s. George Whiting and Renie (Mackey) G.; m. Virginia Ralston, Sept. 3, 1937 (div.); children: Robert C., Nancy McNeil Lowry; m. Marion Gill, Sept. 2, 1966; children: Gill, Mark, Torre, Thomas, John Paul Smitherman. BArch, U. Miami, 1931. Assoc. Russel T. Pancoast, Miami Beach, Fla., 1931-37, Ft. Lauderdale, Fla., 1937-41; ptnr. Gamble, Pownall, Gilroy, Ft. Lauderdale, 1946-66, Gamble, Gilroy, Ft. Lauderdale, 1966-70, Gamble, Gilroy Martin, Ft. Lauderdale, 1970-75; cons. Gamble, Gilroy, Martin, Moul Architects, Ft. Lauderdale, 1980-87; ptnr. Architectural Network (formerly Gamble-Pezeshkan, Architects & Assocs.), Naples, Fla., 1987-93; ret. Pres. Cultural Affairs, Ft. Lauderdale, 1958, Symphony Assn., Ft. Lauderdale, 1960. Served to lt. comdr. USN, 1942-46; PTO. Fellow AIA (emeritus, nat. sec. 1960, 62, mem. jud. com. 1965)); mem. Lauderdale Yacht Club (commodore 1958). Democrat. Episcopalian. Home: Naples Fla. Died Mar. 11, 1994.

GANDHI, RAJIV, former prime minister of India; b. Bombay, Aug. 20, 1944; s. Firoze and Indira G.; m. Sonia Maino, 1968; children: Rahul, Priyanka. Grad. mech. engring., Trinity Coll., Cambridge, Eng., 1965; grad., Imperial Coll., London, 1965. Pilot Indian Airlines, 1972-81; elected to Lok Sabha (Ho. of People of Parliament) from Amethi Uttar Pradesh, 1981, 84; mem. Nat. Exec. of Indian Youth Congress, 1981-83; gen. sec. Indian Nat. Congress, 1983-84; pres. Indian Nat. Congress (now All India Congress Com.), 1984-91; prime minister India, 1984-89, past minister of program implementation, personnel and adminstrv. reforms, and planning, past minister sci. and tech., personnel, and atomic energy and space. Home: New Delhi India Assassinated May 21, 1991.

GANESAN, ADAYAPALAM TYAGARAJAN, geneticist, educator, researcher; b. Madras, India, May 15, 1932; s. Adayapalam Vasudeva Tyagarajan and Savitri G.; m. Ann Katherine Cook, Aug. 3, 1963. B.S., Annamalai U., Madras State, India, 1952, M.A., 1953; Ph.D., Stanford U., 1963. Research fellow Indian Inst., Bangalore, 1953-55; research asst. Indian Agrl. Research Inst., New Delhi, 1955-57; research fellow Carlsberg Lab., Copenhagen, Denmark, 1957-59; successively grad. student, research assoc., asst. prof., assoc. prof. Stanford U., Calif., 1959-76, prof. genetics, 1977-91. Contbr. articles to profl. jours. Charter mem. World Wildlife Fund, U.S.A. Fellow Indian Inst. Sci., 1953-55, Rask-Orsted Found. of Denmark, 1957-59; research career devel. awardee NIH, 1970-75; recipient Calif. Higher Med. Edn. award Am. Lung Assn., 1975-76; sabbatical yr. dept. biochemistry Oxford U., Eng. Mem. AAAS, Genetics Soc. Am. Home: Menlo Park Calif. Died Dec. 1, 1991.

GANILAU, SIR PENAIA KANATABATU, Fijian government official; b. Fiji, July 28, 1918; m. Adi Laisa Delaisomosomo, 1949 (dec. 1971); children: Adi Mei Kainona, Ratu Epeli Gavidi, Adi Lusiana Sivo, Ratu Jone Rakuro, Ratu Josefa Sukuna, Ratu Isoa Fugawai, Ratu Jone Rabici; m. 2d, Adi Davila Liliwaimanu, 1975 (dec. 1984). Student Devonshire course for adminstrn. officers, Wadham Coll., Oxford U., 1947. With Colonial Adminstrn. Svc., 1947, dist. officer, 1948-53; mem. Commonwealth on Fijian Post Primary Edn. in the Colony, 1953; Fijian econ. devel. officer, Roko Tui Cakaudrove, 1956; tour mgr., govt. rep. Fiji Rugby Football tour, N.Z., 1957; dep. sec. for Fijian affairs, 1961-65, minister for Fijian affairs and local govt., 1965-72, leader govt. bus., minister for communications, works and tourism, from 1972, dep. prime minister of Fiji, minister for Fijian affairs and rural devel., gov.-gen., comdr.-in-chief of Fiji, 1983-87, pres., 1987-93; mem. Council of Ministers; ofcl. mem. Legis. Council; chmn. Fijian Affairs Bd.; mem. Fijian Devel. Fund Bd., Native Land Trust Bd., Gt. Council of Chiefs; sr. chief Tovata Confederacy, 1988-93. Served with Fiji Inf. Regt., 1940-46, hon. col. 2d bn., 1973, col., 1979; with Fiji Mil. Forces, 1953-56. Decorated knight Order Brit. Empire, Knight grand class St. Michael and St. George, Knight Companion Royal Victorian Order, Disting. Service Order. Home: Suva Fiji Died Dec. 15, 1993.

GANT, WILLIAM MILTON, state supreme court justice; b. Owensboro, Ky., Nov. 25, 1919; s. Archibald Stuart and Mattie Ellis (Sloane) G.; m. Mary Ellen Price, Dec. 27, 1951; children: Stuart Price, Walter Sloane (dec.). A.B., Transylvania U., 1940; LL.B., U. Ky., 1947. Bar: Ky. 1947, fed. cts. 1947, U.S. Supreme Ct. 1966. Commonwealth atty. 6th Jud. Dist., Owensboro, 1962-76; judge Ky. Ct. Appeals, Frankfort, 1976-83; justice Supreme Ct. Ky., Frankfort, 1983-95. Curator Transylvania U., Lexington, Ky., 1968-95. Served to 1st lt. USAAF, 1942-45. Recipient Disting. Service award Ky. Med. Assn., 1972; recipient Disting. Service award Ky. Council on Crime and Delinquency, 1973. Mem. ABA, Am. Judicature Soc., Ky. Bar Assn., U. Ky. Alumni Assn. (nat. pres. 1958-59, 64-65, Disting. Svc. award). Democrat. Mem. Christian Ch. Home: Owensboro Ky. Died Sept. 10, 1995.

GARBÁTY, MARIE LOUISE, art collector and patron; b. Berlin, Ger., Mar. 9, 1910; widowed. Patron, Met. Opera, N.Y.C. Opera; patron, hon. mem. Allentown (Pa.) Art Mus.; mem. N.Y.C. Opera Guild; fellow in perpetuity Met. Mus. Art; life fellow Mus. Fine Arts, Boston; internat. centennial patron Mus. Fine Arts, Boston; benefactor, life mem. Chrysler Mus., Norfolk, Va.; assoc. mem. Solomon Guggenheim Mus., N.Y.C., co-founder Am. Shakespeare Festival Theater, Stratford, Conn.; friend N.Y.C. Library; mem. Am. Fedn. Art, China Inst. Am. Inc., N.Y.C., Asia Soc., N.Y.C., Art Mus., Palm Beach, Fla.; donations numerous museums, libraries, profl. socs., including Met. Mus. Art, N.Y.C. Deceased. Home: New York N.Y.

GARCIA, JERRY (JEROME JOHN GARCIA), guitarist, composer; b. San Francisco, Aug. 1, 1942; s. Jose and Ruth G.; m. Sarah Katz (div.), daughter: Heather; m. Carolyn Adams (div.), children: Annabelle, Trixie; m. Deborah Koons, Feb. 14, 1994. Played guitar, banjo in folk music duo with Sarah Garcia; musician various groups, 1959-65; founding mem. rock group The Warlocks, 1965, The Grateful Dead, 1966—; Broadway performance Jerry Garcia, Acoustic and Electric, 1987; composer: songs China Cat Sunflower; albums include The Grateful Dead, 1967, Anthem of the Sun, 1968, Aoxomoxoa, 1969, Live Dead, 1969, Workingman's Dead, 1970, American Beauty, 1970, Vintage Dead, 1970, Historic Dead, 1970, Grateful Dead, 1971, Europe, 1972, History of the Grateful Dead, Volume 1: Bear's Choice, 1973, Wake of the Flood, 1973, Skeletons From the Closet, 1974, From the Mars Hotel, 1974, Blues for Allah, 1975, Steal Your Face, 1976, Terrapin Station, 1977, What A Long, Strange Trip It's Been, 1977, Shakedown Street, 1978, Go To Heaven, 1980, Beckoning, 1981, Dead Set, 1981, In The Dark, 1987, Infrared Roses, 1992; solo lp's Hooteroll, 1971, Garcia, 1972, Live at the Keystone, 1973, Compliments of Garcia, 1974, Old & In The Way, 1975, Reflections, 1976, Cats Under the Stars, 1978, Run for the Roses, 1982, (with Ornette Coleman) Virgin Beauty, 1988, (with Grateful Dead and Bob Dylan) Dylan and the Dead, 1989, Built to Last, 1989, Without A Net, 1990, One From The Vault, 1991, Jerry Garcia Band, 1991, (with David Grisman) Garcia/Grisman Acoustic, (with Howard Wales) Hooteroll?; Co-author: Garcia: Signpost to a New Age. Served with U.S. Army, 1959. Band Grateful Dead inducted into Rock & Roll Hall of Fame, 1994. Died August 9, 1995.

GARCIA ROBLES, ALFONSO, Mexican diplomat; b. Mar. 20, 1911; s. Quirino and Theresa Robles Garcia; m. Juana Maria de Szyszlo, 1950; 2 children. LL.B., U. Nacional Autonoma de Mexico, 1933; LL.D., U. Paris, 1937; diploma, Acad. Internat. Law, The Hague, The Netherlands, 1938. Entered Mexican Fgn. Service, 1939—; head dept. internat. orgns., later dir. gen. of Polit. Affairs and Diplomatic Service, 1941-46, dir. div. polit. affairs UN Secretariat, 1946-57, head dept. for Europe, Asia and Africa, Mexican Ministry of Fgn. Affairs, 1957-61, ambassador to Brazil, 1962-64, under-sec. for Fgn. Affairs, 1964-71, permanent rep. to UN, 1971-75, sec. Fgn. Affairs, 1975-76, pres. Preparatory Com. for the Denuclearization of Latin Am., 1964-67, permanent rep. to Disarmament Conf., Geneva, 1977—; chmn. Mexican del. to UN Gen. Assembly on disarmament, N.Y.C., 1978. Author: Le Panaméricanisme et la Politique de Bon Voisinage, 1938; La Question du Petrole au Mexique et le Droit International, 1939; La Sorbona Ayer y Hoy, 1943; México en la Postguerra, 1944; La Conferencia de San Francisco y su Obra, 1946; Política Internacional de México, 1946; Ecos del Viejo Mundo, 1946; El Mundo de la Postguerra, 2 vols., 1946; La Conferencia de Ginebra y la Anchura del Mar Territorial, 1959; La Anchura del Mar Territorial, 1966; The Denuclearization of Latin America, 1967; El Tratado de Tlatelolco.-Génesis, Alcance y Propósitos de la Proscripción de las Armas Nucleares en la América Latina, 1967; México en las Naciones Unidas, 2 vols., 1970; Mesures de Désarmement dans des Zones Particulières: Le Traité visant l'Interdiction des Armes Nucleaires en Amérique Latine, 1971; La Proscripción de las Armas Nucleares en la América Latina, 1975; Seis Años de la Política Exterior de México, 1970-1976; La Conferencia de Revisión del Tratado sobre la no Proliferación de las Armas Nucleares, 1977; 338 Días de Tlatelolco, 1977; La Asamblea General del Desarme, 1979; El Comité de Desarme, 1980. Shared Nobel Peace Prize, 1982. Home: Geneva Switzerland Died Sept. 3, 1991.

GARDNER, R. H. (RUFUS HALLETTE GARDNER, III), retired drama and film critic; b. Mayfield, Ky., July 25, 1918; s. Rufus Hallette and Kathleen (Moorman) G. BA, Tex. Christian U., 1941. Aircraft engr. Glenn L. Martin Co., 1941-49; reporter, feature writer Balt. Sun, 1951-54, drama critic, 1954-84, film critic, 1954-81; vis. lectr. Goucher Coll., 1968; lectr. Humanities Inst., 1976-77; film critic Sta. WMAR-TV, 1976-77, drama critic, 1976-80; lectr. Balt. Film Forum Sem., 1978; drama and film critic Sta. WBJC Pub. Radio, 1981-86;

instr. feature writing dept. mass communications Towson State U., fall 1985. Author: (plays) I.O.U. Jeremiah, 1950, Christabel and the Rubicon, 1969, (books) The Splintered Stage: The Decline of the American Theatre, 1965, Those Years: Recollections of a Baltimore Newspaper Man, 1990. Bd. dirs. Balt. Internat. Film Festival, 1975-81. Mem. Am. Theater Critics Assn., Authors League, Dramatists Guild, Am. Newspaper Guild. Home: Baltimore Md. Died Mar. 4, 1995.

GARLAND, CHARLES STEDMAN, JR., investment banker; b. N.Y.C., Sept. 17, 1927; s. Charles and Aurelia (Stoner) G.; B.A., Yale U., 1949; m. Joan B. Cardwell, Sept. 17, 1954; children: Margaret, Elizabeth, Charles. With Merrill Lynch, Pierce, Fenner & Smith, N.Y.C., 1950-52, Louisville, 1952-54, Alex Brown & Sons, Balt., 1954-90, ptnr., 1964-90. Pres., Balt. Opera Co., 1979-90; trustee Chesapeake Bay Found., 1980-90. Served in USN, 1945-46. Republican. Episcopalian. Clubs: Elkridge, Maryland, Yale, Ausable. Home: Baltimore Md.

GARLINGTON, JAMES CLARKE, lawyer; b. Missoula, Mont, Mar. 24, 1908; s. Osa Clarke and Jessie Olive (Slaughter) G.; m. Nancy Hammatt, Sept. 13, 1933; children—Richard, Suzanne Garlington Winters, Janet Garlington. A.B., U. Mont., 1930, J.D., 1930. Bar: Mont. 1929, U.S. Ct. Appeals (9th cir.) 1930. Ptnr. Pope & Garlington, 1930-35; ptnr. Murphy, Garlington & Pauly, 1939-54; sr. ptnr. Garlington Lohn & Robinson, Missoula, Mont., 1954-95; prof. Mont. U. Law Sch., 1946-60. Served with USNR, 1942-45. Mem. ABA, Mont. Bar Assn. (pres. 1949-50), Am. Law Inst., Am. Coll. Probate Counsel, Sigma Chi, Phi Delta Phi. Republican. Episcopalian. Lodge: Rotary (pres. Missoula 1955-56). Home: Missoula Mont. Died Apr. 1, 1995.

GARMAN, WILLARD HERSHEL, former government official, scientist; b. Indiana County, Pa., Oct. 21, 1912; s. Warren H. and Effie (Berringer) G.; m. Edna Webb, Aug. 25, 1938; children: Shirley Garman Brown, Warren Webb. BS, Pa. State U., 1933, MS, 1934, PhD, 1939. Asst., then assoc. prof. agronomy U. Ga., 1939-42; soil scientist S.C Agrl. Experiment Sta., Clemson, 1942-47; head dept. agronomy U. Ark., 1947-49; prin. soil scientist Experiment Stas. div. USDA, Washington, 1949-54; chmn. Nat. Soil Rsch. Com., 1952-54; chief agriculturist Nat. Plant Food Inst., Washington, 1954-64; v.p. Fertilizer Inst., Washington, 1964-71; sr. chem. specialist AID, Washington, 1971-74, chief crop prodn. div., 1974-76. Contbr. articles to sci. jours. and mags. Lt. USNR, 1944-46, on staff of Fleet Adm. Nimitz, Pearl Harbor and Guam. Fellow AAAS, Soil Sci. Soc. Am. (div. chmn. 1957-58), Am. Soc. Agronomy (bd. dirs. 1953-54, 58-59, pres. so. br. 1952-53, pres. N.E. br. 1964-65); mem. Internat. Soil Sci. Soc., Soil Conservation Soc., Am. Chem. Soc., Cosmos Club, Internat. Club, Sigma Xi, Gamma Sigma Delta, Delta Theta Sigma. Home: Pinehurst N.C. Died Jan. 21, 1995.

GARNSWORTHY, LEWIS SAMUEL, archbishop; b. Edmonton, Alta., Can., July 18, 1922; m. Jean Valance Allen, Aug. 7, 1954; children—Peter, Katherine. B.A., U. Alta., 1943; L.Th., Wycliffe Coll., Toronto, Ont., Can., 1945, D.D. (hon.), 1968; D.D. (hon.), Trinity Coll., Toronto, 1973, Huron Coll., London, Ont., 1976. Ordained deacon Anglican Ch. Can., 1945, priest, 1946; curate, then rector chs. in Ont., 1946, 68; suffragan bishop Anglican Ch. Can. Diocese Toronto, 1968-72, bishop, 1972-79, archbishop of Toronto, 1979-88, met. of Ont., 1971-79. Fellow Coll. Preachers; mem. Albany Club. Home: Don Mills Can.

GARRETT, SYLVESTER, arbitrator; b. Elkins Park, Pa., Dec. 15, 1911; s. Sylvester S. and Mary (Thompson) G.; m. Mary Alexander Yard, Aug. 30, 1938; children—Joan Hickcox, James Yard, John Sharpless. A.B., Swarthmore Coll., 1933; LL.B., U. Pa., 1936. Chmn. Regional War Labor Bd., Phila., 1942-45; vice chmn. Nat. Wage Stblzn. Bd., Washington, 1946; coordinator labor relations Libbey-Owens-Ford Glass Co., Toledo and Pitts. Plate Glass Co., 1946-49; prof. law Stanford U., 1949-51; chmn. bd. arbitration U.S. Steel Co. and United Steelworkers, 1951-79; impartial chmn. U.S. Postal Service and Postal Workers Unions, 1974-79; chmn. Iron Ore Industry Bd. of Arbitration, 1979-89; chmn. arbitration panel Newport News Shipbldg. and United Steelworkers, 1980-96; Disting. vis. prof. Ind. U. of Pa., 1987-89. Author: (with L. Reed Tripp) Management Problems Implicit in Multi-Employer Bargaining, 1950. Mem. citizens assembly Health and Welfare Assn. Allegheny County, 1963-69; Trustee Community Services Pa. Mem. Nat. Acad. Arbitrators (gov. 1956-58, pres. 1963, exec. com. 1964-65, chmn. com. on ethics and grievances 1965-68), Am., Pa. bar assns., Indsl. Relations Research Assn. (counsel 1953-57), Am. Arbitration Assn. (panel arbitrators). Home: Stahlstown PA Died Jan. 11, 1996.

GARRETTE, MARVIN E., newspaper editor; b. Woodstock, Va., Dec. 10, 1938; s. James E. and Clarice I. (Williams) G.; m. Anne Elizabeth Hill, July 21, 1961 (div. 1981); children: Catherine E. Garrette Athaide, Jessica Tucker Garrette Beisel, Sarah Blair; m. Jo Ann Bledsoe, Nov. 4, 1983. B.A. in English Lit., U. Va., 1961, postgrad., 1961-62; postgrad., Am. Press Inst., 1970. Bur. reporter Richmond Times-Dispatch, Va., 1960-64, asst. state editor, 1965-68, spl. projects editor, 1968-70, asst. mng. editor, 1970-82, mng. editor, 1982-92; tchr. U. Richmond, Va. Commonwealth U., Va. Union U., Math-Sci. Ctr. Bd. dirs. Leadership Metro Richmond, 1982-83, Va. High Sch. League Pubs. div., Charlottesville, 1970-92. Ford Found. grantee, 1969. Mem. Soc. of Profl. Journalists (nat. bd. dirs., regional dir. 1980-83), Sigma Delta Chi. Baptist. Club: Bull & Bear. Home: Richmond Va. Deceased.

GARRONE, GABRIEL MARIE CARDINAL, former archbishop of Toulouse; b. Aix-les-Bains, France, Oct. 12, 1901; s. Jean and Josephine (Mathieu) G.; Diploma Advanced Studies in Philosophy; Doctorate Scholastic Philosophy and Theology; licence ès lettres in Philosophie, certificat d'etudes Supérieures de Philosophie. Ordained priest Roman Catholic Ch., 1925; prof., superior Grand Sem. Chambery; archbishop-coadjutor Toulouse, 1947; archbishop of Toulouse and Narbonne, primate Gaule narbonnaise, 1956-66; v.p. Permanent Council Plenary Assembly French Episcopate, 1964-66; pro-prefect Congregation for Cath. Edn. Rome, 1966, prefect, 1968; chargé des Rapports de L'Eglise avec la Culture, 1980; created cardinal, 1967. Decorated grand cross Legion of Honor, Croix de Guerre. Author: Psalms and Prayers; Invitation to Prayer; Lessons on Faith; The Credo's Moral; The Door to Scriptures; Holy Church Out Mother; The Credo's Panorama; There is Your Mother; Catholic Action; Faith and Pedagogy; The Eucharist; Why Pray?; The Nun, Sign of God in the World; Psalms, Prayer for Today; Offers to God and to the World; Lord, Tell Me Your Name; Christian Morals and Human Values; What Must One Believe?; Le Concile, Orientations; Lumen Gentium; Gaudium et spes; Qu'est-ce que Dieu? L'Eucharistie au secours de la foi; Religieuse aujourd'hui? Oui, mais..., 1969; Prier quinze jours avec Vatican II; translations: What God Is; What Theresa of Lisieux Believed; Eucharistic and Belief; Que faut-il faire? Ce que croyait Pascal; L'Eglise 1965-72; la Foi en 1973; la Foi au fil des jours; Le Credo lu dans l'histoire; Pour vous qui sus-je? Aller jusqu'à Dieu; Le Prêtre; Marie, hier et aujourd'hui; Parole et Eucharistie; La Foi tout entière; Je suis le Chemin; Ce que croyait Jeanne Jugan; Ce que croyait Anne-Marie Javouhey; 50 ans de vie d'Eglise; Synode 85; La Communion fraternelle "dernière volontē" du Seigneur: Pour une prēsentation sommaire et ordonnée de la foi. Home: Rome Italy

GARSON, GREER, actress; b. No. Ireland, Sept. 29, 1908; d. George and Nina Sophia (Greer) G.; m. Edward A. Snelson (div.); m. Richard Ney, 1943 (div.); m. E. E. Fogelson, 1949 (dec. 1987). BA with honors, London U.; student, Grenoble U.; HHD (hon.), Rollins Coll., 1950; D of Communication Arts (hon.), Coll. of Santa Fe, 1970; LittD (hon.), Ulster U., 1977. Actress Birmingham (Eng.) Repertory Theatre, 1932-33. Appeared numerous London plays in lead roles; films include Goodbye Mr. Chips, Pride and Prejudice, When Ladies Meet, Blossoms in the Dust, Mrs. Miniver (Acad. award), Random Harvest, Madame Curie, Mrs. Parkington, Julius Caesar, The Law and the Lady, Her Twelve Men, Sunrise at Campobello (Golden Globe award), Strange Lady in Town, The Singing Nun, The Happiest Millionaire; plays include Auntie Mame, Tonight at 8:30, Captain Brassbound's Conversion; also appeared in pioneer British TV and Am. TV. Prin. founding donor Fogelson Forum Dallas Presbyn. Hosp., Fogelson Libr., Greer Garson Theatre, Garson Communications Ctr. and Studios Coll. of Santa Fe, Fogelson Pavillion at Meyerson Symphony Ctr., Dallas; Greer Garson Theatre at So. Meth. U., Dallas. Co-recipient U.S. Dept. of Interior Conservation Svc. award, 1981, many internat. awards. Home: Dallas Tex. Died Apr. 6, 1996.

GARSTON, GERALD DREXLER, artist; b. Waterbury, Conn., May 3, 1925; s. Leonard Alexander and Rose Sarah G.; m. Lois Muriel Freed, July 11, 1948; children: Priscilla Blythe, Joanne Hope. B.A., Johns Hopkins U., 1951. Tchr. Paier Sch. Art, Hamden, Conn., 1974-83, Creative Arts Workshop, New Haven, 1969-84. One-man shows include Creative Arts Workshop, New Haven, 1985, Pucker Safrai Gallery, Boston, 1970-72, 74, 76, 78, 80, 82, 84, 86, 88, 90, 93, Freedman Art Gallery of Albright Coll., Reading, Pa., 1977, Kendall Gallery, Wellfleet, Mass., 1973, Graham Gallery, N.Y.C., 1967, Winfisky Gallery of Salem (Mass.) State Coll., 1970, group shows include Diamonds Are Forever, Artists and Writers on Baseball, N.Y. State Mus., Albany, 1987, Sport Mus., N.Y.C., 1967, Boston Mus. Fine Arts, 1966, A. M. Sachs Gallery, N.Y.C., 1965, Stable Gallery, N.Y.C., 1964, Betty Parsons Gallery, N.Y.C., 1960, represented in permanent collections Harvard U. Fogg Mus., Los Angeles County Mus., William Rockhill Nelson Gallery Art, Kansas City, Mo., New Britain (Conn.) Mus. Am. Art, Phila. Mus. Art, Brandeis U. Rose Mus., Waltham, Mass., Wadsworth Athenaeum, Hartford, Conn., Worcester (Mass.) Art Mus., DeCordova Mus., Lincoln, Mass., Currier Gallery Art, Manchester, N.H., Boston Pub. Libr. Served with USNR, 1943-46. Decorated D.F.C., Air medal with 3 oak leaf clusters. Mem. Artists Equity Assn., Phi Beta Kappa. Home: Bernardston Mass. Died Apr. 2, 1994; interred South Cemetary, Leyton, Mass.

GARTH, THOMAS G., youth organization adminis trator. Pres. Boys and Girls Clubs of Am., Atlanta. Home: Roswell Ga. Died Jan. 3, 1996.

GASSEN, JOSEPH ALBERT, lawyer, former judge; b Louisville, Apr. 15, 1926; s. Albert and Ruth (Bordor Gassenheimer; m. Phyllis Ganey, June 20, 1954; chi dren: Pamela Gassen Alonso, Tod. BS in Commerce, U N.C., 1946; JD, U. Miami, 1949. Bar: Fla. 1949, U.S Dist. Ct. (so. dist.) Fla. 1949, U.S. Ct. Appeals (5th cir 1956, U.S. Ct. Appeals (11th cir.) 1980, U.S. Ct. Mi Appeals 1958, U.S. Supreme Ct 1958. Assoc., Charle Danton, Miami Beach, Fla., 1949-54; atty. Office Pric Stabilization, Miami, 1951-52; sole practice, Miam 1954-58; ptnr. Jepeway & Gassen, Miami, 1958-7 Jepeway, August, Gassen & Pohlig, Miami, 1977-78 August, Gassen, Pohlig and Milstein, Miami, 1978-80 judge U.S. Bankruptcy Ct. So. Dist. Fla., Miami, 1980 84; of counsel Paul, Landy, Beiley & Harper, 1984-86 ptnr. Stroock & Stroock & Lavan, Miami, 1986-88 Mershon, Sawyer, Johnston, Dunwody & Cole, Mia 1988-93. Pres. Family and Children's Svcs., 1973-7 Miami Lighthouse for Blind, 1986-87; past mem numerous civic orgns. Served to lt. USNR, 1943-4 Mem. Nat. Conf. Bankruptcy Judges, Dade County Ba Assn. (pres. 1968-69), Assn. Former Bankruptcy Judge Democrat. Jewish. Lodge: Masons (Miami). Died 199 Home: Miami Fla.

GASSMAN, PAUL GEORGE, chemistry educator; b Buffalo, June 22, 1935; s. Joseph Martin and Florenc Marie (Rautenstrauch) G.; m. Gerda Ann Rozler, Au 17, 1957; children: Deborah, Michael, Vicki, Nanc Amy, Kimberly, Eric. B.S., Canisius Coll., 1957; Ph.D Cornell U., 1960. Asst. prof. Ohio State U., Columbu 1961-66; assoc. prof. Ohio State U., 1966-69, prof 1969-74; chmn. dept. chemistry U. Minn., Mpls., 197 79, prof. chemistry, 1974-88, Regents prof., 1988-9 cons. Ricerca Inc., Smith Kline Beecham, PPG Indu tries. Contbr. articles to profl. jours.; editor 11 book Patentee in field. Alfred P. Sloan fellow, 1967-6 recipient James R. Crowdle Disting. Alumni awar Canisius Coll., 1971, Pres.'s medal, 1991; Nat. Cataly awrd Chem. Mfrs. Assn., 1990. Fellow NAS, AAA Am. Acad. Arts and Scis., Japan Soc. Promotion of Sci mem. Am. Chem. Soc. (pres. 1990, award in petroleu chemistry 1972, Biann award Minn. sect. 1983, Jame Flack Norris award in phys. organic chemistry 198 Arthur C. Cope Scholar award 1986), Chem. So London, Am. Inst. Chemists (Chem. Pioneers awar 1990), Coun. for Chem. Rsch. (chmn. 1986-87). Hom Saint Paul Minn. Died Apr. 21, 1993.

GATES, EDWIN WILDER, physician; b. Nashu N.H., May 18, 1900; s. Edwin Lewis and Alice (Wilde G.; m. Agnes Jessie Cameron, Dec. 22, 1922; 1 so Edwin Wilder. B.S., Colby Coll., 1922, D.Sc. (hon. 1968; M.D., Harvard, 1926. Intern U.S. Marine Hosp S.I., N.Y., 1926-27; resident U.S. Marine Hosp., 192 29; chief medicine Mt. St. Mary's Hosp., 1947-50, chi staff, 1950-54, hon. cons. diabetes, from 1966; chi medicine Niagara Falls (N.Y.) Meml. Hosp., 1950-6 head div. diabetes, 1959-69, hon. chief medicine, fro 1967; dir. Katherine Nye Bartlett Diabetic Teachin Unit, from 1966; instr. medicine Niagara U. Sc Nursing, 1947-50; Established Niagara Falls Diabet Assn., 1954; continuous gen. med. audit Niagara Fal Meml. Hosp., 1955; pub. med. forums Niagara Fal Meml. Hosp. and Mt. St. Mary's Hosp., 1957, div. d abetes Niagara Falls Meml. Hosp., 1959, Dr. Charles F Best Birthplace Trust, Inc., 1959. Author: (with other Diabetes Mellitus: Diagnosis and Treatment, 1964; al articles. Treas. Niagara Falls Community Chest, 194 49; Bd. dirs. Children's Aid Soc., 1933-35, Niagara Fal YMCA, 1933-39. Served with U.S. Army, 1918. Recipient Colby Coll. gavel Colby Coll. Alumni Assn 1968. Fellow ACP; mem. Am. Diabetes Assn. (bd. dir 1955-69, pres. 1967-68, Banting medal 1968), AM Buffalo Acad. Medicine, Niagara County Med. So N.Y. State Med. Soc. (chmn. subcom. diabetes 195 Am., Western N.Y. socs. internal medicine, Phi Be Kappa. Home: Niagara Falls N.Y. Deceased.

GAUTREAUX, MARCELIAN FRANCIS, JR., retir chemical company executive; b. Nashville, Jan. 17, 193 s. Marcelian Francis and Mary Eunice (Terrebonne) G m. Mignon Alice Thomas, Apr. 26, 1952; childre Marcelian III, Marian, Kevin, Andrée. BSChem magna cum laude, La. State U., 1950, MSChemE, 195 PhD in Chem. Engring, 1958, DSc (hon.), 1991. Wi Ethyl Corp., Baton Rouge, 1951-55, 58-86, gen. m dept. R & D, 1968-69, v.p., 1969-74, sr. v.p., 1974-8 advisor to exec. com., 1981-86, also bd. dirs.; instr. L State U., 1955-56, asst. prof. chem. engring., 1956-5 mem. sci. adv. com. Biotech Research Lab., Inc., 198 84. Author in field. Bd. dirs. Baton Rouge Communi Concerts Assn., 1974-85, pres., 1981-85; trustee La. A and Sci. Center, Baton Rouge, 1974-77; mem. La. Sta U. Found., 1978-87; chmn. adv. com. dept. chem. eng ing. La. State U., 1981-83, mem., 1983-86, mem. ac com. Coll. of Engring., 1986-94. Recipient (chart Personal Achievement in Chem. Engring. award Che Engring. Mag., 1968; Charles E. Coates Meml. awa Am. Chem. Soc./Am. Inst. Chem. Engrs., 1976; A Meml. award Chem. Mktg. Research Assn., 1978; B Paper award, 1980, Disting. Delta Chi award 19 charter mem. La. State U. Engring. Hall of Distinctio 1979; named to La. State U. Alumni Hall of Distincti

₹5, Ethyl established Ethyl/Gautreaux chair in chem. ;ring., 1986. Fellow Am. Inst. Chem. Engrs. (Best sented Paper award 1952); mem. Nat. Acad. Engr-, Soc. Chem. Industry, Soc. Engring. Sci. (past dir.), t. Amorphous Studies (sci. adv. com. 1982-86), em. Mktg. Research Assn. (hon.). Roman Catholic. ıbs: Country of La., Baton Rouge Country. Home: :on Rouge La. Died Feb. 13, 1994.

.VENUS, EDWARD RICHARD, banker; b. King-n, Pa., June 13, 1932; s. Edward A. and Bertha (Bel-G.; m. Ruth Madeline James, Apr. 30, 1954; chil-n: Gary, Edward, Paul, James. Student, Wharton ., U. Pa., 1951-54, Wilkes Coll., 1954-61. With First stern Bank N.A., Wilkes-Barre, 1950-93; asst. cashier st Eastern Bank N.A., 1959-62, asst. v.p., 1962-67, ., 1967-72, sr. v.p., cashier, 1972-93; instr. Am. Inst. ıking, 1963-85; cons. Wilkes-Barre Area Voc-Tech. . Automation Com., 1962-93. Bd. dirs. Community unseling Services of N.E. Pa., 1976-93; mem. Luzerne unty Police Automation Com., 1980-88. Recipient sley A. Kuhn Math. award Wyo. Sem. Dean Sch. ., 1950. Mem. Am. Inst. Banking (chpt. pres. 1961- nat. pres. 1972-73), Data Processing Mgmt. Assn., ı. Bankers Assn. (ops. and automation ednl. com. '7-81), Pa. Bankers Assn. (chmn. data processing n. 1969-70), Third Dist. Automated Clearinghouse sn. (dir. 1980-93, pres. 1987), C. of C. Republican. ethodist. Lodge: Masons. Home: Wilkes Barre Pa. ed Nov. 28, 1993.

:BHARD, DAVID, museum director, educator; b. nnon Falls, Minn., July 21, 1927; s. Walter J. and n (Olson) G.; m. Patricia Peeke, July 7, 1954; chil-n: Ellen Jean, Tyra Ann. BA, U. Minn., 1949, MA, 51, PhD, 1957; Doc. degree (hon.) Fine Arts, Otis son Sch. of Art and Design, 1992. Curator, instr. art N.Mex., 1953-55; dir. Roswell (N.Mex.) Mus., 1955- prof. art, dir. art galleries U. Calif., Santa Barbara, 51-80; curator archtl. drawing collection Art Mus., 30-96; bd. dirs. Archtl. Review Co., Santa Barbara; d rsch. in archeology, summers 1949-57; Fulbright of. Tech. U. Istanbul, Turkey, 1960-61; cons. hist. servation, 1970-96. Author: Prehistoric Cave Paint-s of the Diablo Region of Texas, 1960, A Guide to Architecture of Purcell and Elmslie, 1960, A Guide Architecture in Southern California, 1964, R.M. hindler: Architect; Architecture in California, 1868-58, 1968, Kem Weber and the Moderene, 1969, The chfield Building, 1928-1968, 1969, Charles F.A. ysey, Architect, 1970, Architecture in Los Angeles, A mplete Guide, 1985, An Arcadian Landscape: The rdens of A.E. Hanson, 1920-31, 1985, Santa Barbara: Pueblo Viejo, 1986, Romanza: The California chitecture of Frank Lloyd Wright, 1988; co-author: yd Wright, Architect, 1972, High Style Design, itney Museum American Art, 1985, A Guide to chitecture in San Francisco and Northern California, 73, 2d edit., 1986, Indian Art of the Northern Plains, 74, Los Angeles in the 30's, 1989; Bay Area Houses, 76, A Guide to Architecture in Los Angeles and ıthern California, 1977, A Guide to Architecture in nnesota, 1977, 200 Years of American Architectural awing, 1977, A View of California Architecture, 50-1976, 1977, Picturesque California Homes, 1978, e Architecture of Samuel and J.C. Newsom, 1878-08, 1979, The Architecture of Gregory Ain, 1980, lifornia Crazy, 1980, Tulsa Art Deco, 1980, Santa rbara, the Creation of a New Spain in America, 1980, gacy of Minneapolis, 1983, Frank Lloyd Wright in lifornia, 1987, Los Angeles in the 30s, 1989, The nerican Art Deco and Streamine Moderne, 1991, tah Maria Riggs: A Woman Within the California chitectural Scene, 1992, Robert Stacy-Judd: Maya chitecture, The Creation of a New Style, 1993, Build-s of Iowa, 1993, The Architectural Drawings of R.M. hindler, 4 vols., 1993, Los Angeles: An Architectural ide, 1994; editor: California Architects & Architec-e Series; mem. editor com. U. Calif. Press; contbr. icles to profl. jours. Pres. Citizens Planning Assn. nta Barbara County, Inc., 1970-76; vice chmn. His-ic Landmark Commn., Santa Barbara, 1973-96, Ci-ens Planning Assn., 1980-96; bd. dirs. Regional Plan sn., So. Calif., Western Found.; chmn. Montecito chtl. Bd., 1988-89. With AUS, 1945-47; pres. Ham-nds Meadow Preserve, 1990-96. With AUS, 1945-47. sch. grantee NSF; rsch. grantee NEA; rsch. grantee t. Endowment Humanities; Nat. Park Svc. grantee; rd found. grantee study Turkish architecture, 1965; ggenheim Found. fellow, 1980-81. Mem. AIA (hon. t.) 1989, M. Riggs award), Soc. Am. Archaeology, n. Anthrop. Assn., Coll. Art Assn., Soc. Archtl. His-ians (pres. 1980-81, bd. dir.), Archtl. Found. Santa rbara (bd. dirs.). Home: Santa Barbara Calif. Died ar. 3, 1996.

:DDES, LADONNA MCMURRAY, speech edu-or; b. DuQuoin, Ill., May 20, 1935; d. Walter Allen d Cora Ruth (Schwinn) McMurray; m. John Kennedy eddes Jr., Sept. 8, 1973. BS, So. Ill. U., 1957, MS, 61; PhD, U. So. Calif., 1975. Cert. cons. in ethics and rp. compliance Cor Val Inc., Clearwater, Fla. Instr. rtland (Oreg.) State U., 1963-67; asst. prof. Ctrl. ash. State Coll., Ellensburg, 1967-68, Calif. State U., A., 1973-74; justice planner Exec. Office of Staff Svc., ankfort, Ky., 1975-76; staff asst. Ky. Bur. Correc-ns, Frankfort, 1976-78; assoc. prof. Ky. State U., ankfort, 1978-79, dir. Pub. Svc. Inst., 1979-81; chairperson Ky. State U., 1981-83; dean N.W. Mo. State U., Maryville, 1983-86, prof., 1986-94; mgmt. cons., pres. Geddes & Assocs., Frankfort, 1994-95. Author: Intro to Classical Rhetoric, 1991; author poetry (Poet of Merit 1989); contbr. articles to profl. jours. Tutor Adult Basic Edn. Literacy Program, Maryville, Mo., 1987-94; vol. Am. Cancer Soc., 1989-95. Mem. AAUP, NAFE (network dir. 1983-87), Am. Soc. Trial Cons., Assn. for Comm. Adminstrn., Speech Comm. Assn., Am. Soc. Profl. and Exec. Women, Mo. Writers Guild, Speech and Theatre Assn. Mo. (mem. bd. govs. 1992-95, editor jour. 1991-95), Am. Legion Aux., Sigma Kappa, Pi Kappa Delta, Zeta Phi Eta. Home: Frankfort Ky. Died Oct. 1995.

GEE, THOMAS GIBBS, lawyer, retired federal judge; b. Jacksonville, Fla., Dec. 9, 1925; s. James Gilliam and Cecile (Gibbs) G.; m. Deborah Ann Bagg, June 15, 1986; children by previous marriage: Jennifer Gee Updegraf, John Christopher, Mary Cecile, Thomas Gibbs. Student, The Citadel, 1942-43; BS, U.S. Mil. Acad., 1946; LLB, U. Tex., 1953. Bar: Tex. bar 1953. Assoc. Baker & Botts, Houston, 1953-54, Graves, Dougherty, Gee, Hearon, Moody & Garwood (and predecessors), Austin, Tex., 1954; ptnr. Graves, Dougherty, Gee, Hearon, Moody & Garwood (and predecessors), 1955-73; judge U.S. Ct. Appeals, (5th cir.), Austin, 1973-85, Houston, 1985-91; of counsel Baker & Botts, Houston, 1991-93, ptnr., 1993-94. Contbr. articles to profl. jours., publs.; editor-in-chief: Tex. Law Rev, 1952-53. Served with USAAF, 1946-47, with USAF, 1947-50. Mem. Am. Law Inst., Am. Judicature Soc., Am. Acad. Appellate Lawyers, Tex. Bar Found., Order of Coif. Home: Houston Tex. Died Oct. 25, 1994.

GEIGER, RAYMOND ALOYSIUS, advertising executive; b. Irvington, N.J., Sept. 18, 1910; s. Frank A. and Elizabeth (Ollemar) G.; m. Anne Hueber, Sept. 25, 1948; children: Eugene Gregory, Peter Edward, Barbara Elaine, Kenneth C., Michael. A.B., Notre Dame U., 1932; D. Law (hon.), Beaver Coll., 1981, St. Joseph's Coll., Windham, Maine, 1988. With Geiger Bros., Lewiston, Maine, 1932; asst. treas Geiger Bros., Lewiston, 1946-47, sec., treas., 1947-51, pres., 1951-78, chmn. bd., 1978-94; pub., editor Farmers' Almanac, Lewiston, 1934-94; pres. Almanac Publ. Co., Lewiston, 1948-94; chmn. bd. Martin Meyers Co., Phila., William Lynch Assn., Gaithersburg, Md., Geiger Internat., Hato Rey, P.R. Strayer Beitzer Co., York, Pa., Geiger Bros./ West, Rancho Cucamonga, Calif., B&B Advt., Scott City, Kans., N. Donald Edwards Co., Stamford, Conn., K & R Advt., Clarksdale, Miss. Past pres. Assn. Industries of Maine; past dir. New Eng. Council; past mem. bd. govs. St. Joseph's Coll., North Windham, Maine. Served to capt. AUS, 1940-45. Decorated Bronze Star, Purple Heart. Mem. Diary Publs. Internat. (past pres.), Splty. Advt. Assn. (past dir., past pres., elected to Hall of Fame 1978), Lewiston-Auburn C. of C. (past pres.), Nocturnal Adoration Soc. N.J. (founder), Internat. Platform Assn. (past gov.), Bank Mktg. Assn., Airline Passenger Assn. (mem. adv. bd.), Notre Dame Alumni Assn. Club: Nat. Press (Washington) Lodges: Elks, K.C. Home: Lewiston Maine Died Apr. 2, 1994.

GELFOND, MARJORIE PAM, psychologist; b. Long Branch, N.J., Jan. 1, 1948; d. Harold and Ruth (Goldwasser) Edelstein; m. Richard Sanford Gelfond, June 25, 1972; 1 child, Carlen Day. BA, Fairleigh Dickinson U., 1969, MA, 1972; PhD, CUNY, 1988. Psychologist Greystone (N.J.) State Psychiat. Hosp., 1969-72; from instr. to full profl. County Coll. Morris, Randolph, N.J., 1972-92; cons. Morris County Hotline, Denville, N.J., 1972-75, Morris County Hospice, Boonton Twp., N.J., 1979. Contbr. articles to profl. jours. Bd. mem. Dutton Counseling Ctr., Morristown, N.J., 1979-82, Morris County mental Health Assn. (pres.), 1975-76, Instl. Rsch. St. Clare's Hosp., Denville, N.J., 1985-92, Mental Health Adv. Bd., Morristown, N.J., 1978. Recipient Annual Student Rsch. award Assn. for Women in Psychology, 1988. Mem. APA. Jewish. Home: Flanders NJ Deceased May 23, 1992.

GELLHORN, WALTER, law and political science educator, author; b. St. Louis, Sept. 18, 1906; s. George and Edna (Fischel) G.; m. Kitty Minus, June 1, 1932; children—Ellis, Gay. A.B., Amherst Coll., 1927, L.H.D., 1952; LL.B., Columbia U., 1931; LL.D., U. Pa., 1963, U. Akron, 1968, Boston U., 1971, U. Louvain, Belgium, 1972, Rutgers U., 1973, Columbia U., 1976, Georgetown U., 1976, Washington U., 1977, Capital U., 1980. Bar: N.Y., 1932. Law sec. U.S. Supreme Ct. Justice Harlan F. Stone, 1931-32; atty. Office of Solicitor Gen., U.S. Dept. Justice, 1932-33; mem. faculty Columbia U., 1933—, Betts prof. law, 1957-73, Univ. prof., 1973-74, Univ. prof. emeritus, 1974—; regional atty. U.S. Social Security Bd., 1936-38; dir. atty. gen.'s com. on adminstrv. procedure, 1939-41; asst. gen. counsel and regional atty. OPA, 1942-43; spl. asst. to sec. of interior, 1943-44; vice chmn. Nat. War Labor Bd., 2d region, 1944-45, chmn., 1945; mem. coun. Adminstrv. Conf. U.S., 1961-62, 68—; vis. prof. U. Manchester, Eng., 1951, Tokyo U., 1958; James Schouler lectr. Johns Hopkins U., 1941; Edward Douglass White lectr. La. State U., 1956; Oliver Wendell Holmes lectr. Harvard U., 1966. Author: Administrative Law-Cases and Comments, 1940, 8th edit. (with Clark Byse, and Peter L. Strauss, Todd Rakoff and Roy A. Schotland 1987), Federal Administrative Proceedings, 1941, Security, Loyalty, and Science, 1950, Children and Families in the Courts, 1954. Individual Freedom and Governmental Restraints, 1956, Kihonteki Jinken (in Japanese), 1959, American Rights, 1960, When Americans Complain, 1966, Ombudsmen and Others, 1966; (with others) The States and Subversion, 1952, The Freedom to Read, 1956, The Sectarian College and the Public Purse, 1970. Co-recipient Henderson Meml. Prize, 1946, 75; recipient Goldsmith award, 1951, Hillman award, 1957, Columbia Law Alumni medal for excellence, 1971, Learned Hand medal, 1979, Disting. Research award Am. Bar Found., 1988. Fellow Am. Acad. Arts and Scis.; mem. Am. Philos. Soc. (coun. 1970-73, v.p. 1983-86), Assn. Am. Law Schs. (pres. 1963), Nat. Acad. Pub. Adminstrn., Japan Acad. (hon.), Phi Beta Kappa, Alpha Delta Phi (pres. 1955-58), Phi Delta Phi. Home: New York N.Y. Died Dec. 9, 1995.

GEMMA, WILLIAM ROBERT, medical association administrator, educator; b. Clinton, Mass., June 9, 1932; s. James Salvatore and Jessie Elizabeth (Brackett) G.; m. Dianna Patricia Christ, Jan. 23, 1960; children: Janis Michelle, Michael William. BA in Bus. Adminstrn., U. Md., 1962; MHA, U. Minn., 1967; PhD in Preventive Medicine, Ohio State U., 1972. Commd. 2d lt. USAF, 1960, advanced through grades to maj.; resigned, 1974; assoc. adminstr. planning and evaluation USPHS, Rockville, Md., 1974-78, assoc. adminstrv. internat. health, 1978-84; pres. Washington Healthcare Internat., 1984-85; dir. med. affairs U.S. Trading Co., Washington, 1985-87; dir. med. div. ECI Internat., Sterling, Va., 1987-89; pres. Internat. Soc. Emergency Med. Svcs., Chantilly, Va., 1989-95; chmn. pilot study North Atlantic Alliance, Brussels, 1977-82; cons. WHO, Geneva, 1980-83; prof. pub. health and adminstrn. Mem. US Bicentennial, HEW, Washington, 1976. Decorated Order Arts and Sci. (Egypt). Fellow Am. Coll. Healthcare Execs. Roman Catholic. Home: Potomac Md. Died Dec. 2, 1995.

GEOGHEGAN, ELMO LEON, restaurant company executive; b. Kirksville, Mo., Mar. 24, 1927; s. Luke and Katherine Elizabeth (Weber) G.; m. Wilma Rebecca Green, Jan. 26, 1949; children—Elmo Leon, David Lee. Student public schs. With Big Boy Restaurants Am., 1942-94; exec. v.p. Big Boy Restaurants Am., Glendale, Calif., 1968-94; v.p. Marriott Corp. Served with USCGR, 1945-46. Mem. Calif. Restaurant Assn. (dir.). Home: Glendale Calif. Died Nov. 23, 1994.

GEORGE, EARL, composer, conductor, critic; b. Milw., May 1, 1924; s. Adolph Robert and Eleanore Lilly (Werle) G.; m. Margaret Heidner, Sept. 11, 1948; 1 child, Stephen Hubbard. MusB, Eastman Sch. Music, 1946, MusM, 1947, Phd, 1958. Instr. Julius Hartt Music Found., Hartford, Conn., 1948; asst. prof. composition U. Tex., Austin, summer 1948; instr. theory and composition U. Minn., Mpls., 1948-56; prof. Syracuse (N.Y.) U., 1959-88, prof. emeritus, 1988—; music critic Syracuse Herald-Jour., 1961-92; Fulbright lectr. U. Oslo, Norway, 1955-56; condr. Syracuse U. Singers, 1963-69, Syracuse U. Symphony Orch., 1971-80, Syracuse U. Summer Orch., 1971-80. Composer: (orch. compositions) Introduction and Allegro, 1946 (Gershwin prize 1947), A Thanksgiving Overture, 1950 (Boosey and Hawkes award 1950), (chamber composition) Arioso, 1947 (Koussevitzky Commn. award 1947), string quartet (commn. Krasner Quartet 1961), (choral and orch. composition), Missa Brevis, 1950 (Nat. Fedn. Music Clubs award 1950); (operas) Birthdays: two one-act operas, Pursuing Happiness and Another Fourth of July. Recipient James Millikin U. Choral prize, 1947; Guggenheim fellow, 1957. Mem. Am. Music Center, ASCAP. Democrat. Home: Jamesville N.Y. Died Sept. 15, 1994.

GERARD, DAVID E., marketing executive; b. Fall River, Mass., Aug. 30, 1945; s. Irving and Ruth Nita (Sobiloff) G.; m. Arlene Ellen Ramer, May 22, 1971; children: Stefanie, Adam. BA, New Eng. Coll., Henniker, N.H., 1969. Account exec. various radio stas., 1969-74; gen. sales mgr. WJYE(FM), Buffalo, 1974-78, WSHH(FM), Pitts., 1978-80; gen. mgr. WKSW(FM), Cleve., 1980-83; gen. sales mgr. WTOP(AM)/ WTKS(FM), Washington, 1983-84; v.p., gen. mgr. WTIX(AM), New Orleans, 1984-86; pres. Sun Raalo Broadcasting; owner, mgr. WKRT(AM)/WOKW(FM), Cortland, N.Y., 1986-88; pres. Mktg. Specialists, Cortland, 1989—. Chmn. United Way Fund Dr., Cortland County, 1988-89; bd. dirs. Tompkin-Cortland Community Coll. Found., Cortland Downtown Bus. Assn., Cortland City Improvement Corp. (all current). Mem. Cortland County C. of C. (bd. dirs. to date). Home: Cortland N.Y. Died Sept. 26, 1990.

GERARD, WILLIAM A., banker; b. Oklahoma City, June 22, 1940; s. Walter B. and Beryl B. (Baker) G.; m. Janece K. French, Sept. 6, 1960; children: William A., Brian, Melissa. B.S.B.A., U. Tulsa, 1962; M.B.A., U. Pa., 1964. Prodn. supt. Philco-Ford Corp., Phila., 1964-67; prodn. control mgr. Citicorp, N.Y.C., 1967-81; sr. v.p. Securities Industry Automation Corp., N.Y.C., 1981-83; sr. v.p. Chem. N.Y. Corp., N.Y.C., 1983—, Lansdale, 1983—. Republican. Home: Stamford Conn.

GERNSHEIM, HELMUT ERICH ROBERT, photohistorian, writer; b. Munich, Mar. 1, 1913; arrived in Eng., 1937, naturalized, 1946; s. Karl-Theodor and Hermine (Scholz) G.; m. Alison Eames, Mar. 1942 (dec. Mar. 1969); m. Irene Guenin, Oct. 1971. Student art history, U. Munich, 1933-34; Dip., Bavarian State Sch. Photography, Munich, 1936; MSc (hon.), Brooks Inst., Santa Barbara, Calif., 1984; DSc (hon.), U. Bradford, Eng., 1989. Photographer Warburg Inst. Art, London, 1942-45; founder Gernsheim Collection Photography London, 1945-63, U. Tex., 1964-95; lectr. history photography Franklin Coll., Lugano, Switzerland, 1971-72; disting. guest prof. history of art U. Tex., Austin, 1979, Ariz. State U., Tempe, 1982; Regents prof. history of art U. Calif., Riverside, 1984, Santa Barbara, 1985, 89; curator exhbns., London, Lucerne, Goteborg, Stockholm, Amsterdam, Milan, Essen, Cologne, Frankfut, Munich, MOMA, N.Y.C., Rochester, N.Y., Detroit, Austin, numerous others, 1951-84; advisor to the editor Ency. Brittanica, 1968-95; trustee Swiss Found. Photography, Zurich, 1975-81, Alinari Mus. Photography, Florence, Italy, 1985-95. Author: Julia Margaret Cameron, 1948, 75, Lewis Carroll-Photographer, 1949, 68, Roger Fenton, Photographer of Crimean War, 1954, 73, The History of Photography, 1955, 69, 83, and twenty other books; contbr. over 300 articles to newspapers, jours. and art mags. Decorated Cross of Merit, Fed. Republic Germany, 1975; recipient Gold medal Italian Acad. Art, 1980, D.O. Hill medal German Acad. Photography, 1983, Assn. Internat. Photog. Art Dealers award, 1984, Sudek medal Czechoslovak Govt., 1989, Niépce medal Chalon-sur-Saone, France. Fellow Am. Photohistory Soc. (hon.), German Photog. Soc. (Kulturpreis 1959), European Photohistory Soc. (hon. 1985), soc. L.J.M. Daguerre Club (Frankfurt, hon., v.p. Cormeilles-en-Parisis 1989). Home: Castagnola Switzerland Died July 20, 1995.

GERRY, JOHN FRANCIS, federal judge; b. Camden, N.J., Nov. 17, 1925; s. Francis P.; m. Jean June 21, 1952; children: Patricia, Kathleen, Ellen. A.B., Princeton U., 1950; LL.B., Harvard U., 1953. Solicitor Twp. of Mt. Laurel, N.J., 1971-72; judge Camden County Ct., 1972-73, N.J. Superior Ct., 1973-75; judge U.S. Dist. Ct. N.J., 1975-87, chief judge, 1987-94, sr. judge, 1994-95. Mem. ABA, N.J. Bar Assn. Home: Camden N.J. Died Mar. 1995.

GERSCH, HAROLD ARTHUR, physics educator; b. N.Y.C., Jan. 8, 1922; S. Adolph and Marie (Reder) G.; m. Thelma Lee Gardner, Mar. 21, 1947; children: Lee, Harold Jr., Robert. BS in Physics, Ga. Inst. Tech., 1949; PhD, John Hopkins U. Asst. prof. Ga. Inst. Tech., Atlanta, 1953-56, assoc. prof., 1956-62, prof., 1962-70, regent's prof., 1970-87, regent's prof. emeritus, 1987—; vis. lectr. Johns Hopkins U., Balt., 1956-57; vis. prof. U. New Orleans, 1979-80, Oglethorpe U., 1987-88, U.S. Mil. Acad., 1989-90; cons. physics and solid state div. Oak Ridge (Tenn.) Nat. Lab., 1956—, Ford Found., Caracas, Venezuela, 1966. Contbr. over 50 articles to profl. jours. Served in USN, 1940-46. Named NATO Sr. fellow NSF, 1973. Fellow Am. Physical Soc. Republican. Presbyterian. Home: West Point N.Y. Died April 14, 1995.

GERULAITIS, VITAS KEVIN, tennis player; b. Bklyn., July 26, 1954; s. Vitas and Aldona G. Student, Columbia U. Became profl. tennis player, 1974; player for Pitts. Triangles (World Team Tennis), 1974-76; mem. Davis Cup team, 1977-79, BP Cup team, 1973. Established Vitas Gerulaitis Found., 1977. Home: Cleveland Ohio Died Sept. 18, 1994.

GESELL, GERHARD ALDEN, federal judge; b. Los Angeles, June 16, 1910; s. Arnold Lucius and Beatrice (Chandler) G.; m. Marion Holliday Pike, Sept. 19, 1936; children: Peter Gerhard, Patricia Pike. A.B., Yale, 1932, LL.B., 1935. Bar: Conn. 1935, D.C. 1941. With SEC, Washington, 1935-40; tech. adviser to chmn. SEC, 1940-93; acted for Commn. as spl. counsel Temporary Nat. Econ. Com., study legal res. life ins. cos.; mem. Covington & Burling, Washington, 1941-67; judge U.S. Dist. Ct. D.C., 1968-93; sr. judge, 1993; chief asst. counsel Joint Congl. Com. on Investigation Pearl Harbor Attack, 1945-46; Chmn. Pres.'s Com. on Equal Opportunity in the Armed Forces, 1962-64; chmn. com. on adminstrn. of justice D.C. Jud. Council, 1965-67; jud. mem. D.C. Commn. on Jud. Disabilities and Tenure, 1976-81. Co-author: Study of Legal Reserve Life Insurance Cos, 1940, Families and Their Life Insurance, 1940. Recipient Edward J. Devitt Disting. Svc. to Justice award, 1989. Mem. Am. Bar Assn., Am. Law Inst., Am. Coll. Trial Lawyers, Phi Delta Phi, Zeta Psi. Clubs: Lawyers (Washington), Met. (Washington); Casino (North Haven, Maine). Home: Washington D.C. Died Feb. 19, 1993.

GHATTAS, IGNATIUS, clergyman; b. Nazareth, Israel, Dec. 25, 1920. Educated, Holy Savior Sem., Saida, Lebanon. ordained priest, 1946;. consecrated eparch Melkite Diocese of Newton, Mass., 1990. Home: Newton Mass. Died Oct. 11, 1992.

GIALANELLA, PHILIP THOMAS, newspaper publisher; b. Binghamton, N.Y., June 6, 1930; s. Felix and Frances (Demuro) G.; 1 son, Thomas Davis. B.A., Harpur Coll., 1952; M.A., State U. N.Y., 1955. Promotion dir. Evening Press and Sta. WINR-TV, Binghamton, 1957-62; v.p., gen. mgr. Daily Advance, Dover, N.J., 1962-66; v.p. Hartford (Conn.) Times, 1966-70; pres., pub. Newburgh (N.Y.) News, 1970-71; exec. v.p. Hawaii Newspaper Agy., Honolulu, 1971-73, pres., 1974-86; pub. Honolulu Star-Bull., 1975-86; pres. USA Today, 1982-83, pub., 1983; exec. v.p. Honolulu Advertiser, 1986; exec. v.p., chief operating officer Persis Corp., Bellevue, Wash., 1986—, pres. Persis Media div., 1986—; v.p., chief operating officer Northwest Media, Inc., Bellevue, Wash., 1986—, Knoxville (Tenn.) Jour., 1988; chief operating officer Southeast Mags., Inc., Nashville, 1990—; bd. dirs. Capital Investment Co., Hawaii Newspaper Agy. Found., Inc., Hawaii Newspaper Agy., Inc., Waterhouse Properties, Persis Corp., Honolulu Advertiser Inc., N.W. Media, Inc., Knoxville Jour.; v.p., bd. dirs. ASA Properties, Inc., Bay-Area Steuart, Inc., Shiny Rock Mining Corp. Past chmn., memm. exec. com. Nat. Alliaince Businessmen for Hawaii and Micronesia; v.p. Hawaii Newspaper Agy. Found.; mem. Japan-Hawaii Econ. Coun.; bd. govs. East-West Ctr., chmn., 1991; bd. govs. Pacific Asian Affairs Coun.; bd. dirs. Hawaii Theatre Ctr., Honolulu Boy Choir, Honolulu Symphony, Aloha United Way, Aloha coun. Boy Scouts Am., YMCA, Honolulu; mem. adv. group Western Command, U.S. Army. With U.S. Army, 1952-54. Mem. Am. Newspaper Pubs. Assn., Hawaii Pubs. Assn., AP Assn. Calif., AP Assn. Ariz., AP Assn. Hawaii, AP Assn. Nev., Sigma Delta Chi. Roman Catholic. Home: Honolulu Hawaii

GIBB, RICHARD FRASER, aerospace executive; b. Bklyn., Feb. 4, 1945; s. Walter F. and Lucille A. (Gorth) G.; m. Margaret A. Guillory, Feb. 18, 1978; 1 child, Ricardo Barrera. BBA, Nat. U., 1980; grad., Def. Systems Mgmt. Coll., 1992. Logistics mgr. Grumman Aerospace, Bethpage, N.Y., 1972-79; prodn. mgr. Gen. Dynamics, San Diego, 1979-88; ops. dir. Gen. Dynamics, Harlingen, Tex., 1988-92; v.p., launch dir. Martin Marietta, Cape Canaveral, Fla., 1992—. Bd. dirs. Nat. Space Club, Jr. Achievement. Republican. Home: Cocoa Beach Fla. Died Dec. 1, 1994.

GIBBS, JAMES WENRICH, retired glass company executive; b. Canton, Ohio, Dec. 12, 1915; s. Alvin J. and Eva A. (Wenrich) G.; m. Mary Jewel Hellwig, Apr. 12, 1941; children: Sandra Ann Gibbs Chambers, Stephen V., David S. (dec.). BA, Yale U., 1938; post-grad., U. Mich. Law Sch., 1938-39, Wharton Grad. Sch. U. Pa., 1939-40; D of Horological History, Clayton (Mo.) U., 1980. Asst. to pres. Safetee Glass Co., Inc., Phila., 1940-41, v.p., 1942-67, pres., 1967-71, vice chmn. bd., 1971, also bd. dirs. Author: The Dueber-Hampden Story, 1954, The Life and Death of the Ithaca Calendar Clock Company, 1960, Buckeye Horology, 1970, Shaker Clockmakers, Dixie Clockmakers, 1979, Pennsylvania Clocks and Watches: Antique Timepieces and Their Makers, 1984, From Springfield to Moscow: The Complete Dueber Hampden Story, 1986; also articles. Mem. adv. com. Med. Coll. Pa.; trustee Am. Clock and Watch Mus., Bristol, Conn.; elder First Presbyn. Ch., Germantown, Pa. Fellow Royal Soc. Arts, Nat. Assn. Watch and Clock Collectors, Inc. (past pres., Silver Star fellow); mem. Colonial Soc. Pa., Colonial Soc. Mass., Soc. of Mayflower Descs., St. Nicholas Soc., Pa. Soc. Colonial Wars, Cleve. Grays, Colonial Order of Acorn, Dutch Colonial Soc. Del., Ky. Cols., Order of Lafayette, Sovereign Mil. Order Temple Jerusalem, SR, SAR, Vet. Corps Arty., Royal Soc. St. George, Nat. Soc. Sons Colonial New Eng., Newcomen Soc., Nat. Soc. Old Plymouth Colony Descs., Am. Def. Preparedness Assn., Huguenot Soc. Pa., Pa. Hist. Soc., Pilgrim John Howland Soc., Sons St. George, Sons Union Vets. N.J., Valley Forge Hist. Soc., Penn Club, Sons Daus. of Pilgrim Soc., Order Ams. of Armorial Ancestry, Hereditary Order Descs. of Colonial Govs., Order of Descs. Colonial Physicians Chirugiens, Hereditary Order of the First Families of Mass. Home: Philadelphia Pa.

GIBSON, JAMES ISAAC, chemical manufacturing company executive; b. Golden, Colo., Mar. 22, 1925; s. Fred Daniel and May Emma (Borsberry) G.; m. Audrey June Brinley, June 23, 1947; children: James Brinley, David Scott, Robin Lee, Terry Lynn, Cynthia Rae, Holly Jo. BS, U.S. Naval Acad., 1947; BCE, MCE, Rensselaer Poly. Inst., 1950; LLD (hon.), U. Nev., Las Vegas, 1988. Registered profl. engr., Nev., Ariz. Ensign C.E., USN, 1947, advanced through grades to lt., 1953, resigned, 1953; asst. chief engr. Western Electro-Chem. Co., Henderson, Nev., 1953-56; chief engr. Am. Potash and Chem. Corp., Henderson, 1956-61; chief engr. Pacific Engring. and Prodn. Co. Nev., Henderson, 1961-66, exec. v.p., 1966-85, pres., 1985-88, also bd. dirs.; pres. Henderson Ventures, Inc., 1968-88. Mem. assembly Nev. Legis., Carbon City, 1958-66, mem. senate, 1966-88; majority leader Nev. Senate, 1976-88; chmn. council state govts., Lexington, Ky., 1985, vice chmn., 1984, governing bd., 1968-88. Recipient Silver Beaver award Boulder Dam Area council Boy Scouts Am., 1970; named Disting. Nevadan, U. Nev., 1973. Mem. NSPE, Nev. Soc. Profl. Engrs., Sigma Xi. Democrat. Mormon. Home: Henderson Nev.

GIBSON, MARTIN LEROY, JR., journalism educator; b. Colorado City, Tex., Jan. 29, 1934; s. Martin Leroy and Ruth (Hamilton) G.; m. Nancy Louise Westmoreland, Sept. 29, 1956; children: Martin Leroy III, Elizabeth Anne. BA, North Tex. State U., 1955; MSJ, Northwestern U., 1959; PhD, U. Tex., 1973. Sports reporter Galveston (Tex.) Daily News, 1955-5 copy editor Chgo. Tribune, 1959-60, Houston Chronicl 1960-65; instr. journalism North Tex. State U., Dento 1965-69; from asst. prof. to assoc. prof. to pro journalism U. Tex., Austin, 1969—, Phil Warn Regents Prof. of Communications, 1986—; con Freedom Newspapers, Inc., Irvine, Calif., 1980—; own The Newspaper Tuner, Austin, 1980—. Autho (textbook) Editing in the Electronic Era, 1979; contb monthly columns. Served as cpl. U.S. Army, 1956-58 Ottaway fellow, 1981; recipient Fulbright award, 1982 Mem. Soc. Profl. Journalists (local pres. 1972, state pre 1973). Republican. Methodist. Home: Austin Tex.

GIDEON, MIRIAM, composer; b. Greeley, Colo., Oc 23, 1906; d. Abram and Henrietta (Shoninger) G.; m Frederic Ewen, 1949. B.A., Boston U., 1926; M.A Columbia, 1946; D.Sacred Music, Jewish Theol. Sem 1970. Music faculty Bklyn. Coll., 1944-54, Coll. Ci N.Y., 1947-55, Cantors Inst., Jewish Theol. Sem., 195 96, Manhattan Sch. Music, N.Y.C., 1967-96; vis. pro music City Coll., CUNY, 1971-76, prof. emeritus, 197 96. Composer: opera Fortunato, for orch. Symphon Brevis, Lyric Piece for Strings, 2 cantatas, 2 sacred svc in Hebrew, 23 cycles for solo voice and instrument ensemble, works for solo voice and piano, instrument sonatas and suites; recs. orch. and chamber works b Westminster Records, CRI, New World Records, Des Records, Serenus Records; compact disc recs. Ne World, Cambria, Newport Classic; works performed Europe, Far East, U.S. and S.Am. by Internat. So Contemporary Music, League Composers, Londo Prague, Tokyo, Zurich symphony orchs. Recipie Bloch prize for choral work, 1948; Nat. Fedn. Mus Clubs and A.S.C.A.P. award for symphonic musi 1969; Nat. Endowment of Arts grantee, 1974; comm Library of Congress, 1979. Mem. Am. Acad. Arts an Letters, Am. Composers Alliance (bd. govs.), Interna Soc. Contemporary Music (gov.). Home: New Yo N.Y. Died June 18, 1996.

GIDWITZ, JOSEPH LEON, paperboard produc company executive; b. Memphis, Jan. 16, 1905; s. Jacc and Rose (Wolff) G.; Ph.B., U. Chgo., 1928; m. Emi Rose Klein, Sept. 11, 1930; children—Alan, Ralp Betsy. With Lanzit Corrugated Box Co. (merged in Consol. Paper Co. 1963), 1928-63, v.p., 1941-48, pre 1948-63; founder Crandon Paper Mills, Inc. (merge into Consol. Paper Co. 1963), Ft. Madison, Iowa, 195 pres., 1957-63, also dir.; chmn. bd. Consol. Packagin Corp., Chgo., 1963-84, pres., 1973-77, also dir.; v. John Strange Paper Co., 1945-55, pres., 1955-56, chm bd., 1956-69, also dir.; vice chmn. bd., dir., mem. exe com. Helene Curtis Industries, Inc.; vice chmn. bd., d Continental Materials Corp.; dir. Harmony Co., 196 77, chmn. bd., 1971-77. Mem., Founder Council f Jewish Elderly, Chgo., 1971-95, bd. dirs., 1971-95, pre 1971-75, chmn., 1975-76, hon. chmn., 1977-95; mer citizen's bd. U. Chgo., 1971-95, mem. devel. counc 1972-95; mem. Chgo. Symphony Orch. Governing Bc 1973-95; bd. govs. PACE Inst., Chgo., 1977-81; c chmn. social services com. Chgo. Planning Council c Aging and Rehab., 1977-81, chmn. program com., 198 82; mem. adv. council Mayor's Office for Sr. Citize and Handicapped, Chgo., 1978-83, vice chmn. ad com., 1982-83; del. White House Conf. on Aging, 198 Recipient Julius Rosenwald Meml. award Jewish Fed Met. Chgo., 1969, Golden Age Hall of Fame citatio 1971, Spl. Founders Award Trophy, Council Jewis Elderly, 1975. Mem. Fibre Box Assn. (dir. 1956-67 Nat. Paperboard Assn. (dir. 1964-66), Am. Paper Ins Inc. (dir. Paperboard Group 1966-78, mem. exec. cor group 1975-78), Container Indsl. Conf. (founder 1 chmn. and dir. 1948-53), Chgo. Assn. Commerce ar Industry, Chgo. Council on Fgn. Relations, Ill. C. of C Nat. Assn. Mfrs. Clubs: Standard, Mid-Am. (Chgo Died Aug. 8, 1995. Home: Chicago Ill.

GIESECKE, LEONARD FREDERICK, economi educator; b. Houston, Dec. 28, 1937; s. Leona Frederick and Jo-Anna (Tatman) G.; m. Mary Teasle July 13, 1963; children: Marjorie Lyn, Jennif Ann. BA, U. Tex., Austin, 1959, MA, 1967, Ph 1975. Vol. Peace Corps, Philippines, 1961-63; assoc. di Peace Corps, Turkey, 1963-65; teaching asst. dep econs. U. Tex., Austin, 1965-68; asst. prof. dept. econ and bus. Southwestern U., Georgetown, Tex., 1968-7 assoc. prof. dept. econs. and bus. Southwestern U 1975-86, chairperson dept. econs. and bus., 1981-9 prof. dept. econs. and bus., 1986-94, Herbert and Ka Dishman prof., 1990-94; cons. Shell Oil Corp., Austi 1980. Author: American Economic Policy in th Philippines, 1987; contbr. articles to profl. jours. Ch bd. dir. Williamson-Burnet Co. Opportunities, In Georgetown, 1989-91. Danforth assoc. Danfor Found., 1979; recipient William Carrington Finch awa Southwestern U., 1986. Mem. AAUP (pres. Tex. con 1982-84), Am. Econs. Assn., Southwestern Econ Assn., Assn. Evolutionary Econs., Alpha Kappa Psi, Gamma Mu. Democrat. Home: Georgetown Tex. Di Apr. 1994.

GILBERT, FRED IVAN, JR., physician, researcher; Newark, Mar. 5, 1920; s. Fred I. and Gertrude Ol (Lund) G.; m. Helen Ruth Odell, Sept. 21, 1943 (di Jan. 1974); children—Rondi, Kristin, Galen, Geral Fred I. III, Lisa, Cara; m. Gayle Yamashiro, Sept. 1 1978; children—Heidi, John. Jr. cert., U. Hawaii, 194

S., U. Calif.-Berkeley, 1942; M.D., Stanford U., 1946. plomate Nat. Bd. Med. Examiners, Am. Bd. Internal edicine. Intern Stanford-Lane Hosp., San Francisco, 45-46; assoc. clin. prof. medicine Stanford U., Calif., 48-51; internist Straub Clinic and Hosp., Honolulu, 51-95, resident in nuclear medicine, 1979-80; resident neurology U. London, 1960-61; chief medicine ueen's Hosp., Honolulu, 1965-69, now staff; prof. pub. alth and medicine U. Hawaii, Honolulu, 1969-95; ed. dir. Pacific Health Research Inst., Honolulu, 60—; resident in nuclear medicine U. Hawaii and U. alif.-Sacramento, 1978-80; mem. staff St. Francis, uakini, Castle hosps., Honolulu; pres. Hawaii Acad. i., 1959-60, Hawaii Heart Assn., 1959; bd. dirs. ancer Control Cancer Ctr. Hawaii, 1985-86. Contbr. merous articles to profl. jours. Served to capt. U.S. rmy, 1943-48. Recipient Disting. Physician award at. Acad. Practice, 1985. Fellow AAAS, ACP; mem. m. Soc. Nuclear Medicine (pres. Hawaii chpt. 1980-), Am. Coll. Nuclear Physicians, Internat. Health valuation Assn. (pres. 1971-72), AMA, Inst. Medicine Nat. Acad. Sci., Social Sci. Club, Alpha Omega pha. Home: Honolulu Hawaii Died Feb. 5, 1995.

ILBERT, FREDERICK SPOFFORD, JR., executive anager; b. Orange, N.J., Mar. 29, 1939; s. Frederick offord and Annis Burnham (Stearns) G.; m. Margaret ndrus Moon, Sept. 6, 1961; children: Malcolm Anus, Frederick Christopher, Douglas Hamlin. BA in story, Williams Coll., 1961; postgrad., NYU, 1962-66, arvard U., 1968-70. Mgmt. trainee Citibank, N.Y.C., 61, asst. mgr., 1965, asst. v.p., 1969, v.p., 1972-88, v. exec., 1988—; pres. Citicorp Bus., Inc., N.Y.C., 77-82; exec. v.p. Citicorp Indsl. Credit, Inc., Harrison, Y., 1980-88; speaker numerous seminars and confs. ontbr. articles to profl. jours. Mem. rep. Darien Town eeting, 1971-75; treas. Darien YMCA Indian Guides, 72-74; trustee New Canaan Country Sch., 1979-82. ith AUS, 1961-66. Recipient Disting. Community c. award Brandeis U., 1985, Nat. Humanitarian award at. Jewish Ctr. Immunology and Respiratory edicine, 1987. Mem. Nat. Comml. Fin. Assn. (bd. rs. 1977-88, exec. com. 1979-86, v.p. 1980-84, pres. 85, chmn. 1986), Credit Fin. Mgmt. Alumni Assn., appa Alpha. Republican. Presbyterian. Clubs: niversity (N.Y.C.), Wee Burn Country (Darien). ome: Darien Conn.

ILBERT, RICHARD PAUL, judge; b. Balt., Feb. 5, 24; s. Paul Reed and Elsa Katherine (Huse) G.; m. udrey Arlene Rude, Aug. 30, 1944; children: Paul erryl, Richard Joel. AA, U. Balt., 1947, JD, 1950, LM, 1954, LLD (hon.), 1979. Bar: Md. 1950, U.S. ist. Ct. Md. 1950, U.S. Ct. Appeals (4th Cir.) 1956. t. practice Balt., 1952-71; assoc. judge Md. Ct. Spl. ppeals, Annapolis, 1971-76; chief judge Md. Ct. Spl. ppeals, from 1976; adj. prof. Sch. Law, U. Balt., 1981- ; lectr. Am. Acad. Jud. Edn., from 1985. Co-author: aryland Criminal Law and Procedure, 1983, Maryland ort Law Handbook, 1986, Maryland Workmen's ompensation, 1988; contbr. articles to law jours. hmn. Md. Commn. Jud. Disabilities, from 1972. rved with U.S. Army, 1943-46, PTO, 1950-52, ermany. Recipient Disting. Jurist award Sigma Delta appa, 1976; named Alumnus of Yr., 1982. Mem. BA (mem. exec. com. appellate judge's conf. from 87), Council Chief Judges Cts. Appeal (chair 1986-), Appellate Judges Conf. (mem. exec. com. from 87), Hoffberger Ctr. Profl. Ethics, Balt. City Bar ssn., Md. State Bar Assn., Am. Judges' Assn., Am. ricature Soc. Republican. Lutheran. Home: Anapolis Md. Deceased.

ILKESON, ROBERT FAIRBAIRN, retired utility mpany executive; b. Phila., June 26, 1917; s. Fairbairn d Helen L. (Geiger) G.; m. Marie L. Whitwell, Apr. , 1941 (dec. May 1985); children: Katharine, Richard, homas, David, Elizabeth; m. Nancy Brandes, Feb. 28, 88. E.E., Cornell U., 1939. Jr. engr. Phila. Electric o., 1939-40, engr., 1946-51, operating dept., 1953-60, gr. engring. and research, 1960, v.p. engring. and search, 1961-62, exec. v.p., 1962-65, pres., 1965-71, mn. bd., 1971-82, chmn. exec. com., 1973-88; engr. estinghouse Electric Corp., Idaho Falls, Idaho, 1951- . Mem. Nat. Sci. Bd., 1982-88. Served to capt. AUS, 940-45. Mem. IEEE, Sigma Alpha Epsilon. Republin. Episcopalian. Club: Sun City Country. Lodge: asons. Died Mar. 13, 1993. Home: Sun City Ariz.

ILLETT, CHARLES, travel executive; b. Newport, y., Sept. 9, 1915; s. Louis B. and Sarah (Maller) G.; m. rginia Margaret Littmann, June 11, 1949; children: alerie, David, Brian Paul, Peter Guy. B.A., U. Cin., 938. Pub. relations dir. Netherland Plaza Hotel, Cin., 938-39; account exec. Swafford & Koehl Advt. Agy., .Y.C., 1939-40; advt. and sales promotion dir. Hotel ibson, Cin., 1940-41; promotion and pub. relations dir. Y. Conv. and Visitors Bur., N.Y.C., 1946-62; v.p. Y. Conv. and Visitors Bur., 1962-65, exec. v.p., 1966- , pres., 1974-89; cons., 1989-95; mem. travel adv. com. .S. Dept. Commerce, 1963-65, 77-89, nat. adv. com. on wy beautification, 1965-66; del. White House Conf. atural Beauty, 1965; spl. adviser to Discover Am. ravel Orgns., 1967-68, dir., 1968-95; mem. N.Y. State d. Tourist Commrs., 1977-84; chmn. Nat. Urban ourism Coun., 1977-90; mem. adv. bd. Travel and ourism Govt. Affairs, Policy Coun., 1982-95; chmn. ravel and Tourism Awardness Coun., 1988-90. Editor: The Bridge, 1946; writer, lectr. on travel bus. subjects. Mem. pub. affairs com. U.S. Air Force Acad., 1968-71. Served from pvt. to maj. AUS, 1941-46. Decorated Bronze Star; recipient Most Original Travel Idea award Midwest Travel Writers Assn., 1964, Golden Scroll award Broadway Assn., 1977, medal of Amity France, 1980, Am. Traditions award B'nai B'rith Youth Svcs., 1981, Excellence award U. Cin., 1981, N.Y. Gov.'s award for long and disting. svc., The King's Glove award Nat. Assn. Expn. Mgrs., 1988, Berkman Travel Achievement award, 1994; elected to Hall of Leaders of Conv. Liaison Coun., 1985, Am. Soc. of Travel Agts. Hall of Fame, 1988; installed Order of Corte, 1972. Mem. Travel Industry Assn. (dir. 1960-62, pres. 1963-65, chmn. bd. 1965-67, Merit award 1966, Golden Horseshoe award 1972), Internat. Festivals Assn. (dir. 1975-59, sec. 1959-61, sec.-treas. 1966-67), Am. Soc. Travel Agts., Soc. Am. Travel Writers, Pub. Rels. Soc. Am., Internat. Assn. Conv. Burs. (dir. 1968-71, v.p. 1971-72, pres. 1973-74), Travel Industry Assn. Am. (life dir., Nat. Travel Mktg. award 1981). Club: Overseas Press (N.Y.C.). Home: Great Neck N.Y. Died Dec. 4, 1995.

GILLIS, CHRISTOPHER, dancer, choreographer; b. Montreal, Que., Can.. Pvt. studies with, May O'Donnell, Norman Walker, Cindi Green, Sande Shurin. With Paul Taylor Dance Co., N.Y.C., 1976-93. Performances include with May O'Donnell Co., José Limón Co.; choreography for Charlotte Ballet, Am. Ballet Theatre, N.Y. Theatre Ballet; original work Curbs and Corridors premiered at N.Y. City Ctr. Theater, 1990; staged Speaking in Tongues for Paris Opera Ballet; appearances in commls. and films. Home: New York N.Y. Died Aug. 7, 1993.

GILLON, JOHN WILLIAM, lawyer; b. Sherman, Tex., Apr. 24, 1900; s. John William and Lucie (Conner) G.; m. Itzselle L. Cook, July 8, 1930 (dec. Sept. 1977); children: John William, Allen C., Edward J., Paul K., Harvey E., David C.; m. Lillian Millar, Aug. 2, 1981 (dec. Sept. 1988). A.B., Miss. Coll.; LL.B. (Lafferty medal), U. Ky., 1925. Bar: Ky., Ala. 1925. Assoc. Coleman, Spain & Stewart, Birmingham, Ala., 1925-35; mem. firm Spain, Gillon & Young, Birmingham, 1935-66, Spain, Gillon, Riley, Tate & Ansley, 1966-72; of counsel Spain, Gillon, Riley, Tate & Etheredge, 1972-88, Spain, Gillon, Grooms, Blan & Nettles, 1988-92; ret., 1992; mem. adv. com. on revision of probate code State Bar Ala.; dir., sec. Estes Lumber Co., 1939-64; Mem. Jefferson County Jud. Commn., 1953-58; Chmn. Med. Clinic Bd., City of Birmingham, 1966-74; bd. mem. Estate Planning Council, Birmingham, 1967-70. Served with SATC, 1918. Named Outstanding Lawyer, Birmingham Bar, 1983; cited Ala. Law Inst., 1982, 87; inducted Order of Golden Arrow Miss. Coll., 1983. Mem. ABA, Ala. Bar Assn., Birmingham Bar Assn. (exec. com. 1955-57, pres. 1960, chmn. ednl. adv. com. 1966-67), Birmingham C. of C., Miss. Coll. Alumni Assn. (sr. mem., dir. 1973-74), Ala. Law Inst., Birmingham Real Estate Bd. (hon. life), Farrah Law Soc., Order of Coif, Blue Goose, Phi Alpha Delta. Lodge: Lions. Home: Birmingham Ala. Deceased.

GILMORE, JESSE LEE, history educator; b. Grants Pass, Oreg., Jan. 22, 1920; s. Rufus Alva and Eda Augusta (Haberman) G.; m. Chloe Eleanor Anderson, Dec. 21, 1946; children: Cherie Elaine, Eric Franklin. B.A., Willamette U., 1942; M.A., U. Calif. at Berkeley, 1948; Ph.D., U. Calif.-, Berkeley, 1952. Mem. faculty Portland (Oreg.) State U., 1953-93, prof. history, 1967-93; chmn. dept., 1965-75. Served with AUS, 1942-45, ETO, CBI. Mem. Am. Hist. Assn., Orgn. Am. Historians., AAUP. Home: Beaverton Oreg. Died Dec. 17, 1993; cremated.

GILPATRIC, ROSWELL LEAVITT, lawyer; b. Bklyn., Nov. 4, 1906; s. Walter Hodges and Charlotte (Leavitt) G.; m. Margaret Fulton Kurtz, June 18, 1932 (div. Sept. 1945); children: Joan Bradshaw, John Fulton, Elizabeth Leavitt; m. Harriet Heywood, Oct. 25, 1946 (div. Apr. 1958); m. Madelin Thayer Kudner, Sept. 18, 1958 (div. Feb. 1970); m. Paula Melhado Washburn, May 12, 1970 (div. Jan. 1985); m. Miriam R. Thorne, May 2, 1991. A.B. prima academica honoris, Yale, 1928, LL.B., 1931; LL.D., Franklin and Marshall Coll., 1962, Bowdoin Coll., 1963. Bar: N.Y. 1932, U.S. Supreme Ct. 1935, Fed. Ct 1936. Partner Cravath, Swaine & Moore, and predecessor, N.Y.C., 1931-51, 53-61, 64-77; counsel Cravath, Swaine & Moore, and predecessor, 1977-95; chmn. bd. trustees Aerospace Corp., 1960-61; Sterling vis. lectr. law sch. Yale, 1945-46; asst. sec. materiel Air Force, 1951, undersec., 1951-53; dep. sec. Dept. Def., 1961-64; bd. dirs. Eastern Air Lines; dir. emeritus CBS; chmn. bd. Fairchild Camera & Instrument Corp., 1975-77, Fed. Res. Bank N.Y., 1973-75; dir. emeritus Corning Glass Co. Mem. Rockefeller Bros. Spl. Studies Project, 1956-57; mem. council Yale, 1957-63; from trustee, vice chmn. to trustee emeritus Met. Mus. Art; trustee N.Y. Pub. Library, 1963-76. Named Hotchkiss Man of Yr., 1962; recipient citation of merit Yale Law Sch., 1963, Eisenhower award Bus. Execs. for Nat. Security, 1993. Mem. Coun. on Fgn. Rels., River Club, Century Assn., Piping Rock Club, Phi Beta Kappa, Chi Psi. Conglist. Home: New York N.Y. Died Mar. 15, 1996.

GIMBUTAS, MARIJA, archaeologist, educator; b. Vilnius, Lithuania, Jan. 23, 1921; came to U.S., 1949, naturalized, 1955; d. Daniel and Veronica (Janulaitis) Alseika; m. Jurgis Gimbutas, 1942; children: Danute, Živile, Rasa. MA, U. Vilnius, 1942; PhD, U. Tubingen, Germany, 1946; postgrad., U. Heidelberg and Munich, Germany, 1947-49; PhD (hon.), Calif. Inst. Integral Studies, San Francisco, 1988; Vytauas Magnus U., Kaunas, Lithuania, 1993. Research fellow Peabody Mus., Harvard U., Boston, 1955-63; lectr. dept. anthropology Peabody Mus., Harvard U., 1962-63; fellow Center for Advanced Study in Behavioral Scis., Stanford, Calif., 1961-62; prof. European archaeology and Indo-European studies UCLA, 1963-89; fellow Netherlands Inst. for Advanced Studies, 1973-74; project dir. excavations of Neolithic S.E. Europe, Obre, Bosnia, 1967-68, excavations at Sitagroi, N.E. Greece, 1968-69, excavations at Anza, Central Macedonia, 1969-70, at Achilleion, Thessaly, Greece, 1973-74, at Scaloria, nr. Manfredonia, Italy, 1979-80. Author: Die Bestattung in Litauen in der vorgeschichtlichen Zeit, 1946, Prehistory of Eastern Europe, 1956, Ancient Symbolism in Lithuanian Folk Art, 1958, The Balts, 1963, The Bronze Age Cultures of Central and Eastern Europe, 1965, The Slavs, 1971, The Gods and Goddesses of Old Europe, 1974, Neolithic Macedonia, 1976, The Goddesses and Gods of Old Europe, 1982, Die Balten, 1983, Baltai priešistoriniais laikais, 1985; co-editor: (with Colin Renfrew and Ernestine Elster) Excavations at Sitagroi. A Prehistoric Village in Northeast Greece, 1986, The Language of the Goddess, 1989, Achilleion, a Neolithic Village in Northern Greece, 6400-5600 B.C. Monumenta Archaeologica, UCLA, 1989, The Civilization of the Goddess, The World of Old Europe, 1991; editor: Jour. Indo-European Studies, 1973-94, Monumenta Archaeologica, 1976-94. Recipient Woman of Yr. award L.A. Times, 1968; fellow NSF, 1959-60, 68-69, Smithsonian, 1967-71, Kress Found., 1967-72; grantee NEH, 1967, Ahmanson Found., 1973, 85, 92; subject of Festschrift Proto-Indo-European, The Archaeology of Linguistic Problems, 1987. Mem. Soc. Lithuanian Archaeologists (hon.), Lithuanian Acad. Sci. Home: Topanga Calif. Died Feb. 2, 1994.

GIMPEL, JEAN VICTOR, historian; b. Paris, Oct. 10, 1918; s. René and Florence (Duveen) G.; m. P.D. Corre, Jan. 15, 1946; children: Rémy, Olivier, Claire. Swanbourne House Sch., Gt. Britain, 1927-31, Le Rosey, Switzerland, 1931-32, Lycée Louis-Le-Grand, France, 1933-38. Author, medievalist, historian of tech./civilization cycles; lectr. Yale U., U. So. Calif., U. Ottawa, Rochester U., Lehigh U., U. Del., The Royal Oak Found., Albany Inst. History of Art, Carnegie-Mellon U., Alliance Francaise, Ironbridge Gorge Mus., St. George's Chapel, Windsor; cons. UN, 1977-82. Author: The Cathedral Builders, 1958, Against Art and Artists, 1968, The Medieval Machine, 1975, The End of the Future, subtitled The Waning of the Hi-Tech World, 1995, l'Ulime Rapport Sur le Declin de l'Occident, 1986; co-author: Le Moyen Age Pour Quoi Faire?, 1986; editor: René Gimpel's Diary of an Art Dealer; producer TV films including Don't Take It for Granted, 1971. Founder, mem. Models for Rural Devel., 1985, Assn. Villard de Honnecourt, France, 1983, AVISTA Assn. for the Study of Medieval Tech., Sci. and Art, Haverford Coll., 1986; organizer of symposium on Future of the West: Decline or Transformation, U. So. Calif., 1977. Recipient Légion D'Honneur award French Govt., 1946, Médaille de la Résistance, 1946, Croix De Guerre, 1946. Home: London Eng. Died June 16, 1996.

GINGOLD, JOSEF, musician, educator; b. Brest-Litovsk, Russia, 1909; came to U.S., 1920; Pupil, Vladimir Graffman, Eugene Ysayë; MusD (with honors), Ind. U.; D.Music hon., Kent State U., Baldwin-Wallace Coll., Cleve. Inst. Music, New Eng. Conservatory Music. Prof. music Ind. U., disting. prof.; vis. prof. Conservatoire National Superior de Musique, Toho Sch., Tokyo, also others; jury numerous internat. violin competitions, including hon. chmn. Internat. Violin Competition of Indpls. Charter mem., NBC Symphony, concertmaster, soloist, Detroit Symphony Orch., Cleve. Orch.; recs., Columbia, RCA Victor, Fidelio Records. Recipient Robert Foster Cherry Award for Great Teachers, Baylor U., 1993. Home: Bloomington Ind. Died Jan. 1, 1995.

GINSBERG, MITCHELL IRVING, social worker, educator; b. Boston, Oct. 20, 1915; s. Harry J. and Rose (Harris) G.; m. Ida Robbins, Aug. 22, 1948. B.A., Tufts Coll., 1937, M.A., 1938, L.H.D., 1975; M.S.W., Columbia U., 1941, L.H.D., 1986; L.H.D., Adelphi U., 1974; LL.D., U. Md., 1974. Project dir. Peace Corps tng. project in urban community action, Columbia, Venezuela; assoc. prof. Columbia U. Sch. Social Work, 1954-56, prof., 1956, asst. to acting dean, 1958-60, assoc. dean, 1960-66, dean, spl. adv. to pres. on community affairs, 1970-81, prof., dean emeritus, 1981-86, prof. emeritus, 1986—; co-dir. Center for Study Human Rights, 1978—, mem. com. on gen. edn., 1977—; commr. N.Y.C. Dept. Social Services, 1966-67; adminstr. N.Y.C. Human Resources Adminstrn., 1967-70; cons. community action program Office Econ. Opportunity, welfare policy, N.Y.C., 1965-68, Ford Found. Social Welfare Project, 1985—; mem. select panel for promotion child health Office Asst. Sec. for Health, HEW, 1979-81; cons. HEW, Ford Found., 1978—; mem. tech. com. Com. for Nat. Health Ins.; adv. panel nat. ins. subcom. on health Ways and Means Com.,

1975; chmn. Nat. Conf. on Social Welfare Task Force on Title XX Issues, 1976; bd. dirs. Health Security Action Council, 1971—, HIP, 1971-78, Whitney M. Young Meml. Found., 1971—, Health Care Inst.; mem. com. nat. legis. Council on Social Work Edn., 1973-76; trustee Community Service Soc., 1974—; mem. nat. adv. council Hospice, Inc.; mem. task force on cost and financing mental health President's Commn. on Mental Health, 1977; mem. com. on evaluation assistance Greater N.Y. Fund, 1977; mem. N.Y.C. Task Force on Human Services; mem. adv. com. on services to children and families Edna McConnell Clark Found. Editorial adv. bd.: Man and Medicine; adv. bd.: Jour. Inst. Socioeconomic Studies. Served with AUS, 1942-46. Mitchell I. Ginsberg professorship in contemporary urban problems Columbia U. Sch. Social Work established in his honor, 1991. Mem. Nat. Assn. Social Workers (exec. com. N.Y.C. chpt., chmn. social policy and action 1966—, nat. pres. 1971-73, mem. welfare reform task force 1977), AAUP, Nat. Conf. Social Welfare (Distinguished Service award 1975, pres. 1979—), Nat. Acad. Public Adminstrn. (trustee 1978, co-chmn. nat. panel on coordination of services to children and elderly), Nat. Assn. Jewish Center Workers, Am. Pub. Welfare Assn. (chmn. com. social service policy 1975-76, 77, dir. 1974-77), Conf. Deans and Dirs. Schs. Social Work (chmn. 1975-79), Nat. Conf. on Social Welfare, Phi Beta Kappa. Home: 372 Central Park W Apt 9D New York NY 10025-8207 Office: Columbia U Sch Social Wk, 622 W 113th St, New York N.Y. Deceased.

GIORDANO, ANTHONY BRUNO, electrical engineering educator, retired college dean; b. N.Y.C., Feb. 1, 1915; s. Sabino and Natalina (Amato) G.; m. Peggy Cozzi, Dec. 23, 1939; 1 son, Clyde Anton. BEE, Poly. Inst. Bklyn., 1937, MEE, 1939, DEE, 1946; ed. space study program, NASA, summer 1962. Mem. faculty Poly. Inst. N.Y., 1939-95, prof. elec. engring., 1953-95; dean Poly. Inst. N.Y. (Grad. Sch.), 1960-85, grad. dean emeritus, 1985, acting dean engring., 1978-79; scientist OSRD, 1942-45; rsch. supr. Microwave Rsch. Inst., Bklyn., 1945-65; dir. N.E. Radio Astronomy Coun., 1970-95; chmn. engring. adv. com. Bd. Edn., City of N.Y., 1958-60; cons. U.S. AID, 1964-85. Co-author: Network Theory, 1964; contbr. articles to profl. publs.; assoc. editor Jour. Radio Sci., 1967-73. Fellow IRE (chmn. N.Y. sect. 1954-55, regional dir. 1960-62, nat. dir. 1960-62), IEEE (chmn. basic scis. com. 1967-71, chmn. 1967, internat. conv., mem. awards bd. 1972-85, 93-95, life mem. fund com. 1986-90, rep., achievement award edn. soc. 1982-95, chmn., 1989-90, mem. editorial bd. 1990-94, corp. recognition award com. 1989-95, Centennial medal 1984, Sect. I Meritorious Achievement award 1991), Engring Found. of United Engring. (trustee 1968-95, chmn. projects com. 1973-76, chmn. bd. 1979-80, sec. communications soc. 1963-75, chmn. external awards com. 1975-77, chmn. Edison medal awards com. 1978, chmn. Edn. medal awards com. 1981-83), AAAS, AIEE (chmn. basic sci. div. 1955-56, rep. Hoover medal awards com. 1976-84); mem. Am. Soc. Engring. Edn. (chmn. meetings com. Middle Atlantic States sect. 1969-71, chmn. sect. 1971-72, chmn. sr. research award com. 1979-81, dir. zone 1 1973-75, v.p. at large 1974-75, v.p. member affairs 1984-86, chmn. grad. studies div. 1979-80, quality engring. edn. project 1985-87, Western Electric Fund award 1981, Charter Fellow award 1983, pres.-elect 1988-89, pres. 1989-90, W. Leighton Collins award 1987, Internat. Sci. Radio Union, Centennial Medallion Award, 1993), Sigma Xi, Tau Beta Pi, Eta Kappa Nu. Home: Jackson Heights N.Y. Died Oct. 2, 1995.

GISH, LILLIAN, actress; b. Springfield, Ohio; d. James Lee and Mary (Robinson) Gishi. AFD, Rollins Coll.; HHD, Mt. Holyoke Coll.; DFA (hon.), Bowling Green State U., 1976, Middlebury Coll. Debut on stage at 5; appeared in films including Birth of a Nation, Hearts of the World, Broken Blossoms, Way Down East, Orphans of the Storm, La Boheme, Scarlet Letter, Annie Laurie, The Wind, The Enemy, Night of the Hunter, Duel in the Sun, Portrait of Jennie, The Unforgiven, 1960, Follow Me Boys, 1966, The Comedians, 1967, A Wedding, 1978, Thin Ice (TV), 1980, Hambone and Hillie, 1984, Sweet Liberty, 1986, The Whales of August, 1987 (Nat. Bd. Rev. Film Award Best Actress 1987); movies made in Italy include The White Sister, Romola; appeared in plays including Crime and Punishment, 1948, Miss Mabel (title role), 1950, The Curious Savage, 1950, A Trip to Bountiful, Portrait of a Madonna, The Wreck of the 5:25, The Family Reunion (Pulitzer prize), All the Way Home, 1960-61, Romeo and Juliet (role of nurse), 1965, Anya, 1966, I Never Sang for My Father, 1967-68, Too True To Be Good, 1963, A Passage to India, 1963, Uncle Vanya, 1973, A Musical Jubilee, 1975, also TV plays including Twin Detectives, 1976, Sparrow, 1977, Hobson's Choice, 1983; appeared in TV series The Love Boat; toured Europe, Russia, U.S. as lectr. on art films, 1969, 71-73; TV documentary American Masters: Lillian Gish, 1988; Royal Command appearance, Queen Elizabeth the Queen Mother, 1980; author: The Movies, Mr. Griffith and Me, 1969, Dorothy and Lillian Gish, 1973, An Actor's Life for Me, 1987. Recipient hon. Acad. Award, 1971, Handel medallion City of N.Y., 1973, Kennedy Center honors City of N.Y., 1982, Life Achievement award Am. Film Inst., 1984, Dartmouth Film Soc. award, 1990; Dorothy and Lillian Gish Film Theatre on campus Bowling Green (Ohio) State Coll. Home: New York N.Y. Died Feb. 27, 1993.

GIUGGIO, JOHN PETER, newspaper executive; b. Boston, July 5, 1930; s. John Peter and Theresa H. (Gagliard) G.; m. Barbara Savage, May 9, 1953; children: Barbara, John, Patricia, Stephen. B.S. in Bus. Adminstrn, Boston Coll., 1951. With Boston Globe Newspaper, 1945-93, pres., 1978-93; pres., chief oper. officer Affiliated Publs., dir. Trustee Boston Coll. High Sch., Carney Hosp., Emmanuel Coll.; bd. dirs. North Conway (Mass.) Inst. Mem. Boston Coll. Alumni Assn. (pres. 1981-82), Boston C. of C. (dir.), Boston Better Bus. Bur. (assoc. chmn.). Club: Univ. (Boston) (pres.). Home: Cohasset Mass. Died Nov. 17, 1993.

GIVENS, JAMES WALLACE, JR., mathematician; b. Alberene, Va., Dec. 14, 1910; s. James Wallace and Mamie Elizabeth (Hughes) G.; m. Virginia Catherine Shelton, Sept. 16, 1937 (div.); m. Monique Pavel, Feb. 16, 1970 (div.). BS cum laude, Lynchburg (Va.) Coll., 1928; MS, U. Va., 1931; PhD, Princeton U., 1936; DSc (hon.), Lynchburg Coll., 1965. Instr. math. Cornell U., Ithaca, N.Y., 1937-41; instr. to asst. prof. Northwestern U., Evanston, Ill., 1941-46; assoc. prof. math. Ill. Inst. Tech., Chgo., 1946-47; prof. math. U. Tenn., Knoxville, 1947-56; prof. math., chmn. dept. math. Wayne State U., Detroit, 1956-60; prof. math. Northwestern U., Evanston, 1960-79; sr. scientist, dir. applied math div. Argonne (Ill.) Nat. Lab., 1960-75; prof. emeritus math. Northwestern U., 1979—. Recipient Alexander von Humboldt Stiftung award, Bonn, 1974. Fellow AAAS (sec. 1961-64); mem. Am. Math. Assn., Math. Assn. Am., ACM, Soc. for Indsl. and Applied Math. (pres. 1969-70). Home: El Cerrito Calif.

GLAID, ANDREW JOSEPH, III, chemist, educator; b. Pitts., July 14, 1923; s. Andrew J. and Barbara E. (Sommer) G.; m. Mary L. Brown, June 27, 1953; children: Andrew IV, Elaine, Karen, Amy, Mark. B.S., Duquesne U., 1949, M.S., 1950; Ph.D.; NIH fellow, Duke U., 1955. Asst. prof. chemistry Duquesne U., Pitts., 1954-57; asso. prof. Duquesne U., 1957-61, prof., 1961-92, chmn. dept. chemistry, 1975-92. Contbr. research publs. to sci. jours. Mem. Am. Chem. Soc., AAUP. Home: Pittsburgh Pa. Died Feb. 1, 1992.

GLASCO, JOSEPH MILTON, artist; b. Pauls Valley, Okla., Jan. 19, 1925; s. Lowell Marion and Pauline Elizabeth (Suddath) G. Student, U. Tex., 1941-42, Art Students League, N.Y.C., 1948. One-man exhbns. include Perls Gallery, N.Y.C., 1950, Catherine Viviano Gallery, N.Y.C., 1951, 52, 53, 54, 58, 61, 63, 65, 70, Gimpel & Weitzenhoffer Gallery, N.Y.C., 1983; represented in permanent collections, Bklyn. Mus., Albright Mus., Buffalo Mus., Mus. Modern Art, Met. Mus., Newark Mus., Whitney, Mus., Hirshhorn Mus., Princeton Mus. Served with U.S. Army, 1943-46. Mem. Nat. Soc. Lit. and the Arts. Roman Catholic. Home: New York N.Y. Died May 31, 1996.

GLASER, CLAUDE EDWARD, JR., former insurance company executive; b. N.Y.C., Mar. 14, 1919; s. Claude Edward and Hermine (Wolf) G.; m. Alice E. Sommer, Oct. 30, 1948; children: Cathy, Gail, Dianne. LL.B., Fordham U., 1940. Bar: N.Y. 1941. Staff atty. Hartford A&I, N.Y.C., 1946-49; claims mgr. Hartford A&I, White Plains, N.Y., 1949-52; claims mgr. Hartford A&I, N.Y.C., 1952-56, dir., 1981-85; claims mgr. Hartford Ins. Group, N.Y.C., 1956-68; v.p. Hartford Ins. Group, Hartford, Conn., 1968-75, sr. v.p., 1975-85; bd. dirs. N.Y. Underwriters, N.Y.C., Hartford Casualty Co., Hartford Accident and Casualty Co., Twin City Fire Co., Mpls., Hartford Splty. Co., Hartford Ins. Midwest, 1979-85; chmn. bd. govs. Ins. Crime Prevention Inst., Westport, Conn., 1976-77; bd. dirs. Asbestos Claim Facility, Princeton, N.J., 1985-87. Trustee, chmn. Bd. Edn. Eastchester (N.Y.), 1954-63. Served to capt. U.S. Army, 1941-46; served to lt. col. Res., ret. Mem. ABA, N.Y. State Bar Assn., Def. Research Inst., Internat. Assn. Ins. Counsel. Lutheran. Home: Simsbury Conn. Died Mar., 1993.

GLASER, JOSEPH BERNARD, association executive; b. Boston, May 1, 1925; s. Louis James and Dena Sophie (Harris) G.; m. Agathe Maier, Sept. 23, 1951; children: Simeon, Meyer, Sara, John. A.B., UCLA, 1948; J.D., U. San Francisco, 1951; B.H.L., Hebrew Union Coll., 1954, M.H.L., 1956, D.Div., 1980; postgrad. (Merrill Trust grantee), Law Faculty Hebrew U., Jerusalem, 1969-70. Rabbi, 1956; rabbi Temple Beth Torah, Ventura, Calif., 1956-59; regional dir. Union Am. Hebrew Congregations, San Francisco, 1959-71; exec. v.p. Central Conf. Am. Rabbis, N.Y.C., 1971-94; registrar Hebrew Union Coll., Los Angeles, 1956-59, instr. homiletics, 1956-59; instr. Bible, Hebrew Union Coll., Cin., 1954-56; vice chmn. San Francisco Conf. Religion and Peace, 1964-71, San Francisco Conf. Religion and Race, 1963-68; chmn. Clergy Com. Farm Labor Negotiation, 1967-68; chmn. bd. Religion in Am. Life, 1977-82, 87-94, chmn. religious adv. coun.; v.p. Am. Friends of Oxford Centre for Postgrad. Hebrew Studies.; trustee Howard Thurman Ednl. Trust; mem., bd. dirs. Am. Jewish World Svc.; mem. exec. com. Internat. Coordinating Com. on Religion and the Earth. Active Com. 100 for Tibet. With inf. AUS, 1943-46. Decorated Purple heart with oak leaf cluster. Mem. Central Conf. Am. Rabbis, Synagogue Coun. Am. (exec. com.), Union Am. Hebrew Congregations (exec. com., trustee), Conf. of Presidents of Major Jewish Orgns., Jewish Law Assn. Home: Scarsdale N.Y. Died Sept. 21, 1994.

GLASER, KURT, political science educator; b. An
Arbor, Mich., Aug. 19, 1914; s. Otto Charles an
Dorothy Gibbs (Merrylees) G.; m. Florence W. Riddl
Aug. 11, 1939 (div. Aug. 1948); children: Jeffrey, Kris
tin; m. Ingeburg Elfriede Halle, Mar. 8, 1950 (div. Ma
1976); children: Robin, Angela.; m. Dorothy My
Conyers, June 27, 1983. A.B., Harvard U., 1935, A.M
1938, Ph.D., 1941. With Social Security Bd., U.S. Dep
Agr. Washington, 1938-46; with Mil. Govt., German
1946-49; govt. affairs officer Office U.S. High Commn
Frankfurt, Germany, 1949-50; curriculum cons. an
journalist Munich, Germany, 1950-52; exchange office
project dir. Govt. Affairs Inst., Washington, 1952-5
office and mgmt. analyst Records Engring., Inc., Wash
1954-55; asst. prof. U. Md., Germany, 1956-59; lect.
Southern Ill. U., Edwardsville, 1959-60; assoc. pro
Southern Ill. U., 1960-65, prof. govt., 1965-83, pro
emeritus, 1983—; dir. spl. projects Found. Fgn. Affair
Chgo., 1973-84; prof. Tamkang U., Taipei, Taiwa
1983-89, prof. emeritus, 1989—; Fulbright lectr. U. Kie
Fed. Republic of Germany, 1966-67; lectr. Freedom
Found., Valley Forge, Pa., 1978—. Author: Czech
Slovakia: A Critical History, 1961, Der zweite Weltkrie
und die Kriegsschuldfrage, 1964, (with S.T. Posson
Victims of Politics: The State of Human Rights, 197
editor: (with David S. Collier) Found. for Fgn. Affai
series on East-West relations, 1962-69, (with J. Barrat
S. Brand and D.S. Collier) Accelerated Devel. in Sou
Africa, 1974, (with J. Barratt, D.S. Collier and Herma
Mönnig) Strategy for Development, 1976; assoc. edito
Modern Age, 1973—, Plural Societies, 1975-82; mn
editor: Tamkang Jour. Am. Studies, 1984—. Coo
dinator Dynamic Citizenship Forum, St. Louis, 1961-6
Bd. dirs. Found. for Study Plural Socs., 1974-80.
Hoover Inst. grantee, 1968-69. Mem. Univ. Profs. f
Acad. Order (dir. 1975-80). Home: North Dartmou
Mass. Died March 1, 1993.

GLASS, M. MILTON, architect; b. N.Y.C., Jan. 3
1906; s. Louis and Sarah B. (Hertzoff) G.; m. Rose
Schlamowitz, June 12, 1983; children: Joan Doroth
Cantor, Elliott Michael. Student, CCNY, 1925-28, 3
32, Columbia U., 1925-30, N.Y.U., 1930-31, Beaux-Ar
Inst. Design, 1925-31. Draftsman various archtl. office
1925-40; chief draftsman Mayer & Whittlesey (architec
and town planners), 1940-45; partner Mayer, Whittlese
& Glass, 1945-60; sr. partner Glass & Glass, N.Y.C
1960-67, 70-93; instr. site planning Sch. Architectur
Cooper Union, 1961-62. Important works inclu
Master Plan City of Kitimat, B.C., Can.; cons.: In
portant works include Master Plan City of Ashdod, I
rael; apt. houses Butterfield House and The Premie
N.Y.C., Forest Park Crescent, Queens, N.Y. Bd. dir
Citizens Housing and Planning Council N.Y., 1940-8
chmn. com. on community renewal and plannin
criteria, 1963; mem. com. on city planning Citize
Union N.Y., 1962-93; mem. architects adv. com. N.Y.
Housing and Redevel. Bd., 1966-67; mem. adv. co
N.Y. State Commr. Housing and Community Renew
1962-63; chmn. Bd. Standards and Appeals, City N.Y
1967-70; mem. architects' liaison com. N.Y.C. Housin
and Devel. Adminstrn., 1973-75; mem. N.Y.C. Mast
Plumbers License Bd., 1973-82; mem. adv. com. Gra
div. Columbia U. Sch. Architecture, 1950; panel me
of seminars Real Estate Inst., Sch. Continuing Edn
NYU, 1978. Recipient medal of honor N.Y. chpt. AI
1952, Apt. House medal N.Y. chpt. AIA, 1952, 1
Design award Progressive Architecture, 1959, 60, ce
tificate of merit Municipal Arts Soc. N.Y., 1961, 6
Bard award City Club N.Y., 1963, 1st Honor award f
residential design FHA, 1963, award Merit Queens C.
C., 1965. Fellow AIA (sec., chmn. com. on admissio
N.Y. chpt. 1949-50, chmn. civic design com. 1961-6
mem. urban design com. 1970-75), Nat. Inst. Arch
Edn. (trustee, del. to N.Y.C. Fine Arts Fedn. 1974, v.
Fine Arts Fedn. 1982-89, 2d v.p. 1990-93, 1st v.p., 198
93, chmn. com. on nominations to N.Y.C. Art Comm
1974); mem. N.Y. Soc. Architects (dir. 1950-62, 71-9
v.p. 1973, pres. 1973-75), Architects Council N.Y.
(pres. 1973-75, mem. jury to select Mayor's pan
architects for pub. works 1973), N.Y. State Ass
Architects (jury on awards 1971-75, pres. Architec
Council N.Y. 1973-75, dir. 1975-76), Nat. Sculptu
Soc., K.P. Home: New York N.Y. Died July 14, 1993.

GLASSER, MELVIN ALLAN, health policy executiv
consultant; b. N.Y.C., Sept. 6, 1915; s. David C. a
Rae (Startz) G.; m. Esther Kron, June 25, 1939; ch
dren: Stephen, Amy Corey, Robin Hudson. B.S.
CUNY, 1935; postgrad., Columbia U., 1939; L.L.
(hon.), Adelph U., 1951, Tuskegee Inst., 1975. Inves
gator Dept. Welfare, N.Y.C., 1936-39; casework
Jewish Family Welfare Soc., Bklyn., 1937-40; asst. na
dir., field supr. Mil. and Naval Welfare Service, A
Nat. Red Cross, 1940-44; asst. adminstrn. Internat. A
tivities, 1944-49; exec. dir. Mid-Century White Hou
Conf., Children and Youth, Washington, 1949-51; asso
chief U.S. Children's Bur., Washington, 1951-53; exe
v.p. Nat. Found. Infantile Paralysis, Washington, 195
59; adminstrv. dir. Salk Poliomyelitis Vaccine Fie
Trials, Washington, 1955-56; dean, prof Brandeis U
1959-61; dir. Soc. Sec. Dept., Internat. Union, Unit
Automobile, Aero. and Agricultural Impleme
Workers, Detroit, 1961-81, Health Sec. Action Coun
and Com. Nat. Health Ins., Washington, 1981-95; lec
Sch. Pub. Health, U. Mich.; adj. lectr. dept. epidem
ology and pub. health Yale U. Sch. Medicine; pres. a
pointee Nat. Com. 1960 White House Conf. on Childr

d Youth. Author: (with others) Survivor Benefits of ue Collar Workers, 1970, Obstacles in the Pathway to ental Health, 1977; contbr. articles to profl. jours. es. emeritus bd. trustees Tuskegee Inst.; past pres. at. Conf. on Social Welfare, Internat. Fedn. Social orkers, U.S. Com. Internat. Conf. Social Work; past mn. exec. com. Nat. Health Council; U.S. rep. health d welfare Red Cross; mem. adv. com. on health Office Tech. Assessment U.S. Congress, HEW; mem. com. 0 for Nat. Health Ins. Decorated Order of White on Czechoslovakia, Order of Orange Nassau Nether- nds; named Social Worker of the Year Nat. Conf. cial Welfare, 1983. Mem. Inst. of Medicine (council health care task force, past mem. governing council), Nat. cad. Sci., Am. Pub. Health Assn., Am. Pub. Welfare ssn., Nat. Assn. Social Workers, Nat. Conf. Social ork, Group Health Assn. Home: Washington .C. Died Mar. 13, 1995.

LEASON, JAMES ARTHUR, lawyer; b. Cleve., Feb.), 1905; s. M. James and Mary A. (O'Hare) G.; m. elen Mary Nightingale, Feb. 8, 1936 (dec. Apr. 1957); son, Michael Robert; m. Elinor Ferguson, June 6, 959 (dec. Nov. 1975); stepchildren: Sandra (Mrs. Ed arris), Barbara (Mrs. Lawrence C. Phillips), Jeannie E. Irs. Jeffrey Hutzler); m. Anita Wilker, Apr. 9, 77. A.B., Georgetown U., 1928; J.D., Case-Western es. U., 1931. Bar: Ohio 1932. Practiced in Cleve., ecializing in probate, tax, corp. real estate, and ins. w, 1932-41, 46-88; dir. Automatic Auto-Park, Inc., .Y.C.; Bd. govs. Georgetown U., Washington, 1950- 8; mem. senate Georgetown U., 1953-93; Pres. and mdg. brig. gen. emeritus Cleveland Grays, 1960-70; lv. bd. Marycrest Sch., Independence, Ohio, 1950-93. ntered USAAF, 1941; assigned Judge Adv's Dept. dqrs. 2d Air Force, 1943, Colorado Springs, Colo.; in arge Kornberg jewel cases trial judge adv. Watson .M.C. case 1946; col. JAG Corps Res. Decorated onze Star. Mem. ABA (state chmn. jr. bar conf. 937-38, council mem. 6th dist. 1939-40, ho. dels. 1943- 3, mem. standing com. on lawyers in armed forces 974-93, chmn. 1974-76), Bar Assn. Greater Cleve. olden Card mem.), Ohio State Bar Assn. (del. In- rnat. Bar Conf., Madrid 1952, gen. chmn. 86th ann. nv. com. 1966, council of dels. 1980-84), Internat. Bar ssn. (del. conv. 1966), Inter-Am. Bar Assn., Fed. Bar ssn. (pres. Cleve. chpt. 1961-62), Judge Advs. Assn. nat. 1972-92), Am. Soc. Internat. Law, Mil. Order /orld Wars (comdr. Cleve. 1961-62, dir. 1970-93), Am. egion (comdr. Army-Navy Shaker Heights post 54 963-64), VFW (judge adv. post 937 1975-88), Res. Of- cers Assn., Am. U.S. Army. Roman Catholic. Clubs: niversity (Washington); Grays, Georgetown, Cleve. kating, Union (Cleve.); Shaker Heights Country; layhouse. Home: Cleveland Ohio Died 1993.

LEASON, THOMAS W., labor union administrator; N.Y.C., Nov. 8, 1900; s. Thomas William and Mary Quinn) G.; m. Emma Martin (dec. 1961) children: homas W., Jack, Robert E. D. of Laws (hon.), Molloy oll., 1980. Dock worker N.Y.C., 1915, dock supr., 932, worker sugar factory; pres., bus. agt. Checkers' ocal 1346 ILA, N.Y.C.; gen. organizer Internat. Labor nion, N.Y.C., 1953-61, exec. v.p., contract negotiator, 961-63, internat. pres., 1963-92. Mem. fed. adv. ouncil Unemployment Ins., 1983-92; mem. House elect Com. on Hunger, 1984-92; mem. bd. dirs. frican-Am. Labor Ctr., Am. Inst. Free labor Devel.; em. Exec. Councils of the Irish Inst., N.Y., Am. Irish ist. Soc.; grand marshall Saint Patrick's Day Parade, .Y.C., 1984. Recipient Patriotic Civilian Service ward, U.S. Army, 1984, Good Scout award Greater .Y. Council Boy Scouts of Am., 1983, Saint Frances abrini Med. Ctr. award, 1982. Mem. Friendly Sons of . Patrick, Ancient Order of Hibernians (recipient John . Kennedy Meml. award 1982). Home: New York .Y. Died Dec. 24, 1992.

LIKES, ERWIN ARNO, publishing company execu- ve; b. Heide, Belgium, June 30, 1937; came to U.S., 942, naturalized, 1947; s. Morris I. and Gella (Lubow- xi) G.; m. Toni Marlene Brown, June 24, 1959 (div. 982); children: Michael Joseph, Lela Maeve; m. Carol rown Janeway, Mar. 3, 1990. A.B., Columbia U., 959, postgrad., 1960-62; postgrad., U Tübingen, Fed. epublic Germany, 1962-63. Lectr. English and com- arative lit. Columbia, 1960-62, asst. dean coll. 1965- 9; with Basic Books Inc., N.Y.C., 1969-79; exec. v.p. asic Books Inc., 1971-72, pres., pub. 1972-79; also v.p. Iarper & Row, Pubs., Inc., 1975-79, pub., group v.p. r adult trade books, 1976-79; dir. Harper & Row, td., London; sr. v.p. Simon and Schuster, N.Y.C.; ouchstone Books div., 1979-83; pres., pub. Free Press iv. Macmillan Pub. Co., 1983-94; v.p. Macmillan Pub. o., 1983-90, sr. v.p., 1990-94; cons. NEH, Wash- gton, 1971-76; mem. nat. adv. coun. Ctr. for the Book, ibr. of Congress, 1978-94; mem. vis. com. Harvard U. ress, 1989-94, chmn., 1992-94; trustee Columbia U. ress, N.Y.C., 1989-94, mem. exec. com., 1990-94. uthor: Of Poetry and Power, 1964. Woodrow Wilson ellow, 1962-63; German Acad. Austanschdienst fellow, 962-63. Mem. Assn. Am. Pubs. (vice-chmn. gen. pub. iv. 1974-75, chmn. 1975-76, chmn. Freedom to Read om. 1986-90), Phi Beta Kappa. Home: New York .Y. Died May 13, 1994.

ODARD, JAMES MCFATE, retired educational onsultant; b. Kankakee, Ill., Aug. 3, 1907; s. Gerald

Darlington and Sarah (McFate) G.; m. Aura Holton, Dec. 21, 1930; children: Mary Grace, Gerald Holton, Elizabeth Holland. A.B., Park Coll., 1929; A.M., Duke U., 1930; LL.D., Tex. Christian U., 1952; Litt.D., Midwestern U., Tex., 1952; L.H.D., Lander Coll., 1957, St. Ambrose Coll., 1968; Pd.D., Belmont Abbey Coll. 1959; LL.D., Hobart and William Smith Colls., 1963, St. Ambrose Coll., 1969. Instr. Park Coll., 1931-32, Duke U., Durham, N.C., 1933-36; prof. edn., dean coll. Queen's Coll., N.C., 1936-49; exec. sec. commn. colls. and univs. So. Assn. Colls. and Secondary Schs., Atlanta, 1949-54; v.p., dean adminstrn. U. Miami, Coral Gables, Fla., 1954-56, exec. v.p., 1956-60; exec. dir. Council Protestant Colls. and Univs., 1960-66; cons. Inst. Higher Ednl. Opportunity, So. Regional Edn. Bd., Atlanta, 1966-95; cons. Charlotte (N.C.) Mental Hygiene Clinic, 1937-47. Author: Understanding Mar- riage and Family Relations, 1948, The Blue Light, 1964; co- author: Christian Bases of World Order. Mem. So. Assn. Colls. Women, Am. Arbitration Assn., N.C. Mental Hygiene Soc. (bd. 1948-49), Charlotte Mental Hygiene Soc. (pres. 1949), Kappa Delta Pi, Phi Kappa Pni. Presbyn. Clubs: Kiwanis (Charlotte), Executives (Charlotte). Home: Atlanta Ga. Died June 27, 1995.

GODET, MAURICE, mechanical engineer. With Lab de Mechanique des Contacts, Villeurbanne Cedex, France. Recipient Mayo D. Hersey award ASME, 1992. Home: Villeurbanne France Died Oct. 9, 1993.

GODWIN, HARRY, botanist; b. Rotherham, Eng., May 9, 1901; s. Charles William Thomas and Mary Jane (Grainger) G.; M.A., Ph.D., Sc.D., Cambridge U., 1926, 42; m. Margaret Elizabeth Daniels, Sept. 12, 1927; 1 son, David. Fellow Clare Coll., Cambridge (Eng.) U. from 1925, botanist U. Cambridge, from 1923, head sub. dept. quaternary research, 1948-66, head dept. botany, 1960-68; pres. 10th Internat. Bot. Congress, 1964. Mem. Nature Conservancy, London, 1949-54, 65-72. Created knight, 1970; recipient Gold medal Linnean Soc. London, 1966, Prestwich medal Geol. Soc. London, 1951; Gunnar Erdtman medal Polynological Soc. India, 1980; Albrecht Penck medal Deuqua, 1982. Fellow Royal Soc., London (Croonian lectr. 1960); mem. Am. Acad. Arts and Scis. (hon. fgn.), Brit. Ecol. Soc. (pres. 1943), Royal Irish Acad. (hon.), Royal Soc. N.Z. (hon.), Royal Danish Acad. (fgn.), German Acad. Sci. (fgn.), Royal Soc. Uppsala (fgn.), Bot. Soc. Am. (corr.), Bot. Soc. Edinburgh (hon.), Quaternary Research Assn. (hon.), Bot. Soc. Göteborg (corr.), Societas pro Fauna et flora Fennica (fgn.). Author: History of the British Flora, 1956, 75; Fenland: its ancient past and uncertain future, 1978; The Archives of the Peat Bogs, 1981; editor New Phytologist, 1931-61, Jour. Ecology, 1948- 56. Deceased. Home: Cambridge Eng.

GOEBEL, WALTHER FREDERICK, biochemist; b. Palo Alto, Calif., Dec. 24, 1899; s. Julius and Kathryn (Vreeland) G.; m. Cornelia Van Rensselaer Robb, Oct. 23, 1930 (dec. Oct. 1974); children: Cornelia Van Ren- sselaer Bronson, Anne Kathryn Barkman; m. Alice Lawrence Behn, Nov. 12, 1976 (dec. 1989). AB, U. Ill., 1920, AM, 1921, PhD, 1923, scholar in chemistry, 1920- 21, fellow, 1921-23; postgrad., U. Munich, Germany, 1923-24; DS (hon.), Middlebury (Vt.) Coll., 1959; D.Sc. (hon.), Rockefeller U., 1978. Research asst. Rockefeller U., 1924-27, assoc., 1927-34, assoc. mem., 1934-44, mem., 1944-57, prof., 1957-70, prof. emeritus, 1970—. Contbr. monographs, reports and articles on chem. and immunological subjects sci. jours. Mem. Nat. Acad. Scis., Am. Chem. Soc., Am. Soc. Biol. Chemists, Harvey Soc., Am. Assn. Immunologists, Am. Soc. Microbi- ology, Conn. Acad. Sci. and Engring., Gesellschaft für Immunologie (Avery-Landsteiner award 1973), Phi Beta Kappa, Sigma Xi, Phi Lambda Upsilon, Phi Eta. Home: Essex Conn.

GOFRANK, FRANK LOUIS, retired machine tool company executive; b. Detroit, Dec. 23, 1918; s. Louis and Katherine E. (Schweninger) G.; m. Helen J. Rzeznik, Dec. 27, 1945; children: Shirley, Catherine, Ronald. B.A., Walsh Coll., 1950, LL.B. (hon.), 1982. C.P.A., Mich. Staff acct. Parker & Elsholz (C.P.A.s) 1947-48; staff acct. Lyons & Teetzel (C.P.A.s), 1949-50, partner, 1951-58; partner Coopers & Lybrand (C.P.A.s) Detroit, 1959-67; pres. Wilson Automation Co., Warren, Mich., 1967-73; chmn. bd., chief exec. officer Newcor, Inc., Warren, 1973-87; dir. Newcor, Inc. Mem. Mich. Assn. C.P.A.s. Clubs: Country of Detroit, Renaissance; Royal Palm Yacht and Country (Boca Raton, Fla.). Home: Boca Raton Fla. Died Mar. 4, 1995.

GOGGINS, JOHN FRANCIS, dentist, university ad- ministrator; b. Flint, Mich., Oct. 26, 1933; s. King Pierre and Genevieve Adeline (Bouchard) G.; m. Madeleine Alice Murray, Sept. 17, 1960; children: Pa- trick, Colleen, William. Student: U. Notre Dame, 1951- 54; DDS, Marquette U., 1958, MS, 1965. Gen. practice dentistry Flint, 1960-63; instr. Dental Sch. Marquette U., Milw., 1963-65; dean Dental Sch., Marquette U., 1984-92; dir. rsch. ctrs. Grad. Sch., Marquette U., 1992- 94; assoc. dir. collaborative research Nat. Inst. Dental Research, NIH, 1974-81, dep. dir. inst., 1981-83, acting dir., 1982-83, dep. dir., assoc. dir. extramural programs, 1983-84; chmn. fluoridation com. Genesee County Dental Soc., 1961-63. Author articles in field. Served to capt. Dental Corps USAF, 1958-60. postdoctoral fellow USPHS, 1965-66; Recipient Commendation

medal USPHS, 1977, Meritorious Svc. medal USPHS, 1983, Disting. Svc. award Pierre Fouchard Acad. Fellow AAAS, ADA, Am. Coll. Dentists; mem. In- ternat. Assn. Dental Research, Am. Assn. Dental Research, Am. Assn. Dental Schs., Wis. Dental Assn., Greater Milw. Dental Assn., Commd. Officers Assn. USPHS, Omicron Kappa Upsilon. Roman Catholic. Home: Mequon Wis. Died May 24, 1994.

GOIN, JOHN MOREHEAD, plastic surgeon; b. Los Angeles, Mar. 29, 1929; s. Lowell Sidney and Margaret Catherine (Morehead) G.; m. Marcia Stewart Kraft, Mar. 5, 1960; children: Suzanne Jennifer, Jessica Michele. B.A. in Zoology, UCLA, 1951; M.D., St. Louis U., 1955. Diplomate: Am. Bd. Plastic Surgery (dir. 1980-86). Intern U. Calif. Med. Center, San Francisco, 1955-56; asst. resident in surgery U. Calif. Med. Center, 1956-59; asst. resident to chief resident in plastic surgery U. Calif. Med. Center, Los Angeles, 1959-62; fellow in plastic surgery Queen Victoria Hosp., East Grinstead, Sussex, Eng., 1961; pvt. practice specializing in plastic and reconstructive surgery Los Angeles, 1962-95; clin. prof. surgery U. So. Calif.; chief plastic surgery Los Angeles County/U. So. Calif. Med. Center, 1971-80; head div. plastic surgery Children's Hosp. of Los Angeles, 1976-79. Author: (with Marcia Kraft Goin) Changing the Body: Psychological Effects of Plastic Surgery, 1980; Contbr. (with Marcia Kraft Goin) articles to profl. jours. Fellow ACS (gov. 1983- 95); mem. AMA, Calif. Soc. Plastic Surgeons (past pres.), Am. Soc. Plastic and Reconstructive Surgeons (sec. 1979-82, v.p. 1982-83, pres.-elect 1983-84, pres. 1984-85), Am. Soc. Aesthetic Plastic Surgery, Am. Assn. Plastic Surgeons, Pacific Coast Surg. Assn. Republican. Episcopalian. Home: Los Angeles Calif. Died May 16, 1995.

GOLD, AARON ALAN, finance company executive; b. Phila., Oct. 4, 1919; s. Lewis and Rose (Kroll) G.; m. Claire Halpern, Oct. 18, 1942; children: Ross Michael, Joshua S. and Julie B. (twins). Student, Temple U., 1940-42; PhD (hon.), Jewish Theol. Sem. Chmn., chief exec. officer Oxford First Corp., Phila., from 1950; ret. regional dir. Continental Bank, Norristown, Pa.; lectr. Wharton Sch., U. Pa., other univs.; bd. dirs. Ansley Assocs., Inc., Gen. Syndicate Corp., N.J., 1st Capital Trust, Kohala Ranch Assn., Honolulu; ret. sr. advisor Bankers Trust, N.Y.C.; dir. Penn Hudson Fin. Group, Inc., Phila., KM Mgmt. Group Inc., Abington, Pa.; dir. emeritus Manville Corp., Denver. Trustee Lower Ken- sington Environ. Drug Addiction Ctr., Opportunities Industrialization Ctr., Allied Jewish Appeal, Adath Jeshurun Synagogue; chmn. emeritus Kensington Hosp.; chmn. Community Multi-Health Svcs. Found.; bd. dirs. Am. Jewish Com., Am. Technion Soc., Hebrew U., Com. of 70, Phila., Phila. Heart Inst., Cheltenham Art Ctr., Jerusalem Elwyn Inst.; treas Anne Frank Inst. of Phila.; v.p. Haifa U. With U.S. Army, 1942-45. Recipient Cert. of Appreciation Fedn. Allied Jewish Appeal, 1975, B'nai Brith Internat. Humanitarian award, 1979, Cyrus Adler Community Svc. award, 1974, Albert Einstein award Am. Soc. Technion, 1988; named Man of Yr. Am. Jewish Com., 1988. Republican. Jew- ish. Clubs: Ashbourne (Cheltenham, Pa.); Locust (Phi- la.); Port Royal, Hilton Head Island (S.C.). Home: Philadelphia Pa. Deceased.

GOLDBERG, IRVING LOEB, federal judge; b. Port Arthur, Tex., June 29, 1906; s. Abraham and Elsa (Loeb) G.; m. Marian Jessel Melasky, Dec. 30, 1928; children: Nancy Paula (Mrs. Jay L. Todes), Julie Elsa (Mrs. Michael Lowenberg). B.A., U. Tex., 1926; LL.B., Harvard, 1929; L.H.D., Hebrew Union Coll.-Jewish Inst. Religion, 1974; LL.D., So. Methodist U., 1975. Bar: Tex. bar 1929. With Smith Crawford & Combs, Beaumont, Tex., 1929, Harris A. Melasky, Taylor, Tex., 1931; pvt. practice Houston, 1930; house counsel The Murray Co., Dallas, 1932-34; assoc. Martin B. Winfrey, Dallas, 1934, ptnr., 1934-36; ptnr. Thompson, Meek & Goldberg, 1946-50, Goldberg, Akin, Gump, Strauss & Hauer, Dallas, 1950-66; judge U.S. Ct. Appeals 5th Circuit, 1966-95, sr. judge. Past vice chmn. Tex. adv. com. U.S. Commn. Civil Rights; past pres. Jewish Welfare Fedn. Dallas, Dallas Home and Hosp. for Jewish Aged; past nat. v.p. Am. Jewish Com.; Past bd. dirs. Dallas UN Assn., Dallas Council Social Agys., Nat. Conf. Christians and Jews, United HIAS Service, Council Jewish Fedns. and Welfare Funds. Served to lt. USNR, 1942-46. Recipient Brotherhood citation Nat. Conf. Christians and Jews, 1968. Mem. Am., Dallas bar assns. Clubs: Dallas (Dallas), Columbian (Dallas). Home: Dallas Tex. Died Feb. 11, 1995.

GOLDBERG, PAUL JOSEPH, lawyer; b. N.Y.C., July 18, 1937; s. Simon and Grace (Feder) G.; m. Susan M. Gutman, June 16, 1968; 1 son, Scott Barry. A.B., Brown U. 1959; LL.B., Columbia U., 1962. Bar: N.Y. 1963, U.S. Dist. Ct. (so. and ea. dists.) N.Y. 1964, U.S. Tax Ct. 1964, U.S. Ct. Appeals (2d cir.) 1964, U.S. Ct. Appeals (9th cir.) 1985. Assoc. Chester C. Davis, N.Y.C., 1962-68; ptnr. Davis & Cox, N.Y.C., 1968-71, Lea, Goldberg & Spellun, P.C., N.Y.C., 1971-77, Kissam, Halpin & Genovese, N.Y.C., 1977-84, Golenbock and Barell, 1984-91; mem. departmental disciplinary com. 1st Jud. Dept. 1979-81, chmn. hearing panel 1980-81. Mem. ABA (com. on depreciation and investment tax credit tax sect.), N.Y. State Bar Assn. (com. on continuing legal edn.). Died Sept. 23, 1989;

buried Mt. Judah Cemetary. Home: Roslyn Heights N.Y.

GOLDBERGER, HERBERT H., clothing company executive; b. Providence, Dec. 27, 1917; s. Samuel and Bertha (Steiner) G.; m. Phillis V. Finkelstein, June 19, 1941; children: Stephen, Laurie. BA, Brown U., 1939; MBA, Harvard U., 1941. With Clear Weave Hosiery Stores, Boston, 1945-50; exec. v.p. Van's Stores, Boston, 1950-57; pres. Hills Dept. Stores, from 1957; now chmn. Hills Stores Co. (formerly SCOA Industries, Inc.), Canton, Mass. Served with AUS, 1942-45. Home: Canton Mass. Died Dec. 16, 1987.

GOLDFEDER, ANNA, retired research scientist; b. Poland, July 25, 1897; came to U.S., 1931, naturalized, 1940; d. Harry and Tauba (Friedman) G. D.Sc., Karl's U., Prague, Czechoslovakia, 1923; student medicine, Massaryk U., Brno, Czechoslovakia. Research asst. dept. exptl. pathology Masaryk U., 1923-25, assoc. in research dept. physiology, dir. cancer and radio biol. lab; fellow cancer research Vienna, Austria, 1928-29, Lenox Hill Hosp., N.Y.C., 1931; research dept. biol. chemistry Harvard Med. Coll; research dept. bacteriology and immunology Columbia Coll. of Physicians and Surgeons; research dept. biology NYU; research fellow cancer div. Dept. Hosps., N.Y.C., 1934; prin. research scientist, dir. emeritus Cancer and Radio-Biol. Lab., Depts. Health and Hosps., N.Y.C.; research work NYU, prof. biology, dir. Cancer Radiobiol. Research Lab. Contbr. numerous articles to profl. jours. Recipient Damon Runyon Fund for Cancer Research, Gold medal for research on cancer and radiobiology, 1978. Fellow AAAS, N.Y. Acad Scis. (Presdl. Gold medal award 1978), N.Y. Acad. Medicine; mem. Royal Soc. Medicine, Harvey Soc., Am. Assn. for Cancer Research, Soc. for Exptl. Biology and Medicine, Radiol. Research Soc., Radiol. Soc. N.Am. (award). Home: New York N.Y. Died Feb. 15, 1993.

GOLDFELD, STEPHEN MICHAEL, economics educator, university official; b. Bronx, N.Y., Aug. 9, 1940; s. Julius Morris and Ethel (Hammer) G.; m. Laura Heend, July 1, 1962; children: Melanie, Keith. AB, Harvard U., 1960; PhD, MIT, 1963. Sr. economist Council Econ. Advisers, 1966-67; asst. prof. econs. Princeton (N.J.) U., 1963-66, assoc. prof., 1966-69, prof., from 1969, chmn. dept. econs., 1981-85, 90-93, provost, from 1993; vis. prof. U. Cath.de Louvain, 1970-71, U. Calif., Berkeley, 1975-76, Israel Inst. Tech., 1980, European U. Inst., 1990; dir. Cons. in Industry Econs.; mem. Coun. Econ. Advisers, 1980-81; cons. Nat. Indsl. Conf. Bd., Mathematica, Fed. Res. Bd., Brookings Panel on Econ. Activity. Author: Commercial Bank Behavior and Economic Activity, 1966, Precursors in Mathematical Economics, 1968, Nonlinear Methods in Econometrics, 1972, Studies in Nonlinear Econometrics, 1976, The Economics of Money and Banking, 1986, The Economics of Mutual Fund Markets, 1990; assoc. editor Jour. Money, Credit and Banking, 1980-92, Pakistan Devel. Rev., from 1981; contbr. articles to profl. jours. Democratic campaign finance chmn., Princeton, 1969; Bd. dirs. N.J. Ednl. Computing Center, 1969-70. NSF sr. postdoctoral fellow, 1970-71, Guggenheim fellow, 1989-90. Fellow Econometric Soc.; mem. Am. Econ. Assn., Am. Statis. Assn., Am. Finance Assn. Home: Princeton N.J. Deceased.

GOLDIAMOND, ISRAEL, experimental psychologist, educator; b. Ukraine, Nov. 1, 1919; s. Samuel and Clara (Rottenburg) G.; m. Betty Ann Johnson, Feb. 28, 1946; children: Lisa Catherine Plymate, Joe David, Shana Aucsmith. B.A., Bklyn. Coll., 1942; Ph.D., U. Chgo., 1955. Adminstrv. asst. Inst. Design, Chgo., 1947-48; from research asst. to asso. U. Chgo., 1948-55; from asst. to asso. prof. psychology So. Ill. U., 1955-60; prof. psychology Ariz. State U., 1960-63; asso. to exec. dir. Inst. Behavioral Research, 1963-68; from assoc. prof. to prof. psychiatry and psychology (biopsychology) Johns Hopkins Med. Sch., 1965-68; prof. psychiatry and psychology U. Chgo., 1968-90; prof. emeritus, 1990—; clin. fellow Behavior Therapy Research Soc.; staff cons. div. neuropsychiatry Walter Reed Army Inst. Research, 1963-68. Contbr. profl. jours.; Editorial bds.: Jour. Exptl. Analysis Behavior, 1963-68, Jour. Applied Behavior Analysis, 1968-73, Jour. Abnormal Psychology, 1966-74, Communications in Behavior Biology, 1968-71, Behaviorism, 1971-89, Behavior Modification, 1976-83. Served with AUS, 1942-45. Recipient Research Career Devel. award NIMH, 1963-67. Fellow AAAS, Assn. Advancement Behavior Therapy, Am. Psychol. Soc., Am. Psychol. Assn. (v.p. divsn. exptl. analysis behavior 1967-70, bd. dirs. social and ethical responsibility in psychology 1988-90, Am. Psychol. Soc.; mem. AAUP, Psychonomic Soc., Assn. Behavior Analysis (pres. 1977-78), Sigma Xi. Home: Chicago Ill. Deceased.

GOLDING, SIR WILLIAM GERALD, author; b. St. Columb, Cornwall, Eng., Sept. 19, 1911; s. Alec A. and Mildred A. G.; m. Ann Brookfield, 1939; children: David, Judith. B.A., Brasenose Coll., Oxford, Eng., 1935; M.A. hon. fellow, 1966; D. Litt. (hon.), U. Sussex, 1970, U. Kent, 1974, U. Warwick, 1981, Sorbonne, 1981, Oxford U., 1982. Tchr. Bishop Wordsworth's Sch., Wiltshire, Eng., 1940, 45-61. Settlement house work, dir., actor, writer, 1935-39, writer-in-residence, Hollins Coll., 1961-62; author: Poems, 1934, Lord of the Flies, 1954, The Inheritors, 1955, Pincher Martin, 1956, Free Fall, 1959, The Spire, 1964, The Hot Gates, 1965, The Pyramid, 1967, The Scorpion God, 1971, Darkness Visible, 1979 (James Tait Black Meml. prize), Rites of Passage, 1980 (Booker McConnel prize), A Moving Target, 1982, The Paper Men, 1984, An Egyptian Journal, 1985, Close Quarters, 1987, Fire Down Below, 1989; play Brass Butterfly, 1958. Served to lt. Royal Navy, 1940-45. Fellow Royal Soc. Lit., 1955, Companion of Lit., 1981; recipient Nobel prize for lit., 1983; created knight by Queen Elizabeth II, 1988. Home: Cornwall Eng. Died June 19, 1993.

GOLUB, WILLIAM WELDON, lawyer; b. Bklyn, Oct. 7, 1914; s. Joseph and Sarah (Resnek) G.; m. Barbara Lewis, July 3, 1942 (dec.); 1 dau., Joan L. A.B., Columbia U., 1934, J.D., 1937. Bar: N.Y. 1937, U.S. Ct. Appeals (2d cir.) 1944, U.S. Ct. Appeals (3d cir.) 1949, U.S. Supreme Ct. 1953. Assoc. Stanchfield & Levy, N.Y.C., 1937-39; staff atty. Atty. Gen.'s Com. on Adminstrv. Procedure, 1939-40, Trustees, Associated Gas and Electric Corp., N.Y.C., 1940-45; assoc. Shearman & Sterling & Wright, N.Y.C., 1945-53; ptnr. McGoldrick Dannett Horowitz & Golub, N.Y.C., 1953-69; ptnr. Rosenman & Colin, N.Y.C., 1969-87, counsel, 1987-94; cons. govt. agys. Trustee Columbia U., 1981-82, Morris Jumel Mansion, 1990-94. Recipient John Jay award Columbia Coll., Columbia U., 1988, Disting. Achievement award Law Sch., 1993. Mem. ABA, Am. Law Inst., Assn. of Bar of City N.Y., Fed. Bar Council (v.p. 1966-73), Columbia Coll. Alumni Assn. (pres. 1976-78; alumni medal 1972), Columbia Law Sch. Assn (pres. 1978-80), Phi Beta Kappa. Democrat. Clubs: Friars, Bohemians, Collectors (N.Y.C.). Home: New York N.Y. Died Mar. 28, 1994.

GOMBERG, HENRY JACOB, nuclear engineer; b. N.Y.C., Apr. 16, 1918; s. Alexander and Marie (Shuloff) G.; m. Edna M. Cohen, Dec. 28, 1940 (dec. Nov. 1965); children—Richard, Robert; m. Edith Silverglied, June 24, 1967; stepchildren—Stephen, Judith, Eugene Lisansky. B.S.E., U. Mich., 1941, M.S.E., 1943, Ph.D. in Elec. Engring, 1951; Sc.D. (hon.), Albion Coll., 1968. Dir. Mich. Meml.-Phoenix Project, 1959-61; chmn. com. nuclear engring. U. Mich., 1955-58, chmn. dept. nuclear engring., 1958-61, prof. nuclear engring., 1955-61; dep. dir. P.R. Nuclear Center, Mayaquez, 1961-66, dir., 1966-71; pres., chief operating officer KMS Fusion, Inc., Ann Arbor, Mich., 1971, chmn., 1976-80; pres., chief exec. officer KMS Industries, Inc., 1976-78, pres., 1978-80; pres., chmn. Ann Arbor Nuclear Inc., 1981-95; mng. dir. Ann Arbor Nuclear, Israel, Ltd., 1986-95; chmn., CEO Penetron, Inc., 1987-95; chmn., CEO Penetron, Inc., 1987-95; Carnegie vis. prof. U. Hawaii, 1961; cons. Hawaiian Electric Co., Atomic Power Devel. Assocs., Inc., GM Corp., Lockheed Aircraft Co., Nuclear Products Co., Cook Rsch. Labs., ICA, AEC, Nat. Acad. Scis. Chmn. com. research reactors NRC; del. Internat. Conf. Peaceful Uses Atomic Energy, 1955; U.S. rep. Nat. Acad. Sci. to, USSR, 1957. Recipient Henry Russel award U. Mich., 1952. Fellow APHA, AAAS, Am. Nuclear Soc., Radiation Research Soc.; mem. IEEE, Am. Phys. Soc. (com. on fusion Atomic Indsl. Forum), Am. Soc. Engring. Edn., Fusion Power Assn., Sigma Xi, Tau Beta Pi, Eta Kappa Nu, Phi Kappa Phi. Club: Cosmos. Home: Ann Arbor Mich. Died Apr. 8, 1995.

GONZALES, MARJORIE ELAINE, academic dean; b. Bklyn., June 26, 1927; d. Clifford and Marie (Mills) Hyde; m. Joseph Edward Gonzales, Dec. 5, 1948; children: Maria Pavek, Marguerita Elena. BA, Hunter Coll., 1954; MS, Ea. Conn. State Coll., 1971; postgrad., So. Conn. State Coll., 1973, So. Conn. State Coll., 1977. Cert. tchr., elem. and secondary guidance and counseling, intermediate adminstrn. and supervision, Conn. Dean of students New London (Conn.) Bd. Edn., guidance counselor, tchr.; com. mem. Tchr. of Yr. Program, Conn. State Dept. of Edn., 1980-89). Mem. NEA, New London Adminstrs. Edn. Assn., Elem. Middle Sch. Prins. Assn. Conn. (pres. award 1980-89), Conn. Edn. Assn., Phi Delta Kappa. Home: Salem Conn. Died Nov. 9, 1995.

GONZALEZ-TORRES, FELIX, artist; b. 1957. Student, Whitney Mus., 1981, 83; BFA, Pratt Inst., 1983; MFA, NYU, 1987. adj. art instr. NYU, 1987-89, 92, CALARTS, L.A., 1990. One-man shows include Mus. Modern Art, N.Y., 1992, Mus. d'Art Modern de la Ville de Paris, 1996, Galerie Jennifer Flay, Paris, 1993, Mus. in Progress, Vienna, Austria, 1993, Matrix Gallery, U. Calif., 1994, The Fabric Workshop, Phila., 1994, Mus. Contemporary Art, L.A., 1994, Hirschhorn Mus. & Sculpture Garden, 1994, Aldrich Mus. Contemporary Art, 1993, Mus. Modern Art, N.Y., 1993, Studio Oggetto Milan, Italy, 1994, Margo Leavin Gallery, L.A., 1994, Andrea Rosen Gallery, N.Y., 1990, 92-94, Neue Gesellschaft fur Bildende Kunst, Berlin, 1994-95, Guggenheim Mus., N.Y.C., 1995; exhibited work at Mus. Modern Art, N.Y., 1989, Whitney Mus. Am. Art, 1991, Walker Art Ctr., 1992, Mus. Modern Art, N.Y., 1992, San Francisco Mus. Modern Art, 1994. Fellow Nat. Endowment Arts, 1989, 93, Deutscher Akademischer Austauschdienst fellow artist-in-residence program Berlin, 1992; recipient Gordon Matta-Clark Found. award, 1991. Home: New York N.Y. Died Jan. 9, 1996.

GONZALO, JOSE MARIA AGUIRRE, civil engine banker; b. San Sebastian, Spain, Aug. 12, 1897; s. J Maria Aguirre and Hilaria (Gonzalo) Sagastume; Francisca Gonzalez, Nov. 21, 1925 (dec. 1978); childr Carmen (dec.), Jose Maria, Pilar, Beatriz. Civil Engri. degree, Tech. Superior Coll. Rds., Canals and Harbou Madrid, 1921. Founder, chmn., mgr. Agroman Empr Constructora S.A., Madrid, 1927-84; chmn. bd. Ba Guipuzcoano, San Sebastian, from 1941; dir., chmn. Bank Espanol de Credito, Madrid, 1942-84; dir. C Sevillana Electricidad, Madrid and Sevilla, Spain, fr 1951; chmn. bd. Acerinox, Algeciras, Spain, from 19 co-founder, chmn. Inst. Eduardo Torroja Constrn. a Cement, Madrid, 1934-84; chmn. Patronato Cole Univ. est Financieros, Madrid, from 1973; particip tech., constrn. and fin. confs. Patentee in field. Me Spanish Congress, v.p. com., 1968. Decorated Gt. Cr Merito Civil, Gt. Cross Isabel la Catolica, Gt. Cr Cisneros, Gt. Cross Alfonso x el Sabio, Gt. Cross Car III; recipient Golden medal Govt. of Spain, 1967. Me Assn. Progress Mgmt. (bd. dirs.), Found. Europe Culture (bd. govs.). Clubs: Casino Circulo Labra Golf, Sociedad Hipica. Avocations: music; theat literature. Deceased. Home: Madrid Spain

GOOD, BARRY C., financial analyst; b. N.Y.C., Se 27, 1932; s. F. Campbell Good and Vinelia (No Hess; m. Martha L. Byorum, Mar. 10, 1978; childr Hillary H. Stone, Brian C., Ashley C. Student, Yale 1950-52. Fin. analyst Dean Witter and Co., N.Y 1953-65; v.p., fin. analyst Laird Inc., N.Y.C., 1965- mng. dir., fin. analyst Morgan Stanley and Co., N.Y 1973—. Mem. Oil Analysts Group N.Y. (pres. 19 80), Nat. Assn. Petroleum Investment Analysts (dirs. 1980-82), Union Club (gov. 1984—), Maidst Club (East Hampton, N.Y.). Home: Water Mill N.Y.

GOODHUE, FRANCIS ABBOT, JR., lawyer; Needham, Mass., June 11, 1916; s. Francis Abbot a Nora Forbes (Thayer) G.; m. Mary Elizabeth Br May 15, 1948; 1 son, Francis Abbot III. A.B., Harv U., 1937, LL.B., 1940. Bar: N.Y. 1941. Practiced N.Y.C.; mem. firm Dewey, Ballantine, Bushby, Palr & Wood (and predecessor firms), from 1939, partr from 1952, chmn. mgmt. com., 1980-82. Served to comdr. USNR, 1941-46. Republican. Home: N York N.Y. Deceased.

GOODINGS, ALLEN, bishop; b. Barrow-in-Furn Lancashire, Eng., May 7, 1925; s. Thomas Jackson a Ada (Tate) G.; m. Joanne Talbot, Oct. 26, 1959; c dren—Suzanne, Thomas. B.A., Sir George Williams Montreal, Que., Can., 1959; B.D., McGill U., Montr 1959; L.Th., Montreal Diocesan Theol. Coll., 19 D.D. (hon.), 1978. Engr., draftsman in industry, 19 54; ordained to ministry Anglican Ch., 1959; cur then priest chs. in Montreal, 1959-65; rector Ch. of cension, Montreal, 1965-69; dean Cathedral of H Trinity, Quebec, 1969-77; bishop Anglican Diocese Que., 1977-90; asst. bishop Anglican Diocese of Otta 1990—; chaplain Can. Grenadier Guards, Montr 1966-69. Clubs: Cercle universitaire (Quebec), Offi Mess Royal 22d Regt. (Quebec), Garrison (Queb (hon.). Home: Nepean Can.

GOODMAN, ANDREW, business executive; b. N.Y. Feb. 13, 1907; s. Edwin and Belle Dorothy (Lowenste G.; m. Consuelo Manach, Sept. 29, 1935; childr Vivien Malloy, Mary Ann Quinson, Edwin Andr Pamela Lichty. Student, U. Mich., 1924-26. W Bergdorf Goodman, 1926-93, pres., from 1951, chn from 1975, chmn. exec. com.; gen. ptnr. 754 Fifth A Assos. (L.P.), N.Y.C., from 1979; dir. Guardian I Ins. Co., H.M. Rayne, Ltd. of Eng.; hon. dir. Ca Hawley Hale Stores, Inc.; Bd. dirs. Fifth Ave. As trustee Fashion Inst. Tech. Life trustee Fedn. Jew Philanthropies; bd. dirs., trustee United Jewish App v.p. Am. Jewish Com.; bd. dirs. Better Bus. B N.Y.C.; hon. chmn. bd. Nat. Jewish Hosp., Den Served as lt. USN, 1944-46. Recipient Tobe awa 1960; decorated Star of Solidarity Italy). Club: West ester Country (Rye). Home: Rye N.Y. Died Apr. 1993.

GOODMAN, CAROL, lawyer; b. Milford, Mass., N 22, 1945; d. Louis and Ethel (Rosen) G.; divorced child, Elizabeth Sarah Goodman. AB cum lau Barnard Coll., 1966; JD magna cum laude, U. Ma 1974; postgrad., Harvard U., 1973-74. Bar: N.Y. 19 Mass. 1978, Utah 1987, Calif. 1988, U.S. Dist. Ct. and ea. dists.) N.Y. 1975, U.S. Ct. Appeals (2d c 1975, U.S. Dist. Ct. (ea. dist.) U.S. Ct. Appeals (1st c 1978, U.S. Supreme Ct. 1980, U.S. Ct. Appeals (1 cir.) 1986, U.S. Ct. Appeals (9th cir.) 1987, U.S. D Ct. Utah 1987, U.S. Dist. Ct. (cen. dist.) Calif. 19 U.S. Dist. Ct. N Dist. Calif. 1991. Assoc. Paul W Rifkind Wharton & Garrison, N.Y.C., 1974- Goodwin Proctor & Hoar, Boston, 1977-82, LeBo Lamb Leiby & McRae, N.Y.C., 1982-83; ptnr. LeBo Lamb Leiby & McRae, Boston, N.Y.C. and L.A., 19 88, Thelen, Marrin, Johnson & Bridges, Los Ange 1988-92; assoc. Bryan Cave, L.A. and Santa Mon Calif., from 1992; panel atty. Cmty. Law Offices, I N.Y.C., 1974-77. Mem. ABA (com. on regulation fed. securities from 1981, subcom. on litigation fr 1983, sect. on bus. law 1981, mem. task force on insi trading 1984-87, vice-chair task force on securities a tration from 1986, ad hoc com. on proposed SEC R

Practice from 1993, sect. 16 com. from 1992), Boston r Assn. (panel atty. Vol. Lawyers Project from 1977), ass. Bar Assn., L.A. County Bar Assn., Fin. Lawyers nf., Phi Beta Kappa. Democrat. Jewish. Home: San dro Calif. Home: Santa Monica Calif. Deceased.

ODMAN, STANLEY JOSHUA, department store ecutive; b. Montreal, Que., Can., Mar. 23, 1910; came U.S., 1932, naturalized, 1940; s. Issac and Jenny linsweig) G.; m. Alice Therese Hahn, June 16, 1936 c. 1982); children: Ellen, John Edgar; m. Alice dolph, Jan. 6, 1990; stepchildren: David, zabeth. BA, McGill U., 1931, MA, 1932; MBA, rvard U., 1934. With Arco Co., Cleve., 1934-36, .T. Fin. Corp., 1936-42, Interstate Dept. Stores, 42-48; with May Dept. Stores Co., St. Louis, 1948-76, ., 1958-67, pres., 1967-76, chief exec. officer, 1969-76, nn. bd., 1969-76, chmn. exec. com., dir.; pres. mous-Barr Co., St. Louis, 1959-67; owner Top Mgmt. vices, St. Louis, 1976-92. Author: How to Manage a rnaround, 1982; contbr. articles to popular mags. and fl. jours. Treas. Grand Ctr. Inc.; life trustee St. uis Symphony Soc.; mem. emeritus Civic Progress .; bd. dirs. Downtown St. Louis Inc.; bd. dirs. umeier Sculpture Park, Jefferson Meml., Alliance ncaise. Fellow Royal Soc. Arts (London); mem. t. Retail Mchts. Assn., Japan-Am. Soc., Nat. Retail hts. Assn. (Gold Medalist 1982). Clubs: St. Louis, rvard (St. Louis, N.Y.C.); Noonday, Frontenac cquet, Whittemore House, University (St. Louis), stwood Country. Home: Saint Louis Mo. Died Nov. 1992.

ODMAN, WILLIAM I., urban planner, educator; Detroit, June 24, 1919; s. Morris and Bella (Kecner) m. Pearl Meisner, Dec. 28, 1946; children—Ann, borah. A.B., Wayne State U., 1942, M.Pub. Ad- nstrn., 1950; M.City Planning, Mass. Inst. Tech., 52. Planner Detroit City Planning Commn., 1943-50; dent planner Adams, Howard & Greeley, Hartford, nn., 1952-53; dir. rezoning study Boston City Plan- g Bd., 1953-54; asst. prof. city planning Harvard U., 3-56; asso. prof. urban planning U. Ill., Urbana, 6-60, prof., 1960-65, 71-88, emeritus, 1988-95, chmn. t. urban planning, 1965-71, dir. Office Transp. Rsch., 76-79; planning cons., 1955-95; dir. Office Urban nsp. Systems, U.S. Dept. Transp., 1971-73, cons.; s. ICA, Govts. Costa Rica, Iran, U.S. Offices Re- nal Econ. Devel. Mass., Ill., Wis., S.D.; U.S. del. to n. Commn. Europe Colloquium on Urban Transp., 3. Author: Principles and Practice of Urban Plan- g, 1968; Contbr. articles to profl. jours. Mem. bash Valley Interstate Commn., 1966-95. Served with S, 1945. Recipient Merit award Am. Inst. Planners, 9; Fulbright scholar to U.K., 1962-63; Am. Soc.). Adminstrn. fellow, 1971-72. Mem. Am. Planning n., Am. Soc. Planning Ofcls. (edn. council), Am. t. Cert. Planners, Am. Inst. Planners (v.p., past mem. govs., adv. bd. Jour.), Assn. Collegiate Schs. of nning (pres. 1970-71). Home: Urbana Ill. Died Dec. 1995.

ODNER, DWIGHT BENJAMIN, mathematician, eritus educator; b. What Cheer, Iowa, Aug. 15, 1913; William Clifford and Myrtle Elizabeth (Harbour) G.; Mildred E. Wilson, June 29, 1936. B.A. with nors, William Penn Coll., 1934; M.A. (T. Wistar wn fellow), Haverford Coll., 1935; Ph.D., U. Ill., 9. Faculty S.D. State Coll., Brookings, 1937-42, 46; ilty Fla. State U., Tallahassee, 1949-78; prof. math. State U., 1954-78, prof. emeritus math., 1978-95;). dean Fla. State U. (Grad. Sch.), 1953-58; Cons. n. on Accreditation of Armed Services Ednl. Exper- es, 1950-59, Ednl. Testing Service, Princeton, N.J., 5-70; mem. Com. on Undergrad. Program in Math., 6-70, mem. cons. bur., 1963-71; cons., lectr. AID nmer Insts. for Coll. Tchrs., India, 1966, 67; visitor t. for Advanced Study, Princeton, 1971. Math. or: Jour. Communication, 1959-61; Contbr. articles tech. jours. Served with USNR, 1942-46. Mem. th. Assn. Am. (cons. com. on ednl. media 1964, gov. 7-71, cons. bur. 1971-95), Am., London, Edinburgh, ian math. socs., Phi Beta Kappa, Sigma Xi, Phi ppa Phi, Pi Mu Epsilon, Phi Delta Kappa, Chi nma Iota, Lambda Chi Alpha. Presbyn. (elder). me: Tallahassee Fla. Died Sept. 9, 1995.

ODSON, MARK, television producer; b. Sacra- nto, Jan. 24, 1915; s. Abraham Ellis and Fannie oss) G.; children by previous marriages: Jill, athan, Marjorie. BA, U. Calif., 1937. Announcer, scaster, dir. Sta. KFRC, San Francisco, 1938-41; io announcer, dir. N.Y.C., 1941-43; radio dir. U.S. asury War Bond Dr., 1944-45; chmn. bd. Goodson wspaper Group. Formed Goodson-Todman Prodns., 6; originated radio shows Winner Take All, 1946, p the Music, 1947, Hit the Jackpot, 1947-49; creator TV game programs What's My Line, It's News to , The Name's the Same, I've Got a Secret, Two for Money, The Price is Right, Password, Match Game, Tell the Truth, Family Feud, Child's Play, others; ducer TV film series The Web, The Rebel, Richard ne Theater, Branded. Trustee Mus. Broadcasting, 5-92; bd. dirs. Am. Film Inst., 1975-92. Recipient . TV award Gt. Brit., 1951, Emmy award Acad. TV s and Scis., 1951, 52, Sylvania award, Daytime my Lifetime Achievement award., 1989-90. Mem. d. TV Arts and Sci. (pres. N.Y.C. 1957-58), Phi Beta Kappa. Home: New York N.Y. Died Dec. 18, 1992.

GOOSSENS, JOZEF ELISA, personnel director; b. Antwerp, Belgium, Mar. 12, 1943; came to U.S., 1980; s. Johannes Albert and Maria (Janssens) G.; m. Roswitha Anna Winter; children: Anna-Maria, Johanna. BA, Inst. Social Studies, Antwerp, Belgium, 1967. Human resources rep. Usines Renault, Brussels, 1969-71; pers. mgr. Upjohn Belgium, Antwerp, 1971-80; area pers. mgr., Europe Upjohn Internat., Kalamazoo, Mich., 1980-81, labor rels. mgr., 1982-83, dir. employee rels., 1983-85; v.p. human resources Bausch & Lomb, Inc., Rochester, N.Y., 1985—; Avocations: soccer, biking, speaking several fgn. langs. Home: Fairport N.Y.

GORDIMER, NADINE, author; b. Republic of South Africa, Nov. 20, 1923; d.Isidore and Nan (Myers) Gordimer; m. Reinhold Cassirer, Jan. 29, 1954; children: Oriane, Hugo. Ed., Convent Sch., Springs, Republic of South Africa. Author: (story collections) Face to Face, 1949, The Soft Voice of the Serpent, 1952, Six Feet of the Country, 1956, Friday's Footprint, 1960 (W.H. Smith and Son Literary award 1961), Not for Publication, 1965, Livingstone's Companions, 1971, Selected Stories, 1975, Some Monday for Sure, 1976, A Soldier's Embrace, 1980, Town and Country Lovers, 1980, Something Out There, 1984, Crimes of Conscience, 1991, Jump, 1991, Why Haven't You Written?, 1992; (polit. and lit. essays) The Essential Gesture, 1988, Three in a Bed, 1991; (literary criticism) The Black Interpreters, 1973, Writing & Being: Charles Eliot Norton Lectures, 1995; (novels) The Lying Days, 1953, A World of Strangers, 1958, Occasion for Loving, 1963, The Late Bourgeois World, 1966, A Guest of Honour, 1970 (James Tait Black Meml. prize 1973), The Conservationist, 1974 (Booker prize for fiction Nat. Book League 1974), Burger's Daughter, 1979, July's People, 1981, A Sport of Nature, 1987, My Son's Story, 1991, None to Accompany Me, 1994; (other) On the Mines, 1973, Lifetimes Under Apartheid, 1986; editor: (with Lionel Abrahams) Southern African Writing Today, 1967. Decorated comdr. de l'Ordre des Arts et des Lettres (France), 1986; recipient Thomas Pringle award English Acad. South Africa, 1969, CNA award, 1974, 79, 81, 91, Grand Aigle d'Or, 1975, Disting. Svc. in Lit. Commonwealth award, 1981, MLA award, 1982, Nelly Sachs prize (Germany), 1985, Malaparte award (Italy), 1986, Bennett award, 1986, Benson medal, 1990, Nobel Prize for Literature, 1991; Neil Gunn fellowship Scottish Arts Coun., 1981. Fellow Royal Soc. Lit.; mem. AAAS, Com. European Authors, Am. Acad. (hon.), Inst. Arts and Letters (hon.), PEN (v.p).

GORDON, DAVID MICHAEL, economist, educator; b. Washington, May 4, 1944; s. Robert Aaron and Margaret (Shaughnessy) G.; m. Diana Russell Smith, Sept. 7, 1967. BA, Harvard U., 1965, PhD, 1971. Rsch. assoc. Nat. Bur. Econ. Rsch., N.Y.C., 1969-72; lectr. Yale U., New Haven, Conn., 1969-70; asst. prof. econ. New Sch. for Social Rsch., N.Y.C., 1973-79, assoc. prof. econ., 1979-83, prof. econ., from 1984; chair in Am. civilization Ecole des Hautes Études en Sciences Sociales, Paris, 1990-91. Author: Theories of Poverty and Underemployment, 1972 (C Wright Mills award 1973); co-author: Segmented Work, Divided Workers, 1982, Beyond the Waste Land, 1983, After the Waste Land, 1991; editor: Problems in Political Economy, 1977. Mem. steering com. Union for Radical Econs., N.Y.C., 1975-77, 84-85, nominating com. Am. Econ. Assn., Nashville, 1977, 89, bd. of economists L.A. Times, 1986-93. Guggenheim fellow, Guggenheim Found., 1984-85; mem. Inst. for Advanced Study, Princeton, N.J., 1987-88. Mem. Am. Econs. Assn., Union for Radical Polit. Econs., Dem. Socialists Am., Nat. Writers Union. Democrat. Home: New York N.Y. Deceased.

GORDON, EDWARD, music association executive; b. 1930. D.F.A. (hon.), North Central Coll., Naperville, Ill., 1980; MusD (hon.), Cleve. Inst. Music, 1989; LHD (hon.), Rosary Coll., River Forest, Ill. Asso. mgr. Grant Park summer concerts, Chgo. Park Dist., 1958-65; mgr. Grant Park summer concerts, 1965-68; gen. mgr. Ravinia Festival Assn., Chgo., 1968-70; exec. dir. Ravinia Festival Assn., 1970-90, chief operating officer, 1982-90, dir. emeritus, 1990-96, trustee, 1987-90, life trustee, 1991-96; dir. Steans Inst. for Young Artists at Ravinia, 1988-91; Mem. music adv. panel U.S. Dept. State; mem. recommendation bd. Avery Fisher Artist Award program; mem. adv. bd. Van Cliburn Internat. Piano Competition, Internat. Piano Competition, Sydney, Australia, World Piano Competition, London; mem. vis. com. Dept. Music U. Chgo.; chmn. Music panel Arts Club of Chgo.; performed age 9 with Chgo. Symphony under Frederick Stock. Former concert pianist, recitalist, 1992-96. Home: Chicago Ill. Died Apr. 19, 1996.

GORDON, JOHN LUTZ, utility executive; b. Lincoln, Ill., Oct. 10, 1899; s. Frank B. and Marian C. (Lutz) G.; m. Ruth Coddington, Apr. 30, 1928; 1 dau., Marian (Mrs. Jack A. McCann). B.S. in Elec. Engring, Milw. Sch. Engring., 1920, E.E., 1953. Cons. engr. Vaughan & Meyer, Milw., 1920-23; engr. C.A. Shaler Co., Waupun, Wis., 1923-26; with Central Ill. Electric & Gas Co. (now div. of Commonwealth Edison Co.), Rockford, from 1926; chmn. bd. Central Ill. Electric & Gas Co. (now div. of Commonwealth Edison Co.), from 1963. Trustee Rockford Coll.; bd. regents Milw. Sch. Engring.; trustee Rockford Meml. Hosp. Served with AUS, World War I. Mem. Ill. C. of C. (past v.p., chmn. econ. devel. com., dir.), Rockford C. of C. (chmn. indsl. devel. com.), Ill. SAR. Episcopalian. Clubs: Green Valley Country, Old Pueblo, Tucson, Masons (Shriner). Home: Green Valley Ariz. Deceased.

GORDON, KENNETH E., JR., lawyer; b. Welsh, La., Aug. 31, 1942; s. Kenneth Edwin and Lucille (Kimball) G.; m. Judi Higgins, Aug. 6, 1966; children: Cory, Kenneth Bo, Christy, Allison, Casey. BSBA, La. State U., 1964, JD, 1967. Bar: La. 1967, U.S. Dist. Ct. (we. dist.) La. 1967. Assoc. Liskow & Lewis, Lafayette, La., 1969-72, ptnr., 1972-93. Capt. U.S. Army, 1967-69. Roman Catholic. Home: Lafayette La. Died June 7, 1993.

GORDON, MARTIN, publisher, print dealer; b. N.Y.C., Aug. 15, 1939; s. Alexander and Ruth G.; m. Gayle Gunderman, Mar. 13, 1966; children: Kelly, Jeffrey. Assoc. in Applied Sci., Rochester Inst. Tech., 1960, B.S. in Applied Sci, 1961. Pres. Martin Gordon Inc, N.Y.C., 1964-93; gen. ptnr. Sigma Art Fund, N.Y.C., 1971-82. Author, publisher: Gordon's Print Price annuals (on CD-ROM and Book form). Founder In Print Computer Services. Served with AUS, 1952-57. Mem. Art Dealers Assn., Internat. Print Dealers Assn. (founding mem, pres. 1988-90), Pvt. Art Dealers Assn., Appraisers Assn. Am. Jewish. Home: Naples Fla. Died Sept. 15, 1995.

GORDON, MICHAEL, stage and film director, educator; b. Balt., Sept. 6, 1909; s. Paul and Eva (Kunen) G.; m. Elizabeth Cane, Nov. 27, 1939; children: Jonathan Evan, Jane Ellen, Susannah Ruth. B.A., Johns Hopkins U., 1929; M.F.A., Yale U., 1932. Prof., then prof. emeritus theater arts UCLA, 1971-90. Actor, stage mgr., dir. 22 Broadway prodns.; mem., Group Theatre, N.Y.C., 1935-40; dir. Columbia Pictures, 1940-43, dir. prodns. Universal-Internat., Stanley Kramer, 20th Century Fox, Hollywood, 1959-70; 21 films include Underground Agent, 1942, Another Part of the Forest, 1946, An Act of Murder, 1947, I Can Get It for You Wholesale, 1950, Cyrano de Bergerac, 1950, The Secret of Convict Lake, 1951, Pillow Talk, 1959, Portrait in Black, 1960, Boys's Night Out, 1961, Mover Over Darling, 1963, Texas Across the River, 1965, The Impossible Years, 1968; dir. (plays) include Home of the Brave, Male Animal, The Tender Trap. Mem. Dirs. Guild Am., Screen Writers Guild, Acad. Motion Picture Arts and Scis. Home: Los Angeles Calif. Died Apr. 29, 1993; buried Mt. Sinai Cemetary, Los Angeles.

GORDON, RICHARD EDWARDS, psychiatrist; b. N.Y.C., July 15, 1922; s. Richard and Virginia (Ryan) G.; m. Katherine Lowman Kline, Nov. 12, 1949; children: Richard Edwards (dec.), Katherine Lowman Gordon Reed, Virginia Lamborn Gordon Ford, Laurie Lloyd. B.S., Yale U., 1943; M.D., U. Mich., 1945; M.A., Columbia U., 1956, Ph.D., 1961. Diplomate: Am. Bd. Psychiatry and Neurology. Intern City Hosp., N.Y.C., 1945-46; resident in neurology N.Y. Postgrad Hosp., N.Y.C., 1946-47; resident in psychiatry N.Y. Psychiat. Inst., N.Y.C., 1947-48, Manhattan (N.Y.) State Hosp., 1948-49; fellow in psychosomatic medicine and child psychiatry Mt. Sinai Hosp., N.Y.C., 1949-51; practice medicine specializing in psychiatry N.Y.C., 1950-51, Englewood, N.J., 1953-67; mem. staffs Univ. Settlement House, 1950-51, Englewood Hosp., 1953-67, Shands Teaching Hosp., Gainesville, Fla., 1967-94, Gainesville VA Hosp., 1967-76; sr. research psychiatrist, EEG cons. Rockland State Hosp., Orangeburg, N.Y., 1953-54; founder, dir. EEG Clinic Englewood Hosp., 1953, dir. rsch. unit, 1954-60; prof. psychology, cons. psychiatrist Wagner Coll., S.I., N.Y., 1960-67; prof. psychiatry and psychology, dir. Fla. Mental Health Inst., Tampa, 1974-79; assoc. prof. psychiatry, rsch. dir. Multiphasic Health Testing Ctr., U. Fla., Gainesville, 1967-87, emeritus prof. psychiatry Coll. Medicine, 1987-94; adj. prof. clin. psychology U. South Fla., Tampa, 1977-94; founder Mental Health Consultation Center, Hackensack, N.Y., 1956, trustee, 1956-57; founder Community Multiphasic Health Testing Center, Gainesville; mem. N.J. Mental Health Commn., 1957-61; bd. dirs. Biosystems, Inc., Reed Curve, Inc., Applied Digital Tech. Author: Prevention of Postpartum Emotional Difficulties, 1961, (with K.K. Gordon, M. Gunther) The Split-Level Trap, 1961, (with K.K. Gordon) The Blight on the Ivy, 1963, Systems of Treatment for the Mentally Ill: Filling the Gaps, 1981, (with B. Franklin et al) Towards Better Mental Health in New Jersey, 1961, (with C.J. Hursch, K.K. Gordon), Introduction to Psychiatric Research, 1988; contbr. numerous articles to profl. jours. Pres. Kirkwood Environ. Improvement Assn., Gainesville, 1970-75; cons./surveyor Joint Commn. on Accreditation of Hosps., 1980-84. Served to capt. AUS, 1943-45, 51-53. Grantee in field. Fellow Am. Psychiat. Assn. (del. to assembly), Soc. Advanced Med. Systems; mem. AAAS, Fla. Psychiat. Soc. (pres. 1978-79, newsletter editor), Sigma Xi. Club: Yale of Gainesville. Home: Gainsville Fla. Died Jan. 13, 1994.

GORDON, WILLIAM RICHARD, retired investment officer; b. Phila., Nov. 17, 1913; s. William Murray and Lucille Kerzie (Tribble) G.; m. Mary Alice Wagner,

May 20, 1950; children: Anne Morrison Kessler, William Murray, Robert Duff, Douglas Andrew. B.S., U. Pa., 1936. Investment officer U. Pa., Phila., 1936-42; asst. treas. U. Pa., 1942-55, treas., 1955-75, sec. investment bd., 1975-82; asst. instr. accounting, corp. finance, investment banking U. Pa. (Wharton Sch.), 1937-57; pres. Franklin Investment Co., 1975-82; bd. dirs. Fin. Co., Pa. Former commr. Valley Forge State Park.; bd. dirs. Presbyn. Ministers' Fund, Covenant Life Ins. Fund; former trustee Moore Sch. Elec. Engring. Served with 2d Regt., Arty. U.S. Army, 1942-46; capt. Gen. Staff Corps Dept. Army, The Pentagon, 1951-52. Mem. S.R., Soc. Colonial Wars Pa., Soc. War of 1812, St. Andrews Soc. of Phila., Mil. Order Fgn. Wars U.S., Hist. Soc. Pa., Valley Forge Hist. Soc., State Soc. Cin. Pa., Phila. Soc. Promoting Agr., Delta Psi. Presbyterian. Clubs: Philadelphia, St. Anthony (Phila.); Penn. Home: Paoli Pa. Died Dec. 28, 1993.

GORDONE, CHARLES, playwright; b. Cleve., Oct. 12, 1927; s. William Lee and Camille (Morgan) G.; m. Susan Kouyomjian. Ed., Los Angeles City and State Coll., N.Y. U., Columbia U. Dir. in residence Am. Stage, Berkeley, Calif., 1982-85; disting. lectr. in English, theatre and speech Tex. A&M Univ. Actor: Broadway prodn. The Climate of Eden, Mrs. Patterson; off Broadway prodn. The Blacks, Crucifiction, Mice and Men, Fortunato, Rebels and Bugs, Escurial, Liliom; appeared in: off Broadway prodn. No Place to Be Somebody, Of Mice and Men, Mrs. Patterson, The Climate of Eden, Gordone is a Mutha: Carnegie Hall; films Broken Arrow, Street Fight, Heavy Traffic, Angel Heart; author: off Broadway prodn. No Place to Be Somebody (Pulitzer prize for drama 1970), The Last Chord, 1976, also, Gordone is a Muthah; dir.: plays Fortunato, Tobacco Road, Detective Story, Hell Bent for Heaven, Faust, Three Men on a Horse, Moon of the Carabees; assoc. producer: film Nothing But a Man, 1964, Black Like Me; co-founder (with Godfrey Cambridge) film, Com. for Employment of Negro Performers, 1962 (Recipient award Obie award for acting 1964, Vernon Rice award 1970, Drama Desk award, Critic's Circle award 1970, Image award NAACP 1970, Nat. Inst. Arts and Letters 1971). Recipient grant NEH, 1978, D.H. Lawrence fellowship, 1987. Home: College Station Tex. Died Nov. 17, 1995.

GORDONSON, ROBERT MARTIN, retail executive; b. N.Y.C., July 23, 1935; s. Julius and Mildred (Ettinger0 G.; m. Pearl Wunder, Apr. 4, 1965; children: Gary Scott, Judi Michelle, Suzanne Lynn. BS in Acctg., Bklyn. Coll., 1958; postgrad., CCNY, 1965. Accountant Webb and Knapp Inc., N.Y.C., 1955-57, N.Y. and N.J. Lubricant Co., N.Y.C., 1957-58, Lewyt Corp., N.Y.C., 1960-61; chief accountant Masters Inc., Westbury, N.Y., 1961-63, asst. controller, 1963-64, controller, 1964-72, treas., chief fin. officer, 1972-92. Served to lt. U.S. Army, 1958-60. Mem. Nat. Assn. Corp. Treas., Fin. Exec. Inst., Met. Retail Fin. Execs. Assn. Lodge: KP. Home: Jericho N.Y. Died Jan. 1992.

GORIA, GIOVANNI, Italian government official; b. Asti, Piedmont, Italy, July 31, 1943; m. Eugenia Goria; 2 children. Grad. in econs., U. Turin, Italy. Mem. Christian Dem. Party, 1960—; M.P. Italy, Rome, 1976—, econ. advisor to prime minister, 1978-79, sec. budget and econ. planning, 1981-82, minister treasury, 1982-87, prime minister, 1987-88. Home: Rome Italy

GORIN, WILLIAM, retired retail executive; b. Woburn, Mass., Feb. 8, 1908; s. Nehemias and Rebecca (Caban) G.; m. Helaine M. Falkson, May 14, 1945 (dec. Aug. 1971); children: Howard F., Ralph E. LL.B., Boston U., 1928. Bar: Mass. bar 1929. With Almy Stores Inc., Boston, 1928-84; chmn. bd. Almy Stores Inc., until 1984. Trustee Nehemias Gorin Charitable Found. Home: Brookline Mass. Died June 6, 1993.

GORMLEY, BRIAN FRANCIS, advertising executive; b. Norwalk, Conn., Feb. 21, 1945; s. Daniel J. and Helen (Soltes) G.; m. Marlitt Dellabough, Aug. 31, 1986; 1 child, Elona Kassia. BA, Boston Coll., 1967; MA, Fairfield U., 1970; Cert., Sch. Visual Arts, 1978. Dean of students Sch. Visual Arts, N.Y.C., 1973-77; pres. Lake Placid (N.Y.) Sch. of Art, 1977-79; co-dir. arts program XIII Olympic Winter Games, Lake Placid, 1979-81; dir. pub. affairs Calif. Inst. of the Arts., Valencia, 1981-84; pres. Gormley/Takei Inc., Los Angeles, 1984-94, Valencia Airport Shuttles, Los Angeles, 1987-94; bd. dirs. Cons. Consortium, Los Angeles. Author: (poems) Popsicle in My Pocket, 1970. Founder Explorations Art Festival, Los Angeles, 1983; co-founder Los Angeles High Sch. for the Arts, 1985, Chamber Music Los Angeles Festival, 1986, pres. 1987-94, Dance Resource Ctr. Los Angeles, 1987, bd. dirs. 1986-87. Served with USAF, 1968-70. Democrat. Roman Catholic. Home: Santa Clarita Calif. Died Apr. 14, 1994.

GOSHEN-GOTTSTEIN, MOSHE HENRY, philologist, educator; b. Berlin, Sept. 6, 1925; s. Paul M. and Ilse D. (Grand) Gottstein; m. Esther R. Hepner, July 27, 1953; children: Alan M., Jonathan M. MA, Hebrew U., Jerusalem, 1947, PhD, 1951. Prof. bibl. and Semitic philology Hebrew U., Jerusalem, from 1950, dir. Bible project, from 1955; dir. Inst. for Lexicography and Jewish Bible Rsch. Bar Ilan U., Ramatgan, Israel, from 1970; past v.p. World Union Jewish Studies. Author and editor of 20 books and 400 articles. Recipient Israel prize for Jewish studies Ministry of Edn. and Culture, 1988. Mem. World Union for Jewish Studies, Soc. for Bibl. Lit. Home: Jerusalem Israel Deceased.

GOSS, CHARLES HENRY, gas company executive; b. Norwood, Mass., Jan. 9, 1930; s. Charles H. and Ida Maude (May) G.; m. Kathleen Gormican, Oct. 29, 1955; children: P. Elaine, Susan A., Laurel A. Assoc. in Acctg., Bentley Coll., 1952; BSBA, Suffolk U., 1960; MBA, Bryant Coll., 1973. Asst. treas. Valley Gas Co., Cumberland, R.I., 1964-67, treas., 1967-71, v.p., treas., 1971-76, exec. v.p., 1976-77, pres., 1977—, chmn. bd., 1989—; bd. dirs. Pawtucket Mut. Ins. Co. Bd. dirs. R.I. Pub. Expenditure Coun., 1991—; trustee emeritus Old Slater Mill, Pawtucket; mem. grad. adv. com. Bryant Coll., Smithfield. Mem. Am. Gas Assn. (dir., mng. com. 1972-87), New Eng. Gas Assn. (chmn. 1986), Southeastern New Eng. NCCJ (bd. dirs., pres. 1989-91). Home: Cumberland R.I. Deceased.

GOTOH, NOBORU, construction executive; b. Aug. 21, 1916; m. Yoko Gotoh. Grad., Tokyo U., 1940. Pres. Tokyo Corp., 1959-89; chmn. Tokyo Constrn. Co., Ltd.; bd. dirs. Odakyu Electric Railway Co., Ltd., Japan Airlines. Head Japan C. of C., 1984. Home: Tokyo Japan

GOTOVCHITS, GEORGY OLEXANDROVICH, government official, electrical engineering educator; b. Olgopol Village, Vinnitsa, Ukraine, Sept. 17, 1935; s. Olexander Ivanovich and Mariya Mikchailovna (Pomyatyna) G.; m. Larica Yakovlevna Vislouh, July 7, 1957; children: Alla Georgievna, Olexandra Georgievna. Dipolma in elec. engring., Polytech. Inst., Odessa, Ukraine, 1958; diploma (hon.), Presidium Supreme Soviet Ukraine, Kiev, 1987. Engr., electric equipment and automatics, head electro-tech. lab. Progress Plant Chem. and Machine Engring., Berdichev, Zhitomir, USSR, 1958-60; head, electro supt. Progress Plant Chem. and Machine Engring., 1960-62, chief power engr., 1962-71; 1st sec. Berdichev br., for social and econ. devel. Communist Party, USSR, 1971-78; from dep. chmn. to 1st dep. chmn. Exec. Power Com., Zhitomir, Ukraine, 1978-90; chmn. State Com. Ukraine for Population Protection from the Consequences of the Accident at Chernobyl Nuclear Power Plant, Kiev, 1990-91; min. Ministry of the Ukraine for Population Protection from the Consequences of the Accident at Chernobyl Nuclear Power Plant, Kiev, 1990-95; mem. Nuclear Policy Commn. at Pres. of Ukraine, Kiev, 1992-95. Contbr. chpt. to Chernobyl: Five Hard Years, 1992; articles to profl. jours. Secr. party com. organ. Mcpl. Com. Communist Party Ukraine, Berdichev, 1970-78; Col. Russian Army. Recipient 2 orders, 5 medals, Govt. USSR, 1976-85. Home: Kiev Ukraine Died Jan. 3, 1995.

GOUGH, KATHLEEN (ELEANOR KATHLEEN GOUGH ABERLE), research anthropologist; b. Hunsingore, Wetherby, Yorkshire, Eng., Aug. 16, 1925; arrived in Can., 1967; d. Albert and Eleanor (Umpleby) G.; m. Eric John Miller, July 5, 1947 (div. 1950); m. David Friend Aberle, Sept. 5, 1955; 1 child, Stephen Daniel. BA, Girton Coll., Cambridge, Eng., 1946, MA, 1949; PhD, U. Cambridge, 1950. Rsch. fellow Wenner-Gren Found. Anthropology Rsch. Radcliffe Coll., Harvard U., 1953-54; lectr. anthropology U. Manchester, Eng., 1954-55, rsch. assoc., 1960-61; vis. lectr. U. Calif., Berkeley, 1955-56, Wayne State U., Detroit, 1959-60; lectr., rsch. assoc. U. Mich., Ann Arbor, 1956-59; asst. prof. Brandeis U., Waltham, Mass., 1961-63; rsch. assoc. U. Oreg., Eugene, 1963-67; assoc. prof. then prof. Simon Fraser U., Burnaby, B.C., Can., 1967-70; rsch. assoc. U. B.C., Vancouver, Can., 1971-90; field research in South India, 1947-49, 51-53, 64, 76, Socialist Republic of Vietnam, 1976, 82, People's Republic of Kampuchea, 1982; vis. prof. U. Toronto, Can, 1970. Author: Ten Times More Beautiful: the Rebuilding of Vietnam, 1978, Rural Society in Southeast India, 1981, Rural Change in Southeast India, 1950s to 1980s, 1989, Political Economy in Vietnam, 1989; co-author, editor: Matrilineal Kinship, 1961, reprinted 1973, 74, Imperialism and Revolution in South Asia, 1973; mem. editorial bd. Bull. of Concerned Asian Scholarsm 1969-90; contbr. articles to profl. jours. Recipient Outstanding Rsch. award Am. Social Sci. Rsch. Coun., 1963; grantee Am. Soc. Sci. Rsch. Coun., 1954, 58, Social Scis. and Humanities Rsch. Coun. Can., 1974-81, 82-86. Fellow Am. Anthrop. Assn., Royal Anthrop. Inst. (Curl Bequest prize 1953), Royal Soc. Can.; mem. Canadian Assn. Sociology and Anthropology, Canadian Assn. Asian Studies. Home: West Vancouver Can. Died Sept. 8, 1990.

GOULD, MORTON, composer, conductor; b. Richmond Hill, L.I., N.Y., Dec. 10, 1913; s. James and Frances (Arkin) G.; married; four children. Student pub. schs., Richmond Hill. At age 21 conducted and arranged series of programs over Sta. WOR, MBS, Columbia networks; guest condr. major symphony orchs.; concert and radio appearances, Europe, 1966, Australia, 1977, Japan, 1979, major compositions played by Toscanini, Mitropolous, Monteux, Stokowski, Rodzinski, Reiner, Golschmann, others; works include 3 symphonies, Foster Gallery, Concerto for Orchestra, Latin American Symphonette, Spirituals, Cowboy Rhapsody, Lincoln Legend, Interplay, American Salute, American Ballads (commd. by Nat. Endowment for the Arts), (stage show) Billion Dollar Baby, (mus.) Fal River Legend (ballet), (mus. score) Windjammer; composer, condr. Symphony for Band (U.S. Mil. Acad.) 1952, (score for NBC miniseries) Holocaust, 1978 (CBS-TV documentary series) World War I; worl premiere of commd. work, Burchfield Gallery, wit Lorin Maazel and Cleve. Orch., 1981; Composer: In ventions, 1953, Dance Variations, 1953, Showpiece fo Orchestra, 1954, Cinerama Holiday, 1954, Declaration symphonic narrative for orchestra, 1957, Jekyll an Hyde Variations for orchestra, 1957, St. Lawrence Suite 1958, Classical Variations on Colonial Themes (1s performance by Lorin Maazel and Pitts. Symphon Orch.), 1986, Dialogues for Piano and Orchestra, Venic for Double Orchestra, Vivaldi Gallery, Columbia Troubador Music, Soundings, Symphony of Sprituals numerous recs. RCA, Columbia, other labels; made firs digital and direct disc recs. with London Symphony an London Philharm., 1978; commn. Pitts. Youth Orch 1991, Van Cliburn Internat. Piano Competition, 199 Rostropovich and Nat. Symphony, 1991. Recipien Grammy award for best classical record NARAS, 196 numerous Grammy award nominations, Kennedy hono 1994, Pulitzer Prize in music for "String Music", 1995 Mem. ASCAP (pres. 1986-94, pres. emeritus, bd. dirs. Am. Symphony Orch. League (bd. dirs., Gold Bato award 1983), Am. Acad. and Inst. Arts and Letters. Home: Great Neck N.Y. Died Feb. 20, 1996.

GOURLEY, FLETCHER A., dairy company executive b. Dec. 2, 1912; s. Fletcher and Maude (Prather) G.; m Lois Holdren, Aug. 29, 1937; children: Stephen A Barry M. BS in Dairy Industry, Iowa State U., 1937. Mgr. Prairie Farms Dairy, Inc., Carlinville, Ill., 1938-6 gen. mgr., 1962-72, exec. v.p., 1972-88, sr. v.p., 1988— bd. dirs. Carlinville Nat. Bank. Mem. Dairy Shrin Rotary. Lodge: Rotary. Home: Carlinville Ill.

GRADUS, BEN, producer, writer, director; b. Bklyn Jan. 19, 1918; s. Nathan and Anna (Riger) G.; m Esther Terry Stern, Aug. 15, 1945; children: Nyles Ed ward, Lynne M. Student, Bklyn. Evening, 1936-42. Asst. adminstr. Office of War Info., N.Y.C., 1941-4 photographer Sudarg, Inc., N.Y.C., 1945-46; asst. di Affiliated Film Producers, N.Y.C., 1946-48; produce dir. IMPS, Inc., N.Y.C., 1948-56; freelance dir. N.Y.C 1956-57; v.p., dir. Filmways, Inc., N.Y.C., 1957-6 producer, dir., writer ScreenGems, Inc., N.Y.C., 196 64; producer, dir., pres. Dirs. Group, Inc., N.Y.C 1964-80; freelance writer; audio-visual cons. Champio Stamford, Conn., 1979. Author: Directing the Telev sion Commercial, 1981 (Theater Library Assn. awa 1982); producer (film) Crowded Paradise starring Hum Cronyn, 1955 (Emmy award nomination, Gramm award nomination); producer, writer, dir. (26 episode Decision: The Conflicts of Harry S. Truman. Recipie Gold, Silver and Bronze medals various Internat. Fil and TV Festivals, Clio awards. Mem. Writers Gui Am., Dirs. Guild Am., Dramatists Guild. Hom Bedford N.Y. Died Sept. 25, 1990.

GRADY, JOHN FRANCIS, conductor, organist; Great Neck, L.I., N.Y., May 19, 1934; s. John Franc and Florence Annette (Blake) G. B.A., Fordham U 1957; postgrad., Columbia U., 1958, Juilliard Sc Music, 1958-60; Doctorate h.c., State of Michoaga (Mex.), 1974. Ofcl. organist Met. Opera Assn., fro 1964; dir. music St. Patrick's Cathedral, N.Y.C., 1970– head organ dept. Manhattan Sch. Music, 1970-71; Ar judge exams. Conservatory of Nice, France, 1976; Ar judge Internat. Organ Competition Chartres Cathedra France, 1978; organist Internat. Eucharistic Congres Phila., 1976; tchr. organ workshops Gregorian Ins Am., 1968-72, Cathedral Sts. Peter and Paul, 1977-7 79; prof. music history Archdiocesan Sch. Liturgic Music, N.Y.C., 1979-80; organist Internat. Organ Fe tival, First Concert, Toulon, France, 1986; cond Capella Cracoviensis, Cracow, Poland; mem. jury y end exams Nat. Conservatory, Paris, 1990, Region Conservatory, Toulouse, France, 1990. Compose Gloria for Chorus and Orch, 1979; editor, annotato Acts of the Pagan Martyrs by Herbert Musurillo, 195 editor: oratorio Nisi Dominus (G. F. Handel), 1978; re artist Christmas with Renata Scott, 1981, Christm with Canadian Brass, 1981; condr. scene in motion pi ture The Godfather - Part III, 1990; condr., organi ann. concert tours, Europe. Chevalier dans l'Ordre d Arts et Lettres (France). Mem. Nat. Assn. Cathed Organists (founder, past pres.), Am. Guild Organis Broadcast Music Inc. Club: Century, Bohemians Home: New York N.Y.

GRAESE, CLIFFORD ERNEST, retired accounta b. Canova, S.D., Jan. 5, 1927; s. Arthur Edward a Alma M. (Neugebauer) G.; m. LaVonne Marie Boh May 3, 1953; children: Diane, Sally Jo Grae Daugherty, Susan Graese Alfirevic, Larry. B.S., S.D., 1949, LL.D., 1980. C.P.A. With Peat, Marwi Mitchell & Co., Mpls., N.Y.C., 1949-86; audit pt Peat, Marwick, Mitchell & Co., 1958-63, partner charge mgmt. cons., 1963-75; partner in charge counting and auditing Peat, Marwick, Mitchell & C N.Y.C., 1975-77; vice chmn. accounting and audit Peat, Marwick, Mitchell & Co., 1977-85; ret., 198 Mem. Bd. Edn., Saddle River, N.J., 1972-78; trustee S.D. Found., 1979-94, Shrine to Music Mus., 1981- mem. Planning Bd., Saddle River, 1981-85; n campaign treas. Mt. Rushmore Nat. Meml. Soc., 19

. Served with USNR, 1945-46. Mem. Am. Inst. P.A.'s (past chmn. div. profl. ethics). Republican. ıtheran. Clubs: Arrowhead (Rapid City, S.D.); Bay ll Country (Orlando, Fla.); Isleworth (Fla.). Home: indermere Fla. Died July 19, 1994.

RAHAM, ALBERT BRUCE, audiologist, speech and nguage pathologist; b. Oil City, Pa., Aug. 8, 1919; s. lbert Vanderlin and Octavia (Kellogg) G.; m. Mary argaret Zeller, June 4, 1943; children: Janice, ichael. AB, U. No. Colo., 1940; AM, U. Denver, 49; PhD, Northwestern U., 1953. Tchr. high sch. ama Coolidge, Kans., 1940-42; prin. Schofield High h., Schofield Barracks, Hawaii, 1946-48; dir. Speech d Hearing Clinic and Cerebral Palsy Ctr. Bowling reen (Ohio) State U., 1951-52; chief div. audiology, eech and lang. pathology Henry Ford Hosp., Detroit, 52-78; audiology cons. Blue Cross/Blue Shield, Mich.; n. assoc. prof. audiology Wayne State U. Sch. edicine, Detroit, 1979-83; ret., 1988. Editor: Senrineural Hearing Processes and Disorders, 1967. Bd. rs. Detroit Hearing and Speech Ctr., 1956-70, pres., 61-62, 66-67; bd. dirs. Mich. Assn. Better Hearing d Speech, 1967-89, pres., 1976-77; mem. profl. adv. uncil United Cerebral Palsy Assn. Mich., 1960-93, mn., 1968-69; bd. dirs. Nat. Assn. Hearing and eech Agys., 1960-72, 79-81, 1st v.p., 1968-69; mem. eakers bur. United Found., Detroit; survey cons. ›mmn. on Accreditation Rehab. Facilities, 1970-72. ith USAAF, 1942-46. Fellow Am. Speech and aring Assn. (legis. council 1969-75, 78-81); assoc. low Am. Acad. Ophthalmology and Otolaryngology; m. Acad. Rehab. Audiology, Assn. Research in Otoyngology, Am. Audiological Soc. (exec. com. 1974-), Soc. Med. Audiologists, Mich. Speech and Hearing sn. (pres. 1957), Council Exceptional Children; assoc. m. Mich. Otol. Soc. Home: Dearborn Mich. Died ly 16, 1993.

RAHAM, DANIEL ORRIN, retired army officer; b. rtland, Oreg., Apr. 13, 1925; s. John P. and Doris aham; m. Ruth Graham, July 14, 1950 (dec. Sept. 89); children: Daniel Jr., Melanie, Laurie, Douglas, zabeth Julianne, Margaret. B.S., U.S. Mil. Acad., 46. Commd. 2d lt. U.S. Army, 1946, advanced ough grades to lt. gen., 1973, ret., 1976; dep. dir. A, Washington, 1972-74; dir. Def. Intelligence Agy., ashington, 1974-76; prof. U. Miami, Fla., 1976-78; ns. Am. Security Council, Washington, 1978-81; dir. gh Frontier, Inc., Washington, 1981-95. Author: New ategy for the West, 1976; Author: Shall America Be fended, 1979; High Frontier, 1981; A Defense that fends, 1983; We Must Defend America, 1984. publican. Roman Catholic. Died Dec. 31, 1995. me: Arlington Va.

RAHAM, EVARTS AMBROSE, JR., newspaper lumnist; b. St. Louis, Feb. 4, 1921; s. Evarts A. and len (Tredway) G.; m. Perugina Adler, June 30, 1951 c. Apr. 1987); children: Helen, Sarah. B.S., Harvard , 1941. With St. Louis Post-Dispatch, 1941; mng. tor St. Louis Post-Dispatch, 1968-79, contbg. editor, 79-85, columnist, 1985-88. Bd. dirs. Community Sch., Louis, Asso. Harvard Alumni. Served with AUS, 42-46. Home: Saint Louis Mo. Died Mar. 7, 1996.

RAHAM, GLORIA F., nurse educator; b. Angus, br., Apr. 12, 1935; d. H.G. and Ethel A. (White) rling; m. Richard L. Graham, June 19, 1954; chiln: Elizabeth, Jennifer. AS, Donnelly Jr. Coll., 1967; N, U. Kans., Kansas City, 1970; MA, U. Mo., nsas City, 1976. Staff nurse Menorah Hosp., Kansas y, Mo.; sch. nurse Shawnee-Mission Schs., Overland k, Kans.; instr. St. Luke's Hosp. Sch. Nursing, nsas City, Mo. Sec. Community Housing Resource . Mem. Phi Theta Kappa, Phi Delta Kappa. Home: awnee Mission Kans. Died Feb. 27, 1995.

RAHAM, JOHN FINLAYSON, economics educator; Calgary, Alta., Can., May 31, 1924; s. William and zel Marie (Lund) G.; m. Hermioni Sederis, Apr. 30, 56; children: Andrew, James, Johanna, Nicho. B.A. with honours in econs, U. B.C., 1947; A.M. in ons, Columbia U., 1948, Ph.D. in Econs, 1959. Mem. ulty dept. econs. Dalhousie U., Halifax, N.S., nada, 1949-90; prof. Dalhousie U., 1960-90, head ot., 1960-69; Skelton-Clark vis. research fellow een's U., 1963-64; vis. prof. Inst. for Advanced dies, Vienna, 1964; chmn. N.S. Royal Commn. on n., Pub. Services and Provincial-Mcpl. Relations, 71-74, Halifax br. Can. Inst. Internat. Affairs, 1956- mem. econ. adv. panel of minister of fin., 1982-84, ernat. peer rev. com. Fed. Networks of Centres Exence Programme, 1988-90; cons. ednl. fin. Royal mmn. on Edn. and Youth in Newfoundland, 1967-90. uthor: Fiscal Adjustment and Economic Developnt, 1963; gen. editor: Atlantic Provinces Studies, 59-90; contbr. articles to profl. jours. Past chmn. b. Accts. Bd. N.S.; vice chmn. bd. dirs. Art Gallery N.S., 1977-78. 2d lt., arty. and inf. corps Canadian my, 1943-45. Fellow Royal Soc. Can. Can. Council ow, 1968-69; Social Sciences and Humanities search Council sr. fellow, 1979-80. Fellow Royal Can. (v.p. 1977-78); mem. Can. Econs. Assn. (pres. 70-71), Acad. Humanities and Social Scis. of Royal Can. (pres. 1977-78), Canadian Tax Found., Com. the Centres of Excellence, Royal Soc. Adv. Com. of Evaluation of Rsch, Can. 1987-90. Home: Halifax Can. Died Nov. 14, 1990.

GRAIS, SAM S., retail company executive, pharmacist; b. Mpls., Oct. 31, 1906; s. Joseph and Jennie (Kronick) G.; m. Loretta Yager, Oct. 1, 1931; children: MaryJo, Maggie. Pharm. chemist, U. Minn., 1927. cert. pharmacist, Minn. Pres. Gray's Drug Store, St. Paul, 1935-76. Vol. Gov. Perpich's Staff, Mpls.; vice chair Met. Airport Com., Mpls., Govs. Appointments Adv. Com., Mpls.; chair St. Paul Zoning Appeal Bd.; bd. trustees Blue Cross Blue Shield Minn.; pres. Jewish Family Svc.; gov. del. White House Conf. on Aging, 1960-70; v.p. Mt. Sinai Hosp., 1979; pres. coord. Health Care, 1984-87. Recipient Mt. Zion Humanitarian Man of Yr., 1962, Disting. Svcs. award Nat. Govs. Assn., Hon. for dedication to Human Svcs. Reform Nat. Conf. on Social Welfare and Nat. Assn. Social Workers; named OUtstanding Achievement award U. Minn., 1964, WCCO Good Neighbor award, 1964, 89. Mem. Minn. State Pharm. Assn. (pres.), Nat. Assn. Welfare Bd. Mems. (pres.), Nat. Assn. State Health and Welfare (pres.). Democrat. Jewish. Home: Saint Paul Minn.

GRANT, JAMES PINEO, international organization executive; b. Beijing, May 12, 1922; s. John Black and Charlotte (Hill) G.; m. Ethel Henck (dec.); children: John Putnam, James Dickinson, William Joseph; m. Ellan Young, July, 1989. AB, U. Calif., 1943; LLB, JD, Harvard U., 1951; hon. degrees, U. Notre Dame, 1980, Hacetteppe U., 1980, Maryville Coll., 1981, Denison U., 1983, Tufts U., 1983, U. Md., 1986, Clark U., 1987; hon. degree, Georgetown U., 1993; DSc (hon.), Tulane U., 1994. Rep. UNRRA, north China, 1946-47; cons., spl. asst. to dir. U.S. Econ. Aid Mission to China, 1948-49, 50; asso. Covington & Burling, Washington, 1951-54; regional legal counsel for U.S. Econ. Aid Missions in South Asia, 1954-56; dir. U.S. Econ. Aid Mission to Sri Lanka, 1956-58; spl. asst. to dir. Internat. Cooperation Adminstrn., 1958, dep. to dir. ICA, Washington, 1959-62; dep. asst. sec. state for Near Eastern and South Asian affairs, 1962-64; dir. U.S. Econ. Aid Mission to Turkey, 1964-67; asst. adminstr. AID, Washington, 1967-69; pres. Overseas Devel. Council, 1969-79; exec. dir. UNICEF, 1980; hon. prof. Capital Med. Coll. China, 1983. Bd. dirs., trustee Rockefeller Found., 1980-87; bd. dirs. Internat. Vol. Services, Johns Hopkins U. (emeritus), Overseas Devel. Council; trustee, mem. vis. com. Sch. Nutrition, Tufts U. Served as capt. AUS, 1943-45, CBI. Decorated Bronze Star with cluster; Breast Order of Yun Hui (China); recipient Disting. Public Service award AID, 1961; Rockefeller Public Service award, 1980, Boyaca award, Colombia, 1984, Gold Mercury Internat. award, 1984, Presdl. citation Am. Pub. Health Assn., 1985, Alan Shawn Feinstein award Prevention and Reduction of World Hunger Brown U., 1989, E.H. Christopherson Lectureship award, 1990, Diplomatic World Bull. award, 1990, Leonardo d'Oro award, 1990, Community prize Nat. Assn. Italian Municipalities, 1991, Tolstoy award Russian Children's Fund, 1993, Human Rights prize UN, 1993, Hilal-I-Pakistan award Pres. Islamic Republic of Pakistan, 1993, Sri Lanka Ratna award Pres. Sri Lanka, 1994; decorated Command of Nat. Order of Mali, 1989, Gran Cruz of Orden Daniel A. Carrion, Peru, 1991, 1st Class of Order of Sacred Treasure, Japan, 1991, Order of Aguila Azteca, Mexico, 1993, Presdl. Medal of Freedom, 1994. Mem. Soc. Internat. Devel. (pres. 1978-82), Coun. Fgn. Rels., Bar Assn. D.C., North-South Round Table, Soc. for Investigation of Recurrent Events, Cosmos Club (Washington), U.S. of Rome Club. Home: New York N.Y. Died Jan., 1995.

GRAVA, ALFRED H., automotive and business equipment manufacturing company executive; b. 1934. BSME. With Gen. Motors Corp., 1953-73; with Rockwell Internat. Corp., 1973-84; with Sheller-Globe Corp., 1984-95, formerly exec. v.p., pres., chief operating officer. Served with U.S. Army, 1958-59. Home: Auburn Hills Mich. Died July 6, 1995.

GRAVES, NANCY STEVENSON, artist; b. Pittsfield, Mass.. BA, Vassar Coll., 1961; BFA, Yale U., 1961, MFA, 1964; PhD (hon.), Skidmore Coll., 1989; DFA, U. Md., 1992, Yale U., 1992. Numerous one-woman shows, including Whitney Mus. Am. Art, N.Y.C., 1969, Nat. Gallery Can., Ottawa, 1971, Neue Galerie der Stadt Aachen, Ger., 1971, Mus. Modern Art, N.Y.C., 1971, Inst. Contemporary Art, U. Pa., Phila., 1972, La Jolla (Calif.) Mus. Art, 1973, Art Mus. South Tex., Corpus Christi, 1973, André Emmerich Gallery, Inc., N.Y.C., 1974, 77, Janie C. Lee Gallery, Houston, 1977, 78, 83, 84, M. Knoedler & Co., 1979—, Richard Gray Gallery, Chgo., 1981, 86, Gloria Luria Gallery, Bar Harbor Islands, 1983, Greenburg Gallery, St. Louis, 1985, Heland Wetterling Gallery, Stockholm, 1988, 90, Gallery Mukai, Tokyo, 1988, Knoedler Kasmin, London, 1989, Linda Cathcart Gallery, Santa Monica, Calif., 1989, Locks Gallery, Phila., 1991, Meredith Long & Co., Houston, 1991, Irving Galleries, Palm Beach, Calif., 1992, Saff Tech. Arts, N.Y.C., 1992; retrospective show travelled to Albright Knox Gallery, Buffalo, Akron (Ohio) Art Inst., Contemporary Arts Mus., Houston, 1980, Brooks Art Gallery, Memphis, Neuberger Mus., Purchase, N.Y., Des Moines Art Center, Walker Art Center, Mpls., 1981, Hirschorn Mus., Washington, 1987, Modern Mus. Ft. Worth, Santa Barbara Mus., 1987, Bklyn. Mus., 1988; numerous group shows include Whitney Mus. Am. Art, N.Y.C., 1970, 76, 92, Corcoran Gallery Art, Washington, 1971, 76, Parc Floral, Paris, 1971, Neue Gallery, Kassel, Germany, 1972, Serpentine Gallery, London, 1973, Project 74, Colonge, Germany, 1974, Berlin Nat. Gallerie, 1976, Vancouver (B.C.) Art Gallery, Tehran (Iran) Mus. Contemporary Art, 1978, Am. Acad., Rome, 1979, Hudson River Mus., 1979, Helen Foresmand Specer Mus. Art, Kans., 1981, Mus. Fine Arts, Boston, 1982, 87, The Berkshire Mus., 1982, 83, Contemporart Arts Mus., Houston, 1982, Mus. Modern Art, Vienna, Austria, 1983, L.A. County Mus., 1984, Santa Barbara (Calif.) Mus., 1984, Toledo (Ohio) Mus. Art, 1984, Neuberger Mus., 1984, Bklyn. Mus., 1984, 86, Ludwig Mus., Cologne, Nelson-Atkins Mus., 1987, Balt. Mus., 1990, Palace of Budapest, Hungary, 1990, Mus. Fine Arts, Boston, 1992, Bellevue (Wash.) Art Mus., 1993, Mus. Modern Art, N.Y.C., 1994; permanent collections, Mus. Modern Art, N.Y.C., Whitney Mus. Am. Art, N.Y.C., Ludwig Mus., Cologne, Nat. Gallery Can., Ottawa, Des Moines (Iowa) Art Center, La Jolla Mus. Contemporary Art, Art Mus. South Tex., Corpus Christi, Berkeley (Calif.) Mus. Art, Albright-Knox Art Gallery, Buffalo, N.Y., Chgo. Art Inst., Met. Mus. Art, N.Y.C., Hirschorn Mus., Nat. Gallery Art, Washington, Akron (Ohio) Art Mus, Allem Meml. Art Gallery, Oberlin, Ohio, Berkshire Mus. Pittsfield, Birmingham (Ala.) Mus. Art, Bklyn. Mus., Brooks Meml. Art Gallery, Memphis, Corcoran Gallery Art, Washington, Ft. Worth Art Mus., L.A. County Mus., Mus. Contemporary Art, Chgo., Mus. Fine Arts, Houston, Mus. Fine Arts, Dallas, Mus. Modern Art, Vienna, Nelson-Atkins Mus. Art, Kansas City, Neuberger Mus, Purchase, N.Y., Neue Galerie in Alten Kurhaus, Aachen, Pa. Acad. Fine Arts, Phila., St. Louis Art Mus., Solomon R. Guggenheim Mus, N.Y.C., Univ. Art Mus., Berkeley, Calif., Vassar Art Mus., Poughkeepsie, N.Y., Walker Art Ctr., Mpls., Weatherspoon Art Gallery, Greensboro, N.C. . Vassar Coll. fellow, 1971-72; Fulbright-Hayes grantee, 1965-66; Paris Biennale grantee, 1971; Nat. Endowment for Arts grantee, 1972-73; Creative Artist Pub. Service grantee, 1974-75; recipient Skowhegan medal for Drawing and Graphics, 1980, Disting. Artistic Achievement award Yale U. 1985, Disting. award Vassar Coll., 1986, Am. Art award Pa. Acad. Art, 1987. mem. Am. Acad. and Inst. of Arts and Letters. Home: New York N.Y.

GRAY, BASIL, museum curator, Orientalist; b. July 21, 1904; s. Charles and Florence (Elworthy) G.; M.A., Oxford U.; m. Nicolete Binyon, 1933; 2 sons, 2 daus. (1 dec.). Mem. Brit. Acad. excavations in Constantinople, 1928; with Brit. Mus., from 1928, in charge Oriental antiquities, from 1938, dep. keeper, 1940-46, keeper, 1946-69, acting dir. and prin. librarian, 1968; pres. 6th Internat. Congress Iranian Art and Archeology, Oxford, 1972; mem. Reviewing Com. on Export of Works of Art, 1971-79; chmn. exhbn. com. The Arts of Islam, Hayward Gallery, 1976. Mem. vis. com. Ashmolean Mus., Oxford, 1969-79. Recipient Sir Percy Sykes Meml. medal, 1978. Fellow Brit. Acad.; mem. Oriental Ceramic Soc. (pres. 1962-65, 71-74, 77-78), Soc. South Asian Studies (pres. Soc. Afghan Studies 1979-89), Societas Iranologica Europaea (pres. 1983-89). Author: Persian Painting, 1930; (with others) Persian Miniature Painting, 1933; (with Leigh Ashton) Chinese Art, 1935; The English Print, 1937; Persian Painting, New York, 1940; Rajput Painting, 1948; (with others) Commemorative Catalogue of the Exhibition of the Art of India and Pakistan, 1947-48, 1950; Treasures of Indian Miniatures in the Bikanir Palace Collection, 1951; Early Chinese Poettery and Porcelain, 1953; Japanese Screen-paintings, 1955; Buddhist Cave Paintings at Tun-huang, 1959; Treasures of Asia: Persian Painting, 1961; (with D.E. Barrett) Paintings of India, 1963; An Album of Miniatures and Illuminations from the Baysonhori Manuscript of the Shahnameh of Ferdowsi, 1971; The World History of Rashid al-Din, a study of the RAS manuscript, 1979; Sung Porcelain and Stoneware, 1983; Studies in Chinese and Islamic Art, 2 vols., 1985-86; author/editor: The Arts of the Book in Central Asia 1370-1506, 1979; The Arts of India, 1981; editor: Faber Gallery of Oriental Art and Arts of the East Series. Died June 10, 1989. Home: Oxford Eng.

GRAY, GORDON JOSEPH CARDINAL, former archbishop of St. Andrews and Edinburgh; b. Edinburgh, Aug. 10, 1910; s. Francis William and Angela Gray; student St. John's Sem., Wonerish; M.A. with honours, St. Andrews U., D.D. (hon.); D. Univ., Heriot-Watt U. Ordained priest Roman Cath. Ch., consecrated bishop, elevated to cardinal, 1969; asst. priest, St. Andrews, 1935-41; parish priest, Hawick, 1941-47; rector Blairs' Coll., Aberdeen, Scotland, 1947-51; archbishop of St. Andrews and Edinburgh, 1951-85, cardinal, 1969—. Mem. Congregation for Evangelization of Peoples, Congregation of the Sacraments, Congregation of Clerics. Hon. fellow Ednl. Inst. Scotland. Died July 19, 1993; interred St. Mary's Cathedral, Edinburgh. Home: Edinburgh Scotland

GRAY, HENRY DAVID, minister, religious organization administrator; b. Antrim, No. Ireland, Jan. 18, 1908; came to U.S., 1923; s. Nathaniel and Margaret (Lawther) G.; m. Helen Katharine Lorbeer, Aug. 12, 1930; children: Mildred Ellen, David Lawther, Betsey Charisma. B.A. magna cum laude, Pomona Coll., 1930, D.D. (hon.), 1954; M. Div. summa cum laude, Hartford

Theol. Sem., 1933; Ph.D., Edinburgh U., Scotland, 1935; cert. in religious edn., Boston U., 1931; Cert. Theology, Tubingen U., 1935; D. Litt. (hon.), Piedmont Coll., 1976. Ordained minister Congregational Ch., 1935. Numerous positions Congl. Chs., worldwide, 1935-94; mission Congl. Chs., Western Samoa, 1966; dir. 300th anniversary yr. program Old South Ch., Hartford, Conn., 1969-70; minister emeritus Old South Ch., Hartford, 1970-94; dir. summer student study Congl. Ch., Europe, Middle East, worldwide, 1948-70; interim minister Hollywood Congl. Ch., Calif., 1971, North Hollywood Congl. Ch., Calif., 1971-72; dean Am. Congl. Ctr., South Pasadena, Calif., 1972-94; founding mem. Pasadena Coun. Chs., 1947, Nat. Coun. Chs., 1950; bd. dirs. Greater Hartford Coun. Chs., 1956-60; moderator Hampshire Assn. Congl. Christian Chs., 1938-39, L.A. Assn., 1947-48, Conn. Fellowship, 1957-61, 65, Nat. Assn., 1958-59. Author: Young People In Church Work, 1940, A Theology for Christian Youth, 1941, Words For Today, 1944, Under Orders, 1946, Science and Religion, 1946, Primacy of God, 1947, Christian Doctrine of Grace, 1948 (best full length theol. book Ind. Press, London, 1948), The Christian Marriage Service, 1950, Oneonta Guide Book, 1950, 12 edit., 1985, The Upward Call, 1952, Free Church Polity and Unity Report, 1954, Some Christian Convictions, 1955, A Bible Guide to the Holy Land, 1964, Blue Book of Congregational Usage #1, 1965, #2, 1967, Service Book, 1966, South Church Prayers, 1966, God's Torchbearers, 1970, Heart of Oak, Helm of Destiny, 1970, Hollywood Prayers, 1973, Congregational Usage, 1976, 6th edit., 1990, Congregational Worshipbook, 1978, 3d edit., 1990, Pilgrim Fathers Reach the Pacific, 1981, Soundings, 1980, Waymarks, 1983, Plus Ultra, Vol. 1, 1983, Vol. 2, 1985, The Mediators, 1984, The Souls Working Clothes, 1988, 27th edit. What it Means to be a Member of a Congregational Christian Church, 1993, Congregational Worshipbook, 1991; also 8 vols. of lectures and travelog, 1948-70; editor (monthly mag.) The Congregationalist, 1962-66, (monthly mag.) The Pilgrim Highroad, 1939-42, Congregational Jour., 1975-94; contbr. numerous articles to profl. jours., also pamphlets; numerous appearances on TV and radio. Active numerous civic organizations, 1924-70; mem. Hartford City Plan Commn., 1959-70, chmn., 1962-67, 70; mem. Capitol Regional Planning Coun., 1962-67, 70, Conn. Capitol Ctr. Commn., 1966-67, 69-70; organizer Ventura City Environ. Coalition, Calif., 1971; mem. exec. com. Comprehensive Planning Commn., Ventura, Calif., 1973-77; chmn. Cultural Heritage Team, Ventura, 1974-75; pres. South Village, Hartford, 1968-84; mem. Nat. Com. for Scouting, 1939-42; former parliamentarian/vice chmn. Santa Monica Mountains Nat. Commn., Nat. Park Service; founder Congl. World Assembly of Youth, 1949. Recipient numerous awards Boy Scouts Am., Hartford Theol. Sem., Congl. Chs., citation of excellence State of Conn., 1970, Resolution of Profound Appreciation City Council Hartford, 1970, Resolution Commendation award Bd. Suprs. Ventura, 1985, letter of commendation Supt. Nat. Park Service, 1985, citation Conn. Conf. United Ch. Christ, 1985, Spl. Commendation, Internat. Congl. Council, 1987; Gray Hall named in his honor, South Pasadena, Calif., 1955, Hartford, 1960, Alexandroupolis, Greece, 1962, Gray Chapel named for him, Kuzhikode, Kerala, India, 1967, Gray Student Union named for him Lady Doak Coll., Madurai, India, 1967. Fellow Am. Acad. Religion, Royal Anthropol. Inst., Am. Anthropol. Assn.; mem. Soc. Bibl. Lit., Calif. West Congl. Assn. Chs. and Ministers (cons. polity 1984—), Nat. Assn. Congl. Christian Chs. (numerous coms., chmn. coms., offices), Clerics Club, Ventura County Hist. Soc., Calif. Hist. Soc., Nat. Hist. Soc., Am. Congl. Assn. (bd. dirs. 1965-70), United Ref. Ch. History Soc., Brit. Congl. Hist. Circle, Inst. Pacific Studies, Congl. World Assembly Youth (founder, bd. dirs. 1962, chmn. 1985), Congl. Christian Hist. Soc., Congl. Fellowship Conn. (life, exec. com.), Hartford Assn. Congl. Christian Chs. and Ministers (exec. com. 1956-60, citation 1985), Nat. Pilgrim Fellowship (founder, life counselor), Nat. Eagle Scout Assn., Calif. Acad. Scis., West Coast Theol. Club, Conn. Valley Theol. Club, Congl. Mins. Club (Scotland), Pasadena Athletic Club, Wranglers Club, Oneonta Mens Svc. Club (San Gabriel), Nat. World Wildlife Fedn., Sierra Club, Ephebian Soc., Order DeMolay (hon. chevalier), Phi Beta Kappa, Delta Sigma Rho. Republican. Home: Ventura Calif. Died Sept. 3, 1994.

GRAY, NORMAN EUGENE, fire chief; b. Helena, Mont., Nov. 3, 1937; s. Eugene F. and Gladys I. (Lippert) G.; student public schs., Helena, Mont.; m. Sharon A. Weed, Nov. 21, 1959; children—Debra A., Norman Dean. Clk., IRS, Helena, Mont., 1959; firefighter, Helena, 1960—, fire chief, 1979—, tng. officer, 1973-79. Served with USN, 1955-58. Mem. Internat. Assn. Fire Chiefs, Western Fire Chiefs Assn., Mont. State Fire Chiefs Assn. Republican. Club: Elks. Home: Helena Mont.

GRAY, WILLIAM PERCIVAL, judge; b. Los Angeles, Mar. 26, 1912; s. Jacob L. and Catherine (Percival) G.; m. Elizabeth Polin, Nov. 8, 1941; children—Robin Marie, James Polin. A.B., U. Calif. at Los Angeles, 1934; LL.B. cum laude, Harvard, 1939. Bar: Calif. bar 1941. Legal sec. to judge U.S. Ct. Appeals, Washington, 1939-40; with firm O'Melveny & Myers (lawyers), Los Angeles, 1940-41; pvt. practice Los Angeles, 1945-49; partner Gray, Pfaelzer & Robertson, Los Angeles, 1950-66; U.S. dist. judge Central Dist. Calif., 1966—; spl. asst. to atty. gen. U.S., 1958-64; chmn. Calif. Conf. State Bar Dels., 1952. Trustee Ch. of Lighted Window, La Canada. Served from 1st lt. to lt. col. AUS, 1941-45. Fellow Am. Bar Found.; mem. Am. Law Inst., Am. Bar Assn., Los Angeles County Bar Assn. (pres. 1956), State Bar Calif. (bd. govs. 1960-63, pres. 1962-63). Home: Pasadena Calif. Died Feb. 10, 1992.

GRAYSON, SPENCE MONROE, magistrate; b. Savannah, Ga., Dec. 7, 1900; s. William Leon and Lillian (Turner) G.; m. Margaret Armstrong Postell, Dec. 1, 1925 (dec. Mar. 1974); 1 son, William L. II (dec.). Student U.S. Mil. Acad., 1918-19, Ga. Inst. Tech., 1919-20; LLB, U. Ga., 1924. Bar: Ga. 1924, U.S. Dist. Ct. (so. dist.) Ga. Mem. Ga. Ho. of Reps., 1926-45; mem. Ga. Senate, 1944-53, pres. pro tem, 1945-53; city atty. City of Savannah, 1937-47; magistrate U.S. Dist. Ct. So. Dist Ga., from 1970, full-time, from 1981. Recipient Lucas trophy City of Savannah, 1949, Spl. Services award Savannah C. of C., 1949, silver pitcher Ga. Senate, 1952; subject of resolution for services Ga. Senate, 1947, 62; Spence Grayson Day declared by Mayor of Savannah, 1949; bridge named Spence Grayson Bridge, Ga. Dept. Transp., 1962. Mem. Savannah Bar Assn., State Bar Ga. Democrat. Episcopalian. Club: Soc. Colonial Wars. Deceased. Home: Savannah Ga.

GREEN, EARL LEROY, retired biomedical research administrator, geneticist; b. Meadville, Pa., Aug. 7, 1913; s. George Graytric and Iva Pearl (Lewis) G.; m. Margaret Creighton, July 4, 1940. BS, Allegheny Coll., 1935, ScD (hon.), 1960; PhD, Brown U., 1940. Instr. to prof. Ohio State U., Columbus, 1941-56; geneticist US AEC, Washington, 1953-55; dir. The Jackson Lab., Bar Harbor, Maine, 1956-75, ret., 1975. Author: Genetics and Probability in Animal Breeding Experiments, 1981; editor: Biology of the Laboratory Mouse, 1966. Capt. USAAF, 1943-46. Recipient NIH award, 1978, Grad. Achievement award Brown U., 1980. Democrat. Home: Bar Harbor Maine Died Jan. 17, 1995.

GREEN, FRANCIS J., retired bishop; b. Corning, N.Y., July 7, 1906. Ordained priest Roman Cath. Ch., 1932; ordained titular bishop of Serra and aux. bishop of Tucson, 1953; named coadjutor Tucson with right of succession, 1960. Bishop Roman Cath. Ch., Tucson, 1960-1981. Home: Tucson Ariz. Died May 11, 1995.

GREEN, RICHARD R., school superintendent; m. Gwen; 4 children. Student, Augsburg College; Ph.D., Harvard U. School supt. Minneapolis public schools, 1980-88, New York public schools, 1988—. Home: Brooklyn N.Y.

GREEN, ROBERT LAMAR, consulting agricultural engineer; b. Moultrie, Ga., Nov. 15, 1914; s. Louis Pinkney and Bessie (Tillman) G.; m. Frances Cowan, June 7, 1940; 1 son, Robert Lamar. B.S., U. Ga., 1934; M.S., Iowa State Coll., 1939; grad., Command and Gen. Staff Coll., 1944; Ph.D.; fellow Gen. Edn. Bd., Mich. State U., 1953. Registered profl. engr., Ga., Md. Terracing foreman Soil Erosion Service, Athens, Ga., 1934; camp engr. Civilian Conservation Corps., Bartow County, Ga., 1935; jr. agrl. engr. Soil Conservation Service, Lawrenceville and Americus, Ga., 1936-38; work unit conservationist Soil Conservation Service, Lawrenceville, 1939-47; asst. prof. agrl. engring. La. State U., 1947-50, 53-54; agrl. engr. U.S. Spl. Tech. and Econ. Mission to Indonesia (ECA, MSA, TCA, FOA), Djakarta, 1951-53; supt., agrl. engr. S.E. Tidewater Expt. Sta., Dept. Agr., 1954-58; state drainage engr. Md., 1958-73; prof., head dept. agrl. engring. U. Md., 1958-73; coordinator Water Resources Research Center, 1965-79, prof. emeritus agrl. engring., 1979; acting dir. Md. Agrl. Expt. Sta., 1972-76; cons. agrl. engr., Central African Republic, 1979, Guyana, 1981. Contbr. articles to profl. and trade jours. Chmn. Spl. Gov.'s Com. to study shore erosion Md., 1960-66, Spl. Gov.'s Com. for Conservation and Devel. Natural Resources, 1960-66; mem. Md. Water Resources Commn., 1964-85, chmn., 1975-85; chmn. Md. Water Scis. Adv. Bd., 1968-73; bd. suprs. Dorchester County (Md.) Soil Conservation Dist., 1979. Served from 1st lt., cav. to maj., armor AUS, 1941-46; col. Res., ret. Life fellow Am. Soc. Agrl. Engrs. (chmn. D.C.-Md. sect. 1961-62, rep. to NRC 1959-66, dir. 1969-71, rep. Agrl. Research Inst., Nat. Acad. Scis.-NRC 1974-76, del. Pan Am. Union Engrs., hon. v.p. 1972, rep. XII-XVI Congresses, chmn. tech. com. on agrl. and food engring. 1982-84, organizing 1st Pan Am. Congress on Agrl. and Food Engring., XVII conv. in Caracas, 1984, John Deere gold medalist 1988); mem. Sigma Xi, Tau Beta Pi, Phi Kappa Phi, Epsilon Sigma Phi. Episcopalian. Home: Silver Springs Md. Died Oct. 8, 1993; buried Arlington Nat. Cemetary, Arlington, V.A.

GREEN, WARREN HAROLD, publisher; b. Auburn, Ill., July 25, 1915; s. John Anderson Logan and Clara Christina (Wortman) G.; m. Joyce Reinerd, Oct. 8, 1960. Student, Presbyn. Theol. Sem., 1933-34, Ill. Wesleyan U., 1934-36; MB, Southwestern Conservatory, Dallas, 1938; MM, St. Louis Conservatory, 1940, PhD, 1942; HLD (hon.), Southeastern U., New Orleans, 1983; LLD (hon.), Institut de Droit Practique, Limoges, France, 1983; DD (hon.), Calif. Theol Sem., 1980; Litt
(hon.), Confédération Européenne de L' Ord
Judiciaire, France, 1983. Prof. voice, composition, co
ducting and aural theory St. Louis Conservatory, 193
44; program dir. U.S.O., Highland Park, Il
Brownwood, Tex., Orange, Tex., Waukegan, Ill., 194
46; community service specialist Rotary Interna
Chgo., 1946-47; editor in chief Charles C. Thomas, Pub
Springfield, Ill., 1947-66; pub., pres. Warren H. Gree
Inc., St. Louis, 1966-92, Warren H. Green Interna
Inc., 1970-92; sec. John R. Davis Assos., Chgo., 195
92; exec. v.p. Visioneering Advt., St. Louis, 1966-9
mng. dir. Pubs. Service Center, St. Louis, Chgo. ar
Longview, Tex., 1967-92; mng. dir., v.p. InterCo
tinental Industries, Inc., St. Louis, 1976-92; v.p. Epo
Press, St. Louis, 1986-92; cons. U.S., European pub
profl. socs.; lectr. med. publs. Civil War. Contbr. a
ticles to profl. jours., books on Civil War histor
writing, editing. Mem. Mayor's Com. on Water Safet
Met. St. Louis Art Mus., Mo. Bot. Gardens; chief exe
officer Affirmative Action, Inc., St. Louis, 1974-92; pr
Southeastern U., 1984-85, No. Utah U., 1986-9
chancellor Internat. U. Consortium, 1989-92. Recipie
Presdl. citation for outstanding contbn. export expa
sion program U.S., 1973, citation Md. Crime Investati
Com., 1962, citation Internat. Preventive Medic
Found., 1977, citation AMA, 1978. Mem. Civil W
Round Table (v.p. 1969-92), Am. Acad. Criminolog
Am. Acad. Polit. and Social Sci., Am. Assn. Med. Bo
Pubs., Am. Judicature Soc., Great Plains Hist. Soc., C
Mil. Historians, Am. Soc. Personnel Adminstr
University City C. of C. (pres. 1978-88, exec. dir. 198
92), Internat. Assn. Chiefs of Police, Mo. Hist. Soc., I
Hist. Soc., St. Louis Philharmonic Soc., Mo. Botanic
Gardens, St. Louis Art Mus. Clubs: Mo. Athlet
Media, Elks, World Trade, Direct Mktg. St. Louis
Home: Saint Louis Mo. Deceased.

GREENBERG, MELVIN NATHANIEL, lawyer;
Newark, Oct. 22, 1928; s. Irving and Lena (Vinocur) (
m. Elsa Stein, Jan. 20, 1957; children: Dianne, Ca
Anne, Michael Ivan. B.A., N.Y. U., 1949, LL.M
Kennison fellow, 1955; LL.B. with honors, U. Fl
1952, J.D., 1967. Bar: Fla. 1952. Ptnr. Morehea
Forrest, Gotthardt & Greenberg, Miami, Fla., 1955-6
ptnr. Greenberg & Saks, Miami, 1960-67; ptnr., pr
Greenberg, Traurig, Hoffman, Lipoff, Rosen & Quent
P.A., Miami, 1967-90; chmn. Greenberg, Traur
Miami, 1991-93; lectr. bus. law Fla. State U., 1953-5
bd. visitors; adj. prof. law U. Miami, 1966-75, N.Y. U
1978-86; adv. com. N.Y. U. Ann. Inst. Fed. Taxatic
Nat. Citizens Adv. Com. for Support of Med. Edn.,
Miami Inst. Estate Planning; lectr. in field. Trustee
Miami, chmn. vis. com. med. div.; bd. dirs. United W
Dade County, 1986, campaign chmn., 1987; me
Pres.'s Coun. U. Fla.; chmn. Citizens Adv. Bd., Miam
Capt. USAF, 1952-54. Fellow Am. Coll. Tax Couns
mem. ABA, Dade County Bar Assn., Fla. Bar, Grea
Miami Tax Inst., Brickell Club, Royal Palm Ten
Club, Grove Isle Club. Home: Miami Fla. Died Se
12, 1994.

GREENBERG, SIMON, rabbi, education a
homiletics educator; b. Horoshen, Russia, Jan. 8, 19
came to U.S., 1905, naturalized, 1924; s. Morris a
Bessie (Chaidenko) G.; m. Betty Davis, Dec. 13, 19
children: Moshe, Daniel Asher. Student, U. Mir
1920-21; A.B., Coll. City N.Y., 1922; Rabbi, Jew
Theol. Sem., N.Y.C., 1925; Ph.D., Dropsie Coll., Phi
1932; D.D., Jewish Theol. Sem. Am., 1950; postgra
Hebrew U. in Jerusalem, Am. Sch. for Orien
Research, Jerusalem, 1924-25. Rabbi Har Zion Temp
Phila., 1925-46; lectr. Jewish edn. Jewish Theol. Se
1932-41, asso. prof. edn., 1941-48, provost, 1946, pr
edn. and homiletics, 1947-93, acting pres., 1948-49, v
chancellor, v.p. faculties, 1951; dir. U. Judaism, I
Angeles, 1948-58; pres. U. Judaism, 1958-66, pr
emeritus, 1966-93; dir. Sem. Israel Pilot Project, 19
82. Author: Living as a Jew Today, 1939, The Harish
Series, 1942, Ideas and Ideals in the Jewish Prayer Bo
1940, The First Year in the Hebrew School; A Teache
Guide, 1945, The Conservative Movement in Judais
1954, Israel and Zionism, Conservative Approach, 19
Foundations of a Faith, 1968, Words of Poetry, 197
The Ethical in the Jewish and the American Herita
1977, A Jewish Philosophy and Pattern of Life, 19
Year of the Bible: A Guide to Daily Bible Study for
Jewish Community, 1983, Solomon Schechter as a T
ologian, 1987; editor: Ordination of Women as Rab
Studies and Response, 1988, Max Kaduskin—Explo
of the Rabbinic Universe of Discourse and Discovere
Organic Thinking, 1989, Festschrift in Honor of
Robert Gordis, 1991. Bd. dirs. Phila. Psychiat. Hos
pres. Rabbinical Assembly Am., 1937-39; past p
Avukah-Intercoll. Zionist Orgn., Phila. br. Uni
Synagogue, Phila. Bd. Jewish Ministers; mem. nat. e
com. Zionist Orgn. Am., pres. Phila. br., 1941-44, chr
nat. edn. com., 1943-45; exec. dir. United Synago
Am., 1950-53; mem. exec. com. World Zionist Or
1964-68; chmn. United Synagogue Commn. on Jew
Edn., 1962-67; mem. praesidium World Council
Jewish Edn., 1964-68; past mem. chaplains religi
council U. Pa. Recipient Sam Rothberg award Heb
U., 1977; Mordecai M. Kaplan medal U. of Judai
1977; Distinguished Service certificate Religious E
Assn. U.S. and Can.; Sem. medal, 1981; Solon
Schechter award United Synagogue, 1983; Math
Schechter award Women's League Conserva

laism, 1984; hon. citation from The Seminary of laic Studies, Jerusalem, 1988; honored with Turabrew Festschrift, 1989. Fellow Conf. on Sci., ilosophy and Religion. Home: New York N.Y. Died y 26, 1993.

REENBLATT, MILTON, psychiatrist; b. Boston, ne 29, 1914; s. Julius and Sophia (Bolonsky) G.; m. rtrude Anna Rogers, June 10, 1941 (dec. 1985); chiln: David John, Daniel Lawrence; m. Margaret mwey, 1991. A.B. summa cum laude, Tufts U., 35, M.D. cum laude, 1939; Dsc (hon.), U. Mass., 92. Charleton research fellow, instr. physiology Tufts Sch. Medicine, 1939-40, prof. psychiatry, 1963-73, pha Omega Alpha lectr., Bergendahl Meml. lectr., 53; intern gen. medicine Beth Israel Hosp., Boston, 40-41; resident in psychiatry Mass. Mental Health nter, Boston, 1941-42; dir. Electroencephalography b., 1942-63, sr. physician, 1943-45, dir. labs., rsch., 46-63, dir. clin. psychiatry, 1953-57, asst. supt., 1957- practice medicine specializing in psychiatry Boston, 41-73; supt. Boston State Hosp., 1963-67; assoc. clin. of. psychiatry Harvard Med. Sch., 1958-63, lectr. chiatry, 1963-73, lectr. dept. social relations, 1957- Eugene Barrera Meml. lectr. Albany Med. Sch., 55; Israel Strauss Meml. lectr. Hillside Hosp., N.Y.C., 52; lectr. div. psychiatry Sch. Medicine Boston U., 53-73; prof. psychiatry, vice chmn. dept. psychiatry, . social and community psychiatry UCLA, 1973-79, e chmn. dept. psychiatry, 1984-94; asst. dean UCLA h. Medicine), 1977-79; prof., exec. vice chmn. dept. chiatry and biobehavioral scis., dir. Neuropsychiatric t. Hosp. and Clinics UCLA, 1979-84, prof. psychiy emeritus, 1984-94; dir. psychiatry Sepulveda VA sp., 1973-77, 84-86; chief staff VA Med. Ctr. ntwood, 1977-79; chief psychiatry Olive View Med. ., Sylmar, Calif., 1986-92, assoc. dir. psychiatry, 92-94; commr. Mass. Dept. Mental Health, 1967-73; ninstrv. cons. Ventura (Calif.) County Mental Health s., 1994; bd. dirs. Am. Bd. Psychiatry and urology, v.p., 1975, pres., 1976. Author: (with ers) From Custodial to Therapeutic Patient Care in ntal Hospitals, 1955; author, editor: (with others) dies in Lobotomy, 1950, (with Harry C. Solomon) ntal Lobes and Schizophrenia, 1953, (with others) Patient and the Mental Hospital, 1957, (with njamin Simon) Rehabilitation of the Mentally Ill: cial and Economic Aspects, 1959, (with others) The evention of Hospitalization, 1963, Drug and Social erapy in Chronic Schizophrenia, 1965; Editor: (with ers) Mental Patients in Transition, 1961, College dents in a Mental Hospital, 1962, Halfway House: A ciocultural and Clinical Study of Rutland Corner use: A Transitional Aftercare Residence for Female chiatric Patients, 1965, Threat of Impending Diser, 1965, Poverty and Mental Health, 1967, Adolests in a Mental Hospital, 1968, Dynamics of Institunal Change, 1971, Drugs in Combination with Other erapies, 1975, Alcoholism Problems in Women and ildren, 1976, Psychopolitics, 1978, (with R.M. cerra) Hispanics Seek Health Care, 1983, (with A. les and C.M. Pierce) The Mosaic of Contemporary chiatry in Perspective, 1992, (with M. Robertson) melessness: The National Perspective, 1992, (in coloration with P. Rodenhauser) Anatomy of Psychia- Administration: The Organisation in Health and ease, 1992; assoc. editor: Am. Jour. Psychiatry, 1965- referee, 1974-94; assoc. editor: Am. Jour. Social chiatry, 1981-87; editl. bd.: Jour. Studies on Alcohol, 58-92, Psychiatric Opinion, 1962-80, Comprehensive chiatry, 1965-94, New Eng. Jour. Medicine, 1967-70, r. Psychiat. Treatment and Evaluation, 1981-83; tor-in-chief: Seminars in Psychiatry, 1968-74, series tor, 1974-86; assoc. editor: Social Psychiatry, 1972- assoc. editor: Psychiat. Annals, 1975-94. Recipient ghest Disting. award UCLA, 1987. Fellow Am. chiat. Assn. (life, Hofheimer prize 1951, v.p. 1972-73, st pres. No. New Eng. Dist. br., chmn. com. comnity aspects psychiatry, councilor 1966-69, chmn. nmn. on drug safety 1966-68, chmn. council on innal orgn. 1973-76, chmn. ad hoc com. to consider nponent on long range planning 1979, Disting. Sere award 1981, Disting. Psychiat. lectr. 1983, Adnstrv. Psychiatry award 1984, Arnold L. van Ameren award in rehab. 1986, PIA award for Hosp. chiatry 1986), Boston Med. Library, Am. Coll. chiatrists (Disting. Service award 1984), Mass. Soc. search Psychiatry (past pres.), Mass. Med. Soc. (past nn. sect. psychiatry, neurology), Am. Coll. Neurophopharmacology (past pres.), Group for Advancent Psychiatry, Am. Psychopath. Assn. (past pres.), n. Assn. for Social Psychiatry (pres. 1974-76, under's award 1985), World Fedn. Mental Health, n. Coll. Mental Health Adminstrn., So. Calif. chiatric Soc. (Outstanding Achievement award 93). Home: Ventura Calif. Died Nov. 17, 1994.

REENEWALT, CRAWFORD HALLOCK, chemicals cutive; b. Cummington, Mass., Aug. 16, 1902; s. ank Lindsay and Mary Elizabeth (Hallock) G.; m. argaretta Lammot du Pont, June 4, 1926 (dec. Mar. 91); children: Nancy Crawford Frederick, David, awford Hallock. BSChemE, MIT, 1922; DSc, U. l., 1940, Northeastern U., 1950; ED, Rensselaer Poly. t., 1952; LLD (hon.), Columbia U., 1953, Williams ll., 1953, Kenyon Coll., 1958, Kans. State U., Temple 1960, U. Pa., 1961, Swarthmore Coll., 1961, U. tre Dame, 1965, Bowdoin Coll., 1965, Yale U., 1969; ScD (hon.), Boston U., 1953; DCS (hon.), NYU, 1954; DEng. (hon.), Poly Inst. Bklyn., 1954; DSc. (hon.), Phila. Coll. Pharmacy and Sci., 1955, Drexel Inst. Tech., 1961, Hamilton Coll., 1970; LHD (hon.), Jefferson Med. Coll., 1960. With E.I. du Pont de Nemours & Co., 1922-88, asst. dir. exptl. sta., chem. dept., 1939, chem. dir. Grasselli chem. dept., 1942, tech. dir. explosives dept., 1943, asst. dir. devel. dept., 1945, asst. gen mgr. pigments dept., 1945, v.p., 1946-48, pres., 1948-62, chmn. bd., 1962-67, chmn. fin. com., 1967-74, mem. fin. com., 1974-88, hon. chmn. Author: The Uncommon Man, 1959, Hummingbirds, 1960, Bird Song: Acoustics and Physiology, 1968. Trustee emeritus Winterthur Mus., MIT, Carnegie Instn., Longwood Gardens; regent emeritus Smithsonian Instn. Recipient Gold medal Wharton Sch. Alumni Soc., 1952, William Procter prize Sci. Rsch. Soc. Am., 1957, Rsch. medal Am. Soc. Medals, 1958, Poor Richard's Club Gold medal, 1959, Gold medal Econ. Club N.Y., 1961. Mem. Am. Inst. Chem. Engrs. (John Fritz medal 1962, Robert E. Wilson award 1967), Am. Inst. Chemists (Gold medal 1959), Soc. Chem. Industry (Svc. medal 1952, Soc. medal 1963), Am. Acad. Arts and Scis., NAS, Am. Chem. Soc., AAAS, Am. Philos. Soc., Nat. Geog. Soc. (trustee emeritus), Wilmington Club, du Pont Country Club, Theta Chi, Tau Beta Pi. Home: Wilmington Del. Died Sept. 27, 1993.

GREENLEE, JOHN ALDEN, college president; b. Richland, Iowa, Sept. 7, 1911; s. John Amzi and Martha Denny (Logsdon) G.; m. Lillian Ruth Witte, Dec. 13, 1955. BA, U. Iowa, 1930, MA, 1931, PhD, 1934; LLD, Christ Coll., Irvine, Calif., 1988. Prof., asst. to dean scis. Iowa State U., 1940-59; dir. engring. personnel and edn. Collins Radio Co., Cedar Rapids, Iowa, 1959-65; v.p. acad. affairs Calif. State U., Los Angeles, 1965-66; pres. Calif. State U., 1966-79, pres. emeritus, 1980-92; higher edn. cons., 1980-92; Mem. Nat. Commn. on State Workmen's Compensation Laws, 1971-72. Served with USNR, World War II. Decorated Bronze Star. Mem. Phi Delta Kappa, Phi Kappa Phi, Alpha Kappa Psi, Beta Gamma Sigma. Home: South Pasadena Calif. Died Nov. 23, 1992; buried Hampton, Iowa.

GREENWAY, JOHN SELMES, hotel owner; b. Santa Barbara, Calif., Oct. 11, 1924; s. John Campbell and Isabella Dinsmore (Selmes) G. B.A., Yale, 1949; LL.B., U. Ariz., 1954. Owner Ariz. Inn, Tucson, 1958-95. Home: Tucson Ariz. Died Sept. 13, 1995.

GREGG, DAVIS WEINERT, economics educator, financial gerontologist; b. Austin, Tex., Mar. 12, 1918; s. Davis Alexander and Lorene (Murff) G.; m. Mildred Grace McDaniel, May 15, 1942; children: Mary Cynthia, Davis William. B.B.A., U. Tex., 1939; M.B.A., U. Pa., 1940, Ph.D., 1948. Underwriter Aetna Casualty & Surety Co., Hartford, Conn., 1940-41; asst. prof. naval sci. U. Minn., 1945-46; prof. ins. Ohio State U., 1948-49, Grad. Sch. Bus. Stanford, 1949; asst. dean The Am. Coll., Bryn Mawr, Pa., 1949-51; dean The Am. Coll., 1952-53, trustee, 1951-74, life trustee, 1974-93, pres., 1954-82, Disting. prof. econs., 1982-91, prof. emeritus, 1991-93; dir. Boettner Research Inst., 1986-89; founding dir. Boettner Inst. of Fin. Gerontology, 1989-93, chmn. bd. trustees, 1991-93; dir. 1st Internat. Ins. Conf., mem. honors com. Internat. Ins. Soc., Inc.; bd. dirs. Waverly Heights Ltd.; past chmn. Commn. on Ins. Terminology; trustee Kynett Found.; bd. dirs. Bryn Mawr Hosp., 1979-91. Author: An Analysis of Group Life Insurance, 1950, Group Life Insurance, 1964, Insurance Courses Outside the United States, 1960; editor: Life and Health Insurance Handbook, 1959, 3d edit., 1973, World Insurance Trends, 1960, Property and Liability Insurance Handbook, 1965, contbr. chpt. book. Mem. Am. Risk and Ins. Assn. (pres. 1961), Am. Soc. CLUs and ChFCs, Merion Golf Club, Beta Gamma Sigma (Dir.'s Table). Presbyterian (ruling elder). Home: Bryn Mawr Pa. Died Oct. 27, 1993.

GREGOIRE, PAUL CARDINAL, deceased archbishop; b. Verdun, Quebec, Oct. 24, 1911; s. Albert and Marie (Lavoie) G. Student, Seminaire de Sainte-Therese; theol. student, Grand Sem. Montreal, Que., Can.; Ph.D., U. Montreal, Litt.L., M.A. in History, diploma in pedagogy, hon. doctorate, 1969; hon. doctorate, St. Michael's Coll., Winooski Park, Vt., 1970. Ordained priest Roman Cath. Ch., 1937; consecrated bishop, 1961. Dir. Seminaire de Sainte-Therese; prof. philosophy of edn. l'Ecole Normale Secondaire, l'Institut Pedagogique; chaplain of students U. Montreal; aux. to Archbishop of Montreal; vicar gen., dir. Office for Clergy; acting adminstr. diocese; apostolic adminstr. Archdiocese of Montreal, 1967-68, archbishop, 1968-90; elevated to cardinal, 1988, archbishop emeritus; pres. French sect. Episcopal Commn. Ecumenism, Can. Cath. Conf., 1965; presided over numerous diocesan commns., 1965-93. Decorated officer Order of Can. Home: Montreal Can. Died Oct. 30, 1993; interred Cathedral Montreal, Montreal.

GREGORY, DONALD MUNSON, retired lawyer; b. San Francisco, Jan. 21, 1897; s. Warren and Sarah (Hardy) G.; m. Josephine Wallace, May 21, 1924; children: Joan (Mrs. Thomas C. Benet), Donald Munson. AB, U. Calif., Berkeley, 1920; LLB, Harvard U., 1923. Bar: Calif. 1924. Since practiced in San Francisco; mem. firm Chickering & Gregory, from 1926. Del. Commn. for Relief in Belgium, 1916-17. 2d lt. F.A. U.S. Army, 1917-19; lt. col. adj. gen. dept. AUS, 1942-45. Mem. Astron. Soc. Pacific, Am., San Francisco bar assns., State Bar of Calif., Am. Judicature Soc. Clubs: Pacific Union (San Francisco), Sierra (San Francisco), Commonwealth (San Francisco). Home: San Francisco Calif. Deceased.

GREGORY, EDWARD MEEKS, minister; b. Richmond, Va., Sept. 30, 1922; s. George Craghead and Constance (Heath) G.; m. Cornelie Johanna Hogewind-Haalebos, Jun. 17, 1954 (div. Jun. 1959). Grad., St. Christopher's Sch., 1941; AB, U. Va., 1947; MDiv, Episc. Theol. Sch., Cambridge, Mass., 1954; postgrad., George Washington U., 1949, Va. Commonwealth U., 1980, Harvard U., 1981; DMin, U. of South, 1977. Ordained to ministry Episcopal Ch. as priest, 1955. Instr. Staunton (Va.) Mil. Acad., 1947-48; master Episc. High Sch., Alexandria, Va., 1948-51; curate St. Mark's Episc. Ch., Richmond, 1954-69; vicar St. Peter's Episc. Ch., Richmond, 1969-79; chaplain Christchurch Sch., 1980-90, chaplain emeritus, 1990-95; dean East Richmond, 1974-78; diocesan youth dir., 1956-60; diocesan del. Va. Coun. Chs., 1967-73; spiritual adviser Dignity-Integrity/Richmond, 1976-79; mem. Diocesan Dept. Social Rels., 1970-72, Diocesan Lit. Commn., 1973-83; pres. Religious Edn. Coun., Richmond, 1961-62, Richmond Episc. Clericus, 1972-73. Bd. dirs. Vol. Svc. Bur., Richmond, 1960-63, Ednl. Therapy Center, 1964-79, Multiple Sclerosis, 1961-66, Va. Community Devel. Orgn., 1968-75, Va. chpt. ACLU, 1970-71, 76-77, Internat. Coun.; bd. dirs. Va. Coun. Human Rels., 1965-70, treas., 1972-73; bd. dirs. Richmond Planned Parenthood, 1969-74, Richmond chpt. ARC, 1973-79, Richmond United Neighborhoods, 1977-79, Met. Area Resources Clearing House, 1977-79, Ch. Hill Revitalization Team, 1979; bd. govs. Christchurch Sch., Va., 1978-79; pres. Richmond Council Human Relations, 1960-62; pres. Friends' Assn. for Children, 1967-70, bd. dirs., 1975-79; mem. adv. bd. Richmond Model Neighborhood, 1971-73; bd. dirs. Richmond Community Sr. Center, 1975-78, Daily Planet, 1974-79, Alcohol and Drug Abuse Prevention and Tng. Services, 1978-85, Richmond Health Center, 1981-85; vice chmn. Richmond Health Occupations, 1979. Served with Med. Dept. AUS, 1942-46. Decorated Bronze Star. Mem. Richmond Clergy Assn., Jamestown Soc. (gov. 1951-55), Mayflower Soc. (elder Va. co. 1963-81), Va. Hist. Soc., Braintree (Mass.) Hist. Soc., Episcopal Soc. Cultural and Racial Unity (chmn. Richmond 1964-66), Assn. Preservation Va. Antiquities, Valentine Mus., Va. Mus. Fine Arts, Chi Phi. Silhouettist; works exhibited Va. Hist. Soc. Died Jan. 25, 1995. Home: Richmond Va.

GRESHAM, PERRY EPLER, university official, philosophy educator; b. Covina, Cal., Dec. 19, 1907; s. George Edward and Mary Elizabeth (Epler) G.; m. Elsie Stanbrough, Dec. 9, 1926 (dec. Mar. 1947); 1 son, Glen Edward; m. Alice Fickling Cowan, May 6, 1953; 1 dau., Nancy. A.B. summa cum laude, Tex. Christian U., 1931, B.D., 1933, LL.D., 1949; postgrad., U. Chgo., 1932-33, Columbia, 1931-41; Litt.D., Culver-Stockton Coll., 1954, Findlay Coll., U. Cin., 1966, W. Va. U., 1971; L.H.D., Chapman Coll., 1964, Concord Coll.; Ed.D., Transylvania, 1965, Rio Grande Coll.; LL.D., Alderson-Broaddus Coll.; Pd.D., Youngstown U., 1966; D.B.A., Lawrence Inst. Tech., 1973. Prof. philosophy Tex. Christian U., 1936-42; minister U. Christian Ch., Ft. Worth, 1933-42, Seattle, 1942-45; minster Central Woodward Christian Ch., Detroit, 1945-53; feature writer Detroit Free Press, 1950-52; pres. Bethany (W.Va.) Coll., 1953-72, chmn. bd., 1972-76, distinguished prof. philosophy, 1973-94; former adj. prof. U. Wash.; former lectr. U. Mich.; pres. emeritus Bethany (W.Va.) Coll., 1973-94; mem. study com. Commn. on Faith and Order, World Coun. Chs., 1948-60; pres. W.Va. Found. Colls., 1954-58; mem. clergy industry commn. N.A.M., 1957-65; commn. on liberal edn. Assn. Am. Colls., 1963-78 ; chmn. North Central Assn. Colls. and Univs., 1964-66; pres. Internat. Conv. Christian Chs., 1960-61; dir. emeritus Chesapeake & Potomac Telephone Co., Cooper Tire and Rubber Co., Findlay, Ohio.; Wesbanco Corp., 1960-83, pres., 1983; Wheeling Dollar Bank.; bd. dirs. Found. for Econ. Edn., 1960-86, pres., 1983-84, chmn. bd., 1966-68; bd. dirs. Lawrence Inst. Tech., Detroit, John A. Hartford Found., N.Y.C.; fin. agt. for Tudor Monarchs. Author: Incipient Gnosticism in the New Testament, 1933, Disciplines of the High Calling, 1954, The Sage of Bethany, 1960, Answer to Conformity, 1961, Abiding Values, 1972, Campbell and the Colleges, 1973, With Wings As Eagles, 1980, Toasts - Plain, Spicy and Wry, 1986. Mem. Am. Philos. Soc. Internat. Robert Burns Soc., Internat. Platform Assn., Skytop Club (Pa.), Royal Scottish Club (Glasgow), Authors Club (London), Pinehurst Country Club (N.C.), Bermuda Run Country Club (N.C.), Piedmont Club (N.C), Shriners, Masons, Rotary, Alpha Chi. Home: Bethany W.V. Died Sept. 10, 1994.

GRIESEMER, JOHN N., manufacturing executive; b. Mt. Vernon, Mo.; s. Joseph John and Margaret (Arend) G.; m. Kathleen A. Poirot; children: Margaret, Julia, Joseph E., John F., Stephen. BSCE, U. Mo., 1953. Supt. Griesemer Stone Co., Springfield, Mo., 1956-59, v.p., 1959-74, pres., 1974-93; chmn., bd. govs. U.S. Postal Svc., 1986, 88, 90-91, vice chmn., 1990-91, gov. 1984-93; bd. dirs. Boatmen's Nat. Bank of Springfield;

pres. Springfield Bus. Devel. Corp., 1991. Co-chmn. Sprinfield Cath. Schs. Devel. Fund, 1984-86. With USAF, 1953-56, Japan. Mem. Mo. Limestone Producers Assn. (pres. 1963), Na.t Limestone Inst. (chmn. 1974), Nat. Stone Assn. (Dist. Govt. Svc. award 1988). Republican. Roman Catholic. Home: Springfield Mo. Died July 3, 1993.

GRIEVE, HAROLD WALTER, retired interior designer; b. L.A., Feb. 1, 1901; s. Alexander and Maria (Chapman) G.; m. Jetta Goudal, Oct. 11, 1930. Student Los Angeles art schs., 1920-21, Chouinard Sch. Art, 1920-21, Camillo Innocentie, Rome, 1923-24. Art dir. M.P. Studios, 1920-28; art dir. for motion pictures including: Dorothy Vernon of Haden Hall, Lady Windemer's Fan, So This is Paris; interior designer, Los Angeles, now ret.; decorated Colleen Moore Doll House interiors, 1935; interior design work includes homes of George Burns, Jack Benny, Bing Crosby, Erving Thalberg, Norma Schearer, others. Fellow Am. Inst. Interior Designers (life mem., past nat. pres., past local pres.), Acad. of Motion Pictures (founder mem., life mem.), Hist. Soc. So. Calif. Republican. Clubs: Los Angeles Athletic; Beach (Santa Monica, Calif.). Died Nov. 3, 1993. Home: South Gate Calif.

GRIFFIN, MARY ANN, library director; b. Hazleton, Pa., Mar. 6, 1946; d. John and Mary (Kudlick) Timko; m. Joseph Griffin, Dec. 30, 1967. BS, Pa. State U., 1967, MA, 1970; MS, Simmons Coll., 1974, DA, 1980. Libr. asst. Pa. State U., State College, 1970-73; libr. dept. head Tufts U., Medford, Mass., 1974-77; libr. dir. Xavier U., Cin., 1979-84, Villanova (Pa.) U., 1984-95; mem. exec. bd. Tri-State Coll. Libr. Coop., Rosemont, Pa., 1988-92; pres., mem. exec. bd. Greater Cin. Libr. Consortium, 1979-84; trustee PALINET, 1992-95, exec. com., 1992-95, also pres. bd. trustees, 1995; presenter profl. confs. Editor (alumni assn. newsletter) Simmons Libr., 1978-81; contbr. articles to profl. jours. ALA, AAUP, Assn. Coll. and Rsch. Librs. (pres., mem. exec. bd. Delaware Valley chpt. 1985-92, ACRL membership com. 1991-95). Home: Oley Pa. Died Aug. 14, 1995.

GRIFFITHS, IORWERTH DAVID ACE, psychologist, retired educator; Raised Idaho; s. Iorwerth Vivian and Katherine (Lewis) G.; m. Dorothea Ohs. B.S., U. Idaho; M.S., U. Ariz.; Ed.D., No. Colo. U.; postgrad., Wash. State U., U. Minn. lic. psychologist, Calif. Practice in Calif.; with Sears Roebuck & Co., Dick Graves, Inc., Nev. and Idaho; tchr. public schs. Potlatch, Idaho; counselor public sch. Port Townsend, Wash.; dean of students Eastern Ariz. Coll., Thatcher, Reedley (Calif.) Coll.; prof. edn. Calif. State U., Fresno, 1959-83; dir. U.S. Govt. Counselor Tng. Workshops, 1964. Contbr. articles to profl. jours.; co-author: Principles of Retailing, 1956. Named One of 18 All-Time Outstanding Tchrs., Port Townsend Pub. Schs., 1985. Mem. Am. Personnel and Guidance Assn. (membership chmn. 1961-63), Am. Psychol. Assn., NEA, Calif. Personnel and Guidance Assn. (McDaniel award), Nat. Vocat. Guidance Assn., Assn. Counselor Edn. and Supervision, Calif. State Employees Assn., Kings-Tulare Guidance Assn., San Joaquin Valley Guidance Assn., Fresno Counselors Assn., Kappa Delta Pi, Delta Psi Omega, Phi Delta Kappa. Unitarian. Home: Fresno Calif.

GRINKER, ROY RICHARD, SR., psychiatrist, psychoanalyst; b. Chgo., Aug. 2, 1900; s. Julius and Minnie (Friend) G.; m. Mildred Barman, July 24, 1924; children: Roy Richard, Joan Richman. S.B., U. Chgo., 1919; M.D., Rush Med. Coll., 1921. Instr. neurology Northwestern U., 1925; instr. neurology U. Chgo., 1927-29, asst. prof., 1929-31, asso. prof., 1931-35, asso. prof. psychiatry, 1935-36, also chief psychiat. div., 1935-36; chmn. dept. neuropsychiatry, also dir. Inst. for Psychosomatic and Psychiat. Research and Tng., Michael Reese Hosp., Chgo., 1946-76; clin. prof. psychiatry U. Ill., 1951-66; prof. psychiatry Pritzker Med. Sch., U. Chgo., 1969-85, prof. emeritus, 1985-93; sr. ednl. prof. Northwestern U. Med. Sch., 1980-89, sr. ednl. prof. emeritus, 1989-93. Author: 50 Years in Psychiatry; co-author: The Borderline Patient, also numerous other sci. publs.; editor: Mid-Century Psychiatry, Toward a Unified Theory of Human Behavior. Served as student Army Tng. Corps, 1917; col. M.C. 1942-45. Decorated Legion of Merit.; Recipient Maj. Raymonds Longacre award for sci. contbn. to aviation medicine, 1955; Profl. Achievement award U. Chgo. Alumni Assn., 1969; Gold Medal award Soc. Biol. Psychiatry, 1970; Salmon medal N.Y. Acad. Medicine, 1970. Fellow AAAS, N.Y. Acad. Scis., Am. Coll. Neuropharmacology; mem. Am. Psychopathology Assn., Acad. Psychoanalysis (pres. 1961), Am. Assn. Research in Nervous and Mental Diseases, Am. Assn. Neuropathologists, Am. Neurol. Assn., Am. Psychiat. Assn., Am. Psychoanalytic Soc., AMA (editor-in-chief archives neurology, psychiatry 1956-59, archives of gen. psychiatry 1959- 69), Sigma Xi. Club: Standard. Home: Chicago Ill. Died May 9, 1993; interred Chicago, I.L.

GRINKOV, SERGEI, ice skater; m. Ekaterina Gordeeva, 1991; 1 child, Daria. Recipient (all with Ekaterina Gordeeva) 1st Pl. award pairs figure skating World Figure Skating Championships, 1986, 87, 89, 90, Gold medal pairs figure skating Olympic Games, 1988, 94. Home: Davos-Platz Switzerland Died Nov. 20, 1995.

GRISWOLD, ERWIN NATHANIEL, lawyer; b. East Cleveland, Ohio, July 14, 1904; s. James Harlen and Hope (Erwin) G.; m. Harriet Allena Ford, Dec. 30, 1931; children: Hope Eleanor Griswold Murrow, William Erwin. A.B., A.M., Oberlin Coll., 1925; LL.B., Harvard U., 1928, S.J.D., 1929; L.H.D. (hon.), Tufts Coll., 1949, Case Inst. Tech., 1950; LL.D. (hon.), U. B.C., 1949, Brown U., 1950, U. Sydney, U. Melbourne, 1951, Dalhousie U., 1952, Harvard, Amherst Coll., 1953, Columbia U., U. Richmond, 1954, Brandeis U., 1956, U. Mich., 1959, Northwestern U., 1960, U. Toronto, 1962, Williams Coll., 1966, Princeton U., 1968, Oberlin Coll., 1982; D.C.L. (hon.), U. Toronto, 1962, U. Edinburgh, Oxford U., 1964; and numerous other honorary degrees. Bar: Ohio 1929, Mass. 1935, D.C. 1973. With Griswold, Green, Palmer & Hadden, Cleve., 1929; atty. office solicitor gen., spl. asst. to atty. gen. Washington, 1929-34; asst. prof. law Harvard U., 1934-35, prof., 1935-46, dean, Charles Stebbins Fairchild prof. law, 1946-50, dean, Langdell prof. law, 1950-67; solicitor gen. U.S., 1967-73; partner Jones Day Reavis & Pogue, Washington, 1973-91, sr. counsel, 1991-94; mem. U.S. Civil Rights Commn., 1961-67; mem. conf. with Soviet lawyers Lawyers Alliance Nuclear Arms Control, 1983-94. Author: Spendthrift Trusts, 1936, 2d edit., 1947, Cases on Federal Taxation, 1940, 6th edit., 1966, (with others) Cases on Conflict of Laws, 1941, rev. edit., 1964, The Fifth Amendment Today, Law and Lawyers in the United States, Ould Fields, New Corne, 1992. Trustee Oberlin Coll., 1936-94, Bradford Jr. Coll., 1942-49, Tchrs. Ins. and Annuity Assn., 1942-46, Harvard Law Rev. Assn., 1938-67. Fellow Am. Acad. Arts and Scis. (v.p. 1946-48), Brit. Acad. (corr.); mem. ABA (ho. of dels. 1957-85, gold medal 1978), Mass. Bar Assn., Am. Law Inst., Am. Coll. Trial Lawyers, Am. Philos. Soc., Inner Temple (hon. bencher), Harvard Club (N.Y.C.), Burning Tree Club, Cosmos Club, Met. Club (Washington), Phi Beta Kappa. Home: Washington D.C. Died Nov. 19, 1994.

GRIZZARD, LEWIS (M.), JR., newspaper columnist, writer; b. Columbus, Ga., Oct. 20, 1946; s. Lewis McDonald and Christine (Word) G.; married, 1966 (div. 1969); m. Fay Rentz (div. 1976), m. Kathy Tullman, Feb. 10, 1979 (div. 1982). ABJ, U. Ga., 1967. Sportswriter, exec. sports writer Journal, Atlanta, 1968-70; free-lance writer, staff mem. Atlanta Constitution, 1970; sports editor Chgo. Sun-Times, 1970; columnist Atlanta Constitution and Atlanta Journal, 1979-94. Author: (collected columns) Kathy Sue Loudermilk, I Love You, 1979, (collected columns) Won't You Come Home, Billy Bob Bailey?, 1980, (collected columns) Don't Sit Under the Grits Tree With Anyone Else But Me, 1981, (with Loran Smith) Glory! Glory! Georgia's 1980 Championship Season: The Inside Story, 1981, They Tore Out My Heart and Stomped That Sucker Flat, 1982, If Love Were Oil, I'd Be About a Quart Low, 1983, Elvis Is Dead and I Don't Feel So Good Myself, 1986, Shoot Low, Boys-They're Riding Shetland Ponies: In Search of True Grit, 1985, (biography) My Daddy Was a Pistol and I'm a Son of a Gun, 1986, (collected columns) When My Love Returns From the Ladies Room, Will I Be Too Old to Care?, 1987, Don't Bend Over in the Garden, Granny, You Know Them Taters Got Eyes, 1988, Lewis Grizzard on Fear of Flying: Avoid Pouting Pilots and Mechanics Named Bubba, 1989, Lewis Grizzard's Advice to the Newly Wed...and the Newly Divorced, 1989, Chili Dawgs Always Bark at Night, 1989, Getting it On: A Down Home Treasury, 1989, Does a Wild Bear Chip in the Woods? Lewis Grizzard on Golf, 1990, If I Ever Get Back to Georgia, I'm Gonna Nail My Feet to the Floor, 1990, Don't Forget to Call Your Mama-I Wish I Could Call Mine, 1991, Heapin' Helping of the True Grizzard: Down Home Again With Lewis Grizzard, 1991, 1991, I Haven't Understood Anything Since 1962: And Other Nekkid Truths, 1991, You Can't Put No Boogie-Woogie on the King of Rock and Roll, 1992, I Took a Lickin' and Kept on Tickin': And Now I Believe in Miracles, 1993, The Last Bus to Albuquerque, 1994; actor TV including Designing Women; contbr. articles TV, other periodicals. Home: Atlanta Ga. Died Mar. 20, 1994.

GROLNICK, DON, pianist, music arranger, composer, producer. Albums include Weaver of Dreams (leader), (with Bob Berg) Short Stories, (with Brecker Bros.) Collection Volume One, (with Michael Brecker) Don't Try This At Home, Michael Brecker, Now You See It, (with Peter Erskine) Transition, Motion Poet, (with Linda Ronstadt) Simple Dreams, What's New, Lush Life, For Sentimental Reasons, Cry Like A Rainstorm-Howl Like The Wind, (with Steps) Smokin' In The Pit, Step By Step, Paradox, (with Steely Dan) The Royal Scam, Aja, Gaucho, (with James Taylor) Never Die Young, Walking Man, That's Why I'm Here, Flag, Dad Loves His Work. Home: New York N.Y. Died June 1, 1996.

GRONOUSKI, JOHN AUSTIN, university dean, educator; b. Dunbar, Wis., Oct. 26, 1919; m. Mary Metz, Jan. 24, 1948; 2 children. Ph.D. in Econs., U. Wis., 1955; D.H.L. (hon.), Alliance Coll., 1964; LL.D., Fairleigh Dickinson U., 1967, St. Edward's U., 1970, Babson Coll., 1973. Prof. econs. U. Maine, Orono, 1948-50, Wayne State U., Detroit, 1957-59; commr. taxation State of Wis., 1960-63; postmaster gen. U.S. Cabinet Pres. Kennedy and Pres. Johnson, 1963-65; spl. mas U.S. Dist. Ct. Eastern Dist. Wis., 1976-77; ambassad to Poland and U.S. Rep. between U.S. and China, 19 68; dean Lyndon G. Johnson Sch. Pub. Affairs, U. Te Austin, 1969-74, prof. pub. affairs and econs., 1974- Trustee Nat. Urban League, 1968-73, Austin A Urban League, 1977-82, pres., 1982-83; chmn. Bd. ternat. Broadcasting, 1977-81; active Presdl. Stu Commn. Internat. Radio Broadcasting, 1972-73; cont Mich. Tax Study, 1957-58; mem. Austin Area Pvt. dustry Council, 1985-96; chmn. Joint Commn. on M Govt., Austin and Travis County, 1985-87. Served as lt. USAAF, 1942-45. Mem. Nat. Acad. Pub. A minstrn., Polish Inst. Arts and Scis. Am., Inc. (pre Am. Econ. Assn., Nat. Tax Assn. Died Jan. 7, 19 Home: Green Bay Wis.

GROSS, CAROLINE LORD (MRS. MARTIN GROSS), state official; b. Laconia, N.H., May 5, 19 d. William Shepard and Marion (Manns) Lord; Martin L. Gross, Nov. 5, 1960. AB cum laude, Radcl Coll., 1963; MAT, Harvard U., 1964. Rsch. asst. Su Schs., Concord, N.H., 1965-66, N.H. Legis. com. a sessions, Concord, 1966, N.H. Fiscal com. 1967- adminstrv. asst. N.H. gov., Concord, 1969-70; coo N.H. fed. funds, Concord, 1971-72, supr. checkl 1969-84; mem. com. on appropriations N.H. Ho. Reps., 1983-89, clk., 1985-86, div. head, 1987- majority leader, 1989-93. Mem. N.H. Commn. Sta Women, 1972-75; del. N.H. Rep. Conv., 1968-92; le policy asst. N.H. Ho. of Reps., 1974-81; trustee C cord Libr., 1974-77, Granite State Pub. Radio, 1979- Rep. city chmn., Concord, 1980-84; Rep. candid N.H. State Senate, 1980; mem. N.H. Fiscal Com., 19 90; bd. dirs. Cen. N.H. Community Mental He Svcs., 1984-86. Recipient Disting. Svc. award N.H. Assn., 1993, Leadership award N.H. Women's Lob 1993. Mem. Harvard-Radcliffe of N.H. Club (co-p 1981-84). Died Dec. 5, 1994. Home: Concord N.H

GROSS, EARL, artist; b. Pitts., Sept. 1899. Student, Westminster Coll., Carnegie-Mellon Sch. Fine Arts. One-man shows include Macbeth G leries, N.Y.C., 1942, Associated Am. Artists, N.Y. 1945, Atlanta Art Mus., Sarasota Art Assn., Wust Mus., Madison Art Assn., Longboat Key Art Assn., State Mus., Herron Art Inst., New Orleans Acad. Burpee Art Mus., Butler Art Mus., Albuquerque Mus, 1990; exhibited in group shows Manhattan M of Art, 1952, Internat. Water Color Show at Chgo. Inst., Illustrators Club of N.Y.C., Bob-O-Link Coun Club; represented in permanent collections J. Wa Thompson Collection, U.S. Gypsum Co., Carborund Co., Internat. Minerals & Chemicals, Brown & Form Stizell-Weller of Ky., Northern Trust Co., Am. Ho Supply Co., Westclox Co., New Britain Mus. of A Art, Atlanta Art Inst., Reading Mus., Ill. State M Chgo. Art Inst., Chgo. Hist. Soc., Frank Oehlschlea Galleries, Chgo. and Sarasota, Fla., U.S. Air Fo Acad., The Pentagon, Washington, Tavern Club Chgo., U. Mich., Old Northwest Territory Arts S So. Ill. U., Mitsubishi of Japan, Ford Motor Co., numerous pvt. collections including Prime Minister S of Japan and former N.Y. Yankee baseball player DiMaggio, others. Recipient 1st prize Parkersburg Art Ctr., 2d prize Denver Art Show, Cosmopol Mag. Competition, Purchase award Union League C 1959-65, Honorable Mention Terry Art Inst.; nar Official Combat Artist USAF. Mem. Am. Waterc Soc., Arts Club of Chgo., Artists' Guild of Chgo. prize in competition, Best Painting of War Subje Salamagundi Watercolor Club, Phila. Watercolor C Washington Watercolor Club, Madison Wis. League, Nat. Soc. Lit. and the Arts. Home: Al querque N.Mex. Died Mar. 2, 1993.

GROSS, FRITZ A., electronics company executive; Germany, Oct. 8, 1910; came to U.S., 1912, naturaliz 1920; s. Fritz and Anna (Hörmann) G.; m. O Nelson, Aug. 14, 1937; children: Jane, Mar Susan. Grad., Lowell Inst. Tech. MIT, 1930, gr course electronics, 1931; D.Eng. (hon.), Northeast U., 1975. Registered profl. engr., Mass. Design e S.H. Couch Co., Quincy, Mass., 1932-34; with Rayth Co., Lexington, Mass., 1934-93; mgr. heavy electr equipment operations Raytheon Co., 1958-60, vice p gen. mgr. equipment div., 1960-68, v.p. engring., 19 75, tech. cons., 1975-92; tech. adviser radio aids navigation USN, 1946. Recipient certificate of M commendation USN, 1946, Reginald Fessenden aw 1981, Albert A. Michelson award for outstanding and technol. achievement USN League, 1991. Fel IEEE; mem. Am. Soc. Naval Engrs., Armed Fo Communications and Electronics Assn. Ho Westwood Mass. Died Jan. 12, 1993; interred Wes Mass.

GROSSMAN, JOHN HENRY, obstetric gynecologist, educator; b. Rochester, N.Y., Aug. 1914; s. Gustave Adolph and Mabel (Trumeter) A.B., U. Rochester, 1938, M.D., 1941; m. Marya Fryczynski, Nov. 30, 1941; children: John Henry Marja M. Prewitt. Asst. serologist Rochester (N Health Bur., 1940-41; intern surgery New Haven H 1941-42, asst. resident ob-gyn, 1942-43, asso. resid 1943-44, resident ob-gyn, 1944-45; asst. obstetrician gynecologist, mem. faculty Yale U., 1941-43, instr.

, 1943-45; asso. attending obstetrician Bridgeport nn.) Hosp., 1945-56, sr. attending gynecologist and etrician, 1957-70, sr. cons. ob-gyn, 1970-92, pres. chief attending staff, 1960-61; instr. ob-gyn U. lgeport and Bridgeport Hosp. Schs. Nursing, 1945- asst. prof. Coll. Nursing, U. Bridgeport, 1956-92; talk show Here's To Your Health, Sta. WADS, onia, Conn., 1982-92. First v.p. Nichols Village rovement Assn. Recipient Man of Yr. award Am. ion, Trumbull, Conn., 1969; Stanley M. Collins nl. award, 1970; Linking Ring Feature award, 1972; don Magic Circle Silver Wand award, 1981. lomate Am. Bd. Ob-Gyn. Fellow Am. Coll. Obste- ans and Gynecologists (founder, hon. life mem.), Soc. Abdominal Surgeons, Royal Soc. Medicine rseas fellow); mem. Conn. (hon. life), Fairfield nty (hon. life), Bridgeport med. socs., Magicians ld Am., Magic Collectors Assn. (hon. life pres.), Assn. Physicians and Surgeons, Pan Am. Med. 1. (hon. life), New England Magic Collectors Assn. life), Inner Magic Circle (hon. life, MIMC with d Star), Sigma Chi. Clubs: Univ. (Bridgeport); Magic le (London). Feature writer M.U.M. mag., 1958-92, research editor, monthly columnist; feature writer gicol mag., 1959-92; Am. corr. Magic Circular mag., don, 1960-92; mem. Am. Magic Hall of Fame, 1977; br. to books. Died Sept. 8, 1992; buried Nichols etary, Trumbull, Conn. Home: Stratford Conn.

OSZ, KAROLY, government official; b. Miskolc, gary, 1930; m. Éva Csontó; children: Iván, r. Student, Eötvös Lóránd U., Budapest, Hungry. Cen. Apparatus of the Party, Hungary, 1950; of- Hungarian People's Army; head dept. Borsod- uj-Zemplén County Party Com., 1954; mng. editor k-Magyarország Daily, 1958; member polit. staff garian Socialist Workers' Party, sec. com. Hun- an radio and TV, 1962-68, dep. head dept. cen. ., 1968-73, 1st sec. Fejér County Com., 1973, head cen. com., 1974-79, 1st sec. Borsod-Abauj- plén County Com., 1979-84, mem. cen. com., 1980- lst sec. Budapest Party Com., 1984-87, mem. Polit. Com., 1985-96; prime minister Republic of Hun- , 1987-88; gen. sec. cen. com. Hungarian Socialist kers' Party, 1988-89, gen. sec. politburo, 1989. ne: Budapest Hungary Died Jan. 5, 1996.

JBBS, CLIFTON MADISON, economics educator; t. Worth, July 4, 1925; married; 2 children. BBA, ex., 1949, MA, 1955; MA, Harvard U., 1958, PhD cons., 1963. Asst. prof. econs., Mass., 1959-60, ., 1960-65; assoc. prof. econs. U. Tex., Austin, 5-95, Sue Killam prof. in founds. of econs.; mem. com. Hwy. Research Bd., Nat. Acad. Sci.-Nat. arch Council, 1967. Served with USMC, 1943-45, 2, to maj. with res. Mem. Am. Econ. Assn., Am. s. Assn. Home: Austin Tex. Died May 1, 1995.

JNFELD, ERNST, metals company execu- Chmn. Metallurg Inc., N.Y.C. Home: New York Died 1994.

ARDINO, HARRY, actor; b. Bklyn., Dec. 23, . Ed., Haaren High Sch. Movie debut, 1951; ac- (films) including Pork Chop Hill, 1959, Hell is for es, 1962, Madigan, 1968, Lovers and Other ngers, 1969, Red Sky at Morning, 1971, Dirty y, 1971, Capone, 1975, St. Ives, 1976, The En- r, 1976, Roller Coaster, 1977, Matilda, 1978, Any ch Way You Can, 1980, (TV movies) including Only Kill Their Masters, 1972, Indict and Convict, , Street Killing, 1976, Contract on Cherry Street, , Evening in Byzantium, The Sophisticated Gents, , On Our Way, 1985, The Neon Empire, 1989, adway play) Woman of the Year, 1980-81, others; appearances include The Reporter, 1964, The Dick ell Show, Dr. Kildare, The Untouchables, Naked Partners in Crime, 1973, The New Adventures of y Mason, 1973-74, Get Christie Love, 1974, Police y, Studio One, Playhouse 90, The Alcoa Theatre. 1. Acad. Motion Picture Arts and Scis. Home: rly Hills Calif. Died July 17, 1995.

BBINS, KEITH EDMUND, chemical engineering ator; b. Southampton, Eng., Jan. 27, 1937; came to , 1962; m. Pauline Margaret Payne, June 28, 1960; lren: Nick, Vanessa. B.Sc. in Chemistry, Queen y Coll., U. London, 1958; Diploma in Chem. Engr- King's Coll., U. London, 1959, Ph.D. in Chem. ing., 1962. Vis. lectr. U. London, Eng., 1960-62; doctoral fellow U. Fla., Gainesville, 1962-64, asst. , 1964-68, assoc. prof., 1968-72, prof., 1972-76; Briggs prof. engring. Cornell U., Ithaca, N.Y., —, dir. Sch. Engring., 1983-90; vis. cons. theoret- physics divsn., U.K. Atomic Energy Authority, vell, U.K., 1971; vis. prof. physics dept. U. Guelph, -73, 76, U. Kent, Canterbury, Eng., 1975; vis. prof. nistry U. Oxford, 1979-80, 86-87; vis. prof. chem. ing., U. Calif., Berkeley, 1982; vis. prof. Imperial , London, 1978, McCabe lectr. N.C. State U., 1986, say lectr. Tex. A&M, 1989, Dodge lectr. Yale U., , Katz lectr. U. Mich., 1991, Wohl lectr. U. Del., , Merck lectr. Rutgers U., 1992, Olaf Hougen vis. chem. engring., U. Wis., 1993; Miles lectr. U. ., 1995, Merck lectr. U. P.R., 1995; vis. fellow Ful- t Sr. scholar Australian Nat. U., 1993-94; cons. il Oil, 1979, 80, Exxon Engring., 1980-81, Union ide Corp., 1981, Process Simulation Internat., 1982, Nat. Bur. Stds., 1983, BP Rsch., U.K., 1985, 89, Exxon Rsch. and Engring. Co., Clinton, N.J., 1985—, Unilever Rsch., Port Sunlight, U.K., 1985, Linde divsn. Union Carbide Corp., 198, Mobil Rsch., Princeton, 1991, Exxon Chem. Co., 1991, BHP, Melbourne, Australia, 1993, Johnson Matthey, 1994; mem. NAS com. to study formation of Nat. Resource Ctr. for Computing in Chemistry, 1976-77, NRC Assessment Bd. to rev. NIST programs, 1988-91. Mem. editl. bd. Molecular Physics, 1978-87, 95—, Jour. of Chem. Physics, 1995—, Molecular Simulation, 1986—, assoc. editor, 1990—; assoc. editor Am. Int. Chem. Engrs. Jour., 1988-91; editor: Topics in Chem. Engring., Oxford U. Press, 1991—. Recipient best paper ann. award Can. Soc. Chem. Engring., 1973; nemed Eppley Found. fellow Imperial Coll. London, 1970-71, Guggenheim fellow, 1986-87, sr. vis. fellow (SERC award) U. Oxford, 1986-87, vis. fellow (SERC award) Imperial Coll., London, 1994. Mem. NAE, AAAS, Am. Chem. Soc., Am. Inst. Chem. Engrs. (program com. 1974-81, Alpha Chi Sigma award 1986), Am. Inst. Physics, Chem. Soc. (London). Home: Ithaca N.Y.

GUERRI, SERGIO CARDINAL, Vatican City official; b. Tarquinia, Italy, Dec. 25, 1905. Ordained priest Roman Cath. Ch., Mar. 30, 1929; titular archbishop of Trevi, from 1969; elevated to Sacred Coll. Cardinals, 1969; pro-pres. Congregation Pontifical Comm. for State of Vatican City; mem. Congregation Oriental Chs., Congregation Evangelization of Peoples.

GUERRY, ALEXANDER, drug and chemical company executive; b. Chattanooga, Tenn., 1918. B.A. in English, U. South, 1939; M.A. in Bus. and Econs., U. N.C., 1941. With Chattem Drug & Chem. Co., Chattanooga, from 1945, asst. sec., 1946-48, sec., 1948-58, exec. v.p., 1958, pres., from 1958, also dir.; pres., dir. Sports Barn Fitness Ctrs., Chattanooga; dir. Am. Nat. Bank and Trust Co., Chattanooga, Third Nat. Corp. Nashville. Active United Fund of Greater Chattanooga, Community Chest Campaign, ARC Disaster Com.; vestryman St. Paul's Episcopal Ch., Ch. of the Good Shepherd, Lookout Mountain, Tenn.; pres. Episcopal Churchman of Tenn., 1952-53; mem. bishop's council of Diocese of Tenn., 1953-55. Served with U.S. Army, 1941-45. Decorated Silver Star, Legion of Merit, D.F.C. with 4 clusters, Air medal with 2 clusters; recipient numerous tennis, racquetball and handball awards; inducted into Tenn. Sports Hall of Fame, 1982, So. Tennis Hall of Fame, 1984. Mem. U.S. Lawn Tennis Assn. (v.p. so. region), Proprietary Assn. Am., Phi Beta Kappa. Clubs: Chattanooga Tennis. Lodge: Rotary. Home: Chattanooga Tenn. Deceased.

GUJU, JOHN G., physician, educator; b. Youngstown, Ohio, June 13, 1924; s. George and Frances (Ratz) G.; m. Margaret Ann Poole, May 11, 1952; children: John Howard, Paula Jean, Nancy Elissa. BA, Youngstown State U., 1944; MD, Med. Coll. of Wis., 1947. Diplomate Am. Bd. Ob-gyn. Rotating intern Youngstown Hosp., 1947-48, asst. resident in surgery, 1948-49, chief of ob-gyn, 1972-79; resident in ob-gyn Cleve. Met. Gen., 1949-50, U. Hosps., 1950-52; practice medicine specializing in ob-gyn Youngstown, 1955-93; med. dir. Planned Parenthood Fedn., Youngstown, 1960-72; clin. prof. ob-gyn Northeastern Ohio Univs. Coll. Medicine, 1975-93. Mem. youth com. YMCA, 1965-75; bd. dirs. Ohio div. Am. Assn. for Maternal and Child Health, Mahoning County unit Am. Cancer Soc. Capt. USAF, 1953-55. Recipient Alan F. Gutmacher award for service and dedication to Planned Parenthood of Mahoning Valley, 1976. Fellow ACS, Am. Coll. Obstetricians and Gynecologists; mem. AMA, Am. Soc. Abdominal Surgeons, Am. Fertility Soc., Youngstown Soc. Obstetricians and Gynecologists (pres. 1977), Mahoning County Med. Soc. (council 1979-93), Am. Assn. Reproductive Health Profls., Cleve Soc. Obstetricians and Gynecologists, Med.-Dental Bur. Youngstown (pres. 1989-90). Club: Youngstown Country. Lodge: Rotary Internat. Home: Youngstown Ohio Died Jan. 31, 1993; interred Lake Park Cemetary, Youngstown, O.H.

GUNDRUM, JAMES RICHARD, retired minister; b. Muscatine, Iowa, Nov. 30, 1929; s. Otto and Margaret Isabel (Black) G.; m. Frances Ellen Lathrop, June 14, 1954; children—Cameron Michael, David William, Carolyn Anne. B.A., Iowa Wesleyan U., 1951; M.Div., Seabury Western Theol. Sem., Evanston, Ill., 1954, D.D., 1976. Ordained priest Episcopal Ch., 1954; vicar chs. in Western Iowa, 1954-58; rector St. Michael's Ch., Cedar Rapids, Iowa, 1958-69; mission cons. Episcopal Diocese Iowa, 1969-75, canon, 1976—; sec.-treas. Episcopal Gen. Conv., 1975-76; sec. Gen. Conv., Episcopal Ch., 1976-86, sec. exec. council, 1977-86; sec. Domestic and Fgn. Missionary Soc., 1976-86; exec. Office Episcopal Ch. Gen. Conv., 1976-86; dean Calvary Cathedral, Sioux Falls, S.D., 1986-89; ret., 1989; trustee Seabury Western Theol. Sem., 1975-82, Ch. Pension Fund and Affiliates, 1991—; chaplain Cedar Rapids Police Dept., 1961-69. Editor jour., canons gen. conv. Bd. dirs. chmn. personnel com. Cedar Rapids chpt. A.R.C., 1960-64; bd. dirs. Cedar Rapids Mental Health Assn., 1961-65; Mem. Iowa N.G., 1946-48. Recipient Disting. Service Cross St. Michael's Ch., 1968; named Hon. Cedar Rapidian, 1969. Mem. Soc. Advancement Mgmt. Democrat. Club: Rotary (past v.p., dir. Cedar Rapids). Home: Sioux Falls S.D. Died Apr. 22, 1994.

GUNN, MOSES, actor; b. St. Louis, Oct. 2, 1929; s. George and Mary (Briggs) (foster mother, Jewel C. Richie) G.; m. Gwen Landes, July 25, 1966; children: Kirsten Sarah, Justin Moses. A.B., Tenn. State U., 1959; MA, U. Kansas. Former tchr. speech and drama Grambling Coll. Theatrical appearances include The Blacks, 1962-63, In White America, 1963-64, 65, Hard Travelin', 1965, Baal, 1965, Junebug Graduates Tonight, 1965, Measure for Measure, 1966. Day of Absence, 1965, A Hand is on The Gate, 1966, Aaron in Titus Andronicus, 1957, Negro Ensemble Co, 1967-68, Wedding Band, 1967, Song of the Lusitanian Bogey, Summer of the 17th Doll, Daddy Goodness, Kongi's Harvest, Romeo & Juliet, 1968, Cities in Bezique, 1968, To Be Young, Gifted and Black, 1969 ; directed Contributions, 1970, Trial of A. Lincoln, 1971, Twelfth Night, 1971; Othello, Sty of the Blind Pig, 1971, The Poison Tree (Tony award nomination), 1973, 76, The First Breeze of Summer (Obie award), 1975, I Have a Dream, 1976, Our Lan', 1977, Americain Gothic, 1985, Fool for Love, 1985, Boseman and Lena, 1986, A Lesson from Aloes, 1986, Tapman, 1988, King John, 1988, Coriolanus, 1988, Viva Detroit, 1990, Blood Knot, 1991, My Children, My Africa; movie appearances Haunts of the Very Rich, 1972, TV spls. The First Breeze of Summer, 1976, The Women of Brewster Place, The Killing Floor, Perfect Harmony, 1991, Memphis, 1992; TV appearances include Kung Fu, Roots (Emmy nomination), 1977, also series: Good Times, The Cosby Show, Little House on the Prairie, Father Murphy, The Cowboys, Homicide (Emmy citation), 1993 films include Nothing But a Man, 1962, WUSA, 1970, The Great White Hope, 1970, Shaft, 1971, Shaft's Big Score, 1972, Eagle in a Cage, 1972, Hot Rock, 1972, Amazing Grace, 1974, The Iceman Cometh, 1973, Rollerball, 1975, Aaron Loves Angela, Remember My Name, Wild Rovers, 1971, The Ninth Configuration, 1980, Cornbread, Earl and Me, Amityville II, 1982, Firestarter, 1984, The Neverending Story, 1984. Heartbreak Ridge, 1986. Served with AUS, 1954-57. Recipient Obie award, 1967-68, Jersey Jour. for best actor, 1967-68, Image award NAACP, 1982, 86. Mem. Theta Alpha Phi. Home: Guilford Conn. Died Dec. 17, 1993; buried Nut Plains Cemetary, Guilford, C.T.

GUNTER, JOHN BROWN, JR., real estate executive; b. Johnstown, Pa., May 22, 1919; s. John Brown and Mary (Barr) G.; m. Dorothy Mulhollen, July 5, 1942; 1 child, Jerrol Louise. Student, Valley Forge Mil. Acad. Jr. Coll., 1937-39; BS, U. Md., 1941. Exec. dir. Johnstown Cmty. Chest, 1946-48; trainee, mgr. Sears, Roebuck & Co., 1948-52; adminstrv. asst. Penn Traffic Co., Johnstown, 1952-58, contr., 1958-62, asst. treas., 1962-65, sec., 1965-78, corp. v.p. and pres. dept. store divsn., 1976-78; exec. Penn Traffic Co., Johnstown, Pa., 1976-78; pres., dir. Winston Corp., real estate devel., Johnstown, 1979-84; v.p., dir. Johnstown Tribune Pub. Co., 1978-84; chmn., dir. Johnstown Savs. Bank, 1977-94; instr. mgmt. U. Pitts., Johnstown. Comml. panel Am. Arbitration Assn., 1985-94. Served to lt. col. AUS, 1941-46, ETO. Decorated Order Brit. Empire, Bronze Arrowhead. Mem. Nat. Retail Mchts. Assn. (past dir.), Pa. Retailers Assn. (past dir.), Nat. Assn. Realtors, Pa. Assn. Realtors, Mensa, Phi Delta Theta. Republican. Presbyterian. Lodge: Masons. Home: Johnstown Pa. Died Oct. 19, 1995.

GÜNTHER, MARIAN W(ACLAW) J(AN), theoretical physicist; b. Warsaw, Poland, Nov. 27, 1923; came to U.S., 1960; s. Waclaw Henryk and Janina Leona (Wilke) G.; m. Marion Jeanette Koch, Mar. 22, 1976. MS, Jagiellonian U., Cracow, Poland, 1946; PhD, U. Warsaw, 1948, Veniam Legendi, 1951. Postdoctoral fellow U. Leiden, Holland, 1948-50, U. Birmingham, Eng., 1950; asst. prof. U. Warsaw, 1950-53, assoc. prof., 1956-60; assoc. prof. U. Wroclaw, Poland, 1953-56; vis. mem. Inst. for Advanced Study, Princeton, N.J., 1960-61; mem. sci. staff Boeing Sci. Rsch. Labs., Seattle, 1961-64; assoc. prof. of physics U. Cin., 1964-66, prof., 1966-74, prof. emeritus, 1984-94. Contbr. articles to Phys. Rev., Jour. Math. Physics. Recipient cert. of achievement Am. Men and Women of Sci., 1987. Mem. AAAS, N.Y. Acad. Scis. Roman Catholic. Home: Westerville Ohio Died May 22, 1994.

GUPTA, SATISH KUMAR, federal agency executive; b. Karnal, Haryana, India, Sept. 10, 1942; came to U.S., 1970, naturalized, 1978; s. Sham Lal and Vidya (Vidya) G.; m. Purnima Aggarwal, July 11, 1970; children: Arpita, Atul. BA in Applied Math., Panjab U., India, 1968; BS in Mech. Engring. Punjabi U., India, 1968; MS in Indsl. and Mgmt. Engring., CUNY, 1973; MBA, Monmouth Coll., 1978. Registered profl. engr., N.Y., N.J. Project engr. Jabco Industries Ltd., New Delhi; mech. engr., shift supr. Decora Mills, New Delhi, 1969-70; mechanical engr. Bell Telephones, N.Y.C., 1971-73; plant/project engr. Nabisco, Inc., Rio Grande, N.J., 1973-80; program mgr., assembly engr. Tex. Instruments, Inc., Lubbock, Tex., 1980-81; mgr. indsl. engring. Motorola Microsystems, Tempe, Ariz., 1981-87; mgr. engring. small disk div. Control Data Corp., Oklahoma City, 1987-88; dir. engring. and prodn. control div. Office of Nat. Distbn. Mgmt., Gen. Svcs. Adminstrn., Atlanta, 1988-92. Merit scholar Central Govt. of India, 1964. Mem. Am. Soc. Mech. Engrs., India Assn. Phoenix (treas. 1984-86, v.p. 1986-87). Deceased. Home: Clifton Va.

GURNEY, JAMES THOMAS, lawyer; b. Ripley, Miss., Jan. 24, 1901; s. James Andrew and Mary Jane (Shepherd) G.; m. Blanche Johnson, Mar. 5, 1925 (dec.); 1 son, J. Thomas; m. Lannie W. Jones, Jan. 8, 1985. A.B., Miss. Coll., 1919, LL.D., 1972; student, U. Chgo., 1919-20, Columbia U., 1919; LL.B., Cumberland U., Lebanon, Tenn., 1922, J.D., 1968; LL.D., Stetson U., 1970; D.H.L., U. Fla., 1978. Bar: Fla. 1922. Mem. faculty Miss. Woman's Coll., Hattiesburg, 1919-21; and since practiced in Orlando; original counsel Minute Maid Corp. (div. Coca- Cola Co.); gen. counsel Orlando Utilities Commn., 1925-85; dir. emeritus Beneficial Corp.; mem. Fla. Supreme Court com. for redrafting common law rules of procedure, 1945; mem. examining bd. Fla. Parole Commn., 1945; chmn. bd. control Fla. Insts. of Higher Learning, 1945-49, bd. regents. Author: Life Insurance Law of Florida, 1934, Disability Claims Resort to Equity, 1940, World War II Construction of War clauses, 1946; contbr. articles to Fla. Bar Jour. Trustee New Orleans Bapt. Theol. Sem., 1960-67; former bd. dirs. Children's Home Soc. of Fla.; mem. Fla. Council of 100; sponsor for establishment J. Thomas Gurney Elem. Sch. of 1st Bapt. Ch. of Orlando, Fla. Recipient Cert. of Merit U. Fla., 1953; Disting. Svc. award Stetson U., 1958; Disting. Svc. citation New Orleans Bapt. Theol. Sem. and So. Bapt. Found., 1967; award Pres. Ind. Colls. Fla., 1970; Cert. of Appreciation Miss. Coll., 1984. Fellow Am. Bar Found., Am. Coll. Trial Lawyers; mem. ABA (com. on life ins. law, vice chmn. 1944-47, admissions 1944-48, ssn. and adv. spl. com. on pub. relations 1944-46, adminstrv. law 1945, chmn. Fla. membership com. on ins. sect. 1946-48), Fla. State Bar Assn. (pres. 1942-43), Orange County Bar Assn., Am. Life Conv. (legal sect.), Assn. of Life Ins. Counsel (exec. com. 1946-48), Orange County Budget Commn. (chmn. 1935-42), Orlando Community Chest (gen. chmn.), Orlando C. of C. (pres. 1930, nat. council 1940-41, J. Thomas Gurney, Sr. ann. leadership award 1984), Fla. Blue Key (hon.), Newcomen Soc., Alumni Assn. U. Fla. (hon.), Lions Club (dist. gov. 35th dist. Orlando, 1928, University Club (Orlando), Orlando Country Club, Rotary (Orlando) (Paul Harris fellow). Democrat. Baptist. Clubs: Lions (Orlando) (dist. gov. 35th dist. 1928), University (Orlando), Orlando Country (Orlando), Rotary (Paul Harris fellow) (Orlando). Home: Orlando Fla. Died Aug. 31, 1992.

GUTERMUTH, CLINTON RAYMOND, conservationist, naturalist; b. Fort Wayne, Ind., Aug. 16, 1900; s. Henry Christian and Alice Virtue (Zion) G.; m. Ila Bessie Horm, Mar. 4, 1922 (dec. Dec. 3, 1975); m. Marian Schutt Happer, Mar. 21, 1977. Student, U. Notre Dame, 1918-19; grad., Am. Inst. Banking, 1927, postgrad., 1927-28; D.Sc. (hon.), U. Idaho, 1972. Asst. cashier St. Joseph Valley Bank, Elkhart, Ind., 1922-34; dir. div. edn. Ind. Dept. Conservation, Indpls., 1934-40; dir. div. fish and game Ind. Dept. Conservation, 1940-42; Ind. rent dir. OPA, Indpls., 1942-45; exec. sec. Am. Wildlife Inst., Washington, 1945-46; v.p. Wildlife Mgmt. Inst., 1946-71; Chmn. Natural Resources Council Am., 1959-61, hon. mem., 1971; pres., dir. Wildfowl Found. Inc., from 1956; nat. adv. council Pub. Land Law Rev. Commn., 1964-70; Trustee, sec. N.Am. Wildlife Found., Inc., 1945-74; trustee, pres. Stronghold (Sugarloaf Mountain) Inc., from 1947; bd. dirs., pres. World Wildlife Fund, U.S., 1961-73, hon. pres., from 1973; internat. trustee, exec. com. World Wildlife Fund (Internat.), 1971-75; bd. dirs., pres. Nat. Inst. for Urban Wildlife, 1976-85. Author: Official Lake Guide, 1938, Quips and Queries; page on natural history Outdoor Indiana, 1934-42; W.M.I. bi-weekly Outdoor New Bulletin, 1947-50; co-author: W.M.I. bi-weekly The Fisherman's Encyclopedia, 1950, The Standard Book of Fishing, 1950; numerous articles and lectures on various phases of natural resource conservation. Program chmn. ann. N.Am. Wildlife and Natural Resources Conf., 1946-71. Recipient Leopold medal Wildlife Soc., 1957; Fishing Hall of Fame Sportsman's Club Am., 1958; Distinguished Service award Nat. Assn. Soil Conservation Dists., 1958; Meritorious service award Nat. Watershed Congress, 1963; Nat. Service award Keep Am. Beautiful, 1965; Nat. Conservation award Mich. United Conservation Clubs, 1967; Distinguished Service award Nat. Wildlife Fedn., 1969, Jay N. Ding Darling medal, 1987; Horace M. Albright medal Am. Scenic and Historic Preservation Soc., 1970; Order of Golden Ark Prince Netherlands, 1972; elected Hunting Hall of Fame, 1975; recipient Gold medal Camp Fire Club Am., 1977. Fellow AAAS; hon. mem. Am. Com. for Internat. Wildlife Protection; mem. Nat. Rifle Assn. (life, dir. from 1963, pres. 1973-75, life mem. exec. council from 1975), African Safari (Conservation award 1977), Izaak Walton League Am. (life), Outdoor Writers Assn. Am., The Wildlife Soc. (hon., trustee from 1951), Nat. Audubon Soc. (Audubon medal 1982), Wilderness Soc. (life), Am. Fisheries Soc., Internat. Assn. Game Fish and Conservation Commrs. (hon.), Am. Forestry Assn. (hon.), Am. Soc. Range Mgmt., Am. Inst. Biol. Scis., Conservation Edn. Assn., Nat. Parks Assn., Nature Conservancy, The 1001-Nature Trust, World Wildlife Fund, Polar Inst. N.Am., Soil Conservation Soc. Am. (hon.), Arctic Inst. N.Am., Safari Club Internat., Zool. Soc. (N.Y.). Clubs: Masons (32, K.T.), Cosmos, Nat. Press, University (Washington); Explorers, Boone and Crockett (hon. life); Camp Fire (N.Y.C.); Booneville (Ind.) Press (hon.); Elkhart (Ind.) Conservation (hon.); Miami (Fla.) Sailfish; Tanana Valley (Alaska) Sportsmen's (hon.); Outdoor Boating Am. (hon.). Home: Elkhart Ind. Deceased.

GUTHEIL, JOHN GORDON, lawyer; b. N.Y.C., Sept. 10, 1944; s. Emil Arthur and Lilly (Heitlinger) G.; m. Irene Leslie Anderman; June 9, 1968; children: David, Robert. AB, Columbia U., 1965; JD, Harvard U., 1968. Bar: N.Y. 1969. Atty. Javits Trubin Sillcocks & Edelman, N.Y.C., 1969-71, Trubin Sillcocks Edelman & Knapp, N.Y.C., 1971-84; ptnr. Parker Chapin Flattau & Klimpl, N.Y.C., 1984-93; advisor First Am. Title Ins. Co. of N.Y., 1984-93. Mem. N.Y. State Bar Assn. Democrat. Jewish. Home: Ossining N.Y. Died May 12, 1993.

GUTHEIM, FREDERICK, writer, consultant; b. Cambridge, Mass., Mar. 3, 1908; s. August G. and Augusta (Meiser) G.; m. Mary Purdon, June 8, 1935; 1 son, Nicholas. AB, U. Wis., 1931; postgrad., U. Chgo., 1933-35; D Pub. Svc. (hon.), George Washington U., 1979; hon. doctorate, U. Md., 1989. Mem. staff Brookings Instn., 1931-33; with fed. housing and planning agys., 1935-47; asst. dir. French Mission for Reconstrn. and Urbanism, 1946-47; staff writer N.Y. Herald-Tribune, 1947-50; asst. exec. dir. AIA, 1950-53; pvt. practice as planning and hist. preservation cons., from 1953; chmn. internat. cons. Gutheim/Seelig/Erickson, 1971-81; staff dir. Joint Com. on Washington Met. Problems U.S. Congress, 1958-60; pres. Washington Center for Met. Studies, 1960-65, Sr. fellow, 1965-80; producer-dir. exhbns. Mus. Modern Art, 1939, USIA, 1953-58, Nat. Gallery Art, 1956; dir. archtl. rsch. projects U. Mich.; lectr. Cornell U., 1950; vis. prof Williams Coll., 1969; Disting. vis. prof. environ., studies Central Wash. U., 1970; adj. prof. Am. history and civilization, urban and regional planning George Washington U., from 1971, also research cons., dir. grad. program in historic preservation. Author: Houses for Family Living, 1948, (with Coleman Woodbury) Rethinking Urban Redevelopment, 1949, The Potomac, 1949, Housing as Environment, 1953, 100 Years of Architecture in America, 1957, Alvar Aalto, 1960, (with Wilcomb Washburn) The Federal City, Plans and Realities, 1976, Worthy of the Nation, 1977; editor: Frank Lloyd Wright On Architecture, 1941, In The Cause of Architecture, 1975; adv. editor for architecture and planning: Mag. of Art, 1935-40; asst. architecture editor: Federal Guide Series, 1936-37; corr. editor: Urbanistica, 1950-58, Progressive Architecture, 1954-59; Archtl. critic, Washington Post, 1960-62, producer film and TV programs A Fatal Beauty, 1980, Chesapeake Horizons, 1983, The Potomac: American Reflections, 1985. Commr. Upper Montgomery County (Md.) Planning Com., 1950-57; mem. Nat. Capital Regional Planning Council, 1952-57, Pres.'s Council on Pa. Ave, 1962-64, Pres.'s Task Force on Natural Beauty, 1964, U.S. Capitol Master Plan Group, 1976-82; chmn. Nat. Capital Transp. Agy. Bd., 1961-65; mem. Potomac Planning Task Force, Dept. Interior, 1965-67; chmn. Frederick Law Olmsted Sesquicentennial, 1972, Sugarloaf Regional Trails, Md., from 1974, UN Housing and Planning Mission to Zambia, 1965, Nat. Trust Honor Awards Jury, 1982; cons. on environ., habitat confs. UN, 1965-78; mem. Montgomery County Historic Preservation Commn., 1979-81; adviser Nat. Assn. Olmsted Parks, 1980-86. Served with AUS, 1943-45. Decorated Order of Lion Finland; recipient Finlandia Found. award, 1964, Tapiola Medallion, 1974, Calvert prize Md. Hist. Trust, 1976, honor award Nat. Trust Hist. Preservation, 1984, award of merit Am. Assn. State and Local History, 1983, hist. preservation award Mary Washington Coll., 1985, Environment award Md. chpt. Am. Soc. Landscape Architects, 1986, Trustee of Am. award, 1987, Montgomery prize, 1988, Disting. Achievement award Am. Planning Assn., 1988, 90, Hon. award Assn. Collegiate Schs. Architecture, 1990, Louise Du Pont Crowninshield award 1990; Guggenheim Found. fellow, 1965-66; named Hon. Member, Potomac River Basin Consortium, 1985. Fellow U.S. Internat. Council Monuments and Sites; mem. AIA (hon., Medallist 1978, hon. award with Capitol master plan group, 1986), Italian Town Planning Inst. (hon.), Am. Inst. Cert. Planners, Internat. Fedn. for Housing and Planning (mem. coun. from 1977). Club: Cosmos (Washington); 14 W. Hamilton St. (Balt.). Home: Bowie Md. Deceased.

GUTHRIE, GEORGE RALPH, real estate development executive; b. Phila., Mar. 12, 1928; s. George Ralph and Myrtle (Robertson) G.; m. Shirley B. Remmey; children: Mary Elizabeth, Brenda Ann. BS in Econs., U. Pa., 1948. With I-T-E Imperial Corp., Phila., 1948-70; treas. I-T-E Imperial Corp., 1968-69, v.p. fin., 1969-70; pres. N. K. Winston Corp., N.Y.C., 1970-76; exec. v.p. Urban Investment and Devel. Co., Chgo., 1976-78; pres. Urban Investment and Devel. Co., 1978-82, chmn., 1982-88; vice chmn. JMB Instl. Realty Corp., 1987-89; prin. Argyle Enterprises, Chgo., 1989-93; bd. dirs. Zenith Electronics Corp., Chgo. Dock and Canal Trust. Trustee Cornerstone Found.; mem. pres.'s coun. Luth. Social Svcs. Ill.; mem. president's coun., assoc. trustee U. Pa.; past chmn. Chgo. Devel. Coun. Mem. Fin. Execs. Inst., Urban Land Inst. (past trustee), Glen View Club, Jupiter Hills Club, Carlton Club (bd. govs.), Econ. Club, Chgo. Club, Lost Tree Club, Lambda Alpha Internat. Home: Wilmette Ill. Died July 17, 1993.

GUTIERREZ, RAUL, advertising agency executive; Mexico City, Mex., Feb. 18, 1913; s. Raul Gutierr Velasco and Ana (Escalante) de Gutierrez; m. Sylv Wanless, June 12, 1958; children: Fabian, Juanmarc Silvia. Student, Instituto Politecnico Nacional, Mex Film producer Clasa Films Mundiales, Mexico Ci 1945-50; mgr. ARS-UNA Publicistas, Mexico Ci 1945-50; gen. mgr. Publicidad Interamericana, Mexi City, 1951-57; founder, owner Panamericana de Pu licidad, Mexico City, from 1956; merged Ogilvy a Mather Internat., 1969; pres., chmn. bd. Panamerica Ogilvy & Mather, S.A., Mexico City, 1969-85; found Lineas Unidas del Norte; v.p. Instituto de Investig ciones Publicitarias, 1975, Consejo Nacional de la Pu licidad, 1969-72; organizer, lectr. profl. seminars, con in field. Author writings in field. Negotiator Mexic Senate. Served to lt. Mexican Army, 1942-45. Nam Unique Advertiser Life Mag., 1958; interviewed L Mag., 1958. Mem. Asociacion Nacional de la Pu licidad (pres. 1954-56 1st award, 2d award 198 Asociacion Mexicana de Agencias de Publicid (founder 1950, v.p., pres. 1969-72), Colegio de Pu licistas (founder). Club: Club de Golf Chapu Hep (pres.). Home: Naucalpan de Juarez Mexico Died No 1985.

GUTMAN, I. CYRUS, transportation consulta business executive; b. Perth Amboy, N.J., Mar. 1912; s. Leon and Jennie (Levine) G.; m. Mildred Largman, July 21, 1940; children: Harry L., Peg Sheren, Richard J.S. BS in Econs., Johns Hopkins 1932. Dist. mgr. Motor Freight Express, Inc., Phi 1933-40; v.p., treas., gen. mgr. Modern Transfer C Inc., Allentown, Pa., 1940-67, dir. nat. sales, 1967- v.p. Atlantic div. Nat. Resource Recovery Cor 1982—; mem. labor panel Am. Arbitration Ass 1980—; bd. dirs. Eastern Industries, Inc., Wescosvi Pa., 1967-76. Pres. Lehigh County Indsl. Devel. Cor 1959-85, Lehigh's Econ. Advancement Project, In 1960-85; chmn. Lehigh County Indsl. Devel. Authori 1966-82; mem. adv. com. Central Pa. Teamsters Pens and Health and Welfare Funds, 1969-76; mem. n resources com., nat. alumni schs. com. Johns Hopki mem. Lehigh-Northampton Counties Joint Planni Commn., 1962-82; chmn. Allentown Sch. D Authority, 1966-86; mem. Lehigh and Northampt Transp. Authority, 1972-74; chmn. Allentown N Partisan Com. for Local Govt.; mem. Eastern Co Joint Area Com.; assoc. mem. Nat. Jewish Welfare B hon. bd. mem. Allentown Jewish Community C 1986—; exec. com. Citizens for Lehigh County Progre 1965—; chmn. central campaign planning com. Leh Valley Hosps., 1966-67; adv. com. Good Sheph Workshop; adv. bd. Allentown citadel Salvation Arr treas., 1971-80; pres. bd. assocs. Muhlenberg Coll., v 1971-73, pres. 1974-76; bd. assocs. Cedar Crest C 1972—; gen. adv. com. Lehigh County Vocat.-Te Sch., Lehigh County Community Coll., 1977; me Lehigh County Rep. Exec. Com.; trustee Allento Hosp., 1970-82, hon. trustee, 1982-87, hon. mem., 19 hon. Lehigh Valley Hosp. Ctr., 1987—; trustee, Sw Sch., 1977-80; bd. dirs. Lehigh Valley Jr. Achieveme United Fund, Allentown, Jewish Fedn. Allento 1953-60, Wiley House, 1969-80; bd. dirs. Lehigh Va Public TV, Sta. WLVT, 1980—, vice chmn., 1984- chmn. 1989—; past trustee Rabbi Louis Youngerman Found., Internat. Assn. Machinists Lo 1099 Dist. Pension Plan, Phi Sigma Delta Found.; h adv. bd. Lehigh Valley Assn. for Retarded Childr 1969-70; mem. adv. bd. Lehigh Valley Ctr. Performing Arts, 1975-77. Recipient St. Patrick's L award Lehigh Valley, 1961, Civic Svc. commendat Whitehall C. of C.; Golden Deeds award Allento Exchange Club, 1972, Disting. Citizens Sales aw Sales and Mktg. Execs., Allentown and Bethleh 1976, Outstanding Svc. award Lehigh Valley Tra Club, 1978, citation Pa. Ho. of Reps., 1982, City Allentown, 1982, Americanism award Anti-Defamat League and B'nai Brith, 1985, citation Assn. for Bl and Visually Impaired, 1985, citation Lehigh Cou Vocat. Tech. Sch., 1986; Jack Houlihan Commun Vol. award Lehigh County United Way, 1985, Pre proclamation through Gov. Thornburgh, Pa., 19 Cyrus Gutman Scholarship established by Leh County Bus. and Indsl. Community Johns Hopkins 1983; I. Cyrus Gutman Day proclaimed in honor lentown, Bethlehem, Easton, Pa. Mem. Allentown C C. (Disting. Svc. award 1967, past bd. dirs.), Traffic Transp. Assn. Pitts., Met. Traffic Assn. N.Y., Cen. Motor Carriers Assn. (v.p., exec. com.), Pa. Soc., A Trucking Assn. (gov. Regular Common Carrier C 1968), Eastern Labor Adv. Assn. (v.p.), Am. Arbi tion Assn. (labor panel 1980—), Hon. First Defend Johns Hopkins Alumni Assn. (past sec., past pres. Pl area), Lehigh County Hist. Soc. (exec. com. 1968- Nat. Fedn. Temple Brotherhoods, Berkleigh Cour Club (hon. mem., past pres.), Lehigh Valley C Locust Midcity Club, Traffic and Transp. Club, Tr Club Phila., Traffic Club Balt., N.Y. Traffic Club, ingston Club, Masons, B'nai Brith, Omicron D Kappa, Pi Delta Epsilon, Zeta Beta Tau. Home: lentown Pa.

GUYOT, JEAN, former archbishop of Toulouse; Bordeaux, France, July 7, 1905. Ordained priest Ro Catholic Ch., 1932; various offices in Bordeaux Dio titular bishop of Helenopolis, also coadjutor Coutances, 1949; bishop of Coutances, 195

:hbishop of Toulouse, 1966-78; elevated to Sacred ›ll. Cardinals, 1973; mem. de la Congrègation de ›argé et des Séminqires. Decorated oficier Legion d onneur; grande Croix Ordre de Malte. Home: ulouse France

'VYNNE, FRED (FREDERICK HUBBARD 'VYNNE), actor; b. N.Y.C., July 10, 1926; m. Jean ›ynard; 4 children. Attended, Phoenix Sch. Design, Y.; B.A., Harvard U., 1951. Broadway debut in Mrs. :Thing, 1952, Love's Labour's Lost, 1953, The Frogs Spring, 1953, Irma la Douce, 1960, Here's Love, ›63, The Lincoln Mask, 1972; with Am. Shakespeare ›stival in Cat on a Hot Tin Roof 1974, Twelfth Night, ›74, Our Town, 1975, The Winter's Tale, 1975, A ›xas Trilogy, 1976, Angel, 1978, Grand Magic, 1979 ›bie award); appeared in films On the Waterfront, ›54, Munster Go Home, 1966, Luna, 1979, Simon, ›80, Jack-a-Boy, 1980, Cotton Club, 1984, Fatal At- ›ction, 1987, Ironweed, 1987, Shadows and Fog, 1992; ' series Car 54, Where Are You?, 1961-63, The Mun- ›rs, 1964-66, miniseries Kane and Abel, 1985; other ' appearances include Harvey, 1958, The Hasty Heart, ›58, The Old Foolishness, 1961, The Lesson, 1966, ›ancy, 1967, Arsenic and Old Lace, 1969, The Littlest ›gel, 1969, Paradise Lost, 1971, The Police, 1971, ›mes at Sea, 1971, Bound for Freedom, 1976; ›ywriter J. Walter Thompson, 1955-60; author: Best Show, 1958, What's a Nude?, God's First World, ›70, The King Who Rained, 1970, Ick's ABC, 1971, e Story of Ick, 1971, The Sixteen-Hand Horse, 1980. ›me: Los Angeles Calif. Died July 2, 1993.

›AKENSTAD, OTTO, lawyer, insurance company ›cutive; b. Havnik, Norway, Dec. 7, 1901; came to S., 1907, naturalized, 1934; s. Ole and Marie (Olson) ; m. Lillian Peterson, June 30, 1925; children—Dale Ardith L. (Mrs. Harlan Holly), Alan Otto. Student, ›D. Agrl. Coll. Bar: N.D. bar 1926, also Fed. Ct. bars ›26, U.S. Supreme Ct. bar 1926. Mem. firm Burnett, ›rgesen & Haakenstad, Fargo, 1926-1953; spl. atty. S. Dept. Justice, Fargo, 1935-44; co-founder Western ›tes Life Ins. Co., Fargo, 1930; sec. Western States ›e Ins. Co., 1930-44, pres., 1944-68, chmn., 1968-81, ›nn. emeritus, from 1981; dir. Fargo Nat. Bank, N.D., ›53-75. Vice pres. Am. Life Conv., 1948-57, mem. ›c. com., 1957-60, pres., 1960-61; Past mem. bd. ad- ›ssions and budget, past chmn. Fargo United Fund. ›m. Fargo C. of C. (past dir.), N.D. C. of C. (dir. ›55-69), Inst. Life Ins. (dir. 1965-69)), Am. N.D. bar ›ns. Lutheran (trustee). Clubs: Mason (grand master ›D. 1969-70), Lion (past dep. dist. gov.), mem. Red ›oss of Constantine, Fargo Country. Home: Fargo D. Deceased.

›AAS, WALTER A., JR., retired apparel company ›cutive, professional baseball executive; b. San ›ancisco, Jan. 24, 1916; s. Walter Abraham and Elise ›ern) H.; m. Evelyn Danzig, 1940; children: Robert ›, Elizabeth Haas Eisenhardt, Walter J. BA, U. Calif., ›rkeley, 1937; MBA, Harvard U., 1939; hon. degree, ›eaton Coll., 1983. Chief exec. officer Levi Strauss & ›., San Francisco, 1958-76, hon. chmn. exec. com. bd. ›s.; owner, mng. gen. ptnr. Oakland (Calif.) Athletics ›seball Co.; bd. dir. Bank of Am., Bank Am. Corp., ›AL, Inc., Mauna Kea Properties, Pacific Tel. Co.; ›stee The Bus. Enterprise Trust; former bd. dir. Bank Am. Bd. dirs. Nat. Park Found.; mem. adv. coun. ›ading is Fundamental, Inc.; mem. SRI Internat. Adv. ›un.; mem. Nat. Commn. on Pub. Svc; former mem. ›lateral Commn.; former mem. exec. com., former re- ›nal chmn. Nat. Alliance Businessman; former mem. ›esdl. Adv. Coun. for Minority Enterprise, Presdl. ›sk Force on Internat. Devel., 1970, Nat. Ctr. for ›luntary Action, Citizens Commn. on Pvt. Philan- ›opy and Pub. Needs; former mem. vis. com. Harvard ›s. Sch.; former mem. intercollegiate athletics adv. bd. Calif.; former dir. Hunters Point Boys' Club, San ›ancisco Boys' Club, Bay Area Urban League, Mt. ›n Hosp.; campaign chmn. United Bay Area Crusade, ›56, also bd. dirs.; former chmn. Radio Free Europe, ›. Calif.; commr. San Francisco Parking Authority, ›53; former trustee Ford Found., Com. for Econ. ›vel.; former co-chmn. bus. steering com. Nat. ›mbodia Crisis Com. Named a Leader of Tomorrow ›ne mag., 1953, Chief Exec. Officer of Yr. Fin. World ›g., 1976, Alumnus of Yr., U. Calif. at Berkeley, 1984; ›ipient Jefferson award Am. Inst. Pub. Service, 1977, ›umni Achievement award Harvard Grad. Sch. Bus., ›79, Chancellor's award U. Calif. at Berkeley Found., ›82, The Alexis De Tocqueville Society award United ›ay Am., 1985. Mem. Mfrs. and Wholesalers Assn. ›n Francisco, (pres. 1951), Nat. Urban League (former ›.), Phi Beta Kappa, Alpha Delta Phi. Home: San ›ancisco Calif. Died Sept. 20, 1995.

›AASEN, PETER, physics educator; b. Gotha, ›rmany, July 21, 1927; s. Herbert and Ingeborg ›mwer) H.; m. Barbara Kulp, Sept. 12, 1958; children: ›ristine, Elisabeth, Dorothee. PhD, U. Göttingen, ›d. Republic Germany, 1953. Rsch. assoc. U. Chgo., ›54-56; sci. assoc. Max Planck Inst., Stuttgart, Fed. ›public Germany, 1956-58; prof. metal physics U. ›ttingen, from 1959; pres. Acad. Scis. Gottingen, ›80-84. Author: Physical Metallurgy, 1974 (trans. ›eral langs.). Recipient Heyn medal, DGM, 1976, ›F. Mehl medal AIME, 1985, Le Chatelier prize Govt. France, 1987, Humboldt prize Govt of France, 1989. Mem. APS, AIME, Acad. Leopoldina, Nat. Acad. Engring., Academia Europ., Deutsche Gesellschaft Materialk, Deutsche Phys. Gesellschaft. Home: Göttingen Federal Republic of Germany Deceased.

HAASS, ERWIN HERMAN, lawyer; b. Detroit, Feb. 18, 1904; s. Otto C. and Minnie (Peters) H.; m. Virginia Allmand, Oct. 5, 1937; children: Frederick, Robert, Stephen, Susan, Sandra. A.B., U. Mich., 1925, J.D., 1927. Bar: Mich. 1927. Assoc. Race, Haass & Allen, Detroit, 1927-30; partner Hitt, Brewer & Haass, Detroit, 1930-41, Haass, Lungershausen, Frohlich & Lawrence, and predecessors, Detroit, 1941-77; consulting ptnr. Dickinson, Wright, Moon, VanDusen and Freeman, Detroit, 1977-94. Lt. col. AUS, 1942-46. Mem. ABA, State Bar Mich., Detroit Bar Assn., Am. Judicature Soc., Soc. Am. Mil. Engrs. Clubs: Country, Detroit, Detroit Athletic (Detroit), Grosse Pointe (Detroit), Royal Palm Yacht and Country (Boca Raton, Fla.). Home: Pompano Beach Fla. Died June 10, 1994.

HABER, JOYCE, writer, columnist; b. N.Y.C., Dec. 28, 1932; d. John Sanford and Lucille (Buckmaster) H.; m. Douglas S. Cramer, Jr., 1966 (div. 1974); children: Douglas S. III, Courtney Sanford. Student, Bryn Mawr Coll., 1949-50; A.B., Barnard Coll., 1953. Researcher, Time Mag., 1953-63, Los Angeles corr., 1963-66; columnist Los Angeles Times and Los Angeles Times Syndicate, 1966-75; contbg. editor Los Angeles mag., 1977-79; freelance writer. Author: Caroline's Doll Book, 1962, The Users, 1976; contbr.: articles to numerous popular mags. including New West Mag. Home: Beverly Hills Calif. Deceased.

HABERMANN, ARIE NICOLAAS, computer science educator, researcher; b. Groningen, The Netherlands, June 26, 1932; came to U.S., 1968; s. Johan Friedrich and Johanna (Verveen) H.; m. Martha Blom, Oct. 31, 1956; children: Eveline Kilian, Irene, Johan Frederik, Marianne. B.S. in Math. and Physics, Free U., Amsterdam, Netherlands, 1953; M.S. in Math., Free U., 1958; Ph.D. in Applied Math., Tech. U., Eindhoven, Netherlands, 1967. Tchr. math and physics Christelyk Lyceum, Netherlands, 1954-62; lectr. applied math. and programming, also calculus and algebra Tech. U., Eindhoven, 1962-68; vis. research scientist Carnegie-Mellon U., Pitts., 1968-69; assoc. prof. computer sci. Carnegie-Mellon U., 1969-73, prof., 1974-93, head dept. computer sci., 1979-91; dean sch. computer sci., 1988-91; acting dir. SEI Carnegie-Mellon U., 1984-85; asst. dir. NSF, Washington, 1991-93; cons. Siemens Corp., Munich, Fed. Republic Germany, 1980-93, vis. scientist, 1983, cons. N.Am. Philips, 1985-93; mem. sci. adv. com. IBM, 1984-93; mem. adv. bd. for computer sci. NSF, 1983-93; vis. prof. U. Newcastle, Eng., 1973, Tech. U. Berlin, Germany, 1976. Author: Introduction to Operating Systems Design, 1976; (with Troelstra) Transformation Mathematics, 1962; (with Perry) Ada for Experienced Programmers, 1983. Mem. Assn. Computing Machinery, N.Y. Acad. Scis. Home: Pittsburgh Pa. Died Aug. 8, 1993.

HABICHT, JAMES ROBERT, lawyer; b. Worthington, Minn., Oct. 31, 1946; s. Graydon Joshua and Dorothy Carolyn (Klas) H.; m. Valerie Ann Calvin, Aug. 24, 1968; children: Jane, Jennifer, Jeff. AA, Worthington Community Coll., 1966; BA, U. Minn., Morris, 1968; JD, U. Minn., Mpls., 1974. Bar: Minn. 1974, U.S. Ct. Appeals (11th cir.) 1974. Atty. Minn. Power and Light Co., Duluth, 1974-78, sr. atty., 1978-83, gen. counsel, sec., 1983-84, v.p., gen. counsel and sec., from 1984; active legal com. Edison Electric Inst., from 1983. Bd. dirs. St. Mary's Med. Ctr., Deluth, from 1986. Served to sgt. U.S. Army, 1969-71. Methodist. Club: Kitchi Gammi. Home: Duluth Minn. Deceased.

HABYARIMANA, JUVÉNAL, president of Rwanda; b. Rambura, Gisenyi, Rwanda, Mar. 8, 1937; s. Jean-Baptiste Ntibazilikana and Suzanne Nyirazuba; m. Agathe Kanziga, Aug. 17, 1963; 8 children. Student, Coll. St. Paul, Bukavu, Zaire, Lovanium U., Kinshana, Officers Sch., Kigali. Joined Nat. Guard, advanced through grades to comdr.; chief of staff, 1963-65; minister for Nat. Guard, chief staff police, 1965-73; maj. gen., 1973; leader coup to depose Pres. Kayibanda, July 1973; pres. of Rwanda, 1973—; minister nat. def., 1973-91; chmn. OCAM Conf. Heads of State and Govt., 1975. Pres., Com. pour la Paix et l'Unité Nat., 1973-75; leader Mouvement Revolutionnaire nat. pour la Devel., 1975—. Decorated Grand Master, Nat. Order of Rwanda, Grand Cross of Leopold II, Grand Cross of The Order of Leopold, Medal of the Order of the Source of the Nile, Grand Cross of the Nat. Order of Mauritania, Grand Ribbon of the Nat. Order of the Republic of Burundi, Golden Heart (Kenya), 1981; others. Home: Kigali Rwanda

HACKES, PETER SIDNEY, media consultant, freelance television, radio and film performer; b. N.Y.C., June 2, 1924; s. John R. and Ruth (Misch) H.; children: Pamela T. Hackes Thurston, Carole A. Hackes Duckett, Peter Quinn; m. Jessie Malkoff, 1982; 1 stepchild, Jennifer A. Halpern. B.A., Grinnell (Iowa) Coll., 1948, L.H.D. (hon.), 1967; M.A., U. Iowa, 1949; Litt.D. (hon.), Newberry Coll., S.C., 1967. With radio stas. in N.Y., Iowa, Ohio and Ky., 1947-52; Washington corr. CBS, 1952-55; Washington corr. NBC, 1955-86, Dept. Def. corr., 1956-67; anchorman NBC World News Roundup, 1957-61; assignments included White House (Eisenhower through Reagan), House and Senate, 14 Nat. Presdl. nominating convs., every U.S. manned space flight from monkey experiments into shuttle series, Cuban missile crisis, Nixon resignation and Watergate coverup trial, Three Mile Island nuclear accident. World bd. govs. USO; bd. dirs. Wolf Trap Farm Park, Performing Arts, 1975-78; mem. trustees council Met. Washington YMCAs; commr. Nat. Commn. Fire Prevention and Control, 1971-73; bd. visitors Def. Info. Sch., Ft. Benjamin Harrison, Ind. Capt. USNR (ret.). Co-recipient Emmy award for Apollo space flight TV coverage, 1969-70, Peabody award for Second Sunday Series, 1972; recipient NATAS Silver Circle award, 1992. Mem. AFTRA (nat. bd.), SAG, Armed Forces Broadcasters Assn. (bd. dirs.), Radio-TV News Dirs. Assn., Nat. Space Club (founding mem.), Broadcast Pioneers, Washington Quarter Century Broadcasters, Soc. for Preservation and Encouragement of Barbershop Quartet Singing in Am. Home: Washington D.C. Died Apr. 17, 1994.

HACKETT, JOHN FRANCIS, bishop; b. New Haven, Dec. 7, 1911; s. Thomas J. and Anna (Whalen) H. Student, St. Thomas Sem., Bloomfield, Conn., 1929-31, Seminaire St. Sulpice, Issy and Paris, France, 1931-36; LL.D., Fairfield University, 1953, Providence College, 1960. Ordained priest Roman Cath. Ch., 1936; asst. pastor St. Aloysius Ch., New Canaan, Conn., 1936-45; sec. Bishop of Hartford, 1945-52; asst. chancellor Diocese of Hartford, 1945-51, vice chancellor, 1951-52, chancellor, 1953-59, vicar-gen., 1954-90; consecrated titular bishop of Helenopolis in Palaestina; aux. bishop of, Hartford, 1952-86. Home: West Hartford Conn. Died May 30, 1990.

HADLEY, GARLAND RAY, dean, economist; b. Burneyville, Okla., Feb. 14, 1936; s. Raymond Monroe and Jewell Edna (Freeman) H.; m. Ruth Elenore Jicensky, Sept. 3, 1956 (div. 1976); children: Pamela, Valerie, Victoria, David, Elizabeth; m. Kay Lynn Haney, July 15, 1986. BS in Engring., U. Okla., 1961; PhD in Econs., U. Mo., 1975. Exec. v.p. St. Louis Rsch. Coun., 1967-69, Kerr Found., Inc., Oklahoma City, 1970-79; pres. Hadley Enterprises, Inc., Denton, Tex., 1979-83; dean Bus. Sch. Midwestern State U., Wichita Falls, Tex., from 1983. Bd. dirs. Bd. Commerce, Small Bus. Coun., Wichita Falls, from 1986. Mem. Assn. Collegiate Schs. of Bus. (commr. from 1989), Tex. Coun. Bus. Edn. (v.p. from 1984), Am. Econs. Assn., Rotary (bd. dirs. Wichita Falls chpt. from 1988), West Tex. C. of C. (bd. dirs. 1986-88), Phi Delta Kappa, Phi Chi Theta, Omicron Delta Epsilon, Sigma Tau. Presbyterian. Home: Wichita Falls Tex. Deceased.

HADLEY, HENRY LEE, urologist; b. Washington, Aug. 21, 1922; s. Henry Gilbert and Anna Virginia (Hafemayr) H.; m. Bonnie Rae Barnes, Mar. 8, 1945; children: Dean, Jeralyn, Roger, Merrilee. BS, Columbia Union Coll., Takoma Park, Md., 1942; MD, Loma Linda U., 1946. Resident urology Urology Clinic White Meml. Ctr., L.A., 1948-51; chief urology White Meml. Ctr., 1951-70; practice medicine, specialising in urology Loma Linda, Calif., 1951-94; sr. attending physician L.A. Gen. Hosp., 1960-70; chmn., prof. dept. urology Loma Linda Sch. Medicine, 1970-94; chief urology VA Hosp., Loma Linda, 1978-85, San Bernardino County Hosp., 1980-94, Riverside County Hosp., 1988-94. Author: Textbook of Urology, 1960; contbr. articles to profl. jours. Capt. U.S. Army, 1946-48. Mem. Soc. U. Urologists, Am. Urol. Assn., ACS, Internat. Soc. Urology, Loma Linda U. Alumni Assn. (pres. 1980). Home: Redlands Calif. Deceased.

HADLOW, EARL BRYCE, lawyer; b. Jacksonville, Fla., July 29, 1924; s. Earl and Emily (Hadlow) Bryce; m. Nancy Ann Petway, Apr. 5, 1969; children: Richard B., Janet V., Bryce P., Erin. BS, Duke U., 1947, JD, 1950, JD with high honors, 1950. Bar: Fla. 1950. Asst. solicitor Duval County, Jacksonville, 1952-53; ptnr. Mahoney, Hadlow & Adams, Jacksonville, 1953-84; gen. counsel, vice chmn. Barnett Banks Inc., Jacksonville, 1984-90, also bd. dirs., 1984-90; gen. counsel, vice chmn. Home Builders Inc. Svcs., Inc., Jacksonville, 1990-92; bd. dirs. Barnett Bank Trust Co. Contbr. articles to profl. jours. Trustee Jacksonville U. Served with U.S. Army, 1943-46. Fellow Am. Coll. Trust and Estate Counsel; mem. ABA (ho. of dels., mem. com. on scope correlation), Fla. Bar (bd. govs. 1967-72, pres. 1973-74), Jacksonville Bar Assn. (pres. 1966), Am. Bankers Assn. (govt. rels. coun., banking leadership conf.), Assn. Res. City Bankers (govs. rels. coun.), Fla. Bankers Assn. (pres. 1989), Fla. Assn. Bank Holding Cos., Jacksonville C. of C. (pres. 1980), Order of Coif, Phi Delta Phi, Alpha Tau Omega. Republican. Episcopalian. Home: Jacksonville Fla. Died 1992.

HAGELMAN, CHARLES WILLIAM, JR., language professional, educator; b. Houston, Nov. 9, 1920; s. Charles William and Anna Marie (Griffin) H.; m. Elizabeth Drisler Sloan, Sept. 7, 1946; children: Lucy Ann, Charles William III, John Francis. B.A., U. Tex., 1942, Ph.D. (fellow 1952-53), 1956; M.A., Columbia U., 1947; postgrad., Washington U., St. Louis, 1942, Va. Mil. Inst., 1943-44. Part-time instr. English Columbia, 1946-47; instr. Muhlenberg Coll., 1947-51, U. Tex., 1953-55; successively instr., asst. prof., assoc. prof. U. Houston, 1955-59; prof. English, head dept. Lamar State

Coll., Beaumont, Tex., 1959-66; prof. English, assoc. dean humanities Coll. Arts and Scis. U. Toledo, 1966-68; prof. English No. Ill. U., Dekalb, 1968-86; chmn. dept. No. Ill. U., 1968-74, prof. emeritus, 1986—; rsch. affiliate in English Tex. A&M U., 1990—; tech. writing cons., 1956-66; editorial cons. Survival Planning Project Houston-Harris County Area, 1956-57, Business Rev. mag., 1957-59; cons. North Ctrl. Assn. Colls. and Secondary Schs., 1970-80; Lamar State Coll. rep. to So. Humanities Conf., 1961-66. Editor, author: introduction A Vindication of the Rights of Woman, 1966, (with Robert J. Barnes) A Concordance to Byron's Don Juan, 1967; contbr. articles to profl. jours. Served with AUS, 1942-46. Recipient U.S. Steel Co. award for outstanding achievement teaching U. Houston, 1958. Mem. MLA, Midwest Lang. Assn. (exec. com. 1972-74, v.p. 1977-78, pres. 1978-79), South Central Lang. Assn., Keats-Shelley Assn., Byron Soc., Conf. Coll. Tchrs. English (past pres.), Phi Kappa Phi, Sigma Tau Delta. Episcopalian. Home: The Woodlands Tex. Died Dec. 31, 1995.

HAGEMAN, HOWARD GARBERICH, clergyman, former seminary president; b. Lynn, Mass., Apr. 19, 1921; s. Howard G. and Cora E. (Derfler) H.; m. Carol Christine Wenneis, Sept. 15, 1945. Grad., Albany Acad., 1938; A.B., Harvard, 1942; B.D., New Brunswick Sem., 1945; D.D. (hon.), Central Coll., 1957, Knox Coll., Toronto, 1977; Litt.D. (hon.), Hope Coll., 1975; L.H.D., Ursinus Coll., 1975. Ordained to ministry Ref. Ch., 1945. Minister North Ref. Dutch Ch., Newark, 1945-73; pres. New Brunswick Sem., N.J., 1973-85; exchange lectr., South Africa, 1956; lectr. Princeton Sem., Drew U. Author: Lily Among the Thorns, 1952, We Call This Friday Good, 1961, Pulpit and Table, 1962, The Book that Reads You, 1962, Predestination, 1963, That the World May Know, 1965, Advice to Mature Christians, 1965, Easter Proclamation, 1974, Celebrating the Word, 1977, Two Centuries Plus, 1984, Reformed Spirituality, 1986, Posthumous Translation of Pulpit and Table, 1996. Pres. gen. synod Ref. Ch. Am., 1959-60; pres. Friends of New Netherland. Decorated knight comdr. Order of Orange-Nassau (The Netherlands). Mem. N. Am. Acad. Liturgy, Holland Soc. N.Y. (domine), Colonial Order of Acorn, Phi Beta Kappa. Home: New Baltimore N.Y. Died Dec. 20, 1992; interred The GreenWood Cemetary, Brooklyn, N.Y.

HAGGERTY, LAWRENCE GEORGE, business executive; b. Harvey, N.D., Aug. 10, 1916; s. Michael Eugene and Lillian Marie (Evenson) H.; m. Mary Ellen Sweeney, Oct. 17, 1942; children: Michael Eugene, Catherine Ann Lenahan (dec.), Eileen Mary Mundy, Patrick Bernard, Margaret Ellen, Sheila Bridget Mahoney, Maureen Elizabeth Warmuth, Timothy James, Monica Louise Jaekels. B.M.E., Marquette U., 1940. Successively student engr., mgmt. trainee to mgr. mfg. RCA Victor, Indpls., 1940-48; gen. mgr. appliance and parts mfg. divsn. F.L. Jacobs Co., Indpls., Traverse City, Mich., 1948-50; with ITT, 1950-58; successively dir. mfg., v.p. mfg., v.p. and gen. mgr. tech. products div., pres., dir. Capehart-Farnsworth Co., 1950-56; pres., founder Farnsworth Electronics Co., 1956-58; pres., dir., CEO Warwick Electronics Inc. (formerly Warwick Mfg. Corp.), 1958-66; dir. Lawrence G. Haggerty & Assocs., Inc., Chgo., 1967-94; chmn., dir. Haggerty Enterprises, 1978-94, A.R.T. Studio Clay Co., Inc., 1989-94, Tech-Nique Inc., 1991-94; chmn. bd. dirs. Tech-nique, Inc. Trustee Emeritus Marquette U. Decorated Knight Comdr. Equestrian Order of Holy Sepulchre, 1988. Mem. Naples Yacht Club, Quail Creek Country Club (Naples, Fla.), Collier Athletic Club, North Shore Country Club (Glenview, Ill.), Bob O'Link Golf Club (Highland Park, Ill.), Tau Beta Pi, Alpha Sigma Nu, Pi Tau Sigma. Republican. Roman Catholic. Home: Naples Fla. Died May 28, 1994.

HAGSTRUM, HOMER DUPRE, physicist; b. St. Paul, Mar. 11, 1915; s. Andrew and Sadie Gertrude (Fryckberg) H.; m. Bonnie Doone Cairns, Aug. 29, 1948; children: Melissa Billings, Jonathan Tryon. BEE with high distinction, U. Minn., 1935, BS summa cum laude, 1936, MS, 1939, PhD in Physics and Math., 1940, ScD (hon.), 1986. Teaching and research asst. U. Minn., Mpls., 1935-40; research physicist AT&T Bell Labs., Murray Hill, N.J., 1940-85; head surface physics research dept. AT&T Bell Labs., Murray Hill, 1954-78, ret., 1985; cons. dept. physics Stevens Inst. Tech., Hoboken, N.J., 1986-89; vis. prof. Inst. for Solid State Physics, U. Tokyo, Sept.-Dec. 1986, June, July 1989; gen. chmn. Physical Electronics Conf., 1976-80. Author research articles mass spectrometry, microwave magnetrons, surface physics, electron spectroscopy, interaction of ions and metastable atoms with surfaces. Fellow AAAS, Am. Physical Soc. (chmn. div. electron and atomic physics 1957, Davisson-Germer prize 1975); mem. Nat. Acad. Sci., Am. Vacuum Soc (bd. dirs. 1976-78, Welch award 1974), N.Y. Acad. Sci., Sigma Xi, Tau Beta Pi, Eta Kappa Nu. Home: Menlo Park Calif. Died Sept. 7, 1994.

HAGUE, RAOUL, sculptor; b. Constantinople, Mar. 28, 1905; came to U.S., 1921, naturalized, 1930; s. Nazar and Satenig Heukelekian. Student, Robert Coll. Prep. Sch., Constantinople, Iowa State Coll., 1921; Art Inst., Chgo., 1922-25, Beaux-Arts Inst. of Design, N.Y.C., 1926-27, Art Students League, N.Y.C., 1927-28, Courtauld Inst., London, 1950-51. With Fed. Arts Project (Works Progress Adminstrn.), N.Y.C., 1935-39. One-man shows, Egan Gallery, N.Y.C., 1962, (retrospective) Washington Gallery Modern Art, 1964, Xavier Fourcade Gallery, N.Y.C., 1979, 87, Arts Club, Chgo., 1983, Susanne Hilberry Gallery, Birmingham, Mich., 1986, Lennon, Weinberg, Inc., N.Y.C., 1988, 90-91; Galerie Alfred Kren, Cologne, Germany, 1990; exhibited in group shows including Mus. Modern Art, 1933, 56, Curt Valentin Gallery, 1945, Whitney Mus. Am. Art, 1945-48, 89-90, Munson-William-Proctor Inst., Utica, N.Y., 1960, N.Y.C. Coliseum, 1976, Art Inst. Chgo., 1979, Xavier Fourcade Inc., 1980, 82-83, 87, Grey Art Gallery and Study Ctr., NYU, 1981, Lennon, Weinberg, Inc., N.Y.C., 1989, 90, Manny Silverman Gallery, L.A., 1991; represented in permanent collections, Albright-Knox Art Gallery, Mus. Modern Art, Whitney Mus. Am. Art, Met. Mus. Art, Art Inst. Chgo., Hirshhorn Mus. and Sculpture Garden, Washington, Nat. Gallery Art, Washington, San Francsico Mus. Modern Art, J.B. Speed Mus., Louisville, Weatherspoon Art Gallery, Rose Art Mus., Storm King Art Ctr., J.B. Speed Mus., Louisville, Ky. Served as pvt. AUS, 1941-43. Recipient Audubon prize, 1945, Kleinert award, 1956, Guggenheim Meml. award, 1967; grantee Woodstock Found., 1949, Ford Found., 1961, Rothko Found., 1972, Am. Acad. Arts and Letters, 1973. Home: Woodstock N.Y. Died Feb. 17, 1993.

HAHN, RICHARD FERDINAND, lawyer; b. Chgo., May 20, 1909; s. Ernest Theodore and Emily (Sattler) H.; m. Grace Elizabeth Jepsen, Sept. 1, 1935; children: Nancy (Mrs. Noel G. Fischer), Lawrence. B.S., U. Ill., 1930, J.D., 1933. Bar: Ill. bar 1933. Pvt. practice Chgo., 1933-93; ptnr. Halfpenny, Hahn, Roche & Marchese (formerly Halfpenny, Hahn & Roche), Chgo. and Washington, 1934-93. Mem. Woodstock (Ill.) City Council, 1965-67, 73-79; mem., sec. Woodstock Police Commn., 1968-71; mem. Woodstock Indsl. Devel. Commn., 1967-69, Woodstock City Planning Commn., 1957-62, 79-85; mem. Woodstock Community High Sch. Bd., 1952-55, 56-62, pres., 1958-62; Bd. dirs. Woodstock Fine Arts Assn., 1963-67. Mem. Am., Ill., Chgo. bar assns., Am. Judicature Soc., Phi Alpha Delta. Republican. Lodge: Masons. Home: Woodstock Ill. Died June 30, 1993.

HAINES, PERRY VANSANT, cattle company executive; b. Middletown, Ohio, Mar. 14, 1944; s. John Percy and Pendery (Spear) H.; m. Sidonie M. Sexton, 1982; children: Pendery, Caroline. A.B., Princeton U., 1967; M.B.A., Harvard U., 1970. Research asst. Harvard U., 1970-71; cons. Boston Cons. Group, 1971-74; exec. v.p. IBP, Inc. (formerly Iowa Beef Processors), Dakota City, Nebr., 1974-89; dir. IBP, Inc., 1980-89; v.p. Occidental Petroleum, Los Angeles, 1981-87. Served with USMCR, 1967-68. Home: Dakota Dunes S.D. Died 1989.

HAINLINE, FORREST ARTHUR, JR., retired automotive company executive, lawyer; b. Rock Island, Ill., Oct. 20, 1918; s. Forrest Arthur and Marian (Pearson) H.; m. Nora Marie Schrot, July 7, 1945; children: Forrest III, Jon, Patricia, Judith, Brian, David, Nora. AB, Augustana Coll., Rock Island, Ill., 1940; JD, U. Mich., 1947, LLM, 1948. Bar: Ill. 1942, Mich. 1943, Fla. 1970, U.S. Supreme Ct. 1946. Mem. firm Cross, Wrock, Miller & Vieson and predecessor, Detroit, 1948-71, ptnr., 1957-71; v.p., gen. counsel Am. Motors Corp., Detroit, 1971-84, sec., 1972-84, ret. Chmn., Wayne County Regional Interagy. Coordinating Com. for Developmental Disabilities, Mich., 1972-76; chmn. grievance com. U.S. Tennis Assn., 1970-85, mem. exec. com., 1972-74, 83-85, chmn. constn. and rules, 1983-86, mem., legal counsel adult leagues com., 1983-85, 89—, v.p. So. region, 1985-86, parliamentarian, 1991—; arbitrator Men's Internat. Profl. Tennis Coun., 1977-85, Am. Arbitration Assn. (panel arbitrators), 1992—, cert. circuit court mediator, 1992—; pres. Cath. Social Svcs. Oakland County, Mich., 1972-75; mem. exec. com. Western Tennis Assn., 1964—, pres., 1972-73, chmn. constn. and rules com., 1976-84; mem. Men's Internat. Profl. Tennis Council, 1985-87; chmn. Internat. Tennis Fedn. rules com., 1987-90; pres. Western Improvement Assn., 1969-75; bd. dirs. Augustana Coll., 1974-82, sec., 1975-82; bd. dirs. Providence Hosp., Southfield, Mich., 1975-84, sec. 1980, vice chmn., 1981, chmn., 1982, chmn. exec. com., 1983-84. Served to 1st lt. AUS, 1942-46. Named (with family) Tennis Family of Yr., U.S. Tennis Assn., 1974; recipient Outstanding Service award Augustana Coll., 1977; named to Rock Island High Sch. Sports Hall of Fame, 1977, Mich. Amateur Sports Hall of Fame, 1978, Augustana Coll. Sports Hall of Fame, 1980. Mem. ABA, Fed. Bar Assn., Mich. Bar. Assn., Ill. Bar Assn., Fla. Bar Assn., Am. Judicature Soc., Supreme Court Hist. Soc., Augustana Coll. Alumni Assn. (pres. bd. dirs. 1973-74), Phi Alpha Delta. Clubs: Suntide Condominiums, Detroit Tennis, Squash, Island Dunes. Lodge: KC. Home: Stuart Fla.

HALBERT, SHERRILL, retired federal judge; b. Terra Bella, Calif., Oct. 17, 1901; s. Edward Duffield and Ellen (Rhodes) H.; m. Verna Irene Dyer, June 7, 1927; children: Shirley Ellen (Mrs. Stanley J. Eager), Douglas James. A.B., U. Calif. at Berkeley, 1924, J.D., 1927; LL.D., McGeorge Coll. Law, 1962. Bar: Calif. bar 1927. Practiced in Porterville, 1927-41, San Francisco, 1942-44; pvt. practice Modesto, 1944-49; dist. atty. Stanislaus County, 1949; judge Superior Ct. of Calif 1949-54; judge U.S. Dist. Ct. (ea. dist.) Calif., Sacra mento, 1954-89, ret. sr. judge; Chmn. bd. advise McGeorge Sch. Law, Sacramento. Contbg. autho Lincoln for the Ages, 1960, Lincoln: A Contempora Portrait, 1962. Mem. Am. Camellia Soc. (pres. eme itus), Native Sons of Golden West, Nat. Pony Expres Centennial Assn. (pres.), Selden Soc., Calif. Hist. Soc Alpha Chi Rho, Phi Delta Phi. Clubs: Lion (Sacra mento) (hon.), Ambassador's (Sacramento); Book Calif. (San Francisco), Commonwealth (San Francisco) Home: Kentfield Calif. Died May. 31, 1991; interre San Rafael, Calif.

HALDEMAN, HARRY R. (BOB HALDEMAN business consultant, former government official; b. Lo Angeles, Oct. 27, 1926; s. Harry F. and Katherin (Robbins) H.; m. Jo Horton, Feb. 19, 1949; childre Susan Ward, Harry Horton, Peter Robbins, Ann Kur Coppe. Student, U. Redlands, 1944-45, U. So. Cali 1945-46; B.S. in Bus. Adminstrn., UCLA, 1948. A count exec. J. Walter Thompson Co., Los Angeles an N.Y.C., 1949-59; v.p., mgr. Los Angeles office J. Walt Thompson Co., 1960-68; asst. to Pres. U.S., chief Whi House staff, 1969-73; sr. v.p. Murdock Devel. Co., Lo Angeles, 1979-85; pres. Murdock Hotels Corp., 1984-8 chmn. adv. bd. Americom Internat., Inc., Irvine, Cali bd. dirs. Haldeman, Inc., L.A., Family Steak Houses Miami, Inc., Wedgewood Investment Corp., L.A Conductive Rubber Tech., Inc., Seattle. Chief sta Nixon presdl. campaign, 1968. Author: The Ends Power, 1978, THe Haldeman Diaries, 1994. Bd. regen U. Calif., 1965-67, 68-69; trustee Calif. Inst. Arts, 196 68, chmn. bd., 1968; former chmn. bd. trustees Nixo Found.; mem. Commn. White House Fellows, 1969-7 former mem. exec. com., trustee Kennedy Center f Performing Arts. Served with USNR, 1944-46. Mer Beta Theta Pi, Pi Delta Epsilon. Home: Santa Barba Calif. Died Nov. 12, 1993.

HALE, JAMES RUSSELL, religious studies educato minister; b. Phila., Dec. 14, 1918; s. Robert Gifford ar Dorothy Emma (Graham) H.; m. Phyllis Bollinger, Ju 8, 1991; children from previous marriage: Dougl Graham, Dean Edward. A.B., Muhlenberg Coll., 194 B.D., Luth. Theol. Sem., Gettysburg, Pa., 1944, S.T.M 1950; Ed.D., Union Theol. Sem. and Columbia U N.Y.C., 1970. Ordained to ministry Lutheran Ch. Am 1944. Parish pastor Gethsemane and Reformati Luth. chs., Keyport and Long Branch, N.J., 1944-4 Our Savior Luth. Ch., Balt., 1946-50, Redeemer Lut Ch., Ramsey, N.J., 1950-59, St. Paul's Luth. Ch., Co lingswood, N.J., 1959-62; instr. ch. and communi Luth. Theol. Sem., Gettysburg, 1962-63, asst. pro 1963-69, assoc. prof., 1969-70, prof., 1970-84, acti pres., 1989-90, dir. continuing edn., 1990-91, editor Se Bull., 1965-69, dir. advanced studies program, 1975-8 dir. Town and Country Ch. Inst., 1980-85, mem. ad coun., 1985—; cons., 1990—; theologian-in-residen Horthorpe Hall, Leicestershire, Eng., 1980-81; chm acad. com. ch. and soc. Washington Theol. Consortiu 1971-74; bd. dirs. Coun. on Luth. Theol. Edn. in N. 1975-80; vis. prof. Appalachian Ministries Edu Resource Ctr. Berea Coll., Ky., 1986-87, Grad. The Union, Berkeley, Calif., 1987, Luth. Theol. Sem., Phi 1988; cons. Rural Ministry, Area Strategy Studi Social Ministry, Evangelization. Author: To Have a to Hold, 1972, Who are the Unchurched? An E ploratory Study, 1977, rev., 1988, Lutherans and Soc Action, 1979, The Unchurched: Who They Are a Why They Stay Away, 1980, Touching Lives Throu Service, 1994; contbr. articles to profl. jours. Sec., b dirs. Tressler Luth. Social Svcs., Camp Hill, Pa., 197 77, 80-85; chmn. bd. dirs. Tressler Luth. Home f Children: bd. dirs. Adams County Office for Agin 1989—; chmn. Adams County Com. for Family Foc Gettysburg, Pa., 1971-72; del. White House Conf. Aging, 1981; mem. adv. coun. Luth. Social Svcs., Ge tysburg Ctr., 1988—. Served with Civilian Pub. Sv 1942. Case Study Inst. fellow Cambridge, 1973-7 Gerontolgy in Sem. Tng. Program fellow Nat. Interfai Coalition on Aging, 1979; Danforth Found. asso 1963-65; recipient Luth. Brotherhood Faculty Researc 1963-64, 80, award Luth. Ch. Am., 1968-70, 80-8 grants. Mem. Am. Acad. Religion, AAUP, Am. Soci Assn., Religious Rsch. Assn., Soc. Sci. Study Religio Rural Sociol. Democrat. Home: Gettysburg Pa. Di Nov. 5, 1994.

HALEY, GEORGE HENRY, II, management co sultant; b. Oswego, N.Y., Oct. 25, 1917; s. Geor Henry and Alice Kathryn (Horan) H.; B.A., Yale U 1939; LL.B., U. Va., 1942; m. Anne Putney Colema Dec. 18, 1943; children—George Henry, III, Edwa Coleman, Stephen Putney, Anne Putney. Admitted N.Y. bar, 1946; assoc. firm Baldwin, Todd & Leffer N.Y.C., 1945-46; sec. Maxson Foods Systems, In N.Y.C., 1945-47; exec. asst. to operating v.p. Pr Chem. Co., N.Y.C., 1947-49; asst. sec. West Penn El tric Co., N.Y.C., 1949-50; exec. asst. to pres. Vanadiu Corp. Am., N.Y.C., 1950-52; v.p. Ward Howell Asso Inc., mgmt. consultants, N.Y.C., 1952-64; pres. Ha Assocs., Inc., N.Y.C., from 1964, now chmn. Trus United Hosp., Port Chester, N.Y. Served to lt. j.g. US 1942-45. Clubs: Brook, Yale, Racquet and Ten (N.Y.C.); Apawamis, Am. Yacht (Rye, N.Y.); Co Beach and Tennis (Bermuda). Home: Rye N.Y.

IALL, DANIEL RAY ACOMB, social sciences educator; b. Dansville, N.Y., June 17, 1927; s. Daniel Ray comb and Louise (Schudoma) H.; m. Pauline Ruth einkamp, June 3, 1950; 1 dau., Ruth Alice. B.A., Vesleyan U., 1948; M.A., Columbia, 1949, Ed.D., 1958; ostgrad., U. S.C., 1969, U. N.C., 1969. Asst. to dean dminstrn. Newark Coll. Engring., then asst. to pres., 952-59; dir. admissions SUNY Coll.-Geneseo, 1959, rof. econs., 1959-67; dir. summer session, extension v., assoc dean of coll. dean grad. studies, to 1967; rof. econs. Madison Coll., Harrisonburg, Va., 1967-76, ean coll., provost, dir. Center for Econ. Edn.; prof. ons. Trenton (N.J.) State Coll., 1976-83, dean grad. udy, 1976-83, dir. Ctr. Econ. Edn., 1983-90, prof. ocial scis., 1983-95, chmn. econ. dept., 1987-95; exec. r. Eastern Econ. Assn., 1988-91. Trustee, exec. com. J. Coun. on Econ. Edn.; mem. com. on disciplines at. Coun. Social Studies. Named Outstanding Eduator Am., 1971; recipient 2 Nat. awards Joint Council con. Edn., 1987. Fellow Ea. Econ. Assn.; mem. Nat. ssn. Econ. Educators (com. on awards), Phi Delta appa, Kappa Delta Pi (nat. commn. on plans for future, Nat. Leadership award 1987), Delta Sigma Rho, lpha Phi Omega, Sigma Pi, Phi Nu Theta, Phi Chi heta, Pi Gamma Mu, Omicron Delta Epsilon. Home: renton N.J. DIed May 5, 1995.

IALL, EMMETT MATTHEW, university administrator; b. St. Columban, Que., Can., Nov. 29, 1898; s. mes and Alice (Shea) H.; m. Isabel Mary Parker, June 5, 1922; children: Marian Hall Wedge, John E. Grad., Sask., 1919; D.C.L. (hon.), 1964; M.D. (hon.), U. ttawa, 1966; LL.D. (hon.), U. Windsor, 1968, U. Ian., 1968, Queen's U., 1974, Law Soc. Upper Can., 975, Dalhousie U., 1977, York U., 1977, U. Regina, 979; D.S. in Jurisprudence (hon.), Francis Xavier U., ntigonish, N.S., 1974. Bar: Called to Sask. bar 1922, ng's counsel 1935. Pvt. practice law Saskatoon, 1922-7; chief justice Queen's Bench Ct. for Sask., 1957-61; hief justice of Sask., 1961-62; justice Supreme Ct. Can., 962-73; chmn. Royal Commn. Health Services, 1961-4, Com. on Aims and Objectives for Edn. in Ont., 961-95; chancellor U. Guelph, 1971-77; lectr. law U. ask. Coll. Law, 1948-58, mem. univ. senate, 1942-54, niv. chancellor, 1980-95; Goodman lectr. U. Toronto aw Sch., 1975; chief commr. Grain Handling and ransp. Commn., 1975-77; labor arbitrator and conciltor, 1973-95. Trustee St. Paul's Separate Sch. Dist., askatoon, 1937-57, chmn., 1949-59; resident Catholic h. Trustees Sask., 1945-52; exec. com. Sask. Sch. rustees Assn., 1952-57; chmn. bd. St. Paul's Hosp., askatoon, 1947-63. Decorated companion Order Can., 974, knight of malta, 1958, knight Order St. Gregory, 968, knight Holy Sepulchre, 1969; recipient Bronfman ward Am. Public Health Assn., 1966. Hon. mem. U. ask. Faculty Club; hon. nat. pres. Can. Civil Liberties ssn.; Mem. Can. Bar Assn. (v.p. for Sask. 1943-45), aw Soc. Sask. (pres. 1952), Can. Inst. Adminstrn. Juse (dir.), Internat., Commn. Jurists (past pres. Can. ct.). Clubs: Rideau (Ottawa); Saskatoon. Home: askatoon Can. Died Nov. 29, 1995.

IALL, GORDON CLARKE, federal judge; b. Cranrook, B.C., Can., Oct. 3, 1921; s. Watson Smythe and llen (Leitch) H.; m. Agnes Margaret Rife, June 26, 944; children: Nancy Margaret, David Malcolm, ouglas Rife. Student, U. Man., 1941, LLB, 1948. ssoc. Guy, Chappel and Co., Winnipeg, Man., 1948-5; ptnr. Thompson, Dilts, Jones, Hall and Dewar, 956-65; judge Ct. of Queen's Bench, Man., from 1965; ctr. U. Man. Sch. Medicine, Winnipeg, 1954-65; judge t. Appeals for Man., Winnipeg, 1971—. Home: Winpeg Can. Deceased.

IALL, SAM BLAKELEY, JR., federal judge, former ongressman; b. Marshall, Tex., Jan. 11, 1924; s. Sam lakeley and Valerie (Curtis) H.; m. Madeleine Segal, eb. 9, 1946; children: Linda Rebecca Hall Palmer, manda Jane Hall Wynn, Sandra Blake. Student, Coll. Iarshall, 1942; LL.B., Baylor U., 1948. Bar: Tex. 1948. Pvt. practice law Marshall, 1948-76; mem. 94th-98th ongresses, 1st Dist Tex., 1976-85; judge U.S. Dist. Ct. a. dist.) Tex., 1985-94. Past mem. bd. dirs. East Tex. rea council Boy Scouts Am.; past trustee Wiley Coll., Iarshall; past chmn. Marshall Bd. Edn.; past chmn. bd. rs. Harrison County Hosp. Assn., Marshall; mem. bd. evel. Baylor U. Served with USAAF, 1943-45. ecipient Boss of Yr. award Harrison County Legal ecs. Assn., 1965. Mem. Am. Bd. Trial Advocates, BA, Tex. Bar Assn., N.E. Tex. Bar Assn. Harrison ounty Bar Assn. (past pres.), Marshall C. of C. (past res.; Outstanding Citizen award 1970). Democrat. Iem. Ch. of Christ. Lodge: Kiwanis. Home: Marshall ex. Died Apr. 10, 1994.

IALL, WILFRED MCGREGOR, engineering comany executive;; b. Denver, June 12, 1894; s. Frederick olsom and Annie L. (Thompson) H.; m. Anne Gerude Jones, Apr. 4, 1921 (dec. Dec. 1976); children: redrick Folsom, Anne (dec.); m. Louise Hull Claire, ne 23, 1978. B.S., U. Colo., 1916; D.Eng., Tufts U., 955. Engr. hydroelectric constrn. Chas. T. Main Co., 916-17, engr. hydroelectric investigation and design, 920-22; with Chas. T. Main, Inc., 1941—, dir., 1943—, p., 1953-57, pres., chief exec. officer, 1957-72, chmn. d., chief exec. officer, 1972—; Chmn. bd., chief exec. ficer C.T. Main Corp.; chmn. bd., chief exec. officer has. T. Main Internat. Inc., Chas. T. Main N.Y. Inc.; chmn. bd., chief exec. bd. H.P.N. Cons. Inc.; chmn. bd., chief exec. officer Chas. T. Main Mich. Inc., Chas. T. Main Va. Inc., W.M. Hall & Assocs., Inc., Main Constructors Inc., Main Constrn. Mgmt. Inc.; engr. Chrisfield Contracting Co., 1919; supt. constrn., engr. U.G.I. Contracting Co., 1922-28; supt. constrn. Electric Bond & Share Co., 1929-31; cons. engr., 1932-33; engr. charge constrn. TVA, 1933-37; mgr. engring. and constrn. P.R., 1937-41; partner Uhl, Hall & Rich, 1953-62, mng. partner, 1962-80; chmn. bd. Main Erbauer Inc., C.T. Main Constrn Inc., Rite Equipment Co., Inc.; past dir. Arkwright-Boston Mfrs. Mut. Ins. Co.; Past dir. U.S. Com. Large Dams. Bd. dirs. Mass. Soc. Prevention of Blindness. Fellow Am. Soc. C.E.; mem. A.I.M. (fellow pres.'s council 1966), Am. Inst. Cons. Engrs. (past pres. New Eng. sect.), Cons. Engrs. Council New Eng. (past dir.), Soc. Mil. Engrs., Newcomen Soc. (trustee, chmn. Mass. com.), Royal Soc. Encouragement of Arts, Manufacture and Commerce, Engrs. Club (bd. govs.), Mass. Soc. Profl Engrs., Alpha Sigma Phi, Sigma Tau, Tau Beta Pi. Clubs: Metropolitan (N.Y.C.); Country (Brookline, Mass.); Algonquin (Boston), Rotary (Boston) (past dir.), Hamilton Trust (Boston) (past pres.). Home: Boston Mass.

HALLBAUER, ROBERT EDWARD, retired mining company executive; b. Nakusp, B.C., Can., May 19, 1930; s. Edward F. and Lillian Anna (Kendrick) H.; m. Mary Joan Hunter, Sept. 6, 1952; children: Russell, Catherine, Thomas. BS in Mining Engring., U. B.C., 1954. Registered profl. engr., B.C. Various engring. and supervisory positions Placer Devel., Salmo, B.C., 1954-60; mine supr. Craigmont Mines Ltd., Merritt, B.C., 1960-64, mine mgr., 1964-68; v.p. mining Teck Corp., Vancouver, B.C., 1968-79, sr. v.p., 1979-94; pres., CEO Cominco Ltd., Vancouver, 1986-94, also bd. dirs.; ret., 1994; vice chmn. Cominco Ltd. Recipient Edgar A. Scholz medal B.C. and Yukon Chamber of Mines, 1984. Mem. Assn. Profl. Engrs., Can. Inst. Mining, Metallurgy and Petroleum (Inco medal 1992). Home: West Vancouver Can. Died May 10, 1995.

HALLGRIMSSON, GEIR, governor central bank of Iceland; b. Reykjavik, Iceland, Dec. 16, 1925; s. Hallgrimur Benediktsson and Aslaug Geirsdottir Zoega; m. Erna Finnsdottir, 1948; 2 sons, 2 daus. Grad. Reykjavik Coll., 1944; law degree, U. Iceland, 1948; postgrad. in law and econs., Harvard U., 1948-49. Bar: 1951, Supreme Ct. 1957. Sole practice Reykjavik, 1951-59; dir. H. Benediktsson Ltd., 1955-59; mem. Reykjavik City Council, 1954-74, mem. city exec. council, 1954-74, 1st v.p. council, 1958-59, mayor, 1959-72; alt. M.P., 1959-70, prin. mem., 1970—; prime minister, 1974-78; chmn. fgn. affairs com., 1979-83; minister for fgn. affairs, 1983-86. Mem. central com. Independence Party (Sjálfstaedisflokkurinn), 1965-87, chmn., 1973-83; gov. Central Bank Iceland, 1986—. Decorated comdr. with star Order Falcon (Iceland), Grand Cross; Order of the Polar Star (Sweden); comdr. St. Olav (Norway); comdr. 1st class Order Lion (Finland); grand officer Order de Merite (Luxembourg); comdr. Order Dannebrog (Denmark). Home: Reykjavik Iceland

HALLORAN, HARRY RICHARD, contracting company executive; b. Riverside, N.J., July 13, 1902; s. Richard J. and Agnes (Fahy) H.; m. Margaret Schneider, Sept. 8, 1938 (dec. 1980); children: Harry R. Jr., Edward, Richard, Thomas; m. Lorraine Horos, Dec. 1, 1984. BSCE, U. Pa., 1923; D of Comml. Sci. (hon.), Villanova U., 1967; D of Indsl. Rels. (hon.), St. Joseph's U., Phila., 1975. Chmn. bd. dirs. Conduit and Found Corp., Bala Cynwyd, Pa., 1941—; ptnr. N.J. real estate holdings, Deptford, 1956—, Pitman (N.J.) Country Club, 1956—; gen. ptnr. Atlantic City Raceway, 1968-86; vice-chmn. Atlantic City Harness, 1987-88; bd. dirs. City Trusts. Bd. dirs., v.p. Bd. City Trusts, Phila. Recipient Sourin award Cath. Philos. Lit. Inst., Phila., 1979, Alumni award of merit U. Pa. Organized Alumni, 1980, Cresset award Rosemont Coll., 1986. Mem. Assn. Gen. Contractors Am. (treas., life bd. dirs.), Contractors Assn. Eastern Pa. (past pres., chmn. bd. dirs., life bd. dirs.). Republican. Roman Catholic. Clubs: Whitemarsh Valley Country (Lafayette Hill, Pa.) (past pres.); Merion Cricket (Haverford, Pa.); Union (Phila.); N.J. Country. Home: Bryn Mawr Pa.

HALLOWELL, H. THOMAS, JR., retired steel manufacturing company executive; b. Phila., Mar. 22, 1908; s. Howard T. Hallowell and Blanche Nice; m. Dorothy Willits, Apr. 5, 1932; children: Howard T. III, Anne Hallowell Miller, Merrit Willits. BA in Econs., Swarthmore Coll., 1929, LLD (hon.), 1960; LLD (hon.), Spring Garden Coll., 1986; hon. degree, Nat. Inst. Higher Edn., Ireland, 1985. Machine operator Standard Pressed Steel Co., Jenkintown, Pa., 1929-32, gen. supt., 1932-40, plant mgr., 1940-48, exec. v.p., 1948-54; pres. S.P.S. Techs. (formerly Standard Pressed Steel Co.), Jenkintown, 1954-62, chmn., 1962-75, chmn. emeritus, chmn. fin. com., 1985—; pres. Am. Standards Assn., 1956-59; past pres. Montgomery Mfrs. Assn.; past v.p.Nat. Assn. Mfrs. Patentee machine tools and aircraft precision fasteners. Trustee emeritus Swarthmore Coll., Franklin Inst., Pa. State U., William Penn Charter Sch. Republican. Mem. Soc. of Friends. Clubs: Union League (Phila.), Huntingdon Valley Country (Abington, Pa.). Home: Rydal Pa.

HALPERIN, WARREN LESLIE, international aviation executive; b. Bklyn., Apr. 12, 1938; s. Abraham and Bertha Gertrude (Aronowitz) H.; m. Sherry Lee Weshner, Mar. 31, 1968; children: Jonathan David, Justin Edward. PhB, Adelphi U., 1959. Dir. mktg. Faust-Day Inc., Los Angeles, 1969-71; product mgr. Hunt-Wesson Foods, Fullerton, Calif., 1972-74; sr. v.p. Searchmasters Inc., Newport Beach, Calif., 1975-79; ptnr. MCS Assocs., Newport Beach, 1979-83; pres. The Halperin Co. Inc., Newport Beach, 1983-88; exec. v.p. Mercury Savs. and Loan, Huntington Beach, Calif., 1988-89; chmn. bd. dirs. Western Printing Corp., L.A., 1988-89; pres. The Halperin Co. Inc., Dana Point, Calif., 1989-91, CBA Pragmatic USA, Dana Point, 1991-93; dir. gen. internat. ctr. Russian Aviation Trade House, Ltd., Russia, UK, USA, 1993; bd. dirs. Capital Savings & Loan Assn., West Helena, Ark., Aardvark Investments, Ltd., UK, Multi-Nat. Trade House, Ltd., UK. Contbr. articles to profl. jours. and Soviet media. Mem. nat. bd. trusteees Leukemia Soc. Am., N.Y.C., 1980-85; trustee Amigos De Las Americas, Irvine, Calif., 1975-78; pres. Leukemia Soc. Am. Tri-County chpt., Garden Grove, Calif., 1979; founder, bd. dirs. Pragmatik Ltd., Moscow. Named Exec. of Yr. Exec. Mag., 1986. Home: Dana Point Calif. Died Aug. 19, 1993.

HALPIN, CHARLES AIME, archbishop, deceased; b. St. Eustache, Man., Can., Aug. 30, 1930; s. John S. and Marie Anne (Gervais) H. BA, U. Man., 1950; BTh, U. Montreal, 1956; Licentiate Canon Law, Gregorian U., Rome, 1960. Ordained priest Roman Catholic Ch., 1956; named monsignor Roman Cath. Ch., 1969, consecrated bishop, 1973; asst. St. Mary's Cathedral, Winnipeg, Man., 1956-58; vice chancellor, sec. to archbishop Archdiocese Winnipeg, 1960; officialis Archdiocesan Matrimonial Tribunal, 1962; vice-officialis Regional Matrimonial Tribunal, Regina, Sask.; archbishop of Regina, 1973—. Mem. Western Cath. Conf. Bishops (past pres.), Can. Conf. Cath. Bishops (bd. dirs.). Home: Regina Can. Died Apr. 16, 1994.

HALSTEAD, HARRY MOORE, lawyer; b. Washington, Nov. 9, 1918; s. John Harry and Lucinda (Moore) H.; m. Carmella Ann LaRosa, Sept. 7, 1946; children—William, Lucinda, Christina, Concetta. A.B., Rutgers U., 1941; J.D., Yale U., 1948; LL.M., U. So. Calif., 1953. Bar: Calif. bar 1949. Pvt. practice Los Angeles, 1949-95; sr. ptnr. firm Halstead, Baker & Olson, 1959-95; lectr. taxation, estate and trust law. Author several books; contbr. articles to profl. jours. Trustee Linfield Coll., McMinnville, Oreg., 1973-82, S. Pasadena United Methodist Ch. Served to maj. AUS, 1941-46. Mem. Am. Bar Assn. (vice chmn. com. tax and estate planning 1967-77, vice chmn. com. state death taxes 1977-80), State Bar Calif., U. So. Calif. Alumni Assn., Phi Gamma Delta. Clubs: Rutgers So. Calif. (past pres.), Yale of So. Calif. (past pres.), San Marino City, Arcadia Tennis. Home: San Marino Calif. Died Apr. 21, 1995.

HAMBY, A. GARTH, beverage company executive; b. Oneonta, Ala., 1938. B.A. in Journalism, U. Ala., 1959. Reporter Columbus Ledger News, 1959-61; various positions Ga. Power Co., 1961-67; staff rep. pub. rels. dept. Coca-Cola Co., Atlanta, 1967-70, mgr. editorial group pub. rels. dept., 1970-74, asst. to chmn. bd., 1974-78, v.p., sec., dir., corp. external affairs, 1978-79; sr. v.p., sec., dir. corp. external affairs Coca-Cola Co., 1979-80, exec. v.p., sec., 1980-81; exec. v.p. Coca-Cola Co., Atlanta, 1981—. Home: Atlanta Ga. Died July 13, 1993.

HAMCKE, WILLIAM ROBERT, banker; b. N.Y.C., Sept. 16, 1924; s. William Herman and Amelia (Hess) H.; B.B.A., Pace U., 1952; m. Sarah Irvine, May 27, 1950; children: Barbara, Carol. Regional mgr. Ford Motor Co., Dearborn, Mich., 1953-68; controller Pepsi Cola Co., N.Y.C., 1968-69; with Irving Trust Co., N.Y.C., 1969-88, exec. v.p., 1973-88. Served with USAAF, 1942-46. Mem. Fin. Execs. Inst., N.Y. Clearing House. Died July 9, 1988. Home: Stamford Conn.

HAMER, SYLVIA JANE, ballet educator; b. Ann Arbor, Mich., July 9, 1900; d. Melvin Russel and Myrtle D. (Hilliker) Cole; m. Hazell King, Apr. 16, 1918; 1 child, Jay B.; m. Ellsworth Hamer (dec.). Student St. Mary's Abbey, Mills Hill, Eng.; Fellow Degree, Cacchitti Soc., London, 1972. Tchr. and trainer Sylvia Studio, Ann Arbor, from 1934. Founder, bd. dirs. Ann Arbor Civic Ballet, from 1956. Deceased. Home: Ann Arbor Mich.

HAMILTON, CHARLES HENRY, newspaper consultant; b. Webster Springs, W.Va., Nov. 16, 1903; s. Alfred Patton and Cora Jane (Benedum) H.; m. Viola Belle Morrisette, Nov. 3, 1928 (dec. 1963); children: John Alfred, Barbara Morrisette (Mrs. Charles Fraley), Bette (Mrs. Nick Eubank), Viola Lee; m. Muriel Marable Butler, 1964. Grad., Greenbrier Mil. Sch., 1923; A.B., Washington and Lee U., 1926. Reporter Clarksburg Exponent, 1925; sports writer Richmond News Leader, 1926-32, sports editor, 1932-36, city editor, 1936-51, mng. editor, 1951-69, asst. to pres., 1969-74; cons., 1974-90; radio announcer, news commentator sta. WRVA, Richmond, 1927-34; pres. Dixie Profl. Football League, 1935-36; news commentator sta. WRNL, 1939-42; lectr. Am. Press Inst., Columbia,

1946-51; chmn. Va. Associated Press Newspapers, 1956-57; Dir. Fed. Home Loan Bank of Greensboro, 1963, chmn. bd., 1970. Author: Peter Francisco: Soldier Extraordinary; Contbr.: fiction, articles nat. mags., including Sat. Evening Post, Reader's Digest. Chmn. Va. adv. legislative com. unit to rewrite Va. hunting and fishing laws, 1962. Lt. col. AGC U.S. Army Res., 1949-54. Mem. Am. Soc. Newspaper Editors, Va. Press Assn. (pres. 1959, spl. plaque 1971, hon. life mem.), AP Mng. Editors Assn. (dir. 1955-58, bd. regents 1974-94), Am. Legion, Sigma Delta Chi, Lambda Chi Alpha, Delta Sigma Rho, Pi Delta Epsilon, Omicron Delta Kappa. Methodist. Club: Hermitage Country (pres. 1970-74). Home: Richmond Va. Died July 7, 1994.

HAMILTON, SIR (CHARLES) DENIS, newspaper editor-in-chief; b. South Shields, Eng., Dec. 6, 1918; s. Charles and Helena Hamilton; m. Olive Wanless, Dec. 9, 1939; children: Michael, Nigel, Adrian, John. Grad., Middlesbrough High Sch., Eng.; DLitt (hon.), U. Southampton, 1975, City U., 1977; DCL (hon.), U. Newcastle-upon-Tyne, 1979. With editorial staff Evening Gazette, Middlesbrough, 1937-38; with editorial staff Evening Chronicle, Newcastle, Eng., 1938-39, editorial asst. to Viscount Kemsley, 1946-50; editorial dir. Kemsley (now Thompson) Newspapers, 1950-67, editor Sunday Times, 1961-67; editor-in-chief Times Newspapers Ltd., 1967-81, chief exec., 1967-70, chmn., 1971-80; chmn. Times Newspapers Holdings, 1980-81; chmn. Reuters Ltd., 1979-85; chmn. Brit. Com. Internat. Press Inst., 1972-78, pres., 1978-83; pres. Commonwealth Press Union, 1981-83; chmn. Brit. Mus. Pubs. Ltd.; past bd. dirs. Std. Chartered Bank, Evening Gazette Ltd., Newcastle Chronicle and Journal Ltd. Internat. Thomson Orgn. plc. Contbr. articles to jours. Bd. dirs. Brit. Library, 1975-87, IBA, 1981-84; trustee Brit. Mus., 1969—, Henry Moore Found., 1980—, Visnews, 1981-85; gov. Brit. Inst. Florence, 1974—; v.p. mem. exec. com. Great Britain-China Ctr., 1986—; joint sponsor exhibitions Tutankhamun, 1972, China, 1973, U.S. Bicentennial, 1976, Maritime Mus., 1976, Gold of Eldorado, 1978, Vikings, 1980. Served to lt. col. Brit. Army, 1939-45. Decorated Knight, 1976, Order of Merit Grande Officiale (Italy), 1976. Mem. Commonwealth Press Union (pres. 1981-83), Newspaper Publishers' Assn. (mem. council 1950-80, press council 1959-81), Nat. Council for the Tng. of Journalists (chmn. 1957). Clubs: Garrick, Royal Automobile, Grillions. Home: London Eng. Died Apr. 7, 1988.

HAMILTON, JOSEPH HENRY MICHAEL, JR., television producer; b. Los Angeles, Jan. 6, 1929; s. Joseph Henry Michael and Marie (Sullivan) H.; m. Carol Burnett, May 4, 1963 (div.); children: Kathleen, Dana, Joseph Henry Michael III, Jeffrey, Judith, John, Jennifer, Nancy, Carrie, Jody, Erin Kate. Grad., Los Angeles Conservatory Music and Arts, 1951. Musician and singer, 1948-51, engaged as a writer and assoc. TV producer, 1951-57, TV producer, 1957—; prin. producers include: Carol Burnett & Co, Mama's Family, 1982-84, 87. Recipient Emmy awards. Roman Catholic. Clubs: Bel Air Country; Westchester Country (Rye, N.Y.). Home: Los Angeles Calif. Died June 9, 1991.

HAMILTON, MARY LUCIA KERR, retired banker, lawyer; b. Denver, Aug. 3, 1926; d. Henry Hamilton and Helen (Clancy) Kerr; m. William A. Hamilton, June 15, 1957 (dec. Feb. 1989); children: Lucia M., Henry K., John A., Peter D. BS, Simmons Coll., Boston, 1948; JD, U. Toledo, 1958. Bar: Ohio 1958, U.S. Dist. Ct. (no. dist.) Ohio 1959. Sec. United Airlines, Toledo, 1953-55; exec. dir. Toledo Bar Assn., 1955-58; staff atty. Legal Aid Soc., Toledo, 1958-60; assoc. Cobourn, Yager, Smith & Beck, Toledo, 1960-69; trust officer, v.p. Toledo Trust Co., 1969-79; v.p., trust officer First Nat. Bank Toledo, 1979-89, Fifth Third Bank Toledo, N.A. (formerly First Nat. Bank Toledo), 1989-91; retired 1991. Bd. dirs. United Way of Toledo, 1987-90, Sight Ctr., 1987-88; trustee Ohio Bar Found., 1982-87; treas. Maumee Valley Coun. Girl Scouts U.S., 1991-93; bd. dirs. Sunset House, 1992-95. Fellow Ohio Bar Assn. (exec. com. 1987-90), ABA (ho. of dels. 1990-94); mem. Toledo Bar Assn. (pres. 1977-78), Toledo Auto Club (bd. dirs. 1982-95, vice chmn. bd. 1991-92, chmn. 1992-94), Zonta (pres. Toledo club 1986-87), Toledo Club. Roman Catholic. Home: Toledo Ohio Died Nov. 19, 1995.

HAMLIN, MADGE TEMPERANCE SILLS, former gifted education educator; b. Newport News, Va., Sept. 27, 1897; d. James Everett and Fannie Montgomery (Smith) Sills; B.S., Greensboro Coll., 1920; M.A. in History, Columbia U., 1928; m. Paul Mahlon Hamlin, Feb. 18, 1927 (dec. Aug. 1968); 1 dau., Elizabeth Sills Hamlin Hill. Tchr. of English, Kobe, Japan and McIyeire Sch., Shanghai, China, 1921-22; lectr. Nat. Bd. YWCA, various U.S. colls., 1923-25; tchr. gifted children, Garden City, N.Y., 1928-30, Horace Mann Sch. Girls, N.Y.C., 1930-33; founder, benefactor, dir. Hamlin Country Day Sch. for Brilliant Children, Fair Lawn, N.J., 1933-66; organizer, dir. Orchard Sch. for Slow Learning Students, Fair Lawn, 1943-59. Mem. AAUW, DAR, Jamestown Soc., Nat. Soc. Colonial Dames in State N.J. Republican. Congregationalist. Clubs: Montclair Women's; Garden (Montclair and Rossmoor); Women's Nat. Rep. (N.Y.C.). Contbr. articles on travel and edn. to mags. and newspapers; lectr. on influence of

Western civilization on Oriental culture, changing role of women. Deceased. Home: Jamesburg N.J.

HAMNER, HOMER HOWELL, economist; b. Lamont, Okla., Oct. 22, 1915; s. Homer Hill and Myrtle Susan (Edwards) H.; m. Winnie Elvyn Heafner, May 8, 1943 (dec. Aug. 1946); 1 child, Jean Lee (Mrs. Richard L. Nicholson); m. Marjorie Lucille Dittus, Nov. 24, 1947; 1 child, Elaine (Mrs. Alan M. Yard). A.A., Glendale Coll., 1936; A.B., U. So. Calif.; A.B. (Gen. Achievement scholarship 1936-37), 1938, J.D., 1941, A.M., 1947, Ph.D., 1949. Fellow and teaching asst., dept. econs. U. So. Calif., 1945-49; prof. and chmn. dept. econs. Baylor U., 1949-55; editor research com. Baylor Bus. Studies, 1949-55, lectr. summer workshop, 1954; prof., chmn. dept. bus. adminstrn. and cons. U. Puget Sound, Tacoma, Wash., 1955-58; dir. sch. bus. adminstr. and econs. U. Puget Sound, 1959-63, Edward L. Blaine chair econ. history, 1963-94; also occasional lectr. Roman Forums, Ltd., Los Angeles, 1936-40; lectr. Am. Inst. Banking, 1949-50; lectr. Southwest Wholesale Credit Assn., 1949, James Connally AFB, 1950; cons. State of Wash. tax adv. council, 1957-58, State of Wash. Expenditures Adv. Council, 1960. Author: Population Change in Metropolitan Waco, 1950; reviewer, contbr. to Jour. of Finance. Served with U.S. Army, 1941-44. Fellow Found. Econ. Edn., Chgo., Inst. on Freedom, Claremont Men's Coll.; mem. AAUP, Am. Econ. Assn., Southwest Social Sci. Assn. (Tex. chmn. membership com.), Nat. Tax Assn., Am. Finance Assn., Am. Acad. Polit. and Soc. Sci., Order of Artus, Waco McLennan County Bar Assn. (hon.), Phi Beta Kappa, Phi Kappa Phi, Omicron Delta Gamma, Delta Theta Phi, Phi Rho Pi (degree highest achievement 1936). Methodist. Home: Tacoma Wash. Died Jan. 9, 1994.

HAMPTON, LUCILE PAQUIN SMITH (MRS. LAWRENCE CHARLES HAMPTON), artist, educator; b. Dubuque, Iowa, Jan. 7, 1904; d. Albert Hugo and Lola (Lichtenberger) Smith; m. Lawrence Charles Hampton, Dec. 16, 1930 (dec. 1960); children: Lawrence Charles Jr., Nancy Jeanne (Mrs. Merle Willis Asper Jr.), Elizabeth Mary (Mrs. John Erskine). Diploma, Chgo. Acad. Fine Arts, 1923; postgrad., Pasadena (Calif.) City Coll., 1947-48, 64, 67-68, UCLA, 1965-66; BA in Art, Calif. State U., Los Angeles, 1973. Cert. tchr., Calif. Artist advt. dept. Union Lithographing Co., Little Rock, 1923-24; art dir. advt. dept. M. Rich & Bros. Co., Atlanta, 1924-25; head fashion layout artist advt. dept. May Co., Los Angeles, 1925-29; sr. artist advt. dept. David Jones, Ltd., Sydney, Australia, 1929-30; cover designer Women's Budget Mag., Sydney, Australia, 1929-30; fashion illustrator Home Mag., Sydney, 1930; free-lance artist Broadway Dept. Stores and J.W. Robinson & Co. Dept. Stores, Los Angeles, 1930-35; fashion illustrator Robinson Accents Mag., Los Angeles, 1935; freelance artist Lucile Hampton Greeting Cards, San Marino, Calif., 1960-93; head dept. art, tchr. of art essentials and history of art Anoakia Sch. Girls, Arcadia, Calif., 1963-66; substitute tchr. San Marino Unified Sch. Dist., 1973-93. Troop leader Girl Scouts U.S., San Marino, 1948-56, active Girl Scout Leaders' Club, San Marino, 1948-56, pres., 1950-51; active San Marino PTA, 1941-61, exec. bd., 1944-46; mem. San Marino Rep. Women's Club Federated, Opera Guild L.A.; bd. dirs. Euterpe Opera Reading, L.A., 1956-59; guild leader San Marino Community Ch. women. Mem. AAUW (bd. dirs Newport Beach-Costa Mesa br. 1982-83), DAR (regent San Marino chpt. 1960-61), Children Am. Revolution (sr. advisor, sr. pres. El Molino Viejo chpt. 1958-64, social dir. Cotillion Ball 1958-59), PEO (chpt. MK pres. 1955-56), Women's Athletic Club, Pacific Coast Club, San Marino Women's Club, Friday Morning Jrs. Club, Kappa Pi. Republican. Presbyterian. Home: Costa Mesa Calif. Died Dec. 22, 1993; buried Hollywood Meml. Pk. Cemetery, Hollywood, Calif.

HANAI, MASAYA, motor vehicle manufacturing company executive; b. Aug. 1, 1912; m. Motoko Hanai. Ed. Kobe U. Commerce, 1938. Former chmn. Toyota Motor Corp., Aichi, Japan, now sr. adviser; dir. Thailand Motor Co., Ltd. Decorated Medal of Honor with Blue Ribbon. Home: Aichi Japan

HANCOCK, LANGLEY GEORGE, mining and diversified business executive; b. Perth, Australia, June 10, 1909; s. George and Lilian Hancock; m. Hope Margaret Nicholas, Aug. 4, 1947 (dec.); 1 child, Georgina Hope Rinehart. Ed. Hale Sch., Perth; D.Bus.Administrn. (hon.), Hillsdale (Mich.) Coll., 1983. Asst. mgr., then mgr. Mulga Downs Sheep Sta., Western Australia, 1927-34; began prospecting for minerals, 1927, discovered asbestos in Wittenoom Gorge, developed industry, 1936, entered partnership (with E.A. Wright), then sold half of equity to company that became Australian Blue Asbestos Ltd., 1943, asst. mgr. co., 1943-48; became ptnr. (with Wright and Walters) Whim Creek Copper, Mons Cupri Copper, Nunyerry Creek White Asbestos, 1950; made 1st maj. discovery of iron ore in Pilbara, Western Australia, 1952, subsequently discovered over 600 major iron ore deposits; entered into joint iron ore devel. agreement with Texasgulf Inc., 1972; founder Nat. Miner Newspaper, also Westralian Secession Movement, 1974; life governing dir. Hancock Prospecting Pty. Ltd.; dir. Hancock Pilbara Pty. Ltd., Hancock (Nickel) Pty. Ltd., Georgina Hancock (1965) Pty. Ltd., Pilbara Exploration N.L., Ragged Hills Pty. Ltd., Wright Pros-

pecting Pty. Ltd. Author: Wake up Australia, 1979. Contbr. articles on free enterprise to jours. and newspapers. Mem. internat. bd. dirs. Am. U., Washington. Mem. Explorers Club. Died Mar. 27, 1992. Home West Perth Australia

HANDVILLE, ROBERT TOMPKINS, artist, illustrator; b. Paterson, N.J., Mar. 23, 1924; s. Robert Ra_ and Olive (Tompkins) H.; m. Marylee Pollock, Nov. 27 1948; children: Robert C., David C. Cert., Pratt Inst Bklyn., 1948; student, Bklyn. Mus. Art Sch., 1960-64. Asst. art dir. Ruthrauff & Ryan, N.Y.C., 1946-48; artis Kudner Advt. Agy., N.Y.C., 1948-50, Charles E Cooper Studios, N.Y.C., 1950-53; free lance artis Pleasantville, N.Y., 1953-93; mem. faculty Fashion Inst Tech., N.Y.C., 1978-93; mem. Joint Ethics Com N.Y.C., 1983-93; chmn. Artists in the Parks Program Nat. Park Service, Washinton, 1968-70. Designer: U.S Commemorative postal stamps: Yellowstone Nat. Park 1972. Chmn. Pleasantville Community Scholarshi Fund, 1960-68; mem. United Fund Drive, Pleasantville 1960-62. Served with USAF, 1942-46, 50-51. Recipien Ranger Fund Purchase prize Am. Watercolor Soc 1960; recipient Anonymous prize Audubon Artists 1962, Am. Can. award 21st New Eng. Exhbn., 1977 Mario Cooper award Am. Watercolor Soc., 1983. Men Nat. Acad. Design (Sprayer prize 1982), Soc. Illustrator (treas. 1960-64), welfare chmn. 1972-93), An Watercolor Soc. (dir. 1973-75 Pleissner award), Prat Inst. Alumni Soc. (dir. 1970-73). Presbyterian. Home North Eastham Mass. Died Feb. 22, 1993.

HANKE, LEWIS ULYSSES, Latin American histor educator, writer; b. Oregon City, Oreg., Jan. 2, 1905; William U. and Mamie E. (Stevenson) H.; m. Ka_ Gilbert, Aug. 12, 1926; children: Jonathan, Peter, Susar Joanne. B.S., Northwestern U., 1924, M.A., 192_ Ph.D., Harvard U., 1936; Ph.D. (hon.), U. Bahia, Braz 1959, U. Tomas Frias, Potosí, Bolivia, 1965, U. Sevilla Spain, 1966. Instr. history U. Hawaii, Honolulu, 1926 27; instr. history Harvard U., Cambridge, Mass., 1934 39; adj. prof. Am. U. Beirut, 1927-30; staff Library of Congress, Washington, 1939-51, Inst. Latin Am Studies, 1951-58; prof. Latin Am. history U. Tex Austin, 1951-61, Columbia U., N.Y.C., 1961-67, U. Calif., Irvine, 1967-69; Clarence and Helen Haring pro Latin Am. history U. Mass., Amherst, 1969-75; pro emeritus U. Mass., 1975-93; Carnegie lectr., Brazi 1938; James W. Richard lectr. U. Va., 1948; Phi Bet Kappa Soc. vis. lectr., 1961; mem. U.S. nat. cor UNESCO, 1952-54. Author: The First Social Exper ments in America: A Study in the Development of Spanish Indian Policy in the Sixteenth Century, 193_ The Political Theories of Bartolomé de las Casas, 1935 Sixteenth-Century Documents on the Rights of Spain the Indies and the Philippines, 1943, The Spanis Struggle for Justice in the Conquest of America, 194 Bartolomé de las Casas: An Interpretation of His Lif and Writings, 1951, Bartolomé de las Casas: Bookma Scholar, and Propagandist, 1952, Bartolomé de la Casas, Historian: An Essay in Spanish Historiograph 1952, The Imperial City of Potosí: An Unwritte Chapter in the History of Spanish America, 1956, Aris totle and the American Indians: A Study of Rac Prejudice in the Modern World (Tex. Inst. Letter award 1960), 1959, Modern Latin America: Continent Ferment, Vol. I: Mexico and the Caribbean, Vol. II South America, 1959, rev. edit., 1967, Do the Americar Have a Common History?: A Critique of the Bolto Theory, 1964, Bartolomé Arzáns de Orsua y Vela's Hi tory of Potosí, 1965, Contemporary Latin America: Short History; Text and Readings, 1968, Studies on La Casas and on the Struggle for Justice in the Conquest America, 1968, All Mankind is One, 1974, Guide to th Study of United States History Outside the U.S., 194_ 80, 5 vols., 1985; (with Manuel Gimenez Fernande Bartolomé de las Casas, 1474-1566: Bibliography of th Writings on the Life and the Writings of Bartolomé d las Casas, Fondo Histórico y Bibliográfico José Toribi Medina (Santiago de Chile), 1954; editor: Relacione Histórico-Literarias de la América Meridional: Relaci General de la Villa Imperial de Potosí, 1959, Reading in Latin American History: Selected Articles from th Hispanic American Historical Review, Vol. I: To 181 Vol. II: Since 1810, 1966; (with others) Handbook Latin American Studies, 1935-39; Historia de las Indi (History of the Indies), 3 vols., 1951, 2d. edit., 196 (with Gunnar Mendoza) Historia de la Villa Imperial Potosí (History of Potosí), 3 vols., 1965; (with Cels Rodriguez) Los Virreyes Españoles en América duran el Gobierno de la Casa de Austria, 12 vols., 1976-8 Guía de las Fuentes en el Archivo General de Indi para el Estudio de la Administracíon Virreinal Españo de México y en el Peru, 1535-1700, 3 vols., 1977; (wi Gunnar Mendoza and Celso Rodríguez) Guía de l Fuentes en Hispanoamérica para el Estudio de la A ministración Virreinal Española en México y en el Per 1980; compiler: History of Latin American Civilizatio Sources and Interpretations, Vol. I: The Colonial E perience, Vol. II: The Modern Age, 1967, 2d. edit., 19 (abridged edit. Latin America: A Historical reade 1974); contbr. articles to profl. jours. Recipient Ord of the Condor of the Andes, Bolivia, 1965; named ho citizen Municipality of Potosí, Bolivia, 1965; fellow Sc Sci. Research Council, 1937-38; A.S.W. Rosenbac fellow, 1951; grantee Soc. Sci. Research Council, 196 awarded Eloy Antonio de Nebrija-V Centenario prize the University of Salamanca, Spain, 1992. Mem. A ist. Assn. (pres. 1974, Albert Beveridge Meml. fellow)47), Hispanic Soc. Am. (trustee 1961-67), Real cademia de la Historia, Latin Am. Studies Assn. Kalmen Silvert award 1989). Home: Amherst Mass. ied Mar. 26, 1993; interred Amherst, M.A.

ANNAY, N(ORMAN) BRUCE, chemist, industrial search and business consultant; b. Mt. Vernon, Wash., eb. 9, 1921; s. Norman Bond and Winnie (Evans) H.; . Joan Anderson, May 27, 1943; children: Robin, rooke. BA, Swarthmore Coll., 1942, DSc (hon.), 1979; IS, Princeton U., 1943, PhD, 1944; PhD (hon.), Tel viv U., 1978; DSc (hon.), Poly. Inst. N.Y., 1981. With ell Telephone Labs., Murray Hill, N.J., 1944-82; exec. r. materials research div. Bell Telephone Labs., 1967- 3, v.p. research and patents, 1973-82, ret., 1982; rschr. 1 dipole moments and molecular structure, thermionic nission, mass spectroscopy, analysis of solids, solid ate chemistry, semiconductors, superconductors; egents' prof. UCLA, 1976, U. Calif., San Diego, 1979; ons. Alexander von Humboldt Found.; bd. dirs. enum Pub. Co., Gen. Signal Corp., Rohm and Haas o., Alex Brown Cash Res. Fund, Tax-Free Investments rust, Nine Flag Investors Funds. Author: Solid State hemistry, 1967, also articles; editor: Semiconductors,)59, Treatise on Solid State Chemistry, 1974. ecipient Acheson medal, 1976; Perkin medal, 1983; erkeley citation, 1979; Gold medal Am. Inst. Chemists,)86. mem. Nat. Acad. Engring. (past fgn. sec.), Nat. cad. Scis., Am. Acad. Arts and Scis., Mexican Nat. cad. Engring., Electrochem. Soc. (past pres.), Indsl. esearch Inst. (past pres., medal 1982), Dirs. of Indsl. esearch (past chmn.). Home: Port Ludlow Wash. ied June 2, 1996.

ANSEN, MORRIS HOWARD, statistician, former overnment official; b. Thermopolis, Wyo., Dec. 15,)10; s. Hans C. and Maud Ellen (Omstead) H.; m. Mildred R. Latham, Aug. 31, 1930 (dec. Feb. 16, 1983); nildren—Evelyn Maxine, Morris Howard, James Hans, ristine Ellen; m. Eleonore Lamb, Oct. 21, 1986. B.S., . Wyo., 1934; M.A., Am. U., 1940; LL.D., U. Wyo.,)59. Statistician Wyo. Relief Adminstrn., 1934; statis- cian U.S. Bur. of Census, Washington, 1935-43, chief atis. rsch. div., 1944-49, statis. asst. dir., 1949-51, asst. r. statis. standards, 1951-61, assoc. dir. research and evel., 1961-68; sr. v.p. Westat, Inc., 1968-86, chmn. bd. rs., 1986—; instr. statistics grad. sch. Dept. Agr.,)45-50; formerly statis. cons. Nat. Analysts, Inc. Co- uthor: Sample Survey Methods and Theory, 2 vols,)53; Contbr. articles to statis. jours. Recipient Rock- eller Pub. Service award, 1962. Fellow Am. Statis. ssn. (pres. 1960), Royal Statis. Soc. (hon.), AAAS, ist. Math. Statistics (pres. 1953); mem. Internat. Statis. ist. (hon. mem.), Population Assn. Am., Nat. Acad. ci. (com. nat. statistics 1972-76), Internat. Assn. Survey tatisticians (pres. 1973-77), Sigma Xi, Alpha Tau mega, Phi Kappa Phi. Home: Rockville Md. Dec. ct. 9, 1990.

IANSEN, PER KRISTIAN, management consultant; Oslo, Feb. 17, 1932; s. Kristian and Gudrun Marie Nordal) H.; m. Charlotte Berta Kretzschmar, July 18,)64; children: Karin, Christian, Elisabeth. BSCE, tanford U., 1955, MSCE, 1956. Engr., estimator echtel Corp., San Francisco, 1957-67, supt., 1967-72; onstrn. mgr. Bechtel Power Corp., San Francisco,)72-78; mgr. of constrn. Bechtel Power Corp., Ann rbor, Mich., 1978-84; v.p. Bechtel Constrn., Inc., aithersburg, Md., 1984-86; pres. CPH Assocs., Inc., aithersburg, 1987—; mem. industry adv. com. to sch. f constrn. engring. and mgmt. Purdue U., Lafayette, nd., 1982-84. Served as lt. C.E., 1950-53. Mem. SCE, Norwegian Am. C. of C., Constrn. Mgmt. Assn. m., San Francisco Engrs., Montgomery County C. of . Lutheran. Home: Gaithersburg Md.

IANSON, DUANE ELWOOD, sculptor; b. Alexan- ria, Minn., Jan. 17, 1925; s. Dewey O. and Agnes N. Nelson) H.; m. Janice Roche, Aug. 19, 1950; children: raig Curtis, Paul Duane, Karen Liane; m. Wesla Host, une 15, 1968; children: Maja, Duane Elwood. Student, uther Coll., 1943-44, U. Wash., 1944-45; BA, Ma- alester Coll., 1946; MFA, Cranbrook Acad. Art, 1951; HL, Nova U., 1979, LHD, 1985; DFA, Luther Coll., ecorah, Iowa, 1992, Macalester Coll., 1995. Tchr. igh schs. Idaho, 1946-47, Iowa, 1949-50, Conn., 1951- 3; Tchr. high schs. U.S. Army Dependent Schs., ermany, 1953-60, Atlanta, 1960-62; instr. art glethorpe U., 1962-65; asst. prof. Miami-Dade Jr. oll., 1965-69; sculptor associated O.K. Harris Gallery, .Y.C., 1969-90, Marisa del Re Gallery, N.Y.C., 1994- 6. One-man shows include, Würtembergischer unstverein, Stuttgart Germany, 1974, Neue Galerie, achen, Germany, 1974, Akademie der Künste, Berlin,)75, Humleback, Denmark, Lousiana Mus., 1975, dwin A. Ulrich Mus. Art, Wichita, Kans., 1976, U. lebr. Art Galleries, Lincoln, 1976, Des Moines Art enter, Univ. Art Mus. U. Calif.-Berkeley, Portland Art Mus., Oreg., William Rockhill Nelson Gallery, Atkins lus. of Fine Arts, both in Kansas City, Mo., Colo. Fine rts Center, Colorado Springs, Va. Mus. Fine Arts, lichmond, Corcoran Gallery of Art, Washington, all)77, Whitney Mus. Am. Art, N.Y.C., 1978, Jack- onville Art Mus., Fla., 1980, Lowe Art Mus., Miami, la., 1981, Lock Haven Art Mus., Orlando, Fla., 1981, Norton Gallery, Palm Beach, Fla., 1981, O.K. Harris Vorks of Art, N.Y.C., Edwin A. Ulrich Mus. Art, Wichita State U., Kans., travelling exhbn., Isetan Mus. Art, Tokyo, Daimuru Mus., Osaka, Japan, Nagoya City Mus., Japan, Cranbrook Acad. Art, Bloomfield Hills, Mich., Macalester Coll. Art Gallery, St. Paul, Milles-garden, Stockholm, 1986, Auckland (New Zealand) Art Gallery, 1988, City Art Gallery, Wellington, New Zealand, 1989, McDougall Art Gallery, Christchurch, New Zealand, 1989, Dunedin (New Zealand) Pub. Art Gallery, 1989, Waikato Mus. Art and History, Hamilton, New Zealand, 1989, World Design Expn., Nagoya, Japan, 1989, Ft. Lauderdale (Fla.) Mus. Art, 1988, Tampa (Fla.) Mus. Art, 1989, Ctr. for Arts, Vero Beach, Fla., 1989, The Contemporary Mus., Honolulu, 1989, Cranbrook Acad. Art Mus., Bloomfield Hills, Mich., 1990, Philbrook Art Ctr., Tulsa, 1990, Pa. Acad. Fine Arts, Phila., 1990, Brown U. Art Mus., Providence, 1990, Kunsthalle Tubingen, Germany, 1990, Joseph Haubrich, Kunsthalle, Cologne, Germany, 1991, Kunstverein, Hamburg, Germany, 1991, Haus am Waldsee, Berlin, 1991, Neue Gallery Wolfgang Gurlih Mus., Linz, Austria, 1992, Kunsthausverein, Vienna, 1992, Montreal Mus. Fine Arts, 1994, Ft. Worth Art Mus., 1994, Daimuru Mus. Art, Tokyo, 1995, Genichiro-Inokuma Mus. Contemporary Art, 1995, Kagawa and Kintetsu Mus. Art, Osaka, 1995, Marisa del Re Gallery, 1995, Norton Gallery Art, Palm Beach, Fla., 1995. Grantee Ella Lyman Trust, 1963, D.A.A.D. grantee Berlin, 1974; recipient Blair award Art Inst. Chgo., 1974, Fla. prize N.Y. Times, 1985; named Ambassador of Arts, State of Fla., 1983; Duane Hanson Day proclaimed by Broward County, Fla., 1987; named to Fla. Hall of Fame, 1992. Home: Fort Lauderdale Fla. Died Jan. 6, 1995.

HANSON, JOHN KENDRICK, recreational vehicle manufacturing company executive; b. 1913. AA, Waldorf Coll., 1932; BS, U. Minn., 1934; LLD (hon.), Waldorf Coll., 1995. Owner Hanson Furniture Co., 1937-62, Hanson Funeral Home, 1937-62; founder Winnebago Industries Inc., Forest City, Iowa, 1958-96, CEO, 1959-71, 79-81, 90-93, vice chmn. bd. dirs., 1975-79, chmn. bd. dirs., 1959-75, 79-96. Recipient Small Businessman of Yr. award State of Iowa, 1965, Iowa Bus. Hall of Fame award, 1983, Disting. Entrepreneur award Babson Coll., 1984, Disting. Achievment award Recreation Vehicle Industry Assn., 1988, People of Vision award Iowa Soc. to Prevent Blindness, 1984; named to Recreational Vehicle/Motor Home Hall of Fame, 1983, Scandinavian-Am. Hall of Fame, 1990; honored as industry pioneer RYDA, 1995. Home: Forest City Iowa Died June 27, 1996.

HANSON, WILLIAM BERT, physics educator, science administrator; b. Warroad, Minn., Dec. 30, 1923; s. Bert Hanson and Viola Mae Carlquist; m. Wenonah Ann Dahlquist, Mar. 14, 1946 (dec.); children: Bryan, Craig, David, Karen; m. Annelies Ruth Hanlein, Jan. 5, 1996. BAChemE, U. Minn., 1944, MS in Physics, 1949; PhD in Physics, George Washington U., 1954. Rsch. physicist Nat. Bur. Standards, Washington, 1949-54, Boulder, Colo., 1954-56; rsch. scientist Lockheed Missiles and Space Co., Palo Alto, Calif., 1956-62; prof. S.W. Ctr. for Advanced Studies, Dallas, 1962-69, U. Tex. at Dallas, Richardson, 1969-94. Contbr. over 150 articles to sci. jours. Mem. nat. bd. Planned Parenthood, 1970. Lt. USN, 1944-46. Fellow Am. Geophys. Union (John Adam Fleming medal 1985); mem. European Geophys. Union, Internat. Acad. Astronautics. Home: Dallas Tex. Died Sept. 11, 1994.

HANSON, WILLIAM COOK, judge; b. Jefferson, Iowa, May 14, 1909; s. Willis and Pearl Ann (Cook) H.; m. M(arietta) Ruth Hastings, Sept. 18, 1938; children: James W., Thomas D., Jay D., Cynthia G., R. Elaine, Robert B. BA, State U. Iowa, 1933, JD, 1935. Ba: Iowa 1935, U.S. Dist. Ct. Iowa 1935. Pvt. practice law Jefferson, 1935-55; county atty. Greene County, Jefferson, 1939-46; dist. judge 16th Jud. Dist. of Iowa, 1955-62; dist. judge U.S. Dist. Ct. (no. and so. dists.) Iowa, Des Moines, 1962-91, sr. U.S. dist. judge, 1991-95; chief judge U.S. Dist. Ct. (so. dist.) Iowa, 1971-75; mem. Jud. Conf. Com. on Criminal Law, 1975-81. Pres. Jefferson C. of C., 1936. Recipient Bell Tower award Bell Tower Festival Com., 1983; named to Jefferson Alumni Hall of Fame, Alumni Com., 1973. Mem. ABA, Iowa State Bar Assn., Fed. Bar Assn., Greene County Bar Assn., Rotary (Paul Harris fellow 1986), Shriners, Order of Coif. Republican. Methodist. Home: Jefferson Iowa Died June 6, 1995.

HAPALA, MILAN ERNEST, government educator; b. Hranice, Czechoslovakia, Sept. 19, 1919; came to U.S., 1938, naturalized, 1943; s. Vladimir and Marie (Mlcochova) H.; m. M. Adelaide Hamilton, Sept. 6, 1947; children: Milan Ernest Jr., Mary Elizabeth. A.B., Beloit Coll., 1940; A.M., Nebr. U., 1941; Ph.D. in Polit. Sci, Duke, 1956. Mem. faculty Sweet Briar Coll., 1947-90, asso. prof. govt., chmn. div. social studies, 1956-60, 70-73, prof. govt., 1960-92, Carter Glass prof., 1962-90, Carter Glass prof. emeritus, 1990-92, chmn. dept., 1952-63, 65-68, 72-81, dir. Asian studies, 1980-90; instr. Lynchburg (Va.) br. Am. Inst. Banking, 1955-59; vis. lectr. Lynchburg Coll., 1951; vis. prof. U. Va., 1967-68, Randolph-Macon Woman's Coll., 1972; dir. faculty seminar in India U.S. Office Edn., summer 1970; research assoc. Russian and East European Ctr., U. Ill., 1982-83. Author articles, book revs. Chmn. Amherst County Bicentennial Commn. Served with USAAF, 1942-45. Fgn. lang. (Hindi-Urdu) fellow Nat. Def. Fgn. Lang. U. Pa., 1964-65. Mem. Am. Polit. Sci. Assn., Assn. Asian Studies, Assn. Internat. Studies, Am. Assn. Advancement Slavic Studies, AAUP, Czechoslovakian Soc. Arts and Scis., Va. Soc. Sci. (mem. bd. 1966-69), U.S. Assn. for Club of Rome, Phi Beta Kappa. Lodge: Rotary (pres. Amherst 1955). Home: Amherst Va. Died June 20, 1992.

HARBISON, WILLIAM JAMES, lawyer, retired state supreme court justice; b. Columbia, Tenn., Sept. 11, 1923; s. William Joshua and Eunice Elizabeth (Kinzer) H.; m. Mary Elizabeth Coleman, June 14, 1952; children: William Leslie, Mary Alice. Student, The Citadel, 1943-44; B.A., Vanderbilt U., 1947, J.D., 1950. Bar: Tenn. 1950. Spl. justice Tenn. Supreme Ct., Nashville, 1966-67, justice, 1974-90, chief justice, 1980-82, 87-89, pvt. practice, 1950-74, 90—; adj. prof. law Vanderbilt Law Sch., Nashville, 1950—; chmn. civil rules com. Tenn. Supreme Ct., 1965-74. Editor-in-chief: Vanderbilt Law Review, 1949-50. Mem. Metro Nashville Bd. Edn., 1970-74. Served with AUS, 1943-46. Mem. ABA, Tenn. Bar Assn., Nashville Bar Assn. (pres. 1970-71), Order of Coif, Phi Beta Kappa, Rotary, Cedar Creek Club, Cumberland Club. Democrat. Methodist. Home: Nashville Tenn. Died Nov. 20, 1993.

HARDING, VICTOR MATHEWS, lawyer; b. Chgo., July 23, 1908; s. Victor Mathews and Mary M. (Boak) H.; m. Julia Burley, May 25, 1940; children: Julia Harding Weidman, Mary Elizabeth Harding Craft, Katherine DeBlois Harding Bohannon, Victor Clark, Nancy Jane Harding Winter, Burley. A.B. cum laude, Harvard U., 1931, LL.B., 1935; Harvard scholar, Emmanuel Coll., Cambridge U., 1931-32. Bar: Ill. 1935, Wis. 1944. Practiced in Chgo., 1935-42, Milw., 1944-94; with firm Bell, Boyd & Marshall, 1935-42; trial atty. for solicitor U.S. Dept. Labor, 1942-44; mem. firm Whyte, Hirschboeck, S.C., 1944-94; Mem. bd. appeals and bd. health, Village of River Hills, 1948-65; mem. sch. bd. Nicolet High Sch., 1952-57, Mapledale Elem. Sch., 1950-56; mem. com. ct. reorgn. Milwaukee County Bd. Suprs., 1959-60, Joint Com. Bench and Bar to revise rules Circuit Ct. Milwaukee County, 1951-53; Trustee Milw. U. Sch., 1955-63. Mem. ABA, Fed., Wis., Milw. bar assns., Am. Judicature Soc., Legal Club Chgo. Clubs: Town, Wis, Harvard. Home: Milwaukee Wis. Died Nov. 16, 1994.

HARDING, WALTER, retired American literature educator, writer; b. Bridgewater, Mass., Apr. 20, 1917; s. Roy Valentine and Mary Alice (MacDonald) H.; m. Marjorie Brook, June 7, 1947; children: David, Allen, Lawrence, Susan. BS in Edn., Bridgewater (Mass.) State Coll., 1939; MA, U. N.C., 1947; PhD, Rutgers U., 1950; DLitt, SUNY, 1984; DHL, St. Bonaventure, 1994. Instr. Rutgers U., 1947-51; asst. prof. U. Va., 1951-56; from assoc. prof. to disting prof. Am. lit. SUNY-Geneseo, 1956-82, disting. prof. emeritus, 1983-96; dir. SUNY Research Found., 1970-84; lectr. Dept. of State Am. Specialists Program, 1964, 67; bd. dir. Nat. Endowment Humanities seminars, 1976, 77, 79, 83, 84, 85. Author: Days of Henry Thoreau, 1965, The Thoreau Handbook, 1959; editor: (with others) The Thoreau Correspondence, 1958, Variorum Walden, 1963; editor-in-chief: Writings of Thoreau, 1965-73. Fellow Am. Coun. Learned Socs., 1965. Mem. MLA, Thoreau Soc. (pres. 1963, sec. 1941-91, founding sec. 1991-96). Home: Geneseo N.Y. Died Apr. 10, 1996.

HARDY, JEROME SPILMAN, financial executive; b. Manhattan, Kans., Jan. 2, 1918; s. Cleo Clinton and Irene (Johnson) H.; m. Betty St. Clair, Dec. 13, 1946; children: Martha, James, Douglas, Gordon, Quentin. B.S., U. Md., 1939. Mem. hwy. edn. bd. Automotive Safety Found., 1939-43; partner Harris & Hardy (S.A., pub. relations firm), 1946; exec. Doubleday & Co., N.Y.C., 1947-59; v.p. for advt. Doubleday & Co., 1956-59; founder, pub. Time/Life Books, N.Y.C., 1959-64; also v.p. corp.; pub. Life mag., 1964-70; exec. v.p. Dreyfus Corp., 1970, pres., 1970-80; bd. dirs. Ency. Brit., H.S. Stuttman, Essex Life Co. Inc.; chmn. Investment Co. Inst., 1976-78. 1st vice chmn. Salk Inst. Served from pvt. to 1st lt. USAAF, 1943-46. Clubs: University, Sky (N.Y.C.); Augusta Nat. Golf, Pine Valley Golf, Country of New Canaan. Home: New Canaan Conn. Died Dec. 31, 1992.

HARDY, MAURICE G., medical and industrial equipment manufacturing company executive; b. 1931. Dir. European ops. Pall Corp., 1962-72, v.p. European ops., 1972-75; exec. v.p. Pall Corp., Glen Cove, N.Y., 1975-85, pres., COO, 1985-89, pres., CEO, 1989-94, also bd. dirs. Home: Glen Cove N.Y. Died July 10, 1994.

HARE, DAPHNE KEAN, medical association director, educator; b. Palmerton, Pa., Jan. 19, 1937; d. Clare Hibberd and Lucile (Lawrence) Kean; m. Peter Hewitt Hare, May 30, 1959; children: Clare Kean, Gwendolyn Meigs. BA in Physics with honors, Barnard Coll., 1958; MD, Cornell U., 1962. Intern and resident Buffalo Gen. Hosp., 1963-65; NIH fellow SUNY, Buffalo, 1965-68, asst. prof. medicine and biophysics, 1968-76, assoc. prof., 1976-82; assoc. chief of staff for edn. Buffalo VA Med. Ctr., 1975-79, VA clin. investigator, 1972-75; assoc. chief for Grad. Med. Edn. VA Cen. Office, Washington, 1979-82, chief for Med. Edn., 1982-89, dir. Affiliated Residencey Programs Svc., 1989-93; chief Med. Edn. for State of N.Y. VA Med. Ctr., Buffalo, 1993-95, assoc. chief of staff for edn., 1995; mem. NIH tng. grant com., Washington, 1971-75, rsch.-edn. com. Buffalo United Way, 1974-75; cons. Johann Gutenberg U., Mainz, Fed. Republic of Germany, 1969-70, Free U. West Berlin, 1969-70, biol. faculty, Moscow State U., 1989-91, Englehardt Inst. Molecular Biology, Moscow, 1990-93; mgr. Internat. Exch. Programs, Urals State Med. Inst., 1990-95; trustee Biomedical Scis. Exch. Program, Inc., Salisbury Cove, Maine, 1991-95; founder Daphne K. Hare Fund for Russian-Am. Med. Edn. Cooperation, 1991-95; mem. editl. bd. Physiological Revs., 1978-82; founder, co-dir. Internat. Biomedical Agy., Ekaterinburg, Rusia, 1992-95; co-dir. Ednl. Commn. Fgn. Med. Grads. projects in New Ind. States, 1993-95 (awarded $2.4 million U.S. AID grant for med. edn. partnerships in Ukraine and Russia). Contbr. articles to profl. jours. Founder, pres. Buffalo chpt. NOW, 1970-71; bd. dirs. Western N.Y. chpt. ACLU, 1968-76 (chair 1974-78); mem. editorial bd. Signs, N.Y.C., 1974-79; mem. profl. resources com., Am. Med. Women's Assn., 1976-78; mem. exec. coun. Fed. Orgns. for Profl. Women, Wash., 1976-78; v.p. bd. dirs. 1661 Crescent Pl. NW, Inc., Washington, 198-86; mem. legis. com. Am. Women in Sci., Washington, 1986-88; pres. Barnard Class '58, 1993-95. Recipient Rice fellowship Barnard Coll., 1958, Borden prize Cornell U. Med. Coll., 1962, David Worthen Med. Edn. award VA and Assn. Am. Med. Colls., 1991, Meritorious Svc. award, VA, 1993; NIH grants, 1970-73, VA merit rev. grants, 1975-83. Mem. Biophys. Soc. (founder com. on profl. opportunities for women, chair 1973-74), Biophysics Soc. (mem. coun. 1974-77, chair grievance com. 1974-82, exec. com. 1975-77), Assn. Am. Med. Colls. (adv. bd. for women in mgmt. 1979-80). Home: Buffalo N.Y. Died Aug. 3, 1995.

HARE, DAVID, artist; b. N.Y.C., Mar. 10, 1917. Doctorate, Md. Inst. Art. Artist-in-residence Delgado Mus., New Orleans, 1964; vis. instr. sculpture Phila. Coll. Art, 1964-65; vis. artist U. Oreg., Eugene, 1966; with Tamarind Inst., U. N.Mex., Albuquerque, from 1972-92. Sculptor, painter; numerous one-man shows of sculpture and painting, 1941—, including Gallerie Maeght, Paris, 1945, Delgado Mus., New Orleans, 1965, Alessandra Gallery, N.Y.C., 1976, Guggenheim Mus., N.Y.C., 1977, Hamilton Gallery, N.Y.C., 1978, 84, 88, Zolla Lieberman Gallery, Chgo., 1978, Carlson Gallery U. Bridgeport (Conn.), 1982-88, Greunbaumn Gallery, N.Y.C., 1989, Gallery Jillien, Zurich, 1991; numerous group shows 1946— including Gallery Maeght, Venice, France, Whitney Mus. Am. Art, N.Y.C., 1976, Mus. Contemporary Crafts, N.Y.C., 1977, Renwick Gallery, Washington, Rutgers U., New Brunswick, N.J., 1977, Hayward Gallery, London, 1977, Albright Knox Art Gallery, Buffalo, N.Y., 1978, Max Davidson Gallery, N.Y.C., 1980, Hamilton Gallery, N.Y.C., 1980, 83, Contemporary Arts Mus., Houston, 1981, Gruenebaum Gallery, N.Y.C., 1985-88, Tamarind Inst.-U. N.Mex., 1987, Whitney Mus. Art, N.Y.C., 1987, Zabriskie Gallery, N.Y.C., 1987, Ben Shan Gallery, Wayne, N.J., 1988, N.Y. Studio Sch., 1988, Spain, 1989, Bieuvale Internat. II Italy, 1991, Iiac, 1991, Pans, 1991, Maury Silverman Gallery, L.A., 1991, Baurich Coll., 1992, Mus. of Modern Art, 1992, Cross Section, 1992; represented in permanent collections Mus. Modern Art, N.Y.C., Met. Mus., N.Y.C., Whitney Mus. Am. Art, N.Y.C., Bklyn. Mus., Albright-Knox Art Gallery, Buffalo, Guggenheim Mus., N.Y.C., Akron (Ohio) Art Inst., San Francisco Mus. Art, Yale U. Art Gallery, New Haven, Washington U. Gallery of Art, St. Louis, Wadsworth Atheneum, Hartford, Conn., Brandeis U., Mass., Delgado Mus. Art, numerous others, also pvt. collections; sculpture and painting includes The Cronus, Leda and the Swan, Flying Head and Shaman Series, landscapes ; contbg. editor VVV mag., 1942-44, Tages Auzeiger mag., 1989; selected feature articles and revs. in ArtNews, 1971, N.Y. Times, Sat. Rev.,, Arts mag., others. Home: Victor Idaho Died Dec. 21, 1992.

HARING, JOSEPH EMERICK, economist; b. Mansfield, Ohio, July 19, 1931; s. Joseph and Kathryn (Woerner) H.; m. Loreen Carolyn Stuber, June 2, 1956; children: Crystal Janine, Arianne Denise, Elisa Jo, Peter Joseph. B.S., Ohio State U., 1952; Ph.D., Columbia U., 1959. Instr. econs. Columbia U., 1958-59; mem. faculty Occidental Coll., Los Angeles, 1959-77, Richard W. Millar prof. econs. and fin., 1965-77, chmn. dept. econs., 1962-73; econ. planning mgr. Gen. Telephone Co. Calif., Thousand Oaks, 1977-80, planning systems dir., 1980-87; pres., bd. dirs. Calif. Venture Group, 1987-89; chief fin. officer Comet Enterprises, Inc., 1987; pres. Rainier Mfg. Co., 1988-90; Brookings Nat. research prof. econs. S.E. Asia, 1961-62; vis. prof. econs. U. So. Calif., 1964-66, UCLA, 1965, U. Vienna (Austria), 1974, U. Munich (W.Ger.), 1974-75; cons. Govt. Thailand, 1963-64; mem. steering com. So. Calif. Research Council, 1959-73; pres. Pasadena Research Inst., 1959-94; moderator TV series Inside Business, 1970. mem. Calif. State Adv. Com. on Sch. Dist. Budgeting and Fin., 1967-71; pres. Econ. Literacy Council Calif., 1982-86; bd. dirs. Calif. State Univ. Found., 1984-94, vice chmn., 1987-94; pres. Land Econs. Found. Lambda Alpha Internat., 1989; mem. Calif. Mining and Geology Bd., 1971-74. Author: Utility Regulation During Inflation, 1970; The New Economics of Regulated Industries, 1968; Urban and Regional Economics, 1972. Assoc. editor: Jour. Fin. and Quantitative Analysis, 1965-68; Contbr. articles to profl. jours. Served with U.S. Army, 1953-55. Mem. Planning Execs. Inst., N.Am. Soc. Corp. Planners, Am. Econs. Assn., Western Econ. Assn., So. Calif. Econ. Assn. (past pres.), Western Fin. Assn. Econometric Soc., Regional Sci. Assn., So. Calif. Acad. Scis. (editorial bd.), Lambda Alpha. Died June 29, 1994; buried Forrest Lawn, Los Angeles, Ca. Home: Pasadena Calif.

HARKEN, DWIGHT E., cardiologist; b. Osceola, Iowa; m. Anne Hood; children: Alden, Anne. BS, Harvard, MD. Instr. Tufts U.; prof. Harvard U., 1948-1970. Served U.S. Army medical corps, ETO. Founding member, Am. Bd. of Thoracic Surgery; past pres. Assn. for Advancemnt ofMedical Instrumentation. Office: 300 Mount Auburn St Ste 516 Cambridge MA 02138-5600

HARKER, ROBERT IAN, geologist, educator; b. Glasgow, Scotland, Aug. 2, 1926; came to U.S., 1953, naturalized, 1961; s. George Percival and Hilda H.; m. Marina Adele Pundt, June 5, 1955; children: Elizabeth, Jennifer, Alexandra. B.A., Cambridge (Eng.) U., 1949, M.A., 1953, Ph.D., 1954; M.A. (hon.), U. Pa., 1973. Asst. prof. geology Pa. State U., University Park, 1953-56; sr. scientist Johns-Manville Corp., Manville, N.J., 1956-62; pres. Tem-Pres Research Inc. (materials research and devel.), State College, 1962-70; prof. geology U. Pa., Phila., 1970-95; chmn. dept. geology U. Pa., 1974-79, 85-86; cons. in field. Contbr. articles to profl. jours. Sub-lt. Royal Naval Vol. Res., World War II. Fellow Geol. Soc. London, Am. Mineral. Soc.; mem. Mineral. Soc. London. Home: Bala Cynwyd Pa. Died Jan. 6, 1995.

HARKRADER, CARLETON ALLEN, lawyer; b. Bristol, Va., Dec. 17, 1917; s. Charles Johnston and Elva Louise (Moorman) H.; m. Julia Visetti, Jan. 1946 (div. 1949); 1 son, Richard; m. Doris Newman, Feb. 3, 1951; children—Carol, Elva, Deborah. AB, Va. Mil. Inst., 1940; JD, Yale, 1953. Mailer, reporter, editorial writer Bristol Herald Courier, 1934-41; corr. Newsweek mag., Rome; (with Newbold Noyes Jr. interviewed Pope Pius XII on Vatican reaction to atomic bomb), 1945-46; also corr. in Middle East and France, 1945; exec. editor and pub. Bristol Herald Courier and News Bull., 1946-51; appellate atty., legal adviser FTC, 1957-61; ptnr. Wald, Harkrader & Ross (and predecessor firm), Washington, 1961-87; counsel Pepper, Hamilton & Scheetz, 1987—. Maj. AUS, 1941-45; with II Corps on North African landing served in Allied Force Hdqrs. in North Africa and Italy. Decorated Bronze Star medal; recipient Lee Editorial award Va. Press Assn. and Lee Sch. of Journalism, Washington and Lee U. for distinguished editorial writing, 1941. Mem. ABA, Fed. Bar Assn., Va. Bar Assn., D.C. Bar Assn., Sigma Delta Chi, Phi Delta Phi. Democrat. Home: Great Falls Va. Died Jan. 6, 1995.

HARLAN, ROBERT WARREN, retired charitable association executive; b. London Mills, Ill., Jan. 30, 1921; s. Custer and Louella (McElra) H.; m. Effie Louella Henley, Aug. 26, 1945; children: Nancy Jane (Mrs. John Franklin Billings, Jr.), Linda Louella (Mrs. Phillip Ucciferri), Kathryn Louise (Mrs. Steven Hoxmeier), Betsy Ann Haines. B.A., Whittier Coll., 1947; M.A., U. So. Calif., 1955; Ph.D., Ohio State U., 1970. Dir. YMCA's in So. Calif., 1943-61; assoc. exec. Ohio-W.Va. area council YMCA's, Columbus, Ohio, 1961-67; exec. dir. Cen. Atlantic Area and Pacific Region YMCA's, 1967-71; nat. exec. dir. YMCA of U.S.A., N.Y.C., 1971-80; exec. v.p. (Ind. Sector), Washington, 1980-85; former lectr. Whittier Coll. Author: (with others) Thirty Days in the USSR. Past pres. Whittier Community Coordinating Coun.; past trustee Whittier Coll., Am. Humanics Found. Bd.; mem. Coalition Nat. Vol. Orgns. Bd., Nat. Ctr. Charitable Stats. Bd.; bd. dirs. Alpine Community Ctr. Recipient John R. Mott YMCA fellowship, Whittier Coll. Alumni Achievement award. Mem. Assn. Profl. YMCA Dirs. (past pres.), Nat. Assembly of Nat. Vol. Health and Social Welfare Orgns. (past pres.), Non-Profit Mgmt. Assn., Rotary (Rotarian of Yr. award Spring Valley club 1991), Alpine Kiwanis Club. Home: Alpine Calif. Died Jan. 9, 1995.

HARLESS, BYRON BRITTINGHAM, newspaper executive; b. Victoria, Va., May 15, 1916; s. Byron and Laura Belle H.; m. Betty Cabler Keefe, July 4, 1944; 1 dau., Bettina. B.A.E., U. Fla., 1938, M.A.E. (grad. fellow 1938), 1939; postgrad., Columbia U., 1939-41. Research asso. U. Fla., 1938-41, psychologist, 1945-46; pres. Byron Harless, Reid and Assos., Inc. (cons. psychologists), Tampa, Fla., 1946-70; sr. v.p. Knight-Ridder Inc., Miami, Fla., 1970-84, dir., 1984-94; cons. Author: The Measurement of Behavior Problems in High School Students, 1941, also tests. Served with USAAF, 1941-46. Recipient Outstanding Exec. award Tampa chpt. Am. Soc. Sales Execs., 1960. Mem. Am. Psychol. Assn., Southeastern Psychol. Assn., Fla. Psychol. Assn. (Disting. Service award 1955). Episcopalian. Clubs: Riviera Country (Coral Gables); Miami, City (Miami). Home: Miami Fla. Died Mar. 31, 1994.

HARNER, PAUL B., gray iron foundry executive; b. Kutztown, Pa., Oct. 30, 1909; s. John Z. and Katie (Breitensteine) H.; m. Flora A. Schoenley, Nov. 26, 1936; children: Carl J., Mary A. B.A., Franklin an Marshall Coll., 1931; M.B.A., U. Pa., 1932. Wi Union Mfg. Co., Inc., Boyertown, Pa., 1932-68; pre Union Mfg. Co., Inc., 1963-68; with Fashion Hosie Mills, Inc., Boyertown, 1936-68; pres. Fashion Hosie Mills, Inc., 1965-68; pres., dir. Berkmont Industrie Boyertown, 1968-95; chmn. bd. Berkmont Industrie 1974-95; past dir. Farmers Nat. Bank & Trust Co Boyertown. Bd. dirs., past chmn. indsl. com. Unite Chest Bovertown. Mem. Nat. Gray and Ductile Iro Soc. (dir., past sec., citation for service 1968), An Foundrymen's Soc. (dir. Phila. chpt. 1971-72, chm 1975-76), Gray and Ductile Iron Founders Soc. (di 1971-73, sec. 1967-68, treas. 1971-74). Club: Rotaria (past pres. Boyertown). Home: Reading Pa. Died De 23, 1995; interred Boyertown, Pa.

HARPER, LAWRENCE AVERELL, lawyer, educato b. Oakland, Calif., May 18, 1901; s. Fred Fogg Gale an Elizabeth Sarah (Averell) H.; m. Anna Virgin McCune, July 7, 1925; children: Lawrence Verno Virginia Ann, Robert Gale. A.B., U. Calif., 192 A.M., 1924, J.D., 1925; student, King's Coll., U London, 1925-26; Ph.D., Columbia, 1939. Bar: Cal bar 1927. Mem. firm Harper & Harper (specializing customs law), 1928-45, Lawrence, Tuttle & Harpe 1945-54; instr. history U. Calif. at Berkeley, 1928-3 asst. prof., 1939-43, asso. prof., 1943-47, prof., 1947-6 prof. emeritus, 1968—; Mem. council Inst. Early Ar History and Culture, 1969-71. Author: The Englis Navigation Laws, 1939, The Effect of the Navigatic Acts on the Thirteen Colonies, In The Era of the Ame ican Revolution, 1939, Charts and Outlines for Unite States History (2 vols., syllabus series), 1943, 55, Unite We Stand; Divided We Fall in of Mother Country ar Plantations, 1971, also contbr. to hist. and legal book and jours.; Editor: (with F.F.G. Harper) Harper's Cu toms Tariff, 1930; mem. editorial bd.: Am. Jour. Leg History; editorial adv. bd.: Am. History and Lif 1966—; prin. editorial cons. colonial statistics chpt Historic Statistics of U.S, 1960; cons. chpt. coloni statistics, rev. vol., 1975. Guggenheim fellow, 1944-45 Mem. Am. Hist. Assn., Am. Soc. Information Sci., An Econ. History Assn., Am. Soc. for Legal History (v. 1960, dir.), Phi Beta Kappa, Delta Theta Phi. Clu Berkeley Tennis. Home: Orinda Calif.

HARPER, ROY W., federal judge; b. Gibson, Mo July 26, 1905; s. Marvin H. and Minnie (Brooks) H.; r Ruth Butt, July 30, 1941; children: Katherine Brook Harper Connolly, Arthur Murray. A.B., U. Mo., 192 L.L.B., 1929. Bar: Mo. 1929. Mem. tax ins. claims de dept. Shell Petroleum Corp., St. Louis, 1929-30; pv practice law Steele, Mo., 1931-34; mem. firm Ward Reeves, Caruthersville, 1934-47; U.S. dist. judge of Mo Eastern and Western dists. of Mo., 1947-91; ret. Easter Dist. Mo., 1991; sr. judge Eastern and Western Dist Mo., 1971-91; Mem. U.S. Judicial Conf., 1965-77, in tercircuit assignment com., 1968-76, chmn., 1969, ad com. on civil rules, 1971-76; mem. Jud. Panel on Mu tidist. Litigation, 1977-83, Jud. Com. on Air Cond tioning, 1955-56, Com. of Conf. for the purpose giving consideration to changes in Rule 71A(h) of Rul of Civil Procedure and Senate Bill 1958 (82d Cong.) t allow appeals from Interlocutory Orders (1951-56). Chmn. Mo. State Democratic Com., 1946-47; Bd. dir St. Louis unit Shriner's Crippled Children Hosp. Serve with USAAF, 1942-45, PTO, col. Res. Decorate Bronze Star; recipient DeMolay Legion of Honor, 195 Citation of Merit Mo. U. Law Sch., 1963; Partrio award Mo. soc. S.A.R., 1973; George Washingto Honor medal Freedoms Found., 1975. Mem. Am., Mo Pemiscot County bar assns., Order of Coif, Delta The Phi. Democrat. Club: Mason (33 deg., Shriner). Hom Saint Louis Mo. Died Feb. 13, 1994.

HARRAH, ROBERT EUGENE, manufacturing com pany executive; b. Riverside, Washington, May 31, 191 s. William Franklin and Irene Virginia (Clark) H.; m Jayne Ann Knoblock, Aug. 10, 1937; children: Marg Lee, Bonnie Jean. Student, Taft Jr. Coll., 1934-36. Machinist Baash Ross Tool Co., 1936-41; with Ma Island Navy Yard, 1941-42, U.S. Engrs., Panama Cana 1943; owner sawmill and mfg. co., 1943-52, lumber co 1952-68; founder, pres. Remco Hydraulics, Willit Calif., 1957-68; owner, chmn. bd. Harrah Industrie Willits, 1968-93, Microphor Inc., Willits, 1972-8 chmn., chief exec. officer Stanray Corp., Chgo., 1975-7 also dir.; dir., asst. to pres. Abex Corp., 1979-85; di emeritus I.C. Industries; chmn. bd. Hussmann Corp 1984-87, Pneumo Abex Corp., 1985-87, R & J Timbe Co., 1986-92. Mem. Willits Planning Commn., Willi City Council; chmn. bd. trustees Willits High Sch 1949-59; pres. bd. trustees Howard Hosp., 1968-8 governing bd. Ry. Progress Inst. Republican. Club Rotary, Shriners, Masons. Home: Willits Calif. Die June 9, 1993.

HARRINGTON, DONALD C., medical care con sultant; b. Jacksonville,, Oreg., July 28, 1912; s. Joh Charles Fremont and Mary Rhoda (Shinn) H.; m Barbara Vierta Koreck, June 25, 1939; children: Donal F., Thomas M., David C., Robert L. M.D., U. Calif San Francisco, 1939. Diplomate Am. Bd. Ob-Gyn. In tern U. Calif. Hosp., San Francisco, 1938-39, residen 1939-41; chief ob-gyn San Joaquin Co. Hosp., 1945-7 med. care cons.; trustee Calif. Blue Shield, 1961-6 cons. Calif., Dept. Pub. Health, 1957-60; mem. ad com. mental and child health State of Calif., 1957-60; pres. San Joaquin Found. for Med. Care, 1954-70, Am. Assn. of Founds. for Med Care, 1972-73; med. dir. San Joaquin Found. for Med. Care, 1954-73, Computer Scis. Corp., 1978-80; mem. Nat. PSRO Council, 1974-77. Served to maj. USAAC, 1942-46. Recipient Disting. Alumnus award U. Pacific, 1972; Richard & Hinda Rosenthal Found. award ACP, 1978;. Fellow ACS, Am. Coll. Ob-Gyn; mem. San Joaquin County Med. Soc. (pres. 1951), Calif. Med. Assn. AMA, San Francisco Gynecol. Assn. (pres. 1972-73), Pacific Coast Gynecol. Assn., Inst. Medicine of Nat. Acad. Sci. Republican. Methodist. Home: Pioneer Calif. Died Jan. 15, 1993.

HARRINGTON, FRED HARVEY, history educator; b. Watertown, N.Y., June 24, 1912; s. Arthur William and Elsie (Sutton) H.; m. Nancy Howes, Oct. 19, 1935; children: Heather Harrington Monroe, Holly Harrington Szwarek, Hilary Harrington Mandel, Helise Harrington Bucholz, Harvey (dec.). AB with honors, Cornell U., 1933; MA (Frederic Courtland Penfield fellow), NYU, 1934, PhD, 1937, LLD, 1963; LLD (hon.), U. Calif., 1965, Drake U., 1969, Loyola U., Chgo., 1970, U. Wis., Milw., 1982; LHD (hon.), U. Maine, 1966, DePaul U., 1966, Miami U., 1967, Northland Coll., 1969; LittD (hon.), U. Ife, Nigeria, 1969. Instr. history Washington Square Coll., NYU, 1936-37; instr. history U. Wis., 1937-39, asst. prof., 1939-40; prof. history and polit. sci., chmn. dept. U. Ark., 1940-44; asso. prof. history U. Wis., 1944-47, prof., 1947-70, chmn. dept., 1952-55, spl. asst. to pres., 1956-58, v.p. acad. affairs, 1958-62, v.p. univ., 1962, pres., 1962-70, William F. Vilas research prof. history, 1970-82; program adviser in India, Sri Lanka and Nepal for Ford Found., 1971-77; vis. prof. U. W.Va., 1942, Cornell U., 1944, U. Pa., 1949, U. Colo., 1951, Oxford U., 1955; Am. studies seminar U. Kyoto, Japan, 1962; mem. Indo-Am. Subcommn. Edn. and Culture, 1975-80; dir. Carnegie study of role of univ. in adult edn., 1960-77; dir. study Internat. Linkages of Higher Edn., 1976-78; chmn. com. on instnl. coop. Big Ten and Chgo., 1960-62; bd. vis. Air Acad., 1961-64; Wis. chmn. Brotherhood Week NCCJ, 1965; pres. Nat. Assn. State Univs. and Land Grant Colls., 1968-69; mem. Army Adv. Panel on ROTC Affairs, 1963-68; mem. adv. panels AID, 1965-72; bd. dirs. U.S. Ednl. Found. in India, 1971-77, chmn., 1973-77. Author: God, Mammon and the Japanese: Dr. Horace N. Allen and Korean-American Relations (1884-1905), 1944, Fighting Politician: Major General N. P. Banks, 1948, (with M. Curti, R. H. Shryock, T.C. Cochran) An American History (2 vols.), 1950, Hanging Judge, 1951, (with Curti, Shryock, Cochran) History of American Civilization, 1953, The Future of Adult Education: New Responsibilities for Colleges and Universities, 1977. Guggenheim fellow, 1943-44; Ford Faculty fellow, 1955-56; recipient honor award Assn. Indians in Am., 1986. Fellow Wis. Acad. Arts and Letters; mem. Am. Council Edn. (chmn. commn. acad. affairs 1962-65, bd. dirs. 1966-69), Fgn. Policy Assn. (bd. dirs. 1966-68), Nat. Commn. Accrediting (pres. 1966-68), Nat. Assn. Ednl. Broadcasters (bd. dirs. 1965-68), Orgn. Am. Historians (exec. com. 1944-48), Edn. Commn. of States (v.p. 1966-68), Fulbright Alumni Assn. (dir. 1980-84), Phi Beta Kappa, Phi Kappa Phi. Home: Hastings Hdsn N.Y. Died Apr. 8, 1995.

HARRINGTON, GEORGE WILLIAM, chemistry educator; b. N.Y.C., Nov. 13, 1929; s. George Washington and Hedwig Louise (Sommer) H.; m. Patricia Miller, June 4, 1955; children: Steven George, Cathy Louise. B.A., NYU, 1954, Ph.D., 1959. Project engr. Philco Corp. (Lansdale Tube Co.), 1959; prof. chemistry Temple U., Phila., 1959-92, prof. emeritus, 1992-94; assoc. dean Temple U. Grad. Sch., Phila., 1965-68; assoc. dean Temple U. (Coll. Liberal Arts), 1968-71, chmn. dept. chemistry, 1978-81; retired, 1992; Research contractor AEC, 1959-62, Campbell Soup Co., 1963-65. Served with AUS, 1948-52, Korea. Recipient Founders Day award N.Y. U., 1969; grantee Nat. Cancer Inst., NIH, 1975-92. Fellow Am. Inst. Chemists (sr. medal 1955); mem. Am. Chem. Soc. (chmn. phys. sect. Phila. 1969, chmn. analytic sect. 1984, bd. dirs. 1984-86), AAUP, Sigma Xi. Home: Meadowbrook Pa. Died Jan. 11, 1994.

HARRINGTON, JOSEPH, JR., consulting mechanical engineer; b. Riverside, Ill., Sept. 21, 1908; s. Joseph and Cora Agnes (Dunlap) H.; B.S., Mass. Inst. Tech., 1930, D.Sc., 1932; m. Alene Louisa Smith, Sept. 17, 1932; children: Joan Smith, Joseph, Anne Heider. Asst. dir. research United Shoe Machinery Corp., Beverly/Boston, Mass., 1932-55; head mech. engring. dept. Arthur D. Little Inc., Cambridge, Mass., 1955-70; cons. engr. mech. engring., mfg., mgmt. Wenham, Mass., and Cambridge, 1970-86; mem. com. on computer aided mfg. Nat. Acad. Engring., 1977-82, chmn., 1980-82. Selectman Town of Wenham, 1945-50, moderator, 1957-86. Served with C.E., AUS, 1930-40. Registered profl. engr., Mass. Mem. Mass. Moderators Assn. (pres. 1974-76), Mass. Inst. Tech. Alumni Assn., Assn. Integrated Mfg. Tech. (pres. 1970-71), Soc. Mfg. Engrs., Tau Beta Pi. Republican. Author: The Manufacturing Engineer-Today and Tomorrow, 1968; Computer Integrated Manufacturing, 1973; Understanding the Manufacturing Process, 1984. Contbr. articles to profl. publs. Patentee in field. Died June 13, 1986. Home: Westborough Mass.

HARRINGTON, WILLIAM FIELDS, biochemist, educator; b. Seattle, Sept. 25, 1920; s. Ira Francis and Jessie Blanche (Fields) H.; m. Ingeborg Leuschner, Feb. 24, 1947; children: Susan, Eric, Peter, Robert, David. B.S., U. Calif. at Berkeley, 1948, Ph.D., 1952. Research chemist virus lab. U. Calif. at Berkeley, 1952-53; Nat. Found. Infantile Paralysis postdoctoral fellow Cambridge (Eng.) U., 1953-54; Nat. Cancer Inst. postdoctoral fellow Carlsberg Lab., Copenhagen, Denmark, 1954-55; asst. prof. chemistry Iowa State U., 1955-56; biochemist Nat. Heart Inst., 1956-60; prof. biology Johns Hopkins, Balt., 1960—; chmn. dept. biology Johns Hopkins, 1973-83, Henry Walters prof. biology, 1975—; dir. McCollum Pratt Inst., 1973-83, Inst. Biophys. Rsch. on Macromolecular Assemblies, 1989-90; vis. scientist Wiezmann Inst., Rehovot, Israel, 1959, vis. prof., 1970; vis. prof. Oxford U., 1970; Mem. adv. panel physiol. chemistry NIH, 1962-66, adv. panel biophys. chemistry study sect., 1968-72; bd. sci. councillors Nat. Inst. Arthritis and Metabolic Diseases, 1968-72; mem. vis. com. for biology Brookhaven Nat. Lab., 1969-73; adv. bd. Fedn. Advanced Edn. in the Scis., 1975—; adv. coun. Nat. Inst. Arthritis, Muskuloskeletal and Skin Diseases, NIH, 1987-90. Co-editor: Monographs on Physical Biochemistry, 1970—; Bd. editors: Jour. Biol. Chemistry, 1963-68, Mechanochemistry and Motility, 1970-72, Biochemistry, 1971-77, 83—, Jour. Phys. Biochemistry, 1973—, Analytical Biochemistry, 1978—. Fellow Am. Acad. Arts and Sci.; mem. Biophysics Soc., Nat. Acad. Scis., Soc. Biol. Chemists, Phi Beta Kappa, Sigma Xi. Home: Ellicott City Md.

HARRIS, ALFRED PETER, art director, painter; b. Toronto, Ont., Can., Apr. 4, 1932; s. Louis Derwood and Phyllis Ometa (Weir) H. Diploma in Drawing and Painting, Ont. Coll. Art, Toronto, 1955; LLD (honoris causa), Brock U., St. Catharines, Ont., 1985. Display designer T. Eaton Co., Toronto, 1955-57; dir. Rodman Hall Arts Ctr., St. Catharines, 1960—; pres. Ont. Assn. Art Galleries, Toronto, 1971-72; mem. com. monuments Sec. of State, Ottawa, Ont., Can., 1968-69. Exhibited at Windsor Art Gallery, 1977, Gallery Stratford, 1985; one-man shows at Roberts Gallery, 1969-70, 73, 75, 77-79, 81-85, 87, 91. Mem. Can. Art Mus. Dirs. Organ., Ont. Assn. Art Galleries (Fenn award 1987), St. Catharines Club. Home: Saint Catharines Can. Died Dec., 1993.

HARRIS, AURAND, playwright; b. Jamesport, Mo., July 4, 1915; s. George Dowe and Myrtle (Sebastian) H. BA, U. Kansas City, 1936; MA, Northwestern U., 1939; postgrad., Columbia U., 1945-47; LHD (hon.), U. Ind., 1991. Head drama dept. William Woods Coll., Fulton, Mo., 1942-45; drama tchr. Grace Ch. Sch., N.Y.C., 1946-77; tchr. Columbia U. Tchrs. Coll., N.Y.C., summers 1958-63; playwright-in-residence U. Fla., Tallahassee, 1972, U. Tex., Austin, 1976-84, U. Kans., 1979, Calif. State U., Northridge, 1982, Young Audiences, Cleve., 1981-84, Ind. U.-Purdue U., Indpls., 1985, 88, Am. Sch. Madrid, 1986, NYU, 1988-96, U. Hawaii, 1989; assoc. summer theater Cape May, N.J., 1940, Bennington, Vt., 1947, Peaks Island, Maine, 1948, Harwich, Mass., 1963-75; drama tchr. Western Conn. State Coll., Danbury, Conn., summer 1976. Author: (childrens plays) Pinocchio and the Fire-Eater, 1940, Once upon a Clothesline, 1944, Seven League Boots, 1947, Circus Day, 1948 (John Golden award Columbia U. 1945), rev. as Circus in the Wind, 1960, Pinocchio and the Indians, 1949, Simple Simon, 1952, Buffalo Bill, 1953, The Plain Princess, 1954, The Flying Prince, 1958, Junket: No Dogs Allowed, 1959, The Brave Little Tailor, 1960, Pocahontas, 1961, Androcles and the Lion, 1964, Rags to Riches, 1965 (Horatio Alger Newsboy award 1967), A Doctor in Spite of Himself, 1966, The Comical Tragedy or Tragical Comedy of Punch and Judy, 1969, Just So Stories, 1971, Ming Lee and the Magic Tree, 1971, Steal Away Home, 1972, Peck's Bad Boy, 1973, Robin Goodfellow, 1974, Yanke Doodle, 1975, Star Spangled Salute, 1975, The Arkansaw Bear, 1977, Six Plays for Children, 1977, A Toby Show, 1978, Ralph Roister Doister, 1978, Cyrano de Bergerac, 1979, The Romancers, 1979, Candida, 1979, Fashion, 1981, Treasure Island, 1983, The Magician's Nephew, 1984, Ride a Blue Horse, 1986, Huck Finn's Story, 1987, Monkey Magic, 1990, The Pinballs, 1992, Peter Rabbit and Me, 1993, Prince and the Pauper, 1994; (plays) Ladies of the Mop, 1945, The Doughnut Hole, 1947, The Moon Makes Three, 1947, Madam Ada, 1948, And Never Been Kissed, 1950, We Were Young That Year, 1954; co-editor, contbr. Plays Children Love, vol 1, 1981, vol. 2, 1988, Short Plays of Theatre Classics, 1991. NEA grantee, 1976; recipient Seattle Jr. Programs Playwrighting award, 1945, 46, 50, 52, 56, 58, 60, Anderson award Stanford U., 1948, Marburg prize Johns Hopkins U., 1956, Birmingham Jr. Programs award, 1958, 60, 62, Jr. League N.J. award, 1960, North Shore Music Theatre award, 1966, Ohio Theatre Alliance award, 1984, Alumni Achievement award U. Mo., 1987, Sara Spencer Outstanding Contbn. to Children's Theatre award, 1988, Disting. Svc. award Southeast Theatre Assn., 1988, Best Children's Play award Am. Alliance Theatre and Edn., 1990, 92, Alumni Merit award Northwestern U., 1991, Children's Theatre Found. medallion, 1993. Fellow Am. Theatre Assn. (Chorpenning cup 1967, 85). Home: New Orleans La. Died May 6, 1996.

HARRIS, CARMON COLEMAN, judge; b. Boswell, Okla., Nov. 27, 1904; s. William Robberson and Lucy (Coleman) H.; m. Veryl Pauline Fox, Aug. 13, 1932; 1 son, Carmon Coleman. LL.B., U. Okla., 1929. Bar: Okla. bar 1929. Practice in Oklahoma City, 1929-41, 46-49; dist. judge Okla., 1967-84; instr. advocacy Oklahoma City U. Law Sch., 1970-93; vis. lectr. Oklahoma City U. Law Sch. (Sch. Medicine), 1971. Del. to Republican Nat. Conv., 1952; nominee for Congress, 1946, 48; active Rep. Com., 1934-66. Served with AUS, 1941-46; judge adv. staff Comdg. Gen. European Theater 1944-45; prosecutor war crimes trials 1945-46. Decorated Bronze Star medal. Mem. ABA, Oklahoma County Bar Assn., Nat. Conf. State Trial Judges, Okla. Bar Assn. (trustee), Sigma Phi Epsilon, Phi Delta Phi. Clubs: Mason, Lion. Home: Oklahoma City Okla. Died Apr. 18, 1993.

HARRIS, CLAUDE, JR., prosecutor; b. Bessemer, Ala., June 29, 1940; s. Claude Sr. and Lemana (Hogue) H.; m. Barbara Ann Cork, Dec. 31, 1969; children: Jeff, Claude III. BS, U. Ala., 1962, LLB, 1965. Asst. dist. atty. Tuscaloosa, Ala., 1965-76; cir. judge 6th Jud. Cir. Ala., Tuscaloosa, 1977-85; ptnr. Harris, Shields, Braswell & Gunter., Tuscaloosa, 1985-86; mem. 100th-102nd Congresses from 7th dist. Ala., Washington, 1987-94; also coms. 100th Congress from Ala., Washington; U.S. atty. U.S. Dept. of Justice, Birmingham, Ala., 1993-94. Mem. exec. bd. Black Warrior council Boy Scouts Am.; mem. adv. bd., past chmn. Salvation Army, Ala.; chmn. West Ala. Rehab. Ctr., 1986. Recipient Father of Yr. award Tuscaloosa County Cowbelles, 1984, Ala. Gold award Ala. Easter Seal Soc., 1986. Democrat. Home: Tuscaloosa Ala. Died Oct. 2, 1994.

HARRIS, DAVID JOHN, investment company executive, retired; b. Chgo., June 13, 1913; s. David John and Harriet (Aurelius) H.; m. Evelyn Carr, Dec. 19, 1936; children: Carol H. Epkins, Glenn C., John C. BA, U. Chgo., 1935. With Sills, Minton & Co., Chgo., 1935, v.p., 1944, pres., 1945; pres. Fairman, Harris & Co. (merger Fairman & Harris, Inc.), Chgo., 1945-56; resident ptnr. Bache & Co., Chgo., 1956-64; founder, pres. The Chgo. Corp., Chgo., 1964-70; chmn., chief exec. officer The Chgo. Corp., 1970-81, chmn. emeritus, from 1986. Mem. Lake County Dist. 107 Sch. Bd., 1954-57, Rep. Presdl. Task Force, from 1982, Rep. Senatorial Inner Circle, from 1982, U.S. Senatorial Bus. Adv. Bd., from 1983; chmn. Highland Park (Ill.) Community Chest Drive, 1958, Chgo. City Area, U. Chgo. Alumni Fund, 1976-87; trustee Highland Park Hosp., 1958-78; head security industry div. United Way; bd. dirs., treas. The Arthritis Found., 1980-82, mem. exec. com., 1980-87. Mem. Delta Kappa Epsilon. Clubs: The Attic, Chicago, University, Exmoor Country. Home: Highland Park Ill. Deceased.

HARRIS, GEORGE B., federal judge; b. San Francisco, Aug. 16, 1901; s. Bernard Dugan and Gertrude Howard Harris; m. Aileen D. Harris, July 22, 1930; 1 dau., Gail. LL.D., cum laude, U. San Francisco, 1926. Bar: Calif. 1926. Individual practice law, San Francisco, beginning 1926; past assemblyman 27th Dist., San Francisco; judge San Francisco Mcpl. Ct., 1941-46; sr. judge U.S. Dist. Ct. Calif., (No. Dist.) (life appointment by Pres. Harry S. Truman), from 1946. Regent U. San Francisco, 1971. Decorated Knight of Malta, 1962, Knight of St. Gregory, 1966; recipient St. Thomas Moore award, 1966. Mem. Grand Order Knights of Malta. Democrat. Roman Catholic. Deceased. Home: San Francisco Calif.

HARRIS, HARWELL HAMILTON, architect, educator; b. Redlands, Calif., July 2, 1903; s. Frederick Thomas and May Julia (Hamilton) H.; m. Jean Murray Bangs, Feb. 23, 1937. Student, Pomona Coll., 1921-23, Otis Art Inst., 1923-25; D.F.A. (hon.), N.C. State U., 1985. Practice architecture with Richard Neutra, 1929-32; pvt. practice Los Angeles, 1933-51, Austin, Tex., 1951-56; pvt. practice as Harris & Sherwood, Ft. Worth, 1956-57; architect with office in Dallas, 1958-62, Raleigh, N.C., 1962-90; lectr. U. So. Calif., 1945, 1946; vis. critic Columbia, 1943, Yale, 1950, 52; design cons. to Nat. Orange Show, 1950-90; grad. design critic Columbia, 1960-61; prof. architecture N.C. State U., Raleigh, 1962-73; dir. Sch. Architecture, U. Tex., 1951-55; Internat. Exec. Service Corps, North Borneo, 1972, San Salvador, 1977, Singapore, 1978. Sculptor, 1926-29; Prin. works include Lowe House, 1934, Fellowship Park House, 1935, Havens House, 1941, Birtcher House, 1942, Johnson House, 1947, English House, 1950, Chadwick School, 1951, Texas State Fair House, 1954, J. Lee Johnson House, 1956, Am. Embassy, Helsinki, 1957, Havens Meml. Plaza, Berkeley, Calif., 1961, Greenwood Mausoleum, 1959, Dallas Unitarian Ch, 1964, St. Giles Presbyn. Ch, Raleigh, 1969, others; prin. projects include Segmental House for, Revere Copper & Brass Co., 1942, Pottenger Hosp, 1946, Palos Verdes Coll, 1947, Homestyle Found. House for S.W, 1956; drawings in collection of Ctr. for Study Am. Architecture, Austin, Tex.; subject of monograph: Harwell Hamilton Harris, 1985, books: The Second Generation, 1983, Harwell Hamilton Harris: A Collection of His Writings and Buildings, 1965, The Organic View of Design, 1985, Harwell Hamilton Harris: Tracking Life; one-man exhbns. include U. Tex., Austin, 1985, Graham Found., Chgo., 1987, Columbia U., N.Y.C., 1988. Recipient 1st prize Pitts. Glass Inst., 1937, 38; H.H.

Harris fellowship established at U. Tex., 1985. Mem., FAIA, mem., Congrès Internationaux d'Architecture Moderne (sec. Am. chpt. 1932, chpt. for relief and postwar planning 1944), Tau Sigma Delta. Home: Raleigh N.C. Died Nov. 18, 1990.

HARRIS, THOMAS EVERETT, government official, lawyer, retired; b. Little Rock, May 25, 1912; s. Marvin and Ina (Thomas) H.; m. Lucile Hassell, 1935 (div. 1944); children: Marvin Bryan, Ruffin Kirby (dec.); m. Margaret Samson, Aug. 14, 1944; 1 son, Thomas Everett. B.A., U. Ark., 1932; LL.B., Columbia U., 1935. Law clk. to Justice Stone, 1935-36; assoc. firm Covington & Burling, Washington, 1936-37; with Dept. Justice, 1937-41, Office Solicitor Gen., 1939-41; assoc. gen. counsel FCC, 1941-42, OPA, 1942-43; with Bd. Econ. Warfare, 1943; assoc. firm Cahill, Gordon, Zachry & Parlin, N.Y.C., 1943-45; with U.S. Mil. Govt. in, Germany, 1945-46; spl. asst. to atty. gen., alien property div. Dept. Justice, 1947-48; assoc. gen. counsel CIO, 1948-55, AFL-CIO, 1955-75; Mem. Fed. Election Commn., 1975-86. Democrat. Home: Alexandria Va. Died Feb. 6, 1996.

HARRIS, WILLIAM MERL, chemistry educator; b. Los Angeles, Feb. 23, 1931; s. Merl William Evans and Beatrice Theresa (Hawkins) H.; m. Ilse Anneliese Doebrich, Jan. 2, 1957. B.S., UCLA, 1956, Ph.D., 1965; JD, Loyola U., Los Angeles, 1987. Registered patent agt. Mem. tech. staff Hughes Aircraft Co., Culver City, Calif., 1956-59; chemist FDA, Los Angeles, 1964-65; postdoctral research fellow in chemistry UCLA, 1965-66, instr., 1966-70; asst. prof. chemistry Los Angeles Valley Coll., Van Nuys, Calif., 1970-73, assoc. prof., 1973-77, coordinator instrn., 1976-77, prof., 1977—, chmn. dept., 1970—; lectr. chemistry U. Calif.-Santa Barbara., 1968; vis. prof. chemistry UCLA, 1979. Contbr. articles to profl. jours. Served with AUS, 1952-54. Named Outstanding Teaching Asst. UCLA, 1962; Hughes fellow, 1957-59. Mem. Am. Chem. Soc., Royal Soc. Chemistry (Gt. Britain), ABA, State Bar Calif. (intellectual property sect.), Los Angeles Patent Law Assn., Sigma Xi, Phi Lambda Upsilon. Lodge: Masons. Home: Van Nuys Calif. Deceased.

HARRISON, JOAN S(HIRLEY), college dean; b. Orange, N.J., Apr. 29, 1934; d. Harry and Rose (Marshak) Horowitz; m. David Harrison, Mar. 23, 1958; children: Andrew L., Rachel E. AB magna cum laude, Tufts U., 1956; AM, Radcliffe Coll., 1957; MS, Bank St. Coll., N.Y.C., 1982; PhD, The Union Inst., Cin., 1987. Tchr. Weehawken (N.J.) Pub. Schs., 1959-60; faculty Farleigh Dickinson U., Teaneck, N.J., 1960-61, 64-65; program developer, adminstr. Englewood (N.J.) Pub. Schs., 1964-67; asst. dean studies Sarah Lawrence Coll., Bronxville, N.Y., 1973-81, assoc. dean studies, 1981-93, acting assoc. dir. Ctr. for Continuing Edn., 1980-81; dissemination assoc. Englewood Title III Project, 1972; mem. adj. faculty Bank St. Coll., 1981-83, 89, Empire State Coll., 1989, 90; cons. N.Y.C. Bd. Edn., 1982-84. Contbr. articles to profl. jours. Mem. planning bd. met. region Nat. Identification project of Am. Council on Edn., 1980-85. Established Joan Harrison scholarship at Sarah Lawrence Coll., 1992; recipient Am. Coun. on Edn. Nat. Identification award, Westchester Rockland Mentoring award, 1993. Mem. Phi Beta Kappa. Home: Hastings On Hudson N.Y. Died May 31, 1993.

HART, EDWIN JAMES, chemist; b. Port Angeles, Wash., Feb. 7, 1910; s. Fitch James and Josie Anna Elizabeth (Blater) H.; m. Rozella Patricia Clark, June 17, 1939; children: Fitch J., Ann E., John P. B.S., M.S., Wash. State U., 1931; Ph.D., Brown U., 1934; Doktor der Naturwissenschaften Ehren Halber (hon.), Technische U., Berlin, 1984. With L.I. Biol. Lab., 1934-36, U.S. Rubber Co., 1936-48; sr. chemist Argonne Nat. Lab., 1948-75, cons., 1975-89; Brit. Empire Cancer Campaign fellow Mt. Vernon Hosp., Eng., 1961-62; mem. quartermaster dosimetry panel Nat. Acad. Sci., 1955-58, radiobiology com., 1958-64, food irradiation com., 1963-72; del. 2d UN Internat. Conf. on Peaceful Uses Atomic Energy, Geneva, 1958; mem. Internat. Com. on Radiol. Units, 1960-63; cons. Risø Nat. Lab., Denmark, 1967-91; IAEA cons. to Bhabha Atomic Research Centre, Trombay, India, winter 1970; mem. sci. staff U.S. Atoms in Action Program, Tehran, Iran, 1967; vis. prof. Hebrew U., Israel, fall 1967; cons. Lawrence Berkeley Lab., 1976-79, Battelle Pacific Northwest Labs., Richland, Wash., 1990-91; vis. scientist Hahn-Meitner-Institut, Berlin, 1984-89. Author: (with M. Anbar) The Hydrated Electron, 1970. sr. U.S. scientist awardee Alexander von Humboldt Found., W. Ger., 1979-80; recipient Weiss medal Assn. for Radiation Research, Eng., 1975, citation for disting. achievement Brown U., 1983; citation for Disting. Achievement, Washington State U., 1984. Mem. Am. Chem. Soc., AAAS, Soc. Free Radical Research (hon.), Radiation Research Soc., Phi Beta Kappa, Sigma Xi, Phi Kappa Phi, Phi Lambda Upsilon. Home: Port Angeles Wash. Died May 25, 1995.

HART, STEPHEN HARDING, lawyer; b. Denver, Apr. 13, 1908; s. Richard Huson and Elizabeth (Jerome) H.; m. Lorna Rogers, Dec. 30, 1937; children: Richard Huson, James Grafton Rogers, Georgina Hart Martin-Smith. A.B. summa cum laude, Yale U., 1929; postgrad. Harvard U. Law Sch., 1929-30; A.B. (Juris.), New Coll., Oxford, Eng., 1932, A.M., 1938; J.D., U. Denver, 1933. Bar: Colo. 1933. Instr., Denver Law Sch., 1933-35; asst. solicitor Dept. Interior, Washington, 1935-36; assoc. Lewis & Grant, Denver, 1936-47; sr. ptnr. Holland & Hart, Denver, 1947-93; dir. Grassy Creek Coal Co., Colo. Public Expenditure Council, Denver Nat. Bank, Denver U.S. Nat. Bank, United Bank of Denver, United Banks of Colo. Mem. Colo. Ho. of Reps., 1937-39, Colo. Senate, 1939-43; trustee Frederick G. Bonfils Found., 1960-67, Helen G. Bonfils Found., 1961-70; mem. Fgn. Bondholders Protective Council, 1966-81; mem. exec. com. Yale Alumni Bd., 1953-68, Yale Devel. Com., 1956-70; pres. Humphreys Found., 1979-93; trustee Colo. Hist. Soc., 1938-93, pres., 1960-70, chmn., 1971-81, chmn. emeritus, 1981-93. Recipient Yale medal, 1980; Colo. Hist. Soc. named Stephen H. Hart Library in his honor, 1981. Mem. Denver Bar Assn., Colo. Bar Assn. Republican. Episcopalian. Clubs: Univ. Denver Country (Denver); Met. (Washington); Yale, Century Assn., Am. Alpine (N.Y.C.); Brit. Alpine (London). Contbr. articles to profl. jours.; editor Zebulon Pike's Ark. Jour., 1932. Died Nov. 7, 1993. Home: Denver Colo.

HART, WILLIAM MILTON, ophthalmologist, educator; b. St. Clair County, Mo., June 28, 1913; s. Ruben V. and Harriet (Hoskins) H.; m. Ethelwyn Featherstun Stevens, Apr. 14, 1938; children: Juliet Katheryn, William Milton, Sarah Stevens, Ethelwyn Featherstun. AB, S.E. Mo. State Tchrs. Coll., 1937; MS, U. Iowa, 1939; PhD, U. Minn., 1941; MD, Temple U., 1948. Diplomate Am. Bd. Ophthalmology. Mayo Found. fellow in physiology Mayo Clinic, 1939-41; rsch. assoc. dept. ophthalmology U. Iowa, 1941-42; assoc. dept. physiology Jefferson Med. Coll., 1942-44, asst. prof. ophthalmology, 1952-53; asst. prof. biochemistry, clin. asst. ophthalmology Temple U., 1944-49, rsch. assoc. prof. ophthalmology, 1949-52; chief br. ophthalmology Nat. Inst. Neurol. Diseases and Blindness, 1953-54; clin. prof. neuro-ophthalmology U. Md.; Roy E. Mason Disting. prof. ophthalmology, chmn. dept. U. Mo., 1967-79; prof. ophthalmology U. Miss., Jackson, 1979-91, prof. emeritus, 1991-93; chief ophthalmology VA Hosp., Jackson, 1979-91. Surgeon USPHS, 1953-57. Recipient prize Ophthalmology Assn. for Rsch., 1941, Zentmayer award Coll. Physicians Phila., 1946. Fellow ACS, Royal Soc. Medicine; mem. Am. Acad. Ophthalmology, Am. Physiol. Soc., Am. Chem. Soc., Kiwanis, Sigma Xi, Alpha Omega Alpha. Republican. Methodist. Home: Madison Miss. Died Apr. 29, 1993.

HARTL, ALBERT VICTOR, utility executive; b. New Rockford, N.D., Oct. 21, 1911; s. William Robert and Frances (Dusek) H.; m. Ruth Alice Stenquist, June 25, 1935; children: Marlene, Claudeen, Kathleen, Mary Aldeen, Patricia Jean, Albert Vincent. BS in Commerce, U. N.D., 1932. Dep. tax commr. State of N.D., 1934-36; chief acct. N.D. Public Service Commn., 1936-41; with Otter Tail Power Co., 1946-95, exec. v.p., then pres., 1958-75; chmn. bd. Otter Tail Power Co., Bismarck, N.D., 1975-95; dir. Pioneer Mut. Life Ins. Co., Security State Bank, Fergus Falls, Minn.; bd. dirs. Edison Electric Inst., Farm Electrification Council; instr. U. Mary, Bismarck. Trustee Fergus Falls Public Library, 1960-69; dir. CD, Fergus Falls and Otter Tail County, 1949-58; mem. nat. adv. council Boy Scouts Am. With inf. AUS, 1941-46. Decorated Silver Star with oak leaf cluster, Bronze Star with 2 oak leaf clusters; knight of St. Gregory; knight comdr. of Holy Sepulchre; recipient St. George, Silver Beaver, Silver Antelope, Silver Buffalo awards Boy Scouts Am. Mem. Am. Mgmt. Assn. Republican. Roman Catholic. Lodges: Kiwanis, K.C, Elks. Home: Bismark N.D. Died Jan. 9, 1995; interred St. Mary's Cemetery, Bismarck, N.D.

HARTMAN, DONALD T., academic administrator. Exec. officer Pa. State U., Du Bois. Home: Du Bois Pa. Dec. 4/21/93.

HARTMANN, EDWARD GEORGE, historian, educator; b. Wilkes-Barre, Pa., May 3, 1912; s. Louis and Catherine (Jones-Davis) H. A.B., Bucknell U., 1937, A.M., 1938; Ph.D., Columbia U., 1947, M.S. in L.S., 1948. Instr. history Ann-Reno Inst., N.Y.C., 1942-43; asst. prof. Wilkes U., 1946-47; fellow in library, lectr. history CCNY, 1947-48; dir. libraries, mem. faculty Suffolk U., Boston, 1948-58, prof. history, 1956-78, prof. emeritus, 1978-95. Author: The Movement to Americanize the Immigrant, 1948, A History of American Immigration, 1967, Americans from Wales, 1967, History of the Welsh Congregational Church of the City of New York, 1801-1951, 1969, American Immigration, 1979, The Welsh Society of Philadelphia, 1729-1979, 1980, Cymry yn y Cwm: the Welsh of Wilkes-Barre and the Wyoming Valley, 1985, The Ethnic History of the Wyoming Valley, Pennsylvania, 1989, A Classified Bibliography of Welsh Americana, 1993; also articles; editor: Tough 'Ombres, The Story of the 90th Infantry Division, 1944, A Short History of the 357th Infantry Regiment, 1945, Centennial History of the Welsh Baptist Association of Pennsylvania, 1955. Bd. dirs. Nat. Welsh-Am. Found., 1980-95. Served with AUS, 1943-46, ETO; maj. USAF ret. Recipient Heritage medal Nat. Welsh-Am. Found., 1991. Mem. Am. Hist. Assn. (50 yr. mem.), Soc. Am. Historians, Hon. Soc. of Cymmrodorion (London, Eng.) (hon. v.p. 1983-95), Welsh Soc. Phila. (gold medallion 1966), St. David's Soc. N.Y. State (Hopkins medal 1970), Wales Internat. (hon. v.p. 1975-95), Nat. Gymanfa Ganu Assn., Wyo. Hist. and Geol. Soc., German Soc. Pa., 90th Div. Assn., St. David's Soc. Wyoming Valley, Soc. King's Chapel (Boston), Immigration History Soc., Boston Athenaeum, United Oxford and Cambridge U. Club (London), Order Lafayette, Phi Beta Kappa. Home: Estero Fla. Died Oct. 26, 1995; interred at St. Nicholas Cemetery, Wilkes-Barre, Pa.

HARTZ, FRED ROBERT, librarian, educator; b. Annville, Pa., Mar. 31, 1933; s. Jacob and Mary E. (Spearow) H.; m. Emilie Wells Kitzelman, Dec. 30, 1971. BS, Kutztown U., 1954; MSLS, Syracuse U., 1963; postgrad., Drexel U., 1965-67, Temple U., 1968-70; PhD, Occidental U., 1977. Cert. librarian Ga., permanent tchr., Pa. Sch. librarian Fallsington, Pa., 1954-58; sr. librarian Bur. Law and Legis. Reference State Libr. N.J., Trenton, 1960; circulation librarian, head Campus Br. Libr. Rider Coll., Lawrenceville, N.J., 1960-64; asst. prof. libr. sci. and edn. tech. Trenton State Coll., 1964-74; dir. Libr. Media Ctr. pub. high sch., Emmaus, Pa., 1975-76; med. librarian, dir. libr. svcs. Warren (Pa.) State Hosp., 1977-80; librarian DeSoto Correctional Libr., Arcadia, Fla., 1980-82; tech svcs. librarian Ohoopee Regional Libr., Vidalia, Ga., 1982-93; sr. libr. Ga. State Prison, Reidsville, 1994; dir. Pub. Libr. Levittown, Wliingboro, N.J., 1960-64; vis. prof. Vanderbilt U., Peabody U., 1970, No. Mich. U., 1971. Author: (with wife, Emilie K. Hartz) I Sometimes Wish God Had Freddie Hood: A Case History in Psychiatry and Law, 1979, The Library in the Correctional Setting: A Selective, Annotated Bibliography of the Literature of Prison Librarianship 1958-83, 1984, Death Notices From the Vidalia Advance Newspaper 1921-30, 1985, Family Histories in the John E. Ladson Jr., Historical and Genealogical Foundation Library: A Bibliography With Family Name Index, 1986, 2d edit., 1994, Marriage and Death Notices From the Griffin (Georgia) Weekly News and the Griffin Weekly News and Sun 1882-1896, 1987, Genealogical Abstracts from the Georgia Journal, 1809-1818, 1990, vol. 2: 1819-1823, 1992, vol. 3: 1824-1828, 1994; (with Arthur Y. Hoshino) Warren State Hospital, 1880-1980: A Psychiatric Centennial, 1981; (with J.G. Lopez-Cortada; under pseudonym V.E. Schlegelmann) Everything You Always Wanted to Know About Prisons But Could Not Find Out, 1983; (with E.K. Hartz and Michael B. Krimmel) Prison Librarianship: A Selective, Annotated, Classified Bibliography 1945 Through 1985, 1987; contbr. over 40 articles to libr. jours. With U.S. Army, 1958-60. Grantee R.J. Taylor Jr. Found., 1988, 90, 92, 94. Mem ALA, AAUP, Founders Soc. Syracuse U., Ga. Geneal Soc., Beta Phi Mu (hon.). Mem. Schwenkfelder Ch. Home: Vidalia Ga. Died May 17, 1994.

HARVEY, FREDERICK PARKER, advertising agency executive; b. Syracuse, N.Y., Feb. 8, 1920; s. Fred Davey and Grace Aileen (Parker) H.; m. Ann Crowthers, July 20, 1946; children: Ellen Parker, Frederick Crowthers (dec.), John Berry. A.B.-B.J., Syracuse U., 1942, B.S. in Physics, 1943; postgrad., Harvard U., 1944, M.I.T., 1945. Advt. mgr. Sylvania Electric Co., Boston, 1947-52; account exec. Fuller & Smith & Ross, N.Y.C., 1952-59; v.p., account supr. Donahue & Coe Inc., N.Y.C., 1959-63; sr. v.p., corp sec. West, Weir & Bartel, N.Y.C., 1963-68; sr. v.p., mgmt. supr. D'Arcy-MacManus & Masius, N.Y.C., 1968-83; dir. Keene Corp., Am. Heart Assn., Polk County, N.C., Second Wind Hall of Fame; v.p. Thermal Belt Habitat for Humanity, Inc. Elder Larchmont (N.Y.) Ave Ch., 1982-83; pres. bd. trustees Congl. Ch. United Ch. of Christ, Tryon, N.C., 1986-87. Capt Signal Corps, U.S. Army, 1942-46. Elected to Second Wind Hall of Fame, 1987. Mem. Air Force Assn. (exec coun. Iron Gate chpt. 1980-83), Am. Heart Assn. (bd dirs.), Phi Beta Kappa, Sigma Pi Sigma, Sigma Delta Chi. Republican. Home: Tryon N.C. Deceased.

HARVEY, JAMES ROSS, finance company executive; b. L.A., Aug. 20, 1934; s. James Ernest and Loretta Berniece (Ross) H.; m. Charlene Coakley, July 22, 1971; children: Kjersten Ann, Kristina Ross. B.S. in Engring., Princeton U., 1956; M.B.A., U. Calif., Berkeley, 1963. Engr. Chevron Corp., San Francisco, 1956-61; acct. Touche, Ross, San Francisco, 1963-64; chmn. bd. Transam. Corp., San Francisco, 1965-95, bd. dirs.; bd. dirs. Airtouch Comm. Inc., McKesson Corp., Charles Schwab Corp. With U.S. Army, 1958-59. Mem. Bohemian Club, Pacific-Union Club. Home: San Francisco Calif. Died June 6, 1996.

HARVEY, MADELEINE SARA (SALLY), foreign language educator, translator; b. Croydon, Surrey, Eng. Feb. 21, 1946; arrived in New Zealand, 1986; d. George William Newitt and Ivy Cecilia (Bartlett) Harvey. BA in French and Spanish with honors, Monash U., Australia, 1980, PhD in French and Spanish, 1985. With Readheads Advt. Ltd., London, 1966-67, Minitrek Travels, Ltd., Kingston on Thames, Eng., 1968-69; mng dir. expedition on horseback in the Sierra Nevada Aventura Ltd., Spain, 1969-76; tutor in Spanish Monash U., Melbourne, Australia, 1981-85; sr. lectr. U. Auckland, New Zealand, 1986-94, Prince of Asturias chair in Spanish, 1994-95. Author: Carpentier's Proustian Fiction, 1994; co-author: First Year Spanish Workbook and Tape Manual, 1989; editor: Antípodas, 1989; contbd articles to profl. jours. Mem. NAATI (examiner in Spanish Australia 1984-95), New Zealand Soc. Trans lators and Interpreters (coun. mem. 1989-95), Australian Inst. Interpreters and Translators, Assn. Brit. Hispanists, New Zealand Assn. Lang. Tchrs. (sec. 1987-90). Address: Tuakau New Zealand Died, May 2, 1995.

HARWELL, RICHARD BARKSDALE, retired librarian; b. Washington, Ga., June 6, 1915; s. Davis Gray and Helen (Barksdale) H. A.B., Emory U., 1937, B.L.S., 1938; D.Litt., New Eng. Coll., 1966, Wofford Coll., 1987. Asst., Flowers collection Duke U. Library, 1938-40; staff Emory U. Library, 1940-54, asst. librarian, 1948-54; dir. Southeastern Interlibrary Research Facility, 1954-56; dir. publs. Va. State Library, 1956-57; exec. sec. Assn. Coll. and Research Libraries, 1957-61; asso. exec. dir. A.L.A., 1958-61; librarian Bowdoin Coll., Brunswick, Maine, 1961-68, Smith Coll., Northampton, Mass., 1968-70; dir. libraries Ga. So. Coll., Statesboro, 1970-75; curator of rare books and manuscripts U. Ga. Library, 1975-80; bibliog. cons. U. Va. Library, 1953, Boston Athenaeum, 1953; adv. bd. Civil War Centennial Commn.; cons. U. Jordan library, 1966. Author: Confederate Belles-Lettres, 1941, Confederate Music, 1950, Songs of the Confederacy, 1951, Cornerstones of Confederate Collecting, 1953, The Confederate Reader, 1957, More Confederate Imprints, 1957, The Union Reader, 1958; (with R.L. Talmadge) The Alma College Library, 1957; (with E.T. Moore) The Arizona State University Library, 1959; The War They Fought, 1960, Confederate Imprints in the University of Georgia Libraries, 1964, The Confederate Hundred, 1964, Hawthorne and Longfellow, 1966, Brief Candle, The Confederate Theatre, 1973, The Mint Julep, 1975; (with R. W. Willingham) Georgiana; editor: Stonewall Jackson and the Old Stonewall Brigade (J.E. Cooke), 1954, Destruction and Reconstruction (Richard Taylor), 1955, The Committees of Safety of Westmoreland and Fincastle, 1956, Cities and Camps of the Confederate States (FitzGerald Ross), 1958, Kate: The Journal of a Confederate Nurse (Kate Cumming), 1959, Outlines from the Outpost (J.E. Cooke), 1961, Lee (1 vol. abridgement of D.S. Freeman's R.E. Lee), 1961, The Colorado Volunteers in New Mexico, 1862 (O.J. Hollister), 1962, A Confederate Marine, 1963, The Uniform and Dress of the Army and Navy of the Conferate States, 1960, Hardtack and Coffee (John D. Billings), 1960, Two Views of Gettysburg (Sir A.J.L. Fremantle, Frank Haskell), 1964, Washington (1 vol. abridgement D.S. Freeman's George Washington), 1969, Georgia Scenes (A.B. Longstreet), 1975, Margaret Mitchell's Gone with the Wind Letters, 1936-49, 1976, GWTW The Screenplay (Sidney Howard), 1980, Gone With the Wind as Book and Film, 1983, D.S. Freeman's The South to Posterity, 3d edit., 1983, Heros von Borke Memoirs of the Confederate War, Thomas Osborn, (with P.N. Racine) The Fiery Trail, 1986; assoc. editor: Emory Sources and Reprints series, 1948-54; editor: College & Research Libraries, 1962-63; Editorial bd.: Emory U. Quar, 1946-54, Civil War History, 1954-69, Jefferson Davis Papers; Contbr.: Conf. Imprints, 1955, The Lasting South, 1957, Lincoln for the Ages, 1960, The Idea of the South, 1964; articles, revs. to gen. and profl. publs. Bd. dirs. Kittredge Found. Served to lt. USNR, 1943-46. Recipient Award of Distinction Atlanta Civil War Round Table, 1983, Nevins-Freeman award Chgo Civil War Round Table, 1984; Fellow Henry E. Huntington Library, 1951, 67. Mem. Ga. Hist. Soc. (curator 1954-56), Atlanta Hist. Soc. (dir. 1955-56), So. Hist. Soc., ALA, Southeastern Library Assn. (exec. sec. 1952-54), Ga. Library Assn., Am. Antiquarian Soc., Hereward the Wake Soc., Phi Beta Kappa, Sigma Alpha Epsilon. Club: Grolier (N.Y.C.). Died March 3, 1988; interred Resthaven Cemetery, Washington, Ga.

HARWOOD, DOUGLAS AMEND, retired government official; b. N.Y.C., June 17, 1912; s. Brunn and Elsie Amelia (Amend) H.; B.A., Yale U., 1932; postgrad. Columbia, 1934; m. Laura Lucille Turner, Apr. 16, 1952 (div. Nov. 1980); 1 child, Douglas Turner. Exec. asst., liaison officer to Maritime Commn., WPB, 1941-42; regional mgr., asst. dir. devel. N.A.M., 1946-51; cons. Office Civilian Requirements, dir. program planning staff NPA, 1951-52; dir. sales promotion, fleet div. Chrysler Corp., 1952-54; with Mut. Security Program and Fgn. Aid Program, 1955-64, dir. in East Pakistan, 1958-60, head team Fgn. Svc. pers. to Oxford U. African Studies Program, Eng., 1960-61, regional dir. U.S. Mut. Security Program for Equatorial Africa, Congo, 1961-64; sr. market devel. officer, dir. mktg. activities Bur. Internat. Commerce, Dept. Commerce, 1964-68, nat. export sales mgr., dir. global mktg. campaigns, dir. program coordination staff, export devel. activities program, 1968-72, dir. U.S. exhbns., 1972-79; internat. trade cons. govt. and pvt. industry. Served to 1st lt. AUS, 1942-46; PTO. Mem. Internat. Platform Assn., Yale Club (N.Y.C., Washington, Ft. Lauderdale, Fla.). Died Apr. 24, 1995. Home: Pompano Beach Fla.

HASBROUCK, KENNETH EDWARD, professional society administrator; b. Gardiner, N.Y., June 30, 1916; s. Josiah LeFevre and Agnes (Riley) H.; m. Alice Jackson, July 10, 1948; children: Kenneth Edward Jr., Charles Jackson. B in Edn., SUNY, New Paltz, 1946; MA, NYU, 1946. Social studies tchr. various schs., 1941-42, 46-72; pres. Huguenot Hist. Soc., New Paltz, 1960-96, also bd. dirs.; pres. Young-Morse Historic Site, Poughkeepsie, N.Y., 1979-96; historian Ulster County, N.Y., 1960-96. Author: Street of the Huguenots, 1952, History of Gardiner, N.Y., 1955, The Hasbrouck Family in America, Vols. I & II, 1961, Vol. III, 1974, Vol. IV, 1984, Vol. V., 1987, The Bevier Family in America, 1970, Three Hundred Years of the VerNooy Family in America, 1971, The Crispell Family in America, 1976, Vol. II, 1984, Vol. III, 1989, The Giraud-Gerow Family in America: First Four Generations in America, 1981, Vol. II, 1982, Vol. III, 1986; contbr. articles to mags. and newspapers. Named Alumnus of Yr. Coll. New Paltz, 1984. Mem. Huguenot Soc. Am., New England Geneal. Soc., N.Y. Geneal. and Biographical Soc., Holland Soc. N.Y., St. Nicholas Soc., Sons Am. Revolution, Huguenot Hist. Soc., Hasbrouck Family Assn. (pres. 1957-71). Home: New Paltz N.Y. Died May 26, 1996.

HASSAN, WILLIAM EPHRIAM, JR., lawyer; b. Brockton, Mass., Oct. 13, 1923; s. William Ephriam and Matilda (Salemey) H.; m. Rosetta Theresa Amodeo, June 30, 1951; children: William Anthony, Thomas Edward. B.S., Mass. Coll. Pharmacy, 1945, M.S., 1947, Ph.D., 1951; LL.B., Suffolk U., Boston, 1965. Bar: Mass. 1965. Dir. Peter Bent Brigham Hosp., Boston, 1967-78; adj. prof. jurisprudence and hosp. pharmacy Mass. Coll. Pharmacy, 1967-69; v.p. ops., asso. gen. counsel Nat. Med. Care Co., 1968-71; exec. v.p. Brigham and Women's Hosp., Boston, 1978-83, v.p., gen. counsel, 1983-86; ptnr. Hassan & Reardon, P.C., Boston, Mass., 1986-95; mem. faculty Harvard U. Med. Sch., 1968-83; dir. Controlled Risk Ins. Co., Health Providers Ins. Co. Author: Hospital Pharmacy, 5th edit, 1986, Law For the Pharmacy Student, 1971. Chmn. bd. trustees Mass. Coll. Pharmacy; bd. dirs. St. Jude's Children's Research Hosp., 1980-84; hosp. chmn. United Way Mass., 1979; mem. Joint Legis. Commn. Hosp. Charges, 1980; past trustee Emanuel Coll., Boston, Am. U., Beirut. Recipient Disting. Alumni award Mass. Coll. Pharmacy, 1973, Cutler medal Peter Bent Brigham Hosp., 1975. Fellow Am. Coll. Hosp. Adminstrs.; mem. Am. Hosp. Assn., Am. Pharm. Assn., Am. Coll. Apothecaries, Am. Soc. Hosp. Pharmacists, Am. Soc. Pharmacy Law, Am. Soc. Law and Medicine, Mass. Hosp. Assn., Mass. Bar Assn., Boston Bar Assn., Kappa Psi. Home: Newton Mass. Died June 2, 1995.

HASSIALIS, MENELAOS DIMITIOU, mineral engineer; b. N.Y.C., Dec. 25, 1909; s. Dimitri Athanaslou and Maria (Mantsalk) H.; m. Ruth Elizabeth Arnowitz, June 10, 1931 (dec.); children: Joan I. Bucher, Peter John. BA cum laude, Columbia Coll., 1931; MA, Columbia U., 1933; DS (hon.), Bard Coll., 1954. Assoc. mineral engr. Columbia U., N.Y.C., 1944, asst. prof., 1945, assoc. prof., 1947, prof., 1951, Krumb prof., 1954, exec. officer, 1951-87; dir. USAEC Lab. Columbia U., 1951-58, vice chmn. Inst. Study Scis. in Human Affairs, 1966-70; pres. Pacific Uranium Mines Co., 1959-61; Swedish rep., 1960-61; v.p. Tech. Investors Corp., 1961-68; dir. Ambrosia Lakes Uranium Corp., Kerr McGee Nuclear Fules Corp.; chmn. bd. Sandvik Steel Inc., 1973-87; chmn. Disston Corp., 1976; mem. Am. delegation to Geneva Confs., 1955, 58; head UN mission, Turkey, 1964, Spain, 1965. Co-author: Microscopy, 1945, Handbook of Mineral Engineering, 1945; contbr. articles to profl. jours.; patentee in field. Dir., v.p. Valley Hosp., Ridgewood, N.J. Recipient citation govt. Pakistan, 1958, citation Tech. U. W. Berlin, 1968, medal Freiberg Acad., East Germany, 1969, Sch. Engring. and Applied Sci. medal Columbia U., 1990, Reud Econ. award Nat. Inst. for Minerals and Petroleum, 1992, various citations from govts. U.S., Egypt, USSR, Sweden, Italy, Turkey, Eng.; named Knight of Honor and Merit of Malta O.S.J. Fellow Explorers Club (medal); mem. AIME, Am. Chem. Soc., Mineral and Metall. Soc. Am., Soc. Mineral Engrs. Independent. Greek Orthodox. Home: Ridgewood N.J. Died Mar. 17, 1995.

HASTINGS, ROBERT PUSEY, lawyer; b. Los Angeles, May 23, 1910; s. Hill and Mary Garvin (Brown) H.; m. Susan S. Schriber, July 9, 1938 (dec.); 1 child, Susan Hastings Mallory. B.A., Yale U., 1933; LL.B., Harvard U., 1936. Bar: Calif. 1936. Since practiced Los Angeles; counsel Motion Picture div. Office Coordinator Inter-Am. Affairs, 1942-43; partner firm Paul, Hastings, Janofsky & Walker, 1946-81, counsel, 1981-96. Chmn. Calif. campaign USO, 1956-57; pres., chmn. bd. L.A. Civic Light Opera Assn., 1959-65, trustee, 1939-79; sec., trustee Music Ctr. Ops. Co., 1961-65, Harbery Mudd Coll. Sci. and Engring., 1958-85, vice chmn. bd., 1956-80, hon. trustee, 1985-96; chmn. Thacher Sch., 1965-70, trustee, 1938-73, hon. trustee, 1973-96; trustee Friends of Claremont Colls., 1970-96, pres., 1973-75; trustee Friends Huntington Libr. and Art Gallery; bd. overseers Huntington Libr. and Art Gallery; trustee Winston Churchill Found. U.S., 1961-96, Miss Porter's Sch., 1969-73. Decorated Bronze Star medal; Hon. Order British Empire. Mem. Am., Calif., Los Angeles County bar assns., So. Calif. Harvard Law Sch. Assn. (trustee, chmn. 1967-69), Delta Kappa Epsilon. Republican. Episcopalian (vestryman 1968-69, 72-73). Clubs: Chancery (Los Angeles), California (Los Angeles), Sunset (Los Angeles) (past sec., pres. 1970-71), Zamorano (Los Angeles), Lincoln (Los Angeles), Brit. United Services (Los Angeles); Grolier (N.Y.C.). Home: Pasadena Calif. Died May 23, 1996.

HASTRICH, JEROME JOSEPH, bishop; b. Milw., Nov. 13, 1914; s. George Philip and Clara (Dettlaff) H. Student, Marquette U., 1933-35; BA, St. Francis Sem., Milw., 1940, MA, 1941; student, Cath. U. Am., 1941. Ordained priest Roman Cath. Ch., 1941; assigned to Milw. Chancery, 1941; curate St. Ann's Ch., Milw., St. Bernard's Ch., Madison, Wis.; asst. chaplain St. Paul U. Chapel, then U. Wis.; sec. to bishop of Diocese U. Wis., Madison, Wis., 1946-52; chancellor Diocese Madison, Wis., 1952-53; apptd. vicar gen. Diocese Madison, 1953, domestic prelate, 1954, protonotary apos., 1960; aux. bishop, 1963-67, titular bishop of Gurza and aux. of Madison, 1963; pastor St. Raphael Cathedral, Madison, 1967-69; bishop Gallup, N.Mex., 1969-90, ret.; diocesan dir. Confraternity Christian Doctrine, 1946-95, St. Martin Guild, 1946-69; aux. chaplain U.S. Air Force, 1947-67; pres. Latin Am. Mission Program; sec. Am. Bd. Cath. Missions; vice chmn. Bishop's Com. for Spanish Speaking; mem. subcom. on allocations U.S. Bishops Com. for Latin Am.; founder, episcopal moderator Queen of Americas Guild, 1979-95; pres. Nat. Blue Army of Our Lady of Fatima, 1980-95. Mem. Gov. Wis. Commn. Migratory Labor, 1964-95. Club: K.C. (hon. life mem.). Home: Gallup N. Mex. Died May 12, 1995.

HASTY, GERALD RICHARD, retired political science educator, retired army officer, lawyer; b. Pekin, Ill., Apr. 12, 1926; s. Leslie Parke and Bernice Arthene (Brown) H.; BS, Bradley U., 1952; MBA, 1954; postgrad. Harvard U., 1961; MA, Am. U., 1962; PhD, Northwestern U., 1963; LLB, Blackstone Sch. Law, 1968; postgrad., U. Toledo, 1958, U. Maine, 1963, SUNY, Buffalo, 1963, Armed Forces Staff Coll., 1968, Air War Coll., 1965, Harvard Law Sch., 1976; DD (hon.), Am. Fellowship Ch., 1977; LHD, CELO Soc., Mich., 1990; m. Betty Anne Osmundson, June 23, 1951; children: Grant Rutledge, Mark Osmund, Deborah Anne. Bar: Fed. Maritime Commn., 1972, U.S. Ct. Mil. Appeals, 1979. Commd. 2d lt. U.S. Army, 1954, advanced through grades to lt. col., 1966; chief Q.M. Supply div. 7th Logistical Command, Korea, 1961-62; comdg. officer 34th Supply and Service Bn., Vietnam, 1966, also dir. adminstrn. 58th Field Depot; exec. asst. joint logistics rev. bd. Office Sec. Def., Washington, 1969-70; comdg. officer Charleston (S.C.) Army Depot, 1970-72; joint logistics plans officer on staff comdr.-in-chief UN Command, 1972-73; logistics staff officer Joint and Strategic Forces Directorate, Army Concepts Analysis Agy., Bethesda, Md., 1973-74, ret.; asst. prof. pub. adminstrn. George Washington U., Washington, 1964-65, 67, assoc. prof., 1968-69, 73; assoc. prof. polit. sci. Bapt. Coll., Charleston, prof., 1974-87, emeritus prof., 1990; tchr., lectr., various colls., U.S. Korea, Vietnam; vis. prof. Central Mich. U., Webster U., St. Louis, Mo., 1974-87. Counselor, Boy Scouts Am., 1968-91; mem. citizen's adv. and action council to gov. Coastal Carolina Community Pre-release Center, S.C. Dept. Corrections; bd. dirs. Charleston Safety Council; apptd. spl. envoy by gov. for Commonwealth of Pa., 1970; mem. Rep. Nat. Com., 1983-87 (del. S.C. Rep. Conv., 1978, 80, 82, 84, 86; pres. 20th Rep. Precinct, S.C., 1978-86). With AUS, 1944-54. Decorated Legion of Merit with oak leaf cluster, Purple Heart with oak leaf cluster, Congl. Vietnam Vets. medal; recipient Presdl. Achievement award Pres. Ronald Reagan, 1982; Nat. Endowment for Humanities fellow U. Ga., summer 1978; Freedoms Found. at Valley Forge fellow, summers 1984-86. Mem. DAV (life), Charleston Trident C. of C., La. Societe Francaise deBienfaisance de Charleston, Dixie Chpt. 37th Infantry Div. Assn. (charter mem.), Am. Ex-Prisoners of War (nat. chpt.), Navy League, Mil. Order Purple Heart (life), Fed. Exec. Assn. (com. on govt.-wide policy areas), Armed Forces Mgmt. Assn., S.C. Law Enforcement Officers Assn., Nat. Def. Transp. Assn., Am. Bar Assn. (mem. Sr. Lawyers div.), S.C. Polit. Sci. Assn. (exec. council, pres.), Mensa, Internat. Airborne Assn. Vets., Sons Union Vets. of Civil War, Nat. Sourjourners (Ft. Lee chpt.), Heroes of 76 (Ft. Lee chpt.), Masons (32 deg.), Shriners, Kiwanis, Pi Sigma Alpha, Tau Kappa Epsilon, Pi Gamma Mu. Lutheran. Died 1991. Home: Charleston S.C.

HATANAKA, HIROSHI, neurosurgeon; b. Toyama Prefecture, Japan, Apr. 20, 1932; s. Taichi and Hana (Takahashi) H.; m. Anita Louisa Beck, Oct. 15, 1973; children: Elsa, Clara. MD, U. Tokyo, 1957, D of Med. Scis., 1963. Resident in surgery and neurosurgery U. Tokyo Hosp., 1958-62, asst. in surgery, 1963-64; Fulbright scholar, surg. rsch. fellow Harvard U., 1964-67; clin. and rsch. fellow Mass. Gen. Hosp., Boston, 1964-67, vis. fellow neurosurgery, 1971-72; asst. in neurosurgery U. Tokyo Hosp., 1967-73; prof. neurosugery Teikyo U., Tokyo, 1971-94; vis. resident in neurosurgery Montreal Neurol. Inst. and Hosp. at McGill U., summer 1966; disting. vis. prof. Ohio State U., Columbus, 1991-92. Mem. Japanese Cancer Assn., Japanese Surg. Soc., Japanese Congress Neurosurgeons, World Fedn. Neurol. Surgeons, Japan Neurosurg. Soc., Japan Soc. Practicing Surgeons, Internat. Coll. Surgeons, Japan Assn. Cancer Rsch., Asian and Australasian Soc. Neurol. Surgeons, Japan Soc. Cen. Nervous System Computed Tomography, Japan Radiol. Soc., Internat. Soc. Radiology, Japan EEG Soc., Japan Neuropathol. Soc., Japan Neurochemistry Soc., Internat. Soc. for Neutron Capture Therapy (founder, 1st pres. and sec.), Japan Soc. Clin. Imaging (exec. bd.), J.E. Purkyne Czech. Med. Assn. (hon.), Czech Neurosurg. Soc. (hon.). Mem. Society of Friends. Home: Tokyo Japan Died May 14, 1994.

HATCH, JOHN DAVIS, design consultant, art historian; b. Oakland, Calif., June 14, 1907; s. John Davis and Gethel (Gregg) H.; m. Olivia Phelps Stokes, Oct. 14, 1939; children: John Davis VI, Daniel Lindley, James Stokes, Sarah Stokes Saeger. Student, U. Calif., 1926-28; student Far Eastern Studies, Harvard U., 1931; student Near East Studies, Princeton U., summer 1938; student Am. Studies, Yale U., 1940; MA in Classical Studies, St. John's Coll., 1993. Landscape architect Santa Barbara, Calif., 1925, Seattle, 1928; exec. sec. Seattle Art Inst., 1928-29, dir., 1929-31; v.p. Western Assn. Art Museums, 1929-30; surveyed facilities and materials for Far Eastern studies in U.S. and Can., 1931-32, Am. studies in U.S. colls. and univs. for Am. Council Learned Socs., 1938-39; dir. U.S. art projects in New Eng., 1933-34; mem. McDowell Colony, 1938; asst. dir. Isabella Stewart Gardner Mus., Boston, 1932-35, Carnegie Corp., N.Y., 1935-37; founder, adviser So. Negro Colls. Coop. Exhibits Group, 1936-41; founder Am. Artist Depository, 1937, Am. Drawing Ann., 1940, Commn. on Art Studies, 1938; Dir. Albany Inst. History and Art, 1940-48; chmn. Albany-Nijmegen Holland Com., 1948; vis. prof. U. Oreg., 1948-49, U. Calif., summer 1949, U. Mass., summer 1971; dir. Norfolk Mus. Arts and Scis., 1950-59; pres. Phelps Stokes Corp., 1959-62; coordinating adviser, acting chmn. fine arts div. Spelman Coll., Ga., 1964-70; v.p. Nevada Co.; Chmn., founder Old Curtisville, 1965, pres. emeritus, 1981-96; former trustee Lenox Sch., Hoosac Sch.; hon. keeper Cape Henry Light House, Assn. for Preservation Va. Antiquities, 1948-96. Author: American sect. Great Drawings of All Times, 1962, Historic Survey of Painting in Canada, 1946, Historic Church Silver in the Southern Diocese of Virginia, 1952; Editor: Parnassus, 1937-39, Albany County Hist. Assn. Record, 1941-48, Early Am. Industries Chronicle, 1942-49; 100 Am. drawings, Dublin, London, Paris, 1976-77; had pioneer exhibit The Negro Artist Comes of Age, 1943, Painting in Canada, 1944, Thomas Cole, 1942, Outdoor Sculptors of Berkshires, 1978. Donated (with others) Anson Phelps Stokes Ref. Libr. to U. Liberia, 1980. Fellow Morgan Library, Met. Mus. N.Y., Nat. Gallery, Washington. Mem. Master Drawing Assn. (founder, hon. trustee), Am. Drawing Soc. (adv. bd.), Am. Assn. Mus. (founder northeastern conf. 1941, southeastern conf. 1951), Internat. Mus. Assn. (founding), Grolier Club (N.Y.C.), Cosmos Club (Washington), Harvard Mus. Club (Boston), Rotary. Episcopalian. Home: Santa Fe N. Mex. Died May 30, 1996.

HATCHER, MILFORD BURRISS, emeritus surgery educator; b. Macon, Ga., May 5, 1909; s. George Edwin and Kathleen (Ayer) H.; m. Marion Brown Campbell, June 1942; children: Kathleen Hatcher Cook, Milford Burriss Jr. BS magna cum laude, Furman U., 1931; MD, Med. Coll. Ga., 1935; DSc (hon.), Mercer U. Sch. Medicine, 1989. Diplomate Am. Bd. Surgery. Practice medicine specializing in gen. surgery Macon, 1939-41, 46-82; prof., chmn. dept. surgery Mercer U. Sch. Medicine, Macon, 1982-86, prof. and chmn. emeritus, 1986-91; chmn. bd. dirs. Ga. Bank, Macon, 1966-79, co-founder, 1960; co-founder Security Life Ins. Co., Macon, 1954; pres. Med. Assn. Ga., Atlanta, 1960-61. Co-founder Highland Hills Bapt. Ch., Macon, 1954; chmn. task force to establish Mercer U. Sch. Medicine, Macon, 1969, trustee, pres.'s council Mercer U.; chmn. Ga. Med. Polit. Action Com., Atlanta, 1961-63; pres. Med. Coll. Ga. Found. and Alumni Assn., Augusta; mem. Gov.'s adv. com. on cancer, Atlanta, 1986-91, Gov.'s Study Commn. on Indigent; bd. dirs. polit. action com. AMA, Chgo., 1963-64; bd. dirs. Greater Macon C. of C., 1981, Ga. div. Am. Cancer Soc., Atlanta, United Way, Macon. Served to lt. col. M.C., U.S. Army, 1941-46. Recipient Disting. Service award Med. Ctr. Cen. Ga., 1973, Disting. Alumnus award Med. Coll. Ga., 1985, Disting. Service award Med. Assn. Ga. Fellow ACS (cancer liaison), Southeastern Surg. Congress; mem. Internat. Coll. Surgeons (diplomate, regent), Ga. Surg. Soc. (pres. 1986-87), Alpha Omega Alpha. Club: Shield (Macon). Lodge: Rotary. Home: Macon Ga. Died Nov. 22, 1991.

HATCHETT, EDWARD EARL, retired aerospace manufacturing company executive; b. Amarillo, Tex., Aug. 18, 1923; s. Edward Lockett and Cora (Graham) H.; m. Kathryn Farwell, Apr. 27, 1943; 1 dau., Diane Hatchett Sanford. BS in Mgmt. Engring., Tex. A&M U., 1947; cert. exec. program, Stanford U., 1968. Registered profl. engr., Tex. Timestudy engr. Montgomery Ward & Co., Ft. Worth, 1947-49; with Ft. Worth divsn. Gen. Dynamics Corp., 1949-88, v.p. fin., 1970-88; lectr. def. preparedness U.S. Mil. Acad., West Point, N.Y., 1980-82. Div./group chmn. United Way Met. Tarrant County, 1974, 76-79, 81; bd. dirs., adv. council Ft. Worth Salvation Army, 1978-83; co-chmn. spl. gifts div. Tarrant County Salvation Army, 1987; bd. dirs. Casa Mañana Musicals, Ft. Worth, 1980-86, treas., 1984-86; chmn. Ft. Worth 7-County Area Com. for Employer Support of the Guard and Res., 1982-87, vice chmn. Tex., 1986-87; bd. dirs. Longhorn coun. Boy Scouts Am., 1980-90, exec. bd., 1981-90, v.p. fin., 1984-85, treas., 1986, chmn. Scout Show, 1982, 87; mem. Ft. Worth Mayor's Exec. Compensation Pay Com., 1983-84; chmn. Tarrant County Share-In-Freedom U.S. Savs. Bonds, 1967; mem. strategic issues adv. coun. North Tex. Commn., issues mgmt. adv. coun., 1980-83; chmn. gold card div. Tex. Christian U. Fund Campaign, 1981, group chmn. bus. and industry, 1982, group mgr. parents and friends, 1983-84, met. div. mgr., 1985-86; bd. dirs. Internat. Sister Cities Assn. Ft. Worth, 1988-91, chmn. tech. devel. bd. com.; adminstrv. bd. 1st United Meth. Exec. Svc. Corps, 1989-94; mem. Exec. Svc. Corps. Tarrant County, 1990-94, bd. dirs., treas., 1993. Maj. USAAF, 1943-46, 51-53, USAFR to lt. col., 1947-64. Recipient Presdl. citation Am. Soc. Value Engrs., 1974, Silver Beaver award Boy Scouts Am., 1988; named Jimmy Doolittle fellow Aerospace Found. of Air Force Assn., 1984. Mem. Am. Def. Preparedness Assn. (chpt. pres. 1977, nat. bd. dirs. 1975-88, dir. exec. com. 1979-88, mem. nat. exec. com. 1981-87, chmn. nat. fin. com. 1984-87, Outstanding Leadership award 1977), Fin. Execs. Inst. (chpt. bd. dirs. 1976-80, pres. 1979), Air Force Assn. (mem. state adv. coun. 1984-86, fellow Aerospace Found. 1984), Gen. Dynamics Mgmt. Assn., Ft. Worth Air Power Coun., Ft. Worth C. of C. (bd. dirs. 1980-83, 84-88), Greater Ft. Worth Area Civic Leader Assn., Exec. Women Internat. (Exec. of Yr., 1985), Ft. Worth A & M Club (bd. dirs. 1985). Methodist. Home: Fort Worth Tex. Died Jan. 21, 1996.

HATFIELD, WILLIAM EMERSON, chemist, educator; b. Ransom, Ky., May 31, 1937; s. Emerson B. and Pricy Gardner (Hatfield) H.; m. Peggy Ranson, Dec. 17, 1955 (div. 1967); children: Timothy Edward, Robert Bruce, Maryan, Julia, Ellen; m. Jane Alice Cheek, Nov. 22, 1967 (div. 1973). BS, Marshall U., 1958, MS, 1959; PhD, U. Ariz., 1962. Postdoctoral research assoc. U. Ill., Urbana, 1962-63; asst. prof. chemistry U. N.C., Chapel Hill, 1963-67; assoc. prof. U. N.C., 1967-72, prof., 1972-88, Mary Ann Smith prof., 1988-94, adj. prof. Applied Scis., 1988-94, vice chmn. chemistry dept., 1980-85, 87-90, acting chmn. applied scis., 1989-90; vis. scholar Cambridge U., 1978; vis. prof. U. Petroleum and Minerals, Dhahran, Saudi Arabia, 1980, Tata Inst., Bombay, India, 1981, U. Paris-Sud Orsay, 1987, U. Louis Pasteur, Strassburg, 1992; guest prof. Johannes Gutenberg U., Mainz, Fed. Republic Germany, 1982; mem. acad. adv. council GTE Labs, Inc., 1980-81; Am. specialist U.S. Dept. State, 1977; external examiner U. Sierra Leone, 1976-78; cons. in field; dir. NATO Advanced Research Inst., 1978; vis. lectr. U. P.R., 1982; Waite Philip Fishel lectr. Vanderbilt U., 1981; G.O. Doak lectr. N.C. State U., 1981. Author: (with R.A. Palmer) Problems in Structural Inorganic Chemistry, 1971, (with W.E. Parker) Symmetry in Chemical Bonding and Structure, 1974; editor: Molecular Metals, 1979; co-editor (with J.H. Miller Jr.) High Temperature Superconducting Materials, 1988; mem. editorial adv. bd. Jour. Inorganic and Nuclear Chemistry, 1977-82, Inorganic Chemistry, 1988-90; co-editor: (with R.P. Buck, M. Umaña, E. Bowden) Biosensor Technology, 1990. Recipient Disting. Alumnus award Marshall U., 1976; Guggenheim fellow, 1985-86. Mem. AAAS, Am. Chem. Soc. (treas. N.C. sect. 1985-86, chmn. 1988, chmn. inorganic exec. subcom. 1974-82, awards com. 1981-84, 87-89, nominations com. 1992, Charles H. Stone award Carolina-Piedmont sect. 1985, So. Chemist award Memphis sect. 1986, Marcus Hobbs award N.C. sect. 1993), Exams. Inst. (editl. adv. bd. 1986-87), Internat. EPR Soc., Material Rsch. Soc., Marshall U. Alumni Assn., U. Ariz. Alumni Assn., U. N.C. Alumni Assn. (assoc.), Sigma Xi. Democrat. Methodist. Home: Chapel Hill N.C. Deceased.

HAUGE, OLAV H., poet; b. Ulvik in Hardanger, Norway, Aug. 18, 1908; s. Haakon and Katarina (Hakastad) H.; m. Bodil Cappelen. Author: (poetry) Dikt i samling (collected Poems), 1981, 5th edit. 1995; translations: Don't Give Me the Whole Truth, selected poems, translated by Robin Fulton, 1985, Trusting Your Life to Water and Eternity, Twenty Poems by Olav H. Hauge, translated by Robert Bly, 1987, Selected Poems, translated by Robin Fulton, 1990, others; represented in numerous anthologies in different countries. Home: Hardanger Norway Died June 23, 1994; interred Ulvik, Hardanger, Norway.

HAUGEN, EINAR INGVALD, retired language educator, author; b. Sioux City, Iowa, Apr. 19, 1906; s. John and Kristine (Gorset) H.; m. Eva Lund, June 18, 1932; children: Anne Margaret, Camilla Christine. Student, Morningside Coll., Sioux City, 1924-27, Litt.D. (hon.), 1978; B.A., St. Olaf Coll., 1928, D.H.L. (hon.), 1958; M.A., U. Ill., 1929, Ph.D., 1931, Litt.D. (hon.), 1983; Litt.D. (hon.), U. Mich., 1953; M.A. (hon.), Harvard U., 1960; Ph.D. honoris causa, U. Oslo, Norway, 1961, U. Reykjavik, 1971, U. Trondheim, 1972, U. Uppsala, 1976; H.H.D., U. Wis., 1969, Luther Coll., 1975. Asst. prof. Scandinavian Langs. U. Wis., 1931-36, assoc. prof., 1936-38, Thompson prof. Scandinavian langs., 1938-62, Vilas research prof. Scandinavian lang. and linguistics, 1962-64; Victor S. Thomas prof. Harvard U., 1964-75, prof. emeritus, 1975-94; dir. Linguistic Inst., 1943-1944; tchr. army specialized tng. program, 1943-44; cultural relations officer (attaché) Am. embassy, Oslo, 1945-46; guest lectr. U. Oslo, 1938, Fulbright research prof., 1951-52; Fulbright lectr. U. Uppsala, 1976-77; instr. summers U. Minn., 1948, 58, 81, U. Mich., 1949, Georgetown U., 1954, Ind. U., 1964, U. Kiel, 1968; cons. English Lang. Exploratory Com., Tokyo, summer 1958, 1st sem., 1959-60; Guggenheim fellow, 1942-43; spl. State Dept. lectr. U. Iceland, Reykjavik, other Scandinavian univs., 1955-56; pres. IX Internat. Congress Linguists, 1962; mem. Permanent Internat. Com. Linguistics, pres., 1966-72. Author: Beginning Norwegian, 1937, 61, Norsk Amerika (Oslo), 1939, 75, Reading Norwegian, 1940 Norwegian Word Studies, 2 vols., 1941, Voyages t Vinland, 1941, 42, Spoken Norwegian, 1946, (with K.G Chapman), rev. edits., 1964, 82, First Grammatica Treatise, 1950, rev. edit., 1972, Norwegian Language i America: A Study in Bilingual Behavior, 1953, rev. edit. 1969, Bilingualism in the Americas: A Guide t Research, 1957, 2d edit., 1964, Norwegian-English Dic tionary, 1965, 3d edit., 1983, Language Conflict an Language Planning: The Case of Modern Norwegian 1966, The Norwegians in America, 1967, 75, Riksspraak og folkemaal, 1969, Ecology of Language, 1972, Studies 1972, (with T.L. Markey) The Scandinavian Languages 50 yrs. Ling Res, 1972, Bibliography of Scandinavian Languages and Linguistics, 1974, The Scandinavian Languages: An Introduction to their History, 1976 German transl., 1984, (with Eva L. Haugen) Land of th Free, 1978, Björnsön's Vocabulary, 1978, Ibsen' Drama: Author to Audience, 1979, Scandinavia Language Structures,1 982, Oppdalsmaalet, 1982, Blessings of Babel, 1987, Norwegian trans., 1980; editor Dumezil's Gods of the Ancient Northmen, 1973, (wit M. Bloomfield) Language is a Human Problem, 1974 Translated Beyer's History of Norwegian Lit, 1956 Kamban's We Murders, 1970, Koht's Life of Ibsen 1971, Ole Edvard Rølvaag, 1983, (with J. Buckley) Ha Ola og han Per, 1984, More han Ola og han Per, 1988 Immigrant Idealist: Life of Waldemar Ager, 1989, (wit Camilla Cai) Ole Bull, 1992; contbr. to publs. Decorated Order of St. Olaf, 1st class Norway; comd Order of North Star, Sweden; fellow Center Advance Study Behavioral Studies, 1963-64; sr. fellow NEH 1967-68; recipient Nansen award Oslo, 1970, Janck prize Uppsala, 1976. Mem. Am. Acad. Arts and Scis Danish, Icelandic, Norwegian, Swedish acads. sci Royal Norwegian Sci. Soc., Am. Dialect Soc. (pres 1965), Modern Lang. Assn., Linguistic Soc. Am. (pres 1950), Norwegian-Am. Hist. Assn. (bd. editors), others. Home: Belmont Mass. Died June 20, 1994.

HAUSER, PHILIP MORRIS, emeritus sociolog educator; b. Chgo., Sept. 27, 1909; s. Morris and An (Diamond) H.; m. Zelda B. Abrams, Nov. 27, 193 children—William Barry, Martha Ann. Ph.B., U Chgo., 1929, M.A., 1933, Ph.D., 1938; L.H.D Roosevelt U., Chgo., 1967; LL.D., Loyola U., Chgo 1969. Instr. sociology U. Chgo., 1932-37; Lucy Flowe prof. emeritus urban sociology, dir. emeritus Populatio Research Center; sr. fellow East West Population Inst chmn. dept. sociology, 1956-65; chief labor inventor sect. F.E.R.A. and W.P.A., 1934-37; asst. to dir. Stud of Social Aspects of Depression, Social Sci. Researc Council, 1937; asst. chief statistician Nat. Unemploy ment Census, 1937-38; asst. chief statistician for popu lation Bur. of Census, 1938-42, asst. dir., 1942-46, dep dir., 1946-47; acting dir. of U.S. Census, 1950; asst. t sec. Dept. of Commerce, 1945-47; U.S. rep. Populatio Commn. UN, 1947-51; statis. adviser to Govt. Union o Burma, UN Tech. Assistance, 1951-52; expert cons. t sec. of nat. def. Research and Devel. Bd.; statis. advise to govt. Thailand, 1955-56; Walker-Ames prof. U Wash., 1958; vis. Ford prof. Ind. U., 1960, U. Wash 1961, 62; assoc. Leo J. Shapiro and Assocs., Inc., 1977-81; Dir. Family of Selected Funds.; former mem. bd govs. Met. Planning and Housing Council, Chgo.; cons or mem. various coms. re population and vital statistic reporting; former dir. Social Sci. Research Counci research fellow and chmn. internat. adv. com. Population Research Inst. Nihon U., Tokyo, 1981-86. Autho Workers on Relief in U.S., 2 vols, 1939, Movies, Delinquency and Crime, (with Herbert Blumer), 1933, Population Perspectives, 1960, (with Beverly Duncan Housing A Metropolis- Chicago, 1960, The Challenge o America's Metropolitan Population Outlook: 1960-198 1968, (with Patricia Leavey Hodge) Social Statistics i Use, 1975, World Population and Development: Challenges and Prospects, 1979; assoc. editor: Jour. Am Statis. Assn, 1945-49, Am. Jour. Sociology; editor: (wit W.R. Leonard) Government Statistics for Business Use 1946, rev., 1956, Population and World Politics, 195 Urbanization in Asia and the Far East, 1958, The Stud of Population; An Inventory and Appraisal, 1959, (wit O.D. Duncan) Urbanization in Latin America, 196 The Population Dilemma, 1963, 2d edit., 1969, Th Study of Urbanization, 1965, (with Leo F. Schnore Handbook for Social Research in Urban Areas, 196 (with Judah Matras) Differential Mortality in the Unite States: A Study in Socioeconomic Epidemiology, 197 Contbr. articles to profl. jours. Chmn. Adv. Panel o Integration Chgo. Pub. Schs., 1963-64; mem. Ill. Am Negro Emancipation Commn., 1963-65; dir. Task Forc on Edn., White House Conf. to Fulfill These Right 1966; bd. dirs. Nat. Assembly for Soc. Policy an Devel.; pres. Nat. Conf. Social Welfare, 1973-74; mem exec. com. S.E. Asia Devel. Adv. Group. Fellow Am Statis. Assn. (pres. 1962-94), AAAS (sect. v.p. 1959 Am. Assn. for Pub. Opinion Research (chmn. standard com. 1948); mem. AAUP, Population Assn. Am. (pre 1951), Am. Sociol. Assn. (pres. 1967-68), Interna Statis. Inst., Inst. Math. Statistics, Sociol. Researc Assn. (pres. 1961), Nat. Acad. Scis., Am. Acad. Ar and Scis., Am. Philos. Soc., Internat. Union for Sc Study Population, Phi Beta Kappa, Lambda Alpha, Gamma Mu. Home: Chicago Ill. Died Dec. 13, 1994.

HAUSER, STANLEY FILLMORE, bishop; b. Lared Tex., Aug. 7, 1922; s. Stanley Fillmore and Elizabe

Mary (Merriman) H.; m. Madelyn May Horner, June 5, 1947; children: Mary Madelyn, Christine, Stanley, John, Mark. B.A., U. of the South, 1943, D.D. (hon.), 1985; M.Div., Va. Theol. Sem., 1946, D.D., 1980. Ordained priest Episcopal Ch., 1946. Rector Calvary Episcopal Ch., Menard, Tex., 1946-47; priest-in-charge St. James' Episcopal Ch., Fort McKavett, Tex., 1946-47; rector St. John's Episcopal Ch., Sonora, Tex., priest-in-charge Trinity Episcopal Ch., Junction, Tex., 1947-51; rector Zion Episcopal Ch., Charlestown, W.Va., 1951-60, St. Mark's Episcopal Ch., Houston, 1960-68, St. Mark's Episcopal Ch., San Antonio, 1968-79; bishop suffragan Episcopal Diocese W. Tex., San Antonio, 1979—; pres. Community of Chs., San Antonio, 1976-77. Trustee Va. Theol. Sem., Alexandria, 1958-60; bd. trustees U. of the South, Sewanee, Tenn., 1979—; bd. dirs. Amigos de las Americas, Houston, 1975-79. Home: San Antonio Tex.

HAWLEY, JEAN GANNETT, publisher; b. Augusta, Maine, Jan. 16, 1924; d. Guy Patterson and Anne (Macomber) G.; m. Roger Chilton Williams, Oct. 11, 1945 (div. 1952); children: Roger Chilton Jr. (dec.), Guy G., Timothy A.; m. Sumner A. Hawley, Dec. 21, 1970 (dec. Sept. 1993). Student, Bradford Jr. Coll., 1942-43; DBA (hon.), Portland U., 1958; LHD (hon.), Colby Coll., 1959, Nasson Coll., 1959; LLD (hon.), Bates Coll., 1980. Exec. v.p., mgr. nat. advtg. Guy Gannett Comm., Portland, Maine, 1953; pres. Guy Gannett Pub. Co., Portland, Maine, 1954-78, pub., 1959-94, also chmn. bd. dirs. Recipient Deborah Morton award Westbrook Coll., 1965. Home: Boca Raton Fla. Died Sept. 9, 1994.

HAYES, HELEN, actress; b. Washington, Oct. 10, 1900; d. Francis Van Arnum and Catherine Estell (Hayes) Brown; m. Charles MacArthur, Aug. 17, 1928 (dec. Apr. 1956); 1 child, James. Grad., Sacred Heart Acad., Washington, 1917; L.H.D., Hamilton Coll., Clinton, N.Y., 1939, Smith Coll., 1940, Elmira (N.Y.) Coll.; Litt.D., Columbia U., 1949, U. Denver, 1952; D.F.A., Princeton U., St. Mary's Coll. First appeared on stage, age six; mem. Columbia Players, Washington, 4 seasons; toured with Lew Fields and John Drew; mem. A.P.A. Phoenix Repertory Co., from 1966. Stage appearances include Old Dutch, Prodigal Husband, Pollyanna, Penrod, Dear Brutus, Clarence, Bab, To The Ladies, We Moderns, Dancing Mothers, Caesar and Cleopatra, What Every Woman Knows, Coquette, Mr. Gilhooley, Mary of Scotland, 1934, Victoria Regina, 1937-38, Ladies and Gentlemen, 1939-40, Twelfth Night, 1940-41, Candle in the Wind, 1941-42, Harriet, 1943-45, Happy Birthday, 1948, The Glass Menagerie, London, 1948, Farewell to Arms, 1950, Vanessa, 1950, The Wisteria Trees, 1950, Mrs. McThing, 1952, Main-street to Broadway, 1953, Skin of Our Teeth, Europe and U.S., 1955, Harvey, Long Days Journey Into Night, 1971; motion pictures include The Sin of Madelon Claudet (Acad. award 1932), Arrowsmith, My Son John, 1951, Anastasia, 1956, Airport, 1970 (Acad. award Best Supporting Actress 1971), Herbie Rides Again, 1974, Helen Hayes: Portrait of an American Actress, 1974, One of Our Dinosaurs is Missing, 1975, Candleshoe, 1978, Hopper's Silence, 1981; TV shows The Snoop Sisters, 1972-74, played Mrs. Derth in TV revival Barrie's Dear Brutus, 1956, Twelve Pound Look, Mary of Scotland, Skin of Our Teeth, Christmas Tie, Drugstore on a Sunday Afternoon, Omnibus, A Caribbean Mystery, Murder With Mirrors, others; author: (novels) Our Best Years, 1986, Where The Truth Lies, 1988; (autobiography) My Life in Three Acts, 1990. Pres. Am. Nat. Theatre and Acad.; hon. pres. Am. Theatre Wing; 2d v.p. Actors Fund, from 1975-93; chmn. women's activities Nat. Found. for Infantile Paralysis. Recipient best actress award Motion Pictures Acad. Arts and Scis., 1932, Emmy award, 1954, Antoinette Perry award for best actress in Time Remembered, 1958, Medal of City of N.Y., Medal of Arts Finland, Am. Exemplar medal Freedoms Found., 1978, Laetare medal U. Notre Dame, 1979, Medal of Freedom award Pres. of U.S., Nat. Medal of Arts, 1988, Louella Parsons award. Hollywood Women's Press Club, 1990. Republican. Roman Catholic. Home: Nyack N.Y. Died Mar. 17, 1993.

HAYS, DAVID GLENN, retired linguistics educator; b. Memphis, Nov. 17, 1928; s. Oliver Glenn and Adele (de Long) H.; m. Marguerite Frances Thompson, Feb. 4, 1950 (div. 1976); children: Dorothy Adele, Warren Stith, Thomas Glenn; m. Janet Adelson, Oct. 10, 1976. BA, Harvard U., 1951, MA, 1954, PhD, 1956. Social scientist Rand Corp., Santa Monica, Calif., 1954-68; prof. SUNY, Buffalo, 1968-80; owner Metagram, N.Y.C., 1980-90. Author: Evolution of Technology, 1991; contbr. articles to profl. jours. Mem. Internat. Com. on Computational Linguistics (hon., founding chmn. 1964-95). Democrat. Home: New York N.Y. Died July 26, 1995.

HAYS, THOMAS R., electronics executive; b. MacFarlan, W.Va., July 14, 1915; s. William R. and Myra (Wilson) H.; m. Jeane Ligney, May 11, 1945; children: Thomas R. Jr., Sharon Hays Stricchiola, Jeane Anne Hays Nerlino, Bonnie Hays Erlichman. BSEE, Ohio U., 1937; cert., Nothwestern U. Inst. Mgmt., 1959. Registered profl. electrical engr. Student engr. RCA Corp., Camden, N.J., 1937-38, radar and sonar engr., 1938-45; dist. sales mgr. Tube div. RCA Corp., Harrison, N.J., 1946-56; sales mgr. Picture Tube div., Receiving Tube div., Solid State div., Memory Products div. RCA Corp., Somerville, N.J., 1956-60, mktg. mgr. Solid State div., 1960-75; mgr. major accts. RCA Corp., Somerville, 1975-80; pres. Tom Hays, Inc., Madison, N.J., 1980—; realtor Coldwell Banker, 1986—; pres. Tom Hays, Inc., 1980—. Bd. dirs. Madison YMCA, 1982—; bd. dirs., v.p. Madison Meth. Ch., 1985—, pres. bd. trustees, 1988; mem. long range planning com. Morris County Bd. Realtors, 1988—, YMCA, 1989. Republican. Lodge: Rotary (v.p., bd. dirs., 1985—, pres.-elect, 1988, pres., 1989-90). Home: Scottsdale Ariz. Died May 1994.

HAYTON, JACOB WILLIAM, lawyer; b. Carterville, Ill., Mar. 17, 1926; s. James Wesley and Zella (West) H.; m. Beata Mueller, Mar. 17, 1962; 1 son, James Wesley. B.A., U. Chgo., 1946, J.D., 1950. Bar: Ill. 1950, U.S. Supreme Ct. 1981. Since practiced in Chgo.; partner firm Bell, Boyd & Lloyd, 1965-94. Treas. Beacon Neighborhood House, 1952-64, Chgo. Fedn. Settlements, 1959- 62. Mem. ABA, Chgo. Bar Assn., Order of Coif, Phi Beta Kappa. Unitarian. Clubs: University, Legal. Home: Evanston Ill. Died Feb. 14, 1994.

HAYWARD, JANE, museum curator; b. Orange, Conn., Aug. 13, 1918; d. Lawrence Herbert Hayward and Julia Ellen (Woodruff) Elliot. BFA, U. Pa., 1952, MA, 1954; PhD, Yale U., 1958; ArtsD (hon.), Stonehill Coll., 1980. Tech. illustrator Am. Viscose Corp., Phila., 1945-54; rsch. asst. Yale U. Art Gallery, New Haven, 1958-61; instr. Conn. Coll., New London, 1961-64, asst. prof., 1964-67; curator Lyman Allyn Mus., New London, 1961-65; Clawson Mills fellow Met. Mus. Art, N.Y.C., 1967-69, assoc. curator, 1969-74, curator, 1974-94; adj. prof. Columbia U., N.Y.C., 1971-89. Co-author articles in Ency. Britannica, World Book Ency., monographs. Trustee Stonehill Coll., North Easton, Mass., 1972-79. Recipient Monticello prize Yale U., 1956; Am. Coun. Learned Socs. fellow, 1966-67; Cresson scholar Pa. Acad. Fine Arts, 1940, 42. Fellow Internat. Ctr. Medieval Art (life, bd. dirs. 1977-86); mem. Census Stained Glass Windows in Am. (bd. dirs. 1979-94), Coll. Art Assn., Internat. Corpus Vitrearum (Am. rep. 1956-94, pres. Am. bd. 1982-94). Republican. Episcopalian. Home: Riverdale N.Y. Died Oct. 20, 1994.

HAZARD, JOHN NEWBOLD, retired law educator; b. Syracuse, N.Y., Jan. 5, 1909; s. John Gibson and Ada Bosarte (DeKalb) H.; m. Susan Lawrence, March 8, 1941; children: John Gibson, William Lawrence, Nancy, Barbara Peace. Ed., The Hill Sch., 1926; A.B., Yale U., 1930; LL.B., Harvard U., 1934; certificate, Moscow Juridical Inst., 1937; J.S.D., U. Chgo., 1939; LL.D. (hon.), U. Freiburg, 1969, Lehigh U., 1970, Leiden U., 1975, U. Paris, 1977, U. Louvain, 1979, U. Sydney, 1986, Miami U., 1991. Bar: N.Y. 1935, U.S. Supreme Ct. 1945. Fellow Inst. of Current World Affairs (student of Soviet law), 1934-39; asso. with law firm Baldwin, Todd & Young, N.Y.C., 1939-41; dep. dir. U.S.S.R. br. Fgn. Econ. Adminstrn. (and predecessor agys.), 1941-45; adv. on state trading Dept. State, 1945-46; prof. public law Columbia U., 1946-77; Nash prof. law Columbia U., N.Y.C., 1976-77; Nash prof. law emeritus Columbia U., 1977-95; adviser on Soviet law to U.S. chief of counsel for prosecution of Axis criminality, 1945; lectr. Soviet law U. Chgo., 1938-39; lectr. Soviet polit. instns. Columbia U., 1940-41; lectr. internat. politics Fgn. Svc. Ednl. Found., 1944-46; vis. prof. law Yale U., spring 1949, 50, 52, 54, 56; vis. Fulbright prof. U. Cambridge, London Sch. Econs., 1952-53, U. Louvain, Belgium, 1979; vis. prof. U. Tokyo, summer 1956, Grad. Sch. Internat. Studies, Geneva, 1959-60; prof. Luxembourg Comparative Law Faculty, summers 1958-60, Strasbourg Comparative Law Faculty, summers 1962-90; vis. prof. U. Teheran, fall 1966, U. Sydney, 1978, summer 1986; Goodhart prof. Cambridge U., 1981-82; prof. European U. Inst., 1984-85; sr. specialist East-West Center Hawaii, spring 1967; fellow Center for Advanced Study in the Behavioral Scis., 1961-62. Author: Soviet Housing Law, 1939, Law and Social Change in the USSR, 1953, The Soviet System of Government, 1957, Settling Disputes in Soviet Society, 1960, (with I. Shapiro) The Soviet Legal System, 1962, Communists and Their Law, 1969, Managing Change in the USSR, 1983, Recollections of a Pioneer Sovietologist, 1983 (enlarged edit. 1987); editor: Soviet Legal Philosophy, 1951; bd. editors: Am. Slavic and East European Rev; mng. editor, 1951-59; bd. editors: Am. Polit. Sci. Rev, 1950, Am. Jour. Internat. Law, 1956-72, hon. editor, 1974—; bd. editors: Am. Jour. Comparative Law, 1952-89. Dir. and sec. Am. Assn. for the Advancement of Slavic Studies, 1948-60, treas., 1961-65. Recipient Pres.'s Certificate of Merit, 1947. Mem. ABA (vice chmn. internat. and comparative law 1951-58), Assn. of Bar of City of N.Y. (com. on Soviet Affairs 1989-95), Am. Polit. Sci. Assn., Am. Soc. Internat. Law (v.p. 1971-73, hon. v.p. 1973-84, hon. pres. 1984-86), Am. br. Internat. Law Assn. (v.p. 1957-73, pres. 1973-79), Internat. Acad. Comparative Law (pres. 1984-89), Internat. Assn. Legal Sci. (pres. 1968-70), Am. Philos. Soc., Am. Acad. Arts and Scis., World Assn. Law Profs. (co-chmn. 1975-84), Consular Law Soc. (pres. 1986-87), others. Democrat. Episcopalian. Clubs: Century (N.Y.); Wolf's Head. Home: New York N.Y. Deceased April 7, 1995.

HAZELTINE, HERBERT SAMUEL, JR., retired lawyer; b. Huntington Beach, Calif., Dec. 12, 1908; s. Herbert S. and Emma (Phelps) H.; m. Frances Sue Coffin, July 5, 1936; children: Susan, Ann, Lynn. A.B., Stanford U., 1931; LL.D., Harvard U., 1934, U. So. Calif., 1979. Bar: Calif. 1935. Ptnr. Adams, Duque & Hazeltine, L.A., 1945-92. Life trustee Boys' Club Found. So. Calif., U. So. Calif., Chancery Club; bd. dirs. Los Angeles chpt. A.R.C. Served as lt. comdr. USNR, 1942-45. Mem. ABA, Am. Soc. Corp. Secs., Valley Club (Montecito, Calif.), Cypress Point. Home: Santa Barbara Calif. Died May 9, 1993.

HAZEN, JUDI, elementary school educator; b. Syracuse, Kans., Apr. 13, 1943; d. Charles E. and Linda. (Basham) Schoonover; m. Charles Craft Hazen, Dec. 17, 1966; children: Glenn Clifford Hazen, Elizabeth Lyn Hazen. BS, Colo. Woman's Coll., 1961-65. Cert. tchr., Calif. Elem. tchr. Livermore (Calif.) Sch. Dist., 1965-68, sci. tchr., 1982-92; dept. chmn. sci. Junction Middle Sch., Livermore, 1984-92. Named Tchr. of Yr. Livermore Sch. Dist., 1989-92, Outstanding Tchr., Calif. League of Middle Schs., 1993. Mem. NSTA, Calif. Sci. Tchrs. Assn. Home: Livermore Calif. Died Jan. 8, 1996.

HAZLITT, HENRY, author, former editor; b. Phila., Nov. 28, 1894; s. Stuart Clark and Bertha (Zauner) H.; m. Frances S. Kanes, 1936. Student, CCNY, 1912; Litt. D., Grove City Coll., Pa., 1958; LL.D., Bethany Coll., 1961; S.Sc.D., Universidad Francisco Marroquin, Guatemala, 1976. Mem. staff Wall St. Jour., 1913-16; fin. staff N.Y. Evening Post, 1916-18; writer monthly fin. Letter of Mechanics and Metals, Nat. Bank, N.Y.C., 1919-20; fin. editor N.Y. Evening Mail, 1921-23; editorial writer N.Y. Herald, 1923-24; editorial writer The Sun, 1924-25, lit. editor, 1925-29; lit. editor The Nation, 1930-33; editor Am. Mercury, 1933-34; editorial staff N.Y. Times, 1934-46; asso. Newsweek; writer column Bus. Tides, 1946-66; internationally syndicated columnist, 1966-69; co-editor The Freeman, 1950-52, editor-in-chief, 1953. Author: Thinking as a Science, 1916, 69, The Anatomy of Criticism, 1933, A New Constitution Now, 1942, rev. edit., 1974, Economics in One Lesson, 1946, rev. edit., 1979 (10 translations), Will Dollars Save The World?, 1947, Condensed in Reader's Digest, 1948, The Great Idea, 1951, rev. as Time Will Run Back, 1966, The Free Man's Library, 1956, The Failure of the New Economics; An Analysis of the Keynesian Fallacies, 1959, 73, What You Should Know About Inflation, 1960, 65, The Foundations of Morality, 1964, 73, Man vs. The Welfare State, 1969, The Conquest of Poverty, 1973, The Inflation Crisis and How to Resolve It, 1978, From Bretton Woods to World Inflation, 1983; editor: A Practical Program for America, 1932, The Critics of Keynesian Economics, 1960, new edit., 1977, Failure of the New Economics, 1984. Served in A.S., U.S. Army, World War I. Recipient Honor medal Freedoms Found., 1950, 60, 62. Mem. Mont Pelerin Soc. Clubs: Authors (London, Eng.); Century, Dutch Treat, Overseas Press (N.Y.C.). Home: Fairfield Conn. Died July 9, 1993.

HEALY, TIMOTHY STAFFORD, library official; b. N.Y.C., Apr. 25, 1923; s. Reginald Stafford and Margaret Dean (Vaeth) H. B.A., Woodstock Coll., Md., 1946, Ph.L., 1947, M.A., 1948; S.T.L., Facultes St. Albert, Louvain, Belgium, 1954; M.A., Fordham U., N.Y.C., 1957; D.Phil., Oxford U., 1965; M.A., 1979. Joined Soc. of Jesus 1940; ordained Roman Catholic priest, 1953. Instr. Latin and English Fordham Prep. Sch., N.Y.C., 1947-50; instr. English, asst. prof., assoc. prof., prof. Fordham U., 1955-69, exec. v.p., 1965-69; prof. English, vice chancellor for acad. affairs CUNY, 1969-76; prof. English, pres. Georgetown U., Washington, 1976-89, pres. emeritus, 1989-92; pres. N.Y. Pub. Library, 1989-92; mem. Pres.'s Commn. on Fgn. Lang. and Internat. Studies, 1978-79, mem. conf. bd., 1987-92; mem. Middle States Assn. Commn. on Higher Edn., 1976-79; mem. Nat. Adv. Com. on Accreditation and Instl. Eligibility U.S. Dept. Edn., 1981-83, chmn., 1982-83; mem. Council for Fin. Aid to Higher Edn., 1979-85; bd. dirs. Nat. Assn. Ind. Colls. and Univs., 1977-80, 84-87, chmn., 1980; bd. dirs. Am. Coun. on Edn., 1979-85, chmn., 1983-84; mem. U.S. sec. of state's adv. com. on South Africa, 1985-87; trustee Fordham U., 1989-92; bd. visitors grad. ctr. CUNY, 1989-92. Author: John Donne: Ignatius His Conclave, 1969, Georgetown, A Meditation on a Bicentennial, 1989; editor: (with Dame Helen Gardner) John Donne: Selected Prose, 1967; articles to profl. publs. Mem. Folger Com., Folger Shakespeare Libr., 1980-86; bd. dirs. Folger Theatre, 1986-89, African Am. Inst., 1987-92, Covenant House, 1990-92; trustee Regis High Sch., N.Y.C., 1987-92. Kent fellow, 1963-65, Supernumerary fellow St. Cross Coll., Oxford, 1979-92; Am. Council Learned Socs. grantee, 1971. Fellow Am. Acad. Arts and Scis., Soc. for Religion in Higher Edn., 1969; mem. Phi Beta Kappa, Alpha Sigma Nu. Democrat. Home: New York N.Y. Died Dec. 30, 1992.

HEARST, WILLIAM RANDOLPH, JR., editor; b. N.Y.C., Jan. 27, 1908; s. William Randolph and Millicent Veronica (Willson) H.; m. Austine McDonnell, July 29, 1948 (dec. June 1991); children: W.R. Hearst III, John Augustine Chilton. Student, U. Calif., 1925-27; LL.D., U. Alaska. Began career with N.Y. Am., N.Y.C., 1928; as reporter, asst. to city editor, pub. N.Y. Am., 1936-37; pub. N.Y. Jour.-Am., N.Y.C., 1937-56;

served as war corr., 1943-45; chmn. exec. com., dir. Hearst Corp. Bd. dirs. Hearst Found., William Randolph Hearst Found., USO Met. N.Y., House Ear Rsch. Inst. Recipient Pulitzer prize, 1956; Overseas Press Club award, 1958. Mem. UPI Inter-Am. Press Assn. (dir.), Sigma Delta Chi, Phi Delta Theta. Clubs: Madison Square Garden (N.Y.C.); Pacific Union (San Francisco). Home: New York N.Y. Died May 14, 1993.

HECHINGER, FRED MICHAEL, newspaper editor, columnist, foundation executive; b. Nuremberg, Germany, July 7, 1920; came to U.S., 1937, naturalized, 1943; s. Julius and Lilly (Niedermaier) H.; m. Grace Bernstein; children: Paul David, John Edward. Student, NYU, 1937-38; AB, CCNY, 1943; postgrad., U. London, 1945; LLD, Kenyon Coll., 1955; LLD (hon.), Bates Coll., 1963, U. Notre Dame, 1963, Knox Coll., 1966; LHD (hon.), Bard Coll., 1956, Wash. Coll., 1965, Wilkes Coll., 1968, St. Joseph's Coll., 1970, Rider Coll., 1972, Paine Coll., 1972, Trinity Coll., 1973, CCNY, 1977, SUNY, 1986, Marymount Manhattan Coll., 1987, Mercy Coll., 1988, Franklin Pierce Coll., 1990, Conn. Coll., 1991. Corr. London Times Ednl. Supplement, 1946-47; ednl. columnist Washington Post, 1947-50; edn. editor, fgn. corr., cons. to pub. Sunday Herald, Bridgeport, Conn., 1947-50; fgn. corr. Overseas News Agy., 1948-50; spl. writer This Week mag., 1946-59; edn. editor N.Y. Herald Tribune, 1950-56; assoc. pub. The Sunday Herald, Bridgeport, Conn., 1956-59; edn. editor The N.Y. Times, N.Y.C., 1959-69; mem. editorial bd. The N.Y. Times, 1969-77, asst. editorial page editor, 1976, edn. columnist, 1978-90; sr. advisor Carnegie Corp., N.Y.C., 1991-95; pres. N.Y. Times Co. Found., 1977-90; also bd. dirs.; contbg. editor Saturday Rev., 1977-78; adj. prof. CUNY, 1974-78; cons. edn. and cultural relations div. U.S. Mil. Govt., summers 1948, 49; Served with Office Mil. Attache Am. Embassy, London; also with Brit. War Office, 1944-46. Author: New Approaches, 1955, An Adventure in Education, 1956, Worrying About College, 1958, The Big Red Schoolhouse, 1959, A Better Start, 1986, Fateful Choices, 1992; (with Grace Hechinger) Teen-age Tyranny, 1963, Pre-School Education Today, 1966, The New York Times Guide to N.Y.C. Private Schools, 1968, Growing Up in America, 1975; (with Ernest L. Boyer) Higher Education in the Nation's Service, 1981; edn. editor Parents mag., 1957-59; contbr. to Change mag. Pres. N.Y. Times Neediest Cases Fund, 1977-90; mem. Pres.'s Commn. on Fgn. Langs. and Internat. Studies, 1978-79; vice chmn., bd. dirs. Carnegie Corp., 1985-91; bd. dirs. N.Y. Fgn. Policy Assn., Tchrs. Coll., Columbia U.; mem. adv. bd. Yale-New Haven Tchrs. program, Stanford and the Schs. program Stanford U.; co-chair nat. adv. bd. Ctr. for Study of Writing, U. Calif., Berkeley. Recipient Brit. Empire medal, George Polk Meml. award, 1950, 51, 90, Fairbanks award, 1952, Townsend Harris medal, 1968, Soc. Silurians editorial writing award, 1971, 76, Disting. Alumni medal, 1973, Disting. Service award Council Chief State Sch. Officers, Disting. Svc. medal Tchrs. Coll. Columbia U., 1990; Carnegie Found. Advancement of Teaching fellow, 1980-82; recipient Horace Mann Guardian award, 1983, James Bryant Conant award, 1989. Mem. Edn. Writers Assn. (pres. 1956, awards 1948, 49, 52, 64, 68, 73, 74, 76), Century Assn., Phi Beta Kappa. Home: New York N.Y. Died Nov. 6, 1995.

HECK, L. DOUGLAS, diplomat; b. Bern, Switzerland, Dec. 14, 1918; s. Lewis and Dorothy (Tompkins) H.; m. Ernestine Harriet Sherman, Mar. 27, 1972; children: Elizabeth Tompkins, Judith Kingsbury. Grad., Phillips Acad., Andover, Mass., 1937; BA, Yale U., 1941. With Dept. State, Washington, 1943-53; joined Fgn. Svc., 1952; polit. officer Am. consulate gen., Calcutta, India, 1953-56, Am. Embassy, New Delhi, 1956-59; chargé d'affaires Am. Embassy, Kathmandu, Nepal, 1959; dep. chief mission Am. Embassy, Nicosia, Cyprus, 1959-62; polit. counselor Am. Embassy, New Delhi, 1962-65; assigned to Nat. War Coll., 1965-66; country dir. for India, Nepal, Ceylon, and Maldive Islands Dept. State, Washington, 1966-68; consul gen. Am. consulate gen., Istanbul, Turkey, 1968-70; min.-counselor, dep. chief mission Am. embassy, Tehran, Iran, 1970-74; ambassador to Niger Niamey, 1974-76; dir. Office Combat Terrorism, Dept. State, 1976-77; amb. Nepal Kathmandu, 1977-80; mem. Am. del. to coronation of King Birendra of Nepal, 1975. Mem. Diplomatic and Consular Officers Ret. (assoc.), Himalaya Club, Delhi Golf Club, Zeta Psi. Home: Clatskanie Oreg. Died Jan. 13, 1993.

HEFFELBOWER, DWIGHT EARL, engineering services company executive; b. Newton, Kans., Aug. 28, 1925; s. Fred Clifford and Ruby Esther (Garrison) H.; m. Darlene Dorey, Feb. 1, 1948; children: Darl Jay, Kent Lewis, Gail Marie. B.S. in Chem. Engring., Kans. State U., 1949; student, Presbyn. Coll. of S.C., 1943. Engr. Burlington AEC plant Mason & Hanger-Silas Mason Co., Inc., Burlington, Iowa, 1949-56; chief engr. Mason & Hanger-Silas Mason Co., Inc., 1956-63, plant mgr. Iowa Army Ammunition plant, Burlington AEC plant, 1963-73; v.p. Mason & Hanger-Silas Mason Co., Inc., Lexington, Ky., 1973-80; exec. v.p. ops. Mason & Hanger-Silas Mason Co., Inc., Lexington, 1980-86; pres. Mason & Hanger-Silas Mason Co., Inc., 1986-92, chmn., ceo, 1992-94, also dir., 1975-94; v.p. Mason Co., 1986-87, pres., 1987-94, also bd. dirs.; chmn. bd. Mason Techs., Inc., Picayune, Miss.; chmn. bd. DWC Computer Solutions, Inc., Lexington, MCE, Inc.; bd. dirs. Mahco Inc., mason & Hanger Nat., Inc., Huntsville, Ala., Inc., Clute, Tex., Benchmark Electronics, Inc., Versa Tech. Inc., Lexington; mem. external adv. com. Los Alamos (N.Mex.) Nat. Lab. M-Div.; mem. weapons intelligence panel Dept. Energy, 1983, tech. adv. com. on verification of fissile material and nuclear warhead controls, 1991; more. Bd. dirs., v.p. Telford Found., Naples, Fla., 1989-94; trustee Hanger Trust, Lexington, Ky., 1992-94. 2d lt. USAAF, 1943-45. U. Ky. fellow, 1992; named hon. Ky. Coll. Mem. Am. Def. Preparedness Assn. (adv. bd. dirs. 1978-85), Keeneland Assn., Lexington C. of C. Home: Lexington Ky. Died June 23, 1994.

HEGARTY, WILLIAM EDWARD, lawyer; b. N.Y.C., Nov. 18, 1926; s. William Alfred and Mary Johanna (Condon) H.; m. Barbara Meade Fischer, Oct. 26, 1950; children: Katharine Hegarty Bouman, Mary Hegarty Colombo, William, Amanda. AB, Princeton U., 1947; LLB, Yale U., 1950. Bar: N.Y. 1951, U.S. Supreme Ct. 1962, D.C. 1973, Conn. 1989. With Cahill, Gordon & Reindel (and predecessors), N.Y.C., 1950-87, ptnr., 1962-69, sr. ptnr., 1969-87; counsel Mcpl. Art Soc. N.Y., 1988-92. Bd. dirs. Mcpl. Art Soc. N.Y., Florence J. Gould Found., French Inst./Alliance Francaise, Mianus Gorge Preserve, Inc., Mianus River Watershed Coun. With USNR, 1944-46. Decorated Chevalier Legion of Honor, France. Mem. ABA, Am. Bar Found., Assn. of Bar of City of N.Y., Am. Law Inst., Am. Coll. Trial Lawyers, Indian Harbor Yacht Club, India House Club, Princeton Club N.Y. Home: Greenwich Conn. Died Dec. 22, 1992.

HEGENER, MARK PAUL, publisher, clergyman; b. Petoskey, Mich., Apr. 6, 1919; s. John and Anna Marie (Mayer) H. A.B., St. Joseph Sem., Teutopolis, Ill., 1938; postgrad., 1942-46, St. Joseph Sem., Cleve., 1939-42; B.J., Marquette U., 1948. Joined Order of Friars Minor, Roman Catholic Ch., 1938; ordained priest Order of Friars Minor Roman Catholic Ch., 1945; mng. dir. Franciscan Herald Press, Chgo., 1949-86; pub. Franciscan Herald mag., 1955-86; provincial dir. Lay Franciscans, 1949-86. Author: Poverello: St. Francis of Assissi, 1958, Short History of the Third Order of St. Francis, 1963. Pres., founder Mayslake Village Retirement Complex, Oak Brook, Ill., 1962—, Chariton Apts. Retirement Complex, St. Louis, 1968—; founder, trustee Cath. Theol. Union at Chgo., 1968-76; trustee Quincy Coll., 1972-76. Mem. Am. Home Builders Assn., Am. Assn. Homes for Aging, Cath. Press Assn. Home: Hinsdale Ill.

HEGGS, OWEN L., lawyer; b. Cleve., Oct. 1, 1942. BA, Howard U., 1964; JD, Case Western Reserve U., 1967. Bar: Ohio 1967. Ptnr. Jones, Day, Reavis & Pogue, Cleve.; assoc. prof. law Case Western Reserve U., 1974-79. Mem. Order of Coif. Home: Cleveland Ohio Deceased.

HEINEN, CHARLES M., retired chemical and materials engineer. Student, Chrysler Inst.; BSChemE, U. Mich., MSChemE, 1942. Various positions Chrysler Corp., 1934-42, lab. supr. Manhattan project, 1942-45, from materials engr. to dir. dir. emissions/fuel economy and materials engring., 1945-78, former dir. rsch. and materials engring., cons., dir. automotive rsch. group. Recipient Soichiro Honda medal ASME, 1990. Fellow Soc. Automotive Engrs. (fuels and lubricants activities com.), Am. Soc. Metals (com. govt. and pub. affairs, chmn. numerous coms.); mem. Soc. Testing and Materials, U.S. C. of C. (former mem. com. on environment), Engring. Materia Coun., Motor Vehicle Mfg. Assn. U.S. (former mem. quality com.), Coord. Rsch. Coun. (past chmn. group combustion of exhaust gas), Air Pollution Control Assn. Home: Bloomfield Hills Mich. Died Mar. 15, 1994.

HEITZMAN, ROBERT EDWARD, retired materials handling equipment manufacturing company executive; b. Covington, Ky., May 7, 1927; s. Edward John and Philomena (Tegeder) H.; m. Mary Ellen Grom, Aug. 28, 1948; children: Robert Edward, Barbara E., William F. B.S.M.E., U. Cin., 1951. Registered profl. engr., Ohio, N.J., Ky. Internat. engring. mgr. Procter & Gamble Corp., 1951-66; internat. bus. mgr. Allied Chem. Corp., 1966-69; v.p. mfg. Whitehall div. Am. Home Products Corp., 1969-74; sr. v.p. internat. Englehard Industries div. Engelhard Minerals & Chems. Corp., Iselin, N.J., 1975-81; pres., co-owner Buck-El Inc., Murray Hill, N.J., 1982-91. Served with USNR, 1945-46; with AUS, 1947-48. Mem. Greater Newark C. of C. (dir., exec. com. 1978-79), Delta Tau Delta. Home: Lexington Ky. Died Mar. 26, 1995.

HELLER, ROBERT LEO, university chancellor emeritus, geology educator; b. Dubuque, Iowa, Apr. 10, 1919; s. Edward W. and May Olive (Bauck) H.; m. Geraldine Hanson, Sept. 26, 1946; children: Roberta, Katherine, Nancy. B.S., Iowa State U., 1942; M.S., U. Mo., 1943, Ph.D., 1950. Geologist U.S. Geol. Survey, 1943-44; mem. faculty U. Minn., Duluth, 1950-87; prof. geology, chmn. dept. U. Minn., 1960-67, from asst. to provost to assoc. provost, 1965-76, provost, 1977-85, chancellor, 1985-87, chancellor emeritus, 1987-93; dir. NSF earth sci. curriculum project U. Colo., 1963-65; mem. U.S. Nat. Com. Geology, 1977-81; editor Environment Times, 1976-80. Contbr. numerous articles to profl. publs. Vice pres. St. Louis County Heritag and Arts Ctr., 1974-77; vice chmn. Environ. Learnin Ctr., 1987-90, chmn., 1990-93; bd. dirs. Lake Superic Ctr., 1988-93, St. Luke's Hosp. Found., 1987-93; bc dirs. Miller-Dwan Med. Ctr. Fedn., 1973-86, chmn 1984-86. Served to 2d lt. C.E., AUS, 1944-47. Recipient Neil Miner award Nat. Assn. Geology Tchrs 1965, citation of merit Coll. Scis. and Humanities, Iow State U., 1976, Comdrs. medal Order of Lion (Finland 1981, Disting. Alumni award U. Mo., 1988. Mem. Na Assn. Geology Tchrs. (pres. 1976-77), Am. Geol. Ins (v.p. 1977-78, pres. 1978-79, Ian Campbell medal 198 William B. Heroy award 1991), Am. Geol. Inst. Founc (vice chmn. 1984-86, chmn. 1986-92), Coun. Sci. Soc Presidents (vice chmn. 1980-81, chmn. 1981-82), Geo Soc. Am., Paleontol. Soc., AAAS, Am. Assn. Petroleur Geologists, U. Minn. Alumni Assn. (Disting. Svc. awar 1972). Home: Duluth Minn. Died July 11, 1993; ir terred Park Hill Cemetary, Duluth, Minn.

HELLER, WILLIAM F., II, insurance company ex ecutive. AB, Georgetown U., 1960; JD, Cornell U 1963. Bar: N.Y. 1965. V.p., assoc. counsel Tchrs. Ins and Annuity Assn. Am., N.Y.C. Mem. ABA. Home New York N.Y. Died 1991.

HELLIWELL, DAVID LEEDOM, investment com pany executive; b. Vancouver, BC, Can., July 26, 193 s. John Leedom and Kathleen B. (Kerby) H.; m. Mar garet Jeanette Adam, June 2, 1961; children: Kerby C Wendy J., Catherine J., Marnie L., John A. B.A., U B.C., 1957. With Thorne Riddell & Co., 1962-65; div mgr. Steel Bros. Can. Ltd., 1965; v.p., gen. mgr. Stee Bros. Can. Ltd., for B.C., 1967, for Alta., 1969; exec v.p. Steel Bros. Can. Ltd., 1971-73, pres., 1973-78; pres chief exec. officer B.C. Resources Investment Corp Vancouver, 1978-80; chmn. B.C. Resources Investmen Corp., 1980-81; pres. Marin Investments Ltd Vancouver, 1981-86, D.L. Helliwell & Assocs. Ltd Vancouver, 1986-93; bd. dirs. Gwill Industries Ltd Seaboard Life Ins. Co., Can., Mark Anthony Grou Ltd. Fellow Inst. Chartered Accts. of B.C.; mem. Car Inst. Chartered Accts. Anglican. Clubs: Vancouver. Home: Vancouver Can. Died Dec. 30, 1993.

HEMMING, ROY G., writer, magazine editor, broad caster; b. Hamden, Conn., May 27, 1928; s. Benjami Whitney and Anna (Sexton) H. B.A., Yale U., 194 M.A., Stanford U., 1951; grad. cert., U. Geneva, 1950. News editor, program dir. Sta. WAVZ-AM-FM, Nev Haven, 1948-50; writer Voice of Am., 1951-52; wit news dept. NBC, N.Y.C., 1953-54; writer-editor Scholastic Mags., Inc., N.Y.C., 1954-74; publs. dir. Scholastic Internat., 1972-74; editor-in-chief Retiremer Living, also 50 Plus, Whitney Communications Corp N.Y.C., 1975-80; contbg. editor Stereo Rev., 1973-8 from 86, Ovation mag., 1980-88; Gramophone mag from 1992; revs. editor Video Rev., 1980-94; Entertainment Weekly, from 1992; bd. advisers Easter Music Festival, Greensboro, N.C., from 1970; mem Montreux (Switzerland) Internat. Record Award Com 1971-76. Program producer, scriptwriter N.Y Philharm. weekly nat. radio broadcasts, 1979-90, Bosto Symphony Tanglewood broadcasts, 1987; author: Discovering Music: Where to Start on Records and Tape 1974, Movies on Video, 1981, The Melody Lingers On The Great American Songwriters and Their Movi Musicals, 1986, Discovering Great Music on CDs, LP and Tapes, 1988, rev. edit., 1990, 92, 94; co-autho (with David Hajdu) Discovering the Great Singers c Classic Pop, 1991. Mem. Young Republican Club, Nev Haven, 1949-51, N.Y.C., 1951-58. Served with USNR 1945-46. Recipient All-Am. award Ednl. Pubs. Assn 1965, 67. Mem. Nat. Acad. of Recording Arts and Sc Authors Guild (N.Y.C.), N.Y. Sheet Music Soc., N.Y Assn. Cabarets, Duke Ellington Soc., N.Y.C. Club Overseas Press; Deadline (N.Y.C.), Yale (N.Y.C. Stanford of N.Y., N.J., Conn. Home: New York N.Y Deceased.

HENDERSON, JAMES ALEXANDER, financial an banking executive; b. N.Y.C., Feb. 6, 1921; s. James A and Charlotte (Fisher) H.; m. Jean Conway, June 1 1951; children: Elizabeth Barrera, Hilary Ann Henderson Stephens, James Alexander Jr., John Geoffrey. A.B., Hamilton Coll., 1941; postgrad., Columbia 1946-47. With Gen. Electric Co., 1941-42; with Am Express Co., 1947-82, asst. v.p., 1954-57, v.p., 1958-6 sr. v.p., 1964-66, treas., 1966-68, exec. v.p., 1968-8 chmn. bd., dir. Am. Express Pub. Corp., 1968-80; pres dir. Am. Express Can., Inc., 1975-82. Trustee Kno Sch.; former trustee Hamilton Coll. Served with AUS 1942-46, ETO. Decorated Bronze Star. Mem. Internat Golf Assn., River Club, Univ. Club, Nissequogue Gol Club (chmn., gov.). Democrat. Episcopalian. Home Saint James N.Y. Died July 25, 1993.

HENDERSON, JAMES MARVIN, advertising agenc executive; b. Atlanta, Mar. 28, 1921; s. Isaac Harmo and Ruth (Ashley) H.; m. Donna Fern Baade, Apr. 2 1945; children: Linda Dee, James Marvin, Debora Fanchon. Student, Furman U., 1939-40, Clemson Coll 1940-42; also night classes, N.Y.U., 1943-44; B.S., U Denver, 1946; grad., Advanced Mgmt. Program Harvard, 1956. Sales supr. Gen. Foods Corp., N.Y.C 1942-44; account exec. Curt Freiberger Advt. Agy Denver, 1944-46; pres. Henderson Advt., Inc., Green ville, S.C., 1946-95; now founder chmn.; pres. Ne

South Devel. Co. Inc.; pres. Henderson-Saussy Advt., New Orleans, 1966-69; dir. Citizens & So. Nat. Bank, First Fed. Savs. and Loan Assn., Greenville., 1st Fed. of S.C.; Spl. asst. to postmaster gen., 1969-70; adj. prof. Clemson U. and Furman U. Mem. Greenville Youth Commn., 1953-54; chmn. Leadership Greenville Com., 1975, Eisenhower campaign Greenville County, 1952; Republican candidate for lt. gov. S.C., 1970; S.C. state chmn. com. to Re-elect Pres., 1972; adv. bd. Campaign '76 for Pres. Ford, 1976; pres. Greenville Heart Assn.; pres., bd. dirs. Greenville Mental Hygiene Clinic, United Fund.; bd. dirs. Clemson Found.; trustee Converse Coll. Served with AUS, World War II. Named Young Man of Year Greenville, 1954; named to S.C. Bus. Hall of Fame, 1989. Mem. S.C. Jr. C. of C. (past dir.), Greenville Jr. C. of C. (past pres.), Greater Greenville C. of C. (past pres.), Young President's Orgn. (chmn. S.E. chpt.), Greenville Advt. Council (past pres.), Am. Assn. Advt. Agys. (vice chmn. SE region 1954, chmn. SE council 1955, client service com. 1963, nat. dir. 1964, gov. Eastern region 1965, sec.-treas. 1971). Methodist. Lodge: Kiwanis (past pres.). Home: Greenville S.C. Died Oct. 31, 1995.

HENDERSON, ROBERT FRANKLIN, JR., lawyer; b. Denton, Tex., Sept. 19, 1944; s. Robert Franklin and Lois Ann (Wilkins) H.; m. Marina Gloria Sharp, Aug. 23, 1969; 1 child, Charles Andrew. BA, U. Tex., 1967, JD, 1969. Bar: Tex. 1969. Legis. counsel Tex. Legis. Coun., Austin, 1969-77, asst. legal dir., 1977-83, legal dir., gen. counsel, 1983-86; assoc. Hughes & Luce, Austin, 1986-87, ptnr., 1987-94. Mem. ABA, State Bar Tex., Travis County Bar Assn., Met. Club, Univ. Club, Austin Club. Democrat. Methodist. Home: Austin Tex. Died Oct. 12, 1994.

HENIZE, KARL GORDON, astronaut, astronomy educator; b. Cin., Oct. 17, 1926; s. Fred R. and Mabel (Redmon) H.; m. Caroline Rose Weber, June 27, 1953; children: Kurt Gordon, Marcia Lynn, Skye Karen, Vance Karl. Student, Denison U., 1944-45; B.A., U. Va., 1947, M.A., 1948; Ph.D., U. Mich., 1954. Observer U. Mich. Lamont-Hussey Obs., Bloemfontein, Union South Africa, 1948-51; Carnegie postdoctoral fellow Mt. Wilson Obs., Pasadena, Calif., 1954-56; sr. astronomer in charge photog. satellite tracking stas. Smithsonian Astrophys. Obs., Cambridge, Mass., 1956-59; assoc. prof. dept. astronomy Northwestern U., Evanston, Ill., 1959-64, prof., 1964-72; scientist-astronaut NASA Johnson Space Ctr., Houston, 1967-86, sr. scientist, 1986-93; guest observer Mt. Stromlo Obs., Canberra, Australia, 1961-62; prin. investigator astronomy expts. for Gemini 10, 11, 12 and Skylab 1, 2, 3, 1964-78; mem. astronomy subcom. NASA Space Sci. Steering Com., 1965-68; adj. prof. dept. astronomy U. Tex., Austin, 1972-93; team leader NASA Facility Definition Team for Starlab Telescope, 1974-78; chmn. NASA working group for Spacelab Wide-Angle Telescope, 1978-79; jet pilot tng. Vance AFB, Enid, Okla., 1968-69; mem. support crew Apollo 15 and Skylab 1, 2, 3, 1970-73, mission specialist ASSESS 2 Spacelab simulation, 1976-77, mission specialist Shuttle flight 51F (Spacelab 2), 1985. Served with USNR, 1944-46; lt. comdr. Res., ret. Recipient Robert Gordon Meml. award, 1968; NASA medal for exceptional sci. achievement, 1974, Space Flight medal, 1985, Flight Achievement award Am. Astronautical Soc., 1985. Mem. Am., Royal, Pacific astron. socs., Internat. Astron. Union, Phi Beta Kappa. Home: Houston Tex. Died Oct. 5, 1993; interred Mt. Everest, Tibet, China.

HENN, HARRY GEORGE, law educator, writer; b. New Rochelle, N.Y., Oct. 8, 1919; s. Harry Christian and Mollie (Malsch) H. BA summa cum laude, NYU, 1941, JD, 1952; LLB with distinction, Cornell U., 1943. Bar: N.Y. 1944. Assoc. Whitman, Ransom & Coulson, N.Y.C., 1943-53; mem. faculty Cornell U. Law Sch., 1953-85, prof. law, 1957-85, Edward Cornell prof. law, 1970-85, prof. emeritus, 1985-94, Donald C. Brace Meml. lectr., 1978; vis. prof. law Hastings Coll. Law, 1979, NYU, 1983; spl. counsel Cornell U., 1953-56; pres., dir. Cornell Daily Sun, 1966-73; guest lectr. NYU, 1953-78; acting village justice, Cayuga Heights, Ithaca, N.Y., 1965-74; trustee Copyright Soc. U.S., 1953-94, pres., 1961-63; mem. UNESCO panel internat. copyright; also panel cons. gen. revision copyright law; cons. corp. law annotated project Am. Bar Found., 1959-60, 63-64, 68; rsch. cons. N.Y. State Joint Legislative Com. to Study Revision Corp. Laws; also Library of Congress. Author: Copyright Primer (reentitled Henn on Copyright Law), 1979, 2nd edit., 1988, 3rd edit., 1991, Teaching Materials Agency, Partnership and Other Unincorporated Business Enterprises, 1972, 2nd edit., 1985, Teaching Materials on the Laws of Corporations, 1974, supplement, 1980, 2nd edit., 1986; co-author: Laws of Corporations and Other Business Enterprises, 3rd edit., 1983, supplement, 1986; contbr. articles to profl. publs.; editor-in-chief Cornell Law Quar., 1943. Pres. Ithaca Opera Assn., 1968-73, 79-81; trustee South Cen. Rsch. Libr. Coun., 1967-74. Mem. Internat. Gesellschaft für Urheberrecht E.V., N.Y. State Assn. Magistrates, Order of Coif, Phi Beta Kappa, Delta Upsilon, Phi Kappa Phi (chpt. pres. 1964-65), Phi Delta Phi. Home: Jacksonville Fla. Died Oct. 11, 1994.

HENRICI, PETER KARL, mathematics educator; b. Basel, Switzerland, Sept. 13, 1923; s. Hermann and Erika (Muller) H.; m. Eleonore Jacottet, 1951 (div. 1972); children—Christoph, Katherine; m. 2nd Marie Louise Kaufmann, Mar. 1, 1973; 1 child, Andreas. Maturity Gymnasium, 1942; Elec. Engring. diploma, Fed. Inst. Tech., 1948, Math. diploma, 1951, Ph.D. Math., 1953. Research asst. Fed. Inst. Tech., Zurich, 1949-51, prof. math., 1962—; research assoc. Am. U., Washington, 1951-56; prof. math. UCLA, 1956-62; Kenan prof. math U. N.C., Chapel Hill, 1985—. Author 10 books on complex and numerical analysis. Author numerous research papers. Named John v. Neumann lectr. Soc. Indsl. and Applied Math., 1977. Mem. Am. Math. Soc., Math. Assn. Am., Soc. Indsl. Applied Math., Ges. angew. Math. Mech. Avocation: music. Home: Forch Switzerland

HENRY, PAUL BRENTWOOD, congressman; b. Chicago, Ill., July 9, 1942; s. Carl F. and H. I. (Bender) H.; m. Karen Anne Borthistle, Aug. 28, 1965; children: Kara Elizabeth, Jordan Mark, Megan Anne. B.A., Wheaton Coll., 1963; M.A., Duke U., 1968, Ph.D., 1970. Vol. Peace Corps, Liberia, 1963-64; vol. Peace Corps, Ethiopia, 1964-65; instr. polit. sci. Duke U., Durham, N.C., 1969-70; assoc. prof. Calvin Coll., Grand Rapids, Mich., 1970-78; mem. Mich. Ho. of Reps., Lansing, 1979-82, asst. minority floor leader, 1979-82; mem. Mich. Senate, Lansing, 1983-85, 99th-103rd Congresses from 5th (now 3rd) Mich. dist., Washington, 1985-93. Author: Politics for Evangelicals, 1974, (with Stephen V. Monsma) The Dynamics of the American Political System, 1970. Mem. Mich. Bd. Edn., 1975-78; Kent County Republican chmn., Mich., 1975-76. Fellow Duke U., Durham, N.C. Mem. Am. Polit. Sci. Assn. Mem. Christian Reformed Ch. Home: Grand Rapids Mich. Died July 31, 1993.

HENRY, WILLIAM ALFRED, III, journalist, critic, author; b. South Orange, N.J., Jan. 24, 1950; s. William Alfred and Catherine Anne (Elliott) H.; m. Gail Louisa Manyan, Oct. 3, 1981. B.A. (Scholar of the House), Yale U., 1971; postgrad. in History, Boston U., 1973-74. Edn. writer Boston Globe, 1971-72, arts critic, 1972-74, state house polit. reporter, 1974-75, editorial writer, 1975-77; TV editor and columnist Boston Globe, syndicated Field News Service, 1977-80; also weekly book reviewer and occasional nat. and fgn. polit. reporter; critic-at-large N.Y. Daily News, 1980-81; assoc. editor Time mag., N.Y.C., 1981-89, sr. writer, 1989-94, press critic, 1982-85; theater critic, book reviewer Time mag., 1985-94; lectr. Harvard U., MIT, Columbia U., other schs.; mem. faculty Tufts U., 1979, Yale U., 1980; Young Am. Leader traveling fellow EEC, 1977; Poynter fellow in journalism Yale U., 1980; mem. theater panel Mass. Coun. on the Arts, 1977-80; Clarence Derwent, Bayfield, Callaway and Weissberger awards drama judge; Tony awards voter; Pulitzer prize drama judge, 1986-87, chmn., 1989-90, 91-92, 93-94. Prin. author: The Insiders Guide to the Colleges, 1970, 2d edit., 1971, The Blue Football Book, 1971; author: Visions of America: How We Saw the 1984 Election, 1985, TV Special, "Bob Fosse: Steam Heat", PBS Great Performances, 1990, The Great One: The Life and Legend of Jackie Gleason, 1992, In Defense of Elitism, 1994; contbg. author: Great Voices, Small Trumpets: The Media and Minorities, 1980, What's News: The Media in American Society, 1981, Fast Forward, 1983, Pro and Con, 1983, The Road to The White House, 1988, Media Issues and Debate, 3d edit., 1989, Parents Choice Magazine Guide to Video Cassettes for Children, 1989, Jack Benny: The Radio and Television Years, 1991, The Nobel Prize Annual, 1991; contbr. articles to newspapers, mags., encys.; numerous speeches, panels and radio, TV appearances. Mem. task force Mass. Commn. Edn., 1972; historian, bd. dirs. Stone Trust Corp., N.Y.C., 1971-94, Proposition Workshop Inc., Cambridge, 1974-94, Cambridge Ensemble, 1976-80, Leukemia Soc. Greater Boston, 1978-80; mem. adv. bd. Opera Ensemble N.Y., 1985-91; sec. Yale Class 1971, 81-86, coun., 1986-94; rep. to Assn. Yale Alumni, 1986-89; active in fundraising for Yale U., various humane socs., arts groups. Recipient Story of Yr. award New Eng. AP, 1976, Best Feature of Yr. award New Eng. UPI, 1976, Pulitzer prize in criticism, 1980, William Allen White award city, state and regional mags., 1989; co-recipient Pulitzer prize in pub. svc., 1975, UPI New Eng. editorial prize, 1977, Overseas Press Club award, 1990, Emmy award for best info. spl., 1990, Liberty-Unity in Media award Lincoln U., 1991; co-finalist Nat. Mag. award, 1982, 89, 94, Lowell Mellett citation in press criticism, 1984; citation Nat. Conf. of Ams. and Jews, 1991, Gay and Lesbian Alliance Against Defamation, 1990, 91. Mem. ACLU, TV Critics Assn. (founding treas. 1978-79, chmn. spkrs. bur. and profl. edn. 1979-80, bd. dirs. 1980-81), N.Y. Drama Critics Cir. (v.p. 1990-91, pres. 1991-93), Am. Theatre Critics Assn. (awards com. 1993-94). Clubs: St. Botolph (Boston); Book and Snake (New Haven), Elizabethan (New Haven); Yale (N.Y.C.); Players (N.Y.C.). Home: Plainfield N.J. Died June 28, 1994.

HENSHAW, EDGAR CUMMINGS, academic researcher, physician; b. Cin., Dec. 14, 1929; s. Lewis Johnson and Dorothy (Cummings) H.; m. Betty Ann Barnes, Dec. 20, 1958; 1 child, Daniel. AB, Harvard U., 1952, MD, 1956. Intern II and IV Harvard Med. Svc., Boston City Hosp., 1956-57, asst. resident in medicine, 1959-60; rsch. fellow dept. bacteriology Harvard U. Med. Sch., Boston, 1960-62, instr. medicine, 1962-64, assoc. in medicine, 1964-69, asst. prof., 1969-71, assoc. prof., 1971-76; assoc. in medicine Beth Israel Hosp., Boston, 1963-71, asst. physician, 1971-76; prof. oncology in medicine, prof. biochemistry Cancer Ctr. U. Rochester Sch. Medicine and Dentistry, N.Y., 1976-92; asst. dir. basic sci. div. Cancer Ctr., N.Y., 1978-84, assoc. dir. basic sci. div., 1984-92; vis. lectr. Nat. Inst. Med. Rsch., Mill Hill, Eng., 1974-75. Contbr. articles to rsch. jours. Bd. dirs. Rochester br. Cancer Action, Inc., 1978-92. Lt. M.C., USNR, 1957-59. Rsch. grantee Nat. Cancer Inst., 1971-92. Mem. Am. Soc. Biochemists and Molecular Biologists, Am. Assn. Cancer Rsch., Biochem. Soc., Am. Chem. Soc., Rochester Acad. Medicine. Episcopalian. Home: Rochester N.Y. Died Dec. 30, 1992; interred Spring Grove Cemetery, Cin., Ohio.

HENSLEY, EUGENE BENJAMIN, physicist, educator, researcher; b. Augusta, W.Va., Jan. 6, 1918; s. Elbert B. and Anna Francis (Milhoan) H.; m. Elizabeth Selke, June 10, 1954. A.B., Central Meth. Coll., Fayette, Mo., 1947; M.A., U. Mo.-Columbia, 1948, Ph.D., 1951. Mem. staff Research Lab. Electronics, MIT, 1951-53; asst. prof. physics U. Mo., Columbia, 1953-57, assoc. prof. physics, 1957-63, prof., 1963-85; prof. emeritus U. Mo., 1985-92; acting chmn. dept. physics U. Mo., Columbia, 1977-78, assoc. chmn., 1981-85. Contbr. articles to profl. jours. Served with USNR, 1942-46. Recipient research contracts Office of Naval Research, 1953-66; recipient research contracts NSF, 1965-76. Mem. Am. Phys. Soc., AAAS. Mem. Disciples of Christ. Home: Columbia Mo. Died Mar. 16, 1992; interred Meml. Cemetery, Grand Forks, N.D.

HEPBURN, AUDREY, actress; b. Brussels, Belgium, May 4, 1929; d. Joseph Anthony and Baroness Ella (van Heemstra) H.; m. Melchor Gaston Ferrer, Sept. 25, 1954 (div.); 1 child, Sean; m. Andrea Dotti, 1969; 1 child, Luca. Ed., Day Sch., Arnhem, Netherlands, Conservatory of Music, Arnhem; student ballet with, Sonia Gaskel, Amsterdam, Marie Rambert, London. Appeared with Sauce Tartare, also Sauce Piquante, West End, London; appeared in: Cabaret; appeared on TV; actress in: small parts in motion pictures including Nous irons à Monte Carlo; leading roles in: Am. motion pictures Roman Holiday, 1953 (Acad. award as best actress 1954), Sabrina Fair, 1954, War and Peace, 1955, Funny Face, 1956, Love in the Afternoon, 1956; first legitimate play Gigi, N.Y.C., 1951; appeared in: Ondine, N.Y.C. (Tony award), 1954, Producers Showcase; TV, 1957; films Green Mansions, 1958, The Nun's Story, 1959, The Unforgiven, 1960, Breakfast at Tiffany's, 1960, The Children's Hour, 1962, Charade, 1962, My Fair Lady, 1963, Paris When it Sizzles, 1964, How to Steal a Million, 1965, Two for the Road, 1966, Wait Until Dark, 1967, Robin and Marian, 1976, Bloodline, 1979, They All Laughed, 1981, Always, 1989; Gardens of the World (PBS spl.), 1990. Recipient spl. Tony award, 1968, Cecile B. DeMille award Golden Globe Awards, 1990. Home: Beverly Hills Calif. Died Jan. 20, 1993.

HERBERT, GEORGE RICHARD, research executive; b. Grand Rapids, Mich., Oct. 3, 1922; s. George Richard and Violet (Wilton) H.; m. Lois Anne Watkins, Aug. 11, 1945; children: Gordon, Patricia, Alison, Douglas, Margaret. Student, Mich. State U., 1940-42; B.S., U.S. Naval Acad., 1945; D.Sc. (hon.), N.C. State U., 1967; LL.D. (hon.), Duke U., 1978, U. N.C.-Chapel Hill, 1984. Line officer USN, 1945-47; instr. elec. engring. Mich. State U., 1947-48; asst. to dir. Stanford Research Inst., 1948-51, mgr. bus. ops., 1951-55, exec. asso. dir., 1955-56, asst. sec., 1950-56; treas. Am. & Fgn. Power Co., Inc., N.Y.C., 1956-58; pres. Rsch. Triangle Inst., 1958-89, pres. emeritus, 1989-95, vice chmn., 1989-95, also bd. govs.; bd. dirs. CCB Fin. Corp., 1973-95, Duke Power Co., 1977-95; mem. N.C. Bd. Sci. and Tech., 1963-79; mem. tech. adv. bd. U.S. Dept. Commerce, 1964-69, N.C. Atomic Energy Adv. Com., 1964-71; mem. Korea-U.S. joint com. for sci. cooperation Nat. Acad. Scis., 1973-78; mem. bd. sci. and tech. for internat. devel. Nat. Acad. Sci., 1978-81. Bd. dirs. Oak Ridge Assoc. Univs., 1971-73, 78-85, N.C. Biotech. Ctr., 1985-89, Rsch. Triangle Found., 1988-95, Triangle Univs. Ctr. for Advanced Studies, 1976-91; bd. dirs. Microelectronics Ctr. N.C., 1980-89, chmn., 1980-88; trustee Duke U., 1985-93, trustee emeritus, 1993-95. Mem. Sigma Alpha Epsilon. Club: Hope Valley Country. Home: Durham N.C. Died Jan. 14, 1995.

HERBERT, IRA C., food processing company executive; b. Chgo., Oct. 5, 1927; s. Solomon David and Helen (Burstyn) Chizever; m. Lila Faye Ellman, Jan. 6, 1951; children: Carrie Jo, Jeffrey, Fred. BA, Mich. State U., 1950. Account exec. McFarland Aveyard, Chgo., 1951-56; account supr. Edward H. Weiss, Chgo., 1956-63; v.p. McCann Erickson, L.A. and Atlanta, 1963-65; sr. v.p. Coca-Cola U.S.A., Atlanta, 1965-74, pres. food div., 1975-81, exec. v.p., chief mktg. officer, 1981-88, exec. v.p., pres., CEO N.Am. soft dr. sector, 1988-92; bd. dirs. Tex. Commerce Bank, T.C.C. Beverages Ltd., Nat. Data Corp. Served with USAF, 1945-47; with U.S. Army, 1951-52. Mem. Advt. Coun. (dir.), Advt. Edn. Found. (bd. dirs.), Nat. Can and Canning Inst. (bd. dirs.), Capitol City Club, Longboat Key (Fla.) Club, Standard Club, Commerce Club. Jewish. Home: Atlanta Ga. Deceased.

HERINEANU, TEOFIL, archbishop; b. 1925. Bishop Vadu, Fleacu and Cluj, archbishop, 1973-92; Bishop Romanian Orthodox Ch., 1968-92. Home: Bucharest Romania Died Mar. 11, 1992.

HERLIHY, JAMES LEO, playwright, novelist; b. Detroit, Feb. 27, 1927; s. William Francis and Grace (Oberer) H. Student, Black Mountain Coll., 1947-48, Pasadena Playhouse, 1948-50; RCA fellow, Yale Drama Sch., 1956-57. disting. vis. prof. U. Ark., Fayetteville, 1983. Author: (with William Noble) Blue Denim, 1958, The Sleep of Baby Filbertson and Other Stories, 1959, All Fall Down (novel), 1960, Midnight Cowboy (novel), 1965,A Story That Edns With a Scream and Eight Others, 1967, Bad Jo-Jo, 1968, Laughs,1968, Stop You're Killing Me, 1970, The Season of the Witch (novel) 1971; starred in production of The Zoo Story, Paris, 1963; appeared in film, Four Friends,1982. Served with USNR, 1945-46. Home: New York N.Y. Died Oct. 1993.

HERLING, JOHN, newspaperman, publisher; b. N.Y.C., Apr. 14, 1905; s. Morris and Mollie (Konrad) H.; m. Mary Fox, Sept. 16, 1937 (dec. Nov. 1978); 1 stepchild, David Fox Stolberg.; m. Alice Dodge Wolfson, Jan. 24, 1982; 3 stepchildren. A.B., Harvard U., 1928. Publ. sec., also exec. sec. Emergency Com. Strikers Relief of League Indsl. Democracy, 1930-34; asst. editor United Features Syndicate, 1935; Washington corr. Milw. Leader, also other papers, 1936-37; mem. Washington staff Time Inc., 1937; publicity dir. March of Time, 1937-38; dir. Childrens Crusade for Children, 1939-40; asst. sec. New Sch. Social Research, 1940-41; dir. labor and social relations div. Office Inter-Am. Affairs, 1941-46; spl. corr. in Europe for newspapers, 1946; editor, pub. John Herling's Labor Letter, 1950-90; syndicated columnist labor and gen. affairs; lectr. abroad labor affairs for State Dept., 1956, 60, 63, 65. Author: Great Price Conspiracy, 1962, Labor Unions in America, 1964, Right to Challenge, 1972; contbr. magazines. Recipient Journalist award Wash. Newspaper Guild, 1962, 64; Norman Thomas-Eugene V. Debs award, 1978; Eugene V. Debs award Midwest Labor Press Assn., 1984, Disting. Service award Nat. Capital Labor History Soc., 1987, Lifetime Pub. Svc. award Sidney Hillman Found., 1988. Mem. Am. Polit. Sci. Assn., Am. Hist. Soc., Council Fgn. Relations, Authors Guild, Indsl. Relations Research Assn. (pres. Washington chpt. 1955), White House and Congl. Corrs. Assn., Sigma Delta Chi. Clubs: Nat. Press (Washington), Overseas Writers (Washington), Federal City (Washington), Harvard (Washington); Silurians (N.Y.C.). Home: Bethesda Md. Died Feb. 3, 1994; buried Abel's Hill Cemetary, Martha's Vineyard, Mass.

HERMAN, CHARLES ROBERT, opera association executive; b. Glendale, Calif., Feb. 24, 1925; s. Floyd Caves and Anna (Merriken) H. A.B. in German summa cum laude, U. So. Calif., 1949. Asst. to head opera dept. U. So. Calif., Los Angeles, 1949-53; asst. mgr., artistic adminstr. Met. Opera, N.Y.C., 1953-72; gen. mgr. Greater Miami (Fla.) Opera Assn., 1973-85; exec. dir. New World Festival, Inc., Miami, 1979-82. Served with U.S. Army, 1944-46; lt. col. Res. ret. Decorated Army Commendation medal; cavaliere Order of Merit, Italy; officers cross Order of Merit, W.Ger.; Austrian Honor Cross for Sci. and Art 1st class. Mem. Opera Am. (pres. 1983-85). Home: Miami Fla. Died Aug. 19, 1991.

HERNU, CHARLES, French political leader; b. Quimper, France, July 3, 1923; s. Eugene and Laurence (Prost) H. Dir. Le Jacobin, newspaper, 1954; dep. from Rhone dept. French Nat. Assembly, 1956-58, 78-81, dep. from Lyons, 1986—; mayor, Villeurbanne, from 1977; minister of def. French Govt., 1981-86; mem. steering com. French Socialist Party, from 1971. Author: la Colère Usurpée, 1959, Priorité à Gauche, 1969, Soldat Citoyen, 1975, Chroniques d'Attente, 1976, Nous, les Grands, 1980, Defendre la Paix, 1985, Lettre Ouverte à Ceux qui ne veulent pas savoir, 1987. Died Jan. 17, 1990. Home: Villeurbanne France

HEROLD, EDWARD WILLIAM, electrical engineer; b. N.Y.C., Oct. 15, 1907; s. Carl Frederick and Marie (Wollersheim) H.; m. Alexandra Dacis, Aug. 4, 1931; 1 child, Linda Marlene Herold Johnson. B.S., U. Va., 1930; M.S., Poly. Inst. Bklyn., 1942, D.Sc. (hon.), 1961. Registered profl. engr., N.J. Research asst. Bell Telephone Labs., N.Y.C., 1924-26; engr. E.T. Cunningham Co., N.Y.C., 1927-29, RCA, Harrison, N.J., 1930-42; successively mem. tech. staff, dir. tube lab., dir. electronic research lab. RCA Labs., Princeton, N.J., 1942-59; v.p. research Varian Assos., Palo Alto, Calif., 1959-64; dir. tech. RCA Corp., Princeton, 1965-72; cons. electronics, mgmt. and patents, 1972—; bd. dirs. Inst. Radio Engrs., 1956-58, Engring. Found., 1975-78; chmn. bd. Palisades Inst., 1969-84; adv. council elec. engring. dept. Princeton U., 1957-71; cons. Dept. Def., 1950-76. Co-author: Color Television Picture Tubes, 1974; Author 50 tech. articles in field. Fellow IEEE (Founder's medal 1976); mem. Phi Beta Kappa, Sigma Xi. Home: Princeton N.J.

HERRHAUSEN, ALFRED, banker; b. Jan. 30, 1930. Mem. bd. mng. dirs. Deutsche Bank AG, Frankfurt, Fed. Republic Germany, main chmn., dep. chmn. and mem. supervisory bd. of numerous cos. Deceased. Home: Frankfurt Germany

HERRING, REUBEN, retired magazine editor; b. Tifton, Ga., July 14, 1922; s. John Greene and Ruby Leigh (Hewitt) H.; m. Dorothy Lavaine McCorvey, Dec. 2, 1942; children: Carey Reuben, Michael McCorvey (dec.), Daniel Hewitt, Matthew Greene (dec.), Mark Youngblood, Tiria Elizabeth. B.A., U. Ga., 1942. Sports editor Dothan Eagle, Ala., 1945-53; assoc. editor Baptist Sunday Sch. Bd., Nashville, 1953-64, editorial supr., 1964-67, coordinating editor, 1967-83, sr. editor Home Life mag., 1983-87. Author: Two Shall Be One, 1964, Men Are Like That, 1967, Building a Better Marriage, 1975, The Baptist Almanac, 1976 (So. Bapt. Conv. Hist. Commn. award 1976), Your Family Worship Guidebook, 1978, Fire in the Canebrake, 1980, (with Dorothy Lavaine McCorvey Herring) Becoming Friends With Your Children, 1984; For This Cause: The Priorities of Marriage, 1989, A History of the First Baptist Church of Nashville, Tennessee, 1990. Served with U.S. Army, 1942-45. Recipient Career Profl. award Bapt. Sunday Sch. Bd., 1983. Home: Brentwood Tenn. Died July 21, 1993.

HERRMANN, DANIEL LIONEL, retired state chief justice; b. N.Y.C., June 10, 1913; s. Philip and Rose (Schendelman) H.; m. Zelda W. Kluger, Apr. 14, 1940; children: Stephen Eric, Richard Kurt. AB, U. Del., 1935, LLD (hon.), 1976; LLB, Georgetown U., 1939, LLD (hon.), 1981; LLD (hon.), Del. Law Sch., 1978. Bar: D.C. 1938, Del. 1940. Practiced in Wilmington, 1940-51; asst. U.S. atty., 1948-51; asso. judge Superior Ct., Orphans Ct. Del., 1951-58; asso. justice Del. Supreme Ct., 1965-73, chief justice, 1973-85; sr. partner Herrmann, Bayard, Brill & Russell, 1958-65; Disting. vis. prof. Del. Law Sch., 1985—; dir., mem. exec. com. Del. Power & Light Co., 1962-65. Chmn. State Goals Commn., 1960-64; mem. Wilmington Bd. Pub. Edn., 1961-65; chmn. State Planning Commn., 1962-64; Pres. Legal Aid Soc. Del.; pres., chmn. bd. Jewish Fedn. Del., 1956-58; former mem. bd. dirs., exec. com. United Community Fund, Children's Bur. Del., Welfare Council Del., Del-Mar-Va council Boy Scouts Am., Jewish Community Center, Kutz Home for Aging; trustee, v.p. U. Del.; trustee Wilmington Med. Center; bd. mgrs. Wilmington Inst. Free Library. Served to maj. AUS, 1942-46. Recipient Public Service award Del. C. of C., 1981, First Disting. Service award. Fellow Am. Bar Found., Inst. Jud. Adminstrn.; mem. Am., Del. bar assns., Am. Judicature Soc. (dir., Herbert Harley award 1976), Rotary (Pub. Svc. award 1979). Home: Wilmington Del.

HERRNSTEIN, RICHARD JULIUS, psychology educator; b. N.Y.C., May 20, 1930; s. Rezso and Flora Irene (Friedman) H.; m. Barbara Brodo, May 28, 1951 (div. Feb. 1961); 1 child, Julia; m. Susan Chalk Gouinlock, Nov. 11, 1961; children: Max Gouinlock, James Rezso. B.A., CCNY, 1952; Ph.D., Harvard U., 1955. Research psychologist Walter Reed Army Med. Center, Washington, 1956-58; lectr. U. Md., 1957-58; faculty Harvard U., 1958-94, dir. psychol. labs., 1965-67, prof., chmn. dept. psychology, 1967-71. Author: (with E.G. Boring) A Source Book in the History of Psychology, 1965, (with J.C. Stevens and G.S. Reynolds) Laboratory Experiments in Psychology, 1965, I.Q. in the Meritocracy, 1973, (with R. Brown) Psychology, 1975, (with J.Q. Wilson) Crime and Human Nature, 1985, (with Charles Murray) The Bell Curve: Intelligence and Class Structure in American Life, 1994; editor: Psychol. Bull., 1975-81; contbr. articles to profl. jours. Served to 1st lt. AUS, 1956-58. Guggenheim Found. fellow, 1977-78, Sloan Found. fellow, 1982-83. Mem. Am. Acad. Arts and Scis., Phi Beta Kappa, Sigma Xi. Home: Belmont Mass. Died Sept. 13, 1994.

HERSANT, ROBERT JOSEPH EMILE, publications company executive, journalist, editor; b. Vertou, France, Jan. 31, 1920; s. Victor and Juliette (Hugot) H.; married, 8 children. Student Lycées of Rouen and Le Havre, France. Editor, 1945-96; founder, pres.-dir. gen. Groupe de Presse Robert Hersant, Paris, 1950-96; editor/owner of dailies including: Le Figaro, 1975, Presse Océan, Maine Libre, Courrier de l'Quest, Paris Turf, Nord-Eclair, Nord-Matin, Centre-Presse, Le Berry Républicain, L'Eclair de Nantes, La Liberté du Morbihan, France-Soir, 1976-96; editor/owner other publs. including: L'Auto-Jour., Bateaux, La Bonne Cuisine, France-Amérique; owner Le Progrés, Le Dauphine Libéré, 1982-96; pres., dir. gen. Socpresse; pres. adminstrn. Coun. Jours de France, 1989-96; mayor of Ravenel, France, 1953-59; mayor of Liancourt, France, 1967-74; counsel gen. Saint-Just-en-Chaussée, 1954-72. Active Nat. Assembly for l'Oise, 1956-78. Mem. Du Parlement Européen. Died Apr. 21, 1996. Home: Paris France

HERSEY, GEORGE WILLIAM, judge; b. Bar Harbor, Maine, Feb. 11, 1930; s. George William and Mary Laura (Carter) H.; m. Andrea Therese Anderson, Sept. 3, 1971; 1 dau., Laura Therese. B.A. in Psychology, U. Maine, 1952; J.D., Boston U., 1957. Bar: Maine 1957, Fla. 1960. Teaching and research fellow Rutgers U. Law Sch., Newark, 1957-58; ptnr. Masterman & Hersey, Bar Harbor, 1958-59; ptnr. Gunster, Yoakley, Criser, Stewart & Hersey, P.A., Palm Beach, Fla., 1959-79; judge Fourth Dist. Ct. Appeal Fla., West Palm Beach, 1979-85, chief judge, 1985-95. Bd. dirs. Salvation Army, West Palm Beach, Fla., Palm Beec County (Fla.) Community Found. Served to capt. arty U.S. Army, 1952-54. Named Outstanding Profl. Man c Yr., Palm Beach Daily News 1957; Man of Yr., City c Hope, 1977. Mem. ABA, Palm Beach County Ba Assn., Fed. Bar Assn., Palm Beach C. of C. (dir.) Republican. Episcopalian. Club: Kiwanis (Palm Beach) Contbr. chpt., articles to legal publs. Died July 16, 1995 Home: Jupiter Fla.

HERSEY, JOHN, writer; b. Tientsin, China, June 17 1914; s. Roscoe Monroe and Grace (Baird) H.; m Frances Ann Cannon, Apr. 27, 1940 (div. Feb. 1958) children: Martin, John, Ann, Baird; m. Barbara Da Kaufman, June 2, 1958; 1 child, Brook. Student Hotchkiss Sch., 1927-32, Clare Coll., Cambridge (Eng. U., 1936-37; BA, Yale U., 1936, hon. degrees include MA, 1947; LLD, Washington and Jefferson Coll., 195 DHL, Dropsie Coll., 1950; LHD, New Sch. for Socia Research, 1950, Coll. William and Mary, 1987; LittD Wesleyan U., 1954, Bridgeport U., 1964, U. Ne Haven, 1970, Clarkson Coll. Tech., 1972, Syracuse U. 1983, Yale U., 1984, Monmouth Coll., 1986, Albertu Magnus Coll., 1988. Pvt. sec. to Sinclair Lewis, summe 1937; writer for Time mag., editor, 1937-44; sr. edito Life mag., 1944-45; war and fgn. corr. Time, Life, Ne Yorker, 1942-46; fellow Berkeley Coll., Yale U., 195 65; master Pierson Coll., Yale, 1965-70, fellow, 1965-9 lectr. Yale U., 1971-76, vis. prof., 1976-77, adj. prof 1977-84, prof. emeritus, 1984-93; writer in residenc Am. Acad. in Rome, 1970-71; mem. faculty Salzbur Seminar in Am. Studies, 1975; vis. prof. MIT, 1975. Author: Into the Valley, 1943, 89, A Bell for Adanc 1944, Hiroshima, 1946, 85, The Wall, 1950, Th Marmor Drive, 1953, A Single Pebble, 1956, The Wa Lover, 1959, The Child Buyer, 1960, Here to Stay, 196 White Lotus, 1965, Too Far to Walk, 1966, Under th Eye of the Storm, 1967, The Algiers Motel Inciden 1968, The Call, 1985, blues, 1987, Life Sketches, 198 Fling and Ohter Stories, 1990, Antonietta, 1991, Ke West Tales (published posthumously), 1993, man others. Chmn. Conn. Com. for Gifted, 1954-57; mem vis. com. Harvard Grad. Sch. Edn., 1960-65, Loe Drama Center, Harvard, 1980-93; trustee Putney Sch 1953-56, Nat. Citizens' Council for Pub. Schs., 1956-5 Nat. Com. for Support Pub. Schs., 1962-68; del. Whit House Conf. on Edn., 1955, PEN Congress, Toky 1958; commr. Nat. Commn. on New Tech. Uses c Copyrighted Works, 1975-78. Recipient Pulitzer priz for fiction, 1945; Sidney Hillman Found. award, 195 Howland medal Yale, 1952; Hon. fellow Clare Coll Cambridge, 1967. Mem. Authors League Am. (counc 1946-70, 75-93, v.p. 1948-54, pres. 1975-80), Am. Acad and Inst. Arts and Letters (sec. 1962-77, chancell 1981-84), Am. Acad. Arts and Scis., Authors Guil (council 1946-93, chmn. contract com. 1963-87). Home: Key West Fla. Died Mar. 24, 1993; buried Wes Chop Village Cemetery, Martha's Vineyard, Mass.

HERTER, THEOPHILUS JOHN, clergyman, edu cator; b. Kesab, Turkey, June 5, 1913; came to U.S 1919, naturalized, 1926; s. John Michael and Agne Barbara (Schuck) H.; m. Ruth Lillian Birbeck, June 14 1941; 1 child, Philip John. B.A., Haverford Coll., Pa 1945, M.A., 1947; M. Div., Reformed Episcopal Sem Phila., 1945; Th.M., Westminster Theol. Sem., Phila 1965, Th.D., 1966; D.D. (hon.) Reformed Episcopa Sem., 1967. Ordained to ministry Episcopal Ch., 194 Rector, St. Matthews Reformed Episcopal Ch Havertown, Pa., 1943-60; sec., gen. council Reforme Episcopal Ch., Phila., 1948-60, asst. bishop, N.Y.C Phila., 1966-72, bishop, 1972-84, presiding bisho Phila., 1975—. Author: The Abrahamic Covenant in th Gospels, 1966. Home: Havertown Pa.

HERZ, CARL SAMUEL, mathematician; b. N.Y.C Apr. 10, 1930; s. Michael M. and Natalie (Hyman) H m. Judith Scherer, Feb. 28, 1960; children: Rache Nathaniel. B.A., Cornell U., 1950; Ph.D., Princeton U 1953. Instr. Cornell U., 1953-56, asst. prof. math 1956-58, asso. prof., 1958-63, prof., 1963-70; pro McGill U., Montreal, Que., Can., 1970-95, Pete Redpath Prof. Pure Math., 1993-95; dir. Inst. des Sci Mathēmatiques, 1993-95; mem. Inst. Advanced Stud Princeton, N.J., 1957-58; vis. prof. U. Paris, 1962, 6 68, Brandeis U., 1969-70. Alfred P. Sloan fellow, 196 63. Mem. Am. Math. Soc., Can. Math. Soc. (pre 1987-89). Home: Montreal Can. Died May 1, 1995.

HERZIG, CHARLES E., bishop; b. San Antonio, Au 14, 1929. Student, St. Mary's U., St. John's Sem., Ou Lady of the Lake U., San Antonio. Ordained pries Roman Cath. Ch., 1955, consecrated bishop, 1987. Bishop, Tyler, Tex., 1987-91. Home: Tyler Tex. Die Sept. 7, 1991.

HESS, ROBERT DANIEL, psychology and educatio educator; b. Shambaugh, Iowa, Mar. 10, 1920; s. Joh Henry and Allilian (Weavers) H.; m. Betsy N. Muelk June 18, 1949 (div. June 1969); children: Jared A Alyssa N., Devin A., Bradley B. A.B. in Psycholog U. Calif. at Berkeley, 1947; Ph.D. in Human Devel, U Chgo., 1950. Mem. faculty Com. on Human Devel., U Chgo., 1949-67, chmn., 1959-64; dir. Urban Chil Center, 1964-67; fellow Center Advanced Stud Behavioral Scis., Stanford, Calif., 1966-67; Lee L. Jack prof. child edn., prof. psychology Stanford, 1967-8 ednl. cons. Author: (with Gerald Handel) Famil

Worlds: A Psychosocial Approach to Family Life, 1959, (with Judith V. Torney) The Development of Political Attitudes in Children, 1967, (with Virginia Shipman, Jere Brophy, Roberta Bear) The Cognitive Environments of Urban Preschool Child, 1968, (with Decker Walker) Instructional Software: Principles for Design and Use; Editor: (with Roberta M. Bear) Early Education: Current Theory, Research and Practice, 1968. Served with USMCR, 1942-46. Fellow AAAS, Am. Psychol. Assn., Am. Sociol. Assn.; mem. Am. Ednl. Research Assn., Soc. Research Child Devel. Home: Palo Alto Calif. Died June 30, 1993.

HESSE, WILLIAM R., marketing and advertising executive; b. Dayton, Ohio, Jan. 19, 1914; s. Julius R. and Margaret (Reid) H.; m. Anne E., Vandervort, July 3, 1941; children: William R., Carol Anne, Mark Vandervort. AB, U. Cin., 1938. Supr. employment for men Procter & Gamble, Cin.; asst. to sales mgr. Procter & Gamble, 1937-46; v.p. Batten, Barton, Durstine & Osborn, Inc., Pitts. and N.Y.C., 1946-56; sr. v.p. Benton & Bowles, Inc., N.Y.C., 1956-58; exec. v.p. Benton & Bowles, Inc., 1958-61, pres., 1961-68, chief exec. officer, 1965-68; bd. dir., pres., chief exec. officer William R. Hesse Assocs., N.Y.C. and Greenwich, Conn., 1968-75; sr. v.p. Am. Assn. Advt. Agys., Washington, 1975-78, pres., chief exec. officer, 1978; chmn., pres. W.R. Hesse Assocs., Cons., Yarmouth Port, Mass., 1979-94; sec., bd. dir. Advt. Coun.; bd. dir. Nat. Advt. Rev. Com., Advt. Rsch. Found., Traffic Audit Bur.; ptnr. Pacifica Park, Seattle. Mem. mgmt. com. YMCA; mem. adv. bd. Nat. Coffee Assn. Bd.; dirs. Urban League of N.Y. Served as lt. col. Inf. AUS, 1941-45. Recipient Putnam award Nat. Indsl. Advertisers Assn., 1949. Mem. Am. Mgmt. Assn., Am. Assn. Advt. Agys. (bd. dir.-at-large), Royal Soc. Arts (hon. corr.), N.Y. Athletic Club, Cummaquid Golf Club, The Beach Club. Home: Yarmouth Port Mass. Died Nov. 8, 1994.

HESSLER, ROBERT ROAMIE, consulting company executive; b. Toledo, Aug. 23, 1918; s. Roamie C. and Lily (Zenthoefer) H.; m. Winifred J. Graves, Aug. 3, 1940; 1 son, Robert Roamie. BBA, U. Toledo, 1940. Dir. taxes and ins. Willys Overland Motors, Inc., Toledo, 1946-54; gen. mgr. Buggie div. Burndy Corp., Toledo, 1955-60; v.p. Questor Corp., Toledo, 1961-82; ptnr. R & R Cons., Ltd., Toledo, 1983-92; lectr. U. Toledo, 1946-48. Mem. adv. com. George C. Beinke Scholarship Trust; trustee Goerlich Found.; bus. adv. council U. Toledo; bd. dirs. Toledo Zool. Soc. Served to 1st lt. Q.M.C. AUS, 1944-46. Mem. Inst. Mgmt. Accts. (pres. Toledo chpt. 1953-54), Fin. Execs. Inst., Am. Legion, Toledo Club, Masons, Shriners, Jesters. Died Aug. 8, 1992.

HEUMANN, SCOTT FREDRIC, artistic administrator, dramaturge; b. Tulsa, Apr. 19, 1951. BA, Trinity U., San Antonio, 1973; MA, U. Cin., 1975. Sr. editor Performing Arts Mag., Houston, 1977-83; artistic adminstr., dramaturge Houston Grand Opera, 1983—. Contbr. articles to artistic jours. Home: Houston Tex.

HEWETT, ED ALBERT, economist; b. Columbia, Mo., Sept. 2, 1942; s. Edward and Esther Virginia (Lawrence) H.; m. Nancy Anna Maisto, Dec. 29, 1963. Student, Hasting Coll., 1960-62; B.S., Colo. State U., 1964, M.S., 1966; Ph.D. and Cert. in Russian, U. Mich., 1971. From asst. prof. to assoc. prof. econs. U. Tex., Austin, 1971-81; vis. scholar Inst. for World Econs., Budapest, 1974; vis. lectr. dept. econs. U. Pa., Phila., 1977-78; vis. scholar Harvard Russian Rsch. Ctr., Cambridge, Mass., 1979; sr. fellow Brookings Instn., Washington, 1981-91; sr. dir., spl. asst. to the pres. Nat. Security Affairs, Washington, 1991-93; vis. prof. econs. Columbia U., 1987-90; bd. dirs. PlanEcon Inc., Washington; chmn. Nat. Coun. for Soviet and East European Rsch., Washington, 1989-91. Author: Foreign Trade Prices in CMEA, 1974, Energy, Economics and Foreign Policy in the Soviet Union, 1984, Reforming the Soviet Economy: Equality vs. Efficiency, 1988; editor Soviet Economy, 1984-91. Mem. Am. Econs. Assn., Am. Assn. Advancement Slavic Studies, Assn. for Comparative Econ. Systems (exec. com. 1979-81, coun. on foreign rels.). Home: Silver Spring Md. Died Jan. 15, 1993.

HEWLETT, C(ECIL) JAMES, interior designer; b. Russell, N.Y., Apr. 24, 1923; s. Orin Stanley and Grace Josephine (Heffernan) H. Student, U. Md., 1949-51, Syracuse U., 1953-60. Mem. design staff Colony Shop, Syracuse, N.Y., 1952-55, Sagenkahn Co., Syracuse, 1955-61; design dir. Halle Bros. Co., Cleve., 1961-72, Nahan Co., New Orleans, 1973-75; pvt. practice interior design New Orleans, 1975-76;, 1977-88; design dir. Hemenway Co., Inc., New Orleans, 1976-77; owner Hewlett Mack Design Assocs., New Orleans, 1977—; currently lectr. to various profl. groups and nat. convs.; author, tchr. lectr. design philosophy, theory and meaning, human spatial orientation; dir. Inst. for Design Awareness. Contbr. articles to profl. publs. Trustee, chmn. Found. for Interior Design Edn. Rsch., 1970-74, trustee emeritus, 1983—, chmn. futures conf., coll. curricula planning, 1981—; del. Coalition for Nat. Growth Policy, 1971-74; mem. adv. panel Washington Ctr. for Met. Studies, HUD, 1970-74; founder, mem. Nat. Coun. for Interior Design Qualification, 1969-73. With USAAF, 1942-51. Decorated Air medal with 8 oak leaf clusters. Fellow Am. Soc. Interior Designers (position papers com.); mem. Nat. Soc. Interior Designers (pres. 1967-69, chmn. bd. dirs. 1969-71), Interior Design Educators Coun. (hon.), World Future Soc. Home: Chardon Ohio

HEYNS, ROGER WILLIAM, retired foundation executive and educator; b. Grand Rapids, Mich., Jan. 27, 1918; s. Garrett and Rosa (Klooster) H.; m. Esther Gezon, Sept. 20, 1941; children—Michael, John, Daniel. Student Hope Coll., 1936-37; A.B., Calvin Coll., 1940; M. Clin. Psychology, U. Mich., 1942, Ph.D., 1948. Instr. psychology U. Mich., 1947-48, asst. prof., 1948-55, assoc. prof., 1955-57, prof., 1957-65; dean Coll. Lit., Sci. and Arts, 1958-62; v.p. acad. affairs, 1962-65, prof. psychology and edn., 1971; chancellor U. Calif. at Berkeley, 1965-71; pres. Am. Council on Edn., Washington, 1972-77, Stet William and Flora Hewlett Found., 1977-92; mem. Nat. Sci. Bd., 1967-76. Bd. dirs. SETI Inst., World Affairs Coun.; mem. Coun. of Fgn. Rels., 1978-95. Capt. USAF, 1942-46. Recipient outstanding tchr. award U. Mich., 1952, faculty distinguished service award, 1958; Clark Kerr award for outstanding service to edn., 1967; Benjamin Ide Wheeler award as Berkeley's Most Useful Citizen, 1969; Robert C. Kirkwood award for greatest service to N. Calif., 1969. Fellow Am. Psychol. Assn.; chmn. Public Policy Inst. of Calif.; mem. Phi Beta Kappa, Sigma Xi, Phi Kappa Phi. Home: Atherton Calif. Died Sept. 11, 1995.

HIAASEN, CARL ANDREAS, lawyer; b. Benson County, N.D., May 26, 1894; s. Knud O. and Mary (Flaagan) H.; m. Clara Landmark, June 3, 1924 (dec.); 1 son, Kermit Odel (dec.). Student State Tchrs. Coll., Valley City, N.D., 1914-17, U. Ill., 1919-20; J.D., U. N.D., 1922. Bar: Fla. 1923, U.S. Supreme Ct. 1926, U.S. Ct. Claims 1964. Ptnr., McCune, Hiaasen, Crum, Ferris & Gardner, and predecessors, Ft. Lauderdale, Fla, from 1921, sr. ptnr., from 1964. Bd. dirs. Pitts. Theol. Sem., Com. for Chapel of Four Chaplains, Temple U. Served U.S. Army World War I. Fellow Am. Bar Found. (life); mem. ABA, Bar Assn. City N.Y., Order of Coif, Phi Delta Phi, Delta Sigma Rho. Contbr. articles to legal jours. Deceased. Home: Tavernier Fla.

HIBBERT, ELEANOR, author; b. London, 1906; d. Joseph and Alice (Tate) B.; m. G. P. Hibbert. Ed. privately. Writes under the following pseudonyms: Jean Plaidy, Victoria Holt, Philippa Carr, Kathleen Kellow, Ellalice Tate, Elbur Ford, Eleanor Burford; author: (as Jean Plaidy) Together They Ride, 1945, Beyond The Blue Mountains, 1947, Murder Most Royal (and as The King's Pleasure, U.S.), 1949, The Goldsmith's Wife, 1950, Madame Serpent, 1951, Daughter of Satan, 1952, The Italian Woman, 1952, Sixth Wife, 1953, new edit., 1969, Queen Jezebel, 1953, St. Thomas's Eve, 1954, The Spanish Bridegroom, 1954, Gay Lord Robert, 1955, The Royal Road to Fotheringay, 1955, new edit., 1968, The Wandering Prince, 1956, A Health Unto His Majesty, 1956, Here Lies Our Sovereign Lord, 1956, Flaunting Extravagant Queen, 1956, new edit., 1960, Triptych of Poisoners, 1958, new edit., 1970, Madonna of the Seven Hills, 1958, Light on Lucrezia, 1958, Louis the Wellbeloved, 1959, The Road to Compiegne, 1959, The Rise of the Spanish Inquisition, 1959, The Growth of the Spanish Inquisition, 1960, Castile for Isabelle, 1960, Spain for the Sovereigns, 1960, The End of the Spanish Inquisition, 1961, Daughters of Spain, 1961, Katherine, The Virgin Widow, 1961, Meg Roper, Daughter of Sir Thomas More (for children), 1961, The Young Elizabeth (for children), 1961, The Shadow of the Pomegranate, 1962, The King's Secret Matter, 1962, The Young Mary, Queen of Scots, 1962, The Captive Queen of Scots, 1963, Mary, Queen of France, 1964, The Murder in the Tower, 1964, The Thistle and the Rose, 1965, The Three Crowns, 1965, Evergreen Gallant, 1965, The Haunted Sisters, 1966, The Queen's Favourites, 1966, The Princess of Celle, 1967, Queen in Waiting, 1967, The Spanish Inquisition, its Rise, Growth and End (3 vols. in one), 1967, Caroline The Queen, 1968, Katharine of Aragon (3 vols. in one), 1968, The Prince and the Quakeress, 1968, The Third George, 1969, Catherine de Medici (3 vols. in one), 1969, Perdita's Prince, 1969, Sweet Lass of Richmond Hill, 1970, The Regent's Daughter, 1971, Goddess of the Green Room, 1971, Victoria in the Wings, 1972, Charles II (3 vols. in one), 1972, The Captive of Kensington Palace, 1972, The Queen and Lord M, 1973, The Queen's Husband, 1973, The Widow of Windsor, 1974, The Bastard King, 1974, The Lion of Justice, 1975, The Passionate Enemies, 1976, The Plantagenet Prelude, 1976, The Revolt of the Eaglets, 1977, The Heart of the Lion, 1977, The Prince of Darkness, 1978, The Battle of the Queens, 1978, The Queen from Provence, 1979, Edward Longshanks, 1979, The Follies of the King, 1980, The Vow on the Heron, 1980, Passage to Pontefract, 1981, Star of Lancaster, 1981, Epitaph for Three Women, 1981, Red Rose of Anjou, 1982, The Sun in Splendour, 1982, Uneasy Lies the Head, 1982, Myself My Enemy, 1983, Queen of this Realm, 1984, Victoria Victorious, 1985, The Lady in The Tower, 1986, The Courts of Love, 1987, In the Shadow of the Crown, 1988, The Queen's Secret, 1989, The Reluctant Queen, 1990, The Pleasures of Love, 1991, Williams Wife, 1992; (as Eleanor Burford) Daughter of Anna, 1941, Passionate Witness, 1941, Married Love, 1942, When All The World Was Young, 1943, So the Dreams Depart, 1944, Not In Our Stars, 1945, Dear Chance, 1947, Alexa, 1948, The House At Cupid's Cross, 1949, Believe The Heart, 1950, Love Child, 1950, Saint Or Sinner?, 1951, Dear Delusion, 1952, Bright Tomorrow, 1952, When We Are Married, 1953, Leave Me My Love, 1953, Castles in Spain, 1954, Hearts Afire, 1954, When Other Hearts, 1955, Two Loves In Her Life, 1955, Married in Haste, 1956, Begin To Live, 1956, To Meet A Stranger, 1957, Pride of the Morning, 1958, Blaze of Noon, 1958, Dawn Chorus, 1959, Red Sky At Night, 1959, Night of Stars, 1960, Now That April's Gone, 1961, Who's Calling?, 1962, (as Ellalice Tate) Defenders of the Faith, 1956 (under name of Jean Plaidy, 1970), Scarlet Cloak, 1957 (2d edn. under name of Jean Plaidy, 1969), Queen of Diamonds, 1958, Madame Du Barry, 1959, This Was A Man, 1961, (as Elbur Ford) The Flesh and The Devil, 1950, Poison in Pimlico, 1950, Bed Disturbed, 1952, Such Bitter Business, 1953 (as Evil in the House, U.S., 1954), (as Kathleen Kellow) Danse Macabre, 1952, Rooms At Mrs Oliver's, 1953, Lilith, 1954 (2d edit. under name of Jean Plaidy, 1967), It Began in Vauxhall Gardens, 1955 (2d edit. under name of Jean Plaidy, 1968), Call of the Blood, 1956, Rochester-The Mad Earl, 1957, Milady Charlotte, 1959, The World's A Stage, 1960, (as Victoria Holt) Mistress of Mellyn, 1961, Kirkland Revels, 1962, The Bride of Pendorric, 1963, The Legend of the Seventh Virgin, 1965, Menfreya, 1966, The King of the Castle, 1967, The Queen's Confession, 1968, The Shivering Sands, 1969, The Secret Woman, 1971, The Shadow of the Lynx, 1972, On the Night of the Seventh Moon, 1973, The Curse of the Kings, 1973, The House of a Thousand Lanterns, 1974, Lord of the Far Island, 1975, The Pride of the Peacock, 1976, My Enemy the Queen, 1978, The Spring of the Tiger, 1979, The Mask of the Enchantress, 1980, The Judas Kiss, 1981, The Demon Lover, 1982, The Time of the Hunter's Moon, 1983, The Landower Legacy, 1984, The Road to Paradise Island, 1985, Secret for a Nightingale, 1986, The Silk Vendetta, 1987, The India Fan, 1988, The Captive, 1989, The Snare of Serpents, 1990, Daughter of Deceit, 1991, Seven for a Secret, 1992, The Black Opal, 1993; (as Philippa Carr) The Miracle at St Bruno's, 1972, Lion Triumphant, 1974, The Witch from the Sea, 1975, Saraband for Two Sisters, 1976, Lament for a Lost Lover, 1977, The Love Child, 1978, The Song of the Siren, 1979, The Drop of the Dice, 1980, The Adulteress, 1981, Zipporah's Daughter, 1983, Voices in a Haunted Room, 1984, The Return of Gypsy, 1985, Midsummers Eve, 1986, The Pool of St. Branok, 1987, The Changeling, 1989, The Black Swan, 1990, A Time for Silence, 1991, The Gossamer Cord, 1992, We'll Meet Again, 1993, Daughters of England, 1995. Home: London Eng. Died Jan. 18, 1993.

HICKEY, JOSEPH JAMES, ecologist, emeritus educator; b. N.Y.C., Apr. 16, 1907; s. James Bernard and Sarah Theresa (Mooney) H.; m. Margaret Brooks, June 20, 1942 (dec. 1976); 1 child, Susan H. Nehls; m. Lola Alma Gray Gordon, Dec. 26, 1978. BS, NYU, 1930; MS, U. Wis., 1943; PhD, U. Mich., 1949. Research asst. Wis. State Soil Conservation Commn., Madison, 1941-43; research asst. Toxicity Lab., U. Chgo., 1943-44; asst. curator Mus. Zoology, U. Mich., Ann Arbor, 1944-46; fellow Guggenheim Meml. Found., 1946-47; prof. wildlife ecology U. Wis., Madison, 1948-77, prof. emeritus, 1977-93. Author: A Guide to Bird Watching, 1943, 75; (monograph) Survival Studies of Banded Birds, 1952, 72. Editor: Peregrine Falcon Populations, 1969. Contbr. articles to profl. jours. Mem. ad hoc coms. EPA, Nat. Acad. Sci., Wausau Art Mus., Wis. Recipient Arthur A. Allen medal Cornell U., 1976; Spl. Conservation award Nat. Wildlife Fedn., 1976; Chancellor's Teaching award U. Wis., 1976; Eisenmann medal Linnaean Soc. N.Y., 1984; Audubon medal Nat. Audubon Soc., 1984. Fellow AAAS, Am. Ornithologists Union (pres. 1972-73); mem. Ecol. Soc. Am., Cooper Ornithol. Soc., Wildlife Soc (hon., Leopold medal 1972). Home: Madison Wis. Died Aug. 31, 1993.

HICKEY, MARGARET A., editor; b. Kansas City, Mar. 14, 1902; d. Charles L. and Elizabeth (Wynne) H.; m. Joseph T. Strubinger, Oct. 20, 1935 (dec. Oct. 1973). J.D., U. Mo., 1928; LL.D., Cedar Crest Coll., 1952, MacMurray Coll., 1957; L.H.D., Wilson Coll., 1962; Litt.D., St. Mary's Coll. Notre Dame, 1964; D.Ed., Culver-Stockton Coll., 1966; LL.D., U. Mo. at St. Louis, 1975. Bar: bar 1928. Sole practice, 1928-33; founder, dir. Miss Hickey's Sch. for Secretaries, St. Louis, 1933-69; pub. affairs editor Ladies Home Jour., N.Y.C.; apptd. chmn. nat. women's adv. com. and observer Labor-Mgmt. Com., War Manpower Commn., 1942-45; sec. nat. citizens com. U.S. Office Edn.; mem. exec. com. Nat. Social Welfare Assembly; v.p.; mem. adv. bd. Point Four Program, 1950-52; mem. President's adv. com. Vol. Fgn. Aid, AID, 1952-81, vice chmn., 1962-73, chmn., 1973-76; com. White House Conf. Edn.; bd. govs. A.R.C., 1947-53, 55-60, vice chmn. bd., 1947-53, 59-61, dep. to chmn., 1960-73; vice chmn. med. and social adv. com. League Red Cross Socs.; mem. Nat. Manpower Council; mem. bd. Nat. Health Council, 1948-56; mem. President's Nat. Com. White House Conf. Children and Youth, 1960; pres. Nat. Conf. Social Work, 1956-57; chmn. organizing com. Internat. Conf. Social Work, 1966; chmn. Nat. Citizens Council Status Women, 1964-66; mem. commn. social scis. NSF, 1968-69. Mem. bd. overseers Brandeis U.; mem. vis. com. Grad. Sch. Edn., Harvard; trustee Tuskegee Inst. Am. Youth Found.; bd. dirs. Nat. Assn. for Mental Health, 1970-76; active Luce Found. Western Selection Panel for Its Asian Fellows Program, Pub. Adv. Com. Bus. and

Profl. Women's Found. Recipient Benjamin Franklin award for distinguished pub. service journalism, 1953; St. Louis Woman of Achievement award, 1957; Distinguished Alumni award U. Mo. Kansas City, 1972. Mem. Internat. Fedn. Bus. and Profl. Women (chmn. UN com., v.p.), Nat. Fedn. Bus. and Profl. Women (hon. pres.), Am. Newspaper Women's Club, Nat. Fedn. Press Women, Mo. Bar, Women's Bar Assn. Home: Tucson Ariz. Died Dec. 7, 1994.

HICKS, ELE WYATTE, management consultant; b. El Dorado, Ark., May 7, 1926; s. John Wesley and Sara Martha (Wilson) H.; m. Shirley Jean Merrill, July 3, 1947; children: Constance Anne, Victoria Kathleen, Mark Wyatte, David Owen. BA, U. Mo., 1944; MA, U. Mich., 1949. Sales promotion exec. McCannErickson, Inc., N.Y.C., 1947-48; advt. sales promotion mgr. Libbey-Owens-Ford Glass Co., Toledo, 1948-53; v.p., acct. supr. Benton & Bowles, Inc., N.Y.C., 1953-61; exec. v.p., mng. dir. J. Walter Thompson Co., N.Y.C., 1961-76, dir., mem. exec. com.; chmn., dir. Barickman Advt. Inc. (now Doyle Dane Bernbach Inc.), 1976-78; mng. dir., dir. Compton Comm. Inc. (now Saatchi & Saatchi World-wide), N.Y.C., 1978-82; pres. Wyatte Hicks Ptnrs. Inc., Mgmt. Cons., 1982-85; mng. dir. Arthur D. Little, Inc., 1985-87; bd. dirs. Wyatte Hicks Ptnrs., Inc., Rumrill Hoyt, Inc., Klemtner Advt., Inc., Ross Roy Compton NY. subs. Saatchi & Saatchi; mem. N.Y. Advt. Rev. Bd.; lectr., panelist seminars Am. Mgmt. Assn.; leader seminars on high tech. mktg. for McGraw-Hill. With U.S. Army, 1944-47. Decorated Army Commendation medal, Bronze Star, Silver Star. Mem. Am. Assn. Advt. Agys. (bd. govs. 1972-76), Econ. Club N.Y. Republican. Presbyterian. Clubs: New Canaan (Conn.); Field; Genessee Valley (Rochester, N.Y.); Sky (N.Y.C.). Home: Stuart Fla. Died Oct. 16, 1994.

HIGGINS, KENNETH RAYMOND, landscape architect; b. Holyoke, Mass., Nov. 2, 1915; s. Alfred and Lillie (Ritter) H.; student R.I. State Coll., 1934; BS Mass. State Coll., 1937, B in Landscape Architecture, 1939; m. Mary Douthat Smith, Sept. 5, 1942; children: Kenneth Hewlett, Ralph Barton, Janie Lyle. Landscape architect, site planner Richmond (Va.) Field Office Pub. Housing Adminstrn., 1948-51; pvt. practice landscape architecture, Richmond, 1951-76; prin. Higgins Assos., 1976-95. Instr., Richmond Profl. Inst., evenings 1956; cons. in field. Chmn., Richmond Beautification Com., 1954-64; treas. River Rd Citizens Assn., 1956, bd. dirs., 1983-95, pres. 1988-95; bd. dirs. Lewis Ginter Bot. Garden; chmn. Monument Av. Commn., 1969-85. Bd. dirs. Berkeley Thanksgiving Fest. Served to capt. USAAF, 1942-46. Recipient Landscape award Am. Assn. Nurserymen, 1969; Richmond Urban Design award, 1970; Masonry Contractors Assn. Va. award, 1977, Disting. Preservationist award Hist. Richmond Found., 1992. Mem. Am. Soc. Landscape Architects (past Va. chmn., Pres.'s award Potomac chpt. 1968), Landscape Architects Va., U. Mass. Landscape Archtl. Assn., Va. Hist. Soc., Soc. Archtl. Historians, Nat. Trust for Historic Preservation, Eastern Nat. Park and Monument Assn., Assn. for Preservation Va. Antiquities (life), Am. Arbitration Assn. Lambda Chi Alpha. Episcopalian (former vestryman). Club: Country of Virginia. Died Jan. 31, 1995. Home: Richmond Va.

HIGHSMITH, PATRICIA, writer; b. Ft. Worth, Jan. 19, 1921; d. Jay Bernard Plangman and Mary Coates. Attended Barnard Coll.; BA, Columbia U., 1942. Author: (novels) Strangers on a Train, 1950, The Blunderer, 1955, The Talented Mr. Ripley, 1956, Deep Water, 1957, A Game for the Living, 1958, This Sweet Sickness, 1960, The Cry of the Owl, 1962, The Two Faces of January, 1964, The Glass Cell, 1965, A Suspension of Mercy, 1965, Those Who Walk Away, 1967, The Tremor of Forgery, 1969, Ripley Under Ground, 1971, A Dog's Ransom, 1972, Ripley's Game, 1974, Edith's Diary, 1977, The Boy Who Followed Ripley, 1980, People Who Knock on the Door, 1983, Found in the Street, 1986; (short story collections) The Animal Lover's Book of Beastly Murder, 1975, Little Tales of Misogyny, 1977, Slowly, Slowly in the Wind, 1979, The Black House, 1981, Mermaids on the Golf Course, 1985, Tales of Natural and Unnatural Catastrophes, 1987; (non-fiction) Plotting and Writing Suspense Fiction, 1966, 2d edit., 1983. Club: Detection. Home: Zurich Switzerland Died February 4, 1995.

HIGINBOTHAM, WILLIAM ALFRED, physicist; b. Bridgeport, Conn., Oct. 25, 1910; m. Julie Ann Burritt, July 9, 1949 (dec. June 1971); children: Julie Eileen Higinbotham Schletter, Robin Ann Higinbotham Clark, William Burritt; m. Margaret A. Miller, Dec. 19, 1976 (dec. Dec. 1982); m. Edna M. Kinsey, Nov. 26, 1983. A.B., Williams Coll., 1932, D.Sc., 1963; postgrad., Cornell U., 1932-40. Radar research Radiation Lab., Mass. Inst. Tech., 1941-43; with Manhattan Project, Los Alamos, 1943-45; head electronics group Manhattan Project, 1944-45; chmn. Fedn. Am. Scientists, Washington, 1946, 59, 63; exec. sec. Fedn. Am. Scientists, 1947, vice-chmn., 1948, 51; assoc. head electronics div. Brookhaven Nat. Lab., 1947-51, head instrumentation div., 1951-68; sr. physicist Tech. Support Orgn., 1968-84; cons. in field. Patentee over 20 patents on electronic circuits. Higinbotham Hall named in his honor by Fedn. Am. Scientists, 1994. Fellow Am. Phys. Soc., IEEE, Am. Nuclear Soc., AAAS, Inst. Nuclear Materials Mgmt. Invented Higinbotham scaler circuit. Home: Gainsville Ga. Died Nov. 10, 1994.

HILDUM, DONALD CLAYTON, communications educator; b. Plainfield, N.J., Sept. 20, 1930; s. Edward Barkdoll and Isabel (Morrison) H.; m. Priscilla Hunt Ames, July 5, 1952; children: Edward Ames, Robert Morrison, David Waldau. AB, Princeton U., 1952; MA, Harvard U., 1953, PhD, 1960. From instr. to asst. prof. psychology Case Inst. Tech., Cleve., 1956-61; from asst. prof. to prof. psychology Oakland U., Rochester, Mich., 1961-72, chmn. comm. arts, 1975-81, prof. comm. arts, 1972-95; lectr. Fulbright Found. Belgium, Ghent, 1967-68. Editor: Language and Thought, 1967; contbr. articles to profl. jours. Mem. Mich. Assn. Speech Comm., Internat. Network for Social Network Analysis, Internat. Soc. Gen. Semantics, Internat. Comm. Assn., Speech Comm. Assn. Democrat. Unitarian. Home: Rochester Hills Mich. Deceased.

HILFORD, LAWRENCE B., communications company executive; b. N.Y.C., June 17, 1934; s. Norman and Diana Hilford; m. Lynn Sherr, Jan. 11, 1980; children: Jeffrey, Andrew, James. BA, Yale U., 1955; MBA, Harvard U., 1959. Pres. Cartridge Rental Network, N.Y.C., 1972-73; exec. v.p. Viacom Internat., N.Y.C., 1973-77; sr. v.p. Columbia Pictures Industries, N.Y.C., 1979-81; pres., chief exec. officer Sta. CBS/Fox Video, N.Y.C., 1983-85; chmn., chief exec. officer Orion Home Entertainment Corp., N.Y.C., 1986—; adj. prof. program for interactive communications NYU, N.Y.C., 1984-87. Mem. adv. bd. Johns Hopkins U., Balt., 1986—. Home: New York N.Y.

HILL, BARBARA MAE, librarian; b. Keene, N.H., Sept. 19, 1924; d. Gale Earl and Gertrude Wiseman (Reed) Hill; B.E., Keene Tchrs. Coll., 1946; M.S., Simmons Coll., 1952. Tchr. sci. and math. Thayer High Sch., Winchester, N.H., 1946-47; children's librarian Keene Pub. Library, 1947-52; asst. librarian Mass. Coll. Pharmacy and Allied Health Scis., Boston, 1952-58, assoc. librarian, 1958-69, librarian, 1969-90; bd. dirs. Fenway Library Consortium, 1975-90, coordinator, 1982-84; bd. dirs. Fenway Libraries Online, Inc., 1987-90. Mem. Am. Assn. Univ. Profs., Drug Info. Assn., Am. Assn. Colls. Pharmacy (ho. of dels. 1979-80, chmn.-elect libraries-ednl. resources sect. 1981-82, chmn. 1982-83), Med. Library Assn. (chmn. pharmacy group 1965-66, chmn. pharmacy and drug info. sect. 1985-86), Spl. Libraries Assn. (vice chmn. pharm. div. 1972-73, chmn. 1973-74), Kappa Delta Pi, Rho Chi. Died 1990. Home: Boston Mass.

HILL, BENNY (ALFRED HAWTHORN), comedian, television personality; b. Southampton, Eng., Jan. 21, 1925. Veteran of English music halls and girlie revues, early 1950s; began TV career as master of ceremonies on The Service Show, BBC-TV, 1952; later appeared on Show Case, then The Benny Hill Show, BBC-TV; left BBC for Thames TV Ltd., producer of Benny Hill Show; stage revue appearances include: Paris by Night, 1965, Fine Fettle, 1959; film appearances include: Who Done It, 1956, Light Up the Sky, 1960, Those Magnificent Men in Their Flying Machines, 1965, Chitty Chitty Bang Bang, 1968, The Italian Job, 1969; TV film appearance: A Midsummer Night's Dream, 1964. Served with Brit. Army, 3 1/2 yrs. Recipient various awards, including Best TV Comedy award Banff TV Awards Festival, 1982; voted Outstanding TV Personality of Yr., London Daily Mail poll, 1954; named TV Hall of Fame, TV Times (U.K.), 1978-79, named Funniest Man on TV, 1981-82. Died Apr. 20, 1992. Home: London Eng.

HILL, CARL MCCLELLAN, university president; b. Norfolk, Va., July 27, 1907; s. William F. and Sarah A. (Rowe) H.; m. Mary E. Elliott, Sept. 21, 1927 (dec.); 1 dau., Doris E. McGhee; m. Helen C. Rose, Aug. 2, 1970; son, Ernest Rose. B.S., Hampton U., 1931; M.S., Cornell U., 1935, Ph.D., 1941; postgrad., U. Pa., summers 1938-40; LL.D., U. Ky., 1966; D.Sc., U. Louisville, 1975, Eastern Ky. U., 1975. Asst. prof. chemistry Hampton Inst., 1931-41; asso. prof. chemistry Greensboro (N.C.) Agr. and Tech. U., 1941-44; prof. chemistry Tenn. State U., 1944-62, head dept. chemistry, 1944-51; chmn. Sch. Arts and Scis., 1951-58, dean sch., dean faculty, 1958-62; pres. Ky. State U., Frankfort, 1962-75, Hampton (Va.) U., 1967-78; Dir. Crestar Bank. Supt.; chem. research projects TVA, Research Coop., USAF Research and Devel. Command, NSF. Author: General College Chemistry, Laboratory Experiments in Organic Chemistry; Contbr. articles to profl. jours. Bd. commrs. Nat. Commn. Accrediting; mem. Ky. Med. Scholarship Bd., Ky. Authority Ednl. TV, Ky. Council on Pub. Higher Edn.; mem. gen. exec. bd. Presbyn. Ch. U.S.; Bd. dirs. Ky. Heart Assn., Am. Heart Assn., Blue Cross Hosp. Plan, Salvation Army; trustee Stillman Coll., Centre Coll.; mem. bd., exec. com. So. Regional Edn. Bd., 1972-75; sec.-treas. Council on Coop. Coll. Projects, 1964-75; chmn. adv. com. Hampton (Va.) City Coliseum; mem., chmn. Norfolk (Va.) Presbytery Higher Edn. Ministries Com.; mem. nominations com. Synod of Virginias; mem. religion and medicine com. Eastern Va. Med. Sch. Recipient Mfg. Chemists Assn. coll. chem. tchrs. award, 1962. Fellow AAAS, Am. Inst. Chemists, Tenn. Acad. Sci.; mem. Am. Chem. Soc., NEA, N.Y., Ky. acads. sci., Ky. C. of C. (dir.), Sigma Xi, Omega Psi Phi. Lodge: Masons. Home: Hampton Va. Died Apr 4, 1995.

HILL, DANNY EDWARD, lawyer; b. Little Rock Sept. 7, 1947; s. Ralph Edward and Hazel D. (Shepherd) H.; m. Jeannie Louise Owens, Aug. 16, 1969 (div. Sept 1982); children: Roxanne, Danny II; m. Terry Sue Bentley, July 16, 1983; children: Cadie, Elizabeth, Bentley Hallie. BA, Abilene Christian U., 1970; JD, Tex. Tech U., 1973. Bar: Tex. 1973, U.S. Dist. Ct. (no. dist.) Tex 1975, U.S. Ct. Appeals (5th cir.) 1981, U.S. Supreme Ct 1985. Assoc. Shelton & Gilkerson, Lubbock, Tex. 1973-75; asst. dist. atty. 47th Dist. Atty.'s Office Amarillo, 1975-76; pvt. practice Amarillo, 1976-77; state rep. Tex. Ho. of Reps., Austin, 1977-81; ptnr. Miner & Hill, Amarillo, 1977-81; dist. atty. 47th Dist. Atty.'s Office, Amarillo, from 1981. Bd. dirs. March of Dimes from 1982, chmn. 1986-88, Drug Free Schs. and Communities Adv., from 1988; mem. adv. bd. Tex. State Tech. Inst., 1977-82, Panhandle Regional Planning Commn., 1977-82, Tex. Better Rds., 1978-81, Active Texans Against Crime, from 1984, Offender Preparation and Edn. Network, Inc., from 1985, The Found. for a Drug Free Environment, Dispute Resolution Ctr. Mem Tex. State Bar Assn. (adminstrv. law com. 1977-81 penal code and criminal procedure com. from 1990 criminal justice coun. from 1990, asst. sec. from 1992) Nat. Dist. Atty. Assn. (legis. com. from 1990), Tex Dist. Atty. Assn. (bd. dirs. from 1990, sec., treas. from 1990), Tex. Dist. and County Attys. Assn. (legis. affair com. 1981-82, from 86, bd. dirs. from 1988, pres. from 1993), Amarillo Bar Assn. Democrat. Home: Amarillo Tex. Deceased.

HILL, GEORGE WATTS, banker; b. N.Y.C., Oct. 27 1901; s. John Sprunt and Annie Louise (Watts) H.; m Ann McCulloch, Sept. 30, 1924 (dec.); children: George Watts, Ann Dudley, John Sprunt; m. Anne Gibson June 14, 1975. B.S. in commerce, U. of N.C., 1922 student, U. of N.C. Law Sch., 1922-24. Bar: N.C. ba 1924. Pres. Central Carolina Bank & Trust Co., 1932-49, chmn. bd., from 1949; pres. Home Security Life Ins Co., 1934-39, chmn. bd. dirs., 1939-76. Pres. Watt Hosp., 1937-62; Mem. City Council, Durham, 1928-36 Mem. exec. com. American Guernsey Cattle Club, 1934-56; Trustee and mem. exec. com. U. N.C., 1956-72, bd govs., 1972-81; sec. Research Triangle Found. N.C 1958-82; chmn. bd. govs. Research Triangle Inst., from 1959; co-founder N.C. Blue Cross-Blue Shield, 1933 trustee, 1933-74, Leader orgn. coop. mktg. and farm orgns. Served as major AUS, 1943-45. Home: Chapel Hill N.C. Deceased.

HILL, JOHN ALEXANDER, health care and insurance executive; b. Shawnee, Okla., Feb. 24, 1907; s John E. and Mary B. (Cheek) H.; m. Margaret M Mikesell, June 14, 1929; children: Mary, John Jane. A.B., U. Denver, 1928, LL. D., 1965. With Aetna Life Ins. Co. as group rep., Denver, 1928-30; mgr group and pension depts. Aetna Life Ins. Co., Detroit 1930-33; dist. supr. Aetna Life Ins. Co., 1933-36; gen agt. John A. Hill & Assos., Toledo, 1936-58; sr. v.p Aetna Life and Casualty, Hartford, Conn., 1958-62 pres. Aetna Life and Casualty, 1962-70; pres., dir. Hosp Corp. Am., Nashville, 1970-72; vice chmn. Hosp. Corp Am., 1973-74, chmn., 1974-77; former chmn. Am. Lif Ins. Co. N.Y. chmn. bd. govs. Inst. for Living Hartford. Mem. Million Dollar Round Table, Toledo C. of C. (pres. 1953), Beta Theta Pi. Republican. Episcopalian. Clubs: Links (N.Y.C.), University (N.Y.C.) University (Nashville), Belle Meade Country (Nashville) Home: Nashville Tenn. Died April 12, 1994.

HILL, NORMAN JULIUS, publisher, author, editor playwright; b. Bklyn., July 21, 1925; s. Jacob and Ros (Fogel) H.; m. Mary Guest, 1982; children from previous marriage, Emily, Andrew David. B.S.S. cum laude, CCNY, 1947; grad., Am. Acad. Dramatic Arts 1967. Copy chief, account exec. S. Gross & Assocs Norfolk, Va., 1947-48; disc jockey Sta. WLOW Norfolk, 1947; promotion mgr. Sport Mag., N.Y.C 1949-51; promotion dir. Popular Library, Inc., 1951-55 v.p., asst. to pub., 1955-60; founder, pres., editorial di Webster's Red Seal Publs., Inc., N.Y.C., 1960-93 founder, editor Webster's Crosswords mag., 1960-93 v.p. Barkas & Shalit, Inc., N.Y.C., 1962-65; circulation promotion dir. McCall's and Redbook mags., N.Y.C 1965-68; pub. relations dir. McCall Pub. Co., N.Y.C 1968-70; editor Crossword Mags., Popular Library 1963-75, Crossword Mags., CBS Publs., Inc., N.Y.C 1975-87; exec. pub. Genesis Publs., Inc., N.Y.C., 1975-78; cons. McCall's, 1977; editor TV Guide Crossword Mag., 1979-82; editorial cons. Marvel Mags., 1980-82 editor Woman's Day Crosswords Mag., 1981-92; edito Crossword Mags. Diamandi's Communications Inc N.Y.C., 1987-90, Hachette Mags. Inc., N.Y.C., 1990-9 Author: Webster's Crossword Book, 1961, Israel Wi Win, 1970, Marijuana: Teenage Killer, 1970, 165 Temples Desecrated, 1970, The Lonely Beauties, 1971, Fre Sex: a Delusion, 1971, The Violent Women, 197 Modern Dictionary of Synonyms and Antonyms, 197 Webster's Red Seal Crossword Dictionary, 1972, Th Black Panthers, 1972, How to Solve Crossword Puzzle 1974, TV Guide Book of Crossword Puzzles, 6 throug 10, 1979; (play) Love Game (selected for N.Y. Sho Play Festival 1986); contbr.: articles to N.Y. Time Saturday Rev., Variety, Athletic Jour. Served with ir U.S. Army, 1943-46. Recipient cert. of commendatio

UNICEF, 1961, award for outstanding book advertisement Pubs. Weekly, 1955, 56, award for service Boys Clubs Am., 1956, citations Fed. CD Adminstrn., 1954, Theodore Roosevelt Centennial Commn., 1958. Mem. Dramatists Guild, Authors League, Sigma Alpha Mu. Home: New York N.Y. Died Oct. 28, 1993.

HILL, ROLLA B., pathologist; b. Balt., June 11, 1929; s. Rolla B. and Claire (McDowell) H.; children—Claire, Paul, Helen, Holly. B.A., U. Rochester, 1950, M.D., 1955. Mem. pathology faculty Yale U., New Haven, 1959-61, U. Colo., Denver, 1961-69, U. Calif., Davis, 1968-69; chmn. dept. pathology Upstate Med. Center SUNY, Syracuse, 1969-86. Co-author: The Gastrointestinal Tract, 1977, Principles of Pathobiology, 3rd edit, 1980, Environmental Pathology, 1981, The Autopsy: Medical Practice and Public Policy, 1988. Served with M.C. U.S. Army, 1956-58. Mem. AAAS, Am. Assn. Pathologists (pres.), Coun. Acad. Socs. (chmn.), Assn. Pathology Chmn. (pres., first Disting. Svc. award 1986), U.S.-Can. Acad. Pathology, Am. Soc. Clin. Pathologists, Coll. Am. Pathologists, Assn. Am. Med. Colls., Am. Gastroent. Assn. Home: Philo Calif. Died Feb. 12, 1996.

HILLER, LEJAREN ARTHUR, JR., composer, retired educator; b. N.Y.C., Feb. 23, 1924; s. Lejaren and Clara Anita (Plummer) H.; m. Elizabeth Halsey, Apr. 18, 1945; children—Amanda, David. B.A., Princeton U., 1944, M.A., 1946, Ph.D., 1947; M.Mus., U. Ill., 1958. Research chemist E.I. duPont de Nemours & Co., Inc., Waynesboro, Va., 1947-52; research assoc., asst. prof. dept. chemistry U. Ill., Urbana, 1953-58; asst. prof. U. Ill., 1958-61, assoc. prof. music, 1961-65, prof. music, 1965-68; also dir. exptl. music studio; Slee prof. music SUNY-, Buffalo, 1968-81, Birge-Cary prof. music, 1981-84; co-dir. Center for Creative and Performing Arts, 1968-74; lectr. Darmstadt Ferienkurse für Neue Musik, 1963, 65, 69; sr. Fulbright lectr. music, Poland, 1973-74, Brazil, 1980. Author: (with L.M. Isaacson) Experimental Music, 1959, (with R.H. Herber) Principles of Chemistry, 1960, Informationstheorie und Computermusik, 1964; Composer 60 scores written prior to 1980; Minuet and Trio for Six Performers, 1980, Quadrilateral for Piano and Tape, 1981, music for "Chang Fu, the Witch of Moon Mountain," 1982, Three Compositions for Tape, 1983, Tetrahedron for Harpsicord, 1983, Staircase Tango for Piano, 1984, Algorithms III for Nine Instruments and Tape, 1984, Fast and Slow for Saxophone Quartet, 1984, Expo '85 for Multiple Synthesizers, 1985, The Fox Trots Again for Chamber Ensemble, 1985, Metaphors for Guitar Quartet, 1986, Symphony Number 3 for Full Orchestra, numerous others; contbr. articles to profl. jours. Mem. Am. Soc. U. Composers, ASCAP., Am. Music Center. Home: Buffalo N.Y. Died Jan. 26, 1994.

HIMELSTEIN, PEGGY DONN, psychologist; b. Beacon, N.Y., Sept. 21, 1932; d. Leon and Sophie Donn; m. Philip Himelstein, June 1, 1952; children: Steven, Carol, Roger. BS, U. Tex., 1954; MA, U. Tex., El Paso, 1971; PhD, Fla. Inst. Tech., 1983. Lic. psychologist, Tex.; lic. marriage and family therapist, Tex. Dir. Ednl. Devel. Ctr., El Paso, 1971-75; marriage and family therapist El Paso Psychiat. Clinic, 1976-78; instr. in psychology El Paso Community Coll., 1979-82; psychology intern El Paso Ctr. for Mental Health/Mental Retardation Svcs., 1981-82; marriage and family therapist Jewish Family & Children's Svcs., El Paso, 1986-88; pvt. practice El Paso, 1978-94. Mem. APA, Am. Assn. Marriage and Family Therapy (clin.), Soc. Clin. and Exptl. Hypnosis, El Paso Psychol. Assn. (pres. 1981-82), El Paso Assn. for Marriage and Family Therapy (pres. 1989-90), El Paso County Psychol. Soc. (pres. 1992-93), Tex. Psychol. Assn., Southwestern Psychol. Assn., Psi Chi. Home: El Paso Tex. Died June 1, 1994; buried B'Nai Zion cemetary.

HIMENO, EDWARD TORAO, child psychiatrist; b. Honolulu, May 15, 1926; s. Bunzo and Irene Yoshiko (Kudo) H.; B.A., LaSierra Coll., 1950; M.D., Loma Linda U., 1958; m. Miyoko Kusuhara, June 5, 1952; children—Cheryl Aimee, Guy Randall. Intern, Los Angeles County U. So. Calif. Med. Center, 1958-59, resident gen. psychiatry, 1959-62, child psychiatry, 1963-65; practice medicine specializing in child psychiatry, Monterey Park, Calif., 1965—, Cerritos, Calif., 1983—; assoc. prof. psychiatry Loma Linda U. Sch. Medicine, 1967-77, assoc. clin. prof. psychiatry, 1977-80, dir. child psychiatry services, 1967-77; dir. child psychiatry unit Riverside (Calif.) Gen. Hosp., 1972-81; med./clin. dir. Children's Residential Care and Intensive Day Treatment Ctr., Riverside County, Calif., 1981-83; mem. child psychiatry staff Los Angeles County, U. So. Calif. Med. Center, 1962-63, 65-67; cons. Inland Adolescent Clinic, San Bernardino, Calif., 1973-83, Desert Community Mental Health Services, Indio, Calif., 1977-80; cons. child and adolescent unit mental health services San Bernardino County Gen. Hosp., 1973-75; cons. adolescent and young adult program Patton (Calif.) State Hosp., 1968-73, Boy's Republic, Chino, 1970-74, adolescent and adult unit Ingleside Mental Health Center, Rosemead, 1962-81; bd. dirs. Ingleside Mental Health Center, Rosemead, 1974-81, 2d v.p., 1975-81; chmn. med. adv. profl. symposiums, Riverside, Calif., 1979—. Mem. City of Monterey Park Human Relations Commn., 1970. Dist. chmn. Alhambra Monterey Park Council Boy Scouts Am., 1969-70. Served with AUS, 1944-45. Recipient several hons. by various profl. and civic groups. Mem. Japanese Am. Med. Assn. (v.p. 1969, 81-82, sec. 1979-80, pres.-elect 1983-85, pres. 1985-86). Home: Monterey Park Calif.

HIMSWORTH, SIR HAROLD PERCIVAL, physician, researcher; b. May 19, 1905; M.D., U. London, also LL.D.; Dr. honoris causa, Toulouse; LL.D. (hon.), U. Glasgow, U. Wales; D.Sc. (hon.) U. Manchester, 1956, Leeds, 1968, U. West Indies, 1968; Sc.D. (hon.), Cambridge U., 1964. Former prof. medicine U. London; former dir. med. unit Univ. Coll. Hosp. Med. Sch., London, 1939-49; sec., Med. Research Council, 1949-68; chmn. bd. mgmt. London Sch. Hygiene and Tropical Medicine, 1969-76. Author: The Development and Organisation of Scientific Knowledge, 1970, Scientific Knowledge and Philosophic Thought, 1986, The Liver and Its Diseases, 1947; also sci. and med. papers. Fellow Univ. Coll., London; decorated knight comdr. Bath. Fellow Royal Soc., Royal Coll. Physicians, Royal Coll. Radiologists (hon.), Royal Coll. Physicians Edinburgh (hon.), Royal Soc. Medicine (hon.), Royal Coll. Surgeons (hon.), Royal Coll. Pathologists; mem. Belgian Royal Acad. Medicine (hon.), Swedish (hon.), Norwegian med. socs., Am. Acad. Arts and Scis. (fgn. hon.), Royal Soc. Arts and Scis. Gothenburg, Am. Philos. Soc. (fgn. hon.), Assn. Am. Physicians (hon.). Died Nov. 1, 1993; cremated. Home: London Eng.

HIPP, FRANCIS MOFFETT, insurance executive; b. Newberry, S.C., Mar. 3, 1911; s. William Frank and Eunice Jane (Halfacre) H.; m. Mary M. Looper, Nov. 10, 1935 (dec. 1962); children: Mary Elizabeth (dec.), William, John, Mary Jane; m. Shirley A. Mattoon, May 11, 1964. Student, The Citadel, 1929-31; AB, Furman U., 1933, LLD, 1968; LLD, U. S.C., 1964, The Citadel, 1968, Clemson U., 1980, Benedict Coll., 1983, Newberry Coll., 1985; LL.D, Wofford Coll., 1994. With Liberty Life Ins. Co., 1933-95, asst. treas., 1936-41, v.p., 1942, pres., chmn. bd., 1943-95; chmn. bd. Liberty Corp., 1977-95; pres., chmn. bd. Liberty Corp., Greenville, S.C., 1976-77; chmn. exec. com., dir. Cosmos Broadcasting Corp., Greenville; dir. emeritus S.C. Nat. Corp., Columbia, Scana Corp., Columbia.; Mem. S.C. Devel. Bd., 1955-95, chmn., 1959-63; state v.p. Am. Life Conv., 1947-57, mem. exec. com., 1957-63; mem. exec. com. Life Insurors Conf., 1961-64. Trustee S.C. Found. Ind. Colls., The Citadel Devel. Found.; mem. Bus. Partnership Found. of U. S.C., Palmetto Bus. Forum. Recipient Businessman of Yr. award S.C. C. of C., 1980, Order of the Palmetto Gov. of S.C., 1985, 94; named to S.C. Bus. Hall of Fame, 1985. Mem. Newcomen Soc., Kappa Alpha, Beta Gamma Sigma. Presbyn. Clubs: Greenville Country, Poinsett, Green Valley Country, Commerce (Greenville, S.C.), Augusta (Ga.), Nat. Golf. Home: Greenville S.C. Died July 24, 1995.

HIRSCHFIELD, ROBERT S., political science educator; b. St. Louis, Sept. 1, 1928; s. Charles and Rose (Susman) H. AB, Harvard U., 1950, LLB, 1953, MA, 1954; PhD, NYU, 1958. Teaching asst. Harvard U., 1953-54; instr. NYU, 1955-57; instr. Hunter Coll., CUNY, 1958-60, asst. prof., 1961-63, assoc. prof., 1964-66, prof., 1967-85, chmn. polit. sci. dept., 1968-85; CUNY univ. dean for communications, dir. CUNY-TV, 1985-92, dir. internship program, 1968-92. Author: The Constitution and the Court, 1962, The Power of the Presidency, 1968, rev. edit., 1973, 82, Selection/Election: A Forum on the American Presidency, 1982; host, producer TV program Cityscope; editorial dir. Earth Times newspaper. Bd. dirs. N.Y. State Facilities Devel. Corp., from 1979; mem. N.Y.C. Commn. on Status of Women, 1975-81; founding chmn. Univ. Faculty Senate CUNY, 1968-71. Mem. Am. Polit. Sci. Assn., AAUP, Am. Arbitration Assn., Pi Sigma Alpha. Home: New York N.Y. Deceased.

HITCH, CHARLES JOHNSTON, economist, institution executive; b. Boonville, Mo., Jan. 9, 1910; s. Arthur Martin and Bertha (Johnston) H.; m. Nancy Winslow Squire, Mar. 20, 1942; 1 dau., Caroline Rubio. A.A., Kemper Mil. Sch., 1929; B.A. with highest distinction, U. Ariz., 1931, LL.D., 1962; postgrad., Harvard, 1931-32; B.A. with first class honors (Rhodes scholar), Oxford U., 1934, M.A., 1938; D.Sc. in Commerce, Drexel U., 1963; LL.D., U. Pitts., 1968, U. Mo., 1968, George Washington U., 1976; D.Engring., Colo. Sch. Mines, 1979; L.H.D. honoris causa, U. Judaism, 1973; D. Pub. Policy, Rand Grad. Inst., 1985. Began as fellow, praelector, tutor Queen's Coll., Oxford U., 1935-48; gen. editor Oxford Econ. Papers, 1941-48; vis. prof. U. São Paolo, Brazil, 1947; chief econs. div. Rand Corp., Santa Monica, Calif., 1948-61; dir. research program; asst. sec. def. (comptroller), 1961-65; v.p. bus. and finance U. Calif., 1965-66, v.p. of adminstrn., 1966-67, pres. univ., 1968-75; prof. econs. U. Calif. at Berkeley, 1965-75; emeritus; pres. Resources for the Future, 1975-79, also dir.; vis. prof. UCLA, 1949-50; Irving Fisher research prof. Yale, 1957; Staff economist Mission for Econ. Affairs, U.S. Embassy, London, 1941-42; staff economist planning com. WPB, 1942-43; chief stblzn. controls div. Office War Moblzn. and Reconversion, 1945-46; chmn. gen. adv. com. ERDA, 1975-77; mem. Energy Research Advisory Bd. Dept. Energy, 1978-85, Assembly Engring., NRC, 1975-78, Nat. Petroleum Council, 1975-78; mem. advisory council Gas Research Inst., 1976-84, Electric Power Research Inst., 1978-85; mem. Research Coordination Council, Gas Research Inst., 1984-87 ; dir. Aerospace Corp., 1975-82. Author: The Economics of Defense in the Nuclear Age, 1960, Decision Making for Defense, 1965; Editor: Introduction to Economic Analysis and Policy, 1938, Energy Conservation and Economic Growth, 1978. Trustee Asia Found., Center Biotech. Research; bd. dirs. Am. Council on Edn., 1971-74. Served as 1st lt., OSS U.S. Army, 1943-45. Recipient Pub. Service award U.S. Navy, 1965; Phi Beta Kappa vis. scholar, 1977-78; Hon. fellow Queen's Coll., Oxford; Hon. fellow Worcester Coll., Oxford. Fellow AAAS, Am. Acad. Arts and Scis., Nat. Acad. Pub. Adminstrn., Econometric Soc.; mem. Am. Econ. Assn. (v.p. 1965), Royal Econ. Soc., Ops. Research Soc. Am. (council 1955-58, pres. 1959-60), Coun. Fgn. Rels., Phi Beta Kappa. Democrat. Presbyterian. Clubs: Bohemian (San Francisco); Cosmos (Washington). Home: Berkeley Calif. Died September 11, 1995.

HITCH, THOMAS KEMPER, economist; b. Boonville, Mo., Sept. 16, 1912; s. Arthur Martin and Bertha (Johnston) H.; m. Margaret Barnhart, June 27, 1940 (dec. Nov. 1974); children: Hilary, Leslie, Caroline, Thomas; m. Mae Okudaira. Student, Nat. U. Mexico, 1932; A.B., Stanford U., 1934; M.A., Columbia U., 1946; Ph.D., U. London, 1937. Mem. faculty Stephens Coll., Columbia, Mo., 1937-42; spl. study commodity markets Commodity Exchange Adminstrn., Dept. Agr., 1940; acting head current bus. research sect. Dept. Commerce, 1942-43; labor adviser Vets. Emergency Housing Program, 1946-47; economist labor econs. Pres.'s Council Econ. Advisers, 1947-50; dir. research Hawaii Employers Council, Honolulu, 1950-59; sr. v.p., mgr. research div. First Hawaiian Bank, 1959-82; chmn. Hawaii Gov.'s Adv. Com. on Financing, 1959-62; chmn. research com. Hawaii Vistors Bur., 1962-69; chmn. Mayor's Fin. Adv. Com., 1960-68; chmn. taxation and fin. com. Constl. Conv. Hawaii, 1968. Contbr. articles to profl. jours. Trustee Tax Found. of Hawaii, 1955-80, pres., 1968; trustee McInerny Found.; chmn. Hawaii Joint Council Econ. Edn., 1964-68. Served as lt. O.R.C., 1933-38; as lt. USNR, 1943-46. Mem. C. of C. Hawaii (chmn. bd. 1971), Nat. Assn. Bus. Economists, Am., Hawaii econs. assns., Indsl. Relations Research Assn., Am. Statis. Assn., Phi Beta Kappa, Pi Sigma Alpha, Alpha Sigma Phi. Clubs: Waialae Country (pres. 1979), Pacific. Home: Honolulu Hawaii Died August 22, 1989; buried Nat. Meml. Cemetary of the Pacific, Honolulu, Hawaii.

HITCHCOCK, HAROLD BRADFORD, retired biology educator, zoologist; b. Hartford, Conn., June 23, 1903; s. Alfred Marshall and Harriet May (Thompson) H.; m. Martine Cutter, Feb. 20, 1942; children: Susan Hitchcock Kalma, Harriet Hitchcock McNamara, Martha Hitchcock Stewart. BA, Williams Coll., 1926; MA, Harvard U., 1932, PhD, 1938. Instr. to asst. prof. U. Western Ont., London, Can., 1938-43; asst. prof. to prof. Middlebury (Vt.) Coll., 1943-68, chmn. biology dept., 1945-68, Mead prof., 1964-68, prof. emeritus, 1968-95; Dana prof., chmn. biology dept. Bates Coll., Lewiston, Maine, 1969-72, prof. emeritus, 1972-95; vis. prof. Bowdoin Coll., summer 1952; interim prof. Norwich (Vt.) U., fall 1968, U. Hawaii, spring 1969. Am. Acad. Arts and Scis. grantee, 1947, Am. Philos. Soc. grantee, 1949, 51, 52, NSF grantee, 1964; Fulbright rsch. scholar Max Planck Inst., Wilhelmshaven, Germany, 1954; recipient Gerrit S. Miller award N.Am. Symposium on Bat Rsch., 1986. Mem. Am. Soc. Mammology (past dir.). Unitarian. Home: Middlebury Vt. Died Sept. 13, 1995.

HOAGLAND, GORDON W., mathematics educator; b. Nampa, Idaho, Oct. 22, 1936; s. Clyde Mackay and Clara Vivian (Wood) H.; m. Byrnina Louise Burningham, Aug. 1, 1962; children: David, Daniel, Deborah. BS, Brigham Young U., 1966, MS, 1968. Mem. rsch. faculty Oreg. State U., Corvallis, 1968-69; mem. math. faculty Ricks Coll., Rexburg, Idaho, from 1969, dept. chmn., 1979-84, with campus computer planning sect., from 1985; cons. in field. Author: (lab manual) Scientific Programming, 1984; contbr. articles to profl. jours. With U.S. Air N.G., 1954-65. Mem. Am. Math. Assn. for 2 Yr. Colls. (mem. editorial bd. from 1986), Soc. Indsl. and Applied Math., Upper Valley Sq. Dance Club (St. Anthony, Idaho, caller 1978-87), Wagonwheeler Sq. Dance Club (Rexburg, caller from 1969), Pi Mu Epsilon. Republican. Mem. LDS Ch. Home: Rexburg Idaho Deceased.

HOBBS, RANALD PURCELL, publisher; b. Bartlett, N.H., Sept. 14, 1907; s. Don P. and Blanche (Stevens) H.; m. Vera Ingeborg Andren, June 27, 1936; children: Ranald D., Linda A. Young. AB, Dartmouth Coll., 1930. With The Macmillan Co., 1935-43; with Rinehart & Co., Inc., 1943-60, exec. v.p., 1955-60; exec. v.p. Bobbs-Merrill Co., Inc., 1960-61; pres. Hobbs Internat., Inc., 1962-63, Hobbs, Dorman & Co., Inc., 1964-73, Hobbs/Context Corp., 1973-77, Cowles Book Co., Inc., 1968-69; v.p., treas. Moseley Assocs. Inc., 1971-83; Mem. Darien (Conn.) Bd. Edn., 1948-55, chmn., 1950-52; chmn. coll. sect. Am. Textbook Pubs. Inst., 1954-55, bd. dirs., 1956-59, sec., 1957, treas., 1958; regional v.p. United Student Aid Funds, Inc., 1973-77. Bd. govs. Friends of the Libr. of Collier County. Mem. Dartmouth Club. Home: Naples Fla. Died Jan. 28, 1996.

HOBBY, OVETA CULP, newspaper publisher; b. Killeen, Tex., Jan. 19, 1905; d. I.W. and Emma (Hoover) Culp; m. William P. Hobby, Feb. 23, 1931 (dec. 1964); children: William, Jessica (Mrs. Henry Catto Jr.). Student, Mary Hardin Baylor Coll.; L.H.D., Baylor Coll., 1956, Bard Coll., 1950, Lafayette Coll., 1954; LL.D., Baylor U., 1943, Sam Houston State Tchrs. Coll., 1943, U. Chattanooga, 1943, Bryant Coll., 1953, Ohio Wesleyan U., 1953, Columbia U., 1954, Smith Coll., 1954, Middlebury Coll., 1954, U. Pa., 1955, Colby Coll., 1955, Fairleigh Dickinson U., Western Coll.; D.Litt., Colo. Women's Coll., 1947, C.W. Post Coll., 1962. Parliamentarian Tex. Ho. of Reps., 1926-31, 39, 41; research editor Houston Post, from 1931, successively lit. editor, asst. editor, v.p., exec. v.p., editor, 1931-53, editor, pub., 1952-53, pres., editor, 1955-65, chmn. bd., editor, 1965-83; chmn. bd. H&C Communications, Inc., 1978-83, chmn. exec. com., 1983-95; dir. Sta. KPRC AM-TV, 1945-53, 55-69, chmn. bd., 1970-83; chmn. bd., dir. Channel Two TV Co., 1970-83; vice chmn. Channel 5-TV, Nashville; chief women's interest sect. War Dept. Bur. Pub. Relations, 1941-42; apptd. dir. WAAC, 1942; commd. col. AUS, 1943-45; dir. WAC, 1943-45; fed. security adminstr., 1953; sec. HEW, 1953-55. Author: (textbook) Mr. Chairman; syndicated columnist. Sponsor Clark Sch. for Deaf; trustee Eisenhower Birthplace Meml. Park; mem. Pres.'s Com. on Employment for Physically Handicapped, Com. on Civilian Nat. Honors; trustee Eisenhower Exchange Fellowship; bd. dirs. Houston Symphony Soc.; mem. S.W. adv. bd. Inst. Internat. Edn.; mem. Com. of 75, U. Tex.; mem. So. regional com. Marshall Scholarship; mem. Rockefeller Bros. Fund Spl. Studies project; bd. dirs. Com. Econ. Devel.; mem. nat. bd. devel. Sam Rayburn Found.; mem. Crusade for Freedom, Inc.; nat. bd. Eleanor Roosevelt Meml. Found.; trustee Rice U. Decorated D.S.M.; Mil. Merit medal (The Philippines), 1947; recipient Pub. of Yr. award, 1960, Honor award Nat. Jewish Hosp., 1962, Living History award Research Inst. Am., 1960. Mem. Soc. Rehab. Facially Disfigured, So. Newspaper Pubs. Assn. (pres. 1949), Acad. Tex. (charter), Gamma Alpha Chi (hon. vice chmn.). Episcopalian. Clubs: Houston Country, Bayou, Ramada, Jr. League (Houston). Home: Houston Tex. Died Aug. 16, 1995.

HODGKIN, DOROTHY CROWFOOT, chemist; b. Cairo, 1910; m. Thomas L. Hodgkin, 1937 (dec. 1982). Student, Somerville Coll., Oxford, Eng., 1928-32, Cambridge U., 1932-34; ScD (hon.), U. Leeds, U. Manchester, Cambridge U., others, 1932-34; MD (hon.), Modena. Mem. faculty Oxford U., 1934-77, prof. emeritus, 1977-94; chancellor Bristol U., 1988-94. Determined structure of vitamin B12, cholesterol iodide, and penicillin using x-ray crystallographic analysis. Decorated Order of Merit; First Freedom of Beccles; recipient Nobel Prize in chemistry, 1964; Mikhail Lomonosov gold medal, 1982. Fellow Royal Soc. (Royal medal 1956, Copley medal 1976), Australian Acad. Sci., Akad. Leopoldina; mem. Nat. Acad. Scis., Brit. Assn. Advancement of Sci. (pres. 1977-78); fgn. mem. Royal Netherlands Acad. of Sci. and Letters, Am. Acad. Arts and Scis.; hon. fgn. mem. USSR Acad. Scis., Austrian Acad Scis., Norwegian Acad. Scis. Home: Shipton-on Stour Eng. Died July 29, 1994.

HOFFMAN, PHILIP EISINGER, lawyer, real estate company executive; b. N.Y.C., Oct. 2, 1908; s. David S. and Hildegarde (Eisinger) H.; m. Florence L. Lehman, Sept. 9, 1933 (dec.); children: David L., Lynn B. (Mrs. Roger L. Manshel); m. Bee Beham, June 18, 1972. A.B. cum laude, Dartmouth Coll., 1929; LL.B., Yale U., 1932. Bar: N.Y. 1933. Practiced in N.Y.C.; corp. law practice, 1933-42, 45-93; ptnr. Goodell, Hoffman & Spark, 1937-42, Hoffman & Tuck, 1962-93; chmn. exec. com. U.S. Realty & Investment Co., Newark, 1962-93; also dir.; former dir. Comml. Mortgage Co., Ray Miller, Inc., Realty Capital Corp., Ltd., Toronto, Ont., Can.; Mem. N.J. Commn. on Civil Rights, 1969-75, Bipartisan Conf. on Civil Rights, 1960-93, mem. N.J. adv. com., 1964-69; N.J. adv. com. U.S. Commn. on Civil Rights, 1969-75; U.S. rep. Human Rights Commn. UN, 1972-75; chmn. Community Relations Council Essex County, N.J., 1960-63; co-chmn. housing com. Com. of Concern Newark, 1967-69; asst. gen. counsel WPB, Washington, 1942-45; hearing commr. Nat. Prodn. Authority, 1950-53; chmn. coodinating com. Retail Jewelry Industry, 1954-60; chmn. bd. govs. Am. Jewish Com., 1963-67, pres., 1969-73, hon. pres., 1973-93, chmn. nat. exec. bd., 1967-68; hon. chmn. Appeal for Human Relations, 1962-93; mem. exec. com. Nat. Community Relations Adv. Council, 1966-73, Am. Israel Pub. Affairs Com., 1969-73; chmn. adminstrv. council Jacob Blaustein Inst. for Advancement Human Rights, 1975-93; trustee Leonard M. Sperry Research Center, East Orange Gen. Hosp., Jewish Community Council Essex County; chmn. bd. dirs. Nat. Assn. for Visually Handicapped, 1978-79; bd. dirs. Am. Friends of Jerusalem Mental Health Center, 1973-76; bd. govs. Hebrew U. Jerusalem, 1973-93, Internat. League for Human Rights, 1975-93, Com. for Econ. Growth in Israel, 1975; v.p. acad. affairs Am. Friends of Hebrew U., 1978-93. Recipient numerous awards in human relations field. Mem. ABA, Assn. Bar City N.Y., N.Y. County Lawyers Assn., Phi Beta Kappa. Jewish. Clubs: 744 (Newark); Mountain Ridge Country (Caldwell, N.J.). Home: Verona N.J. Died June 6, 1993.

HOFFMAN, ROY A., JR., educator; b. Natchez, Miss., Jan. 31, 1940; s. Roy A. and Mattie L. (Swindle) H.; children: Erik, Amy. BA, Miss. State U., 1962; PhD, U. Ala., Tuscaloosa, 1968. Tchr. Marion County Schs., Hamilton, Ala., 1962-65; instr. Miss. State U., State College, 1965-66; asst. prof. NW Mo. State U., Maryville, 1968-69; prof. Fla. Atlantic U., Boca Raton, 1969-96; pvt. cons., evaluator Dept. Edn., Atlanta, 1972-78; pvt. cons. schs., south Fla., 1971-96; ptnr. consulting firm Psychol. Assocs., south Fla., 1980. Contbr. rsch. articles to profl. jours.; referee Capstone Jour. Edn., 1986-96. Officer, negotiator United Faculty of Fla., 1972-76; mem. Home Assn., Boca Raton, 1970-87. Mem. ASCD, Fla. Ednl. Rsch. Assn., Am. Assn. Colls. of Tchr. Edn. (institutional rep.), Am. Statis. Assn., Am. Philatelic Soc., Bur. Issues Assn. Home: Boca Raton Fla. Died Jan. 26, 1996.

HÖFFNER, CARDINAL JOSEPH, German ecclesiastic; b. Horhausen/Westerwald, Germany, Dec. 24, 1906; s. Paul and Helene (Schug) H.; Dr.Phil., U. Rome, 1929, Dr.Theol., 1932; Dr.Theol., U. Freiburg, 1938, Dr.Sc.Pol., 1941, Dr.Theol. Habil, 1944. Ordained priest Roman Catholic Ch., 1932; consecrated bishop, 1962; elevated to cardinal, 1969; priest in Trier, Germany, 1934-45; prof. pastoral theology and Christian sociology Phil-Theologische Fakultät, Trier, 1945-51; prof. Christian sociology U. Mü nster (Germany), 1951-62; founder, dir. Inst. für Christliche Sozialwissenschafter, 1951; bishop of Münster, 1962-69; archbishop of Cologne, 1969-87; pres. German Bishop's Conf., 1976-87. Former mem. Union Internat. des Etudes Sociales, Brussels, found. com. for U. Bochum, also many working parties and adv. councils. Decorated Grosskreuz des Verdienstordensdens der Bundesrepublik (Germany); Grosskreuz des Verdienstordens (Italy). Author monographs, essays, articles.

HOGAN, CLAUDE HOLLIS, retired lawyer; b. Bishop, Calif., Mar. 2, 1920; s. Claude Hollis and Emma Janet (Slade) H.; m. June Cunningham, June 12, 1946; 1 child, Patricia. A.B., Coll. of Pacific, 1942; LLB., Yale U., 1948. Bar: Calif. 1949. Assoc. Pillsbury, Madison & Sutro, San Francisco, 1948-58, ptnr., 1959-90; retired, 1991. Contbr. articles to profl. jours. Bd. dirs. Ernst D. van Loben Sels- Eleanor Slate van Loben Sels Charitable Found., San Francisco, 1964-94, No. Calif. Grantmakers, 1988-92; pres. Ernst D. van Loben Sels-Eleanor Slate van Loben Sels Charitable Found., 1971-94; mem. San Francisco Lawyers Com. on Urban Affairs, 1973-94, com-chmn., 1978; bd. dirs. Legal Aid Soc. San Francisco, 1974-88; trustee Lawyers Com. for Civil Rights under Law, 1980-94; pres. Child Care Law Ctr., 1985-87, bd. dirs., 1985-87; mem. steering com. Ctr. for Intergrated Svcs., U. Calif., Berkeley, 1991-94. Mem. State Bar Calif. (exec. com. taxation sect. 1975-76, bd. legal specialization 1981-85), ABA, Bar Assn. San Francisco (chmn. taxation sect. 1970, dir. 1978, pres. found. 1983-84), Internat. Fiscal Assn., Am. Judicature Soc., Calif. C. of C. (tax com. 1973-81). Home: San Francisco Calif. Deceased.

HOGARTH, BURNE, cartoonist, illustrator; b. Chgo., Dec. 25, 1911; s. Max and Pauline H.; m. Constance Holubar, June 27, 1953; children: Michael, Richard, Ross. Student Art Inst. Chgo., 1925-27, Chgo. Acad. Fine Arts, 1926-29, Crane Coll., 1928-30, U. Chgo., 1930-32, Northwestern U., 1931-32, Columbia U., 1956-57. Asst. cartoonist to Lyman Young, Tim Tyler's Luck, N.Y.C., 1934; cartoonist Pieces of Eight, McNaught Syndication, N.Y.C., 1935; free lance artist King Features, N.Y.C., 1935-36; staff artist Johnstone Agy., N.Y.C., 1936-37; cartoonist Sunday Color Page, Tarzan, United Feature Syndication, N.Y.C., 1937-50, Sunday page Drago, Post-Hall Syndication, N.Y.C., 1946, Miracle Jones, United Features, N.Y.C., 1948; founder Sch. Visual Arts, N.Y.C., 1947-70, v.p., coord. curriculum, instr., 1947-70; author Watson-Guptill, N.Y.C., 1958-89; instr. Parsons Sch., N.Y.C., 1976-79; pres. Pendragon Press Ltd., N.Y.C., 1975-79; with Art Ctr. Coll. Design, Pasadena, Calif., 1982-96, Otis Art Inst., Parsons Sch. Design, L.A., 1981-96; seminar presenter U. Colo., Boulder; spl. guest German Comics Fair, Cologne, Berlin, 1990; participant traveling exhbn. Sites 1990-92, U.S.; hosted by U.S. Embassy cultural staff, guest and pres. Tarzan Exhibit Am. Cultural Ctr., Brussels, 1995; numerous exhbns. worldwide including Musee des arts decoratives, Louvre, Paris, 1968, 69, Smithsonian Inst., 1990-96, Gallery Karikatury, Warsaw, 1990; one man show Paris, 1967, Bibliotheque Municipale, 1985, Palais de Longchamps, Marseille, France, 1985; group show Gallery Karikatury, Warsaw, Poland, 1990; represented in permanent collections: Smithsonian Instn., Mus. Cartoon Art, U. Colo., U. Wyo., Mus. Art, Gijon, Spain, others. Author: Dynamic Anatomy, 1958, Drawing the Human Head, 1965, Dynamic Figure Drawing, 1970, Drawing Dynamic Hands, 1977, Dynamic Light and Shade, 1981, Dynamic Wrinkles and Drapery, 1991, The Arcane Eye of Hogarth, 1992; creator graphic novels Tarzan of the Apes, 1972, Jungle Tales of Tarzan, 1976, Golden Age of Tarzan, 1979, Life of King Arthur, 1984, The Arcane Eye of Hogarth, 1992; creator, illustrator (with Harry Hurwitz) Morphos the Shapechanger, 1995; author (videocassette) Draw The Human Head, 1989. Trustee NCS Milt Gross Fund., 1980; active 43d Ann. Conf. on World Affairs, Boulder, 1990. Named Best Illustration Cartoonist, Nat. Cartoonists Soc., 1974, 75, 76, Artist of Yr., Pavilion of Humour, 1975; recipient Premio Emil Freixas Silver plaque V-Muestra Internat. Conv., 197 Pulcinella award V-Mostra Internat. del Fumetto, 198 Caran D'Ache Silver plaque Internat. Comics Conv 1984, Adamson Silent Sam award Comics '85 Interna Conv., 1985, Golden Palms award Cesar Illustratic Group, Paris, 1988, Premio Especial award 7th Interna Salon of Humor, Barcelona, Spain, 1989, Golden Lic award Burroughs Bibliophiles, U. Louisville, 199 Bronze trophy German Comics Fair, Cologne, Fe Republic Germany, 1990, L'Age D'Or award Cesar I lustration Group, 1992, Lifetime Achievement awa Kansas City Comic Conv., 1992. Mem. Na Cartoonists Soc. (pres. 1977-79, Reuben Silver plaqu 1993-94), Mus. of Cartoon Art, Am. Soc. Aesthetic Nat. Art Edn. Assn., WHO, Graphic Arts Soc., I ternat. Assn. Authors of Comics and Cartoons. Di Jan. 28, 1996. Home: Los Angeles Calif.

HOGG, HELEN BATTLES SAWYER, astronome educator; b. Lowell, Mass., Aug. 1, 1905; came to Ca 1931; d. Edward Everett and Carrie Myra (Spragu Sawyer; m. Frank Scott Hogg, Sept. 6, 1930; ch dren—Sarah Longley, David Edward, James Scott; n Francis Ethelbert Louis Priestley, Nov. 28, 1985. A.E Mt. Holyoke Coll., 1926, D.Sc. (hon.), 1958; A.M Radcliffe Coll., 1928, Ph.D., 1931; D.Sc. (hon.), U Waterloo, 1962, McMaster U., 1976, U. Toronto, 197 St. Mary's U., Halifax, N.S., 1981; D.Litt. (hon.), S Mary's U.; D. Sci. (hon.), U. Lethbridge, 1985. Lect Smith Coll., Northampton, Mass., 1927; lectr. M Holyoke Coll., South Hadley, Mass., 1930-31, as prof., acting chmn. dept. astronomy, 1940-41; researc assoc. Dominion Astrophys. Obs., Victoria, B.C., Car 1931-34; research assoc. David Dunlap Obs. U Toronto, Ont., Can., 1936—, lectr., 1941-51, asst. pr astronomy, 1951-55, assoc. prof., 1955-57, prof., 195 76, prof. emeritus, 1976—; vis. prof. Harvard U summer 1952; program dir. astronomy NSF, Wash ington, 1955-56. Contbr. articles to profl. jours.; astr nomy columnist Toronto Star, 1951-81. Decorated c ficer, 1968, companion Order of Can., 1976; recipie medal Rittenhouse Astron. Soc., 1967, Centenni medal, 1967, Queen Elizabeth Silver Jubilee meda 1967, Klumpke Roberts award Astron. Soc. Pacifi 1983, Sanford Fleming medal Royal Can. Inst., 198 award of merit City of Toronto, 1985; Obs. of Na Mus. Sci. and Tech. (Ottawa) named in her honor, 198 Mem. Am. Astron. Soc. (councillor 1965-68, Annie Cannon prize 1965-68), Royal Astron. Soc. Can. (pre 1957, hon. pres. 1977-78), Am. Assn. Variable Star O servers (pres. 1940-41), Internat. Astron. Union (pa pres. subcom.), Royal Soc. Can. (pres. sect. 3, 1960-61 Can. Astron. Soc. (1st pres. 1971-72). Club: Universi Women's (Toronto). Home: Richmond Hill Can. Di Jan. 28, 1993; interred Lowell Cemetary, Lowel Ontario.

HOLBROOK, JAY COLLINS, opera company a ministrator; b. Balt., Oct. 13, 1952; s. Frank Weller an Ruth (Collins) H.; B.A. cum laude, U Md., 1973. Pub relations dir. Balt. Opera Co., Inc., 1975-78, asst. ge mgr., 1978-80, gen. mgr., 1980—; part-time facul Johns Hopkins U. Sch. Continuing Studies; mem. ad bd. regional auditions Met. Opera Co. Mem. adv. b Balt. Artscape '82, 83. Recipient award Am. Legio 1967. Mem. Opera Am., Inc. (bd. dirs.), Nat. Ope Inst., Phi Kappa Phi. Democrat. Methodist. Clu Advt., Rotary.

HOLCOMB, MARGUERITE KNOWLES, former ci official, shorthand reporting company executive; Dayton Twp., Mich., Apr. 9, 1913; d. Arthur Russe and Catherine (Biermeyer) Knowles; children: Joyce Holcomb Filius, John F., June A. Student public sch Muskegon and Dayton Twp., Mich. Ofcl. circuit reporter 14th Jud. Circuit, Muskegon, 1943-53; pre Holcomb Reporting Service, Inc., Muskegon, from 195 commr. City of Muskegon, 1975-84, vice-mayor, 197 79, mayor, 1980-82; mem. econ. devel. com. U.S. Co Mayors. Mem. adv. council Ferris State Coll., B Rapids, Mich. Recipient Athena award, State of Mic 1988; named Businesswoman of Yr., Quadrangle Bu and Profl. Women's Clubs 1970, State Small Busines woman of Yr., Mich. Fedn. Bus. and Profl. Women Clubs, 1973, Entrepreneur of Yr., County of Muskego 1984, Mich. Woman Entrepreneur of Yr. Mich. Dep Commerce, 1988. Mem. Nat. Shorthand Reporte Assn., Mich. Shorthand Reporters Assn., Mich. C Reporters Assn. (pres. 1967-68), Muskegon C. of C. (b dirs.) Women's Div. Muskegon C. of C. (pres. 1986-8 treas.), Bus. and Profl. Women's Club (state pres. 196 67), Century Club, Zonta (dir. club). Republican. Home: Muskegon Mich. Deceased.

HOLDEN, REUBEN ANDRUS, retired college pr sident; b. Louisville, Sept. 2, 1918; s. Reuben Andr and Grace (Morgan) H.; m. Elizabeth C. Walker, Ju 23, 1951; children—Grace Morgan, Reuben Andrus 5t George H. Walker, Mary Carter. B.A., Yale U., 194 M.A., 1948, Ph.D., 1951, L.H.D., 1971. Asst. to de of coll. Yale U., 1946-47, asst. to pres., 1947-52, sec. univ., 1953-71; pres. Warren Wilson Coll., Swannano N.C., 1971-86; interim dir. N.C. Ctr. Creative Retir ment, 1988; trustee Conn. Savs. Bank, 1955-71; me adv. coun. fin. aid HEW; civilian aide to Sec. of Arm 1962-68. Bd. dirs. Community Progress, Inc., 1962-6 pres., 1965-68; bd. dirs. Yale-New Haven Hosp., 195 l, New Haven YMCA, 1960-71, Blue Ridge Assembly, 1972-90, Swannanoa Med. Ctr., 1973-81, Asheville Area RC, 1974-79, Asheville United Way, 1977-80, So. Appalachian Highlands Conservancy, 1986-92; trustee Asheville Sch., 1948-74, Hopkins Grammar Sch., 1952-l, Jane Coffin Childs Fund Med. Research, Charles A. Coffin Fund, 1957-71, Ind. Coll. Funds Am., 1976-79, rts Jour., 1980-93, James G.K. McClure Ednl. Fund, 986—, 1991, Warren Wilson Coll., 1988—, Pack Pl. dn., Arts and Sci. Ctr., 1988—, Woodbury Found., 991—, Lewis Rathbun Wellness Ctr., 1993—, Grove rcade Pub. Market Found., 1993—; trustee Edward . Hazen Found., 1966-74, chmn., 1970-73; trustee oote Sch., 1964-71, pres., 1968-71; trustee Asheville rt Mus., 1986-93, v.p., 1989-91; v.p. Ind. Coll. Fund of .C., 1980-86; chmn. Swannanoa Community Council, 981-92. Served with AUS, 1941-46, CBI. Decorated ronze Star, Spl. Breast of Yun Hwei (China); recipient isting. Civilian award U.S. Army. Mem. Culinary ıst. Am. (gov. 1948-73, chmn. 1968-70), Yale-in-China ssn. (trustee 1947-95, pres. 1966-72), Phi Beta Kappa. resbyterian. Clubs: Yale (N.Y.C.), Biltmore (Asheville). Lodge: Rotary. Home: Black Mountain N.C. Died ov. 29, 1995.

HOLDEN, WILLIAM DOUGLAS, surgeon; b. Pittsfield, Mass., Aug. 25, 1912; s. Harry and Katherine C. MacInnis) H.; m. Janet Cobb, Dec. 28, 1936; chilren—John, Frank, Katherine. A.B., Cornell U., 1934, 1.D., 1937. Instr. surgery Case-Western Res. U. Med. ch., 1946-47, sr. instr. surgery, 1947-48, asst. prof., 948-49, asso. prof., 1948-49, Oliver H. Payne prof. urgery, 1950-77, prof. surgery, 1977-85, prof. emeritus, 985-95; dir. surgery Univ. Hosps., Cleve., 1950-77; em. staff Univ. Hosps., 1977-86, mem. hon. staff, 986-95. Contbr. profl. jours. Mem. Am., Central surg. ssns., Soc. U. Surgeons, Soc. Vascular Surgery. Home: Mentor Ohio Died Mar. 3, 1995.

HOLDING, DENNIS HARRY, psychology educator; . London, Dec. 6, 1925; came to U.S., 1968; s. Harry esse and Marion Edith (Goldsmith) H.; m. Margaret Ving, Sept. 13, 1969 (div. 1981); children: Judith Ann, ester Martin; m. Carol Ann Sappenfield, Aug. 11, 981; children: Miles Perry, Brent Timothy. MA in hilosophy, U. Edinburgh, Scotland, 1951, MA in sychology, 1952; PhD in Psychology, U. Durham, ng., 1961. Sci. officer Army Pers. Rsch. Unit, arnborough, Eng., 1952-55; rsch. psychologist dept. ıdsl. health King's Coll., Newcastle, Eng., 1955-60; ctr. psychology U. Leeds, Eng., 1960-66; rsch. fellow ept. psychology U. Exeter, Eng., 1966-68; sr. fgn. rsch. ellow dept. psychology Tulane U., New Orleans, 1968-9; prof. U. Louisville, 1969-93; cons. Am. Inst. Rsch., Vashington, 1973, Human Resources Rsch. Orgn., Ft. nox, Ky., 1985-90. Author: Principles of Training, 965, Psychology of Chess Skill, 1985; editor: Experiental Psychology in Industry, 1969, Human Skills, 2nd dit., 1989; assoc. editor Jour. Motor Behavior, Washgton, 1969-90; gen. editor series John Wiley & Sons, Chichester, Eng., 1977-93. Judge Regional Sci. Fair, ouisville, 1975-93. With Royal Navy, 1943-46. Rsch. rantee Flying Pers. Rsch. Commn., Newcastle, 1955-0, Dept. Sci. Indsl. Rsch., Leeds, 1962-65, Sci. Rsch. Coun., Exeter, 1966-68, NSF, 1968-69. Mem. Exptl. sychology Soc., So. Soc. Philosophy and Psychology, Human Factors Soc. Home: Manlius N.Y. Died Oct. 5, 1993.

HOLIGA, LUDOMIL ANDREW, metallurgical engineer; b. Dayton, Ohio, Dec. 7, 1920; s. Andrew and ntonia Margaret (Sefcek) H.; m. Aryetta Lillian Mernedakis, Feb. 6, 1960; children: David, Carol, Milard, Timothy, Michael. Engr. assoc., Sinclair Coll., 948; B.Sc., Calgary Coll. Tech., 1974, M.M.E., 1975. Cert. mfg. engr. Engr. designer Wright Patterson AFB, Ohio, 1941-54; contract designer Product Design Serices, Inc., Dayton, Ohio, 1955-60; with Dayton Progress Corp., 1961-86, dir. corp. devel., 1972-73, dir. esearch and tech. edn., 1974-86. Research on cutting learances for perforating metals in stamping dies. erved with USAAF, 1942-45, Ohio N.G., 1946-50, AUS, 1951-52. Mem. Soc. Mfg. Engrs. (chmn. tandards com. 1963-72), Ohio Research and Devel. Found., Foremans Club, Am. Metal Stamping Assn. utheran. Home: Dayton Ohio Died Feb. 18, 1995.

HOLLAND, PAUL DELEVAL, lawyer; b. Los Angeles, Feb. 1, 1910; s. Christopher Franklin and ouise (Deleval) H.; m. Claudine Florence Atkins. Student, U. Calif., Los Angeles, 1928-31; A.B., J. So. Calif., 1933, J.D., 1934. Bar: Calif. 1934. Pvt. ractice in Los Angeles, 1934-42, Beverly Hills, 1945-70, os Angeles, Century City, 1970-87. Pres. Sherman Oaks, 1987, Calif. Epilepsy Soc., 1966-70; pres. Epilepsy Found. Am., 1973-75, chmn., 1975-76, hon. life dir., 1980-93; internat. bd. dirs. RP Internat. Mem. ABA, Am. Arbitration Assn., Am. Judicature Soc., Nat. Panel Arbitrators, Los Angeles County Bar Assn, Phi Gamma Delta, Delta Theta Phi. Democrat. Home: Granada Hills Calif. Died Jan. 12, 1993.

HOLLEY, ROBERT WILLIAM, scientist; b. Urbana, Ill., Jan. 28, 1922; s. Charles E. and Viola (Wolfe) H.; n. Ann Dworkin, Mar. 3, 1945; 1 son, Frederick. A.B., J. Ill., 1942; Ph.D., Cornell U., 1947. Fellow Am. Chem. Soc. State Coll. Wash., 1947-48; asst. prof., then ssoc. prof. organic chemistry N.Y. State Agr. Expt. Sta., Ithaca, 1948-57; rsch. chemist plant, soil and nutrition lab. USDA Cornell U., Ithaca, N.Y., 1957-64; prof. biochemistry Cornell U., Ithaca, 1964-69, chmn. dept. biochemistry, 1965-66; resident fellow Salk Inst. Biol. Studies, La Jolla, Calif., 1968-93; mem. biochemistry study sect. NIH, 1962-66; vis. fellow Salk Inst. Biol. Studies; vis. prof. Scripps Clinic and Research Found., La Jolla, 1966-67. Recipient Distinguished Service award U.S. Dept. Agr., 1965, Albert Lasker award basic med. research, 1965; U.S. Steel Found. award in molecular biology Nat. Acad. Scis., 1967; Nobel prize for medicine and physiology, 1968; Guggenheim fellow Calif. Inst. Tech., 1955-56. Fellow AAAS; mem. Am. Acad. Arts and Scis., Am. Soc. Biochem. and Molecular Biology, Am. Chem. Soc., Nat. Acad. Scis., Phi Beta Kappa, Sigma Xi. Home: La Jolla Calif. Died Feb. 11, 1993.

HOLLOWAY, HERMAN M., SR., state senator; b. Wilmington, Del., Feb. 4, 1922; ed. Hampton Inst. Mem. Del. State Senate, 1965-94, chmn. aging com., fed. and state relations com., finance com., grant and aid com. health and social services com. Pres., Polit. Issues League, Inc.; bd. dirs. Walnut St. YMCA. Democrat. Methodist. Clubs: Masons, Elks. Died Mar. 1994. Home: Wilmington Del.

HOLME, THOMAS TIMINGS, industrial engineering educator; b. Frankford, Pa., Mar. 12, 1913; s. Justus Rockwell and Margaret (Mitchell) H.; m. Marjory Evans Walton, July 7, 1936; children: Judith Walton Holme Harrell, Thomas Timings, Penelope Walton. B.S., Lehigh U., 1935, M.S., 1940, I.E. (profl.), 1948; M.A. (hon.), Yale U., 1950; Dr. Engring., Lehigh U., 1970. Registered profl. engr., Pa., Conn. Indsl. engr. E. I. duPont de Nemours & Co., Wilmington, Del. and Fairfield, Conn., 1935-37; asst. prof. mech. engring. Lehigh U., Bethlehem, Pa., 1937-41; assoc. prof. indsl. engring. Lehigh U., 1946-49, prof. indsl. engring., head dept. and dir. curriculum, 1949-50; prof. of indsl. engring., dept. adminstrv. sci. Yale U., 1950-73, emeritus prof., 1973-93, chmn. dept., dir. grad. studies, 1954-63; fellow Trumbull Coll.; cons. U.S. Army Ordnance Corps, 1952-53, 56-57, Hughes Aircraft, 1959, 61-62, Hamilton Standard div. United Aircraft, 1963; nat. exec. sec. Sigma Xi, 1953-69, nat. exec. dir., 1969-81, exec. dir. emeritus, 1981-93 . Mem. Pub. Svc. Commn., Dist. of Fripp Island, S.C., 1983-90, chmn., 1987-88; bd. dirs. Yale Coop., New Haven, exec. com., 1951-72; mem. Yale-Industry Com. of New Haven. Lt. col. U.S. Army, 1941-46, ETO; lt. col. USAR, 1946-53. Recipient U.S. Army Citation medal, Ordnance Certificate of Commendation, Legion of Merit. Mem. Am. Inst. Indsl. Engrs., Am. Soc. Engring. Edn., Newcomen Soc., Sigma Xi, Tau Beta Pi, Pi Tau Sigma, Pi Gamma Mu. Club: Fripp Island (S.C.) Beach and Golf. Home: Fripp Island S.C. Died Dec. 20, 1993.

HOLMEN, (GEORGE) ROBERT, advertising agency executive; b. N.Y.C., May 3, 1933; s. George E. and Katherine J. (Smith) H.; m. Barbara Ann Jordan, Aug. 22, 1959; children: Britt Ann, Robert C., Mark E., Brigitte Ann. BS, Holy Cross Coll., 1955; MBA, Dartmouth Coll., 1960. Account exec. Benton & Bowles, Inc., N.Y.C., 1960-64; with William Esty Co., Inc., N.Y.C., 1964-75, sr. v.p., mgmt. supr., 1970-75; exec. v.p., gen. mgr. McCann Erickson, Inc., N.Y.C., 1975-79; exec. v.p., chief oper. officer Backer & Spielvogel, Inc., N.Y.C., 1979-86; chief exec. officer Backer, Spielvogel and Bates, N.Y.C., 1987-89, also chmn. bd. Trustee Canterbury Sch., New Milford, Conn. Served with USAF, 1955-58. Republican. Roman Catholic. Clubs: Whipporwill (Armonk, N.Y.); Milw. Athletic, Stratton Mountain Country. Home: Armonk N.Y. Died Jan. 23, 1995.

HOLMES, JACK DAVID LAZARUS, historian; b. Long Branch, N.J., July 4, 1930; s. John Daniel Lazarus and Waltrude Helen (Hendrickson) H.; m. Anne Elizabeth Anthony, Sept. 6, 1952 (div. 1965); children: David H., Jack Forrest, Ann M.; m. Martha Rachel Austin, Feb. 11, 1966 (div. 1967); m. Gayle Jeanette Pannell, July 1967 (div. 1970); 1 child, Daniel; m. Stephanie Pasneker, Apr. 10, 1971; 1 child, Sean Burkett. BA cum laude, Fla. State U., 1952; MA, U. Fla., 1953; postgrad., Universidad Nacional Autonoma de Mexico, 1954; Ph.D., U. Tex.-Austin, 1959. Instr. history Memphis State U., 1956-58; asst. prof. McNeese State U., Lake Charles, La., 1959-61; lectr. U. Md., Constantina, Spain, 1962; assoc. prof. U. Ala., Birmingham, 1963-68, prof., 1968-79; hist. cons. 1962—; cons. U.S. Parks Service, 1962, Pensacola Hist. Commn., Fla., 1969-70, New Orleans Cabildo Mus., 1968-73, NEH, 1972-83, Miss. Dept. Archives-History, 1978—, scholar-in-residence, 1986-87, State of Ala., 1980-85, Granadero de Galvez Hidalgo of San Antonio, 1981, State of La., 1983—, Mowa Indians, 1983—, P.K. Yonge Library, U. Fla., 1985-86; substitute tchr. Jefferson County schs., Ala., 1985—. Author: Documentos ineditos para la historia de la Luisiana, 1963; Gayoso, 1965; Honor and Fidelity, 1965; Jose de Evia, 1968; Francis Baily's Journal, 1969; New Orleans: Facts and Legends, 1970; Luis de Onis Memoria, 1969; Guide to Spanish Louisiana, 1970; New Orleans Drinks and How to Mix Them, 1973; History of the University of Alabama Hospitals and Clinics, 1974; The 1779 Marcha de Galvez: Louisiana's Giant Step Forward in the American Revolution, 1974; Galvez, 1981; Stephen Minor, 1983; contbg. author World Book Ency., Acad. Am. Ency., others; editor, dir. La. Collection Series, 1965—; contbr. to numerous hist. books, also articles to U.S. and fgn. hist. jours. Served with inf. AUS, 1951. Created knight cruz de caballero Royal Order Isabel La Catolica, Spain, 1979; Charles W. Hackett fellow, 1959; Am. Philos. Soc. fellow, 1961, 66; Fulbright fellow, 1961-62; Assn. State and Local History grantee, 1966, Nat. Endowment Humanities grantee, 1986-87, numerous others; recipient award of merit, 1978. Mem. Tenn. Squires, So. Hist. Assn. (life), La. Hist. Assn. (dir. 1977-78), Laffite Study Group (pres. 1980-88), Soc. History of Discoveries, Phi Beta Kappa, Phi Kappa Phi, Sigma Delta Pi, Phi Alpha Theta, Pi Kappa Phi. Home: Birmingham Ala.

HOLST, JOHAN JORGEN, Norwegian official, minister of defense of Norway; b. Oslo, Nov. 29, 1937; s. Nils Oluf and Ester (Salvesen) H. Grad. in polit. sci., Columbia U. and U. Oslo, 1965; postgrad., Harvard U. Rsch. assoc. Norwegian Def. Rsch. Establishment, 1963-67; head of rsch. Norwegian Inst. of Internat. Affairs, Oslo, 1960-76, dir., 1981-86, 89-90; state sec. Ministry of Def., Oslo, 1976-79, Ministry of Fgn. Affairs, Oslo, 1979-81; min. of def. Govt. of Norway, Oslo, 1986-89, 90-94. Mem. Norwegian Labor Party. Home: Oslo Norway Died Jan. 13, 1994.

HOLT, VICTORIA, author. Author: (books) Mistress of Mellyn, 1960, Kirkland Revels, 1962, Bride of Pendorric, 1963, Legend of the Seventh Virgin, 1965, Menfreya In the Morning, 1966, The King of the Castle, 1967, The Queen's Confession, 1968, Shivering Sands, 1969, The Secret Woman, 1970, Shadow of the Lynx, 1971, On the Night of the Seventh Moon, 1972, The Curse of the Kings, 1973, The House of a Thousand Lanterns, 1974, Lord of the Far Island, 1975, Pride of the Peacock, 1976, The Devil on Horseback, 1977, My Enemy the Queen, 1978, The Spring of the Tiger, 1979, The Mask of the Enchantress, 1980, The Judas Kiss, 1981, The Demon Lover, 1982, The Time of the Hunters Moon, 1983, The Landower Legacy, 1984, The Road to the Paradise Island, 1985, Secret For a Nightingale, 1986, The Silk Vendetta, 1987, The India Fan, 1988, The Captive, 1989, Snare of Serpents, 1990, Daughter of Deceit, 1991, Seven for a Secret, 1992, The Black Opal, 1993. Home: New York N.Y. Died Jan. 18, 1993.

HOLTER, MARVIN ROSENKRANTZ, physicist, research and development executive; b. Fairport, N.Y., July 4, 1922; s. Frank Marcus and Florence (Zonnevylle) H.; m. Frances Elizabeth Jenkins, July 15, 1955; children: Christine E., Ann F. BS in Physics, U. Mich., 1949, MS in Math., 1951, MS in Physics, 1958. Prof. remote sensing U. Mich., Ann Arbor, 1968-70, head infrared lab., 1964-70; dep. dir. Willow Run lab. U. Mich., Ann Arbor, 1972-73; div. chief earth obs. div. NASA Johnson Space Ctr., Houston, 1970-72; exec. v.p. Environ. Research Inst. Mich., Ann Arbor, 1973-86, sr. v.p., 1986-89; cons. physicist, 1989-93; invited lectr. univs. Stockholm, Upsala, Lund, Sweden, 1969; mem. USAF Sci. Adv. Bd., 1963-79; mem. com. on remote sensing programs for earth resources surveys Nat. Acad. Sci.-NRC, 1973-77; mem. U.S.A.-USSR Working Group on Remote Sensing, 1971-77; advisor Def. Intelligence Agy., 1978-81; mem. U.S. Army Sci. Bd., 1986-92. Coauthor: Fundamentals of Infrared Technology, 1962, Remote Sensing, 1970; editorial bd.: Remote Sensing of Environ., 1968-75. Recipient Exceptional Civilian Service award USAF, 1979; recipient Sci. Achievement award NASA, 1973; co-recipient William T. Pecore award Dept. Interior, 1976, Interpretation award Am. Soc. Photogrammetry, 1969. Mem. Explorers Club, Sigma Xi. Club: Cosmos (Washington). Lodge: Masons. Home: Ann Arbor Mich. Died Oct. 11, 1993.

HOLTZMAN, ERIC, biology educator; b. N.Y.C., May 25, 1939; s. Myron and Jeanne (Robinson) H.; m. Sally Guttmacher, July 14, 1970; 1 son, Benjamin. B.A., Columbia U., N.Y.C., 1959, M.A., 1961, Ph.D., 1964. Prof. biol. scis. Columbia U., N.Y.C., 1967-94, chmn. dept. biol. scis. Author: Cells and Organelles, 3d edit. 1983, Lysosomes: A Survey, 1976. Mem. Am. Soc. Cell Biology (council 1983-94), N.Y. Soc. Electron Microscopists (pres. 1982-83), Histochem. Soc. (pres. 1974-75). Home: New York N.Y. Died Apr. 6, 1994.

HOMSEY, VICTORINE DUPONT (MRS. SAMUEL E. HOMSEY), architect; b. Grosse Pointe Farms, Mich., Nov. 27, 1900; d. Antoin Bidermann and Ethel (Clark) duPont; m. Samuel E. Homsey, Apr. 27, 1929; children—Coleman duPont, Eldon duPont. A.B., Wellesley Coll., 1923; M.Arch., Cambridge (Mass.) Sch. Architecture, 1925. Practice as architect, from 1926; mem. archtl. firm Victorine and Samuel Homsey. Contbr.: Guide to Modern Architecture; major works include Am. Embassy, Tehran, Iran. Mem. exec. com. Greater Wilmington Devel. Council; mem. adv. bd. Historic Am. Bldgs. Survey; mem. Commn. Fine Arts, Washington, from 1976. Recipient 1st prize instl. architecture for Children's Beach House (Lewes, Del.) Pitts. Glass Inst.; regional, state awards for Cambridge Yacht Club Md. Soc. Architects; hon. mention award for design Stubbs Elementary Sch., Wilmington, Del.; hon. mention award for design Sch. Exec. mag. Fellow AIA; mem. NAD (asso.), Colonial Dames. Episcopalian. Club: Wilmington Garden. (Del.). Home: Hockessin Del. Deceased.

HONECKER, ERICH, government official; b. Neunkirchen, Saarland, Aug. 25, 1912; s. Wilhelm H.; m. Edith Baumann, 1947 (div.); 1 dau.; m. Margot Feist, 1953; 1 dau. Mem. Communist Party of Germany, 1929-46, youth sec. central com., 1945, mem. central com., 1946; imprisoned for anti-fascist activity, 1935-45; mem. mng. com. Socialist Unity Party, 1946—; mem. Volkskammer, 1949—; kandidat politburo, central com. Socialist Unity Party, 1950-58, Mitglied, 1958—, 1st sec. central com., 1971-76, gen. sec., 1976-89; mem. State Council, 1971—, chmn., 1976-89; sec. Nat. Def. Council, 1960-71, chmn., 1971-89. Author: From My Life, 1981. Decorated Karl Marx Order, German Democratic Republic, Order of Merit Fatherland in Gold, medal Antifascist Resistance, Held der Sowjet-Union Order of Lenin (USSR).

HONIGBERG, BRONISLAW MARK, zoology educator; b. Warsaw, Poland, May 14, 1920; came to U.S., 1941, naturalized, 1948; s. Zachary Z. and Mary (Laks) H.; m. Rhoda Springer, Feb. 7, 1948; children: Paul Mark, Martin Philip. A.B., U. Calif., Berkeley, 1943, M.A., 1946, Ph.D. (A. Rosenberg research fellow 1949-50), 1950. Instr. to prof. zoology U. Mass., Amherst, 1950-92; chancellor's medalist, lectr. U. Mass., 1975, faculty fellow, 1981-82; asst. prof. Columbia U., summer 1954; rsch. assoc. in pathobiology Sch. Hygiene, Johns Hopkins U., 1958-59; asst. prof. Harvard U., summer 1959; guest investigator lab. parasitic diseases Nat. Inst. Allergy and Infectious Diseases, NIH, 1965-66; guest investigator hon. fellow Ctr. for Tropical Vet. Medicine, U. Edinburgh, 1973-74; vis. scientist Abteilung für Protozoologie, Zoologisches Institut, Universität Bonn, Fed. Republic of Germany, 1982; guest scientist Internat. Ctr. of Insect Physiology and Ecology, Nairobi, Kenya, 1985; vis. scientist Internat. Lab. for Rsch. on Animal Diseases, Nairobi, 1985-86; dir. tng. grants NIH, 1973-87; mem. Internat. Commn. Protozoology, 1965-85, hon. life mem., 1985-92; tropical medicine parasitology study sect. NIH, 1973-77; v.p., chmn. sci. program V, Internat. Congress Protozoology, 1977; v.p. Internat. Symposium on Trichomoniasis, Bialystok, Poland, 1981; hon. pres. Internat. Symposium on Trichomonads and Trichomoniasis, Prague, 1985. Editor Jour. Protozoology, 1971-80, mem. bd. reviewers, 1959-71, 81—; assoc. editor Trans. Am. Micros. Soc., 1966-71; editor N.Am., Parasitology Research (formerly Zeitschrift für Parasitenkunde), 1974-90, mem. editorial bd. 1990—; bd. reviewers Internat. Jour. Parasitology, 1971-74, Acta Tropica, 1977-82; mem. editorial bd. Acta Protozoologica, 1990—; editor (with others) Trichomonads Parasitic in Humans, Springer-Verlag, N.Y., 1989; contbr. articles to profl. jours. Trustee Am. Type Culture Collection, 1966-72, mem. exec. com., 1971-72; mem. U.S. nat. com. Internat. Union Biol. Scis., 1982-88. Recipient Gold medal for human trichomoniasis studies Med. Faculty Comenius U., Bratislava, Czechoslovakia, 1977; Alexander von Humboldt Found. sr. scientist award, 1982; Constantin Janicki medal Polish Parasitol. Soc., 1984; NIH research grantee, 1955—; USPHS spl. research fellow, 1965-66, 73-74. Fellow AAAS, N.Y. Acad. Sci., Royal Soc. Tropical Medicine and Hygiene; mem. Soc. Belge de Médicine Tropicale (corr.), Deutsche Gesellschaft für Parasitologie (corr.), Groupement des Protistologues de Langue Française (hon.), Am. Soc. Zoologists, Am. Soc. Parasitologists, Soc. Protozoologists (pres. 1965-66, hon. mem. 1979), Am. Micros. Soc. (pres. 1964-65), Am. Soc. Tropical Medicine and Hygiene, Biol. Stain Commn., Phi Beta Kappa, Sigma Xi, Phi Kappa Phi. Home: Amherst Mass. Died May 1, 1992; interred Amherst, M.A.

HOOD, DOUGLAS CRARY, retired electronics educator, consultant; b. Toledo, Nov. 26, 1932; s. Douglas Crary and Pauline Edna (Thurston) H.; m. Marlene Carole Ashenfelter, Sept. 14, 1984. BSE, Electronics Inst. Technology, Detroit, 1962; MSD, Brotherhood of White Temple, Sedalia, Colo., 1975. Avionics technician USAF, 1952-56; systems design engr. AT&T, Toledo, 1956-59; customer engr. IBM, Detroit, 1962-66; territory mgr. Mgmt. Assistance Inc., Detroit, 1966-71; owner, mgr. Sonny's Rainbow, Toledo, 1969-84; owner, operator Rainbow Lapidary Art Sch., Toledo, 1971-74; maintenance mechanic Lucas Met. Housing Authority, Toledo, 1984-86; electronics educator, dean dept. engring. Stautzenberger Coll., Toledo, 1987-92; dir. RETS Inst. Tech., Toledo, 1992-94; dept. chair engring. Davis Coll., Toledo, 1994; cons. Midwest Mgmt. Syss., Tecumseh, Miss., 1995-96; master gem cutter and carver, originator of the rainbow cut; cons. Midwest Mgmt. Systems, Tecumseh, 1995-96. Author: various elec. lab. manuals. Mem. IEEE, BOAZ, Am. Soc. for Engring. Educators, Toledo Gem Club (pres. 1970-74), Masons, Shriners. Democrat. Home: Tecumseh Mich. Died Feb. 21, 1996.

HOOD, THOMAS RICHARD, artist, graphic designer, educator; b. Phila., July 13, 1910; s. Thomas Richard and Anne Lovering (Grubb) H. Student, U. Pa., 1929-30; B.F.A. in Advt. Design, Phila. Mus. Coll. Art, 1953. Prof., design coordinator, exhbn. dir. Phila. Coll. Art; dir. Pa. Art Program, 1940-42, Pa. War Services Program, 1943. Exhibited nationally, 1936-95; represented in permanent collections, Phila. Mus., Carnegie Library, Phila. Public Library, N.Y. Public Library, Library of Congress, Phila. Mus. Natural History, Mus. Modern Art, N.Y.C., Bryn Mawr Coll., Yale U., Nat. Portrait Gallery, Smithsonian Instn., also pvt. collections. Served with AUS, 1943-45. Recipient over 60 awards, including Phila. Print Club, 1937, 48, over 60 awards, including Western Pa. Prints, 1940, Soldier Art, 1945, 1st prize Times Herald Exhbn., Washington, 1945, Franklin medal, 1959 (2), 69, 70, award Del. Valley Graphic Arts, 1971, Silver and Bronze medals Art Dirs. Gold medal, 1966, 69, 73, Silver medal, 1971, 73, Neographics Gold, Silver and Bronze medals, 1973, Nat. Graphic Arts Design award U.S. and Can., 1968, (2) 70, Disting. Design award Phila. Coll. Art, 1971, Andy award of Merit, 1973, Neographics Gold Medal, 1976; named to Wisdom Hall of Fame in Edn., 1975. Fellow Internat. Inst. Arts and Letters (life); mem. Am. Color Print Soc. (pres. 1956), Artist Decoys, The Authors, Phila. Art Alliance (chmn. print com. 1977-81), Mus. Modern Art, Phila. Print Club. Club: Peale. Home: Philadelphia Pa. Died July 22, 1995.

HOOVER, EARL REESE, savings association executive, lawyer; b. Dayton, Ohio, Nov. 19, 1904; s. John Jacob and Flora Maude (Brosier) H.; m. Alice Lorene Propst, Dec. 18, 1931; 1 child, Richard Wilson. A.B., Otterbein Coll., 1926, LL.D., 1955; J.D., Harvard U., 1929; LL.D., Salem Coll., 1961. Asst. atty. gen. State of Ohio, Columbus, 1930-31, 32; assoc. Mooney, Hahn, Loeser, Keough & Beam, Cleve., 1933-46; sole practice, Cleve., 1946-50; instr. bus. Fenn Coll. (now Cleve. State U.), 1950-51; law dir. Town of Aurora, Ohio, 1949-50; judge Common Pleas Ct. of Cuyahoga County, Cleve., 1951-69; sr. v.p. Shaker Savs. Assn., Shaker Heights, Ohio, 1969-80, mem. adv. bd. dirs., 1977-80; sr. v.p. Ohio Savs. Assn., 1980—; guest speaker numerous clubs, assns. Author: Cradle of Greatness: National and World Achievements of Ohio's Western Reserve, 1977. Bd. dirs. Cleve. Law Library, 1942-54, Citizens Bur., 1945-53; bd. dirs. Cleve. Roundtable of NCCJ, 1946-52, mem. exec. com., 1950-52, treas., 1950-52, chmn. food industry com Cleve. Health Council, 1942-46; trustee, mem. exec. com. Nationalities Services Ctr., 1953-56; mem. Cleve. Landmarks Commn., 1974- 82; exec. bd. dirs. Greater Cleve. Bicentennial Commn., 1975-76; trustee Cleve. Masonic Library Assn., 1973-83; chmn. pub. relations com. Anti-Tv League of Cleve. and Cuyahoga County, Cleve., 1963-65; trustee Otterbein Coll., 1935-60, chmn. alumni relations and publicity com. of bd. trustees, 1945-60; mem. men's com. Cleve. Playhouse, 1950-57; bd. dirs. Neighborhood Settlement Assn., 1951-58; exec. bd. dirs. Greater Cleve. council Boy Scouts Am., 1956-59, chmn. council's Ct. of Honor, 1949-55, chmn. Newton D. Baker Dist., 1956-59, rep. to Nat. Council, 1957; bd. dir. Cleve. Ch. Fedn., 1955-58, Western Res. Hist. Soc., 1968—, Shaker Hist. Soc., 1969-81, v.p., 1970-71; bd. dirs. Religious Heritage of Am., 1958-59; v.p. Ripon Club (Rep. Club), 1949; mem. exec. Cleve. Civil War Round Table, 1969-70. Named Father of Hall of Fame Otterbein Coll., 1968; recipient Disting. Alumnus award Alumni Assn. of Otterbein Coll., 1970, award for Outstanding Service to Scouting Boy Scouts Am., Southwest Dist., 1972. Mem. Bar Assn. Greater Cleve., Cleve. Bar Assn. (rep. to Council of Dels. of Ohio State Bar Assn. 1937-38, chmn. coms.), Ohio State Bar Assn. (chmn. coms.), Cuyahoga County Bar Assn., Early Settlers Assn. of Western Res. (pres. 1971-72, bd. dirs. 1967—, mem. com. establishing Hall of Fame 1971), Harvard Alumni Assn. of Cleve., Harvard Law Sch. Alumni Assn., Otterbein Coll. Alumni Assn. (nat. pres.). Mem. United Ch. of Christ. Clubs: City (v.p. 1948, bd. dirs. 1946-48), Cleve. Shrine Luncheon (pres. 1959, bd. dirs. 1957-59), Cleve. Advt., Hundred Club (pres. 1938), Republic (bd. dirs. 1940-41, 44-48, pres. 1947). Lodges: Rotary (chmn. projects, emcee civic luncheons), Kiwanis of Cleve. (bd. dirs. Found. 1963-66, v.p. 1965-66), Masons, Shriners, Jesters.

HOPE, CLARENCE CALDWELL, JR., banker, government official; b. Charlotte, N.C., Feb. 5, 1920; s. Clarence Caldwell and Margaret Boyd (Kidd) H.; m. Mae D. Duckworth, Feb. 5, 1944; children: Stephen Douglas, Clarence Caldwell III, Joan Jennings. Diploma, Mars Hill Coll., 1941; B.S., Wake Forest Coll., 1943; diploma, Harvard U. Grad. Sch. Bus. Adminstrn., 1944, Rutgers U. Grad. Sch. Banking, 1953, 56; LLD, Campbell U. With Esso Standard Oil Co., 1946-47; with First Union Nat. Bank N.C., Charlotte, 1947-85; successively br. mgr., mgr. credit dept., asst. cashier, asst. v.p., v.p. First Union Nat. Bank N.C., Dilworth, sr. v.p., 1956-60, exec. v.p., 1960-77, vice chmn. bd., 1977-85, also dir., sec. bd.; sec. commerce State of N.C., 1983-85; dir. FDIC, 1986—; chmn. Neighborhood Reinvestment Corp., 1991—; exec. v.p., dir. 1st Union Corp. Bd. dirs., past pres. Mecklenburg County chpt. ARC, also mem. Southeastern area adv. council, fund vice chmn. for N.C.; mem. social planning council United Appeal; pres. Central Charlotte Assn.; chmn. N.C. Symphony Soc., Inc.; chmn. bd. trustees Wake Forest U.; trustee Pub. Library Charlotte and Mecklenburg Counties; vice-chmn. N.C. Bapt. Hosp.; trustee Annuity Bd. So. Bapt. Conv.; dean for bankers Southwestern Grad. Sch. Banking, So. Meth. U., chmn. bd. found. Lt. USNR, World War II. Mem. Am. Bankers Assn. (mem. governing coun., govt. rels. coun., adminstrv. com.; chmn. com. cooperation with bank regulatory agys., pres. 1979-80), N.C. Bankers Assn. (chmn. legis. com.), Assn. Registere Bank Holding Cos. (chmn. govt. rels. com.), U.S. C. c C. (pub. affairs com.), Charlotte Mchts. Assn. (treas dir., pres., chmn. finance com.), Bankpac (nat. chmn.) Charlotte C. of C., Robert Morris Assocs. (past pres Carolina-Virginias chpt.), Newcomen Soc., Wake Fores U., Central Charlotte Assn. (past pres.), Omicron Delt Kappa, Sigma Phi Epsilon, Beta Gamma Sigma. Bap tist. Clubs: Charlotte Execs., Harvard, Myers Parl Country, City (Charlotte). Home: Charlotte N.C.

HOPPS, SIDNEY BRYCE, lawyer; b. Yale, Mich. May 10, 1934; s. Sidney J. and Betty E. (Bryce) H.; m Ilene P. Morgan, June 20, 1953; children: Paulette Tracy, Erin. B.A., U. Mich., 1957, J.D., 1960. Bar Ohio 1960. Ptnr. Squire, Sanders & Dempsey, Cleve 1960-85, from 87, Cavitch, Familo, Durkin Co. LPA Cleve., 1985-87; mem. Ohio Adv. Bd., Chgo. Title Ins Co. Mem. Greater Cleve. Growth Assn. Mem. Ohi State Bar Assn., Greater Cleve. Bar Assn., Nat. Assn Realtors, Ohio Assn. Realtors, Medina County Bd Realtors, Ohio Roundtable of Real Estate Brokerag Attys., The Club at Soc. Ctr., Phi Beta Kappa, Pl Kappa Phi. Home: Valley City Ohio Deceased.

HORN, THOMAS DARROUGH, education educator b. Iowa City, Iowa, June 26, 1918; s. Ernest and Made line (Darrough) H.; m. Grace Ellen Adams, Aug. 2 1941; 1 child, Diane. B.A., State U. Iowa, 1940, M.A 1946, Ph.D., 1947; student, Cambridge U., Eng., 1945. Tchr. pub. schs. Denver, 1940-42, River Forest, Ill 1942-43; asst. prof. U. No. Iowa, 1947-51; assoc. pro curriculum and instrn. Coll. Edn. U. Tex., Austin, 1951 59, prof., 1959-88; prof. emeritus U. Tex., from 1988 chmn. dept. U. Tex., Austin, 1962-73; vis. lectr. U Pitts., summer 1949, Harvard U., summer 1959, U Mich., 1963; dir. USOE Project, 1964-65, Bi-Cultura Sect., Coll. Edn. Rsch. and Devel. Ctr., 1965-67, Sa Antonio Lang. Rsch. Project, 1967-68, Lang. Rsch Project, 1968-88. Contbr. articles to profl. jours; co author, cons. spelling and reading textbooks, instrn films; editor research monographs, book. Mem. Tex commn. Services to Children and Youth, 1972-82 chmn., 1973-75, vice chmn., 1978-79. Served with U.S Army, 1943-46; to capt. USAFR, 1950-55. Named t Reading Hall of Fame, 1984. Mem. Am. Edn Research Assn. Tchr. Edn. (exec. bd. 1953-59, pre 1957-58), Tex. Assn. for Student Teaching (pres. 1952 53), Tex. Assn. Teacher Educators (Ben Cody Disting Service award, 1986), Internat. Reading Assn. (Sp Service award 1979), Nat. Conf. on Research in Englis (exec. bd. 1957-60, nat. pres. 1958-59), Nat. Counc Tchrs. English (dir. elem. sect. 1965-68), NEA, Na Soc. Study Edn., Phi Delta Kappa, Phi Kappa Phi, Pl Gamma Delta. Home: Austin Tex. Deceased.

HORNUNG, RICHARD, costume designer. Costum designer: (films) Raising Arizona, 1987, China Gir 1987, Less than Zero, 1987, Young Guns, 1988, Patt Hearst, 1988, Miller's Crossing, 1990, Barton Fink 1991, Sleeping with the Enemy, 1991, Doc Hollywood 1991, This Boy's Life, 1992, (with Ann Roth) Dav 1992, Hero, 1993, Natural Born Killers, 1993. Hom Beverly Hills Calif. Died Dec. 30, 1995.

HOROWITZ, VLADIMIR, pianist; b. Kiev, Russi Oct. 1, 1904; s. Samuel and Sophia (Bodik) H.; n Wanda Toscanini, Dec. 21, 1933; 1 dau., Soni (dec.). Ed., Kiev Conservatory; study under, Feli Blumenfeld, Sergei Tarnowsky. Made first appearanc at age 17, Kiev, Russia; made debut Europe, 1925, mad debut in U.S. with N.Y. Philharm., Jan. 1928; conce tours of U.S., 1928—; most recent performances Whi House, 1978, 1986, Royal Festival Hall, London, 198 Japan tour, 1983, USSR tour, 1986. Recipient 2 Grammy awards for best classical performance, instru mental soloist or soloists, 1966-81, 87, for best classica recording, 1987; recipient Best Classical Performance Instrumental Soloist for Kreisleriana Ministry Edn Japanese Govt., 1971, Acad. Award/Classic Best In strumental Soloist, Rec. Geijutsu, 1971, Be Performance Award-Classic Instrumental Soloist CBS SONY, 1970, Prix Mondial du Disque for Kreisleriana 1971, Gold Medal Royal Philharm. Soc., 1972, Gran Prix des Discophiles, 1966; decorated Medal o Freedom; Comdr. Legion of Honor (France); Knigh grand cross Order of Merit (Italy); recipient President Merit award, Nat. Acad. of Recording Artists & Scis 1987, Nat. Medal of Arts, 1990 (awarded posthumou ly). Home: New York N.Y.

HORTON, BERNARD FRANCIS, newspaper edito b. Peabody, Kans., May 26, 1916; s. Frank H. and Lul Elizabeth (Stovall) H.; m. Betty Mildred Wessels, De 20, 1938; 1 son, Gary Francis. BA, U. Wyo., 1938. Owner, editor, pub. Chugwater News (handset weekly Wyo., 1938-42; editor No. Wyo. Daily News, Worlan 1942-43, Rawlins (Wyo.) Daily Times, 1946-49; ass news editor Wyo. Eagle, Cheyenne, 1949-52; news edit Wyo. Eagle, 1952-54, mng. editor, 1955-62, editor, 196 82, columnist, cons., 1982-94; mng. editor Pacific Sta and Stripes, 1946. With AUS, 1943-46; chief pub. re sect. 97th Inf. Divsn. ETO. Mem. Wyo. Press Ass (pres. 1971-72, hon. life mem.). Home: Cheyenne Wy Died Sept. 4, 1994; interred Cheyenne, Wyo.

HOSKINS, ROBERT NATHAN, agribusiness co sultant; b. Keota, Iowa, Feb. 23, 1917; s. Frank A. ar ra E. (Wayman) H.; student U. Mo., 1934-37; B.S., wa State U., 1939; m. Julia L. Jones, July 19, 1946; ildren: Nancy Carol, Mary Susan, Julia Ann, Robert athan. Towerman, Sam A. Baker State Forest, Mo. onservation Commn., 1939, sr. forester, 1940-41; extension forester Fla. Forest Service, 1941-45; indsl. rester Seaboard Air Line R.R. Co. (name changed to eaboard Coast Line R.R. Co. 1967), Richmond, Va., 945-46, gen. forestry agt., 1956-64, gen. indsl. and restry agt., 1964-65, gen. mgr. indsl. devel., 1965-68, st. v.p. containerization and spl. projects, 1968-69, st. v.p. forestry and spl. projects, 1969-79; cons. gribus., 1979—; dir. F.A. Bartlett Tree Expert Co. Iem. core com. Keep Fla. Green, 1946-50, Keep N.C. reen, 1947-49; mem. Gov.'s Adv. Com. on Forestry, a. Economy, 1950-53; mem. adv. com. on forestry rogram in agrl. edn. Va., N.C., S.C., Ga., Fla., Ala., 950-65; mem. adv. com. vocational edn. Va. State Bd. dn., 1950-60; mem. profl. adv. group indsl. devel. ommonwealth Va., 1967-68; mem. staff of resources uture, 1949-50; adviser on forestry edn. So. Regional dn. Bd., 1957-58; southeastern regional chmn. sponsoring com. Nat. Future Farmers Am. Found., 1969-74, ate chmn., Va., 1975-76; mem. nat. adv. com. to sec. gr. on state and pvt. forestry, 1970-73; mem. Va. Agrius. Council; vice chmn. publicity centennial com. Va. ept. Agr. and Commerce, 1977. Pres. Parents' Assn. . Richmond, 1975-76; bd. dirs. Henrico County chpt. RC, 1981-83; mem. Henrico County Republican Com. amed Norfolk's Outstanding Young Man, Norfolk Jr. . of C., 1951, recipient certificate of merit, 1952; cipient Distinguished Service award S.C. Agrl. Tchrs., 953, Alumni Merit award Chgo. Alumni Assn., Iowa ate U., 1954, Key to City, Mayor of Cin., 1960, layor of Phila., 1961, Merit award Fla. Vocational grl. Assn., 1965, Appreciation award Va. Agrl. Tchrs. ssn., 1967, Disting. Service award S.C. Future Farmers m. Assn., 1968, Spl. award for disting. service to onsoring com. Nat. Future Farmers Am., 1971, Hon. ate Farmer degree Tenn. Assn., 1977; Order Palmetto, 973. Mem. Am. (Merit award 1954, awards chmn. 949-54, Disting. Ser. award 1978, Soil Conservation ward Va. chpt. 1978), Ga. (liaison and coordinating m. 1955-56), N.C. (reforestation com. 1951-52), Ala., a. forestry assns., Va. Forests, Fla. Forest and Park ssn., Soc. Am. Foresters, Ry. Tie Assn. (chmn. conrvation com. 1956-58, mem. pub. affairs com. 1977-8), Forest Farmers Assn. (ednl. com. 1957-58), Am. ocat. Assn. (award merit 1958), U.S. (mem. agribus. nd rural affairs com. 1972-75), Soc. of Va. (exec. uncil 1975-93), Fla. State (forestry com. 1952-53), Va. ate (indsl. devel. com. 1965-68), Richmond chambers mmerce. Methodist (finance com. 1962-63). Clubs: Va. ress (Richmond), Soc. of Va. (dir. 1973-75), Hermitage ountry. Author: (with M.D. Mobley) Forestry in the outh, 1956. Editor SCL Forestry Bull., 1945-65. ontbr. articles to profl. jours. Died Oct. 18, 1992; uried Westhampton Meml. Gardens, Richmond. ome: Richmond Va.

IOSMER, CHARLES BRIDGHAM, JR., historian, ducator; b. Naples, Italy, Feb. 23, 1932; s. Charles ridgham and Faye (Durham) H.; m. Jeralyn Prugh, ec. 27, 1955; children: Kathryn, Jonathan rescott. BA, Principia Coll., 1953; MA, Columbia U., 956, PhD, 1961. Tchr. pub. schs., South Huntington, .Y., 1956-59; from instr. to full prof. Principia Coll., lsah, Ill., 1960-93, Jay P. Walker prof. history, 1972-3. Author: Presence of the Past, History of Preservaon, 1965, Preservation Comes of Age, 1981; (with thers) Elsah: A Historic Guidebook. Mem. Ill. Hist. tes Adv. Coun., Springfield, 1969-76; pres. Hist. Elsah ound., 1971-93; chmn. Elsah Zoning Bd., 1973-79. erved with U.S. Army, 1953-55. Named Disting. Asoc., Eastern Nat. Park and Monument Assn., Phila., 981. Mem. Am. Hist. Assn., Orgn. Am. Historians, m. Assn. State and Local History, Soc. Archtl. Historians, Nat. Trust Hist. Preservation. Democrat. hristian Scientist. Home: Elsah Ill. Deceased.

IOSPODOR, ANDREW THOMAS, electronics executive; b. Endicott, N.Y., Jan. 30, 1937; s. Andrew and erna (Yurick) H.; m. Rose Marie Pitarra, June 28, 958; children: Andrew D., Sarah E., Peter J. B.S.M.E., ornell U., 1960; M.S.M.E., Lehigh U., 1963, M.B.A., 967. Product specialist Air Products Inc., Emmaus, a., 1960-66; mgr. RCA, Camden, N.J., 1966-77; dir. ktg. RCA, Burlington, Mass., 1977-79, program mgr. ommand and control, 1979-81, div. v.p., gen. mgr., 981-85; pres., chief exec. officer RCA Am. Communiations, Inc., Princeton, N.J., 1985-87; chmn., chief exec. fficer ARINC, Annapolis, Md., from 1987. Home: iva Md. Deceased.

IOUGH, RICHARD RALSTON, retired communicaons company executive; b. Trenton, N.J., Dec. 13, 917; s. Douglas Ralston and Leola (Moore) H.; m. ane Jackson, Mar. 22, 1941; children: Suzanne, Richard alston, Edith, William, Jane, Robert. B.S. in Engrg., Princeton U., 1939, E.E., 1940; D.Sc. (hon.), Susuehanna U., 1977. Various positions to v.p. Bell elephone Labs., Whippany, N.J., 1940-57; v.p. ops. hio Bell, Cleve., 1959-61; v.p. engring. AT&T, N.Y.C., 961-66, exec. v.p., 1978-82; pres. AT&T Longlines, .Y.C., 1966-78; ret., 1982; dir. Am. Can Co. (now amed Primerica Corp.), Dravo Corp., Alleghany Corp., lidAtlantic Banks, MidAtlantic Nat. Bank, Cyclops ndustries Inc., Midlantic Corp.; chmn. tech. adv. bd. FAA, 1961-66; mem. Def. Sci. Bd., Dept. Def., 1971-74; mem. adv. bd. U.S. Naval Postgrad. Sch., 1967-76; mem. Lower Manhattan adv. bd. Chem. Bank, 1972-76. Trustee Morristown Presbyn. Ch., Morris Jr. Mus., Turrell Fund, Morristown Meml. Hosp., Wilson Coll.; past pres. Madison Bd. Edn., N.J., 1952-59; bd. dirs. United Way of Tri-State, 1978-82; charter trustee Princeton U., 1961-88. Named Outstanding Young Elec. Engr., Eta Kappa Nu, 1947. Fellow IEEE (Alexander Graham Bell medal 1980); mem. NAE, Telephone Pioneers Am. (pres. 1972-73), Princeton Engring. Assn., Phi Beta Kappa, Sigma Xi, Tau Beta Pi. Republican. Presbyterian. Home: Dunbarton N.H. Died July 9, 1992.

HOUGHTON, WILLIAM HENRY, publishing company executive; b. Hartford, Conn., Apr. 13, 1925; s. Henry Ernest and Frances Mary (Plaunt) H.; m. Marion Jensen, Jan. 28, 1959; children: Robert G., Bradley J. BS magna cum laude, Babson Coll., 1949. Comml. mgr. Associated Program Service, Inc., N.Y.C., 1949-52; v.p. mktg. Ency. Brit., Inc., Chgo., 1952-62; exec. v.p. Marketways, Inc., Chgo., 1962-63; pres. Collier Services, Inc., Riverside, N.J., 1963-67; pres., chief exec. officer Macmillan Book Clubs, Inc., N.Y.C., 1967-90; group v.p. Macmillan, Inc., N.Y.C., 1985-90; bd. dirs. Berlitz Pubs., Inc., Gryphon Edition, Inc. Mem. Assn. Am. Pubs., Direct Mktg. Assn., Pres. Assn. Club: Chappaqua (N.Y.) Country. Home: Berkeley Calif. Died 1990.

HOUK, VERNON NEAL, retired public health administrator; b. Dos Palos, Calif., Dec. 16, 1929; s. Guy and Alice Joyce (Woodiwiss) H. Student, San Jose State Coll., 1947-49, U. Calif.-Berkeley, 1949-50; M.D., George Washington U., 1954. Diplomate: Am. Bd. Internal Medicine, Am. Bd. Internal Medicine Pulmonary Disease, Nat. Bd. Med. Examiners. Intern Southern Pacific Gen. Hosp., San Francisco, 1954-55; commd. U.S. Navy, 1955, advanced through grades to comdr., regimental surgeon 4th Marine Fleet, 1955-57; officer in charge, med. officer Amundsen-Scott IGY U.S. Navy, Antarctica, 1957-59; resident, head chest and contagion br. dept. internal medicine U.S. Naval Hosp., Bethesda, Md., 1959-62; head pulmonary disease U.S. Naval Hosp., St. Albans, N.Y., 1962-65, asst. chief medicine, 1965-67; chief pulmonary disease sect. VA Hosp., Houston, Tex., 1967-68; dep. dir. TB div. USPHS Ctr. for Disease Control, Atlanta, Ga., 1968-74, dir. environ. health svcs. divsn., 1974-83, acting dir. ctr. environ. health, 1981-83, dir. Nat. Ctr. Environ. Health and Injury Control, 1983-93; asst. adminstr. USPHS Agy. for Toxic Substances and Disease Registry, Atlanta, 1983-89; asst. surgeon gen. USPHS ATSDR, Atlanta, 1985; sr. advisor for environ. health policy CDC, 1993-94, ret., 1994. Contbr. articles to profl. jours. Recipient sec.'s spl. citation HEW, 1970; commendation medal USPHS, 1980, Disting. Svc. medal, 1985, Outstsanding Svc. medal, 1988, Meritorious Svc. medal, 1992; Eagle award U.S. Dept. Army, 1988, Roger W. Jones award, 1988, William C. Watson Jr. medal of excellence Ctrs. for Disease Control, 1991. Fellow N.Y. Acad. Medicine, Am. Coll. Chest Physicians, A.C.P., N.Y. Acad. Scis.; mem. N.Y. Trudeau Soc., Alpha Omega Alpha. Home: Atlanta Ga. Died Sept. 11, 1994.

HOULTON, LOYCE J., artistic director, choreographer; b. Proctor, Minn., June 13, 1926; d. Andrew and Ragna M. Johnson; m. William H. Houlton, July 28, 1950; children: Laif, Joel, Lise, Andrew. B.A., Carleton Coll., 1946, Hum.D. (hon.), 1981; M.A., NYU, 1950. Mem. dance adv. panel Minn. State Arts Council, 1972-75. Artistic dir. Minn. Dance Theatre, Mpls., 1962-86; prin. choreographer Ballet Mich., 1988, Ballet Austin, Dance Theater of Harlem, A Dancer's Place, New Sch. of Dance; choreographer for Berlin Deutsche Oper Ballet, Washington Ballet, Dayton (Ohio) Ballet, Louisville Ballet, Pacific N.W. Ballet, Pa. Ballet, Pauline Koner Dance Concert, N.Y.C., Tulsa Ballet Co., Royal Winnipeg (Can.) Ballet, Omaha Ballet; video documentary Knoxville Sumemr of 1915; subject of film Loyce; hon. dir. Portraits, Sta. KTCA-TV, PBS; film Carmina Burana, 1991. Recipient Plaudit award Nat. Dance Assn., 1980, Time Life award for Swan Lake, Minn. (choreographer), Spl. Recognition award City Mpls., 1991; Minn. State Arts Bd. choreographic fellow, 1978-79; Nat. Endowment for Arts Class A choreographic fellow, 1988-89, also grantee. Mem. Nat. Assn. Regional Ballet (pres. Mid-States region 1972-73, dir. 1975-95). Home: Minneapolis Minn. Died Mar. 14, 1995.

HOUPHOUËT-BOIGNY, FELIX, president of Republic of Ivory Coast; b. Yamoussoukvo, Ivory Coast, Oct. 18, 1905; m. Marie-Therese Brou; 3 sons, 1 dau. Student, William Ponty Coll. of Gore, Senegal; grad., Fed. Med. Sch. Dakar, Senegal, 1925. Doctor Asst. Medicale, 1925-40; pres. Syndicat Agricole Africain, 1944; mem. French Constituent Assembly, 1945-46, mem. French Nat. Assembly, 1946, 51, 56; minister to French prime minister, 1956-57, minister state, 1957-59, minister pub. health and population, 1957-58, cabinet mem., 1958-59; pres. assembly Ivory Coast Republic, 1958-59, prime minister, councilor French Govt., 1959-60; pres. Council, 1959-60, pres. Republic of Ivory Coast, 1960-93, minister fgn. affairs, 1961, minister interior, edn. and agr., 1963, minister def., 1963-74; pres. Council of Ministers; pres. Reassemblement Democratique Africain, Parti Democratique de la Cote d'Ivoire. Decorated grand cross French Legion of Honor, grand master Nat. Order of Ivory Coast, also others. Home: Abidjan Ivory Coast Died Dec. 7, 1993.

HOUSTON, PEYTON HOGE, retired environmental systems company executive, poet; b. Cin., Dec. 20, 1910; s. George Harrison and Mary Stuart (Hoge) H.; m. Priscilla Moore, Nov. 26, 1942 (div. Jan. 1959); stepchildren: Robert, Russell Stewart; m. Parrish Beaumont Cummings, May 22, 1959; stepchildren: Joseph P. Dobson, Michael Dobson, Laura Parrish Dobson Pool. A.B., Princeton U., 1932. Free lance writer, 1934-41; with Houston & Jolles (mgmt. cons.), N.Y.C., 1941-49, exec. asst., 1941-43, v.p., 1946-49; with The Equity Corp. (and successors Wheelabrator-Frye, The Signal Cos., Allied Signal and the Henley Group), N.Y.C. and Hampton, N.H., 1950-86; asst. to pres. The Equity Corp., 1950-59, v.p., 1959-66; sr. v.p., dir. Gen. United Life Ins. Co. (subs. Equity Corp.), Des Moines, 1967-71; corp. sec. Wheelabrator-Frye, Inc., 1971-81; sec., dir. various subs., corp. sec. The Pullman Co., 1981-88, sec. various subsidiaries. Author: Sonnet Variations, 1962, Occasions in a World, 1969, For the Remarkable Animals, 1970, Arguments of Idea, 1980, The Changes/Orders/Becomings, 1990, Poems on the Shape of the Morning, 1991, Importance of the Unicorn, 1992, XVI Complex Songs at the Borders of Silence, 1993; editor The Garden Prospect, Selected Poems by Peter Yates, 1980. With U.S. Army, 1943-45. Mem. Princeton Club (N.Y.C.), Phi Beta Kappa. Home: Greenwich Conn. Died Mar. 8, 1994.

HOUTS, MARSHALL WILSON, lawyer, author, editor; b. Chattanooga, June 28, 1919; s. Thomas Jefferson and Mary (Alexander) H.; m. Mary O. Dealy, Apr. 27, 1946; children: Virginia, Kathy, Marsha, Patty, Tom, Cindy, Tim. AA, Brevard Jr. Coll., 1937; BS in Law, U. Minn., 1941, JD, 1941. Bar: Tenn. 1940, Minn. 1946, U.S. Supreme Ct. 1967. Spl. agt. FBI, Washington, Brazil, Havana, Boston, 1941-44; ptnr. Palmer & Houts, Pipestone, Minn., 1946-51; mcpl. judge Pipestone, 1947-51; gen. counsel Erle Stanley Gardner's Ct. of Last Resort, Los Angeles, 1951-60; prof. law UCLA, 1954, Mich. State U., East Lansing, 1955-57; adj. prof. Pepperdine U. Law Sch., 1972-80; clin. prof. forensic pathology Calif. Coll. Medicine, U. Calif., Irvine, 1972—; cons. police depts. Creator, editor: TRAUMA, 1959-88; author: Houts: Lawyer's Guide to Medical Proof, 5 vols., 1967, From Gun to Gavel, 1954, From Evidence to Proof, 1956, The Rules of Evidence, 1956, From Arrest to Release, 1958, Courtroom Medicine, 1958, Courtroom Medicine: Death, 3 vols., 1964, Photographic Misrepresentation, 1965, Where Death Delights, 1967, They Asked for Death, 1970, Proving Medical Diagnosis and Prognosis, 14 vols., 1970, Cyclopedia of Sudden, Violent and Unexplained Death, 1970, King's X: Common Law and the Death of Sir Harry Oakes, 1972, Art of Advocacy: Appeals; Art of Advocacy: Cross Examination of Medical Experts, 1980; Courtroom Toxicology, 8 vols., 1981, Who Killed Sir Harry Oakes?, 1988, Jesus' Two Sanhedrin Acquittals—Their Legacies of Due Process of Law, 1989; (with Harold Stassen): Eisenhower: Turning the World Toward Peace, 1990, Cousin Charlie the Crow, 1991. Served with OSS, 1944-46, CBI. Decorated Bronze Arrowhead. Home: Dana Point Calif. Died Nov. 24, 1993.

HOVERMALE, JOHN B., oceanography director. Dir. Naval Oceanographic and Atiyespheric Research Lab., Atmospheric Directorate, Monterey, Calif. Home: Monterey Calif. Died July, 1994.

HOWARD, JANE TEMPLE, author; b. Springfield, Ill., May 4, 1935; d. Robert Pickrell and Eleanor Grace (Nee) H. A.B., U. Mich., 1956; D.Litt. hon., Grinnell Coll., 1979; D.H.L. hon., Hamline U., 1984. Reporter, editor, writer Life mag., 1956-72; vis. lectr. U. Iowa Writers Workshop, 1974, U. Ga. Sch. Journalism, 1975, Yale U., 1976, SUNY-Albany, 1978; James Thurber writer in residence Ohio State U., 1986; notary pub. Author: Please Touch: A Guided Tour of the Human Potential Movement, 1970, A Different Woman, 1973, Families, 1978, Margaret Mead: A Life, 1984; contbr. articles to popular mags. Fellow Soc. Am. Historians, Inc. Home: New York N.Y. Died June 27, 1996.

HOWARD, JOHN TASKER, city planner; b. Paris, June 7, 1911; s. Rossiter and Alice (Woodbury) H.; m. Eleanor M. Robb, 1940 (dec. 1982); children: John T., Jr., Margaret Alice; m. 2nd. Elizabeth C. (Nourse) Frank, 1986. Student, Antioch Coll., 1928-31; B.F.A., Yale U., 1934; B.Arch., M.I.T., 1935, M.C.P., 1936; traveling fellow in regional planning, 1936-37. Research asst. N.E. Regional Planning Commn., Boston, 1935-36; city planner Regional Assn. of Cleve., 1937-42; lectr. in city planning Western Res. U., 1939-49; planning dir. Cleve. City Planning Commn., 1942-49; city planning cons. Boston, Cleve., Hartford, Los Angeles, San Francisco Bay Area, Washing, 1949-89; ptnr. Adams, Howard & Greeley, 1949-63, Adams, Howard & Oppermann, 1964-69; assoc. prof. city planning Mass. Inst. Tech., 1949-57, prof., 1957-73, prof. emeritus, 1973-95, head dept. city and regional planning, 1957-70. Mem. exec. com. Hwy. Research Bd., 1962-68; bd. consultants Eno Found. for Transp., 1962-72, 74-77; mem. Gloucester Capital Improvement Adv. Bd., 1972-92, vice chmn., 1972-92; mem. Downtown Devel. Commn.,

1974-86, chmn., 1980-86, mem. Gloucester Planning Bd., 1981-90, chmn., 1985-89, vice chmn., 1989-90; corporator Addison Gilbert Hosp., 1978-95, trustee, 1980-84, life trustee, 1985-95; trustee Addison Gilbert Found., 1983-89; active Newburyport Planning Bd., 1993-95. Hon. assoc. Cleve. chpt. AIA; recipient Yale medal distinction in Arts, 1959; named Outstanding Young Man of Yr. Cleve. Jr. C. of C., 1942. Mem. Am. Inst. Cert. Planners, Assn. Collegiate Schs. of Planning (pres. 1960), Am. Soc. Planning Ofcls. (dir. 1947-50, medal award 1975), Am. Inst. Planners (pres. 1954-56, Disting. Svc. award 1963), Ohio Planning Conf. (pres. 1948, 60th Anniversary Spl. award 1979, Ohio Planning Pioneer award 1993), Leonard Club of Annisquam (sec. 1981-92, pres. 1980-82). Home: Newburyport Mass. Died Feb. 2, 1995.

HOWE, IRVING, author, historian, critic; b. N.Y.C., June 11, 1920; s. David and Nettie (Goldman) H.; m. Ilana Wiener; 2 children. Grad., CCNY. Tchr. English Brandeis U., 1953-61, Stanford U., 1961-63; prof. English City U. N.Y. at Hunter Coll., 1963-86, Distinguished prof., 1970-86; Christian Gauss seminar chair prof. Princeton U., 1954. Author: Politics and the Novel: A World More Attractive, 1963, Steady Work, 1966, Thomas Hardy, 1967, The Decline of the New, 1969, The Critical Point, 1973, World of Our Fathers, 1976 (Nat. Book award), A Margin of Hope, 1982, Socialism & America, 1985, Socialism and America, 1985, The American Newness, 1986; co-author: The Radical Papers, 1966; editor: periodical Essential Works of Socialism, 1971, The Penguin Book of Modern Yiddish Verse, 1987; co-editor: A Treasury of Yiddish Poetry, 1971; contbr. to N.Y. Times Book Rev. Served with AUS, World War II. Recipient Longview Found. prize for lit. criticism; Nat. Inst. Arts and Letters award; Nat. Book award for history, 1976; Kenyon Rev. fellow for lit. criticism, 1953; Bollingen Found. fellow; Guggenheim fellow, 1971, MacArthur fellow, 1987. Home: New York N.Y. Died May 5, 1993.

HOWE, JACK HOMER, speech communication educator; b. Clarence, Mo., Aug. 20, 1923; s. Warren D. and Goldie Sarah (Howe) H. B.A., Morningside Coll., 1947; LL.B., U. S.D., 1949, M.A., 1949; Ph.D., U. Nebr., 1954. Bar: S.D. 1949. Instr. Southwestern Coll., Kans., 1951-52; lectr. U. Nebr., 1952-54; asst. prof. then assoc. prof. Southwestern Coll., Winfield, Kans., 1954-59; asst. prof. U. Ariz., 1959-60; assoc. prof. Southwestern Coll., 1960-61; asst. prof. then assoc. prof. U. Ariz., 1961-64; vis. prof. U. Calif., Santa Barbara, summer 1964; prof. U. Ariz., 1964-66; vis. prof. Frostburg (Md.) State Coll., 1966-67; prof. Calif. State U., Long Beach, 1967-89, prof. emeritus. Editor: Intercollegiate Speech Tournament Results, 1965-81; calendar editor Jour. of Am. Forensic Assn, 1968-86. Served with U.S. Army, 1943-45. Decorated Purple Heart; recipient Outstanding Service to U. Ariz. award, 1971; Disting. Coaching award U. Utah, 1979; Critic of Yr. award UCLA, 1984; Coach of Yr. award Sacramento City Coll., 1984. Mem. Speech Communication Assn., Am. Forensic Assn. (v.p. 1966-68), Western Forensic Assn. (pres. 1962-64), Pacific S.W. Collegiate Forensic Assn. (pres. 1974-75), Nat. Forensic Assn. (v.p. 1973-77), Western Speech Communication Assn., Cross-Exam. Debate Assn. (exec. sec. 1971-84, pres. 1984-85), Delta Sigma Rho-Tau Kappa Alpha (nat. treas. 1975-79, nat. pres. 1979-81, Disting. Service award 1981). Methodist. Home: Long Beach Calif. Died May 4, 1995.

HOWELL, RICHARD PAUL, SR., transportation engineer; b. Sarasota, Fla., Nov. 20, 1927; s. Paul Augustus and Mary Amanda (Snead) H.; m. Judith Kay Eshelman, Sept. 6, 1958; children: Richard Paul, Thomas Bradford, Robert Greggson, Mary Amanda. BS in Civil Engring., Mich. State U., 1949. Registered profl. engr., Ohio, Mass., R.I., Conn., N.Y., N.J., Pa., Del., D.C., Md. Track supr. to div. engr. Pa. R.R. and successor co. Penn Cen. R.R., 1949-71; chief R.R. engr. to v.p. Parsons DeLeuw, Inc., Washington, 1971-93; dep. gen. mgr. Northeast Corridor Rail Improvement Program, 1978-82; tech. advisor to financing banks Eurotunnel, London, 1989-90; project mgr. So. Calif. Commuter Rail (Metrolink), 1990-93; mem. Mich. State U. Alumni Engring. Coun., 1968-72. Contbr. articles on transp. to profl. publs. Dist. chmn. Md. gubernatorial campaign, 1967. Lt. USNR, 1945-46, Civil Engr. Corps Res. USNR. Recipient Toulmin medal Am. Soc. Mil. Engrs., 1979; named Railroader of Mo., Progressive Railroads, 1979. Mem. Am. Ry. Engring. Assn., Transp. Rsch. Bd., Camp Hill Jr. C. of C. (pres. 1961-62), Masons, Phi Delta Theta. Republican. Presbyterian. Home: Rockville Md. Died July 24, 1993.

HOWLAND, WILLIAM GOLDWIN CARRINGTON, chief justice; b. Toronto, Ont., Can., Mar. 7, 1915; s. Goldwin William and Margaret (Carrington) H.; m. Margaret Patricia Greene, Aug. 20, 1966. BA, LLB, U. Toronto, 1936, Osgoode Hall Law Sch., 1939; LL.D., Queen's U., 1972, U. Toronto, 1981, York U., 1984, Law Soc. Upper Can., 1985; DLitt, Wycliffe Coll., 1985; LLB (hon.), York U., 1991. bar: Ont 1939. Read law with Rowell, Reid, Wright & McMillan, 1936-39; pvt. practice Toronto, 1939-75; assoc. firm McMillan Binch, 1936-75; ptnr. McMillan & Binch, 1948-75; justice of appeal Ct. Appeal, Supreme Ct. Ontario, Toronto, 1975-77; chief justice Ont., 1977-90; bencher Law Soc. Upper Can., 1960, 65, life bencher, 1969-94, treas. (head), 1968-70; gov. Can. Jud. Ctr., 1988-90. Author: Special Lectures, Law Society of Upper Canada, 1951, 60 (with Marriott) Practice in Mortgage Actions in Ontario. Nat. pres. UN Assn. in Can., 1959-60; bd. govs. Upper Can. Coll., 1968-70, 77-90; mem. senate York U., 1968; chmn. adv. council Order of Ont., 1986-90; adv. council Toronto Symphony; trustee Wycliffe Coll., 1975-90. Served to capt. Canadian Army, 1942-45. Decorated comdr. Order St. John, 1984, Order of Ont., 1991, officer Order of Can., 1991; recipient Human Rels. award Can. Coun. Christians and Jews, 1990, Robinette medal Osgoode Hall Law Sch. Alumni Assn., 1993. Mem. Canadian Bar Assn., ABA (hon. mem. Appellate Judge Conf.), Fedn. Law Socs. of Can. (pres. 1973-74), Canadian Inst. Internat. Affairs, Univ. Coll. Alumni Assn. (past pres.), Univ. Coll. Com. U. Toronto, The Advocates Soc. (hon. life), Assn. Provincial Criminal Ct. Judges of Ont. (hon. life), Delta Upsilon, Phi Delta Phi. Anglican. Home: Toronto Can. Died May 13, 1994.

HUANG, SHAO-KU, Chinese government official; b. Hunan, China, June 9, 1901; m. Shu-fang Hou; 3 children. B.Ed., Nat. Peking Normal Univ., 1927. Chief editor Peiping World Daily, 1925-27; pub. Sao Tang Daily, Chungking, 1943-48; minister without portfolio, 1949-54; vice premier, 1954-58, 66-69; minister of fgn. affairs, 1958-60; ambassador to Spain, 1960-62; sec. gen. Nat. Security Council, 1967-79; sr. advisor to Pres. of China, from 1976; pres. Jud. Yuan, 1979-87. Mem. central com. Kuomintang Party, from 1931, mem. central standing com., from 1947. Deceased.

HUBBARD, DAVID ALLAN, minister, educator, religious association administrator; b. Stockton, Calif., Apr. 8, 1928; s. John King and Helena (White) H.; m. Ruth Doyal, Aug. 12, 1949; 1 child, Mary Ruth. BA, Westmont Coll., Calif., 1949; BD, Fuller Theol. Sem., Pasadena, Calif., 1952, ThM, 1954; PhD, St. Andrews U., Scotland, 1957; DD (hon.), John Brown U., 1975; LHD (hon.), Rockford Coll., 1975, Hope Coll., 1990; DLitt (hon.), King Sejong U., Korea, 1985; EdD (hon.), Friends U., 1990; DD (hon.), North Park Coll. & Theol. Sem., 1993. Ordained to ministry Conservative Bapt. Assn., 1952, Am. Bapt. Chs. in the U.S.A., 1984. Lectr. Old Testament studies St. Andrews U., 1955-56; asst. prof. Bibl. studies Westmont Coll., 1957, chmn. dept. Bibl. studies and philosophy, 1958-63; interim pastor Montecito (Calif.) Community Ch., 1960-62; pres., prof. Old Testament Fuller Theol. Sem., 1963-93, pres. emeritus, prof. emeritus Old Testament, 1993-96; exec. v.p. Fuller Evangelistic Assn., 1969-92; Tyndale Old Testament lectr., Cambridge, Eng., 1965, Soc. Old Testament Studies lectr., London, 1971, lectr. numerous U.S. univs., 1973-96. Speaker: internat. radio broadcast The Joyful Sound, 1969-80; author: With Bands of Love, 1968, (with others) Is God Dead?, 1966, Is Life Really Worth Living?, 1969, What's God Been Doing All This Time?, 1970, What's New?, 1970, Does the Bible Really Work?, 1971, Psalms for All Seasons, 1971, Is The Family Here To Stay?, 1971, The Practice of Prayer, 1972, Spanish edit., 1974, Chinese edit., 1979, How To Face Your Fears, 1972, The Holy Spirit in Today's World, 1973, Church—Who Needs It?, 1974, They Met Jesus, 1974, More Psalms for All Seasons, 1975, An Honest Search for a Righteous Life, 1975, Colossians Speaks to the Sickness of Our Time, 1976, Happiness: You Can Find the Secret, 1976, Beyond Futility, 1976, Chinese edit., 1982, Themes from the Minor Prophets, 1977, Strange Heroes, 1977, Galatians: Gospel of Freedom, 1977, Thessalonians: Life That's Radically Christian, 1977, Why Do I Have to Die?, 1978, How to Study the Bible, 1978, What We Evangelicals Believe, 1979, Book of James: Wisdom That Works, 1980, Right Living in a World Gone Wrong, 1981, German edit., 1982, Parables Jesus Told, 1981, (with Bush and LaSor) Old Testament Survey, 1982, The Practice of Prayer, 1982, The Second Coming, 1984, Proclamation 3: Pentecost 1, 1985, Unwrapping Your Spiritual Gifts, 1985, Holy Spirit in Today's World, 1986, Tyndale Commentary: Joel, Amos, 1987, Tyndale Commentary: Hosea, 1989, Communicator's Commentary: Proverbs, 1989, Ecclesiastes, Song of Solomon, WORD 1991; contbg. editor: Eternity mag.; mem. editl. bd. The Ministers' Permanent Library, 1976-92; adv. bd. Evang. Book Club, 1977-86; contbr. articles to dictionaries, mags. Chmn. Pasadena Urban Coalition, 1968-71; mem. Calif. Bd. Edn., 1972-75; bd. dirs. Nat. Inst. Campus Ministries, 1974-78. Personal tribute - festschrift Studies in Old Testament Theology, Word, Inc., 1992. Mem. Catholic Biblical Assn., Nat. Assn. Bapt. Profs. Religion, Nat. Assn. Profs. Hebrew, Am. Acad. Religion, Soc. Bibl. Lit., Soc. for Old Testament Study, Inst. Bibl. Rsch., Assn. Theol. Schs. in U.S. and Can. (exec. com. 1972-80, pres. 1976-78), Fuller Evang. Assn. (trustee 1969-92, exec. v.p. 1969-82). Home: Santa Barbara Calif. Died June 7, 1996.

HUBBARD, STANLEY EUGENE, broadcasting executive; b. Redwing, Minn., June 26, 1897; s. Frank Valentine and Minnie (Ayre) H.; m. Mary Jane Rogers, July 21, 1979; children: Alice Hubbard Liptak, Stanley Stub. Student, St. Paul and Mpls. schs. Founder Ohio Valley Aero Transp. Co., 1919, Sta. WAMD, Mpls., 1923, Sta. KSTP, St. Paul-Mpls.; chmn. bd. emeritus Hubbard Broadcasting Inc., St. Paul. Served with U.S. Army, World War I. Decorated cavaliere Order Crown Italy, 1935; recipient Am. Advt. Fedn. of Minn. Silver medal, 1981, Entrepreneurial award by Minn. Bus. H of Fame, 1982, Nat. Assn. Broadcasters Spirit Broa casting award, 1984; named Minn. Man of Yr. 19 named to Minn. Bus. Hall of Fame, 1985, Broadcasti Hall of Fame, 1991. Mem. Indian Creek Country Cl LaGorce Country Club, Bal Harbour Beach and Ya Club, Somerset Country Club, Town and Country Cl Surf Club, Mpls. Club, Minn. Club. Home: Saint P Minn. Died Dec. 28, 1992.

HUBER, PETER C., diversified chemicals manuf turing company executive; b. 1930. Student, Hamil Coll. With J.M. Huber Corp., Edison, N.J., from 19 v.p., 1959-60, treas., 1960-81, group v.p., treas., fr 1981, then group v.p., vice chmn., chief exec. offic v.p., asst. sec. With USAF, 1951-54. Home: Edis N.J. Deceased.

HUCLES, HENRY BOYD, III, bishop; b. N.Y. Sept. 21, 1923; s. Henry Boyd and Alma Leola (Lew H.; m. Mamie Dalceda Adams, Sept. 18, 1948; childr Henry Boyd IV, Michael Edward. B.S., Va. Union Richmond, 1943; M.Div., Va. Sem., Alexandria, 19 D.D. hon., Va. Sem., 1976. Ordained priest Episco Ch., 1947; parish minister Grace Ch., Millers Tave Va., 1946-49; rector St. George's Ch., Bklyn., 1949- prison chaplain Dept. Corrections, Bklyn., 1954- archdeacon of Bklyn. Episcopal Diocese of L.I., Garc City, N.Y., 1976-81; suffragan bishop Episcopal Dioc of L.I., 1981—; mem. Anglican Council N.Am. a Caribbean, 1982—; hon canon Cathedral of the carnation, Garden City. Vice-pres. Ch. Charity Four Hempstead, N.Y., 1956—. Named Man of Yr. Ki County Med. Soc., Bklyn., 1965. Democrat. Clu Brooklyn; Garden City Golf, Cherry Valley G (Garden City). Home: Garden City N.Y.

HUDDLESON, EDWIN EMMET, JR., lawyer; Oakland, Calif., Jan. 28, 1914; s. Edwin Emmet a Gertrude (Connahan) H.; m. Mary Taeusch, July 1941; children—Michael Stephen (dec.), Edwin Emr III, Mary Catherine. A.B., Stanford U., 1935; LL. Harvard, 1938. Bar: Calif. 1939. Law clk. to Ju A.N. Hand, 1938-39; atty. Office U.S. Solicitor Ge 1939-40; law clk. to Justice Frank Murphy, 1940; spl. projects staff Office Asst. Sec. Intelligence, St Dept., 1946; dep. gen. counsel AEC, 1947-48; mem. fi Cooley, Godward, Castro Huddleson & Tatum, S Francisco, 1949-86, counsel, 1986—; dir. Varian Ass then emeritus dir.; trustee Aerospace Corp., 1960-75, 86, Rand Corp., 1955-65, 66-76, 77-84; trustee Mi Corp., 1957-85, hon., 1986—. Pres. Harvard Law R 1937-38. Trustee Ctr. for Advanced Study in Behavic Scis., 1964-76, 79-85, System Devel. Found., 1957-8 Served to lt. col. AUS, 1941-46, PTO. Decorated gion of Merit; recipient Exceptional Service aw USAF, 1975. Mem. Phi Beta Kappa. Home: Oakla Calif.

HUDNALL, JACK PROWERS, psychology educat b. La Junta, Colo., Oct. 31, 1925; s. Leonard Hyden a Alice (Parsons) H.; m. Irene F. Poe, 1948 (div.); cl dren: Karen, Kathleen, Jack Prowers; m. Helen Ar Heath, 1964; stepchildren: Terry, Doreen, Jeane Howard. Student, Southwestern U., Tex., 1944; B. Colo. Coll., 1947; B.Ed. (Univ. fellow), Wash. State 1950; M.A. (Coll. fellow), Tchrs. Coll., Columbia 1959, postgrad., 1963-64. Sch. psychologist Sea Public Schs., 1949-51; tchr. psychology Edison Te Sch., Seattle, 1951-57; dean Hibbing Jr. Coll., 1959- dean adminstrn. Kingsborough Community Coll., 19 66; founding pres. Bristol Community Coll., 1966- prof. psychology, 1978-81, pres. emeritus, 1981-92; co instr., evaluator community colls. Pres. Greater F River (Mass.) Planning Council, 1967-71; bd. dirs. B tleship Mass. Meml. Com., Fall River, 1974-80, Eas Seals Soc. Mass., 1971-77. Served with USMC, 1944-4 Council for Advancement Secondary Edn. grant 1955-56. Mem. C. of C. of Fall River (dir. 1971-7 Am. Assn. Community and Jr. Colls. (mem. commn Phi Beta Kappa. Democrat. Home: Tucson Ariz. D Oct. 18, 1992.

HUDSON, DEE TRAVIS, anthropologist; b. Denv July 3, 1941; s. Oscar Melvin and Aileen Mae (Gurl H.; m. Janice Ellen Mowers, Aug. 18, 1963; c dren—Lisa Marie and Laura Ann (twins), Mich Scott. A.A., Santa Ana Jr. Coll., 1968; B.A. cum lau Calif. State U.-Long Beach, 1970; M.A., Ariz. State 1973, Ph.D., 1974. Test technician and supr. I Gilfillan Inc., Azusa, Calif., 1964-65; product supp engr. FMA Inc., Los Angeles, 1965-66; computer engr. Calif. Computer Products, Anaheim, Calif., 19 70; curator anthropology, head dept. Santa Barb (Calif.) Mus. Natural History, 1973—; research ass Marine Sci. Inst. U. Calif., Santa Barbara, 1974-81, a research anthropologist dept. anthropology, 1982 cons. and lectr. in field. Served with USN, 1960-64. N trainee, 1970-73; grantee Nat. Endowment Arts, N NEH, Wenner-Gren Found., Smithsonian Instn.; N Acad. Scis. exchange scholar to USSR. Fellow A Anthrop. Assn.; mem. Soc. for Am. Archeology, S Anthrop. Assn. Author: The Holocene Prehistory Old-World Arid-Lands: A Research Appraisal, 19 editor: The Chumash Indians of Southern Califor Selected Readings, 1979; contbr. numerous chpts. books, articles to profl. jours. Home: Santa Barb Calif.

UFFAKER, CARL BARTON, entomologist, searcher, educator; b. Monticello, Ky., Sept. 30, 1914; DeWitt Talmadge and Elizabeth (Wray) H.; m. aralyn Knight, June 16, 1936; children—Ronald W., arry K., Carolyn S. Huffaker Noack, Thomas . B.A., U. Tenn., Knoxville, 1938, M.S., 1939; post-ad., N. C. State U., 1940; Ph.D., Ohio State U., 1942. sst. entomologist U. Del., Newark, 1941-43; assoc. tomologist Inst. Inter-Am. Affairs, Colombia, S. Am.,)43-44; entomologist Inst. Inter-Am. Affairs, Haiti, ominican Republic, 1944-45; entomologist, prof. U. alif.-Berkeley, 1946-85, prof. emeritus, 1985-95; dir. ternat. Ctr. for Biol. Control, U. Calif.-Berkeley, iverside, 1970-84; mem. subcom. U.S. Nat. Com. of ternat. Biol. Program, 1966-70, Internat. Working roup for Biol. Control; mem. ad hoc com. to organize 'estern Hemisphere Sect. of Internat. Orgn. for Biol. ontrol; dir. nat. integrated pest mgmt. project NSF, PA, Dept. Agr., 1972-80; bd. dirs. div. environ. biogy, Internat. Union of Biol. Scis., 1972-76; mem. PA Office of Pesticides ad hoc com. on pest mgmt.,)73-75; mem. study dels. to USSR, 1959, 74, Peoples epublic of China, 1975, 82; cons. UN Environment ·ogram, and Devel. Program; mem. pesticide adv. com. alif. Dept. Food and Agr.; resident-scholar Rockefeller ound. Study and Conf. Ctr., Bellagio, Italy, 1978. Co-thor, co-editor: Biological Control, 1971; Theory and ·actice of Biological Control, 1976; New Technology of st Control, 1980; Ecological Entomology, 1984; also imerous sci. papers. Guggenheim fellow, 1963-64; SF grantee, 1967-79; NIH, USPHS grantee, 1967-73; cipient Levi medal and Jour. Premier award Franklin st., Phila., 1976; Premium award Am. Naturalist Soc. ur., 1983, Wolf Prize in Agriculture, 1994; Berkeley ation U. Calif., 1985; named hon. fellow Royal Enmol. Soc. London, 1983.Wolf Foundation award Wolf oundation, 1994. Fellow AAAS; mem. Internat. Orgn. ol. Control (pres. 1972-76, 78-83), Entomol. Soc. Am. .p. 1980, pres. 1981, governing bd. 1980-82, Woodorth award 1973), Soc. Population Ecology, Ecol. Soc. m., Entomol. Soc. Can., Audubon Soc., Smithsonian ssn., Nat. Acad. Scis., Sigma Xi, Phi Kappa Phi. epublican. Home: Lafayette Calif. Died Oct. 10, 1995.

UFNAGEL, RAYMOND JOSEPH, JR., aerospace id commercial executive; b. Hanover, Pa., Dec. 22,)41; s. Raymond Joseph and Mary Gertrude .awrence) H.; 1 child, Raymond Joseph III. BA in sychology, U. Ariz., 1964; MA in Supervision Mgmt., en. Mich. U., 1974; postgrad., Indsl. Coll. Armed orces, 1976, Nat. War Coll., 1981. Commd. 2d lt. SAF, 1964, advanced through grades to col., 1984; st. for telecommunications command and control Ofe Sec. Air Force, Washington, 1977-79; chief policy id doctrine div. Comdr. in Chief Pacific Hdqrs., 1980- , exec. asst. to dep. comdr. in chief, 1981-84; ret. SAF, 1984; mgr. new bus. staff Command & Control ystems div. Hughes Aircraft Co., Fullerton, Calif., 84-85, mgr. Systems Design Lab., 1985-87, mgr. Pacific id Far East ops., mgr. Advanced Systems Lab., 1987- , mgr. mktg. div. command and control systems div.,)88-91; mng. dir. Hughes airport sys., Calif., from)91. Contbr. articles to profl. publs. Mem. Air Force ssn., Air Traffic Control Assn. (contbr. jour.), Tech. ktg. Soc. Am. Republican. Roman Catholic. Home: naheim Calif. Deceased.

UGHES, (ROBERT) JOHN, journalist, educator; b. eath, Wales, Apr. 28, 1930; s. Evan John and Dellis ay (Williams) H.; m. Vera Elizabeth Pockman; chil-en: Wendy Elizabeth, Mark Evan; m. Peggy Janeane rdan; 1 child, Evan Jordan. Student stationers cos. h., trade sch., London, 1941-46; student, Harvard U.,)61-62; LLD (hon.), Colby Coll. African corr. Christn Sci. Monitor, Boston, 1955-61, asst. fgn. editor,)62-64, Far East corr., 1964-70, mng. editor, 1970, litor, 1970-79, editor, mgr., pub., 1976-79; assoc. dir. SIA, Washington, 1981-82; dir. Voice of Am., Washgton, 1982; asst. sec. of state Dept. of State, Washgton, 1982-85; columnist Christian Sci. Monitor, oston, 1985-95; prof. journalism Brigham Young U., ·ovo, Utah, 1991-95; U.S. del. to Maui conf. on future U.S.-Japan Rels., 1988; mem. Joint Coun. Fgn. Rels./ sia Soc. task force to South Korea, 1986-87; bd. dirs. ılitzer Prize bd., Luce Asian Fellows selection com., ieman Fellows selection com., Harvard U.; chmn. lijah Parish Lovejoy selection com. Colby Coll., laine; judge Sigma Delta Chi awards in journalism; r., cons. News-Jour. Co., Wilmington, Del., 1975-78; lj. prof. journalism Boston U., 1986-87; pres., editor, ib. Concord Comm., Maine, 1989-91; chmn. Pres. ush's Task Force US Govt. Internat. Broadcasting,)91; chmn. Presdl./Congl. Commn. Broadcasting to eople's Republic of China, 1992; mem. Corp. Pub. roadcasting Adv. Commn., 1993; asst. sec.-gen., dir. mm. UN, 1995. Author: The New Face of Africa,)62, Indonesian Upheaval, 1966; dir. radio broadsting Christian Sci. Monitor, prodr. MonitoRadio,)87-89. Recipient Pulitzer Prize for internat. reporting,)65, Best Newspaper Reporting from Abroad award verseas Press Club, 1967; Nieman fellow Harvard U.,)61-62. Mem. Am. Soc. Newspaper Editors (past es.), Pacific Comms. Rsch. Coun., Fgn. Corr. Club ong Kong (pres.). Home: Provo Utah Died Mar. 8,)95.

UGHES, PAULA D., investment company executive; N.Y.C., Sept. 25, 1931; 1 dau., Catherine H. Benton. With Brown & Bigelow, N.Y.C., 1953-61; account exec. Shields & Co., N.Y.C., 1961-72; v.p. Thomson McKinnon Securities Inc., N.Y.C., 1972-78, 1st v.p., dir., 1979—; gov. U.S. Postal Service, 1980—; allied mem. N.Y. Stock Exchange; life trustee Carnegie-Mellon U., chmn. fin. com.; lectr.-instr. Personal Investment Mgmt., NYU; lectr. various schs. and colls.; lectr. Vassar Coll.; speaker New Sch., N.Y.C., panel mem. Wall St. Conf., 1979, 82, 83; bd. govs. Greenwich House, N.Y.C., 1961—. Featured cover articles, Fin. World, 1975, 78, articles in publs., Fortune mag., Wall St. Jour., Pitts. Press, Ariz. Republic, articles to publs., N.Y. Times, articles in publs., N.Y. Post, Indpls. Star; guest, Wall St. Week. Recipient AMITA Golden Lady award in Fin., 1975; recipient Disting. Friend of U. award Carnegie-Mellon U., 1983; named Bus. Woman of Yr. Calif. Bus. Women, 1976. Mem. Women's Forum (dir. 1979-81), Sales Execs. Club N.Y. (treas. 1977-79, dir. 1977—), Fin. Women's Assn., Am. Arbitration Soc., Internat. Assn. Fin. Planners. Republican. Clubs: Duquesne (Pitts.); Shenorock Shore (Rye); Yale (N.Y.C.). Home: New York N.Y.

HUGHES, WILLIAM TAYLOR, physicist, educator; b. Vidor, Tex., Nov. 15, 1936; s. Clarence and Lura (Bunch) H.; m. Ann Greenway Montgomery, June 15, 1965; 1 son, Thomas Abbott. B.S., MA., Ind. U., 1960; Ph.D., Northwestern U., 1967. With Smithsonian Instn., Washington, 1958-59; sr. staff NASA Satellite Sta., Curacao, 1958-59; instr. U. Mo., Columbus, 1963-64; asst. prof. U. W.Va., Charleston, 1964-66; prof. physics and astronomy Bowdoin Coll., Brunswick, Maine, 1967—, head dept., 1972-76; tech. cons. Mem. Gov.'s Adv. Com. on Reactor Safety. Author: Microbiology, 1978, Aspects of Biophysics, 1979; articles. NASA fellow; grantee NSF, Am. Heart Assn., Hearst Found., Am. Cancer Soc. Fellow Royal Astron. Soc. Home: Brunswick Maine Died Apr. 23, 1993.

HUGIN, ADOLPH CHARLES (EUGENE), lawyer, engineer, inventor, educator; b. Washington, Mar. 28, 1907; s. Charles and Eugenie Francoise (Vigny) H. BSEE, George Washington U., 1928; MSEE, MIT, 1930; JD, cert. in patent law and practice, Georgetown U., 1934; cert. radio communication (electronics), Union Coll., 1944; cert., Better Bus. Mgmt. III GE, 1946; LLM, Harvard U., 1947; SJD, Cath. U. Am., 1949; cert. in Christian doctrine and teaching methods, Conf. of Christian Doctrine, 1960; cert. in social svcs. and charity, Ozanam Sch. Charity, 1972. Bar: D.C. 1933, U.S. Ct. Customs and Patent Appeals 1934, U.S. Supreme Ct. 1945, Mass. 1947, U.S. Ct. Claims, 1953, U.S. Ct. Appeals (fed. cir.) 1982; registered U.S. Patent and Trademark Office Atty. Bar, 1933; registered U.S. Treasury Dept. Atty Bar, 1934; registered profl. elec. and mech. engr., D.C. Tchr. French, McKinley Tech. High Sch., Washington, 1923-24; florist and fruit cultivator, 1923-28; examiner U.S. Patent and Trademark Office, 1928; with GE, 1928-46; engr. Meters and Instruments R&D Lab. GE, West Lynn Works, Mass., 1928; engr.-in-charge Insulation Lab. River Works GE, Lynn, Mass., 1929, engr.-in-charge Engine-Electric Drive Devel. Lab., River Works, 1929-30; patent legal asst. GE, Schenectady, N.Y., 1930; patent investigator GE, Washington, 1930-33, patent lawyer, 1933-34; patent lawyer GE, Schenectady, 1934-46, engr.-in-charge section aeros. and marine engring. div., 1942-45, organizer, instr. patent practice course, 1945-46; pvt. practice law, cons. engring. Cambridge and Arlington, Mass., 1946-47; pvt. practice law, cons. engr. Washington and Springfield, Va., 1947-94; assoc. Holland, Armstrong, Bower & Carlson, N.Y.C., 1957; prof. constl. law, civil procedure, intellectual property law and practice, trade regulation and antitrust law, criminal law and procedure, law for engrs. and architects, chmn. student admissions com. Law Sch. Cath. U. Am., Washington, 1949-55. Author: Private International Trade Regulatory Arrangements and the Antitrust Laws, 1949; editor-in-chief Bull. Am. Patent Law Assn., 1949-54; editor notes and decisions Georgetown U. Law Jour., 1933-34, staff, 1930-34; contbr. articles on patents, copyrights, antitrust, radio and air law to profl. jours.; inventor: dynamo-electric machines, insulation micrometer calipers, ecology and pollution controls, musical instruments, dynamometers, heavy-duty inherent constant voltage characteristic generators, water-cooled eddy-current clutches, brakes, and others, granted 12 U.S. patents, several fgn. patents. Mem. Schenectady com. Boy Scouts Am., 1940-42, North Springfield Civic Assn.; charter mem., 1st bd. mgrs. Schenectady Cath. Youth League, 1935-38, hon. life mem., 1945; mem. adv. bd. St. Michael's Parish, Va., 1974-77, lector, commentator, 1969-80; bd. dirs. St. Margaret's Fed. Credit Union, 1963-67, 1st v.p., 1965-67; chmn. St. Margaret's Bldg. Fund, 1954; lectr. St. Margaret's Parish, Md., 1966-69, men's retreat group capt., 1965-68, Parish Coun., 1969-71; mem. legis. com. Schenectady C. of C. Recipient Dietzen Drawing prize George Washington U., 1926, Georgetown U. Law Jour. Key award, 1934, Aviation Law prize Cath. U. Am., 1948, Radio Law prize, 1949, Charities Work award St. Margaret's Ch., 1982; elected to GE Elfun Soc. for Disting. Exec. Svc., 1942. Mem. AIEE, Am. Intellectual Property Law Assn. (life, cert. of Honor for 50 Yrs. Svc. 1980), ABA (life), John Carroll Soc. (life), Nat. Soc. Profl. Engrs., D.C. Soc. Profl. Engrs., St. Vincent de Paul Soc. (St. Margaret's parish conf. v.p. 1949-65, pres. 1965-90, pres. Prince Georges County dist. coun. 1958-61, founding pres. Arlington, Va. Diocesan cen. coun., 1975-77, nat. trustee 1975-77, Frederick Ozanam Top Hat award 1991), Nocturnal Adoration Soc., St. Margaret's Parish Confraternity Christian Doctrine (pres., instr. 1960-61), Washington Archdiocesan Coun. Cath. Men (pres. So. Prince George's County Md. deanery, 1956-58, 65-68), Holy Name Soc. (pres. St. Margaret's parish soc. 1950-52, Prince George's County section 1953, Washington Archdiocesan Union 1953-55), Nat. Retired Tchrs. Assn., Men's Retreat League (Wash. exec. bd. 1954-58), George Washington U. Engring. Soc., Delta Theta Phi law fraternity (E.D. White Senate 1931, mem. emeritus 1974, scholarship key award Georgetown U. Law Sch. 1934). Home: North Springfield Va. Died Dec. 20, 1994.

HUMPHREY, BINGHAM JOHNSON, chemical company executive; b. Proctor, Vt., Feb. 9, 1906; s. Albert Parmlee and Angie T. (Tenney) H.; B.S., U. Vt., 1927, hon. LL.D., 1978; Ph.D., Yale U., 1930; m. Esther R. Stanley, Oct. 25, 1930; children: Eugene B., James R., Sarah. Sr. research chemist Firestone Corp., 1930-42; tech. dir. Conn. Hard Rubber Co., 1942-49; pres. Humphrey-Wilkinson, Inc., 1949-64; pres. The Humphrey Chem. Co., Hamden, Conn., 1964-72, chmn. bd., 1972-88, cons., 1988—; dir. Milfoam Corp. Chmn., Hamden Bd. Edn., 1958-66; trustee U. Vt., 1968-74, chmn. trustees, 1973-74. Mem. Am. Chem. Soc., U. Vt. Nat. Alumni Assn. (pres. 1969-70), Sigma Xi. Clubs: N.Y. Chemists, Rotary. Died Oct. 22, 1991. Home: North Haven Conn.

HUNT, JAMES SIMON WALLIS, television commentator; b. London, Aug. 29, 1947; s. Wallis Glynn and Susan Noel (Davis) H.; m. Sarah Marion Lomax (div.); children: Thomas Ian Wallis, Freddie Alexander. Attended, Wellington Coll., Berkshire, Eng., 1961-65. Racing driver McLaren Racing, London, 1976-78; TV commentator London, 1980—. Formula One World Champion, 1976. Home: London Eng.

HUNT, ROBERT SHERWOOD, educator; b. Postville, Iowa, July 14, 1917; s. Gerald Winslow and Margaret (Sherwood) H.; m. Elaine Marie Hess, Aug. 18, 1948 (div.). A.B., Oberlin Coll., 1939; A.M., Harvard U., 1940; LL.B., Yale U., 1947; S.J.D. (Rockefeller fellow), U. Wis., 1952. Bar: Iowa bar 1948, Ill. bar 1951. From instr. to asst. prof. Coll. Law, U. Iowa, 1947-49; assoc. firm Schiff Hardin and Waite, Chgo., 1950-57; ptnr. Schiff Hardin and Waite, 1957-66; prof. Sch. Law, U. Wash., Seattle, 1966—; assoc. dean Sch. Law, U. Wash., 1970-75; Dir. Security State Bank, Guttenberg, Ia., 1964-71. Author: Law and Locomotives: the Impact of the Railroad on Wisconsin Law in the 19th Century, 1958. Bd. dirs. Mary McDowell Settlement House, Chgo., 1962-66. Served to lt. comdr. USNR, 1940-46, PTO. Mem. Am. Vets. Com. (nat. vice chmn. 1955-56), Am. Bar Assn. Clubs: Corbey Court (New Haven); Cliff Dwellers (Chgo.). Home: Seattle Wash.

HUNT, WALTER L., real estate and petroleum company executive; b. Stacyville, Maine, June 12, 1941; s. Charles O. and Letha W. (Shaw) H.; m. Camilla Kay Sherman, June 8, 1963 (dec. 1993); children: Steven, Ronald, Randal, Kristi, Erica; m. Lynn Ellis Brooks, June 26, 1993. BS, BA, Husson Coll., 1966; MBA, U. Maine, 1973. Acct. Dead River Co., Bangor, Maine, 1966-69, contr. adminstrv. div., 1969-74, asst. treas., 1974-84, treas., sec., 1984-90; v.p., sec. Dead River Co., Bangor, 1987—; fin. cons. Roosevelt Campobello Internat. Park, Campobello Island, N.B., Can., 1975—; bd. dirs. Ea. Maine Healthcare, Bangor, Affiliated Healthcare Systems, Bangor. Trustee Husson Coll., Bangor, 1989—. Mem. Internat. Found. of Employee Benefit Plans, Soc. for Human Resource Mgmt. Republican. Baptist. Home: Dedham Maine Died Jan. 3, 1995.

HUNTER, EDGAR HAYES, architect; b. Hanover, N.H., Aug. 1, 1914; s. Edgar Hayes and Edna H. (Hill) H.; m. Margaret Greenough King, May 8, 1943; children: Christopher King, Margaret Greenough. Grad., Deerfield Acad., 1933; B.A., Dartmouth Coll., 1938, M.A., 1955; M.Arch., Harvard U., 1941. Instr. naval architecture Mass. Inst. Tech., 1941-42; underwater gear design Boston, N.Y. navy yards, 1942-45; partner E.H. & M.K. Hunter, architects-planners, Hanover, N.H., 1945-66; v.p., dir. Raleigh (N.C.) office Lyles, Bissett, Carlisle & Wolff, Columbia, S.C., 1966-69; partner E.H. & M.K. Hunter, architects-planners, Raleigh, 1969-95; v.p. Cricket Corp., Winston-Salem, N.C., 1970-95; prof. architecture Dartmouth, 1946-66; lectr. N.C. State U., 1968-69; archtl. cons. N.C. Higher Edn. Facilities Commn., 1969-70, mem. adv. council, 1968-95; chmn. publ. com; N.C. Architect, 1969-95. Exhibited in Munich, Germany, 1958, traveling exhibit U.S. colls. and museums, 1963-66; Important works include Out Patient Clinic, N.H. State Hosp, 1954, Toll Collectors Sta. and Canopies, Everett and Spaulding turnpikes, N.H., 1955, Lutheran Ch, Hanover, 1962, Arts Center and Sci. Bldg., Colby Jr. Coll, New London, N.H., 1962, Stratton Mountain Site Planning, Vt., 1961, Loon Mountain Ski Area, Lincoln, N.H., 1966, dormitory, Conn. Coll. for Women, New London, 1964, classroom bldg. and dormitories, Bridgton Acad., Maine, 1965, apts. and classroom bldg., Dartmouth Coll., 1958, N.C. State Fair planning, 1970, Sugar Mountain land planning, 1969, Campus Plan for, N.C. Central U., 1971, relocatables, Cricket Corp., 1970; student Internat. Meditation Soc. at Santa Barbara campus, 1972, Happy Inns, N.C. and S.C., Crafts Pavillion at N.C. State Fairgrounds, 1974, Hunter's Creek Townhouses, Raleigh, 1983; co-author: The Indoor Garden: Design Construction, and Furnishing, 1978; illustrator: Own Kitchen and Garden Survival Book, 1978. Mem. Hanover Town Planning Commn., 1964-66; Bd. dirs. Downtown Housing Improvement Corp., Raleigh, 1974-95, Raleigh Chamber Music Guild, Raleigh Children's Theatre. Recipient Progressive Architecture award, 1946, 47; award N.H. State Office Bldg. competition, 1950. Mem. A.I.A. (pres. Raleigh 1973, dir. N.C. chpt. 1973), Newcomen Soc., N.C. Land Use Congress, Internat. Skiing Hist. Assn. (founder, bd. dirs. 1991-95). Presbyterian. Home: Raleigh N.C. Died Mar. 27, 1995.

HUNTER, FRANK HERBERT, broker; b. Pitts., Oct. 22, 1901; s. David Jr. and Elizabeth (Crow) H.; m. Josephine Wittmer, June 15, 1926 (dec.); children: Barbara Josephine Hunter Moore (dec.), David Wittmer, Peter Crow. A.B., Amherst Coll., 1924; J.D., U. Pitts., 1927. Bar: Pa. 1927. Practice law, 1927-28, engaged in securities investment bus., from 1929; with McKelvy and Co., Pitts., 1932-69; partner McKelvy and Co., 1941-69; pres. Parker/Hunter, Inc., 1969-71, chmn. exec. com., 1971-73; bd. govs. N.Y. Stock Exchange, 1962-65. Mem. Investment Bankers Assn. Am. (past chmn. West Pa. group), Allegheny County Bar Assn., Nat. Assn. Securities Dealers (chmn. bd. govs. 1956). Republican. Presbyn. Clubs: Bond (Pitts.), Duquesne (Pitts.); Fox Chapel Golf. Home: Pittsburgh Pa. Deceased.

HUNTER, HOWARD WILLIAM, lawyer, church official; b. Boise, Idaho, Nov. 14, 1907; s. John William and Nellie Marie (Rasmussen) H.; m. Clara May Jeffs, June 10, 1931 (dec. Oct. 1983); children: Howard William (dec.), John Jacob, Richard Allen; m. Inis Berice Egan, Apr. 12, 1990. JD cum laude, Southwestern U., 1939. Bar: Calif. 1939; ordained apostle Ch. of Jesus Christ of Latter-day Sts., 1959, bishop, 1941-47, high councilor, 1947-50. Engaged in banking Calif., 1928-34; practiced law L.A., until 1959; mem. coun. of 12, Ch. Jesus Christ of Latter Day Sts., 1959-94, pres., 1994-95; chmn. bd. dirs. Beneficial Life Ins. Co., Salt Lake City, Watson Land Co., L.A., Heber J. Grant & Co., First Security Corp., First Security Bank of Utah, Continental Western Life Ins. Co., Utah Home Fire Ins. Co.; Deseret Mgmt. Corp. Past pres. Polynesian Cultural Ctr., Hawaii. Mem. Calif. Bar Assn., Utah Bar Assn., Geneal. Soc. Utah (bd. dirs., past pres.). Home: Salt Lake City Utah Died Mar. 4, 1995.

HUNTER, NORMAN L., publishing company art director; b. Eutaw, Ala., Aug. 28, 1932; s. Davis W. and Mary V. (Ray) H.; m. Claudia M. Hunter; children: Derek K., Marc C. Student, Art Inst., Detroit, 1948-49, Soc. Arts and Crafts, Detroit, 1952-55, Art Inst., Chgo., 1955-57. With Johnson Pub. Co., Inc., Chgo., 1955-92, art dir., 1965-92, also co-chmn. art com., staff photographer. Designer books: The Shaping of Black America, Black Defenders of America, 1775-1973, Pictoral History of Black America, Black Power Gary Style, Black Society, 1976, Profiles of Black Mayors in America, DuBois: A Pictoral Biography, 1978, Wade in the Water, 1979, I Wouldn't Take Nothing for My Journey, 1981, others; designer for Fashion Fair Cosmetics, Supreme Life Ins. Co., Sta. WJPC-Radio. Sgt. AUS, Korea. Recipient award for photography Nat. Negro Press Assn. (photograph in Lyndon B. Johnson Libr., 1973), award Washington Art Dir., 1975, Chgo. Book Clinic award, 1977, CEBA award, 1978, 79, 80. Mem. Art Inst. Chgo., Operation PUSH (People United to Save Humanity), NAACP. Home: Chicago Ill. Died Dec. 10, 1992.

HUNTER, ROSS, film producer; b. Cleve., May 6, 1926; s. Isadore and Anna (Rosen) Fuss. MA, Western Res. U., 1942. Sch. tchr. Cleve., 1944-46; actor Columbia Pictures, Hollywood, Calif., 1946-47; producer plays, 1947-50; asst. producer Universal Pictures, Hollywood, 1951-52, assoc. producer, 1952-73; Producer films including Magnificent Obsession, 1953, Madame X, Thoroughly Modern Millie, Midnight Lace, Flower Drum Song, The Chalk Garden, Pillow Talk, Airport, 1970; TV movies include The Money Changer, A Family Upside Down, Suddenly Love, The Best Place to Be. Home: Beverly Hills Calif. Died Mar. 10, 1996.

HUNTING, DAVID D., SR., manufacturing company executive; b. 1892; married. With Steelcase, Inc., Grand Rapids, Mich., 1918-93, v.p., 1943-61, vice chmn., 1961-93; also bd. dirs. Steelcase, Inc.; bd. dirs. Stow-Davis Furniture Co., Inc. Home: Grand Rapids Mich. Deceased.

HUNTINGTON, DAVID CAREW, art history educator; b. Scarsdale, N.Y., Dec. 3, 1922; s. Henry Strong Huntington and Edith Marguerite (Foster) Chamberlin; m. Abbie Gertrude Enders, June 30, 1951; children: Abigail Gertrude, Daniel Lathrop, Caleb Enders. BA, Princeton U., 1947; MA, Yale U., 1953, PhD, 1961. Instr. Smith Coll., Northampton, Mass., 1955-61, asst. prof., 1961-66, assoc. prof., 1966; assoc. prof. U. Mich., Ann Arbor, 1966-73, prof., 1973-90, chmn. dept. history of art, 1985-88; vis. prof. Stanford U., 1983, U. Del., 1989; v.p. Olana Preservation, N.Y.C., 1964-66. Author: The Landscapes of Frederic Edwin Church, 1966, (exhbn. catalogue) Art and the Excited Spirit, 1972, The Quest for Unity: American Art Between World's Fairs, 1876-1893, 1983; mem. nat. adv. bd. Archives of Am. Art, 1980-90; mem. editorial bd. Am. Art Jour., from 1980; editorial adv. bd. Smithsonian Studies in Am. Art, 1986-90; contbr. articles to profl. jours. 2d lt. USAAF, 1943-45. Dixon Ryan fellow N.Y. Hist. Assn., 1963-64, Nat. Humanities Inst. fellow Yale U., 1975-76; Nat. Endowment for the Humanities grantee, 1978, 80. Mem. Coll. Art Assn. Am., Soc. Archtl. Historians, Am. Studies Assn., Victorian Soc. in Am., Am. Studies Assn. Democrat. Mem. Soc. of Friends. Home: Ann Arbor Mich. Died Sept. 30, 1990.

HUNTINGTON, HILLARD BELL, physicist, educator; b. Wilkes-Barre, Pa., Dec. 21, 1910; s. Frederick L. and Gertrude (Bell) H.; m. Ruth Smedley Wheeler, June 24, 1939; children: Frederic Wright, Hillard Griswold, David Champion. B.A., Princeton U., 1932, M.A., 1933, Ph.D., 1941; Dr. honoris causa, U. Nancy I, 1977. Teaching asst. U. Pa., 1941; physics instr. Washington U., 1941-42; staff mem. Radiation Lab., Mass. Inst. Tech., 1942-46; asst. prof. Rensselaer Poly. Inst., Troy, N.Y., 1946-48; assoc. prof. Rensselaer Poly. Inst., 1948-50, prof., 1950-76, chmn. dept. physics, 1961-69, prof. research, from 1976; vis. prof. Yale U., 1960-61, Cornell U., 1968-69; liaison officer Office Naval Research, London, Eng., 1954-55. Fellow Am. Phys. Soc. (chmn. div. solid state physics 1966-67); mem. Fedn. Am. Scientists, Sigma Xi. Home: Troy N.Y. Deceased.

HURLEY, DANIEL FRANCIS, retired labor relations arbitrator; b. Hartford, Conn., Nov. 21, 1911; s. Daniel Cornelius and Catherine Mary (Cunningham) H.; m. Mary Lou Crescence De Wan, Feb. 27, 1943; children: Patricia Lee, Daniel Michael, Tarasia. Student, Trinity Coll., Hartford, Conn., 1929-30, Cleve. Coll. Western Res., 1947-48; LL.B., Northeastern U., 1954. Bar: Mass. bar 1954. Substitute clk. Hartford P.O., 1930-32; moulder Colt Patent Firearms Co., Hartford, 1935-36; labor relations adviser Am. Fedn. Actors, N.Y.C., 1936-39; commr. U.S. Conciliation Service, Dept. Labor, Washington, 1939-41; resident commr. U.S. Conciliation Service, Dept. Labor, Cleve., 1941-44, regional supr. for service, 1944-46; asst. regional dir. U.S. Conciliation Service, Dept. Labor, 1946-47; (entire service trans. to Fed. Mediation and Conciliation Service 1947); regional dir. (entire service trans. to Fed. Mediation and Conciliation Service 1947), Boston, 1948-54; commr. (entire service trans. to Fed. Mediation and Conciliation Service 1947), 1954-78; arbitrator in labor relations, 1978-88; former instr. Univ. Coll., Northeastern U., Boston, ret., 1988. Contbr. articles to profl. jours. Recipient Cardinal Cushing award for excellence labor mgmt. as rep. of pub., 1967. Mem. Indsl. Relations Research Assn. (sec.-treas. Boston chpt. 1968-71), Boston (pres. 1971-72), Fed. bar assns. Roman Catholic. Clubs: K.C. (Cleve.), University (Cleve.). Home: Needham Mass. Deceased.

HURLEY, WILLIAM JOSEPH, lawyer, banker; b. Chgo., May 28, 1926; s. Ira William and Margaret Mary (Reilly) H.; m. Sheila Ann Sullivan, Dec. 28, 1957 (wid. Nov. 1989); children: Michael, Patrick, Anne, Kevin; m. Judith Adele Gardiner, Apr. 12, 1991. Grad., U.S. Mcht. Marine Acad., 1947; J.D. cum laude, U. Notre Dame, 1953. Bar: Ill. 1953. Law clk. to judge Ill. Appellate Ct., 1954-55; practiced law Chgo., 1955-67; counsel, asst. v.p. Talcott Bus. Finance, Chgo., 1968-73; v.p., gen. counsel Pioneer Bank & Trust Co., Chgo., 1974-78; sr. ptnr. Hurley, Kaluck & Schiller, Chgo., Ill., 1978-92; lectr. Ill. Inst. Continuing Legal Edn., 1972-78. Author: Sales and Financing Under Commercial Code, 1973, rev. edit., 1978; assoc. editor: Notre Dame Law Rev., 1952-53. Served to lt. USNR, 1953-54. Mem. ABA, Ill. Bar Assn., Woodstock Country Club, Mich. City Yacht Club. Democrat. Roman Catholic. Home: Chicago Ill. Died June 17, 1992.

HURSKY, JACOB P., Slavic languages and literatures educator; b. Zholdaky, Ukraine, Nov. 4, 1923; came to U.S., 1950; s. Pantelejmon and Hanna (Dziuba) H.; m. Valentina Shkilna, Nov. 15, 1953; children—Alexandra, Tatiana. Ph.M., Ukrainian Free U., Munich, Fed. Republic Germany, 1950; A.M., U. Pa., 1953, Ph.D., 1957. Grad. asst. in Russian Dickinson Coll, Carlisle, Pa., 1951-52; instr. Russian Pa. State U., University Park, 1954-55; asst. prof. Slavic langs. and lit. Syracuse U., N.Y., 1956-62, assoc. prof., 1962-72, prof., 1972-95, assoc. chmn. Slavic langs. and lits. dept., 1976-95; vis. prof. Harvard U., summer 1972, Ukrainian Free U., Munich, Federal Republic Germany, summers 1974-87. Co-editor: Symbolae in honorem Georgii Y. Shevelov, 1971; editor: Tribute to Hryhorij Kytasty, 1980, Studies in Ukrainian Linguistics in Honor of George Y. Shevelov, 1985, also others. George Leib Harrison fellow U. Pa., 1952-53, scholar, 1953-54. Mem. Am. Assn. Tchrs. Slavic and East European Langs., Am. Name Soc., Shevchenko Sci. Soc., Bulgarian Studies Assn., Ukrainian Acad. of Arts and Scis. in U.S. Home: Syracuse N.Y. Died Feb. 28, 1995.

HURWITZ, ALFRED, retired thoracic surgeon; b. Boston, 1908. MD, Johns Hopkins U., 1933. Diplomate Am. Bd. Thoracic Surgery, Am. Bd. Surgery. Intern Beth Israel Hosp., Boston, 1933-34, resident surgery, 1934-38; fellow in thoracic surgery Mass. G Hosp., Boston, 1939. Fellow ACS; mem. AASA AATCVS, Am. Soc. Anesthesiologists, New Eng. Su Soc. Home: Kennebunk Maine Died AUG. 21, 199

HUTCHENS, JOHN KENNEDY, journalist, editor; Chgo., Aug. 9, 1905; s. Martin Jay and Leila (Kenne H.; m. Katherine Regan Morris (dec.); children: An Timothy; m. Marjorie Kohl Brophy (dec.); m. Ruth Brine. AB, Hamilton Coll., 1926, LittD, 1951. porter Daily Missoulian and Sentinel, Missoula, Mo 1926-27; reporter, film critic, asst. drama editor N Evening Post, 1927-28; asst. editor Theatre Arts ma 1928-29, drama critic, 1929-32; drama staff N.Y. Tim 1929-32, 34-38, radio editor, 1941-44; drama cr Boston Evening Transcript, 1938-41; asst. editor N Times Book Rev., 1944-46, editor, 1946-48; book re columnist, reviewer N.Y. Herald Tribune, 1948-56, da book reviewer, 1956-63; mem. editorial bd. Book-of-Month Club, 1963-88. Author: One Man's Monta An Informal Portrait of a State, 1964; edit (anthology) The American Twenties: A Literary norama, 1952; (with George Oppenheimer) The Best the World, 1973, The Gambler's Bedside Book, 197 Mem. Authors Guild, Authors League Am., Du Treat Club (N.Y.C.), Sigma Phi. Democrat. Ho New York N.Y. Died July 22, 1995.

HUTCHINSON, WILLIAM DAVID, federal judge; Minersville, Pa., June 20, 1932; s. Elmer E. a Elizabeth (Price) H.; m. Louise Meloney, 1957; childr Kathryn, William, Louise, Andrew. B.A. magna c laude, Moravian Coll., 1954; J.D., Harvard U., 195 Bar: Pa. Private practice law Pottsville, Pa., 1958- asst. dist. atty. Schuylkill County, Pa., 1963-69, so itor, 1969-72; solicitor Blue Mountain Sch. Dist., C sona, Pa., 1967-81; justice Pa. Supreme Ct., Harrisbu 1982-87; judge U.S. Ct. Appeals (3d cir.), Pottsville, from 1987; chmn. Joint State Govt. Commn. Pa. G Assembly, 1981; mem. Pa. Jud. Council, 1980-82; me Pomeroy Commn. on Unified Jud. System, 1980-8 Mem. Pa. Ho. of Reps., 1973-81, chmn. ethics co 1981; mem. Blue Mountain Sch. Bd., 1963-66 Recipient John Amos Comenius award Moravian C 1982. Mem. ABA, Pa. Bar Assn., Assn. Trial Lawy Am., Pa. Trial Lawyers Assn., Am. Judicature S Schuylkill County Bar Assn. (com. continuing le edn.). Republican. Methodist. Home: Schyulkill Ha Pa. Deceased.

HUTTNER, MARIAN ALICE, library administra b. Mpls., Apr. 10, 1920; d. Frederick August and Hi Christina (Anderson) Huttner; m. Russell R. Ch tensen, Apr. 15, 1950 (div. 1961). BA summa c laude, Macalester Coll., 1941; BS in Library Science, Minn., 1942. Jr. libr. U. Minn., Mpls., 1941-42, li 1942-43, sr. libr., 1943-44, prin. libr. serials, 1944- prin. libr. archives, 1946-53; serials libr. Hamline U., Paul, 1954-56; adult libr. Mpls. Pub. Libr., 1956- rsch. asst., 1961-64, adult group cons., 1964-67, h sociology dept., 1967-69, head main libr. subject dep 1969-75; dep. dir. Cleve. Pub. Libr., 1976-85, inte dir., 1986; automated systems cons., 1987-96; adj. p Case Western Res. U., 1983-84; lectr. Kent State 1982-83. Author: Program for Branches of the Cle land Public Library, 1976; contbr. articles to pr jours. Mem. ALA (reference services com. 1973-7 Minn. Library Assn. (sec. 1961-67), Ohio Library As (awards com. 1984-85). Democrat. Presbyteria Home: Minneapolis Minn. Died Jan., 1996.

HUTTON, WARWICK BLAIR, writer, illustrator; London, July 17, 1939; s. John Campbell and He Sarah (Blair) H.; m. Elizabeth Mills, Aug. 26, 19 children: Hanno, Lily. Illustrator, painter and g engraver, free-lance artist, 1961-94; sr. lectr. Cambric shire (U.K.) Coll. Arts and Tech.; vis. lectr. Mo Coll., 1973-75. Author: Making Woodcuts, 1974, N and the Great Flood, 1977, The Sleeping Beauty, 19 The Nose Tree, 1981 (N.Y. Times award), Beauty a the Beast, 1985, Moses in the Bulrushes, 1986, Jo and the Great Fish, 1986 (Boston Globe/Horn Bo award, N.Y. Times award, Time mag. award), Ad and Eve, 1987, The Tinderbox, 1988, Theseus and Minotaur, 1989 (N.Y. Times award), To Sleep, 19 The Trojan Horse, 1992, Perseus, 1993, Perseph 1994; illustrator: The Silver Cow, 1983, The Selkie G 1986, Tam Lin, 1991. Home: Cambridge Eng. D Sept. 28, 1994.

HU YAOBANG, Chinese government official; Liuyang City, Hunan Province, 1915; m. Li Chao. H orgn. dept. Communist Youth League, 1935, mem. c com., 1936, 49, 1st sec., 1957-64; head orgn. dept. gen. polit. dept. 18th Corps, 1941, dir. polit. dept., 19 head polit. dept. 2d Field Army, 1949; vice ch Taiyuan Mil. Control Commn., 1949; mem. exec. Sino-Soviet Friendship Assn., 1949-54; dir., head and econs. com. North Sichuan People's Admins Office, 1950; polit. commissar North Sichuan Mil. D 1950; mem. SW Mil. and Adminstrv. Com., 1950- sec. New Dem. Youth League, 1952-57; mem. nat. c All-China Fedn. Dem. Youth, 1953-58; vice ch World Fedn. Dem. Youth, 1953-59; mem. standing c Nat. People's Congress, 1954-59, re-elected, 1959, mem. exec. com. All-China Fedn. Trade Unions, 19 57; mem. Cen. Work Com. for Popularization

Standard Spoken Chinese, 1956; vice chmn. Nat. Assn. for Elimination Illiteracy, 1956; mem. 8th Cen. Com. Chinese Communist Party, 1956-67, 11th Cen. Com., 1977, mem. Politburo, 1978, mem. Standing Com., 1980, chmn., 1981-82, mem. Politburo 12th Cen. Com., 1982, mem. Standing Com., 1982-87; mem. standing com. politburo 13th Cen. com., 1987—; acting 1st sec. Shaanxi com. Communist Party, 1965; sec.-gen. Cen. Com., 1978-80, dir. propaganda dept., 1979-80, sec.-gen. secretariat, 1980; 3d sec. Cen. Com. for Inspecting Discipline, 1978-81; gen. sec. Chinese Communist Party, 1980, 82-87. Home: Beijing People's Republic of China

HUYNH TAN PHAT, government official Socialist Republic Vietnam; b. 1913. Formerly editor Thanh-nien; joined Vanguard Youth, 1945; remained in South Vietnam after Geneva Agreement ending anti-French struggle, 1954; sec.-gen. Democratic Party; mem. central com. Nat. Liberation Front, 1964—; pres. Provisional Revolutionary Govt. Republic of South Vietnam, 1969-76, in Saigon, 1975-76; vice premier council of ministers Socialist Republic Vietnam, 1976-82; chmn. State Commn. for Capital Constrn., 1982-83; vice chmn. Council of State, 1982—. Home: Hanoi Socialist Republic of Vietnam

I'ANSON, LAWRENCE WARREN, retired state chief justice; b. Portsmouth, Va., Apr. 21, 1907; s. James Thornton and Emma (Warren) I'A.; m. May Frances Tuttle, Aug. 5, 1933; children: Lawrence Warren, May Frances (Mrs. Peter McCrae Ramsey). AB, Coll. William and Mary, 1928, LLD, 1964; LLB, U. Va., 1931; LLD, Dickinson Law Sch., 1980, Elon Coll., 1986. Bar: Va. 1931. Pvt. practice Portsmouth, 1931-41; atty. Commonwealth of Portsmouth, 1938-41; judge Ct. of Hustings (now Circuit Ct.), 1941-58; justice Supreme Ct. Va., 1958-81, chief justice, 1974-81; mem. Jud. Coun., 1948-70, chmn., 1974-80; chmn. com. that prepared Handbook for Jurors used in all cts. of record in Va.; mem. Coun. Higher Edn. of Va., 1956-59; chmn. Va. Ct. System Study Commn., 1968-71; sponsor Nat. Conf. on Judiciary, 1971; pres., chief exec. officer Beazley Found., Inc., 1981-88, chmn. bd. 1988-90; chmn. bd. Frederick Found., 1988-90; chmn. Conf. Chief Justices, 1979-80; chmn. State-Fed. Coun.; mem. Commn. on Future of Va., 1984-85; bd. dirs. Portsmouth Community Trust, from 1984. Trustee Eastern Va. Med. Sch. Found., 1970-79; tchr. I'Anson Bible Class, 1933-65. Recipient William and Mary Alumni medallion, U. Va. Sesquicentennial award, 1969, Lincoln Harley award Am. Judicature Soc., 1973, Disting. Svc. award Va. Trial Lawyers, 1973, Commonwealth award James Madison U., 1981; named First Citizen Portsmouth, 1946. Fellow Va. State Bar; mem. ABA (com. to implement standards on jud. adminstrn. 1975-78), Va. Bar Assn. (chmn. jud. sect. 1949), SAR (Meritorious Svc. medal 1987), Order of Coif, Phi Beta Kappa (pres. chpt. 1981-82), Pi Kappa Alpha, Omicron Delta Kappa, Phi Alpha Delta. Democrat. Baptist. Clubs: Harbor, Norfolk, Jesters, Nat. Sojourners, Mason (past dist. dep. Va.), Shriner, Kiwanian (past pres. Portsmouth), Moose. Home: Portsmouth Va. Deceased.

IBRAHIMOV, MIRZA AZHDAROGLU, writer; b. Sarab, Iran, Oct. 15, 1911; came to USSR, 1918; s. Azhdar and Zohraa Ibrahimov; m. Primova Sara, July 4, 1938 (dec. 1984); children: Zamira, Sevda, Aidyn, Yilmaz. Student, Leningrad (USSR) State U., 1936. Cert. philologist. Minister Ministry Edn. Azerbaijan, SSR, 1942-44; dep. chmn. Azerbaijan Soviet Socialist Republic Council of Ministers, 1944-48; 1st sec. Azerbaijan Soviet Socialist Republic Writer's Union, 1946-56, 66-72, chmn., 1980-87; sec. USSR Writers' Union, 1946-56, 66-72, 80-87, chmn. Azerbaijan com. for state prizes; chmn. Azerbaijan Soviet Socialist Republic Presidium of Supreme Soviet, 1954-58; dep. chmn. Presidium USSR Supreme Soviet, 1954-58; academician Azerbaijan Soviet Socialist Republic Acad. Scis., 1944—; chmn. soviet Afro-Asian Solidarity Com., 1977-87. Author: Let the Day Come, 1951 (USSR State prize). Dep. USSR Supreme Soviet, 1937—; mem. Azerbaijan Cen. Com. of Communist Party USSR, 1937—. Recipient Hero of Socialist Labor award USSR Supreme Soviet, 1981. Home: Baku USSR

ICHORD, RICHARD HOWARD, lawyer, former congressman; b. Licking, Mo., June 27, 1926; s. Richard Howard and Minda (Curtis) I.; m. Millicent Murphy Koch; children: Richard Howard, Pamela Lee, Kyle. B.S., Mo. U., 1949, J.D., 1952. Bar: Mo. 1952. Instr. bus. law U. Mo., 1950, 51; mem. firm Lay & Ichord, Houston, Mo., 1952-6O; city atty. Houston, 1952; mem. Mo. Ho. of Reps., 1953, speaker pro tem, 1957-58, speaker, 1959-60; mem. 87th-96th Congresses from 8th Mo. Dist.; pres. Washington Indsl. Team, Inc., 1980-84, Legis. Assocs. Internat., 1985-92; mem. firm Winthrop, Koontz, Righter, Clagett & Norquist, 1980-83. Served with A.C. USNR, 1944-46. Mem. VFW, Am. Legion, Houston C. of C. Democrat. Lodges: Masons; Odd Fellows. Home: Fort Washington Md. Died Dec. 1992.

IDRISS, FAROUK SALIM, pediatric cardiovascular-thoracic surgeon; b. Beirut, Jan. 10, 1928; came to U.S., 1953; s. Salim and Souheila (Jaroudi) I.; m. Lorraine Hartwick, Jan. 24, 1958; children: Samir, Rachid, Hamze, Salim. BA, Am. U., Beirut, 1949, MD, 1953. Intern Chgo. Wesley Meml. Hosp., 1953-54, resident in surgery, 1954-58; resident in plastic surgery Cook County Hosp., Chgo., 1955; resident in pediatric surgery Children's Meml. Hosp., Chgo., 1958-59, fellow in surg. rsch., 1959-62; resident in cardiovascular-thoracic surgery Hines VA Hosp., Chgo., 1970-71; prof. surgery Northwestern U. Med. Sch., Chgo. Contbr. articles to profl. jours. Fellow ACS, Am. Acad. Pediatrics, Chgo. Surg. Soc.; mem. Am. Pediatric Surg. Assn., Soc. Thoracic Surgeons, Am. Heart Assn., Am. Assn. Thoracic Surgery. Home: Chicago Ill. Died May 7, 1992.

INCHCAPE, EARL OF (KENNETH JAMES WILLIAM MACKAY), diversified company executive; b. Dec. 27, 1917; s. Earl and Joan I.; m. Aline Thorn Hannay, 1941 (div. 1954); 3 children: m. 2d, Caroline Cholmeley, 1965; 3 children. MA, Trinity Coll., Cambridge, Eng. Chmn., chief exec. Inchcape Plc, 1958-82, life pres., 1982-94; chmn. P & O Steam Navigation Co., 1973-83; dir. Standard Chartered Bank Ltd., Brit. Petroleum Co. Ltd. Pres. Commonwealth Soc. for the Deaf; chmn. Coun. for Middle East Trade, 1963-65; pres. Gen. Coun. Brit. Shipping, 1976-77; prime warden Shipwrights Co., 1967, Fishmongers Co., 1977-78. One of H.M. Commrs. of Lieutenancy for City of London, 1980-94. Died Mar. 17, 1994; interred Glenapp Estate Ayrshire, Scotland. Home: London England

INGERSLEV, FRITZ HALFDAN BENT, acoustics educator; b. Aarhus, Denmark, July 6, 1912; s. Christian and Helga Victorine (Raeder) I.; m. Else Ingeborg Margrethe Heiberg, May 29, 1948; children: Ib Ulrik, Steen Olaf, Dan Philip, Dorrit Margrethe. M in Elec. Engring., Copenhagen Tech. U., 1936, DSc, 1954. Research asst. Copenhagen Tech. U., 1936-41, asst. prof., 1942-53, prof. acoustics, 1954-82, prof. emeritus, 1982-94; engr. acoustics lab. Copenhagen Acad. Tech. Scis., 1941-45, dir., 1945-81. Author: Acoustics in Modern Building Practice, 1949 (Russian translation 1957, Chinese translation 1961), Measurement of Linear and Nonlinear Distortion in Electrodynamic Loudspeakers, 1953; contbr. articles to profl. jours. Recipient Din Ehrennadel Din Deutsches Institut für Normung, 1982, Acoustic Perspective "Homage Volume to Fritz Ingerslev", 1982, Danish Esso prize, 1952, Chr. Moller Sorensen Found. prize, 1961, Finn Henriksen Found. prize, 1969, medal Groupement Acousticiens de Langue Francaise, 1981. Fellow Am. Acoustical Soc., IEEE; mem. Internat. Inst. Noise Control Engring. (pres. 1974-89, Graham Bell medal 1986), Nat. Acad. Engring. (fgn. assn. 1982). Home: Charlottenlund Denmark Died Feb. 5, 1994.

INGRAM, E. BRONSON, oil production equipment industries executive; b. 1931. Grad., Princeton U., 1953. Officer Ingram Oil & Refining Corp., Nashville, 1955-62; with Ingram Corp., Nashville, 1962-78; pres., CEO Ingram Industries, Nashville, 1978-94; chmn., CEO Ingram Industries, Inc., Nashville, 1994-95. With USN, 1953-55. Home: Nashville Tenn. Died June 15, 1995.

INGRAM, WILLIAM TRUITT, sanitation engineer, educator; b. Cleves, O., June 16, 1908; s. Frank and Grace Lillian (Truitt) I.; m. Margaret B. Nelson, 1932; children: Beryl Ingram Crocker, Judith Ingram Nelson, John E., Diane F. Ingram Dennis; m. Filomena T. Lioy, Apr. 19, 1958. B.A., Stanford, 1930; M.P.H., Johns Hopkins, 1942. Diplomate Am. Acad. Environ. Engrs.; profl. engr. N.Y., N.J., Calif., Pa. Office engr. Pacific Gas & Electric Co., San Francisco, 1930-32; recorder U.S. Coast and Geodetic Survey, 1932-33; regional surveyor, supr. Fed. and State Mosquito Control, So. Cal. region, 1933-34; asst. county dir. Cal. Relief Adminstrn., 1934; san. engr. San Joaquin Local Health Dist., 1935-41; regional water works adviser Cal. Bur. San Engring., 1942; asst. regional san. engr. Office Civil Def., 9th region USPHS, 1942-44; camp san. engr. War Refugee Camps Middle East, Brit. Army, USPHS, UNRRA, 1943-44; chief engr. health div. UNRRA, Jugoslav Mission, 1944-46; engring, field asso. Am. Pub. Health Assn., 1947-49; asso. prof. pub. health engring. N.Y. U. Coll. Engring., 1949-54, adj. prof., 1954-73; adj. prof. Poly. Inst. N.Y., 1973-89; cons., 1947—; vis. prof. preventive med. div. Cornell U. Coll. Medicine, 1956-76; adj. prof. environ. engring. N.Y. Med. Coll., 1985-89; lectr. Columbia Sch. Pub. Health; owner Wm. T. Ingram (cons. engr.); mem. Chmn. Engring. Foun. coordinating com. Air Pollution Rsch., 1960-67. Author: The Proposed Sanitary Code- Part III, 1949; chmn. joint editorial bd.: Revision Glossary Water and Wastewater Control Engring., 1962-76; Contbr. to books, also articles to tech. jours.; mem. joint editorial bd.: Revision Glossary Water and Wastewater Control Engring., 1977-81. Recipient Kenneth Allen Meml. award., 1960, Milton T. Hill award, 1976. Fellow AAAS, Am. Pub. Health Assn., Am Soc. Chem. Engring. (chmn. rsch. coun. air resource engring. 1961-73, Am. Soc. Testing and Materials (2d vice chmn. com. D-22 1973-77, award 1976); mem. Am. Soc. Engring. Edn., Am. Indsl. Hygiene Assn., Inter-Am. Assn. San. Engring. (charter), Am. Nat. Standards Inst. (chmn. Z-4 com. 1971-81), Conf. Mcpl. Health Engrs., Am. Water Works Assn., Water Pollution Control Fedn., N.Y. Acad. Sci., Am. Chem. Soc., Assn. Ofcl. Agr. Chemists, Sigma Xi, others. Home: Kenwood Calif.

IONESCO, EUGÈNE, playwright; b. Slatina, Romania, Nov. 13, 1912; s. Eugene and Marie-Therese (Icard) I.; m. Rodika Burileano, July 12, 1936; 1 dau., Marie-France. License es Lettres, Agrege de Lettres. Formerly lectr., critic Bucharest. Author: The Bald Soprano, 1950, The Lesson, 1951, The Chairs, 1952, Le Grandes Chaleurs, 1953, Le Connaissez-vous?, 1953, Le Rhume Onirique, 1953, Le Jeune Fille a marier, 1953, Le Maitre, 1953, The Niece Wife, 1971, The Amedee, or How To Disengage Yourself, 1954, The New Tenant, 1955, The Painting, 1955, Jack, 1955, Improvisation, or The Shepard's Chamelion, 1956, The Future Is in Eggs, 1957, Impromtu pour la Duchesse de Windsor, 1957, Victims of Duty, 1957, Rhinoceros, 1959, Scene a quatre, 1959, The Killer, 1959, Le Jeune Homme a marier, 1960, Apprendre a marcher, 1960, De lire a deux, 1962, Exit The King, 1962, Le Pieton de l'air, 1963, Hunger and Thurst, 1966, Les Salvations, 1970, La Lacune, 1970, The Motor Show, 1970, L'Oeuf dur, pour preparer un oeuf dur, 1970, Ches le docteur, 1970, Le Cocotire en Flammes, 1970, D'Isidione, 1970, Histoire des bandits, 1970, Il t eut d'abord, 1970, Le Cons de Francais pour Americains, 1970, Wipe-Out Games, 1971, Macbett, 1972, Ce Formidable Bordel, 1973, The Man With The Suitcase, 1975, Entre la Vie et le Reve, 1977, Antidotes, 1977; screenplays: Monsieur Tete, 1959, Seven Capital Cities, 1962, La Vase, 1972; teleplays: ballet version The Lesson, 1963; radio plays: The Picture, 1957, Rhinoceros, 1959; books: Ionesco: Les Rhinoceros au theatre, 1960, The Colonel's Photograph, 1962, Notes et contre-notes, 1962, Journal en miettes, 1967 (autobiography), Story Number 1: For Children Under Three Years of Age, 1968, Present Past, Past Present, 1968 (autobiography), Mise en Train: Premiere Anne de francais, 1969, Story Number 2: For Children Under Three Years of Age, 1970, Story Number 3: For Children Over Three Years of Age, 1971, Discours de reception d'Eugene Ionesco a l'Academie francaise et reponse de Jean Dalay, 1971, The Hermit, 1974 (novel); also short stories; illustrator (book) Zouchy et quelques autres histoires, 1989. Decorated chevalier Legion of Honor; recipient Grand Prix du Theatre de la Societe des Auteurs, 1966, Le Prix National du Theatre, 1969, Prix Litteraire de Monaco, 1969, Austrian prize for European literature, 1971, Jerusalem prize, 1973, Ingersoll prize, 1985; Internat. Writers' fellow Welsh Arts Coun., 1973. Mem. Acad. Francaise. Home: Paris France Died Mar. 28, 1994.

IPPEN-IHLER, KARIN ANN, microbiologist, educator; b. Fountain Hill, Pa., Mar. 13, 1942; d. Arthur Thomas and Elisabeth Anne (Wagenplatz) Ippen; m. Garret Martin Ihler, May 2, 1970; children: Elisabeth Emma, Alexander Thomas. BA, Wellesley Coll., 1963; PhD, U. Calif., Berkeley, 1967. Instr. U. Calif., Berkeley, 1967; postdoctoral fellow Harvard U. Med. Sch., Boston, 1967-69, U. Edinburgh, Scotland, 1969-70; asst. prof. U. Pitts., 1971-76; assoc. prof. Tex. A&M U., College Station, 1977-84, interim head dept. med. microbiology, 1987-88, prof. microbiology, from 1984; Mem. NIH Microbial Chemistry Study Sect., 1978-82, NIH Cellular and Molecular Basis of Disease Rev. Com., 1985-89, H. Hughes Doctoral Fellowship program Genetics Panel, 1988, 89, 90, NIH Health Reviewers Res., 1989-93. Mem. editorial bd. Jour. Bacteriology, 1979-93; contbr. rsch. publs., book chpts. and rev. articles to profl. publs. NSF grad. fellow, 1966-67; Harold C. Ernst postdoctoral fellow, 1967-68; Am. Cancer Soc. postdoctoral fellow, 1968-70; grantee NIH, from 1972. Mem. Am. Soc. Microbiology, Genetics Soc. Am. Home: College Station Tex. Deceased.

IRWIN, RICHARD LOREN, systems management association executive; b. Los Angeles, Dec. 8, 1924; s. Loren Wilson and Letty Elizabeth (Tate) I.; m. Martha Louise Sutton, Dec. 15, 1945; children: Martha Jean, Carol Ann. Student, Lockyear's Bus. Coll., 1942-43, 46-48. Cert. assn. exec. Am. Soc. Assn. Execs. Mgr. machine acctg. dept. U.O. Colson Co., Paris, Ill., 1949-55; founder Nat. Machine Accts. Assn. (now Data Processing Mgmt. Assn.), Paris, 1951; internat. pres. Data Processing Mgmt. Assn., Paris, 1954-55, exec. sec., 1955-60; asst. adminstrv. dir. Am. Optometric Assn., St. Louis, 1960-62; exec. dir. Assn. for Systems Mgmt., Cleve., 1962-87, dir. spl. projects, 1987-90. Mem. bd. govs. Shriners Hosp. for Crippled Children; elder Presbyn. Ch. Served with USNR, 1943-46. Named to Hon. Order of Ky. Cols. Mem. Am. Soc. Assn. Execs. (life, cert.), Am. Legion, Masons, Shriners (potentate Al Koran Temple 1991), Elks, Moose. Republican. Home: Berea Ohio Died July 21, 1995.

ISAAC, SOL MORTON, lawyer; b. Columbus, Ohio, Dec. 5, 1911; s. Arthur J. and Bella (Loewenstein) I.; m. Dorothy Durlacher, Dec. 18, 1936 (dec.); children: Beatrice, Frederick Morton, Thomas Durlacher; m. Ilma Rifkin Glaser, Jan. 21, 1984. B.A., Yale U., 1933; J.D., Harvard U., 1936. Bar: Ohio 1936. Since practiced in Columbus; asso. firm James M. Butler, 1936-40, Butler & Isaac, 1940-47, Isaac, Postlewaite, O'Brian and Oman, 1950-72; sr. mem. firm Isaac & Isaac, 1972-76, Isaac, Graham & Nester, 1976-83, Isaac, Brant, Ledman and Becker, 1983-95; Sec., dir. Diamond Milk Products, Inc., 1959-70; chmn. bd. Sunday Creek Coal Co., 1970-71. Bd. dirs. United Community Coun. Columbus and Franklin County, 1958-95, pres., 1969-70; chmn. Gov.'s Survey Com. Mental Health, 1956-57; mem. Ohio

Commn. Children and Youth, 1961-62; mem. coun. on intercultural edn. Columbus Sch. Bd., 1966-68; bd. Ohio Citizens Coun. for Health and Welfare; pres., 1956-59, Family Service Assn. Am., 1953-54; v.p. Nat. Social Welfare Assembly, 1958-60; co-chmn. Nat. Conf. Lawyers and Social Workers, 1961-67; bd. dirs. Columbus Acad., 1947-65, v.p., 1948-59, disting. alumnus award, 1978; bd. dirs., exec. com. Riverside Meth. Hosp., 1965-81; bd. dirs. exec. com. Riverside Meth. Hosp. Found., 1983-89, chmn., 1985-86; bd. dirs. Columbus Area Leadership Lab. Inc., 1974-81, pres., 1979-80; bd. dirs. Nat. Legal Aid and Defender Assn., 1958-60. Lt. USNR, 1943-46. Recipient Brotherhood award Temple Israel, Columbus, 1973, Nat. Guardian of the Menorah award B'nai B'rith, 1974, Mayor's Community Service medal, 1978; Life with Dignity award Heritage House, Columbus, 1980. Fellow Am. Bar Found., Am. Coll. Trust and Estate Counsel; mem. ABA (chmn. sect. family law 1960-61), Ohio Bar Assn. (Ohio Bar medal 1972), Columbus Bar Assn. (pres. 1952-53, Community Service award 1969), Nat. Conf. Social Welfare (pres. 1964-65), The Arts and Edn. Coun. Greater St. Louis (bd. dirs. 1991-95). Home: Saint Louis Mo. Died June 1, 1995.

ISENBURGER, ERIC, artist; b. Frankfurt on Main, Germany, May 17, 1902; came to U.S., 1941, naturalized, 1949; s. Sally R. and Olga (Neumond) I.; m. Jula Elenbogen, Dec. 10, 1927. Student, Art Sch., Frankfurt on Main. One-man shows, Gallery Gurlitt, Berlin, 1933, Gallery Modern, Stockholm, 1934-38, Gallery Wolfgang Gurlitt, Munich, Germany, 1962, Knoedler Galleries, N.Y.C., 1941, 43, 45, 47, 48, 50, 53, 55, Balt. Mus., 1943, DeYoung Meml. Mus., San Francisco, 1945, Springfield (Mass.) Mus., 1945, Colorado Springs Fine Arts Center, 1945, John Herron Art Inst., Indpls., 1946, others; represented in permanent collections, Wadsworth Atheneum, Hartford, Conn., Mus. Tel-Aviv, Israel, Ency. Britannica, Pa. Acad. Fine Arts, Mus. Modern Art, Pa. Acad. Fine Arts, Corcoran Gallery Art, Bezalel Mus. of Jerusalem, John Herron Art Inst., Indpls., M.H. de Young Mus., San Francisco, Miami U. Art Mus., Oxford, Ohio, AAAL, Laguna Beach Art Mus., NAD, Philharmonic Hall, Lincoln Center, others. Recipient prize NAD, 1945, Edwin Palmer Meml. prize, 1957, Henry Ward Ranger Fund purchase, 1957, 80; 3rd prize Carnegie Inst., 1947; Medal of Honor, Pepsi Cola Art competition, 1948; 1st prize and Corcoran gold medal Corcoran Gallery Art, 1949; Thomas Proctor Prize NAD, 1963; Salmagundi Club prize, 1966; Edwin Palmer Meml. prize NAD, 1970; Andrew Carnegie prize, 1972; Aldro T. Hibbard Meml. award, 1976; Florence Brevoort-Eickemeyer prize Columbia U., 1980. Mem. NAD (coun. 1964-67, officer 1975-80, Isaac N. Maynard prize 1991), Audubon Artists (dir. painting 1979, award 1969, 78, 79, Jane Peterson medal and prize 1971, 78, Simex award 1979, Stefan Hirsch Meml. award 1981). Home: New York N.Y. Died Mar. 26, 1994; buried Westchester Hills Cemetery, N.Y.

ISRAEL, FRANKLIN DAVID, architect; b. N.Y.C., Dec. 2, 1945; s. Irving Isadore and Zelda (Carr) I. B.A., U. Pa., 1967; postgrad. Yale U., 1967-68; M.Arch., Columbia U., 1971. Urban designer N.Y.C. Planning Commn., 1968-70; designer Giovanni Pasanella Assocs., N.Y.C., 1971-73; sr. architect Shakestan Pahlavi, Teheran, Iran and London, Llewelyn Davies Assocs., London, 1975-77; lectr. archtl. design UCLA, 1977-83, adj. assoc. prof. Sch. Architecture and Urban Planning, 1983-96. Sponsor, Oppositions, N.Y., 1975; bd. dirs. Archtl. League N.Y., 1978; mem. Com. for Profl. Responsibility, Los Angeles, 1983. William Kinney fellow, 1970; recipient Lucille Snyder award, 1971; Gold medal AIA, 1970; recipient Rome prize, 1973-75; Progressive Architecture award with Llewelyn Davies, 1977. Corr. Gentlemen's Quar. Mag.; contbr. articles to profl. publs. Died June 10, 1996. Home: Los Angeles Calif.

ITALIAANDER, ROLF BRUNO MAXIMILIAN, writer, ethnologist, art director; b. Leipzig, Sachsen, Fed. Republic of Germany, Feb. 20, 1913; s. Curt and Charlotte (Toepfer) I. Attemded, various univs., Leipzig, Berlin and Rome. Writer Hamburg, Fed. Republic of Germany; founder, art dir. Mus. Rade am Schloss Reinbek, Hamburg; vis. prof. Inst. European Studies U. Vienna, 1959, U. Mich., Hope Coll., Kalamazoo Coll., 1961, Am. Negro Univs. and Colls., 1962, U. Bahia, Salvador, Brazil, 1967. Author: Diaboado Jules Lompo: Schwarz Weisser Dialog-Rolf Italiaander und sein Africa-Bild, 1989; also 30 books about Africa, 60 books about modern civilization including religion. Pres. Internat. Translater Congress, Hamburg, 1965. Recipient Disting. Achievement award Hope Coll., Mich., 1976, Order of Merit, Austria, 1977, Fed. Republic of Germany, 1984; named Officer of Honour Legion, Republic Senegal, 1980. Mem. Free Acad. Art Hamburg (co-founder, hon. sec., Hans-Henny Jahnn award 1964), German Translators Union (founder 1954, hon. pres. 1960), Rissho Kosei-kai Japan, Heinrich-Barth Soc. Germany. Home: Hamburg Germany

IVANIER, ISIN, manufacturing company executive; b. Vijnita, Romania, Apr. 9, 1906; s. Jacob and Perl (Weintraub) I.; m. Fancia Herling (dec.); children: Paul, Sydney. Grad., Technion, Haifa, Israel, 1982; DSc (hon.). Chmn., dir. Ivaco, Inc.; dir. Canron Inc.; bd. dirs. Wright's Canadian Ropes Ltd., Bakermet Inc., Docap (1985) Corp. Decorated Order of Can. Club: Montefiore. Home: Montreal Can. Died Sept. 21, 1994.

IVASHKO, VLADIMIR, Soviet government official, economist, engineer. Candidate mem. Cen. Com., Soviet Community Party, Moscow, 1986-89, mem., 1989-94; lst sec. Cen. Com., Ukrainian Communist Party, Kiev, 1989-94. Home: Ukraine Russia Died Nov. 14, 1994.

IVES, DERMOD, lawyer; b. London, Eng., Jan. 23, 1904; came to U.S., 1909, naturalized, 1928; s. Robert Franklin and Mildred (Card) I.; m. Kathleen Christy, May 17, 1928; children: Patricia (Mrs. O. Endicott Perry), Dermod. B.A., Columbia, 1925, J.D., 1928, M.A. in Internat. Law, 1928; LL.D. (hon.), Keuka Coll. Bar: N.Y. 1928. Since practiced in N.Y.C.; ptnr. Windels Marx Davies & Ives (and predecessors), 1938-89, ret., 1989; pvt. practice law N.Y.C. and Greenwich, 1989-92; dir., Chief counsel N.Y. Commn. to Revise Laws of Estates and Trusts, 1961-67. Vice chancellor L.I. Diocese Episcopal Ch., 1954-70, chancellor, 1971-72, adv. eccles. ct., 1958-62, standing com., 1962-72; trustee Jephson Ednl. Trusts No. 1 and No. 2; v.p. Nichols Found. Mem. ABA, N.Y. State Bar Assn., Nassau County Bar Assn. (pres. 1960-61), Assn. Bar City N.Y. Clubs: Stanwich (Greenwich, Conn.); University Glee, University. Home: Greenwich Conn. Died Apr. 30, 1992.

JABARA, PAUL FREDRICK, actor, composer; b. Bklyn., Jan. 31, 1948; s. Saleem and Olga (Azkoul) J. Composer numerous popular songs which earned platinum and gold records including Last Dance, The Main Event, No More Tears (Enough Is Enough), It's Raining Men; producer Barbra Streisand's Broadway Album (Grammy award), numerous others; appeared in Broadway mus. Hair, Jesus Christ Superstar (London Co.), Rocky Horror Show, Rachel Lily Rosenbloom (And Don't You Ever Forget It!); appeared in films including Midnight Cowboy, Medea, Lords of Flatbush, Thank God's It's Friday, others. Recipient Academy award, Grammy award, Golden Globe award. Home: Westport Conn. Deceased.

JACKSON, ELMER MARTIN, JR., former newspaper executive; b. Hagerstown, Md., Mar. 9, 1906; s. Elmer Martin and Blanche Beatrice (Bower) J.; m. Mary W. A. Conard, Aug. 27, 1929 (div.); children: Elmer Martin III, Allen Conard, Pamela Conard; m. Doris C. Grace, Apr. 18, 1972. A.B., St. John's Coll., Annapolis, Md., 1926. Reporter, sports editor, city editor Hagerstown and Annapolis, Md., 1920-30; editor Evening Capital and Md. Gazette, Annapolis, 1933-41; v.p., editor and gen. mgr. Evening Capital and Md. Gazette Newspapers, 1947-69; pres., pub. Anne Arundel Times, 1969-95; owner-pub. Worcester Democrat, Pocomoke City, Md.; gen. mgr., editor Capital-Gazette News, also County News, 1961-69; pres. and pub. Carroll County Times, Westminster, Md., Jackson Printing, Inc., Annapolis and St. Michael's, Md., 1975-95; owner Scott Book Ctr., Annapolis; bd. dirs. Md. Nat. Bank. Author: The Rat Tat, 1927, Annapolis, Three Centuries of Glamour, 1938, (nature study) The Baltimore Oriole, Maryland Symbols, 1964, (genealogy) Keeping the Lamp of Remembrance Lighted, 1985, Beautiful Lady Anne Arundel Calvert, 1989. Past pres. dist. and state press assns.; mem. evaluating commn. Instns. Higher Learning.; gen. chmn. Annapolis Tercentenary Commn., 1949; mem. bd. Fed. Council State Govt., Chgo. Alderman, Annapolis, 1932-36; pres. Anne Arundel County C. of C., 1961-65; del. Md. Legislature, 1937-41; pres. Anne Arundel Pub. Library Assn., 1942-87, life mem., pres. emeritus, 1988; pres. Fine Arts Festival Found.; chmn. Anne Arundel County Econ. Devel. Commn., State Capital Planning Commn.; pres. Md. Gov.'s Prayer Breakfast Soc., 1967-76; life mem. Salvation Army Bd. Comdr. USNR, 1941-47. Named hon. adm. U.S. Naval Acad., 1965, adm. Chesapeake Bay Navy, 1970; recipient Man of Yr. award Anne Arundel County, 1965, Trustee of Yr. award ALA, Dallas, 1984. Mem. Am. Soc. Newspaper Editors, Newcomen Soc., Md. Hist. Soc. (dir.), Naval Acad. Alumni Assn. (assoc.), Mil. Order World Wars (comdr.), Md. Soc. of SAR (pres. 1985-86), Sons Confederate Vets. (camp comdr.), Milit. Order Stars and Bars, Polit. Sci. Club, Sigma Delta Chi. Democrat. Episcopalian. Clubs: Nat. Press (Washington); Annapolis Athletic (past pres.), Annapolitan (sec.-treas.), Thirteen, Annapolis Yacht, Annapolis Roads Golf and Beach, Naval Academy Officers, Naval Academy Golf, Naval Academy Beach, Young Democratic of Anne Arundel County (past pres.); Knights of Golden Circle, Army-Navy (Washington); University, So. Md. Soc, Propeller. Lodges: Elks, Civitan (past pres. and dist. gov. internat. club). Home: Annapolis Md. Dec. July 17, 1995.

JACOBI, KLAUS, government official. Ph.D. in Econs., U. Bern. Mem Gen. Agreement on Tariffs and Trade (GATT), Geneva; dir. U.S.-Swiss relations Fed. Office of Fgn. Econ. Affairs, 1961; dep. chief Swiss delegation Gen. Agreement on Tariffs and Trade, Geneva; head econ. sect. Swiss Embassy, Washington, 1966-68; with Fed. Office Fgn. Econs. Affairs, 1968-73; Swiss ambassador at large for trade negotiations, 1973-84, Swiss ambassador to U.S., 1984—; prof. fgn. econ. policy U. Bern, 1971—. Served as col. Gen. Staff, Sw Armed Forces. Home: Washington D.C. Deceased.

JACOBS, DAVID H, professional baseball team e ecutive. Vice chmn. Cleveland Indians. Home: Clev land Ohio Died Sept. 17, 1992.

JACOBS, KEITH WILLIAM, psychologist, educat b. Ames, Iowa, Feb. 24, 1944; s. Cyril W. and Syl Jacobs; BA, U. No. Iowa, 1968; MA, Eastern Ill. U 1972; PhD, U. So. Miss., 1975; B. in Applied Scien Loyola U., 1993; Adj. instr. psychology Natchez br. So. Miss., 1974-75; asst. prof. psychology Loyola U New Orleans, 1975-79, assoc. prof., 1979-85, prof., fro 1985, chairperson, 1985-90; lectr. psychology Our La of Holy Cross Coll., New Orleans, 1976-80; aux. facul William Carey Coll. Sch. Nursing, New Orleans, 197 80. Active ACLU; exec. bd. Oak Harbor Homeown Assn., 1979-81. Served with U.S. Army, 1968-71. Fell Am. Psychol. Assn., Am. Psychol. Soc. (charter); me Southwestern Psychol. Assn., Midwestern Psych Assn., La. Acad. Scis., Southeastern Psychol. Ass Sigma Xi. Contbr. articles to sci. publs. Deceas Home: Pearlington Miss.

JACOBS, MELVIN, department store executive; 1926, 1926. Grad., Pa. State U., 1947. Mdse. m Bloomingdales, 1947-71; pres. then chmn., chief ex officer federated Miami based div. Burdines, 1972-7 vice chmn., bd. dirs. Federated Dept. Stores Inc., 197 82; former chmn., chief exec. officer Saks and C Louisville, from 1982; chmn., chief exec. officer Sa Fifth Ave. Home: New York N.Y. Died Oct. 6, 1993.

JACOBS, RITA GOLDMAN, retired anesthesiologi b. N.Y.C., Jan. 15, 1927; d. Joseph and Miriam (Fe stein) Goldman; m. David Jack Jacobs, Nov. 28, 19 children: Etta Miriam, MeMe Jacobs Rasmussen. B NYU, 1947; MD, Woman's Med. Coll. Pa., 1951 Diplomate Am. Bd. Anesthesiology. Intern Quee (N.Y.) Gen. Hosp., 1951-52; resident in anesthe Columbia Presbyn. Med. Ctr., N.Y.C., 1952-54, tending anesthesiologist, 1954-58; attending anesthe ologist Meml. Sloan Kettering Cancer Ctr., N.Y. 1958-71; assoc. prof. anesthesiology Cornell Med. Sc N.Y.C., 1968-71; anesthesiologist Berkshire Med. C Pittsfield, Mass., 1971-91; chmn. dept. anesthesiolo Berkshire Med. Ctr., Pittsfield, 1975-84, med. dir. pa clinic, 1986-92; med. dir. Crane Ctr. for Day Surge Berkshire Med. Ctr., Pittsfield, 1984-91; pvt. pract pain mgmt. Pittsfield, 1992; ret., 1992; pres. Berksh Anesthesiologist, PC, Pittsfield, 1975-84, sec., 1984-9 Author, researcher: (scientific exhibit) Use Microhematocrits in Monitoring Changes in Blo Volume During and After Surgery, 1960 (1st Pr Postgrad. Assembly of N.Y. State Soc. of Anesthesio gists); contbr. articles to med. jours. Fellow Am. C Anesthesiologists; mem. AMA, Mass. Med. Soc., Ma Anesthia Assn., Berkshire Dist. Med. Soc. (v.p. 1986- sec. 1988-92, pres.-elect 1992-93), Nat. Abortion Rig Action League, LWV. Democrat. Jewish. Hon Stephentown N.Y. Died Dec. 1, 1993.

JACOBSEN, ROLF, poet; b. Oslo, Mar. 8, 1907; Petra Tendø, 1940; 2 children. Student, U. Oslo formerly journalist for local newspaper, Ham Norway. Author: (poems) Soil and Iron, 1933, Crow 1935, Long-Distance Trains, 1951, Secret Life, 19 The Summer in the Grass, 1956, Letter to the Lig 1960, The Silence Afterwards, 1965, Headlines, 19 Stand Clear of the Doors, Please, 1972, Collect Poems, 1973, Breathing Exercise, 1975, Twenty Poem 1977, Think About Something Else, 1979, Open Night, 1985, All My Poems, 1990. With Norwegi Army, 1927. Recipient Norwegian Critics' prize, 19 Riksmål prize, 1965, Doubloug prize Swedish Aca 1968, Nordic prize, 1989. Mem. Norwegian Ac Lang. and Lit. Home: Hamar Norway Died 199

JACOBSON, LEONARD, architect; b. Phila., Mar. 1921; s. David and Rose (Tollman) J.; m. Joan Ka July 10, 1950; children: Eric, Daniel. B.Arch., U. P 1942, M.Arch., 1947. Registered architect, N.Y., Mas Staff architect various firms N.Y.C., 1947-53; with I. Pei & Ptnrs., N.Y.C., 1953-92, assoc. ptnr., 1968- ptnr. I.M. Pei. & Ptnrs., N.Y.C., 1980-92. Served w AC U.S. Army, 1942-45, Africa, Middle East, Indi Decorated Officier de l'Ordre des Arts et des Lettr France, 1989. Fellow AIA; mem. N.Y. chpt. AIA, A Arbitration Assn. Democrat. Jewish. Home: Briarc Manor N.Y. Died Dec. 26, 1992.

JAFFE, BERNARD MORDECAI, physics educator; N.Y.C., Mar. 7, 1917; s. Allen and Ida (Slavin) J.; Emily May Landes, Apr. 20, 1962. BS, CCNY, 19 PhD, NYU, 1962. Engr. Amperex Electronic Produ Co., N.Y.C., 1940-41; physicist Signal Corps Labs, Monmouth, N.J., 1941-44; engr. Lloyd Rogers & C N.Y.C., 1944-45, Airborne Instrument Labs, N.Y. 1945-46; tutor, lectr. in Physics CCNY, 1946-49, 52- instr. Stevens Inst. Tech., Hoboken, N.J., 1956-59; fr asst. prof. to prof. Adelphi U., Garden City, N.Y., 19 83, emeritus prof. physics, from 1983; asst. prof., ass prof., vis. prof. Columbia U., N.Y.C., 1959-68; vis. a prof., assoc. prof. NYU, N.Y.C., 1961-63. Transla Optical Image Formation and Processing, 1979; paten in field. Fellow Atomic Energy Commn., 1949-5 em. Am. Phys. Soc., Optical Soc. Am., Am. Assn. ysics Tchrs. Home: New York N.Y. Deceased.

FFE, NORA, artist; b. Urbana, Ohio, Feb. 25, 1928; Harry Jefferson and Margaret Elizabeth (McNab) ller; m. Joseph Jaffe, Jan. 19, 1951; children: Lenore Kenneth A. Represented by Virginia Lust Gallery, Y.C. One person shows, Village Art Center, N.Y.C., 53, Sachs Gallery, N.Y.C., 1965, Gallery Lasson odern Art, London, 1970, Open Studio Gallery, inebeck, N.Y., 1978, Vasar Coll., Poughkeepsie, Y., 1979, Pastoral Gallery Art, Easthampton, N.Y., 83, Va. Lust Gallery, N.Y.C., 1990, Montclair State ll., N.J., 1990; exhibited in group shows, Mus. odern Art, N.Y.C., 1961, 64, Pa. Acad. Fine Arts, 54, 67, 68, David Stuart Galleries, Los Angeles, 1969, Mus. Fine Arts, Richmond, 1970, Orpheus As- ading, Stockbridge, Mass., 1971, New Sch. Art ntre, N.Y.C., 1973, Albin Ziegler Gallery, N.Y.C., 73, Grad. Center CUNY, 1978, A.I.R. Gallery, Y.C., 1983-84, Montclair State Coll., N.J., 1986, Soho Gallery, N.Y.C., 1988, WCA, Homage to Adam, no N.Y. Viewing Rm., N.Y., 1990; represented in manent collection, Pa. Acad. Fine Arts, Phila., Finch ll. Mus., N.Y.C., MacDowell Colony, Pan Am. lg., N.Y.C., Univ. Art Mus., U. Calif., Berkeley, lyn. Mus. MacDowell Colony resident, 1969, 70. llock-Krasner Found. grantee, 1991-94. Mem. N.Y. tists Equity Assn. Home: New York N.Y. Died Oct. 1994.

FFE, NORMAN, architect; b. Chgo., Apr. 3, 1932; Sarah Stahl Jaffe; children: Will, Max, Miles. adent, U. Ill., 1950, Chgo. Art Inst., 1953; B.A. in chitecture, U. Calif.-Berkeley, 1957. Registered hitect, N.Y., Calif., Conn., N.C., Pa., N.J., Ga., Ill., x., Mass., Mont., Wash., Va., Colo. Architect, dmore, Owings & Merrill, Chgo., 1956, Marquis & oller, San Francisco, 1957-58, Malone & Hopper, San ancisco, 1958-59, Sleight Assocs., San Francisco, 59-61, Philip Johnson, N.Y.C., 1961-64; prin. Norman Jaffe, Bridgehampton, N.Y., 1964-93; Fellow FAIA, n. Inst. of Archs.; mem. Mayor's Panel N.Y. chitects. Recipient numerous awards for residential sign, including: Archtl. Record, 1964, 71, 77, 78; N.Y. te Assn. Architects, 1975, 80; L.I. chpt. AIA, 1979, 84; N.Y. Masonry Inst., 1984. Mem. AIA. Died ot. 12, 1993; interred East Hampton, N.Y. Home: dgehampton N.Y.

MES, SYDNEY VINCENT, history educator; b. go., Mar. 9, 1929; s. Sydney Vincent and Caroline atrice (Topping) J.; m. Jean Wooster Middleton, July 1950; children—Samuel Wooster, Catherine Ly- A.B. cum laude, Harvard, 1950, A.M., 1951, Ph.D., 58. Instr. history Kent State U., 1956-58; asst. prof. own U., 1959-62, U. Oreg., 1962-65; asso. prof. U. va, Iowa City, 1965-67; prof. history U. Iowa, 1967- chmn. dept., 1970-74, 92-93. Author: A People nong Peoples; Quaker Benevolence in Eighteenth- ntury America, 1963, Colonial Rhode Island-A His- y, 1975; Contbr. articles to profl. jours. Recipient alter Muir Whitehill prize in colonial history, 1984; antee-in-aid Social Sci. Research Council, 1963; antee-in-aid Center for Study History of Liberty in n., 1963-64; Grantee-in-aid Am. Council Learned cs., 1964-65; Grantee-in-aid Nat. Endowment for manities, 1972-74; Grantee-in-aid Charles Warren nter for Studies in Am. History, Harvard U., 1979-80. ellow R.I. Hist. Soc.; mem. Am. Hist. Assn., Orgn. n. Historians, Colonial Soc. Mass., Internat. Commn. History of Rep. and Parliamentary Instns. Home: va City IA.

MESON, WILLIAM JAMES, retired federal judge; Butte, Mont., Aug. 8, 1898; s. William J. and Annie Roberts) J.; m. Mildred Lore, July 28, 1923; children: ary Lucille (Mrs. Walker Honaker), William James, A.B., Mont. U., 1919, J.D., 1922, LL.D., 1952; .D., U. Man., Can., 1954, Rocky Mountain Coll., 59; Dr. Laws, McGeorge Coll. Law, 1965. Bar: ont. 1922. Assoc. Johnston, Coleman and Johnston, lings, 1922-29; mem. Johnston, Coleman & Jameson, 29-40, Coleman, Jameson & Lamey, 1940-57; judge S. Dist. Ct. for Mont., 1957-69, sr. judge, 1969-87; dge Temporary Emergency Ct. Appeals, 1976-87; Bd. s. Nat. Jud. Coll., 1963-64; trustee Nat. Inst. Trial vocacy, 1971-77. Mem. Mont. Ho. of Reps., 1927- Sch. Bd. Trustee, Billings, 1930-32; chmn. Yellow- ne County chpt. A.R.C., 1931-45. Recipient Disting. hievement award Law Sch., Gonzaga U., 1970. llow Am. Bar Found.; mem. ABA (bd. govs. 1943-46, embly del. 1946-53, pres. 1953-54, pres. endowment 51-63, chmn. sect. jud. adminstrn. 1963-64, chmn. spl. n. on adminstrn. criminal justice 1969-73, recipient d medal 1973), Mont. Bar Assn. (pres. 1936- 37), n. Law Inst. (mem. council from 1956), Am. Judica- e Soc. (pres. 1956-58, Herbert Lincoln Harley award 74), Am. Legion, Phi Delta Phi. Methodist. Lodges: asons; Lion (dist. gov. 1941-42). Home: Billings ont. Deceased.

MIESON, HENRY LOUIS, investment executive; Ft. Wayne, Ind., Aug. 28, 1911; s. Henry L. and len May (Jones) J.; m. Georgia Marie Homsher, Dec. 1935; children: Caroline Hagopian, Elizabeth othman, Edward B. AB, George Washington U., 36. Div. mgr. Investors Diversified Service, San Francisco, 1946-53; pres. H.L. Jamieson Inc., San Francisco, 1954-57, Hare's Ltd., N.Y.C., 1957-61, King Merrit & Co., N.Y.C., 1961-63; chmn. bd. Trust Securities Corp., Boston, 1963-67, Winfield & Co., Inc., San Francisco, 1967-73; chmn. Franklin Family of Funds, San Mateo, Calif., 1973-93; bd. dirs. N.W. Life Assurance Co. Am. Served to lt. comdr. USNR, 1943-46. Republican. Clubs: Commonwealth (San Francisco); Peninsula Golf and Country (San Mateo). Home: Menlo Park Calif. Died July 20, 1993.

JANES, G(EORGE) SARGENT, physicist; b. Bklyn., Apr. 12, 1927; s. Warham W. and George Sargent (Leubuscher) J.; m. Ann P. Brown, June 29, 1952; children: William, Thomas, Catherine, George, Susan. BA, Cornell U., 1949; PhD, MIT, 1953. Mem. rsch. staff divsn. nuclear sci. Indsl. Coop., MIT, Cambridge, 1953-56; prin. rsch. scientist Avco Everett (Mass.) Rsch. Lab., 1956-74, v.p. isotope rsch., 1974-82, dir. laser isotope rsch. program, 1974-81, dir. dye laser tech., 1983-87; v.p. rsch. Jersey Nuclear Avco Isotopes, Inc.; vis. scientist, rsch. affiliate, mem. adv. com. MIT Regional Laser Ctr., 1981-93; assoc. Woods Hole Oceanographic Inst., 1983; ind. cons. physics and med. applications of lasers Lincoln, Mass., 1987-93; bd. dirs. Valley Pond Corp., Lincoln. Contbr. articles to profl. jours. Mem. Lincoln Bd. Assessors. Fellow AIAA (assoc.), Am. Phys. Soc.; mem. AAAS, Appalachian Mountain Club (past mem. governing coun.), Sigma Xi. Home: Lincoln Mass. Died Aug. 14, 1993; interred Lincoln Cemetary, Lincoln, Mass.

JANEWAY, ELIOT, economist; b. N.Y.C., Jan. 1, 1913; s. Meyer Joseph and Fanny (Siff) J.; m. Elizabeth Hall, Oct. 29, 1938; children: Michael, William. Ed., Cornell, 1932; grad. student, London Sch. Econs. Former adviser to U.S. presidents; former bus. editor Time mag., N.Y.C., former adviser to editor-in-chief; former cons. bus. trends Newsweek mag.; econ. adviser numerous industries; pub. Janeway Letter; pres., dir. Janeway Pub. & Research Corp., N.Y.C.; chmn., chief exec. officer Classic Rarities Inc., N.Y.C.; chmn. Classic Rarities, Inc. Author: The Struggle for Survival, 1951, reissue, 1968, The Economics of Crisis, 1968, What Shall I Do With My Money?, 1970, You and Your Money, 1972, Musings on Money, 1976, Prescriptions for Prosperity, 1983; contbg. writer to Commonweal, Barron's, N.Y. Times; contbr. numerous publs. Berkeley fellow Yale U. Home: New York N.Y. Died Feb. 8, 1993.

JEGHERS, HAROLD JOSEPH, internist, educator; b. Jersey City, Sept. 26, 1904; s. Albert and Matilda (Gerckens) J.; m. Isabel J. Wile, June 21, 1935; children: Harold, Dee, Sanderson, Theodore. B.S., Rensselaer Poly. Inst., 1928; M.D., Western Res. U., 1932; D.Sc. (hon.), Georgetown U., 1975, Coll. Medicine and Dentistry of N.J., 1976. Intern 5th Med. Svc., Boston City Hosp., 1933-34, resident, 1935-37, physician-in-chief, 1943-46, cons. physician, 1946-66; instr. to assoc. prof. medicine Boston U. Sch. Medicine, 1935-46; prof. and dir. dept. medicine Georgetown U. Sch. Medicine, 1946-56; prof., dir. dept. medicine N.J. Coll. Medicine and Dentistry, Jersey City, 1956-66, emeritus, 1966-90; med. dir. St. Vincent Hosp., Worcester, Mass., 1966-78, emeritus, 1979-90; prof. med. edn. Office Med. Edn. Rsch. and Curriculum Devel., Northeastern Ohio Univs. Coll. Medicine, 1977-86 ; cons. med. edn. St. Elizabeth Hosp., Youngstown, Ohio, 1977-90, Cleve. Health Scis. Libr., Case Western Res. U. and Cleve. Med. Libr. Assn., 1979-86; prof. Tufts U., 1966-74; dir. med. ward svc. Jersey City Med. Ctr., 1958-66; dir. Tufts med. svc. Boston City Hosp., 1969-71; cons. medicine Georgetown U. Sch. Medicine, 1957-59; rep. from A.C.P. to div. med. scis. NRC, 1950-53. Author articles and sects. in books.; developer: Jeghers Med. Index System. Recipient Laetare award Guild of St. Luke, Boston, 1958; Disting. Alumni award Case Western Res. U. Sch. Medicine, 1974. Fellow A.C.P., Am. Soc. for Clin. Investigation; mem. A.M.A., Am. Fedn. for Clin. Rsch., So. Soc. for Clin. Rsch. (v.p. 1948-49), Assn. Am. Physicians, Mass. Med. Soc., Sigma Xi. Home: Marshfield Mass. Died Sept. 21, 1990.

JENKINS, GEORGE W., retail grocery executive; b. 1907. Founder, chmn.-emeritus Publix Super Markets Inc., Lakeland, Fla., 1930-96. Home: Lakeland Fla. Died Apr. 8, 1996.

JENKINS, M. T. PEPPER, anesthesiologist, educator; b. Hughes Springs, Tex., 1917. MD, U. Tex., 1940. Diplomate Am. Bd. Anesthesiology. Intern U. Kans. Hosp., Kansas City, 1940-41; asst. resident internal medicine John Sealy Hosp., Galveston, Tex., 1941-42; resident in surgery Parkland Mem. Hosp., Dallas, 1946-47; asst. resident in anesthesiology Mass. Gen. Hosp., Boston, 1947-48; resident in Anesthesiology Parkland Mem. Hosp., Dallas; McDermott prof. of Anestesiology U. Tex. Southwestern Med. Sch., Dallas; former dir. anesthesiology Children's Med. Ctr., Tex. Scottish Rite Hosp., VA Hosp., Lisbon, Tex.; former cons. anesthesiology Presbyn. Hosp., Baylor U. Med. Ctr., Meth. Hosp., St. Paul Hosp. Lt. comdr. M.C., USNR, 1942-46. Fellow Am. Coll. Anesthesiologists, Faculty of Anaesthetists Royal Coll. Surgeons Eng., Faculty of anaesthetists, Royal Coll. Surgeons Ireland; mem. AMA (Disting. Svc. award 1988), Am. Soc. Anesthesiologists, Am. Coll. Allergists, Am. Urol. Assn., Internat. Anesthesia Rsch. Soc., Australian Soc. Anesthesiology (hon.). Home: Dallas Tex. Died Nov. 21, 1996.

JENKS, HOMER SIMEON, newspaper editor, freelance writer; b. Waltham, Mass., Nov. 13, 1914; s. Willard Irving and Iva Mae (Shepardson) J.; m. Beryl Louise Clinton, Sept. 21, 1940 (dec. 1966); m. Moira Catherine O'Connor, Aug. 19, 1968; 1 dau., Jacqueline Moira. Student, Boston U., 1932-35. City editor Quincy (Mass.) Evening News, 1931-35; staff corr. United Press, Boston, N.Y.C., London, 1935-52; assoc. editor Collier's, 1952-56, Newsweek, 1956-57; exec. news editor Boston Traveler, 1957-62, mng. editor, 1962-64; editor Sunday Herald Traveler, 1964-72; asst. mng. editor Boston Herald Am., 1972-73, assoc. editor, 1976-82; mng. editor Sunday Herald Advertiser, 1973-76; asst. mng. editor Boston Herald, 1983-90; freelance writer, 1990-95; lectr. Simmons Coll., 1977-82. Home: Boston Mass. Died Feb. 23, 1995; interred Scituate, Mass.

JENNER, RICHARD HOWARD, concrete pipe and steel manufacturing company executive; b. Heuvelton, N.Y., Apr. 7, 1930; s. Charles Albert and and Etta Maria (Dewey) J. B.S., Ithaca Coll., 1951. Various adminstrv. positions Ameron, Inc., Monterey Park, Calif., 1957-70; sec.-treas. Ameron, Inc., 1970-77, v.p., 1977-95. Served with USN, 1951-55. Mem. Los Angeles Nat. Assn. Accountants, Risk and Ins. Mgmt. Soc. Club: Los Angeles Stock Exchange. Home: Pasadena Calif. Deceased Dec. 11, 1995.

JERNE, NIELS KAJ, scientist; b. London, England, Dec. 23, 1911; s. Hans Jessen and Else Marie (Lindberg) J.; m. Ursula Alexandra Kohl, 1964; 2 children. Grad., U. Leiden, U. Copenhagen; hon. degrees, U. Chgo., U. Copenhagen, U. Basel, U. Rotterdam, Columbia U. Research worker Danish State Serum Inst., Copenhagen, 1943-55; chief med. officer WHO, Geneva, 1956-62; prof. biophysics U. Geneva, 1960-62; chmn. dept. microbiology U. Pitts., 1962-66; prof. exptl. therapy J.W. Goethe U., Frankfurt, 1966-69; dir. Basel Inst. for Immunology, 1969-80; prof. Inst. Pasteur, Paris, 1981-82; bd. dirs. Paul Ehrlich Inst. Contbr. articles to profl. jours. Del. Nobel prize for medicine, 1984. Recipient Marcel Benoist prize, Berne, 1979, Paul Ehrlich prize, Frankfurt, 1982. Fellow Royal Soc. London; mem. NAS, Danish Royal Soc. Scis. Copenhagen, Am. Philos. Soc., Acad. des Sciences de l'Inst. de France, Am. Acad. Arts and Scis., Croatian Acad. Scis. and Arts Zagreb. Home: Castillon-du-Gard France Died Oct. 7, 1994.

JESSAR, JONATHAN SANDER, public relations executive, consultant; b. Phila., Nov. 27, 1943; s. Joseph and Betty (Salsburg) J.; m. Gayle Harrison, Nov. 10, 1979. B.A., Temple U., 1966. Journalist, Anchorage Daily Times, 1967-69; pub. relations specialist Gen. Foods Corp., White Plains, N.Y., 1969-72; assoc. dir. pub. affairs Soap and Detergent Assn., N.Y.C., 1972-73; sr. v.p. Hill & Knowlton, Washington, 1973-81; exec. v.p., dir. Gray and Co., Washington, 1981-83; exec. v.p., gen. mgr. Burson-Marsteller, Washington, 1983-89; vice chmn. Cassidy and Assocs., Washington, from 1989. Author: Who's There, 1969. Chief of staff for communications Reagan-Bush presdl. campaign, Washington, 1980; communications steering com. Greater Washington Bd. Trade, 1982-87, disting. adv. com. Am. U. Sch. Communications, from 1986. Served with U.S. Army, 1966-69. Recipient Ace High award Arctic Hacks Assn., Anchorage, 1969. Mem. Pub. Relations Soc. Am., Media Found, Pi Lambda Phi. Republican. Clubs: Capitol Hill, International (Washington). Deceased. Home: Easton Md.

JEWETT, PAULINE, Canadian legislator; b. St. Catharines, Ont., Can., Dec. 11, 1922; d. Frederick Coburn and Ethel Mae (Simpson) J. Student, Queen's U., Can., Harvard U., U. London, London Sch. of Econs. Prof. polit. sci. Carleton U., 1955-74; pres. Simon Fraser U., 1974-78; mem. Can. Ho. of Commons, 1963-65, 79—. Mem. New Democratic Party. Home: Burnaby Can.

JOHN, FRITZ, mathematician, educator; b. Berlin, Germany, June 14, 1910; came to U.S., 1935, naturalized, 1941; s. Hermann and Hedwig (Buergel) Jacobsohn-John; m. Charlotte Woellmer; children: Thomas Franklin, Charles Frederic. PhD, Goettingen (Germany) U., 1933; student, Cambridge (Eng.) U., 1934-35; hon. degrees, U. Rome, U. Bath, U. Heidelberg. Asst., the assoc. prof. U. Ky., 1935-42; mathematician Aberdeen Proving Grounds, 1942-45; prof. math. N.Y. U., 1946-94; Courant prof. Courant Inst., 1976-79; dir. Research Inst. Numerical Analysis, Nat. Bur. Standards, 1950-51; spl. research applied math., math. analysis; Sherman Fairchild disting. scholar Calif. Inst. Tech., 1979-80; Josiah Willard Gibbs lectr. Am. Math. Soc., 1975. Author: Plane Waves and Spherical Means, 1955, (with L. Bers and M.S. Schechter) Partial Differential Equations, 1964, (with R. Courant) Introduction to Calculus and Analysis, 1965, Partial Differential Equations, 1978. Recipient G.D. Birkhoff prize in Applied Math., 1973; Rockefeller fellow, 1935, 42; Fulbright lectr. Goettingen U., 1955; Guggenheim travel grantee, 1963, 70; Sr. U.S. Scientist Humboldt award, W. Ger., 1980-81; Benjamin Franklin fellow Royal Soc. Arts; MacArthur fellow, 1984. Mem. Nat. Acad. Scis., Am. Math. Soc. (Steele prize 1982),

AAAS, Math. Assn. Am., Deutsche Akademie der Naturforscher Leopoldina, Sigma Xi. Home: New York N.Y. Died Feb. 1994.

JOHNS, SAMUEL EARL, JR., industrial consultant; b. Brookville, Pa., Mar. 17, 1927; s. Samuel Earl and Alta Lynne (Fonner) J.; m. Molly Margaret Helmheckel, July 6, 1952; children: Alan Ross, Samuel Earl III, Clyde William, Jo Allison. B.S., Clarion State U., 1950. Sta. mgr. Birdwell, Inc. (now div. Seismograph Service Corp.), Tulsa, 1952-58; sr. v.p. tech. Gearhart Industries, Inc., Fort Worth, 1958-95. Author: Basic Electric Log Manual, 1955; contbr. articles to profl. jours.; patentee in field. Served with USN, 1943-46. Republican. Club: Century II (Fort Worth). Home: Fort Worth Tex. Deceased Feb. 21, 1995.

JOHNSON, ANNE MARCOVECCHIO, book publishing executive; b. Staten Island, N.Y., May 22, 1931; d. Martin and Wilhelmina (Baldaccheri) MarcoV.; m. Hugh Johnson, Sept. 25, 1965 (dec. Feb. 1987). BA, Hunter Coll., 1953. Exec. sec. Doubleday & Co., Inc., N.Y.C., 1953-57; exec. sec. Random House, Inc., N.Y.C., 1957-67, asst. to pres., 1967-69, div. v.p., 1969-89, also bd. dirs.; asst. pub. at large John Wiley and Sons, Inc., 1990-93. Bd. dirs. Fund for Free Expression, N.Y.C., 1975, Helsinki Watch, N.Y.C., 1979, Ams. Watch, N.Y.C., 1981; asst. to chmn. Human Rights Watch, 1990-93. Mem. Assn. Am. Pubs. Internat. Freedom to Publish, Essex County Country Club (West Orange, N.J.). Home: Clifton N.J. Died June 13, 1993.

JOHNSON, DAVID ELLIOT, bishop; b. Newark, Apr. 17, 1933; s. Theodore Eames and Frances Lysett (Wetmore) J.; m. Joyce Joanne Evans, Feb. 24, 1958; children: Stephanie Johnson Duensing, Elizabeth Johnson, Scott Johnson. BA, Trinity Coll., 1955; MDiv, Va. Theol. Coll., 1961; postgrad., Coll. Preachers, 1970, 74, 78, 81, 83; DD, Va. Theol. Sem., 1986, Trinity Coll., 1986. Ordained to ministry Episcopal Ch., 1962. Rector Ch. Good Shepherd, Little Rock, 1961-65; vicar St. Martin's, Fayetteville, Ark., 1965-72; chaplain, instr. humanities U. Ark., 1965-72; rector Calvary Ch., Columbia, Mo., 1972-76, St. Boniface Ch., Sarasota, Fla., 1976-85; bishop coadjutor Diocese of Mass., Boston, 1985-86, bishop, 1986-95; chair Dovemass. Trustee Kent (Conn.) Sch., Berkeley Div. Sch. Yale U.; bd. dirs. Boston Ptnrs. in Edn., Nat. Ptnrs. in Edn., Mass. Soc. for Prevention of Cruelty to Children; co-chair Boston Coalition Religious Task Force on Violence and Drugs; mem. steering com. One-to-One. Capt. USAF, 1955-58. Home: Boston Mass. Died Jan. 15, 1995.

JOHNSON, JED JOSEPH, JR., association executive; b. Washington, Dec. 27, 1939; s. Jed Joseph and Beatrice (Luginbyhl) J.; m. Sydney Herlong, Sept. 25, 1965; children: Alice, Sydney. BA, U. Okla., 1961; postgrad. in internat. studies, Johns Hopkins U., 1977-78, 84. Student rep UN Assn., N.Y.C., 1961-62; mem. U.S. Congress, Washington, 1964-66; spl. asst. to dir. Office Econ. Opportunity, Washington, 1967-68; dir. tech. assistance div. EEOC, Washington, 1968-72; cons. Select Com. on Presdl. Campaign Activities, Washington, 1973; exec. dir. U.S. Assn. Former Mems. Congress, Washington, 1974-93; exec. dir. Congl. Study Group on Germany, Washington, 1987-93; cons. Christ Ho., Washington, 1985-93. Contbr. to books: The Japanese Diet and U.S. Congress, 1983, The German Bundestag and the U.S. Congress, 1989. Mem. Cortez Ewing Found., Okla., 1965-66; mem. U.S. Nat. Commn. for UNESCO, Washington, 1962-64; sec. Okla. Congl. Delegation, Washington, 1965-66; mem. Armed Svcs. Com., Washington, 1965-66. Recipient Lasker Found. award UN Assn., 1961, Officer's Cross of Order of Merit, Pres. of Fed. Republic Germany, 1988. Mem. Fed. City Club, Mid-Atlantic Club. Democrat. Mem. Ch. of the Saviour. Home: Alexandria Va. Died Dec. 16, 1993.

JOHNSON, MARVIN DONALD, brewery executive; b. Willcox, Ariz., Nov. 2, 1928; s. Wellington Lott and Hazel Valentine (Bendure) J.; m. Stella C. Pacheco, Feb. 14, 1953; children: Lynn Anne, Marshall Donald, Karen Marie. BS, U. Ariz., 1950, MS, 1957; EdD (hon.), Lincoln Coll., 1970; PhD (hon.), U. Ariz., 1993. Asst. grad. mgr. U. Ariz., 1950-52, dir. student union, 1952-58, dir. alumni assn., 1958-63, v.p. univ relations, 1963-77; adminstrv. v.p. student affairs alumni relations and devel. U. N.Mex., Albuquerque, 1977-85; v.p. corp. affairs Coors Brewing Co., 1985-96; dir. Radio Fiesta, Ariz. Pres., Palo Verde Mental Health Assn., Ariz., 1967-69, Beer Inst. Mgmt. com., 1986-95, Nat. Puerto Rican Coalition Bus. adv. coun., 1991-95; bd. trustees Colo. Jud. Inst., 1991-95, 9 Health Fairs, 1992-95, Cowboy Artists of Am. Mus., 1990-92, adv. bd., 1993-95. Editor: Successful Governmental Relations, 1981. Chmn. Tucson Crime Commn., 1969-71; pres. Catalina coun. Boy Scouts Am., 1966, bd. dirs. Gt. S.W. coun., 1983-85; bd. dirs. Fund for Tucson, 1965-69, Maxwell Mus., 1977-85, Sta. KNME-TV, 1977-85, N.Mex. divsn. Am. Cancer Soc., 1978-85, United Way Albuquerque, 1978-79, 83-85; mem. White House Conf. on Youth, 1971, Gov.'s Film Commn., Ariz., 1971-77; mem. nat. bd. Samaritan Inst., 1987-91; mem. Colo. chpt. Nat. Multiple Sclerosis Soc., trustee, 1987-95, trustee Colo. Bus. Alliance for Youth. Recipient Outstanding Alumni award Future Farmers Am., Ariz., 1964, Outstanding Alumni award Ariz. 4-H, 1970, Silver Antelope award Boy Scouts Am., 1975, Super P.R. award Am. Cancer Soc. N.Mex., 1979, N.Mex. Disting. Pub. Svc. award, 1982, Cmty. Svc., award Red Rocks C.C., 1988, Nat. Western Grand Champion award, 1995, Colo. Sch. of Mines medal, 1995. Mem. Pub. Rels. Soc. Am., Inst. Ednl. Mgmt. (trustee 1972-76), Nat. Assn. State Univs. and Land Grant Colls. (mem. exec. com. 1973-77), Coun. Advancement and Support Edn. (trustee 1976-85, nat. chmn. 1980-81), Newcomen Soc. N. Am., Western Athletic Conf. (chmn. council 1978-79), Ariz. Cattle Growers Assn., Lamplighters Ednl. Round Table, Golden C. of C. (pres. 1988, bd. dirs 1986-89, Civic award 1991), Alpha Zeta, Kappa Kappa Psi, Gamma Sigma Delta, Alpha Kappa Psi, Phi Eta Sigma, Sigma Chi (grand trustee 1973-83, internat. pres. 1983-85). Democrat. Methodist. Club: Denver Rotary. Home: Golden Col. Deceased July 15, 1995.

JOHNSON, RAY, painter; b. Detroit, Oct. 16, 1927. Student, Art Students' League, N.Y.C., Black Mountain Coll. Asso. with Am. Abstract Artists, 1949-52; founded N.Y. Corr. Sch. Art, 1962. Exhibited one-man shows, Willard Gallery, N.Y.C., 1965, 66, 67, Feigen Gallery, Chgo., 1966, 67, Whitney Mus. Am. Art, N.Y.C., 1970, Art Inst. Chgo., 1972, N.C. Mus. Art, Raleigh, 1976; in group shows including, Boylston St. Print Gallery, Cambridge, Mass., 1955, contemporary Arts Assn. Houston, 1959, Batman Gallery, San Francisco, 1961, Pitts. Internat., Carnegie Inst., 1961, AG Gallery, N.Y.C., 1961, Oakland Art Mus., 1963, Mus. Modern Art, N.Y.C., 1966, Finch Coll. Mus. Art, N.Y.C., 1967, Chgo. Mus. Contemporary Art, 1967, Hayward Gallery, London, 1969, U. B.C., 1969; represented in permanent collections, Art Inst. Chgo., Dulin Gallery, Houston Mus. Fine Arts, DeCordova Mus., Lincoln, Mass., Mus. Modern Art, N.Y.C.; pub.: The Paper Snake, 1965. Recipient award Nat. Inst. Arts and Letters, 1966, award for painting Nat. Endowment Arts, 1986. Home: Locust Valley N.Y. Deceased Jan. 14, 1995.

JOHNSON, RAY CLIFFORD, mechanical engineering educator, consultant, writer; b. Canton, Ohio, Aug. 26, 1927; s. Olaf Andreas and Hilma D. (Blomberg) J.; m. Helen Frances Lindgren, July 2, 1949; children: Glen Eric, Barbara Ann, Carol Marie. B.S. with high distinction, U. Rochester, 1950, M.S., 1954, Ph.D., 1983. Registered profl. engr., N.Y., Conn., Mass., Mich., N.J., Ohio. Mech. design engr. Gleason Works, Rochester, N.Y., 1950-51; instr. U. Rochester, 1951-54; sr. design engr. Eastman Kodak Co., 1954-58; asst. prof. mech. engring. Yale, 1958-61; staff engr. IBM Corp., 1961-62; John Woodman Higgins prof. mech. engring. Worcester (Mass.) Poly. Inst., 1962-80, 85-87; Gleason prof. mech. engring. Rochester (N.Y.) Inst. Tech., 1980-85; sr. lectr. mech. engring. U. Rochester, N.Y., 1988-90; lectr. and cons. to major univs. and industries, 1957-95; keynote speaker Symposium on Mech. Design, U. Mex., 1975, 84. vis. fellow mech. engring. U. Salford (Eng.), 1976-77, Nat. Acad. Engring., Mex., 1978-95. Author: Optimum Design of Mechanical Elements, 1961, 80, Mechanical Design Synthesis-Creative Design and Optimization, 1971, 78; also tech. papers. Served with USNR, 1945-46. Recipient Emil Kuichling prize U. Rochester, 1948; Eisenhart award outstanding teaching Rochester Inst. Tech., 1984, Machine Design award Am. Soc. of Manufacturing Engineers, 1995. Fellow ASME; mem. Am. Soc. Engring. Edn., AAUP, Phi Beta Kappa, Sigma Xi, Tau Beta Pi, Pi Tau Sigma, Phi Kappa Phi. Home: Webster N.Y. Died June 28, 1995.

JOHNSON, RAYMOND COLES, insurance executive; b. Bisbee, Ariz., June 19, 1907; s. Ira J. and Carolyn (Coles) J.; m. Alice Elizabeth Abbott, June 21, 1930 (dec. July 21, 1949); children: Carolyn C. Johnson Smith, Eleanor Johnson Palmer; m. Alice Hall Willard, July 16, 1954. B.S. magna cum laude, U. Ariz., 1928, LL.D., 1976. With N.Y. Life Ins. Co., 1927-92; agt. N.Y. Life Ins. Co., Phoenix, 1927-29; asst. mgr. N.Y. Life Ins. Co. (Ariz. br.), 1929-33, mgr., 1933-38; mgr. Los Angeles br. N.Y. Life Ins. Co., 1938-42; supt. agys. home office N.Y. Life Ins. Co., N.Y.C., 1942-43; asst. v.p. N.Y. Life Ins. Co., 1942-49, agy. v.p. and exec. officer, 1949-51, v.p. charge agy. admistrn., 1951-56, v.p. charge agy. affairs, 1956-59, v.p. charge mktg., 1959-62, exec. v.p., 1962-69, dir., 1968-74, vice chmn., 1969-73; pres. Council Fin. Aid to Edn., 1973-78, chmn. exec. com., 1979-92; dir. Western World Ins. Co., Stratford Ins. Co., Tudor Ins. Co. Author: The Achievers, the Art of Self-Management for Success, 1987; contbr. articles mags. and trade jours. Bd. govs. Internat. Ins. Seminars, 1968-92; agy. chmn. Am. Life Conv., 1962; mem. Republican Nat. Fin. Com.; mem., trustee NYU Med. Ctr., 1965; chmn. N.Y. chpt. ARC, 1968-92, United Negro Coll. Fund, Ind. Coll. Funds Am. Recipient U. Ariz. Alumni Achievement award, 1956. Mem. Am. Coll. Life Underwriters (Huebner Gold medal 1979, life trustee), Am. Soc. C.L.U.S., Life Ins. Agy. Mgmt. Assn. (dir., past pres.), Better Bus. Bur. Met. N.Y. (dir. 1968, council 1969), Pilgrims U.S., Newcomen Soc., Knights of Malta, Phi Beta Kappa, Phi Delta Theta, Pi Delta Epsilon, Alpha Kappa Psi. Clubs: University (N.Y.C.); Southampton (L.I., N.Y.); Bath and Tennis (Palm Beach, Fla.), Soc. Four Arts (Palm Beach, Fla.);. Home: West Palm Beach Fla. Died Mar. 13, 1992; interred Woodlawn Cemetery, N.Y.C.

JOHNSON, RICHARD WILLIAM, newspaper ex ecutive; b. Pawnee, Okla., Nov. 25, 1916; s. Ralp Waldo and Ollie May (Colvin) J.; m. Gloria Scott, De 28, 1945; children: Richard, Daniel, Ellen. B.A. Journalism, U. Okla., 1940. Sales rep. Newspaper En terprise Assn., Cleve., 1940-41; Eastern sales mg Newspaper Enterprise Assn., N.Y.C., 1945-63; dir. sp services Newspaper Enterprise Assn., Cleve., 1963-6 v.p. publs. Newspaper Enterprise Assn., N.Y.C., 196 72; sr. v.p. Newspaper Enterprise Assn., 1978-92, Cleve 1972-78; also dir. Newspaper Enterprise Assn., N.Y.C exec. cons. United Media Enterprises, Newspaper En terprise Assn., United Features Syndicate, 1978-81; di Berkley-Small, Inc., Mobile, Ala. Bd. dirs. Soc. Unite Helpers, North Country Freedom Homes. Served wi USNR, 1941-45, PTO. Mem. Inland Daily Press Ass (asso.), So. Newspaper Pubs. Assn. (asso.). Club Cleve. Athletic, Rotary. Home: Morristown N.Y. Die June 29, 1992.

JOHNSON, ROBERT BETHUNE, geography ed cator; b. St. Louis, Mo., Dec. 4, 1920; s. James Forb and Ora (Bethune) J.; m. June Main, Nov. 7, 1942 (de Aug. 1979); children: Kathryn Forbes Allison, Les Main Johnson-Gottesfield; m. Dorothy Ann Roger Mar. 28, 1980 (dec. Jan. 1985). AB, Wash. U., S Louis, 1938; MA, Harvard U., 1947, PhD, 1960. Fellow Syracuse (N.Y.) U., 1946-47; asst. prof. g ography St. Lawrence U., Canton, N.Y., 1949-50; di advt. research Itek Corp., Waltham, Mass., 1959; di programs tempo Gen. Electric Co., Santa Barbar Calif., 1959-61; pres. Prescott (Ariz.) Schole, 1971-7 prof. geography, chmn. dept. Calif. State U. Domenguez Hills, Carson, from 1972, prof. emeritu acting chmn., from 1986; proprietor Johnson Researc Assocs., Santa Barbara, 1961-71; lectr. U. Calif., San Barbara, 1960-63; cons. Santa Barbara County Sch 1962-66. Author/editor: California Patterns on th Land, 5th edit., 1976, Projected World Patterns, 196 70; also articles. Mem. planning adv. com. City of L Angeles, San Pedro, Calif., 1974-82, Citizens Adv. Cor Community Plan, San Pedro, 1974-82, Rep. Cen. Com Los Angeles, 1976-83. Served as cpl. USAAF, 1943-4 capt. U.S. Army, 1951-52. Fellow Am. Geog. Soc mem. Assn. Am. Geographers, Assn. Pacific Coast G ographers, Sigma Xi. Republican. Home: Los Angel Calif. Deceased.

JOHNSON, ROBERT EDWARD, magazine editor; Montgomery, Ala., Aug. 13, 1922; s. Robert and De (Davis) J.; m. Naomi Cole, Dec. 16, 1948; childre Bobbye LaVerne, Janet Bernice, Robert Edwar III. B.A., Morehouse Coll., 1948; M.A., Syracuse U 1952; Litt.D., Miles Coll., 1973. Reporter Atlan Daily World, 1948-49, city editor, 1949-50; asso. edit Jet News mag., Chgo., 1953-54; asst. mng. editor J News mag., 1954-56, mng. editor, 1956-63, exec. edito 1963-95; dir. Project Upward Bound, 1966-68. Bd. di Martin Luther King Jr. Center Social Change, DuSab Mus. Afro-Am. History. Served with USNR, 1943-46 Mem. World Fedn. Scottish Socs., Sigma Delta Ch Alpha Phi Alpha, Alpha Kappa Delta. Clubs: Maso Helms Athletic Found, Chgo. Headline (dir. 1968-70) Home: Chicago Ill. Died Dec., 1995.

JOHNSON, WILLIAM SUMMER, chemistry ed cator; b. New Rochelle, N.Y., Feb. 24, 1913; s. R Wilder and Josephine (Summer) J.; m. Barbara Alle Dec. 27, 1940. Grad., Gov. Dummer Acad., 193 B.A., Amherst Coll., 1936, Sc.D., 1956; M.A., Harva U., 1938, Ph.D., 1940; Sc.D, L.I. U., 1968. Inst Amherst Coll., 1936-37; research chemist Eastma Kodak Co., summer, 1936-39; instr. U. Wis., 1940-4 asst. prof., 1942-44, assoc. prof., 1944-49, Homer A kins prof. chemistry, 1954-60; prof. dept. chemist Stanford U., Calif., 1960-78; Jackson-Wood pr Stanford U., 1974-78, prof. emeritus, 1978-96, chm dept., 1960-69; vis. prof. Harvard U., 1954-55; me exec. bd. Jour. Organic Chemistry, 1954-56; mem. che adv. panel NSF, 1952-56; sec. organic sect. Interna Congress Pure and Applied Chemistry, 1951. Contb chpts. to chemistry books, articles to assn. jours.; me bd. editors: Organic Syntheses, vol. 34, 1954, Jour. A Chem. Soc., 1956-65, Jour. Organic Chemistry, 1954-5 Tetrahedron, 1957-84. Recipient medal Synthetic C ganic Chem. Mfrs. Assn., 1963, Nat. Medal of Sc 1987. Fellow London Chem. Soc.; mem. NAS, A Acad. Arts and Scis., Swiss Chem. Soc., Am. Che Soc. (chmn. organic div. 1951-52, award in synthe organic chemistry 1958, Nichols medal 1968, Rouss prize 1970, Roger Adams award 1977, Arthur C. Co award 1989, Tetrahedron prize 1991), Phi Beta Kapp Sigma Xi. Home: Menlo Park Calif. Deceased.

JOHNSTON, DAVID IAN, manufacturing executi b. Ottawa, Ont., Can., Mar. 11, 1932; s. Wilbur Aus and Florence (Tucker) J.; m. Nancy Hyndman; 7 ch dren. BA, McGill U., 1953, BCL, 1957, LLM, 19 BSc, Sir George Williams U., 1956. European tech. r Canadair, Ltd., 1954-55, solicitor, 1957-64; v.p. le CAE Industries, Ltd., Montreal, Can., 1964-67, ex v.p., 1967-74; pres. Rexcorp. Ltd., 1974-93; v.p., dirs. Aviation Planning Svcs. Ltd., 1974-86; pres. D. Stuart Oil Co., Ltd., 1976-78, chmn. 1978-83; bd. di Dickenson Mines Ltd., 1977-81; chmn. bd. Unit Dr Forge Co., Inc., 1978-93, Amcan Castings Ltd., 19 93, Can. Space Techs., Inc., 1990-93, Impact Industri Inc., 1990-93, Gen. Die & Engring., 1990-93. Cont cles to profl. jours. With RCAF, 1948-52. Mem. t. Internat. Air Law Assn. (past pres.), Can. Bar sn. (bar counsel 1964-66), Que. Bar Assn. (bar unsel 1964-66), Law Soc. Alta., Assn. Can. Gen. unsel (emeritus), Hillside Tennis Club (past pres.), ntreal Badminton and Squash Club, St. James Club ontreal), Hamilton Golf and Country Club, Lambda Alpha (chancellor 1958-64), Tamahaac Club (Anter). Home: Cambridge Can. Died Dec. 13, 1993.

HNSTON, THOMAS JOHN, management contant; b. Oak Park, Ill., Nov. 2, 1922; s. John J. and len J. (Gilmore) J.; m. Elaine Berger, Feb. 16, 1946; dren—Elene Johnston Kapp, Molly, Anne Johnston rdner, Karen, John. B.S., St. Marys Coll., 1943; stgrad., Columbia U., 1943. Personnel analyst Wesn Electric Co. Inc., Chgo., 1946-49; retail personnel r. Montgomery Ward & Co., Chgo., 1949-54; dir. sonnel Panellit Inc., Chgo., 1954-56; assoc. Heidrick Struggles Inc., Chgo., 1956-60, dir. in charge West ast ops., 1960-70; pres., chief exec. officer Heidrick & uggles Inc., San Francisco, Calif., 1970-91;, 1978-91; ir emeritus Heidrick & Struggles Inc., Calistoga, 1-95; bd. dirs. Chalone, Inc. Mem. U. Redland's s.'s Adv. Council, 1968-73; mem. Pres.'s Commn. on ite House Fellows, 1971-76; trustee Robert Louis venson Sch., Pebble Beach, Calif., 1977-95, chmn. bd. ., 1984-95. Served to lt. USNR, 1942-46, PTO. publican. Roman Catholic. Clubs: Calif., University, nandale Golf, San Francisco Yacht. Lodge: Knights Malta. Home: Belvedere Tiburon Calif. Deceased . 23, 1995.

LL, JAMES BYSSE, historian, emeritus educator; June 21, 1918; s. H. H. and Alice Muriel (Edwards) M.A., Oxford U.; student U. Bordeaux (France). low and tutor in politics New Coll., Oxford U., 1946- fellow St. Antony's Coll., 1951-67, fellow emeritus, 57-94, sub-warden, 1951-67; Stevenson prof. internat. tory U. London, 1967-81, emeritus prof., 1981-94; m. Inst. Advanced Study, Princeton, N.J., 1954, 71; prof. history Stanford (Calif.) U., 1958, Sydney ustralia) U., 1979, U. Iowa, 1980; vis. lectr. Harvard 1962. Served with Devonshire Regt. and Spl. Ops. c., 1939-45. Fellow Brit. Acad. Author: The Second ernational, 1955, rev. edit., 1974; Intellectuals in litics, 1960; The Anarchists, 1964, rev. edit., 1979; rope since 1870, 1973, 3d edit., 1983; Gramsci, 1977; e Origins of the First World War, 1984. Died July 12, 94. Home: London Eng.

LSON, ALFRED JAMES, bishop; b. Bridgeport, nn., June 18, 1928; s. Alfred James and Justine zabeth (Houlihan) J. BA, Boston Coll., 1951, MA, 52; BTh., Weston Coll., 1958; MBA, Harvard U., 52; PhD, Gregorian U., Rome, 1970; LHD (hon.), heeling (W.Va.) Jesuit Coll., 1990. Joined S.J., man Cath. Ch., 1946, ordained priest, 1958, bishop, 88; lic. psychologist, Zimbabwe. Tchr. Baghdad aq) Coll., 1952-55; prof., dean Al-hikma U., Baghdad, 52-64; dean Boston Coll., Newton, Mass., 1964-68; n, prof. Sch. Social Workers, Salisbury, Rhodesia, 70-76, St. Joseph U., Phila., 1976-86, Wheeling .Va.) Jesuit Coll., 1986-87; bishop Reykjavik, Iced, 1987—. Chmn. bd. dirs. St. Joseph's Prep Sch., ila., 1979-84; bd. dirs. St. Joseph's U., Phila., 1978-79. em. Knights of Holy Sepulcher. Democrat. Home: ykjavik Iceland Deceased.

NES, CHARLES EDWARD, advertising executive; Mound City, Ill., Oct. 1, 1918; s. William M. and isy D. (Rivers) J.; m. Doris E. Hogendobler, June 26, 38; children—Eleanor Ann, Philip Alan; m. Greta e Houston., Dec. 30, 1955; 1 dau., Emily san. Student, McKendree Coll., Lebanon, Ill., 1936- B.J., U. Mo., 1940. Account supr. Schwimmer & ott (Ins.), Chgo., 1950-52; adminstrv. v.p., dir. Pottsodbury, Inc., 1952-60, pres., chmn. bd., chief exec. cer, 1962-67; sr. v.p. Biddle Advt., 1967-69; chmn. e Anchor Marina, Inc., Gravois Mills, Mo., 1969-93; ner Anchor Advt., Anchor Bus. Communications, avois Mills, 1972—; gen. sales mgr. WHB Radio, nsas City, Mo., 1960-62. Former dir. Greater nsas City Sports Commn.; ambassador Am. Royal. ved as 1st lt. USMC, 1943-46. Former dir. Greater nsas City Sports Commn., Greater Kansas City C. of ambassador Am. Royal. 1st lt. USMC, 1943-46. ub: Masons. Home: Gravois Mills MO. Died Nov. 1994.

NES, EDWARD ELLSWORTH, psychology eduor; b. Buffalo, Aug. 11, 1926; s. Edward Safford and ances Christine (Jeffery) J.; m. Virginia Sweetnam, r. 5, 1947; children: Sarah E., Caroline A., Todd E., nelia G., Jason L., Janet P. A.B., Harvard U., 1949, .D., 1953. Mem. faculty Duke U., 1953-77, prof. ychology, 1961-77, chmn. dept., 1970-73; Stuart prof. ychology Princeton U., 1977-93. Author: Ingratian, 1964, (with H.B. Gerard) Foundations of Social ychology, 1967, (with others) Attribution, 1972, cial Stigma, 1984, Interpersonal Perception, 1990; tor: Jour. Personality, 1954-62; contbr. articles to ofl. jours. Served with AUS, 1944-47. NSF research antee, 1956-93; NIMH spl. fellow, 1963-64; recipient stinguished Sci. Contbn. award Am. Psychol. Assn., 77, Disting. Sci. award Soc. Exptl. Social Psychol., 87; Fellow Center for Advanced Study in Behavioral s., Stanford, Calif., 1963-64, 80-81. Fellow Am. Psychol. Assn., Am. Acad. Arts and Scis.; mem. Soc. Personality Social Psychology (pres. 1988). Home: Princeton N.J. Died July 30, 1993; buried Princton Cemetery, Princeton, N.J.

JONES, HUGH MCKITTRICK, architect; b. St. Louis, Oct. 6, 1919; s. Hugh McKittrick and Carroll (West) J.; m. Elizabeth Siddons Mowbray, Sept. 9, 1940 (dec. July 1978); children: Cynthia Siddons Jones Benjamin, Terry West (Mrs. James Henry Eddy, Jr.), Hugh McKittrick III, Timothy Millard.; m. Margaret Twichell Mowbray, Mar. 17, 1984; stepchildren: Burton Twichell Mowbray, Katharine Siddons Mowbray Michie. B.S., Harvard, 1940, B.Arch., 1942, M.Arch., 1947. Trainee Office Walter Bogner, Cambridge, Mass., 1945-47, Office Douglas Orr, New Haven, 1947-49; architect Jones & Mowbray, New Haven and Guilford, Conn., 1949-54, Office Hugh Jones, Guilford, 1954-87; ret. Office Hugh Jones; corporator, trustee Guilford Savs. Bank, 1954-95, v.p., 1975-77, vice chmn., 1977-95; v.p. Envirland Co., 1976-95. Mem. Guilford Republican Town Com., 1952-84, now assoc.; mem. Guilford Town Planning Commn., 1953-58, chmn., 1956; mem. Regional Planning Agy., 1961-69; rep. Conn. Ho. Reps., 1963-67; mem. Conn. Commn. to Study Metro Govt., 1965-67, Conn. Gov.'s Task Force on Housing, 1971-73; chmn. Regional Housing Council for S. Central Planning Region, 1974-80; mem. Guilford Land Conservation Trust, 1965-95, Guilford Keeping Soc., 1979-95, Guilford Preservation Alliance, 1981-95; pres. Guilford Found., 1976-80, bd. dirs., 1977-82, 83-95. Served to lt. USNR, 1942-46, PTO. Fellow AIA (pres. Conn. chpt. 1962, 63, Nat. dir. 1970-73), Guilford C. of C., Sierra Club, Am. Arbitration Assn. (nat. panel arbitrators 1956-95). Home: Guilford Conn. Deceased May 1, 1995.

JONES, J. KNOX, JR., biologist, educator; b. Lincoln, Nebr., Mar. 16, 1929; s. James Knox and Virginia E. (Bolen) J.; m.Marijane R. Davis, June 24, 1989; children: Amy Sue, Sarah Ann, Laura Lee. B.S., U. Nebr., 1951; M.A., U. Kans., 1953, Ph.D., 1962. Mem. faculty U. Kans., 1959-71; prof. zoology, curator Mus. Natural History, 1968-71, assoc. dir. mus., 1967-71; prof. biol. scis. Tex. Tech U., Lubbock, 1971-86, Horn disting. prof., 1986-92; dean Grad. Sch. Tex. Tech U., 1971-84, assoc. v.p. research, 1972-74, v.p. research and grad. studies, 1974-84; adj. prof. pathology Tex. Tech U. Sch. Medicine, 1973-91; cons. in field. Author monographs, sects. books, articles. Served with U.S. Army, 1953-55. Mem. AAAS, Am. Soc. Mammalogists (pres. 1972-74), Orgn. Tropical Studies (treas. 1974-76), Gulf Univs. Rsch. Consortium (sec. 1979-80), Soc. Systematic Zoology, Tex. Acad. Sci. (editor 1985-92), Southwestern Assn. Naturalists, Sigma Xi, Alpha Tau Omega, Omicron Delta Kappa, Phi Kappa Phi. Home: Lubbock Tex. Died Nov. 15, 1992.

JONES, JENNINGS HINCH, chemical engineering educator; b. Petrolia, Pa., Aug. 19, 1913; s. George Findred and Florence Jennings (Hinch) J.; m. Katherine E. Campbell, Nov. 16, 1940; children: Ellen F. (Mrs. Frank La Belle), Trudy K. B.S., Pa. State U., 1934, M.S., 1937, Ph.D., 1941. Chemist Pa. Coal Products Co., Petrolia, 1934-36; faculty Pa. State U., University Park, 1941-94; prof. chem. engring. Pa. State U., 1964-79, prof. emeritus, 1979-94; cons. in field. Mem. Am. Chem. Soc., Am. Inst. Chem. Engrs., Sigma Xi, Phi Lambda Upsilon. Home: State College Pa. Died Feb. 16, 1994.

JONES, SIR LAURENCE ALFRED, government official; b. Jan. 18, 1933; s. Benjamin Howel and Irene Dorothy Jones; m. Brenda Ann Jones, 1956; 2 children. Grad., RAF Coll., Cranwell, 1953. Jr. officer pilot 208 Squadron in Mid. East, 1954-57; fighter 74 Squadron Weapons Sch., 1957-61; comdr. No. 8 Squadron Aden, 1961-63, No. 19 Squadron RAF Germany, 1967-70; sta. comdr. RAF Wittering, 1975-76, RCDS, 1977; dir. of ops. Air Support MoD, 1978-81, SASO, Strike Command, 1982-84, ACAS, MoD, 1984, ACDS, 1985-86; dir. of ops. ACAS, 1986-87, air mem. for pers., 1987-89; ret., 1989; lt. gov. Isle of Man, Douglas, 1990—. Mem. Royal Air Force Club. Died Sept. 23, 1995.

JONES, LORELLA MARGARET, physics educator; b. Toronto, Ont., Can., Feb. 22, 1943; came to U.S., 1948; d. Donald Cecil and F. Shirley (Patterson) J. BA, Harvard U., 1964; MSc, Calif. Inst. Tech., 1966, PhD, 1968. From postdoctoral fellow to instr. Calif. Inst. Tech., Pasadena, 1967-68; asst. prof. physics U. Ill., Urbana, 1968-70, assoc. prof. physics, 1970-78, prof. physics, 1978—. Author ednl. physics software. Fellow Am. Phys. Soc. (div. particles and fields); mem. AAUP (chpt. pres. 1989-91). Home: Livermore Calif. Died Feb. 9, 1995.

JONES, WARREN LEROY, federal judge; b. Gordon, Nebr., July 2, 1895; S. Lauren and Katherine (Ballengee) J.; m. Edith Ann Le Prouse, Dec. 23, 1921 (dec. Dec. 1989). LLB cum laude, U. Denver, 1924; LLD, Stetson U., 1955; DHL (hon.), La. State U., 1977; DCL, Jacksonville U., 1978. Bar: Colo. 1924, Fla. 1926. Dep. dist. atty. City and County Denver, 1924; mem. Jones, Gandy & Wilson, Denver, 1925; assoc. Fleming, Hamilton, Diver & Lichliter, Jacksonville, 1926-37; mem. Fleming, Hamilton, Diver & Jones, 1938-41; mem. Fleming, Jones, Scott & Botts, 1942-55, sr. mem., 1948-55; judge U.S. Ct. Appeals 5th Cir., 1955-65, sr. judge, 1965-81; sr. judge U.S. Ct. Appeals 11th Cir., 1981—. Sec., dir. Jacksonville Blood Bank, 1942-55. Recipient Lincoln diploma of honor Lincoln Meml. U., 1971. Fellow Am. Coll. Probate Counsel; mem. Fla. C. of C., Jacksonville C. of C. (pres. 1955), SAR, Am. Judicature Soc., Am. Law Inst., ABA, Fla. Bar Assn. (pres. 1944), Jacksonville Bar Assn. (pres. 1939), Nat. Lawyers Club (Washington), Newcomen Soc., Phi Alpha Delta. Episcopalian. Clubs: Timuquana Country, Fla. Yacht, Seminole, River, Ponte Vedra, Civitan (past pres.); Univ. (Jacksonville); Masons (33 deg.), Shriners. Home: Jacksonville Fl.

JORDAN, BARBARA C., lawyer, educator, former congresswoman; b. Houston, Feb. 21, 1936; d. and Arlyne J. BA in Polit. Sci. and History magna cum laude, Tex. So. U.; LLB, Boston U., 1959. Bar: Mass. 1959, Tex. 1959. Pvt. practice, adminstrv. asst. to county judge County of Harris, Tex.; mem. Tex. Senate, 1966-72; pres. pro tem, chmn. Labor and Mgmt. Relations Com. and Urban Affairs Study Com.; mem. 93d-95th congresses from 18th Dist. Tex., 1972-78; mem. com. judiciary, com. govt. ops.; mem. spl. task force 94th Congress; mem. steering and policy com. House Democratic Caucus; Lyndon B. Johnson pub. svc. prof. U. Tex., Austin, 1979-82, Lyndon B. Johnson Centennial chair in nat. policy, 1982—; mem. UN panel on multinat. corps. in South Africa and Namibia; keynote speaker Nat. Dem. Conv., 1976; dir. numerous cos. Author: Barbara Jordan: A Self Portrait, 1979; editor (with Elspeth Rostow) The Great Society: A Twenty-Year Critique; host PBS TV series Crisis to Crisis with Barbara Jordan, 1982; contbr. articles to profl. jours. Trustee Henry J. Kaiser Family Found.; mem. presdl. adv. bd. Ambassadorial Appts., 1979-81; hearings officer Nat. Inst. Edn. Hearings minimum competency testing; founder, bd. dirs. People for the Am. Way. Recipient Eleanor Roosevelt Humanities award State of Israel Bonds, 1984, 21st Charles Evans Hughes Gold medal NCCJ, 1987, Harry S. Truman Pub. Svc. award Harry S. Truman Scholarship Found., 1990, Elmer B. Staats Pub. Svc. Careers award, 1990, Tom C. Clark Equal Justice Under Law award, 1991, Bess Wallace Truman award, 1992, Nat. Civil Rights Mus. Freedom award, 1992, Eleanor Roosevelt Val-Kill award, 1992, 77th Spingarn award NAACP, 1992, Nelson Mandela Health and Human Rights award, 1993; named one of Ten Women of Yr., Time mag., 1976, first choice for Women Who Could Be Appointed to Supreme Ct., Redbook mag., 1979, one among 100 Most Influential Women in Am., Ladies Home Jour., 1980, One of 25 Most Influential Woman in Am., World Almanac, 1986, Best Living Orator, Internat. Platform Assn., 1984, One of Most Influential Women of 20th Century, Nat. Women's Hall of Fame, 1993; inducted into Nat. Women's Hall of Fame, 1990, The African-Am. Hall of Fame, 1993; elected to Tex. Women's Hall of Fame, 1984; 1990 edit. Ann. Survey of Am. Law dedicated in her name, 1990. Fellow Am. Bar Found.; mem. ABA, Tex. Bar Assn., Mass. Bar Assn., Houston Bar Assn., D.C. Bar, NAACP, Delta Sigma Theta. Baptist.

JORGENSEN, JOHN W., steel and aluminum manufacturing company executive; b. 1925; married. BA, Pomona Coll., 1947. With Earle W. Jorgensen Co. Inc., Los Angeles, 1948-90; v.p. Earle M. Jorgensen Co. Inc., Los Angeles, 1962-67, pres., chief adminstrv. officer, mem. exec. com., dir., from 1967, now pres., chief exec. and operating officer. Served with USN, World War II. Home: Los Angeles Calif. Died April 27, 1990.

JORGENSON, WALLACE JAMES, broadcast executive; b. Mpls., Oct. 31, 1923; s. Peter and Adelia Henrietta (Bong) J.; m. Solveig Elizabeth Tvedt, Feb. 24, 1945; children: Peter, Kristin, Mark, Philip, Lisa. Student, St. Olaf Coll., 1941-43, Gustavus Adolphus Coll., 1943; BA, Bowling Green State U., 1944; LHD, Lenoir-Rhyne Coll., 1971. Staff announcer Sta. WCAL, Northfield, Minn., 1941-43; sta. mgr. Sta. KTRF, Thief River Falls, Minn., 1946-48; with Sta. WBT, Charlotte, N.C., 1952-67; v.p., asst. gen. mgr. Sta. WBT, Charlotte, 1966-67; exec. v.p. Jefferson-Pilot Communications Co., Charlotte, 1968-78, pres., 1978-88; also bd. dirs. Jefferson-Pilot Corp., 1978-88; exec. v.p. Hubbard Broadcasting, Inc., 1988-95; chmn. Charlotte br. Fed. Res. Bank, 1984-87; chmn. mgmt. com. Office for Communications, Luth. Ch. in Am., 1978-86; bd. dirs. United Press Editorial Rev. Bd., Washington, 1987-89. Mem. Mus. Broadcasting; pres. United Way campaign, 1984; chmn. Mecklenburg and Union Counties United Way, 1982; bd. govs. ARC, 1977-83; chmn. Red Cross Centennial, 1981; trustee Lenoir-Rhyne Coll., 1963-81, chmn., 1971-77; bd. dirs. Central Piedmont Community Coll. Found., 1980-87; bd. visitors Davidson Coll., 1979-95. Served to 2d lt. USMC, 1943-46, PTO. Recipient Silver medal Charlotte Advt. Club, 1975, Abe Lincoln award So. Bapt. Radio and TV Commn., Dallas, 1976, Communications award N.C. Council Chs., 1976, Harriman award ARC, 1982, Mgmt. award Nat. Editorial Assn., 1987; named Businessman of Yr. Lenoir-Rhyne Coll., 1988. Mem. Broadcast Pioneers, Nat. Assn. Broadcasters (bd. dirs. TV bd. 1983-95, chmn. joint bds. 1987-89), N.C. Assn. Broadcasters (Disting. Svc. award 1981, Hall of Fame 1988), Am. Mgmt. Assn., Assn. Maximum Svc. Telecasters (past chmn.), U.S. C. of C. (bd. dirs. 1986-95, pub. affairs com.), Greater Charlotte C. of C. (past chmn.), TV Info. Office (bd. dirs. 1984-87), TV Bur. Advt., Grandfather Golf and County Club, Carrolwood Village Golf and Tennis Club., Tower Club (founding chmn. 1985-87). Republican. Home: Chapel Hill N.C. Died Feb. 23, 1995.

JORTBERG, RICHARD EDMUND, utility executive; b. Portland, Maine, June 8, 1923; s. Charles Augustus and Adelaide Cecelia (Mahoney) J.; m. Jo Ann Mundy, June 6, 1952; children: Judith, Patricia, Richard Edmund, Michael. BS, U.S. Naval Acad., 1944; MS, George Washington U., 1971. Commd. ensign U.S. Navy, 1944, advanced through grades to capt., 1965; comdr. nuclear attack submarine USS Tullibee, 1959-63, Polaris missile submarine USS Henry L. Stimson, 1965-67, project mgr. deep submergence, Washington, 1969-73, ret., 1973; chief engr. Clinch River Breeder Reactor, Project Mgmt. Corp., 1973-76, gen. mgr. Commonwealth Research Corp., Chgo., 1976-81, dir. nuclear safety Commonwealth Edison Co., Chgo., 1981-84, asst. v.p., 1984-85. cons. nuclear industry, 1986-93. . Pres., Canterbury Improvement Assn., 1982-83. Decorated Bronze Star medal, Legion of Merit with cluster, Purple Heart. Mem. Am. Nuclear Soc., Valley Lo Sports Club, (bd. dirs.), N.Y. Yacht Club, Suntree Country Club, Patrick Yacht Club. Roman Catholic. Died Mar. 15, 1993. Home: Melbourne Fla.

JOSEPH, SIR KEITH SINJOHN, British legislator; b. London, Jan. 17, 1918; s. Samuel and Edna Cicely (Phillips) J.; m. Hellen Louise Guggenheimer, July 6, 1951 (div. 1984); children: James, Emma, Julia, Anna. Ed. Harrow, 1931-36; M.A., Magdalen Coll., Oxford U., 1939; fellow All Souls Coll., 1946-60, 72-94. In bldg. constrn., 1945-59; M.P. for Leeds North East, 1956-94; parliamentary sec. to Ministry Housing and Local Govt., 1959-61; minister of state Bd. Trade, 1961-62; minister housing and local govt., minister for Welsh affairs, 1962-64; sec. state for social services, 1970-74; sec. state for industry, 1979-81; sec. state for edn. and sci., 1981-94; founder, chmn. mgmt. com. Centre for Policy Studies Ltd., 1974-79; dir. Gilbert-Ash Ltd., 1949-59, Drayton Premier Investment Trust Ltd.; dir. Bovis Holdings Ltd., 1951-59, dep. chmn., 1964-70; chmn. Bovis Ltd., 1958-59, founder, 1st chmn. Mulberry Housing Trust, 1965-69. Co-founder, 1st chmn. Found. for Mgmt. Edn., 159. cons. Bovis Ltd. Cable & Wireless plc, Trusthouse Forte plc. Served with Brit. Army, 1939-45. Succeeded to baronetcy, 1944. Jewish. Died Dec. 10, 1994. Home: London Eng.

JUDD, DONALD CLARENCE, sculptor; b. Excelsior Springs, Mo., June 3, 1928; s. Roy Clarence and Effie (Cowsert) J.; children: Flavin Starbuck, Rainer Yingling. Student, Coll. William and Mary, 1948-49, Art Students League, 1949-53; B.S. in Philosophy, Columbia U., 1953, postgrad., 1957-62. Tchr. Bklyn. Inst. Arts and Sci., 1962-64; vis. artist Darmouth Coll., 1966. Author: Complete Writings 1959-75, 1975; one-man shows include Panoras Gallery, 1957, Green Gallery, N.Y.C., 1963, Leo Castelli Gallery, N.Y.C., 1966, 69, 70, 73, 75, 76, 78, 81, 83, 84, Whitney Mus. Am. Art, 1968, Irving Blum Gallery, L.A., 1968, 69, Galerie Bischofberger, Zurich, Switzerland, 1969, Galerie Ileana Sonnabend, Paris, 1969, Galerie Rudolph Zwirner, Cologne, Germany, 1969, Whitechapel Art Gallery, London, 1970, Stedelijk Van Abbemuseum, Eindhoven, The Netherlands, 1970, Folkwang Mus., Essen, Germany, 1970, Konrad Fischer Dusseldorf, Germany, 1970, The Helman Gallery, St. Louis, 1970, Locksley-Shea Gallery, Mpls., 1970, Greenberg Gallery, St. Louis, 1970, Galerie Rolf Rick, Cologne, 1972, 87, 88-89, Galerie Daniel Templon, Paris, 1972, 75, Gian Enzo Sperone and Konrad Fischer, Rome, 1973, Lisson Gallery, London, 1974, 75, Ace Gallery, Venice, Calif., 1974-77, Sable-Castelli Gallery, Toronto, 1976, Mus. Modern Art, Oxford, Eng., 1976, Heiner Friedrich Gallery, N.Y.C., 1977, 78, Cologne, 1977, 79, Munich, 1978, Contemporary Arts Ctr., Cin., 1977, Art Mus. South Tex., 1977, Nationalgalerie, Berlin, 1978, Foyer MGB, Zurich, 1978, Rijksmuseum Kröller-Müller, Otterlo, The Netherlands, 1978, Young-Hoffman Gallery, Chgo., 1978, Akron (Ohio) Art Inst., 1979, Thomas Segal Gallery, Boston, 1979, Galerie Annemarie Verna, Zurich, 1979, 80, 83, 85, 87-88, 90, Newport Harbor Art Mus., Calif., 1981, Larry Gagosian Gallery, L.A., 1982, Margo Leavin Gallery, L.A., 1984, 87, Lia Rumma, Naples, Italy, 1985, Galerie Barbel Grasslin, Frankfurt-au-Main, Germany, 1985, Paula Cooper Gallery, N.Y.C., 1985, 86, 88, 90, Galerie Nachst St. Stephan, Vienn, Austria, 1988, Castello di Rivoli, Italy, 1988, Vivian Horan Fine Art, N.Y.C., 1988, Barbara Krakow and Thomas Segal Galleries, Boston, 1990, Jean Bernier, Athens, Greece, 1990, Soviet Cultural Found., Moscow, 1990, Persons & Lindell Gallery, Helsinki, Finland, 1990, Inkong Gallery, Seoul, Korea, 1991, Shizuoka (Japan) Prefectural Mus. Art, 1992, numerous others; retrospective exhbns. include Leo Castelli Gallery, N.Y.C., 1979, Blum Helman Gallery, N.Y.C., 1983, Max Protech Gallery, N.Y.C., 1984, 101 Spring St., N.Y.C., 1984, 92-93, Galerie Aronowitsch, Stockholm, 1989-90, Gallery Yamaguchi, Osaka, Japan, 1990, Galerie Rolf Rick, Cologne, 1991, St. Louis Art Mus., 1991, Galerie Ryszard Varisella, Frankfurt, Germany, 1991, Jean Bernier, Athens, 1991, Victoria Miro, London, 1991, Galerie Meert Rihout, Brussels, 1992, Gallery Yamaguchi, Osaka, Galerie Tanit, Munich, 1992, Kasseler Kunstverein, Kassel, Germany, 1992, Stedelijk Mus., Amsterdam, 1993-94, Galerie Gmurzynska, Cologne, 1994. Swedish Inst. fellow, 1965, Guggenheim fellow, 1968; NEA grantee, 1967, 76; recipient Skowhegan medal for sculpture Skowhegan Sch. of Painting and Sculpture, 1987, Poses Brandeis U. Creative Arts medal for sculpture, 1987, Stankowski prize Stankowski Found., 1992, 93, Sikkens award Sikkens Found., 1993. Mem. Royal Acad. Fine Arts (fgn. mem.), Littlefield Soc. Home: Marfa Tex. Died Feb. 12, 1994.

JUDSON, LYMAN SPICER VINCENT, author, artist, voice scientist; b. Plymouth, Mich., Mar. 27, 1903; s. Ernest W. and Fannie Louise (Spicer) J.; m. E. Ellen MacKechnie, 1933 (dec. 1964); m. 2d S. Adele H. Christensen, 1968. A.B., Albion Coll., 1925; postgrad., S.E. Mich. U., 1926, U. Iowa, 1929-30, U. So. Calif., 1927, Harvard, 1942, U. San Francisco, Palma, Mallorca, Spain, 1967; M.Sc., U. Mich., 1929; legis. scholar, U. Wis., 1931-33, Ph.D., 1933. Various positions as prof. speech communications and dept. chmn., and as dir. pub. relations and/or dir. fund raising and devel. and long-range planning; chief motion picture and visual edn. divs. OAS, 1946-51; producer ednl. motion pictures "Judson Color Jaunts"; served to comdr. USNR, 1942-65; mem. joint bd. USN tng. films, 1944-46; vis. prof. Latin Am. Affairs Assn. Am. Colls.; speech writer for Hon. Christian A. Herter, 1954-57; staff Supreme Allied Comdr. Atlantic; liaison officer staff Supreme Allied Comdr. Europe and European Hdqrs., dir. gen. NATO, 1953-54; spl. mission Vietnam and 7th Fleet, 1966; TV cons. Johnson Found., 1963-64; devel. and fund raising and long-range planning cons., 1965—. Author: Basic Speech and the Voice Science, 1933, The Fundamentals of the Speaker-Audience Relationship, 1934, Modern Group Discussion, 1935, Manual of Group Discussion, 1936, Public Speaking for Future Farmers, 1936, After-Dinner Speaking, 1937, Winning Future Farmers Speeches, 1939, The Student Congress Movement, 1940, The Monroe Doctrine and the Growth of Western Hemisphere Solidarity (co-author), 1941, Voice Science (co-author), 1942, rev. edit., 1965, The Judson Guides to Latin America (co-author), including Let's Go to Columbia, 1949, Let's Go to Guatemala, 1950, Let's Go to Peru, 1951, Your Holiday in Cuba, 1952, Report of Command Information Bureau 47 on Operation Inland Seas, 1959, The Interview, 1966, The Business Conference, 1969, Vincent Judson: The Island Series, 1973, Solution: PNC and PNCLAND, 1973, The AQUA Declaration, 1976, Happy 60th Birthday, 1982, The Shadow(s), 1983, Constitutional Corporations, 1988, Global Constitutional Corporations, 1991. Mem. Boston Athenaeum (Propr.), Explorers Scout Bd., cabinet mem. bed. mem., exec. com. mem., treas. Twin Lakes council Boy Scouts Am., 1972-73; sustaining mem. Rochester Civic Theatre; sustaining mem. Rochester Art Ctr. Fellow Am. Geog. Soc.; mem. Service Corps Retired Execs. (SCORE), Small Bus. Adminstrn., Inter-Am. Soc. Anthropology and Geography, Soc. Am. Archeology, Am. Soc. Agrl. Scis. Am. Acad. Polit. and Social Scis., Pub. Relations Soc. Am., Am. Speech & Hearing Assn., Archeol. Inst. Am. (pres. Winona-Hiawatha Valley chpt.), AAAS, Am. Micros. Soc., Navy League, Explorer's Club (New York, formerly editor of the Explorers LOG), Sigma Xi (Mayo Found. chpt.), Alpha Phi Omega, Delta Sigma Rho (former nat. sec., nat. editor), Tau Kappa Alpha, Pi Kappa Delta, Sigma Delta Chi (Boston prof. chpt.), Sigma Chi (life mem.). Mem. Clubs: Rotary (Paul Harris fellow); Cosmos (Washington). Home: Rochester Minn.

JULES, MERVIN, artist, educator; b. Balt., Mar. 21, 1912; s. Sidney and Anna (Goldenberg) J.; m. Rita Albers, Apr. 20, 1940; children: Gabriel, Fredrick. Student, Balt. City Coll., 1930, Md. Inst. Fine Arts, 1930-33, Art Students League, 1933-34. Instr. art Fieldston Sch., N.Y.C., 1942-44, Mus. Modern Art, 1943-44, 1946-48, War Vets. Art Center, 1944; vis. artist Smith Coll., 1945-45, asso. prof. art, 1946-63, prof., 1963-94, chmn. art dept., 1963-67; prof., chmn. art dept. CCNY, 1969-94; mem. staff, univ. extension div., dept. edn. Commonwealth Mass., 1950-52; lectr. U. Wis., summer 1951; staff George Vincent Smith Mus., Springfield, 1952-53; lectr. Hillyer Coll., Hartford, Conn., 1953; fellow McDowell Colony, 1938, 61; Yaddo fellow, 1941. One man shows include A.C.A. Gallery, N.Y.C., 1961, A.F.S. Gallery, Binghampton, N.Y., 1971, Ringwood (N.J.) Manor Assn. of Arts, 1973, Galeris Macler, Sarasota, Fla., 1978, 80, Cherry Stone Gallery, Wellfleet, Mass., 1979, Danco Gallery, Florence, Mass, 1979, Century Assn., N.Y.C., 1982; represented in collections including: Met. Mus. art, Mus. Modern Art, Art Inst. Chgo., Mus. Fine Arts of Boston, Portland (Oreg.) Mus., Library Congress, Balt. Mus. Art, Duncan Phillips Gallery, Walker Art Ctr., Tel Aviv Mus., N.Y. Library, La. Art Commn., Fogg Mus., Carnegie Inst., Brit. Mus., 1989, colls. and univs. Bd. dirs. Fine Arts Work Center, Provincetown, Mass.; mem. governing bd. Inst. for Study Art in Edn., Brit. Mus. Recipient Wilson Levering Smith medal, 1939, 41; Purchase prize Balt. Mus. Art, 1941; Purchase prize Mus. Modern Art, 1941; Purchase prize Library Congress, 1945; Purchase prize Bklyn. Mus., 1946; Springfield Art League prize, 1952; 1st prize, 1955; 1st prize Cape Cod Art Assn., 1957; Hollis M. Carlyle purchase prize Eastern States Art Exhbn., 1957; medal CCNY, 1973; McDowell Colony fellow, 1978; grant study in Japan Asian African Study Program, 196 Fellow Royal Soc. Arts; mem. AAUP, Provinceto Art Assn. (trustee, pres. 1985-87), Audubon Artis Nat. Acad., Artists League Am., Com. Art Edn., S Am. Graphic Artists, Artist Equity Assn., Springfi Art League, Boston Printmakers (hon. mention 1 Ann. Exhbn. 1967), Century Assn., Color Print Soc. Phila., Soc. of Am. Etchers, Engravers, Lithograph and woodcutters. Home: New York N.Y. Died July 1994.

JULIA, RAUL, actor; b. San Juan, P.R., Mar. 9, 19 s. Raul and Olga (Arcelay) J.; m. Merel Poloway, Ju 28, 1976; children. BA in Humanities, U. P.R.; stud in drama, Wynn Handman, 1964. Mem. Pho Brand's Theatre Inst., N.Y.C., 1964-94. (Spanish-la prodn.) Life Is A Dream, Astor Playhouse, 1964; N Shakespeare Festival prodns. Macbeth, 1966, 89- Titus Andronicus, summer 1967, Hamlet, 1972, As Y Like It, 1973, King Lear, 1973, The Threepenny Ope 1976, The Cherry Orchard, 1977, The Taming of Shrew, 1978, Othello, 1979; off-Broadway plays: The Cart, 1966, The Memorandum, 1968, No Exit, 19 Your Own Thing, 1968, The Persians, 1970, The E peror of Late Night Radio, 1974, The Robber Brid groom, 1974; Broadway debut, The Cuban Thing, 19 Broadway plays Frank Gagliano's City Scene, 19 Indians, 1969; Broadway plays The Castro Compl 1970, The Two Gentlemen of Verona, 1971, Wher Charley, 1974, Betrayal, 1980, Nine, 1982, Design Living, 1984, Arms and the Man, 1985, Man of Mancha, 1992; rd.-co. prodn. Dracula, 1978, Broadw prodn., 1979; films: The Organization, 1971, Been Do So Long It Looks Like Up To Me, 1971, The Panic Needle Park, 1971, The Gumball Rally, 1976, The E of Laura Mars, 1978, The Escape Artist, 1982, C From The Heart, 1982, Tempest, 1982, Compromisi Positions, 1985, Kiss of the Spider Woman, 1985, T Morning After, 1986, Florida Straits, 1986, Moon O Parador, 1988, Tequila Sunrise, 1988, Romero, 19 Tango Bar, 1989, Mack the Knife, 1989, Presumed nocent, 1990, The Rookie, 1990, The Addams Fam 1991, The Plague, Addams Family Values, 1993, Str Fighter, 1994; TV appearances, Death Scream, Love Life, Mussolini: The Untold Story (mini-series), T Richest Man in the World (mini-series), 1988; TV p appearances Aces UP, CBS, 1974; Rafael the Fixit M series Sesame Street, Pub. Broadcasting System; movie The Alamo: 13 Days to Glory; appeared in Gran Fiesta. Active Internat. Hunger Project. M Hispanic Orgn. Latin Actors. Home: New York N Died Oct. 24, 1994; buried in Puerto Rico.

JULIEN, RICHARD EDWARD HALE, lawyer; Detroit, Mar. 20, 1900; s. Edward H. and Kathe (Heard) J.; m. Sophie Hill, Aug. 30, 1926; c dren—Joan Mary, Richard Edward Hale. A.B., Calif. at Berkeley, 1923; LL.B., Harvard, 1926. Calif. bar 1935. Corporate fiduciary banking N.Y San Francisco, 1927-35; since practiced in San Fran co.; Dir. Travelers Aid Soc. San Francisco, 1963-6 Contbr. articles to banking, legal jours. Life mem. A Bar Assn. (mem. ho. dels. 1952-62, chmn. com. hearing 1960-62, rep. Conf. Lawyers and C.P.A.'s 19 65, mem. bd. govs. 1964-67, assembly del. Ho. of D 1963-66, 71-73); mem. Bar Assn. San Francisco (dirs., chmn. com. judiciary 1958-59), State Bar C (chmn. com. on taxation, com. on Jour. 1958-60), A Law Inst., Practicing Law Inst., Am. Bar Fou (charter life fellow), Am. Judicature Soc., Soc. C Pioneers San Francisco County (v.p.), Am. Legion (p post comdr.), Phi Delta Theta, Phi Alpha Delta (hon Republican. Clubs: Commonwealth of Calif. (past chr sect. on adminstrn. of justice), Harvard, Olympi Home: San Francisco Calif. Deceased.

JULIN, JOSEPH RICHARD, lawyer, educator; Chgo., July 5, 1926; s. George Allan and Je Elizabeth (Carlsten) J.; m. Dorothy Marie Julian, C 18, 1952; children: Pamela, Thomas, Dia Linda. Student, Deep Springs Coll., 1944, Geo Washington U., 1946-49; B.S.L., Northwestern U., 19 J.D., 1952. Bar: Ill. 1952, Mich. 1960. Assoc. f Schuyler, Stough & Morris, Chgo., 1952-57; p Schuyler, Stough & Morris, 1957-59; assoc. prof. law Mich., Ann Arbor, 1959-62, prof. law, 1962-70, as dean, 1968-70; dean, prof. law U. Fla., Gainesvi 1971-80; dean emeritus and prof. law U. Fla., 1980- Chesterfield Smith prof. law, 1985-93; pres., cheif e officer Nat. Conf. Bar Examiners, 1987-90. Auth (with others) Basic Property Law, 1966, 72, 79. Tru Ann Arbor Bd. Edn., 1966-69, pres., 1968-69. Ser with U.S. Army, 1944-46. Fellow Am. Bar Fou mem. Legal Club of Chgo., Mich. Bar Assn., Ill. Assn., Chgo. Bar Assn., Am. Bar Assn. (chmn. sect. legal edn. and admissions to the bar 1977-78), As Am. Law Schs. (pres. 1984), Order of Coif., Phi B Kappa. Republican. Home: Gainesville Fla. Died A 3, 1993.

JUNEJO, MOHAMMAD KHAN, former pri minister of Pakistan; b. Sindhri, Sanghar, Pakist 1932. Educated St. Patrick's Sch., Karachi, Pakist Agr. Inst. Hastings, Eng. Pres. Dist. Local Bd. Sanghar, 1954; mem. West Pakistan Provincial sembly from Sanghar, 1962; apptd. minister W Pakistan cabinet, 1963-69; minister for rys. Pakist

78-79; mem. Pakistani Nat. Assembly, from 1985, ime minister, 1985-88, minister of def., until 1988; tive in health, local govt., coops., works, communica-ns, labor and soc. welfare throughout career; pres. kistan Muslim League, 1985. Lifted state of ergency from Pakistan which was in force for last 20 s. Died Mar. 17, 1993. Home: Islamabad Pakistan

JNKINS, JERRY R., electronics company executive; Ft. Madison, Iowa, Dec. 9, 1937; s. Ralph Renaud d Selma Jeannie (Kudebeh) J.; m. Marilyn Jo hevers, June 13, 1959; children: Kirsten Dianne, aren Leigh. BEE, Iowa State U., 1959; MS in Engr-g. Adminstrn., So. Methodist U., 1968. With def. bus. x. Instruments, Inc., Dallas, 1959-75, asst. v.p., mgr. uipment group, 1975-77, v.p., mgr. equipment group, 77-81, exec. v.p., mgr. data systems and indsl. sys-ns, 1981-85, pres., CEO, 1985-88, chmn, pres., CEO, l. dirs., 1988-96; bd. dirs. Procter and Gamble Co., terpillar Inc., 3M. Trustee So. Meth. U.; bd. dirs. S.-Japan Bus. Coun., Dallas Citizens Coun.; mem. dv. Com. on Trade Policy and Negotiations. Mem. at. Acad. Engring. Home: Dallas Tex. Died May 28, 96.

JRIST, JAMES ALFRED, retired computer services mpany executive; s. Alfred Edward and Rachel raff) J.; m. Janet Calodny, June 28, 1953; children: uis, Carolyn. B.A., Columbia U., 1947, M.B.A., 49. C.P.A., N.Y. Sr. acct. Arthur Young & Co., .Y.C., 1949-51, 53-56; in various fin. positions NBC, 56-65; dir. bus. affairs NBC Films, NBC, N.Y.C., 60-61, NBC News, NBC, N.Y.C., 1961-65; controller olumbia Pictures Corp., N.Y.C., 1965-67; v.p., treas., ief fin. officer John Blair & Co., N.Y.C., 1967-84; sr. p., chief fin. officer, treas. Donovan Data Systems, .Y.C., 1985-87. Served to 1st lt. USAAF, 1943-46; en USAF, 1951-52, CBI, Korea. Mem. Am. Inst. P.A.s, N.Y. State Soc. C.P.A.s, Phi Beta Kappa, Beta amma Sigma. Home: New York N.Y. Died Dec. 19, 91.

ABALEVSKY, DMITRYI BORISOVICH, com-ser; b. St. Petersburg, Dec. 30, 1904; ed. Moscow onservatory; student N.Y. Myaskovsky and A.B. oldenweiser. Prof., Moscow Conservatory, 1939-87; c. Union Soviet Composers, 1951-87; mem. Com-unist Party, 1940-87, mem. USSR Peace com., 1955-, dep. to USSR Supreme Council, from 1966; mem. uncil of dirs. Internat. Soc. for Music Edn., 1961-87, n. pres., 1972-87; v.p. of the Nationality Soviet of the SSR Supreme Council. Named People's Artist of SSR; Hero of socialist labour, 1944, 74; recipient enin prize; State prize, 1946, 49, 51, 80; R.S.F.S.R. ate prize, 1966; decorated Order of Lenin (3), Red anner of Labour, 1966. Mem. Acad. Pedagogical Scis. omposer: 4 symphonies, 2 string quartets, 4 piano ncertos; violin and (2) cello concertos; (cantata) Great otherland, 1942; (operas) Colas Brugnon, 1937, Under re, 1943, Tara's Family, 1950, Nikita Vershinin, 1954, sters, 1969; (films) Petersburg Nights, 1933, Shchors, 39, Marusya's First Year at School, 1948, Mus-rgsky, 1950, Volnitsa, 1956, Sisters, 1957, 18th Year, 58, Gloomy Morning, 1959; 10 Shakespeare sonnets r bass with pianoforte accompaniment, 1953-55, and any other songs and choirs; (symphonic suite) Romeo d Juliet, 1956; (children's cantata) Song of Morning, oring and Peace, 1957; (operetta) Spring Sings, 1957; antata) Lenintsy, 1959; Sonata for Cello and Piano, 62; (oratorio) Requiem, 1964; author 8 books on usic and aesthetics edn. for musicians, teachers and ildren; about 500 articles. Died Feb. 14, 1987. Home: loscow Russia

ÁDÁR, JÁNOS, Hungarian politician; b. Fiume, now ijeka, Yugoslavia, May 26, 1912; ed. secondary sch. em. Young Communists Workers Fedn., 1931, illegal ommunist Party, 1931; an organizer of resistance ovement World War II; dep. police chief, 1945; sec. reater Budapest Party Com., 1945-46; asst. gen. sec. ommunist Party, 1947, dep. gen. sec. Hungarian /orking People's Party (merger Communist Party and ocial Democratic Party), 1948; M.P., Hungary, 1945-l, from 1958; minister internal affairs, 1948; 1st sec. ungarian Socialist Workers Party, 1956-85, gen. sec., 985-88, pres., 1988—; prime minister, 1956-58, 61-65; em. Presdl. Council, from 1965; minister of state, 958-61; mem. C.C., 1956—; mem. Polit. Com., 1956-8. Decorated Hero of Socialist Labor; Hero of Soviet nion; Order of Lenin; recipient Joliot Curie Gold ledal award; Internat. Lenin Peace award. Author: irm People's Power: Independent Hungary, 1958; For e Total Victory of Socialism, 1962; On the Road of enin, 1964; Patriotism and Internationalism, 1968; For e Socialist Hungary, 1972; Selected Speeches and Ar-cles, 1974; On the Road of the Construction of eveloped Socialist Society, 1975; Internationalism, olidarity, Socialist Patriotism, 1977; For Socialism-For eace, 1978; Policy of Alliance-National Unity, 1981; arty, Trade Union, Socialism, 1982; The Renewal of ocialism in Hungary, 1986, Válogatott Müvei, 1 kötet, 957/58 (selected works, vol. 1), 1987. Home: Budapest ungary

AESER, HANS EUGEN, oncologist; b. Berne, witzerland, June 17, 1924; s. Hans Robert and Gertrud Hoechle) K.; m. Rosmary Glanzmann, June 14, 925. MD, U. Med. Sch. Berne, 1951. Asst. dept. pathology U. Berne, 1951, asst. dept. pediatrics, 1952-57, head physician, 1957-63; head labs. U. Inst. for Protein Research, Berne, 1963-64, U. Inst. for Clin. Explt. Cancer Research, Berne, from 1965; lectr. U. Berne, 1972, prof. clin. pathology and oncology, 1981; dir. Inst. Clin./Exptl. Cancer Research, U. Berne, from 1985. Lt. col. Med. Svc. Swiss Army. Recipient Internat. award, Guigoz Inc., 1958, Cancer award, Swiss Nat. Cancer League, 1964, others. Mem. Swiss Pediatric Soc., Swiss Soc. Endocrinology, Swiss Soc. Oncology, Swiss Soc. Clin. Chemistry, Internat. Soc. Pediatric Oncology. Home: Hofwyl Switzerland Deceased.

KAHLES, JOHN FRANK, research company executive; b. Chgo., Sept. 11, 1914; s. Frank Sylvester and Anna (Quint) K.; m. Beatrice Wiesmann, Apr. 13, 1940; children: Bonnie, John, Kathleen, James, Peggy Anne, Michael, Susan. B.S., Armour Inst. Tech., 1936; Ph.D., U. Cin., 1946. Registered profl. engr., Ohio. Assoc. prof. U. Cin., Cin., 1946-51; v.p. Metcut Research Assocs., Inc., Cin., 1951-90, ret., 1990. Editor: Machining Data Handbook 1966-80, 3 edits. Contbr. articles to profl. jours. Bd. dirs. Friars, Cin., 1974-93. Recipient Joseph Whitworth prize Inst. Mech. Engr., London, 1968; Disting. Alumnus award U. Cin., 1972, Friars award, 1992. Mem. Am. Foundrymen's Soc., AIME, Am. Soc. Info. Sci., Am. Soc. for Metals (William H. Eisenman award 1961), ASTM, Internat. Instn. for Prodn. Engring. Research, Engrs. and Scientists of Cin., Soc. Mfg. Engrs. (Research medal 1973), Nat. Acad. Engring. Democrat. Roman Catholic. Home: Cincinnati Ohio Died May 26, 1993.

KAHN, ELY JACQUES, JR., writer; b. N.Y.C., Dec. 4, 1916; s. Ely Jacques and Elsie Plaut Mayer; m. Virginia Rice, 1945 (div. 1969); children: Ely Jacques III, Joseph Plaut, Hamilton Rice; m. Eleanor Munro, 1969; stepchildren: David T.M. Frankfurter, Alexander M. Frankfurter. Grad., Horace Mann Sch., 1933; A.B., Harvard U., 1937; LL.D. (hon.), Marlboro Coll., 1986. Writer, reporter N.Y.C., 1937—; adj. prof. writing Columbia, 1974-75, 81-82. Author: The Army Life, 1942, G. I. Jungle, 1943, McNair: Educator of an Army, 1945, The Voice, 1947, Who, Me? 1949, The Peculiar War, 1952, The Merry Partners, 1955, The Big Drink, 1960, A Reporter Here and There, 1961, The Stragglers, 1962, The World of Swope, 1965, A Reporter in Micronesia, 1966, The Separated People, 1968, Harvard: Through Change and Through Storm, 1969, The First Decade, 1972, (with Joseph P. Kahn) The Boston Underground Gourmet, 1972, Fraud, 1973, The American People, 1974, The China Hands, 1975 (Sidney Hillman prize), Georgia: From Rabun Gap to Tybee Light, 1978, About The New Yorker and Me, 1979, Far-flung and Footloose, 1980, Jock: The Life and Times of John Hay Whitney, 1981, The Staffs of Life, 1985, The Problem Solvers, 1986, Year of Change: More About The New Yorker and Me, 1988, Supermarketer to the World, 1991; contbr.: The New Yorker, other nat. mags. Bd. dirs. Assn. Harvard Alumni, 1969-72. Served with AUS, 1941-45. Recipient Legion of Merit award, Disting. Achievement award Horace Mann Sch., 1981. Mem. Authors Guild Am., Authors League Am., PEN (exec. com. 1976-79), Soc. Am. Historians, Harvard Club (N.Y.C.), Century Assn., Phi Beta Kappa, Kappa Alpha Tau. Home: New York N.Y. Died Mar. 28, 1994.

KAHN, EVERETT FISHER, lawyer, manufacturing corporation executive; b. N.Y.C., Sept. 12, 1924; s. Samuel and Lillian K.; m. Edith S. Adler, Sept. 2, 1951; children: Alison, Lisa, Claudia. A.B., Columbia U., 1947, J.D., 1949. Bar: N.Y. State bar 1950, D.C. bar 1973. Practice law N.Y.C., 1950-53, 67-69; with Bendix Corp. (now Allied Corp. subs. Allied-Signal Corp.), Southfield, Mich., from 1969; govt. relations counsel Bendix Corp. (now Allied Corp. subs. Allied-Signal Corp.), from 1972; sec., dir. Bendix Comml. Service Corp., from 1972, Bendix Field Engring. Corp., from 1972. Served with AUS, 1943-46. Mem. Am. Bar Assn., D.C. Bar Assn., Nat. Security Indsl. Assn. (life). Home: Rockville Md. Deceased.

KAHN, IRVING B., communications executive; b. N.Y.C., Sept. 30, 1917; s. Abraham and Ruth (Baline) K.; m. Elizabeth Heslin, Sept. 17, 1949; children: Ruth, Jean. B.S., U. Ala., 1939. Advt., publicity mgr. Wilby-Kincey theatres, Tuscaloosa, Ala., 1935-38; publicity mgr. orchs., 1938-39; radio contact, advt. and publicity dept. 20th Century Fox, 1939-42, radio mgr., 1945-46; TV program mgr., spl. asst. to Spyros P. Skouras, 1946-51; pres., chmn. TelePrompTer Corp., 1951-71, Irving B. Kahn & Co., 1972-75; pres., chmn. bd. BroadBand Communications, Inc., 1975-94, Choice Cable Corp., 1987-90; chmn. exec. com., dir. Times Fiber Communications, Inc., 1977-80; chmn. bd. Gen. Optronics Corp., 1977-88 , Electro-Optic Devices Corp., 1977-81; dir. Nat. Cable TV Assn., 1965-68; staging cons. Dem., Rep. Nat. Convs., 1952, 56, 60. Pioneered the use of closed-cir. TV for teaching purposes Redstone Arsenal, Huntsville, Ala., the use of large-screen closed-cir. telecasters; co-designer automated electronic audio-visual systems. Served as 1st lt. USAAF, 1942-45. NCTA Larry Boggs Man of Year award, 1970. Mem. Soc. Motion Picture an TV Engrs., Internat. Radio and TV Soc. N.Y., Nat. Cable TV Assn., Am. Rocket Soc., Young Pres. Orgn., Internat. Inst. Communications (trustee 1980-82), Found. of the Dramatists Guild (bd. dirs. 1990-94), Phi Sigma Delta. Clubs: Nat. Press (Washington); Variety of Am. Home: Mamaroneck N.Y. Died Jan. 22, 1994; interred Woodlawn, N.Y.C.

KAISEL, STANLEY FRANCIS, management consultant; b. St. Louis, Aug. 2, 1922; s. Samuel and Dora (Sincoff) K.; m. Mary Ann Shriver, Mar. 2, 1958; children: David Allen, Ann Penland. BSEE, Washington U., St. Louis, 1943; MSEE, Stanford U., 1946, PhD, 1949. Spl. rsch. assoc. Radio Rsch. Lab., Harvard U., Cambridge, Mass., 1943-45; rsch. assoc. Elec. Rsch. Lab., Stanford (Calif.) U., 1946-49, 51-55; rsch. engr. RCA Labs., Princeton, N.J., 1949-51; mgr. engring. microwave tube div. Litton Industries, San Carlos, Calif., 1955-58; pres. Microwave Electronics Corp., Palo Alto, Calif., 1959-69; cons. Albion Assocs., Portola Valley, Calif., 1969-95; mem. vis. com. Sch. Engring., Stanford U. Trustee Woodside (Calif.) Elem. Sch., 1975-81, Nueva Ctr. for Learning, Hillsborough, Calif., 1985-95. Recipient Gold Spike award Stanford U., 1982. Fellow IEEE (chmn. San Francisco sect. 1961-63, bd. dirs. region 6, 1967-68). Jewish. Home: Portola Valley Calif. Died June 22, 1995.

KALBACH, JOHN FREDERICK, electrical engineer, consultant; b. Seattle, Jan. 2, 1914; s. Taylor Patterson and Pauline (Stopplemann) K.; m. Bettina Truesdale Cook, Dec. 28, 1939; children: David Patterson, Jean Louise Kalbach Dent, Paul Douglas. BSEE magna cum laude, U. Wash., 1937. Registered profl. engr., Calif. Rec. equipment designer Seattle Rec. Studios, 1935-37; elec. equipment designer Gen. Electric Co., Ft. Wayne Ind., Schenectady, N.Y. and Lynn, Mass., 1937-47; staff scientist Van de Graff Accelerator, Los Alamos, N.Mex., 1947-51; analog computer designer, engring. mgr. Miller Instruments, Pasadena, Calif., 1951-55; various design mgmt. positions ElectoData and Burroughs Co., Pasadena, 1955-79; cons., owner Kalbach Engring. Assocs., Altadena, Calif., 1979-88; lectr. engring. U. Calif., Berkeley, 1947-48. Contbr. articles to profl. jours.; patentee in field. Fellow IEEE, Inst. Advancement Engring.; mem. Am. Soc. Computing Machinery, Electrostatic Soc. Am. Republican. Club: Electronic. Home: Carmichael Calif. Died Oct. 7, 1988.

KALBFLEISCH, GIRARD EDWARD, federal judge; b. Piqua, Ohio, Aug. 3, 1899; s. Oscar Conrad and Magdalena Margaret (Gerstmeyer) K.; m. Chattie Lenora Spohn, May 1, 1929; m. 2d, Mary Elizabeth Walker Hien, Dec. 23, 1986. LL.B., Ohio No. U., Ada, 1923, LL.D., 1960. Bar: Ohio bar 1924. Pvt. practice Mansfield, Ohio, 1929; pros. atty. Richland County, 1929-33; mcpl. judge Mansfield, 1936-42; judge Ct. Common Pleas, Richland County, 1943-58; sr. U.S. dist. judge for No. Ohio, 1959-90; pres. Common Pleas Judges Assn. Ohio, 1952; mem. Ct. Nisi Prius, Cleve., 1962. Served with S.A.T.C., 1918. Fellow Ohio State Bar Found.; mem. Am. Bar Assn., Fed. Bar Assn., Ohio Bar Assn., Richland County Bar Assn., Soc. Benchers Case Western Res. U. Law Sch. Home: Mansfield Ohio Died Apr. 1, 1990; interred Mansfield, Ohio.

KALINOWSKY, LOTHAR B., neuropsychiatrist; b. Berlin, Dec. 28, 1899; s. Alfred and Anna (Schott) K.; m. Hilda Pohl, Mar. 7, 1925; children: Marion, Ellen. Student univs., Berlin, Heidelberg, Munich, 1917-22; M.D., U. Berlin, 1922, U. Rome, 1934. Diplomate: Am. Bd. Neurology and Psychiatry. Asst. neuropsychiatry univ. hosps. Berlin, Hamburg, Breslau, Vienna, 1922-32; asst. Univ. Hosp. for Nervous and Mental Diseases, Rome, 1933-39; guest physician various European hosps., 1939-40, Pilgrim State Hosp., 1940-43; attending psychiatrist N.Y. Psychiat. Inst. and Hosp., N.Y.C., 1940-58; asso. neurologist Neurol. Inst., N.Y.C., 1940-57; attending psychiatrist St. Vincent's Hosp., N.Y.C., 1957-92; specializing chiefly in somatic treatment in psychiatry, 1938-92; teaching, research asso. psychiatry Coll. Physicians and Surgeons, Columbia U., 1942-58; asso. prof. neuropsychiatry N.Y. Sch. Psychiatry, 1958-92; clin. prof. psychiatry N.Y. Med. Coll., 1961-92; hon. prof. psychiatry Free U. Berlin, 1970-92. Author: (with Paul H. Hoch) Somatic Treatments in Psychiatry, 1961, (with H. Hippius) Pharmacological, Convulsive and Other Somatic Treatments in Psychiatry, 1969, (with H. Hippius and H. E. Klein) Biological Treatments in Psychiatry, 1982; contbr. numerous articles sci. jours. Mem. Brit. Med. Assn., AMA, Am. Psychiat. Assn., Am. Neurol. Assn., N.Y. Acad. Medicine, Internat. League Against Epilepsy, Royal Coll. Psychiatrists (corr.), German Neuropsychiat. Soc. (hon.). Home: New York N.Y. Died June 28, 1992.

KALMANOVITZ, PAUL, brewery company executive. Chmn., chief exec. officer Falstaff Brewing Corp., Corte Madera, Calif.

KAMENKA, EUGENE, historian; b. Cologne, Fed. Republic of Germany, Apr. 3, 1928; arrived in Australia, 1937; s. Sergei and Nadja (Litvin) K.; m. Miriam Mizrahi, 1950 (div. 1964); children: Anat, Eri; m. Alice Erh-Soon Tay, Dec. 18, 1964. BA, U. Sydney, Australia, 1954; PhD, Australian Nat. U., 1964. Research scholar in philosophy Australian Nat. U., Canberra, 1955-57, research fellow in philosophy, 1961-62, research fellow, fellow, sr. fellow, profl. fellow, 1962-74, prof., 1975—; lectr. in philosophy U. of Malaya, Singapore, 1958-59; vis. prof. U. British Columbia, 1986; vis. fellow Trinity Coll., N.Y.C., 1968. Author: The

Ethical Foundations of Marxism, 1962, Marxism and Ethics, 1969, The Philosophy of Ludwig Feuerbach, 1970; editor: A World in Revolution?: The University Lectures 1970, 1970, Paradigm for Revolution? The Paris Commune 1871-1971, 1972, Nationalism-The Nature and Evolution of an Idea, 1973, Community as a Social Ideal, 1982, Utopias, 1987; (with Alice E.-S. Tay) Human Rights, 1978, Justice, 1979, Law-Making in Australia, 1980, Law and Social Control, 1980; (with R. S. Neale) Feudalism, Capitalism and Beyond, 1975; (with Robert Brown and Alice E.-S. Tay) Law and Society-The Crisis in Legal Ideals, 1978; (with Martin Krygier) Bureaucracy, 1979; (with Hon. Mr. Justice F. C. Hutley and Alice E.-S. Tay) Law and the Future of Society, 1979; (with F. B. Smith) Intellectuals and Revolution-Socialism and the Experience of 1848, 1979; (with R. S. Summers and W. Twining) Soziologische Jurisprudenz Und Realistische Utopiae Theorien Des Rechts, 1987; editor, translator: The Portable Karl Marx, 1983. Fellow Acad. Social Scis. in Australia (exec. mem. 1971-74), Australian Acad. Humanities (hon. sec., council 1976-81); mem. Australian Soc. for Legal Philosophy (pres. 1987—). Home: Red Hill Australia

KAMM, JACOB OSWALD, manufacturing executive, economist; b. Cleve., Nov. 29, 1918; s. Jacob and Minnie K. (Christensen) K.; m. Judith Steinbrenner, Apr. 24, 1965; children: Jacob Oswald II, Christian P. A.B. summa cum laude, Baldwin-Wallace Coll., 1940, LL.D., 1963; A.M., Brown U., 1942; Ph.D., Ohio State U., 1948; LL.D., Erskine Coll., 1971. Asst. econs. Brown U., 1942; instr. Ohio State U., 1945; instr. Baldwin-Wallace Coll., 1943-46, asst. prof., 1947-48, assoc. prof., 1948; prof., dir. Baldwin-Wallace Coll. (Sch. Commerce), 1948-53; econ. cons. to U.S. Post Office, 1951; exec. v.p. Cleve. Quarries Co., 1953-55, pres., 1955-67, chmn. bd., CEO, dir., 1967-88; chmn. bd., pres., CEO EFCO Inc., 1985-95; pres., treas., dir. Am. Shipbldg. Co., 1967-69, pres., 1973-74; dir. Nordson Corp., Gradison-McDonald Money Market Fund, Gradison-McDonald Growth Trust, Gradison-McDonald U.S. Treasury Bond Fund, Gradison-McDonald Tax-Exempt Fund, Oatey Co., United Screw and Bolt Corp., MTD Products, Inc.; bd. dirs., chmn. Canefco Ltd. Author: Decentralization of Securities Exchanges, 1942, Economics of Investment, 1951, Making Profits in the Stock Market, 3d rev. edit, 1966, Investor's Handbook, 1954; contbg. author: An Introduction to Modern Economics, 1952, Essays On Business Finance, 1953; weekly columnist econ. affairs Cleve. Plain Dealer, 1964-68; contbg. editor: Webster's New World Dictionary of the American Language; contbr. articles to profl. jours. Exec. bd. Lorain County Met. Park Bd., 1961-66; hon. mem. Mental Health Com., 1964-69; mem. St. Luke's Hosp. Assn., 1967-87; mem. adv. council Cleve. Mus. Natural History, 1967-88; bd. regents State of Ohio, 1969-72; pub. mem. Underground Gas Storage Com. Ohio, 1964-73; chmn. Lorain County Republican Finance Com., 1968-70, mem. exec. com., 1969-70; mem. Ohio Rep. Finance Com., 1969-70; charter life mem. bd. counselors Erskine Coll., 1962-95; life fellow Cleve. Zool. Soc., trustee, 1966-77; trustee Fairview Gen. Hosp., 1966-68; trustee Baldwin-Wallace Coll., 1953-78, mem. exec. and investment coms., 1956-78, chmn. investment com., 1974-78, hon. life trustee, 1979-95; mem. pres.'s club Ohio State U.; mem. com. grad. edn. and research Brown U., 1978-80, Red Cross of Constantine. Recipient Alumni Merit award Baldwin-Wallace Coll., 1956, Wisdom award of honor, and election to Wisdom Hall of Fame, 1970, Pro Mundi Beneficio medal Acad. Humanities, Sao Paulo, Brazil, 1975, Winston Churchill Medal of Wisdom, 1988; named an Eminent Churchill fellow of the Wisdom Soc., 1988; inducted into the Hall of Excellence for the Ohio Found. of Ind. Colls., 1988. Mem. AAUP, Am. Econs. Assn., Royal Econ. Soc., Am. Fin. Assn., Indsl. Assn. North Cen. Ohio (pres. 1960), Ohio Mfrs. Assn. (exec. com. 1970-80), trustee, chmn. bd. trustees 1975-77), Early Settlers Assn. of Western Res. (life), Newcomen Soc. N.Am., Assn. Ohio Commodores, John Baldwin Soc., Ohio Soc. N.Y., Nat. Alumni Assn. Baldwin-Wallace Coll. (pres. 1961-63), Union Club (Cleve.), Duquesne Club (Pitts.), Clifton Club (Lakewood, Ohio), Masons (33 degree), Shriners, Jesters, Valley of Cleve. (treas. emeritus), Phi Beta Kappa, Phi Alpha Kappa, Delta Phi Alpha, Delta Mu Delta, Beta Gamma Sigma. Methodist. Home: Cleveland Oh. Died June 25, 1995.

KANE, ROBERT EDWARD, biologist, educator; b. Erie, Pa., Mar. 22, 1931; s. Edward Thomas and Dorothy Marie (Lavery) K.; m. Nancy Kay Lind, Apr. 11, 1970 (div. June 1976). BS, MIT, 1953; PhD, Johns Hopkins U., 1957. Asst. prof. biochemistry Brandeis U., Waltham, Mass., 1958-61; asst. prof. Dartmouth Med. Sch., Hanover, N.H., 1961-66; assoc. prof. U. Hawaii, Honolulu, 1966-69, prof., 1969—; mem. panel Nat. Inst. Health, Bethesda, Md., 1983-85. Contbr. articles to profl. jours. Recipient Career Devel. award NSF, 1963-66; research grantee NSF, 1958-61, Nat. Inst. Health, 1961—; predoctoral fellow NSF, 1955-57. Fellow AAAS; mem. Am. Soc. for Cell Biology, Internat. Soc. of Devel. Biologists, Sigma Xi. Home: Honolulu Hawaii

KANEMARU, SHIN, Japanese politician; Mem. Ho. of Reps., Japan, re-elected 6 times; minister of constrn., Japan, 1972-73; dir. Nat. Land Agy., then Defence Agy., Japan, until 1978; sec.-gen. Liberal Dem. Party, 1984-92 also former chmn., former chmn. diet policy com.; dep. prime minister, Japan, from 1986. Died March 28, 1996. Home: Tokyo Japan

KANIN, MICHAEL, screenwriter, playwright; b. Rochester, N.Y., Feb. 1, 1910; s. David and Sadie K.; m. Fay Mitchell; 1 child, Josh. Student, Art Students League, N.Y.C., N.Y. Sch. Design. Comml. and scenic artist, musician, entertainer, until 1937. Author screenplays: They Made Her a Spy, 1939; Panama Lady, 1939; Anne of Windy Poplars, 1940; Centennial Summer, 1944; Honeymoon, 1945; When I Grow Up, 1951; The Outrage, 1964; (with Ring Lardner Jr.) Woman of the Year (Acad. Award for Best Original Screenplay 1942), 1941; The Cross of Lorraine, 1942; (with Fay Kanin) Sunday Punch, 1942; My Pal Gus, 1951; Rhapsody, 1953; The Opposite Sex, 1956; Teacher's Pet, 1957 (Acad. Award nomination, Writers Guild nomination), The Right Approach, 1961; The Swordsman of Sienna, 1962; (with Ben Starr) How to Commit Marriage, 1968; dir.: When I Grow Up, 1951; producer: A Double Life, 1947 (2 Acad. Awards); author: (with Fay Kanin) Broadway plays His and Hers, 1954; Rashomon, 1958; The Gay Life; musical, 1961; co-producer: Broadway plays Goodbye My Fancy, 1948; Seidman and Son, 1962. Mem. Writers Guild (bd. dirs. 1943-44, treas. 1944-45), Dramatists Guild, Acad. Motion Pictures Arts and Scis. (documentary com.), Am. Film Inst., Am. Coll. Theatre Festival (playwriting awards program founder), Internat. Sculpture Ctr. Home: Santa Monica Calif. Died Mar. 12, 1993.

KANTOR, SETH, writer, reporter, media affairs specialist; b. N.Y.C., Jan. 9, 1926; s. Arvid and Ella Kathryn (Reisman) K.; m. Anne Blackman, June 7, 1952; children: Susan E. Bank, Amy van Genabeek. Student, Wayne U., 1946-47. Copy boy Detroit AP Bur., 1947; sports editor Lamar (Colo.) Daily News, 1948; feature writer Pueblo (Colo.) Chieftain, 1949; sports desk Denver Rocky Mountain News, 1949; editor, free-lance writer, numerous mags. N.Y.C. and Ft. Worth, 1950-57; reporter Ft. Worth Press, 1957-60, Dallas Times Herald, 1960-62; corr. Scripps-Howard Newspaper Alliance, Washington, 1962-72; corr. Washington Bur., Detroit News, 1972-78; nat. investigative reporter Atlanta Constn., Cox Newspapers, Washington, 1978-81; sr. editor Nation's Bus. Mag., Washington, 1982-83; Washington corr. Austin Am.-Statesman, Cox Newspapers, 1984-91; syndicated reporter N. Am. Newspaper Alliance, 1972-79, N.Y. Times News Service, 1980-81, 84-91; major fgn. reporting assignments included London, Israel, Jordan, Egypt, 1986, Madrid, Kiev, USSR, Moscow, Fed. Republic Germany, Costa Rica, 1987. Author: Who Was Jack Ruby?, 1978, The Ruby Coverup, 1980. Bd. advisors Freedom Found., 1991-93. Recipient numerous profl. awards, including nat. Sigma Delta Chi award for Washington correspondence, 1974; fellow Paul Miller Washington Reporting Fellowship Program, Freedom Found., 1987-88. Mem. Nat. Press Club (bd. govs. 1976-78). Home: Bethesda Md. Died Aug. 17, 1993; interred Judean Gardens, Olney, Md.

KAPLAN, ABRAHAM, philosophy educator; b. Odessa, USSR, June 11, 1918; came to U.S., 1923, naturalized, 1930; s. Joseph and Chava (Lerner) K.; m. Iona Judith Wax, Nov. 17, 1939; children: Karen Eva Kaplan Diskin, Jessica Ariya Kaplan Symonds. B.A., Coll. St. Thomas, 1937; postgrad., U. Chgo., 1937-40; Ph.D., U. Calif., Los Angeles, 1942; D.H.L., U. Judaism, 1962, Hebrew Union Coll., 1971. Instr. NYU, 1944-45; asst. prof. UCLA, 1946-49, assoc. prof., 1949-55, prof., 1955-63, chmn. dept. philosophy, 1952-56; prof. philosophy U. Mich., 1963-72; prof. U. Haifa, Israel, 1972-93; former dean social scis. faculty, chmn. philosophy dept. U. Haifa, 1978-93, Gruenblat prof. social ethics, 1978-93; vis. prof. Harvard U., 1953, 63, 70, Columbia U., 1955, U. Hawaii, 1967-69, Hebrew U., 1970, 72-73, Grad. Sch. Mgmt., UCLA; Andrew Mellon vis. prof. Calif. Inst. Tech., 1977-78; cons. Rand Corp., 1952-64; mem. faculty Brandeis Inst., 1954-62, Hebrew Union Coll., Los Angeles, 1959-62; dir. East-West Philosophers' Conf.; fellow Ctr. Advanced Study in Behavioral Scis., 1960-61, Ctr. Advanced Studies, Wesleyan U., 1962-63, Inst. Social and Behavioral Pathology; vis. fellow Western Behavioral Scis. Inst., 1966. Author: (with H.D. Lasswell) Power and Society, 1950; The New World of Philosophy, 1962; American Ethics and Public Policy, 1963; The Conduct of Inquiry, 1964; Individuality and the New Society, 1970; Love . . . and Death, 1973; In Pursuit of Wisdom, 1976. Bd. editors Inquiry, Oslo, Norway. Guggenheim fellow, 1945-46; Rockefeller fellow, 1957-58. Mem. Am. Philos. Assn. (pres. Pacific div. 1957-58), Israel Philos. Assn. (pres. 1976-93), Am. Soc. Aesthetics, Assn. Legal and Polit. Philosophy, Internat. Assn. Applied Social Scientists (Charter), Assn. Jewish Philosophy, Acad. Psychoanalysis, Nat. Tng. Labs. Home: Los Angeles Calif. Died June 19, 1993.

KAPLAN, JEREMIAH, publisher, editor; b. N.Y.C., July 15, 1926; s. Samuel H. and Fannie (Brafman) K.; m. Charlotte R. Larsen, June 16, 1945; children: Ann Frances, Susanna Ruth, Margaret Jane, David Baruch. Vice pres. Free Press Glencoe, Inc., Ill., 1947-60, pres., 1960-64; editorial dir. gen. pub. div. Crowell-Collier Pub. Co., 1960-62, v.p., 1962-67, sr. v.p., fr 1967; chmn. bd. Sci. Materials, Inc., 1962-63; v Macmillan Co., 1960-63, exec. v.p., 1963-65, pres., 19 73, 77-86, chmn., 1983-87; exec. v.p. Crowell Collier d Macmillan, Inc., 1968-86; head product devel., co mktg. planning Crowell Collier and Macmillan, Ir 1972-93, also bd. dirs.; chmn. Collier Macmillan ternat., from 1973; exec. v.p. and dir. Macmillan, Ir 1979-86; chmn. bd. Macmillan Pub. Co., Inc., 1980- spl. advisor to chmn. Simon & Schuster, Inc., N.Y. 1987, pres., 1987-90; bd. dirs. Franklin Book Progra Inc., Scholastic Publs., Inc., Sage Publs., Inc.; Am. Bc Awards professorial lectr. behavioral scis. Grad. S Bus., U. Chgo., 1960-63. Trustee emeritus Tellad Coll., Stoneleigh-Burnham Sch., U. Rochester; nat. a council Hampshire Coll.; bd. dirs. Equity Libr Theatre, Amested Research Ctr., Nat. Found. Jew Culture, Am. Composer's Orch., U. Pa. Press, M Press. Mem. Poets and Writers, Am. Symphony Or League, Dutch Treat Club, Century Assn. Home: N York N.Y. Died Aug. 10, 1993.

KAPLAN, MARILYN FLASHENBERG, artist; Bklyn.; d. Sander E. and Eva (Novak) Flashenberg; Donald Henry Kaplan, July 11, 1954; children: Dar Alan, Bruce Howard. B.F.A., Syracuse (N.Y.) 1952; M.A. in Art Edn, Columbia U., 1954. E mentary art coordinator Croton (N.Y.) Harmon Scl 1953-54; art cons. Jericho (N.Y.) adult edn., 1960-7 One-woman exhbns. include, Hofstra U., 1966, M Monk Gallery, N.Y.C., 1968, Syosset (N.Y.) Libra 1971, 90, Jericho (N.Y.) Library, 1977, 89, Madis Ave. Gallery, N.Y.C., 1979-83, Isis Gallery, Manhass N.Y., 1986, 88; group exhbns. include NAD, N.Y. 1970, 72, 75, Corcoran Gallery of Art, Washingt 1976, Contemporary Arts Mus., Houston, 1976, Mus. Sci. and Industry, Chgo., Inst. Contemporary A London, 1977, Musée des Arts Decoratifs, Paris, 19 created: poster No More War, 1969; commd. works clude Mass. Blue Cross Blue Shield Hdqrs., 1984; rep. permanent collection, Smithsonian Instn. Recipient Altman award NAD, 1975. Jewish. Home: Jeric N.Y. Died May 6, 1994; buried New Montefiorg Cer tery, PineLawn, N.Y.

KAPLAN, OSCAR JOEL, psychology educator; N.Y.C., Oct. 21, 1915; s. Philip and Rebecca (Uttef) m. Rose Zankan, Dec. 28, 1942; children: Stephen Pa Robert Malcolm, David T.A. A.B., UCLA, 19 M.A., 1938; Ph.D., U. Calif.-Berkeley, 1940. Ins then assoc. prof. psychology So. br. U. Idaho, 1941- asst. prof. psychology San Diego State U., 1946- prof., 1952-94; chmn. dept. psychology San Diego St U., 1950-52, 63-66; dir. center for survey research; a prof. psychiatry Sch. Medicine U. Calif., San Die 1989-94; cons. gerontology USPHS, 1946-50; vis. p pub. health UCLA 1965-66; cons. clin. psychology V 1962-75; dir. rsch. The San Diego Poll, 1986-9 Author: Mental Disorders in Later Life, 2d edit., 19 Psychopathology of Aging, 1979; editorial bd.: Jc Gerontology, 1946-60, 86, 87, VOX MEDICA, 1960- Geriatrics, 1970-80; editor-in-chief: The Gerontolg 1961-66; internat. bd. editors: Gerontology and Ge trics, Amsterdam, 1958-94. Mem. planning com. Nat. Conf. Aging, 1950; mem. Nat. Council on Agi 1954-94, Gov.'s Adv. Com. on Aging, 1963-67; chn San Diego Mayor's Adv. Com. Aging, 1973-81; m Quality of Life Bd., City of San Diego, 1978-8 Recipient Outstanding Prof. award San Diego State 1982, Trustees' Outstanding Prof. award Calif. State System, 1983; Fellow Social Sci. Research Coun 1951; travel fellow NSF, 1954. Mem. Am. Assn. P Opinion Research (council Pacific chpt. 1963), A (pres. div. on maturity and old age 1954-55, Disti Contbrn. award Div. adult devel. and aging 1992 Western Gerontol. Soc. (pres. 1956-57, award for c standing contbns. 1976), Gerontol. Soc. Am. (chn behavioral and social sci. sect. 1951, editor Newsle 1954-60), AAAS (council Pacific div. 1958-59). Hor San Diego Calif. Died Dec. 19, 1994.

KARAMI, RASHID ABDUL HAMID, former pri minister Republic of Lebanon; b. 1921; s. Abdel Har Karami. Ed. Fuad U., Cairo. Minister nat. economy a social affairs, Lebanon, 1954-55; prime minister Lebanon, 1955-56, 58-60, 61-64, 75-76, 84-87, a minister fgn. and expatriates affairs; minister inter 1955-56, minister fin., economy, def. and info., 1958- fin. and def., 1959-60, fin., def. and info., 1975-76, a housing and tourism, 1976. Mem. Nat. Dialogue Co 1975; leader Parliamentary Democratic Front. Su Muslim. Home: Beirut Lebanon

KARANJA, JOSPHAT NJUGUNA, government ficial; b. Feb. 5, 1931. Student, Makarere Co Kampala, Uganda, U. Delhi, Princeton U. Le African Studies Fairleigh Dickinson U., Rutherfo N.J., 1961-62; lectr. African and Modern Europ History U. East Africa, 1962-63; high commr. for Ker London, 1963-70; vice-chancellor U. Nairobi, Ken 1970-79; mem. of parliament Govt. of Kenya, 1986 v.p., 1988-89; bd. dirs. UNITAR; chair, Gen. Accid Ins. Co. (Kenya) Ltd., 1980—.

KARL, MAX HENRY, insurance company executi b. Milw., Feb. 2, 1910; s. Louis and Bertha (Findlin) m. Anita Renee Davis, Nov. 28, 1946; children: Rob Kenneth, Karyn Karl Shwade. BA in Econs., U. W

1931, JD, 1933; D in Comml. Sci. (hon.), U. Wis.-Milw., 1982; LLD, Cardinal Stritch Coll., 1984; LLD with honors, Marquette U., 1985. Bar: Wis. 1933. Practiced in Milw., 1933-57; founder, chmn. exec. com. Mortgage Guaranty Ins. Corp., Milw., 1957-82; chmn. bd., chief exec. officer MGIC Investment Corp., 1974-85; past pres. Mortgage Ins. Cos. of Am.; past mem. adv. com. Fed. Home Loan Mortgage Corp. Chmn. Gov.'s Council on Econ. Devel.; del. Pres.'s Econ. Conf., 1974; v.p. Milw. Redevel. Corp.; Past pres. Milw. Jewish Fedn.; bd. dirs. United Jewish Appeal, Milw. Symphony, United Performing Arts Center, Greater Milw. Com.; chmn. bd. dirs. Touro Coll.; bd. dirs. United Israel Appeal, United Hias Service, Council of Jewish Fedns. and Welfare Funds, N.Y.C., Hillel Acad., Milw., Am. Friends of Hebrew U.; trustee Mt. Sinai Hosp., Milw., Nat. Mutiple Sclerosis Soc.; trustee emeritus Marquette U. Served with USAAF, 1942-45. Recipient House and Home award as one of ten individuals contbg. most to Am. housing, 1962, Golda Meir award, 1973, Vocat. Service award Milw. Rotary Club, 1979, Disting. Service award Wis. Alumni Club of Milw., Gitelson medallion Alpha Epsilon Pi, Headliner of Yr. award Milw. Press Club, 1982; Jabotinsky award State of Israel, 1980; Disting. Service award Wis. Alumni Assn., 1981; Evan P. Helfaer award Wis. chpt. Nat. Soc. Fund Raising Execs., 1982. Mem. Am., Wis., Milw. bar assns., Nat. Assn. Home Builders (Housing Hall of Fame, Roundtable), Beta Gamma Sigma. Jewish. Clubs: Brynwood Country, University. Home: Milwaukee Wis. Died April 19, 1995.

KASINOFF, BERNARD HERMAN, hospital administrator; b. N.Y., Feb. 15, 1920; s. Max and Anna (Miller) K.; m. Helen Jaworski, Oct. 17, 1952; 1 dau., Jessica D. B.A., U. Va., 1942, M.D., 1946. Chief mental hygiene treatment group VA, N.Y.C., 1958-62; dir. Valley Mental Health Center, Staunton, Va., 1962-69; clin. dir. DeJarnette San., 1969-71; supt. Southwestern State Hosp., Marion, Va., from 1971; Pvt. practice neuropsychiatry. Pres. Am. Cancer Soc., Waynesboro, Va., 1970. Served to capt. M.C. AUS, 1947-49. Fellow Am. Geriatrics Soc; mem. AMA, Am. Acad. Clin. Psychiatrists, N.Y. Acad. Sci., Neuropsychiat. Soc. Va. (pres. 1973-74), Med. Soc. Va. (chmn. com. religion and medicine), Am. Psychiat. Assn., Assn. Med. Hosp. Supts. Home: Abingdon Va. Deceased.

KASLÍK, VÁCLAV, producer, conductor, composer; b. Czechoslovakia, Sept. 28, 1917; s. Hynek and Pavla Kaslik; ed. Faculty of Philosophy, Charles U., Prague Conservatory and Conductor's Master Sch. m. Ruzeme Stucesova, Aug. 25, 1942; children—Jirí, Pavel, Ivan. Condr., E.F. Burian Theatre, Prague, 1940-41; asst. dir. Nat. Theatre, Prague, 1941-43, chief opera dir., 1961-65, opera dir., 1966—; chief opera ensemble Opera of May 5th, 1945-48; condr. Smetana Theatre, Prague, 1952-62; condr., Munich and Berlin, Ger., N.Y.C., Moscow, Vienna, Austria, Venice, Italy, Ottawa, Can., Covent Garden, London, Eng.; composer: (operas) Robbers' Ballad, 1944, Calvary, 1950, Krakatit, 1960, Silnice, 1980, A Dead of Governor; (musical) The War with the Jalamaders; (ballets) Don Juan, 1939; Janosik, 1951; Prague Carnival, 1952. producer works for film and TV. Recipient Nat. orders composing and prodn., including Klement Gottwald State prize, 1956; Honored Artist of Czechoslovakia, 1958. Died 1989; buried Pribram, Czech Republic. Home: Soukenicka Czechoslovakia

KATZ, ROBERT ARVIN, lawyer; b. Boston, Jan. 14, 1927; s. Morris Wolf and Freda (Cohen) K.; m. Tracy Oppenheimer, Dec. 28, 1952; children: Terry Alison, Robin Elizabeth, Wendy Arete, Michael Edward. A.B., Harvard, 1946, postgrad., 1947-48; LL.B., Boston U., 1954. Bar: Ill. bar 1954, Conn. bar 1960, N.Y. bar 1966. Practice in Chgo., 1954-59; asso. firm Peebles, Greenberg & Keele (and predecessors), 1954-59; asst. sec. Revlon, Inc., N.Y.C., 1961-65; sec. Joseph E. Seagram & Sons, Inc., N.Y.C., 1965-69; chmn. exec. com., dir. Bevis Industries, Inc., Providence, 1969-72; individual practice law N.Y.C., 1969-72, 75-92; chmn. McGrath Services Corp., 1973-74. Served to ensign USNR, 1944-46. Home: New York N.Y. Died Dec. 20, 1992.

KATZ, SAUL MILTON, economist, social scientist, educator; b. N.Y.C., Apr. 7, 1915; s. Charles L. and Malle (Salop) K.; m. Martha Marie Keller, Sept. 11, 1953; children: Charles, Jonathan, David, Mollie. B.S., Cornell U., 1940, M.S., 1943; M.A., Harvard U., 1949, M.P.A., 1950; Ph.D., Harvard, 1953. Chief food, agr., forestry U.S. Mil. Govt., Germany, 1946-49; chief exports USDA, Washington, 1955-57, program coord. Latin Am., 1957-59; mem. cent. planning staff AID, State Dept., Washington, 1959-61; assoc. prof. econ. and social devel. U. Pitts., 1961-64, prof., 1964-87, prof. emeritus, 1987-95, dir. programs in econ. and social devel., 1963-74, assoc. dean, 1972-73; cons. UN, 1969-95, OAS, 1964-95, AID, 1963-95, various fgn. govts. and industries. Author: Research Guide to Cooperative Farming, 1941, Guide to Modernizing Administration for National Development (translated to Spanish 1965, to Chinese 1968), Systems Approach to Development Administration, 1965, Education for Development Administrators: Character, Form, Content and Curriculum, 1967, Administrative Capability and Agricultural Development, 1970, Quantitative Techniques for National Economic Development Planning, 1972, Striving for the Heavenly Society: The Tactics of Development, 1975, The Regional Organization and Management of Development, 1978, The Regional Organization and Management of Development in Israel, 1981, others. Bd. dirs. Inter-Univ. Consortium on Research and Instn. Bldg.; also chmn. com. systems of Comparative Adminstrn. Group, 1965-95. Served to capt. AUS, 1942-47, ETO. Decorated Bronze Star, Purple Heart; Croix de Guerre avec aguillec (France). Mem. Am. Econ. Assn., Am. Agr. Econ. Assn., Am. Soc. Pub. Adminstrn., Soc. Internat. Devel., Center Inter-Am. Relations, Sociedad Interamericana de Planificacion (Venezuela). Home: Pittsburgh Pa. Died Nov. 28, 1995.

KATZ, STANLEY H., advertising executive; b. Newark, Jan. 2, 1923; s. Charles and Therese (Reif) K.; m. Vivienne Patricia Fox, Nov. 17, 1946; children: Robert N., Douglas D., William L. Student, N.Y. U., 1940-42. V.p., dir. mktg. A. Hollander & Sons, N.Y.C., 1946-53; pres., chief exec. officer Leber Katz Ptnrs., N.Y.C., 1954-56, chmn., chief exec. officer, 1956-86; chmn., chief exec. officer FCB/Leber Katz Ptnrs., N.Y.C., 1986-93; vice chmn., chmn. exec. com. Foote, Cone & Belding, Chgo., 1986-93, also bd. dirs. Contbr. articles to profl. jours. Served with USAAF, 1942-45. Mem. Am. Inst. Mgmt. (president's coun. 1972-78), Am. Assn. Advt. Agys. (gov. N.Y. coun. 1979-83), Friars Club, Lucullus Soc. Club, Royal Danish Yacht Club, N.Y. Yacht Club, Jockey Club. Home: West Orange N.J. Died Jan. 19, 1993.

KAUFFMAN, EWING MARION, pharmaceutical executive, baseball team owner; b. Mo., Sept. 21, 1916; s. John S. and Effie May (Winders) K.; m. Muriel Irene McBrien, Feb. 28, 1962; children: Larry, Sue, Julia. AS, Kansas City Jr. Coll. Founder, chmn. Marion Labs., Inc., Kansas City, Mo., from 1950; now chmn. emeritus Marion Merrell Dow Inc., Kansas City; owner, chmn. Kansas City Royals Baseball Club, 1969-93. Mem. Civic Council, Kansas City.; chmn. Ewing Marion Kauffman Found.; mem. Pres.'s Drug Adv. Coun., Washington. Served to ensign USNR. Recipient Horatio Alger award Am. Schs. and Colls. Assn., Golden Plate award Am. Acad. Achievement, Disting. Eagle award Boy Scouts Am., Nat. Am. Heart award, Harry S. Truman Good Neighbor award, Pres. Bush's 1000 Points of Light award, the Caring award Caring Found., Washington; inducted into the Nat. Sales Hall of Fame. Mem. Kansas City C. of C. (Man of Yr. award 1986). Clubs: Indian Hills Country, Kansas City, Eldorado Country. Home: Kansas City Mo. Died Aug. 1, 1993.

KAUFMAN, KARL LINCOLN, consultant, former state agency administrator; b. Attica, Ohio, 1911; s. S.F. and I. (Huffman) K.; m. Mary Jo Rettig, 1936; children: Karl, James, Robert. B.Sc., Ohio State U., 1933; Ph.D., Purdue U., 1936. Instr., then asst. prof. Wash. State Coll., 1936-40; asso. prof. Med. Coll. Va., 1940-45, prof., head dept., 1945-49; cons. pharm. mfrs.; exec. officer Coll. Pharmacy, Butler U., Indpls., 1949-52; dean Coll. Pharmacy, Butler U., 1952-76; pharm. dir. Ind. Dept. Mental Health, 1976-85; exec. dir. Sci. Edn. Found. of Ind. Inc. 1982-86, sec. 1986-95; project dir. several drug abuse edn. projects. Co-author: American Pharmacy, vol. I, 1945-48, Manual for Pharmacy Aides; Contbr. to: articles to profl. jours. World Book Ency. Past pres. Ind. Health Careers, Inc.; past pres. Comprehensive Health Planning Coun., Marion County Heart Assn.; bd. dirs. Am. Cancer Soc.; past chmn. Internat. Sci. Fair Coun.; founder Sci. Edn. Found. of Ind., Inc., exec. dir., 1982-88; former coord. Ind. Regional Sci. Fairs; past pres. Ind. Interprofl. Health Coun., Cen. Ind. Coun. on Aging; chmn. edn. com. Ind. State Coun. Aging, past pres. Mem. Am., Ind. pharm. assns., Am. Soc. Hosp. Pharms., Am. Chem. Soc., Sigma Xi, Phi Kappa Psi, Rho Chi. Republican. Episcopalian. Clubs: Mason (32), Internat. Torch (internat. past pres.). Home: Indianapolis Ind. Died Nov. 1, 1995.

KAUFOLD, LEROY, aerospace company executive; b. Blackwell, Okla., Sept. 16, 1924; s. Herbert L. and Nora (Johnston) K.; m. Patricia Swanson, Apr. 17, 1943; children: Kim, Mark, Robert. Student, UCLA, 1948-50, U. So. Calif., 1950-52, M.I.T., 1970. With Northrop Avionics, Hawthorne, Calif., 1948-74; chief engr., v.p., and gen. mgr. Northrop Avionics, until 1974; pres. Northrop-Wilcox Electric Co., Kansas City, Mo., 1974-80; corporate v.p. Northrop Co., Century City, Calif., 1975-93; mgmt. cons., 1980-93. Served with USN, 1942-45. Home: Las Vegas Nev. Died June 24, 1993.

KAVKA, GREGORY STEPHEN, philosophy educator; b. Chgo., Oct. 8, 1947; s. Jerome and Georgine (Rotman) K.; m. Virginia Louise Warren, Aug. 12, 1972; 1 child, Amber Kavka-Warren. AB, Princeton U., 1968; PhD, U. Mich., 1973. Asst. prof. philosophy UCLA, 1972-79; assoc. prof. U. Calif., Irvine, 1980-83, prof., 1983-94. Author: Hobbesian Moral and Political Theory, 1986, Moral Paradoxes of Nuclear Deterrence, 1987; mem. editorial bd. Ethics, 1980-94, Jour. Social Philosophy, 1989-94. Fellow Danforth Found., 1968-72, NEH, 1982-83, Am. Coun. Learned Socs.-Ford Found., 1988. Mem. Internat. Hobbes Assn., Am. Philsoph. Assn., Am. Soc. Polit. and Legal Philsophy, Concerned Philosophers for Peace, UCLA Ctr. Internat. and Strategic Affairs. Home: Tustin Calif. Died Feb. 16, 1994.

KAY, ULYSSES SIMPSON, composer, educator; b. Tucson, Jan. 7, 1917; s. Ulysses Simpson and Elizabeth (Davis) K.; m. Barbara Harrison, Aug. 20, 1949; children: Virginia, Melinda, Hillary. B.Mus., U. Ariz., 1938; M.Mus., Eastman Sch. Music, 1940; postgrad., Yale U., 1941-42, Columbia U., 1946-49; Mus. D., Lincoln Coll., 1963, Bucknell U., 1966, U. Ariz., 1969, Dickinson Coll., Carlisle, Pa., 1978; D.H.L., Ill. Wesleyan U., 1969, U.Mo.-Kansas City, 1981. Editorial adviser Broadcast Music, Inc., N.Y.C., until 1968; prof. music Herbert H. Lehman Coll., CUNY, 1968-72, disting. prof., 1972-88; vis. prof. Boston U., 1965, UCLA, 1966-67; Mem. 1st ofcl. del. U.S. composers to USSR Dept. State Cultural Exchange Program, 1958; guest condr. N.Y. Little Symphony, Tucson Symphony, Phila. Orch., 1979. Commd. by Louisville Symphony Orch., Koussevitzky Music Found., DePaur Inf. Chorus, Quincy (Ill.) Fine Arts Soc.; composer: (operas) The Boor, 1955, The Juggler of Our Lady, 1956, The Capitoline Venus, 1970, Jubilee, 1974-76, Frederick Douglass, 1980-85, (ballet) Danse Calinda, 1941, (orchestral music) Oboe Concerto, 1940, 5 Mosaics for chamber orch., 1940, Of New Horizons, overture, 1944, Suite in 5 Movements, 1945, A Short Overture, 1947, Portrait Suite, 1948, Suite for strings, 1949, Sinfonia, 1951, 6 Dances for strings, 1954, Concerto for orch., 1954, Serenade, 1954, Fantasy Variations, 1963, Umbrian Scene, 1964, Markings, 1966, Symphony, 1967, Theatre Set, 1968, Scherzi Musicali for chamber orch., 1969, Aulos for flute and chamber orch., 1971, Quintet Concerto for 5 brass soli and orch., 1975, Southern Harmony, 1976, Chariots, 1979, String Triptych for string orch., 1987, (chamber music) 3 String Quartets, 1953, 56, 61, Piano Sonata, 1940, Quintet for flute and strings, 1947, Piano Quartet, 1949, 5 Portraits for violin and piano, 1972, Guitarra, guitar suite, 1973, rev. 1985, Tromba for trumpet and piano, 1983, Five Winds for wood and quintet, 1984, Pantomime for clarinet, 1986, 2 Impromptus for piano, 1986, Everett Suite for bass trombone, 1988; also vocal works and bank pieces. Served with USNR, 1942-46. Recipient ABC prize, 1946, 3d Ann. Gershwin Contest award, 1947; Prix de Rome scholar Am. Acad. Toma, 1949-52; Alice M. Ditson fellow, 1946; Julius Rosenwald fellow, 1948; Fulbright fellow Italy, 1950-51; Guggenheim fellow, 1964-65. Mem. Corp. of Yaddo, Am. Fedn. Musicians, League of Composers, Nat. Inst. Arts and Letters, Phi Mu Alpha-Sinfonia. Club: Federal City (Washington). Home: Teaneck N.J. Died May 20, 1995.

KEAN, BENJAMIN HARRISON, physician; b. Chgo., Dec. 2, 1912; s. Harrison and Tillie (Rhodes) K.; m. Collette B. Touey, Dec. 26, 1975. A.B., U. Calif., 1933; M.D., Columbia, 1937. Diplomate: Am. Bd. Pathology, Am. Bd. Microbiology. Intern Gorgas Hosp., C.Z., 1937-39; pvt. practice medicine N.Y.C., 1946-93; clin. prof. emeritus tropical medicine and public health Cornell U. Med. Coll.; attending physician N.Y. hosps.; dir. parasitology lab. N.Y. Hosp.; mem. sci. adv. com. tropical diseases program WHO, 1978-80; med. cons. Gen. Motors, Internat. Travelers Health Inst. Author: (with Breslau) Parasites of the Human Heart, 1964, (with Tucker) Traveler's Health Guide, 1965, Traveler's Medical Guide for Physicians, 1966, (with Dahlby) M.D., 1990, (with Sun and Ellsworth) Ophthalmic Parasitology, 1991; also chpts. in books, articles.; co-editor: Tropical Medicine and Parasitology: Classic Investigations, 1978. Served to lt. col. M.C., AUS, 1942-46. Recipient Presdl. award of Golden Heart Philippine Govt., 1968; Egyptian Order of Merit, Govt. of United Arab Republic, 1980. Fellow ACP, Coll. Am. Pathologists; mem. AMA, Royal Soc. Tropical Medicine and Hygiene, Am. Soc. Clin. Pathology, Am., N.Y. socs. tropical medicine, Am. Assn. Pathology and Bacteriology. Home: New York N.Y. Died Sept. 1993.

KEARL, BRYANT EASTHAM, academic administrator, agricultural educator; b. Paris, Idaho, Sept. 21, 1921; s. Chase and Hazel Loveless K.; m. Ruth Warr, Sept. 5, 1941; children: Susan Hoerger, Richard B., Kathryn Marathon, Robert. Student, U. Idaho, 1936-37; B.S., Utah State U., 1941; M.S., U. Wis., 1942; Ph.D., U. Minn., 1951. From instr. to prof. agrl. journalism U. Wis., 1942-52, prof., 1952-89, assoc. dean Grad. Sch., 1963-67, vice chancellor, 1967-70, 78-83, acting chancellor, 1968, dean of univ. outreach, 1984-87, vice chancellor, prof. emeritus, 1989-93; interim dean U. Wis., Wausau, 1990; lectr. U. Minn., 1947-48; Fulbright vis. prof. Friedrich Wilhelms U., Bonn, 1961-62; sr. planning officer U. East Africa, 1964-65; exec. dir. Asia Office Agrl. Devel. Coun., 1970-74; cons. FAO, AID, World Bank; mem. rev. teams Internat. Agrl. Rsch. Ctrs., 1980-81, 89, Rockefeller Found. program rev. com., 1982. Served with USN, 1944-46. Decorated Bronze Star; Rockefeller Found. Study Ctr. resident scholar, 1984; Bundesverdienstkreuz, 1985; Thurburn fellow U. Sydney (Australia), 1986. Mem. Assn. Edn. Journalism, Am. Agrl. Coll. Editors (past pres., Award of Excellence 1992), Alpha Zeta, Epsilon Sigma Phi. Mem. LDS Ch. Home: Madison Wis. Died Sept. 28, 1993.

KEARNEY, RICHARD DAVID, lawyer; b. Dayton, Ky., Jan. 3, 1914; s. David Richard and Mary (Manouge) K.; m. Margaret Helen Murray, Nov. 22,

1944. A.B., Xavier U., 1935; LL.B., U. Cin., 1938. Bar: Ohio 1938. Asst. gen. counsel U.S. High Commr., Germany, 1949-50; dep. U.S. mem. Validation Bd. for German Dollar Bonds, 1953-56; asst. legal adviser European affairs Dept. State, 1956-62, prin. dep. legal adviser, 1962-67; mem. with personal rank of ambassador UN Internat. Law Commn., 1967-77, 1st v.p. commn., 1970, pres. commn., 1972-73, spl. rapporteur for internat. rivers, 1974-78; chmn. Sec. State's Adv. Com. Pvt. Internat. Law, 1964-78; head U.S. del. Conf. Uniform Internat. Sales Law, 1964, The Hague Conf. Pvt. Internat. Law, 1964, 68, 76, conf. on Enforcement Fgn. Judgements, 1966, UN Conf. on Law of Treaties, 1968-69, Inter-Am. Conf. on Human Rights, 1969, UN Conf. on State Succession; pres. Washington Conf. Internat. Wills, 1973; sr. adviser, v.p., mem. exec. com. Am. Soc. Internat. Law, 1978-81; mem. governing council Internat. Inst. for Unification of Pvt. Law, 1968-91. Served to maj. AUS, 1942-46, ETO. Recipient Carr medal State Dept., 1978, Disting. Alumni award U. Cin., 1986. Mem. Am. Acad. Polit. Sci., ABA (medal for contbns. to devel. pvt. internat. law), Fgn. Service Assn., Am. Law Inst., Order of Coif. Democrat. Roman Catholic. Clubs: Landsdowne (London, Eng.); Annapolis Yacht. Home: Mc Lean Va. Died Dec. 18, 1991.

KECK, ROBERT CLIFTON, lawyer; b. Sioux City, Iowa, May 20, 1914; s. Herbert Allen and Harriet (McCutchen) K.; m. Ruth P. Edwards, Nov. 2, 1940 (dec.); children: Robert, Laura E. Simpson, Gloria E. Sauser; m. Lauryne E. George, June 20, 1987. AB, Ind. U., 1936; JD, U. Mich., 1939; LHD, Nat. Coll. Edn., 1973. Bar: Ill. 1939. Assoc. Keck, Mahin & Cate, 1939-46, ptnr., 1946-95; sec., dir. Methode Electronics, Inc. Chmn. bd. trustees Nat. Louis U., 1980-95; trustee Sears Roebuck Found., 1977-79. With USNR, 1943-45. Fellow Am. Coll. Trial Lawyers; mem. ABA, Fed. Bar Assn., Ill. Bar Assn., Chgo. Bar Assn. Seventh Fed. Cir. (past pres.), Phi Gamma Delta. Republican. Methodist. Clubs: Westmoreland Country (Wilmette); Metropolitan, Chgo.; Biltmore Forest Country (Asheville, N.C.); Glen View (Golf, Ill.). Lodge: Masons. Home: Arlington Heights Ill. Died May 23, 1995.

KEEN, MICHAEL JOHN, geophysicist, research scientist; b. Seaford, Eng., Jan. 1, 1935; s. John and Susannah (Bedwell) K.; m. Susan Jane Atkinson, Apr. 27, 1950; children: Alison, Rebecca, Jonathan. BA, Oxford (Eng.) U., Eng., 1957; PhD, Cambridge (Eng.) U., Eng., 1961. Prof. geology, oceanography, physics Dalhousie U., Halifax, N.S., Can., 1971-77, chmn. dept. geology, 1969-77; dir. Atlantic Geosci. Ctr. Atlantic Geosci. Ctr., Geol. Survey of Can., Bedford Inst. Oceanography, Dartmouth, N.S., 1977-88; rsch. scientist Atlantic Geosci. Ctr., Dartmouth, N.S., 1988-93. Author: (textbook) Introduction to Marine Geology; contbr. numerous articles to profl. jours. Fellow Royal Soc. Can., Geol. Assn. Can. (Logan medal 1986, pres. 1979-83); mem. Can. Geophys. Union (pres. 1981-83). Home: Halifax Can. Deceased.

KEENE, CHRISTOPHER, conductor, author, librettist, musician; b. Berkeley, Calif., Dec. 21, 1946; s. James Phillip and Yvonne San Jule Yvette (Cyr) K.; m. Sara Frances Rhodes, Dec. 21, 1967; children: Anthony Alexander, Nicholas Patrick. Ed., U. Calif. at Berkeley, 1963-67. Asst. condr. San Francisco Opera, 1966, San Diego Opera, 1967; mem. conducting staff N.Y.C. Opera, 1969—, music dir., 1982-86, gen. dir., 1989—; music dir. Festival of Two Worlds, Europe, dir., Am.; founder, music dir. L.I. Philharm., 1979-90; music dir. Syracuse (N.Y.) Symphony Orch., 1975-84; music dir., pres. Artpark Buffalo Philharm., 1974-89. Guest condr. Spoleto Festival, 1968, 69, 71, music dir., 1977; mus. dir., Am. Ballet Co., 1969-70; with Santa Fe Opera, 1971, Covent Garden, 1973, N.Y.C. Opera, 1970 (Julius Rudel award), Met. Opera, 1971, Chgo. Symphony, 1976, Berlin Opera, 1976; numerous guest appearances opera cos., maj. symphony orchs., 1972—; mus. dir., pres. Artpark, 1975-89, Syracuse Symphony Orch., 1975-84, L.I. Philharmonic, 1979-89; condr. world premiere Rasputin (Reise), The Most Important Man (Menotti), 1971, Yerma (Villa-Lobos), 1971; condr. N.Y. premiere X, The Life and Times of Malcom X (Davis), Of Mice and Men (Floyd), Akhnaten (Glass); condr. soundtrack Altered States; composer: ballet The Consort, 1970; author: libretto Duchess of Malfi; translator others; works presented include by Roger Sessions, Keith Jarrett, William Schuman, Joseph Schwantner, Michael Tippett, Stephen Douglas, John Corigliano, David Diamond; recs. include Diamonds 5th Symphony, soundtrack for film Altered States. Recipient Ditson Condr.'s award Columbia U., 1991. Home: New York N.Y. Died October 8, 1995.

KEIM, KATHIE MARIE, newspaper editor; b. Orlando, Fla., Nov. 22, 1947; d. Frank Frederick and Althea Detweiler (Leidy) K. BS in Journalism, U. Fla., 1969. Feature writer Sun-Sentinel, Pompano Beach, Fla., 1969; reporter Boca Raton (Fla.) News, 1969-70, Broward Times, Ft. Lauderdale, Fla., 1970-71, Hollywood (Fla.) Sun-Tattler, 1971-73; bur. reporter Ft. Lauderdale News, 1973-74; sportswriter, copy editor Cen. Maine Morning Sentinel, Waterville, 1974—. Mem. Women In Communications. Home: Waterville Maine

KEISER, NORMAN MICHAEL, securities company executive; b. Binghamton, N.Y., Sept. 15, 1919; s. Norman George and Helen Elizabeth (Clinton) K.; m. Louise Knight Belcher, June 26, 1943; children: Michael Lewis, Bruce Norman, Thomas Clinton, Stephen Knight. B.S., Wharton Sch., U. Pa., 1941. Mem. sales staff Armstrong Cork Co., Lancaster and Buffalo, Pa., 1941-42, 45-47; with George D.B. Bonbright Co., Buffalo, 1947-50; exec. v.p. Hugh Johnson & Co., Buffalo, 1950-69, pres., 1969-74, vice chmn., 1974-76; v.p., dir. First Albany Corp., Buffalo, 1977—; exec. v.p., dir. Johnson's Charts, Buffalo, 1949—; pres. Binghamton Credit Corp., N.Y., 1951-80, also dir. Served as aviator USNR, 1942-45. Decorated Navy Cross, Silver Star, D.F.C. (3), Air medal (3). Mem. Beta Gamma Sigma, Phi Gamma Delta. Republican. Home: East Aurora N.Y. Died Dec. 6, 1991.

KEISS, SISTER ISABELLE, academic administrator; b. N.Y.C., Dec. 11, 1931; d. Walter and Sara (Boyle) K.; B.A., Villanova U., 1960; M.A., Cath. U., 1966; Ph.D., Notre Dame U., 1972; postgrad. Harvard U. Grad. Sch. Edn., 1972. Joined Religious Sisters of Mercy, 1952; tchr. English, Bishop Egan High Sch., Levittown, Pa., 1960-63; chmn. English dept. Walsingham Acad., Williamsburg, Va., 1963-65; pres. Gwynedd-Mercy Coll., Gwynedd Valley, Pa., 1971-94. Author: Tender Courage, 1988, Preferential Option for the Poor, 1988; contbr. Dictionary of Christianity in Am., 1989, Relationship Between Trustees and Sponsoring Religious Body, 1991. Bd. dir. North Penn Hosp., 1975, Redeemer Hosp., 1991-94, Assn. Cath. Colls. and Univs., 1990-94; bd. dirs. Mercy Cath. Med. Center, 1975-94, Coll. Misericordia, 1979-88; mem. exec. com. Assn. Mercy Coll., 1990-94. Recipient award Rotary Club, 1980. Died Sept. 1994. Home: Gwynedd Valley Pa.

KELLEHER, THOMAS F., state supreme court justice; b. Providence, Jan. 4, 1923; m. Mary Frances. Grad., Boston U. Sch. Law, 1948. Bar: R.I. bar. Pvt. practice law, probate judge, solicitor Smithfield, R.I.; justice R.I. Supreme Ct.; Mem. Gov.'s Task Force Mental Health, 1963; chmn. Com. on Juvenile Delinquency, 1961. Mem. R.I. Ho. of Reps., 1965-66, dep. majority leader, 1965. Served with USN, 1942-46; capt. USAR ret. Mem. Res. Officers Assn. Home: Barrington R.I. Died July 31, 1995.

KELLERHOUSE, MURIEL ARLINE, theatrical arts educator; b. Halcottsville, N.Y., May 20, 1927; d. William E. and Ethel (Dean) Griffin; m. Kenneth D. Kellerhouse Jr., Aug. 21, 1949; 1 child, Dean Kenneth. BA, SUNY, Albany, 1947, MA, 1953; PhD, Ind. U., 1973. Tchr. speech, English Grand Gorge (N.Y.) Cen. Sch., 1947-60; prof. theater SUNY, Oneonta, 1960-90; bd. dirs. Oneonta Community Theater, 1960-65, Suco-Community Summer Theater, Oneonta, 1965-84. Actress Mo. Summer Theater, Columbia, 1963, in Private History of a Campaign That Failed as directed by Peter Hunt, 1982, in Ruby Moon as directed by Joseph Stillman, 1991. Dem. com. woman, 1980-84. Mem. N.Y. State Theater Edn. Assn. Home: Oneonta N.Y. Deceased.

KELLEY, GLENN E., state supreme court justice; b. St. Edward, Nebr., Apr. 25, 1921; m. Margaret A. Kelley, July 25, 1946; children: Glenn A., David P., Anne L. BS, No. State Coll., 1944; LLB, U. Mich., 1948. Bar: Minn. 1948. Pvt. practice law, 1948-69; judge Minn. Dist. Ct. 3d Jud. Dist., Winona, Minn., 1969-81; assoc. justice Minn. Supreme Ct., St. Paul, 1981—. Served to 1st lt. USAAF, 1942-45. Mem. Nat. Assn. R.R. Trial Counsel, Am. Judicature Soc., Minn. Bar Assn., ABA.

KELLEY, JOHN DENNIS, librarian; b. Nov. 3, 1900; s. John H. and Nora J. (Mullen) K.; m. Mary Agnes Barry, June 29, 1940; children—John H., Thomas B., Dennis J., David B. A.B., Boston Coll., 1922; M.B.A., N.Y.U., 1927. Shoe buyer Nat. Cloak & Suit Co., N.Y.C., 1922-27; mdse. mgr. Gilchrist Co., Boston, 1928-31; office mgr. Carew & McGreenery (investments), 1932-37; librarian, dir. Somerville (Mass.) Pub. Library.; Pres., dir. Central Coop. Bank; corporator Somerset Savs. Bank.; Commr. Div. Pub. Libraries Mass., from 1950. Trustee Somerville Hosp. Mem. ALA, Mass. Library Assn. (past pres.). Club: Boston Review. Lodge: Rotary. Home: Wakefield Mass. Deceased.

KELLEY, VINCENT CHARLES, pediatrician; b. Tyler, Minn., Jan. 23, 1916; s. Charles Enoch and Stella May (Ross) K.; m. Dorothy Jean MacArthur, Sept. 5, 1942; children: Nancy Jean, Thomas Vincent, Richard Charles, William MacArthur, Robert Kenneth, Jean Elizabeth, James Joseph. B.A., U. N.D., 1934, M.A., 1935; B.S. in Edn, U. Minn., 1936, Ph.D. in Biochemistry, 1942, B.S. in Medicine, 1944, M.B., 1945, M.D., 1946. Diplomate: Am. Bd. Pediatrics. Prof. chemistry Emory and Henry Coll., 1941; Rockefeller research fellow U. Minn., 1941-42, Swift fellow in pediatrics, 1948-50, intern in pediatrics, 1945-46, instr., 1949-50; asst. prof. organic chemistry Coll. St. Thomas, 1942-43; asso. prof. pediatrics U. Utah, 1950-58; prof., head div. endocrinology, metabolism and renal disease dept. pediatrics U. Wash., 1958-86, prof. emeritus pediatrics, 1986-94; dir. Utah State Heart Labs., 1953-58. Contbr. numerous articles on biochemistry, pediatrics and endocrinology to profl. jours.; editor: Metabolic, Endocrine and Genetic Disorders of Children, 3 vols., 1974, Practice of Pediatrics, 10 vols., 1958-87, Infections in Children, 1982; mem. editorial bd.: Audio Digest, 1956-72, Med. Digest, 1956-75, Am. Jour. Diseases Children, 1958-69, Internat. Med. Digest, 1960-71. Served with U.S. Army, 1943-45; M.C. USAAF, 1946-48. Recipient E. Mead Johnson award for pediatric research, 1954, Ross Pediatric Edn. award, 1971. Mem. Am. Acad. Pediatrics, AAAS, AAUP, Am. Inst. Biol. Scis., Am. Heart Assn., AMA, Am. Pediatric Soc., Am. Rheumatism Assn., Am. Soc. Nephrology, Internat. Endocrine Soc., N.Y. Acad. Scis., Pan-Am. Med. Assn., Soc. Exptl. Biology and Medicine, Endocrine Soc., Soc. Pediatric Research, Western Soc. Clin. Research, Western Soc. Pediatric Research, Phi Beta Kappa, Sigma Xi, Phi Lambda Upsilon, Phi Eta Sigma, Kappa Kappa Psi. Home: Seattle Wash. Died Mar. 26, 1994; buried Holyrood Cemetery, Seattle, Wash.

KELLIHER, PETER MAURICE, lawyer, arbitrator; b. Chgo., Dec. 23, 1912; s. Edward J. and Catherine (Rooney) K.; m. Virginia Dowdle, Jan. 28, 1942; children: Diane, Peter. A.B., U. Chgo., 1935, J.D., 1937. Bar: Ill. bar 1938. Spl. asst. corp. counsel City Chgo., 1940-41; U.S. commr. conciliation, 1941-42, arbitrator-umpire labor disputes, 1945-88; pres. Kelliher Co., Inc.; developer Hemingway House, Huntington Hills, Algonquin Indsl. Park, One East Superior Office Bldg.; impartial referee Inland Steel Co., Youngstown Sheet & Tube. Past commr. Chgo. Urban Renewal Commn.; bd. dirs. Greater North Michigan Ave. Assn.; mem. fin. com. Holy Name Cathedral, presdl. fact finding bd. Copper Ind. Capt. AUS, 1942-45; spl. agt CIC. Recipient award Chmn. Union Mgmt. Conf. U. Notre Dame, 25th Anniv. award Inst. Indsl. Rels. Loyola U., Heritage of Liberty award Am. Jewish Com. Mem. Nat. Acad. Arbitrators (pres. 1964), Indsl. Rels. Rsch. Assn., Wine and Food Soc., Chgo. Bd. Realtors, Irish Fellowship, Tavern Club (Chgo.), One Hundred Club (Chgo.), Beach Club (Palm Beach).,. Clubs: Tavern (Chgo.), One Hundred (Chgo.); Beach (Palm Beach), Irish Fellowship (bd. dirs.). Home: Chicago Ill. Died, Nov. 9, 1994.

KELLNER, AARON, physician, health facility administrator; b. N.Y.C., Sept. 24, 1914; s. Louis and Rose (Horn) K.; m. Zira DeFries, May 4, 1942; children: David Paul, William DeFries, Charles Horn. BA, Yeshiva Coll., 1934; MPH, Columbia U., 1936; MD, U. Chgo., 1939. Intern Michael Reese Hosp., Chgo., 1939-41; resident Montefiore Hosp., N.Y.C., 1941, Peter Bent Brigham Hosp., Boston, 1942; resident N.Y. Hosp., N.Y.C., 1946, dir. cen. labs., 1948-68, attending pathologist, 1946-92; rsch. fellow Cornell U., N.Y.C., 1947, from asst. prof. to prof. pathology, 1948-86; pres. N.Y. Blood Ctr., N.Y.C., 1964-89. Served to maj. USAF, 1942-46. Mem. Am. Assn. Blood Banks (pres. 1953-54), Am. Heart Assn. (pres. 1960-61, mem. council arteriosclerosis), Council Community Blood Ctrs. (pres. 1974-76). Home: New York N.Y. Died Dec. 11, 1992.

KELLY, GENE CURRAN, dancer, actor, director; b. Pitts., Aug. 23, 1912; s. James Patrick Joseph and Harriet (Curran) K.; m. Betsy Blair, Sept. 22, 1941 (div. 1957); 1 child, Kerry; m. Jeanne Coyne, Aug. 6, 1960 (dec.); children: Timothy, Bridget; m. Patricia Ward, July 1990. AB, U. Pitts., 1933; LHD (hon.), Am. Coll., Paris, 1986. Appeared in N.Y. stage prodns. Leave It To Me, 1938, Hold Your Hats, 1938, Time of Your Life, 1939, One For the Money, 1939, Pal Joey, 1941; dance dir., choreographer N.Y. stage prodns. Hold Your Hats, 1938, The Emperor Jones, 1938, Green Grow the Lilacs, 1939, Billy Rose's Diamond Horseshoe Revue, 1940, Best Foot Forward, 1941; dir. N.Y. stage prodns Flower Drum Song, 1958; films include (as actor) Me and My Girl, 1942, Pilot No. 5, 1942, DuBarry Was a Lady, 1943, Thousands Cheer, 1943, The Cross of Lorraine, 1943, Christmas Holiday, 1944, Ziegfeld Follies, 1945, The Three Musketeers, 1948, The Black Hand, 1949, Summer Stock, 1950, It's a Big Country, 1952, The Devil Makes Three, 1952, Crest of the Wave, 1954, Les Girls, 1957, Marjorie Morningstar, 1958, Inherit the Wind, 1960, Let's Make Love, 1960, What a Way to Go, 1964, The Young Girls of Rochefort, 1968, Forty Carats, 1973, (narrator) That's Entertainment!, 1974, (narrator) That's Entertainment! Part II, 1976, Viva Knievel, 1977, Xanadu, 1980, (narrator) That's Dancing!, 1985; (as actor, choreographer) Cover Girl, 1944, Anchors Aweigh, 1945 (Academy award nomination best actor 1945), Living in a Big Way, 1947, The Pirate 1948, "Slaughter on Tenth Avenue" sequence of Words and Music, 1948, Take Me Out to the Ball Game, 1949, An American in Paris, 1951, Brigadoon, 1954, Deep in My Heart, 1955; (as actor, choreographer, dir.) On the Town, 1949, Singin' in the Rain, 1952, It's Always Fair Weather, 1955, Invitation to the Dance, 1956; (as actor prod., dir.) The Happy Road, 1957; (as dir.) The Tunnel of Love, 1958, Gigot, 1962, A Guide for the Married Man, 1967, Hello, Dolly!, 1969; (as prod., dir.) The Cheyenne Social Club, 1970; television appearances include The Gillette Summer Sports Reel, 1954, Going My Way, 1962-63, The Funny Side, 1971, North and South, 1986, Sins, 1986; author: Take Me Out to the Ball Game, 1948. Served to lt. (j.g.) USNR, 1944-46. Recipient Medal of City of Paris, 1960, Cecil B. DeMille award, 1981, Kennedy Center Honors award, 1982 Lifetime Achievement award Am. Film Inst., 1985; Spl cad. award for Choreography, 1951, Nat. Medal of the rts, 1994. Mem. Chgo. Dance Masters Assn., Screen ctors Guild (v.p.), Phi Kappa. Home: Beverly Hills alif. Died Feb. 2, 1996.

ELLY, HUGH PADRAIC, physics educator; b. oston, Sept. 3, 1931; s. Hugh Patrick and Katherine Mary (Donahue) K.; m. Zita Jean Stanislawski, Apr. 30, 955; children: Timothy, Matthew, Mary, Teresa, ominic, Anne, Patricia, Caroline, Lillian. A.B., arvard U., 1953; M.S., UCLA, 1954; Ph.D., U. Calif.-erkeley, 1963. Elec. engr. Hughes Aircraft Co., Culver ity, Calif., 1952-54; research asst. prof. U. Calif.-San iego, La Jolla, 1963-65; successively asst. prof., assoc. rof., prof. U. Va., Charlottesville, 1965-77, chmn. hysics dept., 1974-78, commonwealth prof., 1977-89; rof.alumni coun. Thomas Jefferson, 1989—; dean aculty Arts and Scis. U. Va., Charlottesville, 1985-89, homas Jefferson prof. alumni coun., 1989-90, provost, 989-91. Contbr. articles to physics jours. Served to st lt. USMC, 1954-57. Fellow Am. Phys. Soc. (chmn. outheastern sect. 1981-82, chmn. div. electron and tomic physics 1984-85); mem. Phi Beta Kappa. Home: harlottesville Va.

ELLY, LUTHER WRENTMORE, JR., physician, ducator; b. Charlotte, N.C., June 9, 1925; s. Luther Vrentmore and Charlotte (Abbott) K.; m. Susan F. owman, Dec. 1, 1956; children: Abbott Bowman, Mary Luther. Student, U. N.C., 1942-44; certificate of nedicine, Sch. Medicine, 1946; M.D., Harvard U., 1948; esearch fellow, Western Res. U. Sch. Medicine, 1954. iplomate: Am. Bd. Internal Medicine (in endocri-ology), Am. Bd. Nuclear Medicine. Intern, then re-ident medicine Univ. Hosps., Cleve., 1948-53; staff hysician Nalle Clinic, Charlotte, N.C., 1955-95; chmn. ept. medicine Charlotte Meml. Hosp., 1964-68; clin. sst. prof. medicine U. N.C. Sch. Medicine, 1966-69, lin. assoc. prof., 1969-72, clin. prof. medicine, 1972-95; Mem. adv. com. aging Family Service Assn. Am., 1961-2; Bd. dirs. Family and Childrens Service Mecklenburg ounty, 1955-61, pres., 1958-61; v.p. Am. Group Prac-ice Assn., 1977, pres., 1979-80; bd. dirs. N.C. Council luman Relations, 1955-60; Pres. Community Health ssn., Charlotte, 1972, Nalle Clinic Corp., 1976-78; roject dir. diabetes cons. and edn. service N.C. Re-ional Med. Program, 1971-73; bd. dirs. Charlotte Drug dn. Center, pres. bd. dirs., 1983-84; mem. med. alumni oun. U. N.C. Sch. Medicine; v.p. med. alumni endow-nent bd. U. N.C., 1986-95. Author articles thyroid and drenal gland function. Bd. dirs. Charlotte Community oncert Assn., 1985, v.p., 1991. Served with USNR, 950-52. Recipient Disting. Service award U. N.C. Sch. Medicine Alumni Assn. Fellow ACP; mem. Endocrine oc., Am. Diabetes Assn., N.C. Diabetes Assn. (pres. 968-69), Am. Acad. Med. Dirs. (dir. 1975-77), Soc. Nuclear Medicine, Am. Coll. Nuclear Physicians, Mecklenburg County Med. Soc. (pres. 1986-87), U. N.C. Med. Alumni Assn. (pres. 1985-86). Home: harlotte N.C. Died Nov. 3, 1995.

ELSO, JOHN MORRIS, retired physicist; b. Punx-utawney, Pa., Mar. 12, 1922; s. John Claude and Helen lverta (Kurtz) K.; m. Nancy Jane Weaver, Jan. 6, 945; 1 dau., Jean Susan. BA in Physics, Gettysburg oll., 1943; MS, Pa. State U., 1945, PhD, 1949. Assoc. rof. elec. engring. Pa. State U., State College, 1949-54; valuation specialist Glenn L. Martin Co., Balt., 1954-5; head space physics (fields) sect. Space Tech. Labs., nc., Redondo Beach, Calif., 1955-62; v.p., dir. research TT Electrophysics Lab., Inc., Columbia, Md., 1962-76; ons. Office of Telecommunications Policy , Exec. Office f the Pres., Washington, 1976-78; chief scientist Signal nalysis Center, Honeywell, Inc., Annapolis, Md., 978-87; vis. asso. prof. Chalmers U. Tech., othenburg, Sweden, 1951-52; mem. Nat. Acad. Scis. om. adv. to Central Radio Propagation Lab. U.S. Bur. tandards, 1963-65; mem. evaluation panel Nat. Astro-omy and Ionosphere Ctr., Arecibo, P.R., 1965-68. uthor: Radio Ray Propagation in the Ionosphere, 964; author articles. Fellow IEEE; mem. SAR, Am. hys. Soc., Am. Geophys. Union, Internat. Union adio Sci. (chmn. U.S. Commn. G 1972-75), Nautical sch. Guild, Suncoast Ship Model Soc., Tampa Bay hip Model Soc., Mensa, Sigma Xi, Sigma Pi Sigma, Pi Mu Epsilon, Phi Sigma Kappa. Home: Hudson Fla. ied Jan. 10, 1994.

EMENY, JOHN GEORGE, mathematics educator; b. udapest, Hungary, May 31, 1926; came to U.S., 1940, aturalized, 1945; s. Tibor and Lucy (Fried) K.; m. Jean lexander, Nov. 5, 1950; children: Jennifer M., Robert . BA, Princeton U., 1947, PhD, 1949, LLD (hon.), 971; DSc (hon.), Middlebury Coll., 1965, Boston Coll., 973, U. Pa., 1975, Bard Coll., 1978, Dickinson Coll., 981; LLD (hon.), Columbia U., 1971, U. N.H., 1972, olby Coll., 1976, Lafayette Coll., 1976, Brown U., 980, Dartmouth Coll., 1981; DSc (hon.), Claremont rad. Sch., 1982; LLD (hon.), Tufts U., 1982; DSc hon.), Rockford Coll., 1983; LLD (hon.), Western Mich. U., 1983, York U., Can., 1984; LHD (hon.), kidmore Coll., 1984; DSc (hon.), City U., London, 989. Asst. theoretical div. Los Alamos Project, 1945-6; asst. teaching and research Princeton, 1946-48; Fine nstr. Office Naval Research fellow math., 1949-51, asst. rof. philosophy, 1951-53; research asst. to Dr. Albert instein, Inst. Advanced Study, 1948-49; prof. math. artmouth Coll., 1953-70, 81-90, adj. prof. math, 1972-81, chmn. math. dept., 1955- 67, Albert Bradley 3d Century prof., 1969-72, pres., 1970-81, prof. math. and computer sci., 1981-90; coordinator ednl. plans and devel., 1967-69; lectr. in Austria, Israel, India, Japan, 1964-65; Vanuxem lectr. Princeton U., 1974; chmn. True BASIC, Inc., Hanover, N.H., 1983— (implemented on a variety of microcomputers); cons. Rand Corp., Santa Monica, Calif., 1953-69; mem. Nat. Commn. Libraries and Info. Sci., 1971-73; mem. regional dir.'s adv. com. HEW, 1971-73. Author: Man and the Computer, Back to BASIC, 1985, 12 other books; co-author: Finite Mathematics with Business Applications: Denumerable Markov Chains; Basic Programming, 1967; contbr. to Ency. Brit., articles to profl. jours.; cons. editor: Jour. Symbolic Logic, 1950-59; assoc. editor: Jour. Math. Analysis and Applications, 1959-70; mem. editorial bd. ABACUS, 1983-88; co-inventor of computer lang. BASIC, Dartmouth Time-Sharing System. Chmn. U.S. Commn. on Math. Instrn., 1958-60; mem. NRC, 1963-66; chmn. Pres.'s Commn. on Accident at Three Mile Island, 1979; mem. Hanover Sch. Bd. (N.H.), 1961-64; Trustee Found. Center, 1970-76, Carnegie Found. Ad-vancement Teaching, 1972-78; bd. dirs. Council for Fin. Aid to Edn., 1976-79; chmn. Consortium on Financing Higher Edn., 1979-80. Served with AUS, 1945-46. Recipient Priestley award, 1976, Edn. award, Am. Fedn. Info. Processing Socs., 1983, N.Y. Acad. Sci. award, 1984, IEEE Computer Pioneer medal, 1986. Mem. Assn. Symbolic Logic, Math. Assn. Am. (chmn. New England sect. 1959-60, mem. bd. govs. 1960-63, chmn. panel biol. and social scis. 1963-64), Am. Math. Soc., Am. Philos. Assn., Am. Acad. Arts and Scis., Century Assn. Club, Phi Beta Kappa, Sigma Xi (nat. lectr. 1967). Home: Etna N.H. Died Dec. 26, 1992.

KEMP, FRANCIS BOLLING, III, banker; b. Greens-boro, N.C., Sept. 10, 1940; s. Francis B. and Billie (Stocks) K.; m. Virginia Wadsworth Millner, Aug. 15, 1964; children: Francis Bolling IV, Elizabeth R. AB cum laude, Davidson Coll., 1963; MBA, Harvard U., 1967. Pres. NCNB Nat. Bank of N.C., 1983-88; corp. exec. v.p. NCNB Corp., 1983-85, pres., 1985—; chmn. NCNB Tex., Dallas, 1988-89; bd. dirs. VISA U.S.A. Inc., VISA Internat. Inc.; chmn. VISA U.S.A., 1988—. Mem. bd. visitors Davidson Coll., 1978-81, trustee, 1988—, bd. dirs.; trustee N.C. Symphony, 1978-84, pres., 1979-80, vice chmn., 1980-81; pres. Spirit Sq. Performing Arts Ctr., 1982-83; bd. dirs. Charlotte Uptown Devel. Corp., 1987-88; pres. Arts and Scis. Coun., 1983-84; bd. dirs. Gov.'s Coun. on Arts and Humanities, 1983-88, Univ. Rsch. Park, 1983-88, Greater Dallas C. of C., 1988—, mem. exec. com.; bd. dirs. Citizens' Coun. Dallas, 1988—; trustee Charlotte Country Day Sch., 1983-85; bd. dirs., mem. exec. com. United Way Cen. Carolinas, Inc., pres.-elect, 1988-89. Served to 1st. lt. U.S. Army, 1963-65. Mem. Charlotte C. of C. (chmn. 1986), Greater Dallas C. of C. (bd. dirs. 1988—), Assn. Res. City Bankers, N.C. Bankers Assn. (pres. 1985-86), N.C. Citizens Bus. and Industry, Phi Beta Kappa, Beta Theta Pi. Republican. Presbyterian. Clubs: Charlotte City, Country of N.C, Quail Hollow Country. Home: Dallas Tex. Died Nov. 23, 1990.

KEMPE, LLOYD LUTE, chemical engineering edu-cator; b. Pueblo, Colo., Nov. 26, 1911; s. Henry Edwin and Ida Augusta (Pittelkow) K.; m. Barbara Jean Bell, June 27, 1938; 1 child, Marion Louise (Mrs. Steven Sanford Palmer). BS in Chem. Engring, U. Minn., 1932, MS, 1938, PhD, 1948. Registered profl. engr., Minn., Mich. Rsch. asst. in soils U. Minn., 1934-35, rsch. accoc., 1940-41, asst. in chem. engring., 1946-48; asst. san. engr. Minn. Dept. Health, 1935-40; instr. bacteriology U. Mich., Ann Arbor, 1948-49; asst. prof. U. Mich., 1949-50, asst. prof. chem. engring. and bacteriology, 1952-55, assoc., prof., 1955-58, prof., 1958-60, prof. chem. engring. and san. engring., 1960-64, prof. chem. engring., 1964-67, prof. chem. engring. and microbiology, 1967-70, prof. emeritus chem. engring., prof. emeritus microbiology and Immunology, 1970-94; asst. prof. food tech. U. Ill., 1950-52. Mem. editl. bd.: Biotech. and Bioengring, 1959-70, Applied Microbi-ology, 1964-94, Food Tech, 1967-69, Jour. Food Sci, 1967-69. Mem. adv. com. on food irradiation Am. Inst. Biol. Scis./AEC; adv. com. on microbiology of foods Nat. Acad. Scis./NRC; adv. com. on botulism hazards HEW/FDA; adv. com. on mil. environ. research Nat. Acad. Scis./NRC. Served to col. AUS, 1941-45. Decorated Bronze Star. Mem. Am. Inst. C.E., Am. Chem. Soc., Am. Soc. Microbiology, Inst. Food Technologists, A.A.A.S., Am. Acad. Environ. Engrs., Water Pollution Control Fedn., Soc. Indsl. Microbi-ology, Sigma Xi, Phi Lambda Upsilon, Tau Beta Pi, Alpha Chi Sigma. Lodges: Masons, Kiwanis. Home: Grand Rapids Mich. Died Oct. 26, 1994.

KENNEDY, EDWIN LUST, retired investment banker; b. Marion, Ohio, May 25, 1904. AB, Ohio U., 1926, LHD (hon.), 1965; postgrad., Ohio State U., Harvard U.; LHD (hon.), Findlay Coll., 1968, Juniata Coll., 1977, Ohio No. U., 1977. Tchr. pub. schs. Ohio; with Lehman Bros., Kuhn, Loeb, Inc., N.Y.C., from 1941; gen. ptnr., ptnr. in charge of oil and gas dept. Lehman Bros., Kuhn, Loeb, Inc. and predecessor firms, N.Y.C., from 1952; now ret.; with Standard and Poor's Co., 1929-32; with bank liquidation staff Pa. Dept. Banking, 1932-36; pvt. investment adviser, 1936-41. Chmn. bd. trustees Ohio U., 1965-66, 74-75; trustee Hiram Coll., 1958—, Ohio U., 1959-75, fundraiser, 1954—, Ohio U. Found., 1956—, Juniata Coll., 1970—, Hampden Sydney Coll., 1982-89; pres. Ohio U. Nat. Alumni Bd. Dirs., 1956-58. Named Vol. of Yr. Coun. for Ad-vancement and Support Edn., 1985. Home: New Vernon N.J.

KENNEDY, ROBERT EMMET, retired new-spaperman; b. Cin., June 6, 1910; s. Robert Emmet and Amelia (Garnier) K.; m. Rosetta Vinson, Oct. 27, 1993 (dec.); children: Jeanne Colleen (Mrs. Theodore Lamb), Robert Emmet. Student, DePaul U., 1928. Police re-porter, later asst. city editor City News Bur., 1929-35; asst. city editor, polit. editor Washington corr., editorial page editor Chgo. Times, 1935-48; editorial writer Chgo. Sun-Times, 1948-50, chief editorial writer, 1950-65, asso. editor, 1965-74; pres. Sea Breeze West Condominium, Inc., Marco Island, Fla., 1974-75. Contbr. to: Marco Island Eagle, 1976-96. Elected sponsor U. Mo. Sch. of Journalism 50th anniversary on recognition of disting. position achieved in the profession of jounalism, 1958. Recipient Aviation Writing award TWA, 1954, Chgo. Coun. on Fgn. Rels. world Understanding award, 1956, Stanley Found. award, 1965, Grenville Clark award, 1968. Mem. Am. Soc. Newspaper Editors, Nat. Conf. Editorial Writers (chmn. 1958), Sigma Delta Chi. Club: Chgo. Press (pres. 1963). Home: Naples Fla. Died Jan. 28, 1996.

KENNEDY, ROSE FITZGERALD (MRS. JOSEPH P. KENNEDY), philanthropist; b. Boston, July 22, 1890; d. John Francis and Josephine Mary (Hannon) Fitzgerald; m. Joseph P. Kennedy, Oct. 7, 1914 (dec. 1969); children: Joseph (dec.), John Fitzgerald (Pres. U.S. 1961-63; dec.), Rosemary, Kathleen (dec.), Eunice (Mrs. Robert Sargent Shriver), Patricia Kennedy Lawford, Robert Francis (dec.), Jean (Mrs. Stephen Smith), EdwardM. Ed., New Eng. Conservatory, Con-vent of the Sacred Heart, Boston, Manhattanville Coll.; LLD (hon.), Manhattanville Coll.; ed., Blumenthal Acad., Valls, The Netherlands; LLD (hon.), Ge-orgetown U., 1977. Author: Times to Remember, 1974. Named Papal Countess Pope Pius XII. Roman Catholic. Home: Hyannisport Mass. Died Jan. 22, 1995.

KENNEY, LOUIS AUGUSTINE, librarian; b. Dorchester, Nebr., Feb. 28, 1917; s. Frank J. and Amelia (Peter) K.; m. Josephine Signer, July 17, 1950; children: Martin, Bonita, Philip, Douglas. A.B., Nebr. State Tchrs. Coll., 1939; B.L.S., U. Ill., 1940, M.S., 1947; postgrad., U. Zurich, Switzerland, 1949-50; Ph.D., U. Md., 1960. Asst. librarian Engring. Library, U. Ill., 1940-41, 46, bibliographer acquisition dept., 1947-48, serials cataloger, 1955-57; acquisition librarian U. Notre Dame, 1948-54; chief tech. services Ill. State Library, 1957-59; chief librarian Air Force Inst. Tech., 1959-60; univ. librarian San Diego State U., 1961-80, univ. librarian emeritus, 1981-93. Author: Frank J. and Amelia Kenney: Their Lives and Times, 1876-1970, 1987, Reviews of Books on the Mental Illnesses: A Col-lection, 1988, Catalogue of the Rare Astronomical Books in the San Diego State University Library, 1988, Frank J. and Amelia Kenney Album of Photographs and Biographical Dictionary, 1991, More Reviews of Books on the Mental Illnesses, 1992. V.p. San Diego Alliance for Mentally Ill, 1985-88, 90-92, pres., 1989. Mem. San Diego Opera Assn., Friends of Malcolm A. Love Libr., San Diego State U.; ALA, Calif. Libr. Assn. (dist. pres. 1965), San Diego State U. Alumni Assn., Phi Alpha Theta, Mortar Bd. Home: San Diego Calif. Died Dec. 10, 1993.

KENNEY, RICHARD ALEC, physiology educator; b. Coventry, Eng., Oct. 4, 1924; came to U.S., 1967; s. Alec and Dorothy Ada (Cooke) K.; m. Bette Gladys Green, Aug. 8, 1959; 1 son by previous marriage, Michael Alec. B.Sc. with honors, U. Birmingham, Eng., 1945, Ph.D., 1947. Lectr. physiology U. Leeds, Eng., 1947-51; with Colonial Rsch. ser., Nigeria, 1951-54; staff mem. WHO, S.E. Asia Region, 1955-60; chmn. physi-ology U. Singapore, 1960-65; reader physiology U. Melbourne, Australia, 1965-67; prof. physiology George Washington U. Med. Center, 1968-90, chmn. dept., 1970-89; tutor physiology Royal Australian Coll. Surgeons, 1965-67. Author: Physiology of Aging; Contbr. articles to profl. jours. Mem. Physiol. Soc. (London), Renal Assn. (London). Club: Cosmos (Washington). Home: Washington D.C. Died Jan. 19, 1995.

KENNY, ALEXANDER DONOVAN, pharmacology educator; b. London, Mar. 4, 1925; came to U.S., 1947; s. Alexander and Alice Astley (Barton) K.; m. Dorothy Marie LeTang, Aug. 19, 1950; children: Alexander Leo, Mary Alice Kenny Sinton, Virginia Ann Kenny Drawe, Peter Donovan. BSc, U. London, 1945, DSc, 1982; PhD, Athenaeum of Ohio, 1950. Sr. chemist Univ. Coll. Hosp., London, 1950-51; chief chemistry lab. Mass. Gen. Hosp., Boston, 1952; research asst. dental sci., instr. Sch. Dental Medicine Harvard U., Boston, 1952-55; assoc. pharmacology Sch. Medicine Harvard U., Boston, 1955-59; assoc. prof. pharmacology W.Va. U. Med. Ctr., Morgantown, 1959-65, prof. pharmacology, 1965-67; prof. pharmacology U. Mo. Med. Ctr., Columbia, 1967-71, prof. biochemistry, 1971-74; prof. pharmacology U. Tex. Med. Br., Galveston, 1974-75; chmn. dept. pharmacology Tex. Tech. U. Health Scis. Ctr., Lubbock, 1976-93; prof. pharmacology, 1976-94;

acting dir. Tarbox Parkinson's Disease Inst., 1976-78, dir., 1978-86, interim research dir., 1986-87; sr. investigator U. Mo. Dalton Research Ctr., 1967-74; cons. NIH, NSF, 1975-87. Author: Intestinal Calcium Absorption and Its Regulation, 1981. Mem. Diocesan Sch. Bd., Amarillo, Tex., 1980-84, pres., 1982-84; pres. Thomas More Cath. Sch. Bd., Lubbock, 1981-83. USPHS fellow; research grantee NIH, USPHS. Mem. Am. Chem. Soc. (div. biol. chemistry), Am. Inst. Nutrition, Am. Soc. Bone and Mineral Rsch., Am. Soc. Pharmacology and Exptl. Therapeutics, Biochem. Soc. (Brit.), Brit. Pharmacol. Soc., Endocrine Soc., Osteoporosis Found., Soc. Endocrinology (Brit.), Soc. Exptl. Biology and Medicine, Lubbock Club. Democrat. Home: Lubbock Tex. Died Apr. 1994.

KENNY, MICHAEL H., bishop; b. Hollywood, Calif., June 26, 1937. Ed., St. Joseph Coll., Mountain View, Calif., St. Patrick's Sem., Menlo Park, Calif., Cath. U. Am. Ordained priest Roman Cath. Ch., 1963; ordained bishop of Juneau, Alaska, 1979-95. Home: Juneau Alaska Died Feb. 20, 1995.

KENT, FREDERICK HEBER, lawyer; b. Fitzgerald, Ga., Apr. 26, 1905; s. Heber and Juanita (McDuffie) K.; m. Norma C. Futch, Apr. 25, 1929; children: Frederick Heber, Norma Futch K. Lockwood, John Bradford, James Cleveland. LLB, J.D., U. Ga., 1926. Bar: Ga. 1926, Fla. 1926. Practiced in Jacksonville, Fla.; of counsel Kent, Ridge & Crawford, Jacksonville, Fla.; chmn. bd. Kent Theatres, Inc.; pres. Kent Enterprises, Inc., Kent Properties, Inc. Chmn. local ARC, 1934, 1950; pres. Jacksonville's 50 Years of Progress Assn., 1951; bd. dirs. YMCA, pres., 1946-50; bd. dirs. Jacksonville Community Chest-United Fund, 1955-59, pres., 1958-59; chmn. Fla. State Plant Bd., 1955-56; bd. control (regents) Fla. Instns. of Higher Learning, 1953-58, chmn., 1955-56; bd. dirs. Riverside Hosp. Assn., 1956-76, pres., 1964-65; chmn. State Jr. Coll. Council, 1962-72; mem. adv. com. Fla. Higher Edn. Facilities Act, 1963, 64; chmn. bd. trustees Fla. Community Coll., Jacksonville, 1965-71; mem. Select Council on Post High Sch. Edn. in Fla., 1967, Fla. Gov.'s Commn. for Quality Edn., 1967; trustee Bolles Sch., Jacksonville, 1954-65, Theatre Jacksonville, 1966-76; chmn. Fla. Quadricentennial Commn., 1962-65; mem. Jacksonville City Council, 1933-1937; mem. Fla. Democratic Exec. Com., 1938-40. Served as lt. USNR, 1942-45. Recipient Distinguished Service award U.S. Jr. C. of C., 1933, Ted Arnold award Jacksonville C. of C., 1961; Fred H. Kent campus Fla. Community Coll. at Jacksonville named in his honor, 1974. Mem. ABA, Internat. Bar Assn., Jacksonville Bar Assn., Jacksonville C. of C., Am. Judicature Soc., Soc. Colonial Wars, Am. Legion, Rotary (pres. 1958-59), Timuquana Country Club (past pres.), Florida Yacht Club, Seminole Club (past pres.), Friars Club, Ye Mystic Revelers, Ponte Vedra Club, River Club, Sigma Alpha Epsilon, Delta Sigma Pi. Republican. Died Sept. 22, 1995.

KERN, FRANK NORTON, lawyer; b. Waymansville, Ind., Feb. 19, 1920; s. Frank W. and Irene (Everdon) K.; m. Minnetta Louise Wooden, Apr. 9, 1944; children: Cynthia Jennifer, Candace. B.A., Ohio Wesleyan U., 1941; M.B.A. with distinction, Harvard, 1943, LL.B. cum laude, 1948. Bar: Ohio 1948, Pa. 1953, N.Y. 1956, D.C. 197. Practiced in Cleve., 1948-51, N.Y.C., 1956-92; assoc. firm Squire, Sanders & Dempsey, Cleve., 1948-51; tax atty. U.S. Steel Corp., Pitts., 1951-54; ptnr. charge tax dept. Reid & Priest, N.Y.C., 1955-80. Mem. Ohio Wesleyan U. Assocs. and Investment Com., 1962-92. Sr. warden Christ's Ch., Rye, N.Y., 1986-92. Served to lt. with USNR, 1943-46. Mem. ABA, Inter-Am. Bar Assn., Phi Beta Kappa. Republican. Episcopalian. Clubs: Met. (Washington); Apawamis (Rye); Sky, Recess (N.Y.). Contbr. articles to profl. jours. Died Aug. 13, 1992. Home: Rye N.Y.

KERR, ROBERT SHAW, bishop; b. Newport, R.I., Aug. 16, 1917; s. Edgar John and Amelia (Shaw) K.; m. Carolyn Brooks Hill, 1945; 2 children. BA, Trinity Coll., Hartford, Conn., 1940; grad., Gen. Theol. Sem., 1943, STB, 1960, ST, 1960. Ordained deacon and priest The Episcopal Ch., 1943. Asst. Cathedral of St. John the Divine, N.Y.C.; master Choir Sch., N.Y.C., 1943-46; rector Vt. parishes, 1946-66; dean Cathedral Ch. of St. Paul, Burlington, Vt., 1966-90; bishop coadjutor Diocese of Vt., 1974, bishop, 1974-90. Home: Burlington Vt. Died 1990.

KERRIGAN, (THOMAS) ANTHONY, writer, translator; b. Winchester, Mass., Mar. 14, 1918; s. Thomas Aloysius and Madeline (Flood) K.; m. Marjorie Burke, Sept. 15, 1935; m. Elaine Gurevitch, Sept. 1, 1951; children: Michael, Antonia, Camilo Jose, Patrick, Elie, Malachy. Licenciado en filosofia y letras, U. Havana, Cuba, 1945, U. Paris, 1952, U. Barcelona, Spain, 1951. Lectr. in Sino-Japanese U. Calif., 1947; translator U. Fla., Gainesville, 1950-51; grantee Bollingen Found., 1961-75; editor, translator Bollingen Found., Princeton U., 1963-75; vis. prof. English State U. N.Y., Buffalo, 1974; vis. prof. Spanish U. Ill., 1977-78; faculty fellow Center Study Man in Contemporary Soc., U. Notre Dame, 1979-84; sr. guest scholar Kellogg Inst. Internat. Studies, 1984-92. Editor, translator: 50 books including 7 vols. the Selected Works of Miguel de Unamuno; Author 3 books poetry. Served with Mil. Intelligence U.S. Army, World War II. Winner Nat. Book award,

1975; finalist, 1974; Translation Center Columbia U. fellow, 1977-78, NEA sr. fellow in lit. grantee, 1988. Fellow Am. Acad. Learned Socs.; mem. Internat. Coun. Transl. Ctr., PEN (Ireland). Home: Notre Dame Ind. Died Mar. 7, 1992; buried U. Notre Dame Cemetery, Notre Dame, Ill.

KESSLER, MARTIN, publishing executive. Pres., pub., editorial dir. Basic Books, Inc., N.Y.C. Home: New York N.Y. Died Feb. 1, 1996.

KESSLER, WAYNE VINCENT, health sciences educator, researcher, consultant; b. Milo, Iowa, Jan. 10, 1933; s. Joseph Edward and Genevieve (Frueh) K.; m. Olive Beatrice Buremaster, Sept., 10, 1953; children: Katherine Marie, Karl Matthew. B.S., N.D. State U., 1955, M.S., 1956; Ph.D., Purdue U., 1959. Asst. prof. pharm. chemistry N.D. State U., Fargo, 1959-60; asst. prof. health physics Purdue U., W. Lafayette, Ind., 1960-64, assoc. prof., 1964-68, prof. bionucleonics, 1968-79, prof. health scis., 1979—; cons. Mead Johnson Inc., Evansville, Ind., 1968-69, Miles Labs., Elkart, Ind., 1970. Author: Cadmium Toxicity, 1974. Fellow Purdue Rsch. Found. , 1957. Fellow AAAS, Acad. Pharm. Scis., Phi Kappa Phi; mem. Health Physics Soc. Presbyterian. Avocations: woodworking; traveling. Died May 9, 1995. Home: Lafayette Ind.

KESTIN, JOSEPH, mechanical engineer, educator; b. Warsaw, Poland, Sept. 18, 1913; came to U.S., 1952, naturalized, 1960; s. Paul and Leah K.; m. Alicja Wanda Drabienko, Mar. 12, 1949; 1 dau., Anita Susan. Dipl. Ing., Engring., U. Warsaw, 1937; Ph.D., Imperial Coll., London, 1945; M.A. ad eundem, Brown U., 1955; D.Sc., U. London, 1966; Dr. h.c., Universite Claude Bernard (Lyon I). Sr. lectr. dept. mech. engring. Polish U. Coll., London, 1944-46; dept. head Polish U. Coll., 1947-52; prof. engring., dir. Ctr. for Energy Studies Brown U., Providence, 1952-84; rsch. prof. Brown U., 1984-93; vis. prof. Imperial Coll., London, 1958, 83-86, Summer Sch. in Jablonna, Warsaw, Polish Acad. Scis., 1973, U. Md., 1983-88; Disting. vis. prof. U. Del., 1989; professeur associe U. Paris, 1966, Université Claude Bernard (Lyon I) and Ecole Centrale de Lyon, 1974; Fulbright lectr. Instituto Superior Tecnico, Lisbon, 1972; spl. lectr. Norges Tekniske, Hogskole, Trondheim, Norway, 1963, 71; lectr. Nobel Com. Berzelius Symposium, 1979; fellow Inst. Advanced Studies, West Berlin; spl. adv. on engring. edn. to Chancellor of U. Tehran, Iran, 1968; chmn. NRC Eval. Panel for Office of Standard Ref. Data of Nat. Bur. Standards, 1976-80, summer sch. on internal variables in thermodynamics and continuum mechanics Internat. Ctr. for Mech. Scis., Udine, Italy, 1988; mem. Eval. Panel for Nat. Measurement Lab. of Nat. Bur. Standards, 1978-80; Numerical Data Adv. Bd., NAS, 1976-80; cons. Nat. Bur. Standards, NATO, Rand Corp.; mem. vis. com. U. Va., Charlottesville, 1964; mem. exec. com. Nat. Bur. Standards Evaluation Panels, 1974-78. Author 5 books on thermodynamics; also 250 research papers in field; translator 5 books on thermodynamics and fluid mechanics; editor-in-chief Dept. Energy Sourcebook on Production of Electricity from Geothermal Energy; tech. editor Jour. Applied Mechanics, 1956-71; mem. editorial bd. Internat. Jour. Heat and Mass Transfer, 1961-71, Heat Transfer-Soviet Research, 1968-93, Heat Transfer-Japanese Research, 1972-93, Mechanics Research Communications, 1973-93, Jour. Non-Equilibrium Thermodynamics, 1976-93, Revue Generale de Thermique, 1975-93, Physica A, 1978-91, Internat. Jour. Thermophysics, 1979-93, Jour. Chem. and Engring. Data, 1980-90; contbr. articles to profl. jours. Recipient Alexander von Humboldt Sr. U.S. Scientist award , 1986. Fellow Inst. Mech. Engrs. (London) (Water Arbitration prize 1949), ASME (task group on energy 1974-76, applied mechanics div. 1967-78, chmn. 1978, nat. nominating com. 1976-78, Centennial medals for research achievements and disting. service, James Harry Potter Gold medal 1981, spl. fellowship Japan), Soc. Promotion of Sci., Internat. Union Pure and Applied Chem. (hon., chmn. subcom. transport properties, 1981-91, fellow 1989, Imperial Coll. Sci., Tech. and Medicine (London); mem. NAE (peer com. mech. engring. 1987-90, memberships com. 1990-93), Am. Soc. Engring. Edn. (chmn. Curtis W. McGraw Research award com. 1976-78), Internat. Assn. Properties of Steam (U.S. del. exec. com. 1954-88, chief of del., 1972-88, pres. 1974-76, hon. fellow 1989), Council Energy Engring. Research, Polish Acad. Scis. (fgn.), Sigma Xi (pres. Brown U. chpt. 1979-84), Tau Beta Pi. Clubs: Univ. (Providence), Faculty Brown U. (Providence). Home: Providence R.I. Died Mar. 16, 1993.

KETTERINGHAM, JOHN M., corporate executive; b. Bournemouth, Dorset, Eng., Mar. 9, 1940; arrived in U.S., 1964; s. Albert James and Margaret Lilian (Grimshaw) K.; m. Susan M. Pattisson, Aug. 4, 1964; children: Emma, Caryn, Michael. BA, Oxford U., Eng., 1961, MA, 1964, D.Phil., 1964. Profl. staff Arthur D. Little Inc., Cambridge, Mass., 1964-76, v.p., 1976-86, sr. v.p., 1986—; bd. dirs. Cambridge Cons. Ltd., Eng., Opinion Research Corp., Princeton, N.J. Author: Breakthroughs, 1986; contbr. chpt. Competitive Strategic Mgmt., 1984, Artificial Lungs, 1978. Mem. AAAS, Am. Mgmt. Assn., Am. Soc. Artificial Internal Organs. Republican. Club: Parkstone Yacht (Poole, Eng.). Home: Lincoln Mass.

KEYS, THOMAS EDWARD, medical library consultant; b. Greenville, Miss., Dec. 2, 1908; s. Thomas Napoleon and Margaret (Boothroyd) K.; m. Elizabeth Schaack, Nov. 2, 1934; children: Thomas Frederick Charles Edward (dec.). A.B., Beloit Coll., 1931, Sc.D 1972; M.A., U. Chgo., 1934. Order asst. Newberry Library, Chgo., 1931-32; asst. librarian Mayo Clinic 1934-35, reference librarian, 1935-42, librarian, 1946-69 sr. library cons., 1969-72; prof. Mayo Found. Grad. Sch Medicine, 1969-72, emeritus, 1972-95; cons., lectr. i field. Author: Applied Medical Library Practice, 195. (with others) Cardiac Classics (later Classics of Cardiology), 1941, 61, 83, History of Surgical Anesthesi 1945, 63, 78, (with A. Faulconer) Foundations of Anesthesiology, 1965, (with Jack Key) Classics of Medica Librarianship, 1980; others; contbr. numerous articles t profl. jours. Bd. regents Nat. Library of Medicine 1959-62. Decorated Knight Order Falcon (Iceland Recipient numerous awards. Fellow Med. Librar Assn., Mayo Found. Soc. for History of Medicine; mem Internat. Soc. History Medicine, Am. Soc. Anesthes ologists (hon.), Anesthesia History Assn. (hon.), Am Osler Soc., Phi Beta Kappa, Beta Phi Mu, Pi Kapp Alpha. Episcopalian. Home: Rochester Minn. Die Oct. 11, 1995.

KHOMEINI, (AYATOLLAH) RUHOLLAI MUSSAVI, political and religious leader of Iran; b Khomein, Iran, May 17, 1900; s. Sayed Mustafa an Hajar (Saghafi) Mussavi; married; 1 son, Sayed Ahmer 3 daus. Tchr. Madresseh Faizieh; leading opponent o Mohammed Reza Shah; led clergy in gen. strike agains Govt. of Shah, 1962; arrested, detained, under hous arrest, 1963; arrested, 1964, exiled to Turkey; exiled i Iraq, 1965; head theol. sch. in Iraq, 1965-78, expelled b Iraqi govt., 1978; in exile in Neauphe-le-Chatea France, 1978-79; returned to Iran, 1979; forced resigna tion of existing govt., apptd. new govt., 1979; returne to City of Qom, 1979; formed spl. militia Army Guardians of Islamic Revolution, 1979; took control Iran, Nov. 1979, named polit. and religious leader l lamic Republic of Iran for life, 1979. Author 21 books Shi'ite Muslim. Home: Qom Iran

KHRISTOV, KHRISTO YANKOV, physicist; b Varna, Bulgaria, June 12, 1915. Grad. physics wi honors, grad. math., Sofia U., 1938; postgrad., U. Par Sorbonne, Moscow U., Nuclear Rsch. Inst., Dubn Soviet Union, 1966. Asst. chmn. nuclear physics an meteorology Sofia U., 1942, asst. prof. theoretic physics, 1946, prof. Physics and Math. Faculty, 195 corr. mem. Bulgarian Acad. Scis., 1951; deputy hea Physics and Math. Faculty Sofia U., 1952, head Physic and Math. Faculty, 1956-58, chmn. nuclear physic 1958-67, dep. rector Kl. Ohridski, 1958, rector K Ohridski, 1972-73, vice chancellor Kl. Ohridski, 197 full mem. Bulgarian Acad. Scis., 1961, dep. dir. Physic Inst., 1964-67, dir. Physics Inst., 1972; dep. dir. Nuclea Rsch. Inst., Dubna, 1967-69; head theory of elem. par ticles sect. Bulgarian Acad. Scis., 1968, head Cosmi Rays Lab., 1968; Bugarian govt. rep. Nuclear Rsc Inst., 1970; dep. chmn. Bulgarian Acad. Scis., 1973-7 founder, dir. Nuclear Rsch. and Nuclear Energy Inst 1973, mem. Presidium, 1977-82; mem. sci. coun. Nuclea Rsch. Inst.; chmn. Soc. Bulgarian Physicists, 1971. Recipient Dimitrov prize, 1952; named Honoured Sc Worker, 1969, People's Sci. Worker, 1972; named l Order of People's Republic of Bulgaria 1st Cl., 197 Order of Georgi Dimitrov, 1985. Home: Sofia Bulgar Died March 20, 1990.

KICHER, THOMAS PATRICK, mechanical enginee educator; b. Johnsonburg, Pa., Oct. 20, 1937; s. Willia Milton and Mary Elizabeth (Divany) K.; m. Janet Ma Logan, July 28, 1962; children: Rita Ann, Paul Thoma Laura Lynn. B.S. in Engring. Sci., Case Inst. Tech 1959, M.S. in Engring. Mechanics, 1962, Ph.D., 1965 Design engr. Douglas Aircraft, 1964-65; asst. pro mech. and aero. engring. Case Western Res. U., Cleve 1965-68, assoc. prof., 1968-78, prof., 1978-86, Arthur Armington prof. engring., 1988-94, chmn. dept. mec and aerospace engring., 1985-92, assoc. dean sci. an engring. Case Inst. Tech., 1974-79, dean Case Sch. En gring., 1992-94; cons. Union Carbide Corp., Medtroni Inc., Chase Brass & Copper Co., Stouffer Foods Corp Westinghouse, Brunswick, 3M, Lubrizol, Parker-Ha nifin, Meyer Products, ProQuip. Fellow AIAA (assoc mem. ASME, Soc. Exptl. Mechanics, Sigma Xi, The Tau (hon.), Tau Beta Pi. Home: Willoughby Hills Oh Died Apr. 1994.

KIDD, DAVID THOMAS, lawyer, retired corporat officer; b. Laramie, Wyo., Feb. 1, 1934; s. David T. an Sarah Lucille (Love) K.; m. Sally Noble, Sept. 1, 195 children: Lynden Louise, David Thomas II. Studen Dartmouth Coll., 1952-55; BA, U. Wyo., 1957, J 1960. Bar: Wyo. 1960, U.S. Dist. Ct. Wyo. 1960, U Ct. Appeals (10th cir.) 1978, U.S. Supreme Ct. 197 Western counsel for natural resources Union Pacif Corp., 1968-88, ret. 1988; pvt. practice law, 1988— mem. U. Wyo. Agenda 2000 Com. Bd. dirs. litigatio Mountain States Legal Found., 1977—, vice chmn 1984-90, chmn., 1990—; judge Municipal Ct., Caspe 1963-68; mem. Wyo. Ho. of Reps., 1963-67; mayo Casper, 1971. Mem. State of Wyo. Commn. on Edn 1983-84, chmn. educator subcom. Mem. ABA, Wyo Bar Assn., Am. Judicature Soc., Am. Counsel Assn Rocky Mountain Mineral Law Found., Rock ountain Oil and Gas Assn. (chmn. legal com. 1982-86, p. Wyo. 1985-87, pres. Petroleum Assn. Wyo. subs. 85-87), Dartmouth Lawyers Assn. Clubs: Casper Pe-oleum. Contbr. articles to profl. jours. Died Sept. 30, 94. Home and Office: Wheatland Wyo.

IENHOLZ, EDWARD, artist; b. Fairfield, Wash., 927; m. Nancy Reddin. Student, State Coll., 1945. ne-man shows include Exodus Gallery, San Pedro, alif., 1958, Ferus Gallery, Los Angeles, 1959, 60, 61, wan Gallery, N.Y.C., 1965, 67, Los Angeles, 1963, 64, , Wide White Space Gallery, Antwerp, Belgium, 1970, , 72, Gemini G.E.L., Los Angeles, 1972, 80, kademie der Kunste, Berlin, Fed. Republic Germany, 973, 78, Stadtischye Kunsthalle Dusseldorf, Fed. epublic Germany, 1973, 77, 89, Centre Nat. d'Art et Culture Georges Pompidou, Paris, 1977, Univ. Art Ius. U. Calif., Berkeley, 1979, Galerie Maeght, Paris, 979, Zurich, Switzerland, 1981, Dibbert Gallery, erlin, 1982, Art Mus. South Tex., Corpus Christi, 982, Contemporary Arts Ctr., Cin., 1982, Newport arbor Art Mus., Newport Beach, Calif., 1982, Braun-ein Gallery, San Francisco, 1982, 84, Mus. Con-mporary Art, Chgo., 1985, L.A. Louver Gallery, enice, 1981, 86, Mus. Moderner Kunst, Mus. des 20 ahrehunderts, Vienna, Austria, inaugural exhbn. ouver Gallery N.Y.C., various others; exhibited in oup shows at Mus. Modern Art, N.Y.C., 1961, 68, wan Gallery, 1962, 64, Oakland Art Mus., Calif., 963, 82, Art Inst. Chgo., 1966, Los Angeles County Ius. Art, 1967, 68, New Sch. Art Ctr., N.Y.C., 1967, unsthalle Nurnberg, Fed. Republic Germany, 1970, enice Biennale, 1977, San Francisco Mus. Modern Art, 982, Whitney Mus. Am. Art, N.Y.C., 1962, 64, 66, 69, , Palm Springs (Calif.) Desert Mus., 1984, Fuller oldeen Gallery, San Francisco, 1984, Hirshhorn Mus. nd Sculpture Garden Smithsonian Instn., Washington, 984, Solomon R. Guggenheim Mus., N.Y.C., 1985, enry Art Gallery U. Wash., Seattle, 1985, Univ. Art allery Calif. State U., Chico, 1985, Seattle Art Mus., 985, Japanese Am. Cultural and Community Ctr., Los ngeles, 1985, L.A. Louver Gallery, 1983, 84, 85, ACE Gallery, Los Angeles, 1986; numerous works eated with Nancy Reddin Kienholz, 1972-94; their ork is subject of various articles and films. Home: Los ngeles Calif. Died June 10, 1994.

IES, CONSTANCE VIRGINIA, nutrition educator, ientist; b. Blue River, Wis., Dec. 13, 1934; d. Guerdon rancis and Gertrude Caroline (Pitts) K. BS, U. Wis., atteville, 1955, MS, U. Wis., Madison, 1960, PhD, 963. Lic. dietitian, Tex.; lic. tchr., Wis. English tchr. othschild-Schofield area schs., Wis., 1955-56; tchr., orarian Pontage High Sch., Wis., 1956-58; research sst. U. Wis., Madison, 1960-63; dietition instr. Madison en. Hosp., Wis., 1960-63; asst. prof. U. Nebr., Lincoln, 963-65, assoc. prof., 1965-68, prof. human nutrition, 968-94. Editor: Bioavailability of Iron, 1983, Bioavai-bility of Calcium, 1985, Bioavailability of Manganese, 987, Bioavailiability of Copper, 1990, Plant Foods for Iuman Nutrition; contbr. articles to profl. jours. ecipient Disting. Alumni award U. Wis., 1974; Dist-ng. Rsch. award Coll. Home Econs. U. Nebr., 1989; rantee Ross-Abbott Labs., 1982. Mem. Am. Chem. oc., Inst. Nutrition, Soc. for Clin. Nutrition, Am. ssn. Cereal Chemists, Am. Dietetics Assn. (registered ietitian), Am. Oil Chemists Assn., Soc. Enteral and arenteral Nutrition, Am. Home Econs. Assn. (Borden ward 1973, Disting. Svc. Award 1987). Congregation-list. Deceased. Home: Lincoln Nebr.

IESLOWSKI, KRYSZTOF, film director; b. Warsaw, oland, June 27, 1941. Student, Sch. Cinema and heatre, Lodz, Poland. Lectr. Faculty Radio and TV, . Silesia, Poland, 1979-82. Works include: (films) First ove, 1974 (Golden Dragon, Internat. Festival of Short ilms 1974), Personnel, 1975 (1st prize Mannheim Germany) Festival 1975), Camera Buff, 1979 (Fipresci rize, Moscow Festival 1979), Blind Chance, 1982, No nd, 1984, A Short Film About Love, 1988, A Short ilm About Killing, 1988 (Spl. Jury prize, Cannes In-ernat. Film Festival 1988, Best Fgn. Feature Film cad. award 1988), City Life, 1990, The Double Life of eronique, 1991, Trois Couleurs: Bleu, 1993, Golden ion Venice, 1993, Silver Bear Berlin, 1994, Blanc, 1994, ouge, 1994 (Prix de la Crititique award for best French ilm 1994, nom. for Acad. award for best dir. and best cript, 1995); (series) Decalogue, 1989; and numerous ocumentaries, short films, TV films. Home: Warsaw oland Died Mar. 13, 1996.

KILKENNY, JOHN F., federal judge, lawyer; b. Ieppner, Oreg., Oct. 26, 1901; s. John Sheridan and Rose Ann (Curran) K.; m. Virginia Brannock, Oct. 14, 931; children: John Michael, Karen Margaret. LLB, . Notre Dame, 1925; LLD (hon.), U. Portland, Oreg., 976. Bar: Oreg. 1926, U.S. Dist. Ct. Oreg. 1927, U.S. t. Appeals (9th cir.), 1933, U.S. Supreme Ct. 1954. Assoc. Raley, Kilkenny & Raley and predecessor firm Raley, Raley & Steiwer, Pendleton, Oreg., 1926-31, tnr., 1931-52; ptnr. Kilkenny, Fabre & Kottkamp, Pendleton, 1952-59; judge U.S. Dist. Ct. Oreg., Por-land, 1959-69; judge, sr. judge U.S. Ct. Appeals (9th ir.), Portland, from 1969; pres., dir. Happy Canyon Co., Pendleton, 1939-40; mem. Oreg. Bd. Bar Ex-aminers, 1951-52. Author: Shamrocks and Shepherds: The Irish of Morrow County, 1969. V.p. Irish-Am. Hist. Soc., 1942-57; charter mem. Oreg. Hist. Soc., 1975-95; trustee U. Portland, Oreg. State Libr., Umatilla County Libr. Recipient Outstanding Citizen award U. Portland, 1967, Disting. Citizen award, 1972, Cert. of Commendation Am. Assn. State and Local History, 1973, Heritage award Oreg. Hist. Soc., 1975, Medal of honor DAR, 1976, Disting. Alumnus award U. Notre Dame and Notre Dame Law Sch., 1985; named hon. lifetime dir. Hist. Soc. U.S. Dist. Ct. Oreg., 1983; John F. Kilkenny U.S. P.O. and Courthouse, Pendleton renamed in his honor, 1984. Fellow Am. Coll. Trial Lawyers, Am. Bar Found.; mem. ABA, Am. Jusicature Soc., Oreg. State Bar Assn. (pres. 1943-44, Award of Merit 1981), Notre Dame Law Assn. (bd. dirs. 1952-72), University Club, Knights of Malta, Elks (life). Repub-lican. Roman Catholic. Home: Portland Oreg. Died Feb. 17, 1995.

KILLEFER, TOM, banker; b. L.A., Jan. 7, 1917; s. Wade and Dorothy (Parks) K.; m. Carolyn Clothier, Apr. 17, 1948; children: Wade II, Caroline, Gail, An-ne. A.B. cum laude, Stanford U., 1938; J.D., Harvard U., 1942; B.C.L., Oxford U., 1947. Bar: Calif. 1946, U.S. Supreme Ct. 1953, D.C. 1954, Mich. 1966. With Lillick, Geary, Wheat, Adams & Charles, Calif. and Washington, 1947-59, ptnr., 1956-59; staff U.S. High Commn. for Germany, 1951-52; exec. dir. Com. Am. Steamship Lines, 1959-60; 1st v.p., vice chmn., dir. Ex-port-Import Bank of Washington, 1960-62; U.S. exec. dir. Inter-Am. Devel. Bank; spl. asst. to Sec. of Treasury, 1962- 66; exec. asst. to v.p. legal affairs Chrysler Corp., Detroit, 1966-67; v.p. finance Chrysler Corp., 1967, v.p. finance, gen. counsel, 1968-75, exec. v.p., 1975-76; pres. U.S. Trust Co., N.Y., 1976; chmn., pres., chief exec. officer U.S. Trust Co., 1976-79, chmn. bd., 1976-82; past chmn. bd. dirs. Detroit br. Fed. Res. Bank of Chgo.; sr. adviser, mem. U.S. del. 1st and 2d ann. meetings Inter-Am. Econ. and Social Coun. Hon. dir. Atlantic Coun. U.S.; former trustee Protestant Episcopal Cathedral Found., Internat. Mgmt. and Devel. Inst.; hon. trustee Com. Econ. Devel.; former trustee Stanford U.; mem. coun. Rockefeller U.; turstee Naval Aviation Mus. Found., Assn. Rhodes Scholars; bd. dirs. Nat. Coun. on Crime and Delinquency, Com-munity Found. Santa Clara County, Lucile Packard Children's Hosp., St. Luke's Hosp., San Francisco. Lt. (s.g.) USNR, 1941-46. Decorated D.F.C. Navy, Air medal, Purple Heart; Order of Merit Peru; recipient nat. award Am. Assn. Coll. Baseball Coaches; Disting. Achievement medal Stanford U. Athletic Bd. Mem. San Franciso Com. on Fgn. Rels., Assn. Gen. Counsel (pres. emeritus), Alibi Club (Washington), Alfalfa Club (Washington), Pacific Union (San Francisco), San Francisco Golf Club, Phi Beta Kappa, Zeta Psi. Epis-copalian. Home: Portola Valley Calif. Died June 16, 1996.

KILLPACK, JAMES ROBERT, bank holding com-pany executive; b. Persia, Iowa, Aug. 11, 1922; s. James Marion and Dorothy (Divelbess) K.; m. Norma Hewett, June 11, 1949; children: James, John, Steven. BS, Miami U., Oxford, Ohio, 1946. CPA, Ohio. With Peat, Marwick, Mitchell & Co., Cleve., 1946-58; treas. Ferro Corp., Cleve., 1958-66; fin. v.p. Island Creek Coal Co., Cleve., 1966-68; dir. corp. planning Eaton Corp., Cleve., 1968-69, v.p. corp. planning, 1969, v.p. adminstrn., 1970, v.p. fin., 1970-78, exec. v.p. fin. and adminstrn., 1978-79; dir. Nat. City Bank, Cleve., from 1979, vice chmn., 1979, pres., 1979-84; dir. Nat. City Corp., Cleve., 1979-93, vice chmn., 1979-80, pres., 1981-86, chmn., chief exec. officer, 1986-87, ret.; bd. dirs. Weatherhead Industries, LDI Corp., Sherwin-Williams Co., Nat. City Corp., Nat. City Bank. With AUS, 1942-45. Mem. AICPA, Fin Execs. Inst. (dir. Cleve. chpt., pres 1970-71), Union Club (Cleve.), Pepper Pike Country Club, The Country Club, Shaker Country Club (Shaker Heights, Ohio), John's Island (Fla.). Mem. Christian Ch. Home: Verno Beach Fla. Died Dec. 26, 1993.

KIMBALL, CHARLES NEWTON, scientific research administrator; b. Boston, Apr. 21, 1911; s. Charles Newton and Josephine Marie (Riley) K.; m. Mary Louise Theis, Oct. 3, 1951; children: John Theis, Susanne Louise. BEE, Northeastern U., 1931, D in Engring. (hon.), 1955; MS in Communications Engring., Harvard U., 1932, ScD, 1934. Rsch. engr. RCA, N.Y.C., 1934-41; instr. Grad. Sch. Engring. NYU, 1940-41; v.p., dir. Aircraft Accessories Corp., Kansas City, 1941-46; tech. dir. rsch. labs. div. Bendix Aviation Corp., Detroit, 1948-50; pres. Midwest Research Inst., Kansas City, Mo., 1950-75, chmn. bd. trustees, 1975-79, pres. emeritus, 1979-94; former dir. TWA, Hallmark Cards. Trustee Com. Econ. Devel. (life), Menninger Found. (life); former chmn. soc. fellows William Rockhill Nelson Gallery Art, Kansas City; former chmn. Greater Kansas City Community Found.; former chmn. adv. council Office of Tech. Assessment, U.S. Congress. Named Mr. Kansas City, 1973. Fellow IEEE; mem. Mo. Squires, Tau Beta Pi, Kansas City Country Club. Home: Shawnee Mission Kans. Died Jan. 8, 1994; buried Forest Hill Cemetery, Kansas City, Kans.

KIM IL-SUNG, president of Democratic People's Republic of Korea; b. Mangyongche, Pyongyang City, Korea, Apr. 15, 1912; s. Kim Hyong Jik and Kang Ban Sok. Founder Down with Imperialism Union, 1926, Korean Communist Youth League, 1927; prisoner, Kirin, China, 1929-30; founder Korean Revolutionary Army, 1930, Korean People's Revolutionary Army, 1932; organizer, leader, anti-Japanese Revolutionary War, 1932-45; founder, chmn. Assn. for Restoration of Fatherland, 1936, Cen. Com. Workers' Party of Korea, 1945, N. Korean Provisional People's Com. 1946, N. Korean People's Com., 1947; founder Korean People's Army, 1948, Gen. Fedn. Trade Unions N. Korea, Worker's Party N. Korea, 1946,; founder, head of state, prime minister Dem. People's Republic Korea, 1948-72; pres., head of state, 1972-94; chmn. Mil. Commn., supreme commdr. Korean People's Army, leader Fatherland Liberation War, 1950-53; organizer, leader socialist transformation of production rels., 1953-58; developer of the country into a socialist Indsl. state, 1957-70; sec. gen. Central Com. Workers' Party Korea, 1966-94, founder; presenter of the policy to expedite the building of socialism and communism to found Demo-catic Confederal Republic of Koryo for realization of independent peaceful reunification at the 6th Party Congress. Originator Juche ideology; author various works. Decorated Marshal Dem. People's Republic Korea, 1953, Hero Dem. People's Republic Korea (3 times), Labor Hero Dem. People's Republic Korea, Generalissimo Dem. People's Republic Korea, Order of Freedom and Independence 1st class, Order of Lenin, 1987, Order of Nat. Flag 1st class, numerous others. Home: Pyongyang Republic of Korea Died 1994.

KIMURA, MOTOO, geneticist; b. Okazaki, Japan, Nov. 13, 1924; s. Issaku and Kana (Kaneiwa) K.; B.Sc., Kyoto U., 1947; Ph.D., U. Wis., 1956, D.Sc. (hon.), 1986; D.Sc., Osaka U., 1956, U. Chgo., 1978; m. Hiroko Mino, Jan. 15, 1957; 1 son, Akio. Asst., Kyoto U., 1947-49; research mem. Nat. Inst. Genetics, Mishima, Japan, 1949-57, lab. head, 1957-64, head dept. popula-tion genetics, 1964-94; vis. prof. U. Pavia (Italy), 1963, 65, U. Wis., 1966, Princeton U., 1969, Stanford U., 1973; vis. mem. U. Wis. Math. Research Center, 1961-62; v.p. 18th Internat. Congress Genetics. Recipient prize Genetics Soc. Japan, 1959; Weldon Meml. prize, 1965; prize Japan Acad., 1978; prize Japan Soc. Human Genetics, 1970; Order of Culture, Govt. Japan, 1976. Mem. Nat. Acad. Scis. (fgn. assoc., John J. Carty Medal for the Advancement of Science, 1987), Am. Acad. Arts and Scis. (fgn. hon.), Genetics Soc. Japan (pres. 1981-84), Japan Acad. Author: Outline of Population Genetics, 1960; Diffusion Models in Population Genetics, 1964; The Neutral Theory of Molecular Evolution, 1983; (with others) An Introduction to Population Genetics Theory, 1970, Theoretical Aspects of Population Genetics, 1971; editor: Future of Man from the Standpoint of Genetics, 1974; Molecular Evolution, Protein Polymorphism and the Neutral Theory, 1982. Died Nov. 13, 1994. Home: Mishima Japan

KINARD, HARGETT YINGLING, financial con-sultant; b. York, Pa., May 29, 1912; s. Henry B. and Edith R. (Yingling) K.; m. Pearl E. Greenhill, Aug. 20, 1932; children: Joan S. (Mrs. Edward J. Mercado), Lois E. (Mrs. Edward Boyd), Gail E. (Mrs. Joseph R. Eastburn). Student, Drexel Inst., Phila., 1928-29; grad., Rider Coll., Trenton, N.J., 1933. C.P.A., Pa. Assoc. firm Lybrand, Ross Bros. & Montgomery, Phila., 1933-51; with Electric Storage Battery Co., Phila., 1951-55; comptroller Electric Storage Battery Co., 1952-55; v.p., treas. Maule Industries, Inc., 1955-58; v.p. finance, 1958-59, financial cons. to various internat. firms, 1959-60; v.p., comptroller First Union Nat. Bank of N.C., Charlotte, 1960-63; sr. v.p., comptroller First Union Nat. Bank of N.C., 1963-65, exec. v.p., comptroller, 1965-71; sr. v.p., treas. 1st Union Nat. Bank Corp., 1968-71; free lance financial cons., 1971-96. Asst. commr. motor vehicles, State of N.C., 1974; asst. sec. N.C. Dept. Transp., 1974-77; Trustee N.C. State Tchrs. and Employees Retirement Fund, 1974-77. Mem. AICPA, Pa. Inst. CPAs. Home: Vero Beach Fla. Died Jan. 3, 1996.

KINCADE, ARTHUR WARREN, banker; b. Chil-licothe, Mo., Aug. 14, 1896; s. John Albert and Flora (Dilley) K.; m. Mary Josephine Igou, Aug. 22, 1917; children: Arthur Warren (dec.), Imogene, Patricia Josephine. Grad. high sch., attended 1 yr. of coll. Of-ficer various banks in Okla. and Tex., 1915-31; pres. W. Tex. Mortgage Loan Co. and its subsidiaries, Amarillo, v.p. First Nat. Bank, Amarillo, 1931-37; exec. v.p. Fourth Nat. Bank, Wichita, Kans., 1937-40; pres. Fourth Nat. Bank, 1940-69, chmn. bd., chief exec. of-ficer, from 1969; chmn. bd. emeritus, cons. Fourth Financial Corp., Wichita. Author articles. Mem. Am. Petroleum Inst., Newcomen Soc., Alpha Kappa Psi (hon.). Club: Masons (K.T.; 32 degree; Shriner). Home: Greenwich Kans. Deceased.

KINCANNON, L. E., petroleum refining company ex-ecutive. Chmn., dir. Rock Island Refining Corp., Indpls. Home: Indianapolis Ind.

KINNEY, ALDON MONROE, JR., business executive, lawyer; b. Cin., May 19, 1921; s. Aldon Monroe and Elsie Marguerite (Griffin) K.; m. Marjorie Ann Aszman, June 13, 1942; children: Gael Maureen Kinney Coleman, Roxanne Kinney Wiley, Aldon Monroe, III. Student, Denison U., 1939-41; AB, U. Cin., 1943, JD, 1948, LLM, 1953. Bar: Ohio 1949, U.S. Supreme Ct. 1952. Ptnr. Jenings & Kinney, Cin., 1949-53; pvt. practice law Cin., 1953-70; counsel, adminstrv. asst. to chmn. A. M.

Kinney, Inc., Cin., 1953-66; chmn. A. M. Kinney, Inc., from 1966, Design Art Corp., Cin., from 1966, Kinvernon Corp., Cin., from 1966, A. M. Kinney Assos., Inc., Chgo., from 1966, Kintech Services, Inc., Cin., from 1969, Walter Kidde Constructors, Inc., N.Y.C., from 1973, Walter Kidde Engrs. Internat., Inc., N.Y.C., from 1973, Vulcan Cin., Inc., from 1975, Kinvernon/ Rudick Assocs., Inc., Cin., from 1992; solicitor, City of Madeira, Ohio, 1953-70; dir. Bank One, Milford, 1961-90. Mem. Newtown (Ohio) Bd. Edn., 1955-57; bd. dirs. Contemporary Arts Center, Cin., 1971-76. Served to sgt. USAAF, 1943-46. Mem. Cin. Bar Assn., Lawyers Club, Engring. Soc. Cin. Clubs: Queen City, Bankers. Home: Cincinnati Ohio Deceased.

KINSELLA, JOHN EDWARD, university dean, food science researcher, educator; b. Wexford, Ireland, Feb. 22, 1938; m. Ruth Ann De Angelis, July 10, 1965; children: Sean, Helen, Kathryn, Kevin. BS in Biology, U. Dublin, 1961; MS in Biology and Biochemistry, Pa. State U., 1965, PhD in Food Biochemistry, 1967. Asst. prof. food biochemistry Cornell U., Ithaca, N.Y., 1967-73, assoc. prof. food chemistry, 1973-77, prof. food chemistry, chmn. food sci. dept., 1977-93, Liberty Hyde Bailey prof. food biochemistry, 1984-93, Gen. Foods Disting. prof. food sci., 1986-88, dir. Inst. Food Sci., 1980-87, SUNY Leading prof., 1987; dean Coll. Agr. and Environ. Scis., dir. Agrl. Exptl. Sta., U. Calif., Davis, 1990-93; cons. U.S. food industry, World Bank, NSF, Brazil, Govt. of Indonesia; mem. food and ntrution bd. Inst. of Medicine, NRC. Author: Fish Oil/ Seafood Health and Disease, 1987, Food Proteins, 1989; editor: Advanced Food and Nutrition Rsch.; contbr. 400 chpts. to books, numerous articles to profl. jours.; patentee protein chemistry and lipid metabolism, immunology cell culture. Recipient Borden Award Borden Found., 1976, Fulbright award, 1984, Phila. Lectureship award, 1986, Atwater award USDA, 1988, Babcock-Hart award, 1987; research grantee NSF, NIH, USDA, various industry assns. Mem. Inst. Medicine of NAS (food and nutrition bd.), AAAS, Am. Chem. Soc. (Agr. and Food Chemistry award 1990, Spencer award 1991), Inst. Food Technologists (exec. com. 1982-85, Am. Inst. Nutrition, Babcock Hart award 1987), Am. Dairy Sci. Assn., Am. Oil Chem. Soc. (Chang award 1991), Internat. Dairy Fedn. Home: El Macero Calif. Died May 2, 1993.

KINZEY, WARREN GLENFORD, anthropology educator; b. Orange, N.J., Oct. 31, 1935; s. Warren Parry and Mildred Irene (Hazzard) K.; m. Trilby Taylor, Mar. 24, 1957 (div. 1977); children: Claudia, Andrea, Monica; m. Julianne L. Kelly, Apr. 16, 1983. BA, U. Minn., 1956, MA, 1958; postgrad., U. Chgo., 1957-60; PhD, U. Calif., Berkeley, 1964. Asst. prof. U. Calif., Davis, 1963-70; assoc. prof. CCNY and Grad. Sch., 1970-83, prof., 1983-94; asst. research anatomist Nat. Ctr. Primate Biology, U. Calif. Davis, 1964-65, planning officer regional med. program Sch. Medicine, 1967-68; chmn. Dept. Anthropology CCNY, 1984-87, dir. Program in Community Health Edn., 1987-88; program dir. phys. anthropology NSF, Washington, 1988-90. Editor: Evolution of Human Behavior: Primate Models, 1987; contbr. articles to profl. jours. NIH rsch. grantee, 1965, 82, Wenner-Gren Found. grantee, 1965, 81, NSF grantee, 1980, 81, 88, 89, 91, 92, 93, World Wildlife Fund grantee, 1986, Earthwatch grantee, 1975-77, 80, 83. Fellow Am. Anthrop. Assn. (program editor biol. anthropology 1983-87), Am. Assn. Phys. Anthropologists (assoc. editor jour. 1986-90), Am. Soc. Primatologists (cons. editor jour. 1984-94), N.Y. Acad. Scis. (chair anthropology sect. 1987-88), Am. Assn. Clin. Anatomists. Unitarian. Home: Tarrytown N.Y. Died Oct. 1, 1994.

KIPPING, VERNON LOUIS, film consultant, marine scientist; b. Cape Girardeau, Mo., Oct. 19, 1921; s. Theodore Frederick and Augusta (Meyer) K.; m. Anna Ruth Uelsmann, Mar. 26, 1944; children: Theodore Paul, John Louis, Douglas Kim. Student, S.E. Mo. State U., 1940-41; AA, Multnomah Coll., 1948; JD, U. San Francisco, 1951. Fingerprint examiner FBI, Washington, 1941-43; with radio communications FBI, Portland, Oreg., 1943-44; spl. employee FBI, Portland, 1946-48; spl. employee San Francisco, 1948-71, 72-76, Chgo., 1971-72; freelance film cons. San Francisco, 1976-94; testified as expert witness Patricia Hearst trial. Owner 19 U.S. and internat. patents motion picture tech., marine sci.; invented means to convert still photos of Patricia Hearst's bank robbery into motion picture and produced said films which were admitted as evidence in Hearst trial. Member San Francisco Neighborhood Libr. Coun., 1989-91; mem. adv. coun. TV Sch. Napa Valley Coll., 1990-94. Sgt. USAAF, 1944-46, PTO. Recipient Spl. prize San Francisco Film Festival, 1967. Mem. AAAS, Soc. Motion Picture and TV Engrs. (program chmn. 1977-79, mgr. 1979-81, membership chmn. 1981-85, spl. events chmn. 1985-88, sec.-treas. 1988-90, chmn. 1990-92, program chair 1994, edn. com. 1990-94, past audiovisual conf. chmn., Citation for Outstanding Svc. 1986), Silicon Valley Engring. Coun., No. Calif. Imperial Owners Club (v.p. 1979-83, pres. 1983-87). Republican. Home: San Francisco Calif. Died Oct. 21, 1994.

KIRCHMAYER, LEON KENNETH, retired electrical engineer; b. Milw., July 24, 1924; s. Henry and Clara (Zenker) K.; m. Olga Temoshok, Dec. 2, 1950; children: Karen Cathleen, Kenneth Lee. B.E.E., Marquette U., 1945; M.S. in Elec. Engring., U. Wis., 1947, Ph.D. in Elec. Engring., 1950; grad. sr. exec. program MIT, 1975. Lab. instr., research asst. Marquette U., 1944-45; exptl. research engr. Cutler-Hammer, Inc., Milw., 1945-46; engring. instr. U. Wis., Madison, 1946-48; with Gen. Electric Co., Schenectady, 1948-84, mgr. system planning and control sect., elec. utility systems engring. dept., 1976-77, mgr. advanced system tech. and planning sect., 1977-84. Author: Economic Operation of Power Systems, 1958; Economic Control of Interconnected Systems, 1959, also numerous articles in profl. jours. Editor 2 books. Patentee in computer control. U. Wis. fellow, 1945; Gerard Swope fellow, 1948; Bernard Price meml. lectr. S. African Inst. Elec. Engrs., 1976; disting. guest India Inst. Elec. Engrs., 1979. Recipient Disting. Svc. citation U. Wis., 1972, Profl. Achievement award Marquette U., 1991. Fellow IEEE (mem. profl. coms.; Centennial medal 1984, Lamme award 1988), ASME (Centennial medal 1980); mem. Nat. Acad. Engring., Internat. Fedn. Automatic Control, Internat. Conf. on Large High-Voltage Electric Systems, Schenectady Profl. Engring. Soc. (named Engr. of Yr. 1966), Sigma Xi, Tau Beta Pi (fellow 1947), Pi Mu Epsilon, Eta Kappa Nu. Died Nov. 12, 1995. Home: Rexford N.Y.

KIRGIS, FREDERIC L., retired lawyer; b. Chicago Heights, Ill., Sept. 25, 1907; s. Frederic and Anne (Smith) K.; m. Kathryn Burrows, June 30, 1933 (dec. Apr. 1980); children: Frederic L., Jerry B. (dec.), Ann Patricia. A.B., U. Ill., 1929, J.D., 1931; J.S.D., Yale, 1936. Bar: Colo. bar 1941. Instr. law U. Ill., 1931-32; Sterling teaching fellow in law Yale, 1932-33; asst. solicitor U.S. Dept. Interior, 1933-36, first asst. solicitor, 1936-40; spl. asst. to U.S. Atty. Gen., 1941-45; ptnr. Gorsuch, Kirgis, Campbell, Walker & Grover, Denver, 1945-79; of counsel Gorsuch, Kirgis, Campbell, Walker & Grover, 1979-95; Mem. adv. council U.S. Pub. Land Law Rev. Commn., 1965-7O. Mem. ABA (chmn. sect. administv. law 1965-66), Colo. Bar Assn., Denver Bar Assn., Order of Coif, Phi Beta Kappa Clubs. Clubs: Denver Country, Denver; Law. Home: Denver Colo. Died March 29, 1995.

KIRK, RUSSELL AMOS, writer, lecturer, editor, foundation president; b. Plymouth, Mich., Oct. 19, 1918; s. Russell Andrew and Marjorie (Pierce) K.; m. Annette Yvonne Courtemanche, Sept. 19, 1964; 4 children. B.A., Mich. State U., 1940; M.A., Duke U., 1941; DLitt, St. Andrews U., Scotland, 1952; hon. degrees include; Litt.D., Boston Coll., St. John's U., Loyola Coll., Balt., Gannon Coll., Central Mich. U., Albion Coll., Grand Valley Coll.; LL.D., Park Coll., Niagara U., Pepperdine U.; L.H.D., Le Moyne Coll.; D.Journalism, Olivet Coll. Pres. Ednl. Reviewer Found., 1960-94; pres. Marguerite Eyer Wilbur Found., 1979-94; vis. prof. various univs.; Fulbright prof., Scotland, 1987; dir. social sci. program Ednl. Rsch. Coun. Am., 1979-85. Contbr. to scholarly and popular publs., U.S., Can., Gt. Britain, Ireland, Germany, Poland, Bulgaria, Russia, Australia, Italy, Norway, Austria, including Sewanee Rev., Contemporary Rev., Dublin Rev., Yale Rev., Jour. History of Ideas, Annals of Am. Acad., N.Y. Times mag., Fortune, Wall St. Jour., History Today, Gen. Edn., The Critic, Kenyon Rev., Nat. Rev., The Month, Southwest Rev., Commonweal, Touchstone, Christianity Today, Queen's Quar., America, Chronicles of Culture, Analysis, Center mag., South Atlantic Quarterly, Crisis, World Rev., Intercollegiate Rev., Fortnightly, Chesterton Rev., The World & I; founder quar. jour. Modern Age; editor quar. Univ. Bookman, 1960-94; author: John Randolph of Roanoke, 1951, 64, 78, The Conservative Mind, 1953, 73, 78, 86, St. Andrews, 1954, A Program for Conservatives, 1954, 89, Academic Freedom, 1955, Beyond the Dreams of Avarice, 1956, 91, The Intelligent Woman's Guide to Conservatism, 1957, The American Cause, 1957, Old House of Fear, 1961, 65, The Surly Sullen Bell, 1965, Confessions of a Bohemian Tory, 1963, The Intemperate Professor, 1965, 88, A Creature of the Twilight, 1966, Edmund Burke, 1967, 88, Political Principles of Robert A. Taft, 1967, Enemies of the Permanent Things, 1969, 84, Eliot and His Age, 1971, 84, Roots of American Order, 1974, 77, 91, The Princess of All Lands, 1979, Decadence and Renewal in Higher Learning, 1978, Lord of the Hollow Dark, 1979, 89, Portable Conservative Reader, 1982, Reclaiming a Patrimony, 1982, Watchers at the Strait Gate, 1984, The Wise Men Know What Wicked Things Are Written on the Sky, 1987, Work and Prosperity, 1989, The Conservative Constitution, 1990, The Politics of Prudence, 1993, America's British Culture, 1993, The Sword of Imagination, 1995; also critical intros. and prefaces to reprints standard scholarly works; editor: Library of Conservative Thought, 1987-94. Recipient Ingersoll prize for scholarly writing, 1984, Presdl. Citizen's medal, 1989, Salvatori prize for hist. writing, 1991; Guggenheim fellow, sr. fellow Am. Coun. Learned Socs., Constl. fellow NEH, disting. fellow Heritage Found. Home: Mecosta Mich. Died Apr. 29, 1994.

KIRKPATRICK, EVRON MAURICE, foundation executive; b. nr. Raub, Ind., Aug. 15, 1911; s. Omer and Lenna Mae (Hain) K.; m. Jeane D. Jordan, Feb. 20, 1955; children: Thomas Reed (dec.), Mary Ellen, Ann Maureen, Douglas J., John E., Stuart A. BA with high honors, U. Ill., 1932, AM, 1933; PhD, Yale U., 1939; LLD, Ind. U., 1977. Instr. polit. sci. U. Minn., 1935-3 asst. prof., 1939-43, assoc. prof., 1943-48, prof., 194 chmn. social sci. div., 1944-48; asst. rsch. dir. rsch. an analysis br. OSS, 1945; asst. rsch. dir. and projects co trol Officer Rsch. and Intelligence, Dept. State, Wash ington, 1946, intelligence program adviser, 1947, chi external rsch. staff, 1948-52, chief psychol., intelligen and rsch. staff, 1952-54, dep. dir. Office Rsch. and I telligence, 1954; exec. dir. Am. Polit. Sci. Assn., 195 81; editorial adviser in polit. sci. Henry Holt & Co 1952-60, Holt Rinehart, and Winston, 1960-68; chm bd. trustees Orgn. Pub. Rsch. Inc., 1955-95; lect Howard U., 1957-61; cons. Nat. Ednl. TV, 1963-6 professorial lectr. Georgetown U., 1959-84; mem. Pres. Commn. on Registration and Voting Participatio 1963-64, Commn. on Presdl. Campaign Debates, 196 64, Presdl. Task Force on Career Advancement, 196 mem. nat. adv. com. on accreditation and instr. eligibility U.S. Dept. Edn., 1987-89. Author: The P ople, Politics and the Politician, 1941, Americ Government, 1942, Survey of American Governmen 1943, (with A.N. Christensen) Running the Countr 1946, Target: The World Communist Propaganda A tivities in 1955, 1956, (with Jeane Kirkpatrick) Ele tions- U.S.A., 1956, Year of Crisis: An Analysis Communist Propaganda Activities in 1956, 195 contbr.: Man and Society, 1938, Essays on the Behav oral Study of Politics, 1962, Perspectives, 196 Foundation of Political Science, 1977, The Past and F ture of Presidential Debates, 1979; editor: World Affair contbr. articles to profl. jours. Trustee Nat. Ctr. Ed Politics, Library Assocs., Georgetown U., 1979-9 trustee Helen Dwight Reid Ednl. Found., 1960-9 treas., 1964-72, pres., 1972-90; dir. Govtl. Affairs Ins 1954-64; mem. adv. com. on fgn. affairs So. Region Edn. Bd., 1952-56; chmn. trustees Inst. Am. Univs France, 1958-95; bd. advisers Hubert H. Humphr Inst., 1978-88; bd. dirs. James Madison Found., 198 95, U.S. Inst. Peace, 1985-95; resident scholar Am. E terprise Inst., 1981-87.Mem. Nat. Arbitration Assn. (b arbitrators 1943-47), Internat. Polit. Sci. Assn. (mem council 1955-67, exec. com. 1958-64), Am. Polit. S Assn., Nat. Acad. Scis. (mem. div. behavioral scis. NR 1963-66, mem. com. internat. relations in behavior NRC 1966-70), Am. Peace Soc. (pres.), Phi Beta Kapp Pi Sigma Alpha (mem. exec. com. 1958-80, pres. 197 76). Died April 26, 1995. Home: Bethesda Md.

KIRKUP, JAMES FALCONER, author; b. Sou Shields, Durham, Eng., Apr. 23, 1923; s. James Harol Joseph and Mary Virginia (Johnson) K.; m. Shimiz Mariko, July 18, 1963; children: Jun, Sachiko, Kenich B.A. with honors, King's Coll., U. Durham, 1951. Vi poet Bath Acad. Art, 1953-56; travelling lectr. Swedis Ministry Edn., 1956-57; prof. English lang. and lit. Salamanca (Spain), 1957-58; prof. English lit. Tohok (Japan) U., 1959-61; vis. prof. Japan Women's U Tokyo, 1964-69; vis. prof., poet in residence Amher (Mass.) Coll., 1968-69; prof. U. Nagoya (Japan), 196 72; Morton vis. prof. internat. lit. Ohio U., Athen 1975-76; playwright in residence Sherman Theatr Univ. Coll., Cardiff, 1975-76; prof. English lit. Kyoto Fgn. Studies, from 1977; lit. editor Orient-West mag Tokyo, 1963-65. Author: (poetry) Indications, 1942, Th Cosmic Shape: An Interpretation of Myth and Legen with Three Poems and Lyric, 1946, The Drowned Sail and Other Poems, 1947, The Creation, 1948, The Su merged Village and Other Poems, 1951, A Corre Compassion and Other Poems, 1952, A Spring Journe and Other Poems, 1954, The Descent into the Cave an Other Poems, 1957, The Prodigal Son: Poems, 195 1959, 1959, Refusal to Conform: Last and First Poem 1963, Japan Marine, 1965, Paper Windows: Poem From Japan, 1968, Japan Physical: A Selection, 196 White Shadows, Black Shadows: Poems of Peace an War, 1970, The Body Servant: Poems of Exile, 197 Broad Daylight, 1971, A Bewick Bestiary, 197 Transmental Vibrations, 1971, Manylined Poem, 197 Zen Gardens, 1973, Scenes From Sutcliffe, 1977, Scen From Sesshu, 1978, Zen Contemplations, 1978, An A tor's Revenge, 1979, The Tao of Water, 1980, Co Mountain Poems, 1980, Dengonban Messages: One-Li Poems, 1980, The Guardian of the Word, 1980, To th Ancestral North: Poems For an Autobiography, 198 The Sense of the Visit: New Poems, 1984, The Guita Player of Zuiganji, 1985, Fellow Feelings, 198 Shooting Stars, 1992, First Fireworks, 1992, Throwbac Poems Towards an Autobiography, 1992, Short Take 1993, Words For Contemplation, 1993, Look At It Th Way!, 1993; (novels) The Love of Others, 1962, Inse Summer, 1971, The Magic Drum, 1972, Gaijin on t Ginza, 1991, Queens Have Died Young and Fair, 199 (plays) Upon This Rock, 1955, Masque: The Triumph Harmony, 1955, The True Mystery of the Nativit 1957, The Magic Drum, 1972; (operas) An Actor Revenge, 1979, Friends in Arms, 1980, The Dama Drum, 1982; (screenplays) Peach Garden, 1954, Tw Pigeons Flying High, 1955, The True Mystery of th Passion, 1960; (autobiography) The Only Child: A Autobiography of Infancy, 1957, Sorrows, Passions, an Alarms: An Autobiography of Childhood, 1959, I, All People: An Autobiography of Youth, 1990, A Po Could Not But Be Gay: Some Legends of My Lo Youth, 1991, Me All Over: Memoirs of a Misfit, 199 (other) These Horned Islands: A Journal of Japan, 196 Tropic Temper: A Memoir of Malaya, 1963, Englan Now, 1964, Japan Industrial: Some Impressions Japanese Industries (2 vols.), 1964-65, Tokyo, 196

Frankly Speaking, 1966, Japan, Now, 1966, Filipinescas: Travels Through the Philippine Islands, 1968, Bangkok, 1968, One Man's Russia, 1968, Aspects of the Short Story: Six Modern Short Stories with Commentary, 1969, Streets of Asia, 1969, Hong Kong and Macao, 1970, Japan Behind the Fan, 1970, Nihon Bungaku Eiyaku No Yuga Na Gijutsu, 1973, Heaven, Hell, and Hari-Kari: The Rise and Fall of the Japanese Superstate, 1974, America Yesterday and Today, 1977, Mother Goose's Britain, 1977, The Britishness of the British, 1978, Eibungaku Saiken, 1980, When I Was a Child: A Study of Nursery Rhymes, 1983, The Glory That Was Greece, 1984, The Mystery and Magic of Symbols, 1987, The Cry of the Owl: Native Folktales and Legends, 1987. Translator: The History of Practice of Magic, 1952, The Vision and Other Poems, 1953, Dark Child, 1954, Ancestral Voices, 1956, The Radiance of the King, 1956, Mother Courage and Her Children, 1957, Evil Eye, 1959, The Girl From Nowhere, 1958, Memoirs of a Dutiful Daughter, 1959, A Summer Gone, 1959, Don Tiburcio's Secret, 1959, The Captive, 1961, It Began In Babel: The Story of the Birth and Development of Races and Peoples, 1961, Dangerous Spring, 1961, The Other One, 1961, The Gates of Paradise, 1962, Trouble in Brusada, 1962, Fast as the Nuno, 1962, Nuno, 1962, The Sins of the Father, 1962, Modern Malay Verse, 1963, Days of Danger, 1963, My Friend Carlo, 1963, Daily Life of the Etruscans, 1964, The Heavenly Mandate, 1964, My Great-Grandfather and I, 1964, Daily Life in the French Revolution, 1964, Immensee, 1965, Tales of Hoffman, 1966, The Little Man, 1966, Red Renard, 1966, From an Old Chronicle, 1967, A Dream of Africa, 1968, Selected Writings of Jules Supervielle, 1968, The Eternal Virgin, 1970, The Hanging Bridge, 1971, Selected Poems of Takagi Kyozo, 1973, Modern Japanese Poetry, 1978, To the Unknown God, 1982, An African in Greenland, 1982, The Bush Toads, 1982, The Little Measure, 1990, A Room in the Woods, 1991, Ito-san, 1991, Painted Shadows, 1991, Vagabond Winter, 1992, All the World's Mornings, 1992, My Micheline, 1993, The Man in the Red Hat, 1993, Worlds ofDifference, 1993, The Compassion Protocol, 1993. Gregory fellow poetry U. Leeds, 1950-52; recipient Atlantic award in lit., 1959; 1st prize Japan PEN contest, 1965; Mildred L. Batchelder award ALA, 1968; Keats prize for poetry 1974; named Ollave Order Bards, Ovates and Druids, 1974; fellow creative writing Sheffield U., 1974-75; hon fellow Inst. Psychophys. Research, Oxford, 1970. Fellow Royal Soc. Lit.; founding fellow Internat. Acad. Poets. Deceased. Home: London Eng.

KIRSTEIN, LINCOLN, ballet promoter; b. Rochester, N.Y., May 4, 1907; s. Louis E. and Rose (Stein) K.; m. Fidelma Cadmus, Apr. 1941. BS, Harvard, 1930. Founder, editor Hound and Horn, 1927-34; established Sch. Am. Ballet, N.Y.C., 1933, former gen. dir., pres. emeritus; former gen. dir. N.Y.C. Ballet. Author: Flesh is Heir, 1932, reprinted, 1975, Dance: A Short History of Theatrical Dancing, 1935, Blast at Ballet, 1938; poems Low Ceiling, 1935; Ballet Alphabet, 1939, Ballet: Bias of Belief, 1983; pub.: Pavel Tchelitchew Drawings, 1947, Elie Nadelman Drawings, 1949, The Classic Ballet, 1952, Rhymes & More Rhymes of a Pfc, 1965, Movement and Metaphor: Four Centuries of Ballet, 1969, W. Eugene Smith, 1970, Elie Nadelman, 1973, New York City Ballet, 1973, Lay This Laurel, 1974, Nijinsky Dancing, 1975, Thirty Years: The New York City Ballet, 1978, George Tooker, 1983, Paul Cadmus, 1983, A. Hyatt Mayor: Collected Writings, 1983, Quarry: A Collection in Lieu of Memoirs, 1986, The Poems of Lincoln Kirstein, 1987, Mosaic: Memoirs, 1994. Recipient Presdl. Medal of Freedom, 1984, N.Y. State Gov.'s Arts award, 1984, Heart of N.Y. award, 1984, Nat. Medal of Arts, 1985. Home: New York N.Y. Died Jan. 5, 1996.

KIVETT, MARVIN FRANKLIN, anthropologist; b. Nebr., Mar. 10, 1917; s. Thomas and Murl (Mark) K.; m. Caroline Ritchey, Sept. 12, 1941; 1 son, Ronald Lee. AB, U. Nebr., 1942, MA, 1951. Archeologist Smithsonian Inst., 1946-49; mus. dir. Nebr. Hist. Soc., Lincoln, 1949-63, adminstrv. dir., 1963-85; dir. Nebr. State Hist. Found., Lincoln, 1963-92. Editor: Nebr. History, 1963-85; contbr. articles to profl. jours. Served with AUS, 1942-46. Home: Lincoln Nebr. Died Dec. 19, 1992.

KLAGSBRUNN, HANS ALEXANDER, retired lawyer; b. Vienna, Austria, Apr. 28, 1909; came to U.S., 1912; s. Hugo and Lili (Brandt) K.; m. Elizabeth Mapelsden Ramsey, Jan. 27, 1934. Student, Vienna Gymnasium, 1922-25; B.A., Yale U., 1929, LL.B., 1932; postgrad., Harvard U. Law Sch., 1932-33. Bar: D.C., U.S. Supreme Ct 1935. Assoc. RFC (and affiliates), 1933-45; exec. v.p., gen. counsel, dir. and mem. exec. com. Def. Plant Corp.; surplus property dir. and asst. gen. counsel RFC; RFC mem. Hancock Contract Settlement Bd. and Clayton Surplus Property Bd. in Office War Mblzn.; dep. dir. Office War Mblzn. and Reconversion, The White House, 1945-46; mem. Army Chem. Corps Reorgn. Com., 1955-56; sr. mem. Klagsbrunn & Hanes (attys.), 1946-68; counsel to successor firm, 1969-83; Mem. Jud. Conf. D.C. Circuit, 1964-66; chmn. com. criminal indigents; mem. U.S. Ct. Appeals Com. on Admissions and Grievances, 1967-74, chmn., 1972-74; mem. task force on U.S. energy policy Twentieth Century Fund, 1976-77; Mem. Health and Welfare Council, bd. dirs., 1958-73, pres., 1961-63; mem. Loudoun County Sanitation Authority, 1959-68, vice chmn., 1965-68; mem. Piedmont (Va.) Environ. Council, 1975-76. Bd. dirs. Friendship House, 1957-68, pres., 1959-68; bd. dirs. Columbia Hosp. for Women, 1964-74, sec., 1966-67, 1st v.p., 1967-68. Recipient Health and Welfare Council Community Service awards, 1961, 63. Mem. Am. Bar Found., Fed. Bar Assn., Am. Arbitration Assn. (nat. panel), Bar Assn. D.C. (chmn. U.S. Ct. Appeals com. 1966-67), ABA (past chmn. coms.), Nat. Planning Assn., A.I.M., Am. Judicature Soc., Newcomen Soc., Phi Beta Kappa, Order of Coif, Phi Beta Kappa Assos., Nat. Symphony Orch. Assn. Clubs: Metropolitan, Yale, Nat. Press, City Tavern; Mory's (New Haven, Ct.). Home: Washington D.C. Died June 23, 1993.

KLANICZAY, TIBOR, literary historian, educator; b. Budapest, Hungary, July 5, 1923; s. Gyula and Gizella (Heyszl) K.; m. Maria Bessenyei, 1949; 2 sons, 1 dau. Dr. h.c. (hon.), U. Tours (France). Lectr., Eotvos Lorand U., Budapest, 1949-57; dep. dir. Inst. Lit. Studies, Hungarian Acad. Scis., 1956-83; vis. prof. Sorbonne, Paris, 1967-68, U. Rome, 1975-79; dir. Ctr. Renaissance Research, Budapest, 1970—; dir. Inst. Lit. Studies, Hungarian Acad. Scis., 1984—. Author: Zrinyi Miklos, 1954, 64; Reneszansz es Barokk, 1961; (with others) History of Hungarian Literature, 1964, Marxizmus es Irodalomtudomany, 1964; co-author, editor: A magyar irondalom tortenete I II, 1964; A mult nagy korszakai, 1973; La crisi del Rinascimento e il Manierismo, 1973; A Manierizmus, 1975; Hagyomanyok ebresztese, 1976; Renaissance und Manierismus, 1977; Pallas magyar ivadékai, 1985, Renesans, Manieryzm, Barok, 1986; editor periodical Irodalomtorteneti Kozlemenyek, 1958-80; mem. adv. bd. Revue de Litterature Comparee, Paris, Can. Rev. Comparative Literature. V.p. Internat. Assn. Hungarian Studies, Budapest. Decorated officier Ordre des Palmes Académiques; cavaliere dell'Ordine al Merito della Republica Italiana; recipient Kossuth prize, 1955; Labour Order of Merit. Fellow Mediaeval Acad. Am. (corr.); mem. Hungarian Acad. Scis., Plish Acad. Scis., Internat. Assn. Comparative Lit., Federation des Sociétés et des Institutes pour l'Etude de la Renaissance, Federation Internationale des Langues et Littératures Modernes, Associazione Internazionale per gli Studi di Lingua e Letteratura Italiana (mem. consiglio direttivo). Home: Budapest Hungary

KLARNET, BETTY, magazine editor. Mng. editor Harper's Bazaar, N.Y.C. Died Sept. 24, 1993.

KLAUS, ELMER ERWIN, chemical engineering educator, consultant; b. Neffsville, Pa., Apr. 19, 1921; s. Elmer Ernest and Esther (Graver) K.; m. Jean Rebecca Hartswick, Sept. 22, 1945; children: Dennis Richard, Diane Gail. B.S., Franklin and Marshall Coll., 1943; M.S., Pa. State U., 1946, Ph.D., 1952. Research asst. Pa. State U., 1943-46, instr., 1946-52, asst. prof., 1952-56, assoc. research prof., 1956-66, prof. chem. engring., 1966-82, M.R. Fenske faculty fellow in chem. engring., 1979-82, prof. emeritus and M.R. Ferske fellow emeritus, 1983-94; cons. Nat. Bur. Standards, 1983-94; chmn. Am. Soc. Lubrication Engrs. ASME Lubrication Conf., 1967; chmn. Gordon Research Conf. Friction Lubrication and Wear, 1976; mem. steering com. for wear and corrosion Office Tech. Assessment, 1976; mem. NRC Com. U.S. Army Basic Rsch., 1977-80; bd. dirs. ACTIS, Inc., (A Computerized Tribology Info. System), 1989. Co-editor: Boundary Lubrication: An Appraisal of World Literature, 1969; assoc. editor: Jour. Lubrication Technology, 1968-79; contbr. articles to profl. jours. Exec. bd. Juniata Valley council Boy Scouts Am., 1965-94. Recipient Pentathalon award Franklin and Marshall Coll., 1943; Outstanding Achievement in rsch. award Pa. State U. Coll. Engring., 1972, Outstanding Svc. award, 1989; Silver Beaver award Juniata Valley council Boy Scouts Am., 1973; ASLE nat. award, 1976; Capt. Alfred E. Hunt medal, Am. Soc. Lubrication Engrs., 1980. Fellow ASME (rsch. com. on lubrication, Mayo D. Hersey award 1982, ASME-Rsch. Com. Tribology innovative rsch. award 1988), Am. Inst. Chemists, Am. Soc. Lubrication Engrs. (hon. mem., dir. 1966-72), Soc. Tribologists and Lubrication Engrs. (rep. to Internat. Tribology Coun. 1989-94, Al Sonntage award 1991); mem. ASTM, Am. Chem. Soc., Am. Inst. Chem. Engrs., Am. Ceramic Soc., Coun. Mech. Failures Prevention Group (chmn. 1976-81), Masons, Sigma Xi, Alpha Chi Sigma, Phi Lambda Upsilon, Sigma Pi Sigma. Mem. United Ch. of Christ. Home: State College Pa. Died July 12, 1994.

KLEIN, FREDERIC WILLIAM, manufacturing executive; b. Boston, Sept. 4, 1922; s. August C. and Maree (Keeling) K.; m. Isobel Marie Pinto, Nov. 4, 1950; children: Kathryn Sanders, Karen Anderson. BS in Marine Engring., U.S. Marchant Marine Acad., Kings Point, N.Y., 1944; BS in Gen. Engring., U. Maine, 1948; diploma, Columbia U., 1979. Registered profl. engr., N.Y. Engr. Ingersoll Rand, N.Y.C., 1948-55; from asst. sales mgr. to v.p., adminstrn. Thomson Industries, Inc., Port Washington, N.Y., 1955-93; dir. Nuclear Equipment Corp., San Carlos, Calif. Contbr. articles to profl. jours. Committeeman Rep. Party, Glen Cove, N.Y., 1989-93; pres. Elsinore Civic Assn., Glen Cover., 1978. Lt. USMC, 1942-44, ETO, PTO. Mem. ASME (Award of Merit 1973, treas. 1970-73, exec. com. 1970-73), Soc. Profl. Engrs., Sales Execs. Club, Am. Mgmt. Assn., Sea Cliff Yacht Club, U.S. Merchant Marine Acad. Officers Club, Navy League. Republican. Episcopalian. Home: Glen Cove N.Y. Died June 1, 1993.

KLIMOVA, RITA, ambassador, economist; b. Jasi, Rumania, Dec. 10, 1931; d. Stanislav and Hana (Coifman) Budin; m. Zdenek Mlynar (div. 1967); children: Milena Bartlova Mlynar, Vladimir Mlynar; m. Zdenek Klima (dec. 1980). Master in Econs., Prague Sch. Econs., 1958; Doctor of Econ. Sci., Econ. Inst., 1966; LDH (hon.), St. John Fisher Coll., 1991. Assoc. prof. dept. econs. Charles U., Prague, Czechoslovakia, 1966-70; freelance translator Prague, 1970-86; amb. to U.S. Washington, 1990-93. Activist Charter 77, 1977-89, Czechoslovak Helsinki Commn., 1986-89, editorial bd. Lidove Nov, 1987-89. Home: Prague Czech Rep. Died Dec., 1993.

KLIMSTRA, WILLARD DAVID, science administrator, zoology educator emeritus, researcher; b. Erie, Pa., Dec. 25, 1919; s. Paul D. and Jessica K.; m. Miriam Brown; children: David Eugene, Kay Klimstra Sweetingham, William B. AA, Blackburn Jr. Coll., 1939; BA, Maryville Coll., 1941; postgrad., U. N.C., 1941-42; MS, Iowa State U., 1948, PhD, 1949. Foreman of consolidation Nat. Munitions Corp., Carrboro, N.C., 1942-45; rsch. fellow, then rsch. assoc. Iowa Coop. Wildlife Rsch. Unit, 1946-49; asst. prof. zoology So. Ill. U., Carbondale, 1949-52, assoc. prof., 1952-59, prof., 1959-83, Disting. prof. zoology, 1983-85, emeritus, 1985, acting chmn. dept., May-Sept., 1961, June-Aug., 1964, dir. grad. studies in zoology, 1973-83, acting dir. Coal Extraction and Utilization Rsch. Ctr., 1976-77, dir. Coop. Wildlife Rsch. Lab., 1951-87; cons. Shawnee Nat. Forest, 1956-87, Ill. Inst. Environment Quality, 1970-78, Ill. Dept. Conservation, 1956-87, Ill. Dept. Bus. and Econ. Devel., 1972-78, Ill. Abandoned Mined Lands Reclamation Coun., 1979-88, Nat. Key Deer Wildlife Refuge, 1970-93, others; mem. conservation com. Ill. Supt. Pub. Instrn., 1956-70; bd. dirs. Ill. Prairie Chicken Found., 1958-68; chmn. Ill. Nature Preserves Commn., 1964-69, 71-79, cons., 1978-83; mem. stripmine reclamation Argonne Nat. Lab., 1972-74; mem. Gov.'s Study Commn. Evaluation Stripmine Reclamation in Ill., 1966-68, Ill. Adv. Coun. Reclamation, 1976-87, Ill. Endangered Species Bd., 1973-87, Ill. Energy Resources Commn., 1979-81; mem. fish and wildlife and pks. nat. scis. adv. com. to Sec. Dept. Interior, 1975-77, mem. study task force U.S. Nat. Wildlife Refuge System, 1977-78; mem. exec. steering com. Sustained Funding for Fish and Wildflie Rsch. at Coll. and Univs., 1979-87; mem. Ill. Wildlife Habitat Commn., 1983-85; maj. advisor 140 master and 17 doctoral students. Recipient Kaplan Rsch. award So. Ill. U. chpt. Sigma Xi, 1974, Alumni citation, Maryville Coll., 1980, Disting. Achievement award Iowa State U. Alumni, 1982, Conservationist award Chevron Corp., 1988, Leadership citation Blackburn Coll., 1989, Disting. Alumni award Blackburn Coll., 1990. Fellow AAAS, Herpetologist League, Ill. Acad. Sci.; mem. Am. Inst. Biol. Scis., Am. Soc. Mammalogists, Ecol. Soc. Am., Nat. Pest Control Assn. (cons. 1966-89), Nat. Audubon Soc., Nat. Wildlife Fedn., Nature Conservancy, Nat. Geog. Soc., Soil Conservation Soc. Am., Wildlife Soc. (hon. life, Profl. award merit Ill. chpt. 1984, Outstanding Book award 1987, Aldo Leopold award 1988), Wilson Ornithol. Soc., Nat. Wildlife Refuge Assn., N.Y. Acad. Sci., Gamma Sigma Delta (literary award 1985), Golden Key (hon.). Home: Cary N.C. Died Feb. 25, 1993.

KLINCK, HAROLD RUTHERFORD, agronomy educator; b. Gormley, Ont., Can., Sept. 24, 1922; s. Roscoe Franklin and Olive Ila (Jennings) K.; m. Isabel Penelope Gilchrist, June 30, 1951; children: John Rutherford, Thomas Daniel, Harold Robert (dec.), Margaret Elizabeth, David Roscoe. B.S.A., Ont. Agrl. Coll., U. Toronto, 1950; M.Sc., McGill U., 1952, Ph.D., 1955. Grad. asst. McGill U., Montreal, Que., 1950-54, lectr. agronomy, 1954-56, asst. prof., 1956-65, assoc. prof., 1965-71, prof. agronomy, 1971-88, prof. emeritus, 1988; acting dean McGill U. (Faculty Agr.), Montreal, Que., 1971-72; acting vice prin. McGill U. (Macdonald Coll.), Montreal, Que., 1971-72. Contbr. articles to profl. jours. Decorated commandeur del'Ordre du Mérite Agronomique; recipient Nuffield Found. travel grant to study at Cambridge Eng., 1961, Commonwealth Found. sci. exchange travel grant to visit Malawi, Africa, 1972, Outstanding Rsch. award Can. Soc. Agronomy, 1989; named Man of Yr. Canadian Seed Trade Assn., 1986. Fellow Agrl. Inst. Can.; mem. Can. Seed Growers Assn. (hon. life), Que. Seed Growers Assn. (hon. life), Master Brewers Assn. (hon.). Home: Colborne Can. Died Mar. 29, 1993.

KLINGBERG, WILLIAM GENE, pediatrician; b. Wichita, Kans., Sept. 17, 1916; s. Harry R. and Ethel (Martin) K.; m. Barbara Jean Hendrickson, June 18, 1941; children: William Gene, Judith Jean, Susan Jane, John David. A.B., Municiple U. of Wichita, 1938; M.D., Washington U., 1943. Diplomate: Am. Bd. Pediatrics. Intern St. Louis Children's Hosp., 1943, resident, 1944-46; asst. prof. to assoc. prof. Washington U. Sch. Medicine, St. Louis, 1947-60; prof. pediatrics W.Va. U., Morgantown, 1960-87, prof. emeritus, 1987-95, chmn. dept. pediatrics, 1960-82; vis. prof. Ankara U., (Turkey), 1957-58. Chmn., campus ministry

Westminster Found., Inc., Morgantown, 1973-95. Served to capt. M.C. U.S. Army, 1945-47. Named Outstanding Tchr. W.Va. U., 1976; named Disting. West Virginian State of W.Va., 1982. Fellow Am. Acad. Pediatrics; mem. Am. Hematology Soc., Va. Med. Assn., AMA, Alpha Omega Alpha. Presbyterian. Home: Morgantown W. Va. Died May 25, 1995.

KLION, STANLEY RING, management consultant; b. N.Y.C., May 9, 1923; s. Samuel M. and Henrietta (Ring) K.; m. Janet Tucker, Dec. 16, 1951; children: Catherine B., Emily J., Jenny T. A.B., Rutgers U., 1942. C.P.A., N.Y. State, D.C. With Peat, Marwick, Mitchell & Co., 1955-86; ptnr. Peat, Marwick, Mitchell & Co., Phila., Boston and N.Y.C., 1960-75; vice chmn. mgmt. cons. dept., dir. Peat, Marwick, Mitchell & Co., N.Y.C., 1975-81; exec. vice chmn. Peat Marwick Internat., 1981-86; with Resource Holdings Ltd., 1986-94; exec. v.p., dir. IRC Inc., Phila., 1967-68; dir. Nash Engring. Co., South Norwalk, Conn., 1967-68, 86-94; mem. audit adv. com. to sec. Navy, Washington, 1972-75; adj. prof. mgmt. Grad. Sch. Bus., N.Y. U., 1978-81; bd. dirs. Circuit City Stores, Inc., Richmond, Va., Parlex Corp., Methuen, Mass., Salant Corp.; trustee Fund Source, N.Y.C., 1987-94, Empire Builders Tax Free Fund, 1990-94; vis. prof., exec.-in-residence, Columbia U. Grad. Sch. Bus., N.Y.C., 1986-94, bd. overseers, 1989-93; trustee Greenwich (Conn.) Libr., 1991-94, treas., 1992-94. Pres. Citizens Council on City Planning, Phila., 1965-67; mem. Wilson Council Woodrow Wilson Internat. Ctr. for Scholars, Washington, 1981-94, chmn, 1988-94. Served as maj. U.S. Army, 1942-46. Mem. Am. Inst. C.P.A.'s (council 1979-80, chmn. MAS exec. com. 1975-78), N.Y. State Soc. C.P.A.'s, AAAS, Phi Beta Kappa. Republican. Jewish. Clubs: Economic, Sunningdale (Scarsdale, N.Y.). Home: Greenwich Conn. Died Apr. 18, 1994.

KLOS, ELMER, film director; b. Brno, Czechoslovakia, Jan. 26, 1910; s. Rudolf and Marie K.; student Faculty of Law Charles U., Prague; m. Anne Vopalka, 1935; 2 children. Dir., Short Film Studios, 1946-47; head creative art staff, scriptwriter Barrandov Feature Film Studio, 1948-74; prof. film and TV faculty Prague U., 1956-70; dir. films: Kidnapped, 1952, Death is Called Engelchen, 1963, Obzalovany, 1964, The Shop on the High Street, 1965, Desire called Anada, 1969. Recipient State prize 2d class, 1960, Gold prize Moscow Internat. Film Festival, 1963, State prize, 1964, Grand Prix Karlovy Vary Internat. Film Festival, 1964, U.S. Acad. award Oscar, 1965, N.Y. Film Critics award, 1967, Selznik prize U.S., 1966. Mem. Czechoslovk Union of Film Artists (pres. 1963-66). Died July 30, 1993. Home: Prague Czechoslovakia

KNAPE, DONALD J., specialty hardware manufacturer; b. Grand Rapids, Mich., 1925; grad. Mich. State U.; married. With Knape & Vogt Mfg. Co., Grand Rapids, 1951—, pres., chief exec. officer, dir., 1966—; dir. Gt. Lakes Fin. Corp., Union Bank & Trust Co. N.A.

KNEBEL, FLETCHER, writer; b. Dayton, Ohio, Oct. 1, 1911; s. A.G. and Mary (Lewis) K.; m. Constance Wood, 1985; child by previous marriage: Jack G. A.B., Miami U., Oxford, Ohio, 1934. With Coatesville (Pa.) Record, 1934, Chattanooga News, 1934-35, Toledo News Bee, 1936, Cleve. Plain Dealer, 1936-50; Washington corr., 1937-50; corr. Washington bur. Cowles Publs., 1950-64; syndicated columnist Potomac Fever, 1951-64. Author: Night of Camp David, 1965, The Zinzin Road, 1966, Vanished, 1968, Trespass, 1969, Dark Horse, 1972, The Bottom Line, 1974, Dave Sulkin Cares!, 1978, Crossing in Berlin, 1981, Poker Game, 1983, Sabotage, 1986; co-author: No High Ground, 1960, Seven Days in May, 1962, Convention, 1964, Before You Sue, 1987. Served as lt. USNR, 1942-45. Mem. Phi Beta Kappa, Sigma Chi. Club: Gridiron. Home: Honolulu Hawaii Died Feb. 26, 1993.

KNIGHT, HARRY W., management and financial consultant; b. Sedalia, Mo., Apr. 20, 1909; s. Harry William and Florence (Lay) K.; m. Agnes Berger, Sept. 15, 1934; children: Kirk Lay, Harry William. AB, Amherst Coll., 1931; postgrad., Harvard U. Grad. Sch. Bus. Adminstrn., 1931-32; MBA, Northwestern U., 1940. With Harris Trust Co., Chgo., 1932-33; sales adminstr. Bauer & Black, 1934-36; fin. dir. City of Winnetka, Ill., 1937-40; city mgr. Two Rivers, Wis., 1941; chief budget sect. War Prodn. Bd., Washington, 1942; asst. chief program control div., munitions assignment bd. Combined Chiefs of Staff, Washington, 1942-45; fin. dir. UNRRA, 1945; sec. fin. com. 3d Council Meeting UNRRA, London, 1945; v.p. Booz, Allen & Hamilton, Inc., 1945-66; chmn. bd. Knight & Gladieux, 1966-73, Hillsboro Assocs., Inc., N.Y., 1973, N.Y.; past bd. dirs. Burlington Industries, Waldorf Astoria, Foxboro, Menlo Venture Capital Fund, Bancroft Racquet Co., Hudson Inst., Products of Asia, Shearson Lehman Appreciation Fund, Shearson Lehman Mgmt. Govt. Fund N.Y., Shearson Small Capital Fund, Shearson Symphony Fund, Shearson Lehman Bros. Intermediate Term Trust, Cigna/Licorny, and others; advisor to Teijin-Seiki of Tokyo, Yendo Assocs. of Tokyo and N.Y. Chmn. Darien Community Fund Dr., 1954; chmn. career conf. Amherst Coll., 1951-54, nat. chmn. capital program, 1962-65, trustee, 1964-81, trustee emeritus, 1981-95; pres. Harvard Bus. Sch. Assn., 1960, chmn. golden anniversary, 1958; chmn. adv. council Sch. Internat. Affairs, Columbia U., 1975-82; chmn. Rep. fin. campaign, Darien, 1952; trustee Com. Econ. Devel., 1968-95, Hampshire Coll., 1968-76, Hudson Inst., 1973-78. Lt. USNR, 1942-45. Recipient Eminent Service medal Amherst Coll. Mem. Fgn. Policy Assn. (bd. dirs. 1955-70), UN Assn. USA (past treas., gov., deputy gov.), Harvard Bus. Sch. Club (N.Y.), Delta Kappa Epsilon. Presbyterian. Clubs: Harvard Bus. Sch. (pres. 1970-71), Univ., Sky (N.Y.C.); Wee Burn Country (Darien, Conn.); Jupiter Island; John's Island Country (Fla.); Pine Valley Golf (N.J.); Sharon Park Country (Menlo Park, Calif.). Home: Menlo Park Calif. Died Jan. 2, 1995.

KNOCK, PETER BENJAMIN, real estate management executive; b. N.Y.C., May 1, 1948; s. Daniel Benjamin and Helen Elizabeth (Olson) K.; m. Signe Sandra Gates, Sept. 12, 1987. BA in Liberal Arts, Coll. of Wooster, 1970, B in Music in Organ Performance, 1970. Dist. mgr. Tishman East Mgmt. Co., N.Y.C., 1982-84; dist. mgr. Wm. A. White/Tishman East, N.Y.C., 1984-85; v.p. Pitt Comml. R.E., Stamford, Conn., 1985-87, L. J. Hooker Internat., Stamford, 1987-89, Grubb & Ellis Co., 1989-91; v.p. Knock Consulting Corp., Harrison, N.Y., 1980-91. Bd. dirs. Child Guidance Ctr, Stamford, 1988-91, Stamford Symphony Assn, 1987-88, Domus Found., 1989-91. Mem. Bldg. Owners and Mgrs. Assn., Nat. Assn. of Corp. Real Estate Execs., Inst. for Real Estate Mgmt., Am. Guild of Organists, Rotary Internat. Republican. Presbyterian. Home: Wilton Conn. Died Feb. 2, 1991.

KNOLL, ERWIN, author, editor; b. Vienna, Austria, July 17, 1931; came to U.S., 1940, naturalized, 1946; s. Carl and Ida (Schaechter) K.; m. Doris Elsa Ricksteen, Mar. 1, 1954; children: David Samuel, Jonathan Robert. B.A., NYU, 1953. Reporter, editor Editor and Publisher mag., N.Y.C., 1948-53; asso. editor Better Schools, N.Y.C., 1956-57; reporter, editor Washington Post, 1957-62; Washington editor Los Angeles Times-Washington Post News Service, 1962-63; Washington corr. Newhouse Nat. News Service, 1963-68; free lance writer, Washington editor The Progressive, 1968-73; editor The Progressive, Madison, Wis., 1973-94; commentator Nat. Pub. Radio, 1980-82; cons. Nat. Commn. on Urban Problems, 1968; host nat. syndicated radio program Second Opinion, 1989-94; panelist MacNeil/Lehrer NewsHour, 1990-94; commentator nat. syndicated radio program Insight, 1994. Author: (with William McGaffin) Anything But the Truth, 1968, Scandal in the Pentagon, 1969; author: No Comment, 1984; editor: (with Judith Nies McFadden) American Militarism, 1970, 1969, War Crimes and the American Conscience, 1970; contbr. articles to mags. Served with AUS, 1953-55. Home: Madison Wis. Died Nov. 2, 1994.

KNOPP, ALBERT J., lawyer; b. Cleve., Dec. 31, 1924. AB, Ohio Wesleyan U., 1947; JD, Cleve. State U., 1961. Bar: Ohio 1961, U.S. Dist. Ct. (no. dist.) Ohio 1962, U.S. Ct. Appeals (6th cir.) 1963, U.S. Supreme Ct. 1973, U.S. Ct. Appeals (10th cir.) 1988. Ptnr. Baker & Hostetler, Cleve. Fellow Am. Coll. Trial Lawyers; mem. ABA, Ohio State Bar Assn., Cleve. Bar Assn., Internat. Assn. Ins. Counsel, Cleve. State U. Alumni Assn. (past pres.), Cleve.-Marshall Law Alumni Assn. Home: Cleveland Ohio Deceased.

KNOUSE, CHARLES ALLISON, osteopathic physician, pathology educator; b. Plattsburg, Mo., Mar. 14, 1921; s. Charles Albert and Alice Susan May (Trout) K.; m. Iris Christine Ehrenreich, May 21, 1944; children: Thea Christine Knouse Price, Charles Allison, Karen Elizabeth Knouse Brungardt, John Arthur. Grad., Emmettsburgh Jr. Coll., Iowa, 1941; student, U. Chgo., 1941-42; D.O., Kansas City Coll. Osteopathy and Surgery, 1949. Diplomate Nat. Bd. Examiners Osteo. Physicians. Gen. practice medicine Howard City, Mich., 1950-55; asst. to editor Am. Osteo. Assn., Chgo., 1955; gen. practice Seattle, 1956; resident Hosps. Kansas City Coll. Osteopathy and Surgery, 1958-61; mem. faculty Kirksville Coll. Osteopathy and Surgery, Mo., 1961-65; mem. staff Kirksville Osteo. Hosp., 1961-65; prof. pathology, chmn. dept. U. Health Scis., Kansas City, Mo., 1965-68; chmn. dept. pathology Meml. Osteo. Hosp., York, Pa., 1968-78; prof. pathology Ohio U. Coll. Osteo. Medicine, 1978-92, dir. lab. services; gen. clinician, cons. forensic pathology Ohio U. Osteo. Med. Ctr. (formerly Ohio U. Med. Assocs. Clinic); mem. vis. faculty W.Va. Sch. Osteo. Medicine, 1975-78, U. New Eng. Coll. Osteo Medicine; cons. pathology Nat. Bd. Examiners for Osteo. Physicians and Surgeons. Contbr. articles to osteo. jours. Mem. bd. elders 1st Christian Ch., Athens, Ohio. With U.S. Mcht. Marine, 1942-44, U.S. Army, 1944-46, ETO. U. Chgo. scholar, 1941. Fellow Am. Osteo. Coll. Pathologists; mem. Am. Osteo. Assn. (lab. surveyor hosp. accreditation, editorial cons. pubs.), Ohio Osteo. Assn., Am. Acad. Osteopathy, AAUP, Am. Assn. Automotive Medicine, Am. Med. Writers Assn., Physicians for Social Responsibility, Psi Sigma Alpha (pres. Grand Council). Mem. Christian Ch. (Disciples of Christ). Home: Athens Ohio Died 1992.

KNOWLES, WARREN PERLEY, former governor, financial corporation executive; b. River Falls, Wis., Aug. 19, 1908; s. Warren P. and Anna Theresa (Deneen) K.; m. Dorothy C. Guidry, Apr. 17, 1943 (di 1968). BA, Carleton Coll., 1930, LLD, 1980; LL.B., U Wis., 1933; LL.D., Marquette U., 1965, Northlan Coll., 1965, Ripon Coll., St. Norberts U., 1975; L.H.D Carroll Coll.; L.H.D. hon. degree, Milton Coll., 197 Lakeland Coll., U. Wis., 1973; D.Eng. (hon.), Milv Sch. Engring., 1981; LLD, Mt. Mary, 1983; D of Pu Svc. (hon.), U. Wis., 1992. Bar: Wis. 1933, admitted practice; diplomate: ICC, U.S. Treasury Dept. Partn Doar & Knowles, New Richmond, 1935-64; lt. go State of Wis., 1954-58, 61-63, gov., 1965-71; chmn. b Heritage Wis. Corp., Milw., 1971-85; pres. Newtc Funds, Milw., 1985-93, also chmn. bd.; bd. dir Midwestern Nat. Ins. Co. Mem. Pres.'s Commn. c Sch. Finance, 1971-72; pres. Univ. Wis. Bd. Regent 1985-89; chmn. Wis. Land Use, 1972-73; mem. Wi Senate, 1940-53, majority floor leader, 1943-53, chm. legis. council, 1947, jud. council, 1951-53; del. Repub lican Nat. Conv., 1948, 56, 60, 64, 68, 72, 76, 80, 8 chmn. Wis. del., 1968, 76; bd. dirs. U. Wis. Found Greater Milw. Commn.; bd. govs. Med. Coll. Wis emeritus mem. bd. trustees Mt. Mary Coll., Milw. Bo Club, St. Francis Hosp. Found.; hon. chmn. Nat. W dlife Found.; trustee Nature Conservatory; chmn. Wi Leukemia Soc.; mem. adv. com. Nat. Multiple Scleros Soc.; bd. dir. Ire Agi Trach found. Served as lt. USNI 1942-46. Mem. Met. Milw. C. of C., Mil. Order Wor Wars, Am., Wis., St. Croix-Pierce County bar assns Assn. Ins. Counsel, Wis. Alumni Assn. (pres. 1952-5 dir.; dir. Alumni Found.), NCCJ, chmn. Wis. chp (1957-58), VFW, Am. Legion, 40 and 8. Republica Clubs: Milw. Athletic, Milwaukee, Univ, Elks. Hom Milwaukee Wis. Died May 1, 1993.

KNUTSON, ELLIOT KNUT, savings and loan assoc ation executive; b. Norma, N.D., May 25, 1924; Engvald and Cora (Knudson) K.; m. Patricia Lom Eaton, Aug. 19, 1944; children: Patrick, Dal Dana. Grad., Mohall (N.D.) High Sch., 1942. Ass v.p. Seattle First Nat. Bank, 1946-62; chmn., chief exe officer Wash. Fed. Savs. & Loan, Seattle, 1962—. Wi USMC, 1943-46. Home: Seattle Wash.

KOCHANOWSKY, BORIS JULIUS, mining co sultant; b. Krasnojarsk, Siberia, Russia, May 4, 190 came to U.S., 1953, naturalized, 1959; s. Julius M. an Maria J. (Borovski) K.; m. Maria E. Chudobba, Sep 1984; 1 child, Vera. Diplom Ingenieur in Mi Surveying, U. Bergakademie, Freiberg, Ger., 192 Diplom Ingenieur; in Mining Engring., 1929; Dr. I genieur in Mining Engring, U. Bergakademie, Claustha Ger., 1955. Coal miner, 1923-29; research asso. Co Bd., Essen, Ger., 1930, U. Bergakademie, Freiber 1930-33; asst. to pres., mgr. mining ops., devel. an research Rheinische Kalksteinwerke Co., German 1933-39; mgr. coal mines Switzerland, 1945-46; mg asphaltite mine Mendoza, Argentina, 1946-48; prof. e gring. and econs. of mining U. Cuyo, San Juan an Mendoza, 1948-53; mem. faculty Pa. State U., 1953-9 prof. mining engring., 1961-67, founder, chmn. miner engring. mgmt. program, 1968-70, prof. emeritus, 197 92; speaker, cons. throughout world. Co-author: Be und Aufbereitungstechnik, Part I, 1933, Part II, 193 Neuzeitliche Sprengtechnik, 1966, also numerous a ticles; inventor mining systems, methods and machines Mem. AIME, Am. Soc. Engring. Edn., AAUP. Hom State College Pa. Died, Dec. 17, 1992.

KOCHEVAR, LEWIS CLAYTON, hydraulics com pany executive; b. Price, Utah, July 18, 1931; s. Josep William and Elva (Prince) K.; m. JoAnn Llewellyn, Ju 28, 1957; children: Mark Llewellyn, Tracy Lynn, Chri tine. BS, Brigham Young U., 1956, MS, 1957. Geol gist Dames & Moore, L.A., 1957-67; with Haskel Inc Burbank, Calif., 1968-92; owner Sandy Hill Glads, Sa Lake City, 1990-95. Cpl. U.S. Army, 1953-55, Austria Mem. N.Am. Gladiolus Coun. (v.p. 1992-95, pres. 199 95). Mem. Ch. Latter-Day Saints. Home: Salt Lak City Utah Died June 6, 1995.

KOCHS, HERBERT WILLIAM, industrial chemic manufacturer; b. Chgo., Mar. 28, 1903; s. August an Adelaide (Petersen) K.; m. Elizabeth Kennedy, 1924; dau., Nancy (Mrs. E. K. Shaw); m. Mildred Swift, De 2, 1928; children: Susan M. (Mrs. W. E. Judevin (dec.), Herbert William, Judith Anne (Mrs. Nelso Shaw); m. Phyllis Anderson, Nov. 10, 1955; m. Pau Leggett, Dec. 28, 1959; children: Justin and Marti (twins). Student, Mass. Inst. Tech., 1920-2 Northwestern U., 1923-24. Sec. Diversey Corp., Chgo 1927-32; v.p. Diversey Corp., 1932-35, pres., 1935-4 chmn., 1943-78, hon. chmn., dir., 1978-93. Past di Nat. Council Crime and Delinquency, pres., 1959-6 hon. v.p., 1964-67; former dir. Grant Hosp.; chmn. b mgrs. Uhlich Childrens Home, 1956-58. Clubs: M.I.T (Chgo.) (past pres.), Chicago Athletic (Chgo.); India Hill (Winnetka, Ill.); American (London, Eng.). Hom Lisle Ill. Died June 5, 1993.

KOENIGSBERG, MARVIN LEE, lawyer; b. Chgo Dec. 10, 1918; s. Isadore and Minnie (Oliff) K.; m. Rit Wilks Volid, June 18, 1980. B.S.L., Northwestern U 1942, J.D., 1942. Bar: Ill. Bar 1942. Lawyer Legal Ai Bur., Chgo., 1942-44; assoc. Gottlieb & Schwart Chgo., 1944-50; ptnr. Friedman & Koven (an predecessors), Chgo., 1950-86; of counsel Rosenthal an Schanfield, Chgo., from 1986; bd. dirs. J.D. Marsha Internat. Inc., Chgo., 1959-79, Marshall Electroni nc., Chgo., 1959-79, Marshall Frankel Found., Chgo., rom 1965. Bd. dirs. Jewish Home for Aged, Chgo. Mem. ABA, Ill. Bar Assn., Chgo. Bar Assn., Decalogue oc., Praetorians, B'nai B'rith (lodge pres. 1952), Tau psilon Rho. Jewish. Home: Chicago Ill. Deceased.

ÖHLER, GEORGES J. F., scientist, immunologist; b. Apr. 17, 1946. Scientist, immunobiologist Max-Planck nstitut fur Immunbiologie, Stübeweg, Fed. Republic Germany. Recipient Nobel prize in Medicine and hysiology, 1984, Albert Lasker Med. Research award, 984. Home: Freiburg Germany Died Mar. 1, 1995.

OJIAN, VARUJAN HAIG, conductor; b. Beirut, Mar. 12, 1935; came to U.S., 1956, naturalized, 1965; s. Haig Awak and Anouche (Der-Parseghian) K. Student 1st prize), Paris Nat. Conservatory, 1947-50; diploma, Curtis Inst. Music, 1959; student, U. So. Calif., 1964. Asst. concertmaster and asst. condr. Los Angeles hilharm., 1965-71; assoc. condr. Seattle Symphony, 972-75; prin. guest condr. Royal Opera, Stockholm, 973-80; music dir. Utah Symphony, Salt Lake City, 980-83, Chautauqua (N.Y.) Symphony, 1981-84, Ballet West, Salt Lake City, 1984-87, Santa Barbara (Calif.) ymphony, 1985-93; faculty dept. music U. Utah, Salt ake City, 1980-83; music dir. Santa Barbara ymphony, 1985-93. Recipient 1st prize Internat. Conducting Competition, Sorrento, Italy, 1972; decorated Order of Lion Finland, 1975, Order of Lion also by ovts. Greece, 1956, Iran, 1955, Lebanon, 1956. Home: Carpinteria Calif. Died Mar. 4, 1993; interred Santa arbara, Calif.

OKENZIE, HENRY FAYETTE, county official; b. Gray's Landing, Pa., July 13, 1918; s. John and Antonia Filimon) K.; BA, U. Denver, 1948; m. Irene Mildred Owens, May 24, 1941; children: Henry Fayette, Antoinette I., John R., Nicholas A. Bus. mgr. athletics J. Denver, 1948-49; dep. clk. Mcpl. Ct. Savannah (Ga.), 952-58; mgr. truck sales Key West Ford, Inc. (Fla.), 961-72; dir. vets. affairs Monroe County, Key West, 972—; exec. sec. Vets. Council Monroe County, 972—. Mem. Monroe County Democratic Exec. Com., 960-69. Served to capt. U.S. Army, 1939-46. Recipient homas H. Gigniallat award, Savannah, 1958. Mem. la. Pub. Rels. Assn. (pres. Fla. Keys/Conch chpt. 977-78), County Vets. Svc. Officers Assn. Fla. (pres. 977-79), Assn. Naval Aviation, Navy League U.S. ife), DAV (life, Savannah chpt. comdr. 1955-56, Key West chpt. comdr. 1971-72, adjutant 1972—), Ret. Officers Assn. (life; pres. chpt. 1981-82), Noncommd. Officers Assn. (life), Nat. Assn. Civilian Conservation Corps Alumni, Nat. Am. Legion Press Assn., Am. Legion (post comdr. 1981-85), Key West C. of C., Henry Kokenzie Polish Legion of Am. Veterans, AMVETS ife), Mil. Order World Wars, Internat. Platform Assn. ife patron), Key West Art and Hist. Soc., Fla. Hist. oc., Polish Inst. Arts and Scis. of Am., Phi Beta Kappa, Omicron Delta Kappa, Pi Gamma Mu. Roman Catholic. Clubs: Elks, Kiwanis (pres. 1985-86), Moose Key West). Lodge: Knights of Columbus. Deceased. Home: Key West Fla.

OLAR, MILTON ANTON, lawyer, corporate executive; b. Chgo., Jan. 18, 1916; s. Frank J. and Josephine Maros) K.; m. Rae Solum, July 4, 1940; children: Caryn Rae, Britton Ward, Christine Edith. B.S.C., Northwestern U., 1937, J.D., 1939. Bar: Ill. 1939, Wis. 1981. Practice law Chgo., 1939-54; atty. U.S. Gypsum Co., Chgo., 1940-42, Butler Bros., Chgo., 1942-59; asst. sec. Butler Bros., 1954-58, gen. devel. mgr., 1954-58, asst. to res., 1958-59; gen. mgr. S.W. region Ben Franklin tores div. City Products Corp. (acquired Butler Bros. 959), Dallas, 1960-62; v.p., sec. City Products Corp., Des Plaines, Ill., 1962-67; pres. Scott Stores div. City Products Corp., Des Plaines, 1967-69, Herst-Allen, 969-72; v.p. City Products Corp., 1972-81; lectr. in eld; cons. OPS, Washington, 1951. Mem. Fed., Am., Wis., Ill., Chgo. bar assns., Am. Soc. Corp. Secs., Assn. Gen. Mdse. Chains (chmn. 1977-79), Lambda Chi Alpha, Phi Delta Phi. Lutheran. Home: Washington sland Wis. Died Jan. 29, 1992.

OLENDA, KONSTANTIN, educator; b. Kamien-Koszyrski, Poland, May 17, 1923; came to U.S., 1946, aturalized, 1951; s. Theodore and Helena K.; m. Paune Moller, June 9, 1962; children: Helena, Christopher. B.A., Rice U., 1950; Ph.D., Cornell U., 1953. Asst. prof. philosophy Rice U., 1953-58, assoc. prof., 958-65, prof., 1965-91, chmn. dept. philosophy, 1968-5, Carolyn and Fred McManis prof. philosophy, 1975-1; Fulbright lectr. U. Heidelberg, 1959-60; vis. prof. U. Tex., Colo. Coll., U.S. Mil. Acad., 1983-84. Author: The Freedom of Reason, 1964, In Defense of Practical Reason, 1969, Ethics for the Young, 1972, Philosophy's Journey, 1974, Religion Without God, 1976, Philosophy n Literature, 1982, Cosmic Religion, 1987, Rorty's Humanistic Pragmatism, 1990; Editor: On Thinking, 979, Organazations and Ethical Individualism, 1989. Mem. Am. Philos. Assn., Southwestern Philos. Soc. pres. 1965), Soc. Advancement of Am. Philosophy, C.S. Peirce Soc., Phi Beta Kappa. Democrat. Home: Houston Tex. Died Dec. 5, 1991.

OLTHOFF, IZAAK MAURITS, chemistry educator; . Almelo, The Netherlands, Feb. 11, 1894; came to J.S., 1927; s. Moses and Rosetta (Wysenbeek) . Ph.D., U. Utrecht, The Netherlands, 1918; D.Sc. (hon.), U. Chgo., U. Groningen, The Netherlands, 1964, Brandeis U., 1974, Hebrew U., Jerusalem, %, U. Ariz., 1985. Asst. in chemistry U. Utrecht, 1915-18, conservator, 1918-24, privatdocent, 1924-27; prof. analytical chemistry, head dept. U. Minn., Mpls., 1927-62; prof. emeritus U. Minn., 1962-93; chmn. com. analytical chemistry NCR; v.p. Internat. Union of Pure and Applied Chemistry, pres. sect. analytical chemistry, chmn. commn. electroanalytical chemistry. Author: Konduktometrische Titrationen, 1923, The Theory of Indicators, 1926, Potentiometric Titrations, 1932, Volumetric Analysis (2 vols.), 1939, (3 vols.), 1958, pH and Electrometric Titrations, 1941, Textbook on Quantitative Inorganic Analysis, 4th edit., 1969, Acid-Base Indicators, 1936, Polarographic Analysis and Amperometric Titrations, 1941-52, Emulsion Polymerization, 1955; assoc. editor Jour. Am. Chem. Soc.; co-editor: Treatise on Analytical Chemistry; contbr. articles to tech. publs. Decorated comdr. Order of Oranje-Nassua, 1947; recipient Anachem award 1961; Polarographic medal Polarographic Soc. Eng., 1964; Hanus medal Czechoslovak Chem. Soc., 1967; Kolthoff gold medal in analytical chemistry Acad. Pharm. Scis., 1967; Albert Einstein award Am. Soc. Technion, 1982; Hall of Fame award Minn. Inventors, 1985, Olin-Palladium award Elecgro Chem. Soc., 1982; Kolthoff Hall at U. Minn. dedicated in his honor, 1973. Fellow AAAS, Royal Soc. Chemistry (hon., Robert Boyle medal 1985); mem. Am. Chem. Soc. (recipient Fisher award analytical chemistry, Minn. award, William H. Nichols medal N.Y. sect., Excellence in Teaching award div. analytical chemistry, 1983), Royal Flemish Acad. Belgium (fgn.), Royal Soc. Sci. and Lettres of Bohemia (corr.), Finnish Chem. Soc. (hon.), Czechoslav Chem. Soc. (hon.), Am. Electrochem. Soc., Dutch Chem. Soc. (hon.), Dutch Pharm. Soc., Nat. Acad. Scis., Am. Acad. Arts and Scis., hon. mem. numerous profl. socs. and assns. Democrat. Unitarian. Home: Minneapolis Minn. Died Feb., 1993.

KOMATSU, YUGORO, steel company executive; b. Kure City, Hiroshima, Japan, Sept. 18, 1920; m. Chieko Wada; children: Keiichiro, Shinjiro. LLB, Imperial U. Tokyo, 1944. With Ministry Internat. Trade and Industry, Tokyo, 1944-76; 1st sec. Japanese Embassy, Bonn, Germany, 1955-60; adminstrv. vice min. Ministry Internat. Trade and Industry, Tokyo, 1974-76; exec. v.p. Kobe Steel Ltd., Tokyo, 1979-83, vice chmn., 1983-84, chmn., 1984-95; advisor Japan C. of C. and Industry, Tokyo, 1977-95; pres. Japan Aluminum Fedn., Tokyo, 1982-83, Materials Process Tech. Ctr., Tokyo, 1992-95; mem. Tax Commn. Prime Mins. Office, 1987-94. Mem. Industry Club Japan. Home: Tokyo Japan Died Dec. 23, 1995.

KONDO, TAKEO, import export company executive; b. Aichi, Japan, 1922. Grad., Tokyo Imperial U., 1944; married. With Kawahishi Airplane Inc., 1944-45, Fuji Seiko Inc., 1946-49; with Mitsubishi Corp., Tokyo, 1949—, pres., chief exec. officer Mitsubishi Intrnat. Corp., N.Y.C., 1982—, also dir. Served with Japanese Navy, 1945-46. Home: New York N.Y.

KONZAL, JOSEPH CHARLES, sculptor; b. Milw., Nov. 5, 1905; s. Frank A. and Sylvia (Baresh) K.; m. Geraldine G. Driscoll, May 20, 1930 (div. June 1957); m. 2d, Theresa Sherman, Oct. 11, 1961. Student, Beaux Arts Inst., N.Y.C., 1926-30, Art Students League, 1926-30, Layton Art Sch., 1925. Tchr. sculpture Bklyn. Mus. Art Sch., 1949-70, Adelphi U., Garden City, N.Y., 1954-70, Newark Sch. Fine and Indsl. Arts, 1960-65, Queens Coll., CUNY, 1969-70, Kent (Ohio) State U., 1971-76. One-man shows include Bertha Schaefer Gallery, N.Y.C., 1960, 63, 65, 67, 70, Adelphi U., Garden City, N.Y., 1965, Kent (Ohio) State U., 1971, Canton (Ohio) Art Inst., 1974, Andre Zarre Gallery, N.Y.C., 1978, 80, New Sch. Social Research, N.Y.C., 1984, Berman/Daferner Gallery, N.Y.C., 1992; group shows include Carnegie Internat., Pitts., 1962, Mus. Modern Art, N.Y.C., 1959, Bklyn. Mus., 1952, 54, 56, 58, 60, Phila. Mus., 1958, 62, 64, 68, N.J. State Mus., Trenton, 1963, 64, 66, Newark Mus., 1960, 63, 66, Aldrich Mus. Contemporary Art, Ridgefield, Vt., 1968, Whitney Mus. Am. Art, N.Y.C., 1948, 60, 62, 64, 66, 68, N.J. Tercentennial Pavilion, N.Y.C. World's Fair, 1964, Cin. Mus., 1958, Galerie Claude Bernard, Paris, 1962, Tate Gallery, London, 1966, Cleve. Mus., 1971, 74, Hemisfair, San Antonio, 1968, New Sch. Social Research, N.Y.C., 1969, Indpls. Mus., 1970, U. Nebr., Lincoln, 1970, Storm King Art Ctr., Mountainville, N.Y., 1971, Blossom Music Ctr., Cuyahoga Falls, Ohio, 1972, Dayton Mus., 1974, Cleve. Art Council, 1974, Albright-Know Mus., Buffalo, 1971, Foley Sq. and Ward's Island, N.Y.C., 1977-78, UN, N.Y.C., 1978, Am. Acad. and Inst. Arts and Letters, N.Y.C., 1981, 82, 83, Queens Coll., N.Y.C., 1984, Kenkeleba Gallery, N.Y.C., 1984-87, Sculptors Guild Annuals, N.Y.C., Hudson Guild, N.Y.C., 1988, Mcpl. Bldg., N.Y.C., 1988, Hofstra Mus., Hofstra U., Hemstead, L.I., 1990, Cast Iron Gallery, N.Y.C., 1991, Sculptors Guild, N.Y.C., 1991; represented in permanent collections (large outdoor sculpture) Canton (Ohio) Art Inst., Storm King Art Ctr., Mountainville, N.Y., Fed. Courthouse, Dayton, Ohio, New Sch. Social Research, N.Y.C., City of Canton, Ohio, (indoor sculpture) Whitney Mus. Am. Art, N.Y.C., N.J. State Mus., Trenton, Tate Gallery, London, Kent State U., Michner Coll., Smithsonian Inst., Washington, Queens Coll., N.Y.C., Norton Gallery Art, West Palm Beach, Fla., Ctr. for Arts, Vero Beach, Fla., Josiah White Exhibit Ctr., Jim Thorpe, Pa., Bishop Ctr. Grays Harbor Coll., Aberdeen Wash., Gen. Svcs. Adminstrn. Art in Architecture Program, Washington, Gen. Svcs. Com. Art in Architecture Divsn., Art & Historic Preservatin Divsn., Pub. Bldg. Lobby; commns. include Am. Heritage (portrait sculptures for mass prodn.), 1958, Gen. Svcs. Adminstrn., U.S.A., Art and Architecture Program, Fed. Ct. House, Dayton, Ohio, large scale outdoor sculpture. Guggenheim fellow John Simon Guggenheim Meml. Found., 1966; grantee Adolph and Esther Gottleib Found., 1982, Pollock-Krasner Found., 1993. Mem. Sculptors' Guild (treas. 1943-61, 83-94, chmn. membership com. 1956-61). Democrat. Home: New York N.Y. Died Nov. 29, 1994.

KOONTZ, RAYMOND, retired security equipment company executive; b. Asheville, N.C., 1912; m. Carol Hamlin; 1 son, Cary Hamlin. With Maguire Industries Inc., 1936-46; with Diebold Inc., Canton, Ohio, from 1947, treas., 1947-51, exec. v.p., treas., 1951-52, pres., chief exec. officer, 1952-78, chmn. bd., chief exec. officer, 1978-82, chmn. bd., 1982-88, chmn., exec. com., bd. dirs., 1988-95, ret., 1995. Mem. Newcomen Soc. N.Am., Canton (Ohio) Club, Brookside Club (Canton), Union Club of Cleve., Congress Lake Club (Hartville, Ohio), Green Boundary Club (Aiken, S.C.). Home: Canton Ohio Deceased.

KOOPMANS, TJALLING CHARLES, economist; b. s'Graveland, Netherlands, Aug. 28, 1910; s. Sjoerd and Wijtske (van der Zee) K.; M.A., U. Utrecht (Netherlands), 1933; Ph.D., U. Leiden (Netherlands) 1936; hon. doctorate econs. Netherlands Sch. Econs., 1963, Catholic U. Louvain, 1967; m. Truus Wanningen, Oct. 1936; children: Anne W., Henry S., Helen J. Came to U.S., 1940, naturalized, 1946. Lectr. Netherlands Econ. U., Rotterdam, 1936-38; specialist fin. sect. League of Nations, 1938-40; research asso. Sch. Pub. and Internat. Affairs, Princeton U., also spl. lectr., sch. bus. N.Y.U., 1940-41; economist Penn Mut. Life Ins. Co., 1941-42; statistician Combined Shipping Adjustment Bd. and Brit. Mcht. Shipping Mission, 1942-44; research asso. Cowles Commn. Research Econs., U. Chgo., 1944-55, asso. prof. econs., 1946-48, prof. econs., 1948-55, dir. research Cowles Commn., 1948-54; prof. econs. Yale U., 1955-81, Alfred Cowles prof. emeritus, 1981—, dir. Cowles Found. for Research in Econs., 1961-67, also fellow of Silliman Coll., Yale U.; Frank W. Taussig prof. econs. Harvard U., 1960-61. Recipient Nobel Meml. award in Econs., 1975. Fellow Econometric Soc. (pres. 1950), Am. Econ. Assn. (pres. 1978, Disting. fellow); mem. Am. Acad. Arts and Scis., Nat. Acad. Scis. Author: Three Essays on the State of Economic Science, 1957. Editor: Statistical Inference in Dynamic Economic Models, 1950; Activity Analysis of Production and Allocation, 1951; co-editor; Studies in Econometric Method, 1953. Contbr. profl. jours. Home: New Haven Conn.

KOREN, STEPHAN, banker; b. Wiener Neustadt, Austria, Nov. 14, 1919; s. Stephan and Maria (Neuhold) K.; m. Marianne Fossek, 1945; children: Elisabeth, Wolfgang, Maria-Anna, Eva Maria, Stephan, Silvia Maria. B.A. in Econs., U. Vienna, 1945, Dr.rer.pol., 1946. Mem. staff Inst. Econ. Research, 1945-65; prof. economy U. Vienna (Austria), 1964; prof., head Econ. Inst., U. Innsbruck (Austria), 1965-67; under-sec. of state Fed. Chancellery Austria, Vienna, 1967, minister of fin., 1968-70; leader Austrian People's Party, Austrian Parliament, Vienna, 1971-78; pres. Austrian Nat. Bank, Vienna, from 1978. Contbr. numerous articles on econ., polit. topics to various publs. Mem. Inst. Advanced Studies (bd dirs. from 1979), Osterreichische Bankwissenschaftliche Gesellschaft (pres. from 1980), Osterreichisches Komitee der Freunde des European Forum Alpbach (pres. from 1960), Osterreichisches Institut fur Wirtschaftsforschung (bd dirs. from 1978). Roman Catholic. Died Jan. 26, 1988; buried Vienna. Home: Vienna Austria

KORODI, ANDRAS, conductor; b. Budapest, Hungary, 1922; student Franz Liszt Acad. (Budapest) under Weiner, Lajtha, Ferencsik. Coach, Budapest State opera, 1945, condr., then prin. condr., 1963-94 ; instr. conducting Franz Liszt Acad., 1957-94 ; chief condr. Budapest Philharmonic Orch.; condr. European orchs.; 1st Hungarian condr. at Bolshoi Theater, Moscow. Died 1986. Home: Budapest Hungary

KOSIKOWSKI, FRANK VINCENT, food scientist, educator; b. Torrington, Conn., Jan. 10, 1916; s. Frank K. and Bertha Samul (Kosikowski); m. Anna Hudak, Oct. 21, 1944; 1 dau., Frances Anne. .S., U. Conn.-Storrs, 1939; M.S., Cornell U., 1941, Ph.D., 1944. Asst. prof. food sci. Cornell U., 1945-47, assoc. prof., 1947-52, prof., 1952-95; tech. devel. officer FAO-UN, Rome, Italy, 1963; vol. Internat. Exec. Service Corp., Tehran, Iran, 1970. Author: Cheese & Fermented Milk Foods, 1966, Advances in Cheese Technology, 1958. Bd. dirs. Bethel Grove Comunity, Ithaca N.Y., 1960. Recipient research awards Am. Diary Sci. Assn., 1955,60; recipient research awards French Govt., 1964, research awards Inst. Food Technologists, 1983, research awards Am. Cultured Dairy Products Inst., 1983. Mem. AAAS, Am.Dairy Sci. Assn., Am. Chem. Soc., Inst. Food Technologists. Roman Catholic. Club: Statler. Home: Ithaca N.Y. Died April 6, 1995.

KOSLER, ZDENEK, conductor; b. Prague, Czechoslovakia, Mar. 25, 1928; s. Malvina and Vaclav K.; student Acad. Music and Dramatic Arts, Prague; m. Jana Svobodova, 1954. Condr. Prague Nat. Theatre, 1951-58; artistic dir. Olomouc Opera, 1958-62; chief Ostrava Opera, 1962-66; asst. condr. N.Y. Philharmonic Orch., 1963-64, F.O.K. Orch., Prague, 1965-67; chief condr. Berlin Komische Opera, 1966-68, Opera of the Slovak Nat. Theatre, Bratislava, 1971-76; condr. Czech Philharm., 1971-81; artistic dir. Prague Nat. Theatre Opera, 1980-86, music dir., 1989-91; numerous concert tours in Japan, U.S.A., Can., and all of Europe. Recipient award for Outstanding Work, 1958, 1st prize and Gold medal D. Mitropoulos Internat. Competition, N.Y., 1963, Artist of Merit, 1974, Nat. Artist, 1984, Order of Labor award, 1988. Died Febr. 7, 1995. Home: Nad Sarkou Czech Republic

KOUNTCHE, SEYNI, president Republic of Niger; b. Fandou, Niger, 1931; grad. French Army Sch., Kati, Mali, Army Sch., St. Louis, Senegal. Joined French Colonial Army, 1949; joined Niger Army, 1961, commd. officer, 1966; dep. chief staff Niger Armed Forces, 1966-73; chief staff, 1973-74; leader coup which overthrew Pres. Diori, 1974; pres. Republic of Niger, pres. Supreme Mil. Council, 1974-87; minister of devel., 1974-76; minister of interior, 1974-76, from 1981; minister of nat. def., 1974-76, 77-87; pres. Council of Ministers, 1977-87. Home: Niamey Niger

KRAESSEL, ALFRED, economics educator; b. Vienna, Austria; came to U.S., 1948; s. Martin and Renate Renee (Goldschlaager) K. BA in Math. Econs., U. Nat. Mayor San Marcos, Lima, Peru, 1941, M Econs. and Social Scis., 1945, D Econs., 1948. Rsch. assoc. Intergovts. Com. on Refugees, N.Y.C. and London, 1946-48; vis. prof. Mich. State U., East Lansing, 1948, U. Rutgers U., New Brunswick, N.J., 1953-56, U. Buffalo, 1957-58; asst. prof., rsch. assoc. U. Chgo., 1949-53; prof. econs. Seton Hall U., South Orange, N.J., from 1956, pres. faculty senate, 1966-68; faculty fellow, historian Princeton (N.J.) U., from 1961;. Author: Development of the Amazon Region of Peru, 1958, Integration of Micro-Economics and Monetary Development, 1972, Modern Microeconomic Theory, 1982. Instr. Greenwich Village Synagogue, N.Y.C., 1965-72; pres. N.J. region Jewish Nat. Fund, Teaneck, 1969-74; hon. vice chmn. Jewish Nat. Fund Am., N.Y.C., 1972-83. Mem. Am. Econ. Assn., AAUP (chpt. pres. 1963-65, 83-88). Republican. Home: West Orange N.J. Deceased.

KRAMER, PAUL JACKSON, plant physiologist, educator, writer, editor; b. Brookville, Ind., May 8, 1904; s. Le Roy and Minnie (Jackson) K.; m. Edith Sara Vance, June 24, 1931; children: Jean Jackson Findeis, Richard Vance. A.B., Miami U., Oxford, Ohio, 1926, D.Litt. (hon.), 1966; M.S., Ohio State U., 1929, Ph.D., 1931, D.Sc. (hon.), 1972; D.Sc. (hon.), U. N.C., 1966; Dr. Honoris Causa, U. Paris VII, 1975. From instr. to prof. botany Duke U., Durham, N.C., 1931-54; James B. Duke prof. Duke U., 1954-74, emeritus prof., 1974-96; dir. Sarah P. Duke Gardens, Duke U., 1945-74; program dir. in regulatory biology NSF, Washington, 1960-61; sr. vis fellow Australian Acad. Sci., Canberra, 1970; mem. vis. com. biology Harvard U., Cambridge, Mass., 1966-71; trustee Biol. Abstracts, Phila., 1965-71. Author: Soil and Plant Water Relationships, 1949, Soil and Plant Water Relationships; A Modern Synthesis (also in Spanish), 1969, Lectures in Tree Physiology (in Chinese), 1982, Water Relations of Plants (also in Russian, Chinese and Japanese), 1983, (with T.T. Kozlowski) Physiology of Trees (also in Russian, Portuguese and Chinese), 1960, Physiology of Woody Plants (in Russian and Chinese), 1979; editor: (with N.C. Turner) Adaptation of Plants to Water and High Temperature Stress, 1980; (with C.D. Raper) Crop Responses to Water and Temperatures Stress in Humid, Temperate Climates, 1983, (with Y. Hashimoto, H. Nonami, and B.R. Strain) Measurement Techniques in Plant Science, 1990, (with T.T. Kozlowski and S.G. Pallardy) Physiological Ecology of Woody Plants, 1991. Recipient award Soc. Am. Foresters, 1961. Fellow AAAS (chmn. sect. G. 1956); mem. Am. Soc. Plant Physiologists (Barnes life mem., pres. 1945, Am. Inst. Biol. Scis. (life, pres. 1964, Disting. Service award 1977), Bot. Soc. Am. (pres. 1964, merit award 1956), Nat. Acad. Scis. (chmn. botany sect. 1968-70), Am. Acad. Arts and Scis., Am. Philos. Soc. Methodist. Clubs: Cosmos (Washington). Home: Chapel Hill N.C. Died May 18, 1996.

KRAMER, RUSSELL ARNOLD, lawyer; b. Maryville, Tenn., Dec. 13, 1918; s. Russell Reed and Alice Gray (Arnold) K.; m. Sara Lee Hellums, Mar. 8, 1942; children: John Reed, Sara Lynne, Randall A. B.A., Maryville Coll., 1940; postgrad., U. Tex., 1941; J.D., U. Mich., 1946. Bar: Tenn. 1942, Pa. 1975. Ptnr. Kramer, Johnson, Rayson, McVeigh & Leake, Knoxville, Tenn., 1947-74; of counsel Kramer, Johnson, Rayson, McVeigh & Leke, Knoxville, Tenn., 1984-93; exec. v.p., dir., gen. counsel Aluminum Co. Am., Pitts., 1974-83. Served to capt. USAAF, 1942-46. Mem. ABA, Tenn. Bar Assn., Knoxville Bar Assn., Am. Judicature Soc. (chmn. 1983). Methodist. Home: Knoxville Tenn. Died July 14, 1993.

KRANCK, ERNST HAKAN, geologist, geographer; b. Birkkala, Finland, Nov. 7, 1898; came to Can., 1948; s. Ernst Albin and Alexandra (Lisitzin) K.; m. Valborg Maria Meinander, Oct. 5, 1930 (dec. 1975); children—Svanta Hakan, Elisabeth Maria, Kate Margareta. M.S., U. Helsinki, 1924, Ph.D., 1929. Asst. prof. U. Helsinki, 1930-45; prof. Comml.Coll., Helsinki, 1932-40; chief geologist Wuoksenniska Co., Finland, 1940-45; prof. U. Neuchatel, Switzerland, 1945-48; prof. dept. geology McGill U., Montreal, Que., Can., 1948-70; mem. research expeditions to Siberia, Tierra del Fuego, Greenland, Can. Arctic. Contbr. articles to profl. jours. Home: Dartmouth Can. Deceased.

KRANZ, MARY ROSARIA, health services administrator; b. Kranzburg, S.D., May 4, 1914; d. Michael M. and Mary M. (Raml) K. BS in Math., No. State Coll., Aberdeen, S.D., 1949; MHA, St. Louis U., 1954; M in Comprehensive Health Planning, The Johns Hopkins U., 1971, D of Pub. Health Adminstrn., 1973; HHD (hon.), Coll. St. Francis, Joliet, Ill., 1985; hon. degree, Mt. Marty Coll., 1992. Tchr., prin. elem. and jr. high schs., S.D., 1932-52; adminstr. Sacred Heart Hosp., Yankton, S.D., 1954-69; health care coord. The Benedictine Health Ctrs., Yankton, 1968-70; assoc. prof. Sangamon State U., Springfield, Ill., 1973-79; assoc. prof., dean grad. studies Coll. of St. Francis, 1979-83, prof., 1983-85; cons. Benedictine Convent, Yankton, 1985-86; pres., chief exec. officer Benedictine Health System, Yankton, 1986-91, cons., 1991-94; mem. chairperson various bds. and coms. Benedictine Health System, 1985-91. Developer grad. prog. Sangamon State U., 1973, Coll. of St. Francis, 1980. Named Chief Exec. Officer of Yr., S.D. Hosp. Assn., 1959; life fellow Am. Coll. Benedictine Convent of the Sacred Heart. Fellow Am. Coll. Halth Execs. (life). Roman Catholic. Home: Yankton S.D. Died Sept. 4, 1994.

KRATZER, GUY LIVINGSTON, surgeon; b. Gratz, Pa., Apr. 24, 1911; s. Clarence U. and Carrie E. (Schwalm) K.; m. Kathryn H. Miller, Jan. 27, 1940; 1 son, Guy Miller. Student, Muhlenberg Coll., 1928-31; M.D., Temple U., 1935; M.S., U. Minn., 1945. Diplomate: Am. Bd. Proctology. Intern Harrisburg Hosp., 1935-36; fellow proctology, surgery Mayo Clinic, 1942-46, fellow surgery, 1949-50; asso. surgeon Pottsville Hosp., 1936-41; assoc. proctologist Allentown (Pa.) Hosp., 1946-94, mem. tumor clinic, 1955-94, chief, dept. proctology, 1958-94; mem. cons. staff Sacred Heart Hosp., 1946-94, chief dept. colon and rectal surgery, 1974-94; clin. assoc. prof. surgery Milton S. Hershey Med. Center, Pa. State U., 1972-75, clin. prof., 1975-94, cons., 1975-94; mem. Pa. Bd. Med. Edn. and Licensure, 1984-94. Author: Disease of the Colon and Rectum, 1985; contbr. numerous articles to med. jours. Pres. Lehigh Valley chpt., bd. dirs. Am. Cancer Soc. Recipient Award for Exceptional Svc. and Significant Contbns. Am. Soc. of Colon and Rectal Surgeons, 1982. Mem. Fellow ACS (pres. S.E. Pa. 1965-66), Am. Proctologic Soc., Internat. Coll. Surgeons; mem. Shelter House Soc., Am. Med. Writers Assn., Pa. Proctologic Soc. (past pres.), Pa. Med. Soc., Am. Med. Authors, Lehigh Valley Med. Soc. (past pres.), Allentown C. of C. (gov.), Lions, Union League. Republican. Evangelical. Home: Allentown Pa. Died 1994.

KRAVITZ, WILLIAM N., lawyer; b. N.Y.C., Sept. 26, 1946; s. Louis I. and Grace (Fox) K.; m. Marilyn H. Piller, Jan. 2, 1971; children: Eric G., Meredyth D., Jordan T. AB, Boston U., 1967; JD, St. John's U., N.Y.C., 1971. Bar: N.Y. 1972, U.S. Dist. Ct. (so. dist.) 1975, U.S. Tax Ct. 1975, U.S. Ct. Appeals (2d cir.) 1975, U.S. Supreme Ct. 1975. Assoc. Fried, Frank, Harris, Shriver & Jacobson, N.Y.C., 1972-76; dep. gen. counsel Bowery Savings Bank, N.Y.C., 1976; assoc. Skadden, Arps, Slate, Meagher & Flom, N.Y.C., 1976-78, ptnr., 1978—. Editor: Employee Benefit Plans: Mergers and Aquisitions, 1983, ESOPs and ESOP Transactions, 1985, Tax-Qualified Employee Benefits-Compensation in Change of Control Situations, 1986, ESOPs: 1988, 1989; edtorial adv. bd. Jour. Pension Planning and Compliance. Mem. ABA (employee benefits com.), N.Y. State Bar Assn. (employee benefits com.), Assn. of Bar of City of N.Y. Home: Oyster Bay N.Y.

KRAYBILL, PAUL NISSLEY, religious official; b. Bainbridge, Pa., June 7, 1925; s. John Rutt and Esther (Nissley) K.; m. Jean Kulp Metz, Dec. 22, 1951; children: Mary Jean, Dale Edward, Linda Sue, Carol Ann, Karen Louise. BA, Eastern Mennonite Coll., 1955. Asst. sec. Eastern Mennonite Bd. Missions and Charities, Salunga, Pa., 1953-58; overseas sec., gen. sec. Eastern Mennonite Bd. Missions and Charities, 1958-70, exec. sec., study commn. on ch. orgn., 1970-71; gen. sec. Mennonite Ch. Gen. Bd., Rosemont, Ill., 1971-77; exec. sec. Mennonite World Conf., 1990-92; pres. Mennonite Health Assn., 1990-92; mem., bd. dirs. Mennonite Christian Leadership Found., Landisville, Pa., 1980-92; sec. Council Mission Bd. Secs., Rosemont, Ill., 1962-74; mem. Presidium Mennonite World Conf., 1967-73; pres. Mennonite Housing Aid, Inc., Lombard, Ill., 1975-81; ordained to ministry, 1981; Mem. exec. com., vice chmn. and trustee Am. Leprosy Missions, Bloomfield, N.J., 1967-80; pres. Tamarack Retirement Residences, Inc., 1985-91. Author: Change and the Church, 1970; Editor: Called to be Sent, 1964, Mennonite World Handbook, 1978. Named Alumnus of the Yr. Eastern Mennonite Coll., 1971. Mem. Am. Soc. Missiology. Home: Goshen Ind. Died Mar. 30, 1993; buried Violett Cemetary, Goshen, I.N.

KREAMER, JOHN HARRISON, lawyer; b. Down Kans., Sept. 12, 1922; s. John Dean and Catheri (Harrison) K.; m. Marion Jane Enggas, July 28, 19 (dec. Feb. 1993); children: Jane Kreamer Meyer, An Kreamer Andersen. A.B., U. Kans., 1946; J.D Harvard U., 1949. Bar: Mo. 1949. Mng. partner Ga & Tucker (and predecessor firms), Kansas City, 1959-9 bd. dirs. Parmelee Industries, Commerce Bank, Coop Transp. Co. Pres., bd. dirs. Mid-Am. Coalition Health Care, 1979-83; bd. dirs., pres. Pub. TV 19, In 1973-78; bd. dirs. Starlight Theater Assn., Mo. Ar Coun., 1975-80, Mid-Am. Arts Alliance, 1978-9 chmn., dir., trustee Midwest Rsch. Inst., 1975-92; chm The Civic Coun., 1982-84; trustee Kansas City Pu Schs. Retirement System, 1979-92, The Menning Found.; mem. oversight com. Nat. Renewable Ener Lab. Served to 1st lt., 83d inf. div., AUS, 1942-45 Decorated Purple Heart, Bronze Star.; named M Kansas City, 1983. Mem. Greater Kansas City C. of (dir. 1964-68, 72-75, v.p. 1964-68), U. Kans. Mem Assn. (pres. 1965-66), Lawyers Assn. K.C. (pres. 196 65), Internat., Am. bar assns., World Assn. Lawye Beta Theta Pi, Pi Sigma Alpha. Clubs: University (pr 1963), Kansas City Country (dir. 1968-70), River Home: Kansas City Mo. Died May 28, 1992.

KREHBIEL, JOHN H., electronics company executiv b. 1906. With Molex, Inc., Lisle, Ill., chmn. bd. dir 1957—. Home: Lisle Ill. Died Nov. 12, 1994.

KRESS, PAUL FREDERICK, political science ed cator; b. Stoughton, Wis., Sept. 10, 1935; s. Frederi Raymond and Mabel Idelia (Paulson) K.; m. Charlo Louise Belshe, Aug. 17, 1959 (dec. Sept. 1988). B.S., Wis.-Madison, 1956, M.S., 1958; Ph.D., U. Cal Berkeley, 1964. Asst. prof. polit. sci. Northwestern U Evanston, Ill., 1964-70; asso. prof. polit. sci. U. N.C Chapel Hill, 1970-75; prof. U. N.C., 1975-82; vis. as prof. U. Hawaii, summer 1967; cons. Naval Resear Lab., San Diego, 1974-75; apptd. guardian ad lit N.C. Ct., 1992-93. Author: Social Science and the Id of Process: The Ambiguous Legacy of Arthur F. Be tley, 1970; mem. editorial bd. Jour. Politics, 1971-7 Social Sci. Research Council fellow, 1962-63. Hom Chapel Hill N.C. Died Mar. 17, 1993.

KRESS, RALPH HERMAN, manufacturing compa executive; b. Lawrence, Mass., July 10, 1904; s. Edwa and Sadie (Welsh) K.; m. Edna Llewelyn Sheridan, Se 9, 1929; 1 son, Edward Sheridan. Student mech. eng ing. and applied math., Lowell Inst., M.I.T., 1937-3 42. Salesman Dodge Truck, Lawrence, 1922-34; sa mgr. Chevrolet Truck Sales, Lawrence, 1934-39; en GM Chevrolet and Fleet div., Detroit, Boston, Was ington, 1939-43; exec. v.p. Dart Truck Co., Kansas Ci Mo., 1950-55; mgr. truck div. Letourneau Westingho Corp., Peoria, Ill., 1955-62; mgr. truck devel. Caterpil Tractor Co., Peoria, 1962-69; exec. v.p. Kress Cor Brimfield, Ill., 1969-95. Contbr. articles to profl. jour Served to maj. U.S. Army, 1943-46. Decorated Legi of Merit. Fellow Soc. Automotive Engrs. (G. Edw Burks Lecture award 1975); mem. Assn. U.S. Army, Mining Assn., Western Mining Assn. Republic Christian Scientist. Club: Rotary. Home: Peoria Died June 28, 1995.

KRETCHMER, NORMAN, obstetrics, pediatrics, n trition educator; b. N.Y.C., Jan. 20, 1923; s. Eman and Sue (Gross) K.; married, 1942; children: Pam Sue, Paul Jay, Steven David. BS, Cornell U., 1944; M U. Minn., 1945, PhD, 1947; MD, SUNY, 1952; D (hon.), Med. Coll. Ohio, Toledo, 1975; doctorat hono causa, U. Bern, Switzerland, 1978. Diplomate Am. B Pediatrics. Asst. physiol. chemistry U. Minn., Mp 1944-47, jr. scientist, 1945-47; asst. prof. biochemis and pathology Coll. Medicine. U. Vt., Burlington, 194 48; res. assoc. pathology L.I. Coll. Med. SUNY, 19 52; Commonwealth fellow medicine, intern Montefi Hosp., N.Y.C., 1952-53; asst. prof. biochemistry a pediatrics Med. Coll. Cornell U., Ithaca, N.Y., 1953- from asst. prof. to assoc. prof. pediatrics, 1956-59; fr prof. to Harold K. Faber prof. Sch. Med. Stanford U Calif., 1959-74, exec. head dept., 1959-69; prof. nutrit U. Calif., Berkeley, 1981-95, chmn. dept. nutritio scis., 1983-88; prof. obstetrics and pediatrics U. Ca San Francisco, 1981-94. Editor-in-chief: Am. Jour. Clin. Nutrition. Fellow Am. Inst. Nutrition. Ho Berkeley Calif. Died Dec. 20, 1995.

KRICK, IRVING PARKHURST, meteorologist; b. S Francisco, Dec. 20, 1906; s. H. I. and Mabel (Royal) m. Jane Clark, May 23, 1930; 1 dau., Marllynn; Marie Spiro, Nov. 18, 1946; 1 son, Irving Parkhu II. BA, U. Calif., 1928; MS, Cal. Inst. Tech., 19 PhD, Calif. Inst. Tech., 1934. Asst. mgr. radio s KTAB, 1928-29; meteorologist, 1930-96; became me staff Calif. Inst. Tech., 1933, asst. prof. meteorolo 1935-38, assoc. prof., prof. and head dept., 1938- organizer, pres. Am. Inst. Aerological Rsch. and Wa Resources Devel. Corp., 1950; pres. Irving P. Krick A socs., Inc., Irving P. Krick, Inc., Tex., Irving P. Kri Assocs. Can. Ltd.; chmn. emeritus, sr. cons. strate Weather Svc: Krick Ctr. Weather R & D, Palm Sprin Calif.; established meteorology dept. Am. Air Lin Inc., 1935, established Internat. Meteorol. Cons. Svc 1946, mng. dir.; cons. in field, 1935-36; mem. sci. ad group Von Kármán Army Air Force, 1945-46. Pian in concert and radio work, 1929-30; Co-author: Sun, S and Sky, 1954; Writer numerous articles on weather analysis, weather modification and forecasting and its application to agrl. and bus. industries. Served as lt. Coast Arty. Corps U.S. Army, 1928-36; commd. ensign USNR, 1938; maj., then lt. col. USAAF, 1943; Weather Directorate, Weather Central Div. unit comdr. of Long Range Forecast Unit A 1942-43; dep. dir. weather sect. U.S. Strategic Air Forces Europe, 1944; chief weather information sect. SHAEF 1945. Decorated Legion of Merit, Bronze Star with Oak leaf cluster U.S.; Croix de Guerre France; recipient Distinguished Service award Jr. C. of C.; chosen one of 10 outstanding men under age 35 by U.S. Jr. C. of C. Fellow AIAA (assoc.), Royal Soc. Arts; mem. AAAS (patron), Royal Meteorol. Soc., Am. Meteorol. Soc., Am. Geophys. Union (supporting mem.), Sigma Xi (supporting mem.). Republican. Home: Pasadena Calif. Died June 20, 1996.

KRIM, ARTHUR B., motion picture company executive, lawyer; b. N.Y.C., Apr. 4, 1910; s. Morris and Rose (Ocko) K.; m. Mathilde Galland, Dec. 7, 1958; 1 child, Daphna. B.A., Columbia U., N.Y.C., 1930, J.D., 1932, LL.D. (hon.), 1982. Bar: N.Y. 1933. With Phillips, Nizer, Benjamin, Krim & Ballon, N.Y.C., 1932-94, sr. ptnr., 1935-78, of counsel, 1978-94; pres. Eagle Lion Films, N.Y.C., 1946-49; chmn. United Artists Corp., N.Y.C., 1951-78; chmn. Orion Pictures Corp., N.Y.C., 1978-94, named founder chmn., chmn. exec. com., 1991; dir. Occidental Petroleum Corp., Los Angeles, Cities Service Corp., Tulsa, Iowa Beef Corp., Iowa City. Editor in chief Columbia Law Rev., 1931-32. Spl. cons. to Pres. U.S., 1968-69; mem. Pres.'s Gen. Adv. Com. Arms Control, 1977-80; chmn. Democratic Nat. Fin. Com., 1966-68, Dem. Adv. Council Elected Ofcls., 1973-76; bd. dirs. Weizmann Inst. Sci., 1948-94, UN Assn., 1961-94, Lyndon Baines Johnson Found., 1969-94, John F. Kennedy Library Found., 1964-94, Arms Control Assn., 1985-94; chmn. bd. trustee Columbia U., 1977-82, chmn. emeritus, 1982-94. Served to lt. col. U.S. Army, 1942-45. Decorated Cavaliere Ufficiale Della award Republic of Italy, Chevalier dans l'Ordre Nat. de la legion d'Honneur (France); recipient Jean Hersholt Humanitarian award Acad. Motion Picture Arts and Scis., 1975. Home: New York N.Y. Died Sept. 21, 1994.

KRIPKE, HOMER, law educator; b. 1912. A.B., 1931; J.D., U. Mich., 1933. Bar: Ohio 1933, Ill. 1934, N.Y. 1945, N.J. 1961. Asst. soliitor SEC, 1939-44; asst. gen. counsel C.I.T. Fin. Corp., 1944-60; practice law, 1933-38, 60-64; gen. counsel Allied Concord Fin. Corp., 1964-66; prof. NYU Sch. Law, 1966-80, U. San Diego, 1981-95; assoc. reporter Rev. Com. on Article 9 of Uniform Comml. Code, 1967-71; mem. Adv. Commn. on Corp. Disclosure, SEC, 1976-77; cons. Am. Law Inst. Fed. Securities Code, 1971-78; mem. Permanent Editorial Bd. for UCC. Mem. Am. Law Inst., Nat. Bankruptcy Conf., Order of Coif. Author: Materials on Consumer Credit, 1970; (with Fiflis and Foster) Accounting for Business Lawyers, 2d edit., 1977, 3d edit., 1985; SEC and Corporate Disclosure: Regulation in Search of a Purpose, 1979; past mem. editorial bd. Mich. Law Rev. Died Jan. 26, 1995. Home: San Diego Calif.

KRITSICK, STEPHEN MARK, veterinarian; b. Cambridge, Mass., Nov. 2, 1951; s. Leo William and Harriet Elizabeth (Stock) K. BS with high honors, Mich. State U., 1973, DVM with high honors, 1974. Intern Angell Meml. Animal Hosp., Boston, 1974-75; assoc. veterinarian Chabot Vet. Hosp., Lexington, Mass., 1975-78; sr. staff clinician ASPCA/Henry Bergh Meml. Hosp., N.Y.C., 1978-79; dir. emergency services The Animal Med. Ctr., N.Y.C., 1979-82; assoc. veterinarian Park East Animal Hosp., N.Y.C., 1982-84; sr. staff clinician ASPCA/Henry Bergh Hosp., N.Y.C., 1984-86; staff clinician Bide-A-Wee Home Assn., N.Y.C., 1986-90; staff vet. Humane Soc. U.S., Washington, 1990-94; veterinarian for Romper Room Show, Sta. WOR-TV, N.Y.C., 1978-87; feature contbr. with People and Pets, Cable News Network, Atlanta, 1980-84; animal sci. editor Good Morning Am., ABC-TV, N.Y.C., 1987-89; host PBS Series The Gentle Doctor: Vet. Medicine, series II, III, and IV, Sta. WEDU-TV, Animal Talk, Independent broadcasters network, Clearwater, Fla. Author: Creature Comforts: The Adventures of a City Vet, 1983, Dr. Kritsick's Tender Loving Cat Care, 1986. Mem. AVMA, AFTRA, SAG, Am. Animal Hosp. Assn., N.Y. State Vet. Med. Soc. Democrat. Home: Hudson N.Y. Died Jan. 16, 1994.

KRIZ, VILEM FRANCIS, photographer, educator; b. Prague, Czechoslovakia, Oct. 4, 1921; came to U.S., 1952; s. Vaclav and Marie (Skruzna) K.; m. Jarmila Veronica Vesela, Nov. 29, 1945; children: Gabriel, Dominica Ursula. Student photography under prof. Jaromir Funke, Josef Ehm and Frantisek Drtikol, State Acad. Graphical Arts, Prague, 1940-46; student, Ecole Cinematographique et Photographique, Paris, 1947. Tchr. photography and art various Calif. colls. including, Holy Names Coll., Oakland, 1964-74, various Calif. colls. including, U. Calif.-Berkeley, 1969-73, various Calif. colls. including; Mills. Coll., Oakland, 1970-74; prof. photography Calif. Coll. Arts and Crafts, Oakland, 1974-91; lectr. in field. Exhibitor photographs, U.S.A., Europe, Japan, 1940—; represented in permanent collections Met. Mus. Art, N.Y.C., Mus. Modern Art, N.Y.C., Internat. Mus. Photography, George Eastman House, Rochester, N.Y., Mus. Fine Arts, Boston, Cin. Art Mus., Mus. Fine Arts, Dallas, Santa Barbara Mus. Art, Calif., San Francisco Mus. Art, Colección XSABA, San Francisco, Oakland Art Mus., New Orleans Mus. Art, Cabinet des Estampes de la Bibliothèque Nationale, Paris, Mus. Dekorativního Umení, Praque; author: Everlasting Beauty, 1939, In Another Time, 1940, They Come Alive Again, 1942, Conversation, Une Invitation au Dialogue, 1963, Kriz: Surrealism and Symbolism, 1971, Sirague City, 1975, Séance, 1979, Vilem Kriz: Photographs, 1979, Gallery Manes, Prague, Czechoslovakia, 1989, retrospective exhbn. Mus. Visual Arts, Prague, 1992. Recipient award of honor Arts Commn. of San Francisco, 1986. Mem. Holy Name Coll. French Honor Soc., Pi Delta Phi. Home: San Francisco Calif. Died Dec. 26, 1994; buried Na Zelene Lisce Cemetery, Prague.

KROL, JOHN CARDINAL, retired archbishop; b. Cleve., Oct. 26, 1910; s. John and Anna (Pietruszka) K. Student, St. Mary's Sem., Cleve., 1937; J.C.B., Gregorian U., Rome, 1939, J.C.L., 1940; J.C.D., Cath. U. Am., 1942; Ph.D., La Salle Coll., 1961; LL.D., John Carroll U., 1955, St. Joseph U., 1961, St. John U., N.Y., 1964, Coll. Steubenville, 1967, Lycoming Meth. Coll., 1966, Temple U., 1964, Bellarmine-Ursuline Coll., 1968, Drexel U., 1970; D.S.T., Villanova U., 1961; L.H.D., Alliance Coll., 1967, Coll. Chestnut Hill (Pa.), 1975, Holy Family Coll., 1977; D.D., Susquehanna U., 1970; D.Theology, U. Lublin (Poland); HHD, Wheeling Coll., 1984. Priest Roman Catholic Ch., 1937, pvt. chamberlain, 1945, domestic prelate, 1951; parish asst., 1937-38; prof. Diocesan Sem.; also chaplain Jennings Home for Aged, 1942-43; vice chancellor Cleve. Diocese, 1943-51, chancellor of diocese, 1951-53, promoter of justice, 1951-53; consecrated bishop, 1953, auxiliary bishop to bishop of Cleve., also vicar gen. Diocese of Cleve., 1953-61; archbishop of Phila., 1961-88; apptd. chmn. bd. trustees The Papal Found., 1988-96; elevated to Sacred Coll. of Cardinals, 1967; undersec. II Vatican Council, 1962-65; mem. Pontifical Commn. Communications Media, 1964-69; chmn. Nat. Cath. Office for Radio and TV, 1963-64, Nat. Cath. Office for Motion Pictures, Cath. Communications Found., 1965-70, Pa. Cath. Conf., 1961-96; v.p. Nat. Conf. Cath. Bishops, 1966-71, pres., 1971-74; vice chmn. U.S. Cath. Conf., 1966-71, pres., 1971-74; mem. adminstrv. bd. and com. Nat. Conf. Cath. Bishops/U.S. Cath. Conf., 1983-86; mem. Pontifical Commn. for Mass Media Communications, 1964-69, Sacred Congregation for Evangelization of Nations, 1967-72, Sacred Congregation for Oriental Ch., 1967-96, Sacred Congregation for Doctrine of Faith, 1973-96; mem. 15 Mem. Council of Cardinals to study and counsel on Vatican finances, 1981; mem. Prefecture of Econ. Affairs of Holy See, 1982; pro.-pres. Extraordinary Synod of Bishops, Rome, 1985. Mem. Pres.'s Nat. Citizens Com. Community Relations; chmn. bd. govs., host 41st Internat. Eucharistic Congress, Phila., 1976; trustee Cath. U. Am., Washington, 1961-71, Nat. Shrine of Immaculate Conception, Cath. League for Religious Assistance to Poland; pres. Center for Applied Research in Apostolate, 1967-70; vice chmn. Com. for Yr. of Bible, 1983; mem. nat. adv. com. Deborah Hosp. Found., 1983; mem. President's Adv. Council for Pvt. Sector Initiatives, 1983-85; mem. council trustees Freedoms Found. at Valley Forge, 1985. Decorated comdr. of cross Order of Merit, Italy; Nat. Order Republic of Chad; recipient gold medal Paderewski Found., 1961; Nat. Human Relations award NCCJ, 1968; Father Sourin award Cath. Philopatrian Inst., 1967; John Wesley Ecumenical award Old St. George's Meth. Ch., 1967; Phila. Freedom medal, 1978; 1st ann. award Angelicum Soc. Am., 1985; Barry award Am. Cath. Hist. Soc., 1985; Copernicus award for advocation of peace throughout world, 1985; Legion of Honor gold medal Chapel of Four Chaplains, 1986; Person of Yr. award Congregation Beth Chaim, Feasterville, Pa., Person the Yr. award Congregation Beth Chaim, Feasterville, Pa., 1985, Shield of Blessed Gregory X Crusader, Nat. Assn. Holy Name Soc., 1986, Bob Hope 5-Star Civilian award Valley Forge Mil. Acad. and Jr. Coll., 1986, Immaculata award Immaculata Coll., 1987. Mem. Canon Law Soc. Am. (pres. 1948-49), Order Sons of Italy (hon.). Home: Philadelphia Pa. Died Mar. 3, 1996.

KROLL, ERNEST, author, editor; b. N.Y.C., Dec. 23, 1914; s. Herman and Nellie (Maas) K.; m. Margaret McHugh, Sept. 24, 1942; 1 child, Dennis. BA, Columbia U., 1936; spl. student, Harvard U., 1941-42. Market researcher Vick Chem. Co., N.Y.C., 1937-38; asst. editor McClure Newspaper Syndicate, N.Y.C., 1938; editor Bettmann Archive, N.Y.C., 1939, Fairchild Publs., N.Y.C., 1940; publicist T.J. Maloney, Inc., N.Y.C., 1940-41; Japanese affairs specialist Dept. State, Washington, 1946-71. Author: (poetry) Cape Horn and Other Poems, 1952 (N.Y. Times 100 best books listing), The Pauses of the Eye, 1955, Fifty Fraxioms, 1973, 15 Fraxioms, 1978, Tattoo Parlor & Other Fraxioms, 1982; editor: (prose) Marianne Moore at The Dial Commissions an Article on the Movies, 1990, Six Letters to An Apprentice, 1992. Served as lt. USN, 1941-45. Two lines from poem "Washington, D.C." in granite floor of Freedom Plaza 13 1/2th St. and Pa. Ave. N.W., Washington, selected by Pa. Ave. Devel. Corp., 1980. Democrat. Home: Washington D.C. Died Apr. 23, 1993; interred Washington, D.C.

KRONE, HELMUT, consultant, former advertising executive; b. N.Y.C., July 16, 1925; s. Otto and Emilie (Lohr) K.; m. Irene Beckmann, Nov. 14, 1970; 1 dau., Kathryn Maria; children by previous marriage: Peter, Lisa, Eric, Mark. Student graphic journalism with, Alexi Brodovitch at New Sch. Social Research. With Doyle Dane Bernbach, Inc., N.Y.C., 1954-69, 72-88, sr. v.p., dir., spl. projects, 1966-69, exec. v.p. creative dir., from 1972; pvt. cons. N.Y.C.; partner Case and Krone, Inc., N.Y.C., 1969-72. Works included in Am. Inst. Graphic Arts 50 Best Advertisements; rep. in: book The 100 Best Advertisements, 1959; created Volkswagen and Avis campaigns. Served with USNR, 1943-46, PTO. Recipient 12 Gold medals N.Y. Art Dirs. Club; elected to Art Dirs. Hall of Fame, 1979, Creative Hall of Fame, 1984. Mem. Am. Inst. Graphic Arts (dir.), Dirs. Guild Am. Home: New York N.Y. Died Apr. 12, 1996.

KROPP, ARTHUR JOHN, public interest organization executive; b. L.I., N.Y., July 30, 1957; s. Arthur John Sr. and Belle Carol (Laning) K. BA, Coll. Wooster, 1979. Asst. dir. PAC, corp. fundraising Rep. Nat. Com., Washington, 1979-82; polit. dir. NSPE, Washington, 1982-84; mem. dir. People for the Am. Way, Washington, 1984-85, v.p., 1986-87, pres., 1987-95; cons. Liberal Party of Can., 1986. Democrat. Lutheran. Home: Washington D.C. Died June 12, 1995.

KRUMM, DANIEL JOHN, manufacturing company executive; b. Sioux City, Iowa, Oct. 15, 1926; s. Walter A. and Anna K. (Helmke) K.; m. Ann L. Klingner, Feb. 28, 1953; children: David Jonathan, Timothy John. B.A. in Commerce, U. Iowa, 1950; postgrad., U. Mich., 1955; D.B.A. (hon.), Westmar Coll., Le Mars, Iowa, 1981; D. Comml. Sci. (hon.), Luther Coll., Decorah, Iowa, 1983. With Globe Office Furniture Co., Mpls., 1950-52; with Maytag Co., Newton, Iowa, 1952-86, v.p., 1970-71, exec. v.p., 1971-72, pres., treas., 1972-74, chief exec. officer, 1974-86; pres., chief exec. officer Maytag Co. Ltd., Toronto, Ont., Can., 1970-93; chmn., chief exec. officer Maytag Corp., Newton, 1986-93; bd. dirs. Centel Corp., Chgo., Snap-On-Tools Corp., Kenosha, Prin. Fin. Group, Des Moines. Mem. bd. of visitors U. Iowa Coll. Bus. Adminstrn.; mem. steering com. for Iowa Endowment 2000 campaign; past chmn. Iowa Natural Heritage Found.; bd. govs. Iowa Coll. Found.; chmn. bd. dirs. Grand View Coll., Des Moines; bd. dirs. Des Moines Symphony Assn., U. Iowa Found., Vocat. Rehab. Workshop for Handicapped Citizens of Jasper County, Iowa, NAM; vice chmn. Iowa Venture Capital Fund, Iowa Bus. Council; mem. com. for econ. devel. Iowa Peace Inst.; trustee FINE Edn. Research Found., 1987-93. Served with USNR, 1944-46. Recipient Oscar C. Schmidt Iowa Bus. Leadership award, 1983; Disting. Achievement award U. Iowa Alumni Assn; named Iowa Bus. Leader of the Yr., 1986. Mem. Am. Mktg. Assn. (past pres. Iowa), Elec. Mfrs. Club, Newton C. of C. (community service award 1980), Maytag Mgmt. Club. Republican. Lutheran. Club: Newton Country. Home: Newton Iowa Died July 1993.

KRUMM, JOHN MCGILL, bishop; b. South Bend, Ind., Mar. 15, 1913; s. William F. and Harriett Vincent (McGill) K. A.A., Pasadena Jr. Coll., 1933; A.B., U. Calif., 1935; B.D., Va. Theol. Sem., 1938, D.D. (hon.), 1974; Ph.D., Yale U., 1948; S.T.D. (hon.), Kenyon Coll., Gambier, Ohio, 1962; D.D. (hon.), Berkeley Div. Sch., Gen. Theol. Sem., 1975; L.H.D. (hon.), Hebrew Union Coll., Cin. Ordained to ministry Episcopal Ch., 1938; vicar Episc. chs., Compton, Lynwood and Hawthorne, Calif., 1938-41; asst. rector St. Paul's Ch., New Haven, 1941-43; rector Ch. of St. Matthew, San Mateo, Calif., 1943-48; dean St. Paul's Cathedral, Los Angeles, 1948-52; chaplain Columbia U., 1952-65; rector Ch. of Ascension, N.Y.C., 1965-71; bishop of So. Ohio, Episc. Ch., 1971-80; suffragan bishop in Europe Paris, 1980-83; assisting bishop Los Angeles, from 1983, St. Paul's Ch., Tustin, Calif., from 1983; vis. lectr. N.T., Berkeley Div. Sch., New Haven, 1942-53; vis. lectr. ch. history Va. Theol. Sem., Alexandria, 1942; instr. Prospect Hill Sch., New Haven, 1942-43; instr. religion U. So. Calif., 1950-52; chmn. clergy div. Univ. Religious Conf., L.A.; pres. San Mateo-Burlingame (Calif.) Coun. Chs., 1947-48, Ch. Fedn. L.A., 1951-52; chmn. nat. coun. Panel of Ams., 1952-61; interim pastor St. James' Ch., N.Y.C., 1990-91; interim bishop in Europe, Paris, 1992; interim rector Trinity Ch., Boston, 1992-93. Author: (with J.A. Pike) Roadblocks to Faith, 1953, Modern Heresies, 1961, The Art of Being a Sinner, 1967, Why Choose the Episcopal Church, 1974, (with others) Denver Crossroads, 1979, Letters from Lambeth, 1988, Flowing Like A River, 1989, The Offensive Cross, 1992. Trustee Mt. Holyoke Coll., 1962-72, Bexley Hall of Colgate-Rochester, Kenyon Coll., Children's Hosp., Cin., 1971-80; chmn. Canterbury Irvine Found., U. Calif., Irvine, 1984-92. Democrat. Clubs: Century Assn. (N.Y.C.); University (Cin.). Home: Tustin Calif. Deceased.

KRUSEN, HENRY STANLEY, investment banker; b. East Orange, N.J., Jan. 13, 1907; s. Henry Addis and Sallie (Scarborough) K.; m. Elizabeth Geary Hoopes, Oct. 24, 1941; 1 dau., Sallie (Mrs. Albert E. Riester). A.B., Cornell U., 1928; postgrad., Sch. Bus., N.Y. U., 1930-52. With Nat. City Co., N.Y.C., 1928-34, Harriman, Ripley & Co., Inc., N.Y.C., 1934-42; with Shearson, Hammill & Co., Inc., 1946-70, sr. v.p., 1964-65, pres., 1966-70; also dir.; chmn. bd. Shearson,

Hammill Mgmt. Co., 1972-73; cons. Shearson Hayden Stone & Co., Inc., 1974-95; former bd. dirs. Wheeling Pitt. Steel Corp., Pitts. Founder Nat. Young Republicans, 1930; chmn. East Orange Rep. City Com., 1939-41; vice chmn. Essex County Rep. Com., 1940-41; Bd. dirs. emeritus, past v.p. Beekman Downtown Hosp., N.Y.C.; trustee emeritus, past chmn. finance com. Union Coll., Cranford, N.J.; past trustee, treas., chmn. finance com. Overlook Hosp., Summit. Served to comdr. USNR, 1943-45. Decorated Legion of Merit. Mem. Ekwanok Country Club (Manchester, Vt.), Phi Kappa Psi. Died Dec. 5, 1995.

KUBINSKI, HENRY ANTHONY, physician, researcher, educator; b. Warsaw, Poland, Jan. 15, 1933; came to U.S.; s. Roman Jan and Ludwika (Helwich) K.; m. Zofia Opara, Mar. 8, 1959; children: Eva, Margaret, Richard. M.D., Univ. Sch. Medicine, Warsaw, Poland, 1955. Rsch. assoc., dept. microbiology Sch. Medicine, Warsaw, Poland, 1954-60; rsch. assoc., instr. Stifung zur Erforschung d. Spinalen Kinderlahmung u.d. Multiplen Sklerose (Heinrich-Pette-Institut), Hamburg, Fed. Republic Germany, 1961-64; rsch. assoc. McArdle Lab. for Cancer Rsch., Madison, Wis., 1964; from asst. to full prof. dept. neurosurgery U. Wis. Sch. Medicine, Madison, 1965-92. Contbr. numerous articles to med. jours. Mem. AAAS, Am. Assn. for Cancer Research, Am. Soc. Microbiology, Am. Soc. Biol. Chemists, Am. Soc. Neurochemistry, Biophys. Soc., N.Y. Acad. Scis., Soc. for Neurosci. Home: Madison Wis. Died Sept. 11, 1992; interred Madison, W.I.

KUDRYK, OLEG, librarian; b. Rohatyn, Ukraine, Dec. 14, 1912; came to U.S., 1949, naturalized, 1954; s. Theodosius and Olga (Spolitakevich) K.; m. Sophie H. Dydynski, Feb. 5, 1944. Diploma, Conservatory Music, Lviv, 1934; LL.M., U. Lviv, 1937, M.A. in Econ. Sci., 1938; postgrad., U. Vienna, 1945-46; M.A. in L.S., U. Mich., 1960; Ph.D. in Polit. Sci., Ukranian Free U., Munich, 1975. Mgr., legal advisor Coop. Agrl. Soc., Chodoriv, Ukraine, 1938-39; mgr. Import-Export Corp., Cracow, Poland, 1940-44; tchr. Comml. Sch., Ulm, Germany, 1946; adminstr. UNRRA and Internat. Refugee Orgn., Stuttgart, Germany, 1947-49; asst. treas., mgr. Self-Reliance Fed. Credit Union, Detroit, 1953-60; rep., cons. Prudential Ins. Co., Detroit, 1955-60; catalog librarian Ind. U., Bloomington, 1960-63, head order librarian, 1963-70, head acquisitions librarian, 1971-82, spl. projects librarian, asst. to assoc. dean, 1982—; lectr. Ukrainian Free U., 1975—; guest lectr. Ind. U. Sch. Library and Info. Sci., 1965—; mem. exec. bd. Olzhych Research Found., 1985—. Contbr. articles to profl. jours.; coordinating editor: Rohatyn, 1989. Grantee Ind. U. Office Research and Advanced Studies Internat. Programs, 1972. Mem. AAUP (chpt. treas., exec. bd. 1976—), ALA, Assn. Coll. Rsch. Librs., Am. Econ. Assn., Am. Acad. Polit. and Social Scis., Ukranian Libr. Assn. Am. (v.p. 1972-75, exec. bd. 1975—), Ukranian Free Acad. Arts and Scis., Shevchenko Sci. Soc., Rohatyn Soc. (pres. cen. com. 1991—). Home: Bloomington Ind. Died Oct. 18, 1994.

KUECHLE, RICHARD THEODORE, mathematics educator; b. Columbus, Ohio, Dec. 9, 1930; s. Theodore Friedrich and Josephine Elizabeth (Koerner) K.; m. Judith Ann Hula, Aug. 16, 1958; children: Jill Evelyn, Scott Richard, Andrea Lynn. BS summa cum laude, Ohio State U., 1952, MA, 1956; MS in Math., U. Mich., 1964; postgrad., U. Colo.; San Jose State U., 1962-63; 76, 78. Math. tchr. and asst. basketball coach Shaker Heights (Ohio) High Sch., 1956-58; math. and sci. tchr. and basketball coach Am. Sch., Berlin, Federal Republic of Germany, 1958-59; math. instr. Heidelberg Coll., Tiffin, Ohio, 1959-62; math. prof. Foothill Coll., Los Altos Hills, Calif., from 1964. Author: Trigonometry: A New Approach, 1984. Lt. USAF, 1953-55. Recipient NSF Acad. Year award, U. Colo. 1962-63, U. Mich. 1963-64. Mem. Nat. Coun. Tchrs. of Math., Calif. Math. Coun. Community Colls. Home: Los Altos Calif. Deceased.

KUEHL, HAL C., retired banker; b. Davenport, Iowa, Mar. 21, 1923; s. Donald J. and Martha A. (Sierk) K.; m. Joyce M. Helms, May 20, 1950; children: Cynthia Ann, David Charles. BBA, U. Wis., 1947, MBA, 1954; postgrad., Grad. Sch. Banking, 1953. CPA, Wis. V.p. Firstar Corp., Milw., 1968-71, exec. v.p., 1971-77, pres., chief adminstrv. officer, 1977-78, pres., chief exec. officer, 1978-86, chmn., chief exec. officer, 1986-88, also bd. dirs.; bd. dirs. First Wis. Nat. Bank, First Wis. Trust Co., Ameritech, Venture Capital Fund, Inc. Trustee Kohler Trust for Arts and Edn. With USNR, 1943-45. Mem. Milw. Club, Bent Pine Club, Milw. Country Club (bd. dirs.), Navy League U.S., Sigma Chi. Episcopalian. Home: Milwaukee Wis. Died July 24, 1995.

KUHN, LUCILLE ROSS, retired naval officer; b. Washington, July 19, 1927; d. Lilburn Joseph and Flora Lee (Perry) K.; A.A. with distinction, George Washington U., 1959, B.A., 1960. Ins. clk. Southwestern Life Ins. Co., Richmond, Va., 1945-48; joined U.S. Navy, 1949, advanced through grades to capt., 1975; woman officer rep. 2d Navy Recruiting Area, Washington, 1963-65; U.S. Naval Security Group, Washington, 1965-68; dir. mil. personnel 12th Naval Dist., San Francisco, 1968-70; mem. staff Office Asst. Sec. Def. for Legis. Affairs, Washington, 1971-74; dir. Officer Candidate Sch., Newport, 1975-77; dir. pay/personnel adminstrv. support system Bur. Naval Personnel, Washington, 1977-79; comdg. officer Recruit Tng. Command, Orlando, Fla., 1979-81; dep. comdr. Navy Recruiting Command, Washington, 1981-84. Aide de camp to Va. govs., 1960-95. Decorated Legion of Merit with gold star, Meritorious Service medal with gold star, Nat. Def. Service medal with bronze star. Mem. Naval Hist. Found., Psi Chi. Died Sept. 22, 1995. Home: Richmond Va.

KUHN, MARGARET (MAGGIE KUHN), organization executive; b. Buffalo, 1905; d. Samuel Frederick and Minnie Louise (Kooman) K. BA, Case-Western Res. U., 1926; hon. degree, Swarthmore Coll., Simmons Coll., Albright Coll., U. Pa., Beaver Coll., U. Mass., 1988, Case Western Res. U., 1989, No. Ill. U., 1990. Formerly with YWCA, Cleve., Phila.; Gen. Alliance Unitarian Women, Boston; later with United Presbn. Ch. U.S.A., N.Y.C.; editor, writer for ch. mag. Social Progress; alt. observer for Presbyns. at UN; ret., 1970; a founder Gray Panthers, Phila., 1971; nat. convener; cons. nat. task force on women United Presbyn. Ch., past 3d v.p. health, edn. and welfare assn.; lectr.; mem. nat. adv. bd. Hospice, Inc.; adv. TV series Over Easy; former mem. Fed. Jud. Nominating Com. Pa. Author: Get Out There and Do Something about Injustice, 1972, Maggie Kuhn on Aging, 1977. Recipient 1st ann. award for justice and human devel. Witherspoon Soc., 1974, Disting. Service award in consumer advocacy Am. Speech and Hearing Assn., 1975, Freedom award Women's Scholarship Assn. Roosevelt U., 1976, ann. award Phila. Soc. Clin. Psychologists, 1976, Peaceseeker award United Presbyn. Peace Fellowship, 1977, Humanist of Yr. award Am. Humanist Assn., 1978. Home: Philadelphia Pa. Died Apr. 22, 1995.

KUHN, THOMAS SAMUEL, history of science educator; b. Cin., July 18, 1922; s. Samuel Louise and Minette (Stroock) K.; m. Kathryn Louise Muhs, Nov. 27, 1948 (div. Sept. 1978); children: Sarah, Elizabeth, Nathaniel; m. Jehane Robin Burns, Oct. 26, 1982. BS summa cum laude in Physics, Harvard U., 1943, MS, 1946, PhD, 1949; LLD, U. Notre Dame, 1973; DHL (hon.), Rider Coll., 1978, Bucknell U., 1979, Linkoping U., Sweden, 1980. With radio research lab. Office Sci. Research and Devel., 1943-45; jr. fellow Harvard U. Soc. Fellows, Cambridge, Mass., 1948-51; asst. prof. gen. edn. and history sci. Harvard U., Cambridge, 1951-56; prof. history sci. U. Calif. at Berkeley, 1961-64; prof. history sci. Princeton (N.J.) U., 1964-68, M. Taylor Pyne prof. history sci., 1968-79; prof. philosophy and history sci. MIT, Cambridge, 1979-83, Laurance S. Rockefeller prof. philosophy, 1983-96; lectr. Lowell (Mass.) Inst., 1951; dir. project sources History Quantum Physics, 1961-64; mem. Inst. Advanced Study, 1972-79. Author: The Copernican Revolution: Planetary Astronomy in the Development of Western Thought, 1957, The Structure of Scientific Revolution, 1962, (with others) Sources for History of Quantum Physics: An Inventory and Report, 1967, The Essential Tension, 1977, Black-Body Theory and the Quantum Discontinuity, 1894-1912, 1978; bd. editors: Dictionary Scietific Biography, 1964-80. Bd. dirs. Social Sci. Research Council, 1964-66. Recipient Howard T. Behrman award Princeton U., 1977, John Desmond Bernal award 4S Soc., 1983, Guggenheim fellowship, 1954-55. Mem. NAS, History Sci. Soc. (George Sarton medal 1982, coun. 1953-68, pres. 1968-70), Am. Acad. Arts and Scis., Am. Philos. Soc., Am. Philos. Assn., Am. Hist. Soc., AAAS, Leopoldina Acad., Philosophy of Sci. Assn. (pres. 1988-96), Acad. Internat. d'Histoire Sci., Phi Beta Kappa, Sigma Xi. Home: Cambridge Mass. Died June 17, 1996.

KUJAWSKI, MARY H., museum director; b. Kofu, Japan, Jan. 12, 1949; d. Stanley G. and Dottie Setsuko (Hagihara) K.; m. Allen F. Roberts, Mar. 29, 1986; 1 child, Seth Michael; 1 stepchild, Avery. BFA in Art History, U. Ill., 1971, MEd, 1972, MA in Art History, 1976. Curatorial and ednl. asst. Krannert Mus. Art-U. Ill., Urbana, 1975-77; lectr. Art Inst. Chgo., 1977-81; lectr. art history U. Mich., Ann Arbor, 1981-88; assoc. chair practice program, asst. dir. and curator of edn. Mus. Art U. Mich., Ann Arbor, 1981-88; dir., curator collections Mus. Art U. Iowa, Iowa City, 1988-90; cons. Nat. Museums of Benin, summer 1987. Author-editor: (catalogues) Margaret Watson Parker, 1982, Earth Magicians, 1985, From Seed Time To Harvest, 1987. Adv. com. UN-USA/Iowa, Iowa City, 1988; slide bank com. Iowa Arts Council, 1988—. Recipient Exhbn. Materials award Mich. Council for the Arts, 1984, School Programs award Mich. Council of Humanities, 1986, 87, 88; grantee Nat. Endowment Arts, 1982. Mem. Am. Assn. Mus., Arts Council of African Studies Assn. (sec.-treas. 1986-88), Coll. Art Assn. (chmn. art on campus com. 1988-90). Home: Iowa City Iowa Died Sept. 2, 1990.

KULL, DOVE MONTGOMERY, former social welfare administrator; b. Perry, Okla.; d. Andrew J. and Polly Ann (McCurry) Montgomery; m. Alexander E. Kull, June 26, 1929; 1 son, John E. BA, U. Okla., 1922, MSW, 1940; MA, Columbia U., 1927; HHD (hon.), U. Alaska, 1988. Social worker United Providence Assn., Oklahoma City, 1921; head English dept. Fairfax (Okla.) High Sch., 1923-26; English instr. ext. div. U. Okla., Norman, 1927-33; prof. Oklahoma City U., 1933-35; social work intake dir. Fed. Emergency Relief Adminstrn., Okla., 1934-35; asst. state dir. intake and cert., asst. dir. employment div. Works Project Adminstrn., Okla., 1935-41, prin. social worker, 1941; head social svc. Campbell-Galbraith Clinic and Coyne Campbell Sanatorium, Okla., 1941; child welfare worker, asst. state supr., state cons. on foster care and adoption Okla. State Dept. Pub. Welfare, 1941-53; sec. community council Okla. Child and Family Welfare Div., 1953-54; welfare dir. Salvation Army, Okla., 1954-58; child welfare worker Anchorage, 1959-61; state child welfare supr. Juneau, Alaska, 1961-67; clin. social worker USPHS Hosp., Kotzebue, Alaska, 1967-69; exec. di. Episc. Ch. Holy Trinity, 1st United Meth. Ch., Juneau, 1969-76. Active sr. housing com. Commr. Community and Regional Affairs, Juneau, 1976; chmn. Sr. Citizens Adv. Bd., Juneau, 1977; del. Internat. Conf. ERA, Houston, 1977; commr. Older Alaska Commn., 1981-89. Named Woman of Yr. Soroptimist Club, 1981, Bus. and Profl. Women's Club, 1981, Sr. Intern Congressman Don Young, 1988; recipient Disting. Svc. award Pioneer and Capital U.S. Jaycees, 1973, Commendation for Svcs. to Elderly Pres. Ronald Reagan, 1982, Citation for Outstanding Contrbns. to Humanity Alaska State Legis., 1987, Andres award Am. Assn. Retired Persons, 1988; Shelter for Victims of Violence named in her honor Aiding Women from Abuse and Rape Emergencies, 1986, Alaskan Sch. Social Work Scholarship (named in her honor) U. Alaska, Anchorage, 1987. Mem. Nat. Assn. Social Workers, Knife and Fork Dinner Club, Blue Pencil, Chi Omega, Theta Sigma Phi, Delta Psi Kappa. Congregationalist. Home: Juneau Ark.

KULWICKI, ALAN, professional stock car driver. 3rd in NASCAR money leaders, 1992. Home: Daytona Beach Fla. Died Apr. 1, 1993.

KUNAYEV, DINMOHAMMED AKHMEDOVICH, Soviet politician and mining engineer; b. Jan. 12, 1912. Ed. Moscow Inst. of Non-Ferrous Metals. Former dir. Kounrad Mine, Kazakh S.S.R.; vice chmn. Council of Ministers Kazakh SSR, 1942-52, chmn., 1955-60, 62-64; 1st sec. Kazakh CP, 1960-62, 1964-86; cand. mem. Politburo Central Com. of CPSU, 1966-71, mem., 1971-87; dep. to Supreme Soviet of the USSR, 1950— and Supreme Soviet of the Kazakh SSR; mem. Presidium of Supreme Soviet of USSR, 1962-93; mem. CPSU Central Com., 1956-87. Hero of Socialist Labour, Order of Lenin (7), Hammer and Sickle Gold Medal (2), Order of the October Revolution 1980, other decorations. Mem Acad. of Scis. of the Kazakh SSR. Died Aug. 22, 1993 Home: Kazakh Kazakhstan

KUNCEWICZOWA, MARIA, writer; b. Samara Russia, Oct. 30, 1897; d. Jozef and Adela Szczepanski m. Jerzy Kuncewicz, 1921; 1 son, Witold. Student Warsaw U., Poland, Jagiellonian U., Cracow, Poland U. Nancy, France. Prof. Polish literature U. Chgo. 1962-70. Books: Przymierze dzieckiem, Twar mezczyzny, Milosc Panienska, Dwa Ksiezyce, Dylizan Warszawski, Cudzoziemka, Dni Powszednie Panstw Kowalskich, Miasto Heroda, Klucze, Zmow Nieobecnych, 1950, Lesnik, 1954, W Domu i w Polsce 1958, Odkrycie Patusanu, 1959, Gaj oliwny, 1961, Do Kichote i nianki, 1966, Tristan, 1967; Fantomy, 197 Natura, 1975, Fantasia Alla Polacca, 1981, Przezrocza 1985. Recipient Literary prize of Warsaw, 1937 Golden Laurel of Polish Acad. Letters, 1937, Pietrza prize, 1966, State prize 1st Class, 1974, Medal of Meri Kosciuszko Found. N.Y., 1972, Medal of Merit Sociét Europeé ne de Culture Warsaw, 1982. Mem. English Am.-Polish PEN Club, Centre Writers in Exi (founder). Home: Kazimieirz Dolny Poland Deceased.

KUNSTLER, WILLIAM MOSES, lawyer, educato lecturer, author; b. N.Y.C., July 7, 1919; s. Monro Bradford and Frances (Mandelbaum) K.; m. Lott Rosenberger, Jan. 14, 1943 (div. Oct. 1975); childre Karin F. Goldman, Jane B. Drazek; m. Margar L.cohen, Oct. 6, 1975; children: Sarah Cohen-Kunstle Emily Cohen-Kunstler. BA, Yale U., 1941; LL Columbia U., 1948. Bar: N.Y. bar 1948, D.C. bar 195 Exec. trainee R.H. Macy & Co., N.Y.C., 1948-49; lec English Columbia U., 1946-50; ptnr. Kunstler, Kunstle Hyman and Goldberg (and predecessor firm), N.Y.C 1949-72, Kunstler & Kuby, N.Y.C., 1992-95; asso prof. law N.Y. Law Sch., 1950-92, Pace U., 1951-6 lectr. New Sch., 1966-68, 80-81; sr. fellow Notre Dan U., 1971. Author: Our Pleasant Vices, 1941, The La of Accidents, 1954, First Degree, 1960, Beyond Reasonable Doubt?, 1961, The Case for Courage, 196 ...And Justice for All, 1963, The Minister and the Ch Singer, 1964, Deep in My Heart, 1966, The Hall-Mi Murder Case, 1980, Trials and Tribulations, 1985, M Life as a Radical Lawyer, 1994, Hints and Allegatior 1994; contbr. book revs. and articles. V.p., bd. di Center for Constl. Rights. Served to maj. AUS, 1941-4 PTO. Decorated Bronze Star medal; recipient Pre award N.Y. State Bar Assn., 1957, Civil Rights awar 1963, 1st award Ohio Radio-Television Inst., 196 Thurgood Marshall Practioner award N.Y. Ass Criminal Def. Lawyers, 1994. Mem. Assn. Bar Ci N.Y., ACLU (dir. 1964-70, nat. council 1968-95, b dirs. nat. emergency civil liberties com. 1968-95), P Beta Kappa, Phi Delta Phi. Home: New York N. Died September 4, 1995.

KUPERSMITH, A. HARRY, lawyer, real estate and financial executive; b. Newark, June 13, 1925; s. David and Bessie (Rubinstein) K.; m. Cynthia Skolnick, Dec. 24, 1947; children: Farrell Preston, Mark Jeffrey, Linda Ellen. Cert., Drury Coll., 1943; B.S. cum laude, NYU, 1948; LL.B., Bklyn. Law Sch., 1954, J.S.D., 1956, J.D., 1968. Bar: N.Y. 1954, U.S. Dist. Ct. (so. dist.) N.Y. 1956. With Kupersmith & Kupersmith (legal, financial, tax and real estate cons.), N.Y.C., 1948-88; practice as atty., tax, real estate and fin. cons. N.Y.C., 1954-88; partner Ramapo Manor Nursing Center, Suffern, N.Y., 1957-75, McQuire-Holiday Motel, 1962-70; pres., chmn. Verson Prodns., Inc., N.Y.C., 1962-67, various real estate instns. and housing devels., 1956-88, Exec. Fin. Planning Corp., N.Y.C., 1956-75; exec. v.p., sec.-treas., dir., mem. exec. com. Del Labs., Inc. (and subs.), N.Y.C., 1962-65; chmn. Computer Systems Medicine and Edn. (and subs.), 1969-71; dir. Ram Group Inc. 1974; gen. counsel Hyfin Credit Union, 1979-86; pres., chmn. Am. Inst. Econ. Growth, N.Y.C., 1965-88; gen. counsel Council Jewish Orgns. in Civil Service, 1973-76; counsel Civil Service-Independent's Party, 1971-84; lectr. Columbia U., 1966-69; lectr., instr. on law, taxes, corporate finance, mergers, acquisitions, housing, real estate, tax shelters; mem. Columbia U. adv. com. nursing home costs for N.Y. State, 1966. Author: An Economic Study of American System, 1956, Tax Havens, 1959, Corporate Finance and Taxes, 1959, Tax Treaties of United States, 1960, United States Industry and Executives Abroad, 1960, Executive Compensation Constructive Receipt, 1961, Corporate Finance and Taxes Defined, 1963, Considerations in Mergers and Acquisitions, 1965, Break Even Techniques, 1965, Men and Their Money, 1966, Nursing Home Industry Review, 1968, Is Nursing Home Business for You?, 1968, Major Health Crisis, 1968, Equity and Venture Capital, 1970, Private Placements, 1970, Capital Growth, 1971, Tax and Investment Shelters, 1971, Investments-Rental Housing vs. Condominiums, 1972, Purchase and Sale of Businesses-Checklist, 1972, Real Estate Partnersips-Government and the Private Investor, 1973, Tax Sheltered Investments, 1973; also articles.; fin. and legal columnist: Drug Trade News, Drug News Weekly, 1965-68. Trustee Martin Revson Trusts, various charitable founds. Served with USAAF, 1943-45. Recipient Wisdom award, 1969. Mem. ABA, Alpha Epsilon Pi, Psi Chi Omega, Beta Gamma Sigma. Home: Bal Harbour Fla. Died Feb. 21, 1993.

KURLAND, PHILIP B., lawyer, educator; b. N.Y.C., Oct. 22, 1921; s. Archibald H. and Estelle (Polstein) K.; m. Mary Jane Krensky, May 29, 1954 (dec. 1992); children: Julie Rebecca, Martha Jennifer, Ellen Sarah; m. Alice Hoag Bator, Feb. 12, 1993. A.B., U. Pa., 1942; LL.B., Harvard U., 1944; LL.D., U. Notre Dame, 1977, U. Detroit, 1982. Bar: N.Y. 1945, Ill. 1972, U.S. Supreme Ct. 1947. Law clk. to judge Jerome N. Frank, 1944-45, Supreme Ct. Justice Felix Frankfurter, 1945-46; atty. Dept. Justice, 1946-47; mem. firm Kurland & Wolfson, N.Y.C., 1947-50; asst. prof. law Northwestern U. Law Sch., 1950-53; mem. faculty U. Chgo., 1953-96, prof. law, 1956-96, William R. Kenan, Jr. prof., 1973-76, William R. Kenan, Jr. Disting. Svc. prof., 1976-92, William R. Kenan, Jr. Disting. Svc. prof. emeritus, 1992-96; counsel Rothschild, Barry & Myers, Chgo., 1972-96; cons. Econ. Stblzn. Agy., 1951-52; chief cons., subcom. on separation of powers U.S. Senate Judiciary Com., 1967-77; cons. U.S. Dept. Justice, 1976; mem. Oliver Wendell Holmes Devise Com., 1975-83. Author, editor: Jurisdiction of Supreme Court of U.S., 1950, Mr. Justice, 1964, Religion and the Law, 1962, Frankfurter: Of Law and Life, 1965, The Supreme Court and the Constitution, 1965, The Great Charter, 1965, Moore's Manual, 1964-70, Moore's Federal Practice, 1964-70, Felix Frankfurter on the Supreme Court, 1970, Mr. Justice Frankfurter and the Constitution, 1971, Landmark Briefs and Arguments of the Supreme Court of the United States, 215 vols., 1975-95, Watergate and the Constitution, 1978, Cablespeech, 1983, The Founders' Constitution, 5 vols., 1987; editor: Supreme Ct. Rev., 1960-89. Trustee Deer Creek Found. of St. Louis, 1983-96. Guggenheim fellow, 1950-51, 54-55. Fellow Am. Acad. Arts and Scis.; mem. ABA, Chgo. Bar Assn. Am. Law Inst., New Brougham Soc. Jewish. Club: Quadrangle (U. Chgo.); U. Pa. (N.Y.); Cliffdweller (Chgo.). Home: Chicago Ill. Died Apr. 16, 1996.

KUSCH, POLYKARP, physicist, educator; b. Blankenburg, Germany, Jan. 26, 1911; came to U.S., 1912, naturalized, 1923; s. John Matthias and Henrietta (van der Haas) K.; m. Edith Starr McRoberts, Aug. 12, 1935 (dec. 1959); children: Kathryn, Judith, Sara; m. Betty Jane Pezzoni, 1960; children: Diana, Maria. B.S., Case Inst. Tech., 1931, D.Sc., 1956; M.S., U. Ill., 1933, Ph.D., 1936, D.Sc. (hon.), 1961; D.Sc. (hon.), Ohio State U., 1959, Colby Coll., 1961, Gustavus Adolphus Coll., St. Peter, Minn., 1962, Yeshiva U., 1976, Coll. of Incarnate Word, 1980, Columbia U., 1983. Engaged as teaching asst. U. Ill., 1931-36; research asst. U. Minn., 1936-37; instr. Columbia U., 1937-41, assoc. prof. physics, 1946-49, prof., 1949-72, chmn. dept. physics, 1949-52, 60-63, acad. v.p. and provost, 1969-72; engr. Westinghouse, 1941-42; research assoc. Columbia U., 1942-44; mem. tech. staff Bell Telephone Labs., 1944-46; prof. physics U. Tex.-Dallas, 1972-93, Eugene McDermott prof., 1974-80, Regental prof., 1980-82, Regental prof. emeritus, 1982-93; rsch. in atomic and molecular beams and optical molecular spectroscopy.

Recipient Nobel prize in physics, 1955, Ill. Achievement award U. Ill., 1975; Fellow; Center for Advanced Study in Behavioral Sciences, 1964-65. Fellow Am. Phys. Soc., AAAS; mem. Am. Acad. Arts and Scis., Am. Philos. Soc., Nat. Acad. Scis. Democrat. Home: Richardson Tex. Died Mar. 20, 1993.

KUSHELOFF, DAVID LEON, journalist; b. N.Y.C., Sept. 23, 1917; s. William and Mollie (Yachnin) K.; m. Roslyn Schlaffer, Sept. 28, 1941; children: Judith Ann, Stephen Gordon, Marjorie Alice. B.S.S., CCNY, 1938. With Washington Times-Herald, 1945-54; with Phila. Bull., 1956-81, book editor, 1977-81. Served with USAAF, 1942-45. Home: Wilmington Del. Died Oct.15, 1995.

KUTNER, LUIS, lawyer. Sole practice law, Chgo. Died Mar. 1, 1993. Home: Chicago Ill.

KUZNETS, SIMON, economist; b. Kharkov, Russia, Apr. 30, 1901; s. Abraham and Pauline (Friedman) K.; m. Edith H. Handler, June 5, 1929; children: Paul, Judith. B.S., Columbia, 1923, M.A., 1924, Ph.D., 1926, D.H.L. (hon.), 1954; D.Sc. (hon.), Princeton, 1951; D.Sc. in Econs. (hon.), U. Pa., 1956, LL.D., 1976; D.Sc., Harvard, 1959; Ph.D. (hon.), Hebrew U. Jerusalem, 1965; LL.D., U. N.H., 1972; D.H.L., Brandeis U., 1975. Social Sci. Research Council Fellow, 1925-27; mem. staff Nat. Bur. Econ. Research, 1927-61; asst. prof. econ. statistics U. Pa., 1930-34, assoc. prof., 1934-35, prof., 1936-54; prof. polit. economy Johns Hopkins, 1954-60; Frank W. Taussig research prof. econs. Harvard, 1958-59, prof. econs., 1960-71; Asso. dir. Bur. Planning and Statistics, WPB, 1942-44. Author: Cyclical Fluctuations, 1926, Secular Movements in Production and Prices, 1930, Seasonal Variations in Industry and Trade, 1933, National Income and Capital Formation, 1938, Commodity Flow and Capital Formation, 1938, National Income, 1941, National Product in Wartime, 1945, National Income: A Summary of Findings, 1946, National Product since 1869, 1946, Shares of Upper Income Groups in Income and Savings, 1953, Six Lectures on the Economic Growth, 1959, Capital in the American Economy, 1961, Postwar Economic Growth, 1964, Economic Growth and Structure: Selected Essays, 1965, Modern Economic Growth, 1966, Economic Growth of Nations, 1971, Population, Capital, and Growth, 1973, Growth, Population, and Income Distribution, 1979; Contbr. articles to econ. jours. Recipient Nobel prize in econs., 1971. Fellow Royal Statis. Soc., Am. Statis. Assn. (pres. 1949), A.A.A.S., Econometric Soc., Brit. Acad. (corr.); mem. Am. Econ. Assn. (pres. 1954), Royal Acad. Scis. Sweden, Am. Philos. Soc., Internat. Statis. Inst., Am. Acad. Arts and Scis., U.S. Acad. Scis. Jewish. Home: Cambridge Mass.

LABOON, JOSEPH THADDEUS, gas company executive; b. Monroe, Ga., Nov. 7, 1920; married. B.S., Ga. Inst. Tech.; 1948; LL.B., Woodrow Wilson Coll. Law, 1952. With Atlanta Gas Light Co., 1939—, v.p., 1962-74, sr. v.p., 1972-76, pres., 1976-86, chief exec. officer, 1980—, chmn., 1986—, dir.; dir. Standard Fed. Savs. and Loan Assn., 1st Nat. Bank Atlanta. Served with USMCR, 1939-75.

LACHS, MANFRED, judge of International Court of Justice; b. Stanis, Poland, Apr. 21, 1914; s. Ignacy and Zofia (Hamerski) L.; m. Fin. Halina, July 31, 1946. LL.M., U. Cracow, Poland, 1936, LL.D., 1937; docteur, U. Nancy, France, 1939; D.Sc.Law, U. Moscow; LL.D., U. Budapest, 1967, Dr. jur. et sc. pd. (honoris causa); LL.D. (hon.), U. Algiers, U. Delhi, U. Nice, U. Bridgeport, U. Bucharest, U. Brussels, U. New Halifax, NYU, SUNY, U. Southampton, U. Sophia, Howard U., U. Vancouver, U. Helsinki, U. London, U. Cracow, U. Dalhousie, U. Vienna, U. Wash., U. Silesia. Prof. Acad. Polit. Scis., Warsaw, Poland, 1949-52; prof. internat. law U. Warsaw, 1952-93; Röling prof. U. Groningen, The Netherlands, 1990; legal adviser Polish Ministry Internat. Affairs, 1947-66, ambassador, 1960-66; judge Internat. Ct. of Justice, 1967-93, The Hague, Netherlands, pres., 1973-76; chmn. Olympic Arbital Tribunal; chmn. legal com. UN gen. assemblies, 1949, 51, 55, vice chmn., 1952; mem. Polish dels. UN Gen. Assemblies, 1946-52, 55-60, 62-66; rep. Poland UN Disarmament Com., 1962-65; rapporteur gen. colloque. Internat. Assn. Juridical Scis., UNESCO, Rome, Italy, 1948, Internat. Law Commn. UN, 1962; chmn. legal com. UN Peaceful Uses of Outer Space, 1962-66; lectr. throughout Europe and U.S. Author: War Crimes, 1945; The Geneva Agreements on Indochina, 1954; Multilateral Treaties, 1958: Polish-German Frontier, 1964; The Law of Outer Space, 1964; The Law of Outer Space-An Experience in Law-Making, 1972; Teachings and Teaching of International Law, 1977; The Teacher in International Law, 1982, 2d edit. 1986; The Development and General Trends of International Law of Our Time, 1984; contbr. over 130 articles in 13 langs. to profl. jours. Dir. Inst. Legal Sci., Polish Acad. Sci. 1961-67; mem. Permanent Ct. Arbitration, The Hague, 1956-93; mem. UN Internat. Civil Service Adv. Bd., 1959-66, UN Internat. Law Commn., 1962-66; adv. council Inst. Air and Space Law McGill U.; council Internat. Inst. Peace and Conflict Research. Recipient award for ednl. achievement Polish Ministry Higher Edn., 1956, award outstanding contbns. devel. rule of law outer space 1962, gold medal, 1966, world jurist

award, 1975, Wateler peace prize, Netherlands, 1976, Copernicus prize, 1984, Britannica award, 1987, 1st Class Prize for Sci. Achievements, Polish Acad. Sci., 1988, Merit medal U. Leyden, The Netherlands. Fellow UN Inst. for Tng. and Rsch. (hon., sr.), Inst. Social Studies, The Hague (hon.); mem. Comité d'Honneur GIPRI, Geneva, Acad. Moral Scis. of Bologna (corr.), Curator Hague Acad. Internat. Law (v.p.), Polish Acad. Scis., Inst. Internat. Law (v-p. 1986-88), Dutch Soc. Scis. (fgn. mem.), Institut de France (corr.), Internat. Acad. Astronautics (hon.), Mexican Acad. Internat. Law (hon.), Indian Soc. Internat. Law (hon.), Am. Soc. Internat. Law (hon.), Internat. Inst. Space Law (pres. 1990). Home: The Hague The Netherlands Died Jan. 14, 1993.

LACKEY, EDWIN K., archbishop. Archbishop Anglican Ch. Can., Ottawa, Ont. Deceased.

LACKEY, LAWRENCE BAILIS, JR., retired architect, urban designer; b. Santa Fe, Nov. 7, 1914; s. Lawrence Bailis and Mary (McFie) L.; children: Merryl, Stephen Byrne. Student in liberal arts, U. N.Mex., 1936; BS in Architecture, U. Mich., 1938; postgrad. (Acad. fellow in town planning; Cranbrook Acad. Art, 1939-41; grad. seminar on computer aids in urban design, M.I.T., 1969. Registered architect, Calif., Alaska. Designer Eliel and Eero Saarinen, Bloomfield Hills, Mich., 1940-41, Wurster, Bernardi & Emmons, San Francisco, 1946-48; architect Skidmore, Owings & Merrill, San Francisco, 1948-54, John Lord King (Architect), San Francisco, 1954-56, John Carl Warnecke & Assos., San Francisco, 1956-59; prin. Lawrence Lackey (Urban Design Cons.), San Francisco, 1959-63, Sasaki, Walker, Lackey & Assos., San Francisco, 1963-65, Lawrence Lackey & Assos., San Francisco and San Rafael, Calif., 1965-75, Lawrence Lackey (Architect), San Rafael, Calif., 1978-91; cons. architect U. Alaska, 1959-71; mem. faculty U. Mont., 1964-71. Designer: preliminary concept Golden Gateway Redevel, San Francisco, 1956, U. N.Mex. Campus Devel. Plan, 1960, U. Mont. Campus Devel. Plan, 1964, Okla. Health Center Devel. Plan, Oklahoma City, 1968, U. Alaska Campus Devel. Plan, 1968, Sci. Teaching Complex Design Concept at, U. Kans. Med. Center, 1970, Creekside Center Complex, San Rafael, 1979. Mem. coordinating com. for redevel. San Francisco C. of C., 1955-58, chmn. com. urban design, 1971. Served as officer USN, 1942-45. Fellow AIA (dir. No. Calif. chpt. 1962); mem. San Francisco Planning and Urban Renewal Assn. (dir., mem. exec. com. 1959-63), San Francisco Planning and Housing Assn. (pres. 1956-59). Home: Sonoma Calif. Died March 12, 1995.

LACY, PETER DEMPSEY, electrical engineer; b. Jacksonville, Fla., Dec. 6, 1920; s. Francis Peter and Nina Elizabeth (Wray) L.; m. Janice Marilyn Cowen, Aug. 5, 1979; children: Eamon, Bridget. B.S. in Elec. Engring. U. Fla., 1942; M.S., Stanford U., 1947, Ph.D. (Sperry fellow 1949), 1952. Rsch. asst. U. Fla., Gainesville, 1938-42; instr. U. Fla., 1942; rsch. asst. Stanford U., 1946-49; cons. Varian Assn., Palo Alto, Calif., 1949; projects leader research and devel. Hewlett-Packard, Palo Alto, 1950-60; founder, chmn. bd. emeritus Wiltron Co., Morgan Hill, Calif., 1960-88. Contbr. articles in field to profl. jours. Served with USN, 1942-46. Fellow IEEE; mem. AAAS, Am. Electronics Assn., Sigma Xi, Phi Kappa Phi. Home: Los Altos Calif. Died Dec. 7, 1992.

LAFFOON, CARTHRAE MERRETTE, management consultant; b. Wilkinsburg, Pa., Jan. 1, 1920; s. Carthrae Merrette and Kittie (Painter) L.; m. Helen Elizabeth Frisk, July 3, 1943; children: Judith Karin (Mrs. Wright), Catharine Elizabeth, Carthrae Merrette III (dec.), Barbara Louise. B.S., Mass. Inst. Tech., 1942. Jr. engr. rsch. lab. Westinghouse Electric Corp., Pitts., 1942-45; asst. project engr. aviation gas turbine div. Westinghouse Electric Corp., South Phila., 1945-47; asst. project engr. Ryan Aero. Co., San Diego, 1947-48; power plant group leader Ryan Aero. Co., 1948-49; jr. engr. San Diego Gas & Electric Co., 1950-53, asst. efficiency engr., 1953-58, asst. sta. chief, 1958-60, mech. engr., 1960-63, chief mech. engr., 1963, v.p. prodn., transmission, 1963-65, v.p. electric, 1965-70, sr. v.p., 1971-76; pres. C.M. Laffoon Cons., 1976-95; pres., dir. Geothermal Generation, Inc., 1976-87, chmn., bd. dirs., 1987-89. Elder Presbyn. Ch. Mem. ASME, Sigma Xi, Tau Beta Pi, Kiwanis. Republican. Home: El Cajon Calif. Died July 19, 1995; buried El Cajon Cemetary.

LA GUMA, JUSTIN ALEXANDER (ALEX LA GUMA), author, journalist; b. Cape Town, South Africa, Feb. 20, 1925; ed. Cape Tech. Sch., Cape Town, London Sch. Journalism. Mem. Nat. Exec. Coloured People's Congress, from 1955; banned from gatherings, under house arrest, confined in solitary, 1962-66, exiled, 1966; freelance writer, London, from 1966; mem. editorial bd. Afro-Asian Writers' Bur., London, from 1968; author: A Walk in the Night, 1962; And a Threefold Cord, 1965; The Stone Country, 1968; In the Fog of the Season's End, 1972; editor Apartheid (anthology), 1972; Time of the Butcherbird, 1978. Mem. Afro-Asian Writers' Assn. (sec.-gen. from 1975). Died Nov. 10, 1985; interred Havanah, Cuba. Home: London Eng.

LAING, RONALD DAVID, psychiatrist, author; b. Glasgow, Scotland, Oct. 7, 1927; m. Jutta; children: Adam, Natasha, Max. M.D., U. Glasgow, 1951. Intern, 1951; conscript psychiatrist Brit. Army, 1951-53; psychiatrist Glasgow Royal Med. Hosp.; tchr. dept. psychol. medicine U. Glasgow, 1953-56; clin. rsch. Tavistock Inst. Human Rels., London, 1956-62; dir. Langham Clinic, London, 1962-65; co-founder Phila. Assn. Kingsley Hall, London, 1964, chmn., 1964-81; speaker various colls. in, U.S., 1970—. Author: The Divided Self, 1960, The Self and Others, 1961, Sanity, Madness and the Family, 1964; (with David G. Cooper) Reason and Violence: A Decade of Sartre's Philosophy, 1950-60, 1964; (with others) Interpersonal Perception, 1966, The Politics of Experience, 1967, The Politics of the Family, 1969, rev. edit., 1971, Knots, 1970, Self and Others, 1970, The Facts of Life, 1976, Do You Love Me?, 1976, Conversations with Adam and Natasha, 1977, Sonnets, 1979, The Voice of Experience, 1982, Wisdom, Madness and Folly, 1985, Paroles D'Enfants, 1989. Home: Going Austria

LAMAR, THOMAS ALLEN, JR., lawyer; b. Rome, Ga., June 20, 1936; s. Thomas Allen and Sarah Eugenia (Bryan) L.; m. Isabelle Eley Collier, July 13, 1963; children: Thomas Allen III, Perrin Collier. BBA, Emory U., 1957, LLB, 1963. Assoc. atty. Sutherland, Asbill & Brennan, Atlanta, 1963-69, ptnr., 1969—. Bd. dirs. Atlanta Speech Sch., 1987—; trustee Ga. Conservancy, Atlanta, 1980-90; mem. class of '77 Leadership Atlanta, 1977; sr. warden All Saint Ch., Atlanta, 1979. Served to lt. j.g. USNR, 1957-60. Mem. ABA, State Bar Ga. (chmn. sect. corp. and banking law 1971-72), Atlanta Bar Assn., D.C. Bar, Lawyers Club Atlanta (pres. 1980-81), Piedmont Driving Club, Alpha Epsilon Upsilon, Beta Gamma Sigma, Kappa Alpha. Episcopalian. Home: Atlanta Ga.

LAMB, GEORGE A., retired university official; b. Pocatello, Idaho, Apr. 3, 1906; s. Luke F. and Mary (Burnell) L.; m. Mary Mellefont, June 25, 1932; children: Mary Anthia Lamb Dorenda, Rose Mary Lamb Malay, Jacqueline Lamb O'Donnell, George Joseph. A.B., U. Portland, 1929, LL.D., 1970; M.S. (Strathcona fellow 1931-32), Yale U., 1932; postgrad., U. Mich., 1932-33. Transp. economist Dept. Agr., 1930-31, 34; teaching fellow U. Mich., 1932-33; mineral economist NRA, 1934-36; transp. economist ICC, 1936-38; economist bituminous coal div. Dept. Interior, 1938-40, chief econs. br., 1940-43, asst. dir. Bur. Mines, 1944-46, dir. Office Coal Research, 1961-63; chief econs. and stats div. Solid Fuels Adminstrn. War, 1943-44; mgr. bus. surveys Pitts. Consol. Coal Co., 1946-61; dir. econ. studies Consol. Coal Co., Pitts., 1963-67; dir. law enforcement edn., dir. research adminstrn. U. Portland, 1967-88, ret., 1989; cons. Nat. Mediation Bd., 1941; mem. Am. Coal Mission to Gt. Britain, 1944; cons. sec. interior, 1950, OPS, 1951-52, cabinet energy study, 1954-56; mem. Am. Coal Team vis. Poland, 1957; U.S. del. ECA Coal Commn., 1959, 60. Contbr. articles to tech. publs. Mem. Am. Statis. Assn., Am. Econ. Assn., AIME, Tau Kappa Epsilon, Beta Gamma Sigma. Roman Catholic. Club: KC. Home: Vancouver Wash. Deceased.

LAMONT, BARBARA GIBSON, librarian; b. Huntington, Ind., Nov. 8, 1925; d. Herbert Donald and Edith (VanAntwerp) LaM. A.B., Coll. William and Mary, 1947; M.A., Radcliffe Coll., 1952; M.S. in L.S, Simmons Coll., 1954. With Harvard Library, 1951-64; head librarian Douglass Coll., Rutgers U., 1964-67; head librarian Vassar Coll., 1967-83, head librarian emeritus, 1983-95. Trustee Southeastern (N.Y.) Library Resources Council, 1967-73. Home: Lagrangeville N.Y. Died Oct. 25, 1995.

LAMONT, CORLISS, philosopher, educator, author; b. Englewood, N.J., Mar. 28, 1902; s. Thomas William and Florence Haskell (Corliss) L.; m. Margaret H. Irish, June 8, 1928 (div.); children: Margaret Hayes (Mrs. J. David Heap), Florence Parmelee (Mrs. Ralph Antonides), Hayes Corliss, Anne Sterling (Mrs. George Jafferis); m. Helen Boyden Lamb, 1962 (dec. July 1975); m. Beth Keehner, July 24, 1986. Grad., St. Bernard's Sch., 1916, Phillips Exeter Acad., 1920; A.B. magna cum laude, Harvard U., 1924; postgrad., New Coll., Oxford (Eng.) U., 1924-25; Ph.D., Columbia U., 1932. Instr. philosophy Columbia, 1928-32, New Sch. Social Rsch., 1940-42; lectr. intensive study contemporary Russian civilization Cornell U., 1943, Social Studies Workshop on Soviet Russia, Harvard Grad. Sch. Edn., 1944; lectr. Columbia Sch. Gen. Studies, 1947-59, Columbia seminar assoc., 1971-91. Editor: Man Answers Death: An Anthology of Poetry, rev. edit., 1952, Dialogue on John Dewey, 1959, Dialogue on George Santayana, 1959, A Humanist Symposium on Metaphysics, 1960, Albert Rhys Williams: In Memoriam, 1962, The Trial of Elizabeth Gurley Flynn by the American Civil Liberties Union, 1968, The Thomas Lamonts in America, 1971, (with Lansing Lamont) Letters of John Masefield to Florence Lamont, 1979, (with Lansing Lamont) Collected Poems of John Reed, 1985, The John Reed Centenary, 1988, Dear Corliss: Letters From Eminent Persons, 1990; author: Issues of Immortality, 1932, The Illusion of Immortality, 5th edit, 1990, You Might Like Socialism: A Way of Life for Modern Man, 1939, The Peoples of the Soviet Union, 1946, A Humanist Funeral Service, 1947, Humanism as a Philosophy, 1949, The Independent Mind, 1951, Soviet Civilization, 1952, Freedom Is As Freedom Does: Civil Liberties in America, 1956, rev. edit., 1990, The Philosophy of Humanism, 7th edit., 1990, Freedom of Choice Affirmed, 1967, A Humanist Wedding Service, 1970, Remembering John Masefield, rev. edit. 1991, Lover's Credo, 1983, Voice in the Wilderness: Collected Essays of Fifty Years, 1974, Yes to Life: Memoirs of Corliss Lamont, 1981, rev. edit., 1991, A Lifetime of Dissent, 1988, Basic Pamphlet Series, 1952—; co-author: syllabus Introduction to Contemporary Problems in U.S, 1929, Russia Day by Day, (with Margaret I. Lamont), 1933; Frequent contbr. to periodicals; speaker radio, TV; vice chmn.: Jour. Philosophy. Bd. dirs. ACLU, 1932-54; pres. Bill of Rights Fund, 1954-69; chmn. Nat. Emergency Civil Liberties Com., 1965—, Nat. Coun.Am.-Soviet Friendship, 1943-46; Candidate for U.S. Senate Am. Labor Party, N.Y., 1952, Independent-Socialist Party, 1958; v.p., mem. exec. bd. Poetry Soc. Am., 1971-74. Recipient of N.Y. City Tchrs. Union Ann. award, 1955, Gandhi Peace award, 1981, Ethics in Action award, 1984, John Phillips award Phillips Exeter Acad., 1986-87. Mem. AAAS, Acad. Polit. Sci., NAACP, Am. Humanist Assn. (pres. emeritus 1992—, John Dewey Humanist award 1972, Humanist of Yr. award 1977), Acad. Am. Poets, PEN, Am. Philos. Assn., UN Assn., Phi Beta Kappa. Clubs: Columbia Faculty (N.Y.C.), Harvard (N.Y.C.). Home: New York N.Y. Died April 26, 1995.

LAMY, PETER PAUL, gerontologist, educator; b. Breslau, Germany, Dec. 14, 1925; s. Rudolf and Luise (Bettinger) L.; m. Angela Pogorilich, Nov. 27, 1952; children: Rudolf, Margaret, Carl. BS in Pharmacy, Phila. Coll. Pharmacy and Sci., 1956, MS, 1958, PhD in Biopharmaceutics, 1964; DSc (honoris causa), Union U., Albany, N.Y., 1988. Instr. pharmacy Phila. Coll. Pharmacy and Sci., 1956-63; instr. pharmacology Woman's Hosp., Phila., 1960-62; asst. prof. pharmacy U. Md., 1963-67, assoc. prof., 1967-72, prof., 1972—, dir. instnl. pharmacy programs, 1968-82, co-dir. profl. experience program, 1970-80; mem. faculty dept. epidemiology and preventive medicine U. Md. Med. Sch., 1974-80; dir. Ctr. Study Pharmacy and Therapeutics for Elderly U. Md. (Med. Sch.), 1982—, prof. epidemiology and preventive medicine, 1985—, prof. family medicine, 1988—; dir. dept. instnl. pharmacy practice U. Md. Hosp., Balt., 1970-77; chmn. dept. pharmacy practice U. Md. Hosp., 1979-87; prof., asst. dean geriatrics U. Md. Sch. Pharmacy, 1987-91, Parke Davis chair in geriatric pharmacotherapy, 1991—; cons. Yager Drug Co., Balt., 1967-87, Levindale Hebrew Geriatic Ctr. and Hosp., Balt., 1972-82, VA Hosp., Balt., 1972-80, John L. Deaton Med. Ctr., 1972-82, VA Med. Ctr., Washington, 1975-86, Ft. Howard, Md., 1978-88, Perry Point, 1983-88; spl. advisor White House Conf. on Aging, 1980-81; mem. Nat. Aging Rsch. Panel, 1981; lectr. psychopharmacology Sch. Nursing, Cath. U. Am., 1973. Author: Prescribing for the Elderly, 1980; reviewer: Jour. Am. Pharm. Assn, 1968-78, Am. Jour. Hosp. Pharmacy, 1972-81, Jour. AMA, 1985—; instl. pharmacy editor: Md. Pharmacist, 1974-76; editor: Elder-Care News; mem. editorial bd.: Hosp. Pharmacy, 1968-79, Drug Intelligence and Clin. Pharmacy, 1978-80, Hosp. Formulary, 1978-79, Jour. Am. Geriatric. Soc., 1983-85, Geriatric Cons., 1982—, Cardiology World News, 1984—, Senior Patient, 1988-91, Welcome News of Hosp. Practice, 1988—; editor: Contemporary Pharmacy Practice, 1978-80; column editor: Geriatrics and Gerontology, Drug Intelligence and Clin. Pharmacy, 1980-86, Geriatrics and Pharmacology, Jour. Gerontol. Nursing, 1984-86; spl. editor Geriatric Drug Therapy, 1985-87; guest editor: Geriatric Clinics; contbr. articles to sci. jours. Vice pres. Catonsville (Md.) Elem. PTA, 1973-74, pres., 1974-75. Served with U.S. Army, 1948-51. Recipient awards Am. Soc. Cons. Pharmacists, Phila. Coll. Pharmacy and Sci., Assn. Gerontology in Higher Edn., 1991; Resolution of Merit, Md. State Senate, 1988. Fellow AAAS, Am. Coll. Apothecaries, Am. Coll. Clin. Pharmacology (chmn. task force on aging 1979-82), Am. Geriatric Soc., Gerontology Soc. Am.; mem. Am. Soc. Hosp. Pharmacists (award), Acad. Pharm. Sci., Am. Pharm. Assn. (Remington Honor medal 1988), Am. Soc. Clin. Pharmacology and Therapeutics, U. Md. Balt. Sch. Pharmacy Alumni (hon. pres.), Sigma Xi, Rho Chi. Home: Baltimore Md. Died Mar. 1994.

LANCASTER, BURT(ON), actor; b. N.Y.C., Nov. 2, 1913; s. James L.; m. Norma Anderson, Dec. 26, 1946 (div. 1969); children: James Steven, William Henry, Susan Elizabeth, Joanne Mari; m. Susan Scherer, Sept. 10, 1990; 1 stepchild, John Martin Scherer. Student, NYU. Formed acrobatic team Lang & Cravat (with Nick Cravat), 1932; performed circuses, carnivals, vaudeville, 1932-39, floor walker lingerie dept., Marshall Field & Co., Chgo., 1939, then salesman haberdashery dept. Appeared in play A Sound of Hunting, N.Y.C., 1945; films include The Killers, 1946, I Walk Alone, 1947, Desert Fury, 1947, Brute Force, Variety Girl, All My Sons, 1948, Sorry, Wrong Number, 1948, Kiss the Blood Off My Hands, 1948, Criss-Cross, 1949, Rope of Sand, 1949, Mister 880, 1950, Flame and the Arrow, 1950, Vengeance Valley, 1951, Jim Thorpe: All American, 1951, Ten Tall Men, 1951, (also co-prodr.) The Crimson Pirate, 1952, Come Back Little Sheba, 1953, South Sea Woman, 1953, From Here to Eternity, 1953, His Majesty O'Keefe, 1954, Apache, 1954, Vera Cruz, 1954, The Rose Tattoo, 1955, The Kentuckian (als dir.), 1954, Trapeze, 1956, The Rainmaker, 1957 Gunfight at OK Corral, 1957, Sweet Smell of Success 1957, (also co-prodr.) Run Silent, Run Deep, 1958 Separate Tables, 1958, The Devil's Disciple, 1959, Th Unforgiven, 1960, Elmer Gantry, 1960 (Acad. award a best actor), The Young Savages, 1961, Judgement a Nuremberg, 1961, Bird Man of Alcatraz, 1962 (Venic Film award for best actor), A Child is Waiting, 1963 The Leopard, 1963, The List of Adrian Messenge 1963, Seven Days in May, 1964, The Train, 1965, Th Hallelujah Trail, 1965, The Professionals, 1966, Th Swimmer, 1968, The Scalphunters, 1968, Castle Keep 1969, The Gypsy Moths, 1969, Airport, 1970, King: A Filmed Record...Montgomery to Memphis, 1969 Lawman, 1971, Valdez is Coming, 1969, Ulzana's Raid 1972, Executive Action, 1973, Scorpio, 1973, (als prodr., co-dir., co-screenwriter) The Midnight Man 1974, Conversation Piece, 1975, 1900, 1975, The Cas sandra Crossing, 1975, The Island of Dr. Moreau, 1976 uffalo Bill and The Indians, 1976, Twilight's Las Gleaming, 1977, 1900, 1977, Go Tell the Spartans, 1978 Zulu Dawn, 1978, Atlantic City, 1981, Cattle Annie an Little Britches, 1981, Local Hero, 1983, The Osterma Weekend, 1983, Fathers and Sons, 1985, Little Treasure 1985, Tough Guys, 1986, Suspect, 1987, Rocke Gibraltar, 1987, The Jeweller's Shop, 1987, Field c Dreams, 1987, Betrothed, 1988; TV mini series O Wings of Eagles, 1985; TV films: Moses the Lawgive 1975, Victory at Entebbe, 1976, Marco Polo, 1984 Scandal Sheet, 1984, Barnum, 1986, Sins of the Fathers 1989, The Phantom of the Opera, 1989, Voyage of Ter ror: The Achille Lauro Affair, 1989, Separate But Equal 1990. Served with spl. services div. Fifth Army AUS 1942-45. Home: Beverly Hills Calif. Died Oct. 20, 1994

LANCASTER, OTIS EWING, engineering educato consultant; b. Pleasant Hill, Mo., Jan. 28, 1909; s Hayden Guard and Ida May (Seaton) L.; m. Hildret Adele Herald, Dec. 5, 1942; children: Elaine Adel Hayden Ewing, Dale Burkham. BS, Central Mo. U Warrenburg, 1929; MA, Mo. U., Columbia, 1934; PhD Harvard U., Cambridge, 1937; aeronautical engr., Cali Inst. of Tech., Pasadena, 1945. Engr. Tchr. High Schs Oak Grove, Independence, Mo., 1929-33; instr. Harvar U., Cambridge, Mass., 1936-37; asst. prof. U. Md., Col lege Park, Md., 1939-42; rsch. div. Bur. Aeronautics Washington, 1945-54; statistician planning staff IRS Washington, 1954-55; dir. econs. and stats. U.S. Pos Office Dept., Washington, 1955-57; westinghouse pro for engring. edn. Pa. State U., University Park, 1957-7 assoc. dean Coll. Engring. Pa. State U., University Park Pa., 1967-74; chief math. and stats. Interstate Commerc Commn., Washington, 1976-80; cons. NASA, Wash ington, 1965-69, FAA, ICC. Co-author: Gas Turbin for Aircraft, 1955; author: Effective Teachng an Learning, 1974; editor: Jet Propulsion Engines, 1959. Served to capt. USN, from 1942. Recipient Meritoriou Civil Svc. award U.S. Navy, 1952. Mem. AIAA ASME, Am. Soc. for Engring. Edn. (pres. 1977-78 Disting. Svc. citation 1982). Home: State College Pa Died Nov. 17, 1992.

LANDAU, ELY, motion picture producer; b. N.Y.C Jan. 20, 1920; m. Edythe Rein, Mar. 13, 1959; children Neil Cary, Les Michael, Jon P., Tina R., Kathy. Ed high sch. Organizer Nat. Telefilm Assos., Inc., N.Y.C 1953; pres., chmn. bd. Nat. Telefilm Assos., Inc., 1953 61; created and formed Am. Film Theatre and El Landau Orgn., 1972. Producer with wife Edie Landau films Long Day's Journey into Night, 1962, The Pawn broker, 1964, The Fool Killer, A Face of War, 1968 The Madwoman of Chailliot, 1969, KING: A Filme Record— Montgomery to Memphis, 1970, The Icema Cometh, 1973, Butley, 1973, Lost in the Stars, 1974 Rhinoceros, 1974, The Homecoming, 1973, A Delicat Balance, 1973, Luther, 1974, Galileo, 1975, Man in th Glass Booth, 1975, In Celebration, 1975, The Gree Tycoon, 1977, Hopscotch, 1980, The Chosen, 1981 Beatlemania, 1981, Separate Tables, 1982, Mr. Halper and Mr. Johnson, 1983, The Holcroft Covenant, 1984. Served with USAAF, World War II. Recipient Georg Foster Peabody award for TV's The Play of the Week recipient Sidney Hillman Found. award, 1960, Sc Christian Leadership spl. Man of Year award, 1970 Image award NAACP, 1970. Home: Los Angeles Cali Died Nov. 5, 1993.

LANDAUER, JAY PAUL, computer informatio scientist; b. N.Y.C., Sept. 25, 1935; s. Ezekiel P. an Mary Annabel (Owings) L.; m. Lorraine Paulin Kopacki, Oct. 15, 1955; children: Stephen Lynda. BSEE, Newark Coll. Engring., 1965; M Com puter Info. Sci., N.J. Inst. Tech., 1984. Jr. engr. Elec tronic Assocs., Inc., Princeton, N.J., 1956-68; sr. eng Electronic Assocs., Inc., West Long Branch, N.J., 1968 83, chief system architect, 1983-90; simulation compute cons., 1990—. Author papers, book chapt. compute topics. Patentee Hydac Computer, 1962. Chmn. Lang tree Troup Boy Scouts Am., Hamilton Sq., N.J., 1966 67; pres. Woodmere Civic Assn., Eatontown, N.J., 1971 72. Mem. IEEE, Soc. for Computer Simulation (sr.). Republican. Lutheran. Home and Office: Brick N.J.

LANDON, SEALAND WHITNEY, lawyer; b Burlington, Vt., Mar. 27, 1896; s. Sealand Whitney an Helen (Weeks) L.; m. Isabelle Morris Miller, June 25 1924; children: Sealand Whitney III, Margot (Mrs. Pau

S. Visher), Richard Warren, Lisa (Mrs. John B. Hewett). B.S. cum laude, Princeton U., 1917; LL.B., Rutgers U., 1925, LL.M., 1926, J.D., 1974; L.H.D., Upsala U., 1977. Bar: N.Y. bar 1926. With Rockwood Sprinkler Co., Worcester, Mass., 1919-21; with Western Electric Co., N.Y.C., 1923-26; prof. law Rutgers U. (N.J. Law Sch.), 1925-35; asso. firm Slayton & Jackson, N.Y.C., 1926-27; mem. firm Hulbert, Heermance & Landon, 1927-31, Swiger, Scandrett Chambers & Landon, 1932-34; atty. AT&T, 1934-37, gen. atty. long lines dept., 1937-51, asst. v.p., asst. sec., 1951-52, sec., asst. to pres., 1952-60, v.p., sec., 1960-61; dir. Nat. Newark & Essex Bank (Midlantic Nat. Bank), Newark, 1962-69, emeritus, 1969-95; public gov. Am. Stock Exchange, 1962-68. Pres. Community Chest Oranges and Maplewood, N.J., 1942-44, treas., 1947-50; past chmn. nat. quota com., vice chmn. nat. budget com. Community Chests and Councils, N.Y., 1948-55; mem. planning bd. and zoning bd. adjustment, West Orange, 1931-54; chmn. bd. mgrs. Llewellyn Park, West Orange, 1937-45, trustee, 1957-95; bd. mem. to survey Dept. Immigration and Naturalization, 1933; asso. counsel Moreland Commn. to investigate guaranteed mortgage and title cos., N.Y. State, 1934; bd. govs. Orange Meml. Hosp., 1946-49; hon. trustee Hosp. Center, Orange, pres., 1950-53, chmn. bd., 1962-65; hon. trustee N.J. Symphony Orch., trustee, 1950-75, chmn. bd., 1960-74; past trustee YMCA of the Oranges; trustee Victoria Found., 1945-79, trustee emeritus, 1979-95, treas., 1950-79; trustee Turrell Fund, 1941-95, pres., 1961-77, chmn. bd., 1977-90; trustee Shelburne Mus., 1957-80, trustee emeritus, 1980-95; chmn. Princeton U. Fund, 1956-62; bd. dirs. Bordentown Mil. Inst., 1930-95, v.p., 1951-71, pres., 1934-51; trustee, v.p. Health Facilities Planning Council N.J., 1965-68; trustee Princeton U., 1958-62, Edison Birthplace Assn., 1967-88; trustee Hosp. Service Plan N.J. (Blue Cross), 1969-85, hon. trustee, 1985-95. Served as capt. CAC, U.S. Army, 1917-19. Recipient citation outstanding citizen of the Oranges and Maplewood N.J., 1953; Greensboro Vt. award, 1984; Outstanding Civic Leader award, Orange, Maplewood and West Essex, N.J., 1985. Mem. Am. Arbitration Assn. (dir. 1929-37, 41-72, chmn. exec. com. 1950-56), Am. Bar Assn., Am. Soc. Corp. Secs. (past v.p., dir.; past pres. N.Y. regional group), Phi Beta Kappa. Republican. Presbyterian. Home: Cannon Beach Oreg. Died Feb. 3, 1995.

LANDY, MAURICE, immunologist; b. Cleve., Mar. 8, 1913; s. Joseph and Rose (Eisenstein) L.; m. Reba Altman, June 1, 1947. A.B., Ohio State U., 1934, M.A., 1934, Ph.D., 1940. Chief biol. labs. SMA Corp., Cleve., 1936-42; chief dept. bacteriology Wyeth Inst., Phila., 1946-47; head typhoid research unit, chief dept. bacterial immunology Walter Reed Army Inst. Research, 1947-56; head immunology sect. Nat. Cancer Inst., 1956-62; chief lab. immunology Nat. Inst. Allergy and Infectious Diseases NIH, Bethesda, Md., 1962-67; chief allergy and immunology br. extramural program Nat. Inst. Allergy and Infectious Diseases NIH, 1967-72; staff adviser Schweizerisches Forschunginstitut, Davos, Switzerland, 1973-79; adviser, devel. biology lab. Salk Inst., La Jolla, Calif., 1985-93; sec. gen. 1st Internat. Congress of Immunology, Washington, 1971. Editor: (with Werner Braun) Bacterial Endotoxins, 1963, Immunological Tolerance, 1969, (with H. Sherwood Laurence) Mediators of Cellular Immunity, 1969, (with Richard T. Smith) Immune Surveillance, 1970, (with J.W. Uhr) Immunologic Intervention, 1971, (with H.O. McDevitt) Genetic Control of Immune Responsiveness, 1972, (with R.T. Smith) Immunobiology of the Tumor-Host Relationship, 1975, (with G. Cudkowicz) Natural Resistance Systems against Foreign Cells, Tumors, and Microbes, 1978, (with N.A. Mitchison) Manipulation of the Immune Response in Cancer, 1978, (with A. L. de Weck) Biochemical Characterization of Lymphokines, 1980, (with E. Skamene and P.A.L. Kongshavn) Genetic Control of Natural Resistance to Infection and Malignancy, 1980, (with Cohen and Oppenheim) Interleukins, Lymphokines and Cytokines, 1983, (with C. Sorg and A. Schimpl) Cellular and Molecular Biology of Lymphokines, 1985; founder: Jour. Cellular Immunology; founder Lymphokines: A Forum for Immunoregulatory Cell Products. Served to capt., San. Corps AUS, 1942-46. Recipient Superior Service award HEW, 1966, AAI award, 1972, Cytokine Internat. Workshops Rsch. award, 1990. Mem. Am. Acad. Microbiology, Am. Assn. Immunologists, Soc. Exptl. Biology and Medicine. Home: La Jolla Calif. Died Apr. 19, 1993.

LANG, FRANCIS HAROVER, lawyer; b. Manchester, Ohio, June 4, 1907; s. James Walter and Mary (Harover) L.; m. Rachel Boyce, Oct. 20, 1934; children: Mary Sue, Charles Boyce, James Richard. A.B., Ohio Wesleyan U., 1929; J.D., Ohio State U., 1932. Bar: Ohio 1932. Practice in East Liverpool, Ohio, 1932-42, 45-96; with War Dept., 1942-45; chmn. bd. First Fed. Savs. & Loan Assn., East Liverpool, 1959-82; former pres., bd. dirs. Walter Lang companies.; hon. bd. dirs. First Nat. Community Bank East Liverpool, Ohio. Past bd. dirs. YMCA, Mary Patterson Meml.; past pres. Columbiana council Boy Scouts Am. regional com., E. Central region; mem. at large Nat. council, 1968-96; bd. dirs. Bd. Global Ministries of United Methodist Ch., 1968-76. Mem. Ohio State Bar Assn., Columbiana County Bar Assn. (past pres.), East Liverpool C. of C. (past pres.), Rotary (past dist. gov.), Masons (33d degree). Methodist. Home: East Liverpool Ohio Died Jan. 12, 1996.

LANG, JENNINGS BENTLY, producer; b. N.Y.C., May 28, 1915; s. Harry and Lillian (Saul) L.; m. Monica Lewis, Jan. 1, 1956; children: Michael Anthony, Robert Bruce, Jennings Rockwell. B.S.S., M.S., St. John's U., 1934, J.D., 1937. Bar: N.Y. 1937. Mem. firm Seligsberg & Lewis, N.Y.C., 1937; agt. Jaffe Agy., 1939-40, partner, v.p., 1942; pres., 1948-50; v.p., head prodn. M.C.A. Television, Universal Television, 1950-69; v.p., producer motion pictures Universal Pictures, 1969-84. Films produced include: Coogan's Bluff, 1968, Winning, 1969, Tell Them Willie Boy is Here, 1970, The Beguiled, 1971, Play Misty for Me, 1971, Slaughterhouse Five, 1972, Charley Varrick, 1973, Breezy, 1973, Earthquake, 1973, Airport '75, 1974, The Front Page, 1974, The Great Waldo Pepper, 1975, The Eiger Sanction, 1975, Airport '77, 1977, House Calls, 1978, Airport '79/The Concorde, 1979, Little Miss Marker, 1979, The Nude Bomb, 1980, Sting II, 1982, Stick, 1983. Bd. dirs. ACLU; bd. dirs. So. Calif. Public Television. Mem. Acad. Motion Picture Arts and Scis., Television Acad. Arts and Scis. Democrat. Clubs: Racquet, Friars. Home: Los Angeles Calif. Died May 29, 1996.

LANGSDORF, ALEXANDER, JR., physicist; b. St. Louis, May 30, 1912; s. Alexander S. and Elsie (Hirsch) L.; m. Martyl S. Schweig, Dec. 31, 1941; children: Suzanne M., Alexandra. B.A., Washington U., St. Louis, 1932; Ph.D., M.I.T., 1937. NRC fellow U. Calif.-Berkeley, 1938; instr. Washington U., 1939-43; physicist Argonne (Ill.) Nat. Lab., 1943-77, sr. physicist, 1947-77; Mem. Dist. 211 High Sch. Bd., 1970-73. Assoc. editor Applied Physics Letters, 1978-91. Recipient Alumni award Washington U., 1958. Fellow Am. Phys. Soc. Home: Schaumburg Ill. Died May 24, 1996.

LANHAM, ELIZABETH, retired management educator; b. Santo, Tex., Mar. 10, 1912; s. James S. and Mina (Latimer) L. B.B.A., Tex. Tech U., 1934; M.B.A., U. Tex., Austin, 1939, Ph.D., 1950. Instr. N.Mex. State Coll., 1939-42; asst. prof. mgmt. U. Ariz., 1942-44; asst. dir. personnel State Farm Ins. Cos., Bloomington, Ill., 1944-47; prof. mgmt. U. Tex., Austin, 1947-78; chmn. dept. mgmt. U. Tex., 1971-76, prof. emeritus, 1978-94, cons. div. extension, 1978-94; cons. in field. Author: Job Evaluation, 1955, Spanish edit., 1962, Japanese edit., 1963, Administration of Wages and Salaries, 1963; author profl. monographs; contbr. articles, revs. to profl. jours. Mem. Sigma Iota Epsilon, Beta Gamma Sigma, Chi Omega. Episcopalian. Home: Austin Tex. Died June 14, 1994; interred Slaton, Tex.

LANNON, JOHN JOSEPH, energy holding company executive; b. Springfield, Ill., Apr. 8, 1937; s. Richard James and Anne (Malone) L.; m. Arlene Joan Mularski, Sept. 2, 1976; children—John Joseph, Susan Kay, Laura Colleen; stepchildren—Kurt Henry, Karen Joan, Lynne Eileen. B.S., U. Ill., 1961; M.B.A., U. Chgo., 1970. C.P.A., Ill. Tax and audit sr. Arthur Andersen & Co., Chgo., 1961-66; with No. Ill. Gas Co., 1966-84, treas., 1973-75, v.p., controller, 1975-77, v.p. central div., 1977-78, v.p., controller, 1978-83, v.p., 1983-84; v.p., controller NICOR Inc., Naperville, Ill., 1978-83, v.p., 1983-84, v.p. fin., 1984-87, sr. v.p., chief fin. officer, 1988-95; dir. Chgo. Community Ventures, Inc., 1975-85, sec., 1976-85; dir. State Bank Saunemin, Ill., NICOR Oil and Gas Exploration. Bd. dirs. Taxpayers Fedn. Ill., 1979-95, chmn., 1988-89. Served with U.S. Army, 1956-58. Mem. Acctg. Rsch. Assn., Am. Gas Assn. (chmn. application acctg. prins. com. 1974-75, mem. acctg. adv. council 1982-95, chmn. 1982-83), Fin. Execs. Inst., Midwest Gas Assn. (chmn. acctg. and fin. sect. 1974-75), Ill. Soc. C.P.A.'s, U. Ill. Coll. Commerce Alumni Assn. (pres. 1977-78), Chgo. Assn. Commerce and Industry, Econ. Club Chgo. Roman Catholic. Home: Naperville Ill. Died 1995.

LANSING, ROBERT HOWELL, actor, director; b. San Diego, June 5, 1928; s. Robert George and Alice Lucille (Howell) Brown; m. Emily McLaughlin, 1956 (div.); 1 child, Robert; m. Garifalia Hardy, 1969 (div.); 1 child, Alice; m. Anne Cecile Erde Pivar, 1981. Ed. pub. schs.; attended, Am. Theatre Wing, 1949-50. Debut as actor on Broadway in Stalag 17, 1951; plays include Richard III, Cyrano de Bergerac, Charley's Aunt, 1953-54, The Lovers, 1956, Cue for Passion, 1958, Suddenly Last Summer, 1958-59, The Great God Brown, 1959, Cut of the Axe, 1960, Antony and Cleopatra, L.A., 1967, Brightower, 1970, Finishing Touches, 1973, The Father, 1973, The O'Neill Sea Plays, 1977, Damien, 1981, The Little Foxes, on Broadway and in London, 1981, Cost of Living, Judith Anderson Theatre, N.Y.C., 1985, John Brown's Body, Williamstown Theatre Festival, 1989, The Sum of Us, 1991; starring roles in motion pictures including Bittersweet Love, 1976, Scalpel, 1977, Acapulco Gold, 1978, Gathering of Eagles, The Grissom Gang, Under the Yum Yum Tree; star TV series 87th Precinct, 1961, Twelve O'Clock High, 1964, The Man Who Never Was, 1966, Automan, 1983, (recurring guest star role as Control) The Equalizer, 1985-89, (recurring guest star) Kung Fu, The Legend, 1992, 93, 94, Firefighters, 1993; numerous other TV appearances including Hotel, The New Alfred Hitchcock Presents, Against the Law, Murder, She Wrote, 1991-92, Law and Order. With U.S. Army, 1946-47. Mem. SAG (bd. dirs., nat. v.p.), Actors Equity Assn., Dirs. Guild Assn., Affiliated TV and Radio Artists, The Players (pres. 1991-93), Acad. Magical Arts (life). Democrat. Home: New York N.Y. Died Oct. 23, 1994.

LANTZ, WALTER, animated cartoon producer; b. New Rochelle, N.Y., Apr. 27, 1900; m. Gracie Lantz. Creator Woody Woodpecker, 1941, Chilly Willy, 1954; started with Gregory La Cava, 1916, with Katzenjammer Kids, Happy Hooligan, Krazy Kat; later producer Col. Heeza Liar for J.B. Bray; producer: joined Universal Pictures, 1928; cartoons for army and navy, ednl. and comml. use; producer first technicolor cartoon for Paul Whiteman's King of Jazz; producer first Woody Woodpecker Show for TV; pres., Walter Lantz Prodns., Inc. (Recipient Acad. award 1979). Star on Hollywood Walk of Fame, 1986; recipient Golden Globe award, Association Internationale du Film d'Animation award. Home: Beverly Hills Calif. Died Mar. 22, 1994.

LARKIN, JANE RITA, brokerage company executive; b. N.Y.C., May 14, 1917; d. Edward Francis and Catherine Veronica (Keenan) L. B.S. with highest honors, St. John's U., N.Y.C., 1938. Br. office ops. mgr. Merrill Lynch, Bklyn., 1942-59; allied mem. N.Y. Stock Exchange, Hirsch & Co., N.Y.C., 1959-70, mem. N.Y. Stock Exchange, 1970-95; allied mem. N.Y. Stock Exchange DuPont Glore Forgan, N.Y.C.; dep. dir. compliance, v.p. Paine Webber, N.Y.C., 1974-95; mem. arbitration panel N.Y. Stock Exchange. Republican. Roman Catholic. Died Nov. 5, 1995. Home: Brooklyn N.Y.

LAROE, EDWARD TERHUNE, III, marine biologist, government official, educator; b. Suffern, N.Y., June 15, 1943; s. Edward Terhune II and Mary Louise (Ritter) LaR.; m. Margaret Ann Engel, Mar. 24, 1964 (div. July 1979); children: Dale Ritter, Tracy Ann; m. S. Elisabeth Sheiry, Aug. 22, 1981. AB in Biology, Stanford U., 1964; MS in Marine Sci., U. Miami, Fla., 1967, PhD Biol. Oceanography, 1970. Rsch. scientist U. Miami, 1970-71; exec. dir. Collier County Conservancy, Naples, Fla., 1971-73; sr. scientist NOAA, Washington, 1973-77; coastal specialist Oreg. Dept. Land Conservation and Devel., Salem, 1975-77; chief Bur. Coastal Zone Mgmt. Fla. Dept. Environ. Regulation, Tallahassee, 1977-79; spl. asst. to asst. sec. Fish, Wildlife and Parks U.S. Dept. Interior, Washington, 1980; dep. chief div. biol. svc. Fish and Wildlife Svc., Washington, 1981-82, chief, 1982-87; dir. coop. rsch. units U.S. Fish and Wildlife Svc., Washington, 1987-94; sr. scientist U.S. Biol. Survey, Washington, 1994—; tech. advisor South Fla. Regional Planning Com., Miami, 1972-73; mem. tech. adv. bd. Fla. Dept. Pollution Control, Tallahassee, 1973; mem. faculty USDA Grad. Sch., Washington, 1982—; del. leader Indo-U.S. Conf. on River Conservation, New Delhi, 1987; U.S. del. Intergovtl. Panel on Climate Change, Moscow, 1989; lectr. Moscow State U., 1991; exec. sec. White House Wetlands Rsch. subcom. FCCSET, 1991—. Co-author: Classification of Wetlands, 1979. Expert witness Environ. Def. Fund, N.Y.C., 1971-75; bd. dirs. Big Cypress Nature Ctr., Naples, Fla., 1972-73; v.p. Fla. Audubon Soc., 1972-73. Recipient Disting. Svc. award Naples Jaycees, 1972, Conservationist of Yr. award Fla. Audubon Soc., 1973, Silver medal Meritorious Svc. Dept. Interior, 1991. Mem. AAAS, Soc. Conservation Biologists, Wildlife Soc., Coastal Soc. (bd. dirs. 1974-79, pres. 1977-78), Natural Areas Assn. (bd. dirs. 1991—), Iron Arrow. Democrat. Home: Arlington Va. Died Oct. 19, 1994.

LARSON, MARTIN ALFRED, author, lecturer; b. Whitehall, Mich., Mar. 2, 1897; s. Alfred and Augusta (Lindblad) L.; m. Lillian Davis, Aug. 9, 1922 (div. June 1933); children: John Alfred, David William; m. Emma Bruder, June 19, 1951. Student, Parsons Bus. Coll., 1916; A.B., Kalamazoo Coll., 1920; M.A. (fellow), U. Mich., 1921, Ph.D., 1923. Mem. faculty Mich. Eastern U., 1923-25, U. Idaho, 1925-27; owner, mgr. Larson Paint Co., Detroit, 1935-50; pres. Martin A. Larson Co., 1946-60; lectr., writer various mags. and periodicals, from 1925; Operator Detroit Open Forum, 1935-48; pres. Detroit Taxpayers Assn., 1942-49; lectr., spl. researcher Americans United, 1964-75; research cons., spl. researcher, weekly columnist Liberty Lobby, from 1967. Author: Milton and Servetus, 1926, The Modernity of Milton, 1927, The Plaster Saint, 1953, The Religion of the Occident, 1959, Wanton Sinner, 1962, Church Wealth and Business Income, 1965, Tax-Exempt Property in Key American Cities, 1965, The Essene Heritage, 1967, The Great Tax Fraud, 1968, (with C. Stanley Lowell) The Churches: Their Riches, Revenues, and Immunities, 1969, Praise the Lord for Tax Exemption, 1969, When Parochial Schools Close, 1972, Tax-Revolt: U.S.A, 1973, Tax-Rebellion: U.S.A, 1974, The Federal Reserve and Our Manipulated Dollar, 1975, (with C. Stanley Lowell) The Religious Empire, 1975, How to Defend Yourself Against the IRS, 1976, The Story of Christian Origins, 1977, The Essence of Jefferson, 1978, How To Save Money on Your Taxes This Year, 1978, How to Establish a Trust and Reduce Taxation, 1978, The Continuing Tax Rebellion, 1979, The Essene-Christian Faith, 1979, The IRS vs. the Middle Class, or How the Average Citizen can Protect Himself Against the Federal Tax Collector, 1980, The Complete Defense Against Income Taxation, 1981, Jefferson: Magnificent Populist, 1981, The Best of Martin Larson, 1982, Tax Revolt: Battle for the Constitution, 1983, New Thought: The Religion of Health, Happiness and

Prosperity, 1984, Tax Revolt: The Battle for the Constitution, 1985, How to Live a Productive Ninety-Year Life, 1985, Newthought Religion, 1987. Recipient Religious Liberty citation Americans United, 1970. Mem. Phoenix Philos. Soc., Am. Humanist Assn., Soc. Religious Humanism, Pi Kappa Delta. Unitarian. Republican. Home: Phoenix Ariz. Deceased.

LASCARA, VINCENT ALFRED, retired naval officer, corporate executive; b. Norfolk, Va., Dec. 24, 1919; s. Joseph and Mary (Caleo) L.; m. Elizabeth Irma Lyons, Feb. 22, 1951; children: Elisa Mary, Vincent Joseph, William Anthony, Virginia Anna. Student, Belmont Abbey Jr. Coll., 1938-40; B.A., Coll. William and Mary, 1942; M.B.A., Stanford U., 1951; postgrad., Naval War Coll., 1967. Commd. ensign USN, 1942, advanced through grades to vice adm., 1976; supply officer U.S.S. Enterprise, 1960-64; dir. inventory control Naval Supply Center, Norfolk, 1964-66; exec. officer Ships Parts Control Center, Mechanicsburg, Pa., 1967-68; comdg. officer Fleet Materials Support Office, Mechanicsburg, 1968-69; asst. comptroller Office Navy Comptroller, Washington, 1969-73; also comdr. Navy Accounting and Fin. Center, 1969-73; comdg. officer Navy Supply Center, Norfolk, 1973-76, vice chief Naval Materiel, 1976-79; v.p. Jonathan Corp., 1981-94; dir. Brown-Boveri Power Equipment. Mem. devel. coun. Va. Inst. Marine Sci., Coll. William and Mary; chmn. bd. dirs. Navy Fed. Credit Union, Washington, Def. Credit Union Coun., Armed Forces Fin. Network, Future of Hampton Roads; chmn. Dolphin Scholarship Found. Home: Virginia Beach Va. Died Feb. 10, 1994.

LASCH, CHRISTOPHER, historian; b. Omaha, June 1, 1932; s. Robert and Zora (Schaupp) L.; m. Nell Commager, June 30, 1956; children: Robert, Elisabeth, Catherine, Christopher. B.A., Harvard U., 1954; M.A., Columbia U., 1955, Ph.D., 1961; L.H.D. (hon.), Bard Coll., 1977, Hobart Coll., 1981. Mem. history faculty Williams Coll., 1957-57, Roosevelt U., Chgo., 1960-61, U. Iowa, 1961-66, Northwestern U., 1966-70; mem. faculty U. Rochester, N.Y., 1970—; Don Alonzo Watson prof. history U. Rochester, 1979—, chmn. dept. history, 1985—; Freud lectr. Univ. Coll., London, 1981. Author: The American Liberals and The Russian Revolution, 1962, The New Radicalism in America, 1965, The Agony of the American Left, 1969, The World of Nations, 1973, Haven in a Heartless World, 1977, The Culture of Narcissism, 1979, The Minimal Self, 1984, The True and Only Heaven, 1991. Grantee Social Sci. Rsch. Coun., 1960, Am. Coun. Learned Socs., 1968, 83, Ford Found., 1974, Guggenheim Found., 1975, NEH, 1988-90; Ctr. for Advanced Study in Behavioral Scis. fellow, 1988-89. Mem. Orgn. Am. Historians., Am. Hist. Assn. Home: Pittsford N.Y. Died Feb. 14, 1994.

LASKER, MARY (MRS. ALBERT D. LASKER), civic worker; b. Watertown, Wis.; d. Frank Elwin and Sara (Johnson) Woodard; m. Paul Reinhardt (div.); m. Albert D. Lasker. A.B. cum laude, Radcliffe Coll.; LL.D., U. Wis.; postgrad., Oxford U.; L.H.D. (hon.), U. So. Calif., U. Calif., Berkeley, Bard Coll., Woman's Med. Coll. Pa., N.Y. U., N.Y. Med. Coll., Jefferson Med. Coll., Phila.; LL.D., Columbia U.; LLD (hon.), Harvard U., 1987. Art dealer; connected with Reinhardt Galleries, N.Y.C.; arranging benefit loan exhbns. outstanding old and modern French masters and selling pictures to collectors and museums Reinhardt Galleries; pres. Albert and Mary Lasker Med. Rsch. Found. Trustee Research to Prevent Blindness, Cancer Research Inst., Leeds Castle Found., John F. Kennedy Ctr. for Performing Arts; hon. chmn. bd. dirs. Am. Cancer Soc.; vice chmn. bd. United Cerebral Palsy Research and Ednl. Found.; bd. dirs. Norton Simon Mus. Chevalier officer French Legion of Honor; recipient Presdl. Medal of Freedom, 1969, Congl. Gold medal, 1989; Albert and Mary Lasker Med. Rsch. Found. established in honor. Home: New York N.Y. Died Feb. 21, 1994; buried Sleepy Hollow Cemetary, Tarrytown, N.Y.

LATHAM, JEAN LEE, writer; b. Buckhannon, W.Va., Apr. 19, 1902; d. George Robert II and Winifred Ethelda (Brown) L. A.B., W.Va. Wesleyan Coll., 1925, Litt.D., 1956; B.D.E., Ithaca Coll., 1928; M.A., Cornell U., 1930; student, W.Va. Inst. Tech., 1942. Head English dept. Upshur County High Sch., 1926-27; substitute tchr. speech W.Va. Wesleyan Coll., 1927; tchr. dramatic and acad. depts. Ithaca Coll., 1928-29; editor in chief Dramatic Pub. Co., Chgo., 1930-36; free lance writer, 1936-41, 45-95; Trainer insps. Signal Corps U.S. War Dept., 1943-45; substitute librarian Warm Springs Found., summer 1951. Playwright: The Blue Teapot, 1932, Old Doc, 1941, Gray Bread, 1941, Senor Freedom, 1941, The Nightmare, 1953; Author: Do's and Don'ts of Drama, 1935, The Story of Eli Whitney, 1953, Medals for Morse, 1954, Carry On, Mr. Bowditch, 1955 (Jr. Literary Guild selection, Newbery Medal, hon. mention Internat. Bd. Books for Young People), Trail Blazer of the Seas, 1956, This Dear Bought Land, 1957 (Jr. Lit. Guild selection 1957), On Stage, Mr. Jefferson, 1958, Young Man in a Hurry; The Story of Cyrus W. Field, 1958, Nutcracker, Puss in Boots, Jack the Giant Killer, Hop O' My Thumb, When Homer Honked, The Dog that Lost His Family, The Cuckoo Who Couldn't Count, The Man Who Never Snoozed, Drake: The Man They Called a Pirate, 1960, Man of the Monitor: The Story of John Ericsson, 1962, The Chagres: Power of the Panama Canal, 1964, Sam Houston: Hero of Texas, 1965, Retreat to Glory, The Story of Sam Houston, 1965, George W. Goethals: Panama Canal Engineer, 1965, The Frightened Hero, 1965, David Glasgow Farragut: Our First Admiral, 1967, The Columbia: Powerhouse of North America, 1967, Anchor's Aweigh: The Story of David Glasgow Farragut, 1968, Far Voyager: The Story of James Cook, 1970, Rachel Carson: Who Loved the Sea, 1973, Who Lives Here?, 1974, What Tabbit the Rabbit Found, 1974, Elizabeth Blackwell: Pioneer Woman Doctor, 1975; Recorded: Carry On Mr. Bowditch (for Talking Books), 1956. Publicity dir. South Pinellas chpt. A.R.C., St. Petersburg, Fla., 1949; Bd. dirs. Friends of U. Miami (Fla.) Library. Mem. Nat. League Am. Pen Women, Women's Aux. U.S. Power Squadron, Phi Kappa Phi, Zeta Phi Eta. Democrat. Methodist. Club: Zonta. Home: Coral Gables Fla. Died June 13, 1995.

LAUFFER, ALICE A., artist, printmaker; b. Frankfort Twp., Ill., Oct. 25, 1919; d. George Albert and Florence Aubina (Gammon) L.; m. William Frederick Schmidt, June 2, 1950; children: Lora, Christine, David, William. Student, Chgo. Acad. Fine Art, 1937-39, Original Hull House workshop, 1940-41, Art Inst. Chgo., evenings 1942-43, 58-63; pupil, Paul Weighardt, Evanston Art Center, 1965-68. Designer Bates Art Industries, Chgo., 1940-42, Eastern Art Products, 1943-46, Printed String, Inc., Chgo., 1956-58; free-lance designer, 1947-56, fine artist, from 1959. One-woman shows: Deer Path Art Gallery, Lake Forest, Ill., 1968, Four Arts Gallery, Evanston, 1971, Chgo. Public Library, 1972, Ill. Arts Council, Chgo., 1975, Artemisia Gallery, 1977, Alonzo C. Mather Hall, Art Inst. Chgo., 1978; group shows include: San Francisco Mus. Art, 1970, No. Ill. U., 1971, Ball State U., Ind., 1972, Minn. Mus. Art, St.Paul, 1968, 73, Dulin Gallery, Knoxville, Ky., 1970, 73, Smithsonian Instn., Washington, 1972, Nat. Gallery Fine Arts, Washington, 1973, 1134 Gallery, Chgo., 1976, Okla. Art Center, Oklahoma City, 1975, 77, Chgo. State U., 1979, Hyde Park Art Ctr., 1978, NAME Gallery, 1979, nat. exhbn. Columbia (Mo.) Coll., 1983; represented in permanent collections: Art Inst. Chgo., Minn. Mus. Art, St. Paul, Mus. Contemporary Art, Chgo., State of Ill. Center Collection at State of Ill. Bldg., Chgo., Gould, Inc., Northwest Industries, Chgo., Block Steel Corp., Kemper Ins. Cos., Borg-Warner Corp., Peat Marwick & Mitchell, Chgo., First Nat. Bank Chgo., City Hall, Winnetka, Ill., artist-in-residence, Blackhawk Mountain Sch. Art, Colo., 1973; rehab., devel. historic indsl. bldg. into artists workspace, residences, from 1978; organizer Rights of Spring exhibit, Northwestern U., 1970, 1st Mid-West Conf. Women Artists, Chgo., 1973, chairperson, coordinator, 4th Mid-West Women's Art Conf., 1983. Recipient James Broadus Clarke award Art Inst. Chgo., 1969, U.S.A. Purchase award Minn. Mus. Art, 1973. Mem. Women's Caucus for Art, Chgo. Women's Caucus for Art (pres. 1983), Chgo. Artists Coalition., Coalition of Women's Art Orgns. (nat. bd. dirs. 1983-84). Club: Arts of Chgo. Home: Chicago Ill. Deceased.

LAUGHLIN, CHARLES VAILL, educator, lawyer; b. Pittsfield, Ill., May 26, 1907; s. Ely Vaill and Anne (Hawker) L.; m. Hope Lorraine Edson, June 5, 1948; 1 son, Richard Vaill. Student, Lenox Coll., 1924-26; LL.B., George Washington U., 1929, A.B., 1930; LL.M., Harvard, 1940; J.S.D., U. Chgo., 1942. Bar: D.C. bar 1929, Ill. bar 1930, Va. bar 1948. With Davies, Jones, Beebe and Busick, Washington, 1929-30, Shanner and Shanner, Chgo., 1931, 32-38, Vedder, Price, Kaufman and Kammholz, Chgo., summer 1952; tchr. polit. sci. Lenox Coll., Hopkinton, Iowa, 1931-32, 38-39; mem. faculty Washington and Lee U., Lexington, Va., 1940-42, 46-77; prof. law Washington and Lee U., 1950-77, prof. emeritus, 1977—; vis. prof. George Washington U., 1960, U. Va., 1961; tchr. classes mil. law U.S. Army Res. program, 1953-60; U.S. commnr., 1962-71, labor arbitrator, 1970—, magistrate, 1971-75; Fulbright lectr. Am. law U., Helsinki, Finland, 1963-64. Contbr. articles to legal jours. Chmn. Va. Republican Com. on Issues, 1957; Republican candidate for Iowa Legislature, 1932; mem. Rockbridge County (Va.) Rep. Com., 1952-59, 64—; mem. Lexington (Va.) Electoral Bd., 1966-72, chmn., 1971-72; del., key note speaker dist. Rep. conv., 1952. Served to capt. Judge Adv. Gen. Corps AUS, 1942-46. Recipient John B. Learner Medal George Washington U., 1929; Charles Vaill Laughlin faculty lounge at Lewis Hall named in his honor. Mem. Am. Law Inst., Order of Coif, Am. Judicature Soc., Judge Advs. Assn., Delta Theta Phi, Acacia. Republican. Presbyterian. Home: Lexington Va. Died Jan. 29, 1985.

LAUN, HAROLD GEORGE, investment banker; b. Elkhart Lake, Wis., Apr. 14, 1905; s. Louis and Adele (Gutheil) L.; m. Mary Rapp, Nov. 8, 1930; children: Mary Georgina, Katherine Louise; m. Margaret Widmark, Feb. 14, 1951. Student, U. Calif. at Berkeley; A.B., U. Wis., 1927. Gen. clk. First Nat. Bank of Chgo., 1927-28; salesman Bonbright & Co., Chgo., 1928-32, Chase, Harris Forbes Co., 1932-33, F.S. Moseley & Co., Chgo., 1933-46; partner F.S. Moseley & Co., 1946-71; account exec. Moseley, Hallgarten and Estabrook, Inc., 1971-93; founder, organizer Technology Fund, 1948; chmn. TV Shares Mgmt. Corp., 1948-54; past dir. Diversey Corp. Past bd. dirs. U. Wis. Found.; trustee Lakeland Coll., Sheboygan, Wis., 1976-93 . Mem. Sigma Phi. Clubs: University; Skokie Country; Mid-Am.; Cliff Dwellers; St. Andrew's (Delray Beach, Fla.). Home: Delray Beach Fla. Died Jan. 22, 1993.

LAVELLE, MICHAEL JOSEPH, economist, academic administrator; b. Cleve., Dec. 28, 1934; s. Michael Joseph and Helen Victoria (Wiejek) L. Student, Xavier U., 1953-57; AB, Loyola U., Chgo., 1958, Licentiate in Philosophy, 1960; PhD in Econs., Boston Coll., 1966; postgrad., Harvard U. Russian Rsch. Ctr., 1963-65; Lic. Theol., Hochschule fur Philosophie und Theologie, Frankfurt, Fed. Republic Germany, 1969. Book rev. editor Rev. Social Economy, 1963-65; dir. social ministry S.J., Detroit, 1970-75, provincial superior, 1977-83; dir. summer urban program John Carroll U., Cleve., 1970, dean Bus. Sch., 1975-77, acad. v.p., 1984-88, pres., 1988-95. Trustee Cleve. Ctr. for Econ. Edn., 1975-88, St. Joseph's U., Phila., 1984-90, Loyola Coll., Balt., 1986-92, Boston Coll., Chestnut Hill, Mass., 1989—, Xavier U., Cin., 1986—, Le Moyne Coll., Syracuse, N.Y., 1993—; mem. Leadership Cleve., 1988-89, Assn. Jesuit Coll. and Univ., 1988—, The Nat. Conf., 1989—, The 50 Club, Cleve., 1988—, A Bus./Clergy Dialogue, Cleve., 1988—. Fgn. Area Fellowship Program fellow, 1963-65. Mem. Am. Assn. for Advancement Slavic Studies, Assn. for Comparative Econ. Studies, Assn. for Social Econs., Union Club. Democrat. Roman Catholic. Home: Cleveland Ohio Died Mar. 25, 1995.

LAVEY, KENNETH HENRY, advertising agency executive, designer; b. Palermo, Calif., Aug. 25, 1923; s. Rudolph Charles and Margaret S. (Williams) L.; m. Joann Lucile Miller, July 11, 1948; children: Brian Benton, Neil Bruce. B.A., Calif. Coll. Arts and Crafts, 1948; grad., Pratt Inst., 1949. With L. W. Frolich (pharm. advt. co.), N.Y.C., 1949-72; creative dir. L. W. Frolich (pharm. advt. co.), 1962-66, sr. v.p., dir. creative planning, 1966-72; co-founder Lavey Wolff Swift, Inc. (health care communications agy.), N.Y.C., 1972; exec. v.p., dir. creative services Lavey Wolff Swift, Inc. (health care communications agy.), from 1972, vice chmn., creative dir.; lectr. Pratt Inst., 1976-77; participant Ten Alumni exhibit, 1962, Fifty Alumni exhibit, 1966; panel mem. Pharm. Advt. Club Seminar. Designer (with Harvard Med. Sch. dept. physiology), anatomical graphics. Served with USAAF, 1943-46. Recipient Student medal for advt. design Pratt Inst., 1949. Mem. Art Dirs. Club N.Y., Am. Ethical Union, Riverdale-Yonkers Ethical Soc. (v.p. 1969-71, 76-77), Riverdale-Yonkers Soc. Ethical Culture (pres. 1990-93). Home: Dobbs Ferry N.Y. Died Apr. 26, 1996.

LAWRENCE, M. LARRY, ambassador; b. Chgo., Aug 16, 1926; s. Sidney A. and Tillie (Astor) L.; m. Shelia; 4 children. B in Sociology, U. Ariz., 1948. Lic. gen contractor; lic. real estate and insurance broker. Chmn. pres., chief exec. officer Del Properties, Inc., 1963-86 chmn., chief exec. officer Hotel del Coronado Corp. Coronado, Calif., 1986-93; U.S. amb. to Switzerland Bern, 1993-96; bd. dirs. Federal Home Loan Bank San Francisco; chmn. bd., chief exec. officer, or ptnr numerous cos. including China Basin Ltd., Coronado Properties, Ltd., Danilo Gardens, Del Properties Inc. Garden Villas Ltd., HDC Properties, Hotel Del Coronado Corp., JKL Ltd., Lawrence-Woodgler Ptnrship. Ltd., Magnolia Gardens Ltd., Poolside Associates, Resort Supply Internat., Ridan Gardens, So Calif. Fin. Ltd., West Coast Fin. Ltd., others. Mem San Diego county Commn. on Bicentennial U.S. Constitution, Exec. Com. Joan Kroc Hospice Ctr., Calif State Commn. on Tourism and Visitor Services, adv. bd U. San Diego Sch. Bus. Adminstrn., Urban Coalition task force com. on housing, Vietnam Vets. Leadership Program of San Diego, archtl. selection com. Convention Ctr. City and County San Diego, San Diego Civic Light Opera Assn., select com. Am.'s Cup Task Force 1987; commr. Calif. Senate Adv. Commn. Cost Control in State Govt., chmn. fin. instns. subcom.; chmn. United Crusade, United Jewish Appeal, Israel Bonds Campaign Tri-Hosp. Dr., San Diego County Charter Rev. Com. bd. dirs. Neighborhood House, World Affairs Council charter life mem. San Diego State U. History Research Ctr.; vice chmn. 1985 Nobel Peace Prize Nominating Commn.; chmn., trustee Citizens United; pres. San Diego Community Service Orgn.; active Dem. coms. Ind. and Calif.; mem. nat. fin. council Dem. Nat. Com. 1978-82, steering com. Re-election Com. Pres. Carter 1979-80, site selection com. 1984 Dem. Nat. Conv. 1982, Dem. Bus. Council, 1982-96, del. selection com Calif. Dem. Party, 1983, nat. adv. bd. Ctr. Nat. Policy 1984; founder Dem. Found. San Diego County, 1986-87 trustee Dem. Party Victory Fund, 1987-88, others. Recipient Alumni Achievement award U. Ariz., 1987 named Man of the Yr., City of Coronado, 1984, San Diego Citizen Yr., 1984; named to Hon. Order Ky Cols. Mem. Navy League, Rest and Aspiration Soc., U San Diego Pres.'s Club (life), Am. Merchant Marine Vet. Assn., Rotary. Home: Bern Switzerland Died Jan 9, 1996.

LAWRENCE, PELHAM BISSELL, corporate executive; b. N.Y.C., Oct. 31, 1945; s. David and Nanc (Wemple) B.; m. Virginia Marie Elsworth, July 4, 196 children: Joseph Pelham, Michael Pelham, Ar Kathryn. A.A., Manatee Jr. Coll., 1966; B.A., U. Fla 1968. C.P.A., Md. Asst. mgr. Chem. Bank, N.Y.C 1971-74; dir. treasury Perdue Farms, Inc., Salisbur d., 1974-77, treas., 1977-80, treas., chief fin. officer, 80-82, v.p. fin., 1982-90, exec. v.p., 1990-91, pres., ief oper. officer, 1991-93; also bd. dirs. Perdue Farms, c. Served to 1st lt. U.S. Army, 1969-71. Decorated rmy Commendation medal. Mem. Am. Inst. C.P.A.s, n. Execs. Inst., Phi Beta Kappa. Roman Catholic. ome: Salisbury Md. Died Jan. 30, 1993.

AWRENCE, SEYMOUR, publisher; b. N.Y.C., Feb. , 1926; s. Jack and Sophie (Luby) L.; m. Merloyd adington, June 21, 1952 (div. Feb. 1984); children: acy, Nicholas. A.B., Harvard, 1948. Editor, pub. of ake, 1945-54; coll. traveler D. Van Nostrand Co., 48-50; coll. traveler, field editor Ronald Press, 1950- ; spl. asst. to editor Atlantic Monthly, 1952-54; asso. itor Atlantic Monthly Press, 1954, dir., 1955-64; v.p. lfred A. Knopf, Inc., 1964; founder Seymour awrence, Inc., 1965, pres., editor in chief, 1965—. ction juror Am. Book Awards, 1981; established The ymour Lawrence Room of Contemporary Literature, Miss., 1992. Clubs: Signet Society (Cambridge, ass.); Harvard (N.Y.C.), Century Assn. (N.Y.C.). ome: Wilton Conn. Deceased.

AWTON, MARY CECILIA, lawyer; b. Washington, ne 2, 1935; d. Frederick Joseph and Cecilia Alice /alsh) L. AB, Seton Hill Coll., Greensburg, Pa., 57; LLD (hon.), Seton Hill Coll., 1972; LLB, Ge- getown U., 1960. Bar: D.C. 1960, U.S. Ct. Appeals).C. cir.) 1960, U.S. Ct. Appeals (9th cir.) 1986, U.S. . Appeals (4th cir.) 1987, U.S. Supreme Ct. 1964. tty. advisor Office of Legal Counsel U.S. Dept. Justice, ashington, 1960-72, dep. asst. atty. gen., 1972-79, unsel Office of Intelligence Policy, 1982-93; gen. unsel Corp. for Pub. Broadcasting, Washington, 1979- ; adminstrv. law officer The White House, Wash- gton, 1980-82; mem. com. on admissions and ievances U.S. Ct. Appeals (D.C. cir.), 1985-92. ustee Seton Hill Coll., 1970-77, 79-88; pres. Westbard ews Condominium, Bethesda, Md., 1982-84, 88-90. ecipient Seal Medallion CIA, 1986, Legal award Assn. Fed. Investigators, 1975. Mem. ABA (council on lminstrv. law 1983-86). Roman Catholic. Home: arta N.J. Died Oct. 1993.

AYTON, JOE, director, choreographer; b. N.Y.C., ay 3, 1931; s. Irving J. and Sadie (Fischer) Lichtman; . Evelyn Russell, Oct. 6, 1959; 1 child, Jeb mes. Grad. high sch. Performer (Broadway) High utton Shoes, 1947, Miss Liberty, 1949, Gentlemen refer Blondes, 1949, Wonderful Town, 1953; chore- rapher: Broadway prodns. Once Upon a Mattress, und of Music, 1959, On The Town, 1959, Green- illow (Tony awd. nom., 1960), Tenderloin, 1960, Sail way, 1961, No Strings, 1962, The Girl Who Came to upper, 1963, Peterpat, 1965, Drat the Cat, 1966, nerry!, 1967, George M! (Tony awd., best chore- graphy, 1969), Dear World, 1968, Scarlett, 1969, Two Two, 1970, Clams on the Half Shell, 1975, Barnum, 80, Bring Back Birdie, 1981, Rock 'n Roll! The First 00 Years, 1982; dir.: Broadway prodn. Harrigan & art, 1985; choreographer: Off-Broadway prodns. On he Town, 1959, Once Upon A Mattress, 1959; touring odn. Gone with the Wind, 1973; prodns. in Eng. in- ude Carol Channing and Her Ten Stout-Hearted Men, 70; choreographer: TV prodns. Mary Martin's Easter pecial, 1959; dir., choreographer: TV prodns. Gershwin ears, 1960, Once Upon A Mattress, 1961, My Name is arbra, 1965, Color Me Barbra, 1966, Jack Jones pecial, 1966, Belle of 14th Street-Barbra Streisand, 67, Flip Side, 1967, Androcles and the Lion, 1968, ebbie Reynolds Special, 1968, Infancy, 1968, Littlest ngel, 1969, Theater of the Deaf, NBC Special, 1967, orelei; U.S. tour, 1973; Raquel Welch, Las Vegas, 73; TV Barbra Streisand, and Other Musical Instru- ents, 1974, World Tour-Carpenters, 1976, A Special livia Newton-John, 1976; choreographer: motion pic- re Thoroughly Modern Millie, 1967, Harry & Walter o to New York; dir.: film Richard Pryor Live on unset Strip, 1982; exec. producer: film Annie, 1982; horeographer: stage show An Evening with Diana oss, Overture, Grand Tour, O.W. for Royal Ballet, ondon, 1970, Double Exposure for City Center Joffrey allet, N.Y.C., 1972, Grand Tour, Houston Ballet, Am. remier and Louisville Ballet, 1986; dir., choreographer: us. stage prodn. Gone With the Wind, London, 1972, ieces of Eight, 1985, Celebration '85, ; U.S. tour, 1973- ; dir.: Lost Colony prodn. Roanoke Island Hist. ssn., from 1965, Nat. Theater of Deaf, Waterford onn.; staged Las Vegas night club acts of, Connie tevens, Diahann Carroll, Dyan Cannon; dir. tours for ionel Richie, 1983, 86-87, Julio Inglesias, 1984, En- elbert Humperdinck, 1984, Joel Grey, 1984, Jeffrey sborne, 1986, dir., choreographer: Bette Midler's lams on the Half-Shell Revue; producer various TV pecials including Diana Ross, 1977, 87, Paul Lynde hristmas Spl., 1977, Mac Davis Christmas Spl., 1977, her, 1978, Carol & Dolly in Nashville, 1979, Paul ynde Goes to the Movies, 1979, Broadway Sings The lusic of Jule Styne, 1987; creator XXIII Summer lympics Closing Ceremonies featuring Lionel Richie, 984; (Recipient Antoinette Perry awards for No trings, 1962, Greenwillow, George M 1969, Emmy ward for My Name is Barbra 1965). Served with AUS, 952-54. Home: Beverly Hills Calif. Died May 5, 1994.

AZAR, IRVING PAUL, lawyer, artists representative; Stamford, Conn., Mar. 28, 1907; s. Samuel Mortimer and Stari (DeLongpre) L.; m. Mary Van Nuys, Jan. 1963. Student, Fordham U., 1926; LL.B., St. Lawrence U., 1931. Bar: N.Y. 1931. Sole practice N.Y.C., until 1935; with Music Corp. Am., 1936-42; artists rep. ser- vice for writers/dirs. for legitimate theatre and motion pictures N.Y.C., Beverly Hills, London and Paris, 1933- 93. Served to capt. USAAF, 1942-45. Home: New York N.Y. Died Dec. 30, 1993.

LEACH, SIR EDMUND RONALD, educator; b. Sidmouth, Eng., Nov. 7, 1910; s. William Edmund Leach; m. Celia Joyce Buckmaster, 1940; children: Louisa, Alexander Bernard. Student, Marlborough Coll., 1923-29; Exhiber., Clare Coll., Cambridge, Eng., 1929; BA, Cambridge U., 1932, MA, 1938; PhD, U. London, 1947. Comml. asst. Butterfield & Swire, Shanghai, People's Republic of China, 1932-37; lectr., reader social anthropology London Sch. Econs., 1947- 53; lectr. Cambridge U., 1953-57, reader, 1957-72, prof., 1972-78; fellow Kings Coll., 1960-66, 79—, provost, 1966-79; anthrop. field research in Formosa, 1937, Kurdistan, 1938, Burma, 1939-45, Borneo, 1947, Ceylon, 1954, 56; mem. Social Sci. Research Council, 1968-71; Malinowski lectr., 1959; Reith lectr., 1967; Frazer lectr., 1982. Author: Social and Economic Or- ganization of the Rowanduz Kurds, 1940, Social Science Research in Sarawak, 1950, Political Systems of High- land Burma, 1954, Pul Eliya: A Village in Ceylon, 1961, Rethinking Anthropology, 1961, A Runaway World?, 1968, Genesis as Myth, 1970, Lévi-Strauss, 1970, Cul- ture and Communication, 1976, L'unité de l'homme et autres essais, 1980, Social Anthropology, 1982; (with D.A. Aycock) Structuralist Interpretations of Biblical Myth, 1983; contbr. articles to profl. jours. Trustee Brit. Mus., 1975-80. Decorated knight Order Brit. Empire; fellow Ctr. for Advanced Study in Behavioral Scis. Stanford U., 1961; sr. fellow Eton Coll., 1966-79. Fellow Brit. Acad.; mem. Royal Anthrop. Inst. (v.p. 1964-66, 68-70, 75—, pres. 1971-74, Curl Essay prize 1951, 57, Rivers medal 1958, Henry Myers lectr. 1966, Huxley lectr. 1980), Assn. Social Anthropologists (chmn. 1966-70), Brit. Humanist Assn. (pres. 1970-72), Am. Acad. Arts and Scis. (fgn. hon.). Home: Bar- rington Eng. Died Jan. 6, 1989.

LEACOCK, PHILIP, film director; b. London, Oct. 8, 1917. Dir.: (films) Riders of the New Forest, 1946, The Brave Don't Cry, 1952, Assignment in London, 1953, The Little Kidnappers, 1954, Escapade, 1955, The Spanish Gardener, 1957, High Tide at Noon, 1957, In- nocent Sinners, 1958, The Rabbit Trap, 1959, Let No Man Write My Epitaph, 1960, Take a Giant Step, 1960, Hand in Hand, 1961, Reach for Glory, 1962, 13 West Street, 1962, The War Lover, 1962, Tamahine, 1964, Adams's Woman, 1970, (TV films) The Birdmen, 1971, When Michael Calls, 1972, The Daughters of Joshua Cabe, 1972, Baffled, 1973, The Great Man's Whiskers, 1973, Dying Room Only, 1973, Key West, 1973, Killer on Board, 1977, Wild and Wooly, 1978, The Curse of King Tut's Tomb, 1980, Angel City, 1980, The Two Lives of Carol Letner, 1981, The Wild Women of Chas- tity Gulch, 1982, Three Sovereigns for Sarah, 1985, (TV series) Gunsmoke, Cimarron Strip, Hawaii 5-O, The Waltons, Family, Paper Chase, Eight is Enough. Mem. Dirs. Guild Am. Home: Pacific Palisades Calif.

LEAREY, FRED DON, telephone company executive; b. Findlay, Ohio, Mar. 7, 1906; s. Fred B. and Iris A. (Galleher) L.; m. Marian E. Van Valkenburgh, Jan. 13, 1935 (dec. Nov. 1981); children: Fred K., Richard N.; m. Mary W. Schoen, Nov. 19, 1983. AB, Ohio Wes- leyan U., 1928. Student engr., lineman, installer, traffic student Ohio Bell Tel. Co., 1928-36, comml. mgr., comml. tng. supr., dist. sales mgr., 1936-43, dir. mktg., 1960-61; with AT&T, N.Y.C., 1943-46; div. comml. mgr., gen. comml. mgr. Ohio Bell Tel. Co., Columbus, 1946-60; pres. Gen. Tel. Co. Fla., Tampa, 1961-71, chmn. bd., 1971, also bd. dirs.; chmn. bd. Bus. Intros. Inc.; bd. dirs. Am. Ship Bldg. Co., MS Orange Co. Past chmn. Civil Service Bd. of Tampa, 1974.; Pres. United Way, 1965-66; bd. dirs. Fla. Council 100, also past chmn.; former trustee New Coll. Found., Sarasota; bd. dirs. Boy Scouts Am.; past interim pres., chmn. bd. U. Tampa. Mem. Tampa C. of C. (past pres.), Com. 100 (past chmn.), Fla. Telephone Assn. (past pres.), Ye Mystic Krewe of Gasparilla. Conglist. Clubs: Rotarian (Tampa) (past dist. gov.), Tampa Yacht and Country (Tampa), Palma Ceia Golf and Country (Tampa), University (Tampa). Home: Tampa Fla. Died Mar. 25, 1993.

LEAVITT, JOAN KAZANJIAN, state health official, physician; b. Boston, Jan. 14, 1926; d. Varaztad Hovannes and Marion V. (Hanford) Kazanjian; m. Don K. Leavitt; children—Mark S., Lynda Donn. A.B., Radcliffe Coll., 1947; M.A., Smith Coll., 1949; M.D., Boston U., 1953. Intern in pediatrics Boston City Hosp., 1953-54, resident in pediatrics, 1954-55; resident in pediatrics Mass. Gen. Hosp., Boston, 1955-56, 57-58; pediatrician Comanche County (Okla.) Guidance Center, 1959; practice medicine specializing in pediatrics Altus, Okla., 1959-64; med. dir. Jackson County (Okla.) Health Dept., 1960-67, Kay County (Okla.) Health Dept., 1967-76; chief maternal and child health service Okla. Health Dept., Oklahoma City, 1976; dep. commr. for personal health services Okla. Health Dept., 1976-77, commr. of health, 1977-93. Mem. AMA, Okla. State Med. Assn., Okla. Public Health Assn., Oklahoma County Med. Soc., Assn. State and Territorial Health Ofcls. (pres. 1985-86), Sigma Xi. Home: Oklahoma City Okla. Died July, 1995.

LEAVITT, JULIAN J., wholesale food company ex- ecutive; b. 1928. Student, Harvard U., 1950. With Springfield Sugar & Products Co., Suffield, Conn., 1953- 96; pres. Home: Suffield Conn. Died Apr., 1996.

LEBOWITZ, HARVEY M., lawyer; b. Balt., Dec. 13, 1929; s. Samuel and Lillian (Caplan) L.; m. Eunice Levin, Aug. 4, 1955; children: Harrison, Bonnie, Fran. LLB, U. Md., Balt., 1954, JD, 1969. Assoc. Hoffberger & Hollander, Balt., 1955-61; ptnr. Gordon, Feinblatt, Rothman, Hoffberger & Hollander, Balt., 1961-79; judge U.S. bankruptcy ct. Dist. Md., Balt., 1979-82; ptnr. Frank, Bernstein, Conaway & Goldman, Balt., 1982-91, Whiteford, Taylor & Preston, Balt., 1991-95; tchr. U. Balt., 1975-79; mem. faculty seminars on bankruptcy, various cities, 1979-95. Author: Ban- kruptcy Deskbook, 1st Edit., 1986, Bankruptcy Deskbook, 2d Edit., 1990; author course material for various seminars. Mem. 4th Cir. Judicial Conf. With U.S. Army, 1954-55. Fellow Am. Coll. Bankruptcy, Md. Bar Found.; mem. ABA, Bankruptcy Bar Assn. Md. (dir. 1989-95, pres. 1994-95), Balt. City Bankruptcy Bar Assn., Assn. Former Bankruptcy Judges, Barristers Club (treas. 1991), E-Streeters Club. Democrat. Jewish. Home: Baltimore Md. Died Nov. 4, 1995.

LECKLIDER, ROBERT WALTER, architect; b. Greenville, Ohio, Nov. 22, 1922; s. David Walter Leck- lider and Ruth Hershey; m. Mary Helen Schmalenberger, Mar. 26, 1950; children: Todd D., Mark A., Amy R. BArch, Miami U., Oxford, Ohio, 1950. Registered architect, Ohio. Job capt. Yount/ Sullivan, Dayton, Ohio, 1950-57; jr. ptnr. Yount/Sul- livan/Lecklider, Dayton, 1957-66; ptnr. Sullivan/Leck- lider/Jay, Dayton, 1966-76; sr. ptnr. Lecklider/Jay Architects, Dayton, 1976—; instr. Sinclair Community Coll., Dayton, 1954-57. Prin. works include Cox In- ternat. Airport, Dayton, Charles F. Kettering Meml. Hosp., Kettering, Ohio, Sinclair Community Coll., Mil- lett Hall, Wright State U., Dayton, Reynolds-Reynolds Computer Bldg., Dayton, Mead Data Cen. Computer Facilities, Dayton, Cedarville (Ohio) Coll. Library, numerous others. Mem. Miami Valley Regional Plan- ning Commn., Dayton, 1969-71; chmn. Planning Commn., Kettering, 1971; bd. dirs. Met. YMCA, Dayton, 1970-79. Served to staff sgt. C.E., U.S. Army, 1943-45. Recipient E.H. Berry award in Architecture, Cin. Architecture Soc., 1950, Beautification award City of Dayton, 1968, Excellence in Design award Ohio Prestressed Council Assn., Columbus, 1976, Singerman award Camp Kern YMCA, Oregonia, Ohio, 1978. Mem. AIA (pres. Dayton chpt. 1958-59), Ohio Soc. Architects (pres. 1975-76), Constrn. Specifications Inst. (pres. Dayton chpt. 1979-80, awards chmn. Great Lakes region 1983-87, nat. awards com. 1987-89). Clubs: En- gineers. (library chmn. 1958), Crestwood (Dayton) (pres. 1972-73). Lodge: Rotary. Home: Dayton Ohio

LEDERER, EDGAR, biochemist, scientist; b. Vienna, Austria, June 5, 1908; immigrated to France, 1933, naturalized, 1938; s. Alfred and Friederike (Przibram) L.; m. Helene Frechet, June 16, 1932; children—Mari- anne, Sylvia, Florence, Pascal, Denis, Aline, Pierre. Dr.phil., U. Vienna, 1930; Dr.es.Sc., Sorbonne, 1938; hon. doctoral degrees U. Aberdeen, U. Liege. Postdoctoral researcher Kaiser Wilhelm Inst., Heidelberg, Germany, 1930-33; dir. research Vitamin Inst., Leningrad, USSR, 1935-37; research asst. Centre National de la Recherche Sci., Paris, 1938-40, mem. sr. research staff, 1945—, dir. research, 1952—, dir. Inst. Chimie des Substances Naturelles, Gif sur Yvette, France, 1960-78; mem. staff Lab. Biochemistry, U. Lyon Faculty Scis., France, 1940-47, Inst. Biologie Physico- Chimique, Paris, 1947-60; assoc. prof. Sorbonne, Paris, 1954-58, prof., 1958—; prof. biochemistry U. Paris, 1956-78. Author books on carotenoids, chro- matography, lipid biochemistry. Served with French Army, World War II. Decorated chevalier Legion of Honor, comdr. Nat. Order Merit (France); recipient Fritzsche award and gold medal Am. Chem. Soc., 1951; Hofmann gold medal German Chem. Soc., 1964; Paul Karrer gold medal Swiss Chem. Soc., 1964; CNRS gold medal, 1974; Tswett medal in chromatography, Houston, 1976; R. Koch gold medal, 1982. Mem. Acad. Scis.; hon. fgm. mem. numerous chem. socs. Research on natural products chemistry and immunochemis- try. Died Oct. 19, 1988. Home: Sceaux France

LEE, MARYAT (MARY ATTAWAY LEE), playwright, director; b. Covington, Ky., May 26, 1923; d. DeWitt Collins and Grace Barbee (Dyer) Lee; student Northwestern U., 1940-41; B.A., Wellesley Coll., 1945; student Middlebury Coll., summer 1944; postgrad. Union Theol. Sem., 1949-50, Columbia U., 1949-51, M.A., 1955; m. David Phillips Foulkes-Taylor, July 4, 1957 (dec. Sept. 1966). Engaged in film editing, 1946-48; instr. Wesleyan Coll., Macon, Ga., 1948-49; transcriber Oral History project Columbia U., 1950-51; asst. to Margaret Mead, 1952-53; writer, dir. DOPE!, a street play, 1951 (pub. in Best Short Plays of 1952-53); producer, founder, playwright Soul and Latin Theater, 1968-70; mem. faculty New Sch. for Social Research, 1965-70; founder, playwright, producer EcoTheater, 1975-89; adj. faculty W.Va. Coll. Grad. Studies, 1978—, presenter Writing Project, 1981; lectr. Shepherd Coll., 1988, Greenbrier Community Coll., 1988; fellow Va. Ctr. for Creative Arts, Sweet Briar, 1979, 86; co-dir. drama and writing workshops Fed. Reformatory for Women, 1972-75; playwright-dir. tng. workshop, Hindman, Ky., Concord Coll., W.Va., Macomb, Ill.; dir. Series of EcoTheater; playwright, dir. tng. workshops., W.Va., Ky., Ill.; developed first indigenous theater network; adv. panel Expansion Arts program Nat. Endowment Arts, 1973-75. Mem. coordinating com. Humanities Ctr. W.Va. Recipient CAP's award, 1970; nat. recognition award Am. the Beautiful Fund, 1985. Rockefeller Found., 1973, DJB Found., 1974, NEA, 1975-89, Humanities Found. W.Va., 1978-89, Arts and Humanities Commn. W.Va., Ky. Arts Council, Ky. Humanities Council; grantee Ill. Humanities, Western Ill. U., Ill. Arts, So. Ill. Arts, Two Rivers Arts, Ill. Inst. for Rural Affairs, Farm Resource Ctr. Mem. Dramatists Guild. Author (plays); Kairos, 1954; Clytemnestra, 1957; Love In 57th Street Gallery, 1960; Four Men & A Monster, 1967, 80; The Tightrope Walker, 1963, 67; Meat Hansom, 1962; FUSE, 1971, 80; (street plays) DOPE!, 1951, Day to Day, After the Fashion Show, The Classroom, Luba; (rural indigenous plays) Ole Miz Dacey, John Henry, The Hinton Play; contbr. articles to profl. publs. and Flannery O'Connor Bull., 1986-89. Developed 1st modern street theater, 1951, and 1st indigenous rural theater network, W.Va., Ky., Ill. and Va. Died Sept. 17, 1989; interred Covington, Ky. Home: Lewisburg W. Va.

LEE, REX E., deceased academic administrator, law educator; b. Los Angeles, Feb. 27, 1935; s. Rex E. and Mabel (Whiting) L.; m. Janet Griffin, July 7, 1959; children: Diana, Thomas Rex, Wendy, Michael, Stephanie, Melissa, Christie. B.A., Brigham Young U., 1960; J.D., U. Chgo., 1963. Bar: Ariz., D.C., Utah. Law clk. Justice Byron R. White, U.S. Supreme Ct., 1963-64; atty. Jennings, Strouss & Salmon, 1964-72, ptnr., 1967-72; founding dean J. Reuben Clark Law Sch., Brigham Young U., Provo, Utah, 1972-81; solicitor gen. U.S.A., Washington, 1981-85; ptnr. Sidley & Austin, Washington, 1985-89; pres. Brigham Young U., Provo, Utah, 1989-96; asst. U.S. atty-gen. in charge civil div. Justice Dept., Washington.; lectr. Am. Inst. Fgn. Trade, 1966-68, U. Ariz. Sch. Law, 1968-72; George Sutherland prof. law Brigham Young U., 1985-96. Mem. gen. bd. Young Men's Mut. Improvement Assn., Ch. of Jesus Christ of Latter-day Saints, 1958-60; bd. dirs. Theodore Roosevelt council Boy Scouts Am., 1967-72. Mem. Am. Law Inst. Home: Provo Utah Died Mar. 11, 1996.

LEE, ROBERT E., government official; b. Chgo., Mar. 31, 1912; s. Patrick and Delia (Ryan) L.; m. Wilma Rector (dec. Sept. 1972); children: Patricia, Robert E., Michael B.; m. Rose Bente. Grad., DePaul U., 1935; hon. doctorates, U. Notre Dame, St. John's U., N.Y.C., St. Bonaventure U. Agt., fiscal asst. to J. Edgar Hoover, FBI, 1939-47; dir. surveys and investigations house appropriations com. U.S. Congress, 1947-53; commr. FCC, 1953—, chmn., 1981—; vice chmn. space conf., Geneva, Switzerland, 1971, Plenipotentiary Conf., Torremolinos, Spain, 1973; organizer, chmn. Com. for Full Devel. All-Channel Broadcasting, Com. for Full Devel. Instrnl. TV Fixed Service; mem. Radio Tech. Commn. for Aeros.; chmn. U.S. del. to World Adminstrv. Tel. & Tel. Conf., 1973, to World Adminstrv. Radio Conf. for Maritime, 1974, to Conf. for Broadcast Satellites, 1977; mem. telecommunications advisory com. Telecommunications Program, U. Notre Dame, South Bend, Ind.; cons. telecommunications Fletcher, Heald & Hildreth. Mem. communications arts advisory council St. John's U.; founder Cath. Apostolate for the Mass Media. Recipient Marconi gold medal, Quarter Century wireless award. Mem. IEEE, Capitol Hill Club, Cosmos Club, Georgetown Club, Washington Club, Press Club, Congressional County Club, Bolling Air Force Officer's Club. Home: Arlington Va.

LEE, ROBERT EDWIN, playwright; b. Elyria, Ohio, Oct. 15, 1918; s. Claire Melvin and Elvira (Taft) L.; m. Janet Waldo, Mar. 29, 1948; children: Jonathan, Lucy. Student, Ohio Wesleyan U., 1935-37, Litt.D., 1962; Litt.D., Coll. Wooster, 1983; LHD, Ohio State U., 1979. Astronomy observer Perkins Observatory, Delaware, Ohio, 1936-37; announcer Sta. WHK-CLE-MBS, Cleve., 1937-38; producer, dir. Young and Rubicam, N.Y.C. and Hollywood, Calif., 1938-42; expert cons. to Sec. of War, 1942-43; v.p. Lawrence & Lee, Inc., 1946-94; prof. playwriting Pasadena (Calif.) Playhouse Coll. Theatre Arts, 1964; adj. prof. dept. theatre arts U. Calif. at Los Angeles, 1966-94; co-founder, pres. Am. Playwrights Theatre, 1973; participant Cultural Exchange Mission to USSR, 1971. TV, radio work (with Jerome Lawrence): prodr., dir., writer Columbia Workshop, 1941-42, Request Performance, 1945-46, Orson Welles Theatre, 1945-46, Favorite Story, 1945-48, Frank Sinatra Show, 1947, The Railroad Hour, 1948-54, Hallmark Hall of Fame, 1949-51, Halls of Ivy, 1950-51, Date with Judy, The Unexpected, Times Square Playhouse, Song of Norway, West Point, Lincoln, The Unwilling Warrior, Shangri-La (adaption), Inherit the Wind (adaption); author plays produced, published (with Jerome Lawrence) Inside a Kid's Head, 1945, Look Ma, I'm Dancin', 1948, The Laughmaker, 1952 (rewritten and produced as Turn on the Night, 1961, The Crocodile Smile, 1970), Inherit the Wind, 1955 (Donaldson award 1955, Variety N.Y. Critics Poll 1975, Outer Circle award 1955, Best Fgn. play Critics award 1960, Brit. Drama critics award 1960, Tony Award nomination 1996), (with Lawrence and James Hilton) Shangri La , 1956, Auntie Mame, 1956, The Gang's All Here, 1959, Only In America, 1959, A Call on Kuprin, 1961, Diamond Orchid, 1965 (rewritten, produced Sparks Fly Upward 1967), Mame, 1966, Dear World, 1969, The Incomparable Max, 1969, The Night Thoreau Spent in Jail, 1970 (screenplay 1976), (as sole author) Ten Days That Shook The World, 1973, Jabberwock, 1972, First Monday in October, 1975 (screenplay 1981), Sounding Brass, 1975, (with Lawrence and Norman Cousins) Whisper in the Mind, 1990, selected plays of Lawrence and Lee (Hardcover) (Collection of 8 previously published works) Ohio State University Press, 1994; plays (unproduced, with Jerome Lawrence) Top of the Mark, Paris, France, Eclipse, Dilly, Some Say Ice, Houseboat in Kashmir, Short and Sweet, The Angels Weep; operas: (with Jerome Lawrence) Auntie Laurie, 1955, Roaring Camp, 1955, Familiar Strangers, 1956; books: Television the Revolution, 1944, Plays By Lawrence and Lee, 1990; recordings (with Jerome Lawrence) Rip Van Winkle, The Cask of Amontillado, A Tale of Two Cities, One God; screenplays (with Jerome Lawrence) My Love Affair With the Human Race, 1962, The New Yorkers, 1963, Joyous Season, 1964, (with John Sinn) Quintus, 1971; Novel by Robert E. Lee, The Lost Letters of General Robert E. Lee, 1993. Recipient New York Press Club award, 1942, Peabody award for best radio program, UN series, 1948, Radio-TV Life award, 1948, 52, Radio TV Mirror award, 1952, 53; Donaldson award best first play, 1955, Outer Critics Circle award, 1955, Variety Critics Poll award, 1955, Moss Hart Meml. award, 1967; citation for disting. svc. to theatre Am. Theatre Assn., 1979, Valentine Davies award Writers Guild Am., 1984, Best Comedy/Drama Spl. award Nat. TV Acad., 1988, Lifetime Achievement award William Inge Festival, Independence Coll., 1988; named to Am. Theatre Hall of Fame, 1990, Coll. of Fellows, 1990; Co-founder Lawwrence & Lee Theatre Research Inst., Ohio State U. 1986. Congregationalist. Home: Encino Calif. Died July 8, 1994; interred Forest Lawn, Hollywood Hills, Calif.

LEE, SOO IK, neurologist, educator; b. Yesan, Choong-Nam, Korea, May 15, 1932; came to U.S., 1964; s. Joo Hyun and Onyo (Jun) L.; m. Ock Kim, Apr. 17, 1962; children: Kyusang, Jean, Sunny Young. Degree in chemistry, Chonbuk Nat. U., Iri, Korea, 1954; MD, Yonsei U., Seoul, 1958, DMSc, 1974. Diplomate Am. Bd. Psychiatry and Neurology and sub. bd. Clin. Neurophysiology, Korean Bd. Internal Medicine. Intern Yonsei U. Severance Hosp., Seoul, 1959-60, resident, chief resident in internal medicine, 1960-64; resident in neurology U. Va. Hosp., Charlottesville, 1964-67, rsch. assoc. in neurology, 1967-68; fellow in clin. EEG Mayo Clinic and Mayo Grad. Sch. Medicine, Rochester, Minn., 1968-69; asst. prof. internal medicine Yonsei U. Coll. Medicine, Seoul, 1969-70, assoc. prof., chmn. neurology, 1972-74, prof., chmn. neurology, 1974; assoc. prof. to prof. neurology U. Va. Sch. Medicine, Charlottesville, from 1974; attending neurologist, dir. EEG and evoked potential lab. U. Va. Hosp., Charlottesville, from 1974; cons. neurologist and electroencephalographer U.S. 8th Army 12th Evacuation Hosp., Seoul, 1971, Salem (Va.) VA Hosp., from 1976; ad hoc reviewer Neurology, Archives of Neurology, Epilepsia; presenter in field. Author: (with F.E. Dreifuss) Epilepsy Case Studies, 1981, Pediatric Epileptology, 1983; contbr. articles to profl. jours. Recipient Am. Korean Found. Hon. scholarship. Fellow Am. Acad. Neurology; mem. AMA, AAAS, Korean Assn. Internal Medicine (exec. dir. 1972-73), Am. Epilepsy Soc. (rules com. 1977-81), Am. EEG Soc. (program com. 1991, evoked potential com. 1978-82, co-chmn. 1980-81), Va. Neurol. Soc. (chmn. cerebral death com. 1979-82, cerebral dealth EEG and EMG com. from 1991), Albemarle County Med. Soc., Va. Med. Soc., So. EEG Soc. Home: Keswick Va. Deceased.

LEFF, CARL, manufacturing company executive; b. N.Y.C., Oct. 23, 1897; s. Max and Sarah (Weinstein) L.; m. Eleanor Wiesen, Jan. 14, 1930; children—Marjorie (Mrs. Morgan Miller), Maxine (Mrs. George Myers). D.D.S., Columbia U., 1919. With Nat. Spinning Co., N.Y.C., from 1919, chmn., from 1978; dir. Beneficial Life Ins. Co. Trustee L.I. Coll. Medicine, 1945-49, Jewish Hosp., Bklyn., from 1926, Fedn. Jewish Philanthropies, United Jewish Appeal, N.Y.C., from 1939. Fellow Brandeis U., from 1966. Clubs: Masons (White Plains, N.Y.), Metropolis Country (White Plains, N.Y.); Palm Beach (Fla.); Country; Harmonie (N.Y.C.). Home: Palm Beach Fla. Deceased.

LEFKOWITZ, LOUIS J., lawyer; b. N.Y.C., July 3, 1904; s. Samuel and Mollie (Isaacs) L.; m. Helen Schwimmer, June 14, 1931; children: Joan (Mrs. Harold Feinbloom), Stephen Allan. LLB cum laude, Fordham U., 1925. Bar: N.Y. 1926. Sole practice N.Y.C.; justice Mcpl. Ct., N.Y.C., 1935, City Ct., N.Y.C., 1954; atty. gen. State of N.Y., Albany, 1957-79; ptnr. Phillips, Nizer, Benjamin, Krim & Ballon, N.Y.C., 1979-96; Mem. N.Y. Assembly, 1928-30; del. Rep. Nat. Conv., 1944, 48, alt. del., 1956. Bd. dirs. Florence Crittenton League; active numerous civic orgns. Mem. ABA, Fed. Bar Assn., Assn. Bar City N.Y., N.Y. County Lawyers Assn., Nat. Assn. Atty. Gens. (pres.), Assn. Lawyers Criminal Cts. Manhattan, Grand St. Boys Assn., Ar Jewish Congress. Jewish. Lodges: K.P., B'nai Brith Home: New York N.Y. Died June 20, 1996.

LE GRANGE, LOUIS, South African politicia lawyer; b. Ladybrand, Aug. 16, 1928; m. Jessie Mara 1952; 4 children. BA in Law, U. South Africa, 195 LLB, 1956; BA in Polit. Sci. with honours, Potch stroomse U., 1964. Bar: South Africa 1956. Ptnr. la firm, Potchefstroom, Union South Africa, 1955—; M. for Potchefstroom, 1966—, dep. min. info. and intern affairs, 1975-78, dep. min. internal affairs, immigrati and pub. works, 1978, min. pub. works and touris 1978-79, min. police and prisons, 1979-80, min. polic 1980-82, min. law and order, 1982-86; speaker Sou African Parliament, 1987—. Patron Western Transva Rugby Union. Mem. Westeern Transvaal Rifle Cl (pres.), South African Nat. Target Shooting Ass (pres.). Home: Cape Town Republic of South Africa

LEHEL, GYORGY, conductor; b. Budapest, Hungar Feb. 10, 1926; s. Laszlo and Klara (Ladanyi) L.; r Zsurzsa Markovits, 1969; 1 son. Ed. Liszt Acad. Mus Budapest, 1942-47; D.Music (hon.), Chgo. Conservato Coll., 1977; m. Zsuzsa Markovits, Dec. 23, 1969. Ch condr., music dir. Budapest Symphony Orch., 1962- condr. concerts, Gt. Britain, Ireland, Belgium, Franc Italy, USSR, Germany, Yugoslavia, Austria, Japa Switzerland, U.S., 1950—. Recipient Liszt prize, 195 62, Kossuth prize, 1973; named merited artist, 196 Home: Budapest Hungary

LEHMANN, JOHANNES THEODOR, mechanic engineering educator; b. Gross-Wandriss, Germar Aug. 10, 1920; s. Martin and Frieda (Daerr) L.; Traute Weber, Aug. 15, 1943; children: Rainer, Angelik Andreas. Diploma in engring., Tech. Hochschu Hannover, Fed. Republic Germany, 1949, D Engrin, 1952; D Engring. (hon.), U. Hannover, 1990. As Tech. Hochschule Hannover, 1949-52; chief engr. Ser ingwerk, Hildesheim, Fed. Republic Germany, 1952-5 sr. asst. Tech. Hochschule Hannover, 1956-59, lect 1959-61, prof., 1961-69, dean, 1965-66; prof. mech. eng ing. Ruhr U., Bochum, Fed. Republic Germany, fro 1969, prorector, 1972-74, dean, 1983-84; hon. pr Shanghai U. Tech., 1985; joint prof. Beijing U., 198 chmn. German Com. for Mechanics, 1987-90. Autho Elemente der Mechanik, 4 vols., 1975-85, Technisc Mechanik, 2 vols., 1987; contbr. numerous articles to s jours. Recipient Kopernikus medal Polish Acad. Sc 1983. Mem. Deutsche Forschungsgemeinschaft (v. 1977-83), Polish Soc. Theoretical Applied Mechani (hon. fgn.), also other sci. orgns. Home: Hannov Germany Deceased.

LEHNHOFF, HENRY JOHN, JR., physician; Lincoln, Nebr., Sept. 13, 1911; s. Henry John and R (Challis) L.; m. JoAnn Milliken, Sept. 16, 1939; ch dren: Henry John III, James Wood. B.A., U. Neb 1933; M.D., Northwestern U., 1938. Diplomate A Bd. Internal Medicine, Am. Bd. Med. Examiners. Inte Kings County Hosp., Bklyn., 1937-39; resident in ternal medicine Mayo Found., Rochester, Minn., 193 42; practice medicine specializing in internal medicir Omaha, from 1946; sr. staff Bishop Clarkson Me Hosp., Nebr. Meth. Hosp.; med. dir. Northwestern B Telephone Co., Omaha, Woodmen of World Life Ir Soc., Omaha; prof. internal medicine U. Nebr. Me Ctr., Omaha, endowed professorship, from 198 Contbr. articles to profl. jours. Served to lt. col. AU 1942-46. Recipient Disting. Service to Medicine awa U. Nebr. Med. Ctr., 1980. Fellow ACP; mem. AM, Nebr. Med. Assn., Am. Soc. Internat. Medicine, A Heart Assn., Royal Soc. Medicine (London), Am. Cc Occupational Medicine, Am. Rheumatism Assn., A Fedn. Clin. Research. Republican. Unitarian. Clu Omaha, Omaha Country. Deceased. Home: Omaha Ne

LEIBSON, CHARLES M., state supreme court justi b. Louisville, KY, June 30, 1929; m. Margaret Le son. LLB cum laude, U. Louisville, 1952; LLM, Va., 1986. Bar: Ky. 1952. Pvt. practice law Louisvil 1954-76; judge Ky. Cir. Ct., Louisville, 1976-82; justi Ky. Supreme Ct., Louisville, 1983-95; lectr. courtroc law U. Louisville Sch. Law, 1969-82; pres. Ky. As Trial Attys., 1965. Chmn. bd. trustees Jefferson Coun Pub. Law Library, 1978-81. 1st lt. JAGC U.S. Arm 1952-54. Named Judge of Yr., Louisville Bar Ass 1979, Ky.'s Outstanding Judge, Ky. Bar Assn., 19 recipient Outstanding State Trial Judge award As Trial Lawyers Am., 1980, Outstanding Svc. award K Pers. Bd., 1982, Disting. Alumni award U. Louisvi Sch. Law, 1984, Outstanding Legal Scholarship awa Brandeis Soc., 1984, Outstanding State Appellate Ju award, Assn. Trial Lawyers Am., 1985; fellow NE 1981. Fellow Internat. Acad. Trial Lawyers; me Louisville Bar Assn., Internat. Acad. Trial Judges, Inr Circle of Advs. Home: Louisville Ky. Died Dec., 199

LEIGH, BEVERLY EUGENE, oil company executi b. Savannah, Ga., Jan. 15, 1924; s. Herbert David a Pauline Catherine (Rehm) L.; m. Mary Pindar, Dec. 1944 (dec. 1968); children: John David, Julia Le West; m. Elizabeth LeHardy, Jan. 30, 1971. U. G 1948, Ga. Inst. Tech., 1950. Analyst U.S. Dept. Co merce, Savannah, Ga., 1953; vice chmn., treas. Colon Oil Industries Inc., Savannah, Ga., 1953-93. Served (j.g.) USNR, 1942-45. Republican. Episcopalian. ome: Savannah Ga. Died Feb. 1993.

EININGER, PAUL MILLER, retired chemistry edu-tor, consultant; b. Mohnton, Pa., Oct. 29, 1911; s. mer S. and Mabel Viola (Miller) L.; m. Miriam Viola achel, June 12, 1937; children: Paul M. Jr., Carol uise, Shirley Ann. BS in Edn., U. Pa., 1932, BS in hem. Engring., 1934, MS in Chemistry, 1936, PhD in ys. Chemistry, 1939. Cert. chemist Am. Inst. hemists. Asst. instr. U. Pa., Phila., 1934-38; chemist u Pont, Niagara Falls, N.Y., 1939-49; asst. prof. emistry Lafayette Coll., Easton, Pa., 1949-54; prof., ad chemistry dept. Albright Coll., Reading, Pa., 1954-; prof. chemistry Moravian Coll., Bethlehem, Pa., 77-78, Lehigh Valley C.C., Schnecksville, Pa., 1978-; cons. Geo W. Ballman Co., Adamstown, Pa., 1954-. Contbr. articles to Jour. Am. Chem. Soc., 1939-70. ol. various roles United Meth. Ch., Mohnton, Pa., 54-95. Mem. Am. Chem. Soc. (sect. chmn. 1934-95), n. Soc. for Metals, Sigma Xi. Home: Reading Pa. ed Oct. 4, 1995.

EINSDORF, ERICH, orchestra conductor; b. Vienna, ustria, Feb. 4, 1912; came to U.S., 1937, naturalized, 42; s. Ludwig Julius and Charlotte (Loebl) L.; m. nne Frohnknecht, Aug. 3, 1939 (div.); children: David, regor, Joshua, Hester, Jennifer; m. Vera Graf., 68. Ed., Vienna; Mus.D. (hon.), Baldwin-Wallace oll., Berea, Ohio, 1945, Rutgers U., 1952; Mus.D. hon. gree, Williams Coll., 1966, Columbia, 1967. Asst. ndr. Salzburg Festival, 1934-37; condr. Met. Opera, til 1943, Cleve. Orch., 1943; music dir. Philharmonic ch., Rochester, 1947-56; dir. N.Y.C. Center Opera, 56, Met. Opera, 1957-62; music dir. Boston mphony Orch., 1962-69; Past mem. Corp. for Pub. oadcasting; past mem. exec. com. John F. Kennedy enter for Performing Arts; mem. Nat. Coun. on Arts. uest appearances with maj. orchs. in, U.S., Europe, cluding, Phila., Los Angeles, St. Louis, New Orleans, pls., Concertgebouw, Amsterdam, Israel ilharmonic, San Francisco Opera, Bayreuth, Holland d Prague festival, London, BBC, London Symphony, rchestre de Paris, Cleve. Orch., Chgo. Symphony, erlin Philharmonic, N.Y. Philharmonic, Vienna mphony; author: Cadenza, The Composer's Advocate, 81; contbr. articles to High Fidelity, Daedalus, N.Y. mes; transcriptions of Brahms Chorale Preludes; cords for RCA Victor, Westminster, Columbia, Decca ondon), E.M.I. Fellow Am. Acad. Arts and Scis.; em. Nat. Endowment Arts. Home: Malverne New ork Died Sept. 11, 1993.

EISHER, WILLIAM RODGER, art institute con-rvator; b. Alden, Mich., Feb. 9, 1941; s. Ralph anklin and Helen Doris (Brewer) L.; m. Doris Louise aycock, Dec. 27, 1967; children: Gregory William, hristina Katherine Park. BA, Mich. State U., 1967, A, 1970, BFA, 1972; postgrad., Intermus. Lab., berlin, Ohio, 1972-74. Asst. conservator painting Nat. allery Art, Washington, 1974-80; head conservation os Angeles County Mus. Art, 1980-85; exec. dir. con-rvation Art Inst. Chgo., 1985-90. Bd. trustees In-rmus. Conservation Assn., Oberlin, Ohio; chmn. Nat. st. Conservation, 1989-92. With USN, 1959-63. DEA fellow, 1968-70. Mem. Nat. Inst. for Conserva-on (vice chmn. 1985-92, bd. dirs. 1982-84, energy com. 977-80, facilities com. 1979-80, environ. standards com. 980-83), Internat. Inst. Conservation Historic and Ar-tic Works, Am. Inst. Conservation Historic and Ar-tic Works, Phi Kappa Phi, Kappa Delta Pi. esbyterian (elder). Home: Evanston Ill. Died Sept. 8, 992.

EITCH, ALMA MAY, city official; b. Fredericksburg, a., Nov. 24, 1924; d. Maurice Andrew Doggett and ora May (Spicer) L.; grad. high sch., Fredericksburg; rious specialized courses U. Va., Va. Poly. Inst. Dep. ommnr. revenue City of Fredericksburg, 1946-69, ommr. revenue, 1970-94; mem. Va. Adv. Legis. ouncil, 1977-78; mem. subcom. Commonwealth Va. evenue Resources and Econ. Commn., 1978. Bd. dirs. redericksburg chpt. ARC, 1960-94, chmn., 1969, redericksburg, Stafford and Spotsylvania chpt. treas., 988-94; sec. Dem. Com. Fredericksburg, 1964; pres., d. dirs. Rappahannock United Way for Fredericksburg, ootsylvania, and Stafford counties, 1979; mem. Our own Fredericksburg, Fredericksburg Area Mus., homas Jefferson Inst., Inc., Friends of the James lonroe Mus., The Met. Opera Guild; trustee Frederick-urg Rescue Squad. Recipient various svc. awards, utstanding Citizenship award Fredericksburg Area C. C., 1979, Clara Barton Honor award Natl. Chmn. olunteers, 1992. Mem. Commrs. Revenue Assn. Va. xec. legis. com., pres. 1979-80), Va. Govtl. Employees ssn. (dir.-at-large 1979-80), League No. Va. Commrs. evenue (pres. 1972), Va. Assn. Local Exec. Constl. fficers (exec. com.), Internat. Assn. Assessing Officers, a. Assn. Assessing Officers, Hist. Fredericksburg ound., Bus. and Profl. Women's Club, Ann Page arden Club (pres. 1980-82, Mary B. Benoit award 977), Altrusa Club. Died June 21, 1994; buried Oak ill, Fredericksburg, Va. Home: Fredericksburg Va.

ELOIR, LUIS FEDERICO, biochemist, educator; b. aris, Sept. 6, 1906; m. Amelie Zuherbuhler de Leloir, 1 au. Ed., U. Buenos Aires; Dr. h.c., univs. Paris, ranada, Cordoba. Research chemist Inst. Biology and Exptl. Medicine, Buenos Aires, Argentina, 1946-47; dir. Inst. Biochem. Research, Campomar, Argentina, 1947—; head dept. biochemistry U. Buenos Aires, Campomar, Argentina, 1962—; mem. directory NRC, Campomar, Argentina, 1958-64. Maj. research includes: isolation of glucose diphosphate, 1948, of uridine diphosphate glucose, 1950, of uridine diphosphate acetylglucosamine, 1953, mechanism of glycogen, 1959, of starch biosynthesis, 1960, isolation of dolechol phosphate from liver, 1970. Recipient Nobel prize for chemistry, 1970. Fgn. mem. Nat. Acad. Scis. (U.S.), Am. Acad. Art and Scis., Am. Philos. Soc.; mem. Argentine Assn. Advancement Sci. (chmn. 1958-59), Nat. Acad. Medicine. Home: Buenos Aires Argentina

LELYVELD, ARTHUR JOSEPH, rabbi; b. N.Y.C., Feb. 6, 1913; s. Edward Joseph and Dora (Cohen) L.; m. Toby Bookholtz, Dec. 26, 1933 (div.); children: Joseph Salem, David Simon, Michael Stephen; m. 2d, Teela Stovsky, Dec. 5, 1964; children: Benjamin (dec.), Robin Beth. AB, Columbia U., 1933; M Hebrew Letters, Hebrew Union Coll., Cin., 1939; DD honoris causa, Hebrew Union Coll.-Jewish Inst. Religion, 1955; LittD (hon.), Cleve. Coll. Jewish Studies, 1986. Rabbi Congregation B'nai Israel, Hamilton, Ohio, 1939-41, Temple Israel, Omaha, 1941-44; pres. Jewish Peace Fellowship, 1941-43; exec. dir. Com. Unity for Palestine, 1944-46, nat. vice chmn., 1944-48; assoc. nat. dir. B'nai B'rith Hillel Founds., N.Y.C., 1946-47; nat. dir. B'nai B'rith Hillel Founds., 1948-56; exec. v.p. Am.-Israel Cultural Found., 1956-58; rabbi Fairmount Temple, Cleve., 1958-86, sr. rabbi emeritus, 1986-96; interim rabbi Temple Emanu-El, Honolulu, 1994-95; founder, bd. dirs. Am. Jewish Soc. for Service, 1941; mem. adv. bd. Pastoral Psychology Inst., Case Western Res. U. Sch. Medicine; B.G. Rudolph lectr. in Judaic Studies, Syracuse U., 1984; lectr. So. African Union for Prog. Judaism, 1985; vis. scholar Oxford Ctr. for Postgrad. Hebrew Studies, Oxford, Eng.; adj. prof. religion Case Western Res. U., 1979-80; Bernard Rich Hollander lectr. in Jewish Thought, John Carroll U., 1980-96; Walter and Mary Tuohy chair in Interreligious Studies, John Carroll U., 1989; sr. teaching fellow Cleve. Coll. Jewish Studies, 1986-96; sec. Joint Rabbinical Com. Conscientious Objectors, 1941-46; Am. vice chmn. World U. Service, 1955-65; nat. pres. Am. Jewish Congress, 1966-72, hon. pres., 1972-96; Goldenson lectr. Hebrew Union Coll.-Jewish Inst. Religion, 1973. Author: Atheism is Dead, 1968, paperback edit., 1970, 2d edit., 1985), The Steadfast Stream, 1995; contbg. author: Religion in the State University, Jewish Heritage Reader, Censorship: For or Against, Punishment: For or Against, Population Control: For or Against; contbr. Universal Jewish Ency., periodicals. Am. chmn. Omaha Fair Employment Practice Coun., 1942-44; pub. panel chmn. WLB 1944; exec. com. Nat. Hillel commn.; gen. chmn. Cleve. Jewish Welfare Fund, 1963; bd. advisors Martin Luther King Ctr. for Social Change. Edward L. Heinsheimer fellow, 1939-41; recipient Centennial medal John Carroll U., 1986; recipient award Western Res. Hist. Soc., 1992. Mem. Commn. on Social Action of Reform Judaism (hon. life), NAACP (hon. exec. com. Cleve. br.), Cen. Conf. Am. Rabbis (exec. bd., nat. v.p. 1973-75, pres. 1975-77), Synagogue Council Am. (nat. v.p. 1975-79, nat. pres. 1979-81), Am. Jewish League Israel (nat. v.p. 1962-84, hon. pres. 1984-96), Nacoms, Phi Beta Kappa, Beta Sigma Rho. Lodge: B'nai B'rith. Home: Cleveland Ohio Died Apr. 15, 1996.

LEMKE, LEROY WALTER, lawyer, state senator; b. Chgo., Sept. 24, 1935; s. Otto Mark and Myrtle Theresa L.; B.S.B.A., Drake U., 1959; J.D., John Marshall Law Sch., 1964; children—Lee Alan, Ronda Lee Lemke Alvarado, Kevin Keith. Bar: Ill. Individual practice law, Chgo., 1973; rep. Ill. Legislature, 1973-75; mem. Ill. State Senate, 1975-87 . Founder, chmn. Ill. Ethnic Heritage Commn. Named Outstanding Senator, Ill. Fedn. Pvt. Univs. and Colls.; Outstanding Legislator, Polish Community Council. Mem. ABA, Ill. Bar Assn., Chgo. Bar Assn., Bohemian Bar Assn., Casimir Pulaski Civic League. Democrat. Home: Chicago Ill.

LENEHAN, WILLIAM THURMAN, English language educator; b. Winnsboro, Tex., May 25, 1930; s. William Allen and Syble (Thurman) L.; m. Angelena Frensley, Aug. 25, 1962; 1 dau., Roma Eileen. B.A., U. Okla., 1955, Ph.D., 1963. Mem. faculty dept. English U. Wis., Madison, 1962-93, prof., 1970-90, prof. emeritus, 1990-93, chmn. dept., 1977-80; chmn. U. Wis. System Basic Skills Task Force, 1978-80, U. Wis. System Basic Skills Task Force (Basic SKills Council), 1980-81, U. Wis. System Testing and Assessment Com., 1987-93. Author: (with Wilma Ebbett) The Writer's Reader, 1967; editor: Alhambra (Washington Irving), 1984; contbr. articles to profl. jours. Served with USAF, 1950-53. Mem. MLA. Home: Madison Wis. Died May 20, 1993.

LENHARTZ, RUDOLF, coal mining executive; b. Buende, Westphalia, Germany, Feb. 10, 1925; Dipl.-Ing., univs. Bonn and Aachen, 1947, Ass.d.B., 1956; m. Gertrud Siekmeier, 1956; 2 children. Mine supt. and engring. mgr. Rheinelbe Bergbau AG, 1956-63, mem. mng. bd., 1965-69; gen. dir. mining ops. Ruhrkohle AG, Essen, W. Ger., 1970-75; chmn. bd. Saarbergwerke AG, Saarbrücken, W. Ger., from 1976; pres. supervisory and adv. bd. Saar-Ferngas AG, Saarbrücken, Saarberg Oel und Handel GmbH, Saarbrücken; mem. mng. com. Gesamtverband des deutschen Steinkohlenbergbaus, Essen, Steinkohlenbergbauverein, Essen; pres. Wirtschaftsvereinigung Bergbau, Bonn; mem. consultative com. European Community Coal and Steel, Brussels; mem. consultative bd. for coal Internat. Energy Agy., Paris. Author tech. articles. Deceased. Home: Saarbrücken Germany

LENIHAN, BRIAN JOSEPH, Irish government official; b. Dundalk, County Louth, Ireland, Nov. 17, 1930; s. Patrick J. and Ann (Scanlon) L.; m. Ann Devine, 1958; 5 children. Student, St. Mary's Coll., Athlone, Ireland; BA, U. Coll., Dublin; LLB, King's Inns Coll., Dublin. Bar: Ireland 1952. Mem. Dail Eireaan (Irish Parliament), Dublin, 1961—; parliamentary sec. to Minister for Lands, Dublin, 1961-64; minister justice Ireland, Dublin, 1964-68, minister edn., 1968-69, minister transport and power, 1969-73, minister fgn. affairs, 1973, 79-81, 87-89, minister fisheries, 1977-79, minister agr., 1982, dep. prime minister, 1987-90, minister for defence, 1989-90. Home: Dublin Ireland Died November 1, 1995.

LENNEBERG, HANS, music librarian, educator; b. Germany, May 16, 1924; came to U.S. 1940; s. Julius and Gisela (Heinemann) L., m. Johanna Kauffman, Sept. 11, 1972; children: Michael, Stephen Sonnenfeld, Peter. AB, Bklyn. Coll.of CUNY, 1952; AM, NYU, 1956, postgrad., 1960; MLS, Pratt Inst., 1962. Instr. music Bklyn Coll. of CUNY, 1956-60; librarian Bklyn. Pub. Libr., 1960-62, asst. head Art and Music div., 1962-63; asst. prof., music librarian U. Chgo., 1963-65, assoc. prof., 1965-85, prof., performing arts librarian, 1985-94. Editor: Modern German Music, Musicology in the Third Reich, 1994, Dissemination of Music, 1994; co-editor: Aspects of Medieval and Renaissance Music, 1956, Jour. Musicol. Rsch.; author: Witnesses and Scholars, 1988, Breitkopf und Hartel in Paris, 1990; contbr. articles to profl. jours. mem. Am. Musicological Soc., Internat. Soc. Music Librs., Music Libr. Assn.. Home: Chicago Ill. Died Sept. 7, 1994.

LEON, EDWARD J., lawyer; b. Chgo., Nov. 4, 1899; s. Murad and Susan (Tann) L.; m. Helen Hall, Sept. 5, 1970; 1 son, Richard Hall. Student, Columbia U., 1920; NYU, 1923. Bar: Conn. 1923, N.Y. 1925, D.C. 1943, U.S. Supreme Ct 1943. Mem. firm. Leon, Weill and Mahony (and predecessors), N.Y.C., 1945-84; counsel Tenzer, Greenblatt, Fallon & Kaplan, N.Y.C., from 1984; Prin. officer Bd. Econ. Warfare, Washington, 1942-43. Pres., dir. Children's Blood Found.; trustee Pop Warner Football Scholars. Mem. Am. Soc. International. Law, Am. Judicature Soc., Am. Bar Assn., New York County lawyers Assn. Clubs: New York Athletic, Winged Foot Golf. Home: New York N.Y. Deceased.

LEONARD, RICHARD MANNING, retired lawyer; b. Elyria, Ohio, Oct. 22, 1908; s. Charles M. and Donna Rae (Russell) L.; m. Doris Frances Corcoran, July 14, 1934; children: Frances (Mrs. Richard Best), Elizabeth. J.D., U. Calif. at Berkeley, 1932. Bar: Calif. bar 1933, U.S. Supreme Ct. bar 1941. Chief atty. Regional Agrl. Credit Corp., 1932-38; gen. practice law San Francisco, 1938-42, 46-55; partner firm Leonard & Dole, San Francisco, 1955-88, ret., 1988; dir. Varian Assos., Palo Alto, Calif., 1948-74; past sec.; dir. Western Gold and Platinum Co., 1955-79, Granger Assos., Palo Alto, 1956-80, also other corps. Author: Belaying the Leader, 1946; Contbr.: also articles to tech. jours. Climbers Guide to Yosemite Valley and Sierra Nevada. Active in conservation projects, 1930-93; mem. Calif. Scenic Hwy. Commn., 1963-69, Calif. Redwood Parks Commn., 1969-93; participant White House Conf. Natural Beauty, 1965; founder, pres. Conservation Law Soc. Am., Sierra Club Found.; founder, trustee Trustees for Conservation; founder, sec. Am. Conservation Films, Varian Found., Forest Genetics Research Found.; vice chmn. commn. on legislation Internat. Union for Conservation Nature, 1963-69; bd. dirs. Save-the-Redwoods League, 1954-93, v.p., 1966-75, pres., 1975-80, chmn., 1980-93; bd. dirs. Sierra Club, 1938-73, pres., 1953-55, hon. pres., 1976-93; bd. dirs. Wilderness Soc., 1948-82, v.p., 1962-63. Served from 1st lt. to maj. AUS, 1942-46, CBI. Decorated Bronze Star; recipient award Calif. Conservation Coun., 1950, Izaak Walton League Am., 1954, Am. Motors Conservation award, 1954, Albright award Am. Scenic and Hist. Preservation Soc., 1972, John Muir award, 1973, Leopold Nature Conservancy, 1984; Redwood Grove in Redwood Nat. Park dedicated to Richard and Doris Leonard, 1993, Redwood Grove in Big Basin Redwood State Park dedicated to Richard and Doris Leonard, 1994. Club: Am. Alpine (hon. mem.). Home: Berkeley Calif. Died July 31, 1993; creamted.

LEONOV, LEONID MAKSIMOVICH, writer; b. Moscow, May 31, 1899; ed. Moscow U. Dep. to Surpeme Soviet, 1970; dir. Pushkin Dom (Pushkin House-U.S.S.R. Acad. Scis., Inst. Russian Lit.), 1972; sec. of bd. USSR Union of Writers; books include: Barsuki, 1924; The Thief, 1927; Sotj, 1930; Skutarevsky, 1932; Road to the Ocean, 1936; The Ordinary Man, 1941; Lenushka, 1943; The Fall of Velikoshumsk, 1944; The Golden Car, 1946; Sazancha, 1959; Mr. McKinley's Flight, 1961; Evgenia Ivanovna, 1963; Plays, 1964; Sot', 1968; The Russian Forest, 1973; In the War Years and After, 1974; Moscow Publicistics, 1976. Recipient State prize, 1942, Lenin prize, 1957; decorated Order of Lenin (four times), Hero of Socialist Labour, Hammer and Sickle Gold medal, Order of Red Banner of Labour, Order of Patriotic War, Merited Worker of Arts of R.S.F.S.R. Died Aug. 8, 1994. Home: Moscow Russia

LEOPOLD, IRVING HENRY, physician, medical educator; b. Phila., Apr. 19, 1915; s. Abraham and Dora (Schlow) L.; m. Eunice Robinson, June 24, 1937; children: Ellen Robinson, John Robinson. BS, Pa. State U., 1934; MD, U. Pa., 1938, DSc, 1943. Diplomate Am. Bd. Ophthalmology (chmn. bd. 1971-72, examiner 1974-81, subcom. impaired vision and blindness 1967-69, task force on ocular pharmacology 1967-69, cons. 1975-79). Intern U. Pa. Hosp., 1938-40; fellow, instr. ophthalmology U. Pa. Hosp., U. Pa. Med. Sch., 1940-45; assoc. Hosp. U. Pa., also U. Pa. Med. Sch., 1945-54; research investigator chem. warfare OSRD, 1941-45; mem. faculty U. Pa. Grad. Sch. Medicine, 1946-64, successively assoc., asst. prof., assoc. prof., 1946-55, prof., head dept. ophthalmology, 1955-64; chief dept. ophthalmology Grad. Hosp., 1955-64; dir. research Wills Eye Hosp., 1949-64, attending surgeon, 1952-64, med. dir., 1961-64, cons. surgeon, 1965-73; chmn. sci. adv. com. Allergan, Inc., 1974, Sr. v.p., 1975; prof., chmn. dept. ophthalmology Mt. Sinai Sch. Medicine, 1965-75; dir. dept. ophthalmology Mt. Sinai Hosp., N.Y.C., 1964-75; prof., chmn. dept. ophthalmology U. Calif. at Irvine, 1975-85, prof. pharmacology, 1982-93, prof. emeritus ophthalmology, 1985-93; clin. prof. ophthalmolgy Coll. Physicians and Surgeons, Columbia, 1964-67; cons. ophthalmologist St. Joseph's Hosp., 1959-64, Albert Einstein Med. Center, 1959-64; Proctor lectr. U. Calif., 1962; Gifford Meml. lectr., Chgo., 1967; Edwin B. Dunphy lectr. Harvard, 1968; Walter Wright lectr. U. Toronto, 1969; Richardson Cross lectr. Royal Soc. Medicine, 1970; Doyne Meml. lectr. Ophthal. Soc. U.K., 1971; DeSchweinitz Meml. lectr., Phila., 1972; Jules Stein lectr. UCLA, 1974; Bedell lectr., Phila., 1975; Edwin B. Dunphy lectr. Harvard, 1975; Francis H. Adler lectr., Phila., 1980, Dwight Towne lectr., Ky., 1979, C.S. O'Brien lectr., New Orleans, 1979; Disting. vis. lectr. Jefferson Med. Coll., 1980, Moorfields Hosp., Eng., 1980, U. Helsinki, Finland, 1980, Third Francis Heed Adler lectr., 1980, 2d ann. Tullos O. Coston lectr., 1981, Sir Stewart Duke-Elder lectr., 1982, Everett R. Viers lectr., Scott and White Clinic and Tex. A&M U. Coll. Medicine, Temple, Tex., 1982, U. Phillipines 1st lectr, 1st Irving H. Leopold lectr. Wills Eye Hosp, 1987-93; Eye Resident Soc., Eye Referral Ctr., 1982, Royal Soc. Medicine lectr., London, 1985; lectr. Internat. Congress Ophthalmology, Japan, 1978, Phillipine Bd. Opthalmology, Charles May lectr. N.Y. Acad. Medicine, 1990; cons. Chem. Warfare Service, U.S. Army, 1948-52, 81; surgeon gen. USPHS, 1952-58, FDA, HEW, 1963; mem. med. adv. com. Orange County chpt. Multiple Sclerosis Soc., 1979-81; chmn. ophthalmology panel U.S. Pharmacopeia, 1960-70, mem. revision panel, 1970-93; chmn. panel drug efficacy in ophthalmology Nat. Acad. Scis.-NRC, 1966-67, 80-93; mem. tng. grants com. USPHS, 1952-58, mem. spl. sensory study sect. research neurol. diseases and blindness, 1954-58; mem. field investigating com. Nat. Inst. Neurol. Diseases and Blindness, 1959-61, mem. neurol. project com., 1961-63, chmn. vision research tng. com., 1967-68; mem. adv. bd. Am. Behcet's Found., Inc., 1980, 81; Expert Agree to Ministry of Health, France, 1981-87; curator ophthalmic pharmaceuticals Found. Am. Acad. Ophthalmology, 1983-89; mem. nat. adv. eye council panel on cataract sect. Nat. Eye Inst. and HEW, 1981-85; mem. med. research and devel. command-chemical welfare U.S. Army, 1981-85. Editor-in-chief: Survey of Ophthalmology, 1958-62; cons. editor, 1962-93; editorial bd.: Am. Jour. Diabetes, 1956-73, Investigative Ophthalmology, 1961-74; assoc. editor: Am. Jour. Ophthalmology, 1984-92; now mem. editorial bd.: assoc. editor Archives of Ophthalmology, 1974-81; cons. Jour. AMA, 1974-81; editorial cons. Jour. Ocular Pharmacology, 1985-92; editor: Ocular Inflammation and Therapeutics, 1981. Trustee Seeing Eye Guide. Recipient Zentmayer award, 1945, 49; honor award Am. Acad. Ophthalmology, 1955, Sr. Hon. award, 1984; Edward Lorenzo Holmes citation and award, 1957; Friedenwald medal Assn. Research Ophthalmology, 1960; Disting. Research award U. Calif., Irvine, Calif., 1980; Disting. Research award U. Calif. Alumni Assn., 1980, Disting. Service to Ophthalmology, 1988; Physician's award Pa. Acad. Ophthalmology and Otolaryngology, 1981; Sir Steward Duke-Elder award, Lederle Medal and Prize for Research in Glaucoma Internat. Glaucoma Congress VI and Am. Soc. Contemporary Ophthalmology, Orlando, Fla., 1982. Mem. N.Y. Acad. Medicine, Am. Ophthal. Soc. (Verhoeff Meml. lectr. 1973, Lucien Howe medal 1974), Am. Acad. Ophthalmology and Otolaryngology (chmn. drug com. ophthalmology 1963-74, Edward Jackson Meml. lectr. 1965, honor guest 1971, 75, Philip M. Corboy Perpetual Excellence award 1988, Disting. Service to Ophthalmology award 1988), Am. Soc. Contemporary Ophthalmology (chief cons. editorial bd. 1981), Assn. Research Ophthalmology (trustee, chmn.), Nat. Soc. Prevention Blindness (dir. 1974-81, v.p., exec. com., hon. bd. dirs.), A.C.S., AAAS, Art Alliance Phila., John Morgan Soc., Coll. Physicians Phila., Am. Diabetes Assn., AMA (chmn. residency rev. com. ophthalmology 1970-72, Physician's Recognition award 1980-87), N.Y. Acad. Sci., Pan Am. Assn. Ophthalmology, Pan Pacific Surg. Assn., Royal Soc. Medicine (London), N.Y. State, N.Y. County, Philadelphia County med. socs., Calif., Orange County med. assns., Orange County Soc. Ophthalmology, Am. Med. Student Assn., Nat. Soc. to Prevent Blindness (hon. bd. dirs. 1986-89), Med. Biochemist Club, Vesper Club, Sigma Xi, Alpha Omega Alpha. Clubs: Medical Biochemists, Big Canyon Country, Balboa Bay. Home: Newport Beach Calif. Died Aug. 2, 1993; interred Pacific View, Newport Beach, Calif.

LEOPOLD, ROBERT LIVINGSTON, psychiatrist, educator; b. Phila., Oct. 5, 1922; s. Simon Stein and Loraine (Livingston) L.; m. Edith Abelmann, Sept. 17, 1944; children: David A., Donald R., William S. A.B., Harvard U., 1944; M.D., U. Pa., 1946; postgrad., Phila. Psychoanalytic Inst., 1949-55. Intern, then resident neurology Grad. Hosp., U. Pa., 1946-50; fellow psychiatry Inst. Pa. Hosp., 1950-51, mem. staff; fellow psychiatry Hosp. U. Pa., 1951-52, mem. staff; practice medicine specializing in psychiatry and psychoanalysis Phila., 1952-67; dir. West Phila. Community Mental Health Consortium, 1967-72; prof. community medicine and psychiatry U. Pa., Phila., 1968-76, prof. psychiatry, 1968-94, chmn. dept. community medicine, 1971-76; psychiatrist-in-chief Phila. Psychiat. Ctr., 1980-82, also mem. staff; cons. psychiatry Am. Friends Service Com., Phila., 1954-94; sr. psychiat. cons. Peace Corps, Washington, 1961-67. Bd. dirs. Eagleville Hosp., Emergency Care Research Found.; chmn. Eagleville Found., 1984-89. Served with AUS, 1943-46. Fellow Am. Psychiat. Assn. (life); mem. AMA, Pa., Philadelphia County med. socs., Am. Psychoanalytic Assn., Internat. Psychoanalytical Assn., Phila. Coll. Physicians, Group Advancement Psychiatry. Home: Haverford Pa. Died Apr. 9, 1994.

LERMAN, LEO, writer, editor in chief; b. N.Y.C., May 23, 1914; s. Samuel and Ida (Goldwasser) L. Student, Feagin Sch. Drama Arts, 1 yr. Author: Leonardo da Vinci: Artist and Scientist, Michaelangelo: A Renaissance Profile, Museum: 100 Years of the Metropolitan Museum of Art (Lotus Club award); contbr. articles to popular mags. including Vogue, House and Garden, Am. Scholar, Saturday Review, Atlantic Monthly; column writer for Dance mag.; features editor Mademoiselle, Vogue; editor-in-chief Vanity Fair; editorial advisor Conde Nast Publs. Mem. Scenic Artists Am. (past pres. costume div.). Home: New York N.Y. Died Aug. 22, 1994.

LERNER, RITA GUGGENHEIM, association executive, information scientist, physicist; b. N.Y.C., May 7, 1929; d. Karl and Fannie (Gottesman) Guggenheim; m. Arnold Lerner, Feb. 14, 1954; children: James, Richard. A.B. cum laude, Radcliffe Coll., 1949; M.A., Columbia U., 1951, Ph.D., 1956. Research assoc. Columbia U., N.Y.C., 1956-64, dir. biol. sci. labs., 1968; mgr. info. analysis Am. Inst. Physics, N.Y.C., 1964-67, mgr. planning and devel., 1969-74, mgr. spl. projects, 1974-79, mgr. mktg. div., 1979-84, mgr. books div., 1985-90; consulting editor VCH Pubs., Inc., from 1990; mem. adv. com. on 108(i) U.S. Copyright Office, 1974-79; cons. editor Hutchinson & Ross, 1975-85. Editor: Encyclopedia of Physics, 1980, 2d edit., 1990, Concise Encyclopedia of Solid State Physics, 1984; contbr. articles to profl. jours. Pres. Ardsley PTA, N.Y., 1955-56. NSF grantee, 1975-80. Fellow AAAS (council, com. on council affairs 1981-84); mem. Assn. Info. Dissemination Ctrs. (pres. 1981-83), Am. Phys. Soc., Am. Chem. Soc., Am. Soc. for Info. Sci., N.Y. Acad. Scis., Sigma Xi. Deceased. Home: Ardsley N.Y.

LESCH, GEORGE HENRY, household products company executive; b. Washburn, Ill., Oct. 10, 1909; s. William and Cora (Held) L.; m. Esther Barrett, Aug. 16, 1935; children: Elizabeth (Mrs. Arthur Ramee), Georgette (Mrs. Mark Copeland). B.S. with honours, U. Ill., 1931; LL.D., Syracuse U., 1964. With Arthur Anderson & Co. (C.P.A.'s), Chgo., 1931-32; with Colgate Palmolive Co., 1932-94; beginning as mem. fgn. dept., successively mem. European auditing staff, treas. Colgate-Palmolive S.A.; pres., v.p. Colgate Palmolive Internat. charge sales and advt., U.K. and Europe, 1932-57; pres. Colgate Palmolive Internat., 1957-60; also dir.; pres., chief exec. officer Colgate-Palmolive Co., 1960-61, chmn. bd., pres., 1961-70, chmn. bd., 1970-75; bd. dirs. Anchor Hocking Co., Bank of N.Y., Am. Sugar Co., Woolworth Co., Uniroyal Co. Trustee Syracuse U. Decorated comdr. Order Merit (Italy). Club: Candlewood Lake (Conn.). Home: Sarasota Fla. Died Sept. 22, 1994.

LESHER, DEAN STANLEY, newspaper publisher; b. Williamsport, Md., Aug. 7, 1902; s. David Thomas and Margaret Eliot (Prosser) L.; m. Kathryn C. Lesher, Nov. 2, 1929 (dec. Mar. 1971); children: Carolyn Lee (dec.), Dean Stanley, Melinda Kay, Cynthia; m. Margaret Louise Lisco, Apr. 2, 1973. BA magna cum laude, U. Md., 1924; JD, Harvard U., 1926. Bar: Mo. 1926. Sole practice Kansas City, 1926-41; gen. counsel Postal Life & Casualty Ins. Co., Kansas City, 1936-41; chmn. bd., pub. East Bay Pub. Co., 1947-60, Lesher Communications, Inc., Walnut Creek, Calif., 1960-93; pres. 31 newspaper owning corps. Contbr. articles to trade publs. Trustee Calif. State Univs. and Colls., 1973-81, 85-93; regent St. Mary's Coll., 1978-82, John F. Kennedy U., 1981-93; mem. Calif. Post-Secondary Edn. Commn., 1979-81. Named News Pub. of Calif., 1977, Best Bus. Leader Walnut Creek Area, 1978, Edn. Pub. of Calif., 1980, Citizen of Yr. Contra Cos County, 1985; recipient Medal of Freedom Valley For, Freedom Found., 1988. Mem. Am. Newspaper Pub Assn., Suburban Newspapers Am. (bd. dirs., Ou standing Pub. award 1982, award named in honor 198 93), Nat. Newspaper Assn. (bd. dirs., spl. award Pres. Reagan & V.P. Bush in White House 198 Walnut Creek (Calif.) C. of C. (pres.), Round H Country Club, Concord Century Club, Harvard Clu Rotary (past dist. gov.), Masons, Phi Kappa Phi, F Delta Theta, Theta Sigma Phi, Sigma Delta Chi. Republican. Home: Orinda Calif. Died May 14, 1993.

LESLIE, WILLIAM H(OUGHTON), minister; Norwalk, Ohio, July 10, 1932; s. William Houghton a Mildred (Wilkinson) L.; m. Adrienne Andrews, July 2 1956 (div. July 1990); children: Laurel, Lisa, Andrew Mark. Student, Bob Jones U., 1950-53; BA wi honors, Wheaton (Ill.) Coll., 1954, MDiv, 1961; M. Northwestern U., 1965, PhD, 1976. Ordained ministry Bapt. Ch., 1957. Sr. pastor 1st Bapt. C Pekin, Ill., 1956-59; asst. pastor Moody Meml. C Chgo., 1959-61; sr. pastor La Salle St. Ch., Chgo., 196 90; sr. assoc. Mid Am. Leadership Found., Chgo., 199 93; frequent retreat and forum speaker. Contbr. artic to profl. jours. Pres. Chgo. Orleans Housing, In 1970-87; bd. dirs. Just Life, Washington, 1986-9 Cabrini-Green Neighborhood Devel. Ptnrs., Chg 1986-89, Kesho Maruno, Chgo., 1988-93; Interna Urban Assocs., Chgo., 1989-93, Community You Creative Learning Experience, Chgo., 1990-93; g Opportunities Internat., Chgo., 1986-93; bd. di Community Renewal Soc., Chgo., 1987-93, pres., 199 Mem. Inst. for Spiritual Companionship (bd. dirs. 198 93), Inst. for Justice Ministries (bd. dirs. 1990-93), A Acad. Religion, Soc. Bibl. Lit., Sem. Consortium f Urban Pastoral Edn. Home: Chicago Ill. Decease

LE SUEUR, MERIDEL, author; b. Murray, Iowa, Fe 22, 1900; d. Winston William Wharton and Marion Sueur; children: Rachel, Deborah. Author fiction, h tory, biography and autobiography, from 1930; auth The Girl, Rites of Ancient Ripening, Harvest, Song f My Time, Worker Writer, Women on the Breadlin North Star Country, I Hear Men Talking, The Lit Spook, Ripening: Selecting Work, 1927-80, 1983, (wi John Crawford) Worker Writers, 1982, Salute to Sprir 1983, Word Is Movement, 1984, Crusaders: The Radic Legacy of Marian and Arthur LeSueur, 1984. Recipie U. Minn. Rockefeller History award, 1955; recipie Nat. Endowment of Arts Eugene Debsaward, 1982 Home: Saint Paul Minn. Deceased.

LEVANDOWSKI, DONALD WILLIAM, geologist; Stockett, Mont., Dec. 20, 1927; s. Anthony and A (Hudak) L.; m. Martha Mary Midlik, June 4, 19 children: Mari Ann, Laura Joan. B.S., Mont. C Mineral Sci. and Tech., 1950; M.S., U. Mich., 19 Ph.D. (Phoenix Meml. fellow), 1956. Cert. profl. ologist, Ind. Research geologist Chevron Oil Fie Research Co., La Habra, Calif., 1955-64; adminst asst. to mgr. exploration research, 1964-65; geophysic Standard Oil of Calif., La Habra, 1965-67; asst. pa chief Dept. Natural Resources, Quebec, Que., summ 1969; assoc. prof. dept. geoscis. Purdue U., W Lafayette, Ind., 1967-75; assoc. head dept. geosc Purdue U., 1970-76, prof., 1975-93, acting head, 197 78, head, 1978-88; ret., 1993; dir. Ind. Mining a Mineral Resources Rsch. Inst., 1980-93. Contbr. te articles to profl. jours. Recipient ERDAS Best S award, 1992, Autometric award for superior pub. imagery interpretation, 1992. Fellow Geol. Soc. A mem. AAAS, Am. Assn. Petroleum Geologists, A Inst. Profl. Geol. Scientists (cert.), Am. S Photogrammetry, Sigma Xi, Phi Kappa Phi. Repub can. Roman Catholic. Club: Explorers. Home: W Lafayette Ind. Died Apr. 8, 1994.

LEVER, WALTER FREDERICK, physician, educat b. Erfurt, Germany, Dec. 13, 1909; emigrated to U. 1935, naturalized, 1941; s. Alexander and Ed (Hirschberg) L.; m. Frances Broughton, 1940 (d 1969); children: Joan (Mrs. Russell Young), Susan (M Richard Siskind); m. Gundula Schaumburg, May 1971; children: Insa Bettina, Mark Alexander. Stude U. Heidelberg, Germany, 1928-30; M.D., U. Leipz Germany, 1934, hon. doctorate, 1990; M.D. (hon.), F U. Berlin, 1984, hon. doctorate, 1983. Diplomate A Bd. Dermatology (spl. competence certification dermatopathology). Intern Cologne (Germany) Hosp., 1934-35, St. John's Hosp., Bklyn., 1936; resid dermatology Mass. Gen. Hosp., Boston, 1936-3 research fellow Mass. Gen. Hosp., 1938-44; from asst. asst. clin. prof. dermatology Harvard Med. Sch., 19 59, lectr., 1959-76; prof. dermatology Tufts U. M Sch, 1959-75, prof. emeritus, 1975-92, chmn. de 1961-75, acting chmn., 1975-78; lectr. dermatol Boston U. Med. Sch., 1978-82; dir. dermatology serv Boston City Hosp., 1961-74; dermatologist-in-chief N Eng. Med. Center Hosps., 1959-78, assoc. staff me 1978-83; bd. consultation Mass. Gen. Hosp., 1959- hon. dermatologist, 1976-83; cons. Robert Br Brigham Hosp., 1949-76; prin. investigator li metabolism USPHS, 1951-65, electron microsco 1962-75; mem. gen. medicine study sect. NIH, 1959- Dohi lectr., Japan, 1963; Pritzker lectr. U. Toron 1976; Novy lectr. U. Calif., Davis, 1977, Pinkus le Wayne U., Detroit, 1987; Hebra lectr. U. Vienna, 198

Author: (with Gundula Schaumburg-Lever) Histopathology of the Skin, 7th edit, 1990, Pemphigus and Pemphigoid, 1965, (with Ken Hashimoto) Appendage Tumors of the Skin, 1969, (with Gundula Schaumburg-Lever) Color Atlas of Histopathology of the Skin, 1988; mem. editorial bd.: Archives of Dermatology, 1963-72, Am. Jour. Dermatopathology, 1979-92. Fellow Am. Acad. Dermatology (past dir.); mem. Soc. Investigative Dermatology (past dir., past pres., hon. mem., Rothman medal 1990), New Eng. Dermatol. Soc., Am. Soc. Dermatopathology (past pres.), Am. Dermatol. Assn., Deutsche Akademie der Naturforscher Leopoldina; hon. mem. Pacific Dermatol. Assn., Austrian (Hebra medal 1989), Brit., Danish, Dutch, Finnish, French, East German, West German, Greek, Indian, Italian, Japanese, Polish, Uruguayan, Venezuelan, Yugoslav Dermatol. Socs. Lutheran. Home: Tubingen Germany Died Dec. 13, 1992.

LEVI, DORO TEODORO, archaeologist; b. Trieste, Italy, June 1, 1898; s. Levi Eduardo and Tivoli Eugenia; m. Anna Cosadinos, Feb. 8, 1928. Grad., Florence U., Italy, 1920; D (hon.), U. Athens, 1988. Prof. U. of Cagliari, Italy, 1935-38; researcher Inst. Advanced Studies, Princeton, N.J., U.S.A., 1938-45; dir Italian Archaelogical Sch., Athens, 1947-77. Author: Price for Archaeology Academia Linc, 1963, Festos e la Civiltā Minoica Part I, 4 vols. 1976-77, Part II 2 vols. 1981, 87-88. Vol. 1st World War, Florence, 1917. Mem. Pontifical Acad., German Archeol. Inst., Greek Archeol. Soc., Acad. Nazionale dei Lincei, Acad. of Athens. Home: Athens Greece Deceased.

LEVI, ROBERT HENRY, department store executive, banker; b. Balt., Mar. 27, 1915; s. Abraham H. and Regina (Ottenheimer) L.; m. Ryda Hecht, Oct. 18, 1939; children: Sandra Jean, Alexander Hecht, Richard Hecht. AB, Johns Hopkins U., 1936, LHD (hon.), 1990. Salesman The Hecht Co. (dept. store), Washington, 1941-42; floor mgr. The Hecht Co. (dept. store), 1942, budget dir., 1945-46, asst. mgr., 1947-49; v.p. The Hecht Co., 1948; exec. v.p. charge corp. affairs, asst. mng. dir. The Hecht Co. Balt. stores, 1950-51, 1st exec. v.p., 1951-55, pres., 1955-68, gen. mgr. Washington area, 1957-59; v.p., mem. exec., finance coms. May Dept. Stores Co., 1959-68, still dir.; chmn. exec. com., dir. Merc.-Safe Deposit & Trust Co., 1968-70, vice chmn. bd., 1970-80, chmn. exec. com., 1980-85; chmn. bd. Catalyst Recovery Internat. Inc., 1978-90; bd. dirs. Hittman Assos., Am. Gen. Ins. Co., Fidelity & Deposit Co. Md., Warburg Pincus Capital Fund. Mem. finance com., bd. dirs. Asso. Jewish Charities; bd. dirs. Jr. Achievement Met. Balt., Fed City Council, Washington; chmn. Greater Balt. Com.; dir. Urban Coalition; vice chmn., dir. Washington Downtown Progress; mem. Urban Renewal Council, Washington; chmn. Downtown Policy Com., D.C.; trustee, past pres. Sinai Hosp.; trustee Johns Hopkins Hosp., Balt., Goucher Coll.; vice chmn. bd. trustees Johns Hopkins U.; mem. adv. com. Am. U. Sch. Bus. Adminstrn., Washington, Fight-Blight Fund, Green Spring Valley Planning Found.; founder, chmn. bd. Balt. Community Found., founding trustee; former trustee Balt. Symphony Orch. Served to lt. USCGR, 1942-45. Decorated comdr. Order Merit Italian Republic; recipient Milton Eisenhower medal listing. svc. Johns Hopkins U., 1987; named to Hall of Fame Balt. City Coll., named Man of Yr., Washington, 1966, Balt., 1990, named Entrepreneur of Yr., Balt., 1990. Mem. Nat. Retail Mchts. Assn. N.Y. (dir.), Am. Retail Fedn. (pres. 1965-67), Center Club, Md. Club, Caves Valley Golf Club, Johns Hopkins Faculty Club. Clubs: Center, Maryland, Caves Valley Golf. Home: Lutherville Timonium Md. Died Feb. 17, 1995.

LEVIN, HARRY, psychology educator; b. Balt., Mar. , 1925; s. Morris and Bessie (Wolfe) L.; m. Deborah B. Stern, Dec. 25, 1946; children: Diane Lynn, David Stern, Rebecca Lee. Student, Johns Hopkins, 1942-43; B.A., U. Md., 1948; M.A., U. Mich., 1949, Ph.D., 1951. Postdoctoral fellow Harvard, 1950-51; asst. prof., rsch. assoc. Lab. Human Devel., 1951-55; vis. assoc. prof. summers Stanford, 1955, 58; mem. faculty Cornell U., 1955-93, prof. child devel. and psychology, 1961-93, chmn. dept. psychology, 1966-72, William R. Kenan, Jr. prof. psychology, 1967-90, William R. Kenan, Jr. prof. psychology emeritus, 1990-93, dean Coll. Arts and Scis., 1974-78; vis. scientist Harvard-Florence (Italy) project; vis. prof. psychology MIT, 1973, U. Bristol, 1987; vis. prof. psychology and edn. Harvard U., 1978-79; cons. to govt. and industry, 1959-93; chmn. psychology panel Com. Internat. Exchange Persons, 1963-66. Author: (with others) Patterns of Child Rearing, 1956, (with J.P. Williams) Basic Studies in Reading, 1970, (with E.J. Gibson) The Psychology of Reading, 1975, The Eye-Voice Span, 1979. Trustee Histadrut Israel Am. Cultural Exchange Inst.; vis. com. Harvard. Served with AUS, 1944-46. Social Sci. Research Council fellow, 1950-51; USPHS fellow, 1961-62. Mem. AAAS, Phi Beta Kappa, Sigma Xi. Home: Ithaca N.Y. Died May 0, 1993; interred Lakeview Cemetery, Ithaca, N.Y.

LEVIN, HARRY (TUCHMAN), retired comparative literature educator, writer; b. Mpls., July 18, 1912; s. Isadore Henry and Beatrice (Tuchman) L.; m. Elena Ivanovna Zarudnaya, June 21, 1939; 1 child, Marina L. (Frederiksen). AB, Harvard U., 1933, mem. Soc. Fellows, jr. fellow, 1934-39, sr. fellow, 1947-66; student, U. Paris, 1934; Litt. D. (hon.), Syracuse U., 1952; LL.D. (hon.), St. Andrews, 1962; L.H.D. (hon.), Union Coll., 1968, Clarkson Coll., 1970; Dr. honoris causa, U. Paris-Sorbonne, 1973; M.A. (hon.), Oxford U., Eng., 1982. Instr., tutor in English Harvard U., 1939-44, assoc. prof., 1944-48; prof. Harvard, 1948-54; prof. English and comparative lit. Harvard U., 1954-60, chmn. dept. comparative lit., 1946-51, 53-54, 61-72, 77-78, chmn. div. modern langs., 1951-52, 55-61, Irving Babbitt prof. comparative lit., 1960-83; emeritus prof. Harvard, 1983-94; lectr. Lowell Lectrs., 1952, Salzburg Seminar, 1953, Gauss seminars, Princeton, 1961; exchange prof. U. Paris, 1953; vis. prof. Tokyo U., 1955, Harvard Ctr. for Renaissance Studies Villa I Tatti, 1989, U. Alcala, 1989; Mrs. William Beckman prof. U. Calif. at Berkeley, 1957; Alexander lectr. U. Toronto, 1958; Patten lectr. Ind. U., 1967; overseas fellow Churchill Coll., Cambridge U., 1967; vis. fellow All Souls Coll., Oxford U., 1974, Folger Inst. seminars, 1980; NEH sr. fellow, 1979; vis. prof. U. P.R., 1981, Chinese U. Hong Kong, 1982; Eastman prof., fellow Balliol Coll., Oxford U., 1982-83; Phi Beta Kappa vis. scholar, 1980-81; chmn. English Inst., 1957; sr. fellow Ctr. Medieval and Renaissance Studies, U. Ariz., 1984; Una lectr. U. Calif.-Berkeley, 1985. Author: The Broken Column: A Study in Romantic Hellenism, 1931, James Joyce: A Critical Introduction, 1941, The Overreacher: A Study of Christopher Marlowe, 1952, Contexts of Criticism, 1957, The Power of Blackness: Hawthorne, Poe, Melville, 1958, The Question of Hamlet, 1959, The Gates of Horn: A Study of Five French Realists, 1963, Refractions: Essays in Comparative Literature, 1966, The Myth of the Golden Age in the Renaissance, 1969, Grounds for Comparison, 1972, Shakespeare and the Revolution of the Times, 1976, Memories of the Moderns, 1980, Playboys and Killjoys: An Essay on the Theory and Practice of Comedy, 1987; Editor: Selected Works of Ben Jonson, 1938, A Satire Against Mankind and Other Poems by the Earl of Rochester, 1942, The Portable James Joyce, 1945, Perspectives of Criticism, 1950, Shakespeare's Coriolanus, 1956, Hawthorne's Scarlet Letter, 1960, Shakespeare's Comedy of Errors, 1965, Veins of Humor, 1972, (with others) Riverside Shakespeare, 1974, Henry James' Ambassadors, 1987; editorial bd.: Comparative Lit., Jour. of History of Ideas, Shakespeare Quar.; Contbr. criticisms to periodicals. Trustee Cambridge Drama Festival. Guggenheim fellow, 1943-44; recipient award Am. Acad. Arts and Letters; Am. Council Learned Soc. award distinguished scholarship in humanities, 1962; decorated chevalier Legion Honor; Huntington Library fellow, 1966; official guest Chinese Acad. Social Scis., 1982. Fellow Am. Acad. Arts and Scis.; mem. Soc. Fellows (acting chmn. 1964-65), Nat. Inst. Arts and Letters, Internat. Assn. U. Profs. English, Fedn. Internat. des Langues et Littératures, Brit. Acad., Am. Philos. Soc., Internat. Comparative Lit. Assn. (v.p. 1963-67), Am. Comparative Lit. Assn. (pres. 1965-68), Acad. of Lit. Studies (v.p. 1973-74), Modern Humanities Research Assn. (pres. 1976), Royal Netherlands Acad. Scis., Phi Beta Kappa. Club: Harvard (N.Y.C.). Died May 29, 1994; interred Wellfleet, M.A.

LEVINE, JOSEPH, conductor; b. Phila., Aug. 14, 1912; s. Harry and Sophia (Raditz) L.; m. Mary Thomas, Feb. 16, 1945; children—Stephen, David. Mus.B. in Conducting and Piano, Curtis Inst. Music, Phila., 1937; pupil, Fritz Reiner and Artur Rodzinski (conducting), Josef Hofmann (piano), Wanda Landowska (harpsichord). Mem. faculty Curtis Inst., 1933-40; asst. condr. Phila. Grand Opera Co., 1938-40; founder, condr. New Center of Music Orch., Phila., 1940-43, Chamber Opera Soc., Phila., 1946-50; faculty Cornish Sch. Allied Arts, Seattle, 1969-73, 76-79. Pianist Phila. Orch., 1940-43, 46-50; condr., USAAF Tactical Air Center Symphonette, 1943-45; piano accompanist with Joseph Szigeti, 1946-50; music dir., condr. Co-Opera Co., Phila., 1947-50, Am. Ballet Theatre, N.Y.C., 1950-58, Omaha Symphony Orch., 1958-69; mem., Cornish Trio, 1969-73, Phila. Duo, 1976-88; music dir., Omaha Civic Opera Soc., 1961-69, Omaha Starlight Theatre, 1961; fgn. tours. under auspices cultural exchange program State Dept., 1950-58; assoc. condr., Seattle Symphony Orch., 1969-73, Hawaii Opera Theatre and Honolulu Symphony Orch., 1973-76; music dir., condr. Bremerton Symphony, 1979-91; co-founder, dir. Bainbridge Island Chamber Music Festival, Wash., 1984-88; Am. condr., Royal Ballet Eng., 1963-65; recorded ballet scores for Capitol Records, 1952-57; author articles. Recipient citations Omaha C. of C., 1960; Dana Coll., 1961; Creighton U., 1962; Key to City Omaha, 1961; Mercian medal Coll. St. Mary, 1967. Club: Rotary. Home: Seattle Wash. Died Mar. 23, 1994.

LEVINSON, JULIUS, lawyer; b. N.Y.C., July 22, 1925; s. Morris and Ida (Wolinsky) L.; m. Shirley Berkowitz, Apr. 6, 1952; children: Annette Naomi, Barry Simpson. BBA, CCNY, 1947; JD, Harvard U., 1950; LLM, NYU, 1960. Bar: N.Y. 1951, U.S. Dist. Ct. (so. dist.) N.Y. 1953. Dir. taxes Colt Industries, Inc., N.Y.C., 1957-61, asst. cont. dir. taxes, 1961-93, asst. v.p. taxes, 1970-93; v.p. taxes Colt Industries, Inc., 1971—. Served with U.S. Army, 1944-46, ATO. Mem. Internat. Assn. Assessing Officers, Mfts. Alliance for Productivity and Innovation (tax coun.), Tax. Execs. Inst., Tax Mgmt. Adv. Bd. Home: New York N.Y. Died Oct. 5, 1993.

LEVITAN, SAR A., economist, educator; b. Shiauliai, Lithuania, Sept. 14, 1914; came to U.S., 1931, naturalized, 1935; s. Osher N. and Yocheved (Rapoport) L.; m. Brita Ann Buchard, Oct. 15, 1946. B.S., CCNY, 1937; M.A., Columbia U., 1939, Ph.D., 1949. Faculty George Washington U., Washington, 1967-94; dir. Ctr. Social Policy Studies, research prof. econs., 1967-94; cons. in field; chmn. Nat. Commn. on Employment and Unemployment Statistics, 1977-79. Author or co-author: Federal Aid to Depressed Areas, 1964, Federal Training and Work Programs in the Sixties, 1969, The Great Society's Poor Law: A New Approach to Poverty, 1969, Blue-Collar Workers, 1970, Big Brother's Indian Programs—With Reservations, 1970, Human Resources and Labor Markets, 1972, 76, 81, Work and Welfare Go Together, 1972, Work Is Here to Stay, Alas, 1973, Old Wars Remain Unfinished: The Veterans Benefit System, 1973, Employment and Earnings Inadequacy, 1974, Still A Dream: The Changing Status of Blacks Since 1960, 1975, Child Care and ABCs Too, 1975, The Promise of Greatness, 1976, Warriors at Work: The Volunteer Armed Force, 1977, More than Subsistence: Minimum Wages for the Working Poor, 1979, Evaluating Federal Social Programs: An Uncertain Art, 1979, What's Happening to the American Family, 1981, 2d rev. edit., 1988, Second Thoughts on Work, 1982, Working for the Sovereign, 1983, Business Lobbies: The Public Good and the Bottom Line, 1983, Beyond the Safety Net: Reviving the Promise of Opportunity in America, 1984, Protecting American Workers, 1986, Working But Poor: America's Contradiction, 1987, A Second Chance: Training for Jobs, 1988, A Proper Inheritance: Investing in the Self-Sufficiency of Poor Families, 1989, Families in Flux, 1990, Programs in Aid of the Poor, 6th edit., 1990, Got to Learn to Earn: Preparing Americans for World, 1991, Spending to Save: Expanding Employment Opportunities, 1992, Enterprise Zones: A Promise Based on Rhetoric, 1992, Evaluation of Federal Social Programs: An Uncertain Impact, 1992, Economies of Rectitude: Necessary But Not Sufficient, 1992, Jobs for Jobs: Toward a Work-Based Welfare System, 1993, The Equivocal Prospects for Indian Reservations, 1993, Educational Reform: Federal Initiatives and National Mandates, 1963-93, Federal Human Resource Policy: From Kennedy to Clinton, 1994, The Displaced vs. The Disadvantaged: A Necessary Dichotomy?, 1994. Served to capt. AUS, 1942-46. Ford Found. grantee, 1962, 67-94. Mem. Am. Arbitration Assn. (labor panel), Fed. Mediation and Conciliation Svc. (labor panel), Indsl. Rels. Rsch. Assn. Home: Washington D.C. Died May 24, 1994.

LEVITT, WILLIAM JAIRD, builder; b. Bklyn., Feb. 11, 1907; s. Abraham and Pauline (Biederman) L.; m. Rhoda Kirshner, Nov. 16, 1929; children: William Jaird, James R.; m. Alice Kenny, Jan., 1959; m. Simone Korchin, Nov. 1969. DCS, St. John's U.; LHD, Yeshiva U.; PhD, Bar Ilan U. Founder-chmn. Levitt & Sons, Inc., until 1969; chmn. bd. William J. Levitt, Inc., Levitt Industries, Inc., Internat. Community Corp. Bd. overseers Albert Einstein Coll. Medicine; bd. dirs. Am. Health Found.; trustee North Shore U. Hosp.; pres. Levitt Found. Served as lt. USNR, 1942-45, PTO. Recipient Frank P. Brown medal Franklin Inst. Pa., 1965. Home: Greenvale N.Y. Died Jan. 28, 1994.

LEVITTAN, SHIRLEY RUTH, former judge; b. N.Y.C., Sept. 8, 1918; d. Nathan William and Winifred (Silverstein) L. BA, Barnard Coll., 1939; Lic. es Lettres, Sorbonne, Paris, 1939; MA, Syracuse U., 1940; LLB, N.Y. Law Sch., 1956. Bar: N.Y. 1956, U.S. Ct. Appeals (2d cir.) 1956, U.S. Dist. Ct. (so. and ea. dists.) N.Y. 1957. Judge Criminal Ct. of City of N.Y., 1969-73; acting justice Supreme Ct. of State of N.Y., N.Y.C., 1973-92. Contbr. articles to profl. jours. Home: New York N.Y. Died Feb. 1992.

LEWIS, GRANT STEPHEN, lawyer; b. N.Y.C., Apr. 27, 1942; s. Arnold R. and Gladys F.; m. Shari J. Gruhn, Sept. 15, 1974; 1 dau., Carrie Ann. A.B., Bates Coll., 1962; J.D., Harvard U., 1965. Bar: N.Y. 1966, U.S. Supreme Ct. 1975, all fed. cir. cts., various fed. dist. cts. With firm LeBoeuf, Lamb, Greene & MacRae (formerly LeBoeuf, Lamb, Leiby & McRae), N.Y.C., 1966-95, ptnr., 1973-95. Mem. ABA, Assn. Bar City N.Y. Clubs: University, Harvard (N.Y.C.). Contbr. articles to profl. jours. Died July 8, 1995. Home: New York N.Y.

LEWIS, HARRY, educational administrator. Exec. sec. NCLA Trade and Tech. Edn. Home: Brooklyn N.Y. Died 1993.

LEWIS, HENRY, conductor; b. Los Angeles, Oct. 16, 1932; m. Marilyn Horne, 1960. Ed. (music scholarship), U. So. Calif. Double-bass player with Los Angeles Philharmonic, later asso. condr. for 3 years, founder, Los Angeles Chamber Orch., 1958, music dir., Los Angeles Opera Co., 1965-68, condr., N.J. Symphony, Newark, 1968-76, condr., Met. Opera, 1972; condr. ballet-cantata: Gershwiniana, La Scala opera house, Milan, 1965; guest condr. maj. world orchs. Served with U.S. Army as condr. 7th Army Symphony, 1955-57. Home: New York N.Y. Died Jan. 26, 1996.

LEWIS, JAMES BERTON, law educator; b. Lenox, Tenn., Oct. 29, 1911; s. Oscar and Maude (Kirby) L.; m. Irene Fogt, Dec. 9, 1961; children: Edward K., Robert

L. Student, Centralia (Wash.) Jr. Coll., 1929-31, Wash. State Coll., 1931; LLB, Columbus U., Washington, 1940. Bar: D.C. 1942, N.Y. 1954. With Treasury Dept., 1931-34, IRS, 1934-42, 45-48; atty. Office Tax Legis. Counsel, Treasury Dept., 1948-52; spl. asst. to chief counsel IRS, 1952-53; assoc. firm Paul, Weiss, Rifkind, Wharton & Garrison, N.Y.C., 1953-55; partner Paul, Weiss, Rifkind, Wharton & Garrison, 1955-82, of counsel, 1982-96; adj. prof. NYU Law Sch., 1962-83; prof. Benjamin N. Cardozo Sch. Law, 1983-96; cons. Am. Law Inst. estate and gift tax, income tax projects; mem. adv. group to commr. IRS, 1976, 87. Author: The Estate Tax, 4th edit, 1979, The Marital Deduction, 1984. Served with USNR, 1942-45. Mem. ABA (vice chmn. publns., sect. taxation 1980-83, chmn. 1984-85), Am. Law Inst., N.Y. State Bar Assn., N.Y. County Lawyers Assn., Assn. Bar City N.Y., D.C. Bar Assn. Democrat. Presbyterian. Club: Masons. Home: New York N.Y. Died May 25, 1996.

LEWIS, JAMES EDWARD, retired chemical company executive, law consultant; b. Ashland, Ky., July 11, 1927; s. Blaine and Hallie Maude (Heal) L.; m. Mary Ann Johnson, Feb. 23, 1952; children: Martha Lewis Innes, Glenna Lewis Rahr, Karen Lewis Hampshire. A.B., Centre Coll. Ky., 1950; M.S., Purdue U., 1954, Ph.D., 1956. Pres. Radiochemistry, Inc., 1956-65; dir. research and devel. United Carbon Co., 1965-70, Ashland Oil, Inc., 1970-74; v.p. research and devel. Ashland Chem. Co., Dublin, Ohio, 1974-79; v.p. Ashland Chem. Co., 1979-88; mayor City of Dublin, 1982-86; lectr., licensor in W. Germany, France, Italy, England, Spain, Denmark, Australia, India, U.S., China, USSR, Japan, Sweden, Korea, Taiwan; mem. Ky. Gov.'s Com. on Nuclear Energy and Space Sci., 1961-65, Ky. Atomic Energy and Space Authority, 1961-65; mem. So. Interstate Nuclear Bd., 1963-65; rep. Indsl. Research Inst., 1967-88, emeritus rep., 1988-93. Contbr. articles to profl. jours. Mem. Dublin Mcpl. Council, 1979-81. Served with U.S. Army, 1944-47. Recipient Preston Carter prize in chemistry, 1950; S. Warfield prize in math., 1950. Mem. Am. Chem. Soc., Licensing Execs. Soc., Landings Club (Savannah), Sigma Xi. Republican. Home: Savannah Ga. Died March 29, 1993.

LEWIS, REGGIE, professional basketball player; b. Balt., Nov. 21, 1965. Student, Northeastern U. Guard Boston Celtics, 1987-93. Named NBA All-Star, 1992. Home: Boston Mass. Died July 27, 1993.

LEWIS, REGINALD F., international financier; b. Balt., Dec. 7, 1942; married; 2 daughters. AB, Va. State U., 1965; JD, Harvard U., 1968. Bar: N.Y. 1970. Assoc. Paul, Weiss, Rifkind, Wharton & Garrison, N.Y.C., 1968-70; ptnr. Lewis & Clarkson, N.Y.C., 1973-89; chmn., CEO TLC Group, LP, N.Y.C., 1983-87, TLC Beatrice Internat. Holdings Inc., N.Y.C., 1987-93. Mem. Assn. of Bar of City of N.Y. (com. on corps.), ABA. Home: New York N.Y. Died Jan. 19, 1993.

LHOTKA, JOHN FRANCIS, physician, educator, anatomist; b. Butte, Mont., May 13, 1921; s. John Francis and Mary (Backowske) L.; m. Lois Katherine Clysdale, Sept. 21, 1951. B.A., U. Mont., 1942; M.S. in Anatomy, Northwestern U., 1948, M.B., 1949, M.D., 1951, Ph.D., 1953. Asst. in anatomy Northwestern U., 1947-50; mem. house staff Mpls. Gen. Hosp., 1950-51; Stain Commn. fellow Northwestern U., summer 1953; asst. prof. anatomy U. Okla. Med. Sch., 1951-55, asso. prof., 1955-69, prof. anatomical scis., 1969-86, prof. emeritus, 1986-93; Active in numis. field, especially medieval coinage of Western Europe. Author: (monographs) Introduction to East Roman Coinage, 1957, 89, Medieval Bracteates, 1958, 89, Medieval French Feudal Coinage, 1966, 90, (with P.K. Anderson) Survey of Medieval Iberian Coinages, 1963, 89; contbr. articles on field histochemistry to profl. jours. Served to 1st lt. CWS USAAF, 1942-46, PTO. Decorated Royal Yugoslav War Cross; recipient 4 Heath medals, Medal of Merit, Farran Zerbe award, initial Newell award Am. Numis. Assn., Donat Cross 1st class Order St. Lazarus of Jerusalem, Order of Augustan Eagle, silver medal Alta and Northwest Ters. Royal Can. Life Saving Soc., Jubilee medal, Alta and N.W. Ters. Royal Can. Life Saving Soc., U. Okal. Media Prodn. award, Medaille de la France Liberty WW II svc. French Govt., 1989, Medaille Commerative de la Reconnaissance, Belgian Govt.,others. Fellow Am. Numis. Soc. (life mem., patron), Royal Numis. Soc. (life mem., hon.), Swiss Numis Soc. (life mem.), Spanish Numis. Soc., Am. Geriatric Soc., Internat. Acad. Pathology, Royal Soc. Health, London, Am. Inst. Chemists, Augustan Soc.; mem. Am. Numis. Assn. (life), Am. Philatelic Soc. (life), Okla. Acad. Sci. (sr.), Okla. State Hist. Soc. (life), Am. Soc. Herpatology and Ichthyology, Co. Mil. Historians, Orders and Medals Soc. Am., Brit. Mus. Soc., Metro. Mus. (N.Y.), Oriental Inst. Chgo., Nat. Rifle Assn. (life endowment), Am. Def. Preparedness Assn. (life), Am. Assn. Anatomists, Histochem. Soc., Am. Soc. Zoology, Biol. Stain Commn., Am. Security Council, Soc. for Exptl. Biology and Medicine, Am. Chem. Soc., Archeol. Inst. Am., E. African Wildlife Soc. (life), Nat. Wildlife Fedn., Am. Soc. Mil. Insignia Collectors, Tokens and Medals Soc., Sigma Xi, Phi Sigma. Clubs: Oklahoma City, Petroleum. Home: Oklahoma City Okla. Died Jan. 4, 1993.

LI, YONGXIN, information company executive; b. Ninghe, Hebei, China, Aug. 10, 1930; s. Shangqiing Li and Zhihong Wang; m. Pei Xia, Dec. 20, 1962; children: Shuo, Tianjian. Student, Qinghua U., Beijing, 1950; BSc, Beijing Inst. Aeronautics, 1954. Engr. 2d Ministry of Machine-Bldg., Beijing, 1954-58, Info. Ctr. 1st Ministry of Machine-Bldg., Beijing, 1958-70; div. head Scientech Info. and Publs. Ministry of Machine-Bldg., Beijing, 1970-82, pres., 1980-90; prof. Hefei Indsl. U., 1987-90, Jilin Indsl. U., Changchon, People's Republic of China, 1987-90; mem. scientech cons. com. Ministry of Machinery & Electronics Industry, 1989. Author numerous rsch. reports. Recipient Prize State Commn. Sci. and Tech., 1986. Mem. Chinese mech. Engr. Soc. (exec.), Chinese Assn. Pubs., Chinese Assn. Translators, World Fedn. Engring. Orgn. Home: Beijing People's Republic of China Died May 12, 1990.

LICHSTEIN, HERMAN CARLTON, microbiology educator emeritus; b. N.Y.C., Jan. 14, 1918; s. Siegfried and Luba (Berson) L.; m. Shirley Riback, Jan. 24, 1942 (dec.); children: Michael, Peter. A.B., NYU, 1939; M.S. in Pub. Health, U. Mich., 1940, Sc.D. in Bacteriology, 1943. Diplomate: Am. Bd. Microbiology. Instr. U. Wis., 1943-46; assoc. prof., then prof. U. Tenn., 1947-50, U. Minn., 1950-61; prof. microbiology, dir. dept. U. Cin. Coll. Medicine, 1961-78, dir. grad. studies microbiology, 1962-78, 81-83, prof. microbiology, 1961-84, prof. emeritus, 1984-95; mem. Linacre Coll., Oxford U., 1976; mem. microbiology tng. com. NIH, 1963-66, microbiology fellowships com., 1966-70; mem. sci. faculty fellowship panel NSF, 1960-63; Herman C. Lichstein disting. lectureship microbial physiology and genetics endowed, 1987. Author: (with Evelyn Oginsky) Experimental Microbial Physiology, 1965; editor: Bacterial Nutrition, 1983; also articles. Mem. Gov. Minn. Com. Edn. Exceptional Child, 1956-57; Bd. dirs. Walnut Hills (Ohio) High Sch. Assn., 1964-66. NRC fellow Cornell U., 1946-47; fellow U. Cin. Grad. Sch., 1965. Fellow AAAS, Am. Acad. Microbiology (gov. 1972-75, chmn. 1973); mem. Am. Soc. Microbiology (hon. 1986), Am. Soc. Biol. Chemistry, Soc. Gen. Microbiology, Assn. Med. Sch. Microbiology Chairmen (council 1970-72, trustee 1974-77), Soc. Exptl. Biology and Medicine, Am. Inst. Biol. Scis., Sigma Xi (pres. Cin. chpt. 1971-73), Phi Kappa Phi, Pi Kappa Epsilon. Home: Cincinnati Ohio Died Jan. 18, 1995.

LIEBENOW, J. GUS, political science educator; b. Berwyn, Ill., May 4, 1925; s. J. Gus Sr. and E. Louise (Leahy) L.; m. Beverly June Bellis, Aug. 2, 1956; children: B. Diane Liebenow Gray, Debra Lynn Liebenow Daly, Jay Stanton, John Stuart. BA summa cum laude, U. Ill., 1949, MA, 1950; postgrad., Harvard U., 1951-52; PhD in Polit. Sci., Northwestern U., 1955. Asst. prof. polit. sci. U. Tex., Austin, 1956-58; asst. prof. polit. sci. Ind. U., Bloomington, 1958-61, assoc. prof., 1961-83, prof., 1983-87, James H. Rudy prof. polit. sci., 1987-90, James H. Rudy prof. emeritus, 1968-72, dean for internat. programs, 1970-72, v.p., dean for acad. affairs, 1972-74; vis. prof. U. Dar es Salaam, Tanzania, 1967, 68, U. Baybreuth, Fed. Republic of Germany, 1987; founding dir. African studies program Ind. U., 1961-72; mem. exec. coun. Internat. African Inst., London, 1977-83; mem. Pres.'s adv. commn. on African affairs U.S. Dept. State, 1969-72; cons. Peace Corps, Fgn. Svc. Inst., Ho. of Reps. subcom. on Africa, Senate subcom. on Africa. Author: Liberia: Evolution of Privilege, 1969, Colonial Rule and Political Development in Tanzania, 1971, African Politics: Crises and Challenges, 1986 (Quincy Wright award 1987), Liberia: Quest for Democracy, 1987 (Edward Wilmot Blyden award 1987, Choice 1988). Staff sgt. U.S. Army, 1943-46, ETO, PTO. Ozias Goodwin fellow Harvard U., 1951-52, rsch. fellow Social Sci. Rsch. Coun., 1953-54, 60-61, Fgn. Area fellow Ford Foun., 1954-56. Founding fellow African Studies Assn. (exec. bd. 1964-64, v.p. 1976-77, pres. 1977-79); mem. AAUP (chpt. pres. Ind. U. 1978-81), Liberian Studies Assn. (founding, mem. editorial bd. 1967-93, first Lifetime Achievement award 1991), Midwest Polit. Sci. Assn. (exec. bd. 1962-65), Soc. Profl. Journalists (Rocking Chair award), African-Caribbean Inst. (bd. advisers 1985-93), Rotary Internat. (Paul Harris fellow), Bronze Tablet (U. Ill.), Phi Beta Kappa (exec. com. Gamma chpt. 1987-93), Phi Kappa Phi, Phi Eta Sigma. Methodist Episcopal. Home: Bloomington Ind. Died June 21, 1993.

LIENHARD, GUSTAV O., foundation executive. Chmn. bd. trustees Robert Wood Johnson Found., Princeton, N.J. Home: Princeton N.J. Died 1987.

LIGHT, WALTER FREDERICK, telecommunications executive; b. Cobalt, Ont., Can., June 24, 1923; s. Herbert and Rosetta Elizabeth (Hoffman) L.; m. Margaret Anne Wylie Miller, July 8, 1950; children: Elizabeth Jean, Janice Catherine. BS with honours, Queen's U., 1949, LLD (hon.), 1981; LLD (hon.), Concordia U., 1980, Dalhousie U., 1985; D in Applied Sci. (hon.), U. Ottawa, 1981; DSc (hon.), Laurentian U., 1984; DEng (hon.), U. Waterloo, 1985. Exec. v.p. ops. Bell Can., Montreal, Que., 1970-74; pres., dir. No. Telecom Ltd., Montreal, 1974-79, pres., chief exec. officer, 1979-82, chmn., chief exec. officer, 1982-84, chmn., 1984-85; bd. dirs. Rockcliffe Rsch. and Tech. Inc., Transtream Inc. Mem. Assos. Carleton U.; fellow Montreal Mus. Fine Arts. Served with RCAF, 1942-45. Decorated Officer, Order of Can., 1986, Order of Ont., 1988. Fellow Engring. Inst. Can., Ca. Acad. Engring. mem. Corp. Engrs. Que., Assn. Profl. Engrs. Ont Mount Royal Club, York Club. Home: Toronto Can Died Feb., 1996.

LIKES, DAVID HENRY, educator, retired air forc officer; b. N.Y.C., Aug. 4, 1914; s. Slyvan Henry an Mamie (Leopold) L.; B.A., Johns Hopkins, 1936; post grad. Harvard U., 1938-39; M.A. (Univ. fellow), Ge orgetown U., 1948, Ph.D., 1949; m. Grace Ann McWil liams, Feb. 28, 1948 (dec. Dec. 1971); children: Davi McWilliams, Lawrence Andrew; m. 2d, Adeline Le Stuckey, July 15, 1972; stepchildren: Elizabeth Stucke Bright, Lauren Stuckey Glass. Commd. 2d lt. USAF 1941, advanced through grades to col., 1945; mem. U.S Mil. North African Mission, Cairo, 1942; assigne Desert Air task force, component USAF Middle Eas 9th Air Force, USAF Middle East, Egypt, 1942-43 mem. Overlord planning staff, London, Eng., 1943-44 assigned 1st Airborne Army, 1944-45; mem. mil. de Potsdam (E. Ger.) Conf., 1945; assigned War Plan div USAF, 1948-51; mem. standing group NATO, Wash ington, 1951-52, U.S. Naval War Coll., 1952-53; mem U.S. Mission to NATO, Paris, 1953-56; mil. air sta planner War Plans Div. Air Staff, Washington, 1956-58 dep. dir. NSC Affairs, Office Sec. Def., 1958-59; mem faculty Nat. War Coll., 1959-61; mem. Aero. Spac Studies Inst., Maxwell AFB, Ala., 1961-63; ret., 1963 prof., chmn. dept. internat. studies Southwestern a Memphis, from 1963; cons. Inst. Internat. Studies U S.C., Islamic and Arabian Devel. Studies Duke U Durham, N.C.; Ford Found. postdoctoral researc fellow Duke U., 1967-68; research fellow Center Middl Eastern Studies, Harvard U., 1975-76; guest lectr. Am Studies Conf., Tamkang, Taipei, Taiwan, 1980, Ins Study U.S.A. and Can., Acad. Scis. USSR, 1981; lect. Inst. Fgn. Policy and Nat. Security, Seoul, 1980. Bd govs. Internat. Group, English Speaking Union. Mem Polit. Sci. Assn., Assn. Asian Studies, Middle Ea Studies Assn., Inst. Naval Procs., Am. Acad. Polit. Sci Internat. Studies Assn., Air Force Assn., Ret. Office Assn., UN Assn. (bd. dirs. Chpt. 1980-83), Nat. Tru Historic Preservation, English Speaking Union, Gol Key Soc., Omicron Delta Kappa, Pi Sigma Alph Clubs: Willowbrook Country (Tyler, Tex.); Harvar (Dallas). Lodge: Rotary. Author: Guerilla Warfar World War II, 1963; Organization of Defense Depart ment, 1963. Contbr. articles to profl. jours. Decease Home: Tyler Tex.

LILLY, FRANK, oncogenetic biomedical researcher; b Charleston, W.Va., Aug. 28, 1930; s. Frank Otho and E Verna (Zimmerman) L.; 1 child, Matthew T. PhD, U Paris, 1959, Cornell U., 1965. Asst. prof. dept. genetic Albert Einstein Coll. Medicine, Bronx, N.Y., 1967-70 assoc. prof., 1970-74, prof., 1974—, chmn. dept., 1976 89; Am. Cancer Soc. rsch. prof. oncogenetics Alber Einstein Coll. Medicine, Bronx, 1989—; mem. bd scientific overseers Jackson Lab., Bar Harbor, Main 1989-94; mem. scientific adv. coun. Cancer Rsch. Inst N.Y.C., 1975-94; mem. scientific adv. com. Wistar Inst Phila., 1979-93. Contbr. 150 scientific articles to prof publs. Mem. Presdl. Commn. on the HIV Epidemi Washington, 1987-88. With U.S. Army, 1952-53. Fellow N.Y. Acad. Scis.; mem. NAS (mem. Com. on Nat. AIDS Strategy 1986-87), Am. Assn. for Canc Rsch. Home: New York N.Y. Died October 14, 1995.

LILLY, JOHN RUSSELL, surgeon, educator; Milw., May 23, 1929; s. John J. and Hazel (Boyer) L m. Roberta J. Hall, 1990; children: John Richar Megan Beth, Grace Eudora. BS, U. Wis., 1951, MD 1954. Diplomate Am. Bd. Surgery, Am. Bd. Thorac Surgery, Am. Bd. Pediatric Surgery. Postgrad. fello pediatric surgery Hosp. for Sick Children, London 1963-64; chief resident pediatric surgery Children Hosp. D.C., Washington, 1964-65, dir. surg. rsch. Rsch Found. of hosp., surg. dir. surg. rsch. Clin. Rsch. Ctr fellow in transplantation U. Colo. Health Scis. Ctr Denver, 1969-70, prof., chief pediatric surgery, 1973-9 acting chmn. dept. surgery, 1980-84; chmn. dept. pedia tric surgery The Children's Hosp., Denver, 1990-9 surg. dir. Pediatric Liver Ctr. U. Colo., 1985-95; mem admissions com. U. Colo. Sch. Medicine, 1987-9 chmn. session adv. bd. chronic liver disease Nat. Ins Diabetes and Digestive and Kidney Diseases, 1988. Guest editor issue on pediatric surgery World Jou Surgery, 1984. Recipient Disting. Surgeon awar Hodgen Soc., 1980, Disting. Faculty award U. Col Sch. Medicine, 1988, Outstanding Tchr. Surgery awar 1989, Disting. Citation, Wis. Med. Alumni Assn., 199 Mem. ACS, Am. Acad. Pediats. (sects. on sur oncology/hematology), Am. Surg. Assn., Am. Pedia Surg. Assn. Home: Denver Colo. Died Feb. 21, 1995.

LINARES, JULIO, Panamanian government ficial. Min. fgn. rels. Govt. of Panama, Panama Ci 1990-93. Home: Panama City Panama Died Oct. 2 1993.

LINCOLN, FRANKLIN BENJAMIN, JR., lawyer; Bklyn., Jan. 18, 1908; s. Franklin Benjamin and An (Ellensberg) L.; m. Helen C. Benz, Oct. 8, 1938; ch dren: Carol Concors, Franklin Benjamin III. AB, Co gate U., 1931, LLD (hon.), 1960; JD, Columbia U 1934. Bar: N.Y. 1934, D.C. 1960, U.S. Supreme C 1944. With Sullivan & Cromwell, N.Y.C., 1934-4 Lundgren, Lincoln & McDaniel, N.Y.C., 1941-59; pr ıalyst Hdqrs. Army Service Forces, Washington, 1943; vilian counsel to fiscal dir. Dept. Navy, 1944-45; asst. c. def., 1959-61; pres. Monroe Internat., Inc., 1961-64; p. Litton Industries, Inc., 1961-64; partner Seward & issel, 1964-66; sr. partner Mudge, Rose, Guthrie & lexander, from 1966, now of counsel; v.p., dir. Cypress ommunications Corp., 1965-69; bd. dirs., chmn. exec. m. Shelter Resources Corp., 1968-70; mem. adv. bd. at. Coun. for Gifted; rep. to Pres. Richard M. Nixon r 1968-69 transition; mem. Pres.'s Fgn. Intelligence dv. Bd., 1969-73. Author: Presidential Transition, 968-1969. Trustee Colgate U., 1967-75, chmn. bd., 975-79; bd. dirs. World Bd. of Trade, 1973-75; bd. rs., chmn. Fed. Home Loan Bank Bd. N.Y., 1972-78. erved to lt. USNR, 1943-44. Recipient Disting. Pub. ervice medal Def. Dept., 1961; Colgate U. Alumni ward for disting. service, 1977. Mem. Phi Beta Kappa, elta Upsilon, Delta Sigma Rho, Phi Delta Phi. epublican. Christian Scientist. Home: Short Hills N.J. ied Nov. 2, 1993; buried St. Stephens Cemetary, lillburn, N.J.

INDER, LIONEL, newspaper editor; b. Ventura, alif., Feb. 8, 1932; s. Dewey and Helen (Buie) L.; m. nn L. Lum, Jan. 23, 1965; children: Lesley, aura. BA, U. N.Mex., 1954; MS in Journalism, orthwestern U., 1960. Reporter Albuquerque ribune, 1956-58; night editor Hollister Publs., ilmette, Ill., 1958-59; copy editor Chgo. Daily News, 959-61; from feature editor to news editor to asst. mng. litor Nat. Observer, Silver Spring, Md., 1961-77; asst., ng. editor Detroit News, 1977-78, mng. editor, 1978-, exec. editor, 1983, editor, v.p., 1983-86, editor, 1986-; editor Memphis Commercial Appeal, 1988-92. erved with U.S. Army, 1954-56. Mem. Am. Soc. ewspaper Editors, Am. Newspaper Pubs. Assn., AP ng. Editors. Methodist. Home: Memphis Tenn. Died ec. 31, 1992.

INDFORS, VIVECA, actress; b. Uppsala, Sweden; me to U.S., 1946, naturalized, 1950; d. Torsten and arin (Dymling) L.; m. George Tabori, July 4, 1954; ildren: John, Lena, Kristoffer. Grad., Gymnasium, ockholm. Founder Berkshire Festival; dir. Sch. Visual rts; tchr. acting workshop Sarah Lawrence Coll., oetry Workshop, N.Y.C., Lehurden Coll., NYU, New h. Gene Frankel Theatre Workshop, others. Joined, oyal Drama Sch. and Theatre, Sweden, 1938; appeared plays in Sweden including: Anne Sophe Hedvig, 1937, rench Without Tears, 1940, Green Pastures, 1941, ood Wedding, 1943, Twelfth Night, 1945, Anna, 1984; wedish films include: Think if I Marry the Minister, 940, Anna Lans, 1941, The Two Brothers, 1941, In eath's Waiting Room, 1942, Appassionata, 1983, hers; plays in the U.S. include: I've Got Sixpence, 952, Anastasia, 1954 (Drama League award), King ear, 1956, Miss Julie, 1956, The Stronger, 1956, The ose Tatoo, 1956, The Golden Six, 1956, I Rise in lame, Cried the Phoenix, 1959, Brouhaha, 1960, Brecht Brecht, 1962, Pal Joey, 1963, A Far Country, 1962-, Postmark Zero, 1965, Merchant of Venice, Strolling layers: Sernora Carrar, Cuba Si, Three Bands and A assion, 1966, The Cretan Woman, 1966, Nigger overs, 1967, Mother Courage, 1970, Dance of Death, 971, I Am A Woman (co-producer, co-arranger, ac-ess), 1974, Touring, 1973, My Mother, My Son, 1978-, Richard III, 1980, Three Boards and a Passion, 981, Kathe Kollwitz, 1982, I Am A Woman, 1982, nna (actress, writer), 1983-93 (N.Y., San Francisco, ppsala, Sweden); film appearances: Night Unto Night, 947, The Adventures of Don Juan, 1947, No Sad Songs r You, 1948, Four Men in a Jeep, 1948 (Berlin Film estival award), Run for Cover, 1953, Captain Dreyfus, 956, I Accuse!, 1958, Weddings and Babies, 1956, No xit (Berlin Festival Silver Bear award 1960), The amned, 1960, Affair of the Skin, 1962, Sylvia, 1964, rainstorm, 1965, Coming Apart, 1969, Puzzle of a ownfall Child, 1971, The Way We Were, 1973, The tronger, The Jewish Wife, An Actor Works, 1974, abu, 1976, Welcome to LA, 1977, A Wedding, 1978, irlfriends, 1978, Voices, 1979, Natural Enemies, 1979, inus, 1979, Creepshow, 1981, Divorce Wars, 1981, lent Madness, 1983, Yellow Pages, 1985, The Sure hing, 1985, (writer, dir.) Unfinished Business, 1986, achel River, 1986 (spl. jury award Sundance Festival, ry award best actress Sundance Festival 1986), Lady eware, 1986, Misplaced, 1989, Luba, 1990, The Ex-rcist III, 1990, Zandalee, 1991, North of Pittsburgh, 991 (Genie Award nomination), A House in the amptons, 1993, Stargate, 1993; TV appearances in-ude: The Bridge of San Luis Rey, 1958, The Idiot, 958, Defenders, 1963, Naked City, 1963, Ben Casey, 964, The Nurses, 1964, F.B.I., Medical Center, The etectives, Marilyn, All My Children, Trapper John, A octor's Story, Hotel, Before Winter Arrives, 1979, laying for Time, 1980, Best Little Girl in the World, 980, For Ladies Only, 1980, Inside the Third Reich, assions, 1985, Billy Grier, 1985, Life Goes On, 1990 mmy award 1990), Last Dance, 1990; European TV ppearances: Frankenstein's Aunt, 1985; theatre prodns. Am A Woman, My Mother, My Son; prod. for coll. ours: Strolling Players, 1966-69; artistic dir., founder, erkshire Theatre Festival; author: Viveka . . . Viveca, n Actress, A Woman, A Life, 1981, I Am A oman..., 1986; author, director: (film) Unfinished usiness, 1985, (play) I, Clara, 1986, Anna, the Gypsy wede, 1986, In Search of Strindberg, 1992. Recipient asaorden, King of Sweden, Best Actress award Berlin Film Festival; named Best Actress of Yr., Internat. Film Awards, Actors Studio award, Emmy Best Actress (guest) in series Life Goes On, 1990. Home: New York N.Y. Died Oct. 1995.

LINDNER, KURT JULIUS, fund management company executive; b. Stettin, Pomerania, Germany, Apr. 10, 1922; came to U.S., 1939; s. Michael and Elsie Lindner; m. Edith Lindner, 1950. C.P.A., Mo. Bookkeeper Louis Greenfield, St. Louis, 1941-42; acct. Jeff K. Stone, St. Louis, 1943-44; with Kessler & Chervitz, St. Louis, 1944-67, ptnr., 1968-70; pres. Lindner Fund, Inc., St. Louis, 1954-93, Lindner Dividend Fund, Inc., St. Louis, 1974-93. Mem. Am. Inst. C.P.A.s. Home: Saint Louis Mo. Died Jan. 4, 1995.

LINDOW, JOHN WESLEY, banker, corporate executive; b. Detroit, June 28, 1910; s. Wesley and Ida Anna (Oetjen) L.; m. Eleanor Niemetta, Aug. 2, 1940; children: John Frederick, Eric Anthony. A.B., Wayne State U., 1931; M.A., George Washington U., 1940. Economist, FCA, 1934; economist U.S. Treasury, 1934-47, asst. dir. research and statistics, 1944-47; with Irving Trust Co., N.Y.C., 1947-75; v.p. charge econs. dept. Irving Trust Co., 1947-55, v.p., head investment adminstrn. div., 1955-68, sec., 1959-70, sr. v.p., 1961-66; exec. v.p. Irving Bank Corp., 1966-70, vice chmn., 1970-72, pres., 1972-75, also bd. dir.; chmn. bd. Nat. Thrift News, Inc., 1976-95; chmn. Dorset Group, 1980-95; former mem. faculty Stonier Grad. Sch. Banking, Rutgers U.; com. tax policies econ. growth. Nat. Bur. Econ. Research; mem. adv. com. to supt. banks N.Y. State, 1973-74; bd. dirs., former mem. exec. com., chmn. research com. Assn. Bank Holding Cos.; occasional cons. Fed. Home Loan Bank Bd. and Sec. of Treasury. Author: Inside the Money Market, 1972; co-author: Determining the Business Outlook, 1954; author articles in banking and finance. Recipient Alumni award Wayne State U., 1953. Mem. Phi Beta Kappa. Home: Manhasset N.Y. Died Feb. 15, 1995.

LINDSAY, GEORGE NELSON, lawyer; b. N.Y.C., Oct. 20, 1919; m. Mary Sloan Dickey, Apr. 13, 1946; children: George Nelson Jr., Louise Dickey, Stephen Whitney, Peter Vliet. BA, Yale U., 1941, LLB, 1947. Bar: N.Y. 1947. Assoc. Debevoise & Plimpton and predecessors, N.Y.C., 1947-54; ptnr. Debevoise & Plimpton (and predecessor firms), N.Y.C., 1955-90; presiding ptnr. Debevoise & Plimpton and predecessors, N.Y.C., 1980-87, of counsel, 1991-93; resident ptnr. Debevoise & Plimpton and predecessors, London, 1989-90; mem. adv. coun. of Africa, Dept. State, 1964-68; mem. exec. com. Lawyers Com. for Civil Rights Under Law, 1969-95, co-chmn. 1969-71. Mem. urban design coun. City of N.Y., 1969-75; bd. dirs. African-Am. Inst., 1969-95, chmn. bd. dirs., 1981-84; trustee, mem. coun. Yale U., 1973-78, 81-86, v.p., 1976-78, 81-86; bd. dirs. Planned Parenthood-World Population, 1965-68, chmn. bd. dirs., 1965-66; trustee Carnegie Endowment for Internat. Peace, 1981-91, vice chmn., 1986-89, hon. trustee, 1991-95; bd. dirs. The Ogilvy Group, Inc., 1962-89, Am. Ditchley Found., 1985-95. Recipient Whitney North Seymour award for civil right, 1988. Fellow Am. Bar Found., N.Y. Bar Found.; mem. ABA, N.Y. State Bar Assn., Assn. of Bar of City of N.Y. (mem. exec. com. 1973-77, chmn. exec. com. 1976-77, v.p. 1977), Am. Judicature Soc., Am. Assn. Internat. Commn. Jurists (bd. dirs. 1969-95, chmn. bd. dirs. 1983-88), Coun. Fgn. Rels., Overseas Devel. Coun. Home: New York N.Y. Died Aug. 8, 1995.

LINDSAY, J(OHN) ROBERT, JR., economics educator; b. Greenville, S.C., Apr. 23, 1925; s. John Robert and Helen Augusta (Morgan) L.; m. Helen Belle Poland, Mar. 24, 1951; children: John Robert, David Allen, John Selman. AB, U. N.C., 1949; AM, Harvard U., 1951, PhD, 1955. Reporter Greenville (S.C.) Piedmont, 1946-48; rsch. asst. Phila. Evening Bull., 1950-51; economist, chief domestic and for. rsch., sr. economist Fed. Res. Bank N.Y., N.Y.C., 1954-64; prof. fin. and econs. Leonard N. Stern Sch. Bus. N.Y. U., N.Y.C., 1964-92; exec. dir. N.Y. State Coun. Econ. Advisors, N.Y.C., 1971-74; dir. econ. rsch. Moreland Act Commn., N.Y.C., 1975-76. Author: Financial Management An Analytical Approach (2nd ed.), 1967. Pres. Ridgewood (N.J.) Symphony Orch., 1987-89; pres. Unitarian Soc. Ridgewood, 1968-70. With USN, 1943-46, PTO. Mem. Am. Econ. Assn., Am. Fin. Assn., Soc. Bus. Ethics., Internat. Trombone Assn. Democrat. Unitarian. Home: Ridgewood N.J. Died Nov. 11, 1992.

LINDSEY, PHILIP HOWARD, association executive; b. Pine Bluff, Ark., Feb. 19, 1929; s. Guy Howard and Thelma Laverne (Bliss) L.; m. Marilyn Rae Swanson, Aug. 6, 1960; children: Vicki Ann, Shari Lee. BA, Temple Coll., 1953; MusB, Am. Conservatory of Music, Chgo., 1956. Corr. Rotary Internat., Evanston, Ill., 1956-58; mgr. exec. svcs. Rotary Internat., 1958-72, div. mgr., 1972-76, asst. gen. sec., 1977-84, assoc. gen. sec., 1984-86, gen. sec., 1986-93. Chmn. orgn. com. United Fund, Evanston, Ill., 1965; bd. dirs. Nat. Found. of Dentistry for the Handicapped, 1980-86; dir., sec., treas. Ill. Found. of Dentistry for the Handicapped, 1983-85. With USN, 1946-47, PTO. Mem. Am. Mgmt. Assn., Am. Soc. Assn. Execs., Chgo. Soc. Assn. Execs. Republican. Baptist. Home: Boaz Ala. Died Feb. 26., 1993.

LINDSEY, ROBERT SOURS, lawyer; b. Dixon, S.D., May 1, 1913; s. Albert Samuel and Ferne (Sours) L.; m. Grace Edith Grimme, Mar. 6, 1943; children: Carol Jeanne Lindsey, Bruce Robert. A.B., Washington U., St. Louis, 1936, LL.B., 1936. Bar: Mo. 1936, Ark. 1943. Practice law St. Louis, 1936-43, Little Rock, 1943-91; partner Wright, Lindsey & Jennings, 1946-85, of counsel, 1985-91; sec., dir. Ferncliff, Inc., 1945-66. Bd. dirs. Presbyn. Village, Inc., 1962-66, 70-76, 78-85, pres., 1972-74; bd. dirs. Met. YMCA, 1962-68, pres., 1965-66; bd. dirs. Presbyn. Found. Ark., Inc., 1962-71, pres., 1966-67; bd. dirs. Ark. Assn. Mental Health, 1960-69, treas., 1963-65; mem. Ark. Merit System Coun., 1967-76, chmn., 1968-69; trustee Ark. Law Sch., Austin Presbyn. Theol. Sem., 1971-77, Ark. Found. Associated Colls., 1975-79, Drs. Hosp., 1980-86; bd. dirs. Shepherd's Ctr., 1981-89. Fellow Am. Bar Found.; mem. ABA, Ark. Bar Assn. (chmn. exec. com. 1965-66, exec. council 1976-77, Outstanding Lawyer award 1969, Outstanding Lawyer-Citizen award 1983), Pulaski County Bar Assn. (pres. 1972-73, Lawyer award, 1988), Internat. Assn. Def. Counsel, Am. Judicature Soc., Am. Counsel Assn., Am. Acad. Hosp. Attys., Phi Delta Phi. Presbyn. Clubs: Little Rock, Exchange, Pleasant Valley Country, Capital. Home: Little Rock Ark. Died Dec. 22, 1991.

LINDUSKA, JOSEPH PAUL, ecologist, consultant; b. Butte, Mont., July 25, 1913; s. Joseph and Helena (Nettik) L.; m. Lilian Ruth Hopkins, Aug. 7, 1936; children: Joanne Ruth Linduska Price, James Joseph. B.A., U. Mont., 1936, M.A., 1938; Ph.D., Mich. State U., 1948. Research ecologist Mich. Dept. Conservation, Lansing, 1940-43, 46-47; research entomologist USDA, Orlando, Fla., 1943-46; chief research-game mgmt. U.S. Fish & Wildlife Service, Washington, 1948-56, assoc. dir., 1966-73; sr. scientist U.S. Fish & Wildlife Service, 1973-74; dir. pub. relations and wildlife mgmt. Remington Arms Co., 1956-66; v.p. for sci. Nat. Audubon Soc., Washington, 1974-78; cons. to environ. orgns.; cons. Nat. Audubon Soc., N.Y.C., 1978-84, others; environ. columnist Kent County News, 1985-93; chmn. bd. Nat. Inst. Urban Wildlife, Columbia, Md., 1982-93; bd. dirs. Wildfowl Found. Author: Ecology of Farm Wildlife, 1950; editor: Waterfowl Tomorrow, 1964; contbr. articles to tech. and popular jours.; feature writer Sports Afield; script writer for TV and movies on conservation subjects. Bd. dirs. Chester-Sassafras Found., Chestertown, Md., 1983-93. Recipient Conservation Service award U.S. Dept. Interior, 1965. Mem. Wildlife Soc. (hon., exec. sec. 1962-65, pres. 1967-68, conservation edn. award 1963, Aldo Leopold award 1984), Outdoor Writers Assn. Am. (bd. dirs. 1960-63, Jade of Chiefs award 1963), Mason-Dixon Outdoor Writers (pres. 1963-65), Boone and Crockett Club (emeritus), Internat. Assn. Fish and Wildlife Agys., Am. Fisheries Soc. Home: Chestertown Md. Died Sept. 1, 1993.

LINK, MAE MILLS (MRS. S. GORDDEN LINK), space medicine historian and consultant; b. Corbin, Ky., May 14, 1915; d. William Speed and Florence (Estes) Mills; m. S. Gordden Link, Jan. 11, 1936. B.S., George Peabody Coll. for Tchrs., Vanderbilt U., 1936; M.A., Vanderbilt U., 1937; Ph.D., Am. U., 1951; grad., Air War Coll., 1965. Instr. social sci. Oglethorpe U., 1938-39; instr. English Drury Coll., 1940-41; assoc. dir. edn. Ga. Warm Springs Found., 1941-42; mil. historian Hdqrs. Army Air Forces, 1943-45, Office Mil. History, Dept. of Army, 1945-51; spl. asst. to surgeon gen., sr. med. historian U.S. Air Force, Washington, 1951-62; cons. in documentation and space medicine historian NASA, Washington, 1962-64; coord. documentation, life scis. historian NASA, 1964-70; rsch. assoc. Ohio State U. Found., 1970-72. Author: Medical Support of the Army Air Forces in World War II, 1955, Annual Reports of the U.S. Air Force Medical Service, 1949-62, Space Medicine in Project Mercury, 1965; (with others) USA/USSR Joint Publ. Foundations of Space Biology and Medicine, 1976; Editor: U.S. Air Force Med. Service Digest, 1957-62; contbr. to Collier's Ency., Ency. Brit., Funk and Wagnall's New Ency., profl. jours. Recipient Meritorious Service award U.S. Air Force, 1955, Ann. Outstanding Performance awards, 1956-62, Outstanding Alumna award Sue Bennett Coll., 1977. Fellow Am. Med. Writers Assn. (past pres. Middle Atlantic region); mem. Aerospace Med. Assn., Air Force Hist. Found. (charter), Internat. Congress History Medicine, Societe Internat. d'Histoire de la Medecine, Planetary Soc. (charter). Republican. Episcopalian. Home: Winchester Va. Died Mar. 18, 1996.

LINNUS, JÜRI, museum director; b. Tartu, Estonian, Jan. 19, 1926; s. Ferdinand and Olga Elisabeth (Mirka) L.; m. Loore Jürilo, Feb. 2, 1952; children: Liivi, Tanel. PhD, Univ. Tartu, 1993. Researcher Estonian Nat. Museum, Tartu, Estonian, 1950-51, scientific sec., 1952-92, rsch. dir., 1976-82, head dept. of FinnoUgric Peoples, 1981-86; lectr. U. Tartu, 1952-92; dir. Museum of Classical Antiquities, Tartu, 1987-95; chmn. Com. Regional Studies, Tartu, 1979-90. Author: Proceedings: Estonian Academy of Sciences, 1973-95, Proceedings: University of Tartu, 1979-95. Mem. founding com. Open Air Mus., Tallinn, Estonia, 1957, Nat. Park at Lahemaa, 1971. Recipient Medal Finnish Soc. Antiquities, 1984, Silver medal Lahemaa Nat. Park, 1986. Mem. Estonian Learned Soc. (chmn. 1994-95), Soc. Mother Tongue. Home: Tartu Estonia Died June 12, 1995.

LINVILLE, THOMAS MERRIAM, engineer; b. Washington, Mar. 3, 1904; s. Thomas and Clara (Merriam) L.; m. Eleanor Priest, Nov. 25, 1939; children: Eleanor, Thomas Priest, Edward Dwight. EE, U. Va., 1926; grad. advanced mgmt. program, Harvard U., 1950; mod. engring. program, UCLA, 1960. Various govt. positions, 1918-26; with Gen. Electric Co., 1926-66, beginning with Advanced Engring. Program, to 1931, successively at corp. level chmn. rotating machines product com., chmn. rotating machines devel. com., staff asst. to mgr. engring., 1926-51, mgr. engring. edn., mgmt. consultation div., 1926-51, mgr. exec. devel., mgr. research operation, mgr. research application and info., 1951-66; chief exec. Linville Co., Engrs., R&D, from 1966; mem. USN tech. missions, Pearl Harbor, 1942, Europe, 1945; mem. NRC, 1960-68. Author books (Linville Books) and papers on elec. machine design and application. Chmn. Schenectady City Planning Commn., 1951; pres. N.Y. State Citizens Com. for Pub. Schs., 1952-53; mem. Gov.'s Council Advancement Research and Devel. N.Y. State, from 1960; pres. Schenectady Mus., 1964-69; chmn. Community Chest, 1964, Devel. Council for Sci., Rensselaer Poly. Inst., 1960-67; vis. com. Norwich U., from 1970, Clarkson U., 1959-65; pres. Mohawk-Hudson council ETV-WMHT Channel 17, 1966-70; bd. dirs. Sunnyview Hosp.; pres. Schenectady Indsl. Devel. Corp., 1967-69. Served to lt. USNR, 1940-42. Recipient Charles A. Coffin award, IEEE Centennial medal, USN Certificate of Commendation; Schenectady Profl. Engrs. Soc. Engr.-of-Year award, 1960. Fellow ASME, AAAS, IEEE (dir. 1953-57, Centennial medal 1984); mem. Nat. Soc. Profl. Engrs. (pres. 1966-67), N.Y. State Soc. Profl. Engrs. (pres. 1954-55), Am. Soc. Engring. Edn., Engrs. Joint Council (dir. 1954-59), N.Y. Acad. Scis., Schenectady C. of C. (past dir., v.p.), Raven Soc., Tau Beta Pi (eminent mem., nat. pres. 1974-76), Theta Tau, Delta Upsilon. Unitarian (pres. 1940-45). Clubs: Rotary, Mohawk, Mohawk Golf. Home: Schenectady N.Y. Deceased.

LIPMAN, EUGENE JAY, rabbi; b. Pitts., Oct. 13, 1919; s. Joshua and Bessie (Neaman) L.; m. Esther Marcuson, July 4, 1943; children: Michael H. (dec.), Jonathan N., David E. AB, U. Cin., 1941; MHL, Hebrew Union Coll., 1943, DD (hon.), 1968. Ordained rabbi, 1943. Rabbi Temple Beth El, Ft. Worth, 1943-44; dir. B'nai B'rith Hillel Found. U. Wash., Seattle, 1949-50; dept. dir. Union of Am. Hebrew Congregations, N.Y., 1951-61; rabbi Temple Sinai, Washington, 1961-85, rabbi emeritus, 1985-94; lectr. in religion Am. U., Washington, 1961-68; lectr. in theology Cath. U. Am., Washington, 1967-79. Author: Yamim Nora'im, 1988; (with A. Vorspan) A Tale of Ten Cities, 1962, Justice and Judaism, 1956; editor: (textbook) The Mishnah, 1970; contbr. numerous articles to profl. jours. and chpts. to books. Pres. Cen. Conf. Am. Rabbis, 1987-89, Interfaith Conf. Met. Washington, 1982-84, Washington Bd. Rabbis, 1971-72; mem. bd. dirs., past pres. Nat. Capitol Area ACLU, 1965-77. Chaplain with armed forces 1944-46, 50-51. Teaching fellow Hebrew Union Coll., 1948-49. Mem. Commn. on Social Action. Democrat. Home: Chevy Chase Md. Died Jan. 14, 1994.

LIPMAN, SAMUEL, musician, music critic; b. San Jose, Calif., June 7, 1934; s. Max and Jane Bessie (Pinsky) L.; m. Jeaneane Jo Dowis, Apr. 18, 1963; 1 child, Edward. BA in Govt., San Francisco State Coll., 1956; MA in Polit. Sci., U. Calif.-Berkeley, 1958; student, L'Ecole Monteux, Hancock, Maine, 1951-57, Aspen Music Sch., 1959-61, Juilliard Sch., N.Y.C., 1959-62, Lev Shorr, Alexander Libermann, Pierre Monteux, Darius Milhaud, Rosina Lhevinne. Concert pianist, 1943-94; teaching asst. polit. sci. U. Calif.-Berkeley, 1957-58; mem. artist faculty Aspen Music Festival, 1972-85, Waterloo Music Festival, Stanhope, N.J., 1976-93; artistic dir. Waterloo Music Festival, 1985-93; music critic Commentary mag., N.Y.C., 1976-94; pub. New Criterion, N.Y.C., 1982-94; exec. com., bd. dirs. Waterloo Found. Arts, 1985-94. Author: Music After Modernism, 1979, The House of Music, 1984, Arguing for Music, Arguing for Culture, 1990, Music and More, 1992; editor: Matthew Arnold, Culture and Anarchy, 1994; contbr. articles to Commentary mag., New Criterion, Times Lit. Supplement, London, Am. Scholar, N.Y. Times Book Rev., others. Pres. Greenhouse Dance Ensemble, N.Y.C., 1981-85; mem. choir com. Congregation Emanu-el, N.Y.C., 1981-94; mem. Nat. Council on the Arts, Washington, 1982-88; treas. Found. for Cultural Rev., Inc., N.Y.C., 1982-94; mem. exec. com. Capital Research Ctr., Washington, 1984-94; chmn. Bradley Commn. funding performing arts in Milw., 1991-92. Nat. Woodrow Wilson fellow, 1956-57; recipient Deems Taylor award ASCAP, 1977, 80. Mem. Am. Fedn. Musicians, Am. Hist. Assn. Democrat. Jewish. Club: Coffee House (N.Y.C.). Home: New York N.Y. Died Dec. 17, 1994.

LIPMAN-WULF, PETER, sculptor, graphic artist; b. Berlin, Apr. 27, 1905; s. Fritz and Lucie (Sinzheimer) Lipman-Wulf; m. Barbara Suzanne VonBolton, Dec. 27, 1961; children: Michèle Stäuble, Ghilia. MA, Acad. Art, Berlin, 1927; M. of Excellence (hon.), Jewish Ctr., Cornell U., 1989. Instr. Academie Colarossi, Paris, 1937-47, CCNY, N.Y.C., 1949-57, Queens Coll., N.Y.C., 1950-56; prof. art Adelphi U., Garden City, N.Y., 1959-72. Contbr. articles to profl. jours.; one man shows include Jewish Mus., N.Y.C., New Sch. for Social Rsch., N.Y.C., Goethe House, Salisbury State Coll., Md., Widener U., Chester, Pa., Rutgers U., New Brunswick, N.J., Slivermine Guild, Conn., Guild Hall, East Hampton, N.Y., Hist. Mus., Riverhead, N.Y., John Jermain Libr., Bridgehampton, N.Y., Vered Gallery, East Hampton, Ctr. for Jewish Living, Cornell U., Ithaca, N.Y., Huntington Pub. Libr., N.Y., Elaine Benson Gallery, Bridgehampton, 1985-87, Denna Presbyn. Ch., Bryn Mawr, Haus Der Kultur, Neu Brandenburg, Germay, 1992, Liberator Gallery, Bridgehampton, 1993, Mairie Lelavendoux, France, 1993; represented in major mus. and pub. instns. in Europe and U.S.; busts of famous condrs. and musicians at Met. Opera, Bruno Walter Auditorium and Music Libr., Juilliard, Manhattan Sch. Music., N.Y.C., Corcoran Gallery, Washington, Munich State Opera, Philharm. and Mus. Hist. Mus., Berlin, Salzburg (Austria) Festspielhaus. Recipient Gold medal Paris, 1937, Olivetti award Silvermine, Conn., 1951, Alfred O. Deshong medal Widner Coll., 1980; fellow John Simon Guggenheim Found., 1949-50; recipient invitation to Yaddo as artist in residence, Saratoga Springs, 1980. Mem. Jimmy Ernst Art Alliance, Silvermine Guild, Artist's Fedn. Home: Sag Harbor N.Y. Died Sept. 26, 1993.

LIPSON, PAUL S., lawyer, deceased; b. N.Y.C., Nov. 1, 1915; s. Joshua and Goldie (Meisel) L.; m. Marcia S. Segerman, Feb. 7, 1971; children: Carol Lipson Wilson, Richard J. B.A., City Coll., N.Y., 1935; LL.B., Columbia U., 1938. Bar: N.Y. 1938. Since practiced in N.Y.C.; ptnr. Blum, Haimoff, Gersen, Lipson, Slavin & Garley, 1968-91, ret., 1991; chmn. law com. Am. Ethical Union, 1976-94. Editor Columbia Law Rev, 1937-38. Trustee Ethical Culture, 1960-94. Served with AUS, 1943-45. Decorated Bronze Star. Mem. ABA, N.Y. State Bar Assn., Assn. of Bar of City of N.Y. Home: Hollywood Fla. Died Dec. 25, 1994.

LISKER, JERRY R., newspaper executive; b. Fall River, Mass., May 8, 1938; s. Arnold and Viola (Archambault) L.; m. Yvette Adler, Feb. 6, 1964; children: Laurie, Andrea, Holly. Student, Columbia U., 1956, San Jose (Calif.) State U., 1957, Idaho State U., 1958-59, U. R.I., 1959-60. Reporter Providence Jour., 1959-61; reporter, then sports editor nat. edit. N.Y. Daily News, 1968-73; exec. sports editor N.Y. Post, 1973-93; pres. Holocto I, Ltd.; mem. Madison Sq. Garden Hall of Fame Commn. Mem. Baseball Writers Assn. Am., Nat. Football Writers Assn., N.Y. Boxing Writers. Club: Friars. Home: New York N.Y. Died Mar. 4, 1993.

LISLE, ROBERT WALTON, real estate executive; b. Butler, Mo., Aug. 18, 1927; s. Henry Harris and Nelle (Walton) L.; m. Donna Moore, Nov. 18, 1950 (dec. Apr. 1993); children: Amy Lisle Albrecht, Thomas W. B.S., U. Mo., 1950, postgrad. Law Sch., 1948-49; grad. Exec. Mgmt. Program, Columbia U., 1972. Vice pres. Prudential Ins. Co., Newark, 1950-82; sr. v.p. real estate investments Travelers Corp., Hartford, Conn., 1982-88; pres. PIC Realty Corp., Newark, 1970-82; chmn. bd., chief exec. officer The Prospect Co., Hartford, 1982-88; chmn. bd. dirs., chief exec. officer The Farnham Corp., Dallas, 1988-93. Mem. real estate adv. bd. NYU, 1982-90. Served with AUS, 1945-46, ETO. Recipient Citation of Merit U. Mo., 1980. Mem. Urban Land Inst. (trustee), Nat. Inst. Bldg. Scis. (dir., treas.), Nat. Assn. Corp. Real Estate Execs., Am. Hotel and Motel Assn., Industry Real Estate Financing Adv. Coun. Presbyterian. Clubs: Bent Tree Country. Home: Dallas Tex. Died Sept. 17, 1993.

LIST, HANS C., manufacturing engineer; b. Graz, Austria, Apr. 30, 1896; s. Hugo and Anna (Raab von Rabenau) L.; m. Elfriede L. Wachter, 1937. Student, Tech. U., Graz, D in Tech. Scis. (hon.), 1963. Designer Grazer Wagon und Maschinenfabrik; prof. Tungchi U., Woosung, China, 1926-32, Tech. U., Graz, 1932-41, Tech U., Dresden, Austria, 1941-45; owner, pres. AVL (inst.) Prof. List Ges. mbH, Graz, from 1945. Co-author, editor: Die Verbrennungskraftmaschine. Recipient Gold medal Assn. Austrian Engrs. & Architects, 1954, Grand medal for Svc., Austrian Republic, 1958, Grand Silver medal for Svcs., 1967, Grand Gold medal for Svcs., 1976, ring of Honor, City of Graz, 1959, title of Citizen of Honor, 1976, Grand Gold medal with Star, Province of Styria, 1976, ring of Honor, 1981, Internat. Tech. Promotion prize Inst. Internat. de Promotion et de Prestige, 1971, Wilhelm Exner medal Austrian Trade Assn., 1971, Hon. Baurat h.c. title Pres. Aus. Republic, 1972. Mem. ASME (Soichiro Honda medal 1991), SAE, ÔAIV, Austrian Acad. of Sci. (Schrôdinger prize 1980), Assn. German Engrs., Conseil Internat. des Machines a Combustion, Rotary Club, Styrian Golf Club. Home: Graz Austria Deceased.

LITTLE, JACK EDWARD, oil company executive; b. Dallas, Sept. 9, 1938. BS, Tex. A&M U., 1960, MS, 1961, PhD, 1966. Dir. prodn. research and exploration research Bellaire Research Ctr., Shell Devel. Co., Houston, 1977; div. prodn. mgr. onshore div. So. region Shell Oil Co., New Orleans, 1978-79; gen. mgr. prodn. western exploration and prodn. region Shell Oil Co., Houston, 1979-80, gen. mgr. Pacific div. western exploration and prodn. ops., 1980-81, v.p. corp. planning, 1981-82, sr. v.p. adminstrn., 1985-86, exec. v.p. exploration and prodn., 1986-94, also bd. dirs.; head Southea Asia div. Shell Internat. Petroleum Co., London, 198 85; pres. Shell Energy Resources, Inc., Newark, De pres., CEO Shell Exploration & Prodn. Co., 1995— mem. equity adv. com. Gen. Electric Investment Corp Stamford, Conn., 1987—; bd. dirs. Am. Petroleum Ins Washington, 1986—. Trustee, mem. exec. com. Unite Way Tex. Gulf Coast, Houston, 1987—; mem. extern adv. com. Tex. A&M Coll. Engring., 1988—. Me Soc. Petroleum Engrs. (chmn. nat. coms. on care guidance, investments and mgmt. and gen. interest 196 81, nat. bd. dirs. 1977-78, bd. dirs. Bakersfield se 1970, bd. dirs. Houston sect. 1969), Nat. Ocean Indu tries Assn. (bd. dirs., mem. exec. com. 1986—), Mi Continent Oil and Gas Assn. (exec. com. 1986—) Baptist. Clubs: Petroleum (bd. dirs. 1987-90), Forum Houston (bd. govs. 1985—), Lakeside Count (Houston, bd. dirs. 1988-91). Home: Houston Te

LITTNER, NER, psychoanalyst, psychiatrist; Toronto, Ont., Can., Nov. 17, 1915; came to U.S., 194 s. Mayer and Emma (Dlugash) L.; 1 child, Edi Littner. BA in Biology, U. Toronto, 1937, MD, 194 grad., Inst. for Psychoanalysis, Chgo., 1954. Diploma Am. Bd. Psychiatry and Neurology. Intern S Vincent's Hosp., L.A., 1940-41; resident in psychiat White Meml. Hosp., L.A., 1941-42, Chgo. State Hosp 1947-49; pvt. practice Chgo., 1951-94; mem. faculty In for Psychoanalysis, 1954-94, founder, dir. child thera program, 1961-81; psychiat. cons. Ill. Child Home a Aid Soc., Chgo., 1958-72, Jewish Children's Bur., Chg 1975-76; mem. Ill. Mental Health Planning Bd., Chg 1971-73. Contbr. numerous articles to med. jours., ch to book. Mem. Motion Picture Appeals Bd., Chg 1962-84; bd. dirs. Jane Addams Ctr., Hull Hou Chgo., 1965-69, Wisdom Bridge Theatre, 1987-88, Vi tory Gardens Theatre, Chgo., 1987-94, Chamber Mu Chgo., 1989-94, Bailwick Reportory Theatre, 1989-9 adv. bd. dirs. Bailwick Theatre, 1989-94; v.p. Citize Com. for Battered Children, Chgo., 1973-77; mem. ad com. Ill. div. ACLU, 1968-94. Recipient Edith L. Lau award Child Welfare League Am., 1959, Citizen of award Ill. Soc. for Clin. Social Work, 1985, award f excellence Nat. Resource Ctr. for Spl. Needs Adoptio 1987. Mem. Am. Psychiat. Assn., Am. Acad. Ch Psychiatry, Am. Psychoanalytic Assn. (cert. in child a adult psychoanalysis), Ill. Psychiat. Soc., Chg Psychoanalytic Soc., Mid Am. Club. Democrat. Je ish. Home: Chicago Ill. Died May 22, 1994.

LIVINGSTON, MOLLIE P., designer; b. N.Y.C.; Abraham and Sarah Parnis; m. Leon Jay Livingston; child, Robert Lewis. Sec.-treas. Parnis Livingston In pres. Mollie Parhis Co., Mollie Parnis Boutique, Mol Parnis at Home. Designer cadet nurses uniform Founder, Dress Up Your Neighborhood awar Jerusalem, 1967—, N.Y.C., 1972—; founder Livingst Awards for Young Journalists, 1980—; founder Mol Parnis Sch. Program for Keeping Surroundings Clea 1975—; overseer Parsons Sch. Design, 1983—. Nam Woman of Yr., Einstein Coll. Medicine, 1985—. Hom New York N.Y.

LIVINGSTON, NANCY, writer; b. Stockton-on-Te County Cleveland, England, Nov. 18, 1935; d. Ha William and Frances (Hewitt) Woolsey; m. David E ward Foster, 1975. actress, 1954-57; sec., 1957- stewardess, 1960-66; prodn. asst. for ind. TV cos., 19 87; writer, 1985-94. Author: The Trouble at Aquitai 1985 (Poisoned Chalice award Crime Writers As 1985), Fatality at Bath and Wells, 1986, Incident Parga, 1987, The Far Side of the Hill, 1987, Death i Distant Land, 1988 (Punch award 1988), Land of O Dreams, 1988, Death in Close-Up, 1989, Mayhem Parva, 1990, Never Were Such Times, 1990, Unwilling to Vegas, 1991. Mem. Crime Writers Assn. (vi chairperson, 1991-92). Home: London Eng. Died O 1994.

LJUBIJANKIC, IRFAN, government official; b. Biha 1952. Grad., Med. Sch. Sarajevo. Min. fgn. affa Govt. of Bosnia-Herzegovina, Sarajevo, 1994-95. Author several sci. and profl. works on medicine a gen. culture. Home: Sarajevo Bosnia-Herzegovina Di May 28, 1995.

LLOYD, RAYMOND GRANN, economist, educat b. Nashville; s. Grant and Johnella (Stewart) L.; Hortense D. Collins, Sept. 18, 1943; 1 dau., Jacqueli Michelle. B.S., Tenn. State U., 1940; M.A., Columb U., 1942; Ph.D., NYU, 1946. Prof. econs., chmn. de Savannah State Coll., 1950-58; dir. div. bus. and pr econs. Tenn. State U., 1958-72; research prof. econ chmn. studies in econs. and bus. U. North Fla., Jac sonville, 1972—; mem. staff Pres.'s Council Econ. A visers, 1970. Editor: Negro Ednl. Rev., 1950—; cont articles to profl. jours. Chmn. Mayor's Adv. Com. Minority Bus. Enterprises; chmn. edn. com. Jacksonvi br. NAACP; elder Woodlawn Presbyn. Ch. Me AAUP, Am. Econ. Assn., Western Econ. Assn Democrat. Home: Jacksonville Fla. Deceased.

LOCKE, JOHN ROBINSON, lawyer; b. San Anton Feb. 10, 1894; s. Jonathan and Brent (Robinson) L.; Grace Walker, Oct. 25, 1921; children: Grace W. (M F. Barton Harvey, Jr.), John Robinson. LL.B., U. V 1915; postgrad., U. Tex., 1915-16. Bar: Tex. 191 With Templeton, Brooks, Napier & Brown, 1916-

ewer & Locke, 1925-26, Kelso, Locke & Lepick (and edecessors), San Antonio, 1927-72, Groce, Locke & ebdon, from 1972; pres. San Antonio Joint Stock Land ank, 1940-48; dir. Frost Nat. Bank.; emeritus dir. First ty Bank of Corpus Christi. Vice pres. San Antonio . Edn., 1938-44; mem. San Antonio Water Bd., 1954- ; mem. San Antonio Pub. Service Bd., 1964-74, chmn., 70-74. Served as 1st lt. F.A. U.S. Army, 1917-19. em. Am., Tex. bar assns. Club: San Antonio Coun- . Home: San Antonio Tex. Deceased.

OCKE, JOHN WHITEMAN, III, manufacturing mpany executive; b. Melrose, Mass., Oct. 17, 1936; s. hn Whiteman Jr. and Lucy (Jones) L.; m. Carol Anne oe, Sept. 5, 1964 (div. 1984); children: Stephanie, ristine, Nancy. BA, Williams Coll., 1959; MBA, arvard U., 1965. CPA, Calif. Auditor Price aterhouse, San Francisco, 1965-68; asst. controller tomat Corp., La Jolla, Calif., 1968-69; auditor Peat, arwick and Mitchell, San Francisco, 1970-71; ad- nstrv. mgr., controller Kaiser Aluminum, Oakland, alif., 1971-81; comml. mgr. Bechtel Group, San ancisco, 1981-84; dir. fin. Gen. Parametric Corp., rkeley, Calif., 1984-87; v.p., controller Di Giorgio orp., San Francisco, 1987-88; v.p. fin., chief fin. officer, .-treas. Vertex, San Francisco, 1988-92; exec. v.p., ief fin. officer Andros Inc., Berkeley, Calif., 1992-95. pointed commr. City of San Francisco, 1990. Served lt. USNR, 1959-63, ret. lt. comdr., 1976. Mem. Am. st. CPA's. Home: San Francisco Calif. Died Feb. 10, 95.

OCKHART, BROOKS JAVINS, retired college dean; Sandyville, W.Va., Feb. 8, 1920; s. Therman Allen d Erna Shirley (Javins) L.; m. Patricia Durrant, July , 1969; 1 son, Jonathan Joseph; children by previous arriage: Patricia (Mrs. Meldon Wolfgang), Lynn Al- . A.B., Marshall U., 1937; M.S., W.Va. U., 1940; .D., U. Ill., 1943. Asst. instr. U. Ill., Urbana, 1940- ; instr. U. Mich., Ann Arbor, 1943-44, 46-48; asst. of. math. Naval Postgrad. Sch., Monterey, Calif., 48-51; assoc. prof. Naval Postgrad. Sch., 1951-55, of., 1955-62, 77-79, dean, 1962-77; ret., 1979; verning bd. Monterey City Schs., 1954-69, pres., 65-67; mem. governing bd. Monterey Peninsula Coll., 54-63, pres., 1960-63. Bd. dirs. Carmel Found., 1989- Lt. (j.g.) USNR, 1944-46. Bd. dirs. Carmel Found., 89-95. Served to lt. (j.g.) USNR, 1944-46. Mem. ath. Assn. Am. (pres. Calif. 1960, sec. 1961-63), Calif. n. Bds. Assn. (dir. 1963-70, pres. 1969), Sigma Xi, Chi a Phi, Kappa Delta Pi. Democrat. Methodist. ome: Monterey Calif. Died Apr. 27, 1995; interred rmel, Calif.

OEB, FRANCES LEHMAN, civic leader; b. N.Y.C., ot. 25, 1906; d. Arthur and Adele (Lewisohn) hman; student Vassar Coll., 1924-26; L.H.D. (hon.), YU, 1977; m. John L. Loeb, Nov. 18, 1926; children: dith Loeb Chiara, John L., Ann Loeb Bronfman, thur Lehman, Deborah Loeb Brice. N.Y.C. commr. UN and Consular Corps, 1966-78. Exec. com. pulation Action Com., Washington; life mem. bd. ildren of Bellevue, Inc., 1974-96; bd. dirs. Internat. esch., Inc., N.Y. Landmarks Conservancy; chmn. bd. st Side Internat. Community Ctr., Inc.; mem. UN vel. Corp., 1972-94; life trustee Collegiate Sch. for ys, N.Y.C.; trustee Cornell U., 1979-88, trustee emer- , 1988-96; trustee Vassar Coll., 1988-96; bd. over- rs Cornell U. Med. Coll., 1983-88 (life mem. 1988- , Inst. Internat. Edn. (life). Mem. UN Assn. (dir.). ubs: Cosmopolitan, Vassar, Women's City (N.Y.C.). ed May 17, 1996.

OEBENSTEIN, WILLIAM VAILLE, research emist, consultant; b. Providence, R.I., Aug. 9, 1914; s. ster and Lillian R. (Marcus) L.; m. Sara Ann Cle- nts, Nov. 12, 1949; children: Linda C., J. Roger, ances L., Cynthia L. BS, Brown U., 1935, MS, 1936, D, 1940. Rsch. chemist Corning Glass Works, Cen- l Falls, R.I., 1940-41, Bone Char Rsch. Project, Inc., ashington, 1946-52; physical chemist Nat. Bureau ndards, Washington, 1952-82; cons. and instr. Silver ring, Md., 1982—. Patentee in field; contbr. 35 ar- es in profl. jours. Maj. U.S. Army, 1941-46, South cific. Recipient Meritorious Svc. medal U.S. Dept. mmerce, Washington, 1958. Fellow Washington ad. Scis. (liaison rep. 1981-82); mem. Am. Chem. Soc. year mem. 1989), Sigma Xi. Jewish. Home: Silver ring Md. Died Mar. 23, 1993.

OEBNER, EGON EZRIEL, physicist; b. Plzen, echoslovakia, Feb. 24, 1924; s. Emil and Josephine oeser) L.; came to U.S., 1947, naturalized, 1952; BA Physics, U. Buffalo, 1950, PhD in Physics, 1955; m. aya S. Sajovics, June 18, 1950; children: Gary Emil, nny Joseph, Mindy Sue. Draftsman, Danek & Co., evec, Czechoslavakia, 1941-42, asst. to chief engr. ezin Waterworks, 1942-44; sr. engr. Sylvania Electric oducts, Inc., Buffalo and Boston, 1952-55; mem. tech. ff RCA Labs., Princeton, N.J., 1955-61; mgr., rsch. ecialist H.P. Assos., Palo Alto, Calif., 1961-65; dept. d, rsch. adviser Hewlett-Packard Labs., 1965-74, lab. oc., 1976-77, mgr. data base mgmt. systems dept., 77-80, mgr. cognitive interface dept., 1980-85, coun- or sci. and tech. 1985—; counselor sci. and technol. airs U.S. embassy, Moscow, 1974-76; lectr. Stanford part-time 1968-74; lectr. U. Calif. at Santa Cruz, 72-74. Mem. N.J. Commn. on Radiation Protection, 1960-62; mem. lay adv. com. on math. Unified Palo Alto Sch. Dist., 1964-66. Bd. dirs. Jewish Center, Princeton, 1957-59. Fellow IEEE; mem. Am. Phys. Soc., Semiotics Soc. Am., Am. Assn. Artificial Intelligence, Am. Optical Soc., AAAS, Sigma Xi, Assn. for Computing Machinery, Cognitive Sci. Soc., N.Y. Acad. Scis., Calif. Acad. Scis., Soc. Hist. Tech., Hist. Sci. Soc., Sigma Alpha Mu. Democrat. Jewish. Club: Palo Alto Hills Golf and Country, Commonwealth. Research in physics, chemistry, electronics, metalurgy, psychology, biophysics, cybernetics, math., sci. policy, linguistics, neural networks, data processing, constitutional law, hist. tech. and hist. sci. Patentee in optoelectronics. Home: Palo Alto Calif.

LOHR, MARY MARGARET, nursing educator, university dean; b. Chgo.; d. Herbert M. and May (Van Patten) L. Diploma, Presbyn. Hosp. Sch. Nursing, Chgo., 1946; BS in Nursing Edn., U. Pitts., 1949; MA, Columbia, 1951, EdD, 1962; postgrad, U. Mich., 1957-58. Staff nurse Downey (Ill.) VA Hosp., 1946-47, head nurse, 1947-48; supr. Downey (Ill.) VA Hosp. (Nursing Service), 1949-50; asst. prof., asso. prof., chmn. dept. psychiat. nursing Coll. Nursing, State U. Iowa, 1951-59; tng. specialist psychiat. nursing Tng. and Manpower br. NIMH, Bethesda, Md., 1961-62; asso. prof. psychiat. nursing Coll. Nursing, U. Ill., Chgo., 1962-66; also chmn. dept. psychiat. nursing; prof., dean Sch. Nursing, U. Va., Charlottesville, 1966-72; dean, prof. Coll. Nursing U. Ill., Chgo., 1972-75, Sch. Nursing, U. Mich., Ann Arbor, 1976-81, Coll. Nursing, Clemson (S.C.) U., 1981-87. Editorial bd.: Perspectives in Psychiat. Nursing, 1962-66; editor psychiat. nursing sect.: Current Concepts in Clin. Nursing, 1966-74; Contbr. articles to profl. jours. Fellow Inst. Medicine Chgo., Am. Acad. Nursing; mem. Nat. League Nursing, Am. Nurses Assn., Soroptimist Club, Sigma Theta Tau, Pi Lambda Theta, Kappa Delta Pi. Home: Tucson Ariz. Died Oct. 19, 1994.

LOHRMAN, JOHN J., manufacturing company executive; b. Ellsworth, Iowa, Mar. 4, 1920; s. Joseph A. and Elizabeth (Crosley) L.; m. Natalie M. Anderson, Aug. 26, 1978; children: James B., Kristine M., David C. Anderson, Andrea Anderson Moriarity. B.Sc., Creighton U., Omaha, 1941; postgrad., U. Pa., 1946-47. Indsl. relations asst., then asst. controller Phila. Transp. Co., 1946-55; assoc. McKinsey & Co., N.Y.C., 1955-57; with RB&W Corp., Mentor, Ohio, 1957-93; v.p. adminstrn. RB&W Corp., 1961-69, exec. v.p., 1969-73, pres., chief exec. officer, 1973-83, chmn. bd., chief exec. officer, 1983-93; bd. dirs. Bank One, Cleve., N.A., Garco Machinery, Inc., Thomas William Lench Holdings Ltd., Lamson and Sessions of Can. Ltd. Trustee Meridia Hillcrest Hosp., Meridia Inst.; chmn. governing bd. Indsl. Fasteners Inst., 1978, chmn., 1988; bd. govs. Employers Resource Council 1980-86. Served to maj. U.S. Army, 1941-46. Recipient Alumni merit award Creighton U., 1980; named to Nat. Insdl. Fastener Show Hall of Fame, 1987. Mem. Kirtland Country Club, Union Club, Chagrin Valley Hunt Club, Audubon Country Club, Wiggins Racket and Yacht Club. Home: Gates Mills Ohio Deceased.

LOMASON, WILLIAM KEITHLEDGE, automotive company executive; b. Detroit, July 12, 1910; s. Harry A. and Elizabeth (Bennett) L.; m. Neva C. Wigle, 1930 (dec. 1965); m. Ruth M. Martin, 1970. AB, U. Mich., 1932, AM, 1933. With Douglas & Lomason Co., Detroit, 1934—; treas. Douglas & Lomason Co., 1943-52, v.p., 1945-50, pres., gen. mgr., 1950-75, chmn. bd., chief exec. officer, 1976-82, chmn. bd., 1982—, also bd. dirs.; pres. Shamrock Air Lines, 1968-76; pres., dir. Douglas y Lomason de Mexico, S.A. de C.V., 1986—. Co-author: When Management Negotiates, 1967. Bd. dirs., mem. exec. com. Nat. Right to Work Com.; bd. dirs. past chmn. and pres. Bus. Council of Ga.; dir. emeritus Mich. Mfrs. Assn. Recipient Man of Yr. award, Carrollton, Ga., 1967; named lt. col. aide de camp Gov.'s Staff, Ga., 1956. Mem. Engring. Soc. Detroit, Econ. Soc. Detroit, Am. Electroplaters Soc., Alpha Chi Rho. Episcopalian. Home: Atlanta Ga.

LONDON, MICHAEL, playwright, artistic director, arts management consultant; b. Columbus, Ohio, Aug. 24, 1951; s. Oscar Basil and Jeannette Marie (Altiere) McGee. Student, Ohio State U., 1969-72, 83, Lamar U., 1975; BA, MA, Columbia Pacific U., 1987; postgrad., Sinclair Coll., 1989-90, Wright State U., 1990-91. Gen. mgr. The Wright Pl., Columbus, 1975-77; mng. dir. Dayton (Ohio) Contemporary Dance Co., 1977-80; exec. dir. Michael London Assocs., Dayton, 1980—; freelance playwright Dayton, 1982—; gen. ptnr. London Group I Prodns., Ltd., Dayton, 1985-91; artistic dir. Am. Theatreworks Found., Dayton, 1986—; mem. Ohio Minority Arts Task Force, Columbus, 1978-85; cons. Acclaim mag., Columbus, 1987-89; playwright Artists in Edn. program, Columbus, 1987—; playwright-in-residence Grandparents Living Theatre, 1990-91; adj. prof. Wright State U., 1991—. Playwright: The Picture Show, 1983, The Homestretch, 1985, SMILE, Chaplain...The One Man Band, 1986, A Shade of Grey, 1987, Le Repas, 1988, My Funeral, 1989, Beyond Freedom, 1990, The Incident at White Rock, 1991, others. Chmn. Jane Reece Neighborhood Assn., Dayton, 1986-88; mem. N. River task force City of Dayton, 1987—; trustee Ballet Met., Inc., 1975-77. Moody scholar Lamar U., 1975. Mem. Assn. Ohio Dance Cos. (trustee 1977-81, 83-84, Trustee award 1984), Dramatists Guild, Authors League of Am., Internat. Soc. Dramatists, Dayton Canoe Club, AFS Internat. Intercultural Programs. Home: Dayton Ohio

LONG, I. A., banker; b. Herndon, Va.; m. Lydia Ann Kimbrough Allen; children: Claxton Allen (dec.), Lydia Ann, Ada White. Ed., U. Va., doctor of Laws, Maryville U. (hon. degree), Am. Inst. Banking. Mem. staff N.Y. br. Royal Bank of Can., 1919-20; asst. cashier Peoples Nat. Bank, Leesburg, Va., 1920-27; v.p. Mercantile Trust Co., St. Louis, 1928-53; pres. S.W. Bank of St. Louis, 1953-77, chmn bd., chief exec. officer, 1977-84, chmn. emeritus, 1984-93. mem. faculty Sch. of Banking, U. Wis. Pres. bd. trustees Mary Inst.; pres. Central Inst. for the Deaf, St. Louis Mcpl. Bond Club, St. Louis Corp. Fiduciaries Assn.; chmn. St. Louis Housing Authority, St. Louis Land Clearance Authority, Citizens Sch. Improvement Com., Fifth War Loan Drive, Met. St. Louis; chmn. emeritus bd. trustees Jefferson Nat. Expansion Meml. Assn.; chmn. emeritus Mo. Hist. Soc.; mem. Mo. Acad. Squires. Named Ky. Col., Ark. Traveler. Recipient Thomas Jefferson award Mo. Hist. Soc. Mem. Investment Bankers Assn. Am. (chmn. Miss. Valley group) (bd. dirs.). Clubs: St. Louis Country, Noonday (past pres.), Racquet (past pres.), Profl. and Bus. Men's of the Hill. Died Nov. 1993; buried Union Cemetery, Leesburg, Va. Home: Saint Louis Mo.

LORD, ANTHONY, retired architect; b. Asheville, N.C., Feb. 17, 1900; s. William Henry and Helen (Anthony) L. BSME, Ga. Sch. Tech., 1922; BFA in architecture, Yale U., 1927. Registered profl. engr., N.C.; registered architect, N.C. Ptnr. Lord and Lord, Architects, Asheville, 1929-33; craftsman of decorative wrought iron Anthony Lord Hand-Forged Iron, Asheville, 1930-35; pvt. practice Asheville, 1935-40; v.p. Six Assocs.-Architects and Engrs., Asheville, 1940-70; ret., 1970. Prin. works include Asheville Citizen-Times Bldg., 1938, dormitories, librs., svc. bldgs., office bldgs., adminstrn. bldgs. for U. N.C., Greensboro, U. N.C., Asheville, Western Carolina U., Montreat-Anderson Coll., Warren Wilson Coll., Swannanoa, N.C., Asheville Sch. for Boys, 1948-70, Am. Enka Corp. lab. and office bldg., 1960-66, first unit, Meml. Mission Hosp., Asheville, 1950; retrospective exhbn. of architecture, ironwork, painting, Asheville Art Mus., 1984. Trustee (emeritus) Pack Meml. Libr., Asheville-Buncombe Libr. System, Asheville, 1943-88, chmn. bd. trustees, 1959-79; bd. advisors Warren Wilson Coll., 1983-93, life mem., 1989; mem. Asheville Tree and Greenway Commn., 1979, hon. mem., 1993; mem. Downtown Devel. Strategies Task Force, 1988-93. Named to Western N.C. Creative Arts Hall of Fame, Asheville, 1988. Fellow AIA; mem. N.C. AIA, Pen and Plate Club (pres. 1958), Downtown Club. Democrat. Home: Asheville N.C. Died Dec. 9, 1993.

LORD, FONCHEN USHER (MRS. WILLIAM WALCOTT LORD), artist; b. St. Louis; d. Roland Green and Florence (Richardson) Usher; AB, Radcliffe Coll., Harvard U., 1933; MA, Washington U., St. Louis, 1935; m. William Walcott Lord, June 12, 1935; children: Fonya Lord Helm, William Pepperell, Carter Usher, Elizabeth Usher Lord Hillman. Exhibited invitational one-woman shows Stetson U., Deland, Fla., 1969, W.Va. Wesleyan Coll., 1970, Avanti Galleries, N.Y.C., 1970, Miami Mus. Modern Art, 1970, Broward Community Coll., Ft. Lauderdale, 1971, Polk Public Mus., 1972, 78, Trend House Gallery, 1972, Fla. So. Coll., 1974, (retrospectiv exhbn.) 1982, Lakeland Civic Center Complex, Theatre Gallery, 1974-93, Miller-King Gallery, Miami, 1975, 76, Artists Gallery, Madeira Beach, Fla., 1978, Russell B. Hicken Fine Arts Ltd., 1979, Winter Haven Cultural Ctr., 1990, U. Tampa, 1982, Polk Community Coll., 1984, Daytona Mus. Arts & Scis., one-woman retrospective, 1988; one-woman invitational Bennett Gallery, Orlando, Fla., 1990, Mennello Gallery, Winter Park, 1990, Lighthouse Gallery, Tequesta, Fla., 1993 (Juried award, 1993); invitational exibits: Fla. Artist Group Area V, Eckerd Coll., 1992, LeMoyne Art Found., Tallahassee, 1992, Gulf Coast Community Coll., Panama City, 1992, Sarasota Visual Arts Center, 1993; exhibited in group shows at Columbia Mus. Art, Columbus Mus. Arts and Crafts, Birmingham Mus. Art, Atlanta High Mus., Norton Gallery, Dulin Gallery Art, Ringling Mus. Art, Butler Inst. Am. Art, Jacksonville Art Mus., Loch Haven Art Ctr., 1990, Biennial, 1983, many others; represented in permanent collections: Fla. Ho. of Reps., City of Lakeland Civic Center, Miami Mus. Modern Art, W.Va. Wesleyan Coll., Lowe Mus. of U. Fla., Fla. So. Coll., Polk Mus. Art, Daytona Mus. Arts and Scis., Tampa (Fla.) Mus. Art, Ctr. for Arts, Vero Beach, Fla., Radcliffe Coll., Cambridge, Mass., New Coll., Sarasota, Pioneer Fed. Savs. and Loan, Northwood Inst., West Palm Beach., Jacksonville Art Mus., Fla. Fed. Savs. Bank, Tampa Tribune, Fla. Pres., Palm Island Corp., Bartow, Fla., 1954-64, Braden River Ranchettes, Bartow, 1964-71; asst. treas. Paris Tanning Co., South Paris, Maine, 1944-48; artist-in-residence Fusion Dance Co., Miami, 1975. Recipient Merit award Fla. State Fair, 1964, Clearwater Art Seminar award, 1961, 63, Sunshine Art Festival award, 1962; Ridge Art ann. competition awards 1963, 65, 66, 67, 70, 73, 85, 90, 92, 93; Chautauqua Nat. award, 1968; award Festival of States Ann., 1965; Sarasota Art Assn. juried awards, 1971, 73, 74, 80, 81, 82, 85, 87, 90; Women's Caucus for

Art (juried award state wide 1993), Cape Coral Nat. award, 1973; Fla. Artist Group awards, 1972, 78, 80, 82, 83, 89, 90, Maitland Art Ctr. Competition, 1990. Fellow Royal Soc. Arts (London); mem. Fla. Artists Group, Zeta Tau Alpha. Episcopalian. Died Aug. 25, 1993. Home: Lakeland Fla.

LOTT, KENCH LEE, JR., banker; b. Selma, Ala., Feb. 3, 1920; s. Kench Lee and Clara Mae (King) L.; children by previous marriage: Barbara Lott Hannan, Betsy Lott Poole, Claire Lott Weathers. B.S. in Commerce, Auburn U., 1941; M.B.A., Wharton Sch., U. Pa., 1947; postgrad., Stonier Sch. Banking, 1954, Grad. Sch. Credit and Fin. Mgmt., Dartmouth Coll., 1962; LLD (hon.), Livingston U., 1989. With 2d Nat. Bank, Houston, 1947-48; with Merchants Nat. Bank, Mobile, Ala., 1948-95; pres. Merchants Nat. Bank, 1972-76, chmn. bd., chief exec. officer, 1976-81; with Southland Bancorp., Mobile, 1972-95; vice chmn. Southland Bancorp., 1972-78, chmn., bd., chief exec. officer, 1978-81; exec. dir. internat. div. First Ala. Bancshares, Inc., 1982-85; bd. dirs. First Ala. of Mobile, Finch Cos., Mobile. Trustee Spring Hill Coll., 1984-90; pres. Mobile Community Found., 1976-80, United Fund of Mobile, 1978-80. Served with F.A. U.S. Army, 1941-46. Decorated Bronze Star, Purple Heart; recipient Disting. Alumni award Auburn U. Sch. Bus., 1977, Pres.'s citation Spring Hill Coll., 1976; named to Ala. Acad. of Honor, 1980, Ala. Sr. Citizens Hall of Fame, 1991. Mem. Auburn U. Alumni Assn. (pres. 1965-67), Omega Delta Kappa (Auburn U. Alumni award 1968), Phi Kappa Phi., Beta Gamma Sigma. Episcopalian. Lodge: Kiwanis (pres. Mobile club 1962). Home: Mobile Ala. Died Jan. 16, 1995.

LOUDEN, JAMES KEITH, management consultant, executive; b. Duquesne, Pa., Mar. 4, 1905; s. George T. and Minnie M. (Zimmerman) L.; m. Genevieve Sybert, June 4, 1932; 1 child, Penelope Ann. B.B.A., Ohio State U., 1928. Supt., indsl. engr. Fostoria Glass Co., Moundsville, W.Va., 1928-33; indsl. engr. Buckeye Steel Castings Co., Columbus, Ohio, 1933-36; supr. standards control div. Owens-Ill. Glass Co., Toledo, 1936-40; dir. indsl. engring. Nat. Supply Co., Pitts., 1940-42; prodn. mgr. glass and closure div. Armstrong Cork Co., Lancaster, Pa., 1942-47; asst. to pres. York Corp., Pa., 1947-55; dir., v.p. asst. to pres. York Corp., 1955-57, vp., gen. mgr. comml. div.; exec. v.p., chief exec. officer, dir. Lebanon Steel Foundry, Pa., 1957-61; v.p. pres.'s profl. assn. Am. Mgmt. Assn., 1963-68, pres., 1968-70, chmn. bd. dirs., pres., 1971-94, also dir.; pres. Corporate Dir., Inc., 1971-94; lectr. summer mgmt. course State U. Iowa, 1939-52; lectr. for profl. socs., ednl. forums in, U.S., Europe, Can. Author: Wage Incentives, 1944, rev, (with J.W. Deegan), 1959) Job Evaluation, (with T.G. Newton), (with J.M. Juran) The Corporate Director, 1967, Making it Happen-The Unit President Concept, 1971, The Effective Director in Action, 1975, Managing at the Top, 1977, Think Like a President, 1981, The Director, 1982. Trustee Princeton Theol. Sem. Fellow Internat. Acad. Mgmt., ASME (Worcester R. Warner medal 1956, chmn. mgmt. divsn. 1949, mem. bd. tech. 1957-62, past chmn., dir.), Am. Mgmt. Assn. (dir., exec. com. mfg. div. planning coun., v.p. 1953-55, gen. mgmt. div. planning coun. 1959-61, v.p. 1961-69), Soc. Advancement Mgmt. (Gilbreth medal 1949, hon. life, pres. 1942); mem. Mfrs. Assn. York (dir., mem. exec. com. 1949-57), SAR, Sigma Phi Epsilon. Republican. Presbyterian. Clubs: Lancaster Country (Pa.), Hamilton (Lancaster); Skytop (Pa.); University (N.Y.C.). Lodges: Masons, Shriners (Lancaster, Pa.). Home: Lancaster Pa. Died Aug. 12, 1994.

LOWELL, JULIET, author; b. N.Y.C., Aug. 7, 1901; d. Max and Helen (Kohut) Loewenthal; m. Leo E. Lowell, Aug. 17, 1922 (dec.); children—Margot, Ross; m. Ben Lowell, 1945. A.M., Vassar Coll., 1922. lectr. Vassar Coll., June 1987. Writer, from 1920, newspaper columnist, lectr.; writer comedy script; appeared on radio programs Underwood Typewriter, Ford Motor Co., Sanka Coffee, also TV shows throughout U.S., Can.; made films for Fox, Warner Bros. motion picture cos., 30 shorts for RKO.; author: Dumb-Belles Lettres, 1933, Dear Sir, 1944, Dear Sir or Madam, 1946, Dear Mr. Congressman, 1948, Dear Hollywood, 1950, Dear Doctor, 1955, 68, Dear Justice, A Book for the Just, the Unjust, and Those Who Just Like to Laugh, 1958, Dear Folks, 1960, Dear Man of Affairs, 1961, Dear VIP, 1963, It Strikes Me Funny, 1964, Boners in the News, 1967, Humor U.S.A, 1968, Dear Candidate, 1968, Racy Tales For Adults and Adultresses, 1969; contbr. article on war humor to Ency. Brit, 1947, articles to nat. mags.; author weekly column Juliet Lowell's Celebrity Letters, Sunday supplement Family Weekly, from 1972. Chmn. book com. N.Y.-Tokyo Sister City Affiliation.; Mem. bd. Hecksher Found. for Children, ID II. Mem. Authors League Am., Internat. Platform Assn., Vassar Alumnae Assn. Clubs: Woman's Press, Overseas Press. Home: Chestnut Hill Mass. Deceased.

LOWRY, ROBERT JAMES, novelist, poet, short story writer; b. Cin., Mar. 28, 1919; s. Beirne Clem and Alma (Collas) L.; m. Bella Alice Cohen, 1941 (div. 1946); m. Frankie Abbe, 1948 (div. 1954); 1 child, David; m. Antoinette LoBianco, 1958 (div. 1965); children: Beirne, Giacomo; m. Mary Louise O'Neill, 1967 (div. 1969). Student, U. Cin., 1937-38. Pub., editor The Little Man Press, Cin., 1938-42; editor, book designer, prodn. mgr. New Directions, N.Y.C., 1945-46; staff writer Time Mag., N.Y.C., 1949-50; reader, editor, copywriter Popular Library, N.Y.C., 1951-56; contbr. book criticism N.Y. Times Sunday Book Rev., N.Y.C., 1951-55, Sat. Rev., N.Y.C., 1951-55; office mgr. Doubleday Book Shop, N.Y.C., 1962; copywriter Cin. Enquirer, 1963; asst. to comml. mgr. Sta. WCPO-TV, Cin., 1963; copywriter Standard Pub., Cin., 1964; staff mem. Writer's Digest Criticism Service, Cin., 1976-79; editorial assoc. Writer's Digest Sch., Cin., 1977-79; personnel cons. Sanford Rose Assocs., Cin., Availability of Western Ohio, Synergistic Search, Sales Cons., Cin.; instr. short story writing U. Cin., 1963. Author: Murderpie, 1939, Hutton Street, 1939, Defense in University City, 1939, Trip to the Bloomin Moon, 1939, I'll Never Be the Same, 1940, The Bad Girl Marie, 1940, Gup: 3 Adventures, 1942, Phisterus, 1943, This Cloud Life, 1943, Hey, Joe!, 1944, The Hey, Joe! Supplement, 1944, War, 1944, Feelthy Pomes, 1945, The Blaze Beyond the Town, 1945, 3, 1945, Casualty, 1946, The Wolf That Fed Us, 1949, The Big Cage, 1949, Happy New Year, Kamerades, 1954, What's Left of April, 1956, The Last Party, 1956, New York Call Girl, 1958, The Prince of Pride Starring, 1959, That Kind of Woman, 1959, The Knife, 1960, Party of Dreamers, 1962, Literature and the Communist State, 1965, New Poems, 1967, Robert Lowry Diary, 1974, The Nut, 1976, Dreams, 1976, A Chronology of My Life Since 1952, 1979, Fun in Gun, 1983, An American Writer at the End of His Life, 1988, Pen & Ink Drawings, 1988, The Race Track of the Dead, 1988, My Confession, 1989, A Story, A Drawing & 2 Poems, 1989, My Doomsday Poem, 1989, A Fantasy Session of My Four Lost Wives, 1989, Life, 1989; contbr. short stories or articles to popular mags. in U.S. and fgn. countries; contbr. book criticisms Chgo. Sun-Times; Robert Lowry collections established at Boston U., U. So. Calif., Kent State U.; translator The Edge of Sunday, 1952; film That Kind of Woman based on short story, 1959. Served with AUS, 1942-45. Story selected for O. Henry Meml. Award Prize Stories, 1950. Home: Cincinnati Ohio Died Dec. 5, 1994.

LOWRY, WILSON MCNEIL, former ballet company executive, foundation executive, writer; b. Columbus, Kans., Feb. 17, 1913; s. Benedict Harrison and Helen Hannah (Graham) L.; m. Elsa Alberta Koch, Aug. 31, 1936; children: Harrison Graham, Hugh (dec.). A.B. magna cum laude, U. Ill., 1934, Ph.D., 1941, Litt.D., 1970. Instr. English U. Ill., 1936-42; writer OWI, 1942-43; expert cons., hdqrs. Army Service Forces, 1943; assoc. editor Dayton (Ohio) Daily News, 1946-47; chief Washington bur. James M. Cox Newspapers, 1947-52; assoc. dir. Internat. Press. Inst., Zurich, 1952-53; dir. Ford Found., 1953-64, v.p., 1964-75; dir. Am. Assembly on Performing Arts, 1977, Am. Assembly on Arts and Pub. Policy, 1984; pres. San Francisco Ballet, 1988-91. Editor: Accent, quar. new lit, 1940-42, The Performing Arts and American Society, 1978, The Arts and Public Policy in the United States, 1985. Served as lt. USNR, 1943-46. Recipient ANTA, Antoinette Perry and John F. Wharton meml. awards in theatre; Am. Assn. Dance Cos. and spl. Capezio awards for disting. service in dance; Nat. Council Arts Adminstrs. award for leadership in visual arts; Am. Assn. Univ. Presses award for disting. services to higher edn.; Disting. Svc. to the Arts award Am. Acad. Arts and Letters, 1992; named hon. mem. Art Students League. Mem. Phi Beta Kappa, Sigma Delta Chi (Distinguished Service award 1948). Democrat. Club: Century Assn. (N.Y.C.). Home: New York N.Y. Died June 6, 1993; buried Sleepy Hollow Cemetery, Tarrytown, N.Y.

LOY, MYRNA, actress; b. Helena, Mont., Aug. 2, 1905; d. David Franklin and Della Williams. Grad., Venice (Calif.) High Sch., Westlake Sch. Girls. Appeared in numerous motion pictures, including Best Years of Our Lives (award World Film Festival, Brussels), 1946, The Bachelor and the Bobby Soxer, 1947, Mr. Blanding Builds His Dream House, 1948, If This Be Sin, Cheaper by the Dozen, 1950, Airport 75, The End, 1979, Just Tell Me What You Want, 1980, others; appeared in stage plays Relative Speaking; TV appearances in Death Takes a Holiday, also, Do Not Fold, Spindle or Mutilate, Indict and Convict, Columbo, Ironsides, Family Affair, The Virginian, The Couple Takes a Wife, It Happened at Lakewood Manor, Summer Solstice, 1981. Organizer Hollywood Film com. U.S. Nat. Commn. for UNESCO, 1948, mem. commn., 1950-54; asst. head welfare activities ARC, N.Y. area, 1941-45; Mem. Am. Assn. UN, Nat. Commn. Against Discrimination in Housing. Recipient Kennedy Ctr. Honor, 1988, Acad. award of Merit, 1990. Home: Los Angeles Calif. Died Dec. 14, 1993.

LUKE, EBEN LIVESEY, chief justice of Botswana; b. Goderich, Sierra Leone, May 7, 1930; s. Samuel Ernest and Rebecca (Cole) L.; m. Rachel Evelyn Macauley, Apr. 18, 1959; 1 child, Pamela. BA in Law with honors, U. Southampton, 1955; BL, Lincoln's Inn (London), 1956. Bar: Sierra Leone. Pvt. practice barrister and solicitor, Freetown, Sierra Leone, 1957-70; notary pub., Sierra Leone, 1968—; judge High Ct., Freetown, 1970-71, justice High Ct., 1971-79, chief justice, 1979-85; justice Gambia Ct. Appeal, Banjul, Gambia, 1972—; chief justice Supreme Ct., Botswana, 1988—; chmn. Jud. and Legal Svc. Commn., Freetown, 1979-85; mem. Com. on Legal Edn. in Africa, Freetown, 1963, Com. on Legal Edn. in Sierra Leone, Freetown, 1964. Bd. truste West African Endowment Fund, 1982-86, West Afric Examinations; mem. Constl. Com., Sierra Leone, 196 Civilian Rule Com., Sierra Leone, 1968, Consl. Re Com., Sierra Leone, 1970. Awarded Officers of t Order of Republic of Sierra Leone, 1978. Mem. Sier Leone Bar Assn. (pres. 1970), Jud. Council of Nat. B Assn. , Freetown Dinner Club, Freetown Golf Clu Royal Overseas League (London), Wilberforce Clu Laboramus (master 1984). Methodist. Home: Loba Botswana

LUTHER, JAMES HOWARD, lawyer, retir pharmaceutical company executive; b. West New Yo N.J., Jan. 27, 1928; s. James Howard and Marga Mary (Leyden) L.; m. Frances Audrey Lynch, July 1951; children: David Gerard, Stephanie Lynch. A magna cum laude, Fordham U., 1948, J.D. cum lau 1951. Bar: N.Y. 1951. Assoc. Donovan, Leisu Newton & Irvine, N.Y.C., 1951-55; with Sterling Dr Inc., N.Y.C., 1955-88, v.p., 1968-78, dir., 1973-88, g counsel, 1976-88, sr. v.p., gen. counsel, 1978-88; g counsel Am. Found. for Pharm. Edn., 1990-92. Me ABA, Nonprescription Drug Mfrs. Assn. (v.p. 1972- dir. 1972-88, chmn. bd. 1985-87). Roman Catholi Home: New York N.Y. Died Mar. 9, 1995.

LUTOSLAWSKI, WITOLD, composer; b. Warsa Poland, Jan. 25, 1913; s. Jozef and Maria (Olszewsk L.; degree in piano State Conservatory Music, Warsa 1936, degree in composition, 1937; hon. doctorate Cle Inst. Music, 1971, Northwestern U., 1972, Warsaw 1973, Lancaster U., 1975, U. Glasgow, 1977, Copernic U., 1980, Durham U., Jagiellonian U. Cracow, Baldw Wallace Coll., Cambridge U., 1987, Royal No. C Manchester, 1987, Belfast U., 1987; Dr.h.c. Cho Music Coll., Warsaw, 1988, New England conservat of Music, Boston, 1990, U. Humaines Scis. Strasbou 1990; DMus (hon.) Duquesne U., Pitts., 1991; m. Ma Danuta Dygat, Sept. 24, 1946. Composer, 1922—; Ce Concerto, 1970, Preludes and Fugue for 13 solo strir 1972, Les espaces du sommeil for baritone and orc 1975, Mi-parti for orch., 1976, Novelette for orch., 19 Double Concerto for oboe, harp and orch., 1980, Th Symphony, 1983, Chairn 1 for chamber orch., 19 Partita for violin and piano, 1984, Chain 2, dialogue violin and orch., 1985, Chain 3 for symphony orc 1986; first public performance orch. piece, 19 performances, Europe, Am., Asia, Australia, Afri tchr. composition Berkshire Music Center, Tanglewo Mass., 1962, Dartington, Devon, Eng., 1963, Swedish Royal Acad. Music, 1965, Aarhus, Denma 1968; condr. orchs. and Choris, 1963—; mem. progr com. Warsaw Autumn Festival, 1956-74. Recipi Warsaw prize, 1948, State Music prize, 1952, 55, Minister Culture prize, 1962, 1st prize Internat. Mu Coun. and Gesellschaft der Musikfreunde, Vienna, 19 Serge Koussevitzky Internat. Rec. award, 1964, Le Sonning Music prize, 1967, Gottfried-von-Herder pr 1967, Internat. du Disque de l'Academie Charles Gr Grand prize, Paris, 1971, Maurice Ravel prize, 19 Sibelius de Wihuri prize, 1973, E. von Siemen's pr 1983, Solidarity prize, 1984, Grawemeyer award musical composition U. Louisville, 1985, gold me Royal Philharm. Soc., 1985, Queen Sofia of Spain pr 1985, Internat. Critics award, 1986, Signature aw Pitts. Symphony Orch., 1991, hon. medal Stockho 1992, Disting. Musician award Inc. Soc. Musici Manchester, 1991; Grammy award, Jurzykowski Fou prize, N.Y., 1966, also others; named Artist of the Hamburg, 1979. Fellow Assn. Norwigian Compos Royal Coll. Music London, Serbian Acad. Sci.; m Acad. Scientiarum et Artium Europea, Polish C posers' Union (hon. mem., recipient prize 1959, Assn. Profl. Cokmposers (hon. London), Royal Swed Acad. Music, Freie Akad. der Künste, Hamb Akademie der Künste, Berlin, Deutsche Akademie Künste zu Berlin, Bayerische Akademie der Schö Künste, Munich, Am. Acad. Arts and Letters, N Inst. Arts and Letters, Royal Acad. Music (Lond Acad. des Beaux Arts (Paris), Acad. Européenne Sciences, des Arts, et des Lettres, Acad. Royale Belgique, Acad. Nazionale de Santa Cecilia (h Rome), Internat. Soc. Contemporary Music (ho Konzert hausgesellschaft Vienna (hon.). Comp symphonic works, vocal music, string quartet. Ho Warsaw Poland

LUX, JOHN H., corporate executive; b. Logansp Ind., Feb. 3, 1918; s. Carl Harrison and Mary Em (Dunn) L.; m. Betty F. Passow, Aug. 27, 1940; child John Ernst, Courtney Rae; m. Bernice Weitzel Bro 1965; m. Linda Merrill Brown, Mar. 2, 1978; child Julia Elizabeth, Jenifyr Claire. B.S., Purdue U., 19 Ph.D., 1942. Asst dir. research and devel. The Ne Co., 1943-46; v.p., cons. Atomic Basic Chems., 1946 dir. research Witco Chem. Co., 1947-50; mgr. product devel. Gen. Electric Co., 1950-52; v.p. S Chem. Co., 1952-55; pres., dir. Haveg Industries, I Wilmington, Del., 1955-66, Haveg Corp., Tou Mgmt. Corp. (P.R.); chmn. bd. Hemisphere Prod Corp. (P.R.), Reinhold Engring. & Plastics Norwalk, Calif., Am. Super-Temperatures Wires pres. Ametek, Inc., 1966-69, chmn. bd., chief exec. ficer, 1969-90, chmn. bd., 1990-93; ret., 1993. M Am. Inst. Chem. Engrs., Am. Chem. Soc., Phi Lam Upsilon. Club: Met. Home: Rancho Santa Fe C Died Jan. 19, 1996.

UYTEN, WILLEM JACOB, astronomer; b. marang, Java, Indonesia, Mar. 7, 1899; came to U.S., ʼ21; s. Jacob and Cornelia M. (Francken) L.; m. Wilnina H. Miedema, Feb. 5, 1930; children: Mona R., nne E., James R. BA, U. Amsterdam, The Netherıds, 1918; PhD, U. Leiden, The Netherlands, 1921; Sc (hon.), Case Western Res., 1967, St. Andrews Coll., otland, 1971. Post-doctoral fellow Lick Obs., San se, Calif., 1921-23; astronomer Harvard Coll., Camidge, Mass., 1923-30; prof., chair dept. astronomy U. inn., Mpls., 1931-67, astronomer emeritus, from 1967. ontbr. numerous articles to profl. jours. Mem. NAS Vatson medal 1964). Home: Minneapolis Minn. eceased.

WOFF, ANDRÉ MICHEL, retired microbiologist, ologist; b. Ainay-le-Chateau, France, May 8, 1902; s. lomon and Marie (Siminovitch) L.; m. Marguerite urdaleix, Dec. 5, 1925. Licence es Scis. Naturelles, ris, 1921, D Med., 1927, D Scis. Naturelles, 1932; n. doctorate, U. Glasgow (Scotland), 1963, U. Chgo., ford (Eng.) U., Belgium, 1964, U. Brussels, 1969, arvard U., 1986. Became fellow Pasteur Inst., Paris, 21, asst., 1925, head lab., 1929, head dept. microbiol. ysiology, 1938; prof. microbiology Faculty Scis., U. rbonne, Paris, 1959-68; head Cancer Research Inst., llejuif, 1968-72; pres. French Family Planning ovement, 1970-74; Researcher nature and function of owth factors, physiology of viruses, induction and pression of viruses, phenomenon of lysogenic bacteria, ent bacterial virus, protozoa nutrition, vitamins as crobial growth factors, vitamin function as co-enme, thermoresistance of viral devel. and virulenza, role fever in fight of animals against viral infections. ıthor: Problems of Morphogenesis in Ciliates: the netosomes in Development, Reproduction and olution, 1950; Biological Order, 1962; also articles. cipient Nobel prize (with François Jacob and Jacques onod) in medicine and physiology, 1965. Fellow yal Soc. (fgn.), Nat. Acad. Scis.; mem. N.Y. Acad. s., Nat. Acad. Scis., Academie des Sciences, 1976. ome: Paris France Died Sept. 30, 1994.

YDICK, LAWRENCE TUPPER, federal judge; b. n Diego, June 22, 1916; s. Roy Telling and Geneva ydick) L.; m. Gretta Grant, Aug 7, 1938; children: etta Grant, Lawrence Tupper; m. Martha Martinez, t. 1969; 1 child, Chip. A.B., Stanford U., 1938, .B. (Crothers law scholar), 1942; Sigma Nu exchange holar, U. Freiburg, Germany, 1938-39; postgrad., arvard U., 1943, Mass. Inst. Tech., 1943-44. Bar: lif. 1946. Since practiced in L.A.; dir. disputes div. th region Nat. War Labor Bd., San Francisco, 1942- asst. to pres., gen. counsel U.S. Grant Export-Imrt, Ltd., L.A., 1946-48; assoc. Adams, Duque & zeltine, L.A., 1948-53, ptnr., 1953-71; U.S. dist. ct. lge Central Dist. Calif., 1971-95. Bd. vis. Stanford w Sch. Lt. USNR, 1943-46. Mem. Am. Law Inst. publican. Home: Laguna Beach Calif. Died Dec. 17, 95.

KE, JAMES PATTERSON, archbishop; b. Chgo., b. 18, 1939. A.B. in Philosophy, Quincy (Ill.) Coll., 63; M.Div. in Theology, St. Joseph Sem., Teutopolis, 1967; Th.D., Union Grad. Sch., Cin., 1981. Joined der Friars Minor, Roman Cath. Ch., 1959, ordained est, 1966, consecrated bishop, 1979. Tchr. religion dua Franciscan High Sch., Parma, Ohio, 1967-68; minstr. Father Bertrand Elem. Sch., Memphis, 1970- pastor St. Thomas Ch., Memphis, 1970-77, Ch. of Benedict the Black, 1977-79; also dir. Newman nter, Grambling (La.) State U., 1977-79; aux. bishop ocese of Cleve., 1979-90, also Episcopal vicar for ban region; apostolic adminstr. Archdiocese Atlanta, 90-91; apptd. archbishop of Atlanta, 1991-92; mem. nominational execs. Interch. Council Greater Cleve., e relations com. Greater Cleve. Roundtable, cons. CC Secretariat Black Caths. (standing com. 1990-92). oord. Black Cath. Hymnal; contbr. articles to reous jours., book chpts. Mem. Guide to Black sources in Greater Cleve., 1990-92. Recipient Martin ther King Jr. awar St. Benedict the Black Sch., 1980, n. Gold Medallion award Black Cath. Ministries and ymen Coun., Diocese of Pitts., 1980, Man of Yr. ard Nat. Assn. Negro Bus. and Profl. Women's Club, 81, Martin Luther King Jr. award Diocese of Newark, 86, others. Mem. NAACP, Nat. Conf. Cath. Bishops gration com., black liturgy subcom. of bishops com. liturgy), U.S. Cath. Conf., Nat. Black Cath. Clergy nf., Ohio Cath. Conf., Urban League, So. Poverty w Center, Bread for the World, Nat. Black Evangelist sn., Pax Christi U.S.A., Nat. Black Cath. Clergy ucus (pres. 1977-79), Pontifical Coun. COR UNUM, t. Adv. Bd., Success Guide. Lodges: Knights St. er Claver, K.C. (4th deg.). Home: Atlanta Ga. Died c. 27, 1992.

NCH, GERALD JOHN, management consultant; b. troit, Feb. 22, 1906; s. Patrick John and Julia Meara) L.; m. Mary Romaine Livernois, July 20, 37 (dec. Jan. 1988); children: Terence, Rose Mary rostoff, Laura Lee Lynch Foley, Gerald John, Julie ne (Mrs. Steven S. Russell); m. Carmela J. Lombadi, v. 4, 1989. AB, Wayne U., 1929, MA, 1935; JD, U. troit, 1933; DBA (hon.), U. Dayton. Bar: Mich. bar 33. Pvt. practice Detroit, 1933-42; dir. war contract minstrn. dept. Fisher Body divsn. GM, 1942-46; dir. contract adminstrn. dept., exec. asst. controller, dir. Washington office; exec. asst. to group exec. tractor and internat. group, dir. Office Def. Products and Govtl. Rels., Ford Motor Co., 1946-56; pres. subs. Office Def. Products and Govtl. Rels. Ford Motor Co. (Aeronutronic Sys., Inc.), 1956-59, v.p., gen. mgr. aeronutronic divsn., 1959-62, group v.p. def. products, 1960-62; chmn. bd. Menasco Mfg. Co., 1962-81; dir., group v.p., cons. to chmn. Colt Industries Inc., Burbank, Calif., 1981-87; mgmt. cons. Pasadena, Calif., 1988-96. Trustee Don Bosco Tech. Inst.; bd. dirs. St. John's Seminary. Mem. Met. Club (Washington), Calif. Club (L.A.), Annandale Club, Ironwood Country Club, Eldorado Club, Univ. Club. Home: Pasadena Calif. Deceased.

LYNCH, RONALD P., financial manager; b. N.Y.C., Nov. 6, 1935; s. Robert Joseph and Mary Louise (Farraher) L.; m. Susan M. Eckert, Apr. 21, 1963; children: Ronald P. Jr., Charles R., Andrew E. BS in Agrl. Econs., Cornell U., 1958. With The Corp. Trust Co., 1959-65; regional sales mgr. Lord, Abbett & Co., 1977-80; western mgr. Lord, Abbett & Co., San Francisco, 1975-77; ptnr. Lord, Abbett & Co., 1977-80, sr. ptnr., 1980-83, chief mktg. and operating officer, 1980-96, dir. asset mgmt., 1983-84, mng. ptnr., 1983-96, also chmn. bd. subs. fund corps. Mem. Cornell U. Council; mem. adv. council S.C. Johnson Grad. Sch. Mgmt., Brunswick Sch.; trustee Greenwich Health Assn., bd. dirs. Mem. Investment Co. Inst. (exec. com., bd. govs., mem. various coms.), Securities Industry Assn., Inc. (mem. investment cos. com. 1985-96, chmn. 1983-85), Nat. Assn. Securities Dealers, Inc (mem. investment cos. com., 1983-96, chmn. bus. conduct com. 1979), Bond Club N.Y. Clubs: Wall Street (N.Y.C.); Field of Greenwich (Conn.), Round Hill; Burlinghame Country (Hillsborough, Calif.); Waynesborough Country (Paoli, Pa.). Home: Greenwich Conn. Died June 26, 1996.

LYON, CECIL BURTON, international organization official; b. S.I., N.Y., Nov. 8, 1903; s. Edmund Burton and Emily (Vyse) L.; m. Elizabeth Sturgis Grew, Oct. 7, 1933; children: Alice E., Lilla Cabot. A.B., Harvard U., 1927. Investment banker N.Y.C., 1927-31; vice consul U.S. fgn. service, Havana, Cuba, 1931, Hong Kong, 1932; 3d sec. embassy Tokyo, 1933, Peiping, China, 1933-38; 3d and 2d sec. Santiago, Chile, 1938-42; with Dept. State, 1942-44; 1st sec. Cairo, 1944-46; spl. asst. to asst. sec. of state for polit. affairs, 1947-48; counselor of embassy Warsaw, Poland, 1948-50; assigned Nat. War Coll., 1950-51; dep. comdt. office U.S. High Commr. for Germany, Berlin, 1951-54; dir. office German affairs State Dept., 1954-55; dep. asst. sec. of state State Dept. (Inter-Am. Affairs), 1955-56; U.S. ambassador to Chile, 1956-58; minister to France, 1958-64; U.S. ambassador to Sri Lanka, 1964-67, Maldive Islands, 1965-67; bd. dirs. Internat. Rescue Com. Hon. bd. dirs. Internat. Rescue com., Henry St. Settlement, N.Y.C, Harris Center for Conservation Edn., Hancock, N.H. Roman Catholic. Clubs: Met. (Washington), Alibi (Washington); Harvard (N.Y.C.), Brook (N.Y.C.). Home: Hancock N.H. Died Apr. 6, 1993.

LYONS, FRANCIS JOSEPH, banker; b. Phila., Nov. 3, 1921; s. John Thomas and Cecilia Catherine (Regan) L.; m. Rose Jordan, Nov. 28, 1953; children—Francis X., Mark J., Mary C. B.S., Georgetown U., 1950; LL.B., 1962. With Riggs Nat. Bank, Washington, 1950-95; v.p. Riggs Nat. Bank, 1968-72, sr. v.p., trust officer, 1972-77, exec. v.p., 1977-84, vice chmn. bd. dirs., 1984-95; mem. Washington Bd. Trade, 1965-95. Treas., trustee Religious Edn. Found., Washington; trustee Trinity Coll., Washington; Served with AUS, 1942-44. Decorated Bronze Star, Purple Heart. Mem. D.C. Bankers Assn. (chmn. fiduciaries 1971-72), Washington Soc. Investment Analysts, Va. Bar Assn. Roman Catholic. Clubs: Metropolitan, 1925 F Street. Home: Vienna Va. Died Aug. 10, 1995.

LYONS, JOSEPH NORMAN, insurance executive; b. Boston, Sept. 5, 1901; s. George Alfred and Alice Antoinette (Sheehan) L.; m. Helen Mary O'Karski, June 27, 1942; children—Joseph Norman, Christie Ann, Mary Candace. Grad., Boston Latin Sch., 1917. With John Paulding Meade Co. (ins.), Boston, 1917-34; founder, pres. Cushing, Lyons, Inc., Boston, from 1934; founder Am. Ednl. Ins. Fund, from 1960; organizer Pilgram Ins. Co., 1960. Trustee Mass. Regional Arthritis and Rheumatism Found.; mem. Fides com. Boston Coll.; trustee Ins. Library Assn. Boston. Fellow Kennedy Libr.; mem. Mass. Brokers Assn. (past dir.). Club: Arundel Beach. Home: Newton Mass. Deceased.

MAAS, JAMES WELDON, psychiatrist; b. St. Louis, Oct. 26, 1929; s. James Werner and Agnes Pohlman (Weldon) M.; m. Joanne Henderson, Dec. 23, 1953 (div. 1972); 1 child, Elizabeth; m. Marilyn S. Loren, Oct. 18, 1972; children: James W., Jonathan W. AB, Wash. U., 1950, MD, 1954. Diplomate Am. Bd. Psychiatry. Sect. head NIMH, Bethesda, Md., 1960-65; prof. psychiatry U. Ill. Med. Sch., Chgo., 1966-72; prof. psychiatry Yale U., New Haven, 1972-82, Hugo A Auler prof., 1976; Hugo A. Auler prof. psychiatry and pharmacology U. Tex. Health Sci. Ctr., San Antonio, 1987-95; vis. scientist Cambridge, Eng. Contbr. articles to profl. jours. and books. Maj. USAF, 1956-58. Grantee NIMH, 1968-95; 1994 award for excellence in psychiatry, Tex. Assn. Psyichiat. Physicians. Fellow Am. Psychiat. Assn. (life), Am. Coll. Neuropsychopharmacology, Davenport Coll., Yale U.; mem. Cosmos Club. Home: San Antonio Tex. Died Jan. 14, 1995.

MAC BRIDE, SEÂN, international government official; b. Paris, France, Jan. 26, 1904; s. John and Maud (Gonne) MacB.; student St. Louis de Gonzague, Paris, 1911-16, Mount St. Benedict, Gorey, Ireland, 1916-18, Nat. Univ., Dublin, 1918; LL.D. (hon.), Coll. St. Thomas, St. Paul, 1975, U. Guelph, 1977, Trinity Coll., U. Dublin, 1978, U. Cape Coast, Ghana, 1978, Fla. So. Coll., 1979, Suffolk U., 1980; Litt.D. (hon.), U. Bradford (Eng.), 1977; m. Catalina Bulfin, Jan. 26, 1926; children—Anna, Tiernan. Called to bar Kings Inn, Dublin; barrister-at-law, 1937, senior counsel, 1943—; admitted to Ghana bar, 1960; figured in leading cases on constitutional law; had extensive practice in High Ct. and Supreme Ct. Founder polit. party Clannna Poblachta (Republican Party), 1946; elected to the Dail Eireann (parliament), 1947-58; minister external affairs Republic of Ireland, 1948-51; pres. Council of Ministers of Council of Europe, 1949-50; v.p. Orgn. European Econ. Cooperation, 1948-51; Irish rep. in Council of Europe Assembly, rapporteur Econ. Commn. Council of Europe, 1954-63; sec.-gen. International Commn. on Jurists, 1963-71; chmn. Exec. Internat. Peace Bur., 1968-74, pres., 1974-88; chmn. Spl. Nongovtl. Orgns. Com. on Human Rights, 1968-74; vice chmn. Congress of World Peace Forces, Moscow, 1973, vice chmn. continuing com., 1973-88; v.p. World Fedn. of UN Assns., 1973; UN commr. for Namibia, 1973-76; asst. sec. gen. UN, 1973-88; pres. Internat. Commn. for Study Communication Problems, UNESCO, Paris, 1977. Trustee Internat. Prisoners of Conscience Fund; cons., chmn. Irish sect. Internat. Commn. Jurists; mem. council European Movement; exec. com. Accra Assembly; v.p. Pan-European Union; expert cons. Pontifical Commn. Justice and Peace, 1966-88; mem. Spl. Nongovtl. Orgns. Com. Disarmament, 1968-88; bd. dirs. Bill of Rights Found. U.S.A., 1976-88. Recipient Nobel Peace Prize, 1974; Lenin Internat. Peace prize, 1977; Am. Medal of Justice, 1978; medal Internat. Inst. Human Rights, 1978; UNESCO medal of merit, 1980; Dag Hammarskjold Peace prize, 1981. Mem. Irish Assn. Civil Liberty, Irish Inland Waterways Assn. (v.p.), Irish UN Assn. (exec. mem.), Amnesty Internat. (a founder, chmn. exec. 1961-74), European Round Table (exec. mem.), Soc. of Irish Foresters, Nuclear Safety Assn. (Ireland) (pres. 1978). Roman Catholic. Author: Civil Liberty, 1947; Ireland's Economy; Our People Our Money; Report on Italian Economic Situation, 1955; Report on Current Economic Situation in Western Europe, 1956. Home: Dublin Ireland

MACDONALD, WALTER E., oil company executive; b. Apr. 11, 1926; (married); 2 children. A.B., Brown U.; J.D., Boston U. V.p. Middle East and marine transp. Mobil Oil Corp. subs. Mobil Corp., N.Y.C., until 1982, exec. v.p. Middle East and marine transp., 1986-93, also bd. dirs.; dir. Arabian Am. Oil Co. Bd. advisers Center for Contemporary Arab Studies, Georgetown U.; mem. adv. council dept. Near Eastern Studies Princeton U.; bd. govs. Middle East Inst.; mem. Pres.'s Council on Near Eastern Studies NYU; trustee Am. U. Cairo. Clubs: Union League, Pinnacle. Home: New York N.Y. Died May 29, 1993.

MACGRATH, C. RICHARD, retired business executive; b. East Orange, N.J., June 20, 1921; s. Charles Halsey and Elizabeth Eugenia (Fowler) MacGrath; m. Nancy Elizabeth Greenwall, Feb. 11, 1955 (dec. Aug. 1980); children: Andrew Alexander, Francis Fowler, Susan Abigail Talcott. AB, Princeton U., 1943. V.p. Lazard Frères & Co., N.Y.C., 1965-85, ret., 1985. Dir. Hosp. for Spl. Surgery, N.Y.C., 1980—, Met. Opera Assn., N.Y.C., 1982—; dir., treas. Greenwall Found., N.Y.C., 1957—; bd. dir., Skowhegan Sch. Painting and Sculputure, N.Y.C., 1965—. Capt. AAF, 1943-46. Mem. SAR, Soc. Colonial Wars, St. Nicholas Soc., Soc. of the Cin., Hugenot Soc., Order of the Magna Carta, River Club, Princeton Club, Mid-Ocean Club, Dublin Lake Club, Kane Lodge. Home: New York N.Y. Died Feb. 19, 1995.

MACGREGOR, ROBERT KEN, construction company executive; b. Malden, Mass., Oct. 30, 1922; s. Herbert and Rose (Williams) MacG.; m. Myla W. Lewis, Dec. 28, 1968; children: Edwin, Lorraine, Marilyn. Student pub. schs., Malden. Owner MacGregor Constrn. Co., Malden, 1946-56; estimator, gen. supt. Sully-Miller Contracting Co., Long Beach, Calif., 1957-68, asst. to pres., 1968-69, v.p., 1969-71, pres., 1971-88, chief exec. officer, chmn. bd., 1988-95; v.p. Koppers Co. Inc., Pitts. Served with USN, 1942-45, ETO. Lodge: Elks. Home: Lakewood Calif. Died Feb. 26, 1995.

MACHEL, SAMORA MOISÉS, president People's Republic of Mozambique; b. Chilembene Village, Limporo Valley, Mozambique, Sept. 1933; trained as male nurse, Hosp. Miguel; m. Grace Simbine, 1975. Nurse, later med. asst. Hosp. Miguel; mil. tng. in Algeria, 1963; organizer tng. camp program, Tanzania; comdr.-in chief army of Frente de Libertaç ã o de Mozambique (FRELIMO) in guerilla war against Portuguese, 1966-74; sec. def. FRELIMO, 1966-74, pres., 1970—; pres. of Mozambique, 1975—. Decorated Order of Sujebator (Mongolia); Order of Friendship; Order of Infante Henrique; Hero of People's Republic of

Mozambique; recipient Lenin Centenary medal, 1970; Joliot Curie Gold medal, 1976 Lenin Peace prize, 1977. Home: Maputo Mozambique

MACINTOSH, ALEXANDER JOHN, lawyer, business executive; b. Stellarton, N.S., Can., July 10, 1921; s. Hugh Ross and Katherine Elizabeth (Stewart) M.; m. Elizabeth Agnes Allen, Apr. 5, 1944; 1 child, Donald Alexander. BA, Dalhousie U., 1942, LLB, 1948; LLD, Brock U., 1987, Dalhousie U., 1992. Bar: N.S. 1948, Ont. 1948; created Queen's counsel 1961. Read law T.D. MacDonald, Q.C., Dep. Atty. Gen., N.S.; ptnr. Blake, Cassels & Graydon, Toronto, 1948-93; mem. Ont. Task Force on Fin. Instns.; bd. dirs. Stelco, Inc., Markborough Properties Inc.; vice chmn. Torstar Corp. Lt. Royal Can. Naval Vol. Res., 1942-45. Clubs: Toronto; York. Home: Toronto Can. Died July 24, 1993.

MACKENZIE, KENNETH VICTOR, physicist; b. Brandon, Man., Can., Aug. 29, 1911; came to U.S., 1923, naturalized, 1939; s. William Franklin and Allie Esther (Stinson) M.; m. Catherine Jane Oleson Morales, Oct. 18, 1968; children by previous marriage: Dorothy Kay Mighell, Robert Bruce, Kenneth Donald, Jessie Jean. Student, Willamette U., 1930-33, DSc, 1983; BS in Math., Physics, U. Wash., 1934, MS in Physics, 1936. Registered profl. engr., Oreg., Wash. Physicist Oreg. State Hwy. Dept., 1936-41; head physicist Puget Sound Magnetic Survey Range USN, Kingston, Wash., 1941-44; assoc. physicist Applied Physics Lab. U. Wash., Seattle, 1944-46; group leader, deep and shallow water propagation Navy Electronics Lab., San Diego, 1946-51, sec. head scattering and oceanography, 1951-55, head shallow water acoustical process sect., 1955-61, chief scientist deep submergence program, 1962-67; sr. physicist acoustic propagation div. Undersea Surveillance and Ocean Sci. Dept. Naval Undersea Ctr. (formerly Navy Electronics Lab.), San Diego, 1967-73; exchange scientist Her Majesty's Underwater Weapons Establishment, Eng., 1961-62; sr. staff scientist, primary adviser sci. and engring. directorate staff U.S. Naval Oceanographic Office, Washington, 1973-76; sr. staff physicist environ. research requirements office Naval Ocean Research and Devel. Activity, Bay St. Louis, Miss., 1976-79; pres. Mackenzie Marine Sci. Cons., San Diego, 1979-93; lectr. Ocean Inst. Qingdao, Shipbuilding Engring. Inst., Harbin, Peking U., Beijing, Nanjing U., 35 others, 1983-93; hon. committeeman Internat. Ocean Devel. Conf., Tokyo, 1971-93; spkr. Joint Oceanographic Assembly IUGG, Edinburgh, Scotland, 1976, Acad. Sci., Beijing, Fifth Def. Agy., Tokyo, 1980; cons. allied govts. and def. industry. Contbr. 175 papers to profl. publs., chpts to books. Recipient Cert. Exceptional Service, Bur. Ordnance, 1945, Cert. Merit, Office Sci. Research, 1945, Navy Electronics Lab. award, 1960, Commendation Navy Unit, 1963, Alumni Citation, Willamette U., 1969, Superior Achievement award Inst. Navigation, 1971, Meritorious Civilian Service award USN, 1979. Fellow Acoustical Soc. Am., Explorers Club, Marine Tech. Soc. (co-founder); mem. Am. Geophys. Union, Am. Phys. Soc., Inst. Navigation (nat. marine chmn. 1965-66, Western regional councilor 1966-68, 73-75), Instrument Soc. Am. (nat. dir. marine scis. div. 1968-70), Navy League, U.S.-China Peoples Friendship Assn., Sigma Xi. Home: La Jolla Calif. Died Aug. 31, 1993; cremated.

MACKINNON, GEORGE E., federal judge; b. St. Paul, Apr. 22, 1906; s. James Alexander Wiley and Cora Blanche (Asselstine) MacK.; m. Elizabeth Valentine Davis, August 20, 1938; children: Catharine Alice, James Davis, Leonard Davis. Student, U. Colo., 1923-24; LL.B., U. Minn., 1929. Bar: Minn. 1929, U.S. Supreme Ct. 1947. Asst. gen. counsel Investors Syndicate, Mpls., 1929-42; engaged pvt. practice law, 1949-53, 58-61; elected mem. Minn. Ho. of Reps. from 29th dist., 1934, 36, 38, 40; mem. 80th Congress, 1947-49, 3d Minn. Dist.; U.S. Atty. for Minn., 1953-58; spl. asst. to U.S. Atty. Gen., 1960; gen. counsel, v.p. Investors Mut. Funds, Mpls., 1961-69; judge U.S. Ct. Appeals for D.C. Cir., 1969-95; pres. judge U.S. Fgn. Intelligence Surveillance Ct. of Rev., 1979-82; U.S. del. UN Congress Prevention of Crime and Treatment of Offenders, 1985; presiding judge div. U.S. Ct. Appeals for Appointment of Ind. Counsels, 1985-92; mem. U.S. Sentencing Commn., 1985-91. Author: Minn. State Reorganization Act, 1939, State Civil Service Law, 1939, Old Age Assistance Act, 1936. Republican nominee for Gov. of Minn., 1958. Served to comdr. U.S. Navy Air Force, 1942-46. Cited for meritorious service by comdr. Air Force U.S. Atlantic Fleet. Mem. ABA, Minn. Bar Assn., Hennepin County Bar Assn., Delta Tau Delta, Phi Delta Phi. Republican. Episcopalian. Clubs: Minneapolis; Lawyers (Washington); Masons (32 deg.). Home: Potomac Md. Deceased May 1, 1995.

MACLAREN, WALTER ROGERS, allergist, educator; b. Yokohama, Japan, Dec. 7, 1910; s. Walter Wallace and Zaidee (Rogers) McL.; m. Dorothy Agnes Goodwin, June 1942 (div. 1970); children: Walter Jr., Jean, Anne, Elizabeth, Catherine; m. Dorothy Hamblen, July 7, 1971. BA, Queens U., 1933; MD, Harvard U., 1938. Diplomate Am. Bd. Allergy and Immunology (bd. dirs., sec. 1978-83). Practice medicine specializing in asthma, allergy and immunology Pasadena, Calif., 1947-94; clin. prof. medicine U. So. Calif. Sch. Med., L.A., 1948-94; dir. Allergy and Immunology Cons. Labs., Inc., Pasadena, 1978-88. Contbr. over 30 articles to profl. jours. Bd. dirs. Pasadena Symphony Orch., 1976-82, Pasadena Chamber Orch., 1984-86. Fellow Am. Acad. Allergy and Immunology, Am. Coll. Allergists, Am. Thoracic Soc., Asthma and Allergy Found. Am., Assn. Clin. Immunology and Allergy (pres.), Pasadena C. of C. (health svcs. com. 1990-94), Sigma Xi. Republican. Club: Valley Hunt (Pasadena). Home: Pasadena Calif. Died Nov. 15, 1994.

MACPHERSON, HERBERT GRENFELL, nuclear engineer; b. Victorville, Calif., Nov. 2, 1911; s. Duncan William and Minnie Belle (Morrison) MacP.; m. Janet Taylor Wolfenden, June 5, 1937; children: Janet Lynne, Robert Duncan. Student, San Diego State Coll., 1928-31; A.B., U. Calif., Berkeley, 1932, Ph.D. in Physics, 1937. Research scientist Nat. Carbon Co., Cleve., 1937-50; asst. dir. research Nat. Carbon Co., 1950-56; dir. reactor programs Oak Ridge Nat. Lab., 1956-64, dep. dir., 1964-70; prof. nuclear engring. U. Tenn., 1970-76; acting dir. Inst. for Energy Analysis, Oak Ridge, 1974-75; cons. Inst. for Energy Analysis, 1975-93; cons. in field. Editor: (with Lane and Maslan) Fluid Fuel Reactor, 1958. Fellow Am. Phys. Soc., Am. Nuclear Soc.; mem. AAAS, Nat. Acad. Engrs., Phi Beta Kappa, Sigma Xi. Clubs: Cosmos, Oak Ridge Country. Home: Oak Ridge Tenn. Died Jan. 26, 1993.

MAGAFAN, ETHEL, artist; b. Chgo., Aug. 10, 1916; d. Peter J. and Julie (Bronick) M.; m. Bruce Currie, June 30, 1946; 1 dau., Jenne Magafan. Student, Colorado Springs Fine Arts Center. guest artist-in-residence Syracuse U., 1976. Painter of 8 murals including Social Security Bldg (now HEW bldg.), Washington, Recorder of Deeds Bldg., Washington, Fredericksburg (Va.) Nat. Mil. Park, 1978; paintings exhibited Carnegie Inst., Corcoran Gallery, Pa. Acad. Fine Arts, NAD, Met. Mus., Denver Art Mus., San Francisco Mus., N.Y. Exhbn., 1950-51, 53, 55, 56, 59, 61, 63, 66, 69, 70, 73, 79, 81, Art Gallery, SUNY, Albany, 1981, Midtown Galleries, N.Y.C., 1984, Smithsonian, 1988, Colo. Springs Fine Arts Ctr., 1989 Nat. Mus. Am. Art, Arvada Ctr. for Arts and Humanities, 1989; represented in permanent collections, including, Springfield (Mo.) Art Mus., Provincetown Art Assn., Met. Mus. Art, Denver Art Mus., Del. Soc. Fine Arts, Des Moines Art Center, Norfolk Mus., Columbia Mus., Butler (Ind.) Inst. Art, Nat. Mus. Women in the Arts, 1987, Albany Inst. of Art & History, Wichita Art Mus., Nat. Mus. Am. Art, Smithsonian Instn.; one-man show Midtown Galleries, N.Y.C., 1987, others; also pvt. collections. John Stacey scholar, 1947; Tiffany fellow, 1949; Fulbright grantee, 1951; Recipient Collectors Am. Art award, 1947, 48; Adele Hyde Morrison prize San Francisco Mus., 1950; hon. mention Am. Painting Today exhbn., Met Mus. Art, 1950; 1st Hallgarten prize NAD, 1951; Ida Wells Stroud award, Am. Watercolor Soc., 1955; purchase prize Nat. Exhbn. Contemporary Arts, 1956; Altman prize for landscape NAD, 1956; Hallmark Art award, 1952; Purchase award, Ball State Tchrs. Coll. Art Gallery, 1958; Columbia (S.C.) Mus., 1959; Portland (Maine) Mus., 1959; 1st award Albany Inst. Art, 1962; Benjamin Altman award NAD, 1964, 73; Andrew Carnegie prize, 1977; award Conn. Acad. Fine Arts, 1965; purchase award Watercolor, U.S.A., Springfield Mus., 1966; Kirk Meml. award NAD, 1967; Berkshire Art Assn. award, 1966, 67, 68, 75; jurors prize Albany Inst. Art, 1969; Grumbacher award, 1970, 75; Hassam Fund purchase, 1970; Arches Paper award Am. Watercolor Soc., 1973; Zimmerman award Phila. Watercolor Soc., 1973; Pres.'s award Audubon Artists, 1974; Emily Lowe award, 1979; Stefan Hirsch Meml. award Audubon Artists Ann., 1976; award Rocky Mountain Nat. Watermedia Exhbn., 1976; Condec award Silvermine Guild Artists, 1978; award, 1979; Silver medal Audubon Artists, 1983; Cooperstown Art Assn. award, 1978, 83; Highwinds award and medal Am. Watercolor Soc., 1983; drawing award Ball State U., 1981; Art of Northeast USA exhibit award Silvermine Guild, 1984; John W. Taylor award Woodstock Artist's Assn. for Drawing, 1985, Harrison Cady award Am. Water Color Soc., 1987, Robert Philipp Meml. award Audubon Artists, 1989, The Grumbacker award Audubon Artists, 1990, Audubon Artists Gold Medal of Honor, 1990, 91, Brobock prize Adirondacks Nat. Exhbn. Am. Watercolors, 1988, Martin Family award Adirondacks Nat. Exhbn. Am. Watercolors, 1990. Mem. NAD (2d v.p. 1975, Benjamin Altman award 1980), Am. Water Color Soc. Home: Woodstock N.Y. Died Apr. 24, 1993; buried Artists' Cemetery, Woodstock, N.Y.

MAGARINOS D., VICTOR, artist; b. Lanus, Buenos Aires, Argentina, Sept. 1, 1924; s. Jose Magarinos D. and Antonia Maria Sanchez; m. Hilda Mans. Student, Escuela Nat. des Artes Visuales. One-man exhbns. include Galería Juan Cristóbal 1950, Inst. Arte Moderno 1950-51; other exhbns. include Mus. Modern Art 1963, El Nuevo Arte Argentino, Walker Art Ctr., Mpls., A Decade of Latin-Am. Art Guggenheim Mus. 1965-66, Mus. Modern Art, N.Y.C., Mus. Nat. Bellas Artes, Mus. Arte Moderno, Buenos Aires, Ctr. Art and Communication, Argentina, Premio d'Italia 1986, Mus. Arte Moderno, Brussels, 1986. Pres. Argentine com. Internat. Assn. Plastic Arts, UNESCO, 1958. Served with Argentine Armed Forces, 1945. Recipient Premio Milano Inst. d'Arte Contemporanea de Milano, 1988, Premio Centauro de Oro Instituido por el Consejo Artistico del Premio Cuatrienal de la Academia de Itali 1988. Mem. Acad. Arti Laboro Perme (Gold medal) Home: Pinamar Argentina

MAGNER, JOHN CRUSE, retired lawyer, consultar b. Dallas, Nov. 10, 1921; s. Harold Joseph and Loui Mary Magner; m. Elizabeth Magner, Oct. 1946; ch dren: Margaret Magner Wetgrove, Robert, Joh Michael, Richard. LLB, So. Meth. U., 1948. Bar: Te 1948. Salesman Continental Supply Co., Ark., La. a Tex., 1938-41; field office mgr. Hunt Oil Co., Dorado, Ark., 1941-44; mem. prodn. dept. land de Sun Oil Co., Dallas, 1944-49; exec. v.p., dir. Row Cos., Inc., Houston, 1949-85, ret., 1985; cons. petroleu Houston, 1985-94. Mem. ABA, Tex. Bar Assn., Te Mid-Continent Oil and Gas Assn., Internat. Assn. Dr ling Contractors, Am. Petroleum Inst., Am. Assn. P troleum Landmen, Houston Assn. Petroleum Landme Home: Houston Tex. Died Jan. 3, 1994.

MAGNER, MARTIN, theatrical producer and direct b. Stettin, Ger., Mar. 5, 1900; came to U.S., 19 naturalized, 1945; s. Max. and Zerlina (Silberstein) M m. Marion Palfi, June 6, 1951. Actor Hamburg kammerspiele, Germany, 1918-20; producer, d Nuremberg, Germany, 1921-27, Breslau, Germar 1928-33, Berlin, 1928-33, Vienna, Austria, 1919- Prague, Czechoslovakia, 1933-39; stage dir. Chgo. Op Co., 1940-41, San Francisco Opera, 1972; producer, d NBC, Chgo. and N.Y.C., 1942-49, CBS, N.Y.C., 19 63; instr., artist-in-residence drama and music U. Chg 1941, Northwestern U., 1942-43, Adelphi Coll., 19 Canisius Coll., 1958; artistic dir. New Theatre Inc., L Angeles, from 1977. Recipient several document awards AMA, Spl. award for maintaining consisten high standards L.A. Drama Critics Circle, 1975, D ing. Lifetime Achievement award L.A. Drama Cri Circle, 1988, Life Time Achievement award Gov. Calif., 1991; recepient The Cross of merit First Cl from the Bundes Repulik of Germany , 1992. M Dirs. Guild Am. Home: Los Angeles Calif. Deceased.

MAGRUDER, RICHARD ALLEN, auth photographer; b. Starkville, Miss., Apr. 1, 1924; Robert Henry and Helen Mildred (Porter) M.; m. M Charles Price; chidlren: Michael Lawrence, Rob Walter, Allen Patrick. Student, U. Tex., 1946- North Tex. State U., 1948-49, Inst. Allende, Mex., 19 53. Staff writer, critic photographer, artist Enterp Newspaper, Beaumont, Tex., 1950-51; tchr., in photography, creative writing Inst. Allende, Mex., 19 54; staff writer, columnist, photographer Tribune N spaper, Galveston, Tex., 1955-56; staff news wri editor, broadcaster NBC Sta. WFAA, Dallas, 1957- co-founder, pres. Allison-Drake Advt., Inc., Dal 1961-63; dir., pres. Allen Richards Advt., Dallas, 19 65, Dallas North Galleries, 1965-66; dir. promotion, ternat. mag. editor Braniff Airways, Inc., Dallas, 19 69; freelance writer, photographer Atlanta, from 19 cons. in field. Author, photographer: Mexico-Mo and Images, 1962, A Snob's Guide to Mexico C 1966; author, illustrator: South American Tourgu 1967; author: Mexico Remembered, 1991; contbr. ticles to L.A. Times, Dallas News, Chgo. Tribu others. With USAAF, 1942-45. Recipient 1st p Best RV Articles RecVee Ind. Assn., Washington, 19 1st prize Best Fgn. Published Article Nat. Tour Coun., Republic Mexico, 1978. Mem. Soc. Am. Tra Writers, Am. Soc. Mag. Photographers. Democra Home: Decatur Ga. Deceased.

MA HAIDE, government official, physician; b. Buff 1910; arrived in People's Republic China, 1933; natu ized, 1949.; Grad. medicine. Physician Commu base, No. Shaanxi Province, People's Republic Ch 1936; joined Chinese Red Army; advisor Ministry Pub. Health, 1950—; mem. 5th Chinese People's P Consultative Conf., 1979; mem. standing com. Chinese People's Polit. Consultative Conf., 1983; dir.-in-chief Welfare Fund for Handicapped, 1984.

MAHONEY, JAMES P., bishop; b. Saskatoon, Sa Can., Dec. 7, 1927. Ordained priest Roman Cath. 1952; bishop Saskatoon, 1967—. Home: Saskat Can. Deceased.

MAHONEY, JUSTIN J., federal judge; b. Troy, N Nov. 7, 1919; m. Mary E. Stevens; children: Mary Ly Justin S., Michael J., Kathleen A., Laurel S. (dec.). U. Toronto, Can., 1940; LLB, Albany Law Sch., 19 Bar: N.Y. 1949, U.S. Supreme Ct. 1962, U.S. Ct. peals (2d cir.) 1969. Assoc. family law firm Troy, 1 61; U.S. atty. U.S. Dist. Ct. (no. dist.) N.Y., Alb 1961-69, referee in bankruptcy, 1969-94. Capt. USN PTO. Decorated Purple Heart, Gold Star, Bronze with valor device. Mem. Fed. Bar Assn. (pres. Em State chpt. 1963-65), N.Y. State Bar Assn., Rensse County Bar Assn., Ret. Officers Assn. Home: Alb N.Y. Died June 10, 1994.

MAIER, HENRY W., mayor; b. Dayton, Ohio, Fe 1918; s. Charles, Jr. and Marie L. (Knisley) M.; Karen Lamb, May 8, 1976; children by previous m age: Melinda Ann Carlisle, Melanie Marie. B.A., Wis., 1940; M.A. in Polit. Sci., U. Wis.-Milw., 19 Mem. Wis. Legislature, 1950-60, floor leader for Se 1953-60; mayor of Milw., 1960-88. Author: Chall to the Cities, 1966. First pres. Nat. Conf. Democ vors, 1976-94; past chmn. nat. adv. com. Health e for the Homeless Program; chmn. nat. Coalition on nan Needs Budget Priorities, 1973-75; mem. Pres.'s . on Youth Employment in the Kennedy Adstrn.; mem. govt. adv. com. on Hwy. Beauty, U.S. t. Commerce in Johnson Adminstrn. Lt. USNR, rld War II, PTO. Named one of 60 most influential in Am. U.S. News and World Report, 1975, 76, of Am.'s top 20 mayors, U.S. News and World ort, 1987; established record of longest tenure of big mayors in U.S. for cities with populations of 500, or more; first occupant of Henry W. Maier Ened Chair in Urban Studies, U. Wis., Milw., 1988-94; pient Disting. Alumni award U. Wis., 1974, disting. an Mayor award Nat. Urban Coalition, 1979-87, ing. Sustained Mayoral Leadership award Nat. an Coalition, 1987, Hubert H. Humphrey award . Conf. Dem. Mayors, 1987, Michael A. diNunzio rd U.S. Conf. Mayors. Mem. U.S. Conf. Mayors s. 1971-72, mem. exec. com., Disting. Pub. Service rd 1984), Nat. League Cities (pres. 1964-65, bd. ., Pres.'s award 1987). Democrat. Home: Delafield . Died July 17, 1994.

INES, CLIFFORD BRUCE, insurance company cutive; b. Tacoma, Wash., Aug. 14, 1926; s. Clifford Lean and Ida Vera (Wardall) M.; m. Mary Jean shall, Sept. 4, 1948; children: Molly, Janet n. Student, Central Coll., Fayette, Mo., 1944-45, U. h., 1945-46; B.S., U. Wash., 1948, LL.B., 1949, J.D., 9. Bar: Wash. 1950. Mem. legal staff Safeco Corp., tle, 1950-62, asso. gen. counsel, 1962-66, gen. nsel, 1966-68, v.p., gen. counsel, 1968-74, sr. v.p., 4-81, pres., chief oper. officer, 1981-86; pres., chief . officer Safeco Corp., 1986-89; dir. Safeco Corp., tle, 1977-93, chmn., chief exec. officer, 1989-92, n. bd. dirs., 1992-93, chmn., 1992-93; exec. v.p., f oper. officer, dir. Gen. Ins. Co. Am., 1974-77, ., 1977-81; exec. v.p. 1st Nat. Ins. Co. Am., 1974-77, ., 1977-81; exec. v.p. Safeco Ins. Co., 1974-77, pres., 7-81. Served with USNR, 1944-46. Mem. ABA, h. Bar Assn., Seattle-King County Bar Assn. (past tee), Washington Athletic Club, Broadmoor Golf), Seattle Golf Club, Columbia Tower Club, Beta ta Pi. Methodist. Home: Seattle Wash. Died May 993.

KKONEN, URHO VEIKKO HENRIK, banker; b. sinki, Finland, Apr. 1, 1919; s. Armas Veikko and Sofia (Lagerlö f) M.; m. Irja Haapanen, Apr. 11, 3; children—Leena Makkonen Linnasalmi, Kari, kki. B.A., U. Helsinki, 1941, M.A., 1942. With nish Diplomatic Service, 1943-57; mem. bd. mgmt. sallis-Osake-Pankki, Helsinki, 1957—; exec. v.p. sinki, 1964-75, pres., 1975-83; chmn. supervisory bd. ma-Repola Oy, Helsinki, 1976—, Perusyhtymä Oy, sinki, 1980—, Huhtamäki Oy, Turku, 1979—. n. Found. Research of Heart Diseases, Helsinki, 2—. Decorated medal of Liberty 1st class, 1940, d cross Order of Lion (Finland), 1978; comdr. er of Dannebrog (Denmark), 1956. Home: Helsinki and

LKIN, MYRON SAMUEL, physicist, management sultant; b. Youngstown, Ohio, Aug. 6, 1924; s. ris and Sarah (Magidson) M.; m. Jocelyn Schoen, 27, 1948; children: Martha, Peter. B.S. in Physics, U., 1948, M.S., 1949, Ph.D., 1951. Nuclear sicist Schlumberg Well Surveying Corp., Ridgefield, n., 1951-52; assoc. dir. Heavy Ion Accelerator Lab., U., 1953-60; program mgr. Minuteman III and n II reentry vehicles Gen. Electric Co., Phila., 1961- program mgr. Manned Orbiting Lab., 1966-68; gen. Manned Orbiting Lab. program, 1968-69; pres. S Corp., Rockville, Md., 1969-71; dep. asst. sec. t. Def., Washington, 1972-73; dir. space shuttle gram NASA, 1973-80; corp. v.p. communications, ronics and space Fairchild Industries, Germantown, , 1980-82; cons. in mgmt., planning and acquisis, 1982-94; pres. Malkin Assocs., Inc., cons. firm in e, def. and environ. issues, 1984-94; CEO Endosat 1991-94. With USMCR, 1943-45. Fellow AIAA oc.); Mem. Phi Beta Kappa, Sigma Xi. Club: Cos- Home: Bethesda Md. Died Oct. 24, 1994.

LLARY, RAYMOND DEWITT, lawyer; b. Lenox, s., Oct. 5, 1898; s. R. DeWitt and Lucy (Walker) m. Gertrude Slater Robinson, Sept. 15, 1923; chil- : R. DeWitt, Richard Walker. A.B., Dartmouth ., 1921; J.D., Harvard U., 1924. Bar: Mass. 1924, 1953. Partner Wooden, Small & Mallary, 1924-31, ary & Gilbert, 1931-51; pvt. practice, counsel to ardson, Dibble & Atkinson, Springfield, Mass., -56, Bulkley, Richardson, Godfrey & Burbank, -64, Wilson, Keyser and Otterman, Chelsea and ford, Vt., 1961-63, Otterman & Allen, Bradford, 1965-70; dir., mem. exec. com. Mass. Mut. Life Ins. 1944-73, Cen. Vt. Pub. Service Corp, 1959-80; ptnr. ary Farm; dir. mem. audit com. Vt. Electric Power 1973-84; numerous other directorships. Chmn. bd. tmen Town of Fairlee, Vt., 1953-57, moderator, -76, mem. planning bd., 1983-86; chmn. Orange nty Tax Appeal Bd., 1964-65; Vt. mem. New Eng. s. Com. on Pub. Transp., 1955; dir. Conn. River ershed Coun., Inc., 1977; trustee emeretus Am. Int. Coll., Hitchcock Found.; trustee Eastern States ., 1942-93, chmn. exec. com., 1943-53, pres., 1953- chmn. bd., 1958-68, hon. chmn. bd. 1968-93, dir. chmn. Vt. bd. trustees, 1975-93; past bd. dirs., pres. Springfield Family Welfare Assn.; chmn. Vt. trustee bd., 1975-93; chmn. Springfield Bd. Pub. Welfare, 1931-34. Enlisted U.S. Army, 1981, assigned to officers tng. unit, Sept. 1988, discharged, 1919, apptd. capt. USAR, 1942, ret., 1945. Recipient citations for outstanding svc. North Atlantic region Future Farmers Am., 1963, U. Conn. Coll. Agrl. Extension Svc., 4-H 1965, achievement award Internat. Assn. Fairs and Expns., 1960, Lifetime Svc. award Ea. States Expn., 1991; co-recipient Master Breeder's award Vt. Holstein-Friesian Assn., 1979, New Eng. States Holstein Friesian Assn., 1969. Mem. New Eng. Fellowship Agrl. Adventurers, Holstein-Friesian Assn. Am. (dir., mem. exec. com. 1957-64, pres., mem. exec. com. 1967-69), ABA, Vt. Bar Assn., Hampden County Bar Assn., Orange County Bar Assn., New Eng. States Holstein Friesian Assn. (pres. 1943-46, dir. 1946-49, Disting. Lifetime Svc. award 1989), Purebred Dairy Cattle Assn. Am. (past pres. and dir.), Am. Legion, Psi Upsilon. Club: Dartmouth (past pres. Hanover area); Exchange (past pres. Springfield).). Home: Bradford Vt. Died Nov. 22, 1993; buried Fairlee, Vt.

MALLE, LOUIS, film director; b. Thumeries, France, Oct. 30, 1932; s. Pierre and Francoise (Beghin) M.; m. Anne-Marie Deschodt (div.); 2 children from previous relationships; m. Candice Bergen, Sept. 27, 1980; 1 child, Chloe. Student, Inst. d'Etudes Politiques, Paris, 1951-53, Inst. des Hautes Etudes Cinematographiques, Paris, 1953-54. Asst. to Jacques Cousteau, 1953-55; coprodr. The Silent World, 1955 (Palme d'Or, Cannes Internat. Film Festival); tech. collaborator with Robert Bresson for Un condamne a mort s'est echappe; dir. films Ascenseur pour l'echafaud, 1957 (Prix Louis-Delluc 1958), Les Amants, 1958 (Spl. Jury prize Venice Film Festival 1968), Zazie dans le metro, 1960, Vie Privee, 1962, Le Feu Follet (Spl. Jury prize Venice Film Festival 1963), Viva Maria, 1965, La Voleur, 1966, William Wilson, 1967, Le Souffle au Coeur, 1971, Lacomb Lucien, 1973, Black Moon, 1975, Pretty Baby, 1978, Atlantic City, 1980, My Dinner with Andre, 1980, Crackers, 1984, Alamo Bay, 1985, Au Revoir Les Enfants (Directing honors Brit. Acad. Film and TV Arts), 1987, Milov En Mai, 1990, Damage, 1992, Vanya on 42nd Street, 1994; also TV short subjects India, 1970. Home: Paris France Home: New York N.Y. Died November 23, 1995.

MALLERS, GEORGE PETER, lawyer; b. Lima, Ohio, Apr. 28, 1928; s. Peter G. and Helen (Daskalakis) M.; m. Rubie Loomis, Feb. 2, 1950; children—Peter G. II, William G., Elaine. B.S., Ind. U., 1951; J.D., Valparaiso U., 1955. Bar: Ind. 1955, U.S. Dist. Ct. (so. and no. dists.) Ind., U.S. Ct. Appeals (7th cir.). Practice law Ft. Wayne, Ind., 1955-94; co-mng. ptnr. Beers, Mallers, Backs & Salin and precedessors, 1955-94; chmn., pres., CEO Mallers & Spirou Enterprises, Inc. Mem. Allen County Police Merit Bd., 1967-77, 88-94; pres. Allen County Young Rep. Club, 1956-58; asst. to Rep. county chmn. Allen County, 1958-92; chmn. City-County Bd. Health, 1980-93. Master Ind. Bar Found.; mem. ABA, Ind. Bar Assn., Allen County Bar Assn. (sec., dir. 1961-63), Am. Judicature Soc., Valparaiso U. Law Sch. Alumni Assn. (nat. pres. 1978-80), Phi Alpha Delta. Home: Fort Wayne Ind. Died 1994.

MALLETTE, ALFRED JOHN, army officer; b. Green Bay, Wis., Nov. 21, 1938; s. Alfred G. and Beatrice Margaret (Stengel) M.; m. Nancy Lee McMillin, Dec. 26, 1960; children: Scott A., Randall J., Nicole L. BS in Math., St. Norbert Coll., DePere, Wis., 1960, BS in Physics, 1961; MS in Engring., Ohio State U., 1968. Commd. 2d lt. U.S. Army, 1961, advanced through grades to lt. gen., 1991; chief Programming Div. Allied Forces, NATO, Brunnsum, The Netherlands, 1977-78; comdr. 8th Signal Bn., Bad Kreuznach, Fed. Republic Germany, 1978-81; dir. tng. devel. U.S. Army Signal Sch., Ft. Gordon, Ga., 1982-83, dir. proponent office, 1983-85; comdr. 93d Signal Brigade, Stuttgart, Fed. Republic Germany, 1985-86; dep. comdg. gen. U.S. Army Signal Sch., Ft. Gordon, 1986-88; dep. dir. info. systems Dept. Army, Washington, 1988-89; comdg. gen. 5th Signal Command, Worms, Fed. Republic Germany, 1989-90, Communications-Elect Command, Ft. Monmouth, N.J., 1990-92; dep. dir. gen. NATO Comm. and Info. Systems Agency, Brussels, 1992-94. Mem. USO, N.Y.C., 1991-92. Mem. Assn. U.S. Army, Armed Forces Communications, Electronics Assn., DAV, Ret. Officers Assn., Indsl. Engring. Honor Soc. of Ohio State U. Roman Catholic. Home: Evans Ga. Died Aug. 15, 1994.

MALMBERG, JOHN HOLMES, physics educator; b. Gettysburg, Pa., July 5, 1927; s. Constantine F. and Margaret Eloise (Dysinger) M.; m. Vilma Ruth Martinus, June 21, 1952 (div. 1992); children: David Gabriel, Lori Ann. BE, Ill. State U., 1949; MS in Physics, U. Ill., 1951, PhD in Physics, 1957. Research, teaching asst. U. Ill., Champaign, 1949-57; staff mem. Gulf Gen. Atomic, San Diego, 1957-69; prof. physics U. Calif., San Diego, 1967—. Contbr. numerous sci. articles to jours.; patentee in field. Served with U.S. Army, 1946. Recipient Tech. Innovation award NASA. Fellow Am. Phys. Soc. (Maxwell prize in plasma physics 1985, award for excellence in plasma physics 1991). Home: Del Mar Calif. Died Nov. 17, 1992.

MANCINI, HENRY, composer; b. Cleve., Apr. 24, 1924; s. Quinto and Anna (Pece) M.; m. Virginia O'Connor, Sept. 13, 1947; children: Christopher, Monica and Felice (twins). Student, Juilliard Inst. Music, 1942; D.Mus. (hon.), Duquesne U., 1977; D (hon.), Mt Saint Mary's Coll., 1980. Pianist, arranger, Tex Beneke Orch., 1945-47, staff composer Universal Pictures, 1952-58; scores include: Glenn Miller Story (nominated for Oscar award), Benny Goodman Story, Touch of Evil, The Hawaiians, The Great Waldo Pepper, 1974, Return of the Pink Panther, 1975, Glass Menagerie, 1987, Sunset, 1988, Welcome Home, 1989, Without a Clue, Physical Evidence, Mother, Mother; scored TV series Peter Gunn, 1958, Mr. Lucky, 1959; with RCA Victor Records, 1959—; recordings include: Days of Wine and Roses, The Blues and the Beat, Mr. Lucky Goes Latin, Combo, Experiment in Terror, Hatari, The Thorn Birds, Our Man in Hollywood, Uniquely Mancini, Dear Heart, In the Pink; (TV series) Newhart, Hotel; author: Sounds and Scores, 1962, (autobiography) Did They Mention the Music?, 1989. Active in Share, Inc., orgn. for mentally retarded children. Recipient (18 nominations) 4 Acad. awards for (score) Breakfast at Tiffany's, (songs) Moon River (with Johnny Mercer), Days of Wine and Roses (lyrics by Mercer), song, socre Victor/Victoria (with Leslie Bricusse); recipient 20 Grammy awards (72 nominations), 2 Emmy award nominations, 1 Golden Globe award (9 nominations), numerous others; named hon. alumni UCLA, 1974, hon. mayor, Northridge, Calif.; Nat. Acad. of Recording Arts & Sciences Lifetime Achievement Award, 1994 (posthumously); more. Mem. Composers and Lyricists Guild Am. (exec. bd.), ASCAP. Home: Beverly Hills Calif. Died June 14, 1994.

MANKIEWICZ, JOSEPH LEO, writer, film director; b. Wilkes-Barre, Pa., Feb. 11, 1909; s. Frank and Johanna (Blumenau) M.; m. Rosa Stradner, July 28, 1939 (dec. 1958); children: Christopher, Thomas; 1 child by previous marriage: Eric; m. Rosemary Matthews, 1962; 1 dau., Alexandra. AB, Columbia U., 1928. Assoc. fellow Yale U., 1979-91. Writer, dir., producer motion pictures, 1929-93 , including Skippy, 1930, If I Had a Million, 1931, Million Dollar Legs, 1932, Manhattan Melodrama, 1934, Fury, 1936, Three Comrades, 1937, Philadelphia Story, 1939, Woman of the Year, 1940, Keys of the Kingdom, 1944, A Letter to Three Wives, 1948, No Way Out, 1950, All About Eve, 1950, 5 Fingers, 1951, Julius Caesar, 1952, Guys and Dolls, 1954; dir.: La Boheme, Met. Opera, 1952; formed Figaro, Inc., 1952; author screenplay, dir. The Barefoot Contessa, The Quiet American, produced by Figaro, Inc.; dir. Suddenly Last Summer, 1959, There Was A Crooked Man, 1969, Sleuth, 1972; writer, dir. The Honey Pot, 1965; pub. All About Eve, a screenplay, 1951, More About All About Eve, a colloquy, 1972. Founding mem., sec. Screen Writers' Guild, 1933. Decorated comdr. Order of Merit (Italy); chevalier Order of Legion of Honor (France); recipient Screen Dirs. Guild Ann. award for directorial achievement, 1949, 50; Screen Writers Guild Ann. award for best Am. comedy, 1949, 50; Acad. Motion Picture Arts and Scis. first award for direction and first award for screen play, 1950, 51, Erasmus. award City of Rotterdam, 1984, D.W. Griffith award for lifetime achievement Dirs. Guild Am., 1986, Alexander Hamilton medal for disting. accomplishment as alumnus Columbia U., Golden Lion award for life time achievement Venice Flim Festival, 1987, Akira Kurosawa award for lifetime achievement San Francisco Internat. Film Festival, 1989. Mem. Acad. Motion Picture Arts and Scis. (life), Screen Dirs. Guild Am. (pres. 1950), Writers Guild Am. (sec. 1933), Bedford Golf and Tennis Club. Home: Bedford N.Y. Died Feb. 5, 1993.

MANKIN, HART TILLER, federal judge; b. Cleve., Dec. 26, 1933; s. Howard Edmonn and Fantine (Tiller) M.; m. Ruth A. Larson, Aug. 14, 1954; children: Margaret, Theodore, Susan. Student, Northwestern U., 1950-52; BA, U. South, 1954, cert. edn. for ministry, 1982; JD, U. Houston, 1960. Bar: Tex. 1960, D.C. 1971, U.S. Supreme Ct. 1968. Pvt. practice Houston, 1960-67; counsel, asst. to pres. Triumph Industries, Houston, 1967-69; gen. counsel GSA, Washington, 1969-71, Dept. Navy, Washington, 1971-73; adminstrv. conf. of U.S. U.S., 1970-71; v.p., gen. counsel Columbia Gas System, Wilmington, Del., 1973-89; assoc. judge U.S. Ct. Vets. Appeals, 1990-96; bd. dirs. Del. Trust Co., 1978-89; adj. prof. Sch. Law Widener U., 1989-90. Bd. dirs. Widener U. Law Sch., Del. Humanities Coun., chmn., 1980-82, Am. Ctr. for Enterprise Edn., Inc., chmn. 1985-89. With USAF, 1954-57. Recipient spl. achievement award GSA, 1970, Disting. Pub. Svc. award Dept. Navy, 1973. Mem. ABA, State Bar Tex., D.C. Bar Assn., Fed. Bar Assn., Maritime Law Assn., U.S., Del. State C. of C. (chmn. 1981-83), Fed. Am. Inn of Ct. (master), Army and Navy Club, U.S. Croquet Assn. Episcopalian. Home: Washington D.C. Died May 28, 1996.

MANLEY, WILLIAM TANNER, economist; b. Bath County, Ky., Aug. 18, 1929; s. Nathan and Flora (Whaley) M.; m. Vertna Jane Alexander, Oct. 30, 1951; 1 son, William Conway. B.S., U. Ky., 1951, M.S., 1955; Ph.D., U. Fla., 1958. Asst. prof. U. Fla., 1958-60, asso. prof., 1960-66; economist Dept. Agr., Washington, 1960-66; dep. dir. mktg. econs. div. Dept. Agr., 1966-68, dir., 1968-73, dir. nat. econ. analysis div., 1973-76; dep.

adminstr. Agr. Mktg. Service, 1976-88; govt. relations advisor Heron, Bruchette, Ruckert and Rothwell Law Firm, Washington, 1988-90; econ. cons. Heron Law Co., Washington, 1990-91, Tuttle and Taylor Law Firm, 1991-96; chmn. U.S. Dept. Agr. Yearbook, 1983; economist Tuttle and Taylor Law Firm, 1991-96. Contbr. articles on econs. of mktg. to profl. jours. Served with USAF, 1951-53. Recipient cert. of merit Dept. Agr., 1963, 69, Superior Service award, 1979, Disting. Service award Nat. Market News Assn., 1979, Meritorious Service medal U.S. Dept. Air Force, 1979, Presdl. Meritorious Exec. Rank award Sr. Exec. Service, 1983, Disting. Out-of-State Alumnus award U. Ky. Agrl. Alumni Assn., 1987, Presdl. Disting. Exec. Rank award Sr. Exec. Service, 1987, Disting. Service award Dept. Agr., 1988. Mem. Internat., So. assns. agrl. economists, Am. Agrl. Econs. Assn., Fed. Exec. Inst. Alumni Assn. (dir. 1976-78), Res. Officers Assn. Methodist. Home: Amelia Island Fla. Died Feb. 5, 1996.

MANN, GOLO, historian; b. Munich, Germany, Mar. 27, 1909; s. Thomas and Katja (Pringsheim) M. Student, U. Munich, U. Berlin, U. Heidelberg. Reader German lit. and history Ecole Normale Supérieure, St. Cloud, France, 1933-35, Rennes U., 1935-36; editor Mass und Wert, Zurich, Switzerland, 1937-40; prof. modern history Olivet Coll., Mich., 1942-43; prof. history Claremont (Calif.) Men's Coll., 1947-57, Stuttgart Tech. Hoshschule, 1960-64. Numerous publications including Vom Geist Amerikas, 1954, Wallenstein, 1971, Gentz, 1973; contbr. articles to profl. jours. With U.S. Army, 1943-46. Recipient Berlin Fontane prize, 1962, Mannheim Schillerpreis, 1964, Büchner prize, 1968, Gottfried Keller preis, 1969, Schiller Gedächtnispreis, 1977, Bayerisches Maximiliansorden for Kunst, 1985, Goethe, 1985; decorated Order of Merit. Mem. Am. Acad. Arts and Scis., Deutsche Acad. for Sprach and Dichtung, Bayerische Acad. Schonen Kunste, Vereinigung Deutscher Wissenschaften. Home: Kilchberg Switzerland Died Apr. 9, 1994.

MANSHIP, CHARLES PHELPS, JR., newspaper executive, retired association executive; b. Baton Rouge, Aug. 13, 1908; s. Charles Phelps and Leora (Douthit) M.; m. Paula Garvey, Aug. 27, 1938. MBA, Harvard, 1932; BJ, U. Mo., 1930; LHD (hon.), La. State U., 1986. Reporter State-Times and Morning Advocate, 1926-27, gen. mgr., 1938-42, pub., 1946-70; advt. salesman Times-Picayune, 1932-34; treas., dir. La. TV Corp., Mobile Video Tapes Co.; pres. Capital City Press; pres. So. Newspaper Pubs. Assn., 1958-59, pres. emeritus, 1959—. Mem. Kappa Alpha. Clubs: Internat. House, Boston (New Orleans); Rotary, Country, City, Country Club of La. (Baton Rouge). Home: Baton Rouge La. Died Sept. 14, 1994.

MANTLE, MICKEY CHARLES, professional baseball player, marketing consultant; b. Spavinaw, Okla., Oct. 20, 1931; s. Elvin Clark and Lovell (Richardson) M.; m. Merlyn Louise Johnson, Dec. 23, 1951; children: Mickey Elvin, David Harold, Billy Giles (dec.), Danny Merle. Grad. high sch. Signed with N.Y. Yankees, 1949, played with Independence (Mo.) farm team, 1949, played with Joplin (Mo.) farm team, 1950, 1st baseman, outfielder, 1951-68, appeared in World Series games, 1951-53, 55-58, 60-64. Inducted into Baseball Hall of Fame Cooperstown, N.Y., 1974. Home: Dallas Tex. Died August 13, 1995.

MANTOVANI, JUANITA MARIE, university dean, educator; b. Chgo., Sept. 18, 1943; d. Norman Bert and Marie Frances (Byczkowski) Watson; A.B. summa cum laude, Marymount Coll., 1965; A.M., UCLA, 1966; Ph.D. in English, U. So. Calif., 1974; m. Robert Albert Mantovani, June 6, 1970. Acting chmn. freshman English program U. So. Calif., 1972-73, asst. dean student affairs, 1973-75, asst. dean humanities, 1975-81, chmn. ethnic studies program, 1980-81, mem. English faculty, 1966-75, mem. adj. faculty, program for study women and men in society, 1975-81; dean undergrad. studies, assoc. prof. English, Calif. State U., Los Angeles, 1981-87, prof., 1987-88; died, 1988; mem. English faculty Long Beach City Coll., 1974-77, Pepperdine U. Liberal Studies Program, 1975-77; lectr., condr. workshops on profl. devel. for women, career devel. and liberal arts edn., images of women and ethnic minorities in lit. and media; video and lecture presentations in field. panelist Nat. Endowment for Humanities Research Seminar on Feminism, 1979. Mem. U. So. Calif. Women in Mgmt. (founder 1979—). Home: Redondo Beach Calif.

MAPELLI, ROLAND LAWRENCE, food company executive; b. Denver, June 10, 1922; s. Herman M. and Della (Borelli); m. Neoma Robinson, Apr. 1942; children: Terralyn Mapelli DeMoney, Geraldine Mapelli Gustafson. Student, Regis Coll., 1959-61; Doctorate (hon.), Regis U., 1994. Owner, operator Mapelli Farms and Ranches, Eaton, Colo., 1960-90; chmn. bd., sr. v.p. Monfort of Colo., Inc., Greeley, 1971-89, pres. energy div., 1983-90, also bd. dirs.; sr. v.p. ConAgra Red Meat Cos., Greeley, 1990-95; bd. dirs. Norwest Banks Colo., Norwest Bank Greeley; bd. dirs., exec. com., 2d v.p. Nat. Western Stock Show; mem. Colo. Agrl. Adv. Com., 1966-73. Chmn. Denver Off-Street Parking Commn., 1960-72; mem. Denver City Coun., 1955-59, Colo. Ho. of Reps., 1961-62, Colo. State Senate, 1962-66; mem. adv. bd. Ft. Logan Mental Health Ctr., 1961-64, St. Anthony's Hosp., 1960-65; bd. dirs. N. Denver Civic Assn., 1955-65, Better Bus. Bur., 1966-69; mem. bd. Ambassadors Loretto Heights Coll., 1960-65; bd. dirs., exec. com. Nat. Western Stock Show, 1966-95; dir. land coun. Colo. State U., 1984-95; mem. Colo. Bus. HIgher Edn. Consortium. 2d lt. USAF, 1942-46, ETO; with USAFR, 1946-55. Recipient Knute Rockne award, 1961, Water for Colo. Conservation award, 1985, Man of Yr. award Colo. Meat Dealers Assn., 1975; named Disting. Citizen of 1994, Long Peak coun. Boy Scouts Am., Colo. Bus. Leader of Yr., 1990. Mem. Nat. Cattlemens Assn., Mountain/Plains Meat Assn. (founder, pres. 1968-69), Colo. Cattle Feeders Assn., Cherry Hills Country Club, Greeley Country Club, Thunderbird Country Club, Denver Athletic Club, Rotary. Roman Catholic. Home: Greeley Colo. Died Jan. 19, 1995.

MARBURY, BENJAMIN EDWARD, anesthesiologist; b. Farmington, Mo., May 23, 1914; s. Benjamin H. and Annie (Eversole) M. A.B., U. Mo., 1939; M.S., La. State U., 1941; M.D., Washington U., St. Louis, 1944. Intern St. Luke's Hosp., St. Louis, 1944-46; asst. resident N.Y. Hosp.-Cornell Med. Center, N.Y.C., 1948-49; mem. staff N.Y. Hosp.-Cornell Med. Center, 1949—; practice medicine specializing in anesthesiology N.Y.C., 1949—; emeritus prof. anesthesiology Cornell U. Med. Coll., N.Y.C., 1948—. Served to capt. M.C. U.S. Army, 1946-48. Mem. AMA, N.Y. Acad. Medicine, N.Y. State Med. Soc., N.Y. County Med. Soc., Am. Soc. Anesthesiology, N.Y. Soc. Anesthesiology. Episcopalian. Club: Univ. (N.Y.C.). Home: Old Lyme Conn. Died Feb. 3, 1995.

MARCH, JOHN WILLIAM, accountant, educator; b. Cleve., Aug. 9, 1923; s. James Herbert and Mildred (MacCorkle) M.; m. Ruth Mary Jaeger, Dec. 16, 1944; children: William J., Roger J., Peter B.; m. Elizabeth Burton, Sept. 17, 1983. B.B.A., U. Wis., 1945. CPA, Wis., Ill. With Arthur Andersen & Co., 1945-78, ptnr., 1956-78, vice chmn. worldwide accounting and audit practice, Chgo., 1970-75, sr. ptnr., 1975-78, now ret.; mem. Fin. Acctg. Standards Bd., 1978-84; adj. prof. Kellogg Grad. Sch. Mgmt., Northwestern U., 1985-88; founding mem. adv. com. Northeastern U. Sch. Pub. Acctg., Boston, 1962. Mem. U. Wis. Found.; exec. com. Bascom Hill Soc., 1977-89; bd. dirs. Hilton Head Orch.; treas. Hilton Head Orch.; treas. Lake Forest Acad., Ill., 1966-70, trustee, 1966-77; mem. corp. Bentley Coll., Waltham, Mass.; mem. nat. adv. coun. U. Fla. Sch. Acctg., 1979-84; gov. mem. Chgo. Orchestral Soc., 1975-78; bd. dirs. U. Wis. Club Chgo., 1985-87, Donors' Forum Chgo., 1976-78; mem. Wellesley Town Meeting, Mass., 1964-65, chmn. adv. and finance com., 1965. Mem. AICPA, Ill. Soc. CPAs, Wis. Soc. CPAs, Am. Acctg. Assn., Inst. Mgmt. Accts., Pinehurst Country Club, Sea Pines Country Club. Presbyterian. Home: Hilton Head Island S.C. Died Dec. 16, 1993.

MARCHIORO, THOMAS LOUIS, surgeon, educator; b. Spokane, Wash., Aug. 1, 1928; s. Americo A. and Gertrude (Dennehy) M.; student Colo. Coll., 1945-46, U. Calif., Berkeley, 1949; B.S. cum laude, Gonzaga U., 1951; M.D., St. Louis U., 1955; m. Karen Byus, Apr. 2, 1956; children: Thomas, John, Elizabeth, Stephen, Joan, Katherine, Robert. Intern St. Mary's Group of Hosps.-St. Louis U. Hosp., 1955-56; resident in gen. surgery Henry Ford Hosp., Dearborn, Mich., 1956-57; resident in gen. and thoracic surgery Colo. Gen. Hosp., Denver, 1957-60, chief resident in surgery, 1961-62; resident Peter Bent Brigham Hosp., Boston, 1958, resident etrangere surgery L'Hopital Leennec, Paris, 1960-61; asst. in surgery U. Colo., 1959-60, instr., 1960-63; asst. prof. surgery, 1963-66, asso. prof., 1966-67; asso. prof. U. Wash., 1967-69, prof., 1969-95, chmn. div. organ transplantation dept. surgery, 1971-95, also vice chmn. dept. surgery; mem. surg. staff U. Wash. Hosp., 1967-95, dir. Transplant Clinic, 1967-95, now attending in transplant surgery Univ. Hosp., Seattle; cons. in surgery to hosps., Seattle; project dir. profl. transplant capability Wash.-Alaska Regional Med. Program, 1972-73, mem. kidney disease adv. com., program services, 1973-95; mem. various profl. coms. and bds., including med. adv. bd. N.W. Kidney Center, nat. renal transplantation adv. group Central Office VA, Chronic Uremia Coordinating Com.; chmn. network 2 End-Stage Renal Disease Network Coordinating Council. Served with USNR, 1945-46. Markle scholar, 1965-71; diplomate Am. Bd. Surgery, Am. Bd. Thoracic Surgery. Fellow A.C.S.; mem. Soc. Univ. Surgeons, Soc. Vascular Surgery, Assn. Acad. Surgery (founding; sec. 1967-72, pres. 1974), Transplantation Soc. (charter; editorial bd. Transplantation 1976-78), Internat. cardiovascular Soc., AAAS, Renal Physicians Assn., European Soc. Surg. Research, Societe Internationale de Chirurgie, N.Y. Acad. Scis., Soc. Golden Pouch, Am. Soc. Nephrology, Pacific Coast Surg. Soc., Seattle, Surg. Soc., Wash. State Med. Soc. (sci. adv. council), King County Med. Soc., Nat. Kidney Found., Am. Heart Assn. (sect. council), Surg. Biology Club III, Am. Soc. Transplant Surgeons (pres. 1976), Am. Surg. Assn., Alpha Omega Alpha, Alpha Sigma Nu. Democrat. Roman Catholic. Research in organ transplantation and preservation, immunobiology, portal circulation, hepatrophic factors, pancreatic function and disease, parathyroid physiology and pathology. Died Feb. 5, 1995. Home: Bellevue Wash.

MARCUS, JACOB RADER, history educator;
Connellsville, Pa., Mar. 5, 1896; s. Aaron and Jen
(Rader) M.; m. Antoinette Brody, Dec. 30, 1925 (de
1 dau., Merle Judith (dec.). AB, U. Cin., 1917, LI
1950; rabbi, Hebrew Union Coll., 1920; PhD, U. Ber
1925; attended, Lane Theol. Sem., 1914, U. Chgo., 19
U. Kiel, 1923; spl. study, Paris and Jerusalem, 1925-
LLD (hon.), Dropsie Coll., 1955; DHL (hon.), Sper
Coll. Judaica, Chgo., 1977, Brandeis U., 1978, Gr
Coll., Phila., 1978, Xavier U., Cin., 1985, Wayne St
U., 1989, Jewish Theological Seminary, 1992. Ins
Bible, rabbinics Hebrew Union Coll., 1920, asst. pr
Jewish history, 1926-29, assoc. prof., 1929-34, pr
Jewish history, 1934-59, apptd. Adolph S. Ochs pr
Jewish history, 1946, Adolph S. Ochs prof. Am. Jew
history, 1959-65, Milton and Hattie Kutz Distinguis
Service prof. Am. Jewish history, 1965-95; dir. A
Jewish Archives, 1947-95, Am. Jewish Periodical Cen
1956-95; v.p. Central Conf. Am. Rabbis, 1947, pr
1949, hon. pres., 1978. Author: The Rise and Dest
of the German Jew, 1934, An Index to Jewish F
schriften, 1937, The Jew in the Medieval World-a Sou
Book, 1938, Communal Sick-Care in the Gern
Ghetto, 1947, Early American Jewry, 2 vols., 1951-
Memoirs of American Jews 1775-1865, 3 vols., 1955-
American Jewry Documents Eighteenth Century, 19
On Love, Marriage, Children...and Death, Too, 19
Studies in American Jewish History, 1969, The Colo
American Jew, 3 vols., 1970, Critical Studies in Am
ican Jewish History, 3 vols., 1971, Israel Jacobson:
Founder of the Reform Movement in Judaism, 19
The American Jewish Woman 1654-1980, The Ameri
Jewish Woman: A Documentary History, 2 vols., 19
United States Jewry, Vol. I, 1989, Vol. II, 1991,
III, 1993, Vol. IV, 1993, To Count a People, 1990, T
I Believe, 1990; editor: The American Jewish Archi
The Concise Dictionary of American Jewish Biogra
2 vols., 1994. Served as 2d lt., 145th Inf. U.S. Ar
1917-19. Recipient Frank L. Weil award Nat. Jew
Welfare Bd., 1955; Lee M. Friedman medal for dist
svc. to history, 1961; honored with publ. Essays
American Jewish History, on 10th anniversary
founding of Am. Jewish Archives, 1958, A Bicenten
Festschrift for Jacob Rader Marcus, 1976, The Writ
of Jacob Rader Marcus, A Bibliographic Record, 19
Mem. Jewish Publ. Soc. Am., Am. Jewish Hist.
(hon. pres.), Am. Acad. Jewish Research, B'nai B'
Phi Beta Kappa. Home: Cincinnati Ohio Died Nov.
1995.

MARION, ANDREW BURNET, lawyer; b. York, S
Apr. 22, 1919; s. John Alexander and Mary (Bur
M.; m. Evelyn R. Cantey, Sept. 20, 1946; child
Evelyn C., Andrew Burnet, Margaret B. A.B. ma
cum laude, U. S.C., 1939, LL.B., 1941. Bar: S.C. 19
Partner firm Savage & Marion, Camden, 1945
partner firm Haynsworth, Perry, Bryant, Marion
Johnstone, Greenville, 1953-86; of counsel Haynswo
Marion, McKay and Guerard, Greenville, 1986-95;
dir. First Bankshares of S.C., First Nat. Bank of S
Carolina Fed. Savs. & Loan Assn.; dir. emeritus
Nat. Bank Corp. Past pres. bd. St. Francis Commu
Hosp., Greenville County Hist. Soc., Greenville
Festival Assn., Community Council; past dir. U.
Ednl. Found. Served to capt. USAAF, 1941-45. M
Am. Law Inst., Am. Judicature Soc., ABA, S.C.
Assn., Wig and Robe, St. Andrews Soc., Cotillon C
Poinsett Club, Palmetto Club, Torch Club, Pine
Hunt Club, Phi Beta Kappa, Omicron Delta Ka
Alpha Tau Omega. Home: Columbia S.C. Died N
20, 1995.

MARKS, ALBERT AUBREY, JR., brokerage h
executive; b. Phila., Dec. 19, 1912; s. Albert A.
Edythe (Lilian) M.; grad. Harrisburg (Pa.) Acad., 1
student Williams Coll., 1928-30; B.S., U. Pa., 1932
Mary Kay Bryan; children—Albert Aubrey, Chris
M., Robert B. Br. office mgr. Newburger & Co., Ph
1934-42, gen. ptnr. Newburger & Co., Atlantic C
N.J., from 1946; sr. v.p. Advest Group Inc., until 1
pres. Atlantic Co. N.J.; dir. Guarantee Bank & T
Co., Atlantic City, Anchor Savs. and Loan Assn.; a
mem. Am., N.Y., Phila., Balt. stock exchanges.
pres. N.J. Mid-Atlantic Farm Show, 1952-54;
Atlantic City Conv. Bur., 1951-54, treas., 1962;
Miss Am. Pageant, 1962-64, chmn. bd., 1966; ch
Boardwalk Adv. Commn.; mem. Bd. Edn., Marg
N.Y.; vice chmn. Com. Adult Edn. So. N.J.;
Atlantic County Community Chest and We
Council, 1953; gen. campaign chmn. Community C
1956; former pres. 4-Club Council; mem. exec. co
Boy Scouts Am., Atlantic County; trustee So.
Devel. Council, 1951-54; mem. N.J. Legis. S
Commn., Securities Adv. Com. N.J. State, Conflict
terest Com. Gov. Betty Bacharach Home Affli
Children; chmn. Com. of 50, Atlantic City, from 1
Atlantic County Improvement Authority, 1975;
Atlantic City Med. Ctr. Found., 1986-89. Served f
2d lt. to lt. col. USAAF, 1942-46. Named Citize
Year, Atlantic City, 1953; Citizen of Decade, Elks, 1
numerous other Man of Yr. awards civic orgns. M
Investment Bankers Assn., Security Traders Assn.,
Assn. Security Dealers, Assn. Stock Exchange Fi
Atlantic City (pres. 1952-53), So. N.J. (chmn. de
council 1951-54) C.'s of C., Atlantic City Center
Assn. (v.p. 1953-54), Mil. Order World Wars (con
nion), Res. officers Assn., Air Force Assn., Newco
Soc., Pa. Soc., Newcomen Soc. Roman Catholic. Cl

sons, Kiwanis (pres. 1954), Press, Haddon Hall :quet, Osborne Beach; Williams, Marco Polo Y.C.). Died Sept. 17, 1989. Home: Margate City N.J.

ARKS, JAMES JOHN, restaurateur, developer; b. go., Aug. 23, 1911; s. Nicholas John and Stella (Gi- M.; B.S., U. Mich., 1935; m. Christine Constance mpary, Nov. 11, 1939; children : Lianna Sandra, ies John. Forestry technician U.S. Forestry Service, 1, Mo., 1934; forest supr. Mich. Conservation Dept., ising, 1934-35; cons. forester, Ann Arbor, Mich., 6-37; owner Martine's Restaurant, Pensacola, Fla., 2-94 , Martine's Ice Cream Co., Pensacola, 1942-94 ; s. Esquire House, Warrington, Fla., 1934-94 , Mar- 's, Pensacola, 1947-94 , Marwood Motors, Pen- ola, 1955-94 , Ky. Fried Chicken, Biloxi and fport, Miss., 1964-94 , Ky. Fried Chicken, Mobile, ., 1964-94 , New Orleans, 1967-94 , Col. Sanders Ky. ed Chicken Corp., 1970-94 ; sec.-treas. Circle Sanita- , Pensacola, 1959-94 . Mem. adv. bd. Fla. Hotel and staurant Commn., 1961-62; mem. bd. Fla. Hospitality 1. Program, 1962-63; chmn., pres. Fla. Tourism uncil, 1962-63; mem. Fla. Council of 100, 1963-94 , n. exec. com.; mem. council advisors U. W.Fla., 5-94 ; advisor to council advisors Univ. System Fla.; n. Baptist Hosp. Health Care Found., 1975-94 , vice in. exec. com., 1976-94; elector Presdl. Electoral l., 1984-94; owner, mgr. Bellview Shopping Ctr., N. afox Plaza Shopping Ctr. Served to comdr. USNR, 7-45. Named Outstanding Fla. Restaurateur, 1964. n. Am. Restaurants Hall of Fame, 1961. Mem. Nat., (pres. 1961-62) restaurant assns., Sales Execs. Club. m. Hellenic Christian Orthodox Ch. (v.p. parish ncil 1976). Rotarian (past local pres., Paul Harris ow). Clubs: Toastmasters; Mobile Country; Pen- ola Country. Died Nov. 23, 1994. Home: Pensacola

RKUS, FRED H., engineering and architectural npany executive; b. Vienna, Austria, May 22, 1927; ie to U.S., 1939; s. Herman Albert and Stephanie ette (Weiner) M.; m. Ruth Kahn, Sept. 4, 1949; dren: Sharon L., Stephen A., Richard D. BSME, U. 1950. Registered profl. engr., Ill., Ind., N.J., Va., g. Mech. engr. Neiler Rich & Bladen, Chgo., 1948- ptnr. Cons. Assocs., Chgo., 1959-64; mng. dir., pres. Epstein and Sons (UK) Ltd., London, 1974-83; h. engr., chief mech. engr. A. Epstein and Sons In- at., Inc., Chgo., 1964-68; project mgr., v.p. A. Ep- 1 and Sons Internat., Inc., Paris, 1968-74; v.p. in- at. ops. A. Epstein and Sons Internat., Inc., Chgo., 3-88, sr. v.p., 1988-94. Mem. Park Forest (Ill.) nning Commn., 1961-68; bd. dirs. Selfhelp Home for d, Chgo., 1991-94. With USN, 1945-46. Democrat. vish. Home: Chicago Ill. Died Dec. 22, 1994.

RQUIS, ROBERT B., architect; b. Stuttgart, many, July 9, 1927; came to U.S., 1937, naturalized, 3; s. Paul Charles and Marianne (Gutstein) M.; m. n Godfrey, Dec. 20, 1950; children: Lisa Lee, Tessa, id. Student, Sch. Architecture, U. So. Calif., 1946- Acad. di Belle Art, Florence, Italy, 1949-50. nder Marquis Assocs. Architects, San Francisco, 3-56; pres. Marquis & Stoller, Architects and Plan- , San Francisco and N.Y.C., 1956-74, Marquis As- ., San Francisco and N.Y.C., 1974-95. Prin. works ide Novato (Calif.) Library (Design award), Sonoma e Coll. Cafeteria, (Instn. Mags. award), housing for rly (Design awards), St. Francis Sq. Co-op, (Design rds), St. Francis Yacht Club, San Francisco (Design rds); energy-conserving Calif. Dept. Justice Office g, Sacramento (Owens Corning Energy award); Am. bassy, San Jose, Costa Rica, Braun Music Bldg, ford U., Primate Ctr. San Francisco Zoo, Aaron land Sch. Music Queens Coll., N.Y.C., Rosa Parks Citizens Housing, San Francisco, (Design awards), h terminal modernization San Francisco Internat. port (design award), Music Sch. Calif. State U., sno, Cmty. Ctr. Recreation & Pks., San Francisco, a Rosa Jr. Coll. Petaluma, Libr./Cmty. Ctr., City of any, Pub. Housing Rehabilitation Sunydale San ncisco, Rockridge Libr., Oakland, City Hall/Cmty. , Orinda; numerous pvt. residences and restoration ects, Works included in publs., exhibited museums. ipient Albert J. Evers environ. award No. Calif. , 1975, Firm award, 1984, Bruner Found. award, , 25-yr. award, over 70 design awards; grantee Nat. owment Arts. Fellow AIA (past chpt. pres., past bd. dirs., past internat. rels. com., bd. dirs., trustee Found. 1984-86, exec. com. Coll. Fellow 1987-91, chancellor 1990, chancellor 1991); mem. Am. itl. Found. (bd. regents 1991-95). Home: San ncisco Calif. Died Jan. 3, 1995.

RRIOTT, JOHN WILLARD, restaurant and motel utive; b. Marriott, Utah, Sept. 17, 1900; s. Hyrum ard and Ellen (Morris) M.; m. Alice Sheets, June 9, ; children: John Willard, Richard Edwin. Grad., er Coll., Ogden, Utah, 1922; A.B., U. Utah, 1926; D. (hon.), Brigham Young U., 1958. Franchise er A. & W. Root Beer Co., Washington, 1926-28; Marriott Corp. (formerly Hot Shoppes, Inc.), 3-64, now chmn., dir.; dir. Riggs Nat. Bank, sapeake & Potomac Telephone Co., Washington Bd. le. Biography: The J. Willard Marriott Story, 1977. 1. commrs. adv. planning bd. Fed. City Council.; govs. United Service Orgns.; chmn. Presdl. In- iral Com., 1969, 73, Honor Am. Com. Recipient Hall of Fame award Am. Restaurant Mag., 1954; Achievement award Advt. Club, 1957; award Am. Marketing Assn., 1959; U. Utah, 1959; Chain Store Age award, 1961; Businessman of Yr. award Religious Heritage Am., 1971; Capt. of Achievement award Am. Acad. Achievement, 1971; Horatio Alger award, 1974. Mem. N.A.M. (dir.), Com. for Econ. Devel. (trustee), Nat. Restaurant Assn. (pres. 1948), Washington Restaurant Assn. (pres. 1939, 43). Mem. Ch. of Jesus Christ of Latter-Day Saints (pres. Washington stake 1948-57). Clubs: Burning Tree (Bethesda, Md.); Indian Creek Country (Miami Beach, Fla.); Bald Peak Colony (Melvin Village, N.H.); Columbia Country (Chevy Chase, Md.); Paradise Valley Country (Ariz.); Washington Admirals (Washington), Capitol Hill (Washington). Home: Washington D.C. Died Aug. 13, 1985; buried Parklawn Cemetery, Bethesda, Md.

MARSHAK, ROBERT EUGENE, physicist, educator; b. N.Y.C., N.Y., Oct. 11, 1916; s. Harry and Rose (Shapiro) M.; m. Ruth Florence Gup, Apr. 18, 1943; children: Ann, Stephen. A.B., Columbia U., 1936; Ph.D., Cornell U., 1939; Ph.D. hon. degree, Utkal U., India, 1977, City U. N.Y., 1979, CCNY, 1980. Instr. dept. physics U. Rochester, N.Y., 1939-43; asst. prof. U. Rochester, 1943-46, asso. prof., 1946-49, prof., 1949-70, chmn. dept. physics and astronomy, 1950-64, Disting. Univ. prof., 1964-70; pres. CCNY, 1970-79, pres. emeritus, 1979-92; Univ. Disting. prof. physics Va. Poly. Inst. and State U., Blacksburg, 1979-87, univ. disting. prof. emeritus, 1987-92; lectr. Harvard Obs., summer 1940; professeur d'Echange (Guggenheim fellow) at Sorbonne, 1953-54; vis. prof. Columbia U., summer 1950, U. Mich., 1952, Tata Inst. Bombay, 1953, French Sch. for Theoretical Physics, 1954, Sch. for Theoretical Physics, Tokyo, 1965; guest prof. at CERN, Geneva; Ford Found. and Guggenheim fellow, 1960-61, Guggenheim fellow, 1967-68, Nobel Found. prof., Sweden, 1970; mem. Inst. Advanced Study, Princeton, spring 1948; physicist radiation lab. Mass. Inst. Tech., 1942-43, Montreal Atomic Energy project, 1943-44; dep. group leader in theoretical physics Los Alamos Sci. Lab., 1944-46; vice chmn. N.Y. State Adv. Com. on Atomic Energy, 1958; Avco vis. prof. Cornell U., 1959; chmn. vis. physics com. Brookhaven Nat. Lab., 1964-65; Niels Bohr vis. prof. Inst. Math. Sci., Madras, India, 1963; lectr. Yalta Internat. Sch., 1966, Hercig Novi Internat. Sch., 1967; head Nat. Acad. Sci. del. to Poland, 1964, to Yugoslavia, 1965; mem. Sloan Fellowship Com., 1967-73; mem. sci. council Internat. Center of Theoretical Physics, Trieste, 1967-75, 84-89; Buhl vis. prof. Carnegie-Mellon U., 1968; trustee N.Y. Law Sch., 1975-79; mem. Solvay Congress, 1967, 82, Pugwash Conf., 1967, U.S.-Japan Com. on Sci.-Cooperation, 1969-72; mem. nat. com. UNESCO, 1970-73; trustee Univ. Research Assn., 1968-70, Atoms for Peace Award, 1958-70; chmn. div. particles and fields, 1970-71; founder Rochester Confs. on High Energy Physics, 1950-92; bd. dirs. Internat. Found. for Sci., Stockholm, 1970-75. Author: Meson Physics, 1952, (with L.I. Schiff and E.C. Nelson) Our Atomic World, 1946, (with E.C.G. Sudarshan) Elementary Particles, 1961, (with Riazuddin and C. Ryan) Theory of Weak Interactions in Particle Physics, 1969, Academic Renewal in the 1970s: Memoirs of a City College President, 1982; assoc. editor: Phys. Rev, 1953-55; editor interscience: Tracts and Monographs in Physics and Astronomy, 1955-70; dir.: Jour. History of Ideas, 1973-80. Recipient A. Cressy Morrison Astron. prize N.Y. Acad. Scis., 1940, J. Robert Oppenheimer Meml. prize, 1982, Alexander von Humboldt award (F.R.G.), 1985-86, Clark Kerr medal U. Calif., Berkeley, 1987; Robert E. Marshak Sci. Bldg. CCNY, 1980 dedicated in his honor. Fellow Am. Phys. Soc. (exec. com. 1968-69, council 1965-69, pres. 1983), AAAS (com. on sci. freedom and responsibility 1983-87); mem. NAS (chmn. adv. com. on sci. exchanges with USSR and Ea. Europe, 1963-66, mem. coun. 1971-74), AAUP, Am. Acad. Arts and Scis. (council 1985-89), Fedn. Am. Scientists (chmn. 1947-48), Am. Philos. Soc., N.Y. Acad. Scis. (life), Coun. Fgn. Affairs, Internat. Union Pure and Applied Physics (past sec. commn. on high energy physics, vice chmn. nat. commn. 1980-82), Phi Beta Kappa (Scholar 1982), Sigma Xi (nat. lectr. 1969). Home: Blacksburg Va. Died Dec. 23, 1992.

MARSHALL, DAVID SAUL, ambassador Singapore to France, Spain and Portugal; b. Singapore, Singapore, Mar. 12, 1908; came to France, 1978; s. Saul Nassim and Flora Ezekiel Mashaal; m. Jean Mary Gray, Apr. 2, 1961; children—Ruth Anna, Sara Elizabeth, Joanna Tamar, Jonathan Mark. LL.B., U. London, 1937; Barrister-at-Law, Middle Temple, London, 1937; LLD (hon.) Nat. U. Singapore, 1987. Cert. notary pub. Adv., solicitor High Ct. Singapore, High Ct. of Malaya and Supreme Ct. of Brunei, 1937-78; chief minister, Singapore, 1955-56; mem. Singapore Legis. Assembly, 1961-63; A.E. and P. to France, 1978—, to Portugal, Spain, 1981—; permanent del. of Singapore to UNESCO, Paris, 1981-85. Chmn. bd. trustees Inst. SE Asian Studies, 1969-74; trustee Jewish Trust Fund, Singapore, 1985—. Served as pvt., Brit. Army, 1942-45; Singapore, POW, Japan. Recipient Datuk Kurnia Johan Pahlawan, Sultan of Pahang, Malaysia, 1970; chevalier de la Legion d'Honneur, France, 1978. Mem. Singapore War Prisoners Assn. (founder, sec. gen.), Internat. C. of C. (ct. of arbitration 1985—). Jewish. Clubs: Cercle de l'Union Interalliée, Travellers (Paris).Died December 12, 1995. Home: Paris France

MARSHALL, GEORGE NICHOLS, minister, author; b. Bozeman, Mont., July 4, 1920; s. James Wallace and Grace (Nichols) M.; m. Barbara Ambrose, June 14, 1946 (div. 1966); 1 child, Charles Hopkinson. AB, Tufts U., 1940, STB, 1941, AM, 1943; MA, Columbia U., 1942; ThM, Harvard U., 1946; PhD, Walden U., 1976; DD, Meadville/Lombard Theol. Sch., 1976. Ordained to ministry Unitarian Ch., 1941. Pastor, Natick, Mass., 1941-43, Plymouth, Mass., 1946-52, Niagara Falls, N.Y., 1952-60; pastor Ch. of Larger Fellowship, Boston, 1960-85, minister emeritus, 1985-93. Author: Church of the Pilgrim Fathers, 1950, Unitarian Universalism as a Way of Life, 1966 (revised as Challenge of A Liberal Faith, 1979, 3d edit., 1988), An Understanding of Albert Schweitzer, 1966, (with David Poling) Schweitzer, A Biography, 1970, new edit., 1989, Facing Death and Grief, 1981, (biography) Buddha, His Quest for Serenity, 1978, 2d edit., 1990, A. Powell Davies and His Times, 1990 (Gustavus Myers award U. Ark. 1991); co-author: Encounters with Eternity, 1986, rev. edit. under title How Different Religions View Death and Afterlife, 1991, Introduction to Hibakusha, 1986. Assoc. dir. dept. extension Unitarian-Universalist Assn., 1960-Assn., 1960-70; treas. Unitarian Ministers Assn., 1954-56; chmn. Unitarian Commn. Ch. and Returning Servicemen, 1944-46; sec. Commn. Unitarian Universalist Union, 1949-53, Council Liberal Chs., 1953-55; pres. Niagara Falls Religious Fellowship, 1950-52. Bd. dirs. N.Y. chpt. Americans for Democratic Action, 1955-56; pres. Niagara County Planned Parenthood Assn., 1953-59, mem. N.Y. State bd., 1955-59; chmn. Unitarian Universalist Commn. Scouting; mem. Boy Scouts Am., 1960-70; del. White House Conf. Against Discrimination, 1958; program chmn. Albert Schweitzer Fellowship, N.Y.C., 1972-93. Capt. USAAF, 1943-46. Recipient Freedom House award of merit, 1949. Mem. Albert Schweitzer World Confedn. (sec.), Am. Friends of Albert Schweitzer. Died Feb. 15, 1993. Home: Chapel Hill N.C.

MARSHALL, J. HOWARD, II, lawyer; b. Phila., Jan. 24, 1905; s. S. Furman and Annabelle (Thompson) M.; m. Eleanor Pierce, June 20, 1931; children: J. Howard III, Pierce; m. Bettye M. Bohanan, Dec. 10, 1961; m. Anna Nicole Smith, 1994. AB, Haverford Coll., 1926, LLD, 1985; JD magna cum laude, Yale U., 1931. Instr. and asst. cruise dir. Floating Univ., 1926-27, cruise dir., 1928-29; asst. dean, asst. prof. law Yale U., 1931-33; mem. Petroleum Adminstrv. Bd., U.S. Dept. Interior, 1933-35; spl. asst. to U.S. atty. gen. and asst. solicitor Dept. Interior, 1933-35; spl. counsel Standard Oil Co. Calif., 1935-37; partner Pillsbury, Madison & Sutro, San Francisco, 1938-44; chief counsel Petroleum Adminstrn. for War, 1941-44, asst. dep. adminstr., 1943-44; gen. counsel U.S. del. to Allied Commn. on Reparations, 1945; ptnr. Meyers, Marshall & Meyers, Washington; Mem. Mil. Petroleum Adv. Bd. to joint chiefs staff, 1944-50, 54-59; pres., dir. Ashland Oil & Refining Co. (and subs. corps.), 1944-51; v.p., dir. Signal Oil & Gas Co., 1952-59, exec. v.p., dir., 1959-60, also subs. and affiliated corps.; pres., dir. Union Texas Natural Gas Corp., 1961-62; dir. Allied Chem. Corp., 1962-68; pres. Union Tex. Petroleum div., exec v.p. Allied Chem. Corp., 1965-67; dir. Tex. Commerce Bank Nat. Assn., Houston; dir., mem. exec. com. M-K-T R.R.; dir. Koch Industries, Inc., Wichita; chmn., dir. Petroleum Corp.; chmn. exec. com., dir. Coastal Corp.; dir. Presidio Oil Co., 1987; cons. sec. interior petroleum def. program, 1950-52. Author (with N.L. Meyers); series monographs Yale Law Jour., 1931, 33. Vice-pres., bd. mgrs. Haverford Coll. Mem. 25 Year Club, Am. Petroleum Inst. (v.p., dir.), Nat. Petroleum Council, Soc. Petroleum Engrs., Am., Calif., Ky. bar assns., AIME, Order of Coif, Beta Rho Sigma. Mem. Soc. of Friends. Clubs: Bohemian (San Francisco), Pacific-Union (San Francisco); 29 (N.Y.C.); River Oaks Country (Houston). Home: Houston Tex. Died Aug., 1995.

MARSHALL, MARY AYDELOTTE, state legislator; b. Cook County, Ill., June 14, 1921; d. John A. and Nell. A. Rice; B.A. with highest honors, Swarthmore Coll., 1942; m. Roger Duryea Marshall, Mar. 3, 1944; children: Nell Aydelotte, Jenny Winslow Marshall Davies, Alice Marie. Economist anti-trust div. Dept. Justice, Washington, 1942-46; mem. Va. Ho. of Dels., 1966-70, 72-92, mem. privileges and elections com., appropriations com., rules com., chmn. counties, cities and towns com., chmn. Legis. Study Commn. on Needs Elderly Virginians, 1973-78; chmn. Legis. Commn. Monitoring Long Term Care, 1983-86; mem. No. Va. Transp. Commn., 1974-80; mem. exec. com. Nat. Conf. State Legislators, 1981-87, also chmn. human svcs. com., chmn. programs and svcs. to states com.; chmn. Task Force on Social Security for Women, Fed. Council on Aging, 1978-81, mem. exec. com., chmn. human resources com. So. Legis. Conf., 1988-90; bd. dirs. Washington Met. Council Govts., 1978, 80, 87, 88, United Srs. Health Corp. Pres., Va. Assn. Mental Health, 1970-73, Va. Fedn. Democratic Women's Clubs, 1971-72; bd. dirs. Nat. Assn. Mental Health, 1972-78; mem. Dem. Central Com. Va., 1976-78. Recipient Achievement award Va. Assn. Mental Health, No. Va. Assn. Mental Health, Va. Fedn. Bus. and Profl. Women's Clubs, Va. Assn. Ind. Retail Gasoline Dealers, No. Va. Retarded Citizens Assn., Arthur Fleming Lecture, Nat. Assn. State Units on Aging, Gov.'s award for Child Care Legis.; named WETA Disting. Woman. Mem. AAUW, LWV. Congregationalist. Clubs: Bus.

and Profl. Women's, No. Va. Dem. Home: Arlington Va.

MARSHALL, SYLVAN MITCHELL, lawyer, former ambassador, television producer; b. N.Y.C., May 14, 1917; s. Louis H. and Kitty Markowitz; m. Mara Byron, Feb. 11, 1951; children: Douglas Wayne, Bradley Ross. B.A., CCNY, 1938; J.D., Harvard U., 1941. Bar: N.Y. State bar 1946, D.C. bar 1953. Mem. firm Garey & Garey, N.Y.C., 1946-51; spl. asst. to chief counsel OPS, Washington, 1951-53; partner firm Granik & Marshall, Washington, 1953-58; spl. dep. atty. gen. N.Y. State, 1946-50; pvt. practice law Washington, 1953-92; sr. ptnr. law firm Marshall, Leon Weill & Mahony; counsel Leon, Weill & Mahony, N.Y.C., 1974-84; sr. Washington ptnr. Marshall, Tenzer, Greenblatt, Fallon & Kaplan, 1984-92; Washington counsel Diamond & Precious Stone Bourse, Idar-Oberstein, W. Ger.; also fgn. embassies; presdl. ambassador to Inauguration of pres. of Mexico, 1976; spl. counsel for internat. affairs to dir. Bowers Mus. for Cultural Art, Santa Ana, Calif. Assoc. producer: Youth Wants to Know and Am. Forum, NBC-TV and radio, 1953-58. Hon. dep. police commr., N.Y.C., 1950-53, hon. consul, Finland. Served from 2d lt. to lt. col. U.S. Army, 1941-46. Decorated knight comdr. Order of Falcon (Iceland), Order of Vasco Nunez de Balboa (Republic of Panama); comdr. Order of Lion (Finland); Order of Taj (Iran); Order Aztec Eagle (Mexico); Order So. Cross (Brazil); Order Ruben Dario (Nicaragua); Order of Lion and Sun (Iran); Nat. Order Merit (Mauritania). Order of Crown (Thailand); Order Strong Right Arm of Kingdom of Gurkhas (Nepal); Order of Republic (Tunisia), Order of the White Elephant (Thailand). Club: Cosmos (Washington). Home: Washington D.C. Died 1992.

MARSHALL, TERRELL, lawyer; b. Little Rock, July 14, 1908; s. J. C. and Jenice (Thomas) Marshall-Small; m. Lourie Darland, Jan. 2, 1927; 1 son, Terrell. LL.B., Ark. Law Sch., 1931, J.D., 1979. Bar: Ark. 1931, U.S. Supreme Ct. 1938. Pvt. practice in Little Rock, 1931-96; atty. Pulaski County Legal Aid Bur., 1938-42. Contbr. to: Birds of Ark, 1951. Bd. dirs. Ark. Property Owners Found.; trustee Ark. Law Sch. Fellow Ark. Bar Found.; mem. ABA, Ark. Bar Assn. (past pres., mem. exec. com.), Pulaski County Bar Assn. (past pres.), Am. Judicature Soc. Club: Lakeside Country (Saline County, Ark.) (past pres.). Home: North Little Rock Ark. Died March 6, 1996.

MARSHALL, THURGOOD, retired U.S. supreme court justice; b. Balt., July 2, 1908; s. William and Norma (Williams) M.; m. Vivian Burey, Sept. 4, 1929 (dec. Feb. 1955); m. Cecilia S. Suyat, Dec. 17, 1955; children: Thurgood, John. A.B., Lincoln U., 1930, LL.D. (hon.), 1947; LL.B., Howard U., 1933, LL.D. (hon.), 1954; LL.D. (hon.), Va. State Coll., 1948, Morgan State Coll., 1952, Grinnell Coll., 1954, Syracuse U., 1956, N.Y. Sch. Social Research, 1956, U. Liberia, 1960, Brandeis U., 1960, U. Mass., 1962, Jewish Theol. Sem., 1962, Wayne U., 1963, Princeton U., 1963, U. Mich., 1964, Johns Hopkins U., 1966, Far Eastern Univ., Manila, 1968, Victoria U. of Wellington, 1968, U. Calif., 1968, U. Otago, Dunedin, New Zealand, 1968. Bar: Md. 1933. Practiced in Balt., 1933-37; asst. spl. counsel NAACP, 1936-38; spl. counsel N.A.A.C.P., 1938-50, dir., counsel legal def. and ednl. fund, 1940-61; U.S. circuit judge for 2d Jud. Circuit, 1961-65; solicitor gen. U.S., 1965-67; justice U.S. Supreme Ct., 1967-91; Civil rights cases argued include Tex. Primary Case, 1944, Restrictive Covenant Cases, 1948, U. Tex. and Okla. Cases, 1950, sch. segregation cases, 1952-53; visited Japan and Korea to make investigation of ct. martial cases involving Negro soldiers, 1951; Cons. Constl. Conf. on Kenya, London, 1960; rep. White House Conf. Youth and Children. Recipient Spingarn medal, 1946; Living History award Research Inst. Mem. Nat. Bar Assn., N.Y. County Lawyers Assn., Am. Bar Assn., Bar Assn. D.C., Alpha Phi Alpha. Episcopalian. Club: Mason (33 deg.). Home: Falls Church Va. Died Jan. 24, 1993.

MARTEKA, VINCENT JAMES, JR., magazine editor, writer; b. Uxbridge, Mass., Jan. 29, 1936; s. Vincent James and Genevieve (Ramian) M.; m. Janet Littler, May 26, 1962; children: Andrew, Peter, Katherine. B.S. in Geology, U. Mass., 1958; M.S., Rensselaer Poly. Inst., 1959. Editor U.S. Geol. Survey, Washington, 1959-60; sci. writer, news editor Sci. Service, Washington, 1961-63; sci. editor My Weekly Reader, children's newspaper, Middletown, Conn., 1964-65; editor Current Sci., sci. mag. jr. high sch. students, Middletown, 1966-95. Author: Bionics, 1965, Mushrooms: Wild and Edible, 1980, also numerous articles (writing awards Edn. Press Assn.); series editor: Our Living World, 12 books, 1993-94. Served with AUS, 1960. Mem. Nat. Assn. Sci. Writers, Mycological Soc. Am., N.Am. Mycological Assn., Nat. Audubon Soc., Mattabeseck Audubon Soc. (pres. 1976). Home: Portland Conn. Died May 31, 1995.

MARTICELLI, JOSEPH JOHN, lawyer, editor; b. Freeland, Pa., Feb. 24, 1921; s. Frank Anthony and Carmela (DiSpirito) M.; m. Alva Mae Aubrey, Oct. 22, 1952; children—Frank Anthony, Barbara Marticelli McGarey. A.B., Lafayette Coll., 1941; LL.B., U. Pa., 1947. Bar: Pa. bar 1948, N.Y. bar 1954, also U.S. Supreme Ct. bar, U.S. Ct. Mil. Appeals bar 1954. Practiced law Freeland, Pa., 1948-53, Rochester, N.Y., 1953-95; mng. editor Lawyers Coop. Pub. Co., Rochester, N.Y., 1980-89, acquisitions editor, 1989; editor Case & Comment; adj. prof. bus. law Monroe Community Coll., Rochester., 1978-85; 1st dep. town atty., Henrietta, N.Y., 1962-76; legis. asst. N.Y. Assembly, 1970-71; counsel to minority N.Y. Senate, 1976-78. Author editor law books; contbr. articles to profl. jours. Chmn. Rep. Town and Country Com., Henrietta, N.Y., 1961; town justice Monroe County, N.Y., 1981-95; pres. Monroe County Magistrates Assn., 1990-91. With AUS, 1942-46. Mem. ABA, N.Y. Bar Assn., Scribes Assn. Legal Writers (pres. 1982-83), Am. Trial Lawyers Assn., Am. Legion (past comdr.). Republican. Roman Catholic. Home: Pittsford N.Y. Died Apr.21, 1995.

MARTIN, DEREK, architect; b. Morpeth, Eng., Mar. 19, 1923; came to came U.S., 1925; s. Albert and Hannah Violet (Cook) M.; m. Elizabeth Graham Bell, Dec. 22, 1951; children: Paula Lee, Derek, Andrew Albert, Peter Bell. B.Arch., Carnegie Inst. Tech., 1948. Registered architect, Pa., N.Y., cert. Nat. Council Archtl. Registration Bds., 1974. Draftsman Kruger Assocs., Los Alamos, 1948; with Various firms, Pitts., 1948-51; chief draftsman Celli-Flynn, McKeesport, Pa., 1951-56; ptnr. Curry & Martin and successor firms Curry, Martin & Taylor and Curry, Martin & Highberger, Pitts., 1956-84; prin. Derek Martin and Assocs., 1985-94. Archtl. works Brashear High Sch., Fallingwater Vistors Ctr., Carnegie Mellon U. dormitories, St. Edmund's Acad., Indiana U. of Pa. Sci. Bldg., Magee Recreation Ctr., Blood Bank Pitts. Bd. dirs. Action Housing, Inc., 1970-80; mem. property com. United Way Agy, Pitts., 1975-79; chmn. selections com. Pa. Dept. Gen. Services, Harrisburg, 1981. Flying officer RCAF, 1942-45. Fellow AIA (dir. 1977-81, Contbn. to Archtl. Profession award Pitts. chpt.); mem. Pa. Soc. Architects (pres. 1973-74), Iron City Fishing (Can. and Pitts., pres. 1981-82). Home: Pittsburgh Pa. Died Feb. 21, 1994.

MARTIN, ERNEST H., theatrical and motion picture executive; b. Pitts., Aug. 28, 1919; s. Samuel and Cecilia (Sklar) Markowitz; m. Nancy Frank (div.); m. Nancy Guild (div.); children: Elizabeth, Cecilia Martin Ford, Polly; m. Twyla Elliott.. A.B., U. Calif. at Los Angeles, 1942. Producer: (with Cy Feuer) stage plays Where's Charley?, 1948, Guys and Dolls, 1950, Can-Can, 1953, The Boy Friend, 1954, Silk Stockings, 1955, Whoop-Up, 1958, How to Succeed in Business Without Really Trying, 1961 (Pulitzer prize for drama), Little Me, 1962, Skyscraper, 1965, Walking Happy, 1966, The Goodbye People, 1968, The Act, 1977; (with Cy Feuer) motion picture Cabaret, 1972 (winner 8 Acad. awards); (motion pictures) Piaf, 1975, A Chorus Line, 1985. Inducted into the Theater Hall of Fame, 1995. Home: Los Angeles Calif. Died May 8, 1995.

MARTIN, GEORGE MAYBEE, lawyer; b. Mohler, Idaho, June 18, 1906; s. George Sylester and Janet Dove (Maybee) M.; m. Elizabeth Harrington Stafford, June 14, 1930; children: Elizabeth Jean, Dorothy Jane, George Stafford, Jonathon Harrington. BSEE, U. Wash., 1928, JD, 1940. Bar: Wash. 1940; registered profl. engr., 1928. Pvt. practice electrical contractor Seattle and Harrah, Wash., 1929-37; gen. merchant Martin & Martin, Harrah, 1930-37; pvt. practice law Yakima, Wash., 1940-94; dep. prosecuting atty. Yakima County, Yakima, 1941-43; ptnr. Martin & Marquis, Yakima, 1975-94. Author (book): Yakima, 1960, Yakima Centennial, 1985; editor: U.S. Post Card Catalog, 1955-60; philatelic columnist. Pres. Maybee Soc.; trustee Yakima Valley Meml. Hosp., Yakima Valley Mus., 1946-94; founder, trustee Yakima Valley Regional Library, 1944-46. Named Distinguished Citizen, Am. Legion, 1969; recipient Others award, Salvation Army, 1976, Silver Beaver, Silver Antelope award Boy Scout Am.; Gov's. Citation Most Disting. Vol., 1989. Mem. ABA, Yakima County Bar Assn. (past pres.), Wash. State Bar Assn., Rotary, Mason, Am. Philatelic Soc. (Luff award 1974). Republican. Presbyterian. Home: Yakima Wash. Died Feb. 21, 1994.

MARTIN, JACQUES CARDINAL, archbishop; b. Amiens, France, Aug. 26, 1908. Ordained priest Roman Cath. Ch., 1934. Elected bishop of Nablus Palestine, 1964; elevated to archbishop, 1986, created cardinal,, 1988. Home: Rome Italy

MARTIN, JOHN J., insurance company executive; b. 1934. BBA, U. Mass., 1956. V.p. Aetna Life Ins. Co., 1978-87, exec. v.p., 1987-88, sr. v.p., 1988—; sr. v.p. Aetna Casualty & Surety Co.; pres., bd. dirs. Aetna Life Ins. & Annuity Co. Home: Hartford Conn. Died June 7, 1992.

MARTIN, MARK, lawyer; b. Shawnee, Okla., June 26, 1914; s. Mark Mehael and Louise (Kraft) M.; m. Marion Norton, Nov. 18, 1939; children: John Harris, Anne. BBA, U. Tex., 1935, LLB, 1937. Bar: Tex. 1937. Practice in Dallas; ptrn. Strasburger & Price and predecessor firms, 1937—; mem. faculty So. Meth. U. Sch. Law, 1938-42; chmn. bd. Def. Rsch. Inst., 1966-70, hon. chmn., 1970—; mem. Tex. Constl. Revision Commn., 1973. Life trustee U. Tex. Law Sch. Found., 1968—; commr. City of University Park, Tex., 1972-74. With USNR, 1942-45. Recipient Disting. Alumnus award U. Tex., 1980, Outstanding Alumnus award Tex. Law Sch., 1983. Fellow Am. Coll. Trial Lawy (regent); mem. ABA (fed. judiciary com.), Tex. Assn. (chmn. bd. 1972-73, Outstanding 50-Yr. Law award 1987), Dallas Bar Assn. (pres. 1967), Tex. As Def. Counsel (pres. 1965-65), Dallas C. of C. (dir. 19 72). Home: Dallas Tex. Died June 13, 1994.

MARTIN, OSCAR THADDEUS, retired lawyer; Springfield, Ohio, Jan. 27, 1908; s. Harrie B. and M garet L. (Buchwalter) M.; m. Dorothy Traquair, J 15, 1937; children: Cecily T., Nancy S. (Mrs. Roger Saunders), David M., Robert M.; m. Lydia Kauffm July 15, 1966. A.B., Princeton, 1929; J.D. cum lau Harvard, 1932. Bar: Ohio 1932. Pvt. prac Springfield, 1932-86; assoc. firm Martin & Corry, 19 40; partner in successor firms and sr. partner Mar Browne, Hull & Harper, 1960-86, ret., 1986; past s bd. dirs. Vernay Labs., Inc., The Kissell Co., Robbin Myers, Inc. Vice pres. nat. council YMCA, 1979- mem. nat. bd., 1958-83; trustee Springfield Fou Springfield Symphony. Mem. ABA, Ohio Bar As Springfield Bar Assn. (past pres.), Am. Law Inst. (l Am. Coll. Probate Counsel, Nat. Assn. Coll. and Un Attys., Phi Beta Kappa. Clubs: Sea Island G Princeton (N.Y.). Home: Saint Simons Island Deceased.

MARTIN, SAMUEL PRESTON, III, physician; East Prairie, Mo., May 2, 1916; s. Samuel Preston Lucy (Simmons) M.; m. Cornelia Ruth Campbell, J 2, 1939; children—Samuel Preston, William Barry, C Susan; m. Dorothy E. Matson, Sept. 5, 1970. M cum laude, Washington U., 1941. Diplomate Am. Internal Medicine. Intern, resident Barnes Hosp., Louis, 1941-44; chief med. resident Duke Hosp., 19 vis. investigator Rockefeller Inst. Med. Research, 19 asso. medicine and microbiology Duke U. Medicine, 1949-50, asst. prof. medicine and micr ology, 1950-53, asso. prof., 1953-56; prof., head d medicine U. Fla., 1956-62, provost Health Center, 19 70; vis. prof. Harvard U. Med. Sch., 1970; p medicine, exec. dir. Leonard Davis Inst. for He Econs., U. Pa., Phila., 1971-78; dir. Robert W Johnson Clin. Scholars Program Leonard Davis Inst. Health Econs., U. Pa., 1975-88; cons. Robert W Johnson Found., 1987-89, L.A. Sch. Bd., 1989-9 Served to capt. AUS, 1944-47. Decorated Order Leopold. Mem. Am. Assn. Physicians, A.C.P., Soc. Clin. Investigation, Am. Assn. Immunologists, Exptl. Biology and Medicine. Home: Philadelphia Died May 2, 1996.

MARTIN, WEBSTER STURTEVANT, maga editor-in-chief; b. Panama, C.Z., Nov. 17, 1948 Vernon Paul and Jean (Webster) M. BA, Sch. Inter Service, Am. U., 1976. Copy editor Internat. He Tribune, Paris, 1970-74; dir. advt. and circula Europe Mag., Washington, 1976-80, mng. editor, 1 82, editor-in-chief, 1982—. Home: Washington D.C

MARTIN, WILLIAM ROBERT, pharmacology cator, physician; b. Aberdeen, S.D., Jan. 30, 192 William E. and Anna Louise (Hawkins) M.; Catherine J. Reynolds, July 2, 1949; children: Cathe Anne, Charles David, Richard Douglas. B.S., Chgo., 1948; M.D., M.S., U. Ill., 1953. Intern C County Hosp., Chgo., 1953-54; instr., then asst. pharmacology U. Ill. Coll. Medicine, Chgo., 1954 neuropharmacologist Nat. Inst. Drug Abuse Addic Rsch. Ctr., Lexington, Ky., 1957-63; dir. center Inst. Drug Abuse Addiction Rsch. Ctr., 1963-77; prof. pharmacology U. Ky. Coll. Medicine, Lexing 1962-77; prof. U. Ky. Coll. Medicine, 1977-93, ch 1977-89, prof. anesthesiology, 1990-93. Editorial Jour. Pharmacology and Exptl. Therapeutics, 1961 adv. bd.: Psychopharmacologia, 1962-81, Pharmacol 1978-93, Pharmacodynamie, 1978-93, Exptl. Neurol 1983-89. Recipient USPHS Commendation me 1966, Meritorious Svc. medal, 1971, Med. Alu award U. Ill., 1977, Nathan B. Eddy Meml. aw NAS, 1977, Professorship award Sterling Drug 1983, Wikler award Nat. Inst. on Drug Abuse, 19 Fellow Coll. Prob. Drug Dependence, Sigma Xi; m AAAS, Am. Soc. Pharmacology and Exptl. Medi Am. Soc. Clin. Pharmacology and Therapeutics, ternat. Brain Rsch. Orgn., Am. Coll. Neuropsy pharmacology, Soc. Neurosci., Internat. Assn. Stud Pain. Home: Midway Ky. Died May 27, 1993; inte Midway, Ky.

MARTINI, EMIL P., JR., wholesale pharmaceu distribution company executive; b. Teaneck, 1928. Grad., Purdue U., 1950. With Bergen Brun Corp., L.A., 1952—; pres., mgr. Bergen Drug Co. L.A., 1956-69, corp. pres., chief exec. officer, 196 chmn., pres., chief exec. officer, 1971-81; chmn., exec. officer Bergen Brunswig Corp. (formerly Be Drug Co. Inc.), L.A., 1981—; also dir. Bergen Drug Inc., L.A.; dir. Bro-Dart Industries, David Janison lyle Corp. Home: Orange Calif.

MARTINI, ROBERT EDWARD, whol pharmaceutical and medical supplies company execu b. Hackensack, N.J., 1932. BS, Ohio State U., 19 With Bergen Brunswig Corp., Orange, Calif., 195 v.p., 1962-69, exec. v.p., 1969-81, pres., 1981-92, 1990—; chmn. Bergen Brunswig Corp., Orange, 19

chmn. exec. com. Bergen Brunswig Corp. Capt. USAF, 1954.

MARTY, FRANCOIS CARDINAL, former archbishop of Paris; b. Pachins, France, May 18, 1904. s. Francois and Zoé Gineste. Ordained priest Roman Cath. Ch., 1930; bishop of St.-Flour, 1952; titular archbishop of Emesa, also coadjutor archbishop of Rheims, 1959; archbishop of Rheims, 1960-68, of Paris, 1968-81; elevated to Sacred Coll. of Cardinals, 1969; titular ch. St. Louis of France; ret. as archbishop, 1981; ordinary for Eastern Rite Catholics in France without ordinaries of their own rites; mem. Congregation Oriental Chs., Congregation Clergy, Sacraments and Divine Worship, Commn. Revision of Code of Canon Law. Home: Villefranche-de-Rouergue France

MARVIN, EARL, lawyer; b. N.Y.C., Mar. 17, 1918; s. Benjamin and Rose Lillian (Salmow) M.; m. Helaine F. Kaplan, Nov. 2, 1941 (div. Jan. 1962); children: Peter F. Benjamin A., Elizabeth C.; m. Eleanor Dreyfus, June 14, 1964. AB, Harvard U., 1938, LLB, 1941, JD, 1967. Bar: Mass. 1941, N.Y. 1942. Assoc. Goldwater & Flynn, N.Y.C., 1946-48; pvt. practice N.Y.C., 1948—; of counsel Goldstein, Schrank, Segelstein & Shays, N.Y.C., 1970—; bd. dirs. Superior Surg. Mfg. Co. Inc., Seminole, Fla., Bleyer Industries Inc., Lynbrook, N.Y. Mem. New York County Lawyers Assn., Harvard Club (N.Y.C.), Inwood Country Club (L.I., N.Y., bd. govs. 1971-73), Countryside Country Club (Clearwater, Fla.). Home: Clearwater Fla.

MASLAND, WILLIAM S., carpet and rug mfg. co. exec.; b. Carlisle, Pa., 1921. With C. H. Masland & Sons, Carlisle, 1945—, asst. sec., 1951-55, sec., tras., 1955-62, exec. v.p., 1962-71, pres., 1971—, also dir.; dir. Okite Corp.

MASON, EDWARD ALLEN, chemistry educator, scientist; b. Atlantic City, Sept. 2, 1926; s. Edward Paul and Olive Margaret (Lorah) M.; m. Ann Courtenay Laufman, July 6, 1952; children: Catherine Hubbard, Stephen Edward, Elizabeth Margaret, Sarah Lois. B.S., Va. Poly. Inst., 1947; Ph.D., MIT, 1951; A.M., Brown U., 1968. Research assoc. MIT, 1950-52; NRC fellow U. Wis., 1952-53; mem. faculty Pa. State U., 1953-55, U. Md., 1955-67; prof. chemistry and engring. Brown U., Providence, 1967-92, emeritus, 1992-94, Newport Rogers prof. chemistry, 1983-92, emeritus, 1992-94, rsch. prof., 1992-94; vis. prof. physics Leiden (Netherlands) U., 1981-82. Author: (with J.T. Vanderslice and H.W. Schamp) Thermodynamics, 1966, (with T.H. Spurling) Virial Equation of State, 1969, (with E.W. McDaniel) Mobility and Diffusion of Ions in Gases, 1973, (with A.P. Malinauskas) Gas Transport in Porous Media: The Dusty-Gas Model, 1983, (with E.W. McDaniel) Transport Properties of Ions in Gases, 1988; assoc. editor: Physics of Fulids, 1963-65, Jour. Chem. Physics, 1964-66; adv. editor: Case Studies in Atomic Physics, 1971-75; editl. bd. Jour. Membrane Sci., 1981-94, Internat. Jour. Thermophysics, 1993-94. Fellow Am. Phys. Soc., Washington Acad. Scis. (Phys. Scis. award 1962), Random Soc.; mem. AAAS, Am. Assn. Physics Tchrs., Sigma Xi, Phi Kappa Phi, Phi Lambda Upsilon. Home: Barrington R.I. Died Oct. 27, 1994.

MASON, PAMELA HELEN, actress, producer, writer; b. London, Mar. 10, 1922; d. Isadore and Helen Spear (Morgan) Ostrer; m. Roy Kellino (div. 1941); m. James Mason (div. 1964); children: Portland, Morgan. Ed. pvt. schs., Eng. Propr. vitamin co., mfr. M's P's Cheese B's and other food products. Author: novels This Little Hand, 1942, Del Palma, 1944, The Blinds Are Down, 1946, Ignoramus Ignormus, 1950, Marriage is the First Step Toward Divorce, The Female Pleasure Hunt; An Anthology of Cat Stories; also articles; appearances include Broadway prodn. Bathsheba, 1969; others, over 20 film appearances; TV films include My Wicked Wicked Ways, 1984; commentator: Pamela Mason TV show, 1960-68, The Weaker Sex, 1969, appearances on all nat. TV talk shows; host talk show, Sta. KABC Radio; columnist Movieline Mag. Home: Beverley Hills Calif. Died June 29, 1996.

MASSA, FRANK, electronics executive; b. Boston, Apr. 10, 1906; s. Ernest Alfred and Maria (Onorati) M.; m. Georgiana Galbraith, June 27, 1936; children: Frank Jr., Robert, Georgiana, Constance, Donald. BSEE, MIT, 1927, MSEE, 1928. Research engr. Victor Talking Machine Co., Camden, N.J., 1928-30; head gov. sound div. RCA-Victor Co., Camden, 1930-40; dir. acoustic research Brush Devel. Co., Cleve., 1940-45; pres. Massa Labs., Inc., Cleve., 1945—; chmn. bd. dirs., engring. cons. Massa Products Corp., Hingham, Mass., 1976—. Author several books in electroacoustics, 1934-40; contbr. articles to profl. jours.; holder 150 patents. Swope fellow MIT, 1927. Fellow IEEE (life), Acoustical Soc. Am. (exec. council); mem. Inst. Radio Engrs. Home: Cohasset Mass.

MASSEE, DAVID LURTON, JR., lawyer; b. Montezuma, Ga., Mar. 8, 1936; s. David Lurton and Minnie McLendon (Fokes) M.; m. Gail Ann Lione, Mar. 22, 1975 (div. Jan. 1983). BA, Emory U., 1958; LLB, U. Va., 1961; LLM in Taxation, NYU, 1965. Bar: Ga. 1960, D.C. 1978. Assoc. Kilpatrick & Cody, Atlanta, 1961-62, 65-70, ptnr., from 1970. Bd. dirs. United Way Met. Atlanta, 1982-88, Met. Atlanta Community Found., from 1984, High Mus. Art, Atlanta, from 1980, Atlanta Coll. Art, 1978-82, Atlanta Alliance Theatre, 1979-85, from 1988; mem. bd. visitors Emory U., from 1989; bd. dirs. St. Luke's Tng. and Counseling Ctr., Inc., from 1989. With USAF, 1962-64. Mem. ABA, State Bar Ga., Atlanta Bar Assn., Am. Coll. Real Estate Lawyers, Lawyers Club Atlanta (pres. 1978-79), Piedmont Driving Club, Capital City Club, Nine O'Clock's Club, Farmington Country Club. Episcopalian. Home: Atlanta Ga. Deceased.

MASSERMAN, JULES HOMAN, neuropsychiatrist, psychoanalyst; b. Chudnov, Poland, Mar. 10, 1905; came to U.S., 1908, naturalized, 1917; s. Abraham and Czerna (Baker) M.; m. Christine McGuire, 1943. M.D., Wayne U., 1931. Diplomate: Am. Bd. Psychiatry and Neurology. Instr., then asst. prof. U. Chgo., 1937-46; asst. prof. neurology and psychiatry Northwestern U. Med. Sch., 1946-48, asso. prof., 1948-52, prof. neurology and psychiatry, 1952-94, co-chmn. dept. psychiatry, 1960-69; dir. edn. Ill. Psychiat. Inst., 1958-62; Roche vis. prof., Australia and N.Z., 1968, China, USSR, Eastern Europe; fellow Center Advanced Study of Behavioral Scis., 1968-69; chmn. Chgo. Psychiat. Council, 1967-69, Ill. Research and Tng. Authority, 1965-68; chmn. council Stone-Brandell Found., 1966-69. Author 18 books in behavioral scis., Psychiatric Odyssey, 424 articles, 16 motion pictures; editor 52 books, jours.; composer, violinist. Pres. Masserman Found. Internat. Accords, 1987-94. Recipient nat. award in pathology Phi Lambda Kappa, 1929; Presdl. award for selective service duty, 1946; Lasker award for research mental hygiene, 1946; Taylor Manor award as psychiatrist of year, 1972; Sigmund Freud award, 1974; Founders award Am. Assn. Social Psychiatry, 1983; Recipient Laughlin award Am. Coll. Psychoanalysts, 1983. Mem. AMA, Am. Psychiat. Assn. (council 1965-68, v.p. 1974-75, sec. 1975-77, pres. 1978-79), Am. Acad. Psychoanalysis (pres. 1956-57), Am. Soc. Biol. Psychiatry (pres. 1956-57), Internat. Assn. Social Psychiatry (hon. life pres. 1969-94), Am. Soc. Group Therapy (pres. 1957-58), Am. Assn. Social Psychiatry (founder 1957, pres. 1973), Am. Acad. Stress Disorders (exec. v.p. 1971-79), Pan Am. Med. Assn. (pres. sect. psychiatry 1983), World Assn. Social Psychiatry (hon. life pres. 1978-94), Masserman Found. for Internat. Accords (pres. 1986-94). Home: Chicago Ill. Died Nov. 6, 1994.

MATA, EDUARDO, conductor; b. Mexico City, Sept. 5, 1942; m. Carmen Cirici Ventallo, Nov. 5, 1968; children: Pilar, Roberto. Student, Nat. Conservatory of Music, 1954-63; studied with Carlos Chavez, 1960-65; student advanced conducting, Tanglewood Sch., 1964. Dir. music Guadalajara Symphony Orch., 1964; dir. music, condr. Orquesta Filarmonica, Nat. U. Mex., 1966-75; condr., advisor music Phoenix Symphony Orch., 1969-77; dir. music Dallas Symphony Orch., 1977-93, condr. emeritus, 1993-95; guest condr. with U.S. orchs. including Boston Symphony, Chgo. Symphony, Cleve. Orch., Pitts. Orch., Detroit Symphony Orch., also orchs. in, South and Cen. Am., Poland, Yugoslavia, Luxembourg, France, Fed. Republic of Germany, Sweden, Eng., Italy, Israel, Australia and Japan. artistic dir. Puebla Music Festival, 1975, Nat. Symphony Mexico City, 1975, San Salvador Festival, 1975, Nat. Opera Mexico City, 1983-85; condr. Casals Festival, 1976; prin. guest condr. Pitts. Symphony, 1989-95. Recipient Elias Sourasky prize, Mex., 1975, Hispanic Heritage award, 1991, 1st Mozart medal Govt. of Mexico, 1991; nominated 2 Grammy awards. Mem. Mex. Soc. Composers, Mex. Union Musicians (Golden Lyre award 1964), Colegio Nacional Ciudad Mexico. Home: Dallas Tex. Died Jan. 4, 1995.

MATCH, ROBERT KREIS, medical center executive; b. N.Y.C., May 8, 1926; s. Philip and Clara (Kreis) M.; children—Gail, Susan, Vicki. Student, N.Y. U., 1943-44, Ohio State U., 1945-46; M.D., SUNY, 1950. Asst. attending surgeon Flower Fifth Avenue Hosp., N.Y.C., 1955-69; asst. attending surgeon Met. Hosp., N.Y.C., 1955-69; staff surgeon L.I. Jewish-Hillside Med. Center, New Hyde Park, N.Y., 1957-77; pres. L.I. Jewish-Hillside Med. Center, 1968-94; med. dir. East Nassau Med. Group, Hicksville, N.Y., 1957-68; prof. community medicine Sch. Medicine, SUNY, Stony Brook; dir. Blue Cross/Blue Shield Greater N.Y. Contbr. articles to various publs. Served with U.S. Army, 1944-45; with USN, 1945-46. Mem. N.Y. State Hosp. Rev. and Planning Council, Hosp. Assn. N.Y. State, Council Teaching Hosps., Assn. Am. Med. Colls. (adminstrv. bd.), Am. Public Health Assn., Group Health Assn. Am. Home: New York N.Y. Died Oct. 6, 1994.

MATHESON, WILLIAM ANGUS, retired manufacturing and public relations executive, consultant; b. Oregon City, Oreg., Aug. 30, 1895; s. Angus and Elizabeth (Williams) M.; m. Maude Moore, Dec. 13, 1917; 1 child, William Angus. Student pub. schs. Sales mgr. Mt. Hood Ice Cream Co., Portland, Oreg., 1921-23, Power Plant Engring. Co., 1923-26, Hart Oil Burner Corp., Phila., 1926-30; br. mgr. Williams Oil-O-Matic Heating Corp., Chgo., 1930-36; N.Y.C. br. mgr. GMSC Delco Appliance Div., 1936-40; v.p., asst. to pres. Williams Oil-O-Matic Heating Corp., 1940, dir., 1940-44, pres., 1944-45; became mgr. Williams Oil-O-Matic div., Eureka Williams Corp., Bloomington, Ill., 1945; gen. sales mgr. Lustron Corp., 1949-50; bus. cons., dir. dealer relations Am. Bildrok Co., Chgo.; pres. Portable Elevator Mfg. Co., Bloomington, 1952-75; pres. Amco div. Dynamics Corp. Am., 1970-75, asst. to pres. parent corp., 1975-87; v.p., dir. Implement Splty. Co., Inc., St. Louis; dir. Am. Foundry & Furnance, Nat. Bank of Bloomington, Lindsay Bros. Co., Mpls., Capital Equipment Co. Author: The Selling Man. Treas. Brokaw Hosp., chmn. bd., 1974-75; mem. exec. com. Oil Heat Inst. Am., Inc.; past pres.; Chmn. McLean County Savs. Bond Com.; nat. asso. Boys Clubs Am.; Chmn. McLean County United Republican Fund; v.p. United Republican Fund. Ill. Served in World War I, May 1917-19. Named to McLean County Republican Hall of Fame. Mem. Farm Equipment Mfrs. Assn. (pres. 1956-57, dir.), Bloomington Assn. Commerce (pres. 1965), Ill. Mfrs. Assn. (dir.). Republican. Presbyn. Clubs: Mason (Chgo.), Rotarian. (Chgo.), Union League (Chgo.), Chicago Athletic (Chgo.); Bloomington Country, Bloomington (Ill.); Ill. Farm Equipment (pres. 1964). Home: Bloomington Ill. Deceased.

MATHEWS, CARMEN SYLVA, actress; b. Phila., May 8, 1918; d. Albert Barnes and Matilde (Keller) M. Student, Bennett Jr. Coll., 1936-38, Royal Acad. Dramatic Art, Eng., 1938, 39. Appeared numerous stage plays; roles include Ophelia in Hamlet, Queen in Richard II, Lady Mortimer in Henry IV, Varya in Cherry Orchard, 1943, Violet in Man and Superman, 1945, Mrs. Sullen in Beaux Strategem, 1945, Miss Ronberry in The Corn is Green, 1946, Miss Neville in She Stoops to Conquer, 1946, Madame Ducotel in My Three Angels, 1952, Mary in Holiday for Lovers, 1957, Candida in Shaw's Candida, 1958, Eileen in Man in Dogsuit, 1958, Lady Utterword in Heartbreak House, 1959-60, Contessa in mus. adapted from Candide, Voltaire, 1956, Ceil in Night Life, 1962, Maria in Lorenzo, 1963, Louise in Zenda, 1963, Queen in Hamlet, 1964, Grandma Hutto in mus. adaptation The Yearling, 1965, Edna in A Delicate Balance, 1966, Bathsheeba in mus. adaptation I'm Solomon, 1967-68, Constance in mus. adaptation Dear World, 1968, Rabbit Run, 1969, Fraulein Schneider in mus. adaptation Cabaret, 1970, Wife in All Over, 1970, Grandma in Ring around the Bathtub, 1971, Gloriani in mus. Ambassador, 1972, Mrs. Aigreville in mus. In Fashion, 1973, Mamita in mus. Gigi, 1974, Arietta in Mornings at Seven, 1974, Mrs. Higgins in Pygmalion, 1975, Mother in Children, 1976, Mrs. Ellis in The Autumn Garden, 1976, Madame Arcati in Blithe Spirit, 1977, Mrs. Tilford in The Children's Hour, Catherine in Arms and the Man, 1979, Fanny Farrelly in Watch on the Rhine, 1980, Cornelia in The Bat, 1980, Betsy Trotwood in mus. David Copperfield, 1981, Cora in Mornings at Seven, 1981, Sarah Delano Roosevelt in Sunrise at Campobello, 1982, Old Lady in Sunday in the Park with George, 1983, Helen in The Road to Mecca, 1984, Mother in Night, Mother, 1985, Grandmother in A Grand Romance, 1985, Mrs. Hardcastle in She Stoops to Conquer, 1986, Cecelia in Autumn Elegy, 1989, Dowager Empress in The Anastasia Game, 1989, Mme. Armfeldt in A Little Night Music, 1990; movie appearances include Butterfield 8, A Rage To Live, Mrs. Boatwright in Sounder, 1971, Fanny Ascher in Daniel, 1983; also in various dramatic TV shows, and other TV show including Judge in TV after sch. spl. To Take A Stand, 1988, role of Lil in MASH, HBO spl. The Last Day in the Life of Brian Darling, 1990, The Best Year of My Life, 1990; recording books for Am. Found. for Blind. Named one of Conn. Outstanding Women United Nations, 1987. Mem. Actors Equity, Screen Actors Guild, AFTRA. Home: Redding Conn. Died Aug., 1995.

MATHIAS, JAMES HERMAN, lawyer; b. N.Y.C., Nov. 12, 1913; s. J. Herman and Alma Rosenstein M.; m. Shirl Seeman, Aug. 2, 1975. B.A., Columbia, 1934, J.D., 1936. Bar: N.Y. State bar 1937. Since practiced in N.Y.C.; mem. firm Cahn & Mathias, 1950-80; individual practice law, 1980-94; asso. prosecutor Internat. Mil. Tribunal, Nuremberg, Ger., 1945. Served to capt., JAGC AUS, 1942-46. Mem. Soc. Strings Inc. (sec. 1955-94), Assn. Bar City N.Y., Confrerie des Chevaliers du Tastevin, Harmonie Club, Phi Beta Kappa. Home: Larchmont N.Y. Deceased.

MATHIAS, MILDRED ESTHER, botany educator; b. Sappington, Mo., Sept. 19, 1906; d. John Oliver and Julia Hannah (Fawcett) M.; m. Gerald L. Hassler, Aug. 30, 1930 (dec.); children: Frances, John, Julia, James (dec.). A.B., Washington U., 1926, M.S., 1927, Ph.D. in Systematic Botany, 1929. Asst. Mo. Bot. Garden, 1929-30; research assoc. N.Y. Bot. Garden, 1932-36, U. Calif., 1937-42; herbarium botanist UCLA, 1947-51, lectr. botany, 1951-55, from asst. prof. to prof., 1955-74, vice chmn. dept., 1955-62, dir. bot. garden, 1956-74, prof. emeritus, 1974—; asst. specialist UCLA Exptl. Sta., 1951-55, asst. plant systematist, 1955-57, assoc. plant systematist, 1957-62; pres. Orgn. Tropical Studies, 1968-70; sec. bd. trustees Inst. Ecology, 1975-77; exec. dir. Am. Assn. Bot. Gardens and Arboreta, 1977-81. Hon. trustee Mo. Botanical Garden, St. Louis, 1989-93. Recipient Medal of Honor Garden Club Am., 1982, Charles Laurence Hutchinson medal Chgo. Hort. Soc., 1988; Mildred E. Mathias Bot. Garden named in her honor, UCLA, 1979; B.Y. Morrison lectr. USDA, 1989. Fellow Calif. Acad. Scis.; mem. AAAS (pres. Pacific div. 1977) Am. Soc. Plant Taxonomy (pres. 1964), Bot. Soc. Am. (Merit award 1973, pres. 1984), Soc. Study of Evolution, Am. Soc. Naturalist, Am. Horticulture Soc.

(Sci. citation 1974, Liberty Hyde Bailey medal 1980). Home: Los Angeles Calif.

MATHIEU, THOMAS JOSEPH, urologist; b. Central Falls, R.I., Sept. 9, 1922; s. Napoleon Joseph and Mary Aurora (Girouard) M.; m. Colomba Rachel Simeone, Sept. 17, 1945; children: Thomas Joseph, Richard, John, Patricia. A.B., Brown U., 1944; M.D., Yale U., 1946. Diplomate Am. Bd. Urology. Intern, R.I. Hosp., Providence, 1946-47; resident Mary Hitchcock Hosp., Hanover, N.H., 1949-52, Mass. Gen. Hosp., Boston, 1952-54; urologist Yakima Urology Clinic, Wash., 1955-95. Served to lt. (j.g.) USN, 1946-49. Mem. AMA, Am. Urology Soc., Am. Assn. Clin. Urologists. Republican. Roman Catholic. Lodge: Rotary. Died Apr. 15, 1995. Home: Yakima Wash.

MATKIN, GEORGE GARRETT, retired banker; b. Ennis, Tex., Jan. 21, 1898; s. George Garrett and Clemens (Loggins) M.; m. Lucile Ross, June 22, 1929 (dec. Feb. 1976); children—Margaret (Mrs. George H. Jackson), Nancy Clemens (Mrs. Raymond Marshall). Student pub. schs., El Paso, Tex. With State Nat. Bank of El Paso (now Nat. Bank El Paso), 1917-87, pres., 1949-67, chmn. bd., 1967-81; sr. chmn. bd. State Nat. Bank of El Paso (now br. M Bank of Dallas), 1981-87; hon. dir. Mountain States Tel. & Tel. Co. Mem. El Paso C. of C. Clubs: Mason (32), El Paso Country, Internat, Coronado. Home: El Paso Tex. Deceased.

MATLOFF, MAURICE, government consultant, author, historian; b. Bklyn., June 18, 1915; s. Joseph and Ida (Glickhouse) M.; m. Gertrude Glickler, Oct. 21, 1942; children: Howard Bruce, Jeffrey Lewis, Jody Matloff Dove. B.A. (N.Y. State scholar 1932-36), Columbia Coll., 1936; M.A. (Harvard-Henry Ware Wales scholar), Harvard, 1937, Ph.D. (Edward Austin fellow, Francis Parkman fellow), 1956; postgrad., Yale, 1943-44. Instr. dept. history Bklyn. Coll., 1939-42, assoc. prof., 1946; sr. historian ops. div. War Dept. Gen. Staff, Washington, 1946-47; sr. historian Hist. div., Dept. Army, Washington, 1947-49; chief strategic plans sect. Office Chief of Mil. History Hist. div., Dept. Army, 1949-60, sr. hist. adviser Post World War II br., 1960-62, chief Current History br., 1962-66, chief Gen. History br., 1966-68, dep. chief historian, 1969-70, chief historian, 1970-73, chief historian U.S. Army Center Mil. History, 1973-81; lectr. U. Md., 1957-71; adj. prof. Am. U., 1965-68, Georgetown U., 1983-93; vis. prof. San Francisco State Coll., summer 1966, U. Calif., Davis, 1968-69, U. Md., 1981-82, Dartmouth Coll., spring 1977, U.S. Mil. Acad., 1982-83; disting. vis. prof. U. Ga., spring 1974; Regents prof. U. Calif., Berkeley, spring 1980; fellow Woodrow Wilson Internat. Center for Scholars, 1981-82; cons. govt. coms.; lectr. Nat. War Coll., Army, Navy and Air war colls., service acads., various univs.; mem. bd. historians U.S. Com. for The Battle of Normandy Mus., 1987-93, adv. coun. Nat. Hist. Intelligence Mus., 1986-93, adv. coun. George C. Marshall Rsch. Found., 1975-93. Author: Strategic Planning for Coalition Warfare, 1941-42, 1953, 1943-44, 1959; gen. editor: Am. Military History, 1969, rev., 1973; mem. adv. editorial bd.: The Public Historian jour, 1980-86; contbr. numerous articles to profl. jours. Served with AUS, USAAF, 1942-46. Sec. Army Study and Research fellow, 1959-60; Meritorious Civilian Service medal, 1965; Dept. Army Outstanding Performance awards, 1972, 74, 75, 76, 78; Dept. Army Exceptional Civilian Service medal, 1981; Dept. Army Outstanding Civilian Service medal, 1983. Mem. U.S. Commn. Mil. History (former trustee), Am. Hist. Assn. (historian, fed. govt. com. 1958-61, First Books program com. 1980-82), Soc. for Mil. History (mem. nominating com. 1970-72, trustee 1976-79), Orgn. Am. Historians, Soc. Historians Am. Fgn. Rels., World War II Studies Assn. (bd. dirs.), Inter-Univ. Seminar on Armed Forces and Soc., Phi Beta Kappa. Home: Rockville Md. Died July 14, 1993; buried King David Falls Ch., Va.

MATSUDA, KAZUHISA, business administration educator; b. Kobe, Japan, Oct. 1, 1924; s. Fusaji and Naoko Adachi; married; 2 children. BS, Kobe U., 1948, DBA, 1962, Hon. Prof. Degree, 1988. Prof. bus. adminstrn. Kobe U., 1963-82, dean, 1982-84; prof. bus. adminstrn. Kobe Gakuin U., 1988-95, dean of econ. faculty, 1991-94. Author: Measurement of Labor-Productivity, 1964, Theory of Labor-Productivity, 1980, Theory of Economic Calculation, 1986, Statistical Analysis of Demand and Supply of Dental Treatment Service in Japan, 1992. Home: Kobe Japan Died Jan. 17, 1995.

MATSUSHIMA, SATOSHI, astronomer, educator; b. Fukui, Japan, May 6, 1923; came to U.S., 1950, naturalized, 1963; s. Kyoyu and Hatsuye (Isaka) M.; m. Reiko Hori, Oct. 25, 1955; children: Peter Koichi, Anne Yuko. B.S., U. Kyoto, 1946; Ph.D., U. Utah, 1954; postgrad., Harvard, 1952-54; Sc.D., U. Tokyo, 1966. Asst. U. Kyoto, 1946-50; research asso. U. Pa., 1954-55; sr. research fellow Paris (France) Obs., 1956-57; research asso. U. Kiel, Germany, 1957-58; asst. prof. physics Fla. State U., 1958-60; assoc. prof. astronomy U. Iowa, 1960-67; prof. astronomy Pa. State U., University Park, 1967-89, prof. emeritus, 1989-92, head dept. astronomy, 1976-89; acting head dept. physics Pa. State U., 1981-82; vis. astronomer Utrecht Obs., Netherlands, 1956; sr. research fellow Calif. Inst. Tech., 1958-60; vis. prof. U. Tokyo, 1965-66, 74, Tohoku U., 1974, U. Kyoto, 1965; cons. U.S. Naval Research Lab., 1963; panel mem. Nat. Acad. Scis.-NRC, 1970-73. Contbr. articles to profl. jours. UNESCO-IAU grantee, 1956-58; German Humboldt Found. fellow, 1957-58; German Astron. Soc. grantee, 1957-58; Research Corp. grantee, 1958; U.S.-Japan Coop. Sci. program fellow, 1965-66; NSF research grantee, 1963-92. Fellow Royal Astron. Soc. Eng.; mem. Am. Astron. Soc., Am. Geophys. Union, Astron. Soc. Pacific, Internat. Astron. Union, Sigma Xi. Home: State College Pa. Died Jan. 31, 1992.

MAUDE, EDWARD JOSEPH, retired banker; b. Orange, N.J., Aug. 6, 1924; s. William L. and Katharine (Vickers) M.; m. Suzanne Norman Fleet, May 21, 1949 (div. 1971); children: Cynthia Vickers, William Lupton III; m. Ann Lang Balmos, 1972. Student, Va. Mil. Inst., 1942; A.B. in Econs., Princeton U., 1948. Asst. v.p. Chem. Bank N.Y. Trust Co., 1948-60; exec. v.p., trustee Community Savs. Bank, Rochester, N.Y., 1960-61; treas. Greenwich Savs. Bank, N.Y.C., 1962-64; pres. trustee Union Sq. Savs. Bank (merger, formed United Mut. Savs. Bank 1969), N.Y.C., 1965-74; chmn., chief exec. Union Sq. Savs. Bank (merger, formed United Mut. Savs. Bank 1969), 1974-82. Trustee Bloomfield (N.J.) Coll., 1975-79; trustee N.C. Downeast chpt. SCORE, 1988-93. Served with inf. AUS, 1942-45, ETO. Episcopalian. Clubs: Princeton, New York, New Bern Golf and Country. Home: New Bern N.C. Died Oct. 13, 1993.

MAUNG MAUNG, lawyer; b. Jan. 31, 1925. Law student, London and Netherlands. Past instr. Yale U.; former chief justice Supreme Ct., Burma, atty. gen., until 1988; pres. Burma, 1988. With Burmese Independence Army, World War II. Home: Rangoon Myanmar Died July 2, 1994.

MAURER, JOSE CLEMENTE CARDINAL, German ecclesiastic; b. Puttlingen, Trier, Mar. 13, 1900. Ordained priest Roman Cath. Ch., 1925. Titular Bishop of Cea, 1950-51; Archbishop of Sucre, Bolivia, 1951-83; elevated to Sacred Coll. of Cardinals, 1967; entitled SS. Redentore e S. Alfonso in via Merulana. Home: Sucre Bolivia

MAURER, LUCILLE DARVIN, state treasurer; b. N.Y.C., Nov. 21, 1922; d. Joseph Jay and Evelyn (Levine) Darvin; m. Ely Maurer, Apr. 29, 1945; children: Stephen Bennett, Russell Alexander, Edward Nestor. Student, U. N.C., Greensboro, 1938-40; BA, U. N.C., Chapel Hill, 1942; MA, Yale U., 1945; DH (hon.), Hood Coll., 1984; HLD (hon.), U. Coll., U. Md., 1990. Economist U.S. Tariff Commn., 1942-43; econ. and market research for pvt. firms, 1957-60; cons. Nat. Center for Ednl. Stats., 1969-70; mem. Md. House of Dels., 1969-87, mem. ways and means com., 1971-87, chmn. joint com. on fed. relations, 1983-87; state treas. State of Md., 1987-96; mem. intergovtl. adv. coun. U.S. Dept. Edn., 1980-82. Del., Md. Constl. Conv., 1967-68; mem. Montgomery County Bd. Edn., 1960-68; trustee Montgomery Community Coll., 1960-68; vice chmn. nat. planning com., advanced leadership program of seminars on edn. and ednl. policy for state legislators Edn. Commn. of States, 1979-81; mem. exec. com. of edn. com. Nat. Conf. of State Legislatures, 1975-84, chmn., 1978-79, chmn. com. on taxes, trade and econ. devel., 1985-86; mem. adv. com. Servicemems. Opportunity Colls., 1978-82; mem. nat. adv. bd. Inst. for Ednl. Leadership, 1979-81; mem. Nat. Com. on Postsecondary Accreditation, 1974-1979; bd. dirs. Montgomery United Way, 1971-76, 84-94; mem. Commn. Higher Edn. of Middle States Assn., 1982-85; mem. Gov.'s Employment and Tng. Coun., 1983-91. Recipient Legislator of Yr. award Md. Assn. for Retarded Children, 1972, John Dewey award Montgomery County Fedn. Tchrs., 1972, Hornbook award Montgomery County Edn. Assn., 1972, Legislator of Yr. award Md. Assn. Counties, 1984, Willis award for outstanding service Md. Assn. Bds. Edn., 1984, Louis B. Brandeis Justice in Govt. award Am. Jewish Congress, 1988, Judge Sarah T. Hughes award for disting. pub. svc. Goucher Coll., 1989, Disting. Pub. Svc. award Md. C. of C., 1989, Nat. Identification Program award Am. Coun. Edn., 1993; named Energy Warrior of Yr., Md. Energy Adminstrn., 1994; inductee Md. Women's Hall of Fame, 1990. Mem. LWV (past dir. Montgomery County, past dir. Md.), AAUW (Internat. Women's Yr. award Silver Spring 1975), NOW (Legis. Excellence award 1981), Bus. and Profl. Women's Club (Woman of Yr. 1984), Nat. Assn. State Treas. (v.p. 1989-90, chmn. legis. com. 1989-91, sr. v.p. 1991-92, pres. 1992-93, Jesse M. Unruh award 1994), Nat. Assn. State Auditors, Comptrs. and Treas. (exec. com. 1988-91, fed./state cash mgmt. reform task force 1988-92), Women Execs. State Govt. (bd. dirs. 1988-92), Women's Equity Action League, Women's Polit. Caucus, Montgomery County Hist. Soc., Order Women Legislators, Delta Kappa Gamma. Jewish. Home: Silver Spring Md. Died June 17, 1996.

MAURER, WESLEY HENRY, retired journalism educator, publisher; b. Bunker Hill, Ill., Jan. 18, 1897; s. Henry P. and Emilia Anna (Boechkler) M.; m. Flossie Wilson, Aug. 31, 1921 (div. May 1943); m. Margaret Elizabeth Weber, Feb. 26, 1944; children: Margaret E., Wesley H. Jr., Marilyn. AB in Bus. and Pub. Adminstrn., U. Mo., 1921, AB in Liberal Arts, 1922, BJ, 1923. News editor Evening Ledger, Mexico, Mo., 1922-24; corr. St. Louis Post Dispatch, Kansas City Sta other newspapers, 1922-24; city editor, editorial write editor Athens (Ohio) Messenger, 1925-28; editorial con various publs., 1938-95, editorial writer, since 1925; in str. Journalism U. Mich., 1924-25; asst. pro journalism, dir. journalism lab. Ohio U., 1925-28; inst U. Mich., 1928-32, asst. prof., 1932-42; acting chmn 1937-38, asso. prof. journalism, 1941-48, exec. sec. dep journalism, 1947, prof., 1948-95, prof. emeritus, chmn dept., 1949-66; mem. exec. com. Coll. Lit., Sci. an Arts, 1949-57, com. on deanship, 1951, mem. sena adv. com. on univ. affairs, 1958-61, chmn. senate adv com. on univ. affairs, 1961; pub. Town Crier, Mackina Island, Mich., 1959-95, Harbor Light, Harbor Spring Mich., 1964-70; editor, pub. St. Ignace (Mich) New 1975-95; univ. rep.; univ. visitor Eng., The Netherlands Germany, Switzerland, Austria, France, Italy, Rom Florence, Greece, Beirut, Egypt, Jerusalem, Vietnam Thailand, The Phillipines, Hong Kong, Korea, Japan Hawaii; pres. Assn. Accredited Sch. and Depts Journalism, 1953-54; pub. relations cons. Essex C Med.-Econ. Research, Windsor, Ont., Can., 1938; con Mainichi Newspapers, Tokyo and Osaka, Japan, 196 U.S. State Dept. specialist, lectr. Ctr. for Advance Studies in Journalism for Latin Am., Quito, Ecuado 1964. Author: series of 12 articles on report of com. o survey of med. service and health agys. for Detroit Fre Press; other Mich. newspapers; series of 3 articles f Canadian Press; sound film on Federal Aid to the Stat for Edn. for Am. Fedn. Tchrs, 1938; sound films O Town is a Neighborhood, for, Community Fund, Chi dren and Youth of Mich., for, Mich. Youth Comm and Mid-Century White House Conf. Organizer, chmn mem. exec. bd. Ann Arbor Citizens' Council; bd. dir Council Am. Affairs and World Events, Detroit, 193 74; lectr. Mott Found., Flint, 1942; asso. organiz Mich. Fedn. Tchrs.; pres., 1936-37, Wesleyan Found 1948. Recipient U. Mich. Distinguished Facult Achievement award, 1961, honor award for disting. sv in journalism U. Mo., 1990; named professor honor causa Universidad Argentina de Periodismo, 1964; in ducted to Mich. Journalism Hall of Fame for Ou standing Contbn. to Journalism, 1987. Mem. Am. So Newspaper Editors (distinguished achievement i journalism, life mem.), AAAS, Am. Assn. Tchr Journalism, AAUP, Am. Fedn. Tchrs. (past pres., sec. ACLU (mem. nat. com.), Jackson Fund for Civil Libe ties. Democrat. Unitarian. Home: Saint Ignace Mic Died June 23, 1995.

MAURO, JOHN BAPTIST, retired marketin researcher; b. St. Margherita Belice, Agrigento, Ital June 20, 1923; came to U.S., 1931; s. Ignazio and Luc (Morreale) M.; m. Dorothy T. Stix, July 19, 1945; chi dren—Janet Lucille, Diane Rose, John Henry, Celes Marie, Andrea Marie, Christopher James. B.S., NYU 1953. Research analyst World-Telegram & Su N.Y.C., 1946-53; research analyst This Week Ma N.Y.C., 1953-57; v.p. research Branham Co., N.Y.C 1957-68; dir. mktg. Family Weekly Mag., N.Y.C., 196 69; dir. research Tampa Tribune, Fla., 1969-73, Med Gen., Inc., Richmond, Va., 1973-86; vis. prof. U. Fla Gainesville, 1970-73; adj. prof. Va. Commonwealth U Richmond, 1979-82, Syracuse U., N.Y., 1981. Autho An Introduction to Boomerangs, 1983, 3d rev. edit 1989, Statistical Deception at Work, 1992; editor: New spaper Research Primer, 1972, 2d edit., 198 Alzheimer's Assoc. Newsletter, Richmond chpt., 198 94; co-editor: Directory of Newspaper Public Servic Programs, 1978, The Question Finder, 1988; creato Newsroom Guide to Polls and Surveys, 1980; contb articles to profl. jours. Bd. dirs. Catholic Virginia Richmond, 1975-79; mem. advt. and mktg. coms. Me Richmond Devel. Council, 1983-85. Served with USM 1943-45, PTO. Decorated D.F.C. Mem. Interna Newspaper Promotion Assn. (Sidney S. Goldish awar 1974, Silver Shovel award 1978, pres. 1976-77, trea 1980-81), Am. Newspaper Pubs. Assn. (news researc com. 1974-82, mktg. com. 1983-84), Newspape Readership Council (chmn. promotion com. 1976-77 Am. Mktg. Assn. (pres. Richmond chpt. 1975-76), V Press Assn. (chmn. promotion com. 1981), Richmond of C. (chmn. research com. 1981-82), U.S. Boomeran Assn. (treas. 1981-85, capt. U.S. team 1984, pres. 198 86). Home: Richmond Va. Died Dec. 11, 1994.

MAUTNER, HENRY GEORGE, chemist; b. Pragu Czechoslovakia, Mar. 30, 1925; came to U.S., 194 naturalized, 1946; s. Frank Thomas and Mar (Neumann) M.; m. Dorothea Johanna Barkemeyer, No 21, 1967; children—Monica Ann, Matthew Erich, A drea Christina. B.S., U. Calif. at Los Angeles, 194 M.S., U. So. Calif., 1950; Ph.D., U. Calif., Berkele 1955; M.A. (hon.), Yale U., 1967. Teaching asst. U Calif., 1951-55; rsch. chemist Productol Co., Santa F Springs, Calif., 1950; faculty Yale U., New Haven, 195 70; prof. dept. pharmacology Yale U., 1967-70, hea sect. medicinal chemistry, 1962-70; prof. biochemist and pharmacology Tufts U. Sch. Medicine, 1970-9 prof. emeritus, 1990-95, chmn. depts., 1970-85; vi scholar Dept. Fine Arts, Harvard U., Cambridge, Mas 1991-92, vis. fellow, 1992-95; vis. fellow dept. organ chemistry U. Uppsala, Sweden, 1962; vis. prof. b ochemistry Max Planck Inst. Biochemistry, Munic 1967-68; vis. prof. biochemistry Bio-Ctr., U. Bas Switzerland, 1985; mem. med. chemistry study se NIH, 1968-72, chmn., 1971-72; mem. neurobiolo panel NSF, 1977-80; vis. prof. biophys. chemistry

Bielefeld, Germany, 1987; mem. sci. adv. com. City of Cambridge; sci. chmn. Children's Sch. Sci., Woods Hole, Mass., 1991-94; mem. corp. Marine Biol. Lab., Woods Hole. Editorial bd. Jour. Med. Chemistry, 1967-70, 76-81; contbr. articles to profl. jours., chpts. to books. Mem. Am. Chem. Soc., Chem. Soc. (London), Am. Assn. Pharmacology, Am. Assn. Cancer Research, Biophys. Soc., Am. Soc. Biol. Chemists. Home: Newton Center Mass. Died April 7, 1995. Buried at Woods Hole, Mass.

MAVES, PAUL BENJAMIN, clergyman, gerontologist; b. Burwell, Nebr., Apr. 21, 1913; s. Benjamin C. and Ellen Alverda (Craun) M.; m. Mary Carolyn Hollman, Sept. 10, 1939; children: Margaret Alverda, David Hollman. A.B., Nebr. Wesleyan U., 1936; B.D., Drew U., 1939, Ph.D., 1949; postgrad, NYU, 1945-46, Harvard U., 1957-58. Ordained minister Meth. Ch., 1940. Pastor Albany, N.Y., 1940-42, Middlebury, Vt., 1942-45; instr. edn. NYU, 1945-46; rsch. assoc. dept. pastoral svcs. Fed. Coun. Chs., 1946-48, acting exec. sec. dept., 1948-49; mem. faculty Drew U., 1949-67, George T. Cobb prof. religious edn., 1956-67; assoc. exec dir., dept. of ednl. devel. Nat. Coun. Chs. of Christ, 1967-70; dir. field edn., prof. ch. adminstrn. St. Paul Sch. Theology, 1970-75; adminstr. Kingsley Manor, L.A., 1975-78; staff assoc. Shepherd's Ctrs. of Am., Kansas City, Mo., 1978-86, sr. cons., 1988-90; dir. Otterbein Gerontology Ctr., Lebanon, Ohio, 1986-88; mem. Nebr. Ann. Conf. Meth. Chs.; del. White House Conf. Aging, 1961; vis. scholar Columbia U., 1964-65; adj. prof. United Theol. Sem., Dayton, Ohio, 1986-91. Author: The Best is Yet to Be, 1951, Understanding Ourselves as Adults, 1959, On Becoming Yourself, 1962, (with J. Lennart Cedarleaf) Older People and the Church, 1949, (with Mary Carolyn Maves) Finding Your Way Through The Bible, 1970, Learning More About The Bible, Exploring How The Bible Came To Be, 1973, Discovering How The Bible Message Spread, 1974; editor: The Church and Mental Health, 1953, Older Volunteers in Church and Community, 1981, A Place to Live in Your Later Years, 1983, Faith for The Older Years, 1986. Home: Lebanon Ohio Died Sept. 15, 1994.

MAY, JOHN LAWRENCE, archbishop; b. Evanston, Ill., Mar. 31, 1922; s. Peter Michael and Catherine (Allare) M. M.A., St. Mary of Lake Sem., Mundelein, Ill., 1945, S.T.L., 1947. Ordained priest Roman Cath. Ch., 1947. Asst. pastor St. Gregory Ch., Chgo., 1947-56; chaplain Mercy Hosp., Chgo., 1956-59; v.p., gen. sec. Cath. Ch. Extension Soc. U.S., 1959-67, pres., from 1967; ord. titular bishop of Tagarbala and aux. bishop, Chgo., 1967-69; pastor Christ The King Parish, Chgo., 1968-69; bishop of Mobile, Ala., 1969-80, archbishop of St. Louis, 1980-94. Mem. Nat. Conf. Cath. Bishops (pres. 1986-94, past v.p.). Home: Saint Louis Mo. Died Mar. 24, 1994.

MAY, ROBERT A., lawyer; b. Grand Rapids, Mich., May 8, 1911; s. Adam F. and Myra Ethel (Shedden) M.; m. Margrethe Holm, Aug. 30, 1934 (dec. Dec. 1970); children: Marcia, Margrethe; m. Virginia L. Salisbury, Mar. 20, 1973. A.B., U. Mich., 1933, J.D., 1936. Bar: Mich. 1936, Ariz. 1941, U.S. Supreme Ct. 1960. Practised law Grand Rapids, 1936-41; practised law Tucson, 1941-86, ret.; sr. ptnr. Robert A. May, P.C. (and predecessors); mem. State Bar Ariz., vice chmn., 1952-53, chmn. group ins. com., 1953-72; co-founder, 1960, chmn. bd. trustees Client's Security Fund, 1961-81; mem. ABA standing com. Clients Security Fund, 1968-73; mem. com. on revision probate code Ariz. State Bar, 1970-72; Ariz. chmn. Joint Editorial Bd. for Uniform Probate Code, 1972-80; mem. com. on revision Ariz. probate code Ariz. Legis. Council, 1970-72; founding mem. Ariz. com. jud. selection, tenure, and discipline, 1957-72, chmn., 1957-67; co-founder So. Ariz. Estates Planning Council, 1956, pres., 1956-58; founder Pima County Bar Assn. Clients Referral Service; co-founder Def. Info. Office, Def. Research Inst. Bd. dirs. St. Luke's in the Desert, 1944-80, pres., 1964-77, pres. emeritus, 1977—, gen. counsel, 1944-82; bd. dirs. St. Luke's Chest Disease Clinic at U. Ariz. Med. Center; bd. dirs. Pima County Legal Aid Soc., 1952-77, emeritus, 1977—, pres., 1958-60; adv. bd. Tucson Med. Center, 1946-49; co-founder Tucson C. of C. Conv. Bur., 1945-74, exec. bd., 1957-67; regional chmn. U. Mich. Law Sch. Fund, 1963-66, mem. nat. com., 1967-72, now emeritus; vice chmn. so. Ariz. mil. base hosps. com. ARC, 1942-45; vice chmn. Citizens Adv. Com. for Pub. Schs., 1944-46; vis. com. U. Mich. Law Sch., 1964-67. Recipient Outstanding Service award Ariz. State Bar Assn., 1977. Fellow Am. Coll. Probate Counsel (bd. regents 1966-69, 73-77); mem. Nat. Coll. Probate Judges (life), Internat. Acad. Law and Sci., Tucson C. of C., Ariz. Pioneers Hist. Soc., ABA (vice chmn. health ins. com. 1958-70, chmn. 1970-72), Am. Bar Found. (life), Internat. Bar Assn., Mich. Bar Assn., Pima County Bar Assn. (pres. 1955-56), Fed. Bar Assn., Fund for Temple Bar (London), So. Ariz. Estate Planning Council (co-founder, pres. 1956), U. Mich. Alumni Assn. (dist. dir. 1943-46), Internat. Assn. Ins. Counsel, Am. Bar Inst., Tucson Council Chs. (mem. exec. bd., chmn. fin. com. 1948-64, pres. 1956-58), Ariz. Council Chs. (v.p. 1956-58), Internat. Acad. Law and Sci., Am. Judicature Soc. (nat. dir. 1963-67), Assn. Ins. Attys., Mich. Alumni Acad. (charter mem.), Phi Sigma Kappa Found., Phi Sigma Kappa (pres. Tucson Alumni Club 1960-74), Alpha Epsilon Mu (hon.). Episcopalian (parish chancellor 1943-78, chancellor emeritus 1978—, vestryman 1943-73, 74-77, rector's warden 1977-78, vice chancellor Ariz. diocese 1959-71). Clubs: Round Table Internat. (pres. 1944-46), Old Pueblo, U. Mich. Alumni (pres. Grand Rapids 1938-41, pres. Tucson 1945-50, 76-77, bd. govs. 1942-79, hon. gov. 1983—, U. Mich. Pres.'s (charter mem.); Inst. for Dirs., Wig and Pen (London). Home: Tucson Ariz.

MAY, ROLLO, psychoanalyst; b. Ada, Ohio, Apr. 21, 1909; s. Earl Tittle and Matie (Boughton) M.; m. Florence DeFrees, June 5, 1938 (div. 1968); children: Robert Rollo, Allegra Anne, Carolyn Jane; m. Ingrid Schöll, 1971 (div. 1978); m. Georgia Miller Johnson, 1988. AB, Oberlin Coll., 1930, HHD (hon.), 1980; BD cum laude, Union Theol. Sem., N.Y.C., 1938; PhD summa cum laude, Columbia U., 1949; DHL (hon.), U. Okla., 1970; LLD (hon.), Regis Coll., 1971; LHD (hon.), St. Vincent Coll., 1972, Mich. State U., 1976, Rockford Coll., 1977, Ohio No. U., 1978, Oberlin Coll., 1980, Sacred Heart U., 1982, Calif. Sch. Profl. Psychology, 1983, Rivera Coll., 1986, Gonzaga U., 1986, Saybrook Inst., 1987; 5 other hon. degrees. Tchr. Am. Coll., Saloniki, Greece, 1930-33; student adviser Mich. State Coll., 1934-36; student counselor CCNY, 1943-44; mem. faculty William Alanson White Inst. Psychiatry, Psychology and Psychoanalysis, 1958-75; lectr. New Sch. Social Research, N.Y.C., 1955-76; tng. fellow supervisory analyst Williams Alanson White Inst. Psychiatry, 1958-94; co-chmn. Conf. on Psychotherapy and Counseling, N.Y. Acad. Scis., 1953-54; vis. prof. Harvard U., summer 1964, Princeton U., 1967, Yale U., 1972; Dean's scholar N.Y. U., 1971; Regents' prof. U. Calif., Santa Cruz, 1973; disting. vis. prof. Bklyn. Coll., 1974-75. Author: Art of Counseling, 1939, Meaning of Anxiety, 1950, rev. edit., 1977, Man's Search for Himself, 1953, Psychology and the Human Dilemma, 1966, Existence: A New Dimension in Psychiatry and Psychology, 1958, Love and Will, 1969, Power and Innocence, 1972, Paulus-Reminiscences of a Friendship, 1973, The Courage to Create, 1975, Freedom and Destiny, 1981, The Discovery of Being, 1983; Editor: Existence: A New Dimension in Psychiatry and Psychology, 1958, Existential Psychology, 2d edit, 1961, Symbolism in Religion and Literature, 1960, My Quest for Beauty, 1985. Trustee Am. Found. Mental Health; bd. dirs. Soc. Arts, Religion and Culture. Recipient award for disting. contbn. to profession and sci. of psychology N.Y. Soc. Clin. Psychology, 1955; Ralph Waldo Emerson award for Love and Will Phi Beta Kappa, 1970; Disting. Contbns. award N.Y. U., 1971; Centennial Medallion St. Peter's Coll., 1972; ann. citation Merrill-Palmer Inst., Detroit, 1973; spl. Dr. Martin Luther King, Jr. award N.Y. Soc. Clin. Psychologists, 1974; Disting. Grad. award Columbia U. Tchrs. Coll., 1975; fellow Branford Coll. Yale U., 1960-94; Whole Life Humanitarian award Whole Life Expn., 1986. Fellow Am. Psychol. Assn. (award for disting. contbn. to sci. and profession of clin. psychology 1971, Gold medal for Disting. Career 1987), Nat. Council Religion Higher Edn., William Alanson White Psychoanalytic Soc. (past pres.); mem. N.Y. State Psychol. Assn. (past pres.). Home: Tiburon Calif. Died Oct. 21, 1994.

MAYER, EUGENE STEPHEN, physician, university administrator; b. Norwalk, Conn., June 5, 1938; s. Eugene O. and Elizabeth B. (Wargo) M.; dau., Erica Lane. B.S., Tufts Coll., 1960; M.D., Columbia U., 1964; M.P.H., Yale U., 1971. Intern Columbia-Presbyn. Hosp., N.Y.C., 1964-65; staff physician Peace Corps, Washington, Turkey, 1965-68; resident in preventive medicine Yale-New Haven Med. Center, 1968-71; mem. faculty dept. family medicine and medicine U. N.C. Sch. Medicine, Chapel Hill, 1971-94; prof. U. N.C. Sch. Medicine, 1976-94; dir. N.C. Area Health Edn. Center Program, 1978-94, asso. dean, 1978-94. Contbr. articles to med. jours. Served with USPHS, 1965-68. Mem. Assn. Am. Med. Colls., AMA, Durham-Orange County Med. Soc., N.C. Med. Soc., N.C. Inst. Medicine, Am. Coll. Preventive Medicine, Phi Beta Kappa. Home: Chapel Hill N.C. Died Nov. 2, 1994.

MAYER, FREDERICK MILLER, retired business executive; b. Youngstown, Ohio, Oct. 8, 1898; s. Rev. Frederick and Carrie Ann (Miller) M.; m. Mildred Katherine Rickard, Nov. 25, 1926 (dec.); children: Frederick Rickard, Elizabeth Ann (Mrs. Boeckman). B.A., Heidelberg Coll., Tiffin, Ohio, 1920, LL.D., 1948; J.D., Harvard U., 1924. Bar: Ohio 1924. Practice in Akron, 1924-26, Youngstown, 1926-32; treas. Continental Supply Co., Dallas, 1932-33; v.p. Continental Supply Co., 1933-45, dir., 1933-55, pres., 1945-56; pres. Continental-Emsco Co. div. Youngstown Sheet and Tube Co., 1957-64; v.p. Youngstown Sheet and Tube Co., 1956-64, mem. exec. com., 1964-69, dir., 1958-69; pres., dir. Continental-Emsco Co., Ltd., Continental-Emsco Co. Compania Anonima, Venezuela, 1956-64, Continental-Emsco Co. de Mexico S.A. de C.V., 1962-64; pres. Fibercast Co. div. Youngstown Sheet and Tube Co., 1960-64; chmn. Continental-Emsco Co. (Gt. Britain), Ltd., Eng., 1957-64; mem. Nat. Petroleum Council, 1961-62; industry advisor U.S. Dept. Commerce. Co-chmn. war fin. com. State of Tex., 1942-46; trustee Dallas Found. for Arts, Heidelberg Coll.; past mem. Dallas Transit Bd., Dallas Park Bd.; hon. trustee Dallas Mus. Fine Art, pres., 1959-61, chmn. bd., 1966-68. With U.S. Army, 1918, WWI. Mem. Am. Petroleum Inst. (past dir.), Mid-Continent Oil and Gas Assn., Petroleum Equipment Suppliers Assn. (hon. dir., past pres.), Ind. Petroleum Assn., Acacia, Huguenot Soc. Ohio, SAR, Brook Hollow Club, Dallas Petroleum Club, Dallas Hunting and Fishing Club, Pi Kappa Delta. Republican. Congregationalist. Home: Dallas Tex. Died Apr. 1, 1993.

MAYER, HAROLD M(ELVIN), geographer, urban planner, educator; b. N.Y.C., Mar. 27, 1916; s. Alexander and Rose (Kreiss) M.; m. Florence Schulson, Mar. 23, 1952; children: Jonathan D., Judith H. BS, Northwestern U., 1936; MS, Washington U., St. Louis, 1937; PhD, U. Chgo., 1943. Zoning specialist Chgo. Land Use Survey, 1939-40; rsch. planner Chgo. Plan Commn., 1940-42, dir. rsch., 1948-50; geographer U.S. Office Strategic Svcs., Washington, 1943-44; chief div. planning analysis Phila. City Planning Commn., 1944-48; asst. prof. to prof. U. Chgo., 1950-68; prof. Kent (Ohio) State U., 1968-74; prof. geography U. Wis., Milw., 1974-94; cons. 1941-94; mem. Chgo. Regional Port Dist. Bd., 1951-53; commr., chmn. transp. com. Northeastern Ill. Planning Commn., Chgo., 1965-68; chmn. port subcommittee Maritime Transp. Rsch. Bd., Washington, 1968-74; v.p. Milw. Bd. Harbor Commrs., 1977-88. Author: The Port of Chicago and the St. Lawrence Seaway, 1957, The Spatial Expression of Urban Growth, 1968, Fifty Years of Professional Geography, 1990, (with others) Chicago, Growth of a Metropolis, 1959, Land Uses in American Cities, 1983; co-editor: Readings in Urban Geography, 1959. Recipient best article award Nat. Coun. Geog. Edn., 1969, teaching award, 1982, book award Geog. Soc. Chgo., 1970. Mem. Am. Inst. Cert. Planners, Assn. Am. Geographers (councillor 1964-67, Anderson medal for applied geography, 1991, Ullman award for transp. 1991), Am. Planning Assn. (past pres. West Lakes), Transp. Rsch. Forum. Died July 23, 1994.

MAYER, J. GERALD, lawyer, business executive; b. N.Y.C., May 2, 1908; s. Charles A. and Lillian P. (Morgan) M.; m. Marian Louese Swayze, July 25, 1931 (dec. 1982); 1 son, Timothy Swayze (dec. 1988); m. Marie Doris Ames, Jan. 1, 1985. Student, Cornell U., 1924-26; BS, George Washington U., 1928; LLB, St. Lawrence U., Canton, N.Y., 1931; LLD (hon.), Hartwick Coll., Oneonta, N.Y., 1962. Bar: N.Y. 1933, D.C. 1950. Engr. Western Electric Co., 1928-33; pvt. practice Schenectady, 1933-41; spl. corp. counsel City of Schenectady, 1937-40; sr. ptnr. Mayer, Kline, Rigby, Washington, 1945; v.p., dir., then exec. v.p. Gen. Instrument Corp., Newark, 1954-63; pres. Colonial (Radio) Network, Inc., Cortland, N.Y., 1947-50; pres., dir. Radio Receptor Corp., 1958-61, Harris Transducer Corp., 1959-63; chmn. Radio Norwich, Inc., N.Y., 1956-81, Gladding Corp., Boston, 1963-84; editor, pub. Cortland Tribune, 1948-50. Served with AUS, 1942-45. Mem. Am., D.C., Fed., N.Y. State bar assns., Adminstrv. Law Assn. Clubs: Kenwood Country; Nat. Press (Washington). Home: Naples Fla. Died Jan. 8, 1994; interred Mosswood Cemetery, Coutit, Mass.

MAYER, JEAN, university chancellor; b. Paris, Feb. 19, 1920; s. André and Jeanne Eugenie (Veille) M.; m. Elizabeth Van Huysen, Mar. 16, 1942; children: André, Laura, John Paul, Theodore, Pierre. BLitt summa cum laude, U. Paris, 1937, BS magna cum laude, 1938, MS, 1939; PhD in Physiol. Chemistry (Rockefeller Found. fellow), Yale U., 1948; Dr. ès Sc. in Physiology summa cum laude, Sorbonne, 1950; hon. degrees; AM, Harvard U., 1965; MD, J.E. Purkyne Coll. Medicine, Prague, Czechoslovakia, 1968; SD, Wittenberg U., 1975; DSc, Mass. State Coll. at Framingham, 1976; DS, Worcester Poly. Inst., 1977, Ball State U., 1981, Med. Coll. Pa., 1982, U. Medicine and Dentistry N.J., 1983, Tokai U., Tokyo, 1985; U. Mass., Amherst; LHD, Northeastern U., 1976, U. Lowell, 1988, Worcester Poly. Inst., 1977, Western New Eng. Coll., 1977, Starr King Sch. for Ministry, 1977, Webster U., 1992; LLD, Curry Coll., 1978; JD, N.E. Sch. Law, 1989; DMus, New Eng. Conservatory, 1990; D honoris causa, Mendeleev Inst. Chem. Tech., Moscow, 1991; DSc (hon.), U. Cape Town, South Africa, 1991; Dr. Pub. Svc. (hon.), U. Health Sci./Chgo. Med. Sch., 1991; DSc, U. Mass., 1992. Fellow Ecole Normale Superieure, Paris, 1939-40, Rockefeller Found. Yale U., New Haven, 1946-48; nutrition officer FAO, UN, 1948-49; from asst. prof. to prof. nutrition Harvard U., 1950-76, lectr. history pub. health, 1961-76; mem. Center for Population Studies, 1968-72, 75-77, co-dir., 1975-76; master Dudley House, 1973-76, hon. master, 1976-93; pres. Tufts U., Medford, Mass., 1976-92, chancellor, 1992-93; Spl. cons. to Pres. U.S., 1969-70; chmn. White House Conf. on Food, Nutrition and Health, 1969; chmn. nutrition div. White House Conf. on Aging, 1971-93; mem. Pres.'s Consumer Adv. Council, 1970-77; mem., vice chmn. President's Commn. on World Food Problems, 1978-80; gen. coordinator U.S. Senate Nat. Nutrition Policy Study, 1974; mem. FAO-WHO Adv. Mission to Ghana, 1959, to Ivory Coast and West Africa, 1960; mem. UNICEF mission to, Nigeria-Biafra, 1969, FAO-WHO Joint Expert Com. on Nutrition, 1961-93; mem. protein adv. group UN, 1973-75; dir. Priorities on Child Nutrition UNICEF, 1973-75; bd. dirs. Monsanto Co., 1970-88, Nat. Intergroup, 1980-90, Sta. WGBH, 1976-93, Lycée Français N.Y.C., 1984-88, Oppenheimer Fin. Corp., 1987-93. Nat. Steel. Adv. bd. Sargent Coll. Boston U., 1955-72; mem. subcom. on med. services U.S. Olympic Com., 1966-70; mem. child health adv. com. Hood

Found., 1964-69, chmn., 1968-69; mem. bd. inquiry on hunger in U.S., Citizens' Crusade against Poverty, 1967; chmn. Nat. Council on Hunger and Malnutrition in U.S., 1968-69; mem. food and nutrition bd. Nat. Acad. Scis., 1973-76. Author: Overweight: Causes, Cost, Control, 1968, Human Nutrition, 1972, A Diet for Living, 1975, Food and Nutrition in Health and Disease, 1977, (with J. Goldberg) Diet and Nutrition Guide, 1990; Editor: (with others) Food and Nutrition in Health and Disease, 1972, U.S. Nutrition Policies in the Seventies, 1973, (with W. Aykroyd) Nutrition Terminology, 1973, Health, 1974, World Nutrition: A U.S. View, 1978, Food and Nutrition in a Changing World (with J. Dwyer), 1979, (with J. Goldberg) Dr. Mayer's Diet and Nutrition Guide, 199, 0also numerous sci. articles.; Asso. editor: Nutrition Revs, 1951-54; nutrition editor: Postgrad. Medicine, 1959-71; editorial bd.: Jour. Applied Physiology, 1960-65, Family Health, 1969-93, Postgrad. Medicine, 1976-84; cons. editor: Environ. Research, 1967-93 , Jour. Nutrition Edn, 1968-70, Geriatrics Digest, 1968-93; syndicated columnist. Bd. dirs. Action for Boston Community Devel., 1964-70; bd. dirs. Am. Kor-Asian Found., 1976-83, French-Am. Found., 1976-83, World Affairs Coun., 1976-86; bd. overseers Shady Hill Sch., Cambridge, Mass., 1965-68; mem. New Eng. Bd. Higher Edn., 1978-93. Capt. French Army, 1940-45. Decorated Croix de Guerre with two palms, Gold Star and Bronze Star, knight Legion of Honor, Resistance medal, Commdr. de l'Ordre de Merite, Luxembourg, 1989, numerous others; recipient Gold medal City of Paris, 1936, Calvert Smith prize Harvard Alumni Assn., 1961, Alvarenga prize Coll. Physicians Phila., 1968, Atwater prize Agrl. Research Adminstrn., 1971; Presdl. citation AAHPER, 1972; Bradford Washburn prize Boston Mus. Sci., 1975; Golden Door award Internat. Inst., 1975; Poiley Gold medal N.Y. Acad. Sci., 1975; Pub. Edn. award Greater Boston chpt. Am. Heart Assn., 1976; gold medal Franklin Inst., 1978; Lemuel Shattuck medal Mass. Public Health Assn., 1980; numerous lectureships including 1st Charles Francis Adams lectr. Tufts U., 1983, 15th McDougall Meml. lectr. FAO, UN, 1987, Carl Perkins Meml. lectr., D.C., 1989, Lowell lectr. Harvard U., 1989. Fellow Am. Acad. Arts and Scis. (coun. 1970-73), AAAS; fgn. mem. French Acad. Scis., French Acad. Medicine; mem. Am. Inst. Nutrition (coun. 1972-75), Am. Physiol. Soc. (editorial bd. 1960-66), Soc. for Nutrition Edn. (pres. 1974-75), Am. Soc. for Clin. Nutrition, Am. Pub. Health Assn. (chmn. food and nutrition sect. 1972-73), Phi Beta Kappa, Sigma Xi, Beta Beta Beta, Delta Omega. Unitarian (chmn. bd. trustees 1st parish, Sudbury, Mass., moderator 1959-66, vestryman 1970-74, sr. warden King's Chapel, Boston 1974-83). Clubs: Harvard (Boston), Somerset (Boston); Annisquam Yacht (Gloucester, Mass.); University (N.Y.C.). Home: Boston Mass. Died Jan. 1, 1993.

MAYER, STEPHEN S., lawyer; b. N.Y.C., May 11, 1952. BA magna cum laude, Hobart Coll., 1974; JD, U. Chgo., 1977. Bar: N.J. 1977, Mich. 1978. Law clerk to Hon. Charles L. Levin Mich. Supreme Ct., 1977-78; mem. Grotta, Glassman & Hoffman, Roseland, N.J. Mem. Phi Beta Kappa. Home: Roseland N.J. Died Dec. 18, 1992.

MAYES, HERBERT RAYMOND, editor, publisher; b. N.Y.C., Aug. 11, 1900; s. Herman and Matilda (Hutter) M.; m. Grace Taub, Dec. 6, 1930; children: Victoria, Alexandra. Editor The Inland Merchant, mag., 1920-24; editor bus. paper div. Western Newspaper Union, 1924-26; editor Am. Druggist, mag., 1926-34, Pictorial Rev., 1934-37; mng. editor Good Housekeeping, 1937-38, editor, 1938-58; editor McCall's, 1959-62; pres. McCall Corp., 1961-65; cons. Norton Simon, Inc., from 1966. Author: Alger, A Biography Without a Hero, 1928, Editor's Choice, 1956, An Editor's Treasury, 1968, The Magazine Maze: A Prejudiced Perspective, 1980. Recipient Editor of Year award Mag. Editors Council, 1960, Distinguished Achievement award in field of periodicals U. So. Calif., 1960, N.Y. Art Dirs. Club medal, 1960, also others; inducted into Pub. Hall of Fame, 1984. Clubs: Book Table, Illustrators Soc, Dutch Treat. Home: New York N.Y. Deceased.

MAYHALL, DOROTHY ANN, museum director, curator of art, sculptor; b. Portland, Oreg., May 31, 1925; d. Nelles Harvey and Dorothy (Gray Orton) M. BFA, U. Iowa, 1950, MFA, MA in Art History, 1952; Diplome Doctorat, Ecole Des Beaux-Arts, Paris, 1953. Exec. dir. jr. coun. Mus. Modern Art, N.Y.C., 1961-65; dir. The Aldrich Mus., Ridgefield, Conn., 1965-71, 79-83, Storm King Art Ctr., Mountainville, N.Y., 1971-75, The Nave Mus., Victoria, Tex., 1976-78; dir. of art The Stamford (Conn.) Mus. and Nature Ctr., 1984-95. Bd. mem. Stamford (COnn.) Arts Coun., 1984-90, Pub. Art Commn., Stamford, 1986-91; chmn. Mayor's Art Gallery, Stamford, 1986-91; mem. art adv. com. Norwalk Community Coll. 1st lt. WAC, 1952-56. Recipient Fulbright scholar Inst. Internat. Edn., Paris, 1952-53. Home: Stamford Conn. Died May 6, 1995.

MAYNARD, ROBERT CLYVE, newspaper editor, publisher, journalist; b. Bklyn., June 17, 1937; s. Samuel Christopher and Robertine Isola (Greaves) M.; m. Nancy Hicks, Jan. 1, 1975; children: Dori J., David H., Alex C. Student, Harvard U., 1966; D.H.L. (hon.), York Coll., 1984, Valparaiso U., 1990, Rockford Coll., 1991; D.F.A. (hon.), Calif. Coll. Arts and Crafts, 1985; D.L. (hon.), Grand View Coll., 1988, Colby Coll., 1991; D.L.L. (hon.), Dominican Coll., San Rafael, Calif., 1991. Reporter Afro-Am. News, Balt., 1956, York (Pa.) Gazette and Daily, 1961-67; reporter Washington Post, 1967-72, assoc. editor/ombudsman, 1972-74, editorial writer, 1974-77; founder, chmn. Inst. for Journalism Edn., 1977-79; editor, pub. Oakland (Calif.) Tribune, 1979-93, owner, 1983-93; syndicated columnist Universal Press Syndicate; commentator TV program This Week with David Brinkley, ABC News; commentator, essayist MacNeil/Lehrer NewsHour; bd. dirs. AP, Pulitzer Prizes. Bd. dirs. Urban Strategies Coun., Mills. Coll.; nat. bd. govs. Media and Society Seminars; trustee Rockefeller Found., Found. Am. Communications; mem. Coll. Prep. Sch. Bd., Oakland, Bethlehem Luth. Ch., West Oakland, Calif.; adv. bd. Grad. Sch. Bus., Stanford U. Nieman fellow Harvard U., 1966. Mem. Council on Fgn. Relations, U.S. Supreme Ct. Hist. Soc., Sigma Delta Chi. Club: Commonwealth (bd. govs.). Home: Oakland Calif. Died Aug. 17, 1993.

MAYS, GERALD AVERY (JERRY MAYS), engineering executive, consultant; b. Dallas, Nov. 24, 1939; s. Avery and Blanche (Ponder) M.; m. Shirley Ann Pike; children: Gerald Avery, Sandra Jo, Sherrie Lynn, Sarah Elisabeth; stepchildren: Donald K. Turner, Bruce R. Turner, Barry K. Turner. B.S. in Civil Engring., So. Methodist U., 1962, postgrad., 1962-63. Registered profl. engr., Tex., Kans., Mo. Laborer, engr. Avery Mays Constrn. Co., Dallas, 1950-63; v.p. Avery Mays Constrn. Co., 1967-71, pres., 1971-84; pres. George A. Fuller Co. of Tex., 1984-87, The Mays Cos., 1987-94; owner Gerald A. Mays, P.E., cons. engrs., 1988-94; football player Kansas City Chiefs, 1961-70; engr. Howard, Needles, Tammen & Bergendoff (cons. engrs.), 1964-67; partner Mays, Flowers, Grady & Burruss Ins.; pres. GAMCO Constructors, Inc., 1972-82. Campaign chmn. Greater Dallas March Dimes, 1973; mem. Dallas Community Relations Bd.; Adv. bd. Dallas Opportunities Industrialization Com., 1972; bd. dirs. Kansas City chpt. ARC, 1969-70, pres. Heart of Am. chpt., 1973; bd. dirs. Baker U., 1970-73; exec. com. Met. Dallas YMCA; chmn. Met. Y Sustaining Fund Campaign, 1976; exec. com. Goodwill Industries Dallas, Goals for Dallas. Recipient football awards All Am. Football League, 1962, 64-68; All Am. Football Conf., 1970; named to All-time Am. Football League Team, All-Time Kansas City Chief Team, Kansas City Chief Hall of Fame, , Young Engr. of Month Kansas City, 1970, Alpha Tau Omega Man of Year, 1970, capt. Kansas City Chiefs, 1963-70. Mem. Salesmanship Club Dallas, Young Pres.'s Orgn., Dallas C. of C., Sigma Tau, Chi Epsilon, Alpha Tau Omega. Home: Highland Village Tex. Died July 17, 1994.

MCAFEE, HORACE J., lawyer; b. Heflin, La., July 17, 1905; s. J. U. and Annie (Reeves) McA.; A.B., So. Meth. U., 1926; J.D., Columbia U., 1931; m. Kathryn Gage, July 6, 1931 (dec. Nov. 1972); children: Mary Ann McAfee Baxter, William Gage, Stuart Reeves; m. 2d, Jane Harrison Shaffer, Aug. 17, 1974 (dec. Mar. 1980); m. 3d, Christine Parker Wright, July 18, 1981. Admitted to N.Y. bar, 1932; with Simpson Thacher & Barlett, attys., N.Y.C., from 1931, ptnr. firm, 1944-54, sr. ptnr., 1954-75; Mem. Irvington Bd. Zoning Appeals, 1951-89, chmn., 1955-89; trustee, sec. Irvington Public Library, 1948-61, pres., 1961-62; dir. St. Faith's House Found., from 1980. Mem. Assn. Bar City N.Y., Am. Bar Assn., N.Y. County Lawyers Assn., Am. Judicature Soc. Republican. Episcopalian. Clubs: Ardsley Curling, Ardsley Country (Ardsley-on-Hudson, N.Y.); Camp Fire Am., Church (N.Y.C.). Deceased. Home: Irvington on Hudson N.Y.

MC AFEE, JERRY, retired oil company executive, chemical engineer; b. Port Arthur, Tex., Nov. 3, 1916; s. Almer McD. and Marguerite (Calfee) McA.; m. Geraldine Smith, June 21, 1940; children: Joe R., William M., Loretta M., Thomas R. B.S. in Chem Engring, U. Tex. at Austin, 1937; Sc.D. in Chem. Engring, Mass. Inst. Tech., 1940; student, Mgmt. Problems for Execs., U. Pitts., 1952. Research chem. engr., rsch. engr. Universal Oil Products Co., Chgo., 1940-43, operating engr., 1944-45; tech. specialist Gulf Oil Corp., Port Arthur, Tex., 1945-50; successively dir. chemistry, asst. dir. research, v.p., asso. dir. research subs., Gulf Research & Devel. Co. Hamarville, Pa., 1950-55; v.p. engring. mfg. dept. of corp. Gulf Oil Corp., 1955-60, v.p., exec. tech. advisor of corp., 1960-64, also dir. planning and econs., 1962-64, sr. v.p., 1964-67, chmn. bd., chief exec. officer, 1976-81; sr. v.p. Gulf Eastern Co., London, 1964-67; exec. v.p. Brit. Am. Oil Co., Ltd., Toronto, Ont., 1967-69; pres., chief exec. officer, dir. Gulf Oil Can. Ltd., 1969-75. Bd. dirs. Am. Petroleum Inst., MIT; mem. exec. com. Allegheny Conf. Community Devel. Fellow Am. Inst. Chem. Engrs. (v.p. 1959, pres. 1960); Mem. Nat. Acad. Engring., Am. Petroleum Inst., Am. Chem. Soc. Presbyterian. Clubs: Duquesne (Pitts.); Fox Chapel Golf; Rolling Rock (Ligonier, Pa.); John's Island, Bent Pine Golf (Vero Beach, Fla.). Home: Vero Beach Fla. Died Oct. 14, 1995; interred John's Island, Vero Beach, Fla.

MC ALLISTER, DONALD, publisher; b. Ithaca, N.Y., July 12, 1902; s. Peter Francis and Margaret (O'Shea) McA.; m. Betty L. Myers, June 30, 1947; children: Donald, Liane Elisabeth. A.B., Cornell U., 1922. With Geyer-McAllister Publs., Inc. (pubs. bus. mags.), N.Y.C., 1922-93; gen. mgr. Geyer-McAllister Publs Inc. (pubs. bus. mags.), 1946-59, pres., 1959-63, chm bd., 1963-93; chmn. bd., chief exec. officer Geye McAllister Internat., Inc.; adv. com. Am. Bus. Press Served with USAAF, 1942-45. Mem. Adminstr Mgmt. Soc., Am. Mgmt. Soc., AIM, Assn. Paid Circ lation Publs. (dir.), Asso. Bus. Publs. (chmn. bd. 195 57); hon. mem., dir. Gift and Decorative Accessori Assn. Am.; hon. mem. Nat. Office Products Assn. Clubs: University (N.Y.C.); Creek (Locust Valle N.Y.); Seawanhaka Corinthian Yacht (Oyster Ba N.Y.). Home: New York N.Y. Died July 22, 1993.

MCANALLY, DON, editor, publisher; b. Sewell, N.J Oct. 27, 1913; s. James C. and Ina (MacLeod) McA Grad. high sch.; m. Edith P. McKinney, Dec. 11, 193 1 child, Shirley M. English. Reporter Woodbury (N.J Daily Times, 1932-45; editor Owens-Ill. Co. publs. N.J. and Ohio, 1945-47; asst. advt. mgr. Libbey-Owen Ford Glass Co., also sales and mgmt. depts. LOF Glas Fibers Co., Toledo, 1947-59; editor Pacific Oil Markete L.A., 1960-66; editor-publisher O&A Marketing New La Canada, Calif., 1966—, The Automotive Booster Calif., 1974—, Calif. Sr. Citizen News, La Canad 1977-84, Calif., Calif. Businesswoman, 1978. Recipie Good Neighbor award Toledo, 1948, award Western O Industry, 1971, Man of Yr. award Pacific Oil Conf 1977, Diamond Pin award Pacific Oil Conf., 198 awards Mobil Dealer Conv., 1968, Douglas Oil Co 1978, Automotive Affiliated Reps., 1979, So. Calif. P troleum Industry Golf and Tennis Tournament, 198 Intermountain Oil Marketers Assn., 1985, Silver Car award Pacific Automotive Show, 1988, Dime-On P Award, 1990 (autobiography) Kisses, Dime-On Pin Twins, Celebrities, and Humor Are My Life, 1990; Mem. Calif. Ind. Oil Marketers Assn., Am. Petroleu Inst. (L.A. basin chpt.), Automotive Hall of Fame (v., So. Calif. chpt. 1984), Nat. Aeronautic Assn., OX Aviation Pioneers, Nat. Speakers Assn., Interna Platform Assn., Petroleum Writers of Am., Lion Masquers Club, Gabby Club, Silver Dollar Clu Roorag Club (L.A.), Greater L.A. Press Club. Hom La Canada Flintridge Calif.

MCBAY, HENRY RANSOM CECIL, chemist, ed cator; b. Mexia, Tex., May 29, 1914; s. William Cec and Roberta (Ransom) McB.; (div. Apr. 1968); childre Michael H.C., Ronald P.W. BS in Chemistry, Wil Coll., 1934; MS in Chemistry, Atlanta U., 1936; PhD Chemistry, U. Chgo., 1945. Prof. Morehouse Coll Atlanta, 1980-87; Fuller E. Callaway prof. chemist Atlanta U., 1982-86, emeritus prof. chemistry, 1986-9 vis. lectr. Howard U., 1973, Dept. Chemistry, U. Md 1974, Dept. Chemistry, U. Atlanta, 1974, Southern U 1976, Washington U., 1979, U. Ala., 1987, The Al A&M U., 1987; invited lectr. Wesleyan U., Middletow Conn., 1993. Contbr. numerous articles to profl. jours Recipient Elizabeth Norten prize for Excellence in Rsc in Chemistry, The U. Chgo., 1944, 45, Outstandin Tchr. award Nat. Orgn. for Advancement Blac Chemists and Engrs., 1976, The Charles H. Herty awar for Outstanding Contbns. to Chemistry from Ga. sec Am. Chem. Soc., 1976, James Flack Norris award fo Outstanding Achievement in Teaching of Chemistr Northeastern Sect. Am. Chem. Soc., 1978, Kimuel A Huggins award in Sci., Bishop Coll., 1980, Beta Kapp Chi Sci. Soc. Lamplighter award. Mem. Am. Chem Soc., Am. Inst. Chemists, Ga. Acad. Sci., Nat. Inst. Sci Home: Atlanta Ga. Died June 23, 1995.

MCCABE, ROBERT ALBERT, wildlife ecology edu cator; b. Milw., Jan. 11, 1914; s. Frank and Matild (Guetlich) McC.; m. Marie Elinor Stanfield, July 1941; children: Colleen, Richard, Thomas, Kevin. BA Carroll Coll., 1939; MA, U. Wis., 1943, PhD, 194 LLD (hon.), Nat. U. Ireland, 1988; DHL (hon.), Carro Coll., Waukesha, Wis., 1989. Arboretum biologist U Wis., Madison, 1943-45, from instr. to full prof. wildli ecology, 1943-84, prof. emeritus, 1984-95, chmn. dept 1952-69; cons. Office Pub. Works, Dublin, Irelan 1970-87; mem. rsch. adv. commn. Wis. Dept. Natur Resources, Madison, 1952-86. Author: Aldo Leopol The Professor, 1987, The Little Green Bird, 1991. Se Wis. Expo. Dept. Bd., West Allis, 1960-66, Wis. Dep Resource Devel., Madison, 1961-63; mem. Dept. In terior Commn. on Lead and Iron Shot Evaluatio Washington, 1973-74; chmn. Nat. Acad. Com. o Vertebrate Pests, Washington, 1967-69. Fulbright prof Ireland, 1969-70; recipient Aldo Leopold medal Th Wildlife Soc., Washington, 1986. Fellow Am Ornithologists Union; mem. The Wildlife Soc. (life, pre 1976-77), Wilson Ornithol. Soc. (life), Brit. Ecol. Soc Brit. Ornithol. Union. Club: Madison Literary. Hom Madison Wis. Died May 29, 1995.

MCCAFFREY, NEIL, publishing executive; b. Ry N.Y., Aug. 29, 1925; s. Cornelius Thomas and Ana tasia Frances (Waterman) McC.; m. Joan Elizabet Melervey, Apr. 10, 1950; children: Maureen, Neil II Eugene V., Roger A., Eileen, Susan. B.A., Fordham U 1950. Employed various positions, 1948-55; edit Doubleday Co., N.Y.C., 1955-61; copywriter Doubleda Co., 1955-61, product mgr., 1960-61; mail order mg Macmillan Co., N.Y.C., 1961-64, dir. advt., 1963-6 founder, pres. Arlington House Pubs., New Rochell N.Y., 1964-78, Conservative Book Club, New Rochell 1964-78; pres. Conservative Book Club, Harrison, N.Y 1982-94; founder, pres. Nostalgia Book Club, Ne

Rochelle, 1968-78, Arlray Advt., New Rochelle, 1972-78; pres. Movie/Entertainment Book Club, Harrison, N.Y., 1978-94; pres. Harrison Assocs. (advt.), Harrison, 1979-94; circulation mgr. Human Events, 1978-83; Direct mail cons. Nat. Republican Congl. Com., 1963-71. Contbr. to: Nat. Rev. Bd. dirs. Am. Conservative Union, 1970-72. Served with USCGR, 1943-46. Mem. Conservation Book Club. Republican. Roman Catholic. Home: Pelham N.Y. Died Dec. 8, 1994.

MC CALL, ABNER VERNON, law educator, retired university administrator; b. Perrin, Tex., June 8, 1915; s. Harry Vernon and Gertrude Elizabeth (Rhoades) McC.; m. Frances Laura Bortle, 1940 (dec. 1969); children: Anne, Bette, Richard, Kathleen; m. Mary W. Russell, 1970. A.B., J.D., Baylor U., 1938; LL.M., U. Mich., 1943. Bar: Tex. 1938. Instr. law Baylor U., 1938-42, prof. law, 1946-59, dean Law Sch., 1948-59, exec. v.p., 1959-61, pres., 1961-81, chancellor, 1981-85; justice Supreme Ct. Tex., 1956; spl. agt. FBI, 1943-46; mem. Tex. Civil Jud. Coun., 1954-84, pres., 1955-58. Pres. Baptist Gen. Couv. Tex., 1963-64; 1st v.p. So. Baptist Conv., 1979, 80, Tex. rep. Edn. Commn. of States, 1968-83, 87-90; pres. Tex. Scottish Rite Found; bd. dirs. Tex. Scottish Rite Hosp. for Children, Nat. Right to Work Com.; chmn. bd. Tex. System Natural Labs., Baylor Med. Found., Leon Jaworski Found., Madison Cooper Found. Mem. State Bar Tex., Assn. Tex. Colls. and Univs. (pres. 1968-69), Ind. Colls. and Univs. Tex. (pres. 1965-71), Philos. Soc. Tex. (pres. 1982). Home: Waco Tex. Died June 11, 1995.

MCCANN, DEAN MERTON, lawyer, former pharmaceutical company executive; b. Ontario, Calif., Mar. 13, 1927; s. James Arthur and Alma Anis (Hawes) McC.; m. Carol Joan Geissler, Mar. 23, 1957. AA, Chaffey Coll., 1948; BS in Pharmacy, U. So. Calif., 1951; JD, U. Calif., San Francisco, 1954; LLM, NYU, 1955. Bar: Calif. 1955; lic. pharmacist, Calif. Pharmacist San Francisco and Ontario, 1951-54; sole practice law Los Angeles, 1955-60; ptnr. MacBeth, Ford & Brady, Los Angeles, 1960-65, McCann & Berger, Los Angeles, 1965-68; v.p., sec. and gen. counsel Allergan Pharms., Inc., Irvine, Calif., 1968-78; sr. v.p., sec., gen. counsel Allergan, Inc., Irvine, 1978-89; pvt. practice Irvine, 1989—; instr. pharmacy law U. So. Calif., Los Angeles, 1956-68; exec. v.p. Pharm. Wholesaler Assn., Los Angeles, 1956-68. Mem., past chmn. bd. counsellors Sch. Pharmacy U. So. Calif., Los Angeles, 1975-96, life mem., past chmn. QSAD centurion, 1963-96. Served with USNR, 1945-46. Fellow Food and Drug Law Inst., 1954-55; recipient Outstanding Alumni Award Sch. Pharmacy U. So. Calif., 1973. Mem. calif. Bar Assn., Orange County Bar Assn., Am. Pharm. Assn., Calif. Pharm. Assn., Orange County Pharm. Assn., U. So. Calif. Pharmacy Alumni Assn. (past pres., Outstanding Alumni award 1973), U. So. Calif. Assocs. (life), Newport Beach Country Club, Balboa Bay Club, Orange County Philharm. Soc., Skull and Dagger Club, Phi Delta Chi. Republican. Home: Newport Beach Calif. Deceased Jan. 1, 1996.

MCCANN, OWEN CARDINAL, archbishop emeritus; b. Woodstock, South Africa, June 26, 1907; s. Edward and Susan Mary (Plint) McC. PhD, Urbanianum; BCom, Cape Town, DLitt (hon.); DHL (hon.) Portland, Maine. Ordained priest Roman Cath. Ch., 1935, titular bishop of Stettorio and vicar apostolic of Cape Town (South Africa), 1950; 1st archbishop of Cape Town, 1951-84, ret., 1984; created cardinal, 1965; titular ch. St. Praxedes. Editor (weekly Cath. newspaper) So. Cross, 1986-92. Died Mar. 26, 1994; interred St. Mary's Cathedral, Cape Town, South Africa. Home: Cape Town S. Africa

MC CARTHY, CHARLES JOSEPH, lawyer, former government official; b. Providence, June 19, 1907; s. John Francis and Mary Elizabeth (Quinn) McC.; m. Gladys Christina McGrail; children: Helen Jacquelyn (Mrs. James F. Hickey), Barbara Ann (Mrs. John J. McCooe), Cormac, William Bernard, Maryellen (Mrs. James A. Jaques III), Dennis Michael. A.B., Providence Coll., 1927; LL.B., Yale U., 1930. Bar: N.Y 1932, R.I 1933, Tenn. 1934, D.C. 1968, U.S. Supreme Ct. 1935. Pvt. practice N.Y.C., 1930-32, Providence, 1932-34; atty. RFC, 1934; legal staff TVA, 1934-67, gen. counsel, 1958-67; prin. McCarthy, Sweeney and Harkaway, P.C. (and predecessor firms), Washington, 1968-86; counsel McCarthy, Sweeney and Harkaway, P.C., 1986-95; spl. asst. to atty. gen. Dept. Justice, 1938-39. Co-author: A Study of the Electric Power Situation in New England, 1970-1990, Transportation Deregulation, 1986; also articles. Mem. Fed. Bar Assn., D.C. Bar Assn. Home: Falls Church Va. Died Feb. 15, 1995.

MCCARTHY, JOSEPH JAMES, trade company executive; b. N.Y.C., Oct. 29, 1923; s. James and Anna (O'Brien) McC.; B.S., Fordham U., 1947. Traffic mgr. Cardinal Export Corp., N.Y.C., 1947-48; dept. mgr. Muller & Phipps (Asia) Ltd., Manila, 1948-49; sales mgr. Far East, Rourke Export Co., Hong Kong, 1949-50; propr. Automotive Supply Co., N.Y.C., from 1950, N.Y.C. Export Internat. Co., from 1959, Export Internat. Komak Corp., N.Y.C., from 1972. Served with U.S. Army, 1943-46. Decorated Purple Heart. Roman Catholic. Deceased. Home: New York N.Y.

MCCARTHY, PATRICK FRANCIS, banker; b. Barnesboro, Pa., June 17, 1901; s. Patrick Francis and Mary Ann (Buggy) McC.; m. Irene Rita Walsh, May 15, 1924 (dec. Apr. 1953); m. Josephine Carlino McCarthy, June 6, 1956. LL.D. (hon.), Indiana U. Pa., 1978; H.H.D. (hon.), St. Francis Coll., 1983. Laborer Barnes & Tucker Coal, Barnesboro, 1913-25; ins. agt. John Hancock Ins. Co., Boston, 1925-30, asst. mgr., 1930-45; gen. agt. Bankers Life, Lincoln, Nebr., 1945-65; pres., chmn. bd. Nat. Bank Commonwealth, Indiana, Pa., from 1965; chmn. bd. Nat. Bank Commonwealth and First Commonwealth Fin. Corp., Indiana, from 1965; dir. Banquest-N.Mex. Corp., Santa Fe, Berkshire Securities, Indiana, Pa. Pres. William Penn council Boy Scouts Am., Indiana, Pa., 1959; pres. Am. Cancer Soc., Indiana, 1955; trustee, pres. bd. Indiana U. Pa., 1960. Recipient Pres.'s Trophy Bankers Life Nebr., 1958; Silver Beaver award Boy Scouts Am., 1965; knighted by Pope John Paul, Knights of St. Gregory, Erie, Pa., 1984. Mem. Pa. Soc. N.Y. Democrat. Roman Catholic. Club: Punxsutawney Country. Lodges: Elks, KC (grand knight) (Punxsutawney, Pa.). Deceased. Home: Punxsutawney Pa.

MC CARTNEY, KENNETH HALL, economist, former college dean; b. Winnipeg, Man., Can., Aug. 28, 1924; came to U.S., 1947, naturalized, 1965; s. Robert and Mabel (Hall) McC.; m. June Lois Palmer, Mar. 20, 1951; children: Kevin Hall, Brian Palmer. B.A., U. Man., 1945; M.A., U. Minn., 1949, Ph.D., 1959; M.S.W. (hon.), Smith Coll., 1973. Instr. United Coll., Winnipeg, 1945-47; instr. U. Minn., 1947-51, 1952-54; spl. lectr. McMaster U., Hamilton, Ont., Can., 1951-52; asst. prof. econs. Smith Coll., Northampton, Mass., 1954-60; assoc. prof. Smith Coll., 1960-64, prof., 1964-83, Robert A. Woods prof., 1983-86, prof. emeritus, 1986-93, dean of faculty, 1978-83, acting dean Sch Social Work, 1971-72, dean, 1972-76, acting pres., July-Nov. 1981; vis. prof. Atlanta U. Center, 1968-69. Home: Fort Myers Fla. Died Nov. 22, 1993.

MCCARTY, PHILIP NORMAN, bank holding company executive; b. Indpls., July 1, 1938; s. Estel E. and Catherine J. (McCafferty) McC.; m. Paula B. Boubeau, May 19, 1962 (div. 1991); 1 child, Carrie Michelle. BBA cum laude, U. Miami, 1960. With Southeast Banking Corp., Miami, 1960-69; asst. v.p. Southeast Banking Corp., 1967-69; sr. v.p., sec. Boatmen's Bancshares, Inc., St. Louis, 1970-94; pres., dir. Boatmen's Life Ins. Co., 1976-94. With U.S. Army, 1961. Mem. Am. Soc. Corp. Secs., Fin. Execs. Inst. Am., Legends Country Club. Republican. Methodist. Home: Ladue Mo. Died July 25, 1994.

MCCLUNG, JOHN ROBINSON, JR., retired advertising company executive; b. Sewanee, Tenn., Sept. 14, 1914; s. John Robinson and Mary Merle (McCall) McC.; m. Edith Logue, Feb. 3, 1944; children: John T., Bonnie McClung Chappa, Marilyn Michele McClung Rositas. BS in Bus. and Journalism, Kans. State U., 1937. Reporter Manhattan (Kans.) Mercury, 1934-36; advt. staff, editor Aetna Life and Casualty Co., Hartford, Conn., 1938-41; account exec., assoc. mgr. Kirschner and Co., San Francisco and Palo Alto, Calif., 1946-65; v.p. Art Blum Agy., San Francisco, 1966; founder, chmn., pres. McClung Advt. Agy., Inc., Palo Alto, 1967-93; ret., 1993. Editor Ins. Adjuster mag., 1963-65, others. Mem. San Francisco Advt. Club, 1946-61. Served to capt. Signal Corps, U.S. Army, 1941-45, PTO. Mem. Adcrafters Club (pres. 1954), Peninsula Advt. Club (bd. dirs. 1971-74), Beta Theta Pi (pres. San Francisco Bay Area Alumni Assn. 1952-54, 63-64, Calif. dist. chief 1954-63, pres. internat. conv. 1965, editor mag. 1977-92), Sigma Delta Chi. Republican. Methodist. Club: Palo. Home: Palo Alto Calif. Deceased.

MCCLURE, ALAN CAMPBELL, naval architect; b. Yonkers, N.Y., Aug. 8, 1923; s. Robert Hirt and Helen (Campbell) McC.; m. Gloria Alice Varley, June 14, 1947; children: Karen, Kent, Gail, Scott, Amy. BS in Naval Architecture and Marine Engring., U. Mich., 1949; MS in Naval Architecture and Marine Engring., MIT, 1950. Registered profl. engr., Tex., Conn. Engring. supr. Gen. Dynamics Corp., Groton, Conn., 1950-62; chief naval architect Project Mohole, Brown & Root, Inc., Houston, 1962-67; sr. naval architect Continental Oil Co., Houston, 1967-71; ptnr., cons. Donhaiser-McClure, Houston, 1971-75; owner, pres. Alan C. McClure Assocs., Inc., Houston, 1975-93; asst. sec. Societe Industrielle D'Electro Metallurgie Tool Co., Houston, 1981-93. Patentee conversion floatable barge into semisubmersible vessel; contbr. articles to profl. jours. including Marine Tech., Ocean Resources Engring., Petroleum Engr. Internat. Served with U.S. Army, 1944-46, ETO. Scholarship Soc. Naval Architects and Marine Engrs., MIT, 1949-50. Fellow Royal Inst. of Naval Architects, Soc. Naval Architects and Marine Engrs. (life, v.p. 1982-84, mem. coun. 1979-84, 88-90, chmn. offshore com., Blakely Smith medalist 1987); mem. Marine Tech. Soc. Republican. Congregationalist. Club: Houston Yacht (Shore Acres, Tex.). Home: Houston Tex. Died May 1, 1993.

MCCOLL, JOHN DUNCAN, consulting company executive; b. London, Ont., Can., Nov. 11, 1925; s. Gordon and Mary Rosamund (Clunis) McC., m. Patricia Amy Ridout, May 29, 1954; children: Pamela, Susan, Gordon. BA, U. Western Ont., 1946, MSc, 1950; PhD, U. Toronto, 1953. Assoc. dir. rsch. Frank W. Horner Ltd., Montreal, Can., 1953-70; v.p. biol. scis. Mead-Johnson Rsch. Ctr., Evansville, Ind., 1970-75; v.p., dir. rsch. Chattem Inc., Chattanooga, 1975-83; pres. McColl Assocs. Inc., Chattanooga, 1983-91; cons. on toxicology, Def. Rsch. Bd. of Can., 1968-72. Contbr. numerous articles to sci. jours.; patentee in field. Mid-South commr. emeritus Clan Donald U.S.A. Inc. Lt. inf. Can. Armed Forces, 1943-46. Nat. Rsch. Studentship Nat. Rsch. Coun. Can., 1949. Mem. Pharmacological Soc. of Can. (sec 1962-63), Soc. of Toxicology of Can. (hon., pres. 1968-69, disting. svc. award 1987), Soc. of Toxicology (charter mem.), Sigma Xi, Torch Club Internat. (Chattanooga). Episcopalian. Home: Chattanooga Tenn. Died July 1991.

MCCOMAS, JAMES DOUGLAS, university president; b. Prichard, W.Va., Dec. 23, 1928; s. Herbert and Nell (Billups) McC.; m. Frances Adele Stoltz; children: Cathleen, Patrick. BS, W.Va. U., 1951, MS, 1960; PhD, Ohio State U., 1962. High sch. tchr., 1951-54, 56-60; asst. prof. to prof., head dept. agrl. and extension edn., prof. ednl. adminstrn. head dept. elem. and secondary edn. N.Mex. State U., 1961-67; dean Coll. Edn. Kans. State U., 1967-69; dean also prof. continuing and higher edn. U. Tenn., 1969-76; pres. Miss. State U., 1976-85, U. Toledo, 1985-88, Va. Poly. Inst. and State U., Blacksburg, 1988-94; field reader U.S. Office Edn.; chmn. Southeastern Manpower Adv. Com.; mem. exec. com. Southeastern Conf.; mem. appeals bd. Nat. Council Accreditation of Tchr. Edn.; pres. Nat. Accreditation Coun. for Agencies Serving the Blind; mem. exec. com. Land Grant Deans Edn.; chmn. com. on equal opportunity Nat. Assn. Land Grant Colls. and State Univs.; assoc. mem. Nat. Manpower Adv. Com., Gov.'s Manpower Adv. Com.; chmn. coun. of presidents State Univs. Miss.; pres. So. Land Grant Colls. and Univs.; chmn. Tenn. Coun. Deans Edn.; mem. Miss. Jr. Coll. Commn.; bd. dirs. Dominon Bancshares Corp.; chmn. Nat. Assn. State & Land Grant Univs.; dir. Va. Ctr. Innovative Tech. Pres. Belmont West Community Assn., Miss. Econ. Coun., East Miss. Coun.; bd. dirs. Toledo Symphony, Toledo Art Mus., Toledo Pub. TV Sta.; sec. pres.'s coun. Nat. Assn. Land Grant and State Univs., chmn. elect; mem. Nat. Coun. on Competitiveness and Acad. Adminstrs.; civilian aide Sec. of Army. With M.C., AUS, 1954-56. Mem. Am. Sociol. Assn., Am. Higher Edn. Assn., Am. Acad. Polit. and Social Sci., Kappa Delta Pi, Gamma Sigma Delta, Alpha Zeta, Omicron Delta Kappa, Phi Kappa Phi, Beta Gamma Sigma. Home: Blacksburg Va. Died Feb. 1994.

MC COMBS, DONALD DWAIN, real estate securities executive; b. Eureka, Mont., Jan. 26, 1922; s. William Elmer and Olive (Schroth) McC.; student U. Calif., Berkeley, 1941-42; m. Amelia De Aloia, Nov. 1982; children: William Henry, David Christopher. Pres., McCombs Securities Co. Inc., Santa Ana, Calif., 1960-95; chmn. bd. D & R Properties Inc., Santa Ana, 1970-95; chmn. bd. McCombs Corp. Trustee, pres. bd. Pomona (Calif.) Unified Schs., 1966-71. Served to lt. USAF, 1942-45. Died July 15, 1995. Home: Laguna Beach Calif.

MC CONKIE, BRUCE REDD, clergyman; b. Ann Arbor, Mich., July 29, 1915; s. Oscar W. and Margaret V. (Redd) McC.; m. Amelia Smith, Oct. 13, 1937; children: Vivian, Joseph F., Stanford S., Mary E., Mark L., Rebecca, Stephen L., Sara J. A.B., U. Utah, 1937, J.D., 1940. Bar: Utah bar 1940. Mem. firm McConkie, Boud, Summerhays & Hess, Salt Lake City, 1940-42; asst. city atty., city prosecutor Salt Lake City, 1940-42; Ordained to ministry Ch. of Jesus Christ of Latter Day Saints, 1946; ch. servicemen's coordinator, 1947-64, gen. authority of ch., from 1946; mem. First Council of 70, 1946-72; mem. council Twelve Apostles, from 1972; pres. So. Australian Mission, Melbourne, Australia, 1961-64. Compiler 3 volumes of doctrines of salvation, sermons and writings of, Joseph Fielding Smith, 1954, 55, 56; Author: Mormon Doctrine, 1958, Doctrinal New Testament Commentary, Vol. 1, The Gospels, 1965; vol. 2, Acts-Philippians, 1970; Vol. 3, Colossians-Revelation, 1972, The Promised Messiah: The First Coming of Christ, 1978, The Mortal Messiah: From Bethlehem to Calvary, Book I, 1979, Book II, 1980, Book III, 1980, Book IV, 1981; The Millennial Messiah-The Second Coming of the Son of Man. Mem. Bd. Edn. Ch. Jesus Christ Latter-day Saints, from 1972; Trustee Brigham Young U., Provo, Utah, from 1972, Ricks Coll., Rexburg, Idaho, from 1973, Ch. Coll. Hawaii, Laie, Oahu, from 1973. Served from 1st lt. to lt. col., M.I. AUS, 1942-46. Home: Salt Lake City Utah Died April 19, 1995; buried City Cemetary, Salt Lake City, U.T.

MCCONNELL, JAMES VERNON, JR., advertising agency executive; b. N.Y.C., June 22, 1938; s. James Vernon and Margot (Murphy) McC.; m. Elizabeth Ann Martin, May 24, 1962; children: Peter C., Christopher J. A.B. in Journalism with honors, U. Pa., 1961. Mgmt. trainee N.W. Ayer & Son, Phila., 1961-64; v.p., account supr. Benton & Bowles, Inc., N.Y.C., 1964-71; with Interpublic Group Cos., N.Y.C., 1971-78; dir. ops. Proeme Campbell Ewald, Sao Paulo, Brazil, 1976-77; group sr. v.p., dir. Doyle Dane Bernbach Inc., N.Y.C., 1978-85; dir., exec. v.p., mng. dir. N.Y. office Campbell-Ewald Co., 1985-87; sr. v.p. internat. account dir. Foote Cone and Belding Inc., N.Y.C., 1987-90; dir. Director's

Studio Inc. Mem. Am. Assn. Advt. Agys. Club: Bedford (N.Y.) Golf and Tennis. Home: Mount Kisco N.Y. Died April 9, 1990.

MCCORD, WILLIAM MAXWELL, social scientist, educator; b. St. Louis, Oct. 24, 1930; s. Don Chylo and Elinor (Maxwell) McC.; m. Arline Fujii, May 8, 1971; children: Geoffrey, Robert, Maxwell, William, Elinor Mary. BA, Stanford U., 1952; PhD, Harvard U., 1955. Instr. social psychology Harvard U., 1955-58; from asst. to assoc. prof. sociology Stanford U., 1958-65, asst. dean Sch. Sci. and Humanities, 1958-61; Lena Gohlman Fox prof. sociology Rice U., 1965-68; prof. sociology Syracuse U., 1968-71; prof., chmn. dept. sociology CUNY, 1971-92; disting. lectr. Polish Acad. Scis., 1961; vis. prof. Am. U. in Cairo, 1964, Nat. U. Singapore, 1984-85; Fulbright prof. Trinity Coll., Dublin, 1977-78; vis. fellow Clare Hall, Cambridge, 1985-86, life mem. 1986-92; resident scholar Bellagio Ctr., 1986. Author: Psychopathy and Delinquency, 1956, Origins of Crime, 1959, Origins of Alcoholism, 1960, The Psychopath, 1964, The Springtime of Freedom, 1965, Mississippi: The Long Hot Summer, 1965, Life Styles in the Black Ghetto, 1969, The Study of Personality, 1969, Urban Social Conflict, 1977, Social Problems, 1977, Power and Equity, 1977, The Psychopath and Mileau Therapy, 1982, Paths to Progress, 1986, Voyages to Utopia, 1990, The Dawn of the Pacific Century, 1991, Contemporary Social Issues, 1991. Mem. President's Com. on Violence, 1965; bd. dirs. Palo Alto chpt. NAACP, 1960-65, Palo Alto Family Svc. Soc., 1960-62, Salvation Army, San Francisco, 1961, Houston Child Guidance Clinic, 1966-68, Bklyn. Sch., 1974-78, Singapore Am. Sch., 1984-85; mem. N.Y. Dem. Com., 1978-89, Rockland (N.Y.) Crime Commn., 1982-89, Conn. Dem. Com., 1990-92; co-founder Rockland chpt. Amnesty Internat., 1987; clk. Conn. meeting Soc. of Friends, 1992. Woodrow Wilson fellow, 1952. Fellow Am. Sociol. Assn.; mem. Internat. Sociol. Assn., Phi Beta Kappa. Mem. Soc. of Friends. Home: New Haven Conn. Died Aug. 9, 1992; buried Rockland Cemetary, Orangeburg, N.Y.

MCCORMICK, JAMES CLARENCE, business consultant; b. Kaufman, Tex., Oct. 5, 1924; s. Clarence Snow and Mabel Ruth (Watkins) McC.; m. Barbara Louise Ostling, Jan. 12, 1947; children: Richard, Sharon, Patricia, Michael, Kelly. B.S., B.B.A., So. Meth. U., 1949. Reporter Dun and Bradstreet, Dallas, 1949-55; with Eppler, Guerin & Turner, Inc., Dallas, 1955-87, vice chmn. bd., 1980-82, gen. dir., 1982-87, mem. exec. com.; pvt. practice bus. cons. Dallas, 1987-95; Author: The Stone Bruise. Mem. bd. advisors Southwestern Bapt. Theol. Sem.; past pres., bd. dirs. Dallas Soc. for Crippled Children, Meth. Bd. for Ch. Ext., Tex. Lit. Bd., Dallas Orthopaedic Found., Family Shelter, YMCA, Salvation Army. Lt. USAAF, 1942-46. Named Disting. Alumni So. Meth. U., 1994. Mem. Nat. Fin. Analysts Fedn., Air Force Assn., Alpha Kappa Psi, Beta Gamma Sigma. Home: Dallas Tex. Died Feb. 21, 1995.

MC CORMICK, WILLIAM BLISS, former mayor Topeka; b. Topeka, June 7, 1927; s. Joseph Bliss and Wilma (Bergundthal) McC.; m. Shirley Westfall, June 9, 1950; children: Timili, Mary, Lory, Jamie, Jennifer. B.B.A., Washburn U., 1952, J.D., 1959. Bar: Kans. 1958. Practiced in Topeka; asst. city atty. City of Topeka, 1959-69, mayor, from 1971. Served with USMC, 1945-47. Mem. Kans., Topeka bar assns., Am. Legion (comdr. post), VFW. Presbyterian. Clubs: Masons, Shriners, Moose. Home: Topeka Kans. Died July 31, 1995.

MC CORMICK, WILLIAM MARTIN, broadcast executive; b. Hackensack, N.J., Dec. 15, 1921; s. John and Delia Theresa (Murphy) McC.; m. Joan Theresa Dowling, June 29, 1957; children: Jean Marie, Patricia, Joan, William Martin. Student, NYU, 1939-43, B.S., 1946; student, Harvard U., 1943-45. Account exec. Sta. WOR, N.Y.C., 1946-54; asst. sales mgr. Sta. WOR, 1955, dir. sales, 1956-59, v.p., dir. sales, 1959-60; pres., gen. mgr. Sta. WNAC-AM and FM and WNAC-TV, Boston, 1960-64; v.p., gen. mgr. Sta. WNAC-TV, 1964-69; area v.p. New Eng. WNAC-TV, 1970-72; pres. McCormick Communications, 1972-85, McCormick Broadcasting Corp., 1986-95; trustee Charlestown Savs. Bank., 1968-83. Bd. dirs. Catholic TV Ctr., 1970-83, ARC, 1970-95; pres. execs. club Greater Boston C. of C., 1965-66, bd. dirs., 1966-68; bd. dirs. Better Bus. Bur., 1966-70. Served with USN, 1941-46. Recipient award Greater Boston C. of C., 1962, citation of merit NCCJ, 1974. Mem. Nat. Assn. Broadcasters, Nat. Radio Broadcasters Assn., New Eng. Broadcasters Assn. Roman Catholic. Clubs: Weston Golf; Oyster Harbors (Osterville, Mass.); John's Island (Vero Beach, Fla.); Wianno (Mass.). Home: Osterville Mass. Died Apr. 23, 1995.

MCCOWEN, MAX CREAGER, retired research scientist; b. Sullivan, Ind., July 4, 1915; s. Roy E. and Ethel G. (Creager) McC.; m. Judy M. Lacefield, July 13, 1985. BS, Ind. State U., 1937, MS, 1938; postgrad., U. Buffalo, 1939, U. Chgo., 1940. Head sci. dept. Edison High Sch., Hammond, Ind., 1938-42; rsch. assoc. Eli Lilly & Co., Indpls., 1946-47, asst. chief parasitology rsch. dept., 1947-48, sr. parasitologist, 1958-65; head parasitology rsch. Lilly Rsch. Ctr. Ltd., Windlesham, Eng., 1965-70; rsch. scientist Lilly Rsch. Labs., Greenfield, Ind., 1970-85; ret. Lilly Rsch. Labs., Greenfield, Ind., 1985; lectr. Marion County Gen. Hosp., Indpls., 1959-70, Ind. U. Sch. Medicine, 1960-70. Elder, First Presbyterian Ch., and First Meridian Heights Presbyn. Ch.; commr. synod assembly United Presbyn. Ch. USA, 1976. Served to lt. USN, 1942-46, to comdr. Res., ret., 1975. Recipient Disting. Alumni award Ind. State U., 1977. Fellow Royal Soc. Tropical Medicine and Hygiene; mem. AAAS, Internat. Coll. Tropical Medicine, Am. Soc. Tropical Medicine and Hygiene, Am. Soc. Parasitologists, Mexican Soc. Parasitology, Soc. Protozologists, Aquatic Plant Mgmt. Soc. (bd. dirs. 1978-81, chmn. local chpts. com. 1979-83, pres. 1984-85, v.p. 1982-83), English Speaking Union, Am. Legion, Lilly Putian Club (sec. 1977-78), Torch Club (pres. 1962-63, bd. dirs. 1975-77), Contemporary Club (bd. dirs. 1975-76), Indpls. Lit. Club (3rd v.p.). Home: Naples Fla. Died July 15, 1994.

MC COY, CLARENCE JOHN, JR., curator; b. Lubbock, Tex., July 25, 1935; s. Clarence John and Marguerite Ceona (McNew) McC.; m. Patsy Ruth Kelly, June 7, 1957; children: John Kelly, Catherine Janet. B.S., Okla. State U., Stillwater, 1957, M.S., 1960; Ph.D., U. Colo., 1965. Instr. zoology Okla. State U., summers 1959-60; research asso. U. Colo. Museum, 1962-64; mem. staff Carnegie Mus., Pitts., 1964-93; curator amphibians and reptiles Carnegie Mus., 1972-93; vis. asst. prof. zoology Ariz. State U., 1969-70; adj. assoc. prof. biology U. Pitts., 1972-93; adj. prof. biology Calif. U. Pa., 1989-93; chmn. herpetology adv. com. Pa. Fish Commn., 1975-93; chmn. amphibian-reptile com. Pa. Biol. Survey, 1979-91; Carnegie Mus. del. Latin Am. Congress Zoology, Montevideo, 1971, Mexico, 1974, Tucuman, 1977, Merida, 1980, Arequipa, 1983. Author: Vertebrates, 1968, Animals of the Islands, 1969, Keys to Mexican Amphibians and Reptiles, 1978, Amphibians and Reptiles in Pennsylvania, 1983; also articles.; editor lizard accounts Catalogue Am. Amphibians and Reptiles, 1967-87, Sci. Publs., Carnegie Mus. Nat. History, 1989-93. Bd. dirs. Western Pa. Conservancy, 1990-93; mem. bd. scientists Chihuahuan Desert Rsch. Inst., 1991-93. NSF fellow, 1961. Mem. AAAS, Am. Soc. Ichthyologists and Herpetologists (gov. 1967-72), Am. Soc. Mammalogists, Herpetologists League (exec. coun. 1965-67, 70-73, v.p. 1984-85, pres. 1986-87), Soc. Systematic Zoology, Soc. Study Amphibians and Reptiles (pres. 1972), Southwestern Assn. Naturalists, Okla. Acad. Sci., Pa. Acad. Sci., Soc. Mexicana Herpetologia, Sigma Xi. Home: Tulsa Okla. Home: Pittsburgh Pa. Died July 7, 1993.

MC CRACKEN, GEORGE HERBERT, magazine publisher; b. Pitts., June 20, 1899; s. George and Anne Elizabeth (Vance) McC.; m. Martha M. Alford, Jan. 22, 1977; children—Judith (Mrs. William M. Clark), George Herbert. B.S., U. Pitts., 1921; Litt.D., Lafayette Coll., 1968; LL.D., Allegheny Coll., 1972; Ed.D. (hon.), Bethany Coll., 1980. Head football coach Allegheny Coll., 1921-23, Lafayette Coll., 1924-35; with Scholastic Mags., Inc., N.Y.C., 1922-95; sr. v.p. Scholastic Mags., Inc., 1954-61, vice chmn. bd., 1961-70, chmn. exec. com., 1971-95, also dir.; founder, 1931 Scholastic Coach mag., pub., 1931-68. Mem. Football Found. Hall of Fame; trustee U. Pitts., Lafayette Coll. Served with U.S. Navy, 1918. Recipient Amos Alonzo Stagg award Am. Football Coaches Assn., 1988. Mem. U. Pitts. Varsity Letter Club, Delta Tau Delta (pres. 1946-48), Omicron Delta Kappa, Beta Gamma Sigma. Presbyn. Clubs: Little, Ocean. Home: Ocean Ridge Fla. Died Mar. 11, 1995.

MCCUNE, SAMUEL KNOX, lawyer; b. Orange, N.J., Dec. 27, 1921; s. Joseph C. and Lucie (Brown) McC.; m. Barbara Campbell, Mar. 5, 1949 (dec. Sept. 1983); children: Helen McCune Gregory, Lucie McCune Van Der Veer; m. Mary Louise McCune, July 25, 1985. AB, Cornell U., 1943; LLB, Columbia U., 1948. Bar: Pa. 1949, U.S. Supreme Ct. 1963. From assoc. to ptnr. Kirkpatrick & Lockhart, Pitts., 1948-93, adminstrv. ptnr., 1983-88. Chmn. Presbyn. Assn. Aging, Pitts., 1954-88; v.p. Borough Council, Fox Chapel, Pa., 1978-90. Served to capt. USAR, 1943-46, ETO. Mem. ABA, Pa. Bar Assn., Allegheny County Bar Assn. Republican. Clubs: Duquesne (Pitts.), Fox Chapel Golf. (sec., bd. dirs. 1975-86); St. Andrews (Delray Beach, Fla., bd. dirs.). Home: Pittsburgh Pa. Died Dec. 8, 1993.

MCDANIEL, DAVID JAMISON, lawyer; b. Portland, Oreg., July 24, 1913; s. David Lester and Harriet LeConie (Jamison) McD.; m. Martha Eyre, Dec. 15, 1961. A.B., Stanford U., 1933; LL.B., Harvard U., 1936. Bar: Calif. 1936, U.S. Dist. Ct. (no. dist.) Calif. 1936, U.S. Ct. Appeals (9th cir.) 1936, U.S. Ct. Appeals (10th cir.) 1958, U.S. Supreme Ct. 1972. Assoc. Shelton, Gray & McWilliams, San Francisco, 1936-41; atty., gen. atty., sr. gen. atty. U.S. Steel Corp. and subs., Calif., 1946-78; sec., bd. dirs. Columbia Iron Mining Co., 1958-63; ptnr. Cotton, Seligman & Ray, San Francisco, 1978-80; ptnr. Jordan, Keeler & Seligman, San Francisco, 1980-81, of counsel, 1981-89; instr., asst. prof. Hastings Coll. Law, 1946-58. Trustee Pacific Sch. Religion, 1978-87, emeritus trustee, 1987-93; trustee Presbyn. Med. Ctr., 1960-64; trustee Mechanics' Inst. of San Francisco, 1961-78, pres., 1974-76; trustee Golden Gate U., 1969-82, life trustee, 1982-93; trustee Regional Cancer Found., 1982-85; regent U. Calif., 1974; bd. dirs. San Francisco YMCA, 1960-73, pres. and chmn., 197 73; pres. San Francisco chpt. English Speaking Unio 1985-87, mem. nat. bd., 1982-86; bd. dirs. Potero H Neighborhood House, 1957-63, pres., 1960-62; dir. N Calif. Rugby Football Union, 1946-52, pres., 1948-4 trustee Yori Wada Found., 1985-93. Served with AU 1941-46; to col. Res. Decorated Bronze Star with oa leaf cluster and V Device. Fellow Am. Bar Found mem. ABA, State Bar Calif., Bar Assn. San Francisc (bd. dirs. 1982-84, award of merit 1984), Am. Judicatu Soc., Ft. Point and Army Mus. Assn. (bd. dirs. 1980-9 pres. 1986-87), Mchts. Exch. Club, Pacific-Union Clu San Francisco Golf Club, Commonwealth Club Cali (bd. govs. 1974-80, pres. 1977), Univ. Club, Queen Club, Lansdowne Club (London), St. Andrew's Soc Order of Coif. Democrat. Presbyterian. Home: Sa Francisco Calif. Died Mar. 18, 1993.

MCDEVITT, DANIEL BERNARD, communication computer and control systems application engineer; Pocatello, Idaho, Apr. 14, 1927; s. Bernard Aloysius an Margaret Helen (Herrmann) McD.; m. MaryAr Bohrer, June 14, 1952. BSEE, U. Idaho, 1950. Regi tered profl. engr., Tex., Ark., Okla. Quality control an value engr. GE, Erie, Phila., 1950-53; sales engr. G Cleve., 1954-56, regional mgr., 1956-59; v.p. mkt Nelson Elec. Mfg. Co., Tulsa, 1959-62; owner Dan McDevitt & Assoc., Tulsa, 1962-95; pres. Progress Er gring., Tulsa, 1965-95, RADIUS Rsch. and Devel. Ins of the U.S., Tulsa, 1963-95; gen. mgr. Manhattar McDevitt-Progress Engring. & Wallace Ltd., Tuls 1975-95; mem. Okla. Coun. Reogranization-State Exe Br., Oklahoma City, 1971-73; advisor Saudi Arabia A Force Acad., Riyad, 1974-77; chmn. Okla. State Con munications Coun., 1972-74; mem. adv. counsel U. SBA. Author: Controlling the Uncontrollable-Mgm Retail, 1969, (pamphlet) A Strategy For U.S. Economic Preeminence, 1985-87; contbr. over 20 articl to Oil & Gas Jour., Am. Engr., Datamation Networ World, Systems. Advisor Okla. State Gov., Oklahom City, 1970-74; chmn. Okla. Coun. on Environmen Oklahoma City, 1970-95, Latah County Dem. Orgn Moscow, Idaho, 1948-50. Officer candidate USMCF 1944-51, South Pacific, Republic of Korea. Recipier Meritorious Achievement award Okla. State Gov., 197 Appreciation medallion Saudi Arabia Air Force Acad 1975. Mem. IEEE, NSPE. Democrat. Roma Catholic. Home: Tulsa Okla. Died Aug. 22, 1995

MCDONALD, BRENDAN JOHN, university pr sident; b. Regina, Sask., Can., May 15, 1930; marrie 1954; 2 children. B.S., St. Cloud State Coll., 195 M.A., U. Minn., 1957; Ph.D. in Higher Edn. A minstrn., Mich. State U., 1967. Registrar, dir. admi sions St. Cloud State Coll., Minn., 1956-65, v.p. ad minstrn. and planning, 1972-73; researcher U. N.D 1966; prof. edn. Mankato State Coll., Minn., 1967-7 asst. acad. v.p., 1967-72; pres. Kearney State Coll Nebr., 1972-82, St. Cloud State U., Minn., 1982—. Trustee fellow Mich. State U., 1967. Home: Saint Clou Minn. Deceased.

MCDONALD, JEANNE GRAY (MRS. JOHN B MCDONALD), television producer; b. Seattle, Sept. 1 1917; d. George Patrick and Mary Edna (Gra Murphy; m. John B. Mc Donald, June 30, 1951; chi dren: Gregory Roland Stoner, Jeanne Eve. Studen Columbia U., 1940, Art Students League, 1940-43, Na Acad. Dramatic Art, 1945. Radio producer, com mentator The Woman's Voice Sta. KMPC, L.A., 194 50; TV producer, commentator, writer The Woman Voice Sta. KTTV-CBS, L.A., 1950-51; TV produce commentator The Jeanne Gray Show Sta. KNXT-T CBS, L.A., 1951-53; West Coast editor Home Sho NBC, L.A., 1955-56; TV film producer documentari and travelogues Virgonian Prodns., L.A., 1953-96. Author: The Power of Belonging, 1978. Women chmn. Los Angeles Beautiful, 1971; mem. Women Aux. St. John's Hosp.; trustee Freedoms Found. Valley Forge, 1966-96, founder, pres. women's chpt Los Angeles County chpt., 1965-66, Western di women's chpt., 1967-68, nat. chmn. 1968-71, nat. chm women vols., 1973-75, hon life mem. Recipient Franci Holmes Outstanding Achievement award, 1949, Silve Mike award, 1948, Emmy award Acad. TV Arts an Scis., 1951, Lulu award Los Angeles Advt. Wome 1952, Genii award Radio and TV Women, 1956, Georg Washington Honor award Freedoms Found. Valle Forge, 1967, honor cert., 1972, Morale award Christian and Jews for Law and Morality, 1968, Exceptional Ser vice award Freedoms Found., 1975, Liberty Belle awar Rep. Women's Club, 1975, Leadership award Lo Angeles City Schs., 1976, Theodore Roosevelt awar USN League, 1986. Mem. Am. Women in Radio an TV, Radio and TV Women So. Calif. (hon., lif founder, 1st pres. 1952), Footlighters (v.p. 1958-59), Lo Angeles C. of C. (bd. dirs. women's div. 1948-54, exe bd., women's div. 1954-66, pres. women's div. 1963-6 hon. past pres. women's div. 1979), L.A. Orphanag Guild, DAR, Les Dames de Champagne, Bel Ai Garden Club, Calif. Yacht Club. Home: Los Angel Calif. Died Jan. 30, 1996.

MCEVOY, CHARLES LUCIEN, printing compan executive; b. Bradford, Pa., Sept. 2, 1917; s. L. Carle an Mary Ellen (McMahon) McE.; m. Rosemary C. Rocc Sept. 2, 1947. A.B., Xavier U., 1938; postgrad., Ge orgetown U., 1938-41; J.D., Chgo. Kent Coll. Law

1950. With Neo Gravure Co. of Chgo., 1947-54, asst. gen. mgr., 1950-52, gen. mgr., 1952-54; v.p. sales The Cuneo Press, Inc., Chgo., 1954-67; exec. v.p. The Cuneo Press, Inc., 1967-73, pres., 1973-88, ret. Served with AUS, 1942-46, PTO. Clubs: Chicago Golf, Chicago Athletic. Home: Chicago Ill. Died Oct. 2, 1993.

MCGEE, NANCY RASCO, education educator; b. Paducah, Ky., May 12, 1938; d. Robert W. and Alberta (Abell) Rasco; m. Bobby J. McGee, June 7, 1959; 1 child, Meghan Elizabeth. BS, Murray State U., 1959, MEd, 1964; EdD, Fla. Atlantic U., 1977. Tchr. Robinson (Ill.) High Sch., 1959-61, Lovell Elem. Sch., Apopka, Fla., 1961-62, Glenridge Jr. High Sch., Winter Park, Fla., 1962-67; from instr. to prof. U. Cen. Fla., Orlando, 1968-92; cons. to numerous workshops on teaching English, 1977-92. Co-author elementary language arts textbook series, 1989; contbr. numerous articles to profl. jours. Mem. Fla. Coun. Tchrs. English (pres. 1989-90, Pres. award 1988), Nat. Coun. Tchrs. English (dir. 1975-92, assembly on adolescent lit. 1982-92, assembly on internat. edn. 1982-92). Home: Winter Park Fla. Died Feb. 2, 1992.

MC GEHEE, CARDEN COLEMAN, banker; b. Franklin, Va., Aug. 11, 1924; s. Clopton Vivian and Laura (Coleman) McG.; m. Caroline Yarnall Casey, Apr. 21, 1951; children: Carden Coleman, Stephen Yarnall, Margaret Fox Verner. Student, Va. Poly. Inst., 1941-43; B.S., U. Va., 1947; postgrad., Rutgers U. Grad. Sch. Banking, 1955-58, Harvard U. Advanced Mgmt. Program, 1970; MA in History, U. Richmond, 1992. With First & Mchts. Nat. Bank, Richmond, Va., 1948-95, asst. trust officer, 1954-56, trust officer, 1956-59, v.p., 1959-62, sr. v.p., 1962, pres., chief adminstrv. officer, 1972-73, chmn. bd., chief exec. officer, dir., 1973-83; chmn. bd., chief exec. officer, dir. First & Mchts. Corp., Richmond, Va., 1974-83; pres. Sovran Fin. Corp., Richmond, Va., 1984-88, chmn. exec. com., 1988-89; chmn. bd. dirs. Sovran Bank N.Am., Richmond, Va., 1986-89; ret., 1989; dir. Chesapeake and Potomac Telephone Co. Va.; mem. adv. bd. Eximbank, Washington, 1986-87; instr. evening div. U. Richmond, 1956-62, Va. Commonwealth U., 1958-64. Pres. United Givers Fund, 1971; bd. visitors Va. Commonwealth U., 1968-78; bd. govs. St. Christophers Sch., 1968-74; bd. sponsors Colgate Darden Grad. Sch. Bus. Adminstrn., U. Va., 1980-95, Sch. Bus. Adminstrn., Coll. William and Mary, 1974-80; v.p., pres. Va. Hist. Soc.; chmn. Retreat Hosp. Served with AUS, 1943-46; maj. Va. N.G. until 1966. Mem. Va. Bankers Assn. (pres. 1980-81), C. of C., St. Andrews Soc., Raven Soc., Beta Theta Pi, Delta Sigma Rho, Omicron Delta Kappa, Phi Alpha Delta, Beta Gamma Sigma, Omicron Delta Upsilon, Phi Alpha Theta. Clubs: Rotarian (pres. Richmond 1971-72), Commonwealth, Country of Va. Home: Richmond Va. Died Feb. 12, 1995.

MCGILL, SAMUEL PEYTON, state senator, automobile dealer, farmer; b. Lincoln County, Ga., Aug. 30, 1914; s. Adolphus Cecil and Lillian Inez (Norman) McG.; student S. Ga. State Coll.; m. Florence Clary, Sept. 22, 1935; children—Sam Clary, Kathryn McGill Lamar. Owner service sta., 1936-38; owner, pres. McGill Truck & Tractor (inc. into McGill's Inc. 1975), 1939—; owner Wilkes County Stockyard, Washington, Ga., 1950—; owner, S.P. McGill Farms, 1942—; dir. Washington Loan & Banking Co. Mem. Washington City Council, 1952-58; mem. Ga. State Senate, chmn. agr. com. Named Wilkes County Citizen of Yr., 1977; recipient Ga. County Agts. award, 1974; Disting. Service award U. Ga. Vet. Sch.; Hon. State FFA Farmer degree. Mem. Ga. Farm Equipment Assn., Ga. Stockyard Assn., Nat. Livestock Mktg. Assn. Democrat. Baptist. Clubs: Lions, Wilkes Country, Atlanta City, Atlanta Athletic. Died Nov. 15, 1988. Home: Washington Ga.

MCGINNIS, ROBERT CAMPBELL, lawyer; b. Dallas, Jan. 1, 1918; s. Edward Karl and Helen Louise (Campbell) McG.; m. Ethel Clift, May 14, 1945; children: Mary, Campbell, John, Robert, Michael. AB, U. Tex., 1938; LLB, Yale U., 1941. Bar: Tex. 1941, Ohio 1942, U.S. Dist. Ct. (no. dist.) Tex. 1948, U.S. Dist. Ct. (we. dist.) Tex. 1950. Assoc. Squires, Sanders & Dempsey, Cleve., 1941-42, Carrington, Gowan, Dallas, 1946-49; ptnr. McGinnis, Lochridge & Kilgore and predecessor firm Powell, Wirtz & Rauhut, Austin, Tex., 1950-95; chmn. Tex. Com. Jud. Ethics, 1972-78; bd. dirs. Republic Bank, Austin. Served to lt. USNR, 1942-46, PTO. Fellow Am. Bar Found.; mem. ABA, Tex. Bar Assn., U.S. Lawn Tennis Assn. (hon. life). Presbyterian. Died Feb. 22, 1995.

MCGLINCHEY, DERMOT SHEEHAN, lawyer; b. N.Y.C., Mar. 21, 1933; s. Patrick J. and Ellen S. McGlinchey; m. Ellen F. Murphy, Aug. 19, 1967; children: Ellen Fiouala, Deirdre Claire. BA, Tulane U., 1954, JD, 1957. Bar: La. 1957, U.S. Dist. Ct. (ea., mid., we. dists.) La. 1957, U.S. Ct. Appeals (5th and 11th cirs.) 1957, U.S. Ct. Appeals D.C. 1984, U.S. Supreme Ct. 1984. Pres. McGlinchey, Stafford, Cellini & Lang, New Orleans, 1974-88; bd. dirs., sec. New Orleans Found. Contbr. articles to profl. jours. Pres. Tulane U. Law Dean's Coun., New Orleans, 1982-84, chmn., 1981-82, mem., 1981—, vice chmn. endowment program Maritime Law Ctr. at Tulane U., bd. dirs.; mem., bd. dirs. Internat. House, 1982-83, World Trade Ctr., 1989—, Project, New Orleans, 1990—; sec. Greater New Orleans Opera Assn., 1985—, campaign chmn., 1989-91, chmn. endowment fund, 1990—; mem. exec. com., vice chmn. Internat. Bus. Com., 1991—, World Trade Ctr. Fellow ABA, La. Bar Found. (chmn. 1986-89); mem. La. Bar Assn. (long range planning com. 1986—), New Orleans Bar Assn., D.C. Bar Assn., Nat. Conf. Bar Founds. (trustee 1986-89, treas. 1989, sec. 1990-91), Fedn. Ins. and Corp. Counsel, Am. Judicature Soc., Def. Rsch. Inst., Inc., Lawyers Adv. Com., Internat. Assn. Def. Counsel, New Orleans Assn. Def. Counsel, La. Assn. Def. Counsel, Maritime Assn. U.S., Tulane U. Alumni Assn. (sec., treas. 1988—, v.p. 1989, 90, pres. elect 1991—, bd. dirs. 1989—), Petroleum Club, Phi Alpha Delta. Roman Catholic. Home: New Orleans La. Died 1993.

MCGOUGH, WALTER THOMAS, lawyer; b. Steubenville, Ohio, June 4, 1919; s. Frank C. and Nellie C. (Curran) McG.; m. Jane Fitzpatrick, Nov. 24, 1949; children: Jane Ellen, W. Thomas Jr., Hugh F., Marita. Student, Duquesne U., 1936-41; LL.B., U. Pitts., 1948. Bar: U.S. Dist. Ct. Pa. 1948. Assoc. Reed Smith Shaw & McClay, Pitts., 1948-58, ptnr., 1958-96, head litigation dept., 1965-79. Case editor U. Pitts. Law Rev. Served to capt. USAAF, 1941-46. Mem. ABA, Am. Law Inst., Pa. Bar Assn., Allegheny County Bar Assn., Am. Judicature Soc. (dir. 1981-88), Acad. Trial Lawyers Allegheny County, 3d Cir. Jud. Conf., Order of Coif. Republican. Roman Catholic. Clubs: Duquesne, Press, Ross Mountain, Pitts. Athletic. Home: Pittsburgh Pa. Died Jan. 22, 1996.

MCGRATH, EARL JAMES, educator; b. Buffalo, Nov. 16, 1902; s. John and Martha Carolyn (Schottin) McG.; m. Dorothy Ann Leemon, May 12, 1944. B.A., U. Buffalo, 1928, M.A., 1930; Ph.D., U. Chgo., 1936; Ph.D. hon. degrees 53 colls. and univs, 1949-93. Mem. faculty U. Buffalo, 1928-45; dean Coll. Liberal Arts, State U. Iowa, 1945-48; prof. U. Chgo., 1948-49; U.S. commr. edn. Office of Edn., FSA, 1949-53; pres., chancellor U. Kansas City, 1953-56; exec. officer Inst. Higher Edn., also prof. higher edn. Tchrs. Coll., Columbia, 1956-68; chancellor Eisenhower Coll., Seneca Falls, 1966-68; dir. Higher Edn. Center, Temple U., 1968-73; sr. cons. Lilly Endowment, Indpls., 1973-76; prof. U. Ariz., 1974-80; chmn. univ. adv. council Western Internat. U., Phoenix, 1978-93; Mem. Fulbright Bd. Fgn. Scholarships, 1949-52; Mem. and former mem. many profl. coms. and commns., local state, nat. and internat. in field of edn. Frequent mem. U.S. govtl. agys. and commns. on study ednl. systems. Author and co-author several books, numerous articles. Trustee Antioch Coll., 1958-61, Muskingum Coll., 1961-64, 68-77, St. Michael's Coll., 1966-75, Buckingham (Eng.) Coll., 1973-76, Warner Pacific Coll., 1972-78; v.p. bd. trustees Western Internat. U., Phoenix, 1980-88, chmn., 1988—; mem. adv. bd. Truman Library. Lt. comdr. USNR, 1942-44. Decorated Knight Order St. John of Jerusalem. Mem. many profl. orgns. and assns. related to field of edn., Cosmos Club (Washington), Old Pueblo Club (Tucson), Tucson Nat. Golf Club, Phi Beta Kappa, Delta Chi, Beta Sigma Pi, Phi Delta Kappa, Delta Phi Alpha, Sigma Xi, Iota Lambda Sigma, Omicron Delta Kappa. Home: Tucson Ariz. Died Jan. 14, 1993.

MC GRATH, JOHN FRANCIS, judge; b. Chgo., Apr. 13, 1926; B.A., Loyola U., Chgo., 1947; J.D., U. Colo., 1950. Bar: Colo. 1950, Ill. 1950; partner firm Kettelkamp, McGrath, Vento, Pueblo, Colo., 1950-67; judge U.S. Bankruptcy Ct., Denver, 1967-89; dep. dist. atty. Pueblo County (Colo.), 1953-57. Pres. Pueblo Symphony, Pueblo Broadway Theatre League. Mem. Colo., Pueblo County (sec.) bar assns., Phi Alpha Delta, Alpha Delta Gamma. Died 1989. Home: Denver Col.

MC GRATH, THOMAS, poet, writer; b. Nov. 20, 1916; m. Eugenia Johnson; 1 son, Tomasito. Student, U. N.D., La. State U., New Coll. Oxford U.; D.Litt. (hon.), U. N.D., 1981. Instr. Colby Coll., Waterville, Maine, 1940-41; asst. prof. Los Angeles State Coll., 1950-54. Author: First Manifesto, 1940, To Walk a Crooked Mile, 1947, Figures from a Double World, 1955; children's books The Beautiful Things; novels The Gates of Ivory, The Gates of Horn, 1957, reprinted 1988, This Coffin Has No Handles, 1985, reprinted 1988; poems Letter to an Imaginary Friend 1962, Parts I and II, 1970, 1957, New and Selected Poems, 1962, The Movie at the End of the World-Collected Poems, 1973, A Sound of One Hand, 1975, Letters to Tomasito, 1976, Open Songs, 1976, Trinc: Praises II, 1979, Waiting for the Angel, 1979, Passages Toward the Dark, 1982, Echoes Inside the Labyrinth, 1983, Letter to an Imaginary Friend, Parts III and IV, 1985, Selected Poems, 1938-88, 1988; contbr. to profl. publs., anthologies. Recipient Shelley Meml. award Poetry Soc. Am., 1989, Lenore Marshall Nation award for Poetry, 1989; Amy Lowell Travelling Poetry scholar, 1965-66; Guggenheim fellow, 1967-68; Bush Found. fellow, 1975-76, 81; Sr. fellow for poetry NEA, 1986. Mem. Assn. Rhodes Scholars, Phi Beta Kappa. Home: Carver Minn. Died Sept. 19, 1990.

MCGREW, THOMAS JAMES, lawyer; b. Wilkes-Barre, Pa., Jan. 21, 1942; s. James Albert and Mary Alice (Cavan) McG.; m. Barbara Weinstein; children: Jessica Lynn, Benjamin Cavan. A.B. cum laude in English Lit. and Philosophy, U. Scranton, 1963; J.D. cum laude, U. Pa., 1970. Bar: D.C. 1970, U.S. Ct. Appeals (D.C., 2d, 4th, 5th, 8th 10th cirs.) 1974, U.S. Supreme Ct. 1974. Vol. Peace Corps, Nigeria, 1964-67; with Arnold & Porter, Washington, 1970-94, ptnr., 1978-94; first holder Disting. Visitor from Practice chair Georgetown U. Law Ctr., 1985-86, adj. prof. fed. econ. regulation and deregulation, 1986-89; chmn. ANALEX Software Devel. Co., 1985-90. Monthly columnist The Legal Times, 1981-84, Adweek mag., 1984-87; contbr. book revs. to profl. jours. Mem. nat. advt. rev. bd. Coun. Better Bus. Bur., 1989-93, chmn. com. on future advt. self-regulation; mem. nat. coun. Returned Peace Corps Vols. Mem. ABA (chmn. subcom. on the law of false and comparative advt.), D.C. Bar Assn., Washington Coun. Lawyers. Home: Chevy Chase Md. Deceased.

MCHENRY, KEITH WELLES, JR., oil company executive; b. Champaign, Ill., Apr. 6, 1928; s. Keith Welles and Jayne (Hinton) McH.; m. Lou Petry, Aug. 23, 1952 (dec. Oct. 1990); children: John, William; m. Dolores Leo, Mar. 21, 1992. B.S. in Chem. Engring, U. Ill., 1951; Ph.D. in Chem. Engring, Princeton U., 1958. With Amoco Corp. (and affiliates), 1955-93; various positions in R & D Amoco Corp., Whiting, Ind., 1955-74; mgr. process research Amoco Oil Co., Naperville, Ill., 1974-75, v.p. research and devel., 1975-89; sr. v.p. tech. Amoco Corp., Chgo., 1989-93; retired, 1993; Hurd lectr. Northwestern U., 1981; Thiele lectr. in fuels engring. U. Utah, 1983, Gerster Meml. lectr. U. Del., 1987; mem. adv. council Catalysis Center, U. Del., Newark, 1978-83, chmn., 1981-82; mem. adv. council Sch. Engring. and Applied Sci., Princeton U., 1976-82; mem. indsl. adv. bd. Coll. Engring., U. Ill., Chgo., 1979-89, chmn., 1984-86; bd. overseers Sch. Bus. Adminstrn., Ill. Inst. Tech., 1983-86; bd. dirs. Indsl. Research Inst., 1982-90, pres., 1988-89; mem. U.S. Nat. Com. World Petroleum Congress, 1975-83. Trustee North Central Coll., Naperville, 1978-94; chmn. area com. Jr. Achievement, 1981-83, 86-88; ordained elder Presbyn. Ch., 1964. Served with U.S. Army, 1946-47. Recipient award Am. Inst. Chem. Engrs., 1988, Univ. Ill., 1989; Gen. Electric fellow, DuPont fellow, 1952-54. Fellow Am. Inst. Chem. Engrs. (editorial bd. jour. 1974-78); mem. Nat. Acad. Engring., Am. Chem. Soc., AAAS, Sigma Xi, Tau Beta Pi. Home: Chicago Ill. Died Jan. 21, 1994.

MCHUGH, JOHN WELLS, architect; b. Springfield, Ohio, June 30, 1918; m. Gillian Wethey, June 23, 1955; children: Patricia, Colin. B.Arch., Notre Dame U., 1941; Diploma, Am. Acad. Fountainbleau, France, 1951. Registered architect, Ohio, N.Mex., Ariz., Colo. Pres. McHugh Lloyd & Assocs., Santa Fe, N.Mex., 1955-95; designer John Gaw Meem, Santa Fe, 1946-55; instr. U. Notre Dame, 1946; arbitrator Am. Arbitration Assn., Santa Fe, 1979-95; sec. N.Mex. Bd. Examiners for Architects, Santa Fe, 1960-69. Chmn. Arts and Humanities Commn.; chmn. Fedn. Rocky Mountain States, 1966-69, N.Mex. Arts Commn., Santa Fe, 1966-69; mem. adv. com. Urban Policy Bd., 1982. Recipient Cert. of Merit N.Mex. Arts Commn., 1970. Fellow AIA (awards for excellence Santa Fe chpt. 1982). Home: Santa Fe N. Mex. Died Apr. 25, 1995.

MC ININCH, RALPH AUBREY, banker; b. Manchester, N.H., June 15, 1912; s. John A. and Gula (Ruiter) McI.; m. Elizabeth B. Farmer, Sept. 16, 1938; children: Richard D., Douglas A. B.S., Harvard U., 1934; grad., Rutgers U. Sch. Banking, 1938. Asst. trust officer Mchts. Nat. Bank, Manchester, 1936-42; pres Mchts. Nat. Bank, 1948-78; chmn. bd. 1st N.H. Bank, N.A. (formerly Mchts. Nat. Bank), 1978-84, Londonderry Bank & Trust Co., 1979-83; examiner Fed. Res. Bank, Phila., 1942-45; v.p., trust officer Union Trust Co., Providence, 1945-48; v.p., treas., trustee Mchts. Savs. Bank, Manchester, 1948-73; former treas., dir. First N.H., Inc.; past dir. First Bank Mortgage, N.H. Ins. Co., Amoskeag Industries, Inc., Laconia Peoples Nat. Bank & Trust Co., N.H., Fed. Res. Bank Boston. Former mem. exec. bd. Daniel Webster council Boy Scouts Am.; past treas. Manchester Inst. Arts and Scis.; past trustee Gale Home, City of Manchester Cemetery Trust Funds, Manchester City Library; trustee emeritus Colby-Sawyer Coll., New London, N.H.; co-trustee Samuel P. Hunt Found.; bd. dirs. Federated Arts of Manchester, 1990, Indsl. Devel. Authority, State of N.H., 1975-91; mem. profl. conduct com. N.H. Supreme Ct., 1979-82. Mem. Manchester C. of C., Am. Automobile Assn. (dir.). Clubs: Rotary, Harvard of N.H, Manchester Country. Home: Manchester N.H. Died March 29, 1993; buried Pine Grove Cemetary, Manchester, N.H.

MC INNIS, MICHAEL L., agricultural studies educator. Asst. prof. agriculture Eastrn Oreg. State Coll., La Grande. Fellow Nat. Assn. Colls. Tchrs. Agriculture 1992. Home: La Grande Oreg. Deceased.

MC KEAN, HUGH FERGUSON, college president, painter, writer; b. Beaver Falls, Pa., July 28, 1908; s. Arthur and Eleanor (Ferguson) McK.; m. Jeannette Genius, June 28, 1945. A.B., Rollins Coll., 1930; M.A., Williams Coll., 1940; Dr. Space Edn., Fla. Inst. Tech., 1963; L.H.D., Stetson U. Coll. Law, 1961; LL.D., U. Tampa, 1970; D.F.A., Rollins Coll., 1972. Instr. art Rollins Coll., Winter Park, Fla., 1932-35; asst. prof.

Rollins Coll., 1935-37, asst. prof., asst. to dir. dept. art, 1937-41, assoc. prof., 1941-45, prof. art, dir. Charles Hosmer Morse Mus. Am. Art, 1942-95, acting pres., 1951-52, pres., 1952-69, pres. emeritus, chancellor, 1969-73; chmn. bd., pres. Charles Hosmer Morse Found., 1976-95; mem. Fla. Fine Arts Coun., 1970-74; pres. Winter Park Land Co. Author: The 'Lost' Treasures of Louis Comfort Tiffany, 1980; works exhibited, Second Nat. Exhbn. Am. Painting, N.Y.C., Soc. The Four Arts, Palm Beach, Fla., 1948, Allied Artists Am. Ann Exhbn., 1949, 4th Southeastern Ann., Atlanta, 1949, numerous ann. exhbns., Fla. Fedn. Art, collections, Tol. Mus. Art U. Va. Trustee Louis Comfort Tiffany Found., 1959-95; charter pres. Channel 24 ETV, Orlando, Fla.; bd. visitors Def. Intelligence Sch., 1968-78. Lt. comdr. USNR, 1942-45. Recipient Decoration Honor Rollins Coll., 1942; Cervantes medal Hispanic Inst. in Fla., 1952; John Young award Orlando Area C. of C., 1967; best work in show Fla. Fedn. Art Ann. Exhbn., 1931, 49; best Fla. landscape, 1949. Mem. Am. Soc. Order of St. John, Nat. Soccer Coaches Am., Omicron Delta Kappa. Clubs: X, Century Assn. (N.Y.C.); Orlando (Fla.) Country; University (N.Y.C.); University (Winter Park). Home: Winter Park Fla. Died May 6, 1995.

MCKEE, OATHER DORRIS, bakery executive; b. Dixon, Miss., Jan. 21, 1905; s. Finis E. and Sarah Ann Elizabeth (Cooper) McK.; m. Anna Ruth King, Aug. 4, 1928; children: Winifred, Ellsworth, Elizabeth, Jack. Student, So. Coll., Collegedale, Tenn. Founder, pres. McKee Baking Co., Collegedale, 1934-71, chmn. bd., 1971-95. Inventor automated bakery equipment. Mem. Tenn. Air Pollution Control Bd., 1971-79; chmn. bd. Hewitt Research Found., 1970-87. Parade marshall Armed Forces Day Parade, 1988. Recipient Alumnus of Yr. award So. Coll., 1978. Mem. Am. Soc. Bakery Engrs., Biscuit and Cracker Mfrs. Assn. (bd. dirs. 1972-95), Am. Bakers Assn. (gov. 1976-86), Profl. and Bus. Men's Assn. (pres. 1966-87), Greater Chattanooga Area C. of C. (bd. dirs. 1978-82, Arthur G. Vieth Meml. award 1979, Community Improvement award 1982, Nat. Heritage award 1985, Mgr. of Yr. award 1987). Republican. Adventist. Club: Mountain City. Lodge: Rotary. Died Oct 27, 1995. Home: Ooltewah Tenn.

MC KENNA, THOMAS JOSEPH, advertising executive; b. Chgo., Oct. 20, 1929; s. Robert Emmet and Helen Elizabeth (Norton) McK.; m. Geraldine M. Bednarz, May 23, 1953 (div. June 1976); children—Terence Patrick, Kathleen Mary, Thomas Joseph Jr. B.A., Northwestern U., 1952. Advt. mgr. farm div. Montgomery Ward, Chgo., 1952-56; mgr. sales promotion Ency. Brit., Chgo., 1956-58, dir. advt. and sales promotion, 1958-61; v.p. Marketways, Inc., Chgo., 1962-63; exec. v.p. Hefter-McKenna Advt., Oak Park, Ill., 1963-69; sr. v.p. creative Douglas Dunhill, Inc., Chgo., 1969-81; pres. McKenna & Erdos, Ltd., Chgo., 1981-91; chmn. McKenna Assocs., Chgo., 1991-95. With USAF, 1951-52. Recipient 29 creative awards Chgo. Assn. Direct Mktg., 1973-84. Mem. Direct Mktg. Assn. (Silver Mailbox award 1975). Home: Chicago Ill. Died Dec. 26, 1995.

MC KINLEY, WILLIAM LESTER, manufacturing company executive; b. Grant, Mich., Mar. 2, 1924; s. Robert B. and Susie (McInnis) McK.; m. Margaret Alice Sheller, Aug. 17, 1946; children—Richard, Michael, Cathleen. Student, Alma (Mich.) Coll., 1942, U. Oreg., 1943; B.A., U. Mich., 1948, LL.B., 1950. Trainee Auto Owners Ins. Co., Lansing, Mich., 1950; with Gerber Products Co., Fremont, Mich., 1950-95; v.p., sec. Gerber Products Co., 1965-68, gen. counsel, 1955-72, exec. v.p., 1971-78, vice chmn., 1978-85, chmn., chief exec. officer, 1985-87, also dir.; dir. Diamond Crystal. Mem. Fremont Pub. Sch. Bd., 1962-69, Gerber Meml. Hosp., 1959-85. Served with AUS, World War II. Mem. Phi Alpha Delta. Conglist. Club: Rotarian. Home: Holland Mich. Died July 17, 1995.

MCLANE, ROBERT DRAYTON, SR., food products executive; b. 1901; married. With McLane Co. Inc., Temple, Tex., chmn., also bd. dirs. Home: Temple Tex. Deceased.

MCLAUGHLIN, JOHN D., food manufacturing and home development executive, retired army officer; b. San Francisco, Dec. 24, 1917; s. John and Lottie (Bruhns) McL.; m. Elizabeth Susan Stumper, July 11, 1946; children: John D., William F., Susan C. Ed., George Washington U.; grad., Armed Forces Staff Coll., 1956, Nat. War Coll., 1959, Advanced Mgmt. Program, Harvard U., 1963; Ph.D. (hon.), Johnson and Wales Coll. Commd. 2d lt. U.S. Army, 1942, advanced through grades to lt. gen.; staff asst. Office Sec. of Def., 1960-61; exec. officer Def. Supply Agy., 1961-63; asst. commandant U.S. Army Q.M. Sch., 1963-65; chief of staff U.S. Army, VietNam, 1965-66; dir. supply U.S. Army Gen. Staff, 1966-67; asst. chief of staff for logistics Pacific Command (CINCPAC), 1967-69; comdg. gen. Quartermaster Center, comdt. U.S. Army Quartermaster Sch., Ft. Lee, Va., 1969-73; comdr. U.S. Theater Army Support Command, Europe, 1973-74; v.p. L.J. Minor Corp., Cleve., 1974-79; pres. L.J. Minor Corp., 1979-83, Piney Springs Devel. Corp.; chmn., chief exec. officer L.J. Minor Corp., 1983-87; pres. L.J. Minor Internat., 1987—; bd. dirs. Sovran Bank, Petersburg, Va.; chmn. bd. Food Am. Corp., GGM Assoc., Inc., McLaughlin Assocs., Inc. Mem. exec. coun. Richmond Boy Scouts Am.; mem. adv. bd. Ednl. Inst. of Am. Culinary Fedn.; trustee Culinary Inst. Am.; pres. U.S. Culinary Team Found.; pres. Q.M. Meml. Found. With AUS, 1934-74. Decorated D.S.M. with oak leaf cluster, Legion of Merit with 4 oak leaf clusters, Bronze Star Medal with 2 oak leaf clusters, Air medal U.S., Distinguished Service Medal Greece; recipient Silver Plate award Internat. Food Service Mfrs. Assn., 1973, Silver Beaver award Boy Scouts Am., 1973. Mem. Quartermaster Assn. (pres. Washington chpt. 1969-70), Harvard Bus. Sch. Alumni Assn., Am. Culinary Fedn., Internat. Foodsvc. Mfrs. Assn., Nat. Restaurant Assn. (Ednl. Found. Diplomates award 1990), Gold and Silver Plate Award Soc., Am. Acad. Chefs (hon. life), Am. Legion, VFW, Mil. Order World Wars, Honorable Order Golden Toque. Clubs: Kiwanis (bd. dirs. Petersburg chpt.), Harvard of Va., Army-Navy. Home: Richmond Va.

MCLAURIN, RONALD DE, political analyst, consultant, author, journalist; b. Oakland, Calif., Oct. 8, 1944; s. Lauchlin De and Marie Annette (Friedman) McL.; m. Joan Adcock, June 11, 1966; children: Leila, Cara. B.A., U. So. Calif., 1965; student, U. Tunis, Tunisia, 1964-65; A.M., Tufts U., 1966, M.A.L.D., 1967, Ph.D., 1973. Instr. Merrimack Coll., North Andover, Mass., 1966-67; mgmt. asst. Office Sec. Def., Washington, 1967-68; asst. for Africa Office Asst. Sec. Def. for Internat. Security Affairs, 1968-69; rsch. scientist Am. Inst. Rsch., Washington, 1969-75; sr. assoc. Abbott Assocs., Inc., Springfield, Va., 1975-94; sec.-treas. Abbott Assocs., Inc., 1985-86, pres., 1986-94; exec. dir. Pacific Century Inst., 1989-91; columnist Diyar newspaper, 1991; internat. rsch. assoc. Inha U., Korea, 1985-95; fellow Ctr. Internat. Devel. U. Md., 1983-86, ptnr. Aurora Ltd., 1986-87; dir. Lau-Mar Ltd., Honolulu, 1981-86, also chmn.; cons. Allen Wayne, Ltd., 1985-86, Am. Insts. Rsch., 1975-76, Analytical Assessments Corp. 1977-79, BDM Corp., 1985-90, Booz Allen & Hamilton, 1989, Bus. Coun. Internat. Understanding, 1984-87, 92-95, CBOL Corp., 1988-95, C&O Resources, 1993-95, Ctr. Advanced Internat. Studies, U. Miami, 1973, Ctr. Advanced Rsch. Inc., 1977-82, Ctr. Strategic and Internat. Studies, Georgetown U., 1981, 84, Grolier, 1990-95, Gulf Cons. Group, 1982-83, Armitage Assocs., 1994-95, Human Resources Rsch. Orgn., 1989, Internat. Cultural Found., 1981, Office Pres. Lebanon, 1984-85, 87, Ministry Def. Lebanon, 1984-85, Washington Embassy Lebanon, 1983-88, Office Crown Prince Jordan, 1982-85, Maison du Futur, 1989-91, Mid. East Assessments Group, 1982-89, Manly, Inc., 1989, Nat. Def. U., 1990-91, Profs. World Peace Acad., 1981, RBI, Inc., 1991, Royal Sci. Soc. (Jordan), 1982-83, Synergy Cons. Ltd., 1990-95, TRW, 1987, Trans Devel. Corp., 1986-87, Univ. Ky. Rsch. Found., 1992-93, Sci. Applications Internat. Corp., 1994-95; Joint Econ. Com. U.S. Congress, 1977-78, Libr. Congress, 1977-78, Office of Asst. Sec. U.S. Dept. Def., 1973, A.R. Wagner and Co., 1976-77; with U. Ky. Rsch. Found., 1992-93. Author: The Middle East in Soviet Policy, 1975, The Art and Science of Psychological Operations, 2 vols., 1976, Foreign Policy Making in the Middle East, 1977, The Political Role of Minority Groups in the Middle East, 1979, Beyond Camp David, 1981, Military Propaganda, 1982, Middle East Foreign Policy: Issues and Processes, 1982, Lebanon and the World in the 1980s, 1983, The Emergence of a New Lebanon: Fantasy or Reality?, 1984, Jordan: The Impact of Social Change on the Tribes, 1984, U.S. Defense Posture in the Pacific, 1987, Alliance Under Tension: Critical Issues in U.S.-Korean Relations, 1988, The Dilemma of Third World Defense Industries: Supplier Controls and Recipient Autonomy, 1989, The U.S. and the Defense of the Pacific, 1989; contbg. editor Mid. East Insight, 1991-95; mem. editorial bd. Exec. Internat. Insight, 1992-95; cons. editor Asia-Pacific Def. Forum, 1976-84; contbr. articles to profl. jours. Mem. Internat. Studies Assn., Inter-Univ. Seminar Armed Forces and Soc., Middle East Inst., Fgn. Policy Research Inst. Psychol. Ops. Soc. Home: Springfield Va. Died June 17, 1995.

MCLEOD, LIONEL E., hospital administrator, medical educator; b. Wainwright, Alta., Can., Aug. 9, 1927; s. Frank E. and Anne (Withnell) McL.; m. Barbara Ann Lipsey, Oct. 18, 1952; children: Laura Jane, Bruce E., Judy Ann, Nancy Joan. BSc, U. Alta., 1949, MD, 1951; MSc, McGill U., 1957. Med. staff, prof. medicine U. Alta Hosp., U. Alta., Can., 1957-68; prof, head Med. U., Calgary, Can., 1968-73; dir. medicine Foothills Hosp., Calgary, Can., 1968-73; dean med. Med. U., Calgary, Can., 1973-81; pres., CEO Univ. Hosp., Can., 1981-94; trustee Med. Foothills Hosp., Calgary, Can.; pres. Alta. Heritage Found. Med. Rsch., 1981-89. V.P. Calgary United Way; bd. dirs. Alta. Heart Found. Markle scholar Med. Sci., 1958-63; named Disting. med. Alumni U. Alta. 1976. Fellow Royal Coll. Physicians and Surgeons Can. (past pres.), Royal Coll. Physicians Edinburgh, Am. Coll. Physicians; mem. Can. Cancer Soc. (dir. Alta. divsn.), Assn. Can. Med. Colls. (past pres.), Can. Soc. Nephrology (past pres.), Can. Coun. Hosp. Accredation (past chmn.), Can. Soc. Clin. Investigation, Centre Club. Home: Vancouver Can. Deceased.

MCLOUGHLIN, WILLIAM GERALD, JR., history educator; b. Maplewood, N.J., June 11, 1922; s. William G. and Florence M. (Quinn) McL.; m. Virginia Ward Duffy, Dec. 25, 1951; children: Helen, Gail, Martha. AB, Princeton U., 1947; MA, Harvard U 1948, PhD, 1953. Carnegie fellow Brown U., Pr vidence, 1954-55, asst. prof. polit. sci. and Am. civic 1955-58, asst. prof. history, 1958-60, assoc. prof., 196 63, prof., 1963-92, Annie McClelland and Willa Prescott Smith chair, 1981-92, chmn. Am. civilizatio program, 1958-60, 73-75; sec. of coun. Inst. Early An History, Williamsburg, Va., 1973-75, chmn. ann. boo prize com., 1973-74. Author: Billy Sunday Was his Re Name, 1955, Billy Graham. Revivalist in a Secular Ag 1958, Isaac Backus and the American Pietistic Trad tion, 1967, The Meaning of Henry Ward Beecher, 197 New England Dissent, 2 vols., 1971 (Melcher price f best book Religion in America 1972), Rhode Island: Bicentennial History, 1978, Revivals, Awakenings an Reform, 1978, Cherokees and Missionaries, 198 Cherokee Ghost Dance and Other Essays on th Southeastern Indians, 1984, Cherokee Renascence, 19 (Wheeler-Voeglin prize Soc. Ethnohistory 1987), Eva and John B. Jones: Champions of the Cherokees, 199 Soul Liberty, 1991, After the Trail of Tears, 1993, Th Cherokees and Christianity, 1994; editor: Charl Grandison Finney: Lectures on Revivals of Religio 1960, (with Robert Bellah) Religion in America, 196 The American Evangelicals, 1968, (with Jack P. Green Preachers and Politicians, 1977, The Diary of Isaa Backus, 3 vols., 1979. Chmn. R.I. affiliate ACLU 1969-70, chmn. free speech com., 1985-92; chmn. R. Com. for Peace in Vietnam, 1970; former chmn. variou PTA's, Providence. 2d lt. F.A., AUS, 1943-46. Fu bright sr. fellow U. London, 1953-54, fellow Gu genheim Found., 1960-61, Harvard Ctr. for Study Liberty, 1960-62, Charles Warren Ctr., Harvard U 1969-70, ACLS, 1971-72, sr. fellow NEH, 1968-6 summer fellow Newberry Libr., 1974. Mem. Am. Ar tiquarian Soc., Soc. Am. Historians, Mass. Hist. Soc. Home: Providence R.I. Died Dec. 28, 1992; interre Swan Point Cemetary, Providence, R.I.

MC MANUS, CHARLES ANTHONY, JR., retire federal official, political and public relations executiv b. Wilkes-Barre, Pa., June 4, 1927; s. Charles Anthon and Mary (Romanoski) McM.; m. Catherine Madison, Sept. 8, 1951; children: Patricia, Catherin Mary, Charles, Susan, William, James. Student, King Coll., Wilkes-Barre, 1946-49, Wyo. Sem. Sch. Bus Kingston, Pa., 1949-51, Temple U., 1953-59. Wi Thiokol Chem. Corp., Trenton, N.J., 1951-52, U.S. Ste Corp., 1952-59; exec. dir. Americans for Constl. Actio Washington, 1959-69; pres., trustee Americans for Co stl. Action, 1969-75; confidential asst. to dep. underse pub. and Congl. affairs Dept. Agr., Washington, 197 77; dir. fin.; polit. action com. Republican Nat. Com 1977-78; public and govt. affairs cons., 1978-80; nat. di Nat. Draft Haig Com., 1979; asst. to insp. gen. Dep Energy, 1981; ret., 1991; dir. Congl. and public affai FERC, 1981-90; dep. asst. adminstr. Congl. and legi affairs SBA, 1990; dep. dir. policy and program analys Dept. Interior, 1991. Bd. dirs. Friends of U.S. Na Arboretum, U.S. Nat. Columns Com. Served wi USNR, 1945-46. Mem. King's Coll. Alumni Assn. Republican. Roman Catholic. Clubs: K.C, Nat. Pres Capitol Hill; Boys and Girls (Bowie, Md.); Off th Record. Home: Bowie Md. Died Nov. 8, 1995.

MCMANUS, WILLIAM JAY, political organizatio executive; b. Mansemond County, Va., Aug. 28, 1900; P.A. and Mary E. (Finn) McM.; m. Georgie Garriso Sept. 19, 1952. BA, Georgetown U., 1924; postgrad Nat. Law U., 1929, U. Wis., Milw., 1959, Harvard U 1965. V.p. pub. rels. and pub. affairs Chesapeake Potomac Telephone Co., Washington, Richmond, Va Charleston, W.Va., and Balt., 1925-65; v.p. Byers McManus Assocs., Inc., Washington, from 1966; treas Rep. Nat. Com., from 1975; bd. dirs. Riggs Nat. Bank Mem. Commn. on White House Fellows; bd. dir Columbia Hosp. for Women, Children's Hosp. Na Med. Ctr., Washington Heart Assn., United Give Fund, Boy Scouts Am., YMCA Found., Nat Histori Trust; pres., bd. dirs. D.C. Soc. for Crippled Childre vice chmn. bd. dirs. D.C. chpt. ARC; v.p. emeritus, b dirs. Fed. City Council; chmn. Decatur House Counci pres. Friendly Sons St. Patrick. Recipient Disting. Se vice award Washington Bd. Trade, 1967, Def. Orienta tion Conf. Assn., 1960, ARC, 1962, Mabel Boarma award ARC, 1971, D.C. Soc. for Crippled Childre 1970, Am. Heart Assn., 1975, Award for Patrioti Civilian Service, U.S. Army, 1983. Mem. Pub. Rela tions Soc. Am., Nat. Geog. Soc., U.S. Navy Leagu Def. Orientation Conf. Assn., Pub. Mems. Assn. Fg Policy. Clubs: Chevy Chase, Met., Columbia, Carlto Nat. Press, Alfalfa, Annapolis Yacht, 1925 F St. (pres. Saints and Sinners (Washington). Home: Washingto D.C. Deceased.

MCMATH, VIRGINIA KATHERINE See ROGERS GINGER

MCMILLAN, JAMES BRYAN, federal judge, retire b. Goldsboro, N.C., Dec. 19, 1916; s. Robert Hunte and Louise (Outlaw) McM.; m. Margaret Blair Mile Feb. 27, 1944 (dec. Mar. 1985); children: James Brya Marjorie Miles Rodell; m. Holly Smith Neaves, Au 23, 1987. Grad., Presbyn. Jr. Coll., 1934; AB, U. N.C 1937; JD, Harvard U., 1940; LLD (hon.), Belmo Abbey Coll., 1982, Davidson Coll., 1984, Johnson C Smith Coll., 1985, U. N.C., 1988, St. Andrews Presby Coll., 1989, U. N.C., Charlotte, 1990; LHD (hon.)

ueens Coll., 1991. Bar: N.C. 1941. Mem. staff N.C. tty.-gen., 1940-42; ptnr. Helms, Mulliss, McMillan & ohnston, Charlotte, 1946-68; judge U.S. Dist. Ct. (we. ist.) N.C., Charlotte, 1968-93; retired, 1993; judge pro em Charlotte City Ct., 1947-51; mem. faculty Nat. Inst. rial Advocacy, Boulder, Colo., 1973-81; instr. trial dvocacy course Harvard Law Sch., 1975-93 , U. N.C. aw Sch., 1976-78, U. Fla. Law Sch., 1978-80; mem. I.C. Cts. Commn., 1963-71. Pres. Travelers Aid Soc., 957-59; bd. visitors Davidson Coll. Lt. USNR, 1942-6, ETO. Recipient Algernon Sydney Sullivan award t. Andrews Presbyn. Coll. Fellow Internat. Acad. rial Lawyers; mem. ABA, 26th Dist. Bar Assn. (pres. 957-58), N.C. Bar Assn. (pres. 1960-61), Am. Judicaire Soc. (dir. 1984-95). United World Federalists, Newcomen Soc., St. Andrews Coll. Alumni Assn. (pres. 965-66), Order of Coif, Golden Fleece, Omicron Delta appa. Democrat. Presbyterian. Home: Charlotte I.C. Died Mar. 4, 1995.

MCMORRIS, GRACE ELIZABETH, banker; b. Aalden, Mass., Feb. 6, 1922; d. John Edward and elma Florence (Swanson) O'Brien; B.A., Boston U., 944; postgrad. Ariz. State U., 1962; m. William Aichael McMorris, May 14, 1944 (dec.); children: Sheila Elizabeth McMorris Christenson, Michael, James, John. Clk., Parlin Meml. Library, Everett, Mass., part-time, 938-40; clk. student post office Boston U., 1941-42; upr. classified advt. desk The Boston Post, 1942-44; ubstitute tchr. public schs., Randolph, Mass., 1956-57; vith Valley Nat. Bank Ariz., Phoenix, 1960-87, trust dminstr., 1969-73, trust officer, 1973-75, asst. v.p., 975-78, v.p., 1978-87, corporate trust mgr., 1977-87, et., 1987. cons. in field, 1988-89. Mem. Am. Soc. Corp. ecs. (pres., treas. Phoenix chpt. 1989-90, v.p.), Pi ambda Sigma (nat. treas. 1947-48). Roman Catholic. Deceased. Home: Chandler Ariz.

MCMURREN, WILLIAM HENRY, construction ompany executive; b. Ontario, Oreg., Oct. 20, 1927; s. erene Elbert and Louise (Baker) McM.; B.S. in Civil Engring., Tex. A & M U., 1950; m. Carlyn Dorothy tenberg, Oct. 17, 1953; children—Catherine Lynn, ohn Henry. With Morrison-Knudsen Co., Boise, Idaho, 955—, exec. v.p., 1969-72, pres., chief exec. officer, 972-84, chmn., chief exec. officer, 1984—, also dir.; dir. st Nat. Bank, Boise, Albertson's, Inc., Boise, Wesnghouse Electric Corp., Pitts. Served with AUS, 1945-6, 50-53. Mem. Am. Bur. Shipping, Soc. Am. Mil. ngrs. (dir.), Moles, Beavers (pres., dir.), Pub. Works Hist. Soc. (trustee). Clubs: Hillcrest Country (Boise); Capitol Hill (Washington). Home: Boise Idaho

MCNAMARA, WILLIAM ALBINUS, utility execuve; b. Superior, Wis., Mar. 1, 1909; s. Bartlett M. and Mary J. (Carpenter) McN.; m. Irene G. Chaltre, June 8, 935; children: William B., Thomas J., John M. B.A. in Commerce, U. Wis., 1930, M.A., 1931, LL.B., 1934. Bar: Wis. 1934. Accountant Frazer and Torbett C.P.A.s), Chgo., 1934-35; sec. bondholders com. Chgo. Title & Trust Co., 1935-36; corp. sec. Curt G. Joa, Inc., Sheboygan Falls, Wis., 1936-37; dir. Curt G. Joa, Inc., 937-92; ptnr. Cavanaugh & McNamara, Madison, Wis., 1937-42, Rieser, Mathy, McNamara & Stafford, Madison, 1942-58; fin. v.p., then v.p. fin. Madison Gas nd Electric Co., 1958-77, chmn. bd., 1977-85, dir., 958-85, chmn.-dir. emeritus, 1984-91; dir. First Fed. Savs. & Loan Assn., Madison, 1985-91; with 1st Fed Savs. Bank, Madison, 1966-85, dir. emeritus 1985-93. Mem. pres.'s council Edgewood Coll., Madison, 1969-2; adv. bd. St. Mary's Hosp. Nursing Sch., 1965-66. Mem. Am. Gas Assn., Wis. Utility Assn., ABA, State Bar Wis. (chmn. taxation sect. 1950-51), Dane County Bar Assn., Greater Madison C. of C. (pres. 1962), Wis. Bus. Econs. Assn. Republican. Roman Catholic. Club: Madison. Lodge: K.C. Home: Clearwater Fla. Died 993.

MCNEIL, GEORGE JOSEPH, painter; b. Bklyn., Feb. 2, 1908; s. James Henry and Julia Anna (Kenney) McN.; m. Dora Tamler, Feb. 8, 1936; children: Helen, ames. Student, Pratt Inst., 1927-29, Art Students League, 1930-31, 32-33, Hans Hofmann Sch. Fine Art, 933-36; BS, Columbia Tchrs. Coll., 1943, MA, 1946, EdD, 1952; DFA (hon.), Pratt Inst., 1985, Md. Inst. Coll. Art, 1988, U. Hartford, 1990. Asst. prof. U. Wyo., 1946-48; assoc. dean, prof. Pratt Inst., 1948-74, rof. emeritus, 1974-95; guest prof. U. Calif.-Berkeley, 956-57; artist-in-residence Tamarind Inst., 1971, 75, 76, 80. One-man exhbns. include Lyceum Gallery, Havana, Cuba, 1941, Egan Gallery, N.Y.C., 1950, 52-54, De Young Mus., San Francisco, 1956, Poindexter Gallery, N.Y.C., 1957, 59, Howard Wise Gallery, N.Y.C., 1960, 62, 64, 67, Univ. Art Mus., Austin, Tex., 1965, Great ones Gallery, N.Y.C., 1966, Des Moines Art Ctr., 969, Pratt Manhattan Ctr., 1973, Landmark Gallery, 975, Berman Gallery, 1977, Terry Dintenfass Gallery, 979, Gruenebaum Gallery, 1981, 83, 85, 87, Ft. Lauderdale Mus., 1982, Knoedler Gallery, 1989, Hirschl and Adler Modern Art Gallery, 1991, Montclair Art Mus., 1991, M. Silverman Gallery, L.A., 1992, N.Y. Studio Sch., N.Y.C., 1993, Rena Bransten Gallery, San Francisco, 1993; group exhbns. include Am. Abstract Artists exhbns., 1935-56, Art Inst. Chgo., 1948, Mus. Modern Art, 1951, Whitney Mus., 1953, 57, 61, 65, Carnegie Internat. exhbns., 1953, 55, 58; represented in permanent collections including Bundy Art Gallery, Waitsfield, Vt., Mus. Modern Art, N.Y.C., Nat. Mus., Havana, Newark Mus., Walker Art Ctr., Mpls., U. Mich. Art Mus., U. Tex. Art Mus., Met. Mus. Art., Whitney Mus. Served with USNR, 1943-46. Recipient Ford Found. purchase, 1963, Nat. Coun. on Arts award, 1966; Guggenheim fellow, 1968. Mem. Am. Inst. Arts and Letters (award 1982). Home: Brooklyn N.Y. Died Jan. 10, 1995.

MCNICHOLS, ROBERT J., federal judge; b. 1922. Student, Wash. State U., 1946-48; J.D., Gonzaga U., 1952. Bar: Wash. 1952. Sr. judge U.S. Dist. Ct. for Eastern Dist. Wash., Spokane. Home: Spokane Wash. Died Dec. 20, 1992.

MCNULTY, PAUL JAMES, business educator, university dean; b. Elmira, N.Y., Feb. 10, 1931; s. Francis James and Marion Agnes (Good) McN.; m. Marian Adella Stever, July 16, 1960 (div. 1977); children: Michael James, Gregory Paul, Clare Elizabeth. B.A., Hobart Coll., 1959; Ph.D., Cornell U., 1965. Research asst. N.Y. State Div. of the Budget, Albany, 1960-61; instr. Cornell U., Ithaca, N.Y., 1964-65; asst. prof. Grad. Sch. of Bus., Columbia U., N.Y.C., 1965-68, assoc. prof., 1968-73, prof., from 1973, vice dean for acad. affairs, from 1985. Author: The Origins and Development of Labor Economics, 1980; contbr. articles to profl. jours. Trustee Jersey City State Coll., 1976-81, chmn., 1980-81; vice chmn. bd. trustees Columbia Jour. World Bus.; co-dir. Columbia Energy Forum; v.p. LEAD Program in Bus., from 1985. Served with U.S. Army, 1951-53. Woodrow Wilson fellow, 1958-59. Mem. Am. Econs. Assn., Hist. Econs. Soc., Assn. Evolutionary Econs., Phi Beta Kappa, Phi Kappa Phi, Beta Gamma Sigma. Home: New York N.Y. Deceased.

MCQUARRIE, GERALD H., savings and loan association executive; b. Minersville, Utah, June 28, 1921; s. Herrick and Lucy Irene (Hall) McQ.; m. Oneida B. Martin, Feb. 22, 1946; children: Sandra Irene, Gerald Brent, Roger Scott. Grad., Compton Coll., 1941. Pres. SouthLand Investment Corp.; co-founder, chief exec. officer, vice chmn. bd. Downey Savs. and Loan Assn., Newport Beach, Calif., also bd. dirs. With USNR, 1945-46, USAF, 1950-52. Mem. LDS Ch. Home: Newport Beach Calif. Died May 30, 1992.

MCRAE, CARMEN, singer. Albums include: By Special Request, 1955, After Glow, 1957, Something to Swing About, 1959, The Great American Songbook, 1972, Live at Birdland West, 1980, Live at Bubba's, 1981, Youre Lookin' at Me, 1983, Carmen Sings Monk, 1990, Sarah - Dedicated To You, 1991, Live at Century Plaza, 1991, The Ultimate Carmen McRae, 1991, Woman Talk, 1991, Here to Stay, 1991, Any Old Time; (with George Shearing) Two for the Road, (with Red Holloway, John Clayton, Paul Humphrey, Jack McDuff, and Phil Upchurch) Fine and Mellow, 1988; film appearances: Hotel, 1967, Jo Jo Dancer, Your Life Is Calling, 1986; TV appearances: Soul, 1976, Sammy and Company, 1976, Carmen McRae in Concert, 1979, From Jumpstreet, 1980, At the Palace, 1981, Billie Holiday: A Tribute, 1981, L.A. Jazz, 1982. Home: Beverly Hills Calif. Died Nov. 10, 1994.

MCVEY, WILLIAM MOZART, sculptor; b. Boston, July 12, 1905; s. Silas R. and Cornelia (Mozart) McV.; m. Leza Marie Sullivan, Mar. 31, 1932. Grad. Cleve. Sch. Art, 1928; student Rice Inst., 1923-25, Acadamie Colarossi and Acadamie Scandinave, Paris, 1929-31; pupil of Dispiau, Paris, 1929-31; Tchr. Cleve. Mus., 1932, Houston Mus., 1936-38, U. Tex., Austin, 1939-46, Ohio State U., Columbus, summer 1946, Cranbrook Art Acad., Bloomfield Hills, Mich., 1946-53; head sculpture dept. Cleve. Inst. Art, 1953-67; vis. sculptor Sch. Fine Arts, Ohio State U., Columbus, 1963-64. Represented in permanent collections IBM, Univ. Mus., Pomona, Calif., Wichita Art Mus., Cleve. Mus., Houston Mus., Syracuse Mus., Cranbrook Mus., Harvard Library, Smithsonian Inst., Yale Library, Nat. Cathedral, Washington, Ariana Mus., Geneva, others; publicly owned works include heroic reliefs and doors San Jacinto Monument, Tex., door FTC, Washington, doors and reliefs Tex. Meml. Mus., reliefs Lakeview Terrace Housing Project, Cleve., heroic grizzly Nat. Hist. Mus., figure Abercrombie Lab., Rice Inst., monument to Davy Crockett, Ozona, Tex., to James Bowie, Texarkana, Tex.; 9 foot bronze of Winston Churchill, British Embassy, Washington; St. Margaret of Scotland and Jan Hus at Washington Cathedral, St. Olga of Russia, Simon de Monfort, Stephen Langton, Sir Edward Coke, Churchill Bay of Nat. Cathedral heroic U.S. Shields Fed. Bldg., Cleve., Jennings Meml., Univ. Circle, Cleve., granite hippo (with Victor Gruen) Eastgate Shopping Ctr., Detroit, 5-ton whale Lincoln Ctr., Urbana, Ill., bronze hippo Cleve. Heights Children's Library, Bell Tower, Hiram Coll., Berry Monument bronze Cleve. Hopkins Airport, panels (with Eero Saarinen) Christ Lutheran Ch., Mpls., bronze of George Washington at Washington Sq., Cleve., head of Churchill, Chartwell, Eng., stainless steel and bronze B clef logo Blossom Music Ctr., numerous others; exhibited honor ct. Paris Grand Salon, 1930, Salon d'Automne, 1931. Chmn. Nat. screening com. Fulbright grants. Served to maj. USAF, World War II. Recipient numerous awards Nat. Sculpture Show, Ceramic Nat., Nat. Archtl. Ceramic, Mich. Acad. Sci. Arts and Letters, Internat. Cultural Exchange Ceramic Exhibit. Fellow Nat. Sculpture Soc.; mem. Coll. Art Assn., Am. Soc. Aesthetics, Internat. Platform Assn., NAD (assoc.). Papers in Archives Am. Art, Smithsonian Inst. Died May 15, 1995. Home: Cleveland Ohio

MCWHIRTER, WILLIAM BUFORD, business consultant; b. Waco, Tex., Aug. 23, 1918; s. Buford and Katherine (McCollum) McW.; A.B.A., Glendale Jr. Coll., 1937; B.A. with honors, U. Calif. Berkeley, 1939; m. Catherine Eugenia Forbes, Sept. 21, 1956. Br. mgr. IBM Corp., San Francisco, 1949-56, dist. mgr. N.Y. area, 1956-57, gen. mgr. supplies div., 1957-59, pres. data systems div., White Plains, N.Y., 1959-62, IBM dir. orgn., 1962-64, pres. indsl. products div., 1964-65; cons. to IBM, other firms, 1966-93; dir. Amdahl Corp., Sunnyvale, Calif., Itel Corp., San Francisco, MHC Corp., N.Y.C. Trustee Mus. of No. Ariz., Scottsdale Meml. Hosp. Found. Served to lt. comdr. USN, 1942-46. Mem. Phi Beta Kappa, Theta Xi. Clubs: San Francisco Sales Executives (pres. 1955-56); Siwanoy (Bronxville, N.Y.); Metropolitan (N.Y.C.); Army-Navy (Arlington, Va.); Phoenix Country; Desert Forest (Carefree, Ariz.); Pauma Valley (Calif.); Desert Mountain Country (Maricopa County, Ariz.). Died Aug. 26, 1993. Home: Carefree Ariz.

MEACHAM, CRAIG LEI, police chief; b. Pasadena, Calif., Mar. 5, 1931; s. William Albert and Edna May (Hornbeck) M.; m. Carolyn June Stentz, Feb. 22, 1971; children: Alan, Pamela, Craig, Janelle, Cynthia. A.A., Rio Hondo Coll., 1964; B.A., Calif. Western U., 1976, M.A., 1976. With Whittier (Calif.) Police Dept., 1955-69, div. comdr., until 1969; cons. criminal justice Gov. Ronald Reagan, 1969-70; dep. chief West Covina Police Dept., 1970-78, chief of police, 1978-95, pub. safety div. mgr., 1981-95; instr. Rio Hondo Coll. With USAF, 1950-54. Mem. Los Angeles County Chiefs of Police Assn. (pres. 1982), San Gabriel Valley Police Chiefs Assn. (pres. 1982), Calif. Police Chiefs Assn. (pres. 1988), Peace Officers Assn. Los Angeles County (pres. 1986-95), San Gabriel Valley Peace Officers Assn. (pres. 1983), West Covina C. of C. (legis. com.). Club: West Covina Lions. Died June 12, 1995. Home: West Covina Calif.

MEADE, EDWIN BAYLIES, retired lawyer; b. Danville, Va., Oct. 30, 1896; s. Julian and Bessie Edmunds (Bouldin) M.; m. Madeline Merle Read, June 23, 1923; children: Edwin Baylies, Frank Opie, Elizabeth Lyne. Student, Danville Sch. for Boys; LL.B., U. Va., 1920. Bar: Va. 1919. Pvt. practice Danville, from 1920; mem. firm Meade, Tate & Daniel, ret., 1989; Mem. Va. Constl. Conv., 1945; mem. Va. Bd. Law Examiners, 1947-50; guest lectr. U. Va. Law Sch., 1951-54; also mem. Bd. Law Rev. Bd. dirs. YMCA, 1951-54, past pres. Served as ensign USNRF, 1918-19. Fellow Am. Bar Found., Am. Coll. Trial Lawyers, Am. Law Found.; mem. U. Va. Alumni Assn. (pres. 1954-55), Va. Bar Assn. (pres. 1956-57), Danville Bar Assn. (past pres.), Order of Cincinnati, Order of Coif, Sigma Nu. Episcopalian. Club: Danville Golf. Home: Danville Va. Deceased.

MEADE, JAMES EDWARD, economist; b. Dorset, Eng., June 23, 1907; s. Charles Hippisley and Kathleen (Cotton-Stapleton) M.; m. Elizabeth Margaret Wilson, Mar. 14, 1933; children—Thomas Wilson, Charlotte Elizabeth Meade Lewis, Bridget Ariane Meade Dommen, Carol Margaret Meade Dasgupta. Student, Oriel Coll., Oxford U., 1926-30, Trinity Coll., Cambridge U., 1930-31; MA, Oxford U., Cambridge U.; Dr. (hon.), U. Basel, U. Hull, U. Bath, U. Oxford; student, U. Glasgow, U. Essex, U. Athens. Fellow, lectr. econs. Hertford Coll., Oxford U., 1930-37; hon. fellow London Sch. Econs.; editor World Econ. Survey, League of Nations, Geneva, 1937-40; mem. econ. sect. Cabinet Secretariat, London, 1940-45, dir., 1945-47; prof. commerce London Sch. Econs., 1947-57; prof. polit. economy Cambridge U., 1957-69, sr. research fellow Christ's Coll., 1969-74; vis. prof. Australian Nat. U., 1956; chmn. Econ. Survey Mission to Mauritius, 1960; chmn. Com. on Structure and Reform of Direct Taxation, 1974-77; gov. Nat. Inst. Econ. and Social Research, 1947—, LSE, 1960-74, Malvern Coll., 1972—. Author: The Rate of Interest in a Progressive State, 1933; Economic Analysis and Policy, 1936; Consumers Credits and Unemployment, 1937; League of Nations World Economic Surveys, 1938 and 1939; Economic Basis of a Durable Peace, 1940; Planning and the Price Mechanism, 1948; The Balance of Payments, 1951; Trade and Welfare, 1955; A Geometry of International Trade, 1952; Problems of Economic Union, 1953; The Theory of Customs Unions, 1955; Control of Inflation, 1958; Neo-Classical Theory of Economic Growth, 1960; Efficiency, Equality and the Ownership of Property, 1964; The Sationary Economy, 1965; The Theory of Indicative Planning, 1967; The Growing Economy, 1968; The Controlled Economy, 1971; The Theory of Economic Externalities, 1973; The Intelligent Radical's Guide to Economic Policy, 1975; The Just Economy, 1976; Stagflation, Vol. I: Wage-Fixing, 1982, Vol. II, Demand Management, 1983, Alternate Systems of Business Organization and of Workers' Renumeration, 1986; Collected Papers: Vols. 1, 2, and 3, 1988, Vol. 4, 1989; Macroeconomic Policy: Inflation, Wealth and the Exchange Rate (jointly), 1989; Agathotopia: The Economics of Partnership, 1989, Liberty, Equality and Efficiency, 1993. Decorated companion Order of Bath; recipient Nobel prize in econs., 1977. Fellow Brit.

Acad.; mem. Royal Econ. Soc. (past pres.), Brit. Assn. (past sect. pres.), Nat. Acad. Scis. (U.S.) (fgn. asso.), Eugenics Soc. (past mem. council), Am. Acad. Arts and Scis. (fgn. hon.), Academia Europaea (emeritus mem.). Home: Cambridge Eng. Died Dec. 22, 1995.

MEADER, RALPH GIBSON, medical administrator; b. Eaton Rapids, Mich., Sept. 6, 1904; s. Robert Eugene and Jennie Editha (Gibson) M.; m. Olive Myrle Root, June 16, 1928; 1 child, Mary Batcheller. A.B., Ohio Wesleyan U., 1925; student, U. Mich., summers 1926, 27, 28; A.M., Hamilton Coll., 1927; Ph.D., Yale U., 1932; LL.D., Phila. Coll. Osteopathy, 1956; Sc.D., Ohio Wesleyan U., 1958. Instr. biology Hamilton Coll., 1925-27; part-time instr. biology Wesleyan U., 1928-29; asst. prof. biology Hamilton Coll., 1927-28; fellow in neuroanatomy Blossom Fund, Yale U. Sch. Medicine, 1929-31; instr. anatomy Yale U. Sch. Medicine, 1931-37, asst. prof., 1937-45, assoc. prof. anatomy, 1945-48; asst. dir. bd. sci. advisors Jane Coffin Childs Meml. Fund for Med. Research, 1942-48; spl. cons. USPHS; as sci. dir. cancer research grants br. Nat. Cancer Inst., 1947-48, chief of br., 1948-60, asso. dir. grants and tng., 1960-65; exec. sec. Nat. Adv. Cancer Council, 1947-65; dep. dir. for research adminstrn. and exec. sec. com. on research Mass. Gen. Hosp., Boston, 1965-76; cons. as asst. to assoc. gen. dir. Mass. Gen. Hosp., 1976-77, cons. grants and contracts, 1977—, also mem. Com. on Research; spl. cons. Nat. Cancer Inst., 1965—; biologist N.Y. State Biol. Survey, 1929-30; mem. biomed. library rev. com. Nat. Library Medicine, 1974-76, chmn., 1975-76, cons., 1976—; cons. Lovelace Med. Found., Albuquerque, 1980-82; Rockefeller Found. fellow in neurology U. Amsterdam, Netherlands, 1938-39. Incorporator Eunice Kennedy Shriver Ctr. for Mental Retardation, Waltham, Mass., 1969—, trustee, 1969-83, pres. bd. trustees, 1977-83; incorporator Spaulding Youth Ctr., Tilton, N.H., 1967—, trustee, 1967-85, pres. bd. trustees, 1972-75, trustee emeritus, 1985—; mem. com. to revise town master plan Town of Sanbornton, N.H. Recipient Superior Service award HEW, 1959; Alumni Disting. Achievement Citation award Ohio Wesleyan U., 1984, (with wife) Goodyear Conservation award of merit, 1988; named (with wife) Conservation Cooperator of Yr., Belknap County, N.H. Conservation Dist., 1988, (with wife) Outstanding Cooperator of Yr., N.H. Assn. Conservation Dists., 1988. Fellow AAAS; mem. Am. Assn. Anatomists, Am. Assn. Cancer Research, Soc. Study of Devel. and Growth, Corp. of Bermuda Biol. Sta. for Research, Inc., N.H. Hist. Soc., Durham Hist. Assn. (N.H.), Nantucket Hist. Soc. (Mass.), Sanbornton Hist. Soc. (v.p., chmn. program com. 1983-85), Phi Beta Kappa, Sigma Xi. Home: Sanbornton N.H. Died May 5, 1995.

MEADOWS, AUDREY, actress; b. Wu Chang, Peoples Republic China; m. Robert F. Six, 1961. Bd. dirs. First Nat. Bank Denver, 1977-96. Appeared in Broadway prodn. Top Banana; on road 2 yrs. with nat. co.: High Button Shoes; lead role in: Jackie Gleason Show; co-star (in role of Alice Kramden) The Honeymooners, CBS; starred in: Play of the Week; co-star Sid Caesar Show, Too Close for Comfort; co-star in eight CBS spectaculars, Dean Martin Spls.; starred in: Hotel, The Love Boat, Murder She Wrote; motion pictures include Rosie, Take Her She's Mine, That Touch of Mink; other TV work includes (series) Uncle Buck, CBS, 1990; author: Love, Alice: My Life as a Honeymooner, 1994. Trustee Pearl Buck Found. Recipient Emmy award for best supporting actress in regular series, 1955, Sylvania award for outstanding contbn. to TV techniques. Home: Los Angeles Calif. Died Feb. 3, 1996.

MEISTER, ALTON, biochemist, educator; b. N.Y.C., June 1, 1922; s. Morris and Florence (Glickstein) M.; m. Leonora Garten, Dec. 26, 1943; children: Jonathan Howard, Kenneth Eliot. B.S., Harvard U., 1942; M.D., Cornell U., 1945. Intern, asst. resident N.Y. Hosp., N.Y.C., 1946; head clin. biochem. research sect. Nat. Cancer Inst., NIH, 1951-55; commd. officer USPHS, NIH, 1946-55; prof. biochemistry, chmn. dept. Tufts U. Sch. Medicine, 1955-67; prof., chmn. dept. biochemistry Cornell U. Med. Coll., N.Y.C., 1967-95; biochemist-in-chief N.Y. Hosp., 1971-95; Vis. prof. biochemistry U. Wash., 1959, U. Calif. at Berkeley, 1961; cons. USPHS, 1964-68; chmn. physiol. chemistry study sect.; mem. com. on growth NRC, 1954; mem. biochemistry study sect. USPHS, 1955-60, biochemistry tng. com., 1961-63; cons. Am. Cancer Soc., 1958-61, 71-74; chmn. U.S. com. Internat. Union Biochemistry, 1960-65, 79-85. Author: Biochemistry of Amino Acids; Mem. editorial bd.: Jour. Biol. Chemistry, 1958-64; assoc. editor, 1976-95; mem. editorial bd.: Biochem. Preparations, 1957-64, Biochemistry, 1962-71, 80-84, Methods in Biochem. Analysis, 1963-87, Biochimica et Biophysica Acta, 1965-77, Ann. Rev. Biochemistry, 1961-65; asso. editor, 1965-95; Editor: Advances in Enzymology, 1969-95; contbr. articles on enzymes, amino acids and glutathione to sci. jours. Recipient Founders award Chem. Industry Inst. Toxicology, 1985. Fellow Am. Acad. Arts and Scis., N.Y. Acad. Sci.; mem. AAAS, NAS, Inst. of Medicine of NAS, Biophys. Soc., Biochem. Soc. London, Chem. Soc. London, Am. Chem. Soc. (Paul-Lewis award enzyme chemistry 1954, chmn. div. biol. chemistry 1965), Am. Assn. Cancer Research, Am. Soc. Biochemistry and Molecular Biology (pres. 1977, William C. Rose award in biochemistry 1984), Japanese Biochem. Soc. (hon.), Royal Acad. Medicine (Spain; hon.), Vitamin Soc. Japan (hon.), Harvey Soc. (hon.), Sigma Xi, Alpha Omega Alpha. Home: New York N.Y. Died Apr. 6, 1995.

MELBO, IRVING ROBERT, retired education educator; b. Gully, Minn., June 20, 1908; s. Hans H. and Hilda J. (Bergdahl) M.; m. Lucile Hays, May 30, 1931; 1 son, Robert Irving; m. Virginia Archer, May 15, 1970. A.B., N.Mex. State Tchrs. Coll., Silver City, 1930, M.A., 1932; Ed.D., U. Calif. at Berkeley, 1934; postgrad., Columbia Tchrs. Coll., 1936-37; LL.D., U. So. Calif., 1975, Pepperdine U., 1975. Prin. pub. elem. schs. Minn., 1927-28; rsch. asst. to pres. N.Mex. State Tchrs. Coll., 1928-30, instr. social sci., supr. student tchrs., 1930-33; staff mem. div. textbooks and publs. Calif. Dept. Edn., Sacramento, 1934-35; dir. dept. research and curriculum Oakland (Calif.) Pub. Sch., 1935-38; dept. supt. and dir. curriculum Alameda Co. Schs., Oakland, 1938-39; prof. ednl. adminstrn. U. So. Calif., Los Angeles, 1939-95; dean U. So. Calif. (Sch. Edn.), 1953-73, dean emeritus, 1974-95, dir. sch. surveys, 1946-95; disting. prof. edn. Pepperdine U., Los Angeles, 1975-80; vis. prof. edn. U. Kans., 1937, 38, U. Utah, 1951, U. Wis., 1953, U. Hawaii, 1956, 60; pres. Melbo Assocs., Inc.; mem. Calif. Bd. Edn. Accreditation Com., 1953-63, chmn., 1960-61; mem. adv. council Ednl. Policies Commn.; mem. citizens mgmt. rev. com. Los Angeles City Schs., 1975; organizer, dir. grad. level programs in edn., Europe, Taiwan, Thailand, Japan, Korea, India, Malawi, 1962; founder Educare, U. So. Calif. Edn. Support Orgn., 1960. Author: Our America, rev. edit, 1948, Social Psychology of Education, 1937, The American Scene, 1942, Young Neighbors in South America, 1944, Our Country's National Parks, vols. 1 and 2, 1941, 50, 61, 64, 73, (with S.P. Poole and T.F. Barton) The World About Us, 1949; contbr. articles to profl. jours. Bd. dirs. S.W. Regional Lab. Ednl. Research; trustee Flintridge Prep. Sch., La Canada, Calif.; mem. exec. com. Univ. Senate, U. So. Calif., 1986-87; mem. Pattern for Sch. Adminstrn. in Calif., 1955, Tchrs. for Metropolis, 1966. Served as lt. USNR, 1943-44, ETO, MTO. Recipient Spl. Freedom Leadership award Freedom Found. at Valley Forge, 1965; Exceptional Service medal USAF, 1968; Irving R. Melbo endowed professorship established in his honor, 1974. Mem. Am. Assn. Sch. Adminstrs., Calif. Congress Parents and Tchrs. (hon. life), Gen. Alumni Assn. U. So. Calif. (hon. life), Ret. Faculty Assn. of U. So. Calif. (pres. 1985-86), Phi Delta Kappa. Home: San Marino Calif. Died Mar. 31, 1995.

MELCZER, JOSEPH TREUHAFT, JR., lawyer; b. Phoenix, Nov. 13, 1912; s. Joseph T. and Hazel (Goldberg) M.; m. Mary Alicia Farrell, Sept. 9, 1947; children: Joseph Treuhaft III, Patricia Ann Kaufman. A.B., Stanford U., 1934, J.D., 1937. Bar: Ariz. 1938. Practiced in Phoenix; partner firm Snell & Wilmer, 1947-89, of counsel, from 1989; dir. Valley Nat. Bank Ariz., 1970-86, emeritus from 1986, Valley Nat. Corp., 1981-86, emeritus from 1986. Sec. Phoenix Thunderbirds, 1946; bd. dirs. Barrow Neurol. Found., Theodore Roosevelt council Boy Scouts Am., Ariz. Hist. Found.; bd. regents emeritus Brophy Coll. Prep.; bd. visitors Stanford U. Law Sch., 1970-72, 79-81. Served to maj. USAAF, 1942-46. Mem. Am., Ariz., Maricopa County bar assns., Am. Judicature Soc. Clubs: Phoenix 20-30 (Phoenix) (pres. 1941), Phoenix Country (Phoenix) (past dir.), Paradise Valley Country (Phoenix) (past dir.), Ariz. (past bd. dirs.). Home: Phoenix Ariz. Deceased.

MELOON, ROBERT A., retired newspaper publisher; b. Davenport, Iowa, July 13, 1928; s. John and Evelyn Mae (Ede) Case; children: Mark Robert, Brian Alfred. Student pub. schs., Davenport. Reporter The Capital Times, Madison, Wis., 1957-71, assoc. editor, 1971-72, mng. editor, 1972-78, exec. editor, 1978-81, gen. mgr., 1981-83, exec. pub., 1983-93; also past bd. dirs., ret., 1993; dir. AP Mng. Editors, 1979; mem. media-law rels. com. State Bar Wis., 1980-89; founding mem., v.p. Wis. Freedom of Info. Coun., 1978-83. Mem. Newspaper Assn. Am., Wis. Newspaper Assn., Inland Press Assn. Unitarian. Home: Madison Wis.

MENAPACE, RALPH CELESTE, JR., lawyer; b. Mt. Carmel, Pa., Nov. 24, 1931; s. Ralph Celeste and Verna Marie (Hudock) M.; m. Nathalie E. Bardong, Dec. 16, 1964; children: Ralph, Nancy, James. B.A., Yale U., 1953, LL.B., 1956. Bar: N.Y. 1957. Assoc. Cahill, Gordon & Reindel, N.Y.C., 1956-65, ptnr., from 1966; counsel, bd. dirs. Mcpl. Art Soc., N.Y.C., 1970—, Central Park Community Fund, from 1975. Mem. Internat. Bar. Assn., N.Y. State Bar Assn., Assn. Bar City N.Y. Home: New York N.Y. Deceased.

MENDELOFF, ALBERT IRWIN, physician, educator; b. Charleston, W.Va., Jan. 29, 1918; s. Morris Israel and Esther (Cohen) M.; m. Natalie Lavenstein, Dec. 19, 1943; children: Henry, John, Katherine. A.B., Princeton U., 1938; M.D., Harvard U., 1942, M.P.H., 1944. Fellow in nutrition Rockefeller Found., 1943-44; nutrition cons. UNRRA mission to Greece, 1944-46; fellow in gastroenterology Evans Meml. Hosp., Boston, 1947-49; asst. prof. medicine and preventive medicine Washington U. Med. Sch., 1949-54, asso. prof., 1955; gastroenterology cons. Barnes Hosp., St. Louis, 1952-55; asso. prof. medicine Johns Hopkins Med. Sch., 1955-70, prof., 1970-93; physician-in-chief Sinai Hosp., Balt., 1955-80; chief research medicine Sinai Hosp., 1980-8 Sr. surgeon Res. USPHS. Editor-in-chief: Am. Jou Clin. Nutrition, 1981-91. Mem. Assn. Am. Physician Am. Soc. Clin. Investigation, Cen. Soc. Clin. Researcl Am. Fedn. Clin. Research, Am. Gastroent. Assn., P Beta Kappa, Alpha Omega Alpha. Home: Baltimo Md. Died Mar. 15, 1993.

MENGEDOHT, LANVILLE HENRY, lawyer; Greenville, S.C., Aug. 14, 1926; s. Lanville H. Sr. an Claudia (Vincent) M.; m. Hazel Porter, Nov. 3, 19 (div. Dec. 1975); children: Lanville H., Jr., Charles F m. Jo Rosebrough, May 17, 1977. BA, The Citad 1950; LLB, U. S.C., 1950. CPCU. V.p. Porter Gen Columbia, S.C., 1951-67; pres. risk mgmt. and fi planning Columbia, 1968-69; v.p. gen. counsel State S.C., Columbia, 1969-72, acting chmn. ins. com., 197 73; v.p., gen. counsel Seibels Bruce & Co., Columbi 1973-89; chmn. bd. S.C. Ins. Guaranty Assn., Columbi 1975-83, S.C. Life & Health Guaranty Assn., Columbi 1983-85; bd. dirs. S.C. Ins. News Service, Columbia Mem. gen. adv. com. Recodification of Ins. Code Columbia, 1985-87; mem. govt. task force Automobi Ins., 1980. Named Boss of Yr., Ins. Women S.C., 1973 Mem. CPCU (pres. S.C. chpt. 1976), Fedn. Ins. Cor Council. Clubs: Palmetto (Columbia); Dram (Columbia) (treas.). Home: Hartsville S.C. Deceased.

MENKART, JOHN, cosmetic company executive; Prague, Czechoslovakia, Aug. 20, 1922; came to U.S 1954, naturalized, 1961; s. Rudolph J. and Milada (Fi cher) M.; m. Margaret White, Apr. 4, 1953; childre Andrew, Deborah; m. Edith L. Chandler, Aug. 2, 196 stepchildren: Elizabeth, David. B.Sc., U. Leeds, Eng 1943, Ph.D., 1946. Research chemist Eng., 1946-5 staff Textile Research Inst., Princeton, N.J., 1954-5 with Gillette Co., 1958-71; pres. Gillette Research Inst 1968-71; v.p. tech. Clairol Inc., Stamford, Conn., 197 76; sr. v.p. Clairol Inc., 1977-87; pres. Shagbark Rsch Inc., 1987—. Author; Mem. editorial bds. profl. jours Mem. bd. mgmt. Stamford Hosp.; bd. dirs. Inds Research Inst., 1979-83. Fellow Textile Inst. G Britain; mem. Cosmetic, Toiletry and Fragrance Ass (chmn. sci. adv. com. 1974-76), Am. Chem. Soc., So Cosmetic Chemists, Univ. Club (N.Y.C.). Hom Greenwich Conn. Died Dec. 9, 1993.

MERCOURI, MELINA (MARIA AMALIA), actres former Greek government official; b. Athens, Greec Oct. 18, 1925; d. Stamatis and Irene M.; ed. Acad. Na Theatre Greece; m. Jules Dassin, 1966. Films includ Stella, 1955, He Who Must Die, 1956, The Gipsy ar the Gentleman, 1955, Never on Sunday, 1960, Topka 1963, Les Pianos Mécaniques, 1964, 10:30 P.M Summer, 1966, Phaedra, 1962, Gaily, Gaily, 196 Promise at Dawn, 1970, Once Is Not Enough, 197 Earthquake, 1974, A Dream of Passion, 1978; stage a pearances include: Ilya, Darling, Lysistrata, 197 Mourning Becomes Electra, A Streetcar Named Desir Helen or the Joy of Living, The Queen of Clubs, Th Seven Year Itch, Sweet Bird of Youth; mem. Gre Parliament for Port of Piraeus, 1977—; minister of cu ture and scis., 1981-89. Author: I Was Born Gree 1971. Recipient Tregene prize, 1984. Home: Athe Greece

MEREDITH, LEWIS DOUGLAS, utility compar executive, consultant; b. Scranton, Pa., May 7, 1905; William S. and Carrie C. (Huff) M.; m. Laura J. Parke Aug. 19, 1935. Student, Bucknell U., 1922-23; A. cum laude, Syracuse U., 1926, A.M., 1927; Ph.D., Ya U., 1933; LL.D., Middlebury Coll., 1975. Inst Syracuse (N.Y.) U., 1925-27; asst. prof. econs. U. V 1927-35; fellow Yale U., 1930-31; instr. Milw. Sta Tchrs. Coll., summer 1932; commr. banking and in State of Vt., 1934-35; investment analyst Nat. Life In Co., Montpelier, Vt., 1935-38, asst. to pres., 1939-4 treas., 1940-44, v.p., 1943—, mem. fin. com., 1938-6 v.p., chmn. fin. com., 1944-47, exec. v.p., chmn. fi com., 1947-66, vice chmn. bd. dirs., chief fin. office 1966-68, mem. dirs. adv. council, 1983—; pres., chi exec. officer Cen. Vt. Pub. Service Corp., Rutland, 196 72, chmn. bd. dirs., 1972-83, mem. dirs. adv. com 1983—, also bd. dirs., 1953-83; chmn. bd. dirs. Con Valley Electric Co. Inc., 1956-83; dir. emeritus Vt. Mu Fire Ins. Co., No. Security Ins. Co., U.S. Air Line Chittenden Trust Co., Vt. Elec. Power Co., Inc corporator Bank of Vt.; lectr. S.S. Huebner Found 1952, Sch. Banking, U. Vt., 1948, 50, 53, 56, als various seminars; cons. State Dept. AID Progran Ecuador, 1965; sec. Vt. Bankers Com., 1932-33; mer residential real estate credit adv. com. Fed. Res. Ban 1950-52; mem. Vt. Merit System Council, 1939-4 chmn., 1940-47; mem. Vt. Council Safety, 1941-46; vi chmn. Vt. War Fin. Commn., 1945; mem. Gov. Housing Adv. Com., 1945, Gov.'s Reapportionme Panel, 1964. Contbg. editor Burlington Free Pres 1933-35; author: Merchandising for Banks, Trust Con panies and Investment Houses, 1935, How to Buy House, 1947; also articles financial mags. Bd. dirs. A soc. Industries Vt., 1969-73; dir. New Eng. Coun., 194 50, v.p., mem. exec. com., 1954-58, pres., 1957-5 chmn. bd., 1959, chmn. com. to study question of tax tion, Vt., 1951-52; mem. Vt. Housing Authority, 197 74; Alumni trustee Syracuse U., 1950-56, 59-60; chm bd. trustees Middlebury Coll., 1967-75, trustee emerit 1975—; trustee Vt. Law Sch., 1983—, Trinity Colleg 1988—, Champlain Coll., 1988— ; corporator Rutlan

Hosp.; bd. govs. Med. Center Hosp. Vt., 1969-73; trustee-at-large Syracuse U., 1966-72, hon. trustee, 1978—; trustee Vt. Arthritis Assn., 1974-77. Recipient honor award Keystone Jr. Coll. Alumni Assn., LaPlume, Pa., 1949, Man of Yr. award, 1979; Arents medal Syracuse U., 1978; Meredith Wing of Starr Library at Middlebury Coll. named in his honor, 1979. Mem. Mortgage Bankers Assn. (gov. 1947-51), Am. Econ. Assn., Vt. Bankers Assn. (hon.), Tex. Mortgage Bankers Assn. (hon. life), Lake Champlain Regional C. of C. (dir. 1977-81, pres. 1981-82), Phi Beta Kappa, Kappa Phi Kappa, Delta Sigma Rho, Phi Kappa Phi. Republican. Conglist. Clubs: Lake Mansfield (Vt.) Trout; University (N.Y.C.); Metropolitan (Washington); Algonquin (Boston); Ethan Allen (Burlington, Vt.); Waikiki Yacht (Honolulu). Lodges: Masons (32 deg.), Shriners. Home: Burlington Vt. Died Dec. 28, 1993.

MEREDITH, RONALD EDWARD, federal judge; b. Clarkson, Ky., Jan. 30, 1946; s. Ralph and Mary (Anderson) M.; m. Joanne Marie Berry, Apr. 23, 1973; children: Kelly, Jaime, Ronee, Mark. BA, Georgetown Coll., Ky., 1967; JD, George Washington U., 1971. Bar: D.C. 1971, Ky. 1971. Minority counsel U.S. Senate Jud. Subcom., Washington, 1971-72; legis. asst. Senator Marlow W. Cook, Washington, 1973-74; ptnr. Kelley & Meredith, Elizabethtown, Ky., 1975-81; U.S. atty. for western dist. Ky., U.S. Dept. Justice, Louisville, 1981-85; judge U.S. Dist. Ct. (we. dist.) Ky., Louisville, 1985-94, chief judge, 1991-94. Trustee Georgetown Coll., 1983-91; deacon Severns Valley Bapt. Ch., Elizabethtown, 1977-85; chmn. 2d congl. dist. Ky. Rep. Com., 1976-80, state campaign chmn., 1979; mem. exec. bd. Old. Ky. coun. Boy Scouts Am., 1982-94. Mem. Fed. Bar Assn., Ky. Bar Assn. Home: Louisville Ky. Died Dec. 1, 1994.

MEREDITH, SCOTT, authors' representative; b. N.Y.C., Nov. 24, 1923; s. Henry and Esta (Meredith); m. Helen Kovet, Apr. 22, 1944; children: Stephen Charles, Randy Beth Meredith Sheer. Educated privately; Litt.D., Mercy Coll., 1983. Writer numerous mag. stories; established Scott Meredith Lit. Agy., Inc., N.Y.C., 1940; pres. Scott Meredith Lit. Agy., Inc., 1942—. Author: Writing to Sell, rev. edits, 1960, 74, 86, Writing for the American Market, 1960, The Face of Comedy, 1961, George S. Kaufman and His Friends, 1974, The Science of Gaming, 1974, Louis B. Mayer and His Enemies, 1986; also stories, novelettes, serials and articles; editor: The Best of Wodehouse, 1949, The Best of Modern Humor, 1951, Bar One Roundup, 1951, The Week-End Book of Humor, 1952, Bar Two Roundup, 1952, The Murder of Mr. Malone, An Anthology of Craig Rice Stories, 1953, Bar Three Roundup, 1954, Bar Four Roundup, 1955, 2d series, 1956, Bar Five Roundup, 1956, (with Ken Murray) The Ken Murray Book of Humor, 1957, Bar Six Roundup, 1957, (with Henry Morgan) The Henry Morgan Book of Humor, 1958, The Best from Manhunt, 1958, The Bloodhound Anthology, 1960, The Fireside Treasury of Modern Humor, 1963, Best Western Stories, 1964, Best Western Stories For Young People, 1965, (with P.G. Wodehouse) The Best of Humor, 1965, A Carnival of Modern Humor, 1966, (with Margaret Truman) Where the Buck Stops, The Harry Truman Memoirs, 1989; contbr. articles on humor to Ency. Brit, 1954-59, articles on fiction writing to Oxford Ency, 1960-61; frequent guest TV, radio shows. Served with USAAF, World War II. Clubs: Three Oaks Tennis (N.Y.C.), Spectator (N.Y.C.), Rare Book Soc. (N.Y.C.). Home: Kings Point N.Y.

MERIAM, HAROLD AUSTIN, JR., lawyer; b. N.Y.C., May 5, 1920; s. Harold Austin and Lola Mary (Olney) M.; m. Joan Anna Chartres (dec. Sept. 1983); children: Harold, Thomas, Stephanie, Elisabeth, Christopher, Peter; m. Helen Patricia Dwyer, Nov. 23, 1984. Student, Fordham U., 1939-41; LLB summa cum laude, Bklyn. Law Sch., 1948. Bar: N.Y. 1949, U.S. Dist. Ct. (ea. and so. dists.) N.Y. 1964, U.S. Ct. Appeals (2d cir.) 1965. Assoc. Wagner, Quillinan, Wagner & Tennant, N.Y.C., 1948-49; mem. faculty Bklyn. Law Sch., N.Y.C., 1949-50; law asst. Charles W. Froessel Assoc. Judge N.Y. State Ct. Appeals, N.Y.C. and Albany, N.Y., 1950-53; assoc. Cullen and Dykman, Bklyn., 1953-64, ptnr., 1965-94; cons. N.Y. State Temporary Commn. on Law of Estates, 1963-66, Commn. on Jud. N.Y. State Constl. Conv., 1967; mem. Commn. to Advise and Consult with Jud. Conf. on Civil Practice Law and Rules, 1969-80. Bd. dirs. Bklyn. Bur. Commun. Svc., 1976-94. Capt USAF, 1942-46. Fellow Am. Coll. Trusts and Estates Counsel; mem. N.Y. State Bar Assn. (chair trusts and estates law sect. 1977-79, v.p. 1981-86), Bklyn. Bar Assn., Bar Assn. Nassau County, Bklyn. Club, Garden City Country Club. Republican. Roman Catholic. Home: Massapequa N.Y. Died Mar. 20, 1994.

MERMELSTEIN, MILTON EMANUEL, lawyer, former department store executive; b. Newark, May 16, 1908; s. Max and Malvina (Weiss) M.; m. Doris Saxe, Dec. 25, 1937; children: John S., Stephen E. A.B., George Washington U., 1930, J.D., 1931; postgrad., Columbia U., 1932; D.C.S. (hon.), St. John's U. Bar: D.C. 1931, N.Y. 1932, N.J. 1938, Mass. 1946. Sr. ptnr. Schwartz, Mermelstein, Burns, Lesser & Jacoby, N.Y.C., 1962-73; counsel Burns Summit Rovins Spitzer & Feldesman (and predecessor firm), 1973-83; chmn., sr. corp. officer Alexander's Inc., N.Y.C., 1969-75, dir. audit com., 1969-85; bd. dirs., mem. exec. com. Irvin Industries, Inc., 1962-82; mem. Boston Stock Exchange. Bd. dirs. Inst. Religion and Health, United Way. Served with USNR, 1944, ETO; comdr. Res. (ret.). Decorated Knight of Malta, Ordine de Cavalieri de Bene; recipient Disting. Alumni Achievement award, Alumni Service award George Washington U., Pope Paul VI Humanitarian award, 1971. Mem. Zeta Beta Tau, Phi Delta Phi. Republican. Jewish. Club: Hollywood (N.J.) Golf. Home: Deal N.J. Died June 21, 1994.

MERO, JUDITH C., lawyer; b. Bridgeport, Conn., Jan. 20, 1941. BS summa cum laude, Boston Coll., 1963; MLS, U. Md., 1973; JD magna cum laude, Georgetown U., 1980, MLT, 1983. Bar: Md. 1980, D.C. 1986. Ptnr. Shulman, Rogers, Gandal, Pordy & Ecker P.A., Rockville, Md.; Trustee Md. Inst. for Continuing Profl. Edn. Lawyers, 1989, sec., 1990-91. Articles editor Am. Criminal Law Review, 1979-80; contbr. articles to profl. jours. Mem. Md. Commn. Phys. Fitness, 1982-87. Mem. ABA (taxation sect., gen. practice sect.), Nat. Acad. Elder Law Attys., Md. Bar Found., Md. State Bar Assn. (taxation sect., sect. coun. 1990—), Women's Bar Assn. Md., Montgomery County Bar Assn. Home: Rockville Md. Died November 1992.

MERRILL, EDWARD CLIFTON, JR., emeritus university president; b. Asheville, N.C., Jan. 29, 1920; s. Edward Clifton and Alice (Tiddy) M.; m. Frances Bonkemeyer, June 2, 1946 (dec. Jan. 1993); children: Susan, Nancy, Ned, Ann. B.A., U. N.C., 1942; M.S., U. Tenn., 1948; Ph.D., George Peabody Coll., 1953; LL.D., Gallaudet U., 1969. Instr. Asheville-Biltmore Coll., 1946- 47; tchr., dean Lee Edwards High Sch., Asheville, 1948-51; instr. George Peabody Coll., also coordinator So. State Coop. Program Ednl. Adminstrn., 1953-55; assoc. prof. edn. Auburn U., 1955-57; summer vis. assoc. prof. edn. Coll. Edn., U. Fla., 1957; prof. edn., assoc. dean grad. studies Coll. Edn., U. Rochester, 1957-60; prof. edn. Coll. Edn., U. N.C., 1960-61; dean Coll. Edn., U. Tenn., 1961-69; pres. Gallaudet U., 1969-83, pres. emeritus, 1983-95; dir. N.Y. Statewide In-Service Program Sch. Adminstrns., 1958-60; mem. N.Y. State Council Adminstrv. Leadership, 1957-60; dir. workshops and insts. U. Rochester, 1957-60; chmn. Assoc. Orgns. Tchr. Edn., 1966; mem. bd. Appalachia Ednl. Labs., Inc., Washington Ednl. TV Assn.; bd. dirs. Deafness Research Found., 1980-83, Nat. Captioning Inst., 1985-95. Co-author: Community Leadership for Public Education, 1955, The Deaf Child in the Public School, 2d edit, 1978; Editor: Better Teaching in School Administration, 1955; Contbr. articles to profl. jours., chpts. to books. Bd. dirs. Nat. Assn. Hearing and Speech Agys., pres., 1971; bd. dirs. Nat. Captioning Inst., Inc., 1983-95, vice-chmn., 1987-91. Recipient Disting. Service award Nat. Assn. of Deaf, 1978; Décoration au Mérite Social World Fedn. of Deaf, 1979; Daniel T. Cloud Leadership award, 1982; Disting. Service award Pres.'s Com. for Employment of the Handicapped, 1983; Disting. Service to Edn. award Council for Advancement and Support of Edn., 1983; Washingtonian of Yr., 1982. Mem. Am. Assn. Sch. Adminstrs. Home: Asheville N.C. Died Jan. 1995.

MERRILL, LINDSEY, music educator; b. Madisonville, Ky., Jan. 10, 1925; s. James E. and Della (Scott) M.; m. Martha Lynn Rowe, June 11, 1948; children: Jonathan Scott, Rebecca Rowe. Mus.B., U. Louisville, 1949; Mus.M., Yale U., 1950; Ph.D., U. Rochester, 1963. Mem. faculty Queen's Coll., N.C., 1950-53, Smith Coll., 1953-56; prof. music Bucknell U., 1957-67, chmn. dept., 1966-67; prof., dir. Sch. Music, dir. Blossom Festival Sch. Kent State U., 1967-75; dean Conservatory Music, U. Mo.-Kansas City, 1975-85; dir. Edn. Found. Ventura, Calif., 1986-95; Music editor Merriam Webster 3d New Internat. Dictionary; cons. in field. Violinist, composer electronic music. Served with AUS, 1943-46. Mem. Pi Kappa Lambda. Home: Ventura Calif. Died April 26, 1995.

MERRISON, ALEXANDER WALTER, physicist and bank director; b. London, Mar. 20, 1924; s. Henry Walter and Violet Henrietta (Mortimer) M.; B.Sc., King's Coll., U. London, 1944; Ph.D., U. Liverpool, 1957; LL.D. (hon.), U. Bristol, 1971; D.Sc. (hon.), U. Ulster, 1976, U. Bath, 1977, Southampton, 1980, Leeds, 1981, Liverpool, 1982; m. Beryl Glencora Le Marquand, 1948 (dec. 1968); children: Jonathan, Timothy; m. Maureen Michele Barry, 1970; children: Andria, Benedict. Researcher, Signals Research and Devel. Establishment, sr. scientific officer rsch. reactor and nuclear physics, Christchurch, 1944-46, AERE, Harwell, 1946-51; Leverhulme fellow, lectr. elementary particle physics U. Liverpool, 1951-57; physicist European Orgn. Nuclear Research CERN, 1957-60; prof. exptl. physics Liverpool U., 1960-69, also dir. Daresbury Nuclear Physics Lab., 1962-69; vice chancellor Bristol U., 1969-84; chmn. Com. of Inquiry into Design and Erection of Steel Box Girder Bridges, 1970-73; mem. Council Sci. Policy. 1967-72, Nuclear Power Adv. Bd., 1973-76; chmn. Royal Commn. Nat. Health Service, 1976-79, Adv. Bd. for Research Councils, 1972-73, chmn. 79-82; chmn. Bristol region Lloyds Bank, 1983-89, also Chmn. Com. Inquiry into Regulation of Med. Profession, 1972-75; vice chmn. S.W. Regional Health Authority, 1973-76; dep. lt. County of Avon, 1974; chmn. Bristol Old Vic Trust, 1971-89, Western Provident Assn., 1984-89; dir. Bristol Evening Post, 1979-89, Bristol Waterworks Co., 1984-89. Chmn. Vice-Chancellors and Principals, 1979-81, Assn. Commonwealth Univs., 1982-83; pres. Coun. of Cern, 1982-85; freeman of the City of London; mem. Coun. Inst. Physics, 1964-66, 1983-89 (pres. 1984-86). Created knight, 1976; recipient Charles Vernon Boys prize Inst. Physics, 1961. Fellow King's Coll., 1973. Fellow Royal Soc., Royal Soc. Arts. Club: Athenaeum (London). Died Feb. 19, 1989; buried Hinton Blewett. Home: Bristol Eng.

MERTES, JOHN ERASMUS, JR., marketing and advertising specialist, retired educator; b. Prague, Okla., Aug. 6, 1913; s. John Erasmus and Mary Nola (Taylor) M.; m. Virginia Alexander; children: Mitchell, Susan. BBA, U. Okla., 1935; MSc, NYU, 1937; MBA, Ind. U., 1952, D of Bus. Adminstrn., 1956. Retailing exec. various cos., 1935-46; acting dir. tng. store, mgr. commissary divsn. Cristobal, Panama Canal Zone, Panama, 1937-44; prof. mktg., advt. U. Okla., Norman, 1946-69; lectr. retailing Ind. U., Bloomington, Ind., 1950-51; dir. MBA grad. studies, prof. mktg. Ea. Ill. U., Charleston, 1969-76; chmn., dir. MBA grad studies, prof. mktg. and advt. U. Ark., Little Rock, 1976-79, prof. emeritus, from 1979; vis. prof. mktg. and mgmt. U. Ill., Chgo., 1966-67; vis. prof. mktg. So. Ill. U., Carbondale, 1968, N.Mex. U., Albuquerque, 1982. Author: Corporate Communications, 1972, Creative Site Evaluation for the Small Retailer, (with John S. Wright) Advertising's Role in Society, 1974; assoc. editor Jour. Mktg., 1975-80; contbr. over 30 articles to profl. publs. Grantee, scholar various instns. Mem. Am. Mktg. Assn. (pres. Oklahoma City chpt. 1950-51), Am. Acad. Advt. (charter, pres. 1967-70), Lions Club, Beta Gamma Sigma, Delta Sigma Pi, Alpha Delta Sigma. Home: Norman Okla. Deceased.

MESERVE, ROBERT WILLIAM, lawyer; b. Chelsea, Mass., Jan. 12, 1909; s. George Harris and Florence Elizabeth (Small) M.; m. Gladys E. Swenson, Oct. 17, 1936 (dec. 1994); children: Roberta Ann Weil, William George, Richard Andrew, John Eric, Jeanne-Marthe. A.B., Tufts Coll., 1931; LL.B., Harvard, 1934; LL.D., Villanova U., 1972, Drury Coll., 1972, Suffolk U., 1972, St. Michael's Coll., 1972, Wm. Mitchell Law Sch., 1977, Tufts U., 1979, Vt. Law Sch., 1984. Bar: Mass. bar 1934. Asst. U.S. atty. Boston, 1936-41, 83-85; lectr. Boston Coll. Law Sch., 1938-40, Harvard Law Sch., 1957-61; assoc., then partner firm Nutter, McClennen & Fish, Boston, 1934-36, 41-43, 46-73; ptnr. firm Newman & Meserve, 1973-78; ptnr. Palmer & Dodge, 1978-83, of counsel, 1986-95; Mem. Mass. Bd. Bar Examiners, 1961-71, sec., 1964-71; chmn. Mass. Bd. Bar Overseers, 1974-78; Mem. sch. com., Medford, Mass., 1936-40, chmn., 1940; by appt. of Chief Justice of the U.S. mem. adv. com. Federal Criminal Rules, 1966-71, adv. com. Federal Civil Rules, 1971-78, adv. com. Admission to Federal Bar Devitt Com. 1977-79, implementation com. Judicial Conf. U.S. Admission Attys. Federal Practiceing Com.; by Presidential appt. Asst. U.S. Atty., Boston, 1936-41, Spl. Asst., 1984-86,. Editor: Harvard Law Rev, 1933-34. Mem. bd. aldermen, Medford, 1941-43; trustee Tufts Coll., 1955-79, chmn., 1965-70, emeritus, 1979-95; pres. Boston Floating Hosp., 1960-65. Served to lt. (s.g.) USNR, 1943-46. Fellow Am. Bar Found. (pres. 1979-80, dir. 1975-95), Am. Coll. Trial Lawyers (pres. 1968-69, bd. regents); mem. ABA (House Dels. 1961-95, past chmn. standing com. fed. Judiciary, pres. 1972-73), Mass. Bar Assn., Mass. Bar Found., Middlesex County Bar Assn., Am. Law Inst., Boston Bar Assn. (past pres.), Am. Acad. Arts and Sci., Inst. Jud. Adminstrn. (pres. 1980-82), Phi Beta Kappa (pres. assocs. 1983-85). Democrat. Unitarian. Home: Winchester Mass. Died Sept. 21, 1995.

METZ, ROBERT ERNEST, lawyer; b. Berkeley, Calif., Nov. 13, 1935; s. Ernest Estel and Margorie Marie (Gallagher) M.; m. Barbro Vera Kullgren, Oct. 3, 1959; children: Elisabeth Barbro Cueto, Annika Marie, Patrick Michael. AB, U. Calif., Berkeley, 1957, LLB, 1963. Bar: Calif. 1963, U.S. Dist. Ct. (no. dist.) Calif. 1964, U.S. Ct. Appeals (9th cir.) 1964. Assoc. Brobeck, Phleger & Harrison, San Francisco, 1963-69, ptnr., 1970-88; sec. Andros Analyzers Inc., Berkeley, 1970-88, Novacor Med. Corp., Oakland, Calif., 1980-88; bd. dirs. Wollongong Group Inc., Palo Alto, Calif. Co-author: Financing California Business, 1976; note and comment editor U. Calif. Law Rev., 1962-63. Served to capt. USAF, 1957-60. Mem. ABA, Calif. Bar Assn., San Francisco Bar Assn., U.S. Council on Intellectual Property, U.S. Council Internat. Bus., Order of Coif. Republican. Club: Olympic (San Francisco). Home: Orinda Calif. Died Nov. 14, 1988.

METZGER, DARRYL EUGENE, mechanical and aerospace engineering educator; b. Salinas, Calif., July 11, 1937; s. August and Ruth H. (Anderson) M.; m. Dorothy Marie Castro, Dec. 16, 1956; children: Catherine Ann, Kim Marie, Lauri Marie, John David. BS in Mech. Engring., Stanford U., 1959, MS, 1960, PhD, 1963. Registered profl. engr., Ariz. Asst. prof. mech. engring Ariz. State U., Tempe, 1963-67, assoc. prof., 1967-70, prof., 1970-92, Regents' prof., 1992-93, prof., chmn. dept., 1974-88, dir. thermosci. research, 1980-88; cons. Pratt & Whitney Aircraft, East Hartford, Conn., 1977-93, Pratt & Whitney Aircraft Can., 1979-93, United Techs. Corp., 1989-93, Garrett Turbine Engine Corp., Phoenix, 1966-77, NASA Lewis Research Ctr., NASA Office of Aeronautics and Space Tech., USAF Aeropropulsion Lab., Worthington Turbine Internat., Solar Turbine Internat., Allied Chem. Corp., Office of Naval Research, Sundstrand Aviation, AT&T, Bell Labs., Calspan Advanced Tech. Ctr., Rocketdyne div. Rockwell Internat., Ishikawajima-Harima Heavy Industries Co., Ltd., Tokyo, United Tech. Corp.; keynote address NATO Adv. Group for Aerospace Research and Develop., Norway, 1985; U.S. del. U.S./China Binat. Workshop on Heat Transfer, Beijing, Xian, Shanghai, 1983, NSF U.S./China Program Dev. Meeting, Hawaii, 1983, NSF/Consiglio Natizionale delle Ricerche Italy Joint Workshop on Heat Transfer and Combustion, Pisa, Italy, 1982; gen. chmn. Symposium on Heat Transfer in Rotating Machinery, Internat. Centre for Heat and Mass Transfer, Yugoslavia, 1982, 92; mem. U.S. sci. com. Internat. Heat Transfer Conf., 1986; mem. NASA Space Shuttle Main Engine Rev. Team, 1986-87, NASA Space Engring. Program External. Task Team, 1987; chair prof. Office of Naval Tech. U.S. Naval Postgrad. Sch., Montery, Calif., 1989. Contbr. articles to profl. jours.; editor: Regenerative and Recuperative Heat Exchangers, 1981, Fundamental Heat Transfer Research, 1980, Heat and Mass Transfer in Rotating Machinery, 1983, Heat Transfer in Gas Turbine Engines, 1987, Compact Heat Exchangers, 1989, A Festschrift for A.L. London, 1990; mem. editorial bd. Internat. Jour. Exptl. Heat Transfer, 1987-93. Ford Found. fellow, 1960, NSF fellow, 1981, ASEE/NASA fellow, 1964-65; recipient Alexander von Humboldt sr. rsch. scientist award Fed. Republic of Germany, 1985, 86, 87, Achievement award ASME, Japan Soc. Mech. Engrs., 1985, Faculty Achievement award Ariz. State U. Alumni Assn., 1987, Grad. Coll. Disting. Rsch. award Ark. State U., 1991; Sonderforschungsbereich grantee U. Karlsruhe, 1988, 89, 90. Fellow ASME (mem. gas turbine com., chmn. heat transfer div. 1982-84, mem. com. on faculty quality 1986), AIAA (assoc. fellow); mem. Soaring Soc. Am., Fed. Aero. Inst. (Internat. Diamond award), Phi Beta Kappa, Sigma Xi, Tau Beta Pi, Pi Tau Sigma, Phi Kappa Phi. Home: Paradise Vly Ariz. Died Aug. 1, 1993.

MEYER, HAROLD LOUIS, mechanical engineer; b. Chgo., June 25, 1916; s. Norman Robert and Martha (Stoewsand) M.; m. Charlotte Alene Tilberg, June 21, 1941 (dec. 1951); 1 child, John C. Nelson. Student, Armour Inst. Tech., Chgo., 1934-42, U. Akron, 1942-44; BA in Natural Sci., Southwestern Coll., Winfield, Kans., 1949; postgrad., Ill. Inst. Tech., 1988, 90; ME in Mech. Engring., 1988. Sales engr. Olsen & Tilgner, Chgo., 1938-39; project engr. Gen. Electric X-Ray, 1939-42, field engr., 1944-46; project engr. Goodyear Aircraft, 1942-44; chief x-ray technologist and therapist William Newton Meml. Hosp., Winfield, 1946-51; sr. design cons. Pollak and Skan, Chgo., 1952-58, cons. design specialist, 1963-68, 92-94; project engr. Gaertner Scientific Co., Chgo., 1958-63; sr. design specialist Am. Steel Foundries, Chgo., 1969-74; cons. Morgen Design, Milw., 1974-76; project engr. Meyersen Engring., Addison, Ill., 1981-92, also bd. dirs.; cons. dir. Miller Paint Equipment, Addison, 1976-87; design cons. R.R. Donnelley, Kraft Foods, Pollak and Skan, 1992-94. Inventor: box sealing sta., 1939, chest x-ray equipment, 1941, G-2 airship, 1943, space program periscope, 1959-62, nuclear fuel inspection and measurement periscope, 1962, beer can filling machine, 1963, atomic waste handling vehicle, 1965, ry. freight car trucks, 1973, hwy. trailer 5th wheels, 1974, motorized precision paint colorant dispensing machines, 1986. Sponsered a family of Cambodian Chinese refugees; mem. Norwood Park (Ill.) Norwegian Old Peoples Home; mem. Family Shelter Svc., Glen Ellyn, Ill. With USNR, 1949-52. Recipient Appreciation award Lioness Club, Glendale Heights, 1985. Mem. AAAS, Chem. Engring. Product Rsch. Panel, Ill. Inst. Tech. Alumni Assn. (new student recruiter 1985-94, Recognition award 1986, 87, honored for 50 yrs. of high standards of profl. activity and citizenship 1988, Emeritus Club award, 1990), Am. Registry of X-Ray Techs. Home: Addison Ill. Died Dec. 30, 1994.

MEYER, JOHN F., insurance company executive. CFO, sr. v.p.-personal ins. fin. Fiemans Fund Insurance Co, Novato, Calif., until 1991, exec. v.p., CFO, 1991-95. Home: Novato Calif. Died Dec. 10, 1995.

MEYER, LEON JACOB, wholesale company executive; b. Chgo., Nov. 12, 1923; s. Joseph and Minnie (Lebovitz) M.; student Lake Forest Coll., 1941-43; B.S., UCLA, 1948; m. Barbara Gene Bothman, Oct. 17, 1948; children: Charles Scott, Mary Anne, John Mark, Ellen Renee. Owner, operator Christopher Distbg. Co., Santa Monica, Calif., 1951-53; pres. J. Meyer & Co., Waukegan, Ill., 1953-80, Western Candy & Tobacco Co., Carpentersville, Ill., 1970-78, Ill. Briar Pipe & Sundry Co., Waukegan, 1963-78; chmn. bd. Phillips Bros. Co., Kenosha, Wis., 1975-85, Ill. Wholesale Co., 1976-89. Served with U.S. Army, 1943-46; PTO. Named Sundry Man of Year, 1976, Candy Distbr. of Yr., 1976; recipient Alex Schwartz Meml. award, 1978. Mem. Nat. Assn. Tobacco Distbrs. (trustee), Ill. Assn. Candy-Tobacco Distbrs. (past chmn. bd.), Federated Merchandising Corp. (past pres.), Internat. Tobacco Wholesaler Alliance (past chmn. bd.), Nat. Automatic Merchandisers Assn., Nat. Candy Wholesalers Assn., UCLA Alumni Club, Waukegan/Lake County C. of C. Clubs: Elks, Eagles. Died March 28, 1990; buried Waukegan, Ill. Home: Highland Park Ill.

MEYER, MARSHALL THEODORE, rabbi; b. N.Y.C., Mar. 25, 1930; s. Isaac and Anita Sarah (Silberstein) M.; m. Naomi Friedman, June 19, 1955; children: Anita Sara, Dodi Daniela, Gabriel Isaac. AB, Dartmouth Coll., 1952, LHD (honoris causa), 1982; M of Hebrew Lit., Jewish Theol. Sem., 1958; postgrad., Hebrew U., Jerusalem, 1955-56, Columbia U., 1957-59, Union Theol. Sem., 1957-59; DST (honoris causa), Jewish Theol Sem. Am., 1981; DD (honoris causa), Kalamazoo Coll., 1985; DHL honoris causa, Hebrew Union Coll., 1990. Ordained rabbi, 1958. Founder, rector Sem. Rabinico Latinoamericano, Buenos Aires, 1962; founder, sr. rabbi Community Bet El, Buenos Aires, 1963; sr. rabbi Congregation B'Nai Jeshurun, N.Y.C.; spl. counsel to chancellor Jewish Theol. Sem. Am., N.Y.C.; Latin Am. dir. World Coun. Synagogues, 1961; founder, dir. Camp Ramah, Cordoba, Argentina, 1964; cons. Secretariat Human Devel. and Family, Dept. Health, Govt. of Argentina; mem. exec. theol. cons. com. Argentine Nat. Inst. Mental Health; mem. internat. editorial adv. com. population reports George Washington U. Med. Ctr.; mem. bd. govs. N.Y. Bd. Rabbis. Editor: Jewish Liturgy, 1968, Social and Religious History of the Jews (Salo W. Baron), 1969, 8 vols.; mem. editorial bd. Cuadernos, 1970—; founder, editor Ediciones Seminario Rabinico Latinoamericano, Maj'shavot; founder, editor: Library of Science and History of Religions, Editorial Paidos. Apptd. to Nat. Commn. for Disappeared Persons, Buenos Aires; founding co-pres. Jewish Movement for Human Rights, Buenos Aires; bd. dirs. Joint Distbn. Com., Am. Com. for Israel Peace Ctr., Am.'s Watch, U.S. Interreligious Com. for Peace in Mid. East, Homes for the Homeless, West Side Community Coun., Witness for Peace, Ctr. on Violence and Human Survival at John Jay Coll. Criminal Justice, Christianity and Crisis, Jewish Fund for Justice, Mazon, Partnership of Faith in N.Y.C., Tucker Found.; other orgns.; bd. visitors Dartmouth Coll.; mem. presdl. commn. Argentine Permanent Assembly for Human Rights; founding mem. higher Inst. Religious Studies in Ecumenical Affairs, Buenos Aires. Decorated Order of Liberator San Martin (Argentina); recipient L'Dor award Internat. B'nai Brith, 1984, Human Rights award New Jewish Agenda, 1985, Maimonides prize Instituto Superior de Estudio Religiosos, 1987, Louis D. Brandeis award Am.-Israeli Civil Liberties Coalition, 1990; sr. fellow Dartmouth Coll., 1951-52, Reynolds fellow, 1955-56, Montgomery fellow, 1991; Merrill fellow, Harvard Sch. Div., 1992. Mem. Rabbinical Assembly, Argentine Inst. Higher Religious Studies (founder). Home: New York N.Y. Died Dec. 29, 1993.

MICKELSON, GEORGE S., governor of South Dakota; b. Mobridge, S.D., Jan. 31, 1941; s. George T. and Madge Mickelson; m. Linda McCahren; children: Mark, Amy, David. BS, U. S.D., 1963, JD, 1965. Ptnr. McCann, Martin and Mickelson, Brookings, S.D., 1968-83, Mickelson, Erickson and Helsper, Brookings, 1983-86; state's atty. Brookings County, 1970-74; mem. S.D. Ho. of Reps., Pierre, 1975-80, speaker pro tempore, 1977-78, speaker, 1979-80; gov. State of S.D., 1987-93; chmn. S.D. Bd. Charities and Corrections, 1980-84. Capt. U.S. Army, 1963-67, Vietnam. Mem. ABA, VFW, S.D. Bar Assn., Assn. Trial Lawyers Am., S.D. Trial Lawyers Assn., Am. Judicature Soc., VFW, Am. Legion. Republican. Methodist. Home: Pierre S.D. Died Apr. 19, 1993; buried Greenwood Cemetary, Brookings, S.D.

MIDDLEKAUFF, ROGER DAVID, lawyer; b. Cleve., May 6, 1935; s. Roger David and Ella Marie (Holan) M.; m. Gail Palmer, Apr. 19, 1963; children: Roger David, Arthur Henry. BChemE, Cornell U., 1957; Cert. Master Engring., 1958; JD cum laude, Northwestern U., 1964. Bar: Ohio 1964, D.C. 1966, U.S. Supreme Ct. 1974. Assoc. Roetzel & Andress, Akron, Ohio, 1964-66, Kirkland, Ellis & Rowe, Washington, Ohio, 1966-69; assoc. Thompson and Middlekauff and predecessor firms, Washington, Ohio, 1969-72, ptnr., 1973-83; ptnr. McKenna, Conner & Cuneo, Washington, Ohio, 1983-89; mem. adv. com. extension service project Dept. Agr., 1976; mem. adv. com. solar energy project ERDA, 1975; observer Codex Alimentarius Commn., FAO/WHO and com. meetings; project rev. group control tech. assessment of fermentation processes, Nat. Inst. Occupational Safety and Health. Co-editor: International Food Regulation Handbook: Policy, Science, Law, 1989; contbr. articles to legal jours.; editor handbooks, Practising Law Inst.; mem. editorial bd. Jour. Regulatory Pharmacology and Toxicology; co-editor: The Impact of Chemistry on Biotechnology, 1988, International Food Regulation Handbook: Science, Policy, Law. Vice chmn. bur. Greater Washington Bd. Trade; trustee Internat. Life Scis. Inst., Nutrition Found., Inc., Risk Sci. Inst.; mem. joint bd. Coun. Com. on Environ. Improvement; chmn. Arthur S. Flemming Awards Commn., 1969-70; vol. gen. counsel Episcopal Found. for Drama, 1976-77, Scotland Community Devel. Assn., 1971-73, Congregations United for Shelter, 1971-73, Iona House, 1974-77; sr. warden St. Columbia's Episc. Ch., Washington, 1975-77; sec., bd. dirs. Episc. Ch. Homes, Washington; chmn. pres.'s chpt. Nat. Capital Area council Nat. Eagle Scout Assn. Served with USN, 1958-61. Recipien Silver Wreath award local chpt. Boy Scouts Am. Mem ABA (chmn. subcom. on food and color additives an pesticide residues, food, drug and cosmetic com. 1977 82), Am. Chem. Soc. (chmn. div. chem. and law 198 sec., treas. biotech. secretariat, 1986-89, mem. exec. com chemistry and the law 1985-89, mem. joint bd. cour environ. improvement), Inst. Food Technologists (exe com. div. toxicology and safety evaluation, 1987-89 Order of Coif. Episcopalian. Clubs: Metropolitan, Ro tary. Home: Bethesda Md. Died Oct. 17, 1989.

MILCINSKI, JANEZ FRAN, university administrato medicine educator; b. Ljubljana, Slovenia, May 3, 191 s. Fran and Marija (Krejci) M.; m. Marija Jeras, Ma 1945 (div. 1952); m. Viktorija Vida Cerv, July 18, 195 children: Metka, Maja. JD, U. Ljubljana, 1936; MD U. Zagreb, Yugoslavia, 1940; D (hon.), U. Ljubljana 1979; MD (hon.), Karl-Marx Univ., Leipzig, Germa Dem. Republic, 1987. Prof., head Inst. for Forensi Medicine, Ljubljana, 1945-83; dean Faculty of Medicin Ljubljana, 1962-64; rector U. Ljubljana, 1973-76; pre Slovenian Acad. Scis. and Arts, Ljubljana, 1976-92. Author: Legal Medicine, Slovenian edit., 1956, Serbo Croatian edit., 1962, Medical Expertise, 1970, 2d vol 1981, Medical Ethics and Deontology, 1982, Years Lik Five Others, 1990. Recipient numerous Europea decorations and awards. Mem. Deutsche Akadem Naturforscher Leopoldina, Yugoslav Assn. Lega Medicine (nat. pres. 1982-83), Internat. Acad. Legal an Social Medicine (pres. 1970-73), Acad. Scis. and Ar SFRY, N.Y. Acad. Scis., Academia Scientiarum et A tium Europaea, Acad. Ligure Scienze e Lettere; ho mem. various European assns. legal medicine, Ordre d St. Fortunat (exec. com. Mainz, Fed. Republic German 1987). Home: Ljubljana Slovenia Died July 28, 199 interred Ljubljana, Slovenia.

MILES, SIR (ARNOLD) ASHLEY, physicia microbiologist; b. Mar. 20, 1904; S. Harry Miles; M.A M.D., Cambridge (Eng.) U. and St. Bartholomew Hosp., London, m. Ellen Margerite Dahl. Demonstrato in bacteriology London Sch. Hygiene, 1929; demon strator in pathology U. Cambridge, 1931; reader i bacteriology Brit. Postgrad. Med. Sch., London, 193 prof. bacteriology U. London, 1937-45, prof. expt pathology, 1952-71, now prof. emeritus; acting di Graham Med. Research Labs., Univ. Coll. Hosp. Me Sch., 1943-45; dir. Med. Research Council wound infe tion unit Nat. Inst. Med. Research, 1942-46; dep. dir 1947-52, dir. dept. biol. standards, 1946-52; dir. List Inst. Preventive Medicine, 1952-71; dep. dir. dept. me microbiology London Hosp. Med. Coll., 1976—; con in field. Created knight, 1966. Fellow Royal Soc., Roy Coll. Physicians, Royal Coll. Pathologists, Soc. Ge Microbiology (hon.) mem. Acad. de Medicine d Belgique (fgn. corr.), Am. Soc. Microbiology, Am. Ass Pathologists, Deutsche Gesellschaft für Hygiene un Mikrobiologie, others. Author: (with Wilson) Topl and Wilson's Principles of Bacteriology and Immunit 1945, 55, 64, 75, 84; contbr. articles to profl. jour Home: London England

MILLAR, MARGARET ELLIS, author; b. Kitchene Ont., Can., Feb. 5, 1915; d. Henry William and Lavin (Ferrier) Sturm; m. Kenneth Millar (pseudonym Ro Macdonald), June 2, 1938 (dec.); 1 dau., Linda Ja (dec.). Student, U. Toronto, 1933-36. Author: The In visible Worm, 1941, The Weak-Eyed Bat, 1942, Th Devil Loves Me, 1942, Wall of Eyes, 1943, Fire Wi Freeze, 1944, The Iron Gates, 1945, Experiment i Springtime, 1947, It's All in the Family, 1948, Th Cannibal Heart, 1949, Do Evil in Return, 1950, Vanis in an Instant, 1952, Rose's Last Summer, 1952, Wiv and Lovers, 1954, Beast in View, 1955, An Air Th Kills, 1957, The Listening Walls, 1959, A Stranger i My Grave, 1960, How Like an Angel, 1962, The Fien 1964, The Birds and the Beasts Were There, 196 Beyond This Point Are Monsters, 1970, Ask for M Tomorrow, 1976, The Murder of Miranda, 198 Mermaid, 1982, Banshee, 1983, Spider Webs, 1986; als writer short stories and TV plays. Recipient Edga award for Beast in View Mystery Writers Am., 195 Woman of Yr. award L.A. Times, 1965, Grandmast award Mystery Writers Am., 1982. Mem. Myste Writers Am. (pres. 1957). Home: Santa Barbara Cal Died Mar. 26, 1994.

MILLER, ALLEN BLAIR, public relations executiv b. Nashville, May 20, 1953; s. Eldon Blair and Patric (Jackson) M. BS in Communications, U. Tenn., 1976 Mktg. dir. Carter & Assoc., Atlanta, 1976-77; mkt rep. Walt Disney World, Orlando, Fla., 1977-79; acc exec., supr. Manning Selvage & Lee, P.R., N.Y.C., 197 84; exec. v.p. Ketchum Pub. Rels., San Francisco, 198 95, also bd. dirs. Chmn. awards com. Pub. Rels. So Am., N.Y.C., 1986-89. Recipient Silver Anvil awar Pub. Rels. Soc. Am., 1987, 88. Mem. Pub. Rels. So Am., San Francisco C. of C. (bd. dirs. 1990-95). Hom San Francisco Calif. Died Nov. 7, 1995.

MILLER, ALVIN VERLE, state senator; b. Cle Lake, Iowa, Feb. 2, 1921; s. Claude Ollin and Cora M (Moorehead) M.; m. Frances Elizabeth Sorensen, Ma 26, 1943; children: Marlene Miller Desing, Marc Miller Kuehler, Danny. Grad. high sch., Clear Lake Rep. State of Iowa, Des Moines, 1973-76, sen., 1977-9 ins. agt. Ventura, Iowa, 1939-89; ret., 1992. Me tions (chmn. Cerro Gordo chpt. 1970-71), Cerro Gordo Mut. Ins. Agts. Assn. (bd. dirs. 1963-89). Democrat. Methodist. Home: Ventura Iowa Died Feb. 9, 1993; buried Ventura Cemetery, Ventura, Iowa.

MILLER, BARBARA STOLER, Sanskrit literature educator, translator; b. N.Y.C.; d. Louis O. and Sara (Cracken) Stoler; 1 child, Gwenn Alison. AB, Barnard Coll., 1962; MA, Columbia U., 1964; PhD, U. Pa., 1968; LHD honoris causa, Mt. Holyoke, 1989. Asst. prof. Oriental studies Barnard Coll., Columbia U., N.Y.C., 1968-72, assoc. prof., 1972-77, prof. Asian and mid. ea. culture, 1977-93, Samuel R. Milbank prof., 1987-93; dir.-at-large Am. Oriental Soc., New Haven, 1981-83; mem. adv. council Smithsonian Instn., 1983-85; chmn. Soc. Fellows in the Humanities, Columbia U., 1986-88. Author: Bhartrihari: Poems, 1967, Phantasies of a Love Thief: The Caurapancasika Attributed to Bilhana, 1971, A Syllabus of Indian Civilization, 1971, Love Song of the Dark Lord: Jayadeva's Gitagovinda, 1977, The Hermit and the Love-Thief: Sanskrit Poems of Bhartrihari and Bilhana, 1978, Exploring India's Sacred Art: Selected Papers of Stella Kramrisch, 1983, Theatre of Memory: The Plays of Kalidasa, 1984, The Bhagavad-Gita: Krishna's Counsel in Time of War, 1986, Yoga: Discipline of Freedom, The Yogasutra of Patanjali, 1993; editor: Songs for the Bride: Wedding Rites of Rural India, 1985; Masterworks of Asian Lit., 1992, The Powers of Art: Patronage in Indian Culture, 1992; scholarly advisor Peter Brooks The Mahabharata, 1988-89; contbr. articles to profl. jours. Recipient Avery Hopwood Writing award Mich., 1959; Woodrow Wilson fellow, 1962; Nat. Def Fgn. Lang. fellow, 1962-63; AAUW grantee, 1965-66; NEH grantee, 1971, 81, 86, 88; Am. Philos. Soc. grantee, 1971; Guggenheim fellow, 1974-75; Mellon fellow, 1976; Am. Inst. Indian Studies fellow, 1974-75; Am. Inst. Indian Studies grantee, 1977; Nat. Council Women award in Higher Edn., 1979; Smithsonian travel grantee, 1981. Mem. Am. Oriental Soc., Assn. Asian Studies (pres. 1990-91), PEN Am. Center, Am. Numis. Soc., Am. Council Learned Socs. (bd. dirs.) Social Sci. Research Council (joint com. South Asia 1982-87, joint com. internat. programs 1988-93). Home: New York N.Y. Died Apr. 19, 1993.

MILLER, BEN NEELY, physician; b. Smyrna, S.C., Dec. 20, 1910; s. Benjamin Neely and Addie Jane (Whitesides) M.; m. Ruth Elizabeth Gambill, Dec. 27, 1938; children: Elizabeth Gambill, Jane Adelaide, Ben Neely. B.S., M.D., Duke U., 1935. Diplomate: Am. Bd. Internal Medicine. Med. resident Duke Hosp., Durham, N.C., 1935-37; instr. U. Ala. Med. Sch., 1937-38; practice of internal medicine Columbia, S.C., 1938-91; vis. lectr. U. S.C., 1967-70; clin. prof. medicine U. S.C. (Sch. Medicine), 1977-91; past chief staff Providence, Baptist, Columbia hosps.; med. cons. S.C. State Hosp., 1938-83, S.C. Dept. Vocat. Rehab. Bd. dirs. United Community Services, 1959-62, public-at-large trustee, 1963-66; med. adv. com. United Health and Med. Research Found. S.C.; mem. S.C. Pollution Control Authority, 1970-73; trustee Duke U. Recipient award S.C. Order of the Palmetto, 1983. Fellow A.C.P., Am. Coll. Allergists, Am. Acad. Allergy; mem. AMA, Southeastern Allergy Assn. (pres. 1955-56), Duke Alumni Assn. (pres. 1960-61), Duke Med. Alumni Assn. (pres. 1955-61), S.C. Med. Assn. (sec. 1962-68, pres. 1970-71), S.C. Soc. Internal Medicine (past pres.), Columbia Med. Soc. (pres. 1950). Presbyterian (elder). Club: Forest Lake Country (Columbia). Home: Lexington S.C. Died Dec. 10, 1995.

MILLER, CRAIG JOHNSON, theatrical lighting designer; b. Hugoton, Kans., Aug. 7, 1950; s. Robert Bruce and Ardis Vernette (Rollins) M. B.S. in Speech, Northwestern U., 1972. Freelance lighting designer: prodns. including Broadway shows On Golden Pond, 1979, Barnum, 1980, The Five O'Clock Girl, 1981, I Won't Dance, 1981, Brothers, 1983, Take Me Along, 1985, Wind in the Willows, 1985, Safe Sex, 1987, Romance, Romance, 1988, Oh, Kay!, 1980, Most Happy Fella, 1992; off-Broadway shows Trixie True, Teen Detective, 1980, Forty Deuce, 1981, Gardenia, 1982, Spookhouse, 1984, Just So, 1985, Smiling Through, 1994; Guthrie Theatre prodns. Romeo and Juliet, 1979, Mary Stuart, 1980, Candide, 1982, The Importance of Being Ernest, 1985, On the Razzle, 1986, Can. Nat. Arts Centre prodn., The History of the American Film, 1979; Stratford Ont. Shakespeare Festival prodn. Waiting for Godot, 1984; resident lighting designer Santa Fe Opera Co., 1979-93, Die Frau Ohne Schatten, Royal Opera, Covent Garden, 1992; dance lighting designer: Boston Ballet, Alvin Ailey Co., Joffrey Ballet, Royal Danish Ballet, Lar Lubovitch Dance Co., Elisa Monte Dance Co., Laura Dean Dance Co. Mem. United Scenic Artists Local 829. Home: New York N.Y. Died June 7, 1994.

MILLER, GERALD RAYMOND, communications educator; b. Muscatine, Iowa, Oct. 18, 1931; s. Raymond Russell and Mabel Anna (Bridges) M.; m. Pearl Ann Parsons, Aug. 2, 1952; children: Patricia Anne Miller Bender, Greg Anthony, Caleb Drew. BA, U. Iowa, 1957, MA, 1958, PhD, 1961. Instr. U. Iowa, Iowa City, 1958-61; asst. prof. U. Washington, Seattle, 1961-62; from asst. prof. to full prof. Mich. State U., East Lansing, 1963-93, Univ. Disting. prof., 1991-93. Author, editor books; contbr. numerous jours. to profl. publs. Served to pvt. U.S. Army, 1952-54, Korea. Recipient Disting. Faculty award Mich. State U., 1973, Joint Resolution of Tribute Mich. Legislature, 1974. Fellow Internat. Communication Assn. (pres. 1979), Am. Psychol. Assn.; mem. Speech Communication Assn. Democrat. Unitarian. Home: East Lansing Mich. Died May 20, 1993; interred Okemos, Mich.

MILLER, JACK RICHARD, federal judge; b. Chgo., June 6, 1916; s. Forest W. and Blanche M.; m. Isabelle M. Browning, Aug. 1, 1942; children: Janice Lee (Mrs. Robert Amott), Mrs. Judy Flynn, James Forrest, Mrs. A.H. Studenmund. A.B. cum laude, Creighton U., 1938, LL.D. (hon.), 1966; M.A., Cath. U., Washington, 1939; J.D., Columbia U., 1946; postgrad., State U. Iowa Coll. Law, 1946; LL.D. (hon.), Loras Coll., 1967, Iowa Wesleyan Coll., 1969, Yonsei U., South Korea, 1976. Bar: Iowa 1946, Nebr. 1946, D.C. 1949. Atty. Office Chief Counsel, IRS, Washington, 1947-48; professorial lectr. taxation George Washington U., 1948; asst. prof. law U. Notre Dame, 1948-49; pvt. practice tax law Sioux City, Iowa, 1949-60; mem. Iowa Ho. of Reps., 1955-56, Iowa Senate, 1957-60; U.S. senator from Iowa, 1961-73; judge U.S. Ct. Customs and Patent Appeals, Washington, 1973-82, U.S. Ct. Appeals (fed. cir.), Washington, 1982—; now sr. judge U.S. Ct. Appeals (fed. cir.). Contbr. numerous articles on tax and patent law to legal periodicals. Served from lt. to lt. col. USAAF, 1942-46; brig. gen. USAF Res. (ret.). Mem. ABA, Iowa, Nebr., D.C. Bar Assns., Am. Law Inst. (life), Am. Patent Law Assn., Am. Legion, VFW, Amvets, KC, Rotary. Home: Tampa Fla. Deceased.

MILLER, J(AMES) GORMLY, retired librarian, educator; b. Rochester, N.Y., Jan. 5, 1914; s. James Billings and Marian (Robinson) M.; m. Mildred Catharine Bevan, Sept. 6, 1939; children: Susan Miller Milligan, James Gormly, Paul B. AB, U. Rochester, 1936; BSLS, Columbia U., 1938. Asst. librarian Rochester Pub. Library, 1938-42; research asst. Bur. Adult Edn., N.Y. State Dept. Edn., 1946; librarian Cornell U.-N.Y. State Sch. Indsl. and Labor Relations, 1946-62, assoc. prof., then prof., 1949-70, 74-77, asst. dir. personnel and budget univ. libraries, 1962-70, libraries dir., 1975-79, librarian, 1979-80, prof. emeritus, 1980-95; acting Univ. librarian Cornell U., 1985-86; dep. chief central library and documentation br. ILO, Geneva, 1970-74; trustee Finger Lakes Library System, 1967-69; pres. bd. trustees South Central Research Library Council, 1980-83, v.p., 1984-85; cons. in field. Author profl. articles, reports. Alderman Ithaca (N.Y.) Common Council, 1959-63, 68; commnr. Ithaca Civil Service Commn., 1964-67. Served with U.S. Army, 1943-46. Mem. Am. Soc. for Info. Sci., ALA, N.Y. State Library Assn., Indsl. Relations Research Assn. Democrat. Anglican. Home: Ithaca N.Y. Died Sept. 12, 1995.

MILLER, JEROME K., retired publisher, copyright law consultant; b. Gt. Bend, Kans., Apr. 18, 1931; s. Walter J. and Kathleen M. (Kliesen) M. BA in History, Emporia State U., 1965; MLS, U. Mich., 1966; MA in History, U. Kans., 1967; EdD, U. Colo., 1976. Bibliographic searcher, cataloger, coord. audiovisual libr. svcs. Boullion Libr., Cen. Wash. U., 1967-74; lectr., then asst. prof. Grad. Sch. Libr. and Info. Sci. U. Ill., Urbana-Champaign, 1975-83, coord. doctoral studies Grad. Sch. Libr. and Info. Sci., 1977-81; pres. Copyright Info. Svcs., 1983-87, Harbor View Publs. Group, Inc., Friday Harbor, Wash., 1988-93. Author: Applying the New Copyright Law: A Guide for Educators and Librarians, 1979, U.S. Copyright Documents: An Annotated Collection for Use by Educators and Librarians, 1980, Using Copyrighted Videocassettes in Classrooms and Libraries, 1984, 2d edit., 1987, The Copyright Directory, 1985, Umbrella Guide to Friday Harbor and San Juan Island, 1988, others; contbr. articles to profl. publs.; producer audio-visual prodns. on copyright. Adv. bd. Ctr. Ecumenical Campus Ministry, Ellensburg, Wash., 1971-73, chmn., 1972-73; lay minister St. Francis parish, Friday harbor, 1985-90, chmn. liturgy com., 1987—, chmn. bldg. com., 1987—, mem. parish coun., 1987—, pres., 1989—; trustee San Juan Island Libr. Dist., 1985—, pres. bd. trustees, 1988—; mem. lay adv. bd. Ellensburg Pub. Schs., 1973-74. Mem. ALA, Libr. and Info. Tech. Assn. (bd. dirs. 1978-81), Am. Assn. Sch. Librs. (editorial com. 1979-82), Assn. Ednl. Communications and Tech. (chmn. copyright taskforce 1974-77, 82-83), Consortium of Univ. Film Ctrs. (charter mem., chmn. copyright com. 1974-76), Wash. Libr. Assn., Wash. Assn. Ednl. Communications and Tech., Ellensburg Kiwanis Club, San Juan Lions Club (bd. dirs. 1986-93, pres. 1991-92, zone chmn. 1992-93), Phi Alpha Theta, Phi Delta Kappa. Home: Friday Harbor Wash.

MILLER, ROBERT JAMES, anthropologist, educator, editor; b. Detroit, Sept. 18, 1923; s. Robert Paul and Desdemona (Jelinek) M.; m. Beatrice Diamond, Nov. 6, 1943; children: Karla M., Erik T., Terin T. Student, India studies U. Pa., 1947; A.B. in Oriental Civilization, U. Mich., 1948; Ph.D. in Anthropology, U. Wash., 1956. Asia research fellow U. Wash., 1948-50, instr. in anthropology, 1950; fellow Inner Asia Project, 1951-52; research anthropologist Inner Mongolia Project, 1955-56; asst. prof. sociology-anthropology Washington U., St. Louis, 1956-59; asst. prof. anthropology U. Wis., Madison, 1959-61; assoc. prof. U. Wis., 1962-64, prof., 1965-88, prof. emeritus, 1988-94, chmn. dept. anthropology, 1965-69, 76-78, prof. South Asian studies, 1959-88; resident dir. Am. Inst. Indian Studies, New Delhi, 1970-72; assoc. dir. Qualitative Systems Analysts Co.; cons. in field. Author: Monasteries and Culture Change in Inner Mongolia, 1959; contbr. numerous articles to profl. publs.; editor: Religious Ferment in Asia, 1974, Robotics: Future Factories, Future Workers. Founding mem. bd. dirs. Council on Understanding of Tech. in Human Affairs. Served with USCG, 1942-44. Social Sci. Research Council fellow, 1952-53; Ford Found. fellow, 1953-55; NSF grantee, 1963-64; Am. Inst. Indian Studies sr. fellow, 1963-64; Smithsonian fellow, 1970-72; Sloan Found. grantee, 1976. Fellow AAAS, Am. Anthrop. Assn.; mem. Assn. Asian Studies, Am. Ethnol. Soc., Soc. Gen. Systems Rsch., Current Anthropology (assoc.), AAUP, Coun. on Anthropology and Edn. (dir. 1980-84, chmn. com. on edn. futures 1981-84), Indian Anthrop. Assn. (founding), Internat. Assn. Buddhist Studies (founding, gen. sec. 1982-86), Am. Radio Relay League, Soc. Wireless Pioneers, Sigma Xi. Home: Camano Island Wash. Dec. Apr. 13, 1994. Buried in Puget Sound and the Ganges River.

MILLER, STEPHEN RABEN, lawyer; b. N.Y.C., Dec. 14, 1928; s. George and Sally (Raben) M.; m. Sara Berman, Dec. 26, 1949 (div. 1982); children: Thomas, Penelope, Ethan; m. Ann Ruth Fox, Jan. 2, 1983. BA, Haverford Coll., 1949; LLB, Yale U., 1952. Bar: N.Y. Ct. of Appeals 1953, Pa. Supreme Ct. 1962. Assoc. Mudge, Stern, Baldwin & Todd, N.Y.C., 1952-58; assoc. Delson, Levin & Gordon, 1959-61, ptnr., 1961; assoc. Dechert, Price & Rhoads, Phila., 1961-63, ptnr., 1963-93. Pres. bd. trustees Green Tree Sch., Phila., 1978-84, trustee, 1973-92; mem. bd. mgrs. Haverford Coll., 1974-86; clk. Radner Friends Meeting, Pa., 1971-73, trustee, 1974-87; commr. Lower Merion Twp., 1990-93. Mem. ABA, Pa. Bar Assn., Phila. Bar Assn. Home: Bryn Mawr Pa. Died 1993.

MILLER, WILLIAM EVANS, JR., retired lawyer; b. Pitts., May 8, 1923; s. William Evans and Elisabeth (Looney) M.; m. Phyllis Evans, Sept. 9, 1950 (dec. Oct. 7, 1982); children: Jonathan, David; m. Sandra Hawkins, June 14, 1986. A.B., Amherst Coll.; LL.B., U. Pa. Bar: Pa. Assoc. Reed Smith Shaw McClay, Pitts., 1949-64, ptnr., 1964-88; ret., 1988. Served to lt. (j.g.) USN, 1943-46, PTO. Mem. Wildwood Club, University Club, Masons. Republican. Christian Scientist. Home: Allison Park Pa. Died Jan. 5, 1996.

MILLIGAN, GEORGE F., bank executive; b. 1934. With Norwest Bank, Des Moines, 1963—, now pres., chief operating officer.

MILLS, HOWARD MCILROY, clergyman, denominational executive; b. Toronto, Ont., Can., Oct. 20, 1935; s. Ralph Shaw and Thora Rosalind (McIlroy) M.; m. Virginia Lee Epes Mills, July 8, 1961; children: Mary Elizabeth, Heather Lee, Alan Stewart Epes. BA, U. Toronto, 1956; MDiv, Emmanuel Coll., 1959; STM, Union Theol. Sem., 1960, PhD, 1970, DD (hon.), 1987; DD (hon.), U. Toronto, Victoria, 1988. Ordained minister United Ch. Can. Univ. chaplain, asst. prof. dept. philosophy Mt. Allison U., Sackville, N.B., 1965-68; assoc. prof. St. Stephen's Coll., Edmonton, Alta., Can., 1969-72; minister St. James-Bond United Ch., Toronto, 1972-74; gen. sec. divsn. ministry personnel and edn. The United Ch. Can., Toronto, 1974-82, gen. sec. of gen. coun., from 1987; pres. United Theol. Sem., New Brighton, Minn., 1983-87; cons. Inter-Ch. Com. Can., 1983; sessional lectr. Emmanuel Coll., Toronto, 1974-76; vis. fellow Inst. Devel. Studies, U. Sussex, U.K., 1981; official advisor edn. WCC, Vancouver, B.C., 1983, chair com. theol. edn.; del. observer Seventh Assembly WCC, Canberra, Australia, 1991; chair task group on structure Can. Coun. Chs., 1991-92; speaker, lectr. in field. Contbr. articles to profl. jours. Planner Project Tandem, from 1985; pres. Chs. Coun. Theol. Edn., from 1990; active Commn. Clergy in Crisis United Ch. Christ USA, 1984-86, Western Coun. Theol. Edn., 1977-80, Programme Commn. Theol. Edn. WCC, 1977-91, N.Am. Ministerial Fellowship, 1976-80, Programme Com. Profl. Ch. Leadership, 1974-81; bd. dirs. Ecumenical Found. Can., coord. com. theol. edn., 1975-82; bd. regents Victoria U., 1974-82. Mem. Can. Theol. Soc., Can. Assn. Pastoral Edn., Soc. Christian Ethics, UN Assn. (Can.), Muskoka Lakes Cottagers Assn., Peppertree Golf and Country Club, Cedar Highlands Ski Club, Eglington United Ch. Deceased.

MILSTEIN, NATHAN, concert violinist; b. Odessa, Russia, Dec. 31, 1904; came to U.S., naturalized, 1942; s. Miron and Maria (Bluestein) M.; m. Therese Weldon, 1945; 1 dau., Maria Bernadette. Student, of P. Stoliarsky, Odessa, of Leopold Auer at Conservatory Music St. Petersburg, of Eugene Ysaye at Brussels. Extensive tours of native country, 1920-26; ann. tours all European countries, U.S. and Can. since 1929, interrupted by World War; several tours, S.Am., Cuba, Mex., North Africa. Recipient Grammy award for classical-instrumental soloist, 1975, Kennedy Ctr. award for Lifetime Achievement, 1987; decorated comdr. Legion of Honor (France); Cross of Honor (Austria). Mem. Acad. St. Cecilia (Italy). Home: London England Died Dec. 21, 1992.

MILTNER, JOHN ROBERT, university official; b. Conneaut, Ohio, Sept. 6, 1946; s. Robert John and

Grace Evelyn (Hall) M.; m. Carol Lee Herd, Oct. 27, 1973; children: William, Kelli, Bryan, Tiffany, Robert. BS, Bowling Green U., 1968; MBA, Pace U., 1981; PhD, The Union Inst., 1990. Cert. fundraising exec. Exploring dir. Boy Scouts Am., Toledo, 1968-72, dir. exploring, N.Y.C., 1975-76, dir. devel., 1977-79, exec. dir. devel. and communications Greater N.Y. councils, 1979-80; mktg. mgr. IBM, Toledo, 1972-73; regional mktg. mgr. Docutel Corp., Boston, 1974; dir. devel. Meml. Sloan-Kettering Cancer Ctr., N.Y.C., 1980-83; vice chancellor U. Calif.-Irvine, 1983-91; pres. Millikin U., Decatur, Ill., from 1991. Mem. exec. com. Irvine Med. Ctr., vice chmn.; bd. dirs. Irvine Health Found., from 1986, Indsl. League Orange County, 1986-87, Orange County coun. Boy Scouts Am., Lincoln Trails coun., from 1991; mem. Charitable Giving Council Orange County, from 1986; dir. Orange County Performing Arts Ctr., 1987-91. Named Outstanding Fund Raising Profl. Internat. Conf. on Philanthropy, 1990. Mem. Nat. Soc. Fund Raising Execs. (cert., dir. from 1977, v.p. 1979-81, pres. 1981-82, vice chmn. nat. bd. 1982-85, chmn.-elect 1985, chmn. 1986-87), Met. Decatur C. of C. (bd. dir. from 1991), Princeton Club, Balboa Bay Club (Newport Beach, Calif.), Country Club Decatur, Decatur Club, Union League Club Chgo., Univ. Club Chgo. Deceased. Home: Venice Fla.

MILTON, JOHN RONALD, English language educator, author; b. Anoka, Minn., May 24, 1924; s. John Peterson and Euphamia Alvera (Swanson) M.; m. Leonharda Allison Hinderlie, Aug. 3, 1946; 1 dau., Nanci Lynn. B.A., U. Minn., 1948, M.A., 1951; Ph.D., U. Denver, 1961. Instr. English and philosophy Augsburg Coll., Mpls., 1949-57; mem. faculty Jamestown (N.D.) Coll., 1957-63, prof. English, chmn. dept., 1961-63; prof. English, U. S.D., Vermillion, 1963-95; chmn. dept. U. S.D., 1963-65; editor S.D. Rev., 1963-95, dir. writing program, 1965-95; vis. prof. N.D. State U., summer 1966, Ind. State U., summer 1966, Bemidji (Minn.) State Coll., 1969; chmn. Dakota Press, publ. U. S.D., 1968-81. Author: (poetry) The Loving Hawk, 1962, Western Plains, 1964, The Tree of Bones, 1965, This Lonely House, 1968, The Tree of Bones and Other Poems, 1973, The Blue Belly of the World, 1974; (novel) Notes to a Bald Buffalo, 1976; (biography) Oscar Howe, 1972, Crazy Horse, 1974; (history) South Dakota: A Bicentennial History, 1977; (criticism) The Novel of the American West, 1980; also interviews, essays, stories, revs., articles; editor: The American Indian Speaks, 1969, Three West, 1970, American Indian II, 1971, The Literature of South Dakota, 1976. Served with U.S. Army, 1943-46. Recipient Gov.'s award for achievement in arts, 1978, Western Am. award, 1984, Western Writers Am. award, 1987, S.D. Hall of Fame Writer of the Year, 1993; Spl. Recognition award S.D. State Hist. Soc., 1978, U. S.D., 1980, S.D. Hist. Assn. award, 1992; Wurlitzer Found. fellow, 1965; Hill Found. grantee, 1966, 69, 70, 81; grantee Whitney Found., 1970, 72, U. S.D., 1963, 64; grantee S.D. Arts Council, 1969, 70, 74, lit. fellowship, 1987; Nat. Endowment Arts writing fellow, 1976-77; fellow S.D. Arts Council, 1987. Mem. Am. Studies Assn. (regional bd. 1957-59), Western Lit. Assn. (pres. 1971, editl. bd. 1966-80, exec. coun. 1966-68), Western History Assn. Home: Vermillion S.D. Died Jan. 28, 1995.

MILTON, LEONARD, electronics manufacturing company executive; b. N.Y.C., July 26, 1917; s. Israel M. and Sadie (Kranes) M.; E.E., Pratt Inst., 1939, D.Sc., 1965; m. Hilda Lozner, Dec. 29, 1946; children: Donn, Ilo, Cindy, Rand. Chief engr. Solar Mfg. Corp., Bayonne, N.J., 1940-46; v.p., chief engr. Filtron Co., Inc., Flushing, N.Y., 1946-56, pres., 1956-70, chmn. bd., 1970-91, pres., chmn. bd., Bethpage, N.Y., 1977-83; dir. Starrett Housing Corp., N.Y.C., 1967-91. Pres. People to People Sports Com., 1966-91; pres. L. Milton Found., 1950-91; bd. govs. St. Huberts Soc. Mem. N.Y. Acad. Scis., IEEE, Tau Beta Pi. Clubs: Shikar Safari, Glen Head Country (L.I.); Explorers, (N.Y.C.). Author: Radio Interference in Aircraft Systems; Radio Interference in Aircraft Electrical and Electronic Systems; Electromagnetic Analysis of the Arctic; Interference Reduction Guide for Design Engineers. Patentee in field. Died Oct. 1, 1991. Home: Great Neck N.Y.

MIMS, THOMAS JEROME, insurance executive; b. Sumter County, S.C., Dec. 12, 1899; m. Valma Gillespie, 1926; children: Thomas Jerome Jr., G. Frank (dec. Apr. 1991). BA, Furman U., 1921. With Rec. and Statis. Corp. N.Y., 1921-29; asst. mgr. Rec. and Statis. Corp. N.Y., Phila., 1922-25; mgr. Rec. and Statis. Corp. N.Y., Indpls., 1925-27, Boston, 1927-29; ins. spl. agt. State of N.J., 1931-32; mgr. Wm. R. Timmons Agy., Greenville, S.C., 1933-94; v.p., sec. Canal Ins. Co., Greenville, 1942-48; pres., dir. Canal Ins. Co., 1948-92, chmn. emeritus, 1992-94; pres., dir. Canal Indemnity Co., Greenville; ptnr. Valetep, Greenville, 1975-94; mem. Legis. Com. To Study Automobile Liability Ins., 1969-70. Emeritus mem. adv. council Furman U., from 1974; mem. adv. bd. S.C. Safety Council, 1969-84, pres., 1970-75, 81-84; bd. dirs. United Way of Greenville, 1970-92, campaign vice chmn., 1975, chmn., 1976, v.p., 1977, pres., 1978, chmn. bd., 1979, hon. bd. dirs., 1981-92; bd. dirs. S.C. United Way, 1981-84; mem. fin. com. 1st Bapt. Ch., Greenville, 1971-94; pres. Rotary Charities, Inc., 1964-65; past mem. bd. dirs. Met. Arts Council; mem. Greenville Little Theatre Council, 1951-85, bus. mgr., 1951-53, 64-66, v.p., 1956-57, 72-73, pres., 1957-58, 73-75; bd. dirs. Greenville Area Mental Health Ctr.; mem. adv. bd. Life Ctr. Named Greenville Jaycee Boss of Yr., 1964, Boss of Yr., Greenville Assn. Ins. Women, 1977, S.C. Vol. of Yr., United Way, 1979, Ins. Co. Man. of Yr., Ind. Ins. Agts. S.C., 1980; named to Honorable Order of Ky. Colonels, 1969; recipient svc. award Internat. Ins. Soc., Paris, 1980. Fellow Pres.'s Coun. AIM; mem. Greenville C. of C. (chmn. community rels. com. 1964-69, dir. 1969-74, pres. 1973, pres. Found. 1973), S.C. C. of C., U.S. C. of C. (ins. com. 1959-61, 64-68), Internat. Ins. Soc. (chmn. bd. dirs. 1983-84, bd. electors, registrar 1984-85, past other coms., named to Hall of Fame, Svc. award 1980), Nat. Assn. Ins. Agts., S.C. Assn. Ins. Agts., Greenville Assn. Ins. Agts. (v.p. 1950-51, pres. 1951-52, chmn. exec. com. 1952-53), Am. Mgmt. Assn., President's Assn., Motor Transp. Assn. (dir. 1973-75, chmn. ins. com. 1951-63), Assn. S.C. Property and Casualty Ins. Cos. (1st v.p. 1961-62, 71-72, pres. 1962-63, 72-73, exec. com. 1961-74), Truck and Heavy Equipment Claims Coun. (charter mem., chmn. membership com.), Internat. Platform Assn., Newcomen Soc., Conf. Bd. Baptist (former pres. Men's Bible Class, 1st Baptist Ch., Greenville, mem. fin. com.). Clubs: World Trade (Atlanta); Poinsett (emeritus), Commerce, Greenville Touchdown, (charter, pres. 1963-64), Clemson IPTAY, City, Furman Paladins (Greenville); Palmetto, Summit (Columbia, S.C.); Short Snout, Palmetto Club, Summit Club. Lodge: Rotary (pres. Greenville 1963-64, v.p. 1964-65). Home: Mauldin S.C. Died Sept. 3, 1994.

MINASY, ARTHUR JOHN, aerospace and electronic detection systems executive; b. N.Y.C., July 19, 1925; s. John and Esther (Horvath) M.; B.S. in Adminstrv. Engring., N.Y. U., 1949, M.S. in Indsl. and Mgmt. Engring., 1952; postgrad. Case Inst. Tech., 1953-55; m. Jayne Marion Leary, June 29, 1946; children: Karen Lynn, Keith Leary, Kathy Jayne. Asst. gen. mgr. Def. div. Bulova Watch Co., Maspeth, N.Y., 1950-53; chief indsl. engr. Standard Products Co., Cleve., 1953-55; gen. mgr. ops. Gruen Industries, Cin., 1955-57; mgmt. cons. Booz-Allen and Hamilton, N.Y.C., 1957-60; mfg. mgr. Sperry Gyroscope Co., Great Neck, N.Y., 1960-62; v.p. ops. Belock Instrument Co., College Point, N.Y., 1962-64; pres. Detection Devices, Inc., Woodbury, N.Y., 1963-94; chmn., chief exec. officer KNOGO Corp., Hauppauge, N.Y., 1966-94; founder, pres. Internat. Electronic Articles Surveillance Mfrs. Assn., Brussels, 1989-93; bd. dirs. KNOGO Italia S.r.l., Milan, Italy, KNOGO SA, Belgium, KNOGO Caribe Inc., Cidra, P.R., KNOGO Australia, KNOGO The Netherlands B.V., KNOGO Switzerland S.A., KNOGO France S.A., KNOGO Denmark APS, KNOGO Deutschland GMBH, KNOGO Scandinavia AB, KNOGO UK Ltd., KNOGO Iberica SA; prin. Arthur J. Minasy Assocs., Mgmt. Cons., 1957-62; adv. bd. Abilities, Inc.; also lectr. in sci. law enforcement and detection systems. Dir., mem. adv. bd. Human Resources Found.; trustee Rehab. Inst. Served with AUS, 1943-46. Decorated Commdr. of Order of the Crown, King of Belgium, 1992; recipient Humanitarian of Yr. award Am. Cancer Soc.; named L.I.'s Entrepeneur of Yr., Inc. Mag., 1990; inductee to Smithsonian Nat. Mus. Am. History, 1991. Mem. Am. Inst. Indsl. Engrs., Internat. Electronic Article Surveillance Mfgrs. Assn. (founder, pres. 1989), Am. Ordnance Assn., Am. Mgmt. Assn., Tau Beta Pi, Alpha Pi Mu. Patentee in field. Died May 9, 1994. Home: Woodbury N.Y.

MINTZ, JEANNE SHIRLEY, government official, Asian affairs specialist; b. N.Y.C., Nov. 30, 1922; d. Nathaniel I. and Jessie G. (Guttentag) Mintz. B.A., Bklyn. Coll., 1943; M.P.A., Harvard U., 1953, Ph.D., 1964. Polit. and econ. analyst, Netherlands Indies govt.-in-exile, N.Y.C., 1943-45; press officer Indonesian delegation to UN, N.Y.C., 1947-51; research assoc. Ctr. for Internat. Studies, MIT, Cambridge, 1953-54; dir. program devel. Asia Soc., N.Y.C., 1957-61; sr. research scientist Spl. Ops. Research Office, Washington, 1964-66; mem. sr. profl. staff Ctr. for Naval Analyses, Arlington, Va., 1966-71, def. research 1971-74; staff specialist for long-range planning Dept. Def., Washington, 1974-82, dir. Far East and So. Hemisphere Affairs, 1983-85, asst. dep. undersec. Asia, Mid. East and So. Hemisphere, 1986-94. Author: Indonesia, in Marxism in Southeast Asia, 1959; Indonesia: A Profile, 1961; Mohammed, Marx and Marhaen, 1965; contbr. numerous articles to profl. jours. Littauer fellow, Harvard, 1951-53. Mem. Assn. for Asian Studies, Council of Harvard Graduate Soc., Exec. Women in Govt. (pres. 1980), Authors Guild, Harvard Alumni Assn. (dir. 1978-81), Harvard Club (dir., Washington 1982-85), Cosmos Club. Jewish. Died Jan 11, 1994. Home: Washington D.C.

MIRANDA Y GOMEZ, MIGUEL DARIO CARDINAL, archbishop of Mexico City; b. Leon, Mex., Dec. 19, 1895. Ordained priest Roman Catholic Ch., 1918. Bishop of Tulancingo, 1937-55; titular archbishop of Selimbria, 1955-56; archbishop of Mexico City and Primate of Mexico, 1956-77; elevated to cardinal, 1969. Entitled Nostra Signora de Guadalupe a Monte Mario. Home: Mexico City Mex.

MIRON, MURRAY SAMUEL, psychologist, educator; b. Allentown, Pa., Aug. 7, 1932; s. Murray R. and Myrtle E. (Hurlbut) M.; m. Helen Kutuchief, July, 1954 (div. June 1972); 1 child, Melinda; m. Cheryl Adamy, Aug. 5, 1973; 1 child, Murray Thomas. MA, U. Ill 1956, PhD, 1960. From asst. prof. to assoc. prof. U Ill., Urbana, 1960-70; prof. Syracuse (N.Y.) U., 195 threat assessor, FBI, Washington, 1972-92, U.S. Dep Energy, Washington, 1980-95, U.S. Dept. State, 198 95. Author: Hostage, 1979; co-author: Cross-Cultur Universals of Affective Meaning, 1976; contbr. 50 a ticles to profl. jours. Negotiatior Onandaga Sheriff Office and Syracuse Police Dept., 1980-84; forensic con Onondaga Dist. Atty., Syracuse, 1992-95. Recipien Gold Badge Internat. Assn. of Chiefs of Police, 1977 Fellow Am. Bd. Forensic Examiners (bd. cert. i document examination and psychol. profiling); men Am. Psychol. Soc., Am. Soc. Indsl. Security, Interna Assn. Bomb Tech. & Investigation. Home: Syracus N.Y. Died July, 1995.

MITCHELL, HENRY CLAY, newspaper columnist; b Washington, Nov. 24, 1923; s. Edward Clay an Katherine (Divine) M.; m. Helen Virginia Hollida May 7, 1949; children—Clay Alexander, Katherin Wood. Student, U. Va., 1941-47. Copyboy Wash ington Star, 1949-51; reporter, critic Comml. Appea Memphis, 1951-66; editor Resorts Mgmt., Memphi 1966, The Delta Rev., Memphis, 1966-70; minor edito Washington Post, 1970-73, columnist, 1973—, writ Earth Man column, 1973—, writer Any Day colum 1976—. Author: The Essential Earthman, 1983, Wash ington: Houses of the Capital, 1984. With USAAF 1942-45. Mem. Royal Hort. Soc. London. Democra Episcopalian. Home: Washington D.C.

MITCHELL, JOSEPH (QUINCY), writer; b Fairmont, N.C., July 27, 1908; s. Averette Nance an Elizabeth Amanda (Parker) M.; m. Therese Dagny E gelsted Jacobsen, Feb. 27, 1931 (dec. Oct. 1980); chi dren: Nora (Mrs. John L.R. Sanborn), Elizabeth (Mr Henry Curtis). Student, U. N.C., 1925-29. Reporte N.Y. World, N.Y.C., 1929-30, N.Y. Herald Tribun 1930-31, N.Y. World Telegram, 1931-38; writer Ne Yorker, N.Y.C., 1938-96. Author: My Ears Are Ben 1938, McSorley's Wonderful Saloon, 1943, Old M Flood, 1948, The Bottom of the Harbor, 1960, Jo Gould's Secret, 1965, (with Edmund Wilson) Apologi to the Iroquois, With a Study of the Mohawks in Hig Steel, 1960, Up in the Old Hotel, 1992. Vestryma Grace Ch., N.Y.C., 1978-84; mem. N.Y.C. Landmark Preservation Commn., 1982-87; mem. restoration com South Street Seaport Mus., 1972-80. Recipient Gol medal for lit. State N.C., 1984, Disting. Alumnus awar U. N.C., 1993, Brendan Gill prize Mcpl. Art Soc., 199 Amb. Book award English-Speaking Union, 1993. Mem. Am. Acad. Arts and Letters, Soc. Archtl. His torians, Soc. Indsl. Archeology, Friends of Cast-Iro Architecture, James Joyce Soc., Gypsy Lore Soc. Clu Century Assn. (N.Y.C.). Died May 24, 1996.

MITCHELL, ROBERT WATSON, publisher; b Randolph, Vt., Oct. 11, 1910; s. Robert J. and Stel (Watson) M.; m. Rita C. Morrissey, Mar. 15, 1935 (de Aug. 1945); children: Margaret (Mrs. William Mather, Jr.), Robert John; m. Virginia Wright Buck ingham, Nov. 27, 1946; children: Thomas S., Mar R. A.B., Dartmouth Coll., 1932; postgrad., Londo Sch. Econs., 1933; L.H.D. (hon.), U. Vt., 1985, Mi dlebury Coll., 1993. Sr. editor, pub., pres. Rutland (Vt Herald, 1942-93; pres. Barre-Montpelier Times-Argu 1964-93; past pres. Rutland Indsl. Devel. Corp. Chm Rhodes Scholarship Com. Named Vt. State C. of C Citizen of Yr., 1986; recipient Extraordinary Vermont award, 1990, Yankee Quill award, 1993, Horace Greel award New Eng. Press Assn., 1994. Mem. Sigma Del Chi. Club: Nat. Press. Home: Rutland Vt. Died Ma 9, 1993.

MITCHELSON, THEO KAY, insurance company ex ecutive; b. Lake City, Fla., Jan. 21, 1925; s. Kay an Lillian Formie (DeVeau) M.; m. Margaret Mari Barber, Sept. 2, 1950; children: Theo Kay Jr., Laur Lisa. BS in Indsl. Mgmt., U. Ala., 1950, postgrad 1950. CPCU; APD in employee rels., tng. and devel sr. profl. in human resource mgmt. Agt. Met. Life In Co., Daytona Beach, Fla., 1950-52; sales rep. Newt Morris Box Co., Jacksonville, Fla., 1952-53; region pers. mgr. State Farm Ins. Cos., Jacksonville, 1953-6 div. mgr., 1967-71; exec. asst. to pres. State Farm In Cos., Bloomington, Ill., 1971-78; dep. regional v.p. Stat Farm Ins. Cos., Monroe, La., 1978-90; cons., speake writer, seminar leader Leadership Devel. Ctr., Jack sonville. Mem. editorial bd. Leaders Digest; contb articles to profl. publs. Mem. adv. bd. Salvation Arm Monroe, 1984-90; founder, sec., bd. dirs. Crimestoppe Ouachita, Monroe, 1985-89; founder, trustee Jac sonville Episcopal High Sch., 1966; pres. bd. dir United Way N.E. La., 1988; adv. bd. dept. gerontolo N.E. La. U., Monroe, 1985-90; bd. dirs. Twin Citi YMCA, Monroe, 1987-90; bd. dirs. Nat. Blue Ridg Conf. on Leadership, 1989—; active numerous oth civic orgns. With USAAF, 1943-46; PTO; 1st lt. U. Army, 1951-52. Recipient Communications an Leadership award Toastmasters Internat., 1978, Distin Svc. to Humanity award Twin City Jaycees, 1983. Mem. Am. Soc. Pers. Adminstrn. (life; nat. pres. 196 Disting. Svc. and Leadership award Jacksonville chp 1963), Soc. CPCUs (nat. edn. com. 1970, award re chpt., Ins. Person of Yr. 1989), Nat. Speakers Ass (charter; cert. profl. speaker), Commerce Execs. Soc. U. Ala., U. Ala. Alumni Assn., Am. Assn. Ret. Person

Sawgrass Country Club (Ponte Vedra Beach, Fla.), Mason (32d deg.), Shriner, Beta Gamma Sigma, Delta Sigma Pi, Pi Kappa Alpha. Home: Ponte Vedra Beach Fla.

MITIN, MARK BORISOVICH, philosopher; b. Zhitomir, Ukraine, July 5, 1901. Ed. Inst. Red Profs., Moscow. In party work, 1929-36; sci. worker Inst. Philosophy, 1936-44; lectr. Higher Party Sch., 1945-50; chief editor For a Lasting Peace, For a People's Democracy, Bucharest, Romania, 1950-56, Question of Philosophy, 1960-67; dep. to USSR Supreme Soviet, 1952-58; mem. staff All-Union Soc. Znania (Knowledge), 1956-60; chmn. sci. council on problems of fgn. ideological movements Acad. Scis. USSR, 1967-87. Author: Hegel and the Theory of Dialectical Materialism, 1932; For Materialist Biological Sciences, 1949; Philosophy of the Contemporary World, 1960; V.I. Lenin and the Pressing Problems of Philosophy, 1971; Philosophy Today, 1975; Problems of Ideological Combat Today, 1976; Philosophy and Progress, 1979. Mem. central com. Communist Party Soviet Union, 1939-61. Decorated Order of Lenin (three times), Order of Red Banner of Labor (three times), Order of Oct. Revolution, Order of Friendship of Peopls; recipient State prize, 1943. Mem. Acad. Scis. USSR. Home: Moscow Russia

MITTERRAND, FRANÇOIS MAURICE MARIE, former president of France; b. Oct. 26, 1916; s. Joseph and Yvonne Lorain; m. Danielle Gouze, Oct. 28, 1944; children: Jean-Christophe, Gilbert. Ed., U. Paris. Dep. to French Parliament, 1946-58, 62-96; minister for ex-service men, 1947-48, sec. state for info., 1948-49, minister for overseas ters., 1950-51; chmn. Union Démocratique et Socialiste de la Résistance, 1951-52; del. Council of Europe, 1953; minister of interior, 1954-55, minister state for justice, 1956-57, senator, 1959-62; pres. Fedn. Democratic and Socialist Left, 1965-68; 1st sec. Socialist Party, 1971-81; vice chmn. Socialist Internat., 1972-81; pres. France, 1981-95; polit. dir. Le Courier de la Nièvre. Author: Le coup d'état permanent, 1964; Ma part de vérité, 1969; Un socialisme du possible, 1970; La rose au poing, 1973; La paille et le grain, 1975; Politique I (in 3 parts), 1977; L'abeille et l'architecte, 1978; Ici et Maintenant, 1980, Politique II, 1981. Served with French Forces, 1939-40; prisoner of war, escaped, later active French Resistance; sec.-gen. Orgn. for Prisoners of War, War Victims and Refugees, 1944-46. Decorated Great Cross Légion d'Honneur, Croix de Guerre, Rosette de la Résistance. Home: Paris France Died Jan. 8, 1996.

MODEL, ELISABETH DITTMANN, sculptor; b. Bayreuth, Bavaria, Bavaria; came to U.S., 1941, naturalized, 1947; d. J. M. and Therese (Fleisher) Dittmann; m. Max Model, Sept. 5, 1922 (dec.); children: Wolfe F. F. Peter. Student, Coll. of Art, Munich, Acad. of Art, Amsterdam, Netherlands; pupil of, M. Kogan, Paris. One-woman exhbns. in, Europe, N.Y.C. and Washington; group exhbns. include, Stedelijk Mus., Amsterdam, Brit.-Am. Art Center, Mus. Fine Arts, Boston Mus. Fine Arts, Phila., Bklyn. Mus., Riverside Mus., Mus. Natural History, N.Y.C., Galleria L'Obelisco, Rome, The Contemporaries, N.Y.C.; represented in permanent collections, Corcoran Gallery, Washington, Ryks-Prenten-Kabinett, Amsterdam, Atheneum Mus., Hartford, Conn., Jewish Mus., N.Y.C., Norfolk Mus., Va., Wichita U., Kans., Hirschhorn Collection, Brandeis U., Newark (N.J.) Mus. Recipient numerous awards, prizes. Mem. Fedn. Modern Painters and Sculptors (v.p.). Home: New York N.Y. Died Nov. 12, 1993.

MOERTEL, CHARLES GEORGE, physician; b. Milw., Oct. 17, 1927; s. Charles Henry and Alma Helen (Soffel) M.; m. Virginia Claire Sheridan, Mar. 22, 1952; children: Charles Stephen, Christopher Loren, Heather Lynn, David Matthew. B.S., U. Ill., 1946-51, M.D., 1953; M.S., U. Minn., 1958; D honoris causa, U. Grenoble, France, 1987. Intern Los Angeles County Hosp., 1953-54; resident in internal medicine Mayo Found., Rochester, Minn., 1954-57; cons. Mayo Clinic, Rochester, 1957-94; chmn. dept. oncology Mayo Clinic, 1975-86; dir. Mayo Comprehensive Cancer Ctr., 1975-86; prof. medicine Mayo Med. Sch., 1972-76, prof. oncology, 1976-94, Purvis and Roberta Tabor prof., 1981-87; mem. oncologic drugs adv. com. FDA; mem. cancer adv. com. AMA; mem. bd. sci. counselors, div. resources, centers and community activities Nat. Cancer Inst.; mem. colorectal cancer adv. com. Am. Cancer Soc. Author: Multiple Primary Malignant Neoplasms, 1966, Advanced gastrointestinal Cancer, Clinical Management and Chemotherapy, 1969; assoc. editor Cancer, 1989-94; mem. editorial bd. Cancer, 1974-94, Cancer Medicine, 1978-83, Current Problems in Cancer, 1978-83, Jour. Soviet Oncology, 1979-83, Cancer Research, 1979-84, Cancer Treatment Rep, 1980-82, Internat. Jour. Radiation Oncology Biol. Physics, 1981-94; Jour. Clin. Oncology, 1986-89, Jour. Med. and Pediatric Oncology, 1986-94. Served with U.S. Army, 1946-47. Decorated Knight of Malta; Walter Hubert lectr. Brit. Assn. Cancer Research, 1976; Ejnar Perman Meml. lectr. Swedish Surg. Assn., 1978; recipient Heath Meml. award M.D. Anderson Hosp., Tex. 1986, Docteur Honoris Causa Republic of France Univ. of Grenoble, 1987, Cancer Research award Assn. of Community Cancer Ctrs., 1987; John S. Lawrence vis. professorship UCLA, 1989, Albert Segaloff vis. professorship Alton Ochsner Med Found., 1989. Mem. Am. Soc. Clin. Oncology (pres. 1979-80, Karnofsky award 1986), Soc. Clin. Trials (dir.), Am. Assn. Cancer Research, Gastrointestinal Tumor Study Group (co-chmn.), AMA, A.C.P., Soc. Surg. Oncology, Am. Gastroenterologic Assn., North Central Cancer Treatment Group (chmn.), Sigma Xi. Home: Rochester Minn. Died June 27, 1994.

MOFFAT, RICHARD HOWE, judge, lawyer; b. Salt Lake City, Dec. 17, 1931; s. David Howe and Muriel (Dods) M.; m. Ann Hope Williamson, June 18, 1955 (dec. Oct. 1990); children: Kathleen Ann, Barbara Lynne, David Richard; m. Marilyn C. Faulkner, Apr. 13, 1991. BS, U. Utah, 1953; JD, Stanford U., 1956. Bar: Utah 1956. Mng. ptnr., pres. Moffat, Welling & Paulsen and predcessor, Salt Lake City, 1956-85; judge 5th Cir. Ct. Utah, Murray, 1985-86, 3d Dist. Ct. Utah, Salt Lake City, 1986-95; chmn. Utah State Jud. Removal Commn., 1977-78. Mem. Salt Lake County Bd. Adjustment, 1980-85, Utah Bd. Water Resources, 1982-85. Mem. ABA, Utah State Bar (commr. 1975-8l), Salt Lake County Bar Assn. (pres. 1969-70, exec. com. 1968-8l), Cottonwood Country Club. Democrat. Home: Seattle Wash. Died Feb. 10, 1995.

MOFFETT, WILLIAM ANDREW, librarian, educator; b. Charlotte, N.C., Jan. 25, 1933; s. Alfred Nisbet and Mary Elizabeth (McLean) M.; m. Deborah Ellen Hoover, May 9, 1958; children: Pamela, Andrew, Charles, Stephanie. BA, Davidson Coll., 1954; MA, Duke U., 1959, PhD, 1968; MLS, Simmons Coll., 1974; LLD (hon.), Davidson Coll., 1992; LittD (hon.), Potsdam Coll., 1993. Chmn. dept. history Charlotte Country Day Sch., N.C., 1959-61; lectr. Alma Coll., Mich., 1964-68; asst. prof. history U. Mass.-Boston, 1968-74; dir. libraries SUNY-Potsdam Coll., 1974-79; prof. history, Azariah Root dir. librs. Oberlin Coll., Ohio, 1979-90; dir. Huntington Libr., San Marino, Calif., 1990-95; cons. in field. Contbr. articles to profl. publs., newspapers. Named Librarian of Yr., Spl. Librs. Assn., 1993, Rsch. Librarian of Yr., Assn. Coll. and Rsch. Librs., 1993; recipient Imroth Meml. award Am. Libr. Assn., 1993, Alumni Achievement award Simmons Coll. Grad. Sch. Libr. and Info. Sci., 1994. Mem. Assn. Coll. and Rsch. Librs. (exec. bd. 1988-91, pres. 1989-90), Grolier (N.Y.) Club, Rowfant Club (Cleve.). Home: Pasadena Calif. Died Feb. 20, 1995.

MOGENSEN, ALLAN HERBERT, retired industrial consultant; b. Paxtang, Pa., May 12, 1901; s. Olaf Einar and Birgitte (Monrad) M.; m. Adele Dean, 1919 (div. 1948); children—Allan Olaf (dec.). Sonia Patricia Mogensen Adsit; m. Giovina Portfolio, 1962. B.S.M.E., Cornell U., 1924. Asst. prof. U. Rochester, N.Y., 1924-30; editor Factory Mag., McGraw Hill Pub. Co., Chgo. and N.Y.C., 1930-33; indsl. cons. Simplification Confs., Lake Placid, N.Y. and Conn., 1933-87; cons. editor Factory Mag., 1933-39. Author: Common Sense Applied to Motion and Time Study, 1931, 32; contbr. articles to profl. publs. Served with U.S. Army, 1944-45. Recipient Gilbreth medal Soc. Indsl. Engrs., 1931. Fellow Inst. Indsl. Engrs. (Taylor Key 1982 Frank and Lillian Gilbreth award Inst. Indsl. Engrs. 1984) mem. Soc. for Advancement of Mgmt. (hon.), Improvement Inst. (mem. adv. bd.). Republican. Home: Lake Placid N.Y. Deceased.

MOLDENHAUER, HOWARD HERMAN, lawyer, banker; b. Charles City, Iowa, Oct. 20, 1929; s. Harry Albert and Grace Ellen (Jensen) M.; m. Mary Lee Grawcock, Sept. 2, 1956; children: Katherine, Elizabeth, James. B.A. with highest distinction, State U. Iowa, 1951; J.D. with distinction, U. Mich., 1956. Bar: Nebr. 1956. Partner firm Miller, Moldenhauer, Morrow & Woodward, Omaha, 1963-65; firm Fitzgerald, Brown, Leahy, McGill & Strom, Omaha, 1965-72; v.p., sec., gen. counsel FirsTier Bank N.A., FirsTier Fin. Inc., 1972-92; spl. asst. atty. gen. of, Nebr., 1963-72; lectr. Creighton U. Law Sch., 1972. Pres. Regency Homes Assn., 1988-90. Served with U.S. Army, 1951-53. Recipient Nebr. State Bar Found. award, 1992; scholarships named in his honor by Phi Beta Kappa, Rotary club, and U. Mich. Law Sch. Fellow Am. Bar Found., Nebr. State Bar Found.; mem. Omaha Bar Assn. (pres. 1972), Nebr. State Bar Assn. (pres. young lawyers sect. 1965, Found. award 1992), Am. Bar Assn., Am. Law Inst., Mich. Alumni Acad. (bd. dirs.), Phi Beta Kappa, Order of the Coif, Omicron Delta Kappa. Republican. Lutheran. Club: Rotary (pres. Omaha 1980). Home: Omaha Nebr. Died June 24, 1992; buried Forest Lawn Cemetery, Omaha, Nebr.

MOLINI, ALBERTO ENRIQUE, chemical engineering educator, researcher; b. Yauco, Puerto Rico, Oct. 25, 1924; s. Tomás Molini and Hercilia Mejia; m. Valentina Ramirez, Nov. 27, 1953; children: José, Deborah, Carmen, Madeleine, Isabel. BSChemE, U. Mich., 1952, MSChemE, 1952, PhD in Chem. Engring., 1957. Registered profl. engr., P.R. Rsch. engr. E. I. DuPont de Nemours and Co., Kinston, N.C., 1956-62, sr. rsch. engr., 1962-65, rsch. assoc., 1965-68; chmn. chem. engring. U. P.R., Mayaguez, 1968-72, prof., from 1979; dir. rum pilot plant U. P.R., Rio Piedras, 1972-77; vis. prof. chem. engring. Carnegie-Mellon U., Pitts., 1978-79; cons. Flanes Cedo Industries, Mayaguez, 1969-71, Pitts. Plate Glass Industries, Guayanilla, P.R., 1969-72, DeMillus and Co., Rio de Janeiro, 1973-75, Destileria Serralles, Inc., Ponce, P.R., 1978-82. Contbr. sci. papers to profl. publs. Mem. Colegio de Ingenieros y Agrimensores of P.R., Instituto de Ingenieros Quimicos de P.R., Am. Inst. Chem. Engrs., Lions, Tau Beta Pi. Roman Catholic. Home: San Germán P.R Deceased.

MOLLISON, RICHARD DEVOL, mining company executive; b. Faribault, Minn., June 7, 1916; s. Allan Edwin and Edna (Devol) M.; m. Elizabeth Ellen Cobb, June 7, 1941; children: Steven Cobb, Ann Elizabeth Mollison Waters, Mark Richard. B.Mining Engring., U. Minn., 1941. Mining engr. various locations, 1941-47; with Texasgulf Inc., 1947-94, v.p., mgr. exploration, 1962-64, v.p. metals div., 1964-72, sr. v.p., 1972-73, pres., 1973-79, vice chmn., 1979-81, chmn., 1981-82; chmn. Kidd Creek Mines Ltd., 1983-86, also bd. dirs. Mem. AIME, Mining and Metall. Soc. Am., Can. Inst. Mining and Metall. Engrs., Tau Beta Pi, Theta Xi. Republican. Clubs: Sky, Mining (N.Y.C.); Riverside Yacht (Conn.); Island Country (Marco Island, Fla.); Classics Country (Naples, Fla.). Home: Marco Island Fla. Died Aug. 2, 1994.

MONAHAN, GEORGE LENNOX, JR., retired air force officer; b. Mpls., Nov. 21, 1933; s. George Lennox and Clara Marie (Weber) M.; m. Mary Kathreen Rockwell, July 20, 1957; children: Cathy, George, Joe, Brian, Andy. B.S., U.S. Mil. Acad., 1955; M.S.E.E., U. N.H., 1965. Commnd. officer U.S. Air Force, advanced through grades to lt. gen.; dir. lightweight fighter Aero Systems Div. U.S. Air Force, Wright-Patterson AFB, Ohio, 1973-75; chief F-16 European Systems Program Office, Brussels, Belgium, 1975-78; asst. DCS systems Air Force Systems Command, Andrews AFB, Md., 1978-80; dir. F-16 fighter program Aero Systems div., Wright-Patterson AFB, Ohio, 1980-83; dir. devel. and prodn. US Air Force Hdqrs., Washington, 1983-86; vice comdr. AF Systems Command, Andrews AFB, Md., 1986-87; prin. dep. asst. sec. for acquistion USAF, 1987-89; dir. Strategic Def. Initiative Orgn., Washington, 1989-90; with Loral, 1991-93. Pres. West Point Soc. of Dayton, Ohio, 1980-83. Ira Eaker fellow Air Force Assn., 1990. Roman Catholic. Home: Falls Church Va. Died Feb. 4, 1993.

MONCION, FRANCISCO, dancer, choreographer; b. Las Vegas, Dominican Republic. Student, Sch. Am. Ballet. Debut with, New Opera Co., 1942; soloist, Internat. Ballet, 1944; also danced on Broadway and with, Ballet Russe de Monte Carlo; soloist, then prin., Ballet Soc. (name changed to N.Y.C. Ballet), 1946—; choreographed: first work Pastorale, for N.Y.C. Ballet, 1957. Died April 1, 1995.

MONROE, BURT LEAVELLE, JR., biology educator; b. Louisville, Aug. 25, 1930; s. Burt L. and Ethelmae (Tuell) M.; m. Rose Louise Sawyer, Dec. 27, 1960; children: Burt Leavelle III, Mark Sawyer. BS, U. Louisville, 1963; PhD, La. State U., 1965. Mem. faculty dept. biology U. Louisville, 1965-94, prof., chmn., 1970-93. Past pres., Louisville Zoo Found., Inc., Louisville Zool. Commn.; bd. trustees past pres. Bernheim Forest Found.; advisor Ky. Nature Preserves Commn. Served to lt. USN, 1953-59. Dept. Interior grantee, 1977-82. Fellow AAAS, Am. Ornithologists Union (past treas., v.p. 1983-84, pres.-elect 1988-90, pres. 1990-92); mem. Cooper Ornithol. Soc., Wilson Ornithol. Soc., Lepidopterists Soc. Republican. Presbyterian. Author: The Birds of Honduras, 1968; co-author Distribution and Taxonomy of Birds of the World, 1990, World Checklist of Birds, 1993, The Birds of Kentucky, 1994; editorial coord. Check-List of North American Birds, 1983; contbr. articles to profl. jours. Died May 14, 1994. Home: Louisville Ky.

MONROE, HERMAN EUGENE, banker; b. Huntsville, Ala., June 5, 1901; s. Daniel C. and Elizabeth (Struve) M.; m. Bessie Landers, Mar. 24, 1927; 1 son, Herman Eugene. Student, Auburn U., 1918-19. Owner, prin. Monroe Bus. Equipment Co., Huntsville, 1922-62; pres. Monroe Bus. Equipment Co., 1962-72, also bd. dirs.; chmn. First Nat. Bank, Huntsville, 1962-86, chmn. bd. emeritus, 1987; past dir. First Ala. Bank Shares Corp., Birmingham, Ala.; past chmn. exec. com., dir. Brown Engring. Co., Huntsville, 1957-67. Chmn. Huntsville Housing Authority, from 1941, chmn. Huntsville Pub. Bldg. Authority, 1960-86, Huntsville Library Bldg. Authority, 1961-86; pres. Huntsville Hosp. Bldg. Authority, 1961-75; chmn. Madison County Bldg. Authority, 1962-75, chmn., from 1975; chmn. Huntsville Planning Commn., 1945-50. Mem. C. of C. Huntsville (past pres., bd. dirs.), Sigma Nu. Home: Huntsville Ala. Deceased.

MONTAGNA, WILLIAM, scientist; b. Roccacasale, Italy, July 6, 1913; s. Cherubino and Adele (Giannangelo) M.; m. Martha Helen Fife, Sept. 1, 1939 (div. 1975); children: Eleanor, Margaret, James and John (twins); m. Leona Rebecca Montagna, Apr. 19, 1980. A.B., Bethany Coll., 1936, D.Sc., 1960; Ph.D., Cornell U., 1944; D. B.S., Universitá di Sassari, 1964. Instr. Cornell U., 1944-45; asst. prof. L.I. Coll. Medicine, 1945-48; asst., assoc. prof. Brown U., 1948-52, prof., 1952-63, L. Herbert Ballou univ. prof. biology, 1960-63; prof., head exptl. biology U. Oreg. Health Scis. Ctr.; dir. Oreg. Regional Primate Rsch. Ctr., Beaverton, 1963-80, ret., director emeritus, 1985-94. Author: The

Structure and Function of Skin, 1956, 3d edit., 1974, Comparative Anatomy, 1959, Nonhuman Primates in Biomedical Research, 1976, Science Is Not Enough, 1980; co-author: Man, 1969, 2d edit., 1973, Atlas of Normal Human Skin, 1991; editor: The Biology of Hair Growth, 1958, Advances in Biology of Skin, 20 vols, The Epidermis, 1965, Advances in Primatology, 1970, Reproductive Behavior, 1974. Decorated Ordine di Cavaliere, 1963, Cavaliere Ufficiale, 1969, Commendatore della Repubblica Italiana, 1975; Italy; recipient spl. award Soc. Cosmetic Chemists, 1957; Gold award Am. Acad. Dermatology, 1958; gold medal for meritorious achievement Universitá di Sassari, 1964; Aubrey R. Watzek award Lewis and Clark Coll., 1977; Hans Schwarzkopf Research award German Dermatol. Soc., 1980. Mem. Acad. Dermatology and Syphilology (hon.), Soc. Investigative Dermatology (pres. 1969, recipient Stephen Rothman award 1972, ann. William Montagna lectr. 1975—), Sigma Xi (Pres. 1960-62). Home: Hillsboro Oreg. Died Nov. 16, 1994.

MONTGOMERY, G(EORGE) FRANKLIN, electrical engineer, consultant; b. Oakmont, Pa., May 1, 1921; s. George Mason and Marie Naomi (Sanner) M.; m. Joan Elizabeth Hartman, Dec. 2, 1967; 1 child, Christopher Mason. BSEE, Purdue U., 1941. Registered profl. engr., D.C. Radio engr. Naval Rsch. Lab., Washington, 1941-44; electronics engr. Nat. Bur. of Standards, Washington, 1946-78; pvt. practice, 1978-95. Invention reviewer Nat. Inst. Standards and Tech., 1978-95; patentee in field. Master sgt. U.S. Army, 1944-46. Fellow IEEE; mem. Audio Engring. Soc. (cons. tech. editor jour.). Home: Washington D.C. Died July 16, 1995.

MONTGOMERY, OWEN THOMAS, analytical chemist, consultant, researcher; b. Louisville, July 14, 1948; s. Owen Thomas and Billie Maxine (Lyon) M.; m. Robin Vela Kimmel, July 3, 1971 (div. 1973). AB in Chemistry, Ind. U., 1975, JD, 1978. Lab. dir. Beck Analytical Svcs., Bloomington, Ind., 1975-80, rsch. dir., 1982-94, tech. supr., 1994-95; cons. Beck Analytical Svcs., Bloomington, 1995-96; sci. CCI-Girdler Catalysts, Louisville, 1980, Reynolds Aluminum, Richmond, Va., 1980-82; cons. Leemore Mining Co., Louisville, 1982-86, Marine Consulting Co., Palm Harbor, Fla., 1986-96. Mem. Am. Assn. Clin. Chemists, Endourological Soc. Home: Palm Harbor Fla. Died May 6, 1996.

MONTOYA, CARLOS GARCIA, guitarist; b. Madrid, Dec. 3, 1903; came to U.S., 1939; s. Juan Garcia and Emilia Montoya; m. Sally MacLean; children: Carlos Jr., Allan. Student of guitar with, Pepe el Barbero. Played in Cafes Cantantes at age 14, then toured in collaboration with singer; made European tour with dancer La Argentina (Antonia Merce), later toured Europe, the Orient, and Ams. singly; appearances at Carnegie Hall, Town Hall, Avery Fisher Hall, N.Y.C. Constitution Hall, Washington, Orch. Hall, Chgo., Music Ctr., L.A., Meml. Opera House, San Francisco, John F. Kennedy Ctr., recent appearances with maj. symphony orchs., playing composition Suite Flamenca; spl. recitals, recs. flamenco music; recorded Carolos Montoya: Flamenco Direct, Vol. I and II for Crystal Clear (now Bainbridge labels CDs). Served with Spanish Army, 1924-27. Decorated encomienda de la Orden del Mérito Civil Spain; recipient keys to N.Y.C., Miami, Fla., Nashville, Honolulu, San Francisco, Order of Civil Merit award The Spanish Chief of State, Madrid, 1973, Ellis Island Medal of Honor, 1986, 87; named hon. citizen Tex., Winnipeg, Man., Can., True Alaskan Sourdough and hon. citizen Alaska, Best Flamenco Guitarist and named to Hall of Fame Guitar Player mag.; Carlos Montoya Day proclaimed by City of Bossier City, La. Mem. Phi Mu Alpha Sinfonia (hon.), Sigma Delta Pi. Home: New York N.Y. Died Mar. 3, 1993.

MOODY, G. WILLIAM, retired aerospace manufacturing company executive; b. Cleveland Heights, Ohio, Nov. 6, 1928; s. John Walter and Anna Barbara (Keck) M. (dec. Apr. 27, 1994); m. Loisjean Kanouse, Sept. 17, 1955; children: Elizabeth Jean, Cynthia Ann, G. William. Student, Ohio U., 1948-49; BSCE, Mich. State U., 1952; Advanced Mgmt. Program, Harvard Grad. Sch. Bus., 1982. Sales engr. Rich Mfg. Corp., Battle Creek, Mich., 1952-55; chief engr. Air Lift Co., Lansing, Mich., 1955-61; product engr. Aeroquip Corp., Jackson, Mich., 1961-62, chief engr. Barco divsn., 1962-68, v.p., gen. mgr., 1968-72, v.p., ops. mgr. AMB divsn., 1972-74, v.p., gen. mgr. aerospace divsn., 1974-81, group v.p. gen. products, 1981-85, pres., 1985-88; v.p. Trinova Corp., 1986-88; ret., 1989; v.p. Denva Group, Jackson, 1992-94; sr. design engr. Clark Floor Machine Co., Muskegon, Mich., 1962; bd. dirs. Nu-Matic Grinders Inc., Cleve., Electronic Sensors Inc., Clawson, Mich., Aeroquip S.A., Aeroquip GmbH, Elm Plating, Jackson. Patentee in field. Gen. chmn. Jackson County campaign United Way, 1976, pres., 1980, bd. dirs., 1976-84, bd. dirs. Mich. affiliate, 1978-82; mem. Planning Commn. North Barrington, Ill., 1967-72; mem. Barrington Area Coun. Govts., 1971-72; trustee, chmn. Foote Meml. Hosp., Jackson; chmn Joint Com. for an Area Hosp., Barrington, 1969-72; trustee, chmn. Physicians Health Plan South Mich.; bd. dirs. Jackson Venture Capital Forum, 1990-94. With U.S. Army, 1946-48. Mem. ASME, Soc. Automotive Engrs., Am. Polit. Items Coll. Soc., Am. Mgmt. Assn., Am. Philatelic Soc., Fluid Power Soc., Jackson C. of C., Town Club (bd. dirs.), Jackson Country Club, Jackson Country Sportsman's Club, Psi Upsilon. Lutheran. Home: Lansing Mich. Died Apr. 27, 1994.

MOOG, HUBERT C., automotive company executive; m. Dorothy Ross, 1944; children—Donna Moog Nussbaum, James Ross, Thomas Hubert. Student in metallurgy Mo. Sch. Mines, 1931-32; B.S. in Metallurgy, U. Wis., 1935. With Moog Automotive, Inc. (and predecessor cos. St. Louis Spring Co. and Moog Industries, Inc.), St. Louis, 1935—, v.p., 1945-53, pres., from 1953, chmn. bd. dirs., 1973-82, chmn. emeritus, 1982—; dir. Mound City Trust Co., Mylee Digital Scis., Inc., Courion Industries, King Adhesive, Blue Cross and Blue Shield of Mo. Bd. dirs. St. Louis Better Bus. Bur., St. Louis Area Regional Commerce and Growth Assn., St. Louis Symphony Soc., St. Louis Regional Indsl. Devel. Commn., Jewish Hosp. St. Louis; trustee Washington U., St. Louis; bd. govs. John Burroughs Sch.; establisher Hubert C. and Dorothy R. Moog Chair in Acctg., Sch. Bus., Washington U., St. Louis. Served with AUS, 1942-45. Mem. Jewish Community Ctrs. Assn., Motor and Equipment Mfrs. Assn. (pres.'s council). Club: Westwood Country (bd. dirs.). Home: Saint Louis Mo.

MOORE, CHARLES WILLARD, architect, educator; b. Benton Harbor, Mich., Oct. 31, 1925; s. Charles Ephraim and Nanette Kathryn (Almendinger) M. B.Arch., U. Mich., 1947; M.F.A., Princeton U., 1956, Ph.D., 1957; M.A. (hon.), Yale U., 1965. Architect Mario Corbett (Architect), 1947-48; architect Joseph Allen Stein (Architect), 1948-49; asst. prof. U. Utah, 1950-52; asst. prof. architecture Princeton U., 1957-59; assoc. prof. U. Calif., Berkeley, 1959-62; chmn. dept. architecture U. Calif., 1962-65, Yale U., New Haven, 1965-69; dean Yale U., 1969-71, prof., 1971-75; prof. architecture UCLA, 1975-85, head dept., 1976-77, 77-80; architect Moore Lyndon Turnbull Whitaker (Architects), 1961-64, Moore Turnbull, San Francisco and New Haven, 1964-70, Charles Moore Assos., Essex, Conn., 1970-76, Moore Grover Harper, Essex, Conn., and Moore Ruble Yudell, Los Angeles, 1976-93; O'Neil Ford Centennial prof. architecture U. Tex., Austin, 1985-93. Author: The Place of Houses, 1974, Dimensions, 1975, Body Memory and Architecture, 1977, The Poetics of Gardens, 1988. Served to capt. U.S. Army, 1952-54. Recipient Topaz medallion for execellence in archtl. edn. AIA/Assn. Collegiate Schs. Architecture, 1989, 25 Yr. award Sea Ranch AIA, 1991; Nat. Endowment Arts grantee, 1975; Guggenheim grantee, 1976-77. Fellow AIA (Gold medal 1991). Democrat. Home: Austin Tex. Died Dec. 16, 1994; interred Monterey, Calif.

MOORE, EMERSON JOHN, bishop; b. N.Y.C., May 16, 1938. Student, Cathedral Coll., N.Y.C., St. Joseph's Sem., N.Y., NYU, Columbia U. Sch. Social Work. Ordained priest Roman Cath. Ch. 1964. Ordained aux. bishop of Curubi and aux. bishop Diocese of N.Y., N.Y.C., 1982-95. Home: New York N.Y. Died Sept. 14, 1995.

MOORE, HERBERT BELL, headmaster; b. Glen Cove, L.I., N.Y., July 30, 1926; s. Lewis Kingsley and Thelma Morton (Bell) M.; m. Martha Marie Fay, June 22, 1951; children: Jeffrey, Janice, Stephen, Susan, Elizabeth, Charles. B.A., Bowdoin Coll., 1947; M.A., Boston U., 1953; Ed.M., Harvard, 1958. Tchr. math., coach Berkshire Sch., Sheffield, Mass., 1947-51; history tchr., coach, pub. relations dir., fund sec. Belmont (Mass.) Hill Sch., 1951-58; headmaster Tilton (N.H.) Sch., 1958-65, Holland Hall Sch., Tulsa, 1965-74, Kent-Denver Country Day Sch., Englewood, Colo., 1974-80; dir. schs. Cranbrook Ednl. Community, Mich., 1980-82; headmaster Tilton (N.H.) Sch., 1982-87, assoc. headmaster, 1987-91; past pres. Ind. Sch. Assn. S.W., Colo. Assn. Ind. Schs. Assn. No. New Eng.; search cons. Carney, Sandoe & Assocs., Boston. Recipient Educator of Yr. award Bowdoin Coll., 1969. Mem. Country Day Sch. Headmasters Assn., Headmasters Assn., Cum Laude Soc. (registrar gen.). Home: Meredith N.H. Died June 29, 1993.

MOORE, JAMES ROBERT, geological oceanographer; b. Temple, Tex., May 18, 1925; s. James Robert and Mary Louise (Petty) M. B.S. with honors, U. Houston, 1951; M.A., Harvard U., 1954; Ph.D., U. Wales, 1964. Research geologist Standard Oil, Ohio, 1951-52; sr. scientist Texaco Research, 1956-66; chief marine geologist U.K.-Irish Sea Project, 1962-64; prof. U. Wis., Madison, 1966-77; also dir. marine lab.; prof., dir. Marine Sci. Inst., U. Alaska, 1977-79; prof. marine studies U. Tex., Austin, 1979-95; cons. in marine mining to internat. cos. and consortia. Editor: Marine Mining, 1976-95; editor-in-chief: Marine Series, 1978-95; Contbr. articles to profl. jours. Served with USNR, 1943-46. Recipient Career Achievement award Underwater Mining Inst., 1989, Outstanding Rsch. award Internat. Mariner Mining Soc., 1989. Mem. Assn. Marine Mining (v.p.), Am. Assn. Petroleum Geologists, Soc. Econ. Mineralogists, Geochem. Soc., Challenger Soc. Oceanography, AAAS, Internat. Assn. Sedimentologists, Sigma Xi. Home: Austin Tex. Died Mar. 25, 1995.

MOORE, PETER INNISFREE, photographer, editor, writer; b. London, Apr. 28, 1932; s. Herbert Samuel and Alma (Chesnut) M.; m. Barbara Kashins, Sept. 23 1961; children: Robin Frances, Rebecca. Student M.I.T., 1952-53, Haverford Coll., 1953-57. Profl photographer contemporary art and performance art 1960-93; artistic dir. Archives Explt. Art, N.Y.C., 1970 93; tech. editor Photomethods mag., 1974-78; sr. edito Modern Photography mag., 1978-89; tchr. New Sch Social Research, N.Y.C., 1972-77, Cooper Union N.Y.C., Germaine Sch. Photography, N.Y.C. Majo shows Grey Art Gallery, Judson Dance Theater, 1982 Lever House, 1978, 81, 86, Light Work Gallery, 1984 Gallery 360 Degree, Tokyo, 1989, Venice Biennale 1990, Alfred Kren Gallery, Cologne, LeCointre/Ozanne Paris, 1991, Walker Art Ctr., Mpls., Gallery Roto Göteborg, Sweden, 1993, Biennale d'Art Contemporair Lyons, 1993; group shows include Bruce Mus Stamford, Conn., Inst. Art and Urban Resources N.Y.C., Maine Photog. Workshop, Eastman House Rochester, N.Y., Photographs pub. in major mags., ar books and histories; contbr. numerous articles o photog. art and tech. to profl. jours. Mem. Am. Soc Mag. Photographers, N.Y. Photohist. Soc., Fluxus. Home: New York N.Y. Died Sept. 28, 1993.

MOORE, RICHARD ANTHONY, diplomat, lawyer b. Albany, N.Y., Jan. 23, 1914; s. John Denis and Julia Frances (Leader) M.; m. Jane Gertrude Swift, Mar. 27 1943 (dec. Nov. 1985); children: Richard Anthony Jr. Matthew, Joseph, Kate, Samuel; m. Esther Horstkott Jantzen, Dec. 29, 1986. BA, Yale U., 1936, LLB, 1939. Bar: N.Y. 1939, D.C. 1976. Atty. Breed, Abbott & Morgan, N.Y.C., 1939-41, Cravath Swaine & Moore N.Y.C., 1942; asst., gen. counsel ABC, N.Y.C., 1946-48 dir. TV, gen. mgr. ABC Western Div., L.A., 1948-51 pres., chief exec. officer Times Mirror Broadcasting Co. L.A., 1951-62; also bd. dirs. Times Mirror Co., L.A. 1956-62; pres., part owner Southwestern Cable Co. other cable systems, L.A., 1962-70; spl. asst. Atty. Gen of U.S., Washington, 1970-71; spl. counsel Pres. of U.S. Washington, 1971-74; counsel Wilner & Scheiner Washington, 1975-89; founder, assoc. producer The McLaughlin Group, Washington, 1981-89; amb. to Ireland Dept. State, Dublin, 1989-92; co-founder, chmn TV Bur. Advt., N.Y.C., 1955-60; pres. TV. Broadcaster of So. Calif., L.A., 1953-55, vice chmn. Nat. Cable TV Assn., 1967-68. Bd. dirs. L.A. Community Chest, 1955-60, L.A. C. of C., 1957-63, Hollywood Bowl, 1952-58 mem. L.A. Mayor's Com. on Human Rights, 1952-56 Pres. Eisenhower's Com. on Nat. Goals, 1955-56; pres Friendly Sons St. Patrick, L.A., 1965; campaign advise Sen. George Murphy, L.A., 1964, Lt. Gov. Robert Finch., L.A., 1966, Pres. Nixon, 1968, Pres. Bush, 1980-88. Capt. USAAF, 1942-46. Decorated Legion of Merit; recipient Emmy award TV Acad., 1984. Mem N.Y. Bar Assn., D.C. Bar Assn., Metropolitan Club Chgo. Club, Cypress Point Club (Pebble Beach), Sunset Club (L.A.), Portmarnock Golf Club (Ireland) Stephen's Green Club (Dublin), Yale Club of N.Y. Home: Washington D.C. Died Jan. 27, 1995.

MOORE, RICHARD DONALD, educator; b. Spokane Wash., Mar. 7, 1924; s. George Walter and Carolyn (Coons) M.; m. Audrey Jean Hauth, Oct. 4, 1946; children—Pamela Ann, Richard Allen, Randall Lee, Jeffrey Thomas. Student, Gonzaga U., 1941-43; M.D., Western Res. U., 1947; postgrad., U. Pa., 1948-49. Instr. pathology Western Res. U., 1952-53, sr. instr., 1953-55 asst. prof., 1955-56; asst. prof. pathology U. Rochester 1956-57, asso. prof. pathology, 1957-67; prof. patholog Western Res. U., 1967-69; prof., chmn. dept. patholog U. Oreg., 1969-86; asst. pathology Univ. Hosps., Cleve 1954-56, 61-69. Contbr. articles to profl. jours. Served with M.C. AUS, 1952-54. Mem. Am. Soc. Expt' Pathology, AAAS, N.Y. Acad. Sci., Internat. Acad Pathology Reticulo Endothelial Soc., Assn. Patholog and Bacteriology, Sigma Xi. Home: Sandy Oregon Died Dec. 11, 1994.

MOORE, SONIA, theatre administrator, researcher; b Gomel, Russia, Dec. 4, 1902; came to U.S., 1940; d Evser and Sophie (Pasherstnik) Shatzov; m. Leo Moore, May 11, 1926 (dec. Mar. 1957); 1 child, Irene Moore Jaglom. Degrees, Reale Conservatorio D Musica Santa Cecilia, Rome, 1939, Reale Accademi Filarmonica, Rome, 1939; student, U. Kiev, U. Moscow Studio Moscow Art Theatre. Dir. Sonia Moore Studio of the Theatre (accredited Nat. Assn. Schs. Theatre) N.Y.C., 1961-95; founder, pres. Am. Ctr. for Stanislavski Theatre Art Inc., 1964-95; artistic dir. Am Stanislavski Theatre, N.Y.C., 1970-95; tchr. Soni Moore Studio, N.Y.C., 1961-95; guest artist lectr demonstrator numerous univs. in U.S. and Can., 1978-95; vis. prof. U. Mo., Kansas City, 1981; TV and radio interviews, 1961-95; convs. presenter, 1982-95; keynote speaker Theater USSR, U. S.C.; lectr. Fordham U 1991, U. N.C., 1989. Dir. numerous off-Broadwa plays, 1960-90, Anna Christie, N.Y.C., 1989, A View from a Bridge, 1990; translator, editor: Stanislavsk Today, 1973, Logic of Speech on Stage, 1976; autho The Stanislavski Method, 1960, The Stanislavski System 1965, 1974, 1984, Training an Actor: The Stanislavsk system in class, 1968, rev. 1979, Stanislavski Reveale The Actor's Complete Guide to Spontaneity on Stage 1991; contbr. articles to Ency. Britannica, Theatre Jour Drama Rev., Secondary Sch. Jour., Players Mag.; cassette lectures on Stanislavski System; videocassett interview by Julie Harris. Founding mem. Nat. Mu Women in the Arts; charter mem. Battle of Normand lus. Recipient Am. Heritage award JFK Library for linorities, N.Y.C., 1974. Mem. ALA, Authors Guild, oc. Stage Dirs. and Choreographers, Am. Theatre ssn., Internat. Biog. Assn., Smithsonian Instn., Assn. or Theatre in Higher Edn. (lectr. convs. N.Y.C. 1989, hgo., 1990), Seattle, 1991, Atlanta, 1992, Phila., 1993, hgo., 1994, Nat. Trust for Hist. Preservation. Home: lew York N.Y. Died May 19, 1995.

IOORE, TERRIS, retired financial educator; b. Haddonfield, N.J., Apr. 11, 1908; s. Robert Thomas and elma Helena (Muller) M.; m. Katrina Eaton Hincks, une 17, 1933; children: Katrina, Henry Winslow lec.). Grad., Storm King Sch., Cornwall, N.Y.; B.A., 'illiams Coll., 1929, LL.D. (hon.), 1979; M.B.A., larvard Grad. Sch. Bus. Adminstrn., 1933, Doctor omml. Sci., 1937; LL.D., U. Alaska, 1967. Treas. and r. William R. McAdams, Inc., Boston, 1940-49; with atterson, Teale and Dennis (accountants), Boston, 945; instr. finance U. Calif. at Los Angeles, 1937-39; res. Boston Mus. of Sci., 1945-48, life trustee, 1972-93; res. U. Alaska, 1949-53, hon. prof. of univ., 1954-72, rof., pres. emeritus, 1973-93; dir. indsl. cooperation U. laine, 1954-55; vis. prof. bus. adminstrn. Colby Coll., 'aterville, Maine, 1955-57; cons. Quartermaster Rsch. nd Engring. Ctr., Natick, Mass., 1957-69, Army Sci. dv. Panel, 1959-69, (U.S. Army Test and Evaluation ommand), 1963-69; explorer Am. expdn. (Sikong xpdn.) which explored, mapped, determined altitude nd made 1st ascent of Mt. Minya Konka, Tibet, China; so mem. various expdns. which made other 1st asents; mem. U.S. Army Alaska Test Expdn., 1942. uthor: chpt. in Modern Airmanship, 1957, Mt. lcKinley, the Pioneer Climbs, 1967; Co-author: chpt. Men Against the Clouds, 1934; Contbr. articles to arious mags. and jours. Sec., research coodinator of laine Coll.-Community Research Program, 1954-57; em. overseers vis. com. in biology Harvard U., 1946-); Mem N.E. Govs.' Com. Pub. Transp., 1954-57. erved as expert cons. to quartermaster gen. 1942-44; ons. Aero. Research Found., 1956. Recipient certifiate of appreciation for outstanding contbn. war effort .M. Gen., 1944, Distinguished Service award USAF r; C.A.P. Fellow Royal Geog. Soc., Am. Geog. Soc. ouncillor 1967-88); mem. N.Y. Acad. Scis. (life), Am. eophys. Union, AAAS, Alpha Kappa Psi, Delta Phi. lubs: Explorers (N.Y.); St. Botolph (Boston); The Alne (London); American Alpine (hon.), Harvard ravellers (hon.), Appalachian Mountain (hon.), Pioners of Alaska (hon.), Mountaineers of Seattle (hon.). ome: Monson Maine Died Nov. 7, 1993.

IOORE, WILLIAM ESTILL, JR., land management nd financial executive; b. Bowling Green, Ky., Dec. 19, 920; s. William E. and Carolyn (Elkin) M.; m. Mararet Jackson Shanks, Mar. 12, 1952; children: Carrol leteer, William Estill III, Marilyn Taylor, Thomas dwin III, James Rogers. B.A., Stanford, 1947. Asst. pres. Tejon Ranch Co., Bakersfield, Calif., 1947-48, p., 1948-58, exec. v.p., 1958-60, pres., 1960-70, chmn. xec. com., 1963-70, exec. cons., 1970—; v.p. Chandlerherman Corp., 1949-56, pres., bd. dirs., 1956-70; pres., d. dirs. Rowland Land Co., 1955-70; chmn. bd. dirs. eritage Investment Corp., 1973—; bd. dirs., mem. xec. com., mem. investment com. T.I. Corp. and Title s. & Trust Co., 1956-84; founding dir. Heritage Savs. Loan Assn., chmn. bd., 1973-79; bd. dirs. San oaquin Valley Oil Producers, Pacific Western Industries nc. Bd. dirs. Tejon-Castac Water Dist., 1961-70; sec. alif. Water Resources Assn., 1960-74, pres., 1974-78, mn. bd., 1978-87, also bd. dirs. and mem. exec. com.; c. Wheeler Ridge-Maricopa Water Dist., Kern ounty, Arvin-Edison Water Dist., 1952-72, Kern ounty, Calif. Irrigation Dist. Assn., Feather River roject Assn., 1955-66; bd. dirs. Kern County Water ommn., 1956—, pres., 1966-76; bd. dirs., exec. cons. ings County Devel. Corp.; bd. dirs. No. Kern Water ist., 1972—, sec., 1977—. Served to lt. col. USMCR, 940-46. Decorated Navy Cross, Silver Star medal, urple Heart. Mem. Philharmonic Assn. Los Angeles, ern County Water Assn. (pres. 1970-73, dir. 1955—), alif. Farm Bur., Calif. Cattlemen's Assn., Calif. C. of ., Bakersfield C. of C., Los Angeles C. of C., Navy eague (v.p., dir. Bakersfield). Republican. Presbyn. lubs: Commonwealth (San Francisco); Annandale Pasadena, Calif.); Food and Wine Soc. (London, Eng.). ome: Bakersfield Calif.

IORAN, THOMAS JOSEPH, retired state supreme ourt justice; b. Waukegan, Ill., July 17, 1920; s. Corneus Patrick and Avis Rose (Tyrrell) M.; m. Mary Jane Vasniewski, Oct. 4, 1941; children: Avis Marie, athleen, Mary Jane, Thomas G. B.A., Lake Forest oll., 1947; J.D., Chgo. Kent Coll. Law, 1950; J.D. on.), Lake Forest Coll., 1977. Bar: Ill. 1977. Inividual practice law Waukegan, Ill., 1950-56; state's ty. Lake County, Ill., 1956-58; probate ct. judge Lake ounty, 1958-61; judge 19th Circuit Ct., Lake and lcHenry counties, Ill., 1961-64; appellate ct. judge 2d ist., Elgin, Ill., 1964-76; justice Supreme Ct. Ill., 1976-2, chief justice, 1988-90; faculty appellate judges eminars NYU; continuing legal edn. seminars La. State . Served with USCG, 1943-45. Mem. ABA, Ill. Bar ssn., Lake County Bar Assn., Inst. Jud. Adminstrn., m. Judicature Soc. Home: Lake Forest Ill. Died Sept. 4, 1995.

MORCH, ERNST TRIER, anesthesiologist, inventor; b. Slagelse, Denmark, May 14, 1908; came to U.S., 1949, naturalized, 1954; s. Ejvind and Gudrun (Trier) M.; m. Eritta Margrethe Hansen, Feb. 13, 1940 (div. 1962); children: Claus T., Sys T., Peter T., Ibi Trier Cieslar. M.D., U. Copenhagen, 1935, Ph.D., 1942; postgrad., Oxford U., 1947. Cons. anesthesia U. Copenhagen, 1942-49; asst. prof. U. Kans. Med. Center, 1950-52; prof. U. Chgo., 1953-58; dir. anesthesia Cook County Hosp., Chgo., 1959-61; pvt. practice anesthesiology Garfield Park Hosp., Chgo., 1961-67; prof., anesthesiologist Rush Presbyterian-St. Luke's Med. Center, Chgo., 1967-78; anesthesiologist Nassau Gen. Hosp., Fernandina Beach, Fla., 1978-88; chief med. staff Nassau Gen. Hosp., 1978, 79; med. cons. Nassau County Detention Facilities, 1979-88, spl. dep. sheriff, 1980; prof. U. Ill., 1969; cons. to Council on Pharmacy and Chemistry of AMA. Author: Chondrodystrophic Dwarfs in Denmark, Sweden and Norway, with Special Reference to Inheritance, 1941, Bandagings, 1942, Anesthesi, 1949, (with Kjerulf-Jensen) How They Came Home from German Concentration Camps, 1945; Contbr.: profl. jours. Ency. Brittanica. Served as lt., M.C. Royal Danish Army, 1937. Decorated for humanitarian work during World War II by Kings of Denmark, Norway and Sweden; recipient Disting. Faculty Alumnus award U. Ill., 1985. Fellow Faculty of Anesthetists of Royal Coll. Surgeons, Sigma Xi; mem. Ill. Soc. Anesthesiologists (pres. 1973-74, distinguished service award 1976, McQuiston award 1985), Chgo. Soc. Anesthesiologists (pres. 1959-60, 67-68), Nassau County Med Soc. (pres. 1981), Soc. d'Anest. et d'Anal. de France (fgn.), Columbiana Soc. Anesthesiology (hon.). Home: Fernandina Beach Fla. Died Jan. 13, 1996.

MORE, PHILIP JEROME, archaeologist, art and antiquities company executive; b. Chgo., Dec. 11, 1911; s. Louis Eli and Anna Leah (Kahn) M.; m. Sylvia Sally Bernstein, Oct. 16, 1937 (div. 1976); children: Andrea More Williams, Michael E., William M. BS, Heidelberg (Germany) U., 1930; postgrad., Ill. Inst. Tech., 1936; LL.D. (hon.), Roosevelt U., 1967; M.B.A., Columbia Pacific U., 1980, Ph.D. in Archeology, 1981. Owner, pres. Feris Flying Service, Chgo., 1936-38; metallurgist Standard Dental Labs., Chgo., 1938-39; project design engr. Birtman Electric Co., Chgo., 1939-50; sr. design engr. Hotpoint div. Gen. Electric Co., Cicero, Ill., 1950-68; dir. purchasing Modern Maid, McGraw Edison, Chattanooga, 1968-76; pres. Choo-Choo Indsls., 1977-79, Things of Beauty, 1979—; cons. on primitive monies to museums and univs.; sponsor numis. studies Roosevelt U., 1966-67; chmn. Roosevelt U. Numis. Library Project. Author: The Lure of Primitive Money, 1960, Odd and Curious Monies of the World, 1963, Primitive Money of the World, Fact and Fantasy, 1981; editorial adv. bd.: Appliance Mag.; contbr. articles on monies and engring. design to profl. jours.; patentee in field. Presdl. appointee Assay Commn., 1965; chmn. Engrs. for Senator Baker, 1972—; chmn. Engrs. for Pres. Carter, 1976; patron Ednl. Librs. to Exodus Trust, San Francisco, Columbia Pacific U., Petaluma, Calif., Hunter Mus. of Art, Houston Mus., MItzpah Congregation, Chattanooga African-Am. Mus., Chattanooga Regional History Mus., B'nai Zion Congregation, Erlanger Med. Ctr., Chattanooga, Howard Sch. Acad. and Tech.; bd. dirs. Chattanooga African Am. Mus., 1990. Decorated Navy Cross; recipient citation for cost saving Gen. Electric Co., 1966. Mem. Gas Appliance Engring. Soc. (pres. 1970-71), Am. Soc. Gas Engrs. (nat. pres. 1975), Indsl. and Sci. Conf. (adv. council appliance design and mfg.), North Shore Coin Club (founder, pres. 1950-58), Chgo. Coin Club (pres. 1964-65), Central States Numis. Soc. (pres. 1965-66), Am. Assn. Ret. Persons (pres. regional br. 1986.). Home: Chattanooga Tenn.

MORFITT, JOHN WINSLOW, laboratory director; b. Malden, Mass., July 4, 1920; s. John Henry and Gertrude (Winslow) M.; m. Elizabeth Nan Hale, Feb. 1, 1947; children: Carolyn E., Susan L., Craig W. BSChemE, Northeastern U., 1943; PhD in Physics, U. Tenn., 1953. Chem. engr., supr. Carbon and Carbide Chem. Co., Oak Ridge, Tenn., 1943-46, 52-55, nuclear criticality experimentalist, 1946-52; mgr. nuclear engring. Gen. Electric Co., Cin. and Idaho Falls, Idaho, 1955-67; mgr. project engring. Idaho Nat. Engring. Lab., Idaho Falls, 1967-76; lab. mgr., chief scientist EG&G, Idaho Falls, 1976—; nuclear criticality cons. Dept. Energy, Oak Ridge and Poartsmouth, Ohio, 1955—. Contbr. articles to profl. jours. Bd. dirs. United Way, Idaho Falls, 1969-75, pres. 1975; bd. dirs. Head Start Program, Idaho Falls, 1978-83; chmn. of trustees Presbyn. Ch. Synod of Pacific, San Francisco, 1974-80. Fellow Am. Nuclear Soc. (bd. dirs. 1972-75); mem. Am. Phys. Soc., Sigma Xi. Home: Idaho Falls Idaho

MORGAN, CHARLES SUMNER, retired association executive; b. Boston, Jan. 23, 1915; s. Charles Russell and Nina (Whitmore) M.; m. Rachel Dean Moore, June 10, 1939; children: Roger W., Andrea D. (Mrs. Thomas E. Weyer). B.S., Tufts U., 1936. Salesman New Eng. Telephone Co., Boston, 1936-38; research asst. Nat. Fire Protection Assn., Boston, 1938-39; field rep. Nat. Fire Protection Assn., 1939-40, mgr. advt., 1940-49, asst. gen. mgr., 1949-68, gen. mgr., 1968-71, pres., chief exec. officer, 1971-80, pres. emeritus, 1980-94. Author: Shipbuilding on the Kennebunk, 1952 (rev. 1970), New England Coasting Schooners, 1963, Public Advocate for Fire Safety, 1977, Coastal Shipping Under Sail, 1978, Master in Sail and Steam, 1981, The Plumstead Lineage, 1982, The Loyalist Connection, 1983, One Morgan Lineage, 1985, Ancestry & Descendants of George Dwight Moore, 1987. Trustee Maine Maritime Mus., 1971-85, chmn. bd. 1983-85, corporator, 1985-87, trustee emeritus, 1987-94, Concord Antiquarian Mus. (v.p. 1981-85, adv. bd. 1986-88); mem. 1st Parish, Concord. Mem. Am. Soc. Assn. Execs. (dir. 1974-77), New Eng. Soc. Assn. Execs. (dir. 1974-77), Conf. Fire Protection Assns. (internat. chmn. 1971-79), Fire Marshals Assn. N.Am. (hon.), Soc. Fire Protection Engrs. (hon.), Order Founders and Patriots of Am., SAR, Concord Antiquarian Soc., New England Hist. Genealogical Soc., Corinthians, Masons. Republican. Home: Concord Mass. Died Aug. 5, 1994.

MORGAN, ROBERT, poet; b. Wales, Apr. 17, 1921; s. William Henry and Else Jane M.; m. Jean Elizabeth Florence; children: Allison Mary, Marion Lesley. Student, Fircroft Coll., 1949-51, Bognor Regis Coll. of Edn., 1951-53, Southampton U., 1969-71. coal miner, 1936-47; tchr. in primary schs., 1951-64; head remedial dept. at secondary sch., Cowplain, Eng., 1964-74; adv. tchr. spl. edn. Gosport (Eng.) Edn. Authority, 1974-80. Author: (poems) The Night's Prison, 1967, Rainbow Valley, 1967, Poems and Extracts, 1968, The Storm, 1974, The Master Miner, 1974, On the Banks of the Cynon, 1976, Voices in the Dark, 1976, The Pass, 1976, Poems and Drawings, 1984, Memoir, 1988, Landmarks, 1989, Saints on Islands, 1991, September Journey, 1991, Attic Poetry, 1991, Reminders, 1992, The Chosen, 1992, Fragments of a Dream, 1992, The Master Miners, 1993, Selected Poems, 1967-77, 1993, Selected Poems, 1978-88, 1993, Selected Poems, 1988-93, 1993, (autobiography) My Lamp Still Burns, 1980, (fiction) The Miner and Other Stories, 1985, (short stories) In the Dark, 1994; exhibited paintings in 17 one-man shows throughout Great Britain. Mem. Welsh Acad., Guild of Anglo-Welsh Writers. Home: Denmead Hampshire Eng. Died Aug. 6, 1994; buried Denmead Cemetery, Waterlooville, Eng.

MORGAN, ROBERT STERLING, st supervisor; b. Choteau, Mont., Aug. 27, 1922; s. James Clarence and Alma Zay (Adams) M.; m. Catharine Adriance Riley, May 17, 1947; children—Douglas, Gail, Richard, Catharine. BS in Forest Mgmt., U. Mont., 1948. Forest Ranger Forest Service St. Joe Nat. Forest, St. Maries, Idaho, 1951-54, Moscow, Idaho, 1954-56; asst. forest supr. St. Joe Nat. Forest, Mont., Idaho, 1956-60; safety tng. officer!O04Forest Service Region 4 St. Joe Nat. Forest, Ogden, Utah, 1960-62; forest supr. Helena Nat. Forest, Ogden, Mont., 1962-74, Bitteroot Nat. Forest, Hamilton, Mont.Y061974—, 1962-74. Recipient Outstanding Environ. Achievement award Romcoe, Denver, 1972, Cert. of Merit Dept. Agr., 1980, Superior Service award Dept. Agr., 1981. Fellow Soc. Am. Foresters; mem. Helena C. of C. (bd. dirs. 1970-74), Bitteroot C. of C. (bd. dirs. 1978-83) Rotary (pres. Helena 1972-73, bd. dirs. Hamilton 1982—). Episcopalian. Home: Hamilton Mont.

MORGAN, WILLIAM WILSON, astronomer, educator; b. Bethesda, Tenn., Jan. 3, 1906; s. William Thomas and Mary McCorkle (Wilson) M.; m. Helen Montgomery Barrett, June 2, 1928 (dec. 1963); children: Emily Wilson, William Barrett; m. Jean Doyle Eliot, 1966. Student, Washington and Lee U., 1923-26; B.S., U. Chgo., 1927, Ph.D., 1931; D.Honoris Causa, U. Cordoba, Argentina, 1971; D.Sc. (hon.), Yale U., 1978. Instr. Yerkes Obs., U. Chgo., Williams Bay, Wis., 1932-36; asst. prof. Yerkes Obs., U. Chgo., 1936-43, asso. prof., 1943-47, prof., 1947-66, Bernard E. and Ellen C. Sunny Distinguished prof. astronomy, 1966-74, prof. emeritus, 1974-94, chmn. dept. astronomy, 1960-66; dir. Yerkes and McDonald Observatories, 1960-63; mng. editor Astrophys. Jour., 1947-52; Henry Norris Russell lectr. Am. Astron. Soc., 1961. Author: (with P.C. Keenan, Edith Kellman) An Atlas of Stellar Spectra, 1943, (with H.A. Abt and J.W. Tapscott) Revised MK Spectral Atlas for Stars Earlier than the Sun, 1978; contbr. research articles to profl. publs.; discoverer (withD. Osterbrock and S. Sharpless) spiral arms of Milky Way Galaxy, 1951. Recipient Bruce gold medal Astron. Soc. Pacific, 1958, Henry Draper medal Nat. Acad. Scis., 1980. Mem. Am. Acad. Arts and Scis., Nat. Acad. Scis.; mem. Pontifical Acads. Scis.; Mem. Royal Danish Acad. Scis. and Letters, Royal Astron. Soc. (assoc. Herschel medal), Nat. Acad. Scis. Argentina, Soc. Royale des Sciences de Liege. Congregationalist. Home: Williams Bay Wis. Died June 21, 1994.

MORI, TAIKICHIRO, business executive; b. Mar. 1, 1904; m. Hanako Mori. Grad., Tokyo Hitotsubashi U., 1928. Pres. Mori Bldg. K.K. Home: Minato-ku Japan Died Jan. 30, 1993.

MORISON, ELTING ELMORE, historian, educator; b. Milw., Dec. 14, 1909; s. George Abbot and Amelia Huntley (Elmore) M.; m. Anne Hitchcock Sims, June 26, 1935; children: Mary, Nicholas, Sarah; m. Elizabeth Forbes Tilghman, 1967. Student, Loomis Inst., 1926-28; A.B., Harvard, 1932, M.A., 1937. Tchr. St. Mark's Sch., 1934-35; asst. dean Harvard, 1935-37; from asst. prof. to Sloan Fellows prof. indsl. mgmt. Mass. Inst. Tech., 1946-67; prof. history Yale, 1967-72; master

Timothy Dwight Coll., 1968-72; chmn. social studies program E.S.I., 1962-72; Killian prof. humanities Mass. Inst. Tech., 1972-95; cons. Houghton-Mifflin Co., 1946-51; Dir. Hitchiner Mfg. Co., Milford, N.H., Upland Farm, Inc., Peterborough, N.H.; Cons. Research and Devel. Bd., Dept. Def., 1946-52. Author: Admiral Sims and the Modern American Navy, 1942, Turmoil and Tradition, A Study of the Life and Times of Henry L. Stimson, 1960, Men, Machines and Modern Times, 1966, From Knowhow to Nowhere, 1974, (with Elizabeth F. Morison) New Hampshire, A History; Editor: The Letters of Theodore Roosevelt, 8 vols, 1951-54, Cowboys and Kings, 1954, The American Style, 1959. Trustee Hampshire Coll., 1966-75, Franklin Pierce Coll., 1978-95; bd. dirs. Center for N.H.'s Future, Concord.; Trustee Council for Critical Skills. Served from lt. (j.g.) to lt. comdr. USNR, 1942-46. Recipient J.H. Dunning prize Am. Hist. Assn., 1942; Francis Parkman prize Soc. Am. Historians, 1960; McKinsey Book award, 1966; Overseas fellow Churchill Coll., Cambridge (Eng.) U., 1976, 80. Fellow Am. Acad. Arts and Scis.; mem. Am. Hist. Assn. Republican. Home: Peterborough N.H. Died Aug., 1995.

MORLEY, RUTH, costume designer. Designer costumes for films including: The Miracle Worker (Oscar nomination), Annie Hall, Kramer vs. Kramer, Superman, One from the Heart, I Ought to Be in Pictures, Hammett, The Chosen, Tootsie; designer costumes for Broadway prodns.: Deathtrap, It's So Nice to be Civilized, A Thousand Clowns, Inherit the Wind, Moon for the Misbegotten, Twice Around the Park and others; designed prodns. for TV including: The Gardner's Son (Emmy nomination), Playing for Time. Died Feb. 12, 1991. Home: New York N.Y.

MOROT-SIR, EDOUARD BARTHELEMY, retired Romance language educator; b. Autun, France, Apr. 1, 1910; s. Francois and Suzanne (Bouteleux) Morot-S.; m. Sept. 12, 1935; children: Anne-Francoise, Catherine. Licence in philosophy, Sorbonne, Paris, 1932, Agregation es lettres, 1934, Doctor es letters, 1947; hon. degree, Syracuse U., 1962, NYU, 1967. Prof. U Bordeaux, France, 1947-50; prof. U. Cairo, 1950-52, U. Lille, France, 1950-57, U. Ariz., 1969-72; prof. U. N.C., Chapel Hill, 1972-83, William Kenan Jr. prof. emeritus of romance lang., 1983-93; exec. sec. Fulbright Commn., Paris, 1952-57; cultural attache and rep. French Univs., French Embassy, 1957-69; pres. Institut Francais de Washington, 1970-93. Author: Negative Thought, 1947, French Thought Today, 1971, The Metaphysics of Pascal, 1975, Literature Francaise, 1968; co-author: From Surrealism to the Empire of Criticism, 1984. Served to lt. Inf., French Army, 1939-40. Decorated War Cross, French Govt., Comdr. Acad. Palms, Ministry of Nat. Edn., Paris, 1960, Comdr. Legion of Honor, France, 1983. Fellow Am. Acad. Arts and Scis.; mem. Am. Assn. Tchrs. French (v.p. 1972-78). Club: The Century. Home: Chapel Hill N.C. Died May 27, 1993.

MORRIS, CARL, artist; b. Yorba Linda, Calif., 1911; s. Curtis W. and Caroline (Babbert) M.; m. Hilda Morris, 1940; 1 son, David. Student, Chgo. Art Inst., 1931-33; exchange scholar, Kunstgewerbeschule, Vienna, 1933-34, Akademie der Bildenden Kuenste, Vienna, 1934-35; fellow, Inst. Internat. Edn. for study in Paris, 1935-36. Instr. Chgo. Art Inst., 1936-38; dir. Spokane Art Center, 1938-39. Executed mural, Post Office, Eugene, Oreg., 1941; one-man shows include Kraushaar Gallery N.Y.C. since 1956, San Francisco Mus. Art, Santa Barbara Mus. Art, Seattle and Portland Art Mus., Palace Legion of Honor, Laura Russo Gallery PHd, OR, Foster/White Gallery, Seattle; retrospective exhbns. includes Portland (Oreg.) Art Mus., 1993; exhbns. in Whitney Mus., Met. Mus., Chgo. Art Inst., Carnegie Internat., Pa. Acad. Fine Arts, Corcoran Gallery, Albright Gallery, Am. Acad. Arts and Letters, Smithsonian Instn., 1974, NAD, 1974, San Francisco Mus. Art, Pitts. Internat. Exhbn., Mus. Modern Art, Nat. Mus. Art, Osaka, Japan; works in permanent collections of: Guggenheim Mus., Stanford U. Mus., San Francisco Mus. Contemporary Art, Wadsworth Atheneum, Met. Mus. Art, Albright-Knox Gallery, Art Inst. Chgo., Krannert Mus., Dayton Art Inst., Walker Art Ctr., Houston Mus. Fine Arts, Portland Art Mus., Whitney Mus. Am. Art, Seattle Art Mus., Denver Art Mus., De Young Mus., Smithsonian Instn., Corcoran Gallery, Toronto Gallery Art, Calif. Palace Legion of Honor, Mus. Modern Art, Modern Art Mus. of Sao Paulo, Brazil, Nat. Gallery Art Hirschhorn Collection, Nat. Acad. Design, Oreg. U. Health Scis., and others; 10 wall paintings commd. for Hall of Religion History now in U. Oreg., 9 paintings Vollum Biomed. Rsch. Ctr.; subject of publs. including Carl Morris (Grace L. McCann Morley), 1960, 100 Artists - 100 Years, Art. Inst. Chgo., 1979, Pacific N.W. Artists & Japan, Nat. Mus. Art Osaka, 1983, 50 N.W. Artists (Bruce Guenther), 1985, Intersecting Light (David Wagoner, 1986, others. Recipient Anne Bremmer Meml. prize San Francisco Mus. Art, Margaret E. Fuller award Seattle Art Mus., Pepsi-Cola bronze award, 1948, Emanuel Walters prize San Francisco Mus. Art, Phelan award Calif., Ford Found. award, 1960, Oreg. Gov.'s award, 1985, Watzek award, 1985, Disting. Svc. award Oreg. Health Sci. U., 1987. Home: Portland Oreg. Died June 3, 1993.

MORRIS, JOHN MCLEAN, surgeon, gynecology educator; b. Kuling, Peoples Republic of China, Sept. 1, 1914; s. DuBois Schanck and Alice Ray (Buell) M; m. Marjorie Stout Austin, Feb. 14, 1951; children: Marjorie, Christina, Constance, Robert, Virginia. AB cum laude, Princeton U., 1936; MD, Harvard U., 1940; MA (hon.), Yale U., 1962. Diplomate Am. Bd. Surgery, Am. Bd. Ob-Gyn. Intern and resident in surgery and gynecology Mass. Gen. Hosp., Boston, 1941-42, 46-47, asst. in surgery, 1947-51; fellow Am. Cancer Soc., Stockholm, Sweden, 1951-52; chief gynecology Yale U. Sch. Medicine, New Haven, 1952-93, assoc. prof. gynecology, 1952-61, acting chmn. dept. ob-gyn, 1960-61, 65-66, prof., 1961-93, John Slade Ely prof., 1969-93; vis. prof. Stanford U. Sch. Medicine, Palo Alto, Calif., 1966-67, U. Tex. M.D. Anderson Hosp., Houston, 1970, UCLA, 1978, U. Tenn. Ctr. Health Sci., Memphis, 1983, Ministry Def. Hosps., Saudi Arabia, 1984, Chang Gung Meml. Hosps., Taiwan, 1987-88; cons. William W. Backus Hosp., Meriden-Wallingford Hosp., Middlesex Meml. Hosp., Milford Hosp., New Britain Gen. Hosp., Stamford Hosp., St. Raphael's Hosp., Uncas-on-Thames Hosp., West Haven VA Hosp., Walter Reed Hosp., Gorgas Hosp., Panama, Tripler Hosp., Honolulu, William Beaumont Hosp., El Paso; trustee, past pres. New Haven br., mem. state cytology com. Am. Cancer Soc.; mem. med. adv. com. on world population Planned Parenthood; mem. human reprodn. unit WHO, Geneva; mem. alumni survey com. Harvard U. Med. Sch.; Holmes lectr. Chgo. Gynecol. Soc., 1986. Author: Endocrine Pathology of the Ovary, 1958; contbr. articles to profl. jours. and chpts. to books. Served as lt. comdr. USN, 1942-46, PTO. Recipient TeLinde award Soc. Gynecol. Surgeons, 1985; Ford Found. research grantee, 1967-72. Fellow ACS, Am. Coll. Ob-Gyn (com. on malignant disease, com. on resident tng., com. on terminology); mem. Am. Gynecol. Soc., Am. Gynecol. and Obstet. Soc. (v.p. 1981-82), Soc. Pelvic Surgeons (sec.-treas. 1961-64, pres. 1974-75), Am. Fertility Soc., Soc. Gynecologic Oncologists (charter), New Eng. Surg. Soc., St. Paul Surg. Soc. (hon.), South Atlantic Assn. Ob-Gyn (hon.), Felix Rutledge Soc. (hon.), George Washington U. Kane-King Obstet. Soc. (hon.), Los Angeles Obstet. and Gynecol. Soc. (hon.), Sigma Xi, Alpha Omega Alpha. Presbyterian. Home: Woodbridge Conn. Died Apr. 8, 1993; buried Grove St. Cemetary, New Haven, C.T.

MORRIS, JOHN MILTON, editorial cartoonist; b. Santa Barbara, Calif., Dec. 19, 1906; s. John Milton and Frances (Raynor) M.; m. Ruth Mitchell, Mar. 2, 1935 (dec.); 1 child, Lee Helen (Mrs. John Phillips). Student, Gardener Art Sch., Los Angeles, 1929, Art Students League, 1932-33. Staff artist Los Angeles Eve. Herald, 1928-30, N.Y. Jour. and Am., 1931-35; with A.P., 1935-87, editorial cartoonist, 1949-56, chief editorial cartoonist, 1956-87; spl. corr. nat. polit. convs., also spl. feature drawings of UN, Presidents of U.S., Washington; tchr. adult edn. courses Horace Greeley Adult Edn. Sch., Chappaqua, N.Y., 1961-63. Chmn. sch. and library com. Town Club, New Castle, N.Y., 1955-56; pres. library bd. trustees, Chappaqua, 1956-61; pres. Chappaqua P.T.A., 1953-54; Bd. dirs. Mus. of the Cartoon, Cartoon Hall of Fame, Greenwich, Conn., 1974-86. Recipient award outstanding cartoon of year Nat. Headliners, 1959; Freedoms Found. award, 1951-52, 54-55, 57, 61-62, 66, 68, 69, 70; Nat. Safety Found. award, 1962; Best Lincoln Day award, 1957; named New Castle Citizen of Year, 1959, one of 4 best editorial cartoonists in U.S. Nat. Cartoonists Soc., 1972. Mem. Assn. Am. Editorial Cartoonists (sec.-treas., 1st v.p., pres. 1970-71), Nat. Cartoonists Soc. (sec. 1970-72). Conglist. (past bd. deacons). Club: Whippoorwill Country (Armonk, N.Y.) (bd. govs. 1960-61). Home: Mission Viejo Calif. Died May 1, 1994.

MORRIS, KENNETH BAKER, mergers, acquisition and real estate executive; b. Bklyn., Feb. 12, 1922; s. Clarence E. and Mabel (Baker) M.; m. Dorothy E. Kohler, Sept. 3, 1960; children: Laura Susan, Sandra Lee. Student bus. adminstrn., Manhattan Coll., 1940-43, B.C.E., 1949; postgrad., Inst. Design, 1959-62, U. Nebr., 1970. Registered profl. engr., N.Y., N.J., Conn., Pa., Mass., Ga., Can. licensed profl. planner, also real estate broker. Asst. to pres., chief engr. Kretzer Constrn. Corp., N.Y.C., 1956-58; cons. engr. Kenneth B. Morris (P.E.), N.Y.C., Augusta, Ga., 1958-61; dir. plant and properties N.Y. U., 1961-66, bus. mgr., 1966-68; v.p. Cooper Union U., N.Y.C., 1968-74; v.p. charge gen. svcs. East River Savs. Bank, N.Y.C., 1974-79; sr. ptnr. cons. Morris Real Estate Co., N.Y.C., 1979—; adj. prof. Pace U., NYU, Fordham U.; Pres., bd. dirs. Grammercy Greenwich Corp., N.Y.C.; bd. dirs. Washington Sq. S.E.; adv. com. Poly. Inst. N.Y.; devel. and fin. adv. com. Cabrini Med. Center. Contbr. articles to mags. and newspapers. Mem. adv. bd., chmn. edn. com. Salvation Army. Served with USAAF, 1943-45. Mem. N.Y. Savs. Bank Assn. (chmn. security com.), Nat. Assn. Real Estate Execs., N.Y. State Real Estate Bd. (city planning com., edn. com., internat. real estate com., taxes and assessments com.), N.Y. State Soc. Real Estate Appraisers, A.I.M., N.Y.C. East Side C. of C. (past pres. and chmn. bd.), Am. Soc. Appraisers (sr. mem.), N.Y. State C. of C. (edn. com.), Lion (1st v.p. club), Am. Arbitration Assn. (nat. panel arbitrators, arbitrator for Am. Stock Exch., City Real Estate Bd.), Nat. Inst. Social Scis., Highlands Country Club.

MORRIS, WILLIAM, editor, author, newspape columnist, radio and TV broadcaster, lexicographer; b Boston, Apr. 13, 1913; s. Charles Hyndman an Elizabeth Margaret (Hanna) M.; m. Jane Frazer, Aug. 1939; m. Mary Elizabeth Davis, Feb. 8, 1947; childre Ann Elizabeth Morris Downie, Susan Jane, John Boyc William Frazer, Mary Elizabeth, Evan Nathanael. AB Harvard U., 1934; postgrad., Bates Coll., 1989, Ariz State U., 1990. Instr. English and Latin, Newman Sch 1935-37; mem. staff coll. dept. G.&C. Merriam Co 1937-43; mng. editor Grosset & Dunlap, 1945-47, exec editor, 1947-53, editor-in-chief, 1953-60; exec. edito Ency. Internat., 1960-62; editor-in-chief Grolie Universal Ency., 1962-64, Am. Heritage Dictionary 1964-72, Xerox Intermediate Dictionary and Weekl Reader Beginning Dictionary, 1971-94. Author: Wil liam Morris on Words for The Bell-McClure Syndicate 1953-68, (with Mary Morris) Words, Wit and Wisdom for LA Times Syndicate, 1968-75, United Featur Syndicate, 1975-83, Morris Assocs., 1983-93; cons editor: Funk & Wagnalls New Standard Dictionary, in ternat. edit., 1954-58, Funk & Wagnalls New Colleg Standard Dictionary, 1958-60; author: It's Easy to In crease Your Vocabulary, 1957, (with Mary Moris) Th Word Game Book, 1959, Dictionary of Word an Phrase Origins, vol. I, 1962, vol. II, 1967, vol. III, 1971 Your Heritage of Words, 1970, Harper Dictionary c Contemporary Usage, 1975, 2d edit., 1984, Morris Dic tionary of Word and Phrase Origins, 1977, 2d edit 1988; editor Words: The New Dictionary, 1947, Berlit Self-Teacher Language Books, 1949-53, Young People' Thesaurus Dictionary, 1971; creator: William Morr Vocabulary Enrichment Program, 1964; contbr. t Newsbreak, Nat. Geog. World, 1987, Harvar symposium on English First movement, 1989. Inc candidate for Vice Pres. U.S., 1976. Served to lt. (j.g U.S. Maritime Service, 1943-45. Mem. ALA, Coll. En glish Assn., Nat. Council Tchrs. English, Mencken Soc (Balt. chpt.), Gallups Island Radio Assn. Clubs: Coffe House, Dutch Treat (pres. emeritus), Harvard, Oversea Press, Silurians, Artists and Writers, Banshees, Th Players (N.Y.C.). Died Jan. 2, 1994.

MORROW, CORNELIUS EARL, urban planne landscape architect; b. Clarksville, Tenn., Apr. 5, 189 s. Cornelius Dotson and Alice (Caroland) M.; m Dorothy Cressler, June 7, 1928 (dec.); children—Wi liam Earl, June. B.A., Vanderbilt U., 1918, M.A., 192 M. of Landscape Architecture and City Plannin Harvard U., 1925. Cert. city planner. Engring. em ployee Regional Plan of New York, N.Y.C., 1925-3 tech. staff mem., 1931-50; sr. ptnr. Morrow Plannin Assn., Ridgewood, N.J., 1948-61; mem. planning servic 20 Planning Bds., N.Y., 1950-65; planning counselo Los Gatos, Calif., from 1965; chmn. planning bd. Tow of Ramapo, N.Y., 1954-65; lectr. city planning CCNY 1959-64. Author: Planning Your Community, 194 contbg. author: Forms and Functions of 20th Centur Architecture, 1952. Served with USN, 1918. Fello Am. Soc. Landscape Architects (sec. 1953-55); mem Am. Inst. City Planning (pres. N.Y. chpt. 1956), Ch Epsilon. Republican. Home: Los Gatos Cali Deceased.

MORROW, EVERETT FREDERIC, financial con sultant, retired banker; b. Hackensack, N.J., Apr. 2 1909; s. John Eugene and Mary Ann (Hayes) M.; m Catherine Gordon, Sept. 18, 1957. Student, Bowdoi Coll., 1926-30, LL.D., 1970; J.D., Rutgers U., 1948. Field sec. NAACP, N.Y.C., 1937-45; writer pub. affai CBS-TV, N.Y.C., 1945-52; exec. asst. Pres. Eisenhowe Washington, 1953-61; v.p. African-Am. Inst., N.Y.C 1962-64, Bank of Am., N.Y.C., 1964-75; exec. asso Ednl. Testing Service, Princeton, N.J., 1975-94; dir. JR Assos., Inc. Author: Black Man in the White Hous 1963, Way Down South Up North, 1973, Forty Years Guinea Pig, 1980. Trustee Phelps-Stokes Fund.; sp ambassador, leader Am. del. to Liberian Sesquicenter nial, 1972. Served to maj. AUS, 1942-46. Mem. Unite Nations Assn., Alpha Phi Alpha, Sigma Pi Phi. Republican. Methodist. Home: New York N.Y. Die April 19, 1994.

MORSE, CARLTON E., author; b. Jennings, La., Jun 4, 1901; s. George Albert and Ora Anna (Grubb) M; m Patricia Pattison DeBall, Sept. 23, 1928; 1 child, Mar Noel. Student, U. Calif., 1919-22. Newspaperma Sacramento Union, 1920-22; with various San Francisc newspapers, Seattle Times; writer NBC, from 193 creator, writer radio series One Man's Family, 1932-5 I Love a Mystery, 1939-42, 43-44, His Honor, th Barber, 1945-46, The Woman in My House, 1951-5 Family Skeleton, 1953-54. Author: Killer at the Whee 1987, A Lavish of Sin, 1987, Stuff the Lady's Hatbo 1988. Home: Woodside Calif. Died May 24, 1993.

MORTIMER, HENRY TILFORD, investment banke b. N.Y.C., June 17, 1916; s. Stanley Grafton an Katharine (Tilford) M.; m. Elise Duggan, Aug. 194 (div. 1951); children: Henry T., Victoria Mortimer d Navacelle; m. Linda M. Metcalfe, Nov. 25, 1965; chil dren: John Metcalfe, Alexander Dudley. A.B., Harvar U., 1939. Assoc. Bank of N.Y., 1947-48; sr. v.p., di Clark Dodge & Co., N.Y.C., 1948-74; sr. v.p. E.F Hutton & Co., Inc., N.Y.C., 1974-93; dir. Chevy Chas Property Co. Ltd., Bermuda, Chevy Chase Fin. Ltd chmn. bd. trustees Derwood Investment Trust. Bd. dir Am. Arab Assn. for Commerce & Industry, N.Y.C

1964-86. Served to lt. col. U.S. Army, 1941-46, ETO. Decorated bronze star with oak leaf cluster; comdr. Order St. John. of Jerusalem. Mem. Pilgrims of Am., English Speaking Union. Republican. Episcopalian. Clubs: Racquet & Tennis, The Brook; Southampton; Travellers (Paris); Whites (London); Metropolitan (Washington). Home: Southhampton New York Died Sept. 6, 1993.

MORTIMER, RUTH, assistant library director; b. Syracuse, N.Y., Sept. 16, 1931; d. Donald Cameron Mortimer and Lillian Ruth Burk; m. John Lancaster, Apr. 13, 1974. AB summa cum laude, Smith Coll., 1953; MS, Columbia U., 1957. Libr. Bklyn. Pub. Libr., 1953-54; asst. in serials Smith Coll. Libr., Northampton, Mass., 1954-56, curator rare books, 1975-94, asst. dir., 1975-94; rare book cataloguer Houghton Libr. Harvard U., Cambridge, Mass., 1957-75; lectr. Art Smith Coll., Northampton, Mass., 1976-94, acting coll. libr., 1991-92; guest curator Smith Coll. Mus. Art, 1979-90; cons. in field. Author: French 16th Century Books, 1964, Italian 16th Century Books, 1974; compiler The Bewildering Thread, 1986; contbg. editor Private Librs. Renaissance England, 1988-94; contbr. articles to books. Recipient John M. Greene award Smith Coll., 1992; Guggenheim fellow Guggenheim Found., 1966; Rosenbach fellow U. Pa., 1984, 85; named Disting. alumni Columbia U., 1991. Mem. ALA, Bibliog. Soc. Am. (pres. 1988-92, co-editor papers), Renaissance Soc. Am. (coun. 1975-81), Grolier Club, Phi Beta Kappa. Home: Williamsburg Mass. Died Jan 31, 1994.

MORTON, CHARLES BRINKLEY, retired bishop, former state legislator, lawyer; b. Meridian, Miss., Jan. 6, 1926; s. Albert Cole and Jean (Brinkley) M.; m. Virginia Roseborough, Aug. 26, 1948; children: Charles Brinkley Jr., Mary Virginia. JD with distinction, U. Miss., 1949; MDiv optime merens, U. South, 1959, DD, 1982. Bar: Miss. 1949, Tenn.; ordained to ministry Protestant Episcopal Ch. as deacon and priest, 1959. Sole practice Senatobia, Miss., 1949-56; mem. Thomas & Morton, Senatobia, Miss., 1952-56, Miss. Ho. of Reps., 1948-52, Miss. Senate, 1952-56; priest-in-charge Ch. of Incarnation, West Point, Miss., 1959-62; rector Grace-St. Luke's Ch., Memphis, 1962-74; dean Cathedral of Advent, Birmingham, Ala., 1974-82; bishop Episcopal Diocese of San Diego, 1982-92, ret., 1992. Contbr. articles to law and hist. jours. Mem. Miss. Commn. Interstate Coop., 1952-56, Miss. State Hist. Commn., 1952-56; past chmn. bd. Bishop's Sch., La Jolla, Calif., Episcopal Community Svcs., San Diego; past trustee Berkeley Div. Sch., Yale U.; active numerous civic and cultural groups. Served with AUS, World War II, Korea; col., chaplain Res. ret. Decorated Silver Star, Bronze Star medal with cluster, Purple Heart, Combat Inf. Badge; recipient Freedoms Found. Honor medal, 1967, 68, 72. Mem. Mil. Order World Wars, Am. Legion (past post comdr.), Phi Delta Phi, Tau Kappa Alpha, Omicron Delta Kappa, Phi Delta Theta. Lodge: Rotary. Home: Memphis Tenn. Died July 13, 1994.

MORTON, WILLIAM GILBERT, banker; b. Fulton, N.Y., Oct. 1, 1906; s. Albert I. and Martha (Gilbert) M.; m. Barbara Link, Jan. 22, 1936; children—William Gilbert, Linda Morton Cote, Albert Harry. MCS, Amos Tuck Sch., 1929. Rep. bond dept. Bankers Trust Co., N.Y.C., 1929-33, L. F. Rothschild & Co., 1933-34; with Onondaga Savs. Bank, Syracuse, N.Y., 1934-79; successively asst. to pres., asst. treas., treas., v.p. Onondaga Savs. Bank, 1934-53, exec. v.p., 1954- 58, pres., 1958-73, chmn., 1973-79, also trustee, 1947-81; Mem. N.Y. State Banking Bd., 1973-76. Mem. alumni council Dartmouth, 1948-52, 55-57, chmn. alumni fund campaign, 1956-58; bd. dirs. Met. Devel. Corp., 1962-86 pres., 1970; adminstrv. bd. Lab. Ornithology, Cornell U., 1972-78. Mem. Savs. Bank Assn. N.Y. (council adminstrn. 1956-62, 64-68, 70-76, 1st v.p. 1970, pres. 1971), Phi Sigma Kappa. Republican. Clubs: Century, Univ., Onondaga Golf and Country, Royal Poinciana Golf (Naples, Fla.); Dartmouth; Club of S.W. Fla. Home: Jamesville N.Y. Died Apr. 18, 1995.

MOSBY, CAROLYN BROWN, state legislator; b. Nashville, May 10, 1932; d. Alvin Thomas and Mary Elizabeth (Snelling) Brown; m. William Edward Jordan, Jr., 1950; 1 son, William Edward; m. John Oliver Mosby, Feb. 5, 1966 (dec. Apr. 1, 1988); 1 dau., Carolyn Elizabeth. Adminstrv. asst. dept. econs. U. Chgo., 1961-80; mem. Ind. Ho. of Reps., 1979-82, Ind. Senate, 1982-90; pres., owner Gary Image Ctr., 1980-90. Former mem. com. on platform accountability Democratic Nat. Com. Recipient Women's Agenda for Action award, 1981, INFO Newspaper awards as Outstanding Citizen in Politics, 1983, in Govt., 1983, Outstanding Citizen award City of Gary, 1983, Ovington award NAACP, 1987; Harvard U. fellow, 1986. Mem. N.W. Ind. Forum (bd. dirs. 1985-88), Gary C. of C. (dir. 1981-83), Nat. Council of Negro Women and Bus. & Profl. Women, Nat. Black Caucus of State Legislators, Nat. Caucus of State Legislatures, Council of State Govts., Sigma Gamma Rho (hon.). Baptist. Mem. editorial bd. AIM mag., 1980-82. Died Jan., 1990. Home: Indianapolis Ind.

MOSHOESHOE, II (CONSTANTINE BERENG SEEISO), King of Lesotho; b. Mokhotlong, Lesotho, May 2, 1938; s. Seeiso Griffith and Mofumahali 'Mabereng; m. Princess Tabitha 'Masentle, 1962; children: Letsie David, Seeiso Semeone, Constance Christina Sebueng. Ed., Roma Coll., Oxford (Eng.) U., 1948-54, Benedictine Coll., Yorkshire, Eng., 1954-57, Corpus Christi Coll., 1957. Paramount Chief of Basutoland, 1960-66, King of Lesotho, 1966-90, 95—, exiled, 1970, 90-92; chancellor Nat. U. Lesotho, 1971. Died January 15, 1996.

MOSKOVITZ, IRVING, lawyer; b. N.Y.C., June 12, 1912; s. David and Sarah (Katz) M.; m. Adele G. Reisner, June 22, 1937; children: Anne Joan Davis, Peter Alan. AB, Columbia Coll., 1932, LLB (Faculty scholar, Kent scholar), 1934. Bar: N.Y. 1935, U.S. Supreme Ct. 1951, D.C. 1965. Law asst. to N.Y. Supreme Ct. justice, 1934-35; assoc. Cook, Nathan, Lehman & Greenman, N.Y.C., 1935-42; dep. and acting chief counsel Bur. Fgn. Funds Control, Treasury Dept., 1942-45; ptnr. Graubard & Moskovitz, N.Y.C., 1949-69, Graubard, Moskovitz & McCauley, Washington, 1963-87; ptnr. Graubard, Moskovitz, Dannett, Horowitz & Mollen, N.Y.C., 1969-86, counsel, 1986-88; counsel Le Boeuf, Lamb, Leiby & MacRae, N.Y.C., 1988-96. Editor Columbia Law Rev., 1932-34. Trustee Marlboro (Vt.) Sch. of Music, 1971-96, chmn. 1987-93, vice chmn. 1993-96, trustee, v.p. Spanel Found, trustee, pres. Friends of Paul Sacher Found., Ginastera Found.; dir. N.Y. Virtuosi. Mem. N.Y. State Bar Assn., Bar Assn. City N.Y. Clubs: Century, Dirs. (London). Home: New York N.Y. Died Apr. 12, 1996.

MOSS, JAMES R., educational administrator, educator; b. Salt Lake City, Apr. 23, 1942; s. Rex F. and Ione (Naegle) M.; m. LaVelle Ridd, July 6, 1965; children: James Jr., John, David, Daniel, Jefferson, Jared, Rachelle. BS, U. Utah, 1966; JD, Stanford U., 1969; AS (hon.), U. Tech. Coll., 1985. Supr. Latter Day Saints Ch. Edn. System, Epsom, Surrey, Eng., 1969-71; div. coordinator Latter Day Saints Ch. Edn. System, London, Eng., 1971-73, Los Angeles, 1973-75; prof. Brigham Young U., Provo, Utah, 1975-86; supt. pub. instrn. State Utah, Salt Lake City, 1986—; mem. Western Interstate Commn. for Higher Edn., Denver, 1986; bd. dirs. Far West Lab. U.S. Dept. Edn., San Francisco, 1987—. Author/editor: The International Church, 1982, Truth Will Prevail, 1987; contbr. articles to mags. and chpts. to books. Mem. Utah Ho. of Reps., Salt Lake City, 1983-86, Utah Jud. Conduct Commn., Salt Lake City, 1983-86; chmn. Utah Jud. Reform Task Force, Salt Lake City, 1985-86; mem. exec. com. Western States Conf. of State Legislators, 1983-86. Mem. MENSA, Phi Alpha Theta, Pi Sigma Alpha, Phi Kappa Phi. Home: Orem Utah

MOSSER, THOMAS JOSEPH, public relations agency executive; b. Plainfield, N.J., Feb. 9, 1944; s. Thomas Franklin and Annette (Pascal) M.; children: Abigail, Thomas Franklin, Kimberly Annette; m. Susan Reilly, Nov. 10, 1980. B.A. in journalism, St. Bonaventure U.; cert. strategic mktg., Harvard Coll. Writer AP, Phila., 1965-66; exec. Burson-Marsteller, N.Y.C., from 1969; vice chmn., COO Burson-Marsteller Worldwide, N.Y.C.; vice chmn., COO, bd. dirs. Young & Rubicam Inc., N.Y.C., exec. v.p., gen. mgr., 1994. Served to lt. USN, 1966-69, Vietnam. Recipient 9 Silver Anvil awards Pub. Rels. Soc. Am., 1969-85. Club: Glen Ridge Country. Home: Caldwell N.J. Died Dec. 10, 1994.

MOSSMAN, HARLAND WINFIELD, emeritus anatomy educator; b. N.Y.C., May 7, 1898; s. Herdmen Xavier and Lucy Barrows (Fuller) M.; m. Ruth Hannah Jackson, June 21, 1924; children: Archie Stanton, Malcolm Herdman, Ardith Rose. BS, Allegheny Coll., 1920; MS, U. Wis., 1922, PhD, 1924. From instr. to prof. anatomy, now prof. emeritus U. Wis., Madison, from 1924. Author: Vertebrate Fetal Membranes, 1987; co-author: Human Embryology, 1945, Mammalian Ovary, 1973. Mem. village bd. Shorewood Hills, Wis., 1946-50. Recipient Henry Gray award Am. Assn. Anatomists, 1987. Fellow AAAS. Democrat. Home: Madison Wis. Deceased.

MOST, HARRY, educator, physician; b. N.Y.C., Sept. 18, 1907; s. Philip and Sarah (Abend) M.; m. Rita Gold, Nov. 20, 1938; children: Susan, Paul. B.S., N.Y.U., 1927, M.D., 1931, D.Sc., 1939; D.T.M.&H., London Sch. Tropical Medicine, 1936. Diplomate: Am. Bd. Preventive Medicine and Pub. Health. Research fellow internat. health div. Rockefeller Found., P.R., Haiti, 1941, Europe, 1950; asst. prof. medicine, asst. prof. clin. pathology N.Y. U. Med. Sch., 1941-46, asso. prof. preventive medicine, 1946-49, prof. tropical medicine, 1949-54, acting chmn. dept. preventive medicine, 1953-54, Hermann M. Biggs prof., chmn. dept. preventive medicine, 1954-76, prof. medicine, 1976-94; lectr. Columbia U., 1942-44; cons. commr. health N.Y. State Dept. Health, 1946-94; dir. tropical disease diagnosis clinic N.Y.C. Dept. Health, 1949-54; vis. lectr. Harvard U. Sch. Pub. Health, 1955-85; vis. physician Bellevue Hosp.; attending physician Univ. Hosp., N.Y.C.; cons. physician Booth Meml. Hosp., N.Y.C., Meadowbrook Hosp., Hempstead, L.I., North Shore Hosp., L.I.; Mem. tropical medicine study sect. USPHS; cons. tropical medicine Surgeon Gen. U.S. USPHS, Marine Hosp., S.I., N.Y., Ellis Island; cons. tropical and internal medicine VA Hosp., N.Y.; cons. Clin. Center. NIH, Communicable Diseases Center, USPHS, Atlanta, Creedmoor State Hosp., Willowbrook State Sch., S.I.; chief cons. tropical medicine VA; lectr. Army Med. Center, 1946-47; cons. schistosomiasis research U.S. Navy; mem. commn. naval med. research NRC; dir. commn. parasitic diseases Armed Forces Epidemiological Bd., 1950; cons. Phelps Meml. Hosp., N.Y. Served to maj. AUS, 1943-46. Decorated Legion of Merit. Fellow N.Y. Acad. Scis., N.Y. Acad. Medicine; mem. Am. Soc. Tropical Medicine (editorial bd.), Am. Soc. Parasitologists, Royal Soc. Tropical Medicine and Hygiene, Nat. Malaria Soc. (editorial bd.), N.Y. Soc. Tropical Medicine (pres. 1963-64), Am. Soc. Clin. Investigation, Am. Pub. Health Assn., AMA, AAAS, Harvey Soc., N.Y. County Med. Soc., Am. Acad. Tropical Medicine, Am. Found. Tropical Medicine, Am. Soc. Tropical Medicine and Hygiene (pres. 1966- 67), Phi Beta Kappa, Sigma Xi, Alpha Omega Alpha, Beta Lambda Sigma; hon. mem. Belgium, Brazilian socs. tropical medicine. Home: New York N.Y. Died Sept. 11, 1994.

MOTTER, DAVID CALVIN, government official, economist; b. New London, Ohio, Feb. 10, 1926; s. Doren M. and Bertha (Potter) M.; m. Margaret Helen Malmfelt, Aug. 12, 1950; 1 child, Catherine Helen. B.A., Baldwin-Wallace Coll., 1950; Ph.D., Vanderbilt U., 1958. Instr. econs. Franklin and Marshall Coll., 1954-56; research fellow Brookings Instn., 1956-57; lectr., then asst. prof. Wharton Sch., U. Pa., 1957-63; sr. economist Office Comptroller Currency, 1963-66, dep. comptroller currency (econs.), 1966-77, dep. controller for interagy. coordination and FDIC asst. to dir., 1977-81, spl. asst. to sr. dep. controller for bank supervision, 1981-85, sr. asst. to chief nat. bank examiner, 1985-92. Author research studies. Mem. W. Phila. Housing Com., 1960-63; pres. Regent Sq. Civic Assn., Phila., 1958-63; Bd. dirs. Fairfax Horsemen's Assn., 1968-71, Animal Welfare League of Fairfax County, 1978-92. Served with USNR, 1944-46. Recipient Meritorious award Treasury Dept., 1972. Mem. Am. Econ. Assn., Am. Fin. Assn., AAUP. Episcopalian. Home: Vienna Va. Died Dec. 24, 1992.

MOTTRAM, ERIC, poet, literature educator. Lectr. in Am. Lit. U. London, 1961-73; founder Inst. U.S. Studies; reader in English and Am. Lit., 1973-83; prof. English and Am. lit. King's Coll., U. London, 1983-95, U. Zurich, U. Malaya, Kuala Lampur, U. Groningen, West Germany, SUNY, Buffalo, Kent State U., Ohio, U. Hyderabad, India, U. Alcala de Henares, Spain. Author: (poetry) Inside the Whale, 1970, Shelter Island and the Remaining World, 1972, The He Expression, 1973, Local Movement, 1973, Two ELegies, 1974, Against Tyranny, 1975, A Faithful Private, 1976, 1922 Earth Raids and Other Poems, 1973-1975, 1976, Homage to Braque, 1976, Spring Ford, 1977, Tunis, 1977, Elegy 15: Neruda, 1978, Windsor Forest: Bill Butler in Memorium, 1979, Precipice of Fishes, 1979, 1980 Mediate, 1980, Elegies, 1981, A Book of Herne, 1975-81, 1981, Interrogation Rooms: Poems 1980-81, 1982, Address, 1983, Three Letters, 1984, The Legal Poems, 1986, Selected Poems, 1989, Peace Projects and Brief Novels, 1989; editor: (with Larry Wallrich) For Bill Butler, 1970, (with others) The Penguin Companion to American Literature, 1971, William Burroughs: The Algebra of Need, 1971, 77, William Faulkner, 1971, Towards Design in Poetry, 1971, Allen Ginsberg in the Sixties, 1972, The Rexroth Reader, 1972, (with William S. Burroughs) Snack, 1975, Paul Bowles: Staticity and Terror, 1977, The Wild Good and the Heart Ultimately: Ginsberg's Art of Persuasion, 1978, (with Gavin Selerie) Jerome Rothenberg, 1984, (with others) The New British Poetry 1968-1988, 1988, Blood on the Nash Ambassador; Investigations in American Cultures, 1989. Died Jan. 1995.

MOUTOUSSAMY, JOHN WARREN, architect; b. Chgo., Jan. 5, 1922; s. Jean Marie and Julia Nettie (Walker) M.; m. Elizabeth Rose Hunt, Mar. 15, 1942; children: John Jr. (dec.), Claude Louis, Jeanne Marie. BSArch, Ill. Inst. Tech., 1948; LLD (hon.), Loyola U., Chgo., 1982. Lic. architect, Ill. Draftsman Schmidt, Garden & Erikson Architects, Chgo., 1950-56; architect PACE Assocs., Chgo., 1956-65; ptnr. Dubin, Dubin and Moutoussamy, Chgo., 1966-83, mng. ptnr., 1983-95; cons. architect Metro. Pier and Exhbn. Authority, Chgo., 1975-95. Trustee Art Inst. Chgo., 1973-95, Loyola U., 1972-81; bd. govs. Sch. Art Inst., 1980-93; vice chmn. Chgo. Plan Commn., 1979-81. Fellow AIA; mem. Wayfarers' Club. Roman Catholic. Home: Chicago Ill. Died May 6, 1995.

MOWERY, BOB LEE, librarian; b. Charlotte, N.C., June 22, 1920; s. Kerr Lee and Ella (Holman) M.; m. Peggy Setzer, Sept. 9, 1945; children: Margaret Mowery Paul, Mary, Robert, John. BA, Catawba Coll., 1941; BS in L.S., U. Chgo., 1947, MA, 1951. Catalogue libr. Dickinson Coll., Pa., 1947-50; libr., head dept. libr. sci. Murray State Coll., 1951-53; libr. McNeese State Coll., 1953-58, Stetson U., 1958-64; dir. librs. Wittenberg U., 1964-83, prof., dir. librs. emeritus, 1983-95; cons., acting dir. libr. Davis & Elkins Coll., 1986-87. Chmn. com. parish edn. Fla. synod Luth. Ch. Am., 1962-64, chmn. com. local arrangements constituting conv., 1962; mem. hist. work com. N.C. Synod., Evang.-Luth. Ch. Am., 1983-92; chmn. com. libr. resources Regional Coun. Internat. Edn.; del. Seminar Current Trends Edn., Yugoslavia, Aug. 1966. Editor La. Libr. Bull., 1955-58; contbr. articles to profl. jours. Trustee DeLand (Fla.)

Pub. Library, Newberry Coll., 1962-64, Springfield Art Center, 1976-81; bd. dirs., treas. Ohio Coll. Libr. Ctr., 1969-74; bd. dirs. Ohionet, 1978-83; pres. Friends of the Henderson County Pub. Library, 1984-86; bd. dirs. Friends of N.C. Pub. Libraries, 1987-93, pres. 1989-91; chmn. Saluda Med. Ctr., 1989-93; bd. dirs. Polk County chpt. ARC, 1992-95. Served with AUS, 1942-46; maj., ret. Nat. Def. Fgn. Lang. fellow, 1967. Fellow Am. Coun. Learned Socs.; mem. Am. Libr. Assn., N.C. Libr. Assn., Bibliog. Soc., Bibliog. Soc. Am., Arthur Machen Soc. (Am.) (pres. 1965-83), Arthur Machen Soc. (Eng., hon. life mem.), Assn. Coll. and Rsch. Libr. (pres. Tristate chpt. 1974-75), Acad. Libr. Assn. Ohio (pres. 1975-76). , Rotary (bd. dirs. Deland club 1961-63), Univ. Club (Springfield), Hendersonville Club. Democrat. Died July 19, 1995. Home: Saluda N.C.

MOYA, (JOHN) HIDALGO, architect; b. Los Gatos, Calif., May 5, 1920; s. Hidalgo and Lilian (Chattaway) Moya; m. Jeniffer Innes Mary Hall, 1947; m. Jean (MacArthur) Conder, 1988; 3 children from previous marriage. Student, Royal W. of Eng. Coll. Art, Archtl. Assn. Sch. Architecture. Pvt. practice architecture, 1946-76; ptnr. Powell, Moya and Ptnrs., London, 1976-94. Prin. works include Churchill Gardens flats, Westminster, 1948-62 (won in open competition), houses and flats at Gospel Oak, St. Pancras, 1954, Vauxhall Park, Lambeth, 1972, Convent Garden, 1983, Houses at Chichester, 1950, Toys Hill, 1954, Oxshott, 1954, Baughurst, Hants, 1954, Skylon for Fest. of Britain 1951 (won in open competition), Brit. Pavilion, Expo 70, Osaka Japan, 1970, Mayfield Sch., Putney, 1955, Plumstead Manor Sch., Woolwich, 1970, dining rms. at Bath Acad. of Art, Corsham, 1970, and Eton Coll., 1974, Mus. of London, 1976, London and Manchester Assurance HQ, near Exeter, 1978, Sch. for Advanced Urban Studies, Bristol U., 1981, Nat. West Bank Shaftesbury Ave., London, 1982, Queens Bldg. RHBNC, Engham, 1986, Queen Elizabeth II Conf. Ctr., Westminster, 1986. Decorated comdr. Order Brit. Empire. Fellow Royal Inst. Brit. Architects (Winning Design award 1946, 50, Bronze medal 1950, 58, 61, Festival of Britain award 1951, Mohlg Good Design in Housing award 1953, 54, Civic Trust awards 1961, Archtl. Design Project award 1965, Archtl. award 1967, Royal Gold medal 1974). Home: Rye Eng. Died Aug. 3, 1994.

MUCKLOW, NEALE HARMON, philosophy educator; b. Albany, N.Y., Aug. 21, 1929; s. Lucian Howe and Marion Eaton (Blakeslee) M.; m. Barbara Jean DeSmidt, Aug. 16, 1951; children: David Hamilton, Roxanne, Nadine M. Cornett. AB, Hamilton Coll., Clinton, N.Y., 1951; PhD, Cornell U., Ithaca, N.Y., 1963. Instr. Hamilton Coll., Clinton, 1953-54; asst. prof. Lycoming Coll., Williamsport, Pa., 1957-64, chmn. dept. philosophy, 1964-69, assoc. prof., 1964-70; assoc. prof. U. Richmond, Va., 1970-74, prof. philosophy, 1974-92, prof. emeritus, 1992-95. Founding mem. Blvd. Civic Assn., Richmond, 1979. Mem. Am. Philos. Assn., South Atlantic Philosophy of Edn. Soc. Presbyterian. Home: Richmond Va. Died Mar. 8, 1995.

MUELLER, JOHN ALFRED, church executive; b. Milw., Apr. 19, 1906; s. Theodore J. and Catherine (Quehl) M.; m. Ruth M. Zehnder, Aug. 16, 1930; children: Annette (Mrs. Milford Brelje), John G. B.E., Concordia Tchrs. Coll., River Forest, Ill., 1927. Instr., minister of music Atonement Luth. Ch., Dearborn, Mich., 1927-42; minister music and edn. Jehovah Luth. Ch., Detroit, 1942-47; field rep. Luth. Laymens League, St. Louis, 1947-50; mem., field services dir. Luth. Laymens League, 1950-95. Composer mus. compositions for choirs and quartettes, 1965. Bd. dirs. Luth. Ch.-Mo. Synod. Recipient Christus Vivit medallion Concordia Theol. Sem., 1974; Disting. Service award Bd. Dirs. Luth. Ch.-Mo. Synod, 1978. Home: Saint Louis Mo. Died Mar., 1995.

MUIR, JEAN ELIZABETH, costume designer; d. Cyril and Phyllis (Coy) M.; m. Harry Leuckert, 1955. D (hon.), RCA, 1981; DLit (hon.), U. Newcastle, 1985; DLitt (hon.), U. Ulster, 1987. Seller, sketcher Liberty & Co., 1950; designer Jaeger Ltd., 1956, Jane & Jane; designer-dir., co-owner Jean Muir Ltd., London, 1967—; mem. art and design com. TEC, 1978-83; mem. bd. for design and art BTEC, 1983—; mem. Design Coun., 1983—. Mem. adv. coun. Victoria and Albert Mus., 1979-83, trustee, 1984—. Recipient Dress of Yr. award Brit. Fashion Writers' Group, 1964, Amb. award for achievement, 1965, trophy Harper's Bazaar, 1965, Maison Blanche Rex Internat. Fashion award, New Orleans, 1967, 68, 74, Churchman's award as fashion designer of yr., 1970, award Neiman Marcus, 1973, svc. award Brit. Fashion Industry, 1984, Hommage de la Mode, Fedn. Française du Prèt-a-porter Feminin, 1985, medal for design Textile Inst., 1987, Bicentennial award Govt. of Australia, 1988. Fellow Royal Soc. Arts, Chartered Soc.. Designers (medal 1987); mem. RDI. Home: London Eng. Died May 28, 1995.

MULLEN, SANFORD ALLEN, physician; b. Tampa, Fla., Jan. 16, 1925; s. Earl and Edith (Allen) M.; m. Minnie Lucille Woodall, Dec. 23, 1945 (dec. Feb. 25, 1983); children: Sanford Allen, Henry Woodall, Michael Hill; m. JoAnn Bonneau Drennon, Oct. 11, 1987. Student, Mercer U., 1943-45; MD, Columbia U., 1949. Diplomate: Am. Bd. Pathology (sub-bds. in clin. pathology, anat. pathology, dermatopathology, blood banking). Intern Grady Meml. Hosp., Atlanta, 1949-50, resident in anatomic pathology, 1950, 53-54; fellow in clin. pathology U. Minn. Hosps., Mpls., 1954-56; pvt. practice medicine specializing in pathology Jacksonville, Fla., from 1956; clin. assoc. prof. U. Fla., 1977-80, clin. prof., from 1980; mem. staff, co-chief dept. pathology U. Hosp. of Jacksonville; mem. staff Bapt. Med. Ctr., Jacksonville, St. Vincent's Med. Ctr., Jacksonville; mem. adv. coun. Nat. Heart, Lung and Blood Inst., 1983-86; mem. Gov.'s Select Com. on Workforce 2000, State of Fla., 1988-91. Mem. nat. bd. govs. Arthritis Found., 1963-64, pres. Duval County div., 1960-61, pres. Fla. chpt., 1963-64; chmn. Jacksonville Mayor's Citizens Adv. Com. on Water Pollution Control, 1965-66, United Fund Campaign; vice chmn. Jacksonville Water Quality Control Bd., 1971-73; vestryman Episcopal Ch., 1967-69, sr. warden, 1969; mem. Health Planning Council N.E. Fla., 1976-77; exec. v.p., med. dir. Fla.-Ga. Blood Alliance, 1970-81, pres., med. dir., from 1982; mem. various adv. coms. Fla. Bd. Health, Fla. Dept. Edn., Fla. C.C. at Jacksonville; mem. adv. bd. Salvation Army, Fla. div., 1971-76; pres. Civic Round Table, 1967-69; rep. Greater Jacksonville Econ. Opportunity Inc., 1966-68; bd. dirs. Jacksonville Symphony Assn., 1970-77, v.p., 1971-73, sec., 1976-77; bd. dirs. Kidney Found. Inc, N.E. Fla. region, 1972-74, Nat. Kidney Found. of Fla., 1986-87; bd. dirs. ARC, Jacksonville Area chpt., 1972-77, 83-86, vice chmn., 1975-77; bd. dirs. Cathedral Found., 1972-76, exec. vice chmn., 1972-76; bd. dirs. Jacksonville Exptl. Health Delivery System Inc., 1973-76, pres., 1973-76; trustee Jacksonville Hosps. Ednl. Program, 1971-76; treas. Exec. Service Corps of NE Fla., from 1984; chmn. task force Jacksonville Look Back Program on AIDS and Blood Transfusions, 1987-91; mem. Fla. Council of 100, from 1983, Jacksonville Art Mus., Cummer Gallery Art; mem. Ye Mystic Revellers, King, 1983; mem. Blue Key. Served with MC USNR, 1950-52; on loan to AUS, USNR, Korea. Recipient Svc. to Mankind West Jacksonville Sertoma Club, 1974, A.H. Robins award for community svc. Fla. Med. Assn., 1973, Cert. of merit, 1990. Fellow Coll. Am. Pathologists (gov. 1966-69, 70-73); mem. AMA (mem. coun. on sci. affairs panel on AIDS 1983-85), AAAS, Am. Acad. Dermatology, Am. Soc. Dermopathology, Am. Soc. Dermatology, Jacksonville Acad. Medicine (pres. 1963, dir. 1966-68, 72-77), Fla. Soc. Pathologists (pres. 1964-66, 72-73, v.p. 1966-67, 73-74), Am. Soc. Clin. Pathologists (councilor Fla. 1962-66), Duval County Med. Soc. (chmn. legis. council 1967, 70-72, dir. 1972, pres. 1974), Fla. Med. Assn. (ho. dels. from 1964, chmn. com. state legis. 1969-75, vice speaker ho. dels. 1976-78, speaker 1978-80, pres.-elect 1980-81, pres. 1981-82, del. to AMA from 1983, mem. task force on AIDS from 1988, chm. com. on priorities and programs 1985, historian from 1988, recipient certificate of merit 1990), So. Med. Assn. (vice-chmn. sect. pathology 1967-68), N.E. Fla. Heart Assn. (dir. 1967-69), Fla. Assn. Blood Banks (dir. 1968-76, pres. 1973-74), Am. Assn. Blood Banks (state rep. of Fla. 1971-72), Am. Blood Commn. (organizing com. 1973-75, bd. dirs. 1975-79), Am. Cancer Soc., Fla. Med. Polit. Action Com. (dir. 1964-65), Am. Soc. Histocompatibility and Immunogenetics, Soc. for Cryobiology, Internat Soc. Blood Transfusions, Jacksonville Zool. Soc. (dir. 1971-77), Jacksonville Area C. of C. (gov. 1966-68, 72-74, chmn. pub. health com. 1965-66, v.p. and treas. 1967, v.p. membership affairs 1968, 69, membership devel., mem. health care cost coalition 1981-86), Fla. Yacht Club, Timuquana Club, River Club, St. Johns Dinner Club (dir. 1967-70, pres. 1969-70), Torch Club (dir. 1968-72, pres. 1971-72), Rotary (pres. Jacksonville chpt. 1970-71), Alpha Tau Omega (pres. Jacksonville alumni 1958-59), Sigma Mu, Gamma Sigma Epsilon, Phi Eta Sigma. Episcopalian. Home: Jacksonville Fla. Deceased.

MÜLLER, HEINER, playwright; b. Eppendorf, Germany, Jan. 9, 1929; m. Inge Müller (dec. 1966). Various positions from bookshop worker, journalist to freelance writer; editor Junge Kunst mag.; staff mem. Berliner-Maxim-Gorki-Theater, 1958-59, Berliner Ensemble, 1970-76, Berliner Volksbühne, 1976-95. Plays include (with Inge Müller) Der Lohndrücker, 1958, Die Korrektur, 1958, Die Umsiedlerin, 1961, Herakles 5, 1966, Philoktet, 1968, Die Aristokraten, 1968, Prometheus, 1969, Arzt wider Willen, 1970, Der Horatier, 1972, Traktor, 1974, Geschichten aus der Produktion 1-2, 1974, Der Bau, 1974, Die Schlacht, 1975, Theater-Arbeit, 1975, Stücke, 1975, Kopien: 3 Versuche, Shakespeare zu tüten, 1977, Leben Gundlings Friedrich von Preussen Lessings Schlaf Traum Schrei, 1979, Germania Tod in Berlin, 1978, Fatzer, 1978, Mauser, 1978, Die Hamletmaschine, 1979, Shakespeare Factory 2, 1980, Der Auftrag, 1980, Verkommenes Ufer Medeamaterial Landschaft mit Argonauten, 1982, Herzstück, 1983, Bildbeschreibung, 1984, Hamletmachine and Other Texts for the Stage, 1984, Wolokolamsker Chaussee 1, 1985, (with Robert Wilson) The Civil Wars: A Tree Is Best Matured When It Is Down, 1985, Anatomie Titus Fall of Rome, 1985, Quai West, 1986, Revolutionsstück, 1988, Stück: Texte über Deutschland 1957-1979, 1989, Kopien 1-2, 1989; (adaptations) Zehn Tage die Welterschütterten (John Reed), 1957, Ödipus Tyrann (Hölderlin), 1968, Wie es euch gefällt (Shakespeare), 1968, Drachenoper (Dessau), 1969, Horizonte (Winterlich), 1969, Wieberkomödie (Müller), 1970, Die Möwe (Chekhov), 1972, Macbeth, 1972, Zement (Gladkov), 1973, Hamlet, 1977, Quartett (de Laclos), 1981, Quai West (Bernard-Marie-Koltès), 1986, Wolokolamsker Chaussee II: Wald bei Moskau (Bek), 1986, Wolokolamsker Chaussee III: Das Duel (Seghers), 1987; numerous other collections of writings. Recipient Heinrich Mann prize, 1959, Erich Weinert medal, 1964, BZ Critics prize, 1970, 76, Lessing prize, 1975. Home: Leipzig Germany Died Dec. 30, 1995.

MULLIGAN, GERALD JOSEPH (GERRY MULLIGAN), composer, arranger, musician, songwriter; b. N.Y.C., Apr. 6, 1927; s. George V.R. and Louise (Shannon) M.; m. Contessa Franca Rota; 1 son, Reed Brown. Studied with, Sam Correnti (saxophone), Johnny Warrington, Gil Evans, Charlie Parker, Duke Ellington (arranging and composition). Arranger, Johnny Warrington, Elliot Lawrence, Sta. WCAU, Phila., Tommy Tucker, Gene Krupa, Claude Thornhill, Kai Winding, Miles Davis; leader Gerry Mulligan Quartet, 1951-96, Concert Jazz Band, 1957-96; artist-in-residence U. Miami, 1974; rec. artist A&M Records, Columbia, Verve, Phillips, World Pacific, Concord, Atlantic, DRG, GRP; solo appearances N.Y. Philharm., London Symphony Orch., La Fenice, Venice, CBC Symphony, Toronto, Can., others; albums include Birth of the Cool, Gerry Mulligan Quartet, The Age of Steam, Litle Big Horn, Walk on Water (Grammy award 1981), Lonesome Boulevard, Mulligan Meets Monk, Mulligan Meets Webster, etc.; orchestral works rec. Symphonic Dreams (Houston Symphony), New American Music, Vol. 1 (The Sea Cliff Chamber Players), What is There To Say, 1994, Re-Birth of the Cool, 1992, Paraiso-Jazz Brazil, 1993, Live In Stockholm, 1995, Jazz 'Round Midnight, 1992, Dream a Little Dream with Ted Rosenthal et al, 1994, Verve Jazz Masters 36, 1994, Dragonfly, 1995. Recipient numerous awards as baritone saxophonist including Conn. Arts award, Hall of Fame award Phila. Music Found., 1990, Viotti Gold medal, Italy, Grammy award Best Big Band performance for Walk on the Water, 1981; Duke Ellington fellow Yale U.; named to Down Beat Hall of Fame, 1993. Mem. ASCAP. Home: Darien Conn. Died Jan. 20, 1996.

MULLIGAN, WILLIAM HUGHES, lawyer, former federal judge; b. N.Y.C., Mar. 5, 1918; s. Stephen Hughes and Jane (Donahue) M.; m. Roseanna Connelly Oct. 20, 1945; children: Anne O'Boyle Mulligan Hartmere, William Hughes, Stephen Edward. A.B. cum laude, Fordham U., 1939, LL.B. cum laude, 1942 LL.D., 1975; LL.D., St. Peter's Coll., Jersey City, 1966 Bklyn. Law Sch., 1972, Iona Coll., 1972, Villanova U. 1974, Pace U., 1979, Suffolk U., 1987; L.H.D., Siena Coll., 1967. Lectr. law Fordham U., 1946-52, assoc prof., 1953-54, asst. dean. prof. law., 1954-56; dean Fordham U. (Law Sch.), 1956-71, Wilkinson prof. law 1961-71; judge U.S. Ct. Appeals, 2d circuit, 1971-81 ptnr. firm Skadden, Arps, Slate, Meagher & Flom N.Y.C., 1981-91; Mem. Law Revision Commn. State N.Y., 1958-71; chmn. exam. bd. Manhattan and Bronx Surface Transit Operating Authority, 1964-71; mem N.Y. State Commn. on Constl. Conv., 1965; mem. adv council Labor and Mgmt. Improper Practices Act, 1968-71; mem. state Commn. Rev. Legislative and Jud. Salaries, 1970-71; mem. Com. Adminstrn. Cts., 1970-71; bd dirs. Fed. Jud. Center, 1979-81; internat. arbitrator legal cons. counsel various state and local coms.; chmn Citizens Com. of Reapportionment Gov. Rockefeller 1964; assoc. chmn. N.Y. State Com. on Sentencing Guidelines, 1984-86. Contbr. articles to profl. publs. Gen. counsel Republican delegation N.Y. State Const Conv., 1967; trustee St. Patrick's Cathedral, 1981-91 trustee Fordham U., 1982-88, trustee emeritus, 1989-96 trustee Cath. Charities, Archdiocese of N.Y., 1985-91 mem. N.Y.C. Bd. Ethics, 1986-87. Served as spl. ag CIC AUS, 1942-46. Recipient St. John de La Sal medal Manhattan Coll., 1967, Learned Hand awar Am. Jewish Com., 1986; Encaenia medal Fordhar Coll., 1966; Fordham Law Alumni medal, 1971; Gol medal N.Y. State Bar Assn., 1982. Mem. Fed. Judge Assn., Am. Judicature Soc. (bd. dirs. 1988-92), Re Lawyers Assn. (hon. nat. chmn. 1987-96), Friendly Son of St. Patrick (pres. 1983-85), Knights of Malt Merchants Club. Roman Catholic. Home: Bronxvil N.Y. Died May 13, 1996.

MULLIN, ROGER WILLIAM, JR., lawyer, form truck manufacturing company executive; b. Bklyn., Jur 2, 1914; s. Roger William and Blanche (Kirchner) M m. Mary Louise Moran, June 2, 1943. A.B., Bkly Coll., 1935; LL.B., Fordham U., 1938; LL.M., Geor Washington U., 1952; LL.D., Allentown Coll., 1977 Bar: N.Y. 1939. Atty. Am. Bankers Assn., 1940-4 staff atty. N.Y. State Jud. Council, 1941-42, 46-48; att firm Gordon, Brady, Caffrey & Keller, N.Y.C., 1948-5 counsel chem. div. NPA, 1950-53; corp. counsel, se Curtis-Wright Corp., 1953-61; v.p., gen. counsel, se Mack Trucks, Inc., 1962-64, v.p. adminstrn. and leg affairs, 1964-67, exec. v.p. adminstrn., 1967-74, vi chmn., 1974-76, chmn. bd., 1976-79; chmn. bd. Copl Cement Co., 1980-89; bd. dirs., mem. exec. co Merchants Nat. Bank, Allentown, 1970-85. Editor chief Fordham Law Rev., 1937-38. Past bd. dirs. A lentown Art Mus., Pa. Stage Co.; past treas., bd. di Allentown and Sacred Heart Hosp. Ctr. Inc.; past pre bd. dirs. Sacred Heart Hosp., Allentown; past trust Allentown Coll., Cedar Crest Coll.; bd. dirs. Allentov Pub. Libr., 1983-95, Allentown Comml. and Ind ᴇvel. Authority, 1983-95; bd. dirs., mem. exec. com. llentown Econ. Devel. Corp., 1985-86. Served to 1st lt. US, 1942-46. Decorated knight of St. Gregory. Mem. llentown-Lehigh County C. of C. Clubs: Lehigh ountry (Allentown), Livingston, Contemporary. odge: Rotary. Home: Allentown Pa. Died May 6, 995.

ɪULLINS, LORIN JOHN, biophysicist, educator; b. ın Francisco, Sept. 23, 1916; s. Harry Hall and Louise Vork) M.; m. Rowena Stetson, Sept. 27, 1946; chil-ren: Carla, Andrew. B.S., U. Calif.-Berkeley, 1937, h.D., 1940. Instr. U. Rochester Sch. Medicine, 1940-3; researcher U. Copenhagen, Naples, Italy, 1947-49; soc. prof. biophysics Purdue U., 1949-59; prof. bi-ɔhysics U. Md. Sch. Medicine, 1960-93; mem. corp. ermuda Biol. Lab., 1951-93; Mem. corp. Marine Biol. ab., Woods Hole, Mass., 1956-77; bd. sci. counselors at. Inst. Neurol. Diseases and Stroke, NIH, 1969-73. ditor: Ann. Rev. Biophysics and Bioengring., 1972-83; ditorial adv. bd.: Molecular Pharmacology, 1965-68, urrents in Modern Biology, 1966-72; editorial bd.: Sci, 950-53, Jour. Neurobiology, 1968-76, Jour. Gen. hysiology, 1968-93, Internat. Jour. Neurosci., 1970-75, ur. Neurosci. Research, 1975-93, Fedn. Proc., 1970-7, chmn., 1971-77. Served to maj. USAAF, 1943-46. ecipient 1978 Orden Andres Bello award Republic of enezuela; 1988 Orden Francisco de Miranda 1st Class, epublic of Venezuela. Fellow AAAS; mem. Am. hysiol. Soc., Biophys. Soc. (council 1968-71, mem. ıbls. com. 1968-93, chmn. 1968-70); mem. Am. Chem. ɔc., Soc. Gen. Physiologists (council 1976-78, chmn. ıbls. com. 1976-84, pres. 1980-81), N.Y. Acad. Sci., ɔc. Exptl. Biology and Medicine, Sigma Xi. Home: hestertown Md. Died Apr. 14, 1993; buried Eastern ıore Vet. Cemetery, Harlock, Md.

ɪULROONEY, CHARLES RICHARD, bishop; b. klyn., Jan. 13, 1906; s. Patrick and Katherine (Gib-ɔns) M. Student, Cathedral Coll., Bklyn., 1921-24; .A., St. Mary's Sem., Balt., 1926; M.A., S.T.B., Cath. . Am., 1930; Ph.D., St. John's U., 1942; LL.D., St. rancis Coll., Bklyn., 1959. Ordained priest Roman ath. Ch., 1930; mem. staff Cathedral Coll., 1932-59, ctor, 1952-59; pres. Cathedral Coll. of Immaculate onception, Bklyn., 1952-59; pastor St. Jerome's Ch., klyn., 1959-72; consecrated bishop Our Lady of erpetual Help Basilica, 1959; auxiliary to bishop of klyn., 1959-81; also titular bishop of Valentiniana. ome: Queens Village N.Y. Died Aug. 5, 1989.

ɪUNFORD, DILLARD, manufacturing company ex-ecutive; b. Cartersville, Ga., May 13, 1918; s. Robert ms and Katherine (Aubrey) M.; m. Danne Brokaw; ildren: Dillard (dec.), Page Shepherd, Mary Aubrey, obert Davis, Henry Allan. BS in Mech. Engring, Ga. st. Tech., 1939. Founder The Munford Co., Atlanta, 946, Munford Do-It-Yourself Store, Atlanta, 1952; es., chief exec. officer The Munford Co., Atlanta, 962; chmn. bd., chief exec. officer Munford Inc. ormerly Atlantic Co.), Atlanta, 1968-93, Leewards reative Crafts subs. Munford Inc., 1985-93; dir. Blount ıc., Garden Svcs. Co., Callaway Gardens and Callaway ound. of Pine Mountains (Ga.). Columnist Marietta aily Jour., The Northside Neighbor, 26 other suburban eeklies. Trustee Ida Cason Callaway Found., Atlanta, orris Brown Coll., LaGrange Coll., Southeastern egal Found., Gannett Found.; mem. Republican Nat. ın. Com.; dir. Manhattan Inst. for Policy Rsch.; bd. ɔvs. 11 Alive Community Svc. Awards. Served to ıpt. AUS, 1942-46. Mem. Young Pres.'s Orgn. (past ternat. pres.), Chief Execs. Forum (past dir.), NAM ast v.p., dir., mem. exec. com.), Atlanta C. of C. (past r.), Homosassa Fishing Club, Piedmont Driving Club, apital City Club, Commerce Club, River Club N.Y.C.), Peachtree Golf, Annabels Club (London), artersville Country Club, Wildcat Cliffs Club (High-nds, N.C.), Rotary, Sigma Alpha Epsilon. Methodist. lubs: Rotary, Piedmont Driving, Capital City, Com-erce; River (N.Y.C.); Peachtree Golf; Annabels ondon); Cartersville Country; Wildcat Cliffs (High-nds, N.C.). Home: Atlanta Ga. Died Sept. 15, 1993.

ɪUÑOZ DUQUE, ANIBAL CARDINAL, archbishop Bogoté; b. Santa Rosa de Osos, Columbia, Oct. 3, 908. Ordained priest Roman Catholic Ch., 1933; shop of Soccoro y San Gil, 1951; bishop of Bu-aramanga, 1952-59; archbishop of Nueva Pamplona, 959-68; titular archbishop of Cariana, also coadjutor chbishop of Bogoté, 1968-72; archbishop of Bogoté, om 1972, now archbishop emeritus; elevated to Sacred oll. of Cardinals, 1973; titlar ch. St. Bartholomew's; il. vicar; mem. Congregation of Sacraments and Divine Vorship, Commn. Revision Code of Canon Law. Died ın. 15, 1987. Home: Bogoté Colombia

ɪUÑOZ VEGA, PABLO CARDINAL, retired chbishop; b. Mira, del Carchi, Ecuador, May 23, 1903; Antonio Muñoz and Josefa Vega; B.Humanities and lassics, Colegio Loyola, Quito, 1922; Filosofía y iencias, Colegio Máximo de San Ignacio, Quito, 1927; .Filosofía, Facultad de Teologia en Oña, Spain, 1931; icencia y Grado Doctoral de Magister Aggregatus, regoriana U., Rome, 1938. Ordained priest Roman ath. Ch., 1933; prof. philosophy Gregoriana U., 1938-5, prof. theology, 1945-50; rector Pontificio Colegio io-Latino-Americano, 1955-57; rector Pontifical regorian U., Rome, 1957-64; titular bishop of Ceramo, 1964-67; archbishop of Quito, 1967-86; elevated to Sacred Coll. of Cardinals, 1969; mem. Sacred Congregation Cath. Edn., Sacred Congregation Religious Life. Author: Introducción a la síntesis de San Agustín, 1945; Causalidad filosófica y determinismo científico, 1946; El estudio del hombre como introducción al problema de o sobrenatural, 1948; Los Problemas de la experiencia mística a la luz del pensamiento agustiniano en Augustinus Magister, 1954; Fe e inteligencia en los orígenes de la ciencia moderna, 1965; Fe y Politica, 1986, Fe y Pensamiento moderno, 1987, Hambre de Dios y Hambre de pan, problema central de la Teología de la liberación, 1987, Nuestra fe en la Eucaristía, 1988, La interpretación filosófica del determinismo científico, de Galileo a Max Planck, 1988.

MUNRO, HAMISH NISBET, biochemist, educator; b. Edinburgh, Scotland, July 3, 1915; came to U.S., 1966, naturalized, 1973; s. Donald and Margaret (Nisbet) M.; m. Edith E. Little, Apr. 5, 1946 (dec. 1987); children: Joan Bruce, Colin Scott, Andrew Fraser, John Michael. B.Sc., U. Glasgow, Scotland, 1936, M.B., 1939, D.Sc., 1956; M.D. with honors, U. Glasgow, 1983; Docteur honoris causa, U. Nancy, France, 1982. Physician, pathologist Victoria Infirmary, Glasgow, 1939-45; lectr. physiology U. Glasgow, 1946-47, sr. lectr., reader biochemistry, 1948-63, prof. biochemistry, 1964-66; prof. physiol. chemistry MIT, Cambridge, 1966-90; prof. medicine and of nutrition Tufts U., Boston, 1979-94; dir. USDA Human Nutrition Research Center on Aging, Tufts U., Boston, 1979-84, sr. scientist, 1984-94. Editor: Mammalian Protein Metabolism, vols. 1-4, 1964-70, Nutrition, Aging and the Elderly, 1989; contbr. articles in field of protein metabolism, molecular biology of iron storage to profl. jours. Recipient Osborn Mendel award Am. Inst. Nutrition, 1968, Borden award, 1978; Bristol-Myers award for disting. achievement in nutrition research, 1981, Rank prize for significant advances in nutrition, 1982, Corson medal of Franklin Inst. Phila., 1988; named to Agr. Research Service Sci. Hall of Fame, 1988. Fellow Royal Soc. Edinburgh, Am. Acad. Arts and Scis., Royal Coll. Physicians London (hon.); mem. Nat. Acad. Sci. U.S., Am. Soc. Biol. Chemists, Am. Inst. Nutrition (pres. 1978-79), Brit. Biochem. Soc. Presbyterian. Home: Glasgow Scotland Died Oct. 28, 1994.

MUNRO, SANFORD STERLING, JR., investment banking company executive; b. Madison, Wis., Mar. 2, 1932; s. Sanford Sterling and Dorothea Irene (Spears) M.; m. Valerie Gene Halbert, Apr. 4, 1956; children: Sanford Sterling, Margaret, Mary, Elizabeth, Peter, Matthew, Andrew. BA, George Washington U., 1957. Mem. profl. staff U.S. Senate, Washington, 1953-61; adminstrv. asst. U.S. Senator Henry M. Jackson, 1961-75; chief of staff Jackson for Pres. Com., 1975-76; govtl. affairs cons. Wenatchee, Wash., 1977; adminstr. Bonneville Power Adminstrn., U.S. Dept. Energy, Portland, Oreg., 1978-81; v.p., nat. dir. pub. power John Nuveen & Co., Inc., Seattle and Chgo., 1981-92; bd. dirs. Cen. Wash. Bank, Wenatchee. Bd. dirs. U.S. nat. com. World Energy Conf.; chmn. U.S. Entity for Columbia River Treaty; mem. Pacific N.W. River Basins Commn., 1978-81; trustee Cen. Wash. U., 1977-83, 85-92, chmn. bd. 1988-90; v.p. Henry M. Jackson Found. With U.S. Army, 1952-53. Mem. Electric Power Rsch. Inst. (vice-chmn. bd. 1978-81), Electric Club Oreg. Democrat. Episcopalian. Clubs: Portland City, Wash. Athletic, Wenatchee Swim and Tennis. Home: Wenatchee Wash. Died Mar. 9, 1992; buried Evergreen Cemetery, Wenatchee, Wash.

MURPHEY, ELWOOD, retired financial service executive; b. Berkeley, Calif., Oct. 9, 1909; s. John Douglass and Clara (Donnel) M.; m. Marjorie Louise Smith, Feb. 14, 1936; children: Barry Thane, Jay Douglass. A.B., U. Calif. at Berkeley, 1930, J.D., 1933. Bar: Calif. 1933. Dep. dist. atty. El Dorado County, Calif., 1933-35; practiced in Oakland, Calif., 1935-60; sec., v.p. law, sr. v.p. ISI Corp., San Francisco, 1960-67, pres., 1967-70, chmn. exec. com., 1970-74, vice chmn. bd., 1974-77, chmn. bd., 1977-86; chmn. bd. ISI Trust Fund, 1967-86; cons. Sigma Mgmt. Svcs., Inc., Wilmington, Del., 1987; inactive mem. State Bar Calif.; inactive mem., pres. Alameda County Bar Assn., 1955. Home: Kensington Calif. Died Jan. 5, 1993.

MURPHY, EDWARD JOSEPH, law educator; b. Springfield, Ill., July 16, 1927; s. Martin J. and Linda A. (Pihlaja) M.; m. Mary Ann Hansen, June 19, 1954; children: Ann, Martin, James, John, Mary, Thomas, Patrick, Michael, Stephen. BS, U. Ill., 1949, LLB, 1951. Assoc. Graham & Graham, Springfield, 1951-54; law clk. Justice Harry B. Hershey, Springfield, 1954-57; assoc. prof. U. Notre Dame (Ind.) Law Sch., 1957-65, prof., 1965-75, acting dean, 1971, Thomas J. White prof., 1975-79, John N. Matthews prof., 1979-95. Author: Life to the Full, 1978, In Your Justice, 1982; co-author: Studies in Contract Law, 1970, 4th edit. 1991, Sales and Credit Transactions Handbook, 1985. With U.S. Army, 1946-47. Roman Catholic. Died July 24, 1995.

MURPHY, FRANKLIN DAVID, physician, educator, publisher; b. Kansas City, Mo., Jan. 29, 1916; s. Franklin E. and Cordelia (Brown) M.; m. Judith Joyce Harris, Dec. 28, 1940; children: Joyce Murphy Dickey, Martha (Mrs. Craig Crockwell), Carolyn (Mrs. Ross Speer), Franklin. A.B., U. Kans., 1936; M.D., U. Pa., 1941. Diplomate: Am. Bd. Internal Medicine. Intern Hosp. U. Pa., 1941-42, instr., 1942-44; instr. medicine U. Kans., 1946-48, dean Sch. Medicine, assoc. prof. medicine, 1948-51, chancellor, 1951-60; chancellor UCLA, 1960-68; chmn. bd., CEO Times Mirror Co., 1968-81, chmn. exec. com., 1981-86; trustee emeritus J. Paul Getty Trust; dir. emeritus Times-Mirror Co. Chmn. Kress Found.; trustee emeritus Nat. Gallery of Art; trustee L.A. County Mus. Art. Capt. AUS, 1944-46. Named One of Ten Outstanding Young Men U.S. Jr. C. of C., 1949; recipient Outstanding Civilian Service award U.S. Army, 1967. Fellow ACP; mem. Phi Beta Kappa, Sigma Xi, Alpha Omega Alpha, Beta Theta Pi, Nu Sigma Nu. Episcopalian. Home: Beverly Hills Calif. Died June 16, 1994; buried Mt. Wash. Cemetery, Kansas City, Mo.

MURPHY, JAMES ALLEN, magazine editor; b. North Platte, Nebr., Aug. 2, 1938; s. Ralph J. and Ruth (Scott) M.; m. Sarah Colby, 1957 (div. 1969); children: Diana Lynne, Jody Ann. BArch, U. Nebr., 1964. Registered architect, Conn. Designer Clark Enersen Ptnrs., Lincoln, Nebr., 1962-64; designer, architect SMS Partnership, Stamford, Conn., 1964-70; profession and industry editor Progressive Architecture, Stamford, 1970-93. Designer schs, coll. and religious bldgs. Mem. profl. adv. com. Coll. Architecture, U. Nebr., 1982-93, adv. coun. Vt. Tech. Sch., Randolph, 1973-80. C0-recipient Neal award Am. Bus. Press., N.Y., 1971, cert. of merit, 1976; Regents scholar U. Nebr., 1957, Margaret Duboard scholar, U. Nebr., 1957, Clark and Enersen scholar, U. Nebr., 1957. Fellow AIA; mem. Nebr. Soc. N.Y. Home: Westport Conn. Died May 16, 1993.

MURPHY, JAMES EMMETT, lawyer, former state legislator; b. Laredo, Mo., Nov. 6, 1910; s. John F. and Ida (Warren) M.; m. Sylvia J. Brassett, May 16, 1944; 1 child, Mary Pat. A.B., William Jewell Coll., 1935; LL.B., George Washington U., 1939. Bar: Mo. bar 1939, Mont. bar 1946. Firm Murphy, Robinson, Heckathorn & Phillips.; Dir. emeritus First Interstate Bank of Kalispell N.A. Author: Half Interest in a Silver Dollar. Mem. Columbia Interstate Compact Commn., 1952-58, chmn. legal com., 1956-58; Mem. Mo. Ho. of Reps., 1939-41; mem. Mont. Ho. of Reps., 1967-73, chmn. judiciary com.; mem. Rep. Nat. Com. for Mont., 1959-72; Mem. Nat. Water Commn.; Trustee Griffis Scholarship Fund, Conrad Mansion. Served with AUS, 1941-46. Mem. N.W. Mont. Bar Assn. (pres. 1951-53), Sigma Nu. Lutheran (v.p.). Club: Mason (32 deg., Shriner). Home: Kalispell Mont. Deceased.

MURPHY, OWEN FRANCIS, public relations executive; b. Long Beach, Calif., Feb. 14, 1927; s. Owen Myers and Gladys Delia (Brace) M.; m. Carolyn Freeman Bugbee, Aug. 8, 1948. BA in Psychology, UCLA, 1947. With Chevron U.S.A. Inc., 1947-87, pub. relations specialist, San Francisco, 1969-71, pub. relations counsel, 1971-72, pub. affairs mgr., Portland, Oreg., 1972-76, Denver, 1977-85, regional v.p. So. Calif., Los Angeles, 1985-87. Pres. emeritus Pres.'s Leadership Class, U. Colo.-Boulder; bd. dirs. Wyo. 4-H Found., Laramie, Colo. Council on Econ. Edn., Boulder. Mem. Greater Los Angeles Visitors and Conv. Bur., Los Angeles chpt. ARC, numerous so. Calif., Colo. and Wyo. non-profit groups. Mem. Overthrust Indsl. Assn. (pres. 1980-87, bd. dirs.), Rocky Mountain Oil and Gas Assn. (dir. 1980-84), Colo. Petroleum Assn. (pres. 1980-84), Wyo. Assn. Vols. in Mgmt. (bd. dirs., chmn. 1985-87), Los Angeles Area C. of C., U. So. Calif. bd. councilors, sch. pub. adminstrn. Republican. Roman Catholic. Died Dec. 7, 1987. Home: Los Angeles Calif.

MURPHY, RICHARD, screenwriter, director; b. Boston; s. John Donahoe and May (Castello) M.; m. Katherine Mauss, Nov. 17, 1942; children: John D. II, Edward Michael. Student, Newman Sch., Lakewood, N.J., 1928-32; A.B., Williams Coll., 1936. Staff writer Lit. Digest, 1936-37; screen writer, 1937-41; contract writer 20th Century Fox, 1945-54; with Columbia Picture Corp., 1954-56; contract writer, dir. 20th Century Fox, 1956-59, writer, dir., 1963-72; writer dir. Columbia Pictures, 1959-62; ltd. ptnr. Daniel Reeves Co., investment brokers, Los Angeles, 1972-83; pres. Cinecom World Enterprises Ltd., 16mm films, Beverly Hills, Calif., 1973-83; mem. exec. bd. Screen Writers Guild, 1949-51, 1st v.p., 1952; mem. exec. bd., bd. dirs. Motion Picture Relief, 1953-93. Author: screenplays Boomerang, 1947, Deep Waters, 1948, Cry of the City, 1948, Panic in the Streets, 1950, U.S.S. Teakettle, 1951, Les Miserables, 1952, The Desert Rats, 1953, Broken Lance, 1954, Compulsion, 1959; author, dir.: Three Stripes in the Sun, 1955, Wackiest Ship in the Army, 1961; adaption: The Last Angry Man, 1960; creator: TV series Our Man Higgins, 1962, Felony Squad, 1966-69; screenplay The Kidnapping of the President, 1980. Served to capt. AUS, 1942-45. Mem. Motion Picture Arts and Scis. Acad. (bd. govs., treas. 1964-68), Writers Guild Am. (treas. 1967-69 Valentine Davies award, pres. screen br. 1969-71), Chi Psi. Clubs: Players (N.Y.), Williams (N.Y.); Beverly Hills Tennis (pres.) (1972-74, 76-78). Home: Beverly Hills Calif. Died May, 1993.

MURPHY, WILLIAM BEVERLY, consumer products executive; b. Appleton, Wis., June 17, 1907; s. S.W. and Hilma (Anderson) M.; m. Helen Brennan, May 28,

1930; children: Robert Blair, Ann Pollock, John Huston, Eric Stevens. B.S. in Chem. Engring., U. Wis., 1928; L.H.D., Pa. Mil. Coll., 1960; LL.D., Lawrence U., 1954, U. Wis., 1963, St. Joseph's Coll., 1965, Rutgers U., 1973; Sc.D., Ursinus Coll., 1970; Engring.D., Drexel U., 1970. Exec. v.p. A.C. Nielsen Co., Chgo., 1928-38; with Campbell Soup Co., 1938-72, exec. v.p., 1949, dir., 1950-80, pres., chief exec. officer, 1953-72; dir. Merck & Co., Inc., 1959-80, AT&T, 1961-78, Internat. Paper Co., 1969-80. Author: Fifty Active Years (Gantt medal 1979). Chmn. Radio Free Europe Fund, 1960-61, Nutrition Found., 1964-65, Bus. Council, 1965-66, Bus. Roundtable, 1972-73; mem. Pub. Adv. Com. on U.S. Trade Policy, Pres.'s Adv. Com. on Labor-Mgmt. Policy, 1964-68, Commn. on Food and Fiber, 1966-67, Commn. on Postal Orgn., 1967-68; mem. hazard adv. com. EPA, 1971-72; hon. trustee Phila. Mus. Art, chmn. capital devel. campaign, 1971-74; chmn. pub. edn. com. Greater Phila. Movement, 1973-74; hon. trustee Acad. Natural Scis. of Phila.; life mem. exec. com. MIT, 1966-72, 76-82, co-chmn. steering com. leadership campaign, 1976-80; life mem. Wis. Alumni Research Found., pres., 1982-86; bd. dirs. Phila. Soc. Promoting Agr., 1981-94, pres., 1985-86. Served WPB, 1942-45. Decorated Presdl. medal for Merit, 1946. Mem. Delta Upsilon, Tau Beta Pi. Republican. Presbyterian. Clubs: Merion Cricket, Philadelphia. Home: Gladwyne Pa. Died May 29, 1994.

MURRAY, EDWARD JAMES, English language educator; b. Bklyn., Apr. 8, 1928; s. Edward James and Catherine Cecilia (Henn) M.; m. Margaret Lisa DeSantis, Sept. 5, 1954 (dec. Aug. 1974); children: Michael, Lisa, Stephen, Monica, Jeanette. BA, Youngstown U., 1962; PhD, U. So. Calif., L.A., 1966. Assoc. prof. English Western Ill. U., Macomb, 1965-68; prof. English and film studies SUNY, Brockport, N.Y., from 1968; vis. prof. Loughborough (England) U., 1985-86. Author: Arthur Miller, Dramatist, 1967, Clifford Odets, 1968, The Cinematic Imagination, 1972, Nine American Film Critics, 1975, Fellini the Artist, 1976, 85, Ten Film Classics, 1978. Sgt. U.S. Army, 1951-53, Korea. Woodrow Wilson fellow Nat. Woodrow Wilson Found., 1962. Mem. United Univ. Professions, N.Y. United Tchrs. Home: Brockport N.Y. Home: North Cohocton N.Y. Deceased.

MURRAY, THOMAS FRANCIS, real estate executive; b. Oxford, Iowa, Oct. 27, 1910; s. Thomas F. and Fern (Hummer) M.; m. Margaret R. Regan, Nov. 11, 1939; children: William R., Robert C., James M. B.S. in Elec. Engring., U. Iowa, 1932. With United Light & Power Engring. and Constrn. Co., 1933-41; with Equitable Life Assurance Soc. U.S., 1946-75, exec. v.p., chief investment officer, chmn. finance com., mem. exec. com., 1973-75, also dir., 1971-75; trustee Franklin Savs. Bank, N.Y.C., 1965-82; trustee, chmn. Equitable Life Mortgage and Realty Investors, 1970-76; dir. Olentangy Mgmt. Co., 1977-82; chmn. Equico Securities, Inc., 1971-75, Equico Lessors, Inc., 1974-75; dir. The Bank of Tokyo Trust Co., 1978-81; dir. Am. Continental Properties, Inc., 1978-95, pres., 1978-82, chmn., 1982-95; dir. N.Y.C. Pub. Devel. Corp., 1973-80, chmn., 1977-79; dir. Allied Stores Corp., 1978-83, Rockefeller Ctr., Inc., 1976-82, PaineWebber Cash Fund, 1978-95, PaineWebber Master Series Inc., 1987-95, Search Am. Corp., 1982-86, Prudential Realty Trust, 1985-95; trustee PaineWebber Tax Exempt Series, 1987-95. Mem. exec. bd. Hutchinson River council Boy Scouts Am., 1960-73, pres., 1971-73; mem. exec. bd. Westchester-Putnam council, 1973-80, mem. adv. council, 1980-95; trustee Urban Land Inst., 1969-95, treas., 1970-73, 1st v.p., 1973-74, pres., 1975-77. Served to lt. col. C.E. AUS, 1941-46. Decorated Legion of Merit. Mem. Real Estate Bd. N.Y., N.Y. Soc. Security Analysts, Am. Soc. Real Estate Counselors, Newcomen Soc., C. of C. U.S.A. (dir. 1974-78). Clubs: University, Economic (N.Y.C.); Leewood Golf (Eastchester, N.Y.) (pres. 1965-67), The Country Club of Naples, Fla. Home: Bronxville N.Y. Died Oct. 10, 1995.

MURRAY, WILLIAM DANIEL, federal judge; b. Butte, Mont., Nov. 20, 1908; s. James E. and Viola E (Horgan) M.; m. Lulu Ann MacDonald, Aug. 24, 1938; children: William Daniel, Gael Ann, Timothy. B.S., Georgetown U., 1932; LL.B., U. Mont., 1936, LL.D. (hon.), 1961. Bar: Admitted Mont. bar 1936. Since practiced in Butte; partner firm of Emigh & Murray, 1936-94; asst. U.S. atty., Butte, 1938-42; U.S. Dist judge Dist. Mont., 1949-94, sr. U.S. dist. judge., 1994. Former chmn. bd. visitors sch. law U. Mont.; mem. bd. regents Gonzaga U.; bd. devel. Georgetown U. Served as lt. UNR, 1942-45. Recipient Barromeo award Carroll Coll., 1960; DeSmet medal Gonzaga U., 1967. Mem. Am., Mont., Silver Bow County bar assns., Bar Assn. D.C. Democrat. Roman Catholic. Home: Butte Mont. Died Oct. 4, 1994.

MUSKIE, EDMUND SIXTUS, lawyer, former secretary of state, former senator; b. Rumford, Maine, Mar. 28, 1914; s. Stephen and Josephine (Czarnecki) M.; m. Jane Frances Gray, May 29, 1948; children—Stephen O., Ellen Muskie Allen, Melinda Muskie Stanton, Martha, Edmund Sixtus. A.B. cum laude, Bates Coll., 1936; LL.B., Cornell U., 1939; hon. degrees, U. N.B., Middlebury Coll., St. Anselm's Coll., William and Mary Coll., U. Md., Alliance Coll., U. N.H., Northeastern U., John Carroll U., Providence Coll., Boston U., Syracuse U., U. Maine, Suffolk U., Bowdoin Coll., Colby Coll., Lafayette Coll., U. Notre Dame, Hanover Coll., George Washington U., U. Buffalo, Nasson Coll., Husson Coll. Bar: Mass. 1939, Maine 1940, U.S. Dist. Ct 1941, N.Y. State 1981, U.S. Supreme Ct. 1981. Practice law Waterville, Maine, 1940, 45-55; gov. of Maine, 1955-59, U.S. senator from Maine, 1959-80; chmn. senate budget com., mem. fgn. relations com., U.S. Senate, chmn. subcom. on intergovtl. relations of senate govt. affairs com., subcom. environ. pollution of environment and pub. works com., subcom. on arms control, asst. majority whip; sec. of state of U.S., 1980-81; ptnr. Chadbourne & Parke, Washington, 1982-96; former mem. Adv. Commn. Intergovtl. Relations; nat. exec. dir. Amvets, 1951; dist. dir. OPS, Maine, 1951-52; Maine chmn. citizens com. for Hoover report, 1950; chmn. Roosevelt Campobello Internat. Park Commn. Author: Journeys, 1972; co-author (with McGeorge Bundy) Presidential Promises and Performances, 1980. Mem. Maine Ho. of Reps., 1948-51, Democratic floor leader, 1949-51; mem. Dem. Nat. Com., 1952-55, Dem. candidate for vice pres. U.S., 1968. Served to lt. USNR, 1942-45. Recipient Laetare medal Notre Dame U., 1981, Presdl. Medal of Freedom, 1981, Former Mems. Congress Disting. Service award, 1981. Mem. Maine Bar Assn., Kennebec County Bar Assn., Waterville Bar Assn., Am. Legion, VFW, Amvets, Phi Beta Kappa, Phi Alpha Delta. Home: Washington D.C. Died March 26, 1996.

MUSSELMAN, PETER ROGERS, university official; b. Balt., Mar. 29, 1928; s. J. Rogers and Paula (Wilson) M. Grad., Phillips Exeter Acad., 1945; B.A., Harvard U., 1949; J.D., Cleve. Marshall Law Sch., 1957. Chartered fin. analyst. With Union Commerce Bank, Cleve., 1949-69; v.p., sec. Union Commerce Bank, 1962-69; sec.-treas. Union Commerce Bank (Union Properities div.), 1963-69; univ. v.p. Case Western Res. U., Cleve., 1969—; dir. Aero Distbrs., Inc., Housing Assocs.; v.p. Village Inc.; trustee CleveTrust Realty Investors; pres. Univ. Circle Research Center Corp., Lorain Dock Co.; v.p. Med. Center Co., 1986-87. Past pres. Cuyahoga County Reward Commn.; v.p. Citizens League; bd. dirs., treas. Cleve. Music Sch. Settlement, 1968-76, trustee, 1968-81; past sec.-treas. Cleve. Clearing House Assn.; chmn. investment com., mem. fin. com. YMCA; mem. finance com. Fedn. Community Planning, Benjamin Rose Inst.; trustee Northeastern Ohio Productivity Improvement Center, John Huntington Fund for Edn. Served with U.S. Army, 1950-52. Life fellow Western Res. Hist. Soc., Cleve. Mus. Art; mem. Inst. Fin. Analysts, Harvard, Hawken Sch., Phillips Exeter alumni assns., Cleve. Soc. Security Analysts (past pres.), Cleve. Bar Assn., Western Res. Archtl. Historians, Nat. Soc. Lit. and Arts. Club: Rowfant. Home: Cleveland Ohio

MYERS, ROBERT LEE, JR., lawyer, banker; b. Camp Hill, Pa., Sept. 15, 1897; s. Robert Lee and Joanna (Bowman) M.; m. Evelyn M. Mentzer, Ont. 16, 1926; children: Robert Lee III, Edward H., Philip N., Virginia E. Myers Meloy. A.B., Dickinson Coll., 1917, M.A., 1921, LL.B., 1921. Bar: Pa. 1921, U.S. Supreme Ct. 1953. Prof. sci., athletic coach Shippensburg (Pa.) State Coll., 1918; prof. law Dickinson Sch. Law, 1923-32; practice law Lemoyne, 1921-80; chmn. Lemoyne Trust Co., 1963-65; chmn. exec. com. Dauphin Deposit Trust Co., 1965-70; dep. atty. gen. Pa., 1935; sec. to Gov. Pa., 1936; chmn. Pa. Unemployment Bd. Rev., 1936-38; sec. banking Pa., 1955-63. Author: (with F.S. Reese) Patton's Commonpleas Practice, 1926. Democratic candidate Pa. Superior Ct., 1935; Bd. dirs. Harrisburg Polyclinic Hosp., 1957-78. Served with Signal Corps, U.S. Army, 1918. Recipient citation of merit Dickinson Sch. Law, 1960. Mem. Nat. Assn. State Bank Suprs. (past pres.), Phi Beta Kappa, Sigma Alpha Epsilon. Presbyterian. Club: Masons. Home: Mechanicsburg Pa. Deceased.

MYHRBECK, SVEN GUNNAR, advertising executive, communications consultant; b. Smaland, Sweden, Oct. 24, 1921; came to U.S., 1923, naturalized, 1929; s. John Waldemar and Anna Kristina (Jorgenson) M.; m. Karen Louise Smith; children: Althea Leslie, Sven Gunnar, Charles John, Kristina May. B.S., M.S. in Mech. Engring, Northeastern U., 1943; postgrad., U.S. Naval Acad., 1943, U. Mich., 1947, Mass. Inst. Tech., 1949. Registered profl. engr., Mass. Project engr. Jackson & Moreland, Boston, 1946-47; founder S. Gunnar Myrbeck & Co., Inc. (indsl. advt.), Norwell, Mass., 1947-87; pres. Tudor II North, Atlantis, Fla.; gen. ptnr. Viking Lands. Author: Dynamic Technical Proposals. Chmn. budget com. Quincy United Fund, 1957-60. Served to lt. comdr. submarines USNR, World War II. Mem. ASME, Am. Bonanza Soc. (charter). Club: Mason (32 deg.). Home: Scituate Mass. Deceased.

MYRER, ANTON OLMSTEAD, author; b. Worcester, Mass., Nov. 3, 1922; s. Raymond Lewis and Angele (Cormack) M.; m. Patricia McFarland Schartle, May 1, 1970. A.B. magna cum laude, Harvard U., 1944. Author: Evil Under the Sun, 1951, The Big War; movie In Love and War, 1957, The Violent Shore, 1962, The Intruder, 1965, Once an Eagle (Book of Month Club and Readers Digest Book Club selection 1968, basis NBC TV series Bestsellers 1977), 1968, The Tiger Waits, 1973, The Last Convertible (Lit. Guild and Readers Digest Book Club selection; NBC-TV miniseries 1979), 1978; A Green Desire, 1982 (main selection of Lit.
Guild). Served with USMCR, 1942-45, PTO. Mer
Authors Guild, PEN, Authors League Am., Signet Soc
Home: Saugerties N.Y. Died Jan. 19, 1996.

NABIYEV, RAKHMAN NABIEVICH, governme
leader; b. 1930. Grad., Tashkent Inst. of Irrigation ar
Mech. Agr., 1954. Chief engr. machine and tractor sta
1954-55, 56-58; dir. maintenance engring. sta., 1959-6
mem. staff Ministry Agr., Tadzhik, Soviet Sociali
Republic, 1960-61, Cen. Com., Tadzhik CP, 1961-6
64-71, Cen. Asian Bur Cen. Com., Communist Par
Soviet Union, 1963-64; min. agr. Tadzhik Sovi
Socialist Republic, 1971-73, min. fgn. affairs, 1973-8
chmn. coun. min., 1973-82; mem. Bur., 1973-93; mer
cen. auditing com. Communist Party Soviet Unio
1976-93; 1st sec. cen. com. Tadzhik Communist Part
1982-93; dep. to USSR Supr. Soviet, 1974-93; pre
Dushanbe, Tadzhikistan, 1992-93. Home: Dushan
Tadzhikistan Died Apr. 1993.

NAGHDI, PAUL MANSOUR, mechanical engineerin
educator; b. Tehran, Iran, Mar. 29, 1924; came to U.S
1944, naturalized, 1948; s. G. H. and A. (Momtaz) N
m. Patricia Spear, Sept. 6, 1947 (dec. Mar. 15, 197
children: Stephen, Suzanne, Sondra. B.S., Cornell U
1946; M.S., U. Mich., 1948, Ph.D., 1951; DSc. (ho
causa), Nat. U. of Ireland, Dublin, 1987; Doctor hono
causa, U. Louvain, Belgium, 1992. From instr. to pro
engring. mechanics U. Mich., 1949-58; prof. engring. sc
U. Calif., Berkeley, 1958-94, chmn. div. appli
mechanics, 1964-69, faculty rsch. lectr., 1994; Mill
prof. Miller Inst. Basic Sci., 1963-64, 71-72, Rosco an
Elizabeth Hughes chair in mech. engring., 1991-94; con
theoretical and applied mechanics, 1953-94; Mem. U.
Nat. Com. on Theoretical and Applied Mechanic
1972-84, chmn., 1979-80; mem. gen. assembly Interna
Union Theoretical and Applied Mechanics, 1978-84
Served with AUS, 1946-47. Recipient Disting. Facul
award U. Mich., 1956, George Westinghouse awa
Am. Soc. Engring. Edn., 1962; Guggenheim fello
1958. Fellow ASME (hon. mem., chmn. appli
mechanics div. 1971-72, mem. com. on honors 1986-9
also chmn. 1991-94, Timoshenko medal 1980), Acou
tical Soc. Am., Soc. Engring. Sci. (bd. dirs. 1963-7
A.C. Eringen medal 1986); mem. NAE, Soc. Rheolog
Sigma Xi. Home: Berkeley Calif. Died July 9, 199
cremated; ashes scattered at sea.

NAGLER, ALOIS MARIA, educator, theatre historia
b. Graz, Austria, Sept. 14, 1907; came to U.S., 193
naturalized, 1944; s. Alois and Auguste (Schupp) N.; r
Erna Scheinberger, Aug. 19, 1933. Dr.phil., U. Gra
1930; M.A. (hon.), Yale, 1960. Lit. editor, theatre cri
for daily paper Vienna, Austria, 1932-38; supr. Cros
Cultural Survey, Intelligence Office, U.S. Navy, 1941-4
mem. faculty Yale, 1946-93, Henry McCormick pro
dramatic history, 1965-93; vis. prof. Columbia, 1960-6
City U. N.Y., 1968-69. Author: Hebbel und die Musi
1928, Sources of Theatrical History, 1952, Shakespeare
Stage, 1958, Theatre Festivals of the Medici, 1964, T
Medieval Religious Stage, 1976, Malaise in der Ope
1980, Misdirection, 1980. Recipient Cross Honor Au
trian Republic, 1967. Mem. Internat. Fedn. Theat
Research (pres. 1959-63), Am. Soc. Theatre Resear
(chmn. 1960-63), Austrian Acad. Arts and Scis. Hom
New Haven Conn. Died Apr. 22, 1993.

NAGY, BARTHOLOMEW STEPHEN, geochemis
educator; b. Budapest, Hungary, May 11, 1927; came
U.S., 1948, naturalized, 1955; s. Stephen and Ma
(Mueller) N.; m. Marjorie Lois Bibey, Feb. 1, 1952;
child, Erika Anne; m. Lois Anne Brach, Aug. 10, 196
1 child, Yvonne Maria. Student, Peter Pazmany U
Budapest, 1945-48; MA, Columbia U., 1950; PhD, P
State U., 1953. With Stanolind Oil & Gas Co., Tuls
1953-55; supr. geophys. research Cities Service Resear
& Devel. Co., Tulsa, 1955-57; assoc. prof. Fordham U
1957-65; vis. assoc. prof. U. Calif., San Diego, 1963-6
assoc. research geochemist, 1965-68; prof. geoscis.
Ariz., Tucson, 1968—; mem. adv. bd. Lunar Sci. Ins
1972; rsch. petroleum and organic geochemistry, x-r
crystallography and analytical chemistry, radioacti
waste containment, carbonaceous meteorites, ar
returned lunar samples; mem. steering com. nucle
waste mgmt. program French Atomic Energy Comm
and European Community, 1991—; chmn. U.S. worki
group internat. geol. correlation program Organics ar
Mineral Deposits, sponsored by UNESCO, 1993—
Author 3 books; contbr. articles in field.; exec. edit
Jour. Precambrian Research. Mem. Geochem. Sc
(counselor 1961-64), Am. Chem. Soc., Internat. Soc. f
Study of Origin of Life. Home: Tucson Ariz. Died No
11, 1995.

NANGLE, THOMAS ROCKWELL, lawyer; b. Ne
Haven, June 14, 1928; s. Benjamin Christie ar
Katharine Robb (Rawles) N.; m. Patricia Hamilt
Littlejohn, Sept. 15 , 1951 (div. 1968); m. Christia
Georgette DuPont, Dec. 14, 1968; children: Thom
Joseph, Emilie Katharine. B.A., Yale U., 1949; LL.
U. Va., 1952. Bar: N.Y. 1953. Assoc. Shearman
Sterling, N.Y.C., 1952-62, ptnr., from 1962. Ep
copalian. Clubs: City of London, Hurlingham. Hor
London Eng. Deceased.

**NASALLI ROCCA DI CORNELIANO, MAR
CARDINAL,** clergyman; b. Piacenza, Italy, Aug.
1903. Ordained priest Roman Catholic Ch., 1927; titu

rchbishop of Anzio, 1969; elevated to Sacred Coll. of ardinals, 1969; titular ch. St. John the Baptist; mem. ongregation of Sacraments and Divine Worship, Congregation Causes of Saints, Secretariat of Non-Believers. ome: Rome Italy

ASH, JOSEPH, discount retail chain company executive; b. 1890. With Gaylords Nat. Corp., Secaucus, .J., from 1933, pres., 1933-66, chmn. bd., from 1966, so dir.; chmn., dir. Towers Stores Inc. Deceased. ome: Secaucus N.J.

ASH, PAUL, academic administrator, consultant, lucator, author, editor; b. Newcastle upon Tyne, Eng.; ame to U.S., 1955, naturalized, 1966; s. William Arthur ad Elsie (Forbes) N.; m. Anne Steere, June 29, 1957; hildren: Christopher Forbes, Jennifer Anne. B.Sc. with onours, London Sch. Econs., 1949; teaching diploma, . London, 1950, acad. diploma in edn., 1952; student, IcGill U., 1952-53; M.Ed., U. Toronto, 1955; Ed.D., arvard, 1959. Tchr. elementary and secondary schs. psom, Kingston, and London, Eng., 1949-52; tchr. ower Can. Coll., Montreal, 1952-55; teaching fellow arvard, 1955-57; asst. prof. edn. Clark U., 1957-59, IcGill U., 1959-62; assoc. prof. Boston U., 1962-66, rof. edn., 1966-84, chmn. dept. humanistic and ehavioral studies, 1974-79, dir. div. humanistic, evelopmental and organizational studies, 1979-82; v.p. r acad. affairs R.I. Sch. Design, 1984-89; mem. faculty ternat. Coll., 1976-93; cons. editor edn. Random ouse, Inc., also Alfred Knopf, Inc., 1965-68, John Viley & Sons, Inc., 1968-76; profl. mem. Nat. Tng. abs. Inst. for Applied Behavorial Sci., 1970-93; mem. at. bd. consultants Nat. Endowment for Humanities, 974-84; cons. Harvard Semitic Mus., 1978-82, Digital quipment Corp., 1980-84; founder, pres. Synergetics ollaborative; vis. prof. edn. Harvard U., 1963-64, ummer, 1973, U. B.C., summer, 1965, U. Calif. at erkeley, summer 1972; Fulbright lectr. U. Chile, 1971; rof. in residence U. Calif. at Santa Barbara, 1971-72; ons. programs tchrs. disadvantaged youth U.S. Office dn., 1967; dir. Polaroid edn. project, 1979-87; spl. ons. to pres., R.I. Sch. Design, 1989-92; mem. faculty each for Am., summer 1990, dean, 1990-92, sr. dean, 993; vis. prof. Tufts U., 1990-91. Author: The Educated Man: Studies in the History of Educational hought, 1965, Culture and the State: Matthew Arnold ad Continental Education, 1966, Authority and reedom in Education: An Introduction to the hilosophy of Education, 1966, Models of Man: Explorations in the Western Educational Tradition, 1968, istory and Education: the Educational Uses of the ast, 1970, A Humanistic Approach to Performance-ased Teacher Education, 1973, Consultants' andbook, 1981; also articles.; Mem. editorial bd.: History Edn. Quar., 1966-80, Harvard Ednl. Rev., 1955-57. res. Civic Edn. Found., 1990—. Served as pilot RAF, 942-46. Mem. ACLU, Nat. Coun. for Nonprofit Bds. ssoc. 1990—), Northeastern Soc. Group sychotherapy, New Eng. Philosophy Edn. Soc. (pres. 967-68), Hist. Edn. Soc. (pres. 1968-69), Philosophy dn. Soc. (exec. bd. 1968-70), Am. Ednl. Studies Assn. xec. council 1968-69, pres. 1971-72), Comparative dn. Soc., Fellowship of Reconciliation. Mem. Soc. of riends. Home: Newton Mass. Died Nov. 12, 1993; uried Mt. Auburn Cemetery, Cambridge, Mass.

ATCHER, WILLIAM HUSTON, congressman; b. owling Green, KY, Sept. 11, 1909; s. J.M. and Blanche Hays) N.; m. Virginia Reardon, June 17, 1937; children: Celeste, Louise. A.B., Western Ky. State Coll., 930; LL.B., Ohio State U., 1933. Bar: Ky. 1934. Pvt. ractice Bowling Green, 1934—; Fed. conciliation ommr. Western Dist. Ky., 1936-37; atty. Warren Co., 937-49; commonwealth atty. 8th jud. dist., 1951-53; em. 83rd-103rd congresses from 2d Ky. Dist., 1953-4. Served as lt. USNR, 1942-45. Mem. Bowling Green ar Assn. (pres.), Am. Legion, Forty and Eight. emocrat. Clubs: Odd Fellow, Kiwanian. Home: owling Green Ky. Died Mar. 30, 1994.

ATHE, DENNIS GERHARDT, ranch executive; b. cobey, Mont., Dec. 12, 1938; s. Michael Henry and araida Sophia (Korf) N.; B.S., St. Benedicts Coll., Atchon, Kans., 1962; M.S., Creighton U., 1966; m. Della Mae Snyder, Dec. 28, 1970; children: Alycia, Michael. harm. detail man Lederle Labs., Am. Cyanamid Co., maha, 1962-64; clin. research coordinator Med. roducts div. 3M Co., St. Paul, 1967; farming, ranching, edstone, Mont., 1967-93; pres. Nathe Ranch Inc., 973-80 ; pres. Wanmdi Kinyan, Inc., 1981-93. Vice-hmn. Mont. Environ. Quality Council, 1977-79, chmn., 979-81 , public mem., 1981-83 ; Mont. State Rep., 977-81, 85-88; Mont. state senator, 1989-93; Mt. Wiche ommr., 1990-93; commr. Interstate Commn. Higher dn., 1990-93; chmn. Sheridan County Planning and nprovement Council, 1973-76; del. Economic Devel. ssn. Eastern Mont., 1973-76; chmn. Three Corners oundary Assn., 1976-77; Democratic Precinct committeeman, 1968-76; vice chmn. Coal Tax Oversight Com., 985-93; mem. Mont. Rural Area Devel. Com., 1976-93, Mont. Western Interstate Commn. Higher Edn.; alternate Mo. River Barge Transp. Com., 1980-93; mem. Gov.'s Groundwater Task Force, 1983-85; bd. suprs. heridan County Conservation Dist., 1969-78; chmn. astern Mont. Range Improvement Com., 1973-78; hmn. Sheridan County Republican Central Com., 1980-3; mem. Mont. Extension Adv. Council, 1980-82 , participant numerous other civic activities. Served with AUS, 1957-58. Mem. Soc. Range Mgmt., (chmn. Mont. Old West regional range program 1975-79), Durum Growers Assn., K.C. Republican. Roman Catholic. Home: Redstone Mt.

NAUMER, HELMUTH JACOB, museum administrator; b. Santa Fe, May 7, 1934; s. Helmuth and Tomee (Reuter) N.; m. Mary Ann Singleton, Sept. 3, 1957 (div. Feb. 1966); children: Karina Anne, Helmuth Karl; m. Carolyn Palmer, Oct. 9, 1966 (div. Nov. 1986); children: Kirsten Anne, Tatiana Elizabeth; m. Sybil Stewart, May 7, 1989. BA, U. N.Mex., 1957; postgrad., U. Minn., 1958. Mgr. Taos Ski Valley, N.Mex., 1958-59; archaeologist Town Creek Indian Mound, Mt. Gilead, N.C., 1959-60; dir. Charlotte Nature Mus., N.C., 1960-62; exec. dir. Fort Worth Mus. Sci. and History, 1962-76, Pacific Sci. Ctr., Seattle, 1976-79; exec. dir., pres. San Antonio Mus. Assn., 1979-86; pres. Mus. N.Mex. Found., 1986-87; officer cultural affairs State of N.Mex., 1987-94; chmn. print media sect. White House Conf. on Children, 1970-71; mem. panel Nat. Endowment for Arts, 1973-76, NEH, 1971-72, Smithsonian Conf. Mus. and Edn., Tex. Arts and Humanities Commn., Nat. Inst. Mus. Svcs., 1984-88; speaker Australian Mus. Assn.; mem. Commn. on Mus. for a New Century, 1982-84. Author: Of Mutual Respect and Other Things, 1977, rev., 1989; contbr. articles to profl. jours. Bd. dirs. High Frontier, 1978-85, 91-94, Dallas-Fort Worth Council Sci. Engring. Socs., 1971-73; internat. bd. trustees Turkish Mus., 1984; bd. trustees Inst. Mus. Svcs., 1988-94; trustees N.Mex. Performing Arts Ctr., 1989-94. Recipient Elsie M.B. Naumberg award Natural Sci. for Youth Found., 1968, Glenda Morgan award for excellence Tex. Hist. Commn., 1986. Mem. Am. Assn. Mus. (chmn. various coms., various offices 1960-94), Mt. Plains Mus. Assn. (regional rep.), Tex. Assn. Mus. (pres. 1969, 71), Art Mus. Assn. (bd. dirs.), Am. Assn. Youth Mus. (pres. 1969, 71), Tex. Inst. Small Mus. Democrat. Home: Santa Fe N.Mex. Died July 25, 1994; interred Glorieta, N.M.

NAVARRE, YVES HENRI MICHEL, author; b. Condom, France, Sept. 24, 1940; s. René and Adrienne (Bax) Navarre. Ed. Lycée Pasteur, Neuilly-sur-Seine, Ecole des Hautes Etudes Commerciales du Nord, U. of Lille. Publicity editor Havas Agy., 1965; creative editor Synergie, 1966-67; head of design Publicis, 1968-69; design dir. B.B.D.O., 1969-70. Author novels including Lady Black, 1971, Evoléne, 1972, Les Loukoums, 1973, Le coeur qui cogne, 1974, Killer, 1975, Niagarak, 1976, Le petit galopin de nos corps, 1977, Kurvenal, 1977, Je vis où je m'attache, 1978, Portrait de Julien devant la fenêtre, 1979, Le temps voulu, 1979, Le jardin d'acclimatation, 1980, Biographie, 1981, Romances sans paroles, 1982, Premières pages, 1983, L'Espérance de beaux voyages, No. 1, 1984, No. 2, 1985, Louise, 1986, Une vie de chat, 1986, Fête Des Mères, 1987, Romans, Un Roman, 1988, Hotel Styx, 1989, La Terrasse des audiences au moment de l'adieu, 1990, Douce France, 1990, Ce sont amis aui vent emporte 1991; playwright: Il pleut, si tuait papalmaman, 1974, Dialogue des sourdes, 1974, Freaks Society, 1974, Champagne, 1974, Les valises, 1974, Histoire d'amour, 1976, La guerre des piscines, 1976, Lucienne de Carpentras, 1976, Les dernieres clientes, 1976, Le Butoir, 1982, September Song, 1982, Le Butoir, 1982, September Song, 1982, Happy End, 1982, Vue imprenable sur Paris, 1982, Villa des fleurs, 1986. Decorated chevalier de l'ordre des Arts et des Lettres, chevalier de l'ordre du Mérite, chevalier de la Légion d'Honneur; recipient Prix Goncourt, 1980. Home: Montreal Can.

NEAHER, EDWARD RAYMOND, federal judge; b. Bklyn., May 2, 1912; s. Charles S. and Mary G. (Mahoney) N.; m. Catherine King, July 29, 1939; children: Nancy Neaher Maas, Rosemary Neaher Niehuss, Virginia Neaher Pape, Edward Raymond Jr. A.B. magna cum laude, Notre Dame U., 1937; LL.B., Fordham U., 1943. Bar: N.Y. 1943, U.S. Supreme Ct. 1960. Spl. agt. FBI, Washington, Balt., Buffalo, N.Y.C., 1943-45; assoc., ptnr. Chadbourne, Parke, Whiteside & Wolff, N.Y.C., 1945-69; U.S. atty. for Eastern Dist. N.Y., Bklyn., 1969-71; U.S. dist. judge Eastern Dist. N.Y., 1971-94; Spl. counsel Republican delegation N.Y. Constl. Conv., 1967; trustee Practising Law Inst., 1976-86, trustee emeritus, 1986-94. Bd. Dirs. N.Y.C. Legal Aid Soc., 1967-69. Jud. fellow Am. Coll. Trial Lawyers; mem. Am., Fed., Bklyn., N.Y. State bar assns., Am. Judicature Soc., Fed. Bar Council, Assn. Bar City N.Y. (chmn. com. on fed. cts. 1966-69), Fordham Law Alumni Assn. (bd. dirs. 1970-85). Club: Notre Dame (N.Y.C.). Home: Fort Myers Fla. Died Apr. 19, 1994.

NEEDHAM, JOSEPH, biochemist, science historian, orientalist; b. 1900; s. Joseph and Alicia N.; m. Dorothy Mary Moyle, 1924 (dec. 1979), m. Lu Gwei-Djen, 1989 (dec. 1991). M.A., Ph.D., Sc. D., Cambridge U.; F.R.S., F.B.A., hon. F.R.C.P.; D.Sc. (hon.), U. Brussels, U. Norwich, Chinese U. Hong Kong; LL.D. (hon.), U. Toronto, U. Salford; Litt.D. (hon.), U. Hong Kong, U. Newcastle upon Tyne, U. Hull, U. Chgo., U. N.C., Wilmington, U. Cambridge, U. Peradeniya, Sri. Lanka; D.Univ. (hon.), U. Surrey; Ph.D. (hon.), U. Uppsala; Companion of Honor awarded by the Queen, 1992 . Fellow Gonville and Caius Coll., Cambridge, 1924-95, librarian, 1959-60, pres., 1959-66 master, 1966-76, sr. fellow, from 1976, emeritus sr. fellow; univ. demonstrator in biochemistry Cambridge U., 1928-33, Sir William Dunn reader in biochemistry, 1933-66, now emeritus; vis. prof. biochemistry Stanford U., 1929; Hitchcock prof. U. Calif., 1950; vis. prof. U. Lyon, 1951, U. Kyoto, 1971, Collège de France, Paris, 1973, U. B.C., Vancouver, 1975; hon. prof. Inst. History of Sci., Peking, 1982, Grad. Sch., Nat. Acad. Natural Scis., Peking, 1984; head Brit. Sci. Mission, China, and sci. counsellor Brit. Embassy, Chungking, adv. to Chinese Nat. Resources Commn., Chinese Army Med. Adminstrn., and Chinese Air Force Research Bur., 1942-46; dir. dept. natural sci. UNESCO, 1946-48; chmn. Ceylon Govt. Univ. Policy Commn., 1958. Recipient Sir William Jones medal Asiatic Soc. Bengal, 1963; George Sarton medal Soc. History of Sci., 1968; Leonardo da Vinci medal Soc. History of Tech., 1968; Dexter award for History of Chemistry, 1979; Nat. award 1st class Chinese Sci. and Tech. Commn., 1988, Fukuoka gold medal, 1990, UNESCO Einstein Gold medal, 1994. Mem. Internat. Union History of Sci. (pres. 1972-74), Nat. Acad. Sci. U.S. (fgn.), Am. Acad. Arts and Scis. (fgn.), Nat. Acad. Scis. China (fgn., 1994), Royal Danish Acad. (fgn.), Internat. Acads. History of Sci. and Medicine, Sigma Xi (hon.). Author: Man a Machine, 1927; The Skeptical Biologist, 1929; Chemical Embryology (3 vols.), 1931; The Great Amphibium, 1932; A History of Embryology, 1934; Order and Life, 1935; Adventures before Birth, 1936; Biochemistry and Morphogenesis, 1942; Time, the Refreshing River, 1943; History is on Our Side, 1945; Chinese Science, 1946; Science Outpost, 1948; Science and Civilisation in China (7 vols. in 30 parts), 1954-95; The Development of Iron and Steel Technology in China, 1958; Heavenly Clockwork, 1960; Within the Four Seas, 1970; The Grand Titration, 1970; Clerks and Craftsmen in China and the West, 1970; Moulds of Understanding, 1976; Celestial Lancets, a history and rationale of Acupuncture and Moxa, 1980; Trans-Pacific Echoes and Resonances—Listening Once Again, 1985; The Hall of Heavenly Records; Korean Clocks and Astronomical Instruments, 1380 to 1780, 1986; editor: Science, Religion and Reality, 1925; Christianity and the Social Revolution, 1935; Background to Modern Science, 1938; Hopkins and Biochemistry, 1949; The Chemistry of Life, 1970, (with Mansel Davies) Selections from the Writings of Joseph Needham, 1990; contbr. articles to profl. jours. Died Mar. 24, 1995. Home: Cambridge Eng.

NEELY, EDGAR ADAMS, JR., lawyer; b. Atlanta, May 8, 1910; s. Edgar A. and Emily Levering (Eckfeldt) N.; m. Ruth Nevenzel, Dec. 17, 1966; children by previous marriage to Claire Graham: Edgar Adams III, Michael G., Alan S., Claire G., Constance L. BA, U. N.C., 1931; LLB, Emory U., 1934. Bar: Ga. 1934, U.S. Supreme Ct. 1963. Practiced Atlanta, 1934-95; chief personnel and labor relations naval contract Arundel Corp., Consol. Engring. Co., Hardaway Contracting Co., 1942-43; asso., then partner Neely, Marshall and Greene, 1934-51; ptnr. Marshall, Greene and Neely, Atlanta, 1951-59, Greene, Neely, Buckley and DeRieux, Atlanta, 1960-66, Neely, Freeman & Hawkins, 1966-76, Neely and Player (and predecessors), Atlanta, 1976-95, Nelson, Mullins, Riley & Scarborough, Atlanta, 1995; mem. legal staff Bell Aircraft, Inc., Marietta, Ga., 1943-45, asst. to mgr., 1945-46; mem. faculty Products Liability Seminars, U. Balt., 1976-77. Author: Gain and Maintain Vibrant Drive from 25 to 95. Good cheer reporter Sta. WSB, 1934-39; chmn. Speakers Bur. Community Chest Fund, ARC, Atlanta, 1930's and 40's; vestryman St. Luke's Episcopal Ch., Atlanta. Named Disting. Alumnus, Emory Univ. Sch. of Law, 1994; recipient six-diamond 60 yr. pin for Norfolk So. Corp. and subs., 1995. Fellow Am. Coll. Trial Lawyers; mem. State Bar Ga., Trial Attys. Am., Nat. Assn. of R.R. Trial Counsel (pres. 1965-66), Ga. Bar Assn. (tradition of excellence award 1984), Internat. Assn. of Defense Counsel, ABA, Atlanta Bar Assn., Lawyers Club Atlanta (Fifty Yr. award 1984), Terminus Tennis Club, Commerce Club, Piedmont Driving Club, Amelia Island Plantation Club, Old War Horse Club (pres. 1986). Clubs: Terminus Tennis, Commerce, Piedmont Driving, Amelia Island Plantation, Old War Horse (pres.). Home: Atlanta Ga. Died Nov. 10, 1995.

NELSON, GEORGE LEONARD, lawyer, newspaper company executive; b. Salt Lake City, Aug. 27, 1897; s. Axel Christian and Josephine (Andersen) N.; m. Ila Emms, Aug. 19, 1925 (dec. Sept. 27, 1973); children: Gayle (Mrs. Donn E. Cassity), George Leonard, Robert Lee; m. Elva S. Heslington, Mar. 20, 1975. Student, George Washington U., 1917, J.D., 1922. Bar: Utah 1922, Ct. Appeals for D.C. 1922, U.S. Supreme Ct. 1957. Ptnr. Romney, Nelson & Cassity (formerly Romney & Nelson), from 1922, now of counsel; dep. county atty. Salt Lake County, 1923-26; pres. Deseret News Pub. Co., Salt Lake City, 1963-66, bd. dirs., 1951-66; v.p., bd. dirs. Newspaper Agy. Corp., 1963-66; Past mem. rules and investigating coms. Utah State Bar. Mem. Citizens Adv. Com. Capital Improvements Salt Lake City.; Trustee Dr. W.H. Groves Latter-day Saints Hosp., 1951-67. Served with USNRF, 1917-19. Mem. Inter-Am. Bar Assn., Am. Coll. Probate Counsel, Phi Delta Phi, Sigma Chi. Mem. Ch. of Jesus Christ of Latter-day Saints (pres. Monument Park stake, now stake patriarch). Home: Salt Lake City Utah Deceased.

NELSON, HARRIET HILLIARD, actress; b. Des Moines, July 18, 1914; d. Roy E. and Hazel Dell

(McNutt) Hilliard; m. Ozzie Nelson, Oct. 8, 1935; children: David Ozzie, Eric Hilliard. Student, St. Agnes Acad. Began as vocalist with Ozzie Nelson's Orch.; appeared on radio programs with Joe Penner, Bob Ripley, Feg Murray, Red Skelton; co-star: (radio program) Adventures of Ozzie and Harriet, Oct. 1944, (TV program) Ozzie and Harriet; actress: (films) including The Falcon, Follow The Fleet, Here Come the Nelsons, (TV show) Ozzie's Girls, 1973, (TV movie) Smash-up on Interstate 5, 1976, (plays) Impossible Years, State Fair; rec. artist: (for TV movie) Brunswick, Vocalian, Victor, Blue Bird. Recipient Nat. Family Week Radio citation by Internat. Council on Christian Family Life, 1947, Genii award Radio and TV Women So. Calif.,1960; named Woman of Yr. in entertainment field, Los Angeles Times; 7 consecutive yrs. Ozzie and Harriet voted best husband-wife team in TV by TV-Radio Mirror Reader's Poll. Home: Laguna Beach Calif. Died Oct. 2, 1994.

NELSON, LEWIS CLAIR, government official; b. Logan, Utah, June 2, 1918; s. Lewis E. and Eleanor (Garrett) N.; m. Mary Dorothy Emmett, Aug. 30, 1941 (dec.); children: David Emmett, Patricia Louise (Mrs. William J. Friend), Judith Ann, Jeffrey Emmett; m. Dottie Groome Hanford, June 8, 1974; children: John Van Hanford III, Joseph G. Hanford. BS, Utah State U., 1939; JD, George Washington U., 1947. Bar: D.C. 1947, Utah 1949, Ohio 1962, N.Y. 1968. Law clk. U.S. Ct. Appeals, 1947-48; mem. firm Moyle & Wanlass, Washington, 1948-51; counsel U.S. Senate Jud. Com., 1951-52; mem. firm Moyle, Nelson & Cotten, Washington, 1952-55; gen. counsel Champion Papers Inc., Hamilton, Ohio, 1955-67; v.p., gen. counsel Champion Internat. Corp. (formerly U.S. Plywood-Champion Papers Inc.), Stamford, Conn., 1967-72; sr. v.p. Champion Internat. Corp., 1972-82, also v.p. subs., dir., 1974-82; commr. Fed. Mine Safety and Health Rev. Commn., Washington, 1982-94. Served to maj. AUS, 1941-46. Mem. ABA (sec. on natural resources law 1960-94, chmn. 1969-70, mem. ho. of dels. 1970-74, 82-92, mem. com. on ethics 1974-80, chmn. 1979-80, treas., gov. 1981-87, mem. sr. lawyers div. coun. 1987-94, coun. govt. and pub. sector lawyers div. 1991-94), D.C. Bar Assn., Utah Bar Assn., Ohio Bar Assn., N.Y. State Bar Assn., Am. Bar Retirement Assn. (bd. dirs.), Assn. Gen. Counsel, Army and Navy Club, Barristers Club, Rotary, Sigma Chi. Home: Mc Lean Va. Died Feb. 3, 1994; interred Logan, Utah.

NELSON, ROBERT HARTLEY, international education executive; b. Berwyn, Ill., Jan. 5, 1921; s. Arthur Axel Reuben and Florence (Lagergren) N.; m. Winifred Harrison, May 5, 1945; children: Richard, Wendy, Steven (dec.), Jonathan, Elizabeth. BA, Knox Coll., 1942; MBA, U. Chgo., 1951. Nat. field sec. Tau Kappa Epsilon frat., 1945-46; sales auditor Maurice L. Rothschild Co., Chgo., 1946-47; with Hammond Corp., Deerfield, Ill., 1947-71; v.p. finance Hammond Corp., 1959-61, v.p., 1961-65, exec. v.p., 1965-71, dir., 1963-71; past dir. Hammond Organ West Export Co., Hammond Organ Europe, Hammond Organ Co., Acoutronics, Inc.; pres. Robert H. Nelson Assocs., Inc., Palatine, Ill., 1972-74; dir. Northwood Inst., U.S.A., Midland, Mich., 1973-74; dir. Exec. Devel. Ctr. U. Ill., Urbana-Champaign, 1976-82; dir. Ctr. for Exec. Devel. Tex. A&M U., College Station, 1982-87; founder ETIME Ednl. Tours, Bryan, Tex., 1987-94; Treas. Village of Inverness, Ill., 1964-65. Trustee, 1969-73; Past trustee Hammond Found.; past trustee alumni gen. chmn., past budget chmn. Knox Coll. Served to capt. USMCR, 1942-45, PTO. Mem. Nat. Assn. Electronic Organ Mfrs. (past dir., pres.), Newcomen Soc. Republican. Presbyterian. Club: Briarcrest Country (Bryan, Tex.). Home: Bryan Tex. Died Feb. 24, 1994.

NELSON, WALDO EMERSON, physician, educator; b. McClure, Ohio, Aug. 17, 1898; s. William and Bertha (Ballmer) N.; m. Margery Harris, June 20, 1928; children: Margery Jane, Mary Ann, William Harris. AB, Wittenberg Coll., 1922, ScD (hon.), 1956; MD, U. Cin., 1926; LHD (hon.), Temple U., 1975; D of Med. Edn. (hon.), Med. Coll. Pa., 1977; HHD (hon.), Med. Coll. Wis., 1981. Diplomate Am. Bd. Pediatrics. Intern Cin. Gen. Hosp., 1926-27; resident pediatrics Cin. Gen. and Children's Hosp., 1927-29; asst. prof. pediatrics U. Cin. Med. Sch., 1932-38, assoc. prof., 1938-40; med. dir. Children's Convalescent Home, Cin., 1931-40; prof. pediatrics Temple U. Med. Sch., Phila., from 1940; chmn. dept. Temple U. Med. Sch., 1940-64; prof. Med. Coll. Pa., 1964-80, emeritus prof., from 1980; attending physician St. Christopher's Hosp. Children, med. dir., 1947-64. Editor: Nelson Textbook of Pediatrics, 4th-14th edits., Jour. Pediatrics, 1959-77; cons. editor, from 1977; contbr. numerous articles to profl. jours. Decorated Order of Mayo Republic of Argentina, 1974, as caballero in Order of Cristobal Colón by Pres. of the Dominican Republic; recipient Gold Medal award Children's Hosp. of Phila., 1985, Procter award Children's Hosp. Med. Ctr. Cin., 1986, Daniel Drake medal Coll. Medicine U. Cinn., 1990, Waldo E. Nelson award St. Christopher's Hosp. for Children, Temple U., 1991. Mem. Am. Acad. Pediatrics, Soc. Pediatric Research, Am. Pediatric Soc. (pres. 1962-63, Howland award 1972), AMA (Jacobi award 1969), Ambulatory Pediatric Assn. (Armstrong award 1984), Pa. Pub. Health Assn., Pa., Phila. County med. socs., Central Soc. Clin. Investigation, Latin Am. Soc. Pediatric Research (hon.). Home: Gladwyne Pa. Deceased.

NELSON, WERNER LIND, agronomist; b. Sheffield, Ill., Oct. 17, 1914; s. Carl Herbert and Ida Josephine (Carlson) N.; m. Clara Jeanette Wilcox, Nov. 16, 1940; children: John Werner, Jean Frances. BS, U. Ill., 1937, MS, 1938; PhD, Ohio State U., 1940. Asst. agronomist U. Idaho, 1940-41, N.C. Soils Research Lab., 1941-42; prof. agronomy N.C. State Coll., 1942-54, in charge soil fertility research, 1951-54; dir. soil testing div. N.C. Dept. Agr., 1949-51; dir. Midwest region Potash & Phosphate Inst., 1955-67, sr. v.p., 1967-85, cons. to pres., 1985-86; adj. prof. agronomy Purdue U., 1973-85; fertilizer industry adv. panel for FAO Freedom from Hunger Campaign, 1961-75; bd. dirs. Council Agrl. Sci. and Tech., 1973-81, Found. Agronomic Research, 1980-85, Potash & Phosphate Inst./TVA Research Com., 1978-85, Soybean Research Adv. Inst., 1982-84; mem. China/U.S.A. Soybean Symposium, 1983. Author: (with S.L. Tisdale, J.D. Beaton and John Havlin) Soil Fertility and Fertilizers, rev., 1966, 75, 85, 93; also chpts. in books; contbr. articles to profl. jours. Recipient Bronze tablet univ. honors U. Ill., 1937; Centennial award Ohio State U., 1973; Merit cert. award Am. Forage and Grassland Council, 1973; cert. distinction Purdue Agrl. Alumni Assn., 1987. Fellow Am. Soc. Agronomy (Agronomic Service award 1964, pres. 1969-70, hon. mem., Werner L. Nelson award established in Agronomic Sci. Found. 1989), AAAS, Soil Sci. Soc. Am. (pres. 1960-61, chmn. group fertilizer com. 1951-52, assoc. editor proc. 1955-59, disting. service award, 1988), Crop Sci. Soc. Am.; mem. Internat. Soil Sci. Soc. (Am. v.p. commn. IV 1960), Ind. Plant Food and Agrl. Chem. Assn. (pres. 1972, Werner L. Nelson award established in his honor 1986), Ind. Soil Soc. (pres. 1955-56), Am. Forage and Grassland Council, Nat. Fertilizer Solutions Assn. (hon., Werner L. Nelson award established in his honor 1985), Farm House, Phi Kappa Phi, Sigma Xi, Gamma Sigma Delta (scholarship award U. Ill. 1937), Alpha Zeta, Phi Eta Sigma. Baptist (chmn. bldg. com. 1960-64). Club: Kiwanis. Home: West Lafayette Ind. Died Nov. 27, 1992.

NEMIR, ROSALEE, pediatrician; b. Waco, Tex., July 16, 1905; d. David and Emma (Shakir) N.; m. Elias J. Audi, July 1934 (dec. 1968); children: Elaine, Alfred, Robert. BA, U. Tex., Austin, 1926; MD, Johns Hopkins U., 1930; ScD (hon.), Colgate U., 1974. Instr. Med. Coll. NYU, N.Y.C., 1933-39, asst. prof., 1939-50, prof., 1959—; vis. prof. microbiology Columbia U. Coll. Physicians and Surgeons, N.Y.C., 1958-59; dir. pediatric rsch. and edn. N.Y. Infirmary, N.Y.C., 1966-73; mem. expert panel on tuberculosis Dept. Health City of N.Y., 1988-89. Contbr. rsch. articles to med. jours. Bd. mgrs. Intercollegiate Br. YMCA, 1954-64, Bklyn. Arthritis and Rheumatism Found., 1954-56, Bklyn. chpt. ARC Greater N.Y., 1973-74; bd. dirs. Bklyn. Kindergarten Soc., 1954—, Willoughby House Settlement, Bklyn., 1955-68, Am. Middle East Rehab., 1971-76, Am. Near East Refugee Aid, 1976-89; trustee Judson Health Ctr., 1963-75; mem. women's com. Boston Symphony Orch., Bklyn., 1950-68, 73; treas. Charles H. Malik Edn. and Loan Fund, 1968-89; rep. Nat. Bicentennial Svc. Alliance, 1975. Decorated medal of Cedars of Lebanon, Republic of Lebanon, 1968; recipient recognition award Bklyn. Kindergarten Soc., 1987, Emily Dunning Barringer award Gouveneur Hosp., 1989, numerous others. Mem. Am. Acad. Pediatrics, Soc. Pediatric Rsch., Am. Pediatric Soc., N.Y. Acad. Medicine, Am. Coll. Chest Physicians, Am. Thoracic Soc., N.Y. Acad. Scis. (hon.)AMA (Physician's Recognitian award 1978), Am. Med. Women's Assn. (Elizabeth Blackwell award 1970), Women's Med. Soc. N.Y. State (Woman of Yr. 1973), Med. Women's Internat. Assn. (hon.), N.Y. County Med. Soc., Soc. Adolescent Medicine, Soc. Alumni Bellevue Hosp., Cosmopolitan Club, Phi Beta Kappa. Home: Lincoln Nebr.

NESBITT, LOWELL, artist; b. Balt., Oct. 4, 1933; s. Frank Eugene and Mildred (Carback) N. B.F.A., Tyler Sch. Fine Arts, Temple U., 1955; student, Royal Coll. Art, London, 1955-56. One-man shows include Balt. Mus. Art, 1958, 69, Franz Bader Gallery, Washington, 1963, Corcoran Gallery Art, 1964, 73, Rolf Nelson Gallery, Los Angeles, 1965, 66, Henri Gallery, Washington, 1965, 66, 67, 69, Howard Wise Gallery, N.Y.C., 1965, 66, Gertrude Kasle Gallery, Detroit, (8 shows) 1966-74, Jefferson Gallery, San Diego, 1967, Tyler Sch. Art, 1967, Galerie Thelen, Essen, Fed. Republic of Germany, 1969, Cologne, Fed. Republic of Germany, 1970, 72, Stable Gallery, N.Y.C., 1968, 69, 70, U. Richmond, 1968, Gimpel Fils Gallery, London, 1971, Gimpel Weitzenhoffer, N.Y.C., 1971, 73, Gimpel & Hanover Galerie, Zurich, Switzerland, 1972, Stefanotty Gallery, N.Y.C., 1973, 74, Galerie Arneson, Copenhagen, Denmark, 1974, Brooke Alexander, Inc., N.Y.C., 1974, Walton Gallery, San Francisco, 1974, Pyramid Gallery, Washington, 1975, Meml. Art Gallery, Rochester, 1975, Andrew Crispo Gallery, N.Y.C., (7 shows) 1976-83, MIT, Cambridge, 1976, Graphis Gallery, Toronto, 1977, Gumps Gallery, San Francisco, 1977, Ulrich Mus. Art, Wichita, 1977, Janus Gallery, Venice, Calif., 1977, Galerie Contacto, Caracas, 1977, Galerie Jöllenbeck, Cologne, 1977, Strong's Gallery, Cleve., 1978, Intown Club, Cleve., 1978, Kent State U., 1978, The Art Contact Gallery, Miami, Fla., 1978, Kornblatt Gallery, Balt., 1978, Selby Mus., Sarasota,
Fla., 1979, McNay Art Inst., San Antonio, 1980, A
drich Mus. Contemporary Art, Ridgefield, Conn., 198
Lyford Cay Gallery, Nassau, Bahamas, 1980, Prof.
Gallery, N.Y.C., Galleri Herder, Falsterbo, Swede
1980, Hull Gallery, Washington, 1980, Fay Gold Ga
lery, Atlanta, 1981, S.W. II Gallery, Dallas, 1981, Butl
Mus. Am. Art, Youngstown, 1982, Mansfield (Ohi
Art Ctr., 1983, Washington and Lee U., 1983, Le
ington, Bayly Art Mus., U. Va., Charlottesville, Atlant
Ctr. for the New Smyrna Beach, Fla., 1983, Okla. Ar
Ctr., Oklahoma City, 1984, Gallery 24, Bay Harbo
Fla., 1984, G. Sander Fine Art, Inc., Daytona Beac
Fla., 1985, Perri Renneth Galleries, Southampton ar
Westhampton, N.Y., 1985, Southampton, 1987, D
Laurenti Gallery, N.Y.C., 1986, 88, Foster Harmo
Gallery, Sarasota, 1986, Images Gallery, Toledo, 198
Temple U., Phila., 1986, Wally Findlay Galleries, Pal
Beach, Fla., 1986, Louis Newman Gallery, Bever
Hills, Calif., 1987, Joy Tash Gallery, Scottsdale, Ari
1987, 88, 89, 91, Dyansen Gallery, San Francisco, 19
and Beverly Hills, 89, Bayley Mus., U. Va., Charlotte
ville, 1990, Martin Lawrence Gallery, Balt., 199
Martin Lawrence Gallery, Palm Springs, Calif., 199
Ctr. for Cultural Arts, Gadsen, Ala., 1990, 1991, Mu
Art, Fort Lauderdale, Fla., 1991, Miami Dade Pub
Libr., 1991, Wessel/O'Connor Gallery, N.Y.C., 199
group shows include Iolas Gallery, N.Y.C., 1964, Stab
Gallery, 1964, Byron Gallery, N.Y.C., 1964, 65, Ni
Contemporary Painters USA, Pan Am. Union, 196
Am. Express Pavillion, N.Y.C World's Fair, 1965, A
of the 50's and 60's, Larry Aldrich Mus., 1965-6
Realism Revisited, Flint (Mich.) Inst. Art, 1966, Herr
Art Inst., Indpls., 1966, Galerie 1900-2000, Paris, 198
Joy Tash Gallery, 1989, Ted Gallery, Albany, 198
Temple U., 1989, Bayly Mus., 1990, U. Va., 1990; pri
exhbns. include Mus. Modern Art, Mexico City, 196
Art of 1964, 1965 and 1966, Larry Aldrich Mus., 196
1st Kent Internat, Kent (Ohio) U., 1967, Contempora
Am. Painting and Sculpture, Krannert Art Mu
Urbana, Ill., 1967, Akron Art Inst., 1967, Galler
Sperone, 2 man, Turin, Italy, 1967, Salone Internat. d
Giovani, Galleria D'Arte Moderna, Milan, Italy, 196
Contemporary Surralists, Los Angeles County Mu
1967, Hofstra U., 1971, Mus. Wuppertal, Fed. Republ
of Germany, 1971, Hausen Fuller Gallery, Sa
Francisco, 1973, Galerie M.E. Theben, Cologne, 197
Fabian Carlson Galerie, Göteburg, Sweden, 197
Corcoran and Corcoran, Miami, 1973, Galerie Ost
gren, Malmo, Sweden, 1972, Gertrude Kasle Galler
1972, Galerie Asonowitsh, Stockholm, 1972, Gale
Aronson, Copenhagen, 1973, Marian Locks Galler
Phila., 1973, group invitational exhbn. drawings ar
watercolors, ICA, 1967, Tokyo (Japan) Biennial, 196
Sao Paolo (Brazil) Biennial, 1967, Cybernetic Se
endipity at ICA, London, 1968, Smithsonian Instr
1969, Jewish Mus., N.Y.C., 1969, Pyramid Galler
Washington, 1971, U. Redlands, Calif., 1975, San Jo
(Calif.) Mus. Art, 1975, Simon-Fraser U., 1975, Ph
brook Art Ctr., Tulsa, 1975, Andrew Crispo Galler
1976, 77, 78, 79, 81, 82, 83, Israel Mus., Jerusale
1979, Md. Inst., Coll. Art, Balt., 1979, Hunt Ins
Carnegie-Mellon U., Pitts., 1979, Am. embass
Moscow, 1979, Okla. Art Ctr., 1979, Kent State U
1980, Am. embassy, Mexico City, 1981, Bayley Mus.,
Va., Charlottesville, 1991; represented in permane
collections, various Am. embassies including Sao Paol
Monrovia and Tanganyika, Tel-Aviv, Israel, Brussel
Belgium, Balt. Mus. Art, Detroit Art Inst., Milw. A
Ctr., Nat. Gallery, Wellington, New Zealand, Corcor
Gallery Art, Goucher Coll., La Jolla (Calif.) Mu
Library of Congress, Yale Art Gallery, Renwick Mus.
Smithsonian Instn., Mus. Modern Art, No. Trust C
Chgo., Phillips Collection, Washington, Hunt Inst. B
Documentation at Carnegie-Mellon U., U. Md., Phi
Mus. Art, Temple U., U. Va., Washington Galle
Modern Art, Art Inst. Chgo., EPA, Washingto
AT&T, N.Y.C. Ctr., Nat. Collection Fine Arts, Na
Gallery Art, Washington, Chase Manhattan Ban
N.Y.C., Florists Trans World Delivery Corp., Mut.
Omaha, Washington, Bank of N.Y., N.Y.C., Ludw
Collection Neue Galerie der Stadt Aachen, German
Thyssen-Bornemisza Collection, Lugano, Switzerlan
Skandinaviska Banken, Göteborg, Ft. Worth Art Ct
Fogg Art Mus., Cambridge, Morris Mus. Arts and Sci
Morristown, N.J., Butler Mus. Am. Art, Youngstow
Ohio, U.S. Dept. Interior, Castel Gandolfo, Rom
World Wildlife Fund, Israel Mus., Fed. Res. Ban
Avery Fisher Hall, Lincoln Ctr. for Performing Ar
Everson Mus. Art, Syracuse, Auchenbach Found., Sa
Francisco, Currier Gallery Art, Manchester, N.H
Portfolios - Collection of U. Md.; also pvt. collections
Served with U.S. Army, 1956-58. Recipient purcha
award for oils and prints Balt. Mus. Art, 1956, Na
Collection Fine Arts, 1969. Home: New York N.
Died July 8, 1993.

NETTING, ROBERT M., anthropology educator;
Racine, Wis., Oct. 14, 1934; s. Robert Jackson ar
Martha Marie (McCorkle) N.; m. Rhonda Marie Gille
Mar. 13, 1993; children from previous marriage: Robe
Frazier, Jessa Forte, Laurel Marthe, Jacqueline A
Frazier. BA English summa cum laude, Yale U., 19
MA Anthropology, U. Chgo., 1959, PhD Anthr
pology, 1963. From asst. prof. to assoc. prof. U. P
1963-72; prof. anthropology U. Ariz., Tucson, 1972-9
Regents' prof. anthropology, 1991-95; field research
Ft. Berthold Reservation, N.D., 1958, Jos Platea
Northern Nigeria, 1960-62, 66-67, 84, 94, Törbel, Vala

Switzerland, 1970-71, 77, Senegal, Ivory Coast, 1977, Portugal, 1982; cons. AID project Stanford U., USDA, USAID Agrl. Devel. Program.; mem. adv. coun. Wenner-Gren Found. Anthropological Rsch., 1982-86, search com. new dir. rsch., 1985-86; mem. com. human dimensions global change commn. behavioral and social scis. and edn. Nat. Rsch. Coun., 1989-91; pres. Internat. Assn. Study Common Property, 1991-92. Author: Hill Farmers of Nigeria; Cultural Ecology of the Kofyar of the Jos Plateau, 1968, Cultural Ecology, 1977, 2d edit., 1986, Balancing on an Alp: Ecological Change and Continuity in a Swiss Mountain Community, 1981, Smallholders, Householders: Farm Families and the Ecology of Intensive Sustainable Agriculture, 1993; editor: Documentary History of the Fox Project, 1948-59, 1960, Ariz. Studies in Human Ecology, 1984-95; contbr. articles to profl. jours. Recipient Robert F. Heizer prize best jour. articles ethnohistory Am. Soc. Ethnohistory, 1987; Ctr. Advanced Study Behavioral Scis. fellow, 1986-87, Guggenheim fellow, 1970-71, NSF grantee, 1958-60, 71, 77-78, 84-87, 94, Nat. Inst. Child Health and Human Devel. Ctr. Population Rsch. grantee, 1974-76, Social Sci. Rsch. Coun. grantee, 1966-67, Ford Found. Fgn. Area Studies fellow, 1960-62, Woodrow Wilson fellow, 1957-58. Fellow Am. Anthropological Assn. (exec. bd. 1981-84); mem. NAS, Am. Ethnological Soc. (councillor 1976-79), Am. Anthrop. Assn. (exec. bd. 1981-84), Soc. Ethnohistory, Phi Beta Kappa. Home: Tucson Ariz. Died Feb. 4, 1995.

NETTLETON, DAVID, religious administrator. Chmn. Gen. Assn. Regular Bapt. Chs., Schaumburg, Ill., from 1988. Home: Schaumburg Ill. Deceased.

NEUMANN, VACLAV, symphony conductor; b. Prague, Sept. 29, 1920; ed. Prague Conservatoire. Former viola player Smetana Quartet; mem. Czech Philharm. Orch.; deputized for Rafael Kubelik, 1948; later conducted orchs. in Karlovy Vary and Brno; condr. Prague Symphony Orch., 1956-63, Czech Philharm., 1964-68; chief condr. Komische Oper, Berlin, 1957-60; conducted 1st performance of The Cunning Little Vixen (Janacek); condr. Leipzig Gewandhaus Orch., also gen. music dir. Leipzig Opera House, 1964-67; condr. Czech Philharm. Orch., 1967-68, chief condr., 1968-90, hon. chief condr., 1990—; chief condr. Stuttgart Opera House, 1970-73; condr. Vienna Philharm., 1987; regularly conducts Vienna Symphonic Orch.; condr. Munich Opera Ensemble, Sweden, 1960, 1970, 71, 72, 74, Romania, 1951, 71, 73, Fed. Republic of Germany, 1962, 65, 67, 71, 73, 74, 75, Yugoslavia, 1970, Bulgaria, 1975, Belgium, 1970, Switzerland, 1970, 75, Spain, 1975, Finland, 1975; conducted many European orchestras including Berlin Philharm., Orchestre National de France, Royal Philharm., Hamburg Philharm., Boston Symphony, N.Y. Philharm. Recipient Nat. prize German Democratic Republic, 1966, honored artist, 1967, nat. artist, 1971, Order of Labour, 1980. Mem. Mahler-Gesellschaft (hon.), Gesellschaft der Musikfreunde (hon.).Died Sept. 2, 1995. Home: Prague Czech Republic

NEUMANN, WILHELM PAUL, chemistry educator; b. Würzburg, Bavaria, Fed. Republic of Germany, Oct. 1, 1926; s. Wilhelm A.E. and Margarete (Bertram) m. Mechtild Maier, Feb. 7, 1959, (wid. 1978); children: Brigitte, Albrecht, Doris; m. Gerda Deutskens, Mar. 21, 1983. Diploma in Chemistry, U. Würzburg, 1949, D degree, 1952. Cert. in Habilitation, Chemistry, U. Giessen, Fed. Republic of Germany. Rsch. and tng. specialist U. Würzburg, 1949-55; asst. rsch. assoc. Max-Planck-Inst. of Coal Research, Mülheim, Ruhr, Fed. Republic Germany, 1955-59; lectr. U. Giessen, Hessen, 1959-65, prof., 1965-68; prof. organic chemistry U. Dortmund, Fed. Republic Germany, 1968-93; pres. of convent, U. Dortmund, head Chem. Dept., 1975-76. Author: The Organic Chemistry of Tin, 1970; contbr. several handbook articles, reviews and over 265 articles to profl. jours. Fellow Japan Soc. for the Promotion of Sci., Tokyo, 1988, Hon. Mem. Soc. Argentina de Investigaciones en Quimica Organica, Argentina, 1987. Mem. Soc. German Chemists (chmn. local section), Rotary (pres. Dortmund chpt. 1986-87). Home: Dortmund Germany Died Aug. 1, 1993.

NEVELS, ZEBEDEE JAMES, physician, surgeon; b. Wewoka, Okla., Nov. 13, 1926; s. Zebedee James and Mary Christine (Meigs) N.; m. Virginia Nell Glass, May 1951; children—Karen Leslie, James Norman. B.A., Kans., 1950; M.D., Howard U., 1958. Diplomate Am. Bd. Surgery. Resident in surgery Mt. Sinai Hosp., Milw., 1960-62; staff VA Hosp., Wadsworth, Kans., 1962-65; chmn. dept. surgery St. Anthony Hosp., Milw., 1973-80; practice medicine and surgery, Milw., 1980—. Served with U.S. Army, 1945-46. Mem. County Med. Soc., State Med. Soc. Wis., Nat. Med. Assn., AMA, Cream City Med. Soc. (pres. 1978-79). Democrat. Baptist. Avocations: fishing; hunting; golf; gardening. Home: Milwaukee Wis.

NEVIUS, BLAKE REYNOLDS, English literature educator; b. Winona, Minn., Feb. 12, 1916; s. Blake Reynolds and Helena (MacLean) N. B.A., Antioch Coll., 1938; M.A., U. Chgo., 1941, Ph.D., 1947. Teaching asst. English dept. U. Ill., 1941-42; mem. faculty UCLA, 1947-94, prof. English, 1961-83, prof. emeritus, 1983-94. Author: Edith Wharton, 1953, Robert Herrick, 1962, Ethan Frome: The Story with Sources and Commentary, 1968, The American Novel: Sinclair Lewis to the Present, 1970, Ivy Compton-Burnett, 1970, Cooper's Landscapes: An Essay on the Picturesque Vision, 1975; editor: Nineteenth-Century Fiction, 1965-71, 80-83, Leatherstocking Tales (J.F. Cooper), 1985. Bd. dirs. Virginia Steele Scott Found. Served with AUS, 1942-45, ETO. Decorated Bronze Star.; Recipient award Humanities Inst., U. Calif., 1967, 71, award for disting. career as editor Conf. Editors of Learned Jours., 1982; Fulbright lectr. Germany, 1953-54; Guggenheim fellow, 1962-63; Rockefeller Ctr. at Bellagio fellow, 1982. Mem. MLA, Internat. Assn. Univ. Profs. English (treas. 1971-74). Democrat. Episcopalian. Home: Minden Nev. Died Oct. 20, 1994.

NEWBERRY, NICK T., insurance company executive. Chmn. Woodmen of the World Life Ins. Soc., Omaha. Home: Omaha Nebr.

NEWHALL, BEAUMONT, historian, photographer; b. Lynn, Mass., June 22, 1908; s. Herbert William and Alice Lillia (Davis) N.; m. Nancy Wynne Parker, July 1, 1936 (dec. 1974); m. Christi Weston, 1975 (div. Feb. 1985). AB cum laude, Harvard U., 1930, AM, 1931, D Art (hon.), 1978; postgrad., U. Paris, 1933, U. London, 1934; DFA (hon.), SUNY, Brockport, 1986. Lectr. Phila. Mus. Art, 1931-32; asst. Met. Mus. Art, 1932-33; librarian Mus. Modern Art, N.Y.C., 1935-42; food editor Wolfe Publs., Rochester, N.Y., 1956-65; contbg. editor Art in Am., 1957-65; curator photography Mus. Modern Art, 1940-42, 45-46; curator Internat. Mus. Photography, George Eastman House, Rochester, N.Y., 1948-58; dir. Internat. Mus. Photography, George Eastman House, 1958-71; vis. prof. art U. N.Mex., Albuquerque, 1971-84; prof. emeritus U. N.Mex., 1984-93; lectr. Black Mountain Coll., 1946-48, U. Rochester, 1954-55, Rochester Inst. Tech., 1956-69; vis. prof. art State U. N.Y. at Buffalo, 1969-71. Author: (with Nancy Newhall) Masters of Photography, 1958, The History of Photography, 1964, 5th edit., 1982, Latent Image, 1967, 83, The Daguerreotype in America, 3d rev. edit, 1976, Airborne Camera, 1969; editor: Photography: Essays & Images, 1980, In Plain Sight, 1983, Supreme Instants: The Photographs of Edward Weston, 1986. Bd. dirs. Civic Music Assn., Rochester, 1963-71. Served to maj. USAAF, 1942-45, ETO. John Simon Guggenheim Found. fellow, 1947, 75, fellow John D. and Catherine T. MacArthur Found., 1984-89. Fellow Royal Photog. Soc. Gt. Britain (hon.), Photog. Soc. Am., Am. Acad. Arts and Scis.; mem. Profl. Photographers Am. (hon. master of photography), Deutsche Gesellschaft für Photographie (corr.). Home: Santa Fe N.Mex. Died Feb. 26, 1993.

NEWMAN, EDWIN STANLEY, lawyer, publishing company executive; b. N.Y.C., Apr. 26, 1922; s. Gordon H. and Rosalind (Zieph) N.; m. Evaline Ada Lipp, Sept. 2, 1945; children: Scott D., Linda S. Newman Perl. BA summa cum laude, CCNY, 1940; LLB, Columbia U., 1943. Admitted to N.Y. State bar, 1943, U.S. Ct. Internat. Trade. Asst. to pres. Am. Jewish Com., 1946-60; ins. co. exec., 1960-69; v.p., gen. counsel Oceana Publs., Inc., Dobbs Ferry, N.Y., 1969-94, exec. v.p., 1994-95, also dir.; past lectr. New Sch. Social Research. Author: Freedom Reader, 1963, Hate Reader, 1964, Law of Philanthropy, 1955, Fundraising Made Easy, 1954, Law of Civil Liberty and Civil Rights, 7th edit., 1987; editor: U.S. Internat. Trade Reports, 1981-95. Chmn. bd. Elmont Jewish Ctr., 1953-57. Served with U.S. Army, 1943-46, 51-52. Named James Kent scholar, 1941, 42, 43. Internat. Bar Assn., Columbia Law Sch. Alumni Assn., Internat. Assn. Jurists (Italian-Am. sect.), Am. Corp. Counsel Assn., Dobbs Ferry Rotary, Phi Beta Kappa. Died June 5, 1995. Home: Dobbs Ferry N.Y.

NEWMAN, FRANK CECIL, legal educator, retired state supreme court justice; b. Eureka, Calif., July 17, 1917; s. Frank J. and Anna (Dunn) N.; m. Frances Burks, Jan. 14, 1940; children: Robert, Julie, Ralph, Carol. A.B., Dartmouth Coll., 1938; LL.B., U. Calif., 1941; LL.M., Columbia U., 1947, J.S.D., 1953; LL.D., U. Santa Clara, 1978. Bar: Calif. 1942. Prof. law U. Calif., Berkeley, 1946-96, dean Sch. Law, 1961-66, Jackson H. Ralston prof. internat. law, 1974-88, prof. emeritus, 1988-96; justice Calif. Supreme Ct., 1977-82; atty. OPA, N.Y.C. and Washington, 1942-43, Office Gen. Counsel Dept. Navy, 1943-46; vis. prof. law schs. Harvard U., 1953-54, U. Wash., summer, 1952, Salzburg Sem. in Am. Studies, Austria, summer, 1954, 64, Inst. Human Rights, Strasbourg, France, summer, 1970, 71, 75, 77, People's U., Beijing, spring, 1985, Global Security Studies program Meiji Gakuin U., Yokohama, spring, 1992, U. San Francisco, 1992-96, Trinity Coll., Dublin, summer, 1993, Golden Gate U., 1994-96, St. Cyril and Methodius U., Macedonia, fall, 1994; cons. OPS, 1951; counsel Gov. Calif. Commn. on Unemployment Compensation, 1952; cons. GAO, 1959, Calif. Agr. and Svcs. Agy., 1975-76; dir. Social Sci. Rsch. Coun., N.Y.C., 1954-58, Fed. Home Loan Bank, San Francisco, 1962-70. Author: (with Stanley S. Surrey) Newman and Surrey on Legislation, 1955, (with Richard B. Lillich) International Human Rights: Problems of Law and Policy, 1979, (with David S. Weissbrodt) International Human Rights: Law, Policy, and Process, 1990, supplement, 1994. Mem. exec. com., chmn. drafting com. Calif. Constn. Revision Commn., 1964-72. Served from ensign to lt. USNR, 1943-46. Mem. Internat. Inst. Human Rights (founding v.p.). Home: Orinda Calif. Died Feb. 18, 1996.

NEWSOM, WILL ROY, former college president; b. Rivera, Calif., Jan. 12, 1912; s. William Charles and Sarah Ann (Mitchell) N.; m. Alice Claire Morgan, Jan. 24, 1931; children: Herbert Charles, Janine, Nina Ann. A.B., Whittier Coll., 1934; M.A., U. So. Calif., 1935, Ph.D., 1939. Grad. fellow U. So. Calif., 1935-39; mem. faculty Whittier Coll., 1939-94, prof. chemistry, 1940-63, chmn. dept., 1940-66, dean coll., 1963-71, v.p., 1971-75, pres., 1975-79, pres. emeritus, 1979-94. Mem. Los Angeles County Air Pollution Adv. Commn., 1944-54; Mem. Whittier City Library Bd., 1954-62, pres., 1956-60; mem. Whittier City Hist. Com., 1969-72. Recipient Shirley Mealer Alumni Service award Whittier Coll., 1962; Honor Scroll award Am. Inst. Chemists, 1979. Mem. Am. Chem. Soc., Pacific S.W. Assn. Chemistry Tchrs. (pres. 1954-55), Whittier Area C. of C. (bd. dirs. 1958-61), Sigma Xi, Phi Lambda Upsilon., Soc. of Friends. Club: Rotarian. Home: Whittier Calif. Died July 8, 1994; interred Rose Hills, Whittier Calif.

NEWSOME, MARY DE SÉVIGNÉ, psychoanalyst; b. South Bend, Ind., Dec. 23, 1929; d. Herman Lafayette and Irene Aurora (de Sévigné) N. BA, U. Chgo., 1950; MD, U. Ill., 1959. Mem. faculty Inst. Psychoanalysis, Chgo., 1989-95; lectr. U. Chgo., 1993-95; assoc. prof. psychiatry Rush Med. Coll., Chgo., 1993-95. Contbr. articles to sci. jours. incl. The Annual of Psychoanalysis, Psychoanalytic Inquiry and Progress in Self Psychology. Home: Chicago Ill. Died Sept. 12, 1995.

NEWTON, DEREK ARNOLD, business administration educator; b. Richmond, Eng., Feb. 18, 1930; s. John Newton and Joan Maude (Garnett) Newton Wright; m. Charlene Dawn LeGrand; 1 child, Lindsay Michelle. A.B., Wabash Coll., 1952; M.B.A., Harvard U., 1962, D. Bus. Adminstrn. (Ford Found. fellow), 1964. Sales mgr. R.H. Donnelley Corp., Washington, 1954-60; lectr. in bus. adminstrn. Harvard U. Sch. Bus., 1964-70; prof. bus. adminstrn. U. Va., 1970-76, Elis and Signe Olsson prof. bus. adminstrn., 1976-82, John Tyler prof. bus. adminstrn., 1982-94; cons. in sales and gen. mgmt. to various U.S. corps. Author: Cases in Sales Force Management, 1970, Sales Force Performance and Turnover, 1973, Think Like a Man, Act Like a Lady, Work Like a Dog, 1979, Sales Force Management, 1982, 2d rev. edit. 1990, Decisions in Marketing, 1989, 2d rev. edit. 1989, Feed Your Eagles, 1991, 2d rev. edit, 1993. Commonwealth of Va. eminent scholar, 1982-94. Home: Crozet Va. Died May 21, 1994; interred Private Garden, Charlottesville, Va.

NGUYEN THI DINH, Vietnamese government official. Vice chmn. State Coun., Hanoi, Socialist Republic Vietnam, 1987-92. Home: Hanoi Vietnam Died Aug. 31, 1992.

NICHOLS, MARY PEROT, writer, educator; b. York, Pa., Oct. 11, 1926; d. Charles Poultney and Dorothy (Leonard) Perot; m. Robert Brayton Nichols, Oct. 11, 1953 (div. 1967); children: Kerstin, Duncan, Eliza. BA in Polit. Sci., Swarthmore Coll., 1948. Reporter, polit. columnist Village Voice, N.Y.C., 1958-66, city editor, columnist, 1968-75; dir. pub. rels. N.Y.C. Parks, Recreation and Cultural Affairs Adminstrn., 1966-68; free-lance journalist, investigative columnist Boston Herald Am., 1975-76; dir. communications Office of Mayor, Boston, 1977-78; pres. Sta. WNYC Radio/TV Communications Group, pub. broadcasting stas. assoc. Nat. Pub. Radio and Pub. Broadcasting System, 1978-80; dir. communications U. Pa., Phila., 1980-83; pres. WNYC Communications Group, N.Y.C., 1984-90; vis. prof. journalism NYU, 1990-91, adj. prof. journalism, 1991-92; adj. prf. social studies N.Y.U., 1992-96; bd. dirs. Citizen's Union. Contbr. articles to various publs., including Barron's, New Republic. Trustee Broadcasting Found. Am., 1978-80, Citizens for Arts in Pa., Parks Coun. N.Y.C., 1969-75; bd. dirs. Citizens Union; mem. adv. bd. Adham Ctr. for TV Journalism, Am. U. in Cairo. Recipient Rosebuds award for investigation of organized crime, journalism rev. More, 1973. Mem. City N.Y. Club, Women's City Club (bd. dirs. 1972-74). Democrat. Home: New York N.Y. Died May 21, 1996.

NICHOLS, OWEN HARVEY, investment company executive; b. Market Harborough, Eng., Feb. 7, 1926; came to U.S., 1948, naturalized, 1968; s. Walter J. and Marguerite (Bull) N.; m. Dorothy Arthur, Oct. 7, 1949 (div.); 1 son, Stuart Arthur; m. Carol Camp, May 14, 1977. Grad. high sch. Trader Balfour Guthrie & Co. Ltd., Dallas, Chgo., San Francisco, 1949-53; mgr. Pillsbury Co., Chgo., 1954-61; sr. v.p. investments Paine Webber, Chgo., 1961-94; Chmn. bd. dirs. Chgo. Bd. Trade, 1971-73; chmn. bd. dirs. Chgo. Bd. Options Exchange, 1972-74, founding chmn., 1974-94. Served with Brit. Army and Royal Navy, 1944-48. Mem. Chgo. Bd. Trade, Hamlet Country Club (Delray Beach, Fla.), Adios Golf Club (Boca Raton, Fla.), Evanston Golf Club. Home: Golf Fla. Died Nov. 1, 1994.

NICHOLS, RICHARD MAURICE, lawyer; b. Peterborough, N.H., May 10, 1905; s. Maurice Herbert and Cora Belle (Wilkins) N.; m. Ruth J. Killian, June 20, 1931; children: Andrew L. James R. A.B., Dartmouth, 1926; LL.B., Harvard U., 1929; LL.D., Babson Coll., 1973. Bar: Mass. 1929. Practiced in

Boston, 1929—. Trustee, past pres. Boston Sci. Museum; former chmn. trustees Babson Coll. Mem. Am., Boston bar assns., Phi Beta Kappa. Home: Neeham Mass. Deceased.

NICHOLSON, GLEN IRA, psychology educator; b. Blairsburg, Iowa, Apr. 21, 1925; s. Willis I. and Berneice (McDaniel) N.; m. Phyllis J. Runge, Aug. 9, 1963; children: Marc, Jonathan, Elisabeth. B.A., U. Iowa, 1948, M.A., 1952, Ph.D., 1963. Prin. high sch. Rowan, Columbus Junction and Marion, Iowa, 1948-61; research asst. U. Iowa, 1961-63; asst., then asso. prof. Wichita State U., 1963-67; asso. prof., head dept. ednl. psychology N.Mex. State U., 1967-69; prof. ednl. psychology U. Ariz., Tucson, 1969-92, prof. emeritus, 1992-94, head dept., 1969-75, dept. head, teaching and tchr. edn. divsn., 1990-91, acting assoc. dean Coll. Edn., 1991-92; div. head Ednl. Founds., 1986-87. Mem. NEA, Phi Delta Kappa. Home: Tucson Ariz. Died Mar. 26, 1994.

NICHTERN, CLAIRE JOSEPH, theatrical producer; b. N.Y.C.; d. Fred and Rebecca (Brumer) Joseph; m. Sol Nichtern, June 4, 1944 (div.); m. Herbert Kallem, Nov. 3, 1977 (div.); children: Judith Nichtern, David Nichtern. Student, NYU, 1951-52. Creative cons. Warner Communications, 1985-94. Casting dir., Phoenix Theatre, 1955-58, prodn. coordinator, 1959-60, asst. to gen. mgr., Playwrights Co., 1958-59; producer: The Banker's Daughter, 1961-62, The Typist and the Tiger, 1962-63, Luv, N.Y.C., 1964-67; producer: Jimmy Shine, 1968-69, The Trial of A. Lincoln, 1971, Santa Anita 42, Chelsea Theatre Ctr., 1975, I Got a Song, 1974, House of Blue Leaves, 1976, Absent Friends, 1976, Cold Storage, 1977-78; dir. admissions: Am. Acad. Dramatic Arts, 1970, producer in residence, 1971-73; assoc. dir.: Circle-in-the-Square, 1973; dir. creative affairs, Warner/ Regency, 1978-79, William Morris Agy., 1979; pres., Warner Theatre Prodns., 1979-85. Recipient Antoinette Perry award, 1965. Mem. League N.Y. Theatres, Assn. Theatrical Press Agts. and Mgrs., Am. Film Inst., Actors Fund. Home: New York N.Y. Died Mar. 26, 1994.

NICKERSON, ALBERT LINDSAY, oil company executive; b. Dedham, Mass., Jan. 17, 1911; s. Albert Lindsay and Christine (Atkinson) N.; m. Elizabeth Perkins, June 13, 1936; children—Christine Morgen, Albert W., Elizabeth Davis, Victoria Tabor. Ed., Noble and Greenough Sch., 1926-29; B.S., Harvard U., 1933, LL.D. (hon.), 1976; LL.D. (hon.), Hofstra U., 1964. Service station attendant Socony-Vacuum Oil Co. (now Mobil Corp.), 1933, dist. mgr., 1940, div. mgr., 1941, asst. gen. mgr. Eastern mktg. div., 1944; dir. Vacuum Oil Co., Ltd. (now Mobil Oil Co., Ltd.), London, Eng., 1945; chmn. bd. Vacuum Oil Co., Ltd. (now Mobil Oil Co., Ltd.), 1946; dir. Socony-Vacuum, 1946-94, v.p., dir., 1951-55, pres., 1955-61, chmn. exec. com., chief exec. officer, 1958-69, chmn. bd., 1961-69; bd. dirs. State St. Investment Co., Federal St. Fund, Fed. Res. Bank N.Y., 1961-66, chmn. bd., 1969-71 ; dir. Placement Bur. War Manpower Commn., 1943; chmn. balance of payments adv. com. Commerce Dept., 1965-66; chmn. Bus. Council, 1967-68. Trustee Internat. House, 1952-62, Am. Mus. Nat. History, 1958-62, 64-69; hon. trustee Brigham and Women's Hosp., Boston, 1977-94, Boston Symphony Orch., 1974-85, Rockefeller U., 1957-86; mem. corp. Harvard, 1965-75, bd. overseers, 1959-65. Mem. Harvard Alumni Assn. (dir.), Bus. Council (chmn. 1967, 68). Republican. Episcopalian. Clubs: Harvard Varsity (Boston), Harvard (N.Y.C.); Harvard (Boston); 25-Year of Petroleum Industry (treas. 1965); Country (Brookline, Mass.). Home: Lincoln Center Mass. Died Aug. 7, 1994.

NICKERSON, EILEEN TRESSLER, psychologist; b. Chgo., Oct. 1, 1927; d. Maurice Shearer and Sybil (Voss) Tressler; m. Richard Gorham Nickerson, June 7, 1957; children: Holly, Wendy, Susan. B.A. with honors, U. Ill., 1949; M.A. U. Minn, 1952; Ph.D., Columbia U., 1961. Counselor Comstock Hall and Jr. Coll. Counseling Office, U. Minn., Mpls., 1949-51; research asst. Sociologiska Instituionen, Uppsala (Sweden) U., 1952-53; mental health cons. Minn. Dept. Public Health, Mpls., 1953-54; research asst. Bd. Higher Edn., N.Y.C., 1954-55; psychology intern VA Hosps., N.Y.C., 1954-57; staff psychologist Boston U. Counseling Center, 1957-59; instr., research asso. social relations dept. Harvard Grad. Sch. Edn., 1958-63, psychologist family relations unit project, 1963-65; cons. psychologist Nordli, Wilson Assos., Worcester, Mass., 1964-71; lectr. psychology Grad. Sch. Edn. and Univ. Coll., Northeastern U., Boston, 1964-71; sr. research asso. Research Inst. for Ednl. Problems, Cambridge, Mass., 1970-71; cons. psychologist Krebs Sch. for Learning Disabilities, Lexington, Mass., 1970-71; supervising project dir. Sch. Consultation Project, Boston U., 1971-74, prof. counseling psychology Sch. Edn., 1971-94, chmn. dept. counseling psychology, 1977-79, 90-94; dir. Ctr. Women's Specialization, Boston U., 1978-94; cons. to various groups; mem. exec. bd. Gifford Sch., Weston, Mass., 1976-78. Author: Helping Children, 1974, Women Today; Tomorrow, 1975, Intervention Strategies for Modifying Sex Stereotypes, 1975, Helping Women, 1978, Action Therapies, 1978, Mothering and Fathering, 1979, Helping Through Action, 1982, Dissertation Handbook, 1985, 92; contbr. numerous articles to various publs. Recipient award Nordli-Wilson Assos., 1969; Milton Fund research award Harvard U., 1961. Fellow APA, Am. Psychol. Soc., Am. Orthopsychiatric Assn., Mass. Psychol. Assn. (exec. bd. 1976-78); mem. Am. Counseling Assn. (exec. coun. 1977-78), Am. Pers. and Guidance Assn., Ea. Psychol. Assn., Greater Boston Pers. and Guidance Assn., Mass. Pers. and Guidance Assn. (pres. 1974-76), Nat. Assn. Sch. Psychologists, Nat. Assn. Psychol. Cons. to Mgmt., New Eng. Pers. and Guidance Conf. (exec. bd. 1976-79), New Eng. Psychol. Assn. (exec. bd. 1981-83, pres. 1983-84), North Atlantic Counselor Educators Assn. (pres. 1977-78), Inter Am. Soc. Psychology, LWV (dir. 1960-67). Home: Hopkinton Mass. Died Apr. 17, 1994; interred Evergreen Cemetary, Hopkinton, M.A.

NIEDERLAND, WILLIAM GUGLIELMO, psychiatrist, psychoanalyst, author; b. Schippenbeil, Germany, Aug. 29, 1904; came to U.S., 1940, naturalized, 1945; s. Abraham and Rosa (Mindes) N.; m. Jacqueline Rosenberg, July 20, 1952; children: James Stanley, Daniel Stewart, Alan Abraham. M.D., U. Wuerzburg, Germany, 1929, Dr. (hon.), 1979; M.D., U. Genoa, Italy, 1934; cert. psychoanalysis, N.Y. Inst. Psychoanalysis, 1953. Intern Beelitz Heilstaetten, Beelitz-Berlin, 1929-30; resident Beelitz Heilstaetten, 1930; public health officer Duesseldorf, Germany, 1930-31; med. dir. Sanatorium Rheinburg, Gailingen, Germany, 1932-33; practice medicine specializing in psychiatry Milan, Italy, 1934-39; ship's doctor Blue Funnel Line, Liverpool, Eng., 1939-40; assoc. prof. mental hygiene U. Philippines, Manila, 1940; pvt. practice psychiatry N.Y.C., 1942-73, Englewood, N.J., 1974-93; practice psychoanalysis, 1953-93; mem. staff Hackensack (N.J.) Gen. Hosp.; tng. psychoanalyst SUNY Downstate Med. Center, 1958-79, clin. prof. psychiatry, 1958-78, clin. prof. psychiatry emeritus, 1978-93; tchr., cons., researcher Hackensack Med. Ctr.and Hosp.; chief psychiat. cons. emeritus Altro Health and Rehab. Services, N.Y.C., 1958-76; lectr. community and psychiat. health, U.S., abroad. Author: Man-Made Plague: A Primer on Neurosis, 1949, The Schreber Case: Profile of a Paranoid Personality, 1974 (translated into 6 langs.), new edit. 1984, After-Effects of the Holocaust, 1980, Trauma and Creativity, 1988 (with Howard F. Stein) Maps from the Mind, 1989; author monographs; contbr. numerous articles to profl. jours. Recipient Ann. award German Med. Assn., 1933, Intercultural Edn. award U. Tampa, 1948, Ann. Rsch. award Mich. Soc. Psychiatry and Neurology, 1970, Gold medal Mt. Airy Psychiat. Found., Denver, 1980, Holocaust Meml. award N.Y. Soc. Clin. Psychologists, 1981, Pioneer Award of the Soc. for Traumatic Studies, 1990. Fellow Am. Psychiat. Assn., Deutsches Dokumentationszuentrum (hon.); mem. AMA (life), Am. Psychoanalytic Assn. (life), Internat. Psychoanalytic Assn. (life), N.Y. Psychoanalytic Soc., N.J. Psychoanalytic Soc., Med. Soc. State N.Y. (life), Psychoanalytic Assn. N.Y. (pres. 1971-73), Fifty Yr. Club Am. Medicine. Jewish. Home: Englewood N.J. Died July 30, 1993.

NIER, ALFRED OTTO CARL, physicist; b. St. Paul, May 28, 1911; s. August Carl and Anna J. (Stoll) N.; m. Ruth E. Andersen, June 19, 1937; children: Janet, Keith; m. Ardis L. Hovland, June 21, 1969. B.S., U. Minn., 1931, M.S., 1933, Ph.D., 1936. Nat. Research fellow Harvard, 1936-38; asst. prof. physics U. Minn., 1938-40, assoc. prof., 1940-43, prof., 1946-80, prof. emeritus, 1980-94; physicist Kellex Corp., N.Y.C., 1943-45. Mem. NAS, AAAS, Am. Phys. Soc., Minn. Acad. Sci., Geochem. Soc., Am. Geophys. Union (William Bowie medal 1992), Am. Philos. Soc., Geol. Soc. Am., Am. Soc. Mass Spectrometry, Soc. Applied Spectroscopy, Am. Acad. Arts and Scis., Royal Swedish Acad. Scis., Max Planck Soc. (Fed. Republic Germany), Sigma Xi. Home: Saint Paul Minn. Died May 16, 1994; buried Acacia Park, St. Paul, Minn.

NIIRANEN, VICTOR JOHANNES, professional society administrator; b. Keewatin, Minn., Apr. 24, 1916. DDS, U. Minn., 1940; postgrad., Honolulu Acad. Art, The Foss Sch. Fine Arts; studies with Lau Chun, Hawaii, Hongkong, China. Commd. lt. jr. grade USN, advanced through grades to capt., ret.; nat. pres. Nat. Soc. Arts and Letters, Honolulu; lectr. in field worldwide. Editor: Yearbook, The Record; contbr. articles to profl. jours. Mem. NSAL. Home: Kaneohe Hawaii Deceased.

NIKOLAIS, ALWIN THEODORE, choreographer; b. Southington, Conn., Nov. 25, 1910; s. John and Martha (Heinrich) N. Student, Bennington Coll., summers 1938-40; pupil of, Hanya Holm, Martha Graham, Doris Humphrey, Charles Weidman, Louis Horst, 1946-48; pvt. music and art study; DFA (hon.), Colo. Coll., 1979; D.F.A. hon., Washington U., St. Louis, 1979; doctorate (hon.), Phila. Coll. Performing Arts, 1984, U. Ill., 1985, U. Utah, 1985. Dir. Nikolais Sch. Dance, Hartford, Conn., 1939-42; dir. dance dept. Hartford U., 1940-42, 46-48; asst. to Hanya Holm N.Y. Studio, 1946-48; dir. Henry St. Playhouse, N.Y.C., 1948-71, Alwin Nikolais Dance Co. (now Nikolais Dance Theatre), N.Y.C., 1953-93; faculty Sarah Lawrence Coll., 1952-54, Columbia Tchrs. Coll., 1953-54, Colo. Coll., summers 1946-49, Conn. Coll., summers 1956-57, U. Utah, summers 1961-63, 65-67; spl. prof. of dance U. Calif., 1982; dir., master tchr. internat. dance course U. Guilford, Eng., 1983; vis. disting. prof. U. N.C., 1983-84; Green Honors prof. Tex. Christian U., 1984; co-dir.
ChoreoArts Assocs., 1973-93, Pro Arts Inc., 1986; mem
nat. screening com. dance Inst. Internat. Edn., 1966-6
chmn., 1967-68; cons. Assoc. Council of Arts, 1966-6
from 1974; theatre arts com. Com. Internat. Exchan
Persons, 1967-68; mem. N.Y. State Council on Art
1967-77; hon. mem., mem. exec. bd. Consul Intern
tional de la Dance, UNESCO; dir. Centre Nationale
Danse Contemporaine d'Angers and Paris, France, fro
1978; bd. dirs. Arts Councils Am., 1974-93, Advs. f
Arts; mem. Artists Com. for Kennedy Ctr. Honor
1981, 87, Internat. Dance Alliance, 1984; choreograph
in residence La Menagerie de Verre, Paris, 1986; mem
first ofcl. Am. artists delegation to Peoples Republic
China, 1981; bd. advisors Congress on Research Danc
1979-93. Choreographer: Kaleidoscope, 1956, Prism
1956, Imago, 1963, Sanctum, 1964, Galaxy, 1965, Run
Canto, 1957, Allegory, 1959, Totem, 1960 (Ann Arb
Festival award in collaboration with Ed Emshwill
1964), Stratus, 1961, Nimbus, 1961, Vaudeville of t
Elements, 1965, Somniloquy, 1967, Triptych, 196
Tent, 1968; (film) Fusion, 1967; (TV) Limbo, 196
Echo, 1969, Structures, 1970, Scenario, 1971, Forepla
1972, Chrysalis; film, 1972, Grotto, 1973, Kyldex, 197
Crossfade, 1974; BBC-TV The Relay, 1971, Temp
1974, Scrolls, 1974, Tribe, 1975, Styx, 1976, Triad, 197
Guignol, 1977, Arporisms, 1977, Castings, 1978, G
lery, 1978, Aviary, A Ceremony for Bird People, 19
(Bronze Hugo Chgo. Internat. Film Festival 198
Count Down, 1979, The Mechanical Organ, 198
Schema, 1980, Talisman, 1981, Five Masks, 1981, Pon
1982, Liturgies, 1983, Persons and Structures, 198
Video Game, 1984, Graph, 1984, Lenny and the Hea
breakers, 1983, L'homme Oisseau, 1985, Illusive Visior
1985, Crucible, 1985, Contact, 1985, Velocities, 198
Arc en Ciel, 1987, Blanc on Blanc, 1987, Hollow Lad
1990, Intrados, 1990; USIA, Nik: An Experience
Sight and Sound, 1974; WHA TV documentary Aviar
1978; European tours, 1968, 69, 71, 74-76, 78, 80, 82-
86, 88, 90; S.Am. tours, 1973, 75, 77, 79, 80, 83, 87,
Japan-Far East tours, 1976, 79, Canada tours 1972,
81, 84, U.S. tours 1940, 1956-93. Served with AU
1942-46. Decorated knight Legion of Honor, Comdr.
l'Ordre des Arts et des Lettres, Paris, 1982; recipie
Dance Mag. award, 1968, Grand Prix Paris Intern
Festival Dance, 1968, Emmy award, 1968, Bitef Thea
award Belgrade, Yugoslavia, 1968, Circulo de Critic
award Chile, 1973, 75, Capezio award, 1982, Samuel
Scripps Am. Dance Festival award, 1985, Mell
Found. award 1975, 85, Ethel H. Barber awa
Northwestern U., 1983, Gold medal Aix en Proven
France, 1985, Gold medal City of Lyon, France, 19
Gold medal City of Arles, France, 1986, Gold me
City of Paris, 1988, Tiffany award N.Y.C., 1988, Vign
Festival award, Italy, 1987, Kennedy Ctr. Alliar
award, 1987, Am. Dance Guild award, 1987, N
Medal of Arts award, 1987; Kennedy Ctr. Lifeti
Achievement Award, 1987; Nat. Council Arts grant
1966, 69-71, 73-75, Nat. Endowment for Arts grant
1966-93; honored with Alwin Nikolais Week
proclamation Gov. Wis., Dec. 1978; Guggenheim fello
1964, 67. Fellow Am. Acad. Arts and Scis.; mem. As
Am. Dance Companies (dir. 1966-67, pres. 1967-6
Nat. Soc. Lit. and Arts, U.S.-Chinese Artist Exchan
Broadcast Music Inc., Soc. des Auteurs et Compositeu
Dramatiques. Home: New York N.Y. Died May
1993.

NILSSON, HARRY, singer, songwriter; b. Bklyn., Ju
15, 1941. In charge computer center Ops. Secu
Pacific 1st Nat. Bank, Van Nuys, Calif., 7 years. Sing
in movie Midnight Cowboy; rec. artist for, RCA;
bums include Nilsson Schmillsson, Little Touch
Schmillsson in The Night, 1973, Son of Schmillss
1972, The Point, The Sandman, 1975, That's The W
It Is, 1976, Knillsson, 1977, Early Times, Greatest H
1978, Nilsson's Greatest Music, 1981, Nilsson Si
Newman, 1989, All-Time Greatest Hits, 1989, Ev
ybody's Talking and Other Hits, 1990; singer: m
sound track Son of Dracula; film sound track Dui
Mon Dei; composer: film sound track Open Y
Window; Bath, 1941, The Puppy Song, Don't Leave M
I Said Goodbye to Me, One, Gotta Get Up, Driv
Along, Down, Jump Into the Fire. Recipient Gram
awards for best popular rock vocal 1969, 72; 3 Album
Year awards for prodn. Stereo Rev.; Thomas A
Edison award for best album of year (Nilsson Schm
son); has 8 gold records, BMI awards; Montreaux F
Festival spl. bd. of merit award for The Point; Atla
Film Festival spl. merit award for The Point. Ho
Agoura Hills Calif. Died Jan. 15, 1994.

**NIXON, PATRICIA RYAN (THELMA CATHERI
NIXON),** wife of former President of United States
Ely, Nev., Mar. 16, 1912; m. Richard Milhous Nix
June 21, 1940; children: Patricia (Mrs. Edward Fi
Cox), Julie (Mrs. Dwight David Eisenhower II). G
cum laude, U. So. Calif., 1937, L.H.D., 1961. X
technician N.Y.C., 1931-33; tchr. high schs. Cal., 1
41; govt. economist, 1942-45. Promoter of world v
humanitarian service, volunteerism in U.S. Decor
grand cross Order of Sun for relief work at time
massive earthquake, 1971; Peru; grand cordon M
Venerable Order Knighthood Pioneers Liberia, 1
named among most admired women George Ga
polls, 1957, 68, 69, 70, 71. Home: New York N.Y. I
June 22, 1993.

IXON, RICHARD MILHOUS, former President of nited States; b. Yorba Linda, Calif., Jan. 9, 1913; s. ancis A. and Hannah (Milhous) N.; m. Thelma atherine Patricia Ryan, June 21, 1940 (dec.); children: atricia (Mrs. Edward Finch Cox), Julie (Mrs. Dwight avid Eisenhower II). A.B., Whittier Coll., 1934; L.B. with honors, Duke U., 1937. Bar: Calif. 1937, S. Supreme Ct. 1947, N.Y. State 1963-69. Practiced w in Whittier, Calif., 1937-42; atty. Office Price Adinstrn., Washington, Jan.-Aug. 1942; mem. 80th-81st ongresses from 12th Calif. Dist.; U.S. senator from alif., 1950-53, v.p. of U.S., 1953-61, Republican ndidate for Pres. of U.S., 1960, Republican nominee r gov. Calif., 1962; counsel firm Adams Duque & azeltine, L.A., 1961-63; mem. firm Mudge Stern aldwin & Todd, N.Y.C., 1963-64; ptnr. firm Nixon udge Rose Guthrie & Alexander, N.Y.C., 1964-68; ected 37th Pres. of U.S., 1968, 72, inaugurated, 1969, , resigned, 1974; hon. chmn. Fund for Democracy and evel., 1992. Author: Six Crises, 1962, RN, 1978, The eal War, 1980, Leaders, 1982, Real Peace, 1984, No ore Vietnams, 1985, 1999: Victory Without War, 88, In the Arena: A Memoir of Victory, Defeat and enewal, 1990, Seize the Moment: America's Challenge a One-Superpower World, 1992, Beyond Peace: The piritual Deficit in America, 1994. Hon. chmn. Boy ubs Am.; trustee Whittier Coll., 1939-68. Served to lt. mdr. USNR, 1942-46, PTO. Mem. Order of Coif. em. Soc. of Friends. Home: New York N.Y. Died or. 22, 1994.

OBLE, SAM, oil and gas producer, trucking company ecutive; b. 1925; married. Formerly with Samedan Oil orp., Noble Drilling Corp., Tulsa; now chmn. bd. oble Affiliates, Inc., Ardmore, Okla. Home: Ardmore kla.

OCE, ROBERT HENRY, neuropsychiatrist, edutor; b. Phila., Feb. 19, 1914; s. Rev. Sisto Julius and adeleine (Saulino) N.; m. Carole Lee Landis, 87. A.B., Kenyon Coll., 1935; M.D., U. Louisville, 39; postgrad., U. Pa. Sch. Medicine, 1947, Langleyrter Neuropsychiat. Inst., 1949, 52. Rotating intern amot Hosp., Erie, Pa., 1939-40; resident psychiatrist arren (Pa.) State Hosp., 1940-41, staff psysician, 1946-; staff physician Met. State Hosp., Norwalk, Calif., 48-50; dir. clin. services Pacific State Hosp., Spadra, lif., 1950-52; dir. clin. services Modesto (Calif.) State osp., 1952-58, asst. supt. psychiat. services, 1958-64; t. practice medicine specializing in neuropsychiatry, 65-73; Mem. faculty postgrad. symposiums in ychiatry for physicians U. Calif., 1958, 66. Author: m) Reserpine Treatment of Psychotic Patients; ntbr. articles to profl. jours. Served from lt. (j.g.) to comdr. M.C. USNR, 1941-46. Recipient Albert and ary Lasker award for integration reserpine treatment entally ill and mentally retarded, 1957; Wisdom award honor, 1970. Life fellow Am. Psychiat. Assn. (sec. 54, 55); fellow Royal Soc. Health; mem. Phi Beta appa, Delta Psi. Episcopalian. Home: Tempe Ariz. ed June 7, 1995.

OLAN, PAUL THOMAS, retired English and manities educator; b. Rochester, N.Y., Apr. 4, 1919; John J. and Anna (Sweeney) N.; m. Peggy Hime, June 1947; children: John Michael, Peter Andrew, zabeth Anne Nolan Fellows. Student, Aquinas Inst. ochester, 1933-37; B.A., Central Ark. U., 1947; M.A., lane U., 1949, Ph.D., 1953. Instr. English, dir. News r. Central Ark. U., 1947; asst. prof. English, dir. pub. ations Centenary Coll. of La., 1949-54; Ford Found. . prof. Ark. State U., 1954-55; prof. English, Dupré of. humanities U. Southwestern La., Lafayette, 1955-. emeritus, 1988-95. Author: Round-The-World ays, 1961, One-Act Plays of Lee Arthur, 1962, aucer for Children, 1963, Writing the One-Act Play, 64, Death For The Lonely, 1964 (Nat. Workshop ayers award), Three Plays by John W. Crawford, 65, Marc Connelly, 1969, Drama Workshop Plays, 69, Describing People, 1970, The Loneliest Game, 71, Hedda Gabler, South, 1972, Last Week I Was nety-Five, 1973, Squeak to Me of Love, 1973, (with nes Burke) Between Hisses 1973, The Highwayman, 75, The Eavesdrop Theatre, 1976, John Wallace awford, 1981, Folk Tale Plays, 1982, Directing the nateur Stage, 1985. Served with USAAF, 1942-45. em. Modern Lang. Assn., Playwrights' Theatre La., n. Studies Assn. Democrat. Home: Lafayette La. ed Mar. 13, 1995.

OLAN, RICHARD JOSEPH, newspaper columnist; Lowell, Mass., Aug. 15, 1918; s. Matthew James and ary Jane (Lendrum) N.; m. Ida Alicia Franceschini, b. 21, 1946 (dec. 1976); children—Richard Matthew, vid Francis; m. Carol Maria Kuzdenyi, Oct. 16, 81. Student, Lowell High Sch. Reporter Couriertizen-Evening Leader, Lowell, Mass., 1936-38; umnist Telegram, Lowell, Mass., 1936, San Francisco aminer, San Francisco, 1946-94. Contbr. articles to ofl. jours. Served to capt. AUS, 1942-46. Recipient der of Mil. Merit award Republic of Philippines, 46. Home: San Rafael Calif. Died Nov. 16, 1994.

OONAN, RAY JOHN, retired newspaper editor; b. lahoma City, May 17, 1914; s. William J. and Myrtle alkbrenner) N.; m. Elizabeth Geer, Mar. 1, 1940; ldren: John, Jeanne, Candy, Phyllis. Student, lahoma City U., 1937-38. Reporter, Daily Oklahoman, 1938-41; reporter, bur. chief St. Louis Star-Times, 1941-51; mem. staff St. Louis Globe-Democrat, 1951-83, city editor, 1966-75, asst. mng. editor, 1975-79, mng. editor, 1979-83; bd. dirs. Mid-Am. Press Inst., 1969-82. Bd. dirs. Met. St. Louis YMCA, 1974-83. Mem. Sigma Delta Chi (pres. St. Louis chpt. 1966-68). Episcopalian. Club: St. Louis Press (pres. 1976-77). Home: Saint Louis Mo. Died May 23, 1994.

NORDLINGER, ERIC ALLEN, political scientist, educator; b. Frankfurt, Fed. Republic of Germany, Sept. 18, 1939; came to U.S., 1946, naturalized, 1951; s. Leo and Kate (Levi) N.; m. Carol Maurine Uhl, Jan. 7, 1978; children: Alexandra, Oliver. B.A. with honors, Cornell U., 1961; M.A., Princeton U., 1963, Ph.D., 1966. Asst. prof. polit. sci. Brandeis U., 1965-70, assoc. prof., 1970-71; assoc. Ctr. for Internat. Affairs Harvard U., 1968-90, assoc. Olin Inst. for Strategic Studies, 1990-94; lectr. govt. Harvard U. Sch. Medicine, 1969-70; asso. prof. polit. sci. Brown U., 1971-73, prof., 1973-94, chmn. dept. polit. sci., 1978-85, assoc. Ctr. for Fgn. Policy Devel., 1988-90; exec. com. Watson Inst. for Internat. Studies, 1989-93. Author: The Working Class Tories: Authority, Deference and Stable Democracy, 1967, Conflict Regulation in Divided Societies, 1972, Decentralizing the City, 1973, Soldiers in Politics: Military Coups and Governments, 1977, On the Autonomy of the Democratic State, 1981; editor: Politics and Society, 1970; mem. editorial bd. Jour. Polit. and Mil. Sociology. NSF grantee, 1968, 74; Ford Found. grantee, 1970; fellow, 1971; Nat. Endowment for Humanities grantee, 1981, Cato Inst. grantee, 1988. Home: Cambridge Mass. Died June, 1994.

NORDSTROM, JAMES F., department store executive; b. 1940; married. BBA, U. Wash., 1962. Various positions Nordstrom, Inc., Seattle, 1960-96, exec. v.p., 1975-78, pres., 1975-78, 1978-96, co-chmn., also bd. dirs. Home: Seattle Wash. Died Mar. 12, 1996.

NORRIS, ROBERT FOGG, physician; b. Wilmington, Del., Dec. 23, 1905; s. Herschel Augustus and Elizabeth Lippincott (Fogg) N.; m. Mary Scattergood, June 13, 1931; children: Anne (Mrs. Baldwin), Victoria (Mrs. Dean). Grad., Phillips Exeter Acad., 1924; AB, Princeton, 1928; MD, U. Pa., 1932. Diplomate: Am. Bd. Pathology. Intern Pa. Hosp., Phila., 1932-34; asst. dir. Ayer Clin. Lab., 1935-41; asst. in pathology Med. Sch. Johns Hopkins U., 1934-35; assoc. William Pepper Lab. Clin. Medicine U. Pa., 1946-50; dir. Wm. Pepper Lab., 1950-68; asst. prof. clin. medicine U. Pa., 1947-48, assoc. prof., 1948-53, prof. clin. pathology, 1953-68, prof. pathology, 1968-74, prof. emeritus, 1974-93; bd. dirs. Penndel Labs., Inc., Ardmore, Pa., 1974-86; cons. in pathology U.S. Naval Hosp., Phila., 1946-68, Princeton (N.J.) Hosp., 1952-68, VA Hosp., Phila., 1965-70. Treas. 6th Congress Internat. Soc. Blood Transfusions, 1956; chmn. Biol. Warfare Def. Com. Phila., 1950-52; asst. dir. div. 5 Phila. Civil Def. Coun., 1952-53; mem. Pa. Disaster Med. Coun., 1959-65; mem. commn. disaster med. services Pa. Med. Soc., 1959-67. From lt. to comdr. USN, 1941-46; capt. Res. ret. Mem. AMA, AAAS, Coll. Am. Pathologists, Am. Soc. Clin. Pathologists, Am. Assn. Pathologists and Bacteriologists, Am. Soc. Microbiologists, Coll. Phys. of Phila., Pa. Assn. Clin. Pathologists (pres. 1969), Pathol. Soc. Phila. (v.p. 1956-57, pres. 1958-59), Pa. Assn. Blood Banks (pres. 1958-59), Internat. Soc. Blood Transfusions (v.p. 1958-64), Pa. Med. Soc. (chmn. commn. blood banks 1947-59), Physiol. Soc. Phila., Phila. County Med. Soc. (chmn. sect. clin. pathology 1953), Sigma Xi, Nu Sigma Nu, Alpha Omega Alpha. Home: Newtown Square Pa. Died Nov. 24, 1993.

NORTON, HOWARD MELVIN, free-lance writer, editor; b. Haverhill, Mass., May 30, 1911; s. Clarence Alfred and Grace Frances (Eckel) N.; m. Marjorie Anderson, July 7, 1940; children: Howard Melvin, Martha (Mrs. Charles P. Izzo, Jr.), Mary, Deborah. B.S.J., U. Fla., 1933. Fgn. corr. in Far East (hdqrs. in Tokyo) for Whaley-Eaton Service, Los Angeles Times, San Francisco Chronicle, Kansas City Star, Phila. Inquirer, 1933-40; Behind-the-News editor Balt. Evening Sun, 1940, 41; fgn. editor Balt. Sun (morning), 1942, war corr., 1943, 44, Washington corr., 1945-50, chief of London bur., 1950-51; chief Moscow bur., 1956-59, Washington bur., 1959-64; mem. nat. staff of U.S. News and World Report, 1964-65, assoc. editor, 1965-70, White House corr., 1970-76; chief Washington bur. Nat. Courier, 1976-77; dir. publs. Nat. Assn. Community Action Dirs., Washington, 1978-82; editorial cons., writer Edison Electric Inst., Washington, 1982-86; free-lance writer, 1987—. Author series of articles on Unemployment Compensation which won Pulitzer Prize for the Balt. Sun, 1947, series of articles exposing deficiencies of Md.'s mental hosps. which resulted in revision of mental health law and legislation appropriation of $28,000,000 to rebuild hosps., 1949; (books) Only in Russia, 1961, The Miracle of Jimmy Carter, 1976, Rosalynn—A Portrait, 1977, When the Angels Laughed, 1977, Good News About Trouble, 1978; editor The Electrification Council Quar. Report, 1983-86. Recipient Centennial award in Journalism U. Fla., 1953; Pacific-Asiatic Service medal, 1945; commendations Army and Navy, 1946; named Disting. Alumnus U. Fla. Coll. Journalism and Communications, 1978. Mem. White House Corrs. Assn., Soc. Profl. Jours., Sigma Delta Chi. Methodist. Clubs: Lakewood Country; Nat. Press (Washington). Home: Wilmington N.C. Died Mar. 12, 1994; interred Oleander Gardens, Wilmington, N.C.

NORVELL, NANCY KATHLEEN, psychologist, educator; b. Atlanta, Aug. 17, 1957; d. Lauren and Lois (Dozier) N.; m. Timothy Lee Boaz, May 20, 1989. BA, U. Va., 1979; MS, Va. Commonwealth U., 1981, PhD, 1984. Diplomate in clin. psychology Am. Bd. Profl. Psychologists; lic. psychologist, Fla. Intern in psychology Brown U., Providence, 1983-84; asst. prof. dept. clin. and health psychology U. Fla., Gainesville, 1984-89; vis. assoc. prof. dept. law and mental health U. South Fla., Tampa, from 1989, assoc. prof. dept. womens studies, from 1991, clin. asst. prof. dept. medicine, div. cardiology, from 1989; pvt. practice Tampa, from 1989; cons. div. cardiology U. Fla., from 1989. Co-author: Facilitating Stress Management, 1990, Stress Management for Law Enforcement, 1990; contbr. over 30 articles to profl. jours. Vol. Ctr. for Women, Tampa, from 1990, Spring Outreach Program for battered women, from 1992; membership com. Mental Health Assn. Hillsborough County, Tampa, from 1990. Mem. APA (Excellence in Cons. Rsch. award 1986), Soc. Behavioral Medicine, Assn. Advancement Behavior Therapy (program com. 1988-90), Fla. Psychol. Assn. (pres. Tampa Bay chpt. 1992), Phi Kappa Phi. Home: Land O'Lakes Fla. Deceased.

NOVER, NAOMI, journalist, editor, author; b. Buffalo; d. B.B. and Rebecca (Shane) Goll; m. Barnet Nover. Student, U. Buffalo; BS, N.Y. State Tchrs. Coll.; MA, George Washington U., 1951. News, features, editorial asst. Buffalo Times; tchr. pub., pvt. schs. Buffalo Park Sch. (demonstration sch. of U. Buffalo), Snyder, N.Y.; music critic Denver Post at Goethe Music Festival, Aspen, Colo.; news corr., columnist Washington Bur. Denver Post; editor, bur. chief Nover News Bur., Washington, 1972—; corr. mission to Europe Portland Oregonian, Italian Peace Treaty Conf., Luxembourg Palace, Paris, Ladybird Johnson trips to nat. parks, 1963; attended various econ. summits; White House corr. Pres. Ford European tour, Switzerland, Spain, Finland, England, France, Germany, Poland, 1975, Pres. Ford trips to China, South Korea, Indonesia, Japan, Philippines, Hawaii, 1978, Pres. Carter trips to India, Saudi Arabia, Israel, Egypt, S.Am., Africa, Eng., Europe, Japan, etc., 1978, Pres. Reagan trips to Peoples Republic of China, Europe, Cen. Am., Caribbean, Iceland, Bali, Indonesia, Finland, 1988, Pres. Bush's trips to Italy, The Vatican, Poland, Hungary, France, NATO, London, Costa Rica, Fed. Republic Germany, Belgium, The Netherlands, 1989, to Finland for Bush-Gorbachev Summit, 1990, Can., Martinique, Bermuda, Paris, London, Athens, Crete, Greece, Ankara, Turkey, Istanbul, Turkey, 1991, Moscow, Kiev, Russia, 1991, Honolulu, Sydney, Australia, Canberra, Australia, Melbourne, Australia, Singapore, Seoul, Korea, Osaka, Japan, Tokyo, 1992, Pres. Clinton trip to UN, N.Y., 1993. Writer, dir. plays produced in Buffalo; participated radio and television plays; producer: nationally syndicated radio program Views and Interviews; author: nationally syndicated feature stories and column Washington Dateline, 1952—; contbr. articles to mags. Formerly active ARC, U.S Treasury War Bonds; chmn. Kalorama area Community Chest, 1947-49; originator embassy participation groups, jr. hostess, chmn., originator embassy tour Goodwill Industries; past chmn., producer program with 1,000 Girl Scouts at Pan Am. Union; past mem. council Girl Scouts U.S.A.; chmn. program com. Columbian Women of George Washington U., 1953-56; nat. chmn. War Nurses Meml.; mem. women's bd. George Washington U. Hosp. Recipient award pin U.S. Treasury Dept.; Silver Eagle award Girl Scouts U.S.A.; chosen to christen ship SS Syosset for vol. and charity activities; named honor citizen Colonial Williamsburg (Va.). Mem. White House Corrs. Assn., State Dept. Corrs. Assn., Congl. Press Galleries Corrs. Assn., U.S. Capitol, AAUW, U.S. Capitol Hist. Soc., U.S. Supreme Ct. Hist. Soc., Founding Friend of Blair House, The Circle of Nat. Gallery of Art, Nat. League Am. Pen Women, Smithsonian Assocs., U.S. Archives, Hist. Preservation, Libr. of Congress Assocs., Women in Radio and TV Assn., Women in Arts Mus., Am. Hist. Assn., Welcome to Washington, Ikebana, Phi Beta Kappa Assocs., Sigma Delta Chi, Pi Lambda Theta (past corr. ofcl. publ., nat. scholastic honors). Died Apr. 22, 1995.

NOWLIN, JOSEPH E., lawyer; b. Arkadelphia, Ark., Aug. 28, 1945. BS, BSBA, U. Ark., 1967; JD, So. Meth. U., 1971. Bar: Tex. 1972. Mem. Gardere & Wynne, Dallas. Editor-in-chief Jour. Air Law and Commerce, 1970-71. 1st lt. U.S. Army, 1969-75. Mem. ABA, State Bar Tex., Tex. Bar Found., Dallas Bar Assn., Phi Alpha Delta, Barristers. Home: Dallas Tex. Died Dec. 24, 1993.

NOYD, R(OY) ALLEN, religious organization administrator; b. Jamestown, N.Y., July 4, 1941; s. Roy Alvin and Carolyn Jane (Van Benthuysen) N.; m. Patricia Ruth Berg, June 9, 1962; children: Scott A., Jeffrey D., Noelle K. Student, Jamestown Community Coll., 1960-62. Ordained to ministry, 1972; cert. behavioral analyst. Assoc. pastor Jamestown (N.Y.) Revival Ctr., 1972-78; pastor Faith Assembly, Jamestown, 1984-85; sr. pastor New Covenant Assembly, Jamestown, 1985-88; gen. sec., treas. Christian Ch. of

N.Am., Transfer, Pa., 1988-94; pres., Jamestown N.Y. Chpt. of Pentecostal Fellowship North Am., 1987-88, v.p., 1985-87. Mem. Nat. Assn. Evangs. (fin. commn.), Nat. Christian Counselors Assn. (regional rep.), Carlson Learning Co. (assoc.), Religious Conf. Mgmt. Assn. Republican. Home: Greenville Pa. Died June 9, 1993; buried Maple Grove Cemetery, Frewsburg, N.Y.

NSENGIYUMVA, VINCENT, archbishop. Archbishop of Kigali Roman Cath.Ch., Rwanda.

NUCCITELLI, SAUL ARNOLD, civil engineer, consultant; b. Yonkers, N.Y., Apr. 25, 1928; s. Agostino and Antoinette (D'Amicis) N.; m. Concetta Orlandi, Dec. 23, 1969; 1 child, Saul A. BS, NYU, 1949, MCE, 1954; DCE, MIT, 1960. Registered profl. engr., N.Y., Mo., Colo., Conn., Mass.; lic. land surveyor, Mo., Colo., Conn., Mass. Asst. civil engr. Westchester County Engrs., N.Y.C., 1949-51, 53-54; project engr. H.B. Bolas Enterprises, Denver, 1954-55; asst. prof., rsch. engr., U. Denver, 1955-58; mem. staff MIT, 1958-60; asst. prof. engring. Cooper Union Coll., N.Y.C., 1960-62; pvt. practice cons. engring., Springfield, Mo., 1962-95; organizer, bd. dirs. Met. Nat. Bank, Springfield; former adviser, bd. dirs. Farm & Home Savs. and Loan Assn. Contbr. articles to profl. jours. Past chmn. Adv. Council on Mo. Pub. Drinking Water; chmn. Watershed Com. of the Ozarks; bd. dirs. YMCA; Greene County Mus. of Ozarks; past chmn. Bd. City Utilities, Springfield; past pres. Downtown Springfield Assn. 1st lt. U.S. Army, 1951-53. Recipient Cert. of Appreciation, Mo. Mcpl. League, 1981; named Mo. Cons. Engr. of Yr., 1973. Fellow ASCE; mem. Nat. Soc. Profl. Engrs., Mo. Soc. Profl. Engrs. (past pres. Ozark chpt.), Boston Soc. Civil Engrs., Am. Concrete Inst., Am. Inst. Steel Constrn., Am. Welding Soc., ASTM, Am. Soc. Mil. Engrs., Springfield C. of C. (past v.p.), Rotary (past pres.). Died Aug. 31, 1995. Home: Springfield Mo.

NUTTEN, WESLEY L, III, lawyer; b. L.A., May 16, 1929; s. Wesley L jr. and Margaret (Cameron) N.; m. Helen Craft, Aug. 29, 1954; children: Kathleen J. Luedeke, Wesley Lawrence, Laura Lynn. BA, Dartmouth Coll., 1951; JD, UCLA, 1958. Atty. Sheppard, Mullin, Richter & Hampton, L.A., 1958-93. Trustee Westridge Sch., 1972-80, Flintridge Prep. Sch., 1976-82, 87-93, pres., 1981, chmn. bd. dirs., 1982; chmn. greater L.A. area Dartmouth Coll. 3d Century Fund, 1969-71; bd. dirs. Harbridge House, 1976-81, mem. Boston-based consulting firm; pres. L.A. Child Guidance Clinic, 1972-75, bd. dirs., 1965-75. Officer USN, 1951-55. Fellow Am. Bar Found., Am. Coll. Trust and Estate Counsel (mem. exec. com., bd. regents 1978-84); mem. ABA (real property, probate and trust law sect. coun. 1977-83), Internat. Acad. Estate and Trust Law, State Bar Calif. (exec. com. of conf. of dels. 1972-75, vice-chmn. 1975), Los Angeles County Bar (chmn. probate and trust law sect. 1971-73, bd. trustees 1975-77), Dartmouth Alumni Club of So. Calif. (pres. 1965), Dartmouth Alumni Coun., Chancery Club, Annandale Golf Club (bd. dirs. 1991-93). Home: Sunland Calif. Died Aug. 8, 1993; buried Forest Lawn Meml. Pk., Hollywood Hills, Los Angeles, Calif.

NUTTING, CHARLES BERNARD, lawyer, educator; b. Iowa City, Dec. 8, 1906; s. Charles C. and Eloise (Willis) N.; m. Mary A. Flannagan, Aug. 17, 1933; children: Catherine (Mrs. Elmer L. Lampe), Elizabeth (Mrs. John D. Verhoeven), Margaret (Mrs. Donald Ralph). B.A., U. Iowa, 1927, J.D., 1930; LL.M., Harvard U., 1932, S.J.D., 1933; LL.D., U. Pitts., 1957, Dickinson Coll. Law, 1960; Litt. D., Geneva Coll., 1957; L.H.D., Seton Hill Coll., 1957. Bar: Iowa 1930, Kans. 1930, U.S. Supreme Ct. 1943, Pa. 1956, D.C. 1964. Practiced with Holmes and Adams, Wichita, Kans., 1930-31; asst. prof. law U. Nebr., Lincoln, 1933-35; asso. prof. U. Nebr., 1936-38, prof., 1938-46; asso. prof. law. U. Tex., Austin, 1935-36; asso. solicitor Dept. Agr., Washington, 1942-46; prof. law, vice dean U. Pitts. Law Sch., 1946-49, dean, 1949-52, vice chancellor, 1952-56; vis. prof. law U. Mich., summer 1948; dir. Buhl Found., Pitts., 1956-60; pres. Action-Housing, Inc., 1957-60; dean Nat. Law Center, George Washington U., 1960-66, prof., 1966-72, emeritus, 1972; prof. Hastings Coll. Law U. Calif., San Francisco, 1972-76; Mem. Fed. City Council, 1960-72, Gov.'s Citizen's Com. Housing, 1956, Pres.'s Conf. Adminstrv. Procedure. Editor: (with F. Reed Dickerson) Cases and Materials on Legislation; Contbr. articles to legal publs. Mem. ABA (vice chmn. adminstrn. law sect 1950-51, chmn. 1951-52), Fed. Bar Assn., Assn. Am. Law Sch. (pres. 1953), Am. Law Inst., Phi Beta Kappa, Order of Coif, Delta Sigma Rho, Phi Delta Phi, Omicron Delta Kappa. Presbyterian. Clubs: Nat. Lawyers (Washington), Cosmos (Washington). Home: Lexington Ky. Died Oct. 23, 1994; interred Iowa City, I.A.

NYAGUMBO, MAURICE, government official; b. Rusape, Zimbabwe, Dec. 12, 1924; married; 5 children. Student, St. Faith's Mission, Zimbabwe, St. Augustine's, Penhalonga, Zimbabwe. Founder, sec. Cen. African Social Club, 1953; founder Youth League in Zimbabwe; sec. Rusape br. African Nat. Congress, 1957; organising sec. Zimbabwe African Nat. Union, 1962; then minister of mines, coop devel. Govt. of Zimbabwe, now sr. minister polit. affairs. Home: Harare Zimbabwe

NYEMASTER, RAY, lawyer; b. Davenport, Iowa, Mar. 23, 1914; s. Jesse Ray and Clara Elva (Stucker) N.; children by previous marriage—Thomas Lee, Martha Merry; m. Martha Jane Backman Jaeger, Dec. 27, 1968; stepchildren—William John Jaeger, Judith Ann Jaeger Hand. Student, Cornell Coll., Mt. Vernon, Iowa, 1931-32; B.A., State U. Iowa, 1936, J.D., 1938. Bar: Iowa bar 1938. Practiced in Des Moines; asso. partner firm Parrish, Guthrie, Colflesh & O'Brien, 1938-68; partner Nyemaster, Goode, McLaughlin, Emery & O'Brien, 1968-95; dir. Vernon Co., Newton, Iowa, Central Life Ins. Co., Des Moines.; Chmn. Iowa Aero. Commn., 1961-73. Bd. dirs. Des Moines Center Sci. and Industry; trustee Cornell Coll., Mt. Vernon, Iowa. Mem. Am., Iowa, Polk County bar assns., Des Moines C. of C. Clubs: Mason (Des Moines) (Shriner, 32 deg., Jester, royal impresario), Rotarian. (Des Moines), Des Moines (Des Moines), Embassy (Des Moines), Wakonda (Des Moines). Home: Des Moines Iowa Died Dec. 7, 1995.

OAKESHOTT, GORDON B(LAISDELL), geologist; b. Oakland, Calif., Dec. 24, 1904; s. Philip S. and Edith May (Blaisdell) O.; m. Beatrice Clare Darrow, Sept. 1, 1929 (dec. 1982); children: Paul Darrow, Phyllis Joy Oakeshott Martin, Glenn Raymond; m. Lucile Spangler Burks, 1986. BS, U. Calif., 1928, MS, 1929; PhD, U. So. Calif., 1936. Asst. field geologist Shell Oil Co., 1929-30; instr. earth sci. Compton Coll., 1930-48; supervising mining geologist Calif. Div. Mines, 1948-56, dep. chief, 1956-57, chief, 1958; dep. chief Calif. Div. Mines and Geology, 1959-72; cons. geologist, 1973-85, ret.; lectr. geology Calif. State U., Sacramento, 1972-73, Calif. State U., San Francisco, 1975. Author: California's Changing Landscapes—A Guide to the Geology of the State, 1971, 2d edit., 1978, Volcanoes and Earthquakes-Geologic Violence, 1975, Japanese edit., 1981, My California: Autobiography of a Geologist with a Tribute to Don Tocher, 1989; contbr. articles to profl. jours. Fellow AAAS, Geol. Soc. Am., Calif. Acad. Sci.; mem. Seismol. Soc. Am., Nat. Assn. Geology Tchrs. (pres. 1970-71, Webb award 1981), Am. Assn. Petroleum Geologists (hon., Michel T. Halbouty Human Needs award 1993), AIME, Mining and Metall. Soc. Am., Peninsula Geol. Soc. (past pres.), Engrs. Club San Francisco, Geol. Soc. Sacramento (past pres.), Peninsula Gem and Geol. Soc. (hon.), Assn. Engring. Geologists (hon.), Earthquake Engring. Research Inst. (past dir.), Am. Inst. Profl. Geologists (emeritus). Home: Walnut Creek Calif.

O'BANNON, HELEN BOHEN, university official; b. Ridgewood, N.J., Aug. 15, 1939; Arthur C. and Lillian (McNamara) Bohen; m. George W. O'Bannon, Sept. 15, 1962; children: Patrick, Colin, Sean, Casey. BA, Wellesley Coll., 1961; MA, Stanford U., 1962; LL.D. (hon.), Beaver Coll., 1984; ArtsD (hon.), Westminster Coll., 1987. Rsch. economist U.S. Treasury, Washington, 1963, 64-65; instr. econs. Robert Morris Coll., Washington, 1970-72; lectr. Chatham Coll., Pitts., 1975, Bryn Mawr (Pa.) Coll., 1981; asst., then assoc. dean Carnegie-Mellon U., Pitts., 1973-76; commr. Pa. Pub. Utility Commn., Harrisburg, 1975-79; sec. Pub. Welfare, Harrisburg, 1979-83; sr. v.p. U. Pa., Phila., 1983—; lectr. program for execs. Carnegie-Mellon U., 1978-82; exec. in residence Bryn Mawr Coll., 1980; adj. prof. Wharton Sch., 1984—. Contbr. articles in field to profl. jours. Bd. dirs. Job Adv. Svc., Pitts., 1977-83, Women in Govt., Carlow Coll., Pitts., 1980-86; mem. adv. coun. Women's Polit. Caucus Allegheny County, 1980-86; trustee Wellesley Coll., 1982-85, Germantown Acad., 1984-86, Planned Parenthood Southeastern Pa., 1984—; mem. Mayor's Econ. Roundtable, 1984—, Pa. Women's Campaign Fund, 1984-87. Named Disting. Dau. of Pa., 1977; recipient Alumnae Achievement award Wellesley Coll., 1980, Women in Govt. award AAUW, 1979. Mem. Nat. Rsch. Coun. (panel on stats. for family assistance and related programs 1983-84, 86-88, transp. rsch. bd. 1977-79), Nat. Assn. Regulatory Commrs. (exec. bd. 1977-79), Wellesley Coll. Alumnae Assn. (pres. 1982-85). Home: Bala Cynwyd Pa. Deceased.

OBERMAN, MOISHE DAVID, magazine publisher; b. Springfield, Ill., Mar. 3, 1914; s. Harry and Ida (Guralnik) O.; student St. Louis Coll. Pharmacy, 1931-33; m. Bobbye Friedman, Oct. 8, 1939; children—Michael Alan, Martin Jay, M.H. William, Marjorie Ann. Scrap metals broker, Springfield, 1937-41; founder Scrap Age Mag., 1944, Mill Trade Jour., 1963, Waste Age Mag., 1969, Encyclopedia of Scrap Recycling, 1976; pres., editor, pub. 3 Sons Pub. Co., Niles, Ill., 1944; pres. Emde Realty Devel. Corp., Springfield, 1957-63; exec. sec. Midwest Scrap Dealers Assn., 1941—; treas. North Shore Investments, Highland Park, Ill., 1968; exec. dir. Springfield Area Devel. and Tourist Commn., 1963-68; mem. Ill. Inst. Environ. Quality Solid Waste Task Force Com., 1971. Pres. Ill. Assn. Jewish Centers, 1934-40; editor congregation publs., treas. North Suburban Synagogue Beth El. Mem. War Production Bd., 1942-44. Recipient Meritorious Service award for outstanding contbns. to iron and steel industry St. Louis Steel Assn., 1961. Mem. Nat. Solid Waste Mgmt. Assn., Am. Pub. Works Assn. (solid waste mgmt. task force), Execs. Inc. (pres. 1963-67), Am. Soc. Assn. Execs., Internat. Platform Assn., Nat. Press Club, Springfield Jr. C. of C. (pres. 1946-47), Springfield Assn. Execs., Springfield Assn. Commerce and Industry. Jewish. Club: B'nai B'rith (sec. 1935-39, pres. 1942-45). Home: Boynton Beach Fla.

OBERT, EDWARD FREDRIC, mechanical engineerin educator; b. Detroit, Jan. 18, 1910; s. Edward and Jess (Funderburg) O.; m. Helen Hadley Whitman, Jan. 1982. B.S., Northwestern U., 1933, M.E., 1934; M.S U. Mich., 1940. Engr. mfg. Western Electric Co Chgo., 1929-30; staff Office Naval Inspection, Chgo 1934-37; prof. mech. engring. Northwestern U., 1937-5 prof. mech. engring. U. Wis., 1958-93, chmn. dep 1963-67; propr. Profl. Engring. Cons.; cons. Nat. Aca Scis., USAF Acad., Denver, Aeromed. Lab. Alaska Committeeman NRC-Nat. Acad. Scis. Autho Thermodynamics, 1948, rev. edit., 1963, Elements Thermodynamics and Heat Transfer, 1949, rev. edi 1962, 80, Internal Combustion Engines, 1950, rev. edi 1968, 73, Concepts of Thermodynamics, 1960; con editor: mech. engr. series of Internat. Textbook C contbr. articles tech. jours. Recipient George We tinghouse award Am. Soc. Engring. Edn., 1953, Edwin Burks award, 1971, U.S. Army cert. of appreci tion for patriotic civilian service, 1970, Benjamin Smi Reynolds award U. Wis., 1973; named hon. mem. I ternat. Mark Twain Soc., 1951, ASME, 1989. Fello ASME (life, Internat. Combustion Engine award 199 Soc. Automotive Engrs. (life); mem. Triangle Fr Sigma Xi, Pi Tau Sigma, Tau Beta Pi. Home: Vero Wis. Died Mar. 23, 1993.

O'BRIEN, PAUL JERRY, newspaper publishing e ecutive; b. Mpls., Apr. 30, 1925; s. John E. and Laure (Carroll) O'B.; divorced; children: John P., James C Thomas R., Joan T. BA, Gonzaga U., 1951. Report Spokane (Wash.) Daily Chronicle, 1947-49; night edit AP, Spokane, 1949-51, bur. mgr., 1951-60; chief of bu AP, Salt Lake City, 1960-63; asst. to pres. Kearn Tribune Corp., Salt Lake City, 1963-84, sec., di 1969—; pub. The Salt Lake Tribune, Salt Lake Cit 1984—; sec., dir. Tele-Communications, Inc., Denve 1970—, Republic Pictures Corp., L.A., 1984—. B regents Gonzaga U., Spokane, 1975-84; bd. dirs. Ho Cross Hosp., Salt Lake City, 1978-87, Utah Sympho Orch., Salt Lake City, 1982—; trustee Holy Cross Hos Found., 1987. Staff sgt. U.S. Army, 1943-45, ETC Decorated D.F.C. Roman Catholic. Home: Salt La City Utah Deceased.

OCHOA, SEVERO, biochemist; b. Luarca, Spain, Se 24, 1905; came to U.S., 1940, naturalized, 1956; Severo and Carmen (Albornoz) O.; m. Carmen Cobian, July 8, 1931. A.B., Malaga (Spain) Coll., 19 M.D., U. Madrid, Spain, 1929; D.Sc., Washington U. Brazil, 1957, U. Guadalajara, Mexico, 1959, W leyan U., U. Oxford, Eng., U. Salamanca, Spain, 19 Gustavus Adolphus Coll., 1963, U. Pa., 1964, Brand U., 1965, U. Granada, Spain, U. Oviedo, Spain, 19 U. Perugia, Italy, 1968, U. Mich., Weizman Inst., Isra 1982; Dr. Med. Sci. (hon.), U. Santo Tomas, Man Philippines, 1963, U. Buenos Aires, 1968, U. Tucum Argentina, 1968; L.H.D., Yeshiva Univ., 1966; LL. U. Glasgow, Scotland, 1959. Lectr. physiology Madrid Med. Sch., 1931-35; head physiol. div. Inst. Med. Research, 1935-36; guest research asst. in phy ology Kaiser-Wilhelm Inst. for Med. Researc Heidelberg, Germany, 1936-37; Ray Lankester inves gator Marine Biol. Lab., Plymouth, Eng., 1937; demo strator Nuffield research asst. biochemistry Oxfo (Eng.) U. Med. Sch., 1938-41; instr., research as pharmacology Washington U. Sch. of Medicine, Louis, 1941-42; research asso. medicine NYU S Medicine, 1942-45, asst. prof. biochemistry, 1945- prof. pharmacology, chmn. dept., 1946-54, prof., chm dept. biochemistry, 1954-76, prof., 1976-93; d inguished mem. Roche Inst. Molecular Biology. Aut publs. on biochem. of muscles, glycolysis in heart a brain, transphosphorylations in yeast fermentati pyruvic acid oxidation in brain and role of vitamin RNA and Protein biosynthesis; genetic code. Decora Order Rising Sun Japan; recipient (with Art Kornberg) 1959 Nobel prize in medicine, Albert G latin medal N.Y. U., 1970, Nat. Medal of Sci., 198 Fellow N.Y. Acad. Scis., N.Y. Acad. Medicine, A Acad. of Arts and Sci., AAAS; mem. NAS, Am. Phi Soc., Soc. for Exptl. Biology and Medicine, Soc. of B Chemists (pres. 1958, editor jour. 1950-60), Intern Union Biochemistry (pres. 1961-67), Biochem. S (Eng.), Harvey Soc. (pres. 1953-54), Alpha Om Alpha (hon.); fgn. mem. German Acad. Nat. Sc Royal Spanish, USSR, Polish, Pullian, Italian, Arg tinian, Barcelona (Spain), Brazilian acads. sci., Ro Soc. (Eng.), Pontifical Acad. Sci., G.D.R. Acad. Sc Argentinian Nat. Acad. Medicine. Home: Madrid Sp Died Nov. 1, 1993; interred Luarca Asturias.

O'CONNOR, FRANCIS JOHN, lawyer; b. N Hampton, Iowa, Mar. 29, 1916; s. Frank A. and M (McNevin) O'C.; m. Marion Rhomberg, June 9, 19 children: Frank R., Gerald R., Karen A., John Kevin T. A.B., U. Iowa, 1937; J.D., Harvard U., 19 LL.D. (hon.), Loras Coll., 1967, Clarke Coll., 197 Bar: Iowa 1940. Practiced in Dubuque; mem. f O'Connor and Thomas P.C., from 1946; ch Grievence Commn. Supreme Ct., Iowa, 1965-75; a county atty., 1942-43; dir. Dubuque Securities Co., A McDonald Mfg. Co., Jacobson Steel Co., E.J. V genthaler Co. Mem. exec. com. Dubuque Indsl. B 1962-66; mem. Iowa Coordinating Council for H High Sch. Edn., 1965-75; trustee U. Iowa Sch. Relig from 1954, pres., 1961-63, v.p., 1967-68; bd. c Archdiocese Dubuque, 1965-89, St. Joseph Ch., 1967

Mt. Olivet Cemetery Assn., 1962-86; corporator, bd. dirs. Clarke Coll., 1967-89; trustee Dubuque Post-War ndsl. Fund, 1946-66, Dubuque Boys Club, 1964-81; bd. regents Loras Coll., 1984-89. Knight of St. Gregory. Fellow Am. Coll. Probate Coun.; Am. Bar Found.; Mem. Am. Bar Assn., Iowa Bar Assn., Dubuque Bar Assn., Am. Judicature Soc., Cath. Order Foresters, Phi Beta Kappa, Beta Theta Pi. Roman Catholic. Clubs: Dubuque Golf and Country (dir. 1945-50, pres. 1945, 56—), Quail Creek (Naples, Fla.); Royal and Ancient St. Andrews, Scotland). Lodges: K.C; Elks. Home: Dubuque Iowa Deceased.

O'CONNOR, ROBERT BARNARD, architect; b. Manhasset, N.Y., Nov. 21, 1895; s. Bernard F. and Anna McH. (Barnard) O'C.; m. Mary Wistar Morris, 924; children—Robert Barnard, Anthony Morris, Fenwick (dec.). A.B., Trinity Coll., 1916, Litt.D., 1976; M.F.A., Princeton U., 1920; D.F.A., Colgate U., 1959. Archtl. practice N.Y.C., from 1921; with Trowbridge & Livingston, Hyde & Shepherd, and Benjamin W. Morris, 1924-29; partner Morris & O'Connor, 1930-42, R.B. O'Connor & W.H. Kilham, Jr., 1943-59; partner rm O'Connor & Kilham, N.Y.C., 1960-68; cons. Kilham, Beder & Chu, 1968-76; Cons. architect N.Y. tock Exchange, 1953-65; supervising architect Princeton U., 1949-54; cons. architect, library Internat. Christian U., Tokyo, 1957-61. Contbr. sect. on museums to Forms and Functions of XXth Century Architecture, 1953, also articles to profl. publs.; prin. archtl. works include Continental Bank & Trust Co, N.Y.C., County Home for Aged, County Office Bldg, Westchester County, N.Y., Avery Mus., Conn. Mut. Life Ins. Bldg, State Savs. Bank, Hartford, Conn., N. Westchster Hosp, Mt. Kisco, N.Y., Firestone Library, Moffett Biol. Research Labs, Chemistry Research Labs, Princeton U., Crane Meml. at, Berkshire Mus., Pittsfield, Mass., alterations and additions to, Met. Mus. Art, N.Y.C., (A. Embury II, asso.), 1940-55, Phoenix Ins. Bldg, Hartford, Old Kenyon Dormitory, Gambier, Ohio, New Library, Math.-Physics Bldg, Arts Center; various dormitories, also Mather Student Center, Trinity oll., Hartford, Conn., Library, U. Louisville, Colgate . Library, Helen Reid Hall, Barnard Coll., N.Y.C.; brary and adminstrn. bldg. N.Y.C. Architect mem. .Y.C. Art Commn., 1965-70; Trustee Trinity Coll., 934-64, emeritus, from 1964; trustee St. Anthony Ednl. found., 1956-71, Oaklands Fund, 1961—; mem. Art commn. Assos., N.Y.C., from 1971, pres., 1976-78; llow Pierpont Morgan Library, from 1976. Served as apt. F.A. AEF, during World War I; chief engr. archtl.) Zone Constructing Q.M. Office, Zone II AUS, 941; in charge all War Dept. constrn. (except fortifica-ons) in N.Y.; in charge all War Dept. constrn. (except rtifications) in N.J.; in charge all War Dept. constrn. xcept fortifications) in Del. Fellow AIA (pres. N.Y. apt. 1943-44, medal of honor N.Y. chpt. 1946); mem. at. Inst. Archtl. Edn., NAD (asso.), Archtl. League Y. (pres. 1956-57), Phi Beta Kappa, Delta Psi. Epispalian. Clubs: Century Assn. (N.Y.C.), St. Anthony N.Y.C.) (pres. 1966-68). Home: Mount Kisco N.Y. eceased.

DEH, AZIZ SALIM, retired oil company scientist; b. azareth, Palestine, Dec. 10, 1925; came to U.S., 1947; Salim Nasr and Kamelah Michele (Audeh) O.; m. onnie Louise Willis, Apr. 21, 1956; children: Susan, nda. B.A., U. Calif.-Berkeley, 1951; M.S., UCLA, 53, Ph.D., 1959. Registered profl. engr., Tex. Sr. esearch assoc. Mobil Research and Devel., Dallas, 76-80, mgr., 1980-94, sr. scientist, 1981-94; dir. Abu nabi Nat. Reservoir Rsch. Found., 1980-89; cons. rof. Stanford (Calif.) U., 1989-94. Contbr. articles to ofl. jours; patentee in field. Recipient Man of Yr. ward News Cir. Mag., 1990. Mem. NAE (elected 87) Soc. Petroleum Engrs. (John Franklin Carll award 84, Outstanding Achievement award 1989), Rsch. c. Am. Home: Plano Tex. Died July 16, 1994.

DONNELL, ALICE LOUISE, lawyer, government icial; b. Stanwood, Wash.; d. John James and Jean-te May (Anderson) O'D. Student, U. Wash., 1932, So. Calif., 1943-44, George Washington U., 1940-42; , George Washington U., 1954; JD (hon.), Western te Law Sch., 1988. Bar: U.S. Dist. Ct. D.C. 1955, S. Ct. Appeals (D.C. cir.) 1955, U.S. Supreme Ct. 54. With staff Atty. Gen. U.S., 1945-49; mem. staff stice Clark, Supreme Ct. of U.S., Washington, 1949- lawyer Fed. Jud. Center, Washington, 1968-90; dir. . inter-jud. affairs and info. services Fed. Jud. Center, 71-90; pvt. practice Dist. of Columbia, 1991-93; sec. as. Nat. Ctr for State Cts., 1971-81; mem. bd. ad-ors Fed. Reformatory for Women, 1968-72, 72-76. ce-chmn. bd. dirs. Potomac Law Sch., Washington, 75-79. Fellow Inst. Jud. Adminstrn. (former v.p.); m. ABA (fellow Am. Bar Found., mem. Lawyers nf. of jud. adminstrn. div., chmn. 1973-74, chmn. fed. com. lawyers conf.), Fed. Bar Assn., Am. Judicature ., Supreme Ct. Hist. Soc. (trustee, v.p.), Phi Alpha lta. Roman Catholic. Home: Washington D.C. Died . 5, 1993.

DONNELL, CLETUS FRANCIS, bishop; b. ukun, Iowa, Aug. 22, 1917; s. Patrick E. and Isabelle (Duffy) O'D. M.A., St. Mary of Lake Sem., Ill., -1; J.C.D., Cath. U. Am., 1945. Ordained priest man Catholic Ch., 1941; asst. pastor Our Lady of rdes Ch., Chgo., 1941-42; vice chancellor Archdi-

ocese of Chgo., 1947-60, vicar, gen. counsel, 1961; apptd. titular bishop Abrittum, aux. bishop Chgo., 1960-67; consecrated bishop, 1960; pastor Holy Name Cathedral, Chgo., 1966; bishop Diocese of Madison, Wis., 1967—; chmn. Am. Bd. Cath. Missions, from 1966, Nat. Catholic Edn. Assn., from 1977. Recipient C. Albert Koob award Nat. Cath. Edn. Assn., 1978. Home: Madison Wis.

O'DONNELL, JOHN FRANCIS, lawyer; b. County Donegal, Ireland, Dec. 7, 1907; came to U.S., 1926, naturalized, 1933; s. Henry J. and Ellen (Kennedy) O'D.; m. Gwynne Large, Feb. 3, 1934; children—John F., Jr., Mary Eileen, Cathleen, Patricia. Student CCNY, 1928-30; LL.B., Fordham U., 1933. Bar: N.Y. 1937, U.S. Dist. Ct. (so. dist.) N.Y. 1942, U.S. Ct. Appeals (2d cir.) 1952. Ptnr. O'Donnell & Schwartz, N.Y.C., 1948—, O'Donnell, Schwartz & Anderson, Washington, 1981—. Mem. Am. Arbitration Assn. (mem. labor law com.). Democrat. Roman Catholic. Home: Katonah N.Y.

O'DONNELL, WALTER GREGORY, lawyer, management educator; b. Cleve., Feb. 3, 1903; s. Walter Thomas and Margaret (McGee) O'D.; m. Angelina M. Oriti, June 10, 1940; children: Charles, Kathleen, Roger, Arleen. LLB, John Marshall Law Sch., Cleve., 1932; BA, Western Res. U., 1932, MA, 1944; PhD, Columbia U., 1959. Bar: Fla. 1925, U.S. Supreme Ct. 1928. Pvt. practice Pinellas County, 1925-30; tchr. Cleve. Pub. High Schs., 1930-35; assoc. prof. Notre Dame Coll., 1935-37; assoc. prof. econs. and polit. sci. John Carroll U., 1937-43; instr. econs. Ohio State U., 1943-47; pvt. practice Tallahassee, 1947-48; assoc. prof. econs. Fla. State U., 1947-48; instr. econs. Columbia U., 1948-51; assoc. prof. indsl. rels. U. Pitts., 1951-52; inst. leader NAM, 1950-51; dir. tng. and exec. devel. Nat. Foremans Inst., 1952-53; mgmt. cons., tng. specialist T.W.I. Found., 1953-54; staff specialist indsl. rels. Lockheed Aircraft, Inc., 1954-56; prof. mgmt. U. Mass., 1956-73, prof. emeritus, 1973—; disting. vis. prof. Mgmt. Bowling Green State U., 1974-76, 78-81; prof. bus. ad-minstrn. in residence U. Conn., Storrs, 1976-78; vis. lectr. Ohio Wesleyan U., summer 1946; vis. assoc. prof. mgmt. Rutgers U., 1954-56; vis. prof. ednl. cons. U. P.R., summer 1961; vis. prof. U. Madrid, 1963; vis. prof. mgmt. U. N.Mex., 1967-68; vis. prof. Bklyn. Poly. Inst., 1968-70; disting. vis. prof. mgmt. Loyola Coll., Balt., 1973, Georgetown U., 1973-74; vis. prof. mgmt. Sch. Adminstrv. Sci., U. Ala.-Huntsville, 1982-86. Author monographs; contbr. articles to profl. jours.; interdis-ciplinary rsch. and pubs. through profl. presentations in global context for integrative gen. mgmt.; numerous contbns. to internat. mgmt. confs., sems. world-wide; pubs. in Spanish, Japanese and German jours. Mem. Cuyahoga County Charter Commn., 1932, Ohio Post War Planning Commn., 1945-46; mem. Rep. Nat. Com., Citizens' Adv. Commn. of Pres. Bush, 1989-90. Ful-bright grantee U. Madrid, 1963. Mem. AAAS, Am. Acad. Mgmt., Inst. Mgmt. Scis. (founder, chmn., exec. sec. Coll. Mgmt. Philosophy 1960-73, reorganizer Coll. Mgmt. Philosophy with series of monographs 1978-80). Democrat. Roman Catholic. Home: Ashfield Mass.

O'DONOGHUE, MICHAEL, producer, director, writer, actor. Appeared in (film) Manhattan, 1979, (TV) Saturday Night Live (also writer), 1975-80, 85-86, (radio) National Lampoon Radio Hour (also writer), 1973; producer, dir. (film) Mr. Mike's Mondo Video (also writer), 1979, (TV) Single Bars, Single Women, 1984; writer (screenplay) Savages, 1972, La Honte de la Jungle (also lyrics), 1975, Gilda Live, (song) Single Women. Home: New York N.Y. Died Nov. 9, 1994.

OGAWA, MASARU, journalist; b. Los Angeles, 1915; s. Kenji Ogawa and Mine Fuijioka; m. Ayame Fukuhara, 1942; 3 children. Ed. UCLA, Tokyo Imperial Coll., Columbia U; D.Litt. (hon.), Lewis and Clark Coll., Portland, Oreg., 1979. With Domei News Agy., 1941-46, Kyodo News Service 1946-48, The Japan Times, 1948—, Chief polit. sect., 1949, asst. mng. editor, 1950, chief editor, 1952, mng. editor, 1958-64, dir., 1959-77, exec. editor, 1964-68, sr. editor, 1968-71, chief editorial writer, 1969-71, editor, 1971-77, advisor, 1977—; chmn. bd. Asia-Pacific Mag., Manila, 1981-85; lectr. Tokyo U., 1954-58; mem. Yoshida Internat. Edn. Found., 1968—, exec. dir., 1972—; mem. Japan Broad-casting Co. overseas program consultative council, 1974-84; dir. Internat. Motion Picture Co., 1970, Am. Studies Found., 1980—, Yoshida Shigeru Meml. Found., 1980—; pres. Pacific News Agy., 1973—. Editorial bd. Media Mag., Hong Kong, 1974. Recipient Vaughn-Ueda prize, 1987. Mem. Japan Editors and Pubs. Assn., Internat. Press Inst., Am.-Japan Soc. (exec. dir. 1980—), Am. Club Tokyo, Tokyo Club (life), Club of Japan (fgn. corr.), Phi Beta Kappa. Avocations: reading; sport. Home: Tokyo Japan

OGDEN, HOWARD ALBERT, librarian; b. N.Y.C., Oct. 20, 1928; s. Howard Albert and Ellen Cecilia (Rogers) O.; m. Patricia Spang, Sept. 2, 1961; children: Carol, Janet, Patricia. AB, U. Pa., 1952; MS in Library Sci., U. N.C., 1973; MPA, Golden Gate U., 1979. Joined U.S. Navy as seaman, 1946, advanced through grades to comdr., 1965; engr. officer U.S.S. Strive, 1952-53; explosive ordnance disposal officer, U.S. and Far East, 1954-58; gunfire control officer U.S.S. Lake Champlain, 1958-59; served on U.S.S. Hale and The

Sullivans, 1959-61; weapons officer, staff comdr. fleet activities Mediterranean, 1962-64; exec. officer U.S.S. Norris, 1964-65; comptroller 5th Naval Dist., Norfolk, Va., 1965-68; exec. officer U.S.S. Sierra, 1968-70; comdg. officer Naval Ordnance Facility, Japan, 1970-72, ret., 1972; dir. Hampton Pub. Library, Va., 1973—; Mem. Libr. Svcs. Constrn. Act Title I adv. com. for continuing edn. Va. State Library, 1977-80, 82-84, also Title III, 1980-85. Mem. City of Hampton Tng. Bd., 1980-84. Mem. ALA, Va. Libr. Assn., Hampton Roads Hort. Soc. Roman Catholic. Club: Va. Masters Swim. Lodge: Hampton Rotary. Died Jan. 18, 1989; interred Hampton, Va. Home: Williamsburg Va.

OHLMAN, CHARLES EDWARD, utilities company executive; b. Peru, Ind., Dec. 11, 1926; s. Walter Edward and Mabel M. (Nicely) O.; m. Lillian Delores DePasquale, Oct. 24, 1953 (dec.); children: Diane, Mark. BS in Elec. Engring., Purdue U., 1951. Registered profl. engr., Ind. Engr. Indpls. Power & Light Co., 1954-71, chief planning engr., 1971-77, asst. v.p. engring. and constrn., 1977-78, v.p. power supply, 1978-79, sr. v.p. consumer services, 1979—. Served to 1st lt. U.S. Army, 1945-46, ETO. Mem. IEEE (sr.), Am. Mgmt. Assn., Indpls. Sci. and Engring. Found., Newcomen Soc., Masons, Scottish Rite, Indpls. Athletic Club, Columbia Club, Hillcrest Country Club, Op-timists. Home: Indianapolis Ind. Deceased.

O'KEEFE, BERNARD JOSEPH, electronics company executive; b. Providence, Dec. 17, 1919; s. John B. and Christina (McNee) O'K.; m. Madeline M. Healey, Nov. 21, 1942; children: Geraldine M., Thomas J., Kathleen J., Carol J. Student, George Washington U., 1937-38; B.E.E., Cath. U. Am., 1941, DST (hon.); DST (hon.), Boston Coll.; Bowdoin Coll.; DCS (hon.), Babson Coll.; D in Engring. Sci. (hon.), Curry Coll.; D in Humane Services (hon.), New Eng. Sch. Law; D in Pub. Service (hon.), Northeastern U. Engr. Gen. Electric Co., 1941-43; with exec. engring. dept. Mass. Inst. Tech., 1946-47; with E G & G Inc., Wellesley, Mass., 1947—; exec. v.p. E G & G Inc., 1960-65, pres., 1965-78, chmn. bd., 1972—; dir. Bank of New Eng., John Hancock Life Ins. Co., Boston Edison Co., LFE Corp., Dennison Mfg. Co., Kurzweil Music Systems, Research & Sci. Inves-tors, Inc. Author: Nuclear Hostages, 1983, Shooting Ourselves in the Foot, 1985. Trustee Lahey Clinic Found.; 1976—, Boston Urban Found., 1968-70, Cath. U. Am., 1968-70, Mus. Sci. 1977-81; dir. Ams. for Energy Independence, 1975—, Associated Industries Mass., 1969-79, John F. Kennedy Library Found., 1984—, World Affairs Council, 1974-78; bd. dirs. Family Counseling and Guidance Ctrs., Inc., Jobs for Mass.; chmn. Citizens for Economy in Govt., 1973-75, Gov's. Mgmt. Task Force, 1975-78, 1979-81; vice chmn. Mass. Bd. Higher Edn., 1966-69; mem. Pres.'s Adv. Council Boston Coll., 1969-73, bd. visitors Boston U., 1965-68, vis. com. Harvard Russian Research Ctr., 1984—, Commerce Tech. Adv. Bd, U.S. Dept. Com-merce, 1969-72., MIT Sea Grant State Industry Adv. Council, 1972-74. Served to lt. (j.g.) USNR, 1943-46. Recipient Ambassador of Indsl. Enterprise award As-sociated Industries Mass., 1984, New Englander of Yr. award, New England Council, 1981; named Dist-inguished Citizen Am. Soc. Pub. Administrn, 1968; Gov.'s Pub. Service fellow, 1974-76. Mem. NAM (chmn. 1982-83, dir. 1976—), Greater Boston C. of C. (dir., past pres.), Mass. Bus. Roundtable (dir. 1973-84), Ctr. for Strategic and Internat. Studies. Home: Way-land Mass. Died July 20, 1989.

OKOSHI, TAKANORI, electronics educator; b. Tokyo, Sept. 16, 1932; s. Makoto and Hisako (Koibuchi) O.; m. Yasuko Hirone, Mar. 29, 1963; children: Asako, Kent, Naoko. B Engring., U. Tokyo, 1955, M Engring., 1957, D Engring., 1960. Lectr. U. Tokyo, 1960-61, assoc. prof., 1961-76, prof. electronics, from 1977, founding dir. Rsch. Ctr. Advanced Sci. and Tech., 1987-89, prof. emeritus, from 1993; founding dir. gen. Nat. Inst. Ad-vanced Interdisciplinary Rsch., Tsukuba, Japan, from 1993; mem. tech. staff Bell Labs, Inc., Murray Hill, N.J., 1963-64; guest prof. Tech. U. Munich, 1972; pres. Japanese com. Union Radio Sci. Internat., Tokyo, 1985, chmn. commn. D, 1987-90, v.p., Brussels, from 1990. Author: Three-Dimensional Imaging Techniques, 1976, Optical Fibers, 1982, Planar Circuits, 1985, Coherent Optical Fiber Communications, 1988; editor-in-chief textbook series, Optoelectronics, from 1983. Recipient The Japan Acad. prize, 1993. Fellow IEEE (M.N. Liebmann Meml. award 1989); mem. Inst. TV Engrs. (pres. 1989-90, Excellent Book award 1975, 85); Inst. Electronics, Info. and Communication Engrs. (pres. 1993-94, Excellent Book award 1978, 83, 84, 90, Achievement award 1979, 83, 86, Disting. Svc. award 1993), Engring. Acad. Japan (v.p. from 1994), Royal Acad. Belgium. Home: Tokyo Japan Deceased.

OLDENDORF, WILLIAM HENRY, physician, edu-cator; b. Schenectady, N.Y., Mar. 27, 1925; s. William Louis and Jane Willard (Shepherd) O.; m. Stella Zabielska, June 24, 1945; children: Eric W., Mark W., William H. Jr. MD, Union U. Albany Med. Coll., 1947; DSc (hon.), Union Coll., Schenectady, 1982, Al-bany Med. Coll., 1982, St. Louis U., 1986. Diplomate Am. Bd. Psychiatry, Am. Bd. Neurology, Am. Bd. Sci. in Nuclear Medicine (dist. founder 1979). Rotating in-tern Ellis Hosp., Schenectady, 1947-48; resident in psychiatry Binghampton Hosp. N.Y. State Dept.Mental Hygiene, 1948-51; clin. fellow in neurology U. Minn. Hosps., Mpls., 1953-55; staff neurology sect. Wadsworth VA Med. Svc., West L.A., 1955-69, chief neurology svc., 1955-57; attending specialist UCLA Hosp. and Clinics, 1960-92; mem. neurology faculty UCLA Sch. Medicine, 1956-92, prof. neurology, 1970-92, prof. psychiatry, 1975-92; hon. rsch. assoc. dept. physiology, Univ. Coll., London, 1965-66; fac. rsch. lectr. UCLA, 1992. Author: Quest for an Image of Brain, 1980, Basics of Nuclear Magnetic Resonance, 1987, MRI Primer, 1991; patentee of 4 neuroimaging apparati; mem. numerous editorial bds. Lt. USNR, 1951-53, AOA 1974. Recipient Albert and Mary Lasker Found. award for clin. med. rsch., 1975, U.S. Pres.' award for disting. fed. civilian svc., Washington, 1985; named Disting. founder Am. Bd. Sci. in Nuclear Medicine, 1979. Fellow AAAS, IEEE (chmn. 1960-61), Am. Acad. Arts and Scis., Am. Acad. Neurology and Soc. of Neuroimaging (pres. 1977-79, Pres.' award 1992), Am. Neurol. Assn. (v.p. 1976-77); mem. NAS, Soc. Nuclear Medicine (trustee 1975-79), Alpha Omega Alpha. Home: Los Angeles Calif. Died Dec. 14, 1992.

OLECK, HOWARD LEONER, legal educator, writer; b. N.Y.C., Jan. 6, 1911; s. Richard and Yvette (Leoner) O.; m. Helen Eugenie Gemeiner, 1941; children: Mrs. Anabel Curtis, Joan Valerie. Grad., Townsend Harris Hall Prep. Sch., 1928; A.B., U. Iowa, 1933; J.D., N.Y. Law Sch., 1938; LL.D., Baldwin Wallace Coll., 1964; Litt.D. (hon.), J. Marshall U., 1967. Bar: N.Y. 1938, Ohio 1957, Fed. 1957. Assoc. prof. N.Y. Law Sch., 1947-56; prof. law, assoc. dean Cleve. State U., 1956-67, dean, 1967-68, 71, Disting. prof. law, 1968-74, Disting. prof. emeritus, 1974-95; prof. law Wake Forest U., Winston-Salem, N.C., 1974-78, Stetson U., St. Petersburg, Fla., 1978-81; adj. prof. Stetson U., 1981-89, prof. emeritus, 1989-95; asst. to editor N.Y. Law Jour., 1946-52; syndicated law columnist Cleve. Plain Dealer, 1959-75, Winston-Salem, Pinellas Rev., other newspapers, 1975-90; cons. to congl. coms. and presdl. commns. Am. Law Inst., pub. svc. groups, Calif., Ill. and Fla. Law Revision Commns., others. Author: Creditors' Rights, 1947, Creditors' Rights and Remedies, 1949, History of Allied Planning of Operations, E.T.O., 1939-45, 1945, Debtor-Creditor Law, 1953, Negligence Investigation Manual, 1953, Negligence Forms of Pleading, 1954, New York Corporations, 1954, Damages to Persons and Property, 1955, Non-Profit Corporations and Associations, 1956, Encyclopedia of Negligence, 2 vols, 1960, Modern Corporation Law, 6 vols, 1960, supplement, 1978, Cases on Damages, 1962, Eye Witness World War II Battles, 1963, Heroic Battles of World War II, 1963, Law for Living, 1967, A Singular Fury, 1968, Law for Everyone, 1971, Nonprofit Corporations, Organization and Associations, 6th edit. (with Stewart), 1994, supplementannually, Primer on Legal Writing, 1974, 4th edit., 1978, National Index to Insurance Laws, 1976, The Lion of Islam, 1977, Nonprofit Organizations Trends, 1977, (with Green and co-editor) Parliamentary Law and Practice for Non-Profit Organizations, 2d edit., 1991, Religious Non-profit Organizations' Problems, 1981, 4th edit., 1990, Oleck's Tort Law Practice Manual, 1982, also War Dept. histories, 1945-46; editor: Directors and Officers Ency. Manual, 1955, Negligence and Compensation Service, 1955-66; National Ins. Law Service, 1962-76, also various jours., 1956-95 ; author: over 300 mag. articles, poems under own and various pen names. Served to maj., tanks AUS, 1942-45, ETO; War Dept. historian. Decorated U.S. and fgn. medals; recipient various bar assn. honors. Mem. St. Petersburg Bar Assn., Am. Trial Lawyers Assn., League Ohio Law Schs. (pres. 1963-64), Scribes (pres. 1972-73), Phi Alpha Delta. Democrat. Unitarian. Home: Saint Petersburg Fla. Died June 2, 1995.

OLIVER, BERNARD MORE, electrical engineer, technical consultant; b. Soquel, Calif., May 27, 1916; s. William H. and Margaret E. (More) O.; m. Priscilla June Newton, June 22, 1946; children: Karen, Gretchen, Eric. AB in Elec. Engring., Stanford U., 1935; MS, Calif. Inst. Tech., 1936, PhD, 1940. Mem. tech. staff Bell Telephone Labs., N.Y.C., 1940-52; dir. R&D, Hewlett-Packard Co., Palo Alto, Calif., 1952-57, v.p. R&D, 1957-81, dir., officer, 1973-81, tech. adviser to pres., 1981; now v.p. emeritus Hewlett-Packard Co., Palo Alto; lectr. Stanford U., 1957-60; cons. Army Sci. Adv. Com., from 1966; mem. sci. and tech. adv. com. Calif. State Assembly, 1970-76. Contbr. articles on electronic tech. and instrumentation to profl. jours.; patentee electronic circuits and devices. Mem. Pres.'s Commn. on the Patent System, 1966, State Senate Panel for the Bay Area Rapid Transit System, 1973; trustee Palo Alto Unified Sch. Dist., 1961-71. Recipient Disting. Alumni award Calif. Inst. Tech., 1972, Nat. Medal of Sci., 1986, Exceptional Engring. achievement medal, NASA, 1990, Pioneer award Internat. Found. Telemetering, 1990; ann. Symposium series est. in his name Hewlett-Packard Labs., 1991. Fellow IEEE (Lamme medal 1977); mem. AAAS, Astron. Soc., Nat. Acad. Sci., Nat. Acad. Engring., Palo Alto Club, Bohemian Club. Republican. Home: Los Altos Calif. Died Nov. 23, 1995.

OLORUNSOLA, VICTOR ADEOLA, political science educator; b. Nigeria, Mar. 23, 1939; married; 3 children. B.A. with high honors, Friends U., 1963; M.A., Ind. U., 1964, Ph.D., 1967. Research asst. Ind. U., 1964-65, lectr. Peace Corps tng. program, 1964-65; asst. prof. Calif. State Coll.-Long Beach, 1967; asst. prof. Iowa State U., Ames, 1967-70, assoc. prof., 1970-75, prof., coordinator grad. studies, 1975-77, prof., chmn. dept. polit. sci., 1977-87; dean Coll. Arts & Scis. Belknap Campus U. Louisville, Ky., from 1987; vis. assoc. prof. Ohio U., 1971; mem. NSF evaluation com. for fellowships in social and behavioral scis., 1976-79, 82-83, mem. evaluation com. for minority fellowships, 1979-81, 82-83; bd. dirs. Partnership for Productivity; cons. Aspen Inst. Humanistic Studies, 1978, 79; cons. famine studies Nat. Ctr. Atmospheric Study, 1974-75. Author: The Politics of Cultural Sub-Nationalism in Africa, 1972, Societal Reconstruction in Two African States, 1977, Soldiers and Power, 1977, State Versus Ethnic Claims: An African Policy Dilemma, 1983; mem. editorial bd. Jour. African Studies, Nigerian Behavioral Scis. Jour. Mem. com. on multi-cultural non-sexist curriculum Ames Sch. Bd., 1977-82, mem. prins.' adv. com., supt.'s adv. com., from 1983. Scholar Inst. Internat. Edn., 1961, Ford Found., 1963-64; Phelps Stokes scholar, 1963; grantee Ford Found., 1965-66, Iowa State U., 1968, 71, Internat. Devel. and Research Ctr., 1971-72, Social Sci. Research Council, 1971-72, Rockefeller Found., 1981, Rothschild Found., 1981; fellow Ford. Mem. Assn. for Advancement Policy Research and Devel. (bd. dirs. 1981), Am. Polit. Sci. Assn. (exec. council 1984-86), Nat. Conf. Black Polit. Scientists, Internat. Studies Assn., African Studies Assn. (exec. com., bd. dirs. 1978-81), Royal African Soc. Eng., Midwest Polit. Sci. Assn. (chmn. nominations com. 1981), Internat. Personnel Mgmt. Assn. Home: Louisville Ky. Deceased.

OLSEN, DAGNE B., state legislator; b. Dalton, Minn., Mar. 19, 1933; d. Glenn F. and Esther J. (Stortroen) Borg; m. Duane D. Olsen, June 25, 1955; children: Deanna, Douglas, Dick. B.S. in Edn., U. N.D., 1955. Cert. life secondary sch. tchr.mem. N.D. Ho. of Reps., 1980-94, chair govt. and vet. affairs com., social services com. Active Manvel Community Betterment Program, 1959-94; vol. chmn., past pres. United Hosp. Aux., Grand Forks; leader 4-H Club; bd. dirs. Agassiz Enterprises Tng. Ctr., Grand Forks, pres., 1982; mem. governing bd. United Hosp.; mem. N.D. Gov.'s Adv. Coun. on Volunteerism, 1984-88; mem. exec. com. N.D. Devel. Disabilities Council, 1982-90, bd. dirs., v.p. Nat. Assn. Devel. Disabilities Councils, 1985-90; mem. pres.' com. on Mental Retardation, 1987-94; pres. Grand Forks County Spl. Edn. Bd.; mem. com. of 100, U. N.D., 1980-94; mem. Nat. Ch. Task Force, 1979-80; mem. Eastern N.D. Dist. Ch. in Soc., 1982-86 ; bd. dirs. Assn. Retarded Citizens N.D., 1966-89; precinct committeewoman, vice chmn. dist. 19 Republican Party, 1974-80; del. N.D. Rep. Conv., 1976, 78, 80, 82, 86, 88, 90, 92, 94, mem. platform com., 1980, Nat. Rep. Conv., 1988; statement of principles com., 1988, issues com., 1988; co-chair N.D. Legislators for Reagan-Bush, 1984; co-vice chmn. N.D. Bush-Quayle campaign, 1988; pres. Transplant Assn., 1993. Recipient Gov.'s Statewide Leadership award for community betterment program, 1964; Outstanding Vol. Service award Office N.D. Gov., 1979; Soil Conservation award N.D. Soil Conservation Dist., 1980; Outstanding Parent award Assn. for Retarded Citizens of N.D., 1977, Mem. of Yr. award 1981; North Central Region Mem. of Yr. award Assn. Retarded Citizens U.S., 1982; named Grand Forks Woman of Yr., 1978; Outstanding Employer of Handicapped, Gov.'s Com. on Employment of Handicapped, 1985; mem. state com. Am. Diabetes Assn. Mem. Nat. Order. Women Legislators, Nat. Rep. Legislators Assn., Am. Legis. Exchange Council, Farm Bur., Am. Agri-Women, N.W. Farm Mgrs. Assn., Am. Legion Aux., Gen. Fedn. Woman's Clubs (past pres. Manvel, state bd.), Pi Lambda Theta, Delta Phi Delta, Delta Zeta. Died Aug. 20, 1994. Home: Manvel N.D.

O'MAHONY, JEREMIAH FRANCIS, financial executive; b. London, Dec. 23, 1946; s. Philip and Maria (Kavanagh) O'M.; m. Mary Josephine Blaney, Jan. 27, 1973; children: Oliver, Ronan, Ruadhri, Theodore, Cressida. With Allerfields, Chartered Accts., London, 1966-70; fin. and cost analyst Esso Petroleum Co., Ltd., London, 1970-71; chief acct., sec. Standard Guarantee Co., Ltd., London, 1971-74; asst. to group fin. dir. UDT Industries, Ltd., London, 1974-79; dir. Ellerman Group, London, 1979-80; from group fin. contr. to vice-chmn., group fin. dir. Ladbroke Group, P.L.C., London, 1980-94. Fellow Inst. Chartered Accts. in Eng. and Wales; mem. Assn. Corp. Treas. Home: Harpenden Eng. Died June 11, 1994.

ONASSIS, JACQUELINE BOUVIER KENNEDY, editor, widow of President of United States; b. Southampton, N.Y., 1929; d. John Vernou III and Janet (Lee) Bouvier; m. John Fitzgerald Kennedy, 35th Pres. of U.S., Sept. 12, 1953 (dec. Nov. 22, 1963); children: Caroline Bouvier Kennedy Schlossberg, John Fitzgerald Jr., Patrick Bouvier (dec. Aug. 1963); m. Aristotle Onassis, Oct. 20, 1968 (dec. Mar. 1975). Grad., Miss Porter's Sch., Farmington, Conn., 1947; student, Vassar Coll., 1947-48, The Sorbonne, Paris, 1949; BA, George Washington U., 1951. Inquiring photographer Washington Times-Herald (now Washington Post and Times Herald), 1952; planned and conducted restoration of decor The White House, 1961-63; cons. editor Viking Press, 1975-77; assoc. editor Doubleday & Co., N.Y.C., 1978-82, editor, 1982-94, now sr. editor. Trust Whitney Mus. Am. Art. Recipient Prix de Paris Vog mag., 1951, Emmy award for pub. service, 1962. Hom Hynannisport Mass. Died May 19, 1994.

O'NEILL, F. J. (STEVE O'NEILL), transporation e ecutive, professional baseball team executive; b. Clev Sept. 18, 1899; m. Nancy. Ed., Campion Coll., Notre Dame. With family trucking and transp. bu (later merged to become Leaseway Transp. Corp. 196 1920s; maj. investor Cleve. Indians, 1960s, chmn. bo with group purchasing N.Y. Yankees, 1973, sold i terest, 1977-78. Home: Cleveland Ohio Deceased.

O'NEILL, THOMAS P., JR., former speaker of U. House of Representatives, former congressman; b. De 9, 1912; s. Thomas P. I and Rose Anne (Tolan) O'N m. Mildred Anne Miller, June 17, 1941; childre Rosemary, Thomas III, Susan, Christopher, Micha Tolan. AB, Boston Coll., 1936; LLD (hon.), Harva U., 1987; also thirty-three other hon. degrees, fro various univs. and colls. Engaged in ins. bus. Ca bridge, Mass.; mem. Cambridge Sch. Com., 1946, 4 mem. Mass. Legislature, 1936-52, minority leader, 194 48, speaker, 1948-52; mem. 83d-87th Congresses 1 dist. Mass., 1953-63, 88th-99th Congresses from 8 dist. Mass., 1963-87; majority whip 88th-97th Co gresses from 8th dist. Mass., 1971-73; majority lead 93d-94th Congresses from 8th dist. Mass., 1973-7 speaker of the house 95th-99th Congresses, 1977-86 Author: (with William Novak) (memoirs) Man of t House, 1987. Decorated Grand Cross, Order Orang Nassau (The Netherlands), 1983; Legion of Hon (France), 1984; recipient Laetare medal Notre Dame U 1980, Presdl. Medal of Freedom, 1991. Democrat Home: Washington D.C. Died Jan. 5, 1994.

ONSTOTT, EDWARD IRVIN, research chemist; Moreland, Ky., Nov. 12, 1922; s. Carl Ervin and Jen Lee (Foley) O.; m. Mary Margaret Smith, Feb. 6, 194 children: Jenifer, Peggy Sue, Nicholas, Joseph. SChemE, U. Ill., 1944, MS in Chemistry, 1948, PhD Inorganic Chemistry, 1950. Chem. engr. Firestone T & Rubber Co., Paterson, N.J., 1944, 46; resear chemist Los Alamos Nat. Lab., 1950-94, guest scientis Patentee in field. Served with C.E., AUS, 1944-46 Fellow AAAS, Am. Inst. Chemists; mem. Am. Che Soc., Electrochem. Soc., N.Y. Acad. Scis., Intern Assn. Hydrogen Energy, Rare Earth Research Conf Izaak Walton League, N.Mex. Acad. Scis., Los Alam Hist. Soc. Republican. Methodist. Home: Los Alam N.Mex. Died Feb. 14, 1995.

OPPENHEIMER, JANE MARION, biologist, h torian, educator; b. Phila., Sept. 19, 1911; d. Jan Harry and Sylvia (Stern) O. B.A., Bryn Mawr Co 1932; Ph.D., Yale U., 1935, postgrad. (Sterling fello 1935-36, Am. Assn. U. Women fellow, 1936-37; Sc (hon.), Brown U., 1976. Research fellow embryology Rochester, 1937-38; faculty Bryn Mawr (Pa.) Co 1938-96, prof., 1953-80, prof. emeritus, 1980-96, acti dean grad. sch., 2d semester, 1946-47; Vis. prof. biolo Johns Hopkins, 1966-67; exchange prof. U. Paris, 196 Author: New Aspects of John and William Hunt 1946, Essays in History of Embryology and Biolo 1967; editor: Autobiography of Dr. Karl Ernst v Baer, 1986; co-editor: Founds. Exptl. Embryology, 19 editor 2d edit., 1974; assoc. editor: Jour. Morpholo 1956-58, Quar. Rev. Biol, 1963-64; mem. editorial b Am. Zoologist, 1965-70, Jour. History Biology, 1967- Quar. Rev. Biology, 1968-75; sect. editor developmen biology: Biol. Abstracts, 1970-73. Mem. history scis. study sect. NIH, 1966-70. Recipient Lucius Wilt Cross medal Yale Grad. Alumni Assn., 1971, K. E. v Baer medal Estonian Acad. Scis., 1992; Guggenhe Meml. Found. fellow, 1942-43, 52-53; Rockefel Found. fellow, 1950-51; NSF postdoctoral fellow, 19 60. Fellow AAAS (sec. sect. L 1955-58, coun. del. se G 1980-83, com. on coun. affairs 1981-82), Am. Ac Arts & Scis., Phila. Coll. Physicians (hon.); mem. A Soc. Zoologists (treas. 1957-59, chmn. div. devel. ology 1967, pres. 1973), Am. Assn. Anatomists, Hist of Sci. Soc. (mem. coun. 1975-77), Am. Assn. Hist Medicine (mem. coun. 1971-74), Am. Soc. Naturalis Soc. for Developmental Biology, Internat. Soc. Developmental Biology, Am. Inst. Biol. Scis. (mem. large governing bd. 1974-77), Internat. Soc. Hist Medicine, Internat. Acad. History of Sci. (Paris) (cor Internat. Acad. History Medicine (Paris), Am. Phi Soc. (coun. 1982-92 , exec. com. 1984-92, sec. 1987-9 Home: Philadelphia Pa. Died Mar 19, 1996.

OPPER, JOHN, painter, educator; b. Chgo., Oct. 1908; m. Jospeh and Mary (Milstein) O.; m. Est Hausman, Mar. 24, 1934; children: Jane, Joseph. rad., Cleve. Sch. Art, 1931; Masters, Case West Reserve U., 1931; EdD, SUNY, 1952. Prof. art W oming U., Laramie,, 1945-47, Columbia U., N.Y 1947-52, U. N.C., Greensboro, 1952-57, NYU, N.Y 1957-74. One man shows include Artists' Gall N.Y.C., 1937, 40, 42, Feragil Gallery, N.Y.C., 1945, Thirty Gallery, Cleve., 1945, San Francisco Mus., 19 Egan Gallery, N.Y.C., 1955, Stable Gallery, N.Y 1959, 60, 62, Grace Borgenicht Gallery, 1966, 68, 73, 78, 79, 84, Vered Gallery, East Hampton, N 1989, 90; exhibited in group shows including Nat. Ac Design, 1933, Met. Mus. Art, N.Y.C., 1941, Art I Chgo., 1941, 42, 44, 47, 48, Pa. Acad. Fine Arts, 1

, Bklyn. Mus., 1941, 42, San Francisco Mus. Art, 45, 46, 47, Weatherspoon Gallery, Greensboro, 1945, ›lo. Springs. Fine Art Gallery, 1946, 47, Denver Art ıus., 1946, Calif. Palace Legion Honor, 1947, Nat. :ad., Washington, 1947, Sacramento Mus. Art, 1947, ›rcoran Gallery Art, 1948, 53, Toledo Mus., 1948, hitney Mus. Am. Art, 1952, Carnegie Inst., 1961, ıle U., 1961, 62, Santa Barbara Calif. Mus., 1964, ıild Hall, East Hampton, N.Y., 1970, Ball State U., 71, Montclair Art Mus., 1977, Cleve. Mus. Art, 1982, eve. Inst. Art, 1990 (Disting. Alumnus award 1990); ›resented in permanent collections including Mus. ›dern Art, N.Y., Whitney Mus. Am. Art, N.Y., Met. ıs. Art, N.Y., Nat. Mus. Am. Art, Washington. :cipient Earnst award Acad. Arts and Letters, 1990, ath award Guild Hall Mus., 1991; fellow Guggenheim ›und., 1968-94. Home: Amagansett N.Y. Died Oct. 4, 95.

RI, KAN, political science educator; b. Osaka, Japan, 1. 28, 1933; s. Tazo and Tamaji (Moriki) O.; m. ruko Horie, Apr. 27, 1961; children: Akemi, Harumi, ›riko. BA cum laude, Taylor U., Upland, Ind., 1956; A, Ind. U., Bloomington, 1958; PhD, Ind. U., 1961. str. Jochi (Sophia) U., Tokyo, 1965-67; assoc. prof. :hi (Sophia) U., 1967-70, prof. polit. sci., 1970-95, :m., faculty Inst. Internat. Relations, 1969-95, dean ıd. sch. Faculty Fgn. Studies, 1985-87; vis. prof. U. ılaya, Kuala Lumpur, Malaysia, 1974-75, U. Mo., ›lumbia, 1975-76 (winter semester), U. Minn., Mpls., ımmer 1978, 88, Princeton (N.J.) U., 1982-83 (fall nester). Author (with Roger Benjamin): Tradition d Change in Postindustrial Japan, 1981; editor Jour. :ernat. Studies, 1978-82; editorial bd. Internat. Studies ıar., 1980-84. Ind. U. fellow, 1960; Matsunaga Sci. ›und. grantee, 1970; Japan Found. grantee, 1974-75. :m. Japanese Polit. Sci. Assn., Japanese Assn. Innat. Relations (councilor 1975-95), Japanese Assn. n. Studies (councilor 1986-95). Home: Tokyo Japan ed Mar. 6, 1995.

RR, ROBERT THOMAS, biologist; b. San ancisco, Aug. 17, 1908; s. Robert Harris and Agnes ›ockburn) O.; m. Dorothy Sutton, June 1934; 1 dau., ıncy Jane (Mrs. Richard A. Davis); m. Dorothy ›wen, Aug. 1942; m. Margaret Barry Cunningham, g. 1972. B.S., U. San Francisco, 1929, D.Sc., 1976; A., U. Calif. at Berkeley, 1931, Ph.D., 1937. search asst. Museum Vertebrate Zoology, U. Calif. at rkeley, 1932-35; wildlife technician U.S. Nat. Park rvice, 1935-36; asst. prof. biology U. San Francisco, 42-48, asso. prof., 1949-54, prof., 1955-64; asst. rator dept. ornithology and mammalogy Calif. Acad. s., San Francisco, 1936-43; assoc. curator Calif. Acad. s., 1944, curator, 1945-75, curator emeritus, 1989-94, ›oc. dir., 1964-75, sr. scientist, 1975-94; vis. prof. ›logy U. Calif. at Berkeley, summer, 1962, spring, 65; Trustee Western Found. for Vertebrate Zoology; m. adv. bd. Point Reyes Bird Obs. Author numerous ›oks and articles in field. Hon. trustee Mountain Lion servation Found. Recipient Alumnus of Yr. award 87. Fellow AAAS (past pres. Pacific div.), Am. nithologists Union, Calif. Acad. Scis. (Fellows' ›dal), Explorers Club; hon. mem. Am. Soc. Mamılogists (past pres.), Cooper Ornithol. Soc. (past s.), San Francisco Mycol. Soc.; mem. Australian ımmal Soc., Biol. Soc. Washington, Nat. Audubon :., Nature Conservancy, Friends of Sea Otter (v.p.). ›me: Larkspur Calif. Died June 23, 1994.

BORN, ROBERT CHESLEY, artist, writer; b. hkosh, Wis., Oct. 26, 1904; s. Albert LeRoy and ice Lydia (Wyckoff) O.; m. Elodie Courter, Mar. 18, 44 (dec. 1994); children; Nicolas Courter, Eliot Wyck-. PhB, Yale U., 1928; student, Brit Acad., Rome, 28, Acad. Scandinav, Paris, 1929. Tchr. Hotchkiss 1., 1930-35; free-lance artist, 1945-95; flight safety ar- U.S. Navy, 1942-85; civilian flight safety artist FAA, 59-85; mem. Pres.'s Com. on Art Edn. in Pub. Schs., 54; chmn. art and architecture com. Yale Council, 53-59. Author: War is No Damn Good, 1946, Low d Inside, 1953, Osborn on Leisure, 1957, The Vul-ians, 1960, Dying to Smoke, 1964, Mankind May ever Make It, 1968, Missile Madness, 1969, An Os-rn Festival of Phobias, 1971, Osborn on Osborn, 84; author, illustrator: Osborn on Conflict, 1984; il-trator books, including: Sense Books, 1941-45; also ıstrator for popular mags.; exhibited Downtown Gal-y, N.Y.C., 1959, 64, 67, USIA graphic arts show, SR, 1963, Carpenter Art Ctr., Cambridge, Mass., 86, Naval Aviation Mus., Washington, 1990; resented by E.L. Stark Gallery, N.Y.C., 1987-94; re-spective exhbn. Beinecke Libr., Yale U., 1992; manent collection Beinecke Libr. Mem. cen. sch. , Salisbury, Conn.; pres. Sharon-Salisbury chpt. ited World Federealists. Lt. comdr. USNR, World ır II. Decorated Legion of Merit; named hon. naval ator #11 U.S. Navy, 1976; recipient Disting. Pub. :. medal sec. U.S. Navy, 1959; assoc. fellow Berkeley ll., Yale U., 1958-90. Mem. ACLU, Scroll and Key, rra Club, Nat. Trust Hist. Preservation, Elizabethan ıb (New Haven). Home: Salisbury Conn. Died Dec. 1994.

BORNE, GREGORY, ballet dancer; b. Louisvil- Grad., Tex. Christian U.; studied dance, N.C. Sch. ts; studied with, Lili Zali of Ballet Pacifica, Calif. ned Ballet Repertory Co. (now Am. Ballet Theatre II), 1974-75; mem. corps de ballet Am. Ballet Theatre, N.Y.C., 1975-79, soloist, 1979-83; joined Nat. Ballet of Can., Toronto, 1983—, soloist, 1983-84, prin., 1984-89; internat. freelance dancer, 1989—; guest artist with Milw. Ballet, Jacob's Pillow, Universal Ballet, 1984-89, Nat. Ballet Can., 1989—, also with San Francisco Ballet, Am. Ballet Theater, Cin. Ballet, Basel (Switzerland) Ballet, Royal Danish Ballet, English nat. Ballet, Universal Ballet Seoul, Republic of Korea. Premiered roles in Glen Tetley's Pierrot Lunaire, Mikhail Barishnykov's Nutcracker, John McFall's Interludes and Robert Desrosier's Blue Snake, David Allan's Masada; other repertory includes: The Sleeping Beauty, Swan Lake, Bayadère, Sphinx, Gemini, Voluntaires, Don Quixote, La Sylphide, Concerto, Serenade, The Four Temperaments, Symphony in C, Elite Syncopations, Onegin, Coppélia, The Merry Widow, Giselle, Song of a Wayfarer, Etudes, others; appeared in feature film Shadow Dancing, 1989, Turning Point, I'm Dancing As Fast As I Can. Winner Bronze medal Sr. Divsn. 1st U.S. Internat. Ballet Competition, Jackson, Miss., 1979. Home: New York N.Y. Died Jan. 8, 1994.

OSBORNE, JOHN JAMES, playwright; b. London, Dec. 12, 1929; s. Thomas Godfrey and Nellie Beatrice (Grove) O.; m. Pamela Lane, June 1951 (div. Aug. 1957); m. Mary Ure (div. 1962); m. Penelope Gilliatt, May 1963 (div. 1968); 1 dau., Nolan Kate; m. Jill Bennett, Apr. 1968 (div. 1977); m. Helen Dawson, 1978. PhD (hon.), Royal Coll. Art, 1970. Co-founder-dir. Woodfall Film Prodns. Ltd., 1958-94; dir. Oscar Lewenstein Plays Ltd., London, 1960-94; coun. mem. English Stage Co., London, 1968-94. Author: (plays) (with Stella Linden) The Devil Inside Him, 1950, (with Anthony Creighton) Personal Enemy, 1955, Look Back in Anger, 1956 (N.Y. Drama Critics Circle award 1958), The Entertainer, 1957, Epitaph for George Dillon, 1958, The World of Paul Slickey, 1959, Luther, 1961 (Tony award best play 1963, N.Y. Drama Critics Circle award 1965), The Blood of the Bambergs, 1962, Under Plain Cover, 1962, Inadmissible Evidence, 1964, A Patriot for Me, 1965 (Evening Standard Drama award 1965), Hotel in Amsterdam, 1968 (Evening Standard Drama award 1968), Time Present, 1968, West of Suez, 1971, A Sense of Detachment, 1972, A Place Calling Itself Rome, 1973, The End of Me Old Cigar, 1975, Watch It Come Down, 1976, Dèjàvu, 1991; (adaptations) A Bond Honoured (La Fianza Satisfecha by Lope de Vega), 1966, Hedda Gabler by Henrik Ibsen, 1972, The Picture of Dorian Gray: A Moral Entertainment by Oscar Wilde, 1975, The Father by August Strindberg, 1989; (screenplays) Look Back in Anger, 1959, The Entertainer, 1960, Tom Jones, 1964 (Academy award best adapted screenplay 1963), Inadmassible Evidence, 1968, The Charge of the Light Brigade, 1968, Moll Flanders, Tomorrow Never Comes, 1978; (teleplays) Billy Bunter, 1952, Robin Hood, 1953, A Matter of Scandal and Concern, 1960, The Right Prospectus, 1970, Very Like A Whale, 1970, The Gift of Friendship, 1972, Jill and Jack, 1974, Almost a Vision, 1960, You're Not Watching Me, Mummy, 1978, Try a Little Tenderness, 1978, Plays for England, 1963, God Rot Turnbridge Wells, 1985; (autobiography) A Better Class of Person, 1981, Too Young to Fight, Too Old to Forget, 1985, Almost a Gentleman, 1991; dir. (play) Meals on Wheels, 1965; actor: (plays) No Room at the Inn, 1948, The Death of Satan, 1956, Cards of Identity, 1956, The Good Woman of Setzuan, 1956, The Apollo de Bellac, 1957, The Making of Moo, 1958, A Cookoo in the Nest, 1974; (films) First Love, 1970, Get Carter, 1971; (TV) The Parachute, 1968, The First Night of Pygmalian, 1969, Brainscrew; editor: Hedda Gabler and Other Plays; contbr. to periodicals, including Encounter, Observer, Times (London). Mem. Writer's Guild Gt. Britain, Garrick Club. Home: Shropshire Eng. Died Dec. 24, 1994.

OSCHMANN, FRITZ WILHELM KARL, oil company executive; b. Hoppenrade, Germany, Oct. 6, 1924; s. Johann and Ella (Mix) O.; m. Siegrid Wilms, Apr. 7, 1951; children: Friedrich, Hilmar. Student Lehrerbildungsanstalt, 1939-43; abitur Oberschule, 1950; Ph.D., U. Munich, 1957. With Mobil Oil Co., Hamburg, Germany, 1948-57, geologist, 1957-68, mgr., 1968-71, gen. mgr., 1971-74, bd. dirs., 1974-75, exploration mgr. MOBIL N.Y., 1975-76; dir. Gelsenberg, Essen, 1976-78; mng. dir. DEMINEX, Essen, 1978-86; pres., chief exec. officer VEBA OEL AG. Mem. German Geol. Soc., German Soc. Mineral Oil and Coal Scis. Died Dec. 13, 1986. Home: Essen Federal Republic of Germany

OSER, BERNARD LEVUSSOVE, food and drug consultant; b. Phila., Feb. 2, 1899; s. Harris E. and Frances (Levussove) O.; m. Clara de Hirsch Kotkin, May 27, 1923; children: Zelda Oser Zelinsky, Alan Stuart. BS, U. Pa., 1920, MS, 1925; PhD, Fordham U., 1927. Diplomate Am. Bd. Indsl. Hygiene, Am. Bd. Nutrition, Am. Bd. Clin. Chemists. Asst. physiol. chemistry Jefferson Med. Coll., 1920-21; biochemist Phila. Gen. Hosp., 1922-26; from asst. dir. to dir., v.p. Food Rsch. Labs. Inc. (predecessor FDRL), 1926-57, from dir. to pres., chmn. bd., 1957-74; cons. Bernard L. Oser Assocs., Bayside, N.Y., 1974-95; adj. prof. Columbia U. Inst. Nutrition Scis., 1959-71. Co-author, collaborator: Practical Physiological Chemistry, 9th, 10th, 11th edits, 1926-31, 1937; co-author and editor: Practical Physiological Chemistry, 12th, 13th edits., 1947, 54, Hawk's Physiological Chemistry, 14th edit., 1965; editorial bd. Analytical Chemistry, 1946-49, Food Tech., 1947-51; Jour. Agr. and Food Chemistry, 1955-58,; sci. editor Food Drug Cosmetic Law Jour., 1957-95, Nutrition Reports Internat., 1974-81; author or co-author over 400 papers and speeches on methods of biological and chemical assay of vitamins, proteins and other nutrients, on the fortification, stabilization and physiological availability of vitamins in pharm. products and fortified foods, on toxicology and safety evaluation of food additives, drugs, pesticides and related chemicals, and on the sci. aspects of food laws and regulations. Trustee Gordon Rsch. Confs., 1954-57; chmn. food sect. Internat. Union Pure and Applied Chemistry, 1961-68; mem. food sci. mission Dept. Agr., 1963, food protection com. NAS-NRC, 1964-71, joint expert com. on food additives FAO-WHO. Recipient Ambassador of Toxicology award Mid-Atlantic chpt. Soc. of Toxicology, 1982. Fellow AAAS, Am. Inst. Chemists, Inst. Food Technologists (pres. 1968-69, Babcock Hart award 1958), N.Y. Acad. Scis., Toxicology Forum, Am. Inst. Nutrition; mem. Am. Chem. Soc. (chmn. div. agrl. and food chemistry 1946-47), Am. Coll. of Toxicology, Am. Coun. on Sci. and Health, Am. Indsl. Hygiene Assn., Am. Inst. of Chemists, Am. Inst. of Nutrition, Am. Soc. of Pharmacology and Exptl. Therapeutics, Assn. of Vitamin Chemists, Nat. Rsch. Coun. (food and nutrition bd.), N.Y. Acad. Medicine (assoc.), N.Y. Inst. Food Technologists (pres. 1968-69), Acad. Toxicological Scis., Soc. of Tech., Teratology Soc., Internat. Soc. Regulatory Toxicology and Pharmacology, Flavor and Extract Mfrs. Assn. (hon.), The Chemists Club (N.Y.), Alpha Epsilon Pi, Sigma Xi (hon.), Phi Tau Sigma (hon.). Home: Teaneck N.J. Died Jan. 21, 1995.

OSTER, GERALD, biophysics educator; b. Providence, Mar. 24, 1918; s. David and Sarah (Arkand) O.; m. Selmaree Greene, May 11, 1973; children: Tatiana, Felix, Alexander. BS, Brown U., 1940; PhD, Cornell U., 1943. Research assoc. M.I.T., 1943-44, Princeton U., 1944-45, Rockefeller Inst., 1945-49; assoc. Birkbeck Coll., London, 1949-50; Rockefeller fellow Royal Instn., London, 1950-51; vis. scientist Sorbonne, Paris, 1951; prof. Poly. Inst. Bklyn., 1951-69; prof. biophysics Mt. Sinai Sch. Medicine, N.Y.C., 1969-88; sr. scientist Environ. Scis. Lab. Bklyn. Coll., 1989-90. Author: Physical Techniques in Biological Research, 1956, The Science of Moiré Patterns, 1964; contbr. numerous articles to profl. jours., art exhbts. moire constrns. Home: New York N.Y. Died Oct. 9, 1993; interred Haiti, West Indies.

OSTROM, THOMAS MARSHALL, psychology educator; b. Mishawaka, Ind., Mar. 1, 1936; s. Alfred Sherman and Marion Esther (Eggleston) O.; m. Diana Forrest, Aug. 30, 1958 (div. Sept. 1977); children: Lisa Gail Webb, Steven Marshall; m. Mary Brickner, Nov. 9, 1991. AB, Wabash Coll., 1958; MA, U. N.C., 1964, PhD, 1964. Prof. psychology Ohio State U., from 1964, dir. social psychology program, 1974-79, 80-85; acting dir. Ctr. Cognitive Sci., 1991-92; vis. prof. U. Bergen, Norway, 1973-74, U. Manheim, Fed. Republic Germany, 1981; lectr. various colls. and univs. Editor: Psychological Foundations of Attitudes, 1968, Person Memory, 1980, Cognitive Responses in Persuasion, 1981; editor Jour Exptl. Social Psychology, 1980-87; contbr. articles to profl. jours. Grantee NSF, 1969-75, Mershon Found., 1967-69, from 90, Office of Naval Rsch., 1977-84. Fellow AAAS, Am. Psychol. Assn., Am. Psychol. Soc.; mem. Soc. Exptl. Social Psychology, Psychonomic Soc., European Assn. Experimental Social Psychology. Democrat. Episcopalian. Home: Hilliard Ohio Deceased.

OTHMER, DONALD FREDERICK, chemical engineer, educator; b. Omaha, May 11, 1904; s. Frederick George and Fredericka Darling (Snyder) O.; m. Mildred Jane Topp, Nov. 18, 1950. Student, Ill. Inst. Tech., Chgo., 1921-23; B.S., U. Nebr., 1924, D.Eng. (hon.), 1962; M.S., U. Mich., 1925, Ph.D., 1927; D.Eng. (hon.), Poly. U., Bklyn., 1977, N.J. Inst. Tech., 1978. Registered profl. engr., N.Y., N.J., Ohio, Pa. Devel. engr. Eastman Kodak Co. and Tenn. Eastman Corp., 1927-31; prof. Poly. U., Bklyn., 1933; disting. prof. Poly. U., 1961-95, sec. grad. faculty, 1948-58; head dept. chem. engring., 1937-61; hon. prof. U. Conception, Chile, 1951; cons. chem. engr., licensor of process patents to numerous cos., govtl. depts., and countries, 1931-95; developer program for chem. industry of Burma, 1951-54; cons. UN, UNIDO, WHO, Dept. Energy, Office Saline Water of U.S. Dept. Interior, Chem. Corps. and Ordnance Dept. U.S. Army, USN, WPB, Dept. State, HEW, Congress, Nat. Materials Advisory Bd., NRC Sci. Adv. Bd., U.S. Army Munitions Command; mem. Panel Energy Advisers to Congress, also other U.S. and fgn. govt. depts.; sr. gas officer Bklyn. Citizens Def. Corps.; lectr. Am. Swiss Found. Sci. Relations, 1950, Chem. Inst. Can., 1944-52, Am. Chem. Soc., U.S. Army War Coll., 1964, Shri RAM Inst., India, 1980, Royal Mil. Coll. Can., 1981; plenary lectr. Peoples Republic of China; hon. del. Engring. Congresses, Japan, 1983; plenary lectr., hon. del. Fed. Republic of Germany, Greece, Mex., Czechoslovakia, Yugoslavia, Poland, P.R., France, Can., Argentina, India, Turkey, Spain, Rumania, Kuwait, Iran, Iraq, Algeria, China, United Arab Emirates; designer chem. plants and processes for numerous corps., U.S., fgn. countries. Holder over 150 U.S. and fgn. patents on methods, processes and engring. equipment in mfg. of pharms., sugar, salt, acetic acid, acetylene, fuel-methanol, synthetic rubber, petrochems., pigments, zinc, aluminum, titanium, also wood pulping, refrigeration, solar and other energy conversion, water desalination, sewage treatment, peat utilization, coal desulfurization, pipeline heating, etc.; contbr. over 350 articles on chem. engring., chem. mfg., synthetic fuels and thermodynamics to tech. jours.; co-founder/co-editor: Kirk-Othmer Ency. Chem. Tech., 17 vols., 1947-60, 24 vols., 2d edit., 1963-71, 26 vols., 3d edit., 1976-84, 4th edit., 25 vols., 1992-95, Spanish edit., 16 vols., 1960-66; editor: Fluidization, 1956; co-author: Fluidization and Fluid Particle Systems, 1960; mem. adv. bd.: Perry's Chem. Engr.'s Handbook; tech. editor: UN Report, Technology of Water Desalination, 1964. Bd. regents L.I. Coll. Hosp., bd. dirs. numerous ednl. and philanthropic instns., engring. and indsl. corps. Recipient Golden Jubilee award Ill. Inst. Tech., 1975, Profl. Achievement award Ill. Inst. Tech., 1978, Award of Honor for Sci. and Tech. Mayor of N.Y.C., 1987, Outstanding Alumnus award U. Nebr., 1989, Citation for Improvement of Quality of Life, Pres. Borough Bklyn., 1989, award for significant contbns. to life Polytechnic U., 1989; named to Hall of Fame, Ill. Inst. Tech., 1981. Fellow AAAS, Am. Inst. Cons. Engrs., Am. Inst. Chemists (Honor Scroll 1970, Chem. Pioneer award 1977), ASME (hon. life, chmn. chem. processes div. 1948-49), N.Y. Acad. Scis. (hon. life, chmn. engring. sect. 1972-73), Instn. Chem. Engrs. (London) (hon. life), Am. Inst. Chem. Engrs. (Tyler award 1958, chmn. N.Y. sect. 1944, dir. 1956-59, Founders award 1991); mem. Am. Chem. Soc. (council 1945-47, E.V. Murphree-Exxon award 1978, hon. life mem.), Soc. Chem. Industry (Perkin medal 1978), Am. Soc. Engring. Edn. (Barber Coleman award 1958), Engrs. Joint Council (dir. 1957-59), Societe de Chimie Industrielle (pres. 1973-74), Chemurgic Council (dir.), Japan Soc. Chem. Engrs., Assn. Cons. Chemists and Chem. Engrs. (award of Merit 1975), Newcomen Soc., Am. Arbitration Assn. (panel mem. or sole arbitrator numerous cases), Deutsche Gesellscaft für Cheme. Apparatewesen (hon. life), Norwegian Club Bklyn., Chemists Club N.Y.C. (pres. 1974-75), Rembrandt Club Bklyn., Sigma Xi (citation disting. research 1983), Tau Beta Pi, Phi Lambda Upsilon, Iota Alpha, Alpha Chi Sigma, Lambda Chi Alpha. Home: Brooklyn N.Y. Died Nov. 1, 1995.

O'TOOLE, JOHN E., advertising executive; b. Chgo., Jan. 17, 1929; m. Phyllis Treadway, 1955; children: Sally, Ellen. BJ, Northwestern U., 1951. With Batten, Barton, Durstine & Osborn, 1953-54, Foote, Cone & Belding, 1954-85; successively copy writer, copy supr., v.p., creative dir. Foote, Cone & Belding, L.A. and Chgo.; pres. Foote, Cone & Belding, N.Y.C., 1969; pres. Foote, Cone & Belding Communications, Inc., N.Y.C., 1970-81, chmn., 1981-85; dir. Am. Assn. Advt. Agys., Washington, 1986-88, pres., 1988-95; dir. Nat. Advt. Rev. Coun.; bd. dirs. John Nuveen Mut. Funds. Author: The Trouble with Advertising, 1981. Served with USMCR, 1951-53; ret. Res. 1956. Home: New York N.Y. Died 1995.

OTT, STANLEY JOSEPH, bishop; b. Gretna, La., June 29, 1927; s. Manuel Peter and Lucille (Berthelot) O. S.T.D., Pontifical Gregorian U., Rome, 1954. Ordained priest Roman Catholic Ch. Bishop Roman Catholic Ch., 1951, aux. bishop, 1976; assoc. pastor St. Francis Cabrini Parish, New Orleans, 1954-57; chaplain La. State U., Baton Rouge, 1957-61; ofcl. Marriage Tribunal, Diocese of Baton Rouge, from 1961; chancellor rector St. Joseph Cathedral, Baton Rouge, 1968-76; aux. bishop of New Orleans, 1976-83, bishop of Baton Rouge (La.), 1983-92; liaison bishop Nat. Coun. Cath. Women. Bd. dirs. ARC, Boy Scouts Am. Mem. Nat. Conf. Cath. Bishops, U.S. Cath. Conf. Democrat. Club: K.C. (state chaplain), Cath. Daus. Am. Home: Baton Rouge La. Died Nov. 28, 1992; interred Cathedral Courtyard, Baton Rouge, L.A.

OTTO, GEORGE JOHN, investment banker; b. San Francisco, June 8, 1904; s. Paul O. and Emma (Shanstrum) O.; m. Marie Kendrick, Oct. 10, 1933; children—Marie L., Elizabeth A., Susan. A.B., U. Calif. at Berkeley, 1926. Bond salesman Mitchum Tully & Co., 1926-35; partner Irving Lundborg & Co., San Francisco, 1935-70; vice chmn. bd. dirs. Clark Dodge Co., Inc., San Francisco, 1970-74; v.p. Paine Webber & Co., 1974-95; dir. Schlage Lock Co.; gov. Stock Exchange Firms; pres. Pacific Coast Stock Exchange, chmn. San Francisco div. Active local council Girl Scouts U.S.A.; trustee World Affairs Council; bd. dirs. Internat. Hospitality Center, Columbia Park Boys Club, Golden Gate Coll., No. Calif. Soc. for Prevention Blindness, San Francisco Ladies Protection and Relief Soc., Palace Fine Arts League. Mem. Investment Bankers Assn. Am. (v.p., gov. Calif. group; past gov.), Brit. Am. C. of C. (dir.). Clubs: Bond (San Francisco) (pres. 1947), Bohemian (San Francisco) (sec., dir. 1956-57), San Francisco Golf (San Francisco), Pacific Union. Home: San Francisco Calif. Died Aug. 31, 1995.

OTTO, GILBERT FRED, zoologist, educator; b. Chgo., Dec. 16, 1901; s. Martin and Fredericka Christina (Rose) O.; m. Loudale Simmons, Dec. 20, 1932; children: Sandra Otto Abbott, Frederick Simmons. AB, Kalamazoo Coll., 1926; MS, Kans. State U., 1927; ScD, Johns Hopkins U., 1929. Instr. Johns Hopkins U., Balt., 1929-31, asst. prof., 1931-42, assoc. prof., 1942-53, asst. dean Sch. of Pub. Health, 1940-47, dir. Parasitology Lab. of Med. Clinics, 1946-53; mgr. Parasitology Rsch. Div. Abbott Labs., North Chicago, Ill., 1953-61; dir. of agrl. and vet. rsch. Abbott Labs., North Chicago, 1961-66; prof. zoology U. Md., College Park, 1966-72, adj. prof., lectr., 1972-80, sr. rsch. assoc., 1980—; lectr. med. entomology Sch. of Hygiene and Pub. Health Johns Hopkins U., 1980-89; cons. Naval Med. Rsch. Inst., 1948-54; mem. sci. adv. bd. biology dept. U. Notre Dame, 1958-67; vis. prof. U. Mich. Biol. Sta., 1946-53; cons. NIH, 1945-50, WHO, 1952-75, FDA, 1941, 77-81; cons. mosquito-borne disease Nat. Acad. Sci., 1983-86; sec. gen. 2d Internat. Congress Parasitology, 1970. Contbr. numerous articles on parasitology to sci. jours; contbr. chpts. to med. and vet. texts. Developer treatment for heartworm in dogs. Chief judge High Sch. Sci. Fairs, Prince Georges County (Md.), 1967-70; trustee B.H. Ransom Meml. Trustee Fund, 1936—, chmn. bd., 1956-73. Named Disting. Alumnus Kalamazoo Coll., 1951, 89, Johns Hopkins U., 1991, Disting. Editor of Yr. Coun. Biology Editors, 1986; recipient Alumni award Johns Hopkins U., 1991, Disting. Vet. Parasitologist, 1992; dedication symposium in his honor Am. Heartworm Soc., 1992. Fellow AAAS, Royal Soc. Tropical Medicine and Hygiene; mem. AVMA (hon. life), Ill. Mosquito Control Assn. (pres. 1960-61; hon. life), Am. Soc. Tropical Medicine, World Assn. Advancement Vet. Parasitology, Am. Soc. Parasitologists (treas. 1937-41, 44, v.p. 1955, pres. 1957; hon. life), Helminthological Soc. Washington (pres. 1936, editor 1952-66; hon. life), Am. Micros. Soc., Am. Heartworm Soc. (hon. life mem.; sec.-treas. 1974-77, asst. editor 1974-77, editor 1977-89, pres. 1977-80), Coun. Biol. Editors (Meritorious award 1986), Johns Hopkins U. Alumni Assn. (Disting. Alumnus award 1991). Home: Vail Colo.

OUKO, ROBERT JOHN, politician; b. Kusumu, Kenya, Mar. 31, 1932; s. Erasto and Susanah Seda Ouku; m. Christabel Akumu Odolla, 1965; 7 children. Grad., Siriba Coll., Haile Sellassie I U., Makarere U. Tchr., 1952-55; with Ministry of African Affairs, Kisii Dist., 1955-58; asst. sec. Fgn. Affairs Dept. Office of the Prime Minister, 1962-63, sr. asst. sec., 1963; permanent sec. Ministry of Fgn. Affairs, 1963-64, Ministry of Works, 1965-69; E. African Minister for Fin. and Adminstrn. Kenya Govt., 1969-70, minister for Common Market and Econ. Affairs, 1970-77, minister of econ. planning and community affairs, 1978-79, minister of fgn. affairs, 1979-83, minister of planning and nat. devel., 1985-87, minister of industry, 1987, minister of fgn. affairs and internat. cooperation, 1988-90; pres. African Assn. for Pub. Adminstrn. and Mgmt., 1971-74; mem. E. African Legis. Assembly, ILO. Contbr. articles to profl. jours.; co-author university textbook on mgmt. Fellow Kenya Inst. Mgmt. Home: Nairobi Kenya Died Feb. 12, 1990; interred Koru.

OVERBY, GEORGE ROBERT, academic administrator; b. Jacksonville, Fla., July 21, 1923; s. Taylor Earl and Virginia (Hewett) O. B.A., Fla. State U., 1951, Ph.D., 1966; M.Ed., U. Fla., 1959, Specialist in Edn., 1963. Tchr. Lake Forest Hills Elem. Sch., 1956-59; tchr. Ribault Secondary Sch., 1961-64; prin. Jacksonville Christian Schs., 1959-61; assoc. prof. Slippery Rock (Pa.) State U., 1966-68, Youngstown (Ohio) State U., 1968-71; prof., chmn. dept. edn. Shelton Coll., Cape Canaveral, Fla., 1971-74; pres. Freedom U., Orlando, Fla., 1974-81, chancellor, 1981-92; chancellor Freedom Sem., Orlando, 1981-92, Freedom Inst., Orlando, 1987-92; Cons. pvt. pub. edn., 1958-92; Mem. Council for Basic Edn.; campus adviser Young Ams. for Freedom, Intercollegiate Studies.; Pres. bd. trustees Christian Enterprises, Inc., 1962-66; adv. bd. Am. Security Council, Inst. Am. Strategy; a founder Center for Internat. Security Studies. Served as aviator USNR, 1943-46. Fellow Intercontinental Biog. Assn. (life), Internat. Inst. Community Service (life); mem. Am. Assn. Higher Edn. (life, charter), NEA (life), AAUP, Am. Assn. Sch. Adminstrs., Nat. Assn. Elementary Sch. Prins., Univ. Profs. for Acad. Order (charter; past dir.), Assn. Supervision and Curriculum Devel., Internat. Assn. for Christian Edn. (founder, pres.), Ednl. Internat. Inc. (founder, pres.), Nat. Council for Social Studies, Am. Assn. Christian Schs., Christian Educators Assn. S.E., Fla. Fedn. Christian Colls. and Univs. (bd. dirs.) Soc. for Study Edn., Citizens for Decent Lit., U.S. Naval Aviation Mus. (life), Assn. Childhood Edn. Internat., Am. Assn. Sch. Adminstrs., Internat. Biog. Assn. (life patron, life fellow), Am. Biog. Inst. Research Assn. (life patron, hon. dir.), Kappa Delta Pi (life), Phi Delta Kappa (life). Home: Orlando Fla. Died Jan. 10, 1992.

OVERBY, LACY RASCO, biotechnology consulting executive; b. Model, Tenn., July 27, 1920; s. Alious William and Oma Catherine (Thomas) O.; m. Elizabeth Mae Hulette, Oct. 1, 1948; children: Megan Stewart, Ross Vincent, Alison Brooke, Alexander Scott. BA, Vanderbilt U., 1941, MS, 1948, PhD, 1951. Prodn. supr. DuPont Corp., Barksdale, Wis., 1941-43; teaching asst. Vanderbilt U., Nashville, 1946-49; from mgmt. positions to div. v.p. Abbott Labs., North Chicago, Ill., 1949-83, cons., 1983-84; v.p. Chiron Corp., Emeryville, Calif., 1983-88; pres. Tech. Exec. Consultants, Alamo, Calif., 1988-94; bd. dirs. Genelex Inc., Seattle, Acrogen, Inc., Oakland, Photonics Inc., Atlanta; cons. Children's Meml. Hosp., Chgo., 1970-73; lectr. in molecular biology Northwestern U., Evanston, Ill., 1968-81. Editor: Viral Hepatitis, 1979, rev. edit., 1983; assoc. editor Jou
Med. Virology, 1977-88, Asian Jour. Clin. Scis., 198
92; contbr. articles to profl. jours.; patentee in field
Chmn. bd. dirs. Am. Cancer Soc., Lake County, Il
1978-82. Served to comdr. USNR, 1943-46; ETO, PTC
Recipient Karl Landsteiner award Am. Assn. Blo
Banks, 1992; DuPont fellow Vanderbilt U., 1948; v
scholar U. Ill., Urbana, 1962-64. Mem. Am. Soc. B
ochemistry and Molecular Biology, Am. Soc. Stu
Liver Diseases, Am. Soc. Microbiology (Pasteur awa
1986), Am. Chem. Soc., Sigma Xi. Episcopalian. Clu
Round Hill Country (Alamo, Calif.). Home: Alan
Calif. Died Dec. 5, 1994.

OVERCASH, REECE A., JR., financial services co
pany executive; b. Charlotte, N.C., June 15, 1926;
Reece A. and Mary Louise (Daniel) O.; m. Christa L
Anderson; children: Susan Kay Overcash-Jenkins, Ma
Ann Austin, Sarah Lee, Alex. BBA, U. N.C., 195(
With Am. Credit Corp., Charlotte, 1952-75, pres., 197
75; pres. Assocs. Corp. N.Am., Dallas, 1975-81, chm
chief exec. officer, 1978-96; dir. Assocs. Corp. N.A
(The Associates), Dallas; chmn. Assocs. First Capi
Corp.; sr. exec. v.p. Gulf & Western Inc., N.Y.C., 198
87; bd. dirs. Duke Power Co., Charlotte, Belo Cor
Dallas, Nat. Gypsum Co., Charlotte. Bd. dirs. Dal
Citizens Council, 1986-88, 1990-92, Sammons Dal
Found., Sammons Found., 1994—; campaign chm
United Way Met. Dallas, 1979, exec. com., 1979-
pres. exec. com., 1981, ; so. cen. regional chmn. Uni
Way Am., 1988-96; v.p. Met. Dallas, 1980-81, pre
from 1981, bd. dirs., 1978-96; bd. dirs. Dallas Coun
Community Coll. Dist. Found., 1977-96, vice chm
1978-79, chmn., 1979-81; mem. consumer adv. coun
Fed. Res. Bd., 1976-78; bd. trustees Dallas Baptist
1986-90; bd. dirs. Circle Ten Council Boy Scouts Ar
1978-86, North Tex. Commn., 1977-96, Better Bus. B
Met. Dallas, 1979-96, Community Council Grea
Dallas, 1981; mem. devel. council U. Dallas Campai
1980; vice chmn. patron gifts com. Dallas Mus. F
Arts, 1980; adv. council Credit Research Ctr., Purd
U., 1980; mem. bus. devel. com. So. Meth. U., 19
mem. strategic planning com. United Way Am., 19
chmn. bd. Dallas United Adv. Coun., 1986-88; exec. b
Cox Sch. Bus. of So. Meth. U., 1983-96; adv. co
Dallas County Treasurer's Office, 1987. Served w
inf., AUS, World War II. Recipient Disting. B
Leadership award U. Tex., Arlington, 1988, Statesm
award Harvard Bus. Sch. Club of Dallas, 1990; nam
Man of Yr., Charlotte, 1972. Mem. Dallas C. of C. (
dirs. 1977-80, 86-89, chmn. adv. com. Leadership Dal
prog. 1979-80, Dallas United prog. 1986), Am. F
Svcs. Assn. (bd. dirs., exec. com. 1966-83, Disting. S
award 1973), Myers Park Country Club, City Cl
(Charlotte), Brookhollow Country Club, Petrole
Club (Dallas). Baptist. Home: Dallas Tex. Died J
19, 1996.

OVERMYER, ROBERT FRANKLYN, astrona
marine corps officer; b. Lorain, Ohio, July 14, 1936,
Rolandus and Margaret (Fabian) O.; m. Katherine El
Jones, Oct. 17, 1959; children: Carolyn Marie, Patri
Ann, Robert Rolandus. B.S. in Physics, Baldwin W
lace Coll., 1958; M.S. in Aeros., U.S. Naval Postgr
Sch., 1964. Commd. 2d lt. U.S. Marine Corps., 19
advanced through grades to lt. col., 1972; comple
aerospace research pilot sch. Edward AFB, 1966;
tronaut with Manned Orbiting Lab. NASA, 1966-
astronaut with Manned Spacecraft Ctr. NAS
Houston, 1969-96; mem. support crew Appolo-So
Test Project, 1973-75; co-pilot on 5th mission Colum
NASA, Houston, 1982; comdr. Spacelab 3 miss
NASA, 1985. Recipient Alumni Merit award Bald
Wallace Coll., 1967. Mem. Soc. Exptl. Test Pilots (
soc.), Sigma Xi. Home: Houston Tex. Died March
1996.

OWENS, J(AMES) CUTHBERT, surgeon, anatom
retired medical educator; b. Bayside, L.I., N.Y., Feb.
1916; s. James Whitfield and Mary Agnes (Hannah)
m. Lila Vollintine, Feb. 23, 1957 (dec. Oct. 1982); c
dren: James W. II (dec.), Ann, Lewis, Jay. BS, C
William and Mary, 1936; MD, Marquette U., 194
Diplomate Am. Bd. Surgery. Intern Cin. Gen. Ho
1941-42; resident Henry Ford Hosp., 1942-43, U
Naval Med. Ctr., Bethesda, Md., 1945-48, Georgeto
U., 1948-50; chief of surgery Colo. State Hosp., Pueb
1951-52; instr. U. Colo. Med. Ctr., 1951-53, asst. p
surgery, 1953-59, assoc. prof., 1959-65, prof., 1965-
surg. head peripheral vascular disease svc., 1952-77,
emergency med. svcs., 1973-80, prof. emeritus, 198
adj. prof. cellular and structural biology U. Co
1986—; mem. staff Univ. Hosp., Gen. Rose Me
Hosp.; cons. VA Hosp., Denver, Fitzsimmons Ho
Denver; mem. com. emergency med. svcs. Nat. Ac
Scis.-NRC, 1966-74; mem. Colo. gov.'s med. adv.
Traffic Safety Coun., 1966-74; mem. Colo. Go
Emergency Med. Svcs. Coun., 1972-77; sec., treas. C
Anat. Bd., 1987-88; grand marshall health sci. c
mencements U. Colo., 1986. Contbr. articles to m
publs. Bd. dirs. Colo. Safety Council, 1968-82. Ser
to lt. comdr. USNR, 1943-48. Decorated Bronze S
recipient citation for med. emergency devel., USP
1972, Disting. Svc. award Emergency Med. Tra
Assn., Colo., 1976, Nat. Notable award City of P
smouth, Va., 1987, Nat. Safety Coun. Surgeons aw
1990. Fellow ACS (mem. com. on trauma 1969
chmn. Colo. com. on trauma 1967-88, Tra

chievement award 1978); mem. AMA (del. com. on nergency med. svcs. 1970-74), Denver Acad. Surgery, enver County Med. Soc. (alt. del. 1990-92, del. 1993-5), Colo. Med. Soc. (Cert. of Svc. 1979), Assn. Am. ed. Colls., Am. Surg. Assn., Denver Clinical and athol. Soc. (hon.), Internat. Cardiovascular Soc., Cen-al Surg. Soc., Soc. Vascular Surgery, Univ. Assn. mergency Med. Svcs. (founding), Am. Trauma Soc. ounding), Am. Assn. Surg. Trauma, Am. Heart Assn., ociete Internat. de Chirurgie, Rocky Mountain Vas-lar Soc., Am. Assn. Clin. Anatomists, Theta Chi elta, Pi Kappa Alpha, Phi Chi. Home: Chapel Hill .C. Died Dec. 3, 1994.

ZAL, TURGUT, president; b. Malatya, Turkey, 1927; Mehmet Siddik and Hafize Ozal; m. Semra Yeginmen; ildren: Ahmet, Zeynep Gonenc, Efe. MSEE, Tech. ., Istanbul, Turkey, 1950. With Elec. Survey Ad-instrn., asst. to gen. dir.; spl. tech. adv. to prime inister Govt. of Turkey, 1965-67; undersec. State anning Orgn., 1967-71; undersec. to prime minister, 979-80, dep. prime minister, 1980-83, prime minister, 983-89, minister of state, from 1980, pres., 1989-93; spl. ojects advisor, sr. economist World Bank, 1971-83; ader Anatavan Partisi (Motherland Party), 1988-93. uthor: Turkey in Europe: And Europe in Turkey, 991. Home: Ankara Turkey Died Apr. 10, 1993.

ACKARD, DAVID, manufacturing company execu-ve, electrical engineer; b. Pueblo, Colo., Sept. 7, 1912; Sperry Sidney and Ella Lorna (Graber) P.; m. Lucile alter, Apr. 8, 1938 (dec., 1987); children: David oodley, Nancy Ann Packard Burnett, Susan Packard rr, Julie Elizabeth Stephens. B.A., Stanford U., 1934, E, 1939; LLD (hon.), U. Calif., Santa Cruz, 1966, atholic U., 1970, Pepperdine U., 1972; DSc (hon.), olo. Coll., 1964; LittD (hon.), So. Colo. State Coll., 973; D.Eng. (hon.), U. Notre Dame, 1974. With acuum tube engring. dept. Gen. Electric Co., henectady, 1936-38; co-founder, ptnr. Hewlett-ackard Co., Palo Alto, Calif., 1939-47, pres., 1947-64, ief exec. officer, 1964-68, chmn. bd., 1964-68, 72-93, mn. emeritus, 1993-96; U.S. dep. sec. defense Wash-gton, 1969-71; dir. Genetech, Inc., 1981-92; bd. dirs. eckman Laser Inst. and Med. Clinic; chmn. Presdl. ommn. on Def. Mgmt., 1985-86; mem. White House i. Coun., 1982-88. Mem. President's Commn. Pers. terchange, 1972-74, President's Coun. Advisors on i. and Tech., 1990-92, Trilateral Commn., 1973-81, irs. Coun. Exploratorium, 1987-90; pres. bd. regents niformed Svcs. U. of Health Scis., 1975-82; mem. U.S.-SSR Trade and Econ. Coun., 1975-82; mem. bd. over-ers Hoover Instn., 1972-96; bd. dirs. Nat. Merit Scho-rship Corp., 1963-69, Found. for Study of Presdl. and ongl. Terms, 1978-86, Alliance to Save Energy, 1977-, Atlantic Coun., 1972-83, vice chmn., 1972-80, Am. nterprise Inst. for Public Policy Rsch., 1978-96, Nat. sh and Wildlife Found., 1985-87, Hitachi Found. Adv. oun., 1986-96; vice chmn. The Calif. Nature Con-rvancy, 1983-90; trustee Stanford U., 1954-69, pres., 958-60, Hoover Instn., The Herbert Hoover Found., avid and Lucile Packard Found., pres., chmn. 1964-96, erbert Hoover Found., 1974-96, Monterey Bay quarium Found., chmn., 1978-96, The Ronald Reagan esdl. Found., 1986-91, Monterey Bay Aquarium Rsch. st., chmn., pres. 1987-96. Decorated Grand Cross of erit Fed. Republic of Germany, 1972, Medal Honor ectronic Industries, 1974; numerous other awards in-uding Silver Helmet Def. award AMVETS, 1973, ashington award Western Soc. Engrs., 1975, Hoover edal ASME, 1975, Gold Medal award Nat. Football ound. and Hall of Fame, 1975, Good Scout award Boy couts Am., 1975, Vermilye medal Franklin Inst., 1976, ternat. Achievement award World Trade Club of San ancisco, 1976, Merit award Am. Cons. Engrs. Council ellows, 1977, Achievement in Life award Ency. itannica, 1977, Engring. Award of Distinction San se State U., 1980, Thomas D. White Nat. Def. award SAF Acad., 1981, Disting. Info. Scis. award Data ocessing Mgmt. Assn., 1981, Sylvanus Thayer award .S. Mil. Acad., 1982, Environ. Leadership award atural Resources Def. Council, 1983, Dollar award at. Fgn. Trade Council, 1985, Gandhi Humanitarium ward, 1988, Roback Award Nat. Contract Mgmt. ssn., 1988, Pub. Welfare Medal NAS, 1989, Chevron onservation Award, 1989, Doolittle Award Hudson st., 1989, Disting. Citizens Award Commonwealth ub San Francisco, 1989, William Wildback award, at. Conf. Standards Labs., Washington, 1990, Ter-nce Keenan Leadership award Grantmakers in Health, 994, John Martin Excellence in Marine Scis. medal anford U., 1994, Nat. Disting. Svc. award Nat. Acads. actice, 1994, Disting. Grantmakers award Coun. on ounds., 1994, Am. Philanthropy award Columbus ound., 1994, Lifetime Achievement award Lemelson-IT, 1995, Excellence medal Free U. of Brussels, 1995, amaritan award Samaritan Counseling Ctr. of Mid-eninsula, 1995, Price/Waterhouse Info. Tech. Leader-ip award for lifetime achievement Computerworld/ nithsonian, 1995; named to Silicon Valley Engring. all of Fame, Silicon Valley Engring. Coun., 1991, ueblo (Colo.) Hall of Fame, 1991. Fellow IEEE ounders medal 1973); mem. Nat. Acad. Engring. ounders award 1979), Instrument Soc. Am. (hon. life-ne mem.), Wilson Council, The Bus. Roundtable, Bus. ouncil, Am. Ordnance Assn. (Crozier Gold medal 70,) Henry M. Jackson award 1988, Nat. Medal Tech. 988, Presdl. Medal of Freedom 1988, Sigma Xi, Phi Beta Kappa, Tau Beta Pi, Alpha Delta Phi (Disting. Alumnus of Yr. 1970). Home: Palo Alto Calif. Died March 26, 1996.

PAGE, JOHN HALL, mining company executive; b. N.Y.C., Mar. 26, 1920; s. Arthur Wilson and Mollie Willis (Hall) P.; m. Susan Channing Simonds, June 5, 1942; children: Susan Trotman, John H., Julia L., Robert W. B.S., Harvard U., 1942. Various mgmt. and pub. relations positions Bell Telephone Co., 1946-61; v.p. Pacific N.W. Bell Telephone, Seattle, 1960-61; exec. v.p. Free Europe, Inc., N.Y.C., 1961-65; asst. to chmn. Inco Ltd., N.Y.C., 1965-73; pres., chief exec. officer Inco U.S., Inc., N.Y.C., 1973-90; dir. GTE Corp., Stamford, Conn., Dexter Corp., Windsor Locks, Conn., Nat. Westminister Bank U.S.A., N.Y.C. Mem. Council Fgn. Relations, N.Y.C.; trustee Youth for Understanding, Washington. Served to lt. USN, 1943-45; PTO. Mem. Am. Iron and Steel Inst. Republican. Died 1990. Home: Huntington N.Y.

PAGE, THORNTON LEIGH, astrophysicist; b. New Haven, Aug. 13, 1913; s. Leigh and Mary Edith Cholmondeley (Thornton) P.; m. Helen Ashbee, Aug. 28, 1938 (div. 1944); 1 dau., Tanya; m. Lou Williams, Aug. 28, 1948; children: Mary Anne, Leigh II. BS, Yale U., 1934; DPhil in Astrophysics (Rhodes scholar for Conn. 1934-37), Oxford (Eng.) U., 1938; MA (hon.), Wesleyan U., Middletown, Conn., 1959; DHC (hon.), U. Cordoba, Argentina, 1969. Chief asst. Oxford U. Obs., 1937-38; from instr. to asst. prof. astronomy U. Chgo., 1938-50; physicist Naval Ordnance Lab., 1941-43; dep. dir. Ops. Research Office, Johns Hopkins, 1950-58; prof. astronomy Wesleyan U., Middletown, 1958-71; dir. Van Vleck Obs., 1959-71; research asso. Manned Spacecraft Center, NASA, 1968-70, E.O. Hulburt Center Space Research, Naval Research Lab., Washington, 1970-76; contract astrophysicist Johnson Space Center, NASA, 1976-93; part-time instr. U. Houston, Clear Lake, 1982-88; mem. for Ops. Research Soc. Am. to NRC, 1960-62; mem. research adv. com. United Aircraft Corp., 1959-72; Smithsonian research asso. Harvard Obs., 1965-67; Nat. Acad. Scis. sr. research asso., 1968-70. Author: Stars and Galaxies, 1962, Wanderers in the Sky, 1965, Neighbors of the Earth, 1965, Origin of the Solar System, 1966, Telescopes, 1966, Starlight, 1967, Evolution of Stars, 1967, Stars and Clouds of the Milky Way, 1968, Beyond the Milky Way, 1969, UFO's, A Scientific Debate, 1972, Far-UV Preliminary Science Report, Apollo 16, 1973, Space Science and Astronomy, 1976, Apollo-Soyuz Experiments in Space, 1977, S201 Catalogue of Far-UV Objects, 1977, S201 Far-UV Atlas of the Large Magellanic Cloud, 1978, S201 Catalogue of Far-UV Objects, 1978, Space Telescope, 1983. Served to comdr. USNR, 1943-46. Decorated Bronze Star, Legion of Merit. Fellow Royal Astron. Soc., AAAS (v.p. sect. D astronomy 1967-68), Am. Astronautical Soc.; mem. Operations Research Soc. Am. (charter, editor, council, v.p.), Astron. Soc. Pacific., Am. Assn. Physics Tchrs., Internat. Astron. Union, Am. Astron. Soc., Internat. Statis. Inst., Sigma Xi. Clubs: Cosmos (Washington); Appalachian Mountain, Explorers. Home: Houston Tex. Died Jan. 2, 1996.

PAGET, ALLEN MAXWELL, investment company executive; b. Karuizawa, Nagano Prefecture, Japan, Sept. 12, 1919; (parents Am. citizens); s. Allen Maxwell and Mary (Baum) P.; m. Dorothy A. Lord, Dec. 22, 1941. BSBA, Lehigh U., 1941. With C. L. Emmert & Co., 1955-58; with Waddell & Reed, Inc., 1958-68, investment mgr., distbr. united group of mutual funds, 1958-68; regional mgr., resident v.p. Waddell & Reed, Inc., Harrisburg, Pa., 1961-68; v.p. Mark Securities, Inc., Camp Hill, Pa., 1968—; chmn. bd. dirs., pres., treas. Penn-Ben, Inc., 1969-83, Paget-San Enterprises, Inc. (Benihana of Tokyo), 1973-83; gen. ptnr. Penn-Ben Ltd. Partnership, 1983—; v.p. Gamma Lambda Corp., 1973-78. Comdr. Supply Corps USN, 1941-55, capt. USNR, ret., 1972. Named Eagle Scout Boy Scouts Am., 1936; recipient Patrick Henry Silver Medallion for Patriotic Achievement, 1989. Mem. Am. Philatelic Soc. (life), Navy League U.S., Res. Officers Assn. (pres. Cent. Pa. chpt. 1972-73), Mil. Order World Wars (comdr. Central Pa. chpt. 1979-82, comdr. Region III 1982-88, staff officer 1988-91, gen. staff emeritus 1991—), The Retired Officers Assn., Internat. Assn. Fin. Counselors (charter), Navy Supply Corps Sch. Alumni Assn. (founding mem.), Capital Region and West Shore Area C. of C., Nat. Sojourners (1st v.p. Cen. Pa. chpt. No. 76, 1987, pres. 1988-89, regional rep. 1990, area rep. 1991-92), Heros of '76, Brown Key Soc., Cen. Pa. Lehigh Alumni (pres. 1966), Cen. Pa. Execs. (bd. dirs. 1985-88), Antique and Classic Car Unit (founder), Rotary (bd. dirs., Paul Harris fellow), Masons (master 1968, lodge treas. 1984-89), KT, Shriners (potentate Zembo temple 1978), Mid Atlantic Shrine Clowns Assn., Internat. Shrine Clown Assn., Pa. Shrine Assn. (pres. 1978-79), Mid Atlantic Shrine Assn. (v.p. 1980-82, pres. 1982-83), Shrine Clowns of Zembo Temple, Tower Soc. of Lehigh U., Tall Cedars Lebanon, Legion of Honor (organizer 1975), Grand Sword Bearer of Grand Lodge Pa., 1988-89, Lamda Mu Sigma (founder Lehigh U. chpt. 1940), Pi Kappa Alpha (treas., E.M. Blanchard Alumni Loyalty award Gamma Lambda chpt. 1991), Alpha Phi Omega, Pi Delta Epsilon. Republican. Presbyterian. Home: Camp Hill Pa. Died Mar. 4, 1992.

PAI, SHIH I., Aeronautical engineer, educator; b. Tatung, Anhwei, China, Sept. 30, 1913; s. Hsi Chuan and Swe Lin (Cha) P.; BS in Elec. Engring., Nat. Central U. China, 1935; MS in Elec. Engring., MIT, 1938; PhD in Aeronautics and Math., Calif. Inst. Tech., 1940; D (hon.) Tech. U. Vienna, 1968; m. Alice Jen-Lan Wang, July 2, 1960; children: Stephen Ming Pai, Sue Pai Yang, Robert Yang Pai, Lou Lung Pai. Prof. aerodynamics Nat. Central U., China, 1940-47; vis. prof. Cornell U., 1947-49; rsch. prof. Inst. Phys. Sci. and Tech. (formerly, Inst. Fluid Dynamics and Applied Math.), U. Md., College Park, 1949-83, prof. emeritus, 1983-96; vis. prof. Tokyo U., 1966, Tech. U. Vienna, 1967, Tech. U. Denmark, 1974, U. Karlsruhe (Germany), 1980-81, U. Paris, 1981; hon. prof. Northwestern Poly. U., Peoples Republic China, 1980-96, Zhejiang U., Peoples Republic China, 1985-96; cons. Gen. Electric Co., N. Am. Aviation, Boeing Co., Martin Co. Served with Chinese Air Force, 1937-40. Guggenheim fellow, 1957-58, sr. scientist fellow NSF, 1966; recipient Alexander von Humboldt award, 1980, Centennial medal A. James Clark Sch. Engring. U. Md., 1994. Fellow Academia Sinica; mem. AIAA, Am. Phys. Soc., German Soc. Applied Math. and Mechanics, Internat. Acad. Astronautics (corr.). Author: 14 tech. books in fluid dynamics, latest being Two-Phase Flows, 1977; Modern Fluid Mechanics, 1981, (with Shijin Lu) The Theroetical and Computational Dynamics of a Compressible Flow, 1991; contbr. over 130 articles to profl. jours.; first to experimentally show the importance of coherent structure in turbulent flow, the authority of jet flow from low speed aerodynamics to hyperionic flow; contbr. modern fluid mechanics including magnetic fluid dynamics, radiation gas dynamics and two phase flows. Died May 23, 1996.

PAIR, PAUL MILTON, computer systems consultant; b. Beatrice, Nebr., Mar. 25, 1898; s. William H. and Mary (Dell) P.; m. Pauline Vaniman, Agu. 3, 1922; children: Maurice V., Marilyn. AB, McPherson Coll., 1922, ScD (hon.), 1988; student, U. So. Calif., summer 1926; MA, U. Wash., 1934, also postgrad. High sch. tchr. history and social studies, Kans., 1922-24; high sch. prin., Okanogan, Wash., 1924-25, Prosser, Wash., 1925-27; supt. Prosser Pub. Schs., 1925-35, Kirkland (Wash.) Pub. Schs., 1935-40; dir. Gregg Coll., Chgo., 1940-50; ednl. dir. Stenographic Machines Inc., 1950-51; head indsl. relations div. Sci. Rsch. Assocs. Inc., from 1951; v.p. Speedwriting Co., N.Y.C., 1952-54; founder Pair Sch. Bus., Inc., Chgo., 1954-57, Automation Inst. Chgo., 1957-68; pres. Automation Inst. Chgo. (acquired by Control Data Corp. 1968), 1957-67; sr. edn. cons. Control Data Corp., 1968-87; cons. Internat. Exec. Service Corps, San Salvador, 1970; dir. Inst. for Cert. Computer Profls., from 1973; founder Pair Sch. Bus., Chgo., 1973; lectr. DeVry Inst. Tech., Phoenix, 1990, Phoenix chpt. Assn. for Systems Mgmt., 1990. Contbr. articles to mags. Mem. Mayor's Commn. Human Relations; sec. Bus. Edn. Found., 1956-60. Co-recipient Award of Merit McPherson Coll., 1962, recipient, 1987; named Vocation Edn. Man of Yr. Goodwill Rehab. Ctr., 1977; Paul M. Pair scholarship created in his honor Control Data Corp./Assn. for Systems Mgmt., Chgo., 1977, Phoenix chpt., 1989, Tarelton State U., 1991, Internat. Soc. for Tech. in Edn., 1991; Paul M. Pair chair created in his honor Glendale (Ariz.) Community Coll., 1989. Mem. Nat. Assn. and Council Bus. Schs., Nat. Bus. Edn. Assn. (pres. 1960-61), Am. Personnel and Guidance Assn., Ill. Pvt. Bus. Schs. (sec. bd.), Office Mgmt. Assn. Chgo., Data Processing Mgmt. Assn. (vice chmn. internat. conf. com. 1973, Computer Sci. Man of Yr. 1973, Gold award 1979, Disting. Info. Sci. award 1983, Diamond award 1985, Double Diamond award 1988, lectr. ann. confs., named to Wall of Fame 1990), Chgo. Guidance and Personnel Assn. (past pres.), Ill. Bus. Schs. Assn. (past pres.), Assn. for Ednl. Data Systems (dir.), Assn. for Systems Mgmt. (emeritus, internat. edn. adv. coun. 1983-86, award of honor 1988), Phi Delta Kappa (60 yr. mem., cert. 1988), Delta Pi Epsilon (hon.). Clubs: North Shore Sunday Evening (exec. v.p.), Ill. Athletic, Rotary, Executives (Chgo.). Home: Phoenix Ariz. Deceased.

PALLOT, E. ALBERT, lawyer, savings and loan executive; b. Russia, June 28, 1908; came to U.S., 1912, naturalized, 1932; s. Nathan Samuel and Sarah Riva (Richmond) P.; m. Hermine Wolfson, Aug. 12, 1962; children: Roxane Pallot Gabai, Suzanne Pallot. JD, Suffolk U., 1932, LLD (hon.), 1978. Bar: Mass. 1932, Fla. 1933. Sole proprieter Pallot & Poppell, and predecessor, Miami, 1952—; founder, former v.p., dir. Citizens Fed. Savs. and Loan Assn., Miami; ret. founder, pres., chmn. bd. Biscayne Fed. Savs. & Loan Assn., Miami; former dir. Central Bank & Trust Co., Central Bank of North Dade; vice chmn. bd., dir. Central Bancorp, Inc.; past chmn. constn. com. Nat. League Insured Savs. Assns.; asst. atty. gen., Fla., 1941-42; lectr. U. Miami Law Sch., 1946-49; spl. atty. Dade County Blue Ribbon Grand Jury, 1953-54; past pres. Fla. Bar Found., 1981-82. Chmn. emeritus Miami Com. on Beautification and Environment, 1958-61, 63-65, 68-94; chmn. Miami Charter Revision Com., 1952-53; former chmn. Met. Miami Mcpl. Bd., 1953-54, 72-94; founding pres. Miami Beach Taxpayers Assn., 1951-53; mem. Pres.'s Com. on Employment of Handicapped, 1972; nat. dir. U.S. Com., Sports for Israel, 1974; founder Mt. Sinai Hosp., Miami Beach, 1972; former v.p., dir., chmn. devel. Fund Cedars of Lebanon Hosp.;

past pres. Greater Miami YMHA; pres. Papanicolaou CAncer Rsch. Found. Inc.; bd. dirs. Papanicolaou Cancer Research Inst., Miami; founder U. Miami. Served as lt. comdr. USNR, World War II. Recipient Man of Year award Beautification Com., 1969, Big Pi award for outstanding achievement Phi Lambda Phi, 1957. Mem. ABA, Fla. Bar Assn. (past chmn. Am. citizenship com.), Dade County Bar Assn., Soc. Founders Papanicolaou Cancer Research Inst., Miami Jr. C. of C. (hon. life), Navy League of U.S. (pres. emeritus, dir. Miami Coun.), Am. Legion (past chmn. citizenship com. Harvey Seeds Post), Westview Country Club, Jockey Club, Bankers Club, Masons (past master), Miami Elks (past exalted ruler), B'nai B'rith (past internat. v.p., hon. chmn. Commn. on Community and Vets. Svc.), Probus (past pres.), Rotary. Home: Miami Fla. Died Oct. 30, 1994.

PALM, ARTHUR CLELAND, advertising agency executive; b. Mansfield, Ohio, Feb. 10, 1907; s. James Arthur and Della (Clel) P.; m. Eleanor Berghoff, Apr. 27, 1929; 1 child, Bruce A. A.B., Western Res. U., 1929. Copy chief Campaigns, Inc., N.Y.C., 1928-36; v.p., gen. mgr. Davey Compressor Co., Kent, Ohio, 1936-41; advt. mgr. Westinghouse Electric Corp., 1941-46; pres. Palm & Patterson, Inc., Cleve., 1946-70; chmn. bd. Palm & Patterson, Inc., from 1970, also dir.; chmn. dir. Paint Corp. Am., Cleve., from 1948. Author short stories, books. Mem. Am. Mktg. Assn., Cleve. Advt. Club, Writers Club Am., Sigma Nu, Sigma Delta Chi, Kappa Kappa Phi. Clubs: Westbrook Country (Mansfield); Rotary, Mid-Day (Cleve.). Home: Novelty Ohio Died Apr. 15, 1989; interred Knollwood, Mayfield Heights, Ohio.

PALMER, ADRIAN B., insurance company executive; b. Chgo., Oct. 23, 1910; m. Gladys Towne Palmer, Feb. 12, 1937; 1 son, Robert. Cons. Rollins Burdick Hunter Co., Chgo. Clubs: Chicago (Chgo.), North Shore Country (Glenview). Home: Lake Forest Ill. Died Feb. 25, 1993.

PALMER, JOHN MARSHALL, lawyer; b. Fairmont, Minn., June 5, 1906; s. John Earl and Winnifred Ann (Ibertson) P.; m. Mary Louise Arntsen, June 28, 1934 (div.); children: Loring Swift, John Edward, Marsha; m. Dorothy Mae Bright, July 27, 1984. B.A., U. Minn., 1928, LL.B., 1931. Bar: Minn. 1931. Assoc. Sweet, Johnson & Sands, Mpls., 1931-32, Stinchfield, Mackall, Crounse, McNally & Moore, Mpls., 1932-42; chief enforcement atty. OPA, St. Paul, 1942-44; ptnr. Stinchfield, Mackall, Crounse & Moore, Mpls., 1944-51, Mackall, Crounse, Moore, Helmey & Palmer, Mpls., 1951-57, Levitt and Palmer, 1957-60, Levitt, Palmer & Bearmon, 1961-65, Levitt, Palmer, Bowen & Bearmon, 1965-68, Levitt, Palmer, Bowen, Bearmon & Rotman, 1968-79; ptnr. Levitt, Palmer, Bowen, Rotman & Share, 1979-82, of counsel, 1982-83; of counsel Briggs & Morgan, 1983-92; sec., dir. Triangle Devel. Co. Mem. ABA, Minn. Bar Assn. (pres. 1955-56), Law Alumni Assn. U. Minn. (past pres., dir.), Am. Coll. Trial Lawyers, Mpls. Club, Phi Gamma Delta, Phi Delta Phi. Congregationalist. Home: Minnetonka Minn. Died Nov. 20, 1995.

PALMER, MELVILLE LOUIS, retired agricultural engineering educator; b. Dobbinton, Ont., Can., Aug. 30, 1924; came to U.S., 1953, naturalized, 1960; s. Louis Grange and Laura Lavina (Peacock) P.; m. Shirley Adams, Aug. 2, 1952; children: Laura, Melanie, Bradley. B.S., U. Toronto, 1950; M.S., Ohio State U., 1955. Asst. dean men Ont. Agrl. Coll., Guelph, 1950-52; asst. mgr. farm machinery United Coop., Toronto, 1952-53; research asst. Ohio Agrl. Expt. Sta., Wooster, 1953-55; extension agrl. engr. Ohio State U., Columbus, 1955-87, prof. agrl. engring., 1970-87, prof. emeritus, 1987-95; cons. Ford Found., 1967. Contbr. numerous articles to tech. jours. Served with RCAF, 1943-46. Inducted into Internat. Drainage Hall of Fame, 1987. Fellow Am. Soc. Agrl. Engrs. (chmn. Ohio sect. 1979, recipient Hancor Soil and Water Engring. award, Gunlogson Countryside Engring. award 1986), Soil and Water Conservation Soc. (pres. All-Ohio chpt. 1973); mem. Ohio Extension Profs. Assn. (pres. 1964), Water Mgmt. Assn. Ohio (Disting. Svc. award 1985), Ohio Land Improvement Contractors (hon. mem., ednl. advisor 1956-87), Gamma Sigma Delta, Epsilon Sigma Phi (Disting. Svc. award 1989). Home: Alexandria Ohio Died Apr. 23, 1995.

PALMER, NORMAN DUNBAR, political scientist, educator, author; b. Hinckley, Maine, June 25, 1909; s. Walter Elmer and Gertrude (Dunbar) P.; m. Evelyn Florence Kalal, Oct. 28, 1944; 1 child, Patricia Lee; m. Gurina McIlrath, Feb. 8, 1992. AB summa cum laude, Colby Coll., 1930, LHD (hon.), 1955; MA (Currier fellow), Yale U., 1932, PhD, 1936. From instr. to assoc. prof. history and govt., chmn. dept. Colby Coll., Maine, 1933-42, 46-47; assoc. prof. polit. sci. U. Pa., Phila., 1947-51; prof. U. Pa., 1951-79, prof. emeritus, 1979-96, chmn. dept., 1949-52, chmn. internat. rels. grad. program, 1959-66; coordinator U. Pa.-U. Karachi project, 1954-59; sr. assoc. Fgn. Policy Research Inst., Phila., 1955-82; dir. Phila. Transnat. Project, 1974-82; vis. prof. internat. relations Columbia U., summer 1950; Fulbright prof. polit. sci. and internat. affairs U. Delhi, India, 1952-53; vis. prof. Swarthmore (Pa.) Coll., 1955; vis. prof. Sch. Advanced Internat. Studies Johns Hopkins U., 1958; vis. prof. Bombay U., 1966-67, U. Hawaii, 1967, Am. U. in Cairo, 1971, Duke U., 1974, Naval Postgrad. Sch., 1976, Grad. Inst. Peace Studies, Kyung Hee U., Seoul, Republic of Korea, 1984, 89, 92; sr. specialist East-West Center, Honolulu, 1966-67; cons. Dept. State, Research Analysis Corp. Author: The Irish Land League Crisis, 1940, 78, (with H.C. Perkins) International Relations: The World Community in Transition, 3d edit., 1969, (with Shao Chuan Leng) Sun Yat-Sen and Communism, 1961, (with others) Studies in Political Science, 1961, The Indian Political System, rev. edit., 1971, (with others) The Indian Ocean: Its Political, Economic and Military Importance, 1972, Elections and Political Development: The South Asian Experience, 1975, The United States and India: The Dimensions of Influence, 1984, (with others) The Art and Science of Politics, 1985, (with others) Fundamentals of Political Science, 1952, (with others) The Idea of Colonialism, 1958, (with others) Leadership and Political Institutions in India, 1958, (with others) Major Governments of Asia, rev. edit., 1963, (with others) The United States and the United Nations, 1964, South Asia and United States Policy, 1966, (with others) Problems of Defense of South and East Asia, 1969; (with others) The Foreign Policy of China, 1972, (with others) Pakistan-The Long View, 1977, (with others) Dynamics of Development: The International Perspective, 1977, (with others) The Subcontinent in World Politics, 1978, 82, (with others) Asian Studies III, 1979; (with others) Changing Patterns of Security and Stability in Asia, 1980, (with others) Great Power Relations, World Order and the Third World, 1981, (with others) South Asian Regional Cooperation, 1985, Westward Watch: The United States and the Changing Western Pacific, 1987, (with others) New Tides in the Pacific, 1987, The New Regionalism in Asia and the Pacific, 1991; contbr. editor Current History, 1949—; editor, contbr.: A Design for International Relations Research, 1970; mem. editorial bd. Orbis, 1957-88, South Asian Studies, 1966—, Asian Affairs, 1974-85, Global Futures Digest, 1980—; contbr. articles to profl. jours. Mem. Citizens Com. for Hoover Report, also Phila. Citizens Charter Com., 1950-51; chmn. Friends of India Com., 1961-68; trustee Princeton in Asia, 1978-82; mem. San Juan County Centennial Com., 1987-88, Bill of Rights Bicentennial Com., 1991. Served to lt. comdr. USNR, 1942-46. Decorated Bronze Star medal.; recipient Honor award Assn. of Indians in Am., 1988, Citizen of Yr. award San Juan County, 1991; Carnegie Endowment Internat. Peace fellow, 1959-60; Coun. Fgn. Rels. rsch. fellow, 1961-62, Guggenheim fellow, 1961-62, Am. Coun. Learned Socs. fellow, 1961-62, 71-72, Am. Inst. Indian Studies fellow, 1966-67, 71-72. Mem. ASPA (internat. com.), Internat. Polit. Sci. Assn., Am. Polit. Sci. Assn. (Council 1954-56), Indian Polit. Sci. Assn. (life), Global Futures Soc., Am. Acad. Polit. and Social Sci. (dir., sec.), Interdependence Council (dir.), Council on Fgn. Relations, Phila. Com. Fgn. Relations, World Affairs Council (dir.), Phila. Council Internat. Visitors (dir.), Assn. Asian Studies, Pa. Polit. Sci. and Pub. Adminstrn. Assn. (exec. council), Fgn. Policy Assn., Nat. Coun. Asian Affairs (pres.), Am. Vets. Com., Am. Legion, Res. Officers Assn., Peace Sci. Soc., Internat. Studies Assn. (pres. 1970-71, life), Internat. Study and Research Inst. (v.p., dir.), Am.-Asian Ednl. Exchange (dir.), Elks, Phi Beta Kappa, Pi Kappa Delta, Alpha Tau Omega. Home: Friday Harbor Wash. Died Feb. 21, 1996.

PANITT, MERRILL, editor; b. Hartford, Conn., Sept. 11, 1917; s. Irving and Anna (Shear) P.; m. Marjorie Hoover, Apr. 2, 1942; 1 son, Jeffrey. B.J., U. Mo. Reporter United Press, 1937-39; pub. rels. ofcl. Mo. Pub. Expenditure Survey, 1939-41; with Triangle Publs., Inc., Phila., 1946-88; TV columnist Phila. Inquirer, 1949-53, adminstrv. asst. to pres., 1948-53; mng. editor TV Guide, 1953-59, editor, 1959-73, editorial dir., 1973-88, contbg. editor, 1988-91; also editorial dir. Television Digest, TV Factbook (trade publs.), 1959-61, Seventeen Mag., 1978-84; editor TV Guide Roundup in 1960. Coauthor: Soldiers' Album, 1946. Trustee, spl. cons. Annenberg Found, 1990-94. Maj. AUS, 1941-46. Recipient medal for disting. service in journalism U. Mo.; Disting. Achievement award in periodicals U. So. Calif.; Gold medal Poor Richard Club of Phila. Home: West Chester Pa. Died Mar. 28, 1994.

PAPANDREOU, ANDREAS GEORGE, prime minister of Greece; b. Chios, Greece, Feb. 5, 1919; s. George and Sophia (Mineiko) P.; m. 2d Margaret Chant, 1951 (div. 1989); 4 children; m. Dimitra Liani, July 13, 1989. MA in Econs., Harvard U., 1942, PhD in Econs., 1943. Teaching fellow and tutor Harvard U., 1942-43, instr., 1943-44, 46-47; assoc. prof. econs. U. Minn., 1947-50; assoc. prof. Northwestern U., 1950-51; prof. U. Minn., 1951-55; prof. U. Calif., Berkeley, 1955-63, chmn. dept. econs., 1956-59; prof. econs. U. Stockholm, 1968-69; prof. econs. York U., 1969-74, dir. research York-Kenya Project, 1969-74; min. to the prime min. Govt. of Greece, 1964, min. of coordination, 1964-65; dep. Greek Parliament, 1964-67; chmn. Panhellenic Liberation Movement, 1968; pres. Panhellenic Socialist Movement, 1974-96; dep. Greek Parliament, 1977-81; leader Main Opposition Party, 1977-81; prime min. Govt. of Greece, 1981-89, 93-96, min. nat. def., 1981-86, also min. edn. and religious affairs; econ. adv. Bank of Greece, 1961-62; dir. Ctr. of Econ. Research, Athens, 1961-64. Author: (with others) An Introduction to Social Science: Personality, Work,
Community, 1953, rev. edits., 1957, 61; (with J.
Wheeler) Competition and its Regulation, 195
Economics as a Science, 1958; A Strategy for Gre
Economic Development, 1962; Fundamentals of Mod
Construction in Macroeconomics, 1962; Introduction
Macroeconomic Models, 1965; Democracy and Nation
Renaissance, 1966; Toward a Totalitarian World?, 196
Man's Freedom, 1970; Greece to the Greeks, 197
Democracy at Gunpoint: The Greek Front, 197
Paternalistic Capitalism, 1972; Project Selection for N
tional Plans, 1974; (with U. Zohar) The Impact A
proach to Project Selection, 1974; Imperialism an
Economic Development, 1975; Transition to Socialism
1977; Toward a Socialist Society, 1977; contbr. chpts.
books; contbr. articles to profl. jours. Fulbright fellow
1959-60; Guggenheim fellow, 1959-60; Wicksell lectr
Stockholm, 1966; Benjamin Fairless lectr. Carnegie
Mellon U., 1969; Edmund Burk Bicentenary lect
Trinity Coll., Dublin, 1970; Woodward lectr. U. B.C
1973. Home: Athens Greece Died June 23, 1996.

PAPEN, FRANK O'BRIEN, banker, state senator;
Dec. 2, 1909; m. Julia Stevenson; 1 child, Miche
Papen-Daniel. LLD (hon.), N.Mex. State U., 1988
Dir. First Nat. Bank Dona Ana County, Las Cruce
N.Mex., 1957-60, exec. v.p., 1957-60, pres., 1960-7
chmn. bd. dirs., chief exec. officer, 1971-82, 88—, pres
chmn. bd. dirs., 1982-87; mem. Ho. of reps. State
N.Mex., 1957-58, senator, 1969-84; vice-chmn. 12 r
gional adv. com. on banking practices and policie
1965-66; mem. adv. com. on fed. legis., 1966; mer
N.Mex. State Investment Council, 1963-67; mer
N.Mex. Dept. Devel. Adv. Council, 1967-68; mer
steering com. Edn. Commn. States; mem. Albuquerq
dist. adv. council SBA; pres. N.Mex. State U. Pres. A
socs. Mem. N.M. Ho. of Reps., 1957-58 (chmn. legi
fin. com. and legis. sch. study com.), N.M. State Senat
1969-84. Recipient Citizen of Yr. award N.Mex. Ass
Realtors, 1966, Branding Iron award N.Mex. State U
1977, The Pres.'s award for Service N.Mex. State U
1983, Regent's medal N.Mex. State U., 1985, N.Me
Sch. Banking Leadership award, 1987, Bob Haynswor
Sportsmanship award Sunland Park Race Track, 1987
Mem. Am. Bankers Assn. (savs. bond chmn. N.Me
1964-66), N.Mex. Bankers Assn. (pres., mem. exec. cor
1965-66), Las Cruces C. of C. (past pres.). Democrat
Lodges: Kiwanis, KC. Home: Las Cruces N.Mex. Di
March 15, 1996.

PAPPAS, HERCULES CHRIS, mining engineer;
N.Y.C., Mar. 23, 1928; s. Hercules and Mildred Loui
P.; m. Lucie Alexandra Wessels, Apr. 6, 1956; childre
Hercules Chris, Audrey Carolyn. A.B., Columbia U
1947, B.S. in Mining Engring, 1948. Mgr. fgn. ops. ra
materials div. Aluminum Co. of Am., Pitts., 1966-7
prodn. mgr. raw materials div. Aluminum Co. of An
1975-80, ops. mgr. raw materials div., 1980-82; dir. i
ternat. Elkem Chems., Pitts., 1982-86; exec. v.p. Hal
(Mining) Inc., Pitts., 1972-73; pres. Compagnie d
Bauxites de Guinee, Pitts., 1973-75, Newmatec In
1986-87, mgmt. cons., 1987-92;. Bd. dirs. Am. Diabet
Assn., Western Pa. affiliate, 1977-83, v.p., 1979-8
Served with C.E. U.S. Army, 1954-56. Mem. AIM
Soc. Mining Engrs., Internat. C. of C. (chmn. co
natural resources U.S. coun. 1979-82), St. Clair Count
Club, Phi Beta Kappa, Tau Beta Pi. Republican. Ep
copalian. Home: Pittsburgh Pa. Died Oct. 30, 1992.

PAPPENHEIMER, ALWIN M(AX), JR., biochemi
immunologist; b. Cedarhurst, N.Y., Nov. 25, 1908;
Alwin Max and Beatrice (Leo) P.; m. Pauline Forb
Sept. 10, 1938; children: Ruth Forbes Brazier, Sar
Ann, John Forbes. S.B., Harvard U., 1929, Ph.I
1932. Instr., tutor biochem. sci. Harvard U., Car
bridge, Mass., 1930-33, prof. biology, 1958-79, mast
Dunster House, 1961-70, researcher biol. labs., 1979-9
NRC fellow Nat. Inst. Med. Research, London, 193
35; sr. chemist Antitoxin and Vaccine Lab., Jamai
Plain, Mass., 1936-39; asst. prof. biochemistry
bacteriology U. Pa., Phila., 1939-41; mem. faculty NY
Coll. Medicine, N.Y.C., 1941-58, prof. microbiolog
chmn. dept., 1956-58; cons. to surgeon gen. Commn.
Immunization, Armed Forces Epidemiol. Bd., Was
ington, 1963-75; mem. regulatory biology panel NS
Washington, 1953-55. Contbr. sects. to books, artic
to profl. jours. Served to lt. col. AUS, 1942-45, PTC
Recipient Eli Lilly award in bacteriology Am. Ass
Microbiology, 1942, Louis L. Seaman award N.Y. Aca
Medicine, 1947, Paul Ehrlich prize and Gold med
1990. Fellow Am. Acad. Arts and Sci., Nat. Acad. Sc
AAAS; mem. Am. Assn. Immunologists (pres. 1954-5
Phi Beta Kappa. Democrat. Club: Cambridge Boa
Home: Watertown Mass. Died Mar. 21, 1995.

PARANDOWSKI, JAN, author; b. Lwow, Russi
May 11, 1895; ed. Lwow U.; m. Irene Parandows
1925; 2 sons, 1 dau. Civil prisoner of war, Russia, 191
19; lit. chmn. Altenberg's Pub. House, Lwow, 1922-
pres. Polish PEN Club, 1933—; editor lit. sect. Poli
Radio, Warsaw, 1935-39; involved in underground
tivity during German occupation, 1939-45; prof. co
parative lit. U. Lublin, 1945-53; author: Aspasie, 19
Deuz Printemps, 1927, Le roi de la vie (Oscar Wild
1929, Les Disque Olympique, 1932, Visites et Renc
tres, 1934, Ciel en flammes, 1936, Trois signes
Zodiaque, 1938, L'heure mediterraneenne, 19
Voyages Litteraires, 1949, Alchimie des Mots, 19
Cadran Solaire, 1952, Essais, 1953, Souvenirs

lhouettes, 1960, (play) Media, 1961, Retour a la Vie, '61, Nuit de Septembre, 1962, Quand j'etais critique eatral, 1963, Feuillets epars, 1965, Acacia, 1967, hers. Decorated gt. cross Order of Polonia; comdr. der Arts and Letters (France); recipient medal of 30th nniversary of People's Poland, 1974; Bronze Olympic edal for novel, 1936; State prize 1st class, 1964. Home: arsaw Poland

ARECATTIL, JOSEPH CARDINAL, retired chbishop; b. Kidangoor, India, Apr. 1, 1912; s. Ittyra d Eliswa (Ittyra) P. Licentiate in Philosophy, Papal m., Kandy, 1936, Th.D., 1941; postgrad., Sacred eart Coll., Thevara, 1945; B.A., Madras U., 1947; D., Windham U., 1970. Ordained priest Roman ath. Ch., 1939. Parish priest, 1941-47; editor Sathyeepam weekly, 1947-53; aux. bishop, 1953; adminstr. postolic, 1956; archbishop of Ernakulam, from 1956, w emeritus, elevated to Sacred Coll. of Cardinals, 69; mem. Pontifical Commns., consultor to Sacred iental Congregation, 1963, mem., 1968; chmn. iental Canon Law Codification Com., 1972; mem. cretariat for Christian Unity, 1970; v.p. Cath. Bishops onf. of India, 1966, pres., 1972; chancellor Pontifical st., Alwaye, 1972; pres. Syro-Malabar Bishops' Conf.; ancellor Dharmaram Pontifical Inst. Theology and ilosophy, Bangalore; founder univ. colls., maj. hosps., nl. trusts, housing projects, irrigation projects, tech. sts., and indsl. concerns. Home: Cochin India eceased.

ARENTE, PIETRO CARDINAL, Italian ecclesiastic; Casalnuovo Monterotaro, Italy, Feb. 16, 1891. dained priest Roman Catholic Ch., 1916. Dir., chiepiscopal Sem. of Naples (Italy), 1916-26; rector of ntifical Urban Coll. of Propagation of Faith, 1934-38, nsultor Congregations of the Holy Office, Council opagation of Faith, 1938-55; archbishop of Perugia, 55-59; titular archbishop of Ptolemais in Thebaide, 59; assessor Sacred Congregations for Doctrine and ith; elevated to cardinal, 1967. Home: Rome Italy

ARK, ROY HAMPTON, communications company ecutive; b. Dobson, N.C., Sept. 15, 1910; s. I.A. and ura Frances (Stone) P.; m. Dorothy Goodwin Dent, t. 3, 1936; children: Roy Hampton, Adelaide ampton Park Gomer. BBA, N.C. State U., Raleigh, 31; LHD (hon.), Keuka Coll., 1967; HHD (hon.), C. State U., 1978; LLD (hon.), Ithaca Coll., 1985, ake Forest U., 1985. Dir. pub. relations Farmers oop. Exchange, N.C. Cotton Growers Coop. Assn., aleigh, 1931-42; founder, editor, pub. Coop. Digest, rm Power, 1939-66; sr. editor Rural Electrification dminstrn., 1936-37; pres., also bd. dirs. RHP Ind. c., Ithaca, 1945-93; pres. Hines-Park Foods, Inc., aca, N.Y., Hines-Park Foods, Ltd., Can. and Duncan nes Inst., Inc., 1949-56, v.p., 1956-63; pres., also bd. s. Avalon Citrus Assocs., Inc., Orlando, Fla., 1962-, Roy H. Park Broadcasting Inc., Greenville, N.C., 62-93, Sta. WDEF-TV-AM-FM, Chattanooga, Tenn., 63-93, Sta. WJHL-TV, Johnson City, Tenn., 1964-93, a. WTVR-TV-AM-FM, Richmond, Va., 1965-93, Sta. NAX-AM, Yankton, S.D., 1968-93, Sta. WUTR-TV, ica-Rome, 1969-93, Sta. WSLS-TV, Roanoke, 1969-, CobbHouse of Rock Hill (S.C.) Inc., 1968, Sta. BMG-TV, Birmingham, 1973-93, Sta. KWJJ-AM/M, 1973-93, Sta. KJJO-AM/FM, Mpls., 1974, Sta. EZX-AM/FM, KWLO/KFMW, Waterloo, Iowa, 87, Sta. WHEN-AM, Syracuse, N.Y., 1976-93, Sta. RHP-FM, Syracuse, 1977-93; chmn., dir. Park Outor Advt. and Park Displays, Ithaca, 1964-88, also bd. s.; pres. Park Outdoor Advt., Inc., Scranton, Pa., 69-84; pres., also bd. dirs. Warner Robins Ga. Inc., 72, Park Newspapers, Inc., Ithaca, 1972-93; and Ga., 72-93, Manassas, Va., 1972-93, Nebraska City, Nebr., 75-93, Brooksville, Fla., 1975-93, Ogdensburg, N.Y., 75-93, Plymouth, Ind., 1977-93, Norwich, N.Y., 1977-, McAlester, Okla., 1978, Macomb, Ill., 1979, ewton, Morganton and Statesville, N.C., 1979, Perry, a., 1980, Mich., 1980, Ark., 1981, Moore County, mberton, Marion and Devils Lake, N.C., 1982, aynesboro, Va., 1983, Medina, N.Y., 1984, Clark ounty, Ind., 1984, Hudson, N.Y., 1985, Ky., 1985, Pa., 86, Iowa, 1986, Blackduck, Minn., 1991; pres., also . dirs. RHP Newspapers Inc., Ithaca, 1973-93, ckport (N.Y.) Pubs. Inc., 1973-93, Kannapolis (N.C.) b. Co., 1978-93; pres., also bd. dirs. State and Aurora c., Broken Arrow, Okla., 1979, Sapulpa, Okla., 1979; mn., chief exec. officer Park Comm., Ithaca, N.Y.; bd. s. Molinos de P.R., Tompkins County Area Devel. rp., Ithaca, First Research Devel. Corp., Ithaca; pres. pstate Small Bus. Investment Co., Ithaca, 1960-66; soc. chmn. laymen's nat. Bible com. Nat. Bible Week, 72; chmn. pub. relations com. N.C. State U. Devel. ouncil, 1963-72, vice chmn. council, 1964-72, chmn., 72-93; trustee Endowment Funds N.C. State U. und., Ithaca Coll., 1973-93, mgr. exec. com., 1977-93, mn. exec. com., 1981-93. Asso. chmn. laymen's nat. ble com. Nat. Bible Week, 1972; chmn. pub. relations m. N.C. State U. Devel. Council, 1963-72, vice chmn. uncil, 1964-72, chmn., 1972-93; trustee N.C. State U., 77-85; bd. dirs. N.C. State U. Found., 1962-66, istee endowment funds; trustee, chmn. exec. com. aca Coll., 1973-93. Recipient spl. citation Am. Inst. oops., 1947; Disting. Service award Tompkins County ited Fund, 1961; Meritorious Service award N.C. ate U. Alumni Assn., 1970; Abe Lincoln award So. pt. Radio-TV Commn., 1971, Gold Plate award Am. Acad. Achievement, 1984; named Country Squire by Gov. N.C., 1953, hon. citizen New Orleans, 1958, hon. citizen Tenn., 1961, Ky. col., 1963, adm. in Gt. Navy Neb., 1961, Soc. Prodigal Son by Gov. N.C., 1964. Mem. N.C. State U. Alumni Assn. (pres. 1960-61, gen. fund chmn. 1962), Pub. Relations Soc. Am., Am. Agrl. Editors Assn., Am. Assn. Agrl. Coll. Editors, Agrl. Relations Council, Sales Execs. Club N.Y.C., Friends Ithaca Coll., Lucullus Circle, Les Amis D'Escoffier Soc., Confrerie de la Chaines des Rotissuers, Antique Automobile Club Am., Va., N.C., Nat. assns. broadcasters, Am., So. newspaper pubs. assns., N.Y. State Pubs. Assn. (pres. 1981), Ga. Press Assn., N.Y. State Pubs. Assn. (dir.), Phi Kappa Phi, Pi Sigma Epsilon, Alpha Phi Gamma, Pi Phi Pi. Presbyn. (ruling elder 1969-93). Clubs: Nat. Press, Capitol (Washington); Sales Execs. (dir. 1980, v.p. 1981-82), N.Y. Athletic, Cornell, Marco Polo (N.Y.C.), Union League (N.Y.C.); City, Capital City, Sphinx (Raleigh); Ithaca Country; Statler (Cornell U.); Commonwealth (Richmond); Shenandoah (Roanoke). Home: Ithaca N.Y. Died Oct. 25, 1993.

PARKER, BARRINGTON DANIELS, federal judge; b. Rosalyn, Va., Nov. 17, 1915; s. George A. and Maude (Daniels) P.; m. Marjorie C. Holloman, Sept. 8, 1939; children: Jason Holloman, Barrington D. A.B. cum laude, Lincoln U., 1936; M.A., U. Pa., 1938; J.D., U. Chgo., 1947. Bar: D.C. Practice law, 1947-69; judge U.S. Dist. Ct. for Dist. D.C., Washington, 1970-93. Mem. ABA, Nat. Bar Assn. Home: Washington D.C. Died June 2, 1993.

PARKER, HAROLD M(ARION), JR., history educator; b. Oklahoma City, Feb. 9, 1923; s. Harold Marion and Fredonia Angie (Nash) P.; m. Constance Eleanor Christensen, May 16, 1946 (div. 1967); 1 child, Howard Mikel; m. Barbara Ann Malin, May 31, 1967; 1 child, Harold Malin. AB, Park Coll., 1944; BD, Louisville Presbyn. Theol. Seminary, 1946, ThM, 1952; ThD, Iliff Sch. of Theology, 1966. Pastor First Presbyn. Ch., Winfield, Kans., 1957-61; instr. Southwestern Coll., Winfield, 1961-66, Friends U., Wichita, Kans., 1966-67; prof. history Western State Coll., Gunnison, Colo., from 1967; with Community Presbyn. Ch., Lake City, Colo., from 1968. Author: Sermons on the Minor Prophets, 1979, Studies in Southern Presbyterian History, 1979; Bibliography of Published Articles on American Presbyterianism, 1901-1980, 1985; contbr. articles to profl. jours. Chmn. Inskip Recreation Commn., Knoxville, Tenn., 1955-57; mem. Bd. Adjustment and Appeals, Gunnison, past chmn. Named Tchr. Yr. Southwestern Coll., 1964, Citizen Yr. Hinsdale County C. of C., 1979; recipient James H. Thornwell award Presbyn. Hist. Found., 1972, 78. Mem. Presbyn. Hist. Soc., Am. Soc. Ch. History., Am. Schs. Oriental Research, Soc. Bibl. Lit., Winfield Oratorio Soc. (chmn. 1960-61), Phi Alpha Theta. Republican. Home: Gunnison Colo. Deceased.

PARKER, ROBERT HALLETT, ecologist; b. Springfield, Mass., Feb. 14, 1922; s. Ralph Coy and Mildred (Hallett) P.; m. Harriet Elizabeth Logan, Dec. 23, 1945; foster children: Joycelene Bryan, Alfred Freeman Bryan, Sandee Jones. Student, Duke U., 1941-43, 49-50; BS, U. N.Mex., 1948, MS, 1949; PhD, U. Copenhagen, 1963. Cert. sr. ecologist, registered profl. geologist. Marine biologist Tex. Game and Fish Commn., Rockport, 1950-57; rsch. ecologist Scripps Inst. Oceanography, U. Calif., LaJolla, 1951-63; resident ecologist Marine Biol. Lab., Woods Hole, Mass., 1963-66; assoc. prof. biology and geology dept. Tex. Christian U., Ft. Worth, 1966-70; pres., chmn. bd. Coastal Ecosystems Mgmt., Inc., Ft. Worth, 1970-94; cons. Humble Oil Co., Houston, 1956-58, Standard Oil Co. N.J., N.Y.C., 1958. Author: Zoo Geography and Ecology of Macro-Invertebrates, 1964, The Study of Benthic Communities, 1975, Benthic Invertebrates in Tidal Estuaries and Coastal Lagoons, 1969; co-author: Marine and Estuarine Environments, Organisms and Geology of the Cape Cod Region, 1967, Sea Shells of the Texas Coast, 1972; contbr. articles to profl. jours. With U.S. Army, 1943-45, ETO. Nat. Acad. Sci. fellow, 1959; recipient Best Abstract award Moscow Oceanographic Congress Nat. Acad. Sci., Moscow, 1966. Fellow Geol. Soc. Am., Explorer's Club N.Y., Tex. Acad. Sci.; mem. AAAS, Am. Assn. Petroleum Geologists (presidential award 1956), Sigma Xi. Republican. Home: Fort Worth Tex. Died Jan. 24, 1994.

PARKER, WILLIAM, baritone; b. Butler, Pa., Aug. 5, 1943. BA in German Langs. and Lit., Princeton U.; studies with, Pierre Bernac, Rosa Ponselle, John Bullock. Albums include Songs of Brahms and Copeland, Pergolesi La Serva Padrona, 1987. Originiator AIDS Quilt Songbook. Recipient 1st prize U.S. Nat. Assn. of Tchrs. of Singing, 1970, 1st prize Paris Competitions, 1971, 1st prize Balt. Competitions, 1970, 1st prize Barcelona (Spain) Competitions, 1975, 1st place award Am. Internat. Competition for Singers. Home: New York N.Y. Died Mar. 29, 1993; interred Butler, P.A.

PARKS, ED H., judge; b. Tulsa, July 21, 1922. BS, U. Tulsa, 1947, LLB, 1950. Bar: Okla. 1950. Asst. atty. Tulsa County, 1953-57; ptnr. Boyd & Parks, Tulsa, 1957-77; judge trial div. Ct. on Jud., Oklahoma City, 1977-84, mem. appellant div., 1985-87; judge Ct. Criminal Appeals (Jud. Dist.) Okla., Oklahoma City, 1984-93; presiding judge Ct. Criminal Appeals (no. dist.) Okla., Oklahoma City, 1985-87, 88-93. Past chmn. Tulsa County Dem. Com. Capt. USMC, World War II, Korea. Fellow Okla. Bar Assn. (law sch. com. 1985-93, indigent com., legal ethics 1991-93, def. 1987-93, chmn. criminal law sect. 1977-79); mem. Assn. Trial Lawyers Am., Okla. Trial Lawyers Assn. (Outstanding State Ct. Judge award 1986, 88, 90), Tulsa Trial Lawyers Assn., Tulsa County Bar Assn. (exec. com. 1975-76, 80-81), Okla. Bar Found. (trustee 1988-93). Home: Tulsa Okla. Died June 6, 1993.

PARSELLS, NORMAN KING, lawyer; b. Stamford, Conn., Dec. 4, 1908; s. Fred Russell and Caroline Louise (King) P.; m. Laura E., Sept. 3, 1938; children: Norman King, Abbe Louise. B.A., Yale U., 1929, LL.B., 1932. Bar: Conn. 1932, U.S. Dist. Ct. Conn., U.S. Ct. Appeals (2d cir.), U.S. Supreme Ct. 1959. Assoc. Marsh, Day & Calhoun, Bridgeport, Conn., 1932-87; now sr. ptnr. Marsh, Day & Calhoun; dir. Sturm, Ruger & Co., Avery Abrasives, Inc., The Producto Machine Co., Baldwin, Pearson & Co., Fairfield Equipment Co. Served to lt. USNR, 1943-46. Fellow Am. Bar Found.; mem. ABA, Am. Law Inst., Conn. Bar Assn., Phi Beta Kappa. Republican. Christian Scientist. Clubs: Brooklawn Country, Fairfield County Hunt. Home: Fairfield Conn. Died 1987.

PARSONS, JAMES BENTON, federal judge; b. Kansas City, Mo., Aug. 13, 1913; s. James B. and Maggie Virgia (Mason) P.; m. Amy Margaret Maxwell, Dec. 24, 1952; 1 son, Hans-Dieter K. B.A., James Millikin U., 1934; student, U. Wis., summers, 1935-39; M.A., U. Chgo., 1946, LL.D., 1949. Bar: Ill. 1949. Successively field agt., asst. to dean men, instr. polit. sci. Lincoln U., Jefferson City, Mo., 1934-38; acting head music dept. Lincoln U., 1938-40; tchr. pub. schs. Greensboro, N.C., 1940-42; mem. firm Gassaway, Crosson, Turner & Parsons, Chgo., 1949-51; tchr. constl. govt. John Marshall Law Sch., Chgo., 1949-51; asst. corp. counsel City of Chgo., 1949-51; asst. U.S. dist. atty., 1951-60; judge superior court Cook County, Ill., 1960-61; judge U.S. Dist. Ct. No. Dist. Ill., 1961-93, now sr. judge. Co-chmn. Ill. Commn. N.Y. World's Fair; chmn. Chgo. Conf. Race and Religion; exec. bd. Chgo. Area council Boy Scouts Am.; Bd. dirs. Trotting Charities, Inc., Chgo. Urban League; trustee Lincoln Acad. Ill., Chgo. Med. Podiatry Hosp.; hon. bd. dirs. Leukemia Research Found., Inc.; nat. bd. trustees Nat. Conf. Christians and Jews; citizens com. U. Ill. Served with USNR, 1942-46. Mem. ABA, Chgo., Ill., Fed., Nat., Cook County bar assns., Ill. Acad. Criminology, N.A.A.C.P., Sigma Pi, Pi Beta Phi, Kappa Alpha Psi. Congregationalist (asst. treas.). Clubs: Standard, Navy League, Covenant (Chgo.). Home: Chicago Ill. Died June 19, 1993.

PARTEE, CECIL A., lawyer, state official; b. Blytheville, Ark., Apr. 10, 1921; m. A.P. Paris; children: Paris I., Cecile A. BS cum laude, Tenn. State U., 1944; JD, Northwestern U., 1946; D (hon.), Kennedy-King Coll., 1973; LHD (hon.), Lake Forest Coll., 1977, Malcolm X Coll., 1978; LLD (hon.), Daniel Hale Williams U., 1977. Pvt. practice, 1947-48, 57-89; asst. state's atty. Cook County, Ill., 1948-56; mem. Ill. Gen. Assembly, Springfield, 1957-77, Ill. Ho. of Reps., Springfield, 1957-67; mem. Ill. State Senate, Springfield, 1967-77, pres. pro-tem, 1971-73, majority leader, 1973-75, pres., majority leader, 1975-77; treas. City of Chgo., 1979-89; Cook County state's atty. State of Ill., Chgo., 1989-90; pvt. practice law Chgo., 1990-94; mem. Chgo. Zoning Bd. Appeals, 1967-76; mem. Dem. Nat. Com., 1972-76; commr. Dept. Human Svcs., City of Chgo., 1977-79. committeeman 20th ward Cook County Dem. Cen. Com., 1972-89, former vice chmn.; mem. adv. bd. Chgo. Area coun. Boy Scouts Am., 1989. Recipient Golden Key award, 1961, Charles F. Armstrong award Fedn. Ind. Colls. and Univs., 1966, 1972, Merit award Northwestern U., 1972, Ada S. McKinley Disting. Svc. award, 1973, award Ill. State Fedn. Labor and Congress Indsl. Orgns., 1974, award Ill. State's Attys. Assn., 1975, award Black Students Union of Lewis U., 1975, award Ill. Credit Union League, 1975, award VFW, 1976, citation Ill. chpt. Disabled Am. Vets., 1976, Humanitarian award Cen. State coun. AFL-CIO, 1976, Disting. Svc. award Ill. Bicentennial Commn., 1976, Man of Yr. award Sigma Gamma Rho, 1977, Nat. Conf. Black Lawyers award, 1977, Outstanding Leadership award League of Black Women, 1977, ann. award Chgo. Pub. Sch. Social Workers, 1977, Imani Black Cath. award, 1978, award Consul Gen. of Republic of China, 1978, award West Garfield Adv. Coun., 1978, Black History Month award Archdiocese Chgo. Cath. Schs., 1979, Brotherhood award Chgo. Conf. for Brotherhood, Inc., 1979, award Bethune-Cookman Coll., 1980, cert. of appreciation Mcpl. Treas. Assn. U.S. and Can., 1981, cert. USAR, 1981, Community Svc. award Englewood Community Health Orgn., 1983, cert. of appreciation Provident Med. Ctr., 1985, Disting. Pub. Svc. Flame of Truth award Anti-Defamation League, 1986, Achievement award Chgo. alumni chpt. Kappa Alpha Psi, 1986, cert. of appreciation Gov. of Ill., 1987, Dedicated Pub. Svc. award State of Ill., 1988, Role Model award Missco Black Cultural Assn., 1988, cert. United Negro Coll. Fund Telethon, 1988; named Chicagoan of Yr. in govt. and politics Chgo. Jr. Assn. Commerce and Industry, 1971, named Most Effective Senator Ill. State Med. Soc., 1971, named to Hon. Order Ky. Cols., 1985, named to 1st All-Pro Mcpl. Mgmt. Team City & State mag., 1986;

Cecil A. Partee Day in Chgo. proclaimed by State of Ill. 1983, Cecil A. Partee Appreciation Day proclaimed by City of Chgo., 1988; commd. Ambass. of Good Will State of Ark., 1986. Mem. ABA, NAACP, Chgo. Bar Assn. (svc. award 1971), Cook County Bar Assn. (award 1972), Urban League (Outstanding Community Svcs. award Chgo. chpt. 1987), Tenn. State U. Alumni Assn. (life mem., Outstanding Alumnus award 1971, M.S. Davis Alumni of Yr. award 1979). Congregationalist. Home: Chicago Ill. Died Aug. 16, 1994.

PARTEN, JUBAL R., petroleum producer; b. Madisonville, Tex., Feb. 16, 1896; s. Wayne Lafayette and Ella Mae (Brooks) P.; m. Patsy E. Puterbaugh, Oct. 31, 1947; 1 son, John Randolph. Student, U. Tex., 1913-17. Entered oil industry, 1919; pres., gen. mgr. Woodley Petroleum Co., Houston, 1922-60; founder, pres. Pan Am. Sulphur Co., Houston, 1947-53; chmn. bd. dirs. Pan Am. Sulphur Co., 1953-60; also dir.; dir. Pure Oil, 1960-65; chmn. bd. dirs. Parten Oil Co.; organizer chmn. bd. dirs.; Woodley Can. Oil Co., Great No. Oil Co., Minn. Pipe Line Co.; chmn., dir. Fed. Res. Bank of Dallas, 1944-54; dir. transp. Petroleum Adminstrn., 1942-44; mem. Nat. Petroleum Council, 1941-50. Chmn. bd. regents U. Tex., 1935-41; organizing dir. Fund for the Republic, Inc., 1953-75; trustee, vice chmn. bd. St. Stephen's Episcopal Sch., Austin, Tex., 1971-82. Served to maj. U.S. Army, World War I. Apptd. mem. Am. Del. to Allied Commn. on Reparations Moscow and Potsdam, 1945; named U. Tex. Most Disting. Alumni, 1987. Mem. Mid-Continent Oil and Gas Assn., Am. Petroleum Inst., Tex. Ind. Producers and Royalty Owners Assn. Democrat. Episcopalian. Clubs: Ramada (Houston), Petroleum (Houston); Oakridge Country (Madisonville, Tex.); Twenty-Five Year. Home: Madisonville Tex. Deceased.

PASAMANICK, BENJAMIN, psychiatrist, educator; b. N.Y.C., N.Y., Oct. 14, 1914; s. Alex and Elizabeth (Moskalik) P.; m. Hilda Knobloch, May 1, 1942 (div. July 1982); m. Lidia Laba, Aug. 27, 1982. A.B., Cornell U., 1936; M.D., U. Md., 1941. Intern State Hosp., Bklyn., 1941, Harlem Hosp., N.Y.C., 1942; resident N.Y. State Psychiat. Inst., 1943; asst. Clinic Child Devel., Yale U., New Haven, 1944-46; chief children's in-patient and out-patient services Neuropsychiat. Inst., U. Mich. Hosp., Ann Arbor, 1946-47; chief children's psychiat. services Kings County Hosp., Bklyn., 1947-50; psychiatrist Phipps Clinic, Johns Hopkins Hosp., Balt., 1952-55, Harriet Lane Home, 1951-55; asst. prof. Johns Hopkins U. Sch. Hygiene and Pub. Health, 1950-52, asso. prof. pub. health adminstrn., 1953-55; prof. psychiatry Ohio State U., 1955-65, adj. prof. sociology and anthropology, 1963-65; clin. prof. psychiatry U. Ill. Coll. Medicine, Chgo., also Chgo. Med. Sch.; asso. dir. research Ill. Dept. Mental Health, 1965-67; pres. N.Y. Sch. Psychiatry, N.Y.C., 1968-72; Sir Aubrey and Lady Hilda Lewis prof. social psychiatry N.Y. Sch. Psychiatry, 1972-84; asso. commr. N.Y. State Dept. Mental Hygiene, 1968-76; adj. prof. psychology NYU, 1968-75, rsch. prof. psychiatry and behavioral scis., 1984-96; rsch. prof. Albany Med. Coll., 1978-80, prof. emeritus, 1980, research prof. med. library scis., 1978-84; clin. prof. preventive and community medicine N.Y. Med. Coll., 1976-77; Cutter lectr. preventive medicine Harvard, 1960; Purkinje lectr. U. Prague, 1963; rsch. adj. prof. epidemiology Sch. Pub. Health and Adminstrv. Medicine, Columbia U., N.Y.C., 1967-77; adj. prof. pediatrics Albany Med. Coll., 1972-77; prof. psychiatry and behavioral sci. Sch. Medicine, SUNY, Stony Brook, 1978-84; mem. com. mental retardation Coun. State Govt.; chmn. com. on standardization of diagnosis WHO; chmn. com. mental health U.S. Com. on Vital and Health Stats.; Percy Bailey lectr. U. Ill.; Lawrence Kolb Sr. lectr. 25th Anniversary NIH. Author 17 books.; contbr. numerous articles to profl. jours.; mem. numerous editorial bds. of professional jours. Recipient Cert. of Recognition for Contbns. to Psychiat. Epidemiology and biostats., Harvard Inst. Psychiat. Epidemiology and Genetics, 1995. Mem. APHA (governing coun. 1956, Rema Lapouse Gold medal 1977), APA (pres. divsn. child, youth and family svcs. 1987), Am. Psychopath. Assn. (Stratton award 1961, pres. 1967, Hamilton medal 1968), Orthopsychiat. Assn. (pres. 1971), Am. Psychiat. Assn. (Hofheimer Rsch. award 1949, 67, Agnes Purcell McGavin award 1986), World Assn. for Psychocial Rehab. (Sci. Distinction award 1994), Am. Anthrop. Assn., Am. Sociol. Assn., Am. Coll. Psychiatrists, Am. Coll. Epidemiologists, Am. Coll. Neuropsychopharmacology, Psychonomic Soc., Soc. Biol. Psychiatry, Acad. Child Psychiatry, Theobald Smith Soc. (founder, pres. 1986-93, sec. 1993), History of Sci. Soc., Soc for Study of Social Problems, others. Home: Schenectady N.Y. Died Jan. 12, 1996.

PASCH, MAURICE BERNARD, lawyer; b. Chilton, Wis., June 17, 1910; s. Jacob and Eva (Leveton) P.; m. Janet Gerhardt, Nov. 26, 1936 (dec. Oct. 1983); children—Ellen, Robert, Suzy. Student, George Washington U., 1932-36; J.D., U. Wis., 1938. Bar: Wis. 1938, U.S. Supreme Ct. 1940. Sec. to U.S. senator, 1932-36; asst. atty. gen. Wis., 1936-40; practice in Madison, Wis., 1940-95; mem. firm Pasch and Pasch.; Dir. Home Savs. & Loan Assn. Mem. Wis. Coordinating Com. for Higher Edn.; Bd. regents U. Wis. Served as lt. USNR, 1942-46. Mem. ABA, VFW, Wis. Bar Assn., Dane County Bar Assn., Mil. Order World Wars (state comdr.), Am. Legion, Navy League (pres.), Nat. Bd. Am. Jewish Com., Comml. Law League Am. (exec. coun.), B'nai B'rith, Masons, Elks, Lions, Madison Club. Jewish (temple pres.). Home: Madison Wis. Died Mar. 1, 1995.

PASLAY, LE ROY CLAY, geophysicist; b. Manhattan, Kans., Dec. 26, 1907; s. Edmond B. and Minerva L. P.; m. Mary Aileen Hull, May 18, 1930; children: Robert Hull, Patricia Louise Paslay Martin. BS in Elec. Engring, Kans. State U., 1930, MS, 1932, DSc (hon.), 1986. Engr. Gen. Electric Co., 1930-31; asst. prof. Kans. State U., Manhattan, 1932-35; dir. rsch. Nat. Geophys. Co., Dallas, 1936-41; chief under water sound div. Naval Ordnance Lab., Washington, 1942-45; prin. ptnr. Marine Instrument Co., Dallas, 1942-95; exec. v.p., dir. Pan Am. Exploration Co., Dallas, 1947-55; pres., dir. Marine Seismic Surveys Inc., Dallas, 1950-63, Marine Geophys. Co. (S.A.), Maracaibo, Venezuela, 1950-61, Marine Petroleum Corp., Dallas, 1957-95; dir. Templeton Growth Fund of Can., Toronto, Ont., Templeton World Fund, Inc., St. Petersburg, Fla., 1978-90; individual trustee Tideslands Royalty Trust, 1954-95; Fla. gov.'s ofcl. rep. Interstate Oil Compact Commn., 1969-70. Patentee in field. Vice mayor Town of Manalapan, Fla., 1959-66, mayor, 1967-70. Recipient U.S. Navy Distinguished Civilian Service award, 1945. Mem. IEEE, Soc. Exploration Geophysicists (Reginald Fessenden award 1976), Am. Water Works Assn. Presbyterian. Clubs: La Coquille (Palm Beach, Fla.); Manalapan (Fla.) Yacht, Manalapan. Home: Lake Worth Fla. Died Sept. 21, 1995.

PASS, JOE, guitarist; b. 1929. Jazz guitarist, 1949-94. Performed as session guitarist with numerous jazz greats including Chet Baker, Bud Shank, Les McCann, Earl Bostic, Duke Ellington, Herb Ellis, Dizzy Gillespie, Oscar Peterson, Ella Fitzgerald; albums include Checkmate, Chops, Complete Catch Me Sessions, For Django, I Remember Charlie Parker, Live at Long Beach City College, Loves Gershwin, Montreux '75, Virtuoso, Portraits of Duke Ellington, (with Herb Ellis) Two for the Road, Summer Nights, 1991. Home: Berkeley Calif. Died May 23, 1994.

PASSOW, AARON HARRY, education educator; b. Liberty, N.Y., Dec. 9, 1920; s. Morris and Ida (Wiener) P.; m. Shirley Siegel, July 2, 1944; children: Michael Joel, Deborah Miriam, Ruth Gertrude. B.A. cum laude, SUNY-Albany, 1942, M.A., 1947; Ed.D. (Romiett Stevens scholar), Columbia U., 1951, MA, 1979. Tchr. sci., math. Stony Point High Sch., N.Y., 1942-43; sci. tchr. Eden Central Sch., N.Y., 1946-48; instr. edn., supr. math. SUNY, Albany, 1948-51; mem. faculty Columbia U. Tchrs. Coll., 1951-91, prof. emeritus edn., 1991-96, prof. edn., 1952-91, Jacob H. Schiff prof. edn., 1972-91, chmn. dept. curriculum and teaching, 1968-77, chmn. com. urban edn., 1965-77, dir. div. ednl. instns. and programs, 1975-80; prof. emeritus, 1991-96; research assoc. Horace Mann-Lincoln Inst. Sch. Experimentation, 1952-65; Fulbright lectr., vis. prof. edn. U. Stockholm, 1967-96 68; vis. prof. Bar-Ilan (Israel) U., 1973, 81, Tel Aviv U., 1981; dir. Study Washington Pub. Schs., 1966-67; ednl. cons., lectr. edn. disadvantaged, edn. gifted and curriculum devel. Coauthor: Organizing for Curriculum Development, 1953, Planning for Talented Youth, 1955, Developing a Curriculum for Modern Living, 1957, Improving the Quality of Public School Programs, 1960; author: Secondary Education for All: The English Approach, 1961; also articles.; editor: Curricular Crossroads, 1962, Education in Depressed Areas, 1963, Education of Disadvantaged: A Book of Readings, 1967, Developing Programs for the Disadvantaged, 1968, Deprivation and Disadvantage: Nature and Manifestations, 1970, Reaching the Disadvantaged Learner, 1970, Urban Education in the 1970s, 1971, Opening Opportunities for Disadvantaged Learners, 1972, The National Case Study: An Empirical Study of 21 National Educational Systems, 1976, Secondary Education Reform: Retrospect and Prospect, 1976, American Secondary Education: The Conant Influence, 1977, The Gifted and the Talented: Their Education and Development, 1979, Education for Gifted Children and Youth, 1980, Reforming the Schools in the 1980s, 1984, Gifted Young in Science: Potential through Performance, 1989, International Handbook of Research and Development of Giftedness and Talent, 1993, Changing Demographics, Changing Schools, 1995. Mem. Englewood Bd. Edn., N.J., 1969-72, pres., 1971. Served to 1st lt. USAAF, 1943-46. Kappa Delta Pi fellow, 1958-59. Mem. NEA (life), ASCD (bd. dirs. 1959-62, chmn. rsch. commn. 1961-63, co-chmn. task force edn. culturally disadvantaged 1964-66), Nat. Soc. Study Edn. (bd. dirs. 1975-96), Met. Assn. Study Gifted (pres. 1957-58), World Coun. for Gifted and Talented Children (hon. bd. dirs. 1979-85, pres. 1985-90, pres. 1987-91), Am. Ednl. Rsch. Assn., Kappa Delta Pi (Lauraete chpt., hon.). Jewish (pres. temple 1966-67). Home: Englewood N.J. Died Mar. 28, 1996.

PATANE, GIUSEPPE, conductor; b. Napoli, Italy, Jan. 1, 1932; s. Franco and Giulia (Caravaglios) P.; m. Rita Saponaro, May 7, 1958 (div.); children: Francesca, Paola. Student, Naples Conservatory. Debuts include Teatro San Carlo, Milan; permanent dir. Landestheater, Linz, Austria, 1961-62, Deutsche Oper Berlin, 1962-72; numerous opera and orchestral recordings: Targa d'Oro, Brescia, Italy, 1970, Bacchetta d'Oro, Parma, Italy, 1973, Grand Prix de Disque, Paris; conducted at La Scala, Milan, Rome, Palermo, Turin, Trieste, Bologna, Verona, Met. Opera, Chgo. Lyric Opera, San Francisc Opera, Cleve. Orch., Vienna State Opera, Paris Opera prin. guest condr. Budapest Philharmonic; condr. Berli Philharmonic, Vienna Philharmonic, Slova Philharmonic. Home: Monte Carlo Monaco

PATERSON, LIN RICHTER, publisher, medica writer; b. Paterson, N.J., Apr. 15, 1936; d. Meyer an Evelyn (Letz) Notkin; m. Howard S. Richter, Dec. 2 1955; children: Michael, Ronni; m. 2d Walter Davi Paterson, Aug. 26, 1982. B.A., Bryn Mawr Coll., 1957 Copy editor W.B. Saunders Co., Phila., 1957-58; fre lance med. editor Boston, 1958-65; med. editor Lahe Clinic Found., Boston, 1965-68; editor med. div. Littl Brown & Co., Boston, 1968-79, med. editor in chie 1979-83; v.p., gen. mgr. book div. Appleton-Century Crofts, East Norwalk, Conn., 1983-84; pres. Appleton Lange (formerly Appleton-Century-Crofts), Ea Norwalk, Conn., 1984-89; pub. Scovill Paterson Inc Norwalk, Conn., 1990-91. Author: (with Fred Be liveau) Understanding Human Sexual Inadequacy, 197 Democrat. Jewish. Home: Norwalk Conn. Died Dec 1991.

PATON, ALAN STEWART, author; Pietermaritzburg, Natal, Republic of South Africa, Ja 11, 1903; m. Dorrie Francis; 2 children; m. 2d, Ann Hopkins, 1969. Student Pietermaritzburg Coll., Nat U.; L.H.D. (hon.), Yale U., La Salle U.; D.Litt. (hon. Kenyon Coll., Rhodes U., Harvard U., Trent U., W lamette U., U. Natal, U. Mich.; D.D. (hon.), Edinburg U.; LL.D. (hon.), U. Witwatersrand. Tchr., 1924-3 prin. Diepkloof Reformatory for African Juvenile D linquents, Johannesburg, 1936-48; pres. Liberal Par South Africa, till 1968; founder Reality mag., 196 books: Cry, the Beloved Country, 1948, Too Late Th Phalarope, 1953, The Land and People of South Afric 1955, South Africa in Transition, 1956, Hope for Sou Africa, 1958, Debbie Go Home (short stories), 196 Hofmeyr, 1965, Instrument of Thy Peace, 1968, Th Long View, 1968, Kontakion for You Departed, 196 musicals: Mkhumbane (Village in the Gully), Aparthe and the Archbishop, 1972, Knocking on the Door, 197 Towards the Mountain (autobiography), Vol. 1, 198 Ah, But Your Land is Beautiful, 1981. Recipie Freedom award, 1960; award Free Acad. of A Hamburg, 1961. Died Apr. 12, 1988. Home: Nat South Africa

PATON, WILLIAM D(RUMMONI M(ACDONALD), pharmacologist, educator; b. May 1917; s. William Paton and Grace Mackenzie P.; schol New Coll., Oxford U., hon. fellow, 1980; BA with 1 class honors, Oxford U., 1938, MA, 1948, DM, 195 BM, BCh, Oxford U., 1942; DSc (hon.), London U 1985, Edinburgh U., 1986; m. Phoebe Margaret Rook 1942. Demonstrator in physiology Oxford U., 1938-3 Goldsmid exhbn. UCH Med. Sch., 1939; editor UC Mag., 1941; house physician UCH Med. Unit, 194 pathologist King Edward VII Sanatorium, 1943-4 mem. sci. staff Nat. Inst. Med. Research, 1944-5 reader in pharmacology Univ. Coll. and UCH Me Sch., 1952-54; prof. pharmacology RCS, 1954-59; pro pharmacology Oxford U., 1959-84; emeritus fellow Ba liol Coll.; dir. Wellcome Inst. History of Medicine, 198 87; del. Clarendon Press; delivered Robert Campb oration, 1957, Clover lectr., 1958; Bertram Lou Abrahams lectr. RCP, 1962; Ivison Macadam lec RCSE, 1973; Osler lectr. RCP, 1978. Author: Man an Mouse: Animals in Medical Research, 1984, 2d edi 1992. Rhodes trustee, 1968-87; Wellcome trustee, 197 87. Knighted, 1979; decorated comdr. Order Brit. E pire, 1968; recipient Fellowes Gold medal, 1941, Beng Meml. prize, 1952, Cameron prize, 1956, Gairdn Found. award, 1959, Gold medal Soc. Apothecari 1976, Osler Meml. medal U. Oxford, 1986, Wellco Gold medal, 1991. Fellow Royal Coll. Physicians, Roy Soc., RSA, FFARCS. Mem. Pharmacol. Soc. (chm editorial bd, 1969-74), Physiol. Soc. (hon. sec. 1951-5 chmn. 1985), Brit. Toxicol. Soc. (chmn. 1982-83), In Study of Drug Dependence, Inst. Animal Technicia (pres. 1969-75), Research Def. Soc. (chmn., Paget lec 1978, Boyd medal 1987); hon. mem. Société Franca d'Allergie, Australian Acad. Forensic Sci.; corr. me German Pharmacol. Soc. Died Oct. 17, 1993. Hom Oxford Eng.

PATRICK, JOHN, playwright; b. Louisville, May 1903; s. John Francis and Myrtle (Osborne) Go gan. Student pvt. schs.; student, Holy Cross Coll., N Orleans, St. Edwards Coll., Austin, Tex., St. Mar Sem., LaPorte, Tex.; DFA (hon.), Baldwin-Walla Coll., 1972, Canisius Coll., 1982; summer stude Harvard U., 1982, Columbia U., 1982. Radio wri NBC, San Francisco, 1933-36; freelance writer, H lywood, Calif., 1936-38. First play, Hell Freeze O appeared N.Y.C., 1936; recent plays include The Ha Heart, 1945, Story of Mary Surratt, 1947, Curio Savage, 1950, Lo and Behold, 1953, Teahouse of August Moon, 1953, Good as Gold, 1957, Everybo Loves Opal, 1961, Everybody's Girl, 1967, Scan Point, 1968, Love Is a Time of Day, 1969, Barrel Full Pennies, 1970, (musical) Lovely Ladies, Kind G tlemen, 1971, Opal Is a Diamond, 1971, Macbeth I It, 1972, The Dancing Mice, 1972, The Savage Dilem 1972, Anybody Out There?, 1972, A Bad Year for T matoes, 1974, Sex on the Sixth Floor, 1974, Love or Three, 1974, Noah's Animals, 1975, Enigma, 1975, Roman Conquest, 1975, Opal's Husband, 1975, Divorce Anyone?, 1976, Suicide Anyone, 1976, People!, 1977, Magenta Moth, 1978, That's Not My Mother, 1978, That's Not My Father, 1978, Girls of the Garden Club, 1979, Opal's Million Dollar Duck, 1979, The Indictments, 1980, Cheating Cheaters, 1985, The Reluctant Rogue, 1986, The Gay Deceiver, 1987, The Green Monkey, 1987; TV play The Small Miracle; movies: Enchantment, President's Lady, Three Coins in the Fountain, 1954, Love Is a Many Splendored Thing, 1955, High Society, 1956, Teahouse of the August Moon, 1956, Les Girls (Royal Command Performance, London), 1957, Some Came Running, 1958, The World of Suzie Wong, 1960, Gigot, 1961, Main Attraction, 1962, Shoes of the Fisherman, 1968: (poetry) Sense and Nonsense, 1989, Dirty Ditties (verse), 1995. Served as capt. with Am. Field Service, India, Burma, 1942-44. Received Pulitzer prize, 1954, N.Y. Drama Critics award, 1954, Perry award, Donaldson award, Aegis Theater Club award, Tony award for play Teahouse of the August Moon, 1954, Fgn. Corr. award, 1957; award for best Am. musical (for Les Girls), Screen Writers Guild, 1957, William Inge award for Lifetime achievement in the Theater, presented by the Gov. of Kans., 1986. Home: Boca Raton Fla. Died November 7, 1995.

PATRICK, JUNE CAROL, psychiatrist; b. Charlotte, Mich., Aug. 29, 1932; d. John and Rachel Irene (Towe) Granstrom; m. Robert Bruce Patrick, Aug. 28, 1955 (dec. Jan. 1981); 1 child, Kathleen Ann. BA, U. Mich., 1954, MA, 1956; DO, Mich. State U., 1978. Diplomate Am. Bd. Psychiatry and Neurology. Staff psychiatrist Milw. County Mental Health Complex, Milw., from 1982; practice medicine specializing in psychiatry Milw. Psychiatric Hosp., Wauwatosa, Wis., from 1982; asst. clin. prof. psychiatry and mental health scis. Med. Coll. of Wis., Milw., 1983—. Mem. NOW, AMA, Am. Psychiat. Assn, Wis. Psychiat. Assn. (women's com. chmn. 1985-86), Am. Osteo. Assn. Home: Alexandria Va. Deceased.

PATRICK, RICHARD MONTGOMERY, aeronautical engineer; b. Rockford, Ill., Sept. 24, 1928; s. Richard Montgomery and May Francis (O'Connor) P.; m. Mary Ann Raliegh, Oct. 20, 1958; children: Elizabeth, Susanne, Richard. Student, Iowa State Coll., 1946-48; B.S., Purdue U., 1950; M.S., 1951; Ph.D., Cornell U.; Ph.D. (Fairchild fellow), 1956. Aero engr. NACA, Langley AFB, 1951, 53; aero. engr. Douglas Aircraft Co., Santa Monica, Calif., 1952; with Avco Everett Research Lab., Mass., 1956-95; chmn. plasma physics com. Avco Everett Research Lab., 1965-95, v.p. directed energy, 1970-95. Contbr. articles to profl. jours. Named Disting. Engring. Alumnus, Purdue U., 1976. Fellow Am. Phys. Soc.; mem. Sigma Xi, Gamma Alpha Rho. Club: Winchester Boat. Home: Winchester Mass. Died Mar. 3, 1995.

PATRY, MARCEL JOSEPH, communications educator, former university dean; b. Beaumont, Que., Can., Jan. 31, 1923; s. Armand R. and Yvonne B. (Marcoux) P. B.A., U. Ottawa, 1945, L.Ph., 1946, M.A., 1947, Ph.D., 1949, L.Th., 1950, D.Ph., 1956. Mem. faculty U. Ottawa, 1950-68; rector St. Paul U., Ottawa, Ont., 1968-77; prof. communications St. Paul U., 1977—, dir. Inst. Social Communications, 1980-84, dean Faculty of Philosophy, 1981-84; mem. coun. adminstrn. Le Droit, Ottawa, 1970-87. Author: Reflexions sur les lois de l'intelligence, 1965, Report of the Rector, 1973. Mem. Can. Assn. Communication, Assn. Ednl. Communications and Tech., Internat. Communication Assn., Internat. Catholic Union Press, World Assn. Christian Communication, Soc. Philosophie de l'Outaouais, Can. Soc. Jacques Maritain. Roman Catholic. Home: Ottowa Can. Deceased.

PATTERSON, CLAIR CAMERON, nuclear chemist, biogeochemist, educator; b. Des Moines, June 2, 1922; s. Claire C. and Vivian (Henney) P.; m. Lorna J. McCleary, Mar. 3, 1944; children: Cameron C., Claire Keister, Charles Warner, Susan Patterson- Hill. BS, Grinnel Coll., 1943; MS, U. Iowa, 1944; PhD, U. Chgo., 1951, postgrad., 1952; hon. degree, Grinnell Coll., 1972, U. Paris, 1977. Geochemist Calif. Inst. Tech., Pasadena, 1952—. Patentee in field; contbr. articles to profl. jours. Recipient Tyler Environmental Prize, 1994, U. Southern Calif. Fellow AAAS; mem. NAS (Lawrence medal) Geochem.Cosmica Arts, Sigma Xi. Home: The Sea Ranch Calif. Died Dec. 5, 1995.

PATTERSON, NEVILLE, state supreme court justice; b. Monticello, Miss., Feb. 16, 1916; s. E.B. P.; m. Catherine Stough; 3 children. LL.B., U. Miss., 1939. Bar: Miss. 1939. Practiced with father Monticello, 1939-41; with legal dept. Fed. Land Bank, New Orleans, 1941; chancellor 15th Chancery Ct. Dist., 1947-63; asst. atty. gen. State of Miss., 1963; justice Supreme Ct. of So. Dist. Miss., 1964—, chief justice, 1977—; Prof. Jackson Sch. Law, from 1966; Chmn. Miss. Jud. Council; past chmn. Miss. Adv. Council on Rule Changes. Served to capt. inf. AUS, 1941-45. Decorated Bronze Star.; recipient Disting. Jurist award Miss. State U., 1984. Mem. Miss. Bar Assn., Conf. of Chief Justices of U.S. (mem. exec. com.), VFW, Am. Legion, 40 and 8. Democrat. Methodist. Clubs: Country of Jackson, Palio. Home: Jackson Miss.

PAUL, WOLFGANG, physics educator; b. Lorenzkirch, Germany, Aug. 10, 1913; s. Theodor and Elisabeth (Ruppel) P.; m. Liselotte Hirsche, 1940 (dec. 1977), m. Doris Waloh, 1979; four children. Diplom, Techn. Hochschule, Berlin, 1937; Habilitation, U. Kiel/ Göttingen, Germany, 1944; Dr. honoris causa, U. Uppsala, U. RWTH Aachen, Germany, U. Thessaloniki, Greece, U. Poznan, Poland; DCL (hon.), U. Kent, UK, 1992. Dozent U. Göttingen, Germany, 1944; ord. prof., dir. Inst. Physics U. Bonn, Germany, 1952-80, now prof. emeritus; pres. Alexander von Humboldt-Stiftung, Bonn, Germany, 1979-89; Dek. Mathemat.-Naturwissenschaft. Fak. U. Bonn, 1957-58, vis. scient. CERN (Centre Européen de Recherche Nucléaire, Genf) 1960-62, chrm. Vorstand der Kernforschungsanlage Jülich, 1963-64, chrm. Wissenshaftlicher Rat, 1963-64, dir. nuclear physics div. CERN, 1965-67, man. dir. DESY, 1971-73, chrm. Wissenschaftlicher Rat v. CERN, 1973-79. Contbr. numerous articles to profl. jours. Pres. Alexander von Humboldt-Stiftung, 1979-89. Recipient Nobel prize in physics, 1989, Robert W. Pohl prize. Mem. German Phys. Soc., European Phys. Soc., German Acad. for Natural Sci. (Leopoldina), Acad. Sci., Order 'Pour le mérite'. Home: Bonn Germany Died Dec. 6, 1993.

PAULING, LINUS CARL, chemistry educator; b. Portland, Oreg., Feb. 28, 1901; s. Herman Henry William and Lucy Isabelle (Darling) P.; m. Ava Helen Miller, June 17, 1923 (dec. Dec. 7, 1981); children: Linus Carl, Peter Jeffress, Linda Helen, Edward Crellin. BS, Oreg. State U., Corvallis, 1922; ScD (hon.), Oreg. State Coll., Corvallis, 1933; PhD, Calif. Inst. Tech., 1925; ScD (hon.), U. Chgo., 1941, Princeton, 1946, U. Cambridge, U. London, Yale U., 1947, Oxford U., 1948, Bklyn. Poly. Inst., 1955, Humboldt U., 1959, U. Melbourne, 1964, U. Delhi, Adelphi U., 1967, Marquette U. Sch. Medicine, 1969; LHD, Tampa U., 1950; UJD, U. N.B., 1950; LLD, Reed Coll., 1959; Dr. h.c., Jagiellonian U., Montpellier (France), 1964; DFA, Chouinard Art Inst., 1958; also others. Teaching fellow Calif. Inst. Tech., 1922-25, research fellow, 1925-27, asst. prof., 1927-29, assoc. prof., 1929-31, prof. chemistry, 1931-64; chmn. div. chem. and chem. engring., dir. Calif. Inst. Tech. (Gates and Crellin Labs. of Chemistry), 1936-58, mem. exec. com., bd. trustees, 1945-48; research prof. (Center for Study Dem. Instns.), 1963-67; prof. chemistry U. Calif. at San Diego, 1967-69, Stanford, 1969-74; pres. Linus Pauling Inst. Sci. and Medicine, 1973-75, 78-94, research prof., 1973-94; George Eastman prof. Oxford U., 1948; lectr. chemistry several univs. Author several books, 1930-94, including How to Live Longer and Feel Better, 1986; contbr. articles to profl. jours. Fellow Balliol Coll., 1948; Fellow NRC, 1925-26; Fellow John S. Guggenheim Meml. Found., 1926-27; Recipient numerous awards in field of chemistry, including; U.S. Presdl. Medal for Merit, 1948, Nobel prize in chemistry, 1954, Nobel Peace prize, 1962, Internat. Lenin Peace prize, 1972, U.S. Nat. Medal of Sci., 1974, Fermat medal, Paul Sabatier medal, Pasteur medal, medal with laurel wreath of Internat. Grotius Found., 1957, Lomonosov medal, 1978, U.S. Nat. Acad. Sci. medal in Chem. Scis., 1979, Priestley medal Am. Chem. Soc., 1984, Chem. Edn. award, 1987, Tolman medal, 1991, award for chemistry Arthur M. Sackler Found., 1984, Vannevar Bush award Nat. Sci. Bd., 1989. Hon., corr., fgn. mem. numerous assns. and orgns. Home: Big Sur Calif. Died Aug. 19, 1994.

PAULSEN, BORGE REGNAR, agricultural cooperative executive; b. San Francisco, July 26, 1915; s. Anton and Christa (Regnar) P.; m. Beverly Ann Gephart, July 3, 1942; children: Lee Ann Paulsen Hanna, R. Anthony, Eric Dana, Carol Louise Paulsen Thomsen. Student Stanford, 1933-35; BS, U. Calif., Berkeley, 1937. Sec., Agrl. Adjustment Adminstrn., Yolo County, Calif., 1937-41; owner, operator Sunset Rice Dryer, Inc., Woodland, Calif., 1946-94; pres. Demeter Corp. Woodland, Agrivest Corp., Woodland; pres. Crane & Cross Books, Inc., Sacramento; dir. emeritus Wells Fargo Bank, 1986-94; dir. Wells Fargo & Co.; farmer, rice grower, 1937-94; farmer walnut orchard; mem. rice research and mktg. com. U.S. Dept. Agr., others; chmn. adv. bd. Berkeley Bank for Coops., 1976. Bd. dirs., v.p. Calif. Rice Research Found., Yuba City, Woodland Meml. Hosp., also former pres.; former pres. Sutter (Calif.) Mut. Water Co.; bd. dirs. Robert Louis Stevenson Sch., Pebble Beach, Calif., Agrl. Council Calif.; adv. bd. Calif. State U., Sacramento; pres. Regnar and Beverly Paulsen Found., 1993. Served with U.S. Army, 1941-46. Recipient Distinguished Service award Calif. Farm Bur., 1974, Outstanding Service award Woodland Meml. Hosp., 1976, Calif. Rice Industry Man of Year award, 1978; named Agribus. Man of Yr., Yolo County Calif. Mem. Rice Rsch. and Mktg. Bd. Calif. (v.p.), Rice Growers Assn. Calif. (pres., chmn. bd. 1968-70), Bean Growers Assn. Calif. (past pres.), Delta Kappa Epsilon. Republican. Episcopalian. Clubs: Commonwealth, Bankers (San Francisco); Rotary Woodland (former pres.); Sutter, Yolo Fliers Country, El Macero Country; Alderbrook Golf and Yacht (Union, Wash.), Grandfathers Club of Am. (Sacramento). Died June 22, 1994. Home: Woodland Calif.

PAUPINI, GIUSEPPE CARDINAL, former archbishop; b. Mondavio, Italy, Feb. 25, 1907. Ordained priest Roman Cath. Ch., 1930; titular archbishop of Sebastopolis in Abasgia, 1956; served in Vatican Diplomatic Corps, 1956-69; internuncio to Iran, 1956-57; nuncio to Guatemala and El Salvadtor, 1958-58, to Colombia, 1959-69; created cardinal, 1969; titular ch. All Saints Ch.; major penitentiary, 1973; mem. Congregation of Causes of Saints, Commn. State of Vatican City. Home: Rome Italy

PAVAN, PIETRO CARDINAL, archbishop; b. Treviso, Italy, Aug. 30, 1903. ordained Roman Cath. Ch., 1928. Proclaimed cardinal, 1985; deacon San Francesco da Paola ai Monti. Home: Rome Italy Died Dec. 26, 1994.

PAVIS, JESSE ANDREW, sociology educator; b. Washington, Sept. 15, 1919; s. Abraham and Ethel (Rein) P.; m. Mary Fleming Bennet, Mar. 9, 1942 (div. Sept. 1963); children: Amaranth, Athar, Arne, Andrea; m. Mary Margaret Monahan, May 9, 1964 (dec. Oct. 1992); children: Deidre, Shira. BA, George Washington U., 1942; MA, Howard U., 1947; PhD, NYU, 1969. Instr. Hofstra U., Hempstead, N.Y., 1948-49; prof. Borough of Manhattan C.C., CUNY, 1964-94; mem. faculty New Sch. for Social Rsch., N.Y.C., 1973-79; researcher Bur. Applied Social Rsch., Columbia U., N.Y.C., 1952-53, Grad. Staff, 1953-54; mem. Cumberland Mental Health Community Ctr., Bklyn., 1977-78; reviewer Contemporary Sociology, Sociology of Sci., 1974; mem. panel Study of Nurse Edn. Needs in So. N.Y., 1964-65. Pres. Pub. Sch. #8 PTA, Bklyn., 1976-80; mem. Parent Coun. Sch. Dist. 13, Bklyn., 1986-90; mem. Bklyn. Child Safety Com., 1976-80. With U.S. Army, 1942-45. Recipient Founders Day award NYU, 1970. Mem. AAAS, Am. Sociol. Soc., N.Y. Acad. Scis., Order of Artus, Pi Gamma Mu. Democrat. Home: Brooklyn N.Y. Died Nov. 15, 1994; cremated Oxford Hills Crematory, Chester, N.Y.

PAYNTER, JOHN PHILIP, conductor; b. Dodgeville, Wis., May 29, 1928; s. Wilfred William and Minnie Elizabeth (Clark) P.; m. Marietta Margaret Morgan, Sept. 10, 1949; children—Bruce David, Megan Elizabeth. B.M., Northwestern U., 1950, M.Mus. in Composition, 1951; LHD, DePaul U., 1992. Mem. faculty Sch. of Music, Northwestern U., 1951-96; prof. conducting, 1974-96; pres. Mid-West Internat. Band and Orch. Clinic. Dir. bands, 1953-96; condr., musical dir., Northshore Concert Band, 1958-96; composer and arranger numerous works. Mem. ASCAP (small awards panel 1988), Am. Bandmasters Assn. (past pres.), Nat. Band Assn. (co-founder, past pres.), World Assn. Symphonic Bands and Ensemble (past pres.), Phi Mu Alpha Sinfonia (life), Phi Eta Sigma, Pi Kappa Lambda. Mem. United Ch. of Christ. Home: Glenview Ill. Died Feb. 4, 1996.

PEACHER, DOUGLAS JOHN, retired retail, catalogue sales company executive; b. Hopkinsville, Ky., Nov. 23, 1912; s. Benjamin F. and Minnie (Adams) P.; m. Gwendolyn Edris Brown, Oct. 12, 1940. LL.B., LaSalle U., Chgo. With Frederick & Nelson Dept. Store, Seattle, 1935-38; with Sears, Roebuck and Co., 1938-66; buyer Sears, Roebuck and Co., Chgo., 1946-50, mgr. mdse. div., 1950-66; pres., dir., chmn. finance com. Simpsons-Sears, Ltd., Toronto, Ont., Can., 1966-76; ret. Simpsons-Sears, Ltd.; pres., dir. Simpsons-Sears Acceptance Co., Ltd., Simpson Sears Properties Ltd.; trustee, mem. investment com. Simpsons-Sears Profit Sharing Retirement Fund; dir. Allstate Ins. Co. Can.; dir. Allstate Life Ins. Co. Can., Inglis Ltd., Photo Engravers & Electrotypes Ltd., Thomson Newspapers Ltd., all Toronto, Westcorp, Inc., Orange, Calif., Western Fin. Savs. Bank; dir., mem. exec. com. Montreal Trust Co., Que., Ins. Co. of the West, San Diego; mem. exec. com., investment com., chmn. audit com. MBR Compensation Com. Hon. trustee George Williams Coll., Downers Grove, Ill.; mem. pvt. support bd. U. Toronto; past mem. res. forces policy bd. Office Sec. of Def., Washington; past nat. bd. dirs., pres. Boys Clubs Can.; bd. dirs. San Diego County council Boy Scouts Am.; bd. dirs., v.p. San Diego Opera Co. Served to maj. gen. USMCR. Mem. Mil. and Hospitaller Order Saint Lazarus of Jerusalem, PTO, Order of St. Lazarus (Knight Comdr.). Clubs: Royal Canadian Mil. Inst. (Toronto), Toronto (Toronto), York (Toronto); Goodwood (Ont.); Army and Navy (Washington); La Jolla Beach and Tennis (Calif.), La Jolla Country; Cuyamaca (San Diego); Ristigouche Salmon (Matapedia, Que.) (pres.). Home: La Jolla Calif. Died Sept. 11, 1995.

PEALE, NORMAN VINCENT, minister; b. Bowersville, Ohio, May 31, 1898; s. Charles Clifford and Anna (DeLaney) P.; m. Ruth Stafford, June 20, 1930; children: Margaret (Mrs. Paul F. Everett), John, Elizabeth (Mrs. John M. Allen). AB, Ohio Wesleyan U., 1920, DD, 1936; STB, Boston U., 1924, AM, 1924, DD (hon.), 1986; DD, Syracuse U., 1931, Duke U., 1938, Cen. Coll., 1964; LHD (hon.), Lafayette Coll., 1952, U. Cin., 1968, Wm. Jewell Coll., 1952; LLD (hon.), Hope Coll., 1962, Brigham Young U., 1967, Pepperdine U., 1979; STD, Millikin U., 1958; LittD, Iowa Wesleyan U., 1958, Ea. Ky. State Coll., 1964, Jefferson Med. Coll., 1955; LHD (hon.), Northwestern U., 1984, Pace U., 1984, Milw. Sch. Engring., 1985, St. John's U., 1985, Marymount Manhattan, 1985; DD (hon.), Boston U., 1986, Mt. Union Coll., 1988; LHD (hon.), Judson Coll., 1988. Ordained to ministry M.E. Ch., 1922; pastor Berkeley, R.I., 1922-24, Kings Hwy. Ch., Bklyn., 1924-27, Univ. Ch., Syracuse, N.Y., 1927-32, Marble Collegiate Ref. Ch., N.Y.C., 1932-84; founder, pub. (with Mrs. Peale) Guideposts mag. Author: A Guide to Confident Living, 1948, The Power of Positive Thinking, 1952, The Coming of the King, 1956, Stay Alive All Your Life, 1957, The Amazing Results of Positive Thinking, 1959, The Tough-Minded Optimist, 1962, Adventures in the Holy Land, 1963, Sin, Sex and Self-control, 1965, Jesus of Nazareth, 1966, The Healing of Sorrow, 1966, Enthusiasm Makes the Difference, 1967, Bible Stories, 1973, You Can If You Think You Can, 1974, The Positive Principle Today, 1976, The Positive Power of Jesus Christ, 1980, Treasury of Joy and Enthusiasm, 1981, Positive Imaging, 1981, The True Joy of Positive Living, 1984; Have a Great Day, 1985; Why Some Positive Thinkers Get Powerful Results, 1986; Power of the Plus Factor, 1987, The American Character, 1988; co-author: (with Ken Blanchard) The Power of Ethical Management, 1988, The Power of Positive Living, 1990, My Favorite Quotations, 1990, This Incredible Century, 1991, My Christmas Treasury, 1991, My Inspirational Favorites, 1992, My Favorite Prayers, 1993, Bible Power for Daily Living, 1993, Positive Thinking Every Day, 1993; co-author: chpt. in Am's. 12 Master Salesmen; writer for various secular and religious periodicals; Tech. adviser representing Protestant Ch. in filming of motion picture: motion picture One Man's Way, based on biography, 1963; film What It Takes To Be A Real Salesman. Trustee Ohio Wesleyan U., Central Coll.; mem. exec. com. Presbyn. Ministers Fund for Life Ins.; mem. Mid-Century White House Conf. on Children and Youth, Pres.'s Commn. for Observance 25th Anniversary UN; pres. Protestant Council City N.Y., 1965-69, Ref. Church in Am., 1969-70; lectr. pub. affairs, personal effectiveness; chaplain Am. Legion, Kings County, N.Y., 1925-27. Recipient numerous awards including: Freedom Found. award, 1952, 55, 59, 73, 74; Horatio Alger award, 1952; Am. Edn. award, 1955; Gov. Service award for Ohio, 1955; Nat. Salvation Army award, 1956; Disting. Salesman's award N.Y. Sales Execs., 1957; Salvation Army award, 1957; Internat. Human Relations award Dale Carnegie Club Internat., 1958; Clergyman of Year award Religious Heritage Am., 1964; Paul Harris Fellow award Rotary Internat., 1972; Disting. Patriot award Sons of Revolution, N.Y. State, 1973; Order of Aaron and Hur Chaplains Corps U.S. Army, 1975; Christopher Columbus award, 1976; All-Time Gt. Ohioan award, 1976; Soc. for Family of Man award, 1981; Disting. Achievement award Ohio Wesleyan U., 1983; Religion in Media Gold Angel award, 1984; Presdl. Medal of Freedom, 1984; 2d Ann. Family Weekly Nat. Treasure award, 1984; Disting. Am. award Sales and Mktg. Execs. Internat., 1985; Theodore Roosevelt Disting. Service award, 1985; World Freedom award Shanghai Tiffin Club, 1985; Napolean Hill Fedn. Gold medal for Literary Achievement, 1985; St. George Assn. Golden Rule award, 1985, Old Hero award NFL, 1987, Adele Rogers St. John Round Table award, 1987, Communicator of the Yr. award Sales and Mktg. Exec. Internat., Little Rock, 1987, Disting. Achievement award Am. Aging, 1987, Grand Cross award Supreme Council, Mother Council of World of 33d and last degree Masons, 1987, Magellan award Circumnavigators Club, 1987, Van Rensselaer Gold medal Masonic Temple Cin., Silver Buffalo award Boy Scouts Am., 1988, Outstanding Alumnus award Ohio Found. of Ind. Coll., 1989, Merit award in Humanities N.Y. Acad, Dentistry, 1989, Pope John XIII award Viterbo Coll., 1989, George M. and Mary Jane Leader Healthcare award, 1989, John Y. Brown award, 1989, Humanitarian of Yr. award Women's Nat. Rep. Club, 1990, Hance award St. Barnabas Health System, 1990, The Samaritan Inst. award, 1990, Caring Inst. award, 1990, Eleanor Roosevelt Val-Kill medal, 1991, Soaring Eagle award Brethren Home Fedn., 1991. Mem. SAR, Blanton-Peale Inst. (founder), Ohio Soc. N.Y. (pres. 1952-55), Episcopal Actors Guild, Am. Authors Guild, Alpha Delta, Phi Gamma Delta (Diamond Owl award 1992). Republican. Clubs: Metropolitan, Union League, Lotos. Lodges: Rotary, Masons (past grand prelate), Shriners, K.T. Home: Pawling N.Y. Died Dec. 24, 1993.

PEANASKY, ROBERT JOSEPH, biochemist, medical educator; b. Menominee, Mich., Oct. 18, 1927; s. Joseph John and Sophia E. (Simeth) P.; m. Elizabeth R. Bender, Sept. 12, 1953; children: Joseph F., Michael J., Paul J., Robert A., John S. B.S. cum laude, Marquette U., 1951, M.S., 1953; Ph.D., U. Wis.-Madison, 1957. NSF trainee Marquette U., Milw., 1957, 58, 60, Dartmouth U., Hanover, N.H., 1959; asst. prof. Marquette U. Med. Sch., Milw., 1960-65, assoc. prof., 1965-67; assoc. prof. U. S.D. Med. Sch., Vermillion, 1967-70, prof., 1970-91, prof. emeritus, 1991—, dept. chmn. 1986-89; vis. scientist U. Ky. Med. Ctr., Lexington, 1965, U. Marseille-aix-en-Provence, 1966-67; vis. prof. Purdue U., West Lafayette, Ind., 1977; participant confs. in field; mem. Great Plains Regional Review and Research Adv. Com., 1969-72. Served to cpl. U.S. Army, 1946-47. USPHS fellow, 1960-62; recipient Career Devel. award USPHS, 1962-67; NIH grantee, 1961-90. Mem. Am. Chem. Soc. (chmn. sect. 1972), Am. Soc. Biochemistry and Molecular Biology, Soc. Exptl. Biology and Medicine (referee editor proceedings 1969-78, mem. council 1976-79), S.D. Acad. Scis. (exec. com. 1983-85), Sigma Xi (pres. local chpt. 1979-80). Democrat. Roman Catholic. Home: Plover Wis.

PEARCE, WILLIAM, manufacturing executive; b. Cin., Oct. 22, 1920; s. Harry Edward and Pearce and Alice Huer; m. Shirley Eleanore Theler, July 19, 1944; children: William Jr., Barbara Ann, Thomas Arthur. Student, Miami U., Oxford, Ohio, 1939-42. Field rep. Coca-Cola Bottling Co., Cin., 1948-55; regional mgr. Coca-Cola Bottling Co., Cleve., 1955-62, N.Y.C., 1962-70; v.p. Coca-Cola Bottling Co. of N.Y., N.Y.C., 1970-82; sr. vp. corp. affairs Coca-Cola Bottling Co. of N.Y., Greenwich, Conn., 1982-86; Pres. N.Y. Soft Drink Assn., N.Y.C., 1985-86, N.J. Soft Drink Assn., Princeton, N.J., 1983-85, N.Y. Food Industry Execs Council, 1980-83, founder. Pres. Nat. Football Found. and Hall of Fame, N.Y.C. Served to lt. USN Air Corps, 1942-46, PTO. Decorated Disting. Flying Cross, Air Medal (3). Republican. Presbyterian. Clubs: Springdale Golf (Princeton, N.J.); Pine Valley Golf (Pine Valley, N.J.). Home: Lawrenceville N.J. Died May 21, 1994.

PEASE, ARCHIE GRANVILLE, newspaper publisher; b. Anoka, Minn., Sept. 25, 1908; s. Thomas Gleason and Mamie (Chase) P.; m. Amy Marie Bridges, June 2, 1934; children: Barbara Pease Reichel, Thomas Bridges. BS, U. Ill., 1931. Tchr., coach New Athens (Ill.) High Sch., 1931-37, Anoka High Sch., 1937-40; adminstrv. asst. to rep. Richard P. Gale U.S. Ho. of Reps., Washington, 1940-42; editor Anoka County Union and Anoka Union Shopper, 1947-51; pres., chief exec. officer Anoka County Union & Shopper, Inc., 1951—; also chief exec. officer Anoka County Union-Shopper; pub. ABC Newspapers. Past mem. Coon Rapids Planning Commn.; bd. dirs. Thurston Found.; mem. long-range planning com. Mercy Hosp.; past chmn., pres. Anoka County chpt. ARC; v.p. Mpls. Aquatennial, 1961-67; mem. Minn. Bd. Edn., 1967-71; past chmn. Anoka County Republican Com.; formerly active numerous civic orgns. Officer AUS, 1942-46, col. USAR, 1930-62, ret. Recipient Silver Beaver award Boy Scouts Am.; Arch Pease Day proclaimed by gov. State of Minn., Sept. 25, 1987. Mem. Nat. Newspaper Assn., Minn. Newspaper Assn. (pres. 1960), Anoka C. of C. (pres. 1965-67), Am. Legion, VFW (life), Minn. Press Club (pres. 1962, former mem. bd. dirs.), Masons, Shriners, Jesters. Baptist. Home: Minneapolis Minn. Died Sept. 1990.

PECK, JOHN W., federal judge; b. Cin., June 23, 1913; s. Arthur M. and Marguerite (Comstock) P.; m. Barbara Moeser, Mar. 25, 1942 (dec. 1981); children—John Weld, James H., Charles E.; m. Janet Alcorn Wagner; 1 stepchild, Gretchen Wagner. AB, Miami U., 1935, LLD, 1966; JD, U. Cin., 1938, LLD, 1965; LLD, Chase Law Sch., 1971; D in Humane Letters, Northern Ky. U., 1993. Bar: Ohio 1938. Partner Peck, Shaffer & Williams, Cin., 1938-61; judge Ct. Common Pleas, Hamilton County, Ohio, 1950, 54; tax commr. State of Ohio, 1951-54; judge Supreme Ct. of Ohio, 1959-60, U.S. Dist. Ct., So. Dist. Ohio, 1961-66; judge U.S. Ct. Appeals, 6th Circuit, 1966—, sr. judge, 1978—; judge Temporary Emergency Ct. Appeals, 1979—; exec. sec. gov. State of Ohio, 1949; lectr. U. Cin. Coll. Law, 1948-70, Salmon P. Chase Coll. Law, 1949-51; mem. com. on adminstrn. criminal law Jud. Conf. U.S., 1971-79. Trustee Miami U., 1959—, emeritus, 1975—; mem. Princeton City Sch. Dist. Bd. Edn., 1958-63, pres. bd., 1963-69. Served to capt. Judge Adv. Gen. Corps AUS, 1942-46. Recipient Gates of Israel medal, 1984, Disting. Alumnus award U. Cin. Coll. Law, 1985, Spirit of '87 award for Liberty through Law, 1987; John Weld Peck Fed. Bldg. named in his honor, 1984. Mem. Cincinnatus Assn. (hon. life), Gyro Club, Beta Theta Phi, Phi Delta Phi. Club: Cin. Lit. Home: Cincinnati Ohio

PECKHAM, HOWARD HENRY, librarian, educator; b. Lowell, Mich., July 13, 1910; s. Herman Algernon and Harriet May (Wilson) P.; m. Dorothy Koth, July 28, 1936; children: Stephen Wilson, Angela Zidana (Mrs. Thomas Hewett). A.B., U. Mich., 1931, A.M., 1933; Litt.D., Olivet Coll., 1975. Chief editorial writer Grand Rapids (Mich.) Press, 1935; curator manuscripts Clements Library of Am. History, U. Mich., 1936-44, lectr. library sci., 1942-46, univ. war historian, 1943-44; dir. Ind. Hist. Bur., Indpls., 1945-53, Clements Library, 1953-77; prof. history U. Mich., 1953-77; cons. Office Naval History, USN Dept., 1966-78. Bassoonist, Hendersonville Symphony, 1977-86; Author: (with R.G. Adams) Lexington to Fallen Timbers, 1942, (with C. Storm) Invitation to Book Collecting, 1946, Pontiac and the Indian Uprising, 1947, Captured by Indians, 1954, The War for Independence, 1958, The Colonial Wars, 1964, The Making of the University of Michigan, 1967, The Toll of Independence, 1974, History of the W.L. Clements Library 1923-73, 1973, Indiana, a Bicentennial History, 1978, Historical Americana, 1980, (juvenile non-fiction) William Henry Harrison, 1951, Nathanael Greene, 1956, Pontiac Young Ottawa Leader, 1963; editor: George Groghan's Journal of 1767, 1939, (with L.A. Brown) Revolutionary War Journals of Henry Dearborn, 1939, Guide to the Manuscript Collections in the Clements Library, 1942, (with S.A. Snyder) Letters From Fighting Hoosiers, 1948, (with C.A. Byrd) Bibliography of Indiana Imprints, 1955, Narratives of Colonial America, 1971, Sources of American Independence, 1978, Ind. Hist. Bull, 1945-53, Liberty's Legacy, 1987; assoc. editor: Am. Heritage quar, 1949-54. Fellow Soc. Am. Archivists (founding mem., mem. council), Am. Assn. State and Local History (pres. 1954-56, mem. council), Am., Miss. Valley hist. assns., Mass. Hist. Soc., Bibliog. Soc. Am., Am. Antiquarian Soc., Adelphic Alpha Pi, Hendersonville Country Club. Congregationalist. Home: Hendersonville N.C. Died July 6, 1995.

PECKHAM, ROBERT FRANCIS, federal judge; b. San Francisco, Nov. 3, 1920; s. Robert F. and Evelyn (Crowe) P.; m. Harriet M. Behring, Aug. 15, 1953 (dec. Apr. 1970); children: Ann Evelyn, Sara Esther; m. Carol Potter, June 9, 1974. AB, Stanford U., 1941, LLB, 1945; postgrad., Yale U., 1941-42; LLD, U. Santa Clara, 1973. Bar: Calif. 1945. Adminstrv. asst. to regional enforcement atty. OPA, 1942-43; pvt. practice Palo Alto and Sunnyvale, 1946-48; asst. U.S. atty., 1948-53, chief asst. criminal div., 1952-53; ptnr. Darwin, Peckham & Warren, San Francisco, Palo Alto and Sunnyvale, 1953-59; judge Superior Ct., Santa Clara County, Calif., 1959-66; presiding judge Superior Ct., 1961-63, 65-66; U.S. dist. judge No. Dist. Calif., 1966-93, chief judge, 1976-88; trustee Foothill Coll. Dist., 1957-59, pres., 1959; mem. bd. visitors Stanford Law Sch., 1969-75, chmn. 1971-72; sr. mem. Am-Asia Law Del. of Asia Found. 1984-85, 87; mem. legal exch. del. vis. various countries South Am., 1989, Mex. and Hungary, 1991; chmn. 9th Cir. Task Force on Dispute Resolution, 1985-91; participant Brit. Fgn. Wilton Park Conf., 1971-74, Eng. State chmn. adv. bd. Friends Outside; coun. mem. Friends of Bancroft Libr., 1981-87. Recipient Brotherhood award NCCJ, 1968, recipient award for alt. dispute resolution leadership Ctr. for Pub. Resources 1984, award for written scholarship, 1985, Award of Merit Stanford Law Sch., 1991. Fellow Am. Bar Found.; mem. ABA (chmn. Nat. Conf. Fed. Trial Judges 1983-84, ho. of dels. 1984-90, assoc. Soviet lawyers exch. delegation 1987-88), Fed. Bar Assn., San Francisco Bar Assn., Santa Clara County Bar Assn. U.S. Jud. Conf. (exec. com. 1987-90, chmn. ad hoc com on cameras in courtroom 1989-91, chmn. com on civil justice reform act of 1990, 1990, advisor fed. cts. study com. 1989-90), Am. Law Inst., Am. Judicature Soc. Calif. Hist. Soc. (trustee 1974-78), Coun. Stanford Law Socs. (chmn. 1974-75), U.S. Dist. Ct. for No. Dist. Calif. Hist. Soc. (chmn. 1979-90), World Affairs Coun. (trustee 1979-85), Phi Beta Kappa, Phi Delta Phi. Home: Palo Alto Calif. Died Feb. 16, 1993; interred Alta Mesa Cemetery, Palo Alto, Calif.

PEDERSEN, HOWARD, vehicle rental and leasing company executive; b. Detroit, July 12, 1931; s. Oscar Henry and Ellen Marie P.; m. Margaret Hudson, June 20, 1953; children—Craig, Lisa, Tom Rob. B.B.A. Gen. Motors Inst., 1954; M.B.A., U. Detroit, 1962. Comptroller Chrysler Chem. Co., Trenton, Mich., 1963-65; with export div. Chrysler Corp., Detroit, 1965-67 fin. exec. Chrysler Corp., 1968; mgr. corp. Profit Forecasting, 1969; comptroller Chrysler Real Estate Co. Troy, Mich., 1970-71; exec. dir. Chrysler Europe London, 1971-75; v.p., corp. officer Norton Simon, Inc. N.Y.C., 1975-78; sr. v.p. acctg. and info. services Avis Inc., N.Y.C., 1978-79; sr. v.p., chief fin. officer Avis Inc., 1979—. Served with U.S. Army, 1954-56. Mem. Engring. Soc., Am. Mgmt. Assn., Nat. Assn. Accountants, Fin. Execs. Inst. Home: Greenwich Conn. Died Sept. 11, 1995.

PEERCE, STUART BERNARD, lawyer; b. N.Y.C. Oct. 18, 1931; s. Jacob Perlmutter and Celia (Alpern) P. m. Lois Peerce; children: Steven L., Marjorie J. Peerce Fuerst, Carol L. A.B., Columbia U., 1952, J.D., 1954. Bar: N.Y. 1954. Assoc. Donovan, Leisure, Newton & Irvine, N.Y.C., 1954-62, ptnr., 1963—. Harlan Fiske Stone scholar, 1952, 53. Mem. ABA, Assn. of Bar of City of N.Y. Home: New York N.Y. Died July 20, 1995.

PELLEGRINO, MICHELE CARDINAL, former archbishop of Turin; b. Centallo/Cuneo, Italy, Apr. 25, 1903. Ordained priest Roman Catholic Ch., 1925. Archbishop of Turin (Italy), 1965-77; elevated to cardinal, 1967. Mem. Congregation of Cath. Edn. Home: Turin Italy

PELLEW, JOHN C., artist; b. Cornwall, Eng., Apr. 9, 1903; came to U.S., 1921, naturalized, 1927; s. Thomas John and Catherine Jane (Jeffrey) P.; 1 dau., Elma Corinne. Student, School Arts, Penzance, Eng. Author: John Pellew Paints Watercolors, 1979; One man shows, Contemporary Arts Gallery, N.Y.C., 1934, 1941, 1948; exhibited Carnegie Internat., Corcoran Art Gallery, Washington, Pa. Acad. Art, Chgo. Art Inst., Nat. Acad. Art. N.Y.C., Whitney Mus., N.Y.C. Bklyn Mus. Detroit Art Inst.; works represented permanent collections, Met. Mus., Bklyn. Mus., Newark (N.J.) Mus. Unio Cultural, São Paulo, Brazil, Columbia U., Butler Mus. of American Art., Charles and Emma Frye Mus. Seattle. Awarded Vezin-James prize Salmagundi Club, 1950, Anders Jordahl prize, 1952, Mischa Lemper award, 1953, Winsor-Newton prize Am. Water Color Soc., 1951, Gold Medal of Honor for water color Allied Artists, 1951, Seeley award (oil) Salmagundi Club N.Y.C., 1964; Butler award Am. Watercolor Soc., 1965 Silver medal, 1970; Antoinette Graves Goetz award 1972; 1st Watercolor award 27th New Eng. Annual 1976. Mem. Am. Water Color Soc. (v.p. 1953, Carolina Stern award 1983, Dolphin fellow), NAD, Allied Artists, Audubon Artists. Club: Salmagundi (N.Y.C.). Home: Norwalk Conn. Died Feb. 26, 1993.

PENNER, WILLIAM A., management consultant; b. Beatrice, Nebr., July 23, 1933; s. Earl E. and Alene (Thomen) P.; m. Barbara Warren (div. 1980); children: William W., George E. BA, Northwestern U., Evanston Ill., 1957; postgrad., U. Chgo. Law Sch., Ill., 1957-58; postgrad. sch. bus., U. Chgo. Law Sch., 1958-59. Security sales A.C. Allyn & Co., Chgo., 1959-64; sales mgr. G.H. Walker & Co., Chgo., 1964-65; exec. v.p., dir. McCormick & Co., Chgo., 1965-74, The Ill. Co., Inc., Chgo.; pres. Washington Capital Group; pres., dir. Nephore Techs. Inc. Nat. trustee Nat. Symphony Orch. Wash., 1988; bd. dirs. Joffrey Ballet. With U.S. Army 1951-53, France. Mem. Econ. Club of Chgo., Assn. for Corp. Growth, Casino Club, U. Club. Republican. Episcopalian. Home: Chicago Ill. Died July 11, 1994.

PENNIMAN, HOWARD RAE, political scientist; b. Steger, Ill., Jan. 30, 1916; s. Rae Ernest and Alethea (Bates) P.; m. Morgia Anderson, Dec. 30, 1940; children: Barbara, Ruth, William, Catherine, Matthew. A.B., La. State U., 1936, M.A., 1938; Ph.D., U. Minn., 1941. Social Sci. Research Council predoctoral field fellow, 1940-41; instr. polit. sci. U. Ala., 1941-42; instr. dept. govt. Yale U., 1942-45, asst. prof., 1945-48; staff CIA, 1948-49; external research staff, asst. chief Dept. State, 1949-52, chief external research staff, 1953-55; staff Psychol. Strategy Bd., 1952-53; chief overseas book div. USIA, 1955-57; prof. govt. Georgetown U., 1957-83, head dept. govt., 1959-63; resident scholar Am. Enterprise Inst., 1971-95; columnist, America, 1958-64, Fulbright research grant, France, 1964-65; cons. Congl. fellowship program Am. Polit. Sci. Assn., 1959; cons. to team observers on presdl. elections in, Vietnam, 1967; election cons. ABC, 1968-95; mem. Presdl. observer teams, El Salvador, 1982, 84, Guatemala, 1985, 88, Philippines, 1986, Taipei, 1989. Author: Sait's American Parties and Elections, rev. edit, 1952, The American Political Process, 1962, Elections in South Vietnam, 1973; Editor: John Locke on Politics and Education, 1947, Britain at the Polls, 1974, 80, France at the Polls, 1975, 78, 81, 86, Canada at the Polls, 1975, 79, 80, 84, Australia at the Polls, 1977, 80, Italy at the Polls, 1978, 81, Ireland at the Polls, 1978, 81, 82, 87, Israel at the Polls, 1977, 81, Switzerland at the Polls, 1979, New Zealand at the Polls, 1980, Greece at the Polls, 1981, Spain at the Polls, 1977, 79, 82; contbr. articles to profl. jours. Del. Md. Constl. Conv., 1967-68, chmn. com. on style; co-chmn. Montgomery County Com. on Drug Abuse, 1969-70; trustee Montgomery Coll., 1971-80. With AUS, 1945-46. Mem. Am. Polit. Sci. Assn. (pres. D.C. chpt. 1958-59), Internat. Polit. Sci. Assn., Phi Beta Kappa, Pi Gamma Mu, Pi Sigma Alpha (nat. pres. 1966, nat. dir. 1975-95, Nat. Capital Area Polit. Sci. Assn. award, 1988), Sigma Delta Chi. Episcopalian. Home: Rockville Md. Died Apr. 13, 1995.

PENNISI, VINCENT RAYMOND, plastic surgeon; b. Jamaica, N.Y., May 13, 1923; s. Vincenzo Pennisi and Mary (Carmela) Sorrentino; m. Madeline Heckeri; children: Madeline Mary Fendler, Vincent Peter, Vinette Marie Ramsay. BS, L.I. U., 1943; DDS, St. Louis U., 1946; MD, Georgetown U., 1950. Intern Mary Immaculate Hosp.; resident in plastic surgery Bronx Vets. Hosp. and St. Francis Meml. Hosp.; pvt. practice San Francisco, 1958—; pres. med. staff St. Francis Meml. Hosp., San Francisco, 1967-69, pres., trustee, 1982-84, past dir. plastic surgery and residency program and burn ctr., dir. Subcutaneous Mastectomy Data Evaluation Ctr.; cons. Letterman Army Med. Ctr. Served to capt. U.S. Army, 1956-58. Fellow Am. Coll. Surgeons; mem. AMA, Calif. Med. Assn., Am. Assn. Plastic Surgeons, Am. Soc. Plastic and Reconstuctive Surgeons. Home: San Francisco Calif.

PENRY, JAMES KIFFIN, physician, neurology educator; b. Denton, N.C., Aug. 21, 1929; s. Robert Lee and Addie Cordelia (Leonard) P.; m. Sarah Doub, Mar. 20, 1955; children: Martin D., Denny K., Edith C. BS magna cum laude, Wake Forest U., 1951, MD, 1955. Diplomate Am. Bd. Psychiatry and Neurology. Commd. 2d lt. USAF, 1955, advanced through grades to maj., 1964; rotating intern Pa. Hosp., Phila., 1955-56; asst. resident in internal medicine and neurology N.C. Bapt. Hosp., Winston-Salem, 1956-58; asst. in neurology Bowman Gray Sch. Medicine, Wake Forest U., 1957-58; asst. resident, then resident in neurology Boston City Hosp., 1958-60; fellow in neurology Harvard Med. Sch., Cambridge, Mass., 1959-60; neurologist, chief neurology svc. USAF Hosp., Maxwell AFB, Ala., 1960-62; chief neurology svc. USAF Hosp., Tachikawa, Japan, 1962-65, Andrews AFB, Md., 1965-66; resigned, 1966; dir. USPHS, Bethesda, Md., 1966-79; dir. Neurol. Disorders Program, chief epilepsy br. Nat. Inst. Neurol. and Communicative Disorders and Stroke, NIH, 1975-79; prof. neurology, assoc. dean for rsch. devel. Bowman Gray Sch. Medicine, Wake Forest U., 1979-89, prof. neurology, sr. assoc. dean for rsch. devel., 1989-93; pres., prof. neurology Epilepsy Inst. N.C., 1993-96; hon. prof. U. Santo Domingo, Dominican Republic, 1987; dir. Comprehensive Epilepsy Ctr., N.C. Bapt. Hosp., Winston-Salem, 1989-93; cons. FDA, 1975-80, Nat. Inst. Neurol. and Communicative Disorders and Stroke, 1979-90, Burroughs Wellcome Co., 1979-90; lectr. in field. Author 30 books and monographs; co-author: (with J.R. Lacy) Infantile Spasms, 1976; (with M.E. Newmark) Photosensitivity and Epilepsy: A Review, 1979, Genetics of Epilepsy: A Review, 1980; editor: Epilepsy: The Eighth International Symposium, 1977; co-editor: (with others) Antiepileptic Drugs, 1972, 3d edit., 1989, Experimental Models of Epilepsy, 1972, Antiepileptic Drugs: Quantitative Analysis and Interpretation, 1978, Advances in Epileptology: (Xth-XIIth) Epilepsy International Symposium, 1980-82, Genetic Basis of the Epilepsies, 1982, Antiepileptic Drug Therapy in Pediatrics, 1983, Idiosyncratic Reactions to Valproate: Clinical Risk Patterns and Mechanism of Toxicity, 1992; editor Merritt-Putnam epilepsy clin. series, 1982-83; mem. editorial bd. Forefronts of Neurology, 1979-96, Metabolic Brain Disease, 1986-90; mem. internat. adv. bd. Advances in Neurology; contbr. numerous articles to profl. jours., book chpts. Decorated Meritorious Svc. medal; recipient Disting. Alumnus award Bowman Gray Sch. Medicine, 1975, 80, 90. Fellow Am. Acad. Neurology; mem. AMA, Am. Neurol. Assn., Am. Epilepsy Soc. (membership com. 1970-71, chmn. constn. com. 1971-72, coun. 1971-73, program com. 1973, nat. pres. 1974, mem. long range planning com. 1978-79, William G. Lennox award 1980, Category I Clin. Rsch. award 1993), Am. Neurol. Assn., Assn. for Rsch. in Nervous and Mental Disease, Am. Electroencephalographic Soc., Ea. Assn. Electroencephalographers, Epilepsy Found. Am. (hon. life, Disting. Svc. award 1975, 25 Yrs. Svc. award 1993, Pearce Bailey award 1979, bd. dirs. 1989-96), Phi Beta Kappa, Alpha Omega Alpha. Home: Thomasville N.C. Died Mar. 31, 1996.

PENUELAS, MARCELINO COMPANY, Spanish language educator; b. El Tovar, Cuenca, Spain, Apr. 20, 1916; came to U.S., 1948, naturalized, 1955; s. Eusebio and Angela (Company) P.; m. Anita Fanjul, Dec. 16, 1950; 1 dau., Anita. B.A., U. Valencia, Spain, 1939, M.A., 1945, M.Ed., 1940; Ph.D., U. Madrid, Spain, 1949. Asst. prof. Spanish lit. U. Denver, 1948-59, asso. prof., 1960-63; vis. prof. Stanford U., 1958-59; asso. prof. U. Wash., Seattle, 1963-67; prof. U. Wash., 1967-86, prof. emeritus, 1986—, chmn. dept. Romance langs. and lits., 1972-81; chmn. devel. com. advanced placement exam. Spanish lit. Coll. Entrance Exam. Bd., 1971-79, chmn., 1978. Author: Lo español en el Suroeste de Estados Unidos, 1965, Mito, literatura y realidad, 1965, Jacinto Benavente, 1968, Introducción a la literature española, 1969, Mr. Clark no toma Coca-Cola, 1960, 69, Conversaciones con Ramón J. Sender, 1970, La obra narrative de Ramón J. Sender, 1971, Cultura hispánica en Estatos Unidos: Los Chicanos, 1978; contbr. articles and short stories to profl. jours. and mags. Mem. MLA, Am. Assn. Tchrs. Spanish and Portuguese. Home: Seattle Wash. Deceased.

PEPPARD, GEORGE, actor; b. Detroit, Oct. 1, 1928. B.A. in Fine Arts, Carnegie Mellon Inst. Broadway appearances include The Girls of Summer, The Pleasure of His Company; appeared in films: The Strange One, Pork Chop Hill, Home From the Hill, The Subterraneans, Breakfast at Tiffany's, How the West Was Won, The Victors, the Carpetbaggers, Operation Crossbow, The Third Day, The Blue Max, Tobruk, Rough Night in Jericho, House of Cards, P.J., What's So Bad About Feeling Good?, Pendulum, The Executioner, Cannon for Cordoba, One More Train to Rob, The Groundstar Conspiracy, Newman's Law, Damnation Alley, Five Days from Home, Fall Down Dead, From Hell to Victory, Battle Beyond Stars, Your Ticket is No Longer Valid, Race to the Yankee Zephyr, Silence Like Glass, The Tigress; TV appearances include Suspicion, U.S. Steel Hour, Alfred Hitchcock Presents, Studio One, Alcoa-Goodyear Playhouse, Hallmark Hall of Fame, (TV films) The Bravos, Banacek, Crisis in Midair, Between Two Loves, Man Against the Mob, Man Against the Mob II, (pilot) Matlock "The PI"; star TV series Banacek, Doctors Hosp., The A Team; author screenplay; dir., prodr., star Five Days From Home, 1978. Home: Beverly Hills Calif. Died May 8, 1994.

PERGAM, ALBERT STEVEN, lawyer; b. N.Y.C., Dec. 23, 1938; s. Irving and Gertrude (Newman) P.; m. Natalie J. Chaliff, Aug. 14, 1965; children: Ilana N., Elizabeth A. B.A. summa cum laude, Yale U., 1960; postgrad., St. John's Coll., Cambridge, Eng., 1960-61; LL.B. magna cum laude, Harvard U., 1964. Bar: N.Y. 1965. Law clk. to judge U.S. Ct. Appeals (2d cir.), 1964-65; spl. asst., asst. atty. gen. civil rights div. U.S. Dept. Justice, Washington, 1965-66; assoc. firm Cleary, Gottlieb, Steen & Hamilton, N.Y.C., 1966-72; ptnr. Cleary, Gottlieb, Steen & Hamilton, 1973-93; resident ptnr. Cleary, Gottlieb, Steen & Hamilton, London, 1980-84. Contbg. author Eurobond Financing, Proc. of So. Meth. U. Inst. on Internat. Fin., 1988, Eurocommercial Paper, Kluwer Studies in Internat. Law, 1989, Internat. Opinions, in Sterba, M.J., Drafting Legal Opinion Letters, 2nd edit. 1992; editorial advisor and contbr. Internat. Fin. Law Rev. Bd. dirs. Yale Alumni Fund. Henry fellow, 1960-61; assoc. fellow Branford Coll., Yale U. Mem. ABA (sect. on bus. law, com. on legal opinions) , Internat. Bar Assn., N.Y. State Bar Assn. (chmn. internat. law and practice sect.), Assn. of Bar of City of N.Y., Elihu Club (New Haven), Elizabethan Club (New Haven), United Oxford and Cambridge Club (London), Phi Beta Kappa. Home: New York N.Y. Died Nov. 21, 1993.

PERKINS, CARROLL MASON, utility executive; b. Green Creek, Ohio, Mar. 11, 1929; s. James Montgomery and Marian (Lund) P.; m. Maxine Joan Corrington, June 24, 1952; children: Michael J., Sherrill L., Timothy C., Jeffrey S. BS, U. Calif.-Berkeley, 1950; MS, Ariz. State U., 1963, PhD, 1975. Agr. statistician USDA, 1951-56; rate analyst, supr. rates, mgr., power service dir., planning, asst. gen. mgr. fin. services, treas. Salt River Project, Phoenix, 1956-85; treas. Salt River Project, 1980-85, assoc. gen. mgr., fin. and info. services, chief fin. officer, 1985-91, gen. mgr., 1991-93; past mem. Mcpl. Securities Rulemaking Bd.; bd. dirs. WEST Assocs. Past bd. dirs. NWYMCA, Heritage Sq. Found.; past pres. Ariz. Lung Assn., Phoenix; mem. Coun. of 100, Ariz. State U. Coll. Bus., Greater Phoenix Leadership, from 1991, Greater Phoenix Econ. Coun.; bd. dirs. Ariz. Town Hall, United for Ariz., Valley of the Sun United Way, Fiscal Accountability and Reform Efforts Commn.; mem. Gov.'s Commn. on Econ. Devel. With USN, 1951-53. Mem. Fin. Execs. Inst., Ariz. Econ. Coun., U.S. Coun. for Energy Awareness, U.S. Energy Assn., Ariz. Reclamation Assn., Am. Public Power Assn. (chmn. rate com. 1971, treas. 1984-93), Navajo Nation Nat. Adv. Bd., Western Energy and Comm. Assn. (bd. dirs.), Ariz. Tax Rsch. Assn. (past bd. dirs.), Ariz. Electric League (bd. dirs. 1974-75), Ariz. Zool. Soc. (bd. dirs.), Phoenix C. of C., Phoenix Kiwanis (bd. dirs. 1979-80). Republican. Methodist. Home: Phoenix Ariz. Died Nov. 21, 1993.

PERKINS, MALCOLM DONALD, lawyer; b. Milton, Mass., Aug. 29, 1914; s. John Forbes and Mary (Coolidge) P.; m. Sheila Delano Redmond, Feb. 1, 1944; children: Malcolm Donald, Sara D., Samuel, William H. AB magna cum laude, Harvard U., 1936, LLB, 1939. Bar: N.Y. 1940, Mass. 1946. Assoc. firm Parker & Duryee, N.Y.C., 1939-41, Herrick & Smith, Boston, 1946-52; partner Herrick & Smith, 1952-85, of counsel, 1985-86; of counsel Condit & Assocs., 1986-95. Pres. bd. trustees Isabella Stewart Gardner Mus., Boston, 1976-91, Milton Acad., 1968-76, Greater Boston Legal Svcs., 1971-74. With USAAF, 1942-46. Mem. Am. Bar Assn., Am. Law Inst., Boston Bar Assn. Club: Tavern (Boston). Home: Milton Mass. Died Mar. 15, 1995.

PERLMAN, DANIEL HESSEL, academic administrator; b. Chgo., Sept. 24, 1935; s. Henry B. and Dorothy (Zimmerman) P.; m. Suzanne Meyer, June 30, 1966; children: Julia, David. B.A., Shimer Coll., 1954, U. Chgo., 1955; M.A., U. Chgo., 1956, Ph.D., 1971. Psychol. counselor Roosevelt U., Chgo., 1961-64, asst. to pres., 1965-70, dir. govt. relations and planning, 1970-72, sec. bd. trustees, 1965-80, prof. edn., 1974-80, dean adminstrn., 1972-80, v.p. adminstrn., 1980; pres. Suffolk U., Boston, 1980-89, Webster U., St. Louis, 1990-94; vis. scholar Harvard U. Grad. Sch. Edn., 1989-90; spl. asst. to dep. commr. higher and continuing edn. HEW, 1977-78; mem. exec. com. Assn. Ind. Colls. and Univs. Mass., 1984-89; mem. commn. on new initiatives Nat. Assn. Ind. Colls. and Univs., 1986-89, commn. on policy analysis, 1993-94. Contbr. articles to profl. jours. Bd. dirs., mem. exec. com. WGBH Ednl. Found., 1982-89; bd. dirs. The Repertory Theatre of St. Louis, Opera Theatre of St. Louis, Dance St. Louis, St. Louis Arts and Edn. Coun., Sta. KETC Pub. TV, St. Louis chpt. NCCJ, United Way St. Louis, NCAA Pres.'s Commn., Beacon Hill Civic Assn., 1980-87; chmn. Higher Edn. Ctr., St. Louis, 1993-94; chmn. good neighbor awards com. NCCJ, Boston, 1980-89; chmn. Boston Higher Edn. Partnership, 1988-89; mem. alumni coun. Inst. Ednl. Mgmt., Harvard U.; mem. internat. adv. com. Interfuture, 1980-89; trustee Boston Plan for Excellence in Pub. Sch., 1988-89; v.p. Greater Boston C. of C., 1988-89. Recipient Disting. Alumnus award Shimer Coll., 1973; sr. Fulbright-hays lectr. Philippines, 1975; fellow Am. Council Edn., 1972-73; Presdl. exchange exec., 1977-78. Mem. Am. Assn. Higher Edn., Am. Assn. U. Adminstrs., Soc. Coll. and Univ. Planning, Soc. Values in Higher Edn., Am. Coun. on Edn. (chmn. exec. com. of coun. of fellows 1984-85, mem. commn. leadership devel. 1981-84, labor/higher edn. coun. 1986-89, commn. for internat. edn. 1993-95), Assn. Urban Univs. (bd. dirs. 1982-89, 91-92), St. Louis Club, Noonday Club. Home: Saint Louis Mo. Deceased.

PERPICH, RUDY GEORGE, governor of Minnesota; b. Carson Lake, Minn., June 27, 1928; s. Anton and Mary (Vukelich) P.; m. Delores Helen Simic, Sept. 4, 1954; children: Rudy George, Mary Susan. A.A., Hibbing Jr. Coll., 1950; D.D.S., Marquette U., 1954. Lt. gov. State of Minn., 1971-76, gov., 1977-79, 83—; v.p., exec. cons. Control Data Worldtech, Inc., Mpls., 1979-82. Mem. Hibbing Bd. Edn., Minn., 1956-62; mem. Minn. Senate, 1962-70. Served to sgt. AUS, 1946-47. Mem. Nat. Govs. Assn. Democrat. Roman Catholic. Home: Saint Paul Minn. Died September 21, 1995.

PERRINE, BEAHL THEODORE, retired lawyer; b. Monticello, Iowa, July 4, 1902; s. John H. and Minnie (Ryan) P.; m. Irene L. Hall, Oct. 27, 1934. Student, U. Mich., 1922-27, J.D., 1927; hon. degree, Mt. Mercy Coll., 1979. Bar: Iowa 1927. Practiced in Cedar Rapids; mem. firm Simmons, Perrine, Albright and Ellwood, from 1943, formerly of counsel; asst. atty. Linn County, 1942-44; former pres. and chmn. bd. Iowa Mfg. Co.; past sec., dir. Amana Refrigeration, Inc.; Regional war Bond dir. Treasury Dept., World War II. Trustee Herbert Hoover Presdl. Library Assn., Mercy Hosp., Cedar Rapids; bd. dirs. Mercy Hosp. Endowment Found.; bd. dirs., chmn. bd. Hall Found.; trustee YMCA, past pres. bd.; former bd. dirs. Episcopal Corp.

Diocese of Iowa. Mem. ABA, Iowa Bar Assn., Linn County Bar Assn. (pres. 1936), Am. Judicature Soc., Cedar Rapids C. of C., Alpha Kappa Lambda, Delta Theta Phi. Clubs: Pickwick, Cedar Rapids Country. Home: Cedar Rapids Iowa Deceased.

PERRY, MARVIN BANKS, JR., retired college president; b. Powhatan, Va., Sept. 29, 1918; s. Marvin Banks and Elizabeth (Gray) P.; m. Ellen Coalter Gilliam, Apr. 6, 1950; children: Elizabeth Gray, Margaret McCluer. A.B., U. Va., 1940; A.M., Harvard U., 1941, Ph.D., 1950; LL.D., Washington Coll., 1967, Washington and Lee U., 1977; D.Litt., Oglethorpe U., 1978. Grad. asst. Harvard, 1946-47; instr. English U. Va., 1947-51, prof. English, dean admissions, 1960-67; asst. prof. English Washington and Lee U., 1951-53, asso. prof., 1953-56, prof., chmn. dept., 1956-60; pres. Goucher Coll., Towson, Md., 1967-73, Agnes Scott Coll., Decatur, Ga., 1973-82; mem. Polish Seminar (Dept. State), U. Krakow, Poland, 1966. Author, editor: Modern Minds, 1949, Nine Short Novels, 1952; Contbr. articles profl. jours. Past trustee Mary Baldwin Coll., Gilman Sch., Bryn Mawr Sch., Md. Acad. Sci., Balt. Symphony Orch.; past trustee Atlanta Arts Alliance, Lovett Sch.; bd. dirs. Sweet Briar Coll. 1982-91; trustee Va. Piedmont Community Coll. Found., 1983-94, Va. Found. for Humanities, 1983-90. Served to lt. USNR, 1942-46; comdr. Res. Mem. MLA, Coll. English Assn. (past dir., past pres. N.C.-Va.), Keats-Shelley Assn. Am., Raven Soc., Phi Beta Kappa, Omicron Delta Kappa, Phi Gamma Delta. Presbyterian (elder). Clubs: Greencroft (Charlottesville); Colonnade (U. Va.); Army and Navy (Washington). Home: Charlottesville N.C. Died Dec. 12, 1994.

PERSKY, JOSEPH H., lawyer; b. Cleve., Dec. 7, 1914; s. Abraham E. and Sylvia (Meisel) P.; A.B. magna cum laude, Case-Western Res. U., 1936, LL.B., 1938; m. Roselyn Diamondstone, Sept. 8, 1940. Admitted to Ohio bar, 1938; mng. assoc. firm Persky, Konigsberg and Shapiro Co., L.P.A., Cleve., 1938—; pres. A.J. Armstrong Co., Inc. of Ohio, Cleve., 1960-82; v.p., sec., dir. Magnetics Internat., Inc., 1969-86; sec., dir. Horizons Research, Inc.; sec., dir. Clark Consol. Industries, Inc., Kidron Body Co. Pres., Cleve. Coll. Jewish Studies, Fairmount Temple; trustee Jewish Community Fedn. Served to lt. USCGR, 1942-45. Mem. Am. Bar Assn., Ohio State Bar Assn., Bar Assn. Greater Cleve., Order of Coif, Phi Beta Kappa. Republican. Jewish. Clubs: Beechmont Country, Commerce, Masons. Home: Cleveland Ohio

PESSEN, EDWARD, historian, author, educator, lecturer; b. N.Y.C., Dec. 31, 1920; s. Abraham and Anna (Flashberg) P.; m. Adele Barlin, Nov. 25, 1940; children: Beth, Abigail, Dinah, Jonathan, Andrew. B.A., Columbia U., 1947, M.A., 1948, Ph.D., 1954. History lectr. CCNY, 1948-54; prof. history Baruch Coll. and Grad. Ctr. CUNY, 1970-72, Disting. prof. history, 1972-92; assoc. prof. history Fisk U., Nashville, 1954-56; prof. history S.I. Community Coll., 1956-70; Edna Gene and Jordan Davidson prof. in the humanities Fla. Internat. U., Miami, 1992; vis. Seagram prof. history U. Toronto, 1979; Fulbright lectr. in Am. history USSR, 1985; vis. prof. history Bochum, Wurzberg, Frankfurt, Munich and Hamburg univs. in Fed. Republic Germany, 1981, U. Lund and Umea, Sweden, 1982. Author: Most Uncommon Jacksonians, 1967, Jacksonian America, 1969, rev. edit., 1978, Riches, Class and Power Before the Civil War, 1973, The Log Cabin Myth: The Social Backgrounds of the Presidents, 1984, Russian edit., 1987, Riches, Class and Power, 1989; author and editor: New Perspectives on Jacksonian Parties and Politics, 1969, Three Centuries of Social Mobility in America, 1974, Jacksonian Panorama, 1976, The Many-Faceted Jacksonian Era, 1977; contbr., co-author more than 75 additional books; mem. editorial bd. N.Y. History, Labor History, Jour. Early Republic; contbr. numerous articles to profl. jours., chpts. to books, Ency. Britannica. Mem. Soc. of Am. Historians. Served with inf. U.S. Army, 1944-45. Decorated Purple Heart, Bronze Star; named Prof. of Yr., Baruch Coll., 1983, 84, 85; SUNY Research Found. grantee, 1968; Guggenheim fellow, 1977; Rockefeller Found fellow, 1978; CUNY Research Found. fellow, 1979. Mem. Am. Hist. Assn., Orgn. Am. Historians, Soc. Historians of Early Am. Republic (adv. bd., pres. 1985-86), Am. Antiquarian Soc., So. Hist. Assn. Home: Brooklyn N.Y. Died Dec. 22, 1992.

PETERS, JOHN EDWARD, advertising agency executive; b. Highland Park, Ill., Aug. 5, 1931; s. John Alexander and Mary Agnes P.; m. Katrina Van Tassel, June 29, 1957; children: Kim, Dirk, Todd, Sara. B.S., Miami U., Oxford, Ohio, 1956; grad., Advanced Mgmt. Program, Harvard U., 1977. With J. Walter Thompson U.S.A., 1956-87; sr. v.p. J. Walter Thompson U.S.A., London, 1972-75; exec. v.p., account dir. J. Walter Thompson U.S.A., N.Y.C., 1975-79; vice chmn. bd. J. Walter Thompson U.S.A., 1980-84, pres., chief operating officer, 1984-87; pres., chief operating officer J. Walter Thompson Co. Worldwide, 1986-87, also dir.; bd. dirs. J. Water Thompson Co.; cons. WPP Group. Mem. bus. adv. council Miami U. Served with AUS, 1952-54. Home: Greenwich Conn. Died. Aug. 5, 1993.

PETERS, ROBERT LEE, architect; b. Brownsville, Tex., Nov. 23, 1920; s. R. Lee and Mary E. (Saunders) P.; m. Helen Frances Smith; children (by previous marriage): Lynn Ellen, Lee Edward, Steven Robert. B.Arch., U. Tex., 1951. Pvt. practice architecture Odessa, Tex., 1953-55; ptnr. Peters & Fields, Odessa and Austin, Tex., 1955-78; pvt. practice Austin, 1979-89; ret., 1990; mem. Odessa City Bldg. Commn., 1958-65, City Tax Equalization Bd., 1963-66; vice chmn. Bldg. Bd. Appeals, 1964-72; mem. adv. council Tex. Dept. Community Affairs, 1972-73. Important works include John Ireland Elementary Sch, Odessa, U. Tex. Land Office Bldg, Ballinger First Nat. Bank, Odessa Family YMCA, Ft. Leaton Restoration, Lake Somerville State Park, Criss Cole Rehab. Center for Blind, Austin, U. Tex. Permian Basin Gymnasium. Precinct chmn. Democratic Party, 1956-58; pres., bd. dirs. Odessa Symphony Assn., Permian Council for Mentally Retarded; bd. dirs. Tex. Fine Arts Soc., Permian Basin Rehab. Center, Austin Symphony Orch. Soc., Umlauf Sculpture Garden. Served with USAAF, 1942-46, PTO. Decorated Air medal; recipient numerous archtl. awards; named Boss of Year Jr. C. of C., 1960. Mem. AIA (past pres., dir. W.Tex. chpt.), Tex. Soc. Architects (past v.p., dir.), Constrn. Specifications Inst. (dir., pres.), Odessa C. of C. (past dir.). Presbyterian. Clubs: Odessa Country, Country of Austin. Lodge: Lions. Home: Austin Tex. Died April 19, 1993.

PETERSMEYER, C(HARLES) WREDE, retired broadcasting executive, venture capitalist; b. L.A., Jan. 28, 1919; s. Harry Frederick and Florence (Quayle) P.; m. Frances Carolyn Gregg, Apr. 12, 1944; children: Susan Calhoun Petersmeyer Henneke, Charles Gregg, Nancy Quayle Petersmeyer Damm. A.B. with honors, U. Calif., 1941; M.B.A. with high distinction, Harvard, 1943. Assoc. McKinsey & Co., 1946-47; asso. J. H. Whitney & Co., 1947-51, partner, 1951-77; founder, chmn. until 1977 of Corinthian Broadcasting Corp., N.Y.; owner sta. KOTV, Tulsa, sta. KHOU-TV, Houston, sta. KXTV, Sacramento, stas.WANE-TV, WANE-AM, Fort Wayne, stas. WISH-TV, WISH-AM, Indpls., TVS Television Network, Funk and Wagnalls, Inc.; past trustee Greenwich Savs. Bank; past dir. Dun & Bradstreet, Carte Blanche, Reuben H. Donnelly Corp. Past trustee Sarah Lawrence Coll., Pine Manor Coll., chmn. bd., 1975-78; chmn. bd. dirs. and overseers Sweet Briar Coll.; bd. dirs. Mid Atlantic Legal Found.; advisor Sprout Funds; chmn. Harvard Bus. Sch. Fund, 1976-78; adv. dir. Met. Opera Assn. Served from pvt. to capt. AUS, 1943-46. Mem. Nat. Assn. Broadcasters (past dir.), Assn. Maximum Service Telecasters (past dir.), Com. Econ. Devel. (hon. trustee), Phi Beta Kappa Assos. (past dir.), Phi Beta Kappa, Delta Kappa Epsilon. Clubs: University, Harvard Bus. Sch. (N.Y.C.); John's Island (Fla.); Augusta (Ga.), Nat. Golf. Home: Vero Beach Fla. Died Apr. 18, 1996.

PETERSON, CARL RUDOLF, lawyer; b. Newark, Apr. 8, 1907; s. Carl Emil Rudolf and Elin (Lindholm) P.; m. Dorothy McNicholas, July 7, 1934; 1 child, Elsa. A.B., Princeton U., 1928; LL.B., Columbia U., 1931. Bar: N.Y. 1932, D.C. 1942. Research asst. Columbia Law Sch., 1931-33; asso. firm Hawkins, Delafield & Longfellow, N.Y.C., 1933-37; with Office Chief Counsel, Bur. Internal Revenue, 1937-42, asst. head legis. and regulation div., 1941-42; ptnr. Alvord & Alvord, Washington, 1942-50, Lee, Toomey & Kent, Washington, 1950-95; lectr. tax and law insts.; condr. occasional seminars Harvard Law Sch., 1950-54; tech. adviser nat. tax com. Fin. Execs. Inst., 1950-95. Contbr. to legal publs. Mem. Am., N.Y. State, D.C. bar assns., Am. Law Inst. Internat. Acad. Law and Sci., Phi Beta Kappa. Clubs: Chevy Chase (Md.); Princeton (Washington), Met. (Washington). Home: Washington D.C. Died June 8, 1995.

PETERSON, GLADE, tenor, opera company director; b. Fairview, Utah, Dec. 17, 1928; s. Golden and Mabel (Mower) P.; m. Mardean Rippon, Dec. 8, 1955; children: Leslie, Kelvin, Michelle. Student U. Utah, 1953; Litt.D. (hon.), So. Utah State Coll., 1978; student Ingenuus Bentzar, Carlos Alexander, Enrico Rosati, Ettore Verna. Debut: Pinkerton in Butterfly, NBC Opera, 1957; debut with Zurich Opera House: Chevalier des Grieux in Manon Lescaut, 1960; deput with Met. Opera, N.Y.C.: Loge in Das Rheingold, 1975; resident mem. Opernhaus Zurich, 1960-75; guest appearances with opera cos. including: Salzburg Fest and Vienna Staatsoper, Austria, Berlin Deutsche Opera, Munich Staatsoper, Stuttgart, W.Ger., La Scala, Milan, Spoleto Fest, Italy, also companies in Belgium, Can., France, Holland, Switzerland; U.S. cos.: Balt., Boston, Dallas, Houston, Phila., Pitts., Portland, San Diego, San Francisco, Santa Fe. Roles include: Don Jose in Carmen, Riccardo in Anna Bolena, Edgardo in Lucia, Faust, Canio in Pagliacci, Turiddu in Cavalleria Rusticana, Ferrando in Cosi fan Tutte, Don Otavio in Don Giovanni, Tamino in Zauberflöte, Prince in Love for Three Oranges, Rodolfo in Boheme, Cavaradossi in Tosca, Riccardo in Ballo in Maschera, Don Carlo, Ernani, Don Alvaro in Forza del Destino, Alfredo in Traviata, Walther in Meistersinger, Loge in Rheingold; also recitalist, guest with symphony orchs.; gen. dir. Utah Opera Co., Salt Lake City, 1976-90; tchr., coach music and drama. Served with M.P., U.S. Army, 1951-53. Scholar, Mannes Sch. Music, 1957; Martha Baird Rockefeller Aid to Musicians scholar for study in Italy, 1960. Mem. Am. Guild Musical Artists. Mormon. Died Apr. 21, 1990. Home: Salt Lake City Utah

PETERSON, J. DWIGHT, investment company executive; b. Decatur, Ind., May 25, 1897; s. John Samuel and Olive (Hale) P.; m. Mary Irene Frisinger, July 19, 1921; children: Patricia (Mrs. Donald C. Danielson), Sally (Mrs. Robert A. Ravensberg), John. A.B., Ind. U., 1919, LL.D. Bond salesman City Trust Co., Indpls., 1919-24; bond salesman City Securities Corp., Indpls., 1924-28; asst. mgr. City Securities Corp., 1928-30, v.p., 1930-34, pres., 1934-63, chmn. bd., 1963-70, 71-79, hon chmn. bd., from 1979; dir. Central Newspapers, Inc. Bd. govs. James Whitcomb Riley Hosp. Found. Served as 2d lt. F.A. U.S. Army, World War I. Mem. SAR Am. Legion, Sigma Chi (past grand consul), Beta Gamma Sigma, Sigma Delta Chi. Republican. Presbyn (elder). Clubs: Columbia, Service, Contemporary, Highland Golf and Country (Indpls.). Lodges: Masons, Rotary. Home: Indianapolis Ind. Deceased.

PETERSON, RONALD LEE, retired educational administrator; b. Balt., Apr. 24, 1931; s. Harold David and Lillian Marie (Sullens) P.; m. Patricia Robbins, Aug. 20 1955; children: M. Douglas, D. Jeffrey, D. Scott. BS in Edn., Towson State U., 1954; MEd, Loyola Coll., 1967. Cert. advanced profl., Md. Tchr. Baltimore County Pub. Schs., Towson, Md., 1954-56; tchr. Balt. City Pub Schs., 1956-64, dept. head, 1964-67, asst. prin., 1967-72 adminstrv. asst., 1972-80, dir. facilities, 1980-89; ret. 1989; pres. Towson State U. Alumni Assn., 1989-95. Treas. polit. campaign, 1978-86. Mem. Towson State U Alumni Assn. (pres. 1989-95), Phi Delta Kappa (pres U. Md. chpt. 1974-75, area coord. 1982-88), Assn. o Sch. Bus. Officials (sect. dir., bd. dirs.). Democrat. Home: Baltimore Md. Died Feb. 21, 1995.

PETRIE, MILTON J., retail company executive; b 1902. With JL Hudson Co., 1923-27; sales mgr. Bernard and Schwartz Cigar Co.; with Red Robin Hosiery Shops, 1927; chmn., pres., chief exec. officer Petrie Stores Corp., Seacuacus, N.J., 1932-94. Died Nov. 6 1994.

PETRIE, ROY H., obstetrician, gynecologist, educator b. Bardwell, Ky., Nov. 9, 1940; s. Randolph Hazel and Glodine (Brown) P. BS, Western Ky. U., 1961; MD Vanderbilt U., 1965; SCD, Columbia U., 1984. Diplomate Am. Bd. Ob-gyn and div. Maternal/Fetal Medicine. Intern U. Rochester, 1965-66; resident Columbia-Presbyn. Med. Ctr., N.Y.C., 1966-70; fellow in perinatal biology U. S.C. Med. Ctr., Los Angeles 1972-73; research assoc. Columbia U., N.Y.C., 1972-73 asst. prof. ob-gyn Coll. Physicians and Surgeon Columbia U., N.Y.C., 1973-79, assoc. prof. ob-gyn dept. dir. med. edn., 1979-84; prof. ob-gyn, dir maternal/fetal medicine Washington U., St. Louis, 1984-92; prof., chmn. dept. ob-gyn. St. Louis U., 1992-96. Author 7 books in field; contbr. over 100 articles o pharmacology and ob-gyn to profl. jours. Served to lt comdr., USNR, 1970-72. Recipient Purdue-Frederic award Am. Coll. of ob-gyn, 1974; named Outstanding Educator Sloane Hosp. for Women, 1979. Mem. Soc for Gynecol. Investigation, Soc. Perinatal Obstetrician (pres. 1984-85, v.p. 1985, sec.-treas. 1981-83), N.Y. Obstetrical Soc., N.Y. Acad. Medicine (pres. ob. sect 1980), N.Y. Perinatal Soc., St. Louis Ob-gyn Soc. Episcopalian. Home: Saint Louis Mo. Died May, 1996.

PETRIK, EUGENE VINCENT, college president; b Little Ferry, N.J., May 25, 1932; s. Ferdinand Vincent and Anna Agnes (Komarek) P.; m. Helen Veliky, Jun 26, 1955; children: John, Mark, Thomas, James. B.S Fairleigh Dickinson U., 1955; M.A., Columbia U., 1957 Ed.D., 1959; postdoctoral student, Stevens Inst. Tech 1961-62. Instr. physics Fairleigh Dickinson U., 1957-59 asst. prof. gen. sci. N.Y. U., N.Y.C., 1959-60; asso. prof Seton Hall U., 1960-65, prof., 1965-68; v.p. Mt. St Mary's Coll., Los Angeles, 1968-73; pres. Bellarmin Coll., Louisville, 1973-91; dir. Commonwealth Life Ins Co., 1981-91, The Cumberland, 1978-91. Author Modern High School Physics, 1959, Inductive Calculus 1967. Mem. adv. council TRY Found., Los Angeles 1971-73; bd. dirs. Louisville-Met. United Way, 1978-87 pres. 1983-85; bd. dirs. Kentuckiana Metroversity, 1973-91, chmn., 1980-82; bd. dirs. Chaminade Prep. Sch., Lo Angeles, 1971-73, Bright Future Child Devel. Ctr Compton, Calif., 1971-73, Louisville Cen. Area, Inc 1976-79, 80-83, Meth. Evang. Hosp., 1984-88, chmn 88-89, Collegiate Sch., 1985-87, Campaign for Greate Louisville, 1988-91; bd. leadership Louisville Found 1979-84, Am. Heart Assn., 1981-82; chmn. Spirit (Louisville Found., 1981; adv. bd. Old. Ky. Hom council Boy Scouts Am., 1979-81. Sci. Manpowe fellow Columbia, 1957, 59; Am. Council Edn. fello acad. adminstrn. internship program, 1966-67. Men Council Ind. Ky. Colls. and Univs. (dir. 1973-91), Ky Ind. Coll. Fund (dir. 1973-91). Club: Rotary (bd. dir Louisville 1979-81, 85-86, pres. 1984-85). Hom Palmyra Ind. Died April 2, 1991; buried Louisvill Calvary Cemetary.

PETRUS, EUGENE FRANCIS, advertising executiv educator; b. Cleve., June 17, 1947; s. Alex Eugene an Margaret (Kazsmere) P.; m. Barbara Jeanne Shabr Aug. 6, 1969 (div. 1979); children: Johathan Scott, Jul Marie, Alexandria Frances; m. Pamela E. Englehaup July 26, 1980. BA, Kent State U., 1969, PhD, 198 MA, U. Okla., 1980. Prof. in sociology Mount Unio Coll., Alliance, Ohio, 1974-78, John Carroll U., Clev land Heights, Ohio, 1978-79, Kent (Ohio) State U

1980-91; pres. Diversa Advt./Mktg., Inc., Kent, 1980-91. Contbr. articles to profl. jours. Bd. dirs. Kent Festival of Trees, 1989. Capt. USAF, 1969-74. Mem. Am. Mktg. Assn., Akron Advt. Club, Aircraft Owners and Pilots Assn., Am. Advt. Fedn., Kent Area C. of C. (pres. Kent area 1989), Rotary. Roman Catholic. Home: Mogadore Ohio Died May 18, 1991.

PETTIT, WILLIAM THOMAS, broadcasting journalist; b. Cin., Apr. 23, 1931; s. William Porter and Kathryn (Neely) P.; m. Patricia M. Barry, Sept. 10, 1989; children by previous marriage: Debra Lynn, Anne Eileen, William James, Robert Thomas. B.A., Iowa State Tchrs. Coll., 1953; M.A., U. Minn., 1958. Reporter WOI-TV, Ames, Iowa, 1953-55, KCRG-TV, Cedar Rapids, Iowa, 1955-56, WCCO-TV, Mpls., 1956-59; reporter NBC News, Phila., 1959-61, N.Y.C., 1961-62, Los Angeles, 1962-67; reporter Pub. Broadcast Lab., 1967-68; reporter NBC News, Los Angeles, 1968-75; reporter NBC News, Washington, 1975-82, exec. v.p., 1982-85; chief nat. affairs, corr. NBC News, 1985-89, corr., London, 1989—, corr. Washington, 1992—. Recipient Emmy award, 1969, 70, 74, Peabody award, 1970, DuPont-Columbia award, 1970, Robert F. Kennedy Journalism award, 1970, 76, Med. Journalism award AMA, 1971, Journalism award Ohio State U., 1990. Mem. AFTRA. Home: Washington D.C. Died December 22, 1995.

PFAFFMANN, CARL, psychology educator; b. Bklyn., May 27, 1913; s. Charles and Anna (Haaker) P.; m. Hortense Louise Brooks, Dec. 26, 1939; children: Ellen Anne, Charles Brooks (dec.), William Sage. Ph.B., Brown U., 1933, M.A., 1935; B.A., Oxford U., Eng., 1937; Ph.D. (Rhodes scholar), Cambridge U., Eng., 1939; D.Sc., Brown U., 1965, Bucknell U., 1966, Yale U., 1972. Research assoc. Johnson Found., U. Pa., 1939-40; instr. psychology Brown U., Providence, 1940-42, asst. prof., 1945-48, assoc. prof., 1949-51, prof., 1951-65; Florence Pirce Grant U. prof. Brown U., 1960; vis. prof. Yale U., New Haven, 1958-59, Harvard U., Cambridge, Mass., 1962-63; nat. Sigma Xi lectr, 1963; v.p. Rockefeller U., N.Y.C., 1965-78, prof., 1965-80, Vincent and Brooke Astor prof., 1980-83; prof. emeritus Rockefeller U., 1983-94; chmn. div. behavioral scis. NRC, 1962-64; chmn. 17th Internat. Congress Psychology, 1963; mem. exec. com. Internat. Union Psychol. Scis., 1966-72; chmn. sect. exptl. psychology and animal behavior Internat. Union Biol. Scis., 1969-76; chmn. com. olfaction and taste Internat. Union Physiol. Scis., 1971-77. Bd. fellows Brown U., 1968-82. Served to comdr. USNR, 1942-45. Recipient Kenneth Craik rsch. award St. John's Coll., Cambridge U., 1968, commemorative medallion NAS-Acad. Scis. USSR, 1989; Guggenheim fellow, 1960-61. Fellow Am. Psychol. Assn. (pres. div. exptl. psychology 1956-57, Disting. Sci. Contbn. award 1963, William James fellow 1989), Am. Psychol. Soc., U.S.-USSR Acads. Sci. (Cooperation medallion), Am. Acad. Arts and Scis.; mem. NAS, Am. Philos. Soc., Soc. Exptl. Psychologists (Howard Crosby Warren medal for rsch. psychology 1960), Am. Physiol. Soc., Ea. Psychol. Assn. (pres. 1958-59). Home: Killingworth Conn. Died Apr. 16, 1994.

PHILIPPS, JOSEPH TIMOTHY, legal educator, lawyer; b. Wheeling, W.Va., Mar. 20, 1940; s. Edwin Emil and Margaret Adelaide (Nesline) P.; m. Sandra Lee Emerson, May 29, 1965; children: Cecelia Marie, Melissa Anne. B.S. in Acctg., Wheeling Coll., 1962; J.D., Georgetown U., 1965; LL.M., Harvard U., 1966. Bar: D.C. 1966, U.S. Dist. Ct. D.C. 1966, U.S. Ct. Appeals (D.C. cir.) 1966, Va. 1983. Prof. law, W.Va. U. Coll. Law, Morgantown, 1966-76; vis. prof. law, Duke U., Durham, N.C., 1976; prof. Loyola Law Sch., Los Angeles, 1977-80, Washington and Lee U., Lexington, Va., 1980-94; prof. in residence Steptoe & Johnson, Washington, 1987; bd. dirs. W.Va. Tax Inst., 1969-76, No. W.Va. Legal Aid Soc., 1974-76; project dir. study W.Va. tax appeals procedures, ABA Ctr. Adminstrv. Justice, 1974; atty.-advisor implementation Postal Reorgn. Act U.S. Postal Service, 1971, 73, 75; spl. asst. atty. gen. W.Va. higher edn. statutes project State of W.Va., 1970; lectr. in field. Ford Found. fellow, Harvard U., 1965; named Outstanding Prof. Coll. Law, W.Va. U. Student Bar Assn., 1969. Mem. ABA (sect. taxation). Democrat. Roman Catholic. Club: Lexington Country. Contbr. articles to law revs. Died Nov. 1994. Home: Lexington Va.

PHILLIPS, ASA EMORY, JR., lawyer; b. Washington, Dec. 7, 1911; s. Asa Emory and Virginia N. (Boyd) P.; m. Anne Wight, 1956; children: Asa Emory III, Anne Crocker (Mrs. Henry McFarlan Ogilby). AB cum laude, Harvard Coll., 1934; JD, Harvard U., 1938. Bar: Mass. 1939, D.C. 1938, Maine 1953, U.S. Supreme Ct. 1944. Sr. partner firm Asa E. Phillips, Jr., Boston, 1952-95; dep. head atty. Compliance div. War Prodn. Bd., Washington, 1942-44; asst. to sec. state and vice pres. U.S., 1945-47. Vice chmn. lawyers div. Greater Boston Community Fund, 1948-50; dist. dir. Federal St. dist., 1947; chmn. Heart Fund for Brookline, 1958-60; chmn. adv. com. Gov. of Commonwealth U.S.S. Mass. Relics, 1965; chmn. com. of mgmt. YMCA, Charlestown, Mass., 1969-71; sec.-treas. Friends of Chamber Music, Inc., 1954-64; chmn. Gov.'s Prayer Breakfast, 1978; mem. council Freedom Trail Found., 1977-95; mem. advisory bd. Salvation Army Greater Boston, 1977-95; bd. dirs. Youth Found., Inc., N.Y.C.; founder, pres. bd. trustees Thomas W. Sidwell Meml. Scholarship, Mrs. Asa E. Phillips Meml. Fund; founder, chmn. bd. trustees Charles Francis Adams Meml. Trophy; trustee Mass. Trustees of Internat. Com. of YMCA for Army and Navy Work, Inc.; corporator Brookline Savs. Bank; mem. overseers com. to visit mil. depts. Harvard U., 1960-66. Served as ensign USN, World War II. Decorated knight Order St. Lazarus; recipient Meritorious Pub. Service citation Sec. Navy, 1960. Mem. ABA (moderator weekly radio broadcasts), Boston Bar Assn., Friends Sch. Alumni Assn. (past pres.), Greater Boston C. of C., Navy League of U.S. (nat. v.p. 1962-68, pres. 1958-77, 1st v.p. Boston council 1977-95, nat. chmn. Navy Day 1965-68, mem. nat. exec. com. 1962-68), Soc. Colonial Wars (treas. 1957-60, gov. Mass. 1963-65, nat. gov. gen. 1969-72), Order Founders and Patriots Am. (gov. Mass. Soc. 1964-95, gov. gen. Gen. Ct. 1972-78), Soc. of Lees of Va. (past nat. v.p.), Huguenot Soc. Mass. (pres. 1966-68, counselor 1985-95), Mass. Com. of Patriotic Socs. (founder, chmn. 1962-95), Soc. of Cin., Roger Williams Family Assn., Soc. Descs. of Colonial Clergy, Order of Lafayette (nat. dir. 1966-95, pres. gen. 1974-95), U.S. Flag Found., Inc. (counselor), SAR (pres. Mass. Soc. 1975-77, Patriot medal 1977, chmn. Ann. Congress 1975, trustee 1977-83, chmn. state pres.' caucus Nat. Soc. 1976-78, nat. trustee 1977-79, historian gen. 1978-80, v.p. gen. 1980-82, Minuteman medal 1981, parliamentarian 1983-95), S.R. (pres. Mass. 1974-95, regional gen. v.p. 1977-78), New Eng. Historic Geneal. Soc., Sovereign Mil. Order, Nat. Smoke, Fire and Burn Inst., Inc. (co-founder, pres. 1973-95), Charitable Irish Soc. (pres. 1985-86, dir. 1986-95), Friends of Ft. Washington, Inc. (sec., treas. 1985-95). Clubs: Country (Brookline); Union, Eastern Yacht, Harvard (Boston); Essex Inst. (Salem); St. Nicholas Soc., Colonial Order of Acorn, N.Y. Yacht, Met., Chevy Chase (Washington); Bar Harbor, Bar Harbor Yacht; Seal Harbor Yacht, Harbor (Seal Harbor); Ends of the Earth. Lodge: Rotary (dir. Boston club 1975-82, pres. 1979-80). Home: Brookline Mass. Died Sept. 24, 1995.

PHILLIPS, JOHN CHARLES, oil company executive, lawyer; b. Metcalfe, Ont., Can., 1921. Student, U. Toronto (Ont.), 1940, Osgoode Hall Law Sch., 1949. Bar: Called to Ont. bar 1949. With Gulf Can. Ltd., Toronto, 1956-85; asst. gen. counsel Gulf Can. Ltd., 1960-64, gen. counsel, 1964-71, v.p., sec., gen. counsel, 1971-76, sr. v.p., 1976-77, exec. v.p., 1977-79, chmn., 1979-85, also dir.; dir. Bank of Nova Scotia, Can. Life Assurance Co. Home: Toronto Can. Deceased.

PHIPPS, GERALD HUGHES, general contractor; b. Denver, Mar. 4, 1915; s. Lawrence and Margaret (Rogers) P.; m. Janet Alice Smith, Sept. 24, 1937 (dec. Sept. 8, 1988); children: Sandra, Karen, Marta; m. Muriel Stokes Magarrell, Apr. 21, 1989. AB, Williams Coll., 1936. Clk., Denver Rio Grande Western R.R. Co., Denver, 1936-37, sec., 1937-39, traffic rep., 1939-42; v.p., treas. Platt Rogers, Inc., Denver, 1946-52; pres. Gerald H. Phipps, Inc., Denver, 1952-84, chmn., 1984-93; v.p., treas. Calif. Electric Power Co., Denver, 1958-63; dir. First Interstate Bank Denver (formerly First Nat. Bank Denver, Intrawest Bank Denver), 1963-85, So. Calif. Edison Co., Rosemead, 1964-85, D&R.G.W. R.R. Co., 1966-84, Rio Grande Industries, 1968-84. Chmn. United Cerebral Palsy Assn. Denver, 1954-55; trustee Colo. Coll., 1966-90, ret.; trustee St. Mary's Acad.; dirs., pres. Colo. Safety Assn., Denver, 1974-75. Served to lt. USN, 1942-46. Mem. Assoc. Gen. Contractors (pres. Colo. Bldg. chpt. 1952-53), Denver C. of C. (bd. dirs. 1974-76, 81-83), Denver Country Club (pres. 1952). Republican. Episcopalian. Died Aug. 6, 1993. Home: Denver Colo.

PHIPPS, MICHAEL CHARLES, library administrator; b. Boone, Iowa, July 6, 1944; s. Russell Lowell and Margaret Jeanne (Lepley) P.; m. Margaret Mary Skold, Oct. 3, 1964 (div. 1980); children: Michael Anthony, Sarah Jeanne. BA in English, U. No. Iowa, Cedar Falls, 1966; MLS, U. Iowa, 1969. Tchr. English, Des Moines Tech. High Sch., 1966-67; dir. Cattermole Meml. Library, Fort Madison, Iowa, 1969-72, Waterloo Pub. Library, Iowa, 1972-83, Omaha Pub. Library, 1983-92; Bd. dirs. Mississippi Valley Film Coop., Quincy, Ill., 1970-72, Films-for-Iowa Library Media Services, 1974-76; mem. Nebr. Adv. Council on Libraries, 1984; mem. Iowa Gov.'s Adv. Council on Library Services, 1976-82. Author: Reference/Information Services in Iowa Public Libraries, 1969; also articles. Cofounder Friends of Waterloo Pub. Library, 1976; mem. Black Hawk County Democratic Central Com., Waterloo, 1979-82; bd. dirs. Friends of Stas. KHKE/KUNI, Cedar Falls, Iowa, 1982-83. Recipient spl. service award Iowa Library Assn., 1975. Mem. ALA (council 1975-79), Nebr. Library Assn. (pres. pub. library sect. 1986), Mountain/Plains Library Assn., Iowa Urban Pub. Library Assn. (sec. 1978-83), ACLU, Met. Opera Guild. Home: Omaha Nebr. Died Oct. 31, 1992.

PHIPPS, PAUL FREDERICK, English language educator; b. St. Louis, Feb. 18, 1921; s. Paris Delbert and Emma Margaretta (Meyer) P.; m. Arline Lois Jass, Feb. 26, 1949; children: Stephen, Elizabeth, Kevin. AB, Valparaiso U., 1949; MA, U. N.C., 1950; PhD in English, Johns Hopkins U., 1961. Dir. composition Johns Hopkins U., Balt., 1953-56; asst. prof. Valparaiso (Ind.) U., 1956-61, assoc. prof., 1961-66, prof., 1966-89, chmn. dept. English, 1966-71, W.G. Friedrich prof. Am. lit., 1986-89, ret., 1989. Contbr. articles to edn. publs. With USN, 1942-46, PTO. Mem. MLA, South Atlantic MLA, S.C. Hist. Soc., Ind. Coll. English Assn. (sec.-treas. 1967-68). Home: Valparaiso Ind. Died Sept. 29, 1993.

PHOENIX, PAUL JOSEPH, steel manufacturing company executive; b. Hamilton, Ont., Can., Feb. 13, 1928; s. Raymond Joseph and Marie (Hagerty) P.; m. Patricia Ruth Kearns, July 11, 1953; children: William, James, Marie, Margaret, Mary Ellen, Jane. B.A., U. Toronto, M.B.A. With Dofasco Inc., Hamilton, 1941—, mgr. quality control, 1964-70, asst. dir. mfg. controls, from 1970, then task force chmn., computerized order entry and prodn. control, v.p. planning, 1973-82, exec. v.p., 1982-83, pres., chief operating officer, 1983-87, pres., chief exec. officer, 1987—, also bd. dirs.; dir. Aberford Resources Ltd., Calgary, Nat. Steel Car, Hamilton. Mem. adv. com. on indsl. mgmt. and tech., Mohawk Coll.; bd. dirs. St. Joseph's Villa, past chmn.; mem. Hamilton Philharm.; past pres. Children's Aid Soc. of Hamilton-Wentworth, 1972; dept. chmn. United Way Campaign. Mem. Am. Inst. Indsl. Engrs. (pres. 1964-65), Am. Mgmt. Assn., Am. Iron and Steel Inst., N.Am. Soc. Corp. Planning, Newman Alumni Soc. (pres. 1967-68), St. Michael's Coll. Alumni Soc. Roman Catholic. Clubs: Burlington Golf and Country; Hamilton Golf and Country, Ancaster.

PHOENIX, RIVER, actor; b. Madras, Oreg., Aug. 23, 1970; s. John and Arlyn P. Films: Explorers, 1985, The Mosquito Coast, 1986, Stand by Me, 1986, Little Nikita, 1988, A Night in the Life of Jimmy Reardon, 1988, Running on Empty (Nat. Bd. Review award best supporting actor, Acad. Award nomination best supporting actor), 1988, Indiana Jones and the Last Crusade, 1989, I Love You to Death, 1990, Dogfight, 1991, My Own Private Idaho, 1991; TV series: Seven Brides for Seven Brothers, 1982-83; TV movies: Robert Kennedy and His Times, Part 3, 1985, Surviving, 1985. Home: Los Angeles Calif. Died Oct. 31, 1993.

PHOUMI VONGVICHIT, government official. Acting pres., vice chmn. Council of Mins. Govt. of Laos, 1986-94; mem. Politburo Lao People's Revolutionary Party. Home: Vientiane Laos Died Jan. 7, 1994.

PIATT, WILLIAM MCKINNEY, III, consulting engineering executive; b. Durham, N.C., Nov. 17, 1918; s. William McKinney and Marion Adele (Sheppard) P.; m. Lois Jewel Keast, Apr. 22, 1943; children: William McKinney IV, Raymond Keast, Joseph Wood. B.S. in Elec. Engring, Lafayette Coll., 1940; postgrad., Rutgers U., 1940-42. Registered profl. engr., N.C., S.C., Ga., Va. Instr. elec. engring. Rutgers U., New Brunswick, N.J., 1942-44; with W.M. Piatt and Co. (Cons. Engrs., and predecessors), Durham, N.C., 1946-95; elec. engr. W.M. Piatt and Co. (Cons. Engrs., and predecessors), 1946-57, ptnr., 1957-64, owner, 1964-66, pres., 1966-95; guest lectr. water supply, waste treatment U. N.C., Duke U. Served to lt. comdr. USNR, 1944-46, 51-53. Fellow ASCE (life), Am. Cons. Engrs. Coun., N.C. Soc. Engrs. (life, pres. 1971, Outstanding Achievement award 1987), Am. Pub. Works Assn. (life); mem. ASTM, Instrument Soc. Am. (sr.), Water Environment Fedn. (life), New Eng. Waterworks Assn. (life), Am. Water Works Assn. (life), Cons. Engrs. Coun. N.C. (pres. 1973-74), N.C. Wildlife Fedn. (dir. 1966-69, v.p. 1970-76), Kiwanis (v.p. 1991, pres.-elect 1992, pres. 1993), Durham Engrs. Club (pres. 1962), Durham County Wildlife Club (pres. 1964-65). Democrat. Christian Scientist. Home: Durham N.C. Died Nov., 1995.

PICACHY, LAWRENCE TREVOR CARDINAL, retired archbishop of Calcutta; b. Darjeeling, India, Aug. 7, 1916; s. Edwin and May (McCue) P.; ed. St. Joseph's Coll. Ordained to ministry Roman Cath. Ch.; rector, headmaster St. Xavier's Coll., Calcutta, India, 1954-60; bishop of Jamshedpur, India, 1962-69; archbishop of Calcutta, India, 1969-88, ret. archbishop, 1988; v.p. Cath. Bishop's Conf. of India, 1972-76, pres., 1976-81; cardinal Sacred Consistory of Pope Paul VI, 1976—. Mem. Rotary. Home: Calcutta India

PICKENS, BUFORD LINDSAY, architectural educator, historian; b. Coffeyville, Kans., Jan. 15, 1906; s. Samuel Milton and Emily (Grigson) P.; m. Jenny Grönner Johnsen, June 2, 1934; children: Lindsay Lloyd, Grigson Buford. B.Arch., U. Ill., 1930; A.M. (fellow), U. Chgo., 1937. Archtl. work Chgo., 1925-28, 30-35; instr. Ohio U., 1937-38; pvt. practice residential architecture, community planning cons., 1938-95; asst. prof. Wayne U., Detroit, 1938-45; prof., dir. Sch. Architecture, Tulane U., 1946-53; prof. Washington U., 1953-74, prof. emeritus, 1974-95; dean Washington U. (Sch. Architecture), 1953-56, dir. campus planning, 1956-63; vis. lectr. U. Minn., summer 1940; cons. Detroit City Planning Commn., 1944-45; Mem. Vieux Carre Commn., New Orleans, 1947-52; mem. Fulbright Adv. Screening Com., 1958-60, Joint AIA/ACSA Award Com., 1976-79. Author: (with others) Pueblo Style and Regional Architecture, 1990; sr. co-author: Washington University in St. Louis: Its Design and Architecture, 1978; editor: Jour. Archtl. Edn., 1955, The Missions of Northern Sonora, 1993; contbr. articles to Am., English, Italian jours. Hist. bldg. commr., Mo.,

1960-73, hist. bldg. commr., St. Louis County, 1964-74. Served U.S. Army as instr. Univ. Tng. Command, 1945, Florence, Italy. Fellow AIA; mem. Soc. Archtl. Historians (pres. 1950), Assn. Collegiate Schs. Architecture (pres. 1957-59), Alpha Rho Chi. Home: Saint Louis Mo. Died June 11, 1995.

PICKENS, MARSHALL IVEY, former hospital administrator, foundation trustee; b. Pineville, N.C., Jan. 23, 1904; s. Cornelius Miller and Emma (Watts) P.; m. Sarah Wakefield, Dec. 17, 1932; children—Lucinda Watts (Mrs. H.B. Lockwood, Jr.), Sarah Wakefield (Mrs. J. Worth Williamson, Jr.), Marshall Ivey. A.B., Duke, 1925, M.A., 1926; LL.D., Davidson Coll., 1962. With Duke Endowment, Charlotte, N.C., 1928—; field rep., asst. sec. Duke Endowment, 1946-61, sec., 1961-66, assoc. dir., 1948-50, dir. hosp. and child care sects., 1950-62, exec. dir. hosp. and child care sects., 1962-66, trustee, 1951—, vice chmn. trustees, 1966-73, chmn., 1973-74, hon. chmn., 1975—; dir. emeritus Duke Power Co. Trustee emeritus Duke U.; past pres. United Way Cen. Carolinas; past pres. Social Planning Council of Charlotte; past pres., bd. mgrs. Meth. Home for Aged; bd. visitors Davidson (N.C.) Coll. Fellow Am. Coll. Hosp. Adminstrs. (hon.); mem. Am., N.C., S.C. hosp. assns., Am. Assn. Hosp. Cons., AIA (hon. assoc. mem.), Newcomen Soc., Omicron Delta Kappa, Pi Kappa Phi. Methodist. Clubs: Charlotte Country (Charlotte), City (Charlotte). Lodge: Rotary (hon.). Home: Charlotte N.C.

PICKUS, ALBERT PIERRE, lawyer; b. Sioux City, Iowa, Aug. 10, 1931; s. Sam G. and Mildred H. (Levy) P.; m. Nancy Ellen Silber, Dec. 17, 1958; children: Miriam I., Peter S., Matthew I. BA, U. Mich., 1953; JD, Case Western Res. U., 1958. Bar: Iowa 1958, Ohio 1958, Mich. 1994. Ptnr. Silber, Pickus & Williams and predecessors, Cleve., 1959-74; ptnr. Squire, Sanders & Dempsey, Cleve., 1974-91, counsel, 1991-93; pvt. consulting practice, Saline, Mich., 1994. Mem. Bd. in Control of Intercollegiate Athletics, U. Mich., 1975-81, 87-93, bd. dirs. Victors Club, Devel. Council, 1976-79, mem. vis. com. Med. Ctr. Alumni Soc., 1978-83, mem. exec. com. Pres.'s Club, 1978-81; mem. fin. com. Cleve. Mt. Sinai Med. Ctr., 1982-85. Mem. ABA, Iowa State Bar Assn., Ohio State Bar Assn., Mich. State Bar Assn., Am. Coll. Real Estate Lawyers, U. Mich.-Ann Arbor Alumni Assn. (pres. 1973-75, dir. for life, cons. to devel. office, Disting. Alumni Svc. award 1972, Presdl. Socs. Svc. citation 1990), Soc. of Benchers. Clubs: Oakwood, Masons (32 degree), Shriners. Died Dec. 29, 1994. Home: Saline Mich.

PIERONI, LEONARD J., engineering and construction company executive; b. 1939. BSChemE, Notre Dame U., 1960; MSChemE, Northwestern U., 1961. With M.W. Kellogg Co., N.Y.C., 1961-70, Rust Engring., N.Y.C., 1970-72; with Parsons, Pasadena, Calif., 1972-77, 78-96, exec. v.p., 1987-90, chmn., chief exec. officer, 1990-96, also dir.; pres. SIP Engring. Inc., 1983-84; mng. dir. Ralph M. Parsons Co. Ltd., London, 1984-85; pres., gen. mgr. Charles T. Main Inc., 1985-87; v.p. sales KTI Corp., 1977-78. Home: La Canada Calif. Deceased.

PIERSON, GEORGE WILSON, history educator; b. N.Y.C., Oct. 22, 1904; s. Charles Wheeler and Elizabeth Granville (Groesbeck) P.; m. Mary Laetitia Verdery, Sept. 10, 1936 (dec. 1982); children: Norah, Laetitia Deems; m. Loueva F. Pflueger, Mar. 24, 1988. B.A., Yale U., 1926, Ph.D., 1933; H.H.D., Merrimack Coll., 1974. Faculty Yale U., 1926-93, prof. history, 1944-46, Larned prof. history, 1946-73, emeritus, 1973-93, also historian of univ., chmn. dept. history, 1956-62, dir. div. humanities, 1964-70; Fellow Davenport Coll., 1933-93. Author: Tocqueville and Beaumont in America, 1938, abridged edit., 1959, Yale College, An Educational History, 1871-1921, 1952, Yale: The University College, 1921-1937, 1955, The Education of American Leaders: Comparative Contributions of United States Colleges and Universities, 1969, The Moving American, 1973, Yale: a short history, 1976, rev. edit., 1979, A Yale Book of Numbers: Historical Statistics of the College and University, 1983, The Founding of Yale: The Legend of Forty Folios, 1988; contbr. American Universities in Nineteenth Century: The Formative Period to The Modern University (editor Margaret Clapp), 1950, Le Second Voyage de Tocqueville en Amérique, 1960; Co-editor: Gustave de Beaumont: Lettres d' Amérique, 1973; editor: Computers for the Humanities?, 1965; contbr. articles to hist., ednl. publs. Guggenheim fellow, 1955-56; Recipient Porter prize Yale U., 1933; Wilbur Lucius Cross medal Yale U. Grad. Sch. Assn., 1973; Alumni medal Yale U., 1975. Fellow Am. Acad. Arts and Scis.; mem. Century Assn., Am. Hist. Assn., Phi Beta Kappa (pres. Yale U. chpt. 1965-73, W.C. DeVane medal 1974, spl. medal and citation 1989). Home: Hamden Conn. Died Oct. 12, 1993; buried Grove Street Cemetery, New Haven, Conn.

PIETTE, LAWRENCE HECTOR, biophysicist, educator, university dean and official; b. Chgo., Jan. 4, 1932; s. Gerald John and Lillian (Bumgardner) P.; m. Mary Irene Harris, Aug. 15, 1957; children: Jeffrey, Martin. B.S., Northwestern U., 1953, M.S., 1954; Ph.D., Stanford U., 1957. Mgr. research biochemistry and biophysics Varian Assos., 1956-65; prof. biophysics U. Hawaii, 1965-92, chmn. dept., 1968-92, dir. Cancer Research Lab., 1970-84; exec. dir. Cancer Center Hawaii, 1974; Chmn. cancer adv. com., regional med. program, research com. Hawaii div. Am. Cancer Soc.; dean. Sch. Grad. Studies Utah State U., Logan, 1984-92; assoc. v.p. research Utah State U., 1984-86, prof. biochemistry, 1984-92. Contbr. articles to profl. jours.; Asso. editor: Jour. Organic Magnetic Resonance. Mem. Am. Chem. Soc., Biophys. Soc., A.A.U.P. Home: Logan Utah Died Nov. 17, 1992.

PILKINGTON, SIR ALASTAIR, business executive, academic administrator; b. Jan. 7, 1920; s. L. G. and Mrs. L. G. Pilkington; ed. Cambridge U.; D.Tech. (hon.), U. Loughborough, 1968; D.Eng. (hon.), U. Liverpool, 1971; LLD (hon.), U. Bristol, 1979; DSc (hon.), U. London, 1979, Alfred U., N.Y., 1990; LLD (hon.) Lancaster U., 1990, Cambridge U., 1991. m. Patricia Nicholls Elliott, 1945 (d. 1977); 2 children; m. Kathleen Haynes, 1978. With Pilkington Bros. Ltd., St. Helens, 1947-95, prodn. mgr. and asst. works mgr., Doncaster, 1949-51, head office, 1952, sub-dir., 1953, exec. dir., 1955-85, dep. chmn., 1971-73, chmn., 1973-80, pres., 1985-95. dep. chmn. Chloride Group Ltd., 1979-95; dir. Brit. Petroleum Co. Mem. Cen. Adv. Coun. Sci. and Tech., 1970-95 , Sci. Rsch. Coun., 1972-95, Brit. Rys. Bd., 1973-76; mem. ct. govs. Adminstrv. Staff Coll., 1973-95; pro-chancellor Lancaster U., 1980-90; chancellor Liverpool U., 1994-95; bd. dirs. Wellcome Found. Ltd. Served with Brit. Armed Forces, 1939-46. Recipient Toledo Glass and Ceramic award, 1963; Mullard medal Royal Soc., 1968; John Scott medal, 1969; Wilhelm Exner medal, 1970; hon. fellow Imperial Coll., 1974; decorated knight Order Brit. Empire. Fellow Royal Soc., Brit. Inst. Mgmt.; mem. Am. Ceramic Soc. Died May, 5, 1995. Home: London Eng.

PINCOFFS, EDMUND LLOYD, philosophy educator; b. Chgo., June 7, 1919; s. Edmund Peter and Rosalind Marie (Posey) P.; m. Mary Elizabeth Zimmerman, Oct. 1, 1948; children: Ruth Posey, Peter, Mary. A.B., U. N.C., 1941; Ph.D., Cornell U., 1957. Partner Maurice Pincoffs Co., Houston, 1946-50; instr. U. Houston, 1955-56, asst. prof., 1956-60, assoc. prof., 1960-65, chmn. dept. philosophy, 1959-65; vis. fellow Princeton, 1962-63; assoc. prof. U. Tex. at Austin, 1965-67, prof., 1967-84, asso. dean Grad. Sch., 1967-68, chmn. dept. philosophy, 1976-80. Author: The Rationale of Legal Punishment, 1966; Quandaries and Virtues, 1986, Philosophy of Law: A Brief Introduction, 1991; editor: The Concept of Academic Freedom, 1975; contbr. articles to profl. jours. Past chmn. Tex. Com. for Humanities. Served with USCGR, 1941-45. Grantee Am. Council Learned Socs., U. Research Inst.; NEH fellow, 1981-82; Nat. Humanities Center fellow, 1982. Mem. Am. Philos. Assn. (v.p. 1991), Southwestern Philos. Assn. (past pres.), Am. Soc. for Polit. and Legal Philosophy, Internat. Assn. for Philosophy of Law and Social Philosophy (past pres. Am. sect.), AAUP (past mem. nat. council, past pres. Tex. conf., past pres. U. Tex. chpt.), ACLU (past dir. Central Tex. chpt.), Omicron Delta Kappa, Phi Kappa Phi, Phi Eta Sigma. Unitarian. Home: Austin Tex. Died Nov. 7, 1991.

PINCUS, MICHAEL STERN, language educator; b. Atlanta, Jan. 18, 1936; s. Bernard M. and Amelia (Stern) P.; m. Jacqueline Kron, June 10, 1956; children: Jonathan D., Gregory K. BA, Union Coll., Schenectady, N.Y., 1957; MA, U. N.C., 1958, PhD, 1961; diploma, U. Madrid, 1960; postgrad., Fairleigh Dickinson U., 1987. Asst. prof. romance langs. Rutgers U., New Brunswick, N.J., 1961-67; assoc. prof. Spanish SUNY, New Paltz, 1967-69; chmn., assoc. prof. Spanish and classics U. N.H., Durham, 1969-72; acting v.p. acad. affairs Mansfield U. Pa., 1976, acting dean grad. studies, 1977, dean liberal arts, 1972-80; dean Mary Baldwin Coll., Staunton, Va., 1980-82; dean coll. liberal arts Fairleigh Dickinson U., Rutherford and Teaneck, N.J., 1982-87; prof., head divsn. classical and modern langs. Coll. of Charleston, S.C., 1987-96; curriculum cons. Computer Horizons Corp., N.Y.C., 1985-86; program evaluation cons. to numerous state and regional accrediting agys., 1969-85. Contbr. numerous articles and reviews to newspapers and profl. jours. Coach Youth Baseball Assn., Mansfield, 1973-80. Mem. Am. Assn. Tchrs. Spanish and Portuguese, MLA, Am. Contract Bridge League (dir. unit 217 1978-80). Home: Folly Beach S.C. Died Mar. 8, 1996.

PINDBORG, JENS JORGEN, oral pathologist; b. Copenhagen, Aug. 17, 1921; m. Iris Garnov, 1994. Student Royal Dental Coll., Copenhagen, U. Ill.; Dr. (hon.), Karolinska Inst., Stockholm, 1973, U. Lund, 1974, U. Oslo, 1976, Witwatersrand U., 1976, U. Helsinki, 1981; LL.D. (hon.), U. Glasgow, 1978, Simmelweiss Med. U., 1985, U. Göteborg, 1986, U. Sheffield, 1988, U. Umeå, 1990, U. Granada, 1994. Instr., rsch. assoc., assoc. prof. Royal Dental Coll., Copenhagen, 1943-59, prof., chmn. dept. oral pathology, 1959-91; head dental dept. U. Hosp., Copenhagen, 1953-91; cons. Danish Nat. Health Service, 1958-66; vis. prof. U. Ill., 1958, 61, Hebrew U., Jerusalem, 1969; WHO vis. prof. in India, 1963-64; dir. Indo-Danish Oral Cancer Control Project, Trivandrum, 1969-78; head collaborating Ctr. under WHO Internat. Reference Ctr. for Oropharyngeal tumours, Agra, India, 1964; head Collaborating Ctr. under WHO Internat. Reference Ctr. for Salivary Gland Tumours London, 1966; vis. prof. Tata Inst. of Fundamental Research Bombay, 1966-94; cons. for Ministry of Health, Uganda, 1966; WHO rsch. expert to New Guinea and Fiji, 1966; dir. WHO Internat. Reference Ctr. on Odontogenic Tumours, 1966, WHO Collaborative Centre on Oral Manifestation of HIV, 1988; WHO cons., Brazil and Colombia, 1967; dir. WHO Internat. Refence Ctr. on Oral Precancerous Conditions, 1967-95, EEC Clearinghouse on the Oral Problems Related to the HIV Infection; WHO cons. on classification of oral diseases; cons. Nat. Inst. Dental Rsch., Bethesda, 1988-88; guest lectr. various univs. Author: The Dentist in Art, 1960; (with R.J. Gorlin) Syndromes of Head and Neck, 1964; Atlas of Disease of the Oral Mucosa, 5th edit., 1993; Pathology of the Dental Hard Tissues, 1970; (with I.R.H. Kramer, H. Torloni) Histological Typing of Odontogenic Tumours, Cysts and Allied Lesions, 1972, (with I.R.H. Kramer, M. Shear) 2d edit., 1992; Histology of the Human Tooth, 1973; Atlas of Disease of the Jaws, 1974; Oral Cancer and Precancer, 1980; others; editor-in-chief Danish Dental Jour., 1963-95, Scandinavian Jour. of Dental Research, 1970-94, Internat. Jour. of Oral Surgery, 1972-75, Community Dentistry and Oral Epidemiology, 1973-88, Journal of Oral Pathology & Medicine, 1989-92; contbr. articles to profl. jours. Recipient E.J. Goddard Oration, Brisbane, 1970; Isaac Schour Meml. award, 1970; Elmer Best award, 1972. Fellow AAAS, Am. Acad. Oral Pathology (hon.), Royal Coll. Surgeons Ireland (hon.), Royal Soc. of London (hon.), Royal Soc. Medicine London (hon.), Royal Coll. Pathologists, Am. Acad. Oral Pathology (hon.); mem. Assn. Hosp. Dentists (pres. 1954-66, Danish Israeli Assn. (pres. 1964-69), Burmese Med. Assn. Died Aug., 1995. Home: Gentofte Denmark

PINE, GRANVILLE MARTIN, lawyer; b. Okmulgee, Okla., Aug. 21, 1915; s. Roswell Dean and Mary Louise (Harder) P.; m. Elide Anna de Teisseyre, Feb. 7, 1976; children: Robert, Donald. A.B., U. Okla., 1936; LL.B., Harvard U., 1939. Bar: N.Y. bar 1941. Ptnr. Morgan, Finnegan, Pine, Foley & Lee, N.Y.C., 1946-86; of counsel Morgan & Finnegan, N.Y.C., 1986—. Home: Vallecchia Italy

PINES, HERMAN, chemistry educator, consultant; b. Lodz, Poland, Jan. 17, 1902; came to U.S., 1928; s. Isaac and Eugenia (Grynfeld) P.; m. Dorothy Mlotek, Aug. 13, 1927; 1 dau., Judith. Chem. engr., Ecole Superieure de Chimie Industrielle, Lyon, France, 1927; Ph.D., U. Chgo., 1935; docteur hon., Universite Claude Bernard, Lyon, 1983. Research chemist Universal Oil Product Co., Riverside, Ill., 1930-45; coordinator exploratory research Universal Oil Products Co., 1945-52; asst. prof. chemistry Northwestern U., 1941-50, assoc. prof., 1950-52, Ipatieff prof., 1953-70, dir. Ipatieff Lab., 1952-70, Ipatieff prof. emeritus, 1970-96; adviser Israeli govt., 1951; chmn. Gordon Research Conf. in Catalysis, 1960; vis. prof. numerous univs. Author: Base-Catalyzed Reactions Chemistry of Hydrocarbons, 1977, The Chemistry of Catalytic Hydrocarbon Conversions, 1981, Genesis and Evolution of the Ipatieff Catalytic Laboratory, 1992; editor: (with D.D. Eley and P.B. Weisz) Advances in Catalysis, 1962-94; patentee in field. Recipient profl. achievement citation U. Chgo. Alumni Assn., 1986, Eugene J. Houdry award Catalysis Soc., 1981. Fellow Am. Inst. Chemists (recipient Chem. Pioneer 1982), Am. Chem. Soc. (recipient Fritzsche 1956, Midwest 1963, Petroleum Chemistry 1981, Murphree 1983), Sigma Xi, Phi Lambda Upsilon. Home: San Rafael Calif. Died Apr. 10, 1996.

PINKNEY, DAVID HENRY, historian; b. Elyria, Ohio, July 2, 1914; s. David Henry and Zaida Margaret (Fulmer) P.; m. Helen Dorothy Reisinger, Nov. 14, 1942 (dec.); children: Janet Sloss, David Henry (dec.). A.B., Oberlin Coll., 1936, H.H.D. (hon.), 1980; M.A., Harvard U., 1937, Ph.D., 1941; Docteur honoris causa, U. Nantes, France, 1980. Research analyst, coordinator info. OSS, Washington and London, 1941-43; asst. prof. history U. Mo., Columbia, 1946-51; assoc. prof. U. Mo., 1951-57, prof., 1957-66, chmn. dept. history, 1956-59; prof. U. Wash., 1966-84, prof. emeritus, 1984-93, Disting. Univ. Lectr., 1977; bd. dirs. Am. Council on Edn., 1979-80. Author: Napoleon III and the Rebuilding of Paris, 1958, The French Revolution of 1830, 1972, The Nineteenth Century, 1978, Decisive Years in France, 1840-1847, 1986, La Révolution de 1830 en France, 1988; co-author: History of France, 1983; editor: A Festschrift for Frederick B. Artz, 1964, French Hist. Studies, 1966-75. Served to lt., j.g. USNR, 1943-46. Fund for Advancement Edn. fellow, 1954-55; Guggenheim fellow, 1960-61; Nat. Endowment for Humanities fellow, 1977-78. Mem. Am. Acad. Arts and Scis., Am. Hist. Assn. (pres. 1980), Soc. French Hist. Studies (pres. 1975-76), Western Soc. French History, Phi Beta Kappa. Home: Seattle Wash. Died May 26, 1993.

PIPAL, FAUSTIN ANTHONY, savings bank executive; b. Chgo., Feb. 15, 1921; s. Frank J. and Agnes (Broz) P.; m. Florence C. Pipal; children by previous marriage: Nancy, Richard, Faustin A., David. J.D., Boston Coll., 1950. Bar: Ill. 1950. From office boy to sr. cost analyst Western Electric Co., 1939-46; with Talman Fed. Savs. & Loan Assn., Chgo., 1950-60; v.p., 1955-60, Gt. Western Savs. & Loan Assn., Calif., 1960-61; resident counsel, treas. LaGrange Fed. Savs. & Loan Assn., Chgo., 1962-86, vice chmn., 1986-93; chmn. bd. St. Paul Bank for Savs., Chgo., 1962-93; former chmn. bd. Renewal Effort Service Corp.; former bd. dirs. Fed.

Savs. and Loan Council Ill. Chmn. bd. Cook County Council Urban Renewal; former trustee Ill. Benedictine Coll., Lisle; bd. dirs. Inst. Rehab. Engring., N.J., Austin Career Edn. Ctr., Nat. Housing Services, Alfred Adler Inst., Chgo., Neighborhood Housing Services of Chgo., Inc. Served with USNR, 1942-45. Mem. Order of Malta. Home: La Grange Ill. Died 1993.

PIPKIN, ALLEN COMPERE, II, mathematician, educator; b. Mena, Ark., May 21, 1931; s. Allen Compere and Leyland (Chambers) P.; m. Ann Brittain, May 26, 1956; children: Janet Louise, Lee Ann, Allen Brittain. Sc.B., MIT, 1952; Ph.D., Brown U., 1959. Research asst. Brown U., Providence, 1955-58; asst. prof. applied math. Brown U., 1960-63, asso. prof., 1963-66, prof., 1966-94; research asso. Inst. for Fluid Dynamics and Applied Math., U. Md., College Park, 1958-60. Author: Lectures on Viscoelasticity Theory, 1972, A Course on Integral Equations, 1991; editorial bd. Soc. Indsl. and Applied Math. Jour. Applied Math., 1970-76, Jour. Eng. Math., 1993-94; contbr. articles to profl. jours. Served with U.S. Army, 1952-54. Guggenheim fellow, 1968; NSF grantee, 1969-94; sr. vis. fellow Sci. Research Council (U.K.), 1978, 82. Mem. Soc. Rheology, Soc. for Natural Philosophy. Home: Rumford R.I. Died Oct. 30, 1994.

PISCATOR, MARIA LEY, educator, author, director, choreographer, playwright; b. Vienna, Austria, Aug. 1, 1900; came to U.S., 1939; d. Edmund V. and Fredericke (von Bronswick) Czada; m. Frank Gerhardt Deutsch, Apr. 10, 1928 (dec. Sept. 1934); m. Erwin Piscator, Apr. 17, 1937 (dec. Mar. 1966). Studied dance with Cerri, Mme. Alevandra, Mme. Egorova, Paris; grad., Handel's Acad., Vienna, Austria; MA, U. Paris, 1933, DLitt, 1935; postgrad., Columbia U., 1950-51. Head choreographer Salzburg (Austria) Festival Max Reinhardt, 1924-29; co-founder Dramatic Workshop New Sch. for Social Research, N.Y.C., 1939-50, chmn., 1939-52; pres. Piscator Found., N.Y.C., from 1967; founder, dir. Junior Dramatic Workshop, 1942-60, Poets Theatre, N.Y.C., 1947, Maria Piscator Inst., N.Y.C., 1954-60, Adirondack Drama Festival, Lake Placid, N.Y., 1949; assoc. dir. Sayville (N.Y.) Playhouse, 1944-46; dir. plays on and off Broadway, in opera houses, schs., workshops and summer theatres; former vis. asst. prof. So. Ill. U., Carbondale, SUNY, Stony Brook; former guest prof. U. Windsor, Can., Park Point Coll., Pitts., others; chmn. March of Dance Series, New Sch. and Rooftop Theatre, 1940-49; chmn. Dance Dept. Dramatic Workshop, New Sch., 1939-52. Stage name Maria Ley; began dance career in 1920, performed with her own company in concert halls and theatres in Europe and South Am.; choreographed Max Reinhardt's prodn. Midsummer Night's Dream, The Imaginary Invalid, A Servant of Two Masters and other plays, Vienna and Salzburg Festivals, 1924-49, first appearance in U.S. as guest star, 1928; stage dir. at Dramatic Workshops, Broadway and Offbroadway for: The Imaginary Invalid, 1942, Romeo and Juliet, 1943-48, Bobino, 1944, The Petrified Forest, 1945, Pinocchio, 1945, Blithe Spirit, 1946, Private Lives, 1946, Emil and the Detectives (own translation of Nights of Wrath), 1947, Tom Sawyer, 1947, Alice in Wonderland, 1948, Ballad of the Mississippi, 1948, Hope of the World, 1948, Two Noh Plays, 1949, A Midsummer Night's Dream, 1947-48, Twilight Crane, 1959-60, Call of the City, 1963-64, Night Talk with a Contemptible Visitor, 1964, The Great Man, 1964, Letters from Chicago, 1964, Circle of Chalk, War and Peace, American Tragedy, The Glass Menagerie, All the Kings Men. The Deputy, The Investigation, all 1968-69, The Debate, 1970, The Death of J.F.K., 1970, Brothers, 1971, The Flies, 1972, Comedy of Errors, A Streetcar Named Desire, 1973; author: (poetry) Das Tanzende Ich (The Dance Within Me), in German, 1924, English, 1930, (essays in French) Theatre au dixhuitieme siecle, 1934, (essay collection) La Canaille au Theatre au XVIII Siecle, (translation from German to French) Hugo von Hoffmansthal's Essai sur Victor Hugo, 1937, (novel) Grace Bennett, 1932, (novel) Lot's Wife, 1954, (one-act play) Lendemain produced at Theatre Champs Elysee, Paris, 1933, (3 act play) Le Chien dangereux, produced at Theatre Madeline, Paris, 1934, (translation from French to German) Armand Salacrou's L'Inconnu d'Arras, 1934, A. Salacrous's Nuits de colere (Nights of Wrath), produced at President's Theater, N.Y.C., 1937, (adaptations of novels for stage) Kleist's Michael Kohlhaas, Kafka's, Metamorphosis, produced at Actor's Studio, 1971, (book) The Piscator Experiment, (autobiography) Mirror People, German edit., 1989. Named to Pres. Circle SUNY, Stony Brook, 1979. Mem. United Fedn. Coll. Tchrs., Actors Equity, Dramatists Guild, Pen Club, Soc. Stage Dirs. and Choreographers. Democrat. Roman Catholic. Home: New York N.Y. Deceased.

PITTENDRIGH, COLIN STEPHENSON, retired biologist, educator; b. Whitley Bay, Eng., Oct. 13, 1918; came to U.S., 1945; s. Alexander and Florence Hemy (Stephenson) P.; married, May 1, 1943; children: Robin Ann., Sandy. BSc in Botany with 1st class honors, U. Durham, Newcastle, Eng., 1940; PhD in Zoology, Columbia U., 1948; DSc (hon.), U. Newcastle-Upon-Tyne, Eng., 1985. From asst. to prof. biology, prof. zoology Princeton (N.J.) U., 1947-69, dean grad. sch., 1965-69; Bing prof. human biology Stanford (Calif.) U., 1969-76, Miller prof. biology, 1980-84; dir. Hopkins Marine Sta. Stanford (Calif.) U., Pacific Grove, Calif., 1976-84; sr. fellow NSF Ctr. for Biol. Tng. U. Va., Charlottesville, 1992-96. Author: (with G.G. Simpson) Textbook of Biology, 1957. Recipient Alexander von Humboldt prize Alexander von Humboldt Found., 1987, Gregor Mendel gold medal Czech Acad. Scis., 1994; Guggenheim fellow, 1959. Mem. NAS, Am. Philos. Soc., Am. Acad. Arts and Scis. Home: Bozeman Mont. Died Mar. 19, 1996.

PLAUT, JAMES SACHS, foundation executive; b. Cin., Feb. 1, 1912; s. Jacob M. and Alice S. (Sachs) P.; m. Mary E. Friedlander, May 24, 1933; children—Susan, Thomas. Student, Auteuil Day Sch., Paris, 1925-26, Taft Sch., Watertown, Conn., 1927-28; A.B., Harvard, 1933, A.M., 1935; D.F.A. (hon.), Wheaton Coll., 1974. Asst. dept. of fine arts Harvard U., 1934-35; asst. to curator of paintings Mus. Fine Arts, Boston, 1935-39; dir. Inst. Contemporary Art, Boston, 1938-56; trustee and dir. emeritus Inst. Contemporary Art, 1956-61; cons. indsl. design for State of Israel; chmn. Exhbn. Services Internat.; dir. devel., trustee New Eng. Aquarium, Boston, New Eng. Conservatory Music; sec. gen. World Crafts Council, 1967-76; pres. Aid to Artisans, Inc., 1976-96; dep. commr. gen. of U.S. to Brussels World Expn., 1958. Author: Steuben Glass, 1948, Oskar Kokoschka, 1948, (with Octavio Paz) In Praise of Hands, 1974; also catalogues for exhbns.; Contbr. to bulls. of art museums, Atlantic Monthly. Vice pres. Old Sturbridge Village, Mass., 1959-61; Gen. chmn. Cambridge Community Fund, 1950 campaign; mem. vis. com. Mus. Fine Arts, Boston, Sch. Artisanry, Boston U.; chmn. vis. com. Wheaton Coll.; mem. council for arts Mass. Inst. Tech. Served with USNR, 1942-46, ETO, North Africa; lt. comdr. Res. Decorated Legion of Merit; Chevalier, Legion d'Honneur; knight 1st Class Order of St. Olav, Norway; comdr. Royal Order of Leopold, Belgium. Clubs: Country (Boston), Badminton and Tennis (Boston); Harvard (N.Y.C.), Century Assn. (N.Y.C.). Home: Westwood Mass. Died Jan. 13, 1996.

PLAYE, GEORGE LOUIS, Romance languages and literature educator; b. Pawtucket, R.I., Mar. 15, 1917; s. Louis Auguste and Lucienne Marie (Tillier) P.; m. Margaret Louise Berg, July 9, 1943; children: Marcia Gail, Stephen Jan; m. Joan Bliss, July 25, 1991. A.B., Brown U., 1939, M.A., 1940; postgrad., Washington U., St. Louis, 1940-41; Ph.D. (fellow), U. Ill., 1949. Mem. faculty Brown U., Providence, 1940-41; instr. U. Chgo., 1946-49, asst. prof., 1949-55, assoc. prof., 1955-68, prof. dept. Romance lang. and lit., 1968-85, prof. emeritus, 1986-92, dir. fin. aid, 1957-59, dean undergrad. students, 1959-71, chmn. com. on disciplines of the humanities, 1971-82; lectr. Ind. U., Bloomington, 1956, 63, 68, 79; cons. Ill. Scholarship Com., 1959-67. Author: Dedicatory Address, 1964, Basic Facts for Reading French, 1959, Reputation of Voltaire in 19th Century France, 1948. Bd. acad. fellows Shimer Coll., 1970-75; trustee Village of Homewood, Ill., 1959-63; mem. Sch. Bd. Dist. 233, Homewood-Flossmoor, Ill., 1965-72; pres. Eastview Civic Assn., 1955-57. Served with U.S. Army, 1942-46. Decorated Bronze Star medal.; Recipient Quantrell Teaching prize, 1959; Irene V. Lichter fellow, 1940-41; others. Mem. MLA, Am. Assn. Tchrs. French, Am. Assn. Tchrs. Italian, Univ. Centers for Rational Alternatives, Phi Beta Kappa. Club: Quadrangle. Home: Raymond N.H. Died Oct. 16, 1992.

PLIMPTON, PAULINE AMES, civic worker, writer; b. N. Easton, Mass., Oct. 22, 1901; d. Oakes and Blanche Ames; B.A., Smith Coll., 1922; m. Francis T.P. Plimpton, June 4, 1926; children: George Ames, Francis T.P., Oakes Ames, Sarah Gay. Pres., House of Industry, 1940-48; bd. dirs. Inst. World Affairs, 1940-74, Pub. Edn. Assn., 1933-44; chmn. United Campaign Fund for Planned Parenthood of Manhattan and Bronx, 1946-49; chmn. Planned Parenthood Fedn. Am. campaign, 1959-60, bd. dirs. 1959-67, 70-73; chmn. United Campaign, 1964; bd. dirs. Planned Parenthood of N.Y.C., 1965-74; rep. Western Hemisphere region Internat. Planned Parenthood Fedn., 1970-73; fund raiser, vol. coun. Philharm. Symphony Soc. N.Y., N.Y. Legal Aid Soc., ARC; mem. adv. coun. Friends of the Columbia Librs., 1986-95. Recipient Planned Parenthood award for devoted service, 1969. Republican. Unitarian. Clubs: Cold Springs Harbor Beach Club, Cosmopolitan, Piping Rock, Ausable (Adirondacks). Contbg. author, editor, compiler Orchids at Christmas, 1975, The Ancestry of Blanche Butler Ames and Adelbert Ames, 1977, Oakes Ames: Jottings of a Harvard Botanist, 1979, The Plimpton Papers: Law and Diplomacy, 1985, A Window on Our World: More Plimpton Papers, 1989, A Collector's Recollections: George Arthur Plimpton, 1993. Died April 15, 1995. Home: New York N.Y.

PLITT, HENRY G., motion picture company executive; b. N.Y.C., Nov. 26, 1918. Student, Syracuse U.; attended, St. Lawrence U. With Paramount Pictures Internat. Corp., United Detroit Theatres; v.p. Paramount Gulf Theatres, New Orleans, pres., gen. mgr.; pres. ABC Films, 1959-65, ABC Great States Inc., 1966; v.p. Prairie Farmer Pubs., 1971, ABC Theatre Holdings Inc., 1974; chmn. Plitt Theatres Inc., 1978-85; now chmn. Showscan Film Corp., Culver City, Calif. With 101st Airbourne div., World War II. Home: Culver City Calif. Died Jan. 26, 1993.

PLOG, FRED, anthropology educator; b. Ft. Monmouth, N.J., July 19, 1944; s. Fred T. and Phyllis (Gessert) P.; m. Gayle Martha Gillham, Apr. 11, 1966; children: Tom, Steve, Amy, Katherine. BA in Econs., Northwestern U., 1966; MA in Anthropology, U. Chgo., 1968, PhD in Anthropology, 1969. Asst. prof. UCLA, 1969-72; assoc. prof. SUNY, Binghamton, 1972-75; prof. Ariz. State U., 1976-81, N.Mex. State U., Las Cruces, 1981—; pres. Past & Future, Inc., Las Cruces, N.Mex. 1979--. Author, editor 24 books; contbr. numerous articles to profl. jours. Fellow Am. Anthrop. Assn., Soc. for Am. Archaeology. Democrat. Roman Catholic. Home: La Mesa Calif.

PLUMB, ROBERT CHARLES, chemistry educator, researcher; b. Springfield, Mass., Jan. 24, 1926; s. William Seley and May Emma (Putnam) P.; m. Vera Francis Baranowski, Apr. 27, 1973. AB in Chemistry, Clark U., 1949; PhD in Phys. Chemistry, Brown U., 1953. Research chemist ALCOA Research, New Kensington, Pa., 1952-56, asst. chief phys. chemistry, 1957-58; NSF fellow Cambridge (Eng.) U., 1956-57; asst., then assoc. prof. Worcester (Mass.) Poly. Inst., 1958-64, prof. chemistry, 1964—, head chemistry dept., 1967-76; rsch. prof. chemistry Brown U., 1990—; vis. prof. Western Australia Inst. Tech., Perth, 1973; acad. cons., 1968—; indsl. cons., 1976—. Columnist Jour. Chem. Edn., 1970-76; also articles to sci. publs.; developer Molecular Dynamics Simulator. Served to sgt. U.S. Army, 1943-45. Delivered Baylis Lectures, U. Western Australia, 1973, Nora Harrington Lecture, Elm's Coll., 1986; recipient Tim award New Eng. Assn. Chemistry Tchrs., 1988. Mem. Internat. Assn. Colloid & Interface Scientists, Am. Chem. Soc. (tour speaker 1965-67, vis. scientist award Western Conn. chpt. 1977), Sigma Xi. Home: Marlborough Mass.

PLUNKETT, ROY J., chemical engineer. AB in Chemistry, Manchester Coll., 1932, DSc (hon.); PhD in Chemistry, Ohio State U., 1936, DSc; DSc, Washington Coll. With dept. organic chem. Jackson Lab. E. I. DuPont de Nemours & Co., Deepwater, N.J., 1936-39, chem. supr. chamber works, 1939-45, supt., 1945-49, supt. Ponsol Colors area, 1949-50, asst. mgr. works, 1950-52; mgr. chem. devel. section dept. organic chems. E. I. DuPont de Nemours & Co., Wilmington, Del., 1952-54, asst. mgr. tech. sect., 1954-57, mgr., 1957-60, dir. rsch. divsn. freon products, 1960-70, dir. ops., 1970-75. Recipient award City of Phila., Soc. Plastics Industry, Nat. Assn. Mfrs., Moissan medal Chem. Soc. France, Holley Medal ASME, 1990; named to Plastics Hall of Fame, 1973, Nat. Inventors Hall of Fame, 1985. Mem. AAAS, AICE, Am. Chem. Soc., Am. Inst. Chemists. Home: Corpus Christi Tex. Died May 12, 1994.

PLYM, LAWRENCE JOHN, manufacturing executive, newspaper publisher; b. Kansas City, Mo., June 28, 1906; s. Francis J. and Jennie (Barber) P.; m. Mary P. Lippincott, Nov. 28, 1933 (dec. 1981); children: Sarah (Mrs. Murray C. Campbell), John Eric, Andrew Joseph.; m. Patricia D. Cunningham, May 27, 1983 (div. 1988). Student, U. Ill., 1928; grad., Babson Inst., 1929. Pres. Kawneer Co., Niles, Mich., 1940-62; pres. Plym Co., Star Pub. Co.; pub. Niles Daily Star; dir. Am. Metal Climax, Inc., N.Y.C., 1st Nat. Bank of Southwestern Mich.; pres. Niles Broadcasting Co. Trustee Lake Forest Acad. Mem. Phi Gamma Delta. Republican. Presbyn. Clubs: Tavern (Chgo.), Chicago (Chgo.), Glen View (Chgo.), Old Elm (Chgo.); Gulf Stream Golf (Delray Beach, Fla.), Country of Florida (Delray Beach, Fla.), Delray Beach Yacht (Delray Beach, Fla.) (commodore). Home: Delray Beach Fla. Died Mar. 12, 1993.

POETTMANN, FREDERICK HEINZ, retired petroleum engineering educator; b. Germany, Dec. 20, 1919; s. Fritz and Kate (Hussen) P.; m. Anna Bell Hall, May 29, 1952; children—Susan Trudy, Phillip Mark. B.S., Case Western Res. U., 1942; M.S., U. Mich., 1944, Sc.D., 1946; grad., Advanced Mgmt. Program, Harvard U., 1966; PhD in Mining Scis. (hon.), Mining U. Leoben, Austria, 1992. Registered profl. engr., Colo., Okla. Research chemist Lubrizol Corp., Wickliffe, Ohio, 1942-43; mgr. production research Phillips Petroleum Co., Bartlesville, Okla., 1946-55; asso. research dir. Marathon Oil Co., 1955-72; mgr. comml. devel. Marathon Oil Co., Littleton, Colo., 1972-83; prof. petroleum engineering Colo. Sch. Mines, 1983-90; retired; cons. in field. Contbr. articles to numerous publs.; co-author, editor 10 books in field; patentee in field. Chmn. S. Suburban Met. Recreation and Park Dist., 1966-71; chmn. Littleton Press Council, 1967-71; bd. dirs. Hancock Recreation Center, Findlay, Ohio, 1973-77. Recipient Halliburton award for outstanding profl. achievement, 1986, Katz medal Gas Processors' Assn., 1993. Fellow AIChE; mem. AIME (hon. mem. 1984, Charles F. Rand Meml. Gold medal 1992, Nat. Acad. Engring, Soc. Petroleum Engrs. (DeGolyer Disting. Svc. medal 1990), Am. Chem. Soc., Am. Petroleum Inst., Sigma Xi, Tau Beta Pi, Alpha Chi Sigma, Phi Kappa Phi, Pi Epsilon Tau. Republican. Home: Littleton Colo. Died July 15, 1995.

POHL, RICHARD WALTER, botanist, educator, curator; b. Milw., May 21, 1916; s. Herman John and Flora Marie (Philipp) P.; m. Marjorie E. Conley, Aug. 15, 1941; children: Katharine E., Richard Wilson, Ann

Marie D. B.S. summa cum laude, Marquette U., 1939; Ph.D., U. Pa., 1947; postgrad., U. Calif., Berkeley, 1952-53. Asst. instr. U. Pa., 1939-42, 45-47; range conservationist Soil Conservation Service, Tex., 1942-45; asst. prof. botany Iowa State U., Ames, 1947-51; assoc. prof. Iowa State U., 1951-56, prof., 1956-93, disting. prof., 1975-93, prof. emeritus, 1986-93, curator Herbarium, 1950-86; research assoc. in botany Field Mus. Natural History, 1968-93. Author: How To Know the Grasses, 1954, 3d edit., 1978, Keys to Iowa Vascular Plants, 1975, Grasses of Costa Rica, 1980; contbr. articles to sci. jours. Served with AUS, 1943. NSF grantee, 1959-84, Fulbright grantee Costa Rica, 1982, 1990, Colombia, 1986. Mem. Internat. Assn. Plant Taxonomy, Am. Soc. Plant Taxonomists (treas. 1959-65, mem. council 1966-72, pres. 1973), Bot. Soc. Am., Am. Inst. Biol. Scis., AAAS, Iowa Acad. Sci. Home: Ames Iowa Died Sept. 3, 1993; cremated.

POLK, LEE, television producer-director, writer; b. Bklyn., Oct. 24, 1923; s. David and Becky (Truskinoff) P.; m. Lois Steinhauer, Jan. 16, 1949 (dec.); children: Bonnie, Joanne, David. Student, N.Y. U., 1946-48. Staff dir. Dumont TV Network, N.Y.C., 1950-55; dir. Sta.-WCBS-TV, N.Y.C., 1955-58; producer-dir. ednl. TV project Sta.-WPIX-TV, N.Y.C., 1958-62; dir. news and public affairs Sta.-WNET-TV, N.Y.C., 1962-70; dir. children's programs Nat. Ednl. TV, N.Y.C., 1970-72, ABC-TV Network, N.Y.C., 1972-76; v.p. King Features TV Prodns., Inc., N.Y.C., 1976-79; v.p. program devel. Gold Key Entertainment, N.Y.C., 1979-80; pres. Polk Communications, N.Y.C., 1980-93; v.p. family programs Revcom TV, N.Y.C., 1986-93; exec. producer Wonder Works Series, PBS; mem. faculty N.Y. U.; instr. New Sch. Social Research; lectr. Fordham U.; cons. TV HEW. Author: (with Eda LeShan) Incredible Television Machine, 1978; contbr. articles on TV to profl. jours. Workshop leader White House Conf. on Children, 1970; moderator of hearings on children's programs FCC, 1972; Mem. Greenburgh Sch. Dist. 7 Bd. Edn., Hartsdale, N.Y., 1970-75; bd. overseers Emerson Coll. Served with USAAF, 1942-46. Recipient Emmy award for Anne of Green Gables, Wonder Works Series, 1986, Christopher award for Anne of Green Gables, 1986; named 1987 Fellow of Internat. Council of NATAS. Mem. NATAS (vice chmn., pres. N.Y.C. chpt. 1976-81, nat. trustee 1977-81, chmn. bd. 1982-84), Nat. Coun. on Families and TV (bd. mem.). Home: New York N.Y. Died Feb. 19, 1993.

POLLACK, HERMAN, international science consultant; b. N.Y.C., Oct. 22, 1919; s. Phillip and Molly (Mareine) P.; m. June Rae Cohen, Nov. 19, 1949. BS in Social Sci., CCNY, 1940; postgrad., Columbia U., 1940-41; MA in Internat. Relations, George Washington U., 1965. With agys. U.S. Govt., 1941-46; with State Dept., 1946-74, chief, mgmt. staff, 1958-61, dep. asst. sec. personnel, 1961-63; assigned Nat. War Coll. (State Dept.), 1963-64, acting dir. Internat. Sci. Affairs, 1964-67, dir. internat. sci. and tech. affairs, 1967-74; cons. to govt., research prof. George Washington U., 1974-90; ret., 1990; mem. commerce tech. adv. bd. CTAB, 1975-77; mem. Weather Modification Adv. Bd., 1977-78, adv. coun. NASA, 1986-90; mem. sci., technol. adv. com. Dept. State. Served with AUS, 1943. Mem. AAAS, NAS (space applications bd. 1988-89). Club: Cosmos (Washington). Home: Silver Spring Md. Died Apr. 13, 1993; buried King David Cemetery, Fairfax, Va.

POLLOCK, MARVIN ERWIN, lawyer; b. N.Y.C., June 3, 1931; s. Benjamin and Roslyn (Dolman) P.; m. Helen Toby Schwartz, May 26, 1967; children: Jennifer, John. AB, U. Pa., 1953; JD, U. Chgo., 1956. Bar: Ill. 1956, N.Y. 1959, N.Mex. 1993, U.S. Dist. Ct. (no. dist.) Ill. 1956, U.S. Dist. Ct. (so. dist.) N.Y. 1960, U.S. Supreme Ct. 1967. Assoc. Altheimer & Gray, Chgo., 1956-58; assoc. Guggenheimer & Untermyer, N.Y.C., 1959-68, ptnr., 1968-85; mem. Herzfeld & Rubin, P.C., N.Y.C., 1986-92; of counsel Montgomery and Andrews, P.A., Santa Fe, 1993-95; pvt. practice, 1995. Author: Resale of Restricted Securities Under SEC Rules 144 and 144A, 1991; author mo. newspaper column, Art and the Law. Mem. ABA, N.Y. State Bar Assn. Died October 9, 1995.

POMPER, VICTOR HERBERT, management consultant; b. White Plains, N.Y., July 17, 1923; s. Anthony Louis and Martha (Manzek) P.; m. Anne Ritchie, 1959; children: Anthony Scott, Michael Louis, Martha Anne. BSEE, MIT, 1948, MS, 1950; grad. advanced mgmt. program, Harvard U., 1973. Registered profl. engr., Mass. Engr. Philco Corp., 1948-49; sales engr. H.H. Scott, Inc., Maynard, Mass., 1950, sales mgr., 1951, asst. gen. mgr., 1952-57, v.p., 1957-59, exec. v.p., 1959-68, pres., dir., 1968-73; pres. Levco, Inc., 1973-81; chmn., pres. Satellite Data Inc, 1981-88; pres. P & L Assocs. Inc., 1989-92; pres. Bio-Behavioral Inst., 1977; instr. Worcester Poly. Inst., 1977. Designer products selected for exhbn. at Milan Triennale, U.S. Pavilion, Brussels Worlds Fair; contbr. articles to tech. jours. Mem. adv. bd. Boston Salvation Army, 1963-69; trustee Childrens Hosp., Fund Urban Negro Devel. Sgt., Signal Corps, AUS, 1943-46. Named one of ten outstanding young men Boston Jr. C. of C., 1959. Mem. Acad. Applied Scis. (v.p., dir. 1963-92), Am. Mgmt. Assn., IEEE (sr.), Acoustical Soc. Am., Am. Inst. Physics, Inst. High Fidelity Mfrs. (dir. 1962-66), Audio Engring. Soc., Am. Assn. Indsl. Mgmt. (pres. Boston 1964-66), Internat. Soc. Gen. Semantics, Soc. Gen. Systems Rsch., Tau Beta Pi, Eta Kappa Nu. Home: Weare N.H. Died May 9, 1992.

PONNAMPERUMA, CYRIL ANDREW, chemist; b. Galle, Sri Lanka, Oct. 16, 1923; came to U.S., 1959, naturalized; s. Andrew and Grace (Siriwardene) P.; m. Valli Pal, Mar. 19, 1955; 1 child, Roshini. BA, U. Madras, 1948; BSc, U. London, 1959; PhD, U. Calif., Berkeley, 1962; DSc, U. Sri Lanka, 1978. Research assoc. Lawrence Radiation Lab., U. Calif., 1960-62; research scientist Ames Research Ctr., NASA, Mountain View, Calif., 1962-70; prof. chemistry U. Md., College Park, 1971-94; dir. Arthur C. Clarke Ctr., Sri Lanka, 1984-86; sci. advisor to pres., Sri Lanka, 1984-94; dir. Inst. Fundamental Studies, Sri Lanka, 1984-91. Author: Origins of Life, 1972; Cosmic Evolution, 1978. Contbr. articles to profl. jours. Pres. Third World Found., 1991. Fellow Royal Inst. Chemistry, Third World Acad. Scis.; mem. Am. Chem. Soc., Astron. Assn., Am. Soc. Biol. Chemists, AAAS, Geochem. Soc., Radiation Research Soc. Home: Washington D.C. Died Dec. 20, 1994.

PONTIKES, KENNETH NICHOLAS, computer leasing company executive; b. Chgo., Mar. 15, 1940; m. Lynne M. Weston, June 21, 1980. BS, So. Ill. U., 1962. With Internat. Bus. Machines, 1961-67; sales dept. OEI Sales Corp., 1967; sales rep. Officer Eletrs Inc., Chgo., 1967-68; mgr. brokerage ops. Data Power Inc., Chgo., 1968-69; pres. Comdisco, Inc., Rosemont, Ill., 1969-76; chmn. bd., pres., chief exec. officer Comdisco, Inc., 1976-94. With USAR, 1963-69. Recipient: Crain's Chgo. Bus. 1991 Exec. of the Year. Home: Des Plaines Ill. Died June 24, 1994; buried Barrington, Ill.

POOLE, JOHN JORDAN, lawyer; b. Fulton County, Ga., May 19, 1906; s. James Stubbs and Etta Ida Lou (Porter) P.; m. Jeannette Harper, July 21, 1931. Ph.B., Emory U., 1927, J.D., 1929. Bar: Ga. 1929. Ptnr. Poole, Pearce, Cooper & Smith Civil law, Atlanta, from 1934; dir. Bass Furniture Co., Peachtree on Peachtree Inn, Simons-Eastern Internat., Inc. Bd. dirs. Atlanta Union Mission Corp. Served as lt. comdr. USNR, 1942-45. Decorated Letter of Commendation. Mem. Am., Ga., Atlanta bar assns. Baptist. Clubs: Optimists (pres. 1949, sec.-treas. 21st dist. 1957), 13, Lawyers, Atlanta Athletic, Commerce (Atlanta). Lodges: Masons, Shriners. Home: Atlanta Ga. Died Dec. 31, 1994.

POPE, WILLIAM KENNETH, bishop; b. Hale, Mo., Nov. 21, 1901; s. William Mumford and Victoria (LaRue) P.; m. Kate Sayle, Mar. 16, 1930; children—Katherine Victoria, Kenneth Sayle. Student, Clarendon (Tex.) Coll., 1917-20; B.A., So. Methodist U., 1922, B.D., 1924, LL.D., 1964; student, Yale Grad. Sch., 1927-29; D.D. (hon.), Southwestern U., Georgetown, Tex., 1937, Hendrix Coll., 1961. Ordained to ministry Methodist Ch., 1925, consecrated bishop, 1960; pastor in Milford, Tex., 1924-26, Breckenridge, Tex., 1929-33, Georgetown, Tex., 1933-36, Springfield, Mo., 1936-40, Austin, Tex., 1940-49, Houston, 1949-60; bishop Ark. area Meth. Ch., 1960-64, Dallas-Ft. Worth area, 1964—; bishop-in-residence Perkins Sch. Theology, So. Meth. U., 1972-76; Mem. gen. bd. evangelism, bd. Christian social concerns Meth. Ch.; mem. program council United Meth. Ch.; chmn. bd. Western Meth. Assembly, Fayetteville, Ark., 1960-64; vis. lectr. Perkins Sch. Theology, So. Meth. U., 1949; del. World Conf. on Life and Work, Oxford, Eng., 1937, World Meth. Conf., Oxford, 1951; vis. preacher Gen. Conf. Meth. Ch. in, Mexico, 1946; rep. Meth. Ch. in U.S. to centennial celebration Methodism in, India, 1956. Author: A Pope at Roam, the Confessions of a Bishop, 1976; Contbr.: Prayer for Today. Pres. Tex. Council Chs., 1968; pres. Tex. Conf. Chs., 1969; Chmn. bd. trustees So. Meth. U., 1971-72. Mem. Lambda Chi Alpha, Theta Phi, Tau Kappa Alpha. Home: Dallas Tex. Deceased.

POPE-HENNESSY, JOHN WYNDHAM, art historian; b. London, Dec. 13, 1913; s. L.H.R. and Dame Una (Birch) P-H. Ed., Downside Sch., Balliol Coll., Oxford (Eng.) U.; LLD (hon.), U. Aberdeen, 1972; hon. doctorate, Royal Coll. Arts, 1973, U. Cattolica, Milan, Italy, 1994; hon. doctorate (posthumously), U. Florence, Italy, 1994. Mem. staff Victoria and Albert Museum, 1938-73, keeper dept. architecture and sculpture, 1954-66, dir., sec., 1967-73; dir. Brit. Mus., 1974-76; consultative chmn. dept. European Paintings Met. Mus. Art, 1977-86; prof. art Inst. of Fine Arts NYU, 1977-92; Slade prof. fine art Oxford U., 1956-57, Cambridge (Eng.) U., 1964-65; Robert Sterling Clark prof. art Williams Coll., Williamstown, Mass., 1961-62; mem. Arts Council, Eng., 1968-76, Ancient Monuments Bd. for Eng., 1969-72; dir. Royal Opera House, 1971-76; adv. bd. dirs. Met. Opera House, 1979-86. Author: Giovanni di Paolo, 1937, Sassetta, 1939, Sienese Quattrocento Painting, 1947, A Sienese Codex of the Divine Comedy, 1947, The Drawings of Domenichino at Windsor Castle, 1948, A Lecture on Nicholas Hilliard, 1949, Paolo Uccello, 1950, rev. edit., 1969, Fra Angelico, 1952, rev. edit., 1974, Italian Gothic Sculpture, 1955, 4th rev. edit., 1996, Italian Renaissance Sculpture,1996, 4th rev. edit., 1985, Italian High Renaissance and Baroque Sculpture, 1963, 4th rev. edit., 1996, Catalogue of Italian Sculpture in the Victoria and Albert Museum, 1964, Renaissance Bronzes in The Kress Collection, 1965, The Portrait in the Renaissance, 1967, Essays on Italian Sculpture, 1968, The Frick Collection, Sculpture, 1970, Raphael, 1970, (with others) Westminster Abbey, 1972, Luca della Robbia (Mitchell prize 1981), 1980, The Study and Criticism of Italian Sculpture, 1981, Benvenuto Cellini, 1985, The Robert Lehman Collection, I: Italian Paintings, 1987, (autobiography) Learning to Look, 1991, The Piero della Francesca Trail, 1991, Donatello Sculptor, 1993, Paradiso: The Illuminations to Dante's Divine Comedy by Giovanni di Paolo, 1993, On Artists & Art Historians: Selected Book Reviews, 1994. Decorated comdr. Brit. Empire; created knight, 1971; named Grand Officer, Republic of Italy, 1988, hon. citizen city of Siena, 1982, hon. citizen City of Florence, 1994, hon. fellow Balliol Coll., Oxford U., Pierpont Morgan Libr., N.Y.; recipient Serena medal Brit. Acad. Italian Studies, 1961, Torch of Learning award Hebrew U., Jerusalem, 1977, Mangia d'Oro, 1982, award Art Dealers Assn. Am., 1984, Premio della Cultura della Presidenza del Consiglio, 1991. Fellow Brit. Acad., Soc. Antiquaries, Royal Soc. Lit., Royal Acad. Arts (hon.); mem. Am. Acad. Arts and Scis., Am. Philos. Soc. (fgn.), Accademia Senese degli Intronati (corr.), Bayerische Akademie der Wissenschaften (corr.), Accademia del Disegno (hon. accademician), Accademia Clementina, Bologna, Ateneo Veneto. Home: Florence Italy Died Oct. 31, 1994; interred Florence, Italy.

POPPELBAUM, WOLFGANG JOHANN, electrical engineering and computer science educator; b. Frankfurt, Germany, Aug. 28, 1924; came to U.S., 1954, s. Hermann and Edith (Baumann) P.; m. Liesel Ida Brueck, Oct. 28, 1982. MS, U. Lausanne, 1948, PhD, 1953. Prin. investigator, charge cir. rsch. group Dept. Computer Sci., U. Ill., Urbana, 1954-89, prof. computer sci., 1963-89, dir. info. engring. lab., 1973-89, prof. emeritus, 1989-93. Author: Computer Hardware Theory, 1972, Stochastic and Deterministic Averaging Processors, 1981; contbr. articles to profl. jours. Recipient 1st prize paper award Pattern Recogn. Soc. Fellow IEEE (chmn. 4.10 com. 1971-72); mem. Swiss Phys. Soc., Am. Phys. Soc., Pattern Recognition Soc., Soc. for Info. Display, Sigma Xi. Home: Urbana Ill. Died Jan. 20, 1993; interred Urbana, Ill.

POPPER, KARL (RAIMUND), author; b. Vienna, Austria, July 28, 1902; s. Simon Siegmund Carl and Jenny (Schiff) P.; m. Josefine Anna Henninger, Apr. 11, 1930 (dec. Nov. 1985). PhD, U. Vienna, 1928; DLitt (hon.), U. London, 1948; LLD (hon.), U. Chgo., 1962, U. Denver, 1966; LittD (hon.), U. Warwick, Eng., 1971, U. Canterbury, New Zealand, 1973; DLitt (hon.), City U. London, 1976, Salford (Eng.) U., 1976, Oxford, 1982; Dr. (hon.), U. Mannheim, Fed. Republic Germany, 1978; Dr. rer. nat. (hon.), U. Vienna, 1978; DLitt (hon.), U. Guelph, Can., 1978; Dr. rer. pol. (hon.), U. Frankfurt, Can., 1979; PhD (hon.), U. Salzburg, Austria, 1979; LittD (hon.), U. Cambridge, Eng., 1980, U. Oxford, 1982; DSc (hon.), Gustavus Adolphus Coll., St. Peter, Minn., 1982, U. London, 1986; PhD (hon.), U. Eichstatt, 1991, U. Madrid, 1991, U. Athens, 1992. Sr. lectr. U. N.Z., 1937-45; reader, then prof. logic and sci. method U. London, 1949-69, emeritus, 1969-94; William James lectr. Harvard U., 1950; Compton Meml. lectr. Washington U., St. Louis, 1965; Henry Broadhead Meml. lectr. U. Christchurch, N.Z., 1973; Herbert Spencer lectr. Oxford U., 1961, 73; Shearman Meml. lectr. U. London, 1961; Romanes lectr. Oxford U., 1972; Darwin lectr., Cambridge U.; fellow Ctr. Advanced Studies, Stanford U., 1956-57, Inst. Advanced Studies, Canberra, Australia, 1962, Vienna, 1964; vis. prof. univs. in U.S., Australia; hon. fellow Darwin Coll., Cambridge, 1980; hon. research fellow dept. history and philosophy of sci. Chelsea Coll., U. London, 1982. Author: Logik der Forschung, 9th edit., 1989, The Open Society and Its Enemies, 14th edit., 1983, The Poverty of Historicism, 9th edit., 1976, The Logic of Scientific Discovery, 13th edit., 1987, Conjectures and Refutations, 10th edit., 1989, Objective Knowledge, 7th edit., 1983, Unended Quest: An Intellectual Autobiography, 7th edit., 1986, Realism and the Aim of Science, 1983, The Open Universe, 1982, Quantum Theory and the Schism in Physics, A World of Propensities, 1990; co-author: The Self and Its Brain, 1977, Auf der Suche nach einer besseren Welt, 4th edit., 1989, Die Zukunft ist offen, 2d edit., 1989. Created knight, 1965; decorated insignia Order of Companions of Honor, Grand Cross with star; recipient prize City of Vienna, 1965, Sonning prize U. Copenhagen, 1973, Lippincott award Am. Polit. Sci. Assn., 1976, Grand Decoration of Honour in gold, Austria, 1976, Dr. Karl Renner prize, Vienna, 1977, Dr. Leopold Lucas prize U. Tubingen, 1981, Internat. prize Catalonian Inst. of Mediterranean Studies, 1989, Kyoto prize Inamori Found., 1992. Fellow Royal Soc., Brit. Acad., London Sch. Econs. (hon.), Darwin Coll. Cambridge U. (hon.); mem. l'Inst. de France; mem. Am. Acad. Arts and Scis. (fgn. hon.), Internat. Acad. Philosophy Sci. (titulaer), Acad. Royale de Belgique (assoc.), Royal Soc. N.Z. (hon.), Acad. Internat. d'Histoire des Scis. (hon.), Deutsche Akademie für Sprache und Dichtung (hon.), Acad. Europeéne des Sciences, des Arts et des Lettres, Soc. Straniero delle Accad. Nazionale dei Lincei, Austrian Acad. Sci. (hon.), Phi Beta Kappa (Harvard U. chpt.). Home: London Eng. Died Sept. 17, 1994.

PORADA, EDITH, archaeologist, educator; b. Vienna, Austria, Aug. 22, 1912. PhD, U. Vienna, 1935; DLitt (hon.), Columbia U., 1989. Mem. faculty Queens Coll.,

1950-58; mem faculty Columbia U., 1958-94, prof. art history and archaeology emeritus, 1982-94; hon. curator seals and tablets Pierpont Morgan Library, 1956-94; lectr. Una's, Berkeley, Mo., 1990. Author: Alt Iran, 1963, The Art of Ancient Iran, 1965; also monographs, articles. Recipient award for disting. achievement Archaeol. Inst. Am., 1977, 1st Internat. Gold Medal award San Marco, 1988, Primo Internazionale i Cavalli d'Oro di San Marco, 1988; Guggenheim fellow, 1983-84. Fellow Am. Acad. Arts and Scis., Brit. Acad. (corr.), Austrian Acad.; mem. Am. Philos. Soc. Home: New York N.Y. Died Mar. 24, 1994.

PORTER, ERIC (RICHARD), actor; b. London, Eng., Apr. 8, 1928; s. Richard John and Phoebe Elizabeth (Spall) P.; ed. Wimbledon Tech. Coll. First profl. appearance Shakespeare Meml. Theatre Co., Arts, Cambridge, Eng.; 1945; 1st appearance in London stage travelling repertory co. St. Joan, King's Hammersmith, 1946; with Birmingham Repertory Theatre, 1948-50; under contract H.M. Tennant, Ltd., 1951-54; appeared in plays The Silver Box, 1951, The Three Sisters, 1951, Thor, With Angels, 1951, Noah, 1951, The Same Sky, 1952, Under the Sycamore Tree, 1952; with Lyric, Hammersmith, 1953, Bristol Old Vic Co., 1954, 55-56, Old Vic Co., 1954-55; Romanoff and Juliet, Piccadilly, 1956, A Man of Distinction, Edinburgh Festival and Princes, 1957; Time and Again, 1957, The Visit, N.Y.C., 1958; Coast of Coromandel, 1959; Rosmersholm, Royal Ct., 1959, Comedy, 1965; under contract Royal Shakespeare Co., 1960-65; Government Inspector, Aldwych, 1966; Stratford Season, 1968; U.S. tour Dr. Faustus, 1969; My Little Boy . . . My Big Girl, Fortune, 1969; The Protagonist, Brighton, 1971; Peter Pan, London Coliseum, 1971; Twelfth Night, St. George's Elizabethean Theatre, 1976 (films) The Fall of the Roman Empire, 1964, The Pumpkin Eater, 1964, The Heroes of Telemark, 1965, Kaleidoscope, 1966, The Lost Continent, 1968. Hands of the Ripper, 1971, Nicholas and Alexandra, 1971, Anthony and Cleopatra, 1972. Hitler, the Last 10 Days, 1973, The Day of the Jackal, 1973, The Belstone Fox, 1973, Callan, 1974, Hennessy, 1975, The 39 Steps, 1978, Little Lord Fauntleroy, 1980, also appeared on TV including The Forsyte Saga, BBC (Best Actor award Guild TV producers and Dirs. 1967), The Jewel in the Crown, 1984, Sherlock Holmes, 1984, Oliver Twist, 1985. Recipient Drama award as best actor of 1959. Club: Buckstone. Deceased. Home: London Eng.

PORTER, HAL, author, playright; b. Albert Park, Victoria, Australia, Feb. 16, 1911; s. Harold Owen and Ida Violet (Ruff) P.; m. Olivia Parnham, 1939 (div. 1943). Student Kensington State Sch., Bairnsdale State Sch., Bairnsdale High Sch. Schoolmaster, Edn. Dept. of Victoria State, 1927-37, Queen's Coll., Adelaide, 1938-41, Prince Alfred Coll., Adelaide, 1942-45, Hutchins Sch., Hobart, 1946-47, Knox Grammer Sch., Sydney, 1947-48, Ballarat Coll., 1948-49, Nijimura Sch., Japan, 1949-51; regional librarian Gippsland and North Central Victoria, 1952-60; author: Short Stories, 1942, The Hexagon, 1956, A Handful of Pennies, 1958, The Tilted Cross, 1961, A Bachelor's Children, 1962, The Tower, 1963, The Watcher on the Cast-Iron Balcony, 1963, The Cats of Venice, 1965, Stars of the Australian Stage and Screen, 1965, The Paper Chase, 1966, The Professor, 1966, The Actors: an Image of the New Japan, 1968, Eden House, 1969, Mr. Butterfry, 1970, Selected Stories, 1971, The Right Thing, 1971, It Could be You, 1972, Fredo Fuss Love Life, 1974, In an Australian Country Graveyard, 1974, The Extra, 1975, Bairnsdale: Portrait of an Australian Country Town, 1977, A Portable Hal Porter, 1979, Seven Cities, 1980, Parker, 1981, The Clairvoyant Goat, 1981, A.M., 1982. Recipient Britannica Literary award, 1976; Commonwealth Literary fellow, 1956, 60, 64, 68, 72, 75-76, 77-81. Deceased. Home: Ballarat Victoria Australia

PORTFOLIO, ALMERINDO GERARD, retired ophthalmologist; b. Union City, N.J., May 10, 1923; s. Pasquale and Angela (Falasca) P.; m. Claire Enright, Nov. 22, 1947; children: Deidre, Almerindo, Drew, Maura, Melissa. B.A., St. Peters Coll., 1943; M.D., N.Y. U., 1947, M.S. in Ophthalmology, 1954. Diplomate: Am. Bd. Ophthalmology. Intern Kings County Hosp., Bklyn., 1947-49; resident in pathology Cleve. City Hosp., 1949-50; resident in ophthalmology N.Y. U.-Bellevue Hosp., N.Y.C., 1951-53; practice medicine specializing in ophthalmology Ridgewood, N.J., 1956-93; mem. staffs Valley Hosp., Ridgewood, N.J., Bellevue and Univ. hosps., N.Y.C.; clin. prof. ophthalmology N.Y. U. Served as capt., M.C. USMC, 1954-56. Fellow A.C.S.; mem. AMA, N.J. Acad. Ophthalmology, Am. Acad. Ophthalmology and Otolaryngology, N.J., Bergen County (N.J.) med. socs. Roman Catholic. Home: Paramus N.J. Died Aug. 28, 1993.

PORTNOFF, COLLICE HENRY, English language educator emeritus; b. San Luis Obispo, Calif., Dec. 9, 1898; d. James H. and Kate E. (Wilson) Henry; m. George E. Portnoff, Aug. 16, 1931; 1 dau., Lisa (Mrs. James Crehan). A.B., U. Calif.-Berkeley, 1921, M.A., 1922; Ph.D., Stanford U., 1927; Carter Meml. fellow, also fellow acad, Am. Acad. in, Rome, 1927-30, M.A., 1930. Instr. Belmont (Calif.) Mil. Acad., 1922-23; teaching asst. Stanford, 1923-27; instr. Ariz. State Coll., Flagstaff, 1930-41; cryptanalyst U.S. Signal Corps, Washington, 1942; translator Allied Mil. Govt., Washington, 1942-43; prof. English Ariz. State U., Tempe, 1945-69; prof. emeritus Ariz. State U., 1969—, chmn. dept., acting head div. lang. and lit., 1957-58, chmn. English dept., 1957-64; Dir. pageant Miracle of the Roses, Scottsdale, Ariz., 1960, gen. chmn., 1961. Author: (play) (with Samuel R. Golding) Naked Came I, 1957, My Close Association With Maria Martinez Sierra, 1993; ofcl. translator: Gregorio and Maria Martinez Sierra, 1947—; editor: (with Stanley Milstein)The History of Otology (Adam Politzer); contbg. editor The Ariz. Republic, Phoenix; co-translator (book rev.): The Cursillo Movement (from Spanish); reviewer Scottsdale Daily Progress, 1978—. Bd. dirs. Phoenix Chamber Music Soc., Valley Shakespeare Theatre; mem. adv. council Greater Phoenix chpt. UNA-USA. Recipient medal for achievement in drama Nat. Soc. Arts and Letters; Distinguished Tchr. award Ariz. State U. Alumni Assn. Mem. AAUP, Ariz. Coll. Assn., Soc. Gen. Semantics, Nat. Soc. Arts and Letters, Washington, Nat. Council Tchrs. English, Conf. Coll. Communication and Composition, Centro Studié E Scambi Internazionali (v.p.), Bus. and Profl. Womens Club Tempe, Cath. Bus. Assn., Am. Translators Assn., Alumni Assn. Am. Acad. in Rome, Rocky Mountain Modern Lang. Assn. (pres. 1964), Pi Sigma, Sigma Delta Pi, Alpha Lambda Delta, Gamma Phi Beta, Phi Kappa Phi. Clubs: Faculty, Women's Faculty (Ariz. State U.); Dinner (Scottsdale), Paradise Valley Country (Scottsdale). Home: Los Angeles Calif.

POSNER, EDWARD CHARLES, telecommunications engineer, educator; b. N.Y.C., Aug. 10, 1933; s. Gustave and Kate (Cohen) P.; m. Sylvia Kouzel, Apr. 26, 1956; children: Joyce K., Steven K. BA, U. Chgo., 1952, MS, 1953, PhD, 1957. Mem. tech. staff advanced studies Bell Labs., N.Y.C., 1956-57; research instr. math. U. Wis.-Madison, 1957-60; asst. prof. math. Harvey Mudd Coll., Claremont, Calif., 1960-61; with Jet Propulsion Lab., Pasadena, Calif., 1961-93; researcher, mgr. Calif. Inst. Tech. Jet Propulsion Lab., Pasadena, 1961-78, mgr. telecommunications planning, 1978-83, chief technologist telecommunications and data acquisition, 1983-93; vis. prof. elec. engring. Calif. Inst. Tech., 1978-93; cons. on seismic signal processing, 1980-93, high definition TV, 1988-93, theft deterrence, 1989-93, radio interference, 1991-93; mem. adv. bd. in comm. Inst. Def. Analyses, Princeton, N.J., 1983-86. Author: (with John Pierce) Introduction to Communication Science and Systems, 1980; editor: (with others) Studies in Combinatorics, 1970; translation editor: Road Traffic Control, 1977; patentee in field. Bd. dirs. Caltech Y, 1978-81; founding chmn. Neural Info. Processing Sys. Found., 1992-93. Fellow IEEE (gov. info. theory group); mem. AAAS, AIAA, Soc. Indsl. and Applied Math. (chmn. So. Calif. sect. 1967-68, 72-73), Am. Math. Soc., Math. Assn. Am., Soc. Exploration Geophysicists, Skeptics, Phi Beta Kappa, Sigma Xi. Died June 15, 1993; buried Mountain View Cemetery, Pasadena, Calif.

POTTER, DENNIS (CHRISTOPHER GEORGE) (CHRISTOPHER GEORGE POTTER), author; b. Joyford Hill, Gloucester, Eng., May 17, 1935; s. Walter and Margaret Potter; m. Margaret Morgan, 1959; 3 children. BA with honours, Oxford (Eng.) U., 1959; hon. fellow, New Coll., Oxford U., 1987. Mem. current affairs staff BBC-TV, London, 1959-61; feature writer, then TV critic London Daily Herald, 1961-64; editorial writer London Sun, 1964; TV critic Sunday Times, 1976-78. Author: (teleplays) The Confidence Course, 1965, Alice, 1965, Stand Up Nigel Barton, 1965, Vote Vote Vote for Nigel Barton, 1965, Where the Buffalo Roam, 1966, Emergency Ward Nine, 1966, Message for Posterity, 1967, A Beast with Two Backs, 1968, The Bonegrinder, 1968, Shaggy Dog, 1968, Moonlight in the Highway, 1969, Angels Are So Few, 1970, Lay Down Your Arms, 1970, Paper Roses, 1971, Casanova (six play series), 1971, Traitor, 1971, Follow the Yellow Brick Road, 1973, A Tragedy of Two Ambitions, 1973, Only Make Believe, 1973, Schmoedipus, 1974, Late Call (TV serial), 1975, Double Dare, 1976, Joe's Ark, 1976, Where Adam Stood, 1976, Pennies from Heaven (TV series), 1978 (Brit. Acad. Film TV Arts award 1978), The Mayor of Casterbridge, 1978, Blue Remembered Hills, 1979 (Brit. Acad. Film TV Arts award 1980), Blade on the Feather, Rain on the Roof, Cream in My Coffee, 1980 (Prix Italia 1982), Tender Is The Night, 1985, The Singing Detective, 1986, Visitors, 1987, Christabel, 1988, Blackeyes, 1989, (screenplays) Pennies from Heaven (from TV series), 1981, Brimstone and Treacle (from stage play), 1982, Gorky Park, 1983, Dreamchild, 1985, Track 29, 1988, (dir., screenplay) Secret Friends, 1992, (plays) Vote Vote Vote for Nigel Barton, 1968, Stand Up Nigel Barton, 1968, Son of Man, 1969, Only Make Believe, 1974, Brimstone and Treacle, 1977, Sufficient Carbohydrate, 1983, Waiting for the Boat, 1984, (novels) Hide and Seek, 1973, Pennies from Heaven, 1982, Ticket to Ride, 1986, Blackeyes, 1987, (non-fiction) The Glittering Coffin, 1960, The Changing Forest: Life in the Forest of Dean Today, 1962. Labour candidate for Pariament from East Hertforshire, 1964. Recipient Writer of Yr. award Writers Guild Great Britain, 1966, 69, Soc. Film and TV Arts award, 1966. Home: Herefordshire Eng. Died June 7, 1994.

POTTER, VINCENT GEORGE, philosophy educator; b. N.Y.C., Oct. 18, 1928; s. Vincent George and Mary Margaret (Hogan) P. AB, Bellarmine Coll., Plattsburg, N.Y., 1953, PhL, 1954; STL, St. Albert De Louvain, Belgium, 1961; PhD, Yale U., 1965. Instr. philosophy St. Peter's Coll., Jersey City, 1954-57; from asst. prof. to dept. chmn. Fordham U., Bronx, 1965-78, rector, Jesuit Community, 1978-83, v.p. for acad. affairs, 1987-92, prof. philosophy, 1992-93, Loyola chair Humanities, 1993—. Author: C.S. Peirce on Norms and Ideals, 1969, Readings in Epistemology: Descartes, Locke, Berkeley, Hume, Kant, 1988, Philosophy of Knowledge, 1989; editor: Doctrine and Experience, 1984; editor-in-chief Internat. Philos. Quar., 1985—; contbr. articles to profl. jours. Trustee Fordham U., 1978-83. Mem. Am. Philos. Assn., Am. Cath. Philos. Assn., Soc. for Advancement of Am. Philosophy, C.S. Peirce Soc. (pres.). Roman Catholic. Home: Bronx N.Y. Died May 3, 1994.

POTTS, M. DEAN, supermarket company executive; b. Blairsville, Pa., Aug. 31, 1926; s. Samuel Merle and Helen (Bergman) P.;. B.S. in Bus. Adminstrn., U. Pitts., 1948; postgrad., NYU Grad. Sch. Bus., 1968-74. V.p. fin., treas. The Great Atlantic & Pacific Tea Co., Montvale, N.J., 1948-77; sr. v.p. fin., treas. First Nat. Supermarkets, Hartford, Conn., 1977-79; treas., sr. v.p., chief fin. officer Golub Corp., Schenectady, N.Y., 1981-95. Mem., past pres. Northeastern Assn. Blind at Albany, Inc., 1985-95; coun. mem. Coll. of Agr. and Tech. SUNY, Cobleskill, 1987-95; adv. bd. Haven of Schenectady, N.Y., 1989. With USAF, 1943-45. Mem. Fin. Execs. Inst., Am. Mgmt. Assn., Food Mktg. Inst. (chmn. electronic funds transfer com. 1988-95). Home: Schenectady N.Y. Died Apr. 26, 1995.

POULOS, PETER PETER, thoracic surgeon, lawyer; b. Orange, N.J., Feb. 18, 1922; s. Peter Spiro and Jennie (Polychronopoulos) P.; m. Helen Siganos, Aug. 22, 1948; children: Paul, John, Eoanna, Maria. BS in Aero. Engring., MIT, 1947; MD, Cornell U., 1952; JD, Rutgers U., Newark, 1989. Bar: N.J. 1990; diplomate Am. Bd. Gen. Surgery, Am. Bd. Thoracic Surgery. Surg. intern Bellevue Hosp., N.Y.C., 1952-53, resident in surgery, 1953-55; NIH rsch. fellow in physiology Cornell Med. Coll., N.Y.C., 1955-56; resident in surgery Manhattan VA Hosp., N.Y.C., 1956-58; resident in thoracic surgery Triboro Hosp., N.Y.C., 1958-60; founder, dir. Heart Inst., Newark, 1960-77; pvt. practice thoracic surgery various hosps. Newark,, Elizabeth and Livingston, N.J., 1977-86; dir. Med. Law Inst., Maplewood, N.J., 1990-95; cons. various law firms, N.J., 1990-95; clin. prof. surgery U. Med. N.J., Newark, 1962-95; lectr. medicine for lawyers Med. Law Inst., Maplewood, 1990-95. Contbr. articles to profl. jours. 1st lt. USAAF, 1943-45, Eng. Decorated Air medal with silver oak leaf cluster. NIH fellow, Cardiovascular Rsch. fellow, Cornell Med. Coll. fellow, 1955-58. Fellow ACS, Am. Soc. Law and Medicine; mem. AMA, N.J. Am. Med. Soc., N.J. Bar Assn., Rsch. Soc., Tau Beta Pi, Sigma Xi. Greek Orthodox. Home: Maplewood N.J. Died Dec. 13, 1994.

POWELL, GEORGE VAN TUYL, lawyer; b. Seattle, May 14, 1910; s. John Havard and Elizabeth Sargent (Gastman) P.; m. Katherine Jaynes, Aug. 22, 1933; children—Jane Powell Thomas, George Van Tuyl, Lisa Katherine. Grad., Phillips Exeter Acad., 1927; A.B., Princeton, 1931; LL.B., U. Wash., 1934. Bar: Wash. bar 1935. Pvt. practice Seattle; counsel Lane Powell Spears Lubersky, 1996. Mem. Wash. Ho. of Reps., 1947-53; Commr. Uniform State Laws, 1952-64; Regent U. Wash., 1965-77. Served to lt. USNR, 1944-46. Mem. ABA (past del.), Wash. Bar Assn. (past bd. govs.), Seattle Golf Club (past pres.), Univ. Club Seattle (past pres.), Rainier Club (Seattle). Home: Seattle Wash. Died April 6, 1996.

POWER, EUGENE BARNUM, microphotographer, business executive; b. Traverse City, Mich., June 4, 1905; s. Glenn Warren and Annette (Barnum) P.; m. Sadye L. Harwick, June 17, 1929 (dec.); 1 child, Philip H. A.B., U. Mich., 1927, M.B.A., 1930, L.H.D., 1971; L.H.D., St. John's U., 1966. With Edwards Bros., Inc., Ann Arbor, Mich., 1930-38, v.p., 1935-38; engaged in expts. with methods and uses of microfilm technique for reprodn. materials for research, 1935; founder Univ. Microfilms (merged Xerox Corp., 1962), 1938-70; dir. Xerox Corp., 1962-68; organized Microfilms, Inc. (as distbn. agency, using microfilm as reprodn. medium for sci. and tech. materials), 1942-62, Projected Books, Inc. (a non-profit corp., for distbn. of reading and entertainment materials in photog. form to physically incapacitated), 1944-70, Eskimo Art, Inc. (non-profit corp.), 1953, Univ. Microfilms, Ltd., London, 1952; dir. Domino's Pizza Inc., Ann Arbor., 1978-92; Past chmn. Mich. Coordinating Council State Higher Edn. Regent U. Mich., 1956-66; del. Internat. Fedn. Documentation Conf., 1939, Paris, 1946, Berne, 1947; pres. Internat. Micrographic Congress, 1964-65, Nat. Microfilm Assn., 1946-54; spl. rep. Coordinator of Info. and Library of Congress, London, 1942, OSS, 1943-45; mem. Nat. Council on Humanities, 1968-74. Author numerous articles. Trustee Carleton Coll., 1966-75, St. John's U., 1966-71; pres., chmn. The Power Found., 1968-93; chmn. Ann Arbor Summer Festival, Inc., 1978-88, chmn. emeritus, 1988-93. Recipient award merit Nat. Microfilm Assn., 1956, fellow, 1963; hon. fellow Magdalene Coll., Cambridge, 1967; hon. fellow Northwestern Mich. Coll., 1967; decorated hon. Knight

Comdr. Order of British Empire Eng., 1977. Mem. U. Mich. Alumni Assn. (Achievement award 1990). Club: Rotary (Paul Harris fellow 1979). Home: Ann Arbor Mich. Died Dec. 6, 1993.

POWERS, RICHARD DALE, agricultural journalism educator; b. Akron, Ohio, Dec. 29, 1927; s. Dale Felton and Jane Isabel (Martin) P.; m. Janet Elizabeth Hoover, June 18, 1951 (dec. May 1966); children: Daniel, Jane; m. Joyce Ann Quigley, May 15, 1969 (div. Nov. 1982); children: Mark, Michele, Andrea, Shara; m. Peggy Krueger, Aug. 20, 1988. B.S. in Agrl., Ohio State U., 1950; M.S., U. Wis., 1952, Ph.D., 1957. Instr. U. Wis., Madison, 1951-57, asst. prof., 1957-60, assoc. prof., 1960-66, prof. argrl. journalism, 1966-95, chmn. dept., 1964-69; vis. prof. Nat. Sch. Agr., Chapingo, Mex., 1969-70. Author: Data Analysis for Social Sciences, 1982; co-author: Agricultural Newswriting; author: ann. reports What's New in Farm Sci., 1951-60. Served with USAF, 1946-48. Recipient Pioneer award Am. Agrl. Editors Assn., 1962; named Disting. Prof. U. Wis Coll. of Agr. and Life Scis., 1982. Home: Austin Tex. Died June 24, 1995.

POZZETTA, GEORGE ENRICO, history educator; b. Great Barrington, Mass., Oct. 29, 1942; s. Attilio Luigi and Mary (Ciolina) P.; m. Sandra Gail Magdalenski, Sept. 17, 1966; children: James, Adrienne. BA, Providence Coll., 1964, MA, 1965; PhD, U. N.C., 1971. Instr. history Providence (R.I.) Coll., 1965-66; teaching assoc. U. N.C., Chapel Hill, 1968-71; from asst. prof. to assoc prof. U. Fla., Gainesville, 1971-84; prof. history U. Fla., 1984-94; lectr. history U. Md. Far East Ext. Div., 1968; edtl. bd. Jour. Am. Ethnic History, Italian Americana, from 1989. Co-author: Immigrant World of Your City, 1987 (award); co-author, editor: The Italian Diaspora, 1992, Shades of the Sunbelt, 1988; editor: American Immigration & Ethnicity (20 vols.), 1991. Served to 1st lt. U.S. Army, 1966-68, Vietnam. Recipient Cavalieri Nell'Ordine Almerito award Italian Govt., 1984; named among oustanding young men of Am. Nat. Jaycees, 1977. Mem. Am. Hist. Assn. (chair prize com. 1988-90, editor quarterly publ. 1993-94), Fla. Hist. Soc. (chair Patrick prize com. 1982-83), Am. Italian Hist. Soc. (pres. 1978-80, edtl. bd.), Southern Hist. Assn. (membership com. 1990-91), Immigration History Soc. (exec. coun. 1982-84, Theodore Saloutos award 1987, edtl. bd.), Orgn. Am. Historians. Democrat. Roman Catholic. Home: Gainesville Fla. Died, Apr. 19, 1995.

PRAEGER, FREDERICK AMOS, book publisher; b. Vienna, Austria, Sept. 16, 1915; came to U.S., 1938; s. Max Meyer and Manya (Foerster) P.; m. Cornelia E. Blach, May 8, 1946 (div. 1959); children: Claudia Elizabeth, Andrea Maxine; m. Heloise Babette Arons, Feb. 5, 1960 (div. 1983); children: Manya Margaret, Alexandra Yael; m. Kellie Masterson, Dec. 1983. Student, U. Vienna, 1933-38, Sorbonne, Paris, 1934; L.H.D. (hon.), U. Denver. Assoc. editor R. Loewit Verlag, Vienna, 1935-38, sports writer; various positions, including jewelry salesman, asst. merchandising mgr. jewelry store chain, 1938-41; civilian head publs. br., info. control div. U.S. Milt. Govt., Hesse, Germany, 1946-48; pres. Frederick A. Praeger, Inc., Pubs., 1950-68; chmn. Phaidon Pubs., Ltd., London; vice chmn., pub. Westview Press, Boulder, Colo., 1975-94; adj. prof. Grad. Sch. Librarianship and assoc. dir. Pub. Inst., 1976, U. Denver. Served to 1st lt. AUS, 1942-46. Decorated Bronze Star. Recipient Carey-Thomas award for creative pub. R.R. Bowker Co., 1957, Austrian Svc. Gold medal, 1990, Austrian Athletic Gold medal, 1990; named hon. grad. U.S. Army Spl. Warfare Sch., 1965. Mem. Internat. Inst. for Strategic Studies, Coun. on Fgn. Rels. Clubs: Meadows Tennis, Flatiron Athletic (Boulder); Denver Track; Cosmos (Washington); Racquet (Vail, Colo.). Home: Boulder Col. Died May 28, 1994.

PRATT, JOHN HELM, federal judge; b. Portsmouth, N.H., Nov. 17, 1910; s. Harold Boswell and Marguerite (Rockwell) R.; m. Bernice G. Safford, Oct. 25, 1938; children: Clare, Lucinda (Mrs. Daniel D. Pearlman), John Helm Jr., Patricia (Mrs. George Moriarty), Mary (Mrs. John Bruadenburg). AB cum laude, Harvard U., 1930, LLB, 1934. Bar: D.C. 1934. Pvt. practice law Washington; ptnr. Morris, Pearce, Gardner & Pratt, 1954-68; asst. counsel Boys Club Greater Washington, 1948-68; U.S. dist. judge, Washington, 1968-95. Chmn. Montgomery County (Md.) Housing Authority, 1950-53; chmn. bd. trustees D.C. Legal Aid Agy., 1967-68; chmn. U.S. Jud. Conf. Com. on Jud. Ethics, 1985-90. Capt. USMCR, 1942-46, PTO. Decorated Bronze Star, Purple Heart; recipient Army citation for civilian svc. in field prosthetics, 1948. Mem. ABA (ho dels. 1963-64), Am. Bar Found., Bar Assn. D.C. (pres. 1963-64), Harvard Law Sch. Assn. (pres. Washington 1952-53), Assoc. Harvard Clubs (pres. 1952-53), Marine Corps Res. Officers Assn. (judge adv. gen. 1961-68), Barristers Club (pres. 1969), Lawyers (pres. 1987), Harvard Club pres. 1949-51), Chevy Chase Club. Democrat. Roman Catholic. Home: Bethesda Md. Died Aug. 11, 1995.

PREATE, ERNEST D., SR., lawyer; b. Pescopagano, Italy, Jan. 10, 1909; s. Dominick J. and Theresa B. (Manzo) P.; m. Anne R. Smith, Feb. 11, 1939; children: Ernest D., Donald L., Robert A., Carlon. AB, Columbia U., 1931; JD, U. Pa., 1934; LHD (hon.), U. Scranton, 1969. Bar: Pa. 1934, U.S. Ct. Appeals (3d cir.) 1957. Ptnr. Levy, Mattes, Preate &McNulty, Scranton, Pa., 1958-66, Levy & Preate, Scranton, 1966-95; dir., gen. counsel Scranton Lackawanna Indsl. Bldg. Co., Lackawanna Indsl. Fund Enterprises, 1982; chmn. Pocono N.E. Devel. Fund, 1984; bd. dir. First Ea. Bank. Pres., Econ.Devel. Coun. N.E. Pa. 1977, MetroAction, Inc., 1981; cited by Greater Scranton Chamber of Commerce for dedicated commitment as Founder and First President (1977) of MetroAction, Inc, a community development corp., June 8, 1983; mem. adv. bd., counsel U. Scranton, 1981; trustee Scranton Prep. Sch., 1982; chmn. bd. dirs. Scranton State Gen. Hosp., 1969; bd. dirs., gen. counsel. Pa. Devel. Credit Corp., 1963-95; "Man of the Year Award", Columbus Day Assn. of Lacka. Co., Pa., 1984; Jesuit "Ignation Award" for outstanding civic business and religious community service, Scranton Preparatory School, 1985; citation from Commonwealth of Pa. House of Reps. for outstanding civic leadership in Northeastern Pa., 1986; chmn. Gov.'s Trial Ct. Nominating Commn., 1986-87. Recipient Lifetime Achievement award Pa. and Am. Planning Assns., 1991; named Disting. Pennsylvanian, William Penn Soc., 1980; named to Bus. Hall of Fame, Jr. Achievement of Northeastern Pa., 1991. Mem. ABA, Pa. Bar Assn. (professionalism com. 1990), Am. Judicature Soc., Lackawanna County Bar Assn., Community Assn. Inst., Scranton C. of C. (bd. dir.), Jud. Conf. 3rd Cir. of U.S. Republican. Roman Catholic. Clubs: Scranton Country, Scranton. Co-author: Pennsylvania Industrial Development Authority Law, 1956. Contbr. articles to profl. jours. Died June 7, 1995. Home: Old Forge Pa.

PRENDERGAST, JOHN PATRICK, accounting company executive; b. Jersey City, Dec. 13, 1927; s. William James and Hannah (Conmy) P.; m. Peg Prendergast, Dec. 27, 1952; children—Kevin, William, Mary Kay, Brian, Sheila; m. Margaret Teresa McGrath. A.B., Fordham U., 1950; M.B.A., NYU, 1957. Ptnr., cons. Arthur Young & Co., N.Y.C., 1961-63, mng. assoc., 1963-66; prin. Arthur Young, N.Y.C., 1966-68, ptnr., 1968—. Track and field ofcl. Olympic Games, Los Angeles, 1984; mem. adv. council Fordham U., Pace U., N.C. Central U., Durham, 1985. Served to lt. USN, 1950-53, Korea; capt. USNR (ret.). Roman Catholic. Clubs: Fordham (pres. 1970-75) (N.Y.C.); Spiked Shoe. Home: Ramsey N.J. Died Feb. 24, 1993.

PRESSLER, HERMAN PAUL, lawyer; b. Austin, Tex., Dec. 12, 1902; s. Herman P. and Veannis (Maddox) P.; m. Elsie W. Townes, Nov. 20, 1928; children—Herman Paul III, Townes Garrett. Student, Va. Mil. Inst, 1919-20; LL.B., U. Tex. at Austin, 1925; grad. advanced mgmt. program, Harvard, 1951. Bar: Tex. bar 1925. Gen. practice Houston, 1925-33, 68-95; mem. law dept. Humble Oil and Refining Co., Houston, 1933-55, dir., 1955-59; v.p., mem. bd. mgmt. Humble Oil and Refining Co. (Humble div.), 1959-60, v.p. pub. relations, 1960-67; dir. Humble Pipe Line Co., 1948-55. Chmn. Houston and Harris County chpt. A.R.C., 1952-54; chmn. emeritus bd. trustees Tex. Children's Hosp.; bd. dirs. Tex. Med. Center, pres., 1976-81; mem. devel. bd. Inst. Texan Cultures; trustee Baylor Coll. Medicine. Mem. Tex. Bar Assn., Miss. Bar Assn., Houston Bar Assn. (pres. 1950-51), Philos. Soc. Tex., Chi Phi, Phi Delta Phi. Republican. Baptist. Clubs: Houston Country (Houston), Petroleum (Houston), Bayou (Houston); Eagle Lake Rod and Gun. Home: Houston Tex. Died May 2, 1995.

PRESTINI, JAMES LIBERO, sculptor, designer, educator; b. Waterford, Conn., Jan. 13, 1908; s. Claude and Angelina (Buzzi) P. BS., Yale, 1930, student Sch. Edn., 1932; student, Ill. Inst. Tech. Inst. Design, Italy, 1953-56. Master Lake Forest (Ill.) Acad., 1933-42; instr. Ill. Inst. Tech. Inst. Design, 1939-46; research engr. Armour Research Found., Chgo., 1943-53; mem. faculty U. Calif. at Berkeley, 1956-93, prof. design architecture, 1962-93; Bauhaus-Archiv research prof. W. Berlin, 1977; cons. univs., research instns. in U.S., India, Germany, 1946-93; co-founder Creators Equity Found., Berkeley, Calif., 1982. Exhbns. prin. U.S. museums and univs., 1938-93; design work featured by Internat. Turned Objects Show, Phila. Exhbn., 1988; represented in permanent collections, Mus. Modern Art, N.Y.C., Cleve. Mus. Art, Art Inst. Chgo., Met. Mus. Art, N.Y.C., San Francisco Mus. Art, Smithsonian Instn., Washington, Buffalo Albright-Knox Art Gallery, Seattle Art Mus., Milw. Art Inst., Mpls. Walker Art Ctr., Chgo. Hist. Soc., U. Calif.-Berkeley Art Mus., U. Ill. Krannert Art Mus., N.Y. Cooper-Hewitt Mus. Design, Bauhaus Archiv Mus., Berlin, Pompidou Centre, Paris, Phila. Mus. Art, Mus. Fine Arts, Boston, Bklyn. Mus., Am. Craft Mus., N.Y.C. Co-recipient Best Research Report prize Internat. Competition Low-Cost Furniture N.Y. Mus. Modern Art, 1949; diploma D'Onore 10th Triennale Milan, Italy, 1954; Am. Iron and Steel Inst. award for excellence in fine art in steel, 1971; award for excellence in craft in steel, 1973; R.S. Reynolds Meml. Sculpture award, 1972; U. Calif. Berkeley award, 1975; Ford Found. grantee, 1962-63; Graham Found. cograntee, 1962; U. Calif. Creative Arts Inst. fellow, 1967-68, 70-71, 73-74; Guggenheim Found. fellow, 1972-73; N.Y. Met. Mus. Art life fellow, 1969; Deutscher Akademischer Austauschdienst grantee Bonn, W. Ger., 1977; elected to Hall of Fame Lake Forest Acad., 1987. Home: Berkeley Calif. Died July 26, 1993.

PRESTON, LEWIS THOMPSON, banker; b. N.Y.C Aug. 5, 1926; s. Lewis Thompson and Prisci (Baldwin) P.; m. Gladys Pulitzer, Apr. 17, 1959; chi dren: Linda Pulitzer Bartlett, Victoria Maria Bartlet Lucile Baldwin, Lewis Thompson, Priscilla Munn, Ele tra. Grad., Harvard U., 1951. With J.P. Morgan & C (merged with Guaranty Trust Co., named Morga Guaranty Trust Co. 1959), N.Y.C., 1951—; vice chm bd., dir. J. P. Morgan & Co. and Morgan Guaran Trust Co., N.Y.C., 1976-78, mem. corporate offic mem. exec. com., 1976-90; pres. J.P. Morgan ar Morgan Guaranty Trust Co., N.Y.C., 1978-80; chm bd., chief exec. officer J. P. Morgan and Morga Guaranty Trust Co., N.Y.C., 1980-90, chmn. exec. com 1991; pres. Internat. Bank Reconstruction and Devel Washington, 1991—; also pres. Internat. Finance Corp Washington, DC, Multilateral Investment Guarant Agency, Washington, DC. With USMC, 1944-46. Mem. Coun. Fgn. Rels., Assn. Res. City Bankers, Broc Club. Republican. Episcopalian. Home: Washingtc D.C. Died May 4, 1995.

PRETE, SESTO, classics educator, researcher; Montefiore, Italy, Sept. 27, 1919; came to U.S., 1956; Settimio Prete and Teresa Ceroni; m. Maria Teres Borgogelli, Dec. 29, 1955; children: Andrew, Charle Cecilia, Elisabeth. Licenza Liceale, Liceo Classic Fermo, Italy, 1938; student, U. Bologna, 1942; Diplom Palaeog., U. Heidelberg, 1943; Ph.D., U. Cologn Germany, 1944, U. Bologna, 1945. Lettore Latin U Bologna, Italy, 1946-53; research scholar Vatica Library, 1953-56; guest prof. U. Calif., Berkeley, 195 55; asst. to assoc. prof. Fordham U., N.Y.C., 1956-6 full prof., 1956-68; prof. dept. of classics U. Kans Lawrence, 1968-92; pres. Internat. Inst. for Humanist Studies, Sassoferrato, 1980-92, Internat. Inst. f Humanistic Studies, "A Poliziano" Mantepulcian 1970-92. Author: P. Terenti Comoediae, 1954, Ricerc sulla Storia del Testo di Ausonio, 1960, The Origin Written Contract with Michelangelo for the Tomb Pope Julius II, 1963, Two Humanistic Anthologie 1964, Galileo's Letter about the Libration of the Moo 1964, Codices Barberiniani Latini 1-150, 1969, Il codi di Columella di Stefano Guarnieri, 1974, Observatio on the History of Textual Criticism in the Medieval ar Renaissance Periods, 1970, Studies in Latin Poets of th Quattrocento, 1978, Decimi Magni Ausonil Oper 1978, Poesie d'amore di G. Pontano, 1979, Tra Filolo e Studiosi della nostra Epoca, 1983; editor: Res Pubblic Litterarum, 1978-92, Studi Umanistici Piceni, 1980-92 Guggenheim fellow, Volkswagen fellow; faculty researc grantee; award Centro Naz. delle Riserche, Humbol Stiftung. Mem. Classical Philos. Assn., Renaissan Soc. Am. Home: Lawrence Kans. Deceased.

PRICE, DON K., JR., political science educator; Middlesboro, Ky., Jan. 23, 1910; s. Don K. and Ne (Rhorer) P.; m. Margaret Helen Gailbreath, Mar. 1936 (dec. Feb. 1970); children: Don C., Linda; m Harriet Sloane Fels, May 8, 1971. A.B., Vanderbilt U 1931; B.A., Oxford U. (Rhodes scholar 1932), 1934, Litt., 1935; D.C.L. (hon.), Oxford U., 1983; L.H.D Case Inst. Tech., 1967, Coll. Wooster, 1972; Litt.D., U Pitts., 1968; LL.D., Centre Coll. Ky., 1961, Syracuse U 1962, Bucknell U., Harvard U., 1970. Reporter, sta editor Nashville Eve. Tennessean, 1930-32; research ass H.O.L.C., and asst. to chmn. Central Housing Com 1935-37; staff mem., com. on pub. adminstrn. Social Sc Research Council, 1937-39; editorial assoc. Pub. A minstrn. Clearing House, 1939-41, asst. dir., 1941-4 assoc. dir., 1946-53; staff mem. U.S. Bur. Budget, 194 46; dep. chmn. Research and Devel. Bd., U.S. Dep Def., 1952-53; assoc. dir. The Ford Found., 1953-5 v.p., 1954-58; prof. govt. Kennedy Sch. Govt. Harvar 1958-80, prof. emeritus, 1980-95, Weatherhead pro pub. mgmt., 1980, Weatherhead prof. emeritus, 1980-9 dean, 1958-77; Eastman prof., fellow Balliol Coll., U Oxford, Eng., 1985-86; trustee Twentieth Century Fun 1965-95, chmn. bd. trustees, 1977-82; bd. trus Vanderbilt U., 1964-95; trustee Rand Corp., 1961-71; s mem. Inst. Medicine of Nat. Acad. Scis., 1979-95; ass to Herbert Hoover (on study of U.S. Presidency und auspices Commn. on Orgn. Exec. Br. Govt.), 1947-4 cons. Exec. Office of Pres., 1961-72; dir. Social Sc Research Council, 1949-52, 64-69; staff dir. Committe on Dept. Def. Orgn., 1953; mem. Pres.'s adv. com. o government orgn., 1959-61; adviser to the King Nepal, Kathmandu, Nepal, 1960. Author: (with Harol and Kathryn Stone) City Manager Government in th United States, 1940, Government and Science, 1954, Th Scientific Estate, 1965, America's Unwritten Constitu tion, 1983; Editor, co-author: The Secretary of Stat 1960. Trustee Rhodes Trust, 1968-78, Weatherhea Found., 1973-95. Served as lt. USCGR, 1943-45. Fellow Am. Acad. Arts and Scis.; mem. Am. Philo Soc., AAAS (bd. dirs. 1959-64, 66-69, pres. 1967), Ph Beta Kappa. Club: Cosmos (Washington). Hom Cambridge Mass. Died July 10, 1995.

PRICE, VINCENT LEONARD, actor; b. St. Louis May 27, 1911; s. Vincent L. and Marguerite (Wilcox) P m. Edith Barrett, 1938 (div.); 1 son, Vincent B.; m Mary Grant, Aug. 28, 1939 (div. 1972); 1 dau., Mar Victoria; m. Coral Browne, 1974. BA, Yale U., 193 student, U. London, Eng., 1934-35; DFA, Calif. Col Arts and Crafts; LLD, Ohio Wesleyan U., 1963. Lect primitive and modern art, letters of Van Gogh. Forme mem. bd. Archives Am. Art; mem. Whitney Museu

Friends Am. Art; former pres. art council U. Calif. at Los Angeles; mem. U.S. Indian Arts and Crafts Bd.; art cons. Sears Roebuck & Co. Author: (autobiography) I Like What I Know, 1958, Book of Joe, 1960, (with Mary Price) Michelangelo Bible, 1964, A Treasury of Great Recipes, 1965, Come into the Kitchen Cook Book, 1969, Treasury of American Art, 1972; editor: (with Ferdinand V. Delacroix) Drawings of Delacroix; stage appearances include Victoria Regina, 1935-37, Mercury Theatre, 1937-38, Outward Bound, 1939-40, Angel Street, 1941-42, Don Juan in Hell, 1952, Cocktail Party, 1951, The Lady's Not For Burning, 1952, Ardele, London, 1975, Diversions and Delights; one-man play as Oscar Wilde, nat. tour, 1977-78, world tour, 1978-82; tour in Charlie's Aunt, 1975; films include Song of Bernadette, 1943, Eve of St. Mark, 1944, Laura, 1944, Leave Her to Heaven, 1945, Shock, 1946, House of Seven Gables, 1940, The Web, 1947, His Kind of Woman, 1951, Dragonwyck, 1946, Three Musketeers, 1948, Champagne for Caesar, 1950, Baron of Arizona, 1950, The House of Wax, 1953, Ten Commandments, 1956, Story of Mankind, 1957, The Big Circus, 1959, Pit and the Pendulum, 1961, Convicts 4, 1962, The Raven, 1962, Masque of The Red Death, 1964, The Last Man On Earth, 1964, Dr. Phibes, 1971, Theatre of Blood, 1974, The Whales of August, 1987, Dead Heat, 1987, Edward Scissorhands, 1991; (cartoon) "Vincent"; (Disney feature cartoon) The Great Mouse Detective; appeared on: radio in The Saint, 1947-50; TV numerous maj. programs including $64,000 Challenge; TV series Time Express, 1979; host: TV series PBS Mystery TV, 1979-87, TV series (Disney Channel) Read Write and Draw, Appreciating Art, Fin. News Network. Former mem. Fine Arts Com., The White House. Recipient L.A. Film Critics award for career achievement, 1992. Home: West Hollywood Calif. Died Oct. 25, 1993.

PRICHARD, ROBERT WILLIAMS, pathologist, educator; b. Jersey City, May 30, 1923; s. George Williams and Mathilde Clara (Engelbrecht) P.; m. Mary Hellen Blankley, Apr. 6, 1946; children: Claudia Cadman Prichard Shepard, Robert Williams. M.D., George Washington U., 1947. Diplomate: Am. Bd. Pathology. Intern D.C. Gen. Hosp., 1947-48; resident Children's, Peter Bent Brigham, Deaconess hosps., Boston, 1948-50, Presbyn. Hosp. and; asst. instr. U. Pa. Sch. Medicine, Phila., 1950-51; from instr. to prof. Bowman Gray Sch. Medicine, Wake Forest U., Winston-Salem, N.C., 1951-95; chmn. dept. pathology Bowman Gray Sch. Medicine, Wake Forest U., 1973-95; med. edn. adv. Am. Embassy, Bangkok, Thailand, 1955-57; mem. Nat. Bd. Med. Examiners. Author: (with Robinson) 20,000 Medical Words, 1972, (with others) Blakiston's Gould Medical Dictionary, 3d edit, 1972; contbr. (with others) numerous articles to profl. jours. Served in U.S. Army, 1944-45. Recipient Teaching Excellence award Bowman Gray Sch. Medicine, 1973, Basic Sci. Teaching award, 1972, 73, 79, 81. Fellow Am. Coll. Lab. Animal Medicine (hon.), Am. Assn. Blood Banks, Am. Assn. Pathologists, Am. Heart Assn., AMA, Am. Soc. Clin. Pathologists, Am. Assn. History of Medicine, Forsyth County Med. Soc., Internat. Acad. Pathology, N.C. Med. Soc., N.C. Soc. Pathologists, Coll. Am. Pathologists, Alpha Omega Alpha, Sigma Xi. Baptist. Clubs: Torch, Old Town. Home: Winston Salem N.C. Died, Jan. 29, 1995.

PRIESTLEY, WILLIAM TURK, architect; b. Yazoo City, Miss., Mar. 3, 1907; s. William Turk and Annola (Beamon) P.; m. Christabel Wheeler, June 11, 1938; children—William Turk, Seymour Wheeler. B.S., Princeton U., 1929; student, N.Y.U. Sch. Architecture, 1930-32, Bauhaus, Dessau, Berlin, Germany, 1932-33; M.Arch., Columbia, 1935. Grad. asst. Columbia Sch. Architecture, 1934-35; tchr. art Dalton Sch., N.Y.C., 1935-37; instr. architecture Cooper Union, 1937-40; asst. prof. architecture Ill. Inst. Tech., 1940-42; prof. architecture, chmn. dept. Western Res. U., 1960-66; mem. Rodgers & Priestley, N.Y.C. and Chgo., 1935-42; with firm Skidmore Owings Merrill, architects, Chgo., 1945-52, PACE Assos. (architects), Chgo., 1952-60; archtl. adviser Western Res. U., 1960-66; with firm Bertrand, Goldberg & Assos., Chgo., 1967-71; pvt. practice of architecture Lake Forest, Ill., 1971-95; Former mem. Fine Art Adv. Com. Cleve. Prin. works include hosps., schs., apts., residences, comml. and indsl. bldgs. Served to maj. USAAF, 1942-45. Fellow AIA. Home: Lake Forest Ill. Died Feb. 10, 1995.

PRIMUS, PEARL, dancer, choreographer; b. Trinidad, British West Indies, Nov. 29, 1919; d. Edward and Emily (Jackson) P.; m. Percival Borde, 1954; 1 child, Onwin. BS Biology, Hunter Coll., 1940; PhD Anthropology, NYU, 1978. Debut appearance N.Y. Young Men's Hebrew Assn., 1943; entertainer Cafe Soc. Downtown, Uptown, 1943-44; Broadway debut with own troupe Belasco Theatre, 1944; featured in revival Show Boat, 1946; toured with own dance co. 1946-47, group renamed Pearl Primus, Percival Borde and Co., 1959; choreographer Hear the Lamb A Crying, 1942, African Ceremonial, 1943, 45, Te Moana, 1943, Shouters of Sobo, 1943, Strange Fruit, 1943, Rock Daniel, 1943, Hard Times Blues, 1943, Jim Crow Train, 1943, The Negro SPeaks of Rivers, 1943, Folk Dance, 1943, Afro-Haitian Play Dance, 1943, Yanvaloo, 1943, Study In Nothing, 1944, Our Sring Will Come, 1944, Slave Market, 1944, Caribbean Conga, 1944, Motherless Child, 1944, Good Night Irene, 1944, Take This Hammer, 1944, Mischevous Interlude, 1944, Wade in the Water, 1944, Gonna Tell God, 1944, Steal Away, 1944, Dark Rhythms, 1944, Mean and Evil Blues, 1945, Twinsome Two Minds, 1945, Just Born, 1945, Scorpio, 1945, Dance of Beauty, 1946, Myth, 1946, Dance of Strength, 1946, War Dance, 1946, Great Getting Up Morning, 1946, Folk Song, 1946, Chamber of Tears, 1946, Emperor Jones, 1947, Trio, 1947, Santos, 1947, The Witch Doctor, 1947, Shango, 1947, Calypso, 1947, Caribbean Carnival, 1948, Fanga, 1949, Prayer of Thanksgiving, 1949, Go Down Death, 1949, Invocation, 1949, Chicken Hop, 1949, American Folk Dance, 1949, Egbo Escapapde, 1950, The Initiation, 1950, Everybody Loves Saturday Night, 1950, Fertility, 1950, Benis Womans War Dance, 1950, Dance of the Fanti Fisherman, 1950, Impinyuza, 1951, Kalenda, 1953, Limbo, 1953, La Jabless, 1954, Mr. Johnson, 1955, Castilian, 1957, Calypso Suite, 1957, Caplypso Revue, 1957, Royal Ishadi, 1958, Temne, 1958, Yoruba Court Dance, 1958, Aztec Warrior, 1958, Ibo, 1958, Earth Magician, 1958, Engagement Dance, 1958, Unesta, 1958, Ntimi, 1959, Whispers, 1960, Story of a Chief, 1960, Naffi Tombo, 1960, Kwan, 1960, Zo Kangai, 1960, Konama, 1960, The Wedding, 1961, The Man Who Would Not Laugh, 1962, To The Ancestors, 1962, Mangbetu, 1963, Zebola, 1963, Life Crises ,1963, Anase, 1965, Village Scene, 1965, My Life, 1965, Masange, 1969, Dance of Lights, 1970, In Honor of a Queen Mother, 1975, Dance of Tattles, 1979, Michael, Row Your Boat Ashore, 1979. 1st artist to be appointed to Am. Dance Festival's Balasaraswati/ Joy Ann Dewey Beinecke chair Disting. teaching, 1991. Home: New Rochelle N.Y. Died Oct. 29, 1994.

PROCTOR, WILLIAM ZINSMASTER, lawyer; b. Des Moines, Nov. 30, 1902; s. Frank and Louise (Zinsmaster) P.; m. Alice S. Bowles, Nov. 24, 1944; children: David J. W., Mary Martha. Student, Drake U., 1920; J.D., U. Mich., 1925. Bar: Iowa 1925. Assoc. Bradshaw, Schenk & Fowler, 1925-35; ptnr. Bradshaw, Fowler, Proctor & Fairgrave, Des Moines, 1935-92; dir. emeritus and gen. counsel emeritus Employers Mut. Casualty Co., Employers Modern Life Co., Emcasco Ins. Co., EMC Ins. Group Inc., Dakota Fire Ins. Co., Bismarck, N.D., Am. Liberty Ins. Co., Birmingham, Ala., Union Mut. Ins. Co. Providence; dir. emeritus Norwest Des Moines N.A. Pres. Des Moines Community Chest, 1956, Des Moines United Community Services, 1957; mem. bd. SSS, 1942-55, Iowa appeal bd., 1955-67; Pres. Des Moines Roadside Settlement, 1950-53; trustee Hawley Welfare Found., 1968-95, chmn., 1974-86; chmn. bd. trustees Preston Ednl. Trust, 1952-86. Mem. ABA, Iowa Bar Assn., Polk County Bar Assn. (pres. 1945), Internat. Bar Assn., Inter-Am. Bar Assn., Am. Judicature Soc., Assn. Bar City N.Y., Fedn. Ins. Counsel. Clubs: Mason (Shriner, Jester), Wakonda, Des Moines (pres. 1953); University (Chgo.). Home: Des Moines Iowa Died Feb. 22, 1995.

PROUDFOOT, ALLIN WHITFIELD, university administrator; b. Chgo., Jan. 23, 1929; s. Alfred C. and Dorothy M. (Whitfield) P.; m. Ruth Ann Shumm, June 3, 1951; children: Alfred, Marcia, Malcolm. B.S.B.A., Northwestern U., 1950, M.B.A., 1961. Vice-pres. brand mgmt. R.J. Reynolds Foods, N.Y.C., 1967-71; pres., chief exec. officer Curtiss Candy Co., N.Y.C., 1971-73; chief exec. officer Coca-Cola Bottling Cos. of Chgo. and Wis., 1973-76; sr. v.p. mktg. Coca-Cola Co., Atlanta, 1976-78; exec. v.p. mktg. Joseph Schlitz Brewing Co., Milw., 1978-80; v.p. univ. devel. Northwestern U., Evanston, Ill., 1980-94. Bd. dirs. Ill. Masonic Med. Ctr., Blowitz-Ridgeway Found.; chmn. bd. Salvation Army of Chgo. Republican. Methodist. Clubs: Chicago, Economic, Glen View, Tavern, Masons. Home: Evanston Ill. Died Apr. 12, 1994.

PROULX, ADOLPHE, clergyman; b. Hanmer, Ont., Can., Dec. 12, 1927; s. Augustin and Marie-Louise (Tremblay) P. B.A., St. Augustine's Sem., Toronto, Ont.; postgrad. in canon law, Rome, Italy, 1958-60. Ordained priest Roman Catholic Ch., 1954; parish priest North Bay and Sudbury, Ont., Can., 1954-57; chancellor Sault Ste. Marie (Ont.) Diocese, 1960-64, aux. bishop, 1965-67; bishop Alexandria (Ont.) Diocese, 1967-74, Gatineau-Hull, Que., Canada, 1974—. Home: Hull Can.

PRUITT, RAYMOND DONALD, physician, educator; b. Wheaton, Minn., Feb. 6, 1912; s. Lyman Burton and Ada (Brandes) P.; m. Lillian Elaine Rasmussen, July 31, 1942 (dec. July 1986); children: Virginia, Kristin, David, Charles. B.S., Baker U., 1933; B.A. (Rhodes Scholar), Oxford U., 1936; M.D., U. Kans., 1939; M.S., U. Minn., 1945; D.Sc. (hon.), Baker U., 1956; L.H.D. (hon.), Hamline U., 1980. Diplomate: Am. Bd. Internal Medicine (cardiovascular diseases). Intern U. Kan. Hosps., 1939-40; fellow medicine Mayo Found., 1940-43, prof. medicine, asso. dir. for med. edn., 1954-59; cons. physician Mayo Clinic, 1943-59; instr. medicine U. Minn., 1945-48, asst. prof., 1948-52, assoc. prof., 1952-55, prof., 1955-59; prof., chmn. dept. medicine Baylor U. Coll. Medicine, 1959-68, v.p. med. affairs, chief exec. officer, 1966-68; dir. Mayo Grad. Sch. Medicine, U. Minn., 1968-75, prof. medicine, 1968-77; founding dean Mayo Med. Sch. U. Minn., 1972-77, emeritus, 1977-93; dir. for medical edn. Mayo Found., 1968-77; prof. medicine Baylor Coll. Medicine, Houston, 1977-78; cons. in residence Meth. Hosp., Houston, 1977-78; prof. medicine Mayo Med. Sch., Rochester, Minn., 1978-81, U. Tenn., Memphis, 1984-93; cons. cardiovascular disease Mayo Clinic, Rochester, 1978-81; mem. Nat. Adv. Research Resources Council, 1969-73; mem. nat. adv. heart council USPHS, 1964-68; mem. Pres.'s Commn. Heart Disease, 1972; chmn. credentials com. council clin. cardiology Am. Heart Assn., 1973-75. Recipient Trustee's medallion for Disting. Svc. Baylor Coll. Medicine, 1988, Founder's Day medallion Baker U., 1989. Mem. Central Clin. Research, AMA, Assn. Profs. Medicine, Assn. U. Cardiologists (pres. 1967), Assn. Am. Physicians, Am. Osler Soc. (pres. 1976-77), Sigma Xi, Alpha Omega Alpha. Methodist. Home: Memphis Tenn. Died, Jan. 14, 1993.

PRUNARET, HENRI, financial executive; b. Union City, N.J., Sept. 3, 1900; s. Henri and Fredricka (Von-Kleinke-Shoppe) P.; m. Mildred Gardinor, Oct. 1, 1924. Student, U. Pa., 1924; student Dipl.Engring, Prussian Staadts U., 1925; Dr.Sci., U. Lyon, 1928. Resident engr. Sonneman Mining, Portage, Pa., 1924-39; combustion engr. H.N. Hartwell & Son, Inc., Boston, 1940-45; v.p. engring. H.N. Hartwell & Son, Inc., 1945-62, pres., treas., from 1962; dir. Ellendick Corp., Flagstaff Corp., H. Harwood & Sons, Inc., J.C. Carson & Co.; v.p., dir. Faris Corp., Inc.; pres., treas. Hartwell Petroleum Corp.; v.p., dir. Inst. Corp. Trustee Gardinor-Prunaret Found., Jenison House Trust; pres., trustee Morse Inst.; trustee The Rivers Country Day Sch., Sir-Sister Trust; pres. bd. trustees Walnut Hill Sch., 1974. Served with Belgian Army, 1917-19. Decorated Legion of Honor Order of Leopold. Mem. AIME, ASME. Republican. Congregationalist. Clubs: Union League, Brae Burn Country, Somerset, Nat. Beagle (pres. 1975-80), Am. Kennel. Home: Natick Mass. Deceased.

PSACHAROPOULOS, NIKOS, theater director, educator; b. Athens, Greece; came to U.S., 1947; s. Konstantin Nicholas and Helen (Mitsakos) P. B.A., Oberlin Coll., 1951; M.F.A., Yale U., 1955; LHD (hon.), Williams Coll., 1974; DFA (hon.), Siena Coll., 1987. Exec. and artistic dir. Williamstown Theatre Festival, 1955—; stage dir. N.Y. Pro Musica, N.Y.C., 1955-70; assoc. prof. Yale U., New Haven, 1955-74, lectr., 1974—. Contbr. articles to profl. jours.; guest dir. Longwharf Theatre, New Haven, Conn., Pasadena (Calif.) Playhouse; dir. play Sweet Bird of Youth.; dir. Broadway play Streetcar Named Desire, 1988, Sweet Bird of Youth, Royal Alexandra Theater, Can., 1988. Bd. dirs. N.Y.C. Opera; bd. dirs. Am. Shakespeare Festival. Mem. Soc. Stage Dirs. and Choreographers, Actor's Equity Assn., Dirs. Guild, Am. Guild Mus. Artists. Home: New York N.Y.

PUGH, WARREN EDWARD, engine company executive; b. Salt Lake City, Dec. 21, 1909; s. William Edward and Eva May (Murphy) P.; m. Leta Vivian Curtis, Sept. 1, 1933; children: Carol Matheson, Lorin K., Donald E. Student, Latter-day Sts. Bus. Coll., Stevens Hennager Coll.; LLD (hon.), U. Utah, 1986. Mgr. Cummins Intermountain Diesel Sales Co., Salt Lake City, 1943-75, chmn. exec. com., 1975-90; also chmn. bd. dirs. Cummins Intermountain Idaho Inc., Boise; pres. Indsl. Devel. and Sales Co., Salt Lake City, 1945-90. Chmn. transp. and pub. safety standing com., 1967-72, edn. subcom. Joint Appropriations Com., 1971-72, senate appropriations com., 1973-90, Utah Hwy. Users Conf.; chmn., trustee Latter-day St. Hosp., Utah Found.; mem. Utah Ho. of Reps., 1959-60, Utah State Senate, 1967-90, U. Utah Nat. Adv. Coun., LDS Ch. Gen. Ch. Audit Com.; majority leader Utah Senate, 1969-70, pres., 1973-74; co-chmn. Senate and Ho. Exec. Appropriation Com., 1973-90; trustee U. Utah Rsch. Inst.; pres. Salt Lake Area C. of C., 1972-73; past mem. LDS Ch. Gen. Sunday Sch. Bd., High Coun. Salt Lake Holladay South Stake LDS Ch.; past bishop Halladay 8th Ward LDS Ch.; past pres. No. Calif. LDS Ch. Mission; patriarch Salt Lake Holladay South Stake LDS Ch. Clubs: Ft. Douglas Hidden Valley Country, Alta (Salt Lake City). Home: Salt Lake City Utah Died April 25, 1990; buried City Cemetary, Salt Lake City, Utah.

PULITZER, JOSEPH, JR., newspaper editor and publisher; b. St. Louis, May 13, 1913; s. Joseph and Elinor (Wickham) P.; m. Louise Vauclain, June 2, 1939 (dec. Dec. 1968); 1 son, Joseph IV; m. Emily S Rauh, June 30, 1973. Grad., St. Mark's Sch., Southborough, Mass., 1932; BA, Harvard U., 1936. Reporter San Francisco News, 1935; mem. staff St. Louis Post-Dispatch, 1936-48, assoc. editor, 1948-55, editor and pub., 1955-86; now chmn. Pultizer Pub. Co. and subs., 1986-93; chmn. Pulitzer Prize Bd., 1955-86; mem. Am. Press Inst., 1956-84; mem. internat. adv. bd. Sing Tao Newspapers Ltd., Hong Kong, 1976-91. Author: A Tradition of Conscience, Proposals for Journalism, 1965; contbr. commentaries and essays to Modern Painting, Drawing & Sculpture Collected by Louise and Joseph Pulitzer, Jr., 3 vols., 1957, 58, 71, vol. IV Modern Painting, Drawing & Sculpture Collected by Emily and Joseph Pulitzer, Jr., 1988. Mem. bd. overseers Harvard U., 1976-82, mem. com. to visit Harvard Art Mus., 1971-75, vice chair, 1976-83, mem., 1984-93; mem. Harvard vis. com. to Univ. Press, 1951; hon. trustee St. Louis Art Mus., 1981-93, commr., 1972-80, mem. adminstrv. bd. control, 1969-72, mem. collections com., 1971-93; chmn. Washington U. com. for the arts, 1968-71, libr. nat. coun., 1987-93; mem. exec. com. St. Louis

Symphony Soc., 1966-93, chmn. music com., 1975-93, trustee 1939-44, 47-93, community outreach com., 1991-93; trustee St. Mark's Sch., 1965-72, St. Louis Country Day Sch., 1960-66. mem. spl. com. acquire works of 18th and 19th century art for White House, 1961; mem. nat. com. raised funds to construct mus. at base of Statue of Liberty Am. Mus. Immigration. Served ensign to lt. USNR, 1942-45. Mem. Am. Newspaper Publishers Assn., Am. Soc. Newspaper Editors, Associated Harvard Alumni (dir.-at-large 1965-68), Internat. Press Inst., Soc. Profl. Journalists, St. Louis Press Club. Home: Saint Louis Mo. Died May 25, 1993.

PULLER, LEWIS B., JR., writer, lawyer; b. 1945; m. Toddy Puller; children: Lewis, Maggie. Grad., Coll. William and Mary, 1967. Author: Fortunate Son: An Autobiography, 1991 (Pulitzer Prize for autobiography 1992). Home: Alexandria Va. Died May 12, 1994.

PUTNAM, ALFRED WYNNE, lawyer; b. Phila., May 27, 1919; s. Alfred and Nancy Wynne (Cook) P.; m. Anne Beale, June 25, 1948; children: Anne Leonard, Alfred Wynne, Edward Beale. A.B., Harvard U., 1940; LL.B., U. Pa., 1947. Bar: Pa. bar 1947. Assoc. firm Hepburn Willcox Hamilton & Putnam (and predecessors), Phila., 1947-95; ptnr. Hepburn Willcox Hamilton & Putnam (and predecessors), 1953-95; sec., bd. dirs. Pa. Warehousing & Safe Deposit Co. Mem. standing com. Episcopal Diocese Pa., 1970-80; pres. Family Svc. Phila., 1956-59, Libr. Co. Phila.; past pres. Chestnut Hill Acad.; bd. dirs. emeritus Fox Chase Cancer Ctr., Am. Oncologic Hosp. Lt. comdr. USNR, 1941-45. Mem. ABA, Pa. Bar Assn., Phila. Bar Assn., Am. Judicature Soc., Juristic Soc., Chevaliers des Tastevin (grand officier), Delta Psi. Republican. Episcopalian. Clubs: Philadelphia (Phila.) (pres. 1976-80), Sharswood Law (Phila.), Racquet (Phila.), Penn. (Phila.), St. Anthony (Phila.); Delphic (Cambridge, Mass.); State-in-Schuylkill, Rabbit. Home: Philadelphia Pa. Died Nov. 12, 1995.

PYE, AUGUST KENNETH, lawyer, educator, university president; b. N.Y.C., Aug. 21, 1931; s. Cyril and Hazel (Forrest) P.; m. Judith Hope King, Feb. 6, 1965; 1 child, Henry Williams. BA, U. Buffalo, 1951; JD, Georgetown U., 1953, LLM, 1955, LLD (hon.), 1978; LHD (hon.), Belmont Abbey Coll., 1979; LLD (hon.), U. Notre Dame, 1990, Alaska Pacific U., 1992, Duke U., 1992. Bar: D.C. 1953, N.C. 1970. Prof. law Georgetown U. Law Center, 1955-66, assoc. dean, 1961-66; prof. law Duke U., 1966-87; dean Law Sch., 1968-70, 73-76, chancellor, 1970-71, 76-82, univ. counsel, 1971-73; pres. So. Meth. U., Dallas, 1987-94; program specialist legal edn. Ford Found., India, 1966-67; chmn. coun. for Internat. Exch. of Scholars, 1985-87; bd. dirs. J. C. Penney Co., Dresser Industries, Inc. Served with AUS, 1953-55. Mem. Am. Law Inst., Assn. Am. Law Schs. (pres. 1977-78), Coun. Fgn. Rels., Army-Navy Club, Tower Club, Energy Club, Phi Beta Kappa. Home: Dallas Tex. Died July 11, 1994.

QUARLES, LEO THOMPSON, utilities company executive; b. Raleigh, N.C., July 1, 1944; s. Walter Greyson and Ida Owen (Hayssen) Q.; m. Beverly Kathryn Abernathy, Sept. 16, 1969; children: Kimberly, Blair, Amy. B.S. in Math., Hampden-Sydney Coll., 1966; M.B.A., East Carolina U., 1969. C.P.A. Auditor Peat Marwick Mitchell & Co., Atlanta, 1969-72; supr. balance sheet and income statement Carolina Power & Light Co., Raleigh, 1972-73, tax acct., 1973-74, tax mgr., 1974-77, asst. treas., 1977-79, treas., from 1979. Presbyterian. Lodge: Rotary. Home: Raleigh N.C. Deceased.

QUELLER, DONALD EDWARD, historian, educator; b. St. Louis, Jan. 14, 1925; s. A.J. and Lee (Straub) Q.; m. Marilyn Lucille Johnson, June 12, 1949 (dec.); children: Kurt, David, Susan, Katherine, Sarah. AB, U. Mich., 1949; postgrad., Stanford Law Sch., 1949-50; MA, U. Mich., 1951; PhD, U. Wis., 1954. With Beloit Coll., 1955-56; faculty U. So. Cal., 1956-68; prof. medieval and renaissance history U. Ill., Urbana, 1968-95. Author: Early Venetian Legislation on Ambassadors, 1966, The Office of the Ambassador in the Middle Ages, 1967, The Fourth Crusade, 1977, Two Studies on Venetian Government, 1977, Medieval Diplomacy and the Fourth Crusade, 1980, The Venetian Patriciate, 1986, Italian transl., 1987; editor: The Latin Conquest of Constantinople, 1971; co-editor: Post Scripta, Essays in Honor of Gaines Post. Chmn. South Pasadena Human Relations Council, 1964-65; chmn. Marilyn Queller Child Care Center. Served with AUS, 1943-46. Fulbright fellow Belgium, 1954-55; Fulbright research fellow Italy, 1962-63; Rockefeller Internat. Relations fellow, 1962-63, 64-65; Guggenheim fellow, 1972-73; Am. Council Learned Socs. grantee-in-aid, 1973; Gladys Krieble Delmas Found. grantee, 1978; Inst. Advanced Study fellow, 1979-80. Fellow Medieval Acad. Am.; mem. Am. Hist. Assn., Medieval Acad. Am., Renaissance Soc. Am. Home: Champaign Ill. Died Sept. 9, 1995.

QUENNELL, PETER, author; b. Bickley, Kent, Eng., Mar. 9, 1905; s. C. H. B. and M. Quennell. Ed., Balliol Coll., Oxford U. Former prof. English lit. Tokyo Bunrika Daigaku. Author: Baudelaire and the Symbolists; A Superficial Journey; Byron: The Years of Fame, Byron in Italy, 1941; Caroline of England, Four Portraits, 1945; Ruskin: The Portrait of a Prophet, 1952; Spring in Sicilly, The Singular Preference, Hogarth's Progress, 1954; The Sign of the Fish, 1960; Shakespeare: The Poet and His Background, 1963; Alexander Pope: the Education of Genius, 1968; Romantic England, 1970; Casanova in London, 1971; Samuel Johnson, his Friends and Enemies, 1972; The Marble Foot, 1976; The Wanton Chase, 1980; Customs and Characters: Contemporary Portraits, 1982, The Pursuit of Happiness, 1989; editor: Aspects of 17th Century Verse; (transl.) Memoirs of the Comte de Gramont; Letters of Madame le Lieven; Memoirs of William Hickey; Byron; A Self Portrait (1798-1824); Mayhew's London Labour and the London Poor, 3 vols.; Marcel Proust: 1871-1922, 1971; Genius in the Drawing Room; Vladimir Nabakov, his Life, his Work, his World, 1979; A Lonely Business: A Self Portrait of James Pope-Hennessy, 1981; editor Cornhill Mag., 1944-51, History Today, 1951-79. Decorated Order Brit. Empire. Home: London Eng. Died Oct. 27, 1993.

QUEST, CHARLES FRANCIS, artist, educator, lecturer; b. Troy, N.Y., June 6, 1904; s. Charles F. and Ann (Hogan) Q.; m. Dorothy Johnson, Sept. 7, 1928. B.F.A., M.F.A., Washington U. Sch. Fine Arts; courses edn., Washington U. Sch. Fine Arts, Paris, 1929. Instr. drawing and art analysis Washington U. Sch. Fine Arts, St. Louis, 1945-71; prof. emeritus. Washington U. Sch. Fine Arts. Executed murals pub. bldgs. libraries, and several large chs., 1930-45; printmaker wood engravings, wood cuts, etchings, copper engraving; painter oil, watercolor, tempera; sculptor crafts stainglass, mosaic; works purchased by Met. Mus. N.Y., Mus. Modern Art N.Y., Chgo. Art Inst., Phila. Art Mus., Library of Congress, St. Louis Art Mus., Bklyn. Mus., Brit. Mus., Victoria and Albert Mus., London, Bibliotheque Nationale, Paris, Nat. Mus., Stockholm, Nat. Mus. Jerusalem, Nat. Gallery Australia, Miss. Mus. Art, Jackson, Toledo Mus., Mint Mus., Charlotte, N.C., Greenville County (S.C.) Mus. Art, and, Hunter Mus. Art, Chattanooga, others; exhibited in 109 mus. and galleries in, U.S., France, Germany, Italy; represented in permanent collections 48 museums including Cleve. Mus. Art, Georgetown U., Washington, Bob Jones U., Greenville, S.C., Hickory (N.C.) Mus. Art, St. John's Mus. Art, Wilmington, N.C.; also oil paintings at, U.S. State Dept. Art in the Embassies Program., Birmingham Mus. Art, Ala., wood engraving at, Del. Art Mus.; exhibit color woodcuts, Am. embassy, Paris, followed by year's tour of France, 1951, one-man shows include Smithsonian Inst., U.S. Nat. Mus., 1951, Maryville Coll. Mus., 1966, Am. Fedn. Arts, 1966, Mint Mus., Charlotte, N.C., 1979, Hampton III Gallery, Greenville, S.C., 1992; exhibited at Boston Mus. Art, Detroit Inst. Art, Cleve. Mus. Art, Fogg Mus. Harvard; two-man shows include Phila. Print Club, Bethesda (Md.) Art Gallery, wood engravings and woodcuts, 1951, altar painting for Old Cathedral St. Louis, 1960 (Recipient 53 prizes 1923-72), print exhbn. Bethesda (Md.) Art Gallery, 1983; permanent exhbn. paintings Charles Quest Gallery of St. Louis. Mem. Soc. Am. Graphic Artists N.Y., Phila. Color Print Soc., So. Vt. Artists, Painters Gallery St. Louis, Hampton III Gallery (Greenville, S.C.). Club: St. Louis (life). Home: Tryon N.C. Died Jan. 1, 1993.

RABIN, YITZHAK, former prime minister of Israel, politician; b. Jerusalem, Mar. 1, 1922; s. Nehemia and Rosa (Cohen) R.; m. Lea Schlossberg, Aug. 23, 1948; 2 children. Student, Kadoorie Agrl. Sch., Kfar Tabor, 1936-40; grad. Staff Coll., Eng., 1953; Ph.D. (hon.), Hebrew U., Jerusalem, 1967, Dropsie Coll., Phila., 1968, Brandeis U., 1968, Yeshiva U., N.Y.C., 1968, Coll. Jewish Studies, Chgo., 1969; U. Miami, 1970, Hebrew Union Coll., Boston, 1971. Palmach commdr., 1943-48, including War Independence; mem. Israel delegation at Rhodes Armistice Negotations, 1949; head tactical ops. Hdqrs., 1950-53; head tng. dept. Israel Def. Force, 1954-56, comdg. officer Northern Command, 1956-59, head manpower br., 1959-60, dep. chief of staff and head Gen. Starr br., 1960-64, chief of staff, 1964-68; amb. of Israel to U.S., Washington, 1968-73; mem. Knesset, 1974—; min. Ministy of Labor, 1974; chmn. Labor Party, 1974-77, 92-95; prime min. Israel, 1974-77, 92-95; minister of communications, 1974-75, min. of Defense, 1984-89, 92-95, min. Ministry of the Interior and Religious Affairs. Recipient Nobel Peace Prize, 1994. Author: The Rabin Memoirs, 1979. Died Nov. 4, 1995. Home: Jerusalem Israel

RADNAY, PAUL ANDREW, physician; b. Szolnok, Hungary, Aug. 6, 1913; came to U.S., 1949, naturalized, 1954; s. Ferenc and Ida (Varsa) R.; m. Eva Balazs, Aug. 6, 1939. MD, U. Szeged, 1937. Diplomate Hungarian Bd. Surgery, Hungarian Bd. Dentistry, Am. Bd. Anesthesiology. Intern Univ. Clinics, Budapest and Szeged, Hungary, 1936-37; chief head and neck surgery outpatient dept. Orszagos Tarsadalom Biztosito Intezet, Budapest, 1945-49; asst. prof. Polyclinic Hosp., Budapest, 1945-49; resident in anesthesiology Queens Gen. Hosp., Jamaica, N.Y., 1953-54; dir. anesthesia sect. cardio-thoracic surgery Montefiore Hosp., Med. Ctr., Bronx, N.Y., 1970-79; cons. Montefiore Hosp., Med. Ctr., Bronx, 1979-83, emeritus attending anesthesiologist, 1983-95; prof. anesthesiology Albert Einstein Coll. Medicine, Bronx, 1981-83, prof. emeritus, 1983-95; prof. respiratory therapy program Manattee Community Coll., Bradenton, Fla. Editor: Anesthetic Considerations for Pediatric Cardiac Surgery, 1980, 2 English, Spanish edits.; contbr. articles to profl. lit. Pres. Am. Hungarian Med. Assn., 1966-67; vice chmn. bd. dirs Am.-Hungarian Found., 1974-90; bd. dirs. Sarasot Opera Assn. Capt. M.C., Hungarian Army, intrmit tantly, 1934-45. Decorated Cross Knighthood Order St Martin, Austria; decorated Cross St. John of Jerusalem Knights of Malta; recipient Disting. Svc. award Am Hungarian Found., 1978, Incentive N.Y. County Med Soc., 1983; recipient Goldzieher award Am.-Hungaria Med. Assn., 1976, also Disting. Svc. award. Fellow Am. Coll. Anesthesiologists, N.Y. Acad. Medicine, N.Y Cardiological Soc., Internat. Coll. Surgeons; mem. Am Soc. Anesthesiologists, N.Y. State Soc. Anesthesiolo gists, N.Y. County Med. Soc., N.Y. State Med. Soc Soc. Cardiovascular Anesthesiologists, Hungarian Soc Anesthesialogists and Intensive Therapists (hon.) Deceased.

RAEDLER, DOROTHY FLORENCE, theatrica director, producer; b. N.Y.C., Feb. 24, 1917; d. Charle Conrad R. and Florence Elizabeth (Radley Raedler. B.A., Hunter Coll., 1942. Producer, dir founder Masque & Lyre, N.Y.C., 1939-52, Am Savoyards, N.Y.C., 1952-68; stage dir. N.Y.C. Oper Co., 1959-65; dir., prodn. coord. City Ctr., Gilbert & Sullivan Co., N.Y.C., 1961-66; dir. V.I. Inst. of Arts 1969-70; assoc. dir. V.I. Council on Arts, 1970; exec dir. St. Croix (V.I.) Sch. Arts, 1970-81, exec. dir., cons 1981-84. Editor: Crowell's Handbook for Gilbert an Sullivan, 1962; dir., co-producer Treemonisha, St. Croi and St. Thomas, V.I., 1988. Pres. St. Croix Anima Welfare Ctr. Inc; bd. dirs. St. James Sch. Arts, N.Y.C 1963-65; dir. media services 14th Legislature of V.I 1981-83. Recipient Contbns. to the Arts award Legis V.I. Mem. N.Y. Gilbert and Sullivan Soc. (hon.). Home: Saint Croix V.I. Died Dec. 11, 1993; cremated.

RAGAN, SAMUEL TALMADGE, newspaper edito publisher, educator, poet laureate; b. Berea, N.C., Dec 31, 1915; s. William Samuel and Emma Clare (Long) R m. Marjorie Usher, Aug. 19, 1939; children: Nancy Ann Talmadge. A.B., Atlantic Christian Coll., 1936 Litt.D., 1972; Litt.D., U. N.C., 1987; D.Letters, Meth Coll., 1980; D.Lit., St. Andrews Coll., 1987. New spaperman in N.C. and Tex., 1936-96; mng. editor author column Southern Accent in Raleigh (N.C.) New and Observer, 1948-69; exec. editor Raleigh News an Observer, also Raleigh Times, 1957-69; editor, pub author column The Pilot, Southern Pines, N.C., 1969 96; sec. N.C. Dept. Arts, Culture and History, 1972-73 conductor program, commentator sta. WTVD, Durham 1969-96; spl. lectr. contemporary issues N.C. State U 1959-68; dir. Writer's Workshop, 1963-96; instr. creativ writing St. Andrews Coll., 1970-96, Sandhills Coll 1969-96; cons. editor St. Andrews Rev., Pembroke Mag Author: (collected poems) The Tree in the Far Pasture 1964, To the Water's Edge, 1971, Journey Int Morning, 1981, In the Beginning, 1985; The Democrati Party: Its Aims and Purposes, 1961, The New Day 1964, Free Press and Fair Trial, 1967, (with Elizabeth S Ives) Back to Beginnings, 1969, In the Beginning (wit Thad Stem Jr.), 1984, A Walk Into April, 1986, Col lected Poems, 1990, Listening for the Wind, 1995 editor: Weymouth Anthology, 1987; contbg. edito World Book Ency., 1964; author articles, poems. Pres Friends Coll., Inc., N.C. State, 1961-62; mem. N.C Library Resources Com., N.C. Govt. Reorgn. Commn 1970-96; moderator N.C. Writers Forum of Charlotte 1963-96; Trustee N.C. Sch. Arts, 1963-72; mem. N.C Adminstrn. of Justice Council, 1964-96, chmn., 1980-83 bd. dirs. N.C. Symphony Soc., 1975-79. Served wi AUS, 1943-46, PTO. Recipient N.C. Tercentenar Poetry award, 1963. Spl. Citation for Contbns. t Journalism Atlantic Christian Coll., North Carolinian Soc. award, 1981, Disting. Svc. medal DAR, 1974, Ed ward Arnold Young award for Poetry, 1965, 72, 91 Morrison award for contbns. to arts N.C., 1976, N.C award for achievements in arts, 1979, R. Hunt Parke award for contbns. to lit., 1987, N.C. Artists award United Arts Coun., 1990, Caldwell award for contbns and achievements in humanities N.C. Humanities Coun 1993; inducted into N.C. Journalism Hall of Fame 1984; appointed Poet Laureate N.C. for life, 1982. Mem. N.C. Lit. Forum (moderator 1956-96), N.C Writers Conf. (chmn. 1962-63), Eastern N.C. Pres Assn. (past pres.), N.C. Press Assn. (pres. 1973-74 Asso. Press Mng. Editors Assn. (dir. gen. chmn. con tinuing studies 1961, sec. 1962, v.p. 1963, pres. 1964 Am. Soc. Newspaper Editors (dir., chmn. freedom o info. com. 1968), Roanoke Island Hist. Soc. (dir.), N.C News Council (past pres.), N.C. Arts Council (chmn 1967-72), Am. Newspaper Pubs. Assn., N.C. Lit. an Hist. Assn. (pres. 1977), Friends of Weymouth (pres 1979-84), Sigma Delta Chi. Democrat. Presbyterian Club: Sandhills Kiwanis (Southern Pines); Builders Cu 1985. Home: Southern Pines N.C. Died May 11, 1996

RAGSDALE, JAMES MARCUS, editor; b. Turlock Calif., July 24, 1938; s. George Alexander and Rub Mabel (Thomas) R.; children: Marc, Meredith David. BA, San Jose (Calif.) State Coll., 1961. Mng editor Solano Rep., Fairfield, Calif., 1961-62; gen. as signment rep. Press Courier, Oxnard, Calif., 1962-64 reporter AP, Charleston, W.Va., 1964-67; corr. in charg AP, Spokane, Washington, 1967-68; news editor AP Seattle, 1968-69; chief of bur. AP, Charleston, 1969-71 Boston, 1971-75; asst. to pub. The Standard-Times, New

Bedford, Mass., 1975-76; editor The Standard-Times, New Bedford, 1976-94; Pulitzer judge Pulitzer Prize, N.Y., 1986-87. Co-chmn. First Night New Bedford, 1987-88, pres., 1989-90; co-chmn. People's Celebration July 4th, 1986-89. Recipient Brotherhood award New Bedford chpt. Prince Henry Soc. Mass., 1993. Mem. Soc. Profl. Journalists (pres. 1983-84), Acad. New England Journalists (Yankee Quill award 1988), Mass. Bar Assn. (co-chmn. bench bar press com. 1984-85). Home: North Dartmouth Mass. Died Aug. 28, 1994.

RAHL, JAMES ANDREW, lawyer, educator; b. Wooster, Ohio, Oct. 8, 1917; s. James Blaine and Harriet (Munson) R.; m. Jean Mayberry, Sept. 5, 1942; 1 child, James Andrew. BS, Northwestern U., 1939, JD, 1942. Bar: Ohio 1942, Ill. 1950, U.S. Supreme Ct. 1962. Atty. OPA, 1942-43; mem. faculty Northwestern U. Law Sch., 1946-94, prof. law, 1953-94, Owen L. Coon prof., 1974-88, prof. emeritus, 1988-94, dir. rsch., 1966-72, dean, 1972-77; counsel Chadwell & Kayser, Chgo., 1952-89; ptnr. Chadwell & Kayser, Brussels, 1963-64; mem. faculty Salzburg Seminar Am. Studies, 1967, 72, 75; Mem. Atty. Gen.'s Nat. Com. to Study Antitrust Laws, 1953-55; mem. White House Task Force Antitrust Policy, 1967-68, UNCTAD Group Experts on Internat. Restrictive Trade Practices, 1973; mem. adv. com. on internat. investment, tech. and devel. Dept. State, 1979-86. Author: (with others) Cases on Torts, 1968, 2d edit., 1977, Advanced Torts, 1977, (with Schwerin) Northwestern University School of Law: A Short History, 1960, Common Market and American Antitrust: Overlap and Conflict, 1970; also articles.; Editor-in-chief: Ill. Law Rev., 1941-42. Served to 2d lt. AUS, 1943-46. Mem. ABA (council anti trust sect. 1965-67), Ill., Bar Assn., Chgo. Bar Assn., Chgo. Council Lawyers, Am. Law Inst., Am. Soc. Internat. Law, Law Club Chgo. (pres. 1976-77). Methodist. Home: Evanston Ill. Died Dec. 29, 1994.

RAINSFORD, GEORGE NICHOLS, college president; b. N.Y.C., June 27, 1928; s. Kerr and Christine (Nichols) R.; m. Jean Wedmore, Sept. 12, 1954; children: Guy, Amy, Anne, Angela, Emily. Grad., Deerfield Acad., 1946; student, Williams Coll., 1946-47; BA cum laude, U. Colo., 1950; postgrad., London Sch. Econs., 1950-51; LLB, Yale U., 1954; MA, U. Denver, 1963; PhD, Stanford U., 1967. Bar: Colo. 1954. Assoc. mem. firm Holme, Roberts, More & Owen, Denver, 1954-56; dir. devel. U. Denver, 1956-63; intern Ellis L. Phillips Found., U. Wash., 1963-64; assoc. dean (Coll. Arts and Scis.); asst. prof. history and law U. Denver, 1967-69; asst. to pres. U. Colo., 1969-71; also assoc. prof. to prof. history; pres. Kalamazoo Coll., 1972-83; pres., prof. Lynchburg Coll., Va., 1983-93; higher ednl. corr. London Times, 1976-78; cons. Ohio Bd. Regents, 1978—; mem. U. Wis. Program Excellence Rev. Bd., 1988—. Author: Congress and Higher Education in the 19th Century, 1972. Trustee Colo. Outward Bound Sch., Denver, 1961—, Va. Episc. Sch., 1985—; mem. Va. World Trade Council, 1988—; mem. Com. on Univ. of the 21st Century, 1988—. Mem. Nat. Assn. Ind. Colls. and Univs. (chmn. 1978-80), Assn. Governing Bds. (chmn. pres.'s com.), Phi Gamma Mu, Phi Alpha Theta, Phi Delta Phi. Home: Lynchburg Va. Deceased.

RAMBO, DACK (NORMAN J. RAMBO), actor; b. Delano, Calif., Nov. 13; s. Lester and Beatrice Rambo. Studies with Lee Strasberg, Vincent Chase. Founder Dack Rambo Prodns. Actor: (TV episodes) Hotel, The Love Boat, Fantasy Island, Charlie's Angels, Wonder Woman, House Calls, The Mississippi, Murder, She Wrote, (TV series) The New Loretta Young Show, 1962-63, The Guns of Will Sonnet, 1967-69, Dirty Sally, 1974, The Sword of Justice, 1978-79, Paper Dolls, 1984, Dallas, 1985-87, All My Children, Never Too Young, (TV pilots) Waikiki, 1980, No Man's Land, 1984, (TV movies) River of Gold, 1971, Hit Lady, 1974, Good Against Evil, 1977, (feature films) Nightmare Honeymoon, 1972, Rich and Famous, 1981, Shades of Love, 1987, Wild Flowers. Mem. Nat. Acad. TV Arts and Scis., Mothers Against Drunk Driving. Home: Earlimart Calif. Deceased.

RAMEY, HENRY JACKSON, JR., petroleum engineering educator; b. Pitts., Nov. 30, 1925; married, 1948; 4 children. B.S., Purdue U., 1949, Ph.D., 1952. Asst. chem. engr. unit ops. lab. Purdue U., 1949, asst. radiant heat transfer from gases, 1951-52; sr. research technologist petroleum prodn. research Magnolia Petroleum Co., Socony Mobil Oil Co., Inc., 1952-55; project engr. Gen. Petroleum Corp., 1955-60; staff reservoir engr. Mobil Oil Co. Div., 1960-63; mem. faculty petroleum engring. dept. Tex. A&M U., 1963-66; prof. petroleum engring. Stanford U., Calif., 1966-93, chmn. dept., 1976-86; cons. Chinese Petroleum Corp., Taiwan, 1962-63, other cos. Contbr. papers, articles to profl. lit.; patentee in field. Served as officer USAAF, 1943-46. Recipient Purdue U. Disting. Engr. award, 1975, Mineral Edn. award AIME, 1987. Mem. Am. Inst. Chem. Engrs., AIME (Ferguson medal 1959), Nat. Acad. Engring. Home: Stanford Calif. Died Nov. 19, 1993.

RAMMELKAMP, JULIAN STURTEVANT, historian, educator; b. Jacksonville, Ill., Aug. 4, 1917; s. Charles Henry and Rhoda Jeannette (Capps) R.; m. Mabel Alvera Tippitt, Feb. 25, 1942; children: David Addison, Julian Charles, Robert Allan. AB, Ill. Coll., 1939; MA, Harvard U., 1947, PhD, 1961. Prof. of history Albion (Mich.) Coll., 1954-84, prof. emeritus, 1984-94. Author: Pulitzer's Post-Dispatch, 1967; contbr. articles to hist. publs. Sgt. U.S. Army, 1941-45. LittD (hon.) Ill. Coll., 1979; D Humanities Albion Coll., 1984. Mem. Am. Hist. Assn., Orgn. Am. Historians, Mo. Hist. Soc., State Hist. Soc. Mo. Democrat. Home: Albion Mich. Died Aug. 24, 1994.

RAMSEY, NORMAN PARK, lawyer, retired federal judge; b. Fairchance, Pa., Sept. 1, 1922; s. Joseph L. and Florence (Bennett) R.; m. Margaret Quarngesser, Apr. 15, 1944 (dec. 1979); children: Margaret S. Ramsey Newman, Mary S. Ramsey Gilvarg, Christine M. Ramsey North, Ann L. Ramsey Grossman; m. Tucky Patz, July 10, 1982. Student, Loyola Coll., Balt., 1939-41; LL.B., U. Md., 1947. Bar: Md. 1946. Law clk. to judge U.S. Dist. Ct., 1947-48; asst. U.S. atty., 1948-50; assoc. Semmes, Bowen & Semmes, Balt., 1951-54; partner Semmes, Bowen & Semmes, 1957-80; asst. atty. gen. Md., 1955, dep. atty. gen. Md., 1955-57; lectr. U. Md. Law Sch., 1951-71; judge U.S. Dist. Ct. Md., 1980-91; sr. judge U.S. Dist. Ct. Md., 1991-92; gen. counsel Semmes, Bowen & Semmes, Balt., 1992-93. Pres., Balt. CSC, 1963-70; pres. Bd. Sch. Commrs., 1975. Served to 1st lt. USMCR, 1943-46. Mem. Bar Assn. Balt. City, ABA (ho. of dels. 1961-81, bd. govs. 1975-78), Md. Bar Assn. (bd. govs. 1965-75, pres. 1973), Order of Coif, Phi Kappa Sigma. Home: Baltimore Md. Died June 15, 1993.

RANDALL, BOB, writer; b. N.Y.C., Aug. 20, 1937; divorced; children: Julia Anne, Edward Gordon. BA, NYU, 1958. Copywriter Marschalk Co., N.Y.C., 1962-72; playwright, novelist, dramatist, 1972-95. Author: (plays) 6 Rms Riv Vu, 1972 (Drama Desk award), Odd Infinitum, 1974, The Magic Show, 1973, David's Mother, 1990, The Fan, 1994, (novels) The Fan, 1975 (Edgar Allen Poe award), The Next, 1977, The Calling, 1980, Last Man On the List, 1990, (films) David's Mother, 1994 (Humanitas award, Emmy award 1994), Zorro, The Gay Blade, 1981; creator: (TV series) On Our Own, 1975-76; producer, head writer: (TV series) Kate and Allie, 1984-88 (Writers Guild Am. award 1986, Humanitus award 1987). Recipient Emmy nomination NATAS, 1975, 84-86, Monitor award, 1985. Mem. Writers Guild Am. (award 1974, 87). Home: New Preston Conn. Died Feb. 11, 1995.

RANDALL, HENRY THOMAS, surgeon; b. N.Y.C., Aug. 29, 1914; s. Henry Thomas and Helen (Nixon) R.; m. Louise Elinor Harman, June 5, 1940; children: Martha Emily, Deborah Anne, Henry Thomas III. AB, Princeton U., 1937; MD, Columbia U., 1941, MScD, 1950; MA, Brown U., 1968. Diplomate: Am. Bd. Surgery, 1951. Surg. intern Presbyn. Hosp., N.Y.C., 1941-42; jr. asst. resident surgery Presbyn. Hosp., 1942, asst. resident surgery, 1945-48, resident surgery, 1949, asst. attending surgeon, 1950-51; instr. surgery Columbia Coll. Phys. and Surg., 1950, asst. prof., 1950-51; asst. vis. surgeon Francis Delafield Hosp., 1950-51; clin. dir. Meml. Hosp., N.Y.C., 1951-61; med. dir., v.p. med. affairs Meml. Hosp., 1961-65, chmn. dept. surgery, 1951-66, attending surgeon, dir. surg. research, 1966-67; surgeon in charge div. surg. research dept. surgery R.I. Hosp., 1967-70, surgeon-in-chief dept. surgery, 1970-79, cons., 1980-91; assoc. surgeon in chief, 1989-91; vis. surgeon James Ewing Hosp., 1951-67; asso. prof. surgery Cornell U. Med. Coll., 1951-54, prof. surgery, 1955-67; prof. med. sci. div. biology and medicine Brown U., 1967-79, prof. med. sci. emeritus, 1979-94; mem. Sloan-Kettering Inst., 1951-67, v.p. clin. affairs, 1961-65. Editor: Manual of Preoperative and Postoperative Care, 1967; Contbr. to textbooks and profl. jours. Served from 1st lt. to maj. M.C. AUS, 1942-45. Decorated Bronze Star with one oak leaf cluster; recipient W.W. Keen award Brown Med. Soc., 1983. Fellow N.Y. Acad. Med., Am. Surg. Assn., A.C.S. (vice chmn. com. pre and postoperative care 1963-65, chmn. 1966-69, com. on continuing edn. 1972-83, pres. R.I. chpt. 1976-78, Disting. Service award 1977); mem. AAAS, James Ewing Soc., R.I. Med. Soc. (Charles L. Hill award 1984), Providence Med. Soc., Am. Cancer Soc. (pres. N.Y.C. div. 1966-67, hon. life mem., Ann. Nat. Divisional award 1985, mem. bd., exec. com. R.I. div., hon. life mem., pres. 1978-80), Soc. Univ. Surgeons (pres. 1959-60), Soc. Clin. Surgery, Harvey Soc., Halsted Soc. (pres. 1963-65), N.Y. Surg. Soc. (pres. 1967), Boston Surg. Soc., New Eng. Surg. Soc., N.Y. Acad. Sci., N.Y. Clin. Soc., N.Y. Cancer Soc. (pres. 1961-62), New Eng. Cancer Soc., Sigma Xi. Club: Brown Faculty (Providence). Home: Bristol R.I. Died May 31, 1994; buried Swan Point Cemetary, Providence, R.I.

RANDT, CLARK THORP, physician, educator; b. Lakewood, Ohio, Nov. 18, 1917; s. Herbert W. and Bessie (Thorp) R.; m. Mary-Louise Paull Mitchell, Jan. 15, 1944; children: Clark Thorp, Dana M., Thomas P. A.B., Colgate U., 1940; M.D., Western Res. U., 1943. Intern, Univ. Hosps., Cleve., 1943-45; resident Neurol. Inst. N.Y., 1947-50; practice medicine, specializing in neurology N.Y.C., 1962-87; asst. in neurology Coll. Physicians and Surgeons, Columbia U., 1949-50; asso. prof. neurology Sch. Medicine, Western Res. U., 1950-59; dir. life sci. NASA, Washington, 1959-61; prof. neurology Sch. Medicine, NYU, 1962-70, prof., chmn. dept. neurology, 1970-87, prof. neurology emeritus, 1988-95; established NASA Ames Research Ctr., Life Sci. Lab., Calif., 1960; dir. Neurology Service, NYU-Bellevue Med. Center, also NYU Hosp.; cons. in neurology N.Y. VA Hosp., 1962-87; dir. life scis. NASA, Washington, 1959-61; chief neurology sect. U.S. Army Psychiat. Center, Mason Gen. Hosp., Brentwood, N.Y.; co-chmn. NASA-DOD bioastronautics coordinating com., Washington, 1960-61. Served to capt. M.C., AUS, 1945-47. Fellow Am. Acad. Neurology; mem. Am. Neurol. Assn., N.Y. Neurol. Soc. (pres. 1967-68), Aerospace Med. Assn. (v.p. 1961-62), Assn. for Research in Nervous and Mental Disease (chmn. bd. trustees 1972-73). Home: Greenwich Conn. Died Nov. 19, 1995.

RANKIN, ALFRED MARSHALL, lawyer; b. Beaver, Pa., July 19, 1913; s. Henry Preston and Annie (Marshall) R.; m. Clara Louise Taplin, Mar. 30, 1940; children: Alfred M. Jr., Thomas T., Claiborne R., Roger F., Bruce T. BS, Yale U., 1936, LLB, 1939. Assoc. Thompson, Hine and Flory, Cleve., 1939-47, ptnr., 1947-91; bd. dirs. NACCO Industries (formerly N.Am. Coal Corp.), Cleve., Hyster-Yale Materials Handling, Inc. Chmn. The Mus. Arts Assn., Cleve.; life trustee Hawken Sch., Cleve.; hon. trustee Western Res. Historical Soc., hon. trustee YMCA of Cleve., Shaker Lakes Regional Nature Ctr. Lt. comdr. USN, 1942-45, PTO. Recipient Grad. award U. Sch., Shaker Heights, Ohio, 1983, Vol.'s award Mayor of Cleve., 1984. Mem. ABA, Ohio Bar Asssn., Cleve. Bar Assn., Chagrin Valley Hunt Club (past pres.), Union Club (past trustee), Kirtland Country Club. Republican. Presbyterian. Home: Chagrin Falls Ohio Deceased.

RANSOM, EDWARD DUANE, lawyer; b. Minot, N.D., Jan. 3, 1914; s. Edward M. and Gladys (Root) R.; m. Margaret E. Phelps, Oct. 6, 1940 (dec. Dec. 1982); children: Edward P., Susan M., Richard M., Mary A.; m. Hazel Hudson, Apr. 28, 1984. Student, Minot State Tchrs. Coll., 1932-34; A.B., U. Mich., 1936, J.D., 1938. Bar: Calif. 1939, U.S. Supreme Ct. 1955, Circuit Ct. Appeals for D.C. and 1st, 2d, 5th and 9th Circuits. Assoc. Lillick, McHose, Wheat, Adams & Charles, San Francisco, 1938-41, 45-95; ptnr. Lillick & Charles, 1950-55, 57-85; gen. counsel Fed. Maritime Bd. and Maritime Administrn., 1955-57; U.S. del. Internat. Maritime Law Conf., 1959, 65, 74, 77. Served as lt. comdr. USN, 1941-45. Mem. ABA (chmn. com. on maritime transp. 1964), Calif. Bar Assn., San Francisco Bar Assn., Maritime Law Assn. (exec. com. 1957-60), San Francisco Legal Aid Soc. (dir. 1966-72), Marine Exchange of San Francisco (pres. 1971-73). Clubs: Propeller of U.S. (pres. chpt. 1975-76), San Francisco, World Trade (San Francisco), Claremont Country (Oakland). Home: Piedmont Calif. Died Mar. 31, 1995.

RANSON, NANCY SUSSMAN, artist; b. N.Y.C., Sept. 13, 1905; d. Bernard and Ida (Jablonsky) Sussman; m. Jo Ranson, Jan. 1927 (dec. 1965); children: Justine Ranson Schachter, Ellen Ranson Adams. Grad., Pratt Inst. Art Sch., 1926, B.F.A., 1974; student, Art Students League, Bklyn. Mus. Art Sch. One-person exhbns. include, George Binet Gallery, N.Y.C., 1948, 50, main br. Bklyn. Pub. Library, 1951, Mexican Govt. Tourist Commn., N.Y.C., 1952, U. Maine, 1964, 78, group shows include, Am. Water Color Soc., 1940, 42, 43, Nat. Assn. Women Artists, 1943-93, Bklyn. Soc. Artists, 1941-62, Am. Soc. Contemporary Artists, 1963-93, Tomorrow's Masterpieces, 1943, Artists for Victory, 1944, Critics Choice show Grand Central Galleries, N.Y.C., 1947, Prize Winners show, 1947, Butler Inst. Am. Art, Youngstown, Ohio, 1950, Audubon Artists, 1950-93, Bklyn. Artists Biennial, Bklyn. Mus., 1950, 54, 56, N.W. Printmakers Internat., 1952, 55, 56, Silvermine Guild Ann., 1956, Nat. Art Gallery N.S.W., Sydney, Australia, 1956, Nat. Exhbn. Contemporary Arts U.S., Pomona, Calif., 1956, N.Y. Soc. Women Artists, 1952-80, Am. Color Print Soc., 1952-90, Pa. Acad. Fine Art, 1957, Whitney Mus. Artists Equity, N.Y.C., 1951, Nat. Soc. Painters in Casein and Acrylic, 1958-93, Color Prints Americas, N.J. State Mus., 1970, other museums and galleries in, U.S., Can., France, Switzerland, India, Japan, Scotland, Eng., Israel, Egypt; represented in permanent collections, Fogg Mus. Art (Harvard U.), rep., Norfolk Art Mus., Brandeis U., U. Maine, Orono, Mexican Govt. Tourist Commn., Mus. City N.Y., Key West (Fla.) Art Hist. Soc., Reading (Pa.) Public Mus., Free Library, Phila., Slater Meml. Mus., Norwich, Conn., Ga. Mus. Art, Athens, Lydia Drake Library, Pembroke, Mass., Butler Inst. Am. Art, Smithsonian Instn. Archives of Am. Art, Washington, Arts and Crafts Inst., Peking, China, permanent collections, also nat. mus., Jerusalem, New Delhi, Tokyo, Sydney, Australia; Slide lectures on art and archaeology around the world, India, Indonesia, Africa, China. Recipient hon. mention in oil Bklyn. Mus., 1946; Eve Clendenin prize, 1953; Nat. Serigraph Soc. award, 1953; Medal of Honor in Graphics, Nat. Assn. Women Artists Ann., 1956; popular painting prize Critics Choice show Grand Central Galleries, 1947; Grumbacher award Bklyn. Soc. Artists, 1954; 1st prize graphics, 1955, 58; Presentation print Bklyn. Soc. Artists, 1962; Joseph Torch award, 1955; Francesca Wood award, 1955; Presentation print Am. Color Print Soc., 1955; 1st prize graphics Nat. Assn. Women Artists, 1958; prize print and drawing exhbn., 1962; Harold Kovner prize Audubon Artists Ann., 1958; Audubon Artists award, 1961; Gramercy prize Nat. Soc. Painters in Casein, 1963; Andrew-Nelson-Whitehead award Am. Soc. Contemporary Artists, 1964; 1st prize graphics, 1970; Barbara Kulicke award acrylics, 1975; Merit award in graphics, 1981; Internat. Women's Yr. award for cultural contbns., 1975-76; prize best silk screen Audubon Ann., 1982; 1st prize in graphics Am. Soc. Contemporary Artists Ann., 1984; MacDowell Found. fellow, 1964. Mem. N.Y. Soc. Women Artists (v.p. 1967-69), Nat. Assn. Women Artists (chmn. fgn. exhbns. 1964-67, chmn. admissions 1969-71, chmn. oil jury 1973-75, chmn. nominations 1975-77, adv. bd. 1977-80, chmn. graphics jury 1980-82), Bklyn. Soc. Artists (corr. sec. 1948-53, pres. 1954-56), Am. Color Print Soc., Audubon Artists (chmn. awards com. 1958, dir. graphics 1970-73, 75-78), Nat. Soc. Painters in Casein and Acrylics (hon. mem. 1990), Artists Equity Assn., Am. Soc. Contemporary Artists (chmn. constn. 1963-83, pres. 1969-71, permanent dir.), Internat. Assn. Art (del. U.S. com. 1964-77, rec. sec. 1977-80). Home: Brooklyn N.Y. Died Jan. 24, 1993.

RAPAPORT, ROBERT M., financial executive; b. Vienna, Austria, July 12, 1931; came to U.S., 1940, naturalized, 1944; s. Gustav H. and Rose (Katz) R.; m. Annette Kohn, Aug. 2, 1953; children: Gary Michael, Steven Mark, Gail Ann, Amy Sue. B.S., U. Mo., 1952. Mgr. Breddo Food Products, Midland Labs., Kansas City, Mo., 1953-60, pres., 1960-67; v.p. Sucrest Corp., N.Y.C., 1967-74; pres., CEO Sucrest Corp., 1974-77; also dir.; internat. commodity exec. E.F. Hutton & Co., N.Y.C., 1977-78; sr. ptnr. Lamborn & Co., N.Y.C., 1978-95; owner, pres. Foote & Jenks, Inc., Camden, N.J., 1981-95; dir. Bestex Corp., Kansas City, Mo. Mem. Am. Soc. Bakery Engrs. and Food Technicians, Am. Soc. Cereal Chemists. Home: Cherry N.J.

RASK, MICHAEL RAYMOND, orthopaedist; b. Butte, Mont., Oct. 24, 1930; s. Barth John and Marguerite Sadie (Joseph) R.; m. Elizabeth Anne Shannon, May 21, 1948; children: Dagny Marguerite Rask-Regan, Badih John, Patrick Henry, Molly Michelle. BS, Oreg. State U., 1951; MD, Oreg. Health Scis. U., 1955; PhD, 1978, U. Humanistic Studies, 1986. Diplomate Am. Bd. Orthopaedic Surgery, Am. Bd. Neurological Orthopaedic Surgery, Am. Bd. Bloodless Surgery, Am. Bd. Medical-Legal Analysts, Am. Bd. Hand Surgery, Am. Bd. Sportsmedicine Surgery, Am. Bd. Spinal Surgery. Intern Kings County Hosp., Bklyn., 1955-56; orthopaedic resident U. Oreg. Med. Sch., Portland, 1959-63; with neurological orthopaedic surgery preceptorships Oreg. Emmanuel Hosp., Portland, 1962-76; pvt. practice in neurol. orthopedic surgery Las Vegas, 1976-94; clin. instr. orthopaedics U. Oreg., 1964-71; prof. Am. Acad. Neurological and Orthopaedic Surgery, 1985-94; editorial reviewer Clin. Orthopaedics & Related Rsch., 1978-94, Am. Med. Reports, 1985-94, Muscle & Nerve, 1987-94, Am. Jour. CranioMandibular Practice. Author: Seminoma, 1970, Orthopod, 1972; editor in-chief: Jour. Neurological Orthopedic Medicine & Surgery, 1976-94; editorial rev. bd. Jour. Craniomandibular Practice; numerous lectures in field. Lectr. Arthritis Found., Las Vegas, 1976-78, cons. orthopaedist Easter Seal Ctr. for Crippled Children & Adults, Las Vegas, 1978-81, med. advisor so. Nev. chpt. Nat. Multiple Sclerosis Soc.; bd. dirs. Gov's. Com. on the Employment of the Handicapped, Nev., 1980-82. Capt. USAF, 1956-63. Fellow Cuban Soc. Orthopaedics Traumatology; mem. Am. Acad. Neurological Orthopaedic Surgeons (hon. 1979, course chmn. 1977-79, pres. 1978, chmn. bd. dirs. 1976-94), Nev. State Pharmacy Assn., Am. Back Soc. (bd. dirs. 1983-88), Semmelweiss Sci. Soc. (pres. Nev. chpt. 1980-94), Am. Fedn. Med. Accreditation (chmn. from 1979), Neurol. Orthopaedic Inst. (chmn. 1979-94), Bd. Neurol. Orthopaedic Surgeons (chmn. 1977-94), Sundry Primary Certifying Bds. (chmn. bd. dirs. 1976-94), Silkworm Club, Caterpillar Club. Democrat. Home: Las Vegas Nev. Died Oct. 18, 1994; cremated.

RATH, GEORGE EDWARD, bishop; b. Buffalo, Mar. 29, 1913; s. Edward F. and Eudora Pearl (Chadderdon) R.; m. Margaret Webber, Apr. 7, 1934; children: Peter F. (dec.), Gail (Mrs. Richard M. Sherk). A.B., Harvard U., 1933; B.D., Union Theol. Sem., 1936; S.T.D., Gen. Theol. Sem., 1964. Ordained deacon Episcopal Ch., 1938, priest, 1939; asst. to chaplain Columbia, 1936-39; asst. chaplain, 1939-41; vicar All Saints' Ch., Millington, N.J., 1941-49; rector All Saints' Ch., 1949-64; suffragan bishop Episcopal Diocese Newark, 1964-70; bishop coadjutor, 1970-73, bishop, 1974-78, ret., 1978; archdeacon Morris County, 1959-64; assisting bishop Episcopal Diocese of Mass., 1982-94. Chmn. bd. trustees Christ Hosp. Jersey City, 1966-79; trustee Cape Cod Mus. Natural History, 1980-85; bd. dirs. Nauset, Inc., 1981-86, 88-93. Mem. Cape Cod (Mass.) Bird Club, Harvard Club of Cape Cod, Montclair (N.J.) Bird Club. Home: East Orleans Mass. Died Noc. 18, 1995.

RATH, HILDEGARD, artist, author, lecturer; b. Freudenstadt, Ger., Mar. 22, 1909; came to U.S., 1948; m. Hermann Gross. Pvt. instrn., with Adolf Senglaub, Stuttgart, 1925, Kunstgewerbeschule, Stuttgart, 1926-27; student, Rustinsches Lehrinstitut, Potsdam, 1928-30, Akademie Der Bildenden, Kunste, Berlin, 1933-37; spl. study with, Lotte Laserstein, Berlin, Otto Manigk, Berlin. Owner, dir. European Sch. Fine Arts, N.Y.C., 1949-54; lectr. art and artists from prehistoric times to present, art socs. and museums, 1960-62; tchr. history of art Great Neck (N.Y.) Pub. Schs. Adult Edn. Program, 1960-62, North Shore Art Assn., Roslyn, N.Y., 1960-61; World field research corr. for movies, children's books, 1967. One-woman shows, Kunsthaus Schaller, Stuttgart, 1927, 41, 46, 59, Washington, 1957, N.Y.C., 1957, 61, 67, 67, 72, Paris, 1963, Manchester, Vt., all shows 1948-89, Nat. Soc. Mural Painters Travelling Exhbn., 1977-86; group shows throughout U.S. and fgn. countries; represented in numerous museums U.S. and Europe; paintings reproduced in Am. Artist, 1963, Enciclopedia Internazionale degli Artisti, 1970-71, Artist Contemporanei, 1982. Recipient Mayor Dr. Blaicher award, Stuttgart, 1941; Grumbacher award of merit Fla. Internat., 1952; award Prix de Paris, 1962; N.Y. Prix de Paris, 1963; Acad. award with gold medal Accademia Italia delle Artie e del Lavoro, 1980; invitation to participate Salon des Nations, Paris, 1983, Centre International d'Art Contemporain, 1986, Paris Artquest, 1986, traveling exhibit, N.Y.C., Los Angeles. Mem. Wurttembergisher Kunstverein Stuttgart, Landesverband Wurttembergischer Kunstler Tubingen (Ger.), So. Vt., N. Shore art assns., Artists Equity N.Y., Knickerbocker Artists N.Y., Nat. Assn. Pub. Sch. Adult Educators, Internat. Platform Assn., Nat. Soc. Mural Painters, Nat. Mus. Women in Arts. Episcopalian. Home: Manchester Center Vt. Died Dec. 12, 1992.

RATNER, MAX, building products company executive, land developer; b. Bialystok, Poland, 1907; m. Betty Ratner; children—Charles, Mark, James, Ronald. J.D., Cleve. Marshall Law Sch. With Forest City Enterprises, Inc., Cleve., 1928—, chmn. bd., 1974—, dir.; pres., bd. dirs. Am. Electrochem. Industries (Frutarom), Ltd., Israel; bd. dirs. Banc One, Cleve. Trustee, past v.p. Jewish Community Fedn.; bd. dirs. Am. Friends Hebrew U., Jewish Theol. Sem., Greater Cleve. Growth Assn., Technion U., Theol. Sem.; trustee Mt. Sinai Hosp.; founder, past bd. dirs. Suburban Hosp.; chmn. bd., past pres. Am.-Israel C. of C. Recipient Scopus award, Eisenman award Am. Friends Hebrew U.; Ohio Gov.'s award, 1980. Home: Cleveland Ohio Died May 31, 1995.

RATNER, SIDNEY, historian, economist, philosopher; b. N.Y.C., June 18, 1908; s. Israel and Olga (Handman) R.; m. Louise Michel Rosenblatt; 1 child, Jonathan. BA, CCNY, 1930; MA, Columbia U., 1931, PhD, 1942. Instr. Sarah Lawrence Coll., Bronxville, N.Y., 1938-39; instr. and lectr. Cooper Union Inst. of Tech., N.Y.C., 1938-41; lectr. history New Sch. for Social Rsch., N.Y.C., 1940; economist Bd. Econ. Warfare, Washington, 1942-44; sr. economist Fgn. Econ. Adminstrn., Washington, 1945; prin. economist, planning div. Office of Fgn. Liquidation U.S. Dept. State, Washington, 1946; asst. prof. Rutgers U., New Brunswick, N.J., 1946-48; assoc. prof. Rutgers U., New Brunswick, 1948-57, prof. history, 1957-78, prof. emeritus, 1978-96; lectr., Kyoto, Japan, 1964, Princeton, N.J., 1956-57. Author: American Taxation, 1942, Taxation and Democracy in America, 1967-80, The Tariff in American History, 1973; co-author: The Evolution of the American Economy, 1980, 2d edit., 1993; editor: The Philosopher of Common Man, 1940, Vision and Action, 1953; editor: (with J. Altman, John Dewey and A.F. Bentley) A Philosophical Correspondence, 1932-51, 1964, (with A.F. Bentley) Inquiry into Inquiries, 1969, (with A.F. Bentley) Makers, Users and Masters, 1954. Co-chmn. Princeton Sakharov Com., N.J., 1986-87. Mem. AAUP, Am. Econ. Assn., Am. Hist. Assn., Econ. History Assn., Conf. on Methods in Philosophy and Scis. (chmn. 1949-50), Inst. N.Y. Acad. Scis., Princeton Human Rights Assn., Soc. for Advancement of Am. Philosophy (H.W. Schneider award 1989). Home: Princeton N.J. Died Jan. 9, 1996.

RAUDSEPP, KARL, bishop; b. Puurmanni, Estonia, Mar. 26, 1980; came to Can., 1948; naturalized, 1950; s. Jaan and Liisa (Gruner) R. m. Ellen Feldmann, July 20, 1935; 4 children. Cand. theol. U. Tartu, Estonia, 1933. Ordained to ministry Estonian Evang. Luth. Church, 1933, dean, 1958, bishop, 1976. Pastor St. Michael Ch., Vandra, Estonia, refugee camps, Fed. Republic Germany; pastor Luth. World Fedn. Svc. to Refugees, St. John's Estonian Ch., Montreal, Que., Can. Author: Marked by Cross, 1982; monographies R.G. Kallas, Arthur Vôôbus; author 3 edits. of sermons in Estonian. Deceased. Home: Toronto Can.

RAUSCHER, FRANK JOSEPH, JR., microbiologist; b. Hellertown, Pa., May 24, 1931; s. Frank J. and Maretta C. (Nauman) R.; m. Margaret Ann Connell, July 30, 1955; children: Mary Agnes, Frank Joseph, Michael Paul, Megan Clare, David Kenneth. B.S., Moravian Coll., 1953; Ph.D., Rutgers U., 1957, Sc.D. (hon.), 1973. Research asst. virology Rutgers U., New Brunswick, N.J., 1955-57, research asso., 1957-58, asst. prof. virology, 1958-59, vis. investigator viral oncology, 1962-67; microbiologist lab. viral oncology Nat. Cancer Inst., Bethesda, Md., 1959-64, head viral oncology sect., 1964-66, chmn. spl. virus cancer program, 1964-70, chief viral leukemia br., 1966-67, asso. sci. dir. viral oncology etiology, 1967-70, sci. dir. etiology, 1970-72, dir. nat. cancer program, 1972-76; sr. v.p. rsch. Am. Cancer Soc., N.Y.C., 1976-88; exec. dir., v.p. Tima, Inc., Stamford, Conn., 1988-92; vis. faculty mem. Trinity Coll., Washington, 1959-70; mem. panel Bd. U.S. Civil Service Examiners, 1965-69; guest lectr. various acad. and comml. groups in U.S. and abroad, 1962-92; chmn. U.S. del. Internat. Agy. Research on Cancer, 1972-76; mem. expert adv. panel on cancer WHO, 1972-77; dir. Whittaker Corp., Los Angeles. Contbr. numerous articles on viral oncology to sci. jours.; mem. editorial bd. Jour. Toxicology and Environ. Health; discovered new murine leukemogenic virus. Trustee Moravian Coll., Bethlehem, Pa., 1971-82. Recipient Superior Service award HEW, 1972, Superior Service award Disting. Service award 1975; Man of Sci. award Achievement Rewards for Coll Scientists Found., 1975; Am. Cancer Soc. Ann. award, 1975; Ann. Charles R. Drew Meml. Cancer award Howard U., 1977; Pap award Papanicolaou Cancer Research Inst. Miami, 1978; Janeway award Am Radium Soc., 1978. Mem. Am. Assn. Cancer Research (dir. 1970), World Soc. Leukemia and Related Diseases, Am. Soc. Clin. Oncology, Am. Acad. Microbiology, AAAS, Theobald Smith Soc., Argentine Acad. Scis (hon.), Nat. Acad. Scis., Am. Assn. Immunologists, Sigma Xi. Roman Catholic. Home: Weston Conn Died Dec. 31, 1992.

RAVELING, DENNIS GRAFF, biology educator; b Devil's Lake, N.D., Feb. 28, 1939; s. Ralph Gordon and Martha Irene (Graff); R. m. Olga Catherine Masnyk Mar. 3, 1962. BA, So. Ill. U., 1960, PhD, 1967; MA U. Minn., 1963. Research scientist Can. Wildlife Service, Winnipeg, Man., Can., 1967-71; asst. prof. dept wildlife-fisheries biology U. Calif., Davis, 1971-74, assoc prof., 1974-80, prof., 1980-91. Contbr. articles to profl jours. Trustee Calif. Wetlands Found. NSF grantee 1963, 73, 75, 77, 78. Fellow AAAS, Am. Ornithologist Union; mem. Am. Soc. Naturalists, Cooper Ornithol Soc., Wildlife Soc., Wilson Ornithol. Soc., Sigma Xi elected fellow of the American Ornithologists union; th Dennis G. Raveling Fellowship established for graduat research by the California Waterfowl Assn.; Dennis G Raveling Endowed Waterfowl Professorship establishe at the U. Cal. Davis. Home: Davis Calif. Died Aug. 12 1991.

RAWLINGS, JAMES SCOTT, architect; b. Richmond Va., June 26, 1922; s. Byrd Lundy and Finetta An (Gardner) R. BS in Architecture, U. Va., 1947; MF in Architecture, Princeton U., 1949. Registere architect, Va., Ind., N.C., S.C. Instr. architecture U Va., Charlottesville, 1947; draftsman, staff architec Marcellus, Wright & Son, Architects, Richmond, 1949 53; founder, ptnr. Rawlings & Wilson, Architects Richmond, 1955-80, pres., chmn., 1980-93, chmn. emer itus, cons., 1993-95. Author: Virginia's Colonia Churches, 1963, Virginia's Ante-Bellum Churches, 1978 Colonial Churches of Virginia, Maryland, Nort Carolina, 1985. Past pres., trustee Va. Found. fo Archtl. Edn.; chmn. Com. for Architecture Rev Richmond, 1967-77; bd. dirs. St. Peter's Parish Ch Restoration Assn., New Kent, Va., 1985-95. Lt. (j.g USNR, 1942-46, PTO. Fellow AIA; mem. Va. Assn Professions, Raven Soc. U. Va., Country Club of Va., F Kappa Alpha. Episcopalian. Home: Richmond Va Died Oct. 27, 1995.

RAY, DONALD PAGE, political economist, associa tion executive, editor; b. Mpls., May 22, 1916; s. Mose and Effie (Page) R. A.B., U. Colo., 1941; Am. Counc Learned Socs. scholar, Cornell U., summer 194 Harvard Yenching Inst., 1941-42; M.A., George Wash ington U., 1947, grad. student, 1949-52. Regiona analyst Far Eastern div., overseas br. office of dir. Offic War Info., 1944-45; asst. dept. econs. George Wash ington U., 1945-47; exec. dir. Nat. Acad. Econs. an Polit. Sci., 1947-59; dir. Nat. Inst. Social and Behaviora Sci., 1959-90, also editor Symposia Studies Series, 1959 90; Asso. editor Social Sci., 1950-55; editor Spl. Pub Series Nat. Acad. Econs. and Polit. Sci., 1953-59. Editor: Trends in Social Science, 1961; Contbr. article and revs. to profl. jours. Fellow AAAS (coun. 1954-62 sec. sect. social, econ. and polit. scis. 1954-62); mem Am. Econ. Assn., U.S. Global Strategy Coun., Harvar Club (Washington), Delta Phi Epsilon, Pi Gamma Mu Omicron Delta Gamma. Presbyterian. Hom Arlington Va. Died June 23, 1992.

RAY, RICHARD EUGENE, osteopath, psychiatrist; b Unionville, Mo., Oct. 7, 1950; s. Richard Raymond an Doris Maxine (Bunyard) R.; m. Elaine Marie Brod Apr. 25, 1986. BS in Biology, N.E. Mo. State U., 197 DO, Kirksville Coll. Osteopathy, 1978. Diplomate Na Bd. Examiners for Osteopathic Physicians & Surgeons cert. ACLS, Am. Heart Assn. Intern Davenport (Iowa Osteopathic Hosp., 1978-79; resident in pediatric Kirksville (Mo.) Osteopathic Hosp., 1979; physicia gen. practice Nat. Health Svc. Corps., Princeton, Mo 1980-81; med. officer U.S. Bur. Prisons Fed. Correc tional Inst., Alderson, W. Va., 1981-82; chief healt programs U.S. Bur. Prisons Fed. Correctional Inst Sandstone, Minn., 1982-83; resident physician i psychiatry Mich Osteopathic Med. Ctr., Detroit, 198 86; staff psychiatrist Alaska Native Med. Ctr. India Health Svc., Anchorage, 1986-88, VA Med. Ctr., She idan, Wyo., 1988-89; chief psychiatrist in chen dependency & psychogeriatrics Moose Lake (Minn Regional Med. Ctr., 1989-92; asst. prof. psychiatry, ass dir. psychiat. med. edn., dir. consultation/liaison svc Chgo. Coll. Osteo. Medicine, 1992-93; staff psychiatris Fergus Falls (Minn.) Regional Treatment Ctr., 1993-9 consulting psychiatrist Northwestern Mental Heal Ctr., Crookston, Minn., 1993-94; dir. psychiat. svc Saginaw (Mich.) County Mental Health Ctr., 1995— chmn. treatment review panel Moose Lake Region Med. Ctr., 1989-92. Lt. comdr. USPHS, 1981-83.

Mem. Am. Osteopathic Assn., Am. Soc. Addiction Medicine, Am Coll. Neuropsychiatrists, Am. Osteopathic Acad. of Addictionology (charter mem.), Kirksville Ostoepathic Med. Sch. Alumni Assn. (life mem.), N.E. Mo. State U. Alumni Assn. (life mem.). Republican. Baptist. Home: Saginaw Mich. Died June 11, 1995.

RAYMOND, VICTOR P., federal official; b. Pueblo, Colo.; s. Clark J. and Barbara J. (Reid) R. BA, U. Mo., 1969; ScD, Johns Hopkins U., 1987. Ops. rschr. nat. ctr. health svcs. rsch. HHS, 1978-82; profl. staff mem. com. vets. affairs U.S. Senate, 1982-85; dep. dir. office congrl. affairs VA, 1985; profl. staff mem. house com. VA U.S House of Reps., 1985-88, staff dir. subcom. hosps. and health care, house com. vets. affairs, 1988-90; dep. dir. Commn. Future Structure Vets. Health Care, 1990-91; assoc. dep. asst. sec. policy Dept. Vets. Affairs, Washington, 1991-93, dep. asst. sec. policy, 1993, asst. sec. policy and planning, 1993-94. Episcopalian. Home: Washington D.C. Died Apr. 1, 1994.

RAYSON, JACK HENRY, dentist, educator, retired; b. Gonzales, Tex., July 22, 1931; s. Jack Henry and Florence (Zint) R.; m. Donna Thornton, Oct. 19, 1957; children: Susan, Scott, David. D.D.S., U. Tex., 1957; M.A., U. New Orleans, 1976. Gen. practice dentistry San Antonio, 1961-62; asst. prof. Baylor Coll. Dentistry, 1962-66, U. Ky. Coll. Dentistry, 1967-69; prof., dean Sch. Dentistry, La. State U., New Orleans, 1969-93; ret., 1993; cons. VA hosps., New Orleans, Biloxi. Author: Synopsis of Complete Dentures, 1977. Served to capt. USAF, 1956-61. Fellow Am. Coll. Dentists; mem. Am., La., New Orleans dental assns., Southeastern Acad. Prosthodontics, Xi Psi Phi, Omicron Kappa Upsilon. Home: Metairie La. Died Nov. 20, 1995.

READ, BENJAMIN HUGER, lawyer, foundation executive; b. Phila., Sept. 14, 1925; s. William Bond and Rachel Biddle (Wood) R.; m. Anne Lowell Keezer, Aug. 2, 1950; children: Benjamin Huger, Dexter K., Mary B. B.A., Williams Coll., 1949; LL.B., U. Pa., 1952. Bar: Pa. 1952. With firm Duane, Morris & Heckscher, Phila., 1952-55; assoc. defender Vol. Defender Assn., Phila., 1955-56; atty. adviser Legal Adviser's Office, State Dept., 1957-58; legis. asst. to Senator Clark of Pa., 1958-63; spl. asst. to sec. state, also exec. sec. Dept. State, 1963-69; acting dir. Woodrow Wilson Internat. Ctr. for Scholars, Smithsonian Instn., 1969, dir., 1969-73; pres. German Marshall Fund of U.S., 1973-77; dep. under-sec. for mgmt. U.S. Dept. State, Washington, 1977-78; under sec. for mgmt. U.S. Dept. State, 1978-81; lawyer, cons., 1981-90; pres. ECOFUND '92, sr. adviser to sec.-gen. of UN 1992 Conf. on Environment and Devel. Bd. dirs. St. Francis Ctrs., Ptnrs. for Dem. Change, Mediation Inst., L.A., Am. Acad. Diplomacy, Ptnrs. for Livable Places, Am. Com. on East-West Rels., Nat. Security Archives. With USMCR, 1943-46. Recipient Disting. Honor award Dept. State, 1981; Disting. Service Cross W. Ger., 1978. Mem. Am. Acad. Diplomacy, Am. Com. on U.S.-Soviet Rels., Nat. Acad. Pub. Adminstrn., Coun. Fgn. Rels., Cosmos Club, Phi Beta Kappa. Home: Washington D.C. Died Mar. 18, 1993.

READE, RICHARD SILL, manufacturing executive; b. Romeo, Mich., Oct. 11, 1913; s. Richard Sill and Ella (Van de Car) R.; m. Arlyne Alice Conger, Apr. 9, 1938; children: William Kent, Todd Conger. B.S. in Mech. Engring., U. Mich., 1934. Mgr. F & B div. Am. Blower Co., Detroit, 1946-51; dir. purchasing Am.-Standard Corp., N.Y.C., 1951-55; pres. Ross Heater Corp., Buffalo, 1955-60; v.p. mfg. (Am.-Standard indsl. div.), Detroit, 1960-64; pres. Crane Can., Ltd., Montreal, Que., Can., 1964-76, Transcar Industries, Inc., Clover, S.C., 1977-92. Mem. Newcomen Soc., Can. Inst. Plumbing and Heating (pres. 1971-72), Chi Phi. Home: Longwood Fla. Died April, 1994.

READING, BONNIE NELSON, lawyer; b. Bklyn., Nov. 13, 1943; d. Edward James Nelson and Frances (Knapp) Connor; m. Paul E. Reading, June 19, 1965 (div. July 1977); children: Eric, Christopher. BA in Russian Linguistics, Cornell U., 1964; JD, Fordham U., 1968. Bar: N.Y. 1971, Calif. 1972. Ptnr. Seltzer Caplan Wilkins & McMahon, San Diego, 1974-95. Bd. dirs. Holiday Bowl, 1984; mem. City of San Diego Park and Recreation Bd., 1988-95, chair, 1990-95. Recipient Daniel T. Broderick award for professionalism, civility and integrity, 1994, Belva Lockwood award for svc. Lawyer's Club, 1992; named Legal Profl. of Yr., 1992. Mem. ABA (family law sect.), Am. Acad. Matrimonial Lawyers, Calif. Trial Lawyers Assn., Calif. State Bar Assn. (family law adv. com. 1980-83, family law exec. com. 1978-81, appellate rev. dept. state bar ct. 1985-87), San Diego County Bar Assn. (v.p. 1982, bd. dirs. 1979-82, chair membership com. 1978-79, clin. edn. program family law 1979, family law sect., cert. spl. sect.), San Diego Trial Lawyers Assn. (bd. dirs. 1983), San Diego County Bar Found. (sec. 1984, bd. dirs. 1983—), Lawyers Club (bd. dirs. 1984). Home: San Diego Calif. Died Sept. 25, 1995.

REARDON, ROBERT JOSEPH, financial corporation executive; b. Cleve., June 9, 1928; s. Arthur E. and Jane (Clark) R.; m. Josephine Carr, July 25, 1953; children: Jane, John, Patricia, Michael (dec.), Mary, Catherine, Daniel, Sarah, Robert. BS in Bus. Adminstrn., U. Mo., 1949. With TV sales dept. Nat. Broadcasting Co., Chgo., 1955-57; sales mgr. WNBC-TV, Hartford, Conn., 1958-59; regional sales mgr. WTCN-TV, Mpls., 1959-61; chmn. bd. Bremer Fin. Svcs., St. Paul, 1973-89; pres., chief exec. officer Bremer Fin. Corp., 1967-89, chmn. bd. dirs., 1988-94; dir. Dakota Bank & Trust, Fargo, N.D., 1st Am. Nat. Bank, St. Cloud, Minn., Drovers 1st Am. Bank, South St. Paul. Trustee Otto Bremer Found., St. Paul, 1967-94; bd. dirs. AHW Corp., Mille Lacs Found., United Way, St. Paul, Catholic Charities, Archdiocese of St. Paul-Mpls., Minn. Coun. on Founds., Mpls.; chmn. bd. Convent of Visitation Sch., St. Paul. Died Jan. 23, 1995. Home: Saint Paul Minn.

RECTOR, RICHARD ROBERT, television executive, producer; b. Sioux Falls, S.D., Oct. 10, 1925; s. Harry David and Naomi Leone (Wilson) R.; m. Marjorie M. Gust, Mar. 10, 1957; children: Christopher, Steven, Tracey. B.S., Northwestern U., 1950. Mgr. CBS Network ops.; dir. ops. for CBS News; program sercice coordinator, unit mgr., producer CBS TV Network, N.Y.C., 1952-61; v.p. VHF, Inc., div. Reeves Broadcasting Corp., 1961-64; pres. Richard R. Rector Prodns., N.Y.C., 1964-65; asst. dir. programming Sta. WCBS-TV, N.Y.C., 1966-69; dir. CBS Network Studios, N.Y.C., 1969-70; v.p. programs and sales planning Viacom, Inc., 1970-71; dir. prodn. planning and sta. liaison Bilingual Children's Television, Oakland, Calif., 1972-75; project dir., exec. producer Over Easy Project, San Francisco, from 1975; pres. Power/Rector Prodns., Inc. Exec. producer: (TV prodns.) Dial M for Music, Camera 3, Am. Mus. Theatre, Sunrise Semester, Pinocchio, The Emperor's New Clothes, Jack and the Beanstalk, Aladdin, (65 programs for Disney Channel) The Scheme of Things; producer: (recs.) Harry Simone Chorale, (mus. concerts on TV) Joan Baez, the Limelighters, Carlos Montoya, (TV drama) Tchin, Tchin, (TV documentaries) Cuban refugees, flights of Scott Carpenter and John Glenn, March of Time series. Pres. Port Washington (N.Y.) Civic Assn., 1960-61, mem. bd. adult edn., Port Washington, 1963-64, mem. adv. bd. dirs. Archdiocesan Communications, citizens adv. com. Dominican Coll.; commr. Calif. State Commn. on Aging, 1991-93 (chmn. long term care and health com.); vice chmn. Marin Commn. on Aging, San Rafael Commn. on Aging. Served with USNR, 1943-46. Mem. Nat. Acad. TV Arts and Scis. (bd. govs. N.Y. 1965-70, treas. 1965-67, trustee 1967-70, pres. San Francisco chpt. 1971-74, trustee 1973-77, nat. vice chmn. 1974-76, chmn. 1976-78, 84-86, coordinator chpt. pres. 1974-77, dir. ATO Found. 1985-87). Presbyterian. Home: San Rafael Calif. Deceased.

REDINGTON, ROWLAND WELLS, physicist, researcher; b. Otego, N.Y., Sept. 26, 1924; s. Raymond Edgar and Sara Jane (Trask) R.; m. Shirley Alice Bennett, June 27, 1947; children: John Bennett, Philip Edgar. ME, Stevens Inst. Tech., 1945; PhD, Cornell U., 1951. Sr. aerodynamicist research div. Curtiss-Wright, Buffalo, 1945; sr. aerodynamicist Cornell U. Aero. Lab., Buffalo, 1946; physicist Gen. Electric Research Lab., Schenectady, N.Y., 1951-66, program mgr., 1966-75, CT program mgr., 1975-79, NMR program mgr., 1979-81, br. mgr., 1981-89, physicist, 1989-91, ret., 1991; adj. prof. Rensselaer Polytech. Inst., Troy, N.Y., 1964-67, U. Calif., San Francisco, 1978-79; mem. grad. clin. faculty U. Calif., San Francisco, 1979-91; cons. adv. group electron devices Dept. of Def., N.Y.C., 1971-77. Contbr. articles to profl. jours.; patentee in field. Commr. Niskayuna Vol. Fire Dept. Coolidge fellow Gen. Electric Corp. Research and Devel., 1985; named Engr. of Yr., Design News, 1989; recipient Indsl. Applications of Physics prize Am. Inst. of Physics, 1989. Fellow Am. Phys. Soc.; mem. Nat. Acad. Engring., Sigma Xi. Home: Niskayuna N.Y. Died June 22, 1995.

REDMOND, WILLIAM ALOYSIUS, state legislator; b. Chgo., Nov. 25, 1908; s. William P. and Gertrude (Crowe) R.; m. Rita Riordan, Mar. 6, 1943; children: Bill, Mary, Colleen. B.S., Marquette U., 1931; J.D., Northwestern U., 1934. Bar: Ill. Mem. Ill. Ho. of Reps., 1959-81; speaker 79th-81st sessions. Chmn. DuPage County Democrats.; mem. Prisoner Rev. Bd., 1982-92. Served to lt. comdr. USNR, 1941-45. Mem. Am., Ill., DuPage County bar assns. Lodges: K.C; Lions. Home: Bensenville Ill. Died Dec. 11, 1992.

REED, DOEL, art educator, etcher; b. Logansport, Ind., May 21, 1894; s. William and Anna and Anderson B.; m. Elizabeth Jane Sparks, Oct. 21, 1920; 1 dau., Martha Jane. Student, Art Acad., Cincinnati, 1916-17, 1919-20, Paris, France, 1926, 1930-31. Prof. emeritus, former chmn. art dept. Okla. State U.; lectr. Assn. of Am. Colls. Art Project.; Phila. Bd. regents Mus. N.Mex.; mem. Hardwood adv. bd. U. N.Mex. Exhibited one-man show, Thomas Gilcrease Inst., Am. History and Art, Tulsa, 1979; works owned by, Bibliotheque Nationale, Paris, Victoria and Albert Mus., London, N.Y. Pub. Library Print Room, Library of Congress, Washington, Honolulu Acad. Fine Arts, Phila. Art Mus., Carnegie Inst. Fine Arts, Seattle Art Mus., Philbrook Art Mus., Okla. State Office Bldg., mural, Met. Mus. Art, N.Y.C., Dayton Art Mus., Butler Art Inst., Youngstown, Rockhill Nelson Mus., Kansas City, Joslyn Art Mus., Omaha, Dallas, Mus. Fine Arts, Houston Art Mus., El Paso Mus. Art, U. Wyo. Art Mus., U. N.Mex. Art Mus., Beaumont Art Mus., Pa. Acad. Art; (Recipient awards: Henry B. Shope, Annual 1949, Appelbaum 1950, Jourdan Memorial, New Orleans 1951, First Prize for Graphics 1951, Audubon Gold Medal of Honor 1951, Purchase award (casein), Joslyn Mus. 1952, Lovis Schwitzer award, L.S. Ayres Purchase award John Herron Art Museum 1952, Black and White award Conn. Acad. Fine Arts 1953, Boston Printmakers award 1953, John Taylor Arms Meml. medal Audubon Artists, N.Y. 1954, M.C. Hewgley Award, Philbrook Art Center 1957, NAD prize 1961, purchase prize DePauw U., Nat. Print Exhbn. 1961, 1st award oils Fine Arts Mus. N.Mex. 1962, Samuel F.B. Morse medal NAD 1965, Cert. of Merit 1980, Gumbacher award Allied Artists Am. 1972, award for achievement and excellence in visual arts Gov. of N.Mex., others.); Author: Doel Reed Makes an Aquatint, 1967; spl. aquatint and 35 proofs for, Soc. Am. Graphic Artists, 1978. Served with 47th Inf., 4th Div., World War I. Mem. Soc. Am. Etchers, Chgo. Soc. Etchers, Ind. Soc. Print Makers, Print Makers Soc. Calif., Allied Artists Am., Nat. Soc. Painters in Casein and Acrylic (Michael M. Engel Meml. award 1978). Home: Taos N. Mex. Deceased.

REED, GEORGE FARRELL, physician; b. Oswego, N.Y., Oct. 25, 1922; s. George C. and Frances (Farrell) R.; m. Jane Margaret Luke, June 28, 1947; children: Sally F., Lucy F., Nancy L., Margaret F. A.B., Colgate U., 1944; M.D., Syracuse U., 1946. Diplomate Am. Bd. Otolaryngology (dir. 1956-86, pres. 1976-79, exec. sec.-treas. 1981-86, sr. councillor 1986-94). Intern Syracuse U. Med. Ctr., 1946-47, USPHS, 1947-49; resident Mass. Eye and Ear Infirmary, Boston, 1949-52; practice medicine specializing in otolaryngology; faculty Harvard Med. Sch., Mass. Eye and Ear Infirmary, 1952-65; prof., chmn. dept. otolaryngology SUNY Upstate Med. Ctr., Syracuse, 1965-76, prof., 1976-94, dean Coll. Medicine, exec. v.p., 1976-86, dean emeritus, prof. otolaryngology, 1986-94; mem. liaison com. on continuing med. edn., 1974-80. Bd. dirs. Clarke Sch. for Deaf, 1957-71. Mem. ACS, AMA, Am. Acad. Otolaryngology (rep. council med. splty. socs., sec. for continuing edn. 1968-80), Am. Laryngol. Assn., Am. Laryngol., Rhinol. and Otol. Assn., Am. Soc. Head and Neck Surgery (pres. 1976-77), Am. Council Otology (pres. 1976-77), Am. Broncho-Esophageal Assn., Soc. Univ. Otolaryngologists (pres. 1975-76), Am. Acad. Facial Plastic and Reconstructive Surgery, Soc. Acad. Chmn. Otolaryngology (sec. 1974-75), Am. Assn. Med. Colls. Home: Fayetteville N.Y. Died Nov. 25, 1994.

REED, GORDON WIES, retired manufacturing executive; b. Chgo., Nov. 20, 1899; s. Frank and Mary Catherine (Wies) R.; m. Naomi Bradley, Sept. 18, 1928; 1 son, Thomas; m. Genevieve Funston, Oct. 7, 1967. B.S., U. Ill., 1922. Vice pres. Hanley Co., Bradford, Pa., 1925-41; pres. Tex. Gulf Producing Co., Houston, 1941-45; chmn. bd. Tex. Gulf Producing Co., 1945-86; dir. AMAX Inc. (formerly Am. Metals Climax, Inc.), Greenwich, Conn., 1966-85; bd. dirs. Putnam Trust Co., Greenwich, Conn.; asst. dir. aluminum magnesium div. W.P.B., 1941-45, spl. asst. to chmn., 1945, spl. asst. to chmn. surplus property bd., 1945; spl. asst. to chief of staff USAF, 1950-60; chmn. Reed Com. on MATS, USAF, 1960; with Assoc. Hosp. Svc. of N.Y., 1947-61. Trustee Greenwich Hosp. Assn. Republican (chmn. Conn. fin. com.). Methodist (chmn. community ch.). Clubs: Round Hill (Greenwich, Conn.), Blind Brook (Port Chester, N.Y.). Home: Greenwich Conn. Deceased.

REED, WILLIAM GARRARD, retired business executive; b. Shelton, Wash., Feb. 3, 1908; s. Mark E. and Irene (Simpson) R.; m. Eleanor Henry, July 11, 1935; children: Susan Henry, William Garrard, Mary Simpson. A.B., U. Wash., 1929; student, Harvard U. Bus. Sch., 1929-30. Former chmn. Crown Simpson Pulp Co., Simpson Timber Co., Simpson Lee Paper Co., Simlog Corp.; former pres. Lumbermen's Merc. Co., State Bank Shelton, Malahat Logging Co., Can.; former exec. v.p. Rayonier, Inc., N.Y.C.; formerly mng. partner Simpson Reed & Co.; former pres. Kamilche Co.; propr. Graysmarsh Farm; dir. Olympia Oyster Co., Simpson Timber Co.; dir. emeritus Boeing Co. Mem. Wash. Rep. Nat. Com., 1940-44; head U.S. del. Econ. Commn. for Europe, 1960; pres. Seattle Found., 1959-61, United Good Neighbor Fund, 1952-53; mem. pres.'s council Calif. Inst. Tech., 1968-70; adv. bd. U. Wash. Grad. Bus. Sch., 1960-70; bd. dirs. Stanford Research Inst., 1957-65, Seattle Art Mus., 1955-73, Harvard Bus. Sch. Assn., 1964-67. Served to lt. comdr. USNR, 1942-45. Decorated Bronze Star. Mem. Psi Upsilon. Episcopalian (sr. warden 1966-68). Clubs: Links (N.Y.C.), Univ. (N.Y.C.); Pacific Union (San Francisco); Univ. (Seattle), Golf (Seattle), Rainier (Seattle). Home: Seattle Wash. Deceased.

REESE, EVERETT D., banker; b. Columbus, Ohio, Jan. 15, 1898; s. David T. and Sarah (Davis) R.; m. Martha Grace Miller, Sept. 4, 1924 (dec. May 1970); children: John Gilbert, Phoebe Lang (Mrs. John D. Lewis), Thekla Alice (Mrs. Donald B. Shackelford), David Everett; m. Pendery Spear Haines, Aug 29, 1971. B.S., Ohio State U., 1919; LL.D., Rutgers U., 1964, Ohio State U., 1971; D.Pub.Service, Ohio No. U., 1968. Instr. sch. commerce Ohio State U., Columbus, 1919-20, Ga. Sch. Tech., Atlanta, 1920-21; part-time instr. Denison U., Granville, Ohio, 1922-23, 39-40; with Park Nat. Bank of Newark, Ohio, from 1921; pres., dir.

Park Nat. Bank of Newark, 1926, chmn. bd., 1956-79, chmn. exec. com., from 1979; chmn. bd. 1st Nat. Bank, Cambridge, Ohio, 1955-73; hon. chmn. 1st Nat. Bank, 1955-73; chmn. bd. First Fed. Savs. & Loan Assn., Newark, 1934-78; chmn. emeritus First Fed. Savs. & Loan Assn., from 1978; chmn. bd. City Nat. Bank & Trust Co., Columbus, 1959-68, First Banc Group of Ohio Co., 1969-73, dir., 1973-78; dir. Suburban Motor Freight, Inc., Liqui-Box, all Columbus; lectr. Sch. Banking U. Wis., 1949-56; mem. faculty Grad. Sch. Banking, Rutgers U., 1950-58; served with Internat. Exec. Service Corps. Trustee emeritus Mt. Carmel Hosp., Columbus, Dawes Arboretum, Newark, Ohio, Denison U., Granville, Ohio, Children's Hosp. of Columbus, Pub. Welfare Found., Washington; trustee Evans Found., Newark., Franklin U., trustee, pres. Columbus Gallery Fine Arts, 1973-75; chmn. exec. com. trustees Piney Woods (Miss.) Country Life Sch.; bd. dirs. Pub. Welfare Found., Inc., Washington; chmn., exec. com. Pres.'s club Ohio State U., 1963-78, chmn. emeritus, from 1978. Recipient Disting. Service award Ohio State U., 1964, Ayres Leadership award Stonier Grad. Sch. Banking, Rutgers U., 1967, Disting. Citizen award Columbus C. of C., Preston Davis award Columbus, Outstanding Citizen of 1979 award Columbus Bd. Realtors. Mem. Ohio Bankers Assn. (pres. 1941-42), Am. Bankers Assn. (pres. 1953-54), Sigma Chi, Phi Alpha Kappa, Delta Sigma Pi, Beta Gamma Sigma, Alpha Kappa Psi. Presbyterian. Clubs: University (N.Y.C.); Lansdowne (London); Columbus, Rocky Fork Hunt and Country, Columbus Country, Athletic, Faculty, Rotary (Columbus); Masons (33 deg.), KT, Shriners. Home: Columbus Ohio Died May 24, 1995.

REGAN, JOHN J., law educator; b. N.Y.C., July 1, 1929; s. John Joseph (dec.) and Catherine (Marshall) R. (dec.); m. Mary O'Connell, Feb. 20, 1971; 1 child, Alycia Cathryn. B.A., Mary Immaculate Coll., 1951; M.A., St. John's U., N.Y., 1963; J.D., Columbia U., 1960, LL.M. Ford Urban Law Fellow, 1970-71), 1971, J.S.D., 1977. Bar: N.Y. 1961, D.C. 1979. Assoc. dean of men, lectr. in law St. John's U., N.Y.C., 1960-62, dean Colls. Liberal Arts and Scis., 1962-68, assoc. prof. law, 1968-70; prof. law Sch. of Law, U. Md., Balt., 1971-78; prof. of law Hofstra U., Hempstead, N.Y., 1978-95, dean Sch. of Law, 1978-82; dir. Inst. Health Law and Policy Hofstra Law Sch., 1995. Author: Law and the Dependent Elderly, 1977, Tax, Estate and Financial Planning for the Elderly, 1985, 95, Your Legal Rights in Later Life, 1989, The Aged Client and the Law, 1990, (with M. Gilfix) Tax, Estate and Financial Planning for the Elderly: Forms and Practice, 1991, 95, Entitlements, 1994. Mem. ABA. Roman Catholic. Home: Garden City N.Y. Died Sept. 1, 1995.

REGENSTEIN, LOUIS, lawyer; b. Atlanta, Feb. 9, 1912; s. Louis and Venia (Liebman) R.; m. Helen Lucile Moses, July 30, 1939; children: Lewis Graham, Jonathan Kent. A.B. cum laude, Harvard U., 1933, J.D. cum laude, 1936; L.H.D. (hon.), Clark Coll., 1986. Bar: Ga. 1935. Assoc. firm Kilpatrick, Cody, Roger, McClatchey & Regenstein, Atlanta, 1936-41, ptnr., 1941-82, of counsel, 1982—; mem. nat. adv. com. Ga. del. White House Conf. on Aging, 1961; lectr. tax insts., 1946—; pres. bd. Atlanta Legal Aid Soc., 1952-53; mem. exec. com. Ga. Republican Party, 1950-58. Editor: Harvard Law Rev, 1935-36; Contbr. articles on taxation to profl. jours. Bd. dirs. Fox Found. Served to lt. col. AUS, 1941-45. Mem. Am., Ga., Atlanta bar assns., Am. Judicature Soc., Nat. Legal Aid and Defenders Assn., World Peace Through Law Center, Atlanta C. of C. (past dir.), Newcomen Soc., Council on Foreign Relations, Atlanta Lawyers Club, Standard Club, Harvard Club, Atlanta City Club (dir.), Commerce Club, Buckhead Club. Home: Atlanta Ga. Died Aug. 15, 1994.

REGGIA, FRANK, electrical engineer; b. Northumberland, Pa., Oct. 30, 1921; s. Nicola and Rachela (DiPhillips) R.; m. Betty Jo Patterson, Jan. 14, 1945; children: James Allen, Daniel Lee. BSEE cum laude, Bucknell U., 1970, MSEE, 1972. Electronic engring. aide rsch. and devel. program microwaves Nat. Bur. Standards, Washington, 1945-48, radio engr., 1949-53; electronic engr. Harry Diamond Labs., Dept. Army, Washington, 1954-59, electronic scientist, 1960-65; elec. engr. Harry Diamond Labs., Dept. Army, Washington and Adelphi, Md., 1966-75, mgr. electronic fuze program, Adelphi, 1976-78; pvt. govt. and industry cons. microwaves Roanoke, Va., 1979—; speaker NATO Microwave Conf. Paris, 1962, Internat. Conf. Microwave Circuitry, Tokyo, 1964, Internat. Conf. Magnetics, Stuttgart, Fed. Republic Germany, 1966, others. Editor Proc. 1971 Internat. Microwave Conf., Washington; author, co-author over 50 articles to profl. jours. 22 patents microwave systems components. Pres. Chevy Chase (Md.) Civic League, 1960-61; scoutmaster, com. chmn. Chevy Chase Coun. Boy Scouts Am. 1962-68; bd. dirs. Post #105 Am. Legion, Bethesda, 1972-75; bd. dirs., trustee, pres. Men's Club St. Andrew Meth. Ch., Bethesda , 1973-78; bus. mgr. Cardinal Chorus, Roanoke, Va., 1982-89. With USN, 1940-45. Decorated Purple Heart. Fellow IEEE (life, editorial bd. Trans on MTT 9 yrs., citation award), AAAS, Wash. Acad. Sci.; mem. Washington Soc. Engrs. (Engr. of Yr. 1952), Washington chpt. MTT Soc. of IEEE (co-founder, life, chmn. 1961), Antenna and Propagation Soc. IEEE, Electron Devices Soc. IEEE, Nat. Assn. Ret. Fed. Employees (Fed. Employee of Yr. award 1978, pres., 1981, officer exec. com. 1978—, v.p. S.W. Va. Area VI 1993-94), Am. Radio Relay League, Tau Beta Pi, NRA, DAV. Democrat. Methodist. Home: Roanoke Va. Died Mar. 13, 1995.

REGHANTI, THOMAS J., transportation equipment manufacturing company executive; b. Milw., 1925; married. B.S., U. Wis., 1950. Saleman to used trailer mgr. Fruehauf div. Fruehauf Corp., Detroit, 1950-66, v.p. used trailers, 1966-68; v.p., gen. sales mgr. Fruehauf Corp., 1968-69; v.p. sales and mktg. Fruehauf Corp., Detroit, 1969-70, corp. v.p., gen. mgr. Fruehauf div., 1970-80, exec. v.p., 1980, pres., dir.; chmn. bd., pres., dir. Fruehauf Can. Inc.; dir. Crane Fruehauf, London, Eng., Henred Fruehauf Pty. Ltd., Johannesburg, South Africa. Served with USAF, 1942-46. Home: Detroit Mich.

REGNERY, HENRY, publisher; b. Hinsdale, Ill., Jan. 5, 1912; s. William Henry and Frances Susan (Thrasher) R.; m. Eleanor Scattergood, Nov. 12, 1938; children: Susan, Alfred S., Henry F. (dec.), Margaret. BS, MIT, 1934; student, U. Bonn., Germany, 1934-36; MA, Harvard U., 1938; LLD (hon.), Mt. Mary Coll., Milw. Staff Am. Friends Service Com., 1938-41; officer Joanna Western Mills Co., 1941-47, past chmn. bd.; founder Henry Regnery Co., 1947, pres., 1947-66, chmn. bd., 1967-1977; founded Gateway Editions, Ltd. (Book publishers), 1977; pres. Regnery Pub., 1977-83, also chmn. bd., 1977-83. Home: Chicago Ill. Died June 18, 1996.

REHM, WARREN STACEY, JR., biophysicist; b. Lancaster, Pa., Oct. 16, 1907; s. Warren Stacey and Grace (Irwin) R.; m. Barbara Campbell, Apr. 17, 1942; 1 dau., Valerie E. (Mrs. Richard Wheelock Lownes). B.S., U. Tex., Austin, 1930, Ph.D., 1935; M.D., U. Chgo., 1941; M.D. (h.c.), U. Uppsala, Sweden, 1975. Research asst. plant physiology U. Chgo., 1935-37; instr. physiology Sch. Medicine, U. Louisville, 1940-42, asst. prof., 1942-45, asso. prof., 1945-48, prof., 1948-58, biophysicist, 1958-61, chmn. dept., 1961-64; prof. physiology and biophysics, chmn. dept. Sch. Medicine, U. Ala., Birmingham, 1964-78; prof. emeritus Sch. Medicine, U. Ala., 1978-94; research prof. medicine U. Louisville Sch. Medicine, 1978-94; cons. Warner-Lambert Pharm. Co., 1965-70. Contbr. sci. papers to books and jours. Recipient Guggenheim award, 1960; Andrès Bello award Govt. of Venezuela, 1981. Mem. AAAS, Physiol. Soc., Soc. Exptl. Biology, Biophys. Soc. Home: Louisville Ky. Deceased.

REICHMANN, RENÉE, real estate corporation officer; m. Samuel Reichmann; children: Albert, Ralph, Paul, Eva, Edward, Louis. Chmn. bd. dirs. Olympia and York Devels., Toronto. Home: Toronto Can.

REID, BENJAMIN LAWRENCE, author, humanities educator; b. Louisville, May 3, 1918; s. Isaac Errett and Margaret (Lawrence) R.; m. Jane Coleman Davidson, July 15, 1942 (dec. Mar. 1993); children: Jane Lawrence (Mrs. Michael A. McAnulty), Colin Way (dec.). A.B., U. Louisville, 1943, D.H.L., 1970; A.M., Columbia U., 1950; Ph.D., U. Va., 1957. Faculty Iowa State Coll., Ames, 1946-48, Smith Coll., Northampton, Mass., 1948-51, Sweet Briar (Va.) Coll., 1951-57; prof. English Mt. Holyoke Coll., 1957-90, Andrew Mellon prof. humanities, 1972-90. Author: Art by Subtraction: A Dissenting Opinion of Gertrude Stein, 1958, William Butler Yeats: The Lyric of Tragedy, 1961, The Man from New York; John Quinn and His Friends (Pulitzer prize 1969), 1968, The Long Boy and Others: Eighteenth Century Studies, 1969, Tragic Occasions: Essays on Several Forms, 1971, The Lives of Roger Casement, 1976, First Acts: A Memoir, 1988, Necessary Lives: Biographical Reflections, 1990; also essays, short stories, verse in lit. rev.; editor: Open Secret: Poems by Colin Way Reid, 1986; co-editor Flag and Feather, Poems by Joyce Horner, 1986. Fulbright Research grantee, 1963-64; Am. Council Learned Socs. fellow, 1966-67; NEH sr. fellow, 1971-72. Mem. AAUP, MLA. Home: South Hadley Mass. Died Nov. 30, 1990.

REID, KATE, actress; b. London, Nov. 4, 1930; d. Walter C. and Helen Isabel (Moore) R.; m. Austin Willis, July 13, 1953 (div. 1962); children: Reid, Robin. Ed., Havergal Coll., Toronto Conservatory Music, U. Toronto; awarded Ph.D.; D.Litt. (hon.), York U., 1970. Stage debut in: Years Ago, Gravenhurst, Ont., Can., summer 1948; toured Eng. as Lizzie in: The Rainmaker; appeared as Catherine Ashland in: The Stepmother, London, 1958; with, Stratford (Ont.) Shakespearean Festival of Can.; appeared in: Othello, 1959, Romeo and Juliet, A Midsummer Night's Dream, 1960, Henry VIII, Love's Labour's Lost, 1961, The Taming of the Shrew, Macbeth, 1962, Juno and the Paycock, 1973, Leaving Home, 1973, Freedom of the City, 1974, Romeo and Juliet, 1974, Cat on a Hit Tin Roof, 1974, Mrs. Warren's Profession, 1976, The Apple Cart, 1976; N.Y.C. debut as Martha in matinee co. of: Who's Afraid of Virginia Woolf?, 1962; appeared in: Cyrano de Bergerac, 1963, Dylan, 1964, Slapstick Tragedy, 1966; appeared on Broadway in Bosoms and Neglect; appeared in play: Death of a Salesman, 1984; appeared in TV series Gavilan, 1982-83; TV movies include: Friendly Persuasion, 1973, Loose Change, 1978, Atlantic City, 1981, Happy Birthday to Me, 1981, Highpoint, 1985. Recipient Order of Can. Home: Toronto Can. Died Mar. 27, 1993.

REIFMAN, WILLIAM J., lawyer; b. Chgo., Mar. 2 1952. BS, U. Ill., 1972; JD, Duke U., 1975. Bar: Ill 1975, U.S. Dist. Ct. (no. dist.) Ill. 1975, U.S. Suprem Ct. 1979, Calif. 1985, U.S. Ct. Appeals (10th cir.) 1985 U.S. Ct. Appeals (9th cir.) 1986, U.S. Ct. Appeals (3c cir.) 1987. Ptnr. Mayer, Brown & Platt, L.A. Home Los Angeles Calif. Died Nov. 20, 1994.

REILLY, GERARD DENIS, judge; b. Boston, Sept 27, 1906; s. Thomas F. and Anne C. (O'Reilly) R.; m Eleanor Fahey, July 15, 1939 (dec.); children: Gerarc Denis (dec.), John Fahey, Margaret Anne Reilly Hef fern.; m. Dorothy K. Owens, Jan. 1982. A.B., Harvard 1927, LL.B., 1933. Bar: Mass. 1933, D.C. 1946. Stat House corr. for the Pawtucket Times, Providence Jour. 1927-29; night copy editor Boston Traveler, 1929-3C asso. firm Goodwin, Procter & Hoar, Boston, 1933-34 reviewing atty. Home Owner's Loan Corp., 1934; be came atty. U.S. Dept. of Labor, 1934, asst. solicitor 1935; adminstr. U.S. Dept. of Labor (Pub. Contract Div.), 1936-37, solicitor, 1937-41; mem. NLRB, 1941 46; mem. firm Reilly, Johns & Zimmerman (an predecessor firms), 1946-70; asso. judge D.C. Ct. Ap peals, 1970-72, chief judge, 1972-76, sr. judge, 1977— Lectr. constl. law Cath. U., 1946-47; counsel Senat com. on labor and pub. welfare, 1947; dir. Reed & Prince Mfg. Co., Worcester, Mass., 1963-70. Fellov Am. Bar Found.; mem. Am., D.C., Boston bar assns. Roman Catholic. Clubs: Nat. Lawyers (Washington) Cosmos (Washington) (pres. 1976-77), Palaver (Wash ington), Harvard (Washington); Bass River Yacht. Home: Washington D.C. Died May 17, 1995.

REILLY, WILLIAM F(RANCIS), lawyer, state publi defender; b. Providence, July 15, 1932; s. Peter P. an Margaret M. (O'Neill) R.; m. Constance P. Hand, Jun 10, 1961; children—Mary E., Karen A., William F. Michael P. A.B., Providence Coll., 1958; LL.B., Bosto U., 1961. Bar: R.I. 1963, U.S. Dist. Ct. R.I. 1966, U.S Ct. Appeals (1st cir.) 1969, U.S. Supreme Ct. 1973 Assoc., Charles J. Rogers, Quinn & Cuzzone, Pro vidence, R.I., 1963—; ptnr. Breslin, Sweeney, Reilly & McDonald, Warwick, R.I., 1970-71; public defende State of R.I., Providence, 1971—; guest lectr. Roge Williams Coll.; mem. R.I. Gov.'s Justice Commn.; mem Spl. Legis. Com.; chmn. com. availability of legal se vices Jud. Planning Council; mem. Bench Bar Adv Com.; mem. Media Adv. Com.; mem. Spl. Legis Commn. to Study Bail. Served to sgt. U.S. Army, 1952 54; Korea. Mem. R.I. Bar Assn., Nat. Legal Aid an Defender's Assn., R.I. Def. Attys. Assn. (founder an 1st pres. 1971-72). Club: K.C. Home: Providence R.I

REITZ, ELMER A., manufacturing company executive b. 1909; married. With Greif Bros. Corp., Delaware Ohio, 1934—, comptroller, 1951-53, sec., then v.p., sec 1953-69, v.p., 1969-70, exec. v.p., from 1970, now chmr fin. com., also bd. dirs. Home: Delaware Ohio Die August, 1994.

RENCHARD, WILLIAM S(HRYOCK), retire banker; b. Trenton, N.J., Jan. 1, 1908; s. John A. an Lillian C. (Smith) R.; m. Alice Marie Fleming, Dec. 1935; children: Jeanie, Christine Renchard Huffmar Cynthia R. French. AB, Princeton U., 1928; DC (hon.), Pace Coll., 1971. Pres. Chem. Bank, N.Y.C 1960-66, chmn. bd., 1966-73, chmn. exec. com., 1973-7 dir., 1960-78, chmn. dirs. adv. com., 1978-82, hon. dir 1982-94; bd. dirs. Amerada Hess Corp., N.Y.C.; ad dir. Borden, Inc., 1989-93. Pres. Manhattan Eye, Ear Throat Hosp., 1969-86, chmn., 1986-94; hon. bd. dir United Hosp. Fund., N.Y.C., 1984-85; trustee emeritu Citizens Budget Commn., N.Y.C., 1985-94. Mem. A falfa Club (Washington), Creek Club (Locust Valle N.Y., bd. govs. 1960-94, pres. 1965-70), Piping Ro Club, Pilgrims Club, Links Club, Lyford Cay Clu (Nassau, the Bahamas). Republican. Episcopalian. Home: Glen Cove N.Y. Died July 4, 1994.

RENSHAW, CHARLES CLARK, JR., retired pu lishing executive; b. Chgo., Aug. 22, 1920; s. Charl Clark and Nanna Lou (Nysewander) R.; m. Elizabe Campbell Fly, Apr. 11, 1953 (div. Jan. 1960); 1 chil Nina (Mrs. Daniel C. Baker III). Student, Hill Sch Pottstown, Pa., 1934-39, Trinity Coll., Hartford, Conn 1939-41. Reporter, feature writer, book critic Chg Herald-Am., 1943-46; assoc. editor Fin. mag., Chgo 1947; writer, articles editor Hearst's Am. Weekl N.Y.C., 1948-61; sr. editor, asst. mng. editor, mn editor World Book Ency. Year Book, Chgo., 1962-6 free-lance writer N.Y.C., 1968-70; sr. editor Nat. W dlife mag., Milw., 1970-72; editor Prism (the Socio-eco Mag. of AMA), 1972-75; editor in chief Socioeco Publs. AMA, Chgo., 1975-78, v.p., editl. dir. non-s publs., 1978-81, v.p., editl. dir. Consumer Books div 1981-85, cons. Office Internat. Medicine, 1988, co group on health policy, 1989-90, cons. group on ele tronic media and consumer affairs, 1990-93; cons. direct mktg. group World Book Ency., Evanston, I 1993-94; cons. Consumer Books divsn. AMA, Chg Ill., 1994-95. Home: Chicago Ill. Died Sept. 5, 1995.

RESNIKOFF, GEORGE JOSEPH, university dea mathematics and statistics educator emeritus; b. N.Y. Mar. 25, 1915; s. Isador and Jenny (Rapaport) R.;

Florence Lisa Herman, Apr. 4, 1943; 1 son, Carl. B.S., U. Chgo., 1950; M.S., Stanford U., 1952, Ph.D., 1955. Assoc. prof. Ill. Inst. Tech., 1957-61, prof., 1961-64; prof. math. and statistics Calif. State U. at Hayward, from 1964, now prof. emeritus, dean of sci., 1969-72, dean grad. studies, 1972-80. Contbr. articles to profl. jours. Served with AUS, 1942-46. Fellow AAAS, Am. Statis. Assn., Inst. Math. Statistics. Home: Oakland Calif. Died Sept. 5, 1994.

RESTON, JAMES BARRETT, retired newspaper publishing executive, author; b. Clydebank, Scotland, Nov. 3, 1909; s. James and Johanna (Irving) R.; came to U.S., 1910; m. Sarah Jane Fulton, Dec. 24, 1935; children: Richard Fulton, James Barrett, Thomas Busey. Student Vale of Leven Acad., Alexandria, Scotland, 1914-20; BS, U. Ill., 1932, LLD (hon.), 1962; LittD, Colgate U., 1951, Oberlin Coll., 1955, Rutgers U., 1957; LLD (hon.), Dartmouth, 1959, N.Y. U., 1961, Boston Coll., 1963, Brandeis U., 1964; LHD, Kenyon Coll., 1962, Columbia, 1963, U. Mich., 1965; LittD, U. N.C., 1968, Williams Coll., 1968; LHD,Harvard, 1970, Stanford, 1972, U. Utah, 1973, Kent State U., 1974, Colby Coll., 1975, Yale U., 1977, Miami U., Oxford, Ohio; hon. degrees U. Md., Northeastern U., 1976, U. Glasgow, 1983. With Springfield (Ohio) Daily News, 1932-33; with publicity dept. Ohio State U., 1933; publicity dir. Cin. Baseball Club, 1934; reporter A.P., N.Y.C., 1934-37, London, 1937-39; reporter London bur. N.Y. Times, 1939-41, Washington bur., 1941-89, chief Washington corr., bur. chief, 1953-64, assoc. editor, 1964-68, exec. editor, 1968-69, v.p., 1969-74, columnist, cons., 1974-89, also dir. N.Y. Times Co., ret., 1989; co-chmn. bd. The Vineyard Gazette, 1968-95. Author: The Artillery of the Press, 1967, Sketches in the Sand, 1967, Washington, 1986, Deadline, 1991. Recipient Pulitzer prize for nat. corr., 1945, nat. reporting, 1957, Overseas Press Club award for interpretation internat. news, 1949, 51, 53, George Polk Meml. award for nat. reporting, 1954; U. Mo. medal, 1961, J.P. Zenger award, 1964, Elijah Parrish Lovejoy award, 1974, fourth Estate award Nat Press Club, 1974; Presdl. Medal of Liberty award, 1986; Helen B. Bernstein Excellence in Journalism award, 1988, Franklin D. Roosevelt Freedom of Speech medal, 1991; decorated Legion d'Honneur (France); ordre National du Mérite (France); Order St. Olav (Norway), Order of Merit (Chile); comdr. Order Brit. Empire. Clubs: Century (N.Y.C.); Chevy Chase (Md.). Died Dec. 6, 1995. Home: Washington D.C.

REVERCOMB, GEORGE HUGHES, federal judge; b. Charleston, W.Va., June 3, 1929; s. Chapman and Sara (Hughes) R.; m. Mary Collins McCall Henderson, Oct. 30, 1960. AB, Princeton (N.J.) U., 1950; JD, U. Va., 1955, LLM in Jud. Process, 1982. Bar: Va. 1955, W.Va. 1956, D.C. 1959, U.S. Supreme Ct. 1964. Pvt. practice Washington and, W.Va. and Va., 1955-56, 59-69; atty. corp. law dept. and legal asst. FCC, Washington, 1956-59; assoc. dep. atty. gen. Dept. Justice, Washington, 1969-70; judge D.C. Superior Ct., 1970-85, U.S. Dist. Ct. D.C., 1985-93; vis. lectr. U. Va. Law Sch., Charlottesville, 1977-85; vice chmn. U.S. Delegation 4th UN Conf. on Prevention of Crime and Treatment of Offenders, Kyoto, Japan, 1970. Served to 1st lt. USAF, 1951-53. Fellow Am. Bar Found.; mem. ABA (chmn. nat. conf. state trial judges 1984-85), D.C. Bar Assn., Va. Bar Assn., W.Va. Bar Assn., Judicial Coun. D.C. Cir., U.S. Dist. Ct. (exec. com. 1988-93), U.S. Judicial Conf. (defender svcs. commn. 1990-93). Presbyterian. Home: Mc Lean Va. Died Aug. 3, 1993; buried Historic Oak Hill Cemetery, Washington, D.C.

REXINE, JOHN EFSTRATIOS, classics educator; b. Boston, June 6, 1929; s. Efstratios John and Athena (Glekas) R.; m. Elaine Lavrakas, June 16. 1957; children: John Efstratios Jr., Athena Elisabeth (Mrs. Stephen L. Hodge), Michael Constantine. AB magna cum laude, Harvard U., 1951, AM, 1953, PhD, 1964; LittD (hon.), Hellenic Coll./Holy Cross Greek Orthodox Sch. of Theology, 1981; Lic. Theol. (hon.), Ctr. Traditionalist Orthodox Studies, 1986. Instr. humanities Brandeis U., 1955-57; from instr. classics to prof. Colgate U., 1957-92, Charles A. Dana prof. classics, 1977-92, chmn. dept. classics, 1964-72, 85-91, dir. div. univ. studies, 1969-72, dir. div. humanities, 1972-84, chmn. dept. classics, slavic and Oriental langs., 1972-73, acting chmn., 1976, assoc. dean faculty, 1973-74, acting dean faculty, 1977-78; dir. Colgate-IBM Corp. Inst. Liberal Arts Program for Execs., 1969-71, 78, 79, 81-86; vis. prof. Greek and classical mythology Coll. Year in Athens, Greece, fall 1972-73; Fulbright-Hays sr. research scholar Am. Sch. Classical Studies, Athens, 1979-80; mem. program bd. div. Christian edn. Nat. Council Chs. Christ, 1969-72; v.p. Inst. for Byzantine and Modern Greek Studies, 1974-93. Author: Solon and His Political Theory, 1958, Religion in Plato and Cicero, 1959, rev. edit., 1968, (with Andreas Kazamias, Paul Nash, Henry Perkinson) The Educated Man, 1965, (with Thomas Spelios, Harry J. Psomiades) A Pictorial History of Greece, 1967, The Hellenic Spirit: Byzantine and Post Byzantine, 1981, An Explorer of Realms of Art, Life and Thought: The Works of Philosopher and Theologian Constantine Cavarnos, 1985; contbg. editor: The Hellenic Chronicle, 1952-93; book rev. editor: Athene, 1957-67, Patristic and Byzantine Rev., 1981-93; book rev. editor: The Orthodox Observer, 1957-72, book rev. columnist, 1972-87; mng. editor Greek Orthodox Theol. Rev., 1959-60, assoc. editor, 1960-67, Diakonia, 1971-84, 86-93; mem. editorial adv. bd. Classical and Modern Literature, 1985-93; asst. editor Helios, 1976-79; editor Classical Outlook, 1977-79; book rev. editor classics and modern Greek: Modern Lang. Jour, 1977-79; contbg. editor Greek Accent, 1983-88; mem. editorial bd. Jour. Modern Hellenism, 1984-85. Trustee Greek Orthodox Theol. Sch., 1955-57. Recipient cert. of disting. service Inst. Internat. Edn., 1984; Danforth Found. Tchr. Study grantee Harvard U., 1959-60; Gold Medal award, Helicon Soc., 1962; Fulbright scholar to Greece, 1951-52; Am. Numis. Soc. fellow, summer 1955; Colgate U. Asian Studies faculty fellow, 1965-66; Archon Didaskalos tou Genous of Ecumenical Patriarchate of Constantinople, 1967; Greek Orthodox Archdiocese award for promotion Greek studies, 1990; Morton E. Spillenger award disting. svc. in classics Classical Assn. of Empire State, 1990, Award of Merit Classical Assn. of Atlantic States, 1992. Mem. Am. Philol. Assn., Mediaeval Acad. Am., Am. Classical League, Classical Assn. Atlantic States, Classical Assn. Empire State (pres. 1987-90), Helicon Soc. (pres. 1956-57), Hellenic Soc. Humanistic Studies (hon.), Hamilton Club (vice chmn. 1985, 89-90, pres. 1986), Phi Beta Kappa, Eta Sigma Phi (trustee 1977-93). Home: Hamilton N.Y. Died Oct. 23, 1993; buried Colgate University Cemetary, Hamilton, N.Y.

REY, ANTHONY MAURICE, hotel executive; b. N.Y.C., Mar. 31, 1916; s. Anthony A. and Madeleine (Lauper) R.; student NYU, 1933-34, L'Ecole Hoteliere, Lausanne, Switzerland, 1934-35; m. Dorothea M. Carley, June 2, 1934; children—Anthony Maurice, Donna Christine, Jamie Elisabeth R. Di Giovanni, Andrea Michele (dec.), Cynthia Anne Higbee. With Waldorf-Astoria Hotel, N.Y.C., 1934-58; gen. mgr., v.p. Astor Hotel, N.Y.C., 1958-65; pres., dir. Chalfonte Haddon Hall, 1965-76; pres. dir. Resorts Internat. Hotel Casino Co., 1976-80, also dir.; v.p. Resorts Internat. Inc., 1979-82, sr. v.p., 1982-86; dir. Bancorp. Atlantic City (N.J.), Guarantee Bank, Atlantic City; sec. E.J.H. Co. Commr., bd. dirs. Atlantic Area council Boy Scouts Am., 1965-87; commr., vice chmn. Atlantic County Improvement Authority, 1965-74; bd. dirs. Miss Am. Pageant, 1966-80; chmn. exec. com. Atlantic City Conv. Bur., 1967-81, chmn. bd., 1975-81; v.p., trustee So. N.J. Devel. Council, 1971-86; chmn. Conv. Liaison Council, 1967-74; bd. dirs. Atlantic County United Fund, 1967-69; trustee Internat. Restaurant and Hotel Union Pension Trust, 1975-76, Am. Hotel Ednl. Inst.; adv. council Culinary Inst. Am., 1980—, Weidner U. Restaurant and Hotel Sch., 1980—, Johnson & Wales Coll. Hotel and Restaurant Sch. Served with USNR, 1942-45. Decorated Bronze Star, Presdl. citation; named N.J. Innkeeper of Year, 1971, Am. Hotel Resort Exec. of 1979, Hotel Man of Yr., State of N.J., 1980; named to Hospitality Hall of Fame, 1969; recipient Arthur Goldman Innkeeper award, 1986, Disting. Citizen award Boy Scouts Am., 1981; Community Services award Anti-Defamation League of B'nai B'rith 1986; hon. dept. fire chief N.Y.C., 1963—. Mem. Greater Atlantic City C. of C. (pres. 1969-71, chmn. bd. 1971-73), N.J. C. of C. (dir. 1973-86), Internat. Hotel Sales Mgmt. Assn., Am. Hotel Motel Assn. (industry adv. council 1974—, trustee Ednl. Inst. 1978-87, Lamplighter award 1986, writer food and beverage manual; chmn. resort com. 1978, chmn. bd. 1979), N.J. Hotel Motel Assn. (pres. 1971-72, chmn. bd. 1972-75, trustee, life mem., Arthur Goldman award 1976), Atlantic City Hotel Assn. (trustee 1976—, pres. 1980-82, chmn. 1982-84, chmn. emeritus 1984), mem. Confrerie dela Chaines des Rotisseurs Bailli, Atlantc City, 1980-87, chmn. emeritus, 1987—. Mem. NYU Hotel and Restaurant Soc. (hon. life), Hotel and Restaurant Mgmt. Soc. Fairleigh Dickenson U. (life), Ednl. Inst. Am. Hotel/Motel (Ambassador at large 1986, cert. hotel administr., cert. food and beverage exec.), Waldorf Astoria Disting. Alumni Assn. (chmn. 1973-88, emeritus 1988), Am. Legion. Episcopalian. Clubs: Skal, Lambs (N.Y.C.); Circus Saints and Sinners (life); Seaview Country (Absecon, N.J.). Home: Smithville N.J.

REYNOLDS, DONALD WORTHINGTON, publisher; b. Ft. Worth, Sept. 23, 1906; s. Gaines Worlie and Anna Louise (Elfers) R. B.J., U. Mo., 1927. Pub. Southwest Times Record, Ft. Smith, Ark., Okmulgee (Okla.) Times, 1940-93, Moberly (Mo.) Monitor-Index, Las Vegas (Nev.) Rev. Jour., 1949-93, Ely (Nev.) Times and Carson City (Nev.) Appeal, 1950-93, Blackwell (Okla.) Jour. Tribune, 1955-93, Chickasha (Okla.) Express, 1956-93, Guthrie (Okla.) Leader, 1958-93, Hawaii Tribune-Herald of Hilo, 1961-93, Pawhuska (Okla.) Daily Jour.-Capital, 1964-93, Guymon (Okla.) Daily Herald, 1966-93, Aberdeen (Wash.) Daily World, 1968, The Daily Report, Ontario, Calif., Northwest Arkansas Morning News, Rogers, Pomona (Calif.) Progress-Bull., Frederick (Okla.) Daily Leader, Borger (Tex.) News Herald, 1977, Pauls Valley (Okla.) Daily Democrat, Wewoka (Okla.) Daily Times, 1967-93, Jacksonville (Tex.) Progress, 1978, Cleburne (Tex.) Times Rev., 1976, Red Bluff (Calif.) Daily News, 1968-93, Booneville (Ark.) Democrat, 1968-93, Holdenville (Okla.) News, 1969-93, Weatherford (Tex.) Democrat, 1967, Washington (Ind.) Times Herald, 1972-93, Sherman (Tex.) Democrat, 1977, Springdale (Ark.) News, Kailua-Kona (Hawaii) West Hawaii Today, 1968-93, Henryetta (Okla.) Freelance, Lompoc (Calif.) Record, Picayune (Miss.) Item, Bartlesville (Okla.) Examiner-Enterprise, Kilgore (Tex.) News Herald, Gainesville (Tex.) Daily Register, Chico (Calif.) Enterprise-Record, Auburn (Wash.) Daily Globe News, Sweetwater (Tex.) Reporter, Glasgow (Ky.) Daily Times, Oskaloosa (Iowa) Herald, Redlands (Calif.) Daily Facts, Vallejo (Calif.) Times-Herald, Poplarville (Miss.) Democrat, Durant (Okla.) Daily Democrat; pres., chief exec. officer Donrey Cablevision, Guymon, Bartlesville, and Blackwell, Okla., Vallejo, Calif.; Pub. Donrey Cablevision, Rogers, Ark.; pres., chief exec. officer Donrey Outdoor, Inc., Las Vegas, Reno, Albuquerque, Spokane, Tulsa, Oklahoma City and Ft. Smith, Donrey Outdoor Advertising, Little Rock, Columbus, Ohio, Amarillo, Tex.; owner, pres. and chief exec. officer radio stas. KEXO, Grand Junction, Colo., radio stas. KBRS, Springdale, Ark., radio stas. KOCM-FM, Newport Beach, Calif., KOLO, Reno, 1955-93, KOLO-TV, Reno, 1954-93, Wichita (Kans.) Donrey Outdoor Co., 1973-93. Hon. disch., maj. M.I. 1945. Awarded Legion of Merit, Bronze Star, Purple Heart, 5 combat stars; Broadcaster of Year award Nev. Broadcasting Assn., 1978. Mem. Nat. Assn. Radio-TV Broadcasters, Am. Soc. Newspaper Editors, So. Newspaper Pubs. Assn., Am. Legion, Sigma Delta Chi, Pi Kappa Alpha. Clubs: Overseas Press (San Francisco); Hillcrest Country (Bartlesville); Tulsa, Dallas Athletic; Hardscrabble Country (Ft. Smith); Prospector's (Reno); Pacific (Honolulu). Home: Fort Smith Ark. Died Apr. 2, 1993.

REYNOLDS, GEORGE LAZENBY, JR., bishop; b. Opelika, Ala., Aug. 18, 1927; s. George Lazenby and Marion Banks (Barnett) R.; m. Barbara Clark, June 9, 1962; children: George III, Katherine. BA, U. South, 1950, DD (hon.), 1985; MDiv, Va. Theol. Sem., 1954, DD (hon.), 1984; PhD, NYU, 1973. Chaplain Sewanee (Tenn.) Mil. Acad., 1954-55; asst. to rector St. Paul's Episcopal Ch., Mt. Lebanon, Pa., 1955-56; priest-in-charge St. Christophers Episcopal Ch., Warrendale, Pa., 1956-62; assoc. sec. leadership tng. div. dept. Christian edn. Exec. Coun. of Episcopal Ch., N.Y.C., 1962-66, adminstr. tng. svcs., 1966-68; rector Christ Episcopal Ch., Glendale, Ohio, 1968-76, St. Stephens Episcopal Ch., Edina, Minn., 1976-85; bishop Episcopal Diocese Tenn., Nashville, 1985—. Chmn. adv. bd. Faith Orgn. in Covenant for Understanding and Svc., Nashville, 1988, 89; mem. Leadership Nashville, 1986—; bd. dirs. St. Andrew's (Tenn.) Sewanee Sch., 1985—; trustee U. South, 1985—. With USN, 1945-46. Mem. Assn. for Creative Change (pres. 1970-72). Home: Nashville Tenn. Died Nov. 3, 1991.

REYNOLDS, MELVIN J. (MEL REYNOLDS), congressman; b. Mound Bayou, Mo., 1952; m. Marisol Reynolds; 1 child, Corean. Grad., U. Ill., Champaign; JD, Oxford U., England. Talk show host Sta. WLS-Radio, Chgo.; asst. prof. Roosevelt U., Chgo.; mem. 103rd-104th Congresses from 2d Ill. dist., 1993—; mem. econ. and ednl. opportunity com. Exec. dir. Community Econ. Devel. and Edn. Found.; founder, pres. Am. Scholars Against World Hunger. Rhodes scholar. Mem. NAACP (exec. com. Chgo. chpt.). Democrat.

RHODES, ANDREW JAMES, medical microbiologist; b. Scotland, Sept. 19, 1911; s. William Thomas and Maud (Innes) R. M.D., U. Edinburgh, 1934. Intern U. Edinburgh, 1934, lectr. bacteriology, 1935-41; prof. bacteriology U. London, 1945; prof. virology U. Toronto, Ont., Can., 1947; practice medicine, specializing in med. microbiology and public health Toronto, 1947-95; med. dir. Public Health Labs., Ont. Govt., Toronto, 1970-76, cons. virology, 1976-78, rabies vaccine for wild life and related rsch., 1979-88. Author: (with C.E. van Rooyen) Virus Diseases of Man, 2 edits, 1940, 48, Text Book of Virology, 5 edits, 1949-68; contbr. (with C.E. van Rooyen) over 200 articles to sci. jours. Decorated Centennial medal Can., 25th Anniversary medal. Life mem. Can. Public Health Assn. (Defries award 1975); mem. Can. Med. Assn. (sr.), Can. Soc. Microbiologists, Royal Soc. Can. Anglican. Home: Toronto Can. Died Feb. 11, 1995.

RIBICOFF, IRVING S., lawyer; b. New Britain, Conn., Apr. 16, 1915; s. Samuel and Rose (Sable) R.; m. Belle Krasne, June 27, 1955; 1 child, Dara K. B.A. summa cum laude, Williams Coll., 1936; LL.B., Yale, 1939. Bar: Conn. bar 1939. Instr. in pub. speaking Williams Coll., 1934-36; atty. reorganization div. SEC, 1939-41; chief price atty. for Conn. OPA, 1942-44; partner Ribicoff & Kotkin (and predecessors), 1941-78; firm Schatz & Schatz, Ribicoff & Kotkin, Hartford, 1978-94; Mem. Hartford County Grievance Com., 1957-61, chmn., 1960-61. Bd. dirs. Law Sch. Fund of Yale, Hartford Festival Music, Hartford Jewish Fedn., Symphony Soc. Greater Hartford; exec. com. Yale Law Sch. Assn.; trustee Greater Hartford YMCA; bus. adv. com. N.E. Colls. Fund. Mem. ABA, Conn. Bar Assn. (mem. fed. practice com. 1967-94, chmn. 1967-69, mem. specialization com. 1969-94, chmn. 1969-74), Hartford County Bar Assn., N.E. Law Inst. (adv. council), Fed. Bar Assn. (Conn. pres. 1964-75), Order of Coif, Phi Beta Kappa. Home: Hartford Conn. Died July 25, 1994.

RICH, BEN ROBERT, aerospace executive, aerothermodynamicist; b. Manila, Philippines, June 18, 1925; came to U.S., 1941; s. Isadore and Annie (Kupfermann) R.; m. Faye Mayer, June 25, 1950 (dec. Aug. 1980); m. Hilda Herman, July 1, 1982; children: Michael D., Karen Rich Erbeck. B.S., U. Calif.-Berkeley, 1949;

M.S., UCLA, 1950; Advanced Mgmt. Program, Harvard U., 1968. Teaching assoc. UCLA, 1949-50; engr. Electro Film, North Hollywood, Calif., 1950; program mgr. advanced devel. projects Lockheed Calif. Co., Burbank, 1965-69, chief engr. advanced design, 1969, chief preliminary design, 1969-71, v.p. advanced design, 1972-75, v.p., gen. mgr. advanced devel. projects, 1975-84; pres. Lockheed Advanced Aeros. Co., Burbank, 1984-91, sr. cons., 1991—; lectr. Wright Bros. AIAA, Royal Aero. Soc., 1988; bd. dirs. Raycomm Transworld Industries, Inc. Recipient Peter Recchia Omni Meml. award 1981, Aviation Week & Space Tech's. Aero/Propulsion Laurel award, 1988, Silver Knight award Nat. Mgmt. Assn., 1989; named Engr. of Yr. San Francisco Engring. Soc., 1981, Alumnus of Yr. UCLA, 1982; Spirit of St. Louis medal Am. Soc. of Mechanical Engineers, 1994. Fellow AIAA (Orgn's. Nat. Aircraft Design award 1972, Sylvanus A. Reed Aeronautics award 1994), Inst. for the Advancement Engring., Nat. Acad. Engring., Inst. Aero. Scis., Tau Beta Pi. Home: Oxnard Calif. Died Jan. 5, 1995.

RICH, CHARLES ALLAN, singer; b. Forrest City, Ark., Dec. 14, 1932; s. Wallace Neville and Helen Margaret (West) R.; m. Margaret Ann Greene, May 25, 1952; children: Renee Annette Rich Bennett, Charles Allan, Laurie, Rich Lee, Jack Michael. Student, U. Ark. Farmer nr. West Memphis, Ark. Appeared in piano bars and clubs, Memphis; session musician, Sun Records, rec. artist, Epic Records; recs. include Behind Closed Doors, 1973 (Gold record), The Most Beautiful Girl (Platinum record, Recipient Grammy award as best country male vocalist 1973, named Male Vocalist of Yr., Country Music Assn. 1973, Entertainer of Yr. 1974, Favorite Country Male Vocalist 1974, Pop Single Male Vocalist, Billboard mag. 1974), Boss Man, Classic Rich, Nobody But You, Silver Linings, American Originals, 1989, Midnight Blue, Pictures and Paintings, 1992, The Complete Smash Sessions, 1992, Unchained Melody, 1992; profile in Smithsonian Inst., 1992. Home: Memphis Tenn. Died July 25, 1995.

RICHARDS, JESS, actor; b. Seattle, Jan. 23, 1943; s. Jack Earl and Permelia (Dunn) Sederholm. Student, U. Wash. Actor (Broadway plays) Meet Me in St. Louis, Barnum, Musical Chairs, A Reel American Hero, Mack and Mabel, Nash at Nine, On the Town (Theatre World award 1972), Two by Two, Blood Red Roses, South Pacific, Walking Happy, (off Broadway) Dames at Sea, One for the Money, Lovesong, The All Night Strut, Lullaby of Broadway, Station J.O.Y., Sing for Your Supper, Josh Logan's Musical Scrapbook, (regional theater) The Tempest, Loot, The Seagull, The Drunkard, A Little Night Music, A Funny Thing Happened On The Way To The Forum, Irma La Douce, Kiss Me, Kate!, Side by Side by Sondheim, The Hasty Heart. Mem. Actors Equity Assn. Home: New York N.Y. Died Nov. 6, 1994.

RICHMAN, DONALD, electronics engineering research scientist; b. N.Y.C., Sept. 15, 1922; s. Max and Rose (Grossman) R.; m. Beatrice Greenfield, Dec. 14, 1947; children: Mark, Steven A., David H., Sharon R. BEE, CCNY, 1943; MEE, Bklyn. Poly., 1948. From engr. to assoc. dir. rsch. Hazeltine Corp., N.Y.C., 1943-62; v.p. Hazeltine Corp., Plainview, L.I., N.Y., 1963; cons. McDonnell Aircraft, St. Louis, 1963-64; pres. Richman Rsch. Corp., L.I., 1965-93; cons. Inst. Def. Analysis, Alexandria, Va., 1965; cons. RCA, United Techs., ITT, Fairchild Corp., Honeywell Corp., Sanders, Sperry Corp., ECR, NCR, Melpar, BBC, Unisys, Hitachi, Matsushita, STL, LCT, SEL, others. Author (with others): Principles of Color TV, 1958; contbr. articles on color TV, signal processing, synchronization, radar to profl. jours.; patentee TV, superregeneration, radar, communications, DC quadricorrelator, synchronous color-killer, demixed (inferred) color highs. Fellow IEEE (V.K. Zworykin TV prize 1957); mem. Sigma Xi, Eta Kappa Nu. Jewish. Home: Dix Hills N.Y. Died June 12, 1993.

RIDGWAY, MATTHEW BUNKER, ret. army officer; b. Fort Monroe, Va., Mar. 3, 1895; s. Thomas and Ruth Starbuck (Bunker) R.; grad. U.S. Mil. Acad., 1917, Inf. Sch., Co. Officers Course, 1925, Advanced Course, 1930, Command and Gen. Staff Sch., 1935, Army War Coll., 1937; m. Mary Anthony, Dec. 13, 1947; 1 son, Matthew Bunker, Jr. (dec.). Commd. lt. U.S. Army, 1917, advanced through grades to gen., 1951; tech. adv. to Gov. Gen., Philippines, 1932-33; asst. chief of staff 6th Corps Area, 1935-36, 2d Army, 1936, dep. chief staff, 1936; asst. chief staff 4th Army, 1937-39; war plans div. War Dept. Gen. Staff, 1939-42; asst. div. comdr. 82d Inf. Div., 1942, comdr., 1942; comdg. gen. 82d Airborne Div., Sicily, Italy, Normandy, 1942-44; comdr. 18th Airborne Corps, Belgium, France, Germany, 1944-45; assigned command Luzon Area Command, Aug. 1945; comdr. MTO, dep. supreme allied comdr. Mediterranean, Oct. 1945-Jan. 1946; sr. U.S. Army mem., chmn. Mil. Staff Com., UN, 1946-48, 49-50; chmn. Inter-Am. Def. Bd., 1946-48; comdr.-in-chief Caribbean Command, 1948-49; dep. army chief of staff; comdg. gen. 8th Army, Korea, 1950-51; comdr.-in-chief Far East Command, comdr.-in-chief, UN Command and Supreme comdr. for Allied Powers, 1951-52; supreme comdr. Allied Powers Europe, 1952-53, Army chief of staff, 1953-55, ret.; dir. Colt Industries. Chmn. bd. trustees Mellon Inst. Indsl. Research, 1955-60. Decorated D.S.C. with oak leaf cluster, D.S.M. with 3 oak leaf clusters, Legion of Merit, Silver Star with oak leaf cluster, 2 Bronze Stars with oak leaf cluster, Purple Heart (U.S.), and numerous fgn. decorations. Clubs: Masons, Duquesne, Pittsburgh; The Brook (N.Y.). Died July 26, 1993. Home: Pittsburgh Pa.

RIDLEY, NICHOLAS, former British secretary of state for trade and industry; b. Newcastle upon Tyne, Eng., Feb., 1929; s. Viscount and Viscountess Ridley; m. Clayre Campbell (div. 1972); 3 children; m. Judy Kendall, 1979. Engring. degree, Balliol Coll., Oxford, 1950. With Brims & Co., Ltd. civil engring. contractors, Newcastle upon Tyne, 1950-59; M.P. for Cirencester and Tewkesbury, 1959-92; parliamentary pvt. sec. to minister of edn., 1962-64; parliamentary sec. to ministry of tech., 1970; parliamentary under-sec. of state Dept. Trade and Industry, 1970; minister of state FCO, 1979-81; fin. sec. to the treasury, 1981-83; sec. of state for transport, 1983-86; sec. of state for environment, 1986-89; sec. of state for trade and industry, 1989-90; del. to Coun. of Europe and WEU, 1962-66; dir. Heenan Group Ltd., 1961-68, Ansonia Fin., 1973-79, Marshall Andrew, 1975-79; chmn.; vice chmn. Conservative Backbench Fin. Com.; mem. Parliamentary Expenditure Select Com., 1974. Named Privy Counsellor in New Yr. Honours List, 1983. Mem. Royal Commn. on Hist. Manuscripts. Conservative. Avocations: painting, fishing, gardening. Died March 4, 1993. Home: Penton Eng.

RIESBECK, JAMES EDWARD, glass company executive; b. Corning, N.Y., Oct. 11, 1942; s. Paul E. and Isadora F. (Quinn) R.; m. Joyce K. Luta, June 8, 1962; 1 child, Bryan. A.A.S., Corning Community Coll., 1962; B.S., U. Ky., 1966; postgrad. Harvard Bus. Sch., 1976. With Corning Glass Works, N.Y., 1966-93, asst. corp. controller, 1977-80, v.p., controller, 1981-93. Mem. Fin. Execs. Inst. Republican. Died June 1993. Home: Corning N.Y.

RIFKIND, SIMON HIRSCH, lawyer; b. Meretz, Russia, June 5, 1901; came to U.S., 1910, naturalized, 1924; s. Jacob and Celia (Bluestone) R.; m. Adele Singer, June 12, 1927 (dec. Apr. 1984); children: Richard Allen, Robert Singer. B.S., CCNY, 1922; LL.B., Columbia U., 1925; Litt.D., Jewish Theol. Sem., 1950; LL.D., Hofstra Coll., 1962, Brandeis U., 1977, CCNY, 1978; J.D., Hebrew U. of Jerusalem, 1980. Bar: N.Y. 1926, Ill. 1957. Legislative sec. to U.S. senator Robert F. Wagner, 1927-33; ptnr. firm Wagner, Quillinan and Rifkind, N.Y.C., 1930-41; fed. judge So. N.Y. Dist., 1941-50; 3d dep. police commr. City of N.Y., 1951; mem. firm Stevenson, Rifkind & Wirtz, Chgo., 1957-61; ptnr. Paul, Weiss, Rifkind, Wharton & Garrison, 1950—; adviser to Gen Eisenhower on Jewish matters in Am. occupation zone, 1945; Herman Phleger vis. prof. law Stanford, 1975; spl. master Colo. River litigation U.S. Supreme Ct.; chmn. Presdl. R.R. Commn., 1961-62; mem. State Commn. Govtl. Operations City N.Y., 1959-61; co-chmn. President's Commn. on Patent System, 1966-67; mem. mayors mediation panel N.Y. City teachers strike, 1963. Mem. Bd. Higher Edn. City N.Y., 1954-66; chmn. adminstrv. bd. Am. Jewish Com., 1953-56, chmn. exec. bd., 1956-59; former chmn. bd., now hon. chmn. exec. com. Jewish Theol. Sem.; bd. dirs. Beth Israel Med. Center, N.Y.C., 1975-86, now emeritus; chmn. bd. Charles H. Revson Found., Inc., 1975-87, bd. dirs., 1987-90; pres. bd. dirs. Tudor Found., Inc., 1945-90; bd. dirs., pres. Norman and Rosita Winston Found., Inc., 1975-87, bd. dirs., 1987-90. Recipient Medal of Freedom, 1946. Mem. Assn. of Bar of City of N.Y., Am. Coll. Trial Lawyers (regent 1967-71, pres. 1976-77), Phi Beta Kappa. Democrat. Jewish. Club: Harmonie (N.Y.C.). Home: New York N.Y. Died November 14, 1995.

RIKER, WILLIAM HARRISON, political science educator; b. Des Moines, Sept. 22, 1920; s. Ben Harrison and Alice (Lenox) R.; m. Mary Elizabeth Lewis, Apr. 24, 1943; children: Katherine, William, Mary. BA, DePauw U., 1942, LittD (hon.), 1979; PhD, Harvard U., 1948; LHD (hon.), Lawrence U., Appleton, Wis., 1975; PhD (hon.), Uppsala U., Sweden, 1977; LHD (hon.), SUNY, Stony Brook, 1986. From asst. prof. to prof. polit. sci. Lawrence Coll., Appleton, Wis., 1948-62; prof. polit. sci. U. Rochester, N.Y., 1962—, now Wilson Prof. polit. sci., chmn. dept. polit. sci., 1962-78, dean Grad. Studies, 1978-83; vis. prof. Washington U., St. Louis, 1983-84. Author: Democracy in the United States, 1953, 64, Theory of Political Coalitions, 1962, Federalism, 1964, Introduction to Positive Political Theory, 1973, Liberalism against Populism, 1982, The Art of Political Manipulation, 1985, The Development of American Federalism, 1987; also numerous articles. Chmn. Rochester Zoning Bd. Appeals, 1966-73. Recipient Grad. Teaching award U. Rochester, 1987, Undergrad. Teaching award, 1988, Duncan Black prize, 1991; Ctr. for Advanced Study in Behavioral Sci. fellow, Stanford U., 1960-61, Fairchild fellow Calif. Inst. Tech., Pasadena, 1973-74, Guggenheim fellow, 1983-84. Mem. NAS, Am. Acad. Arts and Scis., Am. Polit. Sci. Assn. (pres. 1982-83), Pub. Choice Soc. (chmn. 1965-67). Home: Rochester N.Y. Deceased.

RINES, CAROL MARY WILLIAMSON, state and foundation official; b. Boston, Dec. 29, 1943; d. Ralph Woodling and Irene Philomena (Arsenault) Williamson; m. John Hurley, 1964 (div. 1966); m. Robert Harv Rines, Dec. 29, 1972; 1 child, Justice Christopher. A in Bus., Burditt Jr. Coll., Boston, 1967; student, Suffc U., 1968-70; BA in Psychology, Notre Dame Co 1990. Trustee Children's Trust Fund for State of N. Concord, 1986—, chair, Gov.'s appointee, from 19 v.p., bd. dirs. Acad. Applied Sci., Boston, Conco Oxford, Eng., from 1975; pres. N.H. Child and Fam Svcs., from 1990, mem. exec. bd., from 1986; pres. Svc. League of N.H., 1978-79; founding dir. Conco Parents and Children Children's Place, 1980-84; me State Task Force Reach to Recovery, Am. Cancer Sc from 1987. Inventor 2 patents for typewriter automa margin detector, 1978, 80. Mem. Rep. Trust, Was ington, from 1987; grant adminstr. Concord Unit Way, 1986-87; mem. edn. com. Concord Unitarian C 1980-82, fin. com., 1989-90, music com. Mem. Hi land Club, Acad. Applied Sci. Ctr. for Edn. and Dev Alpha Sigma Lamda. Home: Concord N.H. Decease

RING, RODNEY EVERETT, religion educator; Sioux City, Iowa, May 13, 1927; s. Everett Irwin a Pearl Olive (Rubeck) R.; m. Naomi Ruth Korn, Se 11, 1949; children: Alexander Everett, Angela Cath ine. MA, U. Chgo., 1950, PhD, 1954. Pr Muhlenberg Coll., Allentown, Pa., 1950-51, 55-90, Th Coll., Greenville, Pa., 1954-55. Author: Solving Bibli Problems, 1988; editor ELNA bull., 1970-72; cont articles to religious jours. Sgt. U.S. Army, 1946-4 Grantee Muhlenberg Coll., 1964, Mack Trucks In 1967. Mem. Soc. Bibl. Lit., Am. Acad. Religion Home: Kutztown Pa. Died Oct. 25, 1995.

RINGOEN, RICHARD MILLER, manufacturi company executive; b. Ridgeway, Iowa, May 15, 1926 Elmer and Evelyn Louise (Miller) R.; m. Joan Ma Brandt, June 7, 1953; children: David, Jo Daniel. Student, U. Dubuque, Iowa, 1944-45, M quette U., Milw., 1945-46; BSEE with highest disti tion, U. Iowa, 1947, MS, 1948. Rsch. engr. Col Radio, Cedar Rapids, Iowa, 1948-55; v.p. engri Alpha Corp. subs. Collins Radio, Cedar Rapids, 19 59; dir. spl. projects Martin-Marietta Co., Denver, 19 70; v.p., gen. mgr. Ball Bros. Rsch. Corp., Bould Colo., 1970-74; corp. v.p. ops. Ball Corp., Muncie, In 1974-78, chief oper. officer, 1978-80, pres., 1981- chief exec. officer, 1981-91, chmn. bd., 1986-91, also dirs., mem. exec. com., ret.; bd. dirs. Am. Electric Po Co., Inc., Arvin Industries, Inc., Ralston Purina C Am. Nat. Bank, Tokheim Corp.; chief exec. officer Ta Corp., 1973-78; mem. comml. programs adv. c NASA. Patentee in communications, navigation a electronics circuitry. Pres. sch. bd. Arapahoe Cour Colo., 1963-70, past vice chair sch. planning com.; steering com. Arapahoe Jr. Coll., 1969-70; past p United Way of Delaware County, Muncie Symph Assn., Inc.; trustee Hudson Inst., Muncie YMCA; m engring. adv. bd. U. Iowa; past supt. Christian edn. Congregational Ch. Cedar Rapids; bd. dirs. Ball S U. Found., Ball Bros. Found., Meth. Hosp. Indp Keep Am. Beautiful Inc., Minnetrista Cultural Four mem. adv. com. comml. programs NASA. Served w USN. Recipient Bronze award for top chief exec. off in container industry Fin. World, 1982, 84, Chief E Officer Silver award Wall St. Transcript, 1982-83, G award for best chief exec. officer in container indus Wall St. Transcript, 1984; named Industrialist of Ind. Bus. Mag., 1988; Ball Corp. named most innova co. in the packaging industry by Forbes Mag., 198 Mem. Glass Packaging Inst., Can Mfrs. Inst. (ch 1985-86, exec. com. 1986—), Ind. State C. of C. dirs.), Nat. Assn. Mfs. (bd. dirs.). Lodge: Rotary dirs. Muncie club). Home: Boulder Colo. Died July 1993.

RINKER, MARSHALL EDISON, SR., cement concrete company executive; b. Cowan, Ind., Dec. 1904; s. Jacob E. and Alberta May (Neff) R.; m. V Lea Keesling, Nov. 26, 1935 (dec. Mar. 1985); child Marshall Edison Jr., David B., John J.; m. Ruby Ma Stewart, Aug. 27, 1987. Student in teaching, Ball S U., 1921-23; HHD (hon.), Palm Beach Atlantic C 1988. With Rinker Materials Corp. (purchased CSR), 1988; chief exec. officer, chmn. bd. Rin Materials Corp., West Palm Beach, Fla., 1926-88, ch emeritus, 1988-93; CEO, chmn. bd. Rinker Re Corp., West Palm Beach, 1980-88. Chmn., CEO M Rinker Sr. Found., Inc., 1988; chmn. West Palm Be Comty. Chest, 1954; bd. dirs. West Palm Beach c ARC, 1930-50, Fla. East Coast Industries, 1978- trustee emeritus Stetson U., DeLand, Fla.; trustee P Beach Atlantic Coll., West Palm Beach, Fla., 1 chmn. bd. deacons 1st Bapt. Ch., West Palm Be 1960-62. Recipient Free Enterprise medal Palm Be Atlantic Coll., 1985; named John D. MacArthur Leader of Yr., 1985; ednl. instns. named in his h include M.E. Rinker Sr. Sch. Bus. Palm Beach Atla Coll., 1989, M.E. Rinker Sr. Sch. Bldg. Constrn. Fla., 1989, M.E. Rinker Sr. Inst. Tax and Account Stetson U., 1989. Mem. Nat. Concrete Masonry A (bd. dirs., pres. 1954), Nat. Ready Mixed Conc Assn. (pres. 1973, Joseph E. Carpenter award 19 Fla. Concrete and Products Assn. (pres. 1967), W Palm Beach C. of C. (pres. 1954-55), Sigma Lam Chi. Clubs: Everglades, Old Guard Soc., Govs.' ((Palm Beach); Garden of Gods (Colorado Spri Colo.); Ocean Reef (Key Largo, Fla.); River (J ıville, Fla.). Lodge: Rotary (Paul Harris fellow 1988). ome: Palm Beach Fla. Died Apr. 11, 1996.

NZLER, RALPH, museum administrator, folklorist; Passaic, N.J., July 20, 1934; s. Harry Grainger and atrice Pauline (Joseph) R.; m. Kathryn Elizabeth ıghes, Feb. 28, 1970; 1 child, Marni Hoyt. B.A., arthmore Coll., 1956. Dir. field programs, trustee ewport Found., R.I., 1964-67; founding dir. Ctr. Folfe Programs and Cultural Studies Smithsonian Instn., ashington, 1967-82, asst. sec. pub. svc., 1983-90, asst. . emeritus, 1990; mem. exec. com. U.S. Nat. Commn. UNESCO, 1976-81, vice chmn., 1980-81; advisor oan Found., Washington, 1977-81; mem. Pakistan-S. Subcommn. on Edn. and Culture, 1983-94; mem. S. del. 20th Gen. Conf. UNESCO, Paris, 1978; bd. s. Highlander Research and Edn. Ctr., New Market, nn., 1977-94; bd. advisors Foxfire Fund, 1968-78; m. adv. bd. John Edwards Found., UCLA, 1965-94; stee The Ruth Mott Fund, 1988. Author: (with bert Sayers) The Meaders Family, No Ga. Potters, 80, The Korean Onggi Potter, 1987; recorder, editor, notator over 50 ethnographic field recs. of U.S. and rld folk music for Decca, Columbia, Folkways, nguard, and Elektra records, also numerous record . abroad. Recipient Washingtonian of Yr. award ashingtonian mag., 1976; Smithsonian Soc. medal ithsonian Instn., 1977; Mayor's Art award Govt. of C., 1980; Grammy award NARAS, 1988. Fellow n. Folklore Soc.; mem. Anthrop. Soc. Washington, lklore Soc. Greater Washington. Club: Fed. City ashington). Home: Washington D.C. Died July 2, 94.

PLEY, WAYNE EUGENE, JR., lawyer; b. Jackıville, Fla., June 24, 1946; s. Wayne E. and Frances hillips) R.; m. Frances Shutts, Aug. 31, 1968; chilen: Wayne E. III, Frances Caroline. BS, U. Fla., 58; JD, U. Miami, Coral Gables, Fla., 1974. Bar: Fla. 74. Assoc. Rogers, Towers, Bailey, et al, Jacksonville, 74-78; atty. Winn-Dixie Stores, Inc., Jacksonville, 78-91, v.p., gen counsel, sec., 1991-94. Home: Jackıville Fla. Deceased.

TCHIE, LAWRENCE STARR, retired medical rasitologist; b. Glenvil, Nebr., Dec. 9, 1906; s. rfield R. and Bertha (Starr) R.; m. Ethel Allen, Jan. 1932; children: Glennys Ann, Carolyn Starr, Ann zabeth. A.B., Grand Island Coll., Nebr., 1928; M.A., rthwestern U., 1930, Ph.D., 1936. Asst. prof. oman's Coll., U. N.C., 1936-44; research parasitolo- U.S. Army Lab., Tokyo, 1946-56, U.S. Army opical Research Med. Lab., San Juan, P.R., 1956-66, erto Rico Nuclear Ctr., San Juan, 1966-73; dir. P.R. iclear Ctr., San Juan, 1973-76; cons. WHO, Schisomiasis del. to Peoples Republic China. Contbr. ares to profl. jours. Active, Presbyterian Ch.; mem. merous civic orgns.; chmn. bd. Fish of Knox County, nn., 1980-82, Contact, 1982-84. Served to 1st lt. litary Corp, U.S. Army, 1944-47. Recipient cert. of hievement U.S. Army, Isaac Gonzalez-Martinez award R. Com. for Bilharzia Control, Medal of Merit Presdl. ard Philippine Islands. Mem. Am. Soc. Tropical edicine and Hygiene, Am. Soc. Parasitologists. Died y 1, 1989. Home: Oliver Springs Tenn.

THOLZ, JULES, lawyer; b. N.Y.C., Feb. 5, 1925; s. rry and Anna (Levy) R.; children: Adam, ily. AB, Bklyn. Coll., 1948; LLB, Harvard U., 1951; M, NYU, 1958. Bar: U.S. Ct. Appeals (2d cir.) 55, U.S. Dist. Ct. (ea. and so. dists.) N.Y. 1956, U.S. x Ct. 1958, U.S. Supreme Ct. 1960. Ptnr. Kostelanetz tholz Tigue & Fink, N.Y.C., 1963-93; adj. prof. NYU, 73-93; vice chmn. bd., trustee Fed. Bar Counsel, 1975-90-93. Bd. editors Jour. Taxation, 1981-93; contbr. icles to profl. jours. Past pres. Bklyn. Coll. Found. ved with AUS, 1943-46. Decorated Bronze Star. low Am. Coll. Trial Lawyers, Am. Coll. Tax unsel, Am. Bar Found.; mem. ABA (past chmn., spl. viser com. on civil and criminal tax penalties, chmn. n. on spl. investigative techniques, sect. taxation), d. Bar Assn. (past chmn. sanctions-civil and criminal . com.), N.Y. State Bar Assn. (ho. of dels.), N.Y. unty Lawyers Assn. (chmn. com. on taxation 1973-bd. dir. 1974-80). Club: Harvard (N.Y.C.). Home: w York N.Y. Died Sept. 15, 1993.

TTENHOUSE, JOSEPH WILSON, electrical oducts manufacturing company consultant; b. Neo, Mo., Jan. 22, 1917; s. George Eddy and Nannie wart (Morgan) R.; m. Jane Eileen Peterson, June 3, 39; children: Joseph Wilson II, John David, Jane een, Judith Anne, James Jay, Jeffrey Lee. B.S. in ec. Engring, Purdue U., 1939; M.S. in Elec. Engring, Mo., 1949. Registered profl. engr., Mo. Mem. staff lio sta. WBAA, Purdue U., Lafayette, Ind., 1936-39; rious engring. positions James R. Kearney Corp., St. uis, 1939-43; mem. faculty elec. engring. dept. Sch. nes and Metallurgy, U. Mo. at Rolla, 1947-54, assoc. of. elec. engring., 1952-54; tech. dir. hi-voltage uipment div. Joslyn Mfg. and Supply Co., Cleve., 54-65; div. gen. mgr. Joslyn Mfg. and Supply Co., 55-69; group v.p. elec. products Joslyn Mfg. and pply Co., Chgo., 1969-73; pres. Joslyn Mfg. & Supply ., Chgo., 1973-78; chmn. Joslyn Mfg. & Supply Co., 73-79, dir., 1970-79; dir. Hosp. Staffing Services Inc., 83-87; cons. Joslyn Mfg. & Supply Co., 1979-80; pres. . Assos., 1980-94; Guest speaker at meetings of profl. and other socs. Co-author: Electric Power Transmission, 1953; contbr. articles to profl. publs. Mem. indsl. devel. com. City Council, Aurora, Ohio, 1960-62. Served as officer Signal Corps, AUS, 1943-46; maj. Res., ret. Fellow IEEE (mem., chmn. numerous coms.); mem. Nat., Ill. socs. profl. engrs., Am. Soc. Engring. Edn., Conf. Internationale des Grands Reseaux Electriques, Nat. Elec. Mfrs. Assn. (bd. govs. 1970-79, vice chmn. 1974-79), Cleve. C. of C., Sigma Xi, Eta Kappa Nu (nat. adv. bd. 1955-57), Tau Beta Pi, Tau Kappa Alpha, Lambda Chi Alpha. Presbyn. Clubs: Metropolitan, Anvil (Chgo.). Home: Barrington Ill. Died Feb. 12, 1994.

RIVES, ALBERT GORDON, retired lawyer; b. Brimingham, Ala., Apr. 12, 1901; s. John R. T. and Mamie Lillian (Gordon) R.; m. Hester Maude Burchfield, May 22, 1926 (dec. Aug. 4, 1963); m. Margaret Gordon Crawford Jackson, Mar. 9, 1968. LL.B., U. Ala., 1924. Bar: Ala. 1925. Asst. dir. athletics U. Ala., 1924; later practiced in Birmingham; sr. partner firm Rives, Peterson, Pettus, Conway, Elliott and Small, 1936-79, now of counsel. Messenger to Baptist World Congress, Rio de Janeiro, 1960. Served to lt. comdr. USNR, World War II. Mem. Am., Ala., Birmingham bar assns., Internat. Assn. Ins. Counsel, Am. Judicature Soc., SAR, SCV, Ala. Hist. Soc., Phi Alpha Delta, Sigma Chi. Clubs: Bath and Tennis (Palm Beach, Fla.); Mountain Brook; Vestavia Country, The Club (Birmingham). Lodges: Masons, Shriners. Home: Birmingham Ala. Deceased.

ROBBINS, DANIEL, author, art history educator; b. N.Y.C., Jan. 15, 1933; s. David and Ora (Laddon) R.; m. Eugenia Scandrett, Dec. 6, 1959; children: Juliette, Miranda. A.B., U. Chgo., 1951; M.A., Yale U., 1956; student, Inst. Fine Arts, NYU, 1956-58; Ph.D., 1974; Ph.D. Fulbright fellow, Inst. Art and Archaeology, U. Paris, 1958-59. Curator Nat. Gallery Art, Washington, 1960-61, Guggenheim Mus., N.Y.C., 1961-65; dir. Mus. Art, R.I. Sch. Design, Providence, 1965-71, Fogg Art Mus., Harvard, 1971-75; vis. prof. art history Brown U., 1966-71; vis. research prof. art Dartmouth Coll., 1975-80; May I.C. Baker prof. arts Union Coll., Schenectady, 1980-95; sr. fellow Nat. Endowment for Humanities, 1976; vis. prof. Yale U., 1977, Williams Coll., 1978, Hunter Coll., CUNY, 1984, U. Iowa, 1985; vis. mem. Inst. Advanced Study, Princeton, 1986; cons. Vt. Ho. of Reps., 1979; mem. adv. panel mus. program NEA, NEH. Author: Albert Gleizes, 1964, Jacques Villon, 1976, Cubist Drawings, 1978, The Vermont State House, 1980, Edward Koren, Prints and Drawings, 1982, Jean Metzinger, 1985, Walter Murch, 1986, Fernand Léger, 1989, Poons: Creation of the Complex Surface, 1990, Henri Le Fauconnier: A Pioneer Cubist, 1991; contbg. author: Outsider Art, 1994. Trustee Am. Fedn. Arts, Albert Gleizes Found., Paris, 1987-95, Friends of Vt. State House, 1988-95, Can. Ctr. for Architecture, Montreal, Que. Recipient Cubism and Architecture: A Colloquium in Honor of Daniel Robbins, 1993; Guggenheim fellow, 1978. Home: Randolph Vt.

ROBECK, GORDON G(URNEY), environmental engineer; b. Denver, Feb. 3, 1923; s. Martin J. and Anna (Selstad) R.; m. Ephrosinia Yaremko, Feb. 3, 1951; children: John, Paul, Mark. BCE, U. Wis., 1944; SM, MIT, 1950; DSc (hon.), U. Cin., 1985. Commd. officer, san. engr. USPHS, various locations, 1944-74; dir. drinking water research div. U.S. EPA, Cin., 1974-85. Contbr. articles on public health aspects of treating drinking water, nat. drinking water standards to profl. jours., chpts. to books. Recipient Gold medal for exceptional service EPA, 1978, Disting. Service citation U. Wis.-Madison Coll. Engring., 1986. Mem. NAE (mem. water sci. and tech. bd. of NRC 1986-93), ASCE (hon. life, rsch. prize 1965), Am. Water Works Assn. (hon. life mem., outstanding svc. award 1979, rsch. award 1970, Abel Wolman award 1985, numerous publ. awards), Water Pollution Control Fedn. (life). Home: Laguna Hills Calif. Died Feb. 21, 1993.

ROBERTS, ALAN H., psychologist, researcher; b. Chgo., Mar. 2, 1929; s. Carl and Kay (Radford) R.; m. Shirley Boe (div. 1963); children: Kenneth Richard, Karen Elizabeth; m. Myrna Morrison, Mar. 18, 1967; children: Joel Philip, Jennifer Elaine. BA, Mich. State U., 1951, MS, 1952; postgrad., U. Colo., 1953-54; PhD, U. Denver, 1958. Diplomate Am. Bd. Profl. Psychology. Sch. psychologist Colo. Rocky Mountain Sch., Carbondale, 1953-54; from research psychologist to supr. psychology Elgin (Ill.) State Hosp., 1956-69; from asst. to assoc. prof. behavioral sci. N. Mex. Highlands U., Las Vegas, 1960-64; asst. prof. clin. psychology U. Colo., Denver, 1964-65; prof. div. health care psychology U. Minn. dept. phys. medicine and rehabilitation, Mpls., 1966-80, dir. autonomic learning lab., 1973-80, dir. pain clinic and pain treatment program, 1973-80; dir. Behavioral Medicine Program Scripps Clinic and Rsch. Found., La Jolla, Calif., from 1979; co-dir. Anxiety Disorders Clinic Scripps Clinic and Rsch. Found., La Jolla, from 1985, co-dir. Depressive Disorders Clinic, from 1988, head Div. Med. Psychology, from 1989; rsch. assoc. Nat. Tng. Labs., Bethal, Maine, 1955, Group Devel. Labs., U. Colo., Boulder, 1954-55, also teaching assoc.; supr. Walk-In Counseling Ctr., Mpls., 1970-79; mem. rev. bd. St. Peter State Hosp., Minn. Dept. Welfare, 1972-79; adj. faculty mem. San Diego State U., from 1983; vis. prof. Stanford U., Palo Alto, Calif., 1972; assoc. clin. prof. U. Calif., San Diego, from 1983. Contbr. chpts. to books, articles to profl. jours. Served with U.S. Army, 1946-47. Named Sr. Stipend fellow Nat. Inst. Mental Health, NIH, 1962-63. Fellow APA, Am. Psychol. Soc., Acad. Behavioral Medicine Rsch., Soc. Behavioral Medicine; mem. Internat. Assn. Study Pain, Minn. Psychol. Assn. (chmn. legis. com. 1972-73, mem. exec. com. 1974-79, sec. 1976-77, mem. officer 1977-79, life from 1980), Sigma Xi. Home: Encinitas Calif. Deceased.

ROBERTS, EDWARD VERNE, institute administrator; b. San Mateo, Calif., Jan. 23, 1939; s. Verne Walter and Zona Lee (Harvey) R.; m. Catherine Dugan, Sept. 11, 1976 (div. 1983); 1 child, Lee. AA, Coll. San Mateo, 1962; BA, U. Calif., Berkeley, 1964, MA with distinction, 1966, postgrad.; LHD (hon.), Wright Inst., Berkeley, 1981. Teaching assoc. polit. sci. U. Calif., Berkeley, 1964-67, asst. to dean students, specialist removal of attitudinal and archtl. barriers, 1968-69; dir. project handicapped opportunity program for edn. U. Calif., Riverside, 1970-71; cons. student spl. svc. program U.S. Office Edn., Washington, 1969-70; co-founder, instr. Nairobi Coll., East Palo Alto, Calif., 1969-70; prof., dean students Common College, Woodside, Calif., 1971; exec. dir., co-founder Ctr. Ind. Living, Berkeley, 1972-75; dir. State Dept. Rehab., Sacramento, 1975-83; pres. World Inst. Disability, Oakland, Calif., 1983—; trainer Ptnrs. in Policymaking, 1989—, Ptnrs. in Leadership Advanced Tng., Mpls., 1992; trustee Common Coll., 1981—; co-founder, bd. dirs. Wright Inst.; bd. dirs. World Inst. Disability, Internat. Initiative Against Avoidable Disablement, East Sussex, Eng., and Geneva, Project Interdependence. Contbr. articles to profl. jours. Mem. adv. com. pathways to independence United Cerebral Palsy Alameda/Contra Costa County, 1990—, Richmond Unified Sch. Dist. Tech. Task Force, 1991—. Recipient N. Neal Pike prize Boston U., 1990, Disting. Svc. award Pres. U.S., 1991, Just Do It award Devel. Disabilities Commrs., 1991; fellow John D. & Catherine T. MacArthur Fedn., 1985-89. Mem. Disabled People's Internat.-USA (treas., vice chair 1982—), Through the Looking Glass (bd. dirs. 1983—), World Interdependence Fund (bd. dirs. 1990—), Greenlining Coalition, Assn. Severly Handicapped (bd. dirs. 1990—), Assn. Preservation Presdl. Yacht Potomac (bd. govs. 1991—). Democrat. Home: Berkeley Calif. Died Mar. 14, 1995.

ROBERTS, FRANK, state senator; b. Boise, Idaho, Dec. 28, 1915; s. Walter Scott and Mary (Livenzey) R.; m. Louise Charleson (div.); children: Mary Wendy, Leslie; m. Barbara Kay Hughey Sanders, June 29, 1974. BA, Pacific U., 1938; PhM, U. Wisconsin, 1943; PhD, Stanford U., 1955; LLD (hon.), Pacific U., 1990. Prof. Portland (Oreg.) State U., 1946-84; state rep. Oreg. Legis., Salem, 1967-73, state senator, 1975-93. Bd. dirs. Mt. Hood Community Coll. Bd., Gresham, Oreg., 1965-75. Lt. USAAF, 1943-46. Recipient Disting. Svc. award Mt. Hood Community Coll., 1988, E.B. Naughton Civil Liberties award Oreg. ACLU, 1987. Democrat. Home: Portland Oreg. Died Oct. 31, 1993.

ROBERTS, LOUIS WRIGHT, transportation executive; b. Jamestown, N.Y., Sept. 1, 1913; s. Louis Lorenzo and Dora (Wright) R.; m. Mercedes Pearl McGavock, June 8, 1938; children: Louis M., Lawrence E. BA, Fisk U., 1935, LLD (hon.), 1985; MS, U. Mich., 1937, postgrad., 1941; postgrad., MIT, 1946. Teaching asst. Fisk U., Nashville, 1935-36; instr. St. Augustine's Coll., Raleigh, N.C., 1937-40, assoc. prof., 1941-42; assoc. prof. Howard U., Washington, 1943-44; mgr. tube div. Sylvania Elec. Products Inc., Danvers, Salem and Boston, Mass., 1944-50; tube cons. rsch. lab. for electronics MIT, Cambridge, 1950-51, vis. sr. lectr., 1979-80; founder, pres. Microwave Assocs., Inc., Boston, 1950-55; engring. specialist, cons. Bomac Labs., Inc., Beverly, Mass., 1955-59; founder, v.p., dir. METCOM, Inc., Salem, Mass., 1959-67; pres. Elcon Labs., Peabody, Mass., 1962-66; cons. Addison-Wesley Press, Reading, Mass., 1963-67; chief microwave lab. NASA Electronics Rsch. Ctr., Cambridge, 1967-68, chief optics and microwave lab., 1968-70; dep. dir. Office Tech. Transp. Systems Ctr., Cambridge, 1970-72, dir. Office Tech., 1972-77, dir. Office Energy and Environ., 1977-79, dep. dir., 1979, dir. Office Data Systems and Tech., 1980-82, dir. Office Adminstrn., 1982-83, assoc. dir. Office Ops. Engring., 1983-84, acting dep. dir., 1984, acting dir., 1984-85, dir., 1985-89; cons. Battelle Meml. Inst., Columbus, Ohio, 1989-92; coporator Wakefield Savs. Bank, Mass., 1975-90; bd. dirs. Systems Resources Corp. Editor: Electronic Tubes, 1964; author, editor: Handbook of Microwave Measurements, 1966; contbr. articles to profl. jours. Mem. Mass. Gov.'s Commn. on Vocat. Rehab., 1966-68, Positive Program for Boston, 1967-75; pres. Wakefield Coun. Chs., 1967-70; mem. adv. bd. U. Mass., Amherst, 1972-90, Bentley Coll., Waltham, Mass., 1974-90; trustee Univ. Hosp., Boston, 1973-95. Recipient Apollo Achievement award NASA, 1969, Meritorious Achievement award Sec. Transp. 1976, Outstanding Achievement award U. Mich., 1978, Meritorious Exec. award Pres. U.S., 1984. Fellow IEEE; mem. AIAA, AAAS, N.Y. Acad. Sci., Phi Beta Kappa Assocs. (life mem.), Sigma Pi Phi (treas. 1980-85, pres. 1986-89), Nat. Guardsmen Club (pres. 1986-90), Masons. Episcopalian. Home: Wakefield Mass.

ROBERTS, RICHARD HEILBRON, construction company executive; b. Sacramento, Nov. 19, 1925; s. John Montgomery and Mary Lou (Heilbron) R.; m. Jo Anne Sydney Erickson, Feb. 25, 1950; children: Richard, Kurt, Tracy. BSCE, U. Calif., 1949. Registered profl. engr., Calif. Field and resident engr. Calif. Div. Hwys., San Luis Obispo, 1949-51; project and br. mgr. Granite Constrn. Co., Watsonville, Calif., 1951-68, v.p., mgr., 1968-79, pres. engring. constrn. div., 1979-83, exec. v.p., chief operating officer, 1983-89, vice chmn., 1989-95, also bd. dirs. Pres. Nellie Thomas Inst. Learning, 1989-90. Served to corp. U.S. Army, 1944-46. Mem. Soc. Am. Mil. Engrs., Beavers (bd. dirs., pres. 1984, Golden Beaver award 1986, Moles Non-mem. award 1988). Republican. Presbyterian. Clubs: Monterey Peninsula Country (Pebble Beach, Calif.); Silverado Country (Napa, Calif.); Pauma Valley (Calif.) Country. Home: Carmel Calif. Died Aug. 20, 1995.

ROBERTS, RICHARD JAMES, business executive, corporation lawyer; b. Toronto, Ont., Can., Mar. 17, 1922; s. Charles Anthony and Eva Lloy (Lundy) m. Carol Henrietta Hingst, May 4, 1988; children from previous marriage: Mary Virginia, Catherine Elizabeth, Anne Victoria. Barrister and solicitor degree, Osgoode Hall, Toronto, Ont., 1948. Ptnr. Roberts & Anderson, Toronto, Ont., Can., 1948-68; pvt. practice Toronto, Ont., Can., 1968-71; ptnr. Thomson, Rogers, Toronto, 1971-78, Roberts & Drabinsky, Toronto, 1978-81; sec.-treas. Cineplex Odeon Corp., Toronto, 1980-86, sr. v.p., 1986-89; sec. The Live Entertainment Corp., Can., from 1989; lectr. Osgoode Hall Law Sch., Toronto, 1952-62, dir. bar admission course, 1958-70; Queen's counsel, 1959. Capt. Royal Can. Artillery, 1941-46. Decorated Croix de Guerre avec Palme (France); Order of Leopold with palme (Belgium); Clare Brett Martin Meml. scholar, 1948. Mem. Law Soc. Upper Can. (dir. bar admission course 1958-70, chmn. examining bd. 1962-70), Can. Bar Assn., County of York Law Assn., Lawyers' Club of Toronto, Cambridge Club. Home: Toronto Can. Deceased.

ROBERTS, TED, manufacturing executive; b. Mpls., Mar. 28, 1958; s. Walter Glen and Mary Jo (Cronin) R.; m. Lee Ann Gustafson, Nov. 9, 1985. BS in Bus., U. Minn., 1980, MBA in Mktg., 1984. Assoc. pub. Comml. West Mag., Mpls., 1980-82; v.p. mktg. Roberts Automatic Products, Chanhassen, Minn., 1982-95; v.p., dir. Roberts Trading Corp., Des Moines, Iowa. Mem. Nat. Screw Machine Products Assn., N.W. Chi Psi Ednl. Found. (v.p.). Home: Minneapolis Minn. Died Nov., 1995.

ROBERTSON, CHARLES STUART, manufacturing executive; b. Montreal, Que., Can., Mar. 20, 1899; s. Charles James and Margaret Watson (Isaac) R.; m. Elizabeth Cowen Swing, Feb. 1, 1930; children: Charles Stuart, Michael Swing, Philip Swing, Elizabeth Margaret Robertson Whitters. B.B.A. cum laude, Boston U., 1922. Asst. sales mgr. Shapleigh Hardware Co., St. Louis, 1921-22; advt. mgr. C.F. Wing Co., New Bedford, Mass., 1922-23; asst. treas. Morse Driscoll & Co., 1923-25; pres. Robertson Factories, Inc., Taunton, Mass., 1925-73; chmn. bd. Robertson Factories, Inc., 1973-79, chmn. exec. com. from 1979; dir. Glenwood Range Co., Paragon Gear Co. Officer, trustee Morton Hosp., from 1928, Taunton Boys Club, 1927-65; trustee Robertson Trust, Caldeonian Trust. Served with U.S. Army, 1918. Mem. U.S. Indsl. Council (dir. from 1972), Newcomen Soc., Taunton C. of C. Republican. Congregationalist. Clubs: N.Y. Yacht, Falmouth Yacht, Country of Brookline, Woods Hole Golf, Segregansett Golf, 100 of Mass, Rotary. Home: Taunton Mass. Deceased.

ROBIE, WILLIAM RANDOLPH, lawyer, government official; b. Balt., Sept. 15, 1944; s. Fred Smith and Mary Louise (Kent) R. BA, Northwestern U., 1966, JD, 1969. Bar: Ill. 1969, D.C. 1975, U.S. Ct. Mil. Appeals 1971, U.S. Supreme Ct. 1973. Assoc. Hubachek, Kelly, Rauch & Kirby, Chgo., 1969-70; commd. officer U.S. Army JAGC, 1970-74, advanced through grades to capt.; with res., 1974-81; asst. gen. counsel, Office Consumer Affairs, HEW, 1974-75; assoc. dir. legal edn. inst. Civil Service Commn., 1975-78; counsel to assoc. atty. gen. for atty. personnel, 1978-79, dep. assoc. atty. gen., 1979-81, assoc. dep. atty. gen. U.S. Dept. Justice, 1981; dir. Office Atty. Personnel Mgmt., Office Dep. Atty. Gen., U.S. Dept. Justice, Washington, 1981-83; chief immigration judge Exec. Office for Immigration Rev., U.S. Dept. of Justice, Falls Church, Va., 1983—; instr., chmn. adv. bd. Paralegal Studies Project, U. Md. 1976—; liaison mem. Adminstrv. Conf. of U.S., first administrv. judge govt. mem., 1990—. Richard Weaver fellow, 1966-67. Mem. ABA (chmn. standing com. legal assistance mil. personnel 1976-79, chmn. spl. com. delivery of legal services 1979-82, chmn. standing com. lawyers responsibility for client protection 1987-90, chmn. standing com. on legal assts. 1990-91, mem. 1991—), Fed. Bar Assn. (chmn. council on the fed. lawyer 1978-82, dep. sect. coord. for conv. 1982-83, chmn. continuing edn. bd. 1983-84, nat. dep. sec. 1984-85, nat. sec. 1985-86, nat. 2d v.p. 1986-87, nat. 1st v.p. 1987-88, nat. pres. elect 1988-89, nat. pres. 1989-90, chmn. facilities com. 1990—, immediate past nat. pres. 1990-91, chmn. long range planning com. 1991—, del. to ABA ho. of dels. 1991—), Judge Advocates Assn. (dir. 1975—, chmn. field organization com. 1981-85, 2d

v.p. 1986-87, 1st v.p. 1987-88, pres. 1988-89), Ill. Bar Assn., Chgo. Bar Assn., D.C. Bar, Fed. Bar Bldg. Corp. Inc. (v.p., bd. dirs. 1991—), Prettyman-Leventhal Am. Inn of Ct. (founding master, exec. com. 1991—), Shuter's Hill Owners' Assn. (founding pres. 1984-85, bd. dirs. 1984-85, 88—, pres. 1988—), Psi Upsilon (internat. pres. 1984-90, dir. 1969—, internat. sec. 1979-84), Phi Alpha Delta (pres. Melville W. Fuller chpt. 1968-69). Republican. Presbyterian. Club: Nat. Lawyers. Contbr. articles to profl. jours. Deceased. Home: Alexandria Va.

ROBINS, EDWIN CLAIBORNE, SR., retired pharmaceutical company executive; b. Richmond, Va., July 8, 1910; s. Claiborne and Martha (Taylor) R.; m. Lora McGlasson, June 24, 1938; children: Lora Elizabeth Robins Porter, E. Claiborne, Ann Carol Robins Marchant. AB, U. Richmond, 1931; BS, Med. Coll. Va. Sch. Pharmacy, 1933, D in Pharm. Sci., 1958, LLD, 1960. Former chmn. bd. A. H. Robins Co., Inc., Richmond. Trustee emeritus Richmond Meml. Hosp., United Givers Fund, Crippled Children's Hosp.; mem. exec. com.; trustee U. Richmond, past pres. alumni council. Recipient Outstanding Alumnus award MCV Alumni Assn., 1986, Disting. Service award U. Richmond, 1960; Dean M. McCann award Pharm. Wholesalers Assn., 1968; Hugo H. Schaefer medal Am. Pharm. Assn., 1969; Liberty Bell award Richmond Bar Assn., 1970; Sertoma Club award, 1970; Thomas Jefferson award Pub. Relations Soc. Am., 1970; named Pharmacist of Year Va. Pharm. Assn., 1967; Bus. Leader of Year Sales and Mktg. Execs. Richmond, 1969; Disting. Service award Va. State Chamber, 1972; Jackson Davis award for disting. service to higher edn. in Va., 1976; Edward A. Wayne medal for Disting. Service Va. Commonwealth U., 1978; Wall of Fame award, Va. Sports Hall of Fame; Wall of Fame award, 1979; award U. Richmond Athletic Hall of Fame, 1980; Gt. Am. Traditions award B'nai Brith, 1982, Outstanding Alumnus award Med. Coll. Va./Commonwealth U. Sch. Pharmacy, 1983, U. Richmond Paragon medal, 1986, Disting. Citizen award Boy Scouts Am., 1991. Mem. NAM, Am. Pharm. Assn. (hon. pres. 1992), Pharm. Mfrs. Assn. (past chmn.), Va. Mfrs. Assn., Va. Pharm. Assn., Newcomen Soc. N.Am., Richmond C. of C. (past pres.), Med. Coll. Va. Alumni Assn. (past pres., dir.), Phi Beta Kappa, Alpha Kappa Psi, Omicron Delta Kappa, Phi Delta Chi, Kappa Psi, Lambda Chi Alpha, Beta Gamma Sigma (hon.). Baptist (mem. bd. adminstrn.). Clubs: Rotary (past dir.), Commonwealth Forum, Country of Va. Home: Richmond Va. Died July 6, 1995.

ROBINSON, DAVID WALLACE, lawyer; b. Lincolnton, N.C., Nov. 22, 1899; s. David W. and Edith (Childs) R.; m. Elizabeth Gibbes, Jan. 21, 1933; children: Caroline Robinson Ellerbe, David W.; m. Susan Gibbes, Sept. 17, 1955; 1 child, Heyward Gibbes. AB, Roanoke Coll., 1919; AM, LLB, U. S.C., 1921, LLD (hon.) 1963; spl. student Harvard Law Sch., 1921-22; LLD (hon.) Presbyn. Coll., 1941. Bar: S.C. 1921, U.S. Ct. Appeals (4th cir.) 1923, U.S. Supreme Ct. 1933. Adj. prof. Law Sch. U. S.C., Columbia, 1926-32; ptnr. Robinson, McFadden, Moore, Pope, Williams, Taylor & Brailsford and predecessors, Columbia, from 1922; legal cons. Pub. Works Adminstrn., 1939; gen. counsel Fed. Power Commn., 1939-40; legal cons. Bur. Econ. Warfare, 1941-42; ptnr. Gibbes Machinery Co. Trustee Presbyn. Coll., 1960-70; elder Eastminster Presbyn. Ch., Columbia; chmn. bequest com. Presbyn. Ch. U.S.; mem. Columbia Art Mus. Commn., 1956-69; bd. dirs. Carolina Children's Home, Community Chest, Columbia YMCA; state chmn. United Fund; mem. S.C. Edn. Fin. Com., 1950-55; chmn. com. to draft and adopt city mgr. govt., Columbia, 1949-50, Mcpl.-County Consolidation, 1962-63, S.C. legis. com. to study election laws, 1952-54; mem. U. S.C. Chair Endowment Found.; vice chmn. Capitol City Found. Served with U.S. Army, 1918, USAAF, 1942-46. Recipient Disting. Alumnus award U. S.C., 1976. Fellow Am. Coll. Trial Lawyers (regent 1969-73); mem. ABA, S.C. Bar Assn. (pres. 1956). Richland County Bar Assn. (pres. 1947), S.C. State Bar (pres. 1968, recipient DuRant award 1980), Am. Law Inst. (life), Am. Bar Found. (life), Jud. Council S.C. Clubs: Palmetto, Summit, Forest Lake. Lodge: Kiwanis. Deceased. Home: Columbia S.C.

ROBINSON, ROSCOE, JR., army officer; b. St. Louis, Oct. 11, 1928. B.S. in Mil. Engring., U.S. Mil. Acad.; M. in Polit. and Instl. Adminstrn., U. Pitts.; grad., Infantry Sch., AUS Command and Gen. Staff Coll., Nat. War Coll. Commd. 2d lt. U.S. Army, advanced through grades to gen., 1975; comdr. 2d bn., 7th Cav., 1st cav. div. U.S. Army, Vietnam, 1968; comdr. 2d Brigade, 82d Airborne Div., Ft. Bragg, N.C., 1972-73; dep. comdg. gen., then comdg. gen. U.S. Army Garrison, Okinawa, 1973-76; comdg. gen. 82d Airborne div., Ft. Bragg, 1976-78; with Seventh Army, 1978-80; comdg. gen. U.S. Army Japan/IX Corps, 1980-82; U.S. rep. to NATO Mil. Com., 1982-85. Decorated D.S.M. with oak leaf cluster, Silver Star with oak leaf cluster, Legion of Merit with 2 oak leaf clusters, D.F.C., Bronze Star, Air medal (10 awards), Army Commendation medal, Combat Infantryman Badge (2d award). Home: Washington D.C. Died July 24, 1993.

ROBINSON, SHEPARD DOUGLAS, newsletter publisher, author; b. Pitts., Apr. 15, 1925; s. Howard Shepard and Helen (Read) R.; m. Louise Foster Marsh,

Nov. 27, 1951; children: Helen, Marsha, Susan. A[...] Dartmouth Coll., 1949. Police reporter Uniontown (P[...] Morning Herald, 1949-50; copy editor Bergen Eveni[...] Record, Hackensack, N.J., 1950-51; editor, advt. m[...] Carnegie (Pa.) Signal Item, 1952-53; publ., own[...] Schoharie (N.Y.) Rev., 1953-57; asst. to editor Mode[...] Hosp. Mag., Chgo., 1957-58; editor, prodn. mgr. P[...] Ridge (Ill.) Advocate, 1959-62; exec. v.p., chief op[...] officer Barrington (Ill.) Press, 1967-68, editorial dir., [...] mgr. trade mag. div., 1965-68, editor, pub. newspape[...] 1962-68; office mgr. Vance Pub. Co., Chgo., 1969; pu[...] Manufactured Housing Newsletter, Barrington, 1973-[...] columnist Automated Builder, Carpinteria, Cal[...] 1983—. Author: Land Use Guide, 1977, How To Tu[...] Around a Troubled Company, 1979, Manufactur[...] Housing: What It Is, Where It Is, How It Operat[...] 1988; contbr. editor Profl. Builder, 1972-83. With US[...] 1943-46, PTO. Republican. Episcopalian. Home: B[...] rington Ill. Died March 17, 1990.

ROCHE, JOHN P., political science educator; [...] Bklyn., May 7, 1923; s. Walter John and Ruth (Pearso[...] R.; m. Constance Ratcliff Ludwig, June 21, 1947; [...] child, Joanna Ratcliff. AB, Hofstra Coll., 1943; A[...] Cornell U., 1947, PhD, 1949; DLitt, Ripon Coll., 19[...] LLD, U. Mass., 1980; DHL, Tufts U., 1985, Brand[...] U., 1987, Hofstra U., 1989. Instr., asst. prof., as[...] prof. polit. sci. Haverford Coll., 1949-56; prof. polit[...] Brandeis U., Waltham, Mass., 1956-70; Herter pr[...] politics and history Brandeis U., 1970-73, chmn. de[...] politics, 1956-59, 61-65, dean faculty arts and sci[...] 1959-61; chmn. grad. com. Am. Civilization, 1963-[...] Henry R. Luce prof. civilization and fgn. affai[...] academic dean Fletcher Sch. Law and Diploma[...] Medford, Mass., 1973-85; acting dean Fletcher Sch. L[...] and Diplomacy, 1978-79, 85-86, Olin Disting. prof. A[...] Civilization and Fgn. Affairs, 1986-93, prof. emerit[...] 1993-94; dir. Fletcher Media Inst., 1989-94; Fulbrig[...] lectr. France, 1959, Salzburg Seminar; vis. pr[...] Columbia Cornell U., Mass. Inst. Tech., U. Chg[...] Swarthmore Coll.; cons. Senator-Pres. John F. Kenne[...] Vice Pres. Hubert H. Humphrey, Dept. State; spl. co[...] to Pres. U.S., 1966-69; Nat. chmn. Americans [...] Democratic Action, 1962-65; mem. exec. com. C[...] Liberties Union Mass., 1961-66, com. on Prese[...] Danger, 1976-92; mem. Nat. Council on Humaniti[...] 1968-70, Presdl. Commn. on Internat. Broadcastin[...] 1972-73, U.S. Bd. for Internat. Broadcasting, 1974-[...] U.S. Adv. Com. on Arms Control and Disarmame[...] 1982-93, U.S. Nat. Security Edn. Bd., 1993-94; me[...] Subcom. on Prevention of Discrimination and Prot[...] tion of Minorities, UN Human Rights Commn., 19[...] 88; mem. Mass. Adv. Commn., U.S. Civil Rig[...] Commn., 1984-86. Author: (with M.S. Stedman, [...] The Dynamics of Democratic Government, 1954, Cou[...] & Rights, 1961, rev. edit., 1965, The Quest for [...] Dream: Civil Liberties in Modern America, 19[...] Shadow and Substance: Studies in the Theory [...] Structure of Politics, 1964, Origins of American Politi[...] Thought, 1966, American Political Thought: Jefferso[...] the Progressives, 1967, John Marshall, 1967, Sentene[...] to Life: Reflections on Politics, Education and La[...] 1974, (with M.S. Stedman and E. Meehan) T[...] Dynamics of Modern Government, 1966, (with [...] Vidyashanker, J. Hillman) Political Power and Le[...] timacy, 1979, American Nationality, 1607-1978: [...] Overview, 1980, (with Uri Ra'anan) Ethnic Resurge[...] in Modern Democratic States, 1979, National Secur[...] Policy: The Decision-Making Process, 1984, Mode[...] Presidents and the Presidency, 1985, Security Comm[...] ments and Capabilities, 1985; Grinding Axes: Allian[...] Politics in World War II, 1985, The History of Marx[...] Leninist Organizational Theory, 1985; contbg. auth[...] The American Revolution: A Heritage of Change, 19[...] The Legacy of Vietnam, 1976, Encyclopedia of [...] American Constitution, 1986, 1st supplemental v[...] 1991, The USSR Today and Tomorrow, 1987; nati[...] ally syndicated columnist, 1968-82. Trustee Woodr[...] Wilson Ctr. for Scholars, Smithsonian Instn., 1968-[...] Dubinsky Found., 1972-80, Randolph Found., A[...] Polit. Sci. Assn. Endowment; bd. dirs. Internat. Res[...] Com. Staff sgt. USAAF, 1943-46. Recipient Mo[...] Coit Tyler prize Cornell U., 1949; Fellow Rockefel[...] Found., 1954-55, 65-66; Fellow Rockefeller Found. [...] Advancement Edn., 1954-55, Hudson Inst., 1970-9[...] Mem. Am. Polit. Sci. Assn., Soc. Am. Historians, Ma[...] Hist. Soc., Council Fgn. Relations, Phi Beta Kap[...] Sigma Delta Chi, Phi Alpha Theta. Mem. Soc. Frien[...] Clubs: Cosmos, St. Botolph. Home: Weston Mass. D[...] May 6, 1994; interred Weston, M.A.

RODERICK, DAVID MILTON, oil, gas and s[...] corporation executive; b. Pitts., May 3, 1924; s. Mil[...] S. and Anna (Baskin) R.; m. Elizabeth J. Costello, [...] 31, 1948; children: David Milton, Patricia Ann, Thom[...] Kevin. B.S. in Econs. and Finance, U. Pitts. Asst[...] dir. stats. USX Corp. (formerly U.S. Steel Cor[...] N.Y.C., 1959-62; acctg. cons.-internat. projects [...] Corp. (formerly U.S. Steel Corp.), Paris, 1962-64; [...] acctg. USX Corp. (formerly U.S. Steel Corp.), 1964-[...] v.p. internat., 1967-73, chmn. fin. com., dir., 1973-[...] pres., 1975-79, chmn., chief exec. officer, 1979-89, [...] bd. dirs., 1979-89; bd. dirs. Proctor & Gamble Co.; [...] dir. Tex. Instruments, Inc., Aetna Life & Casualty C[...] bd. dirs. Pitts. Pirates; past chmn. Internat. Iron [...] Steel Inst; chmn. U.S.-Korea Bus. Coun. Chmn. [...] ternat. Environ. Bur.; bd. dirs. Allegheny Trails co[...] Boy Scouts Am.; trustee Carnegie-Mellon U. M[...]

lling Rock Club, Laurel Valley Golf Club, Fox apel Golf Club, Duquesne Club, Econ. Club. Home: tsburgh Pa.

DEWALD, PAUL GERHARD, lawyer; b. Newton, s., May 16, 1899; s. Ferdinand Adolph and Elise sche) R.; m. Lillian Young, Aug. 17, 1927 (dec. May 90); children: William Young, Mary Louise (Mrs. d L. Forni), Paul Gerhard. A.B., Ripon Coll., 1921, .D., 1978; LL.B., Harvard, 1924. Bar: Pa. 1924, U.S. preme Ct. Ptnr. firm Buchanan Ingersoll P.C. and decessors, 1930-80, of counsel, 1980-93. Trustee on Coll., 1957-76, chmn. bd., 1965-69. Mem. Am., , Allegheny County bar assns., Am. Law Inst., Phi a Kappa, Pi Kappa Delta, Delta Sigma Rho. publican. Presbyn. Clubs: Harvard-Yale-Princeton tts.), Duquesne (Pitts.). Died May 1, 1993.

EBLING, MARY GINDHART, banker; b. West llingswood, N.J.; d. I.D., Jr. and Mary W. (Simon) ndhart; m. Siegfried Roebling (dec.); children: zabeth (Mrs. D.J. Hobin), Paul. Student bus adnstrn., econs. and fin., U. Pa., econs. and fin., NYU; D (hon.), Ithaca Coll., 1954; DS in Bus. Adminstrn. n.), Bryant Coll.; DSc (hon.), Muhlenberg Coll.; ID (hon.), Wilberforce U.; DFA (hon.), Rider Coll.; S (hon.), St. John's U.; LHD (hon.), Marymount l., Rutgers U., 1987; LLD (hon.) Trenton State l., 1990. Former chmn. bd. Nat. State Bank N.J., men's Bank, Denver, now chmn. emeritus; chmn. Y. World's Fair Corp., 1964-65; dir. Companion Life . Co., N.Y., 1973-91. Mem. adv. com. U.S. commr. . for Expo '67; nat. bd. dirs. U.S.O.; pub. gov. Am. ck Exchange, 1958-62; mem. Regional Adv. Com. on nking Policies and Practices; econ. ambassador State . Chmn., N.J. Citizens for Clean Water, 1969-70; m. Ann. Assay Commn., 1971, Nat. Bus. Council on nsumer Affairs; mem. adv. com. N.J. Museum. Life stee George C. Marshall Research Found., N.J. ntal Service Plan; mem. nat. adv. council Nat. Mule Sclerosis Soc.; trustee Invest-in-America; adv. bd. sn. U.S. Army, civilian aide emeritus to Sec. Army, st Army; bd. govs. Del. Valley Council; chmn. N.J. s. Bond Com.; mem. 4th dist. Adv. Council Naval airs; bd. govs. Swedish Hist. Found.; nat. bd. Jr. hievement Inc.; emeritus mem. def. adv. com. on men in services Dept. Def.; citizens adv. council Com. Status of Women; bd. dirs. Am. Mus. Immigration; nn. N.J. Hospitalized Vets.'s Service; comptroller nton Parking Authority; founder Donnelly Meml. sp. Women's Com. Decorated Royal Order Vasa veden); commendatore Order Star Solidarity (Italy); ipient Brotherhood award NCCJ; Nat. Assn. Ins. men award; Distinguished Service award Marine rps League; Golden Key award N.J. Fedn. Jewish lanthropies; Spirit of Achievement award women's . Albert Einstein Coll. Medicine; Holland award N.J. dn. Women's Clubs; Outstanding Civilian Service dal Dept. Army, 1969; Humanitarian award N.J. ot. Nat. Arthritis Found., 1970; Four Chaplains ard, 1969; Trenton chpt. Nat. Secs. Boss of Year ard, 1969, Internat. Boss of Year award, 1972; lden Plate award Am. Acad. Achievement; Jerusalem ly City of Peace award State of Israel; Dept. of Def. dal for Disting. Pub. Service, 1984, Humanitarian ard Italian-Am. Nat. Hall of Fame, 1989; USO Met. Y. Woman of Yr., 1990, 1st Minutewoman award J. Army & Air Nat. Guard, 1994, others. Mem. Nat. f. Transp. Assn. (life mem.), U.S. Council of I.C.C. ustee), N.J. Conf. Christians and Jews, Swedish lonial Soc., League Women Voters, Am. Inst. nking, N.J. Investment Council, Am. Bankers Assn., . Mayflower Descs., Colonial Daus. 17th Century, enton C. of C., N.J. Firemen's Mut. Benevolent Assn. n. life), DAR, Geneal. Soc. Pa., Bus. and Profl. omen's Club, Daus. Colonial Wars, Pilgrim John wland Soc. Clubs: Zonta, Trenton Country; Colony Y.C.), Sea View Country, Contemporary (Trenton), eenacres Country (Lawrenceville); Overseas Press soc.); Am. Newspaper Women's (assoc.), 1925 F eet (Washington); Union League (Phila.). Died Oct. 1994. Home: Trenton N.J.

DESCH, WILLIAM ROBERT, steel co. exec.; b. rge, Pa., May 20, 1925; s. William V. and Edith M. ; B.S. in Engring. and Bus. Adminstrn., U. Pitts., 50; grad. advanced mgmt. program Harvard U., 1966; Jane Holt. With Jones & Laughlin Steel Corp., Pitts., 46-74, pres., 1970-71, chmn. bd., chief exec. officer, 71-74; pres., chief exec. officer Kaiser Industries, kland, Calif., 1974, vice chmn. bd. chief exec. officer, 74-77; exec. v.p. steel and domestic raw materials U.S. el Corp., Pitts., 1978-79, pres., 1979—, also chief erating officer; dir. Hilton Hotels Corp., Rockwell ternat. Mem. Am. Iron and Steel Inst. Home: Pittsurgh Pa.

OGATNICK, JOSEPH HIRSCH, diplomat, business ecutive, educator; b. N.Y.C., Jan. 26, 1917; s. Morris and Esther Lilian (Shain) R. B.A., U. Iowa; M.A., Pa., Ph.D. Officer Lend-Lease Adminstrn., 1941-45; ptd. fgn. service officer Dept. State, 1945; prin. econ. icer Iceland, 1945-47, North China, 1947-50, Sinpore, Malaysia, 1951-53; dir. commerce and industries U.S. High Commn., Berlin, 1953-54; ret. U.S. High mmn., 1954; prin. Joseph H. Rogatnick and Assocs., nsultants, 1954-61; dir. internat. orgns. div. U.S. pt. Commerce, 1961-62; mgmt. officer internat. ops. Beatrice Foods, 1962-66; pres. Foods & Services A.G., Switzerland, 1962-66; v.p. Pepsico Internat., 1967-68, Hayden Stone, Inc., 1969-70; various acad. activities, 1971-77; prof. internat. mgmt. Boston U., 1978-83; dir. Boston U. in, Brussels, 1978; mem. bd. advisors joint grad. programs Boston U.-Ben Gurion U.; sec., bd. dirs. Palm Beach Round Table, 1988-93; cons. on orgn. and adminstrn. grad. schs. mgmt.; advisor MBA programs Palm Beach Atlantic Coll., West Palm Beach, Fla., Northwood U., Midland, Mich.; mem. U.S. dels. to internat. trade confs. Contbr. numerous articles on econ. devel., ops. mgmt., mktg., fin. fgn. affairs and diplomacy to profl. jours., encys. Alt. mem. Palm Beach (Fla.) Code Enforcement Bd., 1992-93; mem. Palm Beach Civic Assn. Decorated Knight, Order of Falcon Iceland; named Hon. Consul of Luxembourg for Mass., 1980-85, Hon. Consul Emeritus, 1985-87. Mem. Soc. of the Four Arts, Palm Beach C. of C., Palm Beach Lit. Soc., Palm Beach Rotary, Palm Beach Pundits Club. Home: Palm Beach Fla. Died Oct. 27, 1993; interred West Palm Beach, Fla.

ROGERS, DAVID ELLIOTT, physician, educator, author; b. N.Y.C., Mar. 17, 1926; s. Carl Ransom and Helen Martha (Elliott) R.; m. Cora Jane Baxter, Aug. 13, 1946 (dec. Feb. 1971); children: Anne Baxter, Gregory Baxter, Julia Cushing; m. Barbara Louise Lehan, Aug. 26, 1972. Student, Ohio State U., 1942-44, Miami U., Oxford, Ohio, 1944; MD, Cornell U. Med. Coll., N.Y.C., 1948; ScD (hon.), Thomas Jefferson U., 1973, Tufts U., 1982, Morehouse Sch. Medicine, 1985, Mt. Sinai Sch. Medicine, 1986; LHD (hon.), Rush U., 1985; LLD (hon.), U. Pa., 1985; ScD (hon.), Albany Med. Coll., 1990, U. So. Calif., 1993; DSc, U. Pa., 1994. Intern Johns Hopkins Hosp., 1948-49, asst. resident, 1949-50; USPHS postdoctoral fellow div. infectious disease N.Y. Hosp., N.Y.C., 1950-51; chief resident in medicine N.Y. Hosp., 1951-52, attending physician, 1974-94; pres. The Robert Wood Johnson Found., Princeton, N.J., 1972-86; Walsh McDermott Univ. prof. medicine Med. Coll. Cornell U., N.Y.C., 1986-94; sr. advisor The N.Y. Acad. of Medicine, 1990-94; vis. investigator Rockefeller Inst. Med. Research, N.Y.C., 1954-55; Lowell M. Palmer Sr. fellow in medicine Rockefeller Inst. Med. Research and Cornell U. Med. Coll., 1955-57, asst. prof., 1954-56, chief div. infectious diseases, 1955-59; assoc. prof. Cornell U. Med. Coll., 1956-59; prof., chmn. dept. medicine Vanderbilt U., 1959-68; physician-in-chief Vanderbilt U. Hosp., 1959-68; prof., dean med. faculty Sch. Medicine, Johns Hopkins; v.p. univ., med. dir. Johns Hopkins Hosp., 1968-71; Cons. Surgeon Gen., 1958-68, HEW, 1969-72; chmn. sect. Streptococcal-Staphylococcal Disease Commn. Armed Forces Epidemiol. Bd., 1958-69; mem. sci. adv. bd. Mead Johnson Research Center, Evansville, Ind., 1961-68; mem. med. adv. bd. Nat. Bd. Med. Examiners, 1961-64; mem. Tenn. adv. com. U.S. Commn. Civil Rights, 1962-64; mem. adv. com. survey of research and edn. VA-NRC, 1966-68; chmn. nat. sci. adv. council Nat. Jewish Hosp. and Research Center, Denver, 1971-73; mem. sci. adv. bd. Scripps Clinic and Research Found., La Jolla, Cal., 1972-74; vice-chair Nat. Commn. on AIDS, 1989-93; vis. prof. numerous univs. Author: American Medicine: Challenge for the 1980s; mem. editorial bd. Clin. Rsch., 1958-61, Medicine, 1962; editor: Year Book of Medicine, 1966-93. Bd. visitors Charles R. Drew Postgrad. Med. Sch., 1971-94. Served to lt. (s.g.) M.C. USNR, 1952-54. Recipient John Metcalf Polk prize, Alfred Moritz Michaelis prize Cornell U. Med. Sch., 1948; Distinguished Service award Nashville Jr. C. of C., 1960; One of Ten Outstanding Young Men of Year award U.S. Jr. C. of C., 1961; Centennial Achievement award Ohio State U., 1970; award of distinction Cornell Alumni Assn., 1976, John W. Gardner Leadership award, 1991, Disting. Svc. award Hosp. Assn. N.Y. State, 1991, Special Recognition award Am. Coll. Preventive Med., 1993, award City of Medicine, 1993, The John Stearns award for Lifetime Achievement in Medicine, 1994; decorated Royal Order of Cedar Govt. Lebanon, 1972. Master ACP; fellow AAAS, Johns Hopkins Soc. Scholars; mem. AAUP, Am. Fedn. Clin. Rsch., Am. Soc. Clin. Investigation, Assn. Am. Physicians (pres. 1974-75), Assn. Profs. Medicine (sec.-treas. 1965-67), So. Soc. Clin. Rsch., Infectious Disease Soc. Am. (charter), Am. Clin. and Climatol. Assn., Interurban Clin. Club, Coun. Fgn. Rels., Assn. Am. Med. Colls. (Disting. Svc. award, Flexner award 1986), Inst. Medicine (Gustav O. Lienhard award 1993), Cosmos Club, Century Assn., Alpha Omega Alpha. Home: Princeton N.J. Died Dec. 5, 1994.

ROGERS, FRANCES ARLENE, biology educator; b. Northfield, Minn., Jan. 24, 1923; d. Charles James and Mary Gertrude (Still) Ritchey; m. Rodney A. Rogers, July 1, 1956; children: Robert Allen, William David. BA, Drake U., 1944; MS, U. Chgo., 1946; PhD, U. Iowa, 1953. Instr. biology Earlham Coll., Richmond, Ind., 1946-49, U. Iowa, Iowa City, 1951-53; asst. prof. Cornell Coll., Mt. Vernon, Iowa, 1954, Shimer Coll., Mt. Carroll, Ill., 1955-56; lectr. and acting asst. prof. Drake U., Des Moines, 1956-69, asst. prof. to prof., 1969-92; mem. Sci. Educator's Tour of sch./univs. in Europe and Russia, Iowa Acad. Sci., 1972. Author: Outline Text of Comparative Anatomy, 1983. Bd. dirs. Calvin Retirement Community, Des Moines, 1988-92, sec., 1990-92; judge oral presentations Hawkeye Sci. Fair, Iowa, 1969-90. Recipient sci. faculty profl. devel. grant, NSF, 1977-78. Mem. Assn. Midwest Coll. Biology Tchrs., Iowa Acad. Sci., Sigma Xi, Delta Kappa Gamma, Phi Beta Kappa (pres. 1981-82, sec. 1987-92 Gamma of Iowa chpt.), Mortar Bd. Democrat. Presbyterian. Home: Des Moines Iowa Died Nov. 12, 1992.

ROGERS, GINGER (VIRGINIA KATHERINE MCMATH), dancer, actress; b. Independence, Mo., July 16, 1911; d. William Eddins and Lela Emogene (Owens) McMath; m. Edward Jackson Culpepper, 1929 (div. 1931); m. Lew Ayres, 1934 (div. 1941); m. Jack Briggs, 1943 (div. 1949); m. Jacques Bergerac, 1953 (div. 1957); m. G. William Marshall, 1961 (div. 1972). Ed. pub. schs. Began as a child dancer, 1926; stage debut in Ginger and Her Redheads, 1925; vaudeville appearances include The Original John Held Jr. Girl, 1926, Ginger and Pepper, 1928-31; stage appearances include Top Speed, 1929, Girl Crazy, 1930, Love and Let Love, 1951, The Pink Jungle, 1959, More Perfect Union, 1963, Hello, Dolly!, 1965, Our Town, 1972; appeared in motion pictures, 1930—; starred in Young Man of Manhattan, 1930, Queen High, 1930, The Sap From Syracuse, 1930, Follow the Leader, 1930, Honor Among Lovers, 1931, The Tip-Off, 1931, Suicide Fleet, 1931, Carnival Boat, 1932, The Tenderfoot, 1932, The Thirteenth Guest, 1932, Hat Check Girl, 1932, You Said a Mouthful, 1932, Forty Second Street, 1933, Broadway Bad, 1933, Gold Diggers of 1933, 1933, Professional Sweetheart, 1933, A Shreik in the Night, 1933, Don't Bet on love, 1933, Sitting Pretty, 1933, Flying Down to Rio, 1933, Chance at Heaven, 1933, Rafter Romance, 1934, Finishing School, 1934, Twenty Million Sweethearts, 1934, Change of Heart, 1934, Upperworld, 1934, The Gay Divorcee, 1934, Romance in Manhattan, 1934, Roberta, 1935, Star of Midnight, 1935, Top Hat, 1935, In Person, 1935, Follow the Fleet, 1936, Swing Time, 1936, Shall We Dance, 1937, Stage Door, 1937, Having a Wonderful Time, 1938, Vivacious Lady, 1938, Carefree, 1938, The Story of Vernon and Irene Castle, 1939, Bachelor Mother, 1939, Fifth Avenue Girl, 1939, Primrose Path, 1940, Lucky Partners, 1940, Kitty Foyle, 1940 (Academy award best actress 1940), Tom, Dick and Harry, 1941, Roxie Hart, 1942, Tales of Manhattan, 1942, The Major and the Minor, 1942, Once Upon a Honeymoon, 1942, Tender Comrade, 1943, Lady in the Dark, 1944, I'll Be Seeing You, 1944, Weekend at the Waldorf, 1945, Heartbeat, 1946, Magnificent Doll, 1946, It Had to Be You, 1947, The Barkleys of Broadway, 1949, Perfect Strangers, 1950, Storm Warning, 1950, The Groom Wore Spurs, 1951, We're Not Married, 1952, Monkey Business, 1952, Dreamboat, 1952, Forever Female, 1953, Black Widow, 1954, Beautiful Stranger, 1954, Tight Spot, 1955, The First Travelling Saleslady, 1956, Teenage Rebel, 1956, Oh, Men! Oh, Women!, 1957, The Confession, 1964, Harlow, 1965, That's Entertainment!, 1974, That's Dancing!, 1984; TV appearances include (episodic) Dick Powell's Zane Gray Theatre, 1958, The DuPont Show with June Allyson, 1960, Ginger Rogers Show, 1961, The Red Skelton Show, 1962, Ed Sullivan Show, Perry Como Show, Bob Hope Show; (specials) The Ginger Rogers Special, 1958, Carissima, 1959, Bob Hope's Potomac Madness, 1960, The Songs of Irving Berlin, 1962, Rodgers and Hammerstein's Cinderella, 1965; dir. play Babes in Arms, 1987; author: Ginger, 1991. Recipient Kennedy Ctr. Honors, 1992. Home: Medford Oreg. Died Apr. 24, 1995.

ROGERS, HOWARD GARDNER, consultant, photographic company research director emeritus; b. Houghton, Mich., June 21, 1915; s. Gardner and Grace (Phillips) R.; m. Erdna M. Reggio, Jan. 17, 1940; children—Anne Cranford, Peter Nicholas, Mary Phillips Rogers Helmreich, Mark Howard, Lucinda Gardner. Student, Harvard Coll., 1933-35. With Polaroid Corp., Cambridge, Mass., 1936-85; dept. mgr. spl. color photographic research Polaroid Corp., 1954-74, v.p., sr. research fellow, 1976-78, sr. v.p., assoc. dir. research, 1978-80, sr. v.p., dir. research, 1980-85; cons. on photog. systems., light polarizers, 3-D imaging, new polymers. Inventor of instant color photographic systems, dye developers, new light-polarizers and other optical devices. Recipient Wetherill medal Franklin Inst., 1966, Edwin H. Land medal Optical Soc. Am./Soc. for Imaging Sci. and Tech., 1993. Fellow Am. Acad. Arts and Scis., Optical Soc. Am., Soc. for Imaging Sci. and Tech. (hon.), Photographic Hist. Soc. N.E. (hon.), Am. Inst. Chemists; mem. Indsl. Rsch. Inst. (Achievement award 1987). Home: Weston Mass. Died July 29, 1995.

ROGOVIN, MITCHELL, retired lawyer; b. N.Y.C., Dec. 3, 1930; s. Max Shea and Sayde (Epstein) R.; m. Sheila Ann Ender, Jan, 31, 1954; children: Lisa Shea, Wendy Meryl, John Andrew. AB, Syracuse U., 1951; LLB, U. Va., 1954; LLM, Georgetown U., 1959. Bar: Va. 1953, D.C. 1968, N.Y., 1990, U.S. Tax Ct., U.S. Ct. Appeals (1st, 2d, 4th, 5th, 9th, D.C. and fed. cirs.), U.S. Supreme Ct. Chief counsel IRS, Washington, 1964-66; asst. atty. gen. U.S. Dept. Justice, Washington, 1966-69; ptnr. Arnold & Porter, Washington, 1968-76, Rogovin, Huge & Schiller, Washington, 1976-90, Donovan, Leisure, Rogovin, Washington, 1990-95; ret., 1995; spl. counsel CIA, 1975-76, U.S. Civil Svc. Commn., 1980-82; dir. nuclear regulation com. spl. inquiry into Three Mile Island accident NRC, 1979-80; bd. dirs. United So. Assurance Co., Med. Rsch. Legal Def. Fund. Bd. Echo Hill Outdoor Sch.; gen. counsel John Anderson Presdl. Campaign, 1980. Capt. USMC, 1954-58. Mem. Ctr. for

Law and Social Policy (chmn. bd. dirs.), Council on Fgn. Relations, The Wilderness Soc. (governing bd.). Home: Washington D.C. Died Feb. 7, 1996.

ROHRBACK, ROBERT LEE, JR., lawyer; b. Washington, Nov. 17, 1924; s. Robert Lee and Theresa Martha (Morrow) R.; m. Eileen Lenore Reese, Aug. 28, 1948; children: Steven, Karen, Christine, Eric, Kathleen. BSEE, U. Maryland, 1949; JD, Georgetown U., 1952. Bar: Ill. 1958, U.S. Ct. Appeals (7th cir.) Calif. 1953, U.S. Ct. Appeals (fed. cit.) Calif. 1982, U.S. Supreme Ct. 1960. Patent engr. Western Electric Co,, Washington, 1949-50; patent solicitor U.S. Dept. Navy, Washington, 1950-52; patent atty., ptnr. Mason, Kolehmainen, Rathburn & Wyss., Chgo., 1952-87; pvt. practice Mt. Prospect, Ill., 1987-95. Patentee in field. Chmn. bd. trustee, Methodist Ch., Des Plaines, Ill. 1959; pres. Men's Club Methodist Ch., Des Plaines, 1963; precinct capt. Republican Party, Mt. Prospect , Ill. 1964-68. Lt. JG U.S. Navy, 1942-46, 1949-52. Mem. ABA (IPL section, numerous chairs), Optimist Club (pres.),. Home: Barrington Ill. Died Mar. 30, 1995.

ROHRLICH, GEORGE FRIEDRICH, retired social economist; b. Vienna, Austria, Jan. 6, 1914; came to the U.S., 1938; s. Egon Ephraim and Rosa (Tenzer) R.; m. Laura Ticho, Feb. 3, 1946; children: Susannah Ticho Feldman, David Ephraim, Daniel Mosheh. D in Legal Scis., U. Vienna, Austria, 1937, Gold Dr.'s Diploma Law, 1987; PhD (univ. refugee scholar), Harvard U., 1943. Diplomate Consular Acad. Vienna, 1938. Social economist sect. public health and welfare Supreme Comdr. Allied Powers, Tokyo, 1947-50; socioecon. program analyst and developer U.S. Govtl. Policies, 1950-59; sr. staff mem. social security div. ILO, Geneva, 1959-64; vis. prof. social econs. and policy U. Chgo., 1964-67; prof. econs. and social policy Temple U., 1967-81, prof. emeritus, 1981-95; dir. econs. and bus. programs Temple U. Japan, Tokyo, 1987-88; founder, past bd. dirs. Inst. Social Econs. and Policy Rsch.; sr. lectr. Sch. Social Work, Columbia U., 1968-69; dir. rsch. P.R. Commn. Integral Social Security System, San Juan, 1975-76; cons. in field; lectr. USIA, Brazil, 1984; co-dir., Keynoter Nat. Conf. Community Dimensions of Econ. Enterprise, 1984; ILO cons. Govt. Mauritius, 1985. Author: Social Economics—Concepts and Perspectives, 1974; others; editor books, the most recent being: Checks and Balances in Social Security, 1986, Environmental Management: Economic and Social Dimensions, 1976; contbr. articles to profl. publs.; assoc. editor Rev. of Social Economy; editorial adv. bd. Internat. Jour. Social Econs., U.K. Former mem. bd. dirs. Health and Welfare Coun. Greater Phila. Recipient festschrifts Internat. Jour. Social Econs., vol. 10, no. 6/7, 1983, vol. 11, nos. 1/2 and 3/4, 1984; Brookings rsch. tng. fellow, 1941-42; Ford Found. travel grantee, 1966; Fulbright rsch. scholar N.Z., 1980. Mem. AAAS, Assn. Social Econs. (pres. 1978-79, disting. mem. 1983, disting. scholar-Divine award 1989), Am. Econ. Assn., Indsl. Rels. Rsch. Assn. (charter), Internat. Soc. Labor Law and Social Security, Am. Risk and Ins. Assn., Nat. Acad. Social Ins. (elected), Harvard Club of Phila. Democrat. Jewish. Home: Cheltenham Pa. Died Aug. 21, 1995.

ROLLER, DUANE HENRY DUBOSE, historian of science, educator; b. Eagle Pass, Tex., Mar. 14, 1920; s. Duane Emerson and Doris Della (DuBose) R.; m. Marjorie Fair Williamson, Mar. 15, 1942; 1 son, Duane Williamson. A.B. in History of Sci, Columbia, 1941; M.S. in Physics, Purdue U., 1949; Ph.D. in History of Sci. and Learning, Harvard, 1954. Research and teaching asst. physics Purdue U., 1946-49; vis. fellow gen. edn. Harvard U., 1949-50, teaching fellow gen. edn., 1951-54; asst. prof. history of sci., curator DeGolyer Collection U. Okla., Norman, 1954-58, curator History Sci. Collections, 1958-91, curator emeritus, 1991-94, assoc. prof., 1958-62, McCasland prof. history sci., 1962-90, McCasland prof. emeritus, 1990-94, David Ross Boyd prof. history of sci., 1981-90, David Ross Boyd prof. emeritus, 1990-94, asst. dir. spl. collections univ. librs., 1971-78; bd. dirs. U. Okla. Research Inst., 1957-61, v.p., 1967; research assoc. Am. Sch. Classical Studies, Athens, 1970-71, 77-78; Sigma Xi nat. lectr., 1977-79, AAAS/NSF Chautauqua lectr., 1978-82; Chmn. U.S. Nat. Com. History and Philosophy Sci., 1964-65. Author: The De Magnete of William Gilbert, 1959, A Short-title Catalog of the James G. Harlow Collection, 1983, Short-Title Catalog of the History of Science Collections, 1986, Chronological Short-Title Catalog of the History of Science Collections, 1989; Co-author: Foundations of Modern Physical Science, 1959, The Development of the Concept of Electric Charge, 1954, A Checklist of the E. DeGolyer Collection in the History of Science and Technology, 1954, The Catalogue of the History of Science Collections of the University of Oklahoma Libraries, 2 vols, 1976; Editor: Landmarks of Science, 1967-94, Perspectives in the History of Science and Technology, 1971. Lt. comdr. USNR, World War II. Recipient Disting. Service citation U. Okla., 1980; NSF Sr. postdoctoral fellow, 1961-62. Fellow AAAS, Okla. Acad. Sci.; mem. Internat. Acad. History of Sci. (corr.), History of Sci. Soc., Midwest Junto (pres. 1960-61), AAUP, Phi Beta Kappa, Sigma Xi. Home: Norman Okla. Died Aug. 22, 1994; cremated.

ROLLINS, O. WAYNE, diversified services company executive. Chmn., chief exec. officer, dir., Rollins, Inc., Atlanta. Deceased. Home: Atlanta Ga.

ROMANO, JOHN, psychiatrist; b. Milw., Nov. 20, 1908; s. Nicholas Vincent and Frances Louise (Notari) R.; m. Miriam Modesitt, May 13, 1933 (dec. 1989); 1 child, David Gilman. BS, Marquette U., 1932, MD, 1934; DSc (hon.), Med. Coll. Wis., 1971, Hahnemann Med. Coll., 1974, U. Cin., 1979. Diplomate Am. Bd. Psychiatry and Neurology. Asst. biochemistry Marquette U. Sch. Medicine, 1929-30; extern psychiatry Milw. County Asylum for Mental Diseases, 1932-33; intern medicine Milw. County Hosp., 1933-34; asst. psychiatry Yale Sch. Medicine, 1934-35; intern, asst. resident psychiatry New Haven Hosp., 1934-35; Commonwealth Fund fellow psychiatry U. Colo., 1935-38; asst. psychiatrist Colo. Psychopathic Hosp., Denver, 1935-38; fellow neurology Boston City Hosp., 1938-39; Rockefeller fellow neurology Harvard Med. Sch., 1938-39, asst. medicine, 1939-40, instr. medicine, 1940-42; asso. medicine Peter Bent Brigham Hosp., 1939-42; Sigmund Freud fellow psychoanalysis Boston Psychoanalytic Soc., 1939-42; dir. dept. psychiatry Cin. Gen. Hosp., 1942-46; prof. psychiatry U. Cin. Coll. Medicine, 1942-46; psychiatrist in chief Strong Meml. Hosp., Rochester, 1946-71; prof. psychiatry, chmn. dept. U. Rochester Sch. Medicine, 1946-71, distinguished univ. prof. psychiatry, 1968-79, disting. univ. prof. emeritus, 1979-94; lectr. in field; vis. prof. U. Toronto, Ont., Can., 1972; physician-in-residence U.S. Va., 1975-79; qualified psychiatrist N.Y. State Dept. Mental Hygiene, 1954-94: nat. adv. mental health coun. USPHS, chmn. mental health career investigator selection com., 1956-61; chmn. adv. com. human growth and emotion devel. Social Sci. Rsch. Found., 1953; mem. bd. health sci. policy Inst. Medicine, Nat. Acad. Sci., 1985; mem. sci. coun. Nat. Alliance Rsch. on Schizophrenia and Depression, 1985-89 and others. Mem. editorial bd. Jour. Psychiatric Rsch., 1961-78, Schizophrenia Bull, 1971-94; mem. panel of editors: Year Book of Psychiatry and Applied Mental Health, 1972-84; sr. editor The Merck Manual, 15th edit., 1987; contbr. articles to profl. jours. Served as vis. neuropsychiat. cons. 8th Service Command AUS, 1943-44; cons. psychiatry AUS, 1945, ETO. Commonwealth Fund adv. fellow European study, 1959-60; recipient William J. Kerr Lecture award U. Calif., San Francisco, 1972, William C. Menninger Meml. award A.C.P., 1973, Disting. Profl. Achievement award Genesee Valley Psychol. Assn., 1975, Disting. Svc. award Am. Coll. of Psychiatrists, 1987, Sigmund Freud award Am. Assn. Psychoanalytic Physicians, Erik Stromgren medal Aarhus, Denmark, 1981; John Romano Community Residence dedication, Rochester Psychiatric Ctr., 1987. Fellow Acad. Arts and Scis., Royal Coll. Psychiatrists (hon.); mem. Inst. Medicine of NAS (sr.), Assn. Rsch. in Nervous and Mental Disease (1st v.p. 1955), Am. Psychiat. Assn. (Psychiatrist of Yr. Area II award 1976, Disting. Svc. award 1979, Spl. Presdl. Commendation 1994), Physicians for Social Responsibility (adv. bd. Rochester chpt. 1985-94), Am. League Against Epilepsy, Am. Soc. Research Psychosomatic Problems, Nat. Com. Mental Hygiene, Am. Neurol. Assn., AAAS, Am. Soc. Clin. Investigation, Monroe County Soc. Mental Hygiene (dir.), N.Y. Acad. Medicine (Salmon com. on psychiatry and medicine 1970-89, Salmon medal 1984), Phi Beta Kappa (v.p. Iota chpt. 1983-85), Sigma Xi, Alpha Omega Alpha. Unitarian. Clubs: Cosmos (Washington); Fortnightly. Home: Rochester N.Y. Died June 19, 1994.

ROME, HAROLD JACOB, composer; b. Hartford, Conn., May 27, 1908; s. Louis and Ida (Aronson) R.; m. Florence Miles, Feb. 3, 1939; children: Joshua, Rachel. B.A., Yale U., 1929, student Law Sch., 1928-30; B.F.A., Sch. Architecture, 1934. Composer, lyricist: Pins and Needles, produced by Labor Stage, 1937, 39; revue Sing Out the News, produced by Max Gordon, 1938; musical comedy The Little Dog Laughed, produced by Eddie Dowling, 1940; score of Lunch Time Follies; spl. material for Star and Garter (produced by Michael Todd), Ziegfeld Follies, 1943; music and lyrics for Stars and Gripes Army Show produced by Spl. Service Office, Ft. Hamilton and U.S. Army, Call Me Mister, produced by Melvyn Douglas and Herman Levin, 1946; also popular songs Sunday in the Park, All of a Sudden My Heart Sings; and piano suite Opus New York; spl. material for Peep Show, produced by Michael Todd, 1950; music and lyrics for Bless You All, 1950, Wish You Were Here (Logan and Hayward producers), 1952, Fanny (Logan and Merrick producers), 1954, Sing Song Man; children's album And Then I Wrote; music and lyrics Destry (David Merrick and Max Brown producers), 1959; albums Destry Rides Again, 1959, also I Can Get It for You Wholesale, 1962; music and lyrics for The Zulu and The Zayda, 1965, Scarlett, 1970; mus. adaptation of Gone With the Wind, Imperial Theatre, Tokyo, 1970, Drury Lane Theatre, London, 1972, Los Angeles Civic Light Opera, 1973; one man show paintings and songs, Marble Arch Gallery, N.Y.C., 1964, paintings, Bodley Gallery, N.Y.C., 1970. Served with AUS, 1943-45. Recipient Richard Rodgers award ASCAP, 1985, Golden Circle award ASCAP, 1990, Drama Desk award, 1991; named to Songwriters Hall of Fame, 1982, Theatre Hall of Fame, 1992. Mem. Dramatists Guild, AFTRA, ASCAP Golden Circle, Am. Guild Authors and Composers, Composers and Lyricists Guild Am., Yale Club. Democrat. Hom New York N.Y. Died Aug. 26, 1993; interred Westc ester Hills, N.Y.

ROMUALDI, JAMES PHILIP, engineering educatc b. N.Y.C., June 30, 1929; s. Serafino Romualdi and Je (Pesci) Reed; m. Daina M. Mucinieks, June 5, 195 children: Jean Renee and Jessica Anne (twins), Joh Philip. BSCE, Carnegie Inst. Tech., 1951, MSCE, 195 PhD, 1954. Cert. engr., Pa. Engr. Richardson Gord and Assos., summer 1955; rsch. engr. USN Rsch. La summer 1956; from asst. prof to prof. Carnegie Ins Tech., 1955-64, prof. civil engring., 1964-94; pri D'Appolonia Assocs., Pitts., 1958-66; ptnr. GAI Con Inc. (cons. engrs.), Pitts., 1966-81; pres. Romual Davidson & Assocs., Pitts., 1981-94; dir. Transp. Rsc Inst. Carnegie Mellon U., Pitts., 1966-79. Contbr. a ticles to profl. jours.; patentee in field. Fulbright fello Technische Hochschule Karlsruhe, 1954-55. Me ASCE (Young Civil Engr. of Year award Pitts. sec 1968), NSPE, Am. Concrete Inst., Am. Soc. Engrin Educators, Pitts. Athletic Club. Democrat. Hom Pittsburgh Pa. Died Mar. 10, 1994.

ROOSA, ROBERT VINCENT, banker; b. Marquett Mich., June 21, 1918; s. Harvey Mapes and Ru Elizabeth (Lagerquist) Rosa; m. Ruth Grace Amend Mar. 16, 1946; children: Meredith Ann Roosa I derfurth, Alison Ruth Roosa Cluff. A.B., U. Mic 1939, M.A., 1940, Ph.D., 1942, D.Sc. in Bus. A minstrn., 1962; LL.D., Wesleyan U., 1963, Williar Coll., 1974. Tchr. econs. U. Mich., Harvard, Ma Inst. Tech., 1939-43; with Fed. Res. Bank N.Y., 194 60, asst. v.p. research dept., 1953-54, asst. v.p. securiti dept., 1954-56, v.p. research dept., 1956-60; under se for monetary affairs U.S. Treasury, 1961-64; ptr Brown Bros. Harriman & Co., N.Y.C., 1965-93; a visory com. Internat. Finance Corp.; dir. Am. Expre Co., Am. Express Internat. Banking Corp., Owen Corning Fiberglas Corp., Texaco, Inc.; chmn. N. Stock Exchange Advisory Com.; Internat. Capi Market. Author: Federal Reserve Operations in t Money and Government Securities Market, 195 Monetary Reform for the World Economy, 1965, T Dollar and World Liquidity, 1967, (with Milt Friedman) The Balance of Payments; Free Versus Fix Exchange Rates, 1967; Editor: Money, Trade a Economic Growth, 1951. Bd. dirs. Nat. Bur. Eco Research; former vice chmn., trustee Rockefel Found.; chmn. Brookings Instn.; trustee Sloan Ketteri Inst. Cancer Research. Served with AUS, 1943-46 Rhodes scholar Magdalen Coll., 1939. Mem. Coun Fgn. Relations, Conf. Bus. Economists, Am. Eco Assn., Am. Finance Assn. (pres. 1967), UN Assn. (b govs. policy studies), Royal Econ. Soc., Am. Acad. A and Scis., Am. Philos. Soc., Phi Beta Kappa. Clu Harvard, Economic (pres. 1970-71), Links, Pilgrims U.S. (N.Y.C.); Century Association, Cosmos (Was ington); Manursing Island, Apawamis (Westches County). Home: Harrison N.Y. Died Dec. 23, 1993.

ROOT, OREN, lawyer; b. N.Y.C., June 13, 1911; Oren and Aida (de Acosta) R.; m. Daphne Skour Feb. 15, 1947; 4 children. A.B., Princeton U., 19 LL.B., U. Va., 1936; LL.D. (hon.), St. Michael's Co 1963. Bar: N.Y. 1938. Mem. Root, Barrett, Coh Knapp & Smith (and predecessor firms), until 1965; counsel Barrett Smith Schapiro & Simon, 1972-88, Lo Day & Lord, Barrett Smith, 1988-95; counsel Irvi Trust Co., N.Y.C., 1965-72; pres., dir. Charter N. Corp., 1965-70, chmn. bd. dirs., 1970-72; supt. of ban State of N.Y., 1961-64. Author: Persons and Persu sions, 1974; contbr.: periodicals including Sat. Re N.Y. Times Mag. Pres., Nat. Assn. Mental Heal Inc., 1950-52; chmn. Joint Legislature Com. Narcot Study, N.Y., 1956-58; mem. N.Y. Job Devel. Authori 1962-64; spl. asst. to gov. N.Y., 1959-60; chmn. A sociated Willkie Clubs Am., 1940; mem. panel ar trators Am. Arbitration Assn., 1991-95. Lt. com USNR, 1941-45; staff comdr. Fourth Fleet 1942-4 participated in Normandy landings on staff comdr. Ta Force 122 1944. Decorated Croix de Guerre (Franc Cruziero do Sul (Brazil). Mem. N.Y.C. Bar Assn., Na League of U.S., Theodore Roosevelt Assn., Delta P Phi Delta Phi. Republican. Roman Catholic. Hon Bedford N.Y. Died Jan. 14, 1995.

ROPER, SIR CLINTON MARCUS, chief justice the Cook Islands; b. Christchurch, New Zealand, Ju 19, 1921; s. Wilfred Marcus; m. Joan Elsa Turnbull; children. Student, Canterbury U.; LLB, Victoria U Crown solicitor High Ct. New Zealand, Christchurc 1961-68, judge, 1968-85; judge Ct. Appeals, Fiji, 198 87; judge High Ct. Cook Islands, 1985-88, chief justi 1988-94; judge Privy Coun. Ct., Tonga, 1986-90, Appeal, Tonga, 1990-94; chmn. prisons parole b 1970-85, com. inquiry into violence, 1985-87, pris review com., 1987-89. Served New Zealand Arm Forces, 1939-45, World War II. Home: Christchur New Zealand Died Mar. 6, 1994.

ROSBE, WILLIAM LOUIS, lawyer; b. Evanston, I Feb. 17, 1944; s. Robert L. and Margaret H. (Black) 1 child, Kimberly. BA, Yale U., 1966; JD, Cornell 1975. Bar: Va. 1975, U.S. Ct. Appeals (4th cir.) 19 U.S. Supreme Ct. 1979, U.S. Ct. Appeals (D.C. c 1980, D.C. 1981. Ptnr. Hunton & Williams, Richmo Va., 1975—. Asst. gen. coun. Robert E. Lee coun. B

:outs Am., Richmond, Va. Col. USMCR, 1988. lem. ABA (vice chmn. electric power commn. natural sources sect. 1981-87), Va. State Bar (chmn. environ. w sect. 1984-85), Va. Bar Assn., Richmond Bar Assn. ome: Richmond Va. Died Jan. 21, 1995.

OSELLE, RICHARD DONALDSON, industrial, arine and interior designer; b. Garwood, N.J., Nov.), 1916; s. Ernest North and Mary Elizabeth (Donaldon) R.; m. Eunice Calpin, June 28, 1947 (div. Oct. 981); children: Sheryn, Christina, Gail; m. Judith Marie shop, Nov. 13, 1982. Student, St. John's Mil. Acad., 935, Aurora (Ill.) Coll., 1935-37, Bucknell U., 1937-39. Exec. trainee J.J. Newberry Co., N.Y.C., 1939-41, G. ox & Co., Hartford, Conn., 1941-42; materials exeditor Pratt & Whitney Aircraft, Hartford, 1942-43; ec. trainee, indsl. engr. TWA Airline, N.Y.C. and ansas City, 1943-47; with employee rels. staff R.H. lacy, N.Y.C., 1947-49; asst. tng. dir. J.C. Penney Co., .Y.C., 1949-50; owner Roselle Tile Mfr., Seattle, 1950-5; sr. indsl. designer Walter Dorwin Teague Assocs., eattle, 1956-63; owner Roselle Design Internat., Inc., eattle, from 1963; dir. Roselle Design Tours Internat., eattle, 1967-93; internat. bus. developer via confs., from 993. Mem. Am. Soc. Interior Design (nat. edn. chair 972-74), Indsl. Designers Soc. Am. (charter), Internat. ist. Profl. Designers, Master Resources Coun. Internat. ounder, pres.), Soc. Am. Mil. Engrs., Rotary. Republican. Episcopalian. Home: Bellevue Wash. Deceased.

OSENBERG, DENNIS MELVILLE LEO, retired urgeon; b. Johannesburg, South Africa, Jan. 27, 1921; ame to U.S., 1946, naturalized, 1953; s. Nathan and orothy (Lee) R.; m. Jeanna Van der Kar, Jan., 947. BSc with honors, U. Witwatersrand, South frica, 1941, MB, Bch., 1945. Intern Johannesburg en. Hosp., 1946; resident in surgery Tulane U. Ochner Found. Hosp., 1947-51, Children's Hosp., Johanesburg, 1952; asst. thoracic surgeon Biggs Hosp., thaca, N.Y., 1953-54; practice medicine specializing in ardiovascular and thoracic surgery New Orleans, 1955-; sr. surgeon Touro Infirmary, New Orleans, 1955-93; hief dept. cardiovascular and thoracic surgery Touro nfirmary, 1972-85; asst. surgeon Dept. Surgery Tulane ., New Orleans, 1946-50, instr. surgery, instr. thoracic urgery, 1950-57, from asst. prof. to prof., 1957-91, prof. urgery emeritus, 1991—; cons. surgeon Charity Hosp., ew Orleans, 1962-90. With M.C., South African rmy, 1940-45. Fellow ACS; mem. AMA, Am. Coll. hest Physicians, Am. Coll. Cardiology, Am. Heart ssn., Am. Assn. Thoracic Surgery, So. Thoracic Surg. ssn., Internat. Cardiovascular Soc., Am. Thoracic Soc., oc. Thoracic Surgeons, Soc. Vascular Surgery, Internat. oc. Surgery, Royal Soc. Medicine, So. Assn. Vascular urgery. Home: New Orleans La. Died June 15, 1994.

OSENBERG, LEONARD HERMAN, insurance onsultant, retired insurance executive; b. Balt., Dec. 1, 912; s. Henry I. and Laura (Hollander) R.; B.S., arnegie Inst. Tech., 1934; grad. Command and Gen. taff Sch.; m. Edna Mazer, Nov. 20, 1936; children—Theodore M., Victor L., Laurie H., Leonard H. Vith Strasco Ins. Agy., Balt., 1935-82, successively alesman, underwriter, gen. mgr., v.p. fin., 1948-82; dist. gr. Reliance Life Ins. Co., Pitts., 1935-39; state agt. olumbus Mut. Life Ins. Co., 1939-55; founder, pres. hesapeake Life Ins. Co., Balt., 1956-73, chmn. bd., 973-82; v.p. Chesapeake Investment Corp., 1963-68, res., 1968-74; pres. Preferred Equity Ins. Co. Denver, 968-70, chmn. bd., 1970-71; v.p. Chesapeake Fund, 963-68, pres., 1968-74; dir. John L. Deaton Med. ursing Center, Inc., 1968-79, Charles Light Parking, ic., 1968-79, Bayshore Industries, Inc. (Md.), 1949-61; r., mem. exec. com., chmn. fin. com. Nat. City Bank ld., 1967-70; now internat. mgmt. and mktg. cons. to fe ins. industry. Instr. math., physics Night Sch., Balt. ity Coll., 1935-39; instr. civilian pilot tng. program ohns Hopkins U., 1939-42. Commr., Md. Traffic Safety ommn., 1957-67; mem. Gov.'s Commn. to Revise Md. is. Laws, 1960; commr. Md. Pub. Broadcasting ommn., 1967-71, chmn., 1971-87; mem. curricula com. alt. Jr. Coll., 1966-77; mem. Pres. Johnson's Spl. Adv. ouncil for Vocational Edn., 1967-68, Pres.'s Fed. nancial Aid to Higher Edn. Com., 1969-70; pres. Balt. ommunity Concert Assn., 1955-56; chmn. Balt. Adv. ouncil on Vocational Edn., 1970-80; mem. Md. Adv. ouncil on Vocational Edn., 1970-74; mem. Nat. Adv. ommn. on Flammable Fabrics, 1970-73; mem. Md. ommn. to Study Structure and Governance of Edn., 972-73, chmn., 1973-76; asst. sec., dir. Md. Life & ealth Ins. Guaranty Assn., 1972-83; dir. Nat. Asso. fe Cos., 1965-84, pres., 1968-70. Mem. steering com. at. Inst. for Career Edn., 1976-77; bd. advs. Humanies Inst., Inc., 1979-84; trustee Carnegie-Mellon U., 964-70, Sears Scholarship, U. Md., Tau Delta Phi ound., Community Coll. Balt., 1976-84; bd. dirs. Ins. all of Fame; bd. dir., bd. govs. Internat. Ins. Seminars; l. govs. Pub. Broadcasting Service, 1972-77, chmn. vel. com., 1974-77. Served from 2d lt. to capt. SAAF, 1942-45; lt. col. Res., ret. Recipient Outnding Alumni award Carnegie-Mellon U., 1967; Wilm P. White award for outstanding service to the ins. dustry, 1967; Outstanding Alumni award Tau Delta i, 1967. Mem. Inst. Aero. Sci., Inst. Nav., Nat. Assn. fe Cos. (pres. 1968-70). Jewish. Contbr. articles to ins. urs. Lectr. in field. Home: Baltimore Md.

ROSENBERGER, DONALD MARKLEY, hospital consultant; b. Norristown, Pa., Jan. 30, 1913; s. Daniel H. and Jennie K. (Markley) R.; m. Helen Louise Leonardson, June 17, 1941; 1 child, Jane L. A.B., Oberlin Coll., 1934; postgrad., Coll. William and Mary, 1936-37. Adminstrv. intern Pa. Hosp., Phila., 1937-38; adminstrv. asst. Asso. Hosp. Service, Blue Cross, Phila., 1939; adminstr. Clearfield (Pa.) Hosp., 1939-41; dir. Hamot Hosp., Erie, Pa., 1941-49, Maine Gen. Hosp. and Maine Med. Center, Portland, 1949-58; dir. United Hosps. of Newark, including Presbyn., Babies, Hosp. Crippled Children, Newark Eye and Ear hosps., 1958-70; pres. Donald M. Rosenberger & Assos., Inc. (hosp. cons.), 1962—; dir. Interax, Inc., Phila.; v.p. Hosp. Research and Devel. Inst.; cons. USPHS; mem. jury, 1954; A.I.A.'s to judge hosp. architecture; hosp. cons. Am. Pub. Health Assn. Editorial bd.: Quar. Jour. Hosp. Adminstrn., Modern Hosp. Mag. Pres. trustees Beard Sch., Orange, N.J., Morristown-Beard Sch., Morristown, N.J.; chmn. sch. devel. com. and planning bd. Town of Raymond, Maine, also mem. budget com.; v.p. Raymond Waterways Assn.; trustee Blue Cross and Blue Shield N.J.; bd. dirs. So. Maine Sr. Citizens Inc., 1983—; vol. counselor SCORE div. SBA. Fellow Am. Coll. Healthcare Execs., Am. Pub. Health Assn., Soc. Advancement Mgmt. Internat.; mem. Am. Hosp. Assn. (council design and constrn. 1966), N.J. Hosp. Assn. (trustee, chmn. council adminstrv. practice, pres. 1967-68), Maine Hosp. Assn., Pa. Hosp. Assn., hosp. adminstrs. clubs N.Y.C. (pres. 1970-71), N.J., Am. Assn. for Hosp. Planning (dir. 1972-77), Soc. Profl. Mgmt. Consultants (v.p.), N.Y. Acad. Scis. (life), Newcomen Soc., Pa. Soc., Pa. German Soc. Episcopalian. Clubs: Rotarian, Torch. Home: Raymond Maine

ROSENBLUETH, EMILIO, structural engineer; b. Mexico City, Mex., Apr. 8, 1926; s. Emilio and Charlotte (Deutsch) R.; m. Alicia Laguette, Feb. 20, 1954; children: David, Javier, Pablo, Monica. CE, Nat. Autonomous U. Mex., 1948, PhD (hon.), 1985; MS in Civil Engring, U. Ill., 1949, PhD, 1951; PhD (hon.), U. Waterloo, Ont., Can., 1983; postgrad., Nat. Autonomous U. Mex., 1985; PhD (hon.), Carnegie Mellon U., 1989. Surveyor and structural engr., 1945-47; soil mechanics asst. Ministry Hydraulic Resources, also U. Ill., 1947-50; structural engr. Fed. Electricity Commn., also Ministry Navy, 1951-55; prof. engring. Nat. Autonomous U. Mex., 1956-87; prof. emeritus Nat. Autonomous U. Mexico, 1987—; regent Nat. Autonomous U. Mex., 1972-81; pres. DIRAC Group Cons., 1970-77; vice-minister Ministry Edn., 1977-82; pres. Réunion Internationale des Laboratoires d'Essais des Materiaux (RILEM), 1965-66. Co-author: Fundamentals of Earthquake Engineering, 1971; Co-editor: Seismic Risk and Engineering Decisions, 1976; Contbr. to profl. publs. Trustee Autonomous Metropolitana U., 1974-77; mem. working group engring. seismology UNESCO, 1965, UN ad hoc com. Experts Internat. Decade Natural Disaster Reduction, 1987-88, U.S. com. for Decade Natural Disaster Reduction, 1989-90. Recipient M. Hidalgo medal, Mex., 1985, Prince of Asturias prize for sci. and tech., Spain, 1985, Luis Elizondo prize, 1974, Disting. Svc. in Engring. award U. Ill., 1976, Bernardo A. Houssay prize in tech. OAS, 1988, Univ. award for sci. Rsch., 1986; prof. honoris causa Nat. U. Engring., Peru, 1964. Mem. NAS, NAE, Mexican Acad. Sci. Rsch. (pres. 1964-65 Sci. award 1963), Mexican Soc. Earthquake Engring., Mex. Soc. Soil Mechanics (trustee), Internat. Assn. Earthquake Engring. (pres. 1973-77), Mexican Assn. Civil Engrs. (M.A. Urquijo research prize 1977, N. Carrillo rsch. award 1984), N.Z. Soc. Earthquake Engring., Am. Concrete Inst. (hon.), ASCE (W.L. Huber Rsch. prize 1965, Moisseiff award 1966, Alfred M. Freudenthal medal 1976, Nathan M. Newmark medal 1987), Internat. Assn. Earthquake Engring. (pres. 1972-76), Nat. Acad. Arts and Scis. (fgn. assoc.), 3d World Acad. Scis. (bd. dirs.), Sigma Xi. Home: Mexico City Mex. Died Jan. 11, 1994.

ROSENBLUM, ARTHUR HAROLD, pediatric allergist and immunologist; b. Chgo., Feb. 11, 1909; s. Samuel and Mary (Stein) R.; m. Ruth Levine, July 12, 1938; children: Susan, Mary, Laura. SB, U. Chgo., 1930, MS in Physiology, 1932, MD in Physiology with hons., 1933. Diplomate Nat. Bd. Med. Examiners (highest score in nat. 1935), Am. Bd. Pediatrics, Am. Bd. Pediatric Allergy, Am. Bd. Allergy and Immunology. Intern then resident Michael Reese Hosp., Chgo., 1933-35, attending physician pediatric allergy clinic, 1937-66, sr. attending physician pediatric dept., 1966—, dir. allergy sect., 1971-74, co-dir. allergy and immunology div., 1974—; resident Children's Meml. Hosp., Chgo., 1935-36, Mcpl. Contagious Disease Hosp., Chgo., 1936-37; practice medicine specializing in pediatrics and allergy Chgo. area, 1937—; attending physician Infant Welfare dept. City of Chgo., 1937-42; prof. pediatrics Cook County Grad. Sch. Med., Chgo., 1946-58; attending physician pediatric dept., chief nephrology service Cook County Hosp., Chgo., 1946-58; assoc. prof. pediatrics Northwestern U., Chgo., 1950-65; prof. Chgo. Med. Sch., 1965-71; clin. prof. Pritzker Sch. Med., U. Chgo., 1974—; mem. cons. staff St. James Hosp., Chicago Heights, U. Chgo. Hosps. and Clinics, Weiss Meml. Hosp., Chgo. Lt. col. M.C., U.S. Army, 1942-43, PTO. Recipient Long and Devoted Service award Michael Reese Hosp., 1978. Fellow AAAS, Am. Acad. Pediatrics, Am. Acad. Allergy (chmn. penicillin study group 1965-70), Inst. Medicine, Chgo. Med. Soc. of AMA, Am. Assn. Cert. Allergists, Toyal Soc. Health (Great Britain), Internat. Congress Allergology, European Congress Allergology; mem. Chgo. Pediatric Soc. (Disting. Service award 1978, Archibald Hoyne award 1981), Chgo. Allergy Soc. (sec. 1966-67, pres. 1968-69), Internat. Coor. Club of Allergy, Ill. Med. Soc. (chmn. allergy sect. 1964-65, 69-70), Am. Heart Assn., Asthma and Allergy Found. Am. (Chgo. Allergist of Yr. award 1981), U. Chgo. Alumni Assn. (life), Michael Reese Hosp. Alumni Assn. (pres. 1966-67), Phi Beta Kappa, Alpha Omega Alpha. Democrat. Jewish. Home: Chicago Ill.

ROSENBORG, RALPH MOZART, artist; b. N.Y.C., June 9, 1913; s. Mozart Wolfgang and Helena Hedvig (Ohlson) R.; m. Margaret Ann Taylor, Apr. 26, 1951. Pvt. art student, N.Y.C., 1930-33. represented by Synder Fine Art, N.Y.C. More than sixty one-man shows include Eighth Street Playhouse, 1935, Artists Gallery, 1936-38, Willard Gallery, 1939-42, Phillips Meml. Gallery, 1941, Nierendorf Gallery, 1943, Rose Fried Gallery, 1945, Jacques Seligmann Gallery, 1948, 49, 74, Le Roy Davis Galleries, 1952-54, Delacorte Gallery, 1955, Laura Barone Gallery, 1956, Georgette Passedoit Gallery, 1958-59, Albert Landry Gallery, 1960-62, U. Notre Dame Art Mus., 1967, Charles Egan Gallery, 1965, Gallery Schlesinger-Boisante, N.Y.C., 1982, Princeton Gallery Fine Art, 1983, 84, 85, Watercolors, 1940-88, Exhbn. Space, N.Y.C., presented by Princeton Gallery Fine Art, 1988, Snyder Fine Art, N.Y.C., 1991, Abstract woodcuts, etchings, linolium cuts and lithograph of 1940s at Hirschl & Adler, N.Y.C., 1991, 55 Yrs. of Oil and Watercolors painting: A Meml. Exhbn., 1993, Snyder Fine Art, N.YC., selected Oils and Watercolors, Estate Painting, 1994, 95, Acanthus Gallery; exhibited in 300 group shows including: Corcoran Gallery Art, Washington, 1959, San Francisco Mus. Art, 1961, New Britain (Conn.) Mus. Am. Art, 1979, Butler Inst. Am. Art, Youngstown, Ohio, 1979, Sid Deutsch Gallery, N.Y.C., 1978, Art in Embassies Program, 1982-88, Am. Embassy, Asuncion, Paraguay, Cen. S.Am., Lowe Art Mus., U. Miami, Coral Gables, Fla., Terra Mus. Am. Art, Chgo., Jane Voorhees Zimmerli Art Mus., Whitney Mus. Am. Art at Philip Morris, N.Y.C., 1990, Rutgers U., New Brunswick, N.J., 'Abstract Expressionism - Other Dimensions', 1989-90, Nat. Mus. Art, Smithsonian Instn., Washington, Nationale Stichting de Nieuwe Kerk te Amsterdam, The Netherlands, 1990, Utah Mus. Fine Arts, Salt Lake City, 1991, Laguna Gloria Art Mus., Austin, Tex., Montgomery Mus. Fine Arts, Montgomery, Ala., Knoxville, Tenn. Mus. of Art, Meml. Art Gallery of U. Rochester, N.Y., 1992,'Dissenting Voices, The Patricia and Philip Frost Collection, American Abstraction, 1930-45', 1989-90, Herbert F. Johnson Mus. Art, Cornell U., Ithaca, N.Y., Cornell Collects, Modern Am. Art through 1980, 1990, Worcester Art Mus., Worcester, Mass., 1992, Samuel P. Hern Mus., U. Fla., Del. Art Mus., Wilmington, 1992, The Second Wave: Am. Abstraction of the 1930s and 1940s, Selections from the Penny and Elton Yasuna Collection; represented in permanent collections including, Whitney Mus. Am. Art, Guggenheim Mus. Art, Hirshhorn Art Mus., Newark Art Mus., Mus. Modern Art, Collection of Société Anonyme-Yale U. Art Mus., Israel Mus., Snite Art Mus., Notre Dame, Ind., Met. Mus. Art, Seattle Art Mus., Wadsworth Atheneum, Farnsworth Art Mus., Rockland, Maine, Rose Art Mus., Phillips Meml. Gallery, Denver Mus. Art, Detroit Inst. Art, Okla. Mus. Art, Grand Rapids Art Mus., Montclair Mus. Art, Johns Hopkins U. Columbia U. Law Sch., New Sch. Social Research, Princeton (N.J.) U. Art Mus., U. Ga., Finch Coll., NYU, Cornell U., U. Ill.; corp. collections including RCA Radio Corp. Am., Squibb Pharm. Co., Fred Meyer Meml. Trust Coll., Portland, Oreg. Recipient Nat. Council Arts and Humanities award, 1966, Childe Hassem award Am. Acad. Arts and Letters, 1960; Hereward Lester Cooke Found. Art grantee, 1981; Adolph and Esther Gottlieb Found. Art grantee, 1982. Died Oct. 22, 1992.

ROSENSTEIN, LAURENCE S., pharmacologist, toxicologist; b. Phila., Aug. 19, 1943; s. H. and Rosalyn (Slenn) R.; m. Bernice E. Zevin, June 17, 1964; children: Michael, Judith Anne. BSc, Drexel U., 1964, MSc, 1965; PhD, U. Cin., 1970. Supervising toxicologist EPA, Research Triange Park, N.C., 1972-79; mng. toxicologist EPA, Washington, 1979-85, chief br. chem. infor., 1984-85, chief sci. policy staff, 1985-87, chief br. risk analysis, 1987-90; asst. dir. div. antiviral drugs FDA, Rockville, Md., 1990-92, acting deputy dir. antiviral drugs, 1992—; adj. prof. N.C. State U., Raleigh, 1970-77, U. Miami, Coral Gables, Fla., 1970-77; preclin. dir. U.S. AIDS effort, FDA. Contbr. articles to profl. jours. Asst. dir. N.W. Potomac (Md.) Coalition, 1986-90. USPHS predoctoral fellow, 1965-70. Mem. Am. Coll. Toxicology, Internat. Antiviral Soc., Soc. Toxicology. Home: Rockville Md.

ROSENTHAL, BERNARD GORDON, psychologist, educator; b. Chgo., Feb. 3, 1922; s. B.J. and Sonia (Gordon) R.; m. Judith Ann Straka, Sept. 22, 1957; children: Amy, Mark. B.S., Northwestern U., 1942; M.A., Princeton U., 1943, Ph.D., 1944. Instr. Princeton U., 1947-48; asst. prof. U. Chgo., 1948-55; assoc. prof. Howard U.; research assoc., lectr. Harvard, 1957-60; vis. prof. Ill. Inst. Tech., 1964-65, prof. social psychology,

1965-93; prof. psychology Forest Inst. Profl. Psychology, 1980-86, prof. emeritus, 1986-93. Author: The Images of Man, 1971, Development of Self-Identification in Relation to Attitudes towards the Self in the Chippewa Indians, 1974, Von der Armut der Psychologie-und wie ihr Abzuhelfen ware, 1974, (with others) Confrontation: Encounters in Self and Interpersonal Awareness, 1971, In the Search for Community, 1977, Crowding Behavior and the Future, 1983; also articles in sci. and scholarly jours.; Co-editor: The Human Context, 1969-76; exec. editor: Am. Editorial bd, 1971-76; editorial bd.: Existential Psychiatry, 1971-73. Co-chmn. Greater Boston Com. Sane Nuclear Policy, 1959-60; chmn. Greater Ill. Faculty Com. Vietnam, 1965-66. Served with Morale Services Div. War Dept., 1944-45. Mem. Am. Psychol. Assn. (chmn. program com. div. 9 1952-53, chmn. Midwest com. race relations 1951-53), Am. Assn. Humanistic Psychology (chmn. Midwest region 1966-68), AAUP, Phi Beta Kappa, Sigma Xi. Clubs: Princeton (Chgo. and N.Y.C.). Home: Evanston Ill. Died June 16, 1993; interred Los Angeles, Calif.

ROSENTHAL, SAMUEL ROBERT, lawyer; b. Manistique, Mich., June 6, 1899; s. Lazarus and Rachel (Blumrosen) R.; m. Marie-Louise Dreyfus, July 30, 1932; children: Martin Raymond (dec.), Louise (Mrs. James J. Glasser). A.B. summa cum laude, U. Mich., 1921; J.D., Harvard U., 1924; LL.D. (hon.), Grinnell Coll., 1978. Bar: Ill. bar 1925. Since practiced in Chgo.; asso. firm Foreman, Bluford, Steele & Schultz, 1924-26, Sonnenschein Nath & Rosenthal, 1926-36; partner Sonnenschein Carlin Nath & Rosenthal, 1937-94; pres. D and R Fund, Chgo. Pres. bd. edn. Highland Park High Sch., 1955-59; pres. Highland Park Community Chest, 1947-48; Bd. mgrs., life trustee Highland Park Hosp. Found., Michael Reese Hosp. and Med. Center, Ravinia Festival Assn., Newberry Library, Chgo.; trustee Grinnell Coll., 1962-77, Highland Park Pub. Library, 1962-72, 86-94; Fellow Brandeis U., Pierpont Morgan Library. Served lt. U.S. Army, World War I. Mem. ABA, Ill., Chgo. bar assns., Am. Antiquarian Soc., Am. Bar Found., Ill. Bar Found., Chgo. Bar Found., Am. Coll. Probate Counsel, Phi Beta Kappa. Clubs: Mid-America (Chgo.), Mid-Day (Chgo.), Caxton (Chgo.) (pres. 1974-76); Lake Shore Country (Glencoe, Ill.); Grolier (N.Y.). Home: Chicago Ill. Died Nov. 1, 1994.

ROSENTHAL, SOL ROY, preventive medicine educator, researcher; b. Tyktin, Russia; naturalized; s. Harry and Sara E. (Kahn) R.; m. Dorothy Bobinsky, May 26, 1950 (div. 1972); children: Anthony J., Wendy Elizabeth; m. Lucy Donna Lough, Dec. 23, 1972 (div. 1984); children: Sara Lough, Sol Roy Jr. B.S., U. Ill.-Chgo., M.D., M.S., Ph.D. Diplomate Am. Bd. Pathology, Am. Bd. Clin. Pathology. Fellow Inst. Pasteur, France; fellow U. Freiburg, Germany; cons. USPHS, Chgo. Bd. Health; founder, dir. Research Found., Chgo.; dir. Inst. Tb Research, Chgo., Tice Lab., Chgo.; prof. preventive medicine U. Ill.-Chgo.; chmn. Internat. Com. BCG Vaccination Against Cancer and Leukemia. Author: BCG Vaccine: Cancer and Leukemia, 1980, Everybody Can't Be President: A Realistic Approach to Educating; contbr. articles to profl. jours. Originator Tuberculin Tine Test, Risk Exercise. Pres. People to People for Peace; founder, pres. Sr. for Jrs.; bd. dirs. Biennale de Paris; founder, chmn. Academia for the Arts. Mem. Am. Physiol. Soc., Soc. Exptl. Biology and Medicine, Am. Soc. Exptl. Pathology, Am. Thoracic Soc., Scripps Research Council, Sigma Xi, Alpha Omega Alpha. Club: Chicago Literary; Santa Fe Hunt (Rancho Santa Fe). Home: Rancho Santa Fe Calif. Died June 10, 1995.

ROSIER, JAMES LOUIS, English philologist, educator; b. Chgo., Mar. 14, 1932; s. Escol MacFarland and Maudellen (Hamblin) R.; m. Katherine Lee Allen, Sept. 10, 1955; children: Meredith Lee, Paul Carrick, Jessica Holly. Student, De Pauw U., 1949-51; B.A., Stanford U., 1953, Ph.D., 1957; diploma, Freie U. Berlin, West Germany, 1955. Instr. Cornell U., Ithaca, N.Y., 1957-60; asst. prof. Cornell U., 1960-61, U. Mich., Ann Arbor, 1961-63; assoc. prof. English U. Pa., Phila., 1963-68; prof. English philology U. Pa., 1968-92, chmn. grad. studies, 1977-79, mem. Outreach Program for Gifted Students; vis. assoc. prof. U. Chgo., 1965; honors examiner Manhattanville (N.Y.) Coll., 1970-71, Swarthmore (Pa.) Coll., 1972-73, 81-82, 88-89; cons. Binghamton Med. Studies, Can. Coun., Am. Philos. Soc.; external Ph.D. examiner U. Ottawa, 1979, Temple U., 1988; grad. Latin examiner; panelist NEH. Author/co-author: The Vitellius Psalter, 1962, Poems in Old English, 1962, The Norton Reader, 1965-92, Philological Essays, 1970, Old English Language and Literature, 1972, Aldhelm: The Poetic Works, 1985; asst. editor: Middle English Dictionary, 1961-63; mem. editorial bd. Internat. Jour. Lexicography. Bd. dirs. Swarthmore Pub. Library, 1965-69, 1986-92, v.p., 1987-92; bd. dirs. Youth in Action, Chester, Pa.; mem. refugee com. Swarthmore Friends Meeting; mem., chmn. humanities panel Rsch. Found., U. Pa., 1989-91. Baker fellow, 1956-57; Am. Council Learned Socs. grantee, 1960, 72; Am. Philos. Soc. grantee, 1964, 71; Guggenheim fellow, 1964-65; U Pa. Research Found. grantee, 1983; mem. sr. common room Univ. Coll., Oxford (Eng.) U., 1961-92. Fellow Soc. for Values in Higher Edn., Royal Hort. Soc.; mem. Modern Lang. Assn. Am. (chmn. Old English 1961-63), Medieval Acad. Am., Soc. Study Medieval Lang. and Lit., Dictionary Soc. Am. (co-founder, exec. bd. 1977-92, pres. 1985-87, chmn. publs. com. 1988-92), Renaissance Soc. Am. Home: Swarthmore Pa. Died Sept. 7, 1992.

ROSS, EDWIN FRANCIS, health care consultant, former hospital executive; b. Struthers, Ohio, June 19, 1917; s. Edwin Francis and Ethel Marie (Wymer) R.; m. Virginia Kerr, Apr. 26, 1941; children: Richard, David. BS, Mt. Union Coll., 1939; MHA, Washington U., St. Louis, 1949. With Republic Steel Co., Youngstown, Ohio, 1939-40; tchr. public schs. Struthers, Ohio, 1940-42; adminstrv. resident Huron Rd. Hosp., East Cleveland, 1948-49; adminstr. Doctor's Hosp., Cleveland Heights, 1949-53; asst. dir. Univ. Hosp., Cleve., 1953-62; adminstr. U. Nebr. Hosp., Omaha, 1962-66; pres., chief exec. officer Fairview Gen. Hosp., Cleve., 1966-82; health care cons. Cleve., 1983-92; asst. prof. U. Nebr. Coll. Medicine, 1962-66; exec. producer TV series on hosps. and health edn., 1972-81. Pres. Cleve. Area League Nursing. Served with U.S. Army, 1942-47. Mem. Am. Hosp. Assn., Ohio Hosp. Assn., Greater Cleve. Hosp. Assn. (pres. 1972-74, chmn. exec. council 1974-75), Am. Coll. Hosp. Adminstrs. Republican. Presbyterian. Clubs: Masons, Kiwanis. Home: Cleveland Ohio Died Apr. 28, 1992; buried Fairmount Meml. Cemetery, Cleveland, Ohio.

ROSS, JACK LEWIS, psychiatrist; b. Levelland, Tex., Sept. 3, 1932; s. Raymond T. and Mary Ann (Lewis) R.; m. Glenna M. Quillin, July 16, 1960; children: Sarah, Jennifer, Susan, Rebecca. BS, Texas Tech. Coll., 1952; MD, U. Tex., Dallas, 1956. Diplomate Am. Bd. Psychiatry and Neurology; cert. adult and child psychoanalyst. Staff psychiatrist Menninger Found., Topeka, 1962-92; tng. and supervising analyst Topeka Inst. Psychoanalysis, 1979—, dir. 1984-90. Contbr. articles to profl. jours. Served to capt. U.S. Army, 1960-62. Fellow Am. Psychiat. Assn., ACP; mem. Am Psychoanalytic Assn., Alpha Omega Alpha (life). Republican. Methodist. Home: Topeka Kans. Died Apr. 17, 1995.

ROSS, STEVEN J., communications company executive; b. N.Y.C., N.Y., 1927; married. Student, Paul Smith's Coll., 1948. Pres., dir. Kinney Services Inc., 1961-72; pres. Warner Communications Inc., N.Y.C., from 1972, chmn. bd., chief exec. officer, 1972-92; co-chmn., co-chief exec. officer Time Warner Inc., N.Y.C., 1989-90, chmn., co-chief exec. officer, 1990-92; bd. dirs. N.Y. Conv. and Visitors Bur., Mus. of TV and Radio; mem. bd. sports medicine Lenox Hill Hosp. Home: New York N.Y. Died Dec. 20, 1992.

ROSS, STUART TENNENT, surgeon; b. East Hampton, N.Y., Jan. 16, 1907; s. Howard V. and Grace (Conover) R.; m. Jean M. Goodman, June 29, 1933 (div.); 1 child, Jane S.; m. Catherine Klarmann; 1 child, Catherine S. A.B., Columbia, 1927, M.D., 1930. Diplomate Am. Bd. Colon and Rectal Surgery (sec. 1955-68, pres. 1968-69). Intern Meth. Hosp., 1930-32; resident United Hosp., 1932-33; practice medicine Hempstead, N.Y., 1933-46, Garden City, 1946-86; attending proctologist Nassau Hosp., Mineola, N.Y., Mercy Hosp., Rockville, N.Y.; assoc. prof. clin. surgery Sch. Medicine, SUNY, Stony Brook, 1979-93; mem. adv. bd. Med. Specialists. Author: (with Harry E. Bacon) Atlas of Operative Technic, Anus, Rectum and Colon, 1954, (with H.E. Bacon and P. Recio) Proctology, 1956, Synopsis of Anorectal Diseases, 1959, Autobiography of an American Doctor, 1991; assoc. editor: Diseases of Colon and Rectum; editorial cons.: Postgrad. Medicine; contbr. numerous articles to med. jours. Lt. col. M.C., AUS, 1942-46. Decorated Legion of Merit. Fellow ACS, Internat. Coll. Surgeons, Am. Soc. Colon and Rectal Surgeons (pres. 1955), Mexican Proctologic Soc. (hon.), N.Y. Proctologic Soc., Pa. Proctologic Soc., N.J. Proctologic Soc., Pa. Soc. Colon and Rectal Surgery (hon.); mem. AMA (ho. dels.), World Med. Assn., Pan Am. Med. Assn., Mensa, Nassau Surg. Soc. (pres. 1960), Royal Soc. Medicine (Eng.), Am. Cancer Soc. (dir. Nassau divsn.), Internat. Soc. U. Colon and Rectal Surgeons (treas. 1965, v.p. 1986), Pan-Pacific Surg. Assn. Home: Williston Park N.Y. Died Jan. 26, 1993.

ROSSI, BRUNO, physicist; b. Venice, Italy, Apr. 13, 1905; s. Rino and Lina (Minerbi) R.; m. Nora Lombroso, Apr. 10, 1938; children: Florence S., Frank R., Linda L. Student, U. Padua, 1923-25, U. Bologna, 1925-27; hon. doctorate, U. Palermo, 1964, U. Durham, Eng., 1974, U. Chgo., 1977. Asst. physics dept. U. Florence, 1928-32; prof. physics U. Padua, 1932-38; research assoc. U. Manchester, Eng., 1939; research assoc. in cosmic rays U. Chgo., 1939-40; asso. prof. physics Cornell U., 1940-43; prof. physics MIT, from 1946, Inst. prof., 1966-70, Inst. prof. emeritus, from 1970; Mem. staff Los Alamos Lab.; 1943-46, hon. fellow Tata Inst. Fundamental Research, Bombay, India, 1971; mem. physics com. NASA; hon. prof. U. Mayor, San Andres, La Paz, Bolivia. Author: Rayons Cosmiques, 1935, (with L. Pincherle) Lezioni di Fisca Sperimentale Elettrologia, 1936, Lezioni di Fisica Sperimentale Ottica, 1937, Ionization Chambers and Counters, 1949, (with Staub), High Energy Particles, 1952, Optics, 1957, Cosmic Rays, 1964, (with S. Olbert) Introduction to the Physics of Space, 1970, Momenti nella vite di uno Scientiato, 1987, English transl., 1990. Decorated Order of Merit (Italy); recipipient Cresson medal Frankli
Inst., 1974, Nat. Medal of Sci., 1983, Wolf award, 198
Pemio Metteucci Accadamia Nazionle delle Scien
Detto Dei XL, 1992. Mem. AAAS, Am. Acad. Ar
and Scis. (Rumford prize 1976), Nat. Acad. Sci. (spac
sci. bd., astronomy survey com.), Deutsch
Akademieder Naturforscher Leopoldina, Am. Phy
Soc., Am. Inst. Physics, Accademia dei Lincel (Interna
Feltrinelli award 1971), Internat. Astron. Union, Am
Royal astron. socs., Accademia Patavina di Scienz
Letteree Arti, Accademia Ligure di Scienze e Letter
Bolivian Acad. Scis. (corr.), Am. Philos. Soc., Italia
Phys. Soc. (Gold medal 1970), Instituto Veneto
Science, Lettere e Arti, Sigma Xi. Home: Cambrid
Mass. Died Nov. 21, 1994; interred Florence, Italy.

ROSSKAMM, MARTIN, fabric manufacturing con
pany executive; b. 1915. With Fabri-Ctrs. of Am., Inc
Cleve., 1953-95, first pres., chief exec. officer, now chm
bd. dirs. Served with AUS, 1941-45. Home: Hudsc
Ohio Died 1995.

ROTH, JUNE DORIS SPIEWAK, author; b. Have
straw, N.Y., Feb. 16, 1926; d. Harry I. and Ida (Glaze
Spiewak; m. Frederick Roth, July 7, 1945; childre
Nancy, Robert. Student, Pa. State U., 1942-44; grac
Tobé Coburn Sch., 1945; B.A., Thomas Edison Col
1981; M.S., U. Bridgeport, 1982. Merchandising pos
tions N.Y.C., 1944-45; public relations Fred Roth A
socs., N.Y.C., 1959-62; writer, lecturer, syndicate
columnist, 1963—. Author: The Freeze and Plea
Homefreezer Cookbook, 1963, The Rich and Delicio
Low-Calorie Figure Slimming Cookbook, 1964, Ju
Roth's Thousand Calorie Cookbook, 1968, How to U
Sugar to Lose Weight, 1969, Fast and Fancy Cookboo
1969, How to Cook like a Jewish Mother, 1969, T
Take Good Care of My Son: Cookbook for Brid
1969, The Indoor/Outdoor Barbecue Book, 1970, T
Pick of the Pantry Cookbook, 1970, June Roth's Le
Have a Brunch Cookbook, 1971, Edith Bunkers' All
the Family Cookbook, 1972, The On-Your-Own Coo
book, 1972, Healthier Jewish Cookery: The Unsaturat
Fat Way, 1972, Elegant Desserts, 1973, Old-Fashion
Candymaking, 1974, Salt-Free Cooking with Herbs a
Spices, 1975 (R. T. French Tastemaker award), T
Troubled Tummy Cookbook, 1976 (New Jersey Pre
Women first place award 1976), Cooking for Yo
Hyperactive Child, 1977, The Galley Cookbook, 197
MacMeals in Minutes, 1977, The Bagel Book, 1978, T
Economy Cookbook, 1978, The Food/Depressi
Connection, 1978, Aerobic Nutrition, 1981, The Allerg
Gourmet, 1983, Living Better with a Special Diet, 198
The Pasta Lover's Diet Book, 1984, The Executive Su
cess Diet, 1986, Reversing Health Risks, 1988, T
Mood Control Diet, 1990; author nationally syndicat
newspaper column Spl. Diets, 1979—; recipe develop
The Pritikin Program for Diet and Exercise, 1979. Vi
pres. evening group Teaneck (N.J.) br. Nat. Coun
Jewish Women, 1954, pres., 1955, v.p. day group, 195
Recipient Julia Coburn special award, 1970. Me
Authors League Am., Am. Soc. Journalists and Autho
(pres. 1982-83), Newspaper Food Editors and Write
Assn., Am. Med. Writers Assn., Nat. Fedn. Pre
Women, Nat. Press Club, Newspaper Features Coun
(bd. dirs. 1986—). Home: Hackensack N.J.

ROTHBERG, SOL, lawyer, industrialist; b. N.Y.
July 29, 1910; s. Samuel and Ada (Shayne) R.;
Dorothy Platka, Jan. 9, 1938; children: David, Richar
Samuel. LL.B., Ind. U., 1933. Bar: Ind. 1933, U.
Supreme Ct. 1980. Since practiced in Ft. Wayne;
partner firm Rothberg, Gallmeyer, Fruechtenicht
Logan, from 1951, of counsel; chmn. bd. Bowser, In
1960-93, Wabash Smelting, Inc., 1958-93, Gen. Smelti
Co.; dir., counsel NBD Ind. (merger Summit Bank),
Wayne, D & N Micro Products, Ft. Wayne, Compu
Decision Support, Alexandria, Va., chmn. fin. compe
sation com.; former chmn. bd., dir. Summit Labs., In
Founder Ft. Wayne Child Guidance Clinic, 1950, pre
1953; mem. budget and priority coms. Commun
Chest and United Fund, Ft. Wayne, 1949; pres.
Wayne Jewish Fedn., 1949; mem. Econ. Dev
Authority Ind., 1972; now 20 yr. chmn. bd. Ind. E
ployment Devel. Commn.; dir. Allen County Dept. Pu
Welfare, 1936; chmn. United Jewish Appeal, Ft. Way
1953; bd. dirs. Parkview Meml. Hosp. Found.; ad
exec. com. Ind. U. Sch. Bus.; apptd. to bd. di
Midwest Cardiovascular Rsch. Found., 1990. Apptd.
Counsel of Sagamore of the Wabash by Gov. of In
Named Hon. Lt. Gov. State of Ind., 1990. Mem. A
(com. on banking instns. and regulated investment c
taxation sect.), Ind. Bar Assn. (life, bd. dirs. trial se
1958), Allen County Bar Assn. (treas. 1943), Am. Ju
cature Soc., Bar Assn. 7th and 6th Cirs. Fed. Ct. (ho
lt. gov. Ind. chpt. from 1990), Ind. Soc. Chgo., B'
B'rith (pres. Ft. Wayne chpt. 1943), Ind. U. Alum
Assn. (pres. Ft. Wayne chpt. 1934), I Mens Let
Assn., Ft. Wayne Country Club, Quest Club, Tamar
Country Club, Jewish (pres. congregation 1951). Jew
(pres. congregation 1951). Home: Fort Wayne I
Deceased.

ROTHSCHILD, EDWIN ALFRED, lawyer; b. Chg
Oct. 19, 1910; s. Edwin and Hannah (Loeb) R.; m. A
Meyer, Apr. 6, 1939; children: Michael, Jo Ann. A
cum laude, Dartmouth Coll., 1931; LL.B. cum lau
Harvard U., 1938. Bar: Ill. 1938, U.S. Dist. Ct. (
dist.) Ill. 1940, U.S. Supreme Ct. 1960. Asst. advt. m

aurice L. Rothschild, 1931-35; assoc. Mayer, Meyer, ustrian & Platt, Chgo., 1938-41; assoc. Sonnenschein ath & Rosenthal and predecessors, Chgo., 1945-54, nr., 1954-95. Mem. Hyde Park-Kenwood Conservaon Community Coun., Chgo., 1958-93, chmn., 1960-; bd. dirs. S.E. Chgo. Commn., 1956-95; bd. dirs. CLU Ill., 1969-95, pres., 1975-77, v.p., gen. counsel, 77-95; bd. dirs. Met. Planning Coun., Chgo., 1958-95; ustee Inst. Psychoanalysis, Chgo., 1955-82; mem. bd. wish Vocat. Svc., Chgo., 1948-54, pres., 1952-53; bd. rs. Lawyers Com. for Civil Rights Under Law, Chgo., 69-95, sec., 1978-87, co-chmn., 1987-89; bd. dirs. errill's Marauders Assn., 1993-95. Lt. U.S. Army, 41-45. Recipient Disting. Pub. Svc. award Pub. Inrest Law Initiative, 1988, Lifetime Achievement award and for Justice, 1990, ACLU Ill., 1990. Mem. ABA, . Bar Assn., Chgo. Bar Assn. (chmn. com. civil rights 51-53, Chgo. Coun. Lawyers (bd. dirs. 1977-81), iffdwellers Club, Quadrangle Club. Home: Chicago . Died Jan. 10, 1995.

OTHSCHILD, ERNEST LEO, publishing company ecutive; b. Darmstadt, Germany, Sept. 23, 1922; came U.S., 1939, naturalized, 1943; s. David and Auguste evi) R.; m. Edith Margot Chan, Mar. 9, 1952; chilen: Anthony Joseph, Deborah Wilma, Vivian Miriam, ilip Elias. B.A. magna cum laude, NYU, 1948, .A., 1949. Modern lang. editor Am. Book Co., .Y.C., 1951-69; mng. editor Van Nostrand Reinhold ., N.Y.C., 1969-70; exec. editor Van Nostrand Reiold Co., 1970-72; mng. editor D. Van Nostrand Co., 72-78, v.p., editorial dir., 1978-81; editorial dir. msco Sch. Publs., Inc., 1981-94; instr. French NYU, .Y.C., 1951. Pres. Shelter Rock Jewish Ctr., Roslyn, .Y., 1966-68, 89-91; bd. dirs. United Synagogue Am., 81-94; treas. N.Y. Met. Region, 1980-82, v.p., 1982-, 1st v.p., 1992-94. Served with AUS, 1943-45, ETO, TO. Mem. Am. Council on Teaching of Fgn. Langs., m. Assn. Tchrs. of German, Am. Assn. Tchrs. French, m. Assn. Tchrs. Spanish and Portuguese, Phi Beta appa. Home: Roslyn N.Y. Died Jan. 1994.

OTHSCHILD, GEORGE WILLIAM, judge, lawyer; Chgo., Mar. 21, 1917; s. Edwin and Hannah (Loeb) .; m. Valerie Jane Myers, Mar. 16, 1946; children: Jane othschild Jacobsen, John Steven. A.B. cum laude, arvard U., 1939; J.D. cum laude, U. Chgo., 1942. ar: Ill. 1942, N.Y. 1947. Assoc. Root, Ballantine, arlan, Bushby & Palmer, N.Y.C., summer 1942, 46-49; ty., asst. and asso. gen. counsel ECA (and successor ys.), Washington, 1949-55; atty. GATX (formerly en. Am. Transp. Corp.), Chgo., 1955-61, gen. counsel, 61-69, v.p., gen. counsel, 1969-78, sec., dir., 1972-78; l. counsel Steel Project Program, Econ. Devel. Adinstrn., Dept. Commerce, 1979; counsel Coin, Crowley Nord, Chgo., 1979-82; assoc. judge Circuit Ct. of ook County, Chgo., 1983-95; counsel Coin, Crowley & ord, Chgo., 1996. Trustee Hull House Assn. Lt. SNR, 1942-46. Mem. ABA, Ill. Bar Assn., Chgo. Bar ssn. (com. chmn. 1968, 71, 72), Chgo. Council awyers, Order of Coif, Cliff Dwellers (Chgo.), olumbia Yacht Club (Chgo.), Harvard Club (Chgo., .Y.C.), Michigan Shores (Wilmette, Ill.). Home: vanston Ill. Died June 25, 1996.

OUECHÉ, BERTON, writer; b. Kansas City, Mo., pr. 16, 1911; s. Clarence Berton and Nana (Mossman) .; m. Katherine Eisenhower, Oct. 28, 1936; 1 son, radford. B.J., U. Mo., 1933. Reporter Kansas City tar, St. Louis Globe-Democrat, St. Louis Post-Disatch, 1934-44; staff writer New Yorker mag., 1944-94; em. exec. com. Health Research Com. N.Y.C. uthor: Black Weather, 1945, Eleven Blue Men, 1954, he Incurable Wound, 1958, The Last Enemy, 1957, he Delectable Mountains, 1959, The Neutral Spirit, 960, A Man Named Hoffman, 1965, A Field Guide to isease, 1967, Annals of Epidemiology, 1967, What's eft: Reports on a Diminishing America, 1969, The range Man, 1971, Feral, 1974, Fago, 1977, The River orld, 1978, The Medical Detectives, 1980, The edical Detectives II, 1984, Special Places, 1982, Sea to hining Sea: People. Travels. Places., 1986; editor: uriosities of Medicine, 1963. Vice chmn. E. Hampton .I.) Twp. Planning Bd., 1965-70; trustee Guild Hall, . Hampton, Nat. Found. for Infectious Diseases. ecipient Lasker Journalism award for med. reporting, 950, 60, Nat. Council Infant and Child Care ann. ward, 1956, Am. Med. Writers Assn. ann. award, 1963, ournalism award AMA, 1970, W.E. Leidt award Episopal Ch., 1973, J.C. Penney-U. Mo. ann. award, 1978, . Mo. honor award for disting. journalism, 1981, Am. cad. and Inst. Arts and Letters award in lit., 1982, .Y. Pub. Library Literary Lion award, 1985. Fellow ansas City (Mo.) Acad. Medicine; mem. Am. pidemiol. Soc. (hon.), Am. Coll. of Physicians (Lewis homas Communications award, 1987). Clubs: Devon acht (Amagansett N.Y.); Coffee House (N.Y.C.). ome: Amagansett N.Y. Died Apr. 28, 1994; interred magansett, N.Y.

ROUSE, JAMES W., real estate developer, foundation xecutive; b. Easton, Md., Apr. 26, 1914. Student, U. awaii, 1931-32, U. Va., 1932-33; LLB, U. Md., 1937; LD (hon.), Morgan State U., 1968; HHD (hon.), ashington Coll., 1981; LHD (hon.), Johns Hopkins ., 1985, N.J. Inst. of Tech., 1993, Princeton (N.J.) U., 993. Founder, CEO The Rouse Co., 1939-79, chmn. d., 1939-84; founder, chmn. The Enterprise Devel. Co.; founder-chmn. The Enterprise Found.; founder, pres. Am. Coun. To Improve Our Neighborhoods; pres. Urban Am.; founder Nat. Urban Coalition; bd. dirs. Points of Light Found., One to One Found., Jubilee Housing, Inc., Washington., World Times, Inc., The Ryland Group, Inc.; pres. Eisenhower's Adv. Com. on Housing, chmn. subcom.; mem. Pres. Reagan's task force on prvt. sector initiatives, 1982; chmn. nat. housing task force, 1987; founding mem. bus. com. for the arts, bd. dirs. World Policy Inst.; mem. N.Am. adv. bd. Touche, Remnant & Co., London. Bd. trustees emeritus Johns Hopkins U.; former trustee The Conservation Found., Urban Wildlife Rsch. Ctr., Internat. Inst. for Environ. and Devel., The Wilderness Soc.; exec. com. Greater Balt. Com. Lt. (j.g.) USNR, 1942-45. Named to Fortune's Bus. Hall of Fame, 1981, Recipient Presdl. medal of Freedom, Pres. Clinton, 1995. Home: Columbia Md. Died Apr. 9, 1996.

ROUSE, MERL L., insurance executive; b. Urbana, Iowa, Apr. 17, 1909; m. Imogene Rector; children—James, Margaret. Student, Cedar Rapids (Ia.) Bus. Coll. With Inter-Ocean Reins. Co., Cedar Rapids, 1928-34, N.Y.C., 1934-36; asst. sec. Inter-Ocean Reins. Co., 1936-39, sec., 1939, v.p., 1940-46, chmn. bd., 1962-95; (now div. Am. Reins. Co.); v.p., dir. Am. Res. Ins. Co., 1946-51, exec. v.p., 1951-53, pres., 1953-55; pres. Am. Res. Ins. Co. (merged with Am. Reins. Co.), 1955; exec. v.p., dir. Am. Reins. Co., 1955-61, pres., chief exec. officer, 1961-68, chmn. bd., 1968-77, chief exec. officer, 1968-75. Mem. N.Y. Bd. Trade, 1961-95. Mem. Ins. Info. Inst., Nat. Assn. Property and Casualty Reinsurers (founding mem., 1st chmn. 1969). Clubs: Wall Street (bd. govs.), India House, Knickerbocker, N.Y. Athletic (N.Y.C). Home: Stockbridge Mass. Died Jan. 2, 1995.

ROUSSAKIS, NICOLAS, composer, music educator; b. Athens, Greece, June 10, 1934; came to U.S., 1950, naturalized, 1956; s. George and Irene (Sommer) R.; m. Vuka Boyovich, June 5, 1971. BA, Columbia U., 1956, MA, 1960, D in Musical Arts, 1975. Mem. faculty music dept. Columbia U., N.Y.C., 1968-77; assoc. prof. music dept. Rutgers U., New Brunswick, N.J., 1977-94; exec. dir. The Group for Contemporary Music, 1971-85; co-founder, v.p. Am. Composers Orch.; dir. Composers Recs., Inc., 1975-81; panelist Nat. Endowment for Arts, 1982-83, N.Y. State Coun. on the Arts, 1988-91; lectr. in field; appearances on radio shows and Voice of Am. Works include Sonata for Harpsichord, 1967, (for speech chorus and instruments) Night Speech, 1968, Six Short Pieces for Two Flutes, 1969, (for string quartet) Ephemeris, 1979, (for a cappela chorus) Voyage, 1980, (for symphony orch. Nat. Endowment Arts Commn.) Fire and Earth and Water and Air, 1983, (for violin or viola and piano) Pas de deux, 1985, (for trombone, vibraphone and drums) Trigono, 1986, (cantata for chorus, orch. and narrator) The God Abandons Anthony, 1987, (fir small orch.) Mi e Fa, 1991, (for orch.) To Demeter, 1994. Bd. advs. Met. Greek Chorale. Recipient award Nat. Inst. Arts and Letters, 1969; fellow MacDowell Colony, 1964, 65, 67, 68, 69, Ossabaw Island Project, Savannah, Ga., 1966, Yaddo, 1966, 67, 68, 70, N.J. State Council Arts, 1985, 88; grantee Fulbright Found., 1961-63. Mem. Am. Composers Alliance (pres. 1975-81, chmn. bd. govs. 1981-83), Am. Music Ctr. Mem. Greek Orthodox Ch. Home: New York N.Y. Died Oct. 23, 1994; interred Montclair, N.J.

ROUSSIN, ANDRE JEAN PAUL, playwright; b. Marseille, France, Jan. 22, 1911; s. Honore and Suzanne (Gardair) R.; student Inst. Melizan, Marseille; m. Lucienne Deluy, 1947; 1 dau., Jean-Marie. Founder, Le Rideau Gris; plays; Am-stramgam, Une grande fille toute simple, Jean-Baptiste le mal-aime, Le tombeau d'Achille, La sainte famille, La petite hutte, Les oeufs de l'Autruche, Nina, Bobosse, Lorsque l'enfant parait, La main de Cesar, Le mari, la femme et la mort, L'amour fou, La mamma, Une femme qui dit la verité, Les Glorieuses, L'Ecole des autres, Un amour qui ne finit pas, La voyante, la locomotive, on ne sait jamais, Le claque, La Vie est trop courte, La coquine; author adaptations for films. Recipient Officer Legion d'honneur, Commdr. Ordre des arts et des lettres, commdr. Order national du Merite. Mem. Academie Française, Soc. des Auteurs et Compositeurs Dramatiques (pres. 1984, 86). Author essays: Patience et impatiences, 1953, Un contentement raiso-nable, 1965, La boite a couleurs, 1974, Le Rideau rouge, 1982, Rideau Gris et habit vert, 1983. Deceased. Home: Paris France

ROWLAND, ALBERT WESTLEY, education educator; b. Kalamazoo, May 13, 1915; s. Albert and Jesse (Buckalew) R.; m. Belle L. Teutsch, Dec. 21, 1940; children: Thomas Westley, Mary Beth. Ed.D., Mich. State U., 1955; M.A., U. Mich., 1941; B.A., Western Mich. U., 1938. Tchr. Comstock (Mich.) High Sch., 1938-40, Muskegon (Mich.) Sr. High Sch., 1940-42; head speech dept. Alma (Mich.) Coll., 1942-53; editor news service univ. editor Mich. State U., East Lansing, 1953-63; v.p. univ. relations SUNY, Buffalo, 1963-77; mem. faculty SUNY, 1977-95, prof. higher edn., 1977-95; Pres. Am. Coll. Public Relations Assn., 1966-67; vice past trustee Medaille Coll. Gen. editor: Handbook of Institutional Advancement, 1977, 2d edit., 1986. Served with U.S. Navy, 1944-46. Recipient Alice Beeman award Council for Advancement and Support Edn., 1980; President's award Daemen Coll., 1978. Mem. Council Advancement and Support Edn., Am. Assn. Higher Edn., Am. Assn. for Study Higher Edn. Republican. Mem. United Ch. of Christ. Clubs: Lions, Williamsville, New York, Buffalo. Home: East Amherst N.Y. Died July 15, 1995.

ROWLAND, IVAN WENDELL, college dean; b. Pocatello, Idaho, Apr. 1, 1910; s. William N. and Stella M. (Mills) R.; m. Helen Thomas, June 1, 1958; 1 dau., Betty Jo Giles. B.S., Idaho State Coll., 1932; M.S., U. Colo., 1947; Ph.D., U. Wash., 1954. Instr. pub. schs. Ririe, Idaho, also Pocatello, 1933-38; instr. physics Idaho State Coll., 1938-46, prof. pharm. chemistry, 1946-54; dean Idaho State Coll. (Sch. Pharmacy), 1954-56; dean Sch. Pharmacy, U. Pacific, 1956-81, dean emeritus, 1981—, prof. emeritus health care practices, 1981—. Mem. Calif. Pharm. Assns., Rho Chi, Phi Delta Chi (past grand pres.). Clubs: Commonwealth of Calif, Rotary. Home: Newport Oreg.

ROWLING, WALLACE EDWARD, New Zealand diplomat; b. Motueka, South Island, New Zealand, Nov. 15, 1927; m. Glen Elna Reeves, 1951; 3 children. M.A. in Econs., Canterbury U., 1952. Tchr. primary and secondary schs. and univ., New Zealand; officer edn. New Zealand Army; mem. parliament New Zealand, 1962-84; New Zealand ambassador to U.S. Washington, 1985-88; minister finance New Zealand, 1972-74, prime minister of New Zealand, 1974-75, leader opposition, New Zealand, 1975-83, minister fgn. affairs New Zealand, 1974-75. Created Knight, 1983; Fulbright scholar, 1955-56; grantee in U.S., 1967, Europe, 1969. Home: Washington D.C. Died Nov. 15, 1995.

ROY, RADHA RAMAN, physics educator; b. Calcutta, India, Feb. 8, 1921; came to U.S., 1958, naturalized, 1965; s. Debendra Nath and Krishna Kumari R.; children: Manik Ratan, Robin Kumar. B.Sc., U. Calcutta, 1940, M.Sc., 1942; Ph.D., U. London, 1946. Prof. physics, dir. nuclear physics lab. U. Brussels, 1949-57; prof., dir. nuclear physics lab. Pa. State U. University Park, 1958-63; prof. Ariz. State U., Tempe, 1963—; cons. in field. Author: Nuclear Physics, 1967, Photons and Leptons Interactions, 1968, Statistical Physics, 1971; contbr. articles to profl. jours. and encys. Fellow Am. Phys. Soc. Home: Arlington Va.

ROYDEN, HALSEY LAWRENCE, mathematics educator; b. Phoenix, Sept. 26, 1928; s. Halsey Lawrence and June (Slavens) R.; m. Virginia Voegeli, June 15, 1948; children: Leigh Handy, Halsey Lawrence, Constance Slavens. BS, Stanford U., 1948, MS, 1949; PhD, Harvard U., 1951. Mem. faculty Stanford U., 1951-93, prof. math., 1958-93, acting exec. head dept., 1957-58; assoc. dean Sch. Humanities and Scis. Stanford, 1962-65; acting dean Sch. Humanities and Sci. Stanford U., 1968-69, dean Sch. Humanities and Sci., 1973-81; vis. prof. Orta Dogu Teknik Universitesi, Ankara, 1966; Mem. math. scis. div. NRC, 1971-75; mem. adv. com. for research NSF, 1975-77, mem. adv. council, 1978-81; sr. postdoctoral fellow NSF, Swiss Fed. Inst. Tech., Zürich, 1958-59; mem. Inst. for Advanced Study, Princeton, 1969, 82-83, Forschungsinstitut für Mathematik, Zürich, 1979. Author: Real Analysis, 1963; editor: Pacific Jour. Mathematics, 1955-58, 67-69. Recipient Silver medal U. Helsinki, 1970; Guggenheim fellow, 1974. Fellow AAAS; mem. Am. Math. Soc., Math. Assn. Am., Finnish Math. Soc., Am. Inst. Archeology, Phi Beta Kappa, Sigma Xi. Club: Cosmos (Washington). Home: Los Altos Calif. Died Aug. 22, 1993.

ROYLANCE, D. C., lawyer; b. Bismarck, N.D., June 18, 1920; s. William G. and Freda (Zender) R.; m. Joan Stieber, 1954 (dec. 1973); children—Stephen Michael, Kathleen Moore; m. Mary Lou Wagner, 1978. LLB, George Washington U., 1952. Bar: D.C. bar 1952, U.S. Supreme Ct. bar 1960. Of counsel Roylance, Abrams, Berdo & Goodman, Washington. Mem. ABA, Bar Assn. D.C., Am. Intellectual Property Law Assn., Soc. Plastics Engrs., Order of Coif, Phi Alpha Delta. Home: Rockville Md. Died Apr. 16, 1995.

ROZHDESTVENSKY, ROBERT IVANOVICH, poet; b. Kosiha, Altai, Russia, USSR, June 20, 1932; s. Ivan Ivanovich and Vera Paulovna (Fedorova) R.; m. Alla Borisovna Kireeva, Nov. 14, 1953; children: Ekaterina Robertovna, Ksenya Robertovna. Ed., U. Petrozavodsk, USSR, 1950-51, Inst. Lit., Moscow, 1951-56. Writer, 1950-94; spl. corr. Izvestya newspaper, Moscow, 1969-94; mem. jury Cannes Film Festival, France, 1968, 74, 79. Author of more than 90 books on the langs. of the nations of USSR; mem. editl. bd. Smena jour., 1977-94; contbr. numerous working papers and articles to profl. jours; host TV program, Moscow, 1973-87. Dep., Moscow Soviet, 1975; v.p. European Cultural Soc., Venice, Italy, 1981; v.p. Soviet Peace Com., Peace Fund, Moscow, 1981; mem. Union Trade Council, Moscow, 1981, Nat. Olympic Com., 1981. Recipient Golden Laurel Wreath, Struga Poetry Festival, Yugoslavia, 1969; State award for Lit., Moscow, 1979; numerous other state awards for excellence in lit. Mem. Union Soviet Writers (sec. 1970-94), Central Lit. Club (pres. 1980-94). Home: Moscow Russia Died Aug. 19, 1994.

RUB, LOUIS JOHN, savings and loan executive; b. Bklyn., Oct. 2, 1915; s. Louis C. and Paula K. (Knoll) R.; m. Marguerite Gustafson, Sept. 5, 1942; children: Christopher L., Peter M., Timothy F., Marguerite L. B.S. in Accounting; M.B.A., N.Y. U. Asst. sec. East River Savs. Bank, N.Y.C., 1946-49; asst. v.p. East River Savs. Bank, 1949-57; exec. v.p. First Fed. Savs. & Loan Assn., Shreveport, La., 1957-58; v.p. Fed. Home Loan Bank N.Y., N.Y.C., 1958-68; exec. v.p. Fed. Home Loan Bank N.Y., 1968-72; pres. Fed. Home Loan Bank of Pitts., 1973-80; chmn. bd. dirs. Suffolk County Fed. Savs. & Loan Assn., Centereach, N.Y., 1982-83; dir. First Fed. Savs. & Loan Assn. Pitts., 1981-85, U.S Mortgage Ins. Co., Blue Bell, Pa., 1981-86; mem. faculty N.Y. U., 1946-57, 59-63. Club: Duquesne (Pitts.). Home: Pittsburgh Pa. Died Jan. 30, 1996.

RUBIN, CARL BERNARD, federal judge; b. Cin., Mar. 27, 1920; s. John I. and Ethel (Friedman) R.; m. Gloria Weiland, Sept. 23, 1945; children: Marc W., C. Barry, Pam G., Robert S. BA, U. Cin., 1942, JD, 1944, LLD (hon.), 1988. Bar: Ohio 1944. Practiced in Cin., 1944-71; asst. pros. atty. Hamilton County (Ohio), Cin., 1950-60; judge U.S. Dist. Ct. So. Dist. Ohio, 1971-95, chief judge, 1979-90; instr. criminal law Chase Coll. Law, Cin., 1965-67, adj. prof. law, 1987-88; adj. prof. law U. Dayton Coll. Law, 1976; mem. com. on ct. adminstrn. fed. cts. U.S. Jud. Conf., 1975-83; mem. Jud. Coun. 6th Cir., 1985-88. Contbr. articles to legal publs. Mem. 6th Cir. Dist. Judges Assn. (pres. 1977-78). Home: Cincinnati Ohio Died Aug. 2, 1995.

RUBLOFF, BURTON, real estate broker, appraiser; b. Chisholm, Minn., June 1, 1912; s. Solomon W. and Mary R.; m. Patricia F. Williams, July 17, 1943; 1 dau., Jenifer. Grad, Northwestern U., 1940. With Arthur Rubloff & Co. (now Rubloff Inc.), Chgo., 1930—; v.p. Arthur Rubloff & Co. (now Rubloff Inc.), 1947-76, sr. v.p., 1976-94. Bd. dirs. Mcpl. Art League Chgo.; mem. Urbanland Inst. Served with U.S. Army, 1943-46, ETO. Mem. Am. Inst. Real Estate Appraisers (life mem. chpt. 6), Nat. Ill., Chgo. (hon. life mem.) assns. real estate bds., Chgo. Real Estate Bd. (ethics com.), Bldg. Mgrs. Assn. Chgo., Urban Land Inst., Greater State St. Coun. (real estate com.), John Evans Clbu, City Club, Northwestern Club Chgo., Lambda Alpha Internat. (Ely chpt.), Plaza Club. Home: Lake Forest Ill. Died 1994.

RUBNITZ, MYRON ETHAN, pathologist, educator; b. Omaha, Mar. 2, 1924; s. Abraham Srol and Esther Molly (Jonich) R.; m. Susan Belle Block, Feb. 9, 1952; children: Mary Ly Rubnitz Roffe, Peter, Thomas (dec.), Robert. BSc, U. Nebr., 1945; MD, U. Nebr., Omaha, 1947. Diplomate Am. Bd. Pathology. Intern Mt. Sinai Hosp., Cleve., 1947-48; fellow Mt. Sinai Hosp., N.Y.C., 1948-49; resident in pathology Michael Reese Hosp., Chgo., 1949-51; pathologist VA Hosp., Hines, Ill., 1953-56, chief labs., 1956-93, cons., 1993—; assoc. prof. pathology Loyola U. Med. Sch., Maywood, Ill., 1963-70, prof., 1970—; adj. prof. Ill. State U., Normal, 1979—, Coll. St. Francis, Joliet, Ill., 1989—, Ea. Ill. U. Charleston, 1991—, Western Ill. U., Macomb, 1991—; adj. assoc. prof. No. Ill. U., DeKalb, 1979-92; clin. instr. Augustana Coll., Rock Island, Ill., 1991—. Chmn. candidates com. Village Caucus, Winnteka, Ill., 1969-70; bd. dirs. Chgo. Commons Assn., 1968—; mem. New Trier High Sch. Caucus, Winnetka, 1972-74. With AUS, 1943-46, PTO; 1st lt. M.C., U.S. Army, 1951-53. Fellow Am. Soc. Clin. Pathologists, Coll. Am. Pathologists; mem. Internat. Acad. Pathology, Assn. VA Pathologists (pres. 1982-84), Chgo. Pathology Soc., Lake Shore Country Club (Glencoe, Ill.), North Shore Racquet Club, Mich. Shores Club (Wilmette, Ill.). Republican. Jewish. Home: Winnetka Ill.

RUDOLPH, ARNOLD JACK, pediatrician, neonatologist, medical educator; b. Johannesburg, South Africa, Mar. 28, 1918; came to U.S., 1956, naturalized, 1978; s. Chone and Sarah R.; m. Myrna Eunice Marks, Feb. 6, 1951; children: Arlene, Jennifer, Susan, Clifford. M.B. B.Ch., U. Witwatersrand, 1940; postgrad. in neonatology, Harvard U. Med. Sch., Boston, 1956-59. Diplomate Am. Bd. Pediatrics, Am. Bd. Neonatal-Perinatal Medicine. Residency tng. Transvaal Meml. Hosp. for Children, Johannesburg, 1941-46; pvt. practice Johannesburg, 1947-56; asst. prof. pediatrics Baylor Coll. Medicine, Houston, 1961-66, assoc. prof. pediatrics, 1966-70, prof. pediatrics, 1970-95, head neonatology sect., dept. pediatrics, 1971-86, prof. pediatrics dept. ob-gyn., 1973-95, mem. neonatology sect., 1987-95. Contbr. chpts. to books in field; articles to profl. publs. Fellow Am. Acad. Pediatrics, Philippines Pediatric Soc (hon.); mem. AMA, Brit. Med. Assn., Tex. Med. Assn., Harris County Med. Soc., Am. Pediatric Soc., Tex. Pediatric Soc., So. Soc. Pediatric Research, Tex. Perinatal Assn., Houston Pediatric Soc., Nat. Perinatal Assn., Alpha Omega Alpha (hon.). Jewish. Home: Houston Tex. Died July 25, 1995.

RULE, BRENDAN GAIL LONERGAN, psychology educator; b. Bklyn., Nov. 28, 1937; d. Thomas Francis and Katherine Josephine (Roth) Lonergan; m. Stanley Jay Rule, Feb. 17, 1961; children: Stanley, Thomas, Charlene Katherine. BA, U. Calif., 1959; MA, U. Wash., 1961, PhD, 1962. Research asst. U. Calif., Santa Barbara, 1959-60; research trainee VA Hosp., Seattle, 1960-62; extension lectr. U. Wash., 1961-62; session lectr. U. Alta., Edmonton, 1962-63; asst. prof. U. Alta., 1963-68, assoc. prof. psychology, 1968-72, prof., 1972—, dir. Ctr. for Gerontology, 1988—. Contbr. articles to profl. jours. and books. Can. Council fellow. Fellow Am. Psychol. Assn., Can. Psychol. Assn.; mem. Sigma Xi (Gardin Kaplan award 1990). Home: Edmonton Can. Deceased.

RULON, GEORGE WILLIAM, sports association executive; b. Jamestown, N.D., May 9, 1921; s. George William and Kathryn (Mutz) R.; m. Corene Alys Billings, June 26, 1948; children: Jane Marie, Elizabeth Ann Rulon Kehlbeck. B.S., N.D. State U., 1946. Dept. service officer The Am. Legion, Fargo, N.D., 1946-57, dir. membership, Indpls., 1958-61; program coordinator Am. Legion Baseball, Indpls., 1961-89 ; dir. U.S. Baseball Fedn., Hamilton Square, N.J., 1962-89 . Served to 1st lt inf. U.S. Army, 1943-45; ETO. Mem. Am. Baseball Coaches Assn. (exec. com. 1985-89), Nat. Council Youth Sports Dirs. Republican. Roman Catholic. Lodge: Elks. Died Jan. 20, 1989. Home: Indianapolis Ind.

RUSCH, WILLARD VAN TUYL, electrical engineering educator; b. N.Y.C., July 12, 1933; s. Hugo Leonard and Cynthia Katherine (Van Tuyl) R.; m. Joann Foster Garrett, June 22, 1957; children: Leonard, Martha, Willard II, Joseph. BSEE, Princeton U., 1954; MSEE, Calif. Inst. Tech., 1955, PhD, 1959. Instr. Calif. Inst. Tech., Pasadena, 1958-59; asst. prof. U. So. Calif., L.A., 1960-63, assoc. prof., 1963-72, prof., 1972-93; cons. Jet Propulsion Lab. NASA, European Space Agy., numerous aerospace cos., U.S., Europe, 1960-93; vis. scientist Naval Rsch. Lab., Washington, 1962; mem. tech. staff Bell Telephone Labs., Holmdel, N.J., 1966-67; vis. prof. Lab Electromagnetic Theory, Lyngby, Denmark, 1973-74; Sr. Scientist Max Planck Inst. Radioastronomy, Bonn, Germany, 1980-81. Co-author 10 books; contbr. articles to profl. jours.; patentee in field. Recipient Sr. U.S. Scientist prize Von Humboldt Found., 1980; Fulbright scholar U.S. Govt., Germany, 1959-60. Fellow IEEE. Home: Pasadena Calif. Died May 27, 1993.

RUSHKOFF, MARVIN, financial executive, accountant; b. N.Y.C., Nov. 23, 1929; s. Samuel and Sabina (Rittner) R.; m. Sheila Weintraub, June 3, 1956; children: Bennett, Douglas. B.S., N.Y. U., 1951; M.B.A., C.U.N.Y., 1962. C.P.A., N.Y. Acct. Westheimer, Fine, Berger & Co., N.Y.C., 1951-56, sr. acct. S.D. Leidesdorf & Co. (merger Ernst & Whinney), N.Y.C., 1956-62; controller Flicker Vacuum Cleaner Co., Inc., N.Y.C., 1962-64; asst. controller, Mt. Sinai Med. Ctr., 1964-65, controller, 1965-69; assoc. dir. fin., 1969-70, dir. fin., 1970-71, chief fin. officer, v.p. fin., 1971-93, sr. v.p. bus. and fin., 1984-89; asst. prof. clinical admin. med. Mt. Sinai Sch. Med., City U. N.Y., 1970-83, assoc. prof. 1983-93; adjunct asst. prof. Baruch Coll., City U. N.Y., 1971-76; vis. prof. N.Y.U., 1978-82; Formed Marum Rushkoff Assocs.; guest lectr. United Hosp. Fund, 1967-79, Hunter Coll., 1971, Brookdale Continuing Educ. Program, 1979 Co-author: A Guide to Reimbursement Regulations in New York State. Contbr. articles to profl. jours. Served to 1st lt. USAR, Fellow Healthcare Fin. Mgmt. Assn. (recipient award for highest grade on exam. in U.S. and Can., 1968, Follmer award, 1971, Reeves Award 1974, Pres.'s plaque 1974-75, Muncie award 1977); Mem. Healthcare Fin. Mgmt. Assn. (metro N.Y. chpt., pres. 1974, chmn. liaison com. 1981-82), bd. dirs. Am. Healthcare Mgmt., Micro Health Systems; Am. Coll. Hosp. Admins., N.Y. State Soc. C.P.A.s (chmn. com. on health care 1977-78), Am. Inst. C.P.A.s, Hosp. Assn. N.Y. State, Greater N.Y. Hosp. Assn., Fedn. Jewish Philanthropies. Lodge: Kombine K.P. (chancellor comdr. 1965). Died Feb. 4, 1993. Home: Scarsdale N.Y.

RUSSELL, DIANE HADDOCK, pharmacology educator; b. Boise, Idaho, Sept. 9, 1935; d. Grove Marden and Eileen Flora (Gridley) H.; m. Kenneth S. Russell, May 27, 1953 (div. Apr. 1975); children: Shauna, Keri. AA, Boise Jr. Coll., 1961; BS summa cum laude, Coll. Idaho, 1963; PhD, Wash. State U., 1967; postdoctoral student, Johns Hopkins U., 1969. Research chemist Balt. Cancer Research Ctr., 1969-73; assoc. prof. pharmacology dept. pharmacology U. Ariz., Tucson, 1973-76, research assoc. dept. internal medicine, 1973-76, prof. dept. pharmacology, 1976-87, prof. dept. pharmacology, molecular cell biology, 1984-87; prof., head dept. pharmacology and therapeutics U. S. Fla. Coll. Medicine, Tampa, 1988—; mem. Nat. Cancer Inst. Manpower Rev. Com., 1977-81. Mem. editorial bd. Life Scis., N.Y.C., Jour. Immunopharmacology; contbr. numerous articles to profl. jours. Fellow AAAS, Chem. Soc., Endocrine Soc., Am. Soc. Clin. Pharmacology and Exptl. Therapeutics, Soc. Toxicology; mem. Am. Soc. Biol. Chemists, Am. Physiol. Soc., Am. Assn. Cancer Research (bd. dirs. 1979-82), Am. Soc. Cell Biology, Soc. Devel. Biology, Nat. Bd. Med. Examiners (pharmacology sect.), Sigma Xi. Home: Tampa Fla. Home: Tampa Fla.

RUSSELL, EDWIN FORTUNE, lawyer; b. Rochester, N.Y., Aug. 27, 1910; s. Herman and Nell Amelia (Fortune) R.; m. Betty Louise Larson, Aug. 8, 1942; children—Edwin Larson, Sarah Russell Etchart. B.S. in Chem. Engring., U. Mich., 1933, M.S. Chem. Engring., 1933; J.D., N.Y.U., 1938. Bar: N.Y. 1939, U.S. Dist. Ct. (ea. dist.) N.Y., U.S. Ct. Appeals (5th cir.), U.S. Supreme Ct. Assoc. Cullen and Dykman, Bklyn., 193 52, ptnr., 1952—; counsel Village of Bronxville (N.Y. 1961-65, mayor, 1965-67, chmn. zoning bd. appeal 1968-83, justice, 4-yr. term. Chmn. Bronxville Repu lican Village Com., 1979-81. Served to lt. comd USNR, 1942-46. Fellow Am. Bar Found.; mem. N.Y State Bar Assn. (chmn. ho. of dels. 1975-76, pres. 197 77), ABA (ho. of dels. 1976-82, N.Y. State interim de 1981-82), Bklyn. Bar Assn., Westchester Bar Assn., Fe Energy Bar Assn. (pres. 1954), N.Y. State Bar Foun Episcopalian. Clubs: Siwanoy Country (pres. 1973-7 Bronxville); Bklyn., U. Mich. Pres.'s; Nat. Lawye (Washington).Lodge: Masons. Home: Rumson N.J.

RUSSELL, GEORGE FORD, electronics co. exec.; Lynchburg, Va., July 4, 1906; s. Frank and Emi (Ford) R.; S.B., Harvard U., 1928, M.B.A., 1930; Mary Baker, Sept. 4, 1929; children—Mary B., Geor Ford, Mildred. With Tribune Pub. Co., Tacoma, 194 70, pres., 1960-70; pres. Mann-Russell Electronics, Inc Tacoma, Wash., 1936—. Mem. Tacoma Pow Squadron. Presbyterian. Clubs: Tacoma Engrs., Tacom Yacht, Elks. Author: The Electronics of Parall Bonding, 1940; The Principles of Heat Pipes, 1950; Sol Energy Collectors, 1974; contbr. articles to profl. jour patentee in field. Home: Tacoma Wash.

RUSSELL, JAMES SARGENT, retired naval office b. Tacoma, Mar. 22, 1903; s. Ambrose J. and Loel Janet (Sargent) R.; m. Dorothy Irene Johnson, Apr. 1 1929 (dec. Apr. 1965); children: Donald Johnson, Ke neth McDonald (dec. 1993); m. 2d, Geraldine Ha Rahn, July 12, 1966. BS, U.S. Naval Acad., 1926; M Calif. Inst. Tech., 1935. Served with U.S. Mch Marine, 1918-22; commd. ensign U.S. Navy, 1926, a vanced through grades to adm., 1958; naval aviato 1929-65; comdg. officer aircraft sqdn. VP 42, Aleutia and Alaska, 1941-42; chief of staff to comdr. Carri Div. Two, Pacific campaigns of Palau, P.I., Iwo Jim Okinawa, 1944-45; bombing survey, Japan, 194 comdg. officer U.S.S., Bairoko, 1946-47, U.S.S. Cor Sea, 1951-52; with aircraft carrier desk Bur. Aero., 193 41, dir. mil. requirements, 1943-44; dept. dir. mil. a plication AEC, 1947-51; dir. air warfare div. Office Ch Naval Ops., 1952-54; comdr. carrier div. 17 & 5, Pacif Fleet, 1954-55, chief Bur. of Aero., 1955-57; dep. comd Atlantic Fleet, 1957-58, vice chief Naval Ops., 1958-6 comdr. NATO forces in So. Europe, 1962-65, ret., 196 recalled to active duty, 1967, 68, Vietnam; mem. vario Navy adv. bds.; cons. Boeing Co., 1965-79. Decorat D.S.M. with oak leaf cluster, Legion of Merit with tw oak leaf clusters, D.F.C., Air medal (U.S.); grand cro Royal Order King George I (Greece); Grand Ofc Order Republic of Italy; comdr. Legion of Hon (France); Gt. Cross Peruvian Cross of Naval Mer Grand Officer Order of Naval Merit (Brazil); recipie Collier-Trophy, 1956, Russell Trophy Order Daedalians; named to Nat. Mus. of Naval Aviation Ha of Honor, 1990. Fellow AIAA. Died April 14, 199 Home: Tacoma Wash.

RUSSELL, TOMAS MORGAN, lawyer; b. Kankake Ill., Feb. 27, 1934; s. Allie Tomas and Marieta (Kieffer); children: Heather, Hilary. B.S., U. Wis., 196 J.D., 1967. Bar: Ill. 1967, Wis. 1967, U.S. Supreme C 1974, Trial Bar (no. dist.) Ill. Ptnr. Russell & Assoc Chgo.; dir., vice chmn., mem. exec. com. chmn. Ill. Ins for Continuing Legal Edn., 1981-91, chmn. task force c continuing legal edn., 1982-94; founder Ill Captive In Co. Assn.; founder Ill. State Bar Assn. Ins. Risk Rete tion Group, Inc. Author: Illinois Captive Insuran Company Statute. Co-founder, chmn. U. Wis. Law Sc Civil Rights Research Council, 1965-66. Served wi USN, 1953-57. Fellow Chgo. Bar Found. (life), Ill. B found.; mem. ABA (chmn. com. on product safety 197 94), Ill. State Bar Assn. (chmn. jud. adminstrn. se 1981-82, long range planning commn. 1985-94, joint B Assn. com. on jud. compensation), Chgo. Bar Ass (chmn. standing com. on trial bar rules 1981-94, lo range planning commn. 1986-94), Am. Judicature So Law Club Chgo., Legal Club Chgo. (mem. exec. co 1989-90), ACLU, Wis. Bar Assn., Bar Assn. 7th Cir., Wis. Benchers Soc., Urban League Chgo., Better Gov Assn., Businessmen in Pub. Interest, U. Wis. La Alumni Assn. (pres.), Univ. Club, Chgo. Yacht Clu Contbr. articles in field. Died Nov. 3, 1994. Hom Chicago Ill.

RUSTGI, MOTI LAL, physics educator, researcher; Delhi, India, Sept. 29, 1929; s. Misri Lal and Lakshn Devi (Rustgi) R.; m. Kamla Rohatgi, Dec. 10, 195 children: Vinod K., Anil K. M.Sc. in Physics, Delhi U 1951; Ph.D., La. State U., 1957. Research fellow Ind Atomic Energy Commn., Delhi U., 1951-53; resear assoc. Yale U., 1957-60; NRC postdoctoral fellow O tawa; research assoc. Harvard U., 1960-61; read Banaras Hindu U., 1961-63; asst. prof. U. So. Cali 1963-64, Yale, 1964-66; assoc. prof. SUNY-Buffal 1966-68, prof., 1968-92; chmn. numerous coms. SUN Buffalo; vis. prof. SUNY-Stony Brook, spring 1973; vi scientist Oak Ridge Nat. Lab., 1980. Contbr. over 1 articles to Phys. Rev. and other profl. publs. NAS Am. Soc. Engring. Edn. fellow, 1983, 84; USN Am. So Engring. Edn. fellow, 1988, 89, 90, 91. Fellow A Phys. Soc. Home: Buffalo N.Y. Died Nov. 16, 1992.

RUUSUVUORI, AARNO EMIL, architect; b. Kuopi Finland, Jan. 14, 1925; s. Armas Ruusuvuori and Au ımalainen; m. Anna Maria E. Jaameri, 1970; 2 chil-en. Ed., Helsinki Tech. U. Asst. in architecture Hel-ıki (Finland) Tech. U., 1952-59, acting prof. architec-re, 1959-63, prof., 1963-66; prin. own drawing office, 52—; dir. Mus. Finnish Architecture, 1975-78, 83-88; ıte prof. art, 1978-83. Prin. works include Parish ıns: Hyvinkaa Church, 1961, Huutoniemi Ch., 1963, piola Ch., 1964; Printing Works of Weilin and Goos, 64-66; Police Hdqrs., Mikkeli, 1968; Helsinki City ıll renovation, 1961-88; Rauhanummi Chapel, yvinkaa, 1972; Paragon Office Bldg., 1973; REDC dg., Addis Ababa, Ethiopia, 1976; Parate Printing orks, 1979; Hotel Al Rashid, Riyadh, Saudi Arabia, 80; editor Architect-Arkitekten mag., 1952-55, chief itor, 1956-57. Decorated Order of Lion of Finland; cipient Vaino Vahakallio award, 1955; 1st prize award at. Mus., 1987. Fellow AIA (hon.); mem. Finnish ssn. Architects (pres. 1982). Home: Helsinki Finland

UVOLO, FELIX, artist; b. N.Y.C., Apr. 28, 1912; s. elestino and Mary (DeFranco) R.; m. Margaret ancill, 1947; 1 son, Antonio Felix. Student, Art Inst., ıgo., 1930-33. Instr. Art. Inst., Chgo., 1944-47; assoc. of. U. Calif. at Berkeley, 1950-59; prof., 1959-92; ptd. to Inst. Creative Arts, 1964, 71. Represented in exhbns. since 1938; one-man shows include: Durand ıels, N.Y.C., 1947, De Young Mus., San Francisco, 57, Poindexter Gallery, N.Y.C., 1958, 60, U. So. ılif., 1963, Jason Auer Gallery, San Francisco, 1970, uenebaum Gallery, N.Y.C., 1982. Recipient Kearny eml. prize Milw. Mus.; Broadus James Clark prize t. Inst. Chgo.; also William and Bertha Clusmann ize, 1942; William Gerstle prize, 1945; Bremer prize n Francisco Mus., 1942; Virginia Biennial (recom-ended for purchase), 1944; 2d prize Critics Show and Central Galleries, N.Y.C., 1947; Gold medal ılace of Honor, San Francisco; Artist Council prize n Francisco Mus. Art, 1953; prize for painting San ancisco Mus. Art, 1958, 64; 6th ann. prize for awing Graphics award, 1959; 6th ann. prize for awing Graphics award Richmond Art Center; ırchase award San Francisco Hall of Justice, 1967; hers. Home: Sausalito Calif. Died Oct. 10, 1992.

YAN, FRANCES MARY, lawyer, educator; b. Neill, Nebr., Sept. 29, 1920; d. Neil Thomas and ary Loretta (Gallagher) R. B.A., Briar Cliff Coll., 42; J.D., Marquette U., 1947; LL.M., U. Mich., 1948. ar: Wis. bar 1947, U.S. Dist. Ct. bar 1947, U.S. Cir-it Ct. of Appeals bar 1950. Individual practice law ılw., 1949-53; asso. Affeldt & Lichtsinn, Milw., 1954; rtner Lichtsinn, Dede, Anderson & Ryan, Milw., 60-64; Lichtsinn, Dede, Ryan & Haensel, Milw., 64-73; asso. prof. law Creighton U. Law Sch., Omaha, 73-76; prof. Creighton U. Law Sch., 1976-95; vis. of. Sch. Law, Temple U., summer 1977; commnr. ılw. County Circuit Ct., 1972-73. Home: Omaha ebr. Died June 15, 1995.

YAN, HAROLD L., federal judge; b. Weiser, Idaho, ne 17, 1923; s. Frank D.R. and Luella Neibling R.; m. ın Dagres, Feb. 17, 1961; children: Michael C., mothy F., Thomas P. Student, U. Idaho, 1941-43, U. ash., 1943-44, U. Notre Dame, 1944; LL.B., U. Idaho, 50. Bar: Idaho. Atty., 1950-95; pros. atty. Wash-gton County, Idaho, 1951-52; mem. Idaho State nate, 1962-66; judge U.S. Dist Ct. Idaho, 1981-95, ief judge, 1988-92, sr. judge, 1992-95. Mem. Am. Bd. ial Advocates, Idaho Bar Assn., Idaho Assn. Def. ounsel, Idaho Trial Lawyers Assn. Home: Boise Idaho ed Apr. 10, 1995.

YAN, JOHN THOMAS, JR., business executive; b. tts., Mar. 1, 1912; s. John Thomas and Julia (Brown) ; m. Irene O'Brien, Aug. 1, 1939; children: John, III, ene (Mrs. L. Edward Shaw, Jr.), Michael, Daniel, Julia Ars. Robert F. Parker), William. B.S., Pa. State Coll., 34; M.B.A., Harvard U., 1936; D.Sc. (hon.), Du-ıesne U.; LL.D., U. Notre Dame, 1973. Engr. with ine Safety Appliances Co., 1936-38, asst. gen. mgr., 38-40, gen. mgr., 1940-48, exec. v.p. and dir., 1948-53, es., dir., 1953-63, chmn. bd., 1963-90, chmn. exec. m., 1990-95. Mem. exec. com. Allegheny Conf. ommunity Devel.; trustee emeritus U. Notre Dame; ıstee Thomas A. Edison Found.; life dir. Pitts. mphony Soc. Mem. NAS (pres.' circle 1989), ASME, ME, NSPE, Am. Chem. Soc., Am. Soc. Safety ıgrs., Vets. of Safety, Coun. Fgn. Rels., Phi Delta ıeta, Tau Beta Pi, Pitts. Athletic Assn. Roman atholic. Clubs: Pitts. Golf, University, Duquesne; N.Y. acht, Union League (N.Y.C.); Chicago; Metropolitan Vashington); Fox Chapel (Pa.); Rolling Rock igonier, Pa.), Allegheny (Laurel Valley). Lodge: nights of Malta. Home: Pittsburgh Pa. Died July 31, 95.

YDER, JOHN DOUGLASS, electrical engineering ucator; b. Columbus, Ohio, May 8, 1907; s. John dwin and Lucy (Rider) R.; m. Sylvia MacCalla, Sept. 1933; children: Barbara Purves, John MacCal-B.E.E., Ohio State U., 1928, M.S., 1929; Ph.D., wa State U., 1944; D.Eng., Tri-State Coll., 1963. 'ith Gen. Electric Co., 1929-31; in charge elec. and ectronic product research Bailey Meter Co., Cleve., 31-41; prof. elec. engring. Iowa State U., Ames, 1941-; asst. dir. Iowa State U. (Engring. Expt. Sta.), 1947-; prof., head elec. engring. dept. U. Ill., 1949-54; dean gring. Mich. State U., 1954-68, prof. elec. engring., 1968-72; prof. elec. engring. U. Fla., 1979-93; mem. U.S. AID higher edn. study, Brazil, 1967. Author: Electronic Engineering Principles, 1947, Networks, Lines and Fields, 1954, Engineering Electronics, 1967, Electronic Fundamentals and Applications, 1976, Introduction to Circuit Analysis, 1973, Electronic Circuits & Systems, 1976, (with D.G. Fink) Engineers and Electrons, 1984. Recipient Batcher award Radio Club of Am., 1987. Fellow AAAS, IEEE (editor 1958, 59, 63, 64, v.p. 1974, Haraden Pratt award 1978), IRE (pres. 1955); mem. Am. Soc. Engring. Edn. Lodge: Rotary. Home: Ocala Fla. Died July 28, 1993.

SAAL, HUBERT DANIEL, journalist; b. Bklyn., Feb. 23, 1924; s. Theodore Henry and Mary Rebecca (Valins) S.; m. Rollene Waterman (div.); children—Theodora Mathilde, Matthew Adlai, Drusilla Mary. Student, U. Fla., 1941-43; A.B., Yale, 1948; postgrad., Sorbonne, Paris, France, 1948-50, 53-54, Columbia, 1950-51. Free-lance writer Europe, 1948-50, 53-55, N.Y.C., 1955-60; asso. editor Town & Country, 1950-53; instr. U. Miami, Fla., 1960-64; sr. writer Newsweek Mag., 1964-84. Author: The Say-Hey Kid. Served with USAAF, 1943-45. Recipient Deems Taylor award, 1974; Fulbright fellow Paris, 1952-53. Jewish. Home: New York N.Y. Died May 4, 1996.

SAALMAN, HOWARD, architectural historian, educator; b. Stettin, Germany, Feb. 17, 1928; s. Walter Guenter and Gertrude (Robert) S.; m. Jeanne Eloise Farr, July 27, 1954; 1 dau., Daphne Lydia. A.B., CCNY, 1949; M.A., NYU, 1955, Ph.D., 1960. Prof. archtl. history Carnegie-Mellon U., Pitts., 1958-70, Andrew Mellon prof. architecture, 1970-93; emeritus, 1993; vis. prof. U. Calif., Berkeley, 1968, Harvard U., 1969, univs., Berlin, 1973, Bonn, 1979; vis. prof. U. Calif.-Berkeley, Vienna, 1982, Jerusalem, 1987, Heidelberg, 1988, Villa I Tatti, Florence, Italy, 1991. Author: Medieval Architecture, 1962, Medieval Cities, 1968, Haussmann: Paris Transformed, 1971, Filippo Brunelleschi: The Cupola of S. Maria del Fiore, 1980, Filippo Brunelleschi: The Buildings, 1993, others. Fellow Am. Coun. Learned Socs., 1963, Kress Found., 1964, NEH, 1974, 91—, Guggenheim Found., 1984; grantee Am. Philos. Soc., 1966-67, 84-85, 91; recipient Alexander von Humboldt prize, 1992. Mem. Coll. Art Assn. Am., Accademia Nazionale Virgiliana di Scienze Lettere el Arti (corr.), Soc. Archtl. Historians. Democrat. Jewish. Home: Pittsburgh Pa. Died Oct. 19, 1995.

SABATINO, FRANK GEORGE, publisher, consultant; b. Chgo., June 5, 1948; s. John Walter and Marian Lucille (Marzano) S. BA, U. Chgo., 1970. Rsch. assoc. Am. Med. Record Assn., Chgo., 1975-76; exec. editor Quality Rev. Bull., Chgo., 1976-79; staff editor Am. Hosp. Assn., Chgo., 1980-81; mng. editor Hosp. Med. Staff jour. Am. Hosp. Pub. Inc., Chgo., 1981-82, mng. editor Trustee jour., 1982-83, mng. editor Hosps. mag., 1983-85, editor Hosps. mag., 1985-87, v.p. periodicals, 1987-90, asst. to pub., 1990-95; cons. Physicians' Assn. for AIDS Care, Chgo., 1990-91, researcher Ency. Brittanica, 1970-73. Asst. producer (cable TV program) HIV Update; contbr. articles to profl. jours. Vol. Howard Brown Meml. Clinic, Chgo., 1987-95, bd. dirs., 1988. Home: Chicago Ill. Died Jan. 7, 1995.

SABIN, ALBERT BRUCE, physician, scientist, educator; b. Bialystok, Poland, Aug. 26, 1906; s. Jacob and Tillie (Krugman) S.; m. Sylvia Tregillus, 1935; children: Deborah, Amy; m. Heloisa Dunshee de Abranches, July 28, 1972. BS, M.D., NYU, 1931; recipient 40 hon. degress from U.S. and fgn. univs. Research assoc. NYU Coll. Medicine, 1926-31; house physician Bellevue Hosp., N.Y.C., 1932-33; NRC fellow Lister Inst., London, 1934; mem. sci. staff Rockefeller Inst. for Med. Research, N.Y.C., 1935-39; asso. prof. pediatrics U. Cin. Coll. Medicine and Children's Hosp. Research Found., 1939-43, prof. research pediatrics, 1946-60, Disting. Service prof., 1960-71, Emeritus Disting. Service prof., 1971-93; pres. Weizmann Inst. of Sci., Rehovot, Israel, 1970-72; bd. govs. Weizmann Inst. of Sci., 1965-93; cons. U.S. Army, 1941-62; mem. Armed Forces Epidemiological Bd., 1963-69; cons. NIH, USPHS, 1947-73; mem. Nat. Adv. Council Nat. Inst. Allergy and Infectious Diseases, 1965-70; Fogarty scholar Fogarty Internat. Center for Advanced Study in Health Scis., NIH, 1973; mem. adv. com. on med. research Pan Am. Health Orgn., 1973-76; expert cons. Nat. Cancer Inst., 1974; mem. U.S. Army Med. Research and Devel. Adv. Panel, 1974-79; cons. Surgeon Gen., U.S. Army, 1974-93; Disting. Research prof. of biomedicine Med. U. S.C., Charleston, 1974-82, emeritus, 1982-93; sr. expert cons. Fogarty Internat. Ctr., NIH, 1984-86; cons. to asst. sec. for health HEW, 1975-77. Author over 375 papers in field. Bd. govs. Hebrew U. Jerusalem, 1965-93; trustee N.Y. U., 1966-70. Served to lt. col. U.S. Army, 1943-46. Decorated Legion of Merit.; Recipient Antonio Feltrinelli prize in med. and surg. sci. Accademia Nazionale dei Lincei, Rome, 1964; Albert Lasker clin. medicine research award, 1965; gold medal Royal Soc. Health, London, 1969; U.S. Nat. Medal of Sci., 1971; Disting. Civilian Service medal U.S. Army, 1973; Presdl. Medal of Freedom, 1986, Medal of Liberty, 1986, Order of Friendship Among Peoples, USSR, 1986; many other awards. Mem. Nat. Acad. Scis., Am. Acad. Arts and Scis., Assn. Am. Physicians, Am. Pediatric Soc., Infectious Diseases Soc. Am. (pres. 1969), numerous other U.S. and hon. fgn. memberships. Home: Washington D.C. Died Mar. 3, 1993.

SACHAR, ABRAM LEON, university chancellor emeritus; b. N.Y.C., Feb. 15, 1899; s. Samuel and Sarah (Abramowitz) S.; m. Thelma Horwitz, June 6, 1926; children: Howard Morley, Edward Joel (dec.), David Bernard. Student, Harvard U., 1918-19; BA, MA, Washington U., St. Louis, 1920; PhD, Emmanuel Coll., U. Cambridge, Eng., 1923; holder of hon. degrees from 34 colls. and univs. Assoc.in history U. Ill., 1923-29; dir. Hillel Found., U. Ill., 1929-33; nat. B'nai B'rith Hillel Founds. (series of 192 ctrs. on univ. campuses for Jewish students), Champaign, Ill., 1933-48; chmn. Nat. Hillel Found. Commn., 1948-55, hon. chmn., 1955-93; pres. Brandeis U., Waltham, Mass., 1948-68, chancellor, 1968-82, chancellor emeritus, 1982-93; cons. edn. Spl. Commn. on Structure of State Govt., Commonwealth of Mass., 1950; mem. Mass. Com. on Fulbright awards, 1962-69, U.S. Adv. Commn. on Internat. Edn. and Cultural Affairs, 1967-72. Author: A History of the Jews, 1929, 5th edit., 39th printing (Anisfield-Wolf award 1965), Spanish edit., 1943, French edit., 1973, Sufferance Is the Badge, 1939, The Course of Our Times, 1972, 3d edit., 1974, Japanese edit., 3 vols., 1976, A Host at Last, 1977, 2d edit., 1993, The Redemption of the Unwanted, 1983; weekly telecasts Course of Our Times on Nat. Ednl. TV, 1969-74; also articles in jours. of opinion; editor and compiler: Religion of a Modern Liberal, 1983. Bd. govs. Hebrew U., Israel; bd. govs. Ben-Gurion U., Israel; trustee Am. Jewish Hist. Soc., Palestine Endowment Funds, Inc., Jewish Acad. Arts and Scis., Eleanor Roosevelt Meml. Found. Decorated Grosse Verdienstkreuz mit Stern West Germany, 1969; recipient Spirit of St. Louis award St. Louis U., 1977. Fellow Am. Acad. Arts and Scis.; mem. B'nai B'rith, Belmont Club, Harvard Club (Boston), Phi Beta Kappa. Jewish. Died July 24, 1993.

SADOK, LUCJAN, engineering educator; b. Garbow, Poland, Nov. 28, 1941; s. Stanislaw Sadok and Maria Kowalska; m. Barbara Leja, Apr. 25, 1963; 1 child, Marek. MSc, U. Min. and Metall., Krakow, Poland, 1964, PhD, 1970, DSc, 1977. Asst. U. Min. and Metall., Krakow, 1964-71, asst. prof., 1971-77, assoc. prof., 1977-84, prof., 1984-95, vice dean Faculty Metallurgy, 1978-84, 1984-90, head dept. metal forming, 1988-95. Co-author: Teoretyczne Podstawy Technologicznych Procesow Przerobk, 1977, Przerobka Plastyczna, 1986, (textbook) Wybrane Zagadnienia z Ciagarstwa, 1986; editor: Jour. Hutnik, 1988-93. V.p. Sport Club Wisla, Krakow, 1991-95. Recipient Gold Cross of Merit, Pres. of the Nat. Coun., Warsaw, 1979, The Chivalry Cross of Order of Poland's Revival, The Chmn. of People's State Coun., Warsaw, 1985, Medal Ministry of Edn., Min. of Edn., Warsaw, 1987. Mem. Polish Acad. Sci. (pres. 1993), Polish Assn. Metallurgy Engrs. (Silver medal 1988), N.Y. Acad. Sci., Ctrl. Com. for Sci. Degrees. Home: Krakow Poland Died Dec. 22, 1995.

SAGENDORF, BUD (FORREST COWLES SAGENDORF), cartoonist; b. Wenatchee, Wash., Mar. 22, 1915; s. Phillip and Evelyn (Cowles) S.; m. Nadia Crandall, Dec. 17, 1939; children: Martin, Nicki, Bradley. Grad., Santa Monica (Calif.) High Sch., 1934; LHD, Quinnipiac Coll., 1987. Asst. Popeye comic strip E.C. Segar, 1932-38; writer, artist Popeye comic books, games, toys King Features Syndicate, N.Y.C., 1938-58; writer, artist Popeye Sunday & daily newspaper comic feature King Features Syndicate, 1959-94; lectr. history Am. comics various colls. and univs., 1960-80. Author: The Art of Cartooning, 1955, Popeye the First Fifty Years, 1979. Mem. Nat. Cartoonists Soc., Mus. Cartoon Art, Comics Coun., Kiwanis. Republican. Home: Sarasota Fla. Died Sept. 22, 1994; interred Conn.

ST. JACQUES, ROBERT H., food products executive; b. Mar. 3, 1924; s. Emile C. and Marie R. (Messier) St. J.; m. Beverly A. Trussel, June 29, 1975; children: Roberta, Elizabeth, Raymond, David. BME, Cornell U., 1948. Pres. Hayden Mfg. Co., Wareham, Mass., 1948-93; chmn. Ocean Spray Cranberries Inc., Lakeville, Mass., 1984-93; mem. exec. com. Plymouth Savs. Bank., 1975-93. Mgr. community trust funds, Wareham, 1968-89. Sgt. U.S. Army, 1943-46, ETO. Republican. Roman Catholic. Home: Wareham Mass. Died Jan. 17, 1993.

SAKMANN, BERT, physician, cell physiologist. Postdoctoral fellow with Bernard Katz London; asst. prof. Max Planck Inst., Gottingen, Fed. Republic of Germany, from 1974; instr. Marine Biol. Lab. summer courses, Woods Hole, Mass., during 1980's; prof. Max Planck Inst. Für medizinische Forschung, Heidelberg, Fed. Republic of Germany. Co-recipient Nobel Prize in physiology or medicine, 1991. Home: Heidelberg Germany Deceased.

SALAZAR LOPEZ, JOSE CARDINAL, former archbishop; b. Ameca, Mex., Jan. 12, 1910. Ordained priest Roman Cath. Ch., 1934; named titular bishop of Prusiade, 1961, named bishop of Zamora, 1967-70, named archbishop of Guadalajara, 1970-88, created cardinal, 1973. Home: Guadalajara Mexico

SALISBURY, HARRISON EVANS, writer; b. Mpls., Nov. 14, 1908; s. Percy Pritchard and Georgiana

(Evans) S.; m. Mary Hollis, Apr. 1, 1933 (div.); children: Michael, Stephan; m. Charlotte Y. Rand, 1964. A.B., U. Minn., 1930; LL.D., Macalester Coll., 1967, Ursinus Coll., 1971, Columbia Coll., Chgo., 1973, Tufts U., 1985, Amherst Coll., 1985; L.H.D., Md. Inst., 1967, U. Portland, 1971, Carleton Coll., 1976; D. Journalism, Assumption Coll., 1967; post grad. (Montgomery scholar), Dartmouth Coll., 1980; LLD (hon.), Grandview Coll., 1980, Dowling Coll., 1986, Hofstra U., 1992, Occidental Coll., 1992. Reporter Mpls. Jour., 1928-29; corr. United Press, St. Paul, 1930, later Chgo., Washington and N.Y.C.; became London mgr. United Press, 1943, Moscow, 1944; fgn. news editor United Press, 1944-48; Moscow corr. N.Y. Times, 1949-54, mem. N.Y. staff, 1954-63, asst. mng. editor, 1964-72, assoc. editor, 1972-74, editor Op-Ed page, 1970-73. Author: Russia on the Way, 1946, American in Russia, 1955, The Shook Up Generation, 1958, To Moscow and Beyond, 1960, Moscow Journal, 1961, The Northern Palmyra Affair, 1962, A New Russia, 1962, Russia, 1965, Orbit of China, 1967, Behind the Lines-Hanoi, 1967, The Soviet Union-The Fifty Years, 1967, The 900 Days: The Siege of Leningrad, 1969, War Between Russia and China, 1969, The Many Americas Shall Be One, 1971, The Eloquence of Protest (anthology), 1972, To Peking and Beyond, 1973, The Gates of Hell, 1975, Travels Around America, 1976, Black Night, White Snow, 1978, The Unknown War, 1978, Russia in Revolution, 1900-1930, 1978, Without Fear or Favor: The New York Times and Its Times, 1980, One Hundred Years of Revolution, 1983, Journey for Our Times: A Memoir, 1983, The Long March: The Untold Story, 1985, A Time of Change. A Reporters Tale of Our Times, 1988, The Great Black Dragon Fire, 1989, Tianamen Diary: 13 Days in June, 1989, The New Emperors: China in the Era of Mao and Deng, 1992. Recipient Disting. Achievement medal U. Minn., 1955, Pulitzer prize for internat. corr., 1955, George Polk Meml. award fgn. reporting, 1957, 67, Sigma Delta Chi award fgn. corr., 1958, Overseas Press Club Asian award, 1967, Sidney Hillman award, 1967. Mem. Am. Acad. and Inst. Arts and Letters (pres. 1975-76), Authors League (pres. 1980-85), Century Assn. (N.Y.C.), Nat. Press Club (Washington), Theta Delta Chi , Sigma Delta Chi. Home: Taconic Conn. Died July 5, 1993.

SALK, JONAS EDWARD, physician, scientist; b. N.Y.C., Oct. 28, 1914; s. Daniel B. and Dora (Press) S.; m. Donna Lindsay, June 8, 1939; children: Peter Lindsay, Darrell John, Jonathan Daniel; m. Francoise Gilot, June 29, 1970. BS, CCNY, 1934, LLD (hon.), 1955; MD, NYU, 1939, ScD (hon.), 1955; LLD (hon.), U. Pitts., 1955; PhD (hon.), Hebrew U., 1959; LLD (hon.), Roosevelt U., 1955; ScD (hon.), Turin U., 1957, U. Leeds, 1959, Hahnemann Med. Coll., 1959, Franklin and Marshall U., 1960; DHL (hon.), Yeshiva U., 1959; LLD (hon.), Tuskegee Inst., 1964. Fellow in chemistry NYU, 1935-37, fellow in exptl. surgery, 1937-38, fellow in bacteriology, 1939-40; Intern Mt. Sinai Hosp., N.Y.C., 1940-42; NRC fellow Sch. Pub. Health, U. Mich., 1942-43, research fellow epidemiology, 1943-44, research asso., 1944-46, asst. prof. epidemiology, 1946-47; asso. research prof. bacteriology Sch. Medicine, U. Pitts., 1947-49, dir. virus research lab., 1947-63, research prof. bacteriology, 1949-55, Commonwealth prof. preventive medicine, 1955-57, Commonwealth prof. exptl. medicine, 1957-63; dir. Salk Inst. Biol. Studies, 1963-75, resident fellow, 1963-84, founding dir., 1976—, disting. prof. internat. health scis., 1984—; developed vaccine, preventive of poliomyelitis, 1955, cons. epidemic diseases sec. war, 1944-47, sec. army, 1947-54; mem. commn. on influenza Army Epidemiol. Bd., 1944-54, acting dir. commn. on influenza, 1944; mem. expert adv. panel on virus diseases WHO; adj. prof. health scis., depts. psychiatry, community medicine and medicine U. Calif., San Diego, 1970—. Author: Man Unfolding, 1972, The Survival of the Wisest, 1973, (with Jonathan Salk) World Population and Human Values: A New Reality, 1981, Anatomy of Reality, 1983; Contbr. sci. articles to jours. Decorated chevalier Legion of Honor France, 1955, officer, 1976; recipient Criss award, 1955, Lasker award, 1956, Gold medal of Congress and presdl. citation, 1955, Howard Ricketts award, 1957, Robert Koch medal, 1963, Mellon Inst. award, 1969, Presdl. medal of Freedom, 1977, Jawaharlal Nehru award for internat. understanding, 1976. Fellow AAAS, Am. Pub. Health Assn., Am. Acad. Pediatrics (hon., assoc.); mem. Am. Coll. Preventive Medicine, Am. Acad. Neurology, Assn. Am. Physicians, Soc. Exptl. Biology and Medicine, Inst. Medicine (sr.), Phi Beta Kappa, Alpha Omega Alpha, Delta Omega. Home: San Diego Calif. Died June 23, 1995.

SALMON, LOUIS, lawyer; b. Mobile, Ala., Aug. 30, 1923; s. Maurice Louis and Wertie (Williams) S.; m. Elisabeth Echols Watts, June 11, 1948; children: John Houston, Margaret Elisabeth Salmon West. BS, U. Ala., 1943, LLB, 1948; LLD (hon.), U. Ala., Huntsville. Bar: Ala. 1949. Instr. acctg. U. Ala., 1946-48; pub. accountant Smith, Dukes & Buckalew, Mobile, 1949-50; practice in Huntsville, 1950-93; mem. firm Lange, Simpson, Robinson & Somerville and predecessor firms, 1950-93; gen. counsel 1st Ala. Bank of Huntsville; dir. Dunlop Tire Corp., First Ala. Bancshares; past v.p., sec., trustee Huntsville Indsl. Assos. Mem. exec. com. Ala. Rep. Com., 1969-70; past mem. Madison County Rep. Exec. Com., Ala.; pres. Huntsville Indsl. Expan-

sion Com., 1968-70; past bd. dirs. Ala. Christian Coll., Ala. Sports Hall of Fame; mem. pres.'s cabinet U. Ala.; trustee emeritus Randolph Sch.; chmn. bd. trustees U. Ala. Huntsville Found. Decorated Purple Heart; recipient Disting. Svc. award Huntsville U. of C., 1987; inducted into Ala. Bus. Hall of Fame, 1994. Mem. ABA, Ala. Bar Assn., Huntsville Bar Assn., Ala. C. of C. (pres., dir.), Order of Coif, Kappa Alpha, Phi Alpha Delta. Mem. Ch. of Christ. Club: Huntsville Country (past pres.). Lodge: Rotary (past pres.). Home: Hunstville Ala. Died Sept. 26, 1993; buried Maple Hill Cemetary, Huntsville, A.L.

SALOMON, RICHARD, investor; b. N.Y.C., Jan. 9, 1912; s. Emanuel and Mignon (Eckstein) S.; m. Edna Barnes, Nov. 20, 1939; children: Richard E., Robert B., Ralph B. Ph.B., Brown U., 1932, LL.D., 1972. Chief exec. officer Lanvin-Charles of the Ritz (merged into Squibb Corp. 1971), 1936-71; bd. dirs., mem. exec. com. Squibb Corp., 1971-94; mng. ptnr. Riverbank Assocs., N.Y.C.; chancellor Brown U., Providence, 1979-88, chancellor emeritus, 1988-94; also vice-chmn. Spears Benzak Salomon Farrell, N.Y.C. Past chmn. bd. N.Y. Pub. Libr., now chmn. emeritus and vice chmn., nominating com. mem., exec. com. mem.; trustee Lincoln Ctr. Served with Signal Corps U.S. Army, 1942-46. Decorated Bronze Star. Mem. Nat. Acad. Arts and Sci., Century Assn. (N.Y.C.), Century Country Club (Purchase, N.Y.), Hope Club (Providence). Democrat. Home: Stamford Conn. Died July 21, 1994.

SALTZMAN, CHARLES ESKRIDGE, investment banker; b. Zamboanga, Mindanao, Philippines, Sept. 19, 1903; s. Charles McKinley and Mary (Eskridge) S.; m. Gertrude Lamont, May 2, 1931 (div.); 1 son, Charles McKinley; m. Cynthia Southall Myrick, Sept. 25, 1947 (div.); children: Cynthia Myrick Saltzman Motley, Richard Stevens (dec.), Penelope Washburn Saltzman Billings; m. Clotilde Knapp McCormick, Sept. 15, 1978. Student, Cornell U., 1920-21; B.S., U.S. Mil. Acad., 1925; B.A., Oxford (Eng.) U., 1928, M.A., 1933; D.Mil Sci., The Citadel, 1984. Began civilian career with N.Y. Telephone Co., successively comml. engr., comml. asst. mgr., comml. mgr., directory-prodn. mgr., 1930-35; with N.Y. Stock Exchange, 1935-49, beginning as asst. to exec. v.p., later became sec. and v.p.; asst. sec. of state, 1947-49; partner Henry Sears & Co., 1949-56; under sec. of state for adminstrn., 1954-55; partner Goldman, Sachs & Co., N.Y.C., 1956-73, ltd. ptnr., 1973-94; ltd. ptnr. The Goldman Sachs Group, L.P., 1989-94. Bd. mgrs. Seamen's Ch. Inst. of N.Y. and N.J.; trustee Am. Bible Soc., French Inst./Alliance Francaise, George C. Marshall Found.; bd. dirs. Downtown-Lower Manhattan Assn.; hon. bd. dirs. Am. Council on Germany. Served as 2d lt. C.E. U.S. Army, 1925-30; commd. 1st lt., N.Y. N.G. 1930; advanced through grades to lt. col. 1940; on active duty with U.S. Army, 1940-46; serving overseas 1942-46; brig. gen. 1945; relieved from active duty 1946; maj. gen. AUS ret. Decorated D.S.M., Legion of Merit U.S.: Order of Brit. Empire; Croix de Guerre with gold star France; Cross of Merit with swords Poland; Bronze medal Italy; grand officer Order of Crown of Italy; War medal Brazil; comdr. Ouissam Alouitte Morocco; knight Am. soc. of Most Venerable Order of the Hospital of St. John of Jerusalem; Rhodes scholar Magdalen Coll., Oxford U. Mem. English-Speaking Union U.S. (nat. pres. 1961-66, hon. dir.), Assn. Grads. U.S. Mil. Acad. (pres. 1974-78, emeritus pres.), Soc. Cin. (hon.), Kappa Alpha Soc. Methodist. Clubs: University (pres. 1966-70), Union, Century Assn., Pilgrims (N.Y.C.); Met. (Washington). Home: New York N.Y. Died June 16, 1994.

SALTZMAN, HARRY, film producer; b. Can., 1915. Chmn. bd. H.M. Tennent Ltd., Lowndes Prodns. Ltd. Producer 9 James Bond films, other films include Look Back in Anger, The Entertainer, Saturday Night, Sunday, Morning, The Ipcress File, Funeral in Berlin, Billion Dollar Brain, Battle of Britain, Nijinsky. Home: London Eng. Died Sept. 28, 1994.

SAMARITANI, PIER LUIGI, opera set designer, director; b. Novara, Italy, Sept. 29, 1942. Student Accademia de Brea, Milan, Italy, Centre d'Art Dramatique, Paris. Assisted stage designer Lila de Nobili in Paris; set designer: Th du Cymnase, Paris, 1962, Manor for Teatre dell'Opera, Rome, 1964; dance design for Am. Ballet Theatre, 1980; debut as dir. Werther, Florence, 1978; stage designer for many cos. in U.S. and Europe. Exhibited stage designs Spoleto Festival, 1972. Home: Bronx N.Y.

SAMMARTINO, SYLVIA, university co-founder; b. Boston, Dec. 5, 1903; d. Louis J. and Anna E. (Bianchi) Scaramelli; m. Peter Sammartino, Dec. 5, 1933. A.B. Smith Coll., 1925; M.A., Columbia U., 1926; LL.D. (hon.), Kyung Hee U., Korea, 1964; D.H.L. (hon.), Fairleigh Dickinson U., 1966. Tchr. public high sch. N.Y.C., 1927-28, 33-35; treas. Scaramelli & Co., Inc., N.Y.C., 1928-33; ednl. editor Atlantica, 1933-35; circulation mgr. La Voix de France, N.Y.C., 1935-37; registrar Fairleigh Dickinson U., Rutherford, N.J., 1942-50; dir. admissions Fairleigh Dickinson U., 1950-59, dean of admissions, 1959-67. Chmn. N.J. Commn. on Women, 1971; mem. bd. govs. N.Y. Cultural Ctr., 1968-73; mem. exec. com. Restore Ellis Island Commn., 1974-79; pres. Garden State Ballet Found., 1975-80; trustee Newark Symphony Hall, 1976-79, William Carlos Williams Ctr.

for Performing Arts, Rutherford, N.J., 1980-92; truste chmn. Integrity, Inc., 1980-89; trustee, sec.-treas. W liams Inst., 1981-92. Decorated knight Order of Me Italy; comdr. Order Star of Africa Liberia; officer Ord Nat. Ivory Coast; recipient Amita award, 1960; Smi Coll. medal, 1967; President's medal Mercy Coll., 198 Humanitarian award William Carlos Williams Ctr. f the Arts, 1988; named Woman of Yr., Rutherford C. C. Home: Gouldsboro Maine Died Mar. 29, 1992.

SAMUELS, ERNEST, author, educator; b. Chgo., M 19, 1903; s. Albert and Mary (Kaplan) S.; m. Jay Porter Newcomer, Aug. 24, 1938; children: Susann Jonathan, Elizabeth. Ph.B., U. Chgo., 1923, J.D., 192 A.M., 1931, Ph.D., 1942. Bar: Ill. Franklyn Bl Snyder prof. English, Northwestern U., 1942-71; chm English dept., 1964-66; Leo S. Bing vis. prof. U. S Calif., 1966-67; Fulbright lectr. Inter-University Chair Am. Studies, Belgium, 1958-59. Author: Business E glish Projects, 1936, The Young Henry Adams, 19 Henry Adams: The Middle Years, 1958, Henry Adam The Major Phase, 1964, Bernard Berenson: The Maki of a Connoisseur, 1979 (Carl Sandburg award 198 Bernard Berenson: The Making of a Legend, 198 Henry Adams, 1989; editor: Adams, History of t United States, 1967, The Education of Henry Adam 1973, Writings of Henry Adams, 1983, Henry Adam Selected Letters, 1992; mem. editorial bd.: Am. L 1964-71; mem. adv. bd. publ., Adams Papers; ass editor: Letters of Henry Adams, vols. I-III, 1983, vc IV-VI, 1988. Mem. Ill. Commn. of Scholars, 1966-7 Council of Scholars, Library of Congress, 1980-81 Recipient Bancroft award and Parkman award Henry Adams, 1959, Pulitzer prize in biography, 19 Friends of Lit. award for Henry Adams, 1965; Gu genheim fellow, 1955-56, 71-72. Mem. Nat. Coun Tchrs. English (dir. 1956-57), Mass. Hist. Soc. (cor Coll. English Assn. (pres. Chgo. area 1957), Am. Stud Assn. (pres. Wis.-No. Ill. chpt. 1960-61), MLA, T Delta Phi. Home: Evanston Ill. Died Feb. 12, 1996.

SANDIFUR, CANTWELL PAUL, SR., mortga company executive; b. Decatur, Ill., Jan. 15, 1903; Frank Noah and Claira Louise (Iles) S.; m. Jer Evelyn Duling, Dec. 4, 1940; children: C. Paul Jr., M Louise, William F., Ann Elizabeth. LLB, Lewis a Clark Coll., 1930. Ins. agt . Prudential Life In Newark, 1925-27, West Coast Life Ins. Co., Seat Spokane, Wash., 1929-38; owner various business Spokane, 1938-54; chm. bd. Met. Mortgage and Secu ties Co. Inc., Spokane, 1954-95; bd. dirs. subs. M Mortgage & Securities Co. Inc. Chair established in name Ea. Wash. U. Coll. Bus. Aminstrn., 1991. Me Manito Lions Club, Spokane Club. Republican Methodist. Home: Spokane Wa. Died June 2, 1995.

SANGER, ELEANOR, television producer, direct writer; b. Hong Kong, Sept. 15, 1929; d. Richard a Lonni (Wernicke) S.; m. Robert Nelson Riger, June 1950 (div. July 1981); children: Christopher Rob Victoria Riger Phillips, Robert Paris, Charlotte Ri Hull. BA magna cum laude, Smith Coll., 1950; po grad. Russian Inst., Columbia U., 1951-52. Mgr. p affairs Sta. WNBC-TV, N.Y.C., 1957-60; writer A News, N.Y.C., 1967; mgr. client rels., assoc. produ ABC Sports, N.Y.C., 1966-70, staff producer, writ dir., 1973-86; producer Winter and Summer Olymp ABC Sports, 1968, 76, 84; producer Winter Olymp ABC Sports, Lake Placid, N.Y., 1980; producer bobs and luge competition ABC Sports Winter Olymp Calgary, Can., 1988; producer equestrian events N Sports/Summer Olympics, Seoul, Republic of Kor 1988; freelance producer, writer TV documentari 1970; producer, writer Tomorrow Entertainme N.Y.C., 1971-73; adj. lectr. electronic journalism me arts dept. U. Ariz., 1990-93, chmn. adv. bd. media a dept., 1990-93. Assoc. producer The Open Mind, 19 60 (Robert E. Sherwood award 1958), producer, 19 63. Mem. adv. bd. Women's Sports Found. Recipien Emmy awards for Winter and Summer Olympics, 19 Summer Olympics Preview, 1976, Winter Olymp 1980, Summer Olympics, 1984, 88, NCAA Footb 1981, Gold Video award for ABC Funfit with Mary L Retton, Rec. Industry Assn. Am., 1985, Vira award best dir. home video, 1985, Smith Coll. medal, 19 named ABC-YMCA Woman Achiever of Yr., 198 Mem. Acad. TV Arts and Scis., Writers Guild A West, Dirs. Guild Am., Tucson Smith Club (bd. d 1991-93, Smith Coll. medal com. 1991-93), Phi B Kappa. Democrat. Episcopalian. Home: Viney Haven Mass. Died Mar. 7, 1993.

SANKARA, THOMAS, former head of State Burkina Faso. Past minister of info. Upper Volta; pri minister of Upper Volta, 1983, arrested May 1983; coup which deposed Col. Saye Zerbo, Aug. 1983; chr Nat. Council of Revolution, 1983-87; head of State Burkina Faso (formerly Upper Volta), 1983-87. Ser with Army. Home: Ouagadougou Burinka Faso

SAN PEDRO, ENRIQUE, bishop; b. Havana, Cu Mar. 9, 1926; s. Enrique and Maria Anto (Fornaguera) San Pedro. MA in Classical Lit., Coll. Estanislao, Spain, 1947; Licentiate philosophy, Un Pontificia de Comillas, Santander, Spain, 1950; Lic tiate theology, Leopold-Franzens Univ., Innsbru Austria, 1958, STD, 1965; postgrad., Franz -José Univ., Vienna, Austria, 1958-59, 60-64, Pontificio stituto Biblico, Rome, 1963. Ordained priest Roman Cath. Ch., 1957. Lectr. Hebrew Sch. Theology, Colegio de St. Francisco de Borja, Barcelona, Spain, 1963-64; prof. Old Testament St. Pius X Pontifical Coll., Dalat, Vietnam, 1965-75, asst. dean studies, sec. to faculty theology, 1967-72, editor theology digest, 1968-72; prof. Holy Scripture Pacific Regional Sem., Suva, Fiji, 1978-80, head libr., 1979; prof. Holy Scripture and Homiletics St. Vincent de Paul Sem., Boynton Beach, Fla., 1981-85; aux. bishop Diocese of Galveston-Houston, 1986-91; titular bishop Siccesi, 1986-91; co-adjutor bishop Brownsville Diocese, 1991, bishop, 1991-94; bd. dirs. bishop's com. priestly formation, Nat. Cath. Conf. of Bishops-U.S. Cath. Conf., also liaison for Vietnamese migration and refugee svcs., Bishops' com., chmn. Hispanic Affairs com., 1990-93; cons. Bishop's com. on liturgy, sub-com. Hispanic liturgy; mem. exec. bd. Interracial Justice, Nat. Adv. Coun.; lectr. Loyola U., Rome, one semester, 1963-64, St. Thomas Univ., Houston, 1986-87; vis. prof. Sem. de Santo Tomás, Santo Domingo, Dominican Republic, 1976-77, 80-81; instr. permanent deacons program Archdiocese Miami, Fla., 1981-85; guest lectr. Pacific Theol. Coll., Suva, 1978-80; tchr. seminars and courses, Fiji, French Polynesia, Am. Samoa, Miami, Fla., 1978-85; participant Premier Cong. Cath. Internat. des Etudes Biblique, Louvain, Belgium, Congs. Internat. Soc. Study Old Testament, Oxford, Eng., Bonn, Fed. Republic Germany, Uppsala, Sweden. Author: Introducción a la Literatura Profética, 1982, Diez Años Dialogando, 1989, also articles in profl. publs., book revs. Mem. Mayor's AIDS Alliance Adv. Bd., Houston/Harris County, 1986-91; mem. Hispanic AIDS Coalition, Houston Area HIV Health Svcs. Planning Coun., crackdown edn. com. Houston Ind. Sch. Dist., Greater Houston Coalition for Ednl. Excellence, U. Houston Pres.'s Adv. Coun.; trustee Inst. of Religion, Tex. Med. Ctr., Inst. Hispanic Culture Bd. Voc. Guidance Svcs.; bd. dirs. CASA-Child Advocates, Inc., Cath. Univ. Am. Mem. Asia Soc., Nat. Trust Historic Preservation, Vatican Libr. Died July 17, 1994; buried Miami, Fla.

SANTORO, ALEX, infosystems specialist; b. Kansas City, Mo., July 28, 1936; s. Alexander Luke and Mara Louise (Ratkaj) S. BS in Chem., U. Mo., Rolla, 1957; postgrad., U. Kans., 1959; MA in Math., U. Mo., Kansas City, 1965. Dir. computing svc. U. Kans. Med. Ctr., 1966-68; communications programmer United Computing Svc., Kansas City, 1969-71; programmer Trans Tech., Inc., Kansas City, 1971-72; database adminstr. Fed. Res. Bank Kansas City, 1972-84; prin. tech. assoc. Mut. Benefit Life Ins. Co., Kansas City, 1984-91; private cons. Kansas City, 1991-93; rschr./decoder b-ing. Shakespearean works. With U.S. Army, 1959-62. Mem. Assn. for Computing Machinery, AFTRA, Nat. ...on. Soc. Home: Kansas City Mo. Died Nov. 22, 1993.

SANTOSUOSSO, JOSEPH RALPH, manufacturing executive; b. Quincy, Mass, Mar. 14, 1942; s. Frank and ...nne D. (Carbotti) S.; m. Diane Drinkwater, Nov. 9, ...63; children: Laurie, Paul, David. BSME, Worcester ...ly. Inst., 1963, MSME, 1969; MBA in Fin., Ariz. ...ate U., 1973. Registered profl. engr. Mass., N.Y., ...J., Conn. Colo., Fla., Va., N.C., Wash., La. Engr. ...n. Electric Corp., Schenectady, N.Y., 1965-70, ...oneywell Corp., Phoenix, 1970-75; chief engr. ...BASCO Services, Inc., N.Y.C., 1975-85; pres., chief ...c. officer Lockheed Shipbuilding Co., Seattle, 1985-... Anthony Mfg. Co., San Fernando, Calif., 1989—, ...nthony Internat., Inc., 1989—. Mem. adv. com. to ... dirs. N.J. Inst. Tech., Newark, 1983-86. Mem. ...SME, Soc. Naval Architects & Marine Engrs., Am. ...c. Naval Engrs., Sigma Iota Epsilon, Beta Gamma ...ma. Home: Woodinville Wash.

...N YU, president of Burma; b. Prome, Burma, 1919; ...dent U. Rangoon, Commd. officer Burmese Army, ...42, advanced through grades to brig. gen.; mil. sec. to ...ef gen. staff, 1956-59, officer commanding North and ...rthwest mil. areas; mem. Revolutionary Council; dep. ...ef of gen. staff, commdr. land forces; minister fin. and ...enue, 1963; gen. sec. Central Organizing com. ...rmese Socialist Programme Party, from 1965, minister ... planning, fin. and revenue, 1969-72; dep. prime ...nister, 1971-74; minister def., 1972-74; chief gen. staff, ...72-74; sec. Council State, 1974-81, chmn., 1981-88; ... chmn. Socialist Econ. Planning Com., until 1988. ...d January 28, 1996. Home: Rangoon Myanmar

...RAGAT, GIUSEPPE, Italian government official; b. ...t. 19, 1898. Ed., U. degli Studi, Turin, Italy. ...bassador to France, 1945-47; sec. Italian Socialist ...our Party, 1947-64; dep. prime minister Italy, Rome, ...7-49, 54-57, minister merchant marine, 1947-49, ...ister fgn. affairs, 1963-64, former mem. Senate; pres. ...ian Republic, Rome, 1964-71, Social Dem. Party, ...ne, from 1975; life senator. Home: Rome Italy ...eased.

...RGENT, LEON FRANK, lawyer; b. Milw., Jan. 29, ...2; s. Frank H. and Evelyn (Burroughs) S.; m. Mary ...King, May 28, 1927; children: David B., John K., ...abeth (Mrs. J.S. Vazifdar). A.B., Dartmouth Coll., ...3; LL.B., Yale U., 1927. Bar: Mass. 1928. Assoc. ... Warner, Stackpole & Bradlee, Boston, 1927-29, ...ers and Hall, Boston, 1929-50; partner firm Powers ...Hall, Boston, 1950-88; dir. Am. Core Twine Corp., ...2-52, Turgeons, Inc., 1937-74; trustee Winchester Savs. Bank, 1967-75. Author articles on med. malpractice. Trustee Winchester Pub. Library, 1942-57, Alice W. Door Found., 1958-88, Marion L. Decrow Found., 1980-88; trustee, sec., treas. Theodore Edson Parker Found., 1970-88; v.p., dir Winchester Hosp., 1942-49. Fellow Am. Coll. Trial Lawyers; mem. Am., Mass., Boston bar assns., Phi Delta Phi. Club: Winchester Country. Home: Center Sandwich N.H. Died Aug. 17, 1988; interred Center Sandwich, N.H.

SARLAT, NOAH, publisher; b. N.Y.C., July 13, 1918; s. Samuel J. and Mary (Rosenstein) S.; m. Eleanor A. Levy, July 23, 1941; children: Laurie, Ivy Syd. B.A., NYU, 1938. Advt. copywriter Alvin Gardner Co., 1939; sales rep. Look mag., 1940-41, writer book dept., 1945-47; picture editor Reader's Scope mag., 1947-48, Argosy mag., 1948-50; editorial dir. mags. Stag, For Men Only, Man's World, Male, Men, Sportsman, Action for Men, Adventure Life, Triple-Length Adventure, Men in Action, 1950-77; with Rolat Pub. Corp. (pub. Men, True Secrets, Intimate Secrets, Intimate Romances), N.Y.C., 1977-82; asst. to pub. Thomaston Publs., Inc., N.Y.C., 1982-84; editorial dir. Manhattan Living, M.K.L. Ltd., 1984-86; asst. to pub. Larken Communications Inc., 1986-89, editorial cons., 1989; ret., 1989. Free-lance writer, 1947; Compiler, editor: Sintown, U.S.A, 1952, America's Cities of Sin, 1952, How I Made a Million, 1955, Combat, Rogues and Lovers, 1956, This is It, 1957, Women With Guns, 1962, War Cry, 1962, Danger Patrol, 1962; contbr. articles, stories to numerous mags. Served to capt. AUS, 1941-45. Recipient Bronze Star. Jewish. Home: Lake Worth Fla. Deceased.

SATTERLY, JACK, geologist; b. Cambridge, Eng., Sept. 28, 1906; emigrated to Can., 1912; s. John and May Mary Jane (Randall) S.; m. Eileen Sims, Mar. 2, 1935; children: Peter Randall, Elizabeth Hamilton. B.A., U. Toronto, Ont., Can., 1927, M.A., 1928; Ph.D., U. Cambridge, 1931; postgrad., Princeton U., 1931-32. Geologist Loangwa Concessions (N.R.) Ltd., No. Rhodesia, 1933-34, Guysborough Mines Ltd., N.S., 1934-35; instr. dept. geology U. Toronto, 1935-36, lectr., 1936-39; asst. dir. dept. geology Royal Ont. Mus., Toronto, 1936-39; rsch. assoc. dept. mineralogy Royal Ont. Mus., 1971-93; geologist Ont. Dept. Mines, 1939-61, sr. geologist, 1961-67; chief rev. and resources sect., geol. br. Ont. Dept. Mines and No. Affairs, 1967-71. Author: A Catalogue of the Ontario Localities Represented by the Mineral Collection of the Royal Ontario Museum, 1977. Recipient Centennial medal, 1967; Coleman Gold medal in geology U. Toronto, 1927; Royal Ont. Mus. named Jack Satterly Geochronology Lab., 1977; 1851 Exhbn. Overseas scholar, 1929-30, 30-31. Fellow Geol. Assn. Can., Royal Soc. Can.; mem. Can. Inst. Mining and Metallurgy (life), Mineral. Assn. Can. Home: Toronto Can. Died Mar. 1, 1993.

SAUNDERS, JOSEPH FRANCIS, biochemist, retired government official; b. Mt. Pleasant, Pa., Nov. 23, 1950; m. Pauline Claire Dugan; children: Joseph Francis, William Paul. BS, Duquesne U., 1950; MS, Georgetown U., 1955, PhD, 1960. Asst. to head medicine and dentistry br. Office Naval Rsch., Washington, 1952-57, sci. project officer, 1957-59, asst. head, 1959-60, head medicine and dentistry br., 1960-64; biosatellite program scientist and asst. chief of environ. biology, Office of Space Sci. and Applications NASA Hdqurs., Washington, 1964-66; chief environ biology Office Manned Space Flight, Washington, 1966-71; biosatellite program scientist Office Life Scis. Office Manned Space Flight, Washington; coord. U.S.-USSR cancer rsch. activities, mgr. U.S.A.-China Cancer Program, Am. Hungarian Cancer Program, Office Internat. Affairs, Nat. Cancer Inst. NIH, Bethesda, Md., 1973-83, dep. dir., 1973-84; instr. hematology and lab. techniques Bus. Tng. Coll. Pitts., 1950-51; guest scientist Naval Med. Rsch. Inst., 1958-60; mem. several sci. dels. to USSR. Author numerous tech. reports; editor: Bioregenerative Systems, 1968, The Experiments of Biosatellite II, 1971; co-editor: Depressed Metabolism, 1969, U.S.A.-USSR Monograph on Methods of Development in Anticancer Drugs, 1977; editor Immunology in Perspective, 1988; editor, narrator movies on biosatellites; mem. editorial bd. Bioscis. Communications, 1975-78, Year Book of Cancer, 1976-82; coordinating editor Jour. Soviet Oncology, 1980-83. With USNR, 1945-46, 51-52. Recipient Arthur S. Flemming award in sci. 1962, NASA Group Achievement award, 1974, Dirs. award NIH, 1979, Div. Health and Human Svcs. Spl. Achievement award, 1982. Mem. AAAS, Am. Chem. Soc., Am. Physiol. Soc. (mgr. membership and sci. programs dept. 1983-93), Fedn. Am. Socs. Exptl. Biology (exec. officers adv. com. 1986-92), Am. Assn. Immunologists (hon., exec. dir. 1986, mng. editor Jour. Immunology 1986-92), Coun. Biology Editors, Clin. Immunolog. Soc. (hon.), Sigma Xi, Alpha Chi Sigma. Home: Springfield Va. Died June 11, 1993; interred Fairfax Meml. Park, Fairfax, Va.

SAUNDERS, SIR OWEN (ALFRED), mechanical engineer, educator; b. Sept. 24, 1904; s. Aldred George and Margaret Ellen (Jones) S.; ed. Birbeck Coll., London, Trinity Coll., Cambridge (Eng.) U.; m. Marion Isabel McKechney, 1935 (dec. 1980); 3 children; m. 2d Daphne Holmes, 1981. Sci. officer Dept. Sci. and Indsl. Research, 1926; lectr. applied math. physics Imperial Coll., 1932; Clothworkers' Reader in applied thermodynamics U. London, 1937, prof., from 1946, head dept., 1946-65, pro-rector, 1964-67, acting rector, 1966-67, vice chancellor, 1967-69, dean City and Guilds Coll., 1955-64, prof. emeritus; on loan Directorate Tubine Engines, MAP, 1942-45. Pres. Brit. Flame Research Com., British Assn., 1949; chmn. council Royal Holloway Coll., 1971-86; founder Fellowship of Engring., 1976. Author: The Calculation of Heat Transmission, 1932; An Introduction to Heat Transfer, 1950; contbr. articles to profl. jours. Created knight, 1965. Fellow Royal Soc.; hon. mem. Yugoslav Acad., Japan Soc. Mech. Engrs., ASME, Assn. Nat. Acad. Engring. Home: Surrey Eng.

SAUVÉ, JEANNE, former governor general and commander-in-chief of Canada; b. Prud'homme, Sask., Can., Apr. 26, 1922; d. Charles Albert and Anna (Vaillant) Benoît; m. Maurice Sauvé, Sept. 24, 1948; 1 son, Jean-François. Grad., U. Ottawa, D (hon.); diploma in French Civilization, U. Paris, 1952. Nat. pres. Jeunese etudiante catholique, Montreal, 1942-47; asst. to dir. youth sect. UNESCO, Paris, 1951; journalist, broadcaster, 1952-72; bd. dirs. Union des Artistes, Montreal, 1961, v.p., 1968-70; v.p. Canadian Inst. on Pub. Affairs, 1962-64, pres., 1964; mem. Can. Centennial Commn., 1967; gen. sec. Fedn. des Auteurs et des Artistes du Can., 1966-72; mem. Parliament for Ahuntsic, Montreal, 1972-79, Parliament for Laval-des-Rapides, 1980-84; advisor external affairs Sec. of State, 1978-79; min. sci. and tech., then min. environment and communications Govt. of Canada, Ottawa, Ont., 1972-79; speaker Ho. of Commons, Ottawa, 1980-84; gov. gen., comdr.-in-chief of Can., 1984-90. Founder, hon. chmn. Jeanne Sauvé Youth Found., 1990; sworn in mem. Privy Coun. P.C. Companion Order of Can.; decorated comdr. Order of Mil. Merit; recipient La Médaille de la Chancellerie des U. de Paris, Sorbonne U.; 1st woman to hold position of gov. gen. of Can. Fellow Royal Archtl. Inst. Can. (hon.), Royal Soc. Can. (hon.); mem. Inst. for Rsch. on Pub. Policy (founding); Internat. Adv. Council, Power Corp. of Canada, Montreal; Chmn's.Internat. Adv. Council, Americas Soc., New York. Mem. Liberal Party of Can. Roman Catholic. Home: Montréal Can. Died Jan. 26, 1993.

SAVALAS, TELLY ARISTOTELES, actor; b. Garden City, N.Y., Jan. 21, 1926; s. Nicholas Constantine and Christina (Kapsallis) S.; m. Katherine Nicolaides; 1 child, Christina; m. Marilynn Gardner, Oct. 28, 1960; children: Penelope, Candace, Nicholas; m. Julie Hovland, Dec. 22, 1984; children: Christian, Ariana. B.S., Columbia U. Asst. dir. Near East, South Asia and Africa, Info. Service, Dept. State, to 1955; sr. dir. news and spl. events dept., ABC, 1955-58; producer Your Voice of America, 1955-58; dir. Stamford (Conn.) Playhouse, 1958-59. Voice debut as actor Bring Home a Baby, Armstrong Circle Theatre, 1959; appeared in numerous motion pictures including Young Savages, 1961, Cape Fear, 1962, Birdman of Alcatraz, 1962, The Man from the Diners Club, 1963, The New Interns, 1964, Genghis Khan, 1965, The Battle of the Bulge, 1965, The Greatest Story Ever Told, 1965, Beau Geste, 1966, The Dirty Dozen, 1967, The Scalphunters, 1968, Buona Sera, Mrs. Campbell, 1968, The Assassination Bureau, 1969, On Her Majesty's Secret Service, 1969, Crooks and Coronets, 1969, MacKenna's Gold, 1969, Kelly's Heroes, 1970, A Town Called Bastard, 1970, Pancho Villa, 1971, Horror Express, 1972, Inside Out, 1975, Diamond Mercenaries, 1975, Killer Force, 1975, Lisa and the Devil, 1976, Inside Out, 1976, Capricorn One, 1978, Escape to Athena, 1978, The Border, 1979, My Palikari, 1980, Cannonball Run II, 1983, The Dirty Dozen III, 1987, The Secret of the Sahara, Faceless; TV appearances include series The Witness, 1960-61, The Untouchables, 1961, 77 Sunset Strip, 1963, The Fugitive, 1965, Cimarron Strip, 1967, Garrison's Gorrillas, 1967, Combat, 1967, The Marcus-Nelson Murders; TV movie Kojak, 1972, series 1973-78, The Fatal Mission, The Cartier Affair; appeared in TV mini-series The French Atlantic Affair, 1979, Hellinger's Law, 1980; appeared in movie of the week The Belarus File, 1984, Kojak: The Price of Justice, 1987, The Equalizer, 1987, Expedition Titanic, 1987, as Kojak in The ABC Saturday Mystery, 1989, The Commish, 1992; spokesman Ford Motor Co. Served with AUS, World War II. Recipient Peabody award, Emmy awards 1974, 76, People's Choice awards, 1975-76, Freedom Found. award. Greek Orthodox. Home: Universal City Calif. Died Jan 23, 1994.

SAVIT, CARL HERTZ, geophysicist; b. N.Y.C., July 19, 1922; m. Sandra Kaplan, July 6, 1946; children: Mark, Deborah Savit Pearlman, Judith Savit Simon. B.S. with honors, Calif. Inst. Tech., 1942, M.S., 1943, postgrad., 1943-44, 46-48. Statis. cons. Long Range Meteorology Project, U.S. Air Force, 1943-44; assoc. prof. math. San Fernando Valley State Coll., Northridge, Calif., 1959-60; chief math. Western Geophys. Co., Litton Industries, Inc., 1948-60, dir. systems research, 1960-65, v.p. research and devel., 1965-70, sr. v.p., 1971-86; cons. in field, 1986-96; asst. for earth, sea, air sci. to U.S. Pres.'s Sci. Adv.; chmn. Interagy Com. for Atmospheric Scis., 1970-71; mem. panel On-Site Inspection Unidentified Seismic Events, 1961; mem. Pres.'s panels on Disposition of Oil Leasing in the Santa Barbara Channel, Offshore Pollution, 1969; mem. U.S. Initiatives in Transp., 1971; mem. U.S. del. to, USSR, 1971; mem. Assembly Math. and Phys. Scis., Nat. Acad. Scis./NRC, 1977-80; mem. com. on seismology

NAS/NRC, 1971-75, chmn., 1972-74, mem. U.S. nat. com. on tunneling, 1972-75, chmn. subcom. on tech. data and info., 1972-75, mem. panel on earthquake prediction, NAS/NRC, 1973-75, 87-90; dir. Nat. Ocean Industries, Assn., 1972-81, vice chmn. bd., 1973-75, chmn. bd., 1975-76; mem. nat. adv. com. Tex. Marine Biomed. Inst., 1973-78; mem. U.S. Coastal Zone Mgmt. Adv. Com., 1975-78; mem. energy research adv. bd. U.S. Dept. Energy, 1978-81, chmn. com. on geothermal energy, 1979-81; chmn. vis. com. U. Tex. Inst. for Geophysics, 1984—; mem. OCS policy com. Dept. Interior, 1985-89; mem. computer systems tech. adv. com. U.S. Dep. Com., 1989-90, mem. nat. sea grant rev. panel, 1990-94; adj. prof. geophysics Rice U., 1988-94; vis. prof. Netherlands Nat. U. at Utrecht, 1990. Author: Introduction to Geophysical Prospecting; also articles. Served as 2d lt. USAAF, 1944-46. Recipient Litton Advanced Tech. award, 1980; named Inventor of Yr. Houston Intell Property Law Assn., 1988. Fellow Geol. Soc. Am.; mem. European Assn. Exploration Geophysicists, Marine Tech. Soc. (Compass award for disting. achievement 1979), Soc. Exploration Geophysicists (named Classic Author of Geophysics 1960, editor jour. 1967-69, pres. 1971-72, chmn. 43d ann. meeting 1973, Kauffman gold medal 1979, hon. mem.), Acoustical Soc. Am., Am. Mgmt. Assn. (mem. research and devel. council 1974-76), Internat. Assn. Geophys. Contractors (pres. 1973-75 Disting. Achievement award), World Geol. Congress 1989 (hon.), Nat. Acad. Engring., Sigma Xi. Club: Cosmos (Washington). Home: Houston Tex. Died Mar. 21, 1996.

SAWYER, GRANT, lawyer; b. Twin Falls, Idaho, Dec. 14, 1918; s. Harry William and Bula Bell (Cameron) S.; m. Bette Norene Hoge, Aug. 1, 1946; 1 child, Gail. BA, Linfield Coll., 1939; student, U.Nev., Reno, 1940-44; JD, Georgetown U., 1948. Bar: Nev. 1948, D.C. 1948, U.S. Dist. Ct. Nev. 1967, U.S. Ct. Appeals (9th cir.) 1974, U.S. Supreme Ct. 1959. Pvt. practice Elko, Nev., 1948-50; dist. atty. Elko County, Nev., 1950-58; gov. State of Nev., 1959-67; sr. ptnr. Lionel Sawyer & Collins, Las Vegas, 1967-96. Author books and articles on gaming. Mem. bd. regents U. Nev., 1957-58; Dem. nat. committeeman for Nev., 1968-88; chmn. Nev. Commn. on Nuclear Projects, 1985-95; mem. adv. bd. Aid for Aids of Nev., 1987-96; trustee Bluecoats, Inc., 1987-96; mem. exec. com. U. Nev. Las Vegas Found., 1988-96; mem. nat. adv. coun. ACLU, 1988-96; bd. dirs. Nat. Jud. Coll., 1991-94. Pvt. to 1st lt. U.S. Army, 1942-46, PTO. Mem. ABA, Nev. Bar Assn., D.C. Bar Assn., Am. Judicature Soc., Phi Delta Phi. Home: Las Vegas Nev. Died February 19, 1996.

SAWYER, JOHN EDWARD, foundation officer; b. Worcester, Mass., May 5, 1917; s. William Henry and Dorothy (Winslow) S.; m. Anne W. Swift, June 28, 1941; children: Katharine, John, Stephen W., William Kent. AB, Williams Coll., 1939; AM, Harvard U., 1941; LLD (hon.), Amherst Coll., 1961, Wesleyan U., 1962, Williams Coll., 1974, Yale U., 1974, Columbia U., 1985, NYU, 1987, Johns Hopkins U., 1988, Tulane U., 1989. With Dept. State, 1946; jr. fellow Soc. Fellows, Harvard, 1946-49, asst. prof. econ. history, 1949-53; asso. prof. econ. history Yale, 1953-61; pres. Williams Coll., Williamstown, Mass., 1961-73, Andrew W. Mellon Found., N.Y.C., 1975-87; pres. emeritus Andrew W. Mellon Found., 1988-95. Contbr. articles to profl. jours. Trustee Clark Art Inst., Woods Hole Oceanographic Instn., Nat. Humanities Ctr. Served from ensign to lt. USNR, 1942-46; with O.S.S., 1942-45, Washington and overseas. Decorated Bronze Star; recipient Pub. Welfare medal Nat. Acad. Scis., 1988. Fellow Am. Acad. Arts and Scis., Am. Philos. Soc. (councillor); mem. AAAS (dir. 1982-86), Am. Econ. History Assn. (trustee 1956-60), Phi Beta Kappa (Disting. Svcs. to Humanities award 1990). Home: New York N.Y. Died Feb. 7, 1995.

SAYRES, WILLIAM CORTLANDT, anthropologist, educator; b. Detroit, Apr. 5, 1927; s. Cortlandt Whitehead and Doris (Abbott) S.; m. Christine Croneis, July 31, 1951 (dec. Nov. 1970); 1 son, William; m. Juanita Falicia Garcia-Maldonado, Sept. 3, 1971; children: Jason, Nicole, Joel, Rory, Kelli. B.A., Beloit Coll., 1949; M.A., Harvard U., 1951, Ph.D., 1953. Instr. anthropology Yale U., New Haven, 1954-57; research assoc. social scis. N.Y. State Dept. Edn., Albany, 1957-63; assoc. prof. Tchrs. Coll. Columbia U., N.Y.C., 1963-72, prof. edn. Tchrs. Coll., 1972-93, prof. edn. Sch. Internat. and Pub. Affairs, 1983-93, NSF postdoctoral fellow, 1952-53; cons. Ministeries Edn., Lima, Peru, 1963-65, 68-69, Kabul, Afghanistan, 1969-71, 73-76; lectr. U. Santiago, Chile, 1983. Author: Sammy Louis: The Life History of a Young Micmac, 1956, Sonotaw, 1959, Do Good, 1966; co-author: El Maestro y el Desarrollo del Pueblo, 1967; co-editor, author: Social Aspects of Education, 1962; contbr. articles to profl. jours. Named to Athletic Hall of Honor Beloit Coll., 1972. Mem. Phi Beta Kappa, Omicron Delta Kappa, Sigma Xi, Beta Theta Pi. Home: Bogota N.J. Died Feb. 1993; interred North Chatham, N.Y.

SCALI, JOHN ALFRED, journalist; b. Canton, Ohio, Apr. 27, 1918; s. Paul M. and Lucy (Leone) S.; m. Helen Lauinger Glock, Aug. 30, 1945 (div. 1973); children: Donna Claire Scali Bordley, Paula Lucia Scali Wolf, Carla Scali Byrd; m. Denise St. Germain, Mar. 4, 1973. B.S. in Journalism, Boston U., 1942. Reporter Boston Herald, 1942, Boston bur. U.P., 1942-43; war corr. A.P., 1943-44, diplomatic corr. Washington Bur., 1945-61; diplomatic corr. ABC News, Washington, 1961-71; spl. cons. for fgn. affairs to Pres. U.S., 1971-73; U.S. ambassador to UN, N.Y.C., 1973-75; sr. corr. ABC News, Washington, 1975—. mem. adv. council Ariz. Heart Inst., mem. Internat. Heart Inst., Council Am. Ambassadors. Recipient Man of Year award in journalism Boston U., 1965, High Achievement award, 1986, Spl. award Overseas Press Clubs, 1965, Journalism award U. So. Calif., 1964, spl. award Washington chpt. Nat. Acad. Arts and Scis., 1964; John Scali award created by Washington chpt. AFTRA, 1964. Mem. A.F.T.R.A., Council on Fgn. Relations, Sigma Delta Chi. Club: Nat. Press (Washington). Home: Washington D.C. Died October 9, 1995.

SCANNELL, ROBERT E., corporate lawyer; b. N.Y.C., 1939. BS, Holy Cross Coll., 1961; LLB, Columbia U., 1964. Bar: D.C., N.Y. V.p. law, sec. AT&T, N.Y.C. Home: New York N.Y. Died Apr. 4, 1994.

SCARLATO, OREST ALEXANDROVICH, zoologist, researcher, science association director; b. Novorzhev, Pskov, Russia, Aug. 21, 1920; s. Alexander Nickolayevich and Yekaterina (Kobanova) S.; m. Yelena Shamanova, Nov. 28, 1950 (dec. July 1987); 1 child, Sergei Orestovich. Grad. biology faculty, U. Leningrad, 1950, D of Biol. Sci., 1974; kandidat in Biol. Sci., Zool. Inst., Leningrad, 1953. Rschr. Zool. Inst., Russian Acad. Scis., 1953-54, 56-62, sci. sec., 1954-56, asst. dir., 1962-74, dir., 1974-94; mem. presidium St. Petersburg Sci. Ctr., Russian Acad. Scis., 1986-94, mem. Bur. Gen. Biology Dept., Moscow, 1982-94; chmn. Sci. Coun. Regional Nature Mgmt., St. Petersburg, 1980-94. Author: Bivalve Molluscs of Far Eastern Seas of the USSR, 1960, Bivavlve Molluscs of Temperate Latitudes of the Western Pacific Ocean, 1981; editor (serial eds.) Zool. Inst. Fauna of Russia, 1974-94, fauna identification guides, inst. procs. and explorations of seas. Served to lt. co. commr. Russian mil., 1939-45. Recipient Order Banner of Labour, USSR Acad. Sic., 1975, 82, Badge Honour, 1967,Order of Patriotic War, Ministry Def., 1985. Mem. Russian Acad. Scis. (corr.), Russian Geog. Soc., Russian Hydrobiol. Soc., Russian Malacological Soc. Home: Saint Petersburg Russia Died Oct. 13, 1994.

SCARRY, RICHARD MCCLURE, illustrator, author; b. Boston, June 5, 1919; s. John James and Mary Louise Barbara (McClure) S.; m. Patricia Murphy, Sept. 11, 1949; 1 son, Richard. Student, Boston Mus. Sch., 1939-42. Pres. Best Book Club Ever, Random House, Inc., N.Y.C., 1975-93; Died April 30, 1994. Author, illustrator 181 children's books, 1947-94, including Best Word Book Ever, 1963, Best Mother Goose Ever, 1964, I Am a Bunny, (illus. 1963), Busy, Busy World, 1965, Storybook Dictionary, 1966, Best Storybook Ever, 1968, What Do People Do All Day, 1968, Nicky Goes To The Doctor, 1972, Cars and Trucks and Things That Go, 1974, Early Words, 1976, Busiest People Ever, 1976, Best Make-It Book Ever, 1977, Postman Pig and His Busy Neighbors, 1978, Best First Book Ever, 1979, Best Christmas Book Ever, 1981. Served with AUS, 1942-46. Recipient Edgar Allen Poe Spl. award Mystery Writers of Am., 1976. Mem. Authors Guild New York. Clubs: Gstaad (Switzerland) Yacht; Kongelig Dansk Yacht Klub (Copenhagen). Home: Gstaad Switerland Died Apr. 30, 1994.

SCHAAF, C(ARL) HART, economic consultant, writer, former international organization official; b. Ft. Wayne, Ind., Jan. 14, 1912; s. Albert H. and Bertha May (Hart) S.; m. Barbara Joan Crook, Nov. 22, 1945; children: Albert H., Timothy H. Student, U. Montpellier, France, 1930-31, U. Stockholm, 1937-39; B.A., U. Mich., 1935, Ph.D. (Horace H. Rackham fellow), 1940. Instr. polit. sci. CCNY, summer 1940; asso. prof. public adminstrn. Richmond div. Coll. William and Mary, 1940-42; state rationing adminstr. for Va. U.S. OPA, 1942-43; asst. dep. dir. gen., also chief supply for Europe UNRRA, 1944-47; asso. prof. adminstrn. Sch. Bus. and Public Adminstrn., Cornell U., 1947-49; dep. exec. sec. UN Econ. Commn. for Asia and Far East, 1949-54; mem. UN Tech. Assistance Survey Mission to Indonesia, 1950; spl. adviser to UN sec. gen. on relief and support civilian population Korea, 1950-51; resident rep. UN Tech. Assistance Bd., Israel, 1954-57, Phillipines, 1957-59; exec. agt. Com. Coordination Investigations Lower Mekong Basin, UN Econ. Commn., for Asia and Far East, 1959-69; resident rep. UN Devel. Program, Sri Lanka and Republic of Maldives, 1969-74; dep. exec. dir. ops. UN Fund for Population Activities, N.Y.C., 1974-77; team leader Basic Needs Assessment Missions to UN Fund for Population Activities, Nigeria, 1979, Tunisia, 1980, Maldives, 1981, Indonesia, 1984, Egypt, 1985; pres. C. Hart Schaaf Assos., Inc. (cons. econ. and social devel.), 1980-95; Mem. Mekong Adv. Com. Bd., 1969-72. Author: play Partition, 1948; (with Russell H. Fifield) The Lower Mekong: Challenge to Cooperation in Southeast Asia, 1963; Contbr. articles to tech. and acad. jours. Recipient (with Mekong Com.) Ramon Magsaysay award for internat. understanding, 1966, Outstanding Achievement award U. Mich., 1966. Mem. Am. Polit. Sci. Assn., Soc. Internat. Devel. Home: Silver Spring Md. Died Feb. 24, 1995.

SCHAD, THEODORE GEORGE, JR., food compan executive; b. N.Y.C., Mar. 4, 1927; s. Theodore Georg and Helen (Tennyson) S.; m. Karma Rose Cundell, Ma 21, 1957 (dec. June 8 1978); children: Roberta Gay Hil Theodore George III, Olive Schad Smith, Peter Ter nyson; m. Mary Nell Jennings, June 20, 1981. Studen Va. Mil. Inst., 1944-45; BS in Bus. and Econs., Ill. Ins Tech., 1950, MS in Bus. and Econs., 1951. V.p. mkt Great Western Savs. Co., L.A., 1961-63; prin., nat. di mktg., econ. cons. Peat, Marwick, Mitchell, N.Y.C 1964-71; chmn. bd., pres., chief exec. officer Lou An Foods, Inc., Schad Industries, Inc. (formerly Lou An Industries, Inc.), Opelousas, La., 1971-92, Lou Ana I dustries Internat., Opelousas, 1971-84, Schad Industri Internat., Opelousas, 1984-92, Lou Ana Foods of Te Inc., Kingwood, 1986-92, Lou Ana Gardens In Opelousas, 1989-92, TGS Enterprises, Opelousas, 199 92; instr. mktg. and econs. U. Calif., Riverside, U. S Calif., L.A. State Coll., U. Calif., L.A., 1956-63. Pr Assn. Parents Retarded Children, Mamaroneck, N.Y 1970-71; pres. Greater Opelousas C. of C., 1972-73, b dirs. 1973-74, 88-91; bd. dirs. Coun. for Better L Baton Rouge, 1975-80, La. Assn. Bus. and Industr 1980-85; chmn. U.S. Bus. and Indsl. Coun., 1987-91, b dirs., 1979-84, mem. exec. com., 1984-87, 91-92, b dirs. U.S. Indsl. Coun. Ednl. Found., 1987-92; trust Va. Mil. Inst. Found., 1978-88; v.p., mem. exec. b Evangeline area coun. Boy Scouts Am., 1984-85; pr Acadiana R.R. Devel. Dist., 1989-90. Recipient Di ing. Eagle Scout award Boy Scouts Am., 1985, Silv Beaver award, 1990; named Citizen of Yr. City Opelousas, 1979; Paul Harris fellow Rotary, 1987 Mem. Am. Mktg. Assn. (pres. So. Calif. chpt. 1961-6 dir. 1962-63), Greater Opelousas Econ. and Indsl. Cou (bd. dirs. 1988-91), Sertoma (founding pres. Brentwoo Calif. chpt. 1963, named man of yr. Opelousas ch 1978). Republican. Methodist. Home: Opelousas I Died Oct. 24, 1992.

SCHAEFER, EDWARD JOHN, electric company e ecutive; b. Balt., July 10, 1901; s. Michael and Elizab (Planthol t) S.; m. Hildegarde H. Hormel, Dec. 25, 19 children: Patricia, Diane Dorothy. BEE, Joh Hopkins, 1923; DEngring. (hon.), Ind. Inst. Tech. W Franklin Electric Co., Bluffton, Inc., from 1944; dirs. Franklin Electric (Australia) Pty., Ltd., Dan nong, Victoria, First Nat. Bank, Bluffton, Ind. Trus Ind. Inst. Tech.; fellow of bd. trustees Johns Hopkins Recipient Coffin award Gen. Electric Co., 193 Fellow Am. Inst. E.E.; mem. Ft. Wayne Engrs. Cl Tau Beta Pi. Home: Bluffton Ind. Deceased.

SCHAEFFER, PIERRE HENRI MARIE, auth composer; b. Nancy, France, Aug. 14, 1910; s. He and Lucie (Labriet) S.; m. Elisabeth Schmitt, Feb. 1 (dec. June 1941); 1 child, Marie Claire; m. Jacqueline Lisle, Oct. 31, 1962; 1 child, Justine. Student Ec Polytechnique, Paris, 1929-31, Ecole superieure d'el tricite, Paris, 1932-33, Ecole superieure des teleco munications, Paris, 1933-34. Founder Studio d'Es Radiodiffusion Francaise, 1942-45; founder Ra d'Outremer, France, 1950-55; founder, dir. Svc. de Recherche, ORTF, France, 1960-75; founder Groupe Recherche Musique Concrete, France; prof. C servatoire Nat. de Musique, Paris, 1968-76; mem. H Conseil de l'Audiovisuel, France, 1970-75; leader movement to form musique concrete, France, from 19 Composer: Etudes de bruits, 1948; Symphonie pour Homme Seul, 1950; Orphee, 1953; Etude aux Obj 1960; Triedre Fertile, 1975, L'Oeuvre intégrale en 3 1990. author books, essays: Clotaire Nicole, 1938; enfants de coeur, 1949; Traité des Objets Musica 1966; L'Avenir a reculons, 1970; Le gardien de vol (prix Sainte-Beuve 1969), 1969; Machines a c muniquer, vol. 1 Genese des simulacres, 1970, vo Pouvoir et Communication, 1972; La Musique et Ordinateurs, 1971; De l'experience musicale a l'ex ience humaine, 1971; De la Musique concrete a Musique meme, 1977; Les antennes de Jericho, 1 Excusez moi je meurs, 1981; Psychanalyse et Music 1982; Prelude Choral et Fugue, 1981; Faber et Sapi essai, 1986. Decorated chevalier des Palmes acade ques; comdr. Legion d'Honneur; grand officer O Nat. du Merite, comdr. des Arts et des Lettres, McLuhan of Communication, 1989—. Died Aug. 1995. Home: Paris France

SCHAEFLER, LEON, retired lawyer; b. N.Y.C., 2, 1903; s. Morris I. and Kate (Eckstein) S.; m. trude Herbert, June 10, 1927; children—Robe Kathryn. Student, NYU, 1920-21; LL.B., Fordham 1924. Bar: N.Y. bar 1925. Since practiced in that s gen. counsel Fifth Ave. Bank, N.Y.C., 1936-48; Bank of N.Y. (midtown offices); sr. partner firm F & Schaefler, specializing in surrogate and banking of counsel LeBoeuf, Lamb, Leiby & MacRae. Au articles on estate and banking practice. Fellow (h Am. Coll. Probate Counsel (pres. 1959-61, dir. 1957- mem. Fordham Law Alumni Assn. (dir. 1955-5 Club: Univ. Home: New York N.Y. Died Mar. 1994; interred Roselle Park, N.J.

SCHAENEN, LEE JOEL, orchestra conductor Bklyn., Aug. 10, 1925; s. Saul and Julia (Weiss) S. Nell Foster, Oct. 23, 1950. Ed., Columbia Coll., liard Sch. Music, Manhattan Sch. Music. dir. I Opera Ctr. for Am. Artists. Condr., N.Y. City O 1945-53, asst. to, Herbert von Karajan, 1956-57, ondr., Opera Berne, Switzerland, 1959-64, condr., ienna Volksoper, 1965-74, Chgo. Lyric Opera, 1958, 7-91; regular guest condr. Italian radio, Teatro Massimo, Palermo, Tea tro Communale, Florence, ilharmonia Ungarica, 1971-74, Seattle Opera, Florentine Opera, Milw., 1981-86, Utah Opera, Opera Colo.; tistic dir. Opera/Columbus, 1981-84; recs. for eutsche Gramaphone, Melodram, Mus. Heritage Soc. ditor: two operas of Cimarosa, Tales of Hoffmann, vith George London) Leopold Simoneau; accompanist, ach for Giuseppe de Luca, Leonard Warren, Maria allas. Served with AUS, 1943-45. Home: Sanibel land Fla. Died June 17, 1993.

CHAPIRO, MEYER, retired art history educator; b. avly, Lithuania, Russia, Sept. 23, 1904; came to U.S., 07, naturalized, 1914; s. Nathan M. and Fanny delman) S.; m. Lillian Milgram, 1928; children: iriam, Ernest. A.B., Columbia U., 1924, Ph.D., 1929. ectr. dept. fine arts and archaeology Columbia U., 28-36, asst. prof., 1936-46, asso. prof., 1946-52, prof. history, 1952-65; Univ. prof. Columbia, 1965-73; of. emeritus Columbia U., 1973-96; Norton prof. arvard, 1966-67; Slade prof. Oxford U., 1968; lectr. st. Fine Arts, N.Y. U., 1932-36, New Sch. Social ch., 1938-52, Warburg Inst. (London U.), 1947, 57, ollège de France, Paris, 1974, Cornell. U., Ind. U.; llow Ctr. for Advanced Study in Behavioral Scis., anford, 1962-63. Author articles and books on edieval, modern art; mem. bd. editors: Semiotica, Dissent, Jour. History of Ideas; works of art exhibited 1919-, Wallach Art Gallery, Columbia U., 1987. ecorated comdt. de l'Ordre des Arts et des Lettres ance; recipient award for disting. scholarship in manities Am. Council Learned Socs., 1960, ann. eative art award for notable achievement Brandeis U., 66, award for excellence in art history Art Dealers sn. Am., 1973, Mitchell award, 1980; Aby M. arburg prize, Hamburg, 1985; Guggenheim fellow, 39, 1942; MacArthur Found. fellow, 1987. Fellow n. Acad. Arts and Scis., Am.. Philos. Soc., Medieval ad. Am., Am. Inst. Arts and Letters, Brit. Acad. me: New York N.Y. Died Mar. 4, 1996.

CHARRER, BERTA VOGEL, anatomy and neuroscience educator; b. Munich, Dec. 1, 1906; d. Karl and anna V.; widowed. PhD in Zoology, U. Munich, 30; MD (hon.), U. Giessen, Germany, 1976, U. ankfurt, Germany, 1992; DSc (hon.), Northwestern 1977, U. N.C., 1978, Smith Coll., 1980, Harvard U., 32, Yeshiva U., 1983, Mt. Holyoke Coll., 1984, NY, 1985, U. Salzburg, Austria, 1988; LLD, U. gary, Alta., Can., 1982. Research assoc. Research t. for Psychiatry, Munich, 1931-34, Neurol. Inst., ankfurt-am-Main, 1934-37, U. Chgo. Dept. Anatomy, 37-38, Rockefeller Inst., N.Y.C., 1938-40; instr., ow Western Res. U. Dept. Anatomy, Cleve., 1940-46; n Guggenheim fellow U. Colo. Dept. Anatomy, nver, 1947-48, spl. USPHS research fellow, 1948-50; prof. (research) dept. anatomy U. Colo. Sch. dicine, Denver, 1950-55; prof. anatomy Albert Einn Coll. Medicine, 1955-77, acting chmn., 1965-67, 77, disting. prof. emeritus anatomy and neurosci., 78—. Decorated Order of Merit (Free State of varia); recipient Kraepelin gold medal, 1978, F.C. ch award Endocrine Soc., 1980, Nat. Medal Sci., 33. Mem. NAS, Am. Acad. Arts and Scis., Deutsche ad. Naturforscher Leopoldina (Schleiden medal 33), Am. Assn. Anatomists (pres. 1978-79, Henry ay award 1982), Am. Soc. Zoologists (hon. mem.), . Neurosci., Endocrine Soc. (F.C. Koch award 1980). ome: Bronx N.Y. Died July 23, 1995.

HARY, EMANUEL, artist; b. Feb. 27, 1924; s. rold and Aliza S.; m. Judith Schary, Sept. 23, 1951; dren: Abby, David, Anne. Student, Carnegie Inst. h. Sch. Fine Arts, 1945-46, Art Students League, 6-49, Pratt Graphics Ctr., 1962-63, Edwin Dickon, Howard Trafton, Frank Reilly, Ivan Olinsky, oert Hale, Jurgen Fischer. One-man shows, Guild lery, N.Y.C., 1978, 80, 81, group shows, Tel Aviv, an Coll., Bklyn. Mus., Kansas City Country Club za, Mo., U. Mich., U. Miami, Fla., Nassau Comity Coll., Lenox Square Art Festival, Ga., Guild lery, N.Y.; represented in permanent collections, thsonian Nat. Fine Art Collection, Met. Mus. Fine N.Y., Vatican Mus., Rome, Bklyn Mus., Jewish s., N.Y.C., Spertus Mus., Chgo., Madison Art Mus., , Fleming Mus., Vt., Wyo. Art Mus., Laramie, B'nai th Mus., Washington, Mus. of Israel, Jerusalem, s. of Haifa, Israel, Bldg. of Chief Rabbinate, salem, New Britain Mus. Am. Art, Ind. Mus. Am. Ga. Mus. Art, Hofstra U. Mus., Boston Pub. rary, N.Y. Pub. Library, Newark Pub. Library, U. z. Art Mus., Kansas City Art Inst., Library of Cons, in pvt. collections, commns. include, N.Y. rld's Fair Pavillion, Weizmann Inst. Sci., 1964; gned 4 stained glass painted windows for agogue, Rock Hill, N.Y., 1992, wood sculpture, 3, Holocaust Meml., 1994. Home: Rock Hill N.Y. d June 9, 1994.

HERER, ALFREDO VICENTE CARDINAL, bishop; b. Bom Principio, Rio Grande do Sul, zil, Feb. 5, 1903; s. Pedro and Ana Oppermann erer; student Seminario Central de Sao Leopoldo and tificial Gregorian U., Rome. Ordained priest Roman holic Ch., Rome, 1926; pvt. sec. to archbishop of Porto Alegre, Brazil, 1927-33; organizer of Parishes of Tapes and Barra do Ribeiro, 1933-35; parish priest Sao Geraldo, Porto Alegre, 1935-46; aux. bishop of Porto Alegre, 1946; archbishop, 1946-81, archbishop emeritus, 1982-96; elevated to Sacred Coll. of Cardinals, 1969. Died Mar. 10, 1996. Home: Porto Alegre Brazil

SCHIFF, JEROME ARNOLD, biologist, educator; b. Bklyn., Feb. 20, 1931; s. Charles K. and Molly (Weinberg) S. BA in Biology and Chemistry, Bklyn. Coll. (summer scholar invertebrate zoology Woods Hole Marine Biol. Lab.), 1952; PhD in Botany and Biochemistry, U. Pa., 1956. Predoctoral fellow USPHS, 1954-56; fellow Brookhaven Nat. Labs., summer 1956; rsch. assoc. biology Brandeis U., Waltham, Mass., 1956-57, instr., 1957-58, asst. prof., 1958-61, assoc. prof., 1961-65, prof. biology, 1966—, chmn. dept., 1972-75, Abraham and Etta Goodman prof. biology, 1974—; dir. Inst. Photobiology of Cells and Organelles, 1975-87; summer instr. exptl. marine botany Marine Biol. Lab., Woods Hole, Mass., 1971; sr. investigator explt. marine botany Marine Biol. Lab., 1972-74; dir. programs Exptl. Marine Botany, 1974-79; cons. on devel. biology NSF, 1965-68, cons. on metabolic biology, 1982-86; vis. prof. Tel Aviv U., 1972, Hebrew U., 1972, Weizmann Inst., Israel, 1977; mem. biology grant rev. program U.S.-Israel Binat. Sci. Found., 1974—; mem. corp. Marine Biol. Lab., 1972—. Mem. editorial bd. Developmental Biology, 1971-74, Plant Sci., 1972-78, assoc. editor, 1978-81, chief co-editor, 1981—; asst. editor Plant Physiology, 1964-69, adv. editor, 1969-79; mem. editorial com. Ann. Rev. Plant Physiology, 1974-80; contbr. over 180 articles to profl. jours. Carnegie Instn. fellow in plant biology, 1962-63; Recipient Disting. Alumni award Bklyn. Coll., 1972. Fellow AAAS, Am. Acad. Arts and Scis.; mem. Soc. Devel. Biology (sec. 1964-66, mem. exec. com.), Am. Soc. Biol. Chemists, Am. Soc. Plant Physiologists (mem. exec. com. 1972-88, Disting. Svc. award N.E. sect. 1989), Biophys. Soc., Internat. Phycological Soc., Phycological Soc. Am., Soc. Cell Biology, Soc. Gen. Microbiology, Soc. Protozoologists, Am. Soc. Microbiology, Internat. Soc. Devel. Biologists, Brit. Phycological Soc., Am. Soc. Photobiology, Sigma Xi. Home: Waltham Mass. Died July 28, 1995.

SCHILPP, PAUL ARTHUR, philosopher, editor, clergyman; b. Dillenburg, Hessen-Nassau, Germany, Feb. 6, 1897; came to U.S., 1913, naturalized, 1926; s. Hermann and Emilie (Dittmar) S.; m. Louise Gruenholz, Sept. 16, 1918; children: Erna Emilie Schilpp Bimson, Marjorie Elizabeth Schilpp Goodere, Robert Warner, Walter Norman; m. Madelon Golden, July 27, 1950; children: Erich Andrew, Margot Marlene. Student, Humanistic Gymnasium Bayreuth, Bavaria, 1907-13; A.B., Baldwin-Wallace Coll., Berea, Ohio, 1916, Litt.D., 1946; Litt.D., So. Ill. U., 1982; student, Columbia U., summers 1916, 17, Drew Theol. Sem., 1916-17; M.A., Northwestern U., 1922; B.D., Garrett Theol. Sem., 1922; auditor, U. Munich, summer 1928; Ph.D., Stanford U., 1936; L.H.D., Springfield (Mass.) Coll., 1963, Kent State U., 1975. Ordained to ministry Methodist Ch., 1918; pastor Calvary Ch., Terre Haute, Ind., 1918-21; prof. psychology and religious edn. Coll. Puget Sound, 1922-23; assoc. prof. philosophy, acting head dept. Coll. of Pacific, 1923-24, prof. philosophy, 1924-34; 2d chmn. Sch. Social Scis., 1930-34; assoc. prof. German lang. and lit., 1935-36; lectr. philosophy Northwestern U., 1936-37, assoc. prof. philosophy, 1937-50, prof., 1950-65, prof. emeritus, 1965-93; Disting. research prof. continuing edn. So. Ill. U., 1965-82, prof. emeritus, 1982-93; adj. prof. philosophy U. Calif.-Santa Barbara, 1982-87; Mendenhall Found. lectr. DePauw U., 1938; Tully C. Knoles Found. lectr. Coll. Pacific, 1954; Watumull Found. research fellow U. Calcutta, other univs. in India, 1950-51; Ingraham lectr. philosophy and religion Colby Coll., spring 1957; Grady Gammage Meml. lectr. Ariz. State U., 1963; U.S. participant Kant Workshop, U. Cologne, Fed. Republic of Germany, 1963; ofcl. rep. Dept. State, 3d Pakistan Philos. Congress, 1956; co-chmn. So. Ill. U. Einstein Centennial, 1979; Internal Honors lectr. So. Ill. U., Carbondale, 1986; participant Radha Krishnan Centennial Internat. Seminar, Madras (India) Christian Coll., 1988; Radha Krishnan Centennial Celebration lectr. Miami U., Oxford, Ohio, 1988; mem. No. Ill. Conf., United Meth. Ch.; keynote speaker Internat. Seminar, Centennial Birth Celebration, Sarvepalli Radhakrishnan, Madras Christian Coll., India, Feb. 1988. Author: numerous works in field of philosophy, 1928-93, latest being Human Nature and Progress, 1954, The Crisis in Science and Education, 1963, Kant's Pre-Critical Ethics, 1938, 66, 77; contbg. author: This is My Faith (S.G. Cole), 1956, New Frontiers of Christianity (R.C. Raughley), 1962, In Albert Schweitzer's Realms (A. A. Roback), 1962, Religion Ponders Science (E.P. Booth), 1964, The World of Philosophy, 1965, The Critique of War (Robert Ginsberg), 1969, Value and Valuation (J.W. Davis), 1972, Vol. IX, The Philosophy of Karl Jaspers, 1958, Vol. X, Philosophy of C.D. Broad, 1959, Vol. XI, Philosophy of Rudolf Carnap, 1964, La Etica Precritica de Kant, 1966, Vol. XII, Philosophy of Martin Buber, 1967, Vol. XIII, Philosophy of C. I. Lewis, 1968, Vol. XIV, Philosophy of Karl Popper (2 vols.), 1974, Vol. XV, Philosophy of Brand Blanshard, 1980, Vol. XVI, The Philosophy of Jean-Paul Sartre, 1981, Vol. XVI, The Philosophy of Gabriel Marcel, 1984, The Philosophy of W.V. Quine, 1986, The Philosophy of Georg Henrik von Wright, 1988; editor: Albert Einstein: Autobiographical Notes, 1979; Kant-studien; assoc. editor: Religious Humanism; contbr. articles. to philos. jours.; cons. philosophy: Ency. Brit.; invited contbr. The Courage to Grow Old (Phillip L. Berman, editor), 1989. Recipient Disting. Service medal Phi Beta Kappa Assn., Chgo., 1974; Bertrand Russell award Bertrand Russell Soc., 1980. Mem. Am. Philos. Assn. (past pres. cen. div.), other fgn., nat. and state philos. assns. Home: Carbondale Ill. Died Sept. 5, 1993; cremated Estes Park, Colo.

SCHINE, GERARD DAVID, entertainment company executive; b. Gloversville, N.Y., Sept. 11, 1927; s. J. Myer and Hildegarde (Feldman) S.; m. Anna Kristina Hillevi (Rombin), 1957; children: Anna Vidette Angela, Jonathan Mark, Alexander Kevin, Frederick Berndt, Benjamin Axel, William Lance. Grad., Fessenden Sch., West Newton, Mass., 1941, Phillips Acad., Andover, Mass., 1945; A.B., Harvard U., 1949. Pres., gen. mgr. Schine Hotels, 1950-63; exec. v.p. Schine Enterprises, 1952-57, pres., 1957-63; pres. Ski Dek Corp., 1961-67, David Schine & Co., Inc., Mgmt. Internat., Inc., Auto Inns Am., Inc., 1963-72, Ambassador Hotel Co. Los Angeles, 1960-63, 64-67, David Schine & Co. Inc., 1965-82, Schine Music, Myhil Music, Schine Prodns., Los Angeles, Studio TV Services, Inc., Los Angeles, 1980-87, Visual Scis., Inc., 1980-96, High Resolution TV, Inc., 1982-87, High Resolution Scis., Inc., 1987-96. Exec. producer: The French Connection, 1971; writer, producer, dir.: That's Action!, 1977; Author articles and pamphlets. Founding mem. Young Pres.' Orgn., 1950-77; adviser, spl. asst. atty.-gen. U.S. charge subversive activities, 1952; assisted investigation Communist infiltration into UN; chief cons. Senate Permanent Subcom. on Investigations, Com. on Govt. Operations, Jan. to Nov. 1953; directed investigation of Internat. Information Adminstrn., also Voice of America Dept. State, 1953; mem. Los Angeles Citizens Com. for 1960 Democratic Conv.; Trustee Hotel Industry Devel. Fund; past dir. Symphony Club of Miami, Community Concert Assn. Miami Beach, Fla.; past chmn. adv. bd. Conv. Bur., Miami Beach; past mem. citizens adv. com. Hotel Employees Med. Plan; past dir. Com. 1000 for Variety Children's Hosp., Greater Miami Philharmonic Soc., Inc.; nat. bd. trustees City of Hope; past chmn. Miami Beach Com. Opera Guild; trustee Hope for Hearing Fund. Served as lt. U.S. Army Transport Service, 1946-47; with AUS, 1953-55. Mem. Chief Execs. Orgn. Am., Nat. Bus. Aircraft Assn., Aircraft Owners and Pilots Assn., A.I.M. (pres.'s council), So. Fla. Hotel and Motel Assn. (founding pres.), Dade County (Fla.) Devel. Com. Clubs: Lotos; Harvard (N.Y.C.). Home: Beverly Hills Calif. Died June 19, 1996.

SCHLAIFER, ROBERT OSHER, retired business administration educator; b. Vermillion, S.D., Sept. 13, 1914; s. Osher and Mabel (Ellerbroek) S.; m. Geneviève Domergue, June 23, 1940; children: Peter, Renée. AB, Amherst Coll., 1934; PhD, Harvard U., 1940; DBA (hon.), Amherst Coll., 1979. Instr. Harvard U., Cambridge, Mass., 1940-42, asst. prof., 1942-45, 46-51, assoc. prof., 1951-57, prof., 1957-85, prof. emeritus, 1985-94; asst. prof. Pa. State Coll., State College, 1945-46. Author: Probability and Statistics for Business Decisions, 1959, Analysis of Decisions Under Uncertainty, 1969, Development of Aircraft Engines, 1950; (with H. Raiffa) Applied Statistical Decision Theory, 1961. Home: Arlington Mass. Died July 24, 1994.

SCHMIDT, GERNOT GUSTAV, educator; b. Hamburg, Germany, July 29, 1931; s. Gustav and Elisabeth (Weiher) S.; m. Elise Steinwender, Mar. 25, 1966; children: Wignand, Arngard, Herrad. PhD, Free U. Berlin, 1962; Habilitation, U. Bonn, Fed. Republic Germany, 1974. Asst. Tech. U. Berlin, 1963-64, Paedagogische Hochschule, Bonn, 1964-66; asst. U. Bonn, 1966-69, prof., from 1980. Author: Studien zum Germanischen Adverb, 1962, Stammbildung und Flexion der indogermanischen Personalpronomina, 1978. Home: Gönnersdorf Federal Republic of Germany Deceased.

SCHMIDT, HUGO, language educator; b. Vienna, Austria, Jan. 24, 1929; came to U.S., 1952; s. Johann and Maria (Schuster) S.; m. Eleonor Frohnmaier, June 21, 1952 (div. 1978); children: Catherine Schmidt Michael, Eric K. m. Jutta M. Gaedeke, Oct. 26, 1979. M.A., Columbia U., 1954, Ph.D., 1959. Instr. Columbia U., N.Y.C., 1954-59; asst. prof. German Bryn Mawr Coll., Pa., 1959-65, assoc. prof., 1965-67; prof. German U. Colo., Boulder, 1967-93; chmn. dept. Germanic langs. U. Colo., 1968-72, 83-87; dir. summer seminar Nat. Endowment Humanities, Boulder, Colo., 1978. Author: Nikolaus Lenau, 1971; editor: Hofmannsthal's Arabella, 1963; (with others) Brecht's Manual of Piety, 1966, 67, Goldsmith Studies in Comparison, 1989; contbr. articles to profl. publs. Mem. MLA, Am. Assn. Tchrs. German (v.p. 1979-81). Home: Boulder Colo. Died Jan. 10, 1993.

SCHMIT, DAVID HERMAN, priest, religious organization administrator; b. Fairmount, N.D., May 3, 1925; s. Mathias and Matilda Elizabeth (Smith) S. BA in Philosophy and Classical Languages, St. John's U., Collegeville, Minn., 1950; postgrad., St. John's Sem., Collegeville, 1951-54. Ordained priest Roman Cath. Ch., 1951. Asst. pastor St. Mary Parish, Grand Forks, N.D., 1954-61, co-pastor, 1970-75; pastor St. Bernard

Parish, Oriska, N.D., 1961-62; staff Cardinal Muench Sem., Fargo, N.D., 1962-64; pastor St. Vincent DePaul Parish, Leeds, N.D., 1962-70, St. Margaret Mary Parish, Drake, N.D., 1975—; with N.D. Conf. Chs., Bismarck, 1981-86, pres., 1985-86; pres. Diocesan Ecumenical Commn., Fargo, 1981-84. Served with U.S. Army, 1943-45, ETO. Mem. Nat. Assn. Diocesan Ecumenical Officers (bd. dirs. 1982-84). Home: Drake N.D.

SCHMITT, FRANCIS OTTO, neuroscientist, emeritus educator; b. St. Louis, Nov. 23, 1903; s. Otto Franz and Clara Elizabeth (Senniger) S.; m. Barbara Hecker, June 18, 1927 (dec.); children: David (dec.), Robert Hecker, Marion Schmitt Ellis. AB, Washington U., St. Louis, 1924, PhD, 1927; postgrad. (NRC fellow), U. Calif., 1927-28, U. Coll., London, 1928, Kaiser Wilhelm Inst., Berlin-Dahlem, 1928-29; DSc (hon.), Johns Hopkins, 1950, Washington U., 1952, U. Chgo., 1957, Valparaiso U., 1959, Mich. State U., 1968, N.Y. State Med. Coll., 1971, U. Pa., 1981; MD honoris causa, U. Gothenburg, Sweden, 1964; LLD honoris causa, Wittenberg U., 1966, Juniata Coll., 1968. Asst. prof. zoology Washington U., St. Louis, 1929-34; asso. prof. Washington U., 1934-38, prof., 1938-41, head dept., 1940-41; prof. biology Mass. Inst. Tech., 1941, head dept. biology, 1942-55, inst. prof., 1955-69, emeritus, 1973-95; chmn. Neuroscis. Research Found., Inc., 1962-74, trustee, 1974-95, chmn. neuroscis. research program, 1962-74, found. scientist, neuroscis. research program, 1974-95; Mem. Nat. Acad. Scis., 1948-95; mem. Nat. Adv. Health Council, USPHS, 1959-63, Nat. Adv. Gen. Med. Scis. Council, 1969-71; mem. bd. scientific counselors NINCDS, NIH, 1976-79; mem. com. on neurobiology Nat. Acad. Scis.-NRC, 1945, com. on growth, 1946-50, com. on radiation cataracts, 1949-53, com. on atherosclerosis, 1953-54, biol. council, 1954-56; chmn. NIH study sect. on biophysics and biophys. chemistry, 1954-58, other study programs; Holiday lectr., Chgo., 1964, New Orleans, 1966; mem. fellowships for basic research com. Alfred P. Sloan Found., 1971-78; bd. sci. cons. Sloan-Kettering Inst. Cancer Research, 1963-72; bd. sci. adv. com. New Eng. Aquarium, 1967-70; nat. adv. council Marine Biomed. Inst., U. Tex. Med. Br., Galveston, 1973-76; Harvey lectr. N.Y. Acad. Medicine, 1945, Ludwig Kast lectr., 1959; Klopsteg lectr. Northwestern U., 1963; Hooke lectr. U. Tex., Austin, 1965; Iddles lectr. U. N.H., 1975; Ewing Halsell lectr. U. Tex., San Antonio, 1977; Regents lectr. U. Calif., San Diego, 1978; Cecil and Ida Green lectr. U. Tex., Galveston, 1980. Author: The Never- Ceasing Search, 1990; mem. editorial bd. Quar. Rev. Biology, 1961-83, Brain Research, 1966-72, Annual Rev. Biophysics and Bioengring., 1970-73. Trustee Mass. Gen. Hosp., 1947-75, hon. trustee, 1975-95; vis. com. Harvard Div. Sch., 1964-68. Recipient Alsop award Am. Leather Chem. Assn., 1947, Lasker award Am. Public Health Assn., 1956, T. Duckett Jones Meml. award Helen Hay Whitney Found., 1963. Fellow Am. Acad. Arts and Scis. (council 1950-52, 64-65), AAAS, N.Y. Acad. Scis.; mem. Soc. Gen. Physiologists, Histochem. Soc., Am. Philos. Soc. (council 1964-66, v.p. 1972-75), Am. Physiol. Soc., Am. Soc. Zoologists, Soc. Exptl. Biology and Medicine, Soc. Growth and Devel. (treas. 1945-46, pres. 1947), Am. Leather Chem. Assn., Soc. for Neuroscience, Neurochemistry Soc., Internat. Neurochemistry Soc., Biophys. Soc. (councilor), Electron Microscope Soc. Am. (dir. 1944-47, pres. 1949, Disting. Scientist award, 1986), Swedish Royal Acad. Scis., Phi Beta Kappa, Sigma Xi. Home: Weston Mass. Died Oct 3, 1995.

SCHNACKE, ROBERT HOWARD, judge; b. San Francisco, Oct. 8, 1913; s. Carl H. and Elfriede A. (Hanschen) S.; m. June Doris Borina, Sept. 7, 1956 (dec. June 1994). Student, U. Calif. at Berkeley, 1930-32; J.D., Hastings Coll. of Law, 1938. Bar: Calif. 1938. Practiced in San Francisco, 1938-42, 51-53, 59-68; dep. commr. div. corps. San Francisco, State of Calif., 1947-51; chief criminal div. Office U.S. Atty., San Francisco, 1953-58; U.S. atty. No. Dist. Calif., San Francisco, 1958-59; judge Superior Ct., San Francisco, 1968-70, U.S. Dist. Ct. (no. dist.) Calif., San Francisco, 1970-94; Chmn. uniform rules of evidence com. 9th Circuit Jud. Conf., 1963-76. Pres. Guide Dogs for Blind, 1959-62; bd. dirs. Fed. Jud. Ctr., 1975-79; mem. Jud. Panel on Multidist. Litigation, 1979-90. Served with AUS, 1942-46. Mem. Fed. Bar Assn., San Francisco Bar Assn., Am. Judicature Soc., Masons, Burlingame Country Club. Home: San Francisco Calif. Died June 5, 1994.

SCHNEIDER, ALAN, theater director; b. Kharkov, Russia, Dec. 12, 1917; s. Leo Victor and Rebecka (Malkin) S.; m. Eugenie Muckle; 2 children. DHL (hon.), Hofstra U., 1974; DFA (hon.), Williams Coll., 1983; DHL (hon., posthumous), U. Wis., 1990. Dir. Theater Ctr. Juilliard Sch., N.Y.C., 1976-79; prof. drama U. Calif., San Diego, 1979—. Dir. numerous stage plays, including (by Beckett) Waiting for Godot, 1956, Endgame, 1958, Happy Days, 1961, Krapp's Last Tape, 1961, Play, 1964, Film, 1964, Box, 1968, Not I, 1972, Act without Words, 1972, That Time, 1976, Footfalls, 1976, Rockaby, 1981, Ohio Impromptu, 1981, Catastrophe, 1983 (by Edward Albee) American Dream, 1961, Who's Afraid of Virginia Woolf?, 1962, Tiny Alice, 1964, A Delicate Balance, 1966, Quotations from Chairman Mao Tse-Tung, 1968, (by Anderson) You Know I Can't Hear You When the Water's Running, 1967, I Never Sang For My Father, 1968, Inquest, 1970, (by Pinter) Dumbwaiter, 1962, The Collection, 1962, The Birthday Party, 1967, A Kind of Alaska, 1984, (by Edward Bond) Saved, 1970, (by Michael Weller) Moonchildren, 1971, Loose Ends, 1979, (by Gunter Grass) Uptight, 1972, (by E.A. Whitehead) Foursome, 1972, (by Elie Wiesel) The Madness of God, 1974, (by Preston Jones) The Last Meeting of the Knights of the White Magnolia, 1975, Texas Trilogy, 1976; dir. films and TV prodns. including Oedipus the King, 1956, The Life of Samuel Johnson, 1957, The Years Between, 1958, The Secret of Freedom, 1959, (by Archibald McCloud), Waiting for Godot, 1960, Film, 1964, Act Without Words II, 1965, Eh, Joe?, 1966, The Madness of God, 1975. Recipient Antoinette Perry (Tony) award, 1962, Off-Broadway (Obie) award, 1962, Critic Circle award, 1963. Home: Tarrytown N.Y. Died May 3, 1984.

SCHNEIDER, ALEXANDER, violinist, conductor; b. Vilna, Russia, Oct. 21, 1908; came to the U.S., 1932; s. Isak and Chasia (Dainowski) S. Student violin, Vilna Conservatory, Frankfurt Conservatory; studied with, E. Malkin, Adolph Rebner, Carl Flesch, Berlin, Pablo Casals, Prades, France; D.F.A., New Sch. for Social Research, 1965. former mem. faculty U. Calif., Berkeley, U. Wash., U. Chgo., U. Mich., Mills Coll., Stanford U., Chgo. Mus. Coll., Royal Conservatory of Toronto; Mem. exec. bd., v.p., Fromm Music Found. Concertmaster, Symphony Orch., Frankfurt, later, State Opera and Symphony Orch., Saarbrûcken, also, Hamburg, traveled extensively with own string quartet, Germany; with, Budapest String Quartet; toured, Europe, N. Africa, East Indies, Australia, U.S., 1938-50, U.S., S.Am., 1955-93; founder: chamber music concerts Albeneri Trio, U.S. and Can., 1944, (with Ralph Kirkpatrick); formed Sonata Ensemble, 1944; also mem.: concerts with Eugene Istomin; condr.: concerts Dumbarton Oaks Chamber Music Orch; 944 concerts; organized Schneider Quartet, 1952; presented series chamber music concerts N.Y. theaters-in-the round; organized, participated outdoor chamber music concerts Washington Sq., N.Y.C., 1953, 54, also, South Mountain, Pittsfield, Mass., (with pianist Mieczyslaw Horszowski), performed series sonata concerts, 1955, 56, midnight Christmas Eve concert, Carnegie Hall, 1955-93; mus. dir., founder, New Sch. Concerts, N.Y.C., 1956, N.Y. String Orch. Seminar, 1969, organized (with others), Israel Music Festival, 1960-61, guest condr., Boston Symphony, St. Louis Symphony, Israel Philharmonic, Los Angeles Philharmonic, Orch., French Nat. Radio and TV, Paris, Lincoln Center Mostly Mozart Festival, N.Y.C., Met. Mus. Art, Interlochen (Mich.) Acad., asst. mus. dir., Casals Festival, San Juan, P.R., participant ann., Casals Festivals, France, Marlboro Music Festival, Marlboro, Vt. Recipient Elizabeth Sprague Coolidge medal for eminent services to chamber music, 1945, Mayor's Scroll of Appreciation N.Y.C., 1959, Grammy awards (2), Kennedy Ctr. Honor, 1988, award disting. svc. to the arts, Am. Acad. and Inst. of Arts and Letters, 1991. Home: New York N.Y. Died Feb. 2, 1993.

SCHNEIDER, WILLIAM HENRY, army officer; b. San Antonio, Sept. 29, 1934; s. Henry William and Irene (Mooty) S.; m. Barbara Bristol Carver, Aug. 31, 1957; children: Michael W., D. Allen, Catherine S. Hollis, Patricia S. Cade. B.A., St. Mary's U., San Antonio, 1955; M.S.A, George Washington U., 1971; grad., Coll. Naval Warfare, Newport, R.I., 1975. Commd. 2d. lt. U.S. Army, 1955, advanced through grades to lt. gen., 1984; comdr. 1st Bn. 77th Field Artillery 1st Cavalry Div. U.S. Army, Ft. Hood, Tex., 1972-74; comdr. div. arty. then chief of staff 25th inf., div. U.S. Army, Schofield Barracks, HI, 1975-78; dir. pers. and force devel., then chief of staff U.S. Army Materiel Command, Alexandria, Va., 1979-82; comdg. gen. 25th Inf. Div. U.S. Army, Schofield Barracks, 1982-84; dep. CINC U.S. Pacific Command, Hawaii, 1984-87; comdg. gen. 5th U.S. Army, San Antonio, 1987-89; ret., 1989; pres. Tex. Mil. Inst., 1990; bd. dirs. Kelly Field Nat. Bank, Govt. Pers. Mut. Life Ins. Co. Alamo coun. Boy Scouts Am., from 1987; mem. United Way Exec. Com. Decorated Def. Disting. Svc. medal, Army Disting. Svc. medal, Legion of Merit with one oak leaf cluster, Air medal with two oak leaf clusters, , Army Commendation medal with oak leaf cluster; recipient Silver Beaver award Boy Scouts Am., 1987, Good Scout award Boy Scouts Am., Disting. Alumnus award St. Mary's U., 1988. Mem. Assn. U.S. Army (chpt. pres. 1991-92), 25th Inf. Div. Assn. (chpt. pres. 1975-76), Hawaii C. of C. (hon. life). Roman Catholic. Lodge: Rotary. Home: San Antonio Tex. Deceased.

SCHOEN, MAX HOWARD, dentistry educator; b. N.Y.C., Feb. 4, 1922; s. Adolph and Ella (Grossman) S.; m. Beatrice Mildred Hoch, Feb. 5, 1950; children: Steven Charles, Karen Ruth. BS, DDS, U. So. Calif., 1943; MPH, UCLA, 1962, DrPH, 1969. Diplomate Am. Bd. Dental Pub. Health. Pvt. practice dentist L.A., 1947-54; founding ptnr. Group Dental Practice, L.A., 1954-73; prof. dentistry SUNY Sch. Dental Medicine, Stony Brook, 1973-76, pro tem dean, 1974-75; prof. UCLA Sch. Dentistry and Pub. Health, 1976-87, prof. emeritus, 1987-94; vis. prof. U. Conn. Sch. Dental Medicine, Hartford, 1972; assoc. clin. prof. U. So. Calif. Sch. Dentistry, L.A., 1972-73; dir. Maxicare Rsch. and Edn. Found., L.A., 1981-94; cons. Blue Cross Calif., L.A., 1970-90, VA Hosp., Sepulveda, Calif., 1978-88, U.S. Dept. Labor, Washington, 1989; mem. Com. for Nat. Health Ins. Co-author/co-editor: Group Practice and the Future of Dental Care, 1973; contbr. articles profl. jours., book chpts. Mem. adv. com. Health Ca Svcs. Plans, Calif. Dept. Corps., 1980-90, spl. den cons., 1991-95. Capt. AC, U.S. Army, 1943-46, PTC Mem. Nat. Assn. for Pub. Health Policy, Am. Ass Dental Schs., Am. Pub. Health Assn. (v.p. U.S. d 1987, John W. Knutson Disting Svc. award 1990), A Assn. Pub. Health Dentistry (Disting. Svc. award 198 Physicians for Social Responsibility, Group Heal Assn. Am., Inst. Medicine (hon.), Delta Omega. Jewis Home: Los Angeles Ca. Died Dec. 8, 1994.

SCHOENBAUM, SAMUEL, English educator; N.Y.C., Mar. 6, 1927; s. Abraham and Sarah (A schuler) S.; m. Marilyn Turk, June 10, 1946. B. Bklyn. Coll., 1947; M.A., Columbia U., 1949, Ph.I 1953; D. Litt. (hon.), Susquehanna U., 1986, U. Col 1987. Mem. faculty Northwestern U., 1953-75, Fra klyn Bliss Snyder prof. English Lit., 1971-75; Distir prof. English U. City N.Y., 1975-76; Disting. pr Renaissance lit. U. Md., 1976-93, dir. Center Renaissance and Baroque Studies, 1981-96; vis. pr King's Coll., London, 1961, U. Chgo., 1964, Columbia U., 1966, U. Wash., 1968; Hooker Distir vis. prof. McMaster U., Ont., Can., 1986; mem. ac com. Internat. Shakespeare Conf., 1972-96; mem. a coun. Am. Trust for Brit. Libr.; trustee Folger Shak peare Libr., 1974-84; hon. mem. Folger Libr. Rena sance Forum, 1993-96. Author: Internal Evidence a Elizabethan Dramatic Authorship, 1966, Shakespear Lives, 1970, new edit., 1991, William Shakespeare: Documentary Life, 1975 (Distinguished Service awa Soc. Midland Authors 1976), William Shakespeare: Compact Documentary Life, 1977, rev. edit., 19 Shakespeare: The Globe and the World, 1979, Willi Shakespeare: Records and Images, 1981, Shakespe and others, 1985, Shakespeare: His Life, His Langua His Theater, 1990; editor: (with K. Muir) A N Companion to Shakespeare Studies, 1971, Renaissa Drama, 1964-73; mem. editorial bd. Shakespeare Qu Guggenheim fellow, 1956-57, 69-70; Nat. Endowm Humanities Sr. fellowship, 1973-74; recipient Hu ington Library grant, 1959, 67; Newberry Library gr 1958; recipient Friends of Lit. non-fiction award Shakespeare's Lives, 1970. Fellow Royal Soc. (U.K.); mem. Shakespeare Assn. Am. (trustee 1976- 81-96, pres. 1980-81), Internat. Shakespeare Assn. (1988-96), Phi Beta Kappa (hon.). Home: Washing D.C. Died Mar. 27, 1996.

SCHRAG, KARL, artist; b. Karlsruhe, Germany, D 7, 1912; came to U.S., 1938, naturalized, 1944; s. H and Bella (Sulzberger) S.; m. Ilse Szamatolski, June 1945; children: Peter, Katherine. Art student, E Nationale Superieure des Beaux Arts, Paris, 1931- studied with Lucien Simon, Roger Bissiere; student, Student's League of New York; and also student, Ate 17, N.Y.C. Tchr. Bklyn Coll., 1953, Cooper Uni 1954-68; dir. Atelier 17, 1950. Paintings and pr exhibited Art Inst. Chgo., Boston Mus. Fine Arts, M Mus. Art, Mus. Modern Art, Whitney Mus. Am. Mus. Modern Art, Paris, Tate Gallery, London, Inst. Arts, Stockholm, others; one-man shows incl Brussels, 1938, U.S. Nat. Mus., 1945, Kraushaar C leries (19 shows), 1947-95, Phila. Art Alliance, 1952, Ala., 1948, Maine U., 1953, 58, Wagner Coll., N.Y., 1955, Assn. Am. Artists, 1971, 80, 86, 90, Collection Fine Arts, 1972, Bethesda (Md.) Art Gall 1977, Jane Haslem Gallery, Washington, 1987, Bergen Mus. Art, Paramus, N.J., 1993, Sordoni Gallery, Wilkes-Barre, Penn., 1993, Bucknell U., 1 retrospective exhbn. Farnsworth Mus., Rockla Maine, 1992; represented in over 60 pub. collecti including Mus. Modern Art, Whitney Mus. Am. Solomon R. Guggenheim Mus., Met. Mus. Art, Gallery, Washington, Bibliotheque Nationale, P Library of Congress, N.Y. Pub. Library, Phila. M Cleve. Mus., Bklyn. Mus., others. Recipient aw Bklyn. Mus. Print ann., 1947, 50; purchase aw Bradley U., 1952; Erickson prize Soc. Am. Graphic tists, 1962, 64, 67, 77, 80; Lea prize Phila. Print C 1954; Am. Colorprint Soc., 1958, 60, 63, 64; awar retrospective traveling exhbn. by Ford Found., 1 Ford Found. fellowship Tamarind Lithography W shop, 1962; grant Nat. Inst. Arts and Letters, 1 Childe Hassam Purchase Fund award Am. Acad. and Letters, 1969, 73, 77, Andrew Carnegie prize, 19 Mem. NAD (B. Altman prize for landscape paint 1981, 94), At Students League N.Y., Artists Equ Assn. Am. Graphic Artists. Home: New York Died Dec. 10, 1995.

SCHROEDER, ROBERT ANTHONY, lawyer; Bendena, Kans., May 19, 1912; s. Anthony and Na (Bagby) S.; m. Janet Manning, Nov. 21, 1936; 1 c Robert Breathitt. LLB cum laude, U. Kans., 19 Bar: Mo. 1937. Atty. Allstate Ins. Co., Chgo., 1937 assoc. Madden, Freeman, Madden & Burke, Ka City, Mo., 1938-48; ptnr. Swofford, Schroeder & Sh land, Kansas City, 1948-59; pvt. practice law, 195 ptnr. Schroeder & Schroeder, 1967-84; commr. 16th Circuit, 1974-80, Appellate Jud. Commn. of Mo., 1 86; pres., bd. dirs. Roxbury State Bank, Kans., 195 chmn. bd. dirs., 1977-93; chmn. bd. dirs. Rox Bancshares Inc., 1984-93; pres. Douglas County vestment Co., 1967-88; chmn. bd. dirs. Hub State B 1974-82; hon. chmn. Mark Twain Bank Noland, 1 85; regional dir. Mark Twain Bancshares; sr. couns

Mo. Bar, 1987. Author: Twenty-Five Years Under The Missouri Plan, Twenty-Five Years Experience with Merit Judicial Selection in Missouri; editorial bd.: Kan. Bar Jour, 1935-36. Hon. trustee Kansas City Art Inst.; bd. dirs. Mo. Inst. for Justice; mem. dirs. club U. Kans. Williams Ednl. Fund, 1978-81, execs. club, 1981-85, All Am. club, 1986-93. Recipient Disting. Alumnus award U. Kans. Sch. Law; hon. fellow Harry S. Truman Library Inst., disting. charter fellow Kansas City Bar Found.; donor Robert A. Schroeder endowed chair for disting. prof., 1981; established Robert A. Schroeder scholarships and fellowship at U. Kans. Sch. Law.; donor Robert A. Schroeder Scholarship at Midway High Sch., Kans., 1985; Midway High Sch. Track renamed Schroeder Field in his honor, 1991. Fellow Am. Coll. Probate Counsel, Am. Bar Found., Kans. U. Law Soc. (trustee 1970-74); mem. ABA (Mo. chmn. membership com. 1961-65, del. 1966-70, lawyer referral com.), Mo. Bar Found. (v.p. 1965-69, pres. 1969-73), Mo. Bar Assn. (bd. govs. 1959-67), Mo. Bar (exec. com. 1963-67, pres. 1965-66, v.p., pres. found., chmn. legal edn. com. 1964-65, chmn. cts. and judiciary com. 1971-72, mem. bench and bar com. 1970-80, vice chmn. 1970-71; Pres.'s award 1972), Bar Assn. State Kans. (hon. life), Kansas City Bar Assn. (pres. 1957-58, chmn. exec. com., chmn. law day com., chmn. program com. 1968-70, chmn. prepaid legal services com. 1975-76; Achievement award 1976), Am. Judicature Soc. (bd. dirs. 1967-69), Nat. Legal Aid and Defender Assn., U. Kans. Law Alumni Assn. Greater Kansas City (past pres.), Order of Coif, Masons, Delta Tau Delta, Phi Delta Phi. Home: Kansas City Mo. Died March 31, 1993.

SCHULMANN, HORST, central banker; b. Frankfurt/Main, Germany, Apr. 13, 1933; s. Eugen M. and Johanna H. (Hübner) S.; m. Ulrike Wagner, 1973; children: Daniel, Anja. MA in Econs., Johann Wolfgang Goethe U., Frankfurt/Main, Germany, 1958; PhD in Econs., U. Saar, Saarbruecken, Germany, 1964. Sec. gen. German Coun. of Econ. Experts, Wiesbaden, Germany, 1967-69; officer World Bank, Washington, 1970-75; dir. Commn. of European Communities, Brussels, 1975-77; sr. aide German Fed. Govt., Bonn, 1977-82; dep., mng. dir. Inst. Internat. Fin., Washington, 1984-92; pres. Land Ctrl. Bank, Hess, Germany, 1992-94; mem. Ctrl. Bank Coun. of the Bundesbank, Frankfurt/Main, Germany, 1992-94; personal rep. Chancellor Schmidt for Econ. Summits, 1978-82; mem. Monetary Com. of European Communities, 1981-82, chmn., 1982; mem. supervisory bd. Industriekreditbank AG, Düsseldorf, Germany, 1980-85, Volkswagen AG, Wolfsburg, Germany, 1981-82, Veba AG, Düsseldorf, 1981-83. Home: Frankfurt Germany Died Nov. 24, 1994.

SCHWARTZ, BERTRAM, utility executive; b. Bklyn., Sept. 22, 1930; s. Jack and Rae (Becker) S.; m. Isabel Shapiro, Dec. 14, 1969; children: Rachel Lisa, Adam Gabriel. B.S., Lafayette Coll., Easton, Pa., 1952; M.S., Columbia U., 1953. With U.S. AEC, 1953-65, chief chem. processing, 1962-65; asst. to pres. Nuclear Materials and Equipment Corp., Apollo, Pa., 1965-68; with Consol. Edison Co., N.Y.C., 1968—, asst. v.p., 1969-71; v.p. Consol. Edison Co., 1971-75, sr. v.p., 1975-82, exec. v.p., 1982—; dir. Empire State Electric Energy Research Corp.; dir. Atomic Indsl. Forum, Northeast Power Coordinating Council. Named Outstanding Young Engr. AEC, 1963; recipient Superior Performance award, 1964. Jewish. Home: Armonk N.Y.

SCHWARTZ, DAVID LOUIS, lawyer; b. N.Y.C., Dec. 22, 1936; s. Abraham and Anne (Wasserman) S.; m. Nancy Ruth Schnitzer, Sept. 21, 1963; children: Sally Jean, Anne Judith, Daniel Adam. B.A., Columbia U., 1957; LL.B., U. Va., 1960. Bar: Va. 1960, N.Y. 1961. Assoc. Cravath Swaine & Moore, N.Y.C., 1960-68, ptnr., 1969—; mem. real estate adv. com. SEC, 1972. Served with AUS, 1960-61. Mem. Assn. Bar City N.Y., ABA, N.Y. State Bar Assn., Va. State Bar. Home: New York N.Y.

SCHWARTZ, EUGENE M., art collector, patron; b. Butte, Mont., Mar. 18, 1927. Student, New Sch. Social Rsch., NYU, Columbia U., U. Wash. Mem. acquisitions com. Whitney Mus. Am. Art, N.Y.C., 1967-79, 91-95; mem. 20th Century com. Met. Mus. Art, N.Y.C., 1989-95; mem. photog. acquiaitions com. Mus. Modern Art, N.Y.C., 1993-95; collector contemporary Am. art since World War II, chiefly of the sixties: parts of the collection shown as a group at Jewish Mus., Everson Mus. Art, Albany Inst.; individual pieces exhibited at Met. Mus. Art, Mus. Modern Art, Whitney Mus. Am. Art, L.A. County Mus., Tate Gallery, London. Home: New York N.Y. Died Sept. 6, 1995.

SCHWARTZ, FELICE N., social activist, educator; b. N.Y.C., Jan. 16, 1925; d. Albert and Rose (Kaplan) Nierenberg; m. Irving L. Schwartz, Jan. 12, 1946; children: Cornelia Ann, Tony, James Oliver. BA, Smith Coll., 1945; LHD (hon.), Pace U., 1980, Smith Coll., 1981, Marietta Coll., 1989, Chatham Coll., 1990, CUNY Grad. Ctr., 1993, Mt. Holyoke Coll., 1994. Founder, exec. dir. Nat. Scholarship Svc. and Fund for Negro Students, N.Y.C., 1945-51; v.p. prodn. Etched Products Corp., N.Y.C., 1951-54; founder, pres. Catalyst, N.Y.C., 1962-93. Author: Breaking With Tradition: Women and Work, The New Facts of Life, 1992, How To Go To Work When Your Husband Is Against It, Your Children Aren't Old Enough, There's Nothing You Can Do Anyhow, 1968; author numerous articles. Mem. adv. bd. Nat. Women's Polit. Caucus, Nat. Network of Hispanic Women; bd. visitors CUNY Grad. Ctr.; mem. adv. bd. Found. for Student Comm. Woodrow Wilson fellow, 1994-96; recipient Mademoiselle medal for singular achievement in edn., 1949, Disting. Alumnae medal Smith Coll., 1976, Susan B. Anthony award NOW, 1981, Boehm Soaring Eagle award Nat. Women's Econ. Alliance, 1987, Sara Lee Corp. Front Runner award, 1987; named Human Resource Profl. of Yr. Internat. Assn. Pers. Women, 1983. Fellow Nat. Acad. Human Resources; mem. Women's Forum, Inc., Global Bus. Network (Woodrow Wilson vis. fellow). Home: New York N.Y. Died Feb. 8, 1996.

SCHWARTZ, FREDERIC N., business executive; b. Springfield, Mass., Dec. 3, 1906; s. Michael J. and Regina (Burdick) S.; m. Elizabeth Staley, 1935. A.B., Syracuse U., 1931, LL.D., 1963. Chmn. bd., pres. Bristol-Myers Co., until 1965, chmn. bd., 1965-66, chmn. exec. com., 1967-71. Served as lt. col. AUS, 1942-45. Decorated Legion of Merit, 1945. Mem. Delta Kappa Epsilon. Club: River, University (N.Y.C.). Home: New York N.Y. Died Feb. 13, 1995.

SCHWARZ, SANFORD, magazine publisher; b. N.Y.C., Feb. 28, 1920; m. Frances Riley, 1952; m. Charlotte Voelker, Mar. 31, 1977. Advt. dir. Mag. Mgmt. Co., N.Y.C., 1946-52; salesman, then advt. dir. Hillman Periodicals, Inc., N.Y.C., 1952-57; advt. sales exec. Ideal Pub. Corp., N.Y.C., 1957-62; pres. Sanford Schwarz & Co., Inc., N.Y.C., 1962-84, Sterling's Mag., Inc., N.Y.C., 1974-84. Mem. pub. affairs com. Cancer Care Inc. and Nat. Cancer Found., Inc., 1976-80; bd. dirs. Euthanasia Ednl. Council, 1971-74, adviser, 1974-80. With USAAF, 1941-45. Mem. Soc. for Right to Die (dir. 1974-90, treas. 1984-91), Choice in Dying (dir. 1991-94), Players Club, Friars Club. Home: New York N.Y. Died Apr. 13, 1994.

SCHWARZSCHILD, WILLIAM HARRY, JR., banker; b. Richmond, Va., Sept. 19, 1903; s. William Harry and Rosalie (Held) S.; m. Kathryn Emsheimer, Sept. 6, 1945; children: Kathrin, William Harry. A.B., U. Va., 1923; M.B.A., Harvard, 1925. With J. & W. Seligman & Co., 1926-30; v.p. Central Nat. Bank, 1931-41, exec. v.p., 1945-49, pres., 1949-71, chmn. bd., 1967-73, 76-78, also dir.; chmn. bd. Central Nat. Corp., 1971-73, 76-96; dir., mem. exec. com. Central Nat. Bank, Central-Fidelity Banks, Inc., 1921-78. Chmn. Va. Bd. Vocational Rehab., 1964-73; chmn. gen. fund drive Henrico, Richmond, Chesterfield, ARC, 1952; Trustee Richmond Meml. Hosp. Served to lt. comdr. USNR, 1942-45. Decorated Bronze Star. Mem. Richmond C. of C. (pres. 1955-57), Am. Inst. Banking, Phi Beta Kappa. Clubs: Commonwealth, Fishing Bay Yacht, Westwood Racquet. Home: Richmond Va. Died June, 1996.

SCHWEITZER, PIERRE-PAUL, retired banker; b. Strasbourg, France, May 29, 1912; s. Paul and Emma (Munch) S.; m. Catherine Hatt, Aug. 7, 1941; children: Louis, Juliette. Grad., U. Strasbourg, U. Paris, Ecole Libre des Scis. Politiques; LLD, Yale U., 1966, Harvard U., 1966, Leeds (Eng.) U., NYU, 1968, George Washington U., 1972, U. Wales, 1972, Williams Coll., 1973. Insp. Fin. French Treasury, 1936-47; alt. exec. dir. IMF, 1947-48, mng. dir., chmn. exec. bd., 1963-73; sec. gen. Interministerial Com. European Econ. Coop., 1948-49; fin. attache embassy Washington, 1949-53; dir. treasury Ministry Fin., 1953-60; dep. gov. Bank of France, 1960-63, hon. inspecteur général fins., 1974; chmn. bd. Bank Am. Internat. S.A., Luxembourg, 1974-77, Bank Petrofigaz, Paris, 1974-79, Compagnie de Participations et d'Investissements Holding S.A., Luxembourg, 1975-84, Société Financière Internationale de Participations, Paris, 1976-84, Compagnie Monégasque de Banque, Monaco, 1978-88; adv. dir. Unilever N.V. Rotterdam, 1974-84; dir. Banque Pétrofigaz, 1979-91; mem. supervisory bd. Robeco Group, Rotterdam, The Netherlands, 1974-82. Decorated grand croix Legion of Honour, Croix de Guerre, Medaille de la Resistance. Mem. Am. Philos. Soc. Home: Vandoeuvres Switzerland

SCHWINGER, JULIAN, physicist, educator; b. N.Y.C., Feb. 12, 1918; s. Benjamin and Belle (Rosenfeld) S.; m. Clarice Carrol, 1947. A.B., Columbia U., 1936, Ph.D., 1939, D.Sc., 1966; D.Sc. (hon.), Purdue U., 1961, Harvard U., 1962, Brandeis U., 1973, Gustavus Adolphus Coll., 1975; LL.D., CCNY, 1972; D Honoris Causa, U. Paris, 1990; DSc (hon.), U. Nottingham, Eng., 1993, U. Nottingham, 1993. NRC fellow, 1939-40; research assoc. U. Calif.-Berkeley, 1940-41; instr., then asst. prof. Purdue U., 1941-43; staff mem. Radiation Lab., MIT, 1943-46; staff Metall. Lab., U. Chgo., 1943; asso. prof. Harvard U., 1945-47, prof., 1947-72, Higgins prof. physics, 1966-72; prof. physics UCLA, 1972-80, Univ. prof., 1980-94; mem. bd. sponsors Bull. Atomic Sci.; sponsor Fedn. Am. Scientists; J.W. Gibbs hon. lectr. Am. Math. Soc., 1960. Author: Particles and Sources, 1969, (with D. Saxon) Discontinuities in Wave Guides, 1968, Particles, Sources and Fields, 1970, Vol. II, 1973, Vol. III, 1989, Quantum Kinematics and Dynamics, 1970, Einstein's Legacy, 1985; editor: Quantum Electrodynamics, 1958. Recipient C. L. Mayer nature of light award, 1949, univ. medal Columbia U., 1951, 1st Einstein prize award, 1951; Nat. Medal of Sci. award for physics, 1964; co-recipient Nobel prize in Physics, 1965; recipient Humboldt award, 1981, Monie A. Fest Sigma Xi award, 1986, Castiglione di Sicilia award, 1986, Am. Acad. of Achievement award, 1987; Guggenheim fellow, 1970. Mem. AAAS, ACLU, Nat. Acad. Scis., Am. Acad. Arts and Scis., N.Y. Acad. Scis. Home: Los Angeles Calif. Died July 16, 1994.

SCOTT, DAVID C., manufacturing company executive; b. Akron, Ohio, Oct. 21, 1915; m. Eudora A. Vance, 1940 (dec. May 1973); children—Sally Scott Vincent, David C. Jr.; m. Mary M. Donohue, May 23, 1975. B.S., U. Ky., 1940, D.Sc. (hon.), 1971; LL.D. (hon.), Marquette U., 1980, Brescia Coll., Owensboro, Ky., 1985. Owner Inst-Tech. Research, 1942; with Gen. Electric Co., 1945-63; mgr. power tube plant Gen. Electric Co., Schenectady, N.Y., 1954-60; gen. mgr. cathode ray tube dept. Gen. Electric Co., Syracuse, N.Y., 1960-63; v.p., group exec. Colt Industries Inc., 1963-65, exec. v.p., dir., 1965-68; pres. Allis-Chalmers Corp., Milw., 1968-69, chmn. bd., chief exec. officer, 1969-83; pres. David C. Scott Found., Inc.; chmn., dir. Siemens Power Systems, Inc.; bd. dirs. Allis-Chalmers, First Wis. Trust of Fla., Humana, Inc.; former chmn., dir. Fiat-Allis, Siemens-Allis; former dir. Am. Can., First Wis. Corp., Harris Corp., Martin Marietta Corp., The Travelers Corp.; former pres. Egypt-U.S. Bus. Council, Czech-US Bus. Council, Poland-U.S. Bus. Council; former chmn., dir. Nat. Council-U.S.-China Trade; former vice chmn. Sudan-U.S. Bus. Council; former dir. U.S.-USSR Trade and Econ. Council; former chmn. Pres.'s Export Council. Trustee Marquette U.; past trustee Thomas A. Edison Found.; bd. dirs. Rockefeller U. Devel. Council, U. Ky. Devel Council, U. Ky. Coll. Engring. Mem. U. Ky. Alumni Assn. (mem. devel. council). Home: Boynton Beach Fla. Deceased.

SCOTT, ELIZABETH LEONARD, statistics educator; b. Ft. Sill, Okla., Nov. 23, 1917; d. Richard C. and Elizabeth (Waterman) S. B.A., U. Calif., Berkeley, 1939, Ph.D., 1949. Research fellow U. Calif., Berkeley, 1939-49; mem. faculty U. Calif., 1949-88, assoc. prof., 1957-62, prof. stats., 1962-88, emeritus; chmn. dept. stats., 1968-73; asst. dean U. Calif. (Coll. Letters and Sci.), 1965-67, co-chmn. group in biostats., 1972-88; mem. Commn. on Nat. Stats., Nat. Acad. Scis., 1971-77, Commn. on Women in Sci., 1977-82, Commn. on Applied and Theoretical Stats., 1981-84, Oversight Com. on Radioepidemiol. Tables, 1983-85. Research and articles in math. stats. and applications. Fellow Royal Statis. Soc. (hon.), Inst. Math. Stats. (pres. 1977-78, mem. council 1971-74, 76-79); mem. Biometric Soc. (council 1978-81), Am. Astron. Soc., Internat. Astron. Union, Internat. Stats. Inst. (v.p. 1981-83), Internat. Assn. Stats. in Phys. Sci. (sci. sec. 1960-72), Bernoulli Soc. (mem. council 1978-81, pres.-elect 1981-83, pres. 1983-85), Astron. Soc. Pacific, AAAS (chmn. sect. U 1970-71, mem. council 1971-76). Home: Berkeley Calif. Deceased.

SCOTT, HUGH, former senator, retired lawyer; b. Fredericksburg, Va., Nov. 11, 1900; s. Hugh D. and Jane Lee (Lewis) S.; m. Marian Huntington Chase, Apr. 12, 1924 (dec. June 1987); 1 child, Marian Scott Concannon. AB, Randolph-Macon Coll., 1919, LLD, 1955; postgrad., U. Pa., 1917; LLB, U. Va., 1922; LHD, La Salle U., 1955; LLD, Dickinson Coll., 1959, Temple U., 1959, Ursinus Coll., 1960, Phila. Textile Inst., 1960, Washington and Jefferson Coll., 1961, Lebanon Valley Coll., 1962, Lincoln U., 1963, Westminster Coll., 1964, U. Pa., 1966, Waynesburg Coll., 1966, Franklin and Marshall Coll., 1966, Lehigh U., 1968, Albright Coll., 1969, Hanover Coll., 1969, Hahnemann Med. Coll. and Hosp., 1969, Gettysburg Coll., 1970, Drexel U., 1970, Lafayette U., 1971, Dropsie U., 1971, York Coll. of Pa., 1972, William Jewell Coll., 1976; D in Pub. Adminstrn., Suffolk U., 1959; LittD, Phila. Coll. Osteopathy, 1960; DSc, Delaware Valley Coll., 1963; DCL, Susquehanna U., 1966, Union Coll., 1967; LHD, Thomas Jefferson U., 1970, Hebrew Union Coll., 1973; LLD, Rutgers U., 1986. Bar: Va. bar 1921, Pa. bar 1922. Pvt. practice Phila., Washington, 1987; ret., 1987; asst. dist. atty. Philadelphia County, 1926-41; mem. 77th-78th, 79th-85th Congresses, 6th Dist. Pa.; mem. policy com., mem. U.S. Senate, Pa., 1959-77, rep. minority leader, 1969-77; mem. coms. on fgn. relations, judiciary, rules, adminstrn., minority policy com. Civil War Centennial Commn.; vice chmn. Senate Commn. Art and Antiquities; vice chmn. U.S. del. Interparliamentary Union. Author: Scott on Bailments, 1931, How to Go into Politics, 1949, The Golden Age of Chinese Art: The Lively T'ang Dynasty, 1967, Come To The Party, 1968, How To Run for Public Office and Win, 1968; co-author: Politics, U.S.A, 1960. Mem. bd. visitors Naval Acad., 1948, U. Va., 1971-79; bd. regents Smithsonian Instn., USCG Acad., 1963; chmn. bd. visitors Mcht. Marine Acad., 1959; bd. dirs. Georgetown Center Strategic Studies; mem. Oriental art com. Phila. Mus. Art; trustee emeritus Woodmere Art Mus., Phila., Randolph-Macon Coll., Ashland, Va.; chmn. Youth for Understanding; mem. Bd. Fgn. Scholarships, 1977-79; chmn. Rep. Nat. Com., 1948-49; chmn. regional orgn. com. Eisenhower campaign, 1952; chmn. Eisenhower hdqrs. com., mem. rules com., 1954; gen. counsel Nat.

Com., 1955-60; counselor Former Mems. Congress; mem. adv. council New Leadership Fund; chmn. U.S. Senate Study Group, 1982; mem. adv. com. U.S.-Japan Found.; trustee Found. for Hospital and Home Care. With USN, World War II; from lt. to capt. USNR. Decorated comdr. Royal Order of Phoenix (Greece), grand cross Order of El Quetzal (Guatemala), Order of Merit 1st Class (Korea), grand cordon Order of Rising Sun (Japan); recipient Ann. Fgn. Trade award Phila. Fgn. Traders Assn., 1944, Greater Phila. mag. 50th Ann. award, Pa. Assn. Broadcasters' award, 1963, George Washington Honor medal Freedoms Found. at Valley Forge, also numerous Man of the Yr. awards C. of C., service, press, vets. orgns.; named Disting. Pennsyvanian of Yr., William Penn Soc. of Gannon U., 1973, 88. Fellow Am. Bar Found. (hon.); mem. ABA, VFW, Pa. Bar Assn., Phila. Bar Assn., Am. Legion, Amvets, Friendly Sons St. Patrick, Pa. Soc. (N.Y.), Chinese Art Soc. Am., SR, Baronial Order Magna Carta, Mil. Order of the Crusades, Alpha Chi Rho (nat. pres. 1942-46), Phi Beta Kappa, Tau Kappa Alpha, Phi Alpha Delta, Alpha Zeta, Phi Kappa Sigma. Episcopalian. Clubs: Penn, Capitol Hill, Army and Navy, Union League Phila. Lodges: Lions (Germantown), Kiwanis (hon.). Home: Falls Church Va. Died July 21, 1994.

SCOTT, JAMES ALLEN, lawyer; b. Ramseur, N.C., Aug. 1, 1924; s. William Lee and Bertha Alice (Stanbury) S.; m. Patricia Anne Meloy, June 24, 1950; children—Marcy Scott Rule, Allen Jay, Leslie Ann. A.B., Duke U., 1947, LL.B., 1951. Bar: Ohio, N.C. Tax trial atty. IRS Chief Counsel's Office, Cleve., 1951-55; asst. regional counsel IRS Chief Counsel's Office, Richmond, Va., 1955-58, Cleve., 1958-59; ptnr. firm Baker & Hostetler, Cleve., 1959-95. Ch. officer Fairmount Presbyn. Ch., Cleveland Heights, Ohio, 1969-78. Served with USNR, 1943-47. Republican. Home: Aurora Ohio Died May 31, 1995.

SCOTT, JAY, journalist, film critic; b. Oct. 4, 1949; s. Bruce Lee and Muriel Mahala (Chenburg) Beaven; m. Mary Blakeley, Oct. 5, 1968. Student, New Coll., 1967-68, U. N.Mex., 1968-70. Arts editor The Lobo U. N.Mex., Albuquerque, 1970-72; investigative reporter Albuquerque Jour., 1972-75; investigative reporter, arts editor The Albertan, Calgary, Alta., Can., 1975-77; film critic The Globe and Mail, Toronto, Ont., Can., 1977-93; contbr. editor Can. Art, Toronto, Ont., 1984-93; book editor Chatelaine mag., 1988-93. Author: John Nieto, 1989, Changing Woman: The Life and Art of Helen Hardin, 1989, The Prints of Christopher Pratt, 1991; contbg. author: Midnight Matinees, 1985, Take Two, 1985, Pasolini: Between Prophecy and Engima, 1991, Anthology I, 1988, Streets of Attitude; contbr. articles to Village Voice, Premiere, Am. Film, L.A. Times, others. Recipient Silver Gavel, ABA, 1975, award for criticism Nat. Newspaper Assn., Can., 1975, 81, 84, Nat. Mag. award Food Writing Nat. Mag. Awards Found., 1986, Nat. Mag. award Critical Writing, 1988; named Nat. Restaurant Critic of Yr., Nabisco Brands, 1986. Home: Toronto Can. Died July 30, 1993.

SCOTT, WILLARD PHILIP, lawyer, corporate executive; b. Columbus, Ohio, Jan. 8, 1909; s. Wirt Stanley and Mabel Lynne (Rond) S.; m. Lucille Westrom, June 27, 1936 (dec); children: Robert W., David W., Anne L.; m. Virginia J. Field, Oct. 30, 1987. A.B. with honors, Ohio State U., 1930; LL.B. (dean's scholar), Columbia, 1933. Bar: N.Y. 1934, D.C. 1934, Okla. 1969. Ptnr. Oliver & Donnally, N.Y.C., 1938-65; Dir. Am. Potash & Chem. Corp., 1951-94, v.p., 1955-68, vice chmn. bd., 1968-94; v.p., gen. counsel Kerr-McGee Corp., 1968-73, v.p. fin., 1973-75, sr. v.p., 1973-75, cons., 1975-85; gen. counsel Nat. Assn. Mut. Savs. Banks and Savs. Banks Assn. N.Y., 1945-60; counsel bondholders coms. r.r. reorgn. C. & N.-W. Ry., Soo Line, Alton, B. & M. R.R., C., M., St. P. & P. Ry., Fla. East Coast, Central N.J., D. & H. R.R.; dir. 1st Nat. Bank & Trust Co. of Oklahoma City, Transocean Drilling Co. Ltd., Bikita Minerals Ltd. Editor: Business Lawyer, 1958-59; Contbr. articles on corporate law to profl. jours. Trustee, Scarsdale, N.Y., 1951-55, police commr., acting mayor, 1953-55, mayor, 1955-57, mem. bd. appeals, 1957-68; Bd. dirs. Oklahoma City Allied Arts Found., Oklahoma City Symphony Soc.; trustee Okla. Sci. and Arts Found.; bd. advisers Mercy Hosp. Fellow Am. Bar Found., Southwestern Legal Found.; Mem. Internat. Bar Assn. (patron), ABA (commn. on corporate laws 1947-94, chmn. sect. corporate banking and bus. law 1960-61, ho. of dels. 1961-62, chmn. com. ednl. programs), N.Y. Bar Assn., D.C. Bar Assn., Okla. Bar Assn., Am. Law Inst., Assn. Bar City N.Y., Phi Beta Kappa, Phi Kappa Sigma, Phi Delta Phi, Phi Alpha Theta, Pi Sigma Alpha. Republican. Presbyn. Clubs: Union League, Madison Square Garden (N.Y.C.); Metropolitan (Washington); Scarsdale Golf; Oklahoma City Golf and Country (O, Beacon, Whitehall; Univ. (Chgo.); Calif. (L.A.). Home: Oklahoma City Okla. Died July 15, 1994.

SCRIBNER, CHARLES, JR., publisher; b. Quogue, N.Y., July 13, 1921; s. Charles and Vera Gordon (Bloodgood) S.; m. Dorothy Joan Sunderland, July 16, 1949; children: Charles, Blair Sund, John. Student, St. Paul's Sch., 1939; A.B., Princeton, 1943. Advt. mgr. Charles Scribner's Sons, 1946-48, v.p., 1948-50, pres., 1952-77, chmn., 1977-78; chmn. Scribner Book Cos., 1978-95; Pres. Am. Book Pubs. Council, 1966-68. Author: In the Company of Writers: A Life in Publishing, 1991. Trustee Princeton U., 1969-79, Princeton U. Press, 1949-81. Served as lt. USNR, 1943-46, 50-52. Clubs: Racquet and Tennis, Church (N.Y.C.). Home: New York N.Y. Died Nov. 11, 1995.

SCRIBNER, FRED CLARK, JR., lawyer; b. Bath, Maine, Feb. 14, 1908; s. Fred Clark and Emma Amelia (Cheltra) A.; m. Barbara Curtis Merrill, Aug. 24, 1935; children: Fred Clark, Curtis Merrill, Charles Dewey. A.B., Dartmouth Coll., 1930, LL.D., 1959; LL.B., Harvard U., 1933; LL.D., U. Maine, 1958, Colby Coll., 1959, Bowdoin Coll., 1959, U. Vt., 1960; D.D., Gen. Theol. Sem., 1984. Bar: Maine 1933, Mass. 1933, D.C. 1961. Assoc. Cook, Hutchinson, Pierce, and Connell, Portland, Maine, 1933-35; partner Cook, Hutchinson, Pierce, and Connell, 1935-55, Pierce, Atwood, Scribner, Allen, Smith and Lancaster, Portland, 1961-94, Scribner, Hall & Thompson, Washington, 1961-94; dir., gen. counsel, v.p., treas. Bates Mfg. Co., Lewiston, Me., 1946-55; gen. counsel Dept. Treasury, 1955-57, asst. sec. treasury, 1957, under sec., 1957-61; past dir. Sentinel Group Funds, Inc.; mem. commr.'s adv. com. on exempt orgns. Internal Revenue Service; chmn. ad hoc adv. group on presdl. vote for P.R. Pres. Maine Constl. Commn., 1963-64; chmn. Portland Republican City Com., 1936-40, Maine Council Young Rep. Clubs, 1938-40; mem. Maine Rep. State Com., 1940-50 (chmn. exec. com. 1944-50); Rep. nat. committeeman from, Maine, 1948-56; del. Rep. Nat. Conv., 1940, 44, 56, 60, 64, 68; counsel Rep. Nat. Com., 1952-55, 61-73; gen. counsel arrangements com. Nat. Conv., 1956-72; Presdl. elector, 1976; hon. trustee Maine Med. Center, Portland; past bd. dirs. Am. Council Capitol Formation; former pres. bd. trustees Bradford Coll., Haverhill, Mass.; trustee Cardigan Mountain Sch., Canaan, N.H. Recipient Alexander Hamilton award U.S. Treasury; Dartmouth Alumni Council award, 1971; Silver Beaver award Boy Scouts Am. Mem. ABA, Fed. Bar Assn., Maine Bar Assn., Cumberland County Bar Assn., Am. Law Inst., Newcomen Soc. U.S. (clk.), Phi Beta Kappa, Delta Sigma Rho, Alpha Chi Rho. Episcopalian. (mem. standing com., chancellor Diocese of Maine; del. Gen. Conv. P.E. Ch., 1943, 46, 52, 61, 64, 67, 69, 70, 73, 76, 79, 82). Clubs: Capitol Hill (Washington); Portland, Woodfords. Lodges: Kiwanis, Masons (33 deg.). Home: Falmouth Maine Died Jan. 5, 1994.

SCRUGGS, JOHN DUDLEY, landscape architect; b. Flemingsburg, Ky., May 3, 1911. B.A., Berea Coll., 1933; M.L.A., Harvard, 1938. Co-founder, v.p. Scruggs and Hammond, Inc. (Landscape Architects and Planning Cons.), Lexington, Columbus, Ohio and Peoria, Ill., 1946—; vis. critic U. Ky., Harvard; bd. dirs. Hubbard Ednl. Trust. Served with AUS, 1942-46. Fellow Am. Soc. Landscape Architects (chmn. com. on publ rels. 1953-63, com. on biographies of fellows 1976—, coun. of fellows 1982-83); mem. AIA, Lafayette Club, Harvard Club, Lexington Sports Club, Idle Hour Country Club. Home: Nicholasville Ky.

SCURFIELD, RALPH THOMAS, builder, developer, energy company executive; b. Broadview, Sask., Can., Jan. 7, 1928; s. Ralph and Anne Marie (Parsons) S.; m. Sonia Onishenko, July 24, 1954; children: Ralph D., Susan J., Katheryn L., Serge M., Allan P., John W. B.Sc., U. Man., 1948; grad., Advaced Mgmt. Program, Harvard U., 1976. Tchr. Winnipeg, Man., Can.; with Nu-West Group Ltd. (builders and developers, and predecessors), Calgary, Alta.; pres. Nu-West Group Ltd. (builders and developers, and predecessors), 1957-85; dir. Carma Ltd., MICC Investments and Mortgage Ins. Co. Can., Alta. Gas Chems. Ltd.; mem. faculty mgmt. adv. bd. U. Calgary; bd. govs. Banff Centre Continuing Edn. Mem. Housing and Urban Devel. Assn. Can. (past pres.). Mem. United Ch. Can. Clubs: Ranchmen's, Calgary Winter, Calgary Petroleum, Silver Springs Golf and Country. Home: Calgary Can.

SCURLOCK, EDDY CLARK, oil co. exec.; b. Newton, Tex., Jan. 13, 1905; s. R.W. and Ella (Clark) S.; L.H.D., Southwestern U.; D.B.A., Limestone Coll.; m. Elizabeth Belschner, July 17, 1927; 1 dau., Laura Lee (Mrs. Jack Sawtelle Blanton). Founder Scurlock Oil Co., 1936; founder Eddy Refining Co., 1946, now chmn. bd., chief exec. officer; adv. dir. Tex. Commerce Bank, Chem. Bank & Trust. Trustee, Baylor Coll. Medicine, Meth. Hosp., Lon Morris Coll.; bd. dirs. Tex. Med. Center, Inc., Rice U. Assos., Salvation Army, Turner Found. Recipient City of Hope humanitarian award, 1966; Ann. Brotherhood award NCCJ, 1968; Religious Heritage Am. Businessman of Year, 1970; Disting. Service award Tex. Mid-Continent Oil and Gas Assn., 1977; Torch of Liberty award Anti-Defamation League, B'nai B'rith, 1979. Mem. Am. Petroleum Inst. Methodist (bd. stewards). Clubs: River Oaks Country; Petroleum; Houston; El Dorado Country (Palm Springs, Calif.). Died Jan. 17, 1988. Home: Houston Tex.

SEARS, WILLIAM BERNARD, religious organization leader; b. Duluth, Minn., Mar. 28, 1911; s. Frank Cyril and Ethel M. (Wagner) S.; m. Kathleen Fox (dec. 1938); m. Marguerite Reimer, Sept. 29, 1939; children: William, Michael. Student, U. Wis. Broadcaster Sta. WCAU; with local spiritual assemblies N.Y.C. and Johannesburg (Republic of South Africa), 1956-58; chmn. Nat. Spiritual Assembly, south and west Africa; hand of the cause, chief stewart Baha'i Faith. Author, producer internat. quiz BBC; author 10 books. Home: Wilmette Ill. Deceased.

SEATON, EARLE EDWARD, judge; b. Bermuda, Feb. 29, 1924; s. Dudley Earle and Eva Evelyn (Samuels) S,; m. Alberta Thelma Jones, Dec. 24, 1947; children: Elizabeth Wamboi, Dudley Charles (dec.). BS, Howard U., 1945; LlB, London U., 1948; PhD, U. So. Calif., 1966. Barrister, 1948. Pvt. practice advocate Moshi, Tanganyika, 1948-53; lectr. internat. law U. So. Calif., L.A., 1962-63; dir. legal rsch. Ministry Fgn. Affairs, Dares Salaam, Tanzania, 1963-67; judge, high ct. Tanzania, Dares Salaam, 1967-70; minister-counselor Tanzanian Misson to UN, N.Y.C., 1970-72; judge supreme ct. Bermuda, Hamilton, 1972-78; chief justice Republic of Seychelles, Victoria, 1979-89; rapporteur Orgn. African Unity Legal Com., 1964; mem. OAU Mediation Com. on Algeria/Morocco border dispute, 1965-72, E. African Common Market Tribunal, 1969-72; sr. counsel on internat. law and cons. to Milligan, Whyte & Smith, Hamilton, Bermuda, 1989-90; appellate judge, Supreme Ct. of Uganda, 1990-92. Co-author: The Meru Land Case, 1964, Tanzania Treaty Practice, 1969, The Constitutional System of Tanzania, 1981, Law and Social Policy in Seychelles, 1984, Challenges of Dispensing Justice in Africa According to Common Law, 1988. Methodist. Home: Houston Tex.

SEATZ, LLOYD FRANK, former agronomy educator; b. Winchester, Idaho, June 2, 1919; s. William Frank and Emma (Hyder) S.; m. Dorothy Jane Whittle, Aug. 12, 1949; 1 son, William Lloyd. B.S., U. Idaho, 1940; M.S., U. Tenn., 1941; Ph.D., N.C. State U., 1949. Asst. prof. agronomy U. Tenn., 1947-49, assoc. prof., 1949-55; on leave as agronomist and asst. br. chief soils and fertilizer research br. TVA, 1953-55; prof. agronomy U. Tenn., 1955-84, head dept., 1961-84, Clyde B. Austin Disting. prof. agr., 1968-84, prof. emeritus, 1984-95; mem. Bikini Sci. Resurvey Team, 1947; dir. So. Appalachian Sci. Fair, Inc. Contbr. articles to sci. jours., chpts. in books. Served with AUS, 1942-46. Fellow Am. Soc. Agronomy (pres. So. sect.), Soil Sci. Soc. Am.; mem. Am. Soc. Agronomy, Internat. Soc. Soil Sci., Sigma Xi, Phi Eta Sigma, Alpha Zeta, Omicron Delta Kappa, Phi Kappa Phi, Gamma Sigma Delta, Delta Chi. Home: Knoxville Tenn. Died June 21, 1995.

SEBASTIAN, STUART, choreographer; b. Dayton, Ohio, July 26, 1950; s. Virginia (Lorah) S.; B.A. magna cum laude, Am. U., 1976. Profl. dancer, 1965:; prin. dancer Nat. Ballet of Washington, 1972-73; choreographer Met. Opera, Royal Winnipeg Ballet, Washington Ballet, others; speaker for USIA in Russia and Eastern Europe; now dir./prin. choreographer Dayton Ballet, 1980-91; choreographer operas, off-Broadway musicals, ballets. Mem. dance panel Ohio Arts Council. U.S.-U.K. grantee, 1977; Ford Found. scholar 1963-68 scholar Tex. Christian U., 1968-70. Mem. Assn. Ohio Dance Cos. (dir.), Nat. Assn. Regional Ballet (dir.), Am. Guild Mus. Artists. Died Jan. 16, 1991. Home: Akron Ohio

SEEGERS, WALTER HENRY, hematology educator emeritus; b. Fayette County, Iowa, Jan. 4, 1910; s. William and Mary (Wente) S.; m. Lillian Entz, Dec. 31, 1935; 1 child, Dorothy Margaret. B.A., U. Iowa, 1931, M.S., 1932, Ph.D., 1934; D.Sc., Wartburg Coll., 1953; M.D. (hon.), Justus Liebig U., Fed. Republic Germany, 1974; D.Sc. (hon.), Med. Coll. Ohio, 1978. Research fellow U. Iowa, 1931-34, research assoc., 1934-35, 1937-42; research assoc. Antioch Coll., 1936-37; researcher Parke, Davis & Co., Detroit, 1942-45; assoc. prof. physiology Wayne State U. Coll. Medicine, 1945-46, prof., head dept. physiology, 1946-48, prof. physiology and pharmacology, 1948-74, William D. Traitel prof. hematology, 1965-80, emeritus, 1980—, chmn. symposium on blood, 1950-68, dir. Thrombosis Specialized Ctr. of Research, 1972-77; prof. physiology U. Detroit, 1946-51; vis. prof. Baylor U., 1950, 52, U. Uruguay, summer, 1957; vis. scientist, lectr. Rio de Janeiro, 1963; hon. mem. faculty medicine U. Chile; subjects; NSC vis. chair prof. Nat. Taiwan U., 1975 mem. health research facilities sci. rev. com. NIH USPHS, 1966-70; chmn. subcom. blood coagulation NRC, 1950-53, chmn. panel on blood coagulation, 1953-57; mem. Internat. Com. on Hemostasis and Thrombosis, 1954—, Detroit Mayor's Com. Rehab Narcotic Addicts, 1961-73; mem. sci. adv. bd. ARC 1969-72. Author: Prothrombin, 1962; (with E.A. Sharp) Hemostatic Agents, 1948; (with J.M. Dorsey) Living Consciously: The Science of Self, 1959; (with Shirley A. Johnson) Physiology of Hemostasis and Thrombosis 1967; Prothrombin in Enzymology, Thrombosis and Hemophilia, 1967; Blood Clotting Enzymology, 1967 John M. Dorsey Memorabilia, 1982; (with D.A. Walz) Prothrombin and other Vitamin K Proteins, 1986 contbg. author: The Enzymes. Mem. editorial bd.: Am. Jour. Applied Physiology, 1956-63, Am. Jour. Physiology, 1956-63, Circulation Research, 1954-64, Preparative Biochemistry, 1970-80, Thrombosis Research, 1972 Contbr. articles to profl. jours. Bd. regents Wartburg Coll., 1966-80; mem. bd. Ctr. Health Edn., 1961-80 pres., 1969. Co-recipient Ward Burdick award Am. Soc. Clin. Pathologists, 1940, James F. Mitchell Found. Internat. award for heart and vascular research, 1969 recipient Commonwealth Fund Spl. award, 1957, May

Clinic Vis. Faculty cert., 1964, Disting. Service award Lutheran Brotherhood Ins. Soc., 1967, Acad. Achievement award Probus Club, 1963, Research award Wayne chpt. Sigma Xi, 1957, Disting. Service cert. Wartburg Alumni Assn., 1959, Faculty Service award Wayne State U. Alumni, 1971, Wisdom award honor Wisdom Soc., 1970, Mich. Minuteman Gov.'s award, 1973, H.P. Smith award Am. Soc. Clin. Pathologists, 1978; Disting. Grad. Faculty award Wayne State U., 1980, Med. Sch. Disting. Service award, 1980; commendation Stritch Sch. Medicine, Loyola U., 1980. Fellow N.Y. Acad. Scis.; mem. AAAS, Am. Inst. Chemists, Am. Soc. Hematology, Am. Heart Assn., Am. Chem. Soc., Am. Soc. Biol. Chemists, Soc. Exptl. Biology and Medicine, Am. Physiol. Soc., Detroit Physiol. Soc. (hon., pres. 1948, 80), Can. Physiol. Soc., Mich. Acad. Sci., Harvey Soc. (hon.), Chilean Soc. Transfusion and Hematology (hon.), Am. Coll. Clin. Pharmacology and Chemotherapy, Engring. Soc. Detroit, N.Y. Acad. Scis. (hon. life), Med. Soc. Turkey (hon.), Hematology Soc. Turkey (hon.), Mexican Soc. Hematology (hon.), Japanese Soc. Thrombosis and Hemostasis (hon.), Phi Beta Kappa (hon.), Sigma Xi, Alpha Omega Alpha (hon.), Phi Lambda Upsilon, Alpha Chi Sigma, Phi Beta Pi (hon.). Lutheran. Clubs: Torch, Economics (Detroit). Home: Walnut Creek Calif.

SEGATTO, BERNARD GORDON, lawyer; b. Joliet, Ill., July 27, 1931; s. Bernard Gordon and Rose Mary (Fracaro) S.; m. Nancy L. Grady, May 2, 1959; children: Bernard Gordon III, Randall Wayne, Amy Margot. B.A., Beloit Coll., 1953; J.D., U. Ill., 1958. Bar: Ill. 1958. Ptnr. Barber, Segatto, Hoffee & Hines, Springfield, Ill., 1958-94; dir. Rochester State Bank, Ill.; sec., dir. Rochester State BankShares Inc. Contbr. articles to profl. jours. Pres., Little Flower Sch. PTA, Springfield, 1971-73; chmn. adv. bd. Griffin High Sch., Springfield, 1974-82; nat. judge adv. Daus. Union Vets. of Civil War 1861-65, 1972-73, 75-94. Served with AUS, 1953-55. Recipient Real Estate award Lawyers Title Ins. Co. of Richmond, Va., 1958. Mem. ABA, Ill. Bar Assn. (chmn. sch. law com. 1965-66, v.p. jud. adv. polls com. 1974-83), Sangamon County Bar Assn., Am. Arbitration Assn. (arbitrator), Order of Coif, Phi Delta Phi, Sigma Chi. Roman Catholic. Club: Sangamo, Island Bay Yacht (Springfield). Lodge: Rotary. Home: Springfield Ill. Died June 10, 1994.

SEIDENBAUM, ART, newspaper editor, writer; b. N.Y.C., Apr. 4, 1930; s. William George and Lida (Aretsky) S.; m. Judith Weiner, June 14 (div. May 1974); children: Kyle Scott, Kerry Kai; m. Patricia Houser, June 20, 1974. BS, Northwestern U., 1951. Reporter Life mag., N.Y.C., 1955-59; corr. Los Angeles, 1960-61; West Coast Bureau chief Saturday Evening Post, Los Angeles, 1961-62; columnist Los Angeles Times, 1962-78, book editor, 1978-85, opinion editor, 1985--; host; Sta. KCET-TV, Los Angeles, 1965-76; disting. vis. prof. Calif. State U., Dominiguez Hills, 1980. Author: Confrontation on Campus, 1970, This is California, 1975, Los Angeles 200, 1980. Mem. Calif. Council for Humanities, 1977-81. Lt. USN, 1952-55. Recipient award for conbn. to architecture Calif. council AIA, 1965, award for contbn. to lit. Loyola-Marymount U., Los Angeles, 1979. Mem. Soc. Profl. Journalists. Home: Los Angeles Calif.

SEIGLE, JOHN WILLIAM, retired army officer, business executive; b. Cin., May 21, 1929; s. Harry and Cordelia Love (Nicholson) S.; m. Marilyn Anne Johnson, July 15, 1955; children: Sally, John, Gregory. B.S., U.S. Mil. Acad., 1953; M.P.A., Harvard U., 1960, Ph.D., 1967. Commd. 2d lt. U.S. Army, 1953, advanced through grades to maj. gen., 1977; coordinator Army Studies Washington, 1969-71; pres. Combat Arms Tng. Bd., 1972-73; comdr. 2d armored cav. regt. Germany, 1973-74; dep. def. adv. U.S. Mission to NATO Brussels, 1975-77; dep. chief of staff for tng. Hdqrs. U.S. Army Tng. and Doctrine Command Fort Monroe, Va., 1977-79; dep. comdr. Allied Land Forces Southeastern Europe, 1979-80, asst. dep. chief of staff for mil. ops. (joint affairs) Dept. Army, 1980-82, ret., 1982; v.p. bldg. systems sector United Technologies Corp., Hartford, Conn., 1982-87; v.p. planning Sikorsky Aircraft (div. of United Techs. Corp.), Stratford, 1987-94; asst. prof. social scis. U.S. Mil. Acad., 1961-65; pres. Combat Arms Tng. Bd., 1972-73. Trustee Human Resources Rsch. Orgn., George C. Marshall Found.; bd. advisors Patterson Sch. of Diplomacy and Internat. Commerce, U. Ky. Decorated Silver Star, Legion of Merit, D.F.C., D.S.M., Def. Superior Service medal, Bronze Star, Purple Heart. Mem. Council Fgn. Relations, Internat. Inst. Strategic Studies, Army and Navy Club, Kennebunk River Club. Home: Woodbridge Conn. Died Apr. 3, 1994.

SELLINGER, JOSEPH ANTHONY, college president; b. Phila., Jan. 17, 1921; s. Frank and L. Caroline (Wiseman) S. Ph.L., Spring Hill Coll., 1945, B.S. in Chemistry, 1945; postgrad. in theology, Weston Coll., 1948-49, Woodstock Coll., 1949-50; S.T.L., Facultes St. Albert, Louvain, Belgium, 1952. Joined S.J., 1938, ordained priest, Roman Catholic Ch., 1951. Assoc. dean Coll. Arts and Scis. Georgetown U., Washington, 1955-57; dean Georgetown U., 1957-64, sec. corp., intnl. dir., 1957-64; pres., rector Loyola Coll., Balt., 1964-93. Mem. Am. Council Edn. (vice-chmn.), Assn. Higher Edn., Middle States Assn., Nat. Cath. Ednl. Assn., Cath. Theol. Soc., Assn. Am. Colls., Phi Beta Kappa (hon.), Nat. Assn. of Ind. Colls. and Univs. (bd. dirs.). Home: Baltimore Md. Died Apr. 19, 1993.

SELTZER, MILDRED M., gerontologist, educator; b. Cleve., 1921; d. Lafe B. and Libbie (Glickman) Murstein; m. George A. Seltzer, Mar. 29, 1953; children: Judith Ann, Sarah Beth, Lisa Rachael. BA, Miami U., Oxford, Ohio, 1942; MA, U. Chgo., 1944, PhD, 1969. Caseworker social agys., Chgo., 1944-52; instr. sociology Miami U., 1949-51, asst. prof., 1960-69, assoc. prof., 1973-78, prof., 1978-92, acting assoc. provost, 1974-75, assoc. provost for spl. programs, 1975-78, research assoc., assoc. dir. Scripps Gerontology Ctr., 1970-92, dir. edn. and tng., 1980-92, sr. fellow, prof. emerata Scripps Gerontology Ctr., 1992-94. Author: Expected Life History: A Model in Nonlinear Time, Timing: The Significant Common Variable in Both Humor and Aging, Fictive Kin as Companions Through the Adult Years, Humor in Adult Development; author, co-editor: Health and Economic Studies of Older Women, 1989; contbr. articles to profl. jours. Fellow Gerontol. Soc. Am.; mem. Am. Soc. on Aging, Mortar Bd. (hon.), Phi Beta Kappa, Omicron Delta Kappa, Phi Kappa Phi. Home: Oxford Ohio Died Nov. 1994.

SEMONOFF, RALPH PERLOW, lawyer; b. Providence, May 6, 1918; s. Judah C. and Lucy (Perlow) S.; m. Hinda M. Pritsker, Oct. 25, 1942; children: Susan A. Ellen M., Judith W. A.B., Brown U., 1939; LL.B., M.C.L., Harvard U., 1947. Bar: R.I. 1947, U.S. Dist. Ct. R.I. 1948, U.S. Tax Ct. 1949. Partner firm Semonoff & Semonoff, Providence, 1947-60, Levy, Goodman, Semonoff & Gorin, Providence, 1961-85, Licht & Semonoff, 1985-92; mem. R.I. Gov.'s Commn. on Jud. Selection, 1977-85, 91-92; mem. disciplinary com. R.I. Supreme Ct., 1987-92, vice chmn., 1991-92, com. on character and fitness, 1988-91. Editor Harvard U. Law Rev., 1940-41, 46. Pres. Urban League R.I., 1957-61, Citizens League Pawtucket, R.I., 1961-63, Jewish Family and Children's Svc. R.I., 1974-77; chmn. Miriam Hosp., Providence, 1983-85, MIriam Hosp. Found., Providence, 1986-88; bd. dirs. R.I. Legal Svcs., 1969-77. With U.S. Army, 1941-46. Fellow R.I. Bar Found. (bd. dirs., interest on lawyers trust accounts com. 1985-92); mem. ABA, R.I. Bar Assn. (pres. 1978-79, coordinating com. with R.I. Med. Assn.), Pawtucket Bar Assn. (pres. 1963), Am. Law Inst., New Eng. Bar Assn. (bd. dirs. 1979-84). Home: Pawtucket R.I. Died Apr. 2, 1992.

SEMYONOV, JULIAN, editor in chief, writer; b. Moscow, Aug. 10, 1931; s. Landres Alexander Semyon and Nozdrina Nicolaevna Galina; divorced; children: Daria, Olga. D in Afganistan History, Moscow U., 1955. Tchr. Afghani philology Moscow State U., 1955-56; reporter Ogonjek mag., Moscow, 1956-61; editor-in-chief Detectiv and Politic mag., Top Secret mag., Moscow, 1989-93; pres. DEM pub. house, Moscow and Paris, 1987-93. Author numerous novels and scripts including In the Performance of Duty, 1962, Tass is Authorised to Announce, 1987, Seventeen Moments of Spring, 1988, Intercontinental Knot, 1989, No Passport Necessary, 38 Petrovka Street. Capt. Soviet army, 1950-53. Decorated numerous awards USSR, Poland, France, 1985-89. Mem. Internat. Crime Writers' Assn. (hon. pres. 1989-93, dir. Moscow bur. info.), Union of Russian Writers (sec. 1986), N.Y. Acad. Scis., European Acad. Scis. Home: Moscow Russia Died Sept. 14, 1993.

SENDER, STANTON P., lawyer; b. Seattle, Nov. 11, 1932; s. James and Lucile J. S.; m. Michelle R. Vale, Mar. 29, 1973; children: Jason, Todd. AB, Harvard U., 1953, JD, 1956. Bar: U.S. Supreme Ct. 1962, D.C. 1969. Asst. atty. gen. Wash. State, Seattle and Olympia, 1956-61; trial atty. gen. counsel's office I.C.C., Washington, 1961-63; transp. counsel U.S. Senate Commerce Commn., Washington, 1963-69; asst. gen counsel, dir. legal affairs Sears, Roebuck, and Co., Washington, 1969-89; dir. govt. rels. practice group Morgan, Lewis, and Bockius, Washington, 1989-95; adj. prof. Georgetown U., 1970-78. Bd. dirs. (by presdl. appointment) U.S. Railway Assn., 1978-81; treas. Nat. Industrial Transp. League, 1976-88. Recipient Outstanding Coun. award Fed. Bar Assn., 1979, Achievement award Traffic Management mag., 1986, Silver Plaque award Nat. Retail Merchants Assn., 1989 ; named Man of Yr. Nat. Industrial Transp. League, 1986. Mem. ABA (vice chair transp. com. 1989-95), Propeller Club of Washington (bd. govs. 1990-95). Home: Washington D.C. Died Nov. 7, 1995.

SENNSTROM, JOHN HAROLD, manufacturing company executive; b. Schenectady, N.Y., Mar. 15, 1941. B.S. in Indsl. Mgmt., Purdue U., 1965; M.B.A., U. Wash., 1982. Prodn. supr. Haller Inc., Northville, Mich., 1965-69; plant mgr. IPM Corp., Columbus, Ohio, 1969-76; mfg. mgr. Fentron Industries, Seattle, 1976-79; pres. Hytek Finishes Co., Kent, Wash., 1979-84, Fentron Bldg. Products Co., Seattle, 1984-87, Demcon Cons. Co., Redmond, Wash., 1987—. Home: Redmond W. Va.

SERGEL, CHRISTOPHER ROGER, publisher; b. Iowa City, May 7, 1918; s. Roger Louis and Ruth (Fuller) S.; m. Gayle Ritchie; children by previous marriage: Kathryn, Ruth, Christopher Triton, Ingrid, Ann. A.A., U. Chgo., 1939. With Dramatic Pub. Co., Chgo., 1941-93, editor, 1945-93, v.p., 1952-70, pres., 1970-93; capt. schooner on expdn. to South Pacific, 1940, to East Africa, 1947, 49. Playwright, 1938-93; Author: dramatic versions of Lost Horizon, 1942, Winesburg, Ohio, 1958, To Kill a Mockingbird, 1970, Black Elk Speaks, 1975, The Ragtime Dance, 1975, Fame, 1985; others.; contbr. articles to mags. Served to lt. comdr. USMCR, World War II, ETO, PTO. Mem. Dramatists Guild, Drama Desk, Beta Theta Pi. Clubs: Adventurers, Explorers, Cliff Dwellers. Home: Wilton Conn. Died May 7, 1993.

SETTON, KENNETH M., historian, educator; b. New Bedford, Mass., June 17, 1914; s. Ezra and Louise (Crossley) S.; m. Josephine W. Swift, Sept. 11, 1941 (dec. Aug. 1967); 1 son, George Whitney Fletcher; m. Margaret T. Henry, Jan. 4, 1969 (dec. Mar. 1987). A.B., Boston U., 1936, Litt.D. (hon.), 1957; postgrad., U. Chgo., 1936, Harvard U., 1939-40; A.M., Columbia U., 1938, Ph.D., 1941; Dr. Phil. h.c., U. Kiel, Germany, 1979. Instr. classics, history Boston U., 1940-43; assoc. prof. European history U. Man., Can., 1943-45; prof., head dept. history U. Man., 1945-50; Henry C. Lea assoc. prof. medieval history, curator Lea Libr., U. Pa., Phila., 1950-53, Lea prof. history, 1953-54, Lea prof. history, dir. librs., 1955-65, Univ. prof. history, 1962-65; prof. history Columbia U., 1954-55; William F. Vilas rsch. prof. history, dir. Inst. Rsch. in Humanities, U. Wis., 1965-68; prof. history Inst. Advanced Study, Princeton, N.J., 1968-95; vis. lectr. medieval history Bryn Mawr (Pa.) Coll., 1952-53; rsch. fellow Gennadius Libr., Am. Sch. Classical Studies, Athens, Greece, 1960-61; mem. exec. and mng. coms. Am. Sch. Classical Studies, Athens. Author: Christian Attitude Towards the Emperor in the Fourth Century, 1941, 2d edit., 1987, Catalan Domination of Athens, 1311-1388, 1948, rev. edit., 1975; (with Henry R. Winkler) Great Problems in European Civilization, 1954, 2d edit., 1966, Europe and the Levant in the Middle Ages and the Renaissance, 1974, Athens in the Middle Ages, 1975, Los Catalanes en Grecia, 1975, The Papacy and the Levant, 1204-1571, vols. I-IV, 1976, 78, 84, (in Greek) The Byzantine Background to the Italian Renaissance, 1989, Venice, Austria and the Turks in the Seventeenth Century, 1991, Western Hostility to Islam, 1992. Guggenheim Meml. fellow Greece, Italy, 1949, 50; decorated Gold Cross Order George I, Greece; recipient Premi Catalonia Barcelona, 1976, Prix Gustave Schlumberger Paris, 1976, John Gilmary Shea prize Washington, 1979. Fellow Mediaeval Acad. Am. (pres. 1971-72, Haskins medal 1980), Soc. Macedonian Studies (hon.), Am. Acad. Arts and Scis.; mem. Am. Philos. Soc. (John Frederick Lewis prize 1957, 84, 90, v.p. 1966-69, 85-91), Am. Hist. Assn. (award for scholarly distinction 1990), Inst. Catalan Studies (corr.), Phi Beta Kappa. Episcopalian. Home: Hightstown N.J. Died Feb. 18, 1995.

SEVAGIAN, ARAM HAIG, chemist; b. Mattapan, Mass., May 10, 1932; s. Haig Ohanes and Surpoohy Terzian Tarbassian S.; student Northeastern U., 1949-54; BS with honors, Suffolk U., 1960, MA in Edn. (fellow), 1962; postgrad. (NSF grantee) Trinity U., San Antonio, 1968. With E & F King Corp., Norwood, Mass., 1952-53; indsl. diamond dust researcher Raytheon Mfg. Co., Waltham, Mass., 1953-54; chem. analyst Petrochem. div. Nat. Research Corp., Cambridge, Mass., 1957-58; instr. chemistry and physics lab. Suffolk U., Boston, 1959-60, instr. grad. chemistry lab., 1960-62, lectr. chemistry, 1962-66; tchr. chemistry and physics Westwood (Mass.) High Sch., 1960-63, Braintree (Mass.) High Sch., from 1963; cons. on drug identification and chemistry coord., 1972-86. Mem. Citizens Com. Right to Keep and Bear Arms. With U.S. Army, 1955-57. Mem. AAAS, NEA (life), NRA, Mass. Tchrs. Assn., Nat. Sci. Tchrs. Assn., U.S. Naval Inst., U.S. Chess Fedn., Mass. Chess Assn., Mass. Rifle and Pistol Assn., GOAL, Am. Def. Preparedness Assn., Internat. Benchrest Shooters, Nat. Bench Rest Assn., Am. Chem. Soc. (div. chem. edn.), Am. Inst. Physics, Am. Assn. Physics Tchrs., Braintree Edn. Assn., Norfolk County Tchrs. Assn., Mass. Assn. Sci. Tchrs., N.E. Assn. Chemistry Tchrs., Japanese Sword Soc. (life), Am. Legion, Amvets. U.S. Mem. Armenian Apostolic Ch. Clubs: Braintree Rifle and Pistol (dir. jrs. 1974-89), Masons. Died April 22, 1991; buried Mt. Auburn Cemetary, Cambridge, Mass. Home: Milton Mass.

SEVAREID, ARNOLD ERIC, broadcaster, author; b. Velva, N.D., Nov. 26, 1912; s. Alfred and Clare (Hougen) S.; m. Lois Finger, May 18, 1935 (div. 1962); children: Michael and Peter (twins); m. Belen Marshall, 1963 (div. 1974); 1 child, Cristina; m. Suzanne St. Pierre, 1979. A.B., U. Minn., 1935; student, Alliance Francaise, Paris, 1937. Copy boy Mpls. jour., 1931, later reporter; reporter Mpls. Star, 1936-37; reporter, city editor Paris edit. N.Y. Herald Tribune, 1938-39; night editor UP, Paris, 1939; became European corr. Columbia Broadcasting System, 1939; with French Army and Air Force in France and Belgium; broadcast French capitulation from Tours and Bordeaux, has also broadcast news from Asia, Africa, Eng., Holland, Belgium, Luxembourg, Mexico, Brazil; nat. corr. CBS, until 1977; cons., 1977-92. Author: children's book Canoeing with the Cree, 1935; Not So Wild a Dream, 1946, 2d edit., 1976, In One Ear, 1952, Small Sounds in the Night, 1956, This Is Eric Sevareid, 1964; Editor: Candidates, 1960; Contbr. articles to mags. Recipient George Foster Peabody award, 1949, 64, 68, Fourth

Estate award Nat. Press Club, 1984, Emmy award TV Acad. Hall of Fame, 1987. Mem. Radio-TV Corrs. Assn. (past pres.), Sigma Delta Chi. Clubs: Metropolitan, Overseas Writers. Home: Washington D.C. Died July 2, 1992.

SEYMOUR, MARY POWELL, state senator; b. Raleigh, N.C., Apr. 12, 1922; d. Robert C. and Annie (Seymour) Powell; m. Hubert Elmo Seymour, Feb. 3, 1945; children: Hubert Seymour III, Robert John. AA, Peace Coll., Raleigh, 1941; student, Harvard U., 1946-47, U. Mich., 1949-50. Lic. real estate broker. Legal sec., ct. reporter; sec. to dean Harvard U. Grad. Sch. Bus.; adminstnr. med. supply ORD, Greensboro; sec., claims adjustor Social Security; rep. N.C. Gen. Assembly, 1976-84, senator, 1987-88, re-elected 1990; govtl. cons., lobbyist N.C. R.R. Assn., N.C. Bankers Assn., 1985-86; mayor pro tempore City of Greensboro, N.C., 1973-75; mem. Greensboro City Council, 1967-75. Active Tar Heel Triad Girls Scout Coun. Inc., Hayes Taylor YMCA, N.C. Arts Coun., N.C. Parks and Recreation Coun., United Arts Coun.; bd. visitors Peace Coll.; mem. N.C. Inst. Medicine, N.C. Bd. Nat. Conf. Ins. Legis., So. Legis. Conf. Environ. Quality and Natural Resources Com., 1992; mem. transp. adv. coun. Nat. Conf. State Legis. Telecomm. Com., also N.C. law-related edn. bd., women and econ. devel. bd. Named Disting. Alumna, Peace Coll., Woman of Yr., Quota Club; recipient Disting. Svc. award YWCA, Legis. award N.C. Bar Assn., Disting. Svcs. award N.C. Pub. Health, Good Sam award for Legis. for Hearing Impaired, Community Svc. award Bennett Coll., Legis. award N.C. Recreation and Parks, 1984, Eleanor Roosevelt award, Bryant Citizenship award, Dolley Madison award, Disting. Dem. of Yr., 1990. Mem. Women's Profl. Forum, Nat. Order Women Legislators, U.S. Power Squadron. Clubs: O. Henry Womans, Greensboro Council of Garden, Dem. Women, Belews Creek Sailing. Home: Greensboro N.C. Died Aug. 26, 1994.

SHAD, JOHN, investment banker, diplomat; b. Brigham City, Utah, June 27, 1923; s. John Sigsbee and Lillian (Rees) S.; m. Patricia Pratt, July 27, 1952 (dec. Sept. 1988); children: Leslie Anne, Rees Edward. BS cum laude, U. So. Cal., 1947; MBA, Harvard U., 1949; LLB, NYU, 1959; LD (hon.), Rochester U., 1987. From securities analyst to investment banker, 1949-62; with E.F. Hutton Group, Inc., 1963-81, v.p. to vice chmn. bd.; chmn. SEC, Washington, 1981-87; ambassador to The Netherlands, 1987-89; pro bono chmn. Drexel Burnham Lambert Group, N.Y.C., 1989-90; faculty NYU Grad. Sch. Bus. Adminstrn., 1961-62; writer, speaker on Am., The Netherlands and Europe; bd. dirs. Chgo. Bd. Options Exch. Contbr. articles to profl. jours. Bd. dirs. Harvard Bus. Sch. Assocs., Fin. Reporting Inst., Securities Regulation Inst., Nat. Ctr. for Fin. Svcs., Hoover Instn., Nat. Legal Ctr. for the Pub. Interest; chmn. Reagan-Bush N.Y. Fin. Com., 1980. Lt. (j.g.) USNR, 1943-46. Recipient Investment Banker of Year award Fin. mag., 1972, Brotherhood award NCCJ, 1981, Bus. Statesman of Yr. award Harvard Bus. Sch. Club N.Y., 1988, others. Mem. Univ. Club (N.Y.C.), Century Club (N.Y.C.), Harvard Bus. Sch. Club, India House (N.Y.C.), Bohemian Club (San Francisco), Met. Club (Washington), Greenwich Country Club, Chevy Chase Country Club, Beta Gamma Sigma, Phi Kappa Phi, Alpha Kappa Psi. Home: New York N.Y. Died July 7, 1994.

SHAGASS, CHARLES, psychiatrist; b. Montreal, Que., Can., May 19, 1920; came to U.S., 1958, naturalized, 1965; s. Morris and Pauline (Segal) S.; m. Clara Wallerstein, Nov. 1, 1942; children: Carla Louise, Kathryn Sharna, Thomas Alan. B.A., McGill U., Montreal, 1940, M.D., C.M., 1949; M.S., U. Rochester, 1941. Certified in psychiatry, Que. Intern Royal Victoria Hosp., Montreal, 1949-50; resident Royal Victoria Hosp., 1950-53; lectr. McGill U., Montreal, 1952-56, asst. prof. psychiatry, 1956-58; assoc. prof. U. Iowa, Iowa City, 1958-60, prof., 1960-66; prof. Temple U., Phila., 1966-90; prof. emeritus Temple U., from 1990; assoc. chmn. Temple U., Phila., 1981-86, interim chmn., 1986-90; prof. Med. Coll. Pa., Phila., from 1991; asst. psychiatrist Royal Victoria Hosp., 1952-58; psychiat. physician Ea. Pa. Psychiat. Inst., 1966-81; attending psychiatrist Phila. Psychiat. Ctr., from 1982; prof. Med. Coll. Pa., Phila., from 1991; cons. NIMH, Social Security Adminstrs. Author: Evoked Brain Potentials in Psychiatry, 1972; editor: books, including Modern Problems of Pharmacopsychiatry, Vol. 6, 1971, (with others) Psychopathology and Brain Dysfunction, 1977; researcher numerous publs. on brain function in mental illness, 1941. Served with RCAF, 1941-45. USPHS grantee, from 1958. Fellow Royal Coll. Physicians (Can.), Am. Psychiat. Assn., Am. Psychopathol. Assn. (pres. 1974-75, Samuel Hamilton award 1975); mem. Soc. Biol. Psychiatry (pres. 1974-75, Gold Medal award 1977), World Fedn. Socs. Biological Psychiatry (pres. 1981-85, hon. pres. 1991), Am. Coll. Neuropsychopharmacology, Am. EEG Soc., Collegium Internat. Neuro Psychopharmacologicum, Psychiat Rsch. Soc., Group for Advancement Psychiatry, Eastern Assn. Electroencephalographers, Sigma Xi, Alpha Omega Alpha. Democrat. Jewish. Home: Wyncote Pa. Deceased.

SHANE, HAROLD GRAY, educator; b. Milw., Aug. 11, 1914; s. Bert L. and Grace (Gray) S.; m. Ruth Williams, Sept. 1, 1938 (dec.); children: Michael Stewart, Susan Hatker, Patricia Mills, Ann Gray; m. Catherine McKenzie, July 6, 1974. B.E., Milw. State Tchrs. Coll., 1935; M.A., Ohio State U., 1939, Ph.D., 1943. Tchr. Cin. Pub. Schs., 1935-37; prin. Ottawa Hills Elem. Sch., Toledo, 1937-41; supr. elementary edn. State of Ohio, 1941-43; asst. prof. edn. Ohio State U., 1943-46; supt. schs. Winnetka, Ill., 1946-49; prof. edn. Northwestern U., 1949-59; dean Sch. Edn., Ind. U., Bloomington, 1959-65; univ. prof. edn. Sch. Edn., Ind. U., 1965-86, disting. univ. prof. edn., 1967-86, univ. prof. edn. emeritus, 1986-93; cons. U.S. Office Edn., UNESCO, Dept. Def., Danforth Found., Lilly Endowment, IBM, Singer Co., numerous other corps. Author: over 280 books including The Solar System, 1938, Magic of Electricity, 1939, Power Boat Book, 1947, The New Baby, 1948, (with E.T. McSwain) Evaluation and the Elementary Curriculum, 1951, rev. edit., 1958, The American Elementary School, 1953, (with W. A. Yauch) Creative School Adminstration, 1954, The Twins, 1955, Research Helps in Teaching the Language Arts, 1956, Beginning Language Instruction, 1960, (with others) Improving Language Arts Instruction, 1962, Linguistics and the Classroom Teacher, 1967, (with others) Guiding Human Development, 1971; (with others) The Educational Significance of the Future, 1973; The Elementary School in the U.S, 1973, (with Alvin Toffler et al.) Learning for Tomorrow, 1974, The Future of Education, 1975, (with others) The Future As an Academic Discipline, 1975, Issues in Secondary Education, 1976, Curriculum Change: Toward the 21st Century, 1977, (with others) Alternative Educational Systems, 1979, (with M.B. Tabler) Educating for a New Millennium, 1981; Teaching and Learning in a Microelectronic Age, 1987, (with Wilma Longstreet Engle) Curriculum for a New Millennium, 1993; mem. editorial bd. Futures Research Quar., 1986-93, Futurics, 1986-93, Cultural Futures Research, 1986-93; contbr. over 280 articles to popular and profl. jours.; books and articles trans. into 7 langs. including Japanese and Indonesian. Served as officer USNR, 1943-46. Recipient Outstanding Ednl. Journalist award Ed Press, 1974, 83; Disting. Alumnus award Ohio State U., 1980; Kappa Delta Pi Laureate award, 1982. Mem. NEA, ASCD (pres. 1973-74, exec. council 1972-75), Nat. Assn. Nursery Edn., Am. Assn. Sch. Adminstrs., Assn. Childhood Edn., Nat. Soc. Study Edn. (dir. 1968-78), Phi Delta Kappa, Kappa Delta Pi (editorial bd. publs. 1988-90). Home: Bloomington Ind. Died July 12, 1993.

SHANNON, JAMES A., medical investigator, educator; b. Hollis, N.Y., Aug. 9, 1904; s. James A. and Anna (Margison) S.; m. Alice Waterhouse, June 24, 1933; children: Alice, James Anthony. A.B., Holy Cross Coll., Mass., 1925, D.Sc. (hon.), 1952; M.D., NYU, 1929, Ph.D., 1935, D.Sc. (hon.), 1965; D.H.L. (hon.), Albert Einstein Coll. Medicine, 1962; LL.D. (hon.), U. Calif., Berkeley, 1968, Yale U., 1968; D.Sc., Emory U., 1970, Harvard U., 1972; recipient over 25 other hon. degrees from U.S., fgn. instns., 1952-75. Intern Bellevue Hosp., N.Y.C., 1929-31; asst. dept. physiology N.Y. U. Coll. Medicine, 1931-32, instr., 1932-35, asst. prof., 1935-40, asst. prof. dept. medicine, 1941, assoc. prof., 1941-46; dir. research service N.Y. U. med. div. Goldwater Meml. Hosp., 1941-46; dir. Squibb & Sons, Squibb Inst. Med. Research, 1946-49; assoc. dir. in charge research Nat. Heart Inst., 1949-52; assoc. dir. NIH, 1952-55, dir., 1955-68; scholar-in-residence Nat. Library Medicine, 1975-80; prof. biomed. scis., spl. adviser to pres. Rockefeller U., N.Y.C., 1970-75; adj. prof. Rockefeller U., 1975-94; scholar in human biology Eleanor Roosevelt Inst. for Cancer Research, 1977-94; cons. tropical diseases to sec. war, 1943-46; spl. cons. surgeon gen. USPHS, 1946-49, asst. surg. gen., 1952-68; mem. Bd. for Coordination Malarial Studies, chmn. clin. panel, 1943-46; mem. subcom. on shock NRC, 1952-56, NRC exec. com., mem.-at-large, 1954-55, USPHS rep., 1955-63; chmn. panel on malaria Div. Med. Scis., 1951-56; mem. U.S. nat. com. Internat. Union Physiol. Scis., 1955-62; mem. expert adv. panel on malaria WHO, 1956-66, founding mem. adv. com. on med. research, 1959-63; founding mem. adv. com. on med. research Pan Am. Health Orgn., 1962-66; cons. med. affairs AID, 1963-68; cons. Pres.'s Sci. Adv. Com., 1959-65; HEW rep. and vice-chmn. standing com. Fed. Council Sci. and Tech., 1960-68; holder numerous endowed lectureships, various univs. and sci. assns., 1945-94; mem. selection com. Rockefeller Pub. Service awards Princeton U., 1969-73; mem. award selection coms. numerous orgns. and founds.; mem. N.Y.C. Bd. Health, 1970-71; gen. cons. biomed. scis. Merck, Sharpe and Dohme, 1968-76; adv. univ. support program in biomed. scis. R.J. Reynolds Industries Inc., 1978-85. Contbr. articles to profl. jours. Recipient numerous honors and awards, including: Presdl. medal for Merit, 1946; Mendel medal Villanova U., 1961; Rockefeller Pub. Service award, 1964; Disting. Service medal HEW, 1964; Presdl. Disting. Fed. Civilian Service award, 1966; John M. Russel award Markle Found., 1966; 3d Ann. award Hadasash Myrtle Wreath, 1968; Rosenberger medal U. Chgo., 1968; John Phillips Meml. award A.C.P., 1969; Homer W. Smith award Am. Heart Assn., 1969; Nat. Medal Sci., 1974; award for disting. contbns. Soc. Research Adminstrs., 1975; Blue Cross/Blue Shield 50th anniversary award for nat. health achievement, 1980; Award for disting. achievement U. Oreg., 1981; NIH Central Adminstrn. Bldg. (Bldg. 1) dedicated as James A. Shannon Bldg., 1983; Bd. Trustees award Mass. Gen. Hosp., 1986; The Fahray medal The Franklin Inst., 1986, Centennial award Am. Assn. Anatomists, 1987. Fellow Am. Pub. Health Assn., Am. Assn. Hosp. Adminstrs. (hon.); mem. Am. Soc. Pharmacology and Exptl. Therapeutics, Am. Physiol. Soc., Am. Soc. Clin. Investigation, Am. Acad. Arts and Scis., Am. Philos. Soc., Royal Soc. Physicians London, Soc. Exptl. Biology and Medicine, Harvey Soc., Assn. Am. Physicians, AAAS (Philip Hauge Abelson prize 1986), Nat. Acad. Scis. (Pub. Service award 1964, mem. bd. on medicine 1967-70, academic council 1970-73, exec. com. 1970-73), Inst. of Medicine (founding mem. 1970), Nat. Acad. Pub. Adminstrn., ADA (hon.), Am. Hosp. Assn. (hon.), Sigma Xi, Alpha Omega Alpha. Club: Cosmos. Home: Lake Oswego Oreg. Died May 20, 1994.

SHARBAUGH, AMANDUS HARRY, electric company executive; b. Richmond, Va., Mar. 28, 1919; s. Amandus Harry and Jacqueline (Harrison) S.; m. Doris Eitle, Sept. 23, 1940; children: Amandus Harry, Durell Dean. A.B., Case Western Res. U., 1940; Ph.D., Brown U., 1943; postdoctoral, Union U., 1945-55. With Gen. Electric Co., Schenectady, 1942-84; liaison scientist Gen. Electric Co., 1960-63, mgr. dielectrics unit, 1963-73, mgr. plasma physics br., 1973-79, mgr. arc physics and dielectrics, 1979-81, sr. cons., 1981-84; pvt. cons., 1984-94. Contbr. over 100 articles in field to profl. jours.; co-author 4 books in field. Recipient Potter prize Brown U. Fellow IEEE (Dakin award); mem. Nat. Acad. Scis. Conf. Dielectric Phenomena.; Mem. Phi Beta Kappa, Sigma Xi. Democrat. Methodist. Home: Clifton Park N.Y. Died Aug. 15, 1994.

SHARE, WILLIAM FREMONT, newspaper executive; b. Monroe, Wis., Nov. 9, 1926; s. William W. and Zora Belle (Bridge) S.; m. Jeanne Louise Whittemore, Jan. 17, 1948 (dec. Mar. 1988); children: Peter, Brenda Lee, Stephen, Patricia Mary; m. Maxine Eichstedt, Jan. 12, 1991. Attended, U. Wis.-Milw. Ext. Automotive sales mgr. Jour./Sentinel Inc., Milw., 1959-68, mgr. gen. advt., 1968-73; bus. mgr. Milw. Sentinel, 1973-77; v.p. advt. Jour./Sentinel Inc., Milw., 1977-85, sr. v.p. mktg., 1985-90, pres., 1990-95. Mem. Dominican High Sch. Bd., Milw., 1969-71, Better Bus. Bur. Bd., Milw., 1977-85. With USNR, 1945-46, 50-51, WWII, Korea. Mem. Internat. Newspaper Execs. (chair color com. advt. & mktg. 1985-88), Am. Advt. Fedn. (gov. 1979-80), Milw. Advt. Club (pres. 1975-76, Silver medal 1984), Ville du Parc Country Club, Milw. Athletic Club. Roman Catholic. Home: Milwaukee Wis. Died Apr. 12, 1995.

SHARF, DONALD JACK, speech communication educator, researcher; b. Detroit, Aug. 4, 1927; s. Max and Yetta (Spritz) S.; m. Rhoda Lenore Kaine, June 26, 1952; children: Daniel Owen, Ellen. B.A., Wayne State U., Detroit, 1951, M.A., 1952; Ph.D., U. Mich., Ann Arbor, 1958. Editor G&C Merriam Co., Springfield, Mass., 1957-61; asst. prof. SUNY, Buffalo, 1961-64; prof. U. Mich., Ann Arbor, 1964-87, prof. emeritus, 1987-95. Author: (with R. N. Ohdel Macmillan) Phonetic Analysis of Normal and Abnormal Speech, 1992. Served with U.S. Army, 1945-46. Mem. Acoustical Soc. Am., Am. Speech-Lang.-Hearing Assn., Am Assn. Phonetic Scis. (councilor 1983-95). Democrat. Home: Boca Raton Fla. Died June 17, 1995.

SHARITS, PAUL JEFFREY, film artist; b. Denver, Feb. 7, 1943; s. Paul Edward and Florence May (Romeo) S.; BFA in Painting, U. Denver, 1964; MFA in Visual Design, Ind. U., 1966; m. Frances Trujillo. July 28, 1962 (div. 1971); 1 child, Christopher. Instr. art Md Inst. Art, Balt., 1967-70; asst. prof. Antioch Coll. Yellow Springs, Ohio, 1970-73; prof. media State U N.Y., Buffalo, 1973-93; life-long mem. Fluxus, 1965-93 one-man exhbns. include Bykert Gallery, N.Y.C., 1972 74; Galerie Ricke, Cologne, Fed. Republic Germany 1974, 77; Albright-Knox Art Gallery, Buffalo, 1976 Gallery A. Amsterdam, Netherlands, 1977; Galerie Waalkens, Finsterwolde, Netherlands, 1977; Droll Kolbert Gallery, N.Y.C., 1977, Art Gallery Ont. Toronto, 1978; Nina Freudenheim Gallery, 1983-84; retropective of films Centre Georges Pompidou, Paris 1977, Anthology Film Archives, N.Y.C., 1978; rep catalogues, also magazines. Grantee Am. Film Inst. 1968, Ford Found., 1970, 71, Nat. Endowment Arts 1974, Creative Artists Pub. Service, N.Y. State, 1975 78, N.Y. State Council Arts-Nat. Endowment Arts 1976, Whitney Mus., 1984. Died July 8, 1993. Home Buffalo N.Y.

SHARKEY, RAY, actor; b. Bklyn., 1952. Actor: (feature films) Hot Tomorrows, 1976, Stunts, 1977, Paradise Alley, 1978, Who'll Stop the Rain?, 1978, Heart Beat 1979, Willie and Phil, 1980, The Idolmaker, 1980, Love and Money, 1982, Some Kind of Hero, 1982, Body Rock, 1984, duBeat-e-o, 1984, Hellhole, 1985, Wise Guys, 1986, No Mercy, 1986, (TV movie) Behind Enemy Lines, 1985. Mem. Screen Actors Guild, AFTRA. Home: Los Angeles Calif. Died June 11, 1993.

SHARP, MARGERY, author; m. G. L. Castle 1938. B.A. in French with honors, London U. Author: Rhododendron Pie, Fanfare for Tin Trumpets, The Flowering Thorn, Four Gardens, The Nymph and the Nobleman, Sophy Cassmajor, (play) Meeting at Night The Nutmeg Tree, 1937 (play, U.S. 1940, Eng. 194

filmed as Julia Misbehaves 1948), The Stone of Chastity, 1940, Cluny Brown, 1944 (filmed 1946), Britannia Mews, 1946 (filmed 1949), The Foolish Gentlewoman, 1948 (play, London 1949), Lise Lillywhite, 1951, The Gipsy in the Parlour, 1953, The Tigress on the Hearth, 1955, The Eye of Love, 1957, Something Light, 1960, Martha in Paris, 1962, Martha, Eric and George, 1964, The Sun in Scorpio, 1965, in Pious Memory, 1968, Rosa, 1969, The Innocents, 1971, The Beautiful Servants, 1975, Summer Visits, 1977, (short stories) The Lost Chapel Picnic, 1973; author books for children: The Resduers, 1959, Miss Bianca in the Salt Mines, 1966, Lost at the Fair, 1967, Miss Bianca in the Orient, 1970, Miss Biance in the Antarctic, 1977, Miss Bianca and the Bridesmaid, 1972, The Magical Cockatoo, 1974, The Children Next Door, 1974, Bernard the Brave, 1976. Home: London Eng. Died Mar. 14, 1991; interred Aldeburgh, Suffolk.

SHAW, HARRY ALEXANDER, III, manufacturing company executive; b. Tacoma, Sept. 27, 1937; s. Harry Alexander and Gladys (Reynolds) S.; m. Phoebe Jo Crouch, Nov. 27, 1966; children: Harry Alexander IV, Austin R., Christine N. A.B., Dartmouth Coll., 1959. Various sales positions U.S. Steel Corp., 1962-69; nat. sales mgr. Huffy Corp., 1969, mktg. mgr. Ohio Bicycle Div., 1971-73, v.p. mktg., 1973-75, Calif. div. pres., 1975-77; group v.p. Huffy Corp., Dayton, Ohio, 1977-78; with Harvard A.M.P., 1978; pres., chief operating officer Huffy Corp., 1979-82, pres., chief exec. officer, 1982-85, CEO, 1986-93; chmn. Huffy Corp., Dayton, 1993-94; bd. dirs. Baldwin Piano Co., Duriron Co., Soc. Corp., Gen. Corp., Outboard Marine Corp., Dayton Art Inst. Endowment Com. Past trustee Wilberforce U., MIami Valley Hosp.; past pres., bd. trustees Dayton Art Inst.; past sr. warden St. Paul's ch.; past chmn. Dayton area U.S. Olympic Com., United Negro Coll Fund; mem. exec. com., past chmn. Dayton area Progress Coun., Young Pres. Orgn., Bicycle Mfrs. Assn.; mem. cabinet United Way; vice chmn. Am. Recreation Roundtable; bd. dirs. Dayton Area United Way of Am. With USN, 1959-62. Mem. Rotary. Home: Oakwood Mass. Died Sept. 5, 1994.

SHAW, MANFORD AVIS, college chancellor; b. Tremonton, Utah, Nov. 14, 1906; s. N. Edward and LoVisa (Brent) S.; m. Janet Walker, Feb. 4, 1932 (dec. 1950); children: Ann (Mrs. Ian McFarlane), Brent (Mrs. Eugene Foster); m. June Winward, May 6, 1953; children: Michael M. (dec.), Karen (Mrs. G.M. Cordray), Cynthia (Mrs. R. Pitts), Debra (Mrs. F. Benzinger), Avis (Mrs. K. Ravsten). Ph.B., Yale U., 1929; J.D., U. Utah, 1942; LL.D, Westminster Coll., Salt Lake City, 1957. Bar: Utah bar 1942. Salesman Dictaphone Corp., N.Y.C., 1929-32; v.p. E.B. Wicks Co. (realtors), Salt Lake City, 1932-42; pres. Shaw Inc. (realtor), Salt Lake City, 1946-67, Nat. Mortgage Co., Salt Lake City, 1963-65; pres. Westminster Coll., 1968-76, chancellor, 1976-93; trustee, 1936-68, chmn. trustees, 1965-68. Pres. Salt Lake City Bd. Realtors, 1939, Utah Realty Assn., 1940, Utah Sales Exec. Assn., 1941. Served to maj. AUS, 1942-46. Recipient Brotherhood award NCCJ, 1982. Methodist. Clubs: University (Salt Lake City), Cottonwood Country (Salt Lake City). Home: Salt Lake City Utah Died Jan 24, 1993; interred Wasateh Lawn, Salt Lake City, Utah.

SHAY, MARTIN EDWARD, museum director; b. Syracuse, N.Y., Aug. 15, 1948; s. Martin James and Martha Louise (Hess) S.; m. Lynn Ann Rebbeor, Oct. 6, 1979; children: Devin Tremayne, David Martin. BS, SUNY, Oswego, 1971. Tchr. Head Start Program, Syracuse, N.Y., 1971-73; curator Onondaga County Parks, Liverpool, N.Y., 1973-75; asst. interpretive programs N.Y. State Parks, Oswego, 1975-78; coordinator Heritage Found., Oswego, 1978-79; adminstr. Deutschheim State Historic Site, Hermann, Mo., 1979-83; dir. Mo. State Mus., Jefferson City, 1983-92. Chmn. Hermann Arts Coun., 1979-83; mem. Mo. Arts Coun. Touring Com., St. Louis, 1980-83, Mo. Arts Coun. Community Arts Program, St. Louis, 1984-86; bd. dirs. Mo. Citizens for Arts, 1983-92, Capitol City Coun. on Arts, Jefferson City, 1986-91, pres., 1987-90. Recipient award for contbn. to arts Union Electric Co., 1984, Cert. of Appreciation Mo. Arts Edn. Assn., 1989. Mem. Jaycees. Home: Jefferson City Mo. Died Feb., 1992.

SHEAFFER, LOUIS (LOUIS SHEAFFER SLUNG), writer; b. Louisville, Oct. 18, 1912; s. Abraham and Ida (Jacobson) Slung. Student, U. N.C., 1930-31. Reporter, Bklyn. Eagle, 1934-42, 46-47, movie critic, 1947-49, drama critic, 1949-55. Author: O'Neill, Son and Playwright, 1968 (George Freedley award Theater Library Assn. 1969), O'Neill, Son and Artist, 1973 (Pulitzer prize 1974). Guggenheim fellow, 1959, 62, 69; grantee Am. Council Learned Socs., 1960, 62, 82; grantee NEH, 1971-72. Home: Brooklyn N.Y. Died Aug. 7, 1993.

SHEEHAN, JOHN JOSEPH, lawyer; b. Manchester, N.H., Apr. 28, 1899; s. Daniel C. and Mary (Sullivan) S.; m. Ellinor Nielsen, Jan. 8, 1943; children: Karen Ann Lord, Susan Mary Pearsall, Mary Ellinor Sheehan. Student, Georgetown U. Bar: N.H. 1923. Since practiced in Manchester; with Sheehan, Phinney, Bass & Green Assocs., and predecessor firms, 1946-92; U.S. atty. Dist. N.H., 1949-53; Mem. N.H. Ho. of Reps., 1925-28, N.H. Senate, 1931-32; county atty. Hillsborough County, 1933-37; del. N.H. Constl. Conv., 1930, 38, 41, 48, 56-59, 64; pres. pro tem; del. Democratic Nat. Conv., 1936, 40, 48, 60; mem. spl. adv. com. on rules Dem. Nat. Conv., 1956. Local chmn. SSS, 1940-42; chmn. bd. trustees, hon. chmn., trustee, hon. trustee Carpenter Meml. City Library, Manchester; trustee Shaker Village, Inc., 1969-86, Soc. Cen. Trust Fund, 1987-93; hon. fellow John F. Kennedy Libr. Maj. USAAF, 1942-45, ETO (Combat Intelligence officer in campaigns air offensive Europe, Normandy, Nothern France, Rhineland, Cen. Europe and Ardennes 'Battle of the Bulge'). Hon. fellow N.H. Bar Found.; mem. ABA, N.H. Bar Assn. (pres. 1966-67, Disting. Svc. award), Manchester Bar Assn. (pres. 1940-41), Am. Legion, VFW, Amvets, Am. Judicature Soc., Nat. Assn. of R.R. Trial Counsel, N.E. Def. Counsel Assn., N.H., Manchester hist. socs., Nat. Trust for Historic Preservation, Nat. Hist. Soc., Manchester Inst. Arts and Scis., Smithsonian Nat. Assos. Clubs: Manchester Country, K.C. Home: Manchester N.H. Died Apr. 11, 1993.

SHELLENBARGER, MICHAEL ELLSWORTH, architecture educator, researcher; b. Plattsmouth, Nebr., May 20, 1937; s. Clair Ellsworth and Lola Irene (Dow) S.; m. Barbara Ann Bate, Feb. 4, 1968 (div. June 1975). BArch, Iowa State U., Ames, 1960; MArch, Columbia U., N.Y.C., 1966. Registered architect, N.Y. Job capt. Harold Spitznagel & Assoc., Sioux Falls, S.D., 1963-65, I.M. Pei and Ptnrs., N.Y.C., 1966-68; project architect Carlin, Pozzi and Assoc., New Haven, 1968-71; prof. architecture U. Oreg., Eugene, 1971-75; project designer Kaplan and McLaughlin, San Francisco, 1975-77; prof. architecture U. Oreg., Eugene, from 1977; asst. dept. head architecture U. Oreg., Eugene, 1973-75; dir. hist. preservation program U. Oreg., 1986-92. Author, editor: Harmony in Diversity: Architecture...of Ellis Lawrence, 1989; contbr. articles in field. Mem. Hist. Rev. Ordinance Task Force, Eugene, 1986-88; chmn. Sch. Dist. 4J Small Schs. Task Force, Eugene, 1975-76, Eugene Hist. Rev. Bd., 1985-87, 89-92; chmn. awards jury Masonry Inst. Oreg., Portland, 1987. Lt. USN, 1960-63. Mem. Assn. for Preservation Tech., Constrn. History Soc., Soc. for History of Tech. Democrat. Home: Eugene Oreg. Deceased.

SHELTON, HAROLD GARLAND, retired chemical company executive; b. Lynchburg, Va. Feb. 22, 1909; s. James Taylor and Sally (Loving) S.; B.S., Va. Poly. Inst., 1931; m. Marjorie L. Calvert, June 10, 1936 (div. Sept. 1951); children: Clinton C., Marjorie L. Shelton Hillback; m. 2d, Virginia G. Gregory, June 18, 1954; stepchildren: R. William Gregory, David G. Gregory. With Union Carbide Corp., N.Y.C., 1931-45, purchasing agt., 1942-45; with GAF Corp., N.Y.C., 1945-62, v.p., gen. mgr., 1958-61, exec. v.p., 1961-62; v.p. Frank C. Brown & Co., Inc., mgmt. cons., N.Y.C., 1962-67; pres., dir. Trylon Chems., Inc., Lock Haven, Pa., 1967-74; dir. Nucor Corp., Charlotte, N.C., 1965-74, chmn. bd., 1967-74; dir. Phillips Foscue Corp., High Point, N.C., 1970-74, chmn. exec. com., 1973-74. Mem. Club: Surf Golf & Beach. Deceased. Home: North Myrtle Beach S.C.

SHENK, SOL A., retail executive; b. Russia, Oct. 15, 1911. JD, Ohio State U., 1937. Home: Columbus Ohio Died Aug. 31, 1994.

SHEPARD, WILLIAM ALBERT, lawyer, accountant; b. Adel, Ga., Dec. 19, 1920; s. William Marshall and Tempie (Rountree) S. Grad., Mid. Ga. Coll., 1939; BS, U. Ga., 1941; LLB magna cum laude, Oglethorpe U., 1950. Estate tax atty. IRS, Atlanta, 1951-53; pvt. practice law, acct. Valdosta, Ga., 1953-56; fin. mgmt. analyst Pub. Health Svc. Communicable Disease Ctr., Atlanta, 1956-61; Budget analyst FAA, Atlanta, 1961-62; Budget analyst Nat. Communicable Disease Ctr., Atlanta, 1962-68, regional program coord. officer, 1968-79, dep. dir. fin. mgmt. office, from 1979. Sgt. U.S.Army, 1943-46. Mem. Ga. Bar Assn., Fed. Govt. Accts. Assn. Republican. Baptist. Home: Valdosta Ga. Deceased.

SHEPHERD, JOHN CALVIN, lawyer; b. Memphis, June 27, 1925; s. Calvin and Beatrice (Newton) S.; m. Bernice Hines, Sept. 4, 1948; children: J. Michael, William N. Student, Ill. Coll., 1946-48, LLD (hon.), 1979; JD, St. Louis U., 1951; LLD (hon.), No. Ohio U., 1984. Bar: Mo. 1951, Ill. 1962. Assoc. Sievers, Reagan & Schwartz, St. Louis, 1951-53, Haley & Frederickson, St. Louis, 1953-54; ptnr. Evans & Dixon, St. Louis, 1955-70, Coburn, Croft, Shepherd & Herzog, St. Louis, 1970-79; chmn. bd., chief exec. officer Shepherd, Sandberg & Phoenix P.C., St. Louis, 1979-90; ptnr. Armstrong, Teasdale, Schlafly & Davis, St. Louis, 1990-93; chmn. Gov.'s Commn. on Liability Ins., State of Mo., 1986-87. Chmn. bd. overseers Hoover Instn., Stanford, Calif., 1986-88; bd. dirs. Mcpl. Theatre Assn. St. Louis, Barnes Hosp., St. Louis. Served with USMC, 1943-46, PTO. Recipient Disting. Alumnus award Ill. Coll., 1965, Alumni Merit award St. Louis U., 1970; named Hon. Master Bench, Middle Temple, London. Fellow Am. Bar Found., Am. Coll. Trial Lawyers, Internat. Acad. Trial Lawyers; mem. ABA (state del. to Ho. Dels. 1968-73, assembly del. 1974-78, chmn. Ho. Dels. 1978-80, pres. 1984-85), Bar Assn. St. Louis (pres. 1963), Internat. Soc. Barristers, Am. Law Inst., Law Soc. Eng. and Wales (hon.), Order Knights of Malta, Phi Beta Kappa. Republican. Roman Catholic. Clubs: Met. (Washington); Noonday, St. Louis, Mo. Athletic, Bellerive Country (St. Louis). Home: Saint Louis Mo. Deceased.

SHEPPARD, THOMAS FREDERICK, history educator; b. Indpls., June 5, 1935; s. Francis Sherman and Dorothy (White) S.; m. Donna Cox; children: Jocelyn, Allison. AB, Vanderbilt U., 1957; MA, U. Nebr., 1962; PhD, Johns Hopkins U., 1969. Instr. history Western Ky. State U., Bowling Green, 1962-65; asst. prof. Coll. William and Mary, Williamsburg, Va., 1969-71, assoc. prof., 1971-77, prof., 1977—; chmn. dept. history Coll. of William and Mary, 1975-81. Author: Lourmarin in the Eighteenth Century, 1971; contbr. numerous articles and book revs. to profl. publs. Capt. USMCR, 1957-65. Recipient Fellowship for Young Humanists award NEH, France, 1972-73. Home: Williamsburg Va. Died Aug. 1995.

SHERWOOD, RICHARD EDWIN, lawyer; b. L.A., July 24, 1928; s. Benjamin Berkley and Jennie (Goldeen) S.; m. Dorothy Lipsey Romonek, July 25, 1953; children: Elizabeth Deirdre, Benjamin Berkley II. B.A., Yale U., 1949; LL.B., Harvard U., 1952, Sheldon traveling fellow, 1953-54. Bar: Calif. 1953. Law clk. to Justice Felix Frankfurter, U.S. Supreme Ct., 1954-55; with firm O'Melveny & Myers, Los Angeles, 1955-93; ptnr. O'Melveny & Myers, 1964-93; vis. lectr. Yale Law Sch., 1981; vis. prof. Sophia U., Tokyo, 1982; research scholar U. Tokyo, 1982; mem. Calif. Little Hoover Commn., 1961-67, White House Task Force Antitrust Policy, 1967-68. Trustee Los Angeles County Mus. Art, 1964-93, pres., 1974-78, chmn., 1978-92; chmn. overseers RAND Ctr. for Russian and Eurasian Studies, 1986-93; mem. vis. com. Harvard Law Sch., 1969-75, 86-92; trustee Asia Soc., 1978-93, sec., 1989-93; bd. dirs. Ctr. Theatre Group, L.A. Music Ctr., 1980-93, pres., 1982-85, chmn., 1985-87, chmn. exec. com., 1987-93; v.p. Santa Fe Opera, 1992-93, Japanese Am. Cultural and Community Ctr. 2d lt. USAF, 1952-53. Decorated gold rays with rosette Order of Rising Sun (Japan). Mem. ABA, Calif. Bar Assn., Los Angeles County Bar Assn. (chmn. human rights sect. 1970-71), Internat. Inst. for Strategic Studies, Coun. on Fgn. Rels., Internat. Coun., Mus. Modern Art. Home: Beverly Hills Calif. Died Apr. 8, 1993.

SHIBLEY, RAYMOND NADEEM, lawyer; b. State College, Pa., Oct. 7, 1925; s. Jabir and Adma (Hammam) S.; m. Jean Alene Phillips, Mar. 10, 1951 (dec. Oct. 1979). BS in Chemistry, Pa. State U., 1947; LLB, Yale U., 1950. Bar: D.C. 1951, U.S. Ct. Appeals (D.C. cir.) 1951, U.S Ct. Appeals (3rd. cir.) 1955, U.S. Ct. Appeals (10th cir.) 1958, U.S. Ct. Appeals (5th cir.) 1969, U.S. Ct. Appeals (11th cir.) 1981, U.S. Ct. Appeals (6th cir.) 1988, U.S. Ct. Appeals (7th cir.) 1989, U.S. Supreme Ct. 1960. Ptnr. Steptoe & Johnson, Washington, 1950-60, Patterson, Belknap, Farmer & Shibley, Washington, 1960-70, Farmer, Shibley, McGuinn & Flood, Washington, 1970-80, LeBoeuf, Lamb, Greene & MacRae, Washington, 1980-90; of counsel LeBoeuf, Lamb, Leiby & MacRae, Washington, 1991-94; gen. counsel Panhandle Eastern Corp., Houston, 1968-74; alumni fellow Coll. of Sci., Pa. State U., 1987-94. Mem. exec. com. Nat. Campaign for Pa. State U., 1985-90, mem. libr. adv. bd., 1990-94, chmn. mid atlantic region, regional chmn., D.C., Md., Va. and Del., 1986-94; mem. Nat. Devel. Coun., 1991-94; mem. exec. com. Pa. State U., 1991-94; trustee Georgetown Presbyn. Ch. Recipient Disting. Alumni award Pa. State U., 1990. Mem. ABA (coun. pub. utilities sect., 1987-94, chmn. Nat. Gas Com.), Fed. Energy Bar Assn. (pres. 1973-74), Cosmos Club, City Tavern Club, Yale Club of Washington, Order of Coif, Phi Lambda Upsilon, Phi Delta Phi, Alpha Chi Sigma. Republican. Home: Washington D.C. Died July 2, 1994.

SHILTS, RANDY, writer, journalist; b. Davenport, Iowa, Aug. 8, 1951; s. Bud and Norma S. BS, U. Oreg., 1975. Reporter Sta. KQED, San Francisco, 1977-80, Sta. KTVU, Oakland, Calif., 1979-80; staff reporter San Francisco Chronicle, 1981-87, nat. correspondent, 1988—. Author: The Mayor of Castro Street: The Life and Times of Harvey Milk, 1982, And the Band Played On: Politics, People, and the AIDS Epidemic, 1987, Conduct Unbecoming: Gays and Lesbians in the U.S. Military, 1993. Recipient Media Alliance award outstanding nonfiction author, 1982, Gay Acad. Union award outstanding journalist, 1982, Silver medal best nonfiction author Commonwealth Club, 1987, Outstanding Communicator award Assn. Edn. Journalism and Mass Comm., 1988, Outstanding Achivement award Parents and Friends of Lesbians and Gays, 1988, Outstanding Author award Am. Soc. Journalists, 1988. Home: San Francisco Calif.

SHIMAMOTO, GEORGE GENTOKU, architect, architectural engineer; b. Wakayama, Japan, Nov. 15, 1904; s. Gennosuke and Oiwa S.; m. Masayo Mine, Aug. 4, 1934; children: Teruko (Mrs. Herbert Neuwalder), Lily Ayako (Mrs. Wilfred Tashima). B.Sc., Sch. Architecture Poly. Coll. Engring., 1927; postgrad. extension program, Waseda U., Tokyo, Japan, 1928-31. Cons., archtl. advisor Buddhist Mission Am., 1928-39; cons. Golden Gate Internat. Expn., San Francisco, 1939-41; resident project engr. Relocation Center, Topaz, Utah, 1942-44; assoc. firm Kelly & Gruzen

(Architect-Engrs. (name changed to Gruzen & Partners 1964, Gruzen Partnership 1982, Gruzen Samton Steinglass, 1986), N.J. and N.Y.C., 1945-50; sr. assoc., 1951-63, sr. partner, gen. mgr., 1964-73; cons. partner; archtl., archtl. engring. cons. N.Y.C., 1974-94; cons. Toda-Am. Inc., N.Y.C., Archtl. Inst. Japan; hon. advisor Japan Radio House, Ken Zen Martial Arts Sch., N.Y.C. Designer: Horizon House (Design award FHA), Chatham Towers, N.Y.C. (Design award Bard Commn.), Japan House, N.Y.C. (Design award N.Y. State Architects Assn.). Mem. N.Y.C. Housing Task Force.; Chmn. bd. Buddhist Ch., N.Y.C.; bd. dirs. Japanese Am. Help for Aging, Inc.; pres. bd. trustees Bklyn. Botanic Garden, 1983-84. Decorated Order of Rising Sun Japan; recipient citation San Francisco C. of C., citation N.Y.C. Housing Task Force, citation HHFA, cultural award Archtl. Inst. of Japan, 1986. Fellow Archtl. Inst. Japan (citation of services), ASCE (emeritus); mem. A.I.A. (emeritus), Nat. Soc. Profl. Engrs. (emeritus), Am. Soc. Mil. Engrs., Japan Soc. (life, patron), ASTM, Japanese Am. Citizens League (San Francisco), Japanese Am. Assn. N.Y. (v.p. 1974-75, 77-78, chmn. fin. commn. 1975-76, pres. 1979-82, hon. pres. 1983-94, hon. life trustee 1987-94). Buddhist. Clubs: Nippon (N.Y.C.); Haworth (N.J.) Country (chmn. bd.), N.Y. Japanese Lions (charter). Home: Fort Lee N.J. Died Nov. 4, 1994.

SHIMKIN, DEMITRI BORIS, anthropo-geographer, educator; b. Omsk, Siberia, July 4, 1916; came to U.S., 1923; s. Boris Michael and Lydia (Serebrova) S.; m. Edith Manning, Aug. 19, 1943 (dec. Sept. 1984); children: Alexander (dec.), Eleanor Shimkin Sorock; m. Tauby Heller, June 16, 1985. A.B., U. Calif.-Berkeley, 1936, Ph.D., 1939. Johnson scholar, univ. and research fellow U. Calif.-Berkeley, 1937-41; instr. Nat. War Coll., 1946-47, Inst. for Advanced Study, Princeton, 1947-48; research assoc. Russian Research Ctr., Harvard, 1948-53; social sci. analyst, then sr. research specialist U.S. Bur. Census, Washington, 1953-60; prof. anthropology, geography and pub. health U. Ill., Urbana, 1960-85, prof. emeritus, 1985-92; field work in, Wyo., 1937-39, 66, 75, Alaska, 1949, Ill., 1963, 77-82, Miss., 1966-72, 78, 81-83, India, 1978, Tanzania, 1983, 84, 88-89, Israel, 1985, Siberia, 1984; vis. prof. anthropology Harvard U., 1964-65, summer 1970; mem. NRC, 1964-67, U.S. nat. com. Internat. Biol. Program, 1965-69; mem. task force environ. health HEW, 1968-69; mem. task force on civil engring. ASCE, 1975-78. Author: Minerals: A Key to Soviet Power, 1953, (with others) Trends in Economic Growth, 1955, Man's Health and Environment, 1970, The Water's Edge, 1972, The Extended Family in Black Societies, 1978, Anthropology for the Future, 1978, (with Carolyn Sprague) How Midwesterners Cope, 1981, (with others) Studies in North Asiatic Archaeology, Neolithic to Medieval, 1988; contbg. author: Handbook of North American Indians, Vol. II, 1986. Col. AUS; ret. Decorated Legion of Merit; fellow Ctr. Advanced Study Behavioral Scis., 1970-71; sr. Fulbright scholar Kemerovo (USSR) State U., spring 1984. Fellow AAAS, Am. Anthrop. Assn., Soc. for Applied Anthropology (chmn. 1987 program), Royal Anthrop. Inst.; mem. Assn. Am. Geographers, Phi Beta Kappa, Sigma Xi. Methodist. Home: Urbana Ill. Died Dec. 22, 1992; buried Arlington National Cemetary, V.A.

SHIRER, WILLIAM LAWRENCE, author, journalist; b. Chgo., Feb. 23, 1904; s. Seward Smith and Bessie Josephine (Tanner) S.; m. Theresa Stiberitz, 1931 (div. 1970); children: Eileen Inga Dean, Linda Elizabeth Rae; m. Irina Lugovskaya, 1988. A.B., Coe Coll., 1925, Litt. D. (hon.). Journalist, Paris edit. Chicago Tribune, 1925-26; fgn. corr. (Tribune), 1926-33, Universal News Service, 1935-37; became Continental rep. CBS, 1937; war corr., 1939-45, commentator, 1945-47. Author: Berlin Diary, 1941, End of a Berlin Diary, 1947, The Traitor, 1950, Midcentury Journey, 1952, Stranger Come Home, 1954, The Challenge of Scandinavia, 1955, The Consul's Wife, 1956, The Rise and Fall of the Third Reich, 1960 (Nat. Book award 1961), The Rise and Fall of Adolf Hitler, 1961, The Sinking of the Bismarck, 1962, The Collapse of the Third Republic, 1969, Gandhi- A Memoir, 1979, 20th Century Journey- A Memoir of a Life and the Times, (vol. I) The Start, 1976, (vol. II) The Nightmare Years, 1984, (vol.III) A Native's Return, 1990, Love and Hate: The Troubled Marriage of Leo and Sonya Tolstoy, 1994; contbr. articles to Harpers, others. Mem. P.E.N., Authors Guild (pres.), Coun. Fgn. Rels., Soc. Am. Historians, Legion of Honor, Century Club (N.Y.C.), Phi Beta Kappa. Home: Lenox Mass. Died Dec. 28, 1993.

SHKLAR, JUDITH NISSE, political science educator; b. Riga, Latvia, Sept. 24, 1928; came to U.S., 1951; d. Aron and Agnes (Berner) Nisse; m. Gerald Shklar, June 16, 1948; children: David, Michael, Ruth. BA, McGill U., 1949, MA, 1950; PhD, Harvard U., 1955. Instr. polit. sci. Harvard U., Cambridge, Mass., 1956-59; asst. prof. Harvard U., 1959-63, lectr., 1963-70, prof., from 1970, John Cowles prof. govt., from 1980; vis. fellow All Souls Coll., Oxford, U., 1983, Carlyle lectr., 1986; Pitt prof. Am. instns. and history Cambridge U., 1983-84; Storrs lectr. Law Sch., Yale U., 1988; Tanner lectr. U. Utah, 1989. Author: After Utopia, 1957, Legalism, 1964, Men and Citizens, 1969, 85, Freedom and Independence, 1976, Ordinary Vices, 1984, Montesquieu, 1987, The Faces of Injustice, 1990, American Citizenship: The Quest for Inclusion, 1991; contbr. articles to scholarly jours. AAUW fellow, 1955-56; Guggenheim fellow, 1960; MacArthur fellow, 1984. Fellow Am. Acad. Arts and Scis.; mem. Am. Polit. Sci. Assn. (pres. 1989-90), Am. Philos. Soc. Democrat. Home: Cambridge Mass. Deceased.

SHOEMAKER, DAVID POWELL, chemist, educator; b. Kooskia, Idaho, May 12, 1920; s. Roy Hopkins and Sarah (Anderson) S.; m. Clara Brink, Aug. 5, 1955; 1 son, Robert Brink. B.A., Reed Coll., 1942; Ph.D., Calif. Inst. Tech., 1947. Research asst. Calif. Inst. Tech., 1943-45, NRC fellow, 1945-47, sr. research fellow, 1948-51; fellow John Simon Guggenheim Meml. Found. Inst. Theoretical Physics, Copenhagen, Denmark, 1947-48; asst. prof. chemistry Mass. Inst. Tech., Cambridge, 1951-56; asso. prof. Mass. Inst. Tech., 1956-60; prof. MIT, 1960-70; prof. chemistry Oreg. State U., Corvallis, 1970-84, prof. emeritus, 1984-95, chmn. dept. chemistry, 1970-81; vis. scientist Lab. Cristallographie, CNRS, Grenoble, France, 1967, 78-79; vis. lectr. Kemisk Institut, Aarhus, Denmark, June 1979; cons. Exxon Co. U.S.A., Baton Rouge, 1957-86; sec.-treas. U.S.A. Nat. Com. for Crystallography, 1962-64, chmn., 1967-69; mem. vis. com. chemistry dept. Brookhaven Nat. Lab., 1974-79; mem. evaluation panel material scis. div. Nat. Bur. Standards, 1977-79. Author: (with Carl W. Garland, Joseph W. Nibler) Experiments in Physical Chemistry, 1962, 67, 74, 81, 89; Am. co-editor: Acta Crystallographica, 1964-69. Recipient Howard Vollum Sci. and Tech. award Reed Coll., 1986. Fellow AAAS, Am. Phys. Soc.; mem. Am. Chem. Soc., Am. Crystallographic Assn. (pres. 1970), Am. Acad. Arts and Scis., Internat. Union Chrystallography (mem. exec. com. 1972-78), Phi Beta Kappa, Sigma Xi, Phi Lambda Upsilon, Phi Kappa Phi. Home: Corvallis Oregon Died Aug. 24, 1995.

SHORB, EUGENE MURRAY, retired utility executive; b. Cleve., Mar. 6, 1920; s. Charles F. and Beth L. (Murray) S.; m. Harriet Elizabeth Colman, July 14, 1951; children: Janet E., William M., Thomas C. BS in Mech. Engring., Purdue U., 1949. Gas engr. No. Ind. Pub. Service Co., Hammond, 1949-52, various managerial positions, 1952-73, v.p. gas ops., 1973-74, v.p. gas ops. and fuel procurement, 1974-77, sr. v.p. ops., 1977-79, 1st v.p., 1979-81, exec. v.p., chief operating officer, 1981-85, cons. mgmt., 1985-91; bd. dirs. Mercantile Bankorp, Hammond, Mercantile Bank Ind., Hammond. Past officer or bd. dirs. various civic orgns. Served with USNR, 1942-45. Mem. Am. Gas Assn., Ind. Gas Assn. (life, past pres. and bd. dirs.). Republican. Methodist. Home: Munster Ind.

SHORE, DINAH (FRANCES ROSE SHORE), singer, television talk-show hostess; b. Winchester, Tenn., Mar. 1, 1921; d. S.A. and Anna (Stein) S.; m. George Montgomery, Dec. 5, 1943 (div. 1962); children: Melissa Ann, John David; m. Maurice F. Smith, May 26, 1963 (div. 1964). B.A., Vanderbilt U., 1939. dir. Lane Bryant, Inc.; co-sponsor Nabisco Dinah Shore Classic. Became singer, WNEW, N.Y., 1938, joined NBC as sustaining singer, 1938, started contract, RCA-Victor, 1940, star, Chamber Music Soc. of Lower Basin St. program, 1940, joined Eddie Cantor radio program, 1941; star own radio program for Gen. Foods, 1943; entertained Allied Troops ETO, 1944, radio program, Proctor & Gamble; star TV show for Chevrolet, 1951-61; film appearances include Thank Your Lucky Stars, 1943, Make Mine Music, 1946, Follow the Boys, 1963, Oh! God, 1977; hostess show Dinah's Place, NBC-TV, 1970-74, Dinah!, CBS-TV, 1974-79, Dinah! and Friends, from 1979, A Conversation with Dinah, TNN TV, 1989-93; TV appearance Hotel, 1987; Awarded New Star of Radio Motion Picture Daily Poll and World Telegram-Scripts Howard Poll 1940, Best Popular Female Vocalist Motion Picture Daily Fame's Annual Radio Poll 1941-61, Michael Award, Best Female Vocalist, Radio and TV 1950, 51, 52, Billboard Award, Favorite Female Vocalist on Records 1947, Billboard Award, favorite popular female singer in radio 1949, Gallup poll, America's best known and favorite female vocalist 1950, 51, Emmy award, Acad. TV Arts and Sciences 1954, 55, 56, 57, 58, 59, 72, 73, 74, 76, Peabody Award for 1958, Sylvania Award for 1958); Author: Someone's in the Kitchen with Dinah, 1971. Home: Los Angeles Calif. Died Feb. 24, 1993.

SHOUP, WESLEY DALE, publishing company executive; b. Oak Park, Ill., Sept. 24, 1933; s. Jesse George and Clara Elizabeth (Henning) S.; m. Jane J. Lemmerman, June 6, 1957 (div. 1974); children: Mark A., Sandra Ann, Laura Jean; m. Shirley E. Frye. BS, Kans. State U., 1960. From ctrl. dist. mgr. to pub. dir. Wood & Wood Products Mag. Vance Pub. Corp., Chgo., 1961-72, nat. sales mgr. Home Ctr. Mag., 1973-74; pres., bd. dirs. Invincible Machine, Inc., Atlanta, 1974-76; regional mgr. Building Design and Contruction Mag. Cahners Pub. Co., Chgo., 1976-79, assoc. pub. Construction Equipment Mag., 1979-82; created Roads and Bridges Mag., 1982-94; established 4-R Conf. and Roadshow, 1985-94; bd. dirs. The Rd. Info. Programs, Constrn. Industry Mfrs. Assn. With USCG, 1953-57. Recipient Pres. award Asphalt Relaiming/Recycling Assn., 1988. Mem. Const. Ind. Mfrs. Assn. (chmn. mktg. and comm. com. 1987-93), Am. Pub. Works Assn., Am. Road and Transp. Builders Assn., Engring. Soc. W.Pa., Internat. Road Federation, Nat. Assn. County Engrs., Asphalt Recycling Reclaim Assn., Asphalt Emulsion Mfrs. Assn., Am. Bus. Press. Home: Chicago Ill. Died June 10, 1994.

SHUTT, EDWIN HOLMES, JR., consumer products executive; b. St. Louis, July 28, 1927; s. Edwin Holmes and Louise Davenport (Tebbetts) S.; m. Mary Truesdale, Oct. 12, 1953; children: Mary Anne, Edward Truesdale, Amy Louise. BS in Engring., Princeton U., 1950. Mgr. internat. div. for Asia and Latin Am., then v.p. internat. Procter & Gamble Co., Cin., 1968-77; exec. v.p., then pres., chief exec. officer Clorox Co., Oakland, Calif., 1977-81; pres. Tambrands, Inc., Lake Success, N.Y., 1981-89; chief exec. officer Tambrands, Inc., Lake Success, 1982-87, chmn., chief exec. officer, 1987-89; ret., 1989; mem. adv. bd. Bus. Sch., U. Calif., Berkeley, 1980-81; bd. dirs. BTC Diagnostics Inc., 1984-85, 1st Nat. Bank of L.I., 1989-94, Online Resources & Comm. Corp., 1994; mem. arbitration panel N.Y. Stock Exch., 1989-94. Pres. Cin. Coun. World Affairs, 1975-77, Princeton Club So. Ohio, 1976-77; mem. exec. coun. San Francisco Bay Area Boy Scouts Am., 1980-81, exec. bd. Nassau County coun., 1981-94, pres., 1985-89; bd. dirs. Oakland Mus. Assn., 1981, Friends of the Arts, 1986-88, Nat. Assn. Women's Ctrs., 1991-94, L.I. Philharm., 1982-90. Mem. L.I. Assn. (bd. dirs. 1987-90), Grocery Mfrs. of Am. (bd. dirs. 1980, 86-87), Pacific Union (San Francisco), Creek Club, Univ. Cottage (Princeton), Princeton Club of N.Y., Phi Beta Kappa. Republican. Home: Oyster Bay N.Y. Died Dec. 23, 1994.

SIDAROUSS, STEPHANOS (HIS BEATITUDE AND EMINENCE STEPHANOS I), patriarch of Alexandria; b. Cairo, Feb. 22, 1904; s. Sesostris and Clotilde Boghos (Ghali) S.; ed. Jesuits Coll., Cairo, U. Paris and Ecole libre des sciences politiques; Dr.h.c., St. John's U., N.Y.C., Chgo. Vincentian U., 1965. Barrister at law, Cairo, 1926-32; ordained priest Roman Catholic Ch., 1939; dir. sems. in France, 1939-46; rector Coptic Cath. Sem., Tahta, 1946, Tanta, 1947-53, and Maadi, 1953-58 (Egypt); bishop, 1948, patriarch of Alexandria, 1958; elevated to Sacred Coll. Cardinals, 1965; mem. Sacred Congregation of Oriental Chs. Rome, Pontifical Commn. for Code of Canonic Lex, Pontifical Commn. for Oriental Code of Canonic Lex. Home: Cairo Egypt

SIDELLS, ARTHUR F., architect; b. Warren, Ohio, July 4, 1907; s. Byron T. and Mabel Ellen (Luce) S.; m. June Marie Isaly, Nov. 5, 1932; children: Stephen A., Stuart F. BArch, Carnegie Inst. Tech, 1931. Registered architect, Ohio, Pa., Fla., Calif. Pvt. practice Menlo Park, Calif.; vis. lectr. Kent State U.; alumni counselor Carnegie-Mellon U.; mem. Ohio State Bd. Examiners of Architects, 1961-72, pres., 1965, 66, 71; mem. Nat. Coun. Archtl. Registration Bds., 1964-68, chmn. pub. rels. com., chmn. nominating com, exam. com.; mem. Nat. Architect Accrediting Bd., 1967-74, pres., 1972-73, past pres., 1973-74. Prin. works include W.D. Packard Music Hall, Trumbull Regional Campus, Kent State U., Warren Western Reserve High Sch., Riverview Housing for Elderly, St. Joseph Hosp., Second Nat. Bank and Office Tower, Union Savings & Trust Eastwood Br.; contbr. articles to profl. jours. Charter pres. Warren Jaycees, 1933, 1st v.p. Ohio Jaycees, 1937; pres. Warren Rotary Club, 1950, Warren Community Chest, 1950-52. Recipient Sch. Exhibit awards AASA Convs., 1956-61, Spl. citation Pub. Edn., Geneva, Award of Merit Ohio Prestressed Concrete Assn., 1970, Thomas Jefferson medal Nat. Architect Accrediting Bd., 1985; established (with Stephen A. Sidells and Stuart F. Sidells) Carnegie Tradition Scholarship, Carnegie-Mellon U., 1986; Arthur F. Sidells Collection accepted into architecture archives, Carnegie-Mellon U., 1987. Fellow AIA (Ea. Ohio chpt. Gold medal award 1983); mem. SAR, The Buckeye Club (life, pres. 1958). Home: Menlo Park Calif. Died Jan. 3, 1996.

SIGEL, M(OLA) MICHAEL, scientist, medical educator; b. Nieswiez, Poland, June 24, 1920; came to U.S., 1937, naturalized, 1941; s. Zundel and Hinda Lubecka) S.; children: Suzanne Lea Paula, Vicki Adelaide Breina Sigel Sroka, Rachel Delelaw Sarah, Valerie Harriet Louise, David Edward Burl. B.A., U. Tex., 1941; Ph.D., Ohio State U., 1944. Assoc. in virology U. Pa., 1946-50, asst. prof. virology, 1950-53; head virus diagnostic lab. Children's Hosp., Phila., 1946-53; chief reference diagnosis and rsch. unit Center for Disease Control, USPHS, Montgomery, Ala., 1953-55; spl. cons. WHO, Europe, 1956; assoc. prof. U. Miami, Fla., 1955-58; prof. microbiology U. Miami Sch. Medicine, 1958-78, prof. oncology, 1975-78; prof., chmn. microbiology and immunology U. S.C. Sch. Medicine, Columbia, 1978-88, prof., dir. research dept. ophthalmology, 1978-95, disting. prof. microbiology and immunology, 1989-95; disting. prof. emeritus U. S.C. Sch. Medicine, Columbia, S.C., 1993-95; rsch. dir., chmn. rsch. staff Variety Children's Rsch. Found., Miami, 1960-70; rsch. assoc. Lerner Marine Lab., Bimini, Bahamas, 1963-78, Nat. Prostatic Cancer Program, 1976-79; hon. prof. U. W.I., 1960-72; cons. Goodwin Cancer Inst., Coulter Corp.; adj. prof. Fla. Atlantic U., Davie, 1993. Author: (with A. R. Beasley) Viruses, Cells and Hosts, 1962, (with E.H. Cohen) Reticuloendothelial System: Phylogeny/Ontogeny, 1982; editor: Lymphogranuloma Venereum, 1962, Differentiation and Defense Mechanisms in Lower Organisms in Vitro, 1968, (with R. A. Good) Tolerance, Autoimmunity and Aging, 1972; mem. editorial bd. Cancer Rsch., 1969-72, Jour.

Developmental and Comparative Immunology, 1975-95; contbr. articles to profl. jours. Served to col. AUS. Fellow AAAS, N.Y. Acad. Scis.; mem. Am. Soc. Microbiology (pres. So. Fla. br. 1969-70), Soc. Exptl. Biology Medicine (bd. editors), Soc. Pediatric Research, Am. Assn. Immunologists, Soc. Gen. Microbiology, Reticuloendothelial Soc. (counselor, chmn. nat. meeting 1975, pres. 1978-79), Internat. Congress Reticuloendothelial Soc. (co-chmn. 1978 Jerusalem), Am. Zool. Soc. (chmn. div. comparative immunology), Am. Soc. Cell Biology, Am. Assn. Cancer Research, Tissue Culture Assn. (program chmn. 1969-70, counselor-at-large 1974-78), Phi Beta Kappa, Sigma Xi (pres. U. Miami chpt. 1976-77). Home: Pembroke Pines Fla. Died Mar. 18, 1995.

SIGUR, GASTON JOSEPH, JR., political science educator; b. Franklin, La., Nov. 13, 1924; s. Gaston Joseph and Olive (Kribs) S.; m. Estelle Catherine Smotrys, Feb. 4, 1950; children—Christopher, Gaston Joseph, Paul, Katherine Ann, Thomas. B.A., U. Mich., 1947, M.A., 1948, Ph.D., 1957. Asst. dir. U. Mich. Internat. Center, 1952-56; asst. rep. Asian Found., Japan, 1956-59; research scholar Sophia U., Tokyo, 1959-61; acting dir. research and devel. office Asia Found., 1961-62, Afghanistan, 1962-66, Japan, 1966-68, Washington, 1969-72; prof. internat. affairs, dir. Inst. Sino-Soviet Studies, George Washington U., 1972-95; spl. asst. to pres. for nat. security Nat. Security Council, The White House,, 1982-86; asst. sec. for East Asian and Pacific affairs Dept. of State, Washington, 1986-89; Disting. prof. East Asian Studies George Washington U., 1989-95; cons. in field. Author articles, monographs in field; mem. editorial bds. profl. jours. Served with AUS, 1943-46. Mem. Assn. Asian Studies, Internat. House Japan, Japan-Am. Soc. Washington. Clubs: Tokyo American; Cosmos (Washington). Home: Washington D.C. Died Apr. 26, 1995.

SIKES, ROBERT L. F., former congressman; b. Isabella, Worth County, Ga., June 3, 1906; s. Benjamin Franklin and Clara Ophelia (Ford) S.; children: Bobbye Serrene (Mrs. Edward F. Wicke), Robert Keyes. B.S., U. Ga., 1927; M.S., U. Fla., 1929; LL.D., Stetson U., 1969, U. West Fla., 1970; L.H.D., St. Leo Coll., 1969; L.H.D. hon. doctorate, U. Inca Garcilaso de la Vega, Peru, 1970, Hangyang U., Seoul, Korea, 1975; H.H.D. (hon.), Gulf Coast Sem., Fla., 1979. Agrl., indsl. research, 1928-32; published Okaloosa News-Jour., Crestview, Fla., and other newspapers, 1933-46; chmn. Okaloosa County Democratic Com., 1936; mem. Fla. Legislature, 1936-40; mem. 77th-95th Congresses from 1st Fla. Dist., mem. House Appropriations Com.; dir. 1st Bank Crestview, Fla.; chmn. Fla. delegation Dem. Nat. Conv., 1956, 60, mem., 1972; del. Dem. Mid-Term Conf., 1974; Pres. Fla. Press Assn., 1937; mem. Corregidor-Bataan Meml. Commn., 1963; hon. faculty chair govt. Okaloosa-Walton Jr. Coll., Niceville, Fla.; faculty assoc. U. West Fla., Pensacola; bd. visitors U.S. Mil. Acad., CAP, USAF Acad., 1971-74, U.S. Naval Acad., 1975; v.p., dir. Water Resources Congress (formerly Nat. Rivers and Harbors Congress), 1959-71, 1st v.p., 1970-71, exec. com., 1971; del. Pan Am. Roads Conf., Venezuela, 1954, Inter-parliamentary Conf., Poland, 1959, 7th World Forestry Congress, Madrid, Spain, 1966, 6th World Forestry Congress, Buenos Aires, 1972; Congressional adv. U.S. dels. SALT II, Geneva, UN Gen. Assembly Spl. Session on Disarmament, Conf. Com. on Disarmament, Geneva, 1978. N.W. Fla. chmn. Muscular Dystrophy Campaign, 1979; hon. chmn. for Okaloosa County, Am. Heart Assn., 1980; grand marshall Old Spanish Trail Parade, Crestview, Fla., 1980; hon. chmn. United Way of Okaloosa County, 1979, United Way, Pensacola, Fla., 1979; mem. Americana com. Nat. Archives.; chmn. U.S. Air Force Armament Mus. Found. Served with AUS, World War II, ETO; maj. gen. Res. ret. Decorated Legion of Merit; Guatamalan Order Merit, 1961; Peruvian Order of Merit, 1970; recipient Governor's Conservation award, 1960; Fla. award Young Dem. Clubs, 1961; George Washington Meml. award Nat. Rivers and Harbors Congress, 1966; Disting. Service award Water Resources Congress, 1972; Fla. Pub. Service award U.P.I., 1968; Disting. Service awards Am., Fla. forestry assns., 1972; named Hon. State Farmer Fla. Assn. Future Farmers Am., 1967; Disting. Service award Fla. Dept. Agr., 1973; recipient Gen. Louis E. Brereton award Fla. Air Force Assn., 1972; Man of Year award Nat. Fedn. Ind. Businesses, 1972; Cert. of Appreciation Nat. Small Bus. Assn. and Nat. Com. for Small Bus. Tax Reform, 1972; Disting. Service award Nat. Assn. State Foresters, 1972; Fla. West Port Authority Leadership award, 1972; Disting. Alumnus award U. Fla., 1972; J. Sterling Morton award Arbor Day Found., 1973; disting. service awards Fla. V.F.W., 1974; disting. service awards Fla. Bankers Assn., 1975; Patriot's award N.Y. State Res. Officers Assn., 1974; Man of Year awards Forest Farmers Assn., 1974; Man of Year awards H.H. Arnold chpt. Air Force Assn., 1974; spl. commendation Fla. C. of C., 1974; award for disting. service to U.S. Assn. U.S. Army, 1974; disting. service citation Civil Affairs Assn., 1974; resolution of commendation Adj. Gens. Assn., 1974; Square and Compasses award for disting. service Grand Lodge Masons of Fla., 1975; Silver Disting. Achievement award Am. Heart Assn., 1975; cert. of appreciation U.S. Army Ranger Assn., 1976; named Bicentennial Patriot Fla. Bicentennial Commn., 1976; Gold Good Citizen medal SAR, 1978; numerous other honors and awards. Mem. Naval Aviation Mus. Assn. (trustee), Fla. Hist. Soc., Mil. Order World Wars, Am. Legion (Disting. Service award 1962), V.F.W., Nat. Assn. Suprs. (hon.), 40 and 8, Res. Officers Assn. (Disting. Service awards 1958, 66, named to Minute Man Hall of Fame 1964, recipient Man of Year award 1967, Disting. Service award Coast Guard Affairs Com. 1970, Spl. Legis. Counsel 1986-87, hon. chmn. Nat. Conv. Orlando 1987), Ret. Officers Assn. (hon.), Nat. Rifle Assn. (life, dir. 1965-67), Nat. Assn. Master Mechanics and Foremen (hon. mem. Pensacola chpt.), Am. Fedn. Govt. Employees, United Fedn. Postal Clks., Fleet Res. Assn. (hon. life), Navy League (hon. life), Sons Confederate Vets., Am. Soc. Arms Collectors (hon.), SAR (gold good citizenship medal nat. congress 1978), Nat. Security Council (nat. adv. bd. 1979-94), Blue Key (U. Ga. and U. Fla. award), Phi Kappa Phi, Sigma Delta Chi, Alpha Zeta, Phi Sigma, Alpha Gamma Rho.; hon. mem. Order Ahepa (Leadership award 1969), Toastmasters (Communications and Leadership award 1969). Democrat. Methodist. Lodges: Masons; K.P; Elks; Moose; Kiwanis (lt. gov. 1940); Lions hon; Civitan (hon.); Rotary (hon.). Home: Crestview Fla. Died Sept. 28, 1994.

SILBERT, THEODORE H., banker; b. Boston, July 5, 1904; m. Nadia S. Stark, May 6, 1984; 1 child from previous marriage, Arthur Frederick (dec.). LLB (hon.), Bard Coll., Western State U., Anaheim, Calif. With Standard Fin. Corp., 1934-93, pres., 1945-93, bd. dirs., pres., bd. dirs. various subs. cos.; pres., chief exec. officer, dir. Sterling Bancorp. (formerly Standard Prudential Corp.), until 1968, chmn., chief exec. officer, dir., 1968-93; chmn. Sterling Nat. Bank & Trust Co. N.Y.; moderator small bus. Columbia U. Contbr. articles to Harvard Bus. Rev., other bus. publs. Past pres. and former chmn. Assn. Comml. Fin. Cos.; former trustee Bronx-Lebanon Hosp. Ctr.; trustee, founder, chmn. Jewish Assn. for Svcs. for Aged; hon. vice chmn. Anti-Defamation League Nat. Commn.; nat. chmn. Anti-Defamation League Appeal, N.Y.C., nat. treas., mem. exec. com., bd. dirs. N.Y.C. div.; also life mem. Am. Cancer Soc.; bd. dirs., life trustee, mem., bd. dirs., bd. overseers United Jewish Appeal Fedn.; assoc. trustee, mem. pres.'s council Bard Coll., Annandale-on-Hudson, N.Y.; trustee emeritus Brandeis U.; treas., trustee emeritus, Jewish Communal Fund, N.Y.C.; founder Albert Einstein Coll. Medicine; past pres. Soc. Founders; moderator small bus. Columbia U.; trustee Am. Jewish Hist. Soc.; past trustee Park Ave. Synagogue; bd. dirs., mem. exec. com. Jewish Theol. Sem. Am.; bd. dirs. Fashion Inst. Tech., Hebrew Free Loan Soc.; leadership chmn. United Way Harrison, 1987-88. Mem. Fgn. Policy Assn. (assoc.), Def. Orientation Conf. Assn., Assn. Theatrical Press Agts. and Mgrs., Sponsor Ann. Econ. Forecasting Award, Standard Club (Chgo.), Board Room, Harmonie Club, Friars (N.Y.C.), Old Oaks Country Club, Purchase Club (past pres.), Hillcrest Country Club (L.A.). Home: New York N.Y. Died 1993.

SILK, LEONARD SOLOMON, economist, columnist, editor; b. Phila., May 15, 1918; s. Harry Lewis and Ida (Ender) S.; m. Bernice Harriet Scher, June 20, 1948; children: Mark Reuel, Andrew David, Adam Jonathan. AB, U. Wis., 1940, DHL (hon.), 1982; PhD, Duke, 1947, LLD (hon.), 1978; DHL (hon.), Southeastern Mass. U., 1976; LLD (hon.), Montclair State Coll., 1979, Haverford Coll., 1989; DHL (hon.), So. Meth. U., 1987, Dickinson Coll., 1988. Instr. econs. Duke, 1941-42, U. Maine, 1947-48; asst. prof. econs. Simmons Coll., 1948-50; economist HHFA, 1951; asst. econ. commr. U.S. mission to NATO, 1952-54; econs. editor Business Week mag., 1954-69, sr. editor, 1959-69, editor editorial page, chmn. editorial bd., 1967-69; mem. editorial bd. N.Y. Times, 1970-76, columnist, 1970-93; editor Econ. Policy, 1992-95; Ford Found. disting. vis. rsch. prof. Carnegie Inst. Tech., 1965-66; vis. prof. Salzburg Seminar in Am. Studies, 1968; adj. prof. Am. U., 1969-95; sr. fellow Brookings Instn., 1969-95; Disting. prof. Pace U., 1980-95; adj. prof. CUNY, sr. rsch. fellow Ralph Bunche Inst. on U.N., 1992-95; mem. research adv. bd. Com. Econ. Devel., 1978-93; mem. steering group Task Force on War Against Poverty, 1964; cons. Pres.'s Adv. Com. on Labor-Mgmt. Policy, 1962; mem. Carnegie Endowment Seminar on Space, Pres.'s Commn. on Budget Concepts, 1967; chmn. Task Force on Employment and Income Maintenance, 1968-69; cons. U.N. Devel. Program, 1992-95; pres. Nat. Assembly on Social Policy and Devel., 1969-71, N.Y. State Council on Econ. Edn., 1973-75; Disting. scholar-in-residence So. Meth. U., 1985; Disting. lectr. Emory U., 1988; sr. journalist in residence Duke U., 1989; dist. scholar-in-residence, Pace U., 1992-95. Author: Sweden Plans for Better Housing, 1948, Forecasting Business Trends, 1956, The Education of Businessmen, 1960, The Research Revolution, 1960, Veblen, 1966, Economic Commentary, 1967, (with P. Saunders) The World of Economics, 1969, Readings in Economics, 1969, Contemporary Economics: Principles and Issues, 1970, 75, Readings in Contemporary Economics, 1970, (with M.L. Curley) A Primer on Business Forecasting, 1970, Nixonomics, 1972, 74, Capitalism, The Moving Target, 1973; editor: (with Mark Silk) The Evolution of Capitalism, 1973, The Economists, 1976, (with David Vogel) Ethics and Profits, 1976, Economics in Plain English, 1978, 85, (with Rawleigh Warner) Ideals in Collision: The Relationship between Business and the News Media, 1979, (with Mark Silk) The American Establishment, 1980, (with Hedrick Smith et al) Reagan, the Man, the President, 1981, Economics in the Real World, (with George P. Shultz, et al) The Reagan Foreign Policy, 1987, (with Üner Kirdar) A World Fit For People, 1994, Economic Issues Facing the Next President, 1988, The Best From Yank, 1945, Outer Space, Prospects for Man and Society, 1962, Space and Society, 1964, America as an Ordinary Country, 1976, (with Milton Friedman et al) The Business System, 1977. Mem. bd. advisors U. Mass.; trustee Montclair Adult Sch., William Patterson Coll., Joint. Coun. Econ. Edn. Coll. of Atlantic, Mt. Desert Island Biol. Labs., 1991-95; mem. bd. overseers Tuck Sch. Bus. Adminstrn., Dartmouth Coll.; mem. bd. visitors Grad. Sch. CUNY, mem. bd. dirs. Rsch. Found.; mem. bd. visitors Trinity Coll., Duke U., Inst. Policy Scis., Duke U., Duke U. Press, New Sch. Social Rsch.; advisor Lemberg Program in Internat. Econs., Brandeis U.; mem. bd. visitors, mem. vis. com. social scis. U. Chgo. With USAAF, 1942-45. F. Lincoln Cromwell fellow in Sweden Am. Scandinavian Found., 1946; Fulbright rsch. scholar in Norway, 1951; recipient Loeb award disting. bus. and fin. journalism, 1961, 66, 67, 69, 71, 72; G.L. Loeb Meml. award UCLA, 1978; Overseas Press Club citation for fgn. reporting, 1966; Bache award for best bus. reporting, 1972; U. Mo. cert. of outstanding merit, 1967; Poynter fellow in Journalism Yale U., 1974-75; Bonaparte prize Pace U., 1971; Elliott V. Bell award N.Y. Fin. Writers, 1983, Hon. Econs. award Phi Delta Epsilon Baldwin-Wallace Coll., 1986, St. John's U., 1987, TJFR Bus. News Luminary award, 1992. Fellow Nat. Assn. Bus. Economists; mem. Nat. Assembly Social Policy and Devel. (pres.), Am. Econ. Assn., Coun. Fgn. Rels., Century Assn. (mem. bd. mgrs.), Pot and Kettle Club (Hulls Cove, Maine, bd. dirs.), Artus, Phi Beta Kappa, Beta Gamma Sigma (hon. fellow 1989), Phi Kappa Phi. Jewish. Home: Montclair N.J. Died Feb. 10, 1995.

SILLIPHANT, STIRLING DALE, motion picture writer, producer, novelist; b. Detroit, Jan. 16, 1918; s. Leigh Lemuel Silliphant and Ethel May (Noaker) Wellershaus; m. Tiana Du Long, July 4, 1974; children: Stirling, Dayle, Loren (dec.). BA magna cum laude, U. So. Calif., Los Angeles, 1938. Publicity dir. 20th Century-Fox, N.Y.C., 1946-53; screenwriter, independent producer various studios in Hollywood, 1953-96. Screenwriter: (films) Huk, Nightfall, Damn Citizen, Lineup, Village of the Damned, The Slender Thread, In The Heat of the Night, 1968 (Oscar award for best screenplay, Edgar Allen Poe award Mystery Writers Am., Golden Globe award Fgn. Press Assn.), Charly, 1969 (Golden Globe award Fgn. Press Assn.), The New Centurions, 1972, The Poseidon Adventure, 1972 (Writer of Yr. award Nat. Theater Owners Am.), Shaft, 1972 (Image award NAACP), Liberation of Lord Byron Jones, 1973, Murphy's War, 1974, The Towering Inferno, 1974 (Writer of Yr. award Nat. Theater Owners Am.), The Killer Elite, 1975, The Enforcer, 1976, Telefon, 1977, The Swarm, Circle of Iron, When Time Ran Out, Over the Top; prin. writer: (TV series) Naked City, 1960, Route 66, 1960; contbg. writer (TV series) The Chrysler Theater, Alfred Hitchcock Presents, Gen. Elec. Theater, Alcoa-Goodyear Theater; writer: (TV films) Pearl, 1978, Fly Away Home, 1981, Space, 1985, Mussolini, 1986, The Three Kings, 1987; novelist: Maracaibo, 1953, rev. edit., 1987, The Slender Thread, 1971, Pearl, 1980, (John Locke Adventures) Steel Tiger, 1985, Bronze Bell, 1986, Silver Star, 1987. Served to lt. (j.g.) USN, 1943-46. Mem. Writers Guild Am. West, Mystery Writers Assn., Authors League, Phi Beta Kappa. Home: Bangkok Thailand Died April 26, 1996.

SILLMAN, HERBERT PHILLIP, accounting firm executive; b. Detroit, July 18, 1927; s. David and Phyllis (Sumter) S.; m. Maurine R. Shapiro, Mar. 16, 1952; children: Marcie, David, Jonathon. B.S., UCLA, 1949. With Harold Gilbert & Co. (C.P.A.s), Detroit, 1951-54; pnr. Sillman, Kleiman & Thal, Detroit, 1954-69; mng. partner J.K. Lasser & Co., Detroit, 1969-77; assoc. mng. ptnr. internat. Touche Ross & Co., N.Y.C., 1985-89; assoc. mng. ptnr. Internat. Deloitte & Touche, Birmingham, Mich., 1989-91; prin. Sillman Enterprises, Bloomfield Hills, Mich., 1991-95; bd. dirs. Offitbank, N.Y.C., CAPX, Miami, Fla.. Mem. Oak Park Sch. Dist. Bd. Edn., 1963-71, v.p., 1965-67, pres., 1967-69; mem. Oakland County Intermediate Bd. Edn., 1964-70, v.p., 1966-68, pres., 1968-70; mem. edn. com., mem. exec. com., 1st vice chmn. Southeastern Mich. Council Govt., 1969-70; mem. citizens assembly United Community Services Met. Detroit, 1978-95, mem. budget com., 1977-79; mem. budget com. Oakland County Planning Com., 1976-79; bd. dirs. Mich. Colls. Found., 1979-85, Mich. League for Human Services, 1977-80, Jewish Family Service, pres., 1970-73; bd. dirs. Jewish Welfare Fedn., 1972-79, mem. exec. com., 1977-79; bd. dirs. Alvin Ailey Dance Found., 1985-90. Served with USNR, 1945-46. Mem. AICPA (chmn. com. on relations with internat. confs. accts. 1975-77), Mich. Assn. CPAs (chmn. audit com. 1976-77, com. on ins. and pensions 1970-74). Home: Birmingham Mich. Died Sept. 29, 1995.

SILVER, HOWARD FINDLAY, chemical engineering educator; b. Denver, Sept. 16, 1930; s. Ronald Alexander and Marion (Howard) S.; m. Alice Jane Graham, Feb. 4, 1961; children: Ronald Graham, James Howard,

Carol Ann. B.S., Colo. Sch. Mines, 1952; M.S. in Chem. Engring., U. Mich., 1957, Ph.D., 1961. Chem. engr. duPont Co., Buffalo and Chattanooga, 1952-53, 55; research engr. Chevron Research Corp., Richmond, Calif., 1957-58, 61-64; mem. faculty U. Wyo., Laramie, 1964-94; prof. chem. engring. U. Wyo., 1968-92, prof. chem. engring. emeritus, 1992-94; program mgr. fossil fuels and advanced systems Electric Power Research Inst., Palo Alto, Calif., 1974-75. Served with AUS, 1953-55. Mem. Am. Inst. Chem. Engrs., Am. Chem. Soc., Sigma Xi, Tau Beta Pi, Sigma Gamma Epsilon, Phi Lambda Upsilon. Home: Laramie Wyo. Died May 4, 1994; buried Green Hill Cemetery, Laramie, Wyo.

SILVER, JULIUS, lawyer; b. Phila., Dec. 17, 1900; s. Louis and Esther (Miller) S.; m. Roslyn Schiff, July 3, 1929; 1 dau., Enid (Mrs. Winslow). B.A., NYU, 1922, D.C.L. (hon.); J.D., Columbia U., 1924; D.Sc. in Tech. (hon.), Israel Inst. Tech.; D.H.L. (hon.), Jewish Theol. Sem. Am. Bar: N.Y. 1925. Since practiced in N.Y.C.; sr. ptnr. firm Silver & Solomon and predecessor, from 1944; dir. Polaroid Corp., Cambridge, Mass., v.p., chmn. exec. com., from 1937; assoc. counsel com. on banking and currency U.S. Senate, 1932-34. Donor Julius Silver Residence Center, NYU, 1963; founder Julius Silver Inst. Biomed. Engring., Technion U., Israel, 1968; trustee NYU, mem. exec. and finance coms., 1963-75, emeritus, from 1975; trustee Middlesex Coll. (now Brandeis U.), 1946, Jewish Theol. Sem.; pres. Library Corp., 1965-80. Recipient Achievement award NYU Alumni Assn., 1961; Silver Towers named in his honor NYU, 1974; Columbia U. Sch. of Law Julius Silver professorship named in his honor, 1984. Mem. Bar Assn. N.Y.C., N.Y. County Lawyers Assn., Gallatin Soc. (v.p. 1964-68), Phi Beta Kappa, Phi Epsilon Pi (Achievement award 1963), Zeta Beta Tau. Clubs: Old Oaks Country (Purchase, N.Y.); Harmonie. Home: Greenwich Conn. Deceased.

SILVERLIGHT, IRWIN JOSEPH, lawyer; b. Newark, Nov. 10, 1924; s. Benjamin and Rose (Breitkopf) S.; m. Lois S. Cohen, Oct. 30, 1949; children: Than, Scott, Brad. Student, Newark Coll. Engring., 1945-46, John Marshall Coll., 1946-47, John Marshall Coll. Law Sch., 1947-49. Bar: N.J. 1950, V.I. 1971, U.S. Supreme Ct. 1956. Assoc. firm Foreman & Foreman, Elizabeth, N.J., 1950-52; trial counsel Weiner & Weiner, Roselle, N.J., 1952-54; individual practice law Westfield, 1954-62; partner firm Silverlight & Berenson, Westfield, 1962-64, Sachar, Sachar & Bernstein, Plainfield, 1964-69; asst. atty. gen. V.I., 1970-71; partner firm Nichols & Silverlight, St. Croix, V.I., 1971-76; judge Territorial Ct. V.I., St. Croix, 1977-87; judge by designation Dist. Ct. V.I., 1980-83; of counsel Nichols, Newman & Silverlight, St. Croix, V.I., 1987-91; instr. zoning, planning and municipal law Rutgers U. Extension Div., 1967-69. Contbr. to: Legal Aspects of Zoning and Planning, 1968, Opinions of the Attorney General, Virgin Islands, 1970-71. Pres. Progressive Republican Party, St. Croix, 1972-73; trustee Good Hope Sch., St. Croix. Served with USAAF, 1942-45. Decorated Air medal with 4 oak leaf clusters; scholar history U. Ill., 1938, fellow history, 1938-40, faculty fellow Bulter U., 1950-51. Mem. V.I. Bar Assn. (bd. govs. 1975, chmn. legis. and law reform 1974-76, sec. 1990, bd. govs. 1990-91), N.J. Bar Assn., Assn. Trial Lawyers Am., Am. Judges Assn., Am. Judicature Soc., St. Croix C. of C. Jewish. Home: Christiansted V.I. Died May 21, 1991.

SIMMONS, PAUL BARRETT, corporate affairs consultant, deceased; b. Portland, Maine, Feb. 6, 1942; s. J. Donald and Lura Anne (Barrett) S.; m. Joan M. Hoglund, June 12, 1965; 1 son, Charles B. A.B. in Govt., St. Michael's Coll., Winooski Park, Vt., 1964; M.P.A., SUNY-Albany, 1965. Sunday editor Albany Times-Union, N.Y., 1966-68; exec. asst. to commr. N.Y. State Dept. Health, Albany, 1969-72; assoc. commr. N.Y. State Dept. Social Service, Albany, 1972-74; spl. asst. for legislation HEW, Washington, 1975-76; exec. asst. to gov. State of Ill., Springfield, 1977-81; dep. commr. Social Security Adminstrn., Washington, 1981-83; spl. asst. to Pres. for policy devel. Washington, 1983-85; pres. Health Industry Distbrs. Assn., Washington, 1985-87, Simmons Assocs., Inc., Washington, 1988-89; dep. asst. sec. health for communications HHS, Washington, 1990-93; pres. Simons Assocs., Inc., Washington, 1993-94. Republican. Home: Washington D.C. Died Apr. 19, 1994.

SIMMONS, ROBERT FRANCIS, computer science and psychology educator; b. Quincy, Mass., May 14, 1925; s. Timothy Francis and Jacqueline (Eaton) S.; m. Patricia June Enderson, Oct. 12, 1950; children—Sandra, Erin, Steven, Kelly, Darcy. B.A., U. So. Calif., 1959, M.A., 1950, Ph.D., 1954. Behavioral scientist Rand Corp., Santa Monica, Calif., 1956-58; sr. research scientist Systems Devel. Corp., Santa Monica, 1958-68; prof. computer sci. and psychology U. Tex., Austin, 1968-94. Author: Computations from the English, 1984. Mem. Assn. for Computational Linguistics (pres. 1971-72). Home: Austin Tex. Died Nov. 30, 1994.

SIMON, NORTON WINFRED, industrialist; b. Portland, Oreg., Feb. 5, 1907; s. Myer and Lillian (Glickman) S.; m. Jennifer Jones, May 30, 1971; children by previous marriage: Donald Ellis, Robert Ellis (dec.). Student, U. Calif., Berkeley, 1923. Founder, former chief exec. officer Norton Simon Inc., N.Y.C.; founder, chief exec. officer 5 corp. founds. and 1 family found. Los Angeles; former dir., chmn. fin. com. Burlington No., Inc. Mem. Courtauld Inst., London; former mem. Carnegie Commn. on Future of Higher Edn., Nat. Programming Council; mem. Nat. Com. on U.S.-China Relations, Founding Friends of Can.; chmn. bd. dirs. The Founders, Los Angeles Music Center; affiliated Calif. Sch. Profl. Psychology; bd. dirs., trustee Norton Simon Mus., Pasadena, Calif., pres., until 1989; trustee Inst. Advanced Study, Princeton, N.J.; former bd. dirs. Reed Coll., Inst. Internat. Edn., Los Angeles County Mus. Art; former regent U. Calif.; mem. adv. bd. Columbia U.-McGraw Hill Lectures; fellow Pierpont Morgan Library, N.Y.C.; mem., past chmn. Calif. State Transp. Commn. Home: Pasedena Calif.

SIMONIDES, CONSTANTINE B., academic administrator; b. Athens, May 5, 1934; d. Basil C. and Calliope (Constantinides) S.; m. Betty L. Allen, May 5, 1956; children: Edward, Philip, Cynthia. AB in Econs., Boston U., 1958; MBA, Harvard U., 1960. With MIT, Cambridge, Mass., 1960, v.p., 1970-94, sec. of the corp., 1985-94; trustee Babson Coll., Wellesley, 1980-94, Buckingham Browne & Nichols Sch., Cambridge, 1988-94; bd. dirs. Controlled Risk Ins. Co., Cayman Islands, Bay Bank Harvard Trust Co., Cambridge. Mem. Town Meeting of Wellesley, 1975-94; vice chair Wellesley Town Govt. Com., 1993-94. Mem. Harvard Club of Boston, Babson Racquet Club. Home: Wellesley Mass. Died Apr. 24, 1994.

SIMPSON, DON, film producer; b. Anchorage, Alaska, Oct. 29, 1945. Prodn. exec. Paramount, L.A., 1975-77, v.p. prodn., 1977-80, sr. v.p. prodn., 1980-83; co-founder Don Simpson/Jerry Bruckheimer Films, Burbank, Calif., 1983-96. Prodns. include (with Jerry Bruckheimer) Flashdance, 1983, Beverly Hills Cop, 1984, Thief of Hearts, 1984, Top Gun, 1986, Beverly Hills Cop II, 1987, Days of Thunder, 1990, The Ref, 1994, Bad Boys, 1995, Crimson Tide, 1995, Dangerous Minds,1995, The Rock, 1996; film writer: Aloha Bobby and Rose, 1975, Cannonball, 1976. Home: Burbank Calif. Died Jan. 19, 1996.

SIMPSON, WILLIAM BRAND, economist, educator; b. Portland, Oreg., Nov. 30, 1919; s. John Alexander and Janet Christie (Brand) S.; m. Ruth Laura Decker, June 12, 1957. B.A. in Math., Reed Coll., 1942; M.A. in Stats., Columbia U., 1943; Ph.D. in Econs., Claremont Grad. Sch., 1971. Cons. Nat. Def. Mediation Bd., 1941-42, U.S. Dept. Interior, 1942, U.S. War Dept., Tokyo, 1947; head econ. sect. Counter-Intelligence Office, Manila, 1945; spl. rep. Supreme Commander Allied Powers, Japan, 1945-46; exec. dir. Cowles Commn. Research Econs., U. Chgo., 1948-53; co-founder, bd. dirs. Inst. Social and Personal Rels., Oakland, Calif., 1955-61; prof. econs. Calif. State U., L.A., 1958-95; econs. cons. higher edn.; cons. Am. Acad. Asian Studies Grad. Sch., San Francisco, 1956, Japanese Assn. for Rsch. on Forcibly Brought Chinese, 1991-95, Japan Pub. TV, 1993; mentor Reed Coll., 1991-95, mem. nat. adv. coun., 1994-95. Author: Cost Containment for Higher Education, 1991, Special Agent in the Pacific, WWII, 1995, Philosophy of a Concerned Academic, 1995; mng. editor, co-editor Econometrica, 1948-53; editor Managing With Scarce Resources, 1993; contbr. articles to profl. jours. Mem. Philippine arts coun. Pacific-Asia Mus., also mem. Japanese arts coun. Fellow Nat. Social Sci. Rsch. Coun. Mem. ACLU, Econometric Soc. (internat. sec. 1948-52), AAUP (state pres. 1975-76, mem. com. econ. status acad. profession 1976-79, nat. council 1978-81, com. govt. rels. 1982-88, state chmn. com. issues and policy 1981-95), Am. Econs. Assn. (chmn. panel polit. discrimination 1978-80), Am. Assn. Higher Edn., Congress Faculty Assns., Soc. Coll. and U. Planning, United Scottish Socs. So. Calif., Sierra Club (L.A. chpt.), Claremont Grad. Sch. Alumni (coun. 1993-95), Phi Beta Kappa. Democrat. Died Jan. 14, 1995.

SIMS, RILEY V., diversified telecommunications and cable television service corporate executive; b. East St. Louis, Ill., 1903; married. Carpenter, 1924-29; founded with Russell J. Burnup Burnup & Sims, Inc., West Palm Beach, Fla., 1929-93; pres. Burnup & Sims, Inc., Ft. Lauderdale, Fla., 1941-76, chmn. bd., 1968-89, chmn. emeritus, 1989-93, chief exec. officer, to 1971, also dir.; dir. First Fed. Savs. and Loan Assn., Bessemer Trust. Trustee Palm Beach Atlantic Coll.; bd. dirs. Palm Beach Community Found. Recipient Horatio Alger award, Bus. Leader of the Yr. award, Am. Acad. of Achievements Golden Plate award, Disting. Service award Stetson U., Chief award Pres.'s. Ind. Colls. and Univs. of Fla., hon. Phd, 1980. Home: Fort Lauderdale Fla. Died Jan. 13, 1993.

SINCLAIR, GEORGE, telecommunications executive; b. Hamilton, Ont., Can., Nov. 5, 1912; s. Charles Thomson and Elizabeth Gilchrist (MacKenzie) S.; m. Helen Marie Corscadden, Sept. 8, 1951; children: Andrea Joan, Valerie June, Dorothy Elizabeth. B.Sc., U. Alta., 1933, M.Sc., 1935; Ph.D., Ohio State U., 1946, D.Sc. (hon.), 1973. Dir. antenna lab. Ohio State U., Columbus, 1942-47; mem. dept. elec. engring. U. Toronto, 1947-78, prof., 1974-78; chmn. bd. Sinclair Radio Labs., Ltd., Aurora, Ont., 1951-93. Guggenhiem fellow, 1958, Ryerson fellow, 1980; recipient Julian C. Smith Gold medal Engring. Inst. Can., 1980, Manning award, 1988, Disting. Achievement award Antenna Measurement Techniques Assn., 1993. Fellow Royal Soc. Can., IEEE (Gen. A.G.L. McNaughton award 1975); mem. Can. Soc. Elec. Engrs., Assn. Profl. Engrs. Ont. Presbyterian. Club: Kiwanis. Home: North York Can. Died Aug. 16, 1993.

SINCLAIR, STEVEN ALLEN, forest products marketing professional, educator; b. Albemarle, N.C., Jan. 21, 1953; s. Allen and Melba Vann (Cox) S.; m. Karen Elizabeth Weikle, Mar. 11, 1978; children: Brian Christopher, Lindsey Elizabeth. BS, N.C. State U., 1975; PhD, Va. Tech, 1978, MBA, 1985. Intern Weyerhaeuser, Jacksonville, N.C., 1974; rsch. asst. Va. Tech. U., Blacksburg, Va., 1975-78, asst. prof., 1982-84, assoc. prof., 1984-89, prof., 1989-93; asst. prof. U. Minn., St. Paul, 1978-82; adv. com. Appalachian Hardwood Export Ctr., Morgantown, W.Va., 1989-93. Author (book): Forest Products Marketing, 1992; contbr. over 100 articles to profl. jours. Chmn. Christian life com. Blacksburg Bapt. Ch., 1988, fin. com., 1989-92, deacon, 1992. Recipient numerous rsch. grants. Mem. Forest Products Rsch. Soc. (numerous offices, contbg. editor newsletter 1988—, editorial policy com. 1985-89), Soc. Wood Sci. and Tech. (bd. dirs.), Am. Mktg. Assn., Union Forest Rsch. Orgns. (chmn. product mktg. project group), Xi Sigma Pi, Phi Kappa Phi, Gamma Sigma Delta, Beta Gamma Sigma. Home: Blacksburg Va. Died June 11, 1993.

SINDERMANN, HORST, government offical. German Democratic Republic; b. Dresden, Ger., Sept. 5, 1915; married, 2 children. Mem. Communist Union of Youth, Saxony, 1929; polit. imprisonment, 1934-45; chief editor Volksstimme, Chemnitz; chief editor Press Service of Sozialistische Einheitspartei Deutschlands; chief editor dist. paper Freiheit, Halle/Saale, E. Ger.; mem. staff Central Com., Sozialistische Einheitspartei Deutschlands, 1954-63, candidate mem., 1959-63, 1st sec. dist. council, 1963-71, mem., 1963—; candidate mem. Politburo, 1963-67, mem., 1967—; 1st dep. chmn. German Democratic Republic Council Ministers, 1971-73, chmn., 1973-76; vice chmn. Council of State, 1976; mem. Volkskammer, 1963—, pres., 1976—. Decorated Order Karl Marx, Vaterländischer Verdienstorden in silver and gold (2), others. Died Apr. 20, 1990. Home: Berlin Germany

SINGER, MARCUS JOSEPH, biologist, educator; b. Pitts., Aug. 28, 1914; s. Benjamin and Rachel (Gershenson) S.; m. Leah Horelick, June 8, 1938; children: Robert H., Jon Fredric. BS, U. Pitts., 1938; MA, Harvard U., 1940, PhD, 1942. Mem. faculty Harvard Med. Sch., 1942-51, asst. prof. anatomy, until 1951; vis. prof. anatomy L.I. Coll. Medicine, 1950; asso. prof., then prof. zoology and child devel. Cornell U., 1951-61; vis. fellow Dutch Brain Inst., Amsterdam; formerly H.W. Payne prof. anatomy, dir. dept. Case Western Res. U. Sch. Medicine, Cleve., emer. prof.; asso. dir. Devel. Biology Center Case Western Res. U. Sch. Medicine, 1961-94; vis. prof. anatomy Hebrew U., Jerusalem, 1974; Zyskind hon. vis. prof. faculty health scis. Ben Gurion U. Negev, Beersheba, Israel, 1975-76; vis. prof. Gunma U., Japan, 1977; mem. cell biology study sect. NIH, 1971-74, neurology study sect., 1976-94. Author: (with P. Yakovlev) Human Brain in Sagittal Section, 1954, Dog Brain in Section, 1962; editor: Jour. Morphology, 1965-70, asso. editor, 1970-72, Jour. Exptl. Zoology, 1963-68, 70-71, editorial bd., 1970-74; contbr. articles on nervous system, histochemistry regeneration, cytology to profl. publs. Guggenheim fellow Rome, 1967; von Humboldt fellow W. Ger., 1980-81. Fellow Am. Acad. Arts and Scis., Ohio Acad. Sci., AAAS; mem. Am. Neurol. Assn. (asso.), Am. Assn. Anatomists, Soc. Zoologists, Internat. Brain Research Orgn., Assn. Research Nervous and Mental Diseases, Soc. Devel. and Growth, Biol. Stain Commn., Sigma Xi. Home: Cleveland Heights Ohio Died Oct. 8, 1994.

SINGH, ZAIL, former president of India; b. Sandhwan, Faridkot, Punjab, India, May 5, 1916; s. Kishan and Ind (Kaur) S.; m. Pardan Kaur Singh; 1 son, 3 daus. Holds title of Giani (scholar). Leader, movement against autocratic rule in Punjab states; arrested at Faridkot, 1938; founder Faridkot State Congress and launcher Nat. Flag Movement, 1946; formed parallel Govt. in Faridkot State, 1948; pres. State Praja Mandal, 1946-48; revenue minister Patiala and East Punjab States Union (PEPSU) Govt., 1948-49, minister pub. works and agrl., 1951-52; pres. PEPSU Pradesh Congress Com., 1955-56; mem. Rajya Sabha, 1956-62, Punjab Assembly, 1962; minister of State, pres. Punjab Pradesh Congress Com., 1966-72; chief minister of Punjab, 1972-77; pres. Punjab Coop. Union; minister of home affairs, 1980-82, pres. of India, New Delhi, 1982-87. Home: New Delhi India Died Dec. 25, 1994.

SIRNA, ANTHONY ALFRED, III, investment company executive; b. N.Y.C., May 22, 1924; s. Alfred Anthony and Frances Ruth (Lasky) S.; m. Allison Porter, Jan. 12, 1946 (dec. 1971); m. Therese Cooper, Feb. 25, 1972 (dec. 1985); children: Meredith Allison, Corinne Hart, Anthony Alfred IV, Rebecca Cooper, James Cooper; m. Barbara McFadden Cushman, Dec. 20, 1986. B.S. cum laude, Harvard U., 1944, postgrad., 1944-46; postgrad., Columbia U., 1946-47, N.Y. Inst. Finance, 1953. Pres. East 55th St. Corp., N.Y.C., 1946-

; writer, editor Medical Economics, Unicorn Press, Y.C., 1950-53; fin. adviser to chmn. bd. Am. Securi-s Corp., 1953-94, dir., 1956-94; dir. Western Union ternat. Inc., Mangood Corp., Ametek, Inc., Ind. mestone Co., Inc., PCA Internat., Vis. Nurse Svc. Y. Author: (with Allison Sirna) The Wanderings of lward Ely, 1945; contbr. articles to profl. jours. Lt. l. N.Y.C. Aux. Police; capt., trustee Riverview Manor ose Co. 3, Hastings-on-Hudson, N.Y.; Trustee N.Y. oll. Music. Mem. N.Y. Soc. Security Analysts. Clubs: arvard (N.Y.C. and Boston); Westchester Country ye, N.Y.); Riverview Manor Tennis (Hastings-on-udson, N.Y.); Westhampton (N.Y.) Yacht Squadron, esthampton Country; American (London, Eng.). ome: New York N.Y. Died Mar. 24, 1994.

ROIS, RAYMOND, telecommunications adminis-ator; b. St. Epiphane, Que., Can., Jan. 26, 1927; s. eorges Emile and Bernadette (Levesque) S.; m. Yo-nde Landry, Nov. 27, 1948; children: Michele, Renee, arie-Claude, Jean. M.Sc.Com., Laval U., 1948. With ue.-Telephone, Rimouski, 1948—, traffic dir., 1965-66, mml. dir., 1966-67, v.p. ops., 1967-74, pres., chief ec. exec. officer, chmn., 1974-91, chmn. bd., chief exec. ficer, 1991-92, chmn. bd., 1992-94; bd. dirs. Québec éléphone, Trust Gen. du Can., Indsl.-Alliance Life Ins. o., Caisse de dépôt et placement du Québec, Ivanhoé, c., Radio Québec. Gov. Conseil du Patronat du uebec; Laval U. Found., 1985-94; bd. dirs. Que. ymphony Orch., Musee de la Civilisation, Coun. Can. nity. Decorated officer Order of Can., 1991; Col., on. Col. Les Fusiliers du St. Laurent. Mem. Profl. orp. Chartered Adminstrs. Que., Quebec C. of C. (gov. 980-94). Roman Catholic. Club: Golf de Bic. Lodge: .C. (4 deg.). Home: Rimouski Can. Died Sept. 24, 994.

ISK, PHILIP LAURENCE, lawyer; b. Lynn, Mass., ct. 25, 1913; s. Joseph R. and Mary (Casey) S.; m. arbara E. Gardner, July 1, 1947; 1 child, Gardner A.B., Coll. Holy Cross, 1935; JD, Boston Coll., 938. Bar: Mass. 1938, Fed. Ct. 1946. Individual prac-ce law Lynn, 1938-94. Mem. Lynn Sch. Com., 1939-1, Mass. Defenders Com., 1973-94; trustee Mass. Con-nuing Legal Edn., Inc., 1974-78; mem. Mass. Bd. Bar verseers, 1974-79. With U.S. Army, 1943-46. Fellow m. Coll. Trial Lawyers (state chmn. 1969-70), Am. ar Found., Mass. Bar Found. (treas. 1978-94, trustee); em. ABA (ho. of dels. 1963-83, devel. com., chmn. anding com. on forums 1978-81), Mass. Bar Assn. xec. com. 1959-62, bd. dels. 1963-94, pres. 1968-70), ynn Bar Assn. (pres. 1960-62), Essex Bar Assn. (exec. d. 1955-94), Def. Rsch. Inst. (Mass. chmn. 1965-68), lass. Assn. Def. Counsel (pres. 1966-67), Mass. Assn. ank Cousnel, Am. Judicature Soc. (dir. 1976-94), In-ernat. Assn. Ins. Counsel. Home: Swampscott Mass. Deceased.

KELTON, ROBERT BEATTIE, language educator; . Auburn, Mich., Apr. 23, 1913; s. Glen Beattie and rene (Richardson) S.; m. Mary Carmack, June 2, 1940; hildren—Susan, Robert Thomas, Rebecca and Melissa twins). Student, Bay City (Mich.) Jr. Coll., 1934-35; A.B., Eastern Mich. U., 1937; M.A. (univ. scholar 1937-8), U. Mich., 1938, Ph.D. (Horace H. Rackham spl. ellow 1949-50, Am. Council Learned Socs. grantee inguistics Inst. 1950), 1950; postgrad. (Roosevelt fel-ow), U. Brazil, 1942-43; postgrad. (Chilean Govt. fel-ow), U. Chile, 1943; postgrad., U. Salamanca, U. Paris, 972, U. Perugia, 1975. Mem. faculty Auburn (Ala.) J., 1939-76, prof., 1954-76, research prof. comparative inguistics, 1967-76, head dept. fgn. langs., 1954-67; vis. cholar Linguistics Inst., 1967. Contbr. articles, nonographs to profl. jours. Served to lt. USN, 1943-46, o comdr. USNR, ret. 1973. Mem. Nat. Geog. Soc., Modern Lang. Assn., Am. Assn. Tchrs. French, Am. Assn. Tchrs. German, Am. Assn. Tchrs. Spanish and Portuguese, Linguistic Soc. Am., Inst. Internat. Edn. asso.), Nat. Assn. Standard Med. Vocabulary, Am. Mus. Natural History (asso.), Acad. Tamil Culture (as-so.). Home: Auburn Ala. Died Mar. 4, 1996.

SKELTON, THOMAS REGINALD, JR., stage lighting designer; b. North Bridgton, Maine, Sept. 24, 1927; s. Thomas Reginald and Mary Ellen (Anderson) S. B.A., Middlebury Coll., 1950. Assoc. dir., mem. exec. com. Ohio Ballet; assoc. prof. Yale U. Sch. Drama, 1978-81; lighting designer The Joffrey Ballet, N.Y.C.; lectr., mem. bd. trustees Studio and Forum of Stage Design, N.Y.; guest lectr. U. Wash., U. Ohio, NYU, U Akron; bd. visitors N.C. Sch. of Arts. Lighting designer: Broadway prodns., including Oh Dad Poor Dad, Come Summer, Indians, Coco, Mahogany, Bob and Ray, Purlie, Gigi, Shenandoan, All God's Chillun Got Wings, Guys and Dolls, Richard III, The King and I, Camelot, Oklahoma!, Peter Pan, Brigadoon, Fulamina, West Side Waltz, Lena Horne; repertory prodns., including, Boston Opera Co., Yale Repertory Theatre, Am. Shakespeare Festival, Nat. Opera Belgium, Circle in the Square, Nat. Opera Holland, Am. dance Festival, Am. Spoleto Festival, Jones Beach, dance prodns., including, Jose Limon Dance Co., Dancers of Bali, Inbal, Escudero, Mary Anthony Dance Theatre, Paul Taylor Co., The Joffrey, Ballet Folklorico de Mexico, Pearl Lang Co., Merce Cunningham Co., Shankar, Anna Sokolow Co., Nat. Ballet Chile, Ballet of the 20th Century, Grand Ballet Canadienne, Nat. Ballet Can., Pearl Primus Co., The Royal Ballet, Eliot Feld Co., Am. Ballet Theatre, Boston Ballet, Pa. Ballet, Nat. Ballet Australia, Nureyev and Friends, Narkarove Co., Ohio Ballet; ballets, including Parade (Massine), The Green Table (Joos), Astarte (Joffrey), Dancers at a Gathering (Robbins), Scenes From Childhood (Poll), Aurole (Taylor), The Poor's Pavane (Limon), Ket-tentanz (Arpino), Tiller of the Fields (Tudor), Rodeo (DeMille), Rooms (Sokolow), Concerto Barocco (Bal-lenchine), A Footstep of Air (Feld); designer decor and lighting: The Beautiful Bait, Astarte (Joffrey), Sleeping Beauty (Pa. Ballet), The Medium and The Telephone, The Passion Play, Dancers of Bali, Compulsions (Poll); designer staging: Bacalor, Haiti, Arirang, Korea, Feux Follet, Can., Foo Hsing, Formosa; dir.: prodns., in-cluding Turn of the Screw, San Francisco Opera, The Old Maid and the Thief, Comic Opera Players, Come Slowly Eden, Anta Matinee Series, Faces, Berghoff Studio, Carmen, Theatre de la Monaie; author: Handbook of Dance Stagecraft and Lignting, 1955-57. Served with U.S. Army, 1947-48. Recipient Tony award nomination for Indians, 1969-70, for All God's Chillun, 1971-72, for Iceman Cometh, 1985-86, Carbonell award for Peter Pan, 1981. Home: Akron Ohio Died Aug. 9, 1994.

SKRYPNYK, MSTYSLAV STEPAN, archbishop; b. Poltava, Ukraine, Apr. 10, 1898; came to U.S., 1950; s. Ivan and Mariamna (Petlura) S.; m. Ivanna Witkovytsky, Jan. 8, 1921; children: Yaroslav, Tamara Yarovenko, Mariamna Suchoversky. M. Polit. Sci., Sch. Polit. Sci., Warsaw, Poland, 1930; Ph.D. (hon.), Ukrainian Free U., 1951. Acting bishop Pereyaslav, Ukraine, 1942-44; sec. to Council of Bishops in Exile, Offenbach, Germany, 1945-46; bishop Ukrainian Orthodox Ch. Western Europe, 1946-47; archbishop Can. Ukrainian Orthodox Ch., Winnipeg, Man., 1947-50; archbishop, pres. consistory U.S. South Bound Brook, N.J., 1950-71; met. archbishop in Diaspora, 1969-93; met. archbishop Ch. U.S., 1971-93; patriarch of Kiev and all Ukraine, 1990-93; dir. Coop. Union, Halychyna, 1923-26. Dep. mayor Rivne, Volyn, Ukraine, 1930-31; mem. Polish (Seym) Parliament, sec. presidium, mem. fgn. affairs, budget commns., 1931-39, Orthodox Council Volyn, 1932-39. Lt. Russian Army, 1916-17, Ukrainian Nat. Army, 1917-22. Home: South Bound Brook N.J. Died June 11, 1993.

SKRZYPEK, JOSEF, computer science research ad-ministrator. BS, Western New Eng. Coll., 1971; MS, U. Calif., Berkeley, 1974, PhD in Engrng. and Computer Sci., 1979. Rsch. assoc. electronic engrng. and com-puter sci. U. Calif., Berkeley, 1976-79, fellow vision, 1979-80; fellow computers and vision NYU, 1980-81; rsch. engr. Analogic, Inc., 1981-82; assoc. prof. elec-tronics and computer sci. Northeastern U., 1982-85; asst. prof. computer sci. UCLA, from 1985; prin. inves-tigator NSF, 1983-85, Tex. Instruments, 1987-88, Hughes Electronics Rsch. Lab., 1988-89; prof. analog devices Northeastern U., 1983-85; co-pinr. investigator, Def. Adv. Rsch. Project Agy., 1986-88; cons. TRW, from 1987. Officer U.S. Army Res., 1988-91. Mem. IEEE, AAAI, Internat. Conf. Neural Networks. Home: Los Angeles Calif. Deceased.

SKUTT, VESTOR JOSEPH, insurance executive; b. Deadwood, S.D., Feb. 24, 1902; s. Roy N. and Catherine (Gorman) S.; m. Angela Anderson (dec.); children: Donald Joseph (dec.), Thomas James, Sally Jane (Mrs. John G. Desmond, Jr.). LLB, Creighton U., 1923; LLD (hon.), U. Omaha, 1958, U. Nebr. Coll. Medicine, 1964, Creighton U., 1971, Bellevue Coll., 1985, Coll. of St. Mary, 1986; LHD (hon.), U. S.D., 1977. Bar: Nebr. 1923. With Mut. of Omaha Ins. Co., 1924-86, various capacities, chmn. bd., 1953-86, chmn. emeritus, 1986-93; chmn. bd. United of Omaha Life Ins. Co., 1963-86, chmn. emeritus, 1986-93; chmn. bd. Mutual of Omaha Fund Mgmt. Co., 1968-87, chmn. emeritus and founder, 1987-93; founder, chmn. emeritus Companion Life Ins. Co. of N.Y., 1989-93; bd. dirs. emeritus FirsTier Bank, Omaha. Mem. pres.'s com. on Employment of the Handicapped, World Rehabilitation Fund, Inc., Am. Life Conv.; former mem. pres.'s com. Nat Council Boy Scouts Am.; nat. co-chmn. NCCJ, 1978-87; nat. crusade chmn. Am. Cancer Soc., 1967; chmn. Nat. Alliance of Businessmen, 1976-77; Nebr. chmn. United Negro Coll. Fund, 1975, nat. dist-inguished service award, 1977; bd. dirs. Health Ins. Inst., 1972-75, trustee Creighton U., 1968-76, Nat. Little League Found., 1976-93. Recipient Harold R. Gordon Meml. award, 1950; Air Force Exceptional Service medal, 1963; Golden Sword of Hope Am. Cancer Soc., 1966; named Scouting Man of Year, 1971, Man of Year Fedn. Ins. Counsel, 1971; recipient Disting. Nebraska-lander award, 1984, Golden Plate award Am. Acad. Achievement, 1976, Disting. Service award World Rehabilitation Fund, 1983 Silver Buffalo award Boy Scouts Am., 1982, Corp. Leadership award, Nebr. chapter Arthritis Found., 1984; Citations Pres. Gerald Ford, Pres. Jimmy Carter. Mem. Nebr. Bar Assn., Tex. Bar Assn., Okla. Bar. Assn., Internat. Assn. Health Underwriters, Ins. Fedn. Nebr. (former mem. exec. council), Ins. Econs. Soc. Am. Home: Omaha Nebr. Died Feb. 23, 1993.

SLADE, HUTTON DAVISON, educator, microbiolo-gist; b. London, Aug. 6, 1912; came to U.S., 1913, naturalized, 1920; s. Francis and Florence (Davison) S.; m. Eileen Fay Pryor, June 7, 1941; children: Richard Gary, Robert Bryan. B.S., U. Md., 1935, M.S., 1936; Ph.D., Iowa State U., 1942. Research biologist Waller-stein Co., N.Y.C., 1942-43; chief microbiology Rheu-matic Fever Research Inst., Chgo., 1948-57; mem. faculty Northwestern U. Med. Sch., 1957-78, prof. microbiology, 1959-78, prof. emeritus, 1978-93; prof. U. Colo. Dental Sch., Denver, 1978-90; cons. Naval Med. Research Unit 4, Great Lakes, Ill., 1958-70, Office Naval Research, 1967-70; mem. metabolic biology panel NSF, 1966-69; mem. grad. tng. grant. com. NIH, 1967-71, mem. oral biology and medicine study sect., 1976-80; Found. Microbiology lectr., 1971-72; vis. lectr. Oreg. State U., 1972. Mem. editorial bd.: Infection and Im-munity, 1970-80. Mem. sch. bd. 37, Cook County, Ill., 1954-58; Established investigator Am. Heart Assn., 1956-61. Served to maj., Med. Service Corps AUS, 1943-46; col. Res. ret. Recipient Research Career award NIH, 1962-78; research award U. Ala. Internat. Conf. on Cellular, Biochem. and Immunological Properties of Streptococcus Mutans, 1985. Mem. AAAS, Am. Acad. Microbiology (hon.), Am. Soc. Microbiology, Ill. Soc. Microbiology (pres. 1962, Pasteur award 1976). Home: Estes Park Colo. Died Jan. 25, 1993.

SLANER, ALFRED PHILIP, manufacturing company executive; b. Hobart, Okla., Apr. 10, 1918; s. Jacob and Jessie (Roth) S.; m. Luella LaMer, July 13, 1942; chil-dren: Eugenia Ames, Barbara Winslow, Deborah Anderson. B.S., U. Okla., 1939. Exec. trainee Chester H. Roth Co., 1939, v.p., 1942-46, exec. v.p., 1946-56, pres., 1956-58; pres. Kayser Roth Hosiery Co., 1958-76; exec. v.p. Kayser Roth Corp., 1958-60, pres., 1960-76; trustee, chief exec. officer Duplan Corp., N.Y.C., 1976-96; chmn. bd. Vishay Intertechnology Inc.; dir. Scar-sdale (N.Y.) Nat. Bank, Phillips Van Heusen & Loew's Corp. Mem., pres. Bd. Edn. Scarsdale Sch. Dist. 2, 1954-58. Served with USAF, 1941-42. Mem. Nat. Assn. Hosiery Mfrs. (dir., pres. 1954). Democrat. Jewish. Clubs: Quaker Ridge Country, Harmonie, Beach Point. Home: Scarsdale N.Y. Died Mar. 14, 1996.

SLAYTON, DONALD KENT, astronaut, business ex-ecutive; b. Sparta, Wis., Mar. 1, 1924; s. Charles Sherman and Victoria Adelia (Larson) S.; m. Marjory Lunney, May 15, 1955 (div.); 1 son, Kent Sherman; m. Bobbie Jones-Osborn, Oct. 8, 1983. B.Aero. Engrng., U. Minn., 1949; Sc.D. (hon.), Carthage Coll., 1960; D.Eng. (hon.), Mich. Tech. Inst. Served to capt., pilot USAAF, 1942-46; engr. Boeing Aircraft Co., 1949-51; commd. capt. USAF, 1951, advanced to maj., 1959, resigned, 1963; fighter pilot, maintenance officer Calif., Germany, 1952-55; fighter test pilot Edwards AFB, Cal., 1955-59; joined Project Mercury, manned space flight, NASA, 1959, chief astronaut, 1962-63, dir. flight crew ops., 1963-74; mem. crew Apollo-Soyuz pilot docking module, 1975; mgr. Space Shuttle Approach and Landing Test, 1975-77, Space Shuttle Orbital Flight Test, 1978-82; pres. Space Services Inc., 1982-90; dir. space svcs. div. EER, 1991-93; I-F1 Air Racing. Fellow Soc. Exptl. Test Pilots, AIAA, Am. Astronautical Soc.; mem. Order of Daedalians, Am. Fighter Aces. Home: League City Tex. Died June 13, 1993.

SLOAN, MURIEL R, university administratior; b. N.Y.C., Feb. 14, 1926; d. Michael and Kate (Cohen) S. B.A., Hunter Coll., 1947; M.A., Columbia U., 1948; Ph.D., U. Wis., 1958. Acting dir. phys. edn. U. Wis., Madison, 1962-63, chmn. phys. edn. - women, 1971-76, prof. phys. edn., 1968-80; chmn. phys. edn. U. Md., College Park, 1980-82, acting provost div. human and community resources, 1982-83, provost div., 1983-86, asst. vice chancellor, Office of Vice Chancellor of Acad. Affairs andProvost, 1986-95; cons., lectr. Israel Ministry Edn. and Culture, 1964-65. Editor: Perceptual Motor Foundations: A Multidisciplinary Concern, 1968; contbr. articles, papers to profl. jours. Bd. dirs. Nat. Council Women, N.Y.C., 1981-95. Recipient Service Honor award Aquatics Council, AAAHPER, 1971-73. Fellow Am. Acad. Phys. Edn.; mem. Internat. Assn. Phys. Edn. and Sport for Girls and Women (U.S. rep. 1981-84), AAHPER Dance (v.p. elect 1970-71, v.p. 1971-72), Eastern Assn. Phys. Edn. and Sport for Girls and Women (pres. elect 1973-74), Am. Ednl. Research Assn., AAUP, AAUW, Pi Lambda Theta. Club: Zonta Internat. (Prince George's County, Md.). Home: Silver Spring Md. Died Sept. 26, 1995.

SLONIMSKY, NICOLAS, conductor, composer; b. St. Petersburg, USSR, Apr. 27, 1894; came to U.S., 1923, naturalized, 1931; s. Leonid and Faina (Vengerova) S.; m. Dorothy Adlow, July 30, 1931; 1 dau., Electra. Ed., Conservatory of Music, St. Petersburg; D.F.A. (hon.), Northwestern U., 1980. Condr. Pierian Sodality, Harvard, 1928-30; instr. Eastman Sch. Music, Rochester, N.Y., 1923-25, Boston Conservatory Music, 1925-45; instr. Slavic langs. and lits. Harvard U., 1946-47; vis. prof. Colo. Coll., summer 1940, 47-49; lectr. music Simmons Coll., 1947-49, Peabody Conservatory, 1956-57, U. Calif. at Los Angeles, 1964-67; guest condr., Paris, Berlin, Budapest, Havana, San Francisco, Los Angeles, Hollywood, 1931-33, S.A., 1941-42. Concert tours as pianist, Europe, 1921-22, U.S., 1923—, S.Am., 1941-42; wrote for ballet, orch., piano, voice.; author: Music since 1900, 5th edit., 1994, Music of Latin America, 4th edit., 1972, Lexicon of Musical Invective, 1953, Perfect Pitch: A Life Story, 1988, Lectionary of Music, 1989; editor: Internat. Cyclo. of Music and Musicians, 4th-8th edits., 1946-58, Baker's Biog. Dictionary of Musicians, 5th edit., 1958, 6th edit., 1978, 7th edit., 1984, 8th edit., 1991, Concise Baker's Biographical Dictionary of Musicians, 1988, 93; mem. Am. music editorial bd.: Ency. Brit., 1958—; contbr.: ann. music surveys to Ency. Brit. Year Books, 1950-68. Mem. (hon.) Am. Acad. Inst. Arts and Letters. Home: Los Angeles Calif. Died December December 25, 1995.

SLOVO, JOE, South African federal official; b. Lithuania, USSR, 1926; m. Ruth First (dec. 1982); 3 children; m. Helena Dolny. BA, U. Witwatersrand, LLB. Bar: South Africa. Chair South African Communist Party, 1984-87, gen. sec., 1987-91, nat. chair, 1991-95, mem. ctrl. com.; min. housing welfare South Africa, 1994; South African Communist Party rep. Nat. Peace Com., 1991. Co-author: Southern Africa: The Politics of Revolution, 1976; editor Umsebenzi; contbr. articles to The African Communist. Founding mem. Congress Democrats, 1953; mem. Nat. Coordinating Com. Congress Alliance, 1955, Drafing Com. Freedom Charter; organizer Umkhonto weSizwe, 1961, mem. nat. high command, from 1961, chief of staff; mem. revolutionary coun. African Nat. Congress, 1969-83, mem. nat. exec. com., from 1985, mem. polit.-mil. coun., mem. nat. working com.; hon. pres. Nebo Youth Congress; mem. Congress South African Trade Unions, 1992. With South African forces. Home: Johannesburg South Africa Died Jan. 6, 1995.

SLUNG, LOUIS SHEAFFER See SHEAFFER, LOUIS

SMALL, GEORGE MILTON, III, architect; b. Collinsville, Okla., Aug. 13, 1916; s. George Milton and Elsie (Sigmon) S.; m. June Marie Volck, Feb. 20, 1942; children: George Milton III, June Marie. B.Arch., B.S. in Archtl. Engring, U. Okla., 1939; postgrad. with, Mies Van der Rohe, 1946-47. Design architect Perkings & Will, Chgo., 1947, W.H. Deitrick, Raleigh, N.C., 1948-49; founder, owner firm G. Milton Small & Assos., Raleigh, 1949-92; mem. regional pub. adv. panel archtl. and engring. services GSA, 1976. Important works include Student Center and Music Bldg. at N.C. State U, 1972, Med. Soc. N.C. Hdqrs. Bldg, 1971, Carter Football Stadium at N.C. State U, 1967, Raleigh Municipal Bldg, 1960. Vice chmn. Raleigh City Planning Commn., 1950-60, 75-76; mem. Raleigh Bd. Adjustment, 1960-71; Pres. Design Found., N.C. State U., 1966-67. Served to lt. (j.g.) USNR, 1943-45. Fellow AIA. Died May 8, 1992.

SMICK, ELMER BERNARD, minister, educator; b. Balt., July 10, 1921; s. Frank and Marie (Hagert) S.; m. Jane Harrison, Aug. 19, 1944; children: Peter, Karen, Theodore, Rebecca. BA, King's Coll., 1944; STM, Faith Theol. Sem., 1948; PhD, Dropsie Coll., 1951. Ordained to ministry Presbyn. Ch. in Am., 1947. Pastor Evang. Presbyn. Ch., Trenton, N.J., 1947-56; prof. Old Testament langs. Covenant Theol. Sem., St. Louis, 1956-71; prof. Old Testament Gordon Conwell Theol. Sem., South Hamilton, Mass., 1971-91, prof. emeritus, from 1991; vis. prof. Ref. Theol. Sem., Orlando, Fla., from 1991; moderator N.J. Presbytery, Ref. Presbyn. Ch., 1953-54, asst. clk. of synod, 1965; trustee Nat. Presbyn. Missions, 1948-68, World Presbyn. Missions, 1979-81. Author: Archaeology of the Jordan Valley, 1973; editor: The New International Version of the Bible, 1968-78. Named Alumnus of Yr., King's Coll., 1984. Fellow Inst. Bibl. Rsch.; mem. Nat. Assn. Profs. Hebrew, Evang. Theol. Soc. (pres. 1988), Am. Oriental Soc., Soc. Bibl. Lit. Home: South Hamilton Mass. Deceased.

SMILEY, DONALD BURDETTE, retailing executive, lawyer; b. Albany, Ill., Apr. 6, 1915; s. Ralph and Etta (Stafford) S.; m. Dick Cutter, Apr. 10, 1942; children: Margot (Mrs. A.P. Humphrey), Sandra (Mrs. G.B. Weiksner, Jr.), Stafford, Daryl. B.A., Augustana Coll., 1936; J.D., Northwestern U., 1940. Bar: N.Y. 1940, U.S. Supreme Ct. 1945. Asso. Breed, Abbott & Morgan, N.Y.C., 1940-42; with R.H. Macy & Co., Inc., N.Y.C., 1945-94; became sec. and gen. atty. R.H. Macy & Co., Inc., 1953, v.p., treas., dir., 1956-64, exec. v.p., treas., 1964-66, vice chmn., treas., 1966-68, chmn., treas., 1968-71, chmn. bd., chief exec. officer, 1971-80, ret., 1980, dir., 1980-94, chmn. exec. com., 1980-81, chmn. fin. com., 1981-94; dir. Ralston Purina Co., RCA Corp., NBC, Met. Life Ins. Co., Fidelity Union Bancorp., U.S. Steel Corp., N.Y. Stock Exchange, Inc., Texasgulf, Inc., 1966-82. Trustee Met. Mus. Art. Served as lt. USNR, World War II. Mem. Bar Assn. City N.Y., Fgn. Policy Assn. (dir.), N.Y. State Bar Assn., Am. Arbitration Assn., Nat. Retail Mcts. Assn. Order of Coif. Clubs: University (N.Y.C.); River, Round Hill, Indian Harbor Yacht (Greenwich, Conn.); Blind Brook (Port Chester, N.Y.). Home: Greenwich Conn. Died Jan. 9, 1994.

SMILEY, TERAH LEROY, geosciences educator; b. Oak Hill, Kans., Aug. 21, 1914; s. Terah Edward and Frances Angelina (Huls) S.; m. Marie Lemley, July, 1935; 1 child, Terrie Lucille Scheele; m. Winifred Whiting Lindsay, June 10, 1947; children: John, Maureen, Kathlyn; 1 stepchild, Margaret Ann Perry (dec.). Student, U. Kans., 1934-36; M.A., U. Ariz., 1949. With U.S. Nat. Park Service, 1939-41, U.S. Immigration Service, 1941-42; research Lab. of Tree-Ring, U. Ariz., Tucson, 1946-60; dir. Lab. of Tree-Ring, U. Ariz., 1958-60, dir. geochronology labs., 1957-67, head dept. geochronology, 1967-70, prof. geosciences, 1970-96; Gen. chmn. Internat. Conf. on Forest Tree Growth, Tucson, 1960; vice chmn. U.S. Com. on Internat. Assn. for Quaternary Research, Nat. Acad. Sci., 1961-66; gen. chmn. First Internat. Conf. on Palynology, Tucson, 1962; mem. U.S. Com. on Internat. Hydrological Decade, Nat. Acad. Sci., 1964-66; gen. chmn. Internat. Conf. on Arid Lands, Tucson, 1969. Editor: (with James H. Zumberge) Polar Deserts and Modern Man, 1974, The Geological Story of the World's Deserts, 1982; (with Nations, Péwé and Schafer) Landscapes of Arizona, the Geological Story, 1984; contbr. articles to profl. jours. Served with USNR, 1942-45. Research fellow Clare Coll., Cambridge, U., 1970; vis. prof. Kvartärgeologiska Institutionen, Uppsala (Sweden) U., 1970-71; hon. v.p. 2d Internat. Conf. on Palynology, Utrecht, 1966. Fellow AAAS, Geol. Soc. Am., Ariz. Acad. Sci.; mem. Am. Meteorol. Soc., Tree-Ring Soc., Ariz. Geol. Soc. (past pres.), Ariz. Archeol. Soc. (past pres.), Sigma Xi. Home: Tucson Ariz. Died Feb. 29, 1996.

SMITH, ALAN PAUL, plant ecologist and physiologist; b. Madison, N.J., Mar. 31, 1945; s. Glenn Wilson and Ruth Geraldine (Hadley) S. BA, Earlham Coll., 1967; MA, Duke U., 1970, PhD, 1974. Asst. prof. U. Pa., Phila., 1974-81; assoc. prof. U. Miami, Coral Gables, Fla., 1982-87; staff scientist Smithsonian Tropical Rsch. Inst., Balboa, Panama, 1974-93, asst. dir., 1989-93. Contbr. articles to Jour. Ecology, Occologia Biotropica, Nature, Jour. Tropical Ecology. Mem. Am. Soc. Naturalists, Ecol. Soc. Am. Home: Balboa Panama Died Aug. 26, 1993.

SMITH, ALEXIS, actress; b. Penticton, Can., June 8, 1921; m. Craig Stevens, 1944. Ed., Los Angeles City Coll. Actress numerous films, stage plays, 1941—; films include The Lady With Red Hair, 1940, Dive Bomber, 1941, The Smiling Ghost, 1941, Gentleman Jim, 1942, The Constant Nymph, 1942, The Doughgirls, 1944, Conflict, 1945, Rhapsody in Blue, 1945, San Antonio, 1945, Night and Day, 1946, Of Human Bondage, 1946, Stallion Road, 1947, The Woman in White, 1947, The Decision of Christopher Blake, 1948, Any Number Can Play, 1950, Here Comes the Groom, 1951, Undercover Girl, 1952, Split Second, 1953, The Sleeping Tiger, 1955, The Eternal Sea, 1956, The Young Philadelphians, 1959, Once is Not Enough, 1975, Casey's Shadow, 1977, Turning Point, 1977, Tough Guys, 1986, numerous others; stage appearances include Follies, 1971, 72 (Tony award 1972), The Women, 1973, Summer Brave, 1975, Sunset, 1977, Platinum, 1978, The Best Little Whorehouse in Texas, 1979; TV series Hothouse, 1988. Tony nominee, 1981. Home: Burbank Calif. Died June 9, 1993.

SMITH, ALLAN FREDERICK, university administrator; b. Belgrade, Nebr., Dec. 19, 1911; s. Charles Henry and Alice (Kliese) S.; m. Alene Mullikin, June 9, 1939; children: Stephanie, Gregory Allan. A.B. in Edn, Nebr. State Tchrs. Coll., 1933; LL.B. cum laude, U. Nebr., 1940; S.J.D., U. Mich., 1950. Bar: Nebr. bar 1940, Mich. bar 1951. Chief counsel OPA, Washington, 1941-43, 46; assoc. prof. law Stanford, 1946-47; prof. law U. Mich., 1947-94, dean Law Sch., 1960-65, v.p. for acad. affairs, 1965-74, interim pres., 1979-80. Author: Personal Life Insurance Trusts, 1950, (with R. Aigler and S. Tefft) Cases and Materials on Property, rev. edit, 1960, (with L. M. Simes) The Law of Future Interests, 1956, (with Browder and Cunningham) Basic Property Law, 1984. Served with AUS, 1943-45. Fellow Am. Bar Found.; mem. ABA, Mich. Bar Assn., Am. Judicature Soc., Order of Coif, Phi Kappa Phi, Phi Delta Phi. Clubs: University of Mich. Research (Ann Arbor), Lions (Ann Arbor). Home: Ann Arbor Mich. Died Jan. 21, 1994.

SMITH, BILLIE M., retired aircraft company executive; b. Littlefield, Tex., Sept. 4, 1933; s. James W. and Gracie Inez (Ratliff) S.; m. Faye Brewer, May 5, 1985. BS in Math. and Chemistry, Tex. A&I U., 1953. Project engr. Phillips Petroleum Co., McGregor, Tex., 1953-54, 55-58; project mgr., minuteman Thiokol Chem. Corp., Brigham City, Utah, 1958-60; program dir. Titan III United Tech. Corp., Sunnyvale, Calif., 1960-66; mgr. advanced launch systems LTV Aerospace and Def. Co., Mich., 1966-67, chief engr. systems integration, 1967-68, dep. program dir. Lance, 1968-69, v.p. Lance, 1970-72, v.p., gen. mgr., 1972-77; sr. v.p. advanced programs LTV Aerospace and Def. Co., Dallas, 1977-78, sr. v.p. Multiple Launch Rocket System program, 1978-83, sr. v.p., gen. mgr. MLRS div., 1983-85, exec. v.p., gen. missiles and advanced programs div., 1985-89, pres. aircraft products group, 1985-89, ret., 1989. Vice chmn. Dallas County U.S. Savs. Bond Campaign, Dallas, 1986-87, Tarrant County U.S. Savs. Bond Campaign, Ft. Worth, 1987. Served as sgt. U.S. Army, 1954-55. Recipient Outstanding Achievement award Missiles and Rockets Mag., 1965. Mem. Am. Def. Preparedness Assn., Assn. U.S. Army, AIAA, U.S. Field Artillery Assn., Navy League (life), Alphi Chi. Home: Irving Tex. Died May 28, 1992.

SMITH, CYRIL JAMES, pipeline company executive; b. N.Y.C., Aug. 29, 1930; s. Franklin W. and Elizabeth (Cowley) S. A.B., Brown U., 1952; LL.D., U. Va., 1955. Bar: N.Y. bar 1959. With firm Lord, Day & Lord, N.Y.C., 1955-65, Paris, France, 1965-66; resident atty. N.Y.C.; resident atty. Panhandle Eastern Pipe Line Co., Houston, 1966-67, corp. sec., 1967-95, asst. to pres., 1974-77, v.p., 1981-91; v.p., sec. Panhandle Ea Corp., 1981-91, Tex. Ea. Corp., 1989-91; v.p., corp. sec Trunkline Gas Co., ret., 1991. Served with USNR 1956-57. Home: Houston Tex. Died Oct., 1995.

SMITH, DACOSTA, JR., lawyer; b. Weston, W.Va. Apr. 22, 1917; s. DaCosta and Mattie Jane (Callison) S. m. Florence Gray Koblegard, Apr. 12, 1947; children Linda, Marcia, DaCosta III. A.B., W.Va. U., 1937, J.D., 1941. Bar: W.Va. bar 1941. Practiced in Weston dir. Midland Enterprises, Inc., 1956-62, Ohio River Co., 1956-61; trustee, dir. Eastern Gas & Fuel Assos., 1962-74; v.p., gen. counsel Eastern Associated Coal Corp., 1964-74. Served to lt. (s.g.) USNR, World War II. Mem. W. Va., W.Va. State, Lewis County bar assns. Weston C. of C., Kappa Alpha, Phi Delta Phi. Episcopalian. Clubs: Weston Rotary, Deerfield Country. Home: Weston W.Va. Died Jan. 29, 1994.

SMITH, DARWIN EATNA, lawyer, retired manufacturing executive; b. Garrett, Ind., Apr. 16, 1926; s. K Bryant and Hazel (Sherman) S.; m. Lois Claire Archbold, Aug. 19, 1950; children: Steven, Pamela Valerie, Blair. BS in Bus. with distinction, Ind. U. 1950; LLB cum laude, Harvard U., 1955. Bar: Ill. 1955 Assoc. atty. Sidley, Austin, Burgess & Smith, Chgo. 1955-58; with Kimberly-Clark Corp., Neenah, Wis. 1958-91, gen. atty., 1960-91, v.p., 1962-67, v.p. fin. and law, 1967-70, pres., 1970-91, chmn., CEO, 1971-91, ret. 1991. Served with AUS, 1944-46. Home: Irving Texas Died Dec. 28, 1995.

SMITH, DESMOND MILTON, bishop; b. San Ignacio, Cayo, Belize, Mar. 10, 1937; s. Samuel Smith and Almira Young; children: Estel, Victoria, Desmond Dorothy, Owen, Henry. Student, St. John's Sem. Lusaka, Zambia, 1969-71, Coll. of the Resurrection York, Eng., 1976-77; Diploma in Theology, Codrington Coll., Barbados, 1982. Joined Soc. St. Francis, Anglican Ch., 1963; ordained to ministry Anglican Episcopal Ch as deacon, 1970, as priest, 1971, as bishop, 1989. Deacon Diocese of Zambia, 1970; priest Diocese Cen Zambia, 1971; bishop Diocese of Belize, Belize City 1989—. Mem. exec. com. Belize Scout Assn., Belize City, 1990; active Nat. Coun. for Edn., Belmopan Belize, 1991. Fellow Nat. Geog. Soc. Home: Belize City Belize

SMITH, FRANK ACKROYD, biochemical toxicologist, educator, retired; b. Winnipeg, Man., Feb. 14 1919; came to U.S., 1919; s. Frank and Doris A (Babcock) S.; m. Helen Jane McGuire, Apr. 15, 1944 children: Susan Jane, Deborah Ackroyd. BA, Ohio State U., 1940, MSc, 1941, PhD, 1944. Fellow Mellon Inst. for Ind. Rsch., Pitts., 1944, U. Rochester (N.Y.) Manhattan Project, 1944-46, U. Rochester (N.Y.) Atomic Energy Project, 1946-84; instr. toxicology U Rochester (N.Y.) Sch. Medicine & Dentistry, 1946-54 asst. prof. toxicology, 1954-58, assoc. prof. toxicology 1958-84, ret., 1984, part time assoc. prof. toxicology 1984-85, prof. emeritus, 1985-95; cons. WHO, Geneva 1969-73, Nat. Inst. Dental Rsch., NIH, Bethesda, Md. 1969-73, Nat. Rsch. Coun., NAS, Washington, 1971 Workers Compensation Bd., B.C., Vancouver, Conn Dept. Health, U.S. EPA, joint project Delft U. Tech. Ministry of Housing, Phys. Planning and Environment of The Netherlands, Environ. Health Office of the Rotterdam Mcpl. Health Svc.; mem. panel on water fluoridation U.S. Surgeon Gen., Washington. Co-author: Fluorine Chemistry, Vol. III, 1963, Vol. IV 1965; contbr. chpts. to books and articles to profl. jours Vol. Rochester (N.Y.) Mus. and Sci. Ctr. Recipient Adolph Kammer award for merit-in-authorship Am Occupational Med. Assn., 1978. Mem. AAAS, AAUP Am. Chem. Soc., Am. Indsl. Hygiene Assn., Am. Soc for Pharmacology and Experimental Therapeutics, Soc Toxicology (charter), Sigma Xi. Home: Rochester N.Y Died Nov. 9, 1995.

SMITH, GEORGE DUFFIELD, JR., lawyer; b Dallas, Dec. 23, 1930; s. G. Duffield and Gladys (Cassle) S.; m. Ann L. Suggs, Aug. 29, 1956; children Jeanie, Christina, Duffield. B.S. in Bus. Adminstrn., U N.C.-Chapel Hill, 1952; LL.B., So. Meth. U., 1957. Bar Tex. 1957, U.S. Dist. Ct. (no., ea. and western dists.) Tex. 1960, U.S. Ct. Appeals (5th and 10th cirs.) 1983 Assoc. Lyne, Blanchett & Smith, Dallas, 1957-60 Touchstone, Bernays & Johnson, Dallas, 1960-65; ptnr Gardere, Porter & DeHay, Dallas, 1965-79, Gardere & Wynne, Dallas, 1979-89; instr. Internat. Assn. Ins Counsel Trial Acad., 1982. Elder, Highland Park Presbyn. Ch., Dallas; pres. Shakespeare Festival, Dallas 1976; bd. dirs. Hope Cottage, Dallas, Ctr. Pastoral Care & Counseling, 1979-81. Served to capt. USAF, 56 Fellow ABA, Tex. Bar Found.; mem. Tex. Bar Assn (dir. 1985-89), Dallas Bar Assn., Tex. Assn. Def Counsel (pres.), Def. Research Inst. (regional v.p. 1980-83, dir. 1983-86, v.p. pub. relations 1986-88, pres.-elec 1988-89), Internat. Assn. Ins. Counsel, Am. Bd. Trial Advs., Trial Attys. Assn. Am. Republican. Club: Brook Hollow Golf (Dallas). Died Jan. 31, 1989. Home Dallas Tex.

SMITH, GREGORY ALLAN, lawyer; b. Washington Dec. 9, 1945; s. Allan F. and Alene M. (Mullikin) S.; m Barbara M., Jan. 28, 1967; children: Michelle Ann

Risch-Smith, Pamela Cheryl Smith. BA, Princeton U., 1968; JD, U. Wis., 1971. Bar: Wis. 1971, Calif. 1972. Assoc. Pillsbury, Madison & Sutro, San Francisco, 1971-78, ptnr., 1979-89; ptnr. Heller, Ehrman, White & McAuliffe, San Francisco, from 1990. Mem. ABA (tax sect.), Western Pension and Benefits Conf., Calif. State Bar (tax sect., employee benefits com.). Democrat. Home: Berkeley Calif. Deceased.

SMITH, HAROLD HILL, genetics educator; b. Arlington, N.J., Apr. 24, 1910; s. Frederick Harold and Hilda Niles (Burgess) S.; m. Mary Downing, Feb. 11, 1939; children: Frederick, Lucy Smith Keane, Hilda Smith Hodges, Susan Smith Jurs. B.S., Rutgers U., 1931; A.M., Harvard U., 1934, Ph.D., 1936. Asst. geneticist Dept. Agr., Beltsville, Md., 1935-43; assoc. prof., then prof. genetics Cornell U., 1946-56; sr. scientist IAEA, Vienna, Austria, 1958-59; sr. geneticist Brookhaven Nat. Lab., Upton, N.Y., 1956-94; adj. prof. NYU, 1977-94; vis. prof. U. Calif., Berkeley, U. Buenos Aires, 1966; Fulbright lectr. U. Amsterdam, 1953. Editor: Evolution of Genetic Systems, 1972; mem. editorial bd.: Environ. and Exptl. Botany, Jour. Heredity, Mutation Research. Contbr. articles to profl. publs. Served to lt. USNR, 1943-46. Guggenheim fellow, 1953; hon. research asso. Univ. Coll., London, 1966; Nat. Acad. Sci. exchangee with Romanian Acad., 1970. Mem. Am. Genetic Assn. (pres. 1976), Genetics Soc. Am., Bot. Soc. Am., AAAS, AAUP, Tissue Culture Assn., Soc. Developmental Biology, Sigma Phi Epsilon. Clubs: Shoreham Country, Harvard of L.I, Raritan. Home: Shoreham N.Y. Died Oct. 19, 1994.

SMITH, JOHN, politician; b. Sept. 13, 1938; s. Archibald Leitch Smith and Sarah Cameron Scott; m. Elizabeth Margaret Bennett, 1967; 3 children. MA, LLB, Glasgow U.; LLD (hon.), U. Glasgow, 1994. Bar: Scotland, 1967. MP from Lanarkshire North, 1970-83, MP from Monklands East, 1984—, parliamentary pvt. sec. to Sec. State for Scotland, 1974, parliamentary undersec. state, 1974-75; min. of state Dept. Energy, 1975-76, Privy Coun. Office, 1976-78; sec. state for trade, 1978-79; prin. opposition spokesman for trade, prices and consumer protection, 1979-82, energy, 1982-83, on employment, 1983-84, for trade and industry, 1984-87, on treas. and econ. affairs, 1987—; leader Labor Party, 1992—; nat. pres. Indsl. Common Ownership Movement, 1988—. Gov. Ditchley Found., 1987—; hon. bencher Inner Temple, 1993. Home: Edinburgh Scotland

SMITH, JOHN SYLVESTER, retired college president; b. Phila., Aug. 18, 1914; m. Margaret Viola Giebel, Jan. 7, 1938; children: Roy Harold (dec.), Barbara Lynn (Mrs. Thomas Knowles). Student, Muhlenberg Coll., 1932; B.S., Temple U. Tchrs. Coll., 1937; S.T.B. with honors, 1938; M.A., Drew U., 1940, Ph.D., 1948; postdoctoral study, Columbia. Ordained to ministry Methodist Ch., 1938; pastor in Bklyn., 1943-46; Protestant chaplain Bklyn. State Hosp., later N.Y.N.G., 1943-46; asst. to pres. Washington Coll., Chestertown, Md., 1946-51; with Ia. Wesleyan Coll., 1951-53; head dept. philosophy and religion, chmn. div. humanities, then dean of coll.; head dept. philosophy and religion, adminstrv. adviser to pres. Bethune-Cookman Coll., Daytona Beach, Fla., 1953; dean Bethune- Cookman Coll., 1953-54, dean and registrar, 1954-58; dean Dillard U., New Orleans, 1958-59; v.p., univ. dean Ill. Wesleyan U., 1959-62; chmn. div. humanities Findlay Coll., 1962-66; acad. dean, v.p. Lake City (Fla.) Jr. Coll. and Forest Ranger Sch., 1966-67; pres. Fla. Keys Coll., Key West, 1967-79; pastor Presbyn. Kirk of the Keys, Marathon, Fla., 1968-85. Home: Tallahassee Fla. Died Aug. 28, 1992; interred Tallahassee, Fla.

SMITH, KENNETH OWLER, communications educator; b. San Jose, Calif., May 13, 1920; s. William Kenneth and Velma Erin (Owler) S.; m. Patricia Ann Nowack, May 23, 1980. A.B., Stanford U., 1941; M.S., UCLA, 1958, Ed.D., 1967. Editor various newspapers and mags., Calif., 1940-42, 46-49; pub. relations dir. Western Airlines Inc., Los Angeles, Calif., 1950-60; faculty UCLA, Los Angeles, Calif., 1960-64, 67-70; adminstr. U. Calif., Berkeley, Calif., 1965-67; prof. Sch. Journalism U. So. Calif., Los Angeles, Calif., 1970—; dir. Sports Info. Program, Los Angeles, Calif., from 1979; pub. relations/sports info. mgmt. cons. Author: Professional Public Relations, 1968; The Practice of Public Relations, 1969; A Chronology of Sports, 1982; numerous jour. articles. Served with U.S. Army, 1942-46. Recipient Outstanding Faculty award U. So. Calif. 1974-75; Chasqui award Internat. Pub. Relations Assn. 1977. Mem. Pub. Relations Soc. Am. (accredited, Silver Anvil award, 1969, pres. 1977, Educator of Yr. 1979), AAUP, U.S. Olympic Soc., Sigma Delta Chi, Kappa Tau Alpha, Phi Delta Kappa. Club: Univ. So. Calif. Faculty Ctr. Home: Los Angeles Calif. Deceased.

SMITH, LAWRENCE BEALL, artist; b. Washington, Oct. 2, 1909; s. Gerald Karr and Leah (Beall) S.; m. Winn Revere, June 20, 1935; children: Dustin Beall, Leslie Winn, Lochlin Revere. PhB, U. Chgo., 1931; attended, Art Inst. Chgo.; studied with Ernest Thurn, Gloucester, Charles Hopkinson, Boston, Harold Zimmerman, Boston. art instr. Walker Sch. Art, Boston, 1932-36; artist war correspondent WWII. Solo exhbns. include Grace Horn Gallery, Boston, 1940, Assoc. Am. Artists, N.Y.C., 1948, 60, Katonah Mus. Gallery, N.Y., 1955-69, 82, Vose Gallery, Boston, 1962, Narden Gallery, Cross River, N.Y., 1989; exhbns. include Whitney Mus., N.Y.C., 1940, 58, Art Inst. Chgo., 1945, Boston Mus., 1945, Nat. Acad. Design, N.Y.C., 1972, Carnegie Inst. Art, 1972, Wichita Mus., 1981, 87; represented in collections Fogg Mus., Cambridge, Mass., John Herron Art Inst., Indpls., Wichita Art Mus., Andover (Mass.) Mus., Chrysler Mus., Norfolk, Va., Sheridan Swope Art Gallery, Terre Haute, Ind., Mus. City of N.Y., Libr. Cong., Washington, Worcester Found., Shrewsbury, Conn., Met. Mus., N.Y.C., Harvard U., U. Chgo., Colby Coll., MIT, U. Ariz., U. Mo., Brandeis U., West Point, Am. Tobacco Co., Upjohn, Abbott Labs., Lever Bros., Standard Oil; portrait painter univs., corps.; represented in pvt. collections; book illustrator: Tom Jones, Washington Square, Age of Innocence, Anderson's Fairy Tales, Robin Hood, Garland of Fairy Tales; sculpture exhbns. include Katonah Gallery, Maine Coast Galleries, Wichita Mus., Nat. Acad. Design; represented in sculpture collections Worcester Found., Wichita Mus., Round Hill Community Ch., pvt. collections; pvt., mus. collections graphics, lithography, monotype. Recipient Am. Inst. Graphic Arts award, Art Dirs. Club award, Ellen Speyer Sculpture prize Nat. Acad. Design, Purchase prize drawing Norfolk Mus. Home: Cross River N.Y. Died Nov. 2, 1995.

SMITH, MOISHE, artist, printmaker; b. Chgo., Jan. 10, 1929; s. Louis and Esther (Zoob) S.; m. B. Maria Wollmar, July 27, 1964 (div. Aug. 1986); m. Carolyn Waller, June 15, 1991. BA, New Sch. Social Research, 1950; MFA, U. Iowa, 1953, Academica of Florence, Italy, 1959-61; studied with Gigio Morandi, 1959-61. Instr. printmaking So. Ill. U., 1955-59; asst. prof. Stout (Wis.) State U., 1965-66; vis. artist U. Wis., 1966-67, Ohio State U., 1971, U. Iowa, 1971, Utah State U., 1971, U. Calgary, Can., 1974; assoc. prof. U. Wis., Parkside, 1972-77; prof. printmaking Utah State U., Logan, 1977-93. One-man exhbns. include R.M. Light and Co., Boston, 1960, 63, AAA Gallery, N.Y.C., 1965, 74, Jane Halsem Gallery, 1967, 74, 86, Brooks Meml. Art Gallery, Louisville, 1977, Madison Art Ctr., 1978; retrospective Salt Lake Art Ctr., Gayle Weyher Gallery, Salt Lake City, 1988, 90, Yvonne Rapp Gallery, Louisville, 1987, 89, Finch Lane Gallery, Salt Lake City, 1991; group exhbns. include Sao Paulo Internat., 1955, Print Coun. Am., 1959, 62, Bklyn. Mus., 1977, Cracow Internat. Biennale, 1978, 80, 84, 86, 88, Frechen Internat., 1980, 86, Ljubljana Internat., 1981, Grenchen Internat., 1982, Taiwan Internat., 1988; represented in major museums in U.S., Europe, Asia; Absolut Vodka advt. campaign, 1993. Recipient Gov.'s award for art State of Utah, 1993; Fulbright fellow, 1959-61, Guggenheim fellow, 1967-68, Utah Arts Coun. fellow, 1988; Utah State U. grantee, 1978-82. Mem. NAD (academician), Soc. Am. Graphic Artists, L.A. Printmaking Soc. Home: Hyde Park Utah Died July 5, 1993.

SMITH, MORGAN KINMONTH, publishing company executive; b. Morristown, N.J., May 10, 1912; s. Morgan Kinmonth and Sarah C. (Boswell) S.; m. Beatrice Stewart, July 14, 1934; children: Morgan Kinmonth, Helen (Mrs. Brian Taylor), Joan (Mrs. John N. Kidder), Frances deF. (Mrs. Allen Moore), Nancie C. (Mrs. Robert E. Ash, Jr.). Grad., St. Paul's Sch., Concord, N.H., 1930; BS, Yale U., 1934. Prodn. asst. Weyerhaeuser Timber Co., Longview, Everett, Wash., 1934-38; with The Riverside Press subs. Houghton Mifflin Co., Cambridge, Mass., 1938-71, pres., 1966-71, v.p. parent co., 1966-71, also dir., 1952-71; bd. dirs. Middlesex Ins. Co., 1959-74; assoc. mng. dir. Gambit Pubs., Ipswich, Mass., 1971-85; bd. dirs. Concord Bookship Inc., treas. bd. dirs., 1972-93, pres. bd. dirs., 1976-93; dir. Book Mfrs. Inst., 1958-69, pres. 1965-67; gov. Yale U. Press, 1968-86; chmn. bd. govs. 1971-82. Mem. Concord Pers. Bd. 1952-65, chmn., 1956-57, 61-62; trustee Concord Acad., 1947-67, 71-77, pres. 1952-60, v.p., 1971-74; trustee Emerson Hosp., 1947-50, St. Paul's Sch., 1962-66, United Community Svcs. Boston, 1964-67, Douglas Thom Clinic, 1954-73; pres. Douglas Thom Clinic, 1962-64; trustee Little House, 1948-56, pres., 1951-55; vestry Trinity Episcopal Ch., 1947-51; trustee Concord Community Chest, 1947-51, pres., 1947-49; bd. govs. Concord Antiquarian Mus., 1976-80, pres., 1977-79; bd. of overseers DeCordova Mus., 1989-93. Capt. AUS, 1943-45. Mem. Ausable Club (trustee 1965-68, pres. 1968-73, chmn. 1973-78, Tavern Club, Concord Country Club. Republican. Trinity Episcopal Ch. Home: Concord Mass. Died Feb. 21, 1993.

SMITH, OLIVER, theatrical producer, designer; b. Waupun, Wis., Feb. 13, 1918; s. Larue F. and Nina (Kincaid) S. B.A., Pa. State U., 1939; Dr. (hon.), Bucknell U., L.I. U. Master tchr. NYU; co-dir. Am. Ballet Theatre, 1945-80, 90—. Co-producer, designer plays On the Town, 1945, Billion Dollar Baby, 1945, No Exit, 1946, Me and Molly, 1947, Gentlemen Prefer Blondes, 1949, Bless You All, 1950, In The Summer House, 1952, Clearing in the Woods, 1957, Time Remembered, Romulus, 1961, The Night of the Iguana, Lord Pengo, 1962, Barefoot in the Park, 1963, 110 in the Shade, 1963, The Girl Who Came to Supper, 1963, Dylan, 1963, The Chinese Prime Minister, 1964, Ben Franklin in Paris, 1964, Luv, 1964, Poor Richard, 1964, Odd Couple, 1965; designer of musicals Brigadoon, 1946, High Button Shoes, 1946, Miss Liberty, 1949, Paint Your Wagon, 1952, Pal Joey, 1952, On Your Toes, 1955, My Fair Lady, 1956, Candide, 1955, Auntie Mame, 1956, West Side Story (Antoinette Perry award 1958), Jamaica, Destry, Flower Drum Song, Camelot, Beckett; on Broadway Rosalinda, 1942, First Monday in October, Clothes for a Summer Hotel; for Met. Opera Traviata, 1958, Martha, 1961; Hello Dolly, 1963 (Tony award), I Was Dancing, 1964, Candide, 1971, The Little Black Book, 1972, The Time of Your Life, 1972, Lost in The Stars, 1972, Lunch Hour, 1980, Mixed Couples, 1980, A Talent for Murder, 1981, 84, Charing Cross Road, 1982; off-Broadway The Golden Age, 1984; Naughty Marietta, N.Y.C. Opera, 1978; designer movies Band Wagon, 1952, Oklahoma, 1955, Guys and Dolls, 1955, Porgy and Bess; broadway mus. Sound of Music, Unsinkable Molly Brown, 1960; co-dir. Am. Ballet Theatre, 1945-80; designer ballets Rodeo, 1942, Fancy Free, 1943, Fall River Legend, 1946, Swan Lake, Les Noces; exhbns. Pa. State Coll., Mus. Modern Art, Bklyn. Mus., Chgo. Art Inst., Cocoran Gallery, Yale U., interior, Nat. Theatre, Washington; produced On the Town, London, 1962-63. Recipient Donaldson award 1946, 47, 49, 53, Antoinette Perry award 1957, 58, 60, 61, 64, 65, Shubert award 1960, N.Y. Handel medallion 1975; Disting. Alumni award Pa. State U., 1962, Gt. Tchr. award NYU, 1981. Mem. Triangle Soc., Acacia, Nat. Council Arts. Home: New York N.Y.

SMITH, OTIS MILTON, lawyer; b. Memphis, Feb. 20, 1922; s. Samuel M. and Eva Smith; m. Mavis C. Livingston, Dec. 29, 1949; children: Vincent, Raymond, Anthony, Steven. Student, Syracuse U., 1946-47, LLD (hon.), 1978; JD, Catholic U. Am., 1950, LLD (hon.), 1977; LL.D. (hon.), Western Mich. U., 1973, Southwestern, Memphis, 1978, Morgan State Coll., 1978, U. Detroit, 1980, U. Mich., 1983, Detroit Coll. Law, 1985. Bar: D.C., Mich., U.S. Supreme Ct. Mem. Mallory & Smith, Flint, Mich., 1957; asst. pros. atty. Genesee County, Mich., 1955-57; mem. Flint Election Bd., 1956-57; chmn. Mich. Public Service Commn., 1957-59; auditor gen. State of Mich., 1959-61; justice Supreme Ct. Mich., 1961-66; mem. legal staff Gen. Motors Corp., 1967-84, asst. gen. counsel, 1973-74, v.p., 1974-84, assoc. gen. counsel, 1974-77, gen. counsel, 1977-83; of counsel Lewis, White & Clay, Detroit, 1984-94; bd. dirs. Detroit Edison, The Kroger Co.; mem. Adminstrv. Conf. U.S. Bd. dirs. Nat. Urban League, 1973-80, sec. 1979-94; bd. regents U. Mich., 1967-71, bd. govs. Rackham Fund, 1981-94; trustee Oakland U., 1971-77, chmn., 1972-74; v.p. United Found., Detroit, 1973-83; trustee Fisk U., 1973-79, Henry Ford Hosp., 1978-94, Catholic U. Am., 1979-84; bd. dirs. Detroit Symphony Orch., 1980-94, YMCA Met. Detroit, 1976-83; mem. Commn. on Exec. Legis. and Jud. Salaries, 1980-81. Served with AUS, 1942-46. Recipient Disting. Service award Flint Jr. C. of C., 1956, Nat. Alumni award Catholic U. Am., 1961, Silver Beaver award Boy Scouts Am., 1966, Social Responsibility award Opportunities Industrialization Ctrs., 1982. Fellow Am. Bar Found.; mem. ABA (del. 1972-76), Mich. Bar Assn. (bd. commrs. 1968-76), Am. Judicature Soc., Am. Arbitration Assn. (bd. dirs.), Omega Psi Phi (Man of Yr. award 1962). Club: Detroit. Home: Detroit Mich. Died June 29, 1994.

SMITH, PETER BENNETT, banker; b. N.Y.C., Sept. 24, 1934; s. Richard Joyce and Sheila (Alexander) S.; B.A., Yale U., 1956; m. Elizabeth Weinberg, May 10, 1980; children: Marjorie, Alison, Peter, Michael, Madeleine, Hannah, Elizabeth. With J.P. Morgan & Co., 1958-59; with Morgan Guaranty Trust Co., N.Y.C., 1959-96, sr. v.p. mgmt., 1976-79, exec. v.p., 1979-86; chmn. credit policy com., 1986-96; mng. dir. Banco Frances del Rio de la Plata, Buenos Aires, Argentina, 1968-72, Bank Mees & Hope, Amsterdam, Netherlands, 1972-75; pres. Bank Morgan LaBouchere N.V., Amsterdam, 1976; trustee Canterbury Sch., 1986-95, Sharon Conn Hosp.; bd. dirs. Dravo Corp., 1984-90, N.Y.C. Ballet, 1985-92; trustee Marine Corps Command and Staff Coll. Found.; mem. James Madison coun. Libr. Congress. Served to capt. USMCR, 1956-58. Mem. Coun. on Fgn. Rels., Bankers' Roundtable Roman Catholic. Clubs: Economic, Yale (N.Y.C.); Rolling Rock, Sharon Country, Kittansett, Mill Reef. Died Mar. 2, 1996. Home: Sharon Conn.

SMITH, PETER GARTHWAITE, energy consultant; b. July 22, 1923; s. Karl Garthwaite and Fannie (Jones) S.; m. Anne Allerton Ward, Dec. 23, 1950; children—Allerton G., Thomas G., Amy G., Abigail G. A.B., Princeton U., 1948; LL.B., Yale U., 1951. Assoc. Hughes, Hubbard & Reed, N.Y.C., 1951-55; corp. sec. So. Natural Gas Co., Birmingham, Ala., 1963-71; gen. counsel So. Natural Gas Co., Birmingham, 1966-73; exec. v.p. Sonat, Inc., Birmingham, 1973-82, vice chmn., 1984-94, cons., 1984-95; bd. dirs. First Ala. Bank, Birmingham, 1978-92. Chmn. bd. dirs. Ala. Sch. Fine Arts, Birmingham, 1982-88; pres. Met. Devel. Bd., Birmingham, 1982-86; bd. dirs. Episcopal Ch. Found., N.Y.C., 1980-91, Birmingham Turf Club, Inc., 1985-87, Children Can Soar Inc., 1987-89; trustee Ala. Symphony Assn., Birmingham, 1981-85. Served with USAAF, 1943-46. Mem. ABA, Am. Gas Assn. (bd. dirs. 76-80, 82-84), Interstate Natural Gas Assn. (bd. dirs. 1976-84, chmn. bd. dirs. 1983-84), Mid-Continent Oil Gas Assn. (bd. dirs. 1977-84), So. Gas Assn. (bd. dirs. 1974-77), Mountain Brook Club, Downtown Club, Princeton

Club, Nassau Club. Home: Birmingham Ala. Died Aug. 16, 1995.

SMITH, RICHARD FRED, lawyer; b. Detroit, July 7, 1938; s. Fred Charles and Maude Sibley (Haycock) S.; children: Marla, Rosalind. BS, MIT, 1960; JD, Harvard U., 1963. Bar: Tex. 1963. Assoc. Gardere & Wynne, Dallas, 1965-70, ptnr., 1970-90. Mem. Dallas City Coun., 1975-80, Dart Bd., Dallas, 1984-88; vice chmn. Dart Bd., 1986-88; gen. counsel Rep. Party of Tex. Lt. U.S. Army, 1963-65. Mem. ABA, Tex. Bar Assn., Dallas Bar Assn. Methodist. Home: Dallas Tex. Died Jan. 25, 1990.

SMITH, ROBERT LEE, retired civil engineering educator; b. Schaller, Iowa, Oct. 31, 1923; s. Lester Martens and Edith (Bright) S.; m. A. Lucille Johnson, Sept. 6, 1947; children: Barbara Lucille, Milton (dec.), Deborah Lee. B.S., U. Iowa, 1947, M.S., 1948. Research asst. Iowa Inst. Hydraulic Research, Iowa City, 1947-48; asst. prof. dept. applied mechanics U. Kans., Lawrence, 1948-52, Parker prof. water resources, 1962-66, prof., chmn. dept. civil engring., 1967-72, Deane E. Ackers prof. engring., 1970-88; exec. dir. Iowa Natural Resources Council, Des Moines, 1952-55; exec. sec., chief engr. Kans. Water Resources Bd., Topeka, 1955-62; spl. asst. Office Sci. and Tech., The White House, 1966-67; design engr. and hydraulic engr. to numerous firms; water resources cons. Black & Veatch Cons. Engrs., Kansas City, Mo., 1968-95; chmn. com. on water resources rsch. Fed. Coun. for Sci. and Tech.; cons. in field. Contbr. articles to profl. jours. Mem. U.S. Geol. Survey Adv. Com. Water Data for Pub. Use, 1965-89; chmn. commn. on flood ins. research NRC, 1979-82, mem. water sci. and tech. bd., 1982-86, mem. commn. on engring. and tech. systems, 1983-86; trustee Ctr. for Research, Inc., Lawrence, 1981-84. Served with AUS, 1943-46, PTO. Recipient Key Meml. award Kans. Engring. Soc., 1966, Outstanding Engr. award Kans. Engring. Soc., 1967, U.S. Geol. Survey Centennial Plaque, 1980, Ray Linsley award Am. Inst. Hydrology, 1990; U. Kans. Miller Prof. Service award 1985, Disting. Alumni Achievement award U. Iowa, 1990, Disting. Engring. Svc. award U. Kans., 1993. Fellow ASCE (past pres. Kans. sect., Julian Hinds award 1988), AAAS; mem. Nat. Acad. Engring. (elected 1975), NSPE, Kans. Engring. Soc., Am. Water Works Assn., Am. Geophys. Union, Am. Soc. Engring. Edn., Am. Inst. Hydrology (Ray K. Linsley award 1991), Pres.'s Club U. Iowa, Chancellors Club U. Kansas, Masons, Sigma Xi, Delta Chi, Theta Tau, Tau Beta Pi, Chi Epsilon. Republican. Congregationalist. Home: Lawrence Kans. Died Dec. 9, 1995.

SMITH, ROBERT WESTON See WOLFMAN JACK

SMITH, VICTOR EARLE, economist, educator; b. Lansing, Mich., Apr. 9, 1914; s. Earle Baker and Isabelle (Emery) S.; m. E. Margaret French, Nov. 29, 1940; children—David, Michael. A.B., Mich. State Coll., 1935, M.A., 1936; Ph.D., Northwestern U., 1940. Instr. econs. Northwestern U., Evanston, Ill., 1940-42; asst. prof. econs. Yale, 1942-44, Wellesley (Mass.) Coll., 1944-47, Brown U., Providence, R.I., 1947-48; asso. prof. econs. Mich. State U., East Lansing, 1948-53; prof. econs. Mich. State U., 1953-84, prof. foods nutrition, 1963, chmn. dept. econs., 1974-76, prof. emeritus, 1984-95; vis. prof. econs. U. Mich., Ann Arbor, 1963; cons., U.S. Aid Tunisia, 1974, Sierra Leone, 1985, Rwanda, 1986-87. Author: Electronic Computation of Human Diets, 1964, Efficient Resource Use for Tropical Nutrition: Nigeria, 1975; Contbr. articles in field to profl. jours. research grantee Inst. Internat. Agr., 1970; research grantee AID, 1978-81; research grantee study Nigerian rural devel. Midwest Univs. Consortium Internat. Activities, East Lansing, 1966-68; Fund Advancement Edn. faculty fellow, 1954-55; Ford Found. research fellow, 1958-59; NSF research grantee, 1965-67; Rockefeller Found. research grantee, 1968-70. Mem. Am. Econ. Assn., Midwest Econ. Assn., Mich. Acad. Arts Sci., AAUP. Home: Holt Mich. Died July 12, 1995.

SMITH, WARREN BRIERLEY, JR., publishing company executive; b. Binghamton, N.Y., May 26, 1919; s. Warren Brierley and Mary Isabel (Clark) S.; m. Beatrice C. Noehren, Oct. 6, 1942; children: Warren Brierley, Alison Nancy Noehren, David Addison. B.S. in Econs, Wharton Sch., U. Pa., 1940. With Vick Chem. Co., 1940-42, 46-56; engaged in account mgmt. and service Compton Advt., Inc., N.Y.C., 1956-60; v.p. P.F. Collier Co., 1960-62; dir. marketing Crowell-Collier Pub. Co. (now Macmillan, Inc.), 1961-62, v.p., 1962-66, sr. v.p., 1966-67, exec. v.p., 1967-75; dir., 1962-75, sr. v.p., 1975-82; pres. LaSalle Extension U., 1962-68, 71-75, P.F. Collier, Inc., 1980-81, Crowell Internat., 1980-81. Trustee Nat. Home Study Council, bd. dirs., 1962-69, 72-75, pres., 1968, 69; bd. dirs. Westport Transit Dist., Conn., 1981-95, chmn., 1983-95; bd. dirs. Y's Men of Westport, 1983-95, pres., 1985-86; chmn. Westport Little League, 1956-62. Served with AUS, 1943-46. Mem. Beta Gamma Sigma, Pi Gamma Mu, Delta Kappa Epsilon. Home: Westport Conn. Died Nov. 26, 1994.

SMITH, WILBUR COWAN, lawyer; b. Aledo, Ill., July 16, 1914; s. Fred Harold and Anna Elizabeth (Cowan) S.; m. Teressa Phyllis Stout, Sept. 10, 1938; children: Roger Allen, Judith Ellen Smith Adams; m. Florence Ann Mackie, June 21, 1964; 1 dau., Donna Lee Pinkes; step-children: Diane Marie Linhart, Wayne Douglas Griffith, Nancy Ann LaFraugh. Student Colo. U., 1932-33, N.Mex. U., 1933; BA, U. Iowa, 1937; JD, Creighton U., 1954. Bar: Nebr. 1954, U.S. Dist. Ct. Nebr. 1954, U.S. Ct. Appeals (8th cir.) 1974. Salesman Gen. Foods Corp., 1939; civilian chemist U.S. Naval Ordnance, 1942-45; mgr. Omar Flour Mills, 1945-47; account exec. C.A. Swanson & Sons, 1948-49; dist. mgr. Brown-Forman Distillery, 1950-51; adminstrv. asst. to judge Douglas County, 1954-55; asst. city prosecutor Omaha, 1956; sole practice, Omaha, 1956-73; ptnr. Smith & Hansen, Omaha, 1973-93. Pres., North High Sch. PTA, 1959-61, Belvedere Sch., 1954-56, Oak Valley, 1965-67; mem. bldg. com. YMCA, 1954-56; membership com. Boy Scouts Am., 1956-61; county del. Republican Party, 1962-92. Mem. ABA, Nebr. Bar Assn., Omaha Bar Assn., Am. Judicature Soc., Phi Alpha Delta. Methodist. Clubs: Odd Fellows, Masons, Shriners, United Comml. Travelers Protective Assn., Order Eastern Star. Died Sept. 5, 1993. Home: Omaha Nebr.

SMITHSON, ALISON MARGARET, architect, writer; b. Sheffield, Eng., June 22, 1928; d. Ernest Gill and Alison Jessie (Malcolm) G.; m. Peter Denham Smithson, 1949; 3 children. Ed., Sunderland, South Shields, George Watson's Ladies Coll., Edinburgh, U. Durham. Asst. London County Council, 1949-50; pvt. practice architecture with Peter Smithson, 1950-93. Prin. works include Hunstanton Sch., Economist Bldg., London, Robin Hood Gardens, G.L.C. Housing in Tower Hamlets, Garden Bldg. St. Hilda's Coll., Oxford, Arts Barn U. Bath, Small Works, furniture, Fed. Republic Germany; exhbns. include Twenty-four Doors to Christmas, 1979, Christmas and Hogmanay, 1980-81; author: The Tram Rats, The Christmas Tree, Calendar of Christmas, Places Worth Inheriting, An Anthology of Christmas, An Anthology of Scottish Christmas and Hogmanay, Team 10 Primer, Euston Arch; AS in DS, An Eye on the Road, Upper Lawn, Solar Pavilion Folly, St. Jerome: The Study, The Desert, Team 10 Meetings, (novel) Young Girl, (novel) Imprint of India), (with P. Smithson) Urban Structuring Studies, Ordinariness and Light, Without Rhetoric, The Heroic Period of Modern Architecture, The Shift: Monograph, The 1930s, Changing the Art of Inhabitation. Home: London Eng. Died Aug. 14, 1993.

SMOLUCHOWSKI, ROMAN, physicist, emeritus educator; b. Zakopane, Austria, Aug. 31, 1910; came to U.S., 1935, naturalized, 1946; s. Marian and Sophia (Baraniecka) S.; m. Louise Catherine Riggs, Feb. 3, 1951; children: Peter, Irene. MA, U. Warsaw, 1933; PhD, U. Groningen, Holland, 1935. Mem. Inst. Advanced Study, Princeton, 1935-36, instr., research asso. physics dept., 1939-41;; research assoc., head physics sect. Inst. Metals, Warsaw, 1936-39; research physicist Gen. Electric Research Labs., Schenectady, 1941-46; assoc. prof., staff Metals Research Lab., Carnegie Inst. Tech., 1946-50, prof. physics and metall. engring., 1950-56, prof. physics, 1956-60; prof. solid state scis., head solid state and materials Princeton U., 1960-78; prof. astronomy and physics U. Tex., Austin, 1978-96; vis. prof. Internat. Sch. Solid State Physics, Mol, Belgium, 1963, Facultédes Sciences, Paris, 1965-66; lectr. Sch. Planetary Physics, Super-Besse, France, 1972; Fulbright prof. U. Sorbonne-Paris, 1955-56; lectr. Internat. Sch. Solid State Physics, Varenna, Italy, 1957, U. Liège, Belgium, 1956, Faculté des Scis., Paris, 1965-66; vis. prof. NRC of Brazil, 1958-59, Tech. U. Munich, 1974; mem. solid state panel Research and Devel. Bd., Dept. Def., 1949, sec. panel, 1950-61; mem. tech. adv. bd. Aircraft Nuclear Propulsion, 1950; chmn com. on magnetism Office Naval Research, 1952-56; chmn. com. on solids NRC, 1950-61, chmn. solid state scis. panel, 1961-67, chmn. div. phys. scis., 1969-75; mem. space sci. bd. Nat. Acad. Scis., 1969-75, mem. physics survey, 1963-66, 1969-72; adv. com. metallurgy Oak Ridge Nat. Lab., 1960-62, mem. com. on planetary and lunar exploration, 1980-84. Author: (with Mayer and Weyl) Phase Transformations in Nearly Perfect Crystals, 1952, (with others) Molecular Science and Molecular Engineering, 1959, The Solar System—Sun, Planets and Life, 1983; editor: (with N. Kurti) Monograph Series on Solid State, 1957, (with J. W. Wilkins and E. Burstein) Comments in Condensed Matter Physics, (with M. Glazer) Phase Transitions; (with others) Ices in the Solar System, The Galaxy and the Solar System, Radiation Effects and Defects in Solids; editor-in-chief: Crystal Lattice Defects and Amorphous Materials; assoc. editor: Fundamentals of Cosmic Physics; contbr. articles to profl. jours. Chmn. bd. trustees Simon's Rock Coll., 1971-72. Guggenheim Meml. fellow, 1974; fellow Churchill Coll. Cambridge U., Eng., 1974. Fellow Am. Phys. Soc. (chmn. div. solid state physics 1944-46), Am. Acad. Arts and Scis.; mem. AAAS, Internat. Astron. Union, Finnish Acad. Scis. and Letters, Am. Astron. Soc., Mex. Acad. Engring., Brazilian Acad. Scis., Sigma Xi, Alpha Sigma Mu, Pi Mu Epsilon. Home: Austin Tex. Died Jan. 12, 1996.

SMUCK, HAROLD VERNON, retired minister, religious organization administrator; b. Huntington, Ind., Oct. 12, 1920; s. Vaughn M. and Elsie J. (Whiteman) S.; m. Evelyn May Sutton, Aug. 27, 1944; children: Norman, Amelia, Vernon. BRE, Ind. Wesleyan U., 1943; BD, Christian Theol. Sem., 1946; MA, Earlham Coll., 1950. Ordained to ministry Friends United Meeting, 1940. Missionary, pastor, youth sec. Friends United Meeting, 1957-66; sec. World Ministries Commn. Friends United Meeting, Richmond, Ind., 1966-81, Ministry Team leader W. Richmond, 1982-86; clk. Friends World Com. (sect. of the Ams.), Phila., 1989-92, Friends United Meeting, 1993-95. Author: I Do Not Climb This Mountain Alone, 1986, Friends in East Africa, 1987; contbr. articles to jours. in field. Home: Richmond Ind. Died Aug. 23, 1995.

SMULLIN, WILLIAM BROTHERS, radio, televison, cable and newspaper executive; b. Kane, Pa., May 6, 1907; s. William Carrier and Clara E. (Brothers) S.; m. Patricia Duell, Jan. 1, 1945; children—Shirley Lou, William David, Carol Anne, Donald Evan, Patricia Clara. B.A. in Polit. Sci., Willamette U.; postgrad., Harvard U., UCLA, Humboldt State U. V.p., dir. Calif. Oreg. TV, Inc.; founder, sec. Calif. Oreg. Broadcasting; mng. ptnr. Calif. Oreg. Broadcasting Investments, Medford, Oreg., 1933-84; past TV dir. CBS-TV Adv. Bd.; past dir. Oreg. Cable Communications Assn. Past bd. dirs. Humboldt County Fair Bd., Calif., Boy Scouts Am.; past pres. Camp Fire Girls, Humboldt County; mem. adv. bd. U.S. Forestry, Calif.; ch. vestry, sr. warden Episcopal Ch., Humboldt County. Served as communications officer, Calif. State Guard, 1942-44. Recipient Alumni citation Willamette U., 1982; Tom McCall award Oreg. Assn. Broadcasters, 1979; Nat. Gulich award Camp Fire Girls, Paul Harris award Rotary, Presdl. award Oreg. Cable Communications Assn. Mem. IEEE, Am. Forestry Assn., Eureka C. of C. (past pres. bd. dirs.), Nat. Aviation Club, Nat. Assn. Broadcasters (past bd. dirs., Disting. Svc. award, 1990), Calif. Assn. Broadcasters (past pres., bd. dirs.), Sigma Delta Chi. Republican. Clubs: Press and Union, Bohemian, Commonwealth (San Francisco); Ingomar (Eureka); University (Medford). Lodges: Masons, Shriners, Eastern Star. Home: Medford Oreg. Died Jan. 5, 1995.

SNELL, FRANK LINN, lawyer; b. Kansas City, Mo., Dec. 23, 1899; s. Frank Linn and Marie Louise (Genult) S.; m. Elizabeth S. Berlin, Aug. 3, 1927 (dec.); children—Richard B., Kathryn L. LL.B., Kans. U., 1924. Bar: Ariz. 1924. Practiced in Phoenix, from 1927; sr. mem. firm Snell & Wilmer, from 1934; past dir., chmn. bd. Ariz. Pub. Service Co. Chmn. dedication Phoenix Civic Plaza, 1972; past chmn. Phoenix Civic Center Mgmt. Bd.; past chmn. bd., past dir. Am. Grad. Sch. Internat. Mgmt.; hon. bd. dirs. Samaritan Health Services. Recipient Disting. Service award U. Kans., 1964, Disting. Alumnus citation, 1973; Man of Year award Phoenix Advt. Club, 1966; Disting. Achievement award Coll. Bus. Adminstrn., Ariz. State U., 1977; named Disting. Eagle Scout, Boy Scouts Am., 1984, to Ariz. Bus. Hall of Fame, 1987. Mem. Phoenix C. of C. (pres. 1934), Ariz. Nat. Livestock Show Inc. (past pres.), Am., Ariz. bar assns., Internat. Solar Energy Soc. (hon. dir.), Phoenix Fine Arts Assn. (past pres.), Am. Mgmt. Assn. (life). Republican. Presbyterian. Clubs: Phoenix Kiwanis (past pres.), Paradise Valley Country (past pres.). Home: Paradise Valley Ariz. Deceased.

SNELL, GEORGE DAVIS, geneticist, researcher; b. Bradford, MA, Dec. 19, 1903; s. Cullen Bryant and Katharine (Davis) S.; m. Rhoda Carson, July 28, 1937; children: Thomas Carleton, Roy Carson, Peter Garland. B.S., Dartmouth Coll., 1926; M.S., Harvard U., 1928, Sc.D., 1930; M.D. (hon.), Charles U., Prague, 1967; LL.D. (hon.), Colby Coll., 1982; Sc.D. (hon.), Dartmouth Coll., 1974, Gustavus Adolphus Coll., 1981, U. Maine, 1981, Bates Coll., 1982, Ohio State U., 1984. Instr. zoology Dartmouth Coll., 1929-30, Brown U., 1930-31; asst. prof. Washington U., St. Louis, 1933-34; rsch. assoc. Jackson Lab., 1935-73, sci. adminstr., 1949-50, sr. staff scientist, 1957-73, sr. staff scientist emeritus, 1973-96. Author: Search for a Rational Ethic, 1988, (with others) Histocompatibility, 1976; also sci. papers in field; editor: The Biology of the Laboratory Mouse, 1941. Recipient Bertner Found. award in field cancer research, 1962; Griffin award Animal Care Panel, 1962; career award Nat. Cancer Inst., 1964-68; Gregor Mendel medal Czechoslovak Acad. Scis., 1967; Internat. award Gairdner Found., 1976; Wolf Found. prize in medicine, 1978; award Nat. Inst. Arthritis and Infectious Disease-Nat. Cancer Inst., 1978; Nobel prize in medicine (with Dausset and Benacerraf), 1980; NRC fellow U. Tex., 1931-33; NIH health research grantee for study genetics and immunology of tissue transplantation, 1950-73 (allergy and immunology study sect. 1958-62); Guggenheim fellow, 1953-54. Mem. Nat. Acad. Scis., Transplantation Soc., Am. Acad. Arts and Sci., French Acad. Scis. (fgn. asso.), Am. Philos. Soc., Brit. Transplantation Soc. (hon.), Phi Beta Kappa. Home: Bar Harbor Maine Died June 6, 1996.

SNYDER, GUY MAXWELL, photographer; b. Maysville, Mo., Dec. 5, 1899; s. Cornelius Edward and Minnie Irena (Dubbs) S.; m. Myrtle Hampton, July 10 1921; (dec.) 1 child, Aileen Yuille; m. Mary Alice Dexheimer, Dec. 31, 1952; children: Giana Marie Andrews, Aric Nelson. Student, Cen. Bus. Coll., Sedalia Mo., 1919, Kansas City (Mo.) Jr. Coll., 1924. Owner Inter State Studio, Sedalia, 1934. Mem. Profl Photographers Am. Home: Sedalia Mo.

NYDER, JAMES G. (JIMMY THE GREEK) SYNODINOS DIMETRIOS GEORGOS), ddsmaker, columnist; b. Steubenville, Ohio, 1918; narried); 3 children. Former gambler, oddsmaker; ow syndicated columnist with News Am.; founder mmy the Greek Snyder-Pub. Relations; sports analyst 'BS-TV.; appears on NFL Today Show. Author: mmy the Greek, 1975; syndicated columnist. Media ampaign chairperson Nat. Cystic Fibrosis Found.; hairperson N.C. Cystic Fibrosis Found. Home: New 'ork N.Y. Died April 21, 1996.

NYDER, JOHN MENDENHALL, medical adminis-rator, retired thoracic surgeon; b. Slatington, Pa., Aug. , 1909; s. James Wilson and Gertrude Winifred Mendenhall) S.; m. Betty June Wiltrout, Feb. 14, 1942 lec. May 1991); children: Sue Anne Snyder-Alexy, ohn Sanford. BS in Biology, Bucknell U., 1930; MD, J. Pa., 1934; MS in Surgery, U. Minn., 1941. Diplo-nate Am. Bd. Surgery, Am. Bd. Thoracic Surgery. Rotating intern Bryn Mawr (Pa.) Hosp., 1934-35; asst. esident in medicine Univ. Hosps. of Cleve.-Western Res. U., 1935-36; fellow in surgery Mayo Clinic, Rochester, Minn., 1936-41; practiced thoracic surgery 'a., 1945-77; emeritus asst. chief surg. svc., in charge horacic surgery St. Luke's Hosp., Bethlehem, Pa., 1945-7; med. dir. Bur. of Health, Bethlehem, 1981-95; ormerly on staff St. Luke's Hosp., Sacred Heart Mt. 'rexler San.; formerly thoracic surg. cons. Sacred Heart Hosp., Allentown, Pa., Allentown State Hosp., Easton Pa.) Hosp., Gnaden Huetten Hosp., Lehighton, Pa., Muhlenberg Med. Ctr., Bethlehem. Contbr. articles to rofl. jours. Dir. med. sect. Bethlehem CD; mem. Bethlehem Air Pollution Coun.; chmn. Lehigh Valley Med. Adv. Com.; chmn. case finding com. Lehigh Valley TB and Health Assn., pres., 1978-80. Lt. col. J.S. Army, 1942-45, ETO, Col. USAR, 1945-58. Decorated Silver Star, Legion of Merit, Bronze Star. Mem. Masons. Republican. Episcopalian. Home: Lehigh Valley Pa. Died Jan. 15, 1995.

SNYDER, LOUIS LEO, historian, emeritus educator; . Annapolis, Md., July 4, 1907; s. Max and Mollie Faingolos) S.; m. Ida Mae Brown, June 26, 1936. BA, t. John's Coll., 1928; PhD, U. Frankfurt-am-Main, Germany, 1932. Jacob Schiff fellow polit. sci. Columbia J., N.Y.C., 1931-32; spl. corr. from Germany Paris edit. N.Y. Herold-Tribune, 1928-31; mem. faculty CCNY, 1933-77, prof. history, 1953-77, prof. PhD program, 1965-77, prof. history emeritus, 1977-93; vis. lectr. Columbia U., N.Y.C., 1962; Fulbright vis. prof. U. Co-ogne, W. Germany, 1975; Rockefeller scholar Villa Serbelloni, Bellagio, Lake Como, Italy, 1979; cons. psychol. warfare br. War Dept., WWII; hon. dir. N.Y. Tchrs. Pension Assn., 1987. Author: Die persoenlichen und politischen Beziehungen Bismarcks zu Amerikanern, 1932, Race: A History of Modern Ethnic Theories, 1939, German Nationalism: The Tragedy of a People, 1952, The Meaning of Nationalism, 1954, The Age of Reason, 1955, The War: A Concise History, 1939-45, 1961, The Dynamics of Nationalism, 1964, The Making of Modern Man, 1967, The Blood and Iron Chancellor, 1967, The New Nationalism, 1968, Frederick the Great, 1970, Great Turning Points in History, 1971, The Dreyfus Affair, 1971, The Dreyfus Case: A Docu-mentary History, 1973 (Anisfield-Wolf award), Varieties of Nationalism: A Comparative History, 1976, McGraw-Hill Ency. of the Third Reich, 1976; Roots of German Nationalism, 1978, Hitler's Third Reich: A Documentary History, 1982, Global Mini-Nationalisms: Autonomy or Independence, 1982, Louis L. Snyder's Historical Guide to World War II, 1982 (History Book Club selection), National Socialist Germany, 1984, Macro-Nationalisms: A History of the Pan-Movements, 1984, Diplomacy in Iron: The Life of Herbert von Bis-marck, 1985, The Third Reich, 1933-45; A Bib-liographical Guide to German National Socialism, 1987, Hitler's Elite, 1989, Hitler's German Enemies, 1990, Encyclopedia of Nationalism, 1990, Contemporary Na-tionalisms, 1992; co-author: (with R.B. Morris) A Treasury of Great Reporting, 1949; gen. editor: Anvil Van Nostrand-Krieger series of 145 original paperbacks in history and social scis.; assoc. editor: Intellect, 1974-77; mem. editorial bd. Can. Rev. Studies in Nationalism, 1973-93; contbr. articles and revs. to profl. jours. Mem. council Am. Com. on History WWII, 1973-93; bd. dirs. Copyright Clearance Ctr., 1977-93. Served as 1st lt. USAAF, 1943-44. Recipient Alumni award of merit St. John's Coll., Annapolis, Md., 1969; recipient N.J. Writers Conf. citation, 1974, 75, 84, 86, 93; fellow German-Am. Exchange, 1928-29; Ford Found. faculty fellow, 1952-53; Rockefeller Found. grantee, 1965-66; von Humboldt Found. grantee, 1972, 79; named to N.J. Literary Hall of Fame, 1987. Mem. PEN, Am. Arbi-tration Assn. (panelist), Am. Hist. Assn., AAUP, Authors Guild (mem. nat. council 1973-90, bd. dirs., Authors Guild Fund, 1992), Assn. Former German-Am. Exchange Fellows, Ret. Officers Assn., Conf. Group on German Politics, Fulbright Alumni Assn., Phi Beta Kappa, Delta Omicron, Delta Tau Kappa. Home: Princeton N.J. Died Nov. 25, 1993.

SOGIN, HAROLD HYMAN, mechanical engineering educator; b. Chgo., Dec. 14, 1920; s. Samuel and Sadie S.; m. Ruth Joy Reinberg, Dec. 26, 1946; children: Sarah, David W., Cecilia, Daniel. BS in Mech. Engr-ing., Ill. Inst. Tech., 1943, MS, 1950, PhD, 1952. Asst. prof. mech. engring. Ill. Inst. Tech., 1953-55; asst. prof., then assoc. prof. Brown U., 1955-60; prof. mech. engr-ing., chmn. dept. Tulane U., 1978-90, prof. emeritus, 1990-94; cons. in field. Co-editor: Proc. 10th Southeas-tern Seminar Thermal Sciences, 1974. Served with USNR, 1944-46. Grantee NSF, 1962-64, 69-71, 72-75; Grantee NSF Tulane U. Research Council, 1965-66. Fellow AAAS; mem. ASME, Sigma Xi. Jewish. Home: New Orleans La. Died Jan. 23, 1993.

SOILEAU, LOUIS CLAUDMIRE, III, retired oil company executive, consultant; b. Rayne, La., Mar. 7, 1919; s. Louis Claudmire and Marie Blanche (Gaudet) S.; m. Clara Virginia Fremaux, Mar. 7, 1942; children: Mary Blanche Soileau Vehlewald, Louis Claudmire IV, Clara Virginia Soileau Acker. B.S., La. State U., 1941. Roughneck, roustabout, engr. Calif. Co., La., 1945-46, tool pusher, 1947; engr., pioneer in offshore drilling Gulf of Mexico, 1948-50; exec. Richmond Exploration Co., Venezuela, 1950-58, Chevron Oil Co., 1958-77; sr. v.p. Chevron U.S.A., Inc., San Francisco, 1977-84; v.p. Standard Oil Calif., 1981-84. Mem. Outer Continental Shelf Policy Com. Served as maj. U.S. Army, 1941-45, PTO. Decorated Bronze Star; named to Engring. Hall of Distinction, Coll. Engring. of La. State U., 1989. Mem. Am. Petroleum Inst., U.S. C. of C., Mid Con-tinent Oil and Gas Assn., Nat. Ocean Industries Assn. (founding dir.), La. State U. Alumni Fedn. Democrat. Roman Catholic. Home: Rayne La. Died July 13, 1993; buried St. Joseph Cemetary, Rayne, L.A.

SOLANDT, OMOND MCKILLOP, research scientist; b. Winnipeg, Man, Can., Sept. 2, 1909; s. Donald McKillop and Edith (Young) S.; m. Elizabeth McPhedran, Jan. 25, 1941; children: Sigrid, Andrew, Katharine; m. Vaire Pringle, 1972. B.A., U. Toronto, Ont., Can., 1931, M.A., 1933, M.D., 1936, LL.D., 1954; M.A., Cambridge U., Eng., 1939; D.Sci., U. B.C., Can., 1947, Laval U., Can., 1948, U. Man., Can., 1950, McGill U., Can., 1951, St. Francis Xavier U., 1956, Royal Mil. Coll., 1966, U. Montreal, Can., 1967; LL.D., Dalhousie U., Can., 1952, Sir George Williams U., Can., 1966, U. Sask., Can., 1968; D.Eng., U. Waterloo, Can., 1968. Intern Toronto Gen. Hosp., 1937-38; lectr. physiology Cambridge U., Eng., 1939; dir. S.W. London Blood Supplay Depot, 1940; dir. physiol. lab. Armored Fighting Vehicle Sch., 1941; dir. tank sect. Army Oper-ational Rsch. Group, 1942, dep. supt., 1943; supt., 1943; mem. joint mission to evaluate effects atomic bomb U.S. Mil., 1945; chmn. Def. Research Bd., 1946-56; v.p. research and devel. Canadian Nat. Ry., 1957-63; v.p. research and devel., dir. de Havilland Aircraft of Can. Ltd., Huyck Corp., Wake Forest, N.C., 1966-80; chmn. Sci. Council of Can., 1966-72; chancellor U. Toronto, 1965-71; pub. gov. Toronto Stock Exchange, 1971-76; sci. adv. bd. Northwest Territories, chmn., 1975-81; rsch. advisor to the Royal Commn. on the Ocean Ranger Marine Disaster, St. John's, Newfoundland, 1981-85; mgmt. cons. Consultative Group for Internat. Agrl. Research, World Bank, Washington, 1983-84, 87; cons. NSF, Antarctic, 1969 (Svc. medal). Served as col. Canadian Army, 1944-46. Decorated Order of Brit. Empire, 1946, Medal of Freedom with bronze palm, U.S.; Companion Order of Can., 1970; recipient Gold medal U. Toronto, 1936, Profl. Inst. of Can., 1956; Vanier medal Inst. Pub. Adminstrn. Can., 1975; Canadian Operational Research Soc. award of merit, 1983, N.W. Territories, Commnr.'s award, 1983, C.D. Howe award Can. Aeronautics & Space Inst., 1988. Fellow Royal Soc. Can., Royal Coll. Physicians (London); mem. Internat. Ctr. for Insect Physiology and Ecology (bd. govs. 1977-83, chmn. 1983), Internat. Ctr. Diarrhoeal Diseases Research (bd. trustees 1979-82). Canadian Inst. for Radiation Safety (bd. trustees 1982-85), Engring. Inst. Can. (hon.), Can. Physiol. Soc., Can. Operational Research Soc. (pres. 1958-60), Internat. Centre Agrl. in the Dry Areas (bd. trustees 1976-81), Internat. Cetre for Wheat and Maize Improvement (bd. trustees 1976-86). United Ch. of Can. Home: Bolton Can. Died May 12, 1993.

SOLOMON, JOEL MARTIN, retired professional society administrator; b. Malden, Mass., Dec. 25, 1932; m. Carol Natalie Levine, June 5, 1960 (div. 1983); chil-dren: Elaina Raquel, April Monique, Elissa Danielle; m. Eileen Mary Murphy, Feb. 24, 1984. BS, Boston Coll., 1953; SM, Johns Hopkins U., 1957; PhD, U. Wis., 1963. Dir. immunohematology Biologics Standards div. NIH, Bethesda, Md., 1957-60; rsch. fellow ARC, L.A., 1963-64; dir. lab. tng. ARC, Washington, 1964-67; blood bank dir. Bklyn.-Cumberland Med. Ctr., 1967-70; blood products mktg. dir. E. R. Squibb & Sons, Princeton, N.Y., 1970-73; dep. dir., dir. Blood & Blood Products div. FDA, Bethesda, 1974-81; various positions NIH, Bethesda, 1981-88; exec. dir. Am. Assn. Blood Banks, Bethesda, 1991-94. Capt. USPHS, 1957-91. Home: North Potomac Md. Died Dec. 27, 1995.

SOLOMON, RICHARD LESTER, retired psychology educator; b. Boston, Oct. 2, 1918; s. Frank and Rose (Roud) S.; children by previous marriage—Janet Ellen, Elizabeth Grace. AB, Brown U., 1940, MSc, 1942, PhD, 1947, ScD (hon.), 1990. Instr. psychology Brown U., 1946; asst. prof. Harvard U., Cambridge, Mass., 1947-50, assoc. prof., 1950-57, prof. social psychology, 1957-60; prof. psychology U. Pa., Phila., 1960-74, James M. Skinner Univ. prof. sci., 1975-85, prof. emeritus, 1985—; staff OSRD, 1942-45. Mem. AAAS, NAS, Am. Psychol. Assn., Ea. Psychol. Assn. (pres.), Psychonomic Soc. (chmn. governing bd.), Am. Acad. Arts and Scis., Soc. Exptl. Psychologists, Phi Beta Kappa, Sigma Xi. Home: Bartlett N.H. Died Oct. 12, 1995.

SOLT, LEO FRANK, historian, educator; b. Waterloo, Iowa, Oct. 12, 1921; s. Harry E. and Mabel L. (Schneider) S.; m. Mary Ellen Bottom, Dec. 22, 1946; children: Catherine, Susan. B.A., Iowa State Tchrs. Coll., 1943; postgrad., Harvard U., 1943-44; M.A., State U. Iowa, 1948; Ph.D., Columbia U., 1955. Instr. dept. history U. Mass., Amherst, 1952-55; asst. prof. dept. history Ind. U., Bloomington, 1955-60; asso. prof. Ind. U., 1960-64, prof., 1964-94; dean Ind. U. (Grad. Sch.), 1978-87; vis. lectr. U. Wis., summer 1960, Moray House Sch. Edn., Edinburgh, Scotland, summers 1972, 74; mem. nat. selection com. Mellon Grad. Fellowships in the Humanities, 1982-94. Author: Saints in Arms: Puritanism and Democracy in Cromwell's Army, 1959, Church and State in Early Modern England (1509-1640), 1990; contbr. articles on English history to scho-larly jours., book revs. to lit. jours. Served to lt. USNR, 1943-46. Lydia Roberts Traveling fellow, 1951; Gug-genheim fellow, 1961; Folger Library fellow, 1966; Huntington Library fellow, 1967, 79. Mem. Am. Hist. Assn. (v.p. research 1975, chmn. documentary and TV films com. 1970-74), Am. Soc. Ch. History, Indiana Assn. Grad. Schs. (pres. 1987-88), Midwest Assn. of Grad. Schs. (pres. 1983-84), Midwest Conf. Brit. Studies (pres. 1968-70). Home: Bloomington Ind. Died Apr. 18, 1994; cremated.

SOLURSH, MICHAEL, biology educator, researcher; b. L.A., Dec. 22, 1942; s. Louis and Helen (Schwartz) S.; m. Victoria R. Raskin, Mar. 21, 1964; 1 child, Elizabeth. BA, UCLA, 1964; PhD, U. Wash., 1969. Asst. prof. U. Iowa, Iowa City, 1969-73, assoc. prof., 1973-79, prof., 1979—. Mem. Am. Soc. Zoologists (program officer 1990-93), Soc. for Developmental Bi-ologists, Am. Assn. Anatomists (program chairperson 1992-93), Tissue Culture Assn., Am. Soc. for Cell Bi-ology.

SOMMERFELD, RAYNARD MATTHIAS, accounting educator; b. Sibley, Iowa, Aug. 10, 1933; s. Ernest Robert and Lillian Emma (Matthias) S.; m. Barbara Ann Spear, June 9, 1956; children: Andrea Joan, Kristin Elaine. B.S.C., U. Iowa, 1956, M.A., 1957, Ph.D., 1963. Asst. prof. Grad. Sch. Bus., U. Tex., Austin, 1963-66; asso. prof. Grad. Sch. Bus., U. Tex., 1966-68, prof., 1968-72, Arthur Young prof., 1972-76; partner Arthur Young & Co., C.P.A.s, 1976-78; John A. White prof. accounting U. Tex., Austin, 1978-83, Glenn Welsch prof., 1983-84, James Bayless/Rauscher Pierce Refsnes prof., 1984-93, prof. emeritus, 1993-95; mem. Acctg. Edn. Change Com., 1989-92, CPA exam. rev. bd., 1992-95/. Author: Tax Reform and the Alliance for Progress, 1966, (with H. Anderson and H. Brock) An Introduction to Taxation, 1969, rev. edits., 1972, 76-91, (with G.F. Streuling) Tax Research Techniques, 1976, rev. edits., 1981, 89, The Dow Jones-Irwin Guide to Tax Planning, 1974, rev. edits., 1978, 81, Federal Taxes and Management Decisions, 1974 rev. edits., 1978, 81, 83, 85, 87, 89, (with S. Jones), 91, 93, 94, (with H. Anderson, H. Brock, J. Everett) HBJ Federal Tax Course 1984, 1985, 86, Essentials of Taxation, 1990, A Review of Essentials of Taxation, 1990. Served with USAF, 1957-60. Erskine fellow U. Canterbury, New Zealand, 1995. Mem. AICPA, Am. Taxation Assn. (pres. 1975-76, Outstanding Tax Educator award 1993), Tex. Soc. CPAs (bd. dirs. 1969-72, pres. Austin chpt. 1967-68), Am. Acctg. Assn. (pres. 1986-87, Outstanding Acctg. Educator award 1994, Disting. Internat. Vis. Lectr. 1994-95). Lutheran. Home: Austin Tex. Died Aug. 22, 1995.

SOMMERS, ALBERT TRUMBULL, economist, research association executive; b. Milford, Conn., July 30, 1919; s. Robert Edward and Isabel (Faust) S.; m. Jean Marvin Sommers, Dec. 26, 1946; children: Elizabeth, John. A.B., Columbia U., 1939; M.A., N.Y. U., 1949. Ptnr. Boni, Watkins, Jason & Co., N.Y.C., 1947-50; with Conf. Bd., N.Y.C., 1950-94; dir. econ. research Conf. Bd., 1961-72, v.p., 1965-72, sr. v.p., chief economist, 1972-84, sr. fellow, econ. counsellor, 1985-94; pres. Albert T. Sommers & Co., Inc.; econ. adviser Ford Found.; dir. Intercapital Funds, Inc., Grow Group, Inc., Medical Sterilization Inc., Westbridge Capital Corp.; dir. Nat. Bur. Econ. Research; chmn. price adv. com. U.S. Council Wage and Price Stability, 1979-80. Author: The U.S. Economy Demystified, 1985, 3d edit., 1993; editor: The Sommers Letter, 1981-94; contbr. articles to profl. jours. Pres. Port Alert, Inc., Port Washington, N.Y., 1969-71. Served with U.S. Army, 1942-46. Fellow Nat. Assn. Bus. Economists, Internat. Acad. Mgmt.; mem. Am. Econ. Assn., Am. Statis. Assn., Commn. on Law and the Economy. Democrat. Clubs: Univ.; Shelter Rock Tennis. Home: Manhasset N.Y. Died Feb. 20, 1994.

SOMOGYI, JÓZSEF, sculptor, educator; b. Austria, June 9, 1916; s. János and Borbála (Diósy) S.; m. Mária Miske, 1945; children: Mária, Ágnes. Ed., Budapest (Hungary) Coll. Fine Arts, 1941. Tchr. visual arts, 1945-63; prof. Budapest coll. Visual Arts, 1963-93, rector, leading prof. sculpture sect., 1974-87; pres. Assn. Hungarian Artists, 1968-77; mem. Széchenyi-Acad. of Art, 1992-93; lay pres. Hungarian Presbyn. Synod, 1984-92. Exhbns. include World Exhibition, Brussels,

1958 (Grand prize), Venice Biennial, 1971; sculptures include works for civic and cultural bldgs. in Hungary, Austria, Belgium, Poland and Turkey, monuments and sepulchres. Recipient Kossuth prize, 1954, Munkácsy prize, 1956, Merited Artist title, 1966, Eminent Artist title, 1970, Labour Order of Merit, Golden Degree, 1976. Died Jan. 2, 1993.

SOOD, VINOD KUMAR, heavy equipment company executive; b. India, Apr. 24, 1935; m. Lata Sood; 2 sons. BS, Agra U., 1954; CA, India, 1958; SM, MIT, 1964. Various mng. positions Bajaj Elecs. Ltd., 1959-67; with Finning Ltd., 1968-88, v.p. fin., mem. exec. com., 1969-76, exec. v.p., 1976-84, chmn., pres., chief exec. officer, 1984-88, also bd. dirs.; trustee European and Pacific Investment Trust, Toronto; bd. dirs. J.P. Morgan Can. Ltd., Bentall Capital Corp., Conf. Bd. Can. Bd. govs. Bus. Council B.C. Sloan fellow MIT. Clubs: Vancouver, Vancouver Lawn Tennis and Badminton, Can. of Vancouver; Shaughnessy Golf and Country. Home: Vancouver Can. Died Nov. 19, 1988.

SORLING, CARL AXEL, lawyer; b. Moline, Ill., Sept. 13, 1896; s. Jacob Axe and Alma Josephine (Lonnegren) S.; m. Winifred Josephine White, Sept. 15, 1921 (dec. Dec. 1960); 1 dau., Sheila Elizabeth; m. Macon Atnip Johnson, June 4, 1966. LL.B., U. of Mich., 1921, J.D., 1922. Bar: Ill. bar 1922. Engaged in practice of law; now mem. firm Sorling, Northrup, Hanna, Cullen & Cochran. Served as lt., arty. A.E.F., 1917-19. Mem. Am., Ill., Sangamon County, Chgo. bar assns., Alpha Tau Omega, Phi Delta Phi. Lutheran. Clubs: Illini Country (Sprinfield), Sangamo (Sprinfield). Home: Universal City Tex. Deceased.

SÖTÉR, ISTVÁN, novelist literary historian; b. Szeged, Hungary, June 1, 1913; s. István and Jolán (Hreblay) S.; m. Veronika Jasz, 1939. Ed. U. Budapest, 1935, Ecole Normale Supérieure, Paris, 1936; Dr. honoris causa, U. Sorbonne Nouvelle, 1973. Prof. U. Szeged, 1948-52; prof., rector U. Budapest, 1952-83, rector, 1955; dir. Inst. Literary Studies of Hungarian Acad. Scis., 1956-83; rector Lorant Eotvos Univ. Budapest, 1963-66. Author novels and short stories: Walking in the Clouds, 1939, The Robber of the Church, 1942, The Ghost, 1945, The Fall, 1947, The Broken Bridge, 1948, The Eden, 1961, The Lost Lamb, 1974, Bakator, 1976, Tiszta Emma, 1978; Half Circle, 1979; Rings, 1980; author numerous critical essays and hist. monographs. Recipient Kossuth prize, 1954; decorated officier Ordre des Arts et Lettres, banner Order of Hungarian People's Republic. France. Mem. Internat. Comparative Lit. Assn. (pres. 1970-73), Hungarian PEN Club (v.p.), Hungarian Acad. Scis. Home: Budapest Hungary

SOUPHANOUVONG, president of Lao People's Democratic Republic; b. 1902; s. Ouphat Bounkhong. Student engring., Ecole Nat. des Ponts et Chaussees, Paris. Active Nationalist Movement in Laos, 1938—; joined Pathet Lao, fought against French; formed Nationalist Party, Bangkok, 1950; leader patriotic front; minister planning, reconstrn. and urbanism, 1958; arrested, 1959; escaped, 1960, rejoined Pathet Lao forces, became leader; del. Geneva Conf. on Laos, 1961-62; vice premier, min. econ. planning, 1962; absent, then returned, 1974; chmn. Joint Nat. Polit. Council, 1974-75; pres. Lao People's Dem. Republic, 1975-86, 90-91; former pres. Supreme Popular Assembly; mem. politburo, mem. adv. bd. to cen. com. Lao People's Revolutionary Party; chmn. cen. com. Lao Front for Nat. Reconstrn., 1979—, now pres. Recipient Order of Oct. Revolution. Home: Vientiane Laos Died January 9, 1995.

SOWELL, W. R. (BILL SOWELL), aviation company executive; b. Chipley, Fla., Nov. 8, 1920; s. Claude Tee and Eunice (Richardson) S.; student Centenary Coll., 1940-42; grad. Norton Bus. Coll., Shreveport, La., 1942; m. Nadine Martin, Sept. 1942 (div. Feb. 1971); children—J. Donald, Doris Dianne Sowell Preston, Deborah K., Sheri Denise. Owner, pres. Panama Airways, Inc. (now Sowell Aviation Co. Inc.), Panama City, Fla., 1945-53; pilot instr., flying supr. So. Airways, Bainbridge, Ga., 1950-53; founder, prin. owner, chmn. bd. pilot, instr. Sowell Aviation Co., Inc., Panama City, 1954—; chmn. bd. Sowell Aircraft Service, Inc., Panama City, 1964—; founder, pres., owner Pensacola (Fla.) Aviation Inc., 1964-72; airplane and instrument pilot examiner FAA, 1946-79; mem. Panama City Airport Bd., 1959-61, chmn., 1959-61; mem. Fla. Gov.'s Aviation Com., 1972-85, chmn., 1977-79. Served with AC, AUS, 1940-45. Mem. Airplane Owners and Pilots Assn., Quiet Birdmen, Nat. Aviation Transp. Assn., Fla. Aviation Trades Assn. (pres. 1970-72, dir.) Bay County C. of C. (dir. 1956-66, chmn. aviation com. 1962-63). Baptist. Clubs: Rotary, Masons, Shriners, Elks. Died May 20, 1995.

SPADOLINI, GIOVANNI, Italian politician, journalist, educator; b. Florence, Italy, June 21, 1925; s. Guido and Leonella S.; Law degree U. Florence. Writer, Il Messaggero, Rome, 1947-50; polit. editor Gazzetta del Popolo, Turin, Italy, 1950-52, Corriere della Sera, 1955-68; editor Resto del Carlino, 1955-68, Corriere della Sera, 1968-72; prof. contemporary history U. Florence, 1950-94; minister of environ., 1974-76, minister of edn., 1979, prime minister, 1981-82; minister def., 1983-87. Sec., Republican party, 1979-94. Decorated officer Legion of Honor; cavaliere di Gran Groce all'Ordine al Merito della Repubblica; recipient Hemingway Special prize, 1987. Author: Sorel, 1947; Il 1848 realta e leggenda di una rivoluzione, 1948; Ritratto dell' Italia moderna, 1949; Lotta socialein Italia, 1949; Il Papato socialista, 1950; L'opposizione cattolica da Porta Pia al '98, 1954; Giolitti e i cattolici, 1960; I radicali dell'Ottocento, 1962; I repubblicani dopo l'Unita, 1962; Un dissidente del Risorgimento, 1962; Firenze Capitale, 1967; Il Tevere piu largo, 1967; Storia Fiorentina, Carducci nella storia d'Italia; Il Mondodi Giolitti, 1969; Il 20 Settembre nella storia d'Italia, 1971; Autuano del Risorgimento, 1971; L'Italia della Ragione, 1979; L'Italia dei Laici, 1980; Senatore della Repubblica. Died Aug. 5, 1994. Home: Florence Italy

SPAID, JOSEPH SNYDER, banker; b. Syracuse, N.Y., Dec. 22, 1906; s. Clinton A. and Ella (Snyder) S.; m. Mabel Louise Marsh, Sept. 11, 1928; 1 son, Joseph Snyder. Certificate, Am. Inst. Banking, 1930. With City Bank & Trust Co., Syracuse, 1925-29; accountant, auditor Key Bank Central N.Y. (formerly First Trust & Deposit Co.), Syracuse, 1929-33; personnel officer, asst. treas. Key Bank Central N.Y. (formerly First Trust & Deposit Co.), 1943-53, v.p., treas., 1953-60, exec. v.p., 1961-62, dir., 1962-95, pres., 1965-95, chief exec. officer, 1967-95, chmn. bd., 1969-95; cashier, v.p., dir. Citizens Bank, Clyde, N.Y., 1933-43; pres., dir. Key Banks Inc. (formerly First Comml. Banks Inc.), 1972-77, chmn. bd., 1977-80, chmn. exec. com., dir., 1973-95; pres., dir. First Securities Corp.; chmn. Key Trust Co., Albany, N.Y., 1980-82, dir. Mem. Old Erie Canal Park Study Com., 1965-67; chmn. N.Y. State Coll. Forestry Found. Named Man of Year in Syracuse Banking and Finance, 1965; Businessman of Year, 1975; recipient Outstanding Businessman award Syracuse Herald-Jour., Herald-Am., 1975. Mem. Am. Inst. Banking. Episcopalian (former trustee). Clubs: Century (Syracuse); Fair Haven (N.Y.) Yacht; Cavalry (Manlius, N.Y.). Lodge: Masons. Home: Minoa N.Y. Died Nov. 18, 1995.

SPARKS, JACK DAVID, appliance company executive; b. Chgo., Nov. 24, 1922; m. Fredda Sullivan; children: Suzanne, Cinde Marie, Katherine S., Jack David. With Whirlpool Corp., Benton Harbor, Mich., 1940-95, beginning as laborer, successively asst. dir. personnel, sales dept. staff, advt. and promotion mgr., sales mgr., gen. sales mgr., dir. mktg., 1940-59, v.p., 1959-66, group v.p., 1966-77, exec. v.p., 1977-81, vice chmn., chief mktg. officer, from 1981, chmn. bd., chief exec. officer, 1982-87, former pres., dir.; dir. Meredith Corp., Des Moines, Peoples State Bank, St. Joseph, Mich. Formerly chmn. bd. trustees Olivet Coll. Served from pvt. to capt. USAAF, 1941-46. Mem. Mich. Acad. Arts and Scis. Clubs: Racquet (Chgo.); Point O'Woods Golf and Country (Benton Harbor, Mich.). Home: Saint Joseph Mich. Died Dec. 22, 1994.

SPARROW, DONALD, Canadian provincial government official, municipal and farm land assessor and electrician. Student NAIT, SAIT, U. Alberta. Cofounder Sparrow Electric, Ltd., 1960. Chmn. Leduc Recreation Bd.; mem. Province of Alta. Legis. Assembly, Wetaskiwin-Leduc Legis. Assembly, 1982-89; former assoc. minister pub. lands and wildlife, now minister tourism; apptd. minister forestry lands and wildlife, 1986, minister tourism, parks and recreation, 1992. Mem. Leduc C. of C., LIons (pres. 2 terms), Knights of Columbus. Died July 1993. Home: Edmonton Can.

SPEAR, ARTHUR S., toy and game manufacturing company executive; b. 1920. B. in Archtl. Engring., MIT, 1941. Prodn. engr. Artisan Metal Products, 1943-44; prodn. mgr., gen. mgr. Sperry Mfg. Co., 1945-56; plant mgr., gen. mgr. mfg. and distbn. and corp. ops. coordinator Revlon Inc., 1956-64; dir. distbn. Mattel Inc., Hawthorne, Calif., 1964, v.p. ops., 1965, exec. v.p. ops., 1966, pres., 1973, chief exec. officer, 1974, chmn. bd., chief exec. officer, 1978-95, also dir. Served with U.S. Army, 1941-42. Died Dec. 31, 1995. Home: Santa Monica Calif.

SPEARE, ELIZABETH GEORGE, writer; b. Melrose, Mass., Nov. 21, 1908; d. Harry Allan and Demetria (Simmons) George; m. Alden Speare, Sept. 26, 1936; children—Alden, Mary Elizabeth. Student, Smith Coll., 1926-27; A.B., Boston U., 1930, M.A., 1932. Tchr. high sch. English Rockland, Mass., 1933-35, Auburn, Mass., 1935-36. Author: Calico Captive, 1957, The Witch of Blackbird Pond, 1958 (Newbery award), The Bronze Bow, 1961 (Newbery award), Life in Colonial America, 1963, The Prospering, 1967, The Sign of the Beaver, 1983 (Laura Ingalls Wilder award 1989); contbr. articles to mags. Mem. Authors Guild. Home: Tucson Ariz. Died Nov. 14, 1994; buried Union Cemetery, Easton, Conn.

SPECHT, CHARLES ALFRED, business consultant; b. Passaic, N.J., July 30, 1914; s. Alfred F. and Marian A. (Clarke) S.; m. Gertrude A. Morris, Sept. 14, 1940; children: Sara Ann, Sandra Morris. B.B.A., Rutgers U., 1938; postgrad., N.Y. Grad. Sch. Bus. Adminstrn., 1939-40. Clk., bookkeeper Am. Surety Co., N.Y.C., 1933-37; credit analyst Irving Trust Co., 1937-42; staff accountant Price Waterhouse Co., 1942-44; chief accountant DeLaval Steam Turbine Co., Trenton, N.J., 1944-45; works controller Joy Mfg. Co., Franklin, Pa., 1945-50; controller Chas. Pfizer & Co., Inc., Bklyn., 1950-52; dir. Chas. Pfizer & Co., Inc., 1952-55; also pres. Pfizer Internat., fgn. trade subs., 1952-55; fin. analyst Lazard Freres & Co., N.Y.C., 1955-56; pres., dir. Horizons Titanium Corp., 1955-57; v.p., dir. Horizons, Inc., 1955-56; pres., chief exec. officer, dir. Minerals & Chems. Philipp Corp., 1956-63; pres., dir., mem. exec. com. MacMillan Bloedel Ltd., Vancouver, B.C., 1963-68; pres., chief exec. officer, dir., mem. exec. com. Consol. Packaging Corp., Chgo., 1968-73; dir. A.L. Labs Inc.; instr. Rutgers U., 1940-45. Mem. Fin. Execs. Inst. Club: Univ. (N.Y.C.). Home: Bedford N.Y. Died Mar. 19, 1993.

SPELKER, ARNOLD WILLIAM, banker; b. Newark, July 15, 1934; s. William M. and Helen F. (Wilhelm) S.; children: Mark, Scott, Matthew. BS in Acctg., Rutgers U., 1960; MBA, Fairleigh Dickinson U., 1978; postgrad., Harvard U., 1975. CPA, N.J. Sr. acct. KPMG Peat Marwick, N.Y.C., 1960-61; audit supr. Ernst & Young, N.Y.C., 1961-67; dir. op. auditing CBS, Inc., N.Y.C., 1967-70; v.p., asst. controller Chem. Bank, N.Y.C., 1970-81; sr. v.p., CFO U.S. Credit Suisse, N.Y.C., 1981-95; sec., treas. Credit Suisse Investment Corp., Credit Suisse Capital Corp. Mem. parent's adv. coun. Dickinson Coll., 1981-85; mem. pres.'s alumni adv. coun. Fairleigh Dickinson U., 1985-86. Percy H. Johnston scholar Chem. Bank, 1978; recipient Anthony L. Gervino Outstanding Alumni award. Mem. AICPA, N.J. Soc. CPAs, Fin. Execs. Inst. (bd. dirs. 1982-95, pres. N.Y.C. chpt. 1988-89, nat. membership com. 1987-88), Inst. Internat. Bankers (bd. trustees 1986-90), Fairleigh Dickinson U. Alumni Assn. (bd. govs. 1986-90). Home: West New York N.J. Deceased.

SPENCE, HARRY METCALFE, physician, surgeon; b. San Angelo, Tex., Oct. 2, 1905; s. Joseph Jr. and Fannie Lee (Metcalfe) S.; m. Lois G. Ames, Aug. 9, 1940; children: Stephen Ames, Charles Metcalfe. Student, U. Ill.; M.D. cum laude, Harvard, 1930. Diplomate: Am. Bd. Urology. Intern, Free Hosp. for Women, Brookline, Mass., also New Eng. Deaconess Hosp.; surg. and urol. resident Mass. Gen. Hosp., Boston, 1930-34; pvt. practice Ponca City, Okla., 1934-36; urologist, head dept. Dallas Med. and Surg. Clinic, 1936-94; from clin. asst. to clin. prof. urology, past chmn. div. urology Baylor Med. Sch., Southwestern Med. Sch., 1950-94; past chief urology svc. Children's Med. Ctr., Dallas, Parkland Meml. Hosp.; past attending urologist Baylor U. Hosp.; cons. urology to surgeon gen. Brooke Army Hosp., San Antonio. Author numerous sci. papers on urology. Served to comdr. M.C. USNR, 1942-46. Mem. AMA, ACS (regent, past bd. govs.), Am. Assn. Genlto-urinary Surgeons (past pres.), Am. Urol. Assn. (sec., past pres. South Central sect.), Clin. Soc. Genitourinary Surgeons (past pres.), Société Internationale D'Urologie, Brit. Assn. Urol. Surgeons (hon.), Tex. Surg. Soc., Alpha Omega Alpha, Nu Sigma Nu. Club: Corinthian Yacht (Dallas). Home: Dallas Tex. Died May 11, 1994.

SPENCER, JOHN RICHARD, art historian; b. Moline, Ill., Sept. 20, 1923; s. Ora E. and Frances (Lambertson) S.; m. Patricia Ann Brebner, Aug. 12, 1947; children: Stephanie, William, Matthew. B.A., Grinnell Coll., 1947; M.A., Yale U., 1950; Ph.D., 1953; D.F.A. (Hon.), Grinnell Coll., 1972. Mem. faculty Yale U., 1952-57, U. Fla., 1958-62; chmn., dir. Allen Meml Art Mus., Oberlin (Ohio) Coll., 1962-72; dir. mus program Nat. Endowment Arts, Washington, 1972-78 prof., chmn. art dept. Duke U., Durham, N.C., 1978-83 dir. Mus. Art, 1982-86, prof. emeritus, 1993-94. Author: L.B. Alberti on Painting, 1967, Filaete's Treatise on Architecture, 1965, Titian, 1967, Andrea del Castagno and his Patrons, 1991. Served with AUS 1942-45. Decorated Air medal with 3 oakleaf clusters. Fulbright fellow, 1951-52, 56-57; Morse fellow, 1956-57 Nat. Endowment Humanities, sr. fellow, 1967-80; Am Council Learned Socs. grantee, 1950. Mem. Coll. Art Assn., Renaissance Soc. Am. Home: Durham N.C Died July 15, 1994.

SPENDER, SIR STEPHEN K. (HAROLD SPENDER), poet, educator; b. Feb. 28, 1909; s. Edward Harold and Violet Hilda (Schuster) S.; m. Agnes Marie Inez, 1936; m. Natasha Litvin, 1941; 2 children Ed. Oxford U.; D.Litt. (hon.), Montpellier U., Cornell Coll., Loyola U. Co-editor Horizon mag., 1939-41, Encounter, 1953-67; Elliston chair of poetry U. Cin., 1953 Beckman prof. U. Calif., 1959; vis. lectr. Northwestern U., Evanston, Ill., 1963; cons. poetry in English, Library of Congress, Washington, 1965; Clark lectr. Cambridge U., 1966; Mellon lectr., Washington, 1968; Northcliffe lectr. U. London, 1969; pres. English Ctr., PEN Internat., 1975—. Author: 20 Poems; Poems, the Destructive Element, 1934; The Burning Cactus, 1936; Forward from Liberalism, 1937; Trial of a Judge (verse play) 1937; Poems for Spain, 1939; The Still Centre, 1939 Ruins and Visions, 1941; Life and the Poet, 1942; Citizens in War and After, 1945; Poems of Dedication 1946; European Witness, 1946; The Edge of Being, 1949 essay in The God That Failed, 1949; World Within World (autobiography), 1951; Learning Laughter (travels in Israel), 1952; The Creative Element, 1953 Collected Poems, 1954; The Making of a Poem, 1955 Engaged in Writing (stories), 1958; Schiller's Mary ıart (transl.), 1958 (staged at Old Vic 1961); The uggle of the Modern, 1963; Selected Poems, 1965; e Year of the Young Rebels, 1969; The Generous ys (poems), 1971; editor: A Choice of Shelley's Verse, 71; D.H. Lawrence: novelist, poet, prophet, 1973; ve-Hate Relations, 1974; T.S. Eliot, 1975; W.H. ıden: a tribute, 1975; The Thirties and After, 1978; ıth David Hockney) China Diary, 1982; Oedipus Tri-ıgy (transl.), 1983 (staged Oxford Playhouse 1983); ırnals 1939-1982, 1985; Collected Poems 1930-1985, 85; (novel) The Temple, 1988, (poems) Dilphins, 1994. st. Advanced Studies fellow Wesleyan U., 1967; ford U. hon. fellow, 1973; decorated Queen's Gold dal for Poetry, 1971. Mem. Am. Acad. Arts and tters (hon.), Nat. Inst. Arts and Letters (hon.), Phi ta Kappa (hon.). Died 7/16/95. Home: London En-nd

'ERO, STANLEY LEONARD, broadcast executive; Cleve., Oct. 17, 1919; s. Morris B. and Hermine arve) S.; m. Frieda Kessler, June 30, 1946; children: urie, Lisa, Leslie. BS cum laude, U. So. Calif., 1942; stgrad., Cleve. Coll., 1943. Account exec. Sta. HKK, Akron, Ohio, 1946-48, Sta. KFAC, L.A., 48-52; account exec. Sta. KMPC, Hollywood, 1952-v.p., gen. sales mgr., 1953-68, v.p., gen. mgr., 1968-v.p. Golden West Broadcasters. 1978-94; sr. sports ns. Cap Cities, Stas. KMPC and KABC, Hollywood, 94-95. Pres. permanent charities com. entertainment lustry, 1972. With U.S. Maritime Svc., 1942-43. em. So. Calif. Broadcasters Assn. (chmn. 1972), Am. lvt. Fedn. (gov. 1972), Advt. Assn. West, Hollywood of C. (bd. dirs. 1972-90, chmn. bd. dirs. 1985-87), ollywood Advt. Club (bd. dirs. 1972, pres. 1960-61). ome: Encino Calif. Died Oct. 3, 1995.

'ERRY, ROGER WOLCOTT, neurobiologist, edu-tor; b. Hartford, Conn., Aug. 20, 1913; s. Francis B. d Florence (Kraemer) S.; m. Norma G. Deupree, Dec. , 1949; children: Glenn Tad, Jan Hope. AB, Oberlin oll., 1935, M.A., 1937, D.Sc. (hon.), 1982; Ph.D., U. ago., 1941, D.Sc. (hon.), 1976; D.Sc. (hon.), Cam-idge U., 1972, Kenyon Coll., 1979, Rockefeller U., 80; Oberlin Coll., 1982. Rsch. fellow Harvard and erkes Labs., 1941-46; asst. prof. anatomy U. Chgo., 46-52, sect. chief Nat. Inst. Neurol. Diseases of NIH, so asso. prof. psychology, 1952-53; Hixon prof. ychobiology Calif. Inst. Tech., 1954-84, Bd. Trustees of. emeritus, 1984-94; rsch. brain orgn., neuros-cificity, split-brain rsch., hemispheric specialization, nsciousness revolution. Author: Science and Moral iority, 1983, Nobel Prize Conversations, 1985; contbr. ticles to profl. jours. Recipient Oberlin Coll. Alumni ation, 1954, Howard Crosby Warren medal Soc. xptl. Psychologists, 1969, Disting. Sci. Contbn. award n. Psychol. Assn. 1971, Calif. Scientist of Year award alif. Mus. Sci. and Industry, 1972, award Passano ound., 1973, Albert Lasker Basic Med. Rsch. award, 79, co-recipient William Thomas Wakeman Rsch. vard Nat. Paraplegia Found., 1972, Claude Bernard ı. journalism award, 1975, Disting. Rsch. award In-rnat. Visual Literacy Assn., 1979, Wolf Found. prize medicine, 1979, Nobel prize in physiology or edicine, 1981, Realia award Inst. for Advanced Philos. sch., 1986, Mentor Soc. award, 1987, Nat. medal of ı., 1989; William James fellow Am. Psychol. Soc.,1990, isting. Centennial Address award, 1991, Outstanding fetime Contribution award, 1993. Fellow NAS, AAS, Am. Acad. Arts & Scis., Am. Philos. Soc.(Karl ashley award), Am. Neurol. Assn., Royal Soc. (fgn. em.), Pontifical Acad. Scis., USSR Acad. Scis. (fgn. em.). Home: Pasadena Calif. Died Apr. 17, 1994.

PINA, ANTHONY, photojournalist; b. Detroit; s. ostan and Julia (Perry) S.; m. Frances Leto, Mar. 2, 946; children: Costan II, Julia, Kathryn. BA, Detroit st. Tech., 1939; LHD (non.), Siena Heights Coll., 988. Mem. photography staff Detroit Free Press, 946—, chief photographer, 1952-86, spl. asst. to mng. litor, 1986-89, chief photographer emeritus, 1990—. uthor: The Making of the Pope: Pope John XXIII, 962, The Pope and the Council, 1963, This Was the esident: John F. Kennedy, 1964, The Press hotographer, 1968, From a Distant Country: Pope ohn Paul II, 1979, On Assignment: Projects in Photo-ournalism, 1982; numerous one-man exhbns. include etroit Art Inst., 1976, Los Angeles County Mus., 976, Vatican Mus., 1968; mem. spl. Free Press team, 968 (Pulitzer prize). Served with USN, World War II, orea. Decorated Knight, St. Gregory The Great (Pope aul VI); named to Journalist Hall of Fame, Mich. State ., 1989; recipient Gold medallion Pope John XXIII, 962, Silver medallion, 1962, Bronze medallion, 1962, ov.'s Media awrd Concerned Citizens for the Arts, 989, also 482 nat. and internat. photog. awards; Tony pina, Chief Photographer: Four Decades of His News hotography, pub. in his honor Detroit Free Press, 989. Roman Catholic. Home: Bloomfield Hills Mich. ied Jan. 19, 1995.

PIVAK, LAWRENCE EDMUND, television roducer, consultant; b. N.Y.C., June 11, 1900; s. Wil-am B. and Sonya (Bershad) S.; m. Charlotte Beir Ring lec.); children: Judith Spivak Frost (dec.), onathan. AB, Harvard U., 1921; LLD (hon.), Vilberforce U.; DLitt (hon.), Suffolk U.; LHD (hon.), ampa U. Bus. mgr. Antiques mag., 1921-30; asst. to ub. Hunting and Fishing and Nat. Sportsman mags., 1930-33; bus. mgr. Am. Mercury mag., 1934-39, pub., 1939-44, editor, pub., 1944-50; founder Mercury Library-Paperback Books, 1937; originator, founder, pub. Ellery Queen's Mystery mag., 1941-1954, The Mag. of Fantasy and Science Fiction, 1945-54; founder Mercury Mystery Books, Bestseller Mysteries, Jonathan Press Books; originator, pub. Armed Services Paperback Books, 1943; originator, co-founder, producer, moderator program Meet the Press, 1st radio broadcast 1945, 1st TV broadcast 1947; ret., 1975; cons. NBC, 1975—. Recipient 2 Peabody awards, 1991, 2 Emmy awards Nat. Acad. TV Arts and Scis., AP Broadcasters Robert Eunson award, Mass Media award Inst. of Human Relations of Am. Jewish Com., U.S. Conf. Mayors' award, Christopher award; inducted Hall of Fame-Washington chpt. Sigma Delta Chi. Home: Washington D.C. Died Mar. 9, 1994.

SPOEHR, ALEXANDER, anthropologist, retired educator; b. Tucson, Aug. 23, 1913; s. Herman Augustus and Florence (Mann) S; m. Anne Dinsdale Harding, Aug. 2, 1941; children: Alexander Harding, Helene Spoehr Clarke. A.B., U. Chgo., 1934, Ph.D., 1940; D.Sc. (hon.), U. Hawaii, 1952. From asst. curator to curator Field Mus., Chgo., 1940-53; dir. Bishop Mus., Honolulu, 1953-62; prof. Yale U., New Haven, 1953-62; chancellor East-West Ctr., Honolulu, 1962-63; prof. anthropology U. Pitts., 1964-78, prof. emeritus, 1978; U.S. commr. South Pacific Commn., 1957-60; mem. Pacific sci. bd. NRC, Washington, 1955-61, chmn. 1958-61. N.Am. and Pacific ethnological and archaeol. researcher. Contbr. numerous articles to profl. jours. Trustee Bishop Mus., 1981-84; Served to lt. USNR, 1942-45. Recipient Charles R. Bishop medal Bishop Mus., 1991. Fellow Am. Anthropol. Assn. (pres. 1965), AAAS; mem. NAS, Sigma Xi. Home: Honolulu Hawaii Died June 1992.

SPRAGUE, EVERETT RUSSELL, consumer products company executive; b. Inwood, N.Y., Aug. 9, 1915; s. Louie and Eva C. (Davison) S.; m. Karen Olson, Sept. 9, 1967; children—Dian Reed, Linda Kenney, Nancy Chouinard, Russell A. M.E., Stevens Inst. Tech., Hoboken, N.J., 1936, M.S., 1939; D.C.S. (hon.), Am. Internat. Coll., 1978; D. Engr. (hon.), Stevens Inst. Tech., 1988. With Tampax Inc. (named changed to Tambrands, Inc.), Lake Success, N.Y., 1939-88, pres., chief exec. officer, from 1976, chmn., 1981-88, hon. chmn., 1987-95, also dir. Trustee, chmn. bd. dirs. Am. Internat. Coll., Springfield, Mass.; emeritus trustee Stevens Inst. Tech. Fellow Soc. Advancement Mgmt. (profl. mgr. citation Western Mass. chpt. 1960); mem. ASME, Phi Sigma Kappa, Tau Beta Pi. Lodges: Monson Rotary, Masons. Home: Palm City Fla. Died Apr. 20, 1995.

SPRINGER, SIR HUGH WORRELL, government official; b. St. Michael, Barbados, June 22, 1913; s. Charles Wilkinson and Florence Nightingale (Barrow) S.; m. Dorothy Drinan Gittens; children: Richild Diana, Mark Wakefield, Harold Jason, Stephen O'Connor. Student, Harrison Coll., Barbados, 1923-32; BA, Hertford Coll., Oxford U., Eng., 1936, MA, 1944; Barrister at Law, Inner Temple, London, 1938; hon. DSc Social Scis., Laval U., 1958; LLD, U. Victoria, B.C., Can., 1972, U. W.I., 1973, City Univ., London, 1978, U. Manchester, Eng., 1979, U. N.B., 1980, York U., Can., 1980, U. Zimbabwe, 1981, U. Bristol, Eng., 1982, U. Birmingham, Eng., 1983; D. Litt., U. Warwick, Eng., 1974, U. Ulster, 1974, Heriot Watt Univ., 1976, U. Hong Kong, 1977, St. Andrews U., Scotland, 1977; D.C.L., U. Oxford, Scotland, 1980, U. East Anglia, Scotland, 1980. Acting prof. classics Codrington Coll., Barbados, 1938; sole practice law, Barbados, 1938-47; mem. House of Assembly, Barbados, 1940-47, exec. com., 1944-47; gen. sec. Barbados Labour Party, 1940-47; organizer, 1st gen. sec. Barbados Workers' Union, 1940-47; registrar Univ. West Indies, 1947-63, dir. Inst. Edn., 1963-66; acting gov. and comdr.-in-chief Barbados, 1964; dir. Commonwealth Edn. Liaison Unit, London, 1966, Commonwealth asst. sec. gen., 1966-70; sec. gen. Assn. Commonwealth Univs., London, 1970-80; gov.-gen. Barbados, 1984-90; bd. dirs. Sugar Industry Agrl. Bank. Bd. dirs. Hosp. Bd., Edn. Bd., Governing Body Harrison Coll., Queen's Coll., 1938-47; trustee Anglican Ch., 1981-84; chmn. Disciplinary Com. Bar, 1982-84, Nat. Tng. Bd., 1982-84, Income Tax Appeal Bd., 1983-84, Nat. Devel. Found., 1983-84, Mapps Coll., 1983-84, Friends of Scouting, 1983-84, mem. com. of Mgmt. of Assn. Mentally Retarded Children; other vol. service in Jamaica, West Indies, U.K., Ghana, East Africa, South Pacific, UN, Holland. Barbados scholar Harrison Coll., 1931; Guggenheim fellow, 1961-62; Harvard Ctr. for Internat. affairs fellow, 1961-62; sr. vis. fellow All Souls Coll., Oxford, 1962-63, (hon., 1988); Silver medal Royal Soc. Arts, Eng., 1970; Hon. fellow Hertford Coll., 1974; hon. prof. edn. U. Mauritius, 1981; Knight Grand Cross Order St. Michael and St. George; Knight Grand Cross, Royal Victorian Order, 1985; Knight of St. Andrew in Order of Barbados; comdr. Order of Brit. Empire. Anglican. Clubs: Athenaeum, Royal Commonwealth. Home: Saint Peter Barbados Died Apr. 14, 1994; interred St. Michael's Cathedral, Bridgetown.

SPRINGER, JACK G., association executive; b. Norman, Okla., Sept. 11, 1926; s. Charles S. and Mary A. (Goff) S.; m. Doris M. Lebow, Apr. 14, 1945; children: Carol Springer Power, Sheryl Springer Snesko, Jane Springer Oliphant, Cynthia Springer Downs. B.S., U. Okla., 1950. With Pauls Valley (Okla.) C. of C., 1950-51, Seminole (Okla.) C. of C., 1951-53; Bryan-Coll. Station (Tex.) C. of C., 1953-61, Galveston (Tex.) C. of C., 1961-63, W. Tex. Regional C. of C., 1963-71; exec. v.p. Okla. State C. of C., Oklahoma City, 1971-95. Served with U.S. Army, 1944-46. Mem. Assn. Am. C. of C. Execs., Okla. C. of C. Execs. (dir.), Council State Chambers Commerce (past (pres., mem. exec. com.), U.S. C. of C. (c. of c. com.). Home: Oklahoma City Okla. Died Jan. 17, 1995.

SPRINGSTEEN, GEORGE STONEY, JR., former government official; b. N.Y.C., Jan. 7, 1923; s. George S. and Elsa L. (Otto) S.; m. Rosalind Sawyer, May 28, 1955; children: George Sawyer, Martha Louise. B.A., Dartmouth, 1943; M.A., Fletcher Sch. Law and Diplomacy, 1947, M.A.L.D., 1949, Ph.D., 1957. Part-time tchr. econs., history Tufts Coll., 1947-49; internat. economist Dept. State, 1949-58; finance officer, sr. economist Devel. Loan Fund, 1958-61; spl. asst. under sec. state for econ. affairs, 1961, spl. asst. under sec. state, 1961-66, dep. asst. sec. state European affairs, 1966-74; exec. sec. Dept. State and spl. asst. to sec. state, 1974-76, dir. Fgn. Service Inst., 1976-80; ret., 1980; vis. lectr. pub. and internat. affairs Woodrow Wilson Sch., Princeton U., 1982-83, cons., 1980-93; pres. bd. dirs. Internat. Student House, Washington, 1983-87. Served to lt. (j.g.) USNR, 1943-46. Home: Bethesda Md. Died Apr. 24, 1993; buried Arlington Nat. Cemetery.

SPROUT, WILLIAM BRADFORD, JR., architect; b. Natick, Mass., Apr. 4, 1900; s. William Bradford and Margaret (Bigelow) S.; m. Ruth Wilbur, June 1921; m. Sybil Vroom, June 16, 1928; children: Wesley B., William Bradford III, Sarah B. A.B., Harvard U., 1921, M.Arch., 1928. Practice architecture Hingham, Mass., from 1931; staff architect, sec. housing com. John Hancock Mut. Life Ins. Co., 1935-65; archtl. cons. Chmn. Hingham (Mass.) Historic Dists. Commn. Fellow AIA; mem. Boston Soc. Architects (former dir., exec. dir. 1961-62), Mass. Assn. Architects (co-founder, dir., sec.-treas. 1943-74), Constrn. Specifications Inst. (past pres. Boston chpt.), Am. Arbitration Assn. (panel mem. for constrn.), Hingham Yacht Club, Harvard Club of Hingham. Home: Hingham Mass. Deceased.

SPURR, CHARLES LEWIS, medical educator, cancer chemotherapy clinical researcher; b. Sunbury, Pa., Nov. 20, 1913; s. George Clayton and Catherine Irene (Roberts) S.; m. Isabelle Marie Holtzinger, June 18, 1940; children: Charles Lewis, Susanne Spurr Green. B.S., Bucknell U., Lewisburg, Pa., 1935; M.S., U. Rochester, 1938, M.D., 1940. Diplomate, Am. Bd. Internal Medicine. Instr. U. Chgo., 1943-46, asst. prof., 1946-48; assoc. prof. Baylor U., Houston, 1949-57; prof. medicine Bowman Gray Sch. Medicine Wake Forest U., Winston-Salem, N.C., 1957-87, emeritus, 1987-94, dir. Oncology Research Ctr., 1968-82; N.C. nat. del. Am. Cancer Soc., N.Y.C., 1980-82, chmn. bd. N.C. div., 1985-86; chmn. Com. on Cancer, Raleigh, N.C., 1981-85; pres. S.E. Cancer Control Consortium, Inc.; mem. Community Clin. Oncology Program, adv. com. Nat. Cancer Inst., 1988-94; mem. exec. com. Nat. Surg. Adjuvant Project for Breast and Bowel Cancers, 1988-94; mem. investigator Cancer and Leukemia Group B, 1958-80. Contbr. articles to profl. jours. Served to lt. USNR, 1945-52. Named Disting. Internist of Yr., N.C. chpt. ACP, 1990; honoree Charles L. Spurr Prof. Medicine, Bowman Gray Sch. Medicine, Wake Forest U., Charles L. Spurr Ann. Lectureship. Fellow ACP; mem. AMA, Am. Assn. Cancer Edn., Am. Soc. Clin. Oncology, Piedmont Oncology Assn. (chmn. 1976-85), Am. Assn. Cancer Research, Sigma Xi, Alpha Omega Alpha. Club: Old Town. Home: Winston Salem N.C. Died Apr. 1, 1994.

SROLE, LEO, researcher, sociology educator emeritus; b. Chgo., Oct. 8, 1908; s. William and Rebecca (Epstein) S.; m. Esther Hannah Alpiner, Dec. 27, 1941; children: Ira Herschel, Rebecca Yona. B.S., Harvard, 1933; Ph.D., U. Chgo., 1940. Lectr. N.Y. U., 1940-41; prof., chmn. dept. sociology Hobart Coll. (now Hobart and William Smith Colls.), Geneva, N.Y., 1941-42; welfare dir. UNRRA, UNRRA (Landsberg, Germany displaced persons camp), 1945-46; with bur. applied social research Columbia, 1947-48; research dir. ADL B'nai B'rith, 1948-52; prof. sociology Cornell Med. Coll., 1952-59; research prof. Albert Einstein Med. Coll., N.Y.C., 1959-61; prof. sociology SUNY Downstate Med. Center, 1961-65; prof. social scis. dept. psychiatry Columbia Coll. Physicians and Surgeons, 1965-78; prof. emeritus Center for Geriatrics and Gerontology, Faculty Medicine, Columbia U., 1978-93; chief psychiat. research in social scis. N.Y. State Psychiat. Inst., 1966-78; cons. Belgian Ministry of Health, 1970-75, WHO, 1979-93. Author: (with W. Lloyd Warner) Social Systems of American Ethnic Groups, 1945; sr. author: Mental Health in the Metropolis: The Midtown Manhattan Study (designated Citation Classic), 1962, paperback edit., 1975, revised, enlarged edit., 1978; author chpts. in symposium vols.; past assoc. editor: Jour. Social Issues; mem. editorial bd.: Israel Jour. Psychiatry, Am. Sociology Rev., Jour. Psychiat. Evaluation and Treatment; Contbr. articles to sci., gen. periodicals. Served with USAAF as mil. psychologist Air

Surgeon's Office, 1943-45. Hon. fellow Am. Psychiat. Assn.; mem. Internat. Sociol. Assn., Am. Sociol. Assn., AAUP, Soc. for Study Social Problems, Gerontol. Soc., Sigma Xi. Home: Whitestone N.Y. Died May 1, 1993; interred Long Island, N.Y.

STACY, GARDNER W., chemical scientist, educator, lecturer; b. Rochester, N.Y., Oct. 29, 1921; s. Gardner Wesley and May (Roberts) S.; m. Mary Mullen Heydon, Apr. 1, 1967; children: Marcia Ann Stacy Boggs, Anne Elizabeth Heydon Gorham, Richard Neal Heydon, Donald Gardner Stacy, Robert James Stacy. B.S., U. Rochester, 1943; Ph.D., U. Ill., 1946. Rsch. asst. OSRD antimalarial program U. Ill., Urbana, 1943-46; rsch. fellow Cornell U. Med. Sch., N.Y.C., 1946-48; asst. prof. chemistry Wash. State U., Pullman, 1948-55; assoc. prof. Wash. State U., 1955-60, prof., 1960-88, dir. chemistry alumni and industry rels., 1980-88, prof. emeritus, 1988-95; vis. prof. U. Auckland, New Zealand, U. Melbourne, U. New South Wales, Australia, Oreg. State U., U. Hawaii, Ariz. State U., U.S. Mil. Acad., West Point; lectr. on energy crisis, communication skills, improved chem. edn.; mem. various NIH and NSF fellowship and grant panels. Author: Organic Chemistry: A Background for the Life Sciences, 1975; (with Carl Wamser) 2d edit., 1985; contbr. articles to profl. jours. and mags. Bd. dirs. The Cathedral (Episcopal ch.), Spokane, Wash., also cathedral guide, mem. Cathedral chpt.; mem. Brotherhood St. Andrew; bd. dirs., v.p. Cathedral Arts Assn. Recipient Petroleum Rsch. Fund Internat. award Australia and N.Z., 1963-64, Comdr.'s award for Pub. Svc. Dept. Army, 1986; named Outstanding Prof. Alpha Zeta, 1977. Fellow Am. Inst. Chemists, AAAS (nominating com-chemistry sect. C, elected mem at large sect. C); mem. Am. Chem. Soc. (divsns. include chem. edn., organic chemistry, medicinial chemistry 1955-86, profl. relss, councilor Wash.-Idaho border sect. 1957-69, coun. policy com. 1961-69, 78-80, nat., region VI dir. 1970-78, bd, dirs. 1970-80, councilor ex-officio 1970-95, past chmn. coun. com. chem. edn., chmn. bd. com. edn. and students 1972-75, bd. com. pub., profl. and mem. rels., com. on publs. 1977-78, bd. com. on pub. affairs and pub. rels. 1979-80, com. on chem. and pub. affairs 1981-86, cons. to com. 1988-89, subcom. on energy 1979-86, mem. C&EN editorial bd. 1978, 80, mem. council sci. soc. presidents 1978-81, exec. bd. 1979-81, chmn. com. on energy 1980-81, Am. Chem. Soc. nat. pres.-elect 1978, Am. Chem. Soc. nat. pres. 1979, chmn. various profl. confs., host-chmn. internat. meeting, Honolulu 1979, chmn. 7th internat. meeting of chem. soc. presidents, Washington 1979, chmn. Am. Chem. Soc. Presdl. plenary program on energy, Washington 1979), Coun. for Chem. Rsch., Phi Beta Kappa, Sigma Xi, Phi Kappa Phi (emeritus life mem.), Alpha Chi Sigma, Phi Lambda Upsilon, Delta Kappa Epsilon. Home: Spokane Wash. Died Apr. 30, 1995.

STADE, CHARLES EDWARD, architect; b. Des Plaines, Ill, June 28, 1923; s. Chris E. and Martha (Drexler) S.; 1 dau., Ramsey. B.S., U. Ill., 1946; M.F.A., Princeton, 1948; certificate of design, Beaux Art Inst. Design, N.Y.C., 1948; French govt. traveling scholar, 1948. Architect W.J. McCaughev, Park Ridge, Ill., 1945, K. Kassler, Princeton, N.J., 1948; propr. Charles Edward and Assos., Park Ridge, Ill, 1948-81. Author articles in field; prin. works include instl. and related structures. Served with USAAF, 1942-43. Palmer fellow; Princeton fellow; recipient Howard Crosby Butler prize; medal of Prix-de-Emultation of Group Am. Societes des Architects Par Le Govt. Francais. Fellow in Design Am. Soc. Ch. Architects (pres. 1964-66, designs in permanent exhbt.), AIA (award 1956, 57, 62, 63, 65, 67, Excellence in Masonry Architecture award 1972, Outstanding Lighting award 1973, Nat. award for excellence in design 1974). Home: Park Ridge Ill. Deceased.

STAFFORD, WILLIAM EDGAR, author, retired educator; b. Hutchinson, Kans., Jan. 17, 1914; s. Earl Ingersoll and Ruby Nina (Mayher) S.; m. Dorothy Hope Frantz, Apr. 8, 1944; children: Bret William (dec.), Kim Robert, Kathryn Lee, Barbara Claire. BA, U. Kans., 1937, MA, 1946; PhD, State U. Iowa, 1954; LittD, Ripon Coll., 1965; LHD, Linfield Coll., 1970. Faculty Lewis and Clark Coll., Portland, Oreg., 1948-80, prof. English, 1960-80; faculty San Jose (Calif.) State Coll., 1956-57, Manchester (Ind.) Coll., 1955-56; cons. poetry Library of Congress, Washington, 1970. Author: West of Your City, 1960, Traveling Through the Dark, 1962 (Nat. Book award 1963), The Rescued Year, 1966, Eleven Untitled Poems, 1968, Weather: Poems, 1969, Temporary Facts, 1970, Allegiances, 1970, Poems for Tennessee, 1971, In the Clock of Reason, 1973, Someday, Maybe, 1973, Going Places: Poems, 1974, North By West, 1975, Braided Apart, 1976, I Would Also Like to Menion Aluminum: Poems and a Conversation, 1976, Late, Passing Prairie Farm: A Poem, 1976, Stories That Could Be True, New and Collected Poems, 1977, The Design on the Oriole, 1977, All About Light, 1978, A Meeting with Disma Tumminello and William Stafford, 1978, Possinga Creche, 1978, Tuft by Puff. 1978, Two About Music, 1978, Around You, Your Horse and A Catechism, 1979, Absolution, 1980, Things That Happen Where There Aren't Any People, 1980, Unmuzzled Ox, 1980, Sometimes Like a Legend, 1981, A Glass Face in the Rain, 1982, Roving Across Fields: A Conversation and Uncollected Poems 1942-82, 1983, Smoke's Way: Poems From Limited Editions, 1968-81, 1983, Segues: A Correspondence in Poetry, 1984, Listening Deep, 1984, Wyoming, 1985, You Must Revise Your Life, 1986, An Oregon Message, 1987, A Scripture of Leaves, 1989, How to Hold Your Arms When It Rains, 1990, Passwords, 1991, History Is Loose Again, 1991, The Long Sigh the Wind Makes, 1991, My Name is William Tell, 1992, Holding Onto the Grass, 1992; non-fiction Down in My Heart, 1947, Friends to this Ground: A Statement for Readers, Teachers, and Writers of Literature, 1967, Leftovers, A Care Package: Two Lectures, 1973, Writing the Australian Crawl: Views on the Writer's Vocation, 1978, You Must Revise Your Life, 1986, The Mozart Myths: A Critical Reassessment, 1991; regular contbr. to periodicals. Ednl. sec. civilian pub. service sect. Ch. of Brethren, 1943-44; mem. Oreg. bd. Fellowship of Reconciliation, 1959-93. Yaddo Found. fellow, 1956, Guggenheim grantee for creative writing, 1966-67, NEA grantee, 1966, Danforth Found. grantee; recipient short story and poetry prize Oreg. Centennial 1959, Union Civic League award Poetry Mag., 1959, Shelley Meml. award, 1964, Melville Cane award, 1974, Am. Acad. Inst. Arts and Letters Lit. award, 1981. Mem. AAUP, Modern Lang. Assn., Nat. Council Tchrs. English, War Registers League, Modern Poetry Assn. Home: Lake Oswego Oreg. Died Aug. 28, 1993.

STAHL, HENRY GEORGE, lawyer; b. Fremont, Ohio, Apr. 18, 1902; s. John Burton and Florence B. (Fisher) S.; m. Gertrude M. Elmers, Mar. 6, 1926; children: Joyce E. (Mrs. Howard B. Thompson), Florence E. (Mrs. Kenneth Harmon), John B. Student, Tiffin U., 1925, Miami U., Oxford, O., 1923, Bowling Green U., 1924, Ohio No. U., 1926. Bar: Ohio bar 1926. Since practiced in Fremont; mem. firm Stahl, Stahl & Stahl, 1926-51; practice as H.G. Stahl, 1951-92; probate judge, Sandusky County, 1932, 33. Mem. Sandusky County C. of C. (past pres.), ABA, Ohio Bar Assn., Sandusky County Bar Assn. (past pres.), Am. Judicature Soc. Clubs: Mason (past dist. dep.), Elk (past dist. dep.), K.P. (past dist. dep.). Home: Fremont Ohio Died Dec. 18, 1992.

STALEY, AUGUSTUS EUGENE, III, advertising executive; b. Decatur, Ill., Sept. 12, 1928; s. Augustus Eugene Jr. and Lenore (Mueller) S. Student, Northwestern U., 1946-49. Account exec. Ruthrauff & Ryan, Inc., 1950-52; advt. dir. A.E. Staley Mfg. Co., Decatur, Ill., 1952-58; v.p. Dancer-Fitzgerald-Sample, 1958-61, Arthur Meyerhoff Assocs., 1961; exec. v.p. Don Kemper Co., Inc., Chgo., 1961-69; pres., chmn., chief exec. officer SMY Media, Inc., Chgo., 1969—; pres. Advt. Contractors, N.Y.C., 1970-74; chief exec. officer Atwood Richards, Inc., N.Y.C., 1970-86; dir. Mueller Co., Decatur. Sgt. U.S. Army, 1950-60. Clubs: Tavern, Chgo. Athletic (Chgo.), Sky Line (Chgo); Williams (N.Y.C.). Lodges: Masons. Home: Chicago Ill.

STALKER, ALFRED JOSEPH, investment banker; b. Holyoke, Mass., July 5, 1906; s. Alfred W. and Geneva (Kay) S.; m. Hilkka H. S., Dec. 10, 1987. B.S., Syracuse U., 1928. With Pacific Tel. & Tel. Co., Seattle, 1928-29; with Kidder, Peabody & Co., N.Y.C., 1950-95; mgr. dealer relations dept. Kidder, Peabody & Co., 1950-57; gen. partner, dir. West Coast div. Kidder, Peabody & Co., Los Angeles, 1958-67; v.p. Kidder, Peabody & Co., 1967-95. Served to lt. comdr. USNR, 1943-46. Mem. Los Angeles Country Club, Delta Kappa Epsilon. Home: Beverly Hills Calif. Died July 12, 1995.

STALNAKER, ARMAND CARL, former insurance company executive, retired educator; b. Weston, W.Va., Apr. 24, 1916; s. Thomas Carl and Alta (Hinzman) S. B.B.A., U. Cin., 1941; M.A., U. Pa., 1945; Ph.D., Ohio State U., 1951. Asst. prof. bus. Ohio State U., Columbus, 1946-50; with Prudential Ins. Co., 1950-63; adminstrv. v.p., exec. v.p., pres., chmn., chief exec. officer Gen. Am. Life Ins. Co., 1963-86; prof. mgmt. Washington U. Sch. Bus., St. Louis, 1982-91. Mem. Bogey Club, St. Louis Club, Omicron Delta Kappa. Mem. Soc. of Friends. Home: Saint Louis Mo. Died July 1, 1995.

STAMPFL, RUDOLF ALOIS, government official; b. Vienna, Austria, Jan. 21, 1926; came to U.S., 1953, naturalized, 1959; s. Paul Friedrich and Leopoldine (Kittinger) S.; m. Ursula Maria Frieske, Sept. 17, 1956; children: Susanne Maria, Peter Gerhard. B.S., Inst. Tech. Vienna, 1948, M.S., 1950, Ph.D., 1953. Sr. engr. astro electronics br. Army Research and Devel. Labs., Fort Monmouth, N.J., 1953-59; with NASA, Greenbelt, Md., 1959-94; asst. dir. NASA, 1968-73; dir. systems dept. Naval Air Devel. Center, Warminster, Pa., 1973-83; mgr. advanced missions RCA-Astro Space Div., 1983-87; staff dir. ednl. activities IEEE, 1987-92; cons., vis. lectr. aerospace instrumentation systems UCLA, 1964-65; designer Nimbus spacecraft. Author chpts. in books; patentee in field. Served with German Army, 1944-45. Recipient Harry Diamond award, 1967, Pioneer award, 1987. Fellow IEEE, AIAA. Died Oct. 7, 1994.

STANIŠIC, MILOMIR MIRKOV, mathematical physicist, educator; b. Bujacic-Serbia/Yugoslavia, Aug. 19, 1914; came to U.S., 1949, naturalized, 1955; s. Mirko V. and Ana (Bujicic) S.; m. Miroslava, Oct. 2, 1954 (div. Aug. 1962); children: Ana, Michael, Susana. Student, Mil. Officer Acad., Belgrade, Yugoslavia, 1934-37; Cand. Ing., Belgrade U., 1940; Dipl. Ing., Tech., U, Hanover, Germany, 1946, Dr. Ing., 1949; Ph.D., Ill. Inst. Tech., 1958. Scientist Armour Research Found., Chgo., 1950-56; asso. prof. Purdue U., 1956-60, prof., 1960-91; Vis. prof. Johns Hopkins, 1966-67. Mem. Soc. Natural Philosophy, Am. Math. Soc., Am. Phys. Soc., AAUP. Home: West Lafayette Ind. Died Mar. 9, 1991; interred Serbian Orthodox Monastery Gračanica, Third Lake, Ill.

STANLEY, C. MAXWELL, consulting engineer; b. Corning, Iowa, June 16, 1904; s. Claude Maxwell and Laura Esther (Stephenson) S.; m. Elizabeth M. Holthues, Nov. 11, 1927; children: David M., Richard H., Jane S. Buckles. B.S., U. Iowa, 1926, M.S., 1930; L.H.D., Iowa Wesleyan Coll., 1961, Augustana Coll., 1978; H.H.D. (hon.), U. Manila, 1970. Structural designer Byllesby Engrng. & Mgmt. Corp., Chgo., 1926-27; dept. grounds and bldgs. U. Iowa, 1927-28; hydraulic engr. Mgmt. & Engrng. Corp., Dubuque, Iowa, Chgo., 1928-32; cons. engr. Young & Stanley, Inc., 1932-39; partner, pres. Stanley Engrng. Co., Muscatine, Iowa, 1939-66; pres. Stanley Cons., Inc., Muscatine, 1966-71; chmn. bd. Stanley Cons., Inc., 1971-84; pres. HON Industries, Muscatine, 1944-64, chmn. bd., 1964-84 ; pres. Stanley Cons. Ltd. Liberia, 1959-71, dir., 1971-81; mng. dir. Stanley Cons. Ltd. Nigeria, 1960-67, dir., 1967-78; pres. World Press Rev., 1975-84. Author: Waging Peace, 1956, The Consulting Engineer, 1961, 2d edit., 1981, Managing Global Problems, 1979; also articles profl. jours. Trustee Iowa Wesleyan Coll., 1951-84 , chmn., 1963-65; chmn. Strategy for Peace Conf., 1962-84 , Conf. on UN of Next Decade, 1965-84 ; pres. The Stanley Found., 1956-84 ; hon. life bd. dirs. U. Iowa Found., 1966-84 , pres., 1971-75. Recipient Disting. Service award U. Iowa, 1967, Hancher-Finkbine medallion, 1971; Iowa Bus. Leadership award, 1980; named hon. rector U. Dubuque, 1983. Fellow ASCE (Alfred Noble prize 1933, Collingwood prize 1935), IEEE, ASME, Am. Cons. Engrs. Council (chmn. com. fellows 1975, past pres.'s award 1983); mem. Iowa Engrng. Soc. (John Dunlap prize 1943, Marston award 1947, Disting. Service award 1962, hon. mem. 1975, Herbert Hoover Humanitarian award 1979), Nat. Soc. Profl. Engrs. (award for outstanding service 1965, PEPP award 1975), World Federalists U.S.A. (council 1947-84 , pres. 1954-56, 64-66), World Assn. World Federalists (chmn. council 1958-65). Republican. Methodist. Club: Rotary (Paul Harris award 1976). Lodge: Rotary (Paul Harris award 1976). Home: Muscatine Iowa Died Oct. 1984.

STANLEY, WILLIAM, JR., lawyer; b. Laurel, Md., Sept. 30, 1919; s. William and Mary Jane (Gilbert) S.; m. Margaret Fleming Bell, Jan. 15, 1943; m. Janina Hanin, Jan. 14, 1969; children: Amy (Anthony), William III, Robert H., Margaret S. BA, Princeton U., 1941, JD, Harvard U., 1944. Bar: D.C. 1948, Md. 1948. Law clk. U.S. Ct. Appeals D.C. 1948; assoc. Covington & Burling, Washington, 1948-58, ptnr., 1958-92. Served with USNR, 1942-45. Mem. ABA, D.C. Bar Assn. Democrat. Episcopalian. Clubs: Metropolitan, Md. (Balt.). Died May 1992. Home: Washington D.C.

STANTON, EDWARD M., public relations company executive; b. Port Chester, N.Y., Aug. 28, 1921. BJ, Northwestern U., 1943. With Westchester-Rockland Newspapers, N.Y., 1945-47; city editor Women's Wear Daily, 1947-56; pres. Bell & Stanton, Inc., 1956-77, Bell & Stanton, 1956-77, Bell & Stanton div. Manning, Selvage & Lee, Inc., N.Y.C., 1977-96; vice chmn. Manning, Selvage & Lee, 1977-96, vice chmn./N.Y. gen mgr., 1981-82, pres., 1982-96, pres., chief exec. officer, 1985-87, chmn., chief exec. officer, 1987-91, chmn., 1992. Author textbook on retailing, 1955. Mem. SDX, ASAE. Home: New York N.Y. Died Mar., 1996.

STARK, WERNER E., food broker; b. Munich, Feb. 12, 1921; came to U.S., 1938; s. Herman H. and Klara (Rosenfelder) S.; m. Betty (div. 1969); children—Jackie Odom, Larry. B.A., U. Ill., 1942. Chmn. Stark & Co. Farmington Hills, Mich., 1947-95; chmn. bd. dirs. Served with C.I.C., U.S. Army, 1943-47, ETO. Mem Nat. Food Broker's Assn. Club: Detroit Tennis and Squash (pres. 1975-76). Home: West Bloomfield Mich Died July 25, 1995.

STECKLER, WILLIAM ELWOOD, federal judge; b. Mt. Vernon, Ind., Oct. 18, 1913; s. William Herman and Lena (Menikheim) S.; m. Vitallas Alting, Oct. 15, 1938; children: William Rudolph, David Alan. LL.B., Ind. U., 1936, J.D., 1937; LL.D., Wittenberg U., Springfield Ohio, 1958; H.H.D., Ind. Central U., 1969. Bar: Ind. 1936. Pvt. practice Indpls., 1937-50; mem. firm Key & Steckler; pub. counselor Ind. Pub. Svc. Commn., 1949-50; judge U.S. Dist. Ct. (so. dist.) Ind., 1950-95; chief judge. U.S. Dist. Ct. So. Dist., 1954-82; faculty mem for judges confs. Fed. Jud. Ctr., 1973-74. Mem. Ind. Election Bd., 1946-48; chmn. speakers bur. Democratic State Central Com., 1948; bd. dirs. Community Hosp. Indpls.; bd. visitors Ind. U. Sch. Law, Indpls. Served with USNR, 1943. Recipient Man of Yr. award Ind. U. Sch. Law, Indpls., 1970, Disting Alumni Service award 1985; Disting. Alumni Service award Ind. U., 1985. Mem. ABA, Fed. Bar Assn., Ind. Bar Assn., Indpls. Bar Assn., Am. Judicature Soc., Nat. Lawyers Club, Ju

. U.S. (dist. judge rep. from 7th fed. cir. 1961-62, y group pretrial com. 1956-60, pretrial procedure 1960-65, trial practice and procedure com. 1965- :oord. com. for multiple litigation 1966-69, opera- of jury system com. 1969-75, jud. ethics com. 1985- Am. Legion, St. Thomas More Soc. (hon.), Indpls. etic Club, Masons (33 degree), Shriners, Jesters, :r DeMolay, Order of Coif, Sigma Delta Kappa. eran. Home: Indianapolis Ind. Died Mar. 8, 1995.

CKLOW, STEVE, journalist; b. Bklyn., Apr. 3, ; s. Nathaniel and Doris (Truffleman) S.; m. Anne sky, Nov 1, 1986. BA, U. Pa., 1976. Reporter ntic City (N.J.) Press, 1976, Phila. Bulletin, 1976- Washington Star, 1981, Phila. Inquirer, 1981—. pient George Polk award L.I. U., 1988; Spanish guage fellow Nat. Press Club, Cuernavaca, Mex., . Home: Philadelphia Pa. Died Nov. 29, 1994.

EGMULLER, FRANCIS, author; b. New Haven, 3, 1906; s. Joseph F. and Bertha R. (Tierney) S.; m. rice Stein, July 1, 1935 (dec. June 1961); m. Shirley zard, Dec. 22, 1963. Student, Dartmouth Coll., -24; B.A., Columbia U., 1927, M.A., 1928. With ce of War Info., Office of Strategic Svcs., Wash- on and France, 1942-45. Writer under own name pen names Byron Steel, David Keith; author: O Ben Jonson, 1927, Java-Java, 1928, Sir Francis on, 1930, The Musicale, 1930, (with Marie Dresden) America on Relief, 1938, Flaubert and Madame ary, 1939, A Matter of Iodine, 1940, A Matter of ent, 1943, States of Grace, 1946, French Follies, , Blue Harpsichord, 1949, Maupassant: A Lion in Path, 1949, The Two Lives of James Jackson Jarves, , The Grand Mademoiselle, 1956; translator The cted Letters of Gustave Flaubert, 1953, and lame Bovary, 1957, The Christening Party, 1960, Le ou et la Poussiquette, 1961, Apollinaire, Poet ong the Painters, 1963, (with Norbert Guterman) te-Beuve, Selected Essays, 1963, Papillot, Clignot et lo, 1964, Flaubert's Intimate Notebook, 1967, teau, 1970, Stories and True Stories, 1972; transl., or: Flaubert in Egypt, 1973, Your Isadora: the Love y of Isadora Duncan and Gordon Craig, 1974, nce at Salerno, 1978, The Letters of Gustave ibert, 1830-1857, 1980, The Letters of Gustave ibert, 1857-1880, 1982, A Woman, A Man, and Two gdoms: The Story of Madame D'Épinay and the oé Galiani, 1991, (with Barbara Bray) Flaubert-Sand: Correspondence, 1992; contbr. short stories, articles New Yorker. Decorated chevalier French Legion of nor, French Ordre des Arts et Lettres; recipient Red ge Mystery prize, 1940, Nat. Book award, 1971. n. Nat. Inst. Arts and Letters (gold medal 1982), Beta Kappa. Clubs: Century, University (N.Y.C.); colo del Remo e della Vela Italia (Naples). Home: v York N.Y. Died Oct. 20, 1994.

EERE, DOUGLAS VAN, educator; b. Harbor ch, Mich., Aug. 31, 1901; s. Edward Morris and th Ruby (Monroe) S.; m. Dorothy Lou Mac- chron, June 12, 1929; children—Helen Horn, Anne sh. B.S. in Agr, Mich. State U., 1923; A.M., rvard U., 1925, Ph.D., 1931; B.A. (Rhodes scholar), ord U., 1927, M.A., 1953; D.D., Lawrence Coll., 0; L.H.D., Oberlin Coll., 1954, Earlham Coll., 1965; .D., Gen. Theol. Sem., 1967; LL.D., Haverford Coll., 0. Tchr. Onaway (Mich.) High Sch., 1921-22; ulty philosophy Haverford Coll., from 1928, prof., n 1941, also dir. grad. reconstrn. and relief tng., 3-45, Thomas Wistar Brown prof. philosophy, 1950- Thomas Wistar Brown prof. emeritus, from 1964; nicker lectr. Episcopal Theol. Sem., 1938; Ingersoll r. Harvard, 1942; William Belden Noble lectr., 1943; len Tuthill lectr. Chgo. Theol. Sem., 1943; Carew r. Hartford Theol. Sem., 1945; Hoyt lectr. Union eol. Sem., N.Y.C., 1947; Rauschenbusch lectr. chester-Colgate, 1952; Swarthmore lectr., London, 55, Nitobe lectr., Tokyo, 1954; Dana lectr. Carleton ll., 1954, 62; Stone lectr. Princeton Theol. Sem., 1957, aily Hobhouse Meml. lectr., Johannesburg, 1957; rry Emerson Fosdick vis. prof. Union Theol. Sem., 51-62, Auburn lectr., 1961; Maurice Webb lectr. U. tal, South Africa, 1971; Shaffer lectr. Northwestern 1976. Author, editor or translator books relating to d; contbr. to religious publs.; Mem. editorial bd.: ligion in Life, 1961-80. Organizer Quaker Relief Ac- n, Finland, 1945; chmn. Friends World Com., 1964- Quaker observer-del. Vatican Council II, 1963-65, mbeth Conf., London, 1968; Chmn. bd. dirs. Pendle ll Sch. Religion and Social Studies, 1954-70, dir. nmer sch., 5 summers; summer sch. Union Theol. n., 1947, 51; trustee John Woolman Meml., chmn. trustees, 1947-54; trustee Walnwright House, Lewis Stevens Conf. Found. Recipient Alumni award ch. State U., 1947; Annual Upper Room Nat. cita- n, 1981. Mem. Am. Philos. Assn., Assn. Rhodes holars, Am. Theol. Soc. (sec. 1935-42, v.p. 1944-45, es. 1945-46), AAUP, Internat. Fellowship of Recon- iation (chmn. Am. sect. 1954-66), Phi Beta Kappa. em. Soc. Friends (clk. Phila. yearly meeting ministers d elders 1944-47, participant Quaker missions, mem. d. Commn. Chs. Commn. Theologians on Relations Ch. to War, 1944-45, Commn. on Atomic Warfare in ght of Christian Faith, 1945-46. Home: Haverford Pa. ed Feb. 6, 1995.

STEERS, EDWARD, microbiologist; b. Bethlehem, Pa., July 15, 1910; s. John Edward and Elizabeth Louise (Hess) S.; B.S. in Chemistry, Moravian Coll., 1932; M.S. in Biology, Lehigh U., 1937; Ph.D., U. Pa., 1949; m. Mary Mae Hochella, Sept. 26, 1930; children: John Edward, Edward, Mary Elizabeth. Prof., Moravian Coll., Bethlehem, 1932-45; research asso. U. Pa. Sch. Medicine, 1945-49, asso. prof. microbiology in medicine, dir. clin. microbiology William Pepper Lab., Hosp. U. Pa., 1956-63; asso. prof. bacteriology U. Md. Sch. Medicine, 1949-56; prof. bacteriology N.Y. Med. Coll., 1964-66; dir. microbiology Bklyn.-Cumberland Med. Center, 1966-70, dir. labs., 1967-70. Clin. prof. pathology State U. N.Y. Downstate Med. Center, 1966-70, prof. pathology, 1970-74, also dir. clin. labs., chmn. Sch. Med. Tech., 1972-74; prof. dept. biology L.I. U., 1967-70; attending cons. in microbiology and infectious diseases Mercy Hosp., Scranton, Pa., 1974-84, Moses-Taylor Hosp., 1974-84, Community Med. Center, 1974-84. Fellow Am. Acad. Microbiology; mem. Soc. Am. Microbiology, Wayne County (Pa.), Lackawanna (Pa.) hist. socs., Wyo. Hist. and Geol. Soc. Republican. Episcopalian. Contbr. numerous articles to sci. jours. Died Mar. 1990. Home: Paupack Pa.

STEGNER, WALLACE EARLE, author; b. Lake Mills, Iowa, Feb. 18, 1909; s. George Henry and Hilda Emilia (Paulson) S.; m. Mary Stuart Page, Sept. 1, 1934; 1 child, Stuart Page. AB, U. Utah, 1930, LittD, 1968; AM, U. Ia., 1932, PhD, 1935; postgrad., U. Calif., 1932-33, LHD, 1969; LittD, Utah State U., 1972; LLD, U. Sask., 1973; DHL, Santa Clara U., 1979; LittD, U. Wis., 1986, Mont. State U., 1987. Instr. English Augustana Coll., Rock Island, Ill., 1933-34, U. Utah, 1934-37, U. Wis., 1937-39; Briggs Copeland instr. Harvard, 1939-45; prof. English Stanford, 1945-71, Reynolds prof. humanities, 1969-71. Writer, 1934-93; editor in chief: Am. West, 1966-69; Recipient Little Brown & Co. prize for novelette Remembering Laughter 1937, O. Henry 1st prize for short story 1950; author numerous books, 1937-93, including The Women on the Wall, 1950, The Preacher and the Slave, 1950, Beyond the Hundredth Meridian, 1954, The City of the Living, 1956, A Shooting Star, 1961, Wolf Willow, 1963 (Blackhawk award), The Gathering of Zion, 1964, All the Little Live Things, 1967 (Commonwealth Club gold medal 1968), The Sound of Mountain Water, 1969, Angle of Repose, 1971 (Pulitzer prize 1972), The Uneasy Chair: A Biography of Bernard DeVoto, 1974, The Spectator Bird, 1976 (Nat. Book award 1977), Recapitulation, 1979, (with Page Stegner and Eliot Porter) American Places, 1981, One Way To Spell Man, 1982, Crossing to Safety, 1987, The American West as Living Space, 1987, Collected Stories, 1990, Where the Bluebird Sings to the Lemonade Springs, 1992; editor numerous texts and edits.; contbr. articles to mags. Guggenheim fellow, 1950, 52; recipient Robert Kirsch award, 1980. Mem. Am. Inst. & Acad. Arts and Letters, Am. Acad. Arts and Scis. Home: Los Altos Hills Calif. Died Apr. 13, 1993.

STEIGER, CHAUNCEY ALLEN, department store executive; b. Westfield, Mass., Feb. 28, 1893; s. Albert and Izetta (Allen) S.; m. Esther R. Emery, Oct. 3, 1923 (dec.); children—Reynolds E., Elisabeth A.; m. Hazel Clark, Jan. 3, 1947 (dec.). Grad., Phillips Exeter Acad., 1914; B.S., Dartmouth, 1917. With Steiger Co., Springfield, Mass., from 1917; treas. Steiger Co., 1932-66, chmn. bd. dirs., from 1966; treas., dir. Hilbridge Corp., Springfield, from 1940; pres. Steiger Investment Co., Springfield, from 1971; hon. dir. Valley Bank & Trust Co., Springfield. Pres. bd. dirs. Albert Steiger Bldg. Trust, from 1962, Steiger Meml. Fund Ind., from 1953; hon. trustee Wesson Meml. Hosp., Springfield, Springfield Coll., Springfield Library and Mus. Assn., Eastern States Expn., Springfield. Served as ensign USN, World War I. Clubs: Longmeadow Country; Springfield Colony, Dartmouth (Springfield). Lodge: Rotary. Home: East Longmeadow Mass. Deceased.

STEINBERG, DICK, professional football team executive. Gen. mgr., vice pres. N.Y. Jets. Home: Hempstead N.Y. Deceased.

STEINER, PAUL, publishing company executive; b. Vienna, Austria, Jan. 1, 1913; came to U.S., 1939, naturalized, 1945; s. Geza and Ilona (Singer) S.; m. Marianne Esberg, Feb. 15, 1942; 1 son, H. Thomas. Student, U. Vienna, 1938. Asst. to owner, editor in chief Neue Freie Presse, Vienna, 1934-38; owner, chief exec. Chanticleer Press, Inc., N.Y.C., 1950-96; pub. illustrated books in natural history and the arts, pub. Audubon Soc. Field Guide to N.Am. Birds, 2 vols., N.Am. Nature, 16 vols. Recipient Golden Pour le Mérite of City of Vienna, 1986. Home: New York N.Y. Died Mar. 7, 1996.

STEINER, WILLIAM, direct marketing advertising agency executive, consultant; b. N.Y.C., Nov. 4, 1913; s. Bernhard and Regina (Storch) S. B.S. in Mktg. and Journalism, NYU, 1936. Market research dir. Topics Pub. Co., N.Y.C., 1936-40; circulation dir. Scholastic Mags., N.Y.C., 1940-44; promotion dir. Washington Post, 1944-49; bus. mgr. The Am. Girl, N.Y.C., 1949-50; circulation dir. Young Am. Mags. and Films, N.Y.C., 1950-52; pub. Gauden mag., N.Y.C., 1952-54; pres. William Steiner Assocs., Inc., N.Y.C., 1954-85, Steiner/Mauck Direct Inc., 1985-93. Contbr. chpts. to Handbook of Magazine Publishing, 1975, Best of Catalog Age, 1982. Contbr. articles to trade publs. Mem. Direct Mktg. Assn. (judge awards competition, com. mem.), Nat. Bus. Circulation Assn., Fulfillment Mgmt. Assn. (Industry award 1980), Direct Market Creative Guild (treas.), Direct Mktg. Club N.Y. (Leadership award 1982), Women's Direct Response Group (chmn. newsletter com.). Club: NYU (N.Y.C.). Died May 20, 1993. Home: New York N.Y.

STELLA, DANIEL FRANCIS, lawyer; b. Sedalia, Mo., Aug. 1, 1943; s. Frank D. and Martha T. Stella; m. Kaethe Reiff, Aug. 31, 1968; children: Dante, Davidde, Ciara. AB, Holy Cross Coll., 1965; JD, Harvard U., 1968; LLM, London Sch. Econs. and Polit. Sci. (Eng.), 1974. Bar: Mich. 1968, U.S. Dist. Ct. (ea. dist.) Mich. 1968, U.S. Dist. Ct. (we. dist.) Mich., 1977, U.S. Ct. Appeals (6th cir.) 1968, Calif. 1975, U.S. Dist. Ct. (no. dist.) Calif. 1975, U.S. Ct. Appeals (9th cir.) 1975, U.S. Ct. Mil. Appeals 1980. Assoc. Dykema Gossett, Detroit, 1968-69, 77-78, ptnr., 1979-94; assoc. Pillsbury, Madison & Sutro, San Francisco, 1974-76. Mem. Founder Soc., Detroit Art Inst.; pres. Friends Internat. Inst. of Detroit; bd. dirs. Internat. Inst. Detroit, Civic Searchlight of Detroit, Inc.; mem. Sec. of Navy Adv. Com. on naval history. Capt. USNR, 1969-89. Mem. ABA, Calif. Bar Assn., Mich. Bar Assn., Detroit Bar Assn., Holy Cross Coll. Alumni Assn., London Sch. Econs. and Polit. Sci. Soc., Fairlane Club (Dearborn, Mich.), Harvard of Eastern Mich. Club. Died July 15, 1994; buried Holy Sepulchre Archdiocesan Cemetary, Southfield, Mich. Home: Detroit Mich.

STELLAR, ELIOT, physiological psychologist, educator; b. Boston, Nov. 1, 1919; m. Betty E. Stellar. A.B., Harvard U., 1941; M.Sc., Brown U., 1942, Ph.D., 1947; D.Sc. (hon.), Ursinus Coll., 1978, Emory U., 1990; D.H.L. (hon.), Johns Hopkins U., 1983. Formerly asst. prof. psychology Johns Hopkins U.; mem. faculty U. Pa., 1954-93, prof. physiol. psychology, dept. anatomy, 1960-93, dir. Inst. Neurol. Scis.,, 1965-73, provost univ., 1973-78, chmn. anatomy dept., 1990-92, chmn. cell and devel. biology dept., 1992-93; cons. Nat. Inst. Gen. Med. Scis.; mem. sci. adv. bd. U. Wash. Nat. Primate Center; mem. coms. NIH, VA Central Office Adv. Com. Research, NIMH, Carnegie Corp.; com. NAS, Nat. Commn. Protection Human Subjects of Biomed. and Behavioral Research; hon. prof. Tianjin Med. Coll., People's Republic China, 1985. Author: (with C.T. Morgan) Physiological Psychology, (with V.G. Dethier) Animal Behavior; Editor (with J.M. Sprague) series Progress in Physiological Psychology, 1966-73, Jour. Comparative and Physiological Psychology, 1969-74, (with J.R. Stellar) The Neurobiology of Motivation and Reward. Recipient Disting. Achievement award Brown U. Grad. Sch., Disting. Scientist award Internat. Union Physiol. Scis., 1986, Gold medal Am. Psychol. Found. for life achievement in psychol. sci., 1993. Mem. NAS (chmn. human rights com.), APA (chmn. coun. editors), AAAS, Am. Acad. Arts & Scis., Am. Philos. Soc. (pres. 1987-93), Inst. Medicine, Soc. Exptl. Psychologists (Warren medal 1967), Am. Assn. Anatomists, Internat. Brain Rsch. Orgn., Soc. Neurosci. (treas.), Dutch Soc. Scis. (fgn. mem.), Phi Beta Kappa, Sigma Xi. Home: Ardmore Pa. Died Oct. 12, 1993.

STENNIS, JOHN CORNELIUS, former senator; b. Kemper County, Miss., Aug. 3, 1901; s. Hampton Howell and Cornelia (Adams) S.; m. Coy Hines, Dec. 24, 1929 (dec.); children: John Hampton, Margaret Jane (Mrs. Womble). B.S., Miss. State U., 1923; LL.B., U. Va., 1928; LL.D., Millsaps Coll., 1957, U. Wyo., 1962, Miss. Coll., 1969, Belhaven Coll., 1972, William Carey Coll., 1975, Livingston U., 1984. Bar: Miss. Practiced in DeKalb, Miss.; mem. Miss. Ho. of Reps., 1928-32; dist. pros. atty. 16th Jud. Dist., 1931-37; circuit judge, 1937-47; mem. U.S. Senate from Miss., 1947-89, mem. armed services com., chmn. appropriations com.; pres. pro tempore U.S. Senate, 1987-89; exec. in residence Miss. State U., 1989-90. Active in promotion farm youth tng. programs; state chmn. Miss. 4-H Adv. Council. Mem. ABA, Miss. Bar Assn., Phi Alpha Delta, Phi Beta Kappa, Alpha Chi Rho. Presbyterian (deacon). Clubs: Masons, Lions. Home: Mississippi Miss. Died April 23, 1995.

STEPHANOS I, HIS BEATITUDE AND EMINENCE See SIDAROUSS, STEPHANOS

STEPHENS, ROBERT, actor; b. July 14, 1931; s. Rueben and Gladys (Deverell) S.; m. Tarn Basset; 1 dau.; m. Maggie Smith, 1967 (div. 1975); 2 sons; m. Patricia Quinn, Jan. 1995. Educated Bradford Civic Theatre Sch. Mem. English Stage Co., Royal Ct., 1956, Nat. Theatre Co., 1963—; stage appearances include: Sherlock Holmes, N.Y. and Can., 1975, Murderer, 1975, Zoo Story, 1975, Othello, 1976, Pygmalion, L.A., 1979, The Cherry Orchard, 1978, Brand, 1978, The Double Dealer, 1978, Has "Washington" Legs?, 1978, A Midsummer Night's Dream, 1983, Inner Voices, 1983, Cinderella, 1983, The Mystery Plays, 1985, Henry IV-Part I, 1993, Henry IV-Part II, 1993 (Best Actor Olivier award 1993), King Lear, 1993, 94 (Sir John Guelgud award for best actor 1994), Julius Caesar, 1993 (Best Stage Actor award Variety Club 1994); films include: A Taste of Honey, 1962, Cleopatra, 1963, The Small World of Sammy Lee, 1963, The Prime of Miss Jean

Brodie, 1969, The Private Life of Sherlock Holmes, 1970, Travels with my Aunt, 1972, The Asphyx, 1973, Luther, 1974, Puccini, 1984, By the Sword Divided (series), 1984, Hells Bells, 1985, Comrades, 1985, High Season, 1986, Fortunes of War, 1986, Lizzie's Pictures, 1986, Shostokovich, 1987, Empire of the Sun, 1987, The Fruit Machine, 1988, Henry V, 1989, The Bonfire of the Vanities, 1990, The Pope Must Die, 1991, Afraid of the Dark, 1992, Searching for Bobby Fischer, 1992, Century, 1992, Secret Rapture, 1993; television performances include: QB VII, 1974, Kean, 1978, Voyage of Charles Darwin, 1978, Office Story, 1978, Friends in Space, 1979, Suez, 1979, The Executioner, 1980, Adelaide Bartlett (series), 1980, Winter's Tale, 1980, The Double Dealer, 1980, The Trial of Madame Famay, 1980; Alexander the Great, 1980, Holocaust, 1980, Eden End, 1981, The Year of the French, 1981, War and Remembrance, 1986; radio plays include: The Light Shines in the Darkness, 1985, Timon of Athens, 1989. Decorated knight Order of Brit. Empire; recipient Variety Club award for stage actor, 1965. Died Nov. 12, 1995. Home: London Eng.

STERLING, JOHN EWART WALLACE, university chancellor; b. Linwood, Ont., Can., Aug. 6, 1906; came to U.S.,, naturalized, 1947; s. William Sterling and Annie (Wallace) S.; m. Anna Marie Shaver, Aug. 7, 1930; children: William W., Susan Hardy (Mrs. Bernard Monjauze), Judith Robinson (Mrs. Frank Morse). B.A., U. Toronto, 1927; M.A., U. Alta., 1930; Ph.D., Stanford U., 1938; LL.D., Pomona Coll., Occidental Coll., 1949, U. San Francisco, U. Toronto, 1950, U. B.C., Northwestern U., U. Calif., 1958, U. Denver, Loyola U., McGill U., 1961, Columbia U., 1962, McMaster U., 1966, Harvard U., 1968, U. Alta., 1970; D.C.L., Durham U., England, 1953; Litt.D., U. Caen, France, 1957, U. So. Calif., 1960; L.H.D., St. Mary's Coll., 1962, Santa Clara U., 1963, Mills Coll., 1967, U. Utah, 1968. Lectr. history Regina (Sask., Can.) Coll., 1927-28; asst. in history, dir. phys. edn. U. Alta., 1928-30; mem. research staff Hoover War Library, Stanford U., 1932-37, instr. history, 1935-37; asst. prof. history Calif. Inst. Tech., 1937-40, asso. prof., 1940-42, prof. history, 1942-45, Edward S. Harkness prof. of history and govt., exec. com., 1945-48, chmn. faculty, 1944-46; news analyst CBS, 1942-48; dir. Huntington Library, 1948-49; pres. Stanford U., 1949-68, lifetime chancellor, 1968; past dir. Fireman's Fund Am. Ins. Cos., Kaiser Aluminum & Chem. Corp., Shell Oil Co., Tridair Industries, Dean Witter & Co.; Civilian faculty Nat. War Coll., 1947, bd. cons., 1948-52; bd. visitors U.S. Naval Acad., 1956-58, Tulane U., 1960-74; mem. nat. adv. council Health Research Facilities, HEW, 1956-57. Editor: (with H.H. Fisher, X.J. Eudin) Features and Figures of the Past (V.I. Gurko), 1939. Chmn. Commn. Presdl. Scholars, 1965-68; adv. bd. Office Naval Research, 1953-56; chmn Am. Revolution Bicentennial Commn., 1969-70; mem. Ford Internat. Fellowship Bd., 1960, Can.-Am. Com., 1957-74, Am. adv. com. Ditchley Found., Eng., 1962-76; mem. adv. com. fgn. relations U.S. Dept. State, 1965-68; bd. dirs. Council Fin. Aid to Edn., 1967-70; mem. Brit.-N.Am. Com., 1969-74. Decorated knight comdr. Order Brit. Empire, 1976; comdr.'s cross Order Merit Fed. Republic Germany; chevalier Legion d'Honneur France; 2d degree Imperial Order Rising Sun Japan; Grand Gold Badge of Honor for Merits Republic of Austria; Herbert Hoover medal Stanford Alumni Assn., 1964; Clark Kerr award U. Calif., Berkeley, 1969; Uncommon Man award Stanford Assos., 1978; fellow Social Sci. Research Council, 1939-40. Fellow Am. Geog. Soc.; mem. Council on Fgn. Relations, Western Coll. Assn. (pres. 1953), Am., Pacific Coast hist. assns., Assn. Am. Univs. (pres. 1962-64). Clubs: Commonwealth (Palo Alto, San Francisco, N.Y.C., Los Angeles), Bohemian (Palo Alto, San Francisco, N.Y.C., Los Angeles), California (Palo Alto, San Francisco, N.Y.C., Los Angeles), Burlingame Country (Palo Alto, San Francisco, N.Y.C., Los Angeles), Pacific-Union (Palo Alto, San Francisco, N.Y.C., Los Angeles), University (Palo Alto, San Francisco, N.Y.C., Los Angeles) (hon.). Home: Woodside Calif. Deceased.

STERLING, KENNETH, research physician, educator; b. Balt;, July 29, 1920; s. Lee and Frances (White) S.; m. Ruth Yanover; 1 child, Donna. A.B., Harvard Coll., 1940; M.D., Johns Hopkins U., 1943. Diplomate Am. Bd. Internal Medicine. Research fellow in medicine Med. Sch., Harvard U. and Brigham Hosp., Boston, 1949-51; research fellow, then instr. in medicine Yale U., New Haven, 1951-54; asst. prof. medicine SUNY Upstate Med. Ctr., Syracuse, 1954-57; dir. protein research lab. Bronx VA Med. Ctr., N.Y., 1962-95; clin. prof. medicine Columbia U., N.Y.C., 1974-95; mem. endocrinology study sect. NIH, Bethesda, Md., 1973-75; mem. vis. com. for med. dept. Brookhaven Nat. Lab., Upton, N.Y., 1975-78, chmn., 1977-78. Author: Diagnosis and Treatment of Thyroid Diseases, 1975; also chpts., numerous research articles and rev. papers on original use of 51Cr in biology and medicine, turnover in man of labeled albumin, thyroxine and T3, measurement of T3 in serum, mechanism of thyroid hormone action in cells; editorial bd. Endocrinology, 1962-65, Jour. Clin. Endocrinology and Metabolism, 1965-74. Recipient Henry L. Moses award Montefiore Hosp., 1950, 52, 63, William S. Middleton award VA, 1972. Mem. Friends and Parents of Renaissance Project, Inc. Club: Harvard (N.Y.C.). Home: Bronx N.Y. Died Jan. 12, 1995.

STERN, HENRY LOUIS, lawyer, corporate consultant; b. Germany, Jan. 2, 1924; came to U.S., 1938; s. Hugo and Judith (Lypstadt) S.; children: Geoffrey Adlai, Roger Davis. PhB with gen. honors, U. Chgo., 1947, JD, 1950. Bar: Ill. 1950, N.Y. 1956, Calif. 1964. Atty.-adviser SEC, 1950-55; assoc. and ptnr. Mitchell, Silberberg & Knupp, Los Angeles, 1967-80; corp. counsel Holly Corp., N.Y.C. and Azusa, Calif., 1957-67; sr. v.p., gen. counsel, sec. Holly Corp., Dallas, 1980-89; ret., 1989, bd. dirs. and cons., 1989-94. Assoc. editor U. Chgo. Law Rev., 1949-50. Served with AUS, 1943-45. Mem. ABA (com. on fed. securities regulation). Home: San Diego Calif. Deceased.

STERNE, MICHAEL LYON, newspaper editor; b. N.Y.C., Mar. 24, 1936; s. John Christie and Mildred Lyon (Christman) S.; m. Geraldine Ann Savidge, Sept. 25, 1960; children: Evelyn Ann, Christie Savidge. BA, Columbia U., 1958; MA in History, Northwestern U., 1959. Reporter, asst. news editor, asst. city editor N.Y. World Telegram and The Sun, N.Y.C., 1960-65; reporter, interviewer, moderator World at Ten news program Sta. WNET-TV, N.Y.C., 1962-66; from. reporter to assoc. bus. and fin. editor N.Y. Times, 1966-95. Editor: N.Y. Times Guide to Where to Live In and Around New York, 1985; author, narrator TV documentary-Up From H: New Ways Out of Heroin Addiction, 1966. Trustee, v.p. The Chapin Sch., N.Y.C., 1977-90; vestry St. James Episc. Ch., N.Y.C., 1978-81, 83-86, 89-91. Officer Most Venerable Order Hosp. of St. John of Jerusalem. Mem. University Club, Century Assn., Phi Beta Kappa. Home: New York N.Y. Died Nov. 20, 1995.

STERNER, JAMES HERVI, physician, educator; b. Bloomsburg, Pa., Nov. 14, 1904; s. Lloyd Parvin and Nora (Finney) S.; m. Frances Elkavich, Apr. 11, 1932 (div. 1971); children: James R., Susan M., John P.; m. Patricia L. Hudson, 1971. Student, Pa. State Tchrs. Coll., Bloomsburg, 1925; B.S., Pa. State Coll., 1928; M.D., Harvard U., 1932. Diplomate: Am. Bd. Indsl. Hygiene, Am. Bd. Preventive Medicine (chmn. 1961-67). House officer New Eng. Deaconess Hosp., Boston, 1931-32; intern New Eng. Deaconess Hosp., 1932-34; chief resident physician Lankenau Hosp., Phila., 1934-36; dir. lab. indsl. medicine Eastman Kodak Co., Rochester, N.Y., 1936-48; asso. med. dir. Eastman Kodak Co., 1949-50, med. dir., 1951-68; med. dir. Clinton Engring. Works, Tenn. Eastman Corp., Oak Ridge, 1943-45; med. cons. Holston Ordnance Works, Kingsport, Tenn., 1941-43; instr. indsl. medicine and toxicology U. Rochester Sch. Medicine, 1940-50, asso. prof. medicine, 1951-57, clin. asso. prof. medicine, 1958-68, from clin. asso. prof. to clin. prof. preventive medicine and community health, 1951-68; prof. environmental health U. Tex. Sch. Pub. Health, Houston, 1968-75; acting dean U. Tex. Sch. Pub. Health, 1968, asso. dean, 1969-70; clin. prof. occupational medicine U. Calif. Coll. Medicine at Irvine, 1975-85; acting dir. pub. health City Houston, 1970; vis. lectr. indsl. hygiene Harvard U., 1952-56; vis. lectr. indsl. medicine U. Tex. Postgrad. Sch. Medicine, 1954-58; sr. asso. physician Strong Meml. Hosp.; cons. indsl. medicine Genesee Hosp., 1960-68, Rochester Gen. Hosp., 1963-68; adv. med. bd. in Am. Am. Hosp. of Paris, 1958; Mem. interim med. adv. bd. Manhattan Project AEC, 1945-47; mem. radiol. safety sect. and medicolegal bd. Operations Crossroads (Bikini experiment), 1946; cons. indsl. health AEC, 1948-92, mem. adv. com. biology and medicine, 1960-66, mem. gen. adv. com., 1971-74; mem. com. fellowships in indsl. medicine, chmn., 1950-51; mem. com. on toxicol. div. chem. and chem. technol. NRC, 1947-55, 71-74; mem. Nat. Transuranium Registry Adv. Com., chmn., 1969-92; spl. cons. USPHS (chmn. com. on radiation studies), 1951-53; mem. cancer control com. Nat. Cancer Inst., 1957-61; expert adv. panel on occupational health WHO, 1951-92; cons. Nat. Center Health Statistics, 1966-75; mem. com. occupational safety and health ILO; mem. Nat. Council Radiation Protection and Measurements, 1955-68, N.Y. State Gen. Adv. Com. Atomic Energy, 1959-65; environ. health panel Pres.'s Sci. Adv. Com., 1961-65, Nat. Adv. Disease Prevention and Environ. Control Council, 1964-68; chmn. Nat. Air Conservation Commn., 1966-70; mem. adv. environ. panel U.S. Senate Com. on Pub. Works, 1970-75; mem. sci. adv. panel U.S. Ho. of Reps. Com. Pub. Works, 1973-75; environ. health adv. com. EPA, 1975-92. Editorial bd.: Archives Indsl. Hygiene and Occupational Medicine, 1948-54; Contbr. to text books, jours. Recipient Indsl. Health award Houston C. of C., 1954, award N.Y. Acad. Preventive Medicine, 1963; James H. Sterner prof. named in his honor U. Rochester, 1979; Named Disting. Alumni. Bloomsburg U. Pa., 1983. Fellow AAAS, Indsl. Med. Assn. (Knudsen award 1957), Am. Coll. Preventive Medicine (v.p. 1957-58, pres. 1959-60), Am. Pub. Health Assn., Am. Acad. Occupational Medicine (Award of Honor 1959, pres. 1952-53); mem. AMA (chmn. council on occupational health 1961-62, mem. residency rev. com. preventive medicine 1956-61, mem. council environmental and pub. health 1963-73, chmn. 1963-69), Soc. Toxicology, World Med. Assn., Am. Indsl. Hygiene Assn. (Cummings award 1955, pres. 1948-49), Am. Chem. Soc. (councilor 1949-52), Royal Soc. Health, Assn. Tchrs. Preventive Medicine, Radiation Research Soc., Health Physics Soc., NAM (med. adv. com. 1950-68), Mfg. Chemists Assn. (med. adv. com. 1950-57, chmn. environ. health adv. com. 1966-68), Nat. Health Council (pres. 1961), Nat. Tb Assn. (dir.), Aerospac Med. Assn., Air Pollution Control Assn., Interna Assn. Occupational Health (U.S. del. permaner commn.), Phi Kappa Phi, Alpha Omega Alpha. Clu Cosmos. Home: Laguna Beach Calif. Died Aug. 2 1992.

STETSON, JOHN BENJAMIN BLANK, anesthes ologist, educator; b. Chgo., Mar. 18, 1927; s. Lou Blank and Dorothy (Cohen) S.; children: Diana S Dana L., Jonathan O. Student, U. Chgo., 1942-44, 4 47; M.D., Harvard U., 1951. Diplomate: Am. B Anesthesiologists. Intern U. Utah Hosp., 1951-52; r sident Mass. Gen. Hosp.; instr. anesthesiology U. Mich Harvard Med. Sch., Children's Hosp., 1959-65; ass prof., dir. vital function lab. U. Ind. Med. Sch., 1965-6 assoc. prof., asso. dir. dept. anesthesiology Ohio Sta U. Sch. Medicine, 1967-68; dir. clin. pharmacology, a ting med. dir. Strasenburgh Labs., Rochester, N.Y 1968-70; assoc. anesthesiologist Strong Meml. Hosp., Rochester, 1970-76; dir. clin. research Arnar Sto Labs., Inc., 1976-77; prof. Rush Med. Coll., 1977-9 prof. emeritus, 1990-93; cons. Roswell Park Meml. Ins Buffalo, 1968-86; vis. prof. Biomed. Engring., Purd U., 1988-92. Served with USNR, 1944-46. FD grantee, 1973-76. Home: Greencastle Ind. Died Ap 15, 1993.

STEVENSON, DAVID A., materials science educatc b. Albany, N.Y., Sept. 6, 1928; married, 1958; 3 ch dren. BA, Amherst Coll., 1950; PhD in Ph Chemistry, MIT, 1954. Rsch. assoc. metallurgy MI 1953-54, asst. prof., 1955-58; prof. materials sc Stanford (Calif.) U., from 1958; sr. rsch. fellow M Planck Inst. Phys. Chemistry, 1968, 69. Recipient Fr Whipple award Am. Geophysical Union, 1994; Fu bright scholar U. Munich, 1954-55. Mem. Am. Sc Metals, Am. Inst. Mining, Metallurgy and Petroleu Engring., Electrochem. Soc., Sigma Xi. Home: Stanfo Calif. Deceased.

STEVENSON, HENRY MILLER, wildlife research b. Birmingham, Ala., Feb. 25, 1914; s. Henry Munn a Mayme Gene (Fuller) S.; m. Rosa Belle Ard, Nov. 1 1989; children: Nell Stevenson Sanders, Ernest, Hen Jr., James. BA, Birmingham-So. Coll., 1935; MS, Ala., 1939; PhD, Cornell U., 1943. Rsch. assoc. A Coop. Wildlife Rsch. Unit, Auburn, 1943; acting ass prof. U. Miss., Oxford, 1943-44; instr. Memphis Sta Coll., 1944; assoc. prof. Emory (Va.) & Henry Co 1944-46; asst. prof. ornithology Fla. State U., T lahassee, 1946-52, assoc. prof., 1952-65, prof. a curator of birds, 1965-75, prof. emeritus, 1975-9 Beadel rsch. fellow Tall Timbers Rsch. Sta., Tallahass 1975-91. Author: A Key to Florida Birds, 1960, Flori Vertebrates, 1978, Florida Birdlife, 1993; editor F Field Naturalist Jour., 1973-76, currently mem. editor bd.; contbr. more than 200 articles to profl. jours Grantee NRC, 1956, 57, Fla. State U., 1954-57, 60-6 Communicable Disease Ctr. of USPHS, 1961-66, T Timbers Rsch. Sta., 1971-73, 75-80; travel grants A Mus. Natural History, 1981, Field Mus. Natural H tory, 1982. Mem. Am. Ornithologists' Union (elect mem.), Cooper Ornithol. Soc., Ga. State Ornithol. So Ala. Ornithol. Soc. (charter), Fla. Ornithol. Sc (charter, records com., editorial bd.). Methodist. Home: Tallahassee Fla. Died Nov. 4, 1991.

STEVENSON, JOHN O'FARRELL, JR., dean; Bklyn., Oct. 11, 1947; s. John O'Farrell Sr. and Vivi Eslie (Pemberton) S. BA in Math., Fordham U., 19 PhD, MS in Math., Polytechnic U., 1976. Instr. Po Inst., Bklyn.; asst. prof. LaGuardia Community Co Queens, N.Y.; dean Empire State Coll., N.Y.C., 19 80; pres. NSSFNS, N.Y.C., 1980-84; assoc. dean Bro Community Coll., N.Y., 1984-92; Math. pr LaGuardia C.C., 1992-94, assoc. dean, 1992-94. Danforth Found. scholar, 1968; Presdl. scholar, 196 Mem. Soc. for Value in Higher Edn., Am. Assn. Higher Edn., 100 Black Men, Phi Beta Kappa. Democrat. Roman Catholic. Home: Brooklyn N. Died Nov. 24, 1994.

STEWART, CHARLES EDWARD, JR., retired feder judge; b. Glen Ridge, N.J., Sept. 1, 1916; s. Char Edward and Eva (Gay) S.; m. Virginia Louise Brow Jan. 21, 1941; 1 son, Charles Edward III. B. Harvard, 1938, LL.B., 1948. Bar: N.Y. bar, N.J. ba Assoc. firm Dewey, Ballantine, Bushby, Palmer Wood, N.Y.C., 1948-57; partner Dewey, Ballanti Bushby, Palmer & Wood, 1957-72; judge, sr. judge U Dist. Ct., So. Dist. N.Y., N.Y.C., 1972-94. Served capt. AUS, 1942-45. Mem. Assn. of Bar of City N.Y., N.Y., N.J. fed. bar assns. Club: Harvard N. Home: Pawling N.Y. Died Oct. 28, 1994.

STEWART, SAMUEL B., banker, lawyer; b. Chat nooga, Oct. 5, 1908; s. Samuel B. and Dora (Pryor) m. Celeste Dorwin, Apr. 2, 1934; children: Lin Celeste (Mrs. James F. Dickason), James Christoph Dorwin (dec.). A.B., U. Va., 1927; J.D., Columbia 1930; LL.D., Golden Gate U., 1965. Bar: N.Y. 19 Calif. 1947. Assoc. Cravath, de Gersdorff, Swaine Wood, 1930-39; partner Blake & Voorhees (and su cessor firm Blake, Voorhees & Stewart), 1939-47; v. gen. counsel Bank of Am. Nat. Trust & Savs. Assn., S Francisco, 1947-59; exec. v.p., gen. counsel Bank of A Nat. Trust & Savs. Assn., 1959-67, exec. v.p., chief ex officer trust activities, 1962-67, exec. v.p., sr. adminstrv. officer, 1967-69, vice chmn. bd., 1969-70, sr. vice chmn. od., 1970-73; also dir.; vice chmn. bd. Bank Am. Corp., 1969-70, sr. vice chmn. bd., 1970-73, also dir., chmn. gen. trust com., 1969-79; dir. Longs Drug Stores Inc., World Corp.; spl. counsel price adjustment Truman) Spl. Com of U.S. Senate for investigation Nat. Def. Program, 1943-44; Disting. vis. prof. San Francisco State U., 1974. Editor: The Business Lawyer, 1959-60. Trustee Golden Gate U.; trustee Salk Inst., chmn., 1974-85; bd. dirs. No. Calif. Presbyn. Homes Inc., 1983-89; od. govs. San Francisco Symphony, 1974-95, v.p., 1980-95. Recipient Cyril Magnin award, 1979, Jefferson award Am. Inst. Public Service, 1978, Silver Spur award San Francisco Planning and Urban Research Assn., 1980. Mem. Am. Bar Assn. (past chmn. sect. corp. banking and bus. law), Legal Aid Soc. of San Francisco pres. 1963-65), Bar Assn. San Francisco (v.p. 1967), Greater San Francisco C. of C. (pres. 1969-70, chmn. bd. 1971, lifetime contbn. award 1979), Sponsors San Francisco Performing Arts Center (pres. 1973-85), Phi Beta Kappa. Presbyn. (elder). Clubs: Bankers, Bohemian, San Francisco Golf, Silverado Country. Home: San Francisco Calif. Died May 27, 1995.

STIBITZ, GEORGE R(OBERT), research investigator, consultant; b. York, Pa., Apr. 30, 1904; s. George and Mildred Amelia (Murphy) S.; m. Dorothea Lamson, Sept. 1, 1930; children: Mary Stibitz Pacifici, Martha Stibitz Banerjee. Ph.B., Denison U., 1926, Sc.D. (hon.), 1966; M.S., Union Coll., 1927; Ph.D., Cornell U., 1930; Sc.D.(hon.), Keene State Coll., 1978, Dartmouth Coll., 1986. Technician Gen. Electric Co., Schenectady, N.Y., 1927-28; math. engr. Bell Telephone Labs., N.Y.C., 1930-45; tech. aide Nat. Def. Rsch. Com. Office Sci. R&D, 1941-46; cons. in applied math. Burlington and Underhill, Vt., 1945-66; rsch. assoc. Dartmouth Med. Sch., Hanover, N.H., 1964-95, prof. emeritus, 1972-95; cons. in field. Author: Math and Computers, 1957, Math in Medicine, 1966; patentee in field including complex number calculator (Inventors Hall Fame 1983). Recipient Harry Goode award Am. Fedn. Info. Processing, 1965, Piore award IEEE, 1977, medal Babbage Soc., 1982. Mem. AAAS, NAE, Phi Beta Kappa, Sigma Xi. Unitarian. Home: Hanover N.H. Died Jan. 31, 1995.

STIEFEL, FRANK D., lawyer; b. Artesia, Calif., Nov. 3, 1944. AB, U. So. Calif., 1967; JD, U. Calif., Berkeley, 1970. Bar: Calif. 1971. Atty. Meserve, Mumpher & Hughes, Irvine, Calif. Mem. ABA, Orange County Bar Assn., Thurston Soc., Order of Coif. Home: Irvine Calif. Died Feb. 8, 1994.

STILES, JOHN STEPHEN, wholesale distribution executive; b. Green Bay, Wis., Mar. 29, 1913; s. Walter Stephen and Leela (McCurdy) S.; m. Mabel Selberg, May 27, 1939; children: Cynthia Lee Stiles Ross, Stephanie Lynne Stiles Sullivan, Christine Laney Stiles Sylsma. AB, Dartmouth Coll., 1936. With Morley-Murphy Co., Green Bay, Wis., 1936-92, dir., 1942-92, pres., 1953-77, chmn., 1974-92; bd. dirs. Wis. Pub. Svc. Corp., Kellogg Citizens Nat. Bank; exec. com., mem. bd. dirs. Wausau Ins. Co. U.K.; bd. dirs., treas., exec. com. Green Bay Packers. Inc.; founding dir. Am. Nat. Bank of Green Bay, Assoc. Bancorp. Mem. exec. com. Nat. Assn. Congl. Christian Chs., 1973-76; bd. dirs. Wis. Taxpayers Alliance, Bellin Meml. Hosp., Green Bay, 1954-78, vice chmn., 1956-78. Recipient Chancellor's award U. Wis., Green Bay, 1985. Mem. Nat. Wholesale Hardware Assn. (pres. 1957-59), Green Bay C. of C. (v.p. 1958-63), Masons, Rotary (Paul Harris fellow), Phi Kappa Psi (exec. coun. 1935-37). Congregationalist. Home: De Pere Wis. Died Mar. 23, 1992.

STIMPSON, JOHN HALLOWELL, insurance company executive; b. Milo, Maine, Nov. 7, 1926; s. Don H. and Dorrice A. (Clark) S.; m. Valerie B. Smith, June 13, 1953; children: Kevin, Karen, Kimberly. BA, U. Maine, 1950; MBA, U. Pa., 1952; postgrad., Culinary Inst. of Am., 1988-89. C.L.U. Exec. v.p. N.Y. Life Ins. Co., N.Y.C., 1951-87; ret.; bd. dirs. Empire Fidelity Investments Ins. Co., N.Y.C. Trustee Am. Coll., Bryn Mawr, Pa.; mem. alumni bd. Culinary Inst. Am., 1991. Proclaimed Ambassador of Culinary Inst. Am., 1993. Home: Irvington N.Y. Died Jan. 2, 1994; interred Sleepy Hollow Cemetery, North Tarrytown, N.Y.

STIRLING, EDWIN MURDOCH, English educator, critic; b. Chattanooga, June 21, 1940; s. James and Dorothy Lundeen (Pritchett) S.; m. Deborah Grace Whittier, Sept. 14, 1963; children: Matthew, James. BA magna cum laude, U. of the South, 1962; MA, Northwestern U., 1963, PhD, 1972. Instr. U. N.C., Chapel Hill, 1966-69; asst. prof. English, U. of South, Sewanee, Tenn., 1969-76, assoc. prof., 1976-83, prof., 1983—, chmn. dept., 1989-93; civilian adviser Dept. Def., Vietnam, 1969; dir. Sewanee Summer Seminar, 1976-91; mem. bd. trustees St. Andrew's (Tenn.) Sewanee Sch., 1982-84, U. of the South, 1986-89. Mem. Community Coun., Sewanee, 1972-76; mem. exec. com. Franklin County, Tenn. Dem. Party, 1981; del. N.C. Dem. Party Conv., Raleigh, 1968. NEH fellow, 1976, Rye fellow Aspen Inst., 1992. Mem. MLA, AAUP, South Atlantic Modern Lang. Assn., Soc. for Cinema Studies, Phi Beta Kappa. Episcopalian. Home: Sewanee Tenn. Died Dec. 24, 1994.

STOCKS, KENNETH DUANE, energy company executive; b. Newton, Kans., Feb. 5, 1934; s. Clarence Otis and Violette Ruth (Stamm) S.; m. Sue M. Danforth, Sept. 29, 1957; children: Jeffrey A., Gregory W. BS, Kans. State U., 1956; postgrad., Harvard U., 1979. With Conoco, Inc., Houston, 1959-93, adminstrv. trainee, 1959, mgr. planning western hemisphere petroleum, 1973, mgr. adminstrn., 1973-75, v.p. purchasing, 1975-90, v.p., exec. asst. to pres., chief exec. officer, 1990-93; ret., 1993. Pres. bd. dirs. Houston Regional Minority Coun., 1978; bd. mem. Jr. Achievement of S.E. Tex., 1978-93, bd. pres., 1985; sec. Houston POPS Orch., 1985-89. With U.S. Army, 1957-59. Mem. Nat. Assn. Purchasing Mgmt. (exec. steel com. 1976-90). Republican. Methodist. Home: Houston Tex. Died Apr. 1993.

STOCKWELL, OLIVER PERKINS, lawyer; b. East Baton Rouge, La., Aug. 11, 1907; s. William Richard and Lillie Belle (Dawson) S.; m. Roseina Katherine Holcombe, June 24, 1936; 1 child, Angell Roseina (Mrs. William C. Wright). LL.B., La. State U., 1932, J.D., 1968. Bar: La. 1932. Since practiced in Lake Charles; ptnr. firm Stockwell, Sievert, Viccellio, Clements & Shaddock (and predecessor firm), 1933—; Dir. Lakeside Nat. Bank of Lake Charles; past dir. Gulf States Utilities Co.; past mem. jud. council La. Supreme Ct.; past mem. La. Commn. on Law Enforcement and Adminstrn. Criminal Justice; referee bankruptcy U.S. Dist. Ct. (we. dist.) La., 1938-46. Contbr. to La. Law Rev. Pres. Lake Charles Centennial; bd. dirs., mem. exec. com. Council for a Better La., pres., 1972; past bd. dirs. Pub. Affairs Research Council La.; past bd. dirs. La. State U. Found.; past bd. suprs. La. State U., chmn., 1977-78, chmn. emeritus; past chmn. legal services adv. com. La. Joint Legis. Commn. on Intergovtl. Relations.; chmn. Paul H. Hebert Law Ctr. Council La. State U.; mem. Task Force on Excessive Govtl. Regulations. Served to lt. USNR, 1943-45. Rsch. fellow Southwestern Legal Found. Fellow Am. Bar Found., Am. Coll. Trial Lawyers, Am. Coll. Probate Counsel; mem. Inter-Am. Bar Assn., Am. Judicature Soc., Internat. Bar Assn., ABA (past state chmn. jr. bar sect., mem. spl. com. adoption jud. conduct code, chmn. La. membership com., sr. lawyers div.), La. Bar Assn. (past pres.), S.W. La. Bar Assn. (pres. 1942), Mid-Continent Oil and Gas Assn. (exec. com.), Comml. Law League, Internat. Assn. Ins. Counsel, Fedn. Ins. Counsel, Am. Law Inst. (life mem.), La. Law Inst. (past pres., chmn. mineral code com. 1986; chmn. 1987, chmn. emeritus, 1988), Lake Charles C. of C. (past pres., Civic award 1978), State Assn. Young Men's Bus. Clubs (past pres. Lake Charles), La. State U. Law Sch. Alumni Assn. (past pres., Disting. Alumnus award 1989), Order of Coif, Henri Capitant, Kiwanis (Citizen of Yr. award 1990), Pioneer Club, City Club, Lake Charles Country Club, Boston Club of New Orleans, L Club of La. State U. (past pres.), Lambda Alpha, Omicron Delta Kappa. Home: Lake Charles La. Died July 12, 1993; buried at Graceland Cemetery.

STODDART, JACK ELLIOTT, publishing company executive; b. Hamilton, Ont., Can., July 24, 1916; s. Henry Elliott and May (Elliott) S.; m. Ruth Elizabeth Robb, May 9, 1942; children: Jack Elliott, Susan Elizabeth. Student, Westervelt Coll., U. Toronto. With Macmillan Co. of Can., 1936-57; former pres. Gen. Pub. Co., Don Mills, Ont., 1957; pres., pub. Simon & Schuster Can. Ltd. (became PaperJacks Ltd.), 1976; chmn., pres. Stoddart Pub. Ltd., Toronto; dir. Mercor Pub. Ltd. Contbr. articles to profl. jours. Mem. Bd. Trade Met. Toronto. Served with RCAF. Mem. Assn. Can. Pubs. Conservative. Anglican. Clubs: Donalda, Toronto; Wyndemere (Naples, Fla.). Home: Willowdale Can. Deceased.

STOKES, CARL BURTON, ambassador, judge, former mayor, former state legislator; b. Cleve., June 21, 1927; s. Charles and Louise (Stone) S.; m. Shirley Joann Edwards, Jan. 28, 1958 (div. Oct. 1974); children: Carl Burton, Cordi, Cordell; m. Raija Kostadinov, Jan. 3, 1980 (div. 1993); 1 child, Cynthia. B.S. in Law, U. Minn., 1954; LL.B., Cleve. Marshall Law Sch., 1956, also LL.D.; LL.D., Tufts U., U. Cin., St. Francis Coll., Central State U., Wilberforce U., Lincoln U., Union Coll., Livingston Coll., Boston U., Oberlin Coll. Bar: Ohio 1957, N.Y. State bar 1974. Probation officer Cleve. Municipal Ct., 1954-58; presiding and adminstrv. judge Cleve. Mcpl. Ct., 1983-86; asst. prosecutor City Cleve., 1958-62; mayor, 1967-71; mem. Ohio Ho. of Reps., 1962-67; ptnr. Stokes & Stokes, Cleve., 1962-67, Stokes & Character Law Offices, 1980-83, Stokes & Green Law Offices, 1981-83; corr. WNBC, N.Y.C., 1972-80; mem. exec. com. Nat. League Cities, 1968-71, pres. elect, 1970-71; mem. adv. bd. U.S. Conf. Mayors, 1968-71; mem. steering com. Nat. Urban Coalition, 1968-96; adv. com. Urban Am., 1969-71; mem. Ohio Ho. of Reps., 1962-67; mem. policy com. Nat. Democratic Com., 1969-71; hon. chmn. 21st Congl. Dist. caucus, 1970-72; amb. to Republic of Seychelles Dept. of State, 1994-96; adj. prof. dept. polit. sci. Case Western Reserve U., from 1991. Author: The Quality of Our Environment, Promises of Power, 1973; Contbr. articles to profl. jours. Served with AUS, 1945-46, ETO. Recipient numerous awards including Equal Opportunity award Nat. Urban League; fellow Commn. Phila.; Mass. Com. Protestants, Caths. and Jews; Horatio Alger award; Pacesetter award Young People div. Jewish Community Fedn. Chgo.; Chubb fellowYale. Mem. Elks, Gamma Eta Gamma, Kappa Alpha Psi. Club: Elks. Home: Cleveland Ohio Died April 3, 1996.

STOLLER, MORRIS, talent agency company executive; b. N.Y.C., Nov. 22, 1915. B.B.A., CCNY, 1933; LL.B., Bklyn. Law Sch., 1937. C.P.A., Calif. Chmn. William Morris Agy., Beverly Hills, Calif. Mem. Artists' Mgrs. Guild (officer). Home: Beverly Hills Calif.

STOLP, LAUREN ELBERT, speech pathologist; b. Sprague, Wash., July 10, 1921; s. Charles Albert and Sarah Christine (Campbell) S.; m. Nadine McWhorter, Jan. 29, 1946 (dec. 1976); children—Lauren Elyce Stolp Nasseri, Marla Eve Stolp Sullivan; m. Barbara Duncombe Lang, Mar. 3, 1978. Student, U. Wash., 1939-40; A.B., Eastern Wash. State Coll., Cheney, Wash., 1947; M.S., Ind. State U., Terre Haute, 1951. Pvt. practice speech pathology Houston, 1947-49; dir. Stolp Clinic Sch., Houston, 1948-49; pvt. practice speech pathology Roslyn, Pa., 1968-94; instr. spl. edn. Ind. State U., 1949-53; dir. lower and middle schs. Pa. Sch. for Deaf, Phila., 1953-61; prin. middle sch. Pa. Sch. for Deaf, 1961-68; head speech dept. Chestnut Hill Rehab. Hosp., 1970-87, Chestnut Hill Hosp., 1970-92, Northeastern Hosp., 1970-94, Nazareth Hosp., 1976-91, Parkview Hosp., 1980-94; dir. Lauren E. Stolp Assocs., 1976-94, U. Pa. Hosp., 1988-89, Springfield Hosp., 1989-92, Cooper Hosp., Phila., 1991-94; cons. in field. Pres. Upper Moreland High Sch. Home and Sch. Assn., 1964-66. Served with USCGR, 1942-45. Fellow Am. Assn. Mental Retardation; mem. Am., Pa. speech and hearing assns., Am. Acad. Pvt. Practice Speech Pathology and Audiology, A. G. Bell Assn. for Deaf, Orton Soc., Kappa Delta Pi, Phi Delta Kappa. Republican. Episcopalian. Club: Lion (pres. Willow Grove, Pa. 1964-65). Home: Philadelphia Pa. Died Oct. 21, 1994.

STOLZ, PREBLE, legal educator, lawyer; b. 1931. J.D., U. Chgo., 1956. Bar: Calif., 1957. Law clk. to judge U.S. Ct. Appeals (9th cir.), 1956-57; law clk. to Hon. Harold H. Burton, 1957-58; dep. atty. gen. State of Calif., 1958-61; prof. U. Calif. Law Sch.-Berkeley, 1961-96; scholar-in-residence Am. Bar Found., Chgo., spring 1967; vis. prof. Yale U., 1970-71; asst. to Calif. Gov. for Programs and Policies, 1975-76; reporter U.S. Admiralty Rules Com., 1968-72. Mem. Order of Coif. Former editor-in-chief U. Chgo. Law Rev. Died June 11, 1996. Home: Berkeley Calif.

STONE, CHARLES HUDSON, county official; b. Madison, Ala., Oct. 30, 1934; s. Roy Landess and Mae (Hudson) S.; m. Carolyn Phillips; children—Ronda Phillips Stone Myrick, Martha Lynn Stone Hewlett (dec. 1986), Roy Landess. B.A., Auburn U., 1957. Farmer, Gurley, Ala., 1957-77; commr. Madison County Commn., Brownsboro, Ala., 1977—. Developer automated feeder for calves; inventor cotton duster-sprayer; pioneer mulch planting of soy beans. Chmn. Madison County Bd. Equalization, Madison County Com. for Adequate Rural and Community Fire Protection; vice-chmn. Community Resource Devel. Com.; trustee Madison County Sch. System; mem. steering com. Madison County Bd. Edn.; bd. dirs. Huntsville-Madison County Rural YMCA, Huntsville YMCA, Family Counseling Assn., Madison County Recreation Bd., Girl Scouts North Ala. Inc., Madison County Assn. Mental Health, Rocket City Credit Union, Huntsville-Madison County Clean Community System, Rural Sr. Services, Inc., Huntsville 2,000, Huntsville-Madison County Pub. Library Devel. Council; mem. adminstrv. bd. Gurley Methodist Ch.; mem. Huntsville Mus. Art, Ala. Soc. Crippled Children; mem. law planning com. U. Ala.; mem. Auburn U.-Madison County Com., Madison County Health Council. Named Outstanding Young Farmer Madison County, Outstanding Farmers Am., Outstanding Young Farmer Ala., Outstanding Young Farmer Am.; recipient Loyalty award VFW, Achievement awards Nat. Assn. Counties, 1977-85, others. Mem. Artificial Insemination Assn. (pres.), Assn. County Commns. (pres.), Outstanding Farmers Am., Future Farmers Am. (hon.), Madison County Cattlemen's Assn., New C. of C., Gurley Jaycees, Auburn U. Agrl. Alumni. Democrat. Methodist. Club: Huntsville Racquet. Avocations: fishing; hunting; horse back riding; restoring old log cabins. Home: Gurley Ala.

STONE, EZRA CHAIM, theatrical producer and director, educator, actor, writer, farmer; b. New Bedford, Mass., Dec. 2, 1917; s. Solomon and Rose (Meadow) Feinstone; m. Sara F. Seegar, 1942; children: Josef Seegar, Francine Lida. Educated, Oak Lane (Pa.) Country Day Sch., 1928-34; grad., Am. Acad. of Dramatic Arts, N.Y.C., 1935; DFA (hon.), U. Mo., Columbia, 1989. Mem. faculty Am. Theatre Wings Vets. Sch., U. Va. Drama Sch.; ednl. TV cons. Ford Found.; gen. dir., cons. IBM, 1962-86, 91; lectr., tchr. Am. Coll. Theatre Festival, UCLA, Scott Theatre, Ft. Worth, U. Minn., Ariz. Speech and Drama Assn.; vis. prof. theatre arts Calif. State U.-Long Beach, 1973; mem. steering com. Coll. Fellows of Am. Theatre at Kennedy Ctr., Washington, 1989-91; guest artist seminar domestic and overseas tours U.S. Army Music and Theatre Program; guest lectr., adjudicator at numerous instns.; chmn. radio and TV dept. adv. council U. Judaism; pres. and dir. David Library of the Am. Revolution 1979-94; nat. chmn./judge David Library-Am. Coll. Theatre Festival ann. playwriting awards, John F. Kennedy Ctr. of the Performing Arts, Washington, 1974-90; sole adjudicator original mus. theatre student awards, Am. Coll. Theatre Festival/ Kennedy Ctr., 1993; mem. adv. council So. Calif. Ednl. Theatre Assn.; cons. Mt. Vernon Ladies Assn. of Union; dir. My Heart's in the Highlands, U. Va., 1949; prodn. casting asst. George Abbott Prodns. Actor debut in Suppressed Desires (Molnar), YM & YWHA, Phila., 1924, The Flower Seller, Phila. Plays and Players, 1924, Parade, 1935, Ah Wildnerness, Three Men on a Horse, Room Service, Boys From Syracuse; radio debut: Sta. WPEN, Phila., 1924, Horn & Hardart Children's Hour, Sta. WCAU, Phila., Nat. Jr. Theater, Washington, 1931-32, Quality Street, Tale of Two Cities, Last of the Mohicans, Treasure Island; creator character of Bottome in Brother Rat, 1935-38, Sir Epicure Mammon in the Alchemist, 1949; created and played over 600 performances as Henry Aldrich in What a Life, 1938-40; creator role Henry Aldrich in radio serial Aldrich Family, 1938-41, 45-51; also producer-dir. TV program; dir.: (stage prodns.) Reunion in New York, 1939, This is the Army, 1942, How Now Brown Cow, Your Loving Sun (also actor), 1946, Season in the Sun, 1951, Blithe Spirit, 1953; co-starred film Those Were the Days, 1939; Broadway debut as dir. See My Lawyer, 1939; dir. (Broadway prodns.) January Thaw, 1946, Me and Molly, 1948, At War with the Army, 1949, Mark Twain, The Man that Corrupted Hadleyburg, 1951, Count Your Blessings, Blue Danube, 1952, Steve Allen in The Pink Elephant, 1953, Loco, 1953, Ezio Pinza in The Play's the Thing, 1953, Comin' Thru the Rye, 1953, Barrymore Colt One Woman Show, 1953, 8th Observance of the UN, Half in Ernest; producer, dir. program devel. The Hathways, CBS-TV, 1952-54, Affairs of Anatol, ABC-TV, Life With Father, CBS-TV, Love That Guy, CBS, 1952, Debbie Reynolds Show, 1970, I Married Joan, Julia, Tammy, The Munsters, Lost in Space, Karen, Don't Eat the Daisies, Flying Nun, Bob Hope, Bob Newhart; created: Tony Lumpkin in She Stoops to Conquer, 1950; producer-dir. Salvo, N.Y.C.; producer, dir., co-star Sweet Land, Newtown Tricentennial, Pa., 1983; producer-dir. TV programs for, Olsen & Johnson, Ed Wynn, Herb Shriner, Danny Thomas, Fred Allen, Martha Raye, Ezio Pinza, others; actor: Hawaiian Eye, ABC-TV; star Trial of Urial, NBC-TV, Quincy; co-star Munster's Revenge, 1980, Project UFO; dir. Coranado 9, NBC-TV; series Angel, CBS-TV, 1960-61; others; Ann Sothern stage play God Bless Our Bank, Marie Wilson in Fallen Angels; TV dir. series Tammy and The Millionaire; Fantastiks, Pioneer Meml. theatre U. Utah; info. films for LTV Corp., Southwestern Bell Tel. Co., Atlantic Refinery, IBM, General Foods, General Electric, General Motors, Chrysler Motors; The James Stewart Show, Lassie; dir. for ednl. TV: Good Morning Freedom; dir.: Betcha Don't Know, NBC/Children's TV Workshop; dir. for: animated feature The Daydreamer; over 300 documentaries for IBM; dir.: TV shows Bob Cummings, My Living Doll; creator, producer, dir. Golden Wedding Anniversary Tribute to the Lunts, Helen Hayes, Roslind Russell and Fred Astaire ANTA Tributes, 1972; co-star Volpone Music Center Theatre, L.A.; appeared: TV show Hildergarde Withers, ABC-TV, Diana Rigg Show, Julia, actor; Paul Muni biog. picture Emergency; guest star: Eternal Light-Sol Feinstones's America, NBC-TV, 1980; guest artist tours for, U.S. Army Spl. Services; producer, dir. bicentennial documentary The Forty Million; author: Coming Major, 1945, (with Deems Taylor) Puccini Opera Liberté, 1951; concert appearances include Del. Valley Philharm., 1984, Bucks County Singers, 1987; actor Pearl Buck's The Mother, Pearl Buck Found. and Bristol (Pa.) Theatre, 1988, Peony, 1991, The Good Earth, 1992; Old Time Radio Conv. appearances Denver, Cin., Brockton, Kate Smith Foun., Lake Placid, Newark, Shubert Radio Theatre, New Haven, Conn., 1993 recreations of the Aldrich Family, 1991; co-star recreations of Lux Radio Prodn. of You Can't Take It With You, 1990, Norman Corwin's The Plot to Over Throw Xmas (co-star Burgess Meredith); contbr. to mags. Assoc. dir., trustee Am. Acad. Dramatic Arts, also exec. dir. postgrad. center; trustee, awards dir. Sol Feinstone Environ. awards Syracuse U.; bd. dirs. Am. Acad. of Dramatic Arts Alumni Soc., Upper Makefield Hist. Soc., 1989. Master sgt. U.S. Army, 1941-46, USAR, 1945-55. Recipient Grand prize Barcelona Internat. Film Festival, 1971, CINE Golden Eagle award; recipient Golden Mike awrd Golden Radio Buffs of Md., 1981, Silver Mike award Friends of Old Time Radio, 1982; inducted Radio Hall of Fame, 1993. Fellow Am. Theatre Assn.; mem. NATAS, SAG, AFTRA, ANTA (chmn. bd. dirs. ANTA West), Coll. Fellows Am. Theatre (steering com. 1989), Actors Equity Assn. (life), Soc. Stage Dirs. and Choreographers (sec.), Pacific Pioneer Broadcasters, Screen Producers Guild, Am. Guild Variety Artists, Am. Ayrshire Breeders Assn., Newtown Reliance Co. Guild, Writers Guild Am., Army Theatre Arts Assn., Performing Tree So. Calif., Calif. Theatre Coun., Am. Acad. Dramatic Arts Alumni Assn. (bd. dirs.), Dirs. Guild Am. (nat. bd. dirs. 1987-89, ea. dirs. coun. 1979-94). Home: Newtown Pa. Died Mar. 3, 1994.

STONE, GERALD PAUL, engineering company executive; b. Cleve., Dec. 15, 1918; s. Herman and Rose (Simkow) S.; m. Gladys Meyers, May 20, 1950; children: Donald H., Lawrence J. B.Chem. Engring., Coll. City N.Y., 1939; M.Adminstrv. Engring., N.Y. U., 1944, Sc. Engring.D. in Indsl. Engring, 1949; certificate elec. engring. and marine engring., Temple U., 1941; postgrad., Va. Poly. Inst., 1939-40. Registered profl. engr., N.J. Marine, indsl. engr. Navy Dept., 1941-52; pres. G.P. Stone Co., North Bergen, N.J., 1949-93; assoc. prof. mech.-indsl. engring. Poly. Inst. Bklyn., 1952-64, N.J. Inst. Tech.-Newark Coll. Engring., 1966-86; pres. Pub. Research, N.Y.C., 1964-65, G.P. Stone Hosp. Pub. Co., 1967-93; Adj. prof. Coll. City N.Y., Fairleigh Dickinson U., N.Y. U., Pratt Inst., Rutgers U., 1951-93. Author: Management Engineering for Manufacturing, 1967, Programming and Control for Manufacturing, 1968, Improved Driver Education Curriculum, 1972, Hospital Systems Design, 1975, Hospital Unit Processes, 1976, Hospital Training Management; also radio scripts.; Contbr. articles to profl. jours. Active local Boy Scouts Am., Inst. Rehab. Medicine; mem. Mayor of North Bergen's Com. to Relocate N. Hudson Hosp.; mem. com. to combat Huntington's disease Beth Israel Med. Center.; Bd. dirs. N. Hudson Community Center. Recipient commendation sec. navy, 1949. Mem. N.Y. State Soc. Profl. Engrs. (vice chmn. ethical practices com.), Hudson County Soc. Profl. Engrs. (chmn. safety com.), Am. Nat. Standards Inst., AIM, IEEE, AAUP, Am. Inst. Indsl. Engrs. (Greater N.Y. hosp. sect.), Sigma Xi, Phi Lambda Upsilon. Home: North Bergen N.J. Died June 30, 1993.

STONE, MICHAEL P. W., former federal official; b. London, June 2, 1925; married; 2 children. BA, Yale U., 1948; postgrad. law sch., NYU, 1949. Various positions Sterling Vineyards, Napa Valley, Calif., 1964-68, v.p., gen. mgr., dir., 1968-73, pres., dir., 1973-82; dir. U.S. AID Mission in Cairo, 1982-84; dir. Caribbean basin intitiative affairs AID, asst. sec. Dept. of the Army, Washington, 1986-88, undersec., 1988-89, sec., 1989-93; bd. dirs. BEI Electronics, Inc.; chmn. Projects Internat. Assocs., Can. Marconi Co. Home: San Francisco Calif. Died May, 1995.

STONE, WILLIAM C., mathematics educator. BA, Union Coll., 1942; MS, U. Chgo., 1949, PhD, 1952. With Union Coll., Schenectady, N.Y., 1942-44, 51-92, Mary Louise Bailey prof. Home: Schenectady N.Y. Died Apr. 1992.

STORY, GEORGE MORLEY, English language educator, author; b. St. Johns, Nfld., Can., Oct. 13, 1927; m. Laura Alice Stevenson, May 16, 1967; children: Katharine, Lachlan, Simon. Student, Meml. U. Coll., St. John's, Nfld., 1946-48; B.A., McGill U., Montreal, Que., Can., 1950; D.Phil., Oxford U., Eng., 1954. Lectr. in English Meml. U. Nfld., St. John's, 1950-51, asst. prof. English, 1954-59, assoc. prof., 1959-62, prof., 1962-79, Henrietta Harvey prof. English lang. and lit., 1979-94; mem. negotiated grants com. Can. Council, 1970-75; trustee Nfld. Quar. Found., 1982-94. Editor: Sermons of Lancelot Andrews, 1967; co-editor: Sonnets of William Alabaster, 1959, Christmas Mumming in Newfoundland, 1969, A Festschrift for Edgar Ronald Seary, 1976, Dictionary of Newfoundland English, 1982, 2d edit. with supplement, 1990, Early European Settlement and Exploitation in Atlantic Canada, Selected University Orations, 1984; mem. editorial bd. Collected Works of Erasmus, 1974-94, New Oxford English Dictionary, 1984-94; chmn. editorial bd. Jour. Nfld. Studies, 1982-91, Encyclopedia of Newfoundland and Labrador; mem. adv. bd. Australian Nat. Dictionary Centre. Mem. adv. bd. Nat. Library Can.; bd. dirs. Can. Inst. Hist. Microprodns., 1986-89, Nfld Heritage Found.; actice Hist. Sites and Monuments Bd. Can., 1993-94. Decorated Order of Can.; recipient Molson prize Can. Coun., 1977. Fellow Royal Hist. Soc., Soc. Antiquaries, Royal Soc. Can.; mem. Nfld. Hist. Trust (pres. 1969-71), Nfld. Hist. Soc. (pres. 1978-81). Mem. United Ch. Can. Home: Saint John's Can. Died May 26, 1994; interred General Protestant Cemetary, St. John's, Newfoundland.

STOTLAND, EZRA, psychologist, educator; b. N.Y.C., June 9, 1924; s. Isaac and Rose (Chaiken) S.; m. Patricia H. Joyce, July 12, 1963; 1 dau. Sheila; stepchildren: Bruce Hilyer, Barbara Hilyer, Candace Decorah. B.S. in Social Sci, CCNY, 1948; Ph.D. in Social Psychology, U. Mich., 1953. Research assoc. U. Mich., 1953-57; asst. prof. psychology U. Wash., 1957-61, assoc. prof., 1961-64, prof., 1964-85, prof. emeritus, 1985—, dir. soc. and justice program, 1964-88; vis. scientist Battelle N.W., Seattle, 1971-77; co-prin. investigator South Seattle Crime Reduction Program, Seattle Police Dept., 1988-89; cons. VA, VISTA, Crime and Delinquency Ctr. of NIMH, Nat. Inst. Justice, USPHS. Author: Psychology of Hope, 1969 (Behavioral Sci. Book Club selection), (with L. Canon) Social Psychology, 1972, (with A.L. Kobler) Life and Death of Mental Hospital, 1965, End of Hope: A Social-Clinical Study of Suicide, 1964, (with H. Edelhertz, M. Walsh, M. Weinberg) Investigation of White Collar Crime, (1977), (with K. Shaver and S. Sherman) Empathy and Birth Order, 1971, (with R. Mathews, S. Sherman, R. Hansson and B. Richardson) Empathy, Fantasy and Helping, 1978; contbg. author: Advances in Experimental Social Psychology, vol. 4, 1969, (with D. Katz) Psychology: A Study of Science, vol. 3, 1959, (with D. Smith) Urban Policeman in Transition, 1973, Comparative Adminstrative Theory, 1968, Society and War, 1977, Ency. Handbook of Medical Psychology, 1976, Job Stress and the Police Officer, 1976, Internat. Ency. Neurology, Psychiatry, Psychanalysis and Psychology, 1976, (with J. Berberich) Psychology and Criminal Justice; editor (with G. Geis) White Collar Crime: Theory and Research, 1980, (with D. Fleisner, M. Fadon, D Klinger) Community Policing in Seattle ; cons. editor Jour. Research in Crime and Delinquency; contbr. numerous articles to profl. jours. Campaign mgr. Washtenaw County (Mich.) Democratic Com., 1955-56 Bd. dirs. Crisis Clinic of Seattle, 1964-66, Seattle Crim Commn., 1972-78, New Careers, Seattle, 1973-74, Law Enforcement Tng. Bd. of State of Wash., 1978-83 Seattle Mayor's Neighborhood Crime Commn., 1978-87 mem. services adv. com. Wash. State Patrol, 1981-87 Served to sgt. inf. AUS, 1942-46. USPHS Postdoctora fellow, 1961-62; Fulbright fellow, 1969-70. Fellow APA; mem. Soc. Psychol. Study Social Issues (pre 1968, 76-77), Wash. State Assn. Criminal Justice Edu (pres. 1976-77). Home: Bellevue Wash. Deceased.

STOUT, ERNEST GORDON, water ski manufacturin company executive; b. Moran, Kans., Apr. 25, 1913; Raymond Theron and Ival Atena (Boatwright) S.; m Helen Keller Sterling, Feb. 20, 1936 (div. 1973); chi dren: Claudette Stout Blank, Valarie Stout Rerecich; m Lilliam Corrine Stocker, Mar. 31, 1973. BS in Mech Engring., NYU, 1935, MS in Aero. Engring., 1939; cer systems engring., Lockheed Inst., 1965. Registere profl. engr. mech., Calif. Chief naval research Conva div. Gen. Dynamics Corp., San Diego, 1936-55; mg Wash. ops. Ralph M. Parsons Co., Pasadena, Calif 1955-61; div. mgr. advanced design Lockheed Corp Burbank, Calif., 1961-66, dir. transp. systems, 1966-7 pres. Stout-Stocker Assocs., Glendale, Calif., 1974-7 Hydro-Ski Corp., San Diego, from 1978; chmn. seaplan subcom. NASA, 1944-57; cons. Ops. Research, Inc Silver Springs, Md., 1976-82. Author: Hydrodynamic and Hull Design, 1942; contbr. articles to tech. publs designer lst supersonic seaplane; patentee hudro-sl marine vehicle. Bd. dirs. Parkway Manor Home Owne Assn., La Mesa, Calif., from 1983. Served to lt. comd USN, 1944-45 PTO, ETO. Recipient citation achievement NYU, 1955. Fellow AIAA (v.p. 195 Lawrence Sperry award 1941, Sylvanus A. Reed awar 1953); mem. Nat. Security Indsl. Assn. (anti-submarir warfare adv. com. 1954-70), Aerospace Mus., Admiral Club (N.Y.C.), Masons, Tau Beta Pi, Psi Upsilon. Home: La Mesa Calif. Deceased.

STRAHLE, WARREN CHARLES, aerospace enginee educator; b. Whittier, Calif., Dec. 29, 1938; s. Joh Dunn and Josephine Irene (Hoffman) S.; m. Pamell Ann Liles, June 25, 1965 (div. 1969); 1 son, John Curti m. Jane Allen Couch, June 23, 1973 (div. 1988). B.S Stanford U., 1959, M.S., 1960; M.A., Princeton U 1964, Ph.D., 1964. Mem. tech. staff Aerospace Corp San Bernardino, Calif., 1964-67; profl. staff mem. Ins Def. Analysis, Washington, 1967-68; assoc. prof. G Inst. Tech., Atlanta, 1968-71, prof., 1971-74, Regent prof., 1974-94; cons. in field. Reviewer for tech. jours contbr. chpt. to book. Recipient Pendray Aerospac Lit. award, 1985. Fellow AIAA (chmn. tech. con 1969-81 cert. appreciation, jour. editor 1980-82); mer Combustion Inst. (bd. dirs.), Am. Soc. Engring. Edn Sigma Xi (chpt. pres. 1977-78 research award, sustaine research award). Club: Stanford (Ga. chpt.) (pres. 197 75). Home: Atlanta Ga. Died Jan. 1994; interre Atlanta, Ga.

STRANG, MARIAN BOUNDY, librarian; b. Gibso City, Ill., May 5, 1918; d. Ralph Edward and Edr Blackburn (Washburn) Boundy; m. Tom H. Stran Sept. 27, 1943; children—Terry H., Bruce B., Dav R. B.A., U. Wis., 1940, M.L.S., 1941. Libr. Richlar Center, Wis., 1941-42; children's libr. Dearborn (Mich Pub. Libr., 1942-43; asst. libr. Rapides Parish Lib Alexandria, La., 1943-45, Beloit (Wis.) Pub. Libr., 194 46, Fort Knox (Ky.) Libr., 1952-54; libr. Sukiran Lib Okinawa, 1962-64; chief libr. Fort Leonard Wood, M 1964-70; med. libr. U.S. Gen. Wood Army Hosp., Fo Leonard Wood, 1970-88, Med. Libr., Med. Ctr., I dependence, Mo., 1989-95, VA Med. Ctr. Med. Lib Kansas City, Mo., 1989-95, Independence (Mo.) R gional Health Ctr., 1990-95. Mem. ALA, Mo. Libra Assn., Fed. Librarian's Assn., Med. Library Ass AAUN, Bus. and Profl. Women, Delta Zeta. Hom Independence Mo. Died Nov. 12, 1995.

STRASFOGEL, IGNACE, conductor; b. Warsaw, P land, July 17, 1909; came to U.S., 1933, naturalize 1937; s. Ludwig and Salomea (Goldberg) S.; m. Alr Lubin, July 23, 1934 (dec. Apr. 1990); children: Ia Andrew Leigh. Student, Staatliche Akademische Hoc schule für Musik, Berlin. vis. lectr. New Sch. Soc Research, N.Y.C., 1980-94; invited faculty mem. A Inst. Mus. Studies, Graz, Austria, July-Aug., 1989; vited guest composer to Fed. Republic Germany, 199 Accompanist of Joseph Szigeti on world tour, 1927- of Carl Flesch, 1928-30; coach, condr. Opera of Mc Theatre, Duesseldorf, Germany, 1929-30, asst. to ch condrs., Kleiber and Blech, State Opera, Berlin, 1930- composer, condr.: incidental music Fourberies Scapin, Berlin, 1930, Puenktchen und Anton, Deuts Theater, Berlin, 1931; mus. dir.: incidental music Euro A.G, Theater am Kurfuerstendamn, Berlin, 1932; o pianist incidental music, N.Y. Philharmonic Sympho Orch., 1935-44, asst. condr., 1944-45, resigned, 19 apptd. condr., Drs. Orchestral Soc., N.Y.C., 1946, gu condr. Nat. Symphony Orch., Washington, Phila., B falo, 1946, Group Theatre prodn., Johnny Johns accompanist, solo pianist with Lauritz Melchior, 43, broadcast chamber music programs, Perole and varius Quartets, Blaisdell Woodwind Emsemble, network; piano soloist New Friends of Music, Carnegie Hall, 1939, guest condr. Ballet Russe, nberg Concerts, summer 1945, mus. dir. Polonaise -Am. tour), 1942, 1945; condr. reading rehearsals Am. works, N.Y. Philharm. Symphony, 1944-45, Philharm., Carnegie Hall, 1945, Lewisohn Stadium erts, 1944, 45, in New Orleans, Chgo., Toronto, C.; mus. dir.: coast-to-coast tour Brigadoon, 1949- asst. condr., Met. Opera Assn., 1951-60, assoc. r., 1960-94, regular condr. Cin. Summer Opera val, 1959, condr. Met. Opera auditions of Met. a, 1951-55, Met. Opera auditions of air, 1954-57, Opera spring tour, 1957, 69-94, assoc. dir. Kathryn opera courses Met. Opera, until 1972, dir., 1972- orin. condr. Opera du Rhin, Strasbourg, France, 94, debut Met. Opera conducting Eugene Onegin, condr. Met. Opera Summer Concerts, 1965, 68, 71, L.I. (N.Y.) Festival, summer 1965, Vanessa, condr. Grand Theatre, Geneva, Switzerland, 1968; r. Carmen, St. Paul, 1970, Augusta (Ga.) Opera 1969-71, orchesteral concerts, Purbeck Festival, , 1969, 72; music dir. Mozart Opera Festival, C., 1980-81; rejoined Met. Opera, 1982-83; made preparations for Max Reinhardt's prodn. Tales of man, Grosses Schauspielhaus, Berlin, 1931, Of- ach's La Perichole, 1956-57; composer songs based Am. poems; composer String Quartet, 1990; concert ormances at Donnell Library Auditorium, Merklin , Radio WKCR, Columbia U., all N.Y.C., 1984-85; ter classes at Badorb, Germany, Internat. Seminar Opera Studies and Performances, master classes for ers Am. Inst. Mus. Studies, Graz, Austria, July- ., 1989, 90; apptd. dir. of opera dept. Curtis Inst. of sic, Phila., 1986-88; guest-composer at Reck- hausen, Germany, 1990-91; Strasfogel Compositions songs) publ. by Gunnar Music, Inc., 1988; contbr. cles to mags. Recipient State Mendelssohn prize, many, 1926. Mem. N.Y. Singing Tchrs. Assn., CAP. Home: New York N.Y. Died Feb. 6, 1994.

RATTON, HENRY DAVIS, lawyer; b. Pikeville, , Aug. 9, 1925; s. Pem Burton and Minnie M. vis) S.; m. Lois Jean Shipley, June 14, 1947; chil- n: David Carey and Daniel Pemberton (twins), esa Louise. Student, Asbury Coll., 1943, Pikeville l., 1946-47; LL.B., U. Louisville, 1950. Bar: Ky. 0. Ptnr. Stratton, May and Hays, Pikeville, from 0; chmn. Citizens Bank of Pikeville; bd. dirs. London adcasting Co.; chmn. bd. dirs. TransKentucky corp, Campbell County Broadcasting Co., Lawrence unty Broadcasting Co.; chmn. Ky. Continuing Legal n. Commn., 1978-84, Fed. Jud. Selection Commn. ., 1976-85; commr. Nat. Conf. on Uniform State ws, from 1975. Mem. Ky. Crime Commn., 1968-76; dirs., gen. counsel Meth. Hosp., Ky.; regent Eastern . U., 1970-81, chmn. bd. regents, from 84; trustee eville Coll., 1975-89; dir. Gov.'s Scholars Com., from 82. Served with AUS, 1943-46. Fellow ABA (ho. of s. 1975-82), Am. Coll. Trial Lawyers, Am. Coll. Real tate Attys.; mem. Ky. Bar Assn. (pres. 1974-75, pres.- ct. 1975-76, pres. 1976-77, named Oustanding Ky. wyer 1985), Am. Judicature Soc., Ky. Jr. C. of C. p.), Ky. Hist. Soc., Filson Club, Green Meadow Club, llowbrook Club, Jefferson Club, Masons, Phi Alpha lta, Omicron Delta Kappa. Methodist. Home: keville Ky. Deceased.

RATTON, JULIUS ADAMS, retired university esident; b. Seattle, May 18, 1901; s. Julius A. and ura (Adams) S.; m. Catherine N. Coffman, June 14, 35; children: Catherine N., Ann Cary, Laura Student, U. Wash., 1919-20; S.B., MIT, 1923, S.M., 26; Sc.D., Eidgenossische Technische Hochschule, rich, 1928; D. Eng. (hon.), NYU, 1955; Sc.D. (hon.), Francis Xavier, 1957, Coll. William and Mary, 1964, arnegie Inst. Tech., 1965, U. Leeds, Eng., 1967, eriot-Watt U., Edinburgh, Scotland, 1971, Cambridge , Eng., 1972; LL.D., Northeastern U., 1957, Union oll., 1958, Harvard U., 1959, Brandeis U., 1959, arleton Coll., 1960, U. Notre Dame, 1961, Johns opkins U., 1962; L.H.D., Hebrew Union Coll., 1962, klahoma City U., 1963, Jewish Theol. Sem. Am., 1965. Rsch. asst. elec. engring. MIT, 1924-26, asst. prof. elec. ngring., 1928-30, asst. prof. physics, 1930-35, assoc. rof. physics, 1935-41, prof., 1941-51, mem. staff radia- on lab., 1940-45, dir. research lab. electronics, 1944-49, rovost, 1949-56, v.p., 1951-56, chancellor, 1956-59, ac- ng pres., 1957-59, pres., 1959-66; pres. emeritus, 1966- 4; chmn. bd. Ford Found., 196, 1966-71; expert cons. ec. War, 1942-46; mem. U.S. Army Sci. Panel, 1954-56; em. Naval Rsch. Adv. Com., 1954-59; mem. Nat. Sci. d., 1956-62, 64-67; chmn. Comm. on Marine Sci., En- ng. and Resources, 1967-69; mem. Nat. Adv. Com. n Oceans and Atmosphere, 1971-73; life mem. MIT Corp. Author: Electromagnetic Theory, 1941, Science nd the Educated Man, 1966. Life trustee Boston Mus. ci., Carnegie Found. for Advancement of Tchg., 1962- 6, Ford Found., 1955-71, Pine Manor Coll., 1962-71, Rand Corp., 1955-65, Vassar Coll., 1962-70, WGBH Ednl. Found., 1960-66; bd. dirs. Am. Coun. on Edn., 1958-62, Chares Stark Draper Lab., 1973-79, Esso Edn. Found., 1966-70; hon. mem. senate Tech. U. Berlin, 1966. Decorated officer French Legion Honor; cmdr. Order of Boyaca (Colombia); knight comdr. Order of Merit (Fed. Republic Germany); recipient medal for merit, 1946, medal of honor Am. Inst. Radio Engrs., 1957, Disting. Pub. Svc. award USN, 1957, Faraday medal Inst. Elec. Engrs., London, 1961, Boston medal for Disting. Achievement, 1966, citation Marine Tech. Soc., 1969, Man of Yr. award Nat. Fisheries Inst., 1969, Disting. Achievement award Offshore Tech. Conf., 1971, Neptune award Am. Oceaongraphic Inst., 1979, others; hon. fellow Manchester (Eng.) Coll. and Tech., 1963;. Fellow Am. Acad. Arts and Scis., AAAS, Am. Phys. Soc., IEEE (life); mem. Am. Philos. Soc., Nat. Acad. Scis. (v.p. 1961-65), Council Fgn. Relations, Nat. Acad. Engring. (founding), Sigma Xi, Eta Kappa Nu, Tau Beta Pi. Clubs: St. Botolph (Boston); Century Assn. (N.Y.C.). Home: Cambridge Mass. Died June 22, 1994.

STRATTON, LAWRENCE M., college president. P- res. Kutztown State Coll., Pa., until 1987. Home: Kutztown Pa. Died Oct. 29, 1987.

STRAUS, ROBERT WARE, research foundation ex- ecutive; b. Hinsdale, Ill., July 22, 1909; s. Michael W. and Mary (Howe) S.; m. Lenore T. Straus (dec.); chil- dren: Eric T., Nora Ware; m. Eleanor Stone Smol- lar. Student, U. Chgo., 1927; AB, Harvard U., 1931; MSG, U. Grenoble (France), 1939. Ptnr. Benedict, Odquist & Straus, N.Y.C., 1931-39; dir. info. Exec. Of- fice of Pres., Washington, 1939-42; dir. consumer div. U.S. OPA, Washington, 1947-49; pres. Galaxy, Inc., Washington, 1949-87; exec. v.p. Accokeek Found., 1957- 84, pres., 1984—; bd. dirs. Acrylics Research Corp., Melamine Research Corp., Tercentenary Corp., Tricent Corp., Conservation Trust, Puerto Rico; pres. So. Md. Industries, 1947-49. Author: America Builds, 1936, The Case of the Acme Corporation, 1952, A Study Analysis of the Problem of Preserving Recreational and Open Space Lands, 1968, The Possible Dream, 1988; contbr. numerous articles to various profl. jours. Pres., Carrol- sburg Sq. Condominium Assn., Washington; mem. Saving Beautiful Natural Resources of P.R., 1980. Served to comdr. USNR, 1942-47. Recipient E award Dept. Commerce, 1946, Outstanding Contbn. to In- ternat. Commerce award Bur. Internat. Commerce, 1972, Untiring Devotion award Mt. Vernon Ladies Assn. Union, 1973. Mem. Am. Assn. Mus., Am. Assn. for State and Local History, Harvard Club, Nat. Press Club. Democrat. Home: Washington D.C.

STRAUSS, ELLIOTT WILLIAM, educator; b. Blkyn., Jan. 25, 1923; s. Joseph Maxwell and Sonia (Rapoport) S.; m. Gloria Angela Dinella, Aug. 9, 1984; children by previous marriage—William, Monica, Nicholas. A.B., Columbia U., 1944; M.D., NYU, 1949; M.A., Brown U., 1968. Research fellow Harvard Med. Sch., Boston, 1958-61, instr., 1961-65; prof. dept. medicine U. Colo., Denver, 1965-67; prof. dept. biol. and med. sci., Brown U., Providence, 1967—; cons. Dept. HEW, others. Contbr. articles to profl. jours. Served to lt. (s.g.) USNR, 1943-50. Recipient Commendation, NIH, 1959, Career Devel. award, 1961, others. Mem. Am. Gastro. Assn., Am. Soc. Cell Biology. Died Oct. 30, 1987. Home: Cambridge Mass.

STRAUSS, FRANZ JOSEF, government official; b. Munich, Germany, Sept. 6, 1915; s. Franz and Walburga (Schiessl) S.; m. Marianne Zwicknagl, June 4, 1957 (dec. 1984); children: Max-Josef, Franz-Georg, Monika. Ed. U. Munich. Dep. dist. adminstr. Dist. Schongau, 1945, dist. adminstr., 1946-48; mem. German Parliament, 1949-78, Fed. minister for spl. affairs, 1953- 55, for atomic affairs, 1955-56, of defence, 1956-62, Fed. minister of finances, 1966-69; ministerpresident of Bavaria, 1978-88; mem. Bavarian Parliament, 1978- 88. Author: Entwurf für Europa, 1966; Heraus- forderung und Antwort: Ein Programm für Europa, 1968; Zusammenfassung Bundestagsreden, 1969-75; Bundestagsreden und Zeitdokumente, 1974-79; Die Finanzverfassung, 1969; Finanzpolitik-Theorie und Wirklichkeit, 1969; Deutschland, Deine Zukunft, 1975; Signale-Beiträge zur deutschen Politik, 1978; Zur Lage, 1980; Gebote der Freiheit, 1980; Verantwortung vor der Geschichte: Beiträge zur deutschen und internationalen Politik, 1985; Auftrag für die Zukunft: Beiträge zur deutschen und internationalen Politik, 1987; contbr. ar- ticles to profl. jours. Charter mem. Christian Social Union, 1945, sec. gen., 1949, chmn., 1961-88. Served to 2d lt. German Army, 1939-45. Recipient hon. doctorates U. Detroit, Tech. U. Cleve., Kalamazoo Coll., DePaul U., U. Dallas, U. Md., U. Munich.; hon. prof. U. San- tiago, Chile, Ctr. Research and Communications, Manila. Roman Catholic. Died Oct. 3, 1988. Home: Munich Germany

STRENG, FREDERICK JOHN, religion educator; b. Seguin, Tex., Sept. 30, 1933; s. Adolph Carl Sr. and Elizabeth Marie (Hein) S.; m. Ruth Helen Billnitzer, June 6, 1955 (div. 1977); children: Elizabeth Ann, Mark Andrew; m. Bette Sue Blossom, May 23, 1981; stepchildren: Steven Deane, Lisa Deane Evans. BA, Tex. Luth. Coll., 1955; MA, So. Meth. U., 1956; BD, U. Chgo., 1960, PhD, 1963. Asst. prof. U. So. Calif., L.A., 1963-66; assoc. prof. So. Meth. U., Dallas, 1966-74, prof., 1974—; vis. prof. U. Calif., Berkeley, 1973, Harvard U., Cambridge, Mass., 1973, Kwansei Gakuin U., Nishinomiya, Japan, 1986-87; pres. North Tex. Assn. Unitarian Universalist Socs., Dallas, 1990—. Author: Emptiness—A Study in Religious Meaning, 1967, Understanding Religious Life, 3d edit., 1985; editor: (series) Religious Life of Man Series, 1969—; sr. editor: Ways of Being Religious, 1973; co-editor: Spoken and Unspoken Thanks, 1989; contbr. articles to profl. jours. Active various coms. 1st Unitarian Ch. Dallas, 1968—; advisory mem. religious communities task force Dallas Ind. Sch. Dist., 1975—. Recipient Outstanding Prof. award So. Meth. U., 1974, Disting. Alumni award Tex. Luth. Coll., 1988; Fulbright scholar, 1961-62; NEH grantee, 1979. Fellow Ctr. for World Thanksgiving; mem. Soc. for Asian and Comparative Philosophy (pres. 1970-72), Am. Soc. for Study of Religion (pres. 1987- 90), Soc. for Buddhist-Christian Studies (v.p. 1989—), Am. Acad. Religion, Nat. Coun. on Religion and Pub. Edn., Dallas Civil Liberties Union. Home: Dallas Tex.

STRICKLAND, ROBERT, banker; b. Atlanta, May 20, 1927; s. Robert M. and Jessie (Dickey) S.; m. Telside Matthews, July 24, 1953; children: Robert Marion, Douglas Watson, William Logan, Walter Dickey. G- rad., Marist Coll., 1944; BS, Davidson Coll., 1948; LLB, Atlanta Law Sch., 1953. With Trust Co. Ga., Atlanta, 1948-89, v.p., 1959-67, group v.p., 1967, sr. v.p., 1968- 72, sr. exec. v.p., 1972-73, pres., 1973-89; chmn. bd. dirs. Trust Co. Bank, Atlanta, 1974-89, pres. holding co., 1976-89, chmn. bd. dirs. holding co., 1978-89; chmn. bd. dirs., chief exec. officer SunTrust Banks, Inc., 1984-90, chmn. exec. com., 1989-92; mem. and chmn. adv. coun. Trust Co. of Ga., 1992—; bd. dirs., mem. exec. com., chmn. audit com. Life Ins. Co. Ga.; bd. dirs. ING Am. Life Ins. Corp.; bd. dirs., mem. exec. com. Ga. Power Co.; bd. dirs. Oxford Industries. Past pres. United Way Met. Atlanta, chmn. gen. campaign, 1972; past chmn. fin. com., v.p. bd. Piedmont Hosp.; past bd. dirs. Fulton County unit Ga. divsn. Am. Cancer Soc.; trustee emeritus Westminster Schs.; chmn. bd. trustees Emory U.; mem. chmns. coun., past chmn. ctrl. Atlanta Progress, Inc. With AUS, 1950-52. Mem. Am. Bankers Assn. (past state v.p.), Ga. Bankers Assn. (past pres.), Atlanta C. of C. (pres. 1983), Atlanta Arts Alliance (past chmn. bd. dirs., trustee, exec. com.), Piedmont Driving Club (past pres.), Capital City Club, Commerce Club (pres. 1987-90, bd. dirs.), Peachtree Golf Club, Augusta Nat. Golf Club, Sigma Alpha Epsilon. Methodist. Home: Atlanta Ga. Died Nov. 8, 1994.

STRIEDER, JOHN WILLIAM, thoracic surgeon; b. Boston, June 6, 1901; s. Joseph William and Elizabeth Merritt (Robinson) S.; m. Helen Lucille Roberts, Aug. 17, 1935 (dec. Feb. 1961); children: Alison Tennant Strieder Mayher, Helen, Elizabeth Merritt (Mrs. John J. Atwood); m. Denise Jouasset, Aug. 7, 1962. S.B., Mass. Inst. Tech., 1922; M.D., Harvard, 1926. Diplo- mate: Am. Bd. Surgery, Am. Bd. Thoracic Surgery (founder's group; chmn. 1964-66). Intern Boston City Hosp., 1927-29; fellow Univ. Hosp., Ann Arbor, Mich., 1933-35; practice medicine (specializing in thoracic surgery), Boston, 1927-30, 35-76; mem. staff Trudeau Sanatorium, N.Y., 1930-33, Univ. Hosp., Ann Arbor, 1933-35; house surgeon Boston City Hosp., 1927-29, dir. thoracic surgery, 1946-67; house surgeon Boston Lying- in Hosp., 1929-30; asst. resident Trudeau Sanatorium, 1930-33; instr. thoracic surgery U. Mich. Hosp., 1933- 35; instr. surgery Harvard Med. Sch., 1936-40; pvt. practice, 1935-76; cons. thoracic surgery Univ. Hosp., Boston, Newton-Wellesley Hosp., Newton, Mass. Soldiers Home, Chelsea, Mass.; sr. surgeon New Eng. Bapt. Hosp., New Eng. Deaconess Hosp.; surgeon-in- chief Boston Sanatorium, Mattapan, Mass., 1946-66; clin. prof. surgery emeritus Boston U. Sch. Medicine.; John Alexander Meml. lectr., Ann Arbor, 1967; vis. prof. thoracic surgery U. Pa., 1977; John N. Strieder vis. prof. in cardiothoracic surgery Boston U., 1986-93. Mem. editorial bd.: Alexander Monograph Series, 1956- 93; Contbr. articles to profl. jours. Recipient Leonard Wood medal, 1967, Henry Chadwick medal, 1975. Mem. AMA (residency rev. com. thoracic surgery), A.C.S., Am. Assn. for Thoracic Surgery (pres. 1971-72), Soc. Thoracic Surgeons (exec. com.), Am. Cancer Soc., Am. Heart Assn., Am. Thoracic Soc., Am. Lung Assn., New Eng. (v.p. 1966), Boston surg. socs., Aesculapian Club, Harvard Club, The Country Club, Sigma Xi, Lambda Chi Alpha. Home: Chestnut Hill Mass. Died. Oct. 25, 1993.

STRIFFLER, DAVID FRANK, dental public health educator; b. Pontiac, Mich., Oct. 24, 1922; s. Harry Charles and Gemma Scia (Romine) S.; m. Ruth Winifred Lyle, Feb. 5, 1949; children: Stephanie Lynn, Geoffrey David. Student, U. Mich., 1940-43, D.D.S., 1947, M.P.H., 1951. Diplomate Am. Bd. Dental Pub. Health; lic. dentist, Mich., N.Mex. Dir. sch. health Dearborn (Mich.) Pub. Schs., 1951-53; dir. dental health N.Mex. Dept. Pub. Health, Santa Fe, 1953-61; assoc. prof. to prof. dental pub. health and dentistry Sch. Pub. Health and Sch. Dentistry, U. Mich., Ann Arbor, 1961- 86; chmn. dept. community dentistry Sch. Dentistry, U Mich., Ann Arbor, 1962-67; chmn. dept. community health programs Sch. Pub. Health, Ann Arbor, 1978-85; prof. emeritus Sch. Dentistry and Sch. Pub. Health, 1986-95; cons. USPHS, Washington, 1959-95, NIH, Bethesda, Md., 1959-95, Blue Cross and Blue Shield Mich., 1986-90; bd. dirs. Delta Dental Plans of Mich., Lansing, 1971-77, corp. mem., 1977-86; mem. commn. on dental accreditation ADA, Chgo., 1987-89, cons., 1989-90. Co-author: The Dentist, His Practice, and His Community, 1964, 2d edit., 1969, Dentistry, Dental Practice and the Community, 3d edit., 1983; editor: Jour. Pub. Health Dentistry, 1975-86. Served with AUS, 1943-44. Recipient Disting. Service award

N.Mex. Pub. Health Assn., 1960, Disting. Service award Am. Assn. Pub. Health Dentists, 1977, Spl. Merit award Am. Assn. Pub. Health Dentistry, 1986. Fellow Am. Pub. Health Assn. (John W. Knutson Disting. Service award Dental Health sect. 1984); mem. N.Mex. Dental Hygienists Assn. (hon.), Mich. Dental Hygienists Assn. (hon.), Am. Bd. Dental Pub. Health (pres. 1969), Phi Kappa Phi, Delta Omega, Sigma Xi. Democrat. Unitarian. Home: Ann Arbor Mich. Died May 29, 1995.

STRINGER, LOREN FRANK, electronics executive; b. Huntington Park, Calif., Sept. 28, 1925; m. Gretchen Engstrom; children: Lizbeth, Pamela, Frederick, William. BSEE, U. Tex., 1946; MSEE, Calif. Inst. Tech., 1947; PhD in Applied Math., U. Pitts., 1963. From jr. to sr. engr. Westinghouse Industry Engring. Dept., East Pittsburgh, 1947-56; mgr. mill systems devel. Westinghouse Systems Control Div., Buffalo, 1956-58, mgr. product devel., 1958-63; dir. thyristor dr. systems devel. group Westinghouse Electric Co., Buffalo, 1963-64, cons. engr., dir. advanced devel. Westinghouse Systems Control div., 1964-67, mgr. devel. engring. Westinghouse Indsl. Systems div., 1967-72, div. engring. mgr. Westinghouse Indsl. Equipment div., 1972-79, div. engring. mgr. Westinghous Power Electronics and Dr. Systems div., 1979-81, chief engr., 1981-85; pres., chief engr. Stringer Power Electronics Corp., Williamsville, N.Y., 1985-92. Lt. (j.g.) USNR, 1943-46. Life fellow IEEE (Newell power electronics award 1984, Lamme medal 1985); life mem. Assn. Iron and Steel Engrs., Brook Field Country Club. Republican. Home: Clarence N.Y. Died Sept. 19, 1992.

STROTZ, ROBERT HENRY, university chancellor; b. Aurora, Ill., Sept. 26, 1922; s. John Marc and Olga (Koerfer) S.; m. Margaret L. Hanley; children: Vicki, Michael, Frances, Ellen, Ann; stepchildren: Katie, Marcia, Liz. Student, Duke U., 1939-41; B.A., U. Chgo., 1942, Ph.D., 1951; LL.D. (hon.), Ill. Wesleyan U., 1976; LL.D., Millikin U., 1979. Mem. faculty Northwestern U., Evanston, Ill., 1947-94; prof. econs. Northwestern U., 1958-94, dean Coll. Arts and Scis., 1966-70, pres. univ., 1970-85, chancellor, 1985-94; past chmn. Council on Postsecondary Accreditation; Past dir., chmn. Fed. Res. Bank Chgo.; dir. Ill. Tool Works, Inc., Norfolk So. Corp., USG Corp., Mark Controls Corp., First Ill. Corp. Mng. editor: Econometrica, 1953-68; econometrics editor: Internat. Ency. Social Scis, 1962-68; editor: Contributions to Economic Analysis, 1955-70. Bd. dirs., vice chmn. Nat. Merit Scholarship Corp.; bd. dirs. Northwestern Meml. Hosp.; hon. life trustee Field Mus. Natural History, Mus. Sci. and Industry. Served with AUS, 1943-45. Fellow Econometric Soc. (mem. council 1961-67); mem. Am. Econ. Assn., Royal Econ. Soc. Clubs: Comml. (Chgo.), Economic, Univ. (Chgo.), Standard (Chgo.), Tavern (Chgo.), Chgo. (Chgo.); Old Elm (Ft. Sheridan, Ill.); Glen View (Golf, Ill.); Bohemian (San Francisco). Home: Wilmette Ill. Died Nov. 9, 1994; interred Meml. Park, Skokie, Ill.

STRUCKMEYER, FREDERICK CHRISTIAN, JR., state chief justice; b. Phoenix, Jan. 4, 1912; s. Frederick C. and Inez (Walker) S.; m. Margaret Mills, Apr. 17, 1948; children: Frederick C. III, Jan Holly Struckmeyer Zeluff, Karl, Kent. LLB, U. Ariz., 1936. Bar: Ariz. 1936. Pvt. practice law Phoenix, 1936-49; asst. county atty. Maricopa County, 1938-41; judge Superior Ct., 1949-54; justice Ariz. Supreme Ct., 1955-92, chief justice, 1960-61, 66, 71, 80-82;, 1982. 2d lt. to 1st lt., inf. AUS, World War II. Decorated Silver Star, Bronze Star, Purple Heart. Mem. Sigma Nu, Phi Delta Phi. Democrat. Episcopalian. Home: Phoenix Ariz. Died June 22, 1992.

STUART, JOHN M., lawyer, author; b. N.Y.C., Apr. 3, 1927; s. Winchester and Maude Ruth (Marberger) S.; m. Marjorie Louise Browne, Dec. 11, 1954; children: Jane, Alice, Richard. BA, Columbia U., 1948, JD, 1951. Bar: N.Y. 1951, U.S. Supreme Ct. 1955. Assoc., Reid & Priest, N.Y.C., 1951-64, ptnr., 1965—; asst. sec. Minn. Power & Light Co., 1951-64; U.S. judge Fedn. Internationale des Société Magiques at Den Haag, Holland, 1988. Recipient Internat. Brotherhood Magicians award, 1958-60, 1st prize in sci. fiction Phila. Writers Conf., 1958. Mem. ABA, N.Y. County Bar Assn., Sr. Republican. Presbyterian. Author: A Re-examination of the Replacement Fund, 1968; Avoiding Costly Bond Problems, 1980; (with Louis H. Willenken) Utility Mortgages Should be Reexamined, 1984; (with Majorie L. Stuart) (play) Make Me Disappear, 1969; (novel) You Don't Have to Slay a Dragon, 1976. Contbr. articles to mags. Magician, W. German TV magic spl., 1965; appeared in Spy at the Magic Show benefit for Project Hope, Manhasset, N.Y., 1967. Home: Manhasset N.Y.

STUHR, EDWARD PHILLIP, banker; b. Bklyn., May 11, 1905; s. Edward and Dora (Lendell) S.; m. Theresa Cherney, May 29, 1930; children: Edward Philip, David Paul. B.C.S., NYU, 1926. Research dir. Callaway, Fish & Co. (investment bankers), N.Y.C., 1928-41; research officer Fiduciary Trust Co. of N.Y. (investment mgrs.), N.Y.C., 1945-46; v.p. Fiduciary Trust Co. of N.Y. (investment mgrs.), 1947-55, 1st v.p., dir. research, 1956-64, chmn. exec. com., dir. research, 1965-69, chmn. exec. com., 1969-71, hon. dir. Mem. Am. Acad. Polit. Sci. Clubs: Stock Exchange Luncheon (N.Y.C.), Economic (N.Y.C.). Home: Ho Ho Kus N.J. Died May 24, 1993; cremated.

STURMAN, ROBERT HARRIES, neurological surgeon, consultant neurologist; b. Austin, Minn., Jan. 8, 1923; s. Everett Nelson and Hannah (Harries) S.; m. Gloria Weyand, June 24, 1944 (div. Apr. 1980); children: Peter, Everett, Bruce, Jeffrey; m. Ruth Eleanor Synkewecz, Apr. 24, 1980. BA in Chemistry, Colgate U., 1943; MD, Yale U., 1950. Diplomate Am. Bd. Neurol. Surgery, Nat. Bd. Med. Examiners. Intern Waterbury Hosp., Waterbury, Conn., 1950-53; fellow in neurosurgery Hartford Hosp., Hartford, Conn., 1953-54; fellow in neuropathology Yale Univ. Sch. Med., New Haven, Conn., 1954; fellow in neurology Columbia Presbyn. Med. Ctr. N.Y. Neurol. Inst., N.Y.C., 1955; resident in neurosurgery, sr. clin. instr. neurosurgery Univ. Mich. Med. Sch. Univ. Hosp., Ann Arbor, Mich., 1955-56; attending neurosurgeon Waterbury Hosp., Waterbury, Conn., 1959-74, chief neurosurgery, 1974-80; clin. instr. neurosurgery Yale Univ., New Haven, Conn., 1972-80; clin. assoc. neurosurgery Univ. Conn., Hartford, Conn., 1972-80; neurosurgical cons. Detroit Indsl. Clinic, pvt. practice, Detroit, 1980-88, 88—; pvt. consulting Detroit, 1988—; attending assoc. neurol. and neurosurgery, Newington (Conn.) Children's Hosp., 1960-80; cons. Meriden (Conn.) Meml. Hosp. 1958-66, New Milford (Conn.) Hosp., 1956-80, Sharon (Conn.) Hosp., 1956-80, Southbury (Conn.) Tng. Sch., 1956-80; trustee Reading Research, Inc., 1960-65. contbr. to publications in field, 1961-73. Trustee Cerebral Palsy, 1958, Easter Seal Rehab. Ctr., 1968, McTernan Sch., 1963-68; med. adv. bd. Nat. Found., 1960. Lt. (j.g.) USN, 1943-46, PTO. Fellow ACS; mem. Congress Neurol. Surgeons (chmn. pub. rels. com. 1971-72), Am. Assn. Neurol. Surgeons, Mich. State Med. Soc., N.E. Neurosurg. Soc. (trustee 1965-67), Waturbury Med. Soc., New Haven County Med. Soc., Pan Am. Surg. Soc., Pan Pacific Surg. Soc., Soc. Cryosurgery, Wayne County Med. Soc., Conn. State Med. Soc. (chmn. sect. neurosurgery 1970-75), Coun. State Neurosurg. Soc. (socio-econ. com. 1977-80), AMA. Home: Eastpointe Mich. Died Sept. 26, 1994.

STYNE, JULE, composer, producer; b. London, Dec. 31, 1905; came to U.S., 1912, naturalized, 1916; s. Isadore and Anna (Kertman) S.; m. Ethel Rubenstein, 1926 (div. 1951); m. Margaret Brown, 1962; children: Stanley, Norton, Nicholas, Katherine. Student, Chgo. Mus. Coll., Northwestern U., 1927-31. Composer: (film scores) Sailors on Leave, 1941, Sweater Girl, 1942, Priorities on Parade, 1942, Hit Parade of 1943, 1943 (Academy Award nom., best song, 1943), Carolina Blues, 1944, Follow the Boys, 1944 (Academy Award nom., best song, 1944), The Kid From Brooklyn, 1945, Tonight and Every Night, 1945 (Academy Award nom., best song, 1945), Don't Fence Me In, 1945, The Stork Club, 1945, Anchors Aweigh, 1945 (Academy Award nom., best song, 1945), Tars and Spars, 1946, Sweetheart of Sigma Chi, 1946, Earl Carroll Sketchbook, 1946, It Happened in Brooklyn, 1947, Ladies' Man, 1947, Romance on the High Seas, 1947 (Academy Award nom., best song, 1948), Two Guys From Texas, 1948, It's a Great Feeling, 1949 (Academy Award nom., best song, 1948), The West Point Story, 1950, Double Dynamite, 1951, Two Tickets to Broadway, 1951, Meet Me After the Show, 1951, Macao, 1952, Gentlemen Prefer Blondes, 1953, Three Coins in a Fountain, 1954 (Academy Award, best song, 1954), Living It Up, 1954, My Sister Eileen, 1955, How to Be Very, Very Popular, 1955, Bells are Ringing, 1960, Gypsy, 1962, What a Way to Go, 1964, Funny Girl, 1968 (Academy Award nom., best song, 1968); (stage prodns.) Glad to See You, 1944, High Button Shoes, 1947, Gentlemen Prefer Blondes, 1949, Two on the Aisle, 1951, Peter Pan, 1954, Bells are Ringing, 1956, Gypsy, 1959, Do Re Mi, 1960, Subways are Sleeping, 1962, Arturo Ui, 1963, Funny Girl, 1964 (Outstanding Contribution to British Theatre, Anglo-American award, 1966), Hallelujah Baby, 1967 (Tony Awards, best musical and best score, 1968), Darling of the Day, 1968, Look to the Lilies, 1970, Prettybelle, 1971, Sugar, 1972, Lorelei, or Gentlemen Still Prefer Blondes, 1974, (revival) Gypsy, 1974, Hellzapoppin, 1976, Side by Side by Sondheim, 1982, Treasure Island, 1985, (with others) Jerome Robbins' Broadway, 1990, The Red Shoes, 1993; producer: Make a Wish, 1950, Pal Joey, 1952 (Donaldson Award 1952, New York Critics' Circle Award 1952), In Any Language, 1952, Will Success Spoil Rock Hunter?, 1955, Mr. Wonderful, 1956, High Spirits, 1964, Something More, 1964, Jockeys, 1977, Tiebele and Her Dream, 1979; composer, producer: Hazel Flagg, 1953, Say, Darling, 1958, Fade Out-Fade In, 1964. Recipient Drama Desk Award for lifetime of glorious theatre music, 1989-90; Kennedy Center Honors, 1990. Mem. ASCAP, Dramatist Guild Council, Acad. Motion Picture Arts and Sci. Club: Friars. Home: New York N.Y. Died Sept. 20, 1994.

SUDLER, LOUIS COURTENAY, real estate agent, baritone; b. Chgo., Feb. 25, 1903; s. Carroll H. and Susan B. (Culbreth) S.; m. Mary L. Barnes, Feb. 2, 1929 (dec. Oct. 1979); 1 child, Louis Courtenay; m. Virginia Brown, Apr. 21, 1984. Grad., Hotchkiss Sch., 1921; B.A., Yale U., 1925; D.Music (hon.), Southwestern Coll., Winfield, Kans., 1963, Augustana Coll., Rock Island, Ill., 1964, DePaul U., 1972; L.H.D. (hon.), Lake Forest Coll., 1972; D.F.A. (hon.), Northwestern U., 1973; D.Musical Arts (hon.), U. Ill.-Chgo., 1983, Am Conservatory Music, 1986. Founder Sudler & Co., rea estate, Chgo., 1927; leading baritone Chgo. Civic Opera 1945-47; chmn. emeritus, sr. advisor Sudler Marling Chgo., 1985-92; dir. Upper Avenue Bank, 1962-79. Founder, host of Artists' Showcase, NBC-TV, 1960-65 WGN-TV, 1966-74; internat. appearances, 1946-92 guest soloist symphony orchs., concert and marchin bands; soloist inauguration Pres. Eisenhower, 1956; sun Nat. Anthem for Pres.'s Reagan, Ford, Nixon, Johnso and Kennedy; appearances oratorio socs., radio and TV world premieres: Mass (Puccini), Prayer of St. Franci (Arne Oldberg), Abram and Sari (Elinor Remick Warren). Exec. chmn. John Philip Sousa Found.; bd. dirs Chgo. Symphony Orch., pres., 1966-71, chmn., 1971-76 chmn. emeritus, 1976-92. Recipient Peabody award 1968; Flag of Honor, Am. Legion, 1952; Disting. Servic medal State of Ill.; Order of Lincoln; Cross of Honor Internat. Confedn. Music Socs.; Alumnus award Mich State U., 1985; Sanford medal Yale U., 1980; Disting Service to Music award Kappa Kappa Psi, 1985; Cli Dwellers medal; McGaw medal; named Chicagoan c Yr. in arts Chgo. Jr. Assn. of Commerce, 1964; Joh Harvard Citizen of Yr., 1971; Sr. Citizen of Yr. Chgo 1978; Sr. Citizen Hall of Fame Chgo., 1984; Nat. Fedr Music Clubs; Music Mgr. of Yr., Chgo. of Edn.; Mgr. c Yr., Am. Symphony Orch. League; Hon. mem. Chgc Symphony Orch., 1977; Edwin Franko Goldman Meml citation, 1986; Hon. Dir. U. Tex. Longhorn band, 1986 Friends of Lit. citation for Artists' Showcase, 1965 Disting. Service award Lake Forest Fine Arts Allianc 1985; Service award Music Ctr. North Shore, 1986 donor Sudler Flag of Honor and Sudler Cup awards fc Sousa Found.; Sudler Internat. Wind Band Compositio Competition held biennially; Louis Sudler prize in Art endowed at Yale U., Princeton U., Stanford U., Mich State U., Purdue U., Columbia U., Dartmouth Coll Oberlin Coll., Harvard U., Rice U., MIT, John Hopkin U., Duke U., U. Chgo., Emory U. Mem. Nat. Fedr Music Clubs, Friends of Lit., Soc. Colonial Wars, Yal U. Alumni Assn. (Yale medal 1986), Mu Phi Epsilo (hon. bd. dirs. meml. found.). Clubs: Chicago, Cli Dwellers, Saddle and Cycle, Tavern, Arts, Casinc Commercial (Chgo.). Home: Chicago Ill. Died Aug. 25 1992.

SUENENS, LEO JOSEPH CARDINAL, archbishop b. Brussels, Belgium, July 16, 1904; s. Jean and Jeann Janssens; student Coll. Ste. Marie, Brussels, 1915-21 Ph.D., Gregorian U., Rome, 1924, B.C.L., 1927, S.T.D 1929. Ordained priest Roman Cath. Ch., 1927; aux bishop, vicar-gen. Archdiocese of Malines, 1945-61 consecrated bishop, 1945; archbishopof Malines-Brussels, primate Belgium, 1961-79, ret., 1979; elevated t cardinal, 1962; moderator Vatican Council, 1962-65 chancellor Louvain U.; pres. Belgian Bishops Conf 1966-96; mem. Pontifical Commn. for Revision Code c Canon Law. Re-cipient Templeton Found. prize in religion, 1976. Author: Theology of the Legionof Mary 1954, The Right View of Moral Rearmament, 1954, Th Gospel to Every Creature, 1957, Mary, the Mother c God, 1959, The Nun in the World, 1962, Love andControl, 1962, Christian Life Day by Day, 1964, Co responsibility in the Church,1968, A New Pentacost' 1975, Ecumenism and Charismatic Renewal and Socia Action, 1979, Renewal and The Powers of Darkness 1982, Nature and Grace in Vital Unity, 1986, A Controversial Phenomenon: Resting in Spirit, 1987, Spiritua Journey, 1990, Memories and Hopes, 1992, The Hidde Hand of God, Baudouin, King of the Belgians; (wit Archbishop M. Ramsey) The Future of the Christia Church, 1970; (with D. H. Camara) Charismati Renewal and Social Action, 1979. Died May 6, 1996 Home: Brussels Belgium

SULLIVAN, ANNE ELIZABETH, publishing executive; b. N.Y.C., Oct. 23, 1942; d. Eugene Redmond an Anne (Rigney) S.; m. Alan H. Bomser, Oct. 1 1984. BA, Newton (Mass.) Coll., 1964; JD, Fordhar U., 1980. Bar: N.Y. 1981. With permissions dep Farrar, Straus & Giroux, N.Y.C., 1967-74, dir. contrac and copyright dept., 1988-95. Home: New York N.Y Died Nov. 17, 1995.

SULLIVAN, FRANCIS CHARLES, legal educato college dean, lawyer; b. Chgo., Jan. 14, 1927; s. Fran Colby and Mary Cecilia (Burke) S.; m. Dolores Gra June 11, 1955; children: Brian, Eugene, Laurence. B.S Loyola U., Chgo., 1947, J.D., 1949; LL.M., NYU, 196 Bar: Ill. 1950, Tenn. 1986. Ptnr. McKinley, Price & Appleman, Chgo., 1949-56; prof. law Loyola U., Chgo 1956-66; prof. La. State U., 1966-86, assoc. dean, 197 77, dean, 1977-78, prof. law and dean emeritus, 1986— prof., dean C.C. Humphreys Sch. Law, Memphis Sta U., 1985-90, prof. law, dean emeritus, 1989—; distin vis. prof. law U. Okla., 1979, U. San Diego, 1981-8 UCLA, 1985; dir. La. Jud. Coll., 1975-81, Ctr. Crimin Justice, Policy and Mgmt., 1981-82; cons. in field. Author: The Adminstration of Criminal Justice, 196 2d edit., 1968, Evidence, 1969, Louisiana Evidenc 1983, 2d edit., 1984, Louisiana Criminal Justice, 198 2d edit., 1985; contbr. articles to profl. jours. Serve with U.S. Army, 1945-46, 50-52. Named Papal Knigh of Holy Sepulchre; Ford Found. Travel fellow, 1958-5 Ford Found. fellow, 1959-61. Mem. Baton Rouge Ba Assn., Chgo. Bar Assn., Ill. Bar Assn., La. Bar Assn Am. Bar Assn. (recipient award 1978), Tenn. Bar Assn Memphis/Shelby County Bar Assn., Council La Stat

Law Inst., Am. Law Inst., Am. Judicature Soc., Order of Coif, Blue Key. Roman Catholic. Clubs: City of Baton Rouge, Nat. Lawyers, Summit, Chickasaw Country, Camelot; University (San Diego). Home: Memphis Tenn. Deceased.

SULLIVAN, FRANK E., life insurance executive; b. Lowell, Mass., Aug. 17, 1923; s. William H. and (Vera) S.; m. Colette Cleary, June 11, 1949; children: Frank E., Mary, Anne, Robert. BS, Notre Dame U., 1949. CLU. Adminstrv. asst. to football coach Notre Dame U., South Bend, Ind., 1946-52; gen. agt. Am. United Life Ins. Co., South Bend, 1953-74; pres. Mut. Benefit Life Ins. Co., N.J., from 1977, vice chmn.; bd. dirs. St. Joseph Bank & Trust Co., South Bend, Clow Corp., Chgo.; pres. Million Dollar Round Table, 1967; panelist and lectr. in field. Author: Selling Life Insurance for Deferred Compensation, 1962, Setting Goals for Million Dollar Production 1968, The Critical Path to Sales Success, 1970; past chmn. bd. editors: CLU Jour. Past pres. South Bend United Fund, United Community Services South Bend, Health Found. No. Ind., St. Joseph County (Ind.) Urban Coalition. Served with USNR, World War II. Home: Newark N.J. Died Mar. 1, 1993.

SULLIVAN, WALTER SEAGER, editor, author; b. N.Y.C., Jan. 12, 1918; s. Walter Seager and Jeanet E. (Loomis) S.; m. Mary E. Barrett, Aug. 17, 1950; children: Elizabeth Anne, Catherine Ellinwood, Theodore Loomis. B.A., Yale U., 1940, H.L.D., 1969; H.L.D., Newark Coll. Engring., 1973; D.Sc., Hofstra U., 1974, Ohio State U., 1977, U. Ala., 1987, Muhlenberg Coll., 1987. Mem. staff N.Y. Times, 1940-87, fgn. corr. Far East, 1948-50, UN corr., 1951-52, fgn. corr., Germany, 1952-56, chief sci. writer, 1960-62, sci. news editor, 1962-63, sci. editor, 1964-87. Author: Quest for a Continent, 1957, White Land of Adventure, 1957, Assault on the Unknown, 1961, We Are Not Alone, 1964, rev. edit. 1993 (internat. Non-Fiction Book prize 1965), Continents in Motion, 1974, rev. edit. 1991, Black Holes, The Edge of Space, The End of Time, 1979, Landprints, 1984; co-author: The New York Times Guide to the Return of Halley's Comet, 1985; editor: America's Race for the Moon, 1962. Served to lt. comdr. USNR, 1940-46, PTO. Recipient George Polk Meml. award in journalism, 1959, Westinghouse-AAAS award, 1963, 68, 72, Am. Inst. Physics-U.S. Steel Found. award, 1969, James T. Grady award Am. Chem. Soc., 1969, Bradford Washburn award Boston Mus. Sci., 1972, Ralph Coats Roe medal ASME, 1975, Sci. in Soc. Journalism award Nat. Assn. Sci. Writers, 1976, Disting. Public Service award NSF, 1978, Public Welfare medal NAS, 1980, Walter Sullivan award Am. Geophys. Union, 1989, Disting. Pub. Svc. award Conn. Bar Assn., 1990, John Wesley Powell award U.S. Geol. Survey, 1990. Fellow AAAS, Am. Acad. Arts and Scis., Arctic Inst. N.Am.; mem. Am. Geog. Soc. (Daly medal 1973). Home: Riverside Conn. Died Mar. 19, 1996.

SULZBERGER, CYRUS LEO, writer; b. N.Y.C., Oct. 27, 1912; m. Marina Tatiana Lada, Jan. 21, 1942 (dec. 1976); children: Marina Beatrice (Mrs. Adrian Berry), David Alexis. Grad., Harvard, 1934. Columnist N.Y. Times, 1978-93. Author: Sit-Down with John L. Lewis, 1938, The Big Thaw, 1956, What's Wrong with U.S. Foreign Policy, 1959, My Brother Death, 1961, The Test-DeGaulle and Algeria, 1962, Unfinished Revolution, 1965, History of World War II (Am. Heritage History), 1966, A Long Row of Candles, 1969, The Last of the Giants, 1970, The Tooth Merchant, 1973, Unconquered Souls, 1973, An Age of Mediocrity, 1973, The Coldest War, 1974, Postscript with a Chinese Accent, 1974, Go Gentle into the Night, 1976, The Fall of Eagles, 1977, Seven Continents and Forty Years, 1977, The Tallest Liar, 1977, Marina, 1979, How I Committed Suicide, 1982, Such a Peace: The Roots and Ashes of Yalta, 1982, The World and Richard Nixon, 1987, Fathers and Children, 1987, Paradise Regained: A Memoir of a Rebel, 1988. Recipient Pulitzer Prize citation, 1951; award for best consistent reporting from abroad Overseas Press Club Am., 1951; citations for excellence, 1957, 70; award for best book on fgn. affairs, 1973. Club: Metropolitan (Washington). Home: Paris France Died Sept 20, 1993.

SUMNER, ERIC EDEN, retired utility company executive; b. Vienna, Austria, Dec. 17, 1924; came to U.S., 1940, naturalized, 1945; m. Anne-Marie Wiemer, May 24, 1974; children: Eric Eden, Hilary C., Erika, Trevor Anson. B.M.E., Cooper Union, 1948; M.A. in physics, Columbia U., 1953, profl. degree in elec. engring, 1960. With Bell Telephone Labs., Inc., Whippany, N.J., 1948-92, dir. underwater systems lab., 1962-67, exec. dir. div. transmission media, 1967-71, exec. dir. div. loop transmission, 1971-81, v.p. computer tech. and mil. systems area, 1981-84; v.p. ops. systems and network planning Bell Telephone Labs., Inc., Holmdel, N.J., 1984-88, v.p. ops. planning, 1989-92; mem. adv. bd. Ga. Inst. Tech. Sch. Elec. Engring., U. Va. Sch. Engring. Mem. North Caldwell (N.J.) Sch. Bd., 1962-68; pres. Civic Assn., North Caldwell, 1969-71; bd. visitors U. Calif.-Davis. Recipient Computer & Communications prize NEC Corp., 1988. Fellow IEEE (Alexander Graham Bell medal 1978, bd. dirs. 1986-87, pres. elect 1990, pres. 1991); mem. NAE, Communications Soc. (pres. 1982-83), N.J. Inventors Congress and Hall of Fame (pres. 1991-92), Tau Beta Pi, Pi Tau Sigma. Home: Mendham N.J.

SUNDERLAND, PAUL, manufacturing company executive, foundation administrator; b. Omaha, Apr. 24, 1896; s. Lester Thomas and Georgianna (Boulter) S.; m. Avis Marie Peters, Sept. 12, 1920 (dec. Apr. 4, 1962); children: Robert, James Paul; m. Thelma V. Stuart, June 10, 1967. Student, U. Wis., 1916-17, 19-20; LLD (hon.), Drury Coll., 1969. V.p. Ash Grove Cement Co., Springfield, Mo., 1923-46; chmn. of bd. Ash Grove Cement Co., Kansas City, Mo., 1955-67, hon. chmn. bd. Pres. L.T. Sunderland Found., Kansas City. With USN, 1917-18. Mem. Rotary (Springfield and Kansas City, Mo.). Republican. Baptist. Home: Kansas City Mo. Deceased.

SUNDT, THORALF MAURITZ, JR., neurosurgeon, educator; b. Wenonah, N.J., Apr. 3, 1930; s. Thoralf Mauritz and Elinor (Stout) S.; m. Lois Ethelwyn Baker, Oct. 26, 1952; children: Laura E., Thoralf Mauritz, John H. BS with distinction, U.S. Mil. Acad., West Point, N.Y., 1952; postgrad., U. Ariz., Tucson, 1955; MD, U. Tenn., Memphis, 1959. Diplomate: Am. Bd. Neurol. Surgery. Intern John Gaston Charity Hosp., Memphis, 1959-60; resident U. Tenn.-Memphis, 1960-63, Mayo Clinic, 1963-65; prof. neurosurgery Mayo Clinic, Rochester, 1976-92, Vernon F. and Earline D. Dale prof. neurosurgery, 1978, chmn. dept., 1980-92; asst. prof. neurosurgery U. Tenn., Memphis, 1965-68; practice medicine specializing in neurosurgery Rochester; Speakman vis. prof. U. Alta., 1989; Keith lectr. U. Toronto, 1989; Willis lectr. Joint Conf. on Stroke and Cerebral Circulation, 1989; hon. guest Congress Neurol. Surgeons, 1989; hon. pres. Internat. Workshop on Intracranial Aneurysms, Japan, 1989. Mem. editorial bd. Jour. Neurosurgery, 1981-92, editor, 1989-92, chmn. editorial bd., 1986, editor, 1989-92. Served to 1st lt. U.S. Army, 1952-55, Korea. Decorated Bronze Star with oak leaf cluster; recipient Outstanding Alumnus award U. Tenn., 1988, Disting. Alumnus award U.S. Mil. Acad., 1992, Gold medal Internat. Congress of Neurol. Surgeons, 1993; NIH fellow, 1965. Fellow ACS; mem. Inst. Medicine of NAS, Am. Acad. Neurol. Surgeons (pres. 1988-89), Am. Assn. Neurol. Surgeons (chmn. sect. of cerebrovascular surgery, Donaghy lectr. 1989), AMA (resident rev. com. for neurosurgery 1978-92), So. Neurol. Surgery (Grass award 1991), Neurosurg. Soc. Australia (hon.). Republican. Episcopalian. Home: Rochester Minn. Died September 9, 1992.

SUN RA (SONNY BLOUNT (LE SONY'R RA)), jazz musician, orchestra leader; b. Birmingham, Ala.. Student, Ala. A&M Coll. Pianist, composer, arranger, jazz leader Jazz Sci. Arkestra, engagements include Club de Lisa, 1947-48, Grand Terrace, 1953-55, Birdland, 1955-58, all Chgo., Cafe Bizarre, 1961-62, Playhouse, 1962-63, Slugs in Far East, 1966-68, Central Park festivals, 1967-68, The Five Spot, 1975 (all N.Y.C.), Spirit Ho, Newark, 1967-68, Meridian Park festivals, Washington, 1967-68, Newport Jazz Festival, 1973, U. Calif. Jazz Festival, 1973, Ann Arbor Blues and Jazz Festival, 1973-75, Keystone Corner, San Francisco, 1974, U. Pitts., 1975, Antioch Coll., 1975, Kent State U., 1975, Montreux Jazz Festival, 1976, Minn. Inst. Art Auditorium, 1976, U. Va., 1976, Maeight Found concerts, Paris, 1977-80, Lagos Niggria, 1978, jazz showcase, Chgo., 1979, 80, 81, 83, Kennedy Ctr., 1980, Pan-African Festival, Cairo, Egypt, 1982-84, Chgo. Festival, 1983-84, numerous univs. including Houston, Wis. Princeton, Temple, Brandeis, 1980-87, N.Y. Jazz Festival, 1986-87, spl. concerts include: Black Arts Theater, 1965, Avant Garde Festival S.I. Ferry, 1967, Garrick Theater, 1968, Carnegie Hall, 1968, also community concerts sponsored by Haryou-Act, 1968, Afro-Arts Cultural Center Bur. Community Edn., 1968, Mobilization for Youth, 1966, Betterment League Lincoln Sq. Neighborhood Center, 1967 (all N.Y.C.), concert tours for N.Y. State Council Arts, 1966, Esperanto Found. N.Y., 1966; appearances in Europe, 1970, 71, 73, 76, Egypt, 1971, Mexico, 1974, numerous other concerts at art galleries, museums, theater workshops, parks, religious and community orgns., Eastern and Midwestern U.S., Can. and Europe; appeared in movie Space is the Place; recorded, composed (with others) Jazz by Sun Ra, 1956, Fate in a Pleasant Mood, 1960, Futuristic Sounds of Sun Ra, 1961, ESP-Heliocentric Worlds of Sun Ra, vol. 1, 1965, vol. 2, 1966, When Angels Speak of Love, 1965, When Sun Comes Out, 1965, Other Planes of There, 1966, The Magic City, Atlantis, My Brother the Wind, vols. 1 and 2, 1970, Night of the Purple Moon, 1970, Pathways to Unknown Worlds, Deep Purple, Astro Black, The Perfect Man, On the Blue Side, Reflections in Blue, 1987, Blue Delight, 1989, numerous others; author: Umbra; contbr. articles to anthologies Magic City, 1966, Strange Strings, 1967, Nothing Is, 1966. Inducted into Down Beat mag.'s Hall of Fame, 1984. Mem. Infinity, Inc., Sun Dimensions, Outer Spaceways, Inc., Interplanetary Koncepts, Sun Arts, other philos. orgns. Home: Philadelphia Pa.

SURMAN, WILLIAM ROBERT, architect; b. Chgo., May 10, 1926; s. Charles F. and Frances M. (Kadala) S.; m. Joan Marie Jeffers, May 5, 1956; children: William Robert, Robert, Julie, Mary, Thomas. B.S., Rice Inst., 1945; B.S.C.E., Northwestern U., 1948. Architect Pace Assocs., 1957-60, Shaw-Metz & Assocs., 1960-63; pvt. practice architecture, 1963-65; chief architect Graham, Anderson, Probst & White, Chgo., 1965-67; v.p. Graham, Anderson, Probst & White, 1967-68, exec. v.p., 1968-70, pres., chmn. bd., from 1970; now pres. Graham, Anderson, Probst & White, Chgo. Chmn. Bus. Mobilized for Loyola U., 1978-79; chmn. Citizens Bd. Loyola U., 1982-84; trustee Loyola U. Chgo., 1981-90; mem. Glencoe (Ill.) Plan Commn., 1981-83. Served to ensign USNR, 1943-46, PTO; to lt. 1951-53, Korea. Mem. AIA, Nat. Council Archtl. Registration Bds., Ill. Architecture Licensing Bd. Clubs: Economic, Commercial, Arts, Tavern, Executives (dir. 1973-79, pres. 1976-77) (Chgo.); Skokie Country (Glencoe). Home: Glencoe Ill.

SURREY, STANLEY STERLING, lawyer, educator; b. N.Y.C., Oct. 3, 1910; s. Samuel and Pauline (Sterling) S.; m. Dorothy Mooklar Walton, June 6, 1938; 1 son, Scott Stanley. B.S. magna cum laude, CCNY, 1929; LL.B., Columbia U., 1932. Bar: N.Y. 1933, Mass. 1951. Research asst. Columbia Law Sch., 1932-33; atty. Proskauer, Rose & Paskus, N.Y.C., 1933; with NRA, Washington, 1933-35, NLRB, Washington, 1935-37, U.S. Treasury Dept., Washington, 1937-44, 46-47; vis. prof. Calif. Sch. Law, Berkeley, summer 1940; vis. lectr. Columbia Law Sch., summer 1947; prof. law. U. Calif., Berkeley, 1947-50; prof. law Harvard, 1950-61; Jeremiah Smith prof. law, 1958-61, 1969-81, Jeremiah Smith prof. law emeritus, 1981—, also dir. program for internat. taxation, 1953-61; chief reporter Am. Law Inst. income tax project, 1948-61, supr., 1975—; asst. sec. for tax policy Treasury Dept., 1961-69, cons., 1977-81; Mem. Am. Tax Mission to Japan, 1949, 50; spl. counsel U.S. House ways and means King subcom. on internal revenue adminstrn., 1951-52; cons. Treasury Dept., P.R., 1954; spl. adviser UN Expert Group on Tax Matters, 1969—; mem. permanent sci. com. IFA, 1969—. Author: (with others) casebooks in fed. taxation field Federal Income Taxation, Cases and Materials, 2 vols, 1972, 73, 82, Federal Wealth Transfer Taxation, Cases and Materials, 1977, 80, Pathways to Tax Reform, 1973; Contbr. (with others) articles to legal and sailing periodicals. Bd. overseers Florence Heller Sch. Brandeis U., Coll. of V.I.; trustee TIAA, 1972-78. Served as lt. (j.g.) USNR, 1944-46. Decorated Order Sacred Treasure Japan). Fellow Am. Acad. Arts and Scis.; mem. Am. Bar Assn. (council taxation sect. 1958-60), Nat. Tax Assn. (pres. 1979-80), Phi Beta Kappa. Home: Cambridge Mass.

SUSNJARA, GARY M., advertising agency executive; b. N.Y.C., July 29, 1939; s. Michael J. Susnjara and Margaret (Coric) Lappin; m. Mary Angela Pellicane, Apr. 27, 1963; children: Stephanie, Rosemary. BA, Villanova U., 1961, MA, 1963. V.p. DFS Advt., N.Y.C., 1971-76, sr. v.p., 1976-81, pres. N.Y. div., 1981-84; pres., chief operating officer Saatchi & Saatchi DFS, Inc., N.Y.C., 1984-89, cons., 1989-93. Trustee Winthrope U. Hosp., Mineola, N.Y., 1986-93; chmn. N.Y.C. Sport Commn. Found.; bd. dirs. Nat. Crime Prevention Council, Washington, 1983-93. Democrat. Roman Catholic. Home: New York N.Y. Died June 27, 1993.

SUTRO, JOHN ALFRED, lawyer; b. San Francisco, July 3, 1905; s. Alfred and Rose (Newmark) S.; m. Elizabeth Hiss, Oct. 16, 1931; children: Caroline Sutro Mohun, Elizabeth Sutro Mackey, John A., Stephen (dec.). A.B., Stanford U., 1926; LL.B., Harvard U., 1929. Bar: Calif. 1929. Since practiced in San Francisco; with firm Pillsbury, Madison & Sutro, 1929-94, ptnr., 1935-94, adv. ptnr., 1971-94; adv. dir. Bank of Calif. (N.A.), 1976-81; Adv. dir. BanCal Tri-State Corp., 1976-81; past chmn. sr. adv. bd. U.S. Ct. Appeals 9th Cir. Mem. Calif. Commn. on Uniform State Laws, 1968; mem. legal adv. com. Criminal Justice Legal Found.; mem. Calif. Commn. on Interstate Cooperation, 1968; chmn. exec. com. Friends of Stanford Law Libr.; vice chmn. San Francisco Airports Commn., 1970-74; bd. councilors U. So. Calif. Law Ctr., 1972-88; trustee Hastings Law Ctr. Found.; bd. visitors U. Santa Clara Sch. Law, Stanford U. Law Sch., 1967-86; pres., trustee San Francisco Law Libr. (hon. mem.); bd. dirs. St. Luke's Hosp., 1975-85; pres. U.S. Dist. Ct. No. Dist. Calif. Hist. Soc.; v.p. 9th Judicial Cir. Hist. Soc.; mem. USCA 9th Cir. Atty. Admission Fund Com. Served as comdr. USNR, 1940-45. Recipient Navy Disting. Pub. Service award, 1958, ann. award St. Thomas More Soc., 1971, Brotherhood award NCCJ, 1975, Torch of Liberty award Anti-Defamation League of B'nai B'rith, 1980. Fellow Am. Bar Found. (chmn. 1973); mem. Am. Judicature Soc. (dir. 1964-70, exec. com. 1967-70, Herbert Harley award 1974), Navy League (nat. v.p. and dir. 1954-67, mem. nat. adv. council), Calif. Acad. Scis. (trustee 1966-80, hon. trustee 1980-94), Am. Law Inst., Am. Bar Assn. (standing com. fed. judiciary 1968-74, chmn. 1973-74, chmn. com. jud. selection and tenure 1975-78, vice chmn., dir. Nat. Jud. Coll. 1975-80, mem. exec. com. lawyers conf. jud. adminstrn. div., div. council), State Bar Calif. (bd. govs. 1962-66, pres. 1965-66), Bar Assn. San Francisco (pres. 1962, John A. Sutro award for legal excellence 1975), San Francisco C. of C. (pres. 1973, life dir.), Nat. Center for State Cts. (bus. and profl. friends com., independence support fund com., Disting. Service award), Rodeo Cowboys Assn. (life), Phi Alpha Delta. Clubs: Family, Commonwealth (bd. govs. 1957-59), Engineers (San Francisco). Home: San Francisco Calif. Died May 2, 1994.

SUYEMATSU, TOSHIRO, lawyer; b. Oakland, Calif., Aug. 27, 1918; s. Ben T. and Masa (Omaru) S.; m. Marina Franceschi, Sept. 30, 1945 (dec. 1950); m. Ellen Crowley, Apr. 30, 1954. B.A., U. Wyo., 1948, J.D., 1950. Bar: Wyo. 1951, U.S. Supreme Ct. 1970, U.S. Ct. Appeals (9th and 10th cirs.) 1971. Mem. firm Bentley & Suyematsu, Laramie, Wyo., 1951-54; practiced in Cheyenne, Wyo., from 1954; mem. firm Suyematsu and Crowley, 1954-59, Miller, Suyematsu, Crowley, Duncan & Borthwick (and predecessor), from 1959; ct. apptd. U.S. atty. Wyo., 1977, 81; asst. U.S. atty. for Wyo., 1969-89; commnr. Wyo. State Bar. Legal chmn. Boy's State, 1951-52, Girl's State, 1953; govt. appeal agt. U.S. Selective Service, 1967-69; justice of peace, Cheyenne, 1957-58; chmn. Wyo. State Cancer Fund, 1952-54; sponsor Jr. Achievement; scoutmaster Boy Scouts Am., Laramie, Wyo., 1952-53; county treas. Republican Party, 1952; bd. dirs. Legal Services Laramie County, 1968-73. Served with AUS, 1941-46. Decorated Silver Star, Bronze Star, Purple Heart with cluster, Presl. Unit citation with 3 clusters; recipient Outstanding Performance award Dept. Justice, 1970, Dept. Justice dirs.' award, 1976, award of merit Wyo. State Cancer Fund., 1952, 55; named Boss of Yr. Indian Paintbrush chpt. Nat. Secs. Assn., 1976. Mem. Wyo. Bar Assn., Cheyenne Bar Assn. (v.p. 1964, pres. 1966-67), Fed. Bar Assn., UN Soc., Smithsonian Inst. Soc., VFW, DAV, Am. Legion (judge advocate Cheyenne post # 6 1962, Meritorious Svc. award). Home: Cheyenne Wyo. Died June 4, 1994; buried Veterans Cemetery, Casper, Wyo.

SVENDSEN, LOUISE AVERILL, retired curator, art auction company consultant; b. Old Town, Maine, Nov. 22, 1915; d. Albert Guy and Louise Pierce Averill; m. Thoralf Svendsen, 1950 (dec. 1984). BA, Wellesley Coll., 1937; MA, Yale U., 1941, PhD, 1949. Docent Met. Mus. Art, N.Y.C., 1941-42; lectr. dept. edn. Boston Mus. Fine Arts, 1942-43; instr. history of art Duke U., Durham, N.C., 1943-45; instr., asst. prof. Goucher Coll., Balt., 1945-50; asst. prof. Am. U., Washington, 1950-51; lect. Solomon R. Guggenheim Mus., N.Y.C., 1954, asst. curator, 1962-66, curator, 1966-78, sr. curator, 1978-82, curator emeritus, 1983-94; cons. Impressionist Dept. Sotheby's, N.Y.C., 1983-94. Decorated knight 1st class Royal Norwegian Order of St. Olav, Swedish Order of the Polar Star. Mem. Internat. Found. for Art Rsch. (bd. dirs.). Home: New York N.Y. Died Jan. 3, 1994.

SWAN, JOHN CHARLES, library director; b. Elkhorn, Wis., Apr. 12, 1945; s. John Clement and Winifred Jean (Sturtevant) S.; m. Susan Reynolds Crocker, May 1, 1971; children: Matthew Carey, Benjamin Charles. Student, Northwestern U., 1963-66; BA, Boston U., 1967; MA, Tufts U., 1969, PhD, 1975; MLS, Simmons Coll., 1979. Ref. libr. Wabash Coll., Crawfordsville, Ind., 1979-86; head libr. Bennington (Vt.) Coll., 1986-94; part-time instr. English and Am. lit. U. Mass., Boston, Tufts U., Curry Coll., Massasoit Community Coll., U. Mass. Higher Edn. for Prisoners Program, 1970-79; learning librs. asst. lectureship NEH Boston Pub. Libr., 1975, lectureship, 1977. Editor: Music in Boston, 1978; co-author: The Triumph of Pierrot, 1986 (Choice Outstanding Acad. 1986), rev. edit., 1993, The Freedom to Lie, 1989; contbr. articles to profl. jours. Bd. dirs. adult edn. The Tutorial Ctr., Bennington, 1989-93; trustee McCullough Libr., North Bennington, Vt., 1991-94; permanent trustee Bennington Free Libr., 1991-94; bd. dirs. Sage City Symphony, 1992-94. Mem. ALA (chair intellectual freedom round table 1985-86, exec. bd. dirs. 1980-92), ACLU (bd. dirs. Vt. chpt. 1990-92), Vt. Libr. Assn. (chair intellectual freedom com. 1987-93), Ind. Libr. Assn. (chair intellectual freedom com. 1981-86), Granville Bantock Soc. (Ann. award 1983), Baker Street Breakfast Club. Democrat. Mem. Vedantist Ch. Home: Bennington Vt. Died Jan. 26, 1994.

SWANKE, ALBERT HOMER, architect; b. Thomasville, Ga., Nov. 22, 1909; s. John Christian and Stella (Williams) S.; m. Margaret Anne Twaddell, Aug. 11, 1936 (dec. 1968); 1 son, Albert Homer; m. Dorothy Pratt Williams, Feb. 7, 1969. B.S., Ga. Inst. Tech., 1930; student, Beaux Arts Inst. Design, N.Y.C., 1931. Registered architect, N.Y., Conn., D.C., Fla., Ga., Ill., Ind., La., Md., Mass., Minn., Miss., Mo., N.H., N.J., N.C., Ohio, Pa., S.C., Va., Wis. registered profl. planner, N.J. Trainee Flagg, Embury and Ballard, N.Y.C., 1931-35; arch. N.Y. State Ins. Dept., 1936-42, Alfred Easton Poor, 1946; assoc. Walker & Poor, Archs., 1947-52; ptnr. Office of Alfred Easton Poor-Archs./Engrs., N.Y.C., 1952-71, Poor and Swanke & Ptnrs., N.Y.C., 1972-75; mng. ptnr. Poor, Swanke, Hayden & Connell, Archs., 1975-79; sr. ptnr. Swanke Hayden Connell & Ptnrs., 1979-81; cons. Swanke Hayden Connell Archs., 1981-96; trustee, chmn. archtl. rev. bd. Historic Savannah Found.; mem. Village of Larchmont Archtl. Bd. Review, 1963-69, chmn., 1968-69; trustee Larchmont Manor Park Soc., 1962-69, Architects Emergency Com., 1956-76; mem. bd. design Extension of Capitol Project, Washington, 1956-79; alt. mem. coordinating bd. Additional House Office Bldg. Project, Capitol Hill, 1955-60; alt. mem. archtl. adv. bd. Johns Hopkins U., 1961-70. Works include extension of East front of U.S. Capitol, James Madison Meml. Library of Congress Bldg; also restoration Supreme Ct. and Senate Chambers, Washington; Fed. Office Bldg. and Customs Ct., N.Y.C., Home Ins. Co, N.Y.C., Grumman Aircraft Engring. Plant and facilities, Calverton, L.I., N.Y., NATO Airbases at, Dreux and Evreux, France, Queens County (N.Y.) Courthouse and Prison, Hardened Communications Facilities, AT&T Long Lines; addition to, Chgo. Bd. of Trade Bldg.; Hdqrs. Office Bldg of Home Ins. Co., N.Y.C., Public Service Electric & Gas Co., Newark, NML Hdqrs, Milw., Continental Center, N.Y.C., Trump Tower, N.Y.C., 520 Madison Ave. Bldg., N.Y.C.; also numerous banking facilities in, U.S. and abroad; archtl. cons., French-Am. Com. for Restoration of Statue of Liberty. Trustee, mem. exec. com. N.Y. Med. Coll., Flower and 5th Ave. Hosps., 1963-79, Westchester Med. Center Devel. Bd., 1969-73; bd. mgrs. Am. Soc. Prevention Cruelty to Animals, 1976-79, dir. emeritus, 1980-96; mem. Am. Arbitration Assn., 1971-80; mem. archtl. adv. bd. Archdiocese of N.Y., 1979-96. Served as lt. comdr. USNR, 1943-45. Fellow AIA, Am. Soc. Registered Architects; mem. NAD (assoc.), N.Y. Soc. Architects, N.Y. Bldg Congress, Soc. Archtl. Historians, Navy League U.S., Soc. Cincinnati, Phi Sigma Kappa, Pi Delta Epsilon. Republican. Presbyn. Clubs: University (N.Y.C.); Met. (Washington); Boston (New Orleans). Home: New Orleans La. Died Jan. 8, 1996.

SWANN, DONALD IBRAHIM, freelance composer and performer; b. Sept. 30, 1923; s. Herbert William Swann and Naguime Sultan; m. Janet Mary Oxborrow, 1955 (div. 1983); 2 children; m. Alison Smith, 1993. Student, Westminster Sch., Christ Church, Oxford; hons. degree modern lang., Westminster Sch. Contributed music to London revues, including Airs on a Shoestring, 1953-54, as joint leader writer with Michael Flanders; Wild Thyme, musical play with Philip Guard, 1955; in At the Drop of a Hat, 1957, appeared for first time (with Michael Flanders) as singer and accompanist of own songs (this show ran over 2 yrs. in London, was part of Edinburgh Festival, 1959; Broadway, 1959-60; Am. and Can. tour1960-61; tour of Great Britain and Ireland, 1962-63); At the Drop of Another Hat (with Michael Flanders), Haymarket, 1963-64, Globe, 1965; Australia and New Zealand tour, 1964; US tour, 1966-67. Arranged concerts of owwon settings: Set by Swann, An Evening in Crete: Soundings by Swann; Between the Bars: an autobiography in music; A Crack in Time, a concert in search of peace. Musician in Residence, Quaker Study Ctr., Pendle Hill, USA, 1983; has worked in song-writing and performing partnerships with Jeremy Taylor, Sydney Carter, Frank Topping, John Amis; solo entertainments in theatres and concert halls (Stand Clear for Wonders with peace exploration songs). Founded Albert House Press for spl. publs., 1974. Compositions and Publs. include: Lucy and the Hunter, musical play with Sydney Carter; satirical music to Third Programme series by Henry Reed, ghosting for Hilda Tablet; London Sketches with Sebastian Shaw, 1958; Festival Matinis, 1962; Perelandra, music drama with David Marsh based on the novel of C.S. Lewis, 1961-62; Settings of John Betjeman Poems, 1964; Sing Round the Year (Book of New Carols for Children), 1965; The Road Goes Ever On, book of songs with J.R.R. Tolkien,,1968, rev. edn., 1978; The Space Between the Bars: a book of reflections, 1968; Requiem for the Living, to words of C. Day Lewis, 1969; The rope of Love; around the earth in song, 1973; Swann's Way Out: a posthumous adventure, 1974; (with Albert Friedlander) The Five Scrolls, 1975; Omnibus Flanders and Swann Songbook, 1977; Round the Piano with Donald Swann, 1979; (with Alex Davison) The Yeast Factory, music drama, 1979; Alphabetaphon: 26 essays A-Z (illustrated by Natasha Etheridge); songs and operas with Arthur Scholey: The Song of Caedmon, 1971; Singalive, 1978; Wacky and his Fuddlejig (children's musical play), 1978; Candle Tree, 1980; Baboushka (a Christmas cantata), 1980; The Visitors (based on Tolstoy), 1984; Brendan A-hoy! (with Evelyn Kirkhart and Mary Morgan) Mamahuhu (musical play), 1986; Envy (with Richard Crane), 1986. Avocation: going to the launderette. Home: London Eng. Died Mar. 23, 1996.

SWANSON, GUY EDWIN, social scientist, educator; b. Warren, Pa., Oct. 6, 1922; s. Guy Edwin and Minnie Katherine (Haslett) S.; m. Eliane Marie Aerts, Aug. 19, 1977; children—Emily Gray, Elisabeth Huntley, Mary Alice, Sarah Catherine. A.B., U. Pitts., 1943, M.A., 1943; Ph.D., U. Chgo., 1948. Instr. Boston U., 1945-46, Ind. U., 1946-47, U. Chgo., 1947-48; mem. faculty U. Mich., 1948-69; fellow U. Mich. (Center Advanced Study Behavioral Scis.), 1957-58, prof., 1959-69, chmn. dept. sociology, 1961-64; prof. sociology U. Calif., Berkeley, 1969-84, prof. psychology, 1984-95; dir. U. Calif. (Inst. Human Devel.), 1981-88; dir. Social Sci. Research Council, 1961-64. Author: (with Daniel R. Miller) The Changing American Parent, 1958, Inner Conflict and Defense, 1960, The Birth of the Gods, 1960, Religion and Regime, A Sociological Account of the Reformation, 1967, Rules of Descent, Studies in the Sociology of Parentage, 1969, Social Change, 1971, Emotional Disturbance and Juvenile Delinquency, 1980, Ego Defenses and the Legitimation of Behavior, 1988. Guggenheim fellow, 1964-65. Fellow Am. Sociol. Assn., Am. Psychol. Assn., AAAS (v.p. 1968-69). Home: Kensington Calif. Died Feb. 28, 1995.

SWARTZ, RODERICK GARDNER, librarian; b. Fairbury, Nebr., May 25, 1939; s. E. Wayne and Dorine B. (Gardner) S.; m. Marianna Moore, Sept. 1, 1972. B.A., U. Nebr., 1961; M.A., 1962, U. Chgo 1963. Asst. to exec. sec. library adminstrn. div. ALA 1963-64; library cons. Mo. State Library, 1964-66; ass dir. Tulsa City-County Library, 1966-70, asso. dir 1970-72; dep. dir. Nat. Commn. on Libraries and Inf Sci., 1972-74; state librarian Wash. State Librar Olympia, 1975—; mem. faculty U. Okla., 1969-72, U Denver, 1970, Cath. U. Am., 1972-74, Inst. Library an Info. Sci., Tampere, Finland, 1975, U. Wash., 1980— Fulbright fellow, 1975, 80; Council on Librar Resources fellow, 1975. Mem. ALA, Washingto Library Assn. Home: Olympia Wash.

SWAYZE, JOHN CAMERON, SR., news com mentator; b. Wichita, Kans., Apr. 4, 1906; s. Jess Ernest and Christine (Cameron) S.; m. Beulah Ma Estes, Oct. 29, 1932; children: John Cameron Jr Suzanne Louise Patrick. Student, U. Kans., 1925-2 Dramatic Sch., N.Y.C., 1928-29. Mem. editorial sta Kansas City (Mo.) Jour. Post, 1930-40, feature edito 1940; news commentator Stas. KMBC/WHB, 1930-4 mem. news staff Sta. KMBC, 1940-45; news and sp events dir. Western network NBC, Hollywood, Cali 1946-47; radio and television news commentator NB N.Y.C., 1947-56; host Sightseeing with the Swayze N.Y.C., 1950-95; TV comml. spokesman numerou sponsors, N.Y.C., 1956-81; reporter ABC, N.Y.C., 195 95. Author: Art of Living, 1979. Recipient Com mentator award Alfred J. DuPont Found., 1950. Mem Lambs Club, Nat. Press Club, Greenwich Countr Club. Presbyterian. Home: Bal Harbour Fla. Die August 15, 1995.

SWIGART, THEODORE EARL, oil executive; b. A royo Grande, Calif., June 2, 1895; s. Frank W. an Mattie (Rice) S.; m. Erna Patery, Sept. 28, 1918; 1 dau Patricia (Mrs. Curtis R. Inman). A.B., Stanford, 191 Engr., 1918; Engr. spl. officers tng. course, U.S. Nava Acad., 1918. With pipe line dept. Standard Oil Co Calif., 1913-14; Martinez refinery Shell Oil Co., Calif 1915; exploration dept. Shell Oil Co., 1916, prod dept., 1917; petroleum engr. U.S. Bur. Mines, Bartle ville, Okla., 1919-20; asst. to chief petroleum engr. U. Bur. Mines, Washington; supt. Petroleum Expt. Sta Bartlesville, 1923; cons. petroleum engr. Steel Bros. Co., Ltd., London, Attock Oil Co., Ltd., Rawalpind Punjab, India; cons. petroleum engr. Indo-Burma-P troleum Co., Ltd., Yenangyaung, Burma, 1923-24; chi prodn. engr. Shell Oil Co., Calif., 1924-28; asst. ge field supt. in charge prodn., 1928-32, v.p. in charg Tex., N.M., La., Ark.; v.p. in charge Shell Petroleu Corp. (now Shell Oil Co.), 1932-40; pres. Shell Pipe Li Corp., Houston, 1940-54; petroleum adviser Morga Stanley & Co.; chmn., dir. N. Central Oil Corp., 195 72; pres., dir. Ednl. Found., Inc.; past dir. Pilot Fun Commerce Fund, Impact Fund, Industries Trend Fu Inc. Contbr. articles to tech. jours., govt. publs. Pa pres., treas. Houston Museum Fine Arts; trustee Unite Fund Houston and Harris County; past pres. Com munity Chest and Council of Houston and Harris C Tex.; dir., past chmn. Houston Symphony Soc. Mem Tex. Mid-Continent Oil and Gas Assn. (dir., Dis inguished award), Am. Petroleum Inst. (past dir., pa v.p.), Am. Inst. Mining and Metall. Engrs., Am. Ass Petroleum Geologists, Tex. Soc. S.A.R. Clubs: Teja Bayou, River Oaks Country, Eagle Lake Rod and Gu 25 Year Club of Petroleum Industry. Home: Housto Tex. Died Apr. 1, 1993.

SWING, PETER GRAM, music educator; b. N.Y.C July 15, 1922; s. Raymond and Betty (Gram) S.; m Elizabeth Ann Sherman, May 27, 1948; childre Pamela Sherman, Bradford Scott. A.B., Harvard U 1948, A.M., 1951; postgrad., U. Utrecht, Netherland 1951-52; Ph.D., U. Chgo., 1969. Instr., asso choirmaster Rollins Coll., 1952-53; instr. U. Chgo 1953-55; mem. faculty Swarthmore Coll., 1955-89, asso prof., 1959-69, prof., 1969-89, dir. coll. chorus, 1955-8 chmn. dept. music, 1958-74; condr. faculty choir, asso Inst. Advanced Mus. Studies King's Coll., Londo 1989-90; mem. faculty Berkshire Music Ctr., Leno Mass., 1962-86; mem. Nat. Humanities Faculty, 196 70; vis. com. music U. Chgo., 1971-77. Served wi USNR, 1942-46. Fulbright grantee Netherlands, 195 52; Fulbright Sr. Research grantee Belgium, 1970-71 Mem. AAUP, Am. Musicol. Soc. (chmn. Phila. chp 1969-70), Coll. Music Soc., Vereniging voor Nede landse Muziekgeschiedenis, Choral Arts Soc. Phila Musical Fund Soc. Phila., Phi Beta Kappa (hon.). Home: Swarthmore Pa. Died Feb. 16, 1996.

SWINTON, WILLIAM ELGIN, emeritus zoolog educator; b. Kirkcaldy, Scotland, Sept. 30, 1900; s. W liam Wilson and Rachel Hunter (Cargill) S. B.Sc., U Glasgow, Scotland, 1922, Ph.D., 1931, D.Sc., 197 LL.D., U. Toronto, 1975; Litt.D., U. Western On 1977; D.Sc., Queen's U. Ont., 1982. Sci. staff Brit. Mu Natural History, London, 1924-61; head life scis. Roy Ont. Mus., Toronto, 1961-63; dir. Royal Ont. Mu 1963-66; prof. zoology U. Toronto, from 1966, pr emeritus; sr. fellow Massey Coll., Toronto. Auth numerous books.; Contbr. articles to sci. jours. Serv with Royal Navy, 1939. Fellow Royal Soc. Edinburg Royal Soc. Can., Royal Coll. Physicians and Surgeon Acad. Medicine (Toronto); mem. Ont. Med. Ass AAAS, N.Y. Acad. Scis., Am. Assn. Mus., Am. Mu Natural History, Can. Mil. Inst., Am. Inst. Biol. Scis Conservative. Presbyterian. Clubs: Athenaeu ndon); Royal Can. Yacht, Arts and Letters (past .). Home: Toronto Can. Died 1994.

OYER, THOMAS MICHAEL, corporate profes-al; b. Phila., Jan. 14, 1947; s. Harry S. and and y Elizabeth (Salisbury) S.; m. Katherine W. Swoyer, ., 1967; children: Thomas M. Jr., Patrick W., Sarah BA in Sci., U. Notre Dame, 1968; MA in Air and Hygiene, U. N.C., 1969; postgrad., Widener U., 2-74. Controller Roy F. Weston, Inc., West Chester, 1972-80, v.p. mktg., 1980-83, pres., 1983—; adv. dept. sci. U. Pa. With USN, 1969-72. Recipient ting. Performance award Widener U. Sch. Mgmt., 9. Mem. ASME (mem. indsl. adv. bd. 1987—), fl. Svcs. Mgmt. Assn. (pres. 1980-81; founding mem. 6-78), Water Resources Assn. (bd. dirs.). Home: st Chester Pa.

KES, WILLIAM MALTBY, artist; b. Aberdeen, s., Dec. 13, 1911; s. William McQuiston and Eleanor ymond (Johnston) S.; m. Marjorie Tyre, Dec. 24, 1. Studied under, Wayman Adams, 1934-35, Diego era, 1936, John Sloan, 1937, Fernand Leger, 1951. f., artist-in-residence Auburn U., 1942-77, prof. eritus, 1977-92. Author: The Multimetal hography Process, Artist's Proof, vol. 8, 1968, collections of a Lithographile, the Tamarind Papers, l. 6, Number 2, 1983, Diego Rivera and the Hotel forma Murals, Archives of American Art Jour., Vol. Numbers 1 and 2, 1985, (with Taylor Littleton) vancing American Art, Painting, Politics and Cul-al Confrontation at Mid-Century, 1989; contbr. to n. Prize Prints of the 20th Century, 1949, ntmaking Today, 1972, Art of the Print, 1976; one-n exhbns. include Montgomery (Ala.) Mus. Fine ts, 1957, 68, 80, Auburn U., 1967, 73, 75, 81, lumbus (Ga.) Mus. Arts and Crafts, 1958, 68, U. a., 1970, New Orleans U., 1972, U. Miss., 1975; oup exhbns. include Am. Watercolors, Drawings and ints, Met. Mus. Art, 1952, Curators Choice Exhbns., ila. Print Club, 1956; represented in permanent col-tions at Mus. Modern Art, Met. Mus. Art, N.Y.C., n. Art Mus., N.Y., Stedlijk Mus., Amsterdam, Boston us. Fine Arts, Phila. Mus. Art., Nat. Mus. Am. Art, rtland Mus. Art. Served with USAF, 1944-45. Nat. ndowment for the Arts grantee, 1965-66. Mem. Soc. n. Graphic Artists, Scarab, Omicron Delta Kappa, i Kappa Phi. Episcopalian. Home: Auburn Ala. ied Sept. 23, 1992; interred Mt. Airy Ivy Hill, Phila., .

YMONS, JULIAN GUSTAVE, author; b. London, ay 30, 1912; s. Morris Albert and Minnie Louise S.; . Kathleen Clark, Oct. 25, 1941; children: Sarah ouise (dec.), Marcus Richard Julian. Ed. in, London. c. Victoria Elec. Plant Co., 1928-41; advt. copywriter umble, Crowther & Nicholas, 1944-47. Works include oetry Confusions About X, 1938, The Second Man, 944; crime stories The Immaterial Murder Case, 1945, Man Called Jones, 1947, The Broken Penny, 1952, he Paper Chase, 1955, The Colour of Murder, 1957 Crime Writers Assn. award for best book of year), The rogress of a Crime, 1960 (Mystery Writers Am. award or best book of year), The End of Solomon Grundy, 964, The Man Who Lost His Wife, 1970, The Plot gainst Roger Rider, 1973, The Blackheath Poisonings, 978, Sweet Adelaide, 1979, The Detling Secret, 1982, he Name of Annabel Lee, 1983, A Criminal Comedy, 984, The Kentish Manor Murders, 1988, Death's Darkest Face, 1990, Portraits of the Missing, 1991, omething Like a Love Affair, 1992, Playing Happy amilies, 1994; non-fiction A.J.A. Symons, 1950, Charles Dickens, 1951, Thomas Carlyle, 1952, Horatio Bottomley, 1955, A Reasonable Doubt, 1960, The Thir-ies, 1960, reissued as The Thirties and the Nineties, 990, The Detective Story in Britain, 1962, England's Pride, 1965, Picture History of Crime and Detection, 1966 (Mystery Writer Am. spl. award), Bloody Murder, 1972 (Mystery Writers Am. spl. award), rev. edit. 1992, Between the Wars, 1972, Notes from Another Country, 1972, The Hungry Thirties, 1976, The Tell-Tale Heart, 1978, The Great Detectives, 1981, Critical Observations, 1981, Makers of the New, 1987, Criminal Practices, 1994; editor non-fiction An Anthology of War Poetry, 1942, Penguin Classic Crimes Omnibus, 1984, The Es-sential Wyndham Lewis, 1989. Grand master Danish Poe Club, 1978, Swedish Acad. Detection, 1977. Served with Royal Armoured Corps, 1942-44. Fellow Royal Soc. Lit.; mem. Crime Writers Assn. (chmn. 1958-59), Mystery Writers Am. (grand master 1982), Soc. of Authors (chmn. com. of mgmt. 1970-71), Detection Club (pres. 1976-85), The Conan Doyle Soc. (pres. 1989-93), Writers Guild. Home: Walmer Deal Eng. Died Nov. 19, 1994.

SYNGE, JOHN LIGHTON, mathematician, physicist, emeritus educator; b. Dublin, Ireland, Mar. 23, 1897; s. Edward and Ellen (Price) S.; m. Elizabeth Allen, 1918 (dec. 1985); children: Margaret Dryer (dec.), Cathleen Synge Morawetz, Isabel Synge Seddon. B.A., Trinity Coll., Dublin, 1919, M.A., 1922, Sc.D., 1926; LL.D. (hon.), U. St. Andrews, 1966; D.Sc. (hon.), Queen's U., Belfast, Northern Ireland, 1969, Nat. U. Ireland, 1970. Lectr. math Trinity Coll., Dublin, 1920, fellow, prof. natural philosophy, 1925-30; asst. prof. math. Toronto, Ont., Can., 1920-25, prof. applied math., 1930-43; bal-listics mathematician U.S. Strategic Air Forces in Europe, 1944-45; chmn. dept. math. Ohio State U., 1943-46; head dept. math. Carnegie Inst. Tech., 1946-48; sr. prof. Dublin Inst. for Advanced Studies, 1948-72, emeritus, from 1972; vis. lectr. Princeton U., 1939; vis. prof. Brown U., 1941, MIT, summer 1947. Author: Geometrical Optics, 1937; (with B.A. Griffith) Principles of Mechanics, 1942, 3d edit., 1959; editor: (with A. W. Conway) Mathematical Papers of Sir W.R. Hamilton, vol. 1, 1931; (with A. Schild) Tensor Calculus, 1949; Science, Sense and Nonsense, 1951, Geometrical Mechanics and de Broglie Waves, 1954, Relativity: The Special Theory, 1956, 2d edit., 1964, The Relativistic Gas, 1957, Kandelman's Krim, 1957, The Hypercircle in Mathematical Physics, 1957, Relativity: The General Theory, 1960, Talking About Relativity, 1970; research, publs. on devel. geometrical methods in classical mechanics and relativity; constructed (with others) rela-tivistic models of gravitational fields; invented (with W. Prager) hypercircle for boundary value problems of electrostatics, elasticity and hydrodynamics; generalized Hamilton's ray-wave methods with application to de Broglie waves, water waves. Recipient Boyle medal Royal Dublin Soc., 1972. Fellow Royal Soc. London, Royal Soc. Can. (Tory medal 1943); mem. Royal Irish Acad. (pres. 1961-64), Am. Math. Soc., Math. Assn. Am. Home: Blackrock Ireland Deceased.

SZEKELY, JULIAN, materials engineering educator; b. Budapest, Hungary, Nov. 23, 1934; came to U.S., 1966, naturalized, 1975; s. Gyula and Ilona (Nemeth) S.; m. Elizabeth Joy Pearn, Mar. 2, 1963; children: Richard J., Martin T., Rebecca J., Mathew T., David A. BSc, Im-perial Coll., London, 1959; PhD, D.I.C., 1961; DSc, D.I.C., Eng., 1972; Dr honoris causa, Inst. Nat. Polytech. de Grenoble, 1994. Lectr. metallurgy Imperial Coll., 1962-66; asso. prof. chem. engring. State U. N.Y. at Buffalo, 1966-68, prof., 1968-76; dir. Center for Process Metallurgy, 1970-76; prof. materials engring. Mass. Inst. Tech., Cambridge, 1976-95; cons. to govt. and industry; Nelson W. Taylor Meml. lectr. Pa. State U., 1985; John R. Lewis Disting. lectr. U. Utah, 1989; lectr. in field. Author: (with N.J. Themelis) Rate Phe-nomena in Process Metallurgy, 1971, (with W.H. Ray) Process Optimization, 1973, (with J.W. Evans and H.Y. Sohn) Gas-Solid Reactions, 1976, Fluid Flow Aspects of Metals Processing, 1979; (with J.W. Evans and J.K. Brimcombe) Mathematical Modelling of Metals Proces-sing Operations, 1988; editor: Ironmakikng Technology, 1972, The Steel Industry and the Environment, The Steel Industry and the Energy Crisis, 1975; contbr. ar-ticles to profl. jours. Recipient Jr. Moulton medal Brit. Inst. Chem. Engrs., 1964; Extractive Metallurgy Div. Sci. award Am. Inst. Mining and Metall. Engrs., 1973; also Mathewson Gold medal, 1973; Howe Meml. lectr., 1979, Educator award 1991, Extractive Metall. lectr., 1987 ; Sir George Beilby Gold medal Brit. Inst. Chem. Engrs.-Soc. Chem. Industry-Inst. Metals, 1973; Curtis McGraw research award Am. Soc. Engring. Edn., 1974; Profl. Progress award Am. Inst. Chem. Engrs., 1974, TMS Educator award 1991, Alexander von Humboldt-Stiftung Prize, 1992; Charles H. Jennings Meml. award Am. Welding Soc., 1983; John Simon Guggenheim fellow, 1974, TMS fellow, 1993. Mem. Nat. Acad. En-gring., Hungarian Acad. Engring. (hon.). Home: Cam-bridge Mass. Died Dec. 7, 1995.

SZENTAGOTHAI, JANOS, anatomist, educator; b. Budapest, Hungary, Oct. 31, 1912; s. Gustav and Mar-garet (Antal) Schimert; M.D., U. Budapest, 1936; m. Alice Biberauer, June 7, 1938; children: Cathrine (Mrs. Michael Bloch), Claire, (Mrs. Miklos Rethelyi), Chris-tine (Mrs. Tamás Viola). Jr. asst. Budapest U. Med. Sch., 1936-37, sr. asst., 1938-40, prosector, 1941-45, prof. anatomy, head dept., 1963-77; prof. anatomy Pecs U. Med. Sch., 1946-63. Recipient Kossuth State award, 1950, State Award I, 1970. Mem. Hungarian Acad. Scis. (pres. 1977-85), Leopoldina Acad., Nat. Acad. Scis. (U.S.), Acad. Arts and Scis. Author: Die Rolle der Einzelnen Labyrinthrezeptoren bei der Orientation von Augen und Kopf in Raume, 1952; (with B. Flerko, B. Mess, B. Halasz) Hypothalamic Control of the Anterior Pituitary, 1962; (with F.C. Eccles, M. Ito) The Cer-ebellum as a Neuronal Machine, 1967; (with M. Arbib) Conceptual Models of Neural Organization, 1975; also numerous articles. Research on nerve junctions to elucidate circuitry and connectivity in central nervous system, spinal cord pathways and their connetions, structure of simplest reflex paths, pathways and mechanisms of labyrinthine eye-movement reflexes, visual system relay mechanisms, structural basis of nervous inhibition in gen., cerebellar pathways and neuronal machinery of cerebellar cortex, anat. bases of nervous control on endocrine functions, the neuron network of the cerebral cortex. Died Sept. 8, 1994. Home: Budapest Hungary

SZEWALSKI, ROBERT, science educator, consultant; b. Nisko, Poland, Aug. 16, 1903; s. Marc and Barbara Maria (Saalburg) S.; m. Janina Walaszek, Apr. 2, 1947. MS, Tech. U., Lwow, Poland, 1929, D of Tech. Scis., 1935, Habilitation, 1938; D (hon.), Tech. U., Gdansk, Poland, 1977, Tech. U., Poznan, Poland, 1983. From asst. prof. to prof. Tech. U., Lwow, 1927-45; prof. Wroclaw U., 1947-49; prof. Tech. U., Gdansk, 1945, dean shipbuilding dept., 1950-51, rector, 1951-54; dir. Inst. Fluid Flow Machines Polish Acad. Scis., Gdansk, 1953-70; cons. Inst. Fluid Flow Machines, Gdansk, 1970—; vis. prof. Stuttgart U., 1975, Brown U., Pro-vidence, 1976. Author: Theory of Machines, 1954, Ad-vanced Problems in Steam Turbine Engines, 1978; contbr. over 200 sci. papers; inventor high efficiency steam power cycles and tech. Vol. War of In-dependence, 1920. With Polish Air Force, 1939. Decorated Commdr. Polonia Restituta, 1960; recipient Medal of Independence, Cen. Bd., 1928, Gold Medal of Merit, Tchechoslovak Acad. Scis., 1970, Individual 1st Class State prize of Sci., 1980, Medal of Copernicus, Polish Acad. Scis., 1986. Fellow Am. Soc. Mech. Engrs. (life), Inst. Mech. Eng. London; mem. Polish Acad. Scis. (corr. mem. 1952-60, pres. Gdansk br. 1984—), Gdansk Sci. Soc. (full pres. Gdansk br. 1971-73, hon. pres. 1978), Polish French Soc. (v.p. 1960-70). Home: Gdansk Poland Died Feb. 9, 1993.

SZUHAY, JOSEPH ALEXANDER, retired human resources educator; b. Cambridge, Ohio, Feb. 28, 1925; s. David and Barbara (Orosz) S.; m. Joy Naomi Youppi, Nov. 21, 1946; children: Paige Melanie (dec.), Noel Joy (dec.) Brooke Jana. BS in Phys. Edn., U. Iowa, 1953, Cert. in Phys. Therapy, 1954, MS in Anatomy, 1956, PhD in Ednl. Psychology and Rehab. Counseling, 1961. Lic. psychologist, Pa. Recreation therapist Iowa Hosp. for Severely Handicapped Children, Iowa City, 1952-53; instr. Sch. Phys. Therapy U. Iowa, Iowa City, 1954-61; phys. therapist Steindler Orthopedic Clinic-Mercy Hosp., Iowa City, 1959-61; dir. vocat. guidance adult day care program Southeastern Mental Health Ctr. Sioux Falls Coll., 1961-64, lectr. psychology, 1962-64; dir. rehab. counseling program U. Scranton, Pa., 1964-74, prof., chmn. dept. human resources, 1974-89; ret., 1989; vocat. cons. Office Hearings and Appeals-Social Security Adminstrn., 1962-92; commr. HEW (now HHS), 1975-76; ednl. cons. Pa. Bur. Visually Handi-capped, 1968-69; cons. clin. and counseling psychology VA Hosps., 1971-92; cons. adv. coun. on rehab. coun-seling Regional Rsch. Inst. U. Wis., 1974-76; rehab. counseling cons. Coppin State Coll., 1979-81, Lincoln U., 1981-86, U. Vt., 1982, U. Md., Eastern Shore, 1982-86, R.I. U., 1984; mem. rehab. counseling program adv. bd. Pa. State U., 1989-92; mem. manpower task force Gov.'s Comprehensive Vocat. Rehab. Commn., 1967-68; mem. Gov.'s Regional Commn. on Health Care Bill, 1974. Co-author: (with Barry Newhill) Field Investiga-tion and Evaluation of Learning Disabilities (6 vols.), 1981, Health and Medical Manual, 1985; editor: The History of the National Council on Rehabilitation Edu-cation, 1980; book reviewer: Psychiatry and Social Sci. Rev., Bestsellers; contbr. articles to profl. jours. Bd. dirs. Alcoholism and Drug Abuse Coun., Northeastern Pa., 1965-71, pres., 1967-69, chmn. edn. com., 1966, 69, 70; bd. dirs. United Neighborhood Svcs., Lackawanna County, 1965-70, pres., 1968-69; bd. dirs. U. Scranton rep. Allied Services for Handicapped, 1967-78, Lack-awanna County chpt. Nat. Found., 1969-72; bd. dirs., pres. Treatment and Rehab. Ctr., Northeastern Pa., 1970-75; bd. dirs. United Rehab. Svcs., Wilkes-Barre, 1985-92, Scranton and Lackawanna County unit Vis. Nurses Assn., 1972-74, Scranton Mental Health and Mental Retardation Assn., 1971-78, Operation Overcome, Scranton, 1985-92, mem. profl. adv. com., Va. Commonwealth U.; adv. com. Regional Continuing Edn. Programs, 1978-82, Easter Seal Treatment Ctr., Scranton, 1979-92; mem. adv. bd. Traumatic Brain In-jury Project, 1988-92; adv. coun. Successful Partnership Grant Program, United Rehab. Svcs./Scranton Sch. Dis., 1987-90; 2d v.p. Deutsch Inst. Rsch. Rehab. Recreation and Leisure Activities 1986-92, treas. Deutsch Found. 1988-92. Mem. Am. Assn. for Coun-seling and Devel. (chmn. ethics com. 1965-70), Am. Psychol. Assn., Nat. Rehab. Assn., Nat. Council Rehab. Edn. (bd. dir. region II 1969-71, bd. dir. region III 1971-72, 77-83, chmn. legis. com. region III 1972-83), Nat. Council Rehab. Edn. (pres. 1974-75), Pa. Personnel and Guidance Assn., Pa. Rehab. Assn. (bd. dir.), Northeastern Pa. Psychol. Assn., Phi Delta Kappa (treas. U. Scranton chpt. 1970-80). Home: Clarks Summit Pa. Died Oct. 5, 1992.

TAAGEPERA, REIN, social science educator; b. Tartu, Estonia, Feb. 28, 1933; s. Karl and Elfriede Amalie (Erbak) T.; m. Mare Rünk, Oct. 14, 1961; children: Tiina-Kai, Salme, Jaan. B.A.Sc., U. Toronto, 1959, M.A., 1961; Ph.D. in Physics, U. Del., 1965, M.A. in Internat. Relations, 1969. Research physicist duPont Co., Wilmington, Del., 1964-70; mem. faculty U. Calif., Irvine, 1970-94; prof. social sci. U. Calif., 1978-94; dean Tartu U. Sch. of Soc. Scis., Estonia, 1992-94; prof. Tartu U. Sch. of Soc. Scis., Estonia, 1994-95; mem. Estonian Constnl. Assembly, 1991-92, candidate for pres. Estonia, 1992. Co-author: (book) The Baltic States: Years of Dependence, 1940-90, 2d edit., 1993, Seats and Votes: The Effects and Determinants of Electoral Systems, 1989; author: Softening Without Liberalization in the Soviet Union: The Case of Jüri Kukk, 1984, Estonia: Return to Independence, 1993; co-editor: Problems of Mininations: Baltic Perspectives, 1973. Mem. Am. Polit. Sci. Assn., Assn. Advancement Baltic Studies (pres. 1986-88), Social Sci. History Soc. Home: Irvine Ca. Died Oct. 30, 1995.

TABER, LINDA PERRIN, public relations executive; b. Marshalltown, Iowa, Dec. 30, 1941; d. Burr H. Perrin and Luella (Memler); m. Roy Howard Pollack, Oct. 1, 1983; m. Allan D. Taber, Apr. 26, 1969 (div. 1976). B.A., U. Iowa, 1964; M.A., Syracuse U., 1969. Account supr. Ketchum, Macleod & Grove, N.Y.C., 1969-73; v.p. Carol Moberg, Inc., N.Y.C., 1973-78; dir.

Ketchum Pub. Relations, N.Y.C., 1979-83; sr. v.p. Ketchum Pub. Relations, 1983—. Mem. Pub. Relations Soc. Am., The Fashion Group, Women Execs. in Pub. Relations, Women in Communications. Home: New York N.Y. Died Nov. 1, 1994.

TAFT, ROBERT, JR., state official, lawyer, former senator; b. Cin., Feb. 26, 1917; s. Robert A. and Martha (Bowers) T.; m. Blanca Noel, 1939 (dec.); children: Robert A. II, Sarah B. Taft Jones, Deborah Taft Boutellis, Jonathan D.; m. Joan M. Warner, 1978. BA, Yale U., 1939; LLB, Harvard U., 1942. Bar: Ohio, D.C. Of counsel Taft, Stettinius & Hollister, Cin., 1987—; mem. Ohio Ho. of Reps., 1955-62, majority floor leader, 1961-62; mem. 88th Congress at-large from Ohio, 90th-91st Congresses from 1st Ohio Dist.; U.S. senator from Ohio, 1971-76; practice law Washington and Cin., 1977—; . Lt. USNR, 1942-46. Mem. ABA, Ohio Bar Assn., Cin. Bar Assn., D.C. Bar Assn., Camargo Club, Racquet Club, Literary Club, Queen City (Cin.) Club. Camargo, Racquet, Literary, Queen City (Cin.). Home: Cincinnati Ohio

TAGER, HOWARD S., biochemist, researcher, educator; b. Los Angeles, Mar. 31, 1945; s. Max and Lillian (Anderson) T. B.S., UCLA, 1966; Ph.D., U. Mich., 1971. Asst. prof. U. Chgo., 1974-81, assoc. prof., 1981-84, prof., 1984-94, Louis Block prof., chmn., 1985-94; dir. Diabetes Research and Tng. Ctr., Chgo., 1981-94; Med. Scientist Tng. Program, Chgo., 1984-94. Recipient Research Career Devel. award NIH, 1976, Outstanding Citizen of Chgo. award Jaycees, 1981, Mary Jane Kugel award Juvenile Diabetes Found., 1985. Mem. Am. Chem. Soc., Am. Soc. Biol. Chemists, Am. Diabetes Assn. (Lilly award 1983), Sigma Xi. Home: Chicago Ill. Died Sept. 6, 1994.

TAJO, ITALO, opera singer, stage director, lecturer, educator; b. Pinerolo, Italy, Apr. 25, 1915; s. Luigi and Adele T.; m. Inelda Meroni; 1 child, Cecilia. D of Performing Arts honoris causa, U. Cin., 1987. J. Ralph Corbett disting. prof. opera, prof. emeritus opera U. Cin. Conservatory of Music, artist-in-residence; dir. Internat. Opera Festival, Barga, Italy, 1970-75. Rec. artist, HMV, RCA, Telefunken, Cetra-Soria, Decca, EMI, records.; Debut in Rheingold, Turin, 1935; since performed at maj. opera houses throughout world; debut as stage dir.: Mozart and Salieri, Naples, Italy, 1954; internat. opera star and dir. Mem. Nat. Opera Assn., Coll. Coll. Music Soc., McDowell Soc. Roman Catholic. Home: New York N.Y. Died Mar. 29, 1993.

TALBOT, RICHARD BURRITT, veterinarian, educator; b. Waterville, Kans., Jan. 4, 1933; s. Roy B. and Aleta (Stone) T.; m. Mary Jane Hensley, May 24, 1953; children—Richard Lee, Andrea Jean. B.S., Kans. State U., 1954, D.V.M., 1958; Ph.D., Iowa State U., 1963. Diplomate Am. Acad. Vet. Informatics. From instr. to assoc. prof. dept. physiology and pharmacology Coll. Vet. Medicine, Iowa State U., Ames, 1958-65; prof., chmn. dept. physiology and pharmacology U. Ga. Coll. Vet. Medicine, Athens, 1965-68; dean coll. U. Ga. Coll. Vet. Medicine, 1968-75; prof. vet. medicine Va. Poly. Inst. and State U., Blacksburg, 1975—; dean Coll. Vet. Medicine Va. Poly. Inst. and State U., 1975-85; bd. dirs. 1st Va. Bank SW, Hazleton Labs. Corp.; cons. NIH, USDA, FDA. Editor Jour. Vet. Med. Edn. Dist. commr. Boy Scouts Am. Nat. Heart Inst. postdoctoral fellow, 1959. Mem. AVMA (coun. on edn. 1972-80, edn. com. fgn. vet. grads. 1972-82, informatics com. 1990—), Am. Physiol. Soc., Conf. Rsch. Workers Animal Diseases, Nat. Bd. Vet. Med. Examiners, Assn. Am. Vet. Med. Colls., Am. Acad. Vet. Comparative Toxicology, Am. Acad. Vet. Pharm. Therapeutics, Am. Vet. Computer Soc. (pres. 1993—), Sigma Xi, Phi Zeta, Phi Kappa Phi. Presbyterian (elder). Club: Rotary. Home: Blacksburg Va. Died Sept. 8, 1994.

TALLEY, WARREN DENNIS RICK, journalist, broadcaster; b. Pinckneyville, Ill., Aug. 12, 1934; s. Virgil and Hannah (Maxwell) T.; m. Frances Jane Herr, Aug. 9, 1958; children: Wendy Warren, Scott Ryan, Jennifer Jane. B.S. in Journalism, So. Ill. U., 1958. Sports writer Decatur (Ill.) Herald, 1958; sports editor Menlo Park (Calif.) Recorder, 1958-59; reporter UPI, San Francisco, 1959-60; sports editor Rockford (Ill.) Morning Star, also Register Republic, 1960-69; sports editor, columnist Chgo. Today, 1969-74; daily columnist Chgo. Tribune, 1974-79; TV host, interviewer WLS-TV, Chgo.; commentator WLS Radio, Chgo., FNN Sports, L.A.; sports columnist Daily News, Los Angeles, 1979-88; sportstalk host Sta. KABC, Los Angeles, 1980-82; sports host Sta. KVE6 Am. Sports, Las Vegas. Author: (with Jay Johnstone) Temporary Insanity, 1985, Some of My Best Friends Are Crazy, 1990; Over the Edge, 1987, The Cubs of '69, 1989, (with Art Manteris) Super Bookie, 1991; contbr. articles to sports mags. Served with AUS, 1953-55, Korea. Recipient Outstanding Journalism Alumni award So. Ill. U., 1967; Bronze medal Olympic Journalism Assn., 1970; named Ill. Sportswriter of Yr., 1974. Mem. Football Writers Assn., Baseball Writers Assn. Home: Las Vegas Nev. Died Aug. 8, 1995.

TALLMAN, JOHANNA ELEONORE, former library administrator; b. Luebeck, Germany, Aug. 18, 1914; came to U.S., 1923, naturalized, 1930; d. Friedrich Franz and Johanna Cornelia (Voget) Allerding; m. Lloyd Anthony Tallman, May 8, 1954 (dec.). AA, Los Angeles Jr. Coll., 1934; BA, U. Calif., Berkeley, 1936; Cert. in Librarianship, 1937. Asst. librarian San Marino (Calif.) Pub. Library, 1937-38; various positions Los Angeles County Pub. Library, 1938-40, tech. reference librarian, 1940-42; asst. librarian Pacific Aero. Library, Hollywood, Calif., 1942-43; head librarian Pacific Aero. Library, 1943-44; librarian Engring. and Math. Scis. Library, U. Calif., Los Angeles, 1945-73; coordinator phys. scis. libraries U. Calif., Los Angeles, 1962-73; faculty Sch. Library Service, 1961-73; dir. libraries Calif. Inst. Tech., Pasadena, 1973-82; Dir. re-cataloging project U.S. Naval Ordnance Test Sta. Library., China Lake, Calif., 1951; cons. to indsl., research, ednl. instns., 1950-73; mem. trade adv. com. for library assts. Los Angeles Trade Tech. Coll., 1958-73. Author: Check Out a Librarian, 1985. Contbr. articles to profl. jours. Pres. Zonta Club Pasadena, 1976-78, United Svc. Clubs Officers Assn., 1978-79, 88-89, 90-91, Fine Arts Club Pasadena, 1982-84; trustee Pasadena Hist. Soc., 1980-90. Fulbright lectr. Brazil, 1966-67. Mem. ALA (chmn. engring. sch. libraries sect. 1949-50), Calif. Library Assn. (chmn. coll., univ. and research libraries sect. So. dist. 1954), Spl. Libraries Assn. (pres. So. Calif. chpt. 1965-66, chmn. sci.-tech. div. 1969-70), Librarians Assn. U. Calif. (pres. 1971). Home: La Canada Flintridge Calif. Died Nov. 28, 1993.

TAMARU, HIDEHARU, advertising company executive; b. Kagoshima, Japan, Apr. 20, 1914; 3 children. Degree in Lit., Tokyo Univ. Exec. dir. Dentsu Inc., Tokyo, 1965-67, mng. dir., 1967-71, sr. mng. dir., 1971-77, pres., 1977-85. Dir. Fedn. Econ. Orgn., Tokyo, 1977-90; counsellor, chmn. info. com. Tokyo C. of C. and Industry, 1977-90. Mem. Internat. Advt. Assn. (vice chmn. 1978), Japan Advt. Agys. Assn. (pres. 1979), Japan Mktg. Assn. (vice chmn. 1984). Home: Tokyo Japan

TANDY, JESSICA, actress; b. London, Eng., June 7, 1909; d. Harry and Jessie Helen (Horspool) T.; m. Jack Hawkins, 1932 (div. 1942); 1 dau., Susan (Mrs. John Tettemer); m. Hume Cronyn, 1942; children: Christopher Hume, Tandy. Student, Dame Alice Owens Girls Sch., 1919-24, Ben Greet Acad. Acting, 1924-27; LL.D., U. Western Ont., 1974; LHD (hon.), Fordham U., 1985. Dramatic adviser Goddard Neighborhood Center, N.Y.C., 1948. First profl. acting role in: Manderson Girls; later appeared in: London debut in The Rumor, 1929; Comedy of Good and Evil, 1928, Alice Sit-By-The-Fire, 1928, Yellow Sands, 1929; other theatre appearances in Twelfth Night, 1930, Man Who Pays the Piper, Autumn Crocus, Port Said, 1931; various engagements, Old Vic, London, including Midsummer Night's Dream, Hamlet, King Lear, 1933-40; first stage appearance U.S., 1930; on Broadway in Time and Conways, 1938, White Steed, 1939, Yesterday's Magic, 1942, Streetcar Named Desire, 1947, Four Poster, 1951-53, Madame Will You Walk, 1953, The Honeys, 1955, A Day by the Sea, 1955, The Man in the Dog Suit, 1958, Five Finger Exercise, 1959, The Physicists, 1964, Noel Coward in Two Keys, 1974; played in Mpls. Hamlet, Three Sisters, Death of a Salesman, 1963; Foxfire; in The Glass Menagerie; summer theatre prodns. The Caucasian Chalk Circle, 1950-55; appeared: Triple Play, 1958-59, Big Fish, Little Fish, London, 1962; (with husband) reading tour U.S. Face to Face, 1954; A Delicate Balance, 1966-67, The Miser, 1968, Heartbreak House, Shaw Festival, 1968, Tchin-Tchin, Chgo., 1969, Camino Real, Lincoln Center, N.Y.C., 1970, Home, Morosco, N.Y., 1971, All Over, N.Y.C., 1971; (with husband) in) Samuel Beckett festival, Lincoln Center, N.Y.C., 1972, tour Promenade All, 1972-73, Not I, 1973; limited concert recital tour Many Faces of Love, 1974, 75, 76, also Seattle Repertory theatre; tour (with husband) Noel Coward in Two Keys, 1975; appeared in Eve, Stratford (Ont.) Festival, 1976; played Mary Tyrone in Long Day's Journey into Night, Theater London, Ont., Can., 1977; star of The Gin Game, at Long Wharf Theatre, New Haven, 1977, Golden Theatre, N.Y.C., 1978; on tour in U.S., Toronto, London, USSR, 1978-79, Rose, Cort Theater, N.Y.C., 1981; appeared (with husband) in Foxfire, Stratford Festival, Ont., 1980, The Guthrie Theatre, Mpls., 1981, Ahmanson Theatre, Los Angeles, 1985-86, Ethel Barrymore Theatre, N.Y.C., 1982-83; in The Glass Menagerie, Eugene O'Neill Theatre, N.Y.C., 1983-84; off-Broadway in Salonika, 1985; (with husband) in The Petition, Golden Theatre, N.Y.C., 1986; motion pictures include Valley of Decision, 1945, Green Years, 1946, Desert Fox, 1951, Light in the Forest, 1958, The Birds, 1962, Butley, 1973, Honky Tonk Freeway, 1980, The World According to Garp, 1981, Still of the Night, 1981, Best Friends, 1982, The Bostonians, 1983, Cocoon, 1984, Batteries Not Included, 1986, The House on Carroll Street, 1986, Cocoon: The Return, 1988, Driving Miss Daisy, 1989, Fried Green Tomatoes, 1991, Used People, 1992, Camilla, 1994, Nobody's Fool, 1994; TV prodns. Portrait of a Madonna, 1948, Christmas 'Till Closing, 1955, Marriage; series, 1954, The Fallen Idol, 1959, The Moon and Sixpence, 1959, Tennessee Williams' South, Many Faces of Love, 1977, The Gin-Game, 1979, Foxfire, 1987, The Story Lady, 1991, To Dance With the White Dog, 1993 (Emmy nomination, Lead Actress - Special, 1994). Recipient Antoinette Perry award, Twelfth Night Club award for performance in Streetcar Named Desire, 1948, Delia Austria medal for Five Finger Exercise, 1960, bronze medallion (with husband) for performance in The Four Poster Comedia Matinee Club, 1952, Obie award for Not I, 1973, Drama Desk award for Happy Days and Not I, Creative Arts award Brandeis U., 1978, Antoinette Perry (Tony) award for The Gin Game, 1978, Drama Desk award, 1978, Los Angeles Critics award, 1979, Sarah Siddons award, 1979; named to Theatre Hall of Fame, 1979; recipient Antoinette Perry award for Foxfire, 1983, Common Wealth award, 1983, Alley Theatre award, 1987, Acad. Sci. Fiction, Fantasy and Horror Films award for Batteries Not Included, 1987, Franklin Haven Sargeant award Am. Acad. Dramatic Arts, 1988, Emmy award for Foxfire, 1988, Golden Globe award, Silver Bear award Berlin Film Festival, 1990, Baftra award for Driving Miss Daisey, 1991, Nat. medal of Arts Pres. U.S., 1990; nominated for Tony award as best actress in The Petition, 1986; Acad. Award for Driving Miss Daisy, 1990; honoree Kennedy Ctr. Honors, 1986, Antoinette Perry Lifetime Achievement Award, 1994 (with Hume Cronyn). Home: Rego Park N.Y. Died Sept. 11, 1994.

TAPP, JUNE LOUIN, psychology educator; b. N.Y.C.; d. R.B. Louin and Ann Revier-Wacholder. B.A. magna cum laude in Sociology, U. So. Calif., 1951; M.S. in Ednl. Psychology, 1952; Ph.D. in Psychology, Syracuse U., 1963. Registered psychologist, Ill. Instr. ednl. psychology and psychology St. Lawrence U., Canton, N.Y., 1952-55; adminstrv. asst. to dean Moran Crime Inst., 1954-60; asst. instr. in citizenship Maxwell Grad. Sch., Syracuse U., N.Y., 1955-56; tutor in psychology and sociology Albert Schweitzer Coll., Churwalden, Switzerland, 1957-58; asst. prof. psychology Harvey Mudd Coll., Claremont, Calif., 1961-64; organizer behavioral scis. program, 1961-64; lectr., cons. Indian Coll. Youth Project, U. Poona, India, 1963-64; asst. prof., research assoc. com. on human devel. U. Chgo., 1964-67; assoc. prof., research assoc. com. on human devel., 1964-67, assoc. prof. in social scis., 1968-72; co-investigator, project adminstr. Children's Socialization into Compliance Systems, 1965-70; sr. research social scientist Am. Bar Found., Chgo., 1967-72; affiliated scholar, 1972-74; fellow in law and psychology Harvard U. Law Sch., Cambridge, Mass., 1971-72; prof. psychology U. Calif.-San Diego, La Jolla, 1976-78; provost Revelle Coll., 1976-78; chmn. humanities program, 1976-77, chmn. law and society program, 1977-78; prof. child psychology and criminal justice studies, adj. prof. law, adj. prof. family studies U. Minn., Mpls., 1972—; participant U. Calif.-Irvine Mgmt. Inst., 1977; cons. in field; lectr. profl. confs. and symposia. Author: (with F. Krinsky) Ambivalent America: A Psycho-political Dialogue, 1971; (with F.J. Levine) Law, Justice and Individual in Society, 1977. Mem. numerous editorial bds. of profl. jours. Manuscript reviewer for numerous profl. jours. Contbr. articles to profl. jours., chpts. to books. Mem. numerous civic, govtl. and profl. orgns. Recipient numerous civic and profl. awards; grantee in psychology and law from numerous profl. and govtl. agys. and orgns. Fellow Am. Psychol. Assn. (council 1981-84); mem. Am. Psychology-Law Soc. (pres. 1972-73), Soc. Psychol. Study Social Issues (pres. 1978-79), Soc. Research Child Devel., Internat. Assn. Polit. Psychology (council 1979-82), Assn. Advancement Psychology (trustee 1980-84), Interam. Soc. Psychology (v.p. 1985—), Internat. Assn. Cross-Cultural Psychology, Internat. Assn. Philosophy (exec. com. 1974-75), Law and Soc. Assn. (sec. 1973-74, trustee 1980-82), Soc. Exptl. Social Psychology (mem. forum White House Conf. on Children 1970). Home: Minneapolis Minn. Deceased.

TARNOPOLSKY, WALTER SURMA, judge; b. Gronlid, Sask., Can., Aug. 1, 1932; s. Harry and Mary (Surma) T.; children by previous marriage: Mark Andrew, Christina Helen, Alexandra Justine; m. Joanne G. Kramer, Aug. 25, 1973; children: Michelle Raissa, Gregory Jan. BA with honors, U. Sask., Saskatoon, 1953, LLB, 1957; AM in History, Columbia U., 1955; LLM (Newton W. Rowell fellow), U. London, 1962; LLD (hon.), St. Thomas U., 1982, U. Alta., 1986, Trent U., 1986; DCL (hon.), U. Windsor, 1987, York U., 1989. Lectr. in law U. Ottawa, Ont., Can., 1962-63; asst. prof. law U. Sask., 1963-67; assoc. prof. Osgoode Hall Law Sch., York U., Downsview, Ont., 1967-68; v.p. acad. York U., 1972, prof. law, 1972-80; prof., dean of law U. Windsor, Ont., 1968-72; prof., dir. Human Rights Inst., U. Ottawa, 1980-83; justice Ont. Ct. Appeal, 1983—; dep. judge Supreme Ct., N.W.T. Author: The Canadian Bill of Rights, 1966, 2d rev. edit., 1975, Discrimination and the Law in Canada, 1982, rev. edit., 1985; editor: Some Civil Liberties Issues of the 70's, 1975, Canadian Charter of Rights and Freedoms: Commentary, 1983. Vice-chmn. Fed. Electoral Boundaries Commn. for Ont., 1972, 75; mem. UN Human Rights Com., 1977-83, Can. Human Rights Commn., 1978-83; Mem. Can. Consultative Council on Multiculturalism, 1973-77; pres. Can. Civil Liberties Assn., 1977-81. UN Human Rights fellow India; UN Human Rights fellow Malaysia, 1970. Fellow Royal Soc. Can. (chmn. com. on freedom of scholarship and sci. 1987—); mem. Sask. Bar, Law Soc. Upper Can., Can. Bar Assn., Internat. Commn. Jurists (pres. Can. sect. 1985-87), inter-Am.Inst. of Human Rights, Costa Rica (bd. govs. 1981—, African Ctr. for Democracy and Human Rights Studies Gambia (governing coun. 1990). Ukrainian Greek Orthodox. Home: Toronto Can. Deceased.

RT, JERRY GORDON, federal judge; b. Newton ove, N.C., Apr. 15, 1934; s. Gordon G. and Ellen arren) T.; m. Zilphia Britt, June 2, 1956; children: ura Tart Rhodes, Rachel E. BA, Wake Forest U., 55, JD, 1957. Bar: N.C. 1957, U.S. Dist. Ct. (mid. t.) N.C. 1970, U.S. Ct. Appeals (4th cir.) 1974. Ptnr. yle, Boone, Dees and Johnson, Greensboro, N.C., 52-69, Dees, Johnson, Tart, Giles and Tedder, eensboro, 1969-85, Johnson and Tart, Greensboro, 85-86; judge U.S. Bankruptcy Ct., Greensboro, 86—. Capt. USAF, 1958-62. Mem. Nat. Assn. Chpt. Trustees, Nat. Conf. Bankruptcy Judges, N.C. Bar sn., Greensboro Bar Assn., 18th Dist. Jud. Bar Assn. arter bankruptcy and law office mgmt. sect. 1978-80), nkruptcy Coun., Masons (master 1970, treas. 1976-, grand master 1989-90, grand treas. 1991—). epublican. Methodist. Home: Greensboro N.C. Died ly 21, 1995.

ATLOW, RICHARD HENRY, III, civil engineer; b. enver, May 27, 1906; s. Richard Henry and Viletta row) T.; m. Annette Hart, June 18, 1932; children: nnette Beedy Tatlow Ritchie, Richard Henry. B.S., Colo., 1927, C.E., 1933. Engr., partner Harrington Cortelyou, 1929-40; chmn. Abbott, Merkt Internat., c., N.Y.C., 1946-87; chmn., dir. Abbott Merkt rchitects, Inc., 1972—; chmn. bldg. research adv. bd. at. Acad. Sci., 1962-64; mem. com. SST-Sonic Boom, 64-71; v.p. Engrs. Joint Council, 1963-67. Past ustee United Engring.; trustee, pres., 1975-76; bd. rs., v.p. Animal Med. Center, N.Y.C., until 1972. erved to col. C.E., AUS, 1941-46. Decorated Legion of erit. Fellow ASME, ASCE (pres. 1968, dir.); mem. at. Acad. Engring., Am. Inst. Cons. Engrs. (mem. ouncil, past pres.), Newcomen Soc. N.Am. Clubs: osmos (Washington), Chevy Chase (Washington); nion League (N.Y.C.); Shenorock (Rye). Home: carsdale N.Y. Died July 1, 1993.

ATUM, DONN BENJAMIN, entertainment company xecutive; b. L.A., Jan. 9, 1913; s. Frank D. and Terese Murphy) T.; m. Vernette Ripley, Mar. 20, 1937; chilren: Frederic, Donn, Vernette, Forbes, Melantha. A.B. agna cum laude, Stanford U., 1934; postgrad., Loyola ., 1936-38; B.A., Oxford U., Eng., 1936; M.A., Oxford ., 1959; D.B.A., Woodbury Coll., 1953; LL.D. (hon.), epperdine U., 1977; Arts D (hon.), Calif. Inst. Arts, 989. Bar: Calif. 1938. Practice in Los Angeles, 1938-8; ptnr. Lillick, Geary, McHose & Adams, 1945-48; acific coast counsel RCA (and subs.'s), 1942-48; v.p., ir. Don Lee Cos., 1948-51; dir. TV Western div. ABC, 951-54; v.p., mem. exec. com. Walt Disney Prodns. now Walt Disney Co.), Burbank, Calif., 1956-67, dir., 956-92, dir. emeritus, 1992-93, vice chmn., exec. v.p., 967-68, pres., 1968-71, chief exec. officer, 1971-76, hmn. bd., 1971-80, chmn. exec. com., 1980-84; chmn. d. Walt Disney World Co., Burbank, Calif., 1971-80; d. dirs. Western Digital Corp. Trustee New Economy Fund, Small Cap World Fund, Calif. Inst. Arts; chmn. d. John Tracy Clinic. Mem. Acad. Motion Picture Arts and Scis., Acad. TV Arts and Scis., So. Calif., Hollywood Radio and TV Soc. Lodge: The Knights of Malta. Home: Pacific Palisades Calif. Died May 31, 1993.

TAUBMAN, PAUL JAMES, economics educator; b. Fall River, Mass., Dec. 24, 1939; s. Abraham and Lena (Rubin) T.; m. Joan Greenburg, Aug. 19, 1962; children: Geoffry, Rena. BS, U. Pa., 1961, PhD, 1964. Asst. prof. Harvard U., Cambridge, Mass., 1964-65; mem. staff Coun. Econ. Advisers, 1965-66; assoc. prof. dept. econs. U. Pa., Phila., 1966-72, prof., 1972—; rsch. assoc. Nat. Bur. Econ. Rsch., 1977—, head econs. of drugs program, 1988-91. Author: Sources of Inequality of Earnings, 1975, Kinometrics: Determinants of Socioeconomic Success Within and Between Families, 1977. Fellow AAAS (sect. K), Econometric Soc., Internat. Soc. for Twin Studies; mem. Am. Econ. Assn. Deceased.

TAVEL, JAMES WILSON, lawyer; b. Washington, Aug. 17, 1945; s. Ewing Hows and Jean (Wilson) T.; m. Ruth Eifert, Sept. 21, 1973; 1 child, James Cecil. BA in Pub. Affairs, George Washington U., 1967, JD, 1970. Bar: Md. 1971, D.C. 1972, U.S. Supreme Ct. 1974. Legal counsel MCPB-MN CPPC, Silver Spring, Md., 1970-73; ptnr. Beckett, Cromwell & Myers, Bethesda, Md., 1973-85, Linowes & Blocher, Silver Spring, 1985—. Pres. Silver Spring Devel. Coun., 1980-90; mem. Gov.'s Condominium Commn., 1982, 83; assoc. supr. Soil Conservation Dist., 1979-83; chmn. merge coalition Montgomery Effective Regional Growth Effort. Recipient Gov.'s Citation, 1981. Mem. Md. Bar Assn., Montgomery County Bar Assn., Montgomery County Bd. Realtors (assoc.), Suburban Md. Homebuilders Assn. (assoc.), Apt. and Office Bldg. Assn. (assoc.), Montgomery County C. of C. (v.p. legis. affairs 1981-82, 82-83, pres. elect 1983-84, pres. 1984-85, v.p. econ. devel. com. 1989-90), Silver Spring C. of C. (pres. 1981-82, v.p. legis. affairs 1982-83, 83-84, pres. 1985-87), Order of Coif. Democrat. Home: Rockville Md. Deceased.

TAYLOR, SIR GEORGE, botanist; b. Feb. 15, 1904; s. George William and Jane (Sloan) T.; B.Sc. with 1st class honors in Botany, Edinburgh (Scotland) U., 1926, also DSc, Vans Dunlop scholar; LLD (hon.), Dundee, 1972; Dr.Phil. (hon.), Gothenburg, 1958; m. Alice Helen Pendrich, 1929 (dec. 1977); 2 children; m. Norah English (dec. 1967); m. Beryl, Lady Colwyn (dec. 1987); m. June Maitland, 1989. Mem. bot. expdn. to South Africa, Rhodesia, 1927-28; joint leader Brit. Mus. expdn. to Ruwenzori and mountains of East Africa, 1934-35; expdn. to S.E. Tibet and Bhutan, 1938; prin. in Air Ministry, 1940-45; dep. keeper botany Brit. Mus., 1945-50, keeper botany, 1950-56; dir. Royal Bot. Gardens, Kew, Eng., 1956-71; vis. prof. Reading (Eng.) U., 1969-93; dir. Stanley Smith Hort. Trust, 1970-89, cons., 1989-93; Percy Sladen trustee, 1951-81; mem. coun. Nat. Trust, 1961-72, also chmn. gradens com.; mem. coun. RGS, 1957-61, v.p., 1964; mem. Ministry Transport Adv. Com. on Landscaping Treatment of Trunk Rds., 1956-81, chmn., 1969-81; hon. bot. adv. Commonwealth War Graves Commn., 1956-77. VMH, 1956; Fellow Royal Soc., RSE, LS, Royal Hort. Soc. (hon; mem. council 1951-73, v.p. and prof. botany 1974-93, Veitch Gold medal 1963); mem. Linnean Soc. (bot. sec. 1950-56, v.p. 1956), Brit. Assn. Advancement Sci. (gen. sec. 1951-58), Bot. Soc. Brit. Isles (pres. 1955), Internat. Union Biol. Sci. (pres. div. botany 1964-69), Internat. Assn. Plant Taxonomy (pres. 1969-72), Royal Soc. Sci. (Uppsala, Sweden), Royal Bot. Soc. Netherlands (corr.), Bot. Soc. South Africa (hon.), Am. Orchid Soc. (hon.), Worshipful Co. Gardeners (hon. freeman), Royal Caledonian Hort. Soc. (Scottish hort. medal 1986). Clubs: New (Edinburgh, Scotland). Author: An Account of the Genus Meconopsis, 1934, reprinted, 1985; contbr. articles on flowering plants to various periodicals. Died Nov. 13, 1993. Home: Peeblesshire Scotland

TAYLOR, HARRY WILLIAM, physics educator; b. nr. Sturgeon Valley, Sask., Can., Sept. 28, 1925; s. William and Gladys (Evans) T.; m. Wanda Jason, June 18, 1949; children: Allison Leslie, Karen Elizabeth. B.Sc., U. Man., 1951, M.Sc., 1952, Ph.D., 1954. Lectr. U. Man., Winnipeg, 1952-53; fellow NRC, Ottawa, Ont., Can., 1954-55; mem. faculty Queen's U., Kingston, Ont., 1955-61; asst. prof. Queen's U., 1957-61; asso. prof. U. Alta., Edmonton, 1961-65; prof. physics U. Toronto, 1965-91, prof. emeritus physics, 1991-96. Mem. Am. Phys. Soc., Inst. Physics, Inst. Nuclear Engrs., AAAS. Home: Mississauga Can. Died Mar. 30, 1996.

TAYLOR, SIR HENRY MILTON, Bahamas government official; b. Nov. 4, 1903; s. Joseph and Evelyn T.; m. Eula Mae Sisco; 3 stepchildren, 4 daughters from a previous marriage. Mem. Bahamas House of Assembly, from 1949; various political positions, 1949-81; dep. gen. gov. The Bahamas, 1981-82, 84, gen. gov., 1988-94. Author: My Political Memoirs, 1986. Home: Nassau Bahamas Died Feb. 1994.

TAYLOR, MARK, author, educator; b. Linden, Mich., Aug. 15, 1927; s. George Wilton Huebler-Taylor and Constance (Page) Chinery. BA, U. Mich., 1950, MLS, 1952; MEd, U. So. Calif., 1972, PhD, 1976. Asst. libr. Elem. Sch. U. Mich., Ann Arbor, 1950-56; broadcaster Broadcasting Svc. U. Mich., Ann Arbor, 1950-56; dir. young adult svcs. Dayton (Ohio) and Montgomery County Pub. Libr., 1957-60; prof. Sch. Libr. Sci. U. So. Calif., L.A., 1960-70; children's book columnist L.A. Times, 1962-70; producer, performer CBS-Hollywood (Stas. KNXT, KNX-TV) Tell It Again program, L.A., 1962-64; author in residence for schs. and librs., nationwide, 1960-92; founding mem. So. Calif. Coun. Lit. Children and Young People, L.A., 1961. Author: (children's books) Henry series, 1966-88, The Bold Fisherman, 1967, Time for Flowers, 1967, Old Woman and Pedlar, 1969, Old Blue, You Good Dog You, 1970, Wind in my Hand, 1970, Bobby Shafto's Gone to Sea, 1970, Time for Old Magic, 1970, Time for New Magic, 1971, Fisherman and Goblet, 1971, Lamb, Said the Lion, I am Here, 1972, Wind's Child, 1973, Jennie Jenkins, 1975, Case of Missing Kittens, 1978, Young Melvin on the Road, 1980, Cabbage Patch Kids Books (4), 1983, Mr. Pepper Stories, 1984, Care Bear Cousins Books (2), 1984, Case of the Purloined Compass, 1985, Maxie's Mystery Files, 1987 (with Eleanore Hartson), Troll Family Stories (6), Cora Cow Tales (6), Adventures of Pippin (6), San Francisco Cat, 1987, Space Monster Mysteries (with Adams and Hartson), 1987, Beginning-to-Read Fairy Tales (with Hartson), 1987, God, I Listened: The Life Story of Eula McClaney, 1981, (film and TV) President is Missing, Manhattan Magic (The Jeffersons, Lion to Kill, Star Traveler, Summerwind, (textbooks) Understanding Your Language, 1968 (3 vol.), Pathfinder Series, 1978; contbr. articles to profl. jours. Recipient Dutton-Macrae award E.P. Dutton Pub., N.Y.C., 1956, award as author of outstanding series of books So. Cal. Coun. Lit. for Children and Young People, 1977. Mem. ALA, PEN, ASCAP, AFTRA, Reading is Fundamental So. Calif. (chmn. bd. 1984-92), Am. Ctr. Films and TV Children (juror 1985-86), Amnesty Internat., Freedom to Read Found., Internat. Reading Assn., Calif. Libr. Assn., Nat. Coun. Tchrs. English, Assn. Childhhod Edn. Internat., Ohio Libr. Assn., Mich. Libr. Assn., Am. Inst. Graphic Arts, Internat. Folk Music Coun., Am. Fedn. Musicians, Harp Soc. Am., So. Calif. Coun. Lit. Children and Young People (past v.p., founding mem.). Home: Montebello Calif. Died May 16, 1992.

TAYLOR, PETER MATTHEW HILLSMAN, author; b. Trenton, Tenn., Jan. 8, 1917; s. Matthew Hillsman and Katherine T.; m. Eleanor Lilly Ross, June 4, 1943; children: Katherine Baird, Peter Ross. Student, Vanderbilt U., 1936-37, Southwestern Coll., 1937-38; B.A., Kenyon Coll., 1940. Faculty Harvard U., 1946-47; prof. Englishative writing U.Va., Charlottesville, 1967-83; prof. English U. Va., 1967-83; vis. lectr. Ind. U., 1949, Kenyon Coll., 1952-57, Oxford U., 1955, Ohio State U., 1957-63, Harvard U., 1964, 1972-73. Author: A Long Fourth and Other Stories, 1948, A Woman of Means, 1950, The Widows of Thornton, 1954, Happy Families are All Alike, 1959 (Ohioana Book award 1960), Miss Lenora When Last Seen, 1964, The Collected Stories of Peter Taylor, 1969, A Stand in the Mountains, 1968, Presences, 1973, In the Miro District and Other Stories, 1976, The Old Forest and Other Stories, 1985, A Summons to Memphis, 1986 (Pulitzer Prize for fiction 1987), Conservations with Peter Taylor, 1987, The Oracle at Stoneleigh Court, 1993; plays Tennessee Day in St. Louis, 1959, A Stand in the Mountains, 1965. Recipient Nat. Acad. award fiction, 1950; recipient Fulbright award, 1955, 1st prize O. Henry Meml. awards, 1959, Ritz Paris Hemingway prize, 1987, Nat. Acad. Inst. Arts and Letters Gold medal for lit., 1979; Nat. Inst. Arts & Letters grantee in lit., 1952, Rockefeller grantee, 1964; fellow Guggenheim Found., 1950; grantee Ford Found. to study theatre in Eng., 1961. Mem. Nat. Acad. Arts and Letters, Am. Acad. Arts. and Scis. Home: Charlottesville Va. Died Nov. 2, 1994.

TAYLOR, THOMAS HEWITT, JR., construction equipment company executive; b. Cleve., Sept. 23, 1935; s. Thomas Hewitt and Mildred (Sorg) T.; m. Mary Jo Fraley, June 27, 1959 (dec.); children: Kenneth, Marguerite. BA, Amherst Coll., 1957; MBA, U. Pa., 1959. With Ohio Machinery Co., 1959—; treas., then sales mgr. Ohio Machinery Co., Broadview Heights, Ohio, 1964-69; pres. Ohio Machinery Co., 1969—; dir. Dollar Bank divsn. Continental Fed. Savs. & Loan Assn., Cleve., 1972. Trustee St. Luke's Hosp., Cleve., 1976—, Cleve. Music Sch. Settlement; past sr. warden Christ Episcopal Ch., Shaker Heights, Ohio. Mem. Gt. Lakes Caterpillar Dealers Assn. (past pres.), N.E. Caterpillar Dealers Assn. (past pres.), Ohio Equipment Distbrs. Assn. (past pres.), Assoc. Equipment Distbrs. (past pres.), Growth Assn. Cleve., Shriners. Republican. Home: Cleveland Ohio

TEDESKO, ANTON, consulting engineering executive; b. Gruenberg, Germany, May 25, 1903; came to U.S., 1927, naturalized, 1938; s. Victor and Alice (Weiss) T.; m. Sally Murray, June 16, 1938; children: Peter Alden, Suzanne Tedesko Affolter. C.E., Inst. Tech., Vienna, Austria, 1926, D.Sc., 1951; diploma engr., Berlin, 1930; D.Eng. (hon.), Lehigh U., 1966; D.Sc. (hon.), Technol. U., Vienna, 1978. Constrn. engr. Vienna, 1926; with Fairbanks-Morse Co., Chgo., 1927, Miss. Valley Structural Steel Co., Melrose Park, Ill., 1927-28; asst. prof. Inst. Tech., Vienna, 1929; designer dams, bridges, shells, indsl. structures Dyckerhoff & Widmann, Wiesbaden, Germany, 1930-32; with Roberts & Schaefer Co. (engrs.), Chgo., 1932-67; engring. mgr. Roberts & Schaefer Co., Washington, 1943-44; structural mgr. Roberts & Schaefer Co., Chgo., 1944-54; mgr. Roberts & Schaefer Co., N.Y.C., 1955; v.p. Roberts & Schaefer Co., 1956-67; pvt. cons. engring., 1967-94, designer, supr. constrn. arenas, air terminals, bridges, toll roads, indsl. structures, ballistic missile and space rocket launching facilities, wide-span hangars, shell structures, evaluator structural failures, rehab. damaged structures; dir. Thompson-Starrett Co., 1960-61; arbitrator of engring. and constrn. disputes, structural engr. responsible for design rocket assembly and launch facilities for manned lunar landing program Kennedy Space Center, 1962-66; lectr. structural engring. numerous univs.; spl. work shell concrete structures of long span, prestressed concrete; cons. Hdqrs. USAF, 1955-70, to Chief Engr., C.E., U.S. Army, 1970-74, other govt. agys.; mem. various commns. and bds.; moderator engring. confs. Contbr. articles to profl jours. Recipient Alfred Lindau award in field long-span reinforced concrete structures, 1961, Engring. News Record citation, 1966, Johann Joseph Ritter von Prechtl medal, Tech. Univ. of Vienna, Austria, 1994. Fellow ASCE (hon. mem. award 1978); mem. Research Council Performance of Structures, Reinforced Concrete Research Council (exec. com. 1971-94, Arthur J. Boase award 1978), Engrs. Joint Council (metric commn. 1973-80), Am. Concrete Inst. (dir. 1961-64, hon. mem., Henry C. Turner medal for applied innovation and profl. competence, 1987, Phil. M. Ferguson meml. lectr. 1992), Soc. Am. Mil. Engrs., Am. R.R. Engring. Assn., Internat. Assn. Bridge and Structural Engring. (U.S. del. permanent commn. 1965-94, internat. award of merit in structural engring. 1978), Internat. Assn. Shell and Spatial Structures (Hon. Mem. award 1979), Nat. Acad. Engring. Home: Seattle Wash. Died Apr. 2, 1994; interred Lopez Island, Seattle, W.A.

TEITELBAUM, HUBERT I., federal judge; b. Pitts., July 2, 1915; s. Jack and Anna (Wolk) T.; m. Maja Wahrheit, Dec. 2, 1949; children: Hugh, Bruce. AB, U. Pitts., 1937, JD, 1940. Bar: Pa. 1940, U.S. Dist. Ct. 1949, U.S. Ct. Appeals (3d cir.) 1956, U.S. Supreme Ct. 1959. Spl. agt. FBI, 1940-43; atty. U.S. Mil. Govt., Fed. Republic of Germany, 1945-49; pvt. practice law Pitts., 1949-55; 1st asst. U.S. atty., 1955-58; atty. U.S. Dist. Ct. (we. dist.) Pa., 1958-61, judge, 1970-79; mem. ct. adminstrn. com. Jud. Conf. U.S., 1978-87, mem. com. on prisoner litigation, 1981-82; mem. jud. coun. U.S. Ct. Appeals (3rd cir.), 1980-81; adj. prof. law Duquesne U.,

1977-95. Trustee Montefiore Hosp., Pitts., 1963-66, 1969-72, Woodville State Mental Hosp., 1970-73. Capt. AUS, 1944-47; lt. col. Res. Mem. ABA, Fed. Bar Assn., Allegheny County Bar Assns, Am. Law Inst., Am. Trial Lawyers Assn., Allegheny County Acad. Trial Lawyers, U.S. Dist. Judges Assn. for 3d Circuit (pres. 1981-82), Interam. Bar Assn., Fed. Judges Assn. (bd. dirs.), Am. Legion, Order of Coif, Wildwood Golf Club, Amen Corner Club (pres. local chpt. 1979), Variety Club, Nat. Lawyers Club, Pitts. Athletic Assn. Clubs: Wildwood Golf, Amen Corner (pres. 1979), Variety, Nat. Lawyers, Pitts. Athletic Assn. Home: Pittsburgh Pa. Died Jan. 5, 1995.

TEJADA, PAUL, health care administrator; b. N.Y.C., Jan. 12, 1945; s. Nicanor T. and Dorothy Virginia (Doraman) T.; m. Evalyn Lawther Foot, Dec. 30, 1966; children: Dan, Jennifer, Carrie, Melissa. B.A. in Govt., Lake Forest Coll., 1966; M.S. in Hosp. Adminstrn., U. Minn., 1973. Asst. adminstr. Riverview Hosp., Wisconsin Rapids, Wis., 1973-77; adminstr. St. Olaf Hosp., Austin, Minn., 1977-82; adminstr. Alton Meml. Hosp. (Ill.), 1982-94. Bd. dirs. Piasa Council Boy Scouts Am., Alton, Ill., 1983-94, ARC, Alton, 1983-94. Mem. Am. Coll. Hosp. Adminstrs., Am. Mgmt. Assn., Hosp. Fin. Mgmt. Assn., Am. Mktg. Assn. Episcopalian. Lodge: Rotary (Austin, Minn.). Died Feb. 1994. Home: Jackson Mich.

TEMIANKA, HENRI, violinist, conductor; b. Greenock, Scotland, Nov. 19, 1906; came to U.S., 1940; s. Israel and Fanny (Hildebrand) T.; m. Emmy Cowden, Jan. 28, 1943; children: Daniel, David. Ed., Rotterdam, Berlin, Paris; grad., Curtis Inst., 1930; PhD (hon.), DFA (hon.), Pepperdine U., 1986. Founder, artistic dir. Calif. Chamber Symphony Orch., Los Angeles, 1960-92; head violin dept., summer master classes Santa Barbara Music Acad. of West, 1952; artistic adviser Nat. Fedn. Music Clubs; vis. prof. U. Calif. at Santa Barbara, 1960-65; lectr. univs.; prof., music dir. Calif. State U. at Long Beach, 1964-74, prof. emeritus, 1974-92; lectr. UCLA; cons. Ford Found. Debut, N.Y.C., 1928, Europe, 1930, soloist with, John Barbirolli, George Szell, Vaughan Williams, Sir Adrian Boult, Fritz Reiner, Otto Klemperer, also with, Amsterdam Concertgebouw Orch., philharm. orchs. of, Warsaw, The Hague, Rotterdam, London, Brussels, Monte-Carlo, Geneva, Stockholm, Copenhagen, Helsinki; toured, Russia at govt. invitation, 1935, 36, founded, Temianka Chamber Orch., London, 1936, toured, U.S., 1942-92, leader, Paganini String Quartet, 1946-66; produced, wrote, narrated series ednl. motion pictures commd. by, Ednl. TV Center, 1956; guest condr., Los Angeles Philharmonic Orch., 1958-59, 59-60, U.S. tour of 40 concerts with, Temianka Little Symphony, 1960, 61, 64, concert tours, Europe, Orient, S.Am., Can., 1960-92; concert tours with Temianka Virtuosi, U.S. and Hong Kong, 1980, 82, 85; Author: Facing the Music, 1973; contbr. to magazines. Adviser Young Musicians Found. Served with overseas br. OWI, 1942-44. Decorated officier des Arts et Lettres (France). Home: Los Angeles Calif. Died Nov. 7, 1992.

TEMIN, HOWARD MARTIN, medical researcher, educator; b. Philadelphia, Pa., Dec. 10, 1934; s. Henry and Annette (Lehman) T.; m. Rayla Greenberg, May 27, 1962; children: Sarah Beth, Miriam Judith. BA, Swarthmore Coll., 1955, DSc (hon.), 1972; PhD, Calif. Inst. Tech., 1959; DSc (hon.), N.Y. Med. Coll., 1972, U. Pa., 1976, Hahnemann Med. Coll., 1976, Lawrence U., 1976, Temple U., 1979, Med. Coll. Wis., 1981, Colo. State U., 1987, PM Curie, Paris, 1988; U. Medicine Dentistry N.J., 1989; DSc (hon.), Med. and Dental Coll., N.J., 1989; D. honoris causa, U. Pierre et Marie Curie, Paris, 1988. Postdoctoral fellow Calif. Inst. Tech., 1959-60; asst. prof. oncology U. Wis., 1960-64, assoc. prof., 1964-69, prof., 1969-94, Wis. Alumni Rsch. Found. prof. cancer rsch., 1971-80, Am. Cancer Soc. prof. viral oncology and cell biology, 1974-94, H.P. Rusch prof. cancer rsch., 1980-94, Steenbock prof. biol. scis., 1982-94; mem. rsch. policy adv. com. U. Wis. Med. Sch., 1979-83; cons. Office Tech. Assessment Panel on Saccharin, 1977; mem. Internat. Com. Virus Nomenclature Study Group for RNA Tumor Viruses, 1973-75, subcoms. HTLV and AIDS viruses, 1985; mem. virology study sect. NIH, 1971-74, mem. dir.'s adv. com., 1979-83; cons. working group on human gene therapy NIH/RAC, 1984-89, mem. Nat. Cancer Adv. Bd., 1987-94; mem. NAS/IOM Com. for a Nat. Strategy for AIDS, 1986-88, NAS/IOM AIDS activities oversight com., 1988-94, steering com. biomed. rsch. Global Program on AIDS, 1989-90, mem. Global Commn. AIDS, 1991-92, ad hoc vaccine adv. panel NIAID, 1990-91, chmn. adv. com. genertic variation immuno deficiency viruses, vaccine br. div. AIDS, NIAID, NIH, 1988-94, co-chmn. IOM Roundtable for Devel. of Drugs and Vaccines Against AIDS, 1992-94; mem. WHO adv. coun. on HIV and AIDS, 1993; mem. NIAIO HIV rsch. and devel. vaccine working group; co-chair Viral Heteogenicity Focus Group, 1992-94; mem. NAS Report Review Com., 1988-94; mem. fundamental rsch. panel Nat. Conf. on Health Rsch. Principles, 1978; sponsor Fedn. Am. Scientists, 1976-94; mem. Waksman award com. Nat. Acad. Sci., 1976-81; mem. U.S. Steel award Com., 1980-83, chmn., 1982; mem. sci. adv. bd. Coordinating Coun. Cancer Rsch., 1989-94; Disting. lectr. Hermann U., Conn., 1988; Ochoa lectr. Internat. Congress Biochemistry, Prague, 1988; Muller lectr. Internat. Congress Gen., Toronto, 1988; Schultz lectr. Inst. for Cancer Rsch., 1989; Bitterman Meml. lectr., N.Y.C., 1984-94; inaugural lectr. Md. Biotech. Inst., 1990; Abraham White lectr. George Washington U., 1990, Latta lectr. U. Nebr., 1991; bd. dirs. Found. for Adv. Cancer Studies, 1988-94. Assoc. editor: Jour. Cellular Physiology, 1966-77, Cancer Research, 1971-74; exec. editor Molecular Carcinogenesis, 1987; mem. editorial bd.: Jour. Virology, 1971-94, Intervirology, 1972-75, Proc. Nat. Acad. Scis, 1975-80, Archives of Virology, 1975-77, Ann. Rev. Gen., 1983, Molecular Biology and Evolution, 1983-94, Oncogene Research, 1987-94, Jour. AIDS, 1988-94, Human Gene Therapy, 1989, In Vitro Rapid Communication Section, 1984-94, AIDS and Human Retroviruses, 1990-94. Co-recipient Warren Triennial prize Mass. Gen. Hosp., 1971, Gairdner Found. Internat. award, 1974, Nobel Prize in medicine, 1975; recipient Med. Soc. Wis. Spl. commendation, 1971, Papanicolaou Inst. PAP award, 1972, M.D. Anderson Hosp. and Tumor Inst. Bertner award, 1972, U.S. Steel Found. award in Molecular Biology, 1972, Theobald Smith Soc. Waksman award, 1972, Am. Chem. Soc. award in Enzyme Chemistry, 1973, Modern Medicine award for Distinguished Achievement, 1973, Harry Shay Meml. lectr. Fels Rsch. Inst., 1973; Griffuel prize Assn. Devel. Recherche Cancer, Villejuif, 1973, New Horizons lectr. award Radiol. Soc. N.Am., 1968, G.H.A. Clowes lectr. award Assn. Cancer Rsch., 1974, NIH Dyer lectr. award, 1974, Harvey lectr. award, 1974, Charlton lectr. award Tufts U. Med. Sch., 1976, Hoffman-LaRoche lectr. award Rutgers U., 1979, Yoder hon. lectr. award St. Joseph Hosp., Tacoma, 1983, Cetus lectr. award U. Calif., Berkeley, 1984; DuPont lectr. award Harvard U., 1985, Japanese Found. for Promotion Cancer Rsch. lectr. award, 1985, Herz Meml. lectr. award Tel-Aviv U., 1985, Amoros. Meml. lectr. award U. West Indies, 1986, Albert Lasker award in basic med. sci., 1974, Lucy Wortham James award Soc. Surg. Oncologists, 1976, Alumni Disting. Svc. award Calif. Inst. Tech., 1976, Gruber award Am. Acad. Dermatology, 1981, Abraham White award,lectureship George Washington U., 1990; named to Cen. High Sch. Hall of Fame, Phila., 1976; recipient Pub. Health Service Research Career Devel. award Nat. Cancer Inst., 1964-74, 1st Hilldale award in Biolog. Sci. U. Wis., 1986, Braund Disting. vis. prof. award U. Tenn., 1987, Eisenstark lectr. award U. Mo., 1987, 1st Wilmot vis. prof. award U. Rochester, 1987, Sophie Moss lectr. award Hahnemann U., 1991, Latta lectr. award U. Nebr., 1991, Nat. Medal of Sci. NSF, 1992. Fellow AAAS, Am. Acad. Arts and Scis., Wis. Acad. Sci., Arts and Letters, Am. Soc. Microbiology; mem. NAS, Am. Soc. for Therapeutic Radiology and Oncology, Inst. Sci., Am. Philos. Soc., Tissue Culture Assn. (hon.), Royal Soc., Inst. Medicine. Home: Madison Wis. Died Feb. 9, 1994.

TENNEY, CHARLES HENRY, federal judge; b. N.Y.C., Jan. 28, 1911; s. Daniel Gleason and Marguerite Sedgwick (Smith) T.; m. Joan Penfold Lusk, May 14, 1938; children: Patricia Lusk (Mrs. Bernard J. Ruggieri), Charles Henry, Joan Tenney Howard, Marguerite Sedgwick (Mrs. Talton R. Embry), Anne Gleason. Grad., Choate Sch., 1929; A.B., Yale U., 1933, LL.B., 1936. Bar: N.Y. 1937. With firm Breed, Abbott & Morgan, N.Y.C., 1936-51; mem. firm Breed, Abbott & Morgan, 1951-55; commr. investigation N.Y.C., 1955-58; corp. counsel, 1958-61, dep. mayor, city adminstr., 1961-64; U.S. dist. judge So. Dist. N.Y., 1964-94, sr. judge. Mem. N.Y.C. Bd. Ethics, 1960-61. Served to lt. comdr. USNR, 1942-45. Mem. ABA, Fed. Bar Assn., N.Y. State Bar Assn., New York County Bar Assn., Assn. Bar City N.Y., Am. Judicature Soc., Phi Beta Kappa. Home: New York N.Y. Died Nov. 11, 1994.

TERBORGH, BERT, dancer; b. Bennebroek, Netherlands, Mar. 8, 1945; came to U.S., 1975; s. Cornelius Franciscus and Petronella Maria (Berbee) Zwetsloot. Grad., Gymnasium, Haarlem, Netherlands, 1964. Dancer with Scapino Ballet, Australian Dance Theatre and Rotterdam Dance Theater, 1967-72; prin. dancer Bat Dor Dance Co., Israel, 1973-74, Paul Sanasordo and Australian Dance Theater, N.Y.C. and, Australia, 1975; prin. dancer Martha Graham Dance Co., N.Y.C., 1976-82, rehearsal dir., tchr., 1982-87; mem. dance faculty SUNY, Purchase, 1987-96; mem. faculty Martha Graham Ctr., N.Y.C., Neighborhood Playhouse, N.Y.C.; tchr. dance univs., schs., cos., U.S., Europe and Australia. Mem. Am. Guild Mus. Artists. Home: New York N.Y. Died June 21, 1996.

TER-POGOSSIAN, MICHEL MATHEW, radiation sciences educator; b. Berlin, Apr. 21, 1925; naturalized, 1954; s. Michel and Anna (Suratoff) T-P.; m. Ann Garrison Scott, Mar, 3, 1967. BA, U. Paris, 1943, postgrad., 1943-45; postgrad., Inst. Radium, Paris, 1945-46; MS, Washington U., 1948, PhD, 1950. Instr. radiation physics Washington U. Sch. Medicine, St. Louis, 1950-51, asst. prof., 1951-56, assoc. prof., 1956-61, prof., 1961-73, prof. biophysics in physiology, 1964-96, prof. radiation scis., 1973-96; adv. various Dept. Energy and NIH coms.; mem. diagnostic radiology and nuclear medicine study sect., 1979-81. Mem. editorial bd. Am. Jour. Roentgenology, Postgrad. Radiology, Jour. Computer Assisted Tomography, Jour. Nuclear Medicine, Jour. de Biophysique & Medicine Nucleaire; editor: IEEE Trans. on Med. Imaging, 1982-83; patentee in field of radiol. physics. Wendell Scott lectr. Washington U., 1973, Benedict Cassen lectr., 1976, David Gould lectr. Johns Hopkins U., 1977, R.S. Landauer Meml. lectr., 1981, Hans Hecht lectr. U. Chgo., 1981, 2d Ann. Soc. Nuclear Medicine lectr., 1985; recipient Paul C. Aebersold award Soc. Nuclear Medicine, 1777, Herrman L. Blumgart M.D. Pioneer award 1984, Georg Charles de Hevesy Nuclear Medicine Pioneer award Soc. Nuclear Medicine, 1985, Internat. award Gairdner Found., 1993. Fellow Am. Physics Soc., Am. Coll. Radiology (hon.), Acad. Sci. St. Louis; mem. Am. Nuclear Soc., Am. Radium Soc., Radiation Research Soc., Inst. Medicine, Nat. Acad. Sci., Radiol. Soc. N.Am. (New Horizons lectr. 1968). Republican. Home: Saint Louis Mo. Died June 19, 1996.

TERRA, DANIEL JAMES, chemical company executive; b. Phila., June 8, 1911; s. Louis J. and Mary (DeLuca) T.; m. Adeline Evans Richards, Aug. 7, 1937 (dec. 1982); children: Penny Jane (dec.), James D.; m. Judith Anne Farabee, June 27, 1986. BS, Pa. State U., 1931; LLD, MacMurray Coll., 1972; DFA (hon.), Nat. Coll., 1980, U. Ill., 1984. Founder Lawter Internat. Inc., Chgo., 1940; chmn. bd. dirs., CEO Lawter Internat. Inc., 1964-96; amb.-at-large for cultural affairs U.S. Dept. State, 1981-89; chmn. Mercury Fin. Corp., 1989-96; bd . dirs. Lawter Internat. Inc., Mercury Fin. Corp. Founder, chmn., bd. dirs. Terra Mus. Am. Art, Chgo. and Evanston, Ill., Musée Américain Giverny, France; chmn. Terr Found. for Arts; past v.p., mem. exec. com. United Republican Fund Ill., pres., 1973-79; past chmn. Everett Dirksen 500 Club.; nat. fin. chmn. Ronald Reagan for Pres. of U.S. campaign, 1979-80; co-chmn. Pres.'s Task Force for the Arts and Humanities, 1981-82; mem. Pres.'s Com. for Arts and Humanities, 1982-89; bd. dirs. Chgo. Lyric Opera; ex officio trustee Nat. Gallery Art, Washington . Decorated Order of Leopold II (Belgium), comdr. Order Arts and Letters (France; recipient Winthrop Sears medal Chem. Industry Assn., 1972; Distinguished Alumni medal Pa. State U., 1976, Lincoln Acad. medal, Springfield, Ill., 1982. Clubs: Westmoreland Country (Wilmette, Ill.); Chicago (Chgo.), Commercial (Chgo.), Chicago Mid-America (Chgo.), Casino (Chgo.), Indian Hill (Winnetka, Ill.); Nat. Arts (N.Y.C.), Links (N.Y.C.). Home: Chicago Ill. Died June 28, 1996.

TESICH, STEVE, author; b. Titovo Utice, Yugoslavia, Sept. 29, 1942; came to U.S., 1955, naturalized, 1961; s. Radisa and Gospava (Bulaich) T.; m. Rebecca Fletcher, May 24, 1971. BA, Ind. U., 1965; MA, Columbia U., 1967. Freelance writer, 1968-96; author: (plays) The Carpenters, 1970, Lake of the Woods, 1971, Baba Goya, 1972 (Drama Desk award 1973), Gorky, 1975, Passing Game, 1977, Touching Bottom, 1978, Division Street, 1980, Speed of Darkness, 1989, Square One, 1990, On The Open Road, 1992; (novel) Summer Crossing, 1982; (film) Breaking Away, 1979 (Academy award, 1979, N.Y. Film Critics Circle award 1980, Nat. Soc. Film Critics award 1980, Critics Circle Film Sect. award 1980), Eyewitness, 1981, Four Friends, 1981, The World According to Garp, 1982 (Exceptional Film award, Nat. Bd. Rev. 1983), American Flyers, 1985, Eleni, 1985. NDEA fellow, Rockefeller fellow, 1972. Mem. Acad. Motion Picture Arts and Scis. (award 1980), Writers Guild (award 1980), Dramatists Guild, Phi Beta Kappa. Democrat. Home: New York N.Y. Died July 1, 1996.

TEXTER, E(LMER) CLINTON, JR., physician, educator; b. Detroit, June 12, 1923; s. Elmer Clinton and Helen (Rotchford) T.; m. Jane Starke Curtis, Feb. 19, 1949; children: Phyllis Cardew, Patricia Ann, Catherine Jane. B.A. with honors, Mich. State U., 1943; M.D., Wayne State U., 1946; postgrad., U. Detroit, 1946-47, N.Y. U. Postgrad. Med. Sch., 1948-49, Northwestern U., 1959-60, Williams Coll., 1975. Diplomate Am. Bd. Internal Medicine and Gastroenterology. Intern Providence Hosp., Detroit, 1946-47; Heart Assn. research fellow in medicine Cornell U. Med. Coll., N.Y.C., 1948-50; asst. physician to outpatients N.Y. Hosp., N.Y.C., 1949-50; asst. resident medicine 3d div. NYU, Goldwater Meml. Hosp., N.Y.C., 1950-51; instr. medicine Duke U. Sch. Medicine, Durham, N.C.; asst. physician Duke U. Hosp., 1951-53; asso. medicine Northwestern U. Med. Sch., Chgo., 1953-56; asst. prof. medicine Northwestern U. Med. Sch., 1956-61, assoc. prof., 1961-68; prof. physiology adj. U. Tex. S.W. Med. Sch., Dallas, 1969-72; coordinator allied health programs Temple (Tex.) Jr. Coll., 1969-72; prof. medicine, physiology, biophysics Coll. Medicine U. Ark., 1972-95, Jerome S. Levy prof. medicine (gastroenterology), 1985-95, dir. div. gastroenterology, 1972-85; asst. dean Coll. Health Related Professions U. Ark., Little Rock, 1972-73; assoc. dean U. Ark., 1973-75; mem. active staff Univ. Hosp., Little Rock, 1972-95; assoc. chief staff for edn. Univ. Hosp., 1972-75; chief gastroenterology VA Hosp., Little Rock, 1972-79; dir. tng. program in gastroenterology, 1954-65; attending physician Northwestern Meml. Hosp., VA Lakeside Hosp., Chgo., 1953-68; asso. med. dir. Profl. Life & Casualty Co., Chgo., 1965-68; mem. adv. bd. Skokie Valley Community Hosp., 1959-68; chmn. dept. clin. physiology and clin. research ctr., cons. gastroenterology, publs. sects. Scott and White Clinic (Temple Tex.), 1968-72; cons. gastroenterology U.S. Naval Hosp., Great Lakes, 1963-68; cons. William Beaumont Regional Army Med. Center, El Paso, Tex., 1968-95; surgeon gen. U.S. Army, 1970-95; cons. St. Vincent Infirmary, Little Rock, 1973-95, Doctors Hosp., Little ock, Bapt. Med. Center, Little Rock, 1981-95; dir. Ark. Digestive Disease Center, 1975-95; cons. Ark. regional med. program Ark. Health Systems Found., 1972-76, Council on Drugs, 1958-95; mem. select com. on role of dietary fiber in diverticular disease and colon cancer Life Scis. Research Office FASEB, 1980; del. Sino-Am. Conf. on Drug Therapy, Beijing and Shanghai, 1980; vis. prof. U. Fla., 1956, 69, U. Tenn., 1958, Cath. U. Leuven, 1962, 64, 71, 81, U. Zurich, 1964, Karolinska Inst., 1964, U. Gothenburg, 1964, U. Copenhagen, 1964, U. Rome, 1965, 67, 69, U. Ala., 1971. Author: Peptic Ulcer - Diagnosis and Treatment, 1955, Physiology of the Gastrointestinal Tract, 1968, The Aging Gut, 1983; Contbr. articles to profl. jours. Active Ark. Art Center, Ark. Symphony Soc.; bd. dirs. Wayne State Fund, Detroit, 1975-95. Served with USNR, 1947-49. Recipient Disting. Service awards Wayne State U., 1969, 74; Clarence F.G. Brown fellow Inst. Medicine, Chgo., 1953-56. Fellow A.C.P.; mem. AMA (com. on med. rating phys. impairment 1960-64), Am. Gastroent. Assn., Am. Fedn. Clin. Research (chmn. gastroenterology 1956, 63), Stead Scholarship Soc. of Duke U., Am. Med. Writers Assn. (pres. 1973-74), Am. Assn. Study Liver Disease, Am. Soc. Gastrointestinal Edoscopy, Am. Physiol. Soc., Am. Soc. Clin. Pharmacology and Therapeutics (dir. 1971-76), Am. Coll. Gastroenterology (gov. So. region A 1978-79, bd. govs.-Ark 1988-95, nat. affairs com. 1988-95), Gastroenterology Research Group (co-founder 1955, chmn. 1959), Internat. Soc. Gastrointestinal Motility (co-founder 1969, chmn. 1969-61), So. Soc. Clin. Investigation, Central Soc. Clin. Research, William Beaumont Soc. Gastroenterologists, Sigma Xi, Theta Alpha Phi, Delta Chi, Nu Sigma Nu. Episcopalian (lay reader 1968-95, chalicer 1979-95). Clubs: Little Rock, Chancellor's (Little Rock); Literary (Chgo.); John Evans of Northwestern U; Anthony Wayne Soc. (Detroit); Country Club of Va. (Richmond). Home: Little Rock Ark. Died May 4, 1995.

THALER, MARTIN S., lawyer, educator; b. Bklyn., Mar. 22, 1932; s. Philip Paul and Mildred S. T.; m. Mary Kathleen O'Brien, June 30, 1973; 1 child, Megan; children by previous marriage: Diane, Paul, David, Amy. BBA, CCNY, 1953; LLB, Yale U., 1958. Bar: D.C. 1958. Ptnr. Martin, Whitfield, Thaler & Bebchick, Washington, 1961-78, Verner, Liipfert, Bernhard, McPherson & Hand, Washington, 1978-87; ptnr. Weil, Gotshal & Manges, Washington, 1987-90, Budapest, Hungary, 1991-92; lectr. in law and civil procedure George Washington U., 1959-60; adj. prof. uniform comml. code Georgetown U., 1971-78, 84-85, adj. prof. corp. fin., 1980-83, adj. prof. jurisprudence, 1986-91, adj. prof. real estate transactions, 1987-88. Trustee Glenelg (Md.) Country Sch., 1963-71. Cpl. Signal Corps, AUS, 1953-55. Recipient Chales Fahey Disting. Adj. Prof. award Georgetown U. Law Sch., 1990-91. Mem. ABA, Am. Law Inst., Internat. Bar Assn., Bar Assn. D.C. Clubs: Met. (Washington); Yale (N.Y.C.). Home: Clarksville Md. Died Dec. 21, 1992.

THANI, SHEIKH NASIR BIN KHALID AL See AL-THANI, NASIR BIN KHALID

THAYER, STUART WILSON WALKER, lawyer; b. Charleston, W.Va., May 4, 1926; s. Harry G. and Ethel (Wehrle) T.; m. Ann Hart, July 1, 1949; children: Janet Thayer Kiczek, Mark, David, Lucy Thayer Lucero, Peter. A.B., Princeton U., 1947; LL.B., Yale U., 1951. Bar: D.C. 1952, W.Va. 1954, N.Y. 1956. Law clk. to Justice Tom C. Clark U.S. Supreme Ct., Washington, 1951-52; assoc. Covington & Burling, Washington, 1952-54, Spilman, Thomas, Battle & Kolstermeyer, Charleston, W.Va., 1954-56; assoc. Sullivan & Cromwell, N.Y.C., 1956-60, ptnr., 1960-92; retired, 1992. Served to lt. (j.g.) USN, 1944-46. Clubs: India House; Sky (N.Y.C.). Home: New York N.Y. Died Sept. 22, 1992.

THEROS, ELIAS GEORGE, radiology educator and author; b. Grand Island, Nebr., Sept. 28, 1919; s. George Elias Theodoropoulos and Mary Elizabeth (Hoffman) Sherman; m. Ruth Mary Todkill, Feb. 24, 1943; children: George Alexis, William Todkill, Stephanie Ruth Reid. BA in Liberal Arts, UCLA, 1947; MA in Edn., Columbia U., 1948; MD, UCLA, 1957. Diplomate Am. Bd. Radiology. Commd. ensign USNR, 1943, advanced through grades to capt., line and intelligence officer, 1943-57; tng. and curricula officer 11th Naval Dist., San Diego, 1951-53; with USN Med. Corps, 1957-73; intern U.S. Naval Hosp., San Diego, 1957-58; med. officer nuclear submarines USN, 1958-60, submarine squadron and diving med. officer, 1961-62; radiology resident Nat. Naval Med. Ctr., Bethesda, Md., 1962-65; radiology staff tng. officer U.S. Naval Hosp., San Diego, 1965-66; registrar Armed Forces Inst. Pathology, Washington, 1966-73, chief radiopathology div., 1972-73; ret. USN, 1973; chmn. dept. radiologic pathology Armed Forced Inst. Pathology, Washington, 1974-76; prof. radiol. scis., dir. radiol. edn. U. Calif. Med. Ctr., Los Angeles, 1976-79, prof., vice chmn. dept. radiol. scis., 1978-79; I. Meschan Disting. Prof. radiology Bowman Gray Sch. Medicine Wake Forest U., Winston-Salem, N.C., 1979-94; clin. prof. radiology Georgetown U. Sch. Medicine, Washington, 1968-76, U. Nebr. Sch. Medicine, 1970-80, The John Hopkins U. Sch. Medicine, Balt., 1970-76; cons. NIH, 1970-76, U.S. Naval Hosps., 1968-94, U.S. Army Hosps., 1970-94; chmn. com. on self-evaluation and continuing edn. Am. Coll. Radiology, 1968-84. Editor-in-chief Am. Coll. Radiology Continuing Ednl.Syllabi, 1968-88, editor emeritus, 1989-94; reviewer Jour. of Radiol. Soc. North Am., 1973-88; mem. editl. bd. Jour. of Internat. Skeletal Soc., 1975-92, Contemporary Diagnostic Radiology, 1976-91; editorial cons. Critical Revs. in Radiology, 1975-94. Decorated Legion of Merit; recipient Cert. Disting. Service The Armed Forces Inst. Pathology, 1973, Cert. Merit and Outstanding Service USN Surgeon Gen., 1973, Cert. of Merit Univ. Miami Med. Sch., 1973, The Caldwell Medal Am. Roentgen Ray Soc., 1976, Alumni Profl. Achievement award UCLA, 1976, Leo G. Rigler award UCLA, 1978, Cert. of Merit N.Y. Roentgen Soc., 1980, James L. Quinn III Meml. award Wake Forest U., 1982, Gold medal Am. Coll. Radiology, 1986, Gold medal Radiol. Soc. N.Am.,1989, Elias G. Theros ann. radiology rsch. award established by radiology dept. Bowman Gray Sch. Medicine, Wake Forest U., 1990; named Living Legend in Radiology Am. Coll. Radiology, 1988; Elias G. Theros Ctr. and Auditorium for Edn. in Radiologic Pathology dedicated at Armed Forces Inst. of Pathology, Washington, 1994. Hon. fellow Am. Coll. Radiology, Royal Australasian Coll. Radiology, Netherlands Radiol. Soc.; mem. AMA, Am. Roentgen Ray Soc. (Gold medal 1991), Radiol. Soc. North Am., InterAm. Coll. Radiology, Felix Fleischner Internat. Chest Soc. (elected mem.), Internat. Skeletal Soc. (founding mem.); hon. mem. Brazilian Radiol. Soc., Can. Eastern Maritime Province Radiol. Soc., Chgo. Radiol. Soc., Colombian Radiol. Soc., Fla. Radiol. Soc., French-Can. Radiol. Soc., Greek Radiol. Soc., Israeli Radiol. Soc., Ky. Radiol. Soc., Mexican Radiol. Soc., Pacific Northwestern Radiol. Soc., Peruvian Radiol. Soc., Phila. Roentgen Ray Soc., Rocky Mountain Radiol. Soc., Tex. Radiol. Soc., Toronto Radiol. Soc. Home: Advance N.C. Died Nov., 1994.

THIRY, PAUL, architect; b. Nome, Alaska, Sept. 11, 1904; s. Hippolyte A. and Louise Marie (Schwaebele) T.; m. Mary Thomas, Oct. 26, 1940; children—Paul Albert, Pierre. Diploma, Ecole des Beaux Arts, Fontainebleau, France, 1927; A.B., U. Wash., 1928; D.F.A. (hon.), St. Martins Coll., 1970; D.Arts (hon.), Lewis & Clark Coll., 1979. Pvt. practice architecture, 1929—; mem. Thiry & Shay, 1935-39; co-architect war work U.S. Navy Advance Base Depot, Tacoma, Fed. Pub. Housing Adminstrn. projects; community centers and appurtenances Port Orchard, Wash., 1940-44; practice in Salt Lake City, Alaska, Seattle, 1945—; pres. Thiry Architects, Inc., 1971—; architect in residence Am. Acad. in Rome, 1969. Author: (with Richard Bennett and Henry Kamphoefner) Churches and Temples, 1953, (with Mary Thiry) Eskimo Artifacts Designed for Use, 1978; Contbr. articles to profl. jours.; Projects exhibited and illustrated in books and periodicals.; Prin. works include Am. Embassy residence, Santiago, Chile (awarded Diploma Clegio de Arquitectos de Chile 1965); comprehensive plan Seattle Center (awarded A.I.A. citation for excellence in community architecture 1966); Seattle Coliseum (A.I.S.I. awards for design and engring. 1965), (A.I.S.C. award of excellence 1965), Washington State Library (AIA-ALA award 1964), U.S. 4th Inf. (Ivy) Div. Monument, Utah Beach, France, 1969 (hon. citizen Sainte Marie du Mont), Am. Battle Monuments Commn. Meml., Utah Beach, 1984; cons.: comprehensive plan Libby Dam-Lake Koocanusa Project, Mont.; cons. Chief Joseph Dam Powerhouse, Wash.; architect for Visitors Center (C.E. distinguished design award 1970, Chief of Engrs. cert. of appreciation 1974); cons.: New Melones Dam/Reservoir Project, Calif., 1972, Reregulating dam and powerhouse, Libby, Mont., 1977—; others.; works include coll. bldgs., chs., museums, and, govt. projects; also designer fabrics; carpets, furniture. Commnr. City of Seattle Planning Commn., 1952-61, chmn., 1953-54; rep. on exec. bd. Puget Sound Regional Planning Council, 1954-57; chmn. Central Bus. Dist. Study, 1957-60; mem. exec. com. Wash. State Hosp. Adv. Council, 1953-57; architect in charge Century 21 Expn., Seattle, 1957-62; mem. Dept. Interior Historic Am. Bldg. Survey Bd., 1956-61, vice chmn., 1958-61; mem. Joint Com. Nat. Capital, 1961, exec. bd., 1962-72; mem. President's Council Redevel. Pennsylvania Av., Washington, 1962-65; cons. FHA, 1963-67; cons. architect Nat. Capitol, 1964—; mem. Nat. Capital Planning Commn., 1963-75, vice chmn., 1972-75; mem. arts and archtl. com. J. F. Kennedy Meml. Library, 1964; mem. Postmaster Gen.'s Council Research and Engring., 1968-70; mem. Peace Corps Adv. Council, 1982-84. Decorated officier d'Academie with palms France; recipient Paul Bunyan award Seattle C. of C., 1949, Outstanding Architect-Engr. award Am. Mil. Engrs., 1977; named Distinguished Citizen in the Arts Seattle, 1962, Constrn. Man of Year, 1963; Academician N.A.D.; named to Coll. of Architecture Hall of Honor U. Wash., 1987. Fellow A.I.A. (pres. Wash. chpt. 1951-53, preservation officer 1952-62, chancellor coll. fellows 1962-64, chmn. com. nat. capital 1960-64, chmn. com. hon. fellowships 1962-64, Seattle chpt. medal 1984); mem. Nat. Sculpture Soc. (hon., Herbert Adams Meml. medal 1974, Henry Hering medal 1976), Am. Inst. Planners (exec. bd. Pacific N.W. chpt. 1949-52, hon. life), Am. Planning Assn. (hon. life, N.W. chpt. citation 1983), Soc. Archtl. Historians (life mem., dir. 1967-70), Nat. Trust Historic Preservation, Am. Inst. Interior Designers (hon.), Liturgical Conf. (life), Seattle Art Mus. (life), Seattle Hist. Soc. (hon. life), Oreg. Cavemen (hon.), Delta Upsilon, Tau Sigma Delta, Scarab (hon.). Clubs: Cosmos (Washington); Century (N.Y.C.); Architectural League N.Y. Home: Bellevue Wash. Died June 27, 1993.

THOMAS, ABDELNOUR SIMON, software company executive; b. Kfarhoune, Lebanon, Oct. 25, 1913; came to U.S., 1920; s. Simon Thomas and Mary Sawaya-Thomas; m. Eva Maria Balling, Mar. 26, 1951; children: Robert F., David C., Paul J., Simon P., Mary E., Joan T. BS, Holy Cross Coll., 1937; MEd, Boston U., 1939, PhD, 1950. Registered profl. engr., Mass. Prof. math. and math. stats. Boston Coll., 1946-51; founder, dir. rsch. activities A. S. Thomas, Inc., 1955—; vis. prof. MIT. Contbr. Ency. Britanica, numerous. sci. publs. Mem. Nat. Rep. Com., Right to Life. Lt. USNR, 1942-46, PTO. Recipient Forty-One for Freedom award Sec. USN, 1967. Mem. IEEE (life, sr.), Soc. Mfg. Engrs., Numerical Control Soc. Roman Catholic. Home: West Roxbury Mass.

THOMAS, BAILEY ALFRED, food company executive; b. Crisfield, Md.; s. Bailey and Mary H. (Hopkins) T.; children: Frank, John, Gregory. AA in Bus. Adminstrn., U. Balt., 1952. With Libby McNeill & Libby, 1950-51; then with Crosse & Blackwell Co., Balt.; chmn. bd., CEO McCormick & Co. Inc., Sparks, Md.; bd. dirs. Crown Ctrl. Petroleum Corp. Community dir. United Way Ctrl. Md.; mem. Steering Com. Md., Steering Com. Md. Bus. Responsive Govt., adv. bd. William Donald Schaefer ctr. pub. policy U. Balt. Ednl. Found.; bd. govs. The Balt. Goodwill Industries Inc., past pres.; former pres. Buddies Inc.; bd. dirs. Kennedy Inst., Greater Balt. Com.; trustee Loyola Coll., Md. Mem. Am. Spice Trade Assn. (past chmn. indsl. and food service com.), Nat. Assn. Mfrs. (bd. dirs.), Grocery Mfrs. Am., Inc. (bd. dirs.), The Conf. Bd., Inc. Republican. Home: Reisterstown Md. Died July 14, 1994.

THOMAS, BETH EILEEN WOOD (MRS. RAYMOND O. THOMAS), editor; b. North Vernon, Ind., May 12, 1916; d. Fayette J. and Emma J. (Ream) Wood; m. Raymond O. Thomas, Feb. 28, 1941; 1 son, Stephen W. Comml. diploma, Bedford High Sch., 1934; student, Lockyear Bus. Coll., 1936. Sec. WPA, Vincennes, Ind., 1935-36, Evansville, Ind., 1937-38, Indpls., 1939-41; sec. to adj. AAF Storage Depot, Indpls., 1941-44; sec. Coll. Life Ins., Indpls., 1957-58, Indpls. Sch. Bd., 1958-59; classified office mgr. North Side Topics Newspaper, Indpls., 1960-67. Editor: Child Life mag., 1967-71, Brownie Reader, 1971-73, Children's Playmate mag., 1968-91; editorial assoc. Saturday Evening Post, 1971; exec. editorial dir. Jack and Jill mag., 1971-91, Young World mag., 1971-79, Child Life mag., 1971-91, Design mag., 1977-80, Turtle mag. for Presch. Kids, 1979-91, Humpty Dumpty's mag., 1980-91, Children's Digest, 1980-91; editor emeritus juvenile mags., Children's Better Health Inst., 1991-95. Mem. Women in Communications, Indpls. Press Club, Soc. Children's Book Writers. Club: Thetis. Home: Indianapolis Ind. Died May 16, 1995.

THOMAS, DARRELL DENMAN, lawyer; b. Lake Cormorant, Miss., Sept. 10, 1931; s. Darrell Dane and Maggie Adele (McKay) T.; m. Dora Ann Bailey, Feb. 12, 1957 (div. 1988). BS, Memphis State U., 1957; JD, U. Denver, 1960. Bar: Colo. 1960, U.S. Dist. Ct. Colo. 1960, U.S. Supreme Ct. 1967, U.S. Ct. Appeals (10th cir.) 1971. Law clk. to presiding justice U.S. Dist. Ct., Colo., 1960-61; ptnr. Mills & Thomas, Colorado Springs, Colo., 1961-65; pvt. practice Colorado Springs, 1965-96; U.S. commr. U.S. Dist. Ct., 1961-71, U.S. magistrate, 1971-91. Pres. Colorado Springs Symphony, 1979-82; v.p. Colorado Springs Symphony Orch. Found. With U.S. Army, 1952-54. Mem. ABA, Colo. Bar Assn., El Paso County Bar Assn., El Paso Club (dir. 1985-88), Broadmoor Golf Club, Garden of the Gods Club, Masons, Shriner. Republican. Home: Colorado Springs Colo. Died Apr. 8, 1996.

THOMAS, ELWOOD LAUREN, state supreme court justice; b. Council Bluffs, Iowa, July 24, 1930; s. Lauren D. and Atla M. (Fight) T.; m. Susanne Faye Higdon, June 5, 1955; children: Mark, Sandra, Steven. BA, Simpson Coll., 1954; JD, Drake U., 1957. Bar: Iowa 1957, U.S. Dist. Ct. (no. dist.) Iowa 1957, U.S. Dist. Ct. (so. dist.) Iowa 1962, Mo. 1976, U.S. Dist. Ct. (we. dist.) Mo. 1978, U.S. Tax Ct. 1980, U.S. Ct. Appeals (8th cir.) 1982, U.S. Supreme Ct. 1982. Ptnr. Karr, Karr & Thomas, Webster City, Iowa, 1957-61, Qualley & Thomas, Sioux City, Iowa, 1961-65, Shook, Hardy & Bacon, Kansas City, Mo., 1978-91; prof. law U. Mo., Columbia, 1965-78; justice Supreme Ct. Mo., Jefferson City, 1991-95; mem. faculty Mo. Jud. Coll., 1973-95, Nat. Jud. Coll., Reno, 1975-87, Nat. Inst. Trial Advocacy, 1982-83; reporter com. civil jury instrns. Mo. Supreme Ct., 1978-81, chmn., 1981-91; spkr. Citizens Forums Mo. Jud. Sys., 1992. Author: (with others) Missouri Evidence Restated, 1984, Missouri Damages Deskbook, 1987, II Missouri Tort Law, 2d edit., 1990; co-author: Missouri Practice Series-Litigation Guide, 1991. Trustee sch. law U. Mo.-Columbia, 1979-91. Recipient Faculty Alumni award U. Mo.-Columbia, 1971, Disting. Non-Alumni award sch. law U. Mo.-Columbia, 1989, Outstanding Alumni award law sch. Drake U., 1992, Alumni Achievement award Simpson Coll., 1993. Fellow Am. Bar Found.; mem. ABA, Am. Law Inst., Order of Coif, Law Soc. U. Mo. Sch. Law (charter). Methodist. Home: Jefferson City Mont. Died July 30, 1995.

THOMAS, FRANK, JR., physical education educator; b. Meridian, Miss., Oct. 2, 1948; s. Frank and Georgia (Richardson) T. BS, Alcorn State U., 1971; MEd, U. Mo., 1977; Specialist in Edn. degree, Jackson State U., 1978; ArtsD, Mid. Tenn. State U., 1988. Tchr. Providence Edn. Ctr., St. Louis, 1974-75; grad. asst. U. Mo., Columbia, 1975-77, Jackson (Miss.) state U., 1977-78; asst. prof. Phys. Edn. Miss. Valley State U., Itta Bena, Miss., 1978-85; mgr. equipment rm. Mid. Tenn. State U., Murfreesboro, Tenn., 1987-88, grad. asst. in Phys. Edn., 1985-88; assoc. prof. Phys. Edn. Miss. Valley State U., Itta Bena, 1988-90. Dir. Recreation div. Salvation Army Community Ctr., St. Louis, 1974-75. With USAR, 1972-90. Mem. Optimistic Club, Kappa Alpha Psi. Democrat. Baptist. Home: Meridian Miss. Died Nov. 25, 1990.

THOMAS, HENRI, author, poet; b. France, Dec. 7, 1912; s. Joseph and Mathilde Thomas; m. Jacqueline Le Beguec, 1957; 1 child. Student, Strasbourg U. Tchr., until 1939; program asst. French sect. BBC, 1947-58; lectr. in French, Brandeis U., Mass., 1956-60; in charge German dept. Gallimard's Pub. House, Paris, 1960-93. Author: (novels) Le seau à charbon, 1940, Le précepteur, 1942, La vie ensemble, 1943, Les déserteurs, 1951, La nuit de Londres, 1956, La dernière année, 1960, John Perkins (Prix Médicis 1960), Le promontoire (Prix Femina 1961), Le Parjure, 1964, La Relique, 1969, Le Croc des Chiffonniers, 1985, Une Saison Volée, 1986, Un Détour par La Vie, 1988, Le Gouvernement Provisoire, 1989, Le Goût de L'Eternel, 1990, Ai-Je une Patrie, 1991, Le Cinema dans la Grange, 1991, (criticism) La chasse aux trésors, 1961, Tristan Le Dépossédé, 1978, (short stories) La Cible (Prix St. Beuve 1956), Histoires de Pierrot et Quelques Autres, 1960, Sainte Jeunesse, 1972, Les tours de Notre Dame (Prix des Sept, 1979), (essays) Le Porte-A-Faux, 1949, Sous le Lien due Temps, 1963, Le Migrateur, 1983, Le Tableau d'Avancement, 1983, Compté, Pesé, Divisé, 1989, La Joie de Cette Vie, 1991; poetry includes: Póesies complètes, 1970, A Quoi tu penses, 1980, Joueur surpris, 1982, Trézeaux, 1990 (Prix Jules Supervielle 1992); translator works by Goethe, Stifter, Iünger, Shakespeare, Pushkin. Recipient Prix Valéry Larbaud, 1970; decorated chevalier Legion d'honneur. Home: Paris France Died Nov. 3, 1993.

THOMAS, JESS, tenor; b. Hot Springs, S.D., Aug. 4, 1927; s. Charles A. and H. and Ellen (Yocam) T.; m. Violeta Maria de Los Angeles Rios Andino Figueroa, 1974; children: Victor Justin, Lisa, Jess David. A.B., U. Nebr., 1949; M.A., Stanford, 1953; student, Otto Schulmann, San Francisco, 1953-57. Guidance counselor pub. schs. Hermiston, Oreg., 1949-52, Alameda, Cal., 1953-56. Winner San Francisco Opera audition, 1957; profl. debut, Baden State Theatre, Karlsruhe, Germany, 1958, appeared in, Stuttgart, Germany, 1959-64, Bavarian State Opera, Munich, 1959-93, Munich Festival, 1960-93, Bayreuth Festival, 1961-93, Berlin Philharmonic, 1962, Met. Opera Co., 1962-93, Venice, Italy Wagner Festival, 1963, Deutsche Oper, Berlin, 1961-64, Frankfurt Opera, 1963, Salzburg Summer Festival, 1964-93, Vienna State Opera, 1964-93, La Scala Opera, 1965, Opening Night New Met. Opera, 1966, Osaka Japan Festival, 1967, Convent Garden Opera, 1969-93, Salzburg Easter Festival, 1969-93, Paris Grand Opera, 1967-93, San Francisco Opera, 1965-93; sang Tristan in, Covent Garden, Met. Opera, Vienna State Opera, 1971-93, Palacio de Bellas Artes, Mexico City, 1971-93, Casals Festival, 1976-93, Teatro Colon Opera, Buenos Aires, 1976-93, Bolshoi Theatre, Moscow, 1971, appeared in Wagner: The Film, 1983; rec. artist for Angel Records, Deutsche Grammophon, Phillips, RCA, Columbia, N.Y. Philharmonic debut, 1967, Boston Symphony debut, 1967; pub. memoirs Kein Schwert Verhiess Mir Der Vater, 1986. Named Kammersänger Bavarian State Govt., 1963; recipient San Francisco Opera medallion, 1972; named Kammersänger Austrian Govt., 1976; inducted into Acad. Vocal Arts Hall of Fame, Phila., 1986. Mem. Beta Theta Pi, Phi Delta Kappa. Home: Belvedere Tiburon Calif. Deceased.

THOMAS, LEWIS, physician, educator, former medical administrator; b. Flushing, N.Y., Nov. 25, 1913; s. Joseph S. and Grace Emma (Peck) T.; m. Beryl Dawson, Jan. 1, 1941; children: Abigail, Judith, Eliza. BS, Princeton U., 1933, ScD (hon.), 1976; MD, Harvard U., 1937, ScD (hon.), 1986; MA, Yale U., 1969; ScD (hon.), U. Rochester, 1974, U. of Toledo, 1976, Columbia U., Meml. U. Nfld., 1978, U. N.C., Worcester Found., 1979, Williams Coll., 1982, Conn. Coll., U. Wales, 1983, U. Ariz., 1985, L.I. U., 1987, Rockefeller U., U. Ill., U. Minn., 1989; LLD (hon.), Johns Hopkins U., 1976, Trinity Coll., 1980; LHD (hon.), Duke U., 1976, Reed Coll., 1978, Mt. Sinai Sch. Medicine, 1990; LittD (hon.), Dickinson Coll., 1980, Ursinus Coll., 1981, SUNY-Stony Brook, 1983, Drew U., 1983; DMus. (hon.), New Eng. Conservatory Music, 1982; DHL (hon.), NYU Sch. Medicine, 1983; PhD, Weizmann Inst., 1984. Asst. prof. pediatrics Med. Sch. Johns Hopkins U., Balt., 1946-48; assoc. prof. medicine Med. Sch. Tulane U., New Orleans, 1948-50; prof. medicine Med. Sch. Tulane U., 195O; prof. pediatrics and medicine, dir. pediatric research labs. Heart Hosp., U. Minn., Mpls., 1950-54; prof., chmn. dept. pathology NYU Sch. Medicine, 1954-58, prof., chmn. dept. medicine, 1958-66, dean, 1966-69; prof., chmn. dept. pathology Yale U., New Haven, 1969-72, dean, Sch. Medicine, 1972-73; prof. medicine, pathology Med. Sch. Cornell U., N.Y.C., 1973-93, prof. biology Sloan Kettering Inst. div., 1973-93; adj. prof. Rockefeller U., N.Y.C., 1975-93; pres., chief exec. officer Meml. Sloan-Kettering Cancer Ctr., N.Y.C., 1973-80, chancellor, 1980-83; pres. emeritus Meml. Sloan-Kettering Cancer Center, N.Y.C., 1984-93; prof. SUNY-Stony Brook Health Scis. Ctr., 1984-93; scholar-in-residence, Cornell U. Med. Coll., 1988-92; dir. 3d and 4th med. divs. Bellevue Hosp., 1958-66, pres. med. bd., 1963-66; nat. adv. health coun. NIH, 1960-64, nat. adv. child health and human devel. coun., 1964-68; mem. commn. on streptococcal disease Armed Forces Epidemiol. Bd., 1950-62; mem. Pres.'s Sci. Adv. Com., 1967-70, Inst. Medicine, 1971, NAS, 1972-93, mem. coun. and governing bd., 1979-93; chmn. overview cluster subcom. Pres.'s Biomed. Rsch. Panel, 1975-76; mem. Tech. Assessment Adv. Coun., 1980-86; bd. dirs., trustee Squibb Corp. Mem. N.Y.C. Bd. Health, 1956-69; mem. bd. sci. cons. Sloan-Kettering Inst. Cancer Rsch., 1966-72; mem. Sloan-Kettering Inst., 1973-83; bd. dirs. Josiah Macy Jr. Found., 1975-84; bd. sci. advisors Mass. Gen. Hosp., 1970-73, Scripps Clinic and Rsch. Found., 1969-78; bd. dirs., rsch. coun. Pub. Health Rsch. Inst. of City N.Y., 1964-69; bd. overseers Harvard Coll., 1976-82; assoc. fellow Ezra Stiles Coll. Yale U., 1978-82; mem. awards assembly Gen. Motors Cancer Rsch. Found., 1978-83; assoc. fellow Ezra Stiles Coll. Yale U. Author: Lives of a Cell, 1974, Medusa and the Snail, 1979, The Youngest Science, 1983, Late Night Thoughts on Listening to Mahler's Ninth Symphony, 1983, Et Cetera, Et Cetera, 1990, The Fragile Species, 1992; mem. editorial bd. Daedalus, Cellular Immunology, Am. Jour. Pathology. Trustee N.Y.C.-Rand Inst., 1967-71, The Rockefeller U., 1975-88, Draper Lab., 1975-81, John Simon Guggenheim Meml. Found., 1975-85, Mt. Sinai Sch. Medicine, 1979-85, Ednl. Broadcasting Co., 1977-83, Menninger Found., 1980-93; bd. dirs. Lounsbery Found., 1982-93; chmn. bd. Monell Chem. Senses Ctr., 1982-93; bd. advisors Kennedy Inst. Ethics, Georgetown U., 1982-93; trustee Nat. Hospice, 1978-93; mem. bd. overseers U. Pa. Sch. Nursing, 1983-93; adv. council Program in History of Sci. Princeton U., 1982-93; bd. dirs. Am. Friends Cambridge U., 1984-93; mem. adv. com. Aaron Diamond Found., 1985-93; dir. Commonwealth Fund Book Program, 1982-93. Served to lt. comdr. M.C. USNR, 1941-46. Recipient Disting. Achievement award Modern Medicine, 1975, Nat. Book award for Arts and Letters, 1975, Honor award Am. Med. Writers Assn., 1978, Med. Edn. award AMA, 1979, Bard award in medicine and sci. Bard Coll., 1979, Am. Book award, 1981, St. Davids Soc. award, 1980, Woodrow Wilson award Princeton U., 1980, award Cosmos Club, Washington, 1982, Richard Hopper Day award Phila. Acad. Natural Scis., 1985, Lewis Thomas award for communications ACP, 1986, Milton Helpern Meml. award, 1986, Ency. Brit. award, 1986, Alfred P. Sloan Jr. Meml. award, 1987, William B. Coley award Cancer Research Inst., 1987, Gold-Headed Cane award Am. Assn. Pathologists, 1988, Pub. Svc. award Am. Socs. for Exptl. Biology, 1988, Honor award for sci. and tech. Mayor of N.Y.C., 1989, Albert Lasker Pub. Svc. award, 1989, U. Calif. San Francisco Spl. 125th Anniversary medal, City of Medicine award 1990, Loren Eiseley award, 1990, John Stearns award N.Y. Acad. Medicine, 1991, Lewis Thomas prize Rockefeller U., 1993. Fellow Am. Acad. Arts and Scis.; mem. NAS, Am. Acad. and Inst. Arts and Letters, Am. Philos. Assn., Am. Acad. Microbiology, Peripatetic Clin. Soc., Am. Soc. Clin. Investigation, Am. Assn. Immunologists, Soc. Am. Bacteriologists, Assn. Am. Physicians (Kober medal 1983), Am. Pediatric Soc., N.Y. Acad. Scis. (pres.1989), Harvey Soc. (councillor), Scientists' Inst. for Pub. Info (chmn. bd. 1982-88, award for excellence in sci. communication 1982), Council on Fgn. Relations, Interurban Clin. Club, Phi Beta Kappa, Alpha Omega Alpha. Club: Century Assn. Home: New York N.Y. Died Dec. 3, 1993.

THOMAS, LLEWELLYN HILLETH, former physics educator; b. London, Oct. 21, 1903; came to U.S., 1929; s. Charles James and Winifred May (Lewis) T.; m. Naomi Estelle Frech, Sept. 27, 1933; children—James Rhys, Ann Rhonwen Thomas Viele, Margaret Olwen Thomas DeAngelis. D.Sc., Cambridge U., 1965. Fellow Trinity Coll., Cambridge, Eng., 1928-32; asst. prof. Ohio State U., Columbus, 1929-30, assoc. prof., 1930-34, prof., 1934-46; physicist, ballistician Aberdeen Proving Ground, Md., 1943-44; mem. sr. staff Watson Sci. Computing Lab., Columbia U., N.Y.C., 1946-68, prof. physics (hon.), 1950-68, prof. emeritus, 1968—; univ. prof. N.C. State U., Raleigh, 1968-74, prof. emeritus, 1974—. Recipient Davisson-Germer prize Am. Phys. Soc., 1982. Mem. Nat. Acad. Scis. Home: Raleigh N.C. Died Apr. 20, 1992.

THOMAS, PAUL IRVING, author, consultant, retired insurance executive; b. Breton Woods, N.H., Apr. 23, 1906; s. John James and Florence Mary (Simonds) T.; m. Marie Claire Foulkes, Feb. 16, 1935 (dec. Oct. 1980); children: Patricia Anne, Mary Jane; m. Ruth Dee Ward, Feb. 21, 1981. BSCE, U. N.Mex., 1931; cert. in teaching, Rutgers U., 1932; cert., U. Wis., 1966. Registered profl. engr., N.J. V.p. Prentiss B. Reed & Co., Inc., N.Y.C., 1934-47, Associated Reciprocal Exchs., N.Y.C., 1947-56, Kemper Ins. Cos., Chgo., 1956-71 author, free-lance cons. Hendersonville, N.C., 1971— cons. Nat. Com. on Property Ins., Boston, 1982—. Author: How to Estimate Building Losses and Con struction Costs, 1960, 4th rev. edit., 1983, Adjustmen of Property Losses, 1969, 4th edit., 1977, Estimatin Tables for Home Building, 1986, The Contractor's Fiel Guide, 1991. Mem. adv. bd. Ins. Tech. Tng. Inst Dallas, 1981—. Recipient citation of merit Nat. Assn Ind. Ins. Adjusters, 1968, plaque Property Loss Rsch Bur., 1986. Republican. Home: Hendersonville N.C Died May 7, 1994.

THOMAS, ROBERT CHESTER, sculptor, art edu cator; b. Wichita, Kans., Apr. 19, 1924; s. Chester an Alma (Mead) T.; m. Eleanor Louise Brand, July 1 1944; children—Robin Louise, Elizabeth Catherin Studies with Ossip Zadkine, Paris, 1948-49; B.A., U Calif.-Santa Barbara, 1951; M.F.A., Calif. Coll. Ar and Crafts, 1952. Prof. sculpture U. Calif., Sant Barbara, 1954—; executed life size bronze figure U Calif., Santa Barbara, 1967, sculpture J. Magnin stor Century City, 1966, fountain, Montecito, 196 represented in permanent collection Hirshhorn Mus Washington, Whatcom Mus., Bellingham, Wash., San Barbara Mus., U. Calif., Santa Barbara. Served wit USAAF, 1943-46; ETO. Recipient Bronze medal City o Los Angeles, 1949, Silver medal Calif. State Fair, 195 Home: Santa Barbara Calif.

THOMAS, ROSS ELMORE, author; b. Oklahom City, Feb. 19, 1926; s. J. Edwin and Laura (Dea T. B.A., U. Okla., 1949. Reporter Daily Oklahoma Oklahoma City, 1943-44; pub. relations dir. Na Farmers Union, 1952-56; pres. Stapp, Thomas & Wad Inc., Denver, 1956-57; reporter Bonn, Germany, 195 59; rep. Patrick Dolan & Assos., Ltd., Ibadan, Nigeri 1959-61; cons. U.S. Govt., 1964-66. Author: The Co War Swap, 1966, The Seersucker Whipsaw, 1967, Cast Yellow Shadow, 1967, The Singapore Wink, 196 (pseudoname Oliver Bleeck) The Brass Go-Betwee 1969, The Fools in Town are on Our Side, 1970, Th Back-Up Men, 1971, Protocol for Kidnapping, 197 The Procane Chronicle, 1972, The Porkchoppers, 197 If You Can't Be Good, 1973, The Highbinders, 197 The Money Harvest, 1975, Yellow-Dog Contract, 197 Chinaman's Chance, 1978, The Eighth Dwarf, 1979, Th Mordida Man, 1981, Missionary Stew, 1983, Briarpatc 1984, Out on the Rim, 1987, The Fourth Durang 1989, Twilight at Mac's Place, 1990, Voodoo Ltd., 199 Ah, Treachery, 1994. Served with inf. AUS, 1944-46 Recipient Mystery Writers Am. award for best 1st mys tery, 1966, Edgar award, 1967, 85. Home: Malibu Cali Died Dec. 18, 1995.

THOMPSON, DAVID DUVALL, physician; b. Ithac N.Y., June 1, 1922; s. Homer C. and Clara (Smith) T m. Lynn Poucher, Dec. 22, 1945; children: David D Richard M., Catherine R., Peter L. B.A., Cornell U 1943, M.D., 1946. Diplomate Nat. Bd. Med. Examine (treas. 1984-86, mem. spl. com. to space 1989-92). In tern, resident N.Y. Hosp., N.Y.C., 1946-50; head di metabolism N.Y. Hosp., 1957-65, acting physician chief, 1965-66, dir., 1967-87, cons., 1987-95; vis. pro hosp. adminstrn. Cornell U., 1974-95; coordinator clin edn. Cornell U. Med. Coll., 1987-95; trustee Mut. Li Ins. of N.Y. Mem. State Hosp. Rev. and Plannin Coun., 1982-90; trustee Mary Imogene Bassett Hosp Cooperstown, N.Y., chmn. bd. trustees, 1986-94; b overseers Mt. Desert Island Biol. Lab., 1988-95, truste 1990-95. Recipient Lederle Med. Faculty award, 195 57; Otty award, N.Y.C., 1982; Man of Yr., East Mi Manhattan C. of C., 1983; Spl. Tribute award Great N.Y. Hosp. Assn., 1987; Recognition award Ct Alumni Council, 1988. Fellow ACP; mem AMA, Am Physiol. Soc., Harvey Soc., Am. Soc. Clin. Investigatio Assn. Am. Med. Colls., Am. Fedn. Clin. Research, So Med. Adminstrs. (pres. 1977-78), Greater N.Y. Hos Assn. (chmn. 1979), Hosp. Assn. N.Y. State (chm 1980), Am. Skin Assn., Inc. (bd. dirs. 1988-95), Sigm Xi. Home: Tenafly N.J. Died Apr. 13, 1995.

THOMPSON, JESSE JACKSON, former universit educator, clinical psychologist, consultant; b. Sange Calif., July 26, 1919; s. Lewis Elmer and Lucy Ja (Hamilton) T.; m. Clara Lucile Roy, Feb. 4, 1945; chi dren: Lyle Blair, Carolrae, Jon Royal, Mark Alan. BA Santa Barbara State Coll., 1941; MS in Edn., U. S Calif., 1947, PhD, 1957. Lic. psychologist, speec pathologist, Calif. Speech therapist Pasadena (Calif City Schs., 1947-51; coord. spl. svcs Riverside (Calif County Schs., 1951-53, asst. supt. schs., 1953-56; pro communicative disorders Calif. State U., Long Beac 1956-79, dir. ctr. for health manpower edn., 1970-7 pvt. practice in clin. psychology Westminster and San Ana, Calif., 1979-87; coord. mental health svcs. AID Response Program of Orange County, Garden Grov Calif., 1988-89, 90; adv. bd. Speech and Lang. Dev Ctr., Buena Park, Calif., 1966-93, Nat. Coun. YMC 1970-75, Orange County County YMCA's, 1968-7 pres., 1970-72; pres. West Orange County YMCA, 196 72; cons. Orange County Schs., Santa Ana, Calif., 196 71, Child Devel. Clinic, Long Beach, 1961-64, He Start Program, Compton, Calif., 1967-72. Co-autho Talking Time, 2d edit., 1966, Speech Ways, 195 Phonics, 1962, Rhymes for Fingers and Flannel Boar 1962, 87. Pres. Orange County Community Acti Coun., Santa Ana, 1970-71; chmn. bd. dirs. Oran ıty-Long Beach Health Consortium, Santa Ana, ; vol. AIDS Response Program, Garden Grove, ., 1987-93 (Disting. Svc. award 1992), coord. al health svcs., 1988-89, 90; facilitator AIDS stry Ecumenical Network, 1989-93; mem. constitu- com. Southeastern conf. Seventh-Day Adventist 1966-92, vice chmn., 1989-92, chmn., 1992; mem. titution com. PAcific Union conf., 1992-93. Fellow Speech, Lang. and Hearing Assn.; mem. Calif. ch, Lang. and HEaring Assn. (pres. 1959-60, rs 1979), Christian Assn. Psychol. Studies, Assn. ritii Profs., ACLU, Common Cause, People for the Way. Democrat. Home: Westminster Calif. Died 17, 1993.

)MPSON, JOHN THEODORE, communications ultant; b. Decorah, Iowa, Mar. 5, 1917; s. Theodore er and Bertha (Rod) T.; m. Dorothea Mae Green, 3, 1942; children: Jennifer Lynn, Melinda McLean; essie S. Bennett, Feb. 14, 1987. A.B., U. Mich., . With Gen. Electric Co., 1939-58; mgr. distbn. electronics div. Gen. Electric Co., Schenectady, -58; v.p. Raytheon Co., 1958-62; v.p. IT&T, 1962- sr. v.p., 1967-69; pres., chmn. bd., chief exec. officer ance Ross Corp., 1969-70; v.p. Gen Telephone & tronics Internat. Co., 1970-72; cons., dir. various s. Served to lt. (s.g.) USNR, 1943-46. Mem. Delta ilon, Met. Club (N.Y.C.), Greenwich Country Club, an Harbor Yacht Club. Home: Greenwich Conn. d Jan. 12, 1994.

OMPSON, LEE BENNETT, lawyer; b. Miami, an Ter., Mar. 2, 1902; s. P.C. and Margerie Con- ce (Jackson) T.; m. Elaine Bizzell, Nov. 27, 1928; dren: Lee Bennett, Ralph Gordon, Carolyn Elaine s. Don T. Zachritz). B.A., U. Okla., 1925, LL.B., 7. Bar: Okla. 1927. Since practiced in Oklahoma ; spl. justice Okla. Supreme Ct., 1967-68; past sec., counsel, now dir. Mustang Fuel Corp. Past sec. sonic Charity Found. Okla.; past chmn. Okla. anty chpt. ARC, past chmn. resolutions com. nat. v.; founding mem. Dean's Council, U. Okla. Coll. v; past dir. Oklahoma City Symphony Orch., ahoma City Community Fund. Served to col. AUS, 0-46. Decorated Legion. of Merit; recipient Dist- uished Service citation U. Okla., 1971; Rotary ınd. Paul Harris fellow. Fellow Am. Bar Found. st Okla. chmn.), Okla. Bar Found., Am. Coll. Trial vyers (past Okla. chmn.); mem. Oklahoma City C. of (past bd. dirs.), Oklahoma City Jr. C. of C. (past s.), U.S. Jr. C. of C. (past dir., v.p.), ABA (del. 1972, t mem. com. law and nat. security, past mem. spl. n. on fed. ct. procedure), Okla. Bar Assn. (past mem. dels., pres. 1972, Pres.'s award, profl. responsibility mn.), Oklahoma County Bar Assn. (past pres.), r. Record award), Okla. Bar Found. (trustee 1971- 81-84), U. Okla. Alumni Assn. (past mem. exec. n.), U. Okla. Meml. Student Union (past pres., Greek umnus of Yr. award 1982), Oklahoma City Zool. Soc. st bd. dirs.), Am. Judicature Soc., Mil. Order World ırs, Mil. Order Carabao, Am. Legion, Masons (33 gree), Shriners, Jesters, Rotary (past pres., Paul Harris ow), Univ. Club, Men's Dinner Club (past exec. n.), Oklahoma City Golf and Country Club, Beacon ıb, Phi Beta Kappa (Phi Beta Kappa of Yr. 1982), ta Theta Pi (past v.p., trustee). Democrat. Mem. st Christian Ch. (past deacon, life elder). Home: lahoma City Okla. Died July 22, 1994.

HOMSEN, ROSZEL C., federal judge; b. Balt., Aug. , 1900; s. William Edward and Georgie A. (Cathcart) m. Carol Griffing Wolf, June 1, 1929; children: Ge- ge, Grace (Mrs. Richard M. Babcock), Margaret omsen Moler. Ed., Boys Latin Sch., Balt., 1908-15; B., Johns Hopkins, 1919; LL.B., U. Md., 1922; .D., Goucher Coll., 1967. Asso. law firm Soper, wie & Clark (attys.), 1922-27; partner Clark, omsen & Smith, 1927-54; U.S. dist. judge Dist. Md., 54-92, chief judge, 1955-70; sr. judge; judge spl. ct. egional Rail Reorgn. Act of 1973, 1973-92; Instr. mml. law Johns Hopkins, 1933-43; sec. State Bd. Law aminers, 1943-44; instr. law sch. U. Md., 1952-55; em. Jud. Conf. U.S., 1958-64, mem. adv. com. on civil les, 1960-73; mem. com. to implement Criminal Jus- e Act, 1964-74, mem. interim adv. com. on jud. activ- es, 1969-74, mem. com. on adminstrn. criminial law, 70-73, chmn. standing com. on rules of practice and ocedure, 1973-80. Pres. Bd. School Commrs. Balt., 44-54, Alumni Assn. Johns Hopkins, 1947-48; Trustee eritus, past chmn. bd. Goucher Coll.; v.p. Balt. ouncil Social Agys., 1943-46. Served with S.A.T.C., 18. Mem. ABA, Md. Bar Assn. (pres. 1971), Balt. ır Assn., Delta Upsilon, Delta Theta Phi, Phi Beta appa, Omicron Delta Kappa. Club: Hamilton Street alt.). Home: Baltimore Md. Died March 11, 1992.

HOMSON, BRYDEN, conductor; b. Ayr, Scotland. udent Royal Scottish Acad. Music, Staatliche Hoch- hule Musik, Hamburg, Ger. Asst. condr. BBC Scot- sh Orch., 1958-62; condr. Royal Ballet, 1962-64, Den erske Opera, Oslo, 1964-66, Royal Opera, Stockholm, 966; assoc. condr. Scottish Nat. Orch., 1966-68; prin. ondr. BBC No. Symphony Orch., 1968-73; music dir. lster Orch., 1977-85; artistic dir. No. Ireland Opera rust, 1978-79; prin. condr. BBC Welsh Symphony rch., 1979-91 ; prin. condr. R.T.E. Symphony Orch., 983. Died Nov. 14, 1991. Home: London Eng.

THORNBERRY, WILLIAM HOMER, federal judge; b. Jan. 9, 1909; s. William Moore and Mary Lillian (Jones) T.; m. Eloise Engle, Feb. 24, 1945 (dec. Apr. 27, 1989); children: Molly, David, Kate; m. Marian Harris, Feb. 24, 1990. BBA, U. Tex., 1932, LLB, 1936; LLD, Gallaudet U., 1954. Bar: Tex. Assoc. Powell, Wirtz, Rauhut & Gideon, Austin, Tex., 1936; mem. Tex. Ho. of Reps., 1937-40; dist. atty. 53d jud. dist. Travis County, Tex., 1941-42; ptnr. Jones & Thornberry, Austin, 1946-48; mayor pro tem City of Austin, 1947-48; mem. Ho. of Reps. from 10th Tex. dist., 1949-63; judge U.S. Dist. Ct. (we. dist.) Tex., 1963-65; judge U.S. Ct. Appeals for 5th Cir., 1965-95, now senior judge, 1995; mem. com. to implement criminal justice act Jud. Conf., 1964-79, com. on criminal justice act 5th Jud. Coun., 1967. Mem. city coun. City of Austin, 1946-48. Lt. comdr. USN, 1942-46. Recipient Disting. Alumnus award U. Tex., 1965, Silver Beaver award Boy Scouts Am. Mem. ABA, Tex. State Bar Assn., Travis County Bar Assn., Masons (32d degree), Shriners, Kiwanis, Order of Coif. Died Dec. 12, 1995.

THORNEYCROFT, BARON PETER (GEORGE EDWARD THORNEYCROFT), barrister, former politician; b. July 26, 1909; s. George Edward Mervyn and Dorothy Hope T.; m. Sheila Wells Page, 1938 (div. 1949); 1 son; m. 2d, Carla Roberti, 1949; 1 dau. Student Eton, Royal Mil. Acad., Woolwich. Commd. Royal Arty., 1930, resigned commn., 1933; called to bar, Inner Temple, 1935; practised Birmingham (Oxford Circuit), Stafford, 1938-45, Monmouth, 1945-66; parliamentary sec. Ministry of War Transport, 1945; pres. Bd. Trade, 1951-57; chancellor of Exchequer, 1957-58, resigned; minister of Aviation, 1960-62; minister Def., 1962-64; sec. of State for Def., 1964; chmn. Conservative Party, 1975-81; pres. Forte PLC, 1969-81; chmn. BOTB, 1972-74, Pye of Cambridge Ltd., 1967-69, Brit. Res. Ins. Co. Ltd., 1980-87, Gil, Carvajal & Ptnrs. Ltd., 1981—, Cinzano U.K. Ltd., 1982-85; pres. Pirellis Gen. Cable Works Ltd., Pirelli Ltd. Exhbns. of paintings, Trafford Gallery, 1961, 70. Mem. Royal Soc. Brit. Artists. Home: London Eng.

THORPE, JAMES, III, publisher; b. Augusta, Ga., Sept. 10, 1942; s. James and Elizabeth (Daniells) T.; m. Diantha Chrystal, Oct. 18, 1969; 1 child, Elizabeth McLean. B.A., Swarthmore College, Pa., 1964; Ph.D., Yale U., 1968. Instr. dept. English Brandeis U., Waltham, Mass., 1968-69, Hunter Coll., N.Y.C., 1969-73; editor Shoe String Press, Hamden, Conn., 1974-94, pres., 1980-94, chmn. bd., 1982-94. Fulbright Found. fellow, 1964-65; Woodrow Wilson fellow, 1964; Danforth Found. fellow, 1964-68. Home: North Haven Conn. Died Oct. 24, 1994.

THORPE, MERLE, JR., lawyer, foundation executive; b. Washington, Apr. 25, 1917; s. Merle and Lilian I. (Day) T.; m. Sally Sweetser, Nov. 25, 1983. B.A., Yale U., 1938, LL.B., 1941. Bar: D.C. 1941. With Hogan & Hartson, Washington, 1941-94; partner Hogan & Hartson, 1956-82, of counsel, 1982-94; chmn. Atomics, Physics and Sci. Fund, Washington, 1953-65, Columbian Fin. Corp., 1955-65, Shares in Am. Industry, Inc., Washington, 1959-65, Greater Washington Investors, Inc. 1981-88; asst., assoc. gen. counsel Petroleum Adminstrn. Def., 1950-52. Trustee Am. Near East Refugee Aid; pres. Found. for Middle East Peace; bd. govs. Middle East Inst. Served as officer with Intelligence Service, USNR, 1942-46. Mem. Am., D.C. bar assns., Phi Delta Phi. Episcopalian. Clubs: Lawyers (Washington), Chevy Chase (pres. 1969), Metropolitan, Alfalfa, Alibi, Barristers; Pine Valley Golf (Clementon, N.J.); Yale (N.Y.C.). Home: Chevy Chase Md. Died Feb. 13, 1994.

THORSON, THOMAS BERTEL, zoologist, educator; b. Rowe, Ill., Jan. 12, 1917; s. Thomas B. and Hertha (Fylpaa) T.; m. Margaret L. Overgaard, Dec. 31, 1941; children—Sharon M., Joel T. Student, Waldorf Coll., 1934-36; B.A., St. Olaf Coll., 1938; M.S., U. Wash., 1941, Ph.D., 1952. Faculty Yakima (Wash.) Coll., 1946-48, Calif. State U.-San Francisco, 1952-54, S.D. State U., 1954-56; faculty U. Nebr., Lincoln, 1948-50, 56-95; prof. zoology U. Nebr., 1961-82, prof. emeritus, 1982-95, chmn. dept., 1967-71, vice dir. Sch. Biol. Scis., 1975-77. Editor: Investigations of the Ichthyofauna of Nicaraguan Lakes, 1976. Served to capt. USAAF, 1942-46. Fellow AAAS, Explorers Club, Am. Elasmobranch Soc. (disting.); mem. Am. Inst. Biol. Scis., Am. Soc. Zoologists, Am. Soc. Ichthyologists and Herpetologists, Am. Fisheries Soc., Sigma Xi (pres. Nebr. chpt. 1972-74), Phi Sigma. Home: Tualatin Oreg. Died July 4, 1995.

THOTTUMKAL, THOMAS JOSEPH, priest; b. Kerala, India, Dec. 31, 1934; came to U.S., 1987; s. Joseph Chacko and Elizabeth Thomas (Thayil) T. BA, St. Paul Sem., India, 1966; STL, St. Paul U., 1968; ThM, U. Ottawa, Ont., Can., 1968; MA, McMaster U., 1970; ThD, U. Paris, 1971. Ordained priest Roman Catholic Ch., 1958. Prof. liturgy St. Paul Sem., Trichy, India, 1956-58; parish priest, superior Sophia Ashram and St. Joseph Ch., Kuttiadi, Kozhikode, India, 1959-62; novice master, counsellor Congregation Blessed Sacrament, Kerala, 1962-66; chaplain St. Joseph's Mother House, Hamilton, Ont., 1968-71; prof. theology Toronto (Ont.) Sch. Theology, 1971-86; dir. vocations Archdiocese of Toronto, 1975-80; vice rector St. Augustine's Sem., Toronto, 1976-86; pres. Wadhams Hall Sem.-Coll., Ogdensburg, N.Y., 1987—. Author: Nirchalukal, Palai, 1958, Virunnu, Mannanam, 1958, Priesthood and Apostleship, 1973, Ministry, 1982, People's Spirituality, 1983; mem. editorial bd. Jeevadhara, Aleppy, India. Mem. Coll. Theology Soc., Cath. Theol. Soc. Am. Home: Ogdensburg N.Y. Died June 17, 1992.

THRASH, PURVIS JAMES, SR., retired oil field equipment and service company executive; b. Nacogdoches, Tex., Dec. 6, 1927; s. James David and Elsie Marie (Crenshaw) T.; m. Betty Jo Johnston, Mar. 7, 1931; children: Purvis James Jr., Jan Caroline Thrash Beckman, Jill Marie Thrash Denton. BS in Petroleum Engring., Texas A&M U., 1950. V.p. domestic ops. Otis Engring. Corp., Dallas, 1975-80, sr. v.p. mgf., 1980-81, pres., chief exec. officer, 1981-90, chmn. bd., 1981-90, ret., 1990; mem. exec. com. Halliburton Co., Dallas, 1981-90. Author: (with others) Gas Lift Theory and Practice, 1967; contbr. articles to profl. jours.; patentee in field. Bd. dirs. Dallas Jr. Achievement, 1985. Recipient Outstanding Safety Achievement award Safety Coun. of Greater Dallas, 1987, 89. Mem. Am. Petroleum Inst., Soc. Petroleum Engrs., Nat. Oil-Equipment Mfrs. and Dels. Soc., Dallas Petroleum Club. Republican. Methodist. Home: Dallas Tex. Died Oct. 31, 1995.

THREATT, NED LEON, SR., insurance company executive; b. Lancaster, S.C., Apr. 7, 1922; s. Clifford Stephen Sr. and Henrietta Keller (Whaley) T.; m. Sarah Rebecca Boyd, Mar. 10, 1956; children: Jane Mellicent, Sarah Margaret, Ned Leon Jr. BA in Journalism, U. S.C., 1949. Staff reporter The Columbia (S.C.) Record, 1949-54; dir. news Sta. WMSC-Radio, Columbia, 1954-56; research sec. Office of Gov. of S.C., Columbia, 1957-58, exec. sec., 1958-59; dir. publs. Wilbur Smith and Assocs., Columbia, 1959-64; compliance mgr. Colonial Life & Accident Ins. Co., Columbia, 1964-70, asst. v.p., 1970-74, v.p., compliance and govt. relations, 1974-95; mem. life ins. industry adv. com. N.C. Ins. Dept. Mem. Columbia Mus. Art and Scis., 1982-95; trustee Greater Columbia Children's Choir, 1986-95; chmn. bd. trustees Washington St. United Meth. Ch., Columbia, 1987-95. Served as tech. sgt. U.S. Army, 1943-46, ETO. Mem. Assn. S.C. Life Ins. Cos. (treas. 1986-95, mem. exec. com. 1986-95), Soc. Fin. Examiners (assoc., charter mem.), U.S. Life and Health Compliance Assn., Health Ins. Assn. Am. (mem. S.C. state coun., mem. govt. rels. com.), U. S.C. Alumni Assn., Palmetto Club of Columbia. Home: Columbia S.C. Died Aug. 10, 1995.

THURMAN, MAXWELL R., retired army officer; b. High Point, N.C., Feb. 18, 1931. BSChemE, N.C. State U. Commd. officer U.S. Army, advanced through grades to gen., 1983; dir. program analysis and evaluation Office of Chief of Staff, 1977-79; comdr. U.S. Army Recruiting Command, 1979-81, dep. chief of staff for personnel, 1981-83; vice chief of staff Dept. Army, Washington, 1983-87; mem. Joint Chiefs of Staff, Washington, 1983-87; comdg. gen. Army Tng. and Doctrine Command, Ft. Monroe, Va., 1987-89; comdr. in chief U.S. Forces So. Command, Quarry Heights, Republic Panama, 1989-90; ret., 1991; exec.-in-residence N.S. State U., 1993; bd. visitors N.C. State U.; cons. in field. Decorated D.S.M. with 2 oak leaf clusters, Bronze Star with V device with oak leaf cluster, Def. Disting. Svc. medal with oak leaf cluster, N.C. award Pub. Svc., 1992. Mem. Presdl. Panama Canal Consultative Commn., Presdl. Commn. on Assignment of Women in Armed Forces. Home: Alexandria Va. Died Dec. 1, 1995.

TIBBITTS, SAMUEL JOHN, hospital administrator; b. Chgo., Oct. 7, 1924; s. Samuel and Marion (Swanson) T.; m. Audrey Slottelid, Aug. 28, 1949; children: Scott, Brett. B.S., UCLA, 1949; M.S., U. Calif.-Berkeley, 1950. Adminstrv. resident Calif. Hosp., Los Angeles, 1950-51; adminstrv. asst. Calif. Hosp., 1951-52, asst. supt., 1954-59, admistr., 1959-66; chmn. mgmt. com., asst. sec. Luth. Hosp. Soc. So. Calif., 1962-66, pres., 1966-88; chmn. Pacificare Health Systems, 1979-94; chmn. bd. Health Network Am., 1982-94, Am. Healthcare Systems, 1983-88; now chmn. bd. UniHealth America; asst. supt. Santa Monica (Calif.) Hosp., 1952-54; pres. Commn. for Adminstrv. Services in Hosps., 1963, 64, 67, Calif. Health Data Corp., 1968-71; mem. Calif. Health Planning Council and Steering Com., 1968-94, Los Angeles City Adv. Med. Council, 1971, 73, Pres.'s Com. Health Services Industry, Adv. Health Council, Calif., 1973; mem. adv. panel Pres.'s Cost of Living Council, Price Commn. and Pay Bd., Phase II; mem. Calif. Hosp. Commn., 1974-94; mem. adv. bd. programs health service adminstrn. U. So. Calif. Bd. dirs. Calif. Hosp. Med. Center, Martin Luther Hosp., Henry Mayo Newhall Meml. Hosp.; trustee, exec. com. Blue Cross So. Calif., 1966-75. Served with M.C., U.S. Army, 1946-47. Recipient Service to Humanity award Luth. Mut. Life Ins. Co., Outstanding Achievement award Hosp. Council So. Calif., 1972, ACHE Gold Medal award, 1987, CAHHS Award of Merit, 1987; Lester Breslow Disting. lectr., 1983; named assoc. officer most Venerable Order of St. John, 1972. Fellow Am. Coll. Hosp. Adminstrs.; mem. Am. Hosp. Assn. (chmn. council research and planning 1964-67, trustee 1968-70, chmn. bd. trustees 1978, Meritorious Service citation 1973, Trustees' award 1979), San Diego Hosp. Assn. (dir.), Calif. Hosp. Assn. (pres. 1968-69, trustee 1966-70, Ritz E. Heerman award 1960, Award of Merit, 1987),

Hosp. Council So. Calif. (pres. 1961-62), U. Minn. Alumni Assn. Hosp. and Health Care Adminstrn. (hon.), Delta Omega. Home: San Marino Calif. Died Mar. 21, 1994.

TIEN, JOHN KAI, mechanical engineer, educator; b. China, June 4, 1940; came to U.S., 1942; s. Y.S. and T.L. (Lee) T.; m. Noreen, Dec. 18, 1971; children: Jacqueline, John Jr. M in Engrng., Yale U., 1964; MS, Carnegie-Mellon, 1968, PhD, 1969. Rsch. scientist Pratt & Whitney Aircraft, East Hartford, Conn., 1969-72; prof. Columbia U., N.Y.C., 1972-89; Rashid engring. regents chair U. Tex., Austin, from 1989; chmn. U.S. Secretariat System for S&T Devel. of Materials, N.Y.C. Editor: Superalloys, Supercomposites, Superceramics, 1989, Refractory Alloying Elements in Superalloys, 1984, Ultrasonic Fatigue, 1982, Metallurgical Treatises, 1981, Electron and Positron Spectroscopies in Materials Science and Engineering, 1981, Superalloys-Metallurgy and Manufacture, 1976, Alloy and Microstructural Design, 1976. With U.S. Army. Named Outstanding Young Man of Am., U.S. Jr. C. of C., 1980s, Bradley Stoughton Best Young Prof., 1980s; recipient K.C. Li Gold Medal, 1984. Mem. ASTM, ASME, Sigma Xi, Tau Beta Pi, Am. Soc. Metals, MRS. Republican. Lutheran. Home: Marble Falls Tex. Deceased.

TIMLEN, THOMAS MICHAEL, former banker, consultant; b. Jersey City, Oct. 27, 1928; s. Thomas M. and Catherine (Murphy) T.; m. Elizabeth Egli, June 1, 1957 (div. 1975); children: Thomas John, Daniel Karl. AB cum laude, St. Peter's Coll., Jersey City, 1950; LLB, Harvard U., 1953; cert., Stonier Sch. Banking Rutgers U., 1967. Bar: D.C. 1953, N.Y. 1957. With Fed. Res. Bank N.Y., N.Y.C., 1955-90, sr. v.p., 1973-75, exec. v.p., 1975-76, 1st v.p., chief adminstrv. officer, 1976-88, cons., 1988-90; alt. mem. Fed. Open Market Com., 1976-88; chmn. com. fiscal agy. ops. FRS, 1976-80; chmn. com. on automation svcs., 1981-82; bd. dirs. LBS Bank, N.Y.C. Contbg. author: Financial Crisis, 1977. Former trustee Manhattanville Coll., Purchase, N.Y.; chmn. bd. trustees St. Peter's Coll.; mem. bus. adv. coun. Pace U., 1988-91. Mem. Am. Judicature Soc., Downtown-Lower Manhattan Assn., N.Y. Chamber Commerce and Industry, Econ. Club N.Y., Harvard Law Sch. Alumni Assn. Home: New York N.Y. Died Sept 18, 1991.

TIMMERMAN, GEORGE BELL, JR., judge; b. Anderson, S.C., Aug. 11, 1912; s. George Bell and Mary Vandiver (Sullivan) T.; m. Helen Miller DuPre, Feb. 16, 1936. Student, The Citadel, 1930-34, LL.D. (hon.), 1950; LL.B., U. S.C., 1937, J.D., 1970. Bar: S.C. 1937. Practicing atty. Lexington, S.C., 1937-41, 46-55, 59-67; asst. chief trial atty. S.C. Pub. Service Authority, Charleston, 1941; judge 11th Jud. Circuit S.C., 1967-84, spl. circuit judge, 1984-94; lt. gov. State of S.C., 1947-55, gov., 1955-59; pres. S.C. Democratic Conv., 1948, Lexington County Dem. Conv., 1950; S.C. Dem. committeeman, 1952-53; chmn. S.C. del. Dem. Nat. Conv., 1956; Dem. presdl. elector, 1964. Deacon Bapt. Ch. Served with USNR, 1942-46, PTO, In World War II commanded one of the first rocket launcher ships in the Pacific in the Okinawa Operation, having previously volunteered and served in the Naval Armed Guard as a commissioner naval officer. Mem. ABA, S.C. Bar Assn., Am. Judicature Soc., Lexington C. of C., Am. Legion, Assn. Citadel Men (life), Citadel Inn of Ct. (bencher 1984-94), Wig and Robe, Phi Delta Phi, Pi Kappa Phi, Blue Key.; mem. Woodmen of the World. Lodge: Lions. Home: Batesburg S.C. Died Nov. 29, 1994.

TIMMINS, WILLIAM MONTANA, II, management educator; b. Salt Lake City, Mar. 13, 1936; s. William Montana and Mary Brighton T.; m. Theda Laws, Oct. 14, 1960; children: William Montana III, Clark Brighton, Laurel, Sally, Rebekah. BS, U. Utah, 1960, PhD, 1972; MA, Harvard U., 1962; postdoctoral student, UCLA, 1973. Asst. to gov. State of Utah, Salt Lake City, 1966-69; asst. v.p. U. Utah, Salt Lake City, 1969-71; dir. interstate projects Utah Bd. Edn., Salt Lake City, 1971-74; prof. mgmt. Brigham Young U., Provo, Utah, 1974-89; chmn. of bd. TCI, Inc., Paris; vice chmn. Pioneer Valley Hosp., West Valley, Utah, 1985-88; chmn. Mountain View Hosp., Payson, Utah; bd. dirs. Nat. Congress Hosp. Governing Bds., Washington, 1984-88. Author: Career Education (vols. I and II), 1971, Guide to Improved Employee Relations, 1984, International Economic Policy Coordination, 1985, Nonsmoking in the Workplace, 1989; editor: Comprehensive Educational Planning, 1972; contbr. articles to profl. jours. Chmn. Salt Lake County Youth Services Ctr., 1979-80. Recipient Silver Beaver award Boy Scouts Am., 1974, Carnation Silver Bowl Community Services Council, 1978; Redd fellow Redd Ctr. Brigham Young U., 1982. Mem. Utah Hosp. Assn. Salt Lake City (trustee 1985—, Outstanding Trustee award 1988), Am. Soc. Pub. Adminstrn. (bd. dirs. 1983-85, com. mem. 1981-86), Soc. Profls. in Dispute Resolution, Am. Arbitration Assn., Nat. Assn. Civil Service Commrs. (hon., life, pres. 1982-83), Rocky Mountain Pub. Employer Labor Relations Assn. (v.p. 1980-83), Utah Assn. Civil Service Commrs. (pres. 1979-80), Internat. Personnel Mgmt. Assn. (publs. com. 1985—), Phi Kappa Phi. Republican. Mormon. Home: Salt Lake City Utah Died Feb. 1989.

TIMMS, A. JACKSON, lawyer; b. Lock Haven, Pa., July 13, 1938; s. A.B. and Elizabeth (Vaughan) T.; m. Margaret R. Timms, Dec. 28, 1958 (div. 1983); children: Christie E., A. Jackson III, Margaret Shannon; m. Terrie Guille, Aug. 6, 1983; children: Matthew S., Michael G., Kelly V. BA, Yale U., 1960; LLB, U. Va., 1963. Bar: Va. 1964, U.S. Dist. Ct. (ea. dist.) Va., U.S. Ct. Appeals (4th cir.), U.S. Supreme Ct. Ptnr. Seawell, Dalton, Hughes & Timms, Norfolk, Va., 1964-87, Hunton & Williams, Norfolk, from 1987. Mem. ABA, Maritime Law Assn. U.S., Va. Bar Assn., Virginia Beach Bar Assn., Norfolk Portsmouth Bar Assn. Home: Virginia Beach Va. Deceased.

TINBERGEN, JAN, economist; b. The Hague, The Netherlands, Apr. 12, 1903; s. Dirk Cornelis and Jeannette (Van Eek) T.; m. Tine Johanna de Wit, July 19, 1929 (dec.); children: Tine (Mrs. Adriaan M. Van Peski) (dec.), Elsje (Mrs. Maurits J. Barendrecht), Hanneke (Mrs. Steven Hoentjen), Marianne. D. Physics, SLeiden U., 1929; hon. degree D.Econs., univs. of Helsinki, Durham, Amsterdam, Freiburg, Lisbon, Brussels, Strasbourg, Grenoble, Oslo,, 1929, univs. of Paris, Bilbao, Ghent, Kiel, Bordeaux, Turin, Cluj, Cambridge, 1929. Statistician Central Bur. Stats., The Hague, 1929-45; temporarily attached to League of Nations Secretariat, 1936-38; dir. govt. Central planning bur., The Netherlands, 1945-55; prof. The Netherlands Sch. Econs. (now Erasmus U.), Rotterdam, 1933-73; cons. UN, World Bank, The Netherlands, Surinam, UAR, Turkey, Venezuela; research dir. 20th Century Fund, 1960-62. Author: Economic Policy: Principles and Design, 1956, The Design of Development, 1958, Shaping the World Economy, 1962, Lessons from the Past, 1964, Development Planning, 1967, Income Distribution: Analysis and Policies, 1975, Warfare and Welfare, 1987, World Security and Equity, 1990; co-author: Labor Plan, 1935. Recipient Erasmus prize, 1967, Nobel prize econs., 1969, Four Freedoms award Franklin and Eleanor Roosevelt Inst., 1992. Mem. Nat., Royal Dutch, Royal Flemish, Am. Acad. Sci., Brit. Acad. Sci., French Acad. Sci., Econometric Soc., Am. Econ. Assn., Royal Statis. Soc. Mem. Dutch Labor Party. Home: The Hague The Netherlands Died June 9, 1994; interred The Hague, The Netherlands.

TIPTON, CARL WILLIAM, information management and systems engineering company executive, consultant, army officer; b. Manila, Ark., Feb. 27, 1935; s. John William and Flora Mae (Stutts) T.; m. Shirley Ann Sanders, June 1, 1957; 1 child, Carla Ann. BSME, U. Ark., 1958; MS in Logistics Mgmt. with honors, Fla. Inst. Tech., 1979. Commd. 2d lt. U.S. Army, 1958, advanced through grades to brig. gen., 1991; maintenance advisor Saudi Arabian N.G., 1975-76; comdr. 708th Maintenance Bn., Fed. Republic Germany, 1976-78; student Indsl. Coll. Armed Forces, Washington, 1978-79; exec. to comdg. gen. U.S. Army Materiel Command, Alexandria, Va., 1979-82; comdr. 13th Corps Support Command, Ft. Hood, Tex., 1982-85; dir. nat. maintenance point U.S. Army Tank-Automotive Command, Warren, Mich., 1985-86, dep. comdg. gen., 1986-89; comdg. gen. ETO Material Mgmt. and Movement Ctr. U.S. Army, 1989-91; ret., 1991; project dir. TRESP Assocs., Inc., Alexandria, 1991-93; advisor to bd. dirs. Mil. Benefit Assn., Vienna, Va., 1991-93. Mem. Assn. U.S. Army, Am. Def. Preparedness Assn., Soc. Logistics Engrs. Methodist. Home: Woodbridge Va. Died Dec. 3, 1993; buried Arlington Nat. Cemetery, Arlington, Va.

TOBIAS, CHARLES H., lawyer; b. Detroit, 1945. BA, U. Mich., 1967, JD, 1969. Bar: Mich. 1970. Mem. Honigman Miller Schwartz and Cohn, Detroit; chmn. Mich. state adv. com. U.S. Civil Rights Commn., 1985-87. Mem. State Bar Mich. Home: Detroit Mich. Died 1993.

TOBIAS, CHARLES WILLIAM, chemical engineer, educator; b. Budapest, Hungary, Nov. 2, 1920; came to U.S., 1947, naturalized, 1952; s. Karoly and Elizabeth (Milko) T.; m. Marcia Rous, Sept. 10, 1950 (dec. Jan. 1981); children: Carla, Eric, Anthony.; m. Katalin Voros, June 19, 1982. Dipl. in chem. engring, U. Tech. Scis., Budapest, 1942, Ph.D., 1946, Dr (hon), 1992. Registered profl. engr., Calif. Research, devel. engr. United Incandescent & Elec. Co., Ltd., Ujpest, Hungary, 1942-47; instr. phys. chemistry U. Tech. Scis., 1945-46; mem. faculty U. Calif.-Berkeley, 1947-96, prof. chem. engring., 1960-96, chmn. dept., 1967-72, prof. emeritus, 1991-96; faculty sr. scientist Lawrence Berkeley Lab., 1954-96; assoc. research prof. Miller Inst. Basic Sci., 1958-59. Editor: (with Paul Delahay and Heinz Gerischer) Advances in Electrochemistry and Electrochemical Engineering, 1961-64, (with Heinz Gerischer) Advances in Electrochem. Sci. and Engring., 1990-95; mem. editl. bd. Jour. Applied Electrochemistry. Fellow AAAS, Electrochem. Soc. (assoc. editor jour. 1955-90, v.p. 1967-70, pres. 1970-71, Acheson award 1972, hon. mem. 1977-96, Henry B. Linford award for disting. teaching 1982, Vittorio de Nora Diamond Shamrock award 1990); mem. NAE, Hungarian Acad. Scis. (hon.), Am. Chem. Soc., Am. Inst. Chem. Engrs. (Alpha Chi Sigma award 1983, Founders award 1991), Am. Soc. Engring. Edn., Internat. Soc. Electrochemistry (v.p. 1975-76, pres. 1977-78), Deutsche Bunsen-Gesellschaft, Sigma Xi. Home: Orinda Calif. Died Mar. 3, 1996.

TOLLES, WALTER EDWIN, physicist; b. Moline, Ill. Feb. 1, 1916; s. Walter Edwin and Aileen (Sessions) T. m. Gudrun Kercher, June 11, 1939; 1 dau., Mary Wesley. B.S., Antioch Coll., 1939; M.S., U. Minn., 1941 Ph.D., State U. N.Y., Bklyn., 1969. Asst. Kettering Found., Antioch Coll., 1937- 39; teaching asst. U Minn., 1939-42; physicist div. war research Airborne Instruments Lab., Columbia, 1942-45; supr. Airborne Instruments Lab., Inc., 1945-54, head dept. med. and biol. physics, 1954-68; assoc. prof. obstetrics and gynecology Coll. Medicine, State U. N.Y., Bklyn., 1969-78; pres. Applied Sci. Assocs., Inc., 1979-91; Bd. dirs Inst. Oceanography and Marine Biology, 1959. Fellow N.Y. Acad. Scis. (sci. council 1965-93), IEEE (chmn profl. group bio-med. electronics 1959), AAAS; mem Biophys. Soc., Am. Phys. Soc., Am. Soc. Cytology. Home: Fairfield Va. Died Apr. 13, 1993.

TOMLINSON, MILTON AMBROSE, clergyman; b. Cleveland, Tenn., Oct. 19, 1906; s. Ambrose Jessup and Mary Jane (Taylor) T.; m. Ina Mae Turner, Sept. 18 1928; children: Wanda Jean (Mrs. Hugh Ralph Edwards), Carolyn Joy (Mrs. Verlin Dean Thornton). Ed Tenn. pub. schs. Printer, Herald Printing Co., Cleveland, ten years; pastor ch. Henderson, Ky., 1 yr.; gen overseer Ch. of God of Prophecy, Cleveland, 1943-90 gen. overseer emeritus, 1990-95; editor and pub. Th White Wing Messenger; pres. Bible Tng. Inst., chmn trustees. Author: Basic Bible Beliefs. Pres., Tomlinso Home for Children. Home: Cleveland Tenn. Died Apr 26, 1995.

TOMPKINS, JAMES MCLANE, insurance compan executive, government adviser; b. Balt., Jan. 1, 1913; s John Almy and Frederica (McLane) T.; m. Barbar Miller, Nov. 22, 1965. Grad, Phillips Acad., 1931; BA with hons., Yale U., 1935, MA (Pierson Coll. fellow 1940-43), 1943; certificate grad. study labor relations NYU. Dir. undergrad. placement Bur. Appointment instr. Yale U., 1936-40, rsch. fellow, 1937-40; dir. Bur Mil. Service and Information, Yale and Dept. Def. 1940-43; dir. exec. placement, asst. chmn. bd. Vic Chem. Co., N.Y.C., 1943-48; with C.V. Starr & Co Inc., N.Y.C., 1948—, v.p. public affairs, 1968—; cons C.V. Starr & Co., Inc., 1979—, also dir.; dir. Am. Internat. Underwriters Overseas, TAM Sigorta, Turkey chmn. AIU Pakistan, Vt. Accident Ins. Co. Int Uganda Am. Ins. Co., AIU Mediterranean, Inc.; vic chmn. bd. Am. Life Ins. Co., Wilmington, Del.; advise WGM FOG, Norfolk, Va., 1988. Mem. U.S. delegatio UN Conf. Trade and Devel., 1968—; adviser U.S. dele gation OECD, 1969—; mem. U.S. Maritime Transpor Com.; mem. U.S. del. London Diplomatic Conf. Mari time Claims, 1976, Geneva Conf. Multi Modal Trans port, 1975, 77, 78, 79; spl. rep. internat. affairs Internat Ins. Adv. Council, 1967—; pres. James M. Tompkin Co., 1987—; adv. bd. Sta. WMFOG, 1987—; Truste Asia Soc., Samuel Goodyear Scholarship Fund (Yale) chmn. Eisenhower Fellowship Com., Pakistan, 1955-60 mem. Yale Alumni Bd. Recipient Spl. Cert. of Ap preciation Internat. Ins. Adv. Council, 1981-82, Grand Cross Knights Holy Sepulchre. Mem. Yale Alumn Assn. (pres. New Canaan chpt., Yale Class 1935 Alumn Fund rep.), Co. Mil. Historians, Miniature Figure Col lectors Am., Alpha Sigma Phi (past nat. trustee). Clubs Yale (N.Y.C.), India House (N.Y.C.), Sky (N.Y.C.) American (London); Sind (Karachi, Pakistan); Mory' Assn. N.H., Conn. Home: Hartfield Va.

TONHA, PEDRO MARIA, Angola minister of defen se. Min. def. Govt. of Angola, Luanda. Died July 22 1995.

TOOLEY, WILLIAM HENRY, pediatrics educator; b Berkeley, Calif., Nov. 18, 1925; s. William Henry and Margaret (Bailey) T. Student, Carrol Coll.-Helena Mont., 1943-45; M.D., U. Calif., 1949. Intern U.S Naval Hosp., San Diego, 1949-50; pediatrics intern U Calif. Hosps., San Francisco, 1950-51, resident in pedia trics, 1955-56, chief newborn service, 1962-71, chief div pediatric chest disease, 1971-92; sr. staff mem. Cardi ovascular Research Inst., San Francisco, 1968-92, pro pediatrics, 1974-92; mem. sub-bd. perinatal-neonata pediatrics Am. Bd. Pediatrics, 1973-80. Served wit USN, 1943-46, 49-54. John and Mary Markle scholar i acad. medicine, 1963-68. Mem. Am. Acad. Pediatric (com. on fetus and newborn 1968-74, 76-78, chmn. sec on perinatal pediatrics 1975-77, co-editor Standards an Recommendations for Hosp. Care of the Newbor 1977), Soc. for Pediatric Research, Am. Pediatric Soc Soc. Critical Care Medicine, Perinatal Research Soc Soc. for Research in Child Devel., Fleishner Soc., We tern Soc. Physicians, Alpha Omega Alpha. Home: Sa Francisco Calif. Died June 17, 1992.

TOP, FRANKLIN HENRY, JR., physician, researche b. Detroit, Mar. 1, 1936; s. Franklin Henry Sr. an Mary (Madden) T.; m. Lois Elizabeth Fritzell, Sept. 2 1961; children: Franklin H. III, Brian N., Andre M. BS, Yale U., 1957, MD cum laude, 1961. Diplo mate Am. Bd. Pediatrics. Intern, resident, infectio diseases fellow U. Minn. Hosps., Mpls., 1961-6 commd. officer U.S. Army, advanced through grades col.; med. officer, dept. virus diseases Walter Re Army Inst. Research, Washington, 1966-70, chief dep virus diseases, 1973-76, dir. div. communicable diseas and immunology, 1976-79, dep. dir., 1979-81, dir. ar comdt., 1983-87; chief dept. virology Seato Me earch Lab., Bangkok, 1970-73; comdr. U.S.A. Med. earch Inst. of Chem. Def., Aberdeen Proving und, Md., 1981-83; ret. U.S. Army, 1987; sr. v.p. xis Biologics Inc., Rochester, N.Y., 1987-88; exec. , med. dir. MedImmune, Inc., Gaithersburg, Md., n 1988. Contbr. over 40 articles to med. jours. corated Legion of Merit with 2 oak leaf clusters. low Am. Acad. Pediatrics, Infectious Diseases Soc. .; mem. AMA, Am. Assn. Immunologists, Alpha ega Alpha. Home: Rockville Md. Deceased.

RNQUIST, HAROLD EVERETT, insurance comy executive; b. St. Joseph, Mich., Nov. 6, 1918; s. lton Leonard and Lillian Harriet (Pope) T.; m. Mary abeth Gordon, 1958; children: John, Susan, Carolyn, ie. BA in Polit. Sci, U. Calif., Berkeley, 1940; postd., UCLA, 1942. With Johnson & Higgins Calif., 40-48; ins. agt. and broker, 1948-55; v.p. Hollandn. Ins. Co., 1955-56; exec. v.p. Corp. Insurers Seres, 1957-58; pres. New Providence Corp., 1958-78; c. v.p., then pres. Appalachian Ins. Co., 1966-78; s. Affiliated FM Ins. Co., 1971-78; sr. v.p., then exec. . Allendale Mut. Ins. Co., 1972-78; pres., treas. Inn Mountain Mgmt. Corp., Lakeville, Conn., 1978—; s., chief exec. officer, dir. Am. Bristol Ins. Co., Prolence, 1978-80; chmn. bd., pres. Walton Ins. Ltd., milton, Bermuda, 1980-83, also bd. dirs.; chmn. bd., ef exec. officer Sheldon Investments, Ltd., Hamilton, 90—; pres., treas. Indian Mountain Mgmt. (Bermuda) d., Hamilton, 1990—; bd. dirs. Offshore Ins. Mgmt. ., Ft. Worth. Served as officer USNR, 1943-46. em. Delta Phi Epsilon, Pi Sigma Alpha. Clubs: iversity (Providence); Sharon (Conn.) Country. ome: Pembroke Bermuda

ORREY, JOHN GORDON, plant physiologist, edutor; b. Phila., Feb. 22, 1921; s. William Edward and sie Davis (Gordon) T.; m. Norah Jamison Lea-Wilson, ne 1949; children: Jennifer, Joanna, Susan, Sarah, rolyn. BA, Williams Coll., 1942; MA, Harvard U., 47, PhD, 1950. Instr. to assoc. prof. dept. botany U. alif., Berkeley, 1949-60; prof. dept. biology Harvard ., Cambridge, 1960-91; prof., dir. Harvard Forest arvard U., Petersham, Mass., 1984-90, prof. emeritus, 991-93. Author: Plants in Action, 1956, Development Flowering Plants, 1967; editor: Development and unction of Roots, 1976, Biology of Frankia, 1983, pplication of Continuous and Steady-State Methods to oot Biology, 1989. Capt. U.S. Army, 1943-46. Merck . fellow, 1956-57, Guggenheim fellow, 1965-66; Fulight scholar, 1984. Fellow AAAS, Nat. Acad. Sci. ome: Greenfield Mass. Died Jan. 7, 1993; cremated.

OVE, SAMUEL B., biochemistry educator; b. Balt., ly 29, 1921; s. Max George and Sylvia (Gotthelf) T.; . Shirley Ruth Weston, July 22, 1945; children: ichael, Nancy, Deborah. BS, Cornell U., 1943; PhD, . Wis., 1950. Asst. prof. N.C. State U., Raleigh, 1950-5, assoc. prof., 1955-60, prof., 1960-75, William Neal eynolds prof., 1975-94. Fellow AAAS, Am. Inst. of utrition. Home: Raleigh N.C. Died Dec. 31, 1994.

OVSTONOGOV, GEORGIY ALEKSANDROVICH, heatrical director, educator; b. Tbilsi, Georgia, Russia, ept. 28, 1915; s. Aleksandr and Tamara (Papitashvili) .; ed. Lunacharsky Inst. Theatrical Art; m., 2 sons. ctor and asst. dir. Jr. Theatre, Tbilisi, 1931; dir. riboyedov Russian Drama Theatre, Tbilisi, 1938-46, entral Children's Theatre, Moscow, 1946-49, Leninrad Komsomol Theatre, 1950-56; chief dir. Leningrad tate Drama Theatre, 1956—; chmn. directing Leninrad Inst. Theatre, Music and Cinema, 1962—; prodns. nclude: Kremlin Chimes, 1940, School for Scandal, 942, Pompadours, 1954, Irkutsk Story, 1960, Woe from Wit, 1962, Virgin Soil Upturned, 1964, Three Sisters, 964, The Idiot, 1966, Merchants, 1966, Khanuma, 973. Recipient State prize, 1950, 52, 68; named People's Artist, 1957; decorated Order of Lenin (2), Order of Red Banner. Co-editor Theatre monthly; author: Notes on the Theatre, 1960; Talking about Directing, 1962; On Being a Director, 1965; My Thoughts at Large, 1972. Home: Leningrad Russia

TOWEY, MARIE ELIZABETH, nursing administrator, educator; b. Salem, Mass., Jan. 13, 1934; d. Daniel and Mary Catherine (Buckley) Linehan; m. Carroll Francis Towey, Aug. 24, 1957; children: Mary Ellen Towey Roth, Michael Carroll, Kevin James. Diploma Burdett Coll., 1952; R.N., Salem Hosp. Sch. Nursing, 1955; postgrad. Boston Coll. Sch. Nursing, 1956-61; B.S., Salem State Coll., 1975, M.Ed. in Health Counseling and Guidance, 1978. R.N., Mass., Va., D.C, Md., W.Va. Staff nurse Salem Hosp. and Mass. Gen. Hosp., 1955; nursing instr. Salem Hosp. (Mass.), 1955-59, med. nursing supr., 1960-61; staff nurse Twin Oaks Nursing Home, Danvers, Mass., 1961-71, Mt. Pleasant Hosp., Lynn, Mass., 1971; social worker, nurse NIMH Tng. Grant, Malden Ct. Clinic (Mass.), 1972-73; region IV coord. North Shore Coun. on Alcoholism, Danvers, 1973-74; community mental health nurse Danvers-Salem Community Mental Health Resources Unit, Salem, 1974-78; nurse instr. Med. Aid Tng. Sch., Washington, 1978-79, Fairfax County Div. Continuing Edn. med. div., Woodson High Sch. (Va.), 1979-80; dir. nursing and health svcs. ARC, Alexandria, 1980-81; dir. nursing svcs. Med. Pers. Pool, Alexandria, 1981-82, adminstr., 1982-84; adminstr. ambulatory care ctr. Medic 24-Ltd., Baileys Crossroads, Va., from 1984; adminstr. Am. Med. Svcs., Springfield, Va., 1984-85; dir. nursing svc. Camelot Hall Nursing Facility, Arlington, Va., 1985-86, Clinton Convalescent Ctr., Md., 1986; auditing supr., trainor Intracorp, Falls Church, Va., 1986-91; mgr. med. review svcs., nursing coord. FORTIS Corp., Vienna, Va., from 1991; lectr. in field. Co-author planning grant in mental health and mental retardation, 1978. V.p. Mass Soc. of D.C., from 1991; area chmn. Burke Centre Conservancy (Va.), 1981-88; mem. town meeting Danvers Town Govt., 1971-78; pres. Mass. Region IV Mental Health and Mental Retardation Adv. Coun., 1977-78; sec., treas. Mass. Area Bd. Coalition, 1977-78; trustee Danvers State Hosp., 1977-82; community mental health resources devel. unit com. chmn. Danvers-Salem Area Mental Health Retardation Bd., 1973-78, pres., 1975-77; chmn. emergency med. svcs. com. North Shore Coun. on Alcoholism, 1972-76; mem. adv. com. for adult edn. North Shore Region, 1974-75; mem. Danvers Task Force on Deinstitutionalization, 1975-76; bd. dirs. Archdiocesan Coun. Cath. Nurses, 1969-72. Recipient Merit and Appreciation certs. various agys., socs. and hosps. Mem. Am. Nurses Assn. (membership com. from 1983), Va. Assn. Rehab. Nurses, Va. Nurses Assn. (hospitality com. 1983), Va. Assn. Home Health Agys. (chmn. region I legis., rep. 1984-86), D.C. Nurses Assn. (conf. com. 1982), Health Adminstrs. Assn. of Nat. Capitol Area, Salem Hosp. Alumnae Assn. (past treas. and chmn. program 1956-58, 60-64), Alexandria C. of C. Republican. Club: Danvers Garden (pres., chmn. civic beautification 1972-77). Deceased. Home: Fairfax Va.

TOWN, HAROLD BARLING, artist; b. Toronto, Ont., Can., June 13, 1924; s. William Harry and Ellen (Watson) T.; m. Trudella Carol Tredwell, Sept. 7, 1957; children—Heather Allison, Shelley Catherine. Grad., Ont. Coll. Art, 1944; Litt.D. (hon.), York U., Toronto, 1966. Bd. govs. Ont. Coll. Art. Exhibited, Venice Biennale, 1956, 64, 72, Sao Paulo Biennale, 1957, 61, 2d to 6th expn., Gravure, Ljubljana, Yugoslavia, Documenta, Kassel, Germany, 1964, Carnegie Internat., 1964, Arte of Am. and Spain, 1964-65, 1st Brit. Internat. Print Biennale, Bradford, 1968, Can. 101 Edinburgh, Scotland, Internat. Festival, 1968, 7th Biennial Canadian Painting, Ottawa, 1968, Ont. Pavillion, Expo 70, Japan, one-man show, Robert McLaughlin Gallery Civic Centre, Oshawa, 1973, retrospective, 1944-1975 at, Windsor Art Gallery, 1975, retrospective portrait exhbn., 1980; represented in permanent collections including those of, Mus. Modern Art, N.Y.C., Guggenheim Mus., Tate Gallery, London, Stedelijk Mus., Amsterdam, Bklyn. Mus., Detroit Art Inst., Met. Mus. Art, Nat. Gallery Can., York U., others, murals for, St. Lawrence Seaway, Power Dam, Cornwall, Ont., 1958, mural and sculpture, Malton Internat. Airport, Ont., 1962-63, mural, Telegram Bldg., Toronto, 1963, Queen's Park Project, Toronto, 1967, initial opening poster, Ontario Place, Provincial Govt. Can., 1971; (recipient Arno prize Sao Paulo Biennale 1957, internat. prize exhbn. drawings and prints, Lugano, Switzerland 1958, Allied Arts medal Royal Archtl. Inst. Can. 1981, fellow Instituto de Cultura Hispanica-Arte de America y Espana, Madrid 1963); Author: Albert Franck, 1974; Author, illustrator: Enigmas, 1964, Banner and Symbol . . . Founders College, York U, 1965, Silent Stars, Sound Stars, Film Stars, 1971, (with David Silcox) Tom Thomson (The Silence and the Storm), 1977 (Can. Booksellers Assn. award), Murphy the Wonder Dog, 1987; Decor and costumes House of Atreus, Nat. Ballet Co. of Can., 1964, The Drawings of Harold Town, 1969; Columnist Toronto Life Mag.; retrospective Art Gallery of Ont., Toronto, 1986, Can. House Cultural Ctr., London, 1987, Ctr. Culturel Can., Paris, 1987-88, Musée Québec, 1988. Decorated officer Order Can., 1968; recipient Centennial medal, 1967, award of merit for disting. public service City of Toronto, 1979; named hon. fellow Founders Coll., York U., Toronto. Mem. Toronto Art Dirs. Club, Royal Canadian Acad. Home: Toronto Can. Died Dec. 27, 1990.

TOWNLEY, PRESTON, association executive, former dean; b. Mpls., May 10, 1939; s. Francis Reid and Marie Rita (Prestin) T.; m. Marcia Kinnear, June 5, 1962; children: Patrick, Alison, Michael. AB, Harvard U., 1960, MBA, 1962. Staff asst., asst. brand mgr. Procter & Gamble Co., 1962-64; with Gen. Mills, Inc., Mpls., 1964-83; v.p., gen. mgr. Big G div. Gen. Mills, Inc., 1973-76, group v.p. consumer foods, 1976-80, exec. v.p. consumer foods, 1981-83; dean Sch. Mgmt. U. Minn., Mpls., 1984-88; pres., chief exec. officer The Conf. Bd., 1988-94; bd. dir. Donaldson Co., Goodmark Foods Inc., TCF Fin. Corp. Bd. dirs. Sta. KTCA-TV, 1983-88, Cricket Theatre, 1975-81, pres., 1977-79; bd. dirs. St. Paul Chamber Orch., 1977-84, v.p., 1981-84; bd. dirs. Urban Coalition of Mpls., 1980-84. White House fellow, 1967-68. Mem. Coun. Foreign Rels., Harvard Alumni Assn. (regional dir. 1979-82, v.p. 1982-85, 1st v.p. 1987-88, pres. 1988-89), Harvard Club of N.Y.C. (v.p.). Home: New York N.Y. Died Sept. 30, 1994.

TOWNSEND, MAURICE KARLEN, college president; b. Yakima, Wash., Feb. 9, 1926; s. Marion J. and Marie (Karlen) T.; m. Lucille Schoolcraft, Sept. 8, 1956; children: Leslie, Leah, Steven, Bradley. A.B. cum laude, Boston U., 1949; A.M., U. Chgo., 1950, Ph.D., 1954. Lectr. U. Chgo., 1953-56; instr. Ill. Inst. Tech., 1954-56; asst. to dir. Pub. Adminstrn. Clearing House, Chgo., 1954-56; asst. prof. and research asst. U. Va., Charlottesville, 1956-57; mem. field staff Pub. Adminstrn. Service, Chgo., 1957-59; adminstr. Sperry Gyroscope Co., Lake Success, N.Y., 1959-63; acad. dean Moorhead (Minn.) State Coll., 1963-66; dean Stanislaus State Coll., Turlock, Calif., 1966-68; v.p. Ind. State U., Terre Haute, 1969-75; pres. W. Ga. Coll., Carrollton, 1975-93; pres. Gulf So. Conf., 1988-90. Chmn. bd. dirs. So. Atlantic Conf., 1978-79; trustee Ga. Coun. Econ. Edn., 1976-93; mem. dist. com. Carroll County coun. Boy Scouts Am., 1979-80, mem. exec. bd. Atlanta Area coun., 1983-93. With USAAF, 1944-45. Named Hon. Alumnus W. Ga. Coll., 1985. Mem. AAUP, Am. Polit. Sci. Assn., Am. Soc. Pub. Adminstrn., Inst. for Mgmt. Scis., Inst. Coll. and Univ. Adminstrs. of Am. Coun. Edn., Am. Assn. Higher Edn., Am. Assn. Univ. Adminstrs., So. Assn. Colls. and Schs. (mem. commn. colls. 1993, mem. exec. coun. 1993), Ga. Assn. Colls. (v.p. 1987-88, pres. 1988-89), Rotary (Paul Harris fellow), Phi Beta Kappa, Omicron Delta Kappa, Phi Beta Lambda (hon.), Phi Delta Kappa, Pi Sigma Alpha, Phi Delta Theta, Order of Omega, Beta Gamma Sigma, Phi Kappa Phi, Alpha Lambda Delta. Home: Carrollton Ga. Died May 16, 1993.

TRAUTMANN, LES RAYMOND, editor; b. S.I., N.Y., July 18, 1918; s. Henry E. and Bertha (Strofield) T.; m. Virginia Mackoy, Aug. 21, 1943; 1 dau., Julie. BA, Wagner Coll., 1940; MS, Columbia, 1941; LHD, St. Johns U., 1973; LittD, Wagner Coll., 1989. Reporter S.I. Advance, 1940-41, editorial writer, 1946-53, editorial page editor, 1955-60, city editor, 1961-64, editor, 1965-92; editor editorial page St. Petersburg (Fla.) Times, 1954-55. Interview show host, WNYC-TV, 1970-72. Alumni pres. Wagner Coll., 1953-54. Served to capt. AUS, 1942-46. Recipient Distinguished Journalism award Columbia, 1971, Distinguished Citizen award Wagner Coll., 1971, Pres.' medal Coll. Staten Island, 1984. Mem. Am. Soc. Newspaper Editors. Democrat. Home: Staten Island N.Y. Died Feb. 17, 1992; buried Locust Grove Cemetary, Farragut, Iowa.

TREADGOLD, DONALD WARREN, historian, educator; b. Silverton, Oreg., Nov. 24, 1922; s. Frederic Vere and Mina Belle (Hubbs) T.; m. Alva Adele Granquist, Aug. 24, 1947; children: Warren Templeton, Laura Margaret, Catherine Mina. B.A., U. Oreg., 1943; M.A., Harvard U., 1947; D.Phil. (Rhodes scholar 1947), U. Oxford, Eng., 1950. Mem. faculty U. Wash., Seattle, 1949-94; prof. history U. Wash., 1959-93; prof. emeritus U. Wash., Seattle, 1994; chmn. dept. U. Wash., 1972-82, chmn. Russian and East European program, Sch. Internat. Studies, 1983-86, annual faculty lectr., 1980; vis. prof. Nat. Taiwan U., Taipei, 1959; vis. research prof. USSR Acad. Scis., Moscow, 1965, 82, Toyo Bunko, Tokyo, 1968; scholar-in-residence Villa Serbelloni, Bellagio, Italy, 1982; John A. Burns Disting. vis. prof. history U. Hawaii, Manoa, 1986-87; chmn. Far Western Slavic Conf., 1961-62, Conf. on Slavic and East European History of Am. Hist. Assn., 1965, mem. council, 1960-63; chmn. joint com. Slavic studies Social Sci. Research Council and Am. Council Learned Socs., 1962-64; chmn. organizing com. XIV Internat. Congress Hist. Scis., San Francisco, 1975; chmn. program com. III World Congress Soviet and East European Studies, Washington, 1985; mem. acad. council Kennan Inst. for Advanced Russian Studies, 1977-81, chmn., 1986-91; trustee Nat. Council Soviet and East European Research, 1977-84. Author: Lenin and His Rivals, 1955, reprint, 1976, Spanish transl., 1958, The Great Siberian Migration, 1957, reprint, 1976, Twentieth Century Russia, 7th edit, 1990, Malay transl., 1986, The West in Russia and China, 2 vols, 1973, 85, A History of Christianity, 1979, Freedom: A History, 1990; also articles; editor: The Development of the USSR, 1964, Spanish transl., 1969, Soviet and Chinese Communism, 1967, Slavic Review, 1961-65, 68-75, (with P.F. Sugar) A History of East Central Europe, Vols. I, 1993, III, 1994, V, VII-IX, 1974-77, Vol. VI, 1984, (with Lawrence Lerner) Gorbachev and the Soviet Future, 1989. Trustee Bush Sch., 1973-76. Served to capt. AUS, 1943-46. Decorated Bronze Star; recipient E. Harris Harbison award, 1968, Saionji Fgn. Area Studies profl. award, 1991; Ford fellow, 1954-55; Rockefeller grantee, 1959, 61; Guggenheim fellow, 1964-65; Phi Beta Kappa vis. scholar, 1974-75. Fellow Am. Acad. Arts and Scis.; mem. Am. Hist. Assn. (mem. council 1970-73, v.p. Pacific Coast br. 1977-78, pres. 1978-79), Am. Assn. Advancement Slavic Studies (dir. 1968-75, Distinguished Service award 1975, pres. 1977-78, Disting. Contbr. to Slavic Studies award 1988), Am. Assn. Rhodes Scholars, Internat. House of Japan, Phi Beta Kappa (council nominating com. 1973-78, chmn. 1977-78), Sigma Delta Pi. Club: United Oxford and Cambridge U. Home: Seattle Wash. Died Dec. 13, 1994.

TREURNICHT, ANDRIES PETRUS, political official; b. Piketberg, Republic South Africa, Feb. 19, 1921; s. Andries Petrus and Hester Johanna (Albertyn) T.; m. Engela Helena Dreyer, Jan. 18, 1949; children: Elsa, Lise, Elana, Andriette. BA, U. Stellenbosch, Republic South Africa, 1941; MA, U. Capetown, Republic South Africa, 1951, PhD, 1957. Minister religion Dutch Reformed Ch., Republic South Africa, 1946-60, editor die kerkbode, 1960-67, accessor of Synod, 1965-69; editor Hoofstad Perskor, Republic South Africa, 1967-71; mem. parliament Nat. Party, Republic South Africa,

1971-82; dep. minister Republic South Africa Govt., 1976-79, minister, 1979-82; leader Conservative Party, Republic South Africa, 1982-93, Ofcl. Opposition Party, Republic South Africa, 1987-93. Author 17 books; contbr. articles on culture, politics and religion to profl. jours. Decorated Republic South Africa Govt. Home: Pretoria South Africa Died Apr. 22, 1993; buried Old Cemetery, Pretoria, South Africa .

TRIAS, JOSE ENRIQUE, lawyer; b. San Juan, P.R., Nov. 14, 1944; s. Jose and Jane (Grimes) Trias-Monge; children: Alexander J., Margaret K.; m. Julie Noel Gilbert, May 18, 1985. B.A. magna cum laude, Harvard Coll., 1966; LL.B., Yale U., 1969. Bar: P.R. 1970, N.Y. 1971, Mass. 1973, U.S. Ct. Appeals (2d cir.) 1974, U.S. Tax Ct. 1974, U.S. Dist. Ct. (so. dist.) N.Y. 1974, U.S. Ct. Claims 1974, U.S. Supreme Ct. 1980, D.C. 1981, U.S. Ct. Appeals (fed. cir.) 1982. Prof. U. P.R., San Juan, 1969-70; assoc. Paul, Weiss, Rifkind, Wharton & Garrison, N.Y.C., 1971-72, 73-78, ptnr., 1978-91; assoc. Hill & Barlow, Boston, 1972-73; v.p., gen. counsel, sec. Howard Hughes Med. Inst., Chevy Chase, Md., 1992-94; bd. dirs. P.R. Legal Def. and Edn. Fund, Inc., 1978-86, mem. exec. com., 1978-86, vice-chmn., 1980-86; mem. Sheridan Sch. bd. trustees, 1992-94. Woodrow Wilson fellow, 1966; NSF scholar, 1966; John Harvard scholar, 1965. Mem. ABA (adv. bd. internat. human rights trial observer project 1987, govt. submissions com. sect. on taxation 1983-88, affirmative action com. 1984, legal edn. and admission to bar com. 1982-84), N.Y. State Bar Assn. (mem. com. on U.S. activities of fgn. taxpayers 1986-89, com. on tax policy 1987-91), Mass. Bar Assn., D.C. Bar Assn., Colegio de Abogados de P.R., Phi Beta Kappa. Democrat. Home: Bethesda Md. Died May 14, 1994; interred Georgetown, Washington, D.C.

TRIFFIN, BARON ROBERT, economics educator emeritus; b. Flobecq, Belgium, Oct. 5, 1911; emigrated to U.S., 1939, naturalized, 1942; s. Francois and Céline (van Hooland) T.; m. Lois Brandt, May 30, 1940; children: Nicholas, Marc Kerry, Eric. PhB, Louvain U., 1933, Dr. en Droit, 1934, Licencié en Econs., 1935, Dr. honoris causa, 1970; MA in Econs., Harvard U., 1938, PHD in Econs., 1938; Dr. honoris causa, U. New Haven, 1976, Am. Coll. Switzerland, 1982. Lectr. econs. U. Louvain, Belgium, 1938-39; instr. econs. Harvard, 1939-42; chief Latin Am. sect. bd. of govs. FRS, 1942-46; dir. exchange control div. IMF, Washington, 1946-48; head rep. in Europe, observer OEEC Payments Commn., Paris IMF, 1948-49; spl. adviser, alt. U.S. rep. Mng. Bd. European Payments Union European Recovery Adminstrn., Paris, 1949-51; prof. econs. Yale U., 1951-80, Peletiah Perit chair in polit. and social sci., 1958-67, Frederick William Beinecke prof. econs., 1967-80, master Berkeley Coll., 1967-77; prof. emeritus U. Louvain-la-Neuve; vis. prof. Cath. U. Louvain, Belgium, 1977-82; part-time cons. UN Econs. Commns. for Europe, Africa, Asia, Far East, Jean Monnet's Action Com. for U.S. of Europe., Commn. European Communities, other internat. orgns. as CEPAL, Bellagio Group, Ctr. for Arab Unity Studies, Arab Monetary Fund, nat. ministries of fin. and cen. banks Paraguay, Guatemala, Dominican Republic, Ecuador, Israel, others, 1951-93; cons. U.S. State Dept. and Council Econ. Advisers to Pres. Truman, Eisenhower and Kennedy; mem. bd. economists Time Mag. Author: Monopolistic Competition and General Equilibrium Theory, 1940, Monetary and Banking Reform in Paraguay, 1946, Monetary and Banking Legislation of the Dominican Republic, (with H.C. Wallich), 1953, Monetary Reconstruction in Europe, 1952, Europe and the Money Muddle, From Bilateralism to Near- Convertibility, 1947-56, 1957, Gold and the Dollar Crisis, the Future of Convertibility, 1960, The Evolution of the International Monetary System, Historical Reappraisal and Future Perspectives, 1964, The World Money Maze: National Currencies in International Payments, 1966, Our International Monetary System: Yesterday, Today and Tomorrow, 1968, Fate of the Pound, 1969, How to Arrest a Threatening Relapse into the 1930's, 1971; editor (with Rauner S. Masera) Europe's Money: Problems of European Monetary Coordination and Integration, 1984; contbr. numerous articles to profl. jours. Recipient Wells prize in econs. Harvard U., 1940; de Laveleye prize and Gouverneur Cornez prize, Belgium, 1970, First Internat. prize for econs. San Paolo, 1987, Frank E. Seidman disting. award in polit. economy Rhodes Coll., Biancamano Medaille d'ordu mérite european, 1972; decorated Orden del Merito Paraguay, 1944, Commdr. Ordre del Quetzal, Guatamala, 1971, Commdr. Order de la Couronne, Belgium, 1973; conferred title of Baron by King of Belgium, 1989. Mem. World Acad. Art and Sci., Am. Acad. Arts and Scis., Am. Econ. Assn. (v.p. 1967-68), Académie Royale de Belgique, Council Fgn. Relations, Société d'Economie Politique (France and Belgium). Roman Catholic. Home: Louvain Belgium Died Feb. 23, 1993.

TRINH VAN-CAN, JOSEPH-MARIE CARDINAL, archbishop of Hanoi (Vietnam); b. Trac But, Vietnam, Mar. 19, 1921. Ordained priest Roman Catholic Ch., 1949; held various offices in Hanoi archdiocese; ordained titular bishop of Ela (with personal title of archbishop) and coadjutor archbishop of Hanoi, 1978, elevated to Sacred Coll. Cardinals, 1979, Archbishop of Hanoi, 1978—; titular ch. St. Mary in Via. Author: The New Testament (in Vietnamese), 1975, Four Manners of Meditating The Way of the Cross, 1983, Four Ways of Adoration Before The Blessed Sacrament, 1985, (liturgical songs) The Bible (Old and New Testament in Vietnamese), 1987, The Prayer, 1988, Manuel of Seminarists and Priests, 1989; also books of liturgical songs (3), sacraments and benedictions and consolation for the sick. Mem. Congregation: Evangelization of Peoples. Home: Hanoi Vietnam

TROTTER, MILDRED, anatomist, educator; b. Monaca, Pa., Feb. 3, 1899; d. James Robert and Jennie Bruce (Zimmerly) T. A.B., Mt. Holyoke Coll., 1920, D.Sc. (hon.), 1960; M.S., Washington U., St. Louis, 1921, Ph.D., 1924, D.Sc. (hon.), 1980; D.Sc. (hon.), Western Coll. for Women, 1956; postgrad. (NRC fellow), Oxford U., 1925-26. Mem. faculty Washington U., from 1920, prof. gross anatomy, 1946-58, prof. anatomy, 1958-67, prof. emeritus, lectr. in anatomy, from 1967; vis. prof. anatomy Makerere U. Coll., Kampala, Uganda, 1963; cons. Rockefeller Found., 1963; spl. cons. USPHS, 1943-45; anthropologist Schofield Barracks, Hawaii U.S. Dept. Army, 1948-49, Fort McKinley, Philippines, 1951. Contbr. chpts. to books, articles to med. and biol. jours. Recipient Viking Fund medal and award in phys. anthropology, 1956. Mem. Am. Assn. Anatomists (exec. com. 1969-73), Am. Assn. Phys. Anthropologists (pres. 1955-57), Anat. Soc. Gt. Britain and Ireland (life), Am. Anthrop. Assn., Mo. State Anat. Bd. (pres. 1957-67), Anat. Bd. St. Louis (pres. 1941-48, 49-67), Phi Beta Kappa, Sigma Xi, Alpha Omega Alpha. Democrat. Presbyterian. Home: Saint Louis Mo. Deceased.

TROYANOS, TATIANA, opera singer; b. N.Y.C., Sept. 12, 1938; d. Nickolas and Hildagod (Langera) T. Diploma, Juilliard Sch. Music. Debut: N.Y.C. Opera as Jocasta in: Oedipus Rex, 1963, Met. Opera, 1976; appeared at La Scala as Adalgisa in Norma, 1977; singer operas in Hamburg, Fed. Republic of Germany, Berlin, Munich, Vienna, Austria, Salzburg, Austria, Milan, Italy, Rome, Florence, Italy, Palermo, Italy, Paris, Strasbourg, France and London, 1965-75; prin. roles include Carmen, Sextus in Clemenza di Tito, Dido in Dido and Aeneas, Octavian in Der Rosenkavalier, composer in Ariadne auf Naxos, Santuzza in Cavalleria Rusticana; soloist with symphony orchs. including Boston, Cin., Chgo., Los Angeles, Phila., London, N.Y. Philharm.; rec. artist with RCA, Victor Red Seal, Deutsche Grammophon Gesellschaft, EMI, London, Columbia record cos. Juilliard Alumnae scholar. Home: New York N.Y. Died Aug. 21, 1993.

TROYER, JOHN ROBERT, anatomist, educator; b. Princeton, Ill., Feb. 5, 1928; s. Maurice Emanuel and Arvilla Elizabeth (Sprunger) T.; m. Ruth Ann Moore, Aug. 18, 1956; children: David Eric, Susan Elizabeth, Mark Robert, Karen Ruth. AB, Syracuse U., 1949; PhD, Cornell U., 1955. Lab. asst. Cornell U., Ithaca, N.Y., 1949-54; instr. anatomy Sch. Medicine, Temple U., Phila., 1954-59, asst. prof., 1959-63, assoc. prof., 1963-69; John Franklin Huber prof. anatomy and cell biology Temple U., Phila., 1969-93; chmn. dept. anatomy Sch. Medicine, Temple U., Phila., 1979-93, chmn. dept. anatomy and cell biology, 1990-93, co-dir. embryology, neuroanatomy courses rsch. hibernation, 1954-86, researcher in congenital abnormalities, 1968-93; ret., 1993; co-dir. anatomy tng. grant NIH, 1965-70. Contbr. articles to profl. jours., chpts. of books. Elder dir. Christian edn. coun. 1st Presbyn. Ch., Germantown, Pa., 1963-69. Recipient Golden Apple award Student AMA, Temple U., 1967, 69, 72, 76, 78, 81, 84, 90, Lindback award Temple U. Sch. Medicine, 1972, Sowell award, 1981, 93, Outstanding Tchr. award, 1989; NIH grantee, 1962-69; med. sch. yearbooks dedicated to him, 1967, 86, 90. Mem. AAAS, N.Y. Acad. Scis., Am. Assn. Anatomists, Assn. Anatomy Chmns., Am. Soc. Mammalogists, Cajal Club, Hibernation Info. Exch., Sigma Xi (pres. Temple chpt. 1964-65), Alpha Omega Alpha, Gamma Alpha (pres. 1953-54). Democrat. Presbyterian. Home: Philadelphia Pa. Died Sept. 10, 1993, interred George Washington Memorial Park, Plymouth Meeting,P.A.

TRUE, HENRY ALFONSO, JR., entrepreneur; b. Cheyenne, Wyo., June 12, 1915; s. Henry A. and Anna Barbara (Diemer) T.; m. Jean Durland, Mar. 20, 1938; children: Tamma Jean (Mrs. Donald Hatten), Henry Alfonso, III, Diemer D., David L. BS in Indsl. Engring., Mont. State Coll., 1937; PhD in Engring. (hon.), Mont. State U., 1983; LLD (hon.), U. Wyo., 1988. Roustabout, pumper, foreman The Tex. Co., 1937-45, supt. drilling and prodn. for Wyo., 1945-48; mgr. Res. Drilling Co., 1948-51, pres., 1951-59; ptnr. True Drilling Co. and True Oil Co., Casper, Wyo., 1951—; v.p., sec. Toolpushers Supply Co., 1952-53, pres., 1954—; v.p., sec. True Svc. Co., 1953, pres., 1954-70; pres. True Bldg. Corp., 1956-67, Smokey Oil Co., 1975—, Belle Fourche Pipeline Co., 1957—, Black Hills Trucking, Inc., 1977—; owner True Ranches, Inc., 1957-76, pres., 1977-86; pres. True Oil Purchasing Co., 1977-81, True Geothermal Drilling Co., 1981—, True Wyo. Beef, 1987-94; ptnr. Eighty-Eight Oil Co., 1955—, True Geothermal Energy Co., 1981—, True Ranches, 1983—; chmn. Powder River Oil Shippers Svc., Inc., 1963-67; pres. Camp Creek Gas Co., 1964-77; v.p. George Mancini Feed Lots, Brighton, Colo., 1964-72; v.p. Black Hills Marketers, Inc., 1966-72, pres., 1973-80; v.p. White Stallion Ranch, Inc., Tucson, 1965—; pres. Res. Oil Purchasing Co., 1972-73; bd. dirs. Midland Fin. Corp.; former bd. dirs. U. Wyo. Rsch. Corp.; chmn. Hilltop Nat. Bank, 1977—, Mountain Plaza Nat. Bank, 1980-93; mem. exec. com. Wyo. Oil Industry Com., 1958-74, treas., 1958-59, pres. 1960-62; dir. Rocky Mountain Oil Show, 1955; mem. adv. bd. Internat. Oil and Gas Edn. Ctr., 1964—, vice chmn., 1969-73; mem. natural gas adv. coun. Fed. Power Commn., 1964-65, mem. exec. adv. com., 1971-74; mem. exec. co. com. Gas Supply Com., 1965-69, vice chmn., 1967-69; mem. adv. coun. Pub. Land Rev. Commn., 1965-70; dir. U.S. Bus. and Indsl. Coun., 1971—, exec. com., 1974—; mem. Nat. Petroleum Council, 1962— , nat. oil policy com., 1965, vice chmn., 1970-71, chmn., 1972-73; mem. Rocky Mountain Petroleum Industry Adv. Com., Fed. Energy Office, 1973-77; hon. dir. Mountain Bell, bd. advisors, 1965-84; mem. Wyo. Com. Newcomen Soc. U.S., 1974—. Chmn. advance gifts com. United Fund, 1962; nat. assoc. Boys Clubs Am., 1964-69, hon. chmn. local chpt. 1971; trustee Casper Air Terminal, 1960-71, pres. 1964-65, 67-68; mem. research fellows Southwestern Legal Found., 1968—; trustee U. Wyo., 1965-77, pres. bd., 1971-73, mem. adult edn. and community svc. coun., 1961-64, trustee emeritus, 1991—; bd. govs. Western Ind. Colls. Found., 1963-65; nat. trustee Voice of Youth, 1968; bd. dirs., trustee Nat. Cowboy Hall of Fame and Western Heritage Ctr., 1975—, pres. bd., 1978-80, chmn., 1980-82; dir. Mountain States Legal Found., 1977—, exec. com. 1984—, chmn. bd. 1988-90; dir. Nat. Legal Ctr. for the Pub. Interest, 1988-90; steering com. Wyo. Heritage Soc., 1979—, sec.-treas. 1988-91; trustee Buffalo Bill Meml. Assn., 1983-92, emeritus, 1992—; Wyo. state fin. chmn. Reagan-Bush campaign '84. Named Oil Man of Yr., 1959, Disting. Businessman for Small Bus. Mgmt., 1966-67; named to Wisdom Hall Fame, 1970; named Exec. of Yr. Teton chpt. Profl. Secs. Internat., 1985, Hon. Rotarian, Casper Rotary Club, 1990-91; recipient Honored Citizen award, 1964, Casper C. of C., Chief Roughneck of Yr. award, Lone Star Steel award 1965, ann. Indsl. award Wyo. Assn. Realtors, 1965, Pierre F. Goodrich Conservation award Polit. Econ. and Rsch. Ctr., 1982, Oil Man of Century award Casper Centennial Corp., 1989, Heritage award Wyo. Heritage Soc., 1991, Soc. Centennial Alumni Mont. State U., 1992. Mem. Internat. Assn. Drilling Contractors (dir. 1950—), Am. Petroleum Inst. (dir. 1960—, exec. com. 1970—, Gold Medal for Disting. Svc. award 1985), Rocky Mountain Oil and Gas Assn. (treas. 1954-55, v.p. Wyo. 1956-58, dir. 1950—, pres. 1962-63, exec. com. 1954—, hon. mem., 1978), Ind. Petroleum Assn. Am. (v.p. Wyo. 1960-61, exec. com. 1962—, pres. 1964-65, Russell 5, Karney R. Cochran Gt. Am. Producer award 1991), Rocky Mountain Petroleum Pioneers, Wyo. Stockgrowers Assn., Casper Petroleum (dir. 1954), U.S. C. of C. (dir. 1975-81), Casper C. of C., All-Am Wildcatters, 25 Year Club Petroleum Industry (pres. 1979-80), Ind. Petroleum Assn. Mountain States (Rocky Mountain Wildcatter of Yr. award 1982), Petroleum Assn. Wyo. (dir. 1974—), Am. Judicature Soc. (mem. com. justice 1976), Mont. State U. Soc. Centennial Alumni, Masons, Shriners, Elks, Sigma Chi (Significant Sig award, 1981), Beta Gamma Sigma (hon. mem., 1971 Alpha chpt. Wyo.). Republican. Episcopalian (vestry 1960-62). Home: Casper Wyo. Died June 4, 1994.

TRUFFAUT, FRANCOIS, film director; b. Paris, Feb. 6, 1932; s. Roland and Janine (de Monferrand) T.; m. Madeleine Morgenstern, Oct. 29, 1957; children: Laura, Eva, Joséphine. Reporter, motion picture critic Movie Jour. and Arts, 1954-58; dir. motion pictures, 1957—, producer, 1961—; prodns. include Les Mistons, 1958, Les 400 Coups, 1959, Tirez sur le Pianiste, 1960, L'Amour à 20 ans, 1962, Jules et Jim, 1962, La Peau Douce, 1963, Fahrenheit 451, 1966, La Mariée était etait en Noir, 1967, Baisers Volés, 1968; La Sirene du Mississippi, 1969, L'Enfant Sauvage, 1969, Domicile Conjugal, 1970, Les Deux Anglaises et le Continent, 1971, Une Belle Fille comme Moi, 1972, La Nuit Américaine, 1973, L'Histoire d'Adele, 1975, L'Argent de Poche, 1976, L'Homme qui aimait les Femmes, 1977, La Chambre Verte, 1977, L'Amour en fuite, 1978, Le Dernier métro (10 Cesar prize), 1980, La Femme d'a Côté, 1981, Vivement dimanche!, 1983. Recipient Cannes Film Festival prize for Les 400 Coups, 1959; Acad. award as best fgn. lang. film for La Nuit Américaine, 1973. Author: Hitchcock, 1966; Les aventures d'Antoine Doinel, 1970; Les Films de ma vie, 1975; L'Histoire d'Adèle H., 1975; L'Argent de Poche, 1976; L'Homme qui aimait les Femmes, 1977; Hitchcock (édition définitive), 1983. Home: Paris France

TRUONG CHINH (FORMERLY DANG XUAN KHU), former chairman State Council of Vietnam Socialist Republic; b. Nam Dinh, Vietnam, 1907. Sec., Revolutionary League of Vietnamese Youth until 1930, imprisoned by French, 1930-36, worked as journalist, 1936-39, imprisoned, escaped to Yenen, 1939, returned to Vietnam, 1941; sec.-gen. Community Party of Indo-China, later Lao Dong party, 1941-56; chmn. standing com. Nat. Assembly Dem. Republic Vietnam, 1960-76, Nat. Assembly Socialist Rep. Vietnam, 1976-81; pres. State Council, 1981-86; chmn. Nat. Def. Council; chmn. Com. for Drafting Constn. Socialist Republic Vietnam, 1975-76. Sec. gen. Communist Party Vietnam, 1986. Decorated Order of Lenin. Home: Hanoi Socialist Republic of Vietnam

TSATSOS, CONSTANTINE, author, former president of Greece; b. Athens, Greece, July 1, 1899; s. Demetrius and Theodora (Eustratiadi) T.; student Athens U., U. Heidelberg; m. Jeanne Seferiades, June 21, 1930; children: Despina C. (Mrs. Constantine Mylonas), Dora A. (Mrs. Alexander Symeonidi). Prof. social philosophy Athens U., 1933-46; mem. Parliament, 1946-63; minister, 1945-49, 50-51, 56-63; minister of justice, 1967; minister of cultural affairs, 1974; pres. Republic of Greece, 1975-80; mem. Athens Acad., 1961-90; chmn. Com. to Draft New Constn., 1974-75. Mem. Acad. Moral and Polit. Scis. Paris (fgn.), Acad. of Romania, Acad. of Morocco. Author numerous books including: Politics; Greece's Progress; Philosophical Aphorisms; Cicero; Demosthenes; Complete Poetical Works, 1973; Dialogues in a Monastery, 1974; Studies in Aesthetics, 2 vols., 1977; Greece and Europe, 1977; Theory of Art, 1978; Poems of Other Times and Places, 1980; The Unknown Karamanlis, 1984; Latin Poems in Translation, 1985; Life from a Distance, 1985. Died 1990. Home: Athens Greece

TSUCHIYA, TAKUMI, agronomy educator; b. Ajimucho, Oita-Ken, Japan, Mar. 10, 1923; came to U.S., 1968; s. Torao and Masao Tsuchiya; m. Chiyoko Fukushima, Feb. 20, 1953; children: Keiko, Noriko. BAgr, Gifu Ag. Coll., 1943, Kyoto Imperial U., 1947; DAgr, Kyoto U., 1960. Cytogeneticist Kihara Inst. for Biol. Rsch., Yokohama, Japan, 1957-63; postdoctoral fellow U. Man., Winnepeg, Can., 1963-64; cytogeneticist Children's Hosp., Winnepeg, 1964-65; rsch. assoc. U. Manitoba, Winnepeg, 1965-68; assoc. prof. agronomy Colo. State U., Ft. Collins, 1968-73, prof., 1973-92, Univ. Disting. prof., 1991-92; chmn. genetics com. Am. Barley Workers Conf., 1969-92; presenter, lectr. seminars in field. Editor: Barley Genetics Newsletter; co-editor: Chromosome Engineering in Plants: Genetics, Breeding, Evolution, 1991; mem. editorial bd. Cereal Rsch. Communication; contbr. more than 400 articles to sci. jours., chpts. to books. Recipient Oliver P. Pennock Achievement Disting. Svc. award Colo. State U., 1986, Faculty Achievement award Burlington-No., 1987. Fellow Am. Soc. Agronomy, Crop Sci. Soc. Am. (Crop. Sci. Rsch. award 1986, DeKalb Genetics Crop Sci. Disting. Career award 1991), Japan Soc. for Promotion of Sci. (fgn.); mem. Genetics Soc. Japan (hon. fgn.), Am. Genetics Assn., Soc. Econ. Botany, Can. Genetics Soc., Internat. Soc. Cytology (standing collaborator), Sigma Xi (pres. Colo. State U. chpt. 1990, hon. scientist award 1987), Phi Kappa Phi, Gamma Sigma Delta. Home: Fort Collins Colo. Died May 1, 1992.

TUBIS, SEYMOUR, artist, printmaker, sculptor, educator; b. Phila., Sept. 20, 1919. Student, Temple U., 1937-39, Phila. Mus. Sch. Art, 1941-42, Art Students League of N.Y., 1946-49, Academie Grande-Chaumiere, Paris, 1949-50, Instituto d'Arte, Florence, Italy, 1950; student of Hans Hofmann, N.Y.C., 1951. Pvt. tchr. art N.Y.C., Rockport, Mass., 1948-60; tchr. art, summer program Bd. Edn., Great Neck, N.Y., 1949; asst. instr. Art Students League of N.Y., 1948, 49, Bklyn. Mus. Sch. Art, 1950-51; instr. N.Y.C. Adult Edn. Program, 1950-52; head dept. fine arts, instr. printmaking, painting and design Inst. of Am. Indian Arts, Santa Fe, 1963-80; artist-cons. N.Y. World-Telegram and Sun, 1955-59, St. John's Coll., 1960, Mus. of N.Mex., 1960, N.Y. Times, 1960-63. One-man shows include Galerie St. Placide, Paris, 1950, Lowe Found. Galleries, N.Y.C., 1953, 55, Taft Sch., Conn., 1953, La Chapelle Gallery, Santa Fe, 1960, Mus. N.Mex., Santa Fe, 1964, Accents Gallery, Cleve., 1966, U. Calgary (Alta., Can.), 1967, Jamison Galleries, Santa Fe, 1967, N.Mex. State Library, Santa Fe, 1968, Coll. of Santa Fe, 1969, The New West, Albuquerque, 1969, 71, 72, 73, Gallery Contemporary Art, Taos, 1969, Antioch Coll., Balt. and Washington, 1973, Pacific Grove (Calif.) Art Ctr., 1983, Tobey C. Moss Gallery, L.A., 1986-93, Associated Am. Artists, N.Y.C., 1986-93, Warner Roberts Gallery, Palo Alto, 1987, Bluecreek West Gallery, Denver, 1989-92, Masterpiece Gallery, Carmel, Calif., 1992-93, numerous others; exhibited in group shows at Library of Congress, Carnegie Inst., Bklyn. Mus., Pa. Acad. Fine Arts, Dallas Mus. Art, Syracuse U., Royal Soc., London, Eng., Hofstra Coll., Asso. Gallery Art, Detroit, Riverside Mus., N.Y.C., Met. Mus. Art, N.Y.C., Seattle Art Mus., Dept. Interior, Dept. State Embassies Program, Mus. Modern Art, N.Y.C., Mus. of N.Mex., St. John's Coll., Santa Fe, Mus. Internat. Folk Art, Santa Fe, Pa. State Coll., Wichita Art Assn., John F. Kennedy Center for Performing Arts, Washington, also others; represented in permanent collections Library of Congress, Soc. Am. Graphic Artists, Met. Mus. Art, Pa. State Coll., U. Ariz., U. Calgary, Art Students League N.Y., U.S. Dept. Interior, Antioch Coll., Georgetown U., Boston Pub. Library, Worchester (Mass.) Mus. Art, also numerous pvt. collections. Recipient 1st prize in painting, Newspaper Guild N.Y., purchase award Mus. of N.Mex.; rsch. grantee U. Ariz., U. Calif., Santa Barbara; Nat. Endowment Arts grantee, 1980. Mem. Soc. Am. Graphic Artists (1st prize in etching), Art Students League N.Y., Coll. Art Assn. Home: Denver Colo. Died May 15, 1993.

TUCKER, FRED C., JR., investment company executive; b. Indpls., Oct. 25, 1918; s. Fred C. and Bernice (Caldwell) T.; m. Ermajean MacDonald, Sept. 2, 1944; children—Fred C. III, Lucinda Ann. Grad., Lawrenceville Sch., 1936; A.B., DePauw U., 1940; student law, Harvard U., 1940-41; hon. degree, DePauw U., 1984. Pres. F. C. Tucker Co., Inc., Indpls., 1946-86, Tucker Investment Co., Inc., 1986-94; dir. Ind. Nat. Bank, Jefferson Nat. Life Ins. Co., Jefferson Corp.; prin. officer, dir. real estate and devel. cos. Pres. Indpls. Met. YMCA, 1964-65; Ind. chmn. Crusade Freedom, 1954-55; chmn. bd. trustees DePauw U., 1977-80; trustee Arthur Jordan Found., Indpls., Indpls.-Marion County Bldg. Authority. Served as lt. USNR, World War II. Mem. Nat. Inst. Real Estate Brokers (pres. 1966), Indpls. Real Estate Bd. (pres. 1961), Nat. Assn. Realtors (nat. pres. 1972), Arbitration Assn., Am. Soc. Real Estate Counselors, Rep. Vets. Ind., Central Ind. DePauw Alumni Assn. (past pres.), Indpls. C. of C. (pres. 1973-74), Am. Legion (past comdr.), Indian Acad., Delta Tau Delta (past nat. pres.). Methodist. Clubs: Rotary, Meridian Hills Country, Crooked Stick, Indpls. Athletic, Columbia; Royal Poinciana (Naples, Fla.). Home: Indianapolis Ind. Died Dec. 9, 1994.

TUCKER, MORRISON GRAHAM, banker; b. Lincoln, Nebr., May 24, 1911; s. Charles Andrew and Olive Myrtle (Graham) T.; m. Gladys Mae Hartz, Nov. 25, 1944; children: Suzanne, John Graham. AB, Dartmouth Coll., 1932. Asst. nat. bank examiner U.S. Treasury Dept., 1932-36; fed. bank examiner, 1936-38; asst. chief div. exam. Fed. Deposit Ins. Corp., 1939-42; banking adviser to pres. of Philippines, 1944-47; mgr. Latin Am. interests Rockefeller family, 1947-51; chmn. exec. com. Liberty Nat. Bank & Trust Co., Oklahoma City, 1951-69; owner Morrison G. Tucker & Co. (banking and investments); chmn. bd. dirs. First Security Bank & Trust Co., United Bank of Del City. Bd. dirs. Frontiers of Sci. Found.; trustee Oklahoma City U.; pres. alumni council Dartmouth Coll., 1965-66. Served as lt. (j.g.) USNR, 1941-44. Elected to Okla. Hall of Fame, 1978. Mem. Okla. Bankers Assn. (pres. 1974-75), Metropolitan Club (Washington), Univ. Club (N.Y.C.), Oklahoma City Golf and Country Club, Men's Dinner Club (Oklahoma City). Epsicopalian. Home: Oklahoma City Okla. Died May 4, 1994.

TURNBULL, AUGUSTUS BACON, III, university official, public administration educator; b. Atlanta, Mar. 7, 1940; s. Augustus B. and Isabel (Walker) T.; m. Marjorie Hayes Reitz, Nov. 26, 1965. B.A., U. Ga., 1962; Ph.D. in Govt., U. Va., 1967. Asst. press sec. to Gov. Ga., 1964-67; asst. prof. U. Ga., Athens, 1967-71; assoc. prof. pub. adminstrn. Fla. State U., Tallahassee, 1971-81; prof. Fla. State U., 1981—, chmn. dept., 1976-81, assoc. v.p., 1978-81, v.p. acad. affairs, 1981—, provost, 1986—; edn. com. staff dir. Fla. Ho. of Reps., 1974-75; cons. govt. agys. Author: Government Budgeting and PPBS, 1970; contbr. chpt. numerous articles to profl. publs. Active LeMoyne Art Found., Tallahassee, 1972-81, pres., 1979-80; bd. dirs. Tallahassee Symphony, 1980-81, Tallahassee Performing Arts, 1981-82, Your Schs. Found., 1988—; pres. Friends of Leon County Pub. Library, 1983-84, Suwannee area coun. Boy Scouts Am., Leon County Local Planning Agy., 1987-90, Your Schs. Fedn., 1989—. Woodrow Wilson fellow, 1962; Nat. Def. grad. fellow, 1962-64. Mem. Am. Soc. Pub. Adminstrn., Nat. Assn. Schs. Pub. Affairs and Adminstrn. (pres. 1983-84), Nat. Assn. State Univs. and Land Grant Colls. (com. on fed. legis., Com. on edn. and tech.), Ga. Blue Key, Sphinx, Phi Beta Kappa, Phi Kappa Phi, Pi Alpha Alpha (nat. pres. 1986-87). Democrat. Episcopalian. Clubs: Governors, U. Ga. Pres, Fla. State U. Pres. Lodge: Rotary. Home: Tallahassee Fla.

TURNBULL, COLIN MACMILLAN, retired anthropology educator; b. Harrow, Eng., Nov. 23, 1924; came to U.S., 1959, naturalized, 1964; s. John Rutherford and Dorothy Helena (Chapman) T. B.A., Magdalen Coll., Oxford U., 1947, M.A., 1949; diploma in, Social Anthropology, 1956, Litt.B., 1957, D.Phil., 1964; postgrad., London U. Sch. Oriental and African Studies, 1947-49, Banaras Hindu U., India, 1949-51. Assoc. curator Am. Mus. Natural History, N.Y.C., 1959-69; prof. Hofstra U., Hempstead, N.Y., 1969-72, Va. Commonwealth U., Richmond, 1972-75; vis. prof. W.Va. U., Morgantown, 1976; prof. anthropology George Washington U., Washington, 1976-85; adj. prof. N.Y. U., 1963-69, 86 Hunter Coll., N.Y.C., 1964, Vassar Coll., Poughkeepsie, N.Y., 1967-68, vis. prof. SUNY, Buffalo, 1986-87; vis. Randolph disting. prof. Vassar Coll., 1987-88. Author: The Forest People, 1961, The Lonely African, 1962, The Peoples of Africa, 1962, The Mbuti Pygmies, 1965, Wayward Servants, 1965, Tradition and Change in African Tribal Life, 1966, Tibet, 1968, The Mountain People, 1972, Man in Africa, 1976; Music of the Ituri Forest, 1957, Pygmies of the Ituri Forest, 1961, Music of the Rain Forest, 1963; The Mbuti Pygmies: Change and Adaptation, 1983, The Human Cycle, 1983. Served with Royal Navy, 1942-45. Recipient Ann. award Am. Acad. Arts and Letters, Ann. award Nat. Acad. Arts and Letters; grantee Royal Anthrop. Inst.; NSF Nat. Endowment for Humanities. Home: Lancaster Va. Died July 28, 1994.

TURNER, DONALD FRANK, retired lawyer; b. Chippewa Falls, Wis., Mar. 19, 1921; s. Paul and Elizabeth (Catterlin) T.; m. Joan Pearson, Dec. 17, 1955; children: Paul Alfred, Katherine. B.A., Northwestern U., 1941; M.A., Harvard, 1943, Ph.D., 1947; LL.B., Yale, 1950. Bar: D.C. 1951. Law clk. U.S. Supreme Ct., 1950-51; assoc. law firm Cox, Langford, Stoddard & Cutler, Washington, 1951-54; asst. prof. Harvard Law Sch., 1954-57, prof., 1957-65, Bussey prof., 1968-79; of counsel Wilmer, Cutler & Pickering, Washington, 1979-87; prof. law Georgetown U., Washington, 1987-88; sr. fellow Brookings Instn., Washington, 1988-89; ret., 1989; asst. atty. gen. charge anti-trust div. U.S. Dept. Justice, 1965-68. Co-author: Antitrust Policy An Economic and Legal Analysis, 1959, Antitrust Law, vols. 1-5, 1980. Served to lt. USNR, 1942-46. Mem. ABA, Phi Beta Kappa. Home: Washington D.C. Died July 19, 1994.

TURNER, JAMES CASTLE, union official; b. Beaumont, Tex., Nov. 4, 1916; s. James Castle and Lydia (Carley) T.; m. Mary Pauline Curtis, Apr. 14, 1934; children—Vivian, Daniel, Brian, Lisa, Lauran. A.B., Catholic U. Am., 1940. Bus. mgr., bus. rep. local 77 Internat. Union Operating Engrs., Washington, 1940-71; nat. v.p. Internat. Union Operating Engrs., 1956-72, gen. sec.-treas., 1972-75, gen. pres., 1975-85, gen. pres. emeritus, 1985-96; v.p., mem. exec. council AFL-CIO, 1975-85; U.S. rep. ILO, Geneva, 1952, 64, 74, 75, 77. Editor: Internat. Engr, 1972-75. Del. Democratic Nat. Conv., 1952, 56, 60, 64; vice chmn. D.C. Dem. Central Com., 1950-60, 63-67; Dem. nat. commiteeman for, D.C., 1960, 76-96; mem. D.C. City Council, 1967-68; trustee Nat. Urban League, Cath. U. Am., 1974-80; v.p., bd. govs., chmn. exec. com. United Way Am.; pres. Ams. for Energy Independence, 1980. Mem. Nat. Planning Assn. (trustee), Blue Key. Episcopalian. Clubs: Nat. Dem, Nat. Press, Touchdown. Home: Bal Harbour Fla. Died Apr. 13, 1996.

TURNER, LANA (JULIA JEAN MILDRED FRANCES TURNER), actress; b. Wallace, Idaho, Feb. 8, 1921; d. Virgil and Mildred T.; m. Artie Shaw, Feb. 8, 1940 (div.); m. Steven Crane, 1942 (div.); m. Bob Topping (div.); m. Lex Barker (div.); m. Fred May, Nov. 27, 1960 (div.); m. Robert Eaton (div.); m. Ronald Dante. Ed. pub. schs., Presentation Convent, San Francisco. Motion picture actress 1937—; appeared in motion pictures including Love Finds Andy Hardy, 1938, Dramatic School, 1938, Calling Dr. Kildare, Those Glamour Girls, Dancing Co-ed, 1939, Two Girls on Broadway, We Who Are Young, 1940, Ziegfeld Girl, Dr. Jekyll and Mr. Hyde, Honky Tonk, Johnny Eager, 1941, Somewhere I'll Find You, Slightly Dangerous, 1942, Marriage Is a Private Affair, Women's Army, 1944, Keep Your Powder Dry, Week End at the Waldorf, Cass Timberlane, Homecoming, 1947, The Merry Widow, 1951, The Bad and the Beautiful, 1952, Latin Lovers, Flame and the Flesh, Betrayed, The Sea Chase, The Prodigal, Rains of Ranchipur, Another Time, 1958, Imitation of Life, 1959, By Love Possessed, 1961, Bachelor in Paradise, Who's Got the Action, Love Has Many Faces, Madame X, The Big Cube, Persecution, Portrait in Black, Bittersweet Love, 1976; appeared in TV series The Survivors, 1969, Falcon Crest, 1982-83; also numerous theatrical appearances. Author: The Lady, The Legend, The Truth, 1983. Died June 29, 1995.

TURNER, MAURICE THOMAS, JR., police chief; b. Washington, Aug. 13; s. Maurice Thomas and Elizabeth Turner; children: Andre, Jeannine, Eric. Student, Am. U., U. Md.; grad., F.B.I. Nat. Acad. Police officer Met. Police Dept., Washington, 1957-93, lt., 1969-71, capt., 1971-73, dep. chief, 1973-78, asst. chief, head Adminstrv. Services Bur,, 1978-81, chief of police, 1981-93. Bd. dirs. Met. Police Boys' and Girls' Clubs. Served with USMC, 1954-57. Recipient numerous awards and citations. Mem. FBI Nat. Acad., Black Ofcls. Orgn. Home: Washington D.C. Died June 16, 1993.

TURNER, ROBERT LEE, concert hall manager; b. Irvine, Ky., Feb. 14, 1937; s. Charles Ellis and Hazel Louise (West) T.; m. Heidi Antonia Upton, Nov. 14, 1976; children: Jeremy Mark, Christian Upton; children by previous marriage: Brenda LeAnn Turner Burns, Brian Craig. MusB, Stetson U., 1959; MusM, La. State U., 1962. Minister music and edn. 1t Bapt. Ch., Lake City, Fla., 1959-61; uniformed supr. guest relations NBC, N.Y.C., 1961-62; head usher Philharm. Hall, N.Y.C., 1962; asst. mgr. Philharm. Hall, 1963-73; gen. mgr. concert halls Lincoln Ctr. for the Performing Arts, N.Y.C., from 1973; cons. in field. Recipient award of excellence Stetson U. Alumni Assn., 1978. Mem. Internat. Assn. Auditorium Mgrs. (conf. speaker 1977), Internat. Soc. Performing Arts Adminstrs., Assn. Coll. Univ. and Community Arts Adminstrn., Assn. Theatrical Press Agts. and Mgrs, Box Office Mgrs., Internat. Home: New York N.Y. Deceased.

TURNER, WILLIAM KAY, architect, educator; b. Columbia, S.C., Aug. 30, 1933; s. J. Ashby and Grace (Killingsworth) T.; m. Nancy Ann Proctor, Apr. 12, 1957; children: William Michael, Melissa Kay, John Ashby. BS in Architecture, Clemson U., 1955, BArch, 1956; MArch, U. Pa., 1961. Asst. prof. architecture Auburn U., 1961-63, assoc. prof., 1963-64; asst. prof. Tulane U., 1964-68, assoc. prof., 1968-72, prof. architecture, 1972-94, assoc. dean Sch. Architecture, 1970-71, acting dean Sch. Architecture, 1971-72, dean, 1972-80, dir. campus devel., 1983-93; campus architect Rollins Coll., 1982-91, Pacific U., 1990-92; mem. La. Gov.'s Adv. Com. on New Met. Transp. Plan, 1971-78, La. Architects Selection Bd., 1975-76, Nat. Archtl. Accrediting Bd., 1983-86, sec.-treas., 1985-86; project dir. New Orleans and The River, 1973-74. Author: (with James Lamantia) Study of the Proposed Riverfront and Elysian Fields Expressway and an Alternate Proposal, 1965. Bd. dirs. New Orleans Mus. Art, 1975-78; mem. New Orleans City Planning Commn., 1978-81; trustee Historic Faubourg St. Mary Corp., 1982-93, chmn. bd., 1984-85, trustee emeritus, 1993-94. 2d lt., then 1st lt. C.E., U.S. Army, 1956-58. Fellow AIA (bd. dir. New Orleans chpt. 1972-78); mem. Assn. Collegiate Schs. Architecture (pres. 1977-78), Nat. Council Archtl. Registration Bds. Home: New Orleans La. Died Feb. 8, 1994.

TUTTLE, CHARLES EGBERT, publisher, bookseller; b. Rutland, Vt., Apr. 5, 1915; s. Charles Egbert and Helen Sarah (Woolverton) T.; m. Reiko Chiba, Feb. 16, 1952. Grad., Phillips Exeter Acad., 1933; A.B., Harvard, 1937. Pres. Charles E. Tuttle Co., Rutland, from 1938; v.p. Tuttle-Mori Agy., Inc., Tokyo, Japan. Publisher numerous books on, Japan, Asia. Mem. selection com. for, Japan; Mem. selection com. for Eisenhower Exchange Fellowships, 1960-62. Served to capt. AUS, 1942-46. Decorated Order Sacred Treasure, 3d Class (Japan); Recipient commendation Japan Soc. Translators, 1965; Pubs. Assn. for Cultural Exchange (Japan) awards, 1969, 70; Broadcast Preceptor award San Francisco State Coll., 1970; award of merit Vt. Council on the Arts, 1970; John Barnes Pub. of Year award Am. Booksellers Assn., 1970; named Most Successful Grad. Rutland High Sch. 35th reunion, 1967; Internat. Publs. Cultural awards Japan Broadcasting Corp., 1969, 70. Mem. Internat. House Tokyo, Am.-Japan Soc., Vt. Hist. Soc., ALA, Asia Soc., Japan Soc., Asiatic Soc. Japan, Phi Beta Kappa. Clubs: American (Tokyo); Harvard (Boston, N.Y.C.); Army and Navy (Washington). Home: Rutland Vt. Deceased.

TUTTLE, ELBERT PARR, federal judge; b. Pasadena, Calif., July 17, 1897; s. Guy Harmon and Margie Etta (Parr) T.; m. Sara Sutherland, Oct. 22, 1919; children: Elbert Parr, Jane T. (Mrs. John J. Harmon). Student, Punahou Acad., Honolulu, 1909-14; AB, Cornell U., 1918, LLB, 1923; LLD (hon.), Emory U., 1958, Harvard U., 1965, Georgetown U., 1978, Atlanta U., 1984. Bar: Ga. 1923. News and editl. writer N.Y. Evening World, N.Y.C.; also Army and Navy Jour. and Am. Legion Weekly, Washington, 1919; practiced in Atlanta and Washington, 1923-52; mem. firm Sutherland, Tuttle & Brennan; gen. counsel, head legal div. Treasury Dept., 1953-54; judge U.S. Ct. Appeals (5th cir.), 1954-81; chief judge U.S. Ct. Appeals, 1961-67; judge U.S. Ct. Appeals (11th cir.), 1981-96, sr. judge; Chmn. adv. com. on civil rules Jud. Conf. U.S., 1972-78, chmn. adv. com. on jud. activities, 1969-77. Trustee Atlanta Community Chest, 1947-49; v.p. Atlanta Community Planning Council, 1951; Past trustee Interdonominational Theol. Center, Cornell U., Atlanta U., Spelman Coll., Morehouse Coll., Piedmont Hosp. Served to col. F.A., 77th Inf. Div. U.S. Army, 1941-46; comdg. gen. 108th Airborne Div. (res.), 1947-50; brig. gen. U.S. Army Res. Decorated Legion of Merit, Bronze Star, Purple Heart with oak leaf cluster; recipient Presdl. medal of freedom, 1981, Devitt Disting. Svc. to Justice award, 1989. Mem. ABA, Atlanta Bar Assn. (pres. 1948), Atlanta C. of C. (pres. 1949), Phi Kappa Phi, Pi Kappa Alpha (nat. pres. 1930-36), Order of Coif. Episcopalian. Home: Atlanta Ga. Died June 23, 1996.

TVERSKY, AMOS, psychologist; b. Haifa, Israel, Mar. 16, 1937; came to U.S., 1977; s. Joseph and Jenny (Ginzburg) Tversky; m. Barbara Gans, Aug. 30, 1966; children: Oren, Tal, Dona. BA, Hebrew U., Jerusalem, 1961; PhD, U. Mich., 1965; PhD (hon.), U. Goteberg, Sweden, 1985, SUNY, Buffalo, 1987. Lectr. Hebrew U., 1966-69, prof., 1969-77; prof. Stanford (Calif.) U., 1971-96. Co-author: Mathematical Psychology, 1970, Foundations of Measurement, 1971, Judgment Under Uncertainty, 1982. Recipient Marquis award U. Mich., 1965, Disting. Sci. award Am. Psychol. Assn., 1982, MacArthur prize, 1984. Mem. Am. Acad. Arts and Scis., Nat. Acad. Sci. Home: Palo Alto Calif. Died June 2, 1996.

TWEEDIE, LEONARD CHRISTIE, container company executive; b. Chgo., May 4, 1932; s. David and Isabel (Heddle) T.; B.A., Coe Coll., 1953; m. Eathel Darnell, Feb. 19, 1954; children—Sherry Lynn, Jack, Douglas. Mgmt. trainee Am. Boxboard Co., Chgo., 1955-58; regional sales mgr. packaging div. Olin Corp., Joliet, Ill., 1958-68; regional mgr. Time Container, Chgo., 1968-69; gen. mgr. Menasha Corp., Chgo., 1969-70, Neenah, Wis., 1970-74, pres. Hartford Container subs., 1972—, also corp. v.p. and gen. mgr. container div., parent co., 1976—; dir. New Eng. Wooden Ware Co. Cubmaster, 1955-59, 74—, scoutmaster, 1959-60; mem. council Bay Lakes Area Boy Scouts Am., 1983—; pres. PTA, 1974-75. Served with USAF, 1953-55. Mem. TAPPI, Fibre Box Assn. (dir. 1982—), Soc. Packaging and Handling Engrs., Tau Kappa Epsilon. Presbyterian. Clubs: Rotary, Masons, Elks, mem. Order Eastern Star (asso. patron). Home: Oshkosh Wis.

TWIGGS, RUSSELL GOULD, artist; b. Sandusky, Ohio, Apr. 29, 1898; s. William Richard and Fanny (Gould) T.; 1930 (dec. 1952). B.F.A., Carnegie-Mellon U., 1921. Mcht. seaman, 1919-24; departmental asst. Coll. Fine Arts, Carnegie-Mellon U., 1924-74. Exhibited in group shows, Art Inst. Chgo., 1947, Whitney Museum Am. Art, N.Y.C., 1955, Carnegie Inst. Internat., Pitts., 1955-67, Mus. Modern Art, N.Y.C., 1956, Corcoran Gallery Art, Washington, 1957; represented in permanent collections, Whitney Mus. Am. Art, Wadsworth Atheneum, Hartford, Conn., Mus. Art at Carnegie Inst. Internat., Bklyn. Mus., Westmoreland County Mus. Art, Greensburg, Pa.; Subject of book: (Connie Kienzle) Russell Twiggs, 1971. Served with USNR, 1917-1919. Recipient 2d prize for painting Cin. Art Mus., 1955. Mem. Associated Artists of Pitts. (Mrs. Henry J. Heinz, II award 1962, Carnegie Inst. Group prize 1949), Abstract Group of Pitts., Pitts. Plan for Art. Home: Vero Beach Fla. Deceased.

TWITTY, CONWAY, country western entertainer; b. Friarspoint, Miss., Sept. 1; s. Floyd and Velma (McGinnis) Jenkins; children: Mike, Joni, Kathy, Jimmy. Student pub. schs. Rock and roll entertainer, 1958-65, country and western entertainer, 1965-93. Composer numerous songs including: It's Only Make Believe, 1958, Hello Darlin', 1970. Served with U.S. Army 1954-57. Recipient several gold records. Baptist. Home: Hendersonville Tenn. Died June 5, 1993.

TWITTY, HOWARD ALLEN, lawyer; b. Williams, Ariz., Sept. 6, 1909; s. Edgar Montrue and Emilie Marie (Kaiser) T.; m. Zoraida Stoddard, July 26, 1947; children: Hudson Barnes (dec.), Howard Allen, Mary Marie (dec.). A.B., U. So. Calif., 1931, LL.B., 1934. Bar: Calif. 1934, Ariz. 1935. Atty. Indsl. Commn. Ariz., 1935-42; pvt. practice law Phoenix, 1946—; specializing mining law, 1950—; partner Twitty, Sievwright & Mills, 1962—. Author papers on mining law. Served to capt. Q.M.C., AUS, 1942-46. Mem. ABA (chmn. sect. natural resources law 1962-63), state bars Calif., Ariz. Republican. Methodist. Clubs: Arizona, Phoenix Country. Lodges: Masons, Rotary. Home: Phoenix Ariz. Deceased.

TWITTY, JAMES WATSON, artist; b. Mt. Vernon, N.Y., Apr. 13, 1916; s. James Chapman and Amelia Madelon (Lang) T.; m. Anne Marsh Butler, May 18, 1952; children—James Watson, Gary Lee. Student, U. Miami, 1958-59, Art Students League, N.Y.C., 1960-61. Asso. prof. painting Corcoran Sch. Art, Washington, 1964-74; lectr. George Washington U., 1964-74; exchange prof. Leeds Coll. Art, Eng., 1967-68; vis. prof. painting San Antonio Art Inst. One man exhibitions include, Corcoran Gallery Art, Washington, 1966, Lehigh U., Bethlehem, Pa., 1967, David Findlay Gallery, N.Y.C., 1971, 73, 74, 76, 78, 81, McNay Art Inst., San Antonio, 1972, George Washington U., 1975, Bettina Gallery, Zurich, Switzerland, 1977, numerous others; represented in permanent collections, Nat. Gallery Art, Nat. Collection Fine Arts, Corcoran Gallery Art, Balt. Mus. Art, Bklyn. Mus., San Francisco Mus. Art, Dallas Mus. Fine Arts, Mus. Fine Arts, Houston, Minn. Mus. Art, Oxford U., White House and, others. Bd. dirs. No. Va. Art League, 1974-77. Served with USAF, World War II and Korea. Club: Pinehurst Country. Home: Pinehurst N.C. Died Aug. 22, 1995.

ULANHU, former vice president People's Republic of China; b. Suiyan, 1904; m. Yun Liwen. Attended Mongolian-Tibetan Sch., Peking, 1922-24, Far Eastern U., Moscow. Joined Chinese Communist Party, 1925; head edn. dept. Nationalities Inst. under Anti-Japanese Mil. and Polit. Acad., Yenan, 1941; alt. mem. 7th Cen. Com. Communist Party, 1945; chmn. Inner Mongolia People's Govt., 1947-67; comdr. Polit. Commissar Inner Mongolia Mil. Region, People's Librarian Army, 1947-67; mem. Standing Com., Chinese People's Polit. Consultative Conf., 1949, exec. chmn. nat. com., 1978, vice pres., 1978-83; vice minister Nationalities Affairs Commn., 1949, minister, 1954; vice premier State Council, 1954-82; chmn. Nationalities Commn., 1954-67; 2d sec. North China Bur., Cen. Com. Chinese Communist Party, 1965; appointed col. gen., 1955; alt. mem. Politburo, 8th Cen. Com., Chinese Communist Party, 1956-67; criticized and ousted from office in Cultural Revolution, 1967; mem. 10th Cen. Com., Chinese Communist Party, 1973, mem. Cen. Com. and Politburo, 11th Cen. Com., 1977, mem. Cen. Com. and Politburo, 12th Cen. Com., 1982-85; vice chmn. standing com. 4th Nat. People's Congress, 1975-83, permanent chmn. presidium, 5th Nat. People's Congress, 1980, vice chmn. standing com. 7th Nat. People's Congress, 1988—; dir. United Front Work Dept., Chinese Communist Party, 1977-82; mem. Presidium, 12th Congress Chinese Communist Party, 1982; vice pres. People's Republic of China, 1983-88. Home: Beijing Peoples Republic of China

ULLMAN, JOSEPH LEONARD, mathematics educator, researcher; b. Buffalo, Jan. 30, 1923; s. David and Ida (Bir) U.; m. Barbara Eloise Whalley; children: Esther, Ruth, Sara, Katharine. BA, U. Buffalo, 1941; PhD, Stanford U., Palo Alto, Calif., 1949. Instr. U. Mich., Ann Arbor, 1949-51, asst. prof., 1951-58, assoc. prof., 1958-65, full prof., from 1965. Contbr. over 45 articles to profl. jours. Mem. Phi Beta Kappa, Sigma Xi. Home: Chelsea Mich. Deceased.

UNTERKOEFLER, ERNEST L., bishop; b. Phila., Aug. 17, 1917; s. Ernest L. and Anna Rose (Chambers) U. A.B. summa cum laude, Catholic U. Am., 1940, S.T.L., 1944, J.C.D., 1950. Ordained priest Roman Cath. Ch., 1944; asst. pastor in Richmond, Va., 1944-47, 50-54, Arlington, Va., 1947-50; sec. Richmond Diocesan Tribunal, 1954-60; moderator Council Cath. Women and Council Cath. Nurses, 1956-61; sec. Diocean bd. Consultors, 1960-64; founder Cath. Physicians Guild, Richmond, 1957-64; chancellor Richmond Diocese, 1960-64; papal chamberlain, 1961; aux. bishop Richmond; titular bishop Latapolis; vicar gen. Richmond Diocese, 1962-64; bishop of Charleston, S.C., 1964-90; retired, 1990—; promoter IV Synod Diocese Richmond, 1962-64; sec. Nat. Conf. U.S. Bishops, 1966-70, chmn. permanent diaconate com., 1968-71, 74—; chmn. Region IV, 1972-74, mem. adminstrv. com., 1974—; sec. adminstrv. bd. Nat. Cath. Conf., 1966-70; mem. Bishops' Com. on Ecumenical and Inter-religious Affairs, 1965-78, chmn., 1978—; mem. Bishops' Com. on Pastoral Plans and Programs, 2d Vatican Council, 1962-65, Anglican-Roman Catholic subcommns. theology of marriage and mixed marriage; co-chmn. Anglican/Roman Cath. Commn. Theology of Marriage; chmn. Roman Cath.-Presbyn./Reformed Consultation; mem. com. social devel. and world peace U.S. Council Chs., 1971-74; mem. adminstrv. com. and bd. NCCB-USCC, 1978—; mem. Ad Hoc Com. Women in Ch. and Soc., 1971—; co-chmn. Charleston Bicentennial Commn. on Religious Liberty; host bishop for visit of Pope John Paul II to U.S., 1987. Bd. dirs. CARA, 1969—, pres., 1972—; mem. alumni bd. govs. Cath. U. Am. Recipient Pax Christi award St. John's U., Collegeville, Minn., 1970; medal of U. Santa Maria La Antiqua, Panama, 1976; Pacem In Terris award, 1980; decorated grand cross Republic of Panama, 1976. Home: Charleston S.C. Deceased.

UNVERZAGT, GEORGE WILLIAM, JR., judge; b. Chgo., Jan. 18, 1931; s. George William and Margaret Anne (Ziegler) U.; m. Sylvia Helen Rilling, June 6, 1959 (div. June 1980); children: Frederick W., Laura M., William H., Susan M.; m. Elvera Lucille McQueen, Oct. 30, 1982. BA, Elmhurst (Ill.) Coll., 1953; JD, U. Chgo., 1959; cert., Nat. Jud. Coll., Reno, Nev., 1971. Bar: Ill. 1959, U.S. Dist. Ct. (no. dist.) Ill. 1960, U.S. Ct. Appeals (7th cir.) 1960, U.S. Supreme Ct. 1970. Atty. C.B. & Q. Ry. Co., Chgo., 1959-61; assoc. Law Office Charles Popejoy, Glen Ellyn, Ill., 1961-63; ptnr. Popejoy, Bowman & Unverzagt, Wheaton, Ill., 1963-68, Bowman, Unverzagt & Teschner, Wheaton, 1968-70; cir. judge 18th Jud. Cir., DuPage County, Ill., 1970-79; appellate judge 2d Jud. Dist., Elgin, Ill., from 1979; chief judge Cir. Ct. 18th Jud. Cir., 1975-79; presiding judge Appellate Ct. Ill., 2d Dist., 1988-91, chmn. meetings, 1981-82; alt. mem. Ill. Ct. Commn., from 1991. Editor: Illinois Judges Manual, 1984, 88, 92. Alderman City of Elmhurst, 1960-63. 1st lt. U.S. Army, 1953-56. Recipient Alumni Merit award Elmhurst Coll., 1973. Mem. Ill. State Bar Assn. (local govt. sect. coun. from 1990), Ill. Judges Assn. (dir. 1978-86), DuPage Bar Assn. (sec., treas., bd. dirs. 1967-70, hon. pres. 1978-79), Am. Legion, Elks, Masons. Republican. Lutheran. Home: Bloomingdale Ill. Deceased.

UYS, JACOBUS JOHANNES (JAMIE UYS), film director; b. May 30, 1921; s. Victor and Maria (Jacobs) U.; m. Hester Jacoba Van Rooyen, 1945; 3 children. Student, U. Pretoria. Dir. Mimosa Films, 1968-96. Dir.: Daar Doer in die Bosveld, 1950, Fifty-Fifty, 1952, Daar Doer in die Stad, 1953, Money to Burn, 1954, Jabulani Africa, 1954, Die Bosvelder, 1955, Satan's Coral, 1956, Sidney and the Boer, 1957, Rip van Wyk, 1958, Dingaka, 1959, Doodkry is Min, 1960, Lord Oom Piet, 1962, All the Way to Paris, 1964, The Professor and the Beauty Queen, 1967, Lost in the Desert, 1971, Beautiful People, 1973, Funny People, 1976, The Gods must be Crazy, 1980, Funny People II, 1983, The Gods must be Crazy II. Recipient Schlesinger Drum, 1953, Gold medal, Chgo., 1968, Gold Scissors award, 1974, Golden Globe award, 1974, Rapport Oscar, 1975, Grand Prix, Vevey, 1981, Haugesund Grand Prix, 1981, London Film Festival prize, 1981, Chamrousse Grand Prix, 1982. Home: Pretoria South Africa Died Jan. 29, 1996.

VAAS, FRANCIS JOHN, lawyer; b. Newton, Mass., Aug. 22, 1917; s. Joseph Francis and Octavia Mary (Bernhardt) V.; m. Isabel Connelly, Jan. 6, 1969. A.B. summa cum laude, Coll. Holy Cross, 1938; LL.B. magna cum laude, Harvard U., 1948. Bar: Mass. 1948, U.S. Supreme Ct. 1969. Assoc. Ropes & Gray, Boston, 1948-56, ptnr., 1957-95, sr. ptnr. Treas.: Harvard Law Rev., 1947-48. Served to 1st lt. USAF, 1942-46. Mem. ABA, Mass. Bar Assn., Boston Bar Assn. Republican. Roman Catholic. Clubs: Weston Golf (Mass.); Harvard (Boston); KC (Brighton, Mass.). Home: Westwood Mass. Died Apr. 30, 1995.

VAGLIO-LAURIN, ROBERTO, aerospace engineering educator and researcher; b. Milan, Italy, Aug. 7, 1929; came to U.S., 1952, naturalized, 1961; s. Guglielmo and Ester (Singrossi) Vaglio-L.; m. Norma A. Bonaventura, Jan. 4, 1958; children: Stefan J., Marc W. D.Eng., U. Rome, 1950, Dr. Aero. Engring., 1952; Ph.D., Poly. Inst. Bklyn., 1954. Profl. engr. Rome, 1950-52; mem. faculty Poly. Inst. Bklyn., 1955-64, prof. aerospace engring., 1960-64, asst. dir. aerospace research, 1962-64, dir., 1964; mem. staff Inst. Def. Analyses, Arlington, Va., 1964-65; prof. aeros. and astronautics N.Y.U., N.Y.C., 1965-73; prof. applied sci. N.Y.U., 1974-84; chief exec. officer Gen. Applied Sci. Labs., Inc.,

Westbury, N.Y., 1976-77; exec. scientist ORI, Inc., Rockville, Md., 1984-89; corp. sr. scientist Arete Assoc., Arlington, 1989-93; vis. lectr. aerodynamics U. Rome, 1959-93; cons. govt. and indsl. orgns. Contbr. articles to profl. jours. Fellow Am. Inst. Aeros. and Astronautics (asso. editor AIAA Jour. 1967-71, mem. fluid dynamics com. 1964-67); corr. mem. Internat. Acad. Astronautics of Internat. Astronautical Fedn.; mem. Am. Phys. Soc., AAAS, Sigma Xi, Tau Beta Pi. Home: Mc Lean Va. Died Oct. 2, 1993; interred Fairfax Meml. Pk. Cemetery, Fairfax, Va.

VAIVODS, JULIJANS CARDINAL, Latvian ecclesiastic; b. Vorkova, Latvia, Aug. 18, 1895. Ordained priest Roman Cath. Ch., 1918. Chaplain various schs., 1918-23; vicar gen., Liepaja, Latvia, from 1944; apostolic activity curtailed by polit. situation, in exile, 1958-60; vical gen., Riga, Latvia, 1962-64; attended Vatican II, 1964; consecrated titular bishop of Macriana Maior, apostolic adminstr. diocese of Riga and diocese of Liepaja, 1964; elevated to Sacred Coll. of Cardinals, 1983. Author catechetical books and theatrical works for youth. Home: Riga Latvia

VALVANO, JAMES THOMAS, college basketball coach; b. Queens, N.Y., Mar. 10, 1946; s. Rocco and Marie Angela (Vitale) V.; m. Pamela Susan Levine, Aug. 6, 1967; children: Nicole, Jamie, Lee Ann. B.A. in English, Rutgers U., 1967, postgrad., 1968-69. Freshman basketball coach Rutgers U., New Brunswick, N.J., 1967-69; head basketball coach Johns Hopkins U., Balt., 1969-70; asst. basketball coach U. Conn., Storrs, 1970-72; head coach Bucknell U., Lewisburg, Pa., 1972-75; head basketball coach Iona Coll., New Rochelle, N.Y., 1975-80; head coach N.C. State U., Raleigh, 1980-93, dir. athletics, 1986-89; mem. Washington Speaker Bur.; coach: NCAA championship team, 1983, Atlantic Coast Conf. championship team, 1983, 86. Author: Too Soon to Quit, 1983; pub.: Jim Valvano's Guide to Great Eating. Mem. Statue of Liberty Commn., 1986-93. Named Coach of Yr., Hawkeye Rebounders Club Cedar Rapids, Iowa, Medalist Sports Industires St. Louis, Spalding Sporting Goods Co., Ea. Basketball Mag.; named Best of New Generation, Esquire Register, 1984; Atlantic Coach Conf. Coach of Yr., 1988, 89. Roman Catholic. Home: Raleigh N.C. Died Apr. 28, 1993.

VAN ARSDEL, PAUL PARR, JR., allergist, educator; b. Indpls., Nov. 4, 1926; s. Paul Parr and Ellen (Ewing) Van A.; m. Rosemary Thorstenson, July 7, 1950; children: Mary Margaret, Andrew Paul. BS, Yale U., 1946; MD, Columbia U., 1951. Diplomate Am. Bd. Internal Medicine, Am. Bd. Allergy and Immunology. Intern Presbyn. Hosp., N.Y.C., 1951-52; resident in medicine Presbyn. Hosp., 1952-53; research fellow in medicine U. Wash. Sch. Medicine, Seattle, 1953-55, instr. medicine, 1956-58, from asst. prof. to prof. medicine, 1958-94, head allergy sect., 1956-94; spl. fellow in allergy, Boston U., Columbia U., N.Y.C., 1955-56; mem. staff Univ. Hosp., Seattle, chief of staff, 1983-85; assoc. staff Harborview Med. Ctr., Seattle; cons. Children's Hosp., Seattle VA Hosp.; vis. prof. medicine U. London, 1986. Contbr. to profl. publs. V.p., bd. dirs. Community Assn., Iron Springs, Wash., 1980-82. Served with USN, 1945-46. Fellow ACP, Am. Acad. Allergy and Immunology (pres. 1971-72), Royal Soc. Medicine (London); mem. AMA (alt. del. 1972-94), Assn. Am. Med. Colls., Phi Beta Kappa, Sigma Xi, Alpha Omega Alpha. Home: Seattle Wash. Died Jan. 16, 1994; interred Acacia Mausoleum, Seattle, W.A.

VAN BINH, PAUL NGUYEN, archbishop. Archbishop of Ho Chi Minh City Roman Cath. Ch., Vietnam. Died July 1, 1995.

VANCE, SHELDON BAIRD, lawyer, former diplomat; b. Crookston, Minn., Jan. 18, 1917; s. Erskine Ward and Helen (Baird) V.; m. Jean Chambers, Dec. 28, 1939; children: Robert Clarke and Stephen Baird. A.B., Carleton Coll., 1939; J.D., Harvard U., 1942. Bar: Mass. 1942, D.C. 1977, U.S. Supreme Ct. 1977. Practiced in Boston, 1942; assoc. firm Ropes, Gray, Best, Coolidge & Rugg; joined Fgn. Service; econ. analyst, 3d sec. Am. embassy, Rio de Janeiro, Brazil, 1942-46; U.S. vice consul Nice, France and Monaco, 1946-49; U.S. consul Martinique, W.I., 1949-51; Swiss Desk officer, 1951-52; Belgium-Luxemburg desk officer Dept. State, Washington, 1952-54; 1st sec. Am. embassy, Brussels, Belgium, 1954-58; chief personnel placement br. Africa, Middle East and South Asia, 1958-60; student Sr. Seminar in Fgn. Relations, 1960-61; dir. Office Central African Affairs, 1961-62; dep. chief mission Am. embassy, Addis Ababa, Ethiopia, 1962-66; sr. fgn. service insp., 1966-67; U.S. ambassador to Republic of Chad, 1967-69, to Republic of Zaire, Kinshasa, 1969-74; promoted to rank of career minister, 1971; sr. adviser to sec. state, coordinator internat. narcotics matters, also exec. dir. President's Cabinet Com. on Internat. Narcotics Control, Dept. State, 1974-77; ptnr. Vance, Joyce, Carbaugh and Fields, Washington, 1977-87; of counsel Vance, Joyce, Carbaugh & Fields, Washington, 1987-89; bd. dirs. Sun Co. Inc., 1977-87. Vice-chmn. Mayor's Adv. Com. on Drug Abuse, Washington, 1980-91; mem. com. of four internat. experts advising UN Conf. on Narcotic Drugs, 1987; keynote speaker Western Hemisphere Conf. on Narcotic Drugs Inter Parliamentary Union, Carcas, Venezuela, 1987. Mem. Fgn. Svc. Assn., DACOR, Columbia Country Club (Chevy Chase, Md.). Presbyterian. Home: Chevy Chase Md. Died Nov. 12, 1995.

VANDEGRIFT, ALFRED EUGENE, chemical engineer; b. Chanute, Kans., Nov. 10, 1937; s. Alfred Darwin and Alma Louise (Mann) V.; m. Joyce Annette Hermann, Dec. 27, 1959; children: Alfred Gregory, Paige Annette, Scott Eugene, Geoffrey Paul. B.S., U. Kans., 1959; Ph.D., U. Calif., Berkeley, 1963. Assoc. chem. engr. Midwest Research Inst., Kansas City, Mo., 1963-65, sr. chem. engr., 1965-70; sect. mgr., environ. systems Midwest Research Inst., Kansas City, 1970-75; dir. North Star Div., Mpls., 1975-77; dir. econ. and mgmt. sci. div. Midwest Research Inst., Kansas City, 1977-80, v.p. social and engring. systems, 1980-84; pres. MRI Ventures, Inc., 1984-87, Ruf Corp., 1987-88; cons. New Bus. Start-ups, 1988-93; chmn. bd. Ceramic Research Inc., 1985-87; cons., bd. mem. Technitran Internat., 1988-93; also bd. dirs.; mem. adv. bd. FilmTec Inc.; bd. dirs. EnzyTec Inc., Technitran Internat. Ltd.; lectr. U. Mo., Kansas City, 1967-71; adj. prof. U. Mo., Columbia, 1978-86, U. Kans., 1986-93; mem. pvt. sector bd. Solar Energy Rsch. Inst., 1986-89; bd. dirs. Mgmt. Support Group Ltd.; cons. Mid-Am. Mfg. Tech. Ctr., 1991-92. Contbg. author: Gas Cleaning for Air Quality Control, 1975; contbr. articles to profl. jours. Mem. troop com. Boy Scouts Am., 1973, Mayor's Sci. Adv. Com., 1974, adv. bd. Kans. U. Sch. Engring., 1983-93. Standard Oil of Calif. fellow, 1960; Corn Products scholar, 1956-59; recipient Enterprise award Midwest Research Inst.; Council Prin. Scientists, 1975. Mem. AAAS, Am. Inst. Chem. Engrs., Air Pollution Control Assn., Met. Entrepreneuer's Coun., Kansas City C. of C., Tau Beta Pi, Phi Lambda Upsilon. Home: Kansas City Mo. Died July 7, 1993; interred Belton Cemetary, Belton M.O.

VANDIVORT, KEITH WILLIAM, lawyer; b. Toledo, Jan. 3, 1953; s. William D. and Helen L. (Collier) V. BA with honors in Polit. Sci., Northwestern U., 1975; JD cum laude, Georgetown U., 1979. Bar: D.C. 1979. Assoc. Lawler Kent & Eisenberg, Washington, 1979-80; assoc. Dechert Price & Rhoads, Washington, 1980-92, ptnr., 1992-93. Vol. No. Va. AIDS Ministry, Alexandria, 1991-93. Mem. ABA, D.C. Bar Assn., Phi Beta Kappa. Democrat. Methodist. Home: Arlington Va. Died Aug. 15, 1993.

VAN DUSEN, FRANCIS LUND, retired federal judge; b. Phila., May 16, 1912; s. Lewis Harlow and Muriel Mary Leila (Lund) Van D.; m. Rhe Brooke Meserole, June 11, 1942 (dec. Nov. 1976); children: Rhe Van Dusen Jain, Muriel Van Dusen Berkeley, Francis L., Clinton M.; m. Margaret Brooks Goodenough, Aug. 19, 1978. A.B., Princeton U., 1934; LL.B., Harvard U., 1937. Bar: Pa. 1937, U.S. Dist. Ct. (ea. dist.) Pa. 1938, U.S. Ct. Appeals (3d cir.) 1982. Assoc. Dechert Smith & Clark, Phila., 1937-41; atty. Adminstr. Export Control, Washington, 1941; sr. atty. Office Prodn. Mgmt., War Prodn. Bd., Washington, 1942; assoc. Barnes Dechert Price Myers & Rhoads, Phila., 1945-49, ptnr., 1950-55; judge U.S. Dist. Ct. (ea. dist.) Pa., Phila., 1955-67; judge U.S. Ct. Appeals (3d cir.), Phila., 1967-90, sr. judge, 1977-90, ret., 1990. Contbr. articles to profl. jours. Served to lt. comdr. USN, 1942-45, PTO. Decorated Bronze Star (2); recipient Gold Good Citizenship medal SAR, 1973. Mem. Fed. Bar Assn. (Outstanding Pub. Servant award 1977), Jud. Conf. U.S. (mem. probation com. 1963-69, chmn. com. 1971-72, criminal law com. 1969-71), SAR, Navy League U.S. Republican. Episcopalian. Home: Bryn Mawr Pa. Died May 26, 1993.

VAN GELDER, RICHARD GEORGE, retired museum official, zoologist; b. N.Y.C., Dec. 17, 1928; s. Joseph and Clara DeHirsch (Goldberg) Van G.; m. Rosalind Rudnick, July 1, 1962 (dec. 1986); children: Russell Neil, Gordon Mark, Leslie Gail. B.S. with honors, Colo. A&M Coll., 1950; M.S., U. Ill., 1952, Ph.D., 1958. Lab. asst. Colo. A. & M. Coll., 1947-50; teaching asst. U. Ill., 1950-53; research asst. U. Kan., 1954-55, asst. prof., 1955; asst. curator Am. Mus. Nat. Hist., N.Y.C., 1956-61; assoc. curator Am. Mus. Nat. Hist., 1961-69, curator, 1969-86, acting chmn. dept. mammals, 1958-59, chmn. dept., 1959-74; also professorial lectr. Downstate Med. Center, State U. N.Y., 1970-73; lectr., Columbia, 1958-59, asst. prof., 1959-63; with Huachuca Mountain Expdn., summer 1950, Graham Mountain Expdn., summer 1951, Spotted Skunk Expdn., 1953-54, Puritan Expdn., 1957, Uruguay Expdn., 1962-63, Bolivian Expdn., 1964, Bolivian Expdn. II, 1965, Bahama Biol. Survey, 1966, Mozambique Expdn., 1968, S.W. Africa Expdn., 1970, Nyala Expdn., 1971-74, Tsessebe Expdn., 1976-77; Mem. sci. adv. bd. Nat. History Mag., 1958-66, 72-74; mem. adv. bd. Archbold Biol. Sta., Lake Placid, Fla., 1958-74, Global Expdns., Inc., 1985-87; mem. tech. and editorial adv. bd. Population Reference Bur., 1971-75; bd. dirs. Archbold Expdns., Inc., 1965-74, Quincy Bog Natural Area, 1977-94; bd. dirs N.J. Audubon Soc., 1986-89, Okeanos Ocean Research Found., 1987-94; mem. sci. adv. bd. Found. Environ. Edn., 1972; mem. N.J. Non-game and Endangered Species Council, 1982-89. Author: Physiological Mammalogy, 1963, 65, Biology of Mammals, 1969, Animals and Man, 1972, Safari Guide, 1981, Mammals of the National Parks, 1982. Named Honored Alumnus, Coll. Natural Resources, Colo. State U., 1985. Fellow N.Y. Zool. Soc.; mem. Am. Soc. Mammalogists (pres. 1968-70), AAAS, Wildlife Soc., Sigma Xi, Beta Beta Beta, Phi Sigma, Alpha Gamma Rho. Home: Harrington Park N.J. Died Feb. 23, 1994.

VANLANDINGHAM, WILLIAM JENNINGS, banker; b. Louisville, Sept. 10, 1937; s. Zack Jennings and Corinne (Brown) V.; m. Barbara McMillan, Feb. 16; children—William Jennings II, Teri Leigh, Joseph Templeton. Grad. Ga. Tech., 1959; postgrad., Emory U. Law Sch., 1964-67; P.M.D., Harvard U., 1972. Prodn. mgr. Procter & Gamble, Cin. and Dallas, 1962-64; asst. to v.p. Rich's, Inc., Atlanta, 1964-66; pres., chief exec. officer C&S Ga. Corp., Atlanta, from 1966; bd. dirs. Ga. Intercharge Network, Inc. Mem. Atlanta Bd. Edn., 1971-74; bd. dirs. Rsch. Atlanta, Inc., Vol. Atlanta, Ga. Safety Coun., Metro Atlanta chpt. ARC; chmn. bd. trustees Pace Acad.; chmn. Ga. Coun. Econ. Edn.; trustee Ga. Inst. Tech. Found. With USNR, 1959-61. Mem. Ga. Bankers Assn. (bd. dirs.). Methodist. Home: Atlanta Ga. Deceased.

VAN NESS, EDWARD HARRY, association executive; b. Chgo., Apr. 10, 1929; s. George R. and Grace E. (Wikoff) Van N. Student, Loras Coll., 1947-49; Ph.B. magna cum laude, Coll. St. Thomas Aquinas, 1952; M.A. magna cum laude, Aquinas Inst., 1953; postgrad., Loyola U., 1953-54, U. Chgo., 1957-58. Asst. dir. Center for Programs in Govt. Adminstrn., U. Chgo., 1958-59; asso. dir. govt. exec. program N.Y. U., 1959-61; asst. sec. to Gov. Nelson A. Rockefeller, Albany, N.Y., 1961-66; exec. dir. N.Y. State Health Planning Commn., N.Y.C., 1967-73; exec. v.p. Nat. Health Council, N.Y.C., 1973-95; vis. prof. health planning Sloan Inst. Hosp. Adminstrn., Cornell U., 1967-73; lectr. Columbia U., 1968-73; mem. faculty hosp. adminstrn. program Wagner Coll., N.Y.C., 1967-77. Co-editor: Concepts and Issues in Administrative Behavior, 1962. Chmn. Gov.'s Task Force on Universal Health Ins., 1965-70, Gov.'s Planning Com. for Narcotic Addiction Control, 1966-67; exec. sec. N.Y. State Joint Council on Regional Med. Programs, 1967. Served with U.S. Army, 1955-56. Mem. Ind. Sector, Inc., Am. Health Planning Assn., Am. Soc. Assn. Execs., Am. Pub. Health Assn. Home: New York N.Y. Died July 7, 1995.

VAN NORDEN, LANGDON, lawyer; b. N.Y.C., Jan. 12, 1915; s. Ottomar Hoghland and Jeanie Belle (Duncan) Van N.; m. Gloria I. Barnes, June 19, 1948; 1 son, Langdon. Grad., Choate Sch., 1933; A.B., Princeton U., 1937; LL.B., Yale U., 1940. Bar: N.Y. 1941, Conn. 1977. With firm Davis, Polk, Wardwell, Sunderland & Kiendl, N.Y.C., 1940-42, 45-49; with H.A. Caesar & Co., N.Y.C., 1949-93; ptnr. H.A. Caesar & Co., 1951-69; v.p., gen. counsel First Union Comml. Corp., 1970-75; resident counsel firm Winthrop, Stimson, Putnam & Roberts, Stamford, Conn., 1976-89. Pres. Met. Opera Guild, 1953-67; bd. dirs. Met. Opera Assn., chmn., 1975-77; pres. Nat. Orchestral Assn., chmn., 1975-85; trustee Greenwich Country Day Sch., 1968-74. Served to capt. AUS, 1942-45, ETO. Decorated Bronze Star medal. Mem. Yale Law Sch. Assn. (exec. com., past chmn. exec. com.). Clubs: Century Assn. (N.Y.C.); Round Hill (Greenwich, Conn.). Home: Greenwich Conn. Died Jan. 27, 1993.

VAN NOSTRAND, MORRIS ABBOTT, JR., publisher; b. N.Y.C., Nov. 24, 1911; s. Morris Abbott and Margaret Adrianna (Edwards) Van N.; m. Jane Alexander, Dec. 28, 1934 (dec. 1944); children: Pamela George, Patricia Abbott; m. Julia de La Roche Eaton, July 3, 1953; children: Deborah Randall, Abbie Eaton. B.A., Amherst Coll., 1934. With Samuel French, Inc., N.Y.C., 1934-95; sec. Samuel French, Inc., 1948-52, pres., 1952-95; pres. Samuel French Canada, Ltd., Toronto, Ont., 1952-95, Walter H. Baker Co., Boston and Denver, 1952-95, Hugo & Luigi-Samuel French Music Pubs., Inc.; chmn. bd. Samuel French, Ltd., London. Bd. dirs. New Dramatists Com., mem. coun. Friends of Amherst (Mass.) Library. Mem. ANTA (dir.), Chi Phi. Clubs: Amherst, Doubles (N.Y.C.); Nassau Country (Glen Cove) (gov.); Les Ambassadeurs, Clermont (London). Home: New York N.Y. Died Sept. 27, 1995.

VAN PELT, ROBERT, judge; b. Gosper County, Nebr., Sept. 9, 1897; s. Francis M. and Sarah (Simon) Van P.; m. Mildred Carter, June 17, 1925; children: Robert (dec.), Margery Van Pelt Irvin, Samuel. AB cum laude, Doane Coll., 1920, LLD (hon.), 1959; LLB, U. Nebr., 1922, LLD (hon.), 1985; LHD (hon.), Westmar Coll., 1960. Bar: Nebr. 1922. Practiced in Lincoln, 1922- 57; asst. U.S. atty., 1930-34; judge U.S. Dist. Ct. Nebr., Lincoln, 1957-70, sr. judge, from 1970; lectr. Nebr. Law Coll., 1946-57; mem. com. to implement Fed. Magistrates Act; mem. adv. com. jud. activities, adv. com. fed. rules of evidence U.S. Jud. Conf.; apptd. spl. master by U.S. Supreme Ct. in Original Nos. 27, 36, 73, 81, 106 involving boundary disputes affecting the States of Tex., La., Calif., Nev., Ky., Ind., Ohio, Ill. del. Rep. Nat. Conv., 1940, 44, 48; trustee Doane Coll., 1928-68. Mem. Am. Coll. Trial Lawyers, Am. Coll. Probate Counsel, Phi Sigma Kappa, Phi Delta Phi. Congregationalist. Clubs: Lincoln Country, Lincoln Univ. Lodges: Masons (33 deg.), Rotary. Home: Lincoln Nebr. Deceased.

VAN WELL, GÜNTHER WILHELM, retired ambassador; b. Osterath, Germany, Oct. 15, 1922; s. Friedrich and Magda (Hulser) Van W.; m. Carolyn Stevens Bradley, Nov. 9, 1957; children—Kirsten, Mark. M.Econs., U. Bonn, Fed. Republic Germany, 1950, LL.M., %. Jr. barrister Dist. Ct., Dusseldorf, Fed. Republic Germany, 1950-51; 3d and 1st sec. Fgn. Office, Bonn, 1952-54, 59-62; 2d sec. UN Observer's Office, N.Y.C., 1954-59; cousellor Fed. Republic Germany embassy, Tokyo, 1963-67; dir. State Sec. Fgn. Office, Bonn, 1967-81; ambassador to UN and U.S.A. N.Y.C. and Washington, 1981-87; fellow Harvard U., Cambridge, Mass., 1961-62. Contbr. articles to profl. jours. Mem. German Soc. for Fgn. Policy (exec. v.p.), German Juristic Assn., Inst. for East-West Security Studies. Home: Bonn-Bad Godesberg Federal Republic Germany Deceased.

VAN YOUNG, OSCAR, artist, educator; b. Vienna, Austria, Apr. 15, 1906; came to U.S., 1923, naturalized, 1943; s. Emil and Olga (Zimmerman) Van Y.; m. Lilian Finkel (Loli Vann), Apr. 14, 1935; 1 son, Eric Julian. Student, Art Acad., Odessa, Russia, 1918-22; B.A., Calif. State U., Los Angeles, 1958, M.A., 1959. Mem. faculty Pasadena City Coll., 1959-73, Calif. State U., Los Angeles, 1960-63; lectr. in field. One-man shows include, Art Inst. Chgo., 1940, Los Angeles County Mus., 1942, San Francisco Mus. Art, 1943, Pasadena Art Mus., 1945, 51, Santa Barbara Mus., 1946, La Jolla Art Ctr., 1949, Cowie Galleries, Los Angeles, 1953, 57, 61, 66, 71, San Bernardino Valley Coll., 1972, Copenhagen Gallery, Solvang, Calif., 1977, Palm Springs Desert Mus., 1980, Atelier Clemens, Pasadena, Calif., 1980, Zantman Gallery, Palm Desert, Calif., 1983, 90, Ontario (Calif.) Mus. Art, 1983; group exhbns. include Los Angeles County Mus., 1941-61, 80, San Francisco Mus. Art, 1941-45, Pa. Acad. Fine Arts, 1949, Pasadena Art Mus., 1946, 55, Art Inst. Chgo., 1938-46, Corcoran Biennial, Washington, 1941, 47, San Francisco World's Fair, 1940, Ill. State Mus., 1940, 42, 48, Univ. Judaism, Platt Gallery, 1992-93; represented in permanent collections, Los Angeles County Mus., Palm Springs Desert Mus., Ill. State Mus., Laguna Beach (Calif.) Mus. Art, Santa Barbara Mus., Frye Mus., Seattle, Tel Aviv Art Mus., Smithsonian Instn., Washington. Home: Los Angeles Calif. Died Feb. 26, 1993; interred L.A., Calif.

VARNER, JOSEPH ELMER, biology educator, researcher; b. Nashport, Ohio, Oct. 7, 1921; s. George Ezra and Inez Charlotte (Gladden) V.; m. Carol Roberta Dewey, June, 1945 (div. 1971); children—Lee, Lynn, Karen, Beth; m. Jane Elanor Burton, June, 1976. B.Sc., Ohio State U., 1942, M.Sc., 1943, Ph.D., 1949; Docteur Honoris Causa (hon.), Nancy U., France, 1977. Chemist Owens Corning, Newark, 1943-44; analytical chemist Battelle Meml. Inst., Columbus, Ohio, 1946-47; from asst. prof. to prof. biology Ohio State U., Columbus, Ohio, 1950-61; postdoctoral Calif. Inst. Tech., Pasadena, 1953-54; NSF fellow Cambridge U., Eng., 1959-60; research scientist Martin-Marietta, Balt., 1961-65; prof. biochemistry Mich. State U., East Lansing, 1965-73; NSF fellow U. Wash., Seattle, 1971-72; prof. biology Washington U., St. Louis, 1973-95, Am. Cancer Soc. scholar, 1980-81. Author, editor: Plant Biochemistry, 1965, 2d edit., 1976; contbr. articles on plant biology to profl. jours. Fellow AAAS; mem. NAS, Am. Soc. Plant Physiologists (pres. 1969, Stephen Hales Prize 1990), Soc. Developmental Biology (pres. 1986), Am. Acad. Arts and Sci. Home: Saint Louis Mo. Died July 4, 1995.

VASSILEV, ROSA TUSA, journalist, magazine editor; b. Milw.; d. Albert John and Helen (Garippo) Tusa; m. Kyril Vassilev, Aug. 17, 1963 (dec. June 1987). Student, Ala. Coll., 1941. Dir. publicity and edn. Am. Cancer Soc., Milw., 1950-53; reporter Milw. Sentinel, 1953-72; food editor Palm Beach Post, West Palm Beach, Fla., 1972-87; food editor Palm Beach (Fla.) Life, 1972-87, dining out editor, 1987-92. Author: True Grits, 1977. Mem. Confrerie Chaine Rotisseurs, Bailliage Palm Beach. Republican. Roman Catholic. Home: Grosse Pointe Mich. Died Nov. 28, 1992.

VAUGHAN, J(AMES) RODNEY M(ITCHELL), retired industrial scientist, researcher, consultant; b. Margate, Kent, Eng., May 2, 1921; came to U.S., 1957; s. James and Dulcie G. (Chiesman) V.; m. B. Anne H. Blyth, Dec. 18, 1948; children—Peter J., Caroline H., Timothy M. B.A. in Math., Cambridge U., Eng., 1948; M.A., Cambridge U., 1957, Ph.D. in Elec. Engring., 1972. Research engr. Research Lab. of Elec. and Musical Industries, London, 1948-57; sr. engr. Gen. Electric Co., Schenectady, 1957-68, Litton Industries, San Carlos, Calif., 1968-71; chief scientist Litton Industries, 1971-89; pres. Rodney Vaughan Assocs., Inc., Redwood City, Calif., 1989-95; chmn. Microwave Tube Com. (JT-13), Washington, 1964-67; tech. chmn. Microwave Power Tube Conf., Monterey, Calif., 1982. Contbr. articles to profl. jours. Pres., Kopy Kat Ski Club, Scotia, N.Y., 1966, Menlo Players Guild, Menlo Park, Calif., 1978-80. Served to capt. Royal Corps of Signals, Brit. Army, 1940-46. Litton Advanced Tech. award, 1988. Fellow IEEE (assoc. editor Transactions on Electron Devices 1972-76, adminstrv. com. Electron Devices Soc. 1977-84). Club: Oxford and Cambridge (London). Home: Redwood City Calif. Died Feb. 9, 1995.

VAUGHN, CHARLES MELVIN, zoologist; b. Deadwood, S.D., Nov. 23, 1915; s. Roy Francis and May (Smith) V.; m. Mattie Christine Isaacson, Sept. 6, 1941; children: Martha Frances, Richard Charles. B.A., U. Ill., 1939, M.A. (scholar zoology 1939-40), 1940; Ph.D., U. Wis., 1943. Asst. prof., then assoc. prof. zoology Miami U., Oxford, Ohio, 1946-51, prof., chmn. dept. zoology and physiology, 1965-71, prof., 1971-81, prof. emeritus, 1981-93, chmn. dept. zoology, 1971-78, acting dean rsch., 1970-71, interim. assoc. dean rsch. and sponsored programs, 1983-84; instr. parasitology Inst. Tropical Medicine, Bowman Gray Sch. Medicine, 1950-52, sr. parasitologist, 1950-52, assoc. dir. inst., 1951-52; sr. parasitologist, assoc. dir. field service unit Am. Found. Tropical Medicine, N.Y.C., 1952-53; prof. zoology, head dept. U. S.D., 1953-61, prof., chmn. dept., 1961-64, dir. NSF acad. year inst. sci. and math. tchrs. at univ., 1958-64; program dir. coll. and elementary tchr. program inst. sect. NSF, Washington, 1964-65; program dir. acad. year rsch. tng. NSF, 1965, cons., 1965-69; biology specialist AID, 1966, 67; China Med. Bd. fellow, C.A., summer 1956. Served to maj., San. Corps AUS, 1943-46; now col. AUS (ret.). Fellow AAAS (coun. 1976-82, sect. X rep. 1976-84, coun. 1986, sect. Y rep. 1986-90), Ohio Acad. Sci. (pres. 1977-78), Royal Soc. Tropical Medicine and Hygiene; mem. Nat. Assn. Acad. Sci., 1974-93, Am. Soc. Zoologists, Am. Soc. Parasitologists, Am. Microscopical Soc. (pres. 1972-73), Soc. Protozoologists, Am. Soc. Tropical Medicine and Hygiene, Assn. Acads. Sci. (pres. 1971-72), S.D. Acad. Sci. (pres. 1961-62), Assn. Midwestern Coll. Biology Tchrs., Wis. Acad. Scis. Arts and Letters, Res. Officers Assn., Brit. Soc. for Parasitology, Phi Beta Kappa, Sigma Xi, Phi Kappa Phi, Phi Sigma (nat. pres. 1983-93), Kappa Delta Pi, Gamma Alpha, Alpha Phi Omega. Presbyterian. Clubs: Mason, Lion. Home: Oxford Ohio Died Apr. 3, 1993; interred Miami Univ. Sect. Oxford Cemetery, Oxford, Ohio.

VAZQUEZ, SILOS JOSE MACLOVIA, bishop; b. San Louis Potosi, Mex., Nov. 15, 1918; s. Lara Juan and Amada Silos de Vazquez. Humanist, San Luis Potosi Coll., Grad. in Philosophy; Grad. in Philosophy, Roma Pontificia Universidad Gregoriana, Grad. in Theology. Bishop of Autlan Jalisco, Mex. Home: Autlan Jalisco Mex.

VENNING, ELEANOR HILL, retired biochemist; b. Montreal, Que., Can., Mar. 16, 1900; d. George William and Elsie Annette (Kent) Hill; B.A., McGill U., Montreal, 1920, M.S.C., 1921, Ph.D. in Exptl. Medicine, 1933; m. E. A. Venning, June 29, 1929. Assoc. prof. exptl. medicine McGill U., 1950-60, prof., 1960-65; dir. endocrine labs. Royal Victoria Hosp., Montreal, 1950-65. Fellow Royal Soc. Can.; emeritus mem. Can. Soc. Biochemistry, Can. Soc. Physiology, Endocrine Soc. U.S. (Fred Comad Koch award 1962), N.Y. Acad. Scis., Can. Soc. Endocrinology and Metabolism. Contbr. chpts., numerous articles to profl. publs. Deceased. Home: Westmount Can.

VERALDI, LEWIS C., automobile manufacturing company executive; b. Detroit, 1930; married. BSME, Lawrence Inst. Tech., 1968. Various positions Ford Motor Co., Dearborn, Mich., 1949-67, mgr. brakes and chassis frames Product Devel. Group, 1967-69, exec. engr. Product Devel. Group, 1969-71, asst. chief engr., 1971-72, chief assembly engr., 1972-75, v.p. car engring. Ford of Europe, Inc., 1973, corp. v.p., 1975-76, v.p. advanced vehicles div., 1976-80, v.p. advanced vehicle engring. and tech., 1980-82, v.p. luxury and mid-size car engring. and planning, 1982-83, luxury and large car engring. and planning, 1983-86, car programs mgmt., 1986-90. Served with U.S. Army, 1948-49. Mem. Soc. Automotive Engrs.(Eli Whitney Meml. Awd., 1988). Deceased. Home: Dearborn Mich.

VERDIER, PHILIPPE M(AURICE), art historian; b. Lambersart, France, Oct. 5, 1912; came to Can., 1965, naturalized, 1973; s. Georges and Berthe (Fort) V.; m. Patricia Cowles, July 3, 1954; children: Francesca, Lisa, Caroline, Patrick. M.A., Sorbonne, Paris, 1935; mem., Ecole Française de Rome, 1938-39; mem. Agrègè de l'Universitè, Ecole Normale Supèrieure, Paris, 1936. Prof. Institut Français, Barcelona, Spain, 1941, Madrid, 1943-44; prof. Lycèe R. Poincarè, Bar-le-Duc, 1950-51; Henri Focillon fellow Yale U., 1951-52, guest prof., 1959, 61; guest prof. Bryn Mawr Coll., 1952-53, Johns Hopkins U., 1954-65, U. Poitiers, France, 1964; mem. Inst. Advanced Study, Princeton U., 1964-65; titular prof. U. Montrèal, Que., Can., 1965-79, prof. emeritus, 1979-93; curator Walters Art Gallery, Balt., 1953-65, Mus. Art, Carnegie Inst., Pitts., 1963-64; guest prof. Harvard U., 1967, Carleton U., 1972-74; mem. Commission des Programmes Universitaires du Quèbec, 1973-74; acting curator Cleve. Mus. Art, 1979-80; cons. curator Menil Found., Houston, 1980-82; Kress prof. The Nat. Gallery, Washington, 1983-84. Author: (books) Frick Collection Limoges Painted Enamels, 1977, Le Couronnement de la Vierge, 1980, (with others) Animals in Ancient Art, 1981, (with others) Western Decorative Arts, Part I, 1993. U.S. fgn. policy reporter Marshall Plan, 1947-48. Served with French Air Force, 1937-38, 39-40, 45. Decorated Legion of Honor; Arts Council Can. Killam fellow, 1974-76. Mem. Internat. Ctr. Medieval Art, Corpus Vitrearum Medii Aevi, Assn. of Acad. Royale d'Archéologie de Belgique. Roman Catholic. Home: Westerly R.I. Died Sept. 14, 1993.

VERHOOGEN, JOHN, retired geology educator; b. Brussels, Feb. 1, 1912; came to U.S., 1947, naturalized, 1953; s. Rene and Lucy (Vincotte) V.; m. Ilse Goldschmidt, Nov. 28, 1938 (dec. 1981); children: Robert H., Alexis R., Therese, Sylvie. Mining Engr., U. Brussels, 1933; Geol. Engr., U. Liege, 1934; Ph.D., Stanford U., 1936. Asst. U. Brussels, Brussels and Belgian Congo, 1936-39; asst. Fonds Nat. Recherche Sci., Belgian Congo, 1939-40, Mines d'or de Kilo-Moto, Belgian Congo, 1940-43; dir. prodn. Miniere de Guerre, Belgian Congo, 1943-46; assoc. prof. geology U. Calif., Berkeley, 1947-51; prof. U. Calif., 1952-77, prof. emeritus, 1977-93. Author books, articles on petrology, volcanology, geophysics. Guggenheim fellow, 1953-54, 60-61. Mem. Nat. Acad. Scis., Am. Acad. Arts and Scis., Am. Geophys. Union, Geol. Soc. Am. (Day medal 1958). Club: Faculty (Berkeley). Home: Berkeley Calif. Died Nov. 8, 1993.

VERNER, WILLIAM KEMBLE, museum director; b. Phila., June 23, 1935; s. Harry Jacques Jr. and Helen Lucretia (Kirk) V.; m. Abbie Lathrop Sunde, Apr. 28, 1962; children: Victoria Sunde, Alexandra Kirk. AB with high hons., Princeton U., 1957; student, Oxford (Eng.) U., 1956. Adminstrv. asst. Adirondack Mus., Blue Mountain Lake, N.Y., 1962-65, research asst., 1965-68, curator of research, 1968-72, curator, 1972-79; cons. on humanities XIII Olympic Winter Games, Lake Placid, N.Y., 1979-80; cons. dir. Olympic and Winter Sports Mus., Lake Placid, N.Y., 1980-81; pres. Adirondack Mountain Sch., Long Lake, N.Y., 1975-84; editor Adirondack Life mag., Syracuse, N.Y., 1984; dir. Schenectady (N.Y.) Mus., 1985—; cons. in field, N.Y., from 1980; program cons. sta. WCFE-TV, Plattsburgh, N.Y., from 1984. Contbr. articles in field. Chmn. Citizens' Adv. Task Force on Open Space, Adirondack Park Agy., Ray Brook, N.Y., 1978-80; trustee Assn. Protection Adirondacks, Schenectady, from 1986, Fedn. Hist. Services, Troy, N.Y., from 1987. Served with U.S. Army, 1957-60. Exhbn. grantee NEH, 1977-78. Mem. N.Y. State Hist. Assn. (lectr. 1985). Democrat. Home: Schenectady N.Y. Deceased.

VERWOERDT, ADRIAAN, psychiatrist; b. Voorburg, The Netherlands, July 5, 1927; came to U.S., 1953, naturalized, 1958; s. Christopher and Juliana Margaretha (Busch) V.; children: Christopher Earl, Mark Adrian. M.D., Med. Sch. of Amsterdam, 1952. Diplomate: Pan Am. Med. Assn. Rotating intern Touro Infirmary, New Orleans, 1953-54; resident in psychiatry Duke U. Med. Center, Durham, N.C., 1954-55, 58-60; fellow in psychiat. research Duke U. Med. Center, 1960-61, asst. prof. psychiatry, 1963-67, assoc. prof., 1967-71, prof., 1971-95, dir. geriatric psychiatry tng. program, 1966-78; dir. psychiat. residency tng. John Umstead Hosp., Butner, N.C., 1968-80; dir. Geropsychiatry Inst. (John Umstead Hosp.), Butner, N.C., 1980-86; cons. N.C. Dept. Human Resources, 1989-95. Author: Communication with the Fatally Ill, 1966, Clinical Geropsychiatry, 1976, 1st rev. edit., 1981, 2d rev. edit., 90; contbr. articles to profl. jours. Served as capt. M.C. U.S. Army, 1955-57. NIMH Career Tchr. Tng. grantee, 1964-66. Fellow Am. Psychiat. Assn.; mem. Am. Assn. for Geriatric Psychiatry, Am. Psychoanalytic Assn. Home: Durham N.C. Died Sept. 11, 1995.

VEST, GEORGE GRAHAM, lawyer; b. Washington, Mar. 14, 1930; s. John Pinckney Wheeler and Frances Howell (Neville) V.; m. Elizabeth Haskell, Sept. 13, 1958; children: George Graham Jr., Sarah Benson. AB, Brown U., 1952; JD, U. Va., 1958. Bar: D.C. 1959, Conn. 1961. Law clk. to presiding judge US. Ct. Claims, Washington, 1958-60; assoc. Cummings & Lockwood, Stamford, Conn., 1960-67; ptnr. Cummings & Lockwood, Stamford, 1967-94; bd. dirs., v.p., sec. Henry L & Grace Doherty Found., N.Y.C., 1978-94. Cpl. USMC, 1952-55. Cpl. USMC, 1952-55. Mem. ABA, Conn. Bar Assn., Conn. Bar Found. (bd. dirs. 1982, v.p. 1988-92), Stamford Regional Bar Assn., Stamford Tex Assn. (pres. 1975), Conn. Bus. and Industry Assn. (tax sect.), Country Club of New Canaan (Conn.), Landmark Club (Stamford). Republican. Episcopalian. Home: New Canaan Conn. Died Dec. 12, 1994.

VETTER, BETTY MCGEE, commission executive; b. Center, Colo., Oct. 25, 1924; d. William Allen and Bonnie Hunsaker McGee; m. Richard C. Vetter, Sept. 4, 1951; children: David Bruce, Richard Dean, Robert Alan. BA, U. Colo., 1944; MA, Stanford U., 1948; LLD (hon.), Ill. Wesleyan U., 1992. Chemist Shell Devel. Co., Emeryville, Calif., 1944-45; instr. Fresno State Coll., 1948-50, Far Eastern div. U. Calif., 1950-51; adj. prof. Am. U., Washington, 1952-64; part-time U. Va., Arlington, 1952-64, U. Md. Ext. div., College Park, 1960-61; exec. dir. Commn. on Profls. in Sci. and Tech. (formerly Sci. Manpower Commn.), Washington, 1964-94. Editor: Sci., Engring., Tech. Manpower Comments, 1965-94. Served with U.S. Naval Women's Res., 1944-45. Recipient Disting. Svc. award U. Colo., 1990, award Assn. for Women in Sci., 1994. Mem. AAUW, AAAS, Women in Engring. Program Adminstrs. Network (treas. 1992-94). Home: Arlington Va. Died Nov. 18, 1994.

ᐯEVIER, CHARLES, historian, educator, consultant, ıiversity administrator; b. N.Y.C., June 15, 1924; s. 'ax and Sarah (Kramer) V.; m. Marcia Gold, Sept. 7, 952; children: Ann, Ellen, John. B.A., U. Wis., 1948, I.A., 1949, Ph.D., 1953. Instr. U. Wis. Extension at 'ausau, 1951-52, Rutgers U., 1952-54; asst. prof. U. ochester, 1954-59; prof. U. Wis., Milw., 1959-95, vice ıancellor, 1963-69; pres. Adelphi U., 1969-71; exec. p. Univ. Medicine and Dentistry N.J.-N.J. Med. Sch., 971-83, prof. div. social and behavioral sci., dept. sychiatry, 1972-95; faculty cons. Thomas Edison Coll.; ons. Urban Affairs Com. Action, 1968; vis. adj. prof. utgers U. and Essex County Coll. Author: United tates and China, 1906-16; also articles.; editor: A oyage Down the Amur, 1969-71, Flexner—75 Years ater. Trustee Mt. St. Paul Coll., Lexington Sch. for)eaf, North Shore Hosp., 1967-70; bd. dirs. Coun. Iigher Edn. in Newark, N.J. Assn. for Children with Iearing Impairments, WBGO-FM, Newark. With ISAAF, 1943-45. Decorated Air medal. Mem. Am. Iist. Assn., Orgn. Am. Historians, Soc. History Am. 'gn. Rels., Med. History Soc. N.J., AAUP. Home: 'enafly N.J. Died Nov. 9, 1995.

ᐯILELA, AVELAR BRANDAO CARDINAL, rchbishop of Sao Salvador de Bahia; b. Vicosa, Brazil, une 13, 1912. Ordained priest Roman Catholic Ch., 935. Consecrated bishop of Petrolina, 1946; rchbishop, Teresina, Brazil, 1955, Sao Salvador de 3ahia, Brazil, 1971-86; elevated to cardinal, 1973; ardinal primate of Brazil. Died Dec. 19, 1986. Home: ;alvador Brazil

ᐯILLARD, THOMAS LOUIS, actor; b. Waipahu, Hawaii, Nov. 19, 1953; s. Ronald Louis and Diane Ruth MacNaughton) V. Student, Allegheny Coll., Lee Strasberg Inst., Am. Acad. Arts; studies with Warren Robertson. Actor: (stage prodns.) The Winter's Tale, The Zoo Story, Feiffer's People, Butterfingers Angel, Henry V, Vampire Tales, Pagan Holiday, The Happiest Girl in the Whole Wide World, (feature films) Parasite, 1981, Grease II, 1982, Surf II, 1983, Weekend Warriors, 1985, One Crazy Summer, 1985, Heartbreak Ridge, 1986, The Trouble with Dick, 1986, (TV episodes) Rags to Riches, The Golden Girls, Macgruder and Loud, Taxi, (TV series) We Got it Made, 1983-84, (TV movies) Sidney Shorr: A Girl's Best Friend, 1981, High School, U.S.A., 1983, Attack of Fear, 1984; author: (poetry) at the time, 1977, inside outside, 1983; photographer works exhibited at James Turcotte Gallery, Los Angeles, 1983. Mem. Actors' Equity Assn., Screen Actors Guild, AFTRA. Home: North Hollywood Calif. Died Nov. 14, 1994.

VILLECHAIZE, HERVE JEAN PIERRE, actor; b. Paris, Apr. 23, 1943; s. Andre and Eveline (Recchionni) V. Attended, Beaux Art Sch., Paris. Ptnr. Art Students League, N.Y.C. FW Spas, Inc., Mini Autos Corp., Mexico City. Films include The One and Only, The Man with the Golden Gun, The Gang that Couldn't Shoot Straight, Crazie Joe, Forbidden Zone, Airplane II, others; appeared on Broadway in: Elizabeth the First, Gloria Esperanza; mem. Hartford Stage Co. in, Ubu Roi; stage appearances in Rosencrantz and Gilderstern Are Dead, Scuba Duba, Phila. Playhouse, Jack Street, Mark Taper Forum, L.A.; mem. N.Y. City Opera Co. in Rigoletto, Pagliaci, Carrie Nation; starred as Tattoo in TV series Fantasy Island, 1976-83; other TV appearances include Good Morning Am., Johnny Carson Show, Dinah Shore show, Different Strokes, Taxi, The Fall Guy, Shelly Duvall Fairy Tale Theatre, Merv Griffin Show, others; recordings on Children of the World songs: Why, When a Child is Born; exhbns. of paintings in numerous galleries throughout U.S. Founder Venice Anti-Crime Hotline; active Suicide Hotline, Hogars Crea Ctr. for drug and alcohol abuse MacLaren Hall, Green Peace, The Flying Doctors of Mercy, Stop the Madness, Save the Seals, Save the Whales.; bd. dirs. Hathaway House for Children; Sheenway Sch. and Cultural Center. Recipient Art award City of Paris; numerous others. Mem. AFTRA, Wildlife Waystation, Calif. Humane Soc. for Animals, LIGA Internat., Internat. Assn. Chiefs of Police, Nat. Wildlife Assn., St. Joseph's Lakota Council. Home: Burbank Calif. Died Sept. 4, 1993.

VINCENT, LLOYD DREXELL, university president; b. DeQuincy, La., Jan. 7, 1924; s. Samuel and Lila (Dickerson) V.; m. Johnell Stuart, Aug. 30, 1947; children: Drexell Stuart, Sandra. Student, Rice U., 1946-47, 49-50; B.S., U. Tex., Austin, 1952, M.A., 1953, Ph.D., 1960; postdoctoral, Harvard U., summer 1987. Asst. prof. U. Southwestern La., 1953-55, assoc. prof., 1956-58; instr. Tex. A&M U., 1955-56; Danforth Found. tchr. study grantee, NSF Sci. faculty fellow. U. Tex., 1958-59; research scientist Tex. Nuclear Corp., Austin, 1959-60; prof., dir. physics dept. Sam Houston State U., 1960-65, asst. to pres., 1965-67; pres. Angelo State U., San Angelo, Tex., 1967—; co-owner, mgr. ACME Glass Corp., Baytown, Tex., 1947-49; physics cons. Columbia U. Tchrs. Coll., U.S. AID, India, summer 1966; mem. formula adv. com. Tex. Higher Edn. Coordinating Bd., 1975—; chair bd. dirs. Tex. Internat. Edn. Consortium, Inc., 1989-92; bd. dirs. W. Tex. Utilities Co., 1978—; vice chmn. Coun. Pres. of Pub. Sr. Colls. and Univs. Tex., 1980-81; chmn. Coun. Pres. of Lone Star Athletic Conf., 1981-82, 86-87, 93-94; mem. pres. commn. NCAA, 1987-91. Bd. visitors Air U., Maxwell AFB, Ala., 1981-86; mem. adv. com. USAF ROTC, 1989-93, chmn., 1991-93. 2d lt. USAAF, 1942-45. Recipient Meritorious Civilian Svc. award USAF, 1993; named Citizen of Yr., San Angelo C. of C., 1975. Fellow Tex. Acad. Sci.; mem. Am. Phys. Soc., Am. Assn. State Colls. and Univs. (state rep. 1972-74, mem. mission of univ. pres. and chancellors to Malaysia 1986), Am. Assn. Physics Tchrs. (sect. chmn. 1965-67, mem. nat. del. to USSR and China 1983), Assn. Tex. Colls. and Schs. (commn. on colls. 1985—), Rotary, Sigma Xi, Sigma Pi Sigma. Baptist. Home: San Angelo Tex. Died Aug. 5, 1994.

VINCENT-DAVISS, DIANA, law librarian, bibliographer, educator; b. Birmingham, Eng., Jan. 13, 1943; came to U.S., 1965; d. Maxwell Robert and Phyllis Elizabeth (Dain) V.-D.; div.; 1 child, Megan J. Elias. B.A., Cambridge U., Eng., 1965, M.A., 1969; M.L.S., Columbia U., 1972. Reference librarian NYU Sch. Law, N.Y.C., 1973-76, spl. collections librarian, 1976-78, head pub. services, 1978-79, assoc. librarian, 1980-83, librarian, prof. law, 1983-91; lib., prof. Law Sch. Yale U., 1991-93; trustee Procedural Aspects of Internat. Law Inst., Washington, 1985-93. Author, dir. video film Enemies of Books, 1980; contbr. articles to profl. jours. Mem. Am. Assn. Law Librs., Am. Soc. Internat. Law. Home: New Haven Conn. Died Oct. 21, 1994.

VLCEK, JAN BENES, lawyer; b. Chgo., Nov. 16, 1943; s. Anton John and Alice (Benes) V.; m. Ann Lewis, Aug. 23, 1973; children: Elizabeth, Katharine. A.B., Princeton U., 1965; J.D., U. Pa., 1968; M.B.A., George Washington U., 1975. Bar: Fla. 1968, D.C. 1969. Trial atty. CAB, Washington, 1968-69; atty.-advisor Office of Legis., EPA, Washington, 1971-73; assoc. minority counsel Commerce Com. Ho. of Reps., Washington, 1973-76, regulatory programs counsel Energy Com., 1977-78; assoc., then ptnr. Gardner, Carton & Douglas, Washington, 1978-81; with Reagan Energy Transition Team, Washington, 1980-81; ptnr. Sutherland, Asbill & Brennan, Washington, 1981-91; with Bush Transition Team, Washington, 1989; ptnr. Wunder, Diefenderfer, Ryan, Cannon & Thelan (now Wunder, Diefenderfer, Cannon & Thelen, Washington, 1991—; bd. dirs. Nat. Energy Resources Orgn.; with Bush Transition Team, Washington, 1989; fed. rep. Western Interstate Energy Bd., 1990—. Sgt. U.S. Army, 1969-71. Mem. ABA (coun. natural resources, energy and environ. law), Fed. Energy Bar Assn., Capitol Hill Club. Home: Bethesda Md. Deceased.

VOGTLE, ALVIN WARD, JR., retired utility executive; b. Birmingham, Ala., Oct. 21, 1918; s. Alvin Ward and Ollie (Stringer) V.; m. Kathryn Drennen, Apr. 20, 1945 (dec.); children: Kathryn D., Alvin Ward III, Anne Moore Baldwin; m. Rachael Giles, 1966; children: Bryant Wade, William Patrick, Rachel Giles, Robert Jackson. BS, Auburn U., 1939; LLB, U. Ala., 1941. Bar: Ala. 1941. Assoc. firm Martin, Vogtle, Balch & Bingham and predecessor firms, Birmingham, 1941-50; mem. firm Martin, Vogtle, Balch & Bingham and predecessor firms, 1950-62; exec. v.p. Ala. Power Co., 1962-65; exec. v.p., dir. So. Co., 1966-69, pres., dir., 1969-83, chmn. bd., dir., 1983, ret., 1983; dir. Protective Corp., CSX Corp., Union Camp Corp. Trustee YMCA Met. Atlanta. Served from 2d lt. to capt. USAAF, 1941-45. Mem. Ala. Hist. Soc., S.A.R., Soc. Colonial Wars, S.R., Auburn Alumni Assn., Sigma Nu. Episcopalian. Home: Reddick Fla. Died Apr. 10, 1994.

VOIT, FRANZ JOHANN, JR., financial consultant; b. Trübau, Mahren, Germany, July 25, 1932; s. Franz Johann Sr. and Sophie (Wolf) V.; m. Aloisia Pichler, June 3, 1961; children: Wolfgang, Sybille, Harald. Comm. mgr., Tech. Sch. Pforzheim, 1946-49. Tech. mgr. Import/Export, Pforzheim, Fed. Republic of Germany, 1954-76; fin. cons. Import/Export, Fed. Republic of Germany, 1976-95. Decorated Silver medal New Tech. Method, 1973. Home: Pforzhiem Germany Died July 29, 1995.

VOLK, HERMANN CARDINAL, emeritus bishop of Mainz; b. Steinheim, Germany, Dec. 27, 1903; s. Philipp Volk. Dr. phil., U. Fribourg (Switzerland), 1938; Dr. theol., U. Munster (Germany), 1939, Habilitation, 1943. Ordained priest Diocese of Mainz, Roman Catholic Ch., 1927; prof. theology U. Munster, 1946-62; consecrated bishop, 1962; bishop Diocese of Mainz, 1962-82; elevated to cardinal, 1973-88. Author: (collected works) Gesammelte Schriften, 4 vols., 1961-82; numerous other publs. Named hon. citizen City of Steinheim, 1964, City of Mainz, 1975. Died July 1, 1988. Home: Mainz Germany

VOLPI, WALTER MARK, lawyer, diversified company executive; b. N.Y.C., Oct. 4, 1946; s. Walter Joseph and Arlene (Bryant) V.; m. Diana De Rosa, Dec. 13, 1969; 1 son, Mark Joseph. B.A., St. John's U., 1968, J.D., 1974. Bar: N.Y. 1975. Law clk. chief judge N.Y. Ct. Appeals, 1974-76; assoc. Cleary, Gottlieb, Steen & Hamilton, N.Y.C., 1976-80; v.p., gen. counsel Macmillan, Inc., N.Y.C., 1980-85; sec., assoc. gen. counsel Lever Bros., N.Y.C., 1985-86, sr. v.p., gen. counsel, 1986-94. Served to 1st lt. U.S. Army, 1969-71. Mem. ABA, N.Y. State Bar Assn., Am. Law Inst., Assn. of Bar of City of N.Y. Home: New York N.Y. Died Sept. 19, 1994.

VON FRISCH, KARL, zoologist, educator; b. Vienna, Austria, Nov. 20, 1886; s. Anton and Marie (Exner) von F.; ed. univs. Vienna and Munich; Ph.D. (hon.), univs. Berne, Graz, Harvard, Tü bingen, Rostock; D.Sc. (hon.), Fed. Tech. Inst. Zurich; m. Margarete Mohr, 1917; 4 children. Privatdozent, U. Munich, 1912; prof., dir. Zool. Inst., Rostock U., 1921, Breslau, 1923, Munich, 1925, Graz, 1946, Munich, 1950-58. Recipient Magellan prize Am. Philos. Soc.; Kalinga prize, 1959; Nobel prize for medicine/physiology (with K. Lorenz and N. Tinbergen), 1973; decorated Order of Merit. Mem. numerous fgn. acads. sci., Royal Soc. London, Royal Entomol. Soc. London (hon.), Am. Physiol. Soc. (hon.). Author: The Dancing Bees, 1927; Man and the Living World, 1936; Bees, 1950, rev. edit., 1971; Biology, 1952-53; A Biologist Remembers, 1957; The Dance Language and Orientation of Bees, 1965; Animal Architecture, 1974. Home: Munich Germany

VON THURN UND TAXIS, PRINCE JOHANNES, business executive; b. Hofling, Germany, June 5, 1926; s. Prince Karl August and Princess Maria Anna (de Braganca) Thurn und Taxis; grad. High school Regensburg, 1946; pvt. banking studies, 1958; m. Mariae Gloria Gräfin und Herrin von Schönburg, Gräfin und Herrin zu Glauchau und Waldenburg, May 31, 1980; children: Maria Theresia, Elisabeth, Albert Erbprinz. Pres. bd. dirs. banking, brewery, agr. and forestry cos. Head Thurn und Taxis Central Adminstrn. Decorated Order Malta, Rautenkrone. Verdienstorden der Bundesrepublik Deutschland. Mem. 1001 World Wildlife Fund, Wirtschaftsakademie Regensburg. Home: Regensburg Germany

VON WYSS, MARC ROBERT, cement company executive; b. Zurich, Switzerland, Feb. 12, 1931; came to U.S., 1971; s. George H. and Mariejenny A. (Burckhardt) von W.; m. Marina V. Gygi, Sept. 4, 1963; children: George M., Martin C. Grad. in mech. engring. and aerodynamics, Fed. Inst. Tech., Zurich, 1956. Control systems design engr. Svenska Aeroplan AB, Joenkoeping, Sweden, 1957-60; control systems design engr., asst. dept. head Contraves AG, Zurich, 1961-65; sr. v.p. Holderbank Mgmt. & Cons. Ltd., Holderbank, Switzerland, 1966-71; pres., chief exec. officer Holnam Inc. (formerly Dundee Cement Co.), Mich., 1971-93. Home: Ann Arbor Mich. Died Apr. 13, 1993.

VOSPER, ROBERT GORDON, librarian; b. Portland, Oreg., June 21, 1913; s. Chester Vivian and Anna (Stipe) V.; m. Loraine Gjording, Aug. 20, 1940; children: Ingrid, Kathryn, Elinor, Stephen. BA, U. Oreg., 1937, MA, 1939; library certificate, U. Calif., 1940; LLD, Hofstra U., 1967. Jr. librarian U. Calif., 1940-42; asst. reference librarian Stanford U., 1942-44; head acquisitions dept., library UCLA, 1944-48, asst. librarian, 1948-49, assoc. librarian, 1949-52, prof. library sci., 1961-83, prof. emeritus, 1983-94; dir. libraries U. Kans., 1952-61; librarian U. Calif. at Los Angeles, 1961-73; dir. W.A. Clark Meml. Library, 1966-81; Ann. library lectr. U. Tenn., 1957; Walters Meml. lectr. U. Minn., 1959; Fulbright lectr., Italy, 1960; dir. Assn. Research Libraries Farmington Plan Survey, 1957-58; del. Princeton Conf. Internat. Exchanges, 1946, Mexico City Conf. Microfilming Archives, 1949; Sec. Gov.'s Commn. Kans. Territorial Centennial Celebration, 1954-55; mem. NSF Sci. Info. Council, 1965-70; facilities and resources Nat. Library Medicine, 1966-68; vis. com. Mass. Inst. Tech. Library, 1965-72, Stanford U., 1972-78; vis. prof., Columbia U., summer 1967; mem. govt. adv. com. on overseas book and library programs Dept. State, 1970-75. Author or editor: Acquisitions Trends in American Libraries, 1955, The Acquisition of Latin American Library Materials, 1958, European University Libraries, 1964, National and International Library Planning, 1976, Building Book Collections, 1977, Libraries for All, 1980, International Library Horizons, 1989; adv. bd.: Chem. Abstracts, 1965-67; contbr. articles to profl. jours. Bd. dirs. Council on Library Resources, 1968-94; mem. U.S. Com. to UNESCO, 1968-73. Decorated officer Order of Crown of Belgium, 1977; recipient UCLA medal, 1988; Guggenheim fellow, 1959-60; hon. research fellow Sch. Library Studies, Univ. Coll., London, 1973-74. Hon. fellow Internat. Fedn. Library Assns. (v.p. 1971-77, Robert Vosper fellows program estab. in honor 1989); mem. Calif. Library Assn. (chmn. coll. and univ. sect. 1946-47), Mountain Plains Library Assn. (chmn. coll. and univ. sect. 1953-54), Kans. Library Assn., ALA (pres. assn. coll. and reference libraries 1955-56, chmn. bd. acquisition library materials 1954-55, mem. council 1960-72, pres. 1965-66, hon. mem. 1993, J.W. Lippincott award 1985), AAUP, Assn. Research Libraries (chmn. 1963, dir. 1962-64, 69-72), Library Assn. (Gt. Brit.) (hon. v.p. 1974-94), Bibliog. Soc. Am., Phi Beta Kappa. Clubs: Zamorano (Los Angeles), Rounce and Coffin (Los Angeles). Home: Los Angeles Calif. Died May 14, 1994.

VUKASIN, JOHN PETER, JR., federal judge; b. Oakland, Calif., May 25, 1928; s. John P. and Natalie Vukasin; m. Sue D. Vukasin, July 1, 1956; children: John P. III, Kirk E., Alexander G., Kim V. Greer, Karen V. Zeff. AB, U. Calif., 1950, JD, 1956. Bar: Calif. 1956. Commr. Calif. Pub. Utilities Commn., 1969-74, chmn., 1971, 72; judge Superior Ct. of Calif., 1974-83, U.S. Dist. Ct. (no. dist.) Calif., San Francisco, 1983-93; mem. Adminstrv. Conf. of U.S., 1972-75. Contbr. articles to legal jours. With U.S. Army, 1951-

53. Mem. ABA (chmn. pub. utility law sect. 1981-82). Republican. Home: San Francisco Calif. Died Sept. 20, 1993.

WADE, JOHN WEBSTER, law educator, lawyer; consultant; b. Little Rock, Mar. 2, 1911; s. John William and Sarah Vista (Webster) W.; m. Mary Moody Johnson, June 1, 1946; children: John Webster, Mary R. Wade Shanks, William J., Ruth E. Wade Grant. BA, U. Miss., 1932, JD 1934; LLM, Harvard U., 1935, SJD, 1942. Bar: Miss. 1934, Tenn. 1947. Asst. prof. law U. Miss., 1936-38, assoc. prof., 1938-40, prof., 1940-47; prof. Vanderbilt U. Sch. Law, 1947-71, dean, 1952-72, Disting. prof. law, 1971-81, dean and Disting. prof. emeritus, 1981—; vis. prof. U. Tex., 1946-47, Columbia U., 1964-65, U. Mo., 1976-77, Coll. William and Mary, 1981-82, Cornell U., fall 1972, U. Mich., Fall 1982, Pepperdine U., 1983-84, Memphis State U., 1986, U. Hawaii, 1987, Washburn U., fall 1989; uniform laws commr. from Tenn., 1961-92, v.p. Nat. Conf. Commrs. Uniform State Laws, 1977-79; reporter Restatement (Second) of Torts, 1970-81. Trustee (life) Rhodes Coll., Memphis. Capt. USMCR, 1943-45. Decorated Bronze Star; recipient William L. Prosser award for outstanding contbn. of devel. of tort law, 1980. Mem. ABA (honoree for outstanding contbns. in tort and ins. law Torts & Ins. Practice Sect. 1988), Miss. Bar Assn., Tenn. Bar Assn., Nashville Bar Assn., Assn. Order of Coif (nat. pres. 1973-76), Am. Law Inst. (council 1960-70, 82-93). Author: Cases and Materials on Restitution, 2d edit., 1966; Cases and Materials on Torts, 8th edit., 1988; contbr. numerous articles on torts, restitution and other topics to law revs. and other law publs. Died Aug. 24, 1994. Home: Nashville Tenn.

WADLINGTON, JEFF, dancer; b. Pine Bluff, Ark.. Pvt. studies with, Richard Kuch, Richard Gain, Cindi Green, Deborah Lessen; student, N.C. Sch. Arts; scholarship student, Am. Dance Festival. First scholarship apprentice Paul Taylor Sch.; with Paul Taylor Dance Co., N.Y.C., 1986-94. Performances include with May O'Donnell and Joyce Trisler. Home: New York N.Y. Died Sept. 24, 1994.

WAGMAN, FREDERICK HERBERT, librarian, educator; b. Springfield, Mass., Oct. 12, 1912; s. Robert and Rebecca (Gaberman) W.; m. Ruth Jeannette Wagman, Nov. 21, 1941; children: Elizabeth L. Gaidos, William G. A.B. summa cum laude, Amherst Coll., 1933; A.M., Columbia U., 1934, Ph.D., 1942; L.H.D., Amherst Coll., 1958; LL.D. (hon.), Alderson Broaddus Coll., 1967; Litt.D., Luther Coll., 1969. Instr., Columbia Extension, 1933-35; Ottendorfer Meml. fellow NYU, 1935-36; teaching fellow Amherst Coll., 1936-37; instr. U. Minn., 1937-42; head planning unit postal div. U.S. Office Censorship, Washington, 1942-43; head regulations and trg. sect. postal div. U.S. Office Censorship, 1943-45, regulations officer, 1945; successively acting dir. personnel and acting dir. adminstrv. services Library of Congress, 1945-46, asst. dir. reference dept., 1946-47, dir. processing dept., 1947-51, dep. chief asst. librarian, 1951- 52, dir. adminstrn., 1952-53; dir. U. Mich. Library, Ann Arbor, 1953-78; prof. library sci. U. Mich. library, 1953-82; librarian Mich. Acad. Arts, Sci. and Letters, 1953-78; vice chmn. com. mgmt. Wm. L. Clements Library, 1953-78; exec. com. Mich. Hist. Collections, 1953-94; cons. UN Library, 1959-62, Hebrew U. Jerusalem, 1969, various other univs.; mem. exec. com. Nat. Book Com., 1963-64; vice chmn. Nat. Commn. Obscenity and Pornography, 1968-70; pres. Midwest Region Library Network, 1975-76; bd. dirs. Council Library Resources, 1956-91; bd. regents Nat. Library of Medicine, 1967-71. Author: Magic and Natural Science in German Baroque Literature, 1942. Named Hon. Alumnus, U. Mich. Sch. Library Sci. Mem. ALA (pres. 1963-64), Mich. Library Assn. (pres. 1960, hon. mem. 1978), Phi Beta Kappa, Phi Kappa Phi. Democrat. Home: Ann Arbor Mich. Died Mar. 19, 1994.

WAGNER, ROBERT FERDINAND, JR., former city official; b. 1944; s. Robert F. and Susan W. Grad., Harvard U., 1965; postgrad., U. Sussex, Eng.; M.P.A., Princeton U. At-large mem. from Manhattan N.Y.C. Council; chmn. City Planning Commn., N.Y.C., 1977—, dep. mayor, to 1984; pres. Bd. Edn., City of NY, 1986—; chmn. Urban Research Ctr., NYU; adj. prof. NYU, Columbia U.; cons. Twentieth Century Fund. Home: Brooklyn N.Y.

WAHLGREN, OLOF GUSTAF CHRISTERSON, newspaper editor; b. Stockholm, Sept. 21, 1927; s. Christer Fredrik Olof and Jeanne Louise Charlotte (Nyblaeus) W.; B.A., U. Lund, 1951, M.A., 1954, Dr.(ph), 1957; m. Ulla Britt Andersson, July 15, 1955; children: Rebecca, Suzanne, Christer. Mem. staff Sydsvenska Dagbladet, morning paper, Malmö , 1953-87 , dep. dir., 1963-67, chief editor, 1967-87 , mng. dir., 1967-78; mng. dir. Kvällsposten, eve. paper, Malmö , 1963-78; dir. Sydsvenska Dagbladet AB & Kvällspostens AB, 1949-87 , chmn., 1978-87 ; Vice pres. Malmö Mcpl. Com. Art, 1968-76. Initiator, chmn. United Liberal Party movement in So. Sweden, 1964-69. Decorated knight 1st class Order Vasa; comdr. Finnish Order Lion, Icelandic Order Falcon; Order of Merit, Fed. Republic Germany; officer Italian Order Merit; knight Danish Order Dannebrog; officer French Legion of Honor; Knight of Polish Order Polonia Restituta. Mem. Swedish Newspaper Assn. (pres. South Sweden div., dir. 1967-87, hon. chnm. 1987), Internat. Press Inst. (chmn. Swedish nat. com. 1972-82, v.p. 1974-76, pres. 1976-78, hon. mem. 1979), Internat. Fedn. Newspaper Pubs. (exec. bur. com. 1974-84, sec. gen. 1978-84, hon. mem. 1984), World Press Freedom Com. (v.p. 1976-78). Clubs: Travellers (Malmö), Rotary. Author: Contreclock through France. Died Apr. 29, 1990. Home: Malmö Sweden

WAIN, JOHN BARRINGTON, author; b. Stoke-on-Trent, Eng., Mar. 14, 1925; s. Arnold A. and Anne Wain; m. Eirian James, 1960; 3 children. MA, Oxford U.; DLitt (hon.), U. Keele, 1985, U. Loughborough, 1985. Lectr. English lit. U. Reading, 1947-55; freelance writer, lit. critic, 1955-94; Churchill vis. prof. U. Bristol, 1967; vis. prof. Centre Exptl. U., Vincennes, France; George Elliston lectr. on poetry, U. Cin.; prof. poetry Oxford U., 1973-78, fellow Brasenose Coll., 1973-94; dir. 1st Poetry at the Mermaid Festival, London, 1961. Author: (poetry) Mixed Feelings, 1951, Weep Before God, 1961, Letters to Five Artists, 1969, Poems 1949-1979, 1981; (novels) Hurry on Down, 1953, The Contenders, 1958, Strike the Father Dead, 1962, The Smaller Sky, 1967, The Pardoner's Tale, 1978, Young Shoulders (Whitebread award), 1982, Where the Rivers Meet, 1988; (non-fiction) The Living World of Shakespeare, 1964, A House for the Truth, 1972, Samuel Johnson (Heinemann award 1975), 1974, Professing Poetry, 1977; also short stories; editor books on poets, poetry. Decorated companion Order of Brit. Empire; recipient Somerset Maugham award, 1958; James Tait Black Meml. prize, 1974; Whitbread award for fiction, 1982; 1st holder Fellowship in Creative Arts, Brasenose Coll., Oxford U., 1971-72; hon. fellow St. John's Coll., Oxford, 1985-94. Home: London Eng. Died May 24, 1994.

WALDSCHMIDT, PAUL EDWARD, clergyman; b. Evansville, Ind., Jan. 7, 1920; s. Edward Benjamin and Olga Marie (Moers) W. B.A., U. Notre Dame, 1942; student, Holy Cross Coll., Washington, 1942-45; S.T.L., Laval U., Que., Can., 1947; S.T.D., Angelicum U., Rome, Italy, 1948. Ordained priest Roman Catholic Ch., 1946; prof. apologetics and dogmatic theology Holy Cross Coll., 1949-55; v.p. U. Portland, 1955-62, dean faculties, 1956-60, pres., 1962-78; aux. bishop of Portland, 1978-90. Mem. Cath. Theol. Soc. Am. (v.p. 1954-55), NEA, Delta Epsilon Sigma. Club: K.C. (4 deg.). Home: Portland Oreg. Died Oct. 20, 1994.

WALINSKI, NICHOLAS JOSEPH, federal judge; b. Toledo, Nov. 29, 1920; s. Nicholas Joseph and Helen Barbara (Morkowski) W.; m. Vivian Melotti, June 26, 1954 (dec.); children: Marcianne, Barbara, Deanna and Donna (twins), Nicholas Joseph III (dec.). BS in Engring., U. Toledo, 1949, LLB, 1951. Bar: Ohio 1951. Law dir. Toledo, 1953; police prosecutor, 1953-58, mcpl. ct. judge, 1958-64, common pleas ct. judge, 1964-70; judge No. dist. Ohio Western div. U.S. Dist. Ct., Toledo, from 1970; sr. judge, from 1985. Capt. USNR, 1942-48. Recipient Disting. Alumnus award U. Toledo Coll. of Law, 1989, Disting. Alumnus award U. Toledo Law Alumni Assn. Mem. Toledo Bar Assn., Lucas County Bar Assn., Am. Legion, VFW, Cath. War Vets, Toledo Jr. Bar Assn. (Order of Heel 1970). Home: Toledo Ohio Deceased.

WALKER, ERIC ARTHUR, consulting engineer, institute executive; b. Long Eaton, Eng., Apr. 29, 1910; came to U.S., 1923, naturalized, 1937; s. Arthur and Violet Elizabeth (Haywood) W.; m. L. Josephine Schmeiser, Dec. 20, 1937; children: Gail (Mrs. Peter Hearn), Brian. B.S., Harvard U., 1932, M.S., 1933, Sc.D., 1935; LL.D., Temple U., 1957, Lehigh U., 1957, Hofstra Coll., 1960, Lafayette Coll., 1960, U. Pa., 1960, U. R.I., 1962; L.H.D., Elizabethtown Coll., 1958; D.Litt., Jefferson Med. Coll., 1960; D.Sc., Wayne State U., 1965, Thiel Coll., 1966, U. Notre Dame, 1968, U. Pitts., 1970. Registered profl. engr., Pa. Instr. math. Tufts Coll., 1933-34, asst. prof., assoc. prof. elec. engring., 1935-38, head elec. engring. dept., 1935-40; head elec. engring. dept. U. Conn., 1940-43; assoc. dir. Harvard U. Underwater Sound Lab., 1942-45; dir. Ordnance Research Lab., Pa. State U., 1945-52, head elec. engring. dept., 1945-51; dean Sch. Engring. Pa. State U., 1951-56, v.p. univ., 1956, pres., 1956-70; v.p. sci. and tech. Aluminum Co. Am., 1970-76; mem. and past chmn. bd. Inst. for Def. Analysis, 1978-85; exec. sec. Rsch. and Devel. Bd., 1950-51; cons. NRC, 1949-50; mem. and past chmn. com. on undersea warfare; chmn. Pres.'s Com. on Tech. and Distbn. Research for Benefit of Small Bus., 1957; mem. nat. sci. bd. NSF, 1962-68, chmn. nat. sci. bd., 1966-68; chmn. Naval Research Adv. Com., 1963-65, 71-73, Army Sci. Adv. Panel, 1956-58; vice chmn. Pres.'s Com. Scientists and Engrs., 1956-58; adv. panel on engring. and tech. manpower Pres.'s Sci. Adv. Com.; mem. Gov.'s Com. of 100 for Better Edn., 1960-61; bd. dirs. Engring. Found. Contbr. to tech. mags. United bd. visitors U.S. Naval Acad., 1958-60, U.S. Mil. Acad., 1962-64. Recipient Horatio Alger award, 1959, Tasker H. Bliss award Am. Soc. Mil. Engrs., 1959; Golden Omega award Am. Inst. E.E and Nat. Elec. Mfg. Assn., 1962; DoD Pub. Service medal, 1970; Presdl. citation, 1970. Fellow IEEE, Am. Acoustical Soc., Am. Inst. E.E., Am. Phys. Soc.; mem. Am. Inst. Physics, Am. Soc. Engring. Edn. (Lamme award 1965, pres. 1956-57), Pa. Assn. Colls. and Univs. (pres. 1950- 60), Middle States Assn. Colls. and Secondary Schs. (commn. higher edn. 1958-61), Engrs. Joint Council (pres. 1962-63), Nat. Assn. State Univs. and Land-Grant Colls. (exec. com. 1958-62), Nat. Acad. Engring. (pres. 1966-70), Am. Acad. Arts and Scis., Newcomen Soc., Royal Soc. Arts, Duquesne Club, Cosmos Club, Sigma Xi, Tau Beta Pi, Phi Kappa Phi. Home: Hilton Head Island S.C. Died Feb. 17, 1995.

WALKER, GUS A., banker; b. Long Beach, Calif., June 25, 1899; s. Charles Jabez and Carrie D. (Ziegler) W.; m. Cassieta Smith (dec.); children: Richard A., Beverly Walker McLaughlin, Kenneth G., Donald P., David M. Student, U. So. Calif., 1922. Pres. Farmers and Mchts. Bank, Long Beach, 1937-79, chmn. bd., 1979—. Bd. dirs. Metro. Water Dist., Calif., 1943-76; pres. YMCA Greater Long Beach, 1948-51; bd. dirs. Grant Beckstrand Cancer Found., Adelaide Tichenor Clinic. Recipient Horizon award Sr. Care Action Network Found., Long Beach, 1987, Humanitarian award NCCJ, Long Beach, 1989. Mem. Rotary Club Long Beach (pres. 1961-62, Paul Harris fellow), Va. Country Club, Long Beach. Republican. Methodist. Home: Long Beach Calif. Died Jan. 12, 1994.

WALKER, HERMAN, JR., educator, former foreign service officer; b. Nashville, Nov. 21, 1910; s. Herman and Georgia Elizabeth (Graham) W.; m. Betty Friemel, Oct. 17, 1936; 1 son, Steven F.; m. Evelyn Acomb, Jan. 26, 1969. A.B., Duke U., 1931, M.A., 1933, Ph.D., 1937; student, U. Paris, 1934-35; M.A., Harvard U., 1938. Economist, legislative analyst Resettlement Adminstrn., Dept. Agr., 1936-38, 39-46; instr. govt. La. State U., 1938-39; treaty adviser Dept. State, 1946-56, became cons. fgn. service, 1955; 1st sec. U.S. embassy, Paris, 1956-59; vice chmn. U.S. delegation to GATT Tariff Conf., Geneva, 1960-62; chmn. Trade Agreements Com., 1961-62, ret., 1962; cons. Dept. State, 1962-67; vis. prof. Duke U., 1962-63; prof. internat. affairs George Washington U., Army War Coll., 1964-65; chmn. div. history, polit. economy State U. Coll., New Paltz, N.Y., 1965-69; chmn. dept. econs. and polit. sci. State U. Coll., 1969-77, emeritus, 1977-94. Served with USAAF, 1943-45. Rockefeller Found. grantee, 1963-64. Mem. So. Polit. Sci. Assn., Phi Beta Kappa. Home: New Paltz N.Y. Died May 8, 1994.

WALKER, SEBASTIAN, publisher; b. Cheltenham, U.K., Dec. 11, 1942; s. Richard Fife and Christine Maary (Wilkes) W. BA with hons., New Coll., Oxford, 1968. Sales mgr. Chatto and Windus, London, 1970-75; dir. Chaltoo Windows, London, 1977-80, Jonathan Cape; sales mgr. Jonathan Cape, Marshall Cavendish, London, 1975-77; chmn. Walker Books, London, from 1978. Dir. Rambert Dance Co., London, 1987; trustee Music in Country Chs., 1989. Home: London Eng. Deceased.

WALKER, SYDNEY SMITH, JR., actor, educator; b. Phila., May 4, 1921; s. Sydney Smith and Barbara Blakeley (Farrell) W.; m. Catherine Jane Steckle, Feb. 12, 1952 (div. 1956). Student, Hedgerow Theatre Sch., Phila., 1946-47, Conservatoire Nationale de Musique, Paris, 1950. Actor Hedgerow Theatre, Moylan, Pa., 1946-49, Assn. Producing Artists, N.Y.C., 1963-69, Repertory Theater at Lincoln Ctr., N.Y.C., 1970-73; actor, tchr. Am. Conservatory Theatre, San Francisco, 1974-94; actor Olney (Md.) Summer Theatre, summers 1958-63; appeared in Becket, N.Y.C., 1960-61; actor on daytime serials Guiding Light, CBS-TV, N.Y.C., 1969-70, As the World Turns, CBS-TV, N.Y.C., 1971-94, The Secret Storm, CBS-TV, N.Y.C., 1972-74; films Puzzle of a Downfall Child, 1969, The Way We Live Now, 1969, Love Story, 1970, Eye on the Sparrow, 1987, King of Love, 1987, Necessity, 1987, Best Shots, 1987. Served with U.S. Army, 1942-46, ETO. Mem. Actor's Equity Assn., Screen Actors' Guild, AFTRA. Democrat. Home: San Francisco Calif. Died Sept. 30, 1994.

WALL, JOSEPH FRAZIER, historian, educator; b. Des Moines, July 10, 1920; s. Joseph Frazier and Minnie Ellen (Patton) W.; m. Beatrice Mills, Apr. 16, 1944; children: April Ane, Joseph Frazier, Julia Mills. B.A., Grinnell Coll., 1941, LL.D. (hon.), 1978; M.A., Harvard U., 1942; Ph.D., Columbia U., 1951; LL.D. (hon.), Simpson Coll., 1978, Luther Coll., 1982. Faculty Grinnell (Iowa) Coll., 1947-78, 80-90, prof. history, 1957-78, James Morton Roberts honor prof., 1960-61, Parker prof., 1961-78, Earl Strong Disting. prof., 1972-78, chmn. dept. history, 1954-57, 58-60, chmn. div. social studies, 1956-57, 59-60, chmn. div. history, philosophy and math., 1965-66, chmn. faculty, 1966-69, dean coll., 1969-73, Rosenfield prof. pub. affairs, 1980-85; prof. history, chmn. dept. SUNY, Albany, 1978-80, prof. emeritus, 1990-95; spl. assignment to asst. oral history project Columbia, 1957; sr. research Fulbright scholar U. Edinburgh, Scotland, 1957-58; Fulbright prof. U. Gothenburg, Sweden, 1964-65, U. Salzburg, Austria, 1987-88. Author: (with Robert Parks) Freedoms, 1955 (ann. Iowa Civil Liberties Union award 1956), Henry Watterson: Reconstructed Rebel, 1956 (hon. mention John A. Dunning prize 1956), Andrew Carnegie, 1970 (Bancroft prize 1971), Iowa, 1978, Policies and People, 1979, Skibo, 1985, Alfred I. du Pont, 1990 (Pulitzer prize finalist 1991), Andrew Carnegie Reader, 1992. Served to lt. USNR, 1942-46. Mem. AAUP, Iowa Assn. Univ. Profs. (chmn. 1955-56), Am. Hist. Assn., Orgn. Am. Historians (exec. bd. 1974-77), Soc. Am. Historians, Phi Beta Kappa (senator-at-large

1988-94), Sigma Delta Chi. Democrat. Home: Grinnell Iowa Died Oct. 9, 1995.

WALLACE, ARNOLD DELANEY, SR., broadcasting executive; b. Salisbury, Md., Feb. 1, 1932; s. George Linwood Wallace and Margaret Elizabeth (Townsend) Walker; BA, Howard U., 1952; BS magna cum laude, Rutgers U., 1977, postgrad., 1977-95, MA in Mass Communications, Howard U., 1986; m. Theresa Fredericks Brooks, Sept. 27, 1950; children: Deborah, Terry, Arnold Jr., Michael, Stephen, Stephanie. Communications engr. Sta. WCAU-TV, Phila., 1963-72, dir. community affairs, 1972-79; dir. univ. rels. Howard U., 1979-80, gen. mgr. univ. Sta. WHMM-TV, 1980-88; pres., chmn. New Breed Media Group, Inc., 1988-95; co-adj. prof. Rutgers U., 1978-80; adj. prof. Howard U. Sch. of Communications, 1978-95; sec. bd. dirs. Cen. Ednl. Network, 1982-86; co-adj. prof. Montgomery Coll., 1989-95. Mem. Pennsauken (N.J.) Bd. Edn., 1971-95, v.p., 1973-75, pres., 1975-77; bd. dirs. Juvenile Diabetes Found., N.J. Urban League, Phila., Phila. Mayor's Commn. Drug and Alcohol Abuse, Phila. Urban League, N.J. Commn. for Humanities; mem. media com. Crippled Children's Soc. Pa.; mem. bd. mgrs. Anthony Bowen YMCA, Washington. Recipient awards Camden County United Way, Phila. Commn. Human Rights, Assn. Study Afro-Am. Life and History, Chapel of the Four Chaplains, Council Spanish Speaking Orgns., Excellence in Black Media award Bus. Exchange Network, White House Pvt. Sector Initiatives award, 1987. Mem. NATAS, Internat. TV Assn., Negro Airmen Internat. (internat. publicity chmn. 1969-78), Aircraft Owners and Pilots Assn., Nat. Assn. Pub. TV Stas. (sec. bd. trustees 1985-95), World Affairs Coun., Assn. Pub. Broadcasting (sec. bd. trustees 1987-88), Nat. Press Club, Capital Press Club, Washington Area Broadcasters Assn., D.C. C. of C., Alpha Sigma Lambda, Omega Psi Phi. Mem. A.M.E. Ch. Clubs: TV and Radio Advt., Willingboro (N.J.) Country. Lodges: Masons, Shriners, Kiwanis. Author: Broadcast Public Relations, 1979; contbr. articles to mags.; producer, dir. documentary film Journey to Paradise-Barbados; exec. producer (film) 2000 and Beyond, (videotape) James Baldwin At The Capital Press Club. Avocation: flying. Died May 23, 1995. Home: Silver Spring Md.

WALLACE, JOHN KENNARD, manufacturing company executive; b. St. Louis, Nov. 6, 1903; s. Harry Brookings and Mary (Kennard) W.; m. Margaret G. How, Oct. 29, 1929; children: Charles How, Mary Kennard Wallace de Cempaigne, John Kennard. B.A., Yale U., 1927. With Cupples Co. Mfgs., Clayton, Mo., 1927-82, dir., 1933-82, v.p., 1933-42, gen. mgr., 1934-42, pres., 1942-70, chmn. bd., 1970-80; pres. Floyd Charcoal Co., Salem, Mo., 1959-92, Los Angeles Paper Bag Co., 1941-70, Cupples Co., San Francisco, 1953-70, Cupples Products Corp., Mapleswood, Mo., 1946-60; dir. St. Louis Union Trust Co., Mark Twain State Bank, Bridgeton, Mo., Mark Twain Banchares, Clayton. Trustee Taft Sch., Watertown, Conn., 1948-62, Bennett Coll., Millbrook, N.Y., 1962-66. Mem. St. Louis County C. of C. (vice chmn. 1958-62), St. Louis Met. C. of C., Alpha Delta Pi. Methodist. Clubs: Noonday (St. Louis), St. Louis Country (St. Louis), Racquet (St. Louis) (pres. 1941); Clayton; Log Cabin (Ladue) (pres. 1974); Round Table. Home: Saint Louis Mo. Died July, 26, 1992.

WALLACE, KEITH ALTON, legislator, dairy farmer; b. Waterbury, Vt., Feb. 26, 1908; s. James Moses and Florence Ida (Richardson) W.; m. Gladys Helen Pike, Jan. 26, 1942 (dec. May 1985); children: Roaine, Rosina, Kay Alan. BS in Agr., Syracuse U., 1932. mem. State Grange Agr. Com.; pres. Mt. Mansfield Coop. Creamery, Vt. Coop. Coun.; trustee Ea. States Exposition. Pres. Vt. State Sch. Bd. Assn., Vt. Ch. Coun.; auditor Town of Waterbury; sch. dir., town moderator, Harwood Union moderator; mem. Vt. Devel. Commn.; mem. State Senate, 1975-78, Vt. House, 1949-50, 81-86; vice chmn. agr. com. Senate and House; lay leader Meth. Ch.; Vt. storyteller. Recipient Citizenship award Vt. State C. of C., 1975, Vt. Edn. Assn. award, 1975, Sen. George Aiken Agriculturist award, 1989, Award of Recognition Svc. to Vt. Rehab. Corp., 1994; recognized for 59 years of pub. svc. as elected ofcl. to Town of Waterbury; named Future Farmer of Am., 1965; Paul Harris fellow Rotary Internat., 1991. Master Waterbury Grange, Harmony Pomona Grange; mem. Washington County Farm Bur. (pres. 1943-44), Vt. State Farm Bur. (pres., CEO 1953-74), Am. Farm Bur. Fedn. (bd. dirs. 1960-69, chmn. dairy com. 1968-69, Disting. Svc. award 1992). Republican. Methodist. Home: Waterbury Vt. Died June 2, 1995.

WALLACH, IRA, writer; b. N.Y.C., Jan. 22, 1913; s. Morris David and Rose (Sims) W.; m. Devera Sievers, Jan. 25, 1941; 1 dau., Leah B.S.; m. Lillian Opatoshu, June 4, 1970. Student, Cornell. Author: The Horn and the Roses, 1947, How to be Deliriously Happy, 1949, Hopalong-Freud, 1951, Hopalong-Freud Rides Again, 1950, Gutenberg's Folly, 1954, How to Pick a Wedlock, 1956, Muscle Beach, 1959, The Absence of a Cello, 1960, Horatio, 1954, Phoenix 55, 1955, (with A.S. Ginnes) Drink To Me Only, 1958; (anthology) The Courage to Grow Old, 1989; (play) Smiling, the Boy Fell Dead, 1961, The Eye of the Beholder, 1993; (screenplay) Boys' Night Out, 1962, (with George Goodman) The Wheeler-Dealers, (with Peter Ustinov) Absence of a Cello, 1964, Hot Millions (Motion Picture Acad. nomination 1968, Writers Guild of Gt. Britain Best Brit. Comedy Screenplay award, 1968), Five Thousand Years of Foreplay, 1976; (musical) Sweet Mistress, 1976. Mem. Authors Guild Am., Dramatists Guild, Writer's Guild Am., Aircraft Owners and Pilots Assn., P.E.N. Home: New York N.Y. Died Dec. 2, 1995.

WALLHAUSER, GEORGE MARVIN, former congressman, investment executive; b. Newark, Feb. 10, 1900; s. Dr. Henry Joseph Frederick and Rachel Apolonia (Vogt) W.; m. Isabel Towne, May 26, 1926; children: George Marvin, Henry Towne. A.B., U. Pa., 1922; student real estate appraising, Columbia, 1942. With U.S. Realty & Investment Co., Newark, 1928-89, treas., 1947-89, sr. v.p., 1956-89, dir., 1940; mem. 86th-88th Congresses from 12th Dist. of N.J., 1959-65; Chmn. Planning Bd., Maplewood, N.J., 1946-54; mem. Twp. Com. Maplewood, 1954-57; commr. N.J. Hwy. Authority, 1970-75, chmn., 1972-75. Past pres. Bur. Family Service, Oranges and Maplewood. Served with USNRF, World War I. Mem. Am. Legion, Phi Sigma Kappa. Republican. Methodist. Lodges: Masons, Elks. Died Aug. 4, 1993.

WALLIN, JUDITH KERSTIN, pediatrician, educator; b. Paris, Apr. 23, 1938; came to U.S., 1938; d. Theodore Bror and Ella Charlotte (Butler) Wallin. BS in Chemistry, Elizabethtown (Pa.) Coll., 1960; MD, Temple U., 1964. Diplomate Am. Bd. Pediatrics. Intern Bellevue Hosp., N.Y.C., 1964-65, resident specializing in pediatrics, 1965-67, attending pediatrician, 1967—; instr. pediatrics, NYU, 1967-71, asst. prof. clin. pediatrics, 1971-74, assoc. prof., 1974—. Trustee Elizabethtown Coll., 1988—. Recipient Educate for Service through Profl. Achievement award, O.F. Stambaugh Alumni award Elizabethtown Coll., 1978. Home: New York N.Y. Died June 24, 1992.

WALLIS, ROBERT CHARLES, entomologist, epidemiology educator; b. West Burlington, Iowa, Oct. 30, 1921; s. Thomas Frederick and Louise Marie (Leutbecker) W.; m. Grace Eileen McLaughlin, Oct. 17, 1953 (dec. 1980); children—Thomas Frederick, III, Robert Charles, Jr. B.S., Ohio U., 1948, M.S. with honors, 1950; D.Sc., Johns Hopkins U., 1953; M.A. (hon.), Yale U., 1979. Registered profl. entomologist. Grad. fellow in zoology Ohio U., Athens, 1948-50; grad. asst., USPHS fellow in parasitology Johns Hopkins U., Balt., 1950-53; from asst. entomologist to prof. entomology Conn. Agrl. Expt. Sta., New Haven, 1953-63; assoc. prof. epidemiology Yale U., 1963-78, prof. epidemiology, 1978—, chief sect. med. entomology, 1963—; cons. UN/FAO, Rome, 1981—, Internat. Health Cons., Washington, 1984—. Contbr. articles to sci. jours. Patentee in field. Former scoutmaster Boy Scouts Am., 1936-42. Served with U.S. Army, 1942-46, PTO. Fellow Am. Coll. Epidemiologists; mem. Am. Soc. Tropical Medicine and Hygiene, Entomol. Soc. Am. (auditing com.), Entomol. Soc. Washington, Am. Entomol. Soc., Am. Mosquito Control Assn. (research and devel. com.), Am. Soc. Parasitologists, Conn. Entomol. Soc., Northeast Mosquito Control Assn. (sci. advisor), Brit. Soc. for Parasitology (founder), Am. Pub. Health Assn., Am. Inst. Biol. Scis., N.Y. Acad. Scis., Am. Legion, Sigma Xi, Phi Delta Theta. Mem. United Ch. Christ. Avocations: gardening; nature study. Home: North Haven Conn.

WALSH, JAMES PATRICK, JR., pension fund administrator, insurance consultant, actuary; b. Ft. Thomas, Ky., Mar. 7, 1910; s. James Patrick and Minnie Louise (Cooper) W.; m. Evelyn Mary Sullivan, May 20, 1939. Comml. engr. degree, U. Cin., 1933. Cert. pension cons.; enrolled actuary. Acct. Firestone Tire & Rubber Co., also Gen. Motors Corp., 1933-36; rep. ARC, 1937, A.F.L., 1938-39; dir. Ohio Div. Minimum Wages, Columbus, 1939-42; asst. sec.-treas. union label trades dept. A.F.L., Washington, 1946-53; v.p. Pension and Group Cons., Inc., Cin., 1953-93; mem. Pres.'s Commn. Jud. and Congl. Salaries, 1953, Ohio Gov.'s Commn. Employment of Negro, 1940, Hamilton County (Ohio) Welfare Bd., 1955-94; mem. coun. long term illness and rehab Cin. Pub. Health Fedn., 1957-68. Bd. dirs. U. Cin., 1959-67; mem. Library Guild of U. Cin.; bd. govs. St. Xavier High Sch. Alumni Assn., Cin.; trustee Brown Found., Newman Cath. Center, Cin.; mem. Green Twp. Civic Club. Lt. col. AUS, 1942-46; col. Res. ret. Decorated Legion of Merit, Commendation ribbon with two oak leaf clusters; named Ky. col., 1958, Ky. adm., 1968, Ohio commodore, 1985; recipient Disting. Alumni award U. Cin., 1969, Disting. Alumni award Covington Latin Sch., 1983, Insignis award St. Xavier High Sch., 1973, Americanism award Am. Legion, Kevin Barry award Ancient Order of Hiberians, Drummer award Greater Cin. Conv. and Visitor Bur., Selective Svc. System award. Fellow Am. Soc. Pension Actuaries; mem. Am. Acad. Actuaries, Am. Arbitration Assn. (nat. community disputes panel, employee benefit claims panel), Conf. Actuaries Pub. Practice, Marine Corps Res. Officers Assn., Naval Res. Assn., Res. Officers Assn., Am. Legion, VFW, Am. Mil. Retiree Assn., Nat. Assn. Uniform Services, English Speaking Union, Ohio Ret. Officers Assn. (past pres. council), Ret. Officers Assn. (past pres. Cin. chpt. 1973-74), Amvets, Air Force Assn., Ret. Officers Assn. (nat. bd. dirs. 1983-88), Marine Corps League, Nat. Football Found. and Hall of Fame, Am. Fedn. State, County and Employees Union, Naval Order, Internat. Alliance Theatrical Stage Employees (past sgt. at arms), Internat. Hodcarriers, Bldg. and Common Laborers Union, Ins. Workers Internat. Union, Office Employees Internat. Union, Cooks and Pastry Cooks Local, Friendly Sons St. Patrick (past pres.), Covington Latin Sch. Alumni Assn. (past pres.), Soc. for Advancement Mgmt., Defense Supply Assn., Ancient Order Hibernians (past pres.), Assn. U.S. Army (trustee), Am. Ordnance Assn., Soc. Am. Mil. Engrs., Order of Alhambra, Internat. Assn. Health Underwriters, Allied Constrn. Industries, Navy League, Scabbard and Blade, Nat. Council of Cath. Men, Indsl. Relations Research Assn., Green Twp. Rep. Club, Rep. Nat. Com. (life), United Food and Comml. Workers Union, Cursillo, U Cats, Nat. Travel Club, Zoo Soc. of Cin., Seneca County Geneal. Soc., Men of Milford, Cin. Hist. Soc., Intraveler Club, Mil. Order of World Wars, Fraternal Order of Police, Germania Soc., High Frontier, Mature Outlook, Conf. Actuaries in Pub. Practice, Ret. Officers Club. Cen. Ohio, Buckeye State Sheriffs Assn., Butterfield Sr. Citizens Ctr., Nat. Geog. Soc., Millcreek Valley Assn., Alpha Kappa Psi. Republican. Roman Catholic. Clubs: C. Cin. (past pres.), Queen City, American Irish, Insiders, Touchdown, Blue Liners, Roundtable, Scuttlebuts, Newman, Bankers, Mil. (Cin.). Lodges: K.C. (4 deg.), Elks. Home: Cincinnati Ohio Died Jan. 4, 1994.

WALSH, MAURICE DAVID, JR., former librarian, business executive; b. N.Y.C., Dec. 24, 1924; s. Maurice David and Helen Merlyn (Flynn) W.; m. Alice Louise Flynn, Oct. 18, 1952; children—Maud Maureen, Michael Sean, James Liam, Douglas Padraic. B.J., U. Mo., 1949; M.S. in Library Sci, La. State U., 1963; grad., U.S. Army Command and Gen. Staff Coll., 1967. With Jefferson Parish Library, Metairie, La., 1959-80; head librarian Jefferson Parish Library, 1963-80; ret., 1980; area dir. Housing Authority New Orleans, 1980-85; exec. v.p. GTF Enterprises, Inc., 1985-95. Contbr. articles to mil. and libr. publs. and Encyclopedia Americana; vol. broadcaster Radio for the Blind and Print Handicapped, WRBH-FM Radio, New Orleans; co-author (film) The Jefferson Parish Story. Past pres. Pontchartrain Shores Civic Assn.; former bd. dirs. East Jefferson Parish ARC, Vets. Blvd. Bus. Assn. With AUS, 1943-45, 50-52; ret. col. Army Res. Mem. Le Petit Theatre du Vieux Carré, Jefferson Performing Arts Soc., Assn. U.S. Army, First Cav. Div. Assn., 11th Armored Div. Assn. (past v.p.), La. State U. Alumni Assn. (past pres. Greater New Orleans chpt.), Elks, Rotary (Paul Harris fellow), Alpha Delta Sigma. Republican. Roman Catholic. Home: Metairie La. Died Apr. 20, 1995.

WALSH, MICHAEL HARRIES, business executive; b. Binghamton, N.Y., July 8, 1942. B.A. in Econs., Stanford U., 1964; LLB., Yale U., 1969. Bar: Calif. 1970. Asst. dir. admissions Stanford U., 1964-65; White House fellow U.S. Dept. Agr., 1965-66; sr. staff atty. Defenders Inc., San Diego, 1969-72; mem. firm Sheela, Lightner, Hughes, Castro & Walsh, San Diego, 1972-77; U.S. atty. for Calif., 1977-80; exec. v.p. ops. and internat. Cummins Engine Co., Inc., Columbus, Ind., 1980-86; chmn., CEO Union Pacific R.R. Co., Omaha, Nebr., 1986-91; pres. Tenneco Inc., Houston, 1991-92, pres., CEO, 1992, chmn., CEO, 1992-94. Contbr. articles to profl. jours. Mem. State Bar Calif. Home: Houston Tex. Died May 6, 1994.

WALT, ALEXANDER JEFFREY, surgeon, educator; b. Cape Town, South Africa, June 13, 1923; came to U.S., 1961, naturalized, 1966; s. Isaac and Lea (Garb) W.; m. Irene Lapping, Dec. 21, 1947; children: John R., Steven D., Lindsay J. MB, ChB, U. Cape Town, 1948; MS, U. Minn., 1956. Diplomate: Am. Bd. Surgery (bd. dirs. 1976-85, vice chmn. 1983-85). Intern Groote Schuur Hosp. U. Cape Town, 1949-50; resident in surgery Mayo Clinic, Rochester, Minn., 1952-56; surg. registrar St. Martin's Hosp., Bath, Eng., 1956-57; asst. surgeon Groote Schuur Hosp., Cape Town, 1957-61; asst. chief surgery VA Hosp., Dearborn, Mich., 1961-62; chmn. dept. surgery Wayne State U., Detroit, 1966-88; chief of surgery Detroit Receiving Hosp., 1965-80, Harper-Grace Hosps., Detroit, 1972-88; prof. surgery Wayne State U., 1966-90, disting. prof. surgery, 1996. Author: (with R.F. Wilson) Management of Trauma: Pitfalls and Practice, 1975; editor: Early Care of the Injured, 1982. Served with South Africa Armed Forces, 1943-45. Fellow Royal Coll. Surgeons (Can.), Royal Coll. Surgeons (Eng., Hunterian prof. 1969, Moynihan lectr. 1989), ACS (bd. govs. 1975-81, bd. regents 1984-93, chmn. 1991-93, pres. elect 1993-94, pres. 1994-95, scudder orator 1978), Coll. Surgeons of South Africa (hon.), Royal Coll. Surgeons of Edinburgh (hon.); mem. Am. Surg. Assn. (1st v.p. 1990), Cen. Surg. Assn. (pres. 1977-78), Western Surg. Assn. (pres. 1986-87), Soc. Surgery of Alimentary Tract (founder's lectr. 1977, v.p. 1992-93), Am. Assn. Surgery of Trauma (pres. 1976-77), Am. Bd. Med. Specialists (exec. com. 1983-89, treas. 1985-89, v.p.), Internat. Soc. Surgery, Am. Bd. Med. Specialties (pres. 1992-94), Asian Surg. Assn. (hon.), Royal Australasian Coll. Surgeons (hon.), Alpha Omega Alpha. Home: Huntington Woods Mich. Died Feb. 29, 1996.

WALTERMIRE, JIM, secretary of state Montana; b. Choteau, Mont., Feb. 15, 1949; s. Robert and Anne (Luinstra) W.; m. Nancy Serechal. B.S. in Bus. Adminstrn, U. Mont. Engaged in real estate, ranching, constrn. and banking, 1972-75; partner Waltermire & Wicks (investments), Missoula, Mont., 1975-77; commr. Missoula County, 1977-80; sec. of state State of Mont., 1981—; Fellow Union Bank & Trust, Helena, 1970. Recipient Outstanding Young Alumnus award U. Mont., 1985—. Mem. Nat. Assn. Secs. State (pres. 1987). Home: Helena Mont.

WALTHER, JOHN HENRY, banker; b. Hartford, Conn., June 13, 1935; m. Pamela Ball; children: John, Jerome, Joshua. BA in Econs., Wesleyan U., 1957. Pres. N.J. Nat. Bank, Pennington, 1972-76, chief exec. officer, 1976-87, chmn., 1976-92; chmn., CEO BMJ Fin. Corp., Bordentown, N.J., 1992—; chmn. bd. dirs. N.J. Bankers Assn., Princeton, 1980-81; bd. dirs. Am. Bankers Assn., Washington, 1983-84, Fed. Reserve Bank Phila., 1984-86; bd. dirs., mem. exec. com. Assn. Bank Holding Cos., 1985-87. Home: Morrisville Pa. Home: Bordentown N.J. Died April 2, 1995.

WALTON, ERNEST THOMAS SINTON, physicist; b. Dungarvan, County Waterford, Ireland, Oct. 6, 1903; s. J.A. Walton; m. Winifred Isabel Wilson, 1934; 4 children. Student, Meth. Coll., Belfast, Northern Ireland; MSc, Trinity Coll., Dublin, Ireland; PhD, Cambridge (Eng.) U.; DSc (hon.), Queen's U., Belfast, Gustavus Adolphus Coll., Minn., U. Ulster, Northern Ireland; PhD, Dublin City U. Erasmus Smith's prof. natural and exptl. philosophy Trinity Coll., Dublin, 1947-74, fellow emeritus, 1974-95; hon. fellow Inst. Physics, London. Recipient Overseas Research scholar, 1927-30, Sr. Research award, dept. sci. and indsl. research, 1930-34, Clerk Maxwell scholar, 1932-34, Hughes medal, Royal Soc., 1938, Nobel prize for physics, 1951. Fellow Inst. Physics (hon.). Home: Belfast Northern Ireland Died June 25, 1995.

WANAMAKER, SAM, actor, director; b. Chgo., June 14, 1919; s. Maurice and Molly (Bobele) W.; m. Charlotte Holland, 1940; 3 daus. Ed., Drake U., Goodman Theatre Sch. Dir. Jewish Peoples Inst., Chgo., 1939-40. Radio actor, N.Y., 1940-41; also acted in Cafe Crown and Counterattack; actor, dir., 1946-93, artistic dir. New Shakespeare Theatre, Liverpool, Eng., 1957-59; prin. acting roles include: My Girl Tisa, 1947, Christ in Concrete, 1949, Denning Drives North, 1951; films include Taras Bulba, 1962, Those Magnificent Men in Their Flying Machines, 1964, The Spy Who Came In From The Cold, 1965, The Law, 1974, Spiral Staircase, 1974, The Sell-Out, 1976, Voyage of the Damned, 1976, Billy Jack Goes to Washington, 1977, From Hell to Victory, 1978, Death on the Nile, 1978, Private Benjamin, 1980, The Competition, 1980, Irreconcilable Differences, 1984, Raw Deal, 1986, Baby Boom, 1987, A Time to Remember, Guilty by Suspicion, 1991, Pure Luck, 1991, City of Joy, 1991; dir. film Sinbad & the Eye of the Tiger, 1977; actor, producer: play The Watergate Tapes; dir. opera The Ice Break; actor, dir. plays Joan of Lorraine, 1946, The Winter Journey, The Shrike, The Rainmaker, Threepenny Opera, The Big Knife, A Hatful of Rain, A View From the Bridge, Reclining Figure, Othello, The Rose Tattoo, A Far Country, 1961, Macbeth, 1964; dir. plays Gentlemen From Athens, 1948, Goodby My Fancy, 1949, Caesar and Cleopatra, Revival of Gardsman, Children From Their Games, 1962, Case of Libel, 1963; dir. operas King Priam, 1963, Forza del Destino, 1963; dir. and/or actor TV series Cimmarron Strip, TV films The Day the Fish Came Out, 1966, Warning Shot, 1966, The Eliminator, 1967, Custer, The Hawk, Lassiter, Court Martial, The Champions, The Chinese Visitor, 1968, The File of the Golden Goose, 1968, The Executioner, My Kidnapper, My Love, 1980, The Killing of Randy Webster, 1981, Berengers, Baby Boom, 1988; actor, dir. TV shows Holocaust, 1977, Return of the Saint, 1978; actor Blind Love, 1976; founder, exec. dir. Globe Playhouse Trust Ltd., World Centre for Shakespeare Studies Ltd.; actor, dir. numerous films, tv prodns., theatre plays and opera prodns., Britain, U.S., Can., Australia, France, Italy, Yugoslavia and Czechoslovakia, 1975-93. Served with U.S.Army, 1942-45. Home: London Eng. Died Dec. 18, 1993.

WANGLEE, SUVIT, banker; b. Bangkok, Thailand, Dec. 19, 1928; s. Tan Siew Meng and Tongpoon Wanglee; m. Tawara Kanokkul, 1960; 1 child, Saijai. BS in Fin. and Banking, U. Pa., 1957. Sr. exec. v.p. Wang Lee Chan Bank, Bangkok, 1962-73; pres. Nakornthon Bank, Bangkok, 1980-89, CEO, from 1989; chmn. Poonpipat Fin. & Securities, Bangkok, Navajiki Ins. Co., Ltd., Bangkok, Chao Phaya Resort Co., Ltd., Bangkok, Lake Rajada Co., Ltd., Bangkok. Chmn. Bd. of Trade Thailand, Bangkok. Mem. Thai C. of C. (chmn.), U. Thai C. of C. (chmn. trustees). Home: Bangkok Thailand Deceased.

WARD, DONALD BUTLER, minister; b. Boston, June 15, 1919; s. Donald Butler and Emma (Lyons) W.; m. Vera Barbara Bantz, June 10, 1944; children: Vera Margaret Ward McCarty, Laura Ann Ward Mollet, Christopher Donald. Student, Yankton Coll., 1937-39; BS, Northwestern U., 1942; MDiv, U. Chgo., 1959; DD, Lakeland Coll., 1964, Yankton Coll., 1981; LLD, Morningside Coll., 1964. Television account exec. Blair TV Assos., Chgo., 1951-54; mgr. Blair TV Assos., 1954-56; ordained to ministry Congl. Ch., 1959; minister First Congl. Ch. of Ravenswood, Chgo., 1958-60, Kirk of Bonnie Brae, Denver, 1960-62, First Congl. Ch., Evanston, Ill., 1970-79; v.p. Alaska Pacific U., Anchorage, 1979-80; sr. min. 1st Congl. Ch. L.A., 1980-86, min. emeritus, 1986-94; min. Little Stone Ch., Mackinac Island, Mich., 1992-93; commentator Viewpoint (daily radio program), 1978-79. Radio performer-producer, 1942-49, TV performer-producer, 1949-51; author: Not The Scabbard But the Blade, 1965, The Underground Church Is Nonsense, 1969, Master Sermon Series, 1973, Pray Then Like This, 1985, Great Preaching, 1990, William Brewster, My Pilgrim Ancestor, 1990, 93; contbg. editor The Congregationalist; composer: The Bell in the Tower, 1965, Alaska Pacific U. Alma Mater, 1979. Pres. Yankton (S.D.) Coll., 1962-70; past pres. Tri-State Conf., S.D. Found Pvt. Colls.; chmn. bd. Colls. of Mid-Am., Consortium of Ten Colls.; co-chmn. Internat. Congl. Fellowship, 1989-93; bd. dirs. Chgo. Theol. Sem., Sch. Theology, Claremont, Calif., Mental Health Assn. Named Man of Year First Congl. Ch. Evanston, 1956. Fellow Am. Congl. Ctr.; mem. Evanston Hist. Soc., Aircraft Owners and Pilots Assn., Nat. Speakers Assn., Nat. Assn. Congl. Christian Chs. (vice moderator 1993-94), Acad. Magical Arts, L.A. Pianists Club, Univ. Club, Kiwanis, Masons (32d degree), Shriners, Order of Constantine, Sigma Chi (past gov. grand tribune). Home: Bermuda Dunes Calif. Died Sept. 27, 1994.

WARD, LOUIS LARRICK, candy company executive; b. Kansas City, Mo., Nov. 18, 1919; s. Carter William and Fern Alpha (Larrick) W.; m. Adelaide Selby Cobb, Dec. 17, 1955; children—Scott Hardman, Thomas Selby, Linda Larrick. Student, U. Kans., 1937-38; B.S. in Chem. Engring, Stanford, 1941. With Drexel, Harriman & Co., 1946-47, Spencer Chem. Co., 1947-50, Ward Paper Box Co., 1950-60; pres., chmn. bd. Russell Stover Candies, Inc., Kansas City, Mo., 1960-93, bd. dirs. emeritus, 1993-96; retired, 1993; dir. First Nat Bank, Ward Paper Box Co., all Kansas City, Mo. Served with USNR, 1941-46. Mem. Kappa Sigma. Clubs: Kansas City Country (Kansas City, Mo.), River (Kansas City, Mo.), University (Kansas City, Mo.). Home: Kansas City Mo. Died Feb. 10, 1996.

WARD, RICHARD STORER, child psychiatrist, educator emeritus; b. Beirut, Lebanon, Oct. 9, 1920; came to U.S., 1931; s. Edwin St. John and Charlotte Edwards (Allen) W.; m. Adele Marie Zangara, Sept. 2, 1960; children: Steven Henry, Charlotte Canham, Richard Zangara. BA, Amherst Coll., 1942; MD, Columbia U., 1945, postgrad., 1957. Diplomate Am. Bd. Psychiatry and Neurology (child psychiatry cert. com. 1972-80). Intern Babies Hosp., N.Y.C., 1945; resident in psychiatry Stony Lodge, Ossining, N.Y., 1950-51, Psychiat. Inst., N.Y.C., 1951-52; clin. dir. Child Guidance Clinic, Jewish Child Care Assn., Newark, 1952-56, M.B. Child Guidance Inst., Jewish Bd. Guardians, N.Y.C., 1956-60; prof. child psychiatry Emory U., Atlanta, 1960-86, prof. emeritus, 1986—; dir. child unit Parkwood Hosp., Atlanta, 1976-90; pvt. practice psychiatry Atlanta, 1986—. Fellow Am. Psychiat. Assn., Am. Acad. Child Psychiatry, Am. Psychoanalytic Assn.; mem. Am. Orthopsychiat. Assn., Am. Coll. Psychoanalysts. Democrat. Mem. United Ch. of Christ. Home: Atlanta Ga.

WARNE, WILLIAM ELMO, irrigationist; b. nr. Seafield, Ind., Sept. 2, 1905; s. William Rufus and Nettie Jane (Williams) W.; m. Edith Margaret Peterson, July 19, 1929; children: Jane Ingrid (Mrs. David C. Beeder), William Robert, Margaret Edith (Mrs. John W. Monroe). AB, U. Calif., 1927; DEcons (hon.), Yonsei U., Seoul, 1959; LLD, Seoul Nat. U., 1959. Reporter San Francisco Bull. and Oakland (Calif.) Post-Enquirer, 1925-27; news editor Brawley (Calif.) News, 1927, Calexico (Calif.) Chronicle, 1927-28; editor, night mgr. L.A. bur. AP, 1928-31, corr. San Diego bur., 1931-33, Washington corr., 1933-35; editor, bur. reclamation Dept. Interior, 1935-37; on staff Third World Power Conf., 1936; assoc. to reviewing com. Nat. Resources Com. on preparation Drainage Basin Problems and Programs, 1936, mem. editorial com. for revision, 1937; chief of information Bur. Reclamation, 1937-42; co-dir. (with Harlan H. Barrows) Columbia Basin Joint Investigations, 1939-42; chief of staff, war prodn. drive WPB, 1942; asst. dir. div. power Dept. Interior, 1942-43, dept. dir. information, 1943; asst. commr. Bur. Reclamation, 1943-47; apptd. asst. sec. Dept. Interior, 1947, asst. sec. Water and Power Devel., 1950-51; U.S. minister charge tech. cooperation Iran, 1951-55, Brazil, 1955-56; U.S. minister and econ. coord. for Korea, 1956-59; dir. Cal. Dept. Fish and Game, 1959-60, Dept. Agr., 1960-61, Dept. Water Resources, 1961-67; v.p. water resources Devel. and Resources Corp., 1967-69; resources cons., 1969-96; pres. Warne & Blanton Pubs. Inc., 1985-90, Warne Walnut Wrancho, Inc., 1979-96; Disting. Practitioner in Residence Sch. Pub. Adminstrn., U. So. Calif. at Sacramento, 1976-78; adminstr. Resources Agy. of Calif., 1961-63; Chmn. Pres.'s Com. on San Diego Water Supply, 1944-46; chmn. Fed. Inter-Agy. River Basin Com., 1948, Fed. Com. on Alaskan Devel., 1948; pres. Group Health Assn., Inc., 1947-51; chmn. U.S. delegation 2d Inter-Am. Conf. Indian Life, Cuzco, Peru, 1949; U.S. del. 4th World Power Conf., London, Eng., 1950; mem. Calif. Water Pollution Control Bd., 1959-67; vice chmn. 1960-62; mem. water pollution control adv. bd. Dept. Health, Edn. and Welfare, 1962-65, cons., 1966-67; chmn. Calif. delegation Western States Water Council, 1965-67. Author: Mission for Peace-Point 4 in Iran, 1956, The Bureau of Reclamation, 1973, How the Colorado River Was Spent, 1975, The Need to Institutionalize Desalting, 1978; prin. author: The California Experience with Mass Transfers of Water over Long Distances, 1978; editor Geothermal Report, 1985-90. Served as 2d lt. O.R.C., 1927-37. Recipient Disting. Svc. award Dept. Interior, 1951, Disting. Pub. Svc. Honor award FOA, 1955, Order of Crown Shah of Iran, 1955, Outstanding Svc. citation UN Command Korea, 1959, Order of Indsl. Sv. Merit Bronze Star, Korea, 1991. Fellow Nat. Acad. Pub. Adminstrn. (sr., chmn. standing com. on environ. and resources mgmt. 1971-78); mem. Nat. Water Supply Improvement Assn. (pres. 1978-80, Lifetime Achievement award 1984), Internat. Desalination Assn. (founding mem., Lifetime Disting. Service award 1991), Soc. Profl. Journalists, Sutter Club, Nat. Press Club (Washington), Lambda Chi Alpha. Home: Palo Alto Calif. Died Mar. 9, 1996; interred Sacramento, Calif.

WARNS, RAYMOND H., judge; b. St. Paul, July 24, 1920; s. Henry John and Veronica (Jennings) W.; m. Ruth Elenor Fuhrman, Nov. 22, 1947; children—Stephen F., Mark J., Michael T., Raymond H. Student, U. Minn., 1941-42, 45-47; B.S.L., J.D., St. Paul Coll. Law, 1948-52. With law dept. Soo Line R.R., Mpls., 1952-57; with firm Battle, Neal, Harris, Minor & Williams, Charlottesville, Va., 1962-63; with Greyhound Corp., Chgo., 1957-61, 63-69, gen. counsel, 1965; v.p. claims Greyhound Lines, Inc. Greyhound Corp., 1969; gen. atty. Household Finance Corp., 1969-71; U.S. adminstrv. law judge Seattle, 1971-85; retired. Served as pilot USAAF, World War II. Home: Kingston Wash. Died Dec. 6, 1995.

WARTEN, RALPH MARTIN, mathematics educator; b. Bielefeld, Fed. Republic Germany, Jan. 6, 1926; came to U.S., 1948; s. Bernhard and Ernestine (Isaac) Wartensleben; m. Winifred Grace Battelle, Oct. 14, 1950. BS, Bklyn Coll., 1957; MS, Purdue U., 1959, PhD, 1961. Researcher Math. Research Ctr. IBM Corp., Palo Alto, Calif., 1966-68, instr., adv. mathematician fed. systems div., 1961-65; research and teaching asst. Purdue U., Lafayette, Ind., 1957-60; prof. math. Calif. Poly. State U., San Luis Obispo, from 1968. Contbr. articles to profl. jours. Mem. AAAS, Am. Math. Soc., Math. Assn. Am., N.Y. Acad. Scis., Phi Beta Kappa, Sigma Xi, Kappa Mu Epsilon, Alpha Sigma Lambda, Pi Mu Epsilon. Home: San Luis Obispo Calif. Deceased.

WATANABE, MICHIO, Japanese government official; b. Tochigi, Japan, July 28, 1923; married; 2 sons, 1 dau. Educated, Tokyo Comml. Coll. (now Hitotsubashi U.). Salesman, 1945-50; practice as tax lawyer, mem. Prefectural Legislature Tochigi; mem. Ho. of Reps., from 1963; parliamentary vice min. agr. & forestry, dep. sec.-gen. Liberal Dem. Party; chair cabinet com. Ho. of Reps.; min. health & welfare Japan, 1976-77, min. agr., forestry & fisheries, 1978-79, min. fin., 1980-82, min. internat. trade & industry, 1985-86; acting sec.-gen. Liberal Dem. Party, 1984; chair Liberal Dem. Party Policy Rsch. Coun., from 1987; mem. LDP Seirankai; min. fgn. affairs, dep. prime min. Japan. Home: Tokyo Japan Deceased.

WATKINS, ROBERT DORSEY, judge; b. Balt., Sept. 27, 1900; s. Joseph Marion and Harriett Isabelle (Strong) W.; m. Marion Turner, July 1, 1933; 1 dau., Eileen Roberta Dorsey. A.B., Johns Hopkins, 1922, Ph.D., 1925; LL.B., U. Md., 1925. Bar: Md. bar 1925. Since practiced in Balt.; Instr. law sch. U. Md., 1925-68; instr. comml. law Johns Hopkins, 1926-55; U.S. dist. judge Dist. of Md., from 1955, sr. judge. Author: The State as a Party Litigant, 1925. Fellow Am. Coll. Trial Lawyers; mem. ABA, Md. Bar Assn., Balt. Bar Assn. (pres. 1948-49), Order of Coif, Phi Beta Kappa, Omicron Delta Kappa. Home: Baltimore Md. Deceased.

WATSON, JEROME RICHARD, journalist; b. Chgo., May 6, 1938; s. Raja Eminger and Irene (Sutherland) W.; m. Jerilyn Clara Ellis, Feb. 6, 1965; children: Corin Jerome, Miles Girard. A.A., Wright Jr. Coll., 1958; B.S. J., Northwestern U., 1960, M.S. J., 1961. Reporter Chgo. City News Bur., 1960-61; reporter Hollister Newspapers, Wilmette, Ill., 1961-64; reporter Chgo. Sun Times, 1964-93, political editor, columnist, 1972-76, Washington correspondent, 1977-86, Washington bur. chief, 1987-93. Recipient Robert F. Kennedy award Robert F. Kennedy Meml., Washington, 1971, Disting. Service award Sigma Delta Chi, 1982, Publisher's award Chgo. Sun Times, 1985; Nieman fellow Harvard Univ., 1970-71. Mem. The White House Corrs. Assn. (bd. dirs. 1988-91), Gridiron Club. Clubs: Nat. Press, Gridiron. Home: Bethesda Md. Died Dec. 19, 1993.

WATSON, JOHN KING, JR., lawyer; b. Cambridge, Mass., Sept. 20, 1926; s. John King and Viola (Merz) W.; m. Audrey Margaret Williams, Aug. 25, 1951; children: John King III, Audrey Margaret, Jennifer Kathryn, Anne Mary, James King. BA, Harvard U., 1949; LLB, Columbia U., 1952. Bar: N.Y. 1953. Assoc. Lord, Day & Lord, Barrett Smith, N.Y.C., 1952-64, ptnr., 1965-87, counsel, 1987-92; of counsel Cadwalader, Wickersham & Taft, 1994—. Trustee Masters Sch., Dobbs Ferry, N.Y., 1978-84; mem. vis. com. Arms and Armor Dept. MEt. Mus. Art. Pvt. 1st class USMC, 1944-46. Mem. Downtown Assn., Harvard Club

Y.C.), Armor and Arms of N.Y. (pres. 1984-88), rth Fork Country Club, Essex Yacht Club, Old me Country Club. Republican. Home: Essex Conn.

ATSON, JOHN STEVEN, publishing executive; b. bburn-on-Tyne, Eng., Mar. 16, 1916; m. Heba Sylvia Cordova Newbery, Sept. 1, 1942; children—John ilip, Paul Michael Franics. M.A., St. John's Coll., 39; postgrad. Merton Coll., 1941; D.Litt., De Pauw , 1967; D.H.L., St. Andrew's U., 1972; D.H.L., 1972; Hum., Simpson Coll. Sec. to minister fuel and power r Majesty's Govt., Eng., 1942-45; tutor, lectr. Christ ., Oxford, Eng., 1945-66, U. Oxford, 1945-66; prin., s. U. St. Andrews, Scotland, 1945-66; chmn. Scottish ad. Press, Edinburg, Scotland, 1970—. Author: The ign of George III, 1960; A History of the Salters mpany, 1963. Editor: The Law and Working of the nstitution (2 vols.), 1952. Contbr. articles to profl. rs. Dir. Brit. Library Bd., London, 1974-80; war-time : to Ministers of Fuel and Power, London; mem. int U.S./Eng. Ednl. Com. on Ofcl. Commn. Secrets t, 1968. Fellow Christ Ch. Oxford; recipient Silver dal City of Paris, 1967; Gold medal Am. Legion, 78. Fellow Royal Hist. Soc., Royal Soc. Edinburgh. cial Democrat. Mem. Ch. of Eng. Clubs: Royal and cient Golf, New (Edinburgh). Died May 1986. ome: Fife Scotland

ATSON, ROBERT BARDEN, physicist; b. ampaign, Ill., Apr. 14, 1914; s. Floyd Rowe and Esle Jane (Barden) W.; m. Genevieve L. Carter, Oct. 11, 41; children: Ann Barden, Roberta Gail, Douglas arter. AB, U. Ill., 1934; MA, UCLA, 1936; PhD, arvard U., 1941. Teaching asst. UCLA, 1935-36; aching asst., instr. Harvard U., Cambridge, Mass., 36-41, rsch. assoc., 1940-41, rsch. assoc., Underwater ound Lab., 1941-45; from asst. to assoc. prof. physics . Tex., Austin, 1945-60, rsch. assoc., 1946-60; physical is. adminstr. U.S. Dept. of the Army, Washington, 60-76; cons. archtl. acoustics, Austin, 1946-60; rep. to rious nat. and internat. sci. groups U.S. Army, Washgton, 1960-76. Contbr. articles to Jour. Acoustical oc. Am., Jour. Applied Physics. Fellow AAAS (Sci. reedom and Responsibility award 1993), Acoustical oc. Am.; mem. IEEE, Optical Soc. Am., Assn. Am. hysics Tchrs., Wash. Acad. Sci., Sigma Xi, Sigma Pi gma. Home: Mc Lean Va. Died June 4, 1995.

ATSON, THOMAS J., JR., former ambassador, red business executive; b. Dayton, Ohio, Jan. 8, 1914; Thomas J. and Jeanette Kittredge) W.; m. Olive Field awley, Dec. 15, 1941; children: Thomas J. III, Jenette, Olive, Lucinda, Susan, Helen. B.A., Brown U., 937; hon. degrees from following univs., Columbia U.; larvard U., Brown U., Oxford U., Yale U., Cath. U. m., Lafayette Coll., U. Notre Dame, Pace U., Union oll., Rensselaer Poly. Inst., Amherst Coll., Syracuse ., St. Michael's Coll., Winooski, Vt., U. Colo., U. Vt., rinity Coll., Wheaton Coll., Norton, Mass., Bard Coll., nnandale-on-Hudson, N.Y., Colby Coll., Maine. With BM, 1937-40, 46-79, pres., 1952-61, CEO, 1956-71, hmn., 1961-71, chmn. exec. com., 1971-79, dir., chmn. meritus, 1981-93; U.S. ambassador to USSR, 1979-81; d. dirs. Learjet Corp.; mem. Pres.'s Commn. Nat. oals, 1960-61, Pres.'s Adv. Com. Labor-Mgmt. Policy, 961-69, Adv. Com. Troop Info. and Edn., Dept. Def., 962, Pres.'s Task Force on War Against Poverty, 1964-68, Nat. Commn. on Tech., Govt., Automation and Econ. Progress, 1965-66, Pres.'s Commn. on Income Maintenance Programs, 1968-70, Am. Com. on East-West Accord, 1975-78; chmn. gen. adv. com. ACDA, 1978-79. Pres. Greater N.Y. Councils, Boy Scouts Am., 1953-56, pres. Nat. Council, 1964-68; trustee Brown U., 1947-85, vice chancellor, 1979-85, mem. bd. of fellows, 1985-93; trustee Am. Mus. Nat. History, 1955-78, hon. trustee, 1978-93; trustee M.I.T., 1957-62; trustee George C. Marshall Research Found., 1958-89, trustee emeritus, 1989-93; trustee Calif. Inst. Tech., 1960-79, 1981-84, life trustee, 1984-93; trustee Rockefeller Found., 1963-71, John F. Kennedy Library, 1964-93, Mystic Seaport, Inc., 1967-69, 1981-93, Inst. Advanced Study, Princeton, 1968-75, World Wildlife Fund, 1974-78; trustee Mayo Found., 1975-79, 1981-85, emeritus pub. trustee, 1985-93; sr. fellow Woodrow Wilson Nat. Fellowship Found., 1973-79; bd. dirs. Alliance to Save Energy, N.Y.C. Mission Soc., 1981-84, Nat. Exec. Service Corps, 1982-93, Atlantic Council of U.S., 1982-86; mem. Com. of Ams. for the Canal Treaties, 1977-78; citizen regent Smithsonian Instn., 1967-79, regent emeritus, 1981-93. Served to lt. col. USAF, 1940-45. Decorated Air medal; Presdl. medal of Freedom; comdr. Order of Merit, Rep. of Italy; officer Legion of Honor France; officer Order of Leopold II Belgium; comdr. Al Mérito por Servicios Distinguídos Peru; Grand Cross; Equestrian Order of St. Sylvester Vatican; comdr. Royal Order of Vasa Sweden; officer Order of So. Cross Brazil; recipient Silver Antelope, Buffalo, Beaver awards Boy Scouts Am., 1958; Rosenberger medal Brown U., 1968; Gold medal Nat. Inst. Social Scis., 1971; Citation of Merit Salvation Army, 1972; Gold medal Electronic Industries Assn., 1972; Pub. Service award Advt. Council, 1972; Herbert Hoover Meml. award Boys Clubs Am., 1975; Nat. Bus. Hall of Fame award for bus. leadership, 1976; Medallion Sch. of Bus., Coll. of William and Mary, 1976; Pub. Service award Phoenix House, 1981; Internat. Achievement award World Trade Club of San Francisco, 1981; Service to Democracy award Am. Assembly, 1983; Blue Water medal CCA, 1986, Am. Soc. French Legion of Honor medal for Disting. Achievement, 1988, Medal of Achievement Am. Electronic Assn., 1989. Mem. Council on Fgn. Relations, Bus. Council, Internat. C. of C. (trustee U.S. Council 1949-64, chmn. 1955-57), Am. Philos. Soc. (Benjamin Franklin award 1988), Psi Upsilon. Clubs: Links (N.Y.C.), River (N.Y.C.), N.Y. Yacht (N.Y.C.); Metropolitan (Washington); Round Hill, Hope (Providence); Cruising of Am. Home: Greenwich Conn. Died Dec. 31, 1993.

WATTS, HENRY MILLER, JR., stockbroker; b. Phila., Mar. 13, 1904; s. Henry Miller and Laura Esther (Barney) W.; m. Maxine Wieczorek, 1935; m. Anna Harris Pepper, 1952. Grad., St. Paul's Sch., 1921; A.B., Harvard U., 1925. With Robert Glendinning & Co., Phila., 1925-29; mem. N.Y. Stock Exchange, 1929-95, gov., 1958-61, vice chmn. bd. govs., 1961-62, chmn. bd. govs., 1962-65; chmn. bd. Mitchel Schreiber, Watts & Co., Inc., N.Y.C., 1931-82; pres., chmn. bd. Independence Sq. Income Securities Inc., 1972-95; dir. Teradyne Corp., Temporary Investment Fund, Inc., Municipal Fund for Temporary Investment; trustee Trust for Short-Term Fed. Securities; pres., mng. gen. partner Chestnut St. Exchange Fund. Bd. dirs. Muscular Dystrophy Assn. Am., 1965-95, pres., 1968-75, mem. exec. com., 1975-95. Lt. (j.g.) to comdr. USNR, 1941-45, capt. Res. ret. Rector's warden Christ Ch., Phila., 1964-95. Decorated Bronze Star with combat V. Mem. Soc. Cincinnati of Pa. (pres. 1968-71), Mil. Order Fgn. Wars, 1st Troop Phila. City Cav. (hon.). Clubs: Racquet and Tennis (N.Y.C.), Union (N.Y.C.); Philadelphia. Home: Philadelphia Pa. Died Oct. 2, 1995.

WEAVER, JOHN CARRIER, retired university president; b. Evanston, Ill., May 21, 1915; s. Andrew Thomas and Cornelia Myrta (Carrier) W.; m. Ruberta Louise Harwell, Aug. 8, 1940; children: Andrew Bennett, Thomas Harwell. A.B., U. Wis., 1936, A.M., 1937, Ph.D., 1942; LL.D., Mercer U., 1972; L.H.D., Coll. St. Scholastica, 1973; Litt.D., Drury Coll., 1973. Mem. editorial and research staff Am. Geog. Soc. of N.Y., 1940-42; mem. research staff Office of Geographer, U.S. Dept. State, 1942-44; asst. prof. dept. geography U. Minn., 1946-47, assoc. prof., 1947-48, prof., 1948-55; prof. geography, dean Sch. Arts and Sci., Kans. State U., 1955-57; prof. geography, dean grad. coll. U. Nebr., 1957-61; v.p. research, dean grad. coll., prof. geography State U. Iowa, 1961-64; v.p. academic affairs, dean faculties, prof. geography Ohio State U., Columbus, 1964-66; pres., prof. geography U. Mo., 1966-70, U. Wis., 1971; pres. U. Wis. System, 1971-77, emeritus, 1977-95; prof. geography U. Wis. Milw., Madison, Green Bay, 1971-78; hon. prof. geography U. Wis. at Oshkosh; Disting. prof. U. So. Calif., 1977-85, emeritus, 1985-95; exec. dir. Center for Study of Am. Experience, 1978-81, Annenberg Disting. scholar, 1981-82; research cons. Midwest Barley Improvement Assn., Milw., 1946-50; expert cons. to Com. on Geophysics and Geography, Research and Devel. Bd., Washington, 1947-53; mem. adv. com. on geography Office Naval Research, NRC, 1949-52, chmn., 1951-52; vis. prof. U. Oreg., summer 1951, Harvard U., summer 1954; cons. editor McGraw-Hill series in geography, 1951-67; mem. adv. com. to sec. HEW, 1958-62; mem. Mid-Am. State U. Assn., 1959-70, chmn., 1959-61, 70-71; chmn. Council Grad. Schs. U.S., 1961-62; mem. Woodrow Wilson fellow selection com., 1961-70; mem. com. instl. coop. Univs. Western Conf. and Chgo., 1962-66, chmn., 1964-66; pres. Assn. Grad. Schs. in Assn. Am. Univs., 1963-64; Wilton Park fellow Brit. Fgn. Office, 1965, 67, 70, 74, 76; chmn. Nat. Task Force on Future of Pharmacy Edn., 1981-84. Author: Ice Atlas of the Northern Hemisphere, 1946, American Barley Production, A Study in Agricultural Geography, 1950, A Statistical World Survey of Commercial Production, (with Fred E. Lukerman) A Geographical Source book, 1953, The American Railroads, 1958, Minnesota and Wisconsin, 1961; illustrator: Quiet Thoughts, 1971; contbr. articles to books and profl. periodicals; contbg. editor: Geog. Rev, 1955-70. Active Mo. Commn. of Higher Edn., 1966-70, White House Task Force on Priorities in Higher Edn., 1969-70, Edn. Commn. of States, 1971-77; bd. dirs. Harry S. Truman Library Inst. Nat. and Internat. Affairs, 1967-70; trustee Nat. Com. on Accreditation, 1966-76, Johnson Found., Racine, Wis., 1971-77, 81-82, Am. Univs. Field Service, 1971-75, Nat. Merit Scholarship Corp., 1971-77, 80-82; trustee Chadwick Sch., Palos Verdes Peninsula, 1987-93, 94-95, mem. exec. com., 1989-93; mem. citizens' stamp adv. com. to Postmaster Gen., 1981-85; mem. bd. advisors Salvation Army Sch. Officers Tng., Western Ter., 1989-95, mem. U. of So. Calif. pres., 1993-94. Served as lt. (j.g.) USNR, 1944-46; assigned specialist Hydrographic Office, Office of Chief of Naval Ops. Washington. Recipient Vilas medal U. Wis., 1936, Letter Commendation from Chief of Naval Ops., 1946; Carnegie Found. adminstrv. fellow, 1957-58. Fellow Am. Geog. Soc. (governing council 1974-95, John Finley Breeze Morse medal 1986), AAAS; mem Assn. Am. Geographers (council 1949-51, Nat. Research award 1955), Am. Geophys. Union, Arctic Inst. N.Am. (charter asso.), Am. Polar Soc., Internat. Geog. Union, Am. Pharm. Assn. (hon.), Am. Friends of Wilton Park (pres. 1980-81), U. So. Calif. Ret. Faculty Assn. (pres. 1993-94), Phi Beta Kappa, Sigma Xi, Phi Kappa Phi, Delta Sigma Rho, Phi Eta Sigma, Alpha Kappa Psi, Beta Kappa Sigma, Chi Phi. Home: Palos Verdes Peninsula Calif. Died Mar. 10, 1995.

WEBB, E. N., bishop. Bishop of Nev. Ch. of God in Christ, Las Vegas. Home: Las Vegas Nev. Deceased.

WEBER, ALFRED H(ERMAN), physicist, consultant, writer; b. Phila., Jan. 15, 1906; s. Frank Curt and Anna Josephine (Kling) W.; m. Frances Theresa Lever, Dec. 26, 1932 (dec. Nov. 1989); children: Constance Marie, Judith Ann, Christine Frances, Joseph Alfred, Mary Linda, Mark Francis, June Elizabeth. A.B. summa cum laude, St. Joseph's Coll., Phila., 1928, A.M., 1931, D.Sc. (hon.), 1968; Ph.D., U. Pa., 1936. From asst. prof. to prof. physics and math. St. Joseph's Coll., Phila., 1928-39, chmn. dept. physics, 1936-39; asst. prof., assoc. prof. then prof. physics St. Louis U., 1939-74, chmn. dept. physics, 1951-73; prof. physics, space physics U. Ala., Huntsville, 1959-70; lectr. space sci. Washington U., St. Louis, 1960-61; cons. physicist Argonne Nat. Lab., Chgo., 1947-57, pres. Assoc. Midwest Univs., 1960; chief physicist NASA Marshall Space Flight Ctr., Huntsville, 1957-70. Author or contbg. author 7 textbooks; contbr. articles to profl. jours. Grantee in field NSF, AEC, Office Naval Research, Dept. Def., Am. Cancer Soc., others. Fellow Am. Phys. Soc.; mem. Am. Assn. Physics Tchrs., AAUP, Sigma Xi. Home: Sarasota Fla. Deceased.

WEBER, ERNST, engineering consultant; b. Vienna, Austria, Sept. 6, 1901; naturalized, 1936; married, 1936; 2 children. Diploma, Vienna Tech. U., 1924, DSc, 1927; PhD in Physics, U. Vienna, 1926; DSc (hon.), L.I. U., 1963; DEng (hon.), Newark Coll., 1959, U. Mich., 1964, Polytech. Inst. Bklyn., 1969. Research engr. Oesterreichische Siemens-Schuckert-Werke, Austria, 1924-29; research engr. Siemens-Schuckert-Werke, Fed. Republic Germany, 1929-30, vis. prof., 1930-31, research prof. elec. engring., 1931-41; investigator Office of Sci. Research and Devel. Contract, 1942-45; prof. elec. engring., head dept., dir. Microwave Research Inst., 1945-47, pres., 1957-69; emeritus pres. Polytech. U. N.Y., 1969-96; sec. Polytech. Research and Devel. Co., Inc., 1944-52, pres., 1952-60; chmn. div. engring. Nat. Research Council, 1970-74, mem. commn. sociotech. systems, 1974-78, cons., 1978-96. Recipient Howard Coonley medal Am. Standards Assn., 1966, L.E. Grinter award Engrs. Council Profl. Devel., 1978, Nat. Medal of Sci., 1987, Centennial medallion Am. Soc. Engring. Educators, 1993; named to Am. Soc. Engring. Educators Hall of Fame, 1993. Fellow Am. Physical Soc., IEEE (pres. 1959, 63, Founders award 1970); mem. Nat. Acad. Sci., Nat. Acad. Engring. Home: Columbus N.C. Died Feb. 15, 1996.

WEBER, GERALD JOSEPH, federal judge; b. Erie, Pa., Feb. 1, 1914; s. Joseph J. and Ruth M. (Sullivan) W.; m. Berta M. Drechsel, Aug. 21, 1947; children: Thomas, William, Mary. A.B., Harvard U., 1936; LL.B., U. Pa., 1939. Bar: Pa. 1940. Civilian with U.S. Forces, Austria, 1946-47; mem. firm Knox, Weber, Pearson & McLaughlin, Erie, 1957-64; city solicitor Erie, 1951-61; judge U.S. Dist. Ct. Western Dist. Pa., 1964-95. Served with AUS, 1942-45. Decorated Bronze Star. Home: Erie Pa. Deceased.

WEBERMAN, BEN, journalist, editor; b. N.Y.C., Mar. 27, 1923; s. Samuel and Sadie (Wolfe) W.; m. Sylvia Berger, Nov. 15, 1947; children: Nancy Beth Rilander, Lynn Susan Ziven. BS in Math., CCNY, 1943; cert. in Mech. Engring., U. Md., 1944; MBA in Fin., N.Y.U., 1955. Economist Internat. Statistical Bur., N.Y.C., 1946-51; fin. editor Jour. Commerce, N.Y.C., 1951-58, N.Y. Herald Tribune, N.Y.C., 1958-66, Am. Banker Newspaper, N.Y.C., 1966-76; sr. editor columnist Forbes, N.Y.C., 1976-94. Author: Interest Rate Futures, 1982; editor: Dictionary of Banking Terms, 1990. With U.S. Army, 1943-46. Mem. N.Y. Fin. Writers Assn. (pres. 1987). Jewish. Home: New York N.Y. Died Oct. 22, 1994.

WECLEW, THADDEUS VICTOR, dentist, educator; b. Chgo., Oct. 7, 1906; s. Victor Thomas and Mary Mae (Tadrowski) W.; m. Marguerite Helene Pfister, Jan. 1931 (dec. 1964); m. Priscilla Joan Glenicki, Jan. 2, 1965; 1 child, Marilyn Dootson Storm. DDS, U. Ill., 1930, BS, 1987. Lic. dentist Ill. Sole practice dentistry Chgo., 1930-92; asst. prof., cons. U. Ill. Dental Coll., Chgo., 1970-85; cons. and lectr. in field; founder, chancellor Acad. Continuing Edn., 1979-92. Contbr. articles to profl. jours. Bd. dirs. Ill. Good Govt. Inst., 1950-86. Served with USCG, 1945. Named Disting. Alumnus, U. Ill., 1969, Hall of Fame City of Chgo., 1989; decorated officer Ordre Palmes Academique (France); recipient Am. Coll. of Dent Gies award, 1992. Fellow Acad. Gen. Dentistry (founder, pres. emeritus 1965, master, founder, editor jour. 1952-74, editor emeritus 1974-92, exec. dir. 1965-69), Am. Coll. Dentistry, Acad. Dentistry Internat. (hon.), Internat. Coll. Dentistry, Acad. Continuing Edn.; mem. ADA, Ill. State Dental Soc. (disting. mem. 1979), U. Ill. Dental Alumni Assn. (disting. mem., pres. 1967), Nat. Med. and Dental Soc. (disting. mem. 1982), Chgo. Dental Soc. (bd. dirs. 1969-73), Psi Omega, Omicron Kappa Upsilon. Roman Catholic. Home: Chicago Ill. Died Oct. 16, 1992.

WEGNER, HARVEY EDWARD, physicist, consultant; b. Tacoma, Aug. 12, 1925; s. William Godfrey and Pearl

Vivian (Wilson) W.; m. Sally-Ann Christensen, Sept. 15, 1949; children: William A., James F., Linda Sue. BS, U. Puget Sound, 1948; MS, U. Wash., 1950, PhD, 1953. Postdoctoral Brookhaven Nat. Lab., Upton, N.Y., 1953-56; staff mem. Los Alamos Sci. Lab., Los Alamos, N.Mex., 1956-62; sr. scientist Brookhaven Nat. Lab., Upton, N.Y., 1962-92; retired Brookhaven Nat. Lab., Upton, 1992, cons., 1993-94; cons. Brookhaven Nat. Lab., N.Y., 1992-94. Co-author: Quark Matter '83: Proceedings of the Third International Conference on Ultra-Relativistic Nucleus-Nucleus Collisions, 1983. With U.S. Army, 1944-46. Recipient Alexander von Humboldt-Stiftung Sr. Scientist award Germany, 1975-76, 87. Fellow AAAS, Am. Physical Soc.; mem. Am. Assn. Physics Tchrs., Nat. Acad. Sci. (com. mem. comml. aviation safety 1988-92). Republican. Home: La Jolla Calif. Died Nov. 27, 1994.

WEHLE, JOHN LOUIS, brewing company executive; b. Rochester, N.Y., Dec. 21, 1916; s. Louis A. and Elizabeth R. (Rabe) W.; m. Marjorie Strong, Aug. 8, 1942; children: John Louis, Charles S., Henry S. Ed., U. Rochester, Yale U. With Genesee Brewing Co., Rochester, 1939-93; chmn. bd. Genesee Brewing Co., 1969-93; dir; exec. emeritus com. Marine Midland Bank, Rochester. Chmn. bd. Genesee County Mus. Recipient Civic Arts award Rochester, 1977; Bus. Com. Arts award Indpls., 1977. Mem. Landmark Soc. Western N.Y., Yale U., U. Rochester alumni assns. Club: Genesee Valley. Home: Rochester N.Y. Died Nov. 7, 1993.

WEICK, PAUL CHARLES, judge; b. Youngstown, Ohio, Aug. 25, 1899; s. Charles J. and Jane (Guttridge) W.; m. Hilda Rickard, Sept. 28, 1929 (dec. Aug. 1960); 1 son, Paul A.; m. Nelle Edwards, Aug. 15, 1963. LL.B., U. Cin., 1920, LL.D. (hon.), 1965. Bar: Ohio bar 1920. Practice law Akron, Ohio, 1920-56; judge U.S. Dist. Ct. No. Dist. Ohio, 1956-59; judge U.S. Ct. Appeals, 6th Circuit, from 1959, chief judge, 1963-69; mem. Jud. Conf. of U.S., 1963-69; mem. bd. bar examiners Supreme Ct. Ohio, 1946-50. Recipient award Fellows of Ohio State Bar Found., 1965; Centennial award U. Akron, 1970. Mem. ABA, Ohio Bar Assn. (pres. 1950), Akron Bar Assn. (pres. 1942), Am. Judicature Soc., Am. Law Inst., Inst. Jud. Adminstrn., Am., Ohio State bar founds. Home: Akron Ohio Deceased.

WEIGLE, RICHARD DANIEL, retired college president; b. Northfield, Minn., Mar. 9, 1912; s. Luther Allan and Clara (Boxrud) W.; m. Mary Grace Day, Apr. 4, 1942; children: Mary Martha, Constance Day (Mrs. Thomas W. Mann). A.B., Yale U., 1931, A.M., 1937, Ph.D., 1939; student, Yale Div. Sch., 1933-34; LL.D., Washington Coll., 1957, LaSalle Coll., 1958, Wabash Coll., 1960, Coll. Notre Dame Md., 1965, Colo. Coll., 1969; L.H.D., Bard Coll., 1970, St. Francis Coll., 1972, St. Mary's Coll. Md., 1975, U. Md., 1980. Instr. English Yali Union Middle Sch. (Yale-in-China), Changsha, Hunan, China, 1931-33; exec. sec. Yale-in-China, New Haven, Conn., 1934-38; instr., then asst. prof. history, econs. and internat. relations Carleton Coll., Northfield, Minn., 1939-42; staff Office Far Eastern Affairs, Dept. State, 1946-49; pres. St. John's Coll., Annapolis, Md., 1949-80, pres. emeritus, 1980-92; pres. St. John's Coll., Santa Fe, 1961-80; interim pres. St. Mary's Coll. of Md., 1982-83; mem. Anne Arundel County School Bd., 1952-64, pres., 1958-63; chmn. Md. Assn. Bds. Edn., 1961-62; vice chmn. Ind. Coll. Funds Am., 1967-68; chmn. Md. Commn. on Capital City, 1967-77, 85-87, mem., 1980-85; chmn. Loyola-Notre Dame Library Trustees, 1981-88; mem. Md. State Devel. Council Task Force, 1981-85; vice chmn. Md. Hall of Records Commn., 1949-90; dir. St. Mary's City Commn., 1982-92; cons. NEH, 1974-91. Author: Convocatum Est, 1981, The Colonization of a College, 1986, Recollections of a St. John's President, 1949-80, 1988; editor: The Glory Days, 1976; contbr. articles to profl. publs. Trustee Yale-China Assn.; trustee Key Sch., Annapolis, chmn., 1972-74; trustee St. Mary's Coll., Md., 1976-92; active Hist. City Commn., 1974-91. Served with USAAF, 1942-45; hdqrs. G-2, G-3; Served with Chinese Army in India; sec. gen. staff Chinese Combat Command. Mem. Am. Hist. Assn., Md. Hist. Soc., Assn. Am. Colls. (chmn. commn. liberal edn. 1955-57, treas. 1963-66, chmn. 1967-68), Pendennis Mt. Assn., Kiwanis, Rotary, Phi Beta Kappa. Home: Annapolis Md. Died Dec. 14, 1992.

WEIL, LOUIS ARTHUR, JR., newspaper executive; b. Port Huron, Mich., June 26, 1905; s. Louis Arthur and Blanche (Granger) W.; m. Kathryn Ann Halligan, Oct. 20, 1934 (dec. 1986); children: Mary Kay (Mrs. James C. Shook, dec.), Elizabeth Lee Sheridan, Louis Arthur III; m. Mary Langen Auran, Oct. 1988. A.B., U. Mich., 1927. Pres., dir. Federated Publs., Inc., pubs. newspaper in Mich., Ind., Idaho, Wash., 1928-72; editor, pub. Lansing (Mich.) State Jour., 1962-72; pub. Grand Rapids (Mich.) Herald, 1947-58, Lafayette (Ind.) Jour. and Courier, 1954-62; v.p. corporate devel., dir. Gannett Co., Inc., Rochester, N.Y., 1971-94. Recipient Disting. Service to Journalism award U. Minn., 1960. Mem. Inland Daily Press Assn. (pres. 1953), Am. Newspaper Pubs. Assn. (dir. bur. advt. 1952-64, chmn. bur. 1958-60, bd. dirs. assn. 1955-63). Clubs: Lafayette Country, Paradise Valley Country. Lodge: Rotary. Home: Paradise Valley Ariz. Died Jan. 25, 1994.

WEINBERG, ROBERT LEONARD, retired lawyer; b. Balt., May 31, 1923; s. Leonard and Beatrice (Lansburgh) W. Student, Coll. William and Mary, 1940-43; BS, Johns Hopkins, 1952; JD, U. Md., 1949. Bar: Md. 1948. Assoc. Weinberg and Green (attys.), Balt., 1948-52; ptnr. Weinberg and Green (attys.), 1952-94; asst. atty. gen. Md., 1953; instr. labor law and contract law Ea. Coll. (name now U. Balt.), 1954-57, Md. State Bd. C.Cs., 1989-92; ret., 1994. Pres. Comprehensive Housing Assistance, Inc., 1969-71, United Way Cen. Md., 1976-77; v.p. Levindale Hebrew Hosp./Geriatric Ctr., 1971-75, Jewish Hist. Soc. Md., 1980-86; bd. dirs. Sinai Hosp., 1974-86, Associated Jewish Charities Balt., 1980-93, pres. 1991-94,; nat. bd. dirs. NCCJ, co-chmn. Md. region, 1968-70; mem. Policy Studies Inst. Johns Hopkins U., 1984-86, Md. Humanities Coun., 1986-91; bd. dirs. Am. Jewish Hist. Soc., 1982-95, v.p., 1984-90, hon. v.p., 1990-95; v.p. Md. Hist. Soc., 1973-76; others. Mem. ABA, Md. Bar Assn., Balt. Bar Assn., Balt. Bar Found., Am. Judicature Soc. (bd. dirs. 1976-78), Am. Coll. Real Estate Lawyers, Md. Bar Found., Md. C. of C. (v.p. 1981-82), Omicron Delta Kappa, Suburban Balt. Country Club (pres. 1971-74), Ctr. Club (bd. govs., sec., counsel 1962-72). Republican. Jewish. Home: Baltimore Md. Died Oct. 28, 1995.

WEINGARTEN, HILDE (MRS. ARTHUR KEVESS), artist; b. Berlin; came to U.S., 1938, naturalized, 1945; d. Morris and Clara (Leitner) W.; m. Arthur S. Kevess, Jan. 28, 1951 (dec. 1973); children: Ruth, Robert. Student, Art Students League, N.Y.C., 1940-41; grad., Cooper Union Art Sch., 1947, B.F.A., 1976. Solo shows include Carlebach Gallery, N.Y.C., 1949, Brooklyn Heights Gallery, Bklyn., 1962, 68, Contemporary Arts Gallery, N.Y.C., 1962, 66, Cadman Plaza N., Bklyn. Heights, 1971; exhbns. include Corcoran Gallery, Am. Acad. and Inst. Arts and Letters, Seattle Art Mus., Denver Art Mus., Phila. Print Club, Phila. Art Alliance, Bklyn. Mus., N.Y.C., Cleve. Mus. Art, Albright Art Gallery, Rochester Meml. Art Gallery, Dallas Mus. Fine Arts, N.Y. World's Fair, 1965, City Center, Assoc. Am. Artists, ACA Galleries, N.Y.C., NYU, Pratt Graphics Ctr., N.Y.C., Channel 13 Auction, other N.Y.C. galleries, Fujikawa Gallery, Osaka, Japan, Palazzo Vecchio, Florence, Italy; represented in permanent collections Israel Nat. Mus., Jerusalem, Israel, Johnson Mus. Cornell U., Bklyn. Mus., L.I. U., N.Y.C. Pub. Library, 42d St. Print Collection, Fogg Art Mus. Harvard U., Cambridge, Mass., Rose Art Mus. Brandeis U., N.Y.C. Tech. Coll., numerous others; artist, Pratt Graphics Ctr., 1970-86; graphics reproduced in collection poems Tune of the Calliope (Aaron Kramer), song compilation German Folksongs (Arthur Kevess), Women Artists in America II (J.L. Collins). Recipient ann. purchase prize Collectors Am. Art, 1947-65, award for graphics League of Present Day Artists, 1974. Mem. Nat. Assn. Women Artists (Donna Miller Meml. prize for graphics 1975, Akston Found. prize for oil 1980, Dr. and Mrs. I.C. Gaynor award for graphics 1989), Audubon Artists (bd. dirs. 1985-87, Silver medal creative graphics 1981), Paintrs & Sculptors Soc. N.J. (Patrons Art prize oil 1970, Winsor & Newton award oil 1972, Anonymous prize graphics 1973, 1st award graphics 1978, 1st prize mixed media 1985), Am. Soc. Contemporary Artists (bd. dirs. 1983-93, graphics awards 1976, 78, 79, 80, 82, 83, 89), Artists Equity N.Y. (bd. dirs. 1964-72, 90-92). Home: Washington D.C. Died Sept. 8, 1993.

WEINTRAUB, HAROLD M., geneticist; b. Newark, June 2, 1945; married; 2 children. BA, Harvard U., 1967; PhD in Cell Differentiation, U. Pa., 1971, MD, 1973. From asst. to assoc prof. biochem. scis. Princeton (N.J.) U., 1973-77; rschr. dept genetics Fred Hutchinson Cancer Rsch. Ctr., Seattle, 1978-95; mem. study sect. molecular biology NIH; investigator Howard Hughes Med. Inst. Assoc. editor Jour. Cell Biology; asst. editor Science & Cell; contbr. articles to over 180 profl. jours. Scholar Rita Allen Found., 1976-81. Mem. NAS (Richard Lounsberry award, 1991), Am. Acad. Arts and Sci. Home: Seattle Wash. Died Mar. 28, 1995.

WEIR, DON CLAIR, retired physician, educator; b. Grant, Iowa, Mar. 10, 1912; s. Mathew B. and Laura (Liston) W. BS, Creighton U., 1934, MD, 1936. Diplomate: Am. Bd. Radiology. Intern St. Louis City Hosp., 1936-37, asst. resident internal medicine, 1937-39, resident radiology, 1939-41, dir. radiology, 1946-76; dir. X-ray Tech. Sch., William Beaumont Gen. Hosp., 1941-43; dir. radiology 70th Gen. Hosp., 1943-46, St. Marys Hosp., 1960-81; prof., chmn. radiology St. Louis U. Med. Sch., 1969-76; cons. radiologist VA Hosp., St. Louis, Malcolm Bless and Mo. Pacific Hosp. Col. AUS, 1941-46. Fellow Am. Coll. Radiology; mem. AMA, Radiol. Soc. N.Am., St. Louis Med. Soc. (pres. 1962), Am. Roentgen Ray Soc., Sigma Xi, Alpha Omega Alpha. Home: Saint Louis Mo. Died Sept. 20, 1995.

WEIS, SIGFRIED, supermarket chain executive; b. 1916; married. BA, Yale U., 1938. With Weis Markets Inc., Sunbury, Pa., 1938-95, v.p., treas., 1962, pres., 1962-94, also bd. dirs. Home: Sunbury Pa. Died 1995.

WEISBERG, BERNARD, magistrate, federal judge; b. Columbus, Ohio, Dec. 16, 1925; s. Jacob A. and Marie Anne (Bronstein) W.; m. Lois Helen Porges, Aug. 31, 1962; children: Jacob, Joseph, Jerilyn Fyffe, Kiki Ellenby. Student, Ohio State U., 1943; AB with honors, U. Chgo., 1948, JD, 1952. Bar: Ill. 1952, U.S. Supreme Ct. 1964. Law clk. Justice Hon. Tom C. Clark, 1952-53; ptnr. Gottlieb & Schwartz, Chgo., 1953-85; U.S. Magistrate judge U.S. Dist. Ct. (no. dist.) Ill., Chgo., 1985-94. Contbr. articles to profl. jours. Del. Sixth Ill. Constitutional Conv., 1969-70; elected 11th Senatorial Dist., Chgo.; chmn. Govs. Commn. on Individual Liberty and Personal Privacy, 1974-76; mem. exec. com. Ill. Law Enforcement Commn., 1973-77; mem. adv. com. Am. Law Inst., 1965-75, cons. Corp. Gov. Project, 1981-94. Mem. Fed. Bar Assn. (Chgo. chpt. bd. dirs.), Chgo. Bar Assn. (chmn. com. civil rights 1964-66, mem. com. corp. law, mem. com. on securities law, mem. spl. com. on civil disorders), Chgo. Coun. Lawyers (bd. govs. 1984-85). Home: Chicago Ill. Died Jan. 17, 1994.

WEISS, MARVIN, lawyer; b. Jersey City, Oct. 11, 1929; s. William and Malvina (Weinstock) W.; m. S. Henriette, Dec. 19, 1959; children: Stacey Debra Tollin, Mitchell William. BS, NYU, 1951, JD, 1954. Bar: N.Y. 1954, U.S. Dist. Ct. (so. and ea. dists.) N.Y. 1960, U.S. Ct. Appeals (2d cir.) 1962, U.S. Tax. Ct. 1965, U.S. Supreme Ct. 1990. Assoc. Rosling & Eisenberg, Bklyn., 1956-60; ptnr. Eisenberg & Weiss, Bklyn., 1960-77, Moses & Singer, N.Y.C., 1977-79, Olnick, Boxer, Blumberg, Lane & Troy, N.Y.C., 1979-87, Stroock, Stroock & Lavan, N.Y.C., 1987-89, Wilson, Elser, Moskowitz, Edelman & Dicker, N.Y.C., 1989-94. Served with U.S. Army, 1954-56. Mem. ABA, N.Y. State Bar Assn., Bklyn. Bar Assn., Nassau County Bar Assn., N.Y. County Lawyers Assn. Home: North Woodmere N.Y. Died Sept. 21, 1994.

WEITZ, MARTIN MISHLI, minister, religious studies educator; b. Denver, Aug. 2, 1907; s. Joseph and Rachel (Kauffman) W.; m. Margaret Kalach, Aug. 5, 1934; children: Mimi, Jonathan David. Student, Colo. State Coll., 1925-27; BA, U. Cin., 1932; PhD, Hebrew Union Coll., 1959, DD (hon.), 1959; DD (hon.), Lincoln U., 1967; DHL (hon), Colo. No. U., 1964. Diplomate: ordained rabbi. Dir. Hillel Found., Northwestern U., Evanston, Ill., 1934-37, Temple Sholom Religious Sch., Chgo., 1935-37; rabbi Beth Hillel Temple, Kenosha, Wis., 1937-43, B'nai Jeshurun Temple, Des Moines, 1945-48; prof. Drake U., Des Moines, 1946-47; rabbi House of Israel, Hot Springs, Ark., 1949-51, Beth Israel Temple, Atlantic City, N.J., 1951-63, North Shore Synagogue, Syosset, N.Y., 1963-65; dir., prof. Ctr. Interfaith Studies, Lincoln U., Oxford, Pa., 1967-73; rabbi Temple of Israel, Wilmington, N.C., 1974-76; faculty Nat. U., San Diego, Irvine, Mission Viejo, Vista, Anaheim Centers, 1976-91, Saddleback Coll., Mission Viejo, Calif., 1978-92; co-adj. lectr. Rutgers State U., N.J., 1955-61; founder, chmn. bd. Atlantic Community Coll., 1956-63; chmn. subventions com. Central Conf. Am. Rabbis, N.Y.C., 1954-60; part-time chaplain Heritage Pointe, Mission Viejo, Calif., 1991. Author over 100 books, including: Timberline, 1934, Wind Whispers, 1934, (demography) Jewish Community-Studies, 1936, Tercentenary Manual, 1936, Wind-Whispers, 1950, Ten Commandments Today, 1952, Year Without Fear, 1955, Life Without Strife, 1958, Decalogues for Our Day, 1962, Mission to Berlin, 1963, Campus-on-a-Compass, 1969, Mexican Odyssey, 1979; also articles; editor: Hebrew Union Coll. Monthly, 1930-32, Manuals, World Union for Progressive Judaism, 1952-56, The Hour-Glass Mag. Lincoln U., 1968-73. Chmn. Bicentennial Heritage Com., Wilmington, N.C., 1976; mem. Com. on Justice and Peace of Central Conf. Am. Rabbis, N.Y.C., 1951-52; mem. exec. bd. Central Conf., 1951-53; founder, pres. NCCJ, Atlantic City, 1956-61; chmn. Dr. Albert Schweitzer Festival of Culture, San Diego, 1986, Palm Springs, Calif., 1986, 88; chmn. dedication program Chamberlain Hall, Nat. U., San Diego, 1986, Bicentennial of Constn. Celebrity Series, Nat. U., 1987-88; vice chmn. emeritus Inst. Saddleback Community Coll., Mission Viejo, Calif., 1986-92; chairperson U.S. Marine Band, Gym of Saddleback Coll., 1989. Capt. U.S. Army, 1943-46. Recipient citation Tchr. of the Yr. Saddleback Coll., 1982; recipient outstanding faculty award Nat. U., 1983, citation in recognition of help in 100th Anniversary of Orange County, Calif.; dedicated large sect. of Penrose Library to Weitz Library, U. Denver, 1987. Mem. Conf. of Sci. and Ethics (dir. 1977-80), Academians Soc. (pres. 1981-82), Leisure Worlder of Month 1985, Student and Alumni Assn. Hebrew Union Coll. (trustee 1951-55). Lodge: Rotary. Home: Laguna Hills Calif. Died June 22, 1992.

WELCH, CLAUDE EMERSON, surgeon; b. Stanton, Nebr., Mar. 14, 1906; s. John Hayes and Lettie (Phelan) W.; m. Phyllis Heath Paton, Aug. 14, 1937; children: Claude Emerson Jr., John Paton. AB summa cum laude, Doane Coll., 1927, DSc (hon.), 1955; AM in Chemistry, U. Mo., 1928; MD magna cum laude, Harvard U., 1932; DSc, U. Nebr., 1970; DHC (hon.), U. Montevideo, Uruguay, 1982. Asst. instr. organic chemistry U. Mo., 1927-28; surg. resident Mass. Gen. Hosp., Boston, 1932-37, vis. surgeon, 1937-96, chief tumor clinic, 1957-63; clin. prof. surgery Harvard Med. Sch., 1964-72, clin. prof. emeritus, 1972-96; chmn. Bd. Registration in Medicine, Commonwealth of Mass., 1976-81; McLaughlin Gallie vis. prof., hon. fellow Royal Coll. Physicians and Surgeons of Can., 1978-96; Claude E. Welch Professorship in Surgery, Harvard, 1992. Lt. col. M.C., AUS, 1942-45. Decorated Commendation medal; recipient Disting. Service award AMA, 1976, Leader in Am. Medicine award Countway Libr., 1985,

›swell Park medal Buffalo Surg. Soc., 1986. Fellow ernat. Soc. Univ. Colon and Rectal Surgeons (hon.), ston Surg. Soc. (pres. 1965, Bigelow medal 1986, hon. ow); mem. ACS (bd. govs. 1960-63, bd. regents 1963-, pres. 1973-74), Mass. Med. Soc. (pres. 1965), In-nat. Soc. Surgery (pres. U.S. chpt. 1978-80), Soc. rgery Alimentary Tract (pres. 1965), Am. Surg. Assn. 'es. 1976-77), So. Surg. Assn., New Eng. Surg. Assn., n Pacific Surg. Assn. (v.p. 1971-96), James IV Assn. rgeons, N.Y. Soc. Colon and Rectal Surgeons, ırvard Med. Sch. Alumni Assn. (pres. 1972-73), pha Omega Alpha; hon. mem. Coll. Physicians and rgeons, Costa Rica, L.A., Detroit, Kansas City, Portnd, Cen., N.Y., B.C., Chile, St. Paul surg. socs., Que., 'gentina socs. digestive surgery, Am. Soc. Colon and ›ctal Surgeons. Home: Westwood Mass. Died Mar. 9, 96.

ELCH, ROBERT GIBSON, steel industry con-ltant; b. Kewanee, Ill., July 9, 1915; s. Thomas John d Mabel Emily (Bunton) W.; m. Helen Taylor, Mar. , 1940; children: Sherry, Wendy. AB, Stanford U., 37; postgrad., Royal Acad. Dramatic Art. With Dun Bradstreet, Inc., 1937-42; asst. to treas. Henry J. aiser Co., 1942-45; asst. to v.p., gen. mgr. Permanente ›ment Co., 1945-46, Permanente Metals Corp., 1946; gr. distbn. Kaiser Aluminum & Chem. Corp., 1947-54; ec. sec. Steel Service Center Inst. (formerly Am. Steel arehouse Assn.), 1954-57, exec. v.p., 1957-62, pres., ›62-80, vice chmn., 1981, cons., 1981-92; owner Welch sch. Internat., 1981-92; internat. mktg. cons.; lectr. dsl. distbn., trade assn. mgmt., econs. of steel industry; ›m. various govt. adv. coms.; bd. dir. Pitt-Des Moines ›rp., Pitts. Contbr. articles to profl. jours. Bd. dirs. 'stbn. Research Edn. Found.; trustee Freedom Found., alley Forge, Pa. Mem. Am. Iron and Steel Inst., Am. ›c. Assn. Execs. (cert. assn. exec., past mem. exec. ›m., Key award 1970), Am. Soc. Assn. Execs. Found. ast chmn.), Nat. Assn. Wholesale Distbrs. (past mem. ec. com.), U.S. C. of C., Citizens Choice Tax Commn., eve. Mus. Art, Insts. Orgn. Mgmt. (former chmn. bd. gents, exec. com.), Cleve. Soc. Contemporary Art, us. Modern Art (N.Y.C.), Phi Gamma Delta. Clubs: hgo.; Mid Ocean (Bermuda); Met. (N.Y.C.); Garden of ods (Colorado Springs); Mayfield, Union (Cleve.); uquesne (Pitts.); Met. (Washington); LaQuinta Hotel olf (Calif.). Home: La Quinta Calif. Died Mar. 23, ›92.

'ELLINGTON, JOHN STANLEY, lawyer, former ate official; b. Pitts., May 20, 1916; s. John Clifford ıd Mary Simons (Beyer) W.; m. Margaret Hawkins russell, Oct. 25, 1941; children: John Stanley, Mary ıay, Charles Howard. A.B., Allegheny Coll., eadville, Pa., 1937; LL.B., U. Pitts., 1940, J.D., 1968. ar: Pa. 1941, U.S. Supreme Ct. 1965. Atty. Union itle Guaranty Co., Pitts., 1941-42, 45-48; assoc. atty. .S. Army Engrs., Pitts., 1942-43; assoc. atty., asst. sec. a. Gas and Fuel Assocs., Pitts., 1948-53; div. atty., sec. alon div. Textron, Inc., Meadville, 1954-80; chief ›unsel State Treas., Commonwealth of Pa., 1981-89; ›c., dir. Meadville Community Hotel, Inc., 1959-80. d. dirs. Northwestern Pa. chpt. Am. Heart Assn., 977-80; trustee First Presbyterian Ch., Meadville, 1960-5; mem. Meadville Ins. Com., 1976-80; chmn. eadville Airport Commn., 1966-67. Served with inf. US, 1943-45. Decorated Purple Heart. Mem. Am., 'a., Dauphin County bar assns., Meadville Area C. of . (dir., sec. 1972-75), Beta Theta Pi, Phi Delta Phi. ›epublican. Home: Camp Hill Pa. Died Jan. 13, 1995.

VELLIVER, ALBERTUS DELMAR, aerospace ıanufacturing company executive; b. Danville, Pa., Feb. 6, 1934; m. Nancy King; 4 children. BS in Mech. ngring., Pa. State U., 1956; Exec. Bus. Program, tanford U., 1977. With rsch. div. Curtiss-Wright orp., 1956-62; with Boeing Co., Seattle, 1962-94, corp. r. v.p. engring. and tech.; past chmn. NRC aeronautical nd space engring. bd. Contbr. articles to profl. jours. 1em. adv. bd. U. Wash., U. So. Calif., Stanford U., 1IT; mem. indsl. and profl. adv. coun. Coll. Engring. 'a. State U.; mem. adv. com. NSF Coalition of Schs. for xcellence in Edn. and Leadership; bd. dirs. Nat. Ac-ion Coun. for Minorities in Engring. Fellow AIAA, oyal Aeronautic Soc.; mem. NAE. Home: Kent Vash. Died Mar. 1994.

VELLS, BEN HARRIS, retired beverage company ex-cutive; b. Saginaw, Mich., June 11, 1906; s. Ben W. and lorence (Harris) W.; m. Katherine Gladney, June 17, 938; children: Katherine Graves, Ben iladney. Student, Ind. U., 1922-25; A.B., U. Mich., 929, M.A., 1931; L.H.D., Westminster Coll., 1979, U. Mo.-St. Louis, 1983. Tchr. John Burroughs Sch., St. Louis County, 1929-31, 33-38; critic, tchr. U. Mich. Sch. Edn., 1931-33; with Seven-Up Co., St. Louis, 1938-78; ›res. Seven-Up Co., 1965-74, chmn., 1974-78; Chmn. Consumer Research Inst., 1970-77. Pres. St. Louis Symphony Soc., 1970-78, chmn., 1978-84, v.p., 1985-89, ife trustee, 1989-95; pres. Laumeier Internat. Sculpture Park, St. Louis County, 1981-83; mem. community adv. bd. Sta. KWMU-Radio, U. Mo.; hon. life mem. Opera Theatre of St. Louis Bd.; bd. dirs. Community Found., 1977-87, St. Louis Conservatory and Schs. for Arts, 1979-95, 1st St. Forum, 1979-89, Winston Churchill Meml. and Library, Fulton, Mo., Am. Symphony Orch. League, 1987-95, Music Assocs. of Aspen (Colo.), 1979-87, others. Recipient Mo. Arts award, 1984, (with Katherine Gladney Wells) Lifetime Achievement in the Arts award St. Louis Arts and Edn. Coun., 1994. Mem. Nat. Assn. Mfrs. (bd. dirs. 1969-73), Grocery Mfrs. Am. (bd. dirs. 1969-77), St. Louis Symphony Orch. (hon. life), Am. Fedn. Musicians (hon. mem. musicians local), Phi Beta Kappa, Sigma Chi. Clubs: St. Louis, Bellerive Country, Bogey, Noonday, University, Racquet (St. Louis). Lodge: Rotary. Home: Saint Louis Mo. Died July 18, 1995.

WELLS, CECIL HAROLD, JR., consulting engineer; b. San Mateo, Calif., Apr. 21, 1927; s. Cecil H. and Bertha (Teeter) W.; m. Elizabeth Anne O'Leary (dec.); children—Cecilia E. A., Timothy; m. Christina Maria Poelzl; children—Kristy-Sue, Jeff-Dean. Student, Menlo Coll., 1948, San Jose State Coll., 1948, U. Calif., 1949, 52; BCE, U. Santa Clara, 1951, U. Wis., 1980. Registered profl. engr., Calif., Alaska, Ariz., Colo., Mont., Nev., Oreg., Tex., Utah, Wash. Engr. Hall & Pregnoff, San Francisco, 1951-56; engr. Graham Hayes, San Francisco, 1956-58; cons. engr. on bldgs. and structures Cecil H. Wells, Jr. & Assocs., San Mateo, 1953—; pres. 20th Ave. Catering Corp., 1971-72, 2031 Pioneer Ct. Corp., 1958-70; tchr. engring. Menlo Coll., 1948-62; lectr. lateral design of bldgs. Stanford U., 1956-61. Author: Structural Engineering Design for Architects and Design of Buildings for Earthquakes and Wind. Mem. San Mateo County Regional Planning Bd., pres., 1964-65; mem. San Francisco, San Mateo, Santa Clara Tri County Planning Bd., pres., 1959-60; chmn. Elks Charity, 1964-65; mem. Calif. Bay Conservation and Devel. Commn., 1965-67; bd. dirs. Pvt. Fin. Service, Corp., 1988—; mem. Internat. Conf. World Planners, Mexico City, 1964; commr. San Mateo City Planning, 1956-67, chmn., 1958-59, 61-62, 64-67; mem. San Mateo City Govtl. Efficiency Commn., chmn. 1970-72; engr. San Mateo County Harbor Dist., 1969-83; active Boy Scouts Am., mem. exec. bd. county, 1969—, county v.p., exec. bd., 1972-75, chmn. Explorers, 1969-74; pres. Menlo Alumni Council, 1967-68; mem. men's adv. com. LWV, 1970-71, 73-74; trustee Drew Sch., 1972-73; bd. dirs. Purissima Mut. Water Dist., 1968-71, San Mateo County Devel. Assn., 1960—, bd. dirs., 1969—, San Mateo County Growth Policy Council, 1982—. Served with Submarine Svc., USNR, World War II. Named Citizen of Day, Sta. KABL, 1970, 74; recipient 1st place award in apt. design City of Fremont Environ. Design Com., 1973, Silver Beaver award Boy Scouts Am., 1975. Fellow ASCE; mem. ASTM, Structural Engring. Assn. Calif. (sec. 1954-58), Seismol. Soc. Am., Am. Concrete Inst., San Mateo C. of C. (bd. dirs. 1959-89, pres. 1969-72), Applied Tech. Coun., Constrn. Specifications Inst., Earthquake Engring. Rsch. Inst., Internat. Conf. Bldg. Ofcls., Nat. Soc. Profl. Engrs., Am. Soc. Mil. Engrs., Am. Inst. Timber Constrn., Prestressed Concrete Inst., NRA, San Mateo County Hist. Soc., Peninsula Golf and Country Club, Rotary (pres. 1972-73, Paul Harris fellow 1980, bd. dirs. Hacienda chpt. 1988—, Elks (exalted ruler 1966-67, trustee 1967-72, chmn. 1971-72). Club: Peninsula Golf and Country. Lodges: Rotary (pres. 1972-73), Elks (exalted ruler 1966-67, trustee 1967-72, chmn. 1971-72). Home: Los Altos Calif.

WELLS, FRANK G., entertainment company executive, lawyer; b. Mar. 4, 1932. BA summa cum laude, Pomona Coll., 1953; MA in Law, Oxford (Eng.) U., 1955; LLB, Stanford U., 1959. Former vice chmn. Warner Bros. Inc.; ptnr. Gang Tyre & Brown, 1962-69; pres., chief operating officer Walt Disney Co., Burbank, Calif., 1984-94. Co-author: Seven Summits. Trustee Pomona Coll., Nat. History Mus., S. Paul Getty Trust, Calif. Inst. Tech.; mem. bd. overseers for RAND/UCLA Ctr. Study of Soviet Behavior; mem. svcs. polity adv. com. U.S. Trade Regulation; bd. dirs. Rockefeller Found., the Ctr. for Addiction and Substance Abuse, The Yosemite Restoration Trust Svcs. Corp. and Rebuild L.A. 1st lt. U.S. Army, 1955-57. Rhodes scholar, 1955. Mem. ABA, State Bar Calif., L.A. County Bar Assn., Explorers Club, Phi Beta Kappa. Home: Burbank Calif. Died Apr. 3, 1994.

WELLS, JOHN WEST, emeritus geology educator; b. Phila., July 15, 1907; s. Raymond and Maida (West) W.; m. Elizabeth Baker, Dec. 30, 1932; 1 child, Ellen Baker. BS, U. Pitts., 1928; MA, Cornell U., 1930, PhD, 1933. Instr. U. Tex., Austin, 1929-31; instr. to prof. Ohio State U., Columbus, 1938-48; prof. Cornell U., Ithaca, N.Y., 1948-73, emeritus, 1973-94; participant Bikini Island Sci. Resurvey, U.S. Geol. Soc., Washington, 1947, Arno Atoll Expdn., Pacific Sci. Bd., Washington, 1950; researcher U.S. Geol. Survey, Washington, 1946-65. Author 4 books, 165 sci. papers on paleontology, biology, biogeography, history of geology. Recipient James Hall medal N.Y. State Geol. Survey, 1987. Fellow Geol. Soc. Am. (emeritus); mem. Nat. Acad. Sci., Paleontol. Research Inst. (pres. 1961-64), Paleontol. Soc. (emeritus, pres. 1961-62, medal). Home: Ithaca N.Y. Died Jan. 12, 1994.

WELLS, WILLIAM CALVIN, lawyer, insurance company executive; b. Staunton, Va., Nov. 1, 1896; s. John Miller and Sarah (Maslin) W.; m. Pauline Flanery, Feb. 15, 1923; children—Calvin L., Pauline (Mrs. John M. Montgomery, Jr.). A.B., Washington and Lee U., 1917; LL.B., Harvard, 1921. Bar: Miss. bar 1921. Legal dept. A.C.L. R.R., Wilmington, N.C., 1920-21; mem. firm Wells, Stevens & Jones, Jackson, Miss., 1922-30; sr. mem. Wells, Thomas & Wells, Jackson, 1945-68, Wells, Gerald, McLendon, Brand, Watters & Cox, 1968-77, Wells, Moore, Simmons & Stubblefield, 1977—; dir., gen. counsel, exec. com. Lamar Life Ins. Co., 1954-67; chmn. exec. com. First Nat. Bank, Jackson, 1954-67; dir., gen. counsel Downtown Center Corp., Mortgage Bond & Trust Co., Corinth Counce R.R. Co., Miss. Valley Title Ins. Co., Jackson Packing Co.; pres. dir. Fidelity Ins. Co. Am., 1965-73; gen. counsel Hinds-Rankin Met. Water and Sewer Assn., Inc.; div. atty. Gulf, Mobile & Ohio R.R. Co., 1954-73. Served as Lt., A.C. U.S. Army, 1917-19. Mem. Ind. Petroleum Assn. Am., Am. Life Conv., Assn. Ins. Counsel, Internat. Assn. Ins. Counsel, Miss. Colls. Assn., Harvard Law Sch. Assn. Miss. (pres.), Am. Arbitration Assn. (dir.), N.E. Gen. Soc., Am., Miss., Hinds County, Inter-Am., Internat. bar assns., Newcomen Soc. N.Am., Mid-Continent Oil and Gas Assn. (pres. Miss.-Ala. div. 1966-68), Miss. Research and Devel. Council (dir., exec. com.), Jackson C. of C. (dir.), Miss. Bar Found., Nat. Lawyers Club, Am. Judicature Soc., Miss., So. hist. assns., Am. Legion, Kappa Sigma. Presbyn. Clubs: Mason, Kiwanian (past pres.), 100 of Jackson, Knife and Fork, Country of Jackson, Capital City, University, Patio. Home: Jackson Miss. Deceased.

WELSH, MATTHEW EMPSON, former governor; b. Detroit, Sept. 15, 1912; s. Matthew and Inez (Empson) W.; m. Virginia Homann, Sept. 25, 1937; children: Kathryn and Janet (twins). B.S., U. Pa., 1934; student, U. Ind., 1934-36; J.D., U. Chgo., 1937. Bar: Ind. 1937. Since practiced in Vincennes and Indpls.; U.S. atty. So. dist. Ind., 1950-51; rep. Knox County, Ind. Gen. Assembly, 1941-43; Mem. Ind. Senate from Knox and Daviess counties, 1955-59; Democratic floor leader, 1957, 59, gov. Ind., 1961-65; chmn. U.S. sect. Internat. Joint Commn. U.S. and Can., 1966-70; Co-chmn. Ind. Constl. Revision Commn. Democratic Nat. Committeeman from Ind., 1964-66; Democratic nominee Gov. Ind., 1972. Author: View from the Statehouse, 1981. Former trustee Christian Theol. Sem., Indpls., Christian Ch. Found.; Trustee Vincennes U., John A. Hartford Found., Indpls. Found. Served as lt. USNR. Mem. ABA, Ind., Knox County, Marion County bar assns., Phi Delta Phi, Delta Kappa Epsilon. Mem. Christian Ch. (Disciples of Christ). Home: Indianapolis Ind. Died May 28, 1995.

WELZ, CARL JOHN, Christian Science practitioner and teacher; b. San Francisco, Mar. 12, 1913; s. Charles and Henrietta (Groenninger) W.; m. Jerry Beall Hatcher, Dec. 17, 1943; children: Paul Channing, Rebecca Beall; m. Philadelphia Shideler, Oct. 14, 1979. A.B., San Jose State Coll., 1934; M.A., Columbia U., 1939. Tchr. pub. and pvt. schs. Carmichael, Calif., 1935-37, Katonah, N.Y., 1937-39, Montclair, N.J., 1939-40, Avenal, Calif., 1940-41; vice prin. Victory Sch., Stockton, Calif., 1941-42; C.S. practitioner, 1946-92, C.S. tchr., 1958-92. Assoc. editor C.S. Jour., C.S. Sentinel, Herald of C.S., Boston, 1961-67, editor, 1970-75; author: Practical Scientific Christianity, 1983, The Caring Church, 1985; author, editor, pub. The Warm Line newsletter, 1986-92; contbr. articles to C.S. periodicals. Served to maj. USAAF, 1942-46; chaplain USAF, 1951-56. Home: Carmel Calif. Died Oct. 9, 1992.

WENGERD, SHERMAN ALEXANDER, geologist, educator; b. Millersburg, Ohio, Feb. 17, 1915; s. Allen Stephen and Elizabeth (Miller) W.; m. Florence Margaret Mather, June 12, 1940; children: Anne Marie Wengerd Riffey, Timothy Mather Wengerd (dec.), Diana Elizabeth Wengerd Roach, Stephanie Katherine Wengerd Allen. AB, Coll. Wooster, 1936; MA, Harvard U., 1938, PhD, 1947. Registered profl. engr., N.Mex.; profl. geologist; lic. pilot, FAA. Geophysicist, Shell Oil Co., 1937; mining geologist, Ramshorn, Idaho, 1938; Austin teaching fellow Harvard U., 1938-40; rsch. petroleum geologist Shell, Mid-continent, 1940-42, 45-47; prof. geology U. N.Mex., 1947-76; ret., 1976; disting. prof. petroleum geology, 1982; rsch. geologist, 1947-95, Petroleum Ind., 1976-95; past co-owner Pub. Lands Exploration, Inc., Corona and Capitan Oil Cos.; ltd. ptnr. Rio Petro Oil Co., Dallas.; bd. dirs. Capitan Oil & Gas Co. Col. aide-de-camp staff Gov. State N.Mex., 1992. Served to lt. comdr. USNR, 1942-45; capt. Res., ret. Recipient Disting. Alumnus citation Coll. Wooster, 1979. Author chpts. in textbooks and encys., articles in geol. bulls., newsletters. Fellow Geol. Soc. Am., Explorers Club of N.Y., Ret. Officers Assn.; mem. Four Corners Geol. Soc. (hon. life, emeritus mem., pres. 1953), N.Mex. Geol. Soc. (hon. life mem. 1972-95), Albuquerque Geol. Soc. (hon. life mem. 1989-95), Am. Assn. Petroleum Geologists (hon. life, nat. editor 1957-59, pres. 1971-72, chmn. adv. council 1972-73, Presdl. award 1948, Sydney Powers Memorial medal 1992), Am. Petroleum Inst. (acad. mem., exploration com. 1970-72), Am. Inst. Profl. Geologists (state sect. pres. 1970, nat. editor 1965-66), Soc. Econ. Paleontologists and Mineralogists (dir. found. 1982-86), Nat. Aero. Assn. (life), Nat. Assn. Scholars, OX5 Aviation Pioneers (life), Silver Wings Flying Fraternity (life), Thomas L. Popejoy Soc., Naval Res. Assn. (life), Assn. Naval Aviation, Am. Legion (life), VFW (life), U. N.Mex. 21 Club, Sigma Xi, Sigma Gamma Epsilon, Phi Kappa Phi. Died Jan. 28, 1995. Home: Albuquerque N. Mex.

WERT, LUCILLE MATHENA, librarian, educator; b. Sioux City, Iowa, May 24, 1919; d. Arthur Edmund and

Anna Sarah (Harrington) Mathena; m. Charles Allen Wert, Sept. 7, 1942; children: John Arthur, Sara Ann. B.A., Morningside Coll., 1942; B.S. in L.S, Simmons Coll., 1945; M.A., U. Ill., 1963, Ph.D., 1969. Asst. librarian elec. engring. library M.I.T., Cambridge, 1944-45; math., physics and astronomy librarian U. Iowa, Iowa City, 1946-48, U. Chgo., 1948-51; research asst. Grad. Sch. Library Sci., U. Ill., Urbana, 1964-65; research assoc. Grad. Sch. Library Sci., U. Ill., 1966-67, vis. lectr., 1968-69, research asst. prof., 1969-71, research assoc. prof., dir. library research center, 1971-75, assoc. prof., 1975-77, prof. library adminstrn., chemistry librarian, 1977-86, asst. dir. pub. svcs. for phys. scis. & engring., 1981-86, emeritus prof., 1986-95; library cons. Council for Advancement of Small Colls. Editor: Jour. Edn. for Librarianship, 1976-80. Mem. U. Ill. Pres.'s Coun., 1993-95; sustaining fellow Art Inst. Chgo., 1987-95. Recipient Disting. Alumni award Morningside Coll., 1992; U.S. Office of Edn. small rsch. project grantee, 1968-69. Mem. ALA (com. on accreditation site visitors pool 1972-92), Assn. Coll. and Rsch. Librs., Libr. Adminstrn. and Mgmt. Assn., Assn. Libr. and Info. Sci. Edn. (dir. 1974-77), Am. Chem. Soc. (liaison to Spl. Libr. Assn., mem. editorial bd. CHEMTECH 1987-95, chair 1992, chem. info. div awards com. 1988-91), Am. Soc. Info. Scis. (chmn. spl. interest group biology and chemistry 1985-86, spl. interest group steering com. 1987-89), Spl. Librs. Assn. (chmn. chemistry div. 1986-87), Beta Phi Mu. Presbyterian. Home: Champaign Ill. Died Aug. 12, 1995.

WERTHEIMER, SYDNEY BERNARD, lawyer; b. N.Y.C., Apr. 15, 1914; s. Sydney B. and Edna F. (Leimdorfer) W.; m. Jane B. Celler, Nov. 10, 1938; children: Sue Wertheimer Frank, Jill Wertheimer Rifkin. BS in Econs, U. Pa., 1935; LLB, Harvard U., 1938. Bar: N.Y. 1938, U.S. Customs Ct 1970, U.S. Supreme Ct 1976, D.C. Ct. Appeals 1973. Mem. firm Glass & Lynch, N.Y.C., 1938-39; asst. U.S. atty. So. Dist. N.Y., 1939-42; exec. of subs. Schenley Distillers, N.Y.C., 1946-48; from assoc. to ptnr. Weisman, Celler, Spett, Modlin & Wertheimer, N.Y.C., 1947-83; pres. Silas Worth, Inc., 1987-95; former dir. Fedders Corp. Author: (with others) The Draft and You, 1940. Bd. dirs. Am. Red Magen David for Israel, 1951-95, vice chmn., 1988-95, Scarsdale Bd. Edn., N.Y., 1959-62. With USN, 1943-45. Mem. Assn. of Bar of City of N.Y. Club: Quaker Ridge Golf (Scarsdale, N.Y.). Home: Scarsdale N.Y. Died Feb. 21, 1995.

WESBERRY, JAMES PICKETT, religious organization administrator; b. Bishopville, S.C., Apr. 16, 1906; s. William McLeod and Lillian Ione (Galloway) W.; m. Ruby Lee Perry, Sept. 5, 1929 (dec. Dec. 1941); 1 child, James Pickett; m. Mary Sue Latimer, June 1, 1943 (dec. Sept. 7, 1982); m. Alice Margaret Spratlin, Oct. 15, 1983. AB, Mercer U., 1929, MA, 1930, DD, 1957; BD, Newton Theol. Inst., 1931; M of Sacred Theology, Andover Newton Theol. Inst., 1934; postgrad., Harvard U., 1931, Union Theol. Sem., N.Y.C., 1935, 65, Yale U., 1946, So. Bapt. Theol. Sem., 1957, Princeton U., 1958, Oxford U., 1979; LLD, Atlanta Law Sch., 1946; LHD, LaGrange Coll., 1962; LittD, Bolen-Draughan Coll., 1967. Ordained to ministry Bapt. Ch., 1926; pastor Soperton, Ga., 1928-30, Medford, Mass., 1930-31, Kingstree, S.C., 1931-33, Bamberg, S.C., 1933-44; pastor Morningside Bapt. Ch., Atlanta, 1944-75; pastor emeritus Morningside Bapt. Ch., 1975-92; engaged in evangelism, counseling, editing, publishing and chaplaincies, 1975-92; mem. exec. com. So. Bapt. Conv., 1959-65, 74-86, mem. chaplains commn., 1973-79, chmn. adminstrv. com., 1974-79; pres. Ga. Bapt. Conv., 1956-57, 57-58, rec. sec., 1970-92; prof. Mercer U. extension, Atlanta, 1944-53; pres. Highview Nursing Home, Atlanta, 1947-60, chaplain, 1975-92; pres. Nat. Youth Courtesy Found., 1971-92, staff corr. Christian Century, 1951-58; editor column The People's Pulpit; columnist Atlanta Times, 1964-65; chaplain Yaarab Temple, 20 yrs.; chaplain Grand Lodge of Ga. Author: Prayers in Congress, 1949, Every Citizen Has A Right to Know, 1954, The Georgian Literature Commission, 1957, Baptists in South Carolina Before the War Between the States, 1966, Rainbow Over Russia, 1962, Meditations for Happy Christians, 1973, Evangelistic Sermons, 1974, When Hell Trembles, 1974, The Morningside Man (Wesberry's biography by James C. Bryant), 1975, Bread in a Barren Land, 1982, The Lord's Day, 1986; editor: Sunday Mag., 1975-92; editor: Basharet, 1976-77; asst. editor, 1977-92, editor emeritus, 1978-92. Chmn. Ga. Lit. Commn., 1953-74; acting chaplain U.S. Ho. Reps., July-Aug., 1949; mem. Gov.'s Citizens Penal Reform Commn., 1968, Fulton County Draft Bd., 1968-71; bd. dirs. Atlanta Fund Rev. Bd., 1964-70, Grady Met. Girls Club, 1969-72, hon. bd. dirs., Atlanta Union Mission, 1972-92, Dogwood Assn. Festival, 1970-71; trustee Mercer U., 1944-49, 54-57, 72-74, mem. pres.'s coun., 1974-92, also mem. adv. com. Sch. Pharmacy; trustee Atlanta Bapt. Coll., 1964-72, Truett McConnell Coll., Cleveland, Ga., 1960-65; mem. pres.'s council Tift Coll., Forsyth, Ga., 1976-92; bd. mgrs. Lord's Day Alliance U.S., 1971-92, exec. dir. emeritus, 1975-92. Elected Man of the South Dixie Bus. mag., 1972; named to South's Hall of Fame, 1972. Mem. Atlanta Area Mil. Chaplains Assn. (hon.), SAR (state chaplain 1981), Royal Order Scotland. Clubs: Atlanta Harvard, Atlanta Athletic, Atlanta Amateur Movie, Half Century of Mercer U. (past pres.). Lodges: Kiwanis, Masons (Shriner), Lions. Home: Atlanta Ga. Died Dec. 25, 1992.

WESSNER, KENNETH THOMAS, management services executive; b. Swink Springs, Pa., May 1, 1922; s. Thomas Benjamin and Carrie Eva (Whitmoyer) W.; m. Norma Elaine Cook, Jan. 25, 1945; children—Barbara Wessner Anderson, David Kenneth. BS, Wheaton (Ill.) Coll., 1947, LLD (hon.), 1990; HHD (hon.), King's Coll., 1988. Dist. mgr., then mgr. sales promotion Club Aluminum Products Co., 1947-54; with Servicemaster Industries Inc., Downers Grove, Ill., 1954-92, dir. emeritus, adv., 1992—, v.p., 1961, exec. v.p., COO, 1972-73, pres., 1973-81, chief exec. officer, 1975-83, chmn. bd., 1981-90, bd. dirs., servicemaster, 1965-92; pres., chief oper. officer Servicemaster Hosp. Corp. Div., Downers Grove, 1962-72; bd. dirs. Bell Fed. Savs. and Loan Assn., Chgo., 1972-93, Health Providers Ins. Co., 1982-88. Trustee Wheaton (Ill.) Coll., 1972—, chmn. bd., 1982-88; mem. adv. coun. Grad. Sch. Bus., U. Chgo., 1977-86; trustee Chgo. Sunday Evening Club, Health Rsch. and Ednl. Trust, 1985-88, Prison Fellowhsip Ministries. With USAAF, 1943-46. Recipient Outstanding CEO in Svc. Industry award Fin. World mag., 1980, Top CEO in Indsl. Svcs. Indsutry award Wall St. Transcript, 1979-83; named Profl. and Bus. Leader of Yr., Religious Heritage Am., 1981; inducted into Am. Nat. Bus. Hall of Fame, 1991, Health Care Hall of Fame, 1993. Mem. Am. Mgmt. Assn., Am. Hosp. Assn., Beta Gamma Sigma. Clubs: Chgo. Golf (Wheaton); Imperial Golf, Naples Yacht (Fla.). Home: Naples Fla. Deceased.

WEST, ARLEIGH BURTON, retired water resources consultant; b. Hendricks, Minn., July 18, 1910; s. John Earle and Laura Hannah (Larson) W.; m. Edith Eleanor Gustad, Feb. 27, 1943; children: John Burton, Richard Allen. B.A., Hamline U., 1932; grad. student pub. welfare adminstrn., U. Minn., 1933. With Dept. Pub. Welfare, Mpls., 1933-34, Fed. Emergency Relief Adminstrn., Pierre, S.D., 1935; staff Soil Conservation Service, Tech. Coop. Adminstrn., Bur. Indian Affairs, 1936-40; agrl. economist Dept. Agr., 1940-41; with bur. reclamation Dept. Interior, 1941-71; regional dir. Dept. Interior, Boulder City, Nev., 1960-70; asst. to commr. program policy Dept. Interior, 1970-71; cons. water resources, 1971-94. Recipient Distinguished Service award Dept. Interior, 1971. Home: Boulder City Nev. Died Oct. 7, 1994.

WEST, ELMER GORDON, federal judge; b. Hyde Park, Mass., Nov. 27, 1914; s. William Albert Howard and Edith Louise (Hall) W.; m. Viola Kay Cayard, Oct. 30, 1942; children: Roger Gordon, Dan Edward. Student, Northeastern U., 1934-35, Lamar Jr. Coll., Beaumont, Tex., 1935-36; B.S., La. State U., 1941, LL.B., 1942. Bar: La. 1942. Acct. Stone & Webster, 1937-42; mem. firm Long & West, Baton Rouge, 1946-50, Kantrow, Spaht, West & Kleinpeter (and predecessor), Baton Rouge, 1950-61; judge U.S. Dist. Ct. (ea. dist.) La., 1961-67, chief judge, 1967-72; judge U.S. Dist. Ct. (mid. dist.) La., 1972-79, sr. judge, 1979-92; atty. La. Revenue Dept., 1946-48, La. inheritance tax collector, 1948-52; asst. prof., spl. lectr. La. State U. Law Sch., 1947-48; mem. Jud. Conf. U.S., 1971-74, mem. com. on operation jury system, 1972-78. Served to lt. USNR, 1942-45. Mem. ABA, La. Bar Assn., East Baton Rouge Bar Assn., Am. Judicature Soc., Internat. Assn. Ins. Counsel, Nat. Assn. Compensation Claimants Attys., Order of Coif (hon.), Masons, Alpha Tau Omega, Phi Delta Phi. Episcopalian. Home: Baton Rouge La. Died Nov. 2, 1992.

WEST, HOWARD NORTON, retired department store executive; b. N.Y.C., May 3, 1919; s. Abraham D. and Flora (Simpson) W.; m. Caroline E. Dawley, Dec. 15, 1945; 1 child, Andrew D. B.A., Columbia U., 1940. C.P.A., Calif. With Price Waterhouse & Co. (C.P.A's), San Francisco, 1945-52; with Carter Hawley Hale Stores, Inc., Los Angeles, 1952-85; treas. Carter Hawley Hale Stores, Inc., 1963-73, v.p., treas., 1973-76, sr. v.p.-fin., 1976-81, exec. v.p., 1981-85; v.p. Carter Hawley Hale Credit Corp., 1971-76, pres., 1976-85, also dir. Trustee Palos Verdes Peninsula Unified Sch. Dist., 1961-67, pres., 1964-65; trustee Chadwick Sch. (Roessler-Chadwick Found.), 1967-69, treas., 1967-69; trustee, pres. So. Calif. Regional Occupation Center, 1967-69; commr. Ednl. Research Commn. of Calif. Legislature, 1970-72. Served with USNR, 1941-45, PTO. Mem. Am. Inst. C.P.A.s. Home: Santa Monica Calif. Died June 30, 1993.

WESTERMAN, KATY DOROTHEA, former vocational education administrator; b. Swink, Colo., Feb. 16, 1930; d. Orval Ernest and Beatrice Alzina (Cloud) Krout; m. Hugh Abraham Westerman, Oct. 15, 1955 (div. Apr. 1971); children: Vincent Hugh, Theodore Lynn, Michael Darryl Dean, Christopher Wayne, Mark Alan. BA, U. No. Colo., 1954; MEd, Colo. State U., 1979. Tchr. Eagle (Colo.) County High Sch., 1954-57, Sangre De Cristo High Sch., Mosca, Colo., 1957-61, Sierra Grande High Sch., Ft. Garland, Colo., 1961-70; instr., coord. power sewing program San Luis Valley Area Vocat. Sch., Monte Vista, Colo., 1970-74; instr., coord. spl. coop. program Alamosa (Colo.) High Sch., 1974-81; coord. cmty. edn., supr. adult basic edn. and GED Alamosa Pub. Schs., 1981-84; asst. dir. San Luis Valley Area Vocat. Sch., 1984-87; dir. secondary vocat. edn. San Luis Valley, 1988-92; adminstr. Carl Perkins Consortium San Luis Valley Area Vocat. Sch., 1990-92; ret., 1992; instr. Ford Found. Rocky Mountain Area Small High Schs. Project, Mosca, 1957-61; mem. Gov.'s Coun. on Status of Women, Monte Vista, 1971-74; adminstr. Community Recreation Bd., Alamosa, 1981-84; cons. Chinese Spl. Needs Program, People's Republic of China, 1986; sec. Colo. Vocat. Hall of Fame Found., 1979-84, pres., 1988-92. Member Alamosa C. of C., 1986-90; precinct rep. Alamosa County Cen. Dem. Com., 1984-90. Inducted into Colo. Vocat. Hall of Fame, 1994. Mem. NEA, Am. Vocat. Assn., Colo. Vocat. Assn. (sec. new and related svcs. div. 1980-82, pres. elect new and related svcs. div. 1983, pres. 1984-85), Nat. Assn. Vocat. Spl. Needs Pers. (sec. Colo. chpt. 1980-82, pres. elect 1983, pres. 1984-85), Colo. Edn. Assn., Colo. Assn. Vocat. Adminstrs., Colo. Assn. Sch. Execs., Iota Lambda Sigma, Beta Sigma Phi (Woman of the Yr. 1986). Roman Catholic. Home: Alamosa Colo. Died Feb. 25, 1996.

WESTERMAN, SYLVIA HEWITT, journalist, university official; b. Columbus, Ohio; d. Harry James and Grace (Doyle) W. BA, Ohio State U. With Sta. WLW-C, WTVN and WBNS, Columbus, 1954-63; with CBS News, 1963-79, radio TV producer, 1964-67, producer Face the Nation, 1967-74, dep. dir. news, 1974-78, v.p. spl. events and polit. coverage, 1978-79; v.p., exec. asst. to pres. NBC News, N.Y.C., 1979-82; v.p. spl. projects UPI, N.Y.C., 1983-84; pres. Sylvia Westerman Enterprises, N.Y.C.; dir. planning and new programs Fordham Grad. Sch. Bus. Adminstrn., N.Y.C., 1989-95. Recipient Emmy award Nat. Acad. TV Arts and Scis. 1974. Bd. dirs. Ohio State U. Devel. Fund; adv. bd. Critical Difference for Women; coun. advisors Ohio State U. librs.; mem. steering com. Acad. Quality Consortium. Mem. Jr. League Columbus, Cosmopolitan Club, Sigma Delta Chi, Theta Sigma Pi, Kappa Alpha Theta. Home: New York N.Y. Died May 2, 1995.

WESTIN, HAROLD JOSEPH, architectural engineering and construction executive; b. St. Paul, May 6, 1920; s. Joseph Anders and Elsie Karen (Hagstrom) W.; m. Dolores Marion Swanson, May 15, 1943; children: Dee Anne, Cynthia, Rosemary, Amy. BCE, U. Minn.; BS in Law, St. Paul Coll. Law. Registered profl. civil/structural engr. 13 states. Chief field engr. Dravo Corp., Pitts., 1943-44; exec. v.p. Hagstrom Constrn. Co., St. Paul, 1946-56; pres. Harold J. Westin Constructors, Inc., St. Paul, 1957-89, Harold J. Westin Architects and Engrs., P.A., St. Paul, 1963-89; lectr. inst. tech. U. Minn., Mpls., 1950-77; bd. dirs. Hillcrest State Bank, St. Paul, 1964-79; cons. forensic engring. for various counties, municipalities, ednl. and religious insts., from 1950. Author: An Engineer Looks at the Law, 1973, An Engineer Applies the Law, 1972, also series of articles on design responsibilities of architects and engrs., 1975. Bd. dirs. Soc. Profl. Engrs. Found., 1973-75. Served to lt. (j.g.) USNR, 1944-46, PTO. Fellow ASCE (life); mem. Minn. Soc. Profl. Engrs. (chmn. bldg. com. 1975-77), Minn. Soc. Profl. Engrs. (Engr. of Yr. 1973), Nat. Soc. Profl. Engrs. Clubs: U. Minn. Campus, St. Paul Athletic. Home: White Bear Lake Minn. Died May 13, 1989; buried Forest Lawn Meml. Pk., St. Paul, Minn.

WESTON, JACK, actor; b. Aug. 21, 1924. Began career in children's div. Cleve. Playhouse, 1934, appeared in numerous films including: Can't Stop the Music, Stage Struck, Please Don't Eat the Daisies, All in a Night's Work, The Honeymoon Machine, Its Only Money, Palm Springs Weekend, The Incredible Mr. Limpet, Mirage, The Cincinnati Kid, Wait Until Dark, The Thomas Crown Affair, The April Fools, Cactus Flower, A New Leaf, Fuzz, Marco, Gator, The Ritz, Cuba, The Four Seasons, Dirty Dancing; numerous TV show appearances include: Carol Burnett Show, Red Browning of the Rocket Rangers, Gunsmoke, Philco Playhouse, Studio One, Kraft Playhouse, Twilight Zone, The Untouchables; Broadway plays including Break a Leg, Season in the Sun, South Pacific, Crazy October, The Ritz, California Suite, Cheaters. Home: West Hollywood Calif. Died May 3, 1996.

WESTON, THEODORE BRETT, photographer; b. Los Angeles, Dec. 16, 1911; s. Edward and Flora (Chandler) W.; divorced; 1 dau. Freelance photographer Calif. One-man shows include: U. Ariz. Ctr. for Creative Photography, Tucson, 1983, San Francisco Mus. Modern Art, 1983; represented in permanent collections: Mus. Modern Art, N.Y.C., Library of Congress, Washington, Art Inst. Chgo.; photography books: Brett Weston Photographs, Brett Weston Voyage of the Eye; Photographs from Five Decades. Recipient Guggenheim award, 1946. Home: Carmel Calif. Died Jan. 22, 1993.

WHEELER, WILLIAM CRAWFORD, agricultural engineer, educator; b. Maysville, Ga., Feb. 19, 1914; s. James D. and Pearl (Chandler) W.; B.S. in Agrl. Engring., U. Ga., 1940; student U. Tenn., 1941-42; M.S. in Agrl. Engring., Va. Polytech. Inst., 1951; postgrad. Mich State U., 1954-55; m. Annie Adams, May 23, 1942; children—Betty Catherine, James David. Supr. farm Ga. Vocational and Trade Sch., Monroe, 1932-36, instr. farm mechanics, 1940-41; jr. engr. U.S. Dept. Agr. Soil Conservation Service, Monroe; instr. dept. agrl. engrng. U. Tenn., 1941-42, asso. prof. agrl. engring.,

46-53, specializing in rural electrification; prof. agrl. gring. U. Conn., 1953-72, head dept., 1953-69, prof. eritus, 1972—; sabbatical leave for waste disposal idy in Europe and Can., 1969; conducted summer urse in farm mechanics U. Ark., Fayetteville, 1948; rtner Lynwood Devels., Storrs, Conn. Mem. N.E. gional Research Techn. Com. on Poultry Housing, 53-65, Com. on Mechanization of Forage Crops, 54-58; com. on Mechanization of Fruit and Vegetable arvest, 1959-71, Com. on Improvement Efficiency in arvesting Apples, 1966-71; chmn. projects com. Conn. ectrification Council, 1953-66; mem. farm electric rvice com. N.E. Council, 1953-72; mem. water sources Inst. U. Conn., 1964-69. Served as maj. 329th . 83d Div., U.S. Army, 1942-46. Decorated Bronze ar, Purple Heart. Registered engr., Tenn. Fellow Am. c. Agrl. Engrs. (chmn. North Atlantic sect. 1962); em. Am. Soc. Engring. Edn., Nat. Soc. Profl. Engrs., pha Zeta, Scabbard and Blade, Gridiron, Aghon, amma Sigma Delta. Conglist. (chmn. council 1964). uthor articles in field. Died Jan. 25, 1995. Home: tlantic Beach Fla.

HITE, DORIS ANNE, artist; b. Eau Claire, Wis., ly 27, 1924; d. William I. and Mary (Dietz) . Grad., Art Inst. Chgo., 1950. One woman shows, A Galleries, Washington, Bergstrum Art Center and useum, Neenah, Wis., Bradley Gallery, Milw.; exhib-ed in group shows, Ill. Mus., Springfield, 1963, Art lliance, Phila., 1963, Museum Modern Art, N.Y.C., 967, Pa. Acad. Fine Arts, Phila., 1963, 64, 66, Art Inst. hgo., 1963, Met. Museum, 1966, N.A.D., N.Y.C., 962, 63, 64, 65, 67, Butler Inst. Am. Art, Youngtown, hio, 1960, 61, 63, 64, 65, Smithsonian Instn., Wash-gton, 1960, Walker Art Center, Mpls., 1963, 64, ladison (Wis.) Salon Art, 1958-63, 64, Spanish In-rnat. Pavilion, St. Louis, 1969, Utah State U., Logan, 969, 70, Cleve. Inst. Art, Miami (Fla.) U., Chautauqua N.Y.) Art Assn., Soc. Four Arts, Palm Beach, Fla., stituto de arte de Mexico, others; represented in ermanent collection, Butler Inst. Am. Art, Walker Art enter, Milw. Art Center. Recipient grand award Am. Watercolor Soc., 1963, Grumbacker award, 1965, aul Remmy award, 1964; medal of honor Knick-bocker Artists, 1963, Four Arts award Soc. Four Rts, 1963. Mem. NAD (Ranger fund purchase award 965, Obrig award 1967). Home: Cedarburg Wis. Died ept. 5, 1995.

VHITE, F(REDERICK) CLIFTON, public affairs onsultant; b. Leonardsville, N.Y., June 13, 1918; s. rederick H. and Mary (Hicks) W.; m. Gladys Bunnell, une 22, 1940; children: F(rederick) Clifton, A. Carole White Green. AB, Colgate U., 1940; postgrad. Cornell ., 1945-47; degree (hon.) Hillsdale Coll., 1974. Pres., . Clifton White & Assos., Inc., Greenwich, Conn., 961; pres. Pub. Affairs Analysts Inc., N.Y.C., 1970-77; res. DirAction Services, Inc., Greenwich, 1966-70, hmn. bd. 1971-93; pres. Pub. Affairs Counsellors, Inc., N.Y.C., 1957-60; instr. social sci. Cornell U., Ithaca, N.Y., 1945-50; lectr. polit. sci. Ithaca Coll., 1949-51. Chmn. bd. Internat. Found. for Electoral Systems; del res.'s Hwy. Safety Council, 1953; exec. dep. commr. N.Y. State Bur. Motor Vehicles, 1952-55, acting ommr., 1955; mem. adv. council on presdl. selection rookings Instn., Washington, 1971-93; mem. pub. membership inspection team USIA, 1972-93; mem. Agy. or Internat. Devel. Election Observation Team, Costa Rica, 1986; chmn. Presdl. Commn. on Broadcasting to Cuba, 1982; dir. Pub. Affairs Council, Washington, 958-93; mem. Adv. Com. for Broadcasting to Cuba, 988-93; dir. John M. Ashbrook Ctr. Pub. Affairs, dist-ng. vis. prof. Ashland U.; sr. advisor Republican Nat. Chmn., 1983-84. Del. Republican Nat. Conv., 1952, 56, 0, hon. del., 1972; del., chmn. Conv. Coms. Nat. Young Rep. Conv., 1949, 51, 53, 55; pres. N.Y. State Young Reps., 1950-52; spl. asst. N.Y. State Rep. State Chmn., 1950-52; dir. orgn. Nat. Nixon-Lodge Vols., 1960, Nat. Draft Goldwater Com., 1963; nat. dir. Goldwater for Pres. Com., 1963, 64, Citizens for Goldwater-Miller, 1964; campaign mgr. Buckley for Senate, N.Y., 1970; cons. to chmn. Com. to Reelect the Pres., 1972; polit. dir. for Ronald Reagan, Rep. Conv., 1980; sr. adv. Reagan-Bush Presdl. Campaign, 1980; mem. exec. com. Pres.-Elect's Transition Team, 1980; bd. dirs. Ctr. for Democracy at Boston U., Nat. Repub-lican Inst. for Internat. Affairs. Served to capt. USAAF, 1942-45. Decorated Air medal with 3 oak leaf clusters, D.F.C. Mem. Inst. Fiscal and Polit. Edn. (chmn.), Am. Assn. Polit. Cons. (pres. 1970-74), Internat. Assn. Polit. Cons. (dir. 1970-74, pres. 1978), Am. Polit. Sci. Assn., Am. Acad. Polit. and Sci. Assn., Acad. Polit. Sci., SAR, Am. Acad. Polit. and Social Sci. (adv. commn. in-tergovtl. relations 1976-78), Public Members Assn., In-ternat. Found. for Electoral systems (chmn. 1988). Presbyterian (elder). Clubs: Union League (N.Y.C.); Capitol Hill (Washington); Apawamis (Rye, N.Y.); Ashland (Ohio); Army and Navy. Lodge: Masons (32 deg.). Author: (with Joseph Eley) You Should Be a Politician, 1959; (with William J. Gill) Suite 3505, 1967; (with Charles Spiegler) Yes, We Can, 1972; (with Wil-liam J. Gill) Why Reagan Won, 1981. Died Jan. 9, 1993. Home: Greenwich Conn.

WHITE, SIR (VINCENT) GORDON LINDSAY, tex-tile company executive; b. May 11, 1923; s. Charles and Lily May (Wilson) W.; m. Virginia Anne White, 1974; 3 children. Grad., De Aston Sch., Lincolnshire, Eng. Chmn. Welbecson Ltd., 1947-65; dept. chmn. Hanson Trust Ltd., 1965-73; chmn. Hanson Industries N.Am., Iselin, N.J., 1983—; mem. spl. commn. Hanson's Trust's opportunities overseas, 1979-83. Mem. Council for Police Rehab. Appeal, 1985—; bd. dirs. Shakespeare Theatre, Golger Library, Washington, 1985—; bd. dirs., chmn. internat. com. Congl. Award, 1984—; gov. BFI, 1982-84. Served with British mil., 1940-46. Named Knight Comd. Order of the Brit. Empire; St. Peter's Coll. hon. fellow, 1984; recipient Nat. Vol. Leadership award, Congl. award, 1984, Aims of Industry Free En-terprise award, 1985. Clubs: Spl. Forces; Brook, Ex-plorer's (N.Y.C.); Mid-Ocean (Bermuda). Home: Iselin N.J. Deceased.

WHITE, JOSEPH MALLIE, JR., physician, hospital executive; b. Dallas, Dec. 4, 1921; s. Joseph Mallie and Vada (Funderburk) W.; m. Jane Colleen Dennis, Nov. 26, 1950; children: Cynthia Ann White Shaw, Jennifer Sue Karin. B.S., So. Meth. U., 1944; M.D., U. Tex., Dallas, 1947; M.S. in Pharmacology, U. Iowa, 1950. Diplomate: Am. Bd. Anesthesiology. Intern Denver Gen. Hosp., 1947-48; resident U. Iowa Hosp., 1948-51; chmn. dept. anesthesiology U. Okla. Med. Sch., 1956-66; assoc. dean research affairs U. Okla. Med. Center, 1960-64, assoc. dir., assoc. dean, 1964-67; dean U. Okla. Med. Center (Med. Faculty), 1967-68; v.p. academic af-fairs, dean medicine U. Tex. Med. Br., Galveston, 1968-73; provost for health affairs U. Mo.-Columbia, 1973-79; pres. U. Health Scis./Chgo. Med. Sch., 1979-81; med. dir. St. Paul Med. Ctr., Dallas, 1981-93; mem. Liaison Com. on Med. Edn., 1971-78, chmn., 1977-78; mem. Coordinating Council on Med Edn., 1977-79, chmn., 1979. Editor: Clinical Anesthesiology. Served with U.S. Army, 1952-54. Decorated Bronze Star; recipient Dist-inguished Alumnus award U. Tex. Southwestern Med. Sch. at Dallas, 1968. Mem. AMA (chmn. coun. med. edn. 1976-79), Soc. Health and Human Values (pres. 1979-80, Annual Award 1983), Sigma Xi, Alpha Omega Alpha. Home: Dallas Tex. Died Sept. 14, 1993.

WHITE, WALTER PRESTON, JR., lawyer; b. Lynchburg, Va., Apr. 19, 1923; s. Walter Preston and Elizabeth Virginia (Candler) W.; m. Kathryn Mary Whittle, Oct. 12, 1951; children: Edith Rebecca, Amy Patricia. BS in Acctg., U. N.C., 1946, JD, 1949. Bar: N.C. 1949, Fla. 1962, Ga. 1969. Assoc. E.T. Bost, Con-cord, N.C., 1949-51; spl. atty. IRS, Washington, 1951-53; trial atty. IRS, Birmingham, Ala., 1953-56; sr. trial atty. IRS, Jacksonville, Fla., 1956-58, asst. regional counsel, 1958-62; staff asst. to regional counsel IRS, Atlanta, 1968-78; dist. counsel IRS, Atlanta and Miami, Fla., 1978-85; mng. ptnr. Dowling, White & Mooers, Jacksonville, 1962-68; ptnr. Womble Carlyle Sandridge & Rice, Winston-Salem, N.C., 1985-94. Lt. USAAF, 1942-46. Mem. ABA, Fla. Bar Assn. (exec. coun. 1962-68), Ga. State Bar, N.C. Bar Assn., Piedmont Club, Kiwanis. Democrat. Presbyterian. Home: Winston Salem N.C. Died May 8, 1994; interred Concord, N.C.

WHITE, WILLIAM, retired research physicist; b. Millbrook, Ont., Can., Apr. 1, 1928; s. William and Pearl Emma (Lamb) W.; m. Francoise L. Babin, May 28, 1960; children: William Gregory, Gregory Scott, Eric Lachlan. BS in Engring. Physics, Queen's U., Kingston, Ont., 1950; PhD in Nuclear Physics, McGill U., 1961. Dir. rsch. Nuclear Chgo. and G.D. Searle, Des Plaines, Ill., 1962-79, Siemens Gammasonics, Inc., Hoffman Estates, Ill., 1981-93; prin. White R&D Cons., Cary, Ill., 1979-94. Contbr. articles on sci. and rsch. mgmt. to profl. jours. Mem. Soc. Nuclear Medicine. Home: Cary Ill. Died Feb. 9, 1994; buried Crystal Lake Memorial, Crystal Lake, Ill.

WHITFIELD, JACK DUANE, advanced technology services and engineering company executive; b. Paoli, Okla., May 16, 1928; s. Lloyd H. and Ethel (Wigley) W.; m. Marcheta Steward, Sept. 11, 1949; children: Donna W. Dede, Jeffrey, Karen Ortiz. BSAE, U. Okla., 1954; MSME, U. Tenn., 1960; DSc, Royal Inst. Tech., Stockholm, 1972. Registered profl. engr., Tenn. Engr. Gen. Dynamics Convair, Daingerfield, Tex., 1951-54; with Sverdrup Tech. Inc., Tullahoma, Tenn., 1954-95, v.p., 1974-76, exec. v.p., 1976-80, pres., 1981-89, vice chmn., chief exec. officer, 1990-93 (ret.), chmn. bd., 1992-93 (ret.), also bd. dirs.; exec. v.p. Sverdrup Corp., 1985-88, pres., 1989-92; vice-chmn. Sverdrup Corp., Tullahoma, 1993 (ret.); bd. dirs. Tenn. Tech. Bd. Engr-ing. Advisors, Cookeville, 1981-92. Contbr. articles to profl. pubs. Bd. engring. advisors U. Okla., 1981-95; chmn. nat. adv. bd. U. Tenn. Space Inst., Tullahoma, 1985-89; adv. com. Miss. State U., 1992-95. Fellow AIAA (Ground Testing award 1979); mem. Nat. Soc. Profl. Engrs., Tenn. Soc. Profl. Engrs., Sigma Xi. Methodist. Home: Wartrace Tenn. Died Aug. 3, 1995.

WHITMAN, JANE S., lawyer; b. Atlanta, Feb. 6, 1929; d. Henry M. and Elisabeth (Van Ingen) Shaw; m. Robert B. McDermott. BA, William Smith Coll., 1949; JD, U. Mich., 1952. Assoc. McDermott, Will & Emery, Chgo., 1952-61, ptnr., 1961-92. Bd. dirs. Chgo. Found. Women, 1987-92; trustee Lawyers Trust Fund Ill., Chgo., 1987-92. Mem. Am. Coll. Probate Counsel, Chgo. Estate Planning Council, Chgo. Network, Econ. Club, Law Club Chgo. Clubs: Monroe (Chgo.) (bd. govs. 1987-92); Chikaming Country (Lakeside, Mich.); Macatawa Bay Yacht (Mich.). Home: Chicago Ill. Died May 1992.

WHITNEY, GEORGE WARD, lawyer; b. N.Y.C., June 30, 1924; s. Reginald and Muriel Janet (Hall) W.; m. C. Patricia Thayer, June 18, 1949; children: Lynn T., George W., Jonathan, Mark. B.E.E., Rensselaer Poly. Inst., 1949; J.D., George Washington U., 1952. Bar: D.C. 1952, N.Y. 1954, U.S. Ct. Claims 1965, U.S. Ct. Appeals (2d cir.) 1969, U.S. Ct. Appeals (fed. cir.) 1982, U.S. Supreme Ct. 1980. Asst. examiner U.S. Patent Office, Washington, 1948-50; law clk. Gen. Motors Corp., Washington, 1950-52; assoc. Brumbaugh, Graves, Donohue & Raymond, N.Y.C., 1952-60, ptnr., 1960-89; lectr. Vermont Law Sch., 1989-93, Franklin Pierce Law Ctr., 1989-93. U.S. del. Law of Sea Conf., 1981-82; dep. mayor, village trustee, Garden City, N.Y., 1969-72; pres. Citizens Adv. Com. on Edn., Garden City, 1967; pres. Garden City Central Property Owners Assn., 1968-69; chmn., trustee Garden City Library, 1974-80; mem. council Cathedral of the Incarnation, 1983-87. Served with Signal Corps, AUS, 1943-46. Fellow Am. Bar Found.; mem. N.Y. Patent Law Assn. (bd. govs. 1973-76), Am. Patent Law Assn. (pres. 1980-81, bd. mgrs. 1972-73, dir. 1977-82), Am. Intellectual Property Law Assn. (chmn. pub. appointments com. 1983-85, chmn. alternative dispute resolution com. 1989-90), ABA (liti-gation sect., chmn. patent litigation 1977-81, spl. commn. punitive damages 1983-87, chmn. inequitable conduct, misuse and antitrust matter, 1983-85, patent, trademark and copyright sect. chmn. Div. IV 1985-86, chmn. com. patent legis. 1986-88, chmn. judiciary com. 1988-90), Am. Arbitration Assn. (nat. panel arbitrators), Assn. of Bar of City of N.Y. (patents com. 1979-82, Fed. Bar Coun., Fed. Cir. Bar Assn. (jud. selection com. 1985-89), ITC Trial Lawyers Assn., Rensselaer Alumni Coun. (chmn. 1962-64), Downtown Athletic Club (bd. govs. 1970-75), N.Y. Athletic Club, Delta Tau Delta, Phi Alpha Delta. Republican. Episcopalian. Home: Lyme N.H. Died Apr. 30, 1993; buried Old Crtl. Ceme-tery, Chapel Hill, N.C.

WHITNEY, JOHN CLARENCE, lawyer; b. Green Bay, Wis., Feb. 10, 1915; s. John and May (Salvas) W.; m. Helen E. Mayer, May 16, 1942; children: Kathleen A. Whitney Feeney, Robert M., John F. B.A., U. Wis., 1936, LL.B., 1938. Bar: Wis. 1938, U.S. Dist. Ct. (ea. and we. dists.) 1940, 7th Circuit Ct. Appeals 1948. Law examiner Wis. Public Service Commn., 1938-39; assoc. firm Everson, Ryan and Hanaway, Green Bay, Wis., 1939-41; ptnr. Everson, Whitney Everson & Brehm S.C. and predecessors, Green Bay, 1945-94; dir. Morley-Murphy Co. Bd. editors: Wis. Law Rev, 1936-38. Mem. Green Bay Bd. Park Commrs., 1946-55; mem. DePere Police and Fire Commn., DePere, Wis., 1956-61, Wis. Gov.'s Jud. Appointment Rev. Commn., 1978-79; mem. Supreme Ct. com. to draft code of judicial ethics. Served with U.S. Army, 1941; to lt. comdr. USN, 1941-45. Named Young Man of Yr. Jr. C. of C. of Green Bay, 1949. Mem. Brown County Bar Assn. (pres. 1956), State Bar Wis. (pres. 1961-62, chmn. com. to draft long arm statute 1957-59), Am. Bar Assn., Am. Bar Found., Am. Law Inst., Am. Coll. Trial Lawyers, Order of Coif. Republican. Roman Catholic. Club: Oneida Golf and Riding. Home: De Pere Wis. Deceased Feb. 15, 1994.

WHITTEN, CHARLES ARTHUR, geodetic con-sultant; b. Redfield, S.D., Oct. 2, 1909; s. Herbert Wil-liam and Mabel (Hales) W.; m. Brena Evelyn Uber, July 7, 1933; children: William Barclay, David Hart, John Charles. Student, U. Mich., summer 1929; BA, Carthage Coll., 1930, DSc (hon.), 1965; DSc (hon.), U. New Brunswick, Can., 1974; D of Engring. (hon.), Karlsruhe (Germany) U., 1975. Mathematician U.S. Coast and Geodetic Survey, Washington, 1930-46, chief triangulation br., 1946-62, chief electronic computing divsn., 1962, dep. dir. Office Phys. Scis., 1963-65, chief rsch. group, 1965-68, chief geodesist, 1968-72; geodetic cons. Silver Spring, Md., from 1972. Editor: Con-temporary Geodesy, 1959; contbr. articles to profl. jours. Recipient silver and gold medals Dept. Com-merce, 1959, 72, Levallois medal Internat. Assn. Ge-odesy, 1979, Mercherikov medal, 1987. Fellow Am. Geophys. Union (gen. sec. 1967-74, William Bowie medal 1980, Charles Whitten medal 1985); mem. AAAS, Internat. Union of Geodesy and Geophysics (fin. com. 1963-79, pres. 1975-79), Am. Congress on Surveying and Mapping, Cosmos Club (Washington). Lutheran. Home: Silver Spring Md. Deceased.

WHITTEN, JAMIE LLOYD, congressman; b. Cascilla, Miss., Apr. 18, 1910; s. Alymer Guy and Nettie (Early) W.; m. Rebecca Thompson, June 20, 1940; chil-dren—James Lloyd, Beverly Rebecca Merritt. Student lit. and law depts., U. of Miss., 1926-31. Prin. pub. schs., 1931; elected Miss. State Legislature, 1931; elected dist. atty. 17th Dist. of Miss., 1933, reelected, 1935 and 1939; mem. 77th-103rd Congresses from 1st Miss. Dist., 1941-94; chmn. appropriations com., subcom. agrl. 77th-102d Congresses from 1st Miss. Dist. Author: That We May Live. Mem. Beta Theta Pi, Phi Alpha Delta. Democrat. Lodge: Mason. Home: Charleston Miss. Died Sept. 9, 1995.

WICKER, VERONICA DICARLO, federal judge; d. Vincent James and Rose Margaret DiCarlo; m. Thomas Carey Wicker Jr.; children: Thomas Carey III, Catherine Wicker West. B.F.A., Syracuse U., 1952; J.D., Loyola U. of the South, 1966. Bar: La. 1966, U.S Dist. Ct. (ea. dist.) 1968. U.S. magistrate New Orleans, 1977-79; judge U.S. Dist. Ct. (ea. dist.) La., New Orleans, 1979-

94. Mem. vis. com. Loyola U. Law Sch., 1981-92; bd. dirs. Stanley C. Scott Cancer Ctr. Mem. Feb. Bar Assn., La. Bar Assn., New Orleans Bar Assn., Jefferson Parish Bar Aux., Fed. Dist. Judges Assn., Assn. Women Judges, Maritime Law Assn., Justinian Soc. Jurists, Rotary (bd. dirs. New Orleans Club 1989-91, NORFI bd. 1992-94), New Orleans Rotary Fund., Inc., Alpha Delta, Alpha Xi Alpha, Phi Mu. Home: New Orleans La. Died Dec. 10, 1994; buried The Garden of Memories Cemetery, Metairie, La.

WICKES, MARY, actress; b. St. Louis, June 13; d. Frank A. and Mary Isabella (Shannon) Wickenhauser. A.B., D.Arts (hon.), Washington U., St. Louis; postgrad., UCLA, 1972—. Lectr. seminars on acting in comedy Coll. William and Mary, Williamsburg, Va., Washington U. at St. Louis, Am. Conservatory Theatre, San Francisco. Debut at Berkshire Playhouse, Stockbridge, Mass.; appeared in: Broadway plays Stage Door, 1936, Father Malachy's Miracle, 1937, The Man Who Came to Dinner, 1939, Jackpot (musical), 1944, Hollywood Pinafore (musical), 1945, Town House, 1948, Park Avenue (musical), 1946, Oklahoma (revival), 1979, others; numerous appearances in dramatic and musical stock, including St. Louis Mcpl. Opera, Cape Playhouse, Dennis, Mass., Bucks County Playhouse, Pa., Alliance Theater, Atlanta, The Coconut Grove Playhouse, Miami, Fla., Burt Reynolds Theatre, Jupiter, Fla., Fox Theatre, St. Louis, Mark Taper Forum, Ahmanson Theater and Chandler Pavilion, Los Angeles, Am. Shakespeare Festival, Stratford, Conn., Am. Conservatory Theater, San Francisco, Berkshire Playhouse, Mass., 1937-78; film debut in The Man Who Came to Dinner, 1942; other film appearances include Now Voyager, 1942, Higher and Higher, 1943, June Bride, 1948, Anna Lucasta, 1949, On Moonlight Bay, 1951, By the Light of the Silvery Moon, 1952, The Actress, 1953, White Christmas, 1959, The Music Man, 1962, The Trouble with Angels, 1966, Where Angels Go, Trouble Follows, 1968, Touched by Love, 1979, Postcards from the Edge, 1990, Sister Act, 1992, Sister Act II, 1993, Little Women, 1994; TV debut as Mary Poppins: other TV appearances include Studio One, 1946; regular: TV series Doc, Halls of Ivy, Lucy shows, Dennis the Menace, The Canterville Ghost, Murder, She Wrote, Wonderworks (PBS), Twigs, Highway to Heaven, others; co-star ABC series Father Dowling Mysteries, 1989-91. Mem. aux. Hosp. Good Samaritan, L.A.; chmn. Nat. Crippled Children's Soc., Mo., 1969; bd. dirs. Med. Aux. Ctr. for Health Scis., UCLA, 1977-95, St. Barnabas Sr. Ctr., L.A., 1994-95. Recipient numerous awards including Outstanding Actress award Variety Clubs, 1967; awards for vol. work UCLA; Humanitarian award Masons; elected to St. Louis Mcpl. Opera Hall of Fame, 1987; 1st annual Starbiird lectr. Washington U., St. Louis, 1988; nominated best comedy supporting-actress for Sister Act Am. Comedy awards, 1993. Mem. AFTRA, NATAS (Emmy award nomination), SAG, Actors Equity Assn., Acad. Motion Picture Arts and Scis., Phi Mu. Republican. Episcopalian. Home: Los Angeles Calif. Died Oct. 24, 1995.

WICKMAN, PAUL EVERETT, public relations executive; b. Bisbee, Ariz., Aug. 21, 1912; s. Julius and Hilda Wilhelmina (Soderholm) W.; m. Evelyn Gorman, Nov. 22, 1969; children by previous marriage: Robert Bruce, Bette Jane, Marilyn Faye. Student, LaSierra U., Arlington, Calif., 1928-30, Pacific Union Coll., Angwin, Cal., 1931-32; spl. student, Am. U., 1946. Min., 1931-53, Internat. traveler, lectr., writer, 1937-44; assoc. sec Internat. Religious Liberty Assn., 1944-46; travel lectr. Nat. Lecture Bur., 1944-55; exec. sec., dir. internat. radio and TV prodns. Voice of Prophecy Corp., Faith for Today Corp., 1946-53; v.p. Western Advt. Agy., Los Angeles, 1953-55; dir. devel. Nat. Soc. Crippled Children and Adults, Inc., Chgo., 1955-56; exec. dir. Pub. Relations Soc. Am., Inc., N.Y.C., 1956-57; dir. corp. pub. relations Schering Corps., Bloomfield, N.J., 1957-58; pres. Wickman Pharm. Co., Inc., Calif., 1959-83, Paul Wickman Co., 1984-96. Mem. Newport Beach CSC, mem. Orange County Children's Hosp. Fund; trustee Walla Walla (Wash.) Coll., 1989-91. Mem. Newcomen Soc., Pub. Rels. Soc. Am. (accredited), Internat. Platform Assn., Swedish Club (L.A., past pres.), Vikings, 552 Hoag Hosp. Club, Elks, Masons, Shriners, Royal Order Jesters, Kiwanis (past pres. Newport Beach club, lt. gov. div. 41 Cal-Neva Hi 1990-91). Home: Corona Del Mar Calif. Died Mar. 4, 1996.

WIEGAND, C. MONROE, cosmetic company executive; b. Monroe, N.Y., July 1, 1912; s. Karl Wilhelm and Beatric Roxanna (Weygant) W.; m. Emily Ernestine Swanson, July 11, 1933; children: Richard Monroe (dec.), Patricia Randolph, Christine Dale. B.S.M.E., Pratt Inst., 1934. V.p. Avon Products, Inc., N.Y.C., 1953-70; trustee emerita Pratt Inst., Bklyn., 1960-75; trustee Marine America, Inc., Stamford, Conn. Republican. Lodge: Masons. Home: Little Deer Isle Maine Died Nov. 7, 1993.

WIESNER, JEROME BERT, engineering educator, researcher; b. Detroit, May 30, 1915; s. Joseph and Ida (Friedman) W.; m. Laya Wainger, Sept. 1, 1940; children: Stephen Jay, Zachary Kurt, Elizabeth Ann, Joshua A. B.S., U. Mich., 1937, M.S., 1938, Ph.D., 1950. Assoc. dir. U. Mich. Broadcasting Service, 1937-40; chief engr. Acoustical Record Lab., Library of Congress, 1940-42; staff MIT Radiation Lab., Cambridge, Mass., 1942-45, U. of Calif. Los Alamos Lab., 1945-46; mem. faculty MIT, Cambridge, 1946-71, dir. research lab. of electronics, 1952-61, head dept. elec. engring., 1959-60, dean of sci., 1964-66, provost, 1966-71, pres., 1971-80, inst. researcher and prof., 1980-94; spl. asst. to Pres. on sci. and tech., 1961-64; chmn. Pres.'s Sci. Adv. Com., 1961-64; chmn. tech. assessment adv. coun. Office Tech. Assessment, U.S. Congress, 1976-79; bd. dirs. Kenan Sys., Inc., Magnascreen, Rothko Chapel. Author: Where Science and Politics Meet, 1965, ABM: An Evaluation, 1969. Bd. dirs. Weizman Inst. Sci.; trustee Woods Hole Oceanog. Inst., Kennedy Meml. Trust; bd. dirs. MacArthur Found.; life mem. MIT Corp., Cambridge, Carnegie Commn. Recipient Vannevar Bush award NSF, 1992. Fellow IEEE, Am. Acad. Arts and Scis.; mem. NAS (Pub. Welfare medal 1993), Am. Philos. Soc., AAUP, Am. Geophys. Union, Acoustical Soc. Am., Nat. Acad. Engring., MIT Corp. (life), Sigma Xi, Phi Kappa Phi, Eta Kappa Nu, Tau Beta Pi. Home: Watertown Mass. Died Oct. 21, 1994; interred Chilmark, Mass.

WIGNER, EUGENE PAUL, physicist, educator; b. Budapest, Hungary, Nov. 17, 1902; came to U.S., 1930, naturalized, 1937; s. Anthony and Elisabeth (Einhorn) W.; m. Amelia Z. Frank, Dec. 23, 1936 (dec. 1937); m. Mary Annette Wheeler, June 4, 1941 (dec. Nov. 1977); m. Eileen C.P. Hamilton, Dec. 29, 1979. Chem. Engr. and Dr. Engring., Technische Hochschule, Berlin, 1925; hon. D.Sc., U. Wis., 1949, Washington U., 1950, Case Inst. Tech., 1956, U. Chgo., 1957, Colby Coll., 1959, U. Pa., 1961, Thiel Coll., 1964, U. Notre Dame, 1965; D.Sc. (hon.), Technische Universität Berlin, 1966, Swarthmore Coll., 1966, Université de Louvain, Belgium, 1967; Dr.Jr., U. Alta., 1957; L.H.D. (hon.), Yeshiva U., 1963; hon. degrees, U. Liège, 1967, U. Ill., 1968, Seton Hall U., 1969, Cath. U., 1969, Rockefeller U., 1970, Israel Inst. Tech., 1973, Lowell U., 1976, Princeton U., 1976, U. Tex., 1978, Clarkson Coll., 1979, Allegheny Coll., 1979, Gustav Adolphus Coll., 1981, Stevens Inst. Tech., 1982, SUNY, 1982, La. State U., 1985. Asst. Technische Hochschule, Berlin, 1926-27, asst. prof., 1928-33; asst. U. Göttingen, 1927-28; lectr. Princeton U., 1930, part-time prof. math. physics, 1931-36; prof. physics U. Wis., 1936-38; Thomas D. Jones prof. theoretical physics Princeton U., 1938-71; on leave of absence, 1942-45; with Metall. Lab., U. Chgo., 1946-47; as dir. research and devel. Clinton Labs.; dir. CD Rsch. Project, Oak Ridge, 1964-65; Lorentz lectr. Inst. Lorentz, Leiden, 1957; cons. prof. La. State U., 1971-85, ret., 1985; mem. gen. adv. com. AEC, 1952-57, 59-64; mem. math. panel NRC, 1952-54; physics panel NSF, 1953-56; vis. com. Nat. Bur. Standards, 1947-51; mem. adv. bd. Fed. Emergency Mgmt. Agy., 1982-91. Author: (with L. Eisenbud) Nuclear Structure, 1958, The Physical Theory of Neutron Chain Reactors (with A.M. Weinberg), 1958, Group Theory and its Applications to the Quantum Mechanics of Atomic Spectra, 1931, English translation, 1959, Symmetries and Reflections, 1967, Survival and the Bomb, 1969. Decorated medal of Merit, 1946, Order of Banner of Republic of Hungary, Rubies, 1990; recipient Franklin medal Franklin Inst., 1950, citation N.J. Tchrs. Assn., 1951, Enrico Fermi award AEC, 1958, Atoms for Peace award, 1960, Max Planck medal German Phys. Soc., 1961, Nobel prize for physics, 1963, George Washington award Am. Hungarian Studies Found., 1964, Semmelweiss medal Am. Hungarian Med. Assn., 1965, Nat. Sci. medal, 1969, Pfizer award, 1971, Albert Einstein award, 1972, Golden Plate medal Am. Acad. Achievement, 1974, Disting. Achievement award La. State U., 1977, Wigner medal, 1978, Founders medal Internat. Cultural Found., 1982, Medal of the Hungarian Central Rsch. Inst., Medal of the Autonomous Univ. Barcelona, Am. Preparedness award, 1985, Lord Found. award, 1989; named Nuclear Pioneer, Soc. Nuclear Medicine, 1977, Colonel Gov. of La., 1983. Mem. AAAS, Royal Soc. Eng. (fgn.), Royal Netherlands Acad. Sci. and Letters, Am. Nuclear Soc. (first recipient Eugene P. Wigner award 1990), Am. Phys. Soc. (v.p. 1955, pres. 1956), Am. Math. Soc., Am. Assn. Physics Tchrs., Am. Acad. Arts and Scis., Am. Philos. Soc., Nat. Acad. Scis., N.Y. Acad. Scis. (hon. life mem.), Austrian Acad. Scis., German Phys Soc., Franklin Inst., Acad. Sci., Gottingen, Germany (corr.), Hungarian Acad. Sci. (hon.), Austrian Acad. Scis. (hon.), Hungarian L. Eötvös Phys. Soc. (hon.), Sigma Xi. Home: Princeton N.J. Died Jan. 1, 1995.

WILCOX, THOMAS ROBERT, retired bank executive; b. N.Y.C., Aug. 23, 1916; s. NYU and Louisa (Latimer) W.; m. Mary Jane Collette, Mar. 28, 1943; children: Thomas R., Kirby C., Andrew McK. Student, NYU, 1934-38; B.A., Princeton U., 1940. With First Nat. City Bank, 1934-71, beginning as page, successively asst. cashier, asst. v.p., v.p. charge domestic branches, 1954-57, exec. v.p., 1957-67, vice chmn., 1967-71; vice chmn., dir. Blyth Eastman Dillon & Co., Inc., 1971-73; pres. Crocker Nat. Bank, San Francisco, 1974; chmn., chief exec. officer Crocker Nat. Bank, 1974-81, then chmn. exec. com., now ret.; dir. Colgate-Palmolive Co., Hilton Hotels Corp.; trustee Mut. Life Ins. Co. N.Y. Trustee Marine Hist. Assn., Mystic, Conn.; bd. dirs. W.M. Keck Found.; mem. Pan. Am. Internat. Adv. Bd.; gov. Nature Conservancy. Mem. Nat. Golf Links. Clubs: University, Links, N.Y. Yacht, Univ. (N.Y.C.); Bohemian; Shelter Island Yacht (N.Y.). Home: New York N.Y. Died July 19, 1993.

WILENSKI, PETER STEPHEN, diplomat, civil servant; b. Lodz, Poland, May 10, 1939; s. John and Halina (Glass) W.; m. Gail Radford, 1967 (div. 1981); m. Jill Hager. MBBS, Sydney U., Australia, 1962; MA, Oxford U., Eng., 1967; MA in Internat. Affairs, Carleton U., Ottawa, Can., 1969; MPA, Harvard U., 1970; DLitt (hon.), Macquarie U. Registered med. practitioner, Australia, U.K. Prin. pvt. sec. to prime minister Australia, 1972-74; sec. Dept. Labour and Immigration, Australia, 1975; commr. Rev. NSW Govt. Administrn., Sydney, 1977-82; found. prof. Australian Grad. Sch. Mgmt., Sydney, 1977-81; prof. polit. sci. social justice project Australian Nat. U., 1981-83; sec. Dept. Edn. and Youth Affairs, Australia, 1983; chmn. Pub. Svc. Bd., Australia, 1984-87; sec. Dept. Trans. and Communications, Australia, 1987-88, Dept. Fgn. Affairs and Trade, 1992-93; Australian amb. and permanent rep. UN, N.Y.C., 1989-92; Commonwealth Govt. advisor, 1993-94; mem. Australia Coun., 1983-84, Commn. for the Future, Australia, 1986-88, Australian Telecommunications Commn., 1987-88; cons. Orgn. for Econ. Coop. and Devel., Paris, 1980-86; v.p. 46th UN Gen. Assembly. Author: Public Power and Public Administration, 1985, Medical Care Delivery Sytems in China, 1976; co-editor: Decisions, 1981. Pres. Nat. Union Australian U. Students, 1962-33, Abortion Law Reform Assn., Australian Capital Ter., 1970-72, Interim Coun. Chifley U., Sydney, 1986-88; fellow Sydney Univ. Senate, 1963-64, 75-89. Decorated Order of Australia, 1987. Fellow Royal Australian Inst. Pub. Administrn. (councillor 1977-89), Royal Australian Coll. Med. Administrs. (hon.); mem. Australian Inst. Polit. Sci. (dir. 1977-83), Australian Inst. Internat. Affairs, Econ. Soc., Nat. Press Club. Home: Sydney Australia Died Nov. 3, 1994.

WILEY, RICHARD HAVEN, chemist, educator; b. Mattoon, Ill., May 10, 1913; s. John Frederick and Mary Frances (Moss) W.; m. Marybeth Signaigo, Dec. 28, 1940; children: Richard Haven, Frank Edmund. A.B., U. Ill., 1934, M.S., 1935; Ph.D., U. Wis., 1937; LL.B., Temple U., 1943. Fellow Wis. Alumni Research Found., 1935-37; research chemist E.I. duPont de Nemours & Co., Wilmington, Del., 1937-45; asso. prof. chemistry U. N.C., 1945-49; prof. chemistry, chmn. dept. U. Louisville, 1949-65; NSF sr. postdoctoral fellow Imperial Coll., London, 1957-58; vis. prof. grad. div. CUNY, 1963-64, exec. officer chemistry, 1965-68; prof. chemistry Hunter Coll., 1965-79, prof. emeritus, from 1979; vis. scholar Stanford U., 1978-80; vol. employee San Jose State U., 1980-85. Author: (with P.F. Wiley) Pyrazolones, Pyrazolidones and Derivatives, 1963; Editor: (with P.F. Wiley) Five and Six Membered Compounds with Nitrogen and Oxygen, 1963, Pyrazoles, Pyrazolines, Pyrazolidine and Condensed Ring Systems, 1967; asso. editor: Jour. Chem. and Engring. Data, 1966-71; past mem. editorial bd.: Jour. Polymer Sci, Jour. Macromolecular Chemistry; Contbr. to textbook articles on organic and polymer chemistry sci. jours. Fellow AAAS, Am. Inst. Chemists, N.Y. Acad. Scis.; mem. Am. Chem. Soc. (Midwest award St. Louis sect. 1965), N.Y. Acad. Scis., Phi Beta Kappa, Sigma Xi, Phi Eta Sigma, Phi Lambda Upsilon, Phi Kappa Psi. Home: Cupertino Calif. Died March 11, 1996.

WILEY, WILLIAM BRADFORD, publisher; b. Orange, N.J., Nov. 17, 1910; s. William Carroll and Isabel (LeCato) W.; m. Esther T. Booth, Jan. 4, 1936; children: William Bradford II, Peter Booth, Deborah Elizabeth Wiley. A.B., Colgate U., 1932, LL.D. (hon.), 1966. With John Wiley & Sons, Inc., N.Y.C., 1932—; sec., v.p. and sec., exec. v.p., treas. John Wiley & Sons, Inc., 1938-56, pres., 1956-71, chmn., 1971—, dir., 1942—; chmn., dir. John Wiley & Sons, Can., John Wiley & Sons Ltd., Chichester Jacaranda-Wiley, Ltd., Brisbane, Wiley Ea. Ltd., India; mem. mgmt. bd. MIT Press. Trustee emeritus Colgate U., Drew U. Cordier fellow Columbia U. Episcopalian. Clubs: Met. Opera, Players (N.Y.C.); Sakonnet Golf (R.I.), Sakonnet Yacht (R.I.); Baltusrol (N.J.) Golf. Home: Summit N.J.

WILHELM, HARLEY A(LMEY), retired chemist, educator, mechanical engineer; b. Ellston, Iowa, Aug. 5, 1900; s. Bert C. and Anna B. (Glick) W.; m. Orpha E. Lutton, May 29, 1923; children: Lorna Wilhelm Livingston, Max Gene, Myrna Wilhelm Elliott, Gretchen. BA, Drake U., 1923, LLD, 1961; PhD, Iowa State U., 1931. Fellow in chemistry, 1924-25; postdoctoral work U. Mich., Ann Arbor, 1941; tchr. Mapleton (Iowa) H.S., 1923-24, Guthrie Center (Iowa) H.S., 1925-26; prof., coach Intermountain Union Coll., Helena, Mont., 1926-27; semi-pro baseball pitcher Ames (Iowa) Mchts. team, 1930-42; grad. asst. dept. chemistry Iowa State U., Ames, 1927-28, from instr. to prof. chemistry, 1928-45, prof. chemistry, 1945-71, prof. metallurgy, 1963-71; assoc. dir. Ames Lab. of U.S. AEC (now Dept. Energy), 1942-66; prof. emeritus Iowa State U., 1971-95; Manhattan Dist. engr., 1942-66, prin. scientist, 1966-95; AEC del. to Eng., 1949, to Eng. and Europe, 1953, to Argentina and Brazil, 1957; cons. desalinization of water Dept. Interior, 1967; cons. licensing of reactors AEC, Washington, 1968; vis. prof. U. Waterloo, Kitchener Ont., Can., 1969; presenter, cons. in field. Author more than 100 published articles; holder more than 75 patents. Decorated Army-Navy E Flag with 4 stars recipient Gold medal ASME, 1990, Alumni Disting Svc. award Drake U., 1959, Double D. award Nat. D

Club, 1968, Centennial award for svc. Drake U. Alumni Assn., 1981; named to Iowa H.S. Basketball Hall of Fame, 1988, Iowa Inventors Hall of Fame, 1993; metallurgy bldg. Harley A. Wilhelm Hall, Iowa State U., 1986, Centennial Recognition as one of 100 all time great athletes in Bulldog history Drake U., 1991, Chgo. Alumni award Iowa State U., 1949, faculty citation Iowa State U. Alumni, 1969. Fellow Am. Soc. Metals (nat. trustee 1957-60, William Hunt Eisenman award 1962); mem. SAR, Am. Chem. Soc. (gold medal Iowa sect. 1954), Iowa Acad. Sci. (Centennial citation 1975), Rotary Club (Paul Harris fellow 1995), Phi Beta Kappa, Sigma Xi, Phi Lambda Upsilon, Phi Kappa Phi. Died Oct. 7, 1995.

WILHELM, JOSEPH LAWRENCE, archbishop; b. Walkerton, Ont., Can., Nov. 16, 1909; s. John and Magdalena (Uhrich) W. J.C.L., Ottawa U., 1948. Ordained priest Roman Cath. Ch., 1934. Asst., bishop's sec. Hamilton, Ont., 1934-40; chaplain Canadian Army, 1940-45; pastor St. Peter & Paul Ch., Hamilton, 1948-63; aux. bishop of Calgary, Alta., 1963-67; archbishop of Kingston, Ont., 1967-82, ret., 1982. Apptd. col. comdt. Canadian Chaplain Corps., 1982-88. Decorated Mil. Cross. Home: Belleville Can. Died June 25, 1995.

WILKIE, LEIGHTON ALLYN, manufacturing executive; b. Winona, Minn., July 29, 1900; s. Julius C. and Ellen (Leighton) W.; m. Adele Mearns, Feb. 23, 1935; children—Bonnie A. (Mrs. Jon Henricks), Michael L. Student, U. Minn., 1921-22. Founder, chmn. bd. Continental Machines, Inc., Mpls., from 1932; chmn. Contour Saws, Inc., DoAll Co., Des Plaines, Ill., also 50 DoAll sales store corps., prin. cities, from 1942; dir. First Nat. Bank Des Plaines. Author: Your Life in the Machine World. Chmn. Wilkie Bros. Found., Des Plaines.; Bd. dirs. Santa Barbara Mus. Natural History. Mem. Chevaliers du Tastevein, Newcomen Soc. N.Am., Los Rancheros Visitadores (Santa Barbara), Coral Casino Club (Santa Barbara), Birnam Wood Golf Club (Santa Barbara). Home: Santa Barbara Calif. Deceased.

WILKINS, SIR MICHAEL (COMPTON LOCKWOOD), British government official; b. Jan. 4, 1933; s. Eric and Lucy (Lockwood) W.; m. Anne Catherine Skivington, 1960; 1 son, 2 daus. Educated, Mill Hill Sch. Joined as 2d lt. Royal Marines, 1951, advanced through grades to Comdt.-Gen., 1984, ret., 1987; Hon. Col. Exeter U., 1990; lt.-gov., comdr.-in-chief Guernsey, 1990-94. Mem. Royal Yacht Squadron, Army and Navy Club. Home: Saint Peter Port Channel Islands Died Apr. 1994.

WILL, HUBERT LOUIS, federal judge; b. Milw., Apr. 23, 1914; s. Louis E. and Erna (Barthman) W.; m. Phyllis Nicholson, July 23, 1938; children: Jon Nicholson, Wendy (dec.), Nikki, Ami Louise; m. Jane R. Greene, Dec. 20, 1969. A.B., U. Chgo., 1935, J.D., 1937; L.L.D. (hon.), John Marshall Law Sch., 1973. Bar: Wis. 1937, Ill. 1946, U.S. Supreme Ct. 1941. Mem. gen. counsel's staff SEC, Washington, 1937-38; sec. U.S. Senator Robert F. Wagner, 1939; spl. asst. to atty. gen. U.S., 1940-41; asst. to gen. counsel OPA, 1942; tax counsel Alien Property Custodian, 1943; atty. firm Pope & Ballard, Chgo., 1946-48, Nelson, Boodell & Will, Chgo., 1949-61; U.S. dist. judge No. Dist. Ill., 1961-95; Mem. Commn. on Bankruptcy Laws of U.S., 1971-73; mem. com. to consider standards for admission to practice in fed. cts. U.S. Jud. Conf., 1976-79. Contbr. articles legal publs. Chmn. Chgo. Com. Youth Welfare, 1957-61. Served as capt. OSS AUS, 1944-45, chief counterespionage br., ETO. Decorated Bronze Star. Mem. ABA, Fed. Bar Assn., Chgo. Bar Assn., Am. Judicature Soc., Am. Vets. Com., World Vets Fedn. (v.p. coun. U.S.A.). Died Dec. 9, 1995.

WILLENBROCK, FREDERICK KARL, engineer, educator; b. N.Y.C., July 19, 1920; s. Berthold Daniel and Anna Marie (Koniger) W.; m. Mildred Grace White, Dec. 20, 1944. Sc.B., Brown U., 1942; M.A., Harvard U., 1947, Ph.D., 1950. Research fellow, lectr. and asso. dean Harvard U., Cambridge, Mass., 1950-67; provost, prof. faculty engring. and applied sci. SUNY, Buffalo, 1967-70; dir. Inst. Applied Tech., Nat. Bur. Standards, Washington, 1970-76; dean Sch. Engring. and Applied Sci., So. Meth. U., Dallas, 1976-81; Cecil and Ida Green prof. engring. Sch. Engring. and Applied Sci., So. Meth. U., 1976-86; exec. dir. Am. Soc. for Engring. Edn., Washington, 1986-89; asst. dir. Sci., Technol. and Internat. Affairs NSF, Washington, 1989-91; sr. scientist Tech. Adminstrn. Dept. of Commerce, 1992-93; cons. Washington, 1993-95; vis. prof. engring. and pub. policy Carnegie-Mellon U., 1991-92. Contbr. articles to profl. jours. With USNR, 1943-46. Recipient Disting. Engring. award Brown U., 1962; Gold medal U.S. Dept. Commerce, 1975. Fellow IEEE, AAAS; mem. NAE, Sigma Xi, Tau Beta Pi. Home: Reston Va. Died Aug. 24, 1995.

WILLEY, CALVERT LIVINGSTON, association executive; b. Cambridge, Md., Dec. 11, 1920; s. Henry Calvert and Virginia Mae (Mills) W. B.S., U. Md., 1949. Research dir. Clifton Corp., Washington, 1952-53; asst. to exec. dir. Nat. Soc. Profl. Engrs., 1953-56; exec. sec. Am. Soc. Lubrication Engrs., Chgo., 1957-61, Inst. Food Technologists, Chgo., 1961-88; exec. dir. Inst. Food Technologists, 1966-88, exec. dir. emeritus, 1988-94; exec. dir. IFT Found., 1986-88. Served to lt. USNR, WWII and Korea; ret. Fellow AAAS; mem. Am. Soc. Assn. Execs., Council Engring. Soc. Execs. Home: Chicago Ill. Died Apr. 12, 1994; cremated.

WILLIAMS, ARTHUR MIDDLETON, JR., lawyer, retired utility executive; b. Charleston, S.C., Sept. 16, 1914; s. Arthur Middleton and Katherine (Ward) W.; m. Katherine Murphy, Nov. 4, 1943; children: Katherine Elizabeth Williams Mahon, Patricia LaBruce Williams Boykin, Elizabeth Middleton. BS in Textile Chemistry, Clemson U., 1936, LLD (hon.), 1985; JD magna cum laude, U. S.C., 1942, LLD (hon.), 1981; LLD (hon.), Benedict Coll., 1990. Bar: S.C. 1942, U.S. Supreme Ct. 1954. Joined U.S. Army, 1936, served in cav., until 1938; transferred to inactive duty, 1938-42, active duty with armored forces, 1942-43, ret., 1943; practice law Columbia, S.C., 1943-44; with S.C. Electric & Gas Co., Columbia, 1944-82; sr. v.p. S.C. Electric & Gas Co., 1961-66, pres., 1966-77, chief exec. officer, 1967-79, chmn. bd., 1977-82, chmn. emeritus, 1982—, also dir. emeritus; tchr. law Law Sch. U. S.C., 1947-50, 81-84, lectr. history dept., 1989—. Chmn. S.C. Employment Security Commn. Merit System Council, 1950-56; mem. Gov. S.C. Fiscal Survey Commn., 1955, S.C. Commn. Human Affairs, 1971-75, So. Govs. Conf. Peacetime Uses Nuclear Energy, 1955-59; mem. exec. com. So. Interstate Nuclear Bd., 1959-63; sec. S.C. Nuclear Energy and Space Commn., 1962-63; mem. bd. sch. commrs. Dist. 1, Richland County, S.C., 1958-71; mem. U. S.C. Bus. Partnership Found., pres., 1969-71; mem. U. S.C. Law Partnership Bd., pres., 1981—; mem. Carolina Rsch. and Devel. Found., U. S.C., pres., 1980—; mem. exec. com. Ednl. Found., U. S.C.; mem. pres.'s nat. adv. council U. S.C.; mem. Gov.'s Mansion Found.; bd. dirs. United Fund Community Services, Columbia and Richland County, 1955-58, pres., 1956; bd. dirs. Richland County chpt. ARC, 1945-48, Family Welfare Assn. Richland County, 1950-55, Columbia USO, 1948-51; bd. dirs. Carolinas United, 1959-62, exec. com., 1959-62; trustee Porter Gaud Sch., Charleston, 1966-68, Converse Coll., 1971-75, Benedict Coll., 1979-90, Voorhees Coll., 1985-86; bd. dirs. S.C. Episc. Retirement Community at Still Hopes, 1985—, chmn. bd. dirs. 1986-88. Recipient Freedoms Found. award, 1950; Algernon Sydney Sullivan award U. S.C., 1972; Disting. Alumni award, 1975. Mem. S.C. Bar Assn. (v.p. 5th jud. circuit 1954), ABA, Richland County Bar Assn., Columbia C. of C. (dir. 1951-57, 61-64, pres. 1955, nat. counselor 1956), S.C. C. of C. (dir. 1963-66, pres. 1968, chmn. 1969), Edison Electric Inst. (dir. 1973-76, 78-81), Southeastern Electric Exchange (pres. 1970-71, dir. 1966-79), NAM (dir. 1970-73), Phi Beta Kappa, Scabbard and Blade, Blue Key, Phi Psi, Beta Gamma Sigma, Sigma Nu (Centennial award 1969). Episcopalian (vestryman). Clubs: Palmetto (pres. 1967-71, bd. govs. 1959—), Cotillion, Quadrille, Pine Tree Hunt, Centurian, Forest Lake, Summit, Columbia Sailing (Columbia); Winyah Indigo Soc. (Georgetown); Carolina Yacht (Charleston). Home: Columbia S.C.

WILLIAMS, AVON NYANZA, JR., lawyer, state senator; b. Knoxville, Tenn., Dec. 22, 1921; s. Avon Nyanza and Carrie Belle Williams; AB, Johnson C. Smith U., Charlotte, N.C., 1940; LLB, Boston U., 1947, LLM, 1948; LLD (hon.) Fisk U., 1989; DHL (hon.) McHarry Med. Coll., 1990; m. Joan Marie Bontemps, 1956; children: Avon Nyanza, Wendy Janette. Bar: Mass. 1948, Tenn. 1949, U.S. Supreme Ct. 1963. Practice law, Knoxville, 1949-53; ptnr. firm, Nashville, 1953-69; individual practice law, Nashville, 1969—; mem. Tenn. State Senate, 1968—; prof. dental jurisprudence Meharry Med. Coll., 1970-84. Founding mem. Tenn. Voters Coun., 1966—, chmn., 1966-85; founding mem. Davidson County Ind. Polit. Council, 1962—, pres., 1962-66; mem. State Dem. Steering Com., 1964; del. Nat. Dem. Conv., 1972; mem. exec. com. Nashville br. NAACP, 1953-88; elder, trustee St. Andrews Presbyn. Ch., Nashville, 1966—; mem. appeals and rev. com. Meharry Med. Coll., 1970-76; bd. dirs. So. Regional Coun., 1968—, Family and Children's Service, 1956-60. Lt. col. JAGC, U.S. Army Res. Recipient certs. of achievement for civil rights legal work. Mem. ABA, Am. Judicature Soc., Omega Psi Phi, Sigma Pi Phi. Home: Nashville Tenn.

WILLIAMS, DAVID BENTON, advertising agency executive; b. Chgo., May 18, 1920; s. Howard D. and Margaret (Clark) W.; m. Edith Chapin Huntington, Aug. 24, 1943; children—David Huntington, Deborah Benton, Howard Chapin. A.B. magna cum laude, Harvard, 1942. Service detail, media, prodn. Erwin Wasey, Chgo., 1946-47; copy contact Erwin Wasey, Los Angeles, 1947-48, account exec., v.p., 1948-49; v.p. mgmt. Erwin Wasey, N.Y.C., 1949-54; exec. v.p., gen. mgr. Erwin Wasey, 1954-56, pres., 1956; pres. Erwin Wasey, Ruthrauff & Ryan (merger of Erwin Wasey & Co. and Ruthrauff & Ryan), N.Y.C., 1957-65; sr. v.p., dir. Interpub. Group of Cos., Inc., 1965-68, dir.; exec. v.p. Interpub. S.A., 1966-68; sr. v.p. Wilson Haight & Welch (advt.), Hartford, Boston, Greenwich, N.Y.C., Phila., Tampa and Houston, 1969-72; exec. v.p., dir. Wilson Haight & Welch (advt.), 1972-78, pres., dir., 1974-78; dir. Howard Swink Advt. (now Fahlgren & Swink), 1978-84; pres., dir. 1035 Fifth Ave Corp., 1973-95. Served with CIC, U.S. Army. Mem. Apartment Owners Assn. (bd. dirs.), Phi Beta Kappa. Clubs: University, Union (N.Y.C.); Preston Mountain (Kent, Conn.); American (London). Home: New York N.Y. Died Oct. 1, 1995; interred D.C.

WILLIAMS, DONALD SHAND, architect; b. Patchogue, N.Y., Apr. 30, 1930; s. Walter Henry and Florence Hall (Shand) W.; m. Eleanor Jean Kent, June 15, 1952; children—Kent Scott, Karen Williams Seel. B. Arch., Renesselaer Poly. Inst., 1952. Registered architect, Fla., N.C. Intern architect various cos., Calif., N.Y., Fla., 1952-59; ptnr. Wakeling, Levison, Williams and Walker Architects, Clearwater, Fla., 1959-71; pres. Williams & Walker Architects Chartered, Clearwater, 1971-84, Williams Architects Chartered, Clearwater, 1984—. Prin. works include Calvary Bapt. Ch., Clearwater, 1983, Pinellas County Hist. Park, 1976 (Fla. Assn. AIA award 1979). Commr. City of Clearwater, 1967-75, Pinellas Suncoast Transit Authority, 1974—, chmn., 1977-87, Pinellas County Hist. Commn., 1977-89, 92—, chmn., 1988; pres. Jaycees, Clearwater, 1960-61; bd. dirs. Performing Arts Theater and Ctr., Clearwater, 1979-85, 92—. Fellow AIA; mem. Fla. Assn. AIA (medal of honor 1973). Republican. Mem. United Ch. of Christ. Club: Pinellas Rep. Ivory (pres. 1976-78). Lodge: Rotary. Home: Clearwater Fla.

WILLIAMS, GARTH MONTGOMERY, illustrator; b. N.Y.C., Apr. 16, 1912; married; 6 children. Studied, Westminster Sch. Art, Royal Coll. Art, London. Illustrator numerous children's books, including Charlotte's Web, Little House on Prairie series, Cricket in Times Square series, Miss Bianca Books, Stuart Little; writer, illustrator Rabbits' Wedding, Adventures of Benjamin Pink, also others. Recipient Brit. Prix de Rome for sculpture, 1936. Home: New York N.Y. Died May 8, 1996.

WILLIAMS, HARRY LEVERNE, chemical engineering educator; b. Watford, Ont., Can., Nov. 16, 1916; s. Harry Young and Rosa Malinda (Brown) W.; m. Mary Eileen Cawson, Aug. 31, 1946; children: Harvey Thomas Leverne, Jai Joan Mary. B.A., U. Western Ont., 1939, M.Sc., 1940; Ph.D., McGill U., Montreal, 1943. Registered profl. engr., Ont.; chartered chemist. From research chemist to prin. scientist research and devel. div. Polymer Ltd., Sarnia, Ont., 1946-67; prof. chem. engring. and applied chemistry U. Toronto, 1967-82, prof. emeritus, 1982-93; formerly dir. Chem. Engring. Research Cons. Ltd.; cons. in field. Author; patentee in field. Rsch. grantee Nat. Scis. and Engring. Rsch. Coun. Can., Nat. Rsch. Coun. Can., Def. Rsch. Bd. Can., Imperial Oil Enterprises Ltd., Polymer Ltd. Fellow Royal Soc. Can., Chem. Inst. Can. (Dunlop lectr. macromolecular scis. div. 1977), Royal Soc. Chemistry, Inst. Materials, AAAS, N.Y. Acad. Scis., Soc. Plastics Engrs.; mem. Am. Chem. Soc., Soc. Chem. Industry, Sigma Xi. Home: Toronto Can. Died Aug. 10, 1993.

WILLIAMS, JERRE STOCKTON, federal judge; b. Denver, Aug. 21, 1916; s. Wayne Cullen and Lena (Day) W.; m. Mary Pearl Hall, May 28, 1950; children: Jerre Stockton, Shelley Hall, Stephanie Kethley. A.B., U. Denver, 1938; J.D., Columbia, 1941. Bar: Colo. 1941, Tex. 1950, U.S. Supreme Ct. 1944. Instr. U. Iowa Law Sch., 1941-42; asst. prof. U. Denver Law Sch., 1946; mem. faculty U. Tex. Law Sch., Austin, 1946-80; John B. Connally prof. civil jurisprudence U. Tex. Law Sch., 1970-80; judge U.S. Ct. Appeals (5th cir.), 1980-93; mem. faculty Inst. Internat. and Comparative Law San Diego U., Merton Coll. Oxford (Eng.) U., 1977, Magdalen Coll., 1979, Kings Coll., London, Eng., 1981; chmn. Adminstrv. Conf. U.S., 1967-70, pub. mem., 1972-78, sr. conf. fellow, 1980-93; Labor arbitrator, bd. govs. Nat. Acad. Arbitrators, 1964-67, v.p., 1974-75; chmn. Southwestern Regional Manpower Adv. Com., 1964-66; cons. Bur. Budget, 1966-67. Author: Cases and Materials on Employees Rights, 1952, The Supreme Court Speaks, 1956; Editor-in-chief: Labor Relations and the Law, 3d edit, 1965, Constitutional Analysis, 1979. Mem. bd. trustees James Madison Meml. Fellowship Found., 1991-93. Capt. USAF, 1942-46. Mem. ABA (winner Ross Essay contest 1963, chmn. adminstrv. law sect. 1975-76), Am. Law Inst., Inst. Jud. Adminstrn., Internat. Soc. Labor Law & Social Legis., Fed. Bar Assn., Tex. Bar Assn., Assn. Am. Law Schs. (pres. 1980). Methodist. Home: Austin Tex. Died Aug. 29, 1993; buried Texas State Cemetary, Austin, T.X.

WILLIAMS, LANGBOURNE MEADE, retired minerals company executive; b. Richmond, Va., Feb. 5, 1903; s. Langbourne Meade and Susanne Catherine (Nolting) W.; m. Elizabeth Goodrich Stillman, 1930 (dec. 1956); m. Frances Pinckney Breckinridge, 1959 (dec. 1984). A.B., U. Va., 1924; M.B.A., Grad. Sch. Bus. Adminstrn. Harvard, 1926. With Lee, Higginson & Co., N.Y.C., 1926-27; asso. John L. Williams & Sons, Richmond, 1927-30; v.p., treas. Freeport Minerals Co., 1930-33, pres., 1933-58, chmn., 1957-69, chmn. exec. com., 1969-73, hon. chmn., 1973-75; dir. Texaco, Inc., 1958-74, B.F. Goodrich Co., 1938-60, So. Railway, 1957-65; trustee Bank of N.Y., 1941-57. First dir. industry div. ECA (Marshall Plan), Paris, France, 1948; councillor, former chmn. The Conf. Bd.; mem. vis. com. Harvard Bus. Sch., 1933-64; hon. mem. Bus. Council.; hon. mem. bd. govs. Soc. N.Y. Hosp.; hon. trustee George C. Marshall Research Found., Am. Ch. Inst. for Negroes, 1936-57, Va. Inst. Sci. Research, 1959-69;

mem. bd. visitors U. Va., 1963-68, Tulane U., 1954-61. Mem. Harvard Alumni Assn. (past dir.), Va. Hist. Soc. (hon. v.p.), Soc. Fellows U. Va. (hon. life pres.), Soc. of Cincinnati, Assn. Preservation Va. Antiquities, Phi Beta Kappa, Omicron Delta Kappa, Delta Psi. Episcopalian. Clubs: Century (N.Y.C.), Union (N.Y.C.); Metropolitan (Washington); Commonwealth (Richmond), Country of Va. (Richmond); Farmington Country (Charlottesville, Va.). Home: Rapidan Va. Died Sept. 8, 1994.

WILLIAMS, NORMAN, law educator, city planner; b. Chgo., Dec. 26, 1915; s. Norman and Joan (Chalmers) W.; m. Jeanne Tedesche, Nov. 27, 1947; children: Norman Jr., Joan Chalmers, Roger Sidney, Sarah Dorothy. BA, Yale U., 1938, LLB, 1943; postgrad., Corpus Christi Coll., Cambridge, 1938-39, Yale U., 1939-40. Bar: N.Y. 1944. Practice N.Y.C., 1943-48; sr. analyst The Plan for Rezoning N.Y., N.Y.C., 1948-50; from acting dir. to dir. div. of planning, acting chief to chief office of master planning N.Y.C. Dept. of Planning, 1950-60; cons. Outdoor Recreation Resources Rev. Commn., 1961; dir. Guyana Project Joint Ctr. for Urban Studies, Caracas, Venezuela, 1961-62; exec. dir. Gov.'s adv. commn. on transp. State of N.J., 1964-65; mem., vice chmn. Princeton (N.J.) Borough Planning Bd. and Princeton Regional Planning Bd., 1965-75; prof. Vt. Law Sch., 1976-96; prof. urban planning and law U. Ariz., 1978-86; vis. lectr. city planning Columbia U. Architecture Sch., 1951-61, Yale U. Architecture Sch., 1952-61; vis. prof. city planning MIT, 1960, U. Va., 1973; vis. prof. law Rutgers-Newark U., 1965-75, U. Ariz., 1976-78, 87-91, Vt. Law Sch., 1975; prof. urban planning Rutgers U., 1969-75. Note editor, editor-in-chief Yale U. Law Jour., 1942; author: (with others) Vermont Townscape, 1986, American Land Planning Law, 5 vols., 1974-75, 2d edit., 8 vols., 1984-88; contbr. numerous articles to profl. jours. Pres. Citizens Housing and Planning Council N.Y., N.Y.C., 1950; mem. Billings Park Commn., Woodstock, Vt., 1985-92. Mem. Am. Planning Assn. (Disting. Leadership award 1991), Am. Inst. of Cons. Planners. Democrat. Unitarian. Clubs: Yale (N.Y.C.); Lakota (Barnard, Vt.) (bd. dirs. 1977-80, 82-85), Elizabethan, Yale U. (bd. govs. 1937-38). Home: Woodstock Vt. Died Mar. 24, 1996.

WILLIAMS, ROBLEY COOK, former molecular biology educator, researcher; b. Santa Rosa, Calif., Oct. 13, 1908; s. William Claude and Anne Mae (Cook) W.; m. Margery Ufford, June 20, 1931; children—Robley Cook, Grace Elizabeth. A.B., Cornell U., 1931, Ph.D., 1935. Instr. astronomy U. Mich., Ann Arbor, 1935-40, asst. prof., 1940-45, assoc. prof. physics, 1945-48, prof. physics, 1948-50; prof. biophysics U. Calif.-Berkeley, 1950-59, prof. virology, 1959-64, prof. molecular biology, 1964-76, prof. emeritus, 1976-95, assoc. dir. virus lab., 1959-76. Author: Photometric Atlas of Stellar Spectra, 1942, Electron Micrographic Atlas of Viruses, 1974; also numerous articles; patentee in field of evaporated metal films. Mem. U.S. commn. for UNESCO, 1963-69; trustee Deep Springs Coll., Calif., 1968-76. Guggenheim Found. fellow, 1966; recipient Longstreth medal Franklin Inst., 1939, John Scott award City of Phila., 1954, Berkeley citation U. Calif.-Berkeley, 1976. Mem. Nat. Acad. Scis. (council 1960-63), Electron Microscopy Sco. Am. (pres. 1951), Biophys. Soc. (pres. 1958), Am. Acad. Arts and Scis., Sigma Xi. Democrat. Home: Oneonta N.Y. Died Jan. 3, 1995.

WILLIAMSON, JUANITA V., English language educator; b. Shelby, Miss.; d. John M. and Alice E. (McAllister) W. BA, LeMoyne-Owen Coll., 1938; MA, Atlanta U., 1940; PhD, U. Mich., 1961. Asst. prof. English LeMoyne-Owen Coll., Memphis, 1947-56, prof., 1956-94, Disting. Svc. prof., 1980; adj. prof. Memphis State U., 1975-94, linguist, summer 1969, 73, 75; vis. prof. Ball State U., Muncie, Ind., 1963-64, U. Tenn., Knoxville, summer 1975; vis. prof. U. Wis., Milw., summer 73, linguist, summer 1966-67; linguist French Inst. Atlanta U., summer 1963, Hampton (Va.) Inst., summer 1964, U. Ark., Pine Bluff, summer 1981; chmn. English faculty, LeMoyne-Owen Coll., Memphis, 1987-94. Editor: A Various Language, 1971; contbr. articles to profl. jours. Mem. exec. com. United Way, Memphis, 1953-56; cons. Girl Scouts U.S., Memphis, 1956; bd. dirs. Integration Svc., Memphis, 1952-58; mem. exec. com. hist. council United Ch. Christ, 1976. Recipient citation for excellence in edn. Memphis City Council, 1973, Carter G. Woodson award Shelby State Community Coll., 1991; fellow Rockefeller Found., 1949-51, Ford Found., 1954; HEW grantee, 1964-68. Mem. MLA (program com., minority affairs com.), Nat. Council Tchrs. English (coll. sect. exec. com. 1976-79), Am. Dialect Soc. (exec. com. 1979-82), Conf. on Coll. Composition and Communication (exec. com. 1969-71), Delta Sigma Theta. Died Aug. 8, 1993; buried Meml. Park, Memphis, Tenn. Home: Memphis Tenn.

WILLIAMSON, LIZ (ELIZABETH ANNE RAY WILLIAMSON), dancer, choreographer, educator; b. Winston-Salem, N.C.; d. Alexander Hamilton and Maude E. (Young) Ray; m. William Elliott Williamson; 1 child, Wonza Williamson Sinclair. AB, Radcliffe Coll.; MA, NYU. Tchr., Howard U., Tuskegee Inst., Bennett Coll., Greensboro, N.C., Ethical Culture Sch., N.Y.C., The Dalton Sch., N.Y.C.; artist-in-residence Talladega Coll., Ala.; master tchr. in jazz 1st Statewide Dance Conf., Nashville; prof. dance Hostos C.C., CUNY, 1972-73; master tchr. modern and jazz Fla. chpt. Dance Masters Am., Miami Beach, 1971, 1st N.Y. State Coll. and U. Dance Festival, 1971; master tchr. in jazz U. Alta., Edmonton, Can., 1972, Colony Club, N.Y.C., Brick Parish House, N.Y.C.; tchr. Philadanco, Phila., 1988, Internat. Ballet Competition, Jackson, Miss., 1986, 90, Kuopo (Finland) Music and Dance Festival, 1991, Am. Dance Festival Duke U., Durham, N.C., 1989; jazz artist-in-residence Jacob's Pillow, Mass., summer, 1973; chmn. performing and visual arts dept., head dance dept. Dalton Sch., N.Y.C., 1971-74; numerous master classes and workshops; choregrapher Jazz Ballet for Skeel Dancers, Oak Ridge, 1970, Mass. Jazz Ballet, 1970; master tchr. Palucca Sch., Dresden, German Dem. Republic, 1978, Bonn, Fed. Republic Germany, 1978, Les Ballet Jazz, Montreal, Que., Can., 1982; choreographer Dallas Black Dance Co., 1980, Juneau Dance Unltd., Alaska, 1980; vis. tchr. jazz ballet Moderno Enid Sauer Studio, Rio De Janeiro, Brazil, 1977, N.C. Sch. Arts, Winston-Salem, 1973, 74; dancer with Donald McKayle and Alvin Ailey cos., Merry-Go-Rounders, N.Y.C. Appeared in N.Y. City Center's Finian's Rainbow, Carmen Jones; in summer stock The Boy Friend, Show Boat, Follies of 1910, Carnegie Hall, 1960; appeared on Jackie Gleason TV show; films Edge of the City, A Man Called Adam, 1960; rec. artist Hoctor Records. Recipient Elsa Heilich Kempe award Dance Masters Am., 1976, Recognition Achievement award Radcliffe Coll., 1989, Oak Ridge Commemorative medal, 1970, Plaudit award, 1981. Mem. Nat. Assn. Regional Ballet (bd. dirs. 1977-78), New Dance Group (bd. dirs. 1977-78), Soc. Stage Dirs. and Choreographers. Author: Fundamentals of Teaching Modern Dance and Modern Jazz, 1956; editor article on jazz dance Dance mag., 1978, Jazz Gymnastics, Jazz Dance including Aerobic, 1983; contbr. articles to mags. Died Jan. 10, 1996. Home: New York N.Y.

WILLINGHAM, CALDER BAYNARD, JR., novelist, playwright, screenwriter; b. Atlanta, Dec. 23, 1922; s. Calder Baynard and Eleanor (Willcox) W.; m. Helene Rothenberg; m. Jane Marie Bennett; 1953; 4 sons, 2 daus. Ed., The Citadel, 1940-41, U. Va., 1941-43. Author: End as a Man, 1947, Geraldine Bradshaw, 1950, Reach to the Stars, 1951, The Gates of Hell, 1951, Natural Child, 1952, To Eat a Peach, 1955, Eternal Fire, 1963, Providence Island, 1969, Rambling Rose, 1972, The Big Nickel, 1975, The Building of Venus Four, 1977, (screenplays) including Paths of Glory, 1957, One-Eyed Jacks, 1961, The Graduate, 1967, Little Big Man, 1970, Thieves Like Us, 1974, (plays) including End as a Man, 1953. Home: New York N.Y. Died February 19, 1995.

WILLMOT, DONALD GILPIN, business executive; b. Toronto, Ont., Can., Mar. 7, 1916; s. Harold Edward and Florence (Gilpin) W.; m. Ivy Vivian Sutcliffe, Nov. 18, 1939; children: Michael, Wendy, David. B.A.Sc., U. Toronto, 1937; LL.D. (hon.), Brock U., 1989. Engr. Canadian SKF Co. Ltd., Toronto, 1937-38; plant supt. Anthes Imperial Ltd., St. Catharines, Ont., 1939-41; pres., dir. Anthes Imperial Ltd., 1948-68; successively supt., mgr. personnel and pub. relations, asst. to v.p., gen. mgr. Atlas Steels Ltd., Welland, Ont., 1942-48; pres., dir. Molson Industries Ltd., 1968-73; dep. chmn. bd. Molson Cos. Ltd., 1973-74, chmn. bd., 1974-83, hon. chmn., 1983-86, hon. dir., 1986-94; hon. dir. Crown Life Ins. Co., Hayes-Dana Ltd., Bank N.S.; bd. dirs. Tenex Data Corp.; chmn. Aquaterra Corp. Past chmn. bd. govs. Brock U., St. Catharines. Club: Jockey of N.Y. Home: King City Can. Died Jan. 31, 1994.

WILLS, AUDREY ELIZABETH, bank executive; b. Phila., Mar. 28, 1930; d. Theodore A. and Mary C. (Dixon) W. AA, Villanova, 1966. Operations officer First Pa. Bank, Phila., 1961-66, asst. v.p., div. head, 1966-74, v.p., 1974-85, divisional v.p., 1985—; bd. dirs. Del. Valley Bank Methods Assn., Phila.; cons. Fraud Control Bureau, PHila., 1970—, Hurst Assocs., Springfield, Pa., 1986—, L & L Custom Catering Inc., Frederick, Pa., 1980—. Author: Loss Prevention Awareness, 1979; author and exec. producer of film: Tell it to the Judge, 1986; contbr. articles to various publications; editor: Prevention Awareness newsletter. Mem. Phila. Art Mus. Assn., 1975—; mem. New Hanover Civic Assn. (twp. Pa.), 1975-81; mem. Greater Phila. Cultural Alliance, 1976—; mem. Smithsonian Assocs., Washington, 1980—; mem. Paradise (environmental) Watchdogs, Frederick, Pa., 1987; mem. Phila. Clearing House Fraud Commn. (past chmn.); chmn. Women's Achievement Forum Phila. YWCA, 1988-90, trustee 1989, bd. dirs. 1990. Recipient Cert. of Appreciation Dept. Defense USAF Guard and Reserve, 1985, Cert. achievement Women's Forum YWCA of Phila., 1987. Mem. Pa. Bankers Assn., Am. Mgt. Assn., Am. Inst. of Banking, Bank Adminstrn. Inst., Del. Valley Fin. and Security Officer's Assn. Club: Cen. Perklomen Bus. and Profl. Women. Home: Frederick Pa. Died May 28, 1992.

WILMOTTE, RAYMOND M., telecommunications consultant; b. Paris, Aug. 13, 1901; came to U.S., 1932; BA in Mech. Sci., Corpus Christi Coll.; MA in Mech. Sci., Cambridge (Eng.) U., 1929, ScD in Mech. Sci., 1958. With rsch. staff Aircraft Radio Corp., N.J., 1932; prin., cons. broadcasting industry Wilmotte Lab., Washington, 1947-59; program mgr. relay spacecraft (exptl. active communications satellite NASA) RCA, N.J., from 1959; communications specialist FCC, Washington, from 1972; cons. to NAE, RCA, Raytheon, GE, Westinghouse, NASA, 1964-72. Contbr. numerous articles to profl. jours. Patentee (50) in field. Recipient Devel. award Bur. of Ordnance. Fellow IEEE. Home: Washington D.C. Deceased.

WILSON, BASIL WRIGLEY, oceanographic engineering consultant, artist, author; b. Cape Town, Cape, Republic South Africa, June 16, 1909; came to U.S., 1952, naturalized, 1956; s. George Hough and Sarah Anne (Hearn) W.; m. Elizabeth Mary Davenport, Feb. 27, 1941; children—Mary Douglas, Richard Lyman, Gerald Hearn, Derek Wrigley. BS in Civil Engring., U. Cape Town, 1931; M.S. in Ry. Engring., U. Ill., 1939, C.E., 1940; D.Sc. in Engring., U. Cape Town, 1953. Registered profl. engr., South Africa, Tex. Asst. research engr. South African Rys. & Harbours, Johannesburg, Republic South Africa, 1932-52; prof. engring. oceanography Tex. A&M U., College Station, 1953-61; asst. dir. engring. oceanography Nat. Engring. Sci. Co., Pasadena, Calif., 1961-64; dir. engring. oceanography Sci. Engring. Assocs., San Marino, Calif., 1964-68; cons. oceanographic engr. Basil W. Wilson D.Sc., Pasadena, Calif., 1968-96. Editor, author: Berthing and Morring of Ships, 1970, Two Frogs of Olde Japan, 1986, Epics of the Wild, 1996; contbr. numerous papers to engring. jours. and books. Bd. dirs. Pasadena Artist Assocs., 1966. Commonwealth Fund Service fellow, Harkness Found. N.Y., U. Ill., 1938-39, Disting. Alumnus award U. Ill. Alumni Assn., 1987. Fellow Instn. Civil Engrs (overseas premium 1968), ASCE (A.M. Wellington prize 1952, Norman medal 1969, Moffat-Nichol award 1983 hon. mem. 1988), South African Instn. Civil Engrs (instn. award 1959, meritorious rsch. award 1984); mem NAE (emeritus mem. 1984), Am. Geophys. Union Sigma Xi. Home: Pasadena Calif. Died Feb. 9, 1996.

WILSON, EDGAR BRIGHT, chemistry educator; b Gallatin, Tenn., Dec. 18, 1908; s. Edgar Bright and Alma (Lackey) W.; m. Emily Buckingham, June 15 1935 (dec. 1954); children: Kenneth, David, Nina (Nina W. Cornell); m. Therese Bremer, July 25, 1955; children Anne, Paul, Steven. B.S., Princeton U., 1930, D.Sc (hon.), 1981, A.M., 1931; Ph.D., Calif. Inst. Tech., 1933 A.M. (hon.), Harvard U., 1936; D. honoris causa, U Brussels, 1975; D.Sc. (hon.), Dickinson Coll., 1976 Columbia U., 1979, Clarkson Coll., 1983, Harvard U. 1983; Dr. Chem., U. Bologna, 1976. Research fellow Calif. Inst. Tech., 1933-34; jr. fellow Soc. of Fellows Harvard U., 1934-36, asst. prof. chemistry, 1936-39 asso. prof., 1939-46, prof., 1946-79, Theodore William Richards prof. chemistry, 1947-79, prof. emeritus 1979—; research dir. Underwater Explosives Research Lab., 1942-44; chief div. 2 Nat. Def. Research Com. 1944-46; research dir., weapons systems evaluation group Dept. Def., 1952-53. Author: (with Linus Pauling) Introduction to Quantum Mechanics, 1935, Introduction to Scientific Research, 1952, (with P.C Cross, J.C. Decius) Molecular Vibrations, 1955. Hon trustee Woods Hole Oceanographic Instn., 1979—. Recipient Am. Chem. Soc. award, 1937, medal for Merit U.S. govt., 1948, Debye award, 1962; Distinguished Service award Calif. Inst. Tech., 1966; Pauling award 1972; Rumford medal, 1973; Nat. Medal Sci., 1975 Feltrinelli award, 1976; Ferst award Sigma Xi, 1977 Pitts. Spectroscopy award, 1978; Robert A. Welch award, 1978; Willard Gibbs award, 1979; Lippincott medal, 1979; Cresson medal, 1982; Guggenheim fellow 1949-50, 70-71; Fulbright grantee Queen's Coll., Oxford Eng., 1949-50. Mem. Am. Chem. Soc. (Norris award N.E. sect. 1966, Lewis award Calif. sect. 1969, T.W. Richards medal N.E. sect. 1978), Am. Phys. Soc. (Plyler award 1978), Am. Philos. Soc., Am. Acad. Arts and Scis., Internat. Acad., Quantum Molecular Scis., Nat. Acad. Scis., Phi Beta Kappa. Home: Cambridge Mass.

WILSON, H. BRIAN, JR., public relations executive b. Raleigh, N.C., May 13, 1928; s. H. Brian and Kathleen Terrell (Burnside) W.; m. Havel Dolores Mortensen, Nov. 3, 1950 (div. Aug. 1976); children: H Brian Wilson III, Clifford Arthur Wilson. BS in Journalism, W.Va. U., 1951. Assoc. editor Trade Mags., Inc., Cleve., 1954-57; Ea. bur. chief Pen for Pub Co., N.Y.C., 1957-65; mgr. media rels. AMAX, Inc N.Y.C., 1965-69; dir. pub. rels. Susaquehanna Corp Alexandria, Va., 1969-71; fin. pub. rels. mgr. Am. Ca Co., Greenwich, Conn., 1971-74; v.p. corp. rel Pechiney Corp., Greenwich, 1974-92. Bd. dirs. Greenwich Arts Coun., 1983-86. With USN, 1951-53. Mem Nat. Press Club, Aviation/Space Writers Assn., Na Investors Rels. Inst., U.S. C. of C. (pub. affairs com Nat. Assn. of Mfrs. (pub. affairs steering com.). Republican. Baptist. Home: Greenwich Conn. Die Dec. 1992.

WILSON, HILLSMAN VAUGHAN, retired foo company executive; b. Crewe, Va., Dec. 29, 1928; Joseph Henry and Lucy (Vaughan) W.; m. Anne Steua Gantt, May 15, 1965; children: Pamela Hunt, Richa Hillsman, Daniel Vaughan, Robert Vaughan. B.A Coll. William and Mary, 1951; B.C.L., Marshall Wyt Law Sch., 1953. Bar: Va. 1952, Md. 1956. Practiced la Crewe, 1955; with McCormick & Co., Inc., 1955-87, v. fin., 1973-77, exec. v.p., 1977-79, pres., chief operati officer, 1979-87; bd. dirs. McCormick Properties, In various divs. and subs. McCormick & Co. Inc., Ba Life Ins. Co. Former mem. bd. sponsors Loyola Co

Sch. Bus. and Mgmt. Served to 2d lt. F.A. U.S. Army, 1953; to 1st lt. JAGC U.S. Army, 1953-55. Mem. Sigma Nu. Methodist. Club: Balt. Country. Home: Lutherville Timon Md. Died Feb. 14, 1993.

WILSON, OLIN CHADDOCK, astronomer; b. San Francisco, Jan. 13, 1909; s. Olin Chaddock and Sophie (Clary) W.; m. Katherine Elizabeth Johnson, Sept. 3, 1943; children: Nicole, Randall. A.B., U. Calif.-Berkeley, 1930; Ph.D., Calif. Inst. Tech., 1934. Asst. Mt. Wilson Obs., Pasadena, Calif., 1931-36, asst. astronomer, 1936-51, astronomer, 1951-75, astronomer emeritus, 1975-94; war work Calif. Inst. Tech., Pasadena, Calif., 1942-46. Contbr. numerous papers to profl. jours. Recipient Russell Lecture award Am. Astron. Soc., 1977; Bruce medal Astron. Soc. of Pacific, 1984. Democrat. Home: West Lafayette Ind. Died July 13, 994.

WILSON, ORME, JR., retired foreign service officer; . N.Y.C., July 3, 1920; s. Orme and Alice (Borland) W.; m. Mildred Eddy Dunn, Feb. 16, 1950; children: Marshall, Elsie Dunn, Orme III. Student, St. Alban's ch., Washington, 1929-33, St. Mark's Sch., Southborough, Mass., 1933-38; S.B. cum laude, Harvard, 1942; M.A., George Washington U., 1951; diploma, USAF War Coll., 1965. Jr. pilot Pan Am. World Airways, 1946-47, U.S. Army Map Service, 1950; oined Fgn. Service, 1950; vice consul Frankfurt am Main Fed. Republic Germany, 1951-53; vice consul outhampton, Eng., 1953-54; 2d sec. Belgrade, Yugoslavia, 1958-61; 2nd then 1st sec. Athens, Greece, 1961-4; assigned Washington, 1955-57, 65-70; consul gen. Zagreb, Yugoslavia, 1970-74; adviser U.S. Mission to J.N., 1974-77; polit. counselor U.S. Mission to NATO, 977-80; Bd. dirs. Laurel Race Course, Laurel, Md., 968-84. Contbr. to Eastern Europe: Essays in Geographical Problems, 1970. Trustee Bishop Rhinelander ound. for Episcopal Chaplaincy Harvard U. and Radliffe Coll., 1967-71, 76-78, 80-83, hon., 1987—; mem. dv. bd. visitors Mary Baldwin Coll., 1981-90; pres. riends of U. Va. Blandy Exptl. Farm, 1983-86, bd. irs., 1983—, treas., 1986-87; bd. mgrs. Seamen's Ch. nst. N.Y. and N.J., 1984—. lt. USNR, 1942-46. ellow Am. Geog. Soc.; mem. U.S. Tennis Assn. (Prence Cup com.), Thoroughbred Club Am., Va. horoughbred Assn. (bd. dirs. 1982—, treas. 1983-84, p. 1984-89, pres. 1990—), Am. Horse Coun., Internat. awn Tennis Club (N.Y.C. and Brussels), Harvard lub, Brook Club, Racquet and Tennis Club, (N.Y.C.), Metropolitan Club (Washington), Chevy Chase (Wash.). Episcopalian. Home: White Post Va.

WILSON, SAMUEL, JR., architect; b. New Orleans, ug. 6, 1911; s. Samuel and Stella (Poupeney) W.; m. llen Elizabeth Latrobe, Oct. 20, 1951. B.Arch., Tulane ., 1931, LHD, 1990. Architect office Moise H. Goldtein, 1930-33, Historic Am. Bldgs. Survey in La., 1934-5; architect office Richard Koch, 1935-42, assoc., 1945-5; partner Richard Koch & Samuel Wilson Jr., New rleans, 1955-72, Koch and Wilson, Architects, 1972-; lectr. La. architecture Tulane U., 1945-83. Author: Guide to Architecture of New Orleans, 1699-1959, 959, Conversations with Samuel Wilson, Jr.: Dean of rchitectural Preservation in New Orleans (compiled nd edited by Abbye A. Gorin), 1991; editor: Impresions Respecting New Orleans (by Latrobe), 1951, outhern Travels: Journal of John H.B. Latrobe, 1834, 986, The Architecture of Colonial Louisiana: Collected ssays of Samuel Wilson Jr., FAIA; contbr. articles to rofl. publs. Bd. dirs. area council Boy Scouts Am.; bd. irs. Maison Hospitaliere, Friends of Cabildo (pres. bd. 979-81). Served with USCGR, 1942-45. Recipient dward Langley scholarship AIA, 1938; citation Nat. rust for Historic Preservation, 1968; Merit award Am. ssn. State and Local History, 1977; Elizabeth T. erlein award Vieux Carre Commn., 1986; honor award . New Orleans Sch. Urban and Regional Studies, 1986; ecorated comdr. Mil. and Hospitaliere Order St. azarus of Jerusalem., chevalier de l'Ordre des Arts et s Lettres (France), medal honor La. Architects Assn. 987. Fellow AIA; mem. Soc. Archtl. Historians, La. ist. Assn. (pres. 1986), La. Landmarks Soc. (pres. meritus, bd dirs.). Roman Catholic. Club: Boston New Orleans). Home: New Orleans La. Died Oct. 21, 993.

WINGER, HOWARD WOODROW, library educator; Marion, Ind., Oct. 29, 1914; s. Joseph Pendleton and manda Ellen (Shoemaker) W.; m. Helen Margaret ray, Dec. 25, 1941; children—John, Michael, Philip, lizabeth, Robert. A.B. with high distinction, anchester Coll., 1936, LL.D., 1975; B.S., George eabody Coll., 1945; M.S., U. Ill., 1948, Ph.D., 1953. chr. Swayzee High Sch., Ind., 1936-37; copy writer rowell Pub. Co., Springfield, Ohio, 1937-38; tchr. Jefrson Twp. High Sch., Warren, Ind., 1940-42; asst. rarian U. Ill. at Urbana, 1945-50; asst. prof. U. Wis.-adison, 1950-53; asst. prof. Grad. Library Sch., U. hicago, 1953-59, assoc. prof., 59-68, prof., 1968-81, dean, 972-77; Bd. library dirs. Park Forest Pub. Library, Ill., 955-61. Author: Iron Curtains and Scholarship, 1959, even Questions About the Profession' of Librarianship, 962, The Medium Sized Public Library, 1964, Area udies and the Library, 1966, Deterioration and reservation of Library Materials, 1970, Printers and ublishers Devices, 1976, American Library History: 876-1976, 1976, At This Point in Time (verse), 1976;

mng. editor Library Quar, 1961-72, editor, 1979-84. Served with U.S. Army, 1942-44. Mem. ALA (mem. council 1956-60), Assn. of Am. Library Schs. (sec. 1953-56), Beta Phi Mu (internat. pres. 1977), Tau Kappa Alpha. Mem. United Protestant Ch. (chmn. bd. elders 1966-68). Club: Quadrangle (Chgo.). Home: North Manchester Ind. Died Mar. 5, 1995.

WINTER, ROLF GERHARD, physicist, educator; b. Dusseldorf, Germany, June 30, 1928; came to U.S., 1938, naturalized, 1944; s. Julius and Erika (Wolff) W.; m. Patricia Mae Saibel, Jan. 31, 1951; children: Erika Louise, Edward Paul Merritt, James Frederick. BS, Carnegie Mellon U., 1948, MS, 1951, DSc, 1952. Instr., then asst. prof. Western Res. U., 1951-54; asst. prof., then asso. prof. Pa. State U., 1954-64; prof. physics Coll. William and Mary, 1964-87, Chancellor prof. physics 1987-92, chmn. dept., 1966-72; dean of grad. studies Faculty of Arts and Scis., 1981-86; vis. physicist, vis. lectr. Carnegie Mellon U., 1955-56, Oxford (Eng.) U., 1961-62, U. Wis., summer 1963, U. Sask., summer 1976; Swiss Inst. Nuclear Research and U. Zurich, 1979-80, Oxford U., Eng., 1986-87, 91-92; cons. in field, 1955-92. Author: Quantum Physics, 1979, 2d edit., 1986; contbr. articles to profl. jours. Recipient Phi Beta Kappa chpt. faculty award for advancement scholarship, 1967; Knight of Mark Twain award, 1972. Fellow Am. Phys. Soc.; mem. AAUP (chpt. pres. 1975-76), Va. Acad. Sci. Home: Williamsburg Va. Died Dec. 21, 1992.

WINTGEN, DIETER, physicist educator. Prof. dept. physics U. Freiburg, Germany. Recipient Gustav Hertz Preis, Deutsche Physikalische Gesellschaft, 1993. Home: Freiburg Germany Died 1994.

WISHAM, LAWRENCE HERMAN, physician; b. N.Y.C., Jan. 17, 1918; s. William and Sarah (Kagan) W.; m. Shirley D. Schatz, Sept. 24, 1942; 1 dau., Elizabeth. B.S., N.Y. U., 1938; M.D., Chgo. Med. Sch., 1943. Resident Bronx VA Hosp. Phys. Medicine and Rehab., 1948-50; fellow Inst. Rehab. Medicine, 1950-51; dir. dept. phys. medicine and rehab. Brookdale Hosp., Bklyn., 1951-54; asso. dir. dept. rehab. medicine Mt. Sinai Hosp., N.Y.C., 1954-58; dir. Mt. Sinai Hosp., 1958-88; asst. clin. prof. rehab. medicine Columbia Coll. Phys. and Surg., 1956-66; prof. rehab. medicine, chmn. dept. Mt. Sinai Sch. Medicine, 1966-88, prof. emeritus, 1988-93; sr. cons. dept. rehab. medicine Bronx VA Hosp.; spl. research blood flow. Contbr. articles to profl. jours. Served to capt. M.C. AUS, 1944-46, PTO. Fellow Am. Acad. Phys. Medicine and Rehab., N.Y. Acad. Medicine; mem. N.Y. Soc. Phys. Medicine and Rehab. (pres. 1964-65). Home: New York N.Y. Died Dec. 12, 1993.

WITHEY, STEPHEN BASSETT, psychology educator, administrator; b. San Diego, Calif., May 24, 1918; s. Herbert Cookman and Ruth (Bassett) W.; m. Lois Cooley, Apr. 29, 1950; children: Peter B., Michael B. B.S., Asbury Coll., Wilmore, Ky., 1941; M.A., Northwestern U., 1947; postgrad., U. Wash.-Seattle, Seattle, 1947-48; Ph.D., U. Mich.-Ann Arbor, Ann Arbor, Mich., 1952. Program dir. Surbey Research Ctr., Ann Arbor, 1948-76; dir. Survey Research Ctr., Ann Arbor, 1977-82; with dept. psychology U. Mich., Ann Arbor, 1953—, prof., 1960—; research dir. Inst. Social Research, Ann Arbor, 1982—; staff dir. Nat. Assessment of Edn., N.Y.C., 1964-65, cons., 1966-71; chmn. com. on TV and social behavior Social Sci. Research Council, N.Y.C., 1973-77; cons. in field. Author: Big Business as the People See It, 1951, The United States and the United Nations, 1958, Social Indicators of Well Being in America, 1976, 78; author and editor: A Degree and What Else?, 1971. Pres. Ann Arbor Sch. Bd., 1961-67. Served to maj. U.S. Army, 1942-46. Fellow Am. Psychol. Assn.; mem. Am. Sociol. Assn., AAAS, World Future Soc., Sigma Xi, Phi Beta Kappa. Home: Ann Arbor Mich. Deceased.

WITKOP, CARL JACOB, educator, geneticist; b. East Grand Rapids, Mich., Dec. 27, 1920; s. Carl J. and Frances (Miller) W.; m. Mary Worcester, Sept. 3, 1946; children: Carl Gray, Mary Margaret, Martha Frances; m. Maryann Jacobson, Oct. 6, 1966; children: Andrea Jean, Steven Carl, Annake Karine. B.S., Mich. State Coll., 1944; D.D.S., U. Mich., 1949, M.S., 1954. Diplomate Am. Bd. Oral Pathology, (pres. 1985). Commd. asst. dental surgeon USPHS, 1949, advanced through grades to dental dir., 1961; dental officer Nat. Inst. Dental Research, 1950-54; chief human genetic br. Nat. Inst. Dental Research, Bethesda, Md., 1954-66; instr. med. genetics Georgetown U., 1959-65; chmn. div. genetics, prof. U. Minn. Dental Sch., 1966-93, prof. dermatology, 1971-92, prof. emeritus, 1992-93; dir. dermatology Childrens Hosp., Washington, 1955-93, Nat. Found., NIH. Author: Genetics and Dental Health, 1962, Albinism, 1971, (with J.J. Sauk, Jr.) Dental and Oral Manifestations of Hereditary Diseases, 1971. Fellow Am. Acad. Oral Pathology (pres. 1974), AAAS (chmn. sect. on dentistry); mem. ADA, Am. Soc. Human Genetics (sec. 1968-70), Am. Soc. Dermatopathology, Am. Soc. Dermatogenetics, Internat. Pigment Cell Soc. (bd. dirs. 1984-86), Nat. Orgn. for Albinism and Hypopigmentation (chmn. bd. sci. advisors 1984-93) Sigma Xi. Home: Hopkins Minn. Died Mar. 11, 1993.

WITT, ROBERT CHARLES, finance educator; b. Tyndall, S.D., Aug. 24, 1941; s. Emmanuel M. and

Hilda Veronica (Link) W.; m. Laura Gutierrez, May 21, 1974; 1 child, Kristina Monique. BA cum laude, BS with honors, U. S.D., 1964; MS in Actuarial Sci., U. Wis., 1966; MA in Econs., U. Pa., 1968, PhD in Bus. and Applied Econs., 1972. CLU. Teaching asst. U. Wis., Madison, 1965; instr. econs. Augustana Coll., Sioux Falls, S.D., 1965-66; instr. bus. stats. Temple U., Phila., 1969-70; prof. fin. U. Tex., Austin, 1970—; CBA Found. prof., 1980-82, Blades prof., 1982-86, Gus Wortham chaired prof., 1986—, chmn. fin. dept., 1984-88; vis. prof. fin. U. B.C., Vancouver, Can., 1979; advisor U.S. Senate Subcom. on Antitrust and Monopoly, 1969-70, Ill. Ins. Laws Study Commn., 1975-78, Tex. Legis., 1973—, Atty. Gen.'s Office, State of Tex., 1984, Tex. Gov.'s Office, 1989, Tex. Info. Inst., 1982-86, Houston Power and Light, 1989-90, State Bd. of Ins., 1990, 93, U.S. Justice Dept., 1991—, Constrn. Industry Inst., 1989—, Nat. Assn. Ind. Insurers, 1992-93, Tex. Pub. Policy Found., 1994—, also various ins. cos. Assoc. editor Jour. Risk and Ins., 1976-86, 90—, Benefits Quar., 1985-90, Jour. Fin. Svcs. and Rsch., 1989-94; contbg. editor Ins. Abstracts and Revs., 1982—; mem. rsch. and pub. adv. bd., referee Jour. Ins. Issues and Practices, 1977-88; contbr. articles to profl. jours. Bd. govs. Internat. Ins. Soc., 1981—, chmn. rsch. roundtable, 1984-89, chmn. acad. directorate, 1989-91, chmn. bd. moderators, 1991; mem. rsch. bd. S.S. Huebner Found. for Ins. Edn., Wharton Sch., U. Pa., 1983-90; chmn. doctoral awards coms. in bus. and ins. State Farm Cos. Found., 1989—; mem. bd. dirs. Tex. Property and Casualty Ins. Guaranty Assn., 1991-92. Grantee S.S. Huebner Found., Law Found. U. Tex., Ill. Legis., Grad. Sch. Bus. U. Tex., Tex. Atty. Gen., Tex. Legis., Tex. Gov.'s Office, 1989, Nat. Assn. Ind. Insurers, Constrn. Industry Inst., Tex. Pub. Policy Found., 1993-94, Texand for Lawsuit Reform, 1994. Mem. Am. Risk and Ins. Assn. (pres., bd. dirs. 1980-87, Outstanding Feature Aticle award 1974, 76, 85, 86, 93), S.S. Huebner Found. (adminstry. bd. 1987—), Am. Fin. Assn., Am. Econ. Assn., Fin. Mgmt. Assn., Risk Theory Seminar (chmn. 1977), Fin. Execs. Inst. (bd. dirs. 1992—). Home: Austin Tex. Died Feb., 1995.

WITTENMEYER, CHARLES E., lawyer; b. Centerville, Iowa, Sept. 3, 1903; s. Thomas William and Maggie E. (Lantz) W.; m. Dorothy P. Proctor, Mar. 4, 1931; 1 dau., Sheila JoAnn (Mrs. Floyd Darrell Goar). LL.B., Drake U., 1928, J.D. Bar: Iowa 1928, U.S. Supreme Ct 1957. Practiced in Mapleton, 1928-33; practiced in Davenport, 1933-94, city atty., 1944-54. Trustee Fejervary Home.; chmn. Scott County Young Republicans, 1934-36, 2d Dist. Young Reps., 1936-38; chmn. Scott County Rep. Central Com., 1938-56; chmn. Rep. City Central Com., 1944-57, 1st Dist. chmn., 1952-56, Rep. nat. committeeman from, Iowa, 1956-75; del. Rep. Nat. Conv., 1944, 56, 60, 64, 68, 72, chmn. credentials com., 1964, chmn. com. rules and order bus., 1968; pres. Davenport Jaycees. 1936. Mem. SAR, ABA, Iowa Bar Assn. (life), Scott County Bar Assn., Iowa Hist. Soc. (life), Davenport C. of C. (past treas., past dir.), Iowa Farm Bur. Assn., Gen. Soc. War 1812, Masons, Shriners, Davenport Club, Hi-12 Club, Phi Alpha Delta, Phi Gamma Lambda, Theta Nu Epsilon, Helmet and Spurs. Methodist (past trustee ch.). Home: Davenport Iowa Died Aug. 9, 1994.

WITTER, THOMAS WINSHIP, investment banker, broker; b. Oakland, Calif., Nov. 12, 1928; s. Jean C. and Catherine (Maurer) W.; m. Barbara Rogers, June 22, 1951; children—Jane, Susan, Nancy, Barbara, Thomas. B.S., U. Calif. at Berkeley, 1951. Account exec. Dean Witter & Co., San Francisco, 1953-58, ptnr., 1958-68, exec. v.p., 1968—. Hon. dir. Samuel Merritt Hosp., Oakland; regent U. Pacific. Served to 1st lt. USMC, 1951-53. Mem. Bond Club San Francisco, Guardsmen. Clubs: Pacific-Union (San Francisco), Olympic (San Francisco), Bohemian (San Francisco); Claremont Country (Oakland). Home: Piedmont Calif. Died Sept. 23, 1992.

WOELFFER, ELMER AUGUST, veterinarian; b. Waterloo, Wis., Dec. 18, 1897; s. Fredrick G. Woelffer and Bertha E. Huefner; m. Marian Avis Spencer, Dec. 9., 1933; children: Judith, Nancy, Linda. BS, U. Wis., 1922; DVM, Cornell U., 1931. Diplomate Am. Coll. Theriogenologists. Farms mgr. H.P. Hood and Sons, 1931-47; prof. Vet. Coll., Champaign, Ill., 1947-50; v.p. Pabst Farms, Oconomowoc, Wis., 1950-52; cons. bovine reproduction Oconomowoc, 1952-95. Mem. Wis. Vet. Med. Assn., Rotary, Masons, Wis. Holstein Assn. Waukesha County Holstein Assn. Home: Oconomowoc Wis. Died May 8, 1995.

WOLFBERG, DENNIS ALAN, comedian; b. N.Y.C., Mar. 29, 1946; s. Sidney Louis and Frances (Schimmelman) W.; m. Jean Marie McBride, Sept. 8, 1985; children: Daniel Joseph, Matthew James, David Alan. BA, Queens Coll., 1967; MA in Edn. Psychology, St. Johns U., 1974. Tchr. N.Y.C. Bd. Edn., 1967-79; comedian, 1979-94. Recipient Am. Comedy award Acad. Am. Comedy, 1990. Home: Culver City Calif. Died Oct. 3, 1994.

WOLFE, JOHN F., publishing executive. Pub., pres. CEO Columbus (Ohio) Dispatch Mag. Home: Columbus Ohio Died June 10, 1994.

WOLFE, JOHN WALTON, investment banker; b. Columbus, Ohio, Sept. 4, 1928; s. Edgar T. and Alice (Alcorn) W.; m. Norina Vannucci, July 20, 1978; children by previous marriage: Ann M., Robert F., Victoria G., Douglas B. Student, Miami U., Oxford, Ohio, 1946-47. With Ohio Nat. Bank of Columbus, 1948-57; v.p. BancOhio Corp. (bank holding co.), Columbus, 1957-74, also dir.; chmn. bd. Ohio Co., Columbus, 1974—, also dir.; chmn. bd. Dispatch Printing Co., 1975-94; bd. dirs. Columbus Found., RadiOhio Inc., AgLands, WBNS-TV Inc., VideoIndiana Inc., Ohio Equities Inc., Taylor-Woodcraft Inc. Pres. Wolfe Associated Inc., charitable found., Columbus; mem. Ohio Cancer Found.; chmn. Coalition for Cost Effective Health Services. Mem. Nat. Assn. Security Dealers. Clubs: Athletic of Columbus, Buckeye Lake Yacht, Columbus, Columbus Country, Columbus Maennerchor, Muirfield Village Golf, Nat. Press, Press of Columbus. Lodges: Masons, Shriners. Home: Columbus Ohio Died June 10, 1994.

WOLFE, SAMUEL, medical educator; b. Toronto, Ont., Can., June 25, 1923; came to U.S., 1968; s. Louis and Freda (Winograd) W.; m. Mary Vivian Money Wolfe, June 4, 1950; children; Ruth Rebecca, Deborah, Naomi, Lewis Emmanuel. MD, Toronto U., 1950; MPH, Columbia U., 1960, DrPH, 1961. Diplomate Am. Bd. Preventive Medicine. Country doctor, coroner Rural Med. Officer, Saskatchewan, Can., 1951-58; commr. Med. Care Ins. Commn., Saskatchewan, Can., 1962-66; dir. Community Health Svcs., Saskatoon, Can., 1962-68, Health Svcs., Meharry Med. Coll., Nashville, 1968-73; prof. SUNY, Stony Brook, 1973-75; prof. pub. health Columbia U. Sch. Pub. Health, N.Y.C., 1975-91, prof. emeritus pub. health, 1992; cons. Ministry of Health, Teheran, Iran, 1975, Ministry of Health, Kuwait, 1983, Nat. Ctr. Health Svc. Rsch., various locations, 1969-73, 79; pres. Pub. Health Assn. N.Y.C., 1979-80. Co-author: (with R. F. Badgley) Doctors' Strike, 1967, 2d. edit. 1971, The Family Doctor, 1973; editor: Organization of Health Workers and Labor Conflict; contbr. articles to profl. jours. Chmn. Coalition for a Rational Health Policy, N.Y.C., 1979-80; mem. Mayor's Task Force on Pub. Hosps., N.Y.C., 1976. With Royal Can. Army Med. Corps., 1942-45. Rockefeller Found. fellow, N.Y.C., 1959-61; Nat. Ctr. Health Svcs. Rsch. grantee, 1970-77; recipient Haven Emerson medal Pub. Health Assn. N.Y.C., 1981. Fellow Am. Pub. Health Assn. (governing coun. 1986-91), Am. Coll. Preventive Medicine, N.Y. Acad. Medicine. New Democratic Party (Can.). Jewish. Home: Hackensack N.J. Deceased.

WOLFE, WARREN DWIGHT, lawyer; b. Boston, July 30, 1926; s. Louis Julius and Rose (Daniels) W.; m. Caroline M. DuMont, Dec. 29, 1973. B.S. in Journalism, Northwestern U., 1949; M. Internat. Affairs, Columbia U., 1951; J.D. with high honors, U. Toledo, 1959. Bar: Ohio 1959, Mich. 1960. Reporter Wilmington Record, Del., 1951-52; Sunday editor, asst. news editor Middletown Jour., Ohio, 1952-55; copy reader, sect. editor Toledo Blade, 1955-60; assoc. Bugbee & Conkle, Toledo, 1960-64; ptnr. Bugbee & Conkle, 1964-88; of counsel Fuller & Henry, Toledo, 1988-94. Pres. Health Planning Assn. N.W. Ohio, 1970-73; mem. comprehensive health planning adv. coun. Ohio Dept. Health, 1972-75; mem. Ohio Gov.'s Task Force on Health, 1973-74, Lucas County Health Planning Study Com., 1985-94; bd. dirs. N.W. Oho Health Planning, Inc., 1992-94; trustee Toledo Legal Aid Soc., 1968-94, pres., 1973-75; trustee Lucas County unit Am. Cancer Soc., 1964-94, v.p., 1976-81, pres., 1981-83, trustee Ohio div., 1969-70, 85-94, mem. exec. com., 1991-93; mem. sch. mandate study com. Corp. for Effective Govt., 1994-94. With USNR, 1944-46. Mem. ABA, Ohio Bar Assn., Lucas County Bar Assn. (pres. 1966), Toledo Bar Assn. (exec. com. 1969-75), State Bar Mich., Am. Trial Lawyers Assn., Law Alumni Assn. U. Toledo Coll. Law (pres. 1965), Sigma Delta Chi. Club: Toledo Ski (treas. 1972-75, pres. 1975-76). Lodge: Masons. Home: Toledo Ohio Died Nov. 1994.

WOLFF, SHELDON MALCOLM, physician; b. Newark, Aug. 19, 1930; s. Harold D. and Margaret (Turen) W.; m. Lila Leff, May 30, 1956; children: Steven B., Suzanne M., Daniel S. BS, U. Ga., 1952; MD, Vanderbilt U., 1957; D honoris causa, Fed. U., Rio de Janeiro, 1976; DSc honoris causa, Tufts U., 1993, Brandeis U., 1993. Diplomate Am. Bd. Internal Medicine. Clin. assoc. Lab. Clin. Investigation, Nat. Inst. Allergy and Infectious Diseases, NIH, Bethesda, Md., 1960-62; sr. investigator Lab. Clin. Investigation, Nat. Inst. Allergy and Infectious Diseases, NIH, 1963-64, head clin. physiology, 1964-68, clin. dir. and chief, 1968-77; Endicott prof., chmn. dept. medicine Sch. Medicine Tufts U., Boston, 1977—; physician-in-chief New Eng. Med. Center, 1977—. Contbr. chpts. to textbooks, articles to profl. jours. With USPHS, 1960-64, 75-77. Recipient Squibb award, 1976, John R. Phillips award, 1987, Bristol award, 1992, Biomed. Rsch. award Assn. Am. Med. Colls., 1992. Fellow AAAS, ACP (master), Infectious Disease Soc. Am. (pres. 1981), Assn. Am. Physicians, Am. Soc. for Clin. Investigation, Am. Fedn. Clin. Rsch., Am. Clin. and Climatol. Assn., Am. Assn. Immunologists, Assn. Profs. Medicine (Chmn. of Yr. award 1992), Reticulo-Endothelial Soc., Soc. for Exptl. Biology and Medicine, Inst. Medicine, Am. Acad. Arts and Sci., Am. Bd. Internal Medicine (mem. bd. 1976-89, chmn. 1988-89). Home: Wellesley Mass.

WOLFMAN JACK (ROBERT WESTON SMITH), radio personality; b. Bklyn., Jan. 21, 1938; s. Anson Weston and Rosmond (Small) S.; m. Lou Lamb, May 5, 1961; children: Joy Rene, Tod Weston. Grad. high sch., L.I., N.Y.; 1st class lic., Nat. Acad. Broadcasting, Washington. Radio personality, salesman, sta. mgr. Universal Broadcasting, Shreveport, La. and Mpls.; radio personality, salesman, owner U.S. rights Sta. XERF, Del Rio, Tex., 1961-65; radio personality, sta. mgr., owner U.S. rights Sta. XERB, Rosarito Beach, Calif., 1966-71; radio personality Armed Forces Radio, 1970-86, Sta. KDAY, Los Angeles, 1971-73, Sta. WNBC, N.Y.C., 1973-74, 1976-77; first English-speaking radio personality in Japan Sta. FM-Tokyo, 1975-77; radio personality syndicated on 2,177 stations in 53 fgn. countries, 1973—; tv personality-host The Midnight Special, L.A., 1973-82, The Wolfman Jack Show, 24 countries and U.S., 1978-79, The Disco Awards Special, 1979; appears as actor 26 U.S. network tv shows, 1974—; tv personality-host The Rock'N' Roll Palace, 1988—. Appeared in films American Graffiti, 1973, Hanging on a Star, 1976, Dead Man's Curve, 1977, Motel Hell, 1980, Mortuary Academy, 1987; author: Have Mercy!, 1995, (with Byron Laursen) Have Mercy--Confessions of the Original Rock 'n' Roll Animal. Mem. AFTRA, SAG, AGVA, Alliance Can. Cinema, TV and Radio Artists, Rhythm and Blues Found. Republican. Episcopalian. Died July 1, 1995.

WOLFSON, RICHARD FREDERICK, lawyer; b. N.Y.C., Jan. 7, 1923; s. William Leon and Gertrude (Quitman) W.; m. Elaine Cecile Reinherz, June 6, 1954; children: Lisa Reinherz Hess, Paul Reinherz Quitman. B.S., Harvard U., 1942; LL.B., Yale U., 1944. Bar: N.Y. 1945, Fla. 1956. Law clk. to judge U.S. Ct. Appeals 2d Circuit, 1944-45, Justice Wiley Rutledge, U.S. Supreme Ct., Washington, 1945-47; ptnr. Kurland & Wolfson, N.Y.C., 1947-50; assoc. Milton Pollock, N.Y.C., 1950-52; gen. counsel, exec. v.p. Wometco Enterprises, Miami, Fla., 1952-81; ptnr. Stroock & Stroock & Lavan, Miami, Fla., 1982-84; of counsel Kreeger & Kreeger, Miami, Fla., 1985-88, Valdes-Fauli, Cobb, Bischoff & Kriss, Miami, Fla., 1988—; mem. Fla. Bar Commn. on Merit Retention of Judges, 1981; past pres. Ransom-Everglades Sch.; bd. dirs. Ea. Nat. Bank, PMC Capital Inc. Author: (with Kurland) Jurisdiction of the Supreme Court of the United States, 1951; contbr. articles to profl. jours., poetry. Bd. dirs. Miami Philharm. Soc., past pres.; bd. dirs. Opera Guild Greater Miami, treas., chmn. fin. com.; del. givering coun. Am. Jewish Congress, pres. S.E. chpt.; mem. exec.com. Fla. region NCCJ, 1994; trustee Fla. Internat. U. Found. Guggenheim fellow, 1949-50; recipient Disting. Community Service award NCCJ, 1982. Mem. ABA, Dade County Bar Assn., Fla. State Assn., N.Y. State Bar Assn., City Club (Miami), Harvard Club (Miami, N.Y.C.). Democrat. Jewish. Home: Miami Fla. Died Nov. 9, 1994.

WOLKIN, PAUL ALEXANDER, lawyer, former institute executive; b. Phila., Oct. 14, 1917; s. Alex and Anna (Friedman) W.; stepson Rebecca (Likalter) W.; m. Martha Kessler, June 25, 1944 (dec. Dec. 1992); children: Rachel, Adam; m. Diana S. Burgwyn, Dec. 23, 1994. B.A., U. Pa., 1937, M.A., 1938, J.D., 1941. Bar: Pa. 1942, U.S. Supreme Ct. 1947. Law clk. U.S. Ct. Appeals (3d Cir.), Phila., 1942-44; atty. Fgn. Econ. Adminstrn., Washington, 1944-45; asso. gen. counsel French Supply Council, Washington, 1945-46; asst. legal adviser Dept. State, 1946-47; legis. draftsman Phila. Charter Commn., 1948-51; spl. asst. to Phila. Solicitor, 1951; partner firm Wolkin, Sarner & Cooper, Phila., 1951-66; counsel Sarner, Cooper & Stein, Phila., 1966-69, Hudson, Wilf & Kronfeld, Phila., 1971-78, Rawle & Henderson, 1980-81; asst. dir. Am. Law Inst., Phila., 1947-77, exec. v.p., 1977-93, sec., 1979-92, exec. v.p. emeritus, coun., 1993-95; exec. dir. com. on continuing profl. edn. Am. Law Inst.-ABA, 1963-93; sec. permanent editorial bd. Uniform Comml. Code, 1962-93, sec. emeritus, 1993-95; mem. com. specialized pers. Dept. Labor, 1964-69; dir. Pub. Svc. Satellite Consortium, 1980-84. Editor: The Practical Lawyer, 1955-92, founding editor, 1993-95; contbr. articles to profl. jours. Pres. Phila. Child Guidance Center, 1966-72. Recipient Rawle award, 1993. Fellow Am. Bar Found. (life); mem. ABA (spl. com. on standards and codes 1974-80), Am. Law Inst. (coun. 1992-95), Am. Judicature Soc., Jud. Conf. 3d Cir. U.S., Pa. Bar Assn., Phila. Bar Assn. (chair sr. lawyers com. 1994-95), Pa. Bar Inst. (bd. dirs. 1967-75), Order of Coif, Scribes (past pres.). Home: Philadelphia Pa. Died Nov. 9, 1995.

WOMACK, SHARON GENNELLE, librarian; b. Flora, Ill. Dir. Ariz. Libr., Archives and Pub. Records Dept., Phoenix, 1979-93. Died Jan. 28, 1993. Home: Phoenix Ariz.

WOOD, EVELYN NIELSEN, reading dynamics business executive; b. Logan, Utah, Jan. 8, 1909; d. Elias and Rose (Stirland) Nielsen; m. Myron Douglas Wood, June 12, 1929 (dec. May 1987); 1 child, Carolyn Wood Evans. BA, U. Utah, 1929, MA, 1947; postgrad., Columbia U., 1956-57. Tchr. Weber Coll., Ogden, Utah, 1931-32; girls counselor Jordan High Sch., Sandy, Utah, 1948-57, tchr. jr. and sr. high schs., 1948-59; instr. U. Utah, 1957-59; founder, originator Evelyn Wooc Reading Dynamics, 1959-95; tchr. rapid reading U Del., 1961; guest lectr. NEA, 1961, Internat. Reading Assn., Tex. Christian U., 1962; faculty Brigham Young U., research specialist for reading, 1973-74. Author conductor radio programs, 1947; author: (With Marjory Barrows) Reading Skills, 1958, A Breakthrough in Reading, 1961, A New Approach to Speed Reading 1962, Speed Reading for Comprehension, 1962, also articles. Died Aug. 26, 1995.

WOOD, WILLIAM PHILLER, lawyer; b. Bryn Mawr Pa., Oct. 3, 1927; s. Clement Biddle and Emily (Philler W.; m. Maud Isabel Atherton, Dec. 30, 1950 (dec 1976); children: William P., Maude H., Louisa B.; m. 2 Sara Elizabeth Wadsworth, Mar. 19, 1977; stepchildren Jeremy B. Grace Eric W. Grace. A.B., Harvard U. 1949, J.D., 1955. Bar: Pa. 1956. Assoc. firm Morgan Lewis & Bockius, Phila., 1955-64; ptnr. Morgan, Lewi & Bockius, 1964-91, counsel, 1991-95; bd. dirs. McArdl Desco Corp., New Castle, Del. Trustee Grundy Foun. Bristol, Pa., 1980-96, chmn., 1993-95; trustee Genese Valley Conservancy, 1990-96, pres., 1992-96; pres. Phila Mus. of Art, 1976-80, chmn. exec. com., 1980-96, v.p 1972-76, treas., 1968-72; trustee Fairmount Park Ar Assn., 1972-96, v.p., 1985-96; trustee Louis L. Sto Found., Phila., 1969-94, Bryn Mawr Hosp., 1962-76 Phila. Lyric Opera Co., 1960-70; treas. Phila. Art Al liance, 1960-66; pres. La Napoule (France) Art Found Henry Clews Meml., 1984-86, chmn. 1986-96. Served t 1st lt. U.S. Army, 1950-52. Mem. ABA, Pa. Bar Assn Clubs: Phila., State-in-Schuykill, Knickerbocker. Home Chatham Pa. Died Feb. 24, 1996.

WOODALL, NORMAN EUGENE, banker; b. Miss June 10, 1916; s. Albert Edward and Annie (Smith) W m. Virginia Dale Willard, Aug. 12, 1967. BSBA, Miss State U., 1939; postgrad., Am. Inst. Banking, 1962 grad., Sch. Banking of South, La. State U., 1964, Ad vanced Inf. Sch., 1959, Command and Gen. Staff Coll 1965, Indsl. Coll. Armed Forces, 1970. Adjuste Comml. Credit Co., Jackson, Miss., 1939-41; loan ex aminer RFC, Birmingham, Ala., 1946-55; sr. v.p. Firs Nat. Bank Birmingham, 1955-95. Bd. dirs. Birminghar chpt. ARC, 1974-78; treas. Muscular Dystrophy Assn Jefferson County Chpt., 1958, pres. 1959-60. Served t col., infantry AUS, 1941-46, ret. 1972. Decorate Bronze Star with V devise, Legion of Merit. Mem. Re Officers Assn., Assn. U.S. Army, Am. Inst. Banking Miss. State U. Alumni Assn., Birmingham C. of C. S.P in State of Ala. (treas. 1990-91, v.p. 1992-93, pres. 199 94), Ams. Royal Descent, Sovereign Colonial Soc Newcomen Soc. N.Am., Magna Carta Barons, Coloni Order of the Crown, Birmingham Exch. Club (bd. gov 1960-62, 71-72, 75-76, v.p. 1973-74, pres. 1974-75 Vestavia Club (Vestavia Hills, Ala.), The Club, Sigm Chi. Home: Birmingham Ala. Died June 15, 1995.

WOODBRIDGE, HENRY SEWALL, managemer consultant; b. N.Y.C., Sept. 20, 1906; s. George an Harriet (Manley) W.; m. Dorothy Steese White, Jan. 1928 (dec. May 1981); children: Henry Sewall, Anr Sidney (Mrs. William Pickford), Victoria (Mrs. Richar G. Hall). Student, Harvard U., 1923-26. With Stone Webster, Inc., 1926-27; gen. mgr., dir. Raymon Whitcomb, Inc., 1927-40; bus. mgr., asst. to pu Boston Evening Transcript, 1940-41; former v.p. An Optical Co., Southbridge, Mass.; dir. Am. Optical Co 1941-77; pres. Todd-AO Corp., N.Y.C., 1954-58; fi and mgmt. cons., 1958-95; chmn. bd. True Temp Corp., 1960-66, pres., 1964-65; cons. Editoria Gui LTB SA, Rio de Janeiro and São Paulo, Brazil, 1966-8 Barwick Industries, 1967-95, Internat. Horizons, Inc 1975-85, Learning Techs., Inc., 1985-95; pres., mng. di Hillwood Corp., 1966-84; dir.; bd. dirs. Hambro An Bank & Trust Co., Vesper Corp., Union Labor Life In Co. Chmn., Sch. Bldg. Com. Pomfret (Conn.), 1943-4 58-60; mem. Fin. Com. Brookline (Mass.), 1936-3 chmn. Fire, Safety, Pub. Welfare Sub-Com., 1938-3 mem. Conn. Devel. Commn., 1948-55; industry re Nat. War Labor Bd., 1942-45; mem. safety equipme adv. com. WPB, 1942-46; trustee Old Sturbridge Villag 1941-95, chmn., 1965-66; trustee Middlesex Sch., Da Kimball Hosp. Mem. Indsl. Relations Research Assn New Eng. Soc. N.Y. (pres. 1962-65), Soc. Cincinnati State of N.H. (pres. 1989-92). Episcopalian. Club Harvard U., Union (N.Y.C.); Harvard U., Tavern (Bo ton); Harvard U. Faculty (Cambridge, Mass.); Me Cosmos (Washington). Home: Pomfret Conn. Di Nov. 2, 1995.

WOODCOCK, GEORGE, author; b. Winnipeg, Ma Can., May 8, 1912; s. Samuel Arthur and Margar Gertrude (Lewis) W.; m. Ingeborg Hedwig Elisabe Linzer, Feb. 10, 1949. Student, Morley Coll., Londo LLD, U. Victoria, U. Winnipeg; DLitt, Sir George W liams U., U. Ottawa, U. B.C. Broadcaster contb several hundred talks and scripts of plays and doc mentaries to CBC programs; editor of Now, 1940-4 profl. writer, 1946-95; first in Eng. to 1949 and aft wards in Can.; faculty U. Wash., 1954-55; asso. pr English U. B.C., Vancouver, 1956-63; lectr. Asi studies U. B.C., 1963-95; editor Canadian Lit., 1959-7 Author: The White Island, 1940, The Centre Cann Hold, 1943, William Godwin, A Biography, 1946, T Incomparable Aphra: A Life of Mrs. Aphra Behn, 19 The Writer and Politics, 1948, Imagine the South, 1 The Paradox of Oscar Wilde, 1950, A Hundred Years olution: 1848 and After, 1948, The Letters of rles Lamb, 1950, The Anarchist Prince, 1950 (later s. into French), Ravens and Prophets: Travels in stern Canada, 1952, Pierre-Joseph Proudhon, 1956, the City of the Dead: Travels in Mexico, 1956, Incas Other Men: Travels in Peru, 1959, Anarchism, 2, Faces of India, 1964, Asia, Gods and Cities, 1966, Greeks in India, 1966, A Choice of Critics, 1966, Crystal Spirit, 1966 (Gov. Gen. award for Eng. n-fiction), Kerala, 1967, Selected Poems, 1967, The ukhobors, 1968, Canada and the Canadians, 1969, Hudson's Bay Company, 1970, Odysseus Ever urning, 1970, Gandhi, 1971 (U. B.C. medal), Dawn the Darkest Hour: A Study of Aldous Huxley, 2, Herbert Read, The Stream and the Source, 1972, Rejection of Politics, 1972, Who Killed the British pire?, 1974, Amor de Cosmos, 1975, Gabriel mont, 1975 (U. B.C. medal), Notes on Visitations, 6, South Sea Journey, 1976, Peoples of the Coast, 7, Thomas Merton, Monk and Poet, 1978, Faces n History, 1978, The Kestrel and Other Poems, 8, The Canadians, 1979, The World of Canadian iting, 1980, The George Woodcock Reader, 1980, Mountain Road, 1981, Taking it to the Letter, 1, Confederation Betrayed, 1981, Ivan Eyre, 1981, Benefactor, 1982, Letter to the Past, 1982, Collected ms, 1983; British Columbia, a Celebration, 1983, well's Message: 1984 and the Present, 1984, Strange fellows: The State and the Arts in Canada, 1985, Walls of India, 1985, The University of British umbia, 1986, Northern Spring, 1987, Beyond the e Mountain, 1987, The Social History of Canada, 8, Caves in the Desert, 1988, The Marvelous Cen- y, 1988, Powers of Observation, 1989: The Century at Made Us, 1989, British Columbia: A History of Province, 1990, Tolstoy at Yasnaya Polyana and er poems, 1991, The Monk and his Message, 1992, archism and Anarchists, 1992, Power To Us All!, 2, Letter from the Khyber Pass, 1993, George odcock's Introduction to Canadian Poetry, 1993, orge Woodcock's Introduction to Canadian Fiction, 3, The Cherry Tree on Cherry Street and Other ms, 1994, Walking Through the Valley, 1994. cipient Gov. Gen.'s award, 1966, Molson prize, 1973, n. Author's award, 1989; Can. Coun. Travel grantee, 1, 63, 65; Guggenheim fellow, 1951-52, Can. Govt. erseas fellow, 1957-58, Can. Coun. Killam fellow, 70-71, Can. Coun. Sr. Arts fellow, 1975, 78; named eman of City of Vancouver, 1994. Home: Vancouver n. Died Jan. 28, 1995.

OODEN, HOWARD EDMUND, museum director, researcher; b. Balt., Oct. 10, 1919; s. Howard mund and Maria (Barth) W.; m. Virginia Irene rkert, 1941; children: Virginia Lee Wooden Hyde, ward E. BS, Johns Hopkins U., 1946, MA, 1948. tr., dir. edn. St. Paul's Sch., Balt., 1942-50; instr. art Evansville (Ind.), 1953-63; assoc. prof. U. Fla., inesville, 1963-66; mus. dir. Sheldon Swope Art Mus., rre Haute, Ind., 1966-75; mus. dir. Wichita (Kans.) t Mus., 1975-89, dir. emeritus, 1989-95; cons. exhbn. or, numerous locations, 1956-86; art tour guide Eng., ance, Italy, Greece, Germany, U.S.A., 1965-95; assoc. of. Ind. State U., Terre Haute, 1968-75; lectr. Wichita te U., 1980-81. Author: Architectural Heritage of ansville, 1962, Edward Laning-American Realist, 06-81, 1982, Art of the Great Depression, 1985, The- ore Roszak: The Early Works, 1929-43, 1986, Col- ted Essays on 101 Art Works, 1988, Billy Morrow ckson: Interpretations of Time and Light, 1990; co- thor: Aaron Bohrod: Figure Sketches, 1990; contbr. merous articles to profl. publs.; author art catalogues. ulbright teaching fellow Athens (Greece) Coll., 1951- ; research grantee NIH, 1955-65; recipient Gari elchers Meml. medal Artist's Fellowship, Inc., Y.C., 1987. Mem. Internat. Coun. Museums, Am. sn. Mus., Assn. Art Mus. Dirs., Coll. Art Assn Am. emocrat. Mem. Anglican Ch. Home: Wichita Kans. ed Apr. 28, 1995.

OODS, JOHN LUCIUS, management consultant; b. ford, Ohio, Feb. 18, 1912; s. George B. and Helen mith) W.; m. Mary Torkilson, Apr. 2, 1938; children: omas George, Judith Ann, Jean Katharine, John anklin. Student, Am. U., 1929-31; B.S., Northwes- n U., 1933. C.P.A., Ill., Wash., D.C. Asst. cashier ackubin, Legg & Co., 1933-34; accountant Arthur ndersen & Co., 1934-42; office mgr. Bauer & Black, 42-44; controller Amphenol Corp., Broadview, Ill., 44-55; v.p. finance and adminstrn., dir., mem. exec. m. Amphenol Corp., 1955-68; v.p. finance Bunker amo Corp. (combination Amphenol Corp. and Bunker amo Corp.), 1968-71; mgmt. cons. Chgo., 1971-94; dir. ower Products Inc., Valuation Counselors, Inc.; dir., eas. Power Packaging, Inc., 1971-74; pub., dir. orthview (Ill.) Pub. Co., 1950-53; pres., dir. Borg In- estment Co., 1964-71. Author: Ancestry of John L. oods, 1988, Woods-Peden Genealogy, 1991. Mem. lenview Sch. Bd., 1945-51; commr., v.p. Glenview Park d., 1953-60; pres. Northfield Twp. High Sch. Bd. Edn., 47-51, Glen Oak Acres Community Assn., 1947-48. em. Fin. Execs. Inst., Am. Inst. Accts., Ill. Soc. PAs, Am. Mgmt. Assn., Newcomen Soc. N.Am., hgo. Dist. Golf Assn. (dir., treas. 1971-84), Soc. of ayflower Descendants. Republican. Clubs: Mid-Day hgo.), Executives (Chgo.), Union League (Chgo.), conomic (Chgo.); Knollwood (Lake Forest) (pres. 970-73); Wall Street (N.Y.C.). Home: Lincolnshire Ill. Died Aug. 22, 1994; interred Meml. Park Cemetery, Skokie, Ill.

WOODSIDE, ROBERT HANKS, retired banker, financial consulting company executive; b. Perryville, Md., Apr. 8, 1923; s. Amos Harris and Minnie (Milly) W.; m. Gloria D. Nicholson, Sept. 3, 1949; children: Robert H., J. Stephen, John T., Christine G., Anne E. B.S., Temple U., 1947; grad., Stonier Grad. Sch. Banking, 1958. Sr. v.p. Princeton Bank & Trust subs. Horizon Bancorp., Morristown, N.J., 1971-85; owner Worldwide Athletics of Princeton, Inc., Princeton, N.J., R.H.W. Assocs., fin. cons. co.; past dir. Nat. Comml. Finance Conf. Inc.; past instr. Rider Coll. Evening Eve. Sch. Served as ensign USNR, World War II. Mem. Robert Morris Assocs., Sigma Phi Epsilon. Episcopalian. Club: Springdale Golf (Princeton). Home: Princeton N.J. Died Mar. 5, 1995.

WOODWARD, ANNE SPIVEY, museum director; b. Atlanta, Apr. 4, 1949; d. Albert Guy and Jane Davidson (Knapp) S.; m. Roland Henry Woodward, Aug. 11, 1973; children: Elizabeth Rebecca, Hannah Carlisle, Sarah Margaret. BA, Mount Holyoke Coll, 1971; MA, U. Del., 1973. Cert. Mus. Studies. Curatorial cons. Valley Forge (Pa.) State Pk., 1973-76; curatorial cons. Pa. Hist. & Mus. Commn., Harrisburg, 1976-77, field curator, 1977-80; site adminstr. Brandywine Battlefield, Chadds Ford, Pa., 1985-89; mus. dir. Hist. Soc. Del., Wilmington, 1989-96; lectr. in field. Producer: (video) Opening the Door to Freedom,1990. Mem. Am. Assn. Museums, Am. Assn. for State and Local History. Mem. Soc. of Friends. Home: West Chester Pa. Died Apr. 30, 1996.

WOODWARD, MARION KENNETH, lawyer; b. Amarillo, Tex., Apr. 15, 1912; s. Sidney Marion and Lena May (Hicks) W.; m. Maurine Roberta Wallingford, May 31, 1938; 1 child, M. Kenneth Jr. BA, U. Tex., 1933; MA, West Tex. State U., 1940; LLB, U. Tex., 1943. Bar: Tex. 1942. Staff atty. Phillips Petroleum Co., Amarillo, 1945-46; assoc. prof. U. Tex. Law Sch., Austin, 1946-50; prof. U. Tex. Law Sch., 1950-61, Robt. F. Windfohr prof., 1961-82, Robt. F. Windfohr prof. Emeritus, from 1982. Co-author: (with Ernest E. Smith) Probate & Decedents' Estates, 1972, (with William O. Huie & Ernest E. Smith) Oil and Gas Law, 1972, (with Robert Hobbs) Texas Land Titles, 1977; author: (vol 12) West Texas Forms, 1980. With U.S. Army, 1943-45. Named Sterling Fellow Yale U., 1949-50. Fellow Am. Bar Found., acad. fellow Am. Coll. of Probate Counsel; mem. ABA, Tex. Bar Assn., Travis County Bar Assn. Episcopalian. Home: Austin Tex. Deceased.

WOOLF, ROBERT GARY, lawyer; b. South Portland, Maine, Feb. 15, 1928; s. Joseph Rubin and Anna Rose (Glovsky) W.; m. Anne Joy Passman, June 2, 1963; children: Stacey Lee, Gary Evan, Tiffany Jill. A.B., Boston Coll., 1949; J.D., Boston U., 1952; LLD (hon.), Western State U., 1986. Practice law specializing in representation of profl. athletes and entertainers Boston, 1954; mem. NFL Agts. Adv. com. Author: Behind Closed Doors, 1976, Friendly Persuasion, 1990; columnist Nat. Law Jour. Mem. exec. com. Boston coun. Boy Scouts Am., pres.'s coun. Franklin Pierce Coll., Boston U. Nat. Alumni Coun.; dir. Am. Cancer Soc. Boston, U.S. Com. Sports for Israel, Hedwig Yastrzemski Scholarship Fund; bd. dirs. St. Jude's Hosp. Found., Mass. Repertory Co.; trustee Basketball Hall of Fame; chmn. Bob Woolf Am. Internat. YMCA Invitational Basketball Tournament, Jerusalem, (hon.) Juvenile Diabetes Found.; appointed spl. advisor Pres. Reagan's Coun. Phys. Fitness and Sports, 1984. Served with AUS, 1952-54. Recipient Citation of Merit for contribution to sports Commonwealth of Mass., 1974, 84, Masada award State of Israel, 1974, Sportsman of Yr. award B'nai B'rith Temple Emanuel, Newton, Mass., 1983, Temple Emeth, Brookline, Mass., 1984, Boston U. Alumni award, 1985, Boston U. Sch. of Law 's Silver Shingle award, 1987; inducted into Maine Sports Hall of Fame, 1986. Mem. ABA (governing com. on sports and entertainment industries), Comml. Panel of Arbitrators. of Am. Arbitration Assn., Sports Lawyers Assn., Mass. Bar Assn., Mass. Trial Lawyers' Assn., Masons, Shriners, N.Y. Friars Club. Club: Mason (Shriner). Home: Chestnut Hill Mass. Died November 29, 1993.

WOOLFENDEN, WILLIAM EDWARD, art administrator and historian; b. Detroit, June 27, 1918; s. Frederick and Clara (Mackie) W. M.A., Wayne State U., 1942. Asst. curator Am. art Detroit Inst. Arts, 1945-49, dir. edn., 1949-60; asst. dir. Archives Am. Art, Detroit, 1960-62; dir. Archives Am. Art, Smithsonian Instn., N.Y.C., 1962-83; dir. emeritus Archives Am. Art, Smithsonian Instn., 1983-95; mem. spl. faculty Wayne State U., 1945-60; mem. vis. com. Slide and Photograph Dept. Met. Mus. Art; cons. Mus. Services Sothebys. Recipient Alumni award Wayne State U., 1968. Mem. Am. Assn. Mus. Home: Southbury Conn. Died July 19, 1995.

WOOTEN, LOUIS ERNEST, consulting engineer; b. Edgecombe County, N.C., Jan. 22, 1894; s. Amos Monroe and Amanda Millicent (Lewis) W.; m. Edith Rembert Williamson, Aug. 24, 1918; children—Louis Ernest, Edith Wooten Padgette, Sarah Wooten Little, Robert Edward. B.S. in Engring, N.C. State U., 1917, M.S., 1931. Registered profl. engr., N.C. Hwy. engr. N.C. Hwy. Commn., 1919-20; instr., then asso. prof. N.C. State U., Raleigh, 1920-35; regional engr. Farm Security Adminstrn., 1935-36; owner L.E. Wooten (cons. engr.), Raleigh, 1936-48; pres. L.E. Wooten & Co. (cons. engrs.), Raleigh, 1949-73; chmn. bd. L.E. Wooten & Co. (cons. engrs.), from 1949; dir. Cape Fear Feed Products, 1957-58; instr. Yale U., summer 1929. Served to 2d lt., C.E. U.S. Army, 1918-19. Fellow Am. Cons. Engrs. Council (pres. N.C. chpt., nat. dir. 1967-68), ASCE; mem. N.C. Soc. Professions, SAR. Episcopalian. Club: Raleigh Kiwanis. Home: Raleigh N.C. Deceased.

WORDEN, FREDERIC GARFIELD, neuroscientist; b. Syracuse, N.Y., Mar. 22, 1918; s. Vivien S. and Alice Garfield (Davis) W.; m. Katharine Cole, Jan. 8, 1944; children: Frederic, Dwight, Philip, Barbara, Katharine. A.B., Dartmouth Coll., 1939; M.D., U. Chgo., 1942. Diplomate: Am. Bd. Psychiatry and Neurology, Nat. Bd. Med. Examiners. Intern Osler Med. Clinic, Johns Hopkins Hosp., Balt., 1942-43; house officer Henry Phipps Psychiat. Clinic, 1943, house officer to chief resident, 1946-50; asst. in psychiatry, Commonwealth Found. fellow Johns Hopkins Med. Sch., 1946-48; instr. psychiatry, 1949-52; tng. Balt. Psychoanalytic Inst., 1947-53; clin. dir. Sheppard and Enoch Pratt Hosp., Towson, Md., 1950-52; supr. therapy Sheppard and Enoch Pratt Hosp., 1952-53; research psychiatrist, prof. psychiatry Med. Sch., UCLA, 1953-69, head div. adult psychiatry, 1968-69; prof. psychiatry, dir. neuroscis. research program MIT, 1969-83, prof. emeritus, 1983-95; mem. research scientist devel. rev. com. NIMH, 1971-74, mem. bd. sci. counselors, 1975-78; mem. com. on brain scis. NRC, 1971-74; Bd. dirs. Founds. Fund for Research in Psychiatry, 1973-76; bd. overseers Dartmouth Med. Sch., 1979-95; mem. Nat. Adv. Mental Health Council, 1980-83. Author: (with R. Galambos) Auditory Processing of Biologically Significant Sounds, 1972, (with F.O. Schmitt) The Neurosciences: Third Study Program, 1974, (with J.P. Swazey and G. Adelman) The Neurosciences: Paths of Discovery, 1975; also research publs. in psychiatry, neurophysiology. Served to maj. AUS, 1943-46. Fellow Am. Acad. Arts and Scis.; mem. Am. Psychiat. Assn. (chmn. task force on research tng. council on med. edn. and devel.), Soc. for Neurosci. (chmn. program com. 1972), Acoustical Soc. Am., AAAS, Am. Psychoanalytic Assn., UCLA Brain Research Inst., Psychiat. Research Soc., N.Y. Acad. Scis. Club: St. Botolph (Boston). Home: Jamestown R.I. Died June 7, 1995.

WÖRNER, MANFRED, international organization executive; b. Stuttgart, Germany, Sept. 24, 1934; s. Carl and Kläre Wörner; m. Elfie Reinsch, 1982. Student in law, U. Heidelberg, Fed. Republic Germany, U. Paris; Ph.D. in Law, U. Munich, 1961. Parliamentary adviser Baden-Württemberg State Assembly, Fed. Republic Germany, 1962-64; mem. German Bundestag, Bonn., Fed. Republic Germany, 1965-94, Chmn. com. on def., 1976-80, minister of def., 1982-88; dep. chmn. Konrad Adenauer Found., 1970-88; sec. gen. NATO, Brussels, 1988-94. Dep. chmn. Christian Dem. Union parliamentary party, Bundstag, 1969-71, 80-82, chmn. group of Bundestag deps. from Baden-Württemberg, 1970-82; chmn. working group on def. Christian Dem. Union/CSU parliamentary party; mem. nat. exec. Christian Dem. Union, 1973-94. Decorated Grand Cross first class Order of Merit, German govt. Home: Brussels Belgium Died Aug. 12, 1994.

WORONIAK, ALEXANDER, economist, educator; b. Lviv, Ukraine, Feb. 27, 1922; came to U.S., 1950, naturalized, 1955; s. Thomas and Eudoxia (Husar) W.; LL.M., Yoanni Casimiri Universitas, 1939; MS, Columbia U., 1953, postgrad. (Ford Found. scholar), 1955-57; m. Ann Bergkamp. Asst. prof. Yoanni Casimiri U., Poland, 1939-42; subarea dir., legal counselor, sr. researcher U.S. Relief and Rehab. Adminstrn. and Internat. Refugee Orgn., Ger., 1945-50; sr. acct. Gregory V. Collins and Co., 1952-56; researcher, teaching asst. Columbia U., 1956-58; asst. prof. econs. Catholic U. Am., 1958-67, dir. acct. program, 1958-95, chmn. dept. econs. and bus. 1974-88, assoc. prof. 1967-71, ordinary prof. 1971-95; cons., researcher Stanford Research Inst., 1971; cons. Dept. Def. 1981-95. Mem. Philosophy of Edn. Soc. (trustee 1970), Am. Econs. Assn., Am. Statis. Assn., Assn. Comparative Econ. Studies, ALA, Am. Acctg. Assn., Nat. Assn. Accts., Western Econ. Assn., Internat. Studies Assn., Pi Gamma Mu. Ukrainian Catholic. Editor: (with Daniel Spancer) The Transfer of Technology to Developing Countries 1967; author (chpts.) Regional Aspects of Soviet Planning and Industrial Organization, 1973, Technological Transfer in Eastern Europe: Receiving Countries, 1970, The Soviet Union: Seventy Years Later, 1988, Gorbachev's Social Russian Empire: Will the Invisible Hand of Adam Smith Negate the Visible Hand of Vladimir I. Lenin?, 1989, Khozraschet (Economic Accounting) and the Principle of Self-Financing as Criteria of Management Performance Under Perestroika, 1990, Quality and Competetiveness of Manufactured Goods: The Critical Dilemma of Ukranian "Perebudova", 1991, Ukranian Agriculture in Transition- From State Control to Market: Problems and Options, 1992; contbr. articles to profl. jours. Died Feb. 21, 1995. Home: Washington D.C.

WORTIS, JOSEPH, psychiatrist; b. N.Y.C., Oct. 2, 1906; s. Harry and Selina (Brunswick) W.; widowed 1986; children: Henry, Avi, Emily Wortis Leider. BA, NYU, 1927; MD, U. Vienna, Austria, 1932. Diplomate, Am. Bd. Psychiatry. Resident Bellevue Hosp., 1932-34, Johns Hopkins Hosp., 1938-39; prof. SUNY, Stony Brook, 1972-95. Author: Tricky Dick and His Pals, 1949, Soviet Psychiatry, 1950, Fragments of Analysis with Freud, 1952; editor Biol. Psychiatry Jour., 1966-92, Mental Retardation and Devel. Disabilities Rev., 1970-85. Lt. comdr. USPHS, 1943-45. Fellow Internat. Fed. Soc. Biol. Psych. (hon.); mem. Soc. Biol. Psychiatry (pres. 1966-67, Gold medal 1976, Disting. Svc. award 1982), Am. Assn. Mental Deficiency (v.p. 1960-61), Am. Acad. Mental Retardation (pres. 1962-63), Am. Psychiat. Assn., Am. Pub. Health Assn., Internat. Coll. Higher Nervous Activity (sec. 1987-91). Home: Brooklyn N.Y. Died Feb. 22, 1995.

WOZENCRAFT, FRANK MCREYNOLDS, lawyer; b. Dallas, Apr. 25, 1923; s. Frank Wilson and Mary Victoria (McReynolds) W.; m. Shirley Ann Cooper, Nov. 25, 1960; children: Frank McReynolds, Ann Lacey, George Wilson. B.A. summa cum laude, Williams Coll., 1946; LL.B., Yale U., 1949. Bar: Tex. 1950. Law clk. to Justice Hugo L. Black, U.S. Supreme Ct., Washington, 1949-50; mem. firm Baker & Botts, Houston, 1950-60; partner Baker & Botts, 1960-66, 69-90; dir. Rusk Corp.; asst. atty. gen. charge Office Legal Counsel, Dept. Justice, Washington, 1966-69; mem. legal adv. com. N.Y. Stock Exchange, 1978-83; Mem. Commn. Polit. Activity Govt. Employees, 1967; mem. Pres.'s Adv. Panel on Ins., 1967-68; vice chmn. Adminstrv. Conf. U.S., 1968-71, sr. fellow, 1982-94; U.S. rep. Vienna Conf. on Law of Treaties, 1968; vis. fellow Wolfson Coll. Cambridge U., 1989. Mem. exec. bd. Sam Houston Area council Boy Scouts Am., 1959-66, 69—, v.p., 1974-79; past mem. adv. bd. Houston Mus. Fine Arts; past chmn. bd. Assn. Community TV; past mem. bd. govs. Public Broadcasting Service; trustee Hedgecroft Hosp., 1964-66, St. John's Sch., Houston, 1972-79; bd. dirs. Alley Theatre, 1961-66, 73-80. Served to capt. U.S. Army, 1943-46. Decorated Bronze Star. Mem. Am. Law Inst. (coun.), ABA (chmn. sect. adminstrv. law 1973-74, chmn. spl. com. open meetings legislation 1974-75), Houston Bar Assn., Am. Judicature Soc. (bd. dirs. 1988-94), Nat. Assn. Securities Dealers (legal adv. bd. 1988-94) State Bar Tex. (chmn. sect. corp. banking and bus. law 1962-63), Philos. Soc. Tex. (pres. 1989-90), Order of Coif, Gargoyle, Phi Beta Kappa, Phi Delta Theta, Phi Delta Phi, Houston Club (pres. 1984-85), Houston Country Club, Chevy Chase Country Club. Episcopalian. Home: Houston Tex. Died Mar. 25, 1994.

WRAGG, LAISHLEY PALMER, JR., lawyer; b. Pitts., Oct. 11, 1933; s. Laishley Palmer and Irma Grace (Hill) W.; m. Marilyn Jean Smith, Apr. 26, 1957; children: Laishley P., Peter M.B. BBA, U. Mich., 1955; LLB cum laude, Harvard U., 1960; diploma in comparative legal studies, Trinity Hall Coll., Cambridge U., Eng., 1961. Bar: N.Y. 1962, U.S. Supreme Ct. 1974, Conseil Juridique, France 1977, Avocat France, 1992. Assoc. Cravath, Swaine & Moore, N.Y.C., 1961-62, 1965-69, Paris, 1963-65; assoc. Curtis, Mallet-Prevost, Colt & Mosle, N.Y.C., 1969-70, ptnr., 1970-94. Contbr. articles to profl. jours. Mem. U.S. Dept. State ad hoc com. on large constrn. projects; U.S. del. to 15th-20th sessions of UNCITRAL. Lt. USN, 1955-57. Mem. ABA (chmn. subcom. on regional orgns. of com. on internat. instns. law of sect. internat. law and practice), Assn. Bar of City of N.Y., U.S. Coun. Internat. C. of C. (com. on restrictive bus. practices), Inter-Am. Bar Assn., French Am. C. of C., Am. Yacht Club, N.Y. Yacht Club, Royal Ocean Racing Club, Hawks Club, Ekwanok Country Club, Automobile Club France, Duquesne Club, N.Y. Croquet Club. Republican. Presbyterian. Home: New York N.Y. Deceased.

WRAY, KARL, newspaper broker, former newspaper owner and publisher; b. Bishop, Tex., June 8, 1913; s. Ernest Paul and Gertrude (Garvin) W.; m. Flora-Lee Koepp, Aug. 11, 1951; children: Diana, Mark, Kenneth, Norman, Thomas. A.B., Columbia U., 1935. Auditor U.S. Dept. Agr., Washington, also Little Rock, 1935-37; salesman O'Mara & Ormsbee, Inc., N.Y.C., 1937-42; advt. mgr. Lompoc (Calif.) Record, 1947-54; owner, pub. San Clemente (Calif.) Daily Sun-Post, 1954-67, Coastline Dispatch, San Juan Capistrano, Calif., 1956-67, Dana Point (Calif.) Lamplighter, 1966-67; cons. Lear Siegler, Inc., Washington, 1967-68; pub. Daily Star-Progress, La Habra, Calif., 1969-74, Anaheim (Calif.) Bulletin, 1974-86. Mem. Calif. State Park Commn., 1960-64, vice chmn., 1961-62; mem. exec. bd. Orange County coun. Boy Scouts Am., 1961-64, 76-87; mem. citizens adv. com. Orange Coast Coll., 1963-66; bd. dirs. Calif. Newspaper Youth Found., 1974-84; founder, first pres. Freedom Bowl, Inc., Anaheim, Calif., 1981-84, chmn. bd., 1984-86, bd. dirs., 1986-94; authenticated, registered, established Calif. State Hist. Landmarks La Cristianita 1st baptism and Las Flores Asistencia. Mem. Calif. Newspaper Advt. Execs. Assn. (pres. 1952-53), Calif. Newspaper Pubs. Assn. (dir. 1960-64), Am. Theatre Critics Assn., Baseball Writers Assn. Am., Football Writers Assn. Am., Calif. Press Assn., San Juan Capistrano C. of C. (pres. 1966), San Clemente C. of C. (pres. 1956-57), La Habra C. of C. (dir. 1970-74), Anaheim C. of C. (dir. 1974-86). Presbyterian (elder). Home: San Clemente Calif. Died May 28, 1994.

WRIGHT, HAROLD, musician, educator. BM, Curtis Isnt.; studies with Ralph McLane. Prin. clarinet Boston Symphony Orch.; mem. Boston Symphony Chamber Player; prin. clarinet Nat. Symphony, Dallas Symphony; asst. prin. Houston Symphony; former faculty Cath. U., Am. U., and Boston U. First clarinet various orchs. The Casals and Marlboro Festivals; performed wiht many string quartets including Guarneri, Budapest, Juilliard, Cleve., and Fine Arts; soloist Nat. and Boston Symphonies. Home: Boston Mass. Died Aug. 11, 1993.

WRIGHT, JEANETTE TORNOW, college president; b. Milw., Sept. 8, 1927; d. Julius and Ida Tornow; m. Wilfred D. Wright, June 5, 1948. B.A., George Washington U., 1956, M.A., 1959; Ed.D., Boston U., 1967. Lic. psychologist, Mass. Tchr. emotionally disturbed children Arlington County (Va.) Public Schs., Arlington, 1956-58; instr. psychology Bay Path Coll., Longmeadow, Mass., 1958-60, chmn. dept. behavioral sci., 1959-62, dean students, 1960-62, v.p., dean of coll., 1962-79, pres., 1979-94; mem. various evaluation teams, Mass. and Conn.; pres. Nat. Council Ind. Jr. Colls., 1982-83, bd. dirs., 1983-88; bd. dirs. New Eng. Jr. Coll. Coun.; corporator Heritage Bank, 1980-83, dir., 1983-93; ednl. cons. Mem. Gov's. Commn. on Status of Women, 1973-74; chmn. bd. Carew Hill Girls' Club, Springfield, Mass., 1967-70; New Eng. regional chmn., mem. nat. bd. dirs. Girls' Clubs Am., 1970-71; corporator, mem. ethics com. use of human subjects Baystate Med. Ctr., 1980-87, mem. med. care and edn. com., 1981-84; corporator The MacDuffie Sch., 1985-94; bd. dirs. Automobile Club Pioneer Valley, 1977-94, pres., 1987-89; v.p. Springfield Mental Health Assn., 1968-69; bd. dirs. Nat. Assn. Ind. Colls. and Univs., 1988-90. Recipient Golden Boy award Boys' Clubs Am., 1974, Nat. award on Advocacy for Girls' Clubs Am., 1988; named One of Am.'s Most Effective Coll. Pres. in Country, 1986; Fulbright scholar, China, 1986. Fellow Mass. Psychol. Assn.; mem. Am. Psychol. Assn., Am. Personnel and Guidance Assn. (pres. Western Mass. 1961-62), Nat. Coun. Ind. Jr. Colls. (bd. dirs. 1980-94, pres. 1982-83). Home: Longmeadow Mass. Died Mar. 8, 1994.

WRIGHT, SARA-ALYCE PARSON, retired association executive; b. Harrisburg, Pa., Jan. 25, 1918; d. Henry Edwin and Fannie Katherine (Jackson) Parson; m. Emmett Franklin Wright, July 18, 1951. B.S. in Edn, Westchester State Coll., Pa., 1939; MS, U. Pa., 1945; MSW, U. Pitts., 1951; postgrad., Columbia U. Tchrs. Coll., 1960-61; HHD (hon.), North Adams State Coll., 1980. Tchr. Oxford Public Schs., Pa., 1939-41, Harrisburg, Pa., 1941-45; dir. teenage program YWCA, Youngstown, Ohio, 1945-49; nat. cons. teenage programs nat. bd. YWCA, N.Y.C., 1951-63, correlator teenage program, 1963-65; assoc. exec. dir. YWCA, 1965-66; dir. Freeport Youth Service Project of Family Service Assn. of Nassau County, N.Y., 1966-70; sch. community officer Freeport Public Schs., 1970-71; dep. exec. dir. nat. bd. YWCA of the U.S.A., N.Y.C., 1971-74; exec. dir. YWCA of the U.S.A., 1974-84, ret.; nat. adv. com. White House Conf. on Aging. Contbr. articles to profl. jours. Charter mem. bd. dirs. Ind. Sector., ret.; trustee Am. Bible Soc., N.Y.C., United Neighborhood Ctrs. Am., N.Y.C. and Washington; mem. gen. bd. Am. Baptist Chs. in U.S.A.; bd. dirs., exec. com. Family Service Assn. Nassau County, N.Y. Named Disting. Pennsylvanian, 1975; recipient Candace award Nat. Coalition of 100 Black Women, 1982, Equal Opportunity award Nat. Urban League, 1984, Disting. Alumnus award Westchester State Coll. (now Univ.), 1981, Bicentennial Medal Distinction U. Pitts., 1987, Ambassador award YWCA of the U.S.A., 1993. Mem. Nat. Assn. Social Workers, Nat. Assembly of Nat. Vol. Health and Social Welfare Orgns. (past pres.), Nat. Conf. Social Welfare (past dir.), Nat. Center Vol. Action (past dir.), Council Social Work Edn. (ho. of dels.), Nat. Council Negro Women, Nat. Assn. Negro Bus. and Profl. Women, Lambda Kappa Mu (Public Service award 1975), Delta Sigma Theta (Public Service award 1974). Home: Jamaica N.Y. Died Oct. 1994.

WULIGER, ERNEST M., mattress and bedding manufacturing company executive; b. Cleve., Dec. 10, 1920; married. Student, U. Chgo. Chmn., chief exec. officer, dir. Ohio Mattress Co., Cleve., 1982-89; exec. v.p., sec. Ohio-Sealy Mattress Mfg. Co., Cleve., 1953-62, exec. v.p., gen. mgr., 1962-63, pres., chief operating officer, treas., 1963-82. Home: Cleveland Ohio Died Sept. 5, 1992.

WYATT, WILSON WATKINS, lawyer; b. Louisville, Nov. 21, 1905; s. Richard H. and Mary (Watkins) W.; m. Anne Kinnaird Duncan, June 14, 1930; children: Mary Anne, Nancy Kinnaird, Wilson Watkins Jr. J.D., U. Louisville, 1927; LL.D. (hon.), Knox Coll., 1945, U. Louisville, 1948, Centre Coll., 1979, Bellarmine Coll., 1988, Transylvania U., 1989; LHD (hon.), Hanover Coll., 1990. Bar: Ky. 1927. Pvt. practice law Louisville, 1927-41; mayor of Louisville, 1941-45; housing expediter and adminstr. Nat. Housing Agy., 1946; founding ptnr. firm Wyatt, Grafton & Sloss, 1947-80; founding ptnr. firm Wyatt, Tarrant & Combs, 1980-82,
of counsel, 1982-96; lt. gov. of, Ky., 1959-63; Presd'
emissary oil negotiations from Pres. U.S. to Pres. In
donesia, 1963; mem. law faculty Jefferson Sch. Law
1929-35; dir. Courier Jour. and Louisville Times Co
WHAS, Inc., Standard Gravure Co., 1939-86, Ky
Center for Arts Endowment Fund. Presdl. emissary o
negotiations from Pres. U.S. to Pres. Indonesia, 1963
mem. law faculty Jefferson Sch. Law, 1929-35; dir
Courier Jour. and Louisville Times Co., WHAS, Inc
Standard Gravure Co., 1939-86, Ky. Ctr. for Arts En
dowment Fund, 1980-94. Spl. rep. Bd. Econ. Warfare
N. Africa, March-May 1943; chmn. Louisville Me
Area Def. Council (twice awarded citation of Merit)
1942-45; pres. Am. Soc. Planning Ofcls., 1943-44, Ky
Mcpl. League, 1944, Am. Mcpl. Assn., 1945, Louisvill
Area Devel. Assn., 1944-45; pres. Nat. Mcpl. League
1972-75, chmn. council, 1978-81; chmn. Nat. Conf. o
Govt., 1975-78; mem. bd. U.S. Conf. Mayors, 1942-4
mem. Louisville Sinking Fund Commrs., 1936-3
Louisville Com. on Fgn. Relations (chmn. 1940-41)
chmn. Ky. Econ. Devel. Commn., 1960-63; trustee Be
larmine Coll., 1975-82, chmn., 1979-82; trustee U
Louisville, 1950-58, chmn., 1951-55; Ky. chmn
Treasury adv. com. U.S. Savs. Bonds Program, 1948-5
mem. Commn. on Future of South, 1974, 86, Commn
on Operation U.S. Senate, 1975-76; founding chmn. bd
Regional Cancer Ctr. Corp., 1977-84; chmn. Louisvill
Cmty. Found., 1984-92, sr. advisor, 1992-96; vice chmn
Ky. Cancer Commn., 1978-79, Ky. Econ. Devel. Corp
1984-96, Ky. Council Sci. and Tech., 1987-90; foundin
chmn. Leadership Ky., 1984-86, chmn. emeritus; chmn
Judicial Nominating Com. 6th Circuit, 1977-8
Shakertown Roundtable, 1985-96, U. Louisville Found
Devel. Cabinet, 1989-91; founding chmn. Leadershi
Louisville, 1979-81; trustee Bingham Fund for Excel
lence in Teaching, Transylvania U., 1987-96; bd. dir
Nat. Ctr. for Family Literacy, 1989-92, Shakertown a
Pleasant Hill, Ky. Inc., 1990-96; chmn. Gov.'s Highe
Edn. Nominating Com., 1992-93; 1st pres. Young Den
Club, Louisville Jefferson County; nat. chmn. Jefferson
Jackson Day Dinners, 1948, 49; del at large 7 nat. Den
convs., 1944-68; nat. campaign mgr. for Stevenson
1952, co-ordinator campaign divs., 1956; Dem. na
committeeman for Ky., 1960-64; hon. chmn. Louisvil
Encyclopedia. Recipient U.S. Treasury Disting. Servic
award, 1955, Brotherhood award NCCJ, 1974, Gol
Cup for Community Service Louisville Area C. of C
1974; Gov.'s Disting. Service Medallion, 1980; name
Kentuckian of Yr., Sta. WHAS-TV, 1952, Citizen of Y
Louisville Jaycees, 1972, Man of Yr., Louisville Adv
Club, 1973-74, Lawyer of Year, Ky. Bar Assn., 197
Male High Sch. Alumni Hall of Fame, 1976, Lawyer c
Yr., Louisville Bar Assn., 1980, Alumnus of Yr., U
Louisville, 1987, Bus. Hall of Fame, Jr. Achievemen
1994; Ottenheimer award Jewish Community Ctr., 198
Mcpl. Leadership award Ky. Mcpl. League, 198
Brennan-Haly Lecture award U. Louisville, 1989, Cmty
Svc. award Cath. Schs., 1991, Citizen Laureate awar
Younger Woman's Club Louisville, 1991, Firs
Amendment prize Soc. Profl. Journalists, 1991, Wilso
W. Wyatt award established by U. Louisville, 198
Fleur-de-lis award Louisville Forum, 1993. Mem. ABA
Ky. Bar Assn. (sec. 1930-34, commr. 1958), Louisvil
Bar Assn., Am. Law Inst. (life), Ky. C. of C. (dir. 1974
Louisville Area C. of C. (pres. 1972), Pendennis Clu
University Club, Louisville Country Club, Jefferso
Club, Century Club (N.Y.C.), Rotary. Presbyterian.
Home: Louisville Ky. Died June 11, 1996.

WYLIE, CLARENCE RAYMOND, JR., mathemati
educator; b. Cin., Sept. 9, 1911; s. Clarence Raymon
and Elizabeth M. (Shaw) W.; m. Sikri M. Aho, June 2
1935 (dec. 1956); children: Chris Raymond (dec.
Charles Victor; m. Ellen F. Rasor, June 25, 1958. B.S
Wayne State U., 1931, A.B., 1931; M.S., Cornell U
1932, Ph.D., 1934; DSc (hon.), Furman U., 1994, U
Utah, 1995. Instr. Ohio State U., 1934-40, asst. prof
1940-46; cons. mathematican Propeller Lab., Wrigh
Field, Dayton, Ohio, 1943-46; chmn. dept. math. an
acting dean Coll. of Engring., Air Inst. Tech., Wrigh
Field, Dayton, 1946-48; prof. math. U. Utah, Salt Lak
City, 1948-69; chmn. dept. U. Utah, 1948-67; pro
math. emeritus, 1991-95; prof. math. Furman U., Gre
nville, S.C., 1969-78; William R. Kenan, Jr. prof. mat
Furman U., 1971-78, Kenan prof. emeritus, 1978-9
chmn. dept. math., 1970-76; part-time cons. math. Ge
Electric Co., Schenectady, Briggs Mfg. Co., Detroi
Aero Products div. Gen. Motors Corp., Dayto
Humble lectr. in sci. Humble Oil Co., 1955; distin
visitor Westminster Coll., Salt Lake City, 1981; con
mathematician Holloman Air Base, N.Mex., 1955, 56
Author: 101 Puzzles in Thought and Logic, 1958, A
vanced Engineering Mathematics, 6th edit., 1995, I
troduction to Projective Geometry, 1969, (limerick
The Wisdom of Eric Lim, 1974, Differential Equation
1979, The World of Eric Lim, 1991, Strange Havo
poems, 1956, also miscellaneous poetry; other book
papers, articles, pub. in math. jours. Recipient Distin
Alumni award Wayne State U., 1956, Disting. Engrin
Alumni Achievement award, 1985, named to Engrin
Coll. Hall of Fame, 1985; Algernon Sydney Sulliva
award Furman U., 1982; Bell Tower award Furman U
1986. Fellow AAAS; mem. Math. Assn. Am. (chm
Rocky Mountain sect. 1955-56, bd. govs. 1957-60, se
lectr. Southeastern sect. 1983), Am. Math. Soc., A
Soc. Engring. Edn. (chmn. math. div. 1949-50, 1957-5
Utah Acad. Sci. Arts and Letters, S.C. Acad. Sci.,
Beta Kappa, Sigma Xi, Pi Mu Epsilon, Sigma Pi Sigm

Pi Kappa Delta, Delta Sigma Rho, Sigma Delta Psi, Sigma Rho Tau, Phi Kappa Phi, Tau Kappa Alpha. Methodist. Home: Greenville S.C. Died Aug. 31, 1995.

WYMAN, HENRY WALTER, plastic manufacturing company executive; b. Aussig, Czechoslovakia, Feb. 7, 1919; s. Hans and Stella (Parnas) W.; m. Marguerite Ann Streuli, Sept. 30, 1944; children—Alexis Helen, David Christopher Parnas, Carla Marguerite Stel-a. Student elementary, high schs., Czechoslovakia; student, London Sch. Econs., 1939-40, Columbia, 1942-43, extension course N.Y.U., 1943-44. With Pantasote Co., Passaic, N.J., 1942-89, v.p., 1945-60, pres., 1960-83, chmn., 1983-89, also bd. dirs.; ptnr. Eagle Mgmt. Co., Greenwich, Conn., 1960-95; treas. Am. Foam Rubber Co., 1952-54. Bd. dirs. Purchase Community, Inc., 1955-57; chmn. Panwy Found.; bd. dirs., treas. Laymen's Nat. Bible Assn. Mem. Am. Arbitration Assn. (nat. panel arbitration), Photog. Soc. Am., Presidents Profl. Assn., Nat. Exec. Svc. Corps. Lutheran. Clubs: Westchester Color Camera (White Plains, N.Y.); Greenwich (Conn.) Country; Stratton Mountain Country (Bondville, Vt.). Home: Greenwich Conn. Died July 8, 1995.

WYSS, ORVILLE, microbiology educator; b. Medford, Wis., Sept. 10, 1912; s. John and Gertrude (Walther) W.; m. Margaret Bedell, May 31, 1941; children: Ann, Jane, Patti Bess. B.S., U. Wis., 1937; M.S., 1938, Ph.D., 1941. Indsl. research Wallace and Tiernan Co., Belleville, N.J., 1941-45; faculty U. Tex., 1945-93, prof. microbiology, 1948-83, prof. emeritus, 1983-93, chmn. dept. microbiology, 1959-69, 75-76. Author: Elementary Microbiology, 1964, Principles of Biology, 1964, Microorganisms and Man, 1971; also articles microbial physiology; assoc. editor Bacteriological Revs., 1960-66. Antarctic research fellow McMurdo Sound, 1961; Exchange scholar USSR, 1965; Fulbright fellow Sydney, Australia, 1970; Fulbright fellow Kathmandu, Nepal, 1978; Bose lectr. Calcutta U., 1971. Charter fellow Am. Acad. Microbiology (bd. govs.); fellow AAAS; mem. Am. Soc. Biol. Chemists, Am. Soc. Microbiology (pres. 1964-65), Tex. Acad. Sci., Am. Chem. Soc., Brit. Soc. Gen. Microbiology, Sigma Xi (past pres. Tex.), Phi Kappa Phi (past pres. Tex.). Democrat. Unitarian. Home: Pinecliffe Colo. Died Nov. 11, 1993; cremated.

YAGI, YASUHIRO, steel company executive; b. Feb. 5, 1920; married. Grad., Tokyo U., 1943. With Kawasaki Steel Corp., 1943—, exec. dir., 1974-77, mng. dir., 1977-79, v.p., 1979-88, became pres., 1988, now chmn.; v.p. Nikon Tekko Associated. Mem. Japan Metals Acad. (council). Home: Tokyo Japan Died Feb. 1995.

YAMASHIRO, YOSHINARI, steel company executive; b. Tokyo, Feb. 7, 1923; s. Fusa Y.; m. Tsune Y.; children: Noriko, Toru. B. in Politics, Tokyo U. Sch. Law, 1943. Dir. Nippon Kokan K.K., Tokyo, 1976-96, mng. dir., 1978-80, sr. mng. dir., 1980-82, exec. v.p., 1982-85, became pres., 1985, now chmn. bd. Home: Yokohama Japan

YARBOROUGH, RALPH WEBSTER, lawyer, former senator; b. Chandler, Tex., June 8, 1903; s. Charles Richard and Nannie Jane (Spear) Y.; m. Opal Catherine Warren, June 30, 1928; 1 son, Richard Warren. Student, U.S. Mil. Acad., 1 year, Sam Houston State Tchrs. U.; LLB, U. Tex., 1927; LHD, Lincoln Coll., 1965; LLD, St. Edward's U., 1971. Bar: Tex. 1927. Tchr. pub. schs. Tex., 3 yrs; practiced law El Paso, 1927-31; asst. atty. gen. Tex., 1931-34; lectr. law U. Tex., 1935; judge 53d Jud. Dist. of Tex., 1936-41; presiding judge 53d Jud. Dist. of Tex. (3d Adminstrv. Jud. Dist.), 1937-40; U.S. senator from Tex., 1957-71; sole practice Austin, Tex., 1971-96; assoc. prof. polit. sci. U. Tex. at Arlington, 1975; Mem. U.S. Congress delegation 51st Inter-Parliamentary Union Conf., Brasilia, Brazil, 1962, Dublin, Ireland, 1965, Canberra, Australia, 1966, Teheran, Iran, 1966, Palma de Mallorca, Spain, 1967, Lima, Peru, 1968, Vienna, Austria, 1969, Delhi, India, 1969, The Hague, Netherlands, 1970; mem. Tex. Constl. Revision Commn., 1973-74. Contbr. to: Lincoln for the Ages, 1964, Texas Avenue at Main Street, 1964. Author: Frank Dobie; Man and Friend, 1967; foreword Three Men in Texas, 1967, The Public Lands of Texas, 1972, Carrascolendas: Bilingual Education Through Television, 1974. Bd. dirs. Lower Colo. River Authority, 1935-36, State Bd. Law Examiners, 1947-51; mem. Tex. State Library and Archives Commn., 1983; past mem. Abraham Lincoln Sesquicentennial Commn.; past mem. exec. bd. Nat. Civil War Centennial Commn.; Past mem. bd. dirs. Gallaudet Coll. Served as lt. col. AUS, 1943-46, Europe, Japan. Hon. fellow Postgrad. Center Mental Health, N.Y., 1965. Mem. ABA, El Paso Bar Assn., Travis County Bar Assn. (past pres.), Assn. Trial Lawyers Am., Tex. Trial Lawyers Assn., Am. Law Inst., State Bar Tex. (past dir.), V.F.W., Am. Legion, Order of Coif, Acacia, Phi Delta Phi. Democrat. Baptist. Lodges: Masons, Shriners. Home: Austin Tex. Died January 27, 1996.

YATES, PETER, chemistry educator; b. Wanstead, Eng., Aug. 26, 1924; s. Harold Andrew and Kathryn (Wexley) Y.; m. Mary Ann Palmer, Sept. 9, 1950; children: William Palmer Franklin, Thomas Jay Franklin, John Anthony. B.Sc., U. London, 1946; M.Sc., Dalhousie U., 1948; Ph.D., Yale U., 1951. Postdoctoral fellow Harvard U., Cambridge, Mass., 1950-51, mem. faculty, 1952-60; instr. Yale U., New Haven, 1951-52, vis. prof., 1966; prof. chemistry U. Toronto, Ont., Can., 1960-91, Univ. prof., 1986-91, Univ. prof. emeritus, 1991-92; vis. prof. Princeton U., 1977. Fellow Royal Soc. Can., Chem. Inst. Can. (Merck, Sharp & Dohme lectr. 1963, medalist 1984); mem. Am. Chem. Soc. Home: Toronto Can. Died Nov. 16, 1992.

YENDO, MASAYOSHI, architect; b. Yokohama, Japan, Nov. 30, 1920; s. Masanao and Ima (Nakamura) Y.; m. Fumi Matsuzaki, Dec. 25, 1956; 1 child, Masahiko. B.S. in Architecture, Waseda Univ., 1945. With Murano Architect Office, Osaka, 1946-49; pres. M. Yendo Assoc. Architects and Engrs., Tokyo, 1952-94. Important works include: 77th Bank Head Office, 1957; Keio Dept. Store, 1960; Yamaguchi Bank Head Office, 1962; Kashoen Hotel, 1962; Yaizu Plant Yamanouchi Pharm. Co., 1967; Coca-Cola Head Office (Japan), 1971; Yakult Head Office, 1972; Heibonsha Head Office, 1972; Tokyo Am. Club, 1972; Taiyo Fishery Co., Ltd. Head Office, 1973; Seiyu Store Kasugai Shopping Ctr., 1975. Recipient Bldg. Contractors Soc. prize, 1965; Minister of Edn. award of art, 1966. Fellow AIA (hon. 1987); mem. Japan Architects Assn. (pres. 1982-86), Japan Inst. Archtl. (councilor, award 1966). Club: Tokyo Am. Deceased. Home: New York N.Y.

YOUNG, ARDELL MOODY, retired judge, lawyer; b. Ringgold, Tex., Oct. 11, 1911; s. Horace G. and Emma (Garvin) Y.; m. Marjorie Maschal, July 27, 1934; children-Mardelle Fay (Mrs. S.E. Moyers), John Herschel. A.B., U. Okla., 1932, LL.B., 1936. Bar: Okla. 1936, Tex. 1936. 1st asst. dist. atty. Tarrant County, Tex., 1946; partner firm Brown, Herman Scott, Young & Dean, Ft. Worth, 1947-71; judge 153d Dist. Ct., Tarrant County, Tex., 1971-81; counsel Brown, Herman, Scott, Dean & Miles, 1981-89; ret. Brown, Herman, Scott, Dean and Miles, 1989. Served to lt. col. Judge Adv. Gen.'s Dept. AUS, 1941-46. Mem. ABA, Tarrant County Bar Assn., State Bar Tex. (bd. dirs. 1959-62), Am., Tex. Bar Founds., Am. Coll. Trial Lawyers, Masons (33 degree), Shriners, K.T., Phi Alpha Delta. Republican. Presbyterian. Home: Fort Worth Tex. Died Nov. 26, 1993.

YOUNG, C. B. FEHRLER, business executive; b. Birmingham, Ala., May 13, 1908; s. Francis D. Fehrler and Lena Edna (Wells) F.; m. Lois Frances Ellis, Dec. 31, 1934; children: Charles E., Frank B., James T. B.S., Howard Coll., 1930; M.S., Columbia U., 1932, Ph.D., 1935; LL.D., Freed-Hardeman U., 1982. Cons., Nat. So. Products Co., Tuscaloosa, Ala., 1945-52, v.p., 1949-53; pres. Warrior Asphalt Co., Tuscaloosa, 1949-53; founder Auromet Corp., N.Y.C., pres., 1953-56; founder, pres. Ala. So. Warehouse, Inc., Cytho Corp. & M'Lord & M'Lady Cosmetic Co., Douglasville, Ga., 1949-95; founder, pres., chmn. bd. Cracker Asphalt Co. (now Young Refining Corp.), Douglasville, Ga., 1955-95; chmn. bd. Laketon Refining Corp., 1984-87; pres. Universal Home Products, Inc., 1974-84; pres. Energy Explorations, 1976-84; chmn. bd., dir. So. Fed. Savs. & Loan, 1974-80; pres. Cinco, Inc., 1977-95; chmn. bd. Seminole Refining Corp., St. Marks, Fla., 1985-95. Author: Chemistry for Electroplaters, 1947; Surface Active Agents, 1954. contbr. tech. articles to profl. jours. Recipient Engring. Professionalism award, 1987, Boone Noblih award, 1986. Trustee, Freed-Hardeman Coll., Henderson, Tenn., 1978-95, Ga. Christian Found., Inc.; hon. bd. dirs. Ga. Engring. Found., Inc., 1975-95. Mem. Chemist Club, AAAS, Am. Inst. Chem. Engrs., Ind. Refiners Assn. (pres. 1968-69), Douglas County C. of C. (pres. 1957-59), Epsilon Chi, Sigma Xi, Phi Lambda Upsilon. Mem. Church of Christ (elder). Died Mar. 2, 1995. Home: Douglasville Ga.

YOUNG, JOHN HENDRICKS, lawyer; b. Pelham, N.Y., Aug. 12, 1912; s. John Hendricks and Elizabeth (Chatterton) Y.; m. Fredrika Cosden Ritter, Feb. 8, 1967; children: John Hendricks, Anne Payne, Judith S. (Mrs. Richard Geiger). Grad., Phillips Acad., 1930; BA, Yale U., 1934, JD, 1937. Bar: N.Y. 1938. Assoc. firm Carter, Ledyard & Milburn, N.Y.C., 1937-42, 45-47, mem. firm, 1947-82, counsel, 1983-84; of counsel Hughes Hubbard & Reed, N.Y.C., 1985-95; lectr. taxation Practising Law Inst. N.Y., Inst. Continuing Legal Edn., Ga.; dir. Whitney Industries, Inc. Contbr. articles to profl. jours. Trustee Cornelius Vanderbilt Whitney Found. Served to lt. USNR, 1942-45, PTO. Decorated Bronze Star with combat V, 10 battle stars. Mem. ABA, Assn. of Bar of City of N.Y. (lectr.), N.Y. State Bar Assn., Inter-Pacific Bar Assn. (Japan chpt.), Internat. Bar Assn. (Eng. chpt.), Internat. Law Assn. (Am. br.), Lawasia (Australia chpt.), Asia Pacific Lawyers Assn. (Republic of Korea chpt.), World Peace Through Law Center, World Assn. Lawyers (hon. chmn. sect. on taxation), Union Internat. des Avocats (Belgium), Am. Soc. Internat. Law, Internat. Fiscal Assn., Tax Forum, Am. Law Inst., N.Y. Law Inst., Metropolitan Club (N.Y.C.), Yale Club (Miami), Brickell Club (Miami). Home: Bal Harbor Fla. Died Feb. 7, 1995.

YOUNG, LESLIE TOWNER, state legislator, stockbroker; b. N.Y.C., May 26, 1930; s. Leslie Bernard and Constance (Towner) Y.; m. Patricia Cutler, June 18, 1955; children: William, Anne. BA, Yale U., 1952; MS, Columbia U., 1957. Fin. analyst Union Carbide Corp., N.Y.C., 1957-68; v.p., dir. Laird Bissell Meeks, N.Y.C., 1968-74; stockbroker, mgr. Dean Witter Reynolds, Greenwich, Conn., 1974-96; mem. Conn. Ho. of Reps., Hartford, 1984-96. Bd. dirs., pres. New Canaan (Conn.) United Way, 1960s; bd. dirs., v.p. Lower Fairfield Alcohol and Drug Abuse Coun., Stamford, Conn., Weir Farm Heritage Trust, Wilton, Conn.; chmn. Republican Town Com., New Canaan, 1968-74. With U.S. Army, 1953-55. Mem. New Canaan Country Club (greens chmn. 1978-96), New Canaan Exch. Club. Home: New Canaan Conn. Died Mar. 21, 1996.

YOUNG, TERENCE, motion picture director; b. Shanghai, China, June 20, 1915. Ed., Cambridge U. Entered motion picture industry, 1936. Collaborated: screen play Theirs Is the Glory, On the Night of the Fire, On Approval; wrote: screen play Dangerous Moonlight; wrote screen play, directed: The Valley of the Eagles, 1951, They Were Not Divided, 1950; co-dir.: Men of Arnhem, 1944, Storm Over the Nile, 1955, Duel of Champions, 1961, The Dirty Game, 1966; dir.: Corridor of Mirrors, 1948, One Night With You, 1948, Woman Hater, 1948, The Frightened Bride, 1952, Red Beret (Paratrooper), 1953, That Lady, 1954, Safari, 1956, Zarak, 1956, Action of the Tiger, 1957, No Time to Die, 1958, Serious Charge, 1959, Too Hot to Handle, 1960, As Dark as the Night, Black Tights, 1960, Horatio, The Jackals, Dr. No, 1962, From Russia With Love, 1963, The Amorous Adventures of Moll Flanders, 1965, Thunderball, 1965, Triple Cross, 1966, The Poppy Is Also a Flower, 1966, The Rover, 1967, Wait Until Dark, 1967, Mayerling, 1968, The Christmas Tree, 1969, Cold Sweat, 1970, Red Sun, 1972, The Valachi Papers, 1972, Flower of Evil, I Was a Spy, Isadora Duncan, The Klansman, 1974, Jackpot, Bloodline, 1979, You Only Live Twice, 1967, Grand Slam, 1970, War Goddess, 1973, Inchon, 1981, The Jigsaw Man, 1983, Takeover. Served with Guards Armoured Div., World War II. Home: Calabasas Calif. Died Sept. 7, 1994.

YOUNG, VIRGINIA SHUMAN, former mayor of Fort Lauderdale; b. Norfolk, Va., Sept. 16, 1917; d. I.G. and Myrtle (TenBrook) Shuman; m. George F. Young, Mar. 27, 1937 (dec.); children: George William, Nancy Young Smith, Cathy Young Moore. JD (hon.), Nova U., 1986. Co-owner, operator constrn. co., until 1977; vice mayor City of Ft. Lauderdale, 1971-73, 75-81, mayor, 1973-75, 81-85; dir. Landmark Bank, Citizens and Southern, Ft. Lauderdale. Past mem., twice chmn. Broward County Sch. Bd.; pres. Fla. Sch. Bd. Assn., 1965; state and local officer LWV; past mem. Broward County Sch. Trustees; chmn. local sch. bd., 1963, 65; active Sun Dial, Easter Seal Campaign, United Way, Opportunity Ctr., Boy Scouts Am., Girl Scouts U.S.A., Chord, YMCA; past pres. Broward County League of Cities, Fla. League of Cities; former mem. Fla. Gov.'s Council on Criminal Justice, Task Force on Crime and Aged; mem. Met. Planning Orgn., Community Service Council Broward County, Broward Sexual Assault Treatment Ctr.; former mem. Fla. Gov.'s Com. on Edn., Council on Aging, Citizens' Tax Council, Council for Criminal Justice, Council on Community Affairs, Fla. Gov.'s Conf. on Libraries and Info. Planning Com., Adv. Council on Govt. Affairs, Adv. Council on Inter-Govtl. Affairs; former mem. study com. on selection, retention and removal of judges Fla. Bar Assn.; former tchr. Park Temple Meth. Ch.; Downtown Devel. Authority, long range planning com. First United Meth. Ch. Recipient Woman of Yr. award Am. Bus. Women's Assn. Mem. Ft. Lauderdale Hist. Soc., Ft. Lauderdale C. of C., Nat. Assn. Women Bus. Owners, Penwomem, Mangrove Roots of Ft. Lauderdale, Swim Ft. Lauderdale (bd. dirs.), Ft. Lauderdale Beach Assn. Clubs: Soroptimist, Ft. Lauderdale Woman's (past pres.), Women's Exec. Home: Fort Lauderdale Fla. Died Dec., 1994.

YOUSKEVITCH, IGOR, ballet dancer; b. Piriytin, Ukraine, Russia, Mar. 13, 1912; came to U.S., 1939, citizen 1944.; s. Ivan and Sophia (Lipsky) Y.; m. Anna Scarpa, June 27, 1938; 1 child, Maria. Student, Belgrade U., 1930-31; studied ballet with, Nadejda Poliakova, Belgrade, 1931, Olga Preobrajenska, Paris, 1933; hon. doctorate, U. Tex., 1982. Premier danseur noble Ballet Russe de Monte Carlo, toured U.S., 1938-44; premier danseur Am. Ballet Theatre, N.Y.C., 1946-56; artistic advisor, premier danseur Ballet Russe de Monte Carlo, N.Y.C., 1956-58; owner, with wife Igor Youskevitch Sch. Ballet, N.Y.C., 1962-80, Ballet Romantique, N.Y.C., 1963-67; chmn. dance dept. U. Tex., Austin, 1971-82; artistic dir. N.Y. Internat. Ballet Competition, 1984-94; dance cons. Dance Pages Mag., N.Y.C., 1991-94; mem. selection com. Dance Mag. Found., 1990-94. Principal roles include classical ballets, best known for Giselle; Theme and Variations created for him by George Balanchine; (film) Invitation to the Dance, 1952; guest speaker at Kennedy Ctr., 1990, Am. Ballet Theatre, 1990; Snow Maiden created for him by Nijinska; contbr. articles to profl. jours. With USN, 1944-45. Recipient award Dance Mag., 1958, Capezio Found. Dance award, 1991, Gold Medal award for Career Achievement N.Y. Internat. Ballet Competition, 1993, Disting. Artist award Grand Teatro de la Habana, 1993. Russian Orthodox. Home: New York N.Y. Died June 13, 1994; interred East Ridgelawn Cemetery, Clifton, N.J.

YUENGER, JAMES LAURY, journalist; b. Green Bay, Wis., June 13, 1939; s. David Anthony and Carol Jeanette (Haines) Y.; m. Blanche Schulz, Nov. 9, 1963 (div. 1985); 1 child, Jay Noel; m. Mary Catherine Henry, Oct. 5, 1985. BA, St. Norbert Coll., DePere, Wis., 1961. Corr. Moscow Chgo. Tribune, 1971-72, fgn. news editor, 1972-74, corr. London, 1974-76, asst. news editor, 1976-77, roving corr. Middle East, Europe, 1977-81, corr. Poland, 1986-87, editorial writer, 1987-88, nat. news editor, 1988-89, fgn. news editor, 1989-94, sr. writer, 1995; news dir. U. Chgo., 1981-85;. With U.S. Army, 1957-61. Recipient Alumni award humanities St. Norbert Coll., 1977. Mem. Press Club (Chappaquiddick, Mass.), Am. Kite Club. Home: Chicago Ill. Died Aug., 1995.

YUNCKER, BARBARA, science writer; b. Greencastle, Ind.; d. Truman George and Ethel (Claflin) Y. A.B., DePauw U., D.Litt., 1976. Copyreader Wall St. Jour.; various editing positions N.Y. Post; asst. dep. commnr. commerce N.Y. State, 1956-57; medicine and sci. editor N.Y. Post, 1959-84; med. columnist Good Housekeeping mag., 1963-76. Contbr. to nat. mags. Recipient Page One award Newspaper Guild N.Y., 1961; Adolf Meyer award, 1961; Alumni citation DePauw U., 1963; Page One award Newspaper Women's Club N.Y., 1963, 68; Albert Lasker med. journalism award, 1967, 69; Am. Psychiat. Assn. award, 1974; Silurians award, 1975; Matrix award Women in Communications, 1979. Mem. Newspaper Guild (exec. com. local 3 1976-82, v.p. 1981-82, chmn. N.Y. Post unit 1976-79, internat. v.p. 1981-83), Nat. Assn. Sci. Writers, Soc. Journalists and Authors. Democrat. Home: Canaan N.Y. Died Jan. 1, 1996.

ZALESKI, MAREK BOHDAN, immunologist; b. Krzemieniec, Poland, Oct. 18, 1936; came to U.S., 1969, naturalized, 1977; s. Stanislaw and Jadwiga (Zienkowicz) Z. M.D., Sch. Medicine, Warsaw, 1960, Dr. Med. Sci., 1963. Instr. dept. histology Sch. Medicine, Warsaw, 1955-60; asst. prof. Sch. Medicine, 1960-69; research asst. prof. (Henry C. and Bertha H. Buswell fellow) dept. microbiology SUNY, Buffalo, 1969-72; assoc. prof. SUNY, 1976-78, prof., 1978—; vis. scientist Inst. Exptl. Biology and Genetics, Czechoslovak Acad. Sci., Prague, 1965; Brit. Council's scholar, research lab. Queen Victoria Hosp., East Grinstead, Eng., 1966-67; asst. prof. dept. anatomy Mich. State U., East Lansing, 1972-75, assoc. prof., 1975-76. Contbg. author: Transplantation and Preservation of Tissues in Human Clinic, 1966, The Man, 1968, Cytophysiology, 1970, Principles of Immunology, 1978, Medical Microbiology, 1982, Molecular Immunology, 1984; co-author: Immunogenetics, 1983, co-editor: Immunobiology of Major Histocompatibility Complex, 1981; co-translator: Spirit of Solidarity, 1984, Marxism and Christianity: The Quarrel and the Dialogue in Poland (J. Tischner), 1987; mem. editorial com. Immunology Investigations, Polish Jour. of Immunology; contbr. articles to med. jours. Former mem. adv. com. for Internat. Rescue Com., Amnesty Internat., Raul Wallenberg Com. USA; bd. dirs., Permanent Chair Polish Culture, Canisius Coll., Buffalo. NIH grantee, 1976-88; NEH grantee, 1985-87. Mem. Polish Anat. Soc., Transplantation Soc., Internat. Soc. Exptl. Hematology, Ernest Witebsky Center Immunology, Am. Assn. Immunologists, Buffalo Collegium of Immunology, N.Y. Acad. Scis., Solidarity and Human Rights Assn. Roman Catholic. Home: Narberth Pa. Died Dec. 18, 1994.

ZAPFFE, CARL ANDREW, metallurgical engineering consultant; b. Brainerd, Minn., July 25, 1912. BS, Mich. Tech. U., 1933; MS in Metall. Engring., Lehigh U., 1934; ScD, Harvard U., 1939; D Engring. (hon.), Mich. Tech. U., 1960. Registered profl. engr., Md. Metallurgist DuPont Exptl. Sta., Wilmington, Del., 1934-46; rsch. assoc. Battelle Mem. Inst., Columbus, Ohio, 1938-40; rsch. engr. Battelle Mem. Inst., 1940-43; asst. tech. dir. Rustless Iron Steel Corp., Balt., 1943-45; prin., rsch. cons. C.A. Zapffe & Assocs., Balt., 1945-52; metall. engring. cons. Balt., from 1952. Author: Stainless Steels, 1949, Rotary!, 1963, The Archive of Troop 35, 1977, Seven Short Essays On (1-v2/c2)-1/2, 1977, A Reminder on E=mc2, m=mo (1-v2/c2)-1/2, and N=Ne exp t'/gamma tau, 1983, Golden Anniversary of the Dad-Boy Troop, 1983, Kahbe-nagwi-went, The Man Who Lived in Three Centuries, 1983, Paul Bunyan, 1984, Geohydrothermodynamics of a Water Planet I: Quarternary Glaciation Theories, 1984, Oldtimers: Stories of Our Pioneers, vol. 1, 1987, vol. 2, 1989, Indian Days in Minnesota's Lake Region, vol. 1, 1991; contbr. articles to tech. publs.; writer, narrator (ednl. film) Stainless Steel--The Miracle Metal, 1960 (Chris award Columbus Film Festival 1961). Mem. Balt. area coun. Boy Scouts Am., from 1944, scoutmaster, from 1955; founder, historian, Historic Heartland Assn., Brainerd, Minn., from 1970. Recipient Silver Beaver award, Boy Scouts Am., 1958, St. George's award, 1986, numerous awards from profl. orgns., 4 nat. awards for discoveries in metallurgy; Balt. Mayor citation. Fellow Am. Soc. Metals (charter), Am. Inst. Chemists (hon., life); mem. AAAS, Am. Chem. Soc., Am. Geol. Soc., Am. Geophys. Union, Am. Inst. Physicists, Am. Phys. Soc., Am. Soc. Testing and Materials, Am. Welding Soc., Astronomical Soc. of Pacific, Inst. of Metals (Eng.), Internat. Soc. Gen. Relativity and Gravitation, Nat. Assn. Corrosion Engrs., Oceanic Soc., Planetary Soc., Rotary (bd. dirs. 1959-64, pres. 1961-62, Balt. club, hon. Paul Bunyan Axeman from 1950, Brainerd club), Gull Lake Yacht Club (regatta commodore 1968-72, commodore 1971), Sigma Xi, Sigma Phi Epsilon. Home: Baltimore Md. Deceased.

ZAPPA, FRANK, musician, vocalist, composer; b. Balt., Dec. 21, 1940; s. Francis Vincent and Rose Marie Z. Sr.; m. 2nd, Gail Sloatman, 1969; children: Dweezil, Moon Unit, Ahmet Emuukha Rodan, Diva. Student, Chaffey Jr. Coll., 1959. Guitarist, vocalist, composer, founder Mothers of Invention band, 1964-78; pres. Pumpko Industries Ltd., L.A.; founder internat. consulting firm, Why Not?, 1989. Scored film Run Home Slow, 1964; appeared in, scored motion picture 200 Motels, 1971; albums include Freak Out!, 1966, Absolutely Free, 1967, We're Only In It For The Money, 1967, Lumpy Gravy, 1967, Cruisin' with Ruben and the Jets, 1968, Uncle Meat, 1969, Mother Mania, 1969, Hot Rats, 1969, Burnt Weeny Sandwich, 1970, Weasels Ripped My Flesh, 1970, Chungas Revenge, 1970, Live At Fillmore East, 1971, 200 Motels, 1971, Just Another Band From L.A., 1972, The Grand Wazoo, 1972, Waka Jawaka, 1972, Overnite Sensation, 1973, Apostrophe ('), 1974, Roxy and Elsewhere, 1974, One Size Fits All, 1975, Bongo Fury, 1975, Zoot Allures, 1976, In New York, 1978, Studio Tan, 1978, Sheik Yerbouti, 1979, Sleep Dirt, 1979, Orchestral Favourites, 1979, Joe's Garage Act I, 1979, Joe's Garage Acts 2 and 3, 1979, Tinseltown Rebellion, 1981, You Are What You Is, 1981, Shut Up and Play Yer Guitar, 1981, Ship Arriving Too Late, 1982, Baby Snakes, 1983, London Symphony Orhcestra, 1983, The Man from Utopia, 1983, Them or Us, 1984, Boulez Conducts Zappa, 1984, Thing-Fish, 1984, Francesco Zappa, 1984, Frank Zappa Meets the Mothers of Prevention, 1985, Does Humor Belong in Music?, 1986, Jazz From Hell, 1986, Broadway the Hard Way, 1988, Best Bank You Never Heard, 1991, Make a Jazz Noise Here, 1991, Playground Psychotics, 1992, Ahead of Their Time, 1993, The Yellow Shark, 1993; composer chamber works, orchestral compositions; author (with Peter Occhiogrosso) The Real Frank Zappa Book, 1989; producer Frank Zappa's Wild Wild East, short TV bus. news features, 1990. Named Pop Musician of Yr. Down Beat mag., 1970, 71, 72. Home: Los Angeles Calif. Died Dec. 4, 1993.

ZARAGOZA, FRANCISCO, science academy executive. Pres. Acad. Filipina, Manila, The Philippines; pres., dir. Acad. Filipina, Manila.

ZEITER, WILLIAM EMMET, lawyer; b. Harrisburg, Pa., Dec. 1, 1934; s. Jacob David and Maude Elizabeth (Hamm) Z.; m. Jean Palmer Greer, May 22, 1965. BA, Lehigh U., 1955, BSEE, 1956; JD, N.Y. U., 1959. Bar: U.S. Patent Office 1957, Pa. 1960, D.C. 1962, U.S. Supreme Ct. 1963. Acting mgr. Moving the EE-Z Way, Harrisburg, 1956-63; mem. patent staff Bell Tel. Labs., Inc., 1956, 57, 58; asso. firm Morgan, Lewis & Bockius, Phila., 1959-66; mem. firm Morgan, Lewis & Bockius, 1967—, sr. partner, 1975—, mem. exec. com., 1980-82; legal cons. to Ct. Adminstr. Pa., 1972-79; exec. dir. Adv. Com. on Appellate Ct. Rules, 1973-81; mem. Pa. Joint Com. on Documents, 1968—, chmn., 1991—; bd. dirs. Am. Nat. Metric Coun., Washington, 1973-78, vice-chmn., 1975-78; reporter Uniform Metric System Procedure Act; mem. legal adv. panel metric study U.S. Metric Bd., 1979-80; mem. exec. com. Nat. Metric Adv. Panel, U.S. Dept. Commerce, 1969-71, Pa. Dept. State, 1991—; cons. Office Invention and Innovation, Nat. Bur. Standards, 1967-72; mem. ad hoc energy panel Office Tech. Assessment, U.S. Congress, 1975-76; bd. dirs. Burle Industries Inc. Author: West's Pennsylvania Associations Code and Related Materials, 2 vols., 1992; contbr. various articles on legal codification, corp. law, adminstrv. law and metric conversion. Pres. Friends of Logan Sq. Found., 1985-88, bd. dirs., 1984—; trustee Franklin Inst., 1981-88, Lehigh U., 1987—. Recipient Gov.'s citation for drafting Appellate Ct. Jurisdiction Act, 1970, awards for drafting Pa. Jud. Code Allegheny County Bar Assn., 1978; Root-Tilden scholar, 1956-59. Fellow Am. Bar Found.; mem. ABA (chmn. sect. sci. and tech. 1977-78, chmn. conf. sect. chairmen 1978-79, mem. ho. of dels. 1980—, nominating com. 1986-89, bd. govs. 1992—), Pa. Bar Assn., Phila. Bar Assn. (Fidelity award 1979), IEEE, Am. Law Inst. Home: Philadelphia Pa.

ZELAZNY, ROGER JOSEPH, author; b. Cleve., May 13, 1937; s. Joseph Frank and Josephine Flora (Sweet) Z.; m. Judith Alene Callahan, Aug. 20, 1966; children—Devin, Trent, Shannon. B.A., Case Western Res. U., 1959; M.A., Columbia U., 1962. Claims rep. Social Security Adminstrn., 1962-64, policy specialist, 1965-69; profl. writer, 1969—. Books include This Immortal, 1966, Lord of Light, 1967, Creatures of Light and Darkness, 1969, Damnation Alley, 1969, Nine Princes in Amber, 1970, The Guns of Avalon, 1972, To Die in Italbar, 1973, Sign of the Unicorn, 1975, My Name is Legion, 1976, The Hand of Oberon, 1976, The Courts of Chaos, 1978, The Chronicles of Amber (2 vols.), 1979, The Changing Land, 1981; numerous others; also contbr. numerous short stories and articles to mags., anthologies. Recipient Hugo sci. fiction awards, 1966, 68, 76, 82, 86, 87; Nebula award Sci. Fiction Writers, 1966, 76; Prix Apollo, 1972; Balrog award, 1980, 84. Died June 14, 1995.

ZELLER, EDWARD JACOB, physics, astronomy and geology educator, consultant; b. Peoria, Ill., Nov. 6, 1925; s. John George and Mabel Gertrude (Singer) Z. A.B., U. Ill., 1946; M.A., U. Kans., 1948; Ph.D., U. Wis.-Madison, 1951. Research assoc. U. Wis.-Madison, 1951-56; asst. prof. U. Kans., Lawrence, 1956-59, assoc. prof., 1959-63, prof. geology, 1963-91, prof. physics and astronomy, 1969-96. Contbr. numerous articles to profl. jours.; co-inventor identification markings for gemstones and making selective conductive regions in diamond layers. Recipient Antartic Service medal Nat. Acad. Sci., 1966, Group Achievement award NASA, 1983; NSF sr. postdoctoral fellow, Bern, Switzerland, 1962; German Acad. exchange fellow, Munster, Fed. Republic Germany, 1975. Fellow Geol. Soc. Am.; mem. AAAS, Am. Geophys. Union, Explorers Club, Antarctican Soc., Am. Polar Soc., Sigma Xi. Home: Lawrence Kans. Died Jan. 14, 1996.

ZEPPA, ROBERT, surgeon; b. N.Y.C., Sept. 17, 1924; s. Alfred and Angelina (Buscaglia) Z.; m. Cicely M. Lawrence, June 7, 1952; children: Melissa Kay, Scott L. A.B., Columbia U., 1948; M.D., Yale U., 1952. Diplomate: Am. Bd. Surgery. Intern U. Pitts. Med. Center, 1952-53; resident U. N.C., Chapel Hill, 1953-56; prof. surgery U. N.C., 1958-65; prof. surgery and pharmacology U. Miami, Fla., 1965-93; co-chmn. dept. surgery U. Miami, 1966-71, chmn. dept. surgery, 1971-93; chief surg. service VA Hosp., Miami, 1965-72; chief surgery Jackson Meml. Hosp., Miami, 1971-93, pres. med. staff, 1976-78; mem. surgery tng. com. Nat. Inst. Gen. Medicine Scis., 1968-71. Contbr. articles to profl. publs., 3 film presentations. Served to 2d lt., AC U.S. Army, 1943-45, Eng. John and Mary Markle scholar, 1959-64. Mem. A.C.S., AAAS, Am. Gastroent. Assn., Am. Assn. Study Liver Diseases, Am. Surg. Assn., Soc. Surgery Alimentary Tract, Soc. Univ. Surgeons, N.Y. Acad. Scis., So. Surg. Assn., Alpha Omega Alpha. Home: Miami Fla. Died Sept. 2, 1993.

ZETTERLING, MAI ELISABETH, film director, actress, author; b. May 24, 1925; m. Tutte Lemkow, 1944; 1 son, 1 dau.; m. 2d David Hughes 1958 (div. 1977). Ed. Royal Theatre Sch. Drama, Stockholm. Staff of Nat. Theatre, Stockholm, 1943-45; under contract film dir. to Sandrews of Sweden; Swedish stage appearances include: St. Mark's Eve, The Beautiful People, Shadow and Substance, Twelfth Night, Merchant of Venice, Les Mouches, House of Bernada; London stage appearances include: The Wild Duck, The Doll's House, Point of Departure and Restless Heart, The Seagull, Creditors; acted in films: Frenzy, 1944. Frieda 1947, The Bad Lord Byron, 1948, Quartet, 1948, Knock on Wood, 1954, A Prize of Gold, 1955, Seven Waves Away, 1956, Only Two Can Play, 1962, The Main Attraction, 1962, The Bay of St. Michael, 1963; film dir. BBC TV Documentaries; dir., co-writer films: The War Game (1st prize Venice Film Festival 1963), 1963; (feature films) Loving Couples, 1965, Night Games, 1966, Dr. Glas, 1968, The Girls, 1968, Flickorna, 1968; (films) Vincent the Dutchman, We Have Many Names, 1975, The Moon I a Green Cheese, 1976, The Native Squatter, 1977, Lady Policeman, 1979, Of Seals and Men, 1979; (feature film Eng.) Scrubbers, 1983; co-dir. Visions of Eight, 1973 dir., writer (feature film Sweden) Amorosa, 1986 author: (with David Hughes) The Cat's Tale, 1965 Night Games (novel), In the Shadow of the Sun (shor stories), 1975, Bird of Passage (novel), 1976, Rains Ha (children's book), 1979, Ice Island (novel), 1979, Al Those Tomorrows (autobiography), 1985. Home London Eng.

ZHANG, JINGFU, government official of People' Republic of China; b. Beijing, People's Republic c China, 1901. Mem. Chinese Communist Party, fron 1934, alt. mem. 8th Central Com., 1956, mem. 12tl Central Com., from 1982; former vice-minister local in dustry and v.p. sci. and tech. com. People's Republic c China, vice-minister of forestry, 1956-58, criticized an removed from office during Cultural Revolution, 1967 minister of fin., 1975-79, state counsellor, from 1982 minister in charge of state econ. com., 1982-84, mem state fin. and econ. ecom.; gov. and 1st sec. Anhu Provincial Com., 1980-81; 1st polit. commr. Anhui Mil Div., 1980-82. Deceased. Home: Beijing People' Republic of China

ZIEGNER, EDWARD HENRY, retired journalist; b Indpls., Aug. 8, 1920; s. Edward Henry and Pea (McCampbell) Z.; m. Martha Alice McHatton, May 1 1950; children: Anne Virginia, David Edward. Studen Wabash Coll., 1938-39, Ind. U., 1939-41. Statehous reporter Indpls. News, 1946-52, polit. editor, legis. bu chief, 1953-85. Served with U.S. Army, 1942-46. Named to Ind. Journalism Hall of Fame Soc. Prof Journalists, 1990. Mem. Phi Gamma Delta. Democra Presbyterian. Club: Indpls. Press (past v.p., past dir.) Home: Indianapolis Ind. Died June 22, 1993; cremated.

ZILLMANN, ROBERT EDWARD, accountant; b Evanston, Ill., Mar. 16, 1929; s. Emil R. and Dais (Greenland) Z.; m. Marie Frances Vranicar, May 2 1953; children: Barbara Zillmann Park, Er Robert. Student, Lake Forest Coll., 1948-49; B.S Northwestern U., 1952. C.P.A., Ill. Pub. accountar H.C. Goettsche & Co., Chgo., 1952-57; financial exe Abbott Labs., Chgo., 1957-61; operations mgr. Abbo Labs., S.A.R.L., Montreaux, Switzerland, 1962-63; cor ntroller G.D. Searle & Co., Chgo., 1964-67; treas. arsteller, Inc., Chgo., 1968-70; financial v.p. Marller, Inc., 1970-73; asst. treas. Apeco Corp., Evanm, 1973-74; corporate controller Apeco Corp., 1974; ntroller Nat. Assn. Realtors, Chgo., 1974; v.p. finance d adminstrn. Nat. Assn. Realtors, 1975-79; pres. lmann & Co. (C.P.A.s), Chgo., 1979-95. Served with JS, 1946-48. Mem. AICPA (tax div.), Ill. Soc. CPAs, nancial Execs. Inst., Corp. Controllers Inst. Home: enview Ill. Died Aug. 8, 1995.

M, HERBERT SPENCER, author, educator; b. Y.C., July 12, 1909; s. Marco and Minnie (Orlo) Z.; Sonia Elizabeth Bleeker, Jan. 16, 1934 (dec. 1971); ildren: Aldwin Herbert, Roger Spencer; m. Grace ent Showe, June 4, 1978. Student, CCNY, 1927-29; S., M.A., Ph.D., Columbia, 1933-40; D.Sc. (hon.), loit Coll., 1967, Fla. State U., 1977. Instr. sci., mmer play schs., 1926-31; instr. sci. Bklyn. Ethical ılture Sch., 1930-31, N.Y. Ethical Culture Schs., 1932-; tchr. edn. dept., head sci. dept., 1937-45; asso. prof. n. U. Ill., 1950-54, prof. edn., 1954-57; ednl. cons. anhasset Bay Schs., 1946-48, U.S. Fish and Wildlife rvice, 1947-51, Western Pub. Co., 1967-70, Am. iends Service Com., 1968-78; editorial cons. Invidualized Sci. Instrnl. System, 1972-79; pres. ogewinn Corp., 1968-71; Instr. Columbia, 1935-36; mmer field trips, 1937-41; research under Gen. Edn. l. Grant for Comm. on Secondary School Curriculum, ogressive Edn. Assn., 1934-37; adj. prof. edn. U. iami, 1970-82; Mem. Am. Inst. Jr. Activities Com., 38-42, bd. mgrs., 1940-42, v.p., 1942; mem. steering m. Biol. Scis. Curriculum Study and Intermediate is. Curriculum Study, War Dept. (pre-induction tng. ogram), 1942-43; civilian pub. service, 1943-45. uthor/editor over 150 books relating to sci. including fe and Death, 1970, Armored Animals, 1971, Your ain, 1972, Crabs, 1974, Medicine, 1974, Snails, 1975, aves, 1977, Little Cats, 1978, Your Skin, 1979, New oon, 1980, Quartz, 1981, Guide to Trees, 1985, Reps and Amphibians, 1987, Mammals, 1987, Insects, 87, Flowers, 1987, Fishes, 1987; rev. edits. Alligators d Crocodiles, Sharks and others, 1978-87; editor-inief: Our Wonderful World Ency., 1952-63, Golden ncy. Natural Sci., 1960-70; originator, editor: Golden uide Series, 1947-70; ednl. dir.: rev. edits. Artists and riters Press, 1957-69. Recipient Children's Sci. Book wards N.Y. Acad. Scis., 1988. Fellow AAAS; mem. umerous sci. and ednl. socs. Home: Tavernier Fla. ied Dec. 5, 1994.

IMMER, ALBERT ARTHUR, education educator; b. tts., May 20, 1918; s. Albert Peter and Hilda (Volz) ; m. Alma Zimmermann, Mar. 7, 1945; children: lene Lynne, Alyce Lorraine, Alana Leigh. B.S., Pa. ate U., 1942, M.Ed., 1947; Ed.D., U. Pitts., 1951. chr. pub. schs. State College, Pa., 1941-42; music supr. ub. schs. Ford City and Monongahela, Pa., 1946-49; str. U. Pitts., 1949-52; head edn. dept. Susquehanna , 1952-59, dean students, 1959-62; dean, v.p. Bethany oll., Lindsborg, Kans., 1962-66; acting pres. coll. ethany Coll., 1966-67; chmn. dept. edn. Thiel Coll., reenville, Pa., 1967-83, chmn. emeritus, 1983-96; vis. ctr. Bucknell U., Rutgers U., Pa. State U., U. Conn.; el. Gov. Pa. Conf. Edn., 1954. Contbr. articles to rofl. jours. Dir. Snyder County Civii Def., 1952-62; em. Selinsgrove (Pa.) SSS Bd., 1959-62; Nat. del. Luth h. Am., 1956, 60, 62; del. Central Pa. Synod, 1956-62, 4, mem. Christian edn. commn., 1958-62, social welfare ommn., 1960-62, church councilman, Selinsgrove, 1952-2, Lindsborg, 1963-96, City councilman, Selinsgrove, 960-62, Greenville, 1980-88, mem. planning commn., 960-62; fire warden Pa. Forest Commn., 1958-62; Bd. irs. Snyder County chpt. Am. Cancer Soc., 1956-60; d. dirs., fund chmn. Snyder County chpt. A.R.C., 954; bd. dirs. Monongahela Youth Council, 1946-47, Monongahela Concert Bd., 1946-47, Walnut Acres ound., Pa., 1958-62, Lindsborg Community Vol. mbulance Service, 1966-96, Gettysburg Luth. Theol. em., 1974-78. Served with AUS, 1942-46. Mem. NEA, AUP, Music Educators Nat. Conf., Pa. Assn. Liberal Arts Colls. (pres. 1960-61), Pa. Assn. Student Teaching v.p. 1958-59), Nat. Assn. Deans, Rotary, Phi Delta Kappa, Theta Chi, Phi Mu Alpha, Kappa Phi Kappa, Alpha Phi Omega. Home: Greenville Pa. Died Apr. 4, 996.

ZIMMER, NORMAN CUNNINGHAM, architect; b. Denver, Aug. 8, 1924; s. Christian Peter and Vivien Pittam) Z.; m. Marian L. Davis, Oct. 10, 1952; chilren: Jeffery, Gregory, Alexandra, Gabrielle. Student, Portland (Oreg.) Museum Art Sch., 1952. Designer, hen sr. designer Wolff-Phillips, Portland, 1946-54; ptnr. Wolff Zimmer, Portland, 1954-64; sr. ptnr. Wolff, Zimmer, Gunsul, Frasca, Portland, 1964-76, Zimmer, Gunsul, Frasca, 1976-90; prin. Pacific Studios, Portland, 1991-94; vis. prof. U. Oreg. Sch. Architecture, 1964-66; dir. Oreg. Sch. Design, Portland, 1987-90. Prin. works include indsl. complexes for Textronix Inc. in U.S., U.K. and Netherlands, addition to Oreg. State Capitol bldg., Oreg. Hist. Soc. hdqrs. Pres. bd. trustees Portland Art Assn., 1972-73. Served with C.E. AUS, 1943-45. Recipient numerous design awards. Fellow AIA (chmn. com. on architecture for commerce and industry 1969-70, Firm of Yr. award 1990), Arlington Club (Portland), Multnomah Athletic Club (Portland), Founders Club (Portland). Republican. Episcopalian. Home: Portland Oreg. Died Sept. 28, 1994.

ZIMMERMAN, HARRY MARTIN, neuropathologist; b. Vilna, USSR, Sept. 28, 1901; came to U.S., 1909; s. Jacob and Anna (Kaplan) Z.; m. Miriam Gordon, Sept. 2, 1930. BS, Yale U., 1924, MD, 1927; LHD (hon.), Yeshiva U., 1957. Diplomate Am. Bd. Pathology, Am. Bd. Pathology Anatomy. Intern New Haven Hosp., 1927-28, resident, 1928-30; asst. to assoc. prof. pathology Yale U. Sch. Medicine, New Haven, Conn., 1930-43; dir. dept. pathology Montefiore Hosp., Bronx, N.Y., 1946-73, cons. pathology, 1973-95; prof. pathology Coll. Physicians and Surgeons, Columbia U., N.Y.C., 1948-64, Albert Einstein Coll. Medicine, Bronx, 1963-73; assoc. pathologist New Haven Hosp., 1933-43; sr. cons. VA Hosp., Bronx, 1946-72; neuropathology cons. Armed Forces Inst. Pathology, Washington, 1949-73; chmn. research rev. panel Nat. Multiple Sclerosis Soc., 1946-67; mem., chmn. bd counselors Nat. Inst. Neurologic Diseases and Strokes, Bethesda, Md., 1972-77. Editor: (6 vols.) Progress in Neuropathology, 1971-86; contbr. articles to profl. jours. Trustee Am. Cancer Soc., 1961-65; mem. panel on specialization Pres.' Commn. on Health of the Nation, 1952. Served to comdr. USN, 1943-46, PTO. Recipient Hope Chest award Nat. Mutiple Sclerosis Soc., 1971, Max Weinstein award United Cerebral Palsy Found., 1972; named to Order of the Sacred Treasure Emperor of Japan, 1973. Fellow Coll. Am. Pathologists; mem. Am. Assn. Pathologists (gold headed cane award 1982), Assn. Research in Nervous & Mental Diseases (pres. 1964), N.Y. Pathol. Soc. (pres. 1959-61), Am. Neurol. Assn. (hon.). Home: Bronx N.Y. Died July 28, 1995.

ZIMMERMAN, ROBERT EARL, lawyer; b. Kansas City, Mo., Feb. 11, 1928; s. Julius Joseph and Kathryn Bernadine (Highcock) Z.; A.A., Kansas City (Mo.) Jr. Coll., 1947; LL.B., U. Kansas City, 1950; m. Pauline Ann Stephens, Sept. 16, 1950; children: Elaine, David, Mark, Carol. Admitted to Mo. bar, 1950; assoc. firm Madden & Burke, Kansas City, Mo., 1950-51, 53-60; exec. v.p. Stephens Industries, Inc., Kansas City, 1957-63; with Kansas City So. Industries, Inc., 1964-91, successively, atty., gen. atty., asst. gen. counsel, gen. counsel, v.p. and gen. counsel, v.p. law, 1964-82, sr. v.p. law, 1982-91 ; dir. Kansas City So. Ry. Co., La. and Ark. Ry. Co. Served with USMC, 1944-45, with USAF, 1951-53. Mem. ABA, Mo. Bar, Am. Judicature Soc., Kansas City Bar Assn., Lawyers Assn. of Kansas City, Assn. ICC Practitioners. Roman Catholic. Clubs: Hallbrook Farms, Kansas City, Leawood Country, K.C. Died Aug. 9, 1991; buried Mt. Olivet, Kansas City, Mo.

ZIMMERMAN, THEODORE SAMUEL, physician, researcher, educator; b. St. Louis, May 3, 1937; s. Julius Aaron and Rose Bernice (Hammerman) Z.; m. Frances O'Neill, July 29, 1961; children: Grace Ann, Clare Elizabeth. AB magna cum laude, Harvard U., 1959, MD, 1963. Diplomate Am. Bd. Internal Medicine, Am. Bd. Hematology. Intern then resident U. Minn. Hosp., Mpls., 1963-65; with medicine br. NIH, Nat. Cancer Inst., Bethesda, Md., 1965-67; resident in medicine Barnes Hosp., St. Louis, 1967-68; fellow in hematology Case Western Res. U., Cleve., 1968-70; assoc. Scripps Clinic and Research Found., La Jolla, Calif., 1972-74, chief coagulation lab., 1972-88, assoc. prof. immunology, 1974-82, prof., 1982—, mem. hematology staff, 1976—, dir. biomed. research lab., 1974—; assoc. clin. prof. U. Calif. San Diego, La Jolla, 1972—; mem. rev. and adv. coms. NIH, 1974-77, Am. Heart Assn., 1975-77, and others; head div. exptl. hemostats Scripps Clinic and Rsch. Found. Mem. editorial bd. BLOOD, 1981-85, assoc. editor 1987-88; contbr. numerous chpts. to books and articles to profl. jours. Served to lt. comdr. USPHS, 1968-72. Recipient Research Career Devel. award NIH, 1972-77, Merit award Nat. Heart Lung and Blood Inst., 1985. Fellow ACP; mem. Assn. Am. Physicians, Am. Assn. Immunologists, Am. Fedn. Clin. Research., Am. Soc. Clin. Investigation, Am. Soc. Exptl. Pathology, Am. Soc. Hematology (councillor, mem. rev. and adv. coms., Damashek award, 1988), Internat. Soc. Thrombosis and Haemostasis, World Fedn. Hemophilia, Nat. Hemophilia Found. (chmn. med. sci. adv. council). Home: La Jolla Calif. Died Dec. 19, 1988.

ZIRPOLI, ALFONSO JOSEPH, federal judge; b. Denver, Apr. 12, 1905; s. Vincenzo and Stella (Graziani) Z.; m. Giselda Campagnoli, Sept. 19, 1936; children: Sandra Elena, Jane Amanda. AB, U. Calif., Berkeley, 1926, JD, 1928. Bar: Calif. 1928, U.S. Supreme Ct. 1941. Pvt. practice law, 1928-32, 44-61; asst. dist. atty. City and County San Francisco, 1932-33; asst. U.S. atty. No. Dist. Calif., 1933-44; instr. criminal law Hastings Coll. Law, 1945; sr. judge U.S. Dist. Ct. (no. dist.) Calif., San Francisco., 1961-95. Mem. Bd. Suprs. City and County San Francisco, 1958-61. Recipient Star Solidarity, 1953, grand officer Order Merit, 1956; Italy. Fellow Am. Coll. Trial Lawyers; mem. ABA, Fed. Bar Assn., Calif. Bar Assn. Home: San Francisco Calif. Died July 10, 1995.

ZONDERVAN, PETER JOHN (PAT ZONDERVAN), publisher, religious organization executive; b. Paterson, N.J., Apr. 2, 1909; s. Louis and Nellie Petronella (Eerdmans) Z.; m. Mary Swier, May 21, 1934; children: Robert Lee, Patricia Lucille, William J., Mary Beth. Student. pub. schs., Grandville, Mich.; DLitt (hon.), John Brown U., 1969, Lee Coll., 1972; LLD, Campbellsville Coll., Ky., 1985; LHD, Taylor U, Upland, Ind., 1985. Co-founder Zondervan Pub. House, Grandville, Mich., 1931, Grand Rapids, Mich., 1932-93; co-founder Zondervan Corp., Grand Rapids, 1955-93; pres. Grand Rapids Camp of Gideons, 1938-41, chaplain, 1944-46, pres., 1947-48; pres. internat. trustee, 1950-52; v.p. Gideons Internat., 1952-55, pres., 1956-59, treas., 1972-75, chaplain, 1975-78; Bd. dirs. Christian Nationals Evangelism Commn., San Jose, Calif.; bd. dirs. Winona Lake Christian Assembly, Ind., 1937-93, sec., 1961-93; b. dir. Marantha Bible and Missionary Conf., Muskegon, Mich., 1961; organizer, 1st chmn. Christian Businessmen's Com., Grand Rapids, 1942; chmn. com. for city-wide Evangelistic meeting, 1946. Honored with declaration of P.J. Zondervan Day in Grand Rapids, Dec. 1973. Mem. Internat. Platform Assn. Clubs: Lotus (Grand Rapids) (pres. 1949, 65-67); Peninsular of Grand Rapids, Blythefield Country and Golf; Boca Golf (Boca Raton, Fla.). Home: Boca Raton Fla. Died May 6, 1993.

ZUCKERMAN, JOHN VITTO, management educator, consultant; b. Chgo., Sept. 15, 1918; s. Nathan and Tillie (Vitto) Z.; m. Rosalind Kiehnhoff, May 10, 1957 (div. 1978); children: Judith Rochelle Nelson, John Bruce. MA in Psychology, Stanford U., 1948, PhD in Psychology, 1951; student law, U. Houston, 1976-82. Diplomate Am. Bd. Indsl. and Organizational Psychology, Am. Bd. Profl. Psychology. Dir. radio workshop and A-V aids program Stanford (Calif.) U., 1947-48; rsch assoc., instr. film rsch. program Pa. State U., Univ. Park, 1948-49; rsch. asst. dept. psychology Stanford U., 1949-50; aviation psychologist human resources rsch. lab. U.S. Dept. Air Force, Washington, 1950-51; sr. rsch. scientist human resources Rsch. Office, George Washington U., Washington, 1951-55; from dir. indsl. rels. to regional mktg. mgr. Ampex Corp., Redwood City, Calif., 1955-61; from dep. to acting dir. bur. internat. bus. orgn. U.S. Dept. Commerce, Washington, 1961-63; assoc. prof. mgmt. grad. sch. bus. adminstrn. U. So. Calif., 1963-69; prof. mgmt. Coll. Bus. Adminstrn. U. Houston, 1969-93; chair mgmt. dept., U. Houston, 1969-71, dep. dir. Energy Inst, 1973-76; cons. govt., edn. insts. and corps. Contbr. articles to profl. jours. Dir., treas. Houston Ctr. for Humanities, 1977-82; mem. Mayor's Task Force on Energy Policy, 1981, Future Studies com. C. of C., 1973-85. Capt. U.S. Army, 1942-46, PTO. Mem. AAAS, APA, Am. Psychol. Soc., Acad. Applied Sci., Sigma Xi, Beta Gamma Sigma. Home: Houston Tex. Died Aug. 19, 1993.

ZUNIGA, MARCO ANTONIO, physics educator; b. Tegucigalpa, Honduras, Oct. 20, 1942; s. Francisco and Mariana (Izaguirre) Z.; m. Lucy Roberta Barahona, Jan. 2, 1966; children: Marco Antonio, Roberto Francisco, Christian David. BSCE, U. Honduras, 1965; MA in Physics, U. Tex., 1968, PhD in Physics, 1972. Prof. physics U. Honduras, Tegucigalpa, 1973-76, pysics dept. head, 1976-83, grad. dean, 1983-91, geophysics head, 1991-95; chmn. several coms. Coll. of Engrs., Tegucigalph, 1980-86. Contbr. articles to profl. jours. Named Tex. Hon. Citizen Gov. of Tex., 1981; recipient Nat. Sci. award Pres. of Honduras, 1977. Mem. Soc. of Profl. Physicists (pres.), Honduras Physics Soc., Honduras Acad. Scis. (pres. 1984). Roman Catholic. Home: Tegucigalpa Honduras Died May 29, 1995.

ZUTHER, GERHARD HELMUT W., English language educator; b. Berlin, Jan. 12, 1930; came to U.S., 1951, naturalized, 1963; s. Franz and Frieda (Barkemeyer) Z.; m. Edith G. Gilmore, June 25, 1954 (div. 1972); m. 2d Janet E. Riley, Mar. 12, 1983; children by previous marriage: Karen S., Margaret A. B.A. in English, DePauw U., 1953, M.A., 1955; Ph.D., Ind. U., 1959. Instr. German Wabash Coll., Crawfordsville, Ind., 1953-55; instr. English U. Kans., Lawrence, 1958-61, asst. prof., 1961-64, assoc. prof., 1965-69, prof., 1969-87, chmn. dept. English, 1979-84, pres. faculty, 1975-76, 79-80. Compiler: Eine Bibliographie der aufnahme amerikanischer Literatur in deutschen Zeitschriften, 1965. Bd. dirs. Vols. in Ct., 1974-76; bd. dirs. Kans. Vols. in Correction, 1975-76; mem., actor Lawrence Community Theater, 1978-87. DePauw U. scholar, 1951-53; Watkins Faculty fellow, 1962; Alexander von Humboldt fellow, 1964-65. Mem. MLA, Assn. Depts. English, AAUP, Deutsche Gesellschaft fur Amerikastudien, Pi Delta Phi, Delta Phi alpha. Home: Lawrence Kans. Died Nov., 1987.